John Eadie

Cruden's Concordance to the Holy Scriptures

Vol. 1

John Eadie

Cruden's Concordance to the Holy Scriptures
Vol. 1

ISBN/EAN: 9783337315634

Printed in Europe, USA, Canada, Australia, Japan

Cover: Foto ©Lupo / pixelio.de

More available books at **www.hansebooks.com**

CRUDEN'S CONCORDANCE
TO
THE HOLY SCRIPTURES.

EDITED BY

JOHN EADIE, D.D., LL.D.,

PROFESSOR OF BIBLICAL LITERATURE TO THE UNITED PRESBYTERIAN CHURCH, SCOTLAND.

WHOLLY REVISED,

AND PRINTED FROM NEW ELECTROTYPE PLATES EXPRESSLY FOR

HITCHCOCK'S
COMPLETE ANALYSIS OF THE HOLY BIBLE.

Entered, according to Act of Congress, in the year 1869, by A. J. JOHNSON, in the Clerk's Office of the District Court of the United States for the Southern District of New York.

AAH
AARON.
Luke 1:5 wife of daughters of A.
Acts 7:40 saying to A. make gods
Heb. 5:4 called of God, as was A.
7:11 not called after order of A.
9:4 A's rod that budded
AARONITES. 1 Chr. 12:27; 27:17
ABADDON. Rev. 9:11
ABAGTHA. Est. 1:10
ABANA. 2 K. 5:12
ABASE.
Job 40:11 Behold proud, and a.
Is. 31:4 lion will not a. himself
Eze. 21:26 and a. him that is high
Dan. 4:37 in pride is able to a.
ABASED.
Mat. 23:12 exalt, himself be a.
Luke 14:11; 18:14
Phil. 4:12 I know how to be a.
ABASING.
2 Cor. 11:7 offence in a. myself
ABATED.
Gen. 8:3 waters were a. 8:11
Lev. 27:18 he a. from thy estim.
Deut. 34:7 was Moses' force a.
Jud. 8:3 their anger was a.
ABBA.
Mark 14:36 a. Father, all things
Rom. 8:15 we cry, a. Father
Gal. 4:6 crying a. Father
ABDA. 1 K. 4:6; Neh. 11:17
ABDI. 2 Chr. 29:12; Ezr. 10:26
ABDIEL. 1 Chr. 5:15
ABDON. Jud. 12:13; 2 Chr. 34:20
ABED-NEGO. Dan. 1:7; 2:49; 3:23
ABEL, person, or place.
1 Sam. 6:18 stone of A. they set
2 Sam. 20:18 ask counsel at A.
Mat. 23:35 blood of A. Luke 11:51
Heb. 11:4 by faith A. offered
12:24 things than blood of A.
ABEL-BETH-MAACHAH, 1 K. 15:20; 2 K. 15:29
ABEL-MAIM. 2 Chr. 16:4
ABEL-MEHOLAH. Jud. 7:22; 1 K. 19:16
ABEL-MIZRAIM. Gen. 50:11
ABHOR.
Lev. 26:11 soul shall not a. you
15 your soul a. my judgments
30 my soul shall a. you
44 nor will I a. them
Deut. 7:26 shalt utterly a. it
23:7 not a. Edomite, Egyptian
1 Sam. 27:12 his people to a. him
Job 9:31 clothes shall a. me
30:10 they a. me, they flee far
42:6 I a. myself and repent in
Ps. 5:6 Lord will a. bloody man
119:163 I hate and a. lying
Prov. 24:24 nations shall a. him
Jer. 14:21 do not a. us

ABI
Amos 5:10 they a. him
6:8 I a. the excellency of Jacob
Mic. 3:9 yo that a. judgment
Rom. 12:9 a. that which is evil
ABHORRED.
Ex. 5:21 made savor to be a.
Lev. 20:23 therefore I a. them
26:43 their soul a. my statutes
Deut. 32:19 saw it, he a. them
1 Sam. 2:17 men a. the offering
2 Sam. 16:21 art a. of thy father
Job 19:19 inward friends a. me
Ps. 22:24 nor a. affliction
78:59 he greatly a. Israel
89:38 a. hou hast cast off and a.
106:40 that he a. inherit.
Prov. 22:14 a. of the Lord
Lam. 2:7 hath a. his sanctuary
Ezek. 16:25 beauty to be a.
Zec. 11:8 their soul also a. me
ABHORREST.
Is. 7:16 thou a. shall be forsa.
Rom. 2:22 thou that a. idols
ABHORRETH.
Job 33:20 so life a. bread
Ps. 10:3 whom the Lord a.
36:4 mischief on bed, he a. not
107:18 their soul a. meat
Is. 49:7 to him whom nation a.
ABHORRING.
Is. 66:24 an a. to all flesh
ABI.
1 Sam. 8:2 sec. son was A.
1 Chr. 2:24 A. Hezron's wife
7:8 son of Becher, A.
8:10 son of R. was A. Mat. 1:7
ABI-ALBON. 2 Sam. 23:31
ABIATHAR.
1 Sam. 22:20 A. escaped and fled
23:6 when A. son of Ahimelech
9 David said to A. bring, 30:7
2 Sam. 8:17 Zadok and A. 20:25;
1 K. 4:4
1 K. 1:42 King, for him and A.
27 so Solomon thrust out A.
Mark 2:26 in days of A.
ABIB.
Ex. 13:4 out in A. 34:18
23:15 unleav, bread in month
A. 34:18; Deut. 16:1
ABIDAN.
Num. 1:11 A. son of Gid. 2:22
7:60 A. of Benjamin offered, 65
ABIDE.
Gen. 22:5 you here with
Ex. 16:29 a. every man in
Lev. 16:29 a. at door of tabernacle
Num. 8:7 ark shall not a. with
22:21 a. thou with me, but will
2 Sam. 16:18 will his will I a.
Job 24:13 nor a. in paths of light
Ps. 15:1 shall a. in tabernacle
61:4 I will a. in thy tabernacle

ABI
Ps. 7 he shall a. before God
91:1 shall a. under the shadow
Prov. 7:11 her feet a. not in
19:23 shall a. satisfied
Ec. 8:15 shall a. of his labor
Jer. 10:10 not a. his indigna.
42:18 no man a. there, 33; 50:40
Joel 2:11 terrible, who can a. it?
Mic. 5:4 they shall a. for now
Nah. 1:6 can a. in his anger?
Mal. 3:2 whom may a. day of
Mat. 10:11 there a. Mark 6:10;
Luke 9:4
Luke 19:5 I must a. at thy house
24:29 a. with us
John 12:46 not a. in darkness
14:16 Comforter that he may a.
15:4 a. in me, except ye a. 7
6 if a man a. not in me
10 a. in my love, in his love
Acts 27:31 these a. in ship
1 Cor. 3:14 if any man's work a.
7:8 good if they a. even as I
20 let every man a. in same
40 happier if she so a.
Phil. 1:24 to a. in the flesh
1 John 2:24 let that a. in you
27 ye shall a.; 28 children a.
ABIDETH.
2 Sam. 16:3 he a. at Jerus.
Ps. 49:12 man in honor, a. not
55:19 even he that a. of old
125:1 Zion, which a. ever
Prov. 15:31 a. among the wise
Ec. 1:4 the earth a. for ever
John 3:36 wrath of God a.
12:34 heard Christ a.
15:5 he that a. in me bringeth
1 Tim. 2:13 yet he a. faithful
Heb. 7:3 Melchizedek a. a priest
1 Pet. 1:23 word of God which a.
1 John 2:6 he that a. in him ought
14 the word of God a. in you
17 doeth will of God a. for ever
27 the anointing a. in you
3:6 whosoever a. in him
3:14 loveth not brother a. in
24 ye know that he a. in us
2 John 9 whoso a. not in the
ABIDING.
1 Sam. 26:19 from a. in inherit.
1 Chr. 29:15 here is done a.
Luke 2:8 shepherds a. in the field
John 5:38 his word a. in you
1 John 3:15 no murderer hath life a.
ABIEZER.
Jos. 17:2 for children of A.
Jud. 8:2 not A. was gathered?
8:2 better than the vintage of A.
2 Sam. 23:27 A. one of David's
ABI-EZRITE. Jud. 6:11

ABL
ABIGAIL.
1 Sam. 25:3 Nabal's wife A.
27:3 dwelt at Gath with Ahi and A. 30:5; 2 Sam. 2:2
1 Chr. 2:16 sist. Zeruiah and A.
ABIJAH.
2 Chr. 11:18 Rehoboam took A.
Est. 2:15 daughter of A. 9:29
ABIHU.
Ex. 6:23 Aaron's sons Nadab and A. 28:1; Lev. 10:1; Num. 3:2; 26:60; 1 Chr. 6:3; 24:1
24:1 come up A. 9 A. went up
Num. 3:4 A. died bef. Lord, 26:61
ABIJAH, ABIJAM.
1 K. 14:1 A. son of Jero.
31 A. son of Reho. 15:1, 7
1 Chr. 2:10 eighth lot came to A.
1 Chr. 29:1 mother's name A.
ABILITY.
Ezr. 2:69 gave after their a.
Neh. 5:8 after our a. redeemed
Dan. 1:4 had a. to stand in pal.
Mat. 25:15 each accord. to his a.
Acts 11:29 according to a. to send
1 Pet. 4:11 as of the a. God giv.
ABIMELECH.
Gen. 20:2 A. king of Gerar sent
21:22 A. and Phichol spake
26:1 Isaac went unto A.
Jud. 8:31 Gideon's con. bare A.
2 Sam. 11:21 smote A. son of Jer.
1 Chr. 18:16 Zadok and A.
ABINADAB.
1 Sam. 7:1 into the house of A.
16:8 Jesse called A. made him
1 Sam. 6:3 out of house of A.
1 Chr. 13:7
1 K. 4:11 A. had Sol. daughter
ABINOAM. Jud. 4:6; 5:1
ABIRAM.
Num. 16:1 Dathan and A. 26:9
12 sent to call Dath. and A.
K. 16:31 laid founda. in A.
Ps. 106:17 company of A.
ABISHAG. 1 K. 1:15; 2:22
ABSALOM.
2 Sam. 2:6 A. said, I will up
2 Sam. 2:18 three sons, Joab, A. and Asahel, 1 Chr. 2:16
23:18 A. was chief, 1 Chr. 11:20
Luke 18:12 A. view of Edomites
ABIUD. Mat. 1:13
ABJECTS.
Ps. 35:15 the a. gathered
ABLE.
Ex. 18:21 provide a. men
Num. 1:3 a. to go to war, 26:2
13:30 well a. to overcome it
Deut. 16:17 man give as he is a.

CRUDEN'S CONCORDANCE.

ABO

Jos. 23:9 man been a. to stand
1 Sam. 6:20 who a. to stand
1 K. 3:9 who is a. to judge
2 Chr. 2:6 who is a. to build
20:6 none is a. to withstand thee
25:9 Lord is a. to give
Job 41:10 who a. to stand
Prov. 27:4 who a. to stand bef.
Dan. 3:17 our God is a. to deliv.
6:20 God is a. to deliver from
Mat. 3:9 God is a. of these stones
to raise up, Luke 3:8
9:28 believe ye I am a. to do
19:12 he that is a. to receive it
20:22 are ye a. to drink
22:46 no man was a. to answer
Mark 4:33 as they were a. to hear
John 10:29 no man is a. to pluck
Acts 15:10 yoke fathers nor we a.
20:32 word of grace, a. to build
Rom. 4:21 he was a. to perform
11:23 for God is a. to graff them
14:4 God is a. to make him
15:14 ye are a. also to admonish
1 Cor. 3:2 ye were not a. nor yet
10:13 above that ye are a.
2 Cor. 3:6 made us a. ministers of
9:8 God is a. to make all grace
Eph. 3:20 that is a. to do
Phil. 3:21 he is a. to subdue all
2 Tim. 1:12 he is a. to keep that 1
3:7 never a. to come to the know.
15 scriptures a. to make wise.
Heb. 2:18 he is a. to succor them
5:7 to him that was a. to save
7:25 is a. to save to uttermost
11:19 that God was a. to raise
Jam. 1:21 which is a. to save
3:2 a. to bridle the whole body
4:12 one lawgiver a. to save and
Jude 24 to him that is a. to keep
Rev. 5:3 no man was a. to open
13:4 who is a. to make war with
13:16 no man was a. to enter

Be ABLE.
Jos. 1:5 any man be a. to stand
Deut. 7:24 no man be a. to. 11:25
2 Chr. 32:14 should be a. to deliv.
Is. 47:12 thou shalt be a. to profit
Ezek. 33:12 righteous be a. to live
Luke 14:31 be be a. with 10,000
Rom. 8:39 be a. to separate us
1 Cor. 10:13 may be a. to bear
Eph. 3:18 be a. to comprehend
6:11 that ye may be a. to stand
16 ye shall be a. to quench
2 Tim. 2:2 who shall be a. to
Tit. 1:9 may be a. by sound
2 Pet. 1:15 be a. after my decease
Rev. 6:17 who shall be a. to stand

Not be ABLE.
2 K. 18:20 n. be a. to de. Is. 36:14
Ps. 3:1:12 shall not be a. to rise
Ec. 8:17 yet not be a. to find it
Je. 11:11 shall not be a. to put
Jer. 11:11 to escape; 49:10 to hide
Ezek. 7:19 gold shall not be a. to
Luke 13:24 seek, n. be a.; 21:15 to

Not ABLE.
Num. 13:31 we be not a. to go up
14:16 Lord was n. a. Deut. 9:28
Ezr. 10:13 we are not a. to stand
Neh. 4:10 we are not a. to build
Ps. 18:38 wounded not a. to rise
21:11 are not a. to perform
40:12 I am not a. to look up
Amos 7:10 land is not a. to bear
Luke 12:26 not a. to do that is t.
14:29 laid found, and not a. to
John 21:6 not a. to draw for the f.
Acts 6:10 not a. to resist the w.

ABNER.
1 Sam. 14:51 Ner father of A.
17:55 said to A., whose son ?
26:7 but A. and the people lay
14 cried answer thou not A.
2 Sam. 2:14 A. said, let your men
2:23 A. the s. of Ner. 30,32,33,37
4:1 Saul's son heard A. was d.
12 Ish-bosheth in A. sepul.
1 K. 2:5 what Joab did in A.
1 Chr. 26:28 all that A. dedicated
27:21 Jaasiel son of A. rul. of B.

ABOARD.
Acts 21:2 went a. and set forth

ABODE, Substantive.
2 K. 19:27 I know thy a. Is. 37:28
John 14:23 come and make our a.

ABODE, Verb.
Gen. 29:14 Jacob a. with him
49:24 but his bow a. in strength
Ex. 24:16 glory of God a. on Si.
Num. 9:17 cloud a. 18
20 they a. in their tents, 22
11:35 the people a. at Hazeroth

ABO

Num. 20:1 the p. a. Jud. 11:17
22:8 princes of Moab, a. with B.
Deut. 1:46 so ye a. in Kadesh
3:29 we a. in the valley
9:9 I a. in the mount
Jos. 8:9 they a. in their places
8:9 they a. between Bethel
Jud. 5:17 Gilead a. beyond Jor.
Asher a. in his breaches
19:4 Levite a. with him 3 days
20:47 and A. in the rock Rim.
1 Sam. 1:23 the woman a. and g.
7:2 while the ark a. in Kirjath
13:16 Saul and Jona. a. in Gib.
22:6 Saul a.; 22:14.Dav.a.25;26:3
23:18 a. in wood; 2 Sam. 1:1 Zik.
2 Sam. 14:19 Uriah a. in Jerusa.
15:8 vowed while I a. at
1 K. 17:19 a loft where he a.
Mat. 17:22 while they a. in Gal.
Luke 1:56 Mary a. with her a.
8:27 nor a. in any house, but
John 1:32 Spirit and it a. on him
39 they came and a. with him
7:9 he a. in Galilee
8:44 murderer and a. not in t.
11:6 he a. two days still
Acts 1:13 room where a. Peter
14:3 long time a. they speaking
18:3 Paul a. with them and w.
21:7 came and a. with brethren
8 one of Philip and a. with
Gal. 1:18 and a. with Peter

ABODE there, or there ABODE.
Jud. 21:2 people a. there till e.
Ezr. 8:15 there a. we in tents
John 4:40 Jesus a. there two d.
10:40 John bapt. and there a.
Acts 14:28 there they a. long t.
17:14 Silas and Tim. a. there

ABODEST.
Jud. 5:16 why a. among the sh.

ABOLISH.
Is. 2:18 idols he shall utterly a.

ABOLISHED.
Is. 51:6 right shall not be a.
6:6 your works may be a.
2 Cor. 3:13 that which is a.
Eph. 2:15 having a. in his flesh
2 Tim. 1:10 C. who hath a. death

ABOMINABLE.
Lev. 7:21 touch any a. thing
11:43 make yourselves a. with
18:30 commit not these a. cus.
19:7 on the third day, it is a.
20:25 make souls a. by beast
Deut. 14:3 eat any a. thing
1 Chr. 21:6 king's word was a. to
2 Chr. 15:8 put away a. idols
Job. 15:16 much more a. is man
Ps. 14:1 have done a. works
53:1 have done a. iniquity
Is. 14:19 like an a. branch
65:4 broth of a. things is in
Jer. 16:18 carcases of their a.
44:4 this a. thing I hate
Ezek. 4:14 came a. flesh into my
8:10 and behold a. beasts
16:52 sins committed more a.
Mic. 6:10 scant measure that is a.
Tit. 1:16 deny him being a.
1 Pet. 4:3 walked in a. idolatries
Rev. 21:8 unbelieving and the a.

ABOMINABLY.
1 K. 21:26 Ahab did very a.

ABOMINATION.
Gen. 43:32 is an a. to Egyptians
46:34 shepherds is a. to Egyp.
Ex. 8:26 sacrifice the a. of Egyp.
Lev. 7:18 be an a. to you, 19:22,23
11:10 be an a. to you, 12, 20, 23
18:22 womankind it is an a.
Deut. 7:25 it is a. to the Ld. 17:1
26 bring an a. into thy house
12:31 every a. they have done
13:14 such d. is wrought, 17:4
18:12 that do these are a. 22:5
23:18 these are an a. to God
24:4 is an a. before the Lord
25:16 that do unright. are a.
27:15 that maketh a. to Lord
1 K. 11:5 Milcom the a. of Am.
7 Chemosh the a. of Moab
Pr. 3:32 froward is an a.
6:16 seven things are an a.
8:17 wickedness is an a. to Lord
20 froward heart are a.
11:20 lying lips are a. to
13:19 a. to fools to depart

ABO

Prov. 15:8 sacrifi. of w. is a. 21:27
9 of the wicked is an a.
26 of wicked are a. to L.
16:5 one proud in heart is a.
12 a. to kings to commit
17:15 both are an a. to the Lord
20:10 both of them are alike a.
23 weights are an a. to Lord
24:9 the scorner is an a. to men
28:9 even his prayer shall be a.
29:27 unjust man is a. to just,
upright in the way a. to
Is. 1:13 incense is an a. to me
41:24 an a. is he that
44:19 residue thereof an a. f
66:17 eating swine's flesh an a.
Jer. 2:7 my heritage an a.
6:15 they committed a. 8:12
32:35 that they should do this a.
Ezek. 16:50 and committed a.
18:12 to idols and committed a.
22:11 a. with neighbour's wife
33:26 and ye work a.
Dan. 11:31 a. that maketh
12:11 a. that maketh desolate
Mal. 2:11 an a. is committed
Mat. 24:15 a. of desol. Mar. 13:14
Luke 16:15 a. with God
Rev. 21:27 enter that worketh a.

ABOMINATIONS.
Deut. 18:9 not learn to do after a.
32:16 with a. provoked they him
1 K. 14:24 did all a. of nations
2 K. 21:2 a. of heathen, 2 Chr. 33:2.
23:24 a. Jos. put away, 2 Chr. 34:2
2 Chr. 36:8 Jehoiakim and his a.
14 transgressed after all a.
Prov. 26:25 seven a. in his heart
Jer. 44:22 L. could not bear for a.
Ezek. 6:11 alas for all the evil a.
8:6 shalt see greater a. 13, 15
9 wicked a. that they do here
17 light thing to commit a.
9:4 that sigh and cry for the a.
11:18 take away all a. thereof
14:6 your faces from your a.
16:2 Jerusa. to know her a.
18:24 when righteous doth a.
20:4 the a. of their fathers
7 cast ye away a. of eyes
22:2 show her all her a.
36:31 loathe yourselves for a.
44:6 O Israel, let it suffice of a.
Dan. 9:27 overspreading of a.
Rev. 17:4 golden cup full of a.
5 harlots and of a. of earth

Their ABOMINATIONS.
Deut. 20:18 t. a. which have
Is. 66:3 delighteth in their a.
Jer. 7:30 set t. a. in the, 32:34
16:18 recompense t. a. 18:18
Ezek. 11:21 walketh after t. a.
12:16 declare all t. a.
20:8 none did cast away t. a.
33:36 declare to the other t. a.
33:29 desolate because of t. a.
43:8 holy name by t. a.
44:13 bear their shame and t. a.
2 K. 4:3 borrow thee vessels a.
2 Chr. 31:5 as com. came a.
15:25 wandereth a. for bread
Job 18:16 goeth a. tolleth it
Prov. 5:16 be dispersed a.
Is. 24:24 spreadeth a. the earth
Jer. 6:11 on children a.
Lam. 1:20 a. the sword
Mark 1:45 blaze a. the matter
4:22 it should come a.
Luke 1:65 sayings were noised a.
9:17 a. the saying about
Acts 2:6 noised a. the multitude
Rom. 7:3 love of God shed a. in
16:19 your obedience is come a.
See CAST, SPREAD, STAND, SCAT-
TER, WENT.

ABSENCE.
Luke 22:6 betray him in a. of
Phil. 2:12 much more in my a.

ABSENT.
Gen. 31:49 we are a. one from
1 Cor. 5:3 verily as a. in body
2 Cor. 5:6 at home in body are a.
8 willing to be a. from body
9 present or a. accepted
10:1 being a. am bold
11 by letters when a. such
13:2 being a. now I write, 10
Phil. 1:27 I come, or else a.
Col. 2:5 I be a. in the flesh

ABSTAIN.
Acts 15:20 a. from pollutions
29 that ye a. from meats
1 Thes. 4:3 a. from fornication

ABS
ABOVE all gods. See GODS.
ABOVE heaven. See HEAVEN.
Stood ABOVE. See STOOD.

ABOUND.
Prov. 28:20 faithful a. with
Mat. 24:12 iniquity shall a.
Rom. 5:20 the offence might a.
6:1 in sin, that grace may a. ?
15:13 that ye may a. in hope
2 Cor. 1:5 as sufferings a. so
8:7 as ye a. in every thing, see
9:8 make all grace a. to you
Phil. 1:9 love may a. more
4:12 I know how to a. both to a.
17 may a. to your account
18 I have all and a. I am full
1 Thes. 3:12 make you to a. in love
4:1 would a. more and more
2 Pet. 1:8 things be in you and a.

ABOUNDED, ETC., ING.
Prov. 8:24 no fount. a. with
29:22 furious man a. in
Rom. 3:7 of God hath more a.
5:15 grace by J. C. hath a. to
20 sin a. grace did more a.
1 Cor. 15:58 always a. in the
2 Cor. 8:2 poverty a. to riches
Eph. 1:8 he hath a. toward
Col. 2:7 a. therein with thanksg.
2 Thes. 1:3 charity to ea. other a.

ABOUT.
John 7:19 go yet a. to kill me ?
See GONE, ROUND, STOOD, TIME,
WENT.

ABRAHAM with father.
Gen. 26:3 the oath to A. thy f.
24 God of A. thy f. 28:13
82:9 G. of f. A. and God of
20:4:3 took f. A. from
Is. 51:2 look to A. your f.
Mat. 3:9 A. to our f.; Luke 3:8
Luke 1:73 he sware to f. A.
16:24 f. A. have mercy on me
30 nay, f. A. but if one from
John 8:30, 53 our f.
53 greater than f. A. ?
56 f. A. rejoiced to see
Acts 7:2 appeared to f. A.
Rom. 4:1 that A. our f. hath
12 in the steps of faith of f. A.
16 of A. who is f. of us all
Jam. 2:21 A. our f. justified by

ABRAHAM joined with seed.
2 Chr. 20:7 gavest it to seed of A.
Ps. 105:6 O ye s. of A. his
Is. 41:8 thou Israel. the s. of A.
Jer. 33:26 rulers over s. of A.
John 8:33 A.'s s. never in bond.
37 I k. s. but ye seek to kill me
Rom. 4:13 promise not to A. or s.
9:7 they are the seed of A.
11:1 of the s. of A. 2 Cor. 11:22
Gal. 3:16 to A. and s. prom.
3:29 then A., s. and heirs
Heb. 2:16 on him took he s. of A.

ABROAD.
Ex. 12:46 naught of flesh a.
Lev. 18:9 born a. at home or a.
Jud. 12:9 daughters from a.

CRUDEN'S CONCORDANCE. 753

ACC

Thes. 5:22 *a.* from all appear.
Tim. 4:3 com. to *a.* from meats
Pet. 2:11 *a.* from fleshly lusts

ABSTINENCE.
Acts 27:21 after long *a.* Paul stood

ABUNDANCE.
Deut. 33:19 suck of the *a.* of the
1 *Sam.* 1:16 out of *a.* of my
1 *K.* 18:41 sound of *a.* of rain
2 *Chr.* 1:15 spices great *a.*
Job 22:11 *a.* waters cover, 38:34
Ps. 72:7 shall be *a.* of peace
Ec. 5:10 that loveth *a.* with
12 *a.* of the rich not suffer
Is. 15:7 the *a.* they have gotten
47:9 *a.* of thy enchantments
60:5 the *a.* of the sea
66:11 with the *a.* of her glory
Jer. 33:6 reveal *a.* of peace
Ezek. 16:49 *a.* of idleness was
Zec. 14:14 apparel in great *a.*
Mat. 12:34 *a.* of heart, *Luke* 6:45
13:12 have more *a.* 25:29
Mark 12:44 of their *a. Luke* 21:4
Rom. 5:17 receive *a.* of grace
2 *Cor.* 8:2 *a.* of their joy
14 your *a.* a supply, their *a.*
12:7 *a.* of the revelations
Rev. 18:3 thro' *a.* of delicacies

In ABUNDANCE.
Ps. 37:11 delight in *a.* of peace
52:7 in the *a.* of his riches
Luke 12:15 consisteth not in *a.*
2 *Cor.* 8:20 blame us in this *a.*

ABUNDANT.
Ex. 34:6 God *a.* in goodness
Is. 56:12 this day and more *a.*
1 *Cor.* 12:23 bestow more *a.* hon.
24 more *a.* honor to that part
1 *Cor.* 4:15 *a.* grace might
7:15 inward affection is more *a.*
9:12 the administration is *a.*
11:23 labors more *a.* in stripes
Phil. 1:26 rejoicing be more *a.*
1 *Tim.* 1:14 was exceeding *a.*
1 *Pet.* 1:3 his *a.* mercy

ABUNDANTLY.
Gen. 1:20 waters bring forth *a.* 21
8:17 that they may breed *a.*
9:7 multiply, bring forth *a.*
Ex. 1:7 Israel increased *a.*
Num. 20:11 water came out *a.*
1 *Chr.* 22:5 so David prepared *a.*
8 thou hast shed blood *a.*
Job 12:6 whose hand O. bring *a.*
36:28 distil upon man *a.*
Ps. 36:8 *a.* satisfied with fatness
65:10 thou waterest the ridges *a.*
132:15 I will *a.* bless her
145:7 shall *a.* utter the memory
Cant. 5:1 yea drink *a.* O beloved
Is. 15:3 shall howl, weeping *a.*
35:2 blossom *a.* and rejoice
55:7 for he will *a.* pardon
John 10:10 have life more *a.*
1 *Cor.* 15:10 I labored more *a.*
2 *Cor.* 1:12 and more *a.* to you
2:4 love I have more *a.* to you
10:15 according to our rule *a.*
12:15 though the more *a.* I love
Eph. 3:20 able to do exceeding *a.*
1 *Thes.* 2:17 more *a.* to see your
Tit. 3:6 he shed *a.* through
Heb. 6:17 God willing more *a.* to
2 *Pet.* 1:11 be ministered *a.*

ABUSE, ED.
Jud. 19:25 *a.* her all the night
1 *Sam.* 31:4 lest uncircum. *a.* me
1 *Chr.* 10:4
1 *Cor.* 9:18 I *a.* not my power

ABUSERS, ING.
1 *Cor.* 6:9 nor *a.* of themselves
7:31 use this world as not *a.* it

ACCEPT.
Deut. 33:11 and *a.* the work
1 *Sam.* 26:19 him *a.* an offering
2 *Sam.* 24:23 the L. thy God *a.*
Job 13:8 will ye *a.* his person?
10 if ye do secretly *a.* persons
32:21 not *a.* any man's per.
42:8 shall pray, him will I *a.*
Ps. 20:3 and *a.* thy burnt-sac.
82:2 *a.* the persons of the wick.
119:108 *a.* freewill-offerings
Prov. 18:5 not good to *a.* the
Jer. 14:10 Lord doth not *a.* them
12 not *a.* them, *Amos* 5:22
Ezek. 20:40 there will I *a.* them
41 will *a.* you with sweet savor
43:27 and I will *a.* you, saith L.
Mal. 1:8 pleased, or *a.* thy
10 nor will I *a.* an offering
13 should I *a.* this of your h.?
Acts 24:3 we *a.* it always, and

ACC

ACCEPTABLE.
Deut. 33:24 be *a.* to his brethren
Ps. 19:14 med. of my heart be *a.*
69:13 my prayer is in an *a.* time
Prov. 10:32 know what is *a.*
21:3 to do justice is more *a.*
Ec. 12:10 sought *a.* words
Is. 49:8 in an *a.* time have I
58:5 call this an *a.* day
61:2 to proclaim the *a.* yr. of L.
Jer. 6:20 burnt-offerings are n. *a.*
Dan. 4:27 let my counsel be *a.*
Luke 4:19 to preach the *a.* year
Rom. 12:1 holy, *a.* to God
2 that good and *a.* will of God
14:18 is *a.* to God and approved
15:16 of Gentiles might be *a.*
Eph. 5:10 proving what is *a.* unto
Phil. 4:18 sac. *a.* well-pleasing
1 *Tim.* 2:3 *a.* in the sight of God
5:4 good and *a.* before God
1 *Pet.* 2:5 sacrifices *a.* to God
20 this is *a.* with God

ACCEPTABLY.
Heb. 12:28 we may serve God *a.*

ACCEPTANCE.
Is. 60:7 with *a.* on mine altar

ACCEPTATION.
1 *Tim.* 1:15 worthy of all *a.* 4:9

ACCEPTED.
Gen. 4:7 shalt thou not be *a.*
19:21 I have *a.* thee concerning
Ex. 28:38 may be *a.* before
Lev. 1:4 offering shall be *a.* 22:27
7:18 not be *a.* 19:7; 22:23, 25
10:19 should it have been *a.* in
22:21 offering perfect, to be *a.*
1 *Sam.* 18:5 he was *a.* in the sight
25:35 see I have *a.* thy person
Est. 10:3 *a.* of his brethren
Job 42:9 the Lord also *a.* Job
Is. 56:7 their sacrifice shall be *a.*
Jer. 37:20 let our supplication be *a.*
42:2 let our supplication be *a.*
Luke 4:24 no prophet is *a.* in his
Acts 10:35 righteousness is *a.*
Rom. 15:31 service may be *a.*
2 *Cor.* 5:9 or pres. we may be *a.*
6:2 in a time *a.* now is *a.* time
8:12 *a.* according to that a man
17 indeed he a. the exhortation
11:4 gospel which ye have not *a.*
Eph. 1:6 us *a.* in the Beloved

ACCEPTEST.
Luke 20:21 neither *a.* thou

ACCEPTETH.
Job 34:19 *a.* not persons of prin.
Ec. 9:7 for God now *a.* thy works
Hos. 8:13 Lord *a.* them not
Gal. 2:6 God *a.* no man's person
ACCEPTING. See DELIVERANCE

ACCESS.
Rom. 5:2 also we have *a.*
Eph. 2:18 have *a.* to the Father
3:12 boldness and *a.* by faith
ACCHO, *Jud.* 1:31
ACCOMPANY. See SALVATION.

ACCOMPANIED.
Acts 10:23 breth. from Joppa *a.*
11:12 these six brethren *a.* me
20:4 Sopater *a.* Paul into Asia
38 and they *a.* him to the ship
ACCOMPANYING. See ARK of God.

ACCOMPLISH.
Job 14:6 shall *a.* as hireling
Ps. 64:6 they *a.* a diligent
Is. 55:11 it shall *a.* that I please
Jer. 44:25 surely *a.* your vows
Ezek. 6:12 will I *a.* my fury
7:8 will I *a.* mine anger on thee
13:15 *a.* my wrath on the wall
20:8 fury to *a. a.* anger, 21
Dan. 9:2 he would *a.* 70 years
Luke 9:31 should *a.* at Jerusalem

ACCOMPLISHED.
Est. 2:12 da. of purif. *a. Luke* 2:22
Job 15:32 shall be *a.* before
Prov. 13:19 desire *a.* is sweet
Is. 40:2 her warfare is *a.*
Jer. 25:12 70 years are *a.* 29:10
39:16 my words shall be *a.*
Lam. 4:11 Lord hath *a.* his fury
22 punishment of thine iniq. is *a.*
Ezek. 5:13 shall mine anger be *a.*
Dan. 11:36 indignation be *a.*
12:7 *a.* to scatter the power
Luke 1:23 hi. minis. were *a.*
2:6 the days were *a.* that she
21 when eight days were *a.*
12:50 am I straitened till it be *a.*
18:31 concerning Son shall be *a.*
22:37 must yet be *a.* in me

ACC

John 19:28 things were now *a.*
Acts 21:5 had *a.* those days
Pet. 5:9 same afflictions are *a.*
ACCOMPLISHING. See SERVICE.

ACCOMPLISHMENT.
Acts 21:26 *a.* of days of purifica.

ACCORD.
Lev. 25:5 groweth of its own *a.*
Acts 1:14 with one *a.* in prayer
2:1 all with one *a.* in one place
46 daily with one *a.* in temple
4:24 voice to God with one *a.*
5:12 one *a.* in Solomon's porch
7:57 upon Stephen with one *a.*
8:6 with one *a.* gave heed
12:10 opened of his own *a.*
20 but they came with one *a.*
15:25 assembled with one *a.*
18:12 with one *a.* made insur.
19:29 one *a.* into the theatre
2 *Cor.* 8:17 forward of his own *a.*
Phil. 2:2 of one *a.* of one mind

ACCORDING.
Ps. 7:8 judge *a.* to my righteous.
17 praise *a.* to his righteous.
35:7 *a.* to thy mercy remember.
51:1; 106:45; 108:26; 119:124
28:4 give them *a.* to their deeds
33:22 *a.* as we hope in thee
35:24 judge *a.* to thy right.
48:10 *a.* to thy name, so
62:12 to every man *a.* to his
work, *Prov.* 24:12, 29
79:11 *a.* to greatness of
90:11 *a.* to thy fear, so is
103:10 rewarded us *a.* to iniq.
119:25 *a.* to thy word, 28, 41, 58, 65,
76, 107, 116, 154, 169, 170
159 *a.* to thy kindness, *Is.* 63:7
150:2 praise him *a.* to his
Ps. 8:30 speak not *a.* to this
ACCORDING to all. See ALL.
ACCORDING to that.
2 *Cor.* 8:12 *a.* to that a man hath
ACCORDINGLY. See REPAY.

ACCOUNT, Substantive.
Job 33:13 giveth not *a.* of his
2 *K.* 12:4 money of *a.* of ev. man
makest *a.* of him
Ec. 7:27 to find the *a.*
Dan. 6:2 princes might give *a.*
Mat. 14:36 give *a.* thereof
18:23 take *a.* of his servants
Luke 16:2 an *a.* of stewardship
Acts 19:40 give an *a.* of this
Rom. 14:12 *a.* of himself
Phil. 4:17 abound to your *a.*
Phile. 18 put that to mine *a.*
Heb. 13:17 that must give *a.*
1 *Pet.* 4:5 *a.* to him that judgeth

ACCOUNT, ED, ING.
1 *K.* 1:21 shall be *a.* offenders
10:21 silver noth. *a.* of, 2 *Chr.* 9:20
Ps. 22:30 a. for a generation
Is. 2:22 is he to be *a.* of *a.?*
Mark 10:42 *a.* to rule over
Luke 20:35 be *a.* worthy
22:24 should be *a.* greatest
Rom. 8:36 we are *a.* as sheep
1 *Cor.* 4:1 man so *a.* of us
Gal. 3:6 *a.* to him for right.
Heb. 11:19 *a.* that God was able
2 *Pet.* 3:15 *a.* that the long-suff.

ACCURSED.
Deut. 21:23 hanged is *a.* of G.
Jos. 6:17 shall be *a.* it and
18 keep from *a.* thing
7:1 trespass in the *a.* thing
11 taken of the *a.* thing
12 because they were *a.*
destroy the *a.* from
13 there is an *a.* thing in
15 that is taken with *a.* thing
22:20 trespass in *a.* thing
Is. 65:20 100 years old shall be *a.*
Rom. 9:3 could wish myself *a.*
1 *Cor.* 12:3 spirit calleth Jesus *a.*
Gal. 1:8 gospel, let him be *a.* 9

ACCUSATION.
Ezr. 4:6 *a.* against Judah
Mat. 27:37 set over his head *a.*
Mark 15:26 *a.* was of, *Luke* 23:38
Luke 6:7 find an *a.* against him
John 18:29 what *a.* bring ye
Acts 25:18 they brought no *a.*
1 *Tim.* 5:19 receive not an *a.*
2 *Pet.* 2:11 being not a railing *a.*
Jude 9 durst not bring a railing *a.*

ACCUSE.
Prov. 30:10 *a.* not a servant to

ACQ

Mat. 12:10 might *a.* him; *Mar.* 3:2; *Luke* 11:54
Luke 3:14 nor *a.* any falsely
23:2 and they began to *a.* him
14 things whereof ye *a.* him
John 5:45 that I will *a.* you to F.
8:6 might have to *a.* him
Acts 24:2 Tertullus began to *a.*
8 all things whereof we *a.*
13 prove whereof they *a.* me
25:5 with me, and *a.* this man
11 if none, whereof these *a.* me
28:19 aught to *a.* my nation
1 *Pet.* 3:16 falsely *a.* your good

ACCUSED.
Dan. 3:8 Chaldeans *a.* the Jews
6:24 them which had *a.* Daniel
Mat. 27:12 *a.* answered nothing
Mark 15:3 priests *a. Luke* 23:10
Luke 16:1 *a.* that he had wasted
Acts 22:30 certainty wherefore *a.*
23:28 cause whereof they *a.* him
29 perceived to be *a.* of his
25:16 before he which is *a.* have
22 things whereof I am *a.*
Tit. 1:6 not *a.* of riot, or unruly
Rev. 1:10 who *a.* them before
ACCUSER. See CAST DOWN.

ACCUSERS.
John 8:10 those which *a.*
Acts 23:30 com. to his *a.* also
18:14 wine thine *a.* are come
23:35 commanding his *a.* to come
25:16 he have the *a.* face to face
18 against whom, when *a.* stood
2 *Tim.* 3:3 affection, false *a.*
Tit. 2:3 not false *a.* not given to

ACCUSETH, ING.
John 5:45 there is one that *a.* you
Rom. 2:15 thoughts *a.* or exc.
ACCUSTOMED. See DO EVIL.
ACELDAMA. See FIELD.
ACHAIA.
Acts 18:12 Gallio was dep. of A.
27 Apollos to pass into A.
Rom. 15:26 them of A. to make
16:5 Epenetus, first-fruits of A.
1 *Cor.* 16:15 Steph. first-fr. of A.
2 *Cor.* 9:2 A. ready a year ago
11:10 in the regions of A.
1 *Thes.* 1:7 encamples to all in A.
8 sounded not only in A.
ACHAICUS. 1 *Cor.* 16:17
ACHAN, or ACHAR. *Jos.* 7, 22:20; 1 *Chr.* 2:7
ACHIM. *Mat.* 1:14
ACHISH.
1 *Sam.* 21:10 David fled to A. 27:2
12 David was sore afraid of A.
27:9 A. gave him Ziklag
29:2 in the rereward with A.
1 *Kings* 2:40 went to Gath to A.
ACHMETHA. *Ezr.* 6:2
ACHOR.
Jos. 7:26 valley of A. to this
Is. 65:10 valley of A. place for
Hos. 2:15 A. for a door of hope
ACHSAH. *Jos.* 15:16; *Jud.* 1:12
ACHSHAPH.
Jos. 11:1 sent to the king of A.
12:20 king of A. one, 19:25
ACHZIB. *Jos.* 19:29; *Mic.* 1:14
ACKNOWLEDGE, ED.
Deut. 21:17 *a.* son of hated
33:9 nor did he *a.* his brethren
Ps. 32:5 I *a.* my sin unto thee
51:3 I *a.* my transgressions
Prov. 3:6 in all thy ways *a.* him
Is. 33:13 are near, *a.* my might
61:9 all that see shall *a.* them
63:16 Father, tho' Israel *a.* us
64:4 only *a.* thine iniquity
Jer. 3:13 *a.* thine iniquity
14:20 *a.* our wickedness
Dan. 11:39 god, he shall *a.*
Hos. 5:15 they *a.* their offence
Cor. 14:37 let him *a.* the things
16 therefore *a.* to them that
2 *Cor.* 1:13 *a.* unto the end
14 as ye have *a.* us in part

ACKNOWLEDGING, ETH.
2 *Tim.* 2:25 repentance to the *a.*
Tit. 1:1 to the *a.* the truth which
Philem. 6 by the *a.* every good
1 *John* 2:23 he that *a.* the Son

ACKNOWLEDGMENT.
Col. 2:2 to the *a.* of the mystery

ACQUAINT, ED, ING.
Job 22:21 *a.* thyself with him
Ps. 139:3 *a.* with all my ways
Ec. 2:3 *a.* my heart with
Is. 53:3 sorrows, and *a.* with

CRUDEN'S CONCORDANCE.

ADD
ACQUAINTANCE.
2 *K.* 12:5 every man of his *a.*
7 no more money of your *a.*
Job 19:13 mine *a.* are estranged
42:11 all that had been of his *a.*
Ps. 31:11 a reproach to mine *a.*
55:13 mine equal, and mine *a.*
88:8 hast put away mine *a.* far
18 and my *a.* into darkness
Luke 2:44 sought among their *a.*
23:49 all his *a.* stood afar off
Acts 24:23 forbid none of his *a.* to

ACQUIT.
Job 10:14 not *a.* me from mine
Nah. 1:3 L. not at all *a.* wicked

ACRE, S.
1 *Sam.* 14:14 half an *a.* of land
Is. 5:10 ten *a.* of vineyard

ACT.
Is. 28:21 his *a.* his strange *a.*
59:6 and the *a.* of violence
John 8:4 adultery, in the very *a.*

ACTS.
Deut. 11:7 seen the great *a.* of
Jud. 5:11 the righteous *a.*
1 *Sam.* 12:7 all righteous *a.*
2 *Sam.* 23:20 Benaiah who had
done many *a.* 1 *Chr.* 11:22
1 *K.* 10:6 true report of thy *a.*
11:41 the *a.* of Solomon, 2 *Chr.* 9:5
2 *K.* 10:34 the *a.* of Jehu
23:28 the *a.* of Josiah
1 *Chr.* 29:29 the *a.* of David
2 *Chr.* 16:11 the *a.* of Asa
20:34 the *a.* of Jehoshaphat
32:32 *a.* of Hezekiah, 2 *K.* 20:20
Est. 10:2 all the *a.* of his power
Ps. 103:7 his *a.* to the children
106:2 can utter the mighty *a.*
145:4 declare thy mighty *a.* 6:12
150:2 praise him for mighty *a.*

ACTIONS.
1 *Sam.* 2:3 by L. *a.* are weighed

ACTIVITY.
Gen. 47:6 knowest any man of *a.*

ADAM.
Gen. 2:20 A. gave names to all
5:2 and called their name A.
Deut. 32:8 separated sons of A.
Job 31:33 transgressions as A.
Rom. 5:14 death reigned from A.
1 *Cor.* 15:22 for as in A. all die
45 first man A. the last A.
1 *Tim.* 2:13 A. was first formed
14 and A. was not deceived
Jude 14 Enoch the 7th from A.
ADAM. *Jos.* 3:16 the city A.

ADAMANT.
Ezek. 3:9 as an *a.* have I made
Zec. 7:12 heart as an *a.* stone

ADAR.
Ezr. 6:15 finished on 3d day of A.
Est. 3:7 twelfth month A.
13 day of month A. 8:12; 9:1,17
9:15 gathered on 14th day of A.

ADD.
Gen. 30:24 L. shall *a.* to me
Deut. 4:2 not *a.* to, 12:32
29:19 to *a.* drunkenness
1 *K.* 20:6 I *a.* 15 years, *Is.* 38:5
1 *Chr.* 22:14 mayest *a.* thereto
2 *Chr.* 28:13 to *a.* more to sins
Ps. 69:27 *a.* iniquity to iniquity
Prov. 3:2 long life shall they *a.*
30:6 *a.* thou not to his words
Is. 29:1 *a.* ye year to year
30:1 may *a.* sin to sin
Mat. 6:27 can *a.* one cub., *Lu.* 12:25
Phil. 1:16 supposing to *a.* afflict.
1 *Pet.* 1:5 *a.* to your faith virtue
Rev. 22:18 G. shall *a.* to him

ADDED.
Deut. 5:22 and he *a.* no more
1 *Sam.* 12:19 *a.* to all our sins
Jer. 36:32 there were *a.* besides
45:3 Lord hath *a.* grief
Dan. 4:36 majesty was *a.* to me
Mat. 6:33 shall be *a.* to you
Luke 3:20 Herod *a.* yet this
19:11 he *a.* and spake a parable
Acts 2:41 were *a.* 3,000 souls
47 *a.* to the church daily such
5:14 believers were the more *a.*
11:24 people was *a.* to the L.
Gal. 2:6 *a.* nothing to me.
3:19 the law was *a.* because of

ADDER.
Gen. 49:17 Dan shall be an *a.*
Ps. 58:4 the deaf *a.* that stops
91:13 thou shalt tread on the *a.*
140:3 *a.*'s poison is under
Prov. 23:32 stingeth like an *a.*

ADU
ADDETH.
Job 34:37 he *a.* rebellion
Prov. 10:22 he *a.* no sorrow
16:23 wise *a.* learning
Gal. 3:15 disannulleth or *a.*

ADDICTED.
1 *Cor.* 16:15 *a.* themselves

ADJURE, ED.
Jos. 6:26 Joshua *a.* them
1 *Sam.* 14:24 Saul had *a.*
1 *K.* 22:16 how many times shall
I *a.* thee, 2 *Chr.* 18:15
Mat. 26:63 I *a.* thee by the living
Mark 5:7 I *a.* thee by God
Acts 19:13 we *a.* you by Jesus

ADMAH.
Gen. 14:2 Shinab king of A.
Deut. 29:23 the overthrow of A.
Hos. 11:8 make thee as A.

ADMINISTERED.
2 *Cor.* 8:19 *a.* by us to the glory
20 this abundance which is *a.*

ADMINISTRATION, S.
1 *Cor.* 12:5 differences of *a.*
2 *Cor.* 9:12 *a.* of this service

ADMIRATION.
Jude 16 men's persons in *a.*
Rev. 17:6 wondered with great *a.*

ADMIRED.
2 *Thes.* 1:10 to be *a.* in all

ADMONISH, ED.
Ec. 4:13 will no more be *a.*
12:12 by these, my son, be *a.*
Jer. 42:19 certainly I have *a.*
Acts 27:9 Paul *a.* them
Rom. 15:14 to *a.* one another
Col. 3:16 *a.* one another
1 *Thes.* 5:12 over you and *a.* you
2 *Thes.* 3:15 *a.* him as a brother
Heb. 8:5 as Moses was *a.* of God

ADMONITION.
1 *Cor.* 10:11 are written for our *a.*
Eph. 6:4 bring them up in the *a.*
Tit. 3:10 after first and second *a.*

ADO.
Mark 5:39 why make ye this *a.*

ADONI-BEZEK. *Jud.* 1:5

ADONIJAH.
2 *Sam.* 3:4 *a.* son of Haggith
1 *K.* 1:5 A. exalted himself
25 God save king A.
2:21 let Abishag be given to A.
2 *Chr.* 17:8 sent Lev. to teach A.
Neh. 10:16 the people sealed, A.

ADONIKAM. *Ezr.* 2:13; *Neh.* 7:18

ADOPTION.
Rom. 8:15 received the spirit of *a.*
23 waiting for the *a.*
9:4 to whom pertaineth the *a.*
Gal. 4:5 receive the *a.* of sons
Eph. 1:5 predestinated us to *a.*

ADORN, ED, ETH, ING.
Is. 61:10 as a bride *a.* herself
Jer. 31:4 again *a.* with tabrets
Luke 21:5 temple *a.* with goodly
1 *Tim.* 2:9 women *a.* in modest
Tit. 2:10 *a.* the doctrine of God
1 *Pet.* 3:3 whose *a.* not outward *a.*
5 women *a.* themselves
Rev. 21:2 prepared as a bride *a.*

ADRAMMELECH.
2 *K.* 17:31 burnt children to A.
19:37 A. and Sharezer, *Is.* 37:38

ADRAMYTTIUM. *Acts* 27:2

ADRIA. *Acts* 27:27

ADULLAM.
1 *Sam.* 22:1 cave A. 1 *Chr.* 11:15
2 *Sam.* 23:13 came to David to A.
Mic. 1:15 he shall come to A.

ADULTERER, S.
Lev. 20:10 *a.* to death
Job 24:15 the eye of *a.* waiteth
Ps. 50:18 partaker with *a.*
Is. 57:3 seed of *a.* and the whore
Jer. 9:2 for they be all *a.*
23:10 the land is full of *a.*
Hos. 7:4 all *a.* as an oven
7 his *a.* wicked lusts consumed
Luke 18:11 I am not as others, *a.*
1 *Cor.* 6:9 neither *a.* shall inherit
Jam. 4:4 ye *a.* know ye not that

ADULTERESS, ES.
Lev. 20:10 the *a.* put to death
Prov. 6:26 the *a.* will hunt
Ezek. 23:45 judge them as *a.*
Hos. 3:1 a woman yet an *a.*
Rom. 7:3 no *a.* though married

ADV
ADULTEROUS.
Prov. 30:20 the way of *a.* wom.
Mat. 12:39 an *a.* generation, 16:4
Mark 8:38 ashamed in this *a.*

ADULTERY, IES.
Ex. 20:14 thou shalt not com. *a.*
Deut. 5:18; *Mat.* 5:27; 19:18;
Rom. 13:9
Prov. 6:32 commits *a.* lacketh
Jer. 3:8 backsliding Israel com. *a.*
9 committed *a.* with stones
5:7 thou they committed *a.*
7:9 will ye steal and commit *a.*
13:27 I have seen thine *a.*
23:14 they commit *a.* and walk
29:23 they committed *a.*
Ezek. 16:32 a wife that com. *a.*
23:37 with their idols com. *a.*
43 said I to her old in *a.*
Hos. 2:2 *a.* between her breasts
4:2 committing *a.* they break
13 spouses shall commit *a.*
Hos. 4:14 punish when com. *a.*
Mat. 5:28 *a.* in his heart
32 marry her divorced com-
mitteth *a.* 19:9; *Luke* 16:18
15:19 heart proceed *a.* *Mark*
7:21
Mark 10:11 his wife and marry
another com. *a.* *Luke* 16:18
19 not com. *a.* *Lu.* 18:20; *Jas.* 2:11
John 8:3 woman taken in *a.* 4
Rom. 2:22 should not commit *a.*
Jal. 5:19 flesh manifest *a.*
2 *Pet.* 2:14 having eyes full of *a.*

ADVANTAGE, ED, ETH.
Job 35:3 what *a.* will it be
Luke 9:25 a man *a.* if he gain
Rom. 3:1 what *a.* then hath Jew
1 *Cor.* 13:32 what *a.* if the dead
2 *Cor.* 2:11 Satan get an *a.* of us
Jude 16 admiration because of *a.*

ADVENTURE, ED.
Deut. 28:56 not *a.* to set the sole
Jud. 9:17 father *a.* his life far
Acts 19:31 not *a.* into the theatre

ADVERSARY.
Ex. 23:22 be an *a.* to thine *a.*
Num. 22:22 angel *a.* against Bal.
1 *Sam.* 1:6 her *a.* provoked her
29:4 lest in battle he be an *a.*
1 *K.* 5:4 there is neither *a.* nor
11:14 an *a.* to Solomon, 23
25 was an *a.* to Israel
Est. 7:6 *a.* is wicked Haman
Job 31:35 *a.* had written a book
Ps. 74:10 shall *a.* reproach
Is. 50:8 who is mine *a.* let him
Lam. 1:10 the *a.* hath spread out
2:4 with his right hand as an *a.*
4:12 *a.* have entered the gates
Amos 3:11 *a.* be round about
Mat. 5:25 *a.* quickly lest *a.* deliv.
Luke 12:58 goest with thine *a.*
18:3 avenge me of mine *a.*
1 *Tim.* 5:14 give no occas. to *a.*
1 *Pet.* 5:8 your *a.* the devil

ADVERSARIES.
Deut. 32:27 *a.* behave strangely
43 render vengeance to his *a.*
Jos. 5:13 for us, or for our *a.*
1 *Sam.* 2:10 *a.* of L. shall be
Ezr. 4:1 *a.* of Judah heard
Neh. 4:11 *a.* said, they shall not
Ps. 38:20 evil for good are my *a.*
69:19 mine *a.* are all before thee
71:13 that are *a.* to my soul
81:14 my hand against their *a.*
89:42 the right hand of his *a.*
108:4 for my love they are *a.*
20 be the reward of my *a.*
Is. 1:24 I will ease me of my *a.*
9:11 shall set up the *a.* of Rezin
11:13 *a.* of Judah shall be cut off
Is. 63:18 we will repay fury to his *a.*
63:18 our *a.* have trodden down
64:2 name known to thine *a.*
Jer. 30:16 *a.* shall go into cap.
46:10 may avenge him of his *a.*
50:7 their *a.* said, we offend not
Lam. 1:5 her *a.* are the chief
7 *a.* saw her, and did mock
17 his *a.* should be round abt.
2:17 set up the horn of thine *a.*
Mic. 5:9 hand lifted up on *a.*
Nah. 1:2 vengeance on his *a.*
Luke 13:17 *a.* were ashamed
21:15 your *a.* not able to gainsay
1 *Cor.* 16:9 and there are many *a.*
Phil. 1:28 nothing terrified by *a.*
Heb. 10:27 shall devour the *a.*

ADVERSITY, IES.
1 *Sam.* 10:19 saved you of all *a.*

AFF
2 *Sam.* 4:9 my soul out of all *a.*
2 *Chr.* 15:6 vex them with all *a.*
Ps. 10:6 I shall never be in *a.*
31:7 known my soul in *a.*
35:15 in my *a.* they rejoiced
94:13 rest from the days of *a.*
Prov. 17:17 brother born for *a.*
24:10 if thou faint in day of *a.*
Ec. 7:14 day of *a.* consider
Is. 30:20 tho' L. give bread of *a.*
Heb. 13:3 remem. them suffer *a.*

ADVERTISE.
Num. 24:14 I will *a.* thee
Ruth 4:4 I thought to *a.* thee

ADVICE.
Jud. 20:7 your *a.* and counsel
1 *Sam.* 25:33 blessed be thy *a.*
2 *Sam.* 19:43 our *a.* not the first
2 *Chr.* 10:14 after *a.* of young
Prov. 20:18 good *a.* make war
2 *Cor.* 8:10 herein I give my *a.*

ADVISE, ED.
2 *Sam.* 24:13 *a.* and see, 1 *Chr.* 21:12
1 *K.* 12:6 how do ye *a.* that I
Prov. 13:10 well *a.* is wisdom
Acts 27:12 more part *a.* to depart
ADVISEMENT. 1 *Chr.* 12:19

ADVOCATE.
1 *John* 2:1 have an *a.* with the

AFAR, AFAR OFF.
Gen. 37:18 saw Joseph *a. off.*
Ex. 24:1 worship ye *a. off*
Ex. 3:18 noise was heard *a. off*
Neh. 12:43 Jeru. heard *a. off*
Job 36:3 my knowledge from *a.*
25 man may behold it *a. off*
39:29 her eyes behold *a. off*
Ps. 65:5 are *a. off* on the sea
138:6 proud he knoweth *a. off*
139:2 my thoughts *a. off*
Prov. 31:14 bringeth food from *a.*
Is. 23:7 shall carry her *a. off*
66:19 escape to the isles *a. off*
Jer. 23:23 am I not a God *a. off*
30:10 save thee from *a.*
31:10 declare in Isles *a. off*
51:50 remember the Lord *a. off*
Mic. 4:3 strong nations *a. off*
Mat. 26:58 Peter followed *a. off*
Mark 14:54; *Luke* 22:54
27:55 worn. beheld *a. off, Lu.* 15:40
Mark 5:6 he saw Jesus *a. off*
Luke 16:23 seeth Abraham *a. off*
Acts 2:39 promise is to all *a. off*
Eph. 2:17 peace to you *a. off*
Heb. 11:13 seen promises *a. off*
2 *Pet.* 1:9 and cannot see *a. off*
See FAR, STOOD, STOOD.

AFFAIRS.
Ps. 112:5 guide *a.* with discr.
Eph. 6:21 ye may know my *a.*
22 that ye might know our *a.*
Phil. 1:27 I may hear of your *a.*
2 *Tim.* 2:4 entangleth with *a.*

AFFECT, ED, ETH.
Lam. 3:51 eye *a.* my heart
Acts 14:2 their minds evil *a.*
Gal. 4:17 zealously *a.* you
18 good to be zealously *a.*

AFFECTION.
1 *Chr.* 29:3 *a.* to house of God
Rom. 1:31 without natural *a.* 2
Tim. 3:3
2 *Cor.* 7:15 his inward *a.* is more
Col. 3:2 your *a.* on things above
5 mortify inordinate *a.*

AFFECTIONS.
Rom. 1:26 G. gave up to vile *a.*
Gal. 5:24 crucified flesh with *a.*

AFFECTIONATELY.
1 *Thes.* 2:8 *a.* desirous of you
Rom. 12:10 kindly *a.* one to

AFFECTIONED.

AFFINITY.
Ezr. 9:14 join in *a.* with

AFFIRM.
Rom. 3:8 as some *a.* we say
1 *Tim.* 1:7 nor whereof they *a.*
Tit. 3:8 things *a.* constantly

AFFIRMED.
Luke 22:59 hour after another *a.*
Acts 12:15 Rhoda constantly *a.*
25:19 whom Paul *a.* alive

AFFLICT.
Gen. 15:13 shall *a.* them 400 yrs.
31:50 if thou *a.* my daughters
Ex. 1:11 taskmasters to *a.*
22:22 shall not *a.* any widow
Lev. 16:29 shall *a.* your souls, 31;
23:27, 32; *Num.* 29:7
Num. 24:24 ships shall *a.* Ashur
Jud. 16:19 *a.* him, his strength

CRUDEN'S CONCORDANCE.

AFF

2 *Sam.* 7:10 ch'n of wickedness *a.*
1 *K.* 11:39 *a.* seed of David
2 *Chr.* 6:36 turn when thou dost *a.*
1 *K.* 8:35.
Ezr. 8:21 *a.* ours, before God
Job 7:23 Almighty, he *a.*
Ps. 44:2 thou didst *a.* the peo.
55:19 God shall hear and *a.*
119:23 son of wickedness *a.*
:75 they *a.* thy heritage
143:12 all that *a.* my soul
Is. 51 grievously *a.* her
61:33 them that *a.* thee
64:5 for a man to *a.* his soul
64:12 will thou *a.* us very sore?
Lam. 3:33 Lord not *a.* willingly
Amos 5:12 they *a.* the just, they
Nah. 1:12 I will *a.* thee no more
Zep. 8:19 I will undo all that *a.*

AFFLICTED.
Ex. 1:12 more *a.* more grow
2 *Sam.* 22:28 *a.* people wilt save
1 *K.* 2:26 *a.* In all father was *a.*
Job 6:14 to *a.* pity should be
30:11 loosed cord, and *a.* me
34:28 heareth cry of the *a.*
Ps. 18:27 save the *a.* people
22:24 abhorred affliction of *a.*
25:16 I am desolate and *a.*
82:3 do justice to the *a.*
88:7 hast *a.* me with waves
15 I am *a.* and ready to die
90:15 wherein thou hast *a.* us
107:17 fools because of iniq. *a.*
116:10 I was greatly *a.*
119:67 before I was *a.*
71 good that I have been *a.*
75 in faithfulness hast *a.* me
107 am *a.* very much, quicken
129:1 have *a.* me from youth, 2
140:12 L. maintain cause of *a.*
Prov. 15:15 days of the *a.* are evil
22:22 neither oppress *a.* in gate
26:28 lying tongue hateth *a.*
31:5 lest pervert judgment of *a.*
Is. 9:1 lightly *a.* the land
49:13 L. have mercy on his *a.*
51:21 hear now this, thou *a.*
53:4 smitten of God and *a.*
7 and was *a.* yet he opened not
54:11 O thou *a.* tossed with
58:3 have we *a.* our souls
10 if thou satisfy the *a.* soul
60:14 sons of them that *a.* thee
63:9 their affliction he was *a.*
Lam. 1:12 sorrow wherew. L. *a.*
Mic. 4:6 gather her that I have *a.*
Nah. 1:12 *a.* afflict no more
Zep. 3:12 leave an *a.* people
Mat. 24:9 deliver you up to be *a.*
2 *Cor.* 1:6 whether we be *a.* it is
1 *Thes.* 3:10 if she relieved the *a.*
Heb. 11:37 being destitute, *a.*
Jam. 4:9 *a.* and mourn and weep
5:13 is any among you *a.*? let

AFFLICTION.
Gen. 41:52 fruitful in land of *a.*
Ex. 3:17 *a.* of my p. *Acts* 7:34
8:17 out of the *a.* of Egypt
Deut. 16:3 shalt eat bread of *a.*
1 *K.* 22:27; 2 *Chr.* 18:26
28:7 L. heard and looked on *a.*
2 *Sam.* 16:12 L. look on my *a.*
2 *K.* 14:26 Lord saw *a.* of Israel
2 *Chr.* 20:9 cry in *a.* will hear
33:12 Manasseh was in *a.*
Neh. 1:3 remnant are in great *a.*
Job 5:6 *a.* cometh not forth
10:15 confusion see my *a.*
30:16 days of *a.* have taken hold
27 the days of *a.* prevented me
36:8 holden in cords of *a.*
15 delivereth poor in his *a.*
21 chosen rather than *a.*
Ps. 25:18 my *a.* and pain
44:24 and forgettest our *a.*
66:11 laidest *a.* upon our loins
82:9 mourneth by reason of *a.*
108:44 regarded their *a.* when
107:10 bound in *a.* and iron
39 low through *a.* and sorrow
41 setteth poor on high from *a.*
119:50 comfort in my *a.*
92 perished in mine *a.*
153 mine *a.* deliver me
Is. 30:20 L. give water of *a.*
48:10 chosen in furnace of *a.*
63:9 their *a.* he was afflicted
Jer. 16:19 refuge in day of *a.*
30:15 criest thou for thine *a.*
Lam. 1:7 Jerusa. remem'd in *a.*
3:1 that hath seen *a.* by the rod
19 remembering my *a.* and
Hos. 5:15 in *a.* seek me early
Amos 6:6 grieved for *a.* of Jos.
Nah. 1:9 *a.* not rise second time

AFR

Zec. 1:15 helped forward the *a.*
10:11 pass thro' sea with *a.*
Mark 4:17 *a.* ariseth
13:19 shall be *a.* such
Acts 7:11 a dearth and great *a.*
2 *Cor.* 2:4 out of much *a.* I wrote
4:17 light *a.* which is but for
8:2 in a great trial of *a.*
Phil. 1:16 to add *a.* to my
1:14 communicate with in *a.*
1 *Thes.* 1:6 word in much *a.*
3:7 comforted in all our *a.*
Heb. 11:25 rather to suffer *a.*
Jam. 1:27 to visit fatherless in *a.*
5:10 an example of suffering *a.*

AFFLICTIONS.
Ps. 34:19 the *a.* of righteous
132:1 remem'b. David and his *a.*
Acts 7:10 deliver out of all his *a.*
20:23 bonds and *a.* abide me
2 *Cor.* 6:4 approving in *a.*
Col. 1:24 behind of *a.* of Christ
1 *Thes.* 3:3 be moved by these *a.*
2 *Tim.* 1:8 of the *a.* of the gospel
3:11 *a.* which came at Antioch
4:5 watch in all, endure *a.*
Heb. 10:32 great fight of *a.*
33 made a gazing-stock by *a.*
1 *Pet.* 5:9 *a.* accomplished in

AFFRIGHT, ED.
Job 18:20 that went before *a.*
39:22 mocketh at fear and not *a.*
Is. 21:4 fearfulness *a.* me
Mark 16:5 were *a. Luke* 24:37
6 be not *a.* ye seek Jesus
Rev. 11:13 remnant *a.* gave glo.

AFOOT.
Mark 6:33 many ran *a.* thither
Acts 20:13 Paul minding to go *a.*

AFORETIME.
Jer. 30:20 their children as *a.*
Dan. 6:10 he prayed as he did *a.*
Rom. 15:4 things were written *a.*

AFRAID.
Ex. 34:30 were *a.* to come nigh
Lev. 26:6 none make *a. Job* 11:19
Num. 12:8 why not *a.* to speak
1 *Sam.* 4:7 Philistines were *a.*
18:29 yet more *a.* of David
2 *Sam.* 1:14 not *a.* to destroy
22:5 ungodly men made me *a.*
Ps. 18:4.
Neh. 6:9 all made me *a.*
Job 9:28 *a.* of all my sorrows
11:19 none make *a.* thee
13:11 excellency make you *a.*
21 not thy dread make me *a.*
13:24 anguish make him *a.*
18:11 terrors make him *a.*
21:6 when I remember, I am *a.*
23:15 consider, I am *a.* of him
33:7 terror not make thee *a.*
41:25 raiseth hims. mighty *a.*
Ps. 36:3 what time I am *a.*
65:8 dwell are *a.* at thy tokens
77:16 saw thee and were *a.*
83:15 *a.* with thy storm
119:120 *a.* of thy judgments
Is. 17:2 none make them *a. Ezek.*
34:28; *Mic.* 4:4; *Zep.* 3:13.
33:14 sinners in Zion are *a.*
41:5 ends of the earth were *a.*
Jer. 30:10 none make him *a.*
Ezek. 32:26 none made them *a.*
Nah. 2:11.
Dan. 4:5 dream made me *a.*
Jon. 1:5 mariners were *a.*
Mark 5:15 in right mind were *a.*
Luke 8:35.
9:32 and were *a.* to ask him
10:32 as they followed were *a.*
16:8 said any thing, were *a.*
Luke 8:25 being *a.* wondered
Acts 22:26 were all *a.* of Saul
22:3 saw the light and were *a.*
Gal. 4:11 I am *a.* of you lest
1 *Pet.* 3:6 not *a.* with amazem.
2 *Pet.* 2:10 *a.* to speak evil of dig.

Be AFRAID.
Deut. 1:29 nei. be *a.* of them, 31:6
2 *Sam.* 22:46 be *a.* out of close
Ps. 18:45
Job 5:21 not be *a.* of destruction
19:29 be ye *a.* of the sword, for
Ps. 27:1 of whom shall I be *a.*?
Is. 8:12 nor fear ye, nor be *a.*
19:17 shall be *a.* in himself
51:12 shouldest be *a.* of a man
Rom. 13:4 if thou do evil, be *a.*

Not be AFRAID.
Deut. 1:17 not be *a.* of face
7:18 shall not be *a.* of, 20:22
Ps. 3:6 not be *a.* of ten thous.
56:11 not be *a.* what man can do
91:5 not be *a.* for terror by night

AGE

Ps. 112:7 not be *a.* of evil tidings
8 estab'd, he shall not be *a.*
Prov. 3:24 fleet down not be *a.*
Is. 12:2 trust and not be *a.*
31:4 not be *a.* of their voice
Amos 3:6 blown, people not be *a.*
Rom. 13:3 not be *a.* of the power

Be not AFRAID.
Deut. 20:1 be not *a.* of them, *Jos.* 11:6; *Neh.* 4:14; *Jer.* 10:5; *Ezek.* 2:6; *Luke* 12:4
1 *Sam.* 28:13 be not *a.* what saw.
Ps. 49:16 be not *a.* when one is
Prov. 3:25 be not *a.* of sudden
Jer. 1:8 be not *a.* of their faces
Mat. 14:27 it is I, be not *a. Mark* 6:50; *John* 6:20
17:7 Jesus said, Arise, be not *a.*
28:10 be not *a.* go tell brethren
Mark 5:36 ruler, be not *a.* only
Acts 18:9 be not *a.* but speak
1 *Pet.* 3:14 be not *a.* of their

Sore AFRAID.
Num. 22:3 Moab *s. a.* of people
Jos. 9:24 *s. a.* of our lives
1 *Sam.* 17:24 from Goliath *s. a.*
28:20 Saul fell along sore *a.*
31:4 armor-bearer *s. a.* 1 *Chr.* 10:4
Mark 9:6 for they were sore *a.*
Luke 2:9 and they were sore *a.*

Was AFRAID.
Gen. 3:10 thy voice and *w. a.*
Ex. 3:6 Moses *w. a.* to look
Deut. 9:19 I was *a.* of the anger
1 *Sam.* 18:12 was *a.* of David, 15
28:5 saw Philistines, 2 *Sam.* 6:9 David was *a.* of the L.
1 *Chr.* 13:12
Job 3:25 that I was *a.* is come
32:6 I was *a.* and durst not
Dan. 8:17 was *a.* and fell
Hab. 3:2 thy speech and was *a.*
Mat. 2:5 feared me and was *a.*
Mat. 2:22 saw *a.* to go thither
14:30 saw wind boisterous, *w. a.*
25:25 were *a.* and hid thy talent
John 19:8 was the more *a.*
Acts 10:4 Corn'. looked, he *w. a.*

AFRESH.
Heb. 6:6 crucify Son of God *a.*

AFTER.
Jos. 10:14 no day like that *a.* it

AFTER that.
Luke 12:4 *a. t.* have no more that
1 *Cor.* 15:6 *a. t.* was seen of 500

AFTERNOON.
Jud. 19:8 they tarried till *a.*

AFTERWARD, S.
Ps. 73:24 *a.* receive me to glory
Prov. 29:11 keepeth it in till *a.*
Mat. 13:36 shall follow me *a.*
1 *Cor.* 15:23 *a.* that are Christ's
Heb. 12:11 *a.* yieldeth fruit

AGABUS. *Acts* 11:28; 21:10

AGAG.
Num. 24:7 he higher than *A.*
1 *Sam.* 15:9 the people spared *A.*
33 Samuel hewed *A.* in pieces

AGAGITE. See HAMAN.

AGAINST.
Gen. 16:12 hand will be *a.* every
Mat. 10:35 man *a.* his f. *Lu.* 12:53
12:30 he not with me, is *a.* me
Luke 2:34 for a sign spoken *a.*
14:31 cometh *a.* him with 20,000
Acts 19:36 cannot be spoken *a.*
28:22 sect everywh. spoken *a.*

See ANOTHER, GOD, JERUSALEM, ISRAEL, LORD, OVER.

AGAR. Gal. 4:24, 25

AGATE.
Ex. 28:19 third row, *a. 39:12*
Is. 54:12 thy windows of *a.*
Ezek. 27:16 Syria occup. with *a.*

AGE.
Gen. 47:28 *a.* of Jacob 147 years
48:10 eyes of Israel dim for *a.*
Job 5:26 a full *a.* of fifty years
1 *Sam.* 2:33 flower of their *a.*
1 *K.* 14:4 set by reason of *a.*
2 *Chr.* 36:17 that stooped for *a.*
Job 8:26 come to grave in a full *a.*
Job 11:17 inquire of the former *a.*
17:17 thy *a.* clearer than
Ps. 39:5 my *a.* is as nothing
Is. 38:12 my *a.* is departed
Zec. 8:4 with his staff for *a.*
Mark 5:42 *a.* of 12 years. *Luke* 8:42
Luke 2:36 Anna of a great *a.*
3:23 Jesus about 30 years of *a.*
John 9:21 he is of *a.* ask him, 23

AHA

1 *Cor.* 7:36 pass flower of *a.*
Heb. 5:14 strong meat to full *a.*

See OLD, STRICKEN.

AGES.
Eph. 2:7 *a.* to come he might
3:5 other *a.* not made known
21 in church through all *a.*
Col. 1:26 mystery hid from *a.*

AGED.
2 *Sam.* 19:32 Barzillai very *a.*
Job 12:20 the understanding of *a.*
15:10 grey-headed and very *a.*
29:8 the *a.* arose and stood up
32:9 do the *a.* understand
Jer. 6:11 *a.* with him full of days
Tit. 2:2 that the *a.* men be sober
3 the *a.* women he in behavior
Phile. 9 such a one as Paul the *a.*

AGO.
1 *Sam.* 9:20 asses lost 3 days *a.*
1 *K.* 19:25 long *a. Is.* 37:26
Is. 5:11 builded many years *a.*
Mat. 11:21 long *a. Luke* 10:13
Mark 9:21 how long *a.* since this
Acts 10:30 four days *a.* I was
15:7 a good while *a.*
2 Cor. 8:10 be forward a year *a.*
9:2 Achaia was ready a year *a.*
12:2 above fourteen years *a.*

AGONE.
1 *Sam.* 30:13 three days *a.* I fell

AGONY.
Luke 22:44 in an *a.* he prayed

AGREE, ED, ETH.
Amos 3:3 walk except they be *a.*
Mat. 5:25 *a.* with thy adversary
18:19 if two shall *a.* on earth
20:2 had *a.* with labourers
13 not *a.* with me for a penny?
Mark 14:56 witness *a.* not, 59
70 Galilean, and thy speech *a.*
Luke 5:36 out of new, *a.* not
John 9:22 Jews had *a.* already
Acts 5:9 ye have *a.* to tempt
40 and to him they *a.*
15:15 to this *a.* words of proph.
23:20 Jews have *a.* to desire
28:25 *a.* not among themselves
1 *John* 5:8 blood, these *a.* in one
Rev. 17:17 *a.* to give their kingd.

AGREEMENT.
2 *K.* 18:31 *a.* by a pres. *Is.* 36:16
Is. 28:15 with hell are we at *a.*
18 *a.* with hell shall not stand
Dan. 11:6 of north, to make *a.*
2 *Cor.* 6:16 what *a.* hath the

AGRIPPA.
Acts 25:13 A. and Bernice came
24 A. said, I would also hear
26:7 which hope's sake, king A.
28 A. said, almost thou per.

AGROUND.
Acts 27:41 they ran the ship *a.*

AGUE.
Lev. 26:16 appoint burning *a.*

AGUR. *Prov.* 30:1

AH.
Ps. 35:25 *a.* so would we have it
Is. 1:4 *a.* sinful nation, a people
24 *a.* I will ease me of
Jer. 1:6 *a.* Lord God, I cannot
4:10 *a.* Lord thou hast
22:18 *a.* brother, *a.* sister, *a.* L.
32:17 *a.* Lord, thou made
34:5 lament thee, saying *a.* L.
Ezek. 9:8 *a.* Lord, wilt thou
Ezek. 15:20 *a.* thou that

AHA.
Ps. 35:21 *a.* our eye hath seen
40:15 that say unto me *a.*
70:3 turned back that say *a. a.*
Is. 44:16 *a.* I am warm, I have
Ezek. 25:3 saidst *a.* against sanc.
26:2 Tyrus said, *a.* she is brok.
36:2 enemy said, *a.* the ancient places

AHAB.
1 *K.* 16:30, 31; 18:6, 9, 42, 46; 20:13; 21:1, 21, 25, 29; 22:20; 2 *K.* 1:1; 3:5; 8:18, 27; 9:7, 8, 25; 10:11; 21:3, 13
2 *Chr.* 21:13 whored. of ho. of A.
Jer. 29:21 saith the Lord of A.
22 the L. make thee like A.
Mic. 6:16 works of house of A.

AHASUERUS.
Ezr. 4:6 reign of A. wrote
Est. 1:1 is A. which reigned
Dan. 9:1 of Darius, son of A.

AHAVAH. *Ezr.* 8:15, 21, 31

AHAZ.
2 *K.* 16:2 A. was 20 years

756 CRUDEN'S CONCORDANCE.

ALA
1 Chr. 8:35 Mic. Pithon, A. 9:41
2 Chr. 28:19 Judah low, bec. of A.
Is. 1:1 the vision in days of A.
Hos. 1:1; Mic. 1:1.
7:3 go forth to meet A. 10

AHAZIAH
1 K. 22:40 A. his son, 2 K. 8:24
2 K. 1:2 A. fell through
8:29 A. king of Judah, went
10:13 the brethren of A.
2 Chr.; 22:35 Jehosh, join with A.
22:7 destruction of A. was of

AHIAH, 1 Sam. 14:3; 1 K. 4:3

AHIJAH
1 K. 11:29; 12:15; 14:2, 4, 6
15:27 Baasha, son of A.
1 Chr. 2:25 sons of Jerahmeel, A.

AHIKAM
2 K. 22:12 Josiah commanded A.
to inquire, 2 Chr. 34:20
25:22 Gedaliah the son of A.
Jer. 26:24 hand of A. was with
40:6 Gedaliah the son of A.
See GEDALIAH.

AHIMAAZ
1 Sam. 14:50 the daughter of A.
2 Sam. 17:17 Jonathan and A.
18:27 is like the running of A.
1 K. 4:15 A. in Naphtali
1 Chr. 6:8 and Zadok begat A.

AHIMAN
Num. 13:22 A. of the children
Jud. 1:10 Judah slew A.
1 Chr. 9:17 and the porters, A.

AHIMELECH
1 Sam. 21:1 A. was afraid at the
22:9 son of Jesse coming to A.
16 thou shalt surely die A.
26:6 David said to A. who
2 Sam. 8:17 Zadok and A. 1 Chr. 18:16
1 Chr. 24:3 A. of the sons of, 6, 31

AHINOAM, 1 Sam. 14:50; 25:43
AHIO, 2 Sam. 6:3; 1 Chr. 13:7
AHISAMACH, Ex. 35:34

AHITHOPHEL
2 Sam. 15:12 Absalom sent for A.
16:15 came to Jerusal. and A.
21 counsel of A. was as if in
17:7 counsel of A. is not good
15 thus did A. counsel, 23
1 Chr. 27:33 A. was the king's

AHITUB
1 Sam. 22:12 thou son of A.
2 Sam. 8:17 Zadok the son of A.
1 Chr. 18:16

AHOLAH, AHOLIBAH
Ezek. 23:4 Samaria is A., Jerus. A.
36 wilt thou judge A. and A.?
AHOLIAB, Ex. 36:1
AHOLIBAMAH, Gen. 36:2, 5

AI, or HAI
Gen. 13:3 betw. Beth-el and A.
Jos. 7:1 before the men of A.
8:1 up to A. 10:2 greater than A.
Ezr. 2:28 the men of Beth-el and
A. Neh. 7:32
Jer. 49:5 howl, O Heshbon, for A.
AIATH, Is. 10:28

AILED, ETH
Gen. 21:17 what a. thee, Hagar?
1 Sam. 11:5 what a. the people
2 Sam. 14:5 the king said unto
her, what a. thee? 2 K. 6:28
Ps. 114:5 what a. thee, O sea
Is. 22:1 what a. thee now that

AIR
2 Sam. 21:10 birds of the a.
Job 41:16 no a. can come bet.
Prov. 30:19 an eagle in the a.
Ec. 10:20 bird of the a. carry
Mat. 8:20 birds of a. have nests
13:32 birds of thee, lodge in the
Mark 4:34; Luke 9:58
Acts 22:23 threw dust into the a.
1 Cor. 9:26 one that beateth a.
14:9 ye shall speak into the a.
Eph. 2:2 prince of power of the a.
1 Thes. 4:17 meet the L. in the a.
Rev. 9:2 sun and a. were dark
16:17 poured out vial into the a.
See FOWLS.

AJALON, Jos. 10:12

ALARM
Num. 10:5 when ye blow an a. 6
7 blow, but not sound an a.
9 if ye go to war, blow an a.
2 Chr. 13:12 trumpets to cry an a.
Jer. 4:19 O my soul, a. of war
49:2 I will cause an a. of war

ALI
Joel 2:1 an a. in my holy mount.
Zep. 1:16 a. against fenced cities

ALAS
Num. 24:23 a. who shall live
Jud. 6:22 a. ! my brother
2 K. 6:5 a. master, for it was
15 a. master, how shall we do?
Ezek. 6:11 stamp with foot, say a.
Joel 1:15 a. for the day of the L.
Rev. 18:10 a. a. that great, 16,19

ALBEIT
Ezek. 13:7 L. saith, a. I have not
Phile. 19 a. I say not, how thou

ALEXANDER
Mark 15:21 Simon, father of A.
Acts 4:6 Annas, Caiaphas, A.
19:33 they drew A. out of the
1 Tim. 1:20 Hymeneus and A.
2 Tim. 4:14 A. the coppersmith

ALEXANDRIA, ANS
Acts 6:9 of the Libertines and A.
18:24 man, Apollos, born at A.
27:6 centurion found ship of A.

ALIENATE
Ezek. 23:17 her mind was a. from
18 my mind was a. from her as
22 from whom thy mind is a. 28
46:14 not a. first-fruits of land
Eph. 4:18 a. from life of G, thro'
Col. 1:21 that were sometimes a.

ALIKE
1 Sam. 30:24 they shall part a.
Job 21:26 lie down a. in dust
Ps. 33:15 fashion. their hearts a.
139:12 darkn. and light both a.
Prov. 20:10 all things come a. to all
11:6 whe. both shall be a. good
Rom. 14:5 esteemeth ev. day a.

ALIVE
Gen. 7:23 Noah remained a. and
12:12 kill me, and save thee a.
50:20 to save much people a.
Ex. 1:17 men-children a. 18
22 daughter ye shall save a.
22:1 if the theft be found a.
Lev. 10:16 he was angry with
Aaron's sons left a.
Num. 16:33 went down a. into pit
22:33 slain thee, and sav. her a.
31:15 ye saved all the women a.
Deut. 4:4 a. every one this day
5:3 all of us a. here this day
6:24 might pres. us a. this day.
20:16 save a. noth. that breath.
32:30 and I make a. 1 Sam. 2:6
Jos. 8:23 king of A. took they a.
11:10 the Lord hath kept an a.
Jud. 8:19 saved them a. I would
1 Sam. 15:8 he took Agag a.
27:9 left man nor woman a.
2 Sam. 12:18 peace or woe take a.
21:15 Nabob is not a. but dead
2 K. 5:7 G. to kill and make a.?
7:4 if they save us a. we live
10:14 and they took them a.
1 K. 20:18 other 10,000 left a.
Ps. 30:3 L. thou hast kept me a.
Prov. 1:12 swal. a. as the grave
Jer. 49:11 I will preserve a.
Ezek. 13:18 the souls a. that come
19 souls a. that should not live
18:27 he shall save his soul a.
Dan. 5:19 whom would, kept a.
Mark 16:11 heard that he was a.
Luke 15:24 was dead and he a. 32
24:23 angels who said he was a.
Acts 1:3 a. after his passion
9:41 widows, presented her a.
20:12 brought the young man a.
25:19 whom P. affirmed to be a.
Rom. 6:11 a. to God through C.
13 as those a. from the dead
7:9 for I was a. without the law
1 Thes. 4:15 are alive and remain. 17
Rev. 1:18 I am a. forevermore
19:20 cast a. into lake of fire

Keep ALIVE. See KEEP.

Yet ALIVE.
Gen. 43:7 is your father yet a.?

ALL
Gen. 43:27 he get a.? 28 is yet a.
45:26 Joseph is yet a. 28
46:30 See. thou art yet a.
Ex. 4:18 see they be yet a.
Deut. 31:27 I am yet a. with you
2 Sam. 12:18 child yet a. 21, 22
18:14 yet a. in midst of the oak
1 K. 20:32 is yet a.? he is my bro.
Ec. 4:2 than the living yet a.
Ezek. 7:13 sold, although yet a.
Mat. 27:63 said while yet a.

ALL
Gen. 24:56 given a. that he hath
1 Sam. 9:19 tell thee a. in thy h.
30:8 and without fail recover a.
1 K. 20:4 I am thine, and a. I
Neh. 9:6 L. preservest them a.
Job 34:19 they a. are works of his
Ps. 14:3 are a. gone aside, a.
51:19 deliv. him out of them a.
44:17 a. this we come upon us
Prov. 22:2 L. is maker of them a.
Ezek. 20:40 a. of them shall serve
37:24 shall be king to them a.
Dan. 1:19 among a. none like D.
Hos. 5:2 a rebuker of them a.
Mal. 2:10 have we not a. one F.
Mat. 23:8 ye are brethren, a. ye
22:28 for they a. had her
Mark 12:44 a. she had, Lu. 21:4
Luke 4:7 if thou worship me, a.
15:31 son, a. that I have is thine
17:10 when ye have done a. say
John 4:39 told me a. ever I did
13:10 ye are clean, but not a.
17:21 that they a. may be one
Acts 4:33 great grace was on a.
1 Cor. 9:22 a. are yours, ye are
Phil. 4:18 I have a. and abound
2 Tim. 3:11 out of them a. the L.
1 Pet. 3:8 be ye a. of one mind
1 John 2:19 were not a. of us

Above ALL. See ABOVE.

According to ALL.
Gen. 6:22 N. did accor. to a. 7:5
Ex. 31:11 or. Pet. a. commanded
39:31; 39:32, 42; 40:16; Num. 2:34; 8:20; 9:5; 29:40; Deut. 13, 41
Jos. 11:23 took the land ac. to a.
1 K. 8:56 given rest ac. to a. thy
11:37 shall reign ac. to a. thy
22:53 ac. to a. his father had d.
2 K. 23:32; 37; 24:9, 17;
2 Chr. 26:4; 27:2
Neh. 5:19 for good, ac. to a. I h.
Jer. 42:20 ac. to a. L. shall say
42:30 ac. to a. Jehoj. hath done
Eze. 24:24 ac. to a. he hath done

Before ALL.
Gal. 2:14 Peter bef. them a.

For ALL.
Phil. 2:21 for a. seek their own
Heb. 8:11 for a. shall know me
10:10 offering of b. once for a.

In ALL.
Gen. 21:12 in a. Sarah hath said
22 God with thee in a. thou
Deut. 28:9 prosp. in a. that ye do
Ruth 1:30 a. hath dealt bitterly
Eph. 1:23 him that fill. all in a.
Col. 3:11 Christ is all in a.

ALL Night. See NIGHT.

Over ALL.
2 Sam. 3:21 mayest reign over a.
1 Chr. 29:12 thou reignest over a.
Ps. 103:19 kingdom ruleth over a.
Mat. 24:47 ruler over a. Lu. 12:44
John 17:2 giv. him power over a.
Rom. 9:5 over a. God blessed for
10:12 Lord over a. is rich unto

To or Unto ALL.
Ps. 145:9 the Lord is good to a.
Ec. 2:14 one event to a. 9:3, 11
9:2 all things come alike to a.
Is. 26:8 Pharaoh to a. that trust
19:17 Judah shall be unto a.
Luke 12:41 spokest to us, to a.?
Acts 2:39 promise is to a. afar off
4:16 manifest to a. that dwell
Rom. 10:12 rich unto a. that call
10:7 render to a. their dues
1 Tim. 4:16 profit. may app. to a.

Upon ALL.
Rom. 3:22 upon a. them that be.

ALL these.
Gen. 15:10 took to him a. these

ALM
Gen. 42:36 a. these are against me
Ex. 19:1 G. spake a. these words
Job 12:9 know, not that in a. t.
Hab. 2:6 shall not a. t. take up
Mat. 6:33 a. t. shall be, Lu. 12:31

ALL this.
Gen. 41:39 God showed thee a. t.
Deut. 32:27 hath not done a. this
Jud. 6:13 a. this befallen us
1 Sam. 22:15 k. nothing of a. t.
2 Sam. 14; 19 of Joab in a. this?
Job 1:22 a. t. J. sinned not. 2:10
13:1 mine eye hath seen a. this
Ps. 44:17 a. this is come upon us
78:32 for a. this they sinned still
Ec. 8:9 a. this I have I seen and
9:1 a. this I considered in heart
Is. 5:25 for a. this his anger is not
turned 9:12, 17, 21; 10:4
48:6 thou hast heard, see a. this
Jan. 5:22 thou knewest a. this
7:16 asked h. the truth of a. t.
Hos. 7:10 for seek him for a. t.
Mic. 1:5 transgress. of Jac. is a. t.
Mat. 1:22 a. t. was done that pro-
phets be fulfilled 21:4; 26:56
Luke 16:26 a. t. there is a gulf
24:21 a. t. to-day is the third d.

ALL that he had.
Gen. 12:20 T. and a. t. h. h.
13:1 A. out of E. and a. t. h. h.
25:5 Abr. gave a. t. h. h. to
31:21 Jacob fled with a. t. h. h.
39:4 a. t. h. h. into Joseph's h.
5 bl. of the L. was on a. t. h. h.
Mat. 18:25 he sold a. t. he had
Mark 10:50 she spent a. t. she had
12:44 cast in a. t. h. Lu. 21:4

ALL the while.
Job 27:3 a. the w. my breath
See further other usual Substan-
tives;
CONGREGATION DAY, EARTH, IS-
RAEL, MEN, PEOPLE, THINGS, etc.

ALLEGING
Acts 17:3 a. C. must have suf.

ALLEGORY
Gal. 4:24 which things are an a.

ALLELUIAH
Rev. 19:1 great voice say a. 3, 4, 6

ALLOW
Luke 11:48 that ye u. the deeds
Acts 24:15 themselves also a. that
Rom. 7:15 which I do, I a. not

ALLOWED, ETH
Rom. 14:22 that thing wh. he a.
1 Thes. 2:4 as were a. of God

ALLOWANCE
2 K. 25:30 his a. was continual a.

ALLURE
Hos. 2:14 a. her into the wild.
1 Pet. 2:18 they a. through lusts

ALMIGHTY
Gen. 17:1 I am the A. God, walk
28:3 God A. bless thee and make
35:11 I am God a. be fruitful
43:14 God a. give you mercy
49:25 by a. who shall bless thee
Ex. 6:3 appeared by name God a.
Num. 24:4 saw the vision of a. 16
Ruth 1:20 a. hath dealt bitterly
21 the a. hath afflicted me
Job 5:17 deep, not chasten. of a.
6:4 arrows of the a. are with. me
14 forsaketh the fear of the a.
8:3 doth the a. pervert justice?
5 thy supplication to the a.
11:7 find out a. to perfection?
13:3 surely I would speak to a.
15:25 strengtheneth ag. the a.
21:15 a. we should serve him
20 and shall drink the wrath of
22:3 pleasure to a. thou art
17 what the a. do for them?
23 if thou return to the a. thou
25 the a. shall be thy defence
26 have thy delight in the a.
27:10 and the a. troubleth me
24:1 are not hid from the a.
27:2 a. who hath vexed my soul
10 delight himself in the a.
11 b. with a. will I not conceal
29:5 w. the a. was yet with me
31:2 inheritance of a.
35 that the a. would answer me
32:8 inspiration of the a. giveth
33:4 breath of a. hath given me
34:10 far from a. to com. iniq.
12 neither will the a. pervert
35:13 the a. will not regard
37:23 the a. we cannot find him
40:2 contendeth with a. instruct
Ps. 68:14 when a. scattereth k.

CRUDEN'S CONCORDANCE. 757

CRUDEN'S CONCORDANCE.

ANG

Is. 2:3 *a.* the Lord do th take
6:15 the *a.* and honourable he is
19:11 I am the son of *a.* kings
23:7 antiquity is of *a.* days
41:7 I appointed the *a.* people
57:6 done it *a.* laid thy yoke
57:9 awoke as in the *a.* days
Jer. 18:15 stumble from *a.* paths
Ezek. 9:6 began at the *a.* men
Dan. 7:9 the *a.* of days did sit
13 like Son of man came to *a.*
22 till the *a.* of days came

ANCIENTS.

1 *Sam.* 24:13 proverb of the *a.*
Ps. 119:100 more than the *a.*
Is. 3:14 into judgment with *a.*
24:23 L. shall reign bef. his *a.*
Jer. 19:1 of *a.* of people and *a.*
Ezek. 7:26 shall per. from the *a.*
8:12 hast seen what the *a.* do?
27:9 *a.* of Gebal thy calkers

ANCLE-BONES.
Acts 3:7 *a.-b.* received strength.

ANCLES.
Ezek. 47:3 waters were to the *a.*

ANDREW.
Mark 13:3 A. asked privately
John 1:40 which heard was A.

ANDRONICUS. *Rom.* 16:7

ANER. *Gen.* 14:24; 1 *Chr.* 6:70

ANGEL.

Gen. 22:11 *a.* said, Abraham
24:7 send his *a.* before thee, 40
48:16 the *a.* who redeemed me
Ex. 23:20 send *a.* before thee,
23; 32:34; 33:2
Num. 20:16 sent an *a.*
Jud. 13:19 *a.* did wondrously
2 *Sam.* 24:16 the *a.* stretched out his hand, the *a.* 1 *Chr.* 21:15
17 he saw the *a.* that smote
1 *K.* 13:18 *a.* spake by the word
19:5 an *a.* touched Elijah
1 *Chr.* 21:15 U. sent an *a.* to Jeru.
20 Ornan turned and saw the *a.*
27 Lord com. *a.* and he put up
2 *Chr.* 32:21 an *a.* which cut off
Ec. 5:6 bef. *a.* it was an error
Is. 63:9 the *a.* of his presence
Dan. 3:28 God who hath sent *a.*
6:22 sent his *a.* and shut up
Hos. 12:4 had power over the *a.*
Zec. 1:19 that talked, 4:5
3:4 stood before *a.*
Mat. 28:5 *a.* answer. the women
Luke 1:13 *a.* said, fear not, Zach.
19 answered, I am Gabriel
26 in sixth month the *a.* Gab'l
30 the *a.* said, Fear not, Mary
35 *a.* answ. Holy Ghost shall
2:10 *a.* said to the shepherds
13 suddenly with *a.* a multit.
21 so named of the *a.*
22:43 an *a.* strengthening him
John 5:4 *a.* went down at a c. s.
12:29 an *a.* spake to him
Acts 6:15 as the face of an *a.*
7:35 *a.* that appear. in the bush
38 in wilderness with the *a.*
10:7 *a.* which spake to Cornel.
22 warned by a holy *a.* to send
11:13 he had seen *a.* in house
12:8 the *a.* said to Peter, bind
9 true which was done by *a.*
10 the *a.* departed from him
11 sent his *a.* and delivered me
15 then said they, It is his *a.*
23:8 say, neither *a.* nor spirit
9 if an *a.* hath spoken to him
2 *Cor.* 11:14 transf. into *a.* of l.
Gal. 1:8 though we or an *a.*
Rev. 1:1 sig. it by *a.* to John
2:1 *a.* of ch., 8, 12, 18; 3:1, 7, 14
5:2 I saw strong *a.* proclaiming
7:2 *a.* ascending from the east
8:3 *a.* came and stood at the al.
4 ascended out of the *a.* hand
5 *a.* took the censer
7 first *a.* sounded; 8 second *a.*
8:10 third *a.*; 12 fourth *a.*
13 I heard an *a.* flying through
9:1 fifth *a.*; 13 sixth *a.*
11 the *a.* of the bottomless pit
14 sixth *a.* loose the four ang.
10:1 *a.* come down, 18:1; 20:1
5 *a.* which I saw stand on sea
7 in days of voice of seventh *a.*
8 take the book in hand of *a.*
11:15 seventh *a.* sounded
14:6 *a.* fly in the midst of heav.
8 another *a.* saying, Babylon is
19 the *a.* thrust in his sickle
16:1 *a.* poured out vial, 3, 4, etc.
5 *a.* of the waters
17:7 *a.* said, wherefore marvel?
18:21 mighty *a.* took up a stone

ANG

Rev. 19:17 an *a.* standing in the
21:17 of a man, that is of the *a.*
22:16 I Jesus have sent mine *a.*

ANGEL of God.
Ex. 14:19 *a.* of God removed
Jud. 13:6 countn. of *a.* of God
1 *Sam.* 29:9 good as an *a.* of God
2 *Sam.* 14:17 an *a.* of God, 19:27
20 accord. to wisd. of *a.* of G.
Gal. 4:14 rec. me as an *a.* of God

ANGEL of the Lord.
Gen. 16:7 *a.* of the L. found Hag.
22:11 *a.* of the L. called 15
Num. 22:23 *a.* of the L. 25, 27
31 Balaam saw *a.* of Lord
Jud. 5:23 Meroz, said *a.* of L.
6:11 *a.* of the Lord sat under
12 *a.* of L. appeared to G.
21 *a.* of L. put forth end of st.
13:3 *a.* of L. appeared to woman
16 he was an *a.* of L.
20 *a.* of the L. ascended
2 *Sam.* 24:16 *a.* of the L. was by the thresh-pl. 1 *Chr.* 21:15
2 *K.* 19:35 *a.* of the L. smote in camp, *Is.* 37:36
1 *Chr.* 21:12 *a.* of the L. destroy
18 *a.* of the L. commanded G.
30 because of s. of *a.* of the L.
Ps. 34:7 *a.* of the L. encampeth
35:5 let *a.* of the L. chase them
6 let *a.* of the L. perse. them
Zec. 1:12 *a.* of the L. answered
3:5 *a.* of the L. stood by Joshua
6 *a.* of the L. protested
12:8 as the *a.* of the L. before
Mat. 1:20 *a.* of L.ap. in dr. 2:13, 19
24 Jos. did as *a.* of L. had bid.
28:2 *a.* of L. descended
Luke 1:11 Zacharias an *a.* of L.
2:9 *a.* of L. come upon them
Acts 5:19 *a.* of L. opened prison
8:26 *a.* of the L. spake to Philip
12:23 *a.* of the L. smote Herod.

ANGELS.
Gen. 19:1 came two *a.* to Sodom
Ps. 8:5 low. than *a. Heb.* 2:7, 9
68:17 are thousands of *a.*
78:25 man did eat *a.'s* food
91:11 sending evil *a.* among them
Mat. 4:11 *a.* ministered, *Mk.* 1:13
13:39 the reapers are the *a.*
49 the *a.* shall sever the wick.
18:10 their *a.* behold face of G.
24:36 *a.* of heaven, *Mark* 13:32
25:31 all the holy *a.* with him
26:53 twelve legions of *a.*
Mark 8:38 Son of man cometh with the holy *a. Luke* 9:26
12:25 are as the *a.* in heaven
Luke 2:15 as the *a.* were gone
16:22 was carried by the *a.*
20:36 equal unto the *a.*
24:23 also seen a vision of *a.*
John 20:12 seeth two *a.* in white
Acts 7:53 by disposition of *a.*
Rom. 8:38 nor *a.* able to separate
1 *Cor.* 4:9 spect. to world, to *a.*
6:3 that we shall judge *a.*?
11:10 power because of the *a.*
13:1 tongues of men and *a.*
Gal. 3:19 ordained by *a.*
Col. 2:18 in worship. of *a.*
2 *Thes.* 1:7 rev. with mighty *a.*
1 *Tim.* 3:16 of *a.* preached to Ge.
5:21 before *a.* and the elect *a.*
Heb. 1:4 much better than the *a.*
5 to which of the *a.* said he, 13
7 who maketh his *a.* spirits
2:2 word spoken by *a.* steadfast
5 to the *a.* hath not in subject.
16 not nature of *a.* but nature
12:22 innum. company of *a.*
13:2 entertained *a.* unawares
1 *Pet.* 1:12 *a.* desire to look into
3:22 *a.* and powers being subj.
2 *Pet.* 2:4 if God spared not the *a.*
11 whereas greater in power
Jude 6 *a.* kept not first estate
Rev. 1:20 stars *a.* of churches
5:11 voice of many *a.* about him
7:1 four *a.* on the four corners
2 with loud voice to the four *a.*
11 the *a.* stood round the th.
8:13 trumpet of *a.* yet to sound
9:14 loose the four *a.* bound
15 the *a.* were loosed
14:10 torment, in pres. of h. *a.*
21:12 and the gates twelve *a.*

ANGELS of God.
Gen. 28:12 *a.* of G. asc. *John* 1:51
32:1 Jacob went his way, and *a.* of God met him
Mat. 22:30 but as *a.* of God in heaven, *Mark* 12:25

ANG

Luke 12:8 him shall the Son confess before *a.* of God
9 he denied before the *a.* of G.
15:10 in presence of *a.* of God
Heb. 1:6 the *a.* of God worship

His ANGELS.
Job 4:18 *his a.* charged with
Ps. 91:11 give *his a.* charge, *Mat.* 4:6; *Luke* 4:10
103:20 ye *his a.* that excel
104:4 *his a.* spirits, *Heb.* 1:7
148:2 praise ye him all *his a.*
Mat. 13:41 shall send forth *his a.*
16:27 glory of his F. with *his a.*
24:31 *his a.* with a *Mark* 13:27
25:41 fire for devil and *his a.*
Rev. 3:5 will confess before *his a.*
12:7 M. and *his a.* the dragon
9 drag. was cast out, and *his a.*
Rom. 10:19 fool, nation I will *a.*

ANGER.
Gen. 27:45 thy brother's *a.* turn
44:18 let not thine *a.* burn
49:7 cursed be their *a.*
Ex. 32:19 Moses' *a.* waxed hot
Deut. 9:19 I was afraid of the *a.*
13:17 the fierceness of his *a.*
29:24 the heat of this great *a.*?
Jud. 8:3 their *a.* was abated
Job 9:13 G. will not withdraw *a.*
Ps. 21:9 oven in time of thine *a.*
30:5 his *a.* endureth but a mom.
37:8 cease from *a.* and forsake
78:38 no sometimes because of *a.*
90:24 wrathful *a.* take hold
74:1 why doth thy *a.* smoke
78:21 *a.* came up against Israel
88 many a time turn. he his *a.*
49 cast the fierceness of his *a.*
Prov. 15:1 grievous words stir up *a.*
16:14 wrath of a king as mess. *a.*
19:11 discretion deferreth his *a.*
21:14 a gift in secret pacifieth *a.*
22:8 the rod of his *a.* shall fail
27:4 and *a.* is outrageous
29:8 rest in the bosom
Is. 5:25 his *a.* is not turned away.
9:12, 17, 21; 10:4
7:4 fear not for the *a.* of Reziu
10:5 the rod of mine *a.* and staff
25 my *a.* in their destruction
12:1 angry, thine *a.* is turned
13:9 cometh with fierce *a.*
3 day of fierce *a. Lam.* 1:12
30:27 name of L. burn. with *a.*
30 the indignation of his *a.*
42:25 on him fury of his *a.*
48:9 will I defer mine *a.*
66:15 come to render his *a.*
Jer. 2:35 his *a.* shall turn
3:12 cause mine *a.* to fall on you
I will not keep mine *a.*
4:26 cities broken down by his *a.*
7:20 *a.* be poured on this place
18:23 deal with them in time of *a.*
23:20 desolate because of his *a.*
82:31 city, provocat. of his *a.*
37 have driven them in his *a.*
42:18 so wrath of G. on Jerusalem
44:6 mine *a.* was poured forth
49:37 evil on them, my fierce *a.*
Lam. 2:1 his footstool in day of *a.*
6 in the indignation of his *a.*
21 hast thou covered with *a.*
22 the Lord's *a.* none escaped
3:43 thou hast covered with *a.*
4:11 poured out his fierce *a.*
5:22 *a.* against us very wroth.
Ezek. 5:13 thus *a.* be accomplished
7:3 send mine *a.* upon thee
8 accomp. *a.* on thee, 20:8, 21
35:11 will do accord. to thine *a.*
Dan. 9:16 let thine *a.* be turned
Hos. 11:9 not execute fierceness *a.*
14:4 for mine *a.* is turned away
Amos 1:11 his *a.* did tear
Jon. 3:9 God turn from fierce *a.*
Mic. 7:18 his *a.* for ever
7:9 *Mat.* 1:6 who can abide, *p*
Hab. 3:8 the *a.* ag. the rivers
Zep. 3:8 to pour all my fierce *a.*
Mark 3:5 looked on them with *a.*
Eph. 4:31 *a.* be put, *Col.* 3:8

ANGER of the Lord.
Num. 25:4 fierce *a.* of the L.
32:14 to augment *a.* of the L.
Deut. 29:20 *a.* of the L. shall b.
Jud. 2:14 *a.* of the L. against Israel, 20; 3:8; 10:7

ANG

2 *K.* 24:20 thro' the *a.* of the L.
It came to pass, *Jer.* 52:3
Jer. 4:8 *a.* of the Lord is not t.
12:13 fierce *a.* of the L. 25:37
23:20 *a.* of the L. shall not, 30:24
51:45 from *a.* of the L.
Lam. 4:16 *a.* of the L. hath
Zep. 2:2 before *a.* of the L. come
3 hid in day of *a.* of the L.

In ANGER.
Gen. 49:6 *in a.* they slew a man
Deut. 29:23 L. overthrew *in a.*
28 the L. rooted them out *in a.*
Job 9:5 overturn. them *in* his *a.*
18:4 he teareth hims. *in* his *a.*
21:17 distributeth sorrows *in a.*
35:15 he hath visited *in* his *a.*
Ps. 6:1 not *in a. Jer.* 10:24
7:6 in thine *a.* lift up thyself
27:9 put not thy serv. away *in a.*
56:7 *in a.* cast down the people
77:9 *in a.* shut up his mercies?
Is. 13:3 called mighty ones *in a.*
14:6 he that ruled nations *in a.*
32:37 driven them *in* thine *a.*
Jer. 21:5 against you, even *in a.*
33:5 I have slain *in* mine *a.*
Lam. 2:1 Lord covered Zion with a cloud *in* his *a.*
3 cut off *in a.* horn of Israel
3:66 destroy them *in a.*
Ezek. 5:13 execute judgm. *in a.*
13:13 shower *in* mine *a.*
20:30 I gather you *in a.*
43:8 consumed them *in* mine *a.*
Dan. 11:20 destro'd. neither *in a.*
Hos. 13:11 gave a king *in* mine *a.*
Mic. 5:15 execute veng. *in a.*
Hab. 3:12 thresh heathen *in a.*

ANGER kindled.
Ex. 4:14 *a.* of l., *k.* against M.
Num. 11:1 *a.* of the Lord was *k.*
10; 12:9; 22:22
25:3 *a.* of the L. was *k.* against Israel, 32:13; *Jos.* 7:1; 2 *Sam.*
Deut. 6:15 lest *a.* be *k.* against
7:4 so will *a.* be *k.* against yon
29:27 *a.* of the L. *k.* against this
31:17 *a.* be *k.* in that day, *Jos.* 23:16
32:22 *k.* in mine *a. Jer.* 15:14
2 *Sam.* 6:7 *a.* of the Lord was *k.*
against Uzziah, 1 *Chr.* 13:10
19:5 David's *a.* *k.* against
Is. 5:25 *a.* of L. *k.* against
Jer. 17:4 have *k.* a fire in mine *a.*
Zec. 10:3 *a.* ag. the shepherds

Provoke or Provoked to ANGER.
Deut. 32:16 abominations *p.* t. *a.*
21 they have *provoked me to a.*
Jud. 2:12 and *pr.* L. to *a.*
1 *K.* 16:2 *pr.* me *to a.* with sins, 26:33; 1 *Kin.* 14:15
Jer. 8:19 *pr.* me *to a.*
33; *Ezek.* 16:26
2 *K.* 21:15 *pr.* to *a.* since day
22:17 forsaken me that they might *pro.* me *to a.* 2 *Sam.*
34:25; *Jer.* 25:7
Ps. 78:58 *pro.* him *to a.* with high places, 106:29
Prov. 20:2 whoso *pro.* *to a.*
Is. 1:4 *pro.* Holy One of *Is.* — a.
65:3 a people that *pro.* me *to a.*
Jer. 7:19 do they *pro.* me *to a.?*
25:6, 7 *pro. to a.* with works
32:29 *pro. to a.* pouring drink
30 children of Judah *pro.* me *to a.*
Col. 3:21 *pro.* not your chil. *to a.*

Slow to ANGER.
Neh. 9:17 pardon, *slow to a.*
Ps. 103:8 *slow to a.* 145:8
Prov. 15:18 he *s. to a.* appeaseth
16:32 *s. to a.* better than mighty
Joel 2:13 *slow to a.* of great kindness, *Jon.* 4:2
Nah. 1:3 Lord is *sl. to a.*

ANGERED.
Ps. 106:32 *a.* him at waters

ANGLE.
Is. 19:8 all they that cast *a.*
Hab. 1:15 they take up with *a.*

ANGRY.
Gen. 18:30 let not L. be *a.* 32
45:5 be not *a.* that ye sold me
Lev. 10:16 Moses *a.* with Eleaz.
Deut. 1:37 L. *a.* with me 4:21
9:20 L. *a.* very *a.* with Aaron
Jud. 18:25 lest *a.* fellows run on
1 *K.* 8:46 thou be *a.* 2 *Chr.* 6:36
11:9 L. was *a.* with Solomon
2 *K.* 17:18 was *a.* with Israel
Ezr. 9:14 wouldst be *a.* with us
Ps. 2:12 kiss the S., lest he be *a.*
7:11 God is *a.* with the wicked
76:7 when thou art *a.*

CRUDEN'S CONCORDANCE. 759

ANO
Ps. 70:5 how long a. *f* 80:1; 85:5
Prov. 14:17 soon *a.* dealeth fool
21:19 than with an *a.* woman
22:24 friendship with an *a.* man
25:23 so doth an *a.* countenance
29:22 *a.* man stirreth up strife
Ec. 5:6 God he *a.* at thy voice?
7:9 be not hasty in spirit to be *a.*
Cant. 1:6 children were *a.*
Is. 12:1 thou wast *a.* with me
Ezek. 16:42 will be no more *a.*
Jon. 4:1 Jonah was very *a.*
4:4 doest thou well to be *a.?*
9 I do well to be *a.* unto death
Mal. 8:22 is *a.* with brother
Luke 14:21 master of h. being *a.*
15:28 *a.* and would not
John 7:23 are ye *a.* at me *&c.*
Eph. 4:26 be *a.* and sin not
Tit. 1:7 a bishop not soon *a.*
Rev. 11:18 the nations were *a.*

ANGUISH.
Ex. 6:9 not to M. for *a.*
Deut. 2:25 tremble, and be in *a.*
2 *Sam.* 1:9 slay me, for *a.* is come
Job 7:11 I will speak in *a.* of spir.
15:24 *a.* shall make him afraid
Ps. 119:143 and *a.* have taken
Prov. 1:27 when distress and *a.*
Is. 8:22 and behold dimness of *a.*
30:6 into land of trouble and *a.*
Jer. 4:31 the *a.* as of her that
John 16:21 no more her *a.* for joy
Rom. 2:9 tribulation and *a.* upon
2 *Cor.* 2:4 out of *a.* of heart

ANISE.
Mat. 23:23 pay tit. of mint, *a.*

ANNA.
Luke 2:36

ANNAS.
Lu. 3:2; *John* 18:13, 21

ANOINT.
Ex. 28:41 shalt *a.* 30:30; 40:15
28:7 take oil and *a.* him, 40:13
36 shalt *a.* the altar, 40:10
33:26 *a.* the tabernacle, 40:9
Lev. 16:32 whom he shall *a.*
Deut. 28:40 shalt not *a.* thyself
Jud. 9:8 trees went to *a.* a king
15 if in truth ye *a.* me king
1 *Sam.* 9:16 *a.* him captain
15:1 sent me to *a.* thee king
16:3 *a.* him whom I name
12 L. said, Arise, *a.* him
2 *Sam.* 14:2 *a.* not thys. with oil
1 *K.* 1:34 Zadok *a.* him king
19:15 *a.* Hazael king
16 *a.* John, *a.* Elisha
Is. 21:5 princes, *a.* the shield
Dan. 9:24 and *a.* the most Holy
10:3 neither did I *a.* myself
Amos 6:6 *a.* themselves
Mic. 6:15 the olives, but not *a.*
Mat. 6:17 when thou fastest *a.*
Mark 14:8 is come to *a.* my body
16:1 spices that they might *a.*
Luke 7:46 head thou didst not *a.*
Rev. 3:18 *a.* thine eyes

ANOINTED.
Lev. 8:10 *a.* the tabernacle
11 *a.* the altar, *Num.* 7:1
12 A.'s head, and *a.* him
1 *Sam.* 10:1 the L. *a.* thee capt.
15:17 *a.* Saul
16:13 *a.* David, 2 *Sam.* 2:4, 7;
5:8, 17; 12:7; 2 *K.* 9:3, 6, 12;
1 *Chr.* 11:3; 14:8
2 *Sam.* 2:7 Judah have *a.* me k.
3:39 I am weak, though *a.* king
19:20 David arose, and *a.* him...
23:1 David the *a.* of God said
Is. 61:1 *a.* me to preach, *Lu.* 4:18
Ezek. 28:14 *a.* cherub that covers
Luke 7:38 kissed his feet and *a.*
46 this woman hath *a.* my feet
John 9:6 he *a.* the eyes with clay
11 Jesus made clay, and *a.* my
12:3 Mary *a.* feet of Jesus
Acts 4:27 child J. thou hast *a.*
10:38 God *a.* Jesus of Nazar.
2 *Cor.* 1:21 hath *a.* us is God

ANOINTED Ones.
Zec. 4:14 *a.* ones which stand

His ANOINTED.
1 *Sam.* 2:10 exalt horn of *his a.*
12:3 against the L. and *his a.*
5 the L. and *his a.* is witness
2 *Sam.* 22:51 showeth mercy to *his a. Ps.* 18:50
Ps. 2:2 and against *his a.*
20:6 the Lord saveth *his a.*
28:8 saving strength of *his a.*
Is. 45:1 saith L. to *his a.* to C.

Lord's ANOINTED.
1 *Sam.* 16:6 *Lord's a.* is before
24:6 my master, the *Lord's a.*
10 my hand against *Lord's a.*

ANS
1 *Sam.* 26:9 L. *a.* and the guilti.
16 have not kept the *Lord's a.*
2 *Sam.* 1:14 to destroy L. *a.*
19:21 he cursed L. *a.*
Lam. 4:20 *a.* of L. taken

Mine ANOINTED.
1 *Sam.* 2:35 walk before *mine a.*
1 *Chr.* 16:22 touch not *mine a. Ps.* 105:15
Ps. 132:17 a lamp for *mine a.*

ANOINTED with Oil.
1 *Sam.* 1:21 though not *a. with o.*
Ps. 45:7 *a. w. o.* of gladness, *Heb.* 1:9
92:10 I shall be *a. with* fresh *o.*
Mark 6:13 *a. with* oil many sick

Thine ANOINTED.
2 *Chr.* 6:42 turn not away the face of *thine a. Ps.* 132:10
Ps. 84:9 look on face of *thine a.*
89:38 been wroth with *thine a.*
51 footsteps of *thine a.*
Hab. 3:13 salvation with *thine a.*

ANOINTEST.
Ps. 23:5 *a.* my head with oil

ANOINTING.
Ex. 40:15 *a.* everlast. priesthood
Is. 10:27 destroyed bec. of *a.*
1 *John* 2:27 *a.* teacheth all things

ANOINTING Oil.
Ex. 37:29 made the holy *a. oil*
Lev. 8:12 *a. oil* on Aaron's head
10:7 *a. oil* of the L. is upon you
Num. 4:16 Elea. pertaineth *a. oil*
Jam. 5:14 *a.* with *o.* in name of L.

ANON.
Mat. 13:20 *a.* with joy receiv. it
Mark 1:30 mother lay sick and *a.*

ANOTHER.
1 *Sam.* 10:6 shalt he turned to *a.*
Job 19:27 shall behold and not *a. Ps.* 109:8 let *a.* take, *Acts* 1:20
Prov. 31:9 dis. not a secret to *a.*
27:2 let *a.* praise thee, and not
Is. 42:8 my glory not to *a.* 48:11
Is. 62:15 his servants by *a.* name
Hos. 3:3 shalt not be for *a.* man
4:4 let no man reprove *a.*
Mat. 11:3 or do we look for *a.*?
Mark 14:19 *a.* said, Is it I?
Luke 16:7 to *a.* How much owest
2 *Cor.* 11:4 *a.* Jesus, *a.* spirit, or *a.*
Gal. 1:7 which is not *a.* but
6:4 rejoic. in himself, and not in *a.*
Jam. 4:12 that judgest *a.* 10:25

One ANOTHER.
See LOVE.

One against ANOTHER.
1 *Sam.* 2:25 If *one* man *sin a. a.*
Jer. 13:14 dash them *one a. a.*
1 *Cor.* 4:6 puffed up *one a. a.*
Jam. 5:9 grudge not *one a. a.*

One for ANOTHER.
1 *Cor.* 11:33 tarry *one for a.*
Jam. 5:16 pray *one for a.* that ye

ANSWER.
Deut. 20:11 if city make *a.*
1 *Sam.* 24:12 see what *a.* I ret'rn
Job 19:16 and he gave me no *a.*
32:3 found no *a.* and condemn'd
33:12 cry, but none giveth *a. Prov.* 15:1 soft *a.* turneth away
23 hath joy by the *a.* of his
Is. 36:21 answer. him not a word
Cant. 5:6 he gave no *a.*
Mic. 3:7 for there is no *a.* of God
Luke 20:26 marvelled at his *a.*
John 1:22 that we may give *a.*
19:9 Jesus gave him no *a.*
Rom. 11:4 what saith *a.* of God?
1 *Cor.* 9:3 mine *a.* is this
2 *Tim.* 4:16 at my first *a.*
1 *Pet.* 3:15 be ready to give an *a.*
21 the *a.* of a good conscience

ANSWERS.
Job 21:34 in your *a.* remaineth
34:36 his *a.* for wicked men
Luke 2:47 were astonish. at his *a.*

ANSWER, Verb.
Gen. 30:33 righteous. *a.* for me
Deut. 27:15 people shall *a.* amen
1 *K.* 18:24 voice, nor any to *a. Job* 13:22 call thou, and I will *a.*
23:5 the words he would *a.* me
31:14 he visiteth what *a.* him?
32:9 it is in L. be greater, 33:5
40:2 reproveth God, let him *a.*
Ps. 27:7 have mercy and *a.* me
65:5 in right. wilt thou *a.* us?
86:7 will call, thou wilt *a.* me
102:2 when I call *a.* me speedily
108:6 thy right hand, and *a.* me

ANT
Ps. 143:1 in thy faithful. *a.* me
Prov. 15:28 heart studieth to *a.*
22:21 mightest *a.* words of truth
26:5 *a.* a fool accord. to his folly
Is. 14:32 what *a.* the messengers
50:2 was there none to *a.?* 66:4
58:9 shalt thou call. L. will *a.*
Dan. 3:16 not careful to *a.* thee
Hab. 2:1 what *a.* when reproved
Mat. 22:46 no man was able to *a.*
Mark 11:30 heaven or of men? *a.*
14:40 wist they what to *a.*
Luke 11:7 from within shall *a.*
12:11 ye shall *a.* or say
13:25 he shall *a.* I know you not
21:14 not to meditate what ye *a.*
2 *Cor.* 5:12 somewhat to *a.* them
Col. 4:6 how to *a.* every man

I will ANSWER.
Job 13:22 call, *I will a.* 14:15; *Ps.* 91:15; *Jer.* 33:3
Is. 65:24 they could *I will a.*

Not ANSWER.
2 *K.* 18:36 king's commandment was *a.* him *not, Is.* 36:21
Job 9:3 *a.* him one of a thousand
Prov. 1:28 they shall call *I not a.*
20:1 *a.* not a fool accord. to his
22:19 understand, he will *not a.*
Is. 65:12 I called, ye did *not a. Jer.* 7:27 they will *not a.* thee
Luke 14:6 they could *not a.* him
22:68 will *not a.* nor let me go

ANSWERED.
Jud. 8:8 *a.* as men of Succoth *a.*
1 *Sam.* 3:4 he *a.* Here am I, 16
1 *K.* 12:13 the king *a.* roughly,
2 *Chr.* 10:13
18:26 voice, nor any that *a.*
2 *Chr.* 25:9 *a.* the Lord is able
Job 11:2 multit. of words be *a.*
Ezek. 37:3 I *a.* O L. thou knowest
Dan. 2:14 D. *a.* with counsel
Mat. 27:12 he *a.* nothing 14;
Mark 14:61; 15:3, 5; *Luke* 23:9
31 Jesus saw he *a.* discreetly
Acts 22:8 I *a.* Who art thou, L.?
25:8 he *a.* for himself, 26:1

ANSWERED, meant of God.
Gen. 35:3 *a.* me in my distress
Ex. 19:19 M. spake, and G. *a.*
1 *Sam.* 21:1 L. *a.* It is for Saul
1 *Chr.* 21:26 *a.* from heaven by
28 David saw Lord had *a.* him
Ps. 81:7 I. the secret
99:6 on the L. and he *a.* them
118:5 the L. *a.* me and set me
Jer. 23:35 hath the Lord *a.* 37

ANSWERED not.
1 *Sam.* 4:20 *a. not* nor did regard
2 *Sam.* 22:42 looked, but *a.* them *not*
1 *K.* 18:21 people, *a.* him *not*
2 *K.* 18:36; *Is.* 36:21
Jer. 7:13 called, ye *a. not,* 35:17
Mat. 15:23 he *a.* her *not* a word

ANSWEREDST.
Ps. 99:8 thou *a.* them, O Lord
138:3 when I cried thou *a.* me

ANSWEREST.
1 *Sam.* 26:14 *a.* thou not, Abner?
Job 30:20 embold. that thou *a. f*
Mark 14:60; 15:4
John 18:22 *a.* thou the h.-p. so?

ANSWERETH.
1 *Sam.* 28:15 God *a.* me no more
1 *K.* 18:24 God that *a.* by fire
Job 12:1 can God and he *a.* him
Prov. 18:13 that *a.* a matter
23 but the rich *a.* roughly
27:19 as face *a.* to face, so
Ec. 5:20 God *a.* him in the joy
10:19 but money *a.* all things
Gal. 4:25 and *a.* to Jerusalem

ANSWERING.
Luke 23:40 the other *a.* rebuked
Tit. 2:9 not *a.* again

ANT, S.
Prov. 6:6 the *a.* thou sluggard
30:25 *a.* are a people not strong

ANTICHRIST.
1 *John* 2:22 is *a.* that denieth Father and Son
23 whosoever denieth Son
4:3 of *a.* whereof ye heard
2 *John* 7 is a deceiver and an *a.*

ANTIOCH.
Acts 11:19 as far as A. 22
26 called Christians first in A.
13:14 Paul and his comp. from P.
27:19 departed from A. to Jerusalem

ANTIPAS.
Rev. 2:13

ANTIPATRIS.
Acts 23:31

APP
ANTIQUITY.
Is. 23:7 joyous city, whose *a.*

ANVIL.
Is. 41:7 him that smote *a.*

ANY.
Deut. 32:39 nor *a.* that can del.
1 *K.* 18:26 nor *a.* that answered
Job 33:27 If *a.* say, I have sinned
Ec. 4:6 who will show us *a.* good?
Is. 44:8 is no God, I know not *a.*
Amos 6:10 is there yet *a.*
Mark 8:26 nor tell it to *a.* in t.
11:25 have aught against *a. Acts* 9:2 if he found *a.*
See FURTHER, GOD, MAN, MORE.
THING, TIME, WISE.
ANY *while, See* DEAD.

APACE.
See FLEE, FLED.

APART.
Ex. 13:12 every family *a.* 14
Mat. 11:11 into a desert place *a.*
23 mountain *a.* 17:1; *Mark* 9:2
17:19 came the disciples to J. *a.*
Mark 6:31 come ye yourselves *a.*
Jam. 1:21 lay *a.* filthiness

APELLES.
Rom. 16:10

APES.
See PEACOCKS.

APHEK.
1 *Sam.* 4:1 pitched in A. 29:1
1 *K.* 20:30 the rest fled to A.
2 *K.* 13:17 the Syrians in A.

APIECE.
Num. 3:47 five shekels *a.*
17:6 gave him a rod *a.*
Luke 9:3 nor have two coats *a.*
John 2:6 two or three firkins *a.*

APOLLONIA.
Acts 17:1

APOLLOS.
Acts 18:24 A. came to Ephesus
1 *Cor.* 1:12 and I of A. 3:4; 3:5
3:6 I planted, A. watered
4:6 in a figure transferred to A.
Tit. 3:13 bring Zenas and A.

APOLLYON.
Rev. 9:11

APOSTLE.
1 *Tim.* 2:7 I Paul, called to be an *a.*
1 *Cor.* 1:1
11:13 am the *a.* of the Gentiles
1 *Cor.* 9:1 am I not an *a.?* 2
15:9 not meet to be called an *a.*
2 *Cor.* 1:1; *Eph.* 1:1; *Eph.* 1:1:
1:1; *Col.* 1:1
12:12 the signs of an *a.*
1 *Tim.* 2:7 whereto I am ordained an *a.* 2 *Tim.* 1:11
Tit. 1:1 a servant of G. and *a.*
Heb. 3:1 *a.* and high-priest of our

APOSTLES.
Mat. 10:2 names of the twelve *a. Mark* 6:30 the *a.* gathered
Luke 6:13 whom he named *a.*
17:5 the *a.* said, Increase
22:14 down, and the twelve *a.*
24:10 told these things to *a.*
Acts 1:26 with the eleven *a.*
2:43 signs by the *a.* 5:12
5:18 laid their hands on the *a.*
8:1 all scattered except the *a.*
Rom. 16:7 of note among the *a.*
1 *Cor.* 4:9 set forth us the *a.* last
9:5 so *a.* and as brethren
12:28 hath set in church first *a.*
2 *Cor.* 11:5 chiefest *a.* 12:11
13 such are false *a.*
Gal. 1:17 to them *a.* before me
19 other of the *a.* saw I none
Eph. 2:20 built on foundation of *a. and prophets*
4:11 he gave some *a.*
1 *Thes.* 2:6 burdensome as the *a.*
2 *Pet.* 3:2 command. of us the *a.*
17 words spoken by the *a.*
Rev. 2:2 which say they are *a.*
18:20 rejoice over her, ye holy *a.*

APOSTLESHIP.
Acts 1:25 take part of this *a.*
Rom. 1:5 received grace and *a.*
1 *Cor.* 9:2 the seal of mine *a.*
Gal. 2:8 effectually in P. to the *a.*

APOTHECARY.
Ex. 30:25 after art of *a.* 37:29
Ec. 10:1 flies cause ointm. of *a.*

APPAREL.
2 *Sam.* 12:20 D. changed his *a.*
1 *K.* 10:5 attend. of his minis-ters and their *a.* 2 *Chr.* 9:4

APP

L. 3:22 changeable suits of *a.*
4:1 we will wear our own *a.*
63:1 who this glorious in his *a.*
Zep. 1:8 clothed in strange *a.*
Acts 1:10 men stood in white *a.*
10:33 no man's silver or *a.*
1 Tim. 2:9 women in modest *a.*
Jam. 2:2 man come in goodly *a.*
1 Pet. 3:3 or putting on *a.*
See ROYAL.

APPARELLED.
2 Sam. 13:18 daughters were *a.*
Luke 7:25 are gorgeously *a.*

APPARENTLY.
Num. 12:8 will I speak *a.*

APPEAL, ED.
Acts 25:11 I *a.* unto Cesar.
26:32 at liberty, if he had not *a.*
28:19 constrained to *a.* to Cesar

APPEAR.
Gen. 1:9 let the dry land *a.*
Ex. 23:15 none *a.* before me empty, 34:20; Deut. 16:16
34:24 when thou shalt go to *a.*
Deut. 31:11 Israel *a.* before L.
Ps. 42:2 shall I come and *a.*
90:16 work *a.* to thy servants
Cant. 2:12 flowers *a.* on earth
4:1 flock of goats that *a.* 6:5
Is. 1:12 ye come to *a.* before me
Jer. 13:26 that thy shame may *a.*
Ezek. 21:24 doings, your sins *a.*
Mat. 6:16 may *a.* to men to fast
23:28 ye outwardly *a.* righteous
24:30 *a.* the sign of the Son
Luke 11:44 as graves which *a.*
19:11 kingdom of God should *a.*
Acts 26:16 in which I will *a.*
Rom. 7:13 that it might *a.* sin
2 Cor. 5:10 *a.* before judg.-seat
Col. 3:4 Christ our life shall *a.*
1 Tim. 4:15 profiting may *a.*
Heb. 9:24 to *a.* in the presence
24 *a.* the second time
11:3 of things which do *a.*
1 Pet. 4:18 where shall ungod. *a.?*
5:4 when chief Sheph. shall *a.*
1 John 2:28 when he shall *a.*
3:2 not yet *a.* what we shall be, when he shall *a.* we shall
Rev. 3:18 nakedness do not *a.*

APPEAR, *referred to God.*
Lev. 9:4 to-day L. will *a.* 6
16:2 I will *a.* in the cloud
1 Sam. 2:27 *a.* to the house
2 Chr. 1:7 did God *a.* to Solomon
Ps. 102:16 shall *a.* in his glory
Is. 66:5 he shall *a.* to your joy
Acts 26:16 in which I will *a.*

APPEARANCE.
Num. 9:15 as the *a.* of fire, 16
1 Sam. 16:7 looketh on outw. *a.*
Dan. 8:15 the *a.* of a man, 10:18
10:6 his face as *a.* of lightning
John 7:24 accord. to the *a.*
2 Cor. 5:12 which glory in *a.*
10:7 things after the outward *a.*
1 Thes. 5:22 *a.* bstain from all *a.*

APPEARED.
Ex. 4:1 L. hath not *a.* to thee
6:3 I *a.* by name of G. Almighty
1 K. 11:9 had *a.* to Solomon
Jer. 31:3 the L. hath *a.* of old
Mat. 2:7 what time the star *a.*
13:26 then *a.* the tares also
17:3 *a.* Moses and E. Mark 9:4
27:53 holy city, and *a.* to many
Mark 16:9 Jesus *a.* first to Mary
12 he *a.* in another form
14 after he *a.* to the eleven
Luke 1:11 there *a.* to him
9:31 who *a.* in glory, and spake
22:43 *a.* an angel, strengthening
24:34 L. is risen, *a.* to Simon
Acts 7:2 God *a.* to father Abra.
9:17 Jesus, that *a.* to thee in
26:16 I have *a.* for this purpose
27:20 neither sun nor stars *a.*
Tit. 2:11 grace of God hath *a.*
3:4 after the love of God *a.*
Heb. 9:26 he *a.* to put away sin
Rev. 12:1 there *a.* a great w. 3

APPEARETH.
Ps. 84:7 in Zion *a.* before God
Prov. 27:25 the hay *a.*
Jer. 6:1 evil *a.* out of the north
Mal. 3:2 shall stand when he *a.*
Jam. 4:14 life as a vapor that *a.*

APPEARING.
1 Tim. 6:14 keep com. till *a.* L.
2 Tim. 1:10 manifest by the *a.*
4:1 quick and dead at his *a.*
8 to them also that love his *a.*
Tit. 2:13 looking for glorious *a.*

APP

1 Pet. 1:7 to praise at the *a.* of J.

APPEASE.
Gen. 32:20 I will *a.* him

APPEASED, ETH.
Est. 2:1 Ahasuerus *a.*
Prov. 15:18 *a.* to anger, *a.* strife
Acts 19:35 town-clerk had *a.*

APPERTAIN.
Num. 16:30 swallow them, with all that *a.*
Jer. 10:7 for to thee doth it *a.*
See PERTAIN.

APPERTAINED.
Num. 16:32 that *a.* to Korah, 33

APPERTAINETH, ING.
Lev. 6:5 give it to whom it *a.*
Rom. 4:1 Abr. our father, as *a.*

APPETITE.
Job 38:39 fill the *a.* of lions
Prov. 23:2 a man given to *a.*
Ec. 6:7 yet *a.* not filled
Is. 29:8 and his soul hath *a.*

APPII-FORUM. Acts 28:15

APPLE of the eye.
Deut. 32:10 kept him as *a.* of h. e.
Ps. 17:8 keep me as *a.* of eye
Prov. 7:2 law as *a.* of thine eye.
Lam. 2:18 let not *a.* of thine eye
Zec. 2:8 toucheth *a.* of his eye.

APPLE-TREE.
Cant. 2:3 as *a.*-tree among trees
8:5 raised thee up under *a.*-tree
Joel 1:12 and *a.*-tree are withered

APPLES.
Prov. 25:11 like *a.* of gold in pic.
Cant. 2:5 comfort me with *a.*
7:8 smell of thy nose like *a.*

APPLIED.
Ec. 7:25 I *a.* my heart to know
8:9 I *a.* my heart to every work
16 I *a.* heart to know every work

APPLY.
Ps. 90:12 *a.* our hearts to wisd.
Prov. 2:2 *a.* heart to understand
22:17 *a.* thy heart to my know.
23:12 *a.* thy heart to instruction

APPOINT.
Lev. 26:16 will *a.* over you terror
2 Sam. 6:21 to *a.* me ruler
7:10 *a.* a place for my people
Job 14:13 *a.* me a set time
Is. 26:1 will God *a.* for walls
61:3 to *a.* them that mourn in Z.
Jer. 15:3 *a.* over them four kinds
49:19 who is *a.* chosen man, I
50:44 who will *a.* me the time?
Ezek. 21:19 *a.* thee two ways
20 *a.* a way that the sword
Hos. 1:11 they shall *a.* one head
Mat. 24:51 *a.* his portion
Luke 12:46 *a.* his portion
22:29 I *a.* you a kingdom
Acts 6:3 seven men whom we *a.*

APPOINTED.
Num. 9:2 passover in *a.* sea. 3
7 offering of L. in his *a.* season
1 Sam. 13:11 not within the *a.*
1 K. 1:35 *a.* him to be ruler.
20:42 a man *a.* to destruction
Neh. 6:7 thou hast *a.* prophets
9:17 *a.* a captain to return, but
Job 7:3 wearisome nights are *a.*
14:5 thou hast *a.* his bounds
20:29 the heritage *a.* to him
30:23 the house *a.* for all living
Ps. 44:11 like sheep *a.* for meat
78:5 *a.* a law in Israel
79:11 preserve those *a.* to die
102:20 to loose those *a.* to death
Prov. 7:20 come home at day *a.*
8:29 he *a.* the foundations
31:8 as are *a.* to destruction
Is. 1:14 your *a.* feasts my soul
44:7 I *a.* the ancient people
Jer. 5:24 reserveth the *a.* weeks
47:7 sea-shore, there hath he *a.*
Ezek. 4:6 *a.* each day for a year
36:5 and who hath *a.*
Luke 3:13 exact what is *a.* you
10:1 Lord *a.* other seventy
22:29 as Father *a.* me
Acts 1:23:8 two *a.* Joseph and
17:31 he hath *a.* day in which
1 Cor. 4:9 apostles last, *a.* to d.
1 Thes. 3:3 that we are *a.* thereto
5:9 God hath not *a.* us to wrath
2 Tim. 1:11 I am *a.* a preacher
Heb. 3:2 faithful to him that *a.* h.
9:27 *a.* to men once to die
1 Pet. 2:8 whereunto they were *a.*

APPOINTED, *time* and *times.*
1 Sam. 13:8 to set *time* Sam. *a.*

ARE

Job 7:1 an *a.* time to man
14:14 all the days of my *a.* time.
Is. 14:31 be alone in his *a.* time
Jer. 8:7 knoweth her *a.* times
Dan. 8:19 at *time a.* the end
10:1 but the *time a.* was long
27 and be at the *time a.*
29 at the *time a.* shall return
35 it is yet for *a.* time
Hab. 2:3 is yet for *a.* time
Acts 17:26 determ. *times* bef. *a.*
Gal. 4:2 until *time a.*

APPOINTETH.
Ps. 104:19 *a.* moons for seasons
Dan. 5:21 *a.* whomsoever he will

APPOINTMENT.
Job 2:11 made *a.* together to c.

APPREHEND.
2 Cor. 11:32 garrison desir. to *a.*
Phil. 3:12 I may *a.* that for which

APPREHENDED.
Acts 12:4 when he *a.* Peter
Phil. 3:12 I am *a.* of Christ J.
13 count not myself to have *a.*

APPROACH.
Deut. 31:14 thy days *a.* that thou
Job 40:19 his sword to *a.* to him
Ps. 65:4 whom thou causest to *a.*
Jer. 30:21 engaged heart to *a.*
1 Tim. 6:16 in light no man c. *a.*

APPROACHETH, ING.
Is. 58:2 take delight in *a.* God
Luke 12:33 where no thief *a.*
Heb. 10:25 as ye see the day *a.*

APPROVE.
Ps. 49:13 posterity *a.* their say.
1 Cor. 16:3 shall *a.* by your let.
Phil. 1:10 that ye may *a.* things

APPROVED.
Acts 2:22 Jesus, a man *a.* of God
Rom. 14:18 accept to G. *a.* of m.
16:10 Apelles *a.* in Christ
1 Cor. 11:19 they *a.* be made m.
2 Cor. 10:18 commendeth himself is *a.*
13:7 that we should appear *a.*
2 Tim. 2:15 thyself *a.* unto God

APPROVEST, ETH.
Lam. 3:36 subvert a man, *a.* not
Rom. 2:18 *a.* things more excel.

APPROVING.
2 Cor. 6:4 in all things *a.* oursel.

APRON, S.
Gen. 3:7 fig-leaves, made *a.*
Acts 19:12 brought to the sick *a.*

AQUILA. Acts 18:2, 26; Rom. 16:3; 1 Cor. 16:19; 2 Tim. 4:19
AR. Num. 21:28; Deut. 2:9; Is. 15:1

ARABIA.
1 K. 10:15 had kings of A.
Ps. 21:13 the burden upon A.
Jer. 25:24 the cup to kings of A.
Gal. 1:17 I went into A. 4:25

ARABIANS.
2 Chr. 17:11 the A. brought Jeh.
20:7 helped Uzziah ag. the A.
Is. 13:20 nor shall A. pitch tent
Jer. 3:2 as A. in the wilderness
Acts 2:11 Cretes and A. we hear

ARAM.
Gen. 10:22 sons of Sh. Lud, A.
Num. 23:7 B. brought me fr. A.
Mat. 1:3 Esrom begat A. 4
Luke 3:33 Aminadab son of A.
See SYRIA.

ARARAT. Gen. 8:4; Jer. 51:27
ARAUNAH. 2 Sam. 24:16, 23
ARBA. Jos. 14:15; 21:11

ARCHANGEL.
1 Thes. 4:16 with voice of *a.*
Jude 9 Michael the *a.* contend.

ARCHELAUS. Mat. 2:22

ARCHER, S.
Gen. 21:20 Ishmael became an *a.*
49:23 the *a.* sorely grieved him
1 Sam. 31:3 *a.* hit him, 1 Chr. 10:3
Job 16:13 his *a.* comp. me round
Is. 22:3 rulers are bound by *a.*
Jer. 51:3 bendeth let *a.* bend bow

ARCHES.
Ezek. 40:16 windows to the *a.*

ARCHIPPUS. Col. 4:17; Phile. 2
ARCTURUS. Job 9:9; 38:33

ARE,
Num. 15:15 as ye *a.* so stranger
Job 38:35 say to thee, here we *a.*

ARK

Lam. 5:7 sinned, and *a.* not
Mat. 2:18 not conf. bec. they *a.*
Luke 13:25 whence you *a.* 27
John 17:11 may be one as we *a.*
1 Cor. 1:28 things which *a.* not
Rev. 1:19 the things which *a.*

AREOPAGITE. Acts 17:34
AREOPAGUS. Acts 17:19
ARETAS. 2 Cor. 11:32
ARGOB. Deut. 3:4, 13, 14; 1 K. 4:13

ARGUING.
Job 6:25 what doth your *a.* rep.

ARGUMENTS.
Job 23:4 fill my mouth with *a.*

ARIEL.
Ezr. 8:16 I sent for E. and A.
Is. 29:1 woe to A. the city, 2, 7

ARIGHT.
Ps. 50:23 ord. his conversa. *a.*
78:8 that set not their heart *a.*
Prov. 15:2 wise useth know. *a.*
23:31 when it moveth itself *a.*
Jer. 8:6 I heark. they spake not *a.*

ARIMATHEA.
Mat. 27:57 Joseph of A. who was, Mark 15:43; Luke 23:51; John 19:38

ARIOCH.
Gen. 14:1 in the days of A. king
Dan. 2:25 A. brought Daniel

ARISE.
Jos. 1:2 *a.* go over this Jordan
Jud. 5:12 *a.* Barak, lead
2 Sam. 2:14 young men *a.*
1 K. 3:12 any *a.* like thee
1 Chr. 22:16 *a.* be doing
Job 7:4 I *a.* and night be gone?
25:5 doth not his light *a.?*
Ps. 3:7 *a.* O Lord, save me
7:6 *a.* O Lord, in thine anger
12:5 will I *a.* saith the Lord
44:26 *a.* for help, and redeem
68:1 let God *a.* let his enemies
68:10 shall dead *a.* praise thee ?
88:9 waves of sea *a.* thou stilest
102:13 *a.* and have mercy on Z.
Prov. 6:9 *a.* out of thy sleep?
Cant. 2:13 *a.* my love, fair one
Is. 21:5 *a.* ye princes
26:19 my dead body shall *a.*
49:7 kings shall *a.* princes wor.
60:1 *a.* shine, thy light is come
62:4 dead Lord shall *a.* upon thee
Jer. 2:27 in trouble will they say, *a.*
31:6 *a.* ye, let us go up to Zion
Lam. 2:19 *a.* cry out in the night
Dan. 2:39 shall *a.* another kingd.
Amos 7:2 whom shall Jacob *a.* 5
Mic. 2:10 *a.* this is not your rest
4:13 *a.* and thresh. O daughter
7:8 enemy, I fall I shall *a.*
Hab. 2:19 to the dumb stone *a.*
Mal. 4:2 Sun of righteousness *a.*

ARISETH.
1 K. 18:44 *a.* little cloud
Ps. 112:4 to the upright *a.* light
Is. 2:19 *a.* to shake terribly, 21
Mat. 13:21 persec. *a.* Mark 4:17
John 7:52 out of Galilee *a.*
Heb. 7:15 similitude of Melch. *a.*
See SUN

ARISTARCHUS.
Acts 19:29 caught Gaius and A.
20:4 A. accompanied Paul
27:2 one A. a Macedonian
Col. 4:10 A. f.-prisoner, Phile. 24
ARISTOBULUS. Rom. 16:10

ARK.
Gen. 6:14 an *a.* of gopher-wood
7:18 *a.* went on face of waters
Ex. 2:3 took an *a.* of bulrush.
25:16 put into the *a.* the testimony, 21; 40:3, 20
37:1 made the *a.* of shittim-w.
Jos. 3:31 charge shall be the *a.*
4:6; 6:1; 2 Sam. 6:9

CRUDEN'S CONCORDANCE. 761

ARM

1 *Sam.* 6:19 looked into a.
2 *Sam.* 11:11 a. and Israel abide
1 *K.* 4:39 loc. thou barest the a.
8:9 nothing in a. save the two
1 *Chr.* 0:31 the a. had rest
13:3 let us bring again the a.
9 put forth hand to hold the a.
15:1 D. prepared a place for a.
2 *Chr.* 35:4 a. of thy strength,
Ps. 138:6
6:11 whereunto a. hath come
Mat. 24:38 Noah ent. a. *Lu.* 17:27
Heb. 11:7 Noah prepared an a.
1 *Pet.* 3:20 G. waited while the a.
Rev. 11:19 in his temple the a.

Before the ARK.

Ex. 40:5 set altar of gold a.
Jos. 4:7 w. of Jordan cut off a.
7:6 J. fell on his face b. the a.
1 *Sam.* 5:3 D. was fallen be. the a.
1 *Chr.* 16: 37 left *before* the a. A.
2 *Chr.* 5:6 S. and congr. be. the a.

ARK of the Covenant.

Num. 10:33 a. c. of L. went bef.
Jud. 31:26 inside of a. c.
Jos. 4:7 waters cut off before a. c.
Jud. 20:27 a. c. of God was there
1 *Sam.* 4:3 let us fetch the a. c.
2 *Sam.* 15:34 Levites bearing a. c.
1 *Chr.* 17:1 a. c. under curtains
Jer. 3:16 shall my no more, a. c.
Heb. 9:4 tabern. which had a. c.

ARK of God.

1 *Sam.* 3:3 where a. *of G.* was
4:11 a. *of G.* was taken, 17, 22
6:3 if ye send away the o. a.
2 *Sam.* 6:7 there he died before a.
7:2 a. dwelleth within
15:25 a. *of God* into the city
1 *Chr.* 13:12 bring the a. home
15:2 none carry a. *of G.* but L.

ARM.

Ex. 15:16 greatness of thine a.
Deut. 31:20 layeth the a. with
1 *Sam.* 2:31 I will cut off thy a.
and the a. of thy father's h.
2 *Chr.* 32:8 with him is a. of flesh
30:32 sav.st o. that hath
31:22 a. fell from my shoulder
35:9 cry out by reason of the a.
34:15 high a. shall he broken
40:9 hast thou an a. like God?
Ps. 10:15 the a. of the wicked
44:3 nor their own a. save them
77:15 with thy a. red. thy peo.
80:13 then hast a mighty a.
21 mine a. shall strengthen
98:1 his holy a. hath gotten him
Cant. 8:6 as a seal on thine a.
Is. 9:20 the flesh of his a.
33:2 be their a. every morning
40:10 his a. shall rule for him
11 gather the lambs in a.
51:5 shall wait upon me, on
mine a. shall they trust
9 put on strength, O a. of Lord
52:10 hath made bare his holy a.
53:1 to whom is the a. of the L.
revealed? *John* 12:38
50:16 his a. brought salv. 63:5
62:8 hath sworn by the a.
63:12 with his glorious a.
Jer. 17:5 that maketh flesh his a.
31:5 I will fight with a strong a.
Ezek. 4:7 thine a. shall be bare.
31:3 broken a. of Pharaoh
31:17 into hell that were his a.
Dan. 11:6 retain power of the a.
Zec. 11:17 on his a.
Luke 1:51 showed str. with his a.
Acts 13:17 with a high a. brought

AHM, Verb.

1 *Pet.* 4:1 a. yours, with same m.

Stretched-out ARM.

Ex. 6:6 with a s.-*out* a.
Deut. 4:34 assayed to take nation
by a *stretched*-*out* a.
5:15 out thence with a a. 7:19;
26:8; *Jer.* 32:21
2 *Chr.* 6:32 thy *stretched*-*out* a.
Ps. 136:12 a. a. for his mercy
Ezek. 20:33 made earth by s. 32:17
31 I will gather you with s. a.

ARMS.

Gen. 49:24 a. of his hands
Deut. 33:27 the everlasting a.
2 *Sam.* 22:35 how of steel is brok.
by mine a. *Ps.* 18:34
Job 22:9 a. of the fatherless
Ps. 37:17 a. of wicked broken
Prov. 31:17 strengtheneth her a.
Is. 44:12 with strength of a.
49:22 bring thy sons in their a.
51:5 my a. shall judge the peo.

ARO

Ezek. 13:20 tear from your a.
30:22 break Pharaoh's a. 24
24 strength, a. of king of P. 25
Dan. 2:32 and his a. of silver
10:6 his a. like polished brass
11:15 a. of south shall not
22 with the a. of a flood shall
31 a. shall stand on his part
Hos. 7:15 strengthened their a.
11:3 taking them by their a.
Mark 9:36 taken him in his a.
10:16 took them up in his a.
Luke 2:28 S. took G. in his a.

ARMAGEDDON. *Rev.* 16:16

ARMED.

Job 39:21 goeth on to meet a. m.
Ps. 78:9 children of E. being a.
Prov. 6:11 as an a. man. 24:34
Luke 11:21 a strong man a.

ARMENIA. 2 *K.* 19:37; *Is.* 37:38

Jer. 38:12 rotten rags under thy a.
Ezek. 13:18 sew pillows to a.

ARMIES.

Ex. 12:17 your a. out of E.
Num. 33:1 their a. under Mos.
1 *Sam.* 17:10 defy the a. of Israel
26 should defy the a. of God
45 name of God of a. of Israel
Job 25:3 any number of his a. ?
Ps. 44:9 forth with our a.
68:12 kings of a. did flee apace
Cant. 6:13 company of two a.
Is. 34:2 fury upon all their a.
Mat. 22:7 he sent forth his a.
Luke 21:20 Jerus. compa. with a.
Heb. 11:34 to flight a.
Rev. 19:14 a. in heaven followed
19 kings and their a. gathered

1 *Sam.* 17:54 Goliah's a. in his
1 *K.* 22:38 washed his a.
2 *K.* 3:21 all able to put on a.
16:2 a fenced city also and a.
24:13 Hez. showed his precious
things, h. of his a. *Is.* 39:2
2 *Chr.* 28:14 took in that day so
Luke 11:22 a. wherein he
Rom. 13:12 put on a. of light
2 *Cor.* 6:7 approv. by a. of right
Eph. 6:11 put on the a. of God
13 take the whole a. of G.

ARMOR-BEARER.

Jud. 9:34 Abim. called his a.-*b.*
1 *Sam.* 14:7 a. *b.* said, do all that
16:21 David became his a.-*b.*
31:6 Saul died, and his a.-*b.*

ARMORY.

Cant. 4:4 builded for an a.
Jer. 50:25 L. hath opened his a.

ARMY.

Deut. 11:4 he did to the a. of E.
Jud. 9:29 increase thine a.
1 *K.* 20:19 a. like the a. lost
1 *Chr.* 32:21 praise before a.
Cant. 6:4 as a. with banners, 10
Jer. 37:7 I left your a. back
Ezek. 26:18 a. to serve a great
37:10 an exceeding great a.
Dan. 4:35 according to his will
in the a. of heaven
Joel 2:11 his voice before his a.
Acts 23:27 came I with an a.

ARNON.

Num. 21:14 brook of A. 22:36
Deut. 2:24 over the river of A.
Jud. 11:26 by the coasts of A.
Is. 16:2 shall be at fords of A.
Jer. 48:20 tell A. that

AROER.

Num. 32:34 child. of G. built A.
Deut. 2:36; 2 *Sam.* 24:5; 1 *Chr.* 5:8
Is. 17:2 cities of A. are forsaken
Jer. 48:19 inhabitant of A. stand

AROSE.

Gen. 37:7 and lo, my sheaf a.
Ex. 1:8 a. a new king over Eg.
knew not the Lord
Jud. 5:7 until I Deborah a. a mother
28:8 the people a. as one man
Jon. 1:6 a. a. against me
2 *K.* 23:25 aft. him a. there any
Mark 4:39 wrath of the Lord a.
Job 29:8 aged a. and stood up
K. 1:5 sun riseth where bu a.

ART

Dan. 6:19 the king a. early
Mat. 2:14 he a. and took child. 21
8:15 a. and ministered. *Lu.* 4:30
26 he a. and rebuked winds,
Mark 4:39 ; *Luke* 8:24
9:9 a. and follow, 19; *Mark* 2:14
25 the hand, and the maid a.
27:52 saints which slept a.
Mark 9:27 J. lifted him up, he a.
15:30 he a. and came to his f.
Acts 11:19 persec. which a. about
19:28 there a. no small stir
23:7 so said a. a dissension, 10

See nose.

AROSE and went.

1 *Sam.* 2:6 Samuel a. to Eli
1 *K.* 19:21 Elisha a. after Elijah
Jon. 3:3 so Jonah a. to Nineveh
Acts 9:39 Peter a. and went

ARPAD, ARPHAD.

2 *K.* 18:34 gods of A. *Is.* 36:19
19:13 king of A. ? *Is.* 37:13
Is. 10:9 is not Hamath as A. ?
Jer. 40:23 is confounded, and A.

ARPHAXAD.

Gen. 10:22 s. of Shem, A. 11:10
Luke 3:36 was the son of A.

ARRAY.

Job 6:4 terrors of God set in a.
Jer. 50:14 yourselves in a. ag. B.
See BATTLE.

ARRAY, Verb.

Est. 6:9 they may a. the man
Job 40:10 a. thyself with glory
Jer. 43:12 a. himself with land
1 *Tim.* 2:9 not with costly a.

ARRAYED.

Gen. 41:42 Pharaoh a. Joseph
2 *Chr.* 28:15 captives with sp. a.
Mat. 6:29 was not a. like one of these, *Luke* 12:27
Luke 23:11 Herod a. Christ
Acts 12:21 Herod a. in royal app.
Rev. 7:13 these in white
17:4 woman was a. in purple
19:8 to her was granted to be a.

ARROGANCY.

1 *Sam.* 2:3 let not a. come out
Prov. 8:13 pride and a. do I hate
Is. 13:11 cause a. of the proud
Jer. 48:29 M. his loftiness, his a.

ARROW.

Num. 20:16 Jonathan shot a.
2 *K.* 9:24 went out at his h.
13:17 a. of Lord's deliverance
19:32 nor shoot an a. there, *Is.*
37:33
Job 41:28 a. cannot make him
Ps. 11:2 their a. on the string
64:7 an a. sudd. he wounded
91:5 nor afraid for a. that flieth
Prov. 25:18 witness is a sharp a.
Jer. 9:8 tongue as an a. shot out
Lam. 3:12 as a mark for the a.
Zec. 9:14 his a. go forth

ARROWS.

Num. 24:8 through with a.
Deut. 32:23 mine a. upon them
42 mine a. drunk with blood
1 *Sam.* 20:20 will shoot three a.
2 *Sam.* 22:15 sent out a. and scattered them, *Ps.* 18:14
2 *K.* 13:15 take bow and a.
18 take the a. and smote
Job 6:4 a. of Almighty are
Ps. 7:13 ordaineth a. against
21:12 thine a. against them
38:2 thine a. stick fast in me
45:5 a. sharp in heart of enem.
57:4 teeth are spears and a.
58:7 take bow to shoot his a.
64:3 their a. even bitter
76:3 brake he the a. of bow
77:17 thine a. also went abroad
120:4 sharp a. of the mighty
127:4 as a. in hand of a mighty
141:6 shoot thine a. and destroy
Prov. 26:18 man who cast a.
Is. 5:28 whose a. of expert man
7:24 with a. and bows shall m.
21:4 make bright the a.
22:6 Elam bare quiver with a.
21:1 he made his a. bright.
39:3 cause them to pass
9 Israel shall burn bows and a.
Hab. 3:11 light of thine a.

ART, Verb.

Gen. 3:14 thou ? thou ?
Ps. 8:18 so thou art.

ASH

1 *K.* 22:4 as thou a. 2 *K.* 3:7
Jer. 14:22 a. not thou he, O L.
Luke 7:19 a. he that should
Rev. 11:17 a. and w. and a. 16:5

ART, S, Substantive.

Ex. 30:25 ointment after the a.
2 *Chr.* 16:14 spices prep. by a.
Acts 17:29 stones graven by a.
19:19 which used curious a.

ARTAXERXES.

Ezr. 4:7 ; 6:14 ; 7:1, 11, 21
Neh. 2:1 in 20th year of A. wine
5:14 from 20th to 33d year of A.

ARTEMAS. *Tit.* 3:12

ARTIFICER, S.

Gen. 4:22 T. Cain an instr. of a.
1 *Chr.* 29:5 works made by a.
Is. 3:3 away the cunning a.

ARTILLERY.

1 *Sam.* 20:40 Jonath. gave his a.

ASA.

1 *K.* 15:11 A. did right, 2 *Chr.* 14:2,
12, 13 ; 2 *Chr.* 15:8, 17 ; 16:2
1 *Chr.* 9:16 Berechiah, son of A.
2 *Chr.* 14:11 A. cried to the Lord

ASAHEL.

2 *Sam.* 2:18, 21, 32 ; 1 *Chr.* 2:16
3:27 Abner died for blood of A.
23:24 A. was one, 1 *Chr.* 11:26

ASAIAH.

1 *Chr.* 4:36 Jesoniah and A.
6:30 sons of Merari, A. 9:5
2 *Chr.* 34:20 king Josiah sent A.

ASAPH.

2 *K.* 18:18 Joah the son of A. the
recorder, 37 ; *Is.* 36:3, 22
1 *Chr.* 6:39 A. son of, 9:15 ; 13:17
16:7 delivered this psalm to A.
25:1 of the sons of A. 2 ; 26:1
2 *Chr.* 5:12 ; 20:14 ; 29:13 ;
35:15 ; *Ezr.* 2:41 ; 3:10 ; *Neh.*
7:44 ; 11:17, 22 ; 12:35

ASCEND.

Jos. 6:5 people shall a. up
Ps. 2:3 a. into hill, *Rom.* 10:6
135:7 vap. to a. *Jer.* 10:13 ; 51:16
135:8 if I a. up into heaven
Is. 14:13 I will a. to heaven, 14
Ezk. 38:9 a. and come
John 20:17 a. to my Father
Rev. 17:8 shall a. out of pit

ASCENDED.

Jud. 13:20 angel a. in the
Ps. 68:18 thou hast a. on high
Prov. 30:4 hath a. into heaven
John 3:13 no man hath a.
20:17 not yet a. to my Father
Acts 2:34 D. is not a. into the h.
Eph. 4:8 when he a. up
9 that he a. 10 some that a.
Rev. 8:4 smoke of the incense a.
11:12 a. up to heaven

ASCENDETH.

Rev. 11:7 the beast that a. out
14:11 smoke of their torment a.

ASCENDING.

Gen. 28:12 the angels of God a.
1 *Sam.* 28:13 I saw gods a. out
Luke 19:28 before a. up to Jeru.
John 1:51 angels of God a. and
Rev. 7:2 angel a. from the east

ASCENT.

2 *Sam.* 15:30 Dav. went up by the
a. of Olivet
1 *K.* 10:5 and his a. by which he
went up, 2 *Chr.* 9:4

ASCRIBE.

Deut. 32:3 a. ye greatness
Job 36:3 I will a. to my Maker
Ps. 68:34 a. ye strength to God

ASCRIBED.

1 *Sam.* 18:8 to David 10,000

ASENATH. *Gen.* 41:45,50 ; 46:20

ASH.

Is. 44:14 he planteth an a.

ASHAMED.

Gen. 2:25 m. and w. were not a.
Jud. 3:25 a. till they were greatly a.
1 *Chr.* 19:5

as people being a.
8:11 commence until a.
2 *Chr.* 30:15 the priests were a.
Ezr. 9:6 I am a. to lift up
Job 6:20 came, and were a.
11:3 shall no many make a. ?
19:3 not a. to make
Ps. 31:5 and their faces not a.

762 CRUDEN'S CONCORDANCE.

ASH

Ps. 74:21 not oppressed turn a.
Prov. 12:4 she that maketh a.
Is. 22:5 be a. of Ethiopia
24:23 the sun shall be a. when
30:5 a. of a people that could
33:9 L. is a. and hewn down
Jr. 2:26 as thief is a.
6:15 they a. ? at all a. 8:12
8:9 the wise men are a.
14:4 ploughmen were a.
48:13 a. of C. as Is. was a.
Ezk. 16:27 daughters of P. are a.
32:30 terror a. of their might
Luke 13:17 adversaries were a.
16:3 to beg I am a.
Rom. 1:16 not a. of the gospel
5:5 hope maketh not a.
6:21 whereof ye are now a. ?
2 Cor. 7:14 I am not a.
2 Tim. 1:12 neverth. I am not a.
16 O. was not a. of my chain
Ti. 2:11 not a. to call them
11:16 not a. to be called
ASHAMED and confounded. See CONFOUNDED.

Be ASHAMED.
Ps. 6:10 let my enemies be a.
25:3 that wait on thee be a.
let them be a. who transgress
31:1 let me never be a.
17 not be a. wicked be a. 35:26
69:6 wait be a. for my sake
86:17 wh. hate me, may be a.
109:28 let them be a.
119:78 let proud be a.
Is. 1:29 shall be a. of the oaks
23:4 be thou a. O Zidon
26:11 and be a. for their envy
42:17 be greatly a. that trust in
44:9 know, that they may be a.
41 all his fellows shall be a.
45:24 against him shall be a.
65:13 rejoice, ye shall be a.
66:5 and they shall be a.
Jer. 2:36 shalt be a. of Egypt
as refuseded to be a.
12:13 shalt be a. of your rev.
17:13 forsake thee shall be a.
23:11 my persecutors shall be a.
48:13 Moab shall be a. of C.
50:12 your mother shall be a.
Ezek. 16:61 and be a.
43:10 they may be a. of their
Hos. 4:19 be a. bec. of their sac.
10:6 Is. be a. of his own counsel
Joel 1:11 be ye a. O ye husbandm.
2:26 shall never be a. 27
Zec. 9:5 expectation shall be a.
13:4 every one be a. of his vis.
Mark 8:38 be a. of me. Luke 9:26
2 Chr. 9:4 we (that we say not you) should be a.
Phil. 1:20 in nothing I shall b. a.
2 Thes. 3:14 that may be a.
Tit. 2:8 contrary part may be a.
1 Pet. 3:16 may be a. that falsely
Not be, or Be not ASHAMED.
Num. 12:14 she b. a. seven days?
Ps. 25:2 in thee, let me n. b. a.
31:17 let me n. b. a. 119:116
37:19 shall n. b. a. in the evil
119:6 a. when I have respect
46 testimonies, and n. be a.
80 be sound, that I be n. a.
127:5 shall n. be a. but speak
Is. 29:22 Jacob shall not be a.
45:17 a. world without end
49:23 shall not be a. that wait
50:7 like a flint, I shall n. be a.
54:4 for thou shalt not be a.
Zep. 3:11 that day shalt thou a.
Rom. 9:33 believ. shall a. 10:11
2 Cor. 10:8 I should not be a.
2 Tim. 1:8 a. of testimony of L.
2:15 that needeth not be a.
1 Pet. 4:16 as a Chr. let him a.
1 John 2:28 a. before him

ASHDOD.
1 Sam. 5:1 the ark to A. 5
2 Chr. 26:6 wall of A. cit. ab. A.
Neh. 13:23 mar. wives of A. 24
Amos 1:8 ; 3:9 ; Zep.2:4 ; Zec. 9:6

ASHER.
Gen. 30:13 L. called his name A.
49:20 out of A. his bread fat
Deut. 33:24 of A. he said,
Jud. 5:17 A. on the sea-shore

Tribe of ASHER.
Num. 1:41 the tribe of A. 41,500
2:27 the tribe of A. shall
10:26 the host of tribe of A.
13:13 tribe of A. to spy, 31:27
Jos. 19:24 lot for tribe of A. 31
21:6 out of the tribe of A. 30
1 Chr. 6:62,74; Luke 2:36; Rev.7:6

ASK

ASHES.
Gen. 18:27 am but dust and a.
4 the a. without camp
Num. 19:9 gather the a.
1 K. 13:3 and a. poured out
20:38 disguised himself with a.
Est. 4:3 lay in sackcloth and a.
Job 2:8 sat down among the a.
13:12 your remem. like a.
30:19 become like dust and a.
42:6 and repent in dust and a.
Ps. 102:9 eaten a. like bread
147:16 the hoar-frost like a.
Is. 44:20 he feedeth on a.
58:5 to spread a. under him
61:3 to give them beauty for a.
Jer. 6:26 daughter, wallow in a.
25:34 ; 31:40
Ezk. 28:18 bring thee to a. on
Jon. 3:6 king sat in a.
Mal. 4:3 wicked be a. under
Mat. 11:21 repented long ago in sackcloth and a. Luke 10:13
Heb. 9:13 if the a. of a heifer
2 Pet. 2:6 cities of Sodom into a.

ASHTAROTH.
Deut. 1:4 at A. Jos. 9:10 ; 12:4
Jud. 2:13 Is. served A. 10:6
1 Sam. 7:3 strange gods and A. 4
12:10 because we have served A.
31:10 S.'s armor in house of A.
1 K. 11:33 have worshipped A.
1 Chr. 6:71 Gershom was giv. A.

ASHUR, or **ASSUR.**
Gen. 10:11 A. went forth. 22
Num. 24:22 A. shall carry, 24
1 Chr. 2:24 H. wife bare him A.
4:5 A. had two wives, 11 and
Ezr. 4:2 Esar-haddon, king of A.
Ps. 83:8 A. also is joined with
Ezek. 27:23 A. and Chil. 32:22
Hos. 14:3 A. shall not save us

ASIA.
Acts 6:9 of A. disputing Stephen
19:10 all they in A. heard
27 whom all A. worshippeth
1 Pet. 1:1 to strangers scat. in A.
2 K. 4:4 set a. that which
Mark 7:33 a. from the multitude
13:4 laid a. his garments
Heb. 12:1 lay a. every weight

See GO, GONE, TURN, WENT, LAY.

ASK.
Gen. 32:29 w. a. after my name
34:12 a. me never so much dowry and gift, and I will
Deut. 4:32 a. of the days that are
32:7 a. thy father
Jud. 18:5 a. counsel of God
1 Sam. 12:19 this evil to a. us
2:16 why doest thou a. of me
1 K. 2:3 God said. a. what I shall give thee, 2 Chr. 1:7
2 K. 2:9 a. what I shall do
2 Chr. 20:4 J. gathered to a. help
Job 12:7 a. the beasts
Ps. 2:8 a. of me, and I will give
Is. 7:11 a. thee a sign of L. a
12 I will not a. neither tempt
45:11 L. a. of things to come
58:2 they a. ordinances
Jer. 6:16 a. for the old paths
15:5 aside to a. how thou doest
18:13 a. among the heathen
38:14 I will a. thee a thing
50:5 a. the way to Zion
Lam. 4:4 children a. bread
Dan. 6:7 shall a. a petition
Hos. 4:12 people a. counsel
Mic. 4:11 a priests concerning
Hag. 2:11 a. now the law
Mat. 6:8 need of, before ye a.
7:7 a. and it shall be, Luke 11:9
9 his son a. bread, Luke 11:11
11 good things to them that a.
14:7 whatsoever she would a.
16:19 touch. any thing they a.
20:22 what ye a. Mark 10:38
21:22 whatsoever ye a.
22:46 a. him more questions, Mark 12:34; Luke 20:40
Mark 6:22 a. what thou wilt
9:32 afraid to a. him, Luke 9:45
Luke 6:30 goods, a. them not
11:13 Holy S. to them that a.
12:48 of him they will a.
John 1:19 sent priests to a. him
9:21 he is of age, a. him, 23
11:22 whatsoever thou a. of G.
14:13 a. in my name, 14:16
14 if ye a. in my name I will
13:7 abide in me, a. what ye
16:19 were desirous to a.

ASS

John 16:23 ye shall a. me nothing
24 a. and receive that your joy
30 that any should a.
18:21 a. them which heard me
Acts 10:29 I a. for what intent
1 Cor. 14:35 a. their husbands
Eph. 3:20 above all we can a.
Jam. 1:5 lack wisdom, let him a.
6 but let him a. in faith
4:2 ye have not, bec. ye a. not
3 ye a. and rec. not, bec. ye a.
1 John 3:22 we a. we receive
5:14 we a. according to his will
15 heareth us, whatever we a.
16 not unto death, he shall a.

See COUNSEL.

ASKED.
Jud. 5:25 he a. water
13:6 I a. not whence he was
1 Sam. 1:17 petition thou a.
1 K. 3:11 thou a. this thing
2 K. 2:10 hast a. hard thing
Ezr. 5:10 we a. their names
Job 21:29 a. them that go by
Ps. 21:4 he a. life of thee
105:40 people a. he brought
Is. 30:2 not a. at my mouth
41:28 when I a. of them, could
65:1 sought of them that a. not
Dan. 2:10 no king that a.
7:16 a. him the truth
Mat. 16:13 he a. his disciples,
Mark 8:27 ; Luke 9:18
22:23 Sadducees a. him, 35 ;
Mark 9:11 ; 10:2 ; 12:13
Luke 18:40 when near he a.
John 4:10 wouldest have a.
16:24 have ye a. nothing
Rom. 10:20 to them that a. not

ASKELON, or **ASHKELON.**
Jud. 1:18 Judah took G. and A.
14:19 Samson went down to A.
1 Sam. 6:17 for A. one, for Gath
2 Sam. 1:20 in the streets of A.
Jer. 25:20 I made A. and Azzah
47:5 A. is cut off with sword, 7
Amos 1:8 holds sceptre from A.
Zep. 2:4 A. a desolation, 7
Zec. 9:5 A. shall see; A. shall

ASKEST.
Jud. 13:18 why a. after my name?
John 4:9 a. drink of me
18:21 why a. thou me ?

ASKETH.
Ex. 19:14 thy son a. Deut. 6:20
Mic. 7:3 prince a. for a reward
Mat. 5:42 him that a. Luke 6:30
7:8 that a. receiv. Luke 11:10
John 16:5 none n. whither goest
1 Pet. 3:15 a. you a reason of

ASKING.
Ps. 78:18 tempting God by a.
Luke 2:46 a. them questions
John 8:1 they continued a.
1 Cor. 10:25 n. no question, 27

ASLEEP.
Jud. 4:21 Sisera was fast a.
Cant. 7:9 lips of those a. to speak
Jon. 1:5 Jonah was fast a.
Mat. 8:24 he was a. Mark 4:38
26:40 disciples a. Mark 14:37
Acts 7:60 Stephen fell a.
1 Cor. 15:6 but some are fallen a.
18 which are fallen a. in C.
51 not sleep, but be changed
2 Pet. 3:4 since fathers fell a. all

ASNAPPAR. Ezr. 4:10

ASP.S.
Deut. 32:33 wine is venom of a.
Job 20:14 meat is the gall of a.
16 he shall suck poison of a.
Is. 11:8 on the hole of the a.
Rom. 3:13 poison of a.

ASSAULT, ED.
Acts 14:5 an a. made of the G.
17:5 they a. the house of Jason

ASSAY, ED, ING.
Deut. 4:34 hath God a. to take
1 Sam. 17:39 David a. to go
Job 4:2 if we a. to commune
Acts 9:26 Saul a. to join himself
16:7 they a. to go to Bithynia
Heb. 11:29 the Egyptians a.

ASS.
Gen. 22:3 Abrah. saddled his a.
49:14 Issachar is a strong a.
Ex. 13:13 firstling of a. 34:20
23:4 if thou meet enemy's a.
12 thine ox and thine a.
Num. 16:15 not taken one a.
22:25 a. saw the angel, 23, 27
28 opened the mouth of a. 30

ASS

Deut. 22:10 with ox and a.
Jos. 15:18 lighted off her a. Jud.
1:14 ; 1 Sam. 25:23
Jud. 15:16 jawbone of an a.
1 K. 13:28 had not torn the a.
2 K. 6:25 a. head sold for 80 p.
Job 24:3 the a. of the fatherless
Prov. 36:3 a bridle for the a.
Is. 1:3 the a. his master's crib
Jer. 22:19 the burial of an a.
Zec. 9:9 cometh lowly riding on a. the foal of an a. Mat. 21:5
14:15 so be the plague of the a.
Luke 13:15 each loose his a.
14:5 have an a. fallen into pit
John 12:14 had found a young a.
2 Pet. 2:16 dumb a. speaking

See SADDLE.

ASS'S COLT.
Gen. 49:11 binding his a. c.
Job 11:12 born like a wild a. c.
John 12:15 sitting on an a. c.

Wild ASS.
Job 6:5 a. bray when he hath g.
39:5 sent out w. a. free
Jer. 2:24 w. a. used in the w'ness
Hos. 8:9 w. a. alone by himself

ASSES.
Jud. 5:10 ride on w. a.
1 Sam. 8:16 will I take your a.
9:3 a. of Kish were lost, 10:2
2 Sam. 16:1 a. for k. household
1 Chr. 27:30 over a. was Johd.
2 Chr. 28:15 carried feeble on a.
Job 42:12 J. had a thousand she a.
Is. 21:7 he saw a chariot of a.
Ezek. 23:20 flesh as flesh of a.

Wild ASSES.
Job 24:5 as wild a. go they forth
Ps. 104:11 w. a. quench
Is. 32:14 shall be a joy of w. a.
Jer. 14:6 wild a. snuffed wind
Dan. 5:21 dwell. was with w. a.

Young ASSES.
Is. 30:6 riches on young a.
24 y. a. that ear the ground

ASSEMBLE.
Is. 11:12 he shall a. outcasts
45:20 a. and come, and draw n.
48:14 all ye a. yourselves
Jer. 4:5 a. and let us go
8:14 why sit still? a. let us
Ezek. 11:17 I will a. you out of
39:17 a. gather to my sacrifice
Hos. 7:14 a. for corn and wine
Joel 2:16 a. elders, gather
3:11 a. and come. all ye heathen
Amos 3:9 a. on m. Samaria
Mic. 2:12 I will a. O J.
4:6 I will a. her that halteth
Zep. 3:8 I will a. the kingdoms

ASSEMBLED.
1 Sam. 2:22 lay with w. that a.
Ezr. 9:4 a. every one that trem.
Neh. 9:1 ch. of Is. a. with fast.
Est. 9:16 Jews in k.'s provinces
43:9 let the people be a. who
Jer. 5:7 a. by troops in harlot's h.
Mat. 28:12 when a. gave large
John 20:19 disciples a. for fear
Acts 1:4 being a. not to depart
4:31 where they were a.
11:26 w. year a. with church
15:25 it seemed good to us a.

ASSEMBLING.
Heb. 10:25 forsake not the a.

ASSEMBLY.
Gen. 49:6 their a. mine honor
Ex. 12:3 kill a. with hunger
Lev. 4:13 from the eyes of the a.
Deut. 9:10 L. spake out of fire in day of a. 10:4 ; 18:16
1 Sam. 17:47 a. shall know Lord
1 Chr. 30:23 a. took counsel
Ps. 22:16 the a. of the wicked
89:7 feared in a. of the saints
107:32 praise him in a.
111:1 I will praise him in a.
Prov. 5:14 was in all evil in a.
Jer. 6:11 on a. of young men
9:2 an a. of treacherous men
15:17 sat not in a. of mockers
Lam. 2:6 dest. places of the a.
Ezek. 13:9 shall not be in the a.
Acts 19:32 the a. was confused
39 deter, in a lawful a. 41
Heb. 12:23 to the general a.
Jam. 2:2 come to your a. a man

Solemn ASSEMBLY.
Lev. 23:36 eighth day is a. s. a.
Num. 29:35 ; N. 8. 8:18
Deut. 16:8 seventh day s. a. to L.

CRUDEN'S CONCORDANCE. 763

AST
2 *K*. 10:20 a *s. a.* for Baal
2 *Chr.* 7:9 eighth d. made a *s. a.*
Joel 1:14 called a *s. a.* 2:15
Zep. 3:18 sorrowful for the *s. a.*

ASSEMBLIES.
Ps. 68:14 *a.* of violent men
Je. 12:11 *a.* by masters of *a.*
Is. 1:13 calling of *a.*
4:5 create on her *a.* a cloud
Ezek. 44:24 in all mine *a.*
Amos 5:21 not smell in your *a.*

ASSENTED.
Acts 24:9 Jews also *a.*

ASSOCIATE.
Is. 8:9 *a.* and be broken in p.

ASSUAGE, ED.
Gen. 8:1 and the waters *a.*
Job 16:5 mov. of lips should *a.*
6 my grief is not *a.*

ASSURANCE.
Deut. 28:66 shall have none *a.*
Is. 32:17 effect of righteous. *a.*
Acts 17:31 he hath given *a.*
Col. 2:2 full *a* of understanding
1 *Thes.* 1:3 came in much *a.*
H'b. 6:11 to the full *a.* of hope
10:22 draw near in full *a.*

ASSURE.
1 *John* 3:19 shall *a.* our hearts

ASSURED.
Jer. 14:13 give you *a.* peace
2 *Tim.* 3:14 thou hast been *a.*

ASSUREDLY.
Acts 2:36 house of Israel know *a.*
16:10 *a.* gathering, L. called us

ASSYRIA.
Gen. 2:14 toward the east of A.
25:18 dwelt as thou guest to A.
2 *K.* 15:29 cap. to A. 17:6; 18:11
Is. 7:18 that is a land of A.
11:11 recover people from A. 16
19:23 out of Egypt to A. 24, 25
27:13 were ready to perish in A.
Jer. 2:18 in the way of A. ?
Ezek. 27:7 with men of A.
Hos. 7:11 to A. 8:9 up to A.
9:3 eat unclean things in A.
17:6 carried to A. for a present
11:11 dove out of the land of A.
Mic. 5:6 waste the land of A.
7:12 come to thee from A.
Zep. 2:13 destroy A. and Nin.
Zec. 10:10 g. them out of A. 11
See KINGS.

ASTONISHED.
Lev. 26:32 enemies shall be *a.*
1 *K.* 9:8 shall be *a. Jer.* 18:16; 19:8; 42:17; 50:13
Ezr. 9:3 and sat down *a.*
Job 17:8 upright shall be *a.*
18:20 come after shall be *a.*
26:11 pillars of heaven are *a.*
Is. 52:14 many were *a.* at thee
Jer. 2:12 be *a.* O ye heavens
4:9 the priests shall be *a.*
14:9 why be as a man *a.*
Ezek. 3:15 I remained *a.* seven d.
4:17 *a.* one with another
26:16 shall tremble and be *a.*
28:19 know there shall be *a.*
Dan. 3:24 Nebuchadnez. was *a.*
4:19 Daniel was *a.* for one hour
5:9 his lords *a.*
8:27 Daniel was *a.* at the vision
Mat. 7:28 *a.* at his, 22:37; *Mark* 1:22; 6:2; 11:18; *Luke* 4:32
Mark 5:42 *a.* with great astonish.
7:37 beyond measure *a.* 10:26
10:24 disciples were *a.*
Luke 2:47 *a.* at his answers
5:9 was *a.* at draught of fishes
8:56 her parents were *a.* but he
24:22 certain women made us *a.*
Acts 9:6 Saul trembling and *a.*
10:45 which believed were *a.*
12:16 saw Peter, they were *a.*
13:12 deputy believed, being *a.*

ASTONISHMENT.
Deut. 28:28 shall smite with *a.*
37 become an *a.* and a proverb
2 *Chr.* 7:21 shall be an *a.*
29:8 hath delivered them to *a.*
Ps. 60:3 to drink the wine of *a.*
Jer. 8:21 I am black, *a.* hath
25:9 I will make them an *a.* 18
11 land be a desolation and *a.*
29:18 deliver them to be an *a.*
42:18 excera. and an *a.* 44:12
44:22 therei. is your land an *a.*
51:37 Babyl. shall become an *a.*
Ezek. 4:16 drink w. with *a.* 12:19
5:15 an *a.* to the nations
23:33 be filled with cup of *a.*
Zec. 12:4 smite horse with *a.*

AUG
ASTRAY. *See* WENT, GO, GONE.

ASTROLOGERS.
Is. 47:13 let now *a.* star-gazers
Dan. 1:20 ten times better th. *a.*
2:27 cannot the *a.* show
4:7 came in magicians and *a.*
5:7 king cried to bring in the *a.*

ASUNDER. *See* CLEAVE, CUT, DIVIDE, PUT.

ASYNCRITUS. *Rom.* 16:14

ATAD. *Gen.* 50:10, 11

ATE.
Ps. 106:28 *a.* sacrifi. of the dead
Dan. 10:3 I *a.* no pleasant bread
Rev. 10:10 book, and *a.* it up

ATHALIAH.
2 *K.* 8:26 Ahaz. mother was A.
11:1 A. destroyed, 2 *Chr.* 22:10
2 hid Joash from A. 20
1 *Chr.* 8:26 Ben. Shehari. and A.
2 *Chr.* 24:7 the sons of A. 24:11
Ezr. 8:7 Jeshaiah son of A.

ATHENIANS. *Acts* 17:21

ATHENS.
Acts 17:15 bro't Paul to A. 16, 22
18:1 Paul departed from A.
1 *Thes.* 3:1 good to be left at A.

ATHIRST.
Mat. 25:44 when saw we thee *a.*
Rev. 21:6 give to him that is *a.*
22:17 let him that is *a.* come

ATONEMENT.
Ex. 30:16 shall take *a.* money
Lev. 4:20 *a.* for them, 26, 31, 35; 5:6; 6:7; 8:34; 12:8; 14:18; *Num.* 15:25
9:7 make *a.* for thyself, 10:17
16:10 the scape-goat to make *a.*
17 there, when maketh *a.*
34 to make *a.* once a year
23:28 no work, it is a day of *a.*
25:9 day of *a.* make trumpet
Num. 16:46 make *a.* for wrath
31:50 ear-rings to make an *a.*
2 *Sam.* 21:3 wherewith make *a.*
Rom. 5:11 we have rec. the *a.*

ATTAIN.
Ps. 139:6 I cannot *a.* unto it
Prov. 1:5 man of u. *a.* wisdom
Hos. 8:5 they *a.* to innocency ?
Phil. 3:11 might *a.* to resurrec.
Acts 27:12 if they might *a.* to
Rom. 9:30 not *a.* to righteous.

ATTAINED.
Gen. 47:9 not *a.* to days of fath.
31 Is. hath not *a.* to law
Phil. 3:13 I had already *a.*
16 already *a.* let us walk
1 *Tim.* 4:6 whereto thou *a.*

ATTALIA. *Acts* 14:25

ATTEND.
Ps. 17:1 *a.* to my c. 61:1; 142:6
55:2 *a.* to me, I mourn
86:6 *a.* to the voice
Prov. 4:1 *a.* to know understand.
20 son, *a.* to my words, 7:24
5:1 my son, *a.* to my wisdom
1 *Cor.* 7:35 *a.* on Lord

ATTENDANCE.
1 *Tim.* 4:13 give *a.* to reading
Heb. 7:13 gave *a.* at altar

ATTENDED.
Job 32:12 I *a.* none convinced J.
Ps. 66:19 hath *a.* to my prayer
Acts 16:14 she *a.* to things spok.

ATTENDING.
Rom. 13:6 ministers *a.* contin.

ATTENT.
2 *Chr.* 6:40 mine eyes be *a.*
7:15 shall be *a.* to the prayer

ATTENTIVE.
Neh. 1:6 let thine ear now be *a.*
11: *Ps.* 18:2
8:3 people were *a. Luke* 19:48

ATTENTIVELY.
Job 37:2 hear *a.* noise of his v.

ATTIRE.
Prov. 7:10 with *a.* of harlot
Jer. 2:32 a bride forget her *a.* ?
Ezek. 23:15 exceeding in dyed *a.*

AUDIENCE.
Ex. 24:7 and read in *a.*
1 Chr. 28:8 in *a.* of our God
Luke 7:1 in *a.* of the people
20:45 he said in *a.* of disciples
Acts 13:16 ye that fear G. give *a.*
22 and multitude gave *a.* 22:22

AUGHT, *See* OUGHT.

AUGMENT.
Num. 32:14 to *a.* fierce anger

AWA
AUGUSTUS.
Luke 2:1 decree from Cesar A.
Acts 25:21 P. appealed to A. 25
27:1 Julius, a centurion of A.

AUNT.
Lev. 18:14 his wife, she is thy *a.*

AUSTERE.
Luke 19:21 thou art an *a.* man

AUTHOR.
1 *Cor.* 14:33 not *a.* of confusion
Heb. 5:9 became *a.* of salvation
12:2 Jesus, the *a.* and finisher

AUTHORITY, IES.
Prov. 29:2 righteous are in *a.*
Mat. 7:29 having *a. Mark* 1:22
8:9 a man under *a. Luke* 7:8
20:25 exercise *a. Mark* 10:42
21:23 by what *a. Mark* 11:28
Mark 1:27 for with *a.* com. unclean spirits, *Luke* 4:36
13:34 gave *a.* to his servants
Luke 9:1 power and *a.* over
19:17 have thou *a.* over
12:30 deliver him to *a.*
22:25 exercise *a.* called benef.
John 5:27 *a.* to execute judgm.
Acts 8:27 eunuch of great *a.*
9:14 hath *a.* to bind, 26:10, 12
1 *Cor.* 15:24 put down all *a.*
1 *Tim.* 2:2 supplii. for all in *a.*
12 women to usurp *a.* over
Tit. 2:15 rebuke with all *a.*
1 *Pet.* 3:22 and *a.* made subject to
Rev. 13:2 gave him great *a.*

AVAILETH.
Gal. 5:6 Christ cir. *a.* not, 6:15
Jam. 5:16 prayer of right *a.*

AVEN.
Ezek. 30:17 and *A.* fall
Hos. 10:8 high of A. *Amos* 1:5

AVENGE.
Lev. 19:18 thou shalt not *a.*
26:25 *a.* the quarrel of my cov.
Num. 31:2 *a.* Is. of Midianites, 3
Deut. 32:43 *a.* blood of servants
1 *Sam.* 24:12 Lord *a.* me of thee
Is. 1:24 *a.* me of mine enemies
Jer. 46:10 that he may *a.*
Hos. 1:4 will *a.* blood of Jezreel
Luke 18:3 *a.* me of mine adver.
7 shall not God *a.* his own el.
8 he will *a.* them speedily
Rom. 12:19 *a.* not yourselves
Rev. 6:10 dost thou not *a.* our

AVENGED.
Gen. 4:24 Cain be *a.* seven-fold
Jos. 10:13 stayed till peo. had *a.*
Jud. 15:7 yet I will be *a.*
16:28 *a.* of Philis. of my
1 *Sam.* 14:24 that I may be *a.*
18:25 foreskins to be *a.*
25:31 my Lord hath *a.* himself
2 *Sam.* 4:8 hath *a.* my lord
18:19 the Lord hath *a.* him
Jer. 5:9 my soul be *a.* 29; 9:9
Acts 7:24 *a.* him oppressed
Rev. 18:20 God hath *a.* you
19:2 *a.* blood of his servants

AVENGER.
Num. 35:12 from *a. Jos.* 20:3
Deut. 19:6 lest *a.* pursue
12 the elders deliver him to *a.*
Ps. 8:2 mightest still the *a.*
44:16 by r. of the enemy and *a.*
1 *Thes.* 4:6 Lord is *a.* of all such

AVENGETH.
2 *Sam.* 22:48 G. *a.* me, *Ps.* 18:47

AVENGING.
Jud. 5:2 praise L. for *a.* of Isr.

AVERSE.
Mic. 2:8 men from war *a.*

AVOID.
Prov. 4:15 *a.* it, pass not by it
Rom. 16:17 divisions, and *a.*
2 *Tim.* 2:23 unl. questions *a.*
Tit. 3:9 *a.* foolish questions

AVOIDING.
2 *Cor.* 8:20 *a.* this, that no man
1 *Tim.* 6:20 *a.* profane babblings

AVOUCHED.
Deut. 26:17 *a.* the Lord to be
18 *a.* thee to be his people

AWAKE.
Jud. 5:12 *a.* a. Deb., *a. a.* utter
Job 8:6 he would *a.* for thee
14:12 he not come forth, *a.*
Ps. 7:6 for me, 35:23
17:15 I *a.* with thy likeness
44:23 *a.* why sleepest thou
57:8 *a.* my glory, I w. *a.* 108:2
59:4 they prepare, *a.* to help

BAA
Ps. 59:5 O L. *a.* to visit all the
Prov. 23:35 when shall I *a.*
Cant. 2:7 *a.* my love, 3:5; 8:4
4:16 *a.* O north wind
Is. 26:19 *a.* ye that dwell
51:9 *a. a.* put on strength, O arm of the Lord *a.* 52:1
17 *a. a.* stand up, O Jerusalem
Jer. 51:57 perp. sleep, and not *a.*
Joel 1:5 *a.* ye drunkards, weep
Hab. 2:7 *a.* that shall vex thee
19 that saith to the wood, *a.*
Zec. 13:7 *a.* O sword ag. my
Mark 4:38 and they *a.* him
Luke 9:32 when *a.* saw his glory
John 11:11 that I may *a.* him
Rom. 13:11 it is high time to *a.*
1 *Cor.* 15:34 *a.* to righteousness
Eph. 5:14 *a.* thou that sleepest

AWAKED.
1 *Sam.* 26:12 knew it, neither *a.*
1 *K.* 18:27 and must be *a.*
2 *K.* 4:31 the child is not *a.*
Ps. 3:5 I *a.* for L. sustained mb
78:65 L. *a.* as one out of sleep
Jer. 31:26 I *a.* and behold

AWAKEST.
Ps. 73:20 when thou *a.* shalt
Prov. 6:22 when thou *a.* it sha.

AWAKETH, ING.
Ps. 73:20 dream when one *a.*
Is. 29:8 he *a.* and his soul
Acts 16:27 Keeper of the prison *a.*

AWARE.
Cant. 6:12 I was *a.* my soul
Jer. 50:24 O, and was not *a.*
Luke 11:44 over them not *a.*

AWAY.
Is. 1:13 I cannot *a.* with
Luke 23:18 *a.* with this man
John 19:15 *a.* with h., *Acts* 21:36
1 *Cor.* 5:2 *a.* with such a fellow

AWE.
Ps. 4:4 stand in *a.* and sin not
33:8 inhab. of world stand in *a.*
119:161 my heart standeth in *a.*

AWL.
Ex. 21:6 bore his ear with an *a.*
Deut. 15:17 thou shalt take an *a.*

AWOKE.
Mat. 8:25 discip. *a.* h. *Luke* 8:24

AXE.
Deut. 20:19 destroy trees by *a.*
1 *Sam.* 9:48 Abimelech took an *a.*
13:20 went to sharpen *a.*
1 *K.* 6:7 a-head fell into w.
2 *K.* 6:5 *a.*-head fell into w.
Is. 10:15 shall the *a.* boast
Jer. 10:3 cuts a tree with the *a.*
51:20 thou art my battle-*a.*
Mat. 3:10 *a.* is laid, *Luke* 3:9

AXES.
1 *Sam.* 13:21 had a file for the *a.*
2 *Sam.* 12:31 he put them under *a.* of iron, 1 *Chr.* 20:3
Ps. 74:5 fam. as he lifted up *a.*
6 break carved work with *a.*
Jer. 46:22 against her with *a.*
Ezek. 26:9 with *a.* break down

B.

BAALAH. *Jos.* 15:9
BAAL-GAD. *Jos.* 11:17
BAAL-HERMON. *Jud.* 3:3

BAAL.
Num. 22:41 to high places of B.
Jud. 2:13 Is. served B. and Ash.
6:25 down the altar of B. 31
Jud. 6:31 B. and worshipped
10:10 forsaken G. and served B.
19:18 7,000 in Israel which have not bowed to B. *Rom.* 11:4
2 *K.* 10:19 sac. to do for B. 20
hath broken house of B.
17:16 host of heaven served B.
21:3 Manas. reared altars for B.
23:4 bring all the vessels for B.
Jer. 2:8 proph. prophesied by B.
7:9 inc. to B.? 11:13, 17; 32:29
12:16 to swear by B.
19:5 built high places of B.
23:13 prophesied in B.
Hos. 2:8 silver and gold for B.
13:1 Ephraim offended in B.
Zep. 1:1 cut off remnant of B.
BAAL-BERITH. *Jud.* 8:3
BAAL-HAMON. *Cant.* 8:11
BAALI. *Hos.* 2:16

BAALIM.
Jud. 2:11 Is. B.; 3:7; 10:6, 13
8:33 Isr. went whoring after B.
1 *Sam.* 7:4 Israel put away B.

764 CRUDEN'S CONCORDANCE.

BAC
1 K. 18:18 hast followed B.
2 Chr. 17:3 J. sought not to B.
24:7 dedic. things on B. 28:2
33:3 M. reared altars for B.
34:4 brake the altars of B.
Jer. 2:23 have not gone after B.
9:14 have walked after B.
Hos. 2:13 on her days of B. 17

DAALIS. Jer. 40:14
BAAL-MEON. Ezek. 25:9

BAAL-PEOR.
Num. 25:3 Is. joined himself to B. 5; Ps. 106:28; Hos. 9:10
Deut. 4:3 Lord did because of B.
BAAL-PERAZIM. 2 Sam. 5:20;
1 Chr. 14:11
BAAL-SHALISHA. 2 K. 4:42
BAAL-TAMAR. Jud. 20:33
BAAL-ZEBUB. 2 K. 1:2, 16
BAAL-ZEPHON. Ex. 14:2;
Num. 33:7

BAANAH.
2 Sam. 4:6 Rechab and B. esc.
23:29 Heleb the son of B.
1 K. 4:16 B. the son of H.
Ezr. 2:2 D. c. to. Neh. 7:7; 10:27

BAASHA.
1 K. 15:16, 19, 27; 16:1, 6, 11, 12;
21:22; 2 K. 9:9; 2 Chr. 16:3;
Jer. 41:9

BABBLER.
Ec. 10:11 and a b. is no better
Acts 17:18 what will this b. say?

BABBLING, S.
Prov. 23:29 who hath b.?
1 Tim. 6:20 avoiding vain b.
2 Tim. 2:16 profane and vain b.

BABE, S.
Ex. 2:6 behold the b. wept
Luke 1:41 b. leaped in my womb
44, leaped in my womb
2:12 find b. wrapped in swad.
16 the b. lying in a manger
Heb. 5:13 for he is a b.
Ps. 8:2 mouth of b. Mat. 21:16
17:14 leave substance to their b.
Is. 3:4 princes and b. shall rule
Mat. 11:25 rev. t. to b. Luke 10:21
Rom. 2:20 a teacher of b.
1 Cor. 3:1 as unto b. in Christ
1 Pet. 2:2 as new-born b. desire

BABEL. Gen. 10:10; 11:9

BABYLON.
Mat. 1:17 the carrying into B.
Acts 7:43 carry away beyond B.
1 Pet. 5:13 church at B. saluteth
Rev. 14:8 B. is fallen, is fallen
16:19 B. came in remembrance
17:5 B. the mother of harlots
18:10 alas, that city B. 21
See DAUGHTER.

BABYLONIANS. Ezek. 23:15, 17
BABYLONISH. Jos. 7:21
BACA. Ps. 84:6

BACK.
1 K. 14:9 behind t. b. Ezek. 23:35
Ps. 21:12 turn their b.
129:3 ploughed on my b.
Prov. 10:13 rod for b. 19:29; 26:3
Is. 38:17 my sins behind thy b.
50:6 my b. to the smiters
Jer. 2:27 have turned b. unto me
18:17 will show b. not the face
32:33 turned to me b. and not
48:39 turned the b. with shame
Lam. 1:10 how down their b.

BACK, Adjective.
Ex. 33:23 shalt see my b. parts

BACKS.
Neh. 9:26 thy law behind their b.
Ezek. 8:16 their b. toward the
10:12 body, and b. full of
See TURNED.

BACKBITERS.
Rom. 1:30 b. haters of God
BACKBITETH.
Ps. 15:3 that b. not with his
BACKBITING, S.
Prov. 25:23 a b. tongue
2 Cor. 12:20 there be debates, b.

BACKSLIDER.
Prov. 14:14 b. in heart be filled

BACKSLIDING, S.
Jer. 2:19 thy b. shall reprove
3:6 what I. Israel hath done
8 whereby b. Israel com. ad.
3:11 b. Is. hath justified herself
12 return thou O. Israel,
14 O b. children, saith L. 22
5:6 because their b. increased
8:5 back by a perpetual b.

BAL
Jer. 14:7 for our b. are many
31:22 O b. daughter, 49:4
Hos. 4:16 Is. slideth back as a b.
11:7 are bent to b. from me
14:4 I will heal their b. I will

BACKWARD.
Gen. 9:23 b. their faces were b.
49:17 his rider shall fall b.
2 K. 20:10 return b. Is. 38:8
Job 23:8 b. I cannot perceive h.
Ps. 40:14 driven b. that wish me
70:2 turned b. that desire
Is. 1:4 they are gone away b.
28:13 they might go and fall b.
44:25 that turneth wise men b.
59:14 judgm. is turned away b.
Jer. 7:24 went b. not forward
15:6 thou art gone b. therefore
Lam. 1:8 sigheth and turn. b.
John 18:6 went b. and fell to

BAD.
Gen. 24:50 speak b. or good
31:24 to Jacob good or b. 29
Lev. 27:10 a good for b. or b.
Num. 13:9 land if good or b.
24:13 to do either good or b.
2 Sam. 13:22 spake good nor b.
14:17 to discern good or b.
1 K. 3:9 discern good and b.
Mat. 13:48 but cast the b. away
22:10 good and b. and the wed.
2 Cor. 5:10 whether good or b.

BADNESS.
Gen. 41:19 never saw in E. for b.

BADE, EST.
Gen. 27:19 have done as thou b.
Luke 14:9 he that b. thee, 10
16 a supper, and b. many
Acts 11:12 Spirit b. me go
18:21 but b. them farewell

BADGERS.
Ex. 26:14 cov. above of b. skins
35:7 skins dyed red, b. skins
Ezek. 16:10 I shod thee w. b. sk.

BAG.
Deut. 25:13 in thy b. div. weig.
1 Sam. 17:40 sm. stones in a b.
Job 14:17 trans. is sealed in a b.
Pr. 7:20 taken a b. of money
Mic. 6:11 b. of deceitful weights
Hag. 1:6 wages to put in a b. w.
John 12:6 a thief, and had the b.
13:29 because Judas had the b.

BAGS.
2 K. 5:23 two talents in two b.
12:10 they put up in b.
Luke 12:33 prov. b. that wax not

BAHURIM.
2 Sam. 3:16 behind her to B.
16:5 when David came to B.
17:18 came to a house in B.
19:16 a Benj. of B. 1 K. 2:8

BAJITH.
Is. 15:2 he is gone up to B.

BAKE.
Ex. 16:23 that your will b.
Lev. 24:5 and b. twelve cakes
26:26 ten women shall b.
1 Sam. 28:24 woman at E. did b.
Ezek. 4:12 shall b. it with

BAKE-MEATS.
Gen. 40:17 b.-meats for Pharaoh

BAKEN.
1 K. 19:6 was b. on the coals

BAKER.
Gen. 40:1 b. had offended the k.
22 hanged b. as Jo. interpreted
41:10 in ward me and chief b.
Hos. 7:4 oven heated by the b.
6 their b. sleepeth all the n.

BAKERS.
Gen. 40:2 wroth ag. chief of b.
1 Sam. 8:13 daughters to be b.
Jer. 37:21 bread out of b. street

BAKETH.
Is. 44:15 he b. bread, yea, he

BALAAM.
Num. 22:5, 9, 14, 25, 31, 35; 23:4,
30; 24:2, 3, 25; 31:8, 16
Deut. 23:4 Neh. 13:2
Jos. 24:9 B. arose and warred
Jud. 11:25 better than B.?

BAN
Mic. 6:5 remember what B. k.
Rev. 2:14 who taught B. to cast
BALAK.
Jud. 13:40 he is s. ro. yet clean, 41
2 K. 2:23 go up thou b. head
Jer. 16:6 make themselves b.
48:37 every head shall be b.
Ezek. 27:31 make themselves b.
29:18 every head was made b.
Mic. 1:16 make thee b. and poll

BALD-LOCUST.
Lev. 11:22 ye may eat the b.

BALDNESS.
Lev. 21:5 make b. on their head
Deut. 14:1 b. between your eyes
Is. 3:24 inst. of well-set hair, b.
15:2 on heads b. and beard cut
22:12 the Lord did call to b.
Jer. 47:5 b. is come upon Gaza
Ezek. 7:18 b. on their h. Am. 8:10
Mic. 1:16 enlarge thy b.

BALANCE.
Job 31:6 be weighed in even b.
Ps. 62:9 laid in the b. are van.
Prov. 11:1 a false b. 20:23
16:11 just w. and b. are Lord's
Is. 40:12 weighed hills in a b.
15 as a small dust of the b.
46:6 and weighs silver in the b.

BALANCES.
Lev. 19:36 just b. Ezek. 45:10
Job 6:2 calamity laid in the b.
Ezek. 5:1 take b. to weigh
25:7 in the b. and found
Hos. 12:7 b. of deceit
Amos 8:5 falsifying the b.
Mic. 6:11 pure with wicked b. ?
Rev. 6:5 he that sat on h. had b.

BALANCINGS.
Job 37:16 kn. the b. of t. clouds

BALL.
Is. 22:18 will toss thee like a b.

BALM.
Gen. 37:25 Ishmaelites bearing b.
43:11 take a little b. and honey
Jer. 8:22 is there no b. in Gilead?
46:11 to Gilead and take b. O
51:8 howl take b. for her pain
Ezek. 27:17 J. traded in honey b.

BAMAH. Ezek. 20:29

BAND, S.
Lev. 26:13 the b. of your yoke
Jud. 15:14 b. loosed off h. hands
2 K. 23:33 Phar. put Jeh. in b.
Job 38:9 darkness a swaddling b.
31 or loose the b. of Orion?
39:5 the b. of the wild ass?
10 the unicorn with his b. ?
Ps. 2:3 break their b. asunder
73:4 there are no b.
107:14 brake their b. in sunder
Ec. 7:26 snares, hands as b.
Is. 28:22 lest b. be made strong
52:2 loose from b. of thy neck
58:6 loose the b. of wickedness
Jer. 2:20 I have burst thy b.
Ezek. 3:25 shall put b. on thee
4:8 I will lay b. upon thee
34:27 broken the b. of their y.
Dan. 4:15 with a b. of iron, 23
Hos. 11:4 drew them with b.
Zec. 11:7 staves, beauty and b.
14 mine other staff, even b.
Luke 8:29 he brake b.
Acts 16:26 every one's b. were lo.
22:30 loosed Paul from his b.
Col. 2:19 all the body by b.
See BONDS.

BAND, S−companies.
Gen. 32:10 I am become two b.
1 Sam. 10:26 went with him a b.
2 K. 13:21 a man, spied a b.
24:2 L. sent b. of Chaldeans, b.
1 Chr. 12:18 made thee cap. of b.
21 David ag. the b. of rovers
Job 1:17 Chald. made three b.
Ps. 119:61 b. of wicked robbed
Ezek. 12:14 will scatter all his b.
38:22 rain on him and his b.
Hos. 11:4 with b. of a man, Mark 15:16
John 18:3 Judas having re. b.
12 then the b. and the captain
Acts 10:1 b. called the Italian b.
21:31 tid. came to cap. of the b.
27:1 to Jul. cent. of Augustus' b.

BANDED.
Acts 23:12 certain of the Jews b.

BANK.
Gen. 41:17 I stood on the b.
Deut. 4:48 Aroer by the b. of Ar-non, Jos. 12:2; 13:9, 16
2 Sam. 20:15 a b. ag. the city

BAP
2 K. 2:13 E. stood by the b.
19:32 not cast a b. Is. 37:33
Ezek. 47:7 at b. of river
Dan. 12:5 one on this side, other on that side of the b.
Luke 19:23 money into the b.?

BANKS.
Jos. 3:15 Jord. overfl. his b. 4:18

BANNER.
Ps. 60:4 a b. to them that fear
Cant. 2:4 his b. over me was
Is. 13:2 lift ye up a b.

BANNERS.
Cant. 6:4 terr. as an army w. b.

BANISHED.
2 Sam. 14:14 fetch home his b.
14 that his b. be not expelled

BANISHMENT.
Ezr. 7:26 whether to death or b.
Lam. 2:14 have seen causes of b.

BANQUET.
Est. 5:4 Haman come to b. 5, 8
6 to Esther at b. of wine, 7:2
Job 41:6 make a b. of him
Amos 6:7 b. of them that

BANQUET-HOUSE.
Dan. 5:10 came into the b.-h.

BANQUETING, S.
Cant. 2:4 brought me to the b.
1 Pet. 4:3 we walked in lusts, b.

BAPTISM, S.
Mat. 3:7 Pharisees come to his b.
20:22 bap. with b. Mark 10:38
21:25 the b. of J. whence was
it? Mark 11:30; Luke 20:4
Mark 1:4 J. did baptize, and pre.
the b. of repent. Luke 3:3
Luke 7:29 publicans with b. of J.
12:50 a b. to be baptiz. with
Acts 1:22 beginning from b. of J.
10:37 after b. which J. preached
13:24 J. prea. b. of repentance
18:25 Apollos knowing only b.
19:3 they said unto John's b.
4 John bap. with b. of repent.
Rom. 6:4 buried with him by b.
Eph. 4:5 one L., one faith, one b.
Col. 2:12 buried with him in b.
Heb. 6:2 doctrine of b. and lay'g.
1 Pet. 3:21 whereunto, even b.

BAPTIST.
Mat. 3:1 came John b. preaching
11:11 hath not risen a greater
than J. the b. Luke 1:28
12 the days of John the b.
14:2 this is J. the b. is risen
6 give me John the b. head
10:14 art John b. Mark 8:28
17:13 he spake of John the b.
Mark 6:14 John the b. was risen
25 give me head of John the b.
Luke 7:20 John the b. hath sent
33 J. the b. eating nor drink.
9:19 answering said, J. the b.

BAPTIZE.
Mat. 3:11 I b. with w. he shall b.
with Holy Ghost, Mark 1:8;
Luke 3:16; John 1:26
Mark 1:4 J. did b. in wilderness
1:33 he that sent me to b.
1 Cor. 1:17 Ch. sent me not to b.

BAPTIZED.
Mat. 3:6 were b. in J. Mark 1:5
13 then cometh Jesus to b.
14 I have need to be b. of thee
16 J. when he was b. went up
Mark 1:9 Jesus was b. of John
10:39 baptism I am b. withal
16:16 believeth and is b.
Luke 3:7 mult. came to be b.
7:29 came publicans to be b. 7:20
21 Jesus being b. and praying
7:30 lawyers, being not b.
John 3:22 he tarried, and b.
23 and they were b.
4 I J. made and b. more disci.
I thought Jesus himself b. not
10:40 place where J. at first b.
Acts 1:5 b. with water, but ye
shall be b. with H. G. 11:16
2:38 be b. every one of you
41 received his word were b.
8:12 were b. both men and w.
13 Simon, and when he was b.
16 were b. in the name of J.
36 doth hinder me to be b.?
38 P. and eunuch, and he b.
9:18 Saul arose and was b.
10:47 these should not be b.?
48 P. commanded them to be b.
16:15 Lydia when she was b.
33 jailer was b. and all his
18:8 C. believed, and were b.

CRUDEN'S CONCORDANCE. 765

BAR

Acts 19:3 to what were ye b.
5 w. they heard this, were b.
22:16 arise, and be b. and wash
Rom. 6:3 b. into Jesus, b. into
1 Cor. 1:13 b. in the name of P.?
14 I thank God that 1 b. none
16 I b. household of S. not b.
10:2 and were all b. to Moses
12:13 one Spirit b. into one body
15:29 are they b. for the dead
Gal. 3:27 as many as b. into Ch.

BAPTIZEST.
John 1:25 why b. thou

BAPTIZETH.
John 1:33 who b. with the H. G.
3:26 the same b., all men come

BAPTIZING.
Mat. 28:19 t. all nations, b. them
John 1:28 Jordan where J. was b.
31 am I come b. with water
3:23 John was also b. in Enon

BAR.
Neh. 7:3 shut the doors, b. them

BAR, Substantive.
Jud. 16:3 took doors, posts, b.
Amos 1:5 break b. of Damas

BARS.
Deut. 3:5 cit. fenced w. gates and
b. 2 K. 4:13; 2 Chr. 8:5; 14:7
1 Sam. 23:7 a town that hath b.
Job 17:16 to the b. of the pit
38:10 and set b. to the sea
40:18 Beh. his bones b. of iron
Ps. 107:16 b. of iron, Is. 45:2
147:13 strength, b. of thy gates
Prov. 18:19 cont. are like the b.
Jer. 49:31 neither gates nor b.
51:30 Babylon, her b. are brok.
Lam. 2:9 he hath broken her b.
Ezek. 38:11 having gates nor b.
Jon. 2:6 the earth with her b.
Nah. 3:13 fire shall dev. thy b.

BARACHEL. Job 32:2
BARABBAS. Mat. 27; Mark 15;
Luke 23; John 18
BARACHIAS. Mat. 23:35
BARAK. Jud. 4:6, 9; 5:1, 12;
Heb. 11:32

BARBARIAN.
1 Cor. 14:11 a b. and he a b.
Col. 3:11 nei. Greek nor Jew, b.

BARBARIANS.
Acts 28:4 b. saw venomous beast
Rom. 1:14 both to Greeks and b.

BARBAROUS.
Acts 28:2 b. people showed kind

BARBED.
Job 41:7 his skin with b. irons

BARBER.
Ezek. 5:1 take thee a b. razor

BARE –carried.
Ex. 19:4 I b. you on eagle's w.
Deut. 1:31 thy God b. thee as
Is. 53:12 he b. the sin of many
63:9 he b. them all the days
Mat. 8:17 b. our sicknesses
Luke 7:14 they that b. him stood
John 1:26 how, b. what put th.
1 Pet. 2:24 his own self b. our s.

BARE.
Gen. 31:8 the cattle b. speckled
41:27 my wife b. me two sons
Ex. 6:20 Jochebed b. Moses
Jud. 13:2 Manoah's wife b. not
1 Chr. 4:9 Jabez, 1 b. him
Prov. 17:25 bill. to her that b.
22:25 that b. thee shall rejoice
Cant. 6:9 ch. one of her that b.
8:5 that b. thee
Is. 51:2 look unto S. that b. you
Jer. 16:3 mother that b. them
20:14 the day my mother b. me
22:26 cast out mother that b.
50:12 b. you shall be ashamed
Luke 11:27 blessed is w. that b.
23:29 the wombs that never b.

BARE fruit.
Luke 8:8 and b.f. a hundred-fold
Rev. 22:2 tree of life b. f. twelve

BARE rule.
Neh. 5:15 their servants b. r. over

BARE witness, and record.
Mark 14:56 b. f. w. ag. him, 57
Luke 4:22 all b. him w. and won.
John 1:15 b. w. of him, 32, 34
5:33 John b. witness to the truth
12:17 the people with h. b. rec.
19:35 he that saw it b. record
Acts 15:8 kn. the hearts, b. w.
Rev. 1:2 b. r., of the word of God

BAS

BAREST.
Is. 63:19 thou never b. rule over
John 3:26 to whom thou b. witn.

BARE, Adjective.
Lev. 13:45 cl. rent, head b. 55
Is. 32:11 strip ye, make ye b.
47:2 make b. the leg, uncover
52:10 made b. his holy arm
Jer. 13:22 thy heels made b.
49:10 I have made Esau b.
Ezek. 16:7 wast naked and b. 22
39 naked and b. 23:29
Joel 1:7 my fig-tree clean b.
1 Cor. 15:37 shall be, but b. grain

BAREFOOT.
2 Sam. 15:30 went b. and the p.
Is. 20:2 Is. did so, walking b. 3
4 the Egyptians, naked and b.
BAR-JESUS. Acts 13:6
BAR-JONA. Mat. 16:17

BARK.
Is. 56:10 dumb dogs cannot b.

BARLEY.
Ex. 9:31 b. was smitten, for b.
Deut. 8:8 a land of wheat and b.
Jud. 7:13 a cake of b. tumbled
Ruth 1:22 begin. of b. harvest
2:23 winnoweth b. to-night
2 Sam. 11:30 Joab's field, b. there
17:28 Barzillai brought beds, b.
2 K. 4:42 brought 20 loaves of b.
7:1 two meas. of b. for sh. 16, 18
2 Chr. 2:10 20,000 measures of b.
15 wheat, and b. let him send
27:5 Am. gave 10,000 mea. of b.
Job 31:40 let co. grow inst. of b.
Is. 28:25 wheat, and appointed b.
Jer. 41:8 we have treas-ures of b.
Ezek. 4:9 take to thee wh. and b.
12 shalt eat it as b. cakes
13:19 handfuls of b.
Hos. 3:2 for a homer of b.
Joel 1:11 how! for wheat and b.
John 6:9 hath five b. loaves
13 frag. of the five b. loaves
Rev 6:6 meas. of b. for a penny

BARN.
2 K. 6:27 out of the b. floor?
Job 39:12 g. thy seed into the b.
Hag. 2:19 is seed yet in b. vine
Mat. 13:30 g. wheat into my b.
Luke 12:24 no storehouse nor b.

BARNS.
Prov. 3:10 shall thy b. be filled
Joel 1:17 the b. are broken down
Mat. 6:26 nor gather into b.
Luke 12:18 will pull down my b.

BARNABAS.
Acts 4:36; 11:22, 25, 30; 12:25;
13:1, 2, 50; 14:12; 15:2, 12, 37
1 Cor. 9:6 or I only and B. have
Gal. 2:1 I went up with B. 9, 13
Col. 4:10 Marc. sister's son to B.

BARREL, S.
1 K. 17:14 the b. of meal shall
18:33 fill four b. with water

BARREN.
Gen. 11:30 but Sarai was b.
25:21 Reb. b. 29:31 Rachel b.
Ex. 23:26 cast young nor be b.
Jud. 13:2 Man.'s wife was b. 3
1 Sam. 2:5 the b. hath borne sev.
2 K. 2:19 and the ground b.
21 shall not be death, or b.
Job 24:21 evil entreateth the b.
39:6 b. land his dwellings
Ps. 113:9 the b. woman to keep
Prov. 30:16 b. womb not satis.
Cant. 4:2 and none is b. 6:6
Is. 54:1 sing, O b. that didst not
Joel 2:20 drive him into a land b.
Luke 1:7 bec. Elisabeth was b.
36 with her, who was called b.
23:29 blessed are the b. and
Gal. 4:27 rejoice b. that bearest
2 Pet. 1:8 neither b. nor unfruitful

BARS.
Ps. 107:34 fruitful land into b.
BARSABAS. Acts 1:23; 15:22
BARTHOLOMEW. Mat. 10:3;
Mar. 3:18; Lu. 6:14; Acts 1:13
BARTIMEUS. Mark 10:46

BARUCH.
Neh. 3:20 B. son of Zab. repair.
Jer. 32:12; 36:4, 26; 43:3; 45:1
BARZILLAI. 2Sam. 17:27; 19:32,
39; 21:8; 1 K. 2:7; Ezr. 2:61

BASE.
Zec. 5:11 upon her own b.

BASE, Adjective.
2 Sam. 6:22 b. in mine own sight

BAT

Job 30:8 were children of b. men
Is. 3:5 b. against the honorable
Jer. 17:14 kingdom might be b.
39:14 shall he a b. kingdom
Mal. 2:9 I have made you b.
1 Cor. 1:28 b. things G. hath ch.
2 Cor. 10:1 who in presence am b.

BASER.
Acts 17:5 fellows of the b. sort

BASEST.
Ezek. 29:15 Patros b. of kingd.
Dan. 4:17 set, over it b. of men

BASHAN.
Num.21:33; 32:33; Deut. 1:4; 3:1,
3, 4, 10, 11; 4:47; Jos. 13:12
Ps. 22:12 strong bulls of B.
68:15 B. a h. hill, B. why leap. 22
33:9 B. and Carmel shake
Jer. 22:20 lift up thy voice in B.
50:19 feed on Carmel and B.
Ezek. 39:18 fatlings of B.
Amos 4:1 ye kine of B.
Mic. 7:14 let them feed in B.
Nah. 1:4 B. languisheth, Carmel

BASHEMATH.
Gen. 26:34 to wife B. 36:3

BASIN.
1 Chr. 28:17 gold for every b.
John 13:5 he poureth w. into a b.

BASINS.
2 Sam. 17:28 Barzillai brought b.
Jer. 52:19 b. captain took away

BASKET.
Gen. 40:17 in the b. all manner
of bake-meats
Ex. 29:23 b. of unleavened bread.
Lev. 8:2, 26; Num. 6:15, 17
Deut. 26:2 take of 1st fruit in b.
4 put the b. from off thy sh.
17 cursed shall be thy b.
Jud. 6:19 Gid. put flesh in a b.
Jer. 24:2 one b. had good figs
Amos 8:1 a b. of summer fruit, 2
Acts 9:25 w. in a b. 2 Cor. 11:33

BASKETS.
Gen. 40:16 I had three white b.
18 the three b. are three days
2 K. 10:7 their heads in b.
Mat. 14:20 twelve b. Mark 6:43;
Luke 9:17; John 6:13
15:37 brok. meat 7 b. Mark 8:8
16:9 not rememb. how many b.?
10; Mark 8:19, 20

BASTARD.
Deut. 23:2 a b. shall not enter
Zec. 9:6 and a b. in Ashdod
Heb. 12:8 w. chast. them are b.

BAT, S.
Lev. 11:19 b. unclean, Deut. 14:18
Is. 2:20 idols to moles and b.

BATH.
Is. 5:10 ten e. shall yield one b.
Ezek. 45:10 a just ephah, a j. b.
11 ephah and b. of one meas.
14 offer the tenth part of a b.

BATHED.
Is. 34:5 my sword shall be b.

BATHS.
1 K. 7:26 molt, sea cont. 2,000 b.
38 one laver contained 40 b.
2 Chr. 2:10 give 2,000 b. of wine
4:5 the sea held 3,000 b.
Ezr. 7:22 b. of wine, 100 b. oil
Ezek. 45:14 ten b. are a homer
BATH-SHEBA. 2 Sam. 11:3;
12:24; 1 K. 1:15, 31; 2:13

BATTLE.
Deut. 20:3 draw ye nigh, to b.
5 lest he die in the b. 6, 7
1 Sam. 17:28 art come to see b.
47 b. is the L's, 2 Chr. 20:15
26:10 descend into b. and perish
29:4 thou shalt go with me to b.
2 Sam. 11:1 when kings go forth
to b. 1 Chr. 20:1
15 set I Uriah in forefront of b.
19:10 Absalom is dead in b.
23:9 thy peo. b. on b.
20:33 thy serv. into b.of? K. 8:22
22:4 go with me to b. 2 K. 3:7
Job 15:24 a king ready in the b.
39:25 ho suffleth the b. afar off
41:8 remem. the b. do no more
Ps. 18:39 girded with str. to b.
24:8 Lord mighty in b.
55:18 deliv. my soul from th. b.
76:3 br. the shield, and the b.

BEA

Ps. 89:43 not made to st. in the b.
Ex. 9:11 nor b. to the strong
Is. 9:5 every b. of the warrior
13:4 L. must. the host of the b.
22:2 slain are not dead in b.
27:4 set briars ag. me in b.
28:6 turn the b. to the gate
42:25 the strength of the b.
Jer. 8:6 horse rusheth into the b.
18:21 young men be slain in b.
50:22 a sound of b. is in land
Ezek. 7:14 none goeth to the b.
13:5 in the b. in the day of L.
Hos. 1:7 not save them by b.
2:18 break b. out of the earth
10:9 b. in Gibeah not overtake
10:14 strong people in b. array
Joel 2:5 strong, goodly horse in the b.
5 tread their enemies in the b.
Amos 1:14 all nations against J. to b.
1 Cor. 14:8 shall prep. to the b.
Rev. 9:7 like horses prepare to b.
9 chariots running to b.
16:14 b. of that great day, 20:8

Day of BATTLE.
Job 38:23 reserved ag. d. of b.
Ps. 78:9 fight, turned in d. of b.
140:7 covered my head in d. of b.
Prov. 21:31 horse is prep. ag. b.

BATTLE-AXE. See AXE.

BATTLE-BOW.
Zec. 9:10 the b.-bow shall be cut
10:4 out of him came the b.-b.

BATTLES.
1 Sam. 18:17 fight the Lord's b.
25:28 my lord fighteth b. of L.
1 Chr. 26:27 spoils won in b. ded.
2 Chr. 32:8 is God, to fight our b.
Is. 30:32 and in b. of shaking

BATTERING.
Ezek. 4:2 and set b. rams round
21:22 to ap. b. rams ag. gates

BATTLEMENT, S.
Deut. 22:8 a b. for thy roof
Jer. 5:10 take away her b.

DAY.
Zec. 6:3 in fourth chariot b. b.
7 the b. went forth and sought

BAY-TREE.
Ps. 37:35 w. like a green b.-t.

BDELLIUM.
Gen. 2:12 in Havilah there is b.
Num. 11:7 color of manna as b.

BE.
Jud. 6:13 the Lord be with us
2 Chr. 36:23 L. he w. him. Ezr. 1:3
John 3:9 can these things b.?
Rom. 4:17 things which be not
8:31 If G. be for us, who can be
Gal. 4:12 be as I am, for I am

Shall BE, or shall BE.
Ec. 1:9 is that which shall be
Mat. 24:21 ever sh. be, Mark 13:19
Mark 14:19 with you, Luke 9:41
John 14:17 with you, and sh. be
1 John 3:2 appear what we sh. be
Rev. 16:5 and wast, and shalt be

Shall not, or shalt not BE.
Ps. 37:10 shalt not be, Jer. 48:30;
Dan. 11:29; Amos 7:3, 6
Hos. 8:3 shall not be for another
Mat. 16:22 shall not be to thee
20:26 shall not be among you,
Mark 10:43; Luke 22:26

To BE.
Ex. 3:15 that to b. hath already
BEEN. See after BE.

BEACON.
Is. 30:17 left as a b. on the top

BEAM.
Jud. 16:14 went away with the b.
1 Sam. 17:7 spear was like a
weaver's b. 1 Chr. 11:23; 20:5
2 K. 6:2 J. and take thence a b.
5 was felling a b. axe-head
Hab. 2:11 the b. out of the timber
Mat. 7:3 mot b. Luke 6:41, 42
4 a b. is in thine own eye
b. out out the b. Luke 6:12

BEAMS.
Ps. 104:3 b. of ch. in waters
Cant. 1:17 the b. of our house

BEANS.
2 Sam. 17:28 Barzillai brought b.
Ezek. 4:9 unto thee wheat b.

BEAR—carry, or endure.
Gen. 4:13 greater than I can b.
13:6 not able to b. them, 36:7
43:9 let me b. the blame, 44:32
49:15 bowed his shoulder to b.

CRUDEN'S CONCORDANCE.

BEA

Ex. 18:22 shall *b.* the burden
25:27 to *b.*, two table, 27:7; 30:4;
37:5; *Deut.* 10:8; *Jos.* 3:8, 13;
4:16; 2 *Sam.* 15:24
28:12 A. shall *b.* their names
Num. 11:14 *b.* all this, *Deut.* 1:9
14:27 how long *b.* with this
33 children shall *b.* your whoredoms, *Ezek.* 23:35
Deut. 1:31 a man doth *b.* his son
2 *K.* 18:14 put on me, I will *b.*
Ps. 75:3 I *b.* pillars of the earth
89:50 how I do *b.* the reproach
91:12 *b.* thee up, *Mat.* 4:6; *Lu.* 4:11
Prov. 9:12 thou shalt *b.* it
18:14 w. spirit who can *b.* ?
30:21 for four which it cannot *b.*
Is. 1:14 feasts, I am weary to *b.*
46:4 I have made and will *b.* you
7 *b.* him upon the shoulder
52:11 clean that *b.* vessels of L.
Jer. 10:19 and I must *b.* it
17:21 *b.* no burden on Sab. 27
31:19 *b.* the reproach of my y.
44:22 Lord could no longer *b.*
Lam. 3:27 good he *b.* yoke
Ezek. 12:6 in their sight shalt *b.*
16:54 *b.* own shame, 54
34:29 *b.* shame of heath. 36:15
Mic. 6:16 *b.* rep. of my people
7:9 I will *b.* indignation of L.
Zec. 5:10 whither *b.* the ephah ?
6:13 he shall *b.* glory, and rule
Mat. 3:11 shoes not worthy to *b.*
27:32 Simon to *b.* his cross, *Mar.*
15:21; *Luke* 23:26
Luke 14:27 doth not *b.* his cross
18:7 av. his elect, though he *b.*
John 16:12 ye cannot *b.* them
Acts 9:15 vessel to *b.* my name
15:10 nor we were able to *b.*
18:14 reason would I should *b.*
Rom. 15:1 *b.* infirm. of the weak
1 *Cor.* 3:2 hitherto not able to *b.*
10:13 that ye may be able to *b.*
15:49 *b.* the image
2 *Cor.* 11:1 would to G. ye could *b.*
4 ye might well *b.* with him
Gal. 6:2 *b.* one another's burd.
5 shall *b.* his own burden
17 *b.* in my body the marks
Jam. 3:12 fig-tree *b.* ol.-berries ?
Rev. 2:2 canst not *b.* them

BEAR—*bring forth.*
Gen. 17:17 S. 90 years old *b.* ?
18:13 shall I *b.* a child
Jud. 13:3 conceive and *b.* a son
1 *K.* 3:21 not my son I did *b.*
Cant. 4:2 ev. one *b.* twins. 6:6
Is. 7:14 a virgin shall con. and *b.*
54:1 sing, thou that didst not *b.*
Jer. 29:6 that they may *b.* sons
Luke 1:13 Elisab. shall *b.* a son
1 *Tim.* 5:14 marry, *b.* children
BEAR *fruit. See* FRUIT.

BEAR *iniquity.*
Ex. 28:38 A. may *b. in.* of holy
43 A. and his sons *b.* not *in.*
Lev. 5:1 he shall *b.* his *iniq.* 17;
7:18; 17:16; 19:8; 20:17
10:17 given to *b. in.* of the cong.
16:22 shall *b.* all their *in.*
20:19 shall *b.* their *in.* *Num.*
18:1, 23; *Ezek.* 44:10, 12
Num. 14:34 ye shall *b.* your *in.*
Is. 53:11 my righteous servant
shall *b.* their *in.*
Ezek. 4:4 shalt *b.* their *in.* 5, 6
18:20 son shall not *b. in.* of the

BEAR *judgment.*
Ec. 28:30 A. shall *b. j.*
Gal. 5:10 troub. you shall *b.* his *j.*

BEAR *record. See* RECORD.

BEAR *rule.*
Est. 1:22 every man should *b. r.*
in his own house
Prov. 12:24 of diligent *b. r.*
Jer. 5:31 priests *b. r.* by their m.

BEAR *sin.*
Lev. 24:15 shall *b.* his *sin.*
Ezek. 13:49 *b.* the *s.* of your idols
Heb. 9:28 once offered to *b. sin.*

BEAR *witness.*
Ex. 20:16 not *b.* false w. ng. thy,
Deut. 5:20; *Mat.* 19:18; *Rom.* 13:9
1 *K.* 21:10 sons of B. to *b. wit.*
Mark 10:19 not *b. f. w. Luke* 18:20
Luke 11:48 ye *b. wit.* that
John 1:7 came for a wit. to *b. w.*
8 to *b. witness* of that light
3:28 ye *b.* me w. that I said
5:31 if I *b. wit.* of myself
36 *b. witness* of me, 10:25
8:18 I am one that *b. witness*
15:27 ye shall also *b. witness*

BEA

John 18:23 *b. witness* of the evil
37 that I should *b. witness*
Acts 22:5 h.-priest doth *b.* me *w.*
23:11 so must thou *b. w.* at R.
1 *John* 1:2 have seen it, and *b. w.*
5:8 three that *b. witness*

BEAREST,
Ps. 106:4 favor thou *b.* to thy
John 8:13 *b.* record of thyself
Rom. 11:18 *b.* not the root,
Gal. 4:27 rej. barren that *b.* not

BEARETH.
Num. 11:12 a nursing father *b.*
Deut. 29:18 a root that *b.* gall
23 it is not sown, nor *b.* nor
32:11 as an eagle *b.* her young
Job 24:21 entreateth barren th. *b.*
Cant. 6:6 every one *b.* twins
Joel 2:22 for the tree *b.* her fruit
Mat. 13:23 which also *b.* fruit
John 15:2 ev. branch that *b.* not
Rom. 13:4 *b.* not the sword
1 *Cor.* 13:7 charity *b.* all things
Heb. 6:8 which *b.* thorns

BEARETH *rule.*
Prov. 29:2 wicked *b. r.* people m.

BEARETH *witness.*
Job 16:8 my leanness *b. witness*
Prov. 25:18 that *b.* false *wit'ness*
John 5:32 another that *b. wit.*
8:18 the Father *b. witness*
Rom. 8:16 S. *b. w.* with our sp.
1 *John* 5:6 it is the S. that *b. w.*

BEARING.
Gen. 1:29 every herb *b.* seed
16:2 hath restrained me from *b.*
Jos. 3:3 *b.* the ark, 14; 2 *Sam.* 15:24
Ps. 126:6 forth *b.* precious seed
Mark 14:13 *b.* a pitcher of water,
Luke 22:10
John 19:17 he *b.* his cross, went
Rom. 2:15 their conscience *b. w.*
9:1 my con. also *b.* me witness
2 *Cor.* 4:10 *b.* in the body
Heb. 2:4 G. also *b.* them witness
13:13 *b.* his reproach
1 *Tim.* 2:15 be saved in child-*b.*

BEAR, S,
1 *Sam.* 17:34 came a lion and a *b.*
36 thy servant slew lion and *b.*
2 *Sam.* 17:8 chafed as a *b.* robbed
2 *K.* 2:24 came *f.* two shc-*b.*
Prov. 17:12 a *b.* robbed of whelps
28:15 and a ranging *b.*
Is. 11:7 cow and *b.* shall feed
39:11 we roar all like *b.*
Lam. 3:10 he was to me as a *b.*
Dan. 7:5 a second like to a *b.*
Hos. 13:8 as a *b.* bereaved
Amos 5:19 as a man did flee fr. a *b.*
Rev. 13:2 his feet were as of a *b.*

BEARD, S.
Lev. 13:29 plague on head or *b.*
14:9 his hair off his head and *b.*
19:27 mar corners of *b.* 21:5
1 *Sam.* 17:35 caught him by *b.*
21:13 let his spittle fall on *b.*
2 *Sam.* 20:9 Joab took Amasa *b.* to
1 *Chr.* 19:5
10:24 M. trimmed not his *b.*
Ezr. 9:3 hair off my *b.*
Ps. 133:2 on the *b.* even A.'s *b.*
Jer. 7:29 shall also consume *b.*
41:5 men *b.* shaven
48:37 every head bald, *b.* clip.
Ezek. 5:1 to pass on thy *b.*

BEAST.
Gen. 1:24 earth bring forth *b.*
3:1 more subtle than any *b.*
37:20 evil *b.* hath devoured, 33
Ex. 13:12 firstling of a *b.*
22:5 put his *b.* in another
10 deliver any *b.* to his neig.
19 lieth with a *b.* *Lev.* 18:23;
20:15, 16; *Deut.* 27:21
23:29 the *b.* multiply
Lev. 11:47 *b.* that may be eaten
27:9 vow of *b.* if the likeness of any *b.*
Neh. 2:12 save the *b.* I rode on
Ps. 73:22 as a *b.* before thee
147:9 giveth to the *b.* his food
Prov. 12:10 regards life of his *b.*
Ec. 3:19 pre-eminence above *b.*
Is. 43:20 the *b.* shall honor me
63:14 as a *b.* that goeth down
Dan. 4:16 let *b.* heart be given
7:11 till the *b.* was slain
19 the truth of the fourth *b.*
Luke 10:34 on his own *b.*
Acts 28:5 Paul shook off the *b.*
Heb. 12:20 if so much as a *b.*
Rev. 4:7 liveth, like a lion, sec. *b.*
6:3 second *b.* say, Come

BEA

Rev. 11:7 *b.* that ascendeth out of
13:1 a *b.* rise up out of the sea
11 *b.* coming out of the earth
15:2 got the victory over the *b.*
16:13 unclean spirits out of *b.*
17:8 *b.* that was, and is not, 11
16:19 ea. of *b.* and the kings
20:10 the *b.* and false prophet

Every *b.* **BEAST.**
Gen. 1:30 to ev. *b.* I have given
2:19 God formed ev. *b.*
20 Adam gave names to ev. *b.*
3:14 art cursed above every *b.*
8:1 every clean *b.* by sevens, 8
14 and every *b.* after his kind
8:16 every *b.* went out
20 of every clean *b.* be offered
9:2 shall be on every *b.*
5 blood at hand of every *b.*
10 every *b.* I estab. covenant
34:23 shall not ev. *b.* of theirs
Lev. 11:26 ev. *b.* which divideth
the hoof, *Deut.* 14:6
Ps. 50:10 every *b.* of the forest
104:11 give drink to every *b.*
Ezek. 34:8 flock meat to every *b.*
30:17 speak to every *b.*

BEAST, *joined with* **MAN.**
Gen. 6:7 destroy both *m.* and *b.*
Ex. 12:7 move tongue a. *m.* or *b.*
12:12 smite first-born of *m.* and
b. 13:15; *Ps.* 135:8
13:2 first-born of *m.* and *b.* is
Ps. 2:18 cov. for them with *b.*
19:13 *m.* or *b.* it shall not live
36:6 preservest *m.* and *b.*
Jer. 7:20 fury on *m.* and *b.* 21:6;
36:29; *Ezek.* 11:13, 17, 19, 21;
25:13; *Zeph.* 1:3
27:5 I have made *men* and *b.*
31:27 sow J. with seed of *m.* a *b.*
32:43 without *m.* or *b.* 33:10, 12;
36:29; 51:62
50:3 shall depart *m.* and *b.*
Ezek. 38:11 inul. on *m.* and *b.*
Jon. 3:7 let not *m.* nor *b.* taste

Unclean BEAST.
Lev. 5:2 touch any *u. b.* 7:21
27:11 if it be *u. b.* of which, 27

Wild BEAST.
2 *K.* 14:9 *w. b.* in L. 2 *Chr.* 25:18
Job 39:15 forgetteth *w. b.*
Ps. 80:13 *w. b.* doth devour it
Hos. 13:8 the *w. b.* shall tear

BEASTS.
Gen. 31:39 torn of *b. Ex.* 22:31;
Lev. 7:24; 17:15; 22:8
36:6 Esau took all his *b.*
45:17 lade your *b.* and go
Ezr. 1:5 the first-*b.* of *b.*
Lev. 11:2 *b.* eat, *Deut.* 14:4
3 chew cud among *b. Deut.* 14:6
26:6 will rid evil *b.* out of land
Deut. 32:24 will send teeth of *b.*
1 *K.* 4:33 Solomon spake of *b.*
Ezr. 1:4 help him with gold, *b.*
Job 12:7 ask the *b.* they teach
18:3 are we counted as *b.*
37:8 then the *b.* go into dens
Ps. 49:12 the *b.* that perish, 20
104:20 wherein *b.* of forest creep
25 sea, both small and great *b.*
148:10 *b.* and all cattle, praise
Prov. 9:2 hath killed her *b.*
30:30 lion strongest among *b.*
Ec. 3:18 themselves are *b.*
19 befalleth men, before *b.*
Is. 30:6 of *b.* thereof a burnt-off.
46:1 idols on the *b.* and cattle
66:20 upon evil *b.* to my holy
Jer. 9:10 *b.* fled, 12:4 consumed
Ezek. 5:17 send till 14:15
32:4 fill *b.* of whole earth
13 destroy all the *b.* 34:25, 28
Dan. 4:14 *b.* get away
15 his portion be with the *b.*
7:17 four great *b.* are kings
8:4 no *b.* might stand before h.
Joel 1:18 how do the *b.* groan
Hab. 2:17 spoil of *b.*
Zep. 2:15 become a place for *b.*
Zec. 14:15 plague of all these *b.*
Mal. 1:13 offered to me sickh *b.* ?
33:34 A. that ye may set Paul
Rom. 1:23 image made like to *b.*
1 *Cor.* 15:32 I have fought with *b.*
Jam. 3:7 b. is tamed
1 *Pet.* 2:12 as natural brute *b.*
Jude 10 naturally as brutes *b.*
Rev. 4:6 four *b.* full of eyes
8 four *b.* had each six wings
9 when those *b.* give glory
5:6 in midst of four *b.* stood a L.
14 the four *b.* said, Amen
6:1 *b.* saying, Come, 3:5,7

BEA

Rev. 7:11 stood about four *b.*
14:3 sung before the four *b.*
19:4 and four *b.* fell down

BEASTS of the Earth.
Deut. 28:26 carc. meat to all *b.*
1 *Sam.* 17:46 carcasses of P. to *b.*
Job 5:22 nor be afraid of the *b.*
35:11 teacheth us more than *b.*
Ps. 79:2 flesh of thy saints to *b.*
Is. 18:6 they shall he left to *b.*
Jer. 7:33 carc. of peop. meat for *b.*
of the earth, 16:4; 19:7; 34:20
15:3 I will appoint over them *b.*
Acts 10:12 of four-footed *b.* 11:6
Rev. 6:8 kill with hunger and *b.*

BEASTS of the Field.
Ex. 23:11 leave, *b.* may eat
Deut. 7:22 lest *b.* increase
1 *Sam.* 17:44 give thy flesh to *b.*
2 *Sam.* 21:10 nor *b. of the field*
Job 5:23 *b.* shall be at peace
40:20 mountains where *b.* play
Ps. 8:7 put *b.* under his feet
52:20 yea *b.* come to devour
104:11 give drink to ev. *b.*
Is. 56:9 ye *b.* come to devour
Ezek. 29:5 I have given thee for
meat to the *b.* 31:5; 39:4
31:6 under branches *b.* bring
13 on his ruins shall *b.* be
33:27 to *b.* to be devoured
38:20 *b.* shall shake
Dan. 4:12 the *b.* had shadow
25 thy dwelling with *b.* 32
Jer. 13:21 shall mourn with *b.*
4:3 shall land mourn with *b.*
Joel 1:20 *b.* cry also to thee
2:22 ye *b.* pastures

Wild BEASTS.
Lev. 26:22 I will send *w. b.*
1 *Sam.* 17:46 carc. of Phil. to *w. b.*
Ps. 50:11 the *w. b.* are mine
Is. 13:21 *w. b.* shall lie there
22 *wild b.* of the islands
34:14 *w. b. of des.* shall meet with
w. b. of the island, *Jer.* 50:29
Mark 1:13 C. was with the *w. b.*
Acts 10:12 *wt.* were all *w. b.* 11:6

BEAT.
Jud. 9:45 A. *b.* down the city
19:22 sons of B. *b.* at the door
2 *Sam.* 22:43 I *b.* them, *Ps.* 18:42
Ps. 89:23 will *b.* down his foes
Prov. 23:14 *b.* him with the rod
Is. 2:4 *b.* their swords, *Mic.* 4:3
3:15 that ye *b.* my people
27:12 *b.* off from the channel
41:15 mountains, *b.* them small
Joel 3:10 *b.* your ploughshares
Jon. 4:8 the sun *b.* on Jonah
Mat. 7:25 *b.* on house, 27; *Luke*
6:48, 49
21:35 his servants and *b.* one,
Mark 12:3; *Luke* 10:10, 11
Mark 4:37 waves *b.* into the ship
Luke 12:45 begin to *b.*
Acts 16:22 commanded to *b.* them
18:17 took Sosthenes and *b.* him
22:19 *b.* in every synagogue

BEATEN.
2 *Chr.* 34:7 *b.* images to powder
Prov. 23:35 they have *b.* me
Is. 28:27 fitches are *b.* with staff
Jer. 46:5 mighty ones are *b.* down
Mic. 1:7 images shall be *b.*
Mat. 12:9 syna. ye shall be *b.*
Luke 12:47 did not shall be *b.*
Acts 5:40 apostles and *b.* them
10:37 have *b.* us openly
2 *Cor.* 11:25 thrice was I *b.*

BEATEN *Oil.*
Ex. 27:20 *oil b.* *Lev.* 24:2
29:40 hin of *b. oil,* *Num.* 28:5

BEATEST.
Deut. 24:20 when thou *b.* thy ol.
Prov. 23:13 if thou *b.* him

BEATETH.
1 *Cor.* 9:26 as one that *b.* the air

BEATING.
1 *Sam.* 14:10 *b.* down one anoth.
Mark 12:5 *b.* some and killing

BEAUTY.
Ex. 28:2 for glory and *b.*
14:25 praised as Absalom for *b.*
1 *Chr.* 16:29 *b.* of hol. *Ps.* 29:2; 90:9
2 *Chr.* 20:21 head *b.* of holiness
Est. 1:11 the people her *b.*
Job 40:10 array thyself with *b.*
Ps. 27:4 behold the *b.* of the L.
39:11 made his *b.* to consume
43:11 king greatly desire thy *b.*
49:14 their *b.* shall consume
50:2 perfection of *b.*
92:17 the *b.* of Lord be on us

CRUDEN'S CONCORDANCE. 767

BED
Ps. 96:6 and b. in sanctuary
Prov. 6:25 lust not after her b.
26:29 the b. of old is gray bed
31:20 favor is deceitful, b. is v.
Is. 3:24 burning instead of b.
13:10 Babylon the b. of the C.
28:1 b. is a fading flower, 4
5 a diadem of b. to residue
32:17 see the King in his b.
44:13 according to the b.
53:2 no b. that we should desire
61:3 that mourn b. for ashes
Lam. 1:6 Zion all her b. is dep.
2:1 from heaven the b. of Israel
15 men call perfection of b.?
Ezek. 7:20 b. of his ornament
16:14 renown am. heath. for b.
15 didst trust in thine own b.
25 made thy b. to be abhorred
27:3 I am of perfect b. 28:12
4 builders perfected thy b. 11
28:7 swords ag. the b. of thy
17 lifted up because of thy b.
31:8 so tree like Assyrian in b.
32:19 whom dost pass in b.
Hos. 14:6 Israel's b. shall be
Zec. 9:17 how great is his b.
11:7 staves, one I called b. 10

BEAUTIES.
Ps. 110:3 in the b. of holiness

BEAUTIFY.
Ezr. 7:27 king's heart, to b.
Ps. 149:4 b. the meek with salv.
Is. 60:13 b. place of my sanctu.

BEAUTIFUL.
Gen. 29:17 Rachel was b.
Deut. 21:11 am. cap. a b. woman
1 Sam. 16:12 son of a b. country
25:3 Abigail was of a b. count.
2 Sam. 11:2 Bath. was very b.
Est. 2:7 Esther was fair and b.
Ps. 48:2 b. for situation is Zion
Ec. 3:11 every thing b.
Cant. 6:4 thou art b. O my love
7:1 how b. thy feet with shoes
Is. 4:2 the branch of L. be b.
52:1 O Zion, put on thy b. gar.
7 how b. the feet, Rom. 10:15
64:11 and b. house is burnt up
Jer. 13:20 where is thy b. flock?
48:17 broken, and the b. rod
Ezek. 16:12 b. crown on thy head
13 thou wast exceeding b.
23:42 Sabeans put b. crowns
Mat. 23:27 sepulch. which ap. b.
Acts 3:2 at the gate called b. 10

BECAME.
1 Cor. 9:20 to the Jews I b. a Jew
Heb. 7:26 such a High-priest b. us

BECAMEST.
1 Chr. 17:22 thou L. b. their God
Ezek. 16:8 and thou b. mine

BECKONED.
Luke 1:22 Zacharias b. speech.
5:7 they b. to their partners
John 13:21 Peter b. he should ask
Acts 19:33 Alex. b. and would
21:40 P. stood on stairs, and b.

BECKONING.
Acts 12:17 Peter b. unto them
13:16 Paul b. with his hand

BECOME.
Gen. 3:22 man is b. one of us
Ex. 15:2 is b. my salvation, Ps. 118:14; Is. 12:2
32:1 as for M. we wot not what b b. of him, 23; Acts 7:40
Deut. 27:9 art b. the people
Mat. 21:42 is b. the head, Mark 12:10; Luke 20:17; Acts 4:11
John 1:12 to b. the sons of God
2 Cor. 5:17 all things are b. new
Rev. 11:15 b. the kingd. of our L.

BECOMETH.
Ps. 93:5 holiness b. thy house
Prov. 10:4 b. poor that dealeth
17:7 excell. speech b. not a fool
18:7 understand, b. surety
Ec. 4:11 born in his kingd. b.
Mat. 3:15 it b. us to fulfil
13:22 choketh the word, and he b. unfruitful, Mark 4:19
Rom. 16:2 receive P. as b. saints
Phil. 1:27 as b. gospel
1 Tim. 2:10 as b. women
Tit. 2:3 women as b. holiness

BED.
Gen. 47:31 bow. on bedshead b.
49:4 thy father's b. 1 Chr. 5:1
Ex. 21:18 but keepeth b.
1 Sam. 19:13 and laid it in b.
2 Sam. 4:5 who lay on b.
11:2 David arose from his b.
1 K. 1:4 from that b. 6, 16

BEF
2 K. 4:10 set there for him a b.
Job 7:13 my b. shall comfort me
17:13 my b. in the darkness
33:15 slumberings upon the b.
Ps. 4:4 com. with heart on b.
36:4 devis. mischief on his b.
41:3 his b. in his sickness
63:6 I rem. thee upon my b.
132:3 into my b. till I find
139:8 if I make my b. in hell
Prov. 7:16 decked my b. 17
22:27 why take b. from under
26:14 the slothful on his b.
Cant. 1:16 our b. is green
3:1 on my b. I sought him
7 his b. which is Solomon's
6:13 b. is shorter
57:7 on mountain set thy b.
Amos 3:12 in the corner of a b.
Mat. 9:6 thy b. Mark 2:9, 11; John 5:11, 12
Mark 4:21 under a b. Luke 8:16
Luke 11:7 child. with me in b.
17:34 two men in one b.
Rev. 2:22 will cast her into a b.

BED of love.
Ezek. 23:17 came to her in b.

BED of spices.
Cant. 5:13 his cheeks are as a b.
6:2 my beloved is gone to the b.

BED undefiled.
Heb. 13:4 honorable and the b.

BEDAD, Gen. 36:35
BEDAN, 1 Sam. 12:11; 1 Chr. 7:17

BEDCHAMBER.
Ex. 8:3 frogs come into thy b.
2 Sam. 4:7 Ish. lay in his b.
2 K. 6:12 thou speakest in b.
11:2 hid him in b. 2 Chr. 22:11
Ec. 10:20 the rich in b.

BEDS.
Ps. 149:5 sing aloud on b.
57:2 rest in their b. each
Hos. 7:14 they howled on b.
Amos 6:4 lie on b. of ivory
Mic. 2:1 that work evil on b.

BEDSTEAD.
Deut. 3:11 b. was a b. of iron

BEE, S.
Jud. 14:8 swarm of b. in the lion
Ps. 118:12 me about like b.
Is. 7:18 hiss for the b. in As.

BEELZEBUB. Mat. 10:25; 12:24; Mark 3:22; Luke 11:15
Hath BEEN.
Ec. 3:15 which b. b. is now

Have BEEN.
Job 10:19 b. b. as if I had not b.
Is. 66:2 all those things b. b.

not BEEN.
Ob. 16 though they had n. b.

BEER. Num. 21:16
BEER-LAHAI-ROI, Gen. 16:14
BEERSHEBA. Gen. 21:14, 33; 22:19; 26:33; 28:10; 1 K. 19:3

BEETLE.
Lev. 11:22 ye may eat, the b.

BEEVES.
Lev. 22:19 the b. of sheep
Num. 31:28 a tribute of the b.

BEFALL.
Gen. 42:4 lest mischief b. him
38 if mischief b. him, 44:29
49:1 what shall b. you, Deut. 31:29; Jer. 13:1
Deut. 31:17 evils shall b. them
Ps. 91:10 there shall no evil b.
Acts 20:22 things that shall b.

BEFALLEN.
Lev. 10:19 such things have b.
Num. 20:14 travail that hath b.
Deut. 31:21 when troubles are b.
Jud. 6:13 why is all this b.
1 Sam. 28:26 something had b.
Mat. 8:33 what was b.

BEFALLETH.
Ec. 3:19 b. men, b. beasts
2 Sam. 7:17 than all that b. they
Acts 20:19 b. me by lying in wait

BEFORE.
Ps. 16:11 like that b. b. or
Ps. 39:13 spare me b. I go

BEGINNING, Part.
Mat. 14:30 b. to sink, L. save me
20:8 b. from the last
Luke 24:17 all nations, b. at J.
John 8:9 b. at eldest
Acts 1:22 b. from baptism of J.

BEG
Heb. 10:15 aft. that he had said b.
2 Pet. 3:17 know these things b.

Come BEFORE.
Ps. 100:2 c. b. presence
Mic. 6:6 shall I c. b. L.?

BEFORE the people.
Ex. 13:22 pillar of fire from b.
17:5 L. said to Moses, go on b.
34:10 b. all thy p. I will do
1 Sam. 18:13 went out and in b.
Mark 8:6 discip. did set them b.
Luke 20:26 hold of his words b.
Rev. 10:11 prophesy b. people

BEFORE whom.
1 K. 17:1 as the Lord God of Isr. liveth, b. whom I stand, 18:15; 2 K. 3:14; 5:16
Acts 26:26 king b. w. I speak
See further, ALL, ARK, GOD, LORD, MOUNT, STAND, STOOD, WENT.

BEFOREHAND.
Mark 13:11 take no thought b.
2 Cor. 9:5 make up b. your boun.
1 Tim. 5:24 men's s. are open b.
25 good works of some man b.
1 Pet. 1:11 testified b. sufferings

BEFORETIME.
Jos. 20:5 he hated him not b.
2 Sam. 7:10 nor afflict them as b.
Ps. 41:26 b. that we may say
Acts 8:9 Simon which b. used

BEGAN.
Gen. 4:26 b. men call on name
Gen. 10:8 b. to be a mighty one
2 Chr. 34:3 b. to seek after God
Mat. 4:17 Jesus b. to preach
Luke 1:70 been since world b.
14:30 this man b. to build
John 4:52 when he b. to amend
Acts 2:4 since the world b. Acts 3:21; Rom. 16:23
2 Tim. 1:9 in Christ before the world b. Tit. 1:2
Heb. 2:3 at first b. to be spoken

BEGAT.
Prov. 23:24 he thy father that b.
Jer. 16:3 their father that b. them
Dan. 11:6 and he that b. her
Zec. 13:3 and m. that b. him
Jam. 1:18 b. us, 1 John 5:1 loveth him that b.

BEGET.
Gen. 17:20 princes shall he b.
Deut. 4:25 thou shalt b. children
28:41 b. sons
2 K. 20:18 sons thou shalt b. shall they make eunuchs, Is. 39:7
Ec. 6:3 man b. 100 children
2 Chr. take wives, and b. sons
Ezek. 18:10 if he b. a son
14 if he b. a son that seeth

BEGETTEST.
Gen. 48:6 issue which thou b.
Is. 45:10 to his father, what b.

BEGETTETH.
Prov. 17:21 b. a fool, doeth it
23:24 he that b. a wise child
Ec. 5:14 he b. a son

BEGGAR.
Ps. 109:10 let his children b.
Prov. 20:4 sluggard b. in harvest
Luke 16:3 to b. I am ashamed

BEGGAR, LY.
1 Sam. 2:8 lifted b. from dunghill
Luke 16:20 a b. named Lazarus
22 the b. died and was carried
Gal. 4:9 to the b. elements

BEGGED.
Mat. 27:58 b. body of J. Lu. 23:52
John 9:8 he that sat and b.

BEGGING.
Ps. 37:25 seen his seed b. bread
Mark 10:46 Bart. sat b. Lu. 18:35

BEGIN.
Gen. 11:6 this they b. to do, and Jos. 3:7 to magnify
1 Sam. 3:12 I b. I will make
22:15 did I b. to inquire
Neh. 11:17 Mattan. to b. thanks.
Jer. 25:29 b. to bring evil
Ezek. 9:6 and to bury within
13:26 b. to say we have eaten
11:29 behold b. to be mocked
21:28 things b. to come to pass
2 Cor. 3:1 do we b. again
1 Pet. 4:17 judgment must b. at house of G. and if it first b.

BEGINNING, Substantive.
Gen. 49:3 Reuben b. of my st.
Ex. 12:2 the b. of months
Deut. 21:17 is b. of his strength
Job 8:7 thy b. was small
42:12 end of Job more than b.
Ps. 111:10 b. of wis. Prov. 9:10
Prov. 1:7 fear of L. b. of knowl.
17:14 b. of strife, as when one
Ec. 7:8 end of a thing than b.
10:13 b. of words is foolishness
Ec. 6:4:4 since b. of world, men
Mic. 1:13 is b. of sin to daughter
Mat. 24:8 b. of sor. Mark 13:8
21 as was not since b.
Mark 1:1 the b. of the gospel
John 2:11 this b. of miracles
Col. 1:18 who is the b. the first-b.
Heb. 3:14 b. of our confidence
7:3 having neither b. of days
12:20 is worse than the b.
Rev. 3:14 1 am b. 21:6; 22:13
3:14 saith the b. of the creation

At the BEGINNING.
Ruth 3:10 kindness than at b.
1 Chr. 17:9 wicked, waste as b.
Prov. 20:21 in. gotten hastily b.
Is. 1:26 counsellors as at the b.
Dan. 9:23 a. b. of thy supplica.
Mat. 19:4 b. b. made them
John 16:4 I said not to you b.
Acts 11:15 if, G. as on th. a. b.

From the BEGINNING.
Deut. 11:12 eyes of L. on it b.
Ps. 119:160 true from the begin.
Prov. 8:23 I was set up f. b.
Ec. 3:11 no man can find out the work God maketh f. t. b.
Is. 18:2 peop. terrible f. t. b. 7
40:21 been told f. t. b.?
41:26 hath declared f. t. b.?
41:10 declaring the end f. t. b.
46:10 not spoken in secret f. t. b.
Jer. 17:12 high throne f. t. b.
John 6:64 knew f. b. who believ.
8:25 same I said to you f. b.
44 a murderer from the begin.
15:27 have been with me f. b.
Eph. 3:9 f. t. b. of the world
2 Thes. 2:13 God hath f. t. b. begin. chosen you to salvation
2 Pet. 3:4 continue as fr. t. begin.
1 John 2:7 ye have heard b. 3:11
13 known him that is f. t. b.
3:8 the devil sinneth from t. b.
2 John 5 that which we had f. t. b.

In the BEGINNING.
Gen. 1:1 I. t. b. God created b.
Prov. 8:22 the Lord possessed me in the begin. of his way
John 1:1 in the b. was the Word
2 the same was in the b.
Phil. 4:15 know b. of the gospel
Heb. 1:10 L. b. hast laid founda.

BEGINNINGS.
Num. 10:10 b. of your m. 28:11
Ezek. 36:11 bet. than at your b.

BEGINNEST.
Deut. 10:9 thou b. to put sickle

BEGOTTEN.
Num. 11:12 have I b. them?
Deut. 28:8 children b. of them
Jud. 8:30 Gideon had 70 sons b.
Job 38:28 hath b. drops of dew
Ps. 2:7 this day have I b. thee, Acts 13:33; Heb. 1:5; 5:5
Is. 49:21 hath b. me these?
Hos. 5:7 have b. strange children
John 1:14 the only b. of the F.
18 only b. Son, he hath declar.
3:16 he gave his only b. Son
18 not believed in only b. Son
1 Cor. 4:15 b. you through gospel
Philem. 10 Onesi. whom I have b.
Heb. 11:17 A. offered only b. Son
1 Pet. 1:3 b. us again
1 John 4:9 sent his only b. Son
5:1 loveth him b. of him
18 he that is b. of God

First-BEGOTTEN.
Heb. 1:6 he bringeth in first b.
Rev. 1:5 who is f. b. of the dead

BEGUILE.
Col. 2:4 lest any b. you
18 let no man b. you

BEGUILED, ING.
Gen. 3:13 serpent b. me
29:25 wherefore hast thou b.
Jos. 9:22 wherefore have ye b.
2 Cor. 11:3 as the serpent b. Eve

BEH

2 Pet. 2:14 cannot cease from sin, *b.* unstable souls

BEGUN.

Deut. 3:24 *b.* to show thy great.
Mat. 18:24 he had *b.* to reckon
2 Cor. 8:6 had *b.* so would finish
10 for you who have *b.* before
Gal. 3:3 having *b.* in the Spirit
Phil. 1:6 hath *b.* a good work
1 Tim. 5:11 *b.* to wax wanton

BEHALF.

Ex. 27:21 a statute on *b.* of Is.
2 Sam. 3:12 Abner sent on his *b.*
2 Chr. 16:9 sh. hims. strong in *b.*
Job 36:2 yet to speak on God's *b.*
Dan. 11:18 prince for his own *b.*
Rom. 16:19 I am glad on your *b.*
1 Cor. 1:4 I thank God on your *b.*
5:12 to glory on our *b.*
Phil. 1:29 given in *b.* of Christ
1 Pet. 4:16 glorify God on this *b.*

BEHAVE.

Deut. 32:27 lest adversaries *b.*
1 Chr. 19:13 let us *b.* valiantly
Ps. 101:2 I will *b.* wisely
Is. 3:5 child shall *b.* proudly
1 Cor. 13:5 not *b.* unseemly
1 Tim. 3:15 how thou oughtest to *b.* in the house of God

BEHAVED.

1 Sam. 18:5 D. *b.* wisely, 14, 15, 30
Ps. 35:14 I *b.* as he had been f.
131:2 have *b.* and quieted
Mic. 3:4 as they have *b.* ill
1 Thes. 2:10 unblameably we *b.*
2 Thes. 3:7 *b.* not disorderly

BEHAVETH.

1 Cor. 7:36 think he *b.* uncomely

BEHAVIOR.

1 Sam. 21:13 D. changed his *b.*
1 Tim. 3:2 a bishop of good *b.*
Tit. 2:3 women in *b.* as becom.

BEHEADED.

2 Sam. 4:7 Ish. and *b.* him
Mat. 14:10 *b.* John, **Mark.** 6:16, 27; **Luke** 9:9
Rev. 20:4 I saw the souls of *b.*

BEHELD.

Num. 21:9 *b.* serpent of brass
23:21 hath not *b.* iniquity in J.
1 Chr. 21:15 destroying, the L. *b.*
Job 31:26 if I *b.* the sun when
Ps. 119:158 I *b.* transgressors
142:4 I *b.* but there was no man
Prov. 7:7 *b.* among the simple
Ec. 8:17 I *b.* all the work of God
Is. 41:28 I *b.* and there was no man, **Jer.** 4:25
Jer. 4:23 I *b.* the earth
Mark 15:47 *b.* where he was laid, **Luke** 23:55
Luke 10:18 I *b.* Satan as light,
19:41 he *b.* the city and wept
John 1:14 we *b.* his glory
Acts 1:9 they *b.* J. was taken up
17:23 and *b.* your devotions
Rev. 5:6 I *b.* and lo, a lamb
11:12 their enemies *b.* them

BEHEMOTH.

Job 40:15 behold now *b.*

BEHIND.

Is. 38:17 all my sins *b.* thy back
1 Cor. 1:7 ye come *b.* in no gift
2 Cor. 11:5 whit *b.* chiefest, 12:11
Phil. 3:13 forgetting things *b.*
Col. 1:34 fill up what is *b.*
See BEFORE.

BEHOLD.

Gen. 28:15 *b.* I am with thee
Job 1:12 *b.* all he hath
28:28 *b.* the fear of the Lord
40:4 *b.* I am vile what shall I
Ps. 139:8 bed in hell, *b.* thou
Ec. 5:18 *b.* I and chil. **Heb.** 2:13
12:3 *b.* God is my salvation
41:27 way to Zion, *b.* to them
63:1 I said, *b.* me, to a nation
Lam. 1:12 *b.* and see if any sor.
Zec. 5:9 *b.* thy King cometh,
Mat. 21:5; **John** 12:15
Mark 16:6 *b.* place where they
Luke 24:39 *b.* my hands and feet
49 *b.* I send prom. of my Fath.
John 1:29 *b.* the Lamb of God
19:5 Pilate saith, *b.* the man
Acts 9:11 Saul, for, *b.* he prayeth
1 John 3:1 *b.* what manner of love
Rev. 3:20 *b.* I stand at the door
16:15 *b.* I come as a thief
22:7 *b.* I come quickly, 12

BEHOLD I speak, *b.* it is I

BEL

Ezek. 7:10 *b.* the day, *b.* it is come
3:8 *b.* it is come, and it is

Now BEHOLD, *or* BEHOLD now.
Job 16:19 *b.* my witness is in
Jer. 40:4 now *b.* I loose thee
Acts 13:11 *n.* *b.* hand of Lord
20:22 now *b.* I go bound
2 Cor. 6:2 *b. n.* is the accepted t.

BEHOLD it was, BEHOLD there was.
See WAS.

BEHOLD, Verb.

Num. 12:8 similit. of L. shall he *b.*
23:9 from the hills I *b.* him
24:17 shall *b.* him, but not nigh
Deut. 3:27 *b.* it with thine eyes
Job 19:27 shall *b.* and not anoth.
20:9 his place any more *b.* him
23:9 work, but I cannot *b.* him
31:26 his face, who can *b.?*
36:24 magnify his work men *b.*
Ps. 11:4 his eyes *b.* his eyelids
7 doth *b.* the upright
17:2 let thine eyes *b.* things
15 I will *b.* thy face in right.
27:4 to *b.* the beauty of the L.
37:37 perfect, *b.* the upright
46:8 *b.* the works of the Lord
59:4 awake to help me, and *b.*
66:7 his eyes *b.* the nations
80:14 look from heaven, *b.*
91:8 eyes shalt thou *b.* and see
102:19 from heaven did L. *b.*
113:6 he humbleth hims. to *b.*
119:18 mine eyes, that I may *b.*
Prov. 23:33 *b.* strange women
Ec. 11:7 pleasant it is to *b.*
Is. 26:10 will not *b.* the majesty
33:17 *b.* shall *b.* man no more
41:23 do good or evil that we *b.*
63:15:5. from habita. of thy holi.
Jer. 20:4 thine eyes shall *b.*
22:32 nor *b.* the good I will do
32:4 his eyes shall *b.* 34:3
42:2 as thine eyes *b.* us
Lam. 1:18 and *b.* my sorrow
3:50 till Lord *b.* from heaven
5:1 consider and *b.* our reproach
Ezek. 8:9 *b.* wicked abomina.
28:17 that they may *b.*
Dan. 9:18 and *b.* our desolations
Mic. 7:9 I shall *b.* his righteous.
mine eyes shall *b.* her
Hab. 1:3 why canst thou *b.* evil
13 purer eyes than to *b.* evil
Mat. 18:10 their angels *b.* face
Luke 14:29 all that *b.* it mock
21:6 as for those ye *b.* the days
John 17:24 they may *b.* my glory
Acts 7:31 he drew near to *b.* it
32 Moses durst not *b.*
2 Cor. 3:7 Is. could not *b.* face
1 Pet. 2:12 works they shall *b.*
3:2 *b.* your chaste conversation
Rev. 17:8 when they *b.* the beast

BEHOLDEST.

Ps. 10:14 thou *b.* all mischief
Mat. 7:3 *n. b.* mote? **Luke** 6:41
Luke 6:42 *b.* not the beam

BEHOLDETH.

Job 24:18 he *b.* not the way
Ps. 33:13 Lord *b.* all the sons
Jam. 1:24 *b.* himself and goeth

BEHOLDING.

Ps. 119:37 mine eyes from *b.*
Prov. 15:3 *b.* the evil and good
Ec. 5:11 saving the *b.* of them
Mat. 27:55 women *b.*, **Luke** 23:49
Mark 10:21 Jesus *b.* him, loved
Luke 23:35 people stood *b.*
48 *b.* things done, smote breasts
Acts 4:14 and *b.* man healed
23:1 and Paul *b.* the council
2 Cor. 3:18 *b.* as in a glass the g.
Col. 2:5 joying, and *b.* your order
Jam. 1:23 *b.* his natural face

BEHOVED.

Luke 24:46 thus it *b.* Christ
Heb. 2:17 *b.* him to be made

BEING.

Ps. 104:33 I live *b.* 146:2
Acts 17:28 move in, and have our *b.*

BEKAH. **Ex.** 38:26
BEL. **Is.** 46:1; **Jer.** 50:2; 51:44

BELCH.

Ps. 59:7 behold they *b.* out

BELIAL.

Deut. 13:13 children of B.

BEL

Jud. 19:22 certain sons of B.
20:13 the children of B.
1 Sam. 1:16 a daughter of B.
2:12 sons of Eli were sons of B.
10:27 children of B. said, how
25:17 is such a son of B. 25
30:22 then answ. the men of B.
2 Sam. 16:7 come out, man of B.
20:1 a man of B.
23:6 sons of B. shall be as th.
1 *K.* 21:10 two sons of B. 13
2 *Chr.* 13:7 Jerob. children of B.
2 Cor. 6:13 hath Christ with B.?

BELIED.

Jer. 5:12 they have *b.* the L.

BELIEF.

2 Thes. 2:13 of Spirit and *b.*

BELIEVE.

Ex. 4:5 may *b.* L. hath appeared
19:9 may *b.* thee for ever
Num. 14:11 ere they *b.* me?
2 Chr. 20:20 *b.* in the L. his p.
Job 9:16 if I called, would he *b.*
15:22 he *b.* not he shall return
31 deceived trust in van. *b.*
39:12 wilt thou *b.* him he will
Ps. 27:13 fainted unless I *b.*
106:12 I *b.* therefore have I spoken, **2 Cor.** 4:13
119:66 I have *b.* thy command.
Is. 43:10 know and *b.* me
Jer. 12:6 *b.* them not tho' they speak
Hab. 1:5 ye will not *b.*
Mat. 21:25 not *b.* him **Mark** 11:31
24:23 *b.* is C. *b. n.* 26; **Mark** 13:21
Luke 22:67 you will not *b.*
John 3:12 earthly th. and ye *b. n.*
5:38 he hath sent, him ye *b. n.*
47 how shall ye *b.* my words?
6:36 ye have seen me and *b.* not
64 some of you which *b.* not
8:24 if ye *b. n.* I am he, die
45 tell the truth, ye *b.* me not
46 say the truth, why n. *b.* me
10:26 ye *b. n.* bec. not of my s.
37 do not works of F. *b.* me n.
38 yo *b.* not me, be. the works
12:36 could not *b.* because Isa.
47 hear words, and *b.* not
16:9 bec. they *b.* not on me
20:25 into his side, I will *n. b.*
Acts 13:41 if some did not *b.*
15:31 from them that do not *b.*
1 Cor. 10:27 that *b.* not bid to a f.
14:22 sign to them that *b.* not
2 Cor. 4:4 blinded th. *b.* not
1 Tim. 9:13 if we *b.* not, he said.
1 John 4:1 *b.* not every spirit

BELIEVED.

Gen. 15:6 he *b.* counted it. **Rom.** 4:3; **Gal.** 3:6; **Jam.** 2:23
14:31 they *b.* the L. and Moses
Ps. 27:13 fainted, unless I *b.*
106:12 *b.* they his words, spoken, **2 Cor.** 4:13
119:66 I have *b.* thy command.
Is. 53:1 who hath *b.* our report?
John 12:33; **Rom.** 10:16
Dan. 6:23 bec. he *b.* in G.
Jon. 3:5 peo. of Nineveh *b.* G.
Mat. 8:13 *b.* so be it done to thee
21:32 publicans and harlots *b.*
Mark 16:13 neither *b.* they
Luke 1:1 things most surely *b.*
45 blessed is she that *b.* for
John 2:11 his disciples *b.* on him
22 they *b.* the scripture
4:50 the man *b.* word J. spoke
53 the father himself *b.*
5:46 had ye *b.* Moses
7:48 have Pharisees *b.* on him?
8:31 said Jesus to Jews that *b.*
11:45 seen things Jesus did, *b.*
12:11 many of the Jews *b.* on J.
12:37 loveth you, bec. you *b.*
17:8 have *b.* thou didst send me
20 other disciple, saw and *b.*
29 have not seen, and yet *b.*
Acts 2:44 all that *b.* were togeth.
4:4 many wh. h. the word *b.*
32 that *b.* were of one heart
8:12 *b.* Phil. preaching things
13 then Simon himself *b.*
10:45 who *b.* were astonished
11:17 like gift as to us who *b.*
21 a great number *b.* turned
13:12 then deputy *b.*
48 ordained to eternal life *b.*
14:1 both Jews and Greeks *b.*
23 to Lord on whom they *b.*
17:4 *b.* and consorted with Paul
34 certain clave to him and *b.*
18:8 Crispus ch. ruler of syn. *b.*
27 had *b.* through grace
19:2 rec. ye H. G. since ye *b.?*
22:19 I beat them that *b.*
27:11 centur. *b.* master of ship
28:24 some *b.* and some *b.* not
Rom. 4:18 against hope *b.* in h.
13:11 nearer than when we *b.*
1 Cor. 3:5 minis. by whom ye *b.*
15:2 unless ye have *b.* in vain
11 so we preach, and so ye *b.*
Gal. 2:16 we have *b.* in Jesus C.
Eph. 1:13 after ye *b.* ye were
Tit. 1:10 our testim. was *b.*
1 Tim. 3:16 *b.* on in the world
2 Tim. 1:12 whom I have *b.*
Heb. 4:3 we which *b.* do enter
1 John 4:16 *b.* the love of God.

Many BELIEVED.

John 2:23 at the pass. many *b.*
4:39 many of the Samaritans *b.*
11:45 *m.* Jews wh. came to M. *b.*
12:42 chief rulers also many *b.*
Acts 18:8 *m.* Corinth. hearing *b.*

CRUDEN'S CONCORDANCE. 769

BEL
Acts 19:18 m. *b.* confess. their d.

BELIEVED not, *or* not BELIEVED.
Gen. 45:26 b. fainted, he *b. not*
Num. 20:12 ye *b. me not*
Deut. 9:23 and *b.* him *not*
Job 29:24 they *b.* it *not*
Ps. 78:22 they *b. not* in God
  32 *b. not* for his wond. works
106:24 despised land, *b. n.* his w.
Jer. 40:14 but G. *b.* them *not*
Lam. 4:12 world would n. have *b.*
Mat. 21:32 J. came, ye *b.* him *not*
   14 npbr. because they *b. not*
Luke 20:5 say, Why *b.* ye *not?*
24:41 while they *b. not* for joy
John 3:18 because he hath *not b.*
  6:64 Jesus knew who *b. not*
10:25 I told you, and ye *b. not*
12:37 miracles, yet they *b. not*
Acts 9:26 *b. not* he was a disc.
17:5 Jews wh. *b. not*
19:9 were hardened, *b. not*
Rom. 10:14 they have *not b.*
  11:30 times past have *not b.* G.
  31 these also now *not b.*
2 Thes. 2:12 damned who *b. not*
Heb. 3:18 his rest that *b. not*
  11:31 R. per. not with them *b. n.*
Jude 5 destroyed them that *b. n.*

BELIEVERS.
Acts 5:14 *b.* were the more added
1 Tim. 4:12 an example of the *b.*

BELIEVEST.
Luke 1:20 dumb, bec. thou *b. not*
John 1:50 under the fig tree, *b.*
  11:26 never die, *b.* thou this?
14:10 *b.* thou not I am in the F.
Acts 8:37 *b.* with all thy heart
21:27 *b.* thou the prophets?
Jam. 2:19 thou *b.* there is one God

BELIEVETH.
Job 15:22 *b.* not he shall return
Prov. 14:15 simple *b.* every word
Is. 28:16 that *b.* not make haste
Mark 9:23 possible to him that *b.*
16:16 he that *b.* shall be saved,
  he th. *b. not* shall be damn.
John 3:15 *b.* in him, 16
  18 *b. not* is condemned already
  36 *b.* hath everlasting life, 6:47
5:24 *b.* on him that sent me
6:35 *b.* on me shall never thirst
  40 Son, and *b.* on him, hath I.
7:38 *b.* on me, out of his belly
11:25 *b.* though dead, yet shall
  26 *b.* in me shall never die
12:44 *b. not* on me, but on him
  46 whoso *b. not* abide in dark.
14:12 *b.* on me the works
Acts 10:43 *b.* receive remission
Rom. 1:16 of G. to ev. that *b.*
  3:26 justifier of him that *b.* in J.
4:5 that worketh not, but *b.* on
9:33 whoso *b. not* be asha. 10:11
10:4 end of law to ev. one th. *b.*
  10 the heart man *b.* to right.
11:2 one *b.* he may eat
1 Cor. 7:12 a wife that *b. not*
13:7 love *b.* all things
14:24 come in one that *b. not*
2 Cor. 6:15 hath he that *b.*
1 Tim. 5:16 if any that *b.*
1 Pet. 2:6 *b.* shall not be conf.
1 John 5:1 whoso *b.* J. is the C.
  5 overcometh, but he that *b.*
  10 *b.* on the Son; he that *b. n.*
  G. bec. he *b. not* the record

BELIEVING.
Mat. 21:22 ask *b.* ye shall receive
John 20:27 not faithless, but *b.*
  31 that *b.* ye might have life
Acts 16:34 *b.* in God
24:14 *b.* all things written
Rom. 15:13 joy and peace in *b.*
1 Tim. 5:2 that have *b.* masters
1 Pet. 1:8 yet *b.* ye rejoice

BELL.
Ex. 28:31 golden *b.* 39:26
Zec. 14:20 upon the *b.* of horses

BELLOW. *See* BULLS.

BELLOWS.
Jer. 6:29 the *b.* are burnt

BELLY.
Gen. 3:14 on thy *b.* shalt thou go
Lev. 11:42 goeth on the *b.*
Num. 5:21 and thy *b.* to swell
  27:8 turn and wine, through *b.*
Jud. 3:21 dag. thrust it in his *b.*
1 K. 7:20 pomeg. over against *b.*
Job 3:11 when I came out of *b.*
15:2 fill his *b.* with east wind
  35 their *b.* prepareth deceit
20:15 G. shall cast out of his *b.*

BEL
Job 20:20 not feel quietness in *b.*
  23 when about to fill his *b.*
32:19 my *b.* is as wine which
Ps. 17:14 whose *b.* fillest
22:10 from my mother's *b.*
44:25 our *b.* cleaveth to earth
Prov. 13:25 *b.* of wicked
18:8 innermost parts of *b.* 26:22
  20 a man's *b.* shall be satisfied
20:27 inward parts of *b.*
  30 stripes inward parts of *b.*
Cant. 5:14 his *b.* is as br. ivory
7:2 thy *b.* is like wheat
Is. 46:3 borne by me from the *b.*
Jer. 1:5 formed thee in *b.* I k.
51:34 his *b.* with my delicates
Ezek. 3:3 cause thy *b.* to eat
Dan. 2:32 image's *b.* of brass
Jon. 1:17 in *b.* of fish, Mat. 12:40
  2:2 out of the *b.* of hell cried I
Hab. 3:16 my *b.* trembled
Mat. 15:17 into the *b.* and is cast
  out, Mark 7:19
Luke 15:16 his *b.* with the husks
John 7:38 out of his *b.* flow riv.
Rom. 16:18 serve their own *b.*
1 Cor. 6:13 meats for *b.*
Phil. 3:19 whose God is their *b.*
Rev. 10:9 shall make thy *b.* bit.
  10 eaten it, my *b.* was bitter.

BELLIES.
Tit. 1:12 the Cretians are slow *b.*

BELONG.
Lev. 27:24 to whom it did *b.*
Deut. 29:29 secret things *b.* to G.
Ps. 47:9 shields of earth *b.* to G.
68:20 to our God *b.* the issues
Prov. 24:23 these *b.* to the wise
Mark 9:41 bec. ye *b.* to Christ
Luke 19:42 which *b.* to thy p.
1 Cor. 7:32 things *b.* to Lord

BELONGED, EST.
1 Sam. 30:13 to whom *b.* thou?
Luke 23:7 *b.* to Herod's jurisd.

BELONGETH.
Deut. 32:35 to me *b.* vengeance,
Ps. 3:8 *b.* unto God
62:11 power *b.* unto God
Dan. 9:7 righteousness *b.* to thee
  8 to us *b.* confusion of face
Heb. 5:14 strong meat *b.*

BELONGING.
Prov. 26:17 strife *b.* not to him

BELOVED.
Deut. 21:15 two wives, the one *b.*
33:12 *b.* of Lord dwell in safety
Neh. 13:26 *b.* of his G.
10:5 thy *b.* may be *b.* 108:6
127:2 so he giveth his *b.* sleep
Prov. 4:3 only *b.* in sight of m.
Cant. 5:1 drink abundantly, O *b.*
  9 thy *b.* more than another *b.?*
61: whither is thy *b.* gone?
  8:5 cometh leaning on her *b.?*
Dan. 9:23 greatly *b.* 10:11, 19
Hos. 3:1 a woman *b.* of her. fr.
9:16 I will slay the *b.* fruit
Acts 15:25 with *b.* B. and Paul
Rom. 1:7 all in Rome *b.* of God
  9:25 call her *b.* wh. was not *b.*
11:28 are *b.* for Father's sake
16:12 G. Persis who labored
Eph. 1:6 accepted in the *b.*
6:21 T. a *b.* brother, Col. 4:7
4:9 Onesimus, a *b.* brother
  14 Luke the *b.* physician
1 Thes. 1:4 kn. *b.* your election
1 Tim. 6:2 were *b.* they are *b.*
Phile. 16 a servant a brother *b.*
Heb. 6:9 *b.* we are persuaded
2 Pet. 3:8 *b.* be not ig. 16
  15 even as our *b.* brother Paul
1 John 3:2 *b.* now we are the sons
  21 *b.* if our heart condemn
4:1 *b.* believe not every spirit
  7 *b.* let us love one another
3 John 11 *b.* follow not evil,
Jude 20 but ye *b.* building up
Rev. 20:9 they compassed *b.* city

Dearly BELOVED. *See* DEARLY.

My BELOVED.
Cant. 1:14 my *b.* is un. me a clust.
  16 art fair, my *b.* yea, pleasant
2:3 my *b.* is like a roe or a hart
  16 my *b.* is mine, 6:3
17 my *b.* and be like a roe
4:16 let my *b.* come into his g.
5:2 voice of my *b.* 2:8
  5 to open to my *b.* 6 I opened

BEN
Cant. 5:10 my *b.* is, 16 is my *b.*
  6:2 my *b.* is gone
  3 I am my *b.* my *b.* mine, 7:10
7:13 laid up for thee, O my *b.*
Is. 5:1 song of my *b.* touching
Jer. 11:15 my *b.* to do in my b.
Mat. 3:17 this is my *b.* Son, 17:5;
  Mark 1:11; 9:7; Luke 3:22;
  9:35; 2 Pet. 1:17
12:18 my *b.* in whom my soul
Luke 20:13 will send my *b.* Son
Rom. 16:8 greet Amplias my *b.*
1 Cor. 4:14 as my *b.* sons I warn
  17 Tim. my *b.* son, 2 Tim. 1:2
Jam. 1:16 do not err, my *b.* breth.

BELSHAZZAR. Dan. 5:1, 2, 9,
  22, 29, 30; 7:1; 8:1
BELTESHAZZAR. Dan. 1:7;
  2:26; 4:8, 18, 19; 5:12; 10:1

BEMOAN, ED, ING.
Job 42:11 J. Job, and comfort.
Jer. 15:5 who shall *b.* thee, O J.
16:5 neither lament, nor *b.*
22:10 w. ye not for dead, nor *b.*
31:18 heard Eph. *b.* himself
48:17 all ye about him *b.* him
Nah. 3:7 N. who will *b.* them

BENAIAH. 2 Sam. 23:22; 1
  Chr. 11:24; Ezek. 11:1
BEN-AMMI. Gen. 19:38

BENCHES.
Ezek. 27:6 made thy *b.* of ivory

BEND.
Ps. 7:12 wicked *b.* their bow
64:3 *b.* their bows to shoot
Jer. 9:3 they *b.* their tongue
46:9 Lydians, that *b.* the bow
50:14 *b.* bow shoot at her, 29
51:3 bendeth, let the archer *b.*
Ezek. 17:7 vine did *b.* her roots

BENDETH, ING.
Ps. 58:7 when he *b.* his bow
Is. 60:14 that afflicted thee shall
  come *b.* to thee
Jer. 51:3 against him that *b.*

BENEATH.
Ex. 20:4 the earth *b.* Deut. 5:8
Deut. 4:39 earth *b.* there is none
28:13 above only, and not *b.*
Is. 51:6 look on the earth *b.*
John 8:23 ye are from *b.* I above

BENEFACTORS.
Luke 22:25 exer. auth. are call. *b.*

BENEFIT, Verb.
Jer. 18:10 wherewith I *b.* them

BENEFIT, S.
2 Chr. 32:25 Hezekiah rendered
  not according to *b.*
Ps. 68:19 loadeth us with *b.*
103:2 forget not all his *b.*
116:12 render for all his *b.?*
2 Cor. 1:15 have a second *b.*
1 Tim. 6:2 partakers of the *b.*
Phile. 14 *b.* not be of necessity

BENEVOLENCE.
1 Cor. 7:3 render to the w. due *b.*

BEN-HADAD. 1 K. 15:18; 20:2;
  2 K. 6:24; 8:7; 13:3; Jer.
  49:27

BENJAMIN.
Gen. 35:18 the f. called him B.
42:36 J. and will ye take B.
46:21 the sons of B. were B.
  1 Chr. 7:6; 8:1, 40; 9:7; Neh.
  7:7
49:27 B. shall ravin as a wolf
Jud. 3:15 Ehud a B. 2 Sam. 16:11
  beloved of the Lord
Jud. 20:20 went to battle ag't B.
Hos. 5:8 after thee, O B.
Heb. 12:1 which doth so easily *b.*

BENJAMIN with Judah.
Jud. 10:9 to fight J. and B.
1 K. 12:21 speak to the house of J.
  and B. 2 Chr. 11:3
1 Chr. 12:16 came of B. and J.
2 Chr. 15:2 Asa all J. and B.
  Jer. 1:5 fathers of J. and B.
Land of BENJAMIN.
Jud. 21:21 go into l. of B.
1 Sam. 9:16 out of the l. of B.
2 Chr. 17:36 come from l. of B.

Tribe of BENJAMIN.
Num. 1:37 of the l. of B.
13:9 Palti son of R. 21
Jud. 21:17 not cut off fr. B.
Acts 13:21 Saul of the t. of B.
Rom. 11:1 am an I. tribe of B.
Phil. 3:5 stock of Is. tribe of B.

BES
BENJAMITES.
Jud. 19:16 men of pl. were B.
20:35 destroyed of the B.
1 Sam. 22:7 I hear now, ye B.
BENONI. Gen. 35:18

BENT.
Ps. 7:12 *b.* his bow, Lam. 2:4; 3:12
37:14 *b.* their bow to cast down
Is. 5:28 and all their bows *b.*
21:15 for they fled from *b.* bow
Hos. 11:7 my people are *b.*
Zec. 9:13 when I have *b.* J. Judah

BEOR. Gen. 36:32; Num. 22:5;
  24:3; 31:8; Deut. 23:4; Jos.
  13:22; 24:9; 1 Chr. 1:43; Mic.
  6:5
BERACHAH. 1 Chr. 12:3; 2
  Chr. 20:26
BEREA. Acts 17:10, 13; 20:4

BEREAVE.
Ec. 4:8 and *b.* my soul of good
Jer. 15:7 I will *b.* them, 18:21
Ezek. 5:17 send evil beasts, and
  they shall *b.* thee
36:13 no more *b.* them, 14
Hos. 9:12 yet will I *b.* them

BEREAVED.
Gen. 42:36 ye have *b.* of my ch.
43:14 *b.* of my children, I am *b.*
Ezek. 36:13 thou land hast *b.*
Hos. 13:8 meet them as a bear *b.*

BEREAVETH.
Lam. 1:20 abroad the sword *b.*

BERITH. Jud. 9:46
BERNICE. Acts 23:13, 23; 26:30

BERRIES.
Is. 17:6 two or three
Jam. 3:12 fig-tree bear olive *b.*

BERYL.
Dan. 10:6 his body like the *b.*
Rev. 21:20 foundation was *b.*

BESEECH.
Ex. 33:18 I *b.* show me
Num. 12:13 her now, I *b.* thee
70:14 return, we *b.* O God
110:4 O L. I *b.* thee, deliver
118:25 save, I *b.* thee
119:108 accept, I *b.* thee
Jer. 38:20 obey, I *b.* thee
Amos 7:2 forgive I *b.* thee
Jon. 1:14 we *b.* thee O Lord
4:3 take, I *b.* thee, my life
Mat. 8:34 *b.* him dep. Mark 5:17
26:3 I *b.* thee for my son Onesi.
Rom. 12:1 I *b.* you by mercies
2 Cor. 4:16 I *b.* be ye followers
5:20 as tho' God did *b.* you
6:1 we *b.* you rec. not the grace
10:1 I Paul *b.* you by the meek
12:8 I *b.* F. if you, be as I you
Eph. 4:1 pris. of L. *b.* you walk
Phile. 9 yet for love's sake I *b.*
  Heb. 13:19 I *b.* you the rather
1 Pet. 2:11 *b.* as strangers
2 John 5 now I *b.* thee, lady

See BRETHREN.

BESEECHING.
Mat. 8:5 centurion *b.* Luke 7:3
Mark 1:40 leper to him, *b.* him

BESET.
Jud. 19:22 sons of B. *b.* 20:5
Ps. 22:12 bulls of B. have *b.* me
139:5 *b.* me behind and before
Hos. 7:2 doings have *b.* them
Heb. 12:1 which doth so easily *b.*

BESIDE, S.
Gen. 19:12 hast thou here any *b.*
Lev. 18:18 *b.* all this
21:21 *b.* all this
Phile. 19 thine own self *b.*

BESIDE, with self.
Deut. 29:5 *b.* him in thy gates
1 K. 8:21 councillors *b.* Chr. 22:8
Is. 21:2 O Elam, *b.* O Media

BESIEGED.
2 K. 19:24 rivers of *b.* pl. Is. 37:25
Ec. 9:14 a great king and *b.* it
Is. 1:8 Zion is left as a *b.* city
Ezek. 6:12 he that is *b.* by famine

BESOM.
Is. 14:23 the *b.* of destruction

BESOR. 1 Sam. 30:9

CRUDEN'S CONCORDANCE.

BET

BESOUGHT.
Gen. 42:21 *b.* us, we would not
Ex. 32:11 Moses *b.* L. *Deut.* 3:23
2 *Sam.* 12:16 *b.* G. for the child
1 *K.* 13:6 man of God *b.* the L.
2 *K.* 13:4 Jehoahaz *b.* the Lord
2 *Chr.* 33:12 Manasseh in affl. *b.*
Ezr. 8:23 *b.* our God for this
Jer. 26:19 Hezekiah *b.* the Lord
Mat. 8:31 the devils *b.* him, *Mark*
  5:10, 12; *Luke* 8:31, 32
34 *b.* him to depart, *Luke* 8:37
Mark 5:23 Jairus *b. Luke* 8:41
John 4:40 S. *b.* he would tarry
  47 nobleman of Caper. *b.* him
19:38 *b.* he might take the body
Acts 13:42 *b.* that these words
16:15 Lydia *b.* us saying
  39 magistrates *b.* them
21:12 we *b.* him not to go to J.
2 *Cor.* 12:8 for this I *b.* the Lord

BEST.
Ps. 39:5 man at his *b.* state
Luke 15:22 bring forth the *b.*
1 *Cor.* 12:31 covet the *b.* gifts

BESTEAD.
Is. 8:21 pass thro' it hardly *b.*

BESTIR.
2 *Sam.* 5:24 hearest the sound *b.*

BESTOW.
Ex. 32:29 may *b.* on you
Deut. 14:26 *b.* money for what
2 *Chr.* 34:7 they did *b.* on Baalim
Ezr. 7:20 *b.* it out of K.'s treas.
Luke 12:17 to *b.* my fruits
1 *Cor.* 12:23 on these we *b.* more
13:3 though I *b.* all my goods

BESTOWED.
Is. 63:7 ac. to all Lord *b.* on us
John 4:38 to reap whereon ye *b.*
Rom. 16:6 Mary, who *b.* much
1 *Cor.* 15:10 grace *b.* not in vain
1 *Cor.* 1:11 gift *b.* on us by many
8:1 grace *b.* on the churches
Gal. 4:11 lest I *b.* labor in vain
1 *John* 3:1 manner of love F. *b.*

BETHABARA. *John* 1:28

BETHANY.
Mat. 21:17 went into B. 26:6
Mark 11:12; 14:3; *Luke* 10:29
Luke 21:50 led out as far as B.
John 11:1 Lazarus of B. 12:1

BETH-AVEN.
Jos. 7:2 Ai, which is beside B.
1 *Sam.* 14:23 passed over to B.
Hos. 4:15 nor go ye up to B.
5:8 cry aloud at B. after thee
10:5 because of the calves of B.

BETH-CAR. 1 *Sam.* 7:11
BETH-DAGON. *Jos.* 19:27
BETH-DIBLATHAIM. *Jer.* 48:22

BETH-EL.
Gen. 28:19 c. the place B. 35:15
31:13 I am God of B.
35:1 up to B. 3; 6 came to B.
Amos 3:14 will visit altars of B.
4:4 come to B. and transgress
5:5 B. shall come to naught, 6
7:13 proph. not any more at B.
BETH-ELITE. 1 *K.* 16:34
BETHER. *Cant.* 2:17
BETHESDA. *John* 5:2
BETH-EZEL. *Mic.* 1:11
BETH-GAMUL. *Jer.* 48:23
BETH-HACCEREM. *Jer.* 6:1

BETH-HORON.
Jos. 10:11 going down to B.
21:22 gave Lev. B. 1 *Chr.* 6:68
1 *Sam.* 13:18 comp. turned to B.
1 *K.* 9:17 S. built B. 2 *Chr.* 8:5
1 *Chr.* 7:24 Sherah built B.

BETHINK.
1 *K.* 8:47 *b.* them. 2 *Chr.* 6:37

BETH-LEHEMI.
2 *Sam.* 23:15 well of B. 1 *Ch.* 11:17
Mat. 2:1 Jesus born in B. 5, 16
BETH-LEHEM EPHRA-TAH.
Mic. 5:2 B. E. though thou be
BETH-LEHEM JUDAH. *Jud.* 17:7; 19:1, 18; *Ruth* 1:1
BETH-LEHEMITE.
1 *Sam.* 16:1 J. the B. 18; 17:58
2 *Sam.* 21:19 B. slew G. brother

BETH-PEOR.
Deut. 3:29 valley over ag'st B.
4:46 statutes over against B.
34:6 buried Moses over ag'st B.
BETHPHAGE. *Mat.* 21:1; *Mark* 11:1; *Luke* 19:29
BETHSAIDA.
Mat. 11:21 thou, B. 1 *Luke* 10:13

BET

Mark 6:45 disciples go to B. 8:22
Luke 9:10 a desert belong. to B.
John 1:44 Phil. was of B. 12:21
BETH-SHAN. 1 *Sam.* 31:10
BETH-SHEMESH. *Jud.* 1:33;
1 *Sam.* 6:9, 12, 19; 9 *K.* 14;11
BETHUEL. *Gen.* 22:22, 23; 24:24; 28:2

BETHINES.
Gen. 22:31 rose up *b.* and aware
2 *Chr.* 35:15 his messen. rising *b.*
Job 8:5 wouldest seek unto G. *b.*
24:5 as wild asses rising *b.*
Prov. 13:24 chasteneth him *b.*

BETRAY.
1 *Chr.* 12:17 come to *b.* me
Mat. 24:10 shall *b.* one another
26:16 sought opportunity to *b.*
  Mark 14:11; *Luke* 22:6
21 one of you shall *b.* me, *Mark* 14:18; *John* 13:21
46 he is at hand that doth *b.*
Mark 13:12 brother shall *b.* bro.
John 6:64 should *b.* him, 13:11
13:2 into heart of Judas to *b.*

BETRAYED.
Mat. 10:4 J. who *b.* him, *Mark* 3:19
17:22 S. of m. shall be *b.* 20:18;
  26:2, 45; *Mark* 14:41
26:24 Son of man is *b. Mark* 14:21; *Luke* 22:22
  48 he that *b. Mark* 14:44
27:4 I *b.* innocent blood
Luke 21:16 be *b.* both by parents
John 18:2 *b.* him knew the place
1 *Cor.* 11:23 same night he was *b.*

BETRAYERS.
Acts 7:52 of whom ye the *b.*

BETRAYEST, ETH.
Mark 14:42 he that *b.* me
Luke 22:21 hand that *b.* me
48 S. Son of man with a kiss?
John 21:20 is he that *b.* thee?

BETROTH.
Deut. 28:30 shalt *b.* a wife
Hos. 2:19 *b.* thee to me
  20 *b.* to me in faithfulness

BETROTHED.
Ex. 22:16 entice a maid not *b.*
  Deut. 28:28
Lev. 19:20 lieth with a woman *b.*
Deut. 20:7 who hath *b.* a wife
22:23 find a virgin *b.* and lie
  27 *b.* damsel cried, none to save

BETTER.
Gen. 29:19 *b.* I give her to thee
Ex. 14:12 *b.* serv. the Egyptians
Num. 14:3 *b.* to return to E.?
Jud. 8:2 gleanings *b.* than vint.
  11:25 art thou *b.* than Balak
1 *Sam.* 1:8 am not I *b.* than ten s.
  27:1 nothing *b.* than go
1 *K.* 1:47 make name of K. Sol. *b.*
2:32 two men *b.* than he
19:4 am not *b.* than my fathers
21:2 vineyard *b.* than vineyard
2 *K.* 5:12 rivers of Damascus *b.*
2 *Chr.* 21:13 slain brethren *b.* than
Ps. 63:31 praise *b.* than ox
Ec. 2:24 nothing *b.* than to eat
3:22 nothing *b.* than rejoice
4:8 *b.* is he than both they
  9 two are *b.*
6:11 what is man *b.* ?
7:10 former days were *b.*
10:11 and a babbler is no *b.*
Is. 56:5 a name *b.* than of sons
Jer. 26:14 had be slain are *b.*
Dan. 1:20 ten times *b.*
Hos. 2:7 then was it *b.* with me
Amos 6:2 be they *b.* than these
Mat. 6:26 *b.* of the air, are ye not
  b. than they? *Luke* 12:24
12:12 a man *b.* than a sheep?
18:6 *b.* that a millstone, *Mark* 9:42; *Luke* 17:2
Rom. 3:9 are we *b.* than they?
1 *Cor.* 7:38 marriage, doth *b.*
8:8 neither if we eat are we *b.*
9:15 *b.* for me to die
11:17 come together not for *b.*
Phil. 2:3 esteem other *b.* than
Heb. 1:4 much *b.* than the angels
6:9 persuaded *b.* things of you
7:7 the less is blessed of the *b.*
  19 bringing in of a *b.* hope did
22 Jesus of a *b.* testament
8:6 Mediator of a *b.* covenant, established on *b.* promises
9:23 things with *b.* sacrifices
10:34 a *b.* and enduring sub.
11:16 desire a *b.* country

BEW

Heb. 11:35 obtain a *b.* resurrec.
  40 some *b.* thing for us
12:24 *b.* things than that of A.
2 *Pet.* 2:21 *b.* not to have known

BETTER is.
Prov. 15:16 *b. is* little with f. of L.
  17 *b. is* dinner of herbs
16:8 *b. is* a little with right.
  16 *b. is* it to get wisdom
17:1 *b. is* a dry morsel
19:1 *b. is* poor 28:6
27:10 *b. is* a neighbor near
Ec. 4:6 *b. is* handful with quiet
  13 *b. is* a poor wise child than
6:9 *b. is* the sight of the eyes
7:8 *b. is* the end than the beg.
Cant. 4:10 *b. is* thy love

Is BETTER, or is it BETTER.
Jud. 9:2 whether it *b.* all reign
18:19 *is it b.* to be a priest
Ruth 4:15 thy daughter *is b.*
1 *Sam.* 15:22 to obey *is b.*
  28 neighbor that *is b.*
2 *Sam.* 17:14 counsel of H. *is b.*
Ec. 1:19 another that *is b.*
Ps. 37:16 righteous hath *is b.*
63:3 thy loving-kind. *is b.*
84:10 a day in thy courts *is b.*
118:72 *is b.* to me than gold
Prov. 3:14 wisdom *is b.*
8:11 wisdom *is b.* than rubies
19 my fruit *is b.* than gold
12:9 that is despised *is b.*
16:32 that is slow to anger *is b.*
19:22 poor man *is b.* than a liar
27:5 rebuke *is b.* than secret l.
Ec. 6:3 an untimely birth *is b.*
7:1 a good name *is b.* than oint.
3 sorrow *is b.* than laughter,
  by sad. of coun. *is b.* made *b.*
5 the patient in spirit *is b.*
9:4 a liv. dog *is b.* than a d. lion
16 wisdom *is b.* than strength
18 wisd. *is b.* than w. of war
Cant. 1:2 love *is b.* than wine
Luke 5:39 he saith, the old *is b.*
Phil. 1:23 with C. wh. *is* far *b.*

It is BETTER, or BETTER it is.
Ps. 118:8 *it is b.* to trust in L. 9
Prov. 16:19 *b.* to be of humble
21:9 *b.* to dwell in a, 25:24
19 *it is b.* to dwell in the wild.
25:7 *it is* it be said, Come up
Ec. 5:5 *it is* than to vow
7:3 *it is b.* to go to house of m.
5 *b.* to hear reb. of wise men
Rom. 4:3 *it is b.* for me, 8
Mat. 18:8 *it is b.* to enter into life
  halt, 9; *Mark* 9:43, 45, 47
1 *Cor.* 7:9 *b.* to marry than to b.
1 *Pet.* 3:17 *b.* ye suffer for well-d.
5 *b.* to hear reb. of wise men
Rom. 11:23 *b.* not still in unb.
Mat. 26:24 *b.* for, for man *b.*

BIDKAR. 2 *K.* 9:25

BETTERED.
Mark 5:26 she was nothing *b.*

BETWIXT.
Phil. 1:23 I am in a strait *b.* two
*BEULAH.** *Is.* 62:4

BEWAIL.
Lev. 10:6 *b.* the burning L. kind.
Deut. 21:13 and *b.* her father
Jud. 11:37 *b.* my virginity. 38
Is. 16:9 will *b.* with the weep.
2 *Cor.* 12:21 *b.* many who have s.
Rev. 18:9 kings of earth shall *b.*

BEWAILED, ETH.
Jer. 4:31 daughter of Zion that *b.*
Luke 8:52 and all wept and *b.*
23:27 of women which also *b.*

BEWARE.
Gen. 24:6 *b.* bring not my son
Ex. 23:21 *b.* of him, obey his v.
Deut. 6:12 *b.* thou forget L. 8:11
15:9 *b.* there be not a thought
Jud. 13:4 *b.* drink no wine, 18
2 *Sam.* 18:12 *b.* none t. y. mau
Job 36:18 *b.* lest he take thee a.
Prov. 19:25 the simple will *b.*
Is. 8:15 *b.* lest II. persuade
Mat. 7:15 *b.* of false prophets
10:17 *b.* of men. 16:6
16:6 *b.* of the leaven, 11; *Mark* 8:15; *Luke* 12:1
Mark 12:38 *b.* of s. *Luke* 20:46
Luke 12:15 *b.* of covetousness
20:46 *b.* of scribes
Acts 13:40 *b.* lest that come
Phil. 3:2 *b.* of dogs, *b.* of evil w.
Col. 2:8 *b.* lest any man spoil
2 *Pet.* 3:17 *b.* lest being led

BEWITCHED.
Acts 8:9 Simon *b.* the people, 11
Gal. 3:1 who hath *b.* you?

BEWRAY.
Is. 16:3 *b.* not him that wand.

BIN

BEWRAYETH.
Prov. 27:16 oint. of right h. *b.*
29:24 cursing, and *b.* it not
Mat. 26:73 thy speech *b.* thee

BEYOND.
Num. 22:18 B. said, I cannot go
b. the word of the L. 24:13
Deut. 30:13 nor is it *b.* the sea
2 *Sam.* 10:16 *b.* the river, 1 *K.* 14:15; 1 *Chr.* 19:16; *Ezr.* 4:17, 20; 6:6, 8; 7:21, 25; *Neh.* 3:7, 9; *Is.* 7:20; 18:1; *Zep.* 3:10
Mark 6:51 amazed *b.* meas. 7:37
10:14 stretch not *b.* our meas.
Gal. 1:13 *b.* measure I persecut.
1 *Thes.* 4:6 that no man go *b.*

BEYOND *Jordan.* See JORDAN.

BEZALEEL. *Ex.* 31:2; 36:1; 38:22

BEZEK.
Jud. 1:4 slew in B. 10,000 men, 5
1 *Sam.* 11:8 Is. in B. 300,000
BIBBER. See WINE.
BICHRI. 2 *Sam.* 20:1, 2, 6, 22

BID.
1 *Sam.* 9:27 *b.* the servant pass
2 *Sam.* 2:26 *b.* the people return
2 *K.* 5:13 *b.* thee do great thing
10:5 all that thou shalt *b.* us
Zep. 1:7 L. hath *b.* his guests
Mat. 14:28 *b.* me come on the w.
22:9 find *b.* to the marriage
23:3 what they *b.* you observe
Luke 9:61 first *b.* farewell
10:40 *b.* her that she help me
14:12 they also *b.* thee again
1 *Cor.* 10:27 any that bel. not *b.*
2 *John* 10 nor *b.* him God speed

BIDDEN.
1 *Sam.* 9:13 they eat that be *b.*
2 *Sam.* 16:11 for the L. hath *b.*
Mat. 1:24 as angel had *b.* him
22:3 call them that were *b.*
4 tell them *b.* I have prepared
8 they *b.* were not worthy
Luke 7:39 Pharisee who had *b.*
14:7 to those who were *b.*
8 art *b.* lest s more hon. be *b.*
10 art *b.* sit in lowest room
24 none of those men *b.*

BIDDETH, ING.
1 *Sam.* 22:14 goeth at thy *b.*
2 *John* 11 that *b.* him God speed

BIDE.
Rom. 11:23 *b.* not still in unb.

BIDKAR. 2 *K.* 9:25

2 *Sam.* 3:31 David followed tho *b.*
Luke 7:14 and touched the *b.*

BIGTHAN. *Esr.* 2:21; 6:2
BILDAD. *Job* 2:11; 8:1; 18:1;
  25:1; 42:9
BILHAH. *Gen.* 29:29; 35:22, 25

BILL.
Luke 16:6 thy *b.* and write, 7
See DIVORCE.

BILLOWS.
Ps. 42:7 *b.* are gone over, *Jon.* 2:3

BIND.
Num. 30:2 an oath to *b.* his soul
Deut. 6:8 *b.* them for a sign
Jud. 15:10 to *b.* Samson
16:5 *b.* Samson to afflict him
16:11 *b.* me with 7 green with
18:13 will *b.* him with a crown
Job 31:36 I will *b.* it as a crown
38:31 *b.* influence of Pleiades
39:10 canst thou *b.* the unicorn
40:13 *b.* their faces in secret
41:5 wilt thou *b.* Leviathan
Ps. 105:22 to *b.* his princes
118:27 *b.* the sacrifice
149:8 to *b.* their kings
Prov. 3:3 *b.* them about thy neck
6:21 *b.* them upon thy heart
7:3 *b.* them on thy fingers
Is. 8:16 *b.* up the testimony
49:18 *b.* them on thee as a bride
61:1 to *b.* up the broken-hearted
Ezek. 8:15 I will *b.* up broken
Mat. 13:30 *b.* them in bundles
16:19 whatsoever thou shalt *b.*
  18:18
22:13 *b.* him hand and foot
23:4 *b.* heavy burdens grievous
Mark 3:3 no man could *b.* him
Acts 9:14 authority to *b.* all that
12:8 angel said *b.* on sandals
21:11 so shall the Jews *b.*

CRUDEN'S CONCORDANCE. 771

BIT

BINDETH.
Job 5:18 maketh sore and b. up
26:8 he b. up the waters
28:11 he b. floods from overf.
30:18 b. me about as the collar
36:13 hyp. cry not when he b.
Ps. 129:7 he that b. sheaves
147:3 he healeth and b. up
Prov. 26:8 b. a stone in a sling
Is. 30:26 Lord b. up breach

BINDING.
Gen. 49:11 b. his foal to the vine
Acts 22:4 b. and delivering men

BIRD.
Gen. 7:14 every b. went into
Lev. 14:52 cleanse with living b.
Job 41:5 play as with a b.
Ps. 11:1 as a b. to mountain
124:7 our soul is escaped as a b.
Prov. 1:17 in sight of any b.
6:5 as a b. from the fowler
7:23 as a b. hasteth to the snare
26:2 as the b. by wandering
27:8 as a b. that wandereth
Ec. 10:20 b. shall tell the matter
12:4 rise at the voice of the b.
Is. 16:2 as a wandering b.
46:11 ravenous b. from the east
Jer. 12:9 heritage as a speck. b.
Lam. 3:52 chased me like a b.
Hos. 9:11 fly away like a b.
11:11 they shall tremble as a b.
Amos 3:5 a b. fall where no gin
Rev. 18:2 every unclean b.

BIRDS.
Gen. 15:10 the b. divided he not
40:19 the b. shall eat thy flesh
Lev. 14:4 to take two b. alive
Deut. 14:11 clean b. shall eat
2 Sam. 21:10 b. to rest by day
Ps. 104:17 the b. make nests
Ec. 9:12 as b. caught
Cant. 2:12 time of singing of b.
Is. 31:5 as b. flying
Jer. 4:25 b. of heaven were fled
5:27 as a cage full of b. so are
12:4 are consumed and the b.
9 the b. round about
Ezek. 30:4 will gi. thee to rav. b.
39:4 to all b. filled like b. claws
Mat. 8:20 b. have n. Luke 9:58
13:32 b. lodge in the branches
Rom. 1:23 an image like to b.
1 Cor. 15:39 another of b.
Jam. 3:7 every kind of b. is tam.

BIRSHA. Gen. 14:2

BIRTH.
2 K. 19:3 children are come to the b. Is. 37:3
Job 3:16 as a hidden untimely b.
Ps. 58:8 like the untimely b.
Ec. 6:3 untimely b. is better
7:1 better than day of one's b.
Ec. 6:9 shall I bring to the b.
Ezek. 16:3 thy b. is of Canaan
Hos. 9:11 shall fly from the b.
Mat. 1:18 the b. of Jesus Christ
Luke 1:14 shall rejoice at his b.
Gal. 4:19 I travail in b.
Rev. 12:2 she cried, trav. in b.

BIRTHDAY.
Gen. 40:20 which was Ph.'s b.
Mat. 14:6 Herod's b. Mark 6:21

BIRTHRIGHT.
Gen. 25:31 this day thy b.
33 sold his b. to Jacob
34 thus Esau despised his b.
27:36 took away my b.
43:33 first-born ac. to his b.
1 Chr. 5:1 B.'s b. to sons of Jos.
Heb. 12:16 for morsel sold his b.

BISHOP, s.
Phil. 1:1 saints at Philippi, b.
1 Tim. 3:1 desire the office of a b.
2 b. must be blamel. Tit. 1:7
1 Pet. 2:25 to the b. of your souls

BISHOPRICK.
Acts 1:20 his b. let another take

BIT, s.
Ps. 32:9 must be held in with b.
Jam. 3:3 we put b. in horses' m.

BIT, Verb.
Num. 21:6 they b. people
Amos 5:19 and a serpent b. him

BITE.
Ec. 10:8 a serpent shall b.
11 b. without enchantment
Jer. 8:17 serpents, they shall b.
Amos 9:3 serp. and he shall b.
Mic. 3:5 the prophets that b.
Hab. 2:7 rise up that shall b.
Gal. 5:15 if ye b. and devour

BIT

BITETH.
Gen. 49:17 Dan an adder, that b.
Prov. 23:32 it b. like a serpent

BITHYNIA.
Acts 16:7 assayed to go into B.
1 Pet. 1:1 through Asia and B.

BITTEN.
Num. 21:8 it b. when he looks

BITTER.
Gen. 27:34 E. cried with b. cry
Ex. 1:14 made their lives b.
15:23 waters, for they were b.
Deut. 32:24 dev. with b. destru.
32 their clusters are b.
2 K. 14:26 affl. of Isr. it was b.
Job 3:20 why is life given to b.?
13:26 writest b. things
23:2 to-day is my complaint b.
Ps. 64:3 arrows, even b. words
Prov. 5:4 b. as wormwood
27:7 to hungry soul b. thing
Ec. 7:26 more b. than death
Is. 5:20 that put b. for sweet
24:9 strong drink shall be b.
Jer. 2:19 an evil thing and b.
4:18 thy wickedness, it is b.
6:26 make most b. lamentation
31:15 in Ramah, b. weeping
Amos 8:10 the end, as a b. day
Hab. 1:6 b. and hasty nation
Col. 3:19 be not b. against them
Jam. 3:14 if ye have b. envying
Rev. 8:11 men died of waters b.
10:9 it shall make thy belly b.

BITTER with Water.
Num. 5:18 b. w. that causeth
Jam. 3:11 send sweet w. and b.?

BITTERLY.
Jud. 5:23 curse ye b. the inhab.
Ruth 1:20 Almighty hath dealt b.
Is. 22:4 I will weep b.
33:7 amb. of peace shall weep b.
Ezek. 27:30 the pilots shall cry b.
Hos. 12:14 Eph. provoked him b.
Zep. 1:14 the mighty shall cry b.
Mat. 26:75 P. wept b. Luke 22:62

BITTERN.
Is. 14:23 possess. for the b. 34:11
Zep. 2:14 the b. shall lodge

BITTERNESS.
1 Sam. 1:10 Hannah was in b.
15:32 the b. of death is past
2 Sam. 2:26 sword will be b.
Job 7:11 I will complain in the b.
9:18 but filleth me with b.
10:1 I will speak in b. of soul
21:25 another dieth in b. of soul
Prov. 14:10 heart knoweth own b.
17:25 a foolish son is b. to her
Is. 38:15 softly in b. of my soul.
17 for peace I had great b.
Lam. 1:4 afflic., and she is in b.
3:15 he hath filled me with b.
Ezek. 3:14 and I went in b.
21:6 b. sigh before their eyes
27:31 weep for thee with b.
Zec. 12:10 in b. for him as one that is in b. for his first-born
Acts 8:23 art in the gall of b.
Rom. 3:14 full of cursing and b.
Eph. 4:31 let all b. be put away
Heb. 12:15 lest any root of b.

BLACK.
Lev. 13:31 there is no b. hair in it
1 K. 18:45 the heaven was b.
Job 30:30 my skin is b. upon me
Prov. 7:9 in the b. and dark n.
Cant. 1:5 I am b. but comely
6 look not on me, I am b.
5:11 his locks are b. as a raven
Jer. 4:28 shall heavens be b.
8:21 I am hurt, I am b.
14:2 the gates thereof are b.
Lam. 5:10 our skin was b.
Zec. 6:2 in second chariot b. h.
6 b. horses go forth into north
Mat. 5:36 one hair white or b.
Rev. 6:5 and lo, a b. horse
12 the sun became b.

BLACKER.
Lam. 4:8 visage is b. than coal

BLACKISH.
Job 6:16 b. by reason of the ice

BLACKNESS.
Is. 50:3 clothe heavens with b.
Joel 2:6 shall gath. b. Nah. 2:10
Heb. 12:18 ye are not come to b.
Jude 13 to whom is reserved b.

BLADE.
Jud. 3:22 went in after the b.
Job 31:22 from my shoulder-b.

BLA

Mat. 13:26 b. was spr. Mark 4:28

BLAINS.
Ex. 9:9 a boil with b. 10

BLAME.
Gen. 43:9 bear thi b. 44:32
2 Cor. 8:20 no man should b. us
Eph. 1:4 holy and without b.

BLAMED.
2 Cor. 6:3 the ministry be not b.
Gal. 2:11 bec. he was to be b.

BLAMELESS.
Jos. 2:17 be b. of thine oath
Mat. 12:5 prof. Sab. and are b.
Luke 1:6 in ordin. of the L. b.
1 Cor. 1:8 b. in the day of our L.
Phil. 2:15 be b. and harmless
3:6 in the law b.
1 Thes. 5:23 body be preserved b.
1 Tim. 3:2 bishop be b. Tit. 1:7
10 use office of deacon being b.
Tit. 1:6 if any be b. the husband
2 Pet. 3:14 ye may be found b.

BLASPHEME.
2 Sam. 12:14 enemies to b.
1 K. 21:10 didst b. God, 13
Ps. 74:10 shall the enemy b.
Mark 3:28 they shall b.
20 that shall he sp. Holy G.
Acts 26:11 I compelled them to b.
1 Tim. 1:20 may learn not to b.
Jam. 2:7 b. that worthy name
Rev. 13:6 to b. his name

BLASPHEMED.
Lev. 24:11 Israelitish wom. son b.
2 K. 19:6 servants of king of Assyria b. me, 22; Is. 37:6, 23
Ps. 74:18 have b. thy name
Is. 52:5 my name every day is b.
65:7 and b. me on the hills
Ezek. 20:27 your fathers have b.
Acts 18:6 op. themselves and b.
Rom. 2:24 name of God is b.
1 Tim. 6:1 his doctrine be not b.
Tit. 2:5 that the word be not b.
Rev. 16:9 were scorched and b.
11 b. because of their pains
21 b. God because of the hail

BLASPHEMEST, ETH.
Lev. 24:16 whoso b. the Lord
Ps. 44:16 voice of him that b.
Mat. 9:3 scribes said, This m, b.
John 10:36 F. sanctified thou b.

BLASPHEMING.
Acts 13:45 contradicting and b.

BLASPHEMER, s.
Acts 19:37 are not b. of your god.
1 Tim. 1:13 who was before a b.
2 Tim. 3:2 men shall be b.

BLASPHEMY.
2 K. 19:3 a day of b. Is. 37:3
Mat. 12:31 all manner of b. shall be forgiven, but b. against
20:65 heard his b. Mark 14:64
Mark 7:22 out of heart proceed b.
Col. 3:8 now ye also put off b.
Rev. 13:1 upon his heads b.
6 opened his mouth in b.

BLASPHEMIES.
Ezek. 35:12 have heard all thy b.
Mat. 15:19 out of the heart b.
Mark 2:7 man thus speak b.?
3:28 b. they shall blaspheme
Luke 5:21 who is this b. speak.
Rev. 13:5 speaking b.

BLASPHEMOUS.
Acts 6:11 heard him speak b. w.
13 ceaseth not to speak b. w.

BLASPHEMOUSLY.
Luke 22:65 other things b. spake

BLAST.
Ex. 15:8 at b. thy nostrils
Jos. 6:5 a long b. with ram's h.
2 Sam. 22:16 the b. of the breath of his nostrils, Ps. 18:15
2 K. 19:7 a b. on Sen. Is. 37:7
Is. 25:4 the b. of the terrible

BLASTED.
Gen. 41:6 thin ears b. 23, 27
2 K. 19:26 as corn b. Is. 37:27

BLASTING.
Deut. 28:22 smite thee with b.
1 K. 8:37 there be b. 2 Chr. 6:28
Amos 4:9 smitten you with b.
Hag. 2:17 I smote you with b.

BLASTUS. Acts 12:20

BLAZE.
Mark 1:45 b. abroad the matter

BLE

BLEATING, S.
Jud. 5:16 to hear b. of flocks
1 Sam. 15:14 this b. of sheep

BLEMISH.
Ex. 12:5 without b. Lev. 9:3;
14:10; 23:12; Num. 6:14
29:1 two rams with b. Lev. 5:15,
18; 6:6; 9:13; Ezek. 46:4
Lev. 1:3 male without b. 10;
4:23; 22:19
21:17 hath b. not appr. 21:23
22:20 hath a b. Deut. 15:21
21 freewill-offering no b.
24:19 cause a b. in his neighbor
Num. 19:2 a red heifer with. b.
28:3 seven lambs without b.
2 Sam. 14:25 no b. in Absalom
Dan. 1:4 in whom was no b.
Eph. 5:27 holy and without b.
1 Pet. 1:19 of a lamb without b.

BLEMISHES.
Lev. 22:25 b. in them not accept.
2 Pet. 2:13 spots they are and b.

BLESS.
1 Cor. 10:16 cup of bless. we b.

BLESS, God being agent.
Gen. 12:2 I will b. thee, 16:3, 24
3 I will b. them that b. thee
17:16 will b. her, and give thee
22:17 I will b. Heb. 6:14
28:3 b. thee, and multiply thee
32:26 except thou b. me
48:16 b. the lads
49:25 by Alm. who shall b. thee
Ex. 20:24 and I will b. thee
23:25 he shall b. thy bread
Num. 6:24 Lord b. and keep thee
27 on Israel, and I will b. them
24:1 pleased the L. to b. Israel
Deut. 7:13 b. the fruit of thy w.
15:4 no poor, for L. shall b. t.
18 God shall b. thee, 30:16
16:15 bec. Lord shall b. thee
20:15 look down and b. Israel
28:8 b. thee in the land
12 b. all the work of thy hand
33:11 b. Lord his substance
2 Sam. 7:29 to b. the house of thy servant, 1 Chr. 17:27
1 Chr. 4:10 wouldest b. me indeed
Ps. 5:12 wilt b. the righteous
28:9 b. thine inheritance
29:11 b. his people with peace
67:6 our own God shall b. us, 7
115:12 L. will b. us, he will b.
the house of Israel, of Aaron
13 he will b. them that fear L.
128:5 shall b. thee out of Zion
132:15 abundantly b. her prov.
134:3 the Lord b. thee out of Z.
Is. 19:25 L. of hosts shall b.
Hag. 2:19 from this day will I b.
Acts 3:26 sent him to b. you

BLESS, God being the object.
Deut. 8:10 art full, shalt b. Lord
Jud. 5:9 b. the L. Ps. 103:21; 134:1
1 Chr. 29:20 Dav. said, now b. L.
Neh. 9:5 stand up and b. L. for
Ps. 16:7 L. who hath given
26:12 in the cong. will I b. Lord
34:1 b. the Lord at all times
63:4 will I b. thee while I live
66:8 O b. our God
68:26 b. ye God in congregations
103:2 sing to the L. b. his name
103:4 b. his name, 103:1
103:1 b. L. O my soul, 2,22;
104:1, 35
20 b. ye the ang. 21 b. h. hosts
22 b. the Lord all his works
115:18 will b. L. from this time
134:2 lift up your h. b. the L.
145:2 O house of Is.
145:10 O Levi, b. the Lord
145:1 will b. thy name forever
2 every day will I b. thee
10 thy saints shall b. thee
21 b. let all flesh b. his holy n.
Jam. 3:9 therewith b. we God
BLESS, Man agent and object.
Gen. 27:4 b. thee before I die, 25
31 b. me, O my father, 38
34:60 bring them to me, I will b.
49:25 thou shalt bless b. saying
Ec. 12:22 begone, and b. me also
Num. 6:23 on this wise b. Israel
23:20 I have received com. to b.
24 come then not b. them
Deut. 10:8 separ. L. to b. 21:5
27:12 stand on Gerizim, to b.
29:19 heareth curse, to b. him
1 Sam. 9:13 doth b. the sacrifice
2 Sam. 6:20 David returned to b. his household, 1 Chr. 16:43
8:10 Joram his son to b. David
21:3 that ye b. mh. of the Lord

BLO

Jer. 2:34 b. of the poor innocents
18:21 pour out their b. by force
48:10 keepeth his sword from b.
51:35 my b. be on the inh. of C.
Lam. 4:14 pol. thems. with b.
Ezek. 5:17 pestilence and b. pass
9:9 the land is full of b.
14:19 my fury upon it in b.
16:6 when thou wast in thy b.
9:1 I washed away thy b.
38:1 will give thee b. in fury
18:10 sou that is a shedder of b.
13:1 he shall die, his b. shall be
15:10 a vine in thy b.
21:32 thy b. in midst, 22:13
22:3 sheddeth b. in midst of it
24:37 b. is in their hands, 45
24:8 her b. on the top of a rock
28:23 send b. into her streets
32:6 water with thy b. the land
33:6 no b. thou hast not hated b.
even b. shall pursue thee
44:7 the fat and the b.
Hos. 1:4 avenge the b. of Jezreel
4:2 and b. toucheth b.
Joel 2:30 b. fire, pillars of smoke
31 moon turn into b. Acts 2:20
3:21 I will cleanse their b.
Zep. 1:17 their b. poured out
Mal. 9:30 w. with an issue of b.
13 yrs. Mark 5:25; Luke 8:43
16:17 b. hath not revealed it
22:30 in the b. of prophets
33 b. of right. Abel, Luke 11:51
26:28 b. of new test. Mark 14:24
27:6 because it is price of b.
8 called the field of b. Acts 1:19
24 inn. of b. of this just pers.
Luke 13:1 whose b. P. mingled
22:20 test. in my b. 1 Cor. 11:25
44 sweat as great drops of b.
John 1:13 born not of b.
6:54 and drinketh my b. 56
55 and my b. is drink indeed
19:31 forth. came there out b.
Acts 5:28 be to bring this man's b.
15:20 abstain from b. 29; 21:25
17:26 made of one b. all nations
18:6 b. be on your own heads
20:26 pure from b. of all men
1 Cor. 11:27 the body and b.
15:50 flesh and b. cannot inherit
Eph. 6:12 against flesh and b.
Col. 1:20 through b. of his cross
Heb. 2:14 partak. of flesh and b.
9:7 with. his b. which he offered
12 b. of goats, but by his own b.
13 if the b. of bulls sanctifieth
20 the b. of the testament
22 without shedding of b.
10:19 boldest by the b. of Jesus
11:28 and sprinkling of b.
12:4 not yet resisted unto b.
24 b. of sprinkling that speak.
13:11 whose b. is brought into
1 Pet. 1:2 sprinkling of the b.
1 John 1:7 b. of J. C. cleanseth
5:6 came by water and b.
8 the Spirit, water, and b.
Rev. 5:9 redeemed us by thy b.
6:10 avenge our b.
12 and the moon became as b.
7:14 in the b. of the Lamb
8:8 part of sea became b. 16:3
11:6 to turn the waters into b.
12:11 overcame by b. of the L.
11:20 b. came out of winepress
16:6 hast given them b. to drink
18:24 the b. of the prophets
19:2 avenged the b. of his serv.
13 with a vesture dipped in b.
See AVENGER, REVENGER.

BLOOD be upon.
Lev. 20:9 curs. father, his b. Ezek.
11 incest., 13 sodomy, 16 bes-
tiality, 27 wizard, their b. be
u. them
Ezek. 18:13 abom. his b. be upon him
33:5 his b. shall be upon him

BLOOD, with bullock.
Is. 1:11 I del. not in b. of bull.

BLOOD of Christ.
1 Cor. 10:6 com. of b. of C.
Eph. 2:13 made nigh by b. of C.
1 Pet. 1:19 with precious b. of C.
1 John 1:7 the b. of C. cleanseth

BLOOD of the Covenant.
Ex. 24:8 M. said Behold the b.
Zec. 9:11 for thee also by b. of c.
Heb. 10:29 b. of cov. unholy thing
13:20 b. of the everlasting cov.

BLOOD, with eat.
Lev. 3:17 eat neither fat nor b.
7:26 eat no manner of b. 27;
17:14; Deut. 12:16, 23; 15:23

BLO

Lev. 27 eateth b. soul ent off, 17:10
1 Sam. 14:32 eat them with the b.
Ezek. 33:25 ye eat with b.

For BLOOD.
2 Chr. 24:25 for the b. of sons
Ps. 9:12 maketh inquis. for b.
Prov. 1:11 lay wait for b. 18
12:6 are to lie in wait for b.
Mic. 7:2 lie in wait for b.

His BLOOD.
Gen. 37:26 and conceal his b.
42:22 behold his b. is required
Jos. 2:19 his b. be upon his head
2 Sam. 4:11 shall I not req. his b.
1 K. 2:32 shall return his b.
Ezek. 3:18 his b. will I require at
thy hand, 20; 33:4, 6, 8
Hos. 12:14 leave his b. on him
Mat. 27:25 his b. be on us
Acts 20:28 ch. purchased with h. b.
Rom. 3:25 thro' faith in his b.
5:9 justified by his b.
Eph. 1:7 red. thro' his b. Col. 1:14
Heb. 9:12 by his own b. he ent.
13:12 sanct. the people with h. b.
Rev. 1:5 and washed us in his b.

Innocent BLOOD.
Deut. 19:10 that in. b. be not shed
19 put away guilt of in. b. 21:9
21:8 in. b. to thy people's ch.
1 Sam. 19:5 sin against in. b.
1 K. 2:31 take away in. b.
2 K. 21:16 Man. shed in. b. 24:4
Ps. 94:21 they condemn in. b.
106:38 in. b. even b. of sons
Prov. 6:17 hateth hands sh. in. b.
Is. 59:7 haste to shed in. b.
Jer. 7:6 shed not innocent b.
22:17 are to shed innocent b.
26:15 shall surely bring in no. b.
Joel 3:19 bec. they shed inno. b.
Jon. 1:14 L. lay not on us inno. b.
Mat. 27:4 I betrayed innocent b.

Shed BLOOD.
Gen. 9:6 m's b. by m. h. b. be s.
37:22 Reuben said, shed no b.
Lev. 17:4 shed b. shall be cut off
Num. 35:33 cl. of b. s. but by b.
Deut. 21:7 hands not shed this b.
1 K. 2:5 shed b. of war in peace
1 Chr. 22:8 shed b. much b. 28:3
Ps. 79:3 their b. shed like water
10 reveng. b. of thy servants sh.
Prov. 1:16 to shed b. Rom. 3:15
Ezek. 10:39 wo. that a b. 22:4, 6, 9, 12, 27
21:4 guilty in b. th. hast shed, 9
22:25 ye s. b. and shall ye pos.
36:18 for the b. shed
Mat. 23:35 the righteous b. s.
Mark 14:24 this is my b. which
is shed, Luke 22:20
Luke 11:50 b. of all the proph. s.
Acts 22:20 when b. of S. was s.
Rev. 16:6 s. the b. of the saints

Sprinkle BLOOD.
Ex. 29:20 sprinkle b. on altar.
Lev. 1:5, 11; 3:2, 8, 13; 7:2;
17:6; Num. 18:17

BLOOD sprinkled.
Ex. 24:8 M. sp. b. on the people
Is. 63:3 their b. shall be sprinkled
on my garment
Heb. 9:21 he sp. with b.

With BLOOD.
Ex. 30:10 A. make atone, with b.
Lev. 19:26 not eat any thing w. b.
1 K. 2:9 bring thou down with b.
Ps. 106:38 land was pol. with b.
Is. 9:16 sword of L. filled with b.
1 hand shall be soaked with b.
49:26 drunken with their own b.
59:3 hands are defiled with b.
Jer. 19:4 filled with innoc. b.
46:10 drunk with their b.
Lam. 4:14 pol. thems. with b.
Ezek. 38:22 plead ag. him with b.
Hos. 6:8 Gilead polluted with b.
Mic. 3:10 build up Zion with b.
Hab. 2:12 build a town with b.
Gal. 1:16 I conferred not with b.
Heb. 9:22 the law purged with b.
Rev. 8:7 fire, mingled with b.
17:6 the woman drunken w. b.

BLOOD-GUILTINESS.
Ps. 51:14 deliver me from b. g.

BLOODTHIRSTY.
Prov. 29:10 b. th. hate upright.

BLOODY.
Ex. 4:25 a b. husb. art thou, 26
2 Sam. 16:7 Sh. said, Thou b. man
21:1 famine is for S. his b. house
Ps. 5:6 L. will abhor the b. man
26:9 gather not my life with b. m.

BOA

Ps. 55:23 b. m. not live half th. d.
50:2 and save me from b. men
139:19 depart from me, ye b. m.
Ezek. 7:23 full of b. crimes
22:2 wilt thou judge the b. city?
24:6 the b. city, 9; Nah. 3:1
Acts 28:8 lay sick of a b. flux

BLOOMED.
Num. 17:8 A. rod b. blossoms.

BLOSSOM, S.
Gen. 40:10 her b. shot forth
Is. 5:23 b. shall go up as dust

BLOSSOM, ED.
Num. 17:5 the man's rod shall b.
Is. 27:6 Israel shall b. and bud
35:1 desert shall b. as the rose
2 it shall b. abundantly
Ezek. 7:10 the rod hath b.
Hab. 3:17 fig-tree shall not b.

BLOT.
Job 31:7 if any b. hath cleaved
Prov. 9:7 wicked, getteth a b.

BLOT out.
Ex. 32:32 b. me out of thy b.
33 him will I b. out
Deut. 9:14 done that I b. out
25:19 b. out reme. of Amalek
29:20 b. out his name
2 K. 14:27 would b. out name
Ps. 51:1 b. out transgress.
9 b. out all my iniquity
Jer. 18:23 nor b. out their sin
Neh. 4:5 let not their sin be b.
Ps. 69:28 b. out of book of liv.
14 sin of his mother be b. out
Is. 44:22 b. out as a thick cloud
Acts 3:19 bec. they were b. out

BLOTTETH, ING.
Is. 43:25 b. out thy transgress.
Col. 2:14 b. out the handwriting

BLOW, Substantive.
Ps. 39:10 consumed by the b.
Jer. 14:17 with b. a grievous b.

BLOW, Verb.
Ex. 15:10 b. with thy wind
Jud. 7:18 when I b. then b. ye
Ps. 78:26 caused east-wind to b.
147:18 causeth his wind to b.
Cant. 4:16 come, thou south, b.
Ezek. 21:31 will b. ag. thee, 22:21
Hos. 5:8 b. cornet in Gibeah
Hag. 1:9 I did b. upon it
Luke 12:55 see the south-wind b.
Rev. 7:1 that wind should not b.
See TRUMPET.

BLOWETH.
Is. 40:7 b. of the Lord b. on it
51:16 created the smith that b.
John 3:8 wind b. where it listeth
Job 20:26 fire not b. consume

BLOWN.
Ex. 20:4, 30:1, 31, 36; 27:16
2 Chr. 2:7 coming to w. in b. 14
Exc. 1:6 b. hangings, b. marble
8:15 Mordecai in apparel of b.
Ezek. 23:6 Assyr. clothed with b.
See PURPLE, CLOTH, LACE, LOOPS.

BLUENESS.
Prov. 20:30 b. of a wound

BLUNT.
Ec. 10:10 if iron be b. and he

BLUSH.
Ezr. 9:6 I b. to lift up my face
Jer. 6:15 nor could they b. 8:12

BOANERGES. Mark 3:17

BOAR.
Ps. 80:13 b. out of the wood

BOARDS.
Cant. 8:9 inclose her with b.
Acts 27:44 on b. came to land

BOAST, Substantive.
Rom. 2:17 makest thy b. of the law

BOAST, Verb.
1 K. 20:11 not as he
Ps. 44:8 in God we b. all the day
Ps. 49:6 trust in wealth and b.
94:4 workers of iniquity b.
97:7 confounded that b. of idols
Is. 10:15 shall the axe b. itself
61:6 in their glory shall you b.
Rom. 11:18 b. not ag. branches

BOD

2 Cor. 9:2 I A. to them of Maced.
10:15 b. without our measure
16 to b. in another man's line
11:16 receive me that I may b.
Eph. 3:2 b of works, lest any b.

BOASTED.
Ezek. 35:13 with mouth ye h. b.
2 Cor. 7:14 if I have b. any thing

BOASTERS.
Rom. 1:30 b. inventors of evil th.
2 Tim. 3:2 covetous, b. proud

BOASTEST, ETH.
Ps. 10:3 wicked b. of his heart's
52:1 why b. thyself in mischief
Prov. 20:14 then he b.
25:14 whoso b. of a false gift
Jam. 3:5 tongue b. great things

BOASTING, Participle.
Acts 5:36 Theudas b. himself
2 Cor. 10:15 not b. without meas.

BOASTING, Substantive.
Rom. 3:27 where is b. then?
2 Cor. 7:14 our b. before Titus
8:24 show ye the proof of our b.
9:3 lest our b. of you be in vain
4 in this same confidence b.
11:10 no man stop me of this b.
in this confidence of b.
Jam. 4:15 ye rejoice in your b.
John 6:22 no other b. there, Jesus
went not into the b.
23 came other b. from Tiberias
Acts 27:16 work to come by the b.
30 they had let down the b.
32 cut off the ropes of the b.
BOAZ. 1 K. 7:21; 2 Chr. 3:17;
Ruth 2:1, 19; 3:2; 4:1; Lu. 3:32

BOCHIM. Jud. 2:1 camp came up to B. 5

BODY.
Ex. 24:10 as the b. of heaven
1 Sam. 31:12 b. of S. 1 Chr. 10:12
Job 19:17 child.'s sake of my b.
20 worms destroy b.
20:25 and cometh out of the b.
Prov. 5:11 flesh and b. are cons.
Is. 10:18 consume soul and b.
51:23 hast laid thy b. as ground
Ezek. 10:12 whole b. full of eyes
Dan. 7:15 in midst of my b.
Mat. 5:29 b. be cast into hell, 30
6:22 light of b. Luke 11:34; b.
full of light, Luke 11:34, 36
25 thought for b. Luke 12:22
10:28 kill the b. Luke 12:4
14:12 John's discip. took the b.
26:12 this ointment on my b.
26 this is my b. Mark 14:22;
Luke 22:19; 1 Cor. 11:24
27:58 Joseph begged the b. of J.
Mark 15:43; Luke 23:52
Mark 5:29 she felt in her b.
14:8 aforehand to anoint my b.
51 linen cloth cast about his b.
Luke 12:23 b. more than raiment
17:37 b. is, thither the eagles
24:3 found not the b. of Lord
John 28:12 b. of Jesus had him
Rom. 6:6 b. of sin be destroyed
7:4 dead to the law by b. of C.
24 I from the b. of this death
8:10 b. is dead because of sin
13 Spirit mortify deeds of b.
23 the redemption of our b.
1 Cor. 5:3 ab. in b. but present
6:13 b. not for fornica-
tion, but for L. and L. for b.
18 every sin b. is without the b.
19 your b. is temple of H. G.
7:4 no power over her own b.
9:27 I keep under my b. and
10:16 communion of the b. of C.
11:27 guilty of b. and blood
29 not discerning the Lord's b.
12:14 the b. is not one member
15 therefore not of the b. ? 16
17 if whole b. were an eye
19 wh. were the b. ? 20 one b.
27 now ye are the b. of Christ
13:3 I give my b. to be burned
15:35 how raised? with what b.?
37 sowest not that b. that shall
38 God giveth a b. as it hath
44 sown a nat. b. raised spir. b.
2 Cor. 5:8 to be absent from b.
12:2 out of the b. I cannot tell
the edifying of b. of Christ
16 from whom the whole b.
5:23 he is the Saviour of the b.
Phil. 3:21 shall change vile b.
Col. 1:18 head of the b. the ch.
2:11 in putting off the b. of sins

774   CRUDEN'S CONCORDANCE.

BOI

Col. 2:17 shadow, the *b.* is of Ch.
19 from which the *b.* by joints
23 a show of wisdom in neg. *b.*
1 *Thes.* 5:23 your soul and *b.*
Heb. 10:5 a *b.* hast thou prepared
10 offering of the *b. of* Jesus
Jam. 2:16 things needful to *b.*
26 the *b.* without the spirit ·
3:2 to bridle the whole *b.*
3 we turn about their whole *b.*
6 tongue defileth the whole *b.*
Jude 9 disputed about *b.* of M.

Dead BODY.
Num. 19:11 *d. b.* unclean. 16
2 *K.* 8:5 he had restored *d. b.*
Is. 26:19 my *d. b.* sh. they arise
Jer. 26:23 cast his *d. b.* into gra.
36:30 *dead b.* shall be cast out

Fruit of the BODY.
Deut. 28:4 blessed be *f. of thy b.*
18 cursed shall be *fr. of thy b.*
53 shalt eat the *fr. of thy b.*
Ps. 132:11 *f. b.* will I set on thy
Mic. 6:7 *f. of* my *b.* for sin of soul

His BODY.
1 *Sam.* 31:10 fast. *his b.* to wall
Dan. 4:33 *his b.* wet w. dew, 5:21
7:11 beast was slain, and *his b.*
10:6 *his b.* was like the beryl
Luke 23:55 b. how *his b.* was laid
24:23 they found not *his b.*
John 2:21 temple of *his b.*
Acts 19:12 from *his b.* were br.
Rom. 4:19 con. not *h. b.* now d.
1 *Cor.* 6:19 sinneth against *his b.*
7:4 power of *his* own *b.*
2 *Cor.* 5:10 things done in *his b.*
Eph. 1:23 which is *his b.* fulness
Phil. 3:21 like *his* glorious *b.*
Col. 1:24 for *his b.* sake
1 *Pet.* 2:24 bare our sins in *his b.*

In BODY.
Lam. 4:7 *in b.* than rubies
Rom. 6:12 *in* your mortal *b.*
1 *Cor.* 5:3 I verily as absent *in b.*
6:20 glorify God *in* your *b.*
7:34 that she may be holy *in b.*
12:18 members every one *in b.*
25 no schism in the *b.*
2 *Cor.* 4:10 *in b.* the dy. of the L.
that life he manif. *in* our *b.*
5:6 whilst we are at home *in b.*
12:2 whether *in b.* or out *of b.*
Gal. 6:17 I bear *in b.* the marks
Phil. 1:20 be magnified *in* my *b.*
Col. 1:22 *in b.* of his flesh
Heb. 13:3 being yours, *in* the *b.*

One BODY.
Rom. 12:4 members in *one b.*
5 are *one b.* in C. 1 *Cor.* 10:17
1 *Cor.* 6:16 joined to a h. is *one b.*
12:12 as the *b.* is *one*, and hath
13 we are baptized into *one b.*
20 many members, yet *one b.*
Eph. 2:16 rec. both to G. in *one b.*
4:4 there is *one b.* and one S.
Col. 3:15 also called in *one b.*

BODIES.
Job 13:12 your *b.* like *b.* of clay
Ezek. 1:11 wings covered *b.* 23
Dan. 3:27 on *b.* fire had no power
Mat. 27:52 *b.* of saints arose
John 19:31 *b.* should not remain
Rom. 1:24 dishonour their own *b.*
8:11 quicken your mortal *b.*
12:1 your *b.* a living sacrifice
1 *Cor.* 6:15 your *b.* members
15:40 celestial *b.* and *b.*
Eph. 5:28 love wives as own *b.*
Heb. 10:22 *b.* washed with pure
13:11 *b.* of beasts, whose blood

Dead BODIES.
2 *Chr.* 20:24 were *d. b.* fallen
Ps. 79:2 *d. b.* of thy servants
110:6 fill places with *d. b.*
Jer. 31:40 valley of *dead b.*
33:5 to fill them with *d. b.*
34:20 *d. b.* shall be for meat
41:9 Ishm. cast *dead b.* of men
Amos 8:3 *d. b.* in every place
Rev. 11:8 *dead b.* in the street
9 their *dead b.* three days and
a half, nor suffer *d. b.*

BODILY.
Luke 3:22 desc. in a *b.* shape
2 *Cor.* 10:10 *b.* presence is weak
Col. 2:9 fulness of the Godh. *b.*
1 *Tim.* 4:8 *b.* exer. profiteth little

DOIL, S, Substantive.
2 *K.* 20:7 figs on it. *Is.* 38:21
Job 2:7 Satan smote Job with *b.*

BOIL.
Job 41:31 the deep to *b.* like a pot

BON

Is. 64:2 fire causeth waters to *b.*
Ezek. 24:5 make it *b.* well, 46:20

BOILED.
1 *K.* 19:21 yoke of oxen and *b.*
2 *K.* 6:29 so we *b.* my son
Job 30:27 my bowels *b.*

BOISTEROUS.
Mat. 14:30 he saw the wind *b.*

BOLD.
Prov. 28:1 right. are *b.* as a lion
Acts 13:46 P. and Bar. waxed *b.*
Rom. 10:20 Esaias is very *b.*
2 *Cor.* 10:1 being absent, am *b.*
2 wherewith I think to be *b.*
11:21 any is *b.* I am *b.* also
2 *Thes.* 2:2 we were *b.* in our G.
Phile. 8 I might be much *b.* in C.

BOLDLY.
Mark 15:43 Joseph went in *b.*
John 7:26 he speaketh *b.*
Acts 9:27 preached *b.* at Dam.
29 he spake *b.* in name of L. J.
14:3 abode they, speaking *b.*
18:26 Apollos began to speak *b.*
19:8 spake *b.* for three months
Rom. 15:15 written more *b.*
Eph. 6:19 open my mouth *b.*
20 I may speak *b.* as I ought
Heb. 4:16 *b.* to the thr. of grace
13:6 *b.* say, Lord is my helper

BOLDNESS.
Ec. 8:1 *b.* of his face be changed
Acts 4:13 *b.* of Peter and John
29 with all *b.* they may speak
31 spake word of God with *b.*
2 *Cor.* 7:4 great is my *b.* of speech
Eph. 3:12 we have *b.* and access
Phil. 1:20 with all *b.* as always
1 *Tim.* 3:13 they purchase gr. *b.*
Heb. 10:19 *b.* to enter into holiest
1 *John* 4:17 may have *b.* in judg.

BOLSTER.
1 *Sam.* 19:13 goats' hair for *b.* 16
26:7 spear at 3, 11, 12; 16 water

BOND, Adjective.
1 *Cor.* 12:13 one body, *b.* or free
See FREE.

BOND.
Ezek. 20:37 bring you into *b.*
Luke 13:16 from his *b.* on sab.
Acts 8:23 art in the *b.* of iniquity
Eph. 4:3 Spirit, in *b.* of peace
Col. 3:14 charity, *b.* of perfect.

BONDS.
Job 12:18 looseth the *b.* of kings
Ps. 116:16 hast loosed my *b.*
Jer. 5:5 the yoke, and burst the *b.*
27:2 make thee *b.* and yokes
30:8 his yoke, and burst thy *b.*
Nah. 1:13 I will burst thy *b.*
Acts 20:23 that *b.* and affl. abide
23:29 wor. of death or *b.* 26:31
26:14 a certain man left in *b.*
29 as I am, except those *b.*
Eph. 6:20 am an ambass. in *b.*
Phil. 1:7 in *b.* ye are all partak.
13 so my *b.* in C. are manifest
14 waxing confident by my *b.*
16 to add affliction to my *b.*
Col. 4:3 in *b.* 18 rem. my *b.*
2 *Tim.* 2:9 suffer trouble even to *b.*
Phile. 10 begotten in my *b.*
13 in the *b.* of the gospel
Heb. 10:34 compassion of me in *b.*
11:36 others had trial of *b.* and
13:3 rem. them in *b.* as bound

BONDAGE.
Ex. 1:14 bitter with hard *b.*
2:23 Israel sighed by reason of *b.*
13:14 Lord brought us out of the
house of *b.* 20:2; *Deut.* 5:6;
6:12; 8:14; 13:5, 10; *Jos.*
24:17; *Judg.* 6:8
Deut. 26:6 L. laid on us hard *b.*
Neh. 9:17 captain to return to *b.*
Ex. 14:3 rest from thy hard *b.*
Rom. 8:15 received spirit of *b.*
21 from *b.* of corruption
Gal. 4:24 which gendereth to *b.*
3:1 not entangled with y. of *b.*
Heb. 2:15 lifetime subject to *b.*

In, Into, or under BONDAGE.
Ezr. 9:8 reviving in our *b.*
9 God hath not fors. us *in b.*
John 8:33 never *in b.* to any
Acts 7:6 bring them *into b.*
7 to whom they shall be *in b.*
1 *Cor.* 7:15 is not *under b.*
2 Cor. 11:20 man bring you *into b.*
Gal. 2:4 might bring us *into b.*
4:3 *in b.* under the elements
9 ye desire to be *in b.*

BON

Gal. 4:25 answ. to J. which is *in b.*
2 *Pet.* 2:19 is *b.* brought *into b.*

BONDMAID.
Gal. 4:22 one by a *b.* the other

BONDMAN.
Deut. 15:15 wast a *b.* in Egypt,
L. red. thee, 16:12; 24:18, 22
Rev. 6:15 every *b.* hid themselves

BONDMEN.
Lev. 25:44 *b.* shall ye *b.* of the h.
Deut. 28:68 ye sh. be sold for *b.*
2 *K.* 4:1 my two sons to be *b.*
2 *Chr.* 28:10 children of J. for *b.*
Ezr. 9:9 we were *b.* yet God
Est. 7:4 had been sold for *b.*
Jer. 34:13 out of the house of *b.*

BONDSERVICE.
1 *K.* 9:21 a tribute of *b.*

BONDWOMAN.
Gen. 21:10 cast out this *b.* and
her son, *Gal.* 4:30
13 son of *b.* will I make a nat.
Gal. 4:23 son of *b.* born
31 are not children of the *b.*

BONDWOMEN. *See* BONDMEN.

BONE.
Gen. 2:23 this is *b.* of my bones
29:14 art my *b.* and my flesh
Ex. 12:46 neither shall ye break
a *b. Num.* 9:12
2 *Sam.* 5:1 are thy *b.* 1 *Chr.* 11:1
Job 2:5 touch his *b.* and flesh
19:20 my *b.* clear. to my skin
31:22 my arm be bro. from the *b.*
Prov. 25:15 tongue break. the *b.*
Ezek. 37:7 t. gether, *b.* to his *b.*
John 19:36 a *b.* of him sh. n. be b.

BONES.
Ex. 13:19 M. took *b.* of Joseph
Jos. 24:32 *b.* of Joseph buried
1 *Sam.* 31:12 took *b.* of Saul
2 *K.* 13:21 touched *b.* of Elisha
23:14 filled places with *b.*
Chr. 34:5 burnt *b.* of the priests
Job 10:11 hast fenced me with *b.*
Ps. 51:8 *b.* thou hast broken
53:5 G. scattereth the *b.* of him
141:7 *b.* are scat. at grave's m.
Prov. 3:8 marrow to thy *b.*
14:30 the rottenness of the *b.*
15:30 good report maketh *b.* fat
16:24 pleas. words health to *b.*
17:22 broken spirit drieth the *b.*
Ec. 11:5 how the *b.* do grow
See COVENANT.

BOO

Their BONES.
Num. 24:8 Is. shall break *their b.*
1 *Sam.* 31:13 *their b.* buried them
Lam. 4:8 skin cleaveth to *their b.*
Ezek. 32:27 iniquity on *their b.*
Dan. 6:24 bones brake all *their b.*
Mic. 3:2 flesh from *their b.*

BONNETS.
Is. 3:20 L. will take away the *b.*
Ezek. 44:18 shall have linen *b.*

BOOK.
Ex. 17:14 memorial in a *b.*
32:32 blot me out of thy *b.*
33 will I blot out of my *b.*
Num. 21:14 *b.* of the wars
Deut. 17:18 of this law in a *b.*
Jos. 10:13 *b.* of J. 2 *Sam.* 1:18
1 *Sam.* 10:25 S. wrote it in a *b.*
1 *K.* 11:41 *b.* of acts of Solomon
2 *K.* 22:8 Hilk. gave *b.* to Shap.
23:24 perform words in *b.*
Ezr. 4:15 s. may be made in *b.*
Neh. 8:5 Ezra opened the *b.*
Job 19:23 they were prin. in a *b.*
31:35 adver. had written a *b.*
Ps. 40:7 vol. of the *b. Heb.* 10:7
56:8 are they not in thy *b.*?
69:28 blotted out of *b.*
139:16 in thy *b.* all my members
Is. 29:11 as words of a *b.* sealed
12 *b.* is deliv. to him not learn.
18 shall hear words of the *b.*
30:8 now go and note it in a *b.*
34:16 seek ye out of the *b.* of L.
Jer. 30:2 write the words in a *b.*
36:2 roll of a *b.*; 10 read in *b.*
43:1 words in a *b.* from Jerem.
Ezek. 2:9 roll of a *b.* was therein
Dan. 12:1 ev. one writ. in the *b.*
4 O Daniel, seal the *b.*
Nah. 1:1 *b.* of vision of Nahum
Mal. 3:16 a *b.* of remembrance
Mat. 1:1 *b.* of the gen. of Jesus
Luke 3:4 written in the *b.* of *l.*
4:17 deliv. to J. the *b.* of Esaias,
when he opened the *b.*
20 he closed the *b.* and gave it
20:42 in *b.* of Psalms, *Acts* 1:20
Acts 7:42 in *b.* of the prophets
Heb. 9:19 sprinkled the *b.* and
Rev. 1:11 write in a *b.*
3:1 a *b.* written within, on the
2 is worthy to open the *b.* 3
10:2 in his hand a little *b.* open
9 little *b.*; 10 I took the *b.*
20:12 b. was opened, *b.* of life
22:19 if any take from w. of *b.*
See COVENANT.

BOOK of the Law.
Deut. 31:26 *b. of l.* put it in ark
Jos. 1:8 *b. of law* shall not depart
2 *K.* 22:8 I have found *b. of law*
Neh. 8:8 read in the *b. of law*
Gal. 3:10 in *b. of l.* to do them

BOOK of Life.
Phil. 4:3 writ. in the *b. of life*
Rev. 3:5 name out of *b. of l.*
13:8 not writ. in *b. of life*, 17:8
20:12 an. *b.* opened, *b. of life*
15 not written in *b. of life*
21:27 written in L.'s *b. of life*
22:19 part out of the *b. of life*

BOOK of Moses.
2 *Chr.* 23:4 as in *b. of M.* 35:12;
Ezr. 6:18
Mark 12:26 ye not read in *b.*

This BOOK.
Deut. 28:58 if t. *b.* 9 *Chr.* 34:21
2 *K.* 22:13 to the words of *t. b.*
23:3 perf. the words in *this b.*
Jer. 25:13 all that is in *this b.*
51:63 an end of reading *this b.*
John 20:30 not written in *this b.*
Rev. 22:9 keep the say. of *this b.*
10 the sayings of *this b.*
18 plagues in *this b.*
19 things in *this b.*

BOOKS.
Ec. 12:19 of making *b.*
Dan. 7:10 *b.* were op. *Rev.* 20:12
John 21:25 could not cont. the *b.*
Acts 19:19 their *b.* and burned
2 *Tim.* 4:13 bring the *b.* espec.
Rev. 20:12 out of things in *b.*

BOOTH.
Job 27:18 as a *b.* the keeper
Jon. 4:5 Jonah made him a *b.*

BOOTHS.
Gen. 33:17 and Jacob made *b.*
Lev. 23:42 dwell in *b.* seven days
43 I made Is. dwell in *b.*
Neh. 8:14 Isr. should dwell in *b.*

CRUDEN'S CONCORDANCE.   775

BOR

BOOTY, IES.
Jer. 49:32 camels shall he a b.
Hab. 2:7 be for b. unto them
Zep. 1:13 goods shall bec. a b.

BORDER.
Ex. 19:12 touch b. of mount
Deut. 12:20 w. L. enlarge thy b.
1 K. 4:21 Solomon reigned unto b. of Egypt, 2 Chr. 9:26
Ps. 78:54 b. of his sanctuary
Prov. 15:25 establish b. of widow
Is. 37:24 the height of his b.
Jer. 31:17 chil. again to their b.
Joel 3:6 remove them from b.
Amos 1:13 enlarge their b.
6:2 their b. grout. than your b.
Ob. 7 even to the b.
Zep. 2:8 magnified ag. their b.
Mal. 1:4 the b. of wickedness
5 L. will be mag. fr. b. of Isr.
Mark 6:56 if it were but b.
Luke 8:44 touched b. of garment
See EAST, SOUTH.

BORDER, Verb.
Zec. 9:2 H. shall b. thereby

BORDERS.
Ex. 16:35 come to b. Canaan
34:24 I will enlarge thy b.
2 K. 19:23 enter lodg. of his b.
Ps. 74:17 set the b. of the earth
147:14 maketh peace in thy b.
Cant. 1:11 will make b. of gold
Is. 54:12 b. of pleasant stones
Jer. 15:13 thy sins in all thy b.
Ezek. 45:1 be holy in all the b.
Mic. 5:6 treadeth within our b.
Mat. 4:13 in the b. of Zebulun
23:5 enlarge b. of their garments

BORE.
Ex. 21:6 master shall b. his ear
Job 41:2 b. his jaw with thorn?

BORN, for brought forth.
Gen. 17:17 b. him 100 yrs. old, 21:5
Ex. 1:22 every son b. into river
Lev. 19:34 as one b. among
Num. 13:29 one law for him b.
Jos. 8:33 the stranger as he b.
Jud. 13:8 child that shall be b.
2 Sam. 12:14 the child b. shall die
1 K. 3:1 a child shall be b. to the house of David
1 Chr. 22:9 son shall be b. to thee
Job 3:3 day perish wh. I was b.
5:7 yet man is b. to trouble
11:12 b. like a wild ass's colt
13:7 first man that was b.?
38:21 bec. thou wast then b.?
Ps. 22:31 people that shall be b.
58:3 as soon as they be b.
78:6 children that should be b.
87:4 b. there, 6; 5 that man b.
Prov. 17:17 a brother is b.
Ec. 3:2 a time to be b.
4:14 b. in his kingdom
Is. 66:8 nation is a child is b.
66:8 shall a nat. be b. at once?
Jer. 16:3 con. sons and daugh. b.
20:14 cursed be day I was b.
24:26 where not b. shall ye die
Ezek. 16:4 the day thou wast b.
Luke 1:35 thing that shall be b.
2:11 to you is b. this day
John 3:4 be b. when he is old?
5 except a man be b. of water
6 b. of flesh is flesh, that b.
8 so is every one b. of the Sp.
8:41 we be not b. of fornication
9:2 did sin, that he was b. blind
31 wast altogether b. in sins
16:21 for joy that a man is b.
18:37 to this end was I b.
Acts 2:8 wherein we were b.
7:20 which time Moses was b.
22:3 b. in T.; 28 I was free b.
Rom. 9:11 chil. being not yet b.
1 Cor. 15:8 b. out of due time
Gal. 4:23 b. after the flesh, 29
Heb. 11:23 by faith M. when b.
1 Pet. 2:2 as new b. babes desire
1 John 2:29 righte. b. of him
Rev. 12:4 dev. child as soon as b.

BORN again.
John 3:3 except a man be b. a. 5
7 ye must be b. again
1 Pet. 1:23 b. a. not of corruptible
See FIRST-BORN, WITNESS.

BORN of God.
1 John 3:9 b. of G. doth not com. sin
1 John 3:9 of God not com. sin

BOT

1 John 4:7 one that lov. b. of G.
5:1 Jesus is Christ is b. of God
4 whatsoever is b. of God
18 whosoever is b. of God

BORN in the house.
Gen. 15:3 b. in my h. is my heir
Ec. 2:7 had serv. b. in my h.

BORN in the land.
Ex. 12:48 strun. as one b. in l.
Num. 9:14 one ordin. for b. in l.

BORN of a woman, or women.
Job 14:1 man b. of a w.
15:14 b. of a w. that he
25:4 that is b. of a w.
Mat. 11:11 are b. of w. Luke 7:28

BORNE, brought forth.
Gen. 21:7 b. him son in old age
22:24 I have b. three sons
30:20 because I have b. six sons
1 Sam. 2:5 barren hath b. seven
4:20 thou hast b. a son.
Jer. 15:9 b. seven languisheth
10 that thou hast b. me
Ezek. 16:20 thy sons b. to me

BORNE, carried.
Is. 46:3 b. by me from the belly
60:12 he b. upon her sides
Jer. 10:5 they must be b. because
Amos 5:26 have b. tab. of Moloch
Mark 2:3 one sick of palsy was b.
John 20:15 b. him hence tell me
Acts 21:35 was b. of the soldiers
1 Cor. 15:49 b. image of the e.

BORNE, endured.
Job 34:31 I have b. chastisement
Ps. 55:12 then I could have b.
69:7 thy sake I have b. reproach
Is. 53:4 surely he hath b. griefs
Lam. 3:28 hath b. it upon him
5:7 we have b. their iniquities
Ezek. 16:58 hast b. thy lewd.
32:24 b. shame, 30,6; 32:26
Mat. 20:12 b. burden and heat
23:4 griev. to be b. Luke 11:46
Rev. 2:3 hast b. and hast patience

BORROW.
Ex. 3:22 ev. wom. shall b. 11:2
22:14 if a man b. aught
Deut. 15:6 shalt not b. 28:12
2 K. 4:3 go b. thee b. vessels
Mat. 5:42 him that would b.

BORROWED, of Egyptians
2 K. 6:5 master, for it was b.

BORROWER.
Prov. 22:7 b. is servant to lender
Is. 24:2 with lender, so with b.

BORROWETH.
Ps. 37:21 b. and payeth not

BOSOM.
Gen. 16:5 my maid into thy b.
Ex. 4:6 put hand into thy b. 7
Num. 11:12 carry th. in thy b.
Ruth 4:16 Naomi laid it in her b.
1 Sam. 12:3 and lay in his b.
2:20 laid it in her b. and laid her child in my b.
17:19 E. took him out of her b.
Job 31:33 hiding hiding, in my b.
Ps. 35:13 returned to my b.
74:11 thy right hand out of b.
79:12 sevenfold into their b.
89:50 I do bear in my b.
129:7 bindeth sheaves, his b.
Prov. 5:20 emb. b. of stranger?
6:27 man take fire in his b.?
17:23 a gift out of the b.
19:24 his hand in b. 26:15
21:14 a reward in the b.
26:26 resteth in b. of fools
Is. 40:11 the lambs in his b.
65:6 recompense into their b.
7 former work into their b.
Jer. 32:18 iniq. of fathers' b.
Lam. 2:12 soul into mother's b.
Mic. 7:5 lieth in thy b.
Luke 6:38 good m. into your b.
16:22 by angel's into Ab.'s b.
23 in Abrah. and Laz. in his b.
John 1:18 b. of the Father
13:23 leaning on Jesus' b.

BOSOMS.
Job 19:36 thick b. of his bucklers

BOTCH.
Deut. 28:27 smite with the b. 35

BOTTLE.
Gen. 21:14 b. of water gave to H.
15 w. spent in b. 19 filled b.
Jud. 4:19 opened a b. of milk
1 Sam. 1:24 H. took b. of wine
10:3 another carrying b. of w.

BOU

1 Sam. 16:20 Jesse took ab. of w.
Ps. 56:8 my tears into thy b.
119:83 like a b. in the smoke
Jer. 13:12 every b. filled with w.
19:1 a potter's b.; 10 break b.
Hab. 2:15 puttest thy b. to him

BOTTLES.
Jos. 9:4 Gibeonites took wine b.
13 these b. of wine were new
Job 32:19 to burst like new b.
38:37 can stay b. of heaven?
Hos. 7:5 sick with b. of wine
Mat. 9:17 new wine into old b.
else b. break, Mark 2:22;
Luke 5:37, 38

BOTTOM.
Ex. 15:5 they sank into the b.
Job 36:30 covereth b. of the sea
Cant. 3:10 made the b. of gold
Dan. 6:24 they came at b.
Amos 9:3 from my sight in b.
Jon. 2:6 to b. of the mount.
Zec. 1:8 myrtle-trees in b.
Mat. 27:51 veil rent from top to b.
Mark 15:38

BOTTOMLESS.
Rev. 9:1 to him key of the b. pit
2 he opened b. pit, arose smoke
11 had a king, angel of b. pit
11:7 that ascend. out of b. pit
17:8 second out of the b. pit
20:1 an angel hav. key of b. pit
3 cast him into the b. pit

BOUGH.
Gen. 49:22 Joseph is fruitful b.
22 b. 2:48 Abim. cut down a b.
49 cut down every man his b.
Is. 10:33 Lord shall lop b.
17:6 in top of uppermost b.
9 cities be as a forsaken b.

BOUGHS.
Lev. 23:40 b. of goodly trees, b. of
Deut. 24:20 go over the b.
2 Sam. 18:9 mule went under b.
Job 14:9 brought forth a b.
Ps. 80:10 b. like goodly cedars
11 sent out her b. to the sea
Cant. 7:8 take hold of the b.
Is. 27:11 when the b. are with.
Ezek. 17:23 it shall bring forth b.
31:3 his top among thick b. 14
6 nests in his b. Dan. 4:12

BOUGHT.
Gen. 33:19 J. b. field, Jos. 24:32
33:1 Potipher b. Joseph
47:20 Joseph b. all land of E. 23
49:30 Abr. b. 50:13; Acts 7:16
Lev. 27:24 of whom it was b.
Deut. 32:6 father that b. thee?
2 Sam. 12:3 ewe-lamb he had b.
24:24 David b. threshing-floor
1 K. 16:24 O. b. hill Samaria
Neh. 5:16 nor b. we any land
Jer. 32:9 I b. field of Hanameel
Mat. 13:46 sold all, b. that field
21:12 sold and b. in the temple,
Mark 11:15; Luke 19:45
27:7 b. with them potter's field
Mark 15:46 Joseph b. fine linen
16:1 b. sweet spices to anoint
Luke 14:18 have b. a piece of gro.
19 I have b. five yoke of oxen
17:28 drank, they b. and sold
1 Cor. 6:20 ye are b. 7:23
2 Pet. 2:1 deny. L. that b. them

BOUND, actively.
Gen. 22:9 b. Isaac his son
42:24 took Simeon, and b. him
Num. 30:4 had b. her soul
Jud. 15:13 b. Samson with new
withs; 12 ropes; 21 fetters
2 K. 5:23 he b. two talents
17:4 he shut up Hoshea and b.
25:7 Zedekiah with fetters
2 Chr. 33:11 b. Manasseh
36:6 b. Jehoiakim
Prov. 30:4 waters in a garm.
Hos. 7:15 I have b. their arms
Mat. 14:3 b. Mark 6:17
Mat. 27:2 b. Mark 15:1; John 18:12
Luke 13:16 daughter S. hath b.
Acts 12:6 Peter b. with 2 chains
21:33 b. with two chains
22:25 as they b. Paul, 29
23:12 b. themselves, 14, 21
Rev. 20:7 S. at a thousand years

BOUND, passively.
Gen. 39:20 king's pris. are b.
42:19 one of your brethren be b.
Jud. 16:6 mightest be b. 10, 13
Ps. 68:6 bringeth out those b.
107:10 being b. in affliction
Prov. 22:15 foolish. is b. in heart

BOW

Is. 22:3 b. by archers, all are b.
51:1 opening of pris. to them b.
Lam. 1:14 yoke of my tran. is b.
Dan. 3:21 b. in their coats
24 three men b. into furnace?
Mat. 16:19 b. in heaven, 18:18
Mark 15:7 Barabbas which lay b.
John 31:44 b. h. and foot, face b.
18:24 Annas had sent him b.
Acts 9:2 bring them b. 21; 22:5
12:6 Peter b.; 24:27 left Paul b.
20:22 I go b. in the Spirit to J.
21:13 I am ready not to be b.
Rom. 7:2 is b. by the law to her husband, 1 Cor. 7:39
1 Cor. 7:27 b. unto a wife
2 Thes. 1:3 b. to thank God, 2:13
2 Tim. 2:9 word of God is not b.
Heb. 13:3 in bonds, as b. with
Rev. 9:14 loose the angels b.

BOUND with chains.
Ps. 68:6 G. bring. out th. b. w. c.
Jer. 39:7 b. Zed. with c. 52:11
40:1 Jeremiah b. with c.
Nah. 3:10 her great men b. w. c.
Mark 5:4 had been often b. w. c.
Luke 8:29 was kept b. with c.
Acts 21:33 com. P. to be b. w. 2 c.
28:20 for hope of Israel I am b.

BOUND up.
Gen. 44:30 life is b. up in lad's
Is. 1:6 have not been b. up
Jer. 30:13 none to plead, that thou mayest be b. up
Hos. 4:19 wind hath b. her up
13:12 iniq. of Ephraim is b. up
Luke 10:34 he b. up his wounds

BOUND, Substantive.
Gen. 49:26 b. of the everlasting
Job 38:20 take it to the b. there.
Ps. 10:29 the waters set a b.
Jer. 5:22 sand for b. of the sea
Hos. 5:10 them that remove b.

BOUNDS.
Ex. 19:23 b. about the mount
23:31 thy b. from the Red sea
Deut. 32:8 set b. of the people
Job 14:5 b. that he cannot pass
26:10 comp. the waters with b.
Acts 17:26 hast determined the b.

BOUNTY.
2 Cor. 9:5 make up beforeh. y. b.

BOUNTIFUL.
Prov. 22:9 hath a b. eye
Is. 32:5 churl be said to be b.

BOUNTIFULNESS.
2 Cor. 9:11 enriched to all b.

BOUNTIFULLY.
Ps. 13:6 hath dealt b. with me
116:7 Lord hath dealt b.
119:17 deal b. with thy servant
142:7 shalt deal b. with me
2 Cor. 9:6 soweth b. shall reap b.

BOW, Substantive.
Gen. 9:13 set my b. in the cloud
27:3 take thy quiver and b.
48:22 I took of Amorite with b.
49:24 his b. abode in strength
Jos. 24:12 but not with thy b.
2 Sam. 1:22 b. of Jon. turned not
1 K. 22:34 a certain man drew a b. at a venture, 2 Chr. 18:33
2 K. 13:15 take b. and ar. took b.
16 put he hands on king's b.
Job 29:20 my b. was renewed
Ps. 44:6 will not trust in my b.
46:9 he breaketh the b. cutteth
78:3 there brake he arrows of b.
57 aside like a deceitful b.
Is. 41:2 as stubble to his b.
Jer. 6:23 shall lay hold on b.
49:35 I will break the b. of E.
Lam. 2:4 bent his b.
3:13 arrows of his b. in the clou.
Hos. 1:5 I will break b. of Israel
7 I will not save them by b.
2:18 I will break the b.
7:16 they are like a deceitful b.
Amos 2:15 he that handleth b.
Hab. 3:9 b. made quite naked.
Zec. 9:13 filled the b. with Eph.
10 b. of war shall cease
Ezek. 39:9 they shall burn the b.
See BEND, BENT, BATTLE-BOW.

BOWS.
1 Sam. 2:4 the b. of mighty
Neh. 4:16 half of them he b.
Ps. 37:15 b. shall be broken
Is. 5:28 their b. are bent
13:18 their b. shall dash young
Jer. 51:56 every one of their b.
Ezek. 39:9 they shall burn the b.

776 CRUDEN'S CONCORDANCE.

BOW

BOW-SHOT.
Gen. 21:16 as it were a b.-s.

BOW, Verb.
Jos. 23:7 nor b. yourselves to their gods, 2 K. 17:35
2 K. 5:18 I b. in house of Rim.
Job 39:3 b. themselves
Ps. 22:29 to the dust shall b.
72:9 in wilder, sh. b. before him
115:5 b. thy heavens, O Lord
Prov. 5:1 b. thine ear
14:19 evil b. before the good
Ex. 12:3 strong men shall b.
Mic. 6:6 b. myself bef. high G.?
Hab. 3:6 perpetual hills did b.
Eph. 3:14 b. my knees to the F.

BOW down.
Gen. 27:29 nations b. down
37:10 mother, brethren b. down
49:8 father's children shall b. d.
Ex. 11:8 serv. shall b. d. to me
20:5 not b. d. Deut. 5:9
23:24 shalt not b. d. to their g.
Lev. 26:1 any image to b. d. to it
Jud. 2:19 other gods to b. d.
2 K. 5:18 b. d. in house of Rim.
19:16 L. b. d. thine ear, Ps. 86:1
Job 31:10 others b. d. upon her
Ps. 31:2 b. d. th. ear, Prov. 22:17
95:6 worship and b. down
Is. 10:4 without me b. down
46:2 they stoop, they b. down
49:23 kings and queens sh. b. d.
51:23 b. d. that we may go over
58:5 to b. d. head as a bulrush?
60:14 despised thee shall b. d.
65:12 sit b. d. to slaughter
Rom. 11:10 b. d. their back

BOW knee.
Gen. 41:43 before him b. the k.
Is. 45:23 k. shall b. Rom. 14:11
Eph. 3:14 I b. my knee to F.
Phil. 2:10 every knee shall b.

BOWED.
Gen. 43:28 Jos. brethren b.
43:15 Issachar b. shoulder
Jos. 23:16 served other gods, and b. to them, Jud. 2:12, 17
Jud. 5:27 at her feet he b.
2 Sam. 19:14 David b.
22:10 he b. heavens, Ps. 18:9
1 K. 19:18 not b. to B. Rom. 11:4
2 K. 2:15 prophets b. before E.
2 Chr. 7:3 b. upon the pavement
23:22 king and all present b.
Est. 3:5 Mordecai b. not
Mat. 27:29 b. the knee
Luke 24:5 and b. their faces

BOWED down.
Gen. 42:6 J. brethren b. d. 43:28
Jud. 7:6 rest of the people b. d.
Ps. 35:14 I b. d. heavily as one
38:6 I am b. d. greatly,
41:25 soul is b. d. to the dust
57:6 my soul is b. d.
115:14 lips. up all b. d. 146:8
Is. 2:11 haught. of men be b. d.
17 lofti. of man shall be b. d.
21:3 was b. d. at hearing of it
Luke 24:5 and b. their faces

BOWED head.
Gen. 43:28 they b. their heads
Ex. 4:31 they b. their heads and worship. 12:27; Neh. 8:6
34:8 Mos. made haste and b. h.
Num. 22:31 Balaam b. his head
1 Chr. 29:20 b. down their head
2 Chr. 20:18 Jehosh. b. his head
29:30 praises and b. their head
John 19:30 Jesus b. his head

BOWED himself.
Gen. 18:2 A. b. himself, 23:7, 12
19:1 Lot b. himself
33:3 Jacob b. himself 47:31
48:12 Joseph b. himself
Jud. 16:30 S. b. h. with might
2 Sam. 24:20 A. b. h. 1 Chr. 21:21
1 K. 1:23 N. b. h.; 47 king b. h.
42 Adonijah b. h. to king Sol.
2:19 Solomon b. h. to his mother

BOWETH.
Jud. 7:5 that b. on knees
Is. 2:9 m. man b.; 46:1 Bel. b.

BOWING.
Gen. 24:52 Eliezer b. h. to earth
Ps. 17:11 set their eyes, b. down
62:3 as a b. wall shall by
Mark 15:19 spit on him, b. knees

BOWELS.
Gen. 15:4 out of own b. thy heir
25:23 manner of people from b.
43:30 b. did yearn on brother
2 Sam. 7:12 which pro. out of b.
16:11 which came forth of my b.

BRA

2 Sam. 20:10 Jo. sh. Amasa's b.
1 K. 1:26 b. yearned on her son
2 Chr. 21:15 sick. by disease of b.
21:18 smote him in b. 19
32:21 of his own b. slew him
Job 20:14 meat in his b. is turn.
30:27 b. boiled, and rested not
Ps. 22:14 it is melted in my b.
71:6 out of my mother's b.
109:18 come into his b.
Cant. 5:4 b. were moved for him
Is. 16:11 b. sound like a harp
48:19 the offspring of thy b.
49:1 from b. of my mother
63:15 sounding of thy b.
Jer. 4:19 my b. I am pained
31:20 my b. are troubled
Lam. 1:20 b. are troubled, 2:11
Ezek. 3:3 fill thy b. with this roll
7:19 their souls, nor fill their b.
Acts 1:18 J. burst, and all his b.
2 Cor. 6:12 strait, in your own b.
Phil. 1:8 in b. of Christ
2:1 if there be any b.
Col. 3:12 put on b. of mercies
Phile. 7 b. of saints are refreshed
12 rec. him that is my own b.
20 refresh my b. in the Lord
1 John 3:17 shut. up b. of comp.

BOWL.
Jud. 6:38 a b. full of water
Ec. 12:6 or golden b. be broken
Zec. 4:2 candlestick with a b.

BOWLS.
Amos 6:6 that drink wine in b.
Zec. 9:15 shall be filled like b.
14:20 the pots shall be like b.

BOWMEN.
Jer. 4:29 for the noise of the b.

BOX.
2 K. 9:1 take this b. of oil, 3
Mat. 26:7 alaba. b. Mark 14:3
Mark 14:3 brake the b. Luke 7:37

BOX-TREE.
Is. 41:19 set in the desert b.-tree
60:13 glory of Lebanon b.-tress

BOY, S.
Gen. 25:27 the b. grew
Joel 3:3 given a b. for a harlot
Zec. 8:5 shall be full of b.

BOZRAH.
Is. 34:6 hath a sacrifice in B.
63:1 dyed garments from B.
Jer. 48:24 judg. is come upon B.
48:13 B. shall bec. desolation, 22
Amos 1:12 dev. the palaces of B.
Mic. 2:12 put as the sheep of B.

BRACELET, S.
Gen. 24:30 b. on sister's hands
38:18 signet, b. and staff, 25
Ex. 35:22 brought b. Num. 31:50
2 Sam. 1:10 the b. on his arm
Is. 3:19 I will take away the b.
Ezek. 16:11 I put b. on thy hands

BRAKE.
Ex. 32:19 tables out of his hands and b. them, Deut. 9:17
Jud. 7:19 they b. pitchers, 20
16:9 b. withs, 12 b. new ropes
1 Sam. 4:18 Eli fell, his neck b.
1 K. 19:11 a strong wind b. in pieces the rocks
2 K. 11:18 Baal's images b. they
18:4 images, b. brazen serp.
23:14 Jos. b. images, 2 Chr. 34:4
2 Chr. 21:17 Arabians b. into J.
Job 38:8 shut sea wh. it b. forth?
10 b. up for it my decreed place
Ps. 78:3 there b. he the arrows
105:16 b. the whole staff of bread
33 b. trees of their coast
106:29 plague b. in upon them
107:14 b. their bands in sunder
Jer. 28:10 yoke from Jer. b. it
31:32 my covenant they b.
Ezek. 17:16 and covenant he b.
Dan. 2:1 sleep b. from him 34
6:24 the lions b. all their bones
7:7 fourth beast b. in pieces
8:7 ram, and b. his two horns
Mat. 14:19 he blessed and b. and gave the loaves, 15:36; 26:26;
Mark 6:41; 8:6; 14:22; Luke 9:16; 22:19; 24:30; 1 Cor. 11:24
Mark 8:19 I b. the five loaves
14:3 she b. box, and poured
Luke 8:29 he b. the bands
32 they b. not his legs

BRAKE down.
2 K. 10:27 b. down image of Baal
2 Chr. 23:17
11:18 b. down the house of Baal

BRA

2 K. 14:13 b. down w. of J. 2 Chr.
25:23; 36:19; Jer. 39:8; 52:14
23:7 b. d. houses of Sodomites
2 Chr. 26:6 Uzziah b. d. wall of G.
34:4 b. down altars of Baalim

DRAKEST.
Ex. 34:1 first table b. Deut. 10:2
Ps. 74:13 b. heads of dragons, 14
29:7 loaned on thee, thou b.

BRAMBLE, S.
Jud. 9:14 said trees to the b.
15 let fire come out of the b.
Is. 34:13 b. shall come up
Luke 6:44 of a b.-bush grapes

BRANCH.
Num. 13:23 cut a b.
Job 8:16 his b. shooteth forth
14:7 tender b. thereof not cease
15:32 his b. shall not be green
18:16 shall his b. be cut off
29:19 lay all night on my b.
Prov. 11:28 shall flour. as a b.
Is. 4:2 shall b. of the L. be beau.
9:14 Lord will cut off b.
11:1 a b. shall grow out
14:19 cast out like abomina. b.
17:9 cities as an uppermost b.
19:15 work, b. or rush may do
25:5 the b. of terrible ones low
60:21 the b. of my planting
53:2 to David a righteous b.
33:15 cause b. of righteousness
Ezek. 8:17 put b. to their nose
15:2 more than any b. ?
17:3 took the highest b. 22
Dan. 11:7 a b. of her roots
Zec. 3:8 forth my servant the b.
6:12 man whose name is the b.
Mal. 4:1 it shall leave root nor b.
Mat. 24:32 b. yet t. Mark 13:28
John 15:4 every b. that beareth
4 as b. cannot bear fruit
6 he is cast forth as a b.

BRANCHES.
Gen. 40:12 the three b. are three
49:22 bough, whose b. run over
Lev. 23:40 of goodly trees, b.
Job 15:30 shall dry up his b.
Ps. 80:11 sent out her b. to river
104:12 sing among the b.
Is. 16:8 Moab's b. are stretched
17:6 four or five in outmost b.
18:5 he shall cut down the b.
27:10 there lie and consume b.
Jer. 11:16 and b. of it are broken
Ezek. 17:6 spread. vine whose b.
19:10 fruitful and full of b.
14 fire out of a rod of her b.
31:3 not like the Assyrian's b.
36:8 O mount. ye shall shoot b.
Dan. 4:14 cut off his b.
Hos. 11:6 consume Ephraim's b.
14:6 his b. shall spread, and
Joel 1:7 b. thereof are m. white
Nah. 2:2 marred their vine b.
Zec. 4:12 these two olive b. ?
Mal. 13:32 lodge in b. Luke 13:10
Mark 11:8; Mark 11:8; John 12:13
Mark 4:32 shooteth out great b.
John 15:5 I am the vine, ye the b.
Rom. 11:16 if root be holy, so b.
17 if some b. be broken off, 19
18 boast not against the b.
21 spared not the natural b.

BRAND, S.
Jud. 15:5 had set the b. on fire
Zec. 3:2 b. plucked out of fire?

BRANDISH.
Ezek. 32:10 when I b. my sword.

BRASS.
Gen. 4:22 T.-cain instruc. in b. i.
Ex. 25:3 take b. 35:5; 38:24
26:11 make fifty taches of b.
27:2 overlay altar with b. 6
10 b. 19; 38:10 hooks of pillars of b.
30:18 laver of b. and his foot of b.
Lev. 26:19 heaven from earth b.
Num. 31:22 b. i. may abide. fire
Deut. 33:25 shall be iron and b.
Jos. 22:8 ret. with b. and iron
1 K. 7:14 b. i with. weight, 16
2 Chr. 2:7 a cun. man in b. ir. 14
24:12 such as wrought in ir. b.
Job 28:2 iron taken out b.
Is. 48:4 neck ir. sin. and brow b.
60:17 for b. gold, for iron silver
Jer. 6:28 they are b. i. Ezek. 22:18
Ezek. 22:20 gather iron and b.
Dan. 2:35 was iron b. broken, 45
4:15 with band of iron and b. 23
5:4 praised gods of silver, b. i.

Vessels of BRASS.
Jos. 6:19 all b. of b. are consec.
2 K. 25:16 the b. of all these ves. was with. w. Jer. 52:20
Ezek. 27:13 in v. of b. Rev. 18:12

BRAVERY.
Is. 3:18 will take away their b.

BRAWLER, S.
1 Tim. 3:3 bishop must be no b.
Tit. 3:2 to be no b.

BRAWLING.
Prov. 25:24 a b. woman, 21:19

BRAY, ED, ETH.
Job 6:5 doth the wild ass b.
30:7 among the bushes they b.
Prov. 27:22 b. a fool in a mortar

BRAZEN.
2 K. 16:4 brake the b. serpent
25:13 b. sea Chal. Jer. 52:17
2 Chr. 6:13 Sol. made a b. scaf.
12:10 b. shields 11; 1 K. 14:27
15:20 make thee a fenced b. wall
20:2 bulls; Mark 7:4 b. ves.
See ALTAR.

BRE

Dan. 10:6 like in color to pol. b.
Mic. 4:13 will make thy hoofs b.
Ezek. 6:1 were mountains of b.
Mal. 10:9 neither gold nor b.
1 Cor. 13:1 I am as sounding b.
Rev. 1:15 feet like fine b. 2:18
9:20 not worship idols of b.

Iron and BRASS.
Gen. 4:22 T.-cain instruc. in b. i.
Lev. 26:19 heaven from earth b.
Num. 31:22 b. i. may abide. fire
Deut. 33:25 shall be iron and b.
Jos. 22:8 ret. with b. and iron
1 K. 7:14 b. i with. weight, 16
2 Chr. 2:7 a cun. man in b. ir. 14
24:12 such as wrought in ir. b.
Job 28:2 iron taken out b.
Is. 48:4 neck ir. sin. and brow b.
60:17 for b. gold, for iron silver
Jer. 6:28 they are b. i. Ezek. 22:18
Ezek. 22:20 gather iron and b.
Dan. 2:35 was iron b. broken, 45
4:15 with band of iron and b. 23
5:4 praised gods of silver, b. i.

Vessels of BRASS.
Jos. 6:19 all b. of b. are consec.
2 K. 25:16 the b. of all these ves. was with. w. Jer. 52:20
Ezek. 27:13 in v. of b. Rev. 18:12

BREACH.
Lev. 24:20 b. for b. eye for eye.
Num. 14:34 ye shall know my b. of promise
Jud. 21:15 a b. in the tribes
2 Sam. 5:20 forth as b. of waters
6:8 so on Uzzah. 1 Chr. 13:11
1 Chr. 13:8 wheresoever my b.
Job 16:14 with b. upon b.
Ps. 106:23 not Moses stood in b.
Prov. 15:4 perverseness is a b.
Is. 7:6 a b. for us.
30:13 this iniq. shall be as a b.
25 in the day L. bindeth up b.
58:12 called the repairer of the b.
Jer. 14:17 is broken with a b.
Lam. 2:13 thy b. is great
Ezek. 26:10 city wherein a b.

BREACHES.
Jud. 5:17 Asher abode in his b.
1 K. 11:27 rep. b. of city of Dav.
2 K. 12:5 let them repair the b.
6 priests had not repaired the b.
7 why have ye not repaired b.
12:12 he broken the places of b.
22:5 buy timber and hewn st. b.
Is. 22:9 have seen b. of the city
Amos 4:3 shall go out at the b.
9:11 raise up b. thereof

DREAD.
Gen. 14:18 king of S. brought b.
18:5 will fetch a morsel of b.
21:14 Abraham took b. gave H.
25:34 then Jacob grave Esau b.
27:17 savory meat and b. to J.
41:54 in Egypt there was b.
55 cried to Pharaoh for b.
47:15 give us b.; 17 b. for h.
19 buy us and our land for b.
49:20 out of Asher his b. be fat
Ex. 16:4 I will rain b. from heav.
8 in morning, b. to the full, 12
28 sixth day the b. of two days
32 very eon the b. I fed you
23:25 he shall bless thy b.
40:23 he set the b. in order
Lev. 8:26 one wafer he took b.
21:6 not profane name of God, b.
8 sanctify him, offer. b. of God
17 none offer b. of God
21 nigh to offer b. of G. God
22 shall eat b. of God
22:25 a stranger's hand offer b.
24:7 for a memorial, b. offering
Num. 4:7 continual b. be thereon
14:9 people of the land are b.
21:5 soul loatheth this light b.
Deut. 8:3 man doth not live by b. only, Mal. 4:4; Luke 4:4

CRUDEN'S CONCORDANCE. 777

BRE

Deut. 23:4 met you not with b.
29:6 ye have not eaten b. nor
Jos. 9:5 b. was dry and mouldy
 12 this our b. we took hot
Jud. 7:13 a cake of b. tumbled
 8:6 give b. to thy army, 15
 19:5 comfort thy heart with b.
 19 there is b. and wine also
Ruth 1:6 in giving them b.
1 Sam. 2:5 hired out them. for b.
 36 crouch for a morsel of b.
 9:7 the b. is spent in our vessels
 11:4 hallowed b.; 5 b. is com.
 6 priest gave him hallowed b.
 22:13 hast given him b. and
 28:22 let me eat a morsel of b.
2 Sam. 3:29 J. one that lacketh b.
 35 taste b. till sun be down
 9:10 to every one a cake of b
1 K. 13:22 back and hast eaten b.
 17:6 ravens brought b. and flesh
 11 bring me a morsel of b.
2 K. 4:42 brought man of God b.
 18:32 a land of b. Is. 36:17
Neh. 5:14 b. of governor
 9:15 gavest them b. from h.
 13:2 they met not Israel with b.
Job 15:23 wand. abroad for b.
 22:7 withholden b. from hungry
 27:14 not be satisfied with b.
 28:5 out of it cometh b.
 33:20 his life abhorreth b.
Ps. 37:25 his seed begging b.
 78:20 can he give b. *f*
 82:5 with b. of tears
 102:9 eaten ashes like b.
 104:15 b. which stren. man's h.
 132:15 satisfy her poor with b.
Prov. 9:17 b. eaten in secret
 12:9 hon. hims. and lacketh b.
 11 land satisfied with b. 28:19
 22:13 shalt be satisfied with b.
 17 b. of deceit is sweet
 22:9 he giveth of his b.
 31:27 eateth not b. of idleness
Ec. 9:11 nor b. to wise
 11:1 cast thy b. upon the waters
Is. 3:1 away the whole stay of b.
 7 in my house is neither b. nor
 21:14 with their b. him that
 30:20 Lord give b. of adversity
 33:16 his b. shall be given him
 44:15 baketh b. on the coals, 19
 51:14 are that his b. should fail
 55:2 that which is not b.
 10 that it may give b. to eater
 58:7 deal thy b. to hungry?
Jer. 42:14 nor have hunger of b.
Lam. 1:11 they seek b.
 4:4 young children ask b.
 5 we get our b. with peril
Ezek. 4:16 prop. thy b. therewith
 17 they may want b. and water
 16:49 pride, fulness of b. and
 18:7 his b. to the hungry, 16
 44:7 strang. when ye offer my b.
Hos. 2:5 lovers that give me b.
 9:4 sacrifices as b. of mourners
Amos 4:6 given you want of b.
 8:11 not famine of b.
Hag. 2:12 he skirt do touch b.
Mal. 1:7 ye offer polluted b.
Mat. 4:3 st. be made b. Luke 4:3
 6:11 our daily b. Luke 11:11
 7:9 if his son ask b. will he give
 15:24 children's b. Mark 7:27
 33 so much b. *f* Mark 8:4
 16:5 forgot. to take b. Mark 8:14
 11 spake it not concerning b.
 12 not beware of leaven of b.
 26:26 Jesus took b. Mark 14:22
Luke 7:33 Bapt. neither eating b.
 9:3 for your journey, neither b.
 15:17 servants have b. enough
 22:19 took b. gave thanks, 24:30
 24:35 in breaking b.
John 6:7 two him, pennyw. of b.
 32 M. gave you not that b.
 from h. my F. giveth true b.
 35 the b. of God is he
 41 b. which came down, 50
 51 I am the b. of life, 58
 13:18 eateth b. hath lifted
 21:9 fish laid thereon and b.
 13 J. then taketh b. and giveth
Acts 2:42 con. in breaking of b.
 46 break. b. from house to ho.
 20:7 disciples came to break b.
 11 when he had broken b.
 27:35 he took b. and gave th.
1 Cor. 10:16 b. we break is it not
 17 being many are one b.
 11:23 in wh. he was bet. took b.

BRE

2 Cor. 9:10 min. b. to your food
See AFFLICTION.
DREAD-CORN.
Is. 28:28 b.-c. is bruised because
See BASKET, FEAST.
DREAD, with eat.
Gen. 3:19 in sweat of face e. b.
 28:20 if L. give me b. to eat
 31:34 Jacob called broth. to e. b.
 37:25 J.'s brethren sat to e. b.
 42:6 *save* b. he eat
 43:32 Egyptians not e. b. w. H.
Ex. 2:20 that he may e. b.
 16:3 when we eat b. to the full
 15 L. ha. giv. you to e.
 18:12 to e. b. with M.'s *f* in-law
 34:28 e. b. 40 da. Deut. 9:9, 18
Lev. 21:22 shall e. the b. of God
 26:5 ye shall eat b. to the full
Deut. 8:9 eat b. without scarce.
Ruth 2:14 meal-time come eat b.
2 Sam. 9:7 eat b. at my table, 10
 12:21 didst rise and eat b.
1 K. 13:8 nor will I eat b.
 15 come home with me eat b.
2 K. 4:8 const. Elisha to e. b.
 6:22 set b. and w. they may e.
 25:29 did e. b. bef. h. Jer. 52:33
Job 42:11 and did eat b. with Job
Ps. 14:4 people as they e. b. 53:4
 41:9 eat of my b. hath lift. heel
 102:4 I forgot to eat my b.
 127:2 to eat the b. of sorrows
Prov. 4:17 e. b. of wickedness
 9:5 come eat of my b. and drink
 23:6 e. not b. of him hath evil
 23:21 if thy en. hunger give b.
Ec. 9:7 go eat thy b. with joy
Is. 4:1 we will eat our b.
Jer. 5:17 they shall eat up thy b.
 41:1 I did eat b. together in M.
Ezek. 4:13 shall eat defiled b.
 16 they shall eat b. by weight
 12:18 e. b. with quaking; 19 care
 24:17 and eat not b. of men, 22
 44:3 prince sit in it to eat b.
Amos 7:12 thee into J. there e. b.
Ob. 7 eat thy b. have laid a w.
Mal. 1:3:2 w. not when they e. b.
Nah. 2:20 not so much as e. b.
 3:30 buy b. have nothing to e.
 7:2 discip. eat b. with defiled, 5
Luke 14:1 to Phar.'s house to e. b.
 15 he shall e. b. in kingdom
John 6:5 whence shall we buy b.
 23 place where they did eat b.
 31 gave them b. from hea. to e.
 51 if any e. of this b. he shall l.
1 Cor. 11:26 often as ye e. this b.
 27 whosoever shall eat this b.
2 Thes. 3:8 we eat b. for naught?
 12 with quietness they eat b.

Leavened BREAD.
Ex. 13:3 shall not l. b. eaten
 7 no leav. b. Deut. 16:4, 4
Lev. 7:13 he shall offer leavened b.

Loaf, or Loaves of BREAD.
Jud. 8:5 give l. of b. to people
1 Sam. 10:3 ano. car three l. of b.
 4 will give thee two l. of b.
 21:3 five l. of b. my hand
Chr. 16:3 to every one l. of b.

No BREAD.
Gen. 47:13 no b. in all the land
Num. 21:5 no b. and our soul
1 Sam. 21:4 there is no com. b.
 6 no b. there but showbread
 28:20 b. had eaten no b. all day
 30:12 Egyp. had eat no b. 3 days
1 K. 13:9 eat no b. 17,22
2 K. 23:3 no b. for peo. Jer. 52:6
Jer. 38:9 there is no b. in city
Dan. 10:3 I ate no pleasant b.
Mat. 16:7 because we have taken
 no b. 8; Mark 8:16, 17
 26:48 take no scrip, no b.

Piece, or Pieces of BREAD.
1 Sam. 2:36 I may eat a p. of b.
Prov. 6:26 to a p. piece of b.
 28:21 for a p. of b. that man
Jer. 37:21 Jerem. daily a p. of b.
Ezek. 13:19 ye pollute me for p. b.

SHOWBREAD, See
Staff of BREAD.
Lev. 26:26 I have broken b. b.
Ps. 105:16 he brake whole of b.
Ezek. 4:16 break st. b. 5:16; 14:13

Unleavened BREAD.
Ex. 12:18 eat w. u. b. Num. 9:11
 15 sev. days eat unl. b. 13:6, 7;
 23:15; 34:18; Lev. 23:6; Num.
 28:17; Deut. 16:3
Deut. 16:8 six days eat unl. b.
1 Sam. 28:24 witch of E. b. u. b.
Ezek. 45:21 passover of un. b.
Mark 14:12 first day of un. b.

BRE

Luke 22:7 day of u. b. Acts 12:3
Acts 20:6 after days of u. b.
1 Cor. 5:8 with u. b. of sincerity

BREADTH.
Gen. 13:17 through land in b. of it
Deut. 2:5 so much as a foot b.
Jud. 20:16 could sling at a h. b.
Job 37:10 b. of waters is strait.
 38:18 perceived b. of the earth?
Is. 8:8 his wings shall fill the b.
Hab. 1:6 march through b. of la.
Zec. 2:2 measure J. to see tho b.
 5 I see a flying roll, the b.
Eph. 3:18 the b. and length
Rev. 20:9 up on b. of the earth
 21:16 length of city is as the b.

BREAK, Substantive.
2 Sam. 2:32 J. came at b. of day
Acts 20:11 talked till b. of day

BREAK.
Gen. 27:40 b. his yoke off thy n.
Ex. 12:46 b. a bone, Num. 9:12
 34:13 ye shall b. their images
Lev. 22:19 I will b. pride
 30:2 if a man vow, not b. word
Deut. 12:3 shall b. their pillars
1 Sam. 25:10 b. eve. man from m.
Ezr. 9:14 should we again b.
Job 13:25 wilt b. a leaf driven
 39:15 l. wild beast may b. them
Ps. 2:3 b. us b. their bands
 9 b. them with rod of iron
 10:15 b. the arm of the wicked
 58:6 b. their teeth, O God
 80:3] If they b. my statutes
 141:5 which shall not b. my head
Cant. 2:17 until day b. 4:6
Is. 14:25 I will b. the Assyrian
 28:24 b. the clods; 28 nor b. it
 30:14 b. it as of the potter' ves.
 42:3 as a lion so will he b. all
 42:3 reed not b. Mat. 12:20
 58:6 that ye b. every yoke?
Jer. 15:12 iron b. the north. iron
 19:10 b. bottle, so will I b. 11
 49:35 I will b. the bow of Elam
Ezek. 4:16 I will b. the staff of
 bread, 5:16; 14:13
 16:38 as a women that b. wed.
 23:34 shalt b. the sherds
 29:7 hold of thee thou didst b.
 30:18 when I b. yokes of Egypt
 22 will b. Pharaoh's arms. 24
Hos. 1:5 will b. the bow of Israel
 2:18 I will b. the bow of Israel
 10:11 Jacob shall b. his clods
Joel 2:7 and not b. their ranks
Amos 1:5 b. the bar of Damascus
Mic. 3:3 who b. their bones
Zec. 11:11 b. the brotherhood
Mat. 5:19 b. one of least com.
 9:17 the bottles b. and the wine
Acts 20:7 came tog. to b. bread
 21:13 mean ye to b. my heart?
1 Cor. 10:16 bread we b. is it not

BREAK covenant.
Lev. 26:44 I will not b. my cov.
Deut. 31:16 will b. my c. 20
Jud. 2:1 I will never b. my c.
Ps. 89:34 my cov. will I not b.
Jer. 14:21 b. not thy cov. with us
 33:20 if ye can b. my cov.
Ezek. 17:15 b. cov. and be deliv.
Zec. 11:10 I might b. my cov.

BREAK down.
Ex. 23:24 quite b. d. Deut. 7:5
Jud. 8:9 I will b. d. down tower
Neh. 4:3 shall b. d. stone wall
Ps. 74:6 down carved work
Ec. 3:3 a time to b. d.
Is. 5:5 I will b. d. wall of vine.
Jer. 31:28 over them to b. down
 45:4 built I will b. down
Ezek. 13:11 so will I b. down w.
 14 so I will b. down towers of T.
Hos. 10:2 b. down their altars

BREAK forth.
Ex. 19:22 L. b. *f. break into sing-*
 ing, 44:23; 52:9; 54:1
 54:3 b. *f.* into joy ye w. places
 51:3 shall b. *f.* on the right hand
 58:8 then shall thy light b. *f.*
 into light b. *f.* into singing,
 55:12 b. *f.* before you into singing,
Gal. 4:27 b. *f.* that trav. not

BREAK off.
Dan. 4:27 O king, b. *off* thy sins

BREAK out.
Ps. 58:6 b. out the great teeth

BRE

Is. 35:6 shall waters b. out
Hos. 4:2 they b. out and blood, 4
Amos 5:6 lest he b. out like fire

BREAK in pieces.
Job. 19:2 b. me in pieces
 34:24 b. in pieces mighty men
Ps. 72:4 he shall b. in p. the op.
 94:5 they b. in p. thy people
Is. 45:2 I will b. in p. gates of b.
Jer. 51:20 will I b. in pieces n.
 21 with thee b. in p. horse a. r.
 22 b. in p. man, woman
Dan. 2:40 shall it b. in pieces and
 bruise kingdoms, 44
 7:23 shall b. in p. whole earth

BREAK through.
2 K. 3:26 b. th. to king of Edom
Mat. 6:19 th. b. th.; 20 b. not th.

BREAK up.
Jer. 4:3 b. u. yo. f.-gr. Hos. 10:12

BREAKER, S.
Mic. 2:13 b. is come up before
Rom. 1:31 covenant-breakers
 2:25 if thou be a b. of the law

BREAKEST, ETH.
Gen. 32:26 let me go, for day b.
Job 9:17 he b. me with tempest
 12:14 he b. it cannot be built
 16:14 he b. me with breach
 28:4 flood b. out from inhabit.
Ps. 29:5 the ced.; 46:9 b. b. ow
 44:7 thou b. ships of Tar. bick
 119:20 my soul b. for longing
Prov. 25:15 a soft tongue b. the
Ec. 10:8 b. a hedge, a serpent
 11:5 which crushed b. into a viper
Jer. 19:11 as one b. potter's ves.
 22:29 a hammer that b. rock ?
Lam. 4:4 ask bread, no man b.
Dan. 2:40 for as much as iron b.

BREAKING.
Gen. 32:24 wrestled till b. of day
1 Chr. 14:11 like b. forth of wa.
Job 30:14 as a wide b. in of wat.
 41:25 by reason of b. they purify
Ps. 144:14 that there be no b. in
 out; 2:20 b. down walls. of crying
Is. 30:13 whose b. cometh suddenly
 14 b. of the potter's vessel
Ezek. 16:59 oath in b. cov. 17:18
 21:6 with the b. of thy loins
Hos. 13:13 place of b. forth
Luke 21:35 known in b. of bread
Acts 2:42 continued in b. of bre.
 46 b. bread from house to h.
Rom. 2:23 through b. law.

BREAST.
Job 24:9 pluck fatherless from b.
Is. 69:11 shall suck b. of kings
Lam. 4:3 monsters draw out b.
Dan. 2:32 head of gold, his b.
Luke 18:13 publican smote his b.
John 13:25 lying on J.'s b. 21:20

BREASTS.
Gen. 49:25 with blessings of b.
Job 3:12 b. that I should suck
 21:24 his b. full of milk
Ps. 22:9 when on mother's b.
Prov. 5:19 let her b. satisfy thee
Cant. 1:13 all night bet. my b.
 4:5 thy two b. like roe., 7:3
 7:7 b. like clusters of grapes
 8 thy b. as clusters of the vine
 8:1 sucked the b. of my mother
 8 little sister, she hath no b.
 10 and my b. like towers
Is. 28:9 weaned from m. from b.
 66:11 with b. of her consolations
Ezek. 16:7 thy b. are fashioned
 23:3 there were their b. pressed
 8 bruised b. of her virgin.
 21 shalt pluck off thine ow b.
Hos. 2:2 adulteries from b. b.
 9:14 give them dry b.
Joel 2:16 gather those suck the b.
Nah. 2:7 doves tabl. her. on their b.
Luke 23:48 people smote their b.
Rev. 15:6 having their b. girded

BREASTPLATE.
Ex. 25:7 sto. to be set in b. 35:9
 28:1 shall make a b. 15; 39:8

BREATH.
Gen. 2:7 into his nostrils b. of l.
 6:17 to destroy all flesh wherein b.
 7:15 wherein is b.
 22 all in whose nostrils was b.

CRUDEN'S CONCORDANCE.

BRE

2 *Sam.* 22:16 found. discov. at *b.* of his nostrils, *Ps.* 18:15
1 *K.* 17:17 no *b.* left in him
Job 4:9 by *b.* of his nostrils
9:18 not suffer me to take my *b.*
14:10 in whose hand is *b.* of all
15:30 *b.* of his mouth go away
17:1 my *b.* is corrupt, my days
19:17 *b.* is strange to my wife
27:3 while my *b.* is in me
33:4 the *b.* of Alm. hath given
34:14 gather his spirit and *b.*
37:10 by *b.* of God frost is given
41:21 his *b.* kindleth coals
Ps. 33:6 made by the *b.* of his
104:29 takest away *b.* they die
135:17 any *b.* in their mouths
146:4 his *b.* goeth forth
150:6 that hath *b.* praise the L.
Ec. 3:19 they have all one *b.*
Is. 2:22 *b.* in his nostrils
11:4 with *b.* of lips slay wicked
30:8 his *b.* as overflowing str.
31:3 of L, like stream of brim.
33:11 your *b.* as fire shall devour
42:5 giveth *b.* to people upon it
Jer. 10:14 no *b.* in them, 51:17
Lam. 4:20 the *b.* of our nostrils
Ezek. 37:5 *b.* to enter you
6 with skin, and put *b.* in you
8 no *b.* in them; *b.* come, O *b.*
10 the *b.* came they lived
Dan. 5:23 in whose hand thy *b.*
10:17 neither is *b.* left in me
Hab. 2:19 in midst of image
Acts 17:25 giv. to all life and *b.*

BREATHE.

Jos. 11:11 not any left to *b.* 14
Ps. 27:12 such as *b.* out cruelty
Ezek. 37:9 O breath, *b.* on these

BREATHED.

Gen. 2:7 *b.* into nostrils *b.* of life
Jos. 10:40 destroyed all that *b.*
John 20:22 *b.* on them.

BREATHETH, ING.

Deut. 20:16 save alive m. that *b.*
Lam. 3:56 hide not ear at my *b.*
Acts 9:1 Saul yet *b.* thruatenings

BRED.

Ex. 16:20 and it *b.* worms

BREECHES.

Ex. 28:42 make linen *b.* 39:28
Ezek. 44:18 shall have linen *b.*

BREED.

Deut. 32:14 rams of *b.* of Bashan

BREED, ING.

Gen. 8:17 may *b.* abundantly
Zep. 2:9 as Sodom *b.* of nettles

BRETHREN.

Gen. 13:8 no strife, for we be *b.*
19:7 Lot said, *b.* do not so wick.
24:27 Lord led me to master's *b.*
31:23 I. *b.* took each his sword
42:6 *b.* bowed; 13 twelve *b.* 32
45:16 *b.* are c.; 49:5 *b.* of cruel.
Num. 27:7 possess. am, father's *b.*
10 no *b.* give it to his faith's *b.*
Deut. 25:5 if *b.* dwell together
Jos. 6:23 brought out hihab's *b.*
17:4 inheritance among the *b.*
Jud. 9:1 A. went to mother's *b.*
2 *K.* 10:13 we are *b.* of Ahaziah
Chr. 21:2 had *b.* sons of Johos.
Ps. 133:1 *b.* to dwell in unity
Prov. 6:19 soweth discord am. *b.*
17:2 shall have part among *b.*
19:7 *b.* of the poor do hate
Mat. 4:18 Jesus saw two *b.* 21
19:29 hath forsaken houses, *b.*
24:24 indignation ag'st two *b.*
25:25 seven *b.* *Mark* 12:20
28:8 one is Master, ye are *b.*
Mark 10:29 no man hath left *b.*
for my sake, *Luke* 18:29
30 shall receive houses, *b.*
Luke 14:26 hate not children *b.*
16:28 for I have five *b.*
21:16 ye shall be betrayed by *b.*
John 21:23 went among the *b.*
Acts 3:17 *b.* I wot through ignor.
6:3 *b.* look out seven men
7:26 sirs, ye are *b.* ; 9:30 *b.* knew
10:23 *b.* from Joppa accomp.
11:12 six *b.* accompanied me
29 to send relief to the *b.*
12:17 show these things to t. *b.*
14:2 evil affected against the *b.*
15:1 men from Judea taught *b.*
3 caused great joy to all the *b.*
22 and Silas chief among the *b.*
23 and *b.* send greeting to the *b.* of the Gentiles in Antioch
32 exhorted the *b.* 1 *Thes.* 3:14
33 let go in peace from *b.*

BRE

Acts 15:40 re. by *b.* to grace of G.
16:2 Tim. well reported of by *b.*
40 had seen *b.* they comfort.
17:6 drew Jason and certain *b.*
10 *b.* im. sent away Paul, 14
18:18 Paul took leave of the *b.*
27 *b.* wrote to receive Apollos
20:32 *b.* I commend you to God
21:7 Ptolemais, saluted the *b.*
16 to Jerus. *b.* received us
22:5 I received letters to the *b.*
23:5 I wist not, *b.* he was h.-pri.
28:14 where we found *b.*
15 *b.* heard of us
21 any of the *b.* spake harm
Rom. 1:13 not have you ignor. *b.*
11:25; 1 *Cor.* 10:1; 12:1; 1 *Thes.* 4:13
7:1 know ye not, *b.* law hath
8:12 *b.* we are debtors
29 first-born among many *b.*
10:1 *b.* my prayer to God for Is.
12:1 *b.* by the mercies of God
15:30; 16:17; 1 *Cor.* 1:10;
16:15; *Gal.* 4:12; *Heb.* 13:22
1 *Cor.* 1:26 see your calling, *b.*
2:1 I, *b.* when I came to you
3:1 I, *b.* could not speak to you
4:6 these things, *b.*
7:29 *b.* the time is short, 15:50
8:12 ye sin so against the *b.*
9:5 *b.* of the Lord and Cephas
11:2 *b.* that ye remember me
14:26 *b.* when ye come together
13:6 he was seen of above 500 *b.*
58 *b.* be steadfast, *Jam.* 2:5
10:11 I look for him with *b.*
20 the *b.* greet you, *Phil.* 4:21
2 *Cor.* 9:3 I sent *b.* lest our boast.
5 necessary to exhort the *b.*
11:9 *b.* from Macedonia supplied
26 been in perils among false *b.*
13:11 finally, *b.* farewell
Gal. 1:2 *b.* with me to churches
2:4 because of false *b.* brought
Eph. 6:23 peace be to the *b.*
Phil. 1:14 *b.* waxing confident
Col. 1:2 to faithful *b.* in Christ
1 *Thes.* 4:1 we beseech you *b.* 10;
5:12; 2 *Thes.* 2:1
10 to all *b.* in Macedonia
5:15 *b.* pray for us, 2 *Thes.* 3:1
Jud. 21:22 th. *b.* come to comp.
26 greet *b.* with a holy kiss
27 this epistle be read to *b.*
1 *Tim.* 4:6 put the *b.* in remem.
5:1 entreat younger men as *b.*
6:2 because they are *b.*
Heb. 2:11 not ash. to call them *b.*
3:1 holy *b.* consider the apostle
1 *Pet.* 1:22 unfeigned love of *b.*
3:8 love as *b.* be pitiful
1 *John* 3:14 because we love *b.*
16 to lay down our lives for *b.*
3 *John* 3 rej. when *b.* tes. of tru.
5 whatso. thou doest to the *b.*
10 neit. doth he receive the *b.*

His BRETHREN.

Gen. 9:25 servant of serv. to h. *b.*
16:12 he shall dwell in presence of *his b.* 25:18
27:37 *his b.* to him for servants
37:5 a dream and told it to *his b.*
11 *his b.* envied him, his father
38:11 lest he die also as *his b.*
47:12 Joseph nourished *his b.*
49:26 sep. from *b.* *Deut.* 33:16
Ex. 2:11 smiting one of *his b.*
Num. 25:6 to *h. b.* a Midian. w.
27:9 give his inheritance to *h. b.*
Deut. 10:9 L. no part with *his b.*
17:20 not lifted above *his b.*
20:8 lest *his b.* heart faint as
24:7 stealing any of *his b.*
33:9 nor did he acknow. *his b.*
24 let A. be acceptable to *his b.*
Jud. 9:5 Abimelech slew *his b.*
11:3 Jephthah fled from *his b.*
Ruth 4:10 not cut off from *b.*
1 *Sam.* 16:13 anointed h. m. of
22:1 *his b.* and father heard it
30:23 *his b.* and father heard it
1 *Chr.* 4:9 J. more hon. than *h. b.*
5:2 Judah prevailed above *his b.*
7:22 Ephraim mourned *his b.*
25:9 *his b.* and sons twelve
2 *Chr.* 21:4 Jehor. slew all *his b.*
Est. 10:3 accepted of *his b.*
Hos. 13:15 fruitful among *his b.*
Mic. 5:3 rem. of *h. b.* return to I.
Mat. 12:46 *his b.* stood without, *Mark* 3:31; *Luke* 8:19
John 7:5 *his b.* believe in him
Acts 7:13 was made known to *h. b.*
23 into M.'s heart to visit *h. b.*
25 supposed *his b.* understood
1 *Cor.* 6:5 judge between *his b.*
Heb. 2:17 beh. to be like to *his b.*

BRE

Men and BRETHREN.

Acts 1:16 m. *b.* this scripture
2:29 m. *b.* let me fr. speak
37 m. and *b.* what shall we do?
7:2 m. *b.* and fathers, hearken
13:15 m. and *b.* if ye have any
26 m. *b.* children of stock of A.
38 m. and *b.* through this man
13:7 m. and *b.* God made choice
18 James answered, m. and *b.*
22:1 m. and *b.* and fathers
23:1 m. *b.* I have lived in all g.
6 men and *b.* I am a Pharisee
28:17 m. and *b.* though I have committed nothing

My BRETHREN.

Gen. 29:4 my *b.* whence be ye?
37:10 I seek my *b.* tell me
46:31 my *b.* are come, 47;1
Ex. 4:18 let me return to my *b.*
Jos. 2:13 will save alive my *b.*
Jud. 8:19 they were my *b.*
19:23 my *b.* do not so wickedly
1 *Sam.* 30:23 yet me see my *b.*
30:23 ye shall not do so, my *b.*
2 *Sam.* 19:12 ye are my *b.*
28:2 Hear me, my *b.*
Neh. 4:23 my *b.* put off clothes
Job 6:15 my *b.* have dealt deceit.
19:13 put my *b.* far from me
Ps. 22:22 to my *b.* *Heb.* 2:12
69:8 I am a stranger to my *b.*
122:8 for my *b.* sake, I will say
Jer. 12:6 ev. my *b.* *Mark* 3:33
40 m. and my *b.* *Mark* 3:34
3:40 to least of these my *b.*
28:10 tell my *b.* go into Galilee
Luke 8:21 my *b.* are which hear
John 20:17 my *b.* and say
Rom. 9:3 ac. from C. for my *b.*
Jam. 5:10 take my *b.* the prop.

Our BRETHREN.

Num. 20:3 when our *b.* died
1 *Chr.* 13:2 let us send to our *b.*
Neh. 5:5 as flesh of our *b.*
8 have redeemed our *b.* the J.
5:1 cry of people in every city
2 *Cor.* 8:23 our *b.* be inquired of
Rev. 10:12 accuser of our *b.*

Their BRETHREN.

Deut. 18:18 a prophet from *th. b.*
Jud. 21:22 *th. b.* come to comp.
2 *Sam.* 2:26 from following *th. b.*
1 *Chr.* 12:32 *th. b.* at their com.
2 *Chr.* 28:15 brought them to *th. b.*
Neh. 13:13 to distribute to *th. b.*
Job 42:15 inheritance am. *th. b.*
Jer. 41:8 st. them not am. *th. b.*
Heb. 7:5 people that is of *their b.*
Rev. 6:11 *th. b.* should be killed

Thy BRETHREN.

Gen. 27:29 be lord over *thy b.*
37:10 I and *thy b.* come to bow
13 do not *thy b.* feed the flock?
14 wiet. it be well with *thy b.*
48:22 one portion above *thy b.*
49:8 whom *thy b.* shall praise
Deut. 15:7 a poor man of *thy b.*
17:15 from among *t. b.* set king
18:15 raise up a prophet. of *thy b.*
24:14 not oppress poor of *thy b.*
Jos. 2:18 bring *thy b.* home
1 *Sam.* 17:17 take to *thy b.*
Sam. 15:20 take back *thy b.*
2 *Chr.* 21:13 hast slain *thy b.* better than thyself
Jer. 12:6 *thy b.* have dealt treac.
Ezek. 11:15 *thy b.* ev. are thy *b.*
Mat. 12:47 mother and *thy b.* st. with, *Mark* 3:32; *Luke* 8:20
Luke 14:12 call not *thy b.*
22:32 strengthen *thy b.*
Rev. 19:10 I am of *thy b.* 22:9

Your BRETHREN.

Gen. 42:33 leave one of *your b.*
Lev. 10:6 carry *y. b.* from sanct.
6 let *your b.* bewail the burn.
Num. 16:8 *y. b.* ye shall not rule
32:6 *your b.* go to war
18:15 raise up a proph. of *y. b.*
Mat. 6:7 *your b.* what more ye?
5:47 if ye salute *y. b.*

BRI

Acts 3:22 proph. of *your b.* 7:37
1 *Cor.* 6:8 defraud that *your b.*
1 *Pet.* 5:9 same afflic. in *your b.*

BRIDE, S.

1 *Sam.* 8:3 Samuel's sons took *b.*
12:3 hand have I received any *b.*
Ps. 20:10 right hand full of *b.*
Is. 33:15 hands from holding *b.*
Amos 5:12 they take a *b.* and

BRIBERY.

Job 15:34 consume tabor. of *b.*

BRICK, S.

Gen. 11:3 make *b.* had *b.* for st
Ex. 1:14 their lives bitter in *b.*
5:7 give straw to make *b.* 16
8 tale of *b.* lay on them
16 yet deliver the tale of *b.* 19
Is. 9:10 the *b.* are fallen down
65:3 incense on altars of *b.*

BRICKKILN.

2 *Sam.* 12:31 make pass thro' *b.*
Jer. 43:9 hide stones in clay in *b.*
Nah. 3:14 make strong the *b.*

BRIDE.

Is. 49:18 bind them, as a *b.* doth
61:10 as a *b.* adorn. with jewels
62:5 bridegroom rejoic. over *b.*
Jer. 2:32 can a *b.* forget?
7:34 voice of the *b.* 16:9; 25:10
33:11 shall be heard voice of *b.*
Joel 2:16 *b.* go out of her closet
John 3:29 he that hath the *b.* is
Rev. 18:23 voice of *b.* heard
21:2 *b.* adorned for her husband
9 show thee *b.* the Lamb's wife
22:17 Sp. and the *b.* say, Come

BRIDECHAMBER.

Mat. 9:15 can children *b.* mourn
Mark 2:19 child. of *b.* f. *Luke* 5:34

BRIDEGROOM.

Ps. 19:5 as a *b.* coming out
Is. 61:10 as a *b.* decketh himself
62:5 as *b.* rejoiceth over bride
Mat. 9:15 while the *b.* is with them, *Mark* 2:19; *Luke* 5:34
25:1 ten virgins to meet the *b.*
5 *b.* tarried; 6 *b.* cometh, 10
John 2:9 governor called the *b.*
3:29 friend of the *b.* rejoiceth greatly because of the *b.* voi.

See BRIDE.

BRIDLE.

2 *K.* 19:28 *b.* in thy lips, *Is.* 37:29
Job 30:11 have let loose the *b.*
41:13 to him with his double *b.*
Ps. 32:9 must be held with the *b.*
39:1 keep my mouth with a *b.*
Prov. 26:3 a *b.* for the ass
Is. 30:28 a *b.* in jaws of people
Jam. 1:26 and *b.* not his tongue
3:2 able also to *b.* whole body
Rev. 14:20 blood to the horse *b.*

BRIEFLY.

Rom. 13:9 it is *b.* comprehended
1 *Pet.* 5:12 by Sylv. I have writ, *b.*

BRIER.

Is. 55:13 instead of the *b.*
Ezek. 28:24 no more a pricking *b.*
Mic. 7:4 best of them as a *b.*

BRIERS.

Jud. 8:7 tear your flesh with *b.*
16 he took the elders and *b.*
Is. 5:6 there shall come up *b.*
7:23 shall even be for *b.* and
24 shall become *b.* and thorns
25 come thither the fear of *b.*
9:18 wicked. shall devour the *b.*
10:17 devour his *b.* in one day
27:4 set *b.* against me in battle?
32:13 on land shall come up *b.*
Ezek. 2:6 though *b.* be with thee
Heb. 6:8 which beareth *b.* is rej.

BRIGANDINE.

Jer. 46:4 and put on the *b.*
51:3 lifteth up himself in his *b.*

BRIGHT.

Job 37:11 scattereth his *b.* cloud
21 see not *b.* light in the clouds
Cant. 5:14 his belly is as *b.* ivory
Jer. 51:11 make *b.* the arrows
Ezek. 1:13 fire was *b.* and out
21:15 the sword is made *b.*
21 made his arrows *b.*
27:19 iron in thy market
32:8 *b.* lights I will make dark
33:3 lifteth up the *b.* sword
Zec. 10:1 shall make *b.* clouds
Mat. 17:5 a *b.* cloud overshad.
Luke 11:36 *b.* shining of a candle
Acts 10:30 stood in *b.* clothing
Rev. 22:16 *b.* and morning star

BRIGHTNESS.

2 *Sam.* 22:13 thro' *b.* before him were coals kindled, *Ps.* 18:12

BRI

BRI

Job 31:26 moon walking in *b.*
Is. 59:9 we wait for *b.* but walk
60:3 kings to the *b.* of thy rising
19 for *b.* the moon give light
62:1 righteousness go forth as *b.*
Ezek. 1:4 and *b.* was about it, 27
28 so appearance of the *b.* 8:2
10:4 court full of the *b.* of glory
24:7 strangers shall defile thy *b.*
17 hast corrupted by thy *b.*
Dan. 2:31 image, *b.* was excell.
4:36 my *b.* returned unto me
12:3 shine as *b.* of firmament
Amos 5:20 day of L. no *b.* in it
Hab. 3:4 his *b.* was as the light
Acts 26:13 above *b.* of the sun
2 *Thes.* 2:8 the *b.* of his coming
Heb. 1:3 being the *b.* of his glory

BRIM.

Jos. 3:15 dipped in *b.* of water
John 2:7 filled them to the *b.*

BRIMSTONE.

Gen. 19:24 on G. *b.* Luke 17:29
Deut. 29:23 the whole land is *b.*
Job 18:15 *b.* scattered on his hab.
Ps. 11:6 on the wicked snares, fire and *b.* Ezek. 38:22
Is. 30:33 like a stream of *b.*
34:9 dust thereof into *b.*
Rev. 9:17 out of their mouths *b.*
18 third part killed by the *b.*
14:10 shall be tormented with *b.*
19:20 burning with *b.* 20:10
21:8 part in the lake which burneth with fire and *b.*

BRING.

Gen. 6:17 *b.* a flood on the earth
19 two of every sort *b.* into ark
9:14 I *b.* a cloud over earth
18:16 Abra. did *b.* on their way
19 *b.* on A. what he hath spo.
27:12 I shall *b.* a curse on me
42:20 *b.* youngest brother, 34
37 if I *b.* him not, 43:9; 44:32
43:16 *b.* these men home
43:19 take wag. and *b.* your fa.
45:9 *b.* them, and I will bless
Ex. 13:5 L. shall *b.* thee, 11
18:19 mayest *b.* the causes to G.
21:6 master *b.* him to judges
24:19 first of first-fruits *b.* 34:26
23:20 send an angel to *b.* thee
35:5 a willing heart, let him *b.*
30:5 people *b.* more than enough
Num. 14:8 if L. del. in us, will *b.*
14:16 able to *b.* Deut. 9:28
21 Caleb will I *b.* into the land
20:12 ye shall not *b.* this cong.
Deut. 1:17 cause too hard, *b.*
7:1 Lord shall *b.* thee into land
21:12 shalt *b.* her to thy house
b. it, 15 to us that we may, 13
28:7 *b.* Judah to his people
1 *Sam.* 1:22 weaned, I will *b.* him
9:7 said Saul, what *b.* the man?
21 *b.* the portion I gave thee
20:8 why *b.* thee to thy father
2 *Sam.* 3:12 to *b.* all Israel to thee
13 except thou *b.* Michal when
14:10 saith aught, *b.* him to me
19:11 last to *b.* the king back
1 *K.* 8:32 *b.* his way on his head
13:18 *b.* him back to thy house
17:11 *b.* me a morsel of bread
20:33 he said, Go ye, *b.* him
2 *K.* 2:20 *b.* me a new cruse
6:19 *b.* you to whom ye seek
2 *Chr.* 18:29 *b.* an offering
Neh. 13:18 our God *b.* this evil
Job 6:22 did I say, *b.* unto me
10:9 wilt thou *b.* me into dust
14:1 who can *b.* a clean thing
18:14 *b.* him to king of terrors
33:21 thou wilt *b.* me to death
88:30 *b.* back his soul from pit
Ps. 43:3 *b.* me to thy holy hill
60:9 *b.* me into a str. city, 108:10
72:3 shall *b.* peace to people
94:23 *b.* on them their own
Prov. 29:8 scornful *b.* a city
Ec. 3:22 shall *b.* him to see
11:9 God will *b.* thee into judg.
12:14 *b.* every work into judg.
Cant. 8:2 *b.* thee into my m.
Is. 7:17 Lord shall *b.* on thee
15:9 *b.* them in their place
15:9 for I will *b.* more upon I.
23:12 shall *b.* to the ground
43:51 lot *b.* out my righteousness
56:7 will *b.* them to my holy mo.
58:7 *b.* the poor to thy house
60:9 for *b.* thy sons from far
65:4 *b.* their fears upon them
Jer. 3:14 I will *b.* you to Zion
19:21 lest thou *b.* me to nothing

BRI

Jer. 11:8 I will *b.* words of this
17:18 *b.* on them day of evil
31:8 *b.* them from the north
32:42 *b.* on them all the good
33:6 I will *b.* it health and cure
11 shall *b.* sacrifice of praise
48:5 I will *b.* a fear upon them
Ezek. 6:3 *b.* a sword upon you
11:9 *b.* you out of the midst
20:15 I would not *b.* them
21:29 will *b.* on necks of them
23:22 *b.* them against thee on
34:13 *b.* to own, 30:24; 37:21
38:17 *b.* thee against them
Hos. 2:14 and *b.* her to wildern.
Amos 4:1 *b.* and let us drink, 4
Mic. 1:15 will I *b.* an heir to thee
Zec. 8:8 I will *b.* them, and they
Mal. 3:12 be there till I *b.* word
5:23 *b.* thy gift to the altar
17:17 *b.* him to me, *Mark* 9:19
21:2 *b.* them to me, *Mark* 11:2;
Luke 19:30
Mark 7:32 *b.* to him one deaf
Luke 2:10 *b.* good tidings
8:14 *b.* no fruit to perfection
12:11 *b.* you into the synagog.
John 10:16 other sheep I must *b.*
14:26 *b.* all things to remembr.
18:29 what accusation *b.* you?
Acts 5:28 to *b.* this man's blood
7:6 should *b.* them into bondage
9:2 he might *b.* them bound, 21
24:5 I went to *b.* them bound
23:10 to *b.* Paul into the castle
17 *b.* this young man to capt.
1 *Cor.* 1:19 I will *b.* to nothing
28 to *b.* to naught
4:17 *b.* you into remembrance
9:27 body, I *b.* into subjection
16:6 may *b.* me on my journey
1 Cor. 11:26 if a man *b.* you
Gal. 3:24 schoolm. to *b.* us to C.
1 *Thes.* 4:14 sleep, will God *b.*
1 *Pet.* 3:18 he might *b.* us to G.
2 *John* 10 if any *b.* not this doc.
3 *John* 6 if thou *b.* on journey
Rev. 21:24 do *b.* their glory to it
26 *b.* the glory of nations into
See HONE, HITHER.

BRING again.

Gen. 24:6 *b.* not my son *again*, 8
24:15 *b.* thee *b.* into land, 48:21
42:37 I will *b.* him again
Ex. 23:4 *b.* it back to him again
Num. 22:8 I will *b.* word again
Deut. 1:22 *b.* us word again what
22:1 *b.* them again to thy bro.
Jud. 11:9 if ye *b.* me home
19:3 her husb. went to *b.* her
2 *Sam.* 12:23 can I *b.* him again
14:21 *b.* the young man Ab. *d.*
15:8 if Lord *b.* me again to Jerus.
25 *b.* me again and show me
1 *K.* 8:34 forg. and *b.* a. 2 *Chr.* 6:25
13:18 *b.* him with thee to the ark
21:12 what word I shall *b.* a.
2 *Chr.* 2:19 proph. to *b.* above a.
Neh. 9:29 mightest *b.* again
Ps. 68:22 *b.* again from B. I will
b. my people from depths of
Prov. 19:24 as *b.* it to mouth a.
Ec. 3:15 *b.* again what is past
Is. 38:8 *b.* again shadow
46:8 *b.* it *again* to mind
49:5 saith Lord to *b.* Jac. again
52:8 Lord shall *b.* again Zion
Jer. 12:15 will *b.* them a. 50:19
15:19 will I *b.* thee again
16:15 &c. a. to their l. 24:6; 32:37
23:3 *b.* again into their folds
24:4 I will *b.* again Jeremiah, 6
30:3 *b.* again the captivity, 18;
31:23; *Ezek.* 39:25; *Amos* 9:14
32:37 *b.* a captivity of Israel
Ezek. 16:53 when I *b.* a. their
29:14 I will *b.* again captivity
31:16 will *b.* again that driveth
34:4 *b.* again that driven away
Zec. 10:6 *b.* them again, *b.* o.
10 I will *b.* them *a.* out of E.
Mat. 2:8 *b.* word that I may

See CAPTIVITY.

BRING down.

Gen. 42:38 *b.* d. gray h. 44:29, 31
43:7 may, *b.* brother *down* my father
Deut. 9:3 *b.* them *down* before
Num. 22:24 am haughty to *b.* d.
1 *K.* 1:33 Solomon, *b.* d. to G.
2:9 his hoar head *b.* down *d.*
Ps. 18:27 *b.* down high looks
55:23 shalt *b.* d. to pit of dest.
Is. 25:5 shalt *b.* d. the noise
11 he shall *b.* d. their pride

BRI

Is. 25:12 high fort shall he *b. d.*
63:6 *b. d.* their strength to earth
Jer. 40:16 thee *d.* from th. *b.* 4
51:40 will *b.* them *d.* like lambs
Ezek. 26:20 shall *b.* thee down
28:8 shall *b.* thee *d.* to the pit
Hos. 7:12 *b.* them *d.* as fowls
Joel 3:3 *b. d.* to valley of Jehosh,
Amos 3:11 he shall *b. d.* thy str.
9:2 climb to heaven, *b.* them *d.*
Ob. 3 Who shall *b.* me *down*
Acts 23:15 that he *b.* him *down*
20 thou wouldest *b.* *down* Paul
Rom. 10:6 to *b.* Christ *down*

See EVIL.

BRING forth.

Gen. 1:11 earth *b., f.* 24; 20 waters
3:16 in sor. shalt *b. f.* children
18 th. and thist. sh. it *b. f.*
8:17 *b. f.* every living thing
9:7 *b. f.* abundantly in the earth
38:24 *b.* her *f.* let her be burnt
Ex. 3:10 mayst *b. f.* my people Is.
11 who am I that sh. *b. f.* Is.
7:4 I may *b. forth* my armies
Lev. 19:20 *b. f.* old, bec. of new
Num. 20:8 *b. f.* out of the ro.
Jos. 2:3 *b. f.* men come
Jud. 6:18 *b. forth* my present
19:22 *b. f.* man came to thy h.
2 *K.* 19:3 no str. to *b. f. Is.* 37:3
Job 14:9 *b. f.* boughs like a plant
15:35 conc. mischief, *b. f.* vanity
38:32 canst thou *b. f.* Mazzaroth
39:1 the wild goats *b. f.* 2, 3
40:20 mountains *b.* him *f.* food
Ps. 37:6 he shall *b. f.* thy right.
92:14 shall *b. f.* fruit in old age
104:14 *b. f.* food out of earth
147:13 our sheep may *b. f.*
Prov. 27:1 what a day may *b. f.*
Ec. 5:3 should *b. f.* grapes, 4
8:4 I, not *b. f.* children
33:11 conceive chaff, and *b. f.*
41:21 *b. forth* your strong reas.
42:1 he shall *b. f.* judg. to Gen.
3 he shall *b. f.* judgment
66:8 *b. f.* the blind
9 let them *b. f.* their witnesses
45:8 and let them *b. f.* salvation
53:10 water, maketh it *b. forth*
55:10 *b.* *forth*
58:6 conceive mischief and *b. f.*
65:9 I will *b. f.* seed out of J.
23 nor *b. forth* for trouble
66:8 earth to *b. f.* in one day?
9 and not cause to *b. f.*
Jer. 14:2 grow, yea *b. f.* fruit
31:4 I will *b. f.* what he swal.
Ezek. 12:4 shalt *b. f.* thy stuff
17:23 it shall *b. forth* boughs
20:6 to *b.* them *f.* of land of E.
38 *b.* them *f.* out of country
47:12 it shall *b. f.* new fruit
Hos. 9:13 Eph. sh. *b. f.* his chil.
16 though they *b. f.* yet will I
Mic. 4:10 labor to *b. f.* O Zion
7:9 he will *b. of. f.* to the light
Zep. 2:2 before decree *b. f.*
Zec. 3:8 *b. f.* my servant
4:7 *b. f.* headstone with shout.
5:4 *b. f.* a curse, it shall enter
Mat. 1:23 virg. sh. *b. f.* a son, 21
7:18 cannot *b. f.* evil, *Luke* 6:43
Mark 1:20 *b. f.* fruit
Luke 1:31 *b. f.* a son shalt call J.
6:15 having brew'd word *b. f.*
13:22 *b. f.* best robe
John 15:8 it may *b. f.* more fruit
16 I ord. you, should *b. f.* fruit
Acts 12:4 after Easter to *b.* him *f.*
Gen. 7:4 that we shall *b. f.*
5 motions of sin to *b. f.*

BRING in.

Ex. 6:8 *b.* you *into* land
15:17 shalt *b. in* and plant them
23:23 my Angel shall *b.* thee *in*
Num. 15:31 Ill, came, will I *b. in*
Jer. 17:21 *b. in* no burden on sab.
Dan. 2:24 *b.* me before the k.
9:24 to *b.* in everlasting right.
Hag. 1:6 *b.* much and *b.* in little
Luke 5:18 means to *b.* him in
11:31 *b.* to hither the poor
2 *Pet.* 2:1 *b.* in damnable here.

BRING out.

Gen. 42:24 *b.* out of this ho.
38:24 take out *b.* out of this t.
Ex. 6:6 *b.* you *out* from under
13 *b.* chil. of Is. *out* of E. 26, 27;
7:5; 12:51; *Jer.* 31:32
Deut. 22:21 *b.* d. *b.* f. 10:35; both *o.*
Jos. 6:22 *b.* o. thence Rahab
Jud. 6:30 *b. o.* thy son
Is. 25:17 O *b.* me o. of my dis.

BRI

Ps. 142:7 *b.* my soul o. of prison,
143:11 *b.* my soul out of trou.
Is. 42:7 to *b.* o. the prisoners
Ezek. 11:7 *b.* you *out* of midst
20:34 *b.* you o. from peo. 34:13
41 ac. you, when I *b.* you *out*
34:6 *b. f.* out piece by piece
Acts 17:5 sought to *b.* them out

BRING to pass.

Gen. 41:32 God will *b.* it *to p.*
50:20 to *b. t. p.* as at this day
Ps. 37:5 he shall *b.* it *t. p.*
Is. 28:21 *b. to p.* his act
46:11 I will also *b.* it *to p.*

BRING up.

Gen. 46:4 I will *b.* thee up again
Ex. 3:17 I will *b.* you *up* out of
33:12 sayest, *b. up* this people
Num. 20:25 *b. up* Aaron to m. 11.
Jud. 6:13 did not L. *b.* us *up*
1 *Sam.* 19:15 *b.* him *up* in the b.
28:11 he said, *b.* me *up* Samuel
2 *Sam.* 6:2 to *b. up* ark of G. 1 *K.*
8:1, 4; 1 *Chr.* 13:6; 15:3,
14, 25; 2 *Chr.* 5:2, 5
1 *Chr.* 17:5 since I *b. up* Israel
Is. 23:4 nor *b. up* virgins
Jer. 27:22 then will I *b.* them *up*
Ezek. 16:40 *b. up* a company ag.
23:46 I will *b. up* a company
37:6 I will *b. up* flesh on you
Hos. 9:12 they *b. up* children
Rom. 10:7 to *b. up* C, from the d.
Eph. 6:4 *b.* them *up* in nurture

BRINGERS.

2 *K.* 10:5 *b. up* of chil. sent to J.

BRINGEST.

Job 14:3 *b.* me into judgment
Is. 40:9 O *Jer.* that *b.* good tid.
Acts 17:20 *b.* strange things

BRINGETH.

Ex. 6:7 *b.* you from under bund.
Lev. 11:45 L. that *b.* you out
Jud. 8:7 L. *b.* thee into a good
1 *Sam.* 2:6 he *b.* down to the gr.
7 Lord *b.* low, and lifteth up
2 *Sam.* 22:48 *b.* the people under
49 *b.* me forth from mine ene.
Job 12:6 into whose hand L. *b.*
22 *b.* to light shadow of death
12:19 *b.* wrath *b.* punis. of the *sw.*
28:11 thing hid *b.* he to light
Ps. 1:3 *b.* forth his fruit
14:7 when L. *b.* back cap. 53:6
33:10 *b.* coun. of hea. to naught
37:7 *b.* wicked devices to pass
68:6 *b.* out them that are bound
29 *b.* them out of their dist.
80 *b.* them to desired haven
135:7 *b.* wind, *Jer.* 10:13; 51:16
Prov. 10:31 mouth of just *b.* wis.
16:30 moving his lips, he *b.* evil
18:16 gift *b.* him before great men
19:26 son that *b.* reproach
20 delicately *b. up* his servant
25 the fear of man *b.* a snare
31:14 she *b.* her food from a far
Ec. 1:5 to. on them the waters
28:5 down them dwell on h.
*40:23 *b.* the princes to nothing
49:17 *b.* forth chariot and horse
61:11 the earth *b.* forth her bud
Jer. 4:31 *b.* forth her first child
Ezek. 29:16 iniquity to re b.
Hos. 10:1 Is. *b.* forth fruit to him.
Hag. 1:11 which ground *b.* forth
Mat. 3:10 every tree that *b.* not
forth *g.* fruit, 7:19; *Luke* 3:9
7:17 good tree *b.* forth *g.* fruit
12:35 a good man *b.* forth good,
et. b. evil things, *Luke* 6:45
13:23 *b.* forth some a hundred
52 *b.* out of treas. things new
Luke 4:24 the earth *b.* to *h. ye* un.
Luke 6:43 good tree *b. not cor.
Tit. 2:11 grace of G. that *b.* sal.
Heb. 1:6 *b.* first-begot. into world
6:7 the earth *b.* forth herbs
8 *b.* forth sin, and sin *b.*

See TIDINGS.

BRINGING.

Ex. 12:42 observed for L. them
who were restrained from L.
Num. 14:35 by *b. up* a slander
1 *Sam.* 19:10 of *b.* the king, 43
2 *K.* 21:12 I am *b.* such evil
Ps. 126:6 rejoic. *b.* his sheaves
Ezek. 2:9 known in to *b.* forth
Dan. 9:12 upon us great evil

CRUDEN'S CONCORDANCE. 781

BRO

Dan. 7:13 *b.* him near Ancient
9:14 watched evil and *b.* it on
11:6 and they that *b.* her
Hos. 1:4 yo *b* it home
*Mal.*10:18 shall he *b.* before kings,
   Mark 13:9; *Luke* 21:12
12:25 in *b.* to desol. *Luke* 11:17
17:16 *b.* him to disciples
18:24 was *b.* owed 10,000 talents
19:13 *b.* little chil. *Mark* 10:13
Mark 10:13 rebuked those *b.* them
Luke 2:22 *b.* him to Jerusalem
10:34 *b.* him to an inn
John 7:45 have ye not *b.* him?
Acts 5:21 prison to have them *b.*
9:27 *b.* him to apostles
15:3 *b.* on their way
16:20 *b.* them to the magistrates
19:37 *b.* these men, no robbers
20:12 *b.* the young man alive
21:5 they all *b.* us on our way
25:6 commanded Paul to be *b.*
27:24 must be *b.* before Cesar
Rom. 15:31 to be *b.* thither
1 *Cor.* 6:12 not *b.* b. under power
2 *Cor.* 1:16 be *b.* on my way to J.
2 *Tim.* 1:10 *b.* life and immortal.
1 *Pet.* 1:13 grace that is *b.* to you
2 *Pet.* 2:19 of same is he *b.*

BROUGHT again.
Gen. 14:16 Abram *b.* again Lot
Ex. 15:19 L. *b. a.* waters of sea
Deut. 1:25 *b.* us word again
Ruth 1:21 L. *b.* me home again
1 *Sam.* 6:21 Philistines *b.* again
2 *Chr.* 33:13 L. *b.* Manas. a. to J.
Ezek. 34:4 *b. a.* what was driven
39:27 *b.* them *ag.* from the peo.
Heb. 13:20 *b. ag.* from the dead

BROUGHT back.
1 *K.* 13:21 prophet he had *b. back*
2 *Chr.* 19:4 Jehos. *b.* them *b.* to L.
Ps. 83:1 *b. back* the captivity
Ezek. 38:8 land *b. b.* from the sw.

BROUGHT down.
Gen. 39:1 was *b. d.* into Egypt
1 *Sam.* 30:16 *b.* him *d.* they were
Ps. 20:8 they are *b. d.* and fallen
107:12 he *b. d.* their heart
Ps. 5:15 mean man shall be *b. d.*
14:11 thy pomp is *b. down*
13 shall be *b. down* to hell
22:4 shall he *b. d.* speak out
43:14 *b. down* all the nobles
Lam. 2:2 *b.* them *d.* to the gro.
Ezek. 17:24 have *b. d.* high tree
31:18 be *b. d.* with trees of Eden
Zec. 10:11 pride of Assy. be *b. d.*
Mat. 11:23 Capern. *b. d.* to hell;
   Acts 9:30 brethren *b.* him *d.* to C.

BROUGHT forth.
Gen. 1:12 the earth *b. forth* grass
21 waters *b. forth* abundantly
14:18 king of Salem *b. f.* bread
15:5 Lord *b. forth* Abram
19:16 angels *b.* Lot *forth*
41:47 the earth *b. forth* by hand.
Ex. 3:11 *b.* thou hast *b. f.* peop.
16:3 ye have *b.* us *f.* into wild.
29:46 I am L. *b.* them *f.* *Lev.*
   23:43; 26:13, 45
Num. 24:8 God *b.* him *f.*
Deut. 6,12 Lord *b.* thee *f.* 8:14
9:12 people *b. f.* have corrupted
26:8 L. *b.* us *f.* with a mighty h.
8:14 fruits *b. forth.* by an inh.
Jud. 6:8 *b.* you *f.* out of house
2 *Sam.* 22:20 *b.* me *forth* into a
   large place, *Ps.* 18:19
1 *K.* 8:9 forsook Lord who *b. f.*
   their fathers, 2 *Chr.* 7:22
Job 10:18 hast thou *b.* me *f.*
21:30 be *b. f.* to day of wrath
Is. 51:18 *b. forth* falsehood
Is. 43:20 their land *b. f.* frogs
43 *b. forth* his people with joy
Prov. 8:24 no depths, I was *b. f.*
25 before the hills was I *b. f.*
Cant. 8:5 thy mother *b.* thee *f.*
Is. 5:2 I *b. forth* wild grapes
26:18 *b. f.* wind; 43:10 w. *b. f.*
51:18 among sons she hath *b. f.*
66:7 before she trav. she *b. f.*
8 as soon as Z. trav. she *b. f.*
Jer. 2:27 thou hast *b.* me *f.*
11:1 I *b.* them *forth*, 31:13
20:3 Pashur, *b. f. a.* out of stocks
32:21 *b. forth* Israel with signs
50:25 Lord *b. f.* weap. of indig.
51:10 L. hath *b. f.* our right.
Ezek. 12:7 I *b. f.* my stuff by day
14:22 a remnant *b. f.* sons a. d.
Mic. 6:3 which trav. hath *b. f.*
Hag. 2:19 olive-tree hath not *b. f.*
Mal. 1:25 she had *b. f.* first-born

BRO

Mat. 13:8 good gr. *b. f. Mark* 4:8
Luke 1:57 Elizabeth *b. f.* a son
2:7 she *b. f.* her first-born son
12:16 ground of a rich man *b. f.*
Jn. 19:13 Pilate *b. forth* Jesus
Acts 5:19 doors and *b.* them *f.*
12:6 Herod would have *b.* him *f.*
25:17 com. the man to be *b. f.*
Jam. 5:18 earth *b. forth* fruit
Rev. 12:5 she *b. f.* a man-child
13 persecuted woman wh. *b. f.*

BROUGHT in.
Gen. 39:14 *b.* in a Hebrew
47:7 Jos. *b.* in Jacob his father
Deut. 9:4 my right L. *b.* me in
11:29 L. hath *b.* in unto land
Neh. 13:19 no burden *b.* in
Ps. 78:26 *b.* in the south wind
Acts 7:45 *b.* in with Jesus
Gal. 2:4 brethren unawares *b.* in

BROUGHT into.
Num. 16:14 not *b.* us *into* a land
1 *Sam.* 20:8 *b.* thy serv. *into* a cov.
Ps. 22:15 *b.* me *into* dust
Cant. 1:4 king *b.* me *i.* his cham.
Jer. 2:7 *b.* you I. a plen. country
Lam. 3:2 *b.* me *into* darkness
Ezek. 44:7 *b.* in. my sanctuary
Acts 9:8 *b.* him *into* Damascus
21:28 *b.* Greeks *into* the temple
1 *Tim.* 6:7 *b.* nothing *into* world
Heb. 13:11 whose blood is *b. into*

BROUGHT low.
Jud. 11:33 dau. *b.* me very *low*
2 *Chr.* 28:19 Lord *b.* Judah *low*
Job 14:21 they are *b. low*
24:24 are gone and *b. low*
Ps. 79:8 for we are *b.* very *low*
106:43 *b. low* for their iniquity
107:39 *b. low* thro' oppression
116:6 I was *b. low*, he helped
142:6 for I am *b.* very *low*
Ec. 12:4 daug. of music be *b. low*
Is. 2:12 shall be *b. low*
25:5 of terrible ones *b. low*
Luke 3:5 every mountain and hill
   b. low, Is. 40:4

BROUGHT out.
Gen. 15:7 *b.* thee *o.* of Ur of Cha.
43:23 he *b. b.* and unto them
Ex. 13:3 L. *b.* you *out, b.* 14, 16
20:2 L. *b.* thee *out, Lev.* 19:36;
   Num. 15:41; *Deut.* 5:6; *Ps.* 81:10
Lev. 23:43 I *b.* them *o.* 1 *K.* 8:51
Deut. 8:15 that L. *b.* thee *out*
9:28 *b. out* to slay them
Jos. 6:23 *b. out* Rahab and all
24:5 and afterward I *b. o.*
Jud. 13:18 *b.* her *o.* and bolted
2 *Chr.* 23:11 *b. out* the king's son
Ps. 78:16 he *b.* str. *out* of rock
105:43 *b.* his people *out* of Egypt
107:14 *b.* them *out* of darkness
136:11 *b. out* Isr. from among
Jer. 7:32 in the day I L. them *out*
Dan. 5:13 king *b. o.* of Jewry?
Hos. 12:13 prophet L. *b.* Isr. *out*
Am. 2:10 *b.* you *out* of Egypt
Mic. 7:9 *b. o.* me to light
4 *Sam.* 8:8 where they day 1 *b. up*;
   2 *Chr.* 6:5
12:6 L. that *b.* your fathers *up*
1 *K.* 8:1; 1 *Chr.* 15:28; 2 *Chr.* 5:4
11:43 *b. up* the bones of Saul
2 *K.* 17:7 sin, *ag.* L. *b.* them *up*
36 Lord who *b.* you *up*
2 *Chr.* 8:11 Sol. *b.* up dau. of P.
10:6 men *b. up* with him, 10
Neh. 9:18 is thy God *b.* thee *up*
Ec. 2:7 he *b. up* Esther
25 like as when *b. up* with him
Job 31:18 he was *b. up* with me
Ps. 30:3 *b.* up my soul
40:2 he *b. up* out of horrible pit
Prov. 8:30 one *b. up* with him
Lam. 2:22 nourished and *b. up* chil.
13:21 whom hath *b. up* these

BUD

Is. 51:18 her of sons she *b. up*
63:11 he *b.* them *up, Jer.* 2:6
Jer. 11:7 in day I *b.* them *up*
10:14 L. that *b. u.* Israel. 23:7
15 *b. up* Israel from the n. 24:8
Lam. 2:22 those I *b. up* my en.
4:5 *b. up* in scarlet, embrace
Ezek. 19:3 *b. up* one of her whelps
37:13 *b.* you *up* out of your gr.
Amos 2:10 I *b.* you *u.* 3:1; 9:7;
   Mic. 6:4
Jon. 2:6 *b. up* my life from cor.
Luke 4:16 N. where he been *b. u.*
Acts 13:1 I been *b. up* with Herod
22:3 *b. up* at the feet of Gamal.
1 *Tim.* 5:10 widow, if she *b. up*

BROUGHTEST.
Ex. 32:7 people *b.* out have cor.
Deut. 9:28 los. land whence *b. us*
29 inherit, *b.* out, 1 *K.* 8:51
2 *Sam.* 5:2 he *b.* in Isr. 1 *Chr.* 11:2
1 *K.* 8:53 whom *b.* our fathers out
Neh. 9:7 *b.* him forth out of Ur.
15 *b.* forth water out of rock
23 *b.* them into the land
Ps. 60:11 thou *b.* us into the net
12 *b.* us out into a wealthy pl.

BROW.
Is. 48:4 thy neck iron, *b.* brass
Luke 4:29 led him to *b.* of the hill

BROWN.
Gen. 30:32 all *b.* cattle, 33, 40
33 every o. not *b.* accounted st.

BRUISE, Substantive.
Jer. 30:12 L. thy *b.* is incurable
Nah. 3:19 no healing of thy *b*

BRUISES.
Is. 1:6 but wounds and *b.*

BRUISE, Verb.
Gen. 3:15 *b.* thy head, *b.* his heel
Is. 28:28 nor *b.* it with horsemen
53:10 pleased the Lord to *b.* him
Dan. 2:40 as iron shall it *b.*
Rom. 16:20 G. of peace shall *b.* S.

BRUISED.
Lev. 22:24 not offer what is *b.*
2 *K.* 18:21 trusted this *b.* reed
Is. 42:3 a *b.* reed shall he not
break, *Mat.* 12:20
53:5 he was *b.* for our iniquities
Ezek. 23:3 in Egypt *b.* the teats
8 *b.* the breasts of her virginity
Luke 4:18 set at liberty them *b.*

BRUISING.
Ezek. 23:21 in *b.* thy teats by E.
Luke 9:39 the spirit *b.* him

BRUIT.
Jer. 10:22 noise of the *b.* is come
Nah. 3:19 all that hear *b.* of thee

BRUTE. *See* BEASTS.

BRUTISH.
Ps. 49:10 fool and *b.* person
92:6 a *b.* man knoweth not
94:8 understand, ye *b.* am. the peo.
Prov. 12:1 hateth reproof is *b.*
30:2 I am more *b.* than any
Is. 19:11 the counsel of the coun-
sellors of Phar., is become *b.*
Jer. 10:8 they are altogether *b.*
11 men '* *b.* 51:17; 12 pastors
Ezek. 21:31 into the hand of *b.*

BUCKLER, S.
2 *Sam.* 22:31 a *b.* to all that trust
in him, *Ps.* 18:30
1 *Chr.* 5:18 men able to bear a *b.*
12:8 Gadites that could h. *b.*
Ps. 18:2 Lord is my God, my *b.*
33:2 take hold of shield and *b.*
91:4 his truth shall be thy *b.*
Jer. 46:3 order ye *b.* and shield
Ezek. 23:24 set against thee *b.*
26:8 he shall lift *b.* against

BUCKLERS.
2 *Chr.* 23:9 Jehoiada delivered *b.*
Job 15:26 run on bosses of his *b.*
Cant. 4:4 thereon hang a thous. *b.*
Ezek. 35:9 great company with *b.*
39:9 they shall set on fire *b.*

BUD, Substantive.
Job 38:27 *b.* of tender herb
Is. 18:5 when the *b.* is perfect
61:11 as earth bringeth forth a *b.*
Ezek. 16:7 caused thee to multiply
this, 3:7 *b.* shall yield un med
Num. 17:8 Aaron's rod *b.* forth *b.*

BUI

BUD, Verb.
Job 14:9 thr. scent of water. *b.*
Ps. 132:17 horn of David to *b.*
Cant. 7:12 see if pomegranates *b.*
Is. 27:6 Is. shall blossom and *b.*
55:10 maketh the earth to *b.*
Ezek. 29:21 cause horn of Is. to *b.*

BUDDED.
Gen. 40:10 was as though it *b.*
Num. 17:8 A. rod for house of L. *b.*
Cant. 6:11 to see whether pom. *b.*
Ezek. 7:10 pride hath *b.*
Heb. 9:4 ark wherein rod that *b.*

BUFFET.
2 *Cor.* 12:7 mes. of Satan to *b.* me

BUFFETED.
Mat. 26:67 *b.* him, *Mark* 14:65
1 *Cor.* 4:11 to present hour *b.*
1 *Pet.* 2:20 when *b.* for your f.

BUILD, referred to God.
1 *Sam.* 2:35 *b.* him a sure h. 2
   Sam. 7:27; 1 *K.* 11:38
1 *Chr.* 17:10 will *b.* thee a house
25 told w'h *b.* him a house
Ps. 28:5 and not *b.* them up
51:18 *b.* thou the walls of Jer.
69:35 will *b.* the cities of Judah
89:4 *b. up* thy throne to all gen.
127:1 except the L. *b.* the house
147:2 Lord doth *b. up* Jerusalem
Jer. 18:9 con. a nation to *b.* it
24:6 I will *b.* not pull d. 33:28
31:4 I will *b.* thee, O virgin
33:7 I will *b.* Judah and Israel
42:10 if ye abide, I will *b.* you
Ezek. 36:36 that I *b.* ruined pl.
Amos 9:11 *b.* it as in days of old
Mat. 16:18 on this rock *b.* my ch.
26:61 *b.* it in three d. *Mark* 14:58
Acts 15:16 *b.* again tabernacle

BUILD, *Man the Agent.*
Num. 11:4 go to, let us *b.* a city
Num. 32:21 *b.* ye cities
1 *K.* 9:24 then did *b.* Solly.
11:7 Solom. did *b.* a high place
20:19 give Sol. a heart to *b.*
1 *Chr.* 22:19 *b.* ye the sanctuary
2 *Chr.* 14:7 let us *b.* these cities
Ezr. 4:2 let us *b.* with you
Neh. 2:17 let us *b.* the wall
4:3 which they *b.* if a fox go up
10 so we are not able to *b.*
Ec. 3:3 a time to *b. up*
Cant. 8:9 we will *b.* on her
Is. 9:10 fallen, but we will *b.*
45:13 he shall *b.* my city
58:12 *b.* old waste places. 61:4
60:10 sons of strangers. *b.* walls
65:22 not *b.* and another inhabit
Jer. 1:10 set over nations to *b.*
Ezek. 4:2 *b.* a fort against, 21:22
22:25 to *b.* Jerusalem
Amos 9:11 I will *b.* as in days
14 Isr. shall *b.* the waste cities
13 they far off sh. *b.* in temple
9:3 Tyrus did *b.* a stronghold
Zec. 6:12 shall *b.* the temple, 13
15 they are afar off to *b.*
Mal. 1:4 but I will throw d.
Mat. 22:29 ye *b.* tombs of proph.
Luke 11:47, 48
12:28 burns and *b.* greater
14:28 intending to *b.* a tower
30 to *b.* and not able to finish
20:33 word of his grace able
to *b.* you up
Rom. 15:20 lest I *b.* on ano. man's
Gal. 2:18 if I *b.* again things

BUILD, altars, s.
Ex. 20:25 *b.* altar of hewn stone
Num. 23:1 *b.* me here sev. *u.* 24
Deut. 27:5 there *b.* an altar to L.
6 shalt *b.* the *a.* of whole st.
Jos. 22:29 God forbid we sh. *b. a.*

See BEGAN.

BUILD, joined with HOUSE, *s.*
Deut. 25:9 will not *b.* brother's *h.*
28:30, *a* h. *Zep.* 1:13
Ruth 4:11 which two did *b. h.*
2 *Sam.* 7:5 *b.* me *h. Acts* 7:49
Acts 7:13 he shall *b.* h. my n. 1 *Chr.*
   17:12; 22:10; 28:6
1 Chr. 28:2; 2 *Chr.* 6:7
1 K. 2:36 *b. h.* in Jer. to dwell
1 K. 17:12 ; 2:10
22:8 not *b. h.* unto my name

CRUDEN'S CONCORDANCE.

BUI

BUILDED
Gen. 4:17 C. b. city called Enoch
8:20 Noah b. an altar to the L.
10:11 Ashur b. Nineveh and
11:5 L. come to see tower men b.
Jos. 22:16 you b. an altar
1 K. 8:27 house I have b. 43
13:32 houses on wh. Bamah had b.
2 K. 23:13 Solo. b. for Ashtoreth
1 Chr. 24:3 b. must be magnifical
Ezr. 4:13 if city be b. 16
5:8 to the house of great God b
11 we build house b. years ago
15 let the house of G. be b. 5:3
6:14 elders of Jews b. and pros.
Job 21:19 a house he b. not
Ps. 122:3 J. is b. a city compact
Prov. 9:1 wisdom hath b. her b.
24:3 thr. wisdom is a house b.
Ec. 2:4 I b. me houses, I planted
Cant. 4:4 David b. for an armory
Jer. 32:18 city be b. on her heap
Lam. 3:5 he hath b. against me
Ezek. 39:10 wastes shall be b. M.
Luke 17:28 they planted, they b.
Eph. 2:22 in whom ye are b. tog.
1 Pet. 2:5 b. house hath more hou.
4 every house is b. by some m.

BUILDEDST
Deut. 6:10 cities thou b. not

BUILDER, S.
1 K. 5:18 Solomon's and H.'s b.
2 K. 22:6 give it to b. 2 Chr. 34:11
Ezr. 3:10 when b. laid found.
Neh. 4:5 to anger before the b.
Ps. 118:22 stone b. refu. Mat.
21:42; Mark 12:10; Luke 20:17;
Acts 4:11
Ezek. 27:4 thy b. have perfected
Heb. 11:10 city whose b. is God
1 Pet. 2:7 the stone b. disallowed

Master-BUILDER.
1 Cor. 3:10 as a wise ma. b. I have

BUILDEST
Deut. 22:8 b. a new house
Neh. 6:6 for wh. cause b. the wall
Ezek. 16:31 b. thine eminent place
Mat. 27:40 that destroyest the
temple and b. it. Mark 15:29

BUILDETH
Jos. 6:26 cursed be man b. this c.
Job 27:18 b. his house as a moth
Prov. 14:1 wise woman b. her h.
Jer. 22:13 woe to him b. by un.
Hos. 8:14 for. make. b. temples
Amos 9:6 b. his stories in heaven
Hab. 2:12 b. a town with blood
1 Cor. 3:10 another b. thereon

BUILDING, Participle.
1 K. 3:1 and of b. his own house
6:7 no tool of iron heard wh. b.
7:1 seven years in b. it
Ezr. 4:12 b. the rebellious city
Ezek. 17:17 b. forts to cut off
John 2:20 temple was 46 y. in b.
Jude 20 b. up on most holy faith

BUILDING, Substantive.
1 K. 9:1 when Sol. finished the b.
1 Chr. 28:2 made ready for the b.
2 Chr. 3:3 instructed for the b.
Ec. 10:18 slothful, b. decayeth
Ezek. 40:5 measured b. 41:13
46:23 a row of b. round about
1 Cor. 3:9 ye are God's b.
2 Cor. 5:1 we have a b. of God
Eph. 2:21 in whom b. fitly fra.
Heb. 9:11 tabernacle not of th. b.
Rev. 21:18 b. of wall was jasper

BUILDINGS
Mat. 24:1 show him b. of temple
Mark 13:1 see what b. are here, 2

BUILT.
Deut. 13:16 it shall not be b.

BUL

1 K. 22:39 cities that Ahab b.
2 Chr. 14:7 they b. and prospered
b. then a sanctuary therein
26:9 Uzziah b. towers in Jer. 10
27:4 Joth. b. castles and towers
Job 3:14 who b. desolate places
12:14 and it cannot be b. again
22:23 if return shalt be b. up
Ps. 78:69 b. his sanc. like high p.
89:2 mercy shall be b. up
Is. 5:2 b. a tower in the midst
44:26 to Jeru. thou shalt be b.
Jer. 12:16 then shall they be b.
31:4 thou shalt be b. O virgin
32:31 prov. from day they b. it
45:4 which I b. will break d.
Ezek. 16:24 hast b. eminent place
36:14 thou shalt be b. no more
Dan. 4:30 gr. Babylon I have b.
9:25 street shall be b. again
Zec. 8:9 that temple be b.
Mat. 21:33 b. a tower, Mark 12:1
Luke 7:5 hath b. us a synagogue
1 Cor. 3:14 abide wh. he hath b.
Eph. 2:20 b. on found. of apost.
Col. 2:7 rooted and b. up in him
Heb. 3:4 that b. all things is God

BUILT altar.
Ezr. 17:15 b. a. 24:4; 32:5 Aaron
Jud. 6:24 G. b. a.; 21:4 peo. b. a.
1 Sam. 7:17 S. b. a.; 14:35 Saul b.
2 Sam. 24:25 D. b. a. to the Lord
1 K. 9:25 Solo. offered on a. hot.
18:32 with stones Elijah b. a.
2 K. 16:11 Urijah the priest b. a.

BUILT altars.
Num. 23:14 Balak b. seven a.
2 K. 21:4 he b. a. in house of L.
5 b. a. for host of L. 2 Chr. 33:5
2 Chr. 33:15 away a. he had b. in

BUILT city.
Num. 21:27 let city of Sihon be b.
Jos. 19:50 Joshua b. c. and dwelt
1 Chr. 11:8 David b. c. from Millo
Is. 25:2 to be m. c. never be b.
Jer. 31:38 city shall be b. to Lord
Luke 4:29 hill whereon c. was b.

BUILT cities.
Ex. 1:11 b. for Phar. treasure-cit.
Num. 24:13 cities which ye b. not
1 Chr. 14:6 Asa b. fenced c. in J.
17:19 Jehosh. b. cities of store
27:4 Jotham b. c. in mountains
Luke 14:26 c. of J. ye shall be b.

BUILT house, or houses.
Deut. 8:12 when hast b. goodly h.
20:5 what man hath b. new h.
1 K. 3:2 no h. to name of Lord
6:9 Sol. b. h. 14; 8:13 b. h. h.
8:20 have b. a h. for name of L.
44 toward the h. I have b. 48;
2 Chr. 6:34, 38
1 Chr. 17:6 why not h. me a h.?
2 Chr. 6:18 less this h. I have b.?
Amos 5:11 ye b. h. of hewn stone
Hag. 1:2 Lord's h. should be b.
Zec. 1:16 my h. shall be b. in it
Mat. 7:24 b. h. on sand, Luke 6:48
26 b. his h. on sand, Luke 6:49
Acts 7:47 Solomon b. him a h.
1 Pet. 2:5 b. up a spiritual house

BUILT high places.
1 K. 14:23 Jud. b. h. p. and ima.
2 K. 17:9 chil. of Israel b. h. p.
Jer. 7:31 b. h. p. of Tophet; 19:5
32:35 b. h. p. of Baal, 32:35

BUILT wall, or walls.
2 Chr. 27:3 on w. of O. b. much
32:5 Hezekiah b. up w. broken
33:14 Manas. b. w. without city
Ezek. 13:10 one b. up the w.
Dan. 9:25 street b. w. and the w.
Mic. 7:11 thy walls are to be b.

BUL. 1 K. 6:38

BULL.

Job 21:10 their b. gendereth
Is. 51:20 as a wild b. in a net

BULLS
Gen. 32:15 many b. have com-
passed me, strong b.
50:13 will I eat the flesh of b.
68:30 rebuke the multitude of b.
Is. 34:7 with b. shall come down
Jer. 50:11 because ye bellow as b.
52:20 brazen b. under the bases
Ezek. 39:18 eat flesh of b. of E.
Heb. 9:13 blood of b. and goats
10:4 blood of b. take away sins

BULLOCK
Ex. 29:11 kill the b. Lev. 1:5; 8:18
Deut. 33:17 like firstling of b.
Jud. 6:25 take the young b. 26
1 K. 18:33 choose one b. 25

BUR

1 K. 18:33 B. cut tho b. in pieces
Ps. 50:9 no b. out of thy house
69:31 than a b. that hath hor.
Is. 65:25 lion eat straw like b.
Jer. 31:18 a b. unaccus. to yoke

BULLOCK with Sin-offering.
Ex. 29:36 eve. day a b. for sin-o.
Ezek. 43:22 prepare a b. for sin-o.
See BLOOD.

Young BULLOCK.
Lev. 16:3 holy place with a y. b.
Num. 7:15 one y. b. 21, etc. to 81
1 Chr. 13:9 consecrate with y. b.
Ezek. 45:18 y. b. and clea. sanct.
46:6 day of new moon a y. b.

BULLOCKS,
1 Chr. 29:21 offered a thousand b.
Ezr. 6:17 the dedication 100 b.
Ps. 51:19 offer b. on thy altar
66:15 I will offer unto thee b.
Is. 1:11 I delight not in bl. of b.
34:7 the b. shall come down
Jer. 46:21 hired men like fatted b.
50:27 slay all her b. let them go
Ezek. 39:18 drink the blood of b.
Hos. 12:11 they sacrifice b. in G.
See SEVEN.

BULRUSH, ES.
Ex. 2:3 an ark of b.
Is. 18:2 ambas. in vessels of b.
58:5 to bow his head like a b.?

BULWARKS.
Deut. 20:20 b. against the city
2 Chr. 26:15 engines on the b.
Ps. 48:13 mark well her b.
Ec. 9:14 a great king built b.
Is. 26:1 salvation appoint for b.

BUNCH.
Ex. 12:22 take a b. of hyssop
1 Chr. 12:40 Zebulun brought b.
Is. 30:6 treas. upon b. of camels

BUNDLE, S.
Gen. 42:35 every man's b.
1 Sam. 25:29 bound in b. of life
Cant. 1:13 a b. of myrrh is my b.
Mat. 13:30 bind the tares in b.
Acts 28:3 P. gathered a b. of s.

BURDEN.
Gen. 49:14 b. ass. b. in val. in M.
2 Sam. 15:33 biessed be ye b. Saul
1 K. 14:16 b. A. all Isr. mourned
Acts 5:6 the young men b. Aim

BURIED in
Gen. 15:15 b. in a good old age
1 K. 2:10 D. was b. in city of D.
Job 27:15 shall he b. in death.

BURIERS.
Ezek. 39:15 till b. have buried

BUR

Neh. 4:17 bare b. held a weapon
Is. 58:6 to undo the heavy b.
Lam. 3:14 seen for thee false b.
Mat. 23:4 heavy b. Luke 11:46
Gal. 6:2 bear ye one another's b.

BURDENSOME.
Zec. 12:3 Jerusalem a b. stone
2 Cor. 11:9 kept from being b.
12:13 that I was not b. to you
14 I will not be b. to you
1 Thes. 2:6 might been b.

BURIAL.
Ec. 6:3 also that he have no b.
Jer. 22:19 with the b. of an ass
Mat. 26:12 she did it for my b.
Acts 8:2 carried Stephen to his b.

BURIED.
Gen. 23:19 there was Abraham b.
49:31 there they b. Abra. Sarah,
Isaac, Rebekah, there I b.
Num. 11:34 b. the people
20:1 Miriam died, was b. there
33:4 Egyptians b. all first-born
Deut. 10:6 Aaron. there he was b.
Jos. 24:30 bones of J. b. in Shc.
Ruth 1:17 and there will I be b.
2 Sam. 4:12 b. head of Ish-bosh.
21:14 bones of Saul b. in Zelah
1 K. 13:31 wherein man of G. b.
Ec. 8:10 so I saw the wicked b.
Jer. 8:2 nor b. 16:6; 20:6; 25:33
16:4 shall not be lamented nor b.
22:19 be b. with burial of an ass
Ezek. 39:15 till buriers have b.
Luke 16:22 took body and b. it
Luke 16:22 died and was b.
Acts 2:29 D. is both dead and b.
5:9 feet of them which b.
Rom. 6:4 b. with him by baptism
1 Cor. 15:4 that he was d. and b.
Col. 2:12 b. with him in baptism

BURIED him.
Gen. 34:6 he b. him in val. in M.
2 Sam. 2:5 blessed be ye b. Saul
1 K. 14:18 b. h. all Isr. mourned
Acts 5:6 the young men b. him

BURIED in.
Gen. 15:15 b. in a good old age
1 K. 2:10 D. was b. in city of D.
Job 27:15 shall b. b. in death.

BURIERS.
Ezek. 39:15 till b. have buried

BURN.
Gen. 44:18 let not thine anger b.
Ex. 27:20 lamp to b. Lev. 24:2
2 Chr. 2:6 save only to b. sacrif.
13:11 b. to Lord every morning
10:17 b. and devour his thorns
27:4 I would b. them together
40:16 Lebanon is not suf. to b.
Jer. 7:20 my fury shall b.
81:8 so shall they b. odors
36:25 king would not b. roll
Ezek. 24:5 b. also bones under it
11 that the brass of it may b.
39:9 and b. the weapons
Mal. 2:13 b. chariots with fire
Nah. 2:13 I will b. her chariots
Mal. 4:1 that shall b. as oven
Mat. 13:30 in bundles to b. them
Luke 3:17 the chaff he will b.
1 Cor. 7:9 bet. to marry than to b.
2 Cor. 11:29 offend. and I b. not?

BURN joined with fire.
Deut. 5:23 mount. did b. with f.
32:22 a f. shall b. to the lowest
hell, Jer. 17:4
Jos. 11:6 b. chariots with fire
12:3 Ai b. with f.; 14:15 b. the c.
Ps. 79:6 thy jealousy b. like f.?
89:46 thy wrath b. like fire?
Is. 47:14 as stubble f. shall b.
Jer. 4:4 like f. and b.; 21:12
7:21 b. one and. this city with fire
32:29 ; 34:2, 22; 37:8, 10; 38:18
43:13 b. with f. in Eg.; 49:27
Ezek. 5:2 b. with fire a third part
16:41 b. thy h. with f.; 23:47
Mat. 3:12 he will b. up the chaff
unquench. fire, Luke 3:17
Rev. 17:16 eat it, b. her with fire

BURN incense.
Ex. 30:7 A. shall b. sweet i. 8.
1 K. 13:2 Jeroboam stood to b. i.
20:14 shall offer it. b. i. 26:16
1 Chr. 23:13 Aaron sep. to b. i.
2 Chr. 22:19 to b. i. in every city
Jer. 7:9 will ye b. i.?
1 Chr. L. hath chosen you to b. i.
29:11 L. hath chosen you to b. i.
2 Chr. 32:18 forever to b. i.
1 Chr. 2:14 to b. sweet incense
2 Chr. 2:4 one altar and b. inc. on it

CRUDEN'S CONCORDANCE.

BUR
Jer. 7:9 *b. i.* to Baal ? 11:13
44:17 *b. i.* to queen of heaven
Eze. 4:13 *b. incense* on hills
Hab. 1:16 *b. i.* to their dragon
Luke 1:9 Zach. his lot to *b. inc.*

BURNED.
Ex. 3:2 bush *b.* was not cons.
Deut. 9:15 the mount *b.* with fire
Jos. 7:25 *b.* them with fire
2 *Chr.* 31:25 forsaken me *b. inc.*
Esr. 1:10 king's anger *b.* in him
Ps. 39:3 while musing the fire *b.*
Is. 24:6 inhab. of the earth are *b.*
42:25 it *b.* him, laid it not to *b.*
Lam. 2:3 *b. ag. J.* like flaming
John 15:6 withered branches *b.*
Acts 19:19 books, and *b.* them
Rom. 1:27 *b.* in their lust
1 *Cor.* 13:3 th. I give body to *b.*
Heb. 6:8 whose end is to be *b.*
12:18 not come to mount that *b.*
Rev. 1:15 his feet as if they *b.*

BURNETH.
Ps. 46:9 *b.* chariot in the fire
83:14 as the fire *b.,* the wood
97:3 a fire *b.* up his enemies
Is. 9:18 wickedness *b.,* as the fire
44:16 he *b.* part thereof in fire
62:1 salvation as a lamp that *b.*
61:2 as when inciting fire *b.*
67:3 these are a fire *b.* all day
65:5 *b. incense* as if he blessed
Jer. 48:45 him that *b. incense*
Joel 2:3 behind them a flame *b.*
Rev. 21:8 lake which *b.* with fire

BURNING.
Gen. 15:17 a *b.* lamp passed bet.
Lev. 26:16 will appoint *b. ague*
Deut. 28:22 with extreme *b.*
32:24 be devoured with *b. heat*
Job 41:19 out of mo. go *b. lamps*
Ps. 140:10 *b.* coals fall upon them
Prov. 10:27 in his lips as *b.* fire
26:21 as coals up *b.,* coals
21 *b.* lips and a wicked heart
Is. 34:27 name of L. com. far, *b.*
31:9 land shall become *b.* pitch
Jer. 23:9 his word was as a fire *b.*
Ezek. 1:13 appearance like *b. c.*
Dan. 3:6 cast into *b.* furnace, 11
7:9 and his wheels were as *b. f.*
Luke 12:35 loins girded, lights *b.*
John 5:35 John *b.* and shin. light
Rev. 4:5 lamps *b.* before throne
8:8 great mountain *b.* with fire
10 there fell a great star *b.*
19:20 cast alive into a lake *b.*

BURNING, Substantive.
Ex. 21:25 *b.* for *b.* wound for w.
Lev. 10:6 bewail *b.* which Lord
Deut. 29:23 brimstone, salt, *b.*
2 *Chr.* 16:11 great *b.* for him
21:19 people made no *b.* like *b.*
Is. 3:24 be *b.* instead of beauty
4:4 purged Jeru. by spirit of *b.*
9:5 this shall be with *b.,* and *f.*
10:16 under his glory kindle *b.*
33:14 people as the *b.* of lime
Amos 4:11 a firebrand out of *b.*
Rev. 18:9 see smoke of her *b.*

BURNINGS.
Is. 33:14 dwell with everla. *b. ?*
Jer. 34:5 with *b.* of thy fathers

BURNISHED.
Ezek. 1:7 like color of *b.* brass

BURNT.
Gen. 38:24 let her be *b.*
Ex. 3:3 why the bush is not *b.*
Deut. 32:24 be *b.* with hunger
1 *K.* 13:2 men's bones be *b.*
15:13 *b.* her idol, 2 *Chr.* 15:16
2 *K.* 23:16 out of sepul. *b.* them
25:9 *b.* house of the L. 2 *Chr.*
36:19 ; *Jer.* 52:13
Job 30:30 my bones are *b.*
Ps. 102:3 my bones *b.* as hearth
Prov. 6:27 his clothes not be *b. ?*
28 and his feet not be *b. ?*
Jer. 2:15 cities *b.* ; 6:29 believers *b.*
36:28 in the roll Jehoiakim *b.*
51:25 make thee a *b.* mountain
Ezek. 20:17 all faces be *b.* therein
24:10 and let the bones be *b.*
Joel 1:19 the flame *b.* all the trees
Amos 2:1 bec. he *b.* bones of k.
Nah. 1:5 earth is *b.* at his pres.
1 *Cor.* 3:15 man's work be *b.*
Heb. 13:11 *b.* without the camp

BURNT joined with fire.
Lev. 6:30 sin-offer. *b.* in the fire
20:14 if a man take a wife and
her mother, shall be *b. w. f.*
21:9 if daughter of any priest
pro. herself, be *b. with fire*

BUR
Num. 11:1 *fi.* of L. *b.* 3
Deut. 4:11 mountain *b.* with fire
12:31 name and *b.* they *b.* in fire
Jos. 7:15 be taken with accursed
thing be *b.* with fire
Jud. 15:6 *b.* her and fath. with *fi.*
14 cords bec. as flax *b.* with *fi.*
2 *Sam.* 23:7 shall be *b.* with fire
1 *K.* 16:18 *b.* king's house with *f.*
2 *K.* 1:14 fire *b.* up two captains
17:31 Seph. *b.* children in fire
23:11 *b.* chariots of sun with *fire*
25:9 great man's house *b. w. f.*
1 *Chr.* 14:12 gods were *b.* with fi.
2 *Chr.* 28:3 A. *b.* his child. in *fi.*
Neh. 1:3 gates *b.* with *fi.* 2:17
Ps. 80:16 it is *b.* with fire
Is. 1:7 cities are *b.* with *fire*
43:2 walkest thr. fire not be *b.*
64:11 house is *b.* with *fire*
Jer. 38:17 city not be *b.* with *fi.*
49:2 her dau. shall be *b.* with *fi.*
51:32 reeds may have *b.* with *fi.*
58 high gates be *b.* with *fire*
Rev. 18:8 utterly *b.* with *fire*

BURNT Incense.
Ex. 40:27 he *b.* sweet *incense*
1 *K.* 9:25 Solomon *b. i.* upon alt.
12:33 Jerob. offered, and *b. i.*
22:43 people yet *b. i.* 2 *K.* 12:3;
14:4; 15:4, 35
2 *Chr.* 29:7 and have not *b. i.*
Is. 65:7 *b. i.* on the mountains
Jer. 18:15 my people *b. i.*
44:15 that their wives had *b. i.*
Hos. 2:13 she *b. i.* to them
11:2 and *b. i.* to graven images

BURNT-OFFERING.
Gen. 22:7 where is *b.* for a *b.-o. ?*
8 G. will provide lamb for *b.-o.*
Lev. 6:9 law of *b.-o.* 7:37
9:2 ram for *b.-o.* 16:3, 5; 23:18
Num. 7:15 one lamb for *b.-o.* 21
to 81; *Ezek.* 45:15
23:3 stand by thy *b.-o.* 15
28:10 the *b.-o.* of every sabbath
Jos. 22:26 altar not for *b.-o.*
Jud. 13:23 not have rec. a *b.-o.*
1 *Sam.* 7:10 as S. was off. *b.-o.*
13:12 forced myself and off. *b.-o.*
2 *K.* 3:27 offered him for a *b.-o.*
1 *Chr.* 7:1 fire consumed the *b.-o.*
29:24 the *b.-o.* sh. be made
Ps. 40:6 *b.-o.* hast thou not req.
51:16 delightest not in *b.-o.*
19 pl. with *b.-o.* whole *b.-o.*
Is. 40:16 nor beasts th. for *b.-o.*
61:8 L. hate robbery for *b.-o.*
Ezek. 46:13 daily prepare a *b.-o.*

Continual BURNT-OFFERING.
Ex. 29:42 a con. *b.-o. Num.* 28:3,
6, 10, 15, 21, 31 ; 20:11, 16, 19,
24 ; *Ezr.* 3:5 ; *Neh.* 10:33 ;
Ezek. 46:15

Offer BURNT-OFFERING.
Gen. 22:2 take L. *o.* for *b.-o.*
Jud. 11:31 *o.* it up for *b.-o.*
13:16 *b.-o.* offer it to the Lord
1 *Sam.* 6:14 *offer* kine for a *b.-o.*
7:9 *off.* sucking lamb for *b.-o.*
2 *Chr.* 29:27 Hez. com. to *o. b.-o.*
Job 42:8 *o.* for yourselves a *b.-o.*

BURNT-OFFERINGS.
Gen. 8:20 N. offered *b.-o.* on altar
Num. 10:10 trumpets over *b.-o.*
Deut. 12:6 delight in *b.-o.*
1 *K.* 3:15 Solomon offered *b.-o.*
2 *Chr.* 2:1 *b.* a house for *b.-o.*
29:31 not slay all the *b.-o.*
35:11 hasted in offering *b.-o.*
Ezr. 6:9 have need for *b.-o.*
Job 1:5 *o.* acc. to num. to num.
Ps. 50:8 not re. thee for *b.-o.*
66:13 into thy house with *b.-o.*
Is. 1:11 full of *b.-o.* of rams
43:23 small cattle of thy *b.-o.*
56:7 *b.-o.* shall be accepted
Jer. 6:20 *b.-o.* are not acceptable
7:21 put your *b.-o.* to your sacri.
17:26 from south bringing *b.-o.*
19:5 burn sons for *b.-o.* to Baal
Hos. 6:6 knowl. of G. more *b.-o.*
Mic. 6:6 before him with *b.-o. ?*
Mark 12:33 to love neighbor is
more than *b.-o.*
Heb. 10:6 in *b.-o.* for sin

Offer BURNT-OFFERINGS.
2 *Sam.* 24:24 n. *o.* of that cost
me nothing, 1 *Chr.* 21:24
1 *K.* 3:4 1000 *b.-o.* did Solomon *of*
Jer. 33:18 want man to *o. b.-o.*
Amos 5:22 ye *offer* me *b.-o.*

BURNT-SACRIFICE.
Num. 23:6 he stood by his *b.-s.*

BUT
Deut. 33:10 shall put whole *b.-s.*
2 *Sam.* 24:22 oxen for *b.-s.*
1 *K.* 18:38 fire fell and c. *b.-s.*
Ps. 20:3 accept thy *b.-s.*

BURNT-SACRIFICES.
1 *Chr.* 23:31 to offer all *b.-s.*
2 *Chr.* 13:11 morn. and eve. *b.-s.*
Ps. 66:15 I will offer *b.-s.*

BURST up.
Jud. 15:5 foxes *b.* up the shocks
2 *K.* 1:14 fire *b.* up two captains
Job 1:16 fire of God *b. up* sheep
Ps. 74:8 have *b. up* synagogue
106:18 flame *b. up* the wicked
Jer. 9:10 *b. up* none can pass, 12
Mat. 22:7 king *b. up* their city
2 *Pet.* 3:10 earth and w. be *b. up*
Rev. 8:7 third part of trees and
all green grass was *b. up*
Job 32:19 I am ready to *b.* like
Prov. 3:10 *b.* with new wine
Jer. 2:20 I have *b.* thy bands,
5:5; 30:8; *Nah.* 1:13
Acts 1:18 he *b.* asunder in midst

BURSTING.
Is. 30:14 in the *b.* of it a sherd

BURY.
Gen. 23:4 *b.* my d.; 6 *b.* dead, 11:15
47:29 *b.* me not in Egypt, 49:29
50:5 let me go and *b.* my father
6 go up and *b.* thy father, 7
13:26 old proph. came to *b.* him
14:18 Israel shall *b.* him
Ex. 9:10 shall be none to *b.* her
31 this cursed woman *b.* her
35 went to *b.* her
Jer. 7:32 shall *b.* in Tophet, 19:11
14:16 shall have none to *b.* them
Ezek. 39:11 there shall they *b. G.*
13 all the people shall *b.* them
Hos. 9:6 Memphis shall *b.* them
Mat. 8:21 go *b.* father, *Lu.* 9:59
22 dead *b.* their dead, *Lu.* 9:60
27:7 potter's field, to *b.* strang.
John 19:40 manner of J. is to *b.*

BURYING.
Gen. 23:4 *b.* of. *b.* 49:30; 50:13
2 *K.* 13:21 as they were *b.*
Ezek. 39:12 sev. mon. *b.* of them
Mark 14:8 anoint my body to *b.*
John 12:7 against my *b.* she kept

BUSH, ES.
Ex. 3:2 in the *b. Acts* 7:30
4 God called to him out of *b.*
Job 30:4 cut mallows by the *b.*
7 among the *b.* they brayed
Is. 7:19 and rest upon all *b.*
Mark 12:26 have G. in God spake
Luke 6:44 nor of bramble-*b.*
20:37 deaf r. Moses showed at *b.*
Acts 7:35 angel which app. in *b.*

BUSHEL.
Mat. 5:15 a candle and put it un-
der a *b. Mark* 4:21; *Lu.* 11:33

BUSHY.
Cant. 5:11 his locks are *b.*

BUSINESS.
Gen. 39:11 J. went to do his *b.*
Deut. 24:5 nor be charged with *b.*
Jos. 2:14 utter not this our *b.*
Jud. 18:7 had no *b.* with any, 28
Neh. 11:16 over outward *b.*
13:8 let no man know of the *b.*
1 *Chr.* 13:10 wait on their *b.*
23:31 in *b.* of the ambassadors
Neh. 13:30 every one to *b.* his
Job 3:9 that have charge of *b.*
Ps. 107:23 do *b.* in great waters
Prov. 22:29 a man dilig. in his *b.*
Ec. 5:3 through mult. of *b.*
8:16 application to *b.* on earth
Dan. 8:27 I did the king's *b.*
Luke 2:49 about my Father's *b.*
Acts 6:3 may appoint over this *b.*
Rom. 12:11 not slothful in *b.*
1 *Thes.* 4:11 to do your own *b.*

BUSY, IED.
1 *K.* 20:40 as thy serv. was *busy*
2 *Chr.* 35:14 priests of Aar. *b.*

BUSYBODY, IES.
1 *Pet.* 4:15 let none suffer as a *b.*

BUTLER.
Gen. 40:9 *b.* told dream to Jos.
21 restored the chief *b.* to his
41:9 *b.* said, I remem. my faults

BUT
Deut. 33:10 shall put whole *b.-s.*
2 *Sam.* 24:22 oxen for *b.-s.*
1 *K.* 18:38 fire fell and c. *b.-s.*
Ps. 20:3 accept thy *b.-s.*

BUTLERSHIP.
1 *Chr.* 28:31 to offer all *b.-s.*

CAK
BUTTER.
Gen. 18:8 Abra. took *b.* and milk
Deut. 32:14 *b.* of kine
Jud. 5:25 bro. *b.* in lordly dish
2 *Sam.* 17:29 Barzillai brought *b.*
Job 20:17 brooks of honey and *b.*
23:6 I washed my steps with *b.*
Ps. 55:21 smoother than *b.*
Prov. 30:33 churn. of milk bri. *b.*
Is. 7:15 *b.* shall he eat, 22

BUTTOCKS.
2 *Sam.* 10:4 garm. to *b.* 1 *Ch.* 19:4
Is. 20:4 *b.* uncov. to shame of E.

BUY.
Gen. 42:7 fr. Can. to *b.* food, 43:20
47:19 *b.* us and our land
Lev. 25:44 shall *b.* bondmen, 45
Deut. 2:6 ye shall *b.* meat
28:68 and no man shall *b. you*
Ruth 4:5 must *b.* it also of Ruth
2 *Sam.* 24:21 D. said, to *b.* the
thresh.-floor, 24; 1 *Chr.* 21:24
Neh. 10:31 not *b.* it on sabbath
Is. 55:1 *b.* eat, *b.* wine and milk
Jer. 32:7 *b.* my field in Anathoth
44 men shall *b.* fields for money
Mat. 14:15 *b.* victuals, *Mark* 6:36
25:9 go to them that sell, and *b.*
10 went to *b. bridegroom* came
Mark 6:37 sh. we *b.* 200 p. worth
Luke 9:13 *b.* meat for this peo.
22:36 let him sell garm. and *b.*
John 4:8 were gone to *b.* meat
6:5 whence shall we *b.* bread
13 things we have need of
1 *Cor.* 7:30 *b.* as though they pos.
Jam. 4:13 *b.* and sell and get gain
Rev. 3:18 to *b.* of me gold tried
13:17 no man might *b.* or sell

BUY corn.
Gen. 41:57 all came to Jos. to *b. c.*
42:3 Joseph's brethren to *b. c.*
Neh. 5:3 mort. our lands to *b. c.*

BUY poor.
Amos 8:6 may *b.* the *poor* for sil.

BUY truth.
Prov. 23:23 *b. truth,* sell it not

BUYER.
Prov. 20:14 it is naught, saith *b.*
Is. 24:2 as with the *b.* so the *s.*
Ezek. 7:12 let not *b.* rejoice, nor

BUYEST.
Lev. 25:14 and if thou *b.* aught
Ruth 4:5 day *b.* field of Naomi

BUYETH.
Prov. 31:16 consider. field, *b.* it
Mat. 13:44 he selleth all, *b.* field
Rev. 18:11 no man *b.* her mer.

BUZ.
Gen. 22:21 M. bare to Nahor B.
1 *Chr.* 5:14 Jahdo, the son of B
Jer. 25:23 B. to drink the cup

BUZI.
Ezek. 1:3

BUZITE.
Job 32:2, 6

BY and **BY.**
Mat. 13:21 *b. and b.* he is off.
Mark 6:25 give me *b. and b.* head
Luke 17:7 *b. and b.* sit down
21:9 the end is not *b. and b.*

BY-WAYS.
Jud. 5:6 walked through *b.-w.*

BY-WORD.
Deut. 28:37 a *b.* among nations
1 *K.* 9:7 be *b.* among all people
2 *Chr.* 7:20 make this house a *b.*
Job 17:6 made me a *b.* of the
30:9 yea I am their *b.*
Ps. 44:14 a *b.* among heathen

C.

CABINS.
Jer. 37:16 when J. entered into c.

CARUL. 1 *K.* 9:13.

CAGE.
Jer. 5:27 as a *c.* is full of birds
Rev. 18:2 *c.* of every uncl. bird

CAIAPHAS.
Mat. 26:3, 7; *John*
11:49; 18:14, 28.

CAIN.
Gen. 4:5, 15, 25; *Jos.* 15:57.
Heb. 11:4 excel. sacrifice than C.
1 *John* 3:12 not as C. who was of
Jude 11 gone in the way of C.

CAINAN.
Luke 3:36 the son of C. 37

CAKE.
Lev. 8:26 bake twelve c., thereof
Jud. 7:13 a c. tumbled into host
2 *Sam.* 6:19 D. dealt to each a c.

CAL

2 *Sam.* 13:6 Tam. m. couple of *c.*
1 *K.* 17:19 I have not a *c.*
19:6 there was a *c.* baken
Ezek. 4:12 shalt eat it as barley *c.*
Hos. 7:8 Ephr. is a *c.* not turned
See FIGS, UNLEAVENED.

CALAH. *Gen.* 10:12.

CALAMITY, IES.
Deut. 32:35 their *c.* is at hand
2 *Sam.* 22:19 day of *c. Ps.* 18:18
Job 6:2 my *c.* laid in balances
30:13 they set forward my *c.*
Ps. 57:1 until these *c.* be overp.
141:5 my prayer be in their *c.*
Prov. 1:26 I will laugh at your *c.*
6:15 his *c.* shall come suddenly
17:5 he glad at *c.* not be unpun.
19:13 foolish son is *c.* of father
24:22 *c.* shall rise suddenly
27:10 nor go to brother's h. in *c.*
Jer. 18:17 The back in day of *c.*
46:21 day of their *c.* was come
48:16 *c.* of Moab is near to come
49:8 bring *c.* of Esau upon him
32 bring their *c.* from all sides
Ezek. 35:5 shed blood of Israel by sword in day of their *c.*
Ob. 13 sub. in day of their *c.*

CALAMUS.
Ex. 30:23 sweet *c.* 250 shekels
Cant. 4:14 spikenard, saffron, *c.*
Ezek. 27:19 *c.* in market of Tyrus

CALDRON.
1 *Sam.* 2:14 he struck it into *c.*
Job 41:20 smoke, as out of a *c.*
Ezek. 11:3 this city is the *c.* 7
Mic. 3:3 chop them as flesh in *c.*

CALDRONS.
2 *Chr.* 35:13 offering sod in *c.*
Jer. 52:18 *c.* took they away, 19

CALEB.
Num. 13:6, 30; 14:6, 38; 34:19
Jos. 14:13 Josh. gave C. Hebron
15:14 C. drave sons of Anak, 16
1 *Sam.* 25:3 N. was of house of C.
30:14 south of C. burnt Ziklag
CALEB-EPHRATAH. 1 *Chr.* 2:24

CALF.
Gen. 18:7 Abraham fetched a *c.*
Ex. 32:20 Moses burnt *c.*
Deut. 9:16 made you a molten *c.*
Neh. 9:18; *Ps.* 106:19
Job 21:10 their cow casteth not *c.*
Ps. 29:6 maketh to skip like a *c.*
Is. 11:6 *c.* and young lion
27:10 there sh. *c.* feed and lie
Jer. 34:18 when cut *c.* in twain
Ezek. 1:7 their feet like *c.* foot
Hos. 8:5 thy *c.* O S. cast thee off
6 *c.* of Samaria shall be broken
Luke 15:23 bring hither fatted *c.*
27 killed fatted *c.* 30
Acts 7:41 make a *c.* in those days
Rev. 4:7 second beast like a *c.*

CALKERS.
Ezek. 27:9 ancients of Geb. thy *c.*
27 thy *c.* shall fall into seas

CALL.
Gen. 2:19 what A. would *c.* them
Num. 24:20 If the men *c.* thee
Deut. 4:7 God is in all we *c.* for
26 I *c.* heaven and earth to wit. ag. you, 30:19; 31:28
Jud. 21:13 to *c.* peaceably
1 *Sam.* 3:6 thou didst *c.* me, 8
1 *K.* 8:52 hearken in all they *c.*
18:24 *c.* ye on your gods
Job 5:1 *c.* now if any
13:22 *c.* I will answer, 14:15
Ps. 4:1 hear when I *c.* O God
3 the Lord will hear when I *c.*
14:4 who eat my pun. and not
20:9 let king hear us when we *c.*
49:11 *c.* lands after their names
77:6 I *c.* to rem. my song in n.
80:5 plen. In m. to all *c.* on thee
98:6 among them *c.* on name
102:2 when I *c.* answer me sp.
145:18 L. is nigh all that *c.*
Prov. 8:4 to you, O men, I *c.*
9:15 *c.* passengers who go right
31:28 her children *c.* her blessed
Is. 5:20 that *c.* evil good
45:3 *c.* thee by thy name
48:2 *c.* themselves of holy city
13 when I *c.* they stand up
58:5 wilt thou *c.* this a fast
13 *c.* the sabbath a delight
65:15 *c.* his serv. by ano. name
24 before they *c.* I will answer
Jer. 33:3 *c.* to me, I will ans. thee
Lam. 2:15 men *c.* perfection

Hos. 1. 4 L. said, *c.* his n. Jezreel
6 *c.* his name Lo-ruhamah
9 *c.* his name Lo-ammi
7:11 *c.* to Egypt, go to Assy.
Joel 1:14 *c.* a sol. assembly, 2:15
Jon. 1:6 sleeper *c.* on thy God
Zec. 3:10 *c.* ev. man his neighbor
Mal. 3:15 we *c.* the proud happy
Mat. 9:13 not come to *c.* righteous, *Mark* 2:17; *Luke* 5:32
22:3 servants to *c.* them bidden
43 D. in spirit *c.* him Lord
23:9 *c.* no man father on earth
Luke 6:46 why *c.* me Lord
14:13 makest feast *c.* the poor
John 13 13 ye *c.* me Master
Acts 9:14 all *c.* on thy name
16 *c.* over them had evil spi.
24:14 after way they *c.* heresy
Rom. 10:12 to all that *c.* on him
2 *Cor.* 1:23 I *c.* God for a record
2 *Tim.* 2:22 peace wi. th. *c.* on L.
Heb. 2:11 not asha. to *c.* them
10:32 *c.* to remem. former days
Jam. 5:14 let him *c.* the elders
1 *Pet.* 1:17 if ye *c.* on the Father
CALL on the name of the Lord,
Gen. 4:26 began men to *c.* on L.
1 *K.* 18:24 I will *c. L. Ps.* 116:17
2 *K.* 5:11 will come and *c.* on L.
1 *Chr.* 16:8 *c.* upon his name, *Ps.* 105:1; *Is.* 12:4
Joel 2:32 whosoever shall *c.* on *L. Acts* 2:21; *Rom.* 10:13
Zep. 3:9 they may all *c.* on L.
1 *Cor.* 1:2 in every place *c.* L.

Not CALL.
Ruth 1:20 *c.* me not N. *c.* me M.
Ru. 14:4 *c.* not upon the Lord
Is. 31:2 will not *c.* back his w.
Jer. 10:25 fury upon the families that *c.* not on thy name
Luke 14:12 *c.* not thy friends nor
John 15:15 I *c.* you not servants
Acts 10:15 *c.* not common, 11:9
28 not to *c.* any man common

Shall, or shall CALL.
Deut. 30:1 shalt *c.* them to mind
31:19 shalt *c.* people to mour.
Job 14:15 shalt *c.* I will answer
Ps. 50:4 shall *c.* to the heavens
72:17 nations s. *c.* him blessed
Is. 7:14 s. *c.* Immanu. *Mat.* 1:23
41:25 rising of sun shall be *c.*
44:5 s. *c.* himself by name of J.
7 and who, as I, shall *c.* and
55:5 shalt *c.* a nation
58:9 shalt *c.* and L. shall answer
60:14 shall *c.* thee city of Lord
18 shalt *c.* thy walls salvation
61:6 men s. *c.* you min. of our G.
62:12 shall *c.* them holy people
Jer. 3:17 s. *c.* Jor. throne of Lord
19 thou shalt *c.* me, my father
7:27 shalt *c.* to them, not answ.
Hos. 2:16 shalt *c.* me no more B.
Zec. 13:9 they shall *c.* I will hear
Mat. 1:4 s. *c.* them hord. of wick.
3:12 nations shall *c.* you blessed
Mat. 1:21 shalt *c.* his name Jesus
10:25 much more s. *c.* them
Luke 1:13 shalt *c.* his name John
48 generations s. *c.* me blessed
Acts 2:39 as many as the L. s. *c.*
Rom. 10:14 how s. they *c.* on him

Will CALL.
1 *Sam.* 12:17 I will *c.* to Lord.
2 *Sam.* 22:4 I will *c.* Lord, *Ps.* 18:3
Job 27:10 will hypocrite *c.* on G.
Ps. 55:16 I will *c.* on God, 86:7
88:18 quicken us. we will *c.*
116:3 to, I *c.* on him
Is. 22:20 that I *c.* my ser. E.
Jer. 1:15 I will *c.* fam. of north
Rom. 9:25 I w. *c.* them my peo.

CALL upon me.
Ps. 50:15 *c.* u. m. in d. of trouble
91:15 he shall *c.* upon me
Prov. 1:28 *c.* u. m. but I will
Jer. 29:12 then shall ye *c.* u. m.

CALLED.
Gen. 11:9 name of it *c.* Babel
21:17 *c.* to Hagar out of heaven
22:11 *c.* to Abrah. out of heaven
3x:10 not be *c.* any more Jacob
18 his father *c.* him Benjamin
Ex. 8:8 Pharaoh *c.* for Moses, 25 ; 9:27; 10:16, 24 ; 12:31
Deut. 5:1 Moses *c.* all Israel, 29:2
15:2 it is *c.* the Lord's release
28:10 thou art *c.* by name of L.
Jud. 14:15 B. wife, hang us *c.* us
15:17 east away jawb. *c.* place

Jud. 15:18 w. athirst, and *c.* on L.
16:28 Samson *c.* to the Lord
1 *Sam.* 3:9 now *c.* a proph. was *c.*
2 *Sam.* 6:2 name is *c.* by name
12:28 city be *c.* after my name
1 *K.* 1:9 Adonijah *c.* broth. 19, 25
18:3 Ahab *c.* Obadiah the gov.
26 they *c.* on the name of Baal
Ezr. 6:10 Jabez *c.* on God
13:6 whose name is *c.* on it
21:36 David *c.* on Lord
Est. 2:14 except that she were *c.*
4:11 I have not been *c.* to come
Ps. 53:4 they have not *c.* on G.
79:6 kingd. not *c.* on thy name
Is. 43:22 hast not *c.* on me, O J.
48:1 ye, *c.* by the name of Israel
13 O Jacob, my *c.*
51:2 be *c.* trees of righteousness
Lam. 1:16 Jesus who is *c.* Christ
Ezek. 30:29 name is *c.* Bamah
Dan. 5:12 now let Daniel be *c.*
Mat. 1:16 Jesus who is *c.* Christ
13:55 is not his mother *c.* Mary?
18:2 *c.* a little child unto him
20:16 many be *c.* few cho. 22:14
32 Jesus stood still and *c.* them
27:17 shall I release J. *c.* C. 22
Mark 10:49 J. com. him to be *c.*
14:72 P. *c.* to mind word J. said
Luke 1:61 none of thy kind. is *c.*
62 how he would have him *c.*
15:19 worthy to be *c.* thy son, 21
19:15 he com. servants to be *c.*
23:33 place that is *c.* Calvary
John 1:48 before Philip *c.* thee I
4:35 cometh which is *c.* Christ
9:11 a man *c.* Jesus made clay
Acts 9:11 go into str. *c.* Straight
11:26 disciples first *c.* Christians
13:7 *c.* for Barnabas and Saul
18:17 on whom my name is *c.*
19:40 *c.* in quest. for this day's
23:6 I am *c.* in question, 24:21
18 Paul the prisoner *c.* me
Rom. 1:1 P. *c.* to be apos. 1 *Cor.* 1:1
6 are ye also the *c.* of Jesus
7 *c.* to be saints, 1 *Cor.* 1:2
8:17 them art *c.* a Jew
8:29 the *c.* acc. to his purpose
1 *Cor.* 1:9 were *c.* to fellowship
24 *c.* both Jews and Greeks
26 not many noble are *c.*
5:11 *c.* a brother be a fornicator
7:18 *c.* being circum.? is any *c.*
21 art thou *c.* being a servant?
22 wherein he is *c.*
Gal. 1:6 removed from him *c.* you
5:13 ye have been *c.* to liberty
Eph. 2:11 *c.* uncircum. by that *c.*
4:1 vocation wherew. ye are *c.*
4 even as ye are *c.* in one hope
Col. 3:13 to the which ye are *c.*
2 *Thes.* 2:4 exalteth above all *c.*
1 *Tim.* 6:12 *c.* life, wher. art *c.*
20 science falsely so *c.*
2 *Tim.* 1:9 *c.* us with a holy *c.*
Heb. 3:13 while it is *c.* to-day
9:15 they *c.* might rec. promise
11:16 not ash. to be *c.* their God
Jam. 2:7 name by wh. ye are *c.*
1 *Pet.* 2:9 *c.* you out of darkness
21 even hereunto were ye *c.*
3:9 that ye are thereunto *c.*
2 *Pet.* 1:3 that hath *c.* us to glory
1 *John* 3:1 sh. be *c.* the sons of G.
Jude 1 preserved in J. Ch. and *c.*
Rev. 8:11 star is *c.* Wormwood
11:8 city spiritually *c.* Sodom
17:14 they with him are *c.*
19:9 blessed are *c.* to mar. sup.

CALLED, joined with God or Lord.
Gen. 1:5 God *c.* the light Day
5:2 and *c.* their name Adam
Ex. 3:4 God *c.* to him
20 L. *c.* Moses to top of mount
Num. 12:5 L. *c.* Aaron and Mir.
1 *Sam.* 3:4 L. *c.* Samuel, 6, 8, 10
Ps. 50:1 *c.* earth from the rising
Is. 41:2 Lord *c.* him to his foot
42:6 I have *c.* thee in righteous.
49:1 L. hath *c.* me
54:6 *c.* thee as a woman fors.
Ezek. 38:21 sword ag. him in mt.
Hos. 11:1 out of Egypt *c.* my son
Amos 7:4 God *c.* to contend
Acts 16:10 gath. that Lord *c.* us
1 *Cor.* 7:15 G. hath *c.* us to peace
17 L. hath *c.* every one, so let
Gal. 1:15 who *c.* me by grace
1 *Thes.* 2:12 *c.* you to his kingd.
4:7 hath not *c.* us to unclean.
2 *Thes.* 2:14 God *c.* you

CAL

1 *Tim.* 1:9 *c.* us with a holy call.
Heb. 5:4 *c.* of God as was Aaron
10 *c.* of God a high-priest after
1 *Pet.* 5:10 G. who hath *c.* us

He CALLED.
Gen. 26:18 *c.* names as his *f. c.*
Ex. 3:10 *he c.* his name Israel
Ex. 34:16 *c.* to M. out of cloud
2 *K.* 4:36 *c.* to Gehazi, so *he c.*
Ps. 105:16 *he c.* for a famine on
Lam. 1:15 *c.* an assembly
Mat. 10:1 *c.* twelve; 15:10 *mult.*
Mark 1:20 *he c.* them
13:12 Jesus saw her, *he c.*
20:32 Jesus *c.* them
Acts 9:41 had *c.* saints and wid.
10:23 *c.* *he* them in, and lodged
23:23 *he c.* unto him two centur.
Rom. 8:30 *he* also *c.* whom he *c.*
9:24 even us whom *he* hath *c.*
1 *Pet.* 1:15 hath *c.* you is holy
See CALLED the name.

I CALLED, or I have CALLED.
Num. 24:10 I *c.* thee to curse
1 *Sam.* 3:5 El said, I *c.* not. 6
28:15 therefore I have *c.* thee
2 *Sam.* 22:7 in my distress I *c.*
Ps. 18:6; 118:5
Job 9:16 if I had *c.* and he answ.
19:16 I *c.* my servant, no answ.
Pr. 17:6 I have *c.* on thee, for
31:17 not be ashamed, I have *c.*
88:9 I have *c.* daily upon thee
116:4 then *c.* I on name of Lord
Prov. 1:24 I have *c.* and ye ref.
Cant. 5:6 I *c.* him
Is. 13:3 I have *c.* my mighty
41:9 I have *c.* thee from chief
43:1 I *c.* thee by thy name, 45:4
48:15 yea, I have *c.* him
50:2 I *c.* was there none to ans.
51:2 for I *c.* him alone
65:12 I *c.* ye did not a. *Jer.* 7:13
66:4 when I *c.* none did answer
Jer. 35:17 I have *c.* to them, but
Lam. 1:19 I *c.* for my lovers, but
3:55 I *c.* out of the low dungeon
57 drewest near in day I *c.* on
Hos. 11:1 then I *c.* my son out of Egypt. *Mat.* 2:15
Zec. 11:7 one to B., other I *c.*
John 15:15 I have *c.* my friends
Acts 13:2 work wh. I have *c.* them
28:20 have I *c.* for you, to see

CALLED by my name.
2 *Chr.* 7:14 if my people which are *c. by my name* humble
Is. 43:7 even every one *c.* n.
Jer. 7:10 this house *c. b. m. name*, 11, 14, 30 ; 32:34 ; 34:15
25:29 evil on city *c. by n.*
Amos 9:12 remnant of heath. *c. n.*

CALLED by thy name.
1 *K.* 8:43 house *c. b. t. n.* 2 *Chr.* 6:33
Is. 4:1 let us be *c. by t. n.* to take
43:1 I have *c.* thee *by t. n.* 45:4
63:19 were not *c. by thy name*
Jer. 14:9 we are *c. by t. n.*
15:16 am *c. by t. n.* O L. G. of hosts
Dan. 9:18 the city *c. by thy n.*
19 for thy people are *c. n.*

CALLED his name.
Gen. 35:10 *c.* n. Is.; 18 Benoni
4:20 *c.* h. name Enos
4:17 *c.* Jabez; 7:16 Beriah; 23 Ber.
Mat. 1:25 he *c.* his name Jesus
Rev. 19:13 n. is *c.* the word of G.

Sent and CALLED.
Acts 20:17 s. to Ephesus, elders

Shall be CALLED.
Gen. 2:23 *c.* Woman, because
17:5 name *shall be c.* Abraham
21:12 In Isaac *shall thy seed be c. Rom.* 9:7; *Heb.* 11:18
32:28 *shall be c.* no more Jacob
48:6 issue s. *c.* after their broth.
Prov. 16:21 wise in heart *s. c.*
24:8 deviseth evil s. *c.* mischiev.
Is. 4:3 remains. in Jer. *s. c.* holy
9:6 his name *s. be c.* Wonderful
23:5 no more *shall be c.* liberal
32:5 be *c.* the way of holiness
54:5 G. of whole earth *s. be c.*
56:7 *c.* a ho. of prayer, *Mat.* 21:13
Jer. 23:6 *s. c.* L. our righteousness
Zec. 8:3 J. *s. be c.* city of truth
Mat. 2:23 *shall be c.* a Nazarene
5:9 peacemakers *s. c.* the ch. of G.
19 s. *be c.* least in kingdom
Luke 1:32 s. *c.* Son of the Highest
35 holy thing s. *be c.* the Son
60 but *he shall be c.* John
2:23 every male *shall be c.* holy
Rom. 9:26 s. *c.* the children of G.

CRUDEN'S CONCORDANCE. 785

CAL

Shall be CALLED.
Is. 1:26 *s. c.* city of righteousness
47:1 *shalt be c.* no more tender
5 *c*, no more *be c.* a lady of k.
58:12 *t. be c.* repairer of the br.
62:2 *t. be c.* by a new name
4 *s. c.* Hephzi-bah, thy land B.
12 *s. be c.* Sought out, A city n.
Luke 1:76 *t. c.* proph. of Highest
John 1:42 thou *shalt bec.* Cephas

They CALLED.
Num. 25:2 *t. c.* people to sacrifice
Est. 9:26 *they c.* these days Pur.
Ps. 99:6 *t. c.* upon the Lord, and
Jer. 12:6 *t. c.* a multitude
30:17 bec. *t. c.* thee an outcast
Hos. 11:2 as *they c.* them, so they
7 *t. c.* them to Most High
Mat. 10:25 *t. c.* master Beelzebub
Luke 1:59 *t. c.* him Zacharias
John 8:19 *t. c.* parents of him
24 *c. they* man that was blind
Acts 4:18 *t. c.* com. not to speak
5:40 when *t.* had *c.* the apostles
14:12 *they c.* Barnabas Jupiter

Was CALLED.
Is. 48:8 *was c.* a transgressor
Luke 2:21 his name *was c.* Jesus
John 2:2 J. *w. c.* and his discip.
Acts 24:2 *w. c.* forth, Tertullus
1 *Cor.* 7:20 calling wh. he *w. c.*
Heb. 11:8 A. wh. he *w. c.* obeyed
Jam. 2:23 *w. c.* the friend of God
Rev. 19:11 sat on him *w. c.* faith.

CALLEDST, EST.
Jud. 8:1 *c.* us not when wentest
1 *Sam.* 3:5 here am I, thou *c.* me
Ps. 81:7 thou *c.* in trouble
Mat. 19:17 *w. c.* thou me good?
Mark 10:18; *Luke* 18:19

CALLETH.
1 *K.* 8:43 do accor. to all stranger
c. to thee for, 2 *Chr.* 6:33
Job 12:4 *c.* on God, and he ans.
Ps. 42:7 deep *c.* unto deep
147:4 *c.* them, *Is.* 40:26
Prov. 18:6 mouth *c.* for strokes
Is. 21:11 he *c.* to me out of Seir
59:4 none *c.* for justice, nor any
64:7 none that *c.* on thy name
Hos. 7:7 none that *c.* to me
Amos 5:8 *c.* for waters of sea, 9:6
Mat. 27:47 *c.* for E. *Mark* 15:35
Mark 3:13 *c.* to him whom he w.
6:7 *c.* to him the twelve
8:1 Jesus *c.* his disciples
10:49 arise, he *c.* thee
12:37 David *c.* him L. *Luke* 20:44
Lu. 15:6 he *c.* together his friends
9 *c.* her friends and neighbors
20:37 when he *c.* L. the G. of A.
John 10:3 *c.* his sheep by name
11:28 the Master *c.* for thee
Rom. 4:17 *c.* things which be not
9:11 election ns. stand of him *c.*
1 *Cor.* 12:3 by Spirit *c.* Jesus
Gal. 5:8 not of him that *c.*
1 *Thes.* 5:24 faithful is he *c.* you
Rev. 2:20 *c.* herself a prophetess

CALLING, Substantive.
Is. 1:13 *c.* of assemblies I cannot
Ezek. 23:19 *c.* to rem. her youth
Rom. 11:29 *c.* of God without
1 *Cor.* 1:26 ye see your *c.* breth.
7:20 ev. man abide in same *c.*
Eph. 1:18 the hope of his *c.*
4:1 called in one hope of your *c.*
Phil. 3:14 the high *c.* of God
2 *Thes.* 1:11 worthy of this *c.*
2 *Tim.* 1:9 called us w. a holy *c.*
Heb. 3:1 partakers of heavenly *c.*
2 *Pet.* 1:10 your *c.* and election

CALLING, Participle.
Is. 41:4 *c.* gen. from beginning
46:11 *c.* ravenous bird from east
Mat. 11:16 *c.* to fell. *Luke* 7:32
Mark 11:21 P. *c.* to remembrance
Acts 7:59 stoned Stephen *c.* on G.
22:16 thy sins, *c.* on Lord
1 *Pet.* 3:6 S. obeyed A. *c.* him lord

CALM.
Ps. 107:29 maketh storm a *c.*
Jon. 1:11 sea may be *c.* unto us
12 cast me forth, so sea be *c.*
Mat. 8:26 *gr. c. Mark* 4:39; *Lu.* 8:24

CALNEH.
Gen. 10:10 Babel and C.
Amos 6:2 p.ss ye unto C. from

CALNO, *Is.* 10:9
CALVARY, *Luke* 23:33

CALVE, ED, ETH.
Job 21:10 their cow *c.* casteth n.
39:1 mark when hinds do *c.*
50

CAM

Ps. 27:9 make hinds to *c.*
Jer. 14:5 the hind *c.* in the field

CALVES.
1 *Sam.* 6:7 bring *c.* home
1 *K.* 12:28 king made 2 *c.* of gold
32 sacrificing to *c.* he had m.
2 *K.* 10:29 dep. not from gold. *c.*
17:16 ord. priests for the *c.*
Chr. 11:15 ord. priests for the *c.*
13:8 there be with you golden *c.*
Ps. 68:30 rebuke bulls with the *c.*
Hos. 10:5 because of *c.* of Beth.
13:2 that sacrifice kiss the *c.*
14:2 render the *c.* of our lips
Amos 6:4 eat *c.* out of the stall
Mal. 4:2 ye shall grow up as *c.*

CAME.
Gen. 27:35 brother *c. w.* subtilty
32:6 we *c.* to thy brother Esau
Num. 22:9 God *c.* to Balaam, 20
24:2 spirit of God *c.* upon him
Jud. 8:19; 1 *Sam.* 10:10
Deut. 33:2 Lord *c.* from Sinai
Jud. 13:10 man that *c.* other day
1 *Sam.* 2:27 *c.* a man of G. to Eli
4:1 word of Samuel *c.* to all Isr.
2 *Sam.* 22:13 every one that *c.*
1 *K.* 1:42 while he spake *Jon. c.*
4:34 *c.* of all people to hear Sol.
13:10 returned not by way that *c.*
2 *K.* 6:5 one the moss, *c.* he *s.*
10:21 all worshippers of Baal *c.*
17:28 one of priests *c.* to Bethel
10:33 by the way he *c.* return
24:3 at com. of Lord *c.* this on J.
1 *Chr.* 5:9 of Judah *c.* chief ruler
Chr. 11:14 Levites *c.* to Judah
14:14 fear of L. *c.* upon them
25:20 A. not hear, for it *c.* of G.
Est. 1:17 but Vashti *c.* not
Job 3:26 yet trouble *c.*
29:13 him ready to perish *c.*
30:26 I looked for good, evil *c.*
Ps. 18:6 my cry *c.* before him
27:2 when my foes *c.* upon me
78:31 wrath of G. *c.* upon them
88:17 they *c.* about me daily
105:19 until the time his *w. c.*
Ec. 5:15 to go as he *c.* 16
Is. 41:5 ends of earth were af. *c.*
Jer. 7:31 nor *c.* it into my mind,
19:5; 32:35
8:15 for peace, but no good *c.*
44:21 *c.* it not into his mind?
Ezek. 33:22 afore he that *c.* to me.
43:2 glory of G. *c.* from east
Dan. 4:28 all this *c.* on Nebuch.
Amos 5:1 ye know hear lam. of Is. *c.*
Hab. 3:3 G. *c.* from Teman, and
Mat. 8:1 in those days *c. J.* B.
9:1 and *c.* into his own city
Acts 9:3 as he *c.* n. Damascus

CAME nigh.
Mat. 15:29 Jesus *c. n.* to sea of G.
Mark 1:1 when they *c. n.* to J.
Luke 7:12 when he *c. n.* to gate

CAME near.
Ex. 14:20 *c. not n.* other all night
Deut. 1:22 ye *c. n.* to me, 5:23
Jos. 17:4 they *c. n.* bef. El. 21:1
1 *K.* 18:36 Elijah *c. n.* and said
Mat. 42:1 least to the greatest *c. n.*
Zep. 3:1; *Hag.* 1:1 Hag.
Zec. 7:4 *c. w. L.* of hosts, 8:1

CAME nigh.
Mat. 15:29 Jesus *c. n.* to sea of G.
Mark 11:1 when they *c. n.* to J.
Luke 7:12 when he *c. n.* to gate

CAME out.
Gen. 38:28 m. said this *c. o.* first
Ex. 13:5 remember day ye *c. o.* of
Num. 16:27 Dathan and Abiram *c. o.*
2 *Sam.* 6:20 Michal *c. o.* meet D.
18:4 people *c. out* by hundreds
Job 1:21 naked I *c. out* of womb
3:11 when I *c. out* of the belly
5:5 *as c. o.* of my lips
Mat. 8:34 whole city *c. o.*
12:44 return to m. house whence
Lu. ont, Luke 11:24
27:53 they *c. out* found Simon
53 *c. o.* of graves after his res.
Mark 7:31 wo. spirit *c. o.*; 9:26
9:7 a voice *c. out* of the cloud
Luke 1:21 he *c. o.* could not speak
4:35 *c. out* of him, hurt him not
John 16:27 because ye believed I
c. out from God
17:8 that I *c. out* from thee
19:34 forthwith *c. o.* blood
Acts 8:7 unclk. splr. *c. o.* of many
10:18 spirit *c. o.* in *J. c.* Christ
1 *Cor.* 14:36 word of G. *c.* from
Heb. 3:16 not all that *c. o.* of Eg.
Rev. 7:14 these *c. o.* of great trib.

CAME over.
Jos. 4:22 Is. *c. o.* on dry land
Mark 5:1 *c. over* to other side

CAME to pass.

CAM

Dan. 4:28 holy one *c. d.* from b.
Mic. 1:12 evil *c. down* from the L.
Mal. 17:9 as *c. d.* fr. m. *Mark* 9:9
John 3:13 he that *c. d.* fr. heav.
6:38 I *c. down* from heaven
41 bread which *c. d.* 51, 58
Acts 15:1 which *c. down* from J.

CAME forth.
Num. 11:20 *c. we f.* out of Eg. ?
Jud. 14:14 out of eater *c. f.* meat,
out of strong *c. f.* sweetness
2 *Sam.* 16:11 son which *c. f.* of
my bowels seeketh my life
2 *Chr.* 32:21 *c. f.* of his bowels
Prov. 7:15 *c.* I *forth* to meet thee
Ez. 5:15 as he *c. f.* naked
Jer. 20:18 *e.* I *f.* out of womb?
Zec. 10:4 of him *c. f.* the corner
Mark 1:38 for therefore *c. I f.*
John 16:28 I *c. f.* from the Father
19:5 J. *c. f.* wearing the crown

I CAME.
Gen. 30:30 thou hadst before *I c.*
1 *K.* 10:7 I believed not till *I c.*
half was not told, 2 *Chr.* 9:6
Is. 50:2 *I c.* was there no man?
Ezek. 3:15 *I c.* to them of capt.
Mat. 10:34 *I c.* not to send peace
Mark 2:17 *I c.* not to call, *Lu.* 5:32
John 8:14 I know whence *I c.*
42 *I c.* from G. nor *c. I* of mys.
12:27 for this cause *c. I* to h.
47 *I c.* not to judge the world
18:37 for this cause *c. I* into w.
Acts 10:29 *c. I*, as soon as sent f.
20:18 from first day *I c.* into A.
22:11 *I c.* into Damascus
1 *Cor.* 2:1 *I c.* not with excell.
2 *Cor.* 1:23 to spare you *I c.* not
2:3 when *I c.* I sh. have sorrow

CAME in.
Gen. 6:4 sons of God *c. in*
19:5 where men *c. in* to thee
38:18 Judah *c. in* unto her
2 *Sam.* 18:13 David went out and
c. in before the people, 16
2 *Chr.* 15:5 no p. to him that went
Est. 2:14 *c. in* to king no more
Jer. 37:4 Jer. *c. in* and went out
Mat. 22:10 k. *c. in* to see guests
Luke 1:28 angel *c. in* to Mary
7:45 since I *c.* it kissed my feet
Gal. 2:1 who *c. in* privily
1 *Chr.* 17:3 Nathan; 22:8 David
Jer. 1:2 *w. L. c.* to Jer.; 4; 2:1;
14:1; 29:30; 33:1, 19; *Dan.* 9:2
12:8 expressly to *Ezek.* 3:16
1 *K.* 1 Hosea; *Joel* 1:1 Joel
Jon. 1:1 Jon. 3:1; *Mic.* 1:1 Mic.
Zep. 1:1; *Hag.* 1:1 Hag.
Zec. 7:4 *c. w. L.* of hosts, 8:1

CAMEL.
Gen. 24:64 Reb. lighted off the *c.*
Lev. 11:4 not *c.* the *c. Deut.* 14:7
1 *Sam.* 15:3 slay infant, ox, and *c.*
Zec. 14:15 so be plague of *c.*
Mat. 19:24 is easier for a *c. Mark*
10:25; *Luke* 18:25
22:24 strain at a gnat, swallow *c.*

CAMELS.
Gen. 12:16 Abram had *c.*
24:19 draw water for thy *c.* 44
30:41 J. had much cattle, *c.*
31:17 J. set his sons *c.* furniture
Jud. 6:5 Midianites came with *c.*
7:12 their camels as *c.* on the s.
1 *Sam.* 27:9 David took away *c.*
30:17 save 400 which rode on *c.*
1 *K.* 10:2 to Jer. with *c. 2 Chr.* 9:1
Job 1:3 his subst. was 3,000 *c.*
17 Chaldeans fell upon the *c.*
42:12 he saw *a channel* of Eg.
Is. 21:7 saw a chariot of *c.*
30:6 treasures on bunches of *c.*
60:6 mult. of *c.* shall cover thee
Jer. 49:20 shall take their *c.*
Ezek. 25:5 Rabbah a stable for *c.*
3:4 ruin, *c. c.* ride, *Mark* 1:6

CAMEST.
Gen. 10:8 Hagar, whence *c.* thou
Num. 22:37 wherefore, thou not
Deut. 11:10 *nd, day c.* out of Eg.
Jud. 11:1 rem. day *c.* out of E.
17:28 why *c.* thou down hither

CRUDEN'S CONCORDANCE.

CAN
2 *Sam.* 15:20 whereas *c.* but yes.
1 *K.* 13:9 nor return by way *c.* 17
14 man of God that *c.* from J.?
2 *K.* 19:28 I will turn thee back
   by way thou *c. Is.* 37:29
Neh. 6:13 *c.* down, mount. flowed
Jer. 1:5 before thou *c.* forth out of
   the womb I sancti. thee
Ezek. 32:2 *c.* forth with thy rivers
Mat. 9:13 friend, how *c.* in hit.
John 6:25 Rabbi, when *c.* hither
16:30 we believe thou *c.* from G.
Acts 9:17 in the way as thou *c.*
CAMON. *Jud.* 10:5

CAMP.
Ex. 14:19 ang. of L. went bef. *c.*
32:17 a noise of war in *c.*
27 *c.* slay every man brother
33:6 proclaimed through the *c.*
Lev. 24:10 strove together in *c.*
Num. 4:5 when *c.* setteth forw.
11:1 con. in utmost parts of *c.*
26 Eld. and Med. prophes. in *c.*
Deut. 23:14 in midst of thy *c.*
Jos. 6:18 made *c.* of Isr. a curse
Jud. 13:25 spirit of God began to
   move Samson in the *c.*
21:8 none to the *c.* from Jabesh
1 *Sam.* 4:6 noise of shout in the *c.*
17:17 run to *c.* to thy brethren
2 *K.* 6:8 in such a place be my *c.*
7:7 left *c.* as it was, fled for life
8 when these lepers came to *c.*
19:35 angel of L. smote in *c.* of
   Assyr. 185,000, *Is.* 37:36
Ps. 78:28 let it fall in midst of *c.*
106:16 envied M. also in the *c.*
Ezek. 4:2 set the *c.* also against it
Joel 2:11 for his *c.* is very great
Rev. 20:9 compassed *c.* of saints

CAMP, Verb.
Is. 29:3 I will *c.* against thee
Jer. 50:29 bend the how *c.* ag. it
Nah. 3:17 *c.* in hedges in cold day

CAMPED.
Ex. 19:2 Israel *c.* before mount

Into the CAMP.
1 *Sam.* 4:7 God is come *into c.*

Out of the CAMP.
Ex. 19:17 M. brought people *o. c.*
Lev. 10:4 your brethren *out c.*
24:23 had cursed *out c.*
Num. 14:44 M. departed not *o. c.*
13:46 shall *c. o. c.* of Phil.
Heb. 13:11 beasts burnt *w. the c.*
13 go forth to him *w. the c.*

CAMPS.
Num. 10:2 trum. for journey of *c.*
Amos 4:10 stink of your *c.* come

CAMPHIRE.
Cant. 1:14 my beloved is as *c.*
4:13 thy plants an orchard of *c.*

CAN.
Mat. 27:65 as sure as you *c.*
John 15:4 no more *c.* ye except
Rom. 8:7 subject to law, nor *c.* be

How CAN.
John 3:9 said, h. *c.* these th. be?
Acts 8:31 h. *c.* I exc. some guide?

CANA.
John 2:1 marriage in C. 11
4:46 Jesus came again into C.
21:2 Thomas and Nath. of C.

CANAAN.
Gen. 9:18, 22, 25; 10:15; 28:1
Ex. 15:15 the inhabitants of C.
Jud. 3:1; 4:2, 23; 5:19
Ps. 106:38 to the idols of C.
135:11 smote all kingdoms of C.
Is. 19:18 speak language of C.
Zep. 2:5 C. I will destroy thee
Mat. 15:22 a woman of C. cried

Land of CANAAN.
Gen. 12:5 to go into *land of* C.

CANAANITE.
Gen. 12:6; 15:21; 24:3; 34:30
Ex. 23:28 drive out C. 33:2; 34:11
Num. 21:3 deliv. up C. *Neh.* 9:24
Mat. 10:4 Simon the C. *Mark* 3:18

CANAANITES. 1 *Chr.* 2:3
CANDACE. *Acts* 8:27

CANDLE.
Job 18:6 his *c.* be put out
21:17 *c.* of wicked put out?
29:3 his *c.* shined on my head
Ps. 18:28 thou wilt light my *c.*
Prov. 20:27 spirit of man is *c.*
24:20 *c.* of wicked be put out
31:18 *c.* goeth not out by night
Jer. 25:10 from them light of *c.*
Mat. 5:15 put *c.* under a bushel,
   Mark 4:21; *Luke* 8:16; 11:33
Luke 11:36 bright shining of *c.*
15:8 a *c.* and sweep the house
Rev. 18:23 *c.* shine no more
22:5 need no *c.* nor light of sun

CANDLES.
Zep. 1:12 will search Jer. with *c.*

CANDLESTICK.
Ex. 25:31 make *c.* 37:17; *Num.* 8:4
40:24 put *c.* in tent of congress.
Lev. 24:4 lamps on *c.* continually
Num. 3:31 their charge shall be *c.*
2 *K.* 4:10 let us set for him a *c.*
1 *Chr.* 28:15 gold for every *c.*
2 *Chr.* 13:11 set they in order *c.*
Dan. 5:5 wrote over ag. the *c.*
Zec. 4:2 behold a *c.* all of gold
11 olive-trees on right side of *c.*
Mat. 5:15 on a *c.* it giveth
   light to all. *Luke* 8:16; 11:33
Mark 4:21 not be set on *c.?*
Heb. 9:2 first wherein was the *c.*
Rev. 2:5 else I will remove thy *c.*

CANDLESTICKS.
1 *K.* 7:49 *c.* of p. gold, 2 *Chr.* 4:7
Jer. 52:19 he took away the *c.*
Rev. 1:14 two *c.* standing bef. G.
See SEVEN.

CANE.
Is. 43:24 brought me no sweet *c.*
Jer. 6:20 *c.* from far country

CANKER, ED.
2 *Tim.* 2:17 will eat as *c.*
Jam. 5:3 your gold and silver is *c.*

CANKER-WORM.
Joel 1:4 *c.* eat, and *c.-w.* left. 2:25
Nah. 3:15 like *c.-w.* make thyself
   many as the *c.-w.*
16 *c.-w.* spoileth and fleeth

CANNOT.
Is. 1:13 calling of assemblies I *c.*
Jer. 14:6 *c.* I do with you
Luke 16:26 from hence to you *c.*

CANST.
Mat. 8:2 thou *c.* make me clean
Mark 9:22 if thou *c.* do any thing

CAPERNAUM. *Mat.* 4:13; 8:5;
11:23; 17:24; *Luke* 4:23; 10:15;
John 2:12; 4:46; 6:17, 24, 59
CAPITOL. *Amos* 9:1; *Amos* 3:7

CAPPADOCIA.
Acts 2:9 dwellers in C. we hear
1 *Pet.* 1:1 strangers throughout C.

CAPTAIN.
Gen. 37:36 sold him to Potiph. *c.*
40:4 *c.* charged Jos. with them
Num. 14:4 make a *c. Neh.* 9:17
Jos. 5:14 as *c.* of host of the L.
15 *c.* of the L. host said to Jos.
Jud. 4:2 *c.* of Jabin's host was
   Sisera, 7; 1 *Sam.* 12:9
11:6 said to Jephthah, be our *c.*
11 made him *c.* over them
1 *Sam.* 9:16 anoint him *c.* 10:1
13:14 Lord com. him to be *c.*
17:18 carry th. ten cheeses to *c.*
22:2 David became *c.* over them
2 *Sam.* 5:2 shalt be *c.* over Israel
8 he shall be c. 1 *Chr.* 11:6
10:18 if thon he not *c.* of the thr.
23:19 Abishai was therefore *c.*
2 *K.* 16:16 Isr. made Omri *c.* king
1 *Chr.* 11:6 king sent a *c.* with fifty
4:13 wouldest be spo. for to *c.?*
5:1 Naaman *c.* of host of Syria
9:5 an errand to thee, O *c.*
15:25 Pekah a *c.* of his conspired
18:24 face of one *c. Is.* 36:9
20:5 Hezekiah *c.* of my people
25:8 Nebuzar-adan. *c. Jer.* 52:12
1 *Chr.* 11:21 honorable, he was *c.*
27:5 for 3d month Benaiah
3 *Chr.* 13:12 God himself is our *c.*
Jer. 37:13 a *c.* Irijah took Jer.
51:27 appoint a *c.* against her
John 18:12 band and *c.* took Jes.
Acts 5:26 *c.* with officers brought
Heb. 2:10 *c.* of their salvation

CAPTAINS.
Ex. 15:4 chosen *c.* are drowned
Deut. 1:15 I made wise men *c.*

CAP
1 *Sam.* 8:12 he will appoint him *c.*
22:7 son of Jesse make you *c.*
9 *Jam.* 18:5 *c.* charge con. Achish
23:8 that sat chief among the *c.*
1 *K.* 2:5 what Joab did to the *c.*
20:24 kings away, and put *c.*
22:38 when *c.* perceived he was
   not the king, 2 *Chr.* 18:32
1 *Chr.* 11:15 three of 30 *c.* went
2 *Chr.* 33:11 brought on them *c.*
Job 39:25 the thunder of the *c.*
Jer. 13:21 taught them to be *c.*
51:23 I will break in pieces *c.*
57 I will make drunk her *c.*
Ezek. 21:22 *c.* to open the mouth
23:6 *c.* all desirable men, 12, 23
Mark 6:21 a supper to *c.*
Luke 22:4 J. communed with *c.*
Rev. 19:18 may eat the flesh of *c.*

CAPTIVE.
Gen. 14:14 brother was taken *c.*
34:29 their wives took they *c.*
Ex. 12:29 unto first-born of *c.*
2 *K.* 5:2 bro. away a little m.
6:22 those thou hast taken *c.*
Is. 49:21 I am desolate, a *c.*
24 shall lawful *c.* be delivered
51:14 *c.* exile hasteneth
52:2 loose thys. O *c.* dau. of Z.
Amos 6:7 *c.* with first that go *c.*
2 *Tim.* 2:26 taken *c.* by him

Carry or carried CAPTIVE,
   or CAPTIVES.
Gen. 31:26 *car.* my daughters *c.*
Num. 24:22 until A. *car.* thee *c.*
1 *K.* 8:46 *car.* them *c.* 2 *Chr.* 6:36
47 they bethink thems. in land
   whither *carried c.* 2 *Chr.* 6:37
2 *K.* 15:29 T.-pilneser *car.* them *c.*
16:9 *c.* peo. of Damas. *c.* to Kir
17 *Chr.* 5:6 king of Assyria *c. c.*
2 *Chr.* 25:12 10,000 did Judah *c. c.*
28:5 *car.* a great multitude *c.*
8 *Is. car. c.* of brethren 200,000
Ps. 106:46 pitied of th. *c.* them *c.*
137:3 *c.* us *c.* required a song
Jer. 13:17 Lord's flock is *car. c.*
19 J. shall he wholly *c.* away *c.*
20:4 shalt *c.* them *c.* to Babylon
24:5 acknowledge them *car. c.*
29:4 saith the Lord to all *car. c.*
14 bring you into place whence
   I caused you to be *car. c.*
41:10 Ishm. *c. c.* all the residue
43:12 *carry* the Egyptians *c.*
52:29 *c. c.* from Jer. 832 persons
30 *c. c.* of the Jews 745 persons
Ezek. 6:9 nations whither he *c.*
Dan. 11:8 also *c. c.* into Egypt
Amos 1:6 her, they *c. c.* captivity
Ob. 11 in day strangers *car. c.*

Carrying CAPTIVE.
Jer. 1:3 to *car.* of Jerusalem *c.*

Lead, or led CAPTIVE.
Jud. 5:12 *lead* thy captivity *c.*
1 *K.* 8:48 return unto thee in land
   of enemies which *l.* them *c.*
2 *Chr.* 30:9 shall find compassion
   before them that *lead c.*
Ps. 68:16 *led* captiv. *c. Eph.* 4:8
Nah. 2:7 Huzzab shall be *led c.*
Luke 21:24 shall he *led* away *c.*
2 *Tim.* 3:6 lead *c.* silly women

CAPTIVES.
Num. 31:9 women of Midian *c.*
19 brought *c.* 19 purify youre.
Deut. 21:11 am. *c.* a beauti, wo.
32:42 drunk with blood of *c.*
1 *Sam.* 30:5 David's two wives *c.*
2 *K.* 24:14 from Jerus. 10,000 *c.*
28:11 deliver the *c.* again
13 ye shall not bring in *c.*
Is. 14:2 take them *c.* whose *c.*
20:4 the Ethiopians *c.*
45:13 go and let my *c.* go for price
61:1 liberty to the *c. Luke* 4:18
Jer. 48:46 thy sons and d. are *c.*
50:33 took them *c.* hold them
Ezek. 1:1 as I was among *c.*
16:53 captivity of thy *c.*
Dan. 2:30 found a man of *c.* of J.

CAPTIVITY.
Ex. 28:17 first row a *c.* 39:10
L. 54:12 make thy gates of *c.*
Ezek. 28:13 and *c.* thy covering

CARCASE.
Lev. 5:2 touch *c.* unclean thing
11:8 *c.* not touch, *Deut.* 14:8
Deut. 28:26 *c.* be meat to fowls
Jos. 8:29 should take his *c.*
Jud. 14:8 to see *c.* of lion honey
1 *K.* 13:22 thy *c.* not come
24 a lion stood by *c.*
2 *K.* 9:37 *c.* of Jez. be as dung
Is. 14:19 cast out as a *c.* trodden
Mat. 24:28 *c.* is there will eagles

CARCASSES.
Gen. 15:11 fowls came on *c.*
Lev. 11:11 *c.* in abomination, 26
26:30 cast your *c.* on *c.* of idols
Num. 14:29 *c.* shall fall in wilder.
1 *Sam.* 17:46 I will give *c.* of Ph.

CAR
Ezr. 9:7 have been delivered to *c.*
Neh. 1:2 Jews wh. were left of *c.*
4:4 for a prey in land of their *c.*
Est. 2:6 Mordecai carried with *c.*
Job 42:10 L. turned the *c.* of Job
Ps. 14:17 Lord bring back *c.* 53:1
78:61 deliv. his strength into *c.*
126:1 when L. turned *c.* of Z.
4 turn again our *c.* O L. as str.
Is. 5:13 my peo. are gone into *c.*
22:17 carry thee with mighty *c.*
46:2 themselves are gone into *c.*
Jer. 15:2 for the *c.* to the *c.* 43:11
29:14 I will turn away your *c.*
30:3; 32:44; 33:7, 11, 26
20 hear all of *c.* ; 28 *c.* is long
22 taken up a curse by all *c.*
31 send to all them of *c.*
30:10 seed from land of *c.* 46:27
34:11 hath Moab gone into *c.*
Lam. 1:3 Judah is gone into *c.*
5 her children are gone into *c.*
3:14 discov. to turn away thy *c.*
4:22 no more carry thee into *c.*
Ezek. 1:2 fifth y. of Jehoiac. *c.*
3:11 get to them of *c.* and speak
11:25 I spake to them of *c.* all
12:7 my staff, as stuff for *c.*
16:53 bring again their *c.* the *c.*
   of Sodom and Samaria
25:3 went into *c.* thou saidst
33:21 in 12th year of *c.* one saw.
39:23 house of Isr. went into *c.*
40:1 in the 25th year of our *c.*
Dan. 6:13 D. of the *c.* of Judah
11:33 shall fall by *c.* many days
Hos. 6:11 returned *c.* of my peo.
Ob. 20 *c.* of this host, *c.* of Jer.
Mic. 1:16 gone into *c.* from thee
Hab. 1:9 gather *c.* as the sand
Zep. 2:7 shall turn away *c.* 3:20
Zec. 6:10 take of them of the *c.*
Rom. 7:23 *c.* to the law of sin
2 *Cor.* 10:5 into *c.* every thought
See CAPTIVE.

Bring CAPTIVITY.
Ps. 53:6 when God *b.* back *c.*
Jer. 30:18 *b.* ag. *c.* of Jacob's t.
31:23 I shall *b.* again them *c.*
48:47 *bring* again *c.* of Moab
49:6 I will *b.* again *c.* of Ammon
39 will *bring* again *c.* of Elam
Ezek. 29:14 *b.* again *c.* of Egypt
39:25 now will I *b.* again *c.* of J.
Joel 3:1 I *b.* again *c.* of Judah
Amos 9:14 *b.* again *c.* of my peo.

Children of CAPTIVITY.
Ezr. 4:1 *c. c.* builded temple
10:7 proclamation to the *c. c.*
16 *c. c.* of *c.* did so, all were sep.
Dan. 5:13 which art *c. c.* of Ju.

Go into CAPTIVITY.
Deut. 28:41 sons and daugh. *g. c.*
Jer. 20:6 and house shall *go c.*
22:22 thy lovers shall *go into c.*
30:16 adver. every one shall *go c.*
46:19 O daugh. furnish to *go c.*
48:7 Chem. shall *c.* ; 49:3 king
Ezek. 12:4 go as they that *go c.*
30:17 these cities shall *go into c.*
18 Egypt, her dau. shall *go c.*
Amos 1:5 people of S. shall *go c.*
15 their king shall *go into c.*
5:5 Gilgal shall surely *go into c.*
27 I cause you to *go into c.*
7:17 Is. shall surely *go into c.*
9:4 they go *c.* before enemies
Mic. 1:16 city shall *go into c.*
Rev. 13:10 lead. *into c.* shall *go c.*

Out of CAPTIVITY.
Ezr. 2:1 went up *o. c. Neh.* 7:6
6:21 come *out c.* kept the feast
8:35 come *out c.* offered

CARBUNCLE, S.
Ex. 28:17 first row a *c.* 39:10
Is. 54:12 make thy gates of *c.*
Ezek. 28:13 and *c.* thy covering

CARCASE.
Lev. 5:2 touch *c.* unclean thing
11:8 *c.* not touch, *Deut.* 14:8
Deut. 28:26 *c.* be meat to fowls
Jos. 8:29 should take his *c.*
Jud. 14:8 to see *c.* of lion honey
1 *K.* 13:22 thy *c.* not come
24 a lion stood by *c.*
2 *K.* 9:37 *c.* of Jez. be as dung
Is. 14:19 cast out as a *c.* trodden
Mat. 24:28 *c.* is there will eagles

CARCASSES.
Gen. 15:11 fowls came on *c.*
Lev. 11:11 *c.* in abomination, 26
26:30 cast your *c.* on *c.* of idols
Num. 14:29 *c.* shall fall in wilder.
1 *Sam.* 17:46 I will give *c.* of Ph.

CRUDEN'S CONCORDANCE. 787

CAR

Is. 5:25 their *c.* torn in streets
34:3 stink come up out of *c.*
66:24 *c.* of them transgressed
Jer. 7:33 *c.* of this people be meat for fowls, 16:4; 19:7
16:18 filled mine hab. with the *c.*
Ezek. 6:5 lay *c.* of Isr. before Id.
48:9 *c.* of their kings far from
Nah. 3:3 a great number of *c.*
Heb. 3:17 *c.* fell in wilderness

CARCHEMISH.
2 *Chr.* 35:20 to fight against C.
Is. 10:9 is not Calno as C. ?
Jer. 46:2 river Euphrates in C.

CARE.
1 *Sam.* 10:2 father left *c.* of asses
2 *K.* 4:13 careful with all this *c.*
Jer. 49:31 the nation without *c.*
Ezek. 4:16 shall eat bread with *c.*
Luke 10:34 he took *c.* of him
35 said, Take *c.* of him
1 *Cor.* 9:9 God take *c.* for oxen ?
12:25 same *c.* one for another
2 *Cor.* 7:12 *c.* for you might ap.
8:16 same earnest *c.* in Titus
11:28 *c.* of all the churches
1 *Tim.* 3:5 how take *c.* of church
1 *Pet.* 5:7 casting your *c.* on him

CARE, ED.
2 *Sam.* 18:3 if we flee, not *c.* for
Ps. 142:4 no man *c.* for my soul
Luke 10:40 *c.* that my sister left
John 12:6 he *c.* for the poor
Acts 18:17 G. *c.* for none of those
1 *Cor.* 7:21 a servant? *c.* not
Phil. 2:20 natur. *c.* for your state
2 *K.* 4:13 thou hast been *c.* for us
Jer. 17:8 *c.* in year of drought
Dan. 3:16 we are not *c.* to answer
Luke 10:41 *c.* about many things
Phil. 4:6 be *c.* for nothing, but
10 *c.* but lacked opportunity
Tit. 3:8 *c.* to maintain good w.

CAREFULLY.
Deut. 15:5 thou *c.* hearken to L.
Mic. 1:12 inha. of M. waited *c.*
Phil. 2:28 I sent him the more *c.*
Heb. 12:17 sought it *c.* with tears

CAREFULNESS.
Ezek. 12:18 drink water with *c.*
19 shall eat their bread with *c.*
1 *Cor.* 7:32 have you without *c.*
2 *Cor.* 7:11 what *c.* it wrought

CARELESS.
Jud. 18:7 saw how they dwelt *c.*
Is. 32:9 hear, ye *c.* daughters
10 ye *c.* women ; 11 ye *c.* ones
Ezek. 30:9 *c.* Ethiopians afraid

CARELESSLY.
Is. 47:8 thou that dwellest *c.*
Ezek. 39:6 fire am. them dwelt *c.*
Zep. 2:15 rejoicing city dwelt *c.*

CARES.
Mark 4:19 *c.* of this world choke
Luke 8:14 chok. with *c.* and rich.
21:34 overcharged with *c.* of life

CAREST, ETH, ING.
Deut. 11:12 a land which L. *c.*
Mat. 22:16 *c.* thou for any man
Mark 4:38 *c.* thou not we perish
12:14 art true, and *c.* for no man
John 10:13 hireling *c.* not for sh.
1 *Cor.* 7:32 is unmarried *c.* 34
33 is married, *c.* for world, 34
1 *Pet.* 5:7 for he *c.* for you

CARMEL.
1 *Sam.* 25:2 posses. in C. 7, 40
1 *K.* 18:19 gather all Is. to mt. C.
Cant. 7:5 head u. thee is like C.
Is. 33:2 excellency of C.
Jer. 46:18 as C. by the sea
Amos 1:2 C. shall wither, 9:3
Mic. 7:14 in the midst of C.

CARMELITE.
1 *Sam.* 30:5 N. C. 2 *Sam.* 2:2; 3:3
2 *Sam.* 23:35 Hezrai C. one of D.
CARMI. *Gen.* 46:9; *Jos.* 7:1;
1 *Chr.* 2:7; 4:1

CARNAL.
Rom. 7:14 I am *c.* sold under sin
8:7 *c.* mind is enmity against G.
15:27 to minister to *c.* things
1 *Cor.* 3:1 unto *c.* even to babes
3 are yet *c.* ; 4 are ye not *c.* ?
9:11 if we reap your *c.* things
2 *Cor.* 10:4 w. of warfare not *c.*
Heb. 7:16 law of *c.* commandment
9:10 stood in *c.* ordinances

CARNALLY.
Lev. 18:20 not lie *c.* with n. wife
19:20 lieth *c.* with a bondmaid

CAR

Num. 5:13 man lie with her *c.*
Rom. 8:6 *c.* minded is death

CARPENTER, S.
2 *Sam.* 5:11 c. to D. 1 *Chr.* 14:1
2 *Chr.* 24:12 hired *c. Ezr.* 3:7
Is. 41:7 *c.* encouraged goldsmith
44:13 *c.* stretcheth out his rule
Jer. 24:1 *c.* he carried away, 29:2
Mat. 13:55 is not this the *c.* son?
Mark 6:3 is not this the *c.*

CARPUS. 2 *Tim.* 4:13

CARRIAGE, S.
1 *Sam.* 17:22 David left his *c.*
Is. 10:28 Michmash laid up *c.*
46:1 your *c.* were heavy laden
Acts 21:15 we took up our *c.*

CARRY.
Gen. 50:25 *c.* up my b. *Ex.* 13:19
Ex. 33:15 pres. go not, *c.* us
Lev. 10:4 *c.* your breth. out of *c.*
Num. 11:12 *c.* them in bosom
Deut. 14:24 too long to *c.* it
Jos. 4:3 *c.* the twelve stones
1 *Sam.* 20:40 *c.* them to the city
2 *Sam.* 19:18 *c.* king's household
1 *K.* 18:12 spirit of L. sh. *c.* thee
2 *K.* 4:19 *c.* him to his mother
9:2 *c.* John to an innerchamber
17:27 *c.* thith. one of the priests
1 *Chr.* 15:2 none ought to *c.* ark
23:26 L. no more *c.* tabernacle
2 *Chr.* 35:6 *c.* him to B. *Jer.* 39:7
9:4 spring, of those *c. a.* 10:6
Jer. 29:4 caused to be *c. a.*
Jam. 2:33 wind *c.* them away
Mark 8:10 No was *c. a.* into cap.
Mat. 1:11 about time *c. a.* to B.
Mark 15:1 *c.* Jesus *a.* to Pilate
1 *Cor.* 12:2 G. *c. a.* dumb idols
Gal. 2:13 Barnabas *c. a.*
Rev. 12:15 be *c. a.* of flood
17:3 *c.* me *a.* in spirit, 21:10

CARRIEST, ETH, ING.
Job 21:18 as chaff storm *c.* away
27:21 east wind *c.* him away
Ps. 78:9 Ephraim *c.* bows turned
90:5 them away with flood
Mat. 1:17 till the *c.* into Babylon
Rev. 17:7 mystery of beast th. *c.*

CART.
1 *Sam.* 6:7 makes a new *c.* and
2 *Sam.* 6:3 set ark on a new *c.*
1 *Chr.* 13:7 Uzzah drave the *c.*
Is. 28:28 corn with wheel of *c.*
Amos 2:13 as a *c.* is pressed

CART-ROPE.
Is. 5:18 draw sin as with a *c.-r.*

CART-WHEEL.
Is. 28:27 nor is *c.-w.* turned

CARVED, ING, INGS.
Ex. 31:5 Bezaleel in *c.* 35:33
Jud. 18:18 fetched the *c.* image
1 *K.* 6:18 cedar within was *c.*
2 *Chr.* 33:7 *c.* image in house G.
31:4 Josiah cut down *c.* images
Ps. 74:6 they break *c.* work
Prov. 7:10 my bed with *c.* work

CAS

Ezek. 37:1 *c.* me out in Sp. of L.
Dan. 1:2 *c.* into land of Shinar
Hos. 10:6 also *c.* unto Assyria
12:1 and oil is *c.* into Egypt
Joel 3:3 *c.* into your temples
Luke 7:12 dead man *c.* out
16:22 was *c.* by the angels
24:51 was *c.* up into heaven
Acts 3:2 one lame from womb *c.*
5:5 young man *c.* Ananias out
7:16 fathers were *c.* to Sychem
8:2 *c.* Stephen to his burial
21:34 com. to be *c.* into castle
Eph. 4:14 *c.* with every wind
Heb. 13:9 *c.* with divers doctrines
2 *Pet.* 2:17 *c.* with a tempest
Jude 12 clouds without water *c.*
See **CAPTIVE.**

CARRIED away.
Gen. 31:18 J. *c. a.* all his cattle
26 *c. a.* thy daughters
1 *Sam.* 30:2 *c.* them *a.* 18.
2 *K.* 17:6 *c.* Is. into Assyria, 23
11 heathen whom the L. *c. a.*
28 one of priests they had *c. a.*
24:14 *c. a.* all Jerusalem
15 *c. a.* Jehoiachin to Babylon
25:21 so Judah was *c. a.* out of
1 *Chr.* 5:26 *c. a.* the Reubenites
6:15 when L. *c. a.* J. and Jerus.
9:1 *c. a.* for their transgression
2 *Chr.* 14:13 Asa *c.* away, 21:17
Ezr. 2:1 been *c. a. Neh.* 7:6
9:4 spring, of those *c. a.* 10:6
Jer. 29:4 caused to be *c. a.*
Jam. 2:33 wind *c.* them away
Mark 8:10 No was *c. a.* into cap.
Mat. 1:11 about time *c. a.* to B.
Mark 15:1 *c.* Jesus *a.* to Pilate
1 *Cor.* 12:2 G. *c. a.* dumb idols
Gal. 2:13 Barnabas *c. a.*
Rev. 12:15 be *c. a.* of flood
17:3 *c.* me *a.* in spirit, 21:10

CASE, S.
Ex. 5:19 did see were in evil *c.*
Ps. 144:15 happy p. in such a *c.*
Mat. 5:20 in no *c.* enter kingdom
19:10 *c.* of man be so with wife
1 *Cor.* 7:15 bondage in such *c.*

CASEMENT.
Prov. 7:6 looked through my *c.*

CASIPHIA. *Ezr.* 8:17

CASSIA.
Ex. 30:24 of *c.* 500 shekels
Ps. 45:8 garments smell of *c.*
Ezek. 27:19 *c.* in thy market

CAST, passive.
Job 18:8 he is *c.* into a net
7:6 me *c.* into a dead deep
1:40 id let them be *c.* into fire
Prov. 16:33 the lot is *c.* into lap
Ec. 3:5 covering *c.* over all
Is. 22:18 *c.* thee into a country
24:22 as pris. *c.* into dungeon
Jer. 22:28 J. *c.* a despised idol
26:23 *c.* his dead body into gr.
28:17 is into fire, *Ezek.* 15:4
38:6 *c.* Jerem. into dungeon, 9
41:7 Ishmael *c.* them into pit
Lam. 3:53 *c.* a stone upon me
Ezek. 11:16 I have *c.* them far off
23:35 *c.* me behind thy back
28:17 I will *c.* thee to ground
Dan. 3:20 *c.* them into furnace
21 did not we *c.* three into fire
6:24 *c.* them into den of lions
Jon. 2:3 *c.* me into the deep
Mic. 4:7 I will make her *c.* off
7:19 *c.* all their sins into sea
Nah. 3:6 I will *c.* filth on thee
2 *Cor.* 4:9 *c.* down, not destroyed
Rev. 8:8 as a great mount. burn.
12:13 dragon saw *c.* to earth
19:20 both *c.* alive into the lake
20:10 the devil was *c.* into lake
14 death and hell *c.* into lake
15 not found in book of life, *c.*

CAST, active.
Gen. 31:38 she-goats have not *c.*
37:20 *c.* him into some pit
39:7 *c.* eyes on Joseph
Ex. 1:22 every son *c.* into river
4:3 he *c.* rod on the ground
15:4 Ph. chariots he *c.* into sea
25 had *c.* tree into the waters
22:31 flesh torn, *c.* it to the dogs
21:26 nothing *c.* their young
25:12 *c.* 4 rings, 37:3, 13 ; 38:5
32:19 Moses *c.* tables out
Num. 35:23 *c.* it on him
Deut. 29:28 L. *c.* into an. land
Jos. 8:29 *c.* king of Ai at gate
10:27 *c.* them into cave
Jud. 9:53 a woman *c.* a piece of millstone, 2 *Sam.* 11:21
1 *Sam.* 18:11 S. *c.* javelin, 20:33
2 *Sam.* 16:6 S. *c.* stones at Dav.
18:17 *c.* Absalom into a pit
1 *K.* 7:46 *c.* them, 2 *Chr.* 4:17
14:9 *c.* me behind thy back
19:19 E. *c.* his mantle on him
2 *K.* 2:16 *c.* him on some mount.
21 spring, and *c.* salt in there
3:25 *c.* each his stone
4:41 meal he *c.* into the pot
6:6 he *c.* in stick, iron swam
9:25 *c.* into portion of N. 26
13:21 *c.* into sepulchre of Elisha
23 *c.* from his presence as yet
19:18 *c.* gods into fire, *Is.* 37:19
32 *c.* a bank ag. it, *Jer.* 37:33
Neh. 9:26 *c.* law behind
Est. 3:7 *c.* Pur, 9:24
Job 20:23 shall *c.* fury of wrath
27:22 God shall *c.* upon him
30:19 hath *c.* me into mire
40:11 *c.* abroad rage of wrath
Ps. 55:3 they *c.* iniquity on me
22 *c.* thy burden on the Lord
14:7 *c.* fire into thy sanctuary
78:49 *c.* on them his wrath
Prov. 1:14 *c.* in thy lot among us
Ec. 11:1 *c.* thy bread on waters
Is. 2:20 shall *c.* his idols to bats
Jer. 38:17 have *c.* all my sins behind
26:23 *c.* Urijah's body into graves
38:23 *c.* it into fire on hearth
38:6 *c.* Jerom. into dungeon, 9
41:7 Ishmael *c.* them into pit
Lam. 3:53 *c.* a stone upon me
Ezek. 11:16 I have *c.* them far off
23:35 *c.* me behind thy back
28:17 I will *c.* thee to ground
Dan. 3:20 *c.* them into furnace
21 did not we *c.* three into fire
6:24 *c.* them into den of lions
Jon. 2:3 *c.* me into the deep
Mic. 4:7 I will make her *c.* off
7:19 *c.* all their sins into sea
Nah. 3:6 I will *c.* filth on thee

CAS

John 3:24 not yet *c.* into prison
Acts 27:26 *c.* on a certain island
Rev. 8:7 hail and fire *c.* on earth
8 mountain burning *c.* into sea
12:13 dragon was *c.* into earth
19:20 both *c.* alive into the lake
20:10 the devil was *c.* into lake
14 death and hell *c.* into lake
15 not found in book of life, *c.*

CAST away.
Lev. 26:44 I will not *c.* them *a.*
2 *Sam.* 1:21 shield of mighty *c. a.*
2 *K.* 7:15 vessels Syrians *c. a.*
2 *Chr.* 29:19 vessels Ahaz *c. a.*
Job 8:4 *c.* them *a.* for transgress.

788 CRUDEN'S CONCORDANCE.

CAS

Job 8:20 G. will not c. a. perfect
Ps. 2:3 c. a. their cords
51:11 c. me not a. from presence
Ec. 3:5 a time to c. a. stones, 6
Is. 5:24 because they have c. a.
30:22 c. a. as menstruous cloth
31:7 c. a. his idols of silver
41:9 chosen and not c. thee a.
Jer. 7:29 out thy hair and c. it a.
33:26 c. a. seed of Jacob
Ezek. 18:31 c. a. all transgress.
20:8 did not c. a. abominations
Hos. 9:17 God will c. them a.
Mat. 13:48 but c. the bad away
Luke 9:25 if a man be c. away
Rom. 11:1 God c. a. his people?
2 not c. away people
Heb. 10:35 c. not a. your confid.

CASTAWAY.

1 Cor. 9:27 lest I myself be a c.

CAST down.

Ex. 7.10 Aaron c. down his rod
Jos. 10:11 L. c. d. great stones
Jud. 6:28 Baal was c. down
1 K. 18:42 Elijah c. himself d.
2 Chr. 25:8 G. hath power to c. d.
12 c. them d. from top of rock
Neh. 6:16 c. d. in their own eyes
Job 18:7 counsel sh. c. him d.
22:29 when men are c. down
29:24 my count. they c. not d.
41:9 be c. d. at sight of him?
Ps. 17:13 disap. him, c. him d.
36:12 they are c. down
37:14 bent bow to c. d. needy
24 shall not be utterly c. d.
42:5 c. d. O my soul? 11; 43:5
6 my soul is c. d. within me
56:7 in thine anger c. d. people
62:4 consult to c. him down
99:44 c. his throne d. to ground
102:10 lifted me up, and c. d.
Prov. 7:26 c. d. many wounded
Js. 28:2 shall c. d. with his hand
1 Cor. 6:15 shall be c. down, 8:12
Lam. 2:1 c. d. the beauty of Isr.
Ezek. 6:14 c. d. your slain
19:12 thy mother was c. d.
31:16 when I c. d. Assyrian d.
32:18 wail for E. and c. her d.
Dan. 7:9 the thrones were c. d.
8:7 he-goat c. d. ram to the gr.
10 it c. d. some of host
12 c. down truth to ground
11:12 he shall c. d. ten thous.
Mat. 4:6 c. thyself d. Luke 4:9
15:30 c. them d. at Jesus' feet
27:5 he c. d. pieces of silver
Luke 4:29 c. Jesus d. headlong
2 Cor. 4:9 c. d. but not destroyed
7:6 that comforteth those c. d.
2 Pet. 2:4 c. angels down to hell
Rev. 12:10 the accuser is c. d.

CAST forth.

Neh. 13:8 I c. forth household
Ps. 144:6 c. f. lightning
Jer. 22:19 Jehoi. c. f. beyond g.
Ezek. 32:4 c. thee f. on op. field
Hos. 14:5 c. f. his roots at Leb.
Jon. 1:15 c. f. Jonah into sea
Mark 7:26 c. f. devil
John 15:6 he is c. f. as a branch

CAST lots.

Lev. 16:8 a. lots on the two g.
Jos. 18:10 Joshua c. lots in Sh.
1 Sam. 14:42 c. l. but. me and Jon.
1 Chr. 26:13 c. l. as well small
Ps. 22:18 c. l. upon my vesture.
Mat. 27:35; John 19:24
Jl. 3:3 c. lots for my people
Ob. 11 foreigners c. l. on Jer.
Jon. 1:7 c. lots that we may k.
Nah. 3:10 c. l. for her hon. men

CAST off.

2 K. 23:27 I will c. off Jerusa.
1 Chr. 28:9 c. thee off forever
2 Chr. 11:14 J. had c. them off
Job 15:33 c. off his flower
Ps. 43:2 why dost c. me off?
44:9 but thou hast c. off, 60:1, 10; 89:38; 108:11
23 Lord c. us not off for ever
71:9 c. me not off in old age
74:1 why hast c. us off for ever?
77:7 will Lord c. off for ever?
94:14 not c. o. his p. Lam. 3:31
Jer. 26:16 I will c. Hananiah off
31:8 c. off seed of Isr. 33:24
Lam. 2:7 L. hath c. off his altar
Hos. 8:3 Is. hath c. off thing good
5 thy calf, O Sam. c. thee off
Amos 1:11 bec. he c. off all pity
Zec. 10:6 tho' I not c. them off
Acts 22:23 and c. off their clothes
Rom. 13:12 let us c. off works

CAS

1 Tim. 5:12 c. off their first faith

CAST out.

Gen. 21:10 c. o. this bondwoman
Ex. 34:24 c. out the nations
Lev. 18:24 nations 1 c. o. 20:23;
Deut. 7:1
Deut. 9:17 c. tables out
1 K. 9:7 this house will I c. out
of my sight, 2 Chr. 7:20
21:26 Amorites c. out, 2 K. 16:3
2 K. 10:25 captains c. them out
17:20 c. them out, 24:20
2 Chr. 13:9 have ye not c. out
27:19 to c. us out of thy posses.
Neh. 1:9 there were of you c. out
Job 20:15 c. them out of his belly
39:3 they c. out their sorrows
Ps. 5:10 c. them out in trans.
18:42 did c. them out as dirt in
44:2 afflict. people, and c. th. o.
60:8 will I c. out my shoe, 108:9
78:55 he c. out the heathen, 80:8
Prov. 22:10 c. out the scorner
Is. 14:19 art c. out of thy grave
26:19 earth shall c. out the dead
34:3 their slain shall be c. out
56:7 that thou bring poor c. out
60:5 c. you out for my name's k.
Jer. 7:15 c. you out of my sight
8:19 our dwellings have c. us o.
15:1 c. out of my s, 23:39; 52:3
16:13 will I c. you out
22:26 I will c. thee out
28:3 dead body shall be c. out
31:34 Nebuch. hath c. me out
Ezek. 16:5 wast c. o. in open field
28:16 c. thee out of mountain
Amos 8:8 c. out and drowned
Mic. 2:9 women have ye c. out
Zep. 3:15 hath c. o. thine enemy
Zec. 1:21 to c. out horns of Gen.
9:4 Lord will c. her out
Mat 5:13 unsav. c. o. Luke 14:35
7:5 first c. out beam, Luke 6:42
22 in thy name c. out devils?
8:12 child. of kingdom be c. out
16 c. out spirits with his word
31 if thou c. us out suffer us
9:33 devil was c. o. dumb spake
10:1 power against spir. to c. o.
8 raise dead, c. out devils
12:24 c. o. but by B. Luke 11:18
26 if Satan c. out Satan
28 by spirit of God c. o. devils
15:17 and is c. out into draught
17:19 we c. him o.? Mark 9:28
21:12 Jesus c. o. all that sold,
Mark 11:15; Luke 19:45
8½e. c. v. Mark 12:8; Luke 20:15
Mark 1:34 c. o. m. dev. 39; 6:13
3:15 have power to c. out devils
23 how can Satan c. o. Satan?
16:9 out of whom c. 7 devils
17 shall c. out devils
Luke 6:22 c. out your name
11:20 with finger of G. c. o. dev.
13:32 I c. out devils and do cures
20:12 wounded him c. him out
John 6:37 I will in no wise c. out
9:34 reach 1s? they c. him out
12:31 pr. of this world be c. out
Acts 7:19 c. out their young
21 when Moses was c. out
58 c. Stephen out and stoned
16:37 c. out tackling of ship
Gal. 4:30 c. out the bondwoman
Rev. 12:9 great dragon was c. out
15 serpent c. out water, 16

Lord CAST out.

1 K. 14:24 L. c. o. bef. ch. of Isr.
2 K. 16:3; 2 Chr. 28:3; 33:2
Jer. 17:8 L. c. o. before Is. 21:2
Zec. 2:4 behold L. will c. her out

CAST up.

2 Sam. 20:15 c. up bank ag. city
Is. 57:14 c. ye up, pre. way, 62:10
20 whose waters c. up mire
Jer. 18:15 in way not c. up
50:26 c. her up as heaps
Lam. 2:10 c. up dust, Ezek. 27:30
Dan. 11:15 shall c. up a mount

CASTEST, ETH.

Job 15:4 yea thou c. off fear
21:10 cow c. not her calf
Ps. 50:17 c. my words behind
78:16 c. them into destruction
88:14 why c. thou off my soul
147:6 Lord c. the wicked down
17 he c. forth his ice
Prov. 10:3 c. away subst. of w.
19:15 slothful, c. into deep sleep
21:24 c. down strength
26:18 a madman c. firebrands
Jer. 6:7 as she c. out wickedness

CAT

Mat. 9:34 he c. out devils, Mark 3:22; Luke 11:15
1 John 4:18 per. love c. out fear
3 John 10 c. them out of church
Rev. 6:13 fig-tree c. untimely figs

CASTING.

Ex. 15:1 c. himself down
Job 6:21 ye see my c. down
Ps. 74:7 by c. down dwelling-p.
89:39 profaned crown by c. it
Mic. 6:14 thy c. down be in mid.
Mat. 27:30 c. lots, John 19:24
Mark 9:38, c. out dev. Luke 9:49
Luke 21:2 wid. c. in two mites
Rom. 11:15 if c. away be recou.
2 Cor. 10:5 c. down imaginations
1 Pet. 5:7 c. all your care on him

CASTLE.

1 Chr. 11:5 David took c. of Zion
7 David dwelt in c. city of D.
Prov. 18:19 like bars of a c.
Acts 21:34 Paul to be carried into
the c. 37; 22:24; 23:10
23:16 entered into c. told Paul

CASTLES.

Gen. 25:16 names by their c.
Num. 31:10 burnt their goodly c.
2 Chr. 17:12 Jehoshaphat built c.
27:4 in the forest built c.

CASTOR. See SIGN.

CATCH.

1 K. 20:33 men did hastily c.
Ex. 7:12 we shall c. them alive
Ps. 10:9 in wait to c. the poor
35:8 let his net c. himself
109:11 extor. c. all he hath
Jer. 5:26 set a trap they c. men
Ezek. 19:3 it learned to c. prey, 6
Hab. 1:15 c. them in their net
Mark 12:13 to c. him in his wo.
Luke 5:10 from henceth. c. men
11:54 to c. something

CATCHETH.

Mat. 13:19 c. what was sown
John 10:12 wolf c. the sheep

CATERPILLAR, S.

1 K. 8:37 if any c. 2 Chr. 6:28
Ps. 78:46 their increase to c.
105:34 ne spake, and c. came
Is. 33:4 like gathering of c.
Jer. 51:14 with men as c.
27 horses come up as rough c.
Joel 1:4 c.-w. left hath c. eaten
2:25 restore years c. hath eaten

CATTLE.

Gen. 1:25 God make the c.
3:14 art cursed above all c.
8:1 God remembered c. in ark
9:10 establish covenant with c.
13:2 Abram was rich in c.
31:9 taken away c. of your fath.
43 these c. are my c. and all
34:5 his sons were with his c.
46:32 their trade to feed c.
47:6 make them rulers over c.
17 Joseph gave bread for c.
Ex. 9:4 sever. bet. c. of Is. and c.
20 and c. flee into the houses
12:29 smote first-born of c.
Num. 3:41 take c. of Levi
20:19 c. drink, I will pay for it
32:4 land for c. and thy servants
Job 36:33 c. concerning vapor
Ps. 50:10 c. on a thousand hills
104:14 grass to grow for the c.
148:10 all c. praise the Lord
Ec. 2:7 great and small c.
Is. 7:25 for treading of lesser c.
43:23 not brought me small c.
46:1 their idols were upon c.
Jer. 9:10 nor hear voice of the c.
Ezek. 34:17 judge bet. c. 20;22
Hag. 1:11 for a drought upon c.
Zec. 2:4 for multitude of c.
13:5 man taught me to keep c.
Luke 17:7 servants feeding c.
John 4:12 dr. thereof, and his c.

Much CATTLE.

Gen. 30:43 Jacob had much c.
Ex. 12:38 out of Egy. with m. c.
Num. 32:1 Reuben had much c.
Jos. 22:8 ye have much c.
2 Chr. 26:10 Uzziah had much c.
Jon. 4:11 Nin. wherein is m. c.

Our CATTLE.

Gen. 34:23 shall not also go
47:16 give your c. will give
Num. 32:16 sheepfolds for o. c.
26:19 kill our c. with thirst
Neh. 10:36 bring first-born of o. c.

Their CATTLE.

Gen. 31:9 shall not their c.
33:3 nah. for 2. Jos. 14:4
46:5 Midian. came with t. c.

CAU

1 Sam. 23:5 brought away ., c.
Ps. 78:48 he gave up their c.
107:38 sull. not their c. to dec.
Jer. 40:32 a booty, t. c. a spoil

Thy CATTLE.

Gen. 30:29 thy c. was with me
31:41 served thee 6 years for t. c.
Ex. 9:19 and gather t. c.
20:10 t. c. do any w. Deut. 5:14
34:19 firstling among thy c.
Lev. 25:7 sub. be meat for thy c.
Deut. 11:15 send grass for thy c.
28:4 fruit of t. c. 11; 30:9
51 he shall eat fruit of thy c.
Is. 30:23 L. c. feed in large past.

Your CATTLE.

Gen. 47:16 bread for your c.
Deut. 3:19 y. c. in. c. Jos. 1:14
7:14 be barren among your c.

CAUGHT.

Gen. 22:13 behind him a ram c.
Ex. 4:4 and c. the serpent
Num. 31:32 prey men had c.
Jud. 8:14 c. young man of Suc.
21:23 danced, whom they c.
1 Sam. 17:35 I c. him by his bea.
2Sam. 2:16 c. every one his fellow
18:9 Absalom's head c. hold of
1 K. 1:50 Adon. c. hold on altar
2:28 J. c. hold on horns of altar
11:30 Ahijah c. her garment
2 K. 4:27 she c. Elisha by feet
2 Chr. 22:9 they c. Ahaziah
Prov. 7:13 so she c. him
Jer. 50:24 O Babylon, thou art c.
Mat. 11:31 Jesus c. Peter
21:39 the husbandmen c. him
Mark 12:3 they c. the servant
Luke 8:29 oftentimes it c. him
John 21:3 that night c. nothing
Acts 6:12 Stephen and c. him
8:39 the spirit c. away Philip
16:19 they c. Paul and Silas
26:21 the J. c. me in the temple
27:15 when ship wes. we let
2 Cor. 12:2 I knew a man c. up
4 he was c. up into paradise
16 crafty I c. you with guile
1 Thes. 4:17 we shall be c. up to.
Rev. 12:5 child was c. up to God

CAUL, S.

Ex. 29:13 a. above the liver, 22;
Lev. 3:4, 10, 15, 4:9; 7:4; 8:16, 25; 9:10, 19
Is. 3:18 will take away their c.
Hos. 13:8 rend c. of their heart.

CAUSE, Substantive.

Ex. 22:9 c. of both before judges
23:2 nor speak in a c. to decline
3 counten. a poor man in his c.
6 wrest judg. of poor in his c.
Num. 16:11 for which c. thou
and all thy company are ga.
27:5 Moses brought c. before L.
Deut. 1:17 the c. too hard for you
1 Sam. 17:29 is there not a c.?
23:39 L, pleaded c. of my rep.
2 Sam. 13:16 there is no c.
15:4 hath any c. might come
1 K. 8:45 maintain their c. 49, 59;
2 Chr. 6:35, 39
11:27 c. that he lift up his hand
12:15 c. was fr. L. 2 Chr. 10:15
1 Chr. 21:8 a c. of tresp. to Is. ?
19:22 to 10 what c. shall come
Job 5:8 would I commit my c.
13:18 I have ordered my c.
23:4 order my c. before him
29:16 c. I know not I searched
31:13 if I did despise c. of serv.
Ps. 9:4 hast maintained my c.
35:23 awake to my c. my God
140:12 Lord will maintain the c.
Prov. 18:17 he first in his own c.
29:9 debate thy c. with neighbor
29:7 considereth c. of poor
31:8 for the dumb in the c.
Ec. 7:10 say not, what is the c.
Is. 1:23 not c. of widow come
41:21 produce your c. saith Lord
51:22 God that pleadeth the c.
Jer. 5:28 judge not c. of fatherl.
11:20 to thee revealed my c.
29:13 unto thee I opened my c.
26:16 he judged the c. of poor
Lam. 3:36 w. a man in his c.
59 seen my wrong, jud. my c.
Jon. 1:7 for whose c. 8
Mat. 5:32 saving for c. of forni.
19:3 put away his wife for ev. c.
Luke 23:22 no c. of death in him
Acts 10:21 c. where, ye are come
13:38 found no c. of death
28:18 was no c. of death in me
2 Cor. 4:16 which c. we faint not
5:13 we be sober, it is for yo. c.

CAU

2 Cor. 7:12 his c. that h. done w.
Phil. 2:18 same c. do yo joy
2 Tim. 1:12 for which c. I suffer
Heb. 2:11 c. he is not ashamed to
Plead CAUSE.
1 Sam. 24:15 Lord plead my c. Ps. 35:1; 43:1; 119:154
Ps. 74:22 plend thine own c.
Prov. 22:23 will plead their c.
23:11 plead their c. with thee
31:9 p. the c. of poor and needy
Jer. 30:13 none to plead thy c.
50:34 Lord thor. plead their c.
51:36 behold I will plead thy c.
Mic. 7:9 until he plead my c.
For this CAUSE.
Ex. 9:16 f. t. c. raised up Ph.
John 12:27 f. t. c. came I
18:37 f. t. c. came I into the w.
Rom. 12:6 f. t. c. I will confess
1 Cor. 11:30 f. this c. many
Eph. 3:14 f. this c. I bow
1 Thes. 2:13 f. this c. thank we
1 Tim. 1:16 f. t. c. I obtained
Heb. 9:15 f. this c. he is med.
1 Pet. 4:6 f. t. c. was gospel pr.
Without CAUSE.
1 Sam. 19:5 slay D. without a c.
Job 2:3 to destroy him without c.
9:17 multipli. my wounds w. c.
Ps. 7:4 that w. c. is my enemy
25:3 that transgress w. c.
35:7 as c. dig. a pit without c.
19 w. c. 69:4; John 15:25
109:3 fought ag. me with. a c.
119:78 perv. with me with. a c.
161 persecuted me with. c.
Prov. 1:11 lurk for innocent w. c.
3:30 st. not with a man with. c.
23:29 hath wounds without c.
24:28 be not witness without c.
Ez. 52:4 oppressed them w. c.
Lam. 3:52 chased me sore w. c.
Ezek. 14:23 have not done w. c.
Mat. 5:22 angry with bro. w. c.
CAUSE.
Gen. 45:1 c. every man to go out
Num. 16:5 will c. him to come
Deut. 1:38 c. to inh. 3:28; 31:7
12:11 c. his name to dwell there
2 Sam. 13:13 c. my shame to go
Est. 3:13 c. to perish, 8:11
Job 6:24 c. me to understand
34:11 c. every man to find
Ps. 10:17 wilt c. thine ear
67:1 c. his face to sh. 80:3, 7, 19
76:8 c. judgment to be heard
143:8 c. me to hear
Prov. 4:16 unless c. some to fall
Ye. 5:6 to e. thy flesh to sin
Cant. 8:13 voice, c. me to hear it
s. 3:12 lead c. thee to err, 9:16
27:6 c. them of Jacob take root
30:30 c. his glor. voice be heard
42:2 nor c. his voice to be heard
58:14 c. thee to ride on high
61:11 c. righteousness to spring
62:9 and not c. to bring forth
Jer. 3:12 not c. mine anger
7:8 c. to dwell in this place, 7
13:27 c. people forget my name
31:2 I want to c. him to rest
9 c. to walk by rivers of waters
Lam. 3:32 but though he c. grief
Ezek. 30:37 c. to pass under rod
34:15 I will c. them to lie down
36:12 c. men to walk upon you
Dan. 9:17 G. c. thy face to shine
Joel 3:11 thither c. mighty ones
Hab. 1:3 why c. me behold
Mat. 10:21 c. par. to be put to d.
Mark 13:12; Luke 21:16
Rom. 16:17 mark them c. divi.
Col. 4:16 c. it be read in church
CAUSE to cease. See CEASE.
CAUSED.
Gen. 2:21 Lord c. a deep sleep
20:13 God c. me wander
Deut. 34:4 the land c. thee
2 Chr. 16:20 c. all to stand to it
Ezr. 6:12 c. his name to dwell
Job 31:16 c. eyes of widow
Ps. 66:12 c. men to ride over
119:49 on which c. me to hope
Is. 19:14 have c. Egypt to err
63:11 Sp. of Lord c. him to rest
Jer. 12:14 c. my people to inher.
13:11 c. to cleave house of Isr.
23:21 c. you to trust in a lie
32:23 thou hast c. all this evil
did I little ones have, a cry
Zec. 3:4 c. thy iniquity to pass
Mal. 2:8 c. many to stumble
John 11:37 c. this man not died
Acts 15:3 c. great joy to brethren

CEA

2 Cor. 2:5 if any have c. grief
CAUSELESS.
1 Sam. 25:31 hast shed blood c.
Prov. 26:2 curse c. shall not co.
CAUSES.
Ex. 18:19 bring c. to God
25 hard c. brought to Moses
Deut. 1:16 c. between brethren
Jer. 3:8 c. whereby backsliding
Lam. 3:58 pleaded c. of my soul
Lam. 4:22:1 c. the Jews caught me
CAUSEST.
Job 30:22 c. me to ride on wind
Ps. 65:4 blessed c. approach thee
CAUSETH.
Job 30:3 spirit of under. c. me
37:13 c. it come for correction
Ps. 135:7 he c. vapors to ascend,
Jer. 10:13; 51:16
Prov. 10:5 son c. sh. 17:2; 19:26
17:2 rule over a son c. shame
19:27 Instruction that c. to err
28:10 c. righteous to go ast.
Mat. 5:32 c. her to commit adul.
2 Cor. 2:14 which c. us triumph
9:11 c. through us thanksgiving
1 Chr. 26:16 lot came by the c.
CAUSEWAY.
Cant. 7:9 c. lips of those asleep
Jer. 20:10 in c. you to return
CAVE, S.
Gen. 19:30 Lot dwelt in a c. he
23:19 buried Sarah in the c.
49:29 bury me in the c.
Jos. 10:16 kings hid in a c. 17
Jud. 6:2 Israel made c.
1 Sam. 13:6 Israel did hide in c.
22:1 David escaped to the c.
24:10 delivered thee in the c.
1 K. 18:4 prophets hid in c. 13
19:9 Elijah came to a c. and
Ezek. 32:27 die that be in the c.
John 11:38 it was a c. a stone
Heb. 11:38 they wandered in c
CEASE.
Gen. 8:22 day and night not c.
Num. 8:25 age of fifty years, c.
11:25 prophesied, did not c.
17:5 to c. the murmurings
Deut. 15:11 poor shall never c.
32:26 remnrth. of them to c.
Jos. 22:25 child. c. from fearing
Jud. 15:7 after that I will c.
20:28 up. up. or shall I c. f
1 Sam. 7:8 c. not to cry to G.
2 Chr. 16:5 let his work c.
Ezr. 4:23 to c. by force
Neh. 6:3 why should the work c.
Job 3:17 c. from troubling
10:20 my days few f c. then
14:7 tender branch will not c.
Ps. 37:8 c. from anger
46:9 he maketh wars to c.
89:44 hast made his glory to c.
Prov. 10:27 c. to hear instruction
20:3 an honor to c. from strife
22:10 and reproach shall c.
23:4 c. from thy wisdom.
Ec. 12:3 grinders c. bec. few
Is. 1:16 c. to do evil
2:22 c. ye from man whose br
10:25 and indignation shall c.
16:10 vintage shouting to c.
17:3 fortress c. from Ephraim
21:2 all the sighing made to c.
33:1 shalt c. to spoil, be spoiled
Jer. 14:17 let tears not c.
17:8 nor c. from yielding fruit
31:36 seed of Israel shall c.
Lam. 2:18 apple of thine eye c.
Ezek. 6:6 that your idols may c.
7:24 pomp of the strong to c.
12:23 will make this proverb c.
23:27 make thy lewdness to c.
30:10 multitude of Egypt to c.
13 his magnificence to c.
18 pomp of her str. c. 32:28
Amos 7:5 Lord c. I beseech thee
Acts 13:10 not c. to pervert right
1 Cor. 13:8 tongues they shall c.
Eph. 1:16 I c. not to give thanks
Col. 1:9 not c. to pray for you
2 Pet. 2:14 cannot c. from sin
CAUSE to CEASE.
Ezr. 4:5 could not c. then c.
Neh. 4:11 cause the work to c.
Ps. 85:4 cause thine anger to c.
Prov. 18:18 c. contentions to c.
Is. 13:11 c. arrog. of proud to c.
30:11 cause H. O. of Israel to c.
Jer. 7:34 c. mirth in J. to c.
36:29 cause to c. man and beast
48:35 c. to c. him that offereth
Ezek. 33:48 cause lewdness to c.

CEI

Ezek. 20:13 cause n. of songs to c.
30:13 cause their images to c.
34:10 c. to c. from feeding, 25
Dan. 9:27 shall c. oblation to c.
11:18 cause reproach offered to c.
Hos. 1:4 c. to c. kingdom of Isr.
CEASED.
Gen. 18:11 it c. to be with Sarah
Jud. 2:19 c. not from their d.
5:7 inhabitants of villages c.
1 Sam 2:5 that were hungry c.
25:9 in name of David and c.
Jer. 4:24 then c. work of house
Job 32:1 three men c. to answer
Ps. 35:15 did tear me and c. not
77:2 my sore ran and c. not
Is. 14:4 opp. c. golden city c.
Lam. 5:14 elders have c.
15 the joy of our heart is c.
Mat. 14:32 w. c. Mark 4:39; 6:51
Luke 7:45 not c. to kiss my feet
11:1 was praying, when he c.
Acts 5:42 c. not to preach Jesus
20:1 after uproar was c. Paul
31 three years I c. not to warn
21:14 not be persuaded, we c.
Gal. 5:11 offence of cross c.
Heb. 4:10 c. from his own works
10:2 not have c. to be offered
1 Pet. 4:1 hath c. from sin
CEASETH.
Ps. 12:1 for the godly man c.
49:8 redemption precious, it c.
Prov. 26:20 talebearer, strife c.
Is. 16:4 the spoiler c.
24:8 tabrets c. joy of the harp c.
33:8 the wayfaring man c.
Lam. 3:49 eye trickleth, c. not
Acts 6:13 c. not to speak blasph.
CEASING.
1 Sam. 12:23 sin in c. to pray
Acts 12:5 prayer made without c.
Rom. 1:9 c. make m. 1 Thes. 1:3
1 Thes. 2:13 we think G. w. c.
5:17 pray without c.
2 Tim. 1:3 without c. I have re.
CEDAR.
2 Sam. 7:2 I dwell in house of c.
7 why build ye not house of c.
1 K. 4:33 he spake from the c.
5:8 I will do thy desire once. c.
2 K. 14:9 sent to c. 2 Chr. 25:18
Job 40:17 moveth tail like a c.
Ps. 92:12 righteous grow like c.
Cant. 1:17 beams of our house c.
8:9 inclose her with boards of c.
Ez. 41:19 in wilderness the c.
Jer. 22:14 it is celled with c.
15 because closest thyself in c.
23:11 shall be a goodly c.
27:24 chest is made of c. among
31:3 Assyrian was a c.
Zep. 2:14 shall uncover c. work
Zec. 11:2 howl, for c. is fallen
CEDAR-TREES.
Num. 24:6 as c. tabernac. as c.-t.
2 Sam. 5:11 H. sent c.-t. to Dav.
1 K. 5:6 they hew me c.-t.
10 11, gave Solomon c.-t. 9:11
2 K. 19:23 cut down tall c.-t.
1 Chr. 14:1 David prepared c.-t.
17:6 built him house of c.-t.
22:4 c.-t. in abundance, 4
2 Chr. 1:15 c.-t. as sycamore, 9:27
2:8 send me c.-t. out of Lebanon
Ezr. 3:7 gave money for c.-t.
Is. 9:10 change them into c.
37:24 I will cut down c. choice c.
44:14 herewith him down c.
Jer. 22:7 cut down thy choice c.
33 makest thy nest in the c.
Ezek. 31:8 c. in garden
Zec. 11:1 fire may devour thy c.
CEDARS of Lebanon.
Jud. 9:15 bramble dev. c. of L.
Ps. 104:16 c. of Leb. he planted
Is. 2:13 Lord on all c. of Leb.
14:8 c. of Leb. rejoice at thee
Ezek. 27:5 c. from Leb. to make
CEDRON. John 18:1

CER

Jer. 22:14 it is c. with cedar
Hag. 1:4 to dwell in c. houses?
CEILING.
1 K. 6:15 he built walls of the c.
CELEBRATE.
Lev. 23:32 even c. sabbath, 41
Is. 38:18 death cannot c. thee
CELESTIAL.
1 Cor. 15:40 c. bodies, glory of c.
CELLARS.
1 Chr. 27:28 over the c. of oil
CENCHREA.
Acts 18:18 shorn his head in C.
Rom. 16:1 serv. of church at C.
CENSER, S.
Lev. 10:1 sons of Aaron took c.
16:12 a c. full of burning coals
Num. 16:6 take ye c. 17
39 Eleazar took the brazen c.
Ezek. 8:11 with every man his c.
Heb. 9:4 holiest had the golden c.
Rev. 8:3 angel having a golden c.
5 angel took the c. and filled it
CENTURION, S.
Mat. 8:5 came unto him a c.
8 c. said, L. I am not worthy
27:54 when c. saw earthquake
Luke 7:2 c. servant was sick
23:47 c. saw what was done
Acts 10:1 Cornelius was a c.
22 Cornelius the c. a just man
21:32 immediately took c.
22:26 when the c. heard that
23:17 Paul called one of the c.
25 he called to him two c.
24:23 command. a c. to keep P.
27:1 J, a c. of Augustus' band
11 c. believ. m. more than P.
43 c. willing to save Paul
28:16 delivered the prisoners
CEPHAS.
John 1:42 shalt be called C.
1 Cor. 1:12 I am of C. 3:22
9:5 broth. of the L. and C. 15:5
Gal. 2:9 James, C. and John
CEREMONIES.
Num. 9:3 passover accord. to c.
CERTAIN, sure.
Deut. 13:14 c. men children of D.
17:4 carried away c. poor
Jer. 41:5 came c. from Shechem
52:15 carried away c. poor
Dan. 8:27 D. was sick c. days
Mat. 20:20 desiring c. thing
Mark 14:57 c. bare false witness
Luke 5:12 he was in a c. city
11:27 a c. woman lift up voice
18:9 parable to c. who trusted
24:22 c. women made us aston.
24 c. with us went to sepulchre
John 5:4 went at a c. season
Acts 9:10 Saul c. days with disc.
10:48 Peter to tarry c. days
19:1 to v. c. c. of the church
15:24 which went from us
17:28 as c. of your own poets
Rom. 15:26 to make a c. contrib.
Gal. 2:12 before c. came from J.
Heb. 2:6 one in a c. place testified
4:4 in c. place of seventh day
7 he limiteth a c. day, saying
10:27 c. looking for of judgm.
Jude 4 c. men crept in unawares
A CERTAIN man. See MAN.
CERTAIN, sure.
Deut. 13:14 the thing c. 17:4
1 K. 2:37 kn. for c. 42; Jer. 20:15
Dan. 2:45 the dream is c.
Acts 25:26 no c. thing to write
1 Cor. 4:11 no c. dwelling-place
1 Tim. 6:7 it is c. we can carry
CERTAINLY.
Gen. 18:10 will c. return to thee
26:28 saw c. L. was with thee
42:7 c. knew he would say
Ex. 3:12 c. I will be with thee
22:4 it found in his h. and c.
1 Sam. 20:9 if I knew c. evil
23:26 c. make my lord a sure
1 K. 1:30 so will I c. do this day
2 K. 8:10 thou mayest c. recover
2 Chr. 18:27 If c. return in peace
Jer. 8:8 in c. in vain made he it
13:9 he c. I have spoken to
44:17 c. do what goeth out
Lam. 2:16 c. this is the day looked
Dan. 11:10 c. come and over. 13
Luke 23:47 c. this was a man
CERTAINTY.
Jos. 23:13 c. Lord will no more
1 Sam. 23:23 with the c.

CILA

Prov. 22:21 *c.* of words of truth
Dan. 2:8 *c.* ye would gain time
Luke 1:4 know *c.* of those things
Acts 22:30 would have known *c.*

CERTIFY, IED.
Ezr. 4:14 we have *c.* the king
16 *c.* king that if city be built
Gal. 1:11 I *c.* you the gospel

CESAR.
Mat. 22:17 tribute to C. *Mark* 12:14; *Luke* 20:21, 22
Luke 2:1 a decree from C.
John 19:12 not C.'s friend; ag. C.
Acts 17:7 dec. of C. 25:8, 11, 21
Phil. 4:22 they that are of C.

CESAREA.
Mat. 16:13 into coasts of C.
Mark 8:27 into the towns of C.
Acts 8:40; 9:30; 10:24; 22:23; 25:4

CHAFED.
2 *Sam.* 17:8 they be *c.* as a bear

CHAFF.
Job 21:18 as *c.* storm carrieth
Ps. 1:4 like the *c.* which wind
35:5 be as *c.* before the wind
Is. 5:24 as flame consumeth *c.*
17:13 nations be chased as *c.*
29:5 terrible ones shall be as *c.*
33:11 conc. *c.* and bring forth
41:15 shall make the hills as *c.*
Jer. 23:28 what is *c.* to the wheat
Dan. 2:35 *c.* of threshing floor
Hos. 13:3 as *c.* driven with w.
Zep. 2:2 day pass as the *c.*
Mat. 3:12 b. up the *c. Luke* 3:17

CHAIN.
Gen. 41:42 put a gold *c.* about his neck, *Dan.* 5:7, 16, 29.
Cant. 4:9 ravished me with one *c.*
Lam. 3:7 he made my *c.* heavy
Ezek. 7:23 *c.* land is full of crim.
10:11 I put a *c.* on thy neck
Acts 28:20 for hope bound with *c.*
2 *Tim.* 1:16 O. not ashamed of *c.*
Rev. 20:1 angel *c.* in his hand

CHAINS.
Jud. 8:26 *c.* about camels' necks
1 *K.* 6:21 *c.* of gold before oracle
Ps. 119:8 to bind kings with *c.*
Prov. 1:9 instruction shall be *c.*
Cant. 1:10 neck comely with *c.*
Is. 3:19 L. will take away thy *c.*
40:19 goldsmith casteth silver *c.*
43:14 come after thee in *c.*
Jer. 40:4 l. thee this day from *c.*
Ezek. 19:4 brought him with *c.*
8 they put him in ward in *c.*
Mark 5:3 no not with *c.*
Acts 12:7 Peter's *c.* fell off
2 *Pet.* 2:4 deliv. into *c.* of dark.
Jude 6 reserved in everlasting *c.*
See BOUND.

CHALCEDONY.
Rev. 21:19 foundation was a *c.*

CHALCOL.
1 *K.* 4:31 Sol. was wiser than C.
1 *Chr.* 2:6 sons of Z. Heman, C.

CHALDEA.
Jer. 50:10 C. shall be a spoil
51:24 to inhabitants of C. 35
Ezek. 16:29 thy fornication to C.
23:16 messeng. to them into C.

CHALDEAN.
Ezr. 5:12 them into hand of C.
Dan. 2:10 such things at any C.

CHALDEANS.
Job 1:17 C. made out three bands
Is. 23:13 C. the Assyrian foun.
Dan. 1:4; 2:2; 3:8; 4:7; 5:7, 11
Hab. 1:9 lo, I raise up the C.
Acts 7:4 out of the land of the C.

CHALDEES.
2 *K.* 24:2 of the C. 25:4, 10, 26
2 *Chr.* 36:17 the king of the C.
Is. 13:19 Bab. the beauty of C.

CHALK-STONES.
Is. 27:9 stones of altar as *c.-s.*

CHALLENGETH.
Ex. 22:9 another *c.* to be his

CHAMBER.
Gen. 43:30 J. entered into his *c.*
Jud. 15:1 my wife into the *c.*
16:9 in wait abiding in *c.* 12
2 *K.* 4:11 Elisha turned into *c.*
Neh. 13:5 prepared for Tobiah *c.*
Ps. 19:5 as bridegroom out of *c.*
Cant. 3:4 *c.* of her conceived me
Jer. 36:10 book in *c.* of Gemariah
20 laid roll in *c.* of Elishama
Ezek. 40:13 *c.* prospect to south
Dan. 6:10 windows open in his *c.*

CHA

Joel 2:16 bridegr. go forth of *c.*

Inner CHAMBER.
1 *K.* 20:30 Benh. came into in. *c.*
22:25 carry *c.* 2 *Chr.* 18:24
2 *K.* 9:2 carry Jehu into *inner c.*

Little CHAMBER.
2 *K.* 4:10 a *little c.* on the wall
Ezek. 40:7 *little c.* one reed, 13

Side CHAMBER.
Ezek. 41:5 every *side c.* four cub.

Upper CHAMBER.
2 *K.* 1:2 (thro' a lattice in *u. c.*
23:12 altars on top of *upper c.*
Acts 9:37 Dorcas in *u.* of *upper c.*
39 P. when come into *upper c.*
20:8 many lights in *upper c.*

CHAMBERS.
1 *K.* 6:5 against the wall built *c.*
1 *Chr.* 9:26 porters over *c.* 23:28
Job 9:9 maketh *c.* of the south
Ps. 104:3 beams of *c.* in waters
13 watereth hills from *c.*
118:30 in the *c.* of their kings
Prov. 7:27 down to *c.* of death
24:4 by knowledge *c.* be filled
Cant. 1:4 brought me into his *c.*
Is. 26:20 *c.* and shut thy doors
Jer. 22:13 buildeth *c.* by wrong
14 his wide house and large *c.*
35:2 Rechabites into one of *c.*
Ezek. 8:12 in *c.* of his imagery
21:14 sword entereth privy *c.*
42:13 holy *c.* where priests eat
Mat. 24:26 he is in secret *c.*

CHAMBERING.
Rom. 13:13 *c.* and wantonness

CHAMBERLAIN, S.
2 *K.* 23:11 Nathan-melech the *c.*
Est. 1:10 seven *c.* that served
2:21 king's *c.* were wroth
Acts 12:20 Blastus the king's *c.*
Rom. 16:23 Erastus *c.* salutoth

CHAMELEON.
Lev. 11:30 the unclean, the *c.*

CHAMOIS.
Deut. 14:5 ye shall eat, the *c.*

CHAMPAIGN.
Deut. 11:30 in *c.* over against G.

CHAMPION.
1 *Sam.* 17:4 there went out a *c.*
51 saw their *c.* was dead

CHANCE.
1 *Sam.* 6:9 *c.* that happened to us
Ec. 9:11 time and *c.* happeneth
Luke 10:31 by *c.* a priest came
1 *Cor.* 15:37 it may *c.* of wheat

CHANCELLOR.
Ezr. 4:8 Rehum the *c.* 9, 17

CHANGE.
Gen. 45:22 each *c.* to Ben. five *c.*
Jud. 14:12 *c.* of garments, 13
2 *K.* 5:5 took ten *c.* of raiment
22 two *c.* of garments
23 bound two *c.* of garments
Job 10:17 *c.* and war are ag. me
14:14 I wait till my *c.* come
Ps. 55:19 no *c.* they fear not
Prov. 24:21 them given to *c.*
Heb. 7:12 of necessity a *c.* of law

CHANGE, Verb.
Lev. 27:10 he shall not *c.* it
Job 17:12 *c.* the night into the day
Ps. 102:26 as vesture *c.* them
Is. 9:10 will *c.* them into cedars
Jer. 2:36 so much to *c.* thy way?
13:23 can Ethiopian *c.* his skin
Dan. 7:25 think to *c.* times
Hos. 4:7 *c.* their glory to shame
Hab. 1:11 shall *c.* the customs
Rom. 1:26 women did *c.* the use
Gal. 4:20 I desire to *c.* my voice
Phil. 3:21 O. shall *c.* our vile b.

CHANGED, ETH.
Gen. 31:7 your father *c.* wages
41:14 Joseph *c.* his raiment
Lev. 13:16 flesh turn and be *c.*
55 plague have not *c.* his color
1 *Sam.* 21:13 *c.* behavior before
2 *Sam.* 12:20 Dav. *c.* his apparel
2 *K.* 24:17 *c.* name to Zedekiah
25:29 *c.* prison gar. *Jer.* 52:33
Job 30:18 is my garment *c.*
Ps. 15:4 sweareth to hurt, *c.* not
102:26 as a vesture *c. Heb.* 1:12
106:20 *c.* their glory to an ox
Ec. 8:1 bold. of face shall be *c.*
Is. 24:5 *c.* the ordinance

CHA

Jer. 2:11 *c.* their gods, my people
48:11 and his scent is not *c.*
Dan. 2:21 he *c.* the time of the gold *c.*
Ezek. 5:6 hath *c.* my judgments
Dan. 2:9 to speak till time be *c.*
21 he *c.* times and seasons
3:19 form of his visage was *c.*
27 coats *c.* nor smell of fire
4:16 heart be *c.* from man's
6:8 writing that it be not *c.*
15 no decree may be *c.*
Mic. 2:4 *c.* portion of my people
Rom. 1:23 *c.* barbarians *c.* their m.
25 *c.* glory of uncor. God
Rom. 1:23 *c.* truth of God into a lie
1 *Cor.* 15:51 we shall all be *c.* 52
2 *Cor.* 3:18 *c.* into same image
Heb. 7:12 for priesthood being *c.*

CHANGEST, ED, countenance.
Job 14:20 *c.* his *c.* and sendest
Dan. 5:6 king's *c.* was *c.* 9
7:28 my *countenance c.* in me
Ez. 19:23 *c.* us, saying

CHANGERS, S.
Mat. 21:12 tables of money *c.*
Mark 11:15; *John* 2:14, 15

CHANGING.
Ruth 4:7 manner concerning *c.*

CHANNEL, S.
2 *Sam.* 22:16 *c.* of the s. *Ps.* 18:15
Is. 8:7 shall come up over his *c.*
27:12 beat of from *c.* of the riv.

CHANT.
Amos 6:5 *c.* to sound of the viol

CHAPEL.
Amos 7:13 it is the king's *c.*

CHAPITER, S.
Ex. 36:38 *c.* with gold, 38:28
38:17 overlaying of *c.* 19
2 *K.* 17:10 of brass, 2 *K.* 25:17;
2 *Chr.* 4:12, 13; *Jer.* 52:22

CHAPMEN.
2 *Chr.* 9:14 what *c.* brought

CHAPPED.
Jer. 14:4 because the ground is *c.*

CHARGE, Substantive.
Gen. 26:5 Abraham kept my *c.*
28:6 Isaac gave Jacob a *c.*
Num. 6:13 Moses and Aaron gave
9:18 kept *c.* of the L. 23
27:23 Joshua a *c. Deut.* 31:23
Jos. 22:3 Reubenites kept *c.*
2 *Sam.* 18:5 *c.* concerning Abs.
1 *K.* 11:28 Jeroboam ruler over *c.*
2 *K.* 7:17 Lord *c.* of the gate
1 *Chr.* 9:27 boc. *c.* was on them
Neh. 7:2 Hanani *c.* over Jerus.
Job 34:13 *c.* over the earth ?
Jer. 35:11 *c.* things I knew not
Jer. 30:12 *c.* concerning Jeremiah
47:7 seeing L. hath given it *c.*
Ezek. 9:1 have *c.* over the city
44:8 not kept *c.* of holy things
15 kept *c.* of my sanctuary
48:11 my *c.* went not astray
Acts 7:60 lay not sin to their *c.*
8:27 had *c.* of treasure
16:24 rec. *c.* thrust into prison
23:29 to his *c.* worthy of death
Rom. 8:33 to *c.* of God's elect ?
1 *Cor.* 9:18 gospel without *c.*
1 *Tim.* 1:18 *c.* I commit to thee
2 *Tim.* 4:16 not be laid to their *c.*
See KEEP.

Give CHARGE.
Num. 27:19 *give* Joshua a *c.*
Deut. 31:14 call J. *give* him a *c.*
2 *Sam.* 14:8 I will *give c.* con. thee
1 *Chr.* 22:12 L. *give* thee wis. and *c.*
Ps. 91:11 *g.* ang. *c. Mat.* 4:6;
Luke 4:10
1 *Tim.* 5:7 these things *give* in *c.*
6:13 *give* thee *c.* in sight of God

CHARGE, Verb.
Ex. 19:21 go down *c.* the people
Cant. 2:7 I *c.* dau. 3:5; 5:8; 8:4
5:9 that thou dost so *c.* us
Mark 9:25 I *c.* thee, come out
1 *Tim.* 1:3 *c.* that they teach no
5:7 these things *c.* them
21 I *c.* thee bef. God; 2 *Tim.* 4:1
6:17 *c.* them that are rich

CHARGEABLE.
2 *Sam.* 13:25 not all go, lest be *c.*
Neh. 5:15 governors were *c.*
2 *Cor.* 11:9 I was *c.* to no man
1 *Thes.* 2:9 we would not be *c.*
2 *Thes.* 3:8 might not be *c.* to any

CHARGED.
Gen. 26:11 Abimelech *c.* his peo.
28:1 Isaac called J. and *c.* him
40:4 captain *c.* Jos. with them
49:29 Jacob *c.* his sons, and said

CHA

Ex. 1:22 Pharaoh *c.* his people
1:16 I *c.* your judges
34:5 bor be *c.* with holiness
27:11 Moses *c.* people same day
1 *Sam.* 14:27 heard not when S. *c.*
2 *Sam.* 18:12 bearing, king *c.*
1 *K.* 2:1 David *c.* Solomon
13:9 so *c.* me by word of Lord
2 *Chr.* 36:23 *c.* me to b. *Ezr.* 1:2
Job 1:22 nor *c.* God foolishly
4:17 angels he *c.* with folly
Ezr. 32:13 I *c.* Baruch saying
35:8 obeyed Jonadab in all he *c.*
Mat. 9:30 *c.* that no man know it,
Mark 8:43; *Luke* 9:21
11:16 J. *c.* not to make known
Mark 7:36 *c.* not to tell, 8:30; 9:9;
Luke 5:14; 8:56
10:48 *c.* him should hold peace
1 *Thes.* 2:11 *c.* every one of you
1 *Tim.* 5:16 let not church be *c.*

CHARGEDST.
Ex. 19:23 *c.* us, saying

CHARGER, S.
Num. 7:13 offering silver *c.* 19–79
85 each *c.* of silver 130 shekels
Ezr. 1:9 one thousand *c.*
Mat. 14:8 head in a *c. Mark* 6:25

CHARGES.
2 *Chr.* 8:14 Levites to their *c.*
31:17 twenty years in their *c.*
35:2 set priests in their *c.*
Acts 21:24 be at *c.* with them
1 *Cor.* 9:7 warfare at his own *c.* ?

CHARGING.
Acts 16:23 *c.* jailer to keep safely
2 *Tim.* 2:14 *c.* strive not about w.

CHARIOT.
Gen. 41:43 ride in second *c.*
Ex. 14:25 Lord took off *c.* wheels
1 *K.* 18:44 prep. thy *c.* get down
20:25 number *c.* for *c.*
22:35 the blood ran into *c.*
2 *K.* 2:11 appeared *c.* of fire
12 cried, *c.* of Israel, 13:14
5:21 from *c.* to meet Gehazi
9:16 J. rode in *c.* ; 27 smite in *c.*
28 carried him in a *c.* 23:30
2 *Chr.* 35:24 took him out of *c.*
Ps. 46:9 burneth the *c.* in fire
76:6 *c.* and horse cast into *c.*
Cant. 3:9 *c.* of wood of Lebanon
Is. 21:7 saw a *c.* of asses
22:18 *c.* shall I break in pieces *c.*
Mic. 1:13 bind *c.* to swift beast
Zec. 6:2 first *c.* red horses
9:10 cut off *c.* from Ephraim
Acts 8:29 join thyself to this *c.*
38 commanded *c.* to stand still

His CHARIOT.
Gen. 46:29 J. made ready *his c.*
Ex. 14:6 Ph. made ready *his c.*
Jud. 4:15 Sisera lighted off *his c.*
5:28 *his c.* so long in coming
1 *K.* 12:18 to *his c.* 2 *Chr.* 10:18
22:34 to driver of *his c.*
2 *K.* 5:9 Naaman came with *h. c.*
9:21 went out each to *his c.*
24 Jehoram sunk down in *h. c.*
10:16 made him ride in *his c.*
Jer. 4:13 *his c.* like whirlwind
Acts 8:28 in *his c.* read Esaias

CHARIOT-CITIES.
2 *Chr.* 1:14 placed in *c.-c.*
8:6 Solomon built all *c.-c.*
9:25 bestowed the *c.-c.*

CHARIOT-HORSES.
2 *Sam.* 8:4 hou. *c.-h.* 1 *Chr.* 18:4
2 *K.* 7:14 they took two *c.-h.*

CHARIOT-MAN.
2 *Chr.* 18:33 to *c.-m.* turn thy h.

CHARIOTS.
Gen. 50:9 went with Joseph *c.*
Ex. 14:7 Pharaoh took 600 *c.*
28 waters covered all the *c.*
15:4 Ph.'s *c.* cast into sea, 19
Jos. 17:16 *c.* of iron 18; *Jud.* 1:19; 4:3
Jud. 5:28 wheels of his *c.*
1 *Sam.* 8:11 king appoint for his *c.*
13:5 to fight Israel 30,000 *c.*
2 *Sam.* 1:6 the *c.* followed Saul
1 *K.* 10:26 Solomon had 1,400 *c.*
22:33 captains of *c.* saw Jeh.
2 *K.* 13:7 left but ten *c.*
14 *c.* of Israel, and *c.* of Ahn.
Ps. 68:17 *c.* of God are 20,000
Cant. 6:12 my soul like *c.* of Am.
Is. 2:7 nor any end of their *c.*
22:18 *c.* of thy glory be shame
31:1 woe to them that trust in *c.*
37:24 by mul. of *c.* am I come
66:15 with *c.* like whirlwind,
Jer. 4:13; *Dan.* 11:40

CRUDEN'S CONCORDANCE. 791

CHA

Jer. 47:3 at rushing of his *c.*
Ezek. 23:24 against thee with *c.*
26:10 walls shake at noise of *c.*
Joel 2:5 like noise of *c.* shall leap
Mic. 5:10 I will destroy thy *c.*
Nah. 2:3 *c.* shall be with torches
4 *c.* shall rage in the streets
3:3 I will burn her *c.* in smoke
Hag. 2:22 I will overthrow the *c.*
Rev. 9:9 sound of wings as of *c.*

CHARIOTS *with horses.*
Deut. 11:4 he did to *h.* and *c.*
20:1 seest *horses* and *c.* fear not
Jos. 11:6 hough their *h.* burn *c.*
9 Josh. burnt their *c.* with fire
2 *Sam.* 15:1 Absal. pre. *h.* and *c.*
1 *K.* 20:1 Samaria with *c.* and *h.*
2 *K.* 6:17 mount. full of *c.* and *h.*
7:6 to hear a noise of *h.* and *c.*
10:2 with you *c.* and *horses*
Ps. 20:7 trust in *c.* some in *h.*
Cant. 1:9 comp. to *h.* in Phar. *c.*
Is. 66:20 bring brethren in *c.*
Jer. 17:25 princes in *c.* 22:4
46:9 come up, ye *h.* rage ye *c.*
50:37 on their *horses* and *c.*
Ezek. 26:7 Tyrus Neb. with *c.*
39:20 at table with *h.* and *c.*
Nah. 3:2 *h.* and jumping *c.*
Hab. 3:8 thy *c.* of salvation
Rev. 18:13 buys their *h.* and *c.*

CHARITABLY.
Rom. 14:15 now walkest not *c.*

CHARITY.
1 *Cor.* 8:1 but *c.* edifieth
13:1 and have not *c.* 4, 13
4 *c.* suffereth long, *c.* env. not
13 faith, hope, *c.* greatest is *c.*
14:1 let all be done with *c.*
Col. 3:14 above all put on *c.*
1 *Thes.* 3:6 good tidings of your *c.*
2 *Thes.* 1:3 *c.* to each other
1 *Tim.* 1:5 end of command. is *c.*
2:15 if continue in faith and *c.*
4:12 example in *c.* in spirit
2 *Tim.* 2:22 follow righteous. *c.*
3:10 known my life, faith, *c.*
Tit. 2:2 aged men be sound in *c.*
1 *Pet.* 4:8 fervent *c. c.* cover sins
5:14 greet with a kiss of *c.*
2 *Pet.* 1:7 brotherly kindness *c.*
3 *John* 6 borne witness of thy *c.*
Jude 12 spots in your feasts of *c.*
Rev. 2:19 I know thy works, *c.*

CHARMED.
Jer. 8:17 wh. will not be *c.*

CHARMER, S.
Ps. 58:5 not hearken to *c.*

CHARRAN. *Acts* 7:2, 4

CHASE.
Lev. 26:8 shall *c.* a hundred, 36.
Deut. 32:30 *c.* 1,000, *Jos.* 23:10
Ps. 35:5 angel of L. *c.* them

CHASED, ETH, ING.
Deut. 1:44 Amorites *c.* you
Jud. 9:40 Abimelech *c.* him
Neh. 13:28 I *c.* him from me
Job 18:18 he *c.* out of the world
20:8 he *c.* as a vision of night
Prov. 19:26 *c.* away his mother
Is. 13:14 shall he as the *c.* roe
17:13 they shall be *c.* as chaff
Lam. 3:52 *c.* me sore like a bird

CHASTE.
2 *Cor.* 11:2 pres. you as *c.* virgin
Tit. 2:5 young women be *c.*
1 *Pet.* 3:2 your *c.* conversation

CHASTEN.
2 *Sam.* 7:14 *c.* with rod of men
Ps. 6:1 *c.* me in hot displ. 38:1
Prov. 19:18 *c.* son while hope
Dan. 10:12 *c.* thyself before God
Rev. 3:19 I rebuke and *c.*

CHASTENED.
Deut. 21:18 they have *c.* him
Job 33:19 is *c.* also with pain
Ps. 69:10 *c.* my soul
73:14 and *c.* every morning
118:18 Lord hath *c.* me sore
1 *Cor.* 11:32 *c.* that we be not
2 *Cor.* 6:9 as *c.* and not killed
Heb. 12:10 for a few days *c.* us

CHASTENEST, ETH, ING.
Deut. 8:5 *c.* his son, so L. *c.* thee
Job 5:17 *c.* of Almighty, *Prov.* 3:11; *Heb.* 12:5
Ps. 91:12 bless. is whom thou *c.*
Prov. 13:24 lov. him, *c.* betimes
Is. 26:16 *c.* was on them
Heb. 12:6 whom Lord loveth he *c.*

CHE

Heb. 12:7 if ye end. *c.* what son
11 no *c.* seemeth to be joyous

CHASTISE, ED, ETH.
Lev. 26:28 I will *c.* seven times
Deut. 22:18 elders shall *c.* him
1 *K.* 12:11 I will *c.* you with scorpions, 14; 2 *Chr.* 10:11, 14
14:6 he that *c.* heathen
Jer. 31:18 *c.* me, and I was *c.*
Hos. 7:12 I will *c.* them as cong.
10:10 I should *c.* them
Luke 23:16 *c.* him and release, 22

CHASTISEMENT.
Deut. 11:2 have not seen the *c.*
Job 34:31 I have borne *c.*
Is. 53:5 *c.* of our peace
Jer. 30:14 with *c.* of a cruel one
Heb. 12:8 with. *c.* then bastards

CHATTER.
Is. 38:14 so did I *c.*

CHEBAR. *Ezek.* 1:1, 3; 3:15, 23; 10:15, 20

CHECK.
Job 20:3 heard *c.* of my reproach

CHECKER-WORK.
1 *K.* 7:17 Hir. made nets of *c.*

CHEDORLAOMER. *Gen.* 14:4
1 *K.* 22:24 Zed. smote Mic. on *c.*
Job 16:10 smitten me on the *c.*
Lam. 3:30 *c.* to him that smiteth
Mic. 5:1 smite the judge on the *c.*
Mat. 5:39 right *c.* turn other
Luke 6:29 to him smiteth one *c.*

CHEEKBONE.
Ps. 3:7 smitten enemies on *c.*

CHEEKS.
Cant. 1:10 thy *c.* comely
5:13 his *c.* are as a bed of spices
Is. 50:6 my *c.* to them
Lam. 1:2 her tears are on her *c.*

CHEEKTEETH.
Joel 1:6 he hath *c.* of a great lion

CHEER.
Deut. 24:5 shall *c.* up his wife
Ec. 11:9 thy heart *c.* thee
Good CHEER.
Mat. 9:2 son, be of g. *c.*
14:27 be of g. *c. Mark* 6:50
John 16:33 be of g. *c.* I have
Acts 23:11 be of good *c.* Paul
27:22 to be of good *c.* 25, 36

CHEERFUL.
Jud. 9:13 which *c.* God and man

CHEERFULLY.
Prov. 15:13 a *c.* countenance
Zec. 8:19 be to Judah *c.* feasts
9:17 corn make young men *c.*
2 *Cor.* 9:7 God loveth a *c.* giver

CHEERFULLY.
Acts 24:10 *c.* answer for myself

CHEERFULNESS.
Rom. 12:8 showeth mercy with *c.*

CHEESE, S.
1 *Sam.* 17:18 carry ten *c.* to capt.
2 *Sam.* 17:29 *c.* of kine for David
Job 10:10 curdled me like *c.*

CHEMARIM. *Zep.* 1:4

CHEMOSH.
Num. 21:29 O people of C.
Jud. 11:24 what C. giveth?
1 *K.* 11:7, 33; *Jer.* 48:7, 13, 46

CHENAANAH. 1 *K.* 22:24;
2 *Chr.* 18:23.

CHENANIAH. 1 *Chr.* 15:22 C. chief of Lev. 27

CHERETHITES. *Ezek.* 25:16
1 *Sam.* 30:14 invasion on the C.
2 *Sam.* 8:18 the C. 20:23; 1 *Chr.* 18:17.
Zep. 2:5 woe unto nation of C.

CHERISH, ED, ETH.
1 *K.* 1:2 let her *c.* him, and lie
4 damsel *c.* the king
Eph. 5:29 *c.* flesh, as L. church
1 *Thes.* 2:7 as a nurse *c.* children

CHERITH. 1 *K.* 17:3.

CHERUB.
Ex. 25:19 *c.* on one end *c.* 37:8
2 *Sam.* 22:11 on a *c. Ps.* 18:10
Ezek. 9:3 gone up from a *c.*
10:14 first face was face of a *c.*
28:16 destroy thee, O covering *c.*
41:18 every *c.* had two faces

CHERUBIM.
Gen. 3:24 placed at the east *c.*

CHI

Ex. 37:7 made two *c.* of gold
1 *K.* 8:25 both the *c.* of one meas.
8:7 *c.* covered ark, 2 *Chr.* 5:8;
Heb. 9:5
2 *Chr.* 3:10 most holy house two *c.*
Ezek. 10:16 *c.* went wheels went
19 the *c.* lifted wings, 11:22
Between the CHERUBIM.
Ex. 25:22 from *b.* two *c.*
Num. 7:89 *betw.* the two *c.*
1 *Sam.* 4:4 wh. dw. *bet. c.* 2 *Sam.* 6:2; 2 *K.* 19:15; *Is.* 37:16
Ps. 80:1 dwellest *bet. c.* shine
99:1 he sitteth *bet. l. c.*
Ezek. 10:2 fire from *bet. t. c.* 6
7 hand from *betw.* the *c.*

CHESED. *Gen.* 22:22

CHESNUT-TREE, S.
Gen. 30:37 Jac. took rods of *c.*
Ezek. 31:8 *c.-t.* not like his bran.

CHEST, S.
2 *K.* 12:9 a *c.* and bored a hole
2 *Chr.* 24:8 at king's com. made *c.*
Ezek. 27:24 thy merchants in *c.*

CHEW, ED, ETH.
Lev. 11:4 *c.* the cud, *Deut.* 14:7
7 *c.* not the cud, *Deut.* 14:8
Num. 11:33 ere flesh *c.* wrath

CHICKENS.
Mat. 23:37 hen gathereth her *c.*

CHIDE.
Ex. 17:2 people did *c.* why *c.*
Jud. 8:1 Eph. did *c.* with Gid.
Ps. 103:9 he will not always *c.*

CHIDING.
Ex. 17:7 Meribah, because of *c.*

CHIEF.
Gen. 40:22 restored the *c.* butler
22 but he hanged the *c.* baker
Num. 3:32 Eleazar *c.* over the *c.*
2 *Sam.* 23:18 Abishai was *c.*
1 *Chr.* 5:2 of Judah came *c.* ruler
11:6 smit. Jebusites be *c.* Joab
18:17 the sons of David were *c.*
26:10 though not first-born *c.*
27:3 rulers *c.* in the trespass
29:22 taketh away heart of *c.*
29:25 chose out their way, sat *c.*
40:19 behemoth is *c.* of ways
Ps. 78:51 *c.* of strength, 105:36
137:6 Jerusalem above my *c.* joy
Prov. 1:21 crieth in *c.* places
16:28 whisperer sep. *c.* friends
Is. 14:9 hell stirreth up *c.* once
Jer. 13:21 taught them as *c.* over
31:7 shout among *c.* of nations
Lam. 1:5 her adversaries are *c.*
Dan. 11:41 *c.* of children of Am.
Amos 6:1 *c.* of the nations
Mat. 20:27 whosoever will be *c.*
23:6 love *c.* seats, *Mark* 12:39
Mark 6:21 supper to his *c.* estates
Lu. 11:15 cast, out devils thro' *c.*
14:1 house of one of *c.* Pharisees
7 they chose *c.* rooms, 20:46
22:26 he *c.* as he that serveth
John 12:42 *c.* rulers many believ.
Acts 14:12 he was the *c.* speaker
17:4 of *c.* women not a few
Eph. 2:20 *c.* corner-st. 1 *Pet.* 2:6
1 *Tim.* 1:15 of whom I am *c.*
1 *Pet.* 5:4 *c.* Shep. shall appear

CHIEF captain.
2 *Sam.* 5:8 he shall be *c.* and cap.
Acts 21:31 came to *c. captain*
32 saw *c. captain* he came
24:7 *c. captain* Lys. came upon us
22 *c.* shall come, I will know
CHIEF captains.
2 *Sam.* 23:8 sat *c.* among the *c.*
2 *Chr.* 8:9 he. *c.* of Solomon's *cap.*
Rev. 6:15 *c. c.* hid themselves
CHIEF fathers.
Num. 31:26 *c. f.* of the congreg.
1 *Chr.* 9:34 *c. fathers* of Levites
24:31 *c. fathers* of priests
26:32 2,700 *c. f.* 11, made rulers
Chr. 26:12 number of *c. fathers*
Ezr. 1:5 rose up *c. fath.* of Jud.
Neh. 7:70 *c.* of *f.* gave to work, 71
Jos. 22:14 *c. h.* a prince was sent

CHIEF house.
Jos. 22:14 *c. h.* a prince was sent

CHI

2 *K.* 25:18 took *c.* pr.
1 *Chr.* 27:5 Benaiah a *c. priest*
29:22 anointed Z. to be, *c. priest*
2 *Chr.* 19:11 Amariah *c. priest*
26:20 Azariah *c. p.* looked on
CHIEF priests.
Ezr. 10:5 *c. p.* and all Israel
Mat. 16:21 suffer of the *c. priests*
26:47 multitude from *c. priests*
27:12 accu. of *c. p. Mark* 15:3
41 *c. p.* mocking, *Mark* 15:31
Mark 14:1 *c. p.* sought, 55; *Mat.* 26:59; *Luke* 9:22; 22:1
Luke 23:23 voices of *c. p.* prev.
John 7:32 *c. p.* sent officers, 18:3
Acts 9:14 auth. from *c. p.* 26:10
23:30 commanded *c. p.* to appear

CHIEF prince, or princes.
1 *Chr.* 7:40 children of A. *c.* of *p.*
Ezek. 38:2 Gog *c. prince*, 3; 39:1
Dan. 10:13 Michael one of *c. p.*

CHIEF singer, or singers.
Neh. 12:46 in days of D. *c.* of *s.*
Hab. 3:19 to *c. singer* on instru.

CHIEFEST.
1 *Sam.* 2:29 yoursel. fat with *c.*
9:22 Sam. made sit in *c.* place
2 *Chr.* 32:33 in *c.* of sepulchres
Cant. 5:10 the *c.* among 10,000
2 *Cor.* 11:5 *c.* apostles, 12:11

CHIEFLY.
Rom. 3:2 *c.* because to them
Phil. 4:22 *c.* they of Cesar's h.
2 *Pet.* 2:10 *c.* them walk after fl.

CHILD.
Gen. 21:16 not see death of *c.*
37:30 *c.* is not, and I whither
42:22 do not sin against the *c.*
Ex. 2:8 maid called *c.* mother
22:22 not afflict any fatherless *c.*
Jud. 11:34 his daughter, only *c.*
13:8 teach us what we do to *c.*
1 *Sam.* 1:25 brought the *c.* to Eli
3:8 Eli perc. L. had called *c.*
2 K. 3:25 divide living *c.* in two
14:3 what shall become of *c.*
22 soul of the *c.* came
2 K. 4:31 told *c.* is not awaked
35 *c.* sneezed, *c.* opened eyes
Prov. 22:13 correction from *c.*
Ec. 4:8 hath neither *c.* nor bro.
1 second *c.* that shall stand
Is. 3:5 *c.* shall behave proudly
7:16 before *c.* know to refuse
8:4 before *c.* know to cry
11:8 *c.* put hand on cockatrice
65:20 *c.* shall die 100 years old
Jer. 4:31 bring forth her first *c.*
31:20 Eph. is he a pleasant *c.?*
44:7 cut off man, woman, and *c.*
Mat. 10:21 deliver *c.* to death
17:18 *c.* was cured from that h.
18:2 a little *c.*
Luke 1:59 came to circumcise *c.*
1:66 what manner of *c.*
76 *c.* called prophet of Highest
80 *c.* grew, waxed strong, 2:40
2:27 parents brought in *c.* Jesus
3:28 look on my son, only *c.*
John 4:49 come down ere *c.* die
16:21 as soon as delivered of *c.*
Acts 4:27 against thy holy *c.* J.
30 done by name of thy *c.* J.
13:10 Saul said, Thou *c.* of devil
Rev. 12:4 to devour her *c.* as soon
5 her *c.* was caught up to God

A CHILD.
Gen. 18:13 bear a *c.* who am old?
44:20 and a *c.* of his own age
Ex. 2:2 a goodly *c. Heb.* 11:23
1 *Sam.* 2:18 *c.* girded with linen
1 *K.* 3:25 a *c.* born to house of D.
Job 3:3 flesh fresher than a *c.*
Prov. 20:11 a *c.* is known
22:6 train up a *c.* in way he
15 foolish. b. in heart of *a c.*
23:13 *a c.* left to himself
at bringing up *a c.* from *c.*
Ec. 4:13 better *a c.* wise *c.* than
10:16 when thy king is *a c.*
Is. 10:19 *a c.* may write
Jer. 1:6 for I am *a c.* 7
30:15 a man *c.* is born to thee
Hos. 11:1 Is. *a c.* I loved him
Mark 9:21 he said of *a c.*
10 *c.* took *c.* set it, *Luke* 9:47
Luke 1:7 hath no *c.* 2 I spake as *a c.*
Tim. 3:15 no long as he is *a c.*

792 CRUDEN'S CONCORDANCE.

CHI

2 *Tim.* 3:15 from a c. known sc.
Heb. 11:11 S. deliv. of a c. past a.
Rev. 12:5 a man c. to rule nations

Little CHILD.
1 *K.* 3:7 I am but a *l, c.*
11:17 H. fled being yet a *little c.*
2 *K.* 5:14 the flesh of a *little c.*
Is. 11:6 a *little c.* shall lead them
Mat. 18:2 J. called a *little c.* to him
5 receive one such *l. c.* in my
Mark 10:15 whoso not rec. kingdom of G. as *lit. c. Luke* 18:17

No CHILD.
Gen. 11:30 Sarai had *no c.*
Lev. 22:13 priest's dau. have *n. c.*
Deut. 25:5 brother die, have *n. c.*
2 *Sam.* 6:23 Michal had *no c.*
2 *K.* 4:14 verily she hath *no c.*
Luke 1:7 they had *no. c. hot. E.*
Acts 7:5 when he had *no c.*

Sucking CHILD.
Num. 11:12 beareth *sucking c.*
Is. 11:8 *suck. c.* play on hole
49:15 woman forget *suck. c.*
Lam. 4:4 tongue of *suck. c.*

This CHILD.
Luke 2:17 told concerning *this c.*
34 *t. c.* is set for fall and rising
9:48 receive *t. c.* in my name

With CHILD.
Gen. 16:11 Hagar thou art *w. c.*
19:36 daughters of Lot *with c.*
38:24 T. thy daughter is *w. c.*
25 whose these are, am I *w. c.*
Ex. 21:22 hurt a woman *w. c.*
1 *Sam.* 4:19 Phin. wife was *w. c.*
2 *Sam.* 11:5 B. said, I am *w. c.*
2 *K.* 8:12 wilt rip up their woman *with c.* 15:16
Ec. 11:5 h womb of her *w. c.*
Is. 26:17 *with c.* that draweth
18 we have been *with c.*
54:1 that didst not trav. *with c.*
Jer. 30:6 whc. a man trav. *w. c.*
31:8 the woman *with c.*
Hos. 13:16 *with c.* shall be rip.
Amos 1:13 rip. up woman, *w. c.*
Mat. 1:18 *with c.* of the H. Ghost
23 a virgin shall be *with c.*
24:19 woe to them that are *w. c.*
Luke 2:5 Mary, great *with c.*
1 *Thes.* 5:3 travail on wom. *w. c.*
Rev. 12:2 and she being *with c.*

Young CHILD.
1 *Sam.* 1:24 the *c.* was young
Mat. 2:8 search dilig. for *y. c.*
13 take *young c.* and his moth.

CHILD-BEARING.
1 *Tim.* 2:15 shall be saved in c.-b.

CHILDHOOD.
1 *Sam.* 12:2 before you from c.
Ec. 11:10 c. and youth are vanity

CHILDISH.
1 *Cor.* 13:11 I put away c. things

CHILDLESS.
Gen. 15:2 seeing I go c.
Lev. 20:20 they shall die c.
1 *Sam.* 15:33 as thy sword made women c. so thy mother be c.
Jer. 22:30 write ye this man c.
Luke 20:30 sec. took her, died c.

CHILDREN.
Gen. 3:16 In sorrow bring forth c.
16:2 I may obtain c. by her
25:22 the c. struggled within her
30:1 give me c. or I die
31:8 c. God hath given
43:8 thy father's c. shall bow
Ex. 20:5 iniq. of fath. on c. 34:7;
Num. 14:18; *Deut.* 5:9
21:4 c. shall be her masters
Num. 13:28 saw c. of Anak there
26:11 c. of Korah died not
Deut. 9:2 before c. of Anak?
13:13 c. of Belial are gone out
14:1 ye are the c. of the Lord
23:8 c. begotten of them
24:16 fath. not put to death for c. nor c. for fath. 2 *Chr.* 25:4
32:20 c. in whom there is no f.
33:24 Asher he blessed with c.
Jud. 8:18 resembled c. of king
20:13 deliver us the c. of Belial
1 *Sam.* 2:5 she that hath many c. is waxed feeble
2 *Sam.* 7:10 c. of wickedness nffl. any more, 1 *Chr.* 17:9
1 *K.* 21:13 came in two c. of Bel.
2 *K.* 2:24 she-bears tare 42 c.
10:13 c. of king c. of queen
14:6 c. of murderers, 2 *Chr.* 25:4
17:34 as Lord com. c. of Jacob
19:3 c. are come to b. *Is.* 37:3

CHI

1 *Chr.* 2:30 Seled died without c.
32 and Jether died without c.
4:27 Shimei's bro. not many c.
16:13 ye c. of Jacob, *Ps.* 105:6
2 *Chr.* 19:7 to Jeroboam c. of B.
25:7 L. is not with all c. of E.
Ezra 10:44 by whom had c.
Neh. 9:23 c. multipliedst as stars
Job 19:17 I entreated for c. sake
Ps. 8:6 c. of fools, yea c. of base
41:34 king over all c. of pride
Ps. 17:14 they are full of c.
34:11 come ye c. hearken to me
69:8 am alien to my mother's c.
72:4 be shall save c. of needy
78:6 c. wh. sh. be born might
82:6 all of you c. of Most High
53:3 holpen c. of Lot, Selah
102:28 c. of thy serv. continue
113:9 barren to be mother of c.
127:3 c. are a heritage of Lord
4 as arrows in hand, so are c.
137:7 remember, c. of Edom
148:12 old men and c. praise L.
149:2 let c. of Zion be joyful
Prov. 4:1 hear, ye c. the instruction, 5:7; 7:24; 8:32
17:6 glory of c. are their fathers
31:28 her c. call her blessed
Ec. 6:3 if a man beget 100 c.
Cant. 1:6 my mother's c. angry
Is. 1:2 brought up c. they reb.
4 c. that are corrupters
2:6 in the c. of strangers
3:4 give c. to be their princes
12 c. are their oppressors
8:18 c. Lord hath giv. *Heb.* 2:13
13:18 eyes shall not spare c.
21:17 mighty of c. of K. dimin.
23:4 nor bring forth c.
30:1 woe to rebellious c.
9 lying c. c. will not hear law
38:19 father to c. make known
47:8 neither know loss of c.
9 loss of c. widowhood
49:20 c. shalt have, shall say
54:1 are c. of desolate than c. of married wife, *Gal.* 4:27
57:4 are ye not c. of transgr.
5 slaying the c. in the valleys
63:8 c. that will not lie
66:8 Zion brought forth c.
Jer. 3:14 O backsliding c. 22
19 how put thee among the c.
4:22 my people are sottish c.
6:11 pour it out on c. abroad
7:18 c. gather wood, fathers
9:21 death entered to cut off c.
15:7 I will bereave them of c.
31:15 R. weep for c. *Mat.* 2:18
Lam. 2:20 shall the women eat c.
5:13 c. fell under the wood
Ezek. 2:4 are impudent c.
20:21 the c. rebelled against me
23:30 c. talking against thee
47:22 to strangers that beget c.
Dan. 1:4 c. in whom was no blem
17 four c. God gave knowledge
Mic. 1 Michael shall stand for c.
Hos. 1:2 take c. of whoredoms
2:4 not have mercy on her c.
11:10 c. shall tremble
12:3 breaking forth of c.
Joel 2:16 gather c. and those
23 be glad, then, ye c. of Zion
Amos 9:7 c. of the Ethiopians?
Mic. 1:16 poll thee for delicate c.
2:9 H. I will punish king's c.
Mal. 4:6 heart of fathers to c. c. to fathers. *Luke* 1:17
Mat. 2:16 Herod slew all the c.
3:9 to raise up c. *Luke* 3:8
5:45 be the c. of your Father
8:12 but the c. shall be cast out
9:15 c. of bridechamber mourn, *Mark* 2:19; *Luke* 5:34
10:21 c. sg. parents, *Mark* 13:12
11:19 justi. of her c. *Luke* 7:35
13:38 good seed are c. of kingd.
15:26 c. bread, *Mark* 7:27
17:26 then are the c. free
19:29 forsaken c. *Mark* 10:29
20:20 mother of Zebedee's c.
21:15 saw c. crying in temple
Mark 7:27 let the c. first be filled
28 dogs eat of the c. crumbs
Luke 1:16 c. of Is. shall turn
7:32 c. sitting in markets
11:7 c. are with me in bed
13 know how to give good g.
13:34 would I have gathered c.
16:8 c. of this world are wiser than c. of light
18:29 left c. for kingdom of G.
19:44 c. within thee
20:29 seven breth. first c. died
31 seven took her, died also, and left no c.
34 the c. of this world marry
John 8:39 were Abraham's c.
Acts 3:25 ye are c. of prophets
Rom. 8:17 if c. then heirs, heirs
9:7 seed of Abra. are they all c.
11 the c. being not yet born
1 *Cor.* 14:20 not c. in understand.
Cor. 12:14 c. not lay up

CHI

Gal. 3:7 of faith, are c. of Abra.
4:3 when c. were in bondage
25 Jeru. in bondage with her c.
31 we are not c. of bondwoman
Eph. 1:5 to the adoption of c.
2:2 in c. of disobedience
3 were by nature c. of wrath
4:14 we be no more c. tossed
5:1 followers of God as dear c.
6 wrath on c. of dis. *Col.* 3:6
6:1 c. obey your par. *Col.* 3:20
4 *Tim.* 5:4 if any widow have c.
10 if she brought up c.
Heb. 2:14 as c. are partakers
12:5 speaketh to you as c.
1 *Pet.* 1:14 as obedient c.
2 *Pet.* 2:14 cursed c.
2 *John* 1 to elect lady and her c.
13 c. of elect sister greet thee
Rev. 2:23 I will kill her c.

See AMMON, CAPTIVITY.

CHILDREN of Benjamin.
Jud. 20:13 c. of B. would not
2 *Sam.* 2:25 c. of B. gathered
1 *Chr.* 12:16 c. of B. to hold to D.
Jer. 6:1 O ye c. of B. gather

Children's CHILDREN.
Gen. 45:10 thou and thy c. c.
Ex. 34:7 iniq. of fathers on c. c.
2 *K.* 17:41 served images *child. c.*
Ps. 103:17 righteousness to c. c.
128:6 shalt see c. c.
Prov. 13:22 inherit. to his c. c.
17:6 *child. c.* crown of old men
Jer. 2:9 with your c. c. will I pl.
Ezek. 37:25 and c. c. for ever

Fatherless CHILDREN.
Ps. 109:12 to favor his f. c.
Jer. 49:11 leave thy f. c.

CHILDREN of God.
Mat. 5:9 peacemakers c. of God
Luke 20:36 c. of God being c.
John 11:52 in one the c. of God
Rom. 8:16 we are the c. of God.
21 glor. liberty of the c. of G.
9:8 c. of the flesh, not c. of G.
26 called c. of the living God
1 *John* 3:10 c. of G. manifest, c. of d.
5:2 know we love c. of God

His CHILDREN.
Gen. 18:19 Abra. will com. h. c.
Deut. 17:20 pro. days and his c.
32:5 is not spot of his c.
33:9 nor knew his c.
1 *Sam.* 13:9 seven c. grew with h. c.
Ez. 6:19 give a light, and to h. c.
2 *Chr.* 28:3 burnt h. c. after h.
33:6 his c. to pass through fire
Job 5:4 his c. are far from safety
17:5 eyes of his c. shall fail
19:18 h. shall seek to please
21:19 iniquity for his c.
27:14 if his c. be multiplied
Ps. 69:30 if his c. forsake
103:13 as a father pitieth his c.
109:9 let his c. be fatherless
10 let his c. be vagabonds
Prov. 14:26 his c. shall have ref.
20:7 are blessed after him
Hos. 9:13 shall bring forth his c.
John 4:12 his c. drank thereof
1 *Thes.* 2:11 ch. you as fath. h. c.
1 *Tim.* 3:4 his c. in subjection

CHILDREN of Israel.
Ex. 1:7 c. of I. were fruitful
12 grieved bec. of the c. of I.
2:25 God looked on c. of *Israel*
4:31 heard L. had visited c. of I.
6:13 c. of I. o. of Eg. 26, 27; 12:51
28:43 I will meet with c. of I.
Lev. 25:55 c. of I. are servants
Num. 14:10 gl. of L. ap. bef. c. I.
Jos. 7:12 c. I. not stand bef. ene.
2 *Sam.* 21:9 Gib. not c. of I.
1 *K.* 9:22 c. of Is. make bondm.
2 *Chr.* 8:9 Sol. none c. I. bondm.
Neh. 2:5 our c. as their children
9:1 c. of I. were assem. fasting
13:19 in blood be on our c.

CHILDREN of promise.
Rom. 8:8 c. prom. counted
Gal. 4:28 as Isaac, are c. of prom.

Strange CHILDREN.
Ps. 144:7 rid me from str. c. 11
Hos. 5:7 have begotten *strange c.*

Their CHILDREN.
Gen. 31:43 can I do to *their c.?*
Ex. 4:10 may teach *their c.*
22 might be well with *their c.*
31:13 *their c.* may learn
2 *K.* 8:12 thou wilt dash *their c.*
17:31 burnt *their c.* to the gods
41 c. c. served images
2 *Chr.* 20:13 before L. with *th. c.*
25:4 he slew not *their c.*
Job 21:11 *their c.* dance
Ps. 78:6 show *their c.*

CHILDREN of men.
1 *Sam.* 26:19 if c. m. cursed be
2 *Sam.* 7:14 the stripes of c. m.
1 *K.* 8:39 knowest hearts of c. of men, 2 *Chr.* 6:30
Ps. 11:4 his eyelids try c. of men
12:1 faith. fail from amon. c. m.
14:2 heaven upon c. m. 53:2
36:7 c. m. put trust under sha.
45:2 fairer than the c. of men
90:3 return ye c. of men
107:8 works to c. m. 15, 21, 31
115:16 given to c. of men
Prov. 15:11 hearts of c. of men
Lam. 3:33 doth not grieve c. m.
Dan. 3:8 wherever *thec. of. m.*

Men-CHILDREN.
Ex. 1:17 midw. saved men. c.
34:23 men-c. shall app. bef. L.

Men, Women, and CHILDREN.
Deut. 3:6 in B. we dest. m. w. c.
31:12 gather men, and c.
Ezra 10:1 great cong. of m. w. c.
Mat. 14:21 eaten, were 5,000 m. beside women and c. 15:38

My CHILDREN.
Gen. 30:26 give me my c.
31:43 these c. are my c. and
42:36 me ye have ber. of my c.
43:14 if bereaved of my c. I am
Ex. 21:5 I love my master my c.
1 *K.* 20:7 he sent to me for my c.
Job 29:5 my c. were about me
Is. 49:21 I have lost my c.
Jer. 10:20 my c. gone forth of me
Lam. 1:16 my c. are desolate
Ezek. 16:21 thou hast slain my c.?
Luke 11:7 my c. are with me
2 *Cor.* 6:13 speak as to my c.
3 *John* 4 hear my c. walk in truth

No CHILDREN.
Gen. 16:1 Sarai bare him *no c.*
30:1 Rachel saw she bare *no c.*
1 *Sam.* 1:2 but Hannah had *no c.*
Mat. 22:24 having *no c. Mark* 12:19; *Luke* 20:31; seven left

Our CHILDREN.
Gen. 31:16 riches ours and *our c.*
Num. 14:3 that *our c.* be a prey
Deut. 29:29 bel. to us and *our c.*
Jos. 22:24 c. might sp. to *our c.*
25 your c. make o. c. cease
Mat. 27:25 his blood be on *our c.*
Neh. 5:5 *our c.* as their children

CHILDREN of promise.
Rom. 8:8 c. prom. counted
Gal. 4:28 as Isaac, are c. of prom.

CRUDEN'S CONCORDANCE. 793

CHO

Ps. 78:4 not hide them from *t. c.*
6 and declare them to *their c.*
90:16 let thy glory appear to *t. c.*
132:12 I. *c.* sh. sit on thy throne
Is. 13:16 *t. c.* be dashed to pieces
Jer. 17:2 *t. c.* remember altars
18:21 deliver *their c.* to famine
30:20 *t. c.* shall he as aforetime
32:18 into bosom of *their c.*
39 good of them and *their c.*
47:3 not look back to *their c.*
Lam. 4:10 have sodden *their c.*
Ezek. 20:18 I said to *their c.*
23:39 when had slain *their c.*
37:25 they and *their c.* sh. dwell
Hos. 9:12 *l. c.* yet I will bereave
Joel 1:3 your *c.* tell *t. c.* and *t. c.*
Mic. 2:9 from *their c.* taken
Zec. 10:7 *l. c.* shall see it
9 live with *their c.* and turn
Acts 13:33 same to us *their c.*
1 Tim. 3:12 ruling *their c.* well
Tit. 2:4 women to love *their c.*

Thy CHILDREN.
Deut. 4:40 w. with *thy c.* 12:25, 28
6:7 shalt teach them to *thy c.*
30:2 thou and *thy c.* obey with
Jos. 14:9 be thine and *thy c.*
1 Sam. 16:11 are here all *thy c.*
1 K. 8:4 if *thy c.* take heed
2:25 *thy c.* take h. 2 Chr. 6:16
2:23 thy wives and *thy c.*
2 K. 10:30 *thy c.* of fourth gen.
2 Chr. 21:14 L. shall smite *thy c.*
Job 8:4 if *thy c.* have sinned
Ps. 45:16 inst. of fathers be *thy c.*
73:15 offend ag. gen. of *thy c.*
128:3 *thy c.* like olive-plants
132:12 if *thy c.* keep covenant
147:13 blessed *thy c.* within thee
Is. 49:17 *thy c.* shall make haste
25 and I will save *thy c.*
54:13 all *thy c.* be taught of L.
and great be peace of *thy c.*
Jer. 5:7 *thy c.* have forsaken me
31:17 that *thy c.* come again
38:23 bring out *thy c.* to Chald.
Ezek. 16:36 by the blood of *thy c.*
Hos. 4:6 I will also forget *thy c.*
Mat. 23:37 how oft. would I have gath. *thy c.* Luke 13:34
Luke 19:44 lay *thy c.* within thee
2 John 4 *thy c.* walking in truth

Your CHILDREN.
Ex. 12:26 *your c.* shall say
22:24 *your c.* shall be fatherless
Lev. 26:22 beasts rob you of *y. c.*
Deut. 1:39 *your c.* shall go in
11:2 I speak not with *your c.*
19 ye shall teach *your c.*
21 days of *your c.* be multiplied
24:16 con. *your c.* to observe
Jos. 4:22 then let *your c.* know
1 K. 9:6 if *y. c.* turn from fol. me
1 Chr. 28:8 inh. to *y. c. Ezr.* 9:12
2 Chr. 30:9 *your c.* shall find
Ps. 115:14 you and *your c.*
Jer. 2:30 have I smitten *y. c.*
Mat. 7:11 gifts to *y. c. Luke* 11:13
12:27 by whom do *y. c.* cast out
Luke 23:28 weep for *y.* and *y. c.*
Acts 2:39 is to you and *y. c.*
1 Cor. 7:14 were *your c.* unclean
Eph. 6:4 pro. not *y. c. Col.* 3:21

Young CHILDREN.
Job 19:18 *young c.* despised me
Lam. 4:4 *y. c.* ask bread
Nah. 3:10 *young c.* were dashed
Mark 10:13 brought *y. c.* to him
Acts 7:19 they cast out *y. c.*

CHILEAB. 2 Sam. 3:3
CHILION. Ruth 1:2, 5
CHILMAD. Ezek. 27:23

CHIMHAM.
2 Sam. 19:37 C. let him go, 38, 40
Jer. 41:17 habitation of C.

CHIMNEY.
Hos. 13:3 be as smoke out of *c.*

CHIOS. Acts 20:15
CHISLEU. Neh. 1:1; Zec. 7:1

CHITTIM.
Num. 24:24 from coasts of C.
Is. 23:1 from the land of C. 12
Jer. 2:10 pass over the isles of C.
Ezek. 27:6 ivory out of isles of C.
Dan. 11:30 ships of C. shall come

CHIUN. Amos 5:26
CHLOE. 1 Cor. 1:11

CHODE.
Gen. 31:36 Jacob *c.* with Laban
Num. 20:3 people *c.* with Moses

CHOICE.
1 Sam. 9:2 Saul a *c.* young man
2 Sam. 10:9 *c.* of Is. 1 Chr. 19:10

CHO

2 Chr. 25:5 300,000 *c.* men
Cant. 6:9 *c.* one of her that bare
Acts 15:7 God made *c.* among us

CHOICEST.
Is. 5:2 planted with the *c.* vine
22:7 *c.* valleys full of chariots

CHOKE.
Mat. 13:22 deceitfulness of riches *c.* the word, Mark 4:19

CHOKED.
Mat. 13:7 thorns *c. Mar.*4:7; Lu.8:7
Mark 5:13 *c.* in sea, Luke 8:33
Luke 8:14 and are *c.* with cares

CHOLER.
Dan. 8:7 he-goat moved with *c.*
11:11 k. of south moved with *c.*

CHOOSE, as an act of God.
Num. 16:7 man L. doth *c.* be holy
Deut. 7:7 did not *c.* you because
12:5 place Lord shall *c.* 11, 14, 18, 26; 14:23, 24, 25; 15:20;
16:2, 6, 7, 15, 16; 17:8, 10;
18:6; 26:2; 31:11; Jos. 9:27
17:15 king, whom Lord shall *c.*
1 Sam. 2:28 did I *c.* him of all
2 Sam. 16:18 and this people *c.*
21:6 hang in G. whom L. did *c.*
1 K. 14:21 the city the L. did *c.*
Neh. 9:7 God who didst *c.* Abram
Ps. 25:12 teach in way he shall *c.*
47:4 he shall *c.* our inheritance
Is. 14:1 Lord will yet *c.* Israel
49:7 Holy One of Israel shall *c.*
66:4 I will *c.* their delusions
Zec. 1:17 Lord shall *c.* Jer. 3:12

CHOOSE.
Deut. 23:16 in place he shall *c.*
30:19 therefore *c.* life that both
Jos. 24:15 *c.* this day whom serve
1 Sam. 17:8 *c.* you a man for you
Job 9:14 *c.* out my words to reason
34:4 let us *c.* to us judgment
33 or whether thou *c.*
Prov. 1:29 did not *c.* fear of L.
3:31 *c.* none of his ways
Is. 7:15 know to *c.* good, 16
56:4 eunuchs *c.* things
58:5 *c.* wherein I del. not
Ezek. 21:19 *c.* a place *c.* it
Phil. 1:22 what I shall *c.* I wot n.

CHOOSEST, ETH, ING.
Job 7:15 my soul *c.* strangling
15:5 thou *c.* tongue of crafty
Ps. 65:4 blessed is man thou *c.*
Is. 40:20 *c.* a tree will not rot
41:24 abomination is he *c.* you
Heb. 11:25 to suffer affliction

CHOP.
Mic. 3:3 *c.* bones of my people

CHORAZIN. Mat. 11:21; Lu.10:13

CHOSE.
Ex. 18:25 Moses *c.* able men
Deut. 4:37 he *c.* their seed, 10:15
Jos. 8:3 J. *c.* 30,000 mighty
Jud. 5:8 they *c.* new gods
1 K. 8:16 *c.* no city to build a house, 2 Chr. 6:5
1 Chr. 28:4 Lord *c.* me before all
Job 29:25 I *c.* out their way
Ps. 78:67 *c.* not tribe of Ephr.
68 but *c.* the tribe of Judah
70 he *c.* David also his servant
Ezek. 20:5 in the day I *c.* Israel
Luke 6:13 he *c.* twelve apostles
Acts 6:5 *c.* Stephen, full of faith
13:17 G. of Israel *c.* our fathers
15:40 Paul *c.* Silas and departed

CHOSEN.
Gen. 16:5 him *c.* cause to come
Jos. 8:2 have *c.* you the Lord
1 Sam. 8:18 king ye have *c.* 12:13
1 K. 3:8 hast *c.* a great people
8:44 toward city thou hast *c.*
1 K. 16:13 children of J. *c.* ones
Job 36:21 *c.* rather than affliction
Ps. 33:12 *c.* for his inheritance
89:3 covenant with my *c.*
19 I exalted one *c.* out of people
105:6 ye of Jacob, his *c.*
B forth his *c.* with gladness
23 had not Moses his *c.* stood
26 I may see good of thy *c.*
Prov. 16:16 rather *c.* than silver
22:1 a good name rather *c.*
Is. 43:20 to give drink to my *c.*
65:15 name a curse to my *c.*
66:3 have *c.* their own ways

CHR

Jer. 8:3 death shall be *c.* rather
49:19 who is a *c.* man, 50:44
Mat. 20:16 but few *c.* 22:14
Mark 13:20 elect whom hath *c.*
Luke 10:42 M. hath *c.* good part
Acts 1:24 whether thou hast *c.*
9:15 for he is a *c.* vessel to me
Rom. 16:13 Rufus *c.* in Lord
1 Cor. 8:19 *c.* of churches to trav.
2 Tim. 2:4 *c.* him to be a soldier
1 Pet. 2:9 ye are a *c.* generation
Rev. 17:14 they are called, and *c.*

CHOSEN of God.
Luke 28:35 if C. the *c.* of God
Acts 10:41 witnesses *c.* bef. of G.
1 Pet. 2:4 living stone *c.* of God

God hath CHOSEN.
Deut. 12:21 G. *h. c.* to put, 16:11
21:5 G. *h. c.* to minister
1 Chr. 29:1 Sol. whom al. G. *h. c.*
Acts 22:14 G. of fathers *h. c.*
1 Cor. 1:27 G. *h. c.* foolish th. G.*h. c.*
28 things despised G. *h. c.*
2 Thes. 2:13 G. from begin. *h. c.*
Jam. 2:5 h. not G. *c.* poor of w.

I have CHOSEN.
1 K. 11:13 for. sake which *I h. c.*
2 K. 21:7; 23:27; 2 Chr. 6:6
32 J. *h. c.* out of all tribes
Neh. 1:9 *I h. c.* to set my name
Ps. 119:30 *I h. c.* way, 173
Is. 41:8 Jacob whom *I have c.*
9 *I have c.* and not cast away
43:10 my serv. L. J. *Mat.* 12:18
44:1 Israel whom *I h. c.* 2 Josh.
49:10 *I have c.* thee in fur.
56:5 the bed that *I have c.* P 6
Hag. 2:23 *I have c.* thee
John 13:18 whom *I have c.*
15:16 ye have not *c.* me, *I h. c.*
19 *I have c.* you out of world

Lord hath CHOSEN.
Deut. 7:6 *L.h.c.* thee to b. 14:2
18:5 *L. h. c.* him out of all
1 Sam. 10:24 see ye him *L. h. c.*
16:10 Samuel said, *L. h.* not *c.*
1 Chr. 28:4 *Lord hath c.* Judah
5 *L.h. c.* Sol. to sit on throne, 10
2 Chr. 29:11 *L. h. c.* you to serve
Ps. 105:26 *L.* whom he had *c.*
132:13 *L. c.* Zion; 135:4 *L. h. c. J.*
Jer. 33:24 two families *L. h. c.*
Zec. 3:2 *L.* that *c. J.* rebuke thee
Eph. 1:4 acc. as he *hath c.* us

CHOSEN men.
Jud. 20:16 700 *c.* m. left-handed
2 Chr. 13:3 Ab. with 400,000 *c. m.*
Jeroboam with 800,000 *c. m.*
Ps. 78:31 smote *c. m.* of Israel
Acts 15:22 to send *c. men*, 25

CHRIST.

Mat. 2:4 where C. sh. be born
16:16 thou art C. the Son
23:8 one is Master, even C. 10
24:5 saying I am C. *Mark* 13:6;
26:68 prophesy to us, thou C.
Mark 9:41 bec. ye belong to C.
15:32 let C. descend from cross
Luke 2:26 before he had seen C.
4:41 devils knew he was C.
23:35 save thyself and us
39 if C. save thyself and us
24:26 ought not C. to have suff.
46 it behooved C. to suffer
John 4:25 Mes. cometh called C.
7:27 C. cometh, 31
41 C. come out of Galilee?
42 C. cometh of seed of David
9:22 did confess he was C.
12:31 heard it, abideth for ever
Acts 2:33 would raise up C. to sit
3:18 showed *c.* should suffer
8:5 Philip preached C. to them
9:20 straightway preached C.
17:3 C. must needs have suff.
26:23 C. should suffer
Rom. 5:6 in due time C. died
8 yet sinners, C. died for us
9:1 C. was raised from dead
c. I being raised dieth no m.
7:4 by the body of C.
8:9 have not the spirit of C.
10 if C. be in you, body is d.
11 raised up C. from dead
14:9 answered Rom.?
15:3 even C. pleased not himself
5 of whom C. came
10:1 C. is end of law for right.
4 to bring C. down from above
11:7 then shall C. profit nothing
12:5 and like for whom C. died
14 in these things serveth *c.*
15:3 *C.* pleased not himself
7 us *c.* also received us

CHR

Rom. 15:18 wh. C. not wrought
not where C. was named
16:5 Epenetus first-fruits to C.
1 Cor. 1:23 we preach C. cruc'f.
24 C. the power of God, and
3:23 ye are C. and C. is God's
5:7 C. our passover sacrificed
8:11 perish, for whom C. died
9:21 under law to C. that I m.
10:4 and that Rock was C.
9 nor let us tempt C.
15:3 how C. died for our sins
13 if C. be preached
10 rise not, is not C. raised
17 not raised, faith is v.
23 in his order, C. first-fruits
2 Cor. 3:4 thro' C. to God-ward
3:16 known C. after flesh
6:15 what concord C. with B.
Gal. 2:20 C. liveth in me
21 if C. is dead in vain
3:13 C. redeemed us from curse
24 schoolmaster to br. us to C.
29 if ye be C.'s, then Abr.'s seed
4:7 heir of God through C.
19 till C. be formed in you
5:1 wherewith C. m. us free
2 if C. circum. C. profit nothing
4 C. is of none effect unto you
24 that are C. have crucified
Eph. 2:12 without C.
3:17 that C. may dwell by faith
4:13 which is the head, even C.
20 ye have not so learned C.
5:2 as C. also loved us
14 C. shall give thee light
23 as C. is head of the church
24 as church is subject to C.
25 love wives as C. loved ch.
32 concerning C. and church
6:5 singlen. of heart as to C.
Phil. 1:15 some preach C.
16 preach C. of contention
18 C. is preached, and I rejoice
20 C. be magnified in my body
21 for me to live is C.
2:11 that they may win C.
4:13 I can do all through C.
Col. 2:8 world, and not after C.
3:1 C. sitteth on right hand
4 C. who is our life shall ap.
11 but C. is all and in all
13 as C. forgave you, so do ye
24 for ye serve the Lord C.
Heb. 3:6 C. as a son
5:5 so C. glorified not himself
3:11 C. a high-priest of good
24 C. was once offered to bear
1 P. 2:21 C. also suffered for us
3:18 C. once suffered for sins
4:1 as C. suffered in the flesh
1 John 4:3 confess not C. is C.
4:15 is come power of his C.

Against CHRIST.
Acts 4:26 kings gath. *a.* his C.
1 Cor. 8:12 brethren, ye sin *a.* C.
1 Tim. 5:11 wax wanton *a.* C.

By CHRIST.
2 Cor. 1:5 aboundeth *by* C.
Gal. 2:17 to be justified *by* C.
Eph. 3:21 glory in church *by* C.

For CHRIST.
1 Cor. 1:17 C. sent me not to b.
4:10 we are fools *for* C. sake
2 Cor. 4:5 as God *for* C. sake
5:20 ambassadors *for* C.
12:10 in distresses *for* C.
Phil. 3:7 I counted loss *for* C.
2 Thes. 3:5 patient waiting *for* C.

Jesus, *with* CHRIST.
Mat. 1:16 J. called C. 27:17, 22
John 1:17 and truth by J. C.
17:3 may know thee, and J. C.
Acts 2:38 in name of J. C.
3:6 in name of J. C. rise up
20 J. C. who was preached
5:42 ceased not to preach J. C.
8:12 Philip preach. things conc.
17 believed J. C. is Son of God
18 in name of J. C. come out
10:36 preaching peace by J. C.
17:3 Jesus I preach to you is C.
18:5 testified that Jesus was C.
28 by scripture, Jesus was C.
19:4 should believe on C. Jesus
Rom. 1:1 serv. of J. C. 1:1
25:6 is he called of Jesus C.
3 many called of Jesus C.
6 thro' the faith of Jesus C.
2:16 secrets of men by J. C.
3:22 by faith of J. C.
21 redemption in Jesus C.

CHR

Rom. 5:15 gr. by one man J. C.
17 reign in life by one J. C.
6:3 baptized into *Jesus* C.
8:1 to them in C. *Jesus*
2 C. J. made me free
16:3 my helpers in C. *Jesus*
1 *Cor.* 1:1 J. C. 2 *Cor.* 1:1; *Eph.* 1:1
2 call on name of J. C.
4 grace given you by J. C.
30 of him are ye in C. *Jesus*
2:2 save J. C. crucified
4:15 in C. J. have I begotten
2 *Cor.* 4:6 in face of J. C.
5:18 reconciled us by J. C.
13:5 that *Jesus* C. is in you
Gal. 2:16 justified by faith of J. C.
3:14 blessings on G. through J. C.
28 ye are all one in C. *Jesus*
4:14 one as an angel, as C. J.
Eph. 2:6 heav. places in C. J.
20 J. C. chief corner-stone
Phil. 1:8 I in bowels of *Jesus* C.
2:5 mind in you, was in C. J.
11 J. C. is Lord to glory of G.
21 seek not th. wh. are J. C.
3:8 for excellency of C. J.
12 I am apprehended of C. J.
4:19 riches in glory by C. J.
Col. 2:6 rec. C. J. so walk ye
1 *Tim.* 1:15 C. J. ca. to save sin.
2:5 one mediator, the man C. J.
6:13 C. *Jesus* who witnessed
2 *Tim.* 1:9 grace given us in C. J.
13 faith and love in C. *Jesus*
Phile. 1:9 P. a priso. of J. C. 9, 23
Heb. 13:8 *Jesus* C. the same yes.
1 *John* 1:7 blood of *Jesus* C.
2:1 an advocate *Jesus* C.
5:6 by water and blood J. C.
20 even in *Jesus* C.

Lord Jesus CHRIST.
Acts 11:17 believed on L. J. C.
15:11 through grace of L. J. C.
16:31 believe on L. J. C.
20:21 faith toward L. J. C.
Rom. 5:1 p. with G. thro' L. J. C.
11 joy in God through L. J. C.
6:23 eternal life through L. J. C.
8:39 love of G. in C. J. our L
13:14 put ye on the L. J. C.
16:20 grace of L. J. C. be w. you,
24; 2 *Cor.* 13:14; *Gal.* 6:18
1 *Cor.* 1:7 coming of our L. J. C.
8:6 one L. J. C. by whom are
15:57 victory thro' our L. J. C.
10:22 if any love not L. J. C.
2 *Cor.* 1:2 from G. and L. J. C.
Gal. 1:3; *Eph.* 1:2; *Col.* 1:2
8:9 ye know grace of L. J. C.
Gal. 6:14 in cross of L. J. C.
Eph. 1:3 Father of L. J. C.
17 God of L. J. C.
1 *Thes.* 1:3 hope in L. J. C.
2:19 in presence of L. J. C.
3:13 at coming of L. J. C.
5:23 pres. to coming of L. J. C.
2 *Thes.* 2:1 by coming of L. J. C.
16 our L. J. C. who hath
1 *Tim.* 5:21 I charge thee before L. J. C. 2 *Tim.* 4:1
2 *Tim.* 4:22 L. J. C. be with thy
2 *Pet.* 1:11 kingdom of L. J. C.
3:18 in knowledge of L. J. C.

In CHRIST.
Acts 24:24 concerning faith in C.
Rom. 9:1 I say the truth in C.
12:5 many, are one body in C.
16:7 were in C. before me
9 Urbane our helper in C.
10 Apelles approved in C.
1 *Cor.* 3:1 as unto babes in C.
4:10 but ye are wise in C.
15:18 asleep in C.
19 in this life hope in C.
22 in C. all be made alive
2 *Cor.* 1:21 establish us in C.
2:14 to triumph in C.
17 in sight of God speak in C.
3:14 veil is done away in C.
5:17 in C. he is a new creature
19 in C. reconciling the world
20 in C. stead, be reconciled
12:2 a man in C. 14 years
19 we speak boldly in C.
Gal. 1:22 to churches of J. in C.
3:17 confirmed of G. in C.
27 as many as baptized in C.
Eph. 1:3 spiritual bless. in C.
10 in one all things in C.
12 who first trusted in C.
20 in C. when he raised
3:6 his promise in C.
Phil. 1:13 my bonds in C.
2:1 if any consolation in C.
Col. 2:5 your faith in C.
1 *Thes.* 4:16 dead in C. rise first

CHR

1 *Tim.* 2:7 I speak the truth in C.
1 *Pet.* 3:16 good conversation in C.

In CHRIST.
Mat. 24:23 h. is C. *Mark* 13:21
Mark 12:35 C. is son. *Luke* 20:41
Luke 2:11 a Saviour, wh. is C.
23:2 saying, that he is C.
John 7:41 said this is the C.
9:22 Saul proving this is C.
17:3 *Jesus* I preach to you is C.
Rom. 8:34 it is C. that died
1 *Cor.* 1:13 is C. divided?
7:22 being free i t C. servant
11:3 head of every man is C.
12:12 are one body, so is C.
15:13 if dead rise not, is C. 16
2 *Cor.* 10:7 if any trust he is C.
Phil. 1:21 to live is C.
Col. 1:27 is C. in you hope

Of CHRIST.
Mat. 11:2 John heard works of C.
22:42 what think ye of C.?
Rom. 8:9 any have not S. of C.
35 sep. us from love of C.?
14:10 judgment-seat of C.
1 *Cor.* 1:17 cross of C. be made
8:16 we have the mind of C.
6:15 your bodies members of C.
10:16 communion of blood of C.
11:1 be foll. of me as I of C.
3 the head of C. is God
12:27 ye are the body of C.
2 *Cor.* 1:5 as sufferings of C.
2:10 forgave I it in person of C.
15 we are a sweet savor of C.
3:3 epistle of C. ministered
4:4 light of gospel of C. shine
5:14 love of C. constraineth us
8:23 they are glory of C.
10:1 by the meekness of C.
5 bringing to obedience of C.
11:10 the truth of C. is in me
12:9 power of C. *Rev.* 12:10
13:3 proof of C. speaking
Gal. 1:10 be servant of C.
2:16 be justified by faith of C.
6:12 persecution for cross of C.
Eph. 2:13 by the blood of C.
3:4 in mystery of C.
8 the unsearchable riches of C.
19 love of C. which passeth
4:7 measure of gift of C.
5:5 inheritance in king. of C.
6:6 as servants of C.
Phil. 1:10 till the day of C.
29 it is given in behalf of C.
2:16 rejoice in the day of C.
30 work of C. nigh to death
3:18 enemies of the cross of C.
Col. 1:24 afflictions of C.
2:2 mystery of God, and of C.
17 but the body is of C.
3:16 let the word of C. dwell
4:3 to speak the mystery of C.
2 *Tim.* 2:19 the name of C.
Heb. 3:14 made partakers of C.
9:14 more, blood of C. purge
11:26 reproach of C. greater
1 *Pet.* 1:11 Spirit of C. did signify
19 with precious blood of C.
4:13 partakers of C. sufferings
14 reproached for name of C.
Rev. 20:6 priests of G. and of C.

That CHRIST.
John 1:25 if thou be not that C.
6:69 sure that thou art that C.

The CHRIST.
Mat. 16:20 he was the C.
26:63 whether thou be the C.
Mark 8:29 saith, thou art the C.
14:61 the C. son of the B.?
Luke 3:15 whether he were t. C.
9:20 Peter said thou art the C.
22:67 saying art thou the C.
John 1:20 I am not the C.
4 found the Messias, the C.
3:28 I said I am not the C.
4:20 is not this the C.?
42 this is indeed the C. 7:26
7:41 others said, this is the C.
10:24 be the C. tell us plainly
11:27 I believe thou art the C.
20:31 believe *Jesus* is the C.
1 *John* 2:22 *Jesus* is the C.
5:1 believeth *Jesus* is the C.

With CHRIST.
Rom. 6:8 if we be dead with C.
8:17 then joint-heirs with C.
Gal. 2:20 I am crucified with C.
Eph. 2:5 quickened us tog. w. C.
Phil. 1:23 a desire to be with C.
Col. 2:20 if dead with C.
3:1 if risen w. C. seek things

CHU

Col. 3:3 your life is hid with C.
Rev. 20:4 reigned with C.

CHRISTIAN, S.
Acts 11:26 called c. at Antioch
26:28 almost pers. me to be a c.
1 *Pet.* 4:16 if any suffer as a c.

CHRISTS.
Mat. 24:24 false c. *Mark* 13:22

CHRONICLES.
1 *Chr.* 27:24 number put in c.
Est. 6:1 to bring the book of c.
See BOOK.

CHRYSOLITE.
Rev. 21:20 seventh found. a c.

CHRYSOPRASUS.
Rev. 21:20 tenth foundation a c.

CHURCH.
Mat. 16:18 on this rock b. my c.
18:17 tell it to the c.
Acts 2:47 added to c. daily such
5:11 great fear came on c.
8:1 persecution against c.
11:26 assembled with the c.
14:23 ordained elders in every c.
27 had gathered c. together
15:3 brought on way by the c.
22 it pleased elders with the c.
18:22 when he had saluted c.
Rom. 16:5 greet c. in their house
1 *Cor.* 4:17 as I teach in every c.
14:4 prophesieth edifieth c.
5 that c. may receive edifying
23 if c. be come into one place
16:19 c. in their house
Eph. 1:22 head over all to the c.
3:10 known by c. wisdom of G.
5:24 as c. is subject to Christ
25 as Christ loved the c.
27 might present a glorious c.
32 cherisheth it, as Lord the c.
32 speak concern. Christ and c.
Phil. 3:6 persecuting the c.
4:15 no c. communicated
Col. 1:18 head of the body the c.
24 for his body's sake, the c.
4:16 salute c. in Laodicea
15 *Nymphas* ho.
Phile. 2 c. in thy house
Heb. 12:23 to c. of first-born
1 *Pet.* 5:13 c. at Babylon saluteth
Acts 15:5 needful to c. them
21:21 they ought not to c.

CIRCUMCISED.
Gen. 17:10 every man-child be c.
14 not c. shall be cut off
26 Abraham was c. and Ishm.
34:15 every male c.
Ex. 12:48 be c. keep passover
Jos. 5:3 c. children of Isr.
Jer. 9:25 punish all c. with uncir.
Acts 15:1 except c. not saved, 24
16:3 Paul c. Timothy
Rom. 4:11 though not c.
1 *Cor.* 7:18 being c.? in uncircumcision? let him not be c.
Gal. 2:3 Titus compelled to be c.
5:2 if c. C. shall profit nothing
6:12 they constrain you to be c.
13 they c. keep not the law
Phil. 3:5 c. eighth day
Col. 3:11 in whom also ye are c.

CIRCUMCISING.
Luke 2:21 days accomp. for c.

CIRCUMCISION.
John 7:22 M. gave unto you c.
23 if on the sabbath receive c.
Rom. 2:25 c. profiteth, if thou keep the law; thy c. is made
28 nor is that c. the heart
3:30 shall justify c. by faith
4:9 this blessedness on c. only?
10 when he was in c.? not in c.
1 *Cor.* 7:19 c. is keeping of com.
Gal. 2:9 they should go unto c.
5:6 neither c. availeth. 6:15
11 and I, if I yet preach c.
Eph. 2:11 by that called c.
Phil. 3:3 c. which worship God
Col. 3:11 c. without hands, by c.
3:11 there is nei. c. nor uncir.

Of CIRCUMCISION.
Ex. 4:26 bloody hus. bec. of c.
Acts 7:8 Abrah. covenant of c.
10:45 they of c. were astonished
11:2 of c. contended with Peter
Rom. 3:1 what profit of c.?
4:11 he received the sign of c.
12 of c. to them of c.
15:8 J. C. was a minister of c.
Gal. 2:7 gospel of c. com. to Pe.
2:8 in Peter to apostleship of c.
Col. 4:11 who are of the c. salute
Tit. 1:10 unruly, especially of c.

CRUDEN'S CONCORDANCE. 795

CIT

CIRCUMSPECT, LY.
Ex. 23:13 in all things be *c*.
Eph. 5:15 see that ye walk *c*.

CISTERN, S.
2 K. 18:31 drink ev. one of his *c*.
Prov. 5:15 drink of thine own *c*.
Ec. 12:6 wheel broken at the *c*.
Is. 36:16 every one of own *c*.
Jer. 2:13 hewed out *c*, of brok. *c*.

CITY.
Gen. 4:17 Cain builded a *c*.
11:4 build *c*. and a tower
5 Lord came down to see *c*.
8 they left off to build the *c*.
18:26 find fifty righteous in *c*.
24:25 came upon the *c*. boldly
Num. 21:28 flame is gone from *c*.
Deut. 2:36 not one *c*. too strong
3:4 not a *c*. we took not from
13:15 smite inhabit. of that *c*.
Jos. 3:16 very far from *c*. Adam
6:3 compass the *c*. six days, 7
14 burnt *c*, Deut. 13:16 Jos. 8:8,
19; Jud. 1:8; 13:27
8:2 lay ambush for *c*. behind
20 smoke of *c*. ascended to h.
15:13 *c*. of Arba, which *c*. is II.
19:50 gave Joshua *c*. he asked
Jud. 6:27 he feared men of *c*.
9:45 *c*. and sowed it with salt
20:40 flame of the *c*. ascended
Ruth 1:19 all the *c*. was moved
4:11 for *c*. of my people know
1 Sam. 1:3 out of *c*. yearly to w.
4:13 told it, all the *c*. cried out
8:22 every man to his *c*. 1 K.
22:36; Ezr. 2:1; Neh. 7:6
28:3 Israel b. him in his own *c*.
2 Sam. 12:1 two men in one *c*.
15:2 of what *c*, art thou ?
19:37 I may die in my own *c*.
20:19 seekest to destroy a *c*.
1 K. 1:45 so that *c*. rang again
11:32 *c*. I have chosen, 36
2 K. 6:19 neither is this the *c*.
11:20 and the *c*. was in quiet
21:10 *c*. Jer. was besieged, 25:2
2 Chr. 13:8 *c*. was destroyed of *c*.
19:5 and he set judges *c*. by *c*.
30:10 posts passed from *c*. to *c*.
32:18 that they might take *c*.
Ezr. 4:12 building rebellions *c*.
Neh. 2:3 why not sad, *c*. waste, 5
11:9 Judah was second over *c*.
Ed. 8:15 the *c*. Shushan rejoiced
Ps. 48:2 *c*. of gr. king. Mat. 5:35
53:6 go round about the *c*. 14
72:16 they of *c*. shall flourish
107:4 found no *c*. to dwell in
122:3 Jerusalem as a *c*. compact
127:1 except the Lord keep *c*.
Prov. 8:3 crieth at entry of *c*.
10:15 his strong *c*. 18:11
11:10 the *c*. rejoiceth
11 by blessing of upright *c*.
16:32 than he that taketh a *c*.
25:28 like a *c*. broken down
29:8 scornful bring *c*. into snare
Ec. 9:14 there was a little *c*.
15 poor wise man delivered *c*.
Is. 1:26 *c*. of right. faithful *c*. 21
11:31 howl, O gate, cry O *c*.
17:1 Damascus from being a *c*.
19:2 shall fight, *c*. against *c*.
24:10 *c*. of confusion is broken
33:20 Zion *c*. of our solemnities
60:14 shall call thee *c*. of Lord
62:12 a *c*. not forsaken
Jer. 3:14 take you one of *c*.
4:29 *c*. shall flee for the noise
19:12 make this *c*. as Tophet
25:29 *c*. called by my name
32:24 come to *c*. and *c*. is given
38:2 he *c*. was broken up, 52:7
46:8 I will destroy the *c*.
48:25 how *c*. of praise not left
Lam. 1:1 how doth *c*. sit solitary
3:15 *c*. men call perf. of beauty
Ezek. 4:1 portray *c*. Jerusalem
7:23 the *c*. is full of violence
9:1 that have charge over *c*.
4 go thro' midst of *c*. Jerusa.
9 *c*. is full of perverseness
10:2 coals of fire over the *c*.
27:32 what *c*. is like Tyrus
33:21 saying, the *c*. is smitten
48:35 name of *c*. be, L. is there
Dan. 9:18 *c*. called by thy na. 19
Hos. 6:8 G. *c*. of th. work iniq.
Amos 4:7 to rain on one *c*.
8 one *c*. to another
5:3 *c*. that went up by thous.
Mic. 6:9 Lord's voice crieth to *c*.
Hab. 2:12 stablish a *c*. by iniq.
Zep. 3:1 woe to the oppressing *c*.
Zec. 8:3 Jerusalem a *c*. of truth
5 streets of *c*, be full of boys

Zec. 14:2 the *c*. shall be taken
Mat. 5:14 a *c*. set on hill cannot
35 Jerusalem is *c*. of great King
8:34 *c*. came out to meet Jesus
10:11 whatsoever *c*. ye enter
15 that *c*. Mark 6:11; Luke 10:12
11:20 all the *c*. was moved
22:7 king burnt up their *c*.
23:34 persecute from *c*. to *c*.
Mark 1:33 *c*. was gathered
5:14 told it in the *c*. Luke 8:34
Luke 2:3 taxed, ev. one to own *c*.
7:12 much people of *c*. with her
19:41 he beheld the *c*. and wept
23:51 he was of Arimathea a *c*.
John 4:39 many of th., *c*. believed
Acts 8:8 was great joy in that *c*.
13:44 almost whole *c*. to h.
16:12 in that *c*. certain days
17:5 set all the *c*. in an uproar
19:29 *c*. was filled with confus.
21:30 all the *c*. was moved
Heb. 11:10 *c*. that hath found.
16 hath prepared for them a *c*.
13:29 the *c*. of the living God
19:14 we have no continuing *c*.
Jam. 4:13 will go into such a *c*.
Rev. 20:9 comp. the beloved *c*.
21:14 wall of *c*. had foundations
18 the *c*. was pure gold
23 *c*. had no need of the sun

Bloody CITY.
Ezek. 22:2 judge the bloody *c*. ?
24:6 bloody *c*. 9; Nah. 3:1

Defenced CITY.
Is. 25:2 of a defenced *c*. a ruin
27:10 the d. *c*. shall be desolate
Jer. 1:18 thee this day a d. *c*.

CITY of David.
2 Sam. 5:9 *c*. of D. 1 Chr. 11:7
6:10 remove ark into *c*. of D.
12 brought ark into *c*. of D. 16
1 K. 2:10 D. was buried in *c*. D.
3:1 Sol. brought her to *c*. of D.
8:1 out of *c*. of D. 2 Chr. 5:2.
11:43 bur. in *c*. D. 2 Chr. 9:31
14:31 R. bur. *c*. D. 2 Chr. 12:16
15:8 bur. A. *c*. of D. 2 Chr. 14:1
22:50 J. bur. *c*. D. 2 Chr. 21:1
2 K. 8:24 J. bur. *c*. D. 2 Chr. 21:20
9:28 A. was buried in *c*. of D.
12:21 J. bur. *c*. D. 2 Chr. 24:25
14:20 Amaziah; 15:7 Azariah
15:38 Jot. 2 Chr. 27:9; 28:27 Ahaz
2 Chr. 24:16 bur. Jeh. in *c*. of D.
Is. 22:9 breaches of *c*. of D.
29:1 woe to A. *c*. where David
Luke 2:4 Joseph went to *c*. of D.
11 born in *c*. of D. a Saviour

Elders, with CITY.
Deut. 19:12 elders of his *c*.
21:6 elders of that *c*. next
20 say to *c*. of *c*. our son is
22:17 cloth before elders of *c*.
23:6 elders of his *c*. shall call
Jos. 20:4 let. him cause to *c*. of *c*.
Jud. 8:16 Gideon took elders of *c*.
Ruth 4:2 took ten men of *c*. of *c*.
Ezr. 10:14 elders of every *c*.

Every CITY.
2 K. 3:19 every *c*. fenced *c*.
1 Chr. 31:19 of sons of A. in *c*. *c*.
Jer. 4:29 every *c*. shall he forsak.
48:8 spoiler shall come on *c*. *c*.
Mat. 12:25 a *c*. divided ag. itself
Luke 13:1 two into every *c*.
Acts 15:21 in *c*. *c*. them that p.
36 visit brethren in every *c*.
20:23 H. G. witnesseth in *c*. *c*.
Tit. 1:5 ordain elders in every *c*.

Fenced CITY.
2 K. 10:2 with you a fenced *c*.
17:9 tower of watchmen to f. *c*.
2 Chr. 11:23 he dispersed of chil.

CITY of God.
Ps. 46:4 make glad *c*. of God
48:1 to be praised in *c*. of God
8 *c*. of God will establish it
87:3 glorious things spoken of
thee, O *c*. of God
Heb. 12:22 *c*. of living God
Rev. 3:12 name of *c*. of my God

Great CITY.
Gen. 10:12 Resen a great *c*.
Jos. 10:2 Gibeon was great *c*.
Neh. 7:4 *c*. was large and great
Jer. 22:8 done thus to great *c*.
Jon. 1:2 Nineveh that g. *c*. 3:2
3:3 N. was an exceeding g. *c*.
Rev. 11:8 in street of great *c*.
14:8 Bab. g. *c*. 18:10, 16, 19, 21
16:19 great *c*. was divided
17:18 woman 13 that great *c*.
21:10 he showed me that g. *c*.

Holy CITY.
Neh. 11:1 Jerusalem the holy *c*.
18 46:2 call themselves of holy *c*.
52:1 put on beau. garm. O h. *c*.
Dan. 9:24 seventy w. on thy h. *c*.
Mat. 4:5 devil taketh him to h. *c*.
27:53 went to h. *c*. and appeared
Rev. 11:2 holy *c*. shall they tread
21:2 I John saw the h. *c*. coming
22:19 take his part out of h. *c*.

In, or into the CITY.
Gen. 19:12 hast in the *c*. bring
Deut. 20:14 all in the *c*. take
28:3 blessed shalt be in the *c*.
16 cursed shalt be in the *c*.
Jos. 6:21 destroyed all in the *c*.
8:19 into *c*. and set it on fire
Jud. 1:24 entrance into *c*.
2 Sam. 15:25 car. back ark into *c*.
27 return into the *c*.
1 K. 14:11 dieth of Jerob. in *c*.
12 when thy feet enter into *c*.
16:4 that dieth of Baasha in *c*.
2 K. 7:4 we will enter into the *c*.
12 catch them, get into *c*.
Ps. 31:21 showed me his marvellous
kindness in a strong *c*.
55:9 seen violence in the *c*.
Prov. 1:21 in *c*. wisdom uttereth
Ec. 7:19 mighty men in the *c*.
8:10 wicked were forgotten in *c*.
Is. 24:12 in the *c*. is left deso.
Jer. 14:18 if I enter into the *c*.
38:9 no more bread in the *c*.
52:6 famine was sore in the *c*.
Lam. 1:19 gave up ghost in *c*.
Hos. 11:9 not enter into the *c*.
Joel 2:9 run to and fro in the *c*.
Amos 3:6 be blown in the *c*. shall
there be evil in a *c*.
7:17 thy wife be harlot in *c*.
Zec. 3:4 J. began to enter into *c*.
Mat. 9:1 came into his own *c*.
10:5 *c*. of the Samaritans
11 into whatsoever *c*. ye enter
26:18 go into *c*. to such a man
Mark 14:13 into the *c*. Acts 9:6
28:6 every one into his *c*.
Mark 14:13 into the *c*. a waterer
18:2 there was in a *c*. a judge
22:10 ye are entered into *c*.
24:49 tarry ye in *c*. of Jerusalem
John 4:8 disciples gone into *c*.
Acts 11:5 in the *c*. of Joppa
14:20 he came into the *c*.
21:30 with him in the *c*.
21:12 synagogues nor in the *c*.
2 Chr. 11:26 in perils in the *c*.
Rev. 22:14 through gates into *c*.

CITY of the Lord.
Ps. 101:8 cut off all wicked doers
from *c*. of the Lord.
Is. 60:14 call thee *c*. of Lord

Out of the CITY.
Gen. 44:4 gone out of the *c*.
Ex. 9:29 soon as I am out of *c*.
33 Moses went out of the *c*.
Jud. 1:24 saw man come *o*. of *c*.
2 Sam. 18:3 succor us out of *c*.
20:16 wise woman out of the *c*.
Job 24:12 groan from out of *c*.
Jer. 39:4 king went o. of *c*. 52:7
Ezek. 48:30 are goings *o*. of the *c*.
Mat. 4:10 go forth out of the *c*.
Mat. 21:17 went out of the *c*.
Mark 11:19 he went out of *c*.
Luke 4:29 thrust him out of *c*.
9:5 go out of *c*. shake off dust
Acts 7:58 cast Steph. out of the *c*.
14:19 drew him out of *c*.
16:13 we went out of the *c*.
21:5 brought us out of the *c*.

CITY of Refuge.
Num. 35:25 rest. him to *c*. of ref.
Jos. 21:13 *c*. of r. 1 Chr. 6:57
21 Shech.; 27 Golan; 32 Kod.

This CITY.
Gen. 19:11 I. will destroy this *c*.
20 this *c*. is near to flee unto
21 I will not overthrow this *c*.
Jos. 6:26 buildeth this *c*.
Jud. 19:11 into this *c*.
1 Sam. 9:6 in this *c*. a man of 11.
1 K. 2:19 this *c*. is pleasant
8:44 pray toward this *c*. 2 Chr. 6:34
13:32 cast off this *c*. Jerusalem
81 def. *c*. Mat. c. 3:7:35; 38:6
23:27 cast off this *c*. Jerusalem
2 Chr. 6:34 pray toward this *c*.
Ezr. 4:13 if this *c*. be builded, 16
Neh. 13:18 bring evil on this *c*.

CIT

Jer. 6:6 this is the *c*. to be visited
17:25 this *c*. shall remain
12:8 will make this *c*. desolate
15 bring on this *c*. all the evil
20:5 deliver strength of this *c*.
21:9 abideth in this *c*. shall die
10 set my face against this *c*.
22:8 why L. done thus unto *c*.
26:6 I will make this *c*. a curse
15 innocent blood on this *c*.
27:17 this *c*. be laid waste
32:3 give *c*. to Chald. 28; 34:2
31 this *c*. been as a provocation
33:5 hid my face from this *c*.
34:22 cause them return to *c*.
38:17 this *c*. shall not be burnt
39:16 words on this *c*. for evil
Ezek. 11:3 this *c*. is the caldron, 7
Mat. 10:23 persecute in this *c*.
Acts 18:10 much people in this *c*.
22:3 brought up in this *c*. at feet

Without CITY.
Gen. 19:16 men set Lot with. *c*.
Num. 35:5 measure from w. *c*.
Rev. 14:20 w.-press trodden w. *c*.

CITIES.
Gen. 19:29 when God destroy, *c*.
35:5 terror of God on *c*. round
47:21 he rem. people to *c*.
Num. 13:19 what *c*. they dwell in
35:8 give of his *c*. to Levites
Deut. 2:37 nor to *c*. in mountains
3:19 abide in *c*. I have given you
6:10 to give thee goodly *c*.
19:5 flee to one of these *c*.
Jos. 10:19 suf. h. not to enter *c*.
11:13 as for *c*. still in strength
19:6 described it by *c*. in a book
Jud. 20:48 set on fire *c*.
21:23 they repaired the *c*.
1 Sam. 31:7 Israelites forsook *c*.
2 Sam. 24:12 our God, *c*. of our *c*.
19:13
1 K. 9:12 Hiram came to see *c*.
20:34 *c*. father took I restore
2 Chr. 3:28 dwelt in desolate *c*.
Ps. 9:6 O enemy, destroyed *c*.
Ec. 6:11 Until *c*. be wasted
14:21 nor fill world with *c*.
19:18 day shall five *c*. in E.
33 he hath despised the *c*.
64:10 thy holy *c*. a wilderness
Jer. 2:15 his *c*. are burnt
28 number of thy *c*. 11:13
13:19 *c*. of south be shut up
20:17 those *c*. into captivity
32:44 virgin, to those thy *c*.
49:13 *c*. be perpetual wastes
50:32 I will kindle fire in his *c*.
Ezek. 26:19 like *c*. not inhabited
30:17 *c*. be desolate in midst *c*.
39:9 thy *c*. shall burn with fire
Hos. 8:14 send fire upon his *c*.
11:6 sword shall abide on his *c*.
Amos 4:8 three *c*. to one for wat.
Mic. 5:14 so will I destroy thy *c*.
Zep. 3:6 their *c*. are destroyed
Zec. 1:17 my *c*. shall yet spread
Mat. 10:23 not have gone over *c*.
11:1 to preach in their *c*.
20 to upbraid *c*. he done strange *c*.
1 Pet. 2:6 *c*. of S. and G. to ashes
Jude 7 *c*. about them in like m.
Rev. 16:19 *c*. of the nations fell

All CITIES.
Num. 21:25 Is. took all these *c*.
Jos. 21:34; 34:1; Jos. 10:39
21:10 burnt their *c*. Jud. 20:48
Deut. 20:15 thus do to all *c*. afar
Jos. 11:14 all *c*. of kings dew r.
21:19 all *c*. of Aaron were 13 *c*.
41 all *c*. of Levites were 48 *c*.
Num. 18:6 came out of all *c*.
2 Sam. 8:8? I came to all *c*. of liv.
Neh. 10:37 tithes in all the *c*.
Jer. 4:26 all the *c*. broken down
31:21 in all *c*. habita. of sheph.
Hos. 13:10 save thee in all thy *c*.
Acts 3:40 he preached in all *c*.

Defenced CITIES.
Is. 3:21 Sennacherim up. def. *c*.
37:26 to lay waste defenced *c*.
Jer. 4:5 go to fortified *c*. 8:14
34:7 def. *c*. *c*. remained of J.

Fenced CITIES.
Num. 13:17 king dwelleth
Deut. 3:5 *c*. fenced with high w.
9:1 to heaven, Jos. 14; 11:12
Jos. 10:20 entered into fen. *c*.
1 Sam. 6:18 both fenced *c*.
2 Chr. 11:5 fenced *c*. in Judah
17:2 *c*. of north in fenced *c*.
Hos. 8:14 J. multiplied fenced *c*.

CRUDEN'S CONCORDANCE.

CLA

Zep. 1:16 day of alarm ag. f. c.

CITIES of Judah.
2 Sam. 2:1 I go up to c. of J. ?
2 K. 23:8 burnt inc. in c. of J.
1 Chr. 6:57 sons of Aaron c. of J.
2 Chr. 17:7 to teach in c. of J. 13
19:5 set judges in the c. of J.
22:2 gather Lev. out of c. of J.
Neh. 11:3 in c. of Judah each
Ps. 60:35 will build c. of Judah
Is. 40:9 c. of Jud. behold your G.
44:26 c. of J. ye shall be built
Jer. 1:15 fam. of north ag. c. of J.
4:16 voice against c. of J.
7:17 what they do in c. of J.
9:11 c. of J. des. 10:22 ; 34:22
11:12 c. of Judah cry to gods
32:44 witness in the c. of Judah
33:10 man and beast in c. of J.
13 in the c. of Ju. shall flocks
44:6 fury kindled in c. of Jud.
21 incense yo burn in c. of J.
Zec. 1:12 not mercy on c. of J.

CITIES of Refuge.
Num. 35:6 six c. for ref. 13, 14
11 ap. c. of refuge, Jos. 20:2
1 Chr. 6:67 to sons of K. of c. r.

Six CITIES.
Jos. 15:59 mount. of Jud. six c.

CITIES, with Suburbs.
Lev. 25:34 sub. of c. not be sold
Num. 35:2 give to L. sub. for c.
Jos. 21:3 to Levites c. with s.

CITIES, with Villages.
1 Sam. 6:18 c. and of country v.
Mat. 9:35 J. went about all c. and villages teaching, Luke 13:22
Mark 6:56 into villages or c.

CITIES, with waste.
Lev. 26:31 your c. waste, 33
Is. 61:4 shall be laid waste
Ezek. 6:6 in dwell. c. shall be w.
19:7 w. their c. ; 35:4 thy c. w.
30:35 w. c. are become fenced
36 w. c. be filled with flocks
Amos 9:14 build the waste c.

Your CITIES.
Ps. 1:7 your c. are burnt
Jer. 40:10 dwell in your c.

CITIZEN, S
Luke 15:15 prodigal joined to c.
19:14 his c. hated him, and
Acts 21:39 a c. of no mean city
Eph. 2:19 fellow-c. with saints

CLAD.
1 K. 11:29 Jerob. had c. himself
Is. 59:17 c. with zeal as a cloak

CLAMOR, OUS.
Prov. 9:13 a foolish woman is c.
Eph. 4:31 let all c. be put away

CLAP hands.
Job 27:23 shall c. their hands
Ps. 47:1 c. your h. all ye people
98 let the floods c. their hands
Is. 55:12 trees of field c. their h.
Lam. 2:15 c. their h. at thee
Nah. 3:19 bruit of thee c. hands

CLAPPED, ETH.
2 K. 11:12 c. their hands
Ezek. 25:6 hast c. thy hands
Job 34:37 c. his hands among us

CLAVE, cleft.
Gen. 22:3 A. c. wood for bur.-off.
Num. 16:31 ground c. asunder
Jud. 15:19 God c. hollow in jaw
1 Sam. 6:14 c. wood of cart
Ps. 78:15 c. rocks, Is. 48:21

CLAVE, adhered.
Gen. 34:3 his soul c. to Dinah
Ruth 1:14 R. c. to mother-in-law
2 Sam. 20:2 3nd. c. to their king
23:10 till his hand c. to sword
K. 11:2 Sol. c. to these in love
2 K. 18:6 Hezekiah c. to the Lord
Neh. 10:29 c. to their brethren
Acts 17:34 certain men c. to Paul

CLAUDA. Acts 27:16
CLAUDIA. 2 Tim. 4:21

CLAWS.
Deut. 14:6 the cleft into two c.
Dan. 4:33 his nails like bird's c.
Zec. 11:16 he shall tear their c.

CLAY.
Job 4:19 dwell in houses of c.
10:9 hast made me as the c.
13:12 are like to bodies of c.
27:16 prepare raiment as c.
33:6 I am formed out of c.
38:14 it is turned as c. to seal
Ps. 40:2 up out of the miry c.
Is. 29:16 esteem. as potter's c.

CLE

Is. 41:25 as potter treadeth c.
45:9 c. say to him fashioneth it
64:8 we the c. thou our potter
Jer. 18:4 vessel made of c. marred
6 as c. is in the potter's hand
43:9 stones, hide them in c.
Dan. 2:33 his feet, part c. 34, 42
Nah. 3:14 go into c. and tread
Hab. 2:6 ladeth with thick c.
John 9:6 he made c. of spittle
15 he put c. on mine eyes
Rom. 9:21 potter power over c.?

CLAY-GROUND.
1 K. 7:46 into c.-g. 2 Chr. 4:17

CLEAN.
Lev. 23:22 not make c. riddance
Jos. 3:17 c. over Jordan, 4:1, 11
Ps. 77:8 is his mercy c. gone
Is. 24:19 earth is c. dissolved
Joel 1:7 he hath made it c. bare
2 Pet. 2:18 those c. escaped

CLEAN, Adjective.
Gen. 8:20 took of every c. beast
35:2 be c. and change garments
Lev. 7:19 all c. shall eat thereof
10:10 difference betw. c. 11:47;
20:25; Ezek. 22:26; 44:23
16:30 be c. from all your sins
22:4 not eat holy things till c.
Num. 19:18 a c. person take hys.
Deut. 12:15 c. may eat, 15:22
1 Sam. 20:26 surely he is not c.
Job 11:4 flesh come ne. be c. 14
15 wash in snow and be c.
13 he saith, Wash and be c.
Job 11:4 I am c. in thine eyes
14:4 c. thing out of an unclean ?
15:14 what is man to be c. ?
15 heavens not c. in his sight
25:4 he be c. born of a woman
33:9 I am c. without transgr.
Prov. 16:2 c. in his own eyes
Ps. 9:2 alike to c. and unclean
Is. 1:16 wash ye, make you c.
28:8 so there is no place c.
52:11 be ye c. that bear vessels
Jer. 13:27 wilt not be made c. ?
Ezek. 36:25 sprinkle c. water on
Mat. 8:2 thou canst make me c.
Mark 1:40; Luke 5:12
3 thou c. Mark 1:41; Lu. 5:13
23:25 c. the outside, Luke 11:39
Luke 11:41 all things are c.
John 13:11 Ye are not all c.
15:3 ye are c. through the word
Acts 18:6 own hands, I am c.
Rev. 19:8 linen, c. and white, 14

CLEAN hands.
Job 9:30 make hands never so c.
17:9 c. hands shall be stronger
Ps. 24:4 he that hath c. hands

CLEAN heart.
Ps. 51:10 create in me a c. heart
73:1 God is good to such of c. h.
Prov. 20:9 made my heart c. ?

Is CLEAN.
Lev. 13:13 he c. 17, 37, 39
Ps. 19:9 fear of the Lord is c.
Prov. 14:4 no oxen are, crib is c.
John 13:10 but is c. every whit

Pronounce CLEAN.
Lev. 13:6 pronounce him c. 14:7

Shall be CLEAN.
Lev. 11:36 wh. is water s. be c.
12:8 she s. be c. 15:28; 13:58 it s. be c.
14:20 be s. be c. 53; 15:13; 17:15;
22:7; Num. 19:12, 19
Num. 31:24 shall be c. Ezek. 36:25
Ps. 51:7 hyssop and I shall be c.

CLEANNESS.
2 Sam. 22:21 c. of my hands recompensed me, Ps. 18:20
25 c. in his eyesight, Ps. 18:24
Amos 4:6 give you c. of teeth

CLEANSE.
Ex. 29:36 c. the alt. Lev. 16:19
Num. 8:6 take Lev. and c. them
2 Chr. 29:15 c. house of Lord, 16
22 Levites should c. it.
Ps. 19:12 c. from secret faults
Mic. 1:4 valleys wh. he c. as wax
Cant. 2:14 that art in c.

CLE

1 John 1:9 c. us from unrighi.

CLEANSED.
Lev. 14:14 to be c. 17, 18, 23, 28
Num. 35:33 land cannot be c.
Jos. 22:17 we are not c.
2 Chr. 29:18 c. all the house of L.
30:19 his heart though not c.
34:5 Josiah c. Judah and Jerus.
Neh. 13:9 they c. the chambers
Job 33:9 what profit if I be c.
Ps. 73:13 c. my heart in vain
Ezek. 22:24 art the land not c.
44:26 he is c. reck. seven days
Dan. 8:14 then sanctuary be c.
Mat. 8:3 his leprosy was c.
11:5 lepers are c. Luke 7:22
Mark 1:42 leprosy dep. he was c.
Luke 4:27 none c. save Naaman
17:17 were not ten c. but where
Acts 10:15 what God hath c. 11:9

CLEANSETH, ING.
Job 37:21 fair the wind c. them
Prov. 20:30 blueness of a wo. c.
1 John 1:7 bl. of Jesus Christ c.
Mark 1:44 offer for c. Luke 5:14

CLEAR.
Gen. 44:16 how shall we c. ours.
Exod. 34:7 by no means c. guilty
2 Sam. 23:4 c. shining after rain
Ps. 51:4 c. when thou judgest
Cant. 6:10 c. as the sun
Is. 18:4 like a c. heat on herbs
Amos 8:9 darken earth in c. day
Zec. 14:6 light shall not be c.
2 Cor. 7:11 ap. yourselves to be c.
Rev. 21:11 c. as crystal, 22:1
18 pure gold like to c. glass
Job 11:17 shalt be c. than noon

CLEARING.
Num. 14:18 no means c. guilty
2 Cor. 7:11 what c. of yourselves

CLEARLY.
Job 33:3 utter knowledge c.
Mat. 7:5 c. to pull, Luke 6:42
Mark 8:25 and saw every man c.
Rom. 1:20 from creation c. seen

CLEARNESS.
Exod. 24:10 body of heaven in c.

CLEAVE.
Lev. 1:17 c. it with the wings
Ps. 74:15 didst c. the fountain
Hab. 3:9 c. the earth with rivers
Zec. 14:4 mount shall c. in midst
Gen. 2:24 shall c. to his wife,
Mat. 19:5; Mark 10:7
Deut. 4:4 ye that did c. to the L.
10:20 to him shalt thou c. 11:22 ;
13:4 ; 30:20; Jos. 22:5
Jos. 23:8 c. to Lord your God
Job 38:38 the clods c. together
Ps. 101:3 hate work, not c.
102:5 my bones c. to my skin
137:6 let my tongue c. to roof
Jer. 14:1 c. to house of Jacob
13:11 caused to c. to me Is.
Ezek. 3:26 make thy tongue c.
Dan. 2:43 not c. one to another
11:34 c. to them with flatteries
Acts 11:23 heart c. to Lord
Rom. 12:9 c. to that wh. is good

CLEAVED.
2 K. 3:3 J. c. to Jeroboam's sins
Job 29:10 their tongue c. to roof
31:7 blot hath c. to my hands

CLEAVETH.
Job 16:20 my bone c. to my skin
Ps. 22:15 tongue c. to my jaws
41:8 an evil disease c. to him
44:25 our belly c. to the earth
119:25 my soul c. to the dust
Jer. 13:11 as girdle c. to loins
Lam. 4:4 tongue of suck. child c.
Luke 10:11 dust of city which c.

CLEAVETH, divideth.
Deut. 14:6 beast that c. the cleft
Job 16:13 he c. my reins asunder
Ps. 141:7 as when our c. wood
Ec. 10:9 wood he endangered

CLEFT.
Mic. 1:4 valleys sh. be c. as wax

CLEFTS.
Cant. 2:14 that art in c.
Is. 2:21 to go into c. for fear
Jer. 49:16 dw. in the c. Ob. 3
Am. 6:11 smite house with c.

CLEMENCY.
Acts 24:4 hear us of thy c.

CLEMENT. Phil. 4:3
CLEOPAS. Lu. 24:18; Jo. 19:25

CLERK.
Acts 19:35 town c. had appeased

CLO

CLIFT, S.
Ex. 33:22 will put thee in a c.
2 Chr. 20:16 come by c. of Ziz
Job 30:6 to dwell in c. of valleys
Is. 57:5 sla. children under c.

CLIMB, ED, ETH.
1 Sam. 14:13 Jonathan c. up
Jer. 4:29 they shall c. up rocks
Joel 2:7 c. wall like men of war
9 they shall c. up on houses
Amos 9:2 though c. up to heaven
Luke 19:4 Zaccheus c. up a tree
John 10:1 c. up some other way

CLIPPED.
Jer. 48:37 every beard shall be c.

CLOAK.
Is. 59:17 clad with zeal as a c.
Mat. 5:40 let him have c. also
Luke 6:29 taketh c. forbid not
John 15:22 no c. for their sin
1 Thes. 2:5 nor used c. of covet.
2 Tim. 4:13 c. I left at Troas
1 Pet. 2:16 lib. for c. of malicious.

CLODS.
Job 7:5 clothed with c. of dust
21:33 c. of valley be sweet
38:38 c. cleave fast together
39:24 J. ploughm. break the c.
Jos. 10:11 J. shall break his c.
Joel 1:17 seed is rotten under c.

CLOSE.
Num. 5:13 kept c. from husband
2 Sam. 22:46 afraid out of their c. places, Ps. 18:45
1 Chr. 12:1 David kept himself c.
Job 28:21 kept c. from fowls
Jer. 42:16 follow c. after you
Amos 9:11 c. up the breaches
Luke 9:36 they kept it c.

CLOSED.
Num. 16:33 earth c. upon them
Is. 1:6 they have not been c.
29:10 Lord hath c. your eyes
Dan. 12:9 the words are c. up
Jon. 2:5 the depth c. me around
Mat. 13:15 eyes c. Acts 28:27
Luke 4:20 and he c. the book

CLOSER.
Prov. 18:24 a friend sticketh c.

CLOSEST.
Jer. 22:15 thou c. thyself in ced.

CLOSET, S.
Joel 2:16 bride go out of her c.
Mat. 6:6 prayest, enter thy c.
Luke 12:3 spok. in the ear in c.

CLOTH.
Num. 4:8 spread a c. of scarlet
Mat. 22:17 spread c. hof. elders
1 Sam. 19:13 M. uov. im. with c.
21:9 sword is wrapt in a c.
2 Sam. 20:12 cast a c. on Amasa
2 K. 8:15 Hazael took a thick c.
32:22 as a menstruous c.
Mat. 9:16 new c. Mark 2:21
27:59 wrapped it in a linen c.
Mark 14:51 linen c. about body

CLOTHE.
Ex. 40:14 his sons and c. them
Ed. 4:4 raiment to c. Mordecai
Ps. 132:16 c. priests-with salva.
18 his enemies c. with shame
Prov. 23:21 drowsiness c. with
Is. 22:21 c. him with thy robe
48:18 shalt c. thee with them
50:3 c. heavens with blackness
Ezek. 26:16 c. with trembling
34:3 c. you with the wool
Hag. 1:6 ye c. but none warm
Zec. 3:4 I will c. thee
Mat. 6:30 if God so c. the grass, much more c. you, Lu. 12:28

CLOTHED.
Gen. 3:21 coats of skins, c. them
Lev. 8:7 Moses c. A. with robe
1 Sam. 1:24 c. with scarlet
1 Chr. 21:16 Israel c. with sack.
2 Chr. 6:41 priests c. with salv.
18:9 king of Israel and Judah c.
28:15 c. all that were naked
Ez. 4:2 king's gate c. with
Job 7:5 my flesh c. with worms
10:11 c. me with skin and flesh
29:14 righteousness it c. me
39:19 c. his neck with thunder ?
Ps. 35:26 be c. with sh. 109:29
132:1 Lord is c. with majesty
104:1 thou art c. with honor
108:18 c. himself with cursing
132:9 priests be c. with right.
Prov. 31:21 c. with scarlet
Is. 61:10 c. me with garm. of sal.
Ezek. 16:10 c. thee wi. broidered

CRUDEN'S CONCORDANCE.

COM

Ps. 42:2 when shall I c. and app.
50:3 our God shall c. and not
65:2 unto thee shall all flesh c.
80:2 and c. and save us
86:9 all nations shall c.
102:2 when wilt thou c. to me
109:17 loved cursing, so let it c.
119:41 let thy mercies c. 77
Ec. 9:2 all things c. alike
Cant. 2:10 love, c. away, 13
Is. 13:5 c. from a far country
5 day of L. c. as destruction
21:12 inquire ye, return, c.
26:20 c. my people, enter
33:4 your G. will c. with veng.
40:10 will c. with strong hand
41:25 raised up one, he shall c.
44:7 things coming, and shall c.
45:20 assem, and c. draw near
24 even to him shall men c.
51:11 redeemed shall c. to Z.
53:1 c. ye to the waters, c. ye
3 c. unto me, hear
59:20 Redeemer shall c. to Z.
60:3 Gentiles c. to thy light, 5
66:18 Lord will c. with fire
Jer. 2:31 will c. no more to thee
3:22 we c. to thee
4:22 wherefore c. these things
17:15 word of Lord? let it c.
40:4 seem good to c. if ill to c.
46:16 as Carmel so shall he c.
48:4 who shall c. unto me?
Lam. 1:4 none c. to solemn fea.
Ezek. 21:27 till he c. whose right
33:31 c. to thee as the people
33 it will c. then shall know
36:8 they are at hand to c.
Hos. 6:1 c. let us return to Lord
3 he shall c. to us as the rain
13:13 time to seek L. till he c.
Joel 1:15 as destruction sh. it c.
2:31 he, terrible day of Lord c.
Hab. 2:3 it will c. and not tarry
Zec. 1:21 what c. these to do?
14:5 God shall c. and all saints
Mal. 3:1 the Lord ye seek shall c.
Mat. 2:6 out of thee c. Governor
6:10 thy kingdom c. Luke 11:2
8:9 c. and he cometh, Luke 7:8
11 many shall c. from the east
11:3 he that sh. c.? Luke 7:19, 20
23 c. all ye that labor
16:24 if any man will c. after me
17:10 Elias must first c. ? 11
19:14 then shall the end c.
42 know not hour Lord doth c.
23:31 c. ye blessed of my Father
Mark 8:34 if any will c. after me,
Luke 8:23; 14:27
12:14 child, to c. Luke 18:16
Luke 10:1 place whither he w. c.
17:20 when kingdom should c.
19:13 occupy till I c.
22:18 till king. of God shall c.
John 1:39 he saith, c. and see
3:20 baptizeth, and all men c.
5:14 lest worse thing c. to thee
40 ye will not c. to me that ye
6:37 F. giveth shall c. to me
44 no man can c. except F. 65
7:34 I am, thither ye cannot c.
37 if any man thirst, let him c.
8:14 ye cannot tell whence I c.
18:18 before it c. that when c.
14:18 I will c. unto you
23 and we will c. unto him
17:11 I c. to thee, 13
21:22 I will he tarry till I c. 23
Acts 1:11 this Jesus shall so c. as
2:20 before great day of Lord c.
8:24 pray ye for these things c.
9:38 he would not delay to c.
13:40 lest that c. upon you
16:9 c. over into Macedonia
17:4 believe on him should c.
22:22 Moses did say should c.
Rom. 3:8 do evil th. good may c.
1 Cor. 4:5 judge nothing till L. c.
11:26 show L.'s death till he c.
34 will I set in order when I c.
2 Cor. 1:15 I was minded to c.
12:20 for I fear, lest when I c.
2 Thes. 1:10 shall c. to be glori.
2:3 except c. a falling away
1 Tim. 4:8 life now is, and to c.
2 Tim. 4:3 time will c. they will
Heb. 4:16 c. boldly to throne.
7:25 able to save them c. to God
10:37 he that shall c. will c.
Rev. 3:3 else I will c. on thee
11 I c. quickly, 22:7, 20
6:1 saying, c. and see, 3, 5, 7
22:17 and let him athirst c.

COME again.
Gen. 28:21 so that I c. ag.

COM

Ex. 14:26 waters c. a. on E.
Jud. 6:9 I c. a. in peace
13:8 let man of God c. again
1 K. 2:41 Shimei was c. again
12:5 thr. d. and c. a. 2 Chr. 10:5
17:21 let this child's soul c. a.
Ps. 126:6 he shall c. again
Prov. 3:28 say not, Go and c. a
Luke 10:35 I c. ag. will repay
John 14:3 I will c. aga. and rec.
28 I go away, and c. a.
2 Cor. 2:1 not c. a. in heaviness
12:21 I c. a. God will humble
13:2 if I c. a. I will not spare

COME down.
Gen. 45:9 saith Jos. c. d. to me
Ex. 3:8 I am c. d. to deliver
19:11 Lord will c. d. on Sinai
Num. 11:17 I will c. d. and talk
Deut. 28:24 it shall c. d.
Jud. 7:24 c. d. against Midian.
1 Sam. 23:11 S. c. d.? will c. d.
20 according to desire
2 K. 1:4 not c. d. from, 6, 16
9 thou man of God c. down
Neh. 6:3 I cannot c. d.
Ps. 7:16 c. d. on his own pate
72:6 shall c. down like rain
144:5 bow thy heavens and c. d.
Is. 47:1 c. down O virgin
64:1 that thou wouldst c. d.
Jer. 21:13 who shall c. d. ag. us?
48:18 c. down from thy glory
Ezek. 26:15 prin. of sea shall c. d.
30:6 pride of power shall c. d.
Joel 3:11 thy mighty ones too. c. d.
Mat. 24:17 on house-top not c. d.
27:40 c. d. fr. cr. 42; Mark 15:30
Mark 19:5 J. said, Zaccheus c. d.
John 4:49 c. down ere child die

COME forth.
Gen. 15:4 c. f. of thy bowels
1 Sam. 14:11 Hebrews c. f.
1 K. 2:30 saith the king, c. forth
Is. 10:25 they, let mine c. forth
49:20 if I shall c. f. as gold
Ps. 17:2 let my sentence c. f.
88:8 I cannot c. forth
Is. 11:1 c. f. rod out stem of J.
41:2 c. f. forth of waters of J.
Jer. 46:9 let mighty men c. forth
Ezek. 21:19 twain c. forth
Dan. 3:26 ye serv. of God, c. f.
Joel 3:18 a fountain shall c. forth
Mic. 5:2 out of thee c. forth ruler
Mat. 15:18 c. f. from heart
Mark 9:25 c. f. by prayer
Luke 12:37 will c. f. and serve
John 5:20 c. f. they done good
11:43 he cried, Lazarus, c. forth
Acts 7:7 shall c. f. and serve me

COME hither.
Gen. 15:16 the fourth gen. c. h.
Jud. 16:2 Samson c. hither
1 Sam. 10:22 man should c. h.
16:11 not sit down till he c. h.
2 Sam. 20:16 say to Joab, c. h.
Prov. 25:7 bet. he said, c. up h.
Dan. 3:26 servants of G. c. h.
John 4:16 call husband and c. h.
Acts 17:6 turned world, are c. h.
Rev. 4:1 c. up hither 11:12; 17:1;
21:9

COME in or into.
Gen. 19:31 not a man to c. in
24:31 c. in thou blessed of Lord
31:24 thou madest c. in
Deut. 31:2 I can no more c. in
Jos. 14:11 my strength to c. in
1 K. 1:14 I will c. in after thee
3:7 I know not how to c. in o.
13 c. in thou wife of Jeroboam
15:17 any to go out or c. in
2 K. 4:4 when c. in, shut door
11:9 each his men to c. in and
2 Chr. 1:10 and c. in before peo.
16:1 none go out or c. in to A.
23:6 c. into house, save priests
Neh. 2:7 till I c. into Jerus.
Est. 6:5 said, let Haman c. in
24:7 king of glory c. in, 9
Ok! for the waters are c. in
96:8 and c. into his courts
Is. 19:1 Lord shall c. into Egypt
10:33 Assyrian sh. c. into L.
24:10 no more c. in
35:10 kings of Judah c. in
51:50 Jerus. c. into your mind
Mic. 5:5 Assyrian shall c. into
Mat. 10:27 Son of man sh. c. in
24:3 many sh. c. in my name
Mark 13:6; Luke 21:8
23:51 Son of man shall c. in
Luke 11:33 wh. c. in may see

COM

Luke 12:46 c. in a d. he look. n.
14:23 compel them to c. in
John 5:43 I am c. in my Father's
name, if another shall c.
6:14 prophet, that sh. c. 11:27
Acts 10:15 c. into my house
Rom. 11:25 fulness of G. be c. in
1 Cor. 14:23 c. in those unlearned
24 if c. in one believeth not
Jam. 2:2 there c. in a poor man
Rev. 3:20 c. in to him, and sup

COME near.
Gen. 20:4 Abim. had not c. n.
Ex. 16:9, say c. n. bef. the L.
Num. 16:5 cause him to c. near
1 Sam. 10:20 tribes to c. near
Jer. 32:9 lest they c. n. thee
19:169 let my cry c. near
Is. 41:1 c. near to judgment
48:16 c. ye near hear ye this
50:8 mine adversary? c. near
Ezek. 40:46 c. near to L. to min
41:15 c. near to be minister
Mal. 3:5 c. near to you to judg.
Luke 19:41 c. near be hohold city
Acts 23:15 or over he c. near

COME nigh.
Ex. 34:30 were afraid to c. n.
Lev. 10:3 be sanc. in c. n. nigh
Luke 10:9 kingdom of G. c. n. 11

COME not.
Ex. 14:2 they shall not c. nigh
Num. 16:12 we will n. c. np, 14
Jos. 3:4 c. not near them are c.
22:7 ye c. not among nations
Deut. 12:29 Joab would not c.
2 K. 19:32 king of Assyria not c.
into city, 33; Is. 37:33, 34
2 Chr. 35:21 I c. not against thee
Jer. 10:8 not c. within
Job 13:16 hypocrite n. c. before
Ps. 32:6 they shall not c.
69:27 let them not c. into
91:7 it shall not c. nigh thee
Prov. 5:8 c. not nigh door of b.
Is. 7:17 L. shall bring da. ys not c.
32:10 gathering shall not c.
54:14 terror shall not c. near
65:5 which say, c. not near me
Ezek. 14:16 things shall not c.
Hos. 4:15 c. not ye unto Gilgal
9:4 soul shall n. c. into house
Zec. 14:18 if fam. of E. c. not
Mat. 22:3 and they would not c.
Luke 2:3 not c. for pr. Luke 8:19
Luke 14:20 married, I cannot c.
John 5:24 not c. into condemn.
40 not c. that ye might
7:34 thither ye cannot c. 36
16:7 the Comforter will not c.
1 Cor. 4:18 as tho. I would not c.

COME out.
Gen. 15:14 c. o. with substance
17:6 kings c. out of thee, 35:11
Num. 11:20 it c. out at nostrils
12:4 c. out ye three to tabern.
20:5 people c. out of Egypt, 11
Deut. 28:7 c. out one way
Jud. 9:29 in. army and c. out
1 Sam. 11:3 to-mor. will c. out, 10
24:14 after whom is king c. out?
2 Sam. 16:7 c. out, bloody man
1 K. 6:1 480th year after Isr. c. o.
20:17 men c. out of Samaria
2 K. 5:11 he would c. out to me
18:31 agree, and c. out, Is. 36:16
Ps. 14:7 O that salva. c. out of Z.
68:31 princes shall c. out of E.
Nah. 1:11 one c. out imagineth
Mat. 5:26 c. out till thou have
Mark 14:48; Luke 22:52
Mark 1:25 c. o. of him, Luke 4:35
5:8 c. out unclean, Luke 8:29
7:11 Christ c. out of Galilee?
Acts 16:18 to c. out of her
Rom. 11:26 c. out of Zion Deliv.
2 Cor. 6:17 c. out from among
Rev. 16:13 spirits c. out of drag.
18:4 c. out of her, my people

COME to pass.
Num. 11:23 my word c. to p.
Deut. 13:2 wonder c. to pass
Jos. 23:14 all c. to pass
Jud. 13:12 M. said, words c. to p.
21:3 why is this c. to pass
1 K. 13:32 saying shall c. to pass
Is. 7:7 not stand, nor c. to p.
14:24 so shall it c. to p.
49:9 former things are c. to p.
Jer. 32:24 has spoken is c. to p.
Ezek. 12:25 I speak shall c. to p.
24:14 spoken, it shall c. to p.

COM

Dan. 2:29 what shall c. to p.
Zec. 6.15 this shall c. to p.
7:13 c. to pass that as he cried
Mat. 24:6 these must c. to pass
Mark 11:23 th. he saith sh. c. to p.
13:29 ere these things c. to p.
Luke 2:15 see this thing c. to p.
21:7 when these c. to pass ? 28
24:12 wond. at what was c. to p.
18 not known things c. to pass
John 13:19 c. to p. may b. 14:29
Rev. 1:1 must shortly c. to pass

COME short.
Rom. 3:23 all c. sh. of glory of G.
Heb. 4:1 seem to c. short of it

COME together.
Job 9:32 should c. t. in judgment
19:12 troops c. t. against me
Jer. 3:18 c. t. out of land of north
Joel Israel and Judah shall c. t.
Acts 1:6 wh. they were c. t. 28:17
10:27 he found many c. together
19:32 knew not wherefore c. t.
21:22 multitude must needs c. t.
1 Cor. 7:5 c. together again
11:17 you c. t. not for the better
14:23 if whole church be. c. t.
34 ye c. not t. to condemna.
26 c. to. every one of you hath

COME up.
Ex. 19:24 c. up thou and Aaron
24:12c. up to me into mount
33:5 I will c. up in a moment
34:3 no man shall c. up with
Num. 20:8 why c. up out of E.
Jos. 10:6 c. up to us quickly
Jud. 1:3 Jud. said c. up with me
16:18 Lords c. up, 9
15:10 why are ye c. up ag. us?
16:18 Del. sent, c. up this once
Jam. 14:10 if they say c. up
17:25 seen man that is c. up
1 K. 1:35 then c. up after him
20:22 will c. up against thee
2 K. 18:25 am I c. u. 1s. 36:10
50 7:9 to grave c. up no more
Prov. 25:7 better said, c. up
Is. 8:7 c. up over his channels
14:8 no feller is c. up against us
Jer. 40:19 he shall c. up, 50:44
22 shall c. up and fly as eagle
Ezek. 38:16 c. up ag. my people
Hos. 1:11 shall c. up out of land
13:15 wind of the L. shall c. up
Ob. 21 saviors shall c. up on Z.
Zec. 14:17 whose will not c. up
18 if family of Egypt c. not up
Acts 8:31 Philip to c. up and sit
10:4 Cornel. the alms are c. up
Rev. 4:1 c. up hither, 11:12

COME, passive.
Gen. 6:13 the end of all flesh is c.
18:5 are ye c. to your servant
21 accord, to cry is c. to me
Ex. 3:9 cry of Israel is c. to me
Num. 22:11 there is a people c.
Jos. 5:14 as captain am I c.
Jud. 16:2 Samson is c. hither
1 Sam. 4:7 G. is c. into the camp
9:16 bec. their cry is c. to me
2 K. 8:7 man of God is c. hither
Jer. 9:19 after all that is c.
Job 38:25 thing I feared is c. 4:5
Ps. 44:17 all this is c. on us, yet
53:6 O that salvation were c.
55:5 fear, and trembling are c.
69:2 I am c. into deep waters
102:13 yea, the set time is c.
Is. 10:28 he is c. to Aiath
56:1 my salvation near to c.
60:1 shine, for thy light is c.
61:2 year of my redeemed is c.
63:3 therof. this is c. on van
5 0:27 their day is c.
31 thy day is c. I will visit thee
51:13 on waters, thy end is c.
Lam. 4:18 our end is c.
5:1 remomb. what is c. upon no
Ezek. 7:2 an end is c. on land, 6
6 the morning is c. upon thee
10 day, behold it is c. 39:8
21:25 whose day is c. 29
Dan. 9:13 all this evil is c. on us
Amos 8:2 the end is c. on Israel
Mic. 1:9 c. to gate of my people
10:28 kingdom of God is c.
14:11 Son of man is c. to save
14:41 hour is c.
11:28 Master is c. and calleth
12:23 J. answ. the hour is c. 17:1
Cor. 13:10 when that perf. is c.
Col. 1:6 which gospel is c. to you
1 John 4:3 that confesseth n. C.
is c. in the flesh, 2 John 7

CRUDEN'S CONCORDANCE. 799

COM

1 *John* 5:20 we k. Son of G. is *c.*
I am COME, *or* **am I COME**
Ex. 18:6 *I* Jethro am *c.* to thee
Num. 22:38 Bal. said. lo, *I am c.*
2 *Sam.* 14:32 am *I c.* fr. Gesh. ?
Ps. 60:2 *I am c.* into deep wat.
Ec. 1:16 lo, *I am c.*
Dan. 9:23 *I am c.* to show, 10:14
10:12 *I am c.* for thy words
Mat. 5:17 *I am c.* to destroy law
9:13 *I am* not *c.* to call right.
10:34 not *I am c.* to send peace
35 *I am c.* to set at variance
Luke 12:51 *I am c.* to give peace ?
John 1:31 therefore am *I c.*
5:43 *I am c.* in my F.'s name
7:28 *I am* not *c.* of myself
9:39 for judgment *I am c.*
10:10 *I am c.* th. might ha. life
12:46 *I am c.* a light into world
16:28 *I am c.* again I leave wor.

COME, *joined with* **Time.**
Gen. 30:33 answer in *t.* to *c.*
Ex. 13:14 asketh in *time* to *c.*
Deut. 6:20 ; *Jos.* 4:6, 21
Ps. 102:13 the set *time* is *c.*
Prov. 31:25 rejoice in *t.* to *c.*
Cant. 2:12 *t.* of sing. of birds *c.*
Is. 13:22 her *time* is near to *c.*
30:8 he for *time* to *c.*
42:23 will hear for *time* to *c.* ?
Ezek. 7:7 *t.* is *c.* 12; *Hag.* 1:2 not *c.*
Luke 9:51 *t. c.* he sh. be received
Gal. 4:4 when fulness of *t. w. c.*
1 *Tim.* 6:19 founda. aga. *t.* to *c.*
1 *Pet.* 4:17 *t.* is *c.* judgm. must b.

Yet COME.
Deut. 12:9 not yet *c.* to the rest
John 2:4 my hour is not yet *c.*
7:6 my time is not yet *c.*
30 hour was not yet *c.* 8:20
11:30 J. was not yet *c.* into town
Rev. 17:10 the other is not yet *c.*

COMELINESS.
Is. 53:2 hath no form nor *c.*
Ezek. 16:14 perfect through my *c.*
27:10 they of Lud set fo. thy *c.*
Dan. 10:8 my *c.* into corruption
1 *Cor.* 12:23 more abundant *c.*

COMELY.
1 *Sam.* 16:18 David a *c.* person
Job 41:12 con. his *c.* proportion
Ps. 33:1 praise is *c.* for, 147:1
Prov. 30:29 four are *c.* in going
Ec. 5:18 it is *c.* for one to eat
Cant. 1:5 I am black, but *c.*
10 cheeks are *c.* with jewels
4:3 thy speech is *c.*
6:4 art *c.* O my love, as Jerus.
Is. 4:2 the fruit shall be *c.*
Jer. 6:2 daugh. of Zion to a *c.* w.
1 *Cor.* 7:35 I speak for that *c.*
12:24 *c.* parts have no need

COMERS.
Heb. 10:1 *c.* thereunto perfect

COMEST.
Deut. 28:6 blessed when thou *c.*
19 cursed when thou *c.* in
Jud. 17:9 Mic. said, whence *c.*
18:17 old man said, whence *c.*
1 *Sam.* 16:4 *c.* peacea. ? 1 *K.* 13:18
17:45 thou *c.* to me w. a sword
2 *K.* 5:25 whence *c.* th. Gehazi ?
Job 1:7 whence *c.* thou ? 2:2
Jon. 1:8 whence *c.* thou ?
Mat. 3:14 and *c.* thou to me ?
Luke 23:42 wh. *c.* into thy king.

COMETH.
Deut. 23:13 that *c.* from thee
1 *Sam.* 4:3 when ark *c.*
9:6 all he saith *c.* surely to pass
10:8 *c.* not to king's table
Job 38:19 wh. then *c.* wisdom ?
Ps. 30:5 but joy *c.* in morning
75:6 promotion *c.* not from east
98:13 for he *c.* to judge
118:26 blessed is he *c.* in name
121:2 my help *c.* from the Lord
Ec. 4:14 he *c.* in with vanity
Cant. 2:8 he *c.* leaping on moun.
Is. 13:9 day of L. *c.* with wrath
30:27 name of L. *c.* from far
63:1 Zion thy salvation *c.*
63:1 who is this *c.* from Edom
Jer. 17:6 not see when good *c.*
43:11 *c.* he shall smite Egypt
Lam. 3:37 and it *c.* to pass
Ezek. 38:18 *c.* in your mind
21:7 because it *c.* behold it *c.*
24:21 when this *c.* kn. I am L.
33:31 they come as people *c.*
33 when this *c.* to pass, then
Dan. 12:12 *c.* to 1,335 days

COM

Joel 2:1 day of L. *c.* 2; *Zec.* 14:1;
1 *Thes.* 5:2
Mal. 4:1 day *c.* that shall burn
Mat. 3:11 he that *c.* after is mig.
Mark 1:7; *Luke* 3:16
5:37 more than these *c.* of evil
8:9 *c.* and he *c.* , *Luke* 7:8
21:5 thy king *c.* , *John* 12:15
9 blo. is he *c.* in name of Lord.
Mark 11:9; *Luke* 13:35; 19:38
25:19 after long time Lord *c.*
Mark 8:38 when he *c.* in glory
9:12 Elius *c.* first and restoreth
14:43 while he spake *c.* Judas
Luke 6:47 whoso *c.* to me, and
12:37 he *c.* shall find watching
40 *c.* at an hour ye think not
43 when he *c.* shall find
55 will he heat, and it *c.*
17:20 *c.* not with observation
19:36 *c.* shall he find faith
John 3:6 canst not tell wh. it *c.*
20 nor *c.* to the light
4:21 woman, hour *c.* 23; 16:32
6:35 *c.* to me never hunger, 37
45 learned of Father, *c.* to me
7:27 *C. c.* no man knoweth, 31
42 Christ *c.* of seed of David
9:4 night *c.* no man can work
14:6 no man *c.* to Father but
16:32 hour *c.* ye shall be scat.
Acts 10:33 when hee, and *c. speak*
1 *Cor.* 15:24 then *c.* the end
2 *Cor.* 11:28 beside wh. *c.* on me
1 *Thes.* 5:3 day of L. *c.* as a thief
Heb. 11:6 *c.* to G. must believe
Jude 14 L. *c.* with 10,000 saints
Rev. 1:7 he *c.* with clouds
17:10 *c.* continue a short space

COMETH down.
Is. 55:10 rain *c. d.* from heaven
John 6:33 he *c. down,* 50
Jam. 1:17 every good gift *c. d.*
Rev. 3:12 new Jeru. which *c. d.*

COMETH forth.
Ex. 4:14 *c. forth.* to meet thee
Jud. 11:31 *c. forth* of doors
1 *Sam.* 11:7 *c.* not *f.* after S.
Job 5:6 affliction *c.* not *forth*
14:2 he *c. forth* like a flower
Is. 28:29 this also *c. forth*
Ezek. 33:30 what word *c. forth*
Mic. 1:3 L. *c. f.* out of his place

COMETH nigh.
Num. 1:51 stranger that *c.* n. be put to death, 3:10, 38; 18:7

COMETH out.
Deut. 28:57 young one *c.* out
Is. 26:21 Lord *c.* out of his place
42:5 earth, and what *c.* out
Mat. 15:11 *c.* out of mouth, this defileth a man, *Mark* 7:20

COMETH up.
1 *Sam.* 28:14 an old man *c. up*
Cant. 8:5 *c. up* from wilderness ?
Jer. 46:7 that *c. up* as a flood ?
50:3 out of north *c. up* a nation

COMFORT.
Gen. 5:29 shall *c.* us conc. work
Job 6:10 then should I yet have *c.*
10:20 alone that I may take *c.*
76 let kindness be for my *c.*
Ps. 119:50 my *c.* in affliction
76 let kindness be for my *c.*
Ezek. 16:54 thou art a *c.* to them
Mat. 9:22 be of good *c.* , *Luke* 8:48
Mark 10:49 be of *g. c.* he calleth
Acts 9:31 walking in *c.* of H. G.
Rom. 15:4 *c.* of the scriptures
1 Cor. 14:3 speaketh to *c.*, and *c.*
2 *Cor.* 1:3 blessed be God of all *c.*
4 *c.* wherewith we are comfort.
7:4 I am filled with *c.*
13 were comforted in your *c.*
Phil. 2:1 if any *c.* of love
19 of good *c.* when I know
Col. 4:11 been *c.* to me

COMFORT, Verb.
Gen. 5:29; as concerning work
18:12 my Lord *c.* your hearts
37:35 sons rose to *c.* him
Jud. 19:5 *c.* heart with bread, 8
2 *Sam.* 10:2 David sent to *c.* him
1 *Chr.* 7:22 came to *c.* him
Job 2:11 friends came to *c.* him
7:13 say, My bed shall *c.* me
9:27 if I say, I will *c.* myself
21:34 how *c.* ye me in vain
Ps. 23:4 thy staff, they *c.* me
71:21 shalt *c.* me on every side
119:82 when wilt thou *c.* me ?
Cant. 2:5 *c.* me with apples
Is. 22:4 labor not to *c.* me
40:1 *c.* ye, ye my people

COM

Is. 51:3 L. shall *c.* Zion, *c.* was.
19 by whom shall I *c.* thee ?
61:2 to *c.* all that mourn
66:13 so will I *c.* you in Jeru.
Jer. 8:18 when I would *c.* myself
16:7 nor man tear to *c.* them
31:13 I will *c.* and make rejoice
Lam. 1:2 hath none to *c.* her, 17
21 there is none to *c.* me
2:13 equal, that I may *c.* thee ?
Ezek. 14:23 *c.* when ye see ways
Zec. 1:17 Lord shall yet *c.* Zion
10:2 they *c.* in vain
John 11:19 to *c.* them concerning
2 *Cor.* 1:4 may be able to *c.* them
2:7 ye ought rather to *c.* him
Eph. 6:22 might *c.* your hearts
Col. 4:8 and *c.* your hearts
1 *Thes.* 3:2 to *c.* you conc. faith
4:18 *c.* one another
5:11 wherefore *c.* yourselves
2 *Thes.* 2:17 L. J. *c.* your hearts
14 *c.* the feeble-minded

COMFORTABLE.
2 *Sam.* 14:17 w. of L. now be *c.*
Zec. 1:13 L. answ. with *c.* words

COMFORTABLY.
2 *Sam.* 19:7 speak *c.* to thy serv.
2 *Chr.* 30:22 spake *c.* to Levites
32:6 not captains, and spake *c.*
Is. 40:2 speak *c.* to Jerusalem
Hos. 2:14 I will speak *c.* to her

COMFORTED.
Gen. 24:67 Isaac was *c.*
37:35 Jacob refused to be *c.*
38:12 Judah was *c.*
50:21 Joseph *c.* his brethren
Ruth 2:13 for hast *c.* me
2 *Sam.* 12:24 David *c.* Bath-sheba
13:39 he was *c.* concerning A.
Job 42:11 brethren *c.* him.
Ps. 77:2 my soul refused to be *c.*
86:17 bec. Lord, hast *c.* me
119:52 and have *c.* myself
Is. 49:13 God *c.* his people, 52:9
54:11 Oh thou afflicted not *c.*
66:13 shall he *c.* in Jerusalem
Jer. 31:15 Rachel refused to be *c.*
Ezek. 5:13 fury to rest, I w. be *c.*
14:22 be *c.* concerning
31:16 all that drink water be *c.*
32:31 Pharaoh shall be *c.*
Mat. 2:18 not be *c.* bec. were not
5:4 mourn, for they shall be *c.*
Luke 16:25 he is *c.* thou from.
John 11:31 the Jews which *c.* her
Acts 20:12 brought man alive, *c.*
Rom. 1:12 I may be *c.* with you
1 *Cor.* 14:31 and all be *c.*
2 *Cor.* 1:4 we are *c.* of God
7:6 God *c.* us by coming of Titus
7 consola. wh. he was *c.* in you
13 we are *c.* in your comfort
Col. 2:2 hearts be *c.* being knit
1 *Thes.* 2:11 know how he *c.* you
3:7 we were *c.* in our affliction

COMFORTEDST.
Is. 12:1 and thou *c.* me.

COMFORTER, S.
2 *Sam.* 10:3 sent *c.* 1 *Chr.* 19:3
Job 16:2 miserable *c.* are ye all
Ps. 69:20 I looked for *c.* but
Ec. 4:1 oppressed, had no *c.*
16 *c.* that should relieve is far
Nah. 3:7 whence shall I seek *c.*
John 14:16 give you another *C.*
26 *C.* which is the Holy Ghost
15:26 when the *C.* is come
16:7 *C.* will not come

COMFORTETH.
Job 29:25 as one that *c.* mourners
Is. 51:12 I am he that *c.* you
66:13 as one his mother *c.* so
2 *Cor.* 1:4 who *c.* us in tribula.
7:6 God that *c.* those cast down

COMFORTLESS.
John 14:18 I will not leave you *c.*

COMFORTS.
Ps. 94:19 thy *c.* delight my soul
Is. 57:18 and restore *c.* to him.

COMING.
Gen. 30:30 skew my *c.*
Num. 22:36 heard of Balaam's *c.*
Jud. 5:28 chariot so long in *c.* ?
1 *Sam.* 16:4 trembled at his *c.*
22:6 thy *c.* in with me is good
Is. 14:9 moved to meet thee at *c.*
2 *K.* 19:27 know thy *c.* , *Is.* 37:28
Ps. 37:13 seeth his day is *c.*
121:8 L. shall preserve thy *c.* in
Ec. 4:14 things *c.* let them know
Jer. 8:7 observe time of their *c.*
Mic. 2:15 accord. to days of thy *c.*

COM

Mal. 3:2 abide day of his *c.* ?
4:5 before *c.* of the great day
Mat. 16:28 till see Son of man *c.*
24:3 shall be sign of thy *c.* ?
27 *c.* of Son of man be, 37, 39
30 Son of man *c.* 26:64; *Mark* 13:26; 14:62; *Luke* 21:27
48 Lord delayed *c.* , *Luke* 12:45
25:27 at *c.* received my own,
Luke 19:23
Mark 6:31 many *c.* and going
Luke 19:5 continual *c.* she w. me
John 5:7 I am *c.* another step.
15 hour is *c.* 28; 10:12 wolf *c.*
Acts 7:52 before *c.* of Just One
9:28 Saul was with them *c.* in.
13:24 preached before his *c.*
15:23 that are Christ's at his *c.*
16:17 glad of *c.* of Stephanas
2 *Cor.* 7:6 G. comf. us by *c.* of T.
7 not by his *c.* only
Phil. 1:26 abundant, by my *c.*
1 *Thes.* 2:19 rejoicing at his *c.* ?
3:13 unblameable at *c.* of Lord
4:15 which remain to *c.* of L.
5:23 blameless to *c.* of our Lord
2 *Thes.* 2:1 we beseech by *c.* of L.
8 destroy with brightness of *c.*
9. *c.* is after working of Satan
Jam. 5:7 be patient to *c.* of Lord
8 for *c.* of Lord draweth nigh
1 *Pet.* 2:4 *c.* as unto a live stone
2 *Pet.* 1:16 power and *c.* of L. J.
3:4 the promise of his *c.* ?
12 hasting to *c.* of day of God
1 *John* 2:28 not be ash. at his *c.*
Jam. 5:11 another beast *c.* up
21:2 new Jer. *c.* down from G.

COMINGS.
Ezek. 43:11 show them the *c.* in

COMMAND, Substantive.
Job 39:27 eagle mount at thy *c.*

COMMAND, Verb.
Gen. 18:19 Ab. will *c.* children
Ex. 18:23 and God *c.* thee so
Num. 8:8 I will hear what L. *c.*
Is. 6 the thing Lord doth *c.*
Deut. 28:8 Lord *c.* blessing
32:46 *c.* children to observe
Jos. 11:15 so did Moses *c.* Joshua
Ps. 42:8 L. *c.* his loving-kindness
44:4 *c.* deliverance for Jacob
Is. 45:11 work of my hands, *c.*
Jer. 27:4 *c.* to say to masters
Lam. 1:10 *c.* should not enter
Mat. 19:7 why did Moses *c.*
27:64 *c.* sepulchre be made sure
Mark 10:3 what did Moses *c.* you
Luke 8:31 not *c.* to go into deep
9:54 *c.* fire to come down
Acts 8:29 we straitly *c.* you
15:5 to *c.* to keep law of Moses
2 *Thes.* 3:4 will do things we *c.*
6 we *c.* you in name of Lord
12 such we *c.* and exhort
1 *Tim.* 4:11 these things *c.*

I COMMAND.
Ex. 7:2 all *I c., Jer.* 1:7, 17
34:11 obs. what *I c.* , *Deut.* 12:28
Lev. 25:21 *I* will *c.* my blessing
Deut. 4:2 not add to word *I c.* you
7:11 wh. *I c.* 8:11 ; 10:13; 11:8, 27 ; 13:18 ; 32:46
21:18 *I c.* thee to do this, 22
30:16 *I c.* thee this day love L.
Jer. 11:4 do all which *I c.* you
Amos 9:9 *I* will *c.* and sift house
Mat. 15:14 if ye do what *I c.* you
17 *I c.* you, that ye love
Acts 16:18 *I c.* thee In na. of J.

COMMANDED.
Gen. 50:12 J.'s sons did as he *c.*
Ex. 1:17 did not as *c.*
19 *Ex.* 1:18 *c.* pass, 3:8
Num. 3:16 he *c.* child, of I. did as L. *c.*
29 *c.* oheyed my voice in all *I c.*
1 *Sam.* 20:29 *c.* me to be business
2 *K.* 17:27 know thy *c.* L. 21:8
16:26 according to all what *I c.*
2 *Chr.* 8:14 so had David *c.*
33:8 any I *c.* Judah to work Lord
Neh. 13 Hezekiah ; 13:16 Manas.
Est. 4:17 Mord. did as Esther *c.*
8:9 writ. accor. to all Mord. *c.*
Job 38:12 hast thou *c.* morning
Ps. 33:9 *c.* and it stood
7:35 and to *c.* *c.* O people
Mat. 14:19 *c.* multitude to sit,
Mark 6:39
Luke 8:4 to park *c.* him to be hold
21:6 disciples did as Jesus *c.*

CRUDEN'S CONCORDANCE.

COM

Mat. 28:20 teac. to observe all I *c.*
Luke 9:21 *c.* them to tell no man
Acts 25:6 Festus *c.* Paul to be b.
1 *Cor.* 14:34 *c.* to be under obed.
1 *Thes.* 4:11 work as we *c.*
Heb. 12:20 not endure the *c.*

God COMMANDED.
Gen. 6:22 according to all. *G. c.*
7:9 as *God* had *c.* 16; 21:4;
Deut. 20:17; *Jos.* 10:40
Deut. 5:32 observe to do as *God c.*
8:1 *God c.* to teach 20; 12:3
20:16 day *God c.* thee to keep
1 *Chr.* 14:16 David did as *God c.*
Ezr. 7:23 whatsoever is *c.* by *G.*
Ps. 68:28 *God* hath *c.* thy str.
Acts 10:33 all *c.* thee of God
2 *Cor.* 4:6 God who *c.* light shine

Lord COMMANDED.
2 *Sam.* 24:19 D. went up as *L. c.*
Ps. 106:34 whom *L. c.* them
131:3 for there *L. c.* blessing
Lam. 1:17 *L.* hath *c.* concern. J.
Acts 13:47 turn to Gent. so *L. c.*

Lord *or* God COMMANDED, *implicitly*
Ex. 23:15 as I *c.* in time ap.
Deut. 17:3 I have not I *c.* thee?
Jer. 19:5; 23:32; 29:23
Jos. 1:9 have not I *c.* thee? be
1 *K.* 11:10 *c.* Sol. concerning this
1 *Chr.* 16:15 word he *c.* to 1000 generations, *Ps.* 105:8
Ps. 7:6 awake to judgm. hast *c.*
33:9 he *c.* and it stood fast
119:4 *c.* hath *c.* his covenant
119:4 *c.* us to keep thy precepts
138 testimonies hast *c.* are r.
148:5 he *c.* they were created
Is. 13:3 *c.* my sanctified ones
34:16 for my mouth it hath *c.*
45:12 heavens and host have I *c.*
Jer. 7:31 I *c.* not, 19:5; 32:35
Lam. 2:17 he *c.* in days of old
Ezek. 9:11 I have done as thou *c.*
24:18 I did in morn. as *c.* 37:10
Zec. 1:6 words I *c.* did they not
Mal. 4:4 rem. law I *c.* in Horeb
Luke 14:22 Lord, I *c.* is done as *c.*
Acts 10:42 he *c.* us to preach

Moses COMMANDED.
Deut. 31:20 turn from way I *c.*
33:4 *Moses c.* us a law, even
Jos. 1:7 observe to do all *Moses c.*
22:2 ye have kept all *Moses c.*
Mat. 8:4 offer the gift *Moses c.*
Mark 1:44 of. for thy cleansing things *Moses c. Luke* 5:14
John 8:5 *Moses c.* such he stoned

COMMANDEDST.
Neh. 9:14 thou *c.* them precepts
Jer. 32:23 done nothing thou *c.*

COMMANDER.
Is. 55:4 and *c.* to the people

COMMANDEST.
Jos. 1:16 all thou *c.* us we will do
18 not hearken in all thou *c.*
Jer. 32:23 done nothing of all *c.*
Acts 23:3 *c.* me to be smitten

COMMANDETH.
Num. 32:25 will do as my lord *c.*
Job 9:7 *c.* sun, and it riseth not
37:12 may do whatever he *c.*
Lam. 3:37 when *L. c.* not?
Mark 1:27 *c.* spirits, *Luke* 4:36
Acts 17:30 *c.* all men to repent

COMMANDING.
Gen. 49:33 Jacob an end of *c.*
Mat. 11:1 Jesus made end of *c.*

COMMANDMENT.
Ex. 34:32 *c.* all L. had spoken
Num. 15:31 broken *c.* be cut off
23:20 have received *c.* to bless
27:14 rebelled against my *c.*
Deut. 30:11 this *c.* I command
1 *K.* 2:43 why hast not kept *c.*
1 *Chr.* 13:32 were at their *c.*
28:21 people will be at thy *c.*
2 *Chr.* 19:10 betwixt law and *c.*
30:12 one, heart to do *c.* of king
31:5 as soon as *c.* came abroad
Ezr. 8:17 I sent with *c.* to Iddo
10:3 of those tremble at *c.*
Neh. 11:23 king's *c.* conc. them
Est. 1:12 refused to come at *c.*
3:3 why transgressest king's *c.?*
9:1 when king's *c.* drew nigh
Job 23:12 nor gone back from *c.*
Ps. 119:96 *c.* exceeding broad
147:15 forth his *c.* upon earth
Prov. 6:23 the *c.* is a lamp
8:29 waters run not pass his *c.*
13:13 feareth *c.* be rewarded
19:16 keepeth *c.* keepeth soul
Ec. 8:5 keepeth *c.* feel no evil

COM

Jer. 35:14 obey their father's *c.*
Dan. 3:22 king's *c.* was urgent
9:23 the *c.* came forth, and I am
Hos. 5:11 he walked after *c.*
Mal. 2:1 O priests, *c.* is for you
4 I have sent this *c.* to you
Mat. 15:3 transgress *c.* of God?
6 the *c.* of God of no effect
22:36 which is the great *c.*
38 this is great *c. Mark* 12:30
Mark 7:8 laying aside *c.* of God
9 full well ye reject *c.* of God
12:31 no *c.* greater than these
Luke 15:29 nor transgressed I *c.*
23:56 rested sab. accord. to *c.*
John 10:18 this *c.* I received of
12:49 a *c.* what I should say
50 his *c.* is life everlasting
14:31 Father gave me *c.* so I do
15:12 *c.* that ye I. 1 *John* 3:23
14:21 *c.* we gave no such *c.*
23:30 gave *c.* to his accusers
Rom. 7:8 occasion by the *c.* 11
9 *c.* came, sin revived
10 *c.* which was ordained to l.
12 *c.* is holy, just, and good
13:9 if any other *c.* it is
16:26 accord. to *c.* of everl. God
1 *Cor.* 7:6 I speak this, not of *c.*
2 *Cor.* 8:8 not by *c.* but by occa.
Eph. 6:2 first *c.* with promise
1 *Tim.* 1:1 by *c.* of *G. Tit.* 1:3
5 end of the *c.* is charity out of
Heb. 7:16 after law of a carnal *c.*
18 disannulling of the *c.*
11:23 not afraid of king's *c.*
2 *Pet.* 2:21 turn from holy *c.*
3:2 mindful of *c.* of us apos.
1 *John* 2:7 but an old *c.*
3:23 this is his *c.*
4:21 this *c.* have we from him,
2 *John* 4 received a *c.* from Fath.
6 this is the *c.*

Give *or* given COMMANDMENT.
Ex. 25:22 I will *give* in *c.*
Deut. 1:3 Lord had *g.* him in *c.*
Ezr. 4:21 *g. c.* till sno. *c.* be *g.*
Ps. 71:3 hast *given c.* to save
Lam. 23:11 hath *g. c.* against city
Nah. 1:14 *L.* hath *g. c.* conc. thee
John 11:57 *g. c.* if any knew

Keep COMMANDMENT.
See KEEP.

COMMANDMENT of the Lord.
Num. 24:13 can. go bey. *c. of L.*
1 *Sam.* 12:14 against *c. of the L.*
15 but rebel ag. *c. of the L.*
13:13 hast not kept *c. of the L.*
15:13 S. said, I perf. *c. of the L.*
24 I have trans. *c. of the L.*
2 *Sam.* 12:9 despised *c. of the L.*
1 *K.* 24:3 at *c. of L.* came on J.
2 *Chr.* 26:25 was *c. of the Lord*
Ps. 19:8 the *c. of the Lord* is pure
1 *Cor.* 7:25 I have no *c. of the L.*

New Commandment.
John 13:34 a new *c.* I give
1 *John* 2:7 no *c.* 8 a *new c.*
2 *John* 5 not as tho' I wrote a *c.*

Rebelled against the COMMANDMENT.
Num. 27:14 rebelled against my *c.*
Deut. 1:26 ye r. *a. c. of L.* 43
9:23 then ye r. *a. the c. of Lord*
Lam. 1:18 I have reb. ag. his *c.*

COMMANDMENTS.
Gen. 26:5 Abraham kept my *c.*
Ex. 15:26 if give ear to his *c.*
34:28 ten *c. Deut.* 4:13; 10:4
Lev. 4:13 against any *c.* 27
5:17 commit any forbidden *c.*
27:34 these are *c. L.* command
Num. 15:39 rem. all *c.* of Lord
Deut. 8:11 in not keeping his *c.*
11:13 if you shall hearken to my *c.* 28:13; *Jud.* 3:4
27 if ye will obey the *c. of L.*
28 if ye will not obey the *c.*
1 *Sam.* 15:11 Saul not perf. my *c.*
1 *K.* 11:34 b. he hath kept my *c.*
14:8 David who kept my *c.*
18:18 ye have forsaken the *c.*
K. 17:16 they left all the *c.*
19 Judah kept not *c.* of the L.
18:6 kept his *c.* which he com.
1 *Chr.* 28:8 keep all the *c.*
Ezr. 9:10 have forsaken thy *c.*
14 sh. we again break thy *c.*
Neh. 9:16 heark. to thy *c.*
9:29 testi. if they keep not my *c.*
119:10 not wander from *c.*

COM

Ps. 119:19 hide not thy *c.* from me
35 to go in path of thy *c.*
47 I will delight in thy *c.*
66 for I have believed thy *c.*
73 that I may learn thy *c.*
86 *c.* are faithful; 151 truth
98 through *c.* made me wiser
127 I love thy *c.*; 131 I longed
143 *c.* my delights; 172 right.
166 done thy *c.*; 176 not forget
Prov. 2:1 will hide my *c.*
7:1 lay up my *c.* with thee
10:8 wise in heart will rec. *c.*
Is. 48:18 hadst hearkened to *c.*
Mat. 5:19 whoso. break least *c.*
15:9 teach. *c.* of men, *Mark* 7:7
22:40 on these two *c.* hang law
Mark 10:19 thou knowest *c.*
Luke 18:20
Luke 1:6 walking in *c.* blameless
John 14:21 he that hath my *c.*
15:10 if I keep my *c.* shall abide
1 *Cor.* 7:19 nothing, but keep. *c.*
14:37 things I write you are *c.*
Col. 2:22 *c.* and doctr. of men
1 *Thes.* 4:2 ye know *c.* we gave
2:4 keepeth not *c.* is a liar
3:24 that keepeth *c.* dwelleth
2 *John* 6 this is love, walk after *c.*

Do COMMANDMENTS.
Num. 15:40 *do* all my *c.*
Deut. 6:25 to *do* all *c.* 15:5
1 *Chr.* 28:7 to *do* my *c.*
Ps. 103:18 that rem. his *c.* to *do*
111:10 understanding that *do c.*
Rev. 22:14 blessed are they *do c.*

Not do COMMANDMENTS.
Lev. 26:14 if ye will *not do c.*

See KEEP.

COMMEND.
Luke 23:46 into thy hands I *c.*
Acts 20:32 breth. I *c.* you to God
Rom. 3:5 iniquity, *c.* right. of G.
16:1 I *c.* unto you Phebe
2 *Cor.* 3:1 we begin again to *c.*
5:12 for we *c.* not ourselves
10:12 compare with some that *c.*

COMMENDATION.
2 *Cor.* 3:1 need we epistles of *c.*

COMMENDED.
Gen. 12:15 princes *c.* Sarai
Prov. 12:8 man *c.* ac. to wisd.
Ec. 8:15 then I *c.* mirth
Luke 16:8 Lord *c.* unjust steward
2 *Cor.* 12:11 have been *c.* of you

COMMENDETH.
Rom. 5:8 God *c.* his love tow. us
1 *Cor.* 8:8 meat *c.* us not to God
2 *Cor.* 10:18 *c.* himself is approv.

COMMENDING.
2 *Cor.* 4:2 *c.* ourselves

COMMISSION, S.
Ezra 8:36 delivered the king's *c.*
Acts 26:12 as I went with *c.*

COMMIT.
Ex. 20:14 not *c.* adult. *Deut.* 5:18;
Mat. 5:27; 19:18; *Rom.* 13:9
Lev. 5:17 *c.* things forbidden
18:29 *c.* any of these abomin.
Num. 5:6 *c.* any sin that men *c.*
Deut. 19:20 *c.* no more such evil
2 *Chr.* 21:11 J. to *c.* fornication
Job 5:8 would I *c.* my cause
Ps. 31:5 thy hand I *c.* my spirit
37:5 *c.* thy way to the Lord
Prov. 16:3 *c.* thy works unto Lord
12 to kings to *c.* wickedness
Is. 22:21 I will *c.* thy government
Jer. 44:7 why *c.* ye this evil?
Ezek. 8:17 *c.* abomina. they *c.* h.
16:43 shalt not *c.* this lewdness
22:9 in midst of thee *c.* lewdness
Hos. 5:6 priests *c.* lewdness
7:1 for they *c.* falsehood
Luke 12:48 *c.* worthy of stripes
16:11 *c.* the true riches?
John 2:24 Jes. did not *c.* himself
Rom. 1:32 *c.* such worthy of d.
2:2 is ag. them *c.* such things
2:4 dost thou *c.* sacrilege?
1 *Cor.* 10:8 not let us *c.* fornica.
1 *Tim.* 1:18 charge I *c.* to thee
2 *Tim.* 2:2 to faithful men
Jam. 2:9 respect to persons ye *c.*
1 *Pet.* 4:19 *c.* keeping of souls
1 *John* 3:9 born of God, not *c.* sin
Rev. 2:14 taught Is. to *c.* fornica.
20 my servants to *c.* fornica.

See ADULTERY.

COMMIT Iniquity.
2 *Sam.* 7:14 *c.* i. I will chasten

COM

Job 34:10 Almighty he sh. *c. i.*
Jer. 9:5 weary th. to *c. iniquity*
Ezek. 3:20 right. and *c. i.* 33:13

COMMIT trespass.
Lev. 5:15 if a soul *c. t.* thro' ig.
Num. 5:12 if a man's wife *c. tres.*
31:16 caused Israel to *c. trespass*
Jos. 22:20 Achan *c.* a *trespass*

COMMIT whoredom, *or* whoredoms.
Lev. 20:5 that *c. w.* with Molech
Num. 25:1 to *c. w.* with dau. of M.
Ezek. 16:17 *c. w.* with images
34 followeth to *c. whoredom*
20:30 *c.* ye *w.* after their abo.?
23:43 will they *c. w.* with her
Hos. 4:10 *c. w.* and not increase
13 your daugh. shall *c. w.* 14

COMMITTED.
Gen. 39:6 *c.* all he hath to my h.
22 *c.* to Joseph the pris'oners
Lev. 20:23 *c.* these and I abhorr.
Jud. 20:6 *c.* lewdness in Israel
1 *K.* 8:47 we have *c.* wickedness
14:22 with sins they *c.*
Jer. 2:13 my people *c.* two evils
5:30 a horrible thing is *c.*
16:10 what is our sin we have
41:3 *c.* to provoke me, 9
Ezek. 16:26 hast also *c.* fornica.
51 nor Sam. *c.* half of thy sins
18:21 from sins he *c.* 22, 28
23:3 *c.* whored. in Eg. in youth
7 *c.* her whoredoms with them
33:16 none of his sins he *c.*
Hos. 1:2 land hath *c.* great who.
4:18 they have *c.* whoredom
Mark 15:7 who had *c.* murder
Luke 12:48 have *c.* much, of him
John 3:22 *c.* all judgment to Son
Acts 8:3 *c.* them to prison
25:11 if I have *c.* any th. worthy
25 found he *c.* nothing worthy
27:40 *c.* themselves to the sea
28:17 *c.* nothing against people
Rom. 3:2 *c.* were *c.* oracles of God
2 *Cor.* 5:19 *c.* to us word of recon.
12:21 lasciviousness they *c.*
Gal. 2:7 gospel of the uncircum.
was *c.* to me, 1 *Tim.* 1:11
1 *Tim.* 6:20 what is *c.* to thee
2 *Tim.* 1:12 to keep what I *c.*
Jam. 5:15 if he *c.* sins be forgiv.
1 *Pet.* 2:23 *c.* himself to him jud.
Jude 15 ungodly deeds they *c.*
Rev. 17:2 have *c.* forni. 18:3, 9

See ABOMINATIONS.

COMMITTED Iniquity.
Ps. 106:6 we have *c. iniquity*
Ezek. 33:13 *iniqui. c.* he shall die
Dan. 9:5 *c. i.* and done wickedly

COMMITTED trespass.
Jos. 7:1 Is. *c. t.* in accurs. thing
22:16 what *t.* is this ye have *c.*
31 because not *c.* this *t.* aga. L.
Ezek. 15:8 have *c. t. I* will make
20:27 in that they *c. t.* ag. me

COMMITTEST, ETH, ING.
Ps. 10:14 *c.* himself to thee
Ezek. 8:6 abomination Is. *c.*
33:15 without *c.* iniquity, 18
Hos. 4:2 by lying, *c.* adultery
5:3 O Ephraim, *c.* whoredom
John 8:34 *c.* sin, is servant of sin
1 *Cor.* 6:18 *c.* fornication sinneth
1 John 3:4 *c.* sin transgresseth l.
8 he that *c.* sin is of the devil

COMMODIOUS.
Acts 27:12 the haven was not *c.*

COMMON.
1 *Sam.* 21:4 there is no *c.* bread
Ec. 6:1 there is an evil, it is *c.*
Jer. 31:5 eat them as *c.* things
Ezek. 23:42 with men of *c.* sort
Acts 2:44 had all things *c.* 4:32
10:14 eaten any thing *c.* 11:8
1 *Cor.* 10:13 no temptation but *c.*
28 should not call any man *c.*
Tit. 1:4 my son after *c.* faith
Jude 3 to write of *c.* salvation

COMMON people.
Lev. 4:27 if any of *c.* people
Mark 12:37 *c. peo.* heard him

COMMONLY. *See* REPORTED.

COMMONWEALTH.
Eph. 2:12 aliens from the *c.* of Is.

COMMOTION, S.
Jer. 10:22 a great *c.* out of north
Luke 21:9 when ye hear of *c.* be

COMMUNE.
Ex. 25:22 there *c.* with thee
1 *Sam.* 18:22 *c.* with D. secretly

CRUDEN'S CONCORDANCE. 801

COM

COM
1 *Sam.* 19:3 I will c. with my fa.
Job 4:2 if assay to c. with thee
Ps. 4:4 c. with your own heart
64:5 c. of laying snares privily
77:6 night I c. with my heart

COMMUNED.
Gen. 23:8 Abra.; 34:6 Hamor, 8
42:24 Joseph; *Jud.* 9:1 Abim.
1 *Sam.* 9:25 Samuel; 25:39 David
1 *K.* 10:2 the queen of Sheba c.
with Solomon, 2 *Chr.* 9:1
2 *K.* 22:14 c. with Huldah
Ec. 1:16 I c. with my own heart
Dan. 1:19 king c. with them
Luke 6:11 c. what do to Jesus
24:15 while c. Jesus drew nigh
Acts 24:26 Felix c. the oftener

COMMUNICATE.
Gal. 6:6 c. to him that teacheth
Phil. 4:14 c. with my affliction
1 *Tim.* 6:18 be willing to c.
Heb. 13:16 and to c. forget not

COMMUNICATED.
Gal. 2:2 c. to them that gospel
Phil. 4:15 no church c. with me.

COMMUNICATION, S.
2 *Sam.* 3:17 A. had c. with elders
2 *K.* 9:11 ye know his c.
Mat. 5:37 let your c. be yea, yea
Luke 24:17 what manner of c.
1 *Cor.* 15:33 evil c. corrupt good
Eph. 4:29 no corrupt c. Col. 3:8
Phile. 6. c. of thy faith effectual

COMMUNING.
Gen. 18:33 left c. with Abraham
Ex. 31:18 an end of c. on Sinai

COMMUNION.
1 *Cor.* 10:16 c. of blood, c. of body
Cor. 6:14 wh. c. light with dark.
13:14 c. H. G. be with you all

COMPACT.
Ps. 122:3 Jerusalem is a city c.

COMPACTED.
Eph. 4:16 the whole body c.

COMPANY, Substantive.
Gen. 32:8 E. come to the one c.
33:8 c. of nations be of thee
Num. 16:16 thou and all thy c.
40 be not as Korah and his c.
22:4 this c. lick up all round
26:9 strove in c. of Korah, 27:3
Jud. 9:37 another c. by plain
18:23 comest with such a c. *?*
1 *Sam.* 30:15 bring me to this c. *?*
2 *K.* 5:15 his c. came to Elisha
9:17 he spied the c. of Jehu
2 *Chr.* 21:24 Syrians with small c.
Job 16:7 made desolate all my c.
34:8 in c. with workers of iniq.
Ps. 55:14 to house of God in c.
68:30 rebuke the c. of spearmen
106:17 covered c. of Abiram
24 fire was kindled in their c.
Prov. 29:3 keepeth c. with harl.
Cant. 1:9 to a c. of horses in Ph.
6:13 as it were c. of two armies
Ezek. 16:40 bring a c. against thee
23:46 I will bring a c. on them
32:22 Ashur is there and her c.
38:7 prepare, thou and thy c.
Hos. 6:9 so c. of priests murder
Luke 2:44 supposs. him c. of his.
6:17 and c. of his disciples
23 separate you from their c.
9:14 sit by fifties in a c.
38 a man of the c. cried out
21:22 a woman of our c. made
Acts 4:23 went to their own c.
10:28 unl. for a Jew to keep c.
15:22 to send chosen men of c.
17:5 gathered a c. and set city
21:8 we of Paul's c. departed
Rom. 15:24 filled with your c.
1 *Cor.* 5:11 not to keep c. with
2 *Thes.* 3:14 have no c. with him
Heb. 12:22 an innum. c. of angels
Rev. 18:17 c. in ships afar off

Great COMPANY.
Gen. 50:9 with Joseph a great c.
2 *Chr.* 9:1 queen of S. with g. c.
20:12 no might ag. this great c.
Ps. 68:11 g. was c. of those pub.
Jer. 31:8 great c. return thither
Ezek. 17:17 Pharaoh with great c.
John 6:5 saw a great c. come
Acts 6:7 g. c. of priests obedient

COMPANY, Verb.
1 *Cor.* 5:9 not to c. with fornic.
Acts 1:21 which have c. with us

COMPANIES.
Jud. 7:16 300 into three c.
1 *Sam.* 11:11 Saul put in three c.
13:17 spoilers in three c.

COM

COM
2 *K.* 5:2 Syrians gone by c.
Neh. 12:31 c. gave thanks, 40
Job 6:19 the c. of Sheba waited
Is. 21:13 O ye travelling c.
57:13 let thy c. deliver thee
Mark 6:39 to make all sit by c.

COMPANION.
Ex. 32:27 slay every man his c.
Jud. 14:20 S.'s wife to c. 15:6
1 *Chr.* 27:33 Hushai king's c.
Job 30:29 I am a c. to owls
Ps. 119:63 c. to all that fear thee
Prov. 13:20 c. of fools be destroy.
28:7 c. of riotous shameth fath.
24 same is c. of a destroyer
Mal. 2:14 she is thy c. wife of
Phil. 2:25 Epaph. my c. in labor
Rev. 1:9 I John your c. in tribu.

COMPANIONS.
Jud. 11:38 went with c.
14:11 thirty c. to be with him
Job 35:4 will answer thee and c.
41:6 c. make a banquet of him?
Ps. 45:14 her c. shall be brought
122:8 for my c. sake I will say
Cant. 1:7 aside by flocks of thy c.
8:13 c. hearken to thy voice
Is. 1:23 princes c. of thieves
Ezek. 37:16 Judah and for c. 17
Dan. 2:17 Dan. made known to his c.
Acts 19:29 caught Paul's c.
Heb. 10:33 c. of them so used

COMPARABLE.
Lam. 4:2 sons of Zion c. to gold

COMPARE, ED, ING.
Ps. 89:6 who in heaven c. to L. *?*
Prov. 3:15 not be c. 8:11
Cant. 1:9 I have c. thee
Is. 40:18 wh. likeness c. to him *?*
46:5 to whom will ye c. me
Rom. 8:18 to be c. with the glory
1 *Cor.* 2:13 c. spiritual things
2 *Cor.* 10:12 c. ours. with some
that com. c. themse.; amongst

COMPARISON.
Jud. 8:2 I done in c. of you *?* 3
Hag. 2:3 in your eyes in c. of it
Mark 4:30 with what c. shall we

COMPASS.
2 *Sam.* 5:23 but fetch a c. behind
2 *K.* 3:9 fetched a c. of 7 days
Prov. 8:27 c. on face of the deep
Is. 44:13 marketh it with c.
Acts 28:13 fetched a c. to Rheg.

COMPASS, Verb.
Num. 21:4 c. the land of Edom
Jos. 6:3 ye shall c. the city
7 c. it, let the king, 2 *Chr.* 33:7
Job 16:13 his archers c. me about.
40:22 willows of brook c. him
Ps. 5:12 with favour c. as a shield
7:7 congregation c. thee about
17:9 deadly enemies who c. me
26:6 so will I c. thine altar
32:7 c. me with songs of deliv.
10 trust, in Lord mercy c. him
49:5 iniquity of my heels c. me
140:9 as far head of those c. me
142:7 the righteous shall c. me
Is. 50:11 c. yoursel. with sparks
Jer. 31:22 a wom. shall c. a man
Hab. 1:4 wicked c. righteous
Mat. 23:15 for ye c. sea and land
Luke 19:43 thine enemies shall c.

COMPASSED.
Deut. 2:1 we c. Seir many days
Jos. 6:11 so the ark c. the city
Jud. 11:18 c. the land of Edom
16:2 they c. Samson in
1 *Sam.* 23:26 Saul c. David and
2 *Sam.* 18:15 ten c. about Abs.
22:6 c. me ab. *Ps.* 18:5
2 *K.* 6:15 behold a host c. city
2 *Chr.* 21:9 Edomites which c.
Job 19:6 God c. me with net
16:10 c. wasters with his band
Ps. 17:11 now c. us in our steps
22:12 bulls c. me; 16 dogs
Lam. 3:5 c. me with gall and
Luke 21:20 when ye see J. c. with
Heb. 5:2 himself, with infirmity

COMPASSED about.
Ps. 18:4 c. ab. *Ps.* 18:5
Ps. 88:3 c. about me
2 *K.* 6:15 behold a host c.
2 *Chr.* 22:1 about Jehoshaph.
Ps. 40:12 iniquit. c. me about
109:3 c. me about with words of
118:10 all nations c. me about
11 they c. me about, 12
Jon. 2:3 billows c. me about
Luke 8:23 c. about with a cloud

COMPASSED.
2 *K.* 5:1 Syrians c. city about
2 *Chr.* 4:3 c. about Jehoshaph.
Ps. 48:12 beheld, c. Zion about
116:10 all nations c. me about
Prov. 11:13 of a faithful spirit c.
12:23 prudent c. knowledge
Jer. 50:2 publish and c. not

COMPASSEST, ETH.
Gen. 2:11 c. Havilah; 13 Ethio.

CON

CON
Ps. 73:6 pride c. them as a chain
139:3 thou c. my path, and
Hos. 11:12 Ephraim c. with lies

COMPASSION.
1 *K.* 8:50 give them c. before
2 *Chr.* 30:9 children shall find c.
Mat. 9:36 Jesus moved with c.
14:14; *Mark* 1:41; 6:34
18:27 lord was moved with c.
1 *Pet.* 3:8 hav. c. one of another
1 *John* 3:17 shut. his bowels of c.

Full of COMPASSION.
Ps. 78:38 he being full of c.
86:15 G. *f.* of c. 111:4; 112:4; 145:8

Have or had COMPASSION.
Ex. 2:6 babe wept, she had c.
Deut. 13:17 L. may h. c. on thee
30:3 Lord will have c. on thee
1 *Sam.* 23:21 for ye have c. on me
1 *K.* 8:50 they may h. c. on them
2 *Chr.* 36:15 had c. on his people
17 Chaldees had no c. on man
Is. 49:15 she not have c. on son
Jer. 12:15 I will have c. on them
Lam. 3:32 he have c. *Mic.* 7:19
Mat. 15:32 c. on mult. *Mark* 8:2
18:33 c. on thy fellow-servant
20:34 so Jesus had c. on them
Mark 5:19 how L. had c. on thee
9:22 have c. on us and help us
Luke 7:13 L. saw her, he had c.
10:33 Samaritan had c. on him
15:20 father had c. and ran and
Rom. 9:15 will have c. on whom
Heb. 5:2 can have c. on ignorant
10:34 had c. of me in my bonds
Jude 22 of some have c. making

COMPASSIONS.
Lam. 3:22 because his c. fail not
Zec. 7:9 show c. ev. man to bro.

COMPEL.
Mat. 5:41 c. thee to go a mile go
Mark 15:21 c. one Simon to bear
Luke 14:23 c. them to come in

COMPELLED, EST.
2 *Chr.* 21:11 c. Judah thereto
Mat. 27:32 him c. to bear cross
Acts 26:11 c. them to blaspheme
Gal. 2:3 c. to be circumcised
14 c. Gentiles to live as Jews?

COMPLAIN, ED, ING.
Num. 11:1 c. it displeased Lord
Jud. 21:22 bre. come to us to c.
Job 7:11 I will c. in bitterness
31:38 the furrows thereof c.
Ps. 77:3 I c. and my spirit was
144:14 be no c. in our streets
Lam. 3:39 doth a living man c. *?*

COMPLAINERS.
Jude 16 these are murmurers, c.

COMPLAINT.
1 *Sam.* 1:16 abundance of my c.
Job 7:13 couch shall ease my c.
9:27 if I say, I will forget my c.
10:1 I will leave c. on myself
21:4 is my c. to man *?*
23:2 even today is my c. bitter
Ps. 55:2 I mourn in my c.
142:2 I poured out my c.
Acts 25:7 c. against Paul

COMPLETE.
Lev. 23:15 seven sabbaths be c.
Col. 2:10 and ye are c. in him
4:12 that ye may stand c. in all

COMPOSITION.
Ex. 30:32 may like it after c. 37

COMPOUND, ETH.
Ex. 30:25 an ointment c.
33 whosoever c. any like it

COMPREHEND.
Job 37:5 doeth he, we cannot c.
Eph. 3:18 able to c.

COMPREHENDED.
Is. 40:12 c. dust of the earth
Rom. 13:9 it is briefly c. in this

CONCEAL, ED, ETH.
Gen. 37:26 bro. and c. his blood
Deut. 13:8 nor shalt thou c. him
Job 6:10 I have not c. the words
27:11 Almighty will I not c.
41:12 I will not c. his parts
Ps. 40:10 not c. thy loving-kind.
Prov. 11:13 of a faithful spirit c.
12:23 prudent c. knowledge
Jer. 50:2 publish and c. not

CONCEIT, S.
Prov. 18:11 as high wall in own c.

CON

CON
Prov. 26:5 he be wise in own c.
12 a man wise in his own c. *?*
16 sluggard wiser in own c.
28:11 rich is wise in own c.
Rom. 11:25 in your own c.
12:16 be not wise in own c.

CONCEIVE.
Gen. 30:38 c. when came to drink
Jud. 13:3 shalt c. and bear a son,
7; *Luke* 1:31
Job 15:35 c. mischief, *Is.* 59:4
51:5 in sin did mother c. me
Is. 7:14 a virgin shall c. and
33:11 c. chaff; 59:13 c. falsehood
Heb. 11:11 Sarah rec. str. to c.

CONCEIVED.
Gen. 4:1 Eve c.; 17 Cain's wife c.
16:4 Hagar c.; 21:2 Sarah c.
25:21 Reb. c.; 29:32 Leah, 33
30:5 Bilhah c.; 23 Rachel c.
39 flocks c.; 38:3 Shuah c.
38:18 Tamar c.; *Ex.* 2:2 Joch. c.
Lev. 12:2 have c. seed, and borne
Num. 11:12 have I c. all this *?*
1 *Sam.* 1:20 Hannah c. 2:21
2 *Sam.* 11:5 Bath-sheba c.
2 *K.* 4:17 Shun.; *Is.* 8:3 proph.
Job 3:3 there is a man-child c.
Ps. 7:14 c. mischief, brought
Cant. 3:4 chamber of her c. me
Jer. 49:30 c. a purpose ag. you
Hos. 1:3 Gomer c.
2 c. hath done shamefully
Mat. 1:20 c. in her is of Holy G.
Luke 1:36 Elizabeth hath c. a son
2:21 so named before he was c.
Acts 5:4 c. this in thy heart *?*
Rom. 9:10 Rebecca had c.
Jam. 1:15 when lust hath c.

CONCEPTION.
Gen. 3:16 multiply thy c.
Ruth 4:13 the Lord gave her c.
Hos. 9:11 glory flee from the c.

CONCERN, ETH.
Ps. 138:8 L. perfect that c. me
2 *Cor.* 11:30 c. mine infirmities

CONCERNING.
Gen. 19:21 accepted thee c. this
Num. 10:29 spoken good c. Isr.
1 *K.* 11:10 command him c. this
Ec. 7:10 inquire wisely c. this
Is. 29:7 therefore I cried c. this
Ezek. 21:28 saith L. c. Ammon,
47:14 c. which lifted my hand
Luke 24:27 exp. things c. him.
41 written in Psalms c. me
Acts 13:34 as c. he raised him
Rom. 9:5 as c. flesh Christ came
11:28 as c. gospel enemies for
2 *Cor.* 11:21 I sp. as c. reproach
Phil. 4:15 as c. giving and recei.
1 *Thes.* 5:18 will of God in C. c.

CONCISION.
Phil. 3:2 beware of the c.

CONCLUDE.
Rom. 3:28 c. a man is justified

CONCLUDED.
Acts 21:25 touching Gent. we c.
Rom. 11:32 c. them all in unbel.
Gal. 3:22 hath c. all under sin

CONCLUSION.
Ec. 12:13 hear c. of matter

CONCORD.
2 *Cor.* 6:15 what c. Ch. with D.

CONCOURSE.
Prov. 1:21 crieth in place of c.
Acts 19:40 give acc. of this c.

CONCUBINE.
Jud. 19:2 c. played the whore
9 arose and divided her, 20:6
20:4 I and my c. to lodge
2 *Sam.* 3:7 unto my father's c. *?*
21:11 what Rizpah c. of Saul

CONCUBINES.
Gen. 25:6 to sons of c. gave gifts
2 *Sam.* 5:13 David took more c.
19:5 Abs. went in to father's c.
19:5 and the lives of thy c.
20:3 king put his c. in ward
2 *Chr.* 11:21 took threescore c.
Est. 2:14 Shaashgaz kept c.
Cant. 6:8 there are eighty c.
9 and c. they praised her
Dan. 5:3 c. drank in them, 23

CONCUPISCENCE.
Rom. 7:8 sin wr. all manner of c.
Col. 3:5 mortify evil c.
1 *Thes.* 4:5 not in the lust of c.

CONDEMN.
Ex. 22:9 whom judges shall c.

51

CRUDEN'S CONCORDANCE.

CON

Deut. 3:1 judges shall c. wicked
Job 9:20 my mouth shall c. me
10:2 I will say, Do not c. me
34:18 wilt th. c. him most just?
40:8 wilt thou c. me, that
Ps. 37:33 nor c. him
94:21 they c. innocent blood
109:31 those that c. his soul
Prov. 12:2 wick. devices will he c.
Is. 50:9 who is he shall c. me?
54:17 that rise against thee c.
Mat. 12:41 shall c. it, *Luke* 11:32
42 queen of south shall c. it
23:14 c. him to d. *Mark* 10:33
Luke 6:37 c. not, sh. not be con.
John 3:17 his Son to c. the world
8:11 neither do I c. thee, go
2 *Cor.* 7:3 I speak not this to c.
1 *John* 3:20 If our heart c. us
21 If our heart c. us not, we

CONDEMNATION.
Luke 23:40 thou art in same c.
John 3:19 c. that light is come
5:24 believeth, not come into c.
Rom. 5:16 judgment by one to c.
18 judgment came to c.
8:1 there is no c. to them in C.
1 *Cor.* 11:34 come not together, to c.
2 *Cor.* 3:9 minist. of c. be glory
1 *Tim.* 3:6 lest he fall into c. of
Jam. 3:1 receive the greater c.
5:12 be nay, lest ye fall into c.
Jude 4 of old ordained to this c.

CONDEMNED.
Job 32:3 yet had c. Job
Ps. 109:7 judged, let him be c.
Amos 2:8 they drink wine of c.
Mat. 12:7 not have c. guiltless
37 by thy words shalt be c.
27:3 J. when he saw he was c.
Mark 14:64 c. him to be guilty
Luke 21:26 delivered him to be c.
John 3:18 believ. on him, is not
c. believ. not, is c. already
8:10 hath no man c. thee?
Rom. 8:3 for sin c. sin in flesh
1 *Cor.* 11:32 not be c. with world
Tit. 2:8 speech that cannot be c.
3:11 sinneth, being c. of hims.
Heb. 11:7 by which he c. world
Jam. 5:6 c. and killed the just
9 grudge not, lest ye be c.
2 *Pet.* 2:6 c. with overthrow

CONDEMNEST, ETH, ING.
1 *K.* 8:32 c. wicked
Job 15:6 own mouth c. thee
Prov. 17:15 he that c. the just
Acts 13:27 fulfilled them in c. him
Rom. 2:1 judgest thou c. thyself
8:34 who is he that c.?
14:22 c. not himself in thing

CONDESCEND.
Rom. 12:16 c. to men of low est.

CONDITION, S.
1 *Sam.* 11:2 on this c. make cov.
Luke 14:32 desireth c. of peace

CONDUCT, ED.
2 *Sam.* 19:15 c. king over Jor. 31
40 people of Judah c. king
Acts 17:5 that c. Paul brought
1 *Cor.* 16:11 but c. him in peace

CONDUIT.
2 *K.* 18:7 stood by, *Is.* 36:2
20:20 how the made a pool and c.
Is. 7:3 to meet Ahaz at end of c.

CONFECTION.
Ex. 30:35 make a c. after art

CONFECTIONARIES.
1 *Sam.* 8:13 your dau. to be c.

CONFEDERACY.
Is. 8:12 c. to whom people say c.
Ob. 7 men of thy c. brought

CONFEDERATE.
Gen. 14:13 these c. with Abram
Ps. 83:5 they are c. against thee
Is. 7:2 Syria is c. with Ephraim

CONFERENCE.
Gal. 2:6 they in c. added nothing

CONFERRED.
1 *K.* 1:7 Adonijah c. with Joab
Acts 4:15 c. among themselves
25:12 Festus, when he had c.
Gal. 1:16 I c. not with flesh and

CONFESS.
Lev. 5:5 c. he hath sinned
16:21 c. over him all the iniq.
26:40 if they c. their iniquity
Num. 5:7 they shall c. their sin
1 *K.* 8:33 c. thy name, 35; 2 *Chr.* 6:24, 26
Neh. 1:6 c. sins of children of Is.
Job 40:14 c. thy hand can save
Ps. 32:5 I said, I will c. my tr.

CON

Mat. 10:32 c. me before, *Lu.* 12:8
John 9:22 if c. that he was Christ
12:42 did not c. him, lest they
Acts 23:8 but Pharisees c. both
24:14 I c. after the way
Rom. 10:9 c. with thy mouth
14:11 every tongue shall c.
15:9 c. to thee among Gentiles
Phil. 2:11 every tongue should c.
Jam. 5:16 c. your faults
1 *John* 1:9 if we c. our sins
4:15 c. Jesus is the Son of God
1 *John* 7 c. not Jesus Christ
Rev. 3:5 c. his name bef. my Fa.

CONFESSED, ETH, ING.
Ezr. 10:1 Ezra had c. weeping
Neh. 9:2 stood and c. their sins
Prov. 28:13 whoso c. and forsak.
Dan. 9:23 c. my sin and the sin
Mat. 3:6 baptized c. their sins
John 1:20 c. I am not the Christ
Acts 19:18 many c. and showed
Heb. 11:13 c. they were strangers
1 *John* 4:2 spirit that c. Christ
3 c. not Jesus Christ is come

CONFESSION.
Jos. 7:19 and make c. to God
2 *Chr.* 30:22 offer. and making c.
Ezr. 10:11 make c. to the Lord
Dan. 9:4 I prayed and made c.
Rom. 10:10 with mouth c. is m.
1 *Tim.* 6:13 witnessed a good c.

CONFIDENCE.
Jud. 9:26 Shech. put c. in Gaal
2 *K.* 18:19 what c. is this? *Is.* 36:4
Job 4:6 is not this thy fear, thy c.
31:24 fine gold thou art my c.
Ps. 65:5 art c. of all the earth
118:8 than put c. in man
9 than to put c. in princes
Prov. 3:26 Lord shall be thy c.
14:26 fear of Lord is strong c.
21:22 strength of c.
25:19 c. in unfaithful
Is. 30:15 is c. be your strength
Jer. 48:13 ashamed of B. their c.
Ezek. 28:26 shall dwell with c.
29:16 E. be no more c. of Israel
Mic. 7:5 put ye not c. in a guide
Acts 28:31 preaching with all c.
2 *Cor.* 1:15 in this c. minded
2:3 c. that my joy is the joy
7:16 that I have c. in you
8:22 great c. I have in you
10:2 the c. I think to be bold
11:17 as foolishly in this c.
Eph. 3:12 access with c. by faith
Phil. 1:25 having this c.
3:3 we have no c. in the flesh
4 I might have c. in flesh
2 *Thes.* 3:4 c. in L. touching you
Phile. 21 c. in thy obedience
Heb. 3:6 if we hold fast c.
14 beginning of our c. stedfast.
10:35 cast not away your c.
1 *John* 2:28 we may have c.
3:21 then have we c. toward G.
5:14 the c. we have in him

CONFIDENCES.
Jer. 2:37 Lord rejected thy c.

CONFIDENT.
Ps. 27:3 in this I be c.
Prom. 14:16 fool rageth and is c.
Rom. 2:19 art c. thou art a guide
2 *Cor.* 5:6 we are always c.
8 c. and willing to be absent
9:4 ashamed in same c. boasting
Phil. 1:6 c. of this very thing
14 waxing c. by my bonds

CONFIDENTLY.
Luke 22:59 c. affirmed, This fel.

CONFIRM.
Ruth 4:7 manner to c. all things
1 *K.* 1:14 I will c. thy words
Is. 35:3 c. feeble knees
Ezek. 13:6 they would c. the w.
Dan. 9:27 c. cov. for one week
11:1 I stood to c. him
Rom. 15:8 c. promises made
1 *Cor.* 1:8 also c. you to the end
2 *Cor.* 2:8 ye would c. your love

CONFIRMATION.
Phil. 1:7 in the c. of the gospel
Heb. 6:16 an oath for c. is an end

CONFIRMED.
2 *Sam.* 7:24 c. to thyself Israel
1 *K.* 14:5 as soon as king was c.
1 *Chr.* 14:2 Lord had c. him k.
16:17 c. same to J. *Ps.* 105:10
Est. 9:31 Esther c. matt. of Pur.
Dan. 9:12 words he spake

CON

Acts 15:32 exhorted and c. them
1 *Cor.* 1:6 testim. of C. c. in you
Gal. 3:15 if c. no man disannul.
17 the covenant that was c.
Heb. 2:3 was c. to us by them
6:17 he c. it by an oath

CONFIRMETH, ING.
Num. 30:14 bonds on her, he c.
Deut. 27:26 cursed be he c. not
Is. 44:26 c. word of his servant
Mark 16:20 c. the word
Acts 14:22 c. souls of disciples
15:41 Syria c. the churches

CONFISCATION.
Ezr. 7:26 judgm. be exec. to c.

CONFLICT.
Phil. 1:30 same c. ye saw in me
Col. 2:1 knew what c. I have

CONFORMABLE.
Phil. 3:10 made c. to his death

CONFORMED.
Rom. 8:29 c. to image of his Son
12:2 be not c. to this world

CONFOUND.
Gen. 11:7 c. their language, 9
Jer. 1:17 lest I c. thee before
1 *Cor.* 1:27 to c. the wise, 1 c.

CONFOUNDED.
2 *K.* 19:26 inhab. were c. *Is.* 37:27
Job 6:20 c. bec. they had hoped
Ps. 35:4 be c. that seek my soul
69:6 let not those seek L. be c.
71:13 be c. that are adversaries
24 are c. that seek my heart
83:17 let them be c. for ever
97:7 c. be all that serve images
129:5 let all he c. that hate Zion
Is. 1:29 c. for the gardens
19:9 that weave net-work be c.
37:27 inhabitants were c.
Jer. 9:19 bec. we have forsaken
10:14 founder c. by image, 51:17
14 be c. that persecute me
46:24 dau. of E. c. ; 48:20 Moab
49:23 Hamath is c.; 50:2 Bel.
50:12 your mother be sore c.
51:47 Babylon whole land be c.
51 c. bec. we heard reproach
Ezek. 16:52 be thou c. bear 63
Mic. 7:16 nations c. at their m.
Zec. 10:5 riders and horses be c.
Acts 2:6 multitude were c.
9:22 Saul c. Jews at Damascus

Ashamed and CONFOUND- ED.
Ps. 40:14 ash. c. seek soul, 70:2
Is. 24:23 moon be ash. sun c.
41:11 inc. ag. thee be a. and c.
45:16 idol mak. be a. and c.
54:4 not be ashan. neither c.
Jer. 14:3 noh. and lit. ones a. c.
15:9 borne seven been a. and c.
22:22 shall be ashamed and c.
31:19 ash. yea c. bec. I did bear
Ezek. 36:32 be a. c. O. for your w.
Mic. 3:7 seers be a. diviners c.

Not CONFOUNDED.
Ps. 22:5 were not c.
Is. 45:17 her c. worlds with. end
57:7 God will help, I not be c.
1 *Pet.* 2:6 believeth shall not be c.

CONFUSED.
Is. 9:5 battle is with c. noise
Acts 19:32 the assembly was c.

CONFUSION.
Lev. 18:23 c. beast to lie, it is c.
20:12 they have wrought c.
1 *Sam.* 20:30 chosen D. to thy c.
Ezr. 9:7 delivered to c. of face
Job 10:15 I am full of c.
Ps. 35:4 to c. that devise
44:15 my c. is bef. me, before me
70:2 to c. that desire my hurt
71:1 let me never be put to c.
109:29 cover with their c.
Is. 24:10 the city of c. is broken
30:3 trust in shadow of Egypt c.
34:11 stretch on it line of c.
41:29 their molten images are c.
45:16 makers of idols go to c.
61:7 for c. they shall rejoice in
Jer. 3:25 and our c. covereth us
7:19 provoke to the c.
20:11 everl. c. never be forgot
Dan. 9:7 belongeth c. of faces, 8
Acts 19:29 city was filled with c.
1 *Cor.* 14:33 God not author of c.
Jam. 3:16 where strife is, is c.

CONGEALED.
Ex. 15:8 depths were c. in sea

CONGRATULATE.
1 *Chr.* 18:10 his welfare, and c.

CON

CONGREGATION.
Lev. 10:17 to bear iniquity of c.
16:33 atonement for all the c.
Num. 1:16 the renowned of c.
14:27 bear with this evil c.?
15:15 one ordinance be for c.
16:21 sep. yours. from this c.
45 get you up from am. this c.
47 Aaron ran into midst of c.
27:16 Lord set a man over c.
33:12 bef. c. for judg. *Jos.* 20:6
27:21 c. gath. as one man
31:5 came not up with c. to L.
1 *K.* 12:20 called Jeroboam to c.
Ps. 10:8 himself sep. from c.
Neh. 13:1 Moab. not come into c.
Job 15:34 c. of hypoc. desolate
30:28 and I cried in the c.
Ps. 1:5 nor sinners in c. of right.
22:22 midst of c. will I praise
26:5 hated the c. of evil-doers
35:18 speak righteousness, O c.?
74:2 rem. c. thou hast purch.
19 forget not the c. of thy poor
75:2 when I receive the c.
82:1 G. standeth in c. of mighty
89:5 thy faithfulness in c.
107:32 exalt him also in c.
111:1 praise the Lord in c.
Prov. 5:14 in midst of c.
21:16 remain in c. of the dead
Is. 14:13 will sit on mount of c.
Jer. 6:18 O c. what is among
30:20 c. be established before
Lam. 1:10 not enter into c.
Hos. 7:12 chas. them as their c.
Joel 2:16 sanctify the c.
Acts 13:43 when c. was broken

All the CONGREGATION.
Lev. 8:3 gather all the c.
16:17 at noment for all the c.
Num. 16:3 all the c. are holy
22 be wroth with all the c.?
20:27 sight of all the c. *Jos.*
Num. 20:29 wrath fell on all the c.
1 *K.* 8:14 king blessed all the c. 55
1 *Chr.* 29:20 all the c. blessed L.
2 *Chr.* 23:3 a. t. c. made covenant
29:6 all the c. worshipped
Neh. 5:13 all the c. said, Amen
8:17 all the c. come again

Elders of the CONGREGATION.
Lev. 4:15 e. of c. shall lay hands

Great CONGREGATION.
1 *K.* 8:65 Sol. held feast, and all
the c. 2 *Chr.* 7:8; 30:13
Ezr. 10:1 assem. to him a gr. c.
22:25 pr. be of thee in g. c.
35:18 give thee thanks in g. c.
40:9 preached right. in g. c.
10 not conc. truth from great c.

CONGREGATION of Israel.
Lev. 4:13 if c. of Is. sin
2 *Chr.* 24:6 accord. to com. of c. I.

CONGREGATION of the Lord.
Num. 16:3 you above c. L.
27:17 c. of L. Lord. not as sheep
Deut. 23:1 not en. c. of L. 2, 3
Mic. 2:5 in c. L. Lord
23:8 in sight of c. L.

Tabernacle of the CONGREGATION.
Ex. 29:44 sanctify t. of t. c.
40:34 a cloud cov. tent of the c.
35 M. not able to enter t. of c.
Lev. 1:3 at door of the t. c. 23, 25
8:9 Levites before t. of the c.
12:4 come out to t. of t. c.
14:10 glory of L. ap. in t. of c.
18:4 charge of taber. of the c.
Deut. 31:14 pres. yours. in t. of c.
Jos. 18:1 set up t. c. at Shi.
1 *K.* 8:4 bro. up the t. 2 *Chr.* 5:5
2 *Chr.* 1:3 there was t. of the c.

See DOOR.

Tent of the CONGREGATION.
Num. 10:3 tent of the c. finished
40:34 a cloud cov. tent of the c.
35 M. not able to enter t. of c.

Whole CONGREGATION.
Ex. 16:2 w. c. of Isr. murmured
Num. 3:7 keep charge of whole c.
Jos. 22:18 wroth with w. c.
Jud. 21:13 wh. c. sent to Benj.
2 *Chr.* 6:3 king blessed whole c.
Ezr. 2:64 whole c. 42,360. *Neh.* 7:66
Prov. 26:26 he showed bef. w. c.

CONGREGATIONS.
Ps. 26:12 in c. will I bless L.
68:26 bless ye God the c.
74:4 enemies roar in thy c.

CONIAH. *Jer.* 22:24, 28; 37:1

CRUDEN'S CONCORDANCE. 803

CON
CONQUER.
Rev. 6:2 conquering and to *c.*
CONQUERORS.
Rom. 8:37 we are more than *c.*
CONSCIENCE.
John 8:9 convicted by own *c.*
Acts 23:1 I have lived in good *c.*
24:16 a *c.* void of offence
Rom. 2:15 *c.* bearing witness
9:1 my *c.* bearing witness
13:5 be subject for *c.* sake
1 *Cor.* 8:7 with *c.* of idol eat it
10 weak *c.* be emboldened
12 wound weak *c.* ye sin
10:25 no question for *c.* sake, 27
28 eat not, for his and *c.* sake
29 *c.* I say, not thine own, but
2 *Cor.* 1:12 testimony of our *c.*
4:2 com. to every man's *c.*
1 *Tim.* 1:5 and of a good *c.*
19 holding faith and a good *c.*
3:9 mystery of faith in pure *c.*
4:2 *c.* seared with a hot iron
2 *Tim.* 1:3 whom I serve with *c.*
Tit. 1:15 but their *c.* is defiled
Heb. 9:9 as pertaining to *c.*
14 purge *c.* from dead works
10:2 worshippers no more *c.*
22 sprinkled from an evil *c.*
13:18 trust we have good *c.*
1 *Pet.* 2:19 for *c.* endure grief
3:16 having a good *c.*
21 but the answer of a good *c.*
CONSCIENCES.
2 *Cor.* 5:11 manifest in your *c.*
CONSECRATE.
Ex. 29:9 *c.* A. and sons, 30:30
32:29 *c.* yourselves this day to L.
1 *Chr.* 29:5 *c.* his service to Lord
Ezek. 43:26 shall *c.* themselves
Mic. 4:13 I will *c.* their gain
CONSECRATED.
Jud. 17:5 M. *c.* one of sons, 12
1 *K.* 13:33 whosoever would, he *c.*
2 *Chr.* 26:18 yourselves to Lord
31 *c.* things six hundred oxen
31:6 tithe of holy things *c.*
Heb. 7:28 Son, who is *c.* evermore
10:20 by a living way *c.* for us
CONSECRATION, S.
Ex. 29:22 for it is a ram of *c.*
Lev. 7:37 this is law of the *c.*
8:28 *c.* for sweet savor to Lord
31 with bread in basket of *c.*
33 days of your *c.* be at end
Num. 6:9 defiled head of his *c.*
CONSENT, ED, ING.
Gen. 34:21 only let us *c.* to them
Deut. 13:8 shalt not *c.* to him
1 *K.* 20:8 hearken not, nor *c.*
Ps. 50:18 sawest thief, thou *c.*
Prov. 1:10 entice thee, *c.* th. not
Dan. 1:14 so he *c.* in this matter
Luke 23:51 same had not *c.*
Acts 8:1 *c.* to his death, 22:20
18:20 to tarry longer, he *c.* not
Rom. 7:16 I *c.* to law
1 *Tim.* 6:3 *c.* not to whole, words
CONSENT, Substantive.
1 *Sam.* 11:7 came out with one *c.*
Ps. 83:5 consulted with one *c.*
Hos. 6:9 of priests murder by *c.*
Zep. 3:9 serve him with one *c.*
Luke 14:18 one *c.* to make excuse
1 *Cor.* 7:5 ex. with *c.* for a time
CONSIDER.
Deut. 4:39 *c.* it in thy heart
32:29 wise in *c.* latter end
Jud. 18:11 *c.* what ye have to do
1 *Sam.* 12:24 *c.* how great things
25:17 *c.* what thou wilt do
Job 11:11 will he not then *c.* it?
23:15 I *c.* I am afraid of him
31:27 would not *c.* his ways
37:14 *c.* wondrous works of God
Ps. 5:1 *c.* my meditation
9:13 *c.* my trouble
8:3 when I *c.* thy heavens
13:3 *c.* and hear, 45:10
25:19 *c.* my enemies
37:10 diligently *c.* his place
48:13 *c.* her palaces, that ye
64:2 *c.* this, ye that forget God
64:9 wisely *c.* of his doing
119:95 I will *c.* thy testimonies
153 *c.* mine affliction, deliver
159 *c.* how I love thy precepts
Prov. 6:6 go to ant, *c.* her ways
23:1 *c.* what is before thee
24:12 that pondereth heart *c.* it?
Ec. 5:1 *c.* not that they do evil
7:13 *c.* work of God, who can
14 in day of adversity *c.*
Is. 1:3 my people doth not *c.*

CON
Is. 14:16 shall narrowly *c.* thee
18:4 *c.* in my dwelling-place
41:20 that they may see, and *c.*
43:18 nor *c.* the things of old
52:15 not heard shall they *c.*
Jer. 2:10 *c.* if there be such thing
23:20 in the latter days ye sh. *c.*
it perfectly, 30:24
Lam. 2:20 *c.* to whom done this
5:1 O Lord, *c.* our reproach
Ezek. 12:3 it may be they will *c.*
Dan. 9:23 and *c.* the vision
Hos. 7:2 *c.* not that I remember
Hag. 1:5 *c.* your ways, 7
2:15 I pray *c.* from this day, 18
Mat. 6:28 *c.* the lilies, *Lu.* 12:27
Luke 12:24 *c.* the ravens
John 11:50 nor *c.* it is expedient
Acts 15:6 elders came to *c.* of this
2 *Tim.* 2:7 *c.* and L. give thee
Heb. 3:1 brethren *c.* the Apostle
7:4 *c.* how great this man was
10:24 let us *c.* one another
12:3 *c.* him endured such con.
CONSIDERED, EST.
1 *K.* 8:47 have *c.* things
Job 1:8 hast thou *c.* Job? 2:3
Ps. 31:7 hast *c.* my trouble
Prov. 24:32 then I *c.* it well
Ec. 4:1 I *c.* all the oppressions
4 again I *c.* all travail, and
9:1 all this I *c.* to declare this
Jer. 33:24 *c.* not people have spo.
Acts 12:12 when Peter had *c.*
Rom. 4:19 *c.* not his body dead
CONSIDERETH, ING.
Ps. 33:15 he *c.* all their works
41:1 blessed is he *c.* the poor
Prov. 21:12 *c.* house of wicked
28:22 *c.* not poverty shall come
22:7 righteous *c.* cause of poor
31:16 she *c.* a field, buyeth it
Is. 44:19 none *c.* to say, I burnt
57:1 none *c.* right, is tak. away
Ezek. 18:14 *c.* and doeth not, 28
Gal. 6:1 *c.* lest also be tempted
Heb. 13:7 *c.* end of their conver.
CONSIST, ETH.
Luke 12:15 life *c.* not in abund.
Col. 1:17 by him all things *c.*
CONSOLATION.
Jer. 16:7 nor give them cup of *c.*
Luke 2:25 Simeon waiting for *c.*
6:24 woe to you rich, rec. yo. *c.*
Acts 4:36 interpreted, son of *c.*
15:31 they rejoiced for the *c.*
Rom. 15:5 God of *c.* grant you
2 *Cor.* 1:5 our *c.* aboundeth by C.
6 afflicted for your *c.* comforted
7 so ye be partakers of the *c.*
7:7 *c.* wherewith he was comf.
Phil. 2:1 if any *c.* in Christ
2 *Thes.* 2:16 given us everlast. *c.*
Phile. 7 joy and *c.* in thy love
Heb. 6:18 might have strong *c.*
CONSOLATIONS.
Job 15:11 are *c.* of God small
21:2 and let this be your *c.*
Is. 66:11 with breasts of her *c.*
CONSORTED.
Acts 17:4 *c.* with Paul and Silas
CONSPIRACY.
2 *Sam.* 15:12 Absalom's *c.* strong
2 *K.* 12:20 all *c.* against Joash
14:19 *c.* ag. A. 2 *Chr.* 25:27
15:15 acts of Shallum and *c.*
17:4 found *c.* in Hoshea
Jer. 11:9 *c.* among men of Judah
Ezek. 22:25 a *c.* of her prophets
Acts 23:13 forty which made *c.*
CONSPIRATORS.
2 *Sam.* 15:31 Ahith. is among *c.*
CONSPIRED.
Gen. 37:18 *c.* ag. Jos. to slay him
1 *Sam.* 22:13 *c.* thou and son of J.
1 *K.* 15:27 Baasha *c.* ag. Nadab
16:9 Zimri *c.* against Elah, 16
2 *K.* 9:14 John *c.* against Joram
10:9 I *c.* against my master
15:10 Shallum *c.* ag. Zechariah
25 Pekah *c.* against Pekahiah
21:23 serv. of Amon *c.* ag. him
24 *c.* against him, 2 *Chr.* 33:25
2 *Chr.* 24:21 *c.* against Jehoiada
25 *c.* mine affliction, deliver
Neh. 4:8 *c.* all to come and fight
Amos 7:10 Amos hath *c.* ag. thee
CONSTANT, LY.
1 *Chr.* 28:7 if he be *c.* to do com.
Prov. 21:28 he heareth, speaketh *c.*
Acts 12:15 she *c.* affirmed it was
Tit. 3:8 I will thou affirm *c.*
CONSTELLATIONS.
Is. 13:10 *c.* thereof

CON
CONSTRAIN, ED, ETH.
2 *K.* 4:8 women *c.* him to eat
4:24 28 the spirit in me *c.* me
Mat. 14:22 J. *c.* disc. *Mark* 6:45
Luke 24:29 *c.* him, saying, Abide
Acts 16:15 Lydia *c.* us to come
28:19 I was *c.* to appeal to
2 *Cor.* 5:14 love of Christ *c.* us
Gal. 6:12 *c.* you to be circum.
CONSTRAINT.
1 *Pet.* 5:2 oversight, not by *c.*
CONSULTATION.
Mark 15:1 chief priests held a *c.*
CONSULT, ED, ETH.
1 *K.* 12:6 Rehoboam *c.* 8
1 *Chr.* 13:1 D. *c.* with captains
2 *Chr.* 20:21 Jeh. *c.* with people
Neh. 5:7 then I *c.* with myself
Ps. 62:4 *c.* to cast him down
83:3 *c.* against hidden ones
5 have *c.* with one consent
Ezek. 21:21 king of B. *c.* images
Dan. 6:7 presidents and capt. *c.*
Mic. 6:5 rem. what Balak *c.*
Hab. 2:10 *c.* shame to thy house
Mat. 26:4 *c.* might take Jesus
Lu. 14:31 *c.* w. able with 10,000
John 12:10 *c.* to put L. to death
CONSULTER.
Deut. 18:11 a *c.* with spirits
CONSUME.
Ex. 33:3 lest I *c.* thee in way, 5
Deut. 5:25 this fire will *c.* us
7:16 shalt *c.* all the people
28:38 locust shall *c.* it, 42
32:22 fire kindled in anger *c.*
Jos. 24:20 *c.* after done you good
1 *Sam.* 2:33 to *c.* thine eyes
2 *K.* 1:10 let fire *c.* thy fifty, 12
Job 13:31 fire *c.* tabern. of brib.
20:26 a fire not shown *c.* him
31:19 and heat *c.* snow waters
Ps. 37:20 *c.* into smoke shall *c.*
39:11 his beauty to *c.* away
49:14 their beauty *c.* in grave
Is. 7:20 L. shall *c.* the beard
10:18 *c.* glory of his forest
27:10 shall calf *c.* branches
Jer. 42:27 fire *c.* fat of Ben-ha
49:10 shall *c.* his branches
21:25 sword is furbished to *c.*
22:15 I will *c.* thy filthiness
24:10 kindle fire *c.* the flesh
35:12 they are giv. us to *c.*
Dan. 2:44 it shall *c.* these kingd.
Hos. 11:6 sword *c.* his branches
Zep. 1:2 I will *c.* all off land
3 I will *c.* man and beast
Zec. 5:4 in house and *c.* it
14:12 tongue shall *c.* away
2 *Thes.* 2:8 whom L. shall *c.*
Jam. 4:3 may *c.* it on your lusts
CONSUME them.
Ex. 32:10 that I may *c.* t. 12
Num. 16:21 *c.* t. in a moment, 45
Deut. 7:22 mayest not *c.* t.
Neh. 9:31 not utterly *c.* them
Ps. 59:13 *c.* t. in wrath, *c.* them
Jer. 8:13 I will utterly *c.* t.
14:12 I will *c.* them by sword
Ezek. 20:13 fury on them to *c.* t.
Luke 9:54 fire to *c.* them
CONSUMED.
Gen. 19:15 be *c.* in the iniquity
17 escape to mount, lest be *c.*
31:40 in day drought *c.* me
38:24 behold, Judah was *c.*
Ex. 3:2 bush *c.* not
Num. 11:1 fire *c.* them as uncible
Ps. 6:7 mine eye is *c.*
39:10 my honor *c.* 102:3
90:10 *c.* by blow of thy hand
71:13 let them be *c.* that are

CON
Ps. 73:19 utterly *c.* with terrors
78:63 fire *c.* their young men
90:7 we are *c.* by thine anger
104:35 let sinners be *c.* out of
118:87 almost *c.* me upon earth
119 my zeal hath *c.* me, becau.
Prov. 5:11 flesh and body are *c.*
Is. 16:4 oppressors *c.* out of land
29:20 the scorner is *c.* and all
64:7 *c.* us because of iniquities
Jer. 5:3 *c.* refused correction
6:29 lead is *c.*; 12:4 beasts
30:18 should be *c.* with shame
36:23 till all the roll was *c.*
44:18 we have been *c.* by sword
Lam. 2:22 those I swad. enemy *c.*
3:22 of Lord's mercies not *c.*
4:16 anger of Lord doth *c.*
Ezek. 5:12 with famine *shall* be *c.*
13 and ye *shall* be *c.*
Dan. 2:35 *ch.* be no more *c.*
Joel 1:4; 2:3 *Le.* left
Nah. 1:10 heap of dry stub.
Mal. 3:6 sons of Jacob are not *c.*
Gal. 5:15 ye be not *c.*
Shall be CONSUMED.
Num. 14:35 wilder. sh. they be *c.*
17:13 shall we be *c.* with dying
1 *Sam.* 12:25 ye *s. be c.*
Is. 1:28 that forsake L. sh. be *c.*
66:17 eat swine's flesh, *s. be c.*
Jer. 16:4 *s. be c.* by sw. 44:12, 27
Ezek. 5:12 with famine *shall be c.*
13:14 and ye *shall be c.*
34:29 *sh.* be no more *c.*
47:12 nor *shall* fruit thereof be *c.*
Dan. 11:16 land which *shall be c.*
CONSUMED, with till or until.
Deut. 2:15 *until c.*, *Jos.* 8:8
until he have *c.* thee
Jos. 10:20 slaying them till *c.*
1 *Sam.* 15:18 *until* they be *c.*
2 *Sam.* 22:38 I turned not *until* I
had *c.* them, *Ps.* 18:37
1 *K.* 22:11 push Syr. u. *c.* them
2 *K.* 13:17, 19; 2 *Chr.* 18:10
Ezr. 9:14 angry *till* hadst *c.* us
Jer. 9:16 send a sword *till* I have
c. them, 24:10; 27:8; 49:37
CONSUMETH, ING.
Deut. 4:24 a *c.* fire, *Heb.* 12:29
9:3 L. goeth bef. thee as a fire
Job 13:28 he *c.* as a garment that
22:20 remnant of them fire *c.*
31:12 fire that *c.* to destruction
Is. 5:24 as the flame *c.* chaff
CONSUMMATION.
Dan. 9:27 desolate until *c.*
CONSUMPTION.
Lev. 26:16 appoint over you *c.*
Deut. 28:22 smite thee with *c.*
Is. 10:22 *c.* dec. shall overflow
23 the Lord shall make a *c.*
28:22 I have heard from L. a *c.*
CONTAIN.
1 *K.* 8:27 heaven of heav. cannot
c. thee, 2 *Chr.* 2:6; 6:18
John 21:25 world not *c.* the books
1 *Cor.* 7:9 if cannot *c.* marry
CONTAINED, ETH, ING.
Ezek. 23:32 thy sister's cup *c.*
Rom. 2:14 by nat. thi. *c.* in law
Eph. 2:15 abol. law *c.* in ordin.
1 *Pet.* 2:6 it is *c.* in scripture
CONTEMN, ED, ETH.
Ps. 10:13 wicked *c.* God?
15:4 eyes a vile person is *c.*
107:11 *c.* counsel of Most High
Cant. 8:7 substance would be *c.*
Is. 16:14 glory of Moab be *c.*
Ezek. 21:10 lit *c.* rod of my son
CONTEMPT.
Est. 1:18 thus arise too much *c.*
Job 12:21 *c.* on princes, *Ps.* 107:40
31:31 *c.* of families terrify me
Ps. 119:22 remove from me *c.*
123:3 we are ex. filled with *c.*
4 soul filled with *c.* of proud
Prov. 18:3 wicked com. then *c.*
12:8 into *c.* the honorable
Dan. 12:2 awake to everlast. *c.*
CONTEMPTIBLE.
Mal. 1:7 say, table of Lord is *c.*
12 meat *c.* 2:9 I made you *c.*
2 *Cor.* 10:10 his speech *c.*
CONTEMPTUOUSLY.
Ps. 31:98 speak *c.* against right.
CONTEND.
Deut. 2:9 neither *c.* in battle, 24
c. not with them
33:8 will you *c.* for him?
Prov. 28:4 such as keep law *c.*
Ec. 6:10 may *c.* with him
Is. 49:25 I will *c.* with thee
50:8 who will *c.* with me?

CRUDEN'S CONCORDANCE.

CON

Is. 57:16 I will not c. for ever, nor
Jer. 12:5 how c. with hor—?
18:19 to voice of them that c.
Amos 7:4 Lord called to c. by fire
Mic. 6:1 c. thou bef. the mount.
Jude 3 earnestly c. for the faith

CONTENDED.
Neh. 13:11 c. I with rulers, 17
Job 31:13 servants when they c.
Is. 41:12 not find them that c.
Acts 11:2 they of circum. c. with

Job 10:2 show me wherefore c.

CONTENDETH.
Job 9:3 that c. with Almighty
Prov. 29:9 if wise c. with foolish

CONTENDING.
Jude 9 when c. with the devil

CONTENT.
Gen. 37:27 sell him, brethren c.
Lev. 10:20 heard that, he was c.
Jos. 7:7 would we had been c.
2 *K.* 6:3 one said, Be c. and go
Job 6:28 now therefore be c.
Prov. 6:35 nor will he rest c.
Mark 15:15 Pilate willing to c.
Luke 3:14 be c. with your wages
Phil. 4:11 in every state to be c.
1 *Tim.* 6:8 raiment, let us be c.
Heb. 13:5 be c. with such things
3 *John* 10 not c. with prating

CONTENTION.
Prov. 13:10 by pride cometh c.
17:14 leave off c. before it be
18:6 a fool's lips enter into c.
22:10 cast out scorner, c. sh. go
Jer. 15:10 borne me a man of c.
Hab. 1:3 that raise up c.
Acts 15:39 the c. was so sharp
Phil. 1:17 preach Christ of c.
1 *Thes.* 2:2 speak gospel with c.

CONTENTIONS.
Prov. 18:18 casteth c. to cease
19 c. like bars of a castle
19:13 c. of a wife, 27:15
22:10 who hath c. ?
1 *Cor.* 1:11 there are c. am. you
Tit. 3:9 avoid c. and strivings

CONTENTIOUS.
Prov. 21:19 with c. woman
26:21 a c. man to kindle strife
27:15 dropping and c. woman
Rom. 2:8 to them that are c.
1 *Cor.* 11:16 if any seem to be c.

CONTENTMENT.
1 *Tim.* 6:6 godli. with c. is gain

CONTINUAL.
Ex. 29:42 be a c. burnt-offering
2 *Chr.* 2:4 for c. show-bread
Prov. 15:15 merry heart a c. feast
Is. 14:6 smote with a c. stroke
Jer. 48:5 c. weeping shall go up
Ezek. 39:14 men of c. employm.
Luke 18:5 lest by her c. coming
Rom. 9:2 c. sorrow in my heart
See BURNT-OFFERING.

CONTINUALLY.
Gen. 6:5 imagination was evil c.
Ex. 28:30 on heart before L. c.
1 *Chr.* 16:11 seek his face c.
Job 1:5 thus did Job c.
Ps. 34:1 his praise be c. 71:6
35:27 c. L. be mag., 40:16; 70:4
38:17 sorrow c. before me
40:11 truth c. preserve me
42:3 c. say, Where is thy God?
44:15 confusion c. before me
52:1 burnt-office. c. before me
Song whereunto I may c. resort
6 my praises be c. of thee
14 but I will hope c. and yet
73:23 I am c. with thee, thou
74:23 the tumult increaseth c.
109:15 let them be before L. c.
119:44 shall I keep thy law c.
109 my soul is c. in my hand
117 respect to thy statutes c.
140:2 c. are gathered for war
Prov. 6:14 deviseth mischief c.
21 bind them c. on thy heart
Is. 21:8 c. upon the watch-tower
49:16 thy walls are c. before me
51:13 hast feared c. because
52:5 my name c. is blasph.
58:11 L. shall guide thee c.
60:11 gates shall be open c.
65:3 provoketh me to anger c.
Jer. 6:7 before me c. is grief
Lam. 3:14 c. whom serves c. 20
Hos. 12:6 wait on thy God c.
Ob. 16 heathen drink c.
... 3:19 thy wick. passed c. ?

CON

Luke 24:53 c. in temple
Acts 6:4 ourselves c. to prayer
12:6 c. on this very thing
Heb. 7:3 abideth a priest c.
10:1 sacrifices year by year c.
13:15 the sacrifice of praise c.

CONTINUANCE.
Deut. 28:59 plag. and of long c.
Ps. 139:16 in c. were fashioned
Is. 64:5 in those is c.
Rom. 2:7 patient c. in well-doing

CONTINUE.
Ex. 21:21 if he c. a day or two
1 *Sam.* 12:14 c. following the L.
13:14 thy kingdom not c.
2 *Sam.* 7:29 it may c. for ever
1 *K.* 2:4 L. may c. word he spake
Job 15:29 neither substance c.
17:2 are c. in their provocation?
Ps. 36:10 O c. thy loving-kind.
49:11 that their houses shall c.
102:28 children of thy serv. c.
119:91 c. according to the ordin.
Is. 5:11 c. till night, till wine
Jer. 32:14 may c. many days
Dan. 11:8 c. more years than k.
Mat. 15:32 c. now three days
John 8:31 if ye c. in my word
15:9 c. ye in my love
Acts 13:43 to c. in grace of God
14:22 exhorting to c. in faith
26:22 I c. unto this day
Rom. 6:1 shall we c. in sin
11:22 if thou c. in his goodness
Gal. 3:5 tenth of gospel might c.
Phil. 1:25 I shall c. with you all
Col. 1:23 if ye c. in the faith
4:2 c. in prayer, and watch
1 *Tim.* 2:15 if they c. in faith
4:16 doctrine, c. in them
2 *Tim.* 3:14 c. in things hast
Heb. 7:23 not suffer to c.
13:1 let brotherly love c.
Jam. 4:13 c. there a year
1 *Pet.* 2:4 this, c. as they were
1 *John* 2:24 ye shall c. in the Son
Rev. 13:5 power to c.
17:10 he must c. a short space

CONTINUED.
Ruth 1:2 Daniel c. to year of C.
Luke 6:12 c. all night in prayer
22:28 ye c. with me in tempt.
Acts 1:14 these c. in prayer
2:42 stead. in apostles' doc.
8:13 Simon c. with Philip
20:7 P. c. speech until midnight
Heb. 8:9 c. not in my covenant
1 *John* 2:19 no doubt c. with us

CONTINUETH, ING.
Job 14:2 as shadow, and c. not
Jer. 30:23 a c. whirlwind. It
Gal. 3:6 c. daily with one ac.
1 *Tim.* 5:5 c. in supplications
Ech. 7:24 because he c. ever
13:14 we have no c. city, but
Jam. 1:25 perfect law, c. in it

CONTRADICTING.
Acts 13:45 with envy c. blasph.

CONTRADICTION.
Heb. 7:7 without c. less is blessed
12:3 endured such c. of sinners

CONTRARIWISE.
2 *Cor.* 2:7 c. rather to forgive him
Gal. 5:7 c. when saw gospel was
1 *Pet.* 3:9 railing, but c. blessing

CONTRARY.
Lev. 20:24 will I walk c. 28, 41
Est. 9:1 though turned to c.
Mat. 14:24 for the wind was c.
Acts 17:7 these do c. to decrees
18:13 to worship God c. to law
23:3 to be smitten c. to the law
26:9 c. to the name of Jesus
Rom. 11:24 grafted c. to nature
16:17 c. to doctrine ye learned
Gal. 5:17 c. one to the other
Col. 2:14 handwriting c. to us
1 *Tim.* 1:10 c. to sound doctrine
Tit. 2:8 he of a c. part be ashm.

CONTRIBUTION.
Rom. 15:26 c. for the poor saints

CONTRITE.
Ps. 34:18 such as of c. spirit
51:17 c. heart, wilt not despise
Is. 57:15 of a c. and humble
heart of the c. ones
66:2 of c. spirit and trembleth

CONTROVERSY.
Deut. 17:8 being matters of c.

COP

Deut. 19:17 between whom c. is
21:5 by their word c. be tried
25:1 if there be a c. betw. men
2 *Sam.* 15:2 that had a c. came
2 *Chr.* 19:8 set the Levites for c.
Is. 34:8 year of recom. for c.
Jer. 25:31 hath c. with nations
Ezek. 44:24 in c. they shall stand
Hos. 4:1 L. hath a c. with inhab.
12:2 Lord hath a c. with Judah
Mic. 6:2 L. hath c. with people
1 *Tim.* 3:16 with. c. great is mys.

CONVENIENT, LY.
Prov. 30:8 with food c. for me
Jer. 40:4 it seemeth c. to go, 5
Mark 6:21 a c. day was come
14:11 might c. betray him
Acts 24:25 a c. season, I will call
Rom. 1:28 to do things c. not c.
1 *Cor.* 16:12 time c. will c. time
Eph. 5:4 talking, nor jesting, c.
Phile. 8 to enjoin thee that c.

CONVERSANT.
Jos. 8:35 strangers c. am. them
1 *Sam.* 25:15 long as we were c.

CONVERSATION.
Ps. 37:14 as be of upright c.
50:23 ordereth his c. aright
2 *Cor.* 1:12 in godly sinc. had c.
Gal. 1:13 ye have heard of my c.
Eph. 2:3 had our c. in times past
4:22 concerning the former c.
Phil. 1:27 c. as becometh gospel
3:20 for our c. is in heaven
1 *Tim.* 4:12 be an example in c.
Heb. 13:5 c. be without covet.
7 considering end of their c.
Jam. 3:13 show out of a good c.
1 *Pet.* 1:15 in all manner of c.
18 not redeemed from vain c.
2:12 c. honest among Gentiles
3:1 may be won by c. of wives
2 while they behold chaste c.
16 falsely accuse your good c.
2 *Pet.* 2:7 vexed with the filthy c.
3:11 to be in all holy c.

CONVERSION.
Acts 15:3 declaring c. of Gentiles

CONVERT, ED.
Ps. 51:13 sinners be c. unto thee
Is. 6:10 lest c. and be healed
60:5 abundance of sea be c.
Mat. 13:15 be c. Mark 4:12
18:3 c. and become as children
Luke 22:32 when c. strengthen
John 12:40 be c. *Acts* 28:27
Acts 3:19 repent ye and be c.
Jam. 5:19 do err, and one c. him

CONVERTETH, ING.
Ps. 19:7 law is perfect, c. soul
Jam. 5:20 he which c. a sinner

CONVERTS.
Is. 1:27 her c. be redeemed with

CONVEY, ED.
1 *K.* 5:9 I will c. them by sea
Neh. 2:7 c. me over till I come
John 5:13 Jesus c. himself away

CONVICTED.
John 8:9 c. by their own conscience

CONVINCE, ED, ETH.
Job 32:12 none of you c. Job
John 8:46 which of you c. me
Acts 18:28 mightily c. the Jews
1 *Cor.* 14:24 he is c. of all, is
Tit. 1:9 be able to c. gainsayers
Jam. 2:9 c. of law as transgres.
Jude 15 to c. all that are ungodly

CONVOCATION.
Ex. 12:16 a holy c. *Lev.* 23:7, 24, 35; *Num.* 28:18; 29:1
Num. 28:26 first-fruit a holy c.

CONY, IES.
Lev. 11:5 c. chew. cud, *Deut.* 14:7
Ps. 104:18 a refuge for the c.
Prov. 30:26 the c. a feeble folk

COOK, S.
1 *Sam.* 8:13 daughters to be c.
9:23 Sam. said to the c. Bring

COOL.
Gen. 3:8 walking in c. of day
Luke 16:24 and c. my tongue

COPIED.
Prov. 25:1 men of Hezekiah c.

COPPER.
Ezr. 8:27 two vessels of fine c.

COPPERSMITH.
2 *Tim.* 4:14 Alexander the c. did

COPULATION.
Lev. 15:16 seed of c. 17, 18

COR

COPY.
Deut. 17:18 write a c. of law
Jos. 8:32 c. of law of Moses
Ezr. 4:11 c. of letter sent, 5:6
2 *K.* 3:14 c. of writing, 8:13

COR.
Ezek. 45:14 a bath out of c.

CORAL.
Job 28:18 no mention made of c.
Ezek. 27:16 Syria merchant in c.

CORBAN.
Mark 7:11 it is c. that is, a gift

CORD.
Job 4:15 let spies down by a c.
Job 30:11 he hath loosed my c.
41:1 dr. out tongue with a c.?
Ec. 4:12 threefold c. not quickly
12:6 or ever silver c. be loosed
Mic. 2:5 a c. by lot in the congr.

CORDS.
Jud. 15:13 Samson with new c.
Job 36:8 in c. of affliction
Ps. 2:3 let us cast away their c.
11:2(?) bind the sacrifice with c.
129:4 hath cut c. of the wicked
140:5 proud have hid c. for me
Prov. 5:22 with c. of his sins
Is. 5:18 draw iniquity with c.
33:20 any of the c. be broken
Jer. 10:20 spoiled, and all my c.
Hos. 11:4 drew with c. of a man
John 2:15 a scourge of small c.

CORIANDER.
Ex. 16:31 c. seed, *Num.* 11:7

CORINTH.
Acts 18:1 after, Paul came to C.
19:1 while Apollos was at C.
1 *Cor.* 1:2; 2 *Cor.* 1:23
2 *Tim.* 4:20 Erastus abode at C.

CORINTHIANS.
Acts 18:8 of the C. 2 *Cor.* 6:11

CORMORANT.
Lev. 11:17 owl and c. *Deut.* 14:17
Is. 34:11 c. possess it. *Zep.* 2:14

CORN.
Gen. 41:57 all came to buy c.
42:2 in Egypt, *Acts* 7:12
27:28 stacks of c. be consum.
Lev. 2:16 barn part of beaten c.
23:14 ear bread nor parched c.
Num. 18:27 of threshing-floor
Deut. 16:9 put sickle to c.
25:4 not muzzle ox treadeth c.
1 *Cor.* 9:9; 1 *Tim.* 5:18
Jos. 5:11 did eat of old c. 12
? *Jud.* 3:7 lie down at heap of c.
1 *Sam.* 17:28 bring parched c.
25:18 Abigail took of parched c.
2 *K.* 19:26 blasted c. *Is.* 37:27
Neh. 5:2 we take up c. for them
Job 5:26 as a shock of c. cometh
24:6 reap every one c. in field
39:4 young grow up with c.
Ps. 65:9 thou preparest them c.
13 the valleys covered with c.
72:16 handful of c. in the earth
78:24 given of the c. of heaven
Prov. 11:26 with c. people curse
Is. 17:5 harvestman gather. c.
61:10 and c. of my floor
62:8 no more give c. to enemies
Ezek. 36:29 I will call for c. and
Hos. 2:9 I will take away my c.
7:14 Ephraim loveth to tread c.
14:7 shall revive as the c. and
Joel 1:10 for the c. is wasted
17 the c. is withered
Am. 8:5 that we may sell c.
9:9 like as c. sifted in sieve
Hag. 1:11 after that the fall c.
John 12:24 except c. of wheat

Ears of CORN.
Gen. 41:5 seven ears of c. came
Lev. 2:14 offer green ears of c.
Ruth 2:2 glean c. ears of c.
2 *K.* 4:42 brought full ears of c.
Job 24:24 cut off as ears of c.
Mat. 12:1 to pluck ears of c. *Mark* 2:23; *Luke* 6:1

CORN-FLOOR.
Hos. 9:1 reward on every c.-fl.

Standing CORN.
Ex. 22:6 so that the c. be consum.
Deut. 23:25 stand. c. of neighbor
Jud. 15:5 foxes go into c. c.

CORN and wine.
Gen. 27:28 G. gave plenty of c. w.
37 with c. and w. I sust. him
Deut. 7:13 bless thy c. and wine

CRUDEN'S CONCORDANCE.

COR

Deut. 11:14 gather in thy *c. w.*
12:17 tithe of thy *c. w.* 14:23
18:4 first fruit of *c. w.* and wine
28:51 leave thee *c. and wine*
33:28 J. shall be on land of *c. w.*
2 *K.* 18:32 laud of *c. w. Is.* 36:17
2 *Chr.* 31:5 first-fruits of *c. w.*
32:28 storehouses for *c. and w.*
Neh. 5:11 part of *c. and wine*
10:39 offer, of *c. and w.* 13:5, 12
Ps. 4:7 in time *c. w.* increased
Lam. 2:12 Where is *c. and w.?*
Hos. 2:8 I gave her *c. and wine*
22 the earth shall hear *c. w.*
7:14 assemble for *c. and wine*
Joel 2:19 I will send you *c. a. w.*
Hag. 1:11 drought on *c. and w.*
Zec. 9:17 *c.* make men cheer. *w.*

CORNELIUS. *Acts* 10:1, 7, 25, 31

CORNER.
Lev. 21:5 nor shave off *c.* of beard
2 *Chr.* 28:24 altars in every *c.*
Ps. 118:22 is head stone of *c.*
Prov. 7:8 passing near her *c.*
12 she lieth in wait at every *c.*
21:9 better to dwell in *c.* 25:24
Is. 30:20 thy teachers into a *c.*
Jer. 31:38 city built to gates of *c.*
48:45 devour *c.* of Moab
51:26 nor take a stone for a *c.*
Ezek. 46:21 in every *c.* of court
Amos 3:12 in S. in *c.* of a bed
Zec. 10:4 out of him came *c.*
Mat. 21:42 same is bec. head of *c.*
Ps. 118:26; *Mark* 12:10; *Luke*
20:17; *Acts* 4:11; 1 *Pet.* 2:7
Acts 26:26 was not done in a *c.*

CORNER-GATE.
Zec. 14:10 be inhabited to *c.-g.*

CORNER-STONE, S.
Job 38:6 who laid *c.-s.* thereof?
Ps. 144:12 daughters as *c.-stone*
Is. 28:16 in Zion a *c.-s.* 1 *Pet.* 2:6
Eph. 2:20 Christ being chief *c.-s.*

CORNERS.
Lev. 19:9 not reap the *c.* 23:22
27 not round *c.* of your heads
Num. 24:17 smite *c.* of Moab
Deut. 32:26 I will scatter into *c.*
Job 1:19 smote four *c.* of house
Is. 11:12 gather disp. from four *c.*
Jer. 9:26 I will punish all in utter most *c.* 25:23; 49:32
Ezek. 7:2 end is come upon four *f.*
43:20 put blood upon four *c.*
Mat. 6:5 they love to pray in *c.*
Acts 10:11 knit at four *c.* 11:5
Rev. 7:1 four angels on four *c.*

CORNET.
1 *Chr.* 15:28 ark with sound of *c.*
Ps. 98:6 of *c.* make a joyful noise
Dan. 3:5 time ye hear *c.* 15
Hos. 5:8 blow ye the *c.* in Gibeah

CORNETS.
2 *Sam.* 6:5 David played on *c.*
2 *Chr.* 15:14 shouting with *c.*

CORPSE, S.
2 *K.* 19:35 all dead *c. Is.* 37:36
Nah. 3:3 no end of their *c.* they
Mark 6:29 took up John's *c.* and

CORRECT.
Ps. 39:11 *c.* man for iniquity
91:10 shall not be *c.?*
Prov. 29:17 *c.* thy son
Jer. 2:19 own wickedness *c.* thee
1 2:14 O Lord, *c.* me but with
30:11 *c.* thee in measure 46:28

CORRECTED, ETH.
Job 5:17 happy is man God *c.*
Prov. 3:12 whom L. loveth he *c.*
23:13 servant not be *c.* by words
Heb. 12:9 fathers which *c.* us

CORRECTION.
Job 37:13 rain whether for *c.*
Prov. 3:11 not. be weary of his *c.*
7:22 goeth as a fool to the *c.*
15:10 *c.* grievous to him
22:15 rod of *c.* drive it from him
23:13 withhold not *c.* from child
Jer. 2:30 children received no *c.*
5:3 have refused to receive *c.*
7:28 nation receiveth not *c.*
Hab. 1:12 establish them for *c.*
Zep. 3:2 she received not *c.*
2 *Tim.* 3:16 scrip. profitable for *c.*

CORRUPT, Adjective.
Gen. 6:11 the earth also was *c.* 12
Job 17:1 my breath is *c.*
Ps. 14:1 they are *c.* 53:1; 73:8
38:5 my wounds are *c.* because
Prov. 25:26 as a *c.* spring
Ezek. 20:44 not accor. to *c.* doings
23:11 in her inordinate love

COU

Dan. 2:9 ye have prep. *c.* words
Mal. 1:14 sacrificeth a *c.* thing
Mat. 7:17 a *c.* tree evil fruit
18 *c.* tree good fruit, *Luke* 6:43
12:33 or else make tree *c.* and
Eph. 4:22 put off the old man *c.*
29 let no *c.* communication
1 *Tim.* 6:5 disputings of men of *c.*
2 *Tim.* 3:8 men of *c.* minds

CORRUPT, Verb.
Deut. 4:16 lest ye *c.* yours. 25
31:29 after my death ye will *c.*
Dan. 11:32 sh. he *c.* by flatteries
Mal. 2:3 I will *c.* your seed
Mat. 6:19 moth and rust doth *c.*
20 moth nor rust doth *c.*
1 *Cor.* 15:33 evil communica. *c.*
2 *Cor.* 2:17 that *c.* the word
Jude 10 in those things they *c.*
Rev. 19:2 *c.* earth with her forn.

CORRUPTED, ETH.
Gen. 6:12 all flesh had *c.* his way
Ex. 32:7 people have *c.* themselves, *Deut.* 9:12; 32:5
Ezek. 16:47 *c.* more than they
28:17 hast *c.* thy wisdom
Hos. 9:9 deeply *c.* themselves
Zep. 3:7 and *c.* their doings
Mal. 2:8 *c.* covenant of Levi
Luke 12:33 nor moth *c.*
2 *Cor.* 7:2 wronged *c.* no man
11:3 your minds be *c.*
Jam. 5:2 your riches are *c.*

CORRUPTERS.
Is. 1:4 children that are *c.*
Jer. 6:28 they are all *c.*

CORRUPTIBLE.
Rom. 1:23 image like to *c.* man
1 *Cor.* 9:25 to obtain a *c.* crown
15:53 *c.* must put on incorrup.
1 *Pet.* 1:18 not redeemed with *c.*
23 born again, not of *c.* seed
3:4 be in that which is not *c.*

CORRUPTING.
Dan. 11:17 dau. of women in *c.*

CORRUPTION.
Lev. 22:25 their *c.* is in them
2 *K.* 23:13 right of mount of *c.*
Job 17:14 I said to *c.* my father.
Ps. 16:10 nei. suffer thy H. One to see *c. Acts* 2:27; 13:35
49:9 live and not see *c.*
Is. 38:17 deliv. it from pit of *c.*
Dan. 10:8 comeliness into *c.*
Jon. 2:6 br. up my life from *c.*
Acts 2:31 nei. his flesh did see *c.*
13:34 no more to return to *c.*
36 David saw *c.*
37 whom God raised saw no *c.*
Rom. 8:21 from bondage of *c.*
1 *Cor.* 15:42 is sown in *c.* raised
50 *c.* inherit incorruption
Gal. 6:8 of the flesh reap *c.*
1 *Pet.* 1:4 escaped the *c.* that is
2:12 perish in their own *c.*
19 they are servants of *c.*

COST.
2 *Sam.* 19:42 eaten of king's *c.*?
21:24 offer of that *c.* nothing
1 *Chr.* 21:24 b. offering without *c.*
Luke 14:28 and counteth the *c.*

COSTLINESS.
Rev. 18:19 made rich by her *c.*

COSTLY.
1 *K.* 7:9 all these were of *c.* stones
John 12:3 took spikenard, *c.*
1 *Tim.* 2:9 not with *c.* array

COTES.
2 *Chr.* 32:28 Hezekiah made *c.*

COTTAGE.
Is. 1:8 dau. of Zion is left as a *c.*
24:20 earth be removed like a *c.*
Zep. 2:6 coasts be *c.* for sheph.

COUCH, ES.
Gen. 49:4 Reuben went to my *c.*
Job 7:13 I say my *c.* shall ease
Ps. 6:6 I water *c.* with tears
Amos 3:12 in Damascus on a *c.*
6:4 that stretch upon their *c.*
Luke 5:19 filling with his *c.*
24 arise take up thy *c.* and go
Acts 5:15 laid sick folks on *c.*

COUCH, ED.
Job 38:40 when they *c.* in dens
Gen. 49:9 Judah *c.* as a lion
Num. 24:9 he, he lay as a lion

COUCHETH, ING.
Gen. 49:14 a strong ass *c.* down

COU

Deut. 33:13 deep that *c.* beneath
Ezek. 25:5 a *c.* place for flocks

COULD.
Ps. 37:36 but he *c.* not be found
Jer. 15:1 *c.* not be toward this p.
Mark 9:18 they *c.* not, *Lu.* 9:40
14:8 she hath done what she *c.*

COULTER.
1 *Sam.* 13:20 sharpen each his *c.*

COUNCIL.
Ps. 68:27 princes of J. and *c.*
Mat. 5:22 Raca, in danger of *c.*
12:14 Pharisees held a *c.*
26:59 *c.* so, false wit. *Mark* 14:55
Mark 15:1 *c.* bound Jesus
Luke 22:66 led Jesus into their *c.*
John 11:47 gather *c. Acts* 5:21
Acts 4:15 com. to go out of *c.*
5:27 and set them before *c.*
34 stood up in *c.* a Pharisee
41 departed from *c.* rejoicing
6:13 brought Stephen to *c.*
22:30 he com. their *c.* to appear
23:15 ye with *c.* sig. to captain
24:20 evil in me, while before *c.*

COUNCILS.
Mat. 10:17 del. to *c. Mark* 13:9

COUNSEL.
Ex. 18:19 I will give thee *c.*
Num. 27:21 Eleazar ask *c.*
31:16 *c.* of Balaam to trespass
Deut. 32:28 a nation void of *c.*
Jos. 9:14 asked not *c.* at the L.
Jud. 20:7 give here your *c.*
2 *Sam.* 15:31 *c.* of A. foolishness
16:23 all *c.* of Ahith. with D.
17:14 defeated good *c.* of Ah.
20:18 surely ask *c.* at Abel
1 *K.* 1:12 let me give thee *c.*
12:8 forsook *c.* 2 *Chr.* 10:8
2 *K.* 6:8 took *c.* with his servants
18:20 I have *c.* for war, *Is.* 36:5
1 *Chr.* 10:13 died for asking *c.*
2 *Chr.* 22:5 Ahaziah after their *c.*
25:16 art thou made of king's *c.*
Neh. 4:15 brought our *c.* to naught
Neh. 5:13 *c.* of froward headlong
10:3 shine on *c.* of the wicked
12:13 hath *c.* and understand.
21:16 *c.* of wicked is far, 22:18
38:2 darkeneth *c.* by words?
42:3 hideth *c.* without knowl. ?
Ps. 1:1 not in *c.* of ungodly
14:6 shamed the *c.* of poor
16:7 who hath given me *c.*
20:4 the Lord fulfil all thy *c.*
31:13 they took *c.* against me
33:10 *c.* of heathen to naught
55:14 we took sweet *c.* together
64:2 from secret *c.* of wicked
73:24 guide me with thy *c.*
83:3 crafty *c.* against thy people
106:13 waited not for his *c.*
43 provoked him with their *c.*
107:11 contemned *c.* of M. High
Prov. 8:14 *c.* is mine, and wisd.
11:14 where no *c.* is, people fall
12:15 hearkeneth to *c.* is wise
19:20 hear *c.* receive instruction
20:5 *c.* in man like deep water
18 purpose established by *c.*
21:30 no wisdom nor *c.*
21:6 by wise *c.* shalt make war
27:9 friend by hearty *c.*
Is. 5:19 *c.* of Holy One
7:5 taken evil *c.* against thee
11:2 spirit of *c.* rest upon him
19:3 I will destroy *c.* of Egypt
11 *c.* of counsellors brutish
23:8 hath taken this *c.* ag. T.?
28:29 which is wonderful in *c.*
25:15 to hide *c.* from Lord
30:1 with whom took he *c.*?
44:26 performeth *c.* of his mes.
Jer. 18:18 nor *c.* perish from wise
21 knowest all their *c.* ag. me
19:7 make void the *c.* of Judah
32:19 mighty God, great in *c.*
38:15 if I give *c.* wilt not thou
49:7 is *c.* perished from prudent?
30 king of Babylon taken *c.*
Ezek. 7:26 *c.* perish from ancients
11:2 give wicked *c.* in this city
28:4 in thy wisdom thou hast *c.*
Hos. 4:12 my people ask *c.*
10:6 *c.* shall take from him
Mic. 4:12 they know not *c.*
Acts 18:18 nor *c.* perished
Hab. 2:10 consulted shame *c.*
Mark 3:6 *c.* ag. his, *John* 11:53
Luke 7:30 *c.* of God ag. them
23:51 not consented to *c.*
John 11:53 took *c.* to put him
Acts 2:23 by determinate *c.*
5:33 they took *c.* to slay them
38 if this *c.* be of men
9:23 Jews took *c.* to kill him

COU

Acts 27:42 soldiers' *c.* to kill pris.
Eph. 1:11 after *c.* of his own will
Heb. 6:17 immutability of his *c.*

COUNSEL, of God, or *take.*
Jud. 18:5 said, Ask *c. of God*
20:18 chil. of Is. asked *c. of G.*
1 *Sam.* 14:37 Saul asked *c. of G.*
Ps. 33:11 *c. of L. Prov.* 19:21
Is. 19:17 hoc. of the *c. of Lord*
Jer. 23:18 stood in *c. of Lord*
49:20 hear *c. of Lord,* 50:45
Luke 7:30 rejected *c. of God*
Acts 2:23 determinate *c. of God*
20:27 to declare all *c. of God*

My COUNSEL.
2 *Chr.* 25:16 not heark. to *my c.*
Job 29:21 kept silence at *my c.*
Prov. 1:25 set at naught *my c.*
30 they would none of *my c.*
Is. 46:10 *my c.* shall stand
11 executeth *my c.*
Jer. 23:22 had stood in *my c.*
Dan. 4:27 O king, let *my c.* be

Own COUNSEL.
Job 18:7 his *own c.* cast down
Hos. 10:6 ashamed of his *own c.*

Take COUNSEL.
Neh. 6:7 come now, let us *take c.*
Ps. 2:2 rulers *t. c.* against Lord
13:2 how long *t. c.* in my soul
71:10 wait for my soul, *take c.*
16:3 *take c.* execute judgment
83:5 that *take c.* but not of me
45:21 yea, let them *take c.*

COUNSEL, LED.
2 *Sam.* 16:23 which Ahith. *c.*
17:15 Ahithophel *c.* thus I *c.* 21
Job 26:3 how *c.* him hath no wis.
Ex. 8:31 *c.* thee to keep
Rev. 3:18 I *c.* to buy of me gold

COUNSELLOR.
2 *Sam.* 15:12 D.'s *c.* 1 *Chr.* 27:33
1 *Chr.* 26:14 Zechariah a wise *c.*
27:32 Jonathan was a *c.*
2 *Chr.* 22:3 Athaliah was his *c.*
Is. 3:3 Lord taketh away *c.*
9:6 be called Wonderful, *C.*
40:13 or who being his *c.* hath
41:28 for I beheld, was no *c.*
Mic. 4:9 is thy *c.* perished?
Nah. 1:11 out of thee a wicked *c.*
Mark 15:43 *J.* a *c. Luke* 23:50
Rom. 11:34 hath been his *c.*

COUNSELLORS.
2 *Chr.* 22:4 *c.* after father's death
Ezr. 4:5 hired *c.* against them
7:14 sent of king and his sev. *c.*
28 ext. mercy to me before *c.*
Job 3:14 at rest with *c.* of earth
12:17 leadeth *c.* away spoiled
Ps. 119:24 thy testimonies my *c.*
Prov. 11:14 multitude of *c.* 24:6
12:20 to *c.* of peace is joy
15:22 in multitude of *c.* estab.
Is. 1:26 restore thy *c.* as at begin.
19:11 wise *c.* of Pharaoh brutish
Dan. 3:27 the king's *c.* saw these
4:36 my *c.* sought unto me
6:7 all the *c.* have consulted

COUNSELS.
Job 37:12 turned about by his *c.*
Ps. 5:10 fall by their own *c.*
81:12 walked in their own *c.*
Prov. 1:5 shall attain to wise *c.*
12:5 *c.* of wicked are deceit
22:20 excellent things in *c.?*
Is. 25:1 *c.* of old are faithful
47:13 wearied in mul. of thy *c.*
Jer. 7:24 nor *c.* of their own
Mic. 6:16 because of their own *c.*
1 *Cor.* 4:5 manifest *c.* of heart

COUNT.
Lev. 23:15 *c.* from morrow after
23:27 let *c.* years of sale, 50
Num. 23:10 can *c.* dust of Jacob
1 *Sam.* 1:16 *c.* not me dan. of B.
Job 13:13 multi-*c.* me a stranger
31:4 doth not he *c.* all my steps
Ps. 87:6 L. *c.* when he writeth
139:22 *c.* them mine enemies
Mic. 6:11 shall I *c.* them pure?
Acts 26:2 neither *c.* I my life
Phil. 3:8 I *c.* all loss, *c.* but dung
2 *Thes.* 1:11 *c.* you worthy
3:15 *c.* him not as an enemy
2 *Tim.* 6:1 *c.* masters worthy of
Phile. 17 if thou *c.* me a partner
Jam. 1:2 *c.* it joy when ye fall
5:11 we *c.* happy which endure
2 *Pet.* 2:13 *c.* it pleasure to riot

CRUDEN'S CONCORDANCE.

COU

2 *Pet.* 3:9 as some men *c.* slackn.
Rev. 13:18 *c.* number of beast

COUNTED.
Gen. 15:6 *c.* it to him *Ps.* 106:31;
  Rom. 4:3; *Gal.* 3:6
30:33 he *c.* stolen with me
31:15 are we not *c.* strangers
1 *K.* 3:8 cannot be *c.* for multi.
1 *Chr.* 21:6 Benjamin *c.* he not
Neh. 13:13 were *c.* faithful
Job 18:3 whore. are we *c.* as beas.
41:29 darts are *c.* as stubble
Ps. 44:22 we are *c.* as sheep for
88:4 *c.* with them go to the pit
Prov. 17:28 hold, peace is *c.* wise
97:14 be *c.* a curse to him
Is. 5:28 hoofs be *c.* like flint
32:15 field be *c.* for a forest
53:18 where is he *c.* towers
40:15 nations *c.* as small dust
17 nations *c.* less than nothing
Hos. 8:12 wore *c.* as strange
Mat. 14:5 *c.* him. *Mark* 11:32
Luke 21:36 *c.* worthy to escape
Acts 5:41 rejoice, were *c.* worthy
19:19 burn books, and *c.* price
Rom. 2:26 uncir. be *c.* for circ.
4:5 his faith is *c.* for right,
9:8 child. of promise *c.* for seed
Phil. 3:7 those I *c.* lost for Christ
2 *Thes.* 1:5 *c.* worthy of kingdom
1 *Tim.* 1:12 he *c.* me faithful
5:17 elders *c.* worthy
Heb. 3:3 *c.* worthy of more glory
7:6 he whose descent is not *c.*
10:29 *c.* blood of cov. unholy
See ACCOUNTED.

COUNTETH, ING.
Job 19:11 *c.* me of enem. 33:10
Ec. 7:27 *c.* one by one, to find
Luke 14:28 and *c.* the cost

COUNTENANCE, Verb.
Ex. 23:3 neither *c.* a poor man

COUNTENANCE.
Gen. 4:5 Cain was wroth, *c.* fell
31:2 Jacob beheld *c.* of Laban
5 father's *c.* not toward me
Num. 6:26 lift up his *c.* on thee
Deut. 28:50 a nation of fierce *c.*
Jud. 13:6 his *c.* like *c.* of angel
1 *Sam.* 1:18 her *c.* no more sad
16:7 look not on his *c.* or height
12 David was of beau. *c.* 17:42
2 *Sam.* 14:27 Tam.
2 *K.* 8:11 he settled his *c.* on II.
Neh. 2:2 why is thy *c.* sad
3 why not *c.* sad, when city
Job 14:20 thou changest his *c.*
29:24 light of *c.* cast not down
Ps. 4:6 lift light of thy *c.* on us
10:4 pride of *c.* not seek God
11:7 *c.* doth behold upright
21:6 made him glad with thy *c.*
42:5 praise for help of his *c.*
11 who is health of my *c.* 43:5
4:3 light of thy *c.* did save
80:16 perish at rebuke of thy *c.*
89:15 walk in light of thy *c.*
90:8 secret sins *c.* in light of thy *c.*
Prov. 15:13 maketh a cheerful *c.*
16:15 in light of king's *c.* is life
25:23 so angry *c.* a backbiting
27:17 so man sharpeneth *c.* of
Ec. 7:3 by sadness of *c.*
Cant. 2:14 see *c.* thy *c.* is comely
5:15 his *c.* is as Lebanon
Is. 3:9 *c.* doth witness ag. them
Ezek. 27:35 be troubled in their *c.*
Dan. 5:6 king's *c.* was changed
6 king's *c.* fierce *c.* stand up
Mat. 6:16 as hypocrites, of sad *c.*
28:3 *c.* like lightning, *Luke* 9:29
Acts 2:28 full of joy with thy *c.*
2 *Cor.* 3:7 not behold Mo. for *c.*
Rev. 1:16 *c.* was as sun shineth
See CHANGED.

COUNTENANCES.
Dan. 1:13 let our *c.* be looked on
15 their *c.* appeared fairer and

COUNTERVAIL.
Est. 7:4 not *c.* the k.'s damage

COUNTRY.
Gen. 24:4 thou shalt go to my *c.*
20:26 not be so done in our *c.*
30:25 that I may go to my *c.*
43:33 lord of *c.* said unto us
Num. 13:18 born in *c.* shall do
32:1 *c.* Lord smote before Israel
Deut. 26:3 come into *c.* L. sware
Jos. 2:2 to search out the *c.* 3
7:3 go up and view the *c.*
Jud. 11:21 Isr. possessed that *c.*
16:24 the destroyer of our *c.*
Ruth 1:2 came into *c.* of Moab
2 *Sam.* 15:23 all the *c.* wept

COU

1 *K.* 22:27 Syrians filled the *c.*
2 *K.* 3:20 *c.* filled with water
Is. 1:7 *c.* is desolate, cities burnt
22:18 like a ball in a large *c.*
Jer. 22:10 not see his native *c.*
31:8 bring them from north *c.*
48:21 judgment upon plain *c.*
50:9 an assembly from north *c.*
Ezek. 20:38 bring them forth of *c.*
25.9 glory of *c.* Beth-jeshimoth
Jon. 4:2 when yet in my *c.*
Mat. 9:31 his fame in all that *c.*
Mark 5:10 not send fb. out of *c.*
14 told it in the *c. Luke* 8:34
15:15 joined to cit. of th. *c.*
Acts 12:20 their *c.* was nourished
27:27 they drew near to some *c.*
Heb. 11:9 as in a strange *c.*
14 plainly that they seek a *c.*
15 been mindful of that *c.*
16 desire better *c.* a heavenly

Far COUNTRY.
Jos. 9:6 we be come from *f. c.* 9
1 *K.* 8:41 out of a far *c.* for thy
sake, 2 *Chr.* 6:32
2 *K.* 20:14 fr. *f. c.* fr. Bab. *Is.* 39:3
Prov. 25:25 good news from *f. c.*
Is. 13:5 from *f. c.* to destroy
46:11 *c.* exec. counsel from *far c.*
Jer. 4:16 witchers come fr. *far c.*
8:19 because of them in a *far c.*
Mat. 21:33 householder went into
far c. Mark 12:1
25:14 a man trav. into a *far c.*
Luke 15:13 journey into a *far c.*

Own COUNTRY.
Lev. 16:29 one of own *c.* 24:22
1 *K.* 10:13 went to her *o. c.*
11:21 I may go to my *own c.*
22:36 every man to *own c.*
Jer. 51:9 every one into his *o. c.*
Mat. 8:19 dep. into their *own c.*
13:57 without honor save in his
o. c. Mark 6:4; *Luke* 4:24
Mark 8:1 came into his *own c.*
John 4:44 proph. no honor in *o. c.*

Thy COUNTRY.
Gen. 12:1 out of *thy c. Acts* 7:3
32:9 return to *t. c.* and kindred
Num. 20:17 let us pass thro' *t. c.*
Jon. 1:8 what is *thy c.?*
Luke 4:23 do here in *thy c.*

COUNTRY Villages.
1 *Sam.* 6:18 both of *c. villages*

COUNTRYMEN.
2 *Cor.* 11:26 in perils by own *c.*
1 *Thes.* 2:14 like things of your *c.*

COUNTRIES.
Gen. 26:3 to thy seed these *c.* 4
41:57 all *c.* came to buy corn
1 *Chr.* 22:5 glory through *c.*
2 *Chr.* 17:10 fear of G. on all *c.*
Ezr. 3:8 because of people of *c.*
4:20 which ruled over all *c.*
Ps. 110:6 wound over many *c.*
Is. 8:9 give ear ye of far *c.*
Jer. 23:3 I will gather my flock
out of all *c.* 8; 32:37
28:8 prophesied against many *c.*
Ezek. 5:5 Jerusalem in midst of *c.*
6 changed statutes more th. *c.*
6:8 when scattered through *c.*
11:16 I scattered them among
c. little sanctuary in *c.*
17 out of *c.* 20:31, 41
22:4 a mocking to all *c.*
23:7 to perish out of *c.*
29:12 disperse through *c.* 36:19
33:10 these two *c.* shall be mine
Dan. 11:40 he shall enter into *c.*
42 forth his hand upon the *c.*
Luke 21:21 that are in *c.* enter

COUPLED.
1 *Pet.* 3:2 conversation *c.* with f.

COURAGE.
Jos. 2:11 nor any more *c.* in any
2 *Chr.* 15:8 took *c.* put away idols
Dan. 11:25 stir up *c.* ag. king
Acts 28:15 thanked God took *c.*

Good COURAGE.
Num. 13:20 *good c.* bring fruit
Deut. 31:6 strong and of *good c.* 7,
23; *Jos.* 1:6, 9, 18; 10:25; 1
Chr. 22:13; 28:20
2 *Sam.* 10:12 be of *g. c.* 1 *Chr.*
19:13; *Ezr.* 10:4; *Is.* 41:6
Ps. 27:14 be of *g. c.* he shall stre.
thy heart, 31:24

COURAGEOUS, LY.
Jos. 1:7 be *c.* 23:6; 2 *Chr.* 32:7
2 *Sam.* 13:28 be *c.* valiant
2 *Chr.* 19:11 deal *c.*

COV

Amos 2:16 be *c.* shall flee naked

COURSE.
1 *Chr.* 27:1 of övery *c.* 24,000
2 *Chr.* 5:11 did not wait by *c.*
Ezr. 3:11 sang together by *c.*
Ps. 82:5 foundations out of *c.*
Jer. 8:6 every one turned to his *c.*
23:10 their *c.* is evil, their force
Luke 1:5 Zacharias *c.* of Abia
8 in the order of his *c.*
Acts 13:25 John fulfilled his *c.*
16:11 with straight *c.* 21:1
20:24 finish my *c.* with joy
21:7 finished *c.* from Tyre
1 *Cor.* 14:27 by three, by *c.*
2 *Thes.* 3:1 may have free *c.*
2 *Tim.* 4:7 I have finished my *c.*
Jam. 3:6 on fire the *c.* of nature
See WATERCOURSE.

COURSES.
Jud. 5:20 the stars in their *c.*
2 *Chr.* 23:8 the Levites into *c.*
31:2 Hezekiah appointed *c.*
35:10 Levites stood in their *c.*

COURT.
Ex. 27:9 shalt make the *c.*
40:8 thou shalt set up the *c.*
2 *K.* 20:4 afore Isaiah was into *c.*
2 *Chr.* 20:5 Jehosh. bef. new *c.*
24:21 stoned Zechariah in *c.*
29:16 brought unclean. into *c.*
Est. 6:5 beh. H. standeth in *c.*
Is. 34:13 shall be a *c.* for owls
Jer. 32:12 Jeremiah stood in *c.*
36:3 stand in *c.* of Lord's house
32:2 Jeremiah was shut up in *c.*
of prison, 33:1; 39:15
Ezek. 8:7 brou. me to door of *c.* 16
10:3 the cloud filled inner *c.*
40:17 to outward *c.* 42:1; 46:21
28 he brought me to inner *c.*
43:5 brought me to inner *c.*
46:21 in every cor. of *c.* was a *c.*
Amos 7:13 and it is the king's *c.*
Rev. 11:2 *c.* without the temple.

COURTS.
2 *K.* 21:5 built altars for hosts of
heav. in two *c.* 2 *Chr.* 33:5
1 *Chr.* 23:28 office to wait in *c.*
28:6 Solomon shall build my *c.*
2 *Chr.* 23:5 all the people be in *c.*
Ps. 65:4 he may dwell in thy *c.*
84:2 soul fainteth for *c.* of Lord
92:13 flourish in *c.* of our God
96:8 bring offering come into *c.*
100:4 enter his *c.* with praise
116:19 pay vows in the *c.* of
135:2 ye that stand in the *c.* of
Is. 1:12 to tread my *c.?*
62:9 drink it in *c.* of holiness
Ezek. 9:7 fill *c.* with the slain
Zec. 3:7 shalt also keep my *c.*
Luke 7:25 delicately in king's *c.*

COURTEOUS, LY.
Acts 27:3 Julius *c.* entreated P.
28:7 and Publius lodged us *c.*
1 *Pet.* 3:8 love as brethren, be *c.*

COUSIN, S.
Luke 1:36 thy *c.* Elisabeth
1:58 her *c.* heard how

COVENANT.
Gen. 9:12 tok. of *c.* 13, 17; 17:11
17:4 my *c.* is with thee
14 hath broken my *c.*
Ex. 31:16 sab. a perpetual *c.*
34:28 wrote upon tables the *c.*
Lev. 26:15 that ye break my *c.*,
c. I *c.* to perform all the people
Deut. 4:13 dec. unto you his *c.*
23 lest ye forget *c.* of Lord
31 Lord not forget *c.*
5:2 Lord made *c.* with us
9:9 tables of the *c.* tables of *c.*
15 because ye have forsaken *c.*
31:20 they will break my *c.*
Jud. 2:1 I will never break *c.*
1 *Sam.* 20:8 thy serv. in *c.* of L.
1 *K.* 19:10 Israel forsaken *c.* 14
20:34 went thee as. with this *c.*
2 *K.* 13:23 bec. of *c.* with Abrah.
22:1 read *c.* in hearing of people
stood to *c.* 2 *Chr.* 34:31
1 *Chr.* 16:15 be mindful of his *c.*
2 *Chr.* 15:12 into *c.* to seek Lord
15:20 dedied *c.* of priestho.
Ps. 25:14 will show them his *c.*
44:17 neither dealt fal. in thy *c.*
50:16 take my *c.* in thy mouth
55:20 he hath broken his *c.*
74:20 respect to *c.* for dark pla.

COV

Ps. 78:37 neit. were stead. in his *c.*
80:28 my *c.* st. fast with him
34 my *c.* will I not break, nor
89 made void *c.* of thy servant
111:5 ever be mindful of his *c.*
0 commanded his *c.* for ever
Prov. 2:17 forgetteth *c.* of her G.
Is. 24:16 *c.* with death be disan.
33:8 broken *c.* he hath despised
42:6 for *c.* of people, 49:8
54:10 nor *c.* of my peace be rem.
56:4 eunuchs hold of my *c.* 6
59:21 as for me this is my *c.*
Jer. 11:2 hear ye words of *c.* 6
3 cursed obeyeth not w. of *c.*
14:21 break not thy *c.* with us
22:9 bec. they have forsaken *c.*
31:32 which my *c.* they break
33:20 if you can break *c.* of day
21 my *c.* be broken with Da.
25 if my *c.* be not with day
31:18 not performed words of *c.*
50:5 join to L. in perpetual *c.*
Ezek. 16:8 into a *c.* with thee
59 in breaking *c.* 17:18
61 give th. for daugh. not by *c.*
17:15 or break *c.* and be deliv.?
16 whose *c.* he brake
19 my *c.* he hath broken, it
20:37 bring you into bond of *c.*
44:7 they have broken my *c.*
Dan. 9:27 confirm *c.* for one week
11:22 also the prince of *c.*
28 his heart he against holy *c.*
30 indignation against holy *c.*
32 do wickedly against *c.*
Hos. 10:4 falsely in making a *c.*
Zec. 11:10 I might break my *c.*
Mat. 26:4 my *c.* ho with Levi. 5
8 ye have corrupted *c.* of Levi
10 by profaning *c.* of fathers
14 she is the wife of thy *c.*
3:1 messenger of *c.* delight in
Acts 3:25 children of *c.* G. made
7:8 gave him *c.* of circumcision
Rom. 1:31 *c.* breakers
11:27 this is my *c.* when I take
Gal. 3:15 tho' it be but a m.'s *c.*
17 the *c.* confirmed bef. of God
Heb. 8:6 mediator of a better *c.*
7 if first *c.* had been faultless
9 they continued not in my *c.*
9:1 first *c.* had also ordinances
4 and the tables of the *c.*
See ARK, BLOOD, BREAK.

Book of the COVENANT.
Ex. 24:7 Moses took *book of c.*
2 *K.* 23:2 Josiah read all the w.
of *book of c.* 2 *Chr.* 34:30

Establish COVENANT.
Gen. 6:18 *establish* my *c.* 9:9
17:7 est. *c.* bet. me and Abra.
19 *esta. c.* with I. and seed, 21
Ezek. 16:60 *e.* to thee an *overl. c.*

Everlasting COVENANT.
Gen. 9:16 I may remember *c. e.*
17:13 your flesh for *everlast. c.*
19 *c.* with Isaac for an *ever. c.*
2 *Sam.* 23:5 an *ever. c.* ordered
1 *Chr.* 16:17 confirmed to Israel
for an *everlast. c. Ps.* 105:10
Is. 24:5 have broken *everlast. c.*
55:3 *c. e.* w. you, 61:8; *Jer.* 32:40
Ezek. 37:26 *everlast. c.* with them
Heb. 13:20 thro' blood of *ever. c.*

**Keep, keepeth, or kept COVE-
NANT.**
Gen. 17:9 thou shalt *keep* my *c.*
Ex. 19:5 if ye will *keep* my *c.*
Deut. 7:9 God wh. *k. c.* th. 1 *K.*
8:23; 2 *Ch.* 6:14; *Neh.* 1:5; 9:32
Kep. words of this *c.* and do
33:9 they have *kept* thy *c.*
1 *K.* 11:11 hast not *k. c. Ps.* 78:10
Ps. 25:10 no such as *k. c.* 103:18
132:12 if thy child. *keep* my *c.*
Ezek. 17:14 by *k. of c.* it might
Dan. 9:4 *keep c.* and mercy

Made COVENANT.
Gen. 15:18 same day L. *m. c.*
21:27 Abra. and Abim. *m. c.* 32
Deut. 5:2 L. *m. c.* with us in H.
3 *m.* not *c.* with fa. *Heb.* 8:9
29:1 besides *c.* he *made* in Ho.
31:16 will break my *c.* I *made*
Jos. 24:25 Joshua *m. c.*
1 *Sam.* 18:3 J. and D. *m. c.* 23:18
20:16 J. *m. c.* with house of D.
1 *K.* 8:21 ark w. is *c.* of L. he *m.*
20:34 Ahab *made c.* with Benj.
K. 11:4 Jehoiada *m. c.*
17 *made c.* bet. Lord and king
23:3 *made* with you not forget
Ezr. 10:3 *m. c.* with God
Job 31:1 *m. c.* with mine eyes
Ps. 50:5 that have *made c.* with
83:5 with one consent they *m. c.*
89:3 *m. c.* with my chosen
Jer. 34:8 after king had *m. c.*
13 I *m. c.* with fathers
15 *made c.* before me, 18
Dan. 9:27 *c.* with many, for one
1 *Chr.* 11:3 David *m. c.* with eld.

CRUDEN'S CONCORDANCE. 807

COV

1 *Chr.* 16:15 mind. of *c.* he made with A. *Neh.* 9:8; *Ps.* 105:9
2 *Chr.* 31:7 *c.* he bad m. with D.
23:3 m. a *c.* with king Joash
Job 31:1 m. a *c.* with mine eyes
Ps. 50:5 m. a *c.* with me
50:3 made a *c.* with my chosen
Is. 28:15 m. a *c.* with death
57:8 enlarg. thy bed and m. a *c.*
Jer. 11:10 broke *c.* I m.
31:32 not ac. to *c.* I m. with th.
34:8 Zed. m. *c.* with people, 15
13 I made a *c.* with your fath.
15 ye had made *c.* before me
Ezek. 17:13 *made* a *c.* with him

Make COVENANT.
Gen. 17:2 m. *c.* bet. me and thee
26:28 m. *c.* with thee, 31:44
Ex. 28:38 m. no *c. Deut.* 7:2
34:10 I m. *c.* before thy people
12 m. *c.* with inhabitants, 15
Deut. 29:14 nor with yon m. *c.*
1 *Sam.* 11:2 on this cond. I m. *c.*
2 *Chr.* 29:10 in my he. to m. a *c.*
Neh. 9:38 we *make* a sure *c.*
Job 41:4 will he m. a *c.*
Jer. 31:33 this is the *c.* I will m.
Heb. 8:10; 10:16
Ezek. 34:25 m. *c.* of peace, 37:26
Hos. 2:18 m. *c.* for them.
12:1 do m. *c.* with Assyrians

New COVENANT,
Jer. 31:31 n. *c.* with Is. *Heb.* 8:8
Heb. 8:13 a *new c.* the first old
12:24 mediator of the *new c.*

Remember COVENANT.
Gen. 9:15 I will r. my *c. Lev.* 26:42; *Ezek.* 16:60
Lev. 26:45 for their sakes *r. c.*
Ps. 105:8 he hath *r.* his *c.* 106:45
Amos 1:9 rem. not the broth. *c.*
Luke 1:72 and to *rem.* his holy *c.*

COVENANT of Salt.
Lev. 2:13 salt of *c.* to be lacking
Num. 18:19 it is a *c. of s.*
2 *Chr.* 13:5 to David by *c. of salt*

Transgressed, ing COVENANT.
Deut. 17:2 wickedness in *t.* his *c.*
Jos. 7:11 *trangressed* my *c.*
15 because he *t. c.* of the Lord,
Jud. 2:20; 2 *K.* 18:12
23:16 ye have *trans. c.* of Lord
Jer. 34:18 men that *trans.* my *c.*
Hos. 6:7 like men *trans.* the *c.*
8:1 they have *trans.* my *c.*

COVENANTED.
2 *Chr.* 7:18 as I have *c.* with D,
Hag. 2:5 word I *c.* with you
Mal. 26:15 *c.* for thirty pieces.
Luke 22:5 *c.* to give him money

COVENANTS.
Rom. 9:4 to whom pertaineth *c.*
Gal. 4:24 two *c.* one from Sinai
Eph. 2:12 strangers from *c.*

COVER,
Ex. 33:22 *c.* thee while I pass
Num. 22:5 they *c.* face of earth
Deut. 23:13 *c.* wh. com. from thee
33:12 shall *c.* him all the day
1 *Sam.* 24:3 S. went to *c.* his feet
Neh. 4:5 *c.* not their iniquity
Job 16:18 earth, *c.* not my blood
21:26 worms shall *c.* them
22:11 waters *c.* thee, 38:34
40:22 the shady trees *c.* him
Ps. 91:4 *c.* thee with his feath.
104:9 they turn not to *c.* earth
109:29 *c.* with own confusion
132:11 darkness shall *c.* me
140:9 mischief of lips *c.* them
Is. 11:9 waters *c.* sea, *Hab.* 2:14
11:11 worms *c.* thee
22:17 L. will surely *c.* thee
26:21 earth no more *c.* her s.a.n
30:1 *c.* with a covering, but
58:7 naked, that thou *c.*
59:6 nor *c.* themsel. with works
60:2 darkness shall *c.* the earth
6 multi. of camels shall *c.* thee
Jer. 46:8 I will *c.* the earth
Ezek. 7:18 horror shall *c.* them
12:6 thou shalt *c.* thy face
14 he shall *c.* his face, that
24:7 pour. it not on the gr. to *c.*
17 *c.* not thy lips,
22 ye shall not *c.* your lips
26:10 horses, their dust *c.* thee
19 when waters shall *c.* thee
30:18 so for her a cloud *c.* her
32:7 I will *c.* the heaven, sun
37:6 *c.* you with skin and
38:9 he like cloud to *c.* land, 16
Hos. 2:9 flax given to *c.* her
10:8 mount. *c.* us, *Luke* 23:30

COV,

Ob. 10 shame shall *c.* thee
Mic. 3:7 shall all *c.* their lips
7:10 shame *c.* her said to me
2:17 violence of L. *c.* thee
Hab. 2:17 violence of L. *c.* thee
Mark 14:65 and *c.* his face
1 *Cor.* 11:7 man not to *c.* head
1 *Pet.* 4:8 charity *c.* mult. of sins

COVERED.
Gen. 7:19 mountains were *c.* 20
9:23 *c.* naked. of their father
24:65 Rebekah *c.* herself
38:14 Tam. *c.* her with a veil
Ex. 14:28 waters *c.* chariots
15:5 the depths *c.* them
10 the sea *c.* them, *Jos.* 24:7
24:15 a cloud *c.* the mount. 16
37:9 *c.* with wings mercy-seat
40:21 veil *c.* ark of testimony
Num. 4:20 when holy things *c.*
Deut. 32:15 art *c.* with fatness
Jud. 4:18 Jael *c.* Sisera, 19
1 *Sam.* 19:13 Mich. *c.* the image
28:14 old man cometh up *c.*
1 *K.* 1:1 *c.* David with clothes
8:7 cher. *c.* the ark, 1 *Chr.* 5:8
Job 15:27 *c.* his face with fatness
23:17 I *c.* not before the darkness
31:33 if I *c.* my transgressions
Ps. 44:15 shame of face *c.* me
19 *c.* us with shadow of death
65:13 valleys *c.* over with corn
68:13 w. of dove *c.* with silver
71:13 *c.* with reproach that seek
86:45 hast *c.* him with shame
106:17 *c.* company of Abiram
139:13 *c.* me in mother's womb
Prov. 26:23 a potsherd *c.* with
26 whose hatred is *c.* by deceit
Ec. 6:4 his name *c.* with dark.
Is. 6:2 with twain he *c.* his face
2:10 the seers hath he *c.*
51:16 I have *c.* thee in shadow
61:10 *c.* me with robe
Jer. 51:42 she is *c.* with waves
Lam. 2:1 *c.* dau. of Z. with clo.
3:16 he hath *c.* me with ashes
43 hast *c.* with anger
44 *c.* thyself with a cloud
Ezek. 1:11 two wings *c.* bod. 23
16:8 and *c.* thy nakedness
10 I *c.* thee with silk
18:7 and hath *c.* the naked, 16
24:8 her blood should not be *c.*
27:7 blue and purple *c.* thee
31:15 I *c.* the deep for him
37:8 and skin *c.* them above
Jon. 3:8 and beast he *c.* with sa.
Hab. 3:3 his glory *c.* heavens
Mat. 8:24 was *c.* with waves
10:26 nothing *c.* that shall not
be revealed, *Luke* 12:2
1 *Cor.* 11:6 the woman be not *c.*

COVERED face.
Gen. 38:15 Tamar had *c.* her *face*
2 *Sam.* 19:4 but David *c.* his *face*
Est. 7:8 they *c.* Haman's *face*
Ps. 69:7 shame hath *c.* my *face*
Prov. 24:31 nettles *c. face* there.
Is. 6:2 with twain he *c.* his *face*
Jer. 51:51 shame hath *c.* our *fac.*

Head COVERED.
2 *Sam.* 15:30 David had his *h. c.*
Est. 6:12 Haman, his *head c.*
Ps. 140:7 *c.* my *head* in battle
Jer. 14:3 and *c.* their *heads*
1 *Cor.* 11:4 ev. man praying, *h. c.*

COVERED sin
Ps. 32:1 *sin* is *c. Rom.* 4:7
83:2 thou hast *c.* all their *sin*

COVEREDST.
Ps. 104:6 *c.* it with deep
Ezek. 16:18 ht. garm. and *c.* them

COVEREST.
Deut. 22:12 vesture wherewith *c.*
Ps. 104:2 *c.* thyself with light

COVERETH.
Num. 22:11 *c.* face of the earth
Jud. 3:24 surely *c.* his feet
Job 9:24 *c.* faces of judges
15:27 *c.* his flesh with fatness
36:30 he *c.* bottom of the sea
32 with clouds he *c.* the light
Ps. 73:6 violence *c.* as garment
147:8 *c.* heaven with clouds
Prov. 10:6 vio. *c.* the mouth, 11
12 love *c.* all sins
12:16 prudent man *c.* shame
17:9 transgression seek. love
28:13 *c.* his sins, shall not pros.
Ezek. 31:15 our confusion *c.* us
Mal. 2:16 for one *c.* violence
Luke 8:16 candle *c.* it with ves.

CRA

COVERING, Participle.
Ex. 25:20 *c.* mercy-seat with
Num. 4:5 shall take down *c.* veil
Ezek. 28:16 O *c.* cherub
Mal. 2:13 *c.* the altar with tears

COVERING, Substantive.
Gen. 20:16 thee a *c.* of the eyes
Ex. 22:27 it is his *c.* for his skin
Lev. 13:45 put *c.* on upper lip
1 *Sam.* 17:19 *c.* over well's mou.
Job 22:14 thick clouds *c.* to him
24:7 naked have no *c.* in cold
26:6 destruction hath no *c.*
31:19 any poor without *c.*
Ps. 105:39 he spread cloud for *c.*
Cant. 3:10 he made *c.* of purple
Is. 22:8 discovered *c.* of Judah
28:7 *c.* cast over all people
30:20 *c.* narrower, than can wr.
30:1 with *c.* not of my Spirit
22 ye shall defile *c.* of images
50:3 I make sackcloth their *c.*
Ezek. 28:13 precious stone thy *c.*
1 *Cor.* 11:15 hair is given for *c.*
See BADGER.

COVERINGS.
Prov. 7:16 deck. my bed with *c.*
31:22 maketh herself *c.* of tap.

COVERS.
Ex. 25:29 make *c.* 37:16
Num. 4:7 put *c.* to cover withal

COVERT.
2 *K.* 16:18 *c.* for the sabbath,
Ahaz took down
Job 38:40 when lions abide in *c.*
40:21 behemoth lieth in *c.* of
Ps. 61:4 trust in *c.* of thy wings
Is. 4:6 a tabernacle for a *c.*
16:4 be thou a *c.* from spoiler
32:2 a man bec. from tempest
Jer. 25:38 forsaken his *c.*

COVET.
Ex. 20:17 thou shalt not *c. Deut.* 5:21; *Rom.* 7:7; 13:9
Mic. 2:2 they *c.* fields and take
1 *Cor.* 12:31 but *c.* the best gifts
14:39 *c.* to prophesy

COVETED.
Jos. 7:21 then I *c.* them, and
Acts 20:33 I *c.* no man's silver
1 *Tim.* 6:10 while some *c.* after

COVETETH.
Prov. 21:26 *c.* all the day long
Hab. 2:9 woe to him *c.* evil cov.

COVETOUS.
Ps. 10:3 wicked blesseth *c.*
Luke 16:14 Phari. who were *c.*
1 *Cor.* 5:10 yet not altog. with *c.*
11 *c.* with such not to eat
6:10 nor *c.* inherit, *Eph.* 5:5
1 *Tim.* 3:3 bishop must not be *c.*
2 *Pet* 2:14 exer. with *c.* practices

COVETOUSNESS.
Ex. 18:21 men hating *c.*
Ps. 119:36 incline not heart to *c.*
Prov. 28:16 hateth *c.* sh. prolong
Is. 57:17 for iniquity of his *c.*
Ezek. 33:31 heart goeth after *c.*
Hab. 2:9 that coveteth an evil *c.*
Luke 12:15 take heed and beware *c.*
Rom. 1:29 filled with all *c.*
2 *Cor.* 9:5 as a matter not of *c.*
Eph. 5:3 *c.* let it not be named
Col. 3:5 mortify *c.* wh. is idola.
1 *Thes.* 2:5 nor used cloak of *c.*
Heb. 13:5 conver. be without *c.*
2 *Pet.* 2:3 through *c.* make mer.

COW.
Num. 22:28 *c.* or ewe, sh. not kill
Is. 11:7 *c.* and the bear shall feed
Ezek. 4:15 given thee *c.* dung for
Amos 4:3 every *c.* at that before

COZBI. *Num.* 25:15, 18

CRACKLING.
Ec. 7:6 *c.* of thorns under pot

CRACKNELS.
1 *K.* 14:3 take with thee *c.*

CRAFT.
Dan. 8:25 cause *c.* to prosper
Mark 14:1 take him by *c.*
Acts 18:3 he was of same *c.*
19:27 not only our *c.* is in dan.
Rev. 18:22 whatsoever *c.* he be

CRAFTINESS.
Job 5:13 in their *c.* 1 *Cor.* 3:19

CRE

Luke 20:23 he perceived their *c.*
2 *Cor.* 4:2 not walking in *c.* nor
Eph. 4:14 carried by cunning *c.*

CRAFTY.
Job 5:12 he disap. devices of *c.*
15:5 thou choosest tongue of *c.*
2 *Cor.* 12:16 being *c.* I caught

CRAFTSMAN.
Deut. 27:15 the work of the *c.*
Rev. 18:22 no *c.* be found.

CRAFTSMEN.
2 *K.* 24:14 carried away *c.* 16
1 *Chr.* 4:14 for they were *c.*
Neh. 11:35 the valley of *c.*
Acts 19:24 no small gain to *c.*
38 *c.* have matter against any

CRAG.
Job 39:28 eagle abideth on *c.*

CRANE.
Is. 38:14 like *c.* so did I chatter
Jer. 8:7 *c.* obs. time of coming

CRASHING.
Zep. 1:10 great *c.* from hills

CRAVED, ETH.
Prov. 16:26 for his mouth *c.* it
Mark 15:43 Joseph *c.* body of J.

CREATE,
Ps. 51:10 *c.* in me a clean heart
Is. 4:5 *c.* on every d.-p. a cloud
45:7 *c.* darkness, I *c.* evil
57:19 I *c.* the fruits of the lips
65:17 I *c.* new heavens
18 rejoice in that which I *c.*

CREATED.
Gen. 1:1 in the begin. God *c.* he.
21 God *c.* great whales
27 God *c.* man to his own image, male and female, 5:2
2:3 in it rested from all he *c.*
6:7 will destroy man I have *c.*
Deut. 4:32 day God *c.* man
Ps. 89:12 porth and south he *c.*
102:18 people to be *c.*
104:30 forth spirit they are *c.*
148:5 com. and they were *c.*
Is. 40:26 hath *c.* these things
43:1 O Jacob
7 I have *c.* him for my glory
45:8 I the Lord have *c.* it
12 I have *c.* man upon it
18 he *c.* it not in vain
48:7 *c.* now, not from begin.
54:16 have *c.* smith, *c.* waster
Jer. 31:22 L. hath *c.* a new thing
Ezek. 21:30 judge where wast *c.*
28:13 in day thou wast *c.*
15 from day thou wast *c.*
Mal. 2:10 hath not one God *c.*
Mark 13:19 creation G. *c.*
1 *Cor.* 11:9 man *c.* for the wom.
Eph. 2:10 workmanship *c.* in C.
3:9 who *c.* all things by Jes. C.
4:24 God is *c.* in righteousness
Col. 1:16 were all things *c.*
3:10 after image of him *c.* him
1 *Tim.* 4:3 G. *c.* to be received
Rev. 4:11 hast *c.* all things, for thy pleasure are and were *c.*
10:6 who *c.* heaven and the

CREATETH.
Amos 4:13 *c.* w. L. is his name

CREATION.
Mark 10:6 from *c.* male and fe.
13:19 as was not from the *c.*
Rom. 1:20 from *c.* are clearly
8:22 that whole *c.* groaneth
2 *Pet.* 3:4 continue as from the *c.*
Rev. 3:14 beginning of *c.* of God

CREATOR,
Ec. 12:1 remember *c.* in youth
Is. 40:28 *c.* of ends of the earth
43:15 I am the Lord, *c.* of Israel
Rom. 1:25 creature more than *c.*
1 *Pet.* 4:19 as to a faithful *c.*

CREATURE.
Gen. 1:20 bring forth moving *c.*
Lev. 11:46 this is law of every *c.*
Mark 16:15 gospel to every *c.*
Col. 1:23
Rom. 8:19 expectation of *c.*
20 *c.* made subject to vanity
21 *c.* be delivered from bond.
39 any *c.* able to separate us
2 *Cor.* 5:17 he is a new *c.*
Gal. 6:15 nor avail, but new *c.*
Col. 1:15 first born of every *c.*
1 *Tim.* 4:1 every *c.* of G. is good
Heb. 4:13 any *c.* not manifest
Rev. 8:13 every *c.* in heaven

808 CRUDEN'S CONCORDANCE.

CRO

Living CREATURE.
Gen. 1:21 God created every l. c.
24 let earth bring forth liv. c.
2:19 Adam called every liv. c.
9:10 cov. with every living c.
12 between me and ev. l. c. 15
Lev. 11:46 law of every living c.
Ezek. 1:20 spirit of l. c. 21; 10:17
10:15 l. c. I saw by Chebar, 20

CREATURES.
Is. 13:21 houses full of doleful c.
Jam. 1:18 of first-fruits of his c.
Rev. 8:9 third of c. in sea died

Living CREATURES.
Ezek. 1:5 likeness of four lis. c.
14 l. c. ran, returned as light.
19 l. c. went the wheels went
3:13 noise of wings of living c.

CREDITOR, S.
Deut. 15:2 c. that lendeth shall
2 K. 4:1 c. to take my two sons
Is. 50:1 to which of my c.
Luke 7:41 c. had two debtors

CREEK.
Acts 27:39 discovered a certain c.

CREEP.
Lev. 11:31 unclean all that c.
Ps. 104:20 beasts of forest c.
2 Tim. 3:6 of this sort c. into

CREEPETH.
Gen. 1:25 every thing that c. 26
30 given to every thing c. herb
7:8 c. went in two and two, 14
21 of thing that c.
8:17 bring forth every thing c.
19 whatsoever c. went forth
Lev. 11:41 that c. shall be an abomination, 42, 44; 20:25
Deut. 4:18 of any thing that c.

CREEPING thing, s.
Gen. 1:26 dominion over ev. c. t.
Lev. 5:2 unclean c. thing
11:21 ye eat, of every c. thing
22:5 of whoso, toucheth any c. t.
Deut. 14:19 c. thing that flieth
1 K. 4:33 he spake of c. t. fishes
Ps. 104:25 c. things innumerable
148:10 all c. things praise the L.
Ezek. 8:10 form of c. t. portrayed
38:20 all c. t. shake at my pres.
Hos. 2:18 covenant with c. things
Hab. 1:14 men as c. things
Acts 10:12 P. saw c. things, 11:6
Rom. 1:23 like to c. things

CREPT.
Jude 4 certain c. in unawares

CRESCENS. 2 Tim. 4:10
CRETE. Acts 27:7, 13, 21; Tit. 1:5
CRETES. Acts 2:11
CRETIANS. Tit. 1:12

CREW.
Mat. 26:74 the cock c. Mar. 14:68;
Luke 22:60; John 18:27

CRIB.
Job 39:9 unicorn abide by thy c.?
Prov. 14:4 no oxen are c. is clean
Is. 1:3 ass know, his master's c.

CRIED. See after cry.

CRIME, S.
Job 31:11 his is a heinous c.
Ezek. 7:23 land is full of bloody c.
Acts 25:16 conc. c. laid ag. him
27 not to signify the c. laid

CRIMSON
2 Chr. 2:7 cun. to work in c. 14
3:14 he made the veil of c.
Is. 1:18 your sins be like c.
Jer. 4:30 thou clothest with c.

CRIPPLE.
Acts 14:8 being a c. from womb

CRISPING-PINS.
Is. 3:22 L. will take away c.-p.

CRISPUS. Acts 18:8; 1 Cor. 1:14

CROOK-BACKED.
Lev. 21:20 c.-b. not approach

CROOKED.
Deut. 32:5 are a c. generation
Job 26:13 formed the c. serpent
Ps. 125:5 aside to their c. ways
Prov. 2:15 whose ways are c.
Ec. 1:15 c. not be m. stra. 7:13
Is. 27:1 pun. lev. that c. serpent
40:4 c. be made, 42:16; Luke 3:5
43:2 make the c. places straight
59:8 have made them c. paths
Phil. 2:15 midst of a c. nation

CROP.
Lev. 1:16 he shall pluck away c.

CRO

CROPPED.
Ezek. 17:4 c. off top of y. twigs, 22

CROSS.
Mat. 10:38 taketh not his c. is not worthy of me, Luke 14:27
16:24 c. and follow me, Mark 8:34; Luke 9:23
27:32 compelled to bear c. Mark 15:21; Luke 23:26
40 if S. of God come down from the c. 42; Mark 15:30, 32
John 19:17 bearing c. went forth
19 wrote title, and put it on c.
25 stood by the c. his mother
31 not remain on c. on sabbath
1 Cor. 1:17 lest c. be of none ef.
18 preaching of c. foolishness
Gal. 5:11 offence of the c. ceased
6:12 suf. persecution for c. of C.
14 should glory, save in the c.
Eph. 2:16 reconcile both by c.
Phil. 2:8 obedient to death of c.
3:18 are enemies of c. of Christ
Col. 1:20 through blood of c.
2:14 nailing it to his c.
Heb. 12:2 endured the c.

CROSS-WAY.
Ob. 14 nor have stood in c.-w.

CROUCH, ETH.
1 Sam. 2:36 c. for piece of silver
Ps. 10:10 he c. and humbleth

CROW, CROWING. See COCK.

CROWN.
Ex. 25:25 a golden c. to border
29:6 holy c. upon the mitre
Lev. 8:9 on his forefront holy c.
21:12 c. of anointing is
2 K. 11:12 c. on J. 2 Chr. 23:11
Est. 1:11 Vashti with c. royal
Job 31:36 bind it as a c. to me
Ps. 89:39 hast profaned his c.
132:18 upon himself c. flourish
Prov. 4:9 c. of glory deliver
12:4 a virtuous woman is a c.
14:24 c. of wise is their riches
16:31 hoary head is a c. of glory
17:6 children's child. c. of old
27:24 c. endure to every genera.
Cant. 3:11 behold S. with the c.
Is. 28:1 woe to the c. of pride
5 shall be for a c. of glory
62:3 shalt also be a c. of glory
Jer. 13:18 c. of glory come down
Ezek. 21:26 take off the c.
Zec. 9:16 as the stones of a c.
John 19:5 J. wearing c. of thorns
1 Cor. 9:25 a corruptible c.
Phil. 4:1 beloved, my joy and c.
1 Thes. 2:19 our c. of rejoicing
2 Tim. 4:8 c. of righteousness
Jam. 1:12 he shall rec. c. of life
1 Pet. 5:4 shall receive c. of glory
Rev. 2:10 give thee a c. of life
3:11 that no man take thy c.
6:2 a c. was given to him

CROWN of gold.
Ex. 25:11 c. of g. round about,
24; 30:3; 37:2; 11, 12, 26
Est. 8:15 Mordecai with c. of g.
Ps. 21:3 c. of g. on his head

CROWN, with Head.
Gen. 49:26 on c. of Joseph's h.
Deut. 33:20 teareth arm with c.
2 Sam. 1:10 the c. on his head
from h. 1 Chr. 20:2
14:25 sole to c. of h. Job 2:7
Est. 2:17 king set c. on her h.
6:8 c. royal set upon his head
Job 19:9 taken c. from my head
Is. 3:17 smite with a scab c. of h.
28 broken c. of thy head
48:45 c. of h. of tumultuous ones
Lam. 5:16 c. fallen from our head
Ezek. 16:12 beautiful c. on thy h.
Mat. 27:29 put c. of thorns, Mark 15:17; John 19:2
Rev. 12:1 c. of twelve stars
14:14 on his head a golden c.

CROWNED.
Ps. 8:5 hast c. him with glory
Prov. 14:18 c. with knowledge
Cant. 3:11 his mother c. him
Nah. 3:17 thy c. are as locusts
2 Tim. 2:5 not c. except he strive
Heb. 2:9 Jesus c. with glory

CROWNEDST.
Heb. 2:7 c. him with glory and

CROWNEST, ETH.
Ps. 65:11 c. year with thy goods
103:4 c. thee with lovingkindness.

CROWNING.
Is. 23:8 against Tyre the c. city

CROWNS.
Ezek. 23:42 besa, c. on their h.

CRY

Zec. 6:11 make c. ; 14 c. to Helem
Rev. 4:4 elders had c. of gold
10 cast their c. before throne
9:7 on locusts' heads were c.
12:3 dragon having seven c.
13:1 upon his horns ten c.
19:12 on his head many c.

CRUCIFY.
Mat. 20:19 to Gentiles, to c. him
23:34 some of them ye shall c.
27:31 to c. him, Mark 15:20
Mark 15:13 cried again c. him, 14
Luke 23:21 c. him, c. John 19:6, 15
Heb. 6:6 S. of God afresh

CRUCIFIED.
Mat. 26:2 bet. to be c. Luke 24:7
27:22 said, Let him be c. 23
26 del. him to be c. John 19:16
35 c. him, John 19:23
38 thieves c. 44; Mark 15:32;
Luke 23:33; John 19:18
28:5 Jesus w. was c. Mark 16:6
John 19:20 where Jesus was c. 41
Acts 2:23 by wicked hands c.
36 made J. whom ye c. L. 4:10
Rom. 6:6 old man is c. with him
1 Cor. 1:13 was Paul c. for you?
23 preach Christ c. unto Jews
2:2 Jesus Christ and him c.
8 not have c. Lord of glory
2 Cor. 13:4 for c. through weak.
Gal. 2:20 I am c. with Christ
3:1 Chr. set forth c. among you
5:24 are Christ's have c. flesh
6:14 by whom the world is c.
Rev. 11:8 where Lord was c.

CRUEL.
Gen. 49:7 wrath, for it was c.
Ex. 6:9 for c. bondage
Deut. 32:33 c. venom of asps
Job 30:21 art become c. to me
Ps. 25:19 hate me with c. hatred
71:4 deliver out of hand of c.
Prov. 5:9 thou give years to c.
11:17 he c. troubleth own flesh
12:10 mercies of wicked are c.
17:11 c. messenger be sent
27:4 wrath is c.
Cant. 8:6 jealousy is c.
Is. 13:9 day of Lord cometh c.
19:4 Egyptians give to c. lord
Jer. 6:23 they are c. 50:42
Lam. 4:3 daughter of my peo. c.
11:36 trial of c. mockings

CRUELLY.
Ezek. 18:18 bec. he c. oppressed

CRUELTY.
Gen. 49:5 instruments of c.
Jud. 9:24 c. to sons of Jerubbaal
Ps. 27:12 such as breathe out c.
74:20 are full of habitations of c.
Ezek. 34:4 with c. ye ruled them

CRUMBS.
Mat. 15:27 eat of c. Mark 7:28
Luke 16:21 to be fed with the c.

CRUSE.
1 Sam. 26:11 take the c. of water
12 so David took the c. 16
1 K. 14:3 take a c. of honey
17:12 I have a little oil in c.
14 nor c. of oil fail 16
19:6 Elijah had c. of water
2 K. 2:20 bring me a new c.

CRUSH.
Job 39:15 forgetteth foot may c.
Lam. 1:15 to c. my young
3:34 to c. all the prisoners
Amos 4:1 which c. the needy

CRUSHED.
Lev. 22:24 not offer what is c.
Num. 22:25 ass c. Balaam's foot
Deut. 28:33 and c. alway
1 Sam. 12:3 c. I ? whom deft.
Job 5:4 are c. in the gate
39:3 . breaketh into a viper
Jer. 51:34 Nebuch. hath c. me.

CRY, Substantive.
Gen. 18:21 accord. to c. come up
Ex. 2:23 their c. came up, 3:9
3:7 I have heard their c.
11:6 be a great c. in all Egypt
12:30 there was great c. in Eg.
Neh. 5:1 a g. c. of the people
Acts 23:9 so said, arose a great c.

Hear CRY.
Ex. 22:23 I will hear their c.
22:23 if I hear a cry, hear
Jer. 14:12 I will not h. their c.
23:16 hear c. in the morning

CRIES.
Jam. 5:4 c. of them that reaped

CRY, Verb.
Ex. 5:8 idle therefore they c.
22:23 if I hear afflict any they c.
32:18 voice of them that c.
Lev. 13:45 and c. Unclean
Jud. 10:14 go c. to the gods
2 Chr. 32:9 c. in affliet. with her
Job 30:20 I c. thou dost not hear
24 they c. in his destruction
35:9 oppressed to c. they c. out
12 they c. none giveth answer
36:13 c. not when he bindeth
38:41 his young ones c. to God
Ps. 22:2 I c. in the daytime
27:7 O Lord, when I c. 28:2
28:1 to thee will I c.
34:17 righteous c. Lord heareth
56:9 when I c. mine enem. turn
57:2 I will c. to God most high
61:2 from end of earth will I c.
66:3 be merciful, for I c. daily
89:26 shalt c. thou art my father
141:1 Lord I c. make haste
147:9 to young ravens which c.
Prov. 8:1 doth not wisdom c. and
21:13 shall c. but not be heard
Is. 8:4 before child c. My father
13:22 beasts of islands shall c.
14:31 c. O city, thou Palestina
15:4 and Heshbon shall c. and
32:7 their valiant ones shall c.
34:14 satyr shall c. to fellow
40:2 c. to Jerus. warfare accom.
6 voice said, c. what shall I c.?
42:2 he shall not c. nor lift voice
13 he shall c. yea, prevail
14 I c. like travailing woman
46:7 one shall c. to him, yet can
58:9 c. he shall say, Here I am
65:14 shall c. for sorrow of heart
Jer. 2:2 go and c. in ears of Jer.
3:4 wilt not from this time c.
4:5 blow trumpet, c. gather
11:11 though they c. to me
12 c. to gods
14 not hear when c. Ezek. 8:18
22:20 go up to Lebanon, and c.
25:34 and c. 48:20; Zec. 11:2
31:6 watchmen on Ephraim c.
47:2 forbear to c. mark me
20:15 shake, when wounded c.
27:30 c. bitterly for Tyrus
Hos. 8:2 Israel c. to me, my God

CRUDEN'S CONCORDANCE. 809

CRI

Joel 1;19 Lord, to thee will I c.
 20 the beasts c. unto thee
Jon. 3;8 man and beast c. to G.
Mic. 3;5 bite with tooth, c. peace
Nah. 2;8 c. but none look back
Zep. 1;14 mighty sh. c. bitterly
Zec. 1;14 angel said, c. thou
Mat. 12;19 not strive nor c.
Luke 18;7 avenge elect, which c.
Rom. 8;15 whereby we c. Abba
Gal. 4;27 c. that travailest not

CRY against.
Deut. 15;9 c. to L. a. thee, 24;15
2 Chr. 13;12 to c. alarm ag. you
Job 31;38 if my land c, ag. me
Jon. 1;2 go to Nineveh, c. ag. it

CRY aloud.
1 K. 18;27 Elijah said, c. aloud
Job 19;7 I c. aloud but no judgm.
Ps. 55;17 at noon will I c. aloud
Is. 24;14 c. aloud from the sea
54;1 break forth into sing. c. a.
58;1 c. aloud spare not
Hos. 5;8 c. a. at Beth-a. after
Mic. 4;9 why c. a. ? is there no

CRY to the Lord.
1 Sam. 7;8 cease not to c. for us
Ps. 107;19 c. to the Lord, 28
Is. 19;20 c. to L. bec. of oppres.
Joel 1;14 sanctify fast, c. to the L.
Mic. 3;4 c. to the L. he will not

CRY out.
1 Sam. 8;18 ye shall c. out
Job 19;7 I c. out of wrong,
35;9 c. c. by r. of arm of mighty
Is. 12;6 c. out and shout
15;4 soldiers of M. shall c. out
5 my heart shall c. out for M.
Jer. 2;9 wonder, c. out, and cry
Jer. 48;31 I will c. out for Moab
Lam. 2;19 c. out in the night
Amos 3;4 y. lion c. out of den ?
Hab. 1;2 I c. out to thee
2;11 stone shall c. out of wall
Mark 10;47 c. out, Have mercy
Luke 19;40 stones would c. out

CRIED.
Gen. 27;34 E. c. with bitter cry
"1;15 he heard that I c.
41;55 c. to Pharaoh for bread
Num. 11;2 c. to Moses
Deut. 22;24 dam. bec. she c. not
27 damsel c. and none to save
Jud. 5;28 mother c. through lat.
7;21 all the host ran, and c.
10;12 ye c. and I delivered you
1 Sam. 17;8 G. c. to armies of Isr.
20;37 Jonathan c. after lad, 38
2 Sam. 20;16 then c. a wise w.
22 c. to my G. he did hear
1 K. 13;2 c. against altar, 4, 21
18;28 c. aloud and cut them,
2 K. 2;12 Elisha c. My father
6;5 he c. Alas, it was borrowed
8;5 woman c. to king for house
11;4 Athaliah c. Treason
1 Chr. 5;20 c. to God in the battle
2 Chr. 32;20 Isaiah c. to heaven
Neh. 9;27 they c. thou heard, 28
Job 29;12 I delivered poor that c.
29;5 they c. as after a thief
Ps. 18;6 in my distress I c. to G.
41 c. but none to save them
22;5 they c. and were delivered
24 c. unto him, he heard
30;2 O Lord I c. to thee
8 I c. to thee O Lord and made
31;22 heartiest sup, when I c.
31;8 this poor man c. and the L.
66;17 I c. with my mouth, 77;1
88;1 I c. day and night
13 I c. O Lord, in the morning
119;145 I c. with whole heart
130;1 out of the depths have I c.
138;3 I c. thou answeredst
Jer. 6 I meared at voice of him c.
30;7 have I c. concerning this
Jer. 4;20 destru. on destru. is c.
Ezek. 9;8 I fell on my face, and c.
10;13 it was c. to them
Dan. 6;20 he c. O Daniel
Jon. 7;14 not c. to me with heart
Jon. 1;5 mariners c. cv. man to
2;2 I c. by reason of afflict'ion to
L. out of belly of hell, c. I
Zec. 7;13 as he c. and they would
not hear, so they c.
Mat. 14;30 Peter c. Lord save me
20;31 c. the more, Have mercy,
Mark 12;26 spirit c. and rent him
John 7;37 Jesus c. If any thirst
Acts 18;32 some c. one th. 21;31,
22;21 whereof they c. ag. him
Rev. 10;3 he c. seven thunders
13;2 and she c. travailing

CUB

Rev. 14;18 c. to him that had sic.
14;2 he c. mightily, 13
19 they c. weeping and wailing

CRIED to the Lord.
Ex. 8;12 Moses c. to the L. 15;25;
17;4; Num. 12;13
14;10 Israel c. to the Lord, Jud.
3;9, 15; 4;3; 6;7; 10;1
Num. 20;16 we c. to the Lord he
heard, Deut. 26;7
Jos. 24;7 c. to the L. he put dark.
1 Sam. 7;9 S. c. to the L. 15;11
2 Chr. 13;14 they c. to the L. Ps.
107;6, 13; Jon. 1;14
14;11 Asa c. to the Lord
Ps. 3;4 I c. to the L. 120;1; 142;1
Lam. 2;18 c. to L. O dau. of Z.

CRIED with a loud voice.
1 Sam. 28;12 En-dor c. w. l. v.
2 Sam. 19;4 D. c. w. l. v. O Abes.
2 Chr. 32;18 c. w. l. v. in J. lang.
Mat. 27;46 ninth hour J. c. w. l. v.
50; Mark 15;34, 37; Luke
23;46; John 11;43
Mark 1;26 evil spirit c. w. a l. v.
Acts 7;60 S. c. w. a loud voice
16;28 Paul c. with a loud voice
Rev. 6;10 c. w. a l. v. How long
7;2 angel c. w. l. v. 10;3; 10;17
10 stood bef. Lamb c. w. l. v.

CRIED out.
1 Sam. 4;13 city c. out ; 5;10 Ek.
1 K. 22;32 Jehosh. 2 Chr. 18;31
Jer. 20;8 I c. out I cried violence
Mat. 8;29 spirits c. out, Luke 4;33
Mark 6;49 blind men c. out
Mark 1;23 unclean spirit c. out
9;21 father c. out, Luke 9;38
15;13 c. o. again, Mat. 27;23;
Luke 23;18 ; John 19;6
Acts 19;28 c. out Great is D. 34
22;22 c. and threw dust
23;6 Paul c. out I am a Pharisee

CRIEST, ETH.
Gen. 4;10 brother's blood c.
Ex. 14;15 where. c. thou to me ?
22;27 when he c. I will hear
1 Sam. 25;11 David c. to the king ?
Job 24;12 soul of wounded c.
Ps. 72;14 del. needy when he c.
84;2 c. out for living God
Prov. 1;20 wisdom c. 8;3 ; 9;3
2;3 if thou c. after knowledge
8, 26;17 as a woman c. out
40;3 that c. in the wilderness
57;13 c. let companies deliver
Jer. 12;8 my heritage c. ag. me
31;15 why c. thou
Mic. 6;9 Lord's voice c. to city
Mat. 15;23 for she c. after us
Luke 9;39 he c. out
Rom. 9;27 Esa.as also c.
Jam. 5;4 hire of labourers c.

CRYING.
1 Sam. 4;14 Eli heard noise of c.
5 Sam. 13;19 Tamar went on c.
Job 39;7 nor reg. he c. of driver
Prov. 19;18 soul spare for his c.
30;15 horseleech hath, c. Give
Is. 22;5 day of c. to mountains
24;11 a c. for wine in streets
65;19 of c. no more heard in her
Jer. 48;3 of c. be from Horonaim
72;4 c.? the heedstone with c.
Mat. 3;3 covering altar with c.
1;3; Luke 3;1; John 1;23
21;15 children c. in the temple
21;26 c. out, Men of Israel, help
36 multitude, away with him
Gal. 4;6 a. Abba, Father
Heb. 5;7 prayers with strong c.
Rev. 21;4 no more death, nor c.

CRYSTAL.
Job 28;17 and c. cannot equal it
Ezek. 1;22 as color of terrible c.
21;11 light of city clear as c.
22;1 a pure river, clear as c.

CUBIT.
Deut. 3;11 after the c. of a man
Ezek. 43;13 the c. is a c.
Mat. 6;27 one c. to stat. Lu. 12;25

CUBITS.
Gen. 6;15 length of the ark 300 c.
1 K. 6;2 length of the house 60 c.
2 K. 14;13 brake wall of Jerusalem 400 c.
Neh. 3;13 door was of 2 Chr. 25;6
Est. 5;14 gallows 50 c. high, 7;9
Ezek. 40;23 gate to gate 100 c.
45;17 the settle fourteen c.

CUR

Dan. 3;1 height of image 60 c.
John 21;8 were from land, 200 c.
Rev. 21;17 wall of city 144 c.

CUCKOO.
Lev. 11;16 c. ab. Deut. 14;15

CUCUMBERS.
Num. 11;5 we remember the c.
Is. 1;8 as lodge in garden of c.
CUD. See CHEW and CHEWETH.

CUMBERED, ETH.
Luke 10;40 c. about much serv.
13;7 why c. it the ground ?

CUMBRANCE.
Deut. 1;12 I alone bear your c. ?

CUMMIN.
Is. 28;25 doth he not scatter c.
27 on c. but c. is beaten
Mat. 23;23 ye pay tithe of c.

CUNNING.
Gen. 25;27 Esau was a c. hunter
Ex. 31;4 to devise c. works
Ezra. 16;18 son of J. c. in play.
1 Chr. 25;7 c. in songs, were 288
2 Chr. 2;13 I sent a c. man of H.
Ps. 137;5 right hand forget I c.
Cant. 7;1 work of a c. workman
Is. 3;3 take away c. artificer
40;20 he seeketh a c. workman
Jer. 9;17 send for c. women
10;9 all the work of c. men
Dan. 1;4 children c. in knowl.
Eph. 4;14 car. by c. craftiness

CUNNINGLY.
2 Pet. 1;16 c. devised fables

CUP.

Gen. 40;11 Phar.'s c. in my hand
41;2 silver c. in sack's mouth
2 Sam. 12;3 drank of his own c.
Ps. 11;6 he portion of their c.
16;5 L. is the portion of my c.
23;5 my c. runneth over
75;10 waters of a full c. wrung
"558 in hand of Lord is a c.
116;13 I will take c. of salvation
Prov. 23;31 giveth his color in c.
Is. 51;17 hast drunk the c. the
dregs of the c. of trembling
22 taken out of thy hand c. of
Jer. 16;7 give c. of consolation
25;15 take wine c. of this fury
17 took I c. at Lord's hand
28 they refuse c. at thy hand
49;12 judgment not to drink c.
51;7 Babylon be a golden c.
Lam. 4;21 c. also pass through t.
Ezek. 23;31 her c. into thy hand
32 drink of thy sister's c. deep
Hab. 2;16 c. of L. right hand
Zec. 12;2 Jerus. c. of trembling
Mat. 10;42 c. of c. wat. Mark 9;41
20;23 to drink c. Mark 10;38
23 indeed of my c. Mark 10;39
25;35 make clean outside of c.
26 cleanse first that within c.
26;27 he took the c. gave thanks,
Mark 14;23 ; Luke 22;17, 20;
1 Cor. 11;25.
39 let this c. pass from me,
Mark 14;36 ; Luke 22;42
42 if c. may not pass from me
Luke 22;20 this c. is new testament in my bl. 1 Cor. 11;25
John 18;11 c. Father hath given
1 Cor. 10;16 c. of blessing
21 cannot drink c. of L. and c.
11;25 as often as ye drink of c.
27 drink c. of Lord unworthily
Rev. 14;10 without mixt. into c.
16;19 to her c. of his wrath
17;4 woman having golden c.
18;6 fill to her double
Jer. 15;10 every one doth c. me
Mat. 2;3 I will c. your blessings
Mt. 5;11 M. th. that c. Lu. 6;28
Jam. 4;9 laugh, be turned to m.

CUP-BEARER.
Neh. 1;11 I was the king's c.-b.

CUP-BEARERS.
1 K. 10;5 saw c.-b. 2 Chr. 9;4

CUPS.
1 Chr. 28;17 pure gold for the c.
Is. 22;24 hang of the vessels of c.
Jer. 35;5 Rechabites took aw. c.
Mark 7;4 as washing of c. 8

CURDLED.
Job 10;10 c. me like cheese ?

CURE, Substantive.
Jer. 33;6 I will bring it c.

CURE, ED.
Jer. 33;6 I will c. them, and
Hos. 5;13 could he not c. you
Mat. 17;16 disciples, not c. him
18 child c. very hour
Luke 7;21 same hour he c. many
9;1 gave power to c. diseases
John 5;10 Jesus said to the c.

CUR

CURES.
Luke 13;22 I do c. to-day

CURIOUS, LV.
Ex. 21;8 c. girdle, 27, 28; 29;5;
39;5; Lev. 8;7
35;32 and to devise c. works
Ps. 139;15 c. wrought in lowest
Acts 19;19 that used c. arts

CURRENT.
Gen. 23;16 c. money with mer.

CURSE, Substantive.
Gen. 27;12 bring c. on me
Num. 5;18 bitter water that causeth the c. 19, 22, 24, 27
27 woman be c. am. h. peo.
Deut. 11;26 a bless. and c. 30;1
28 a c. if ye will not obey
29 and put the c. upon Ebal
23;5 c. into blessing, Neh. 13;2
27;13 this c. of this c.
Jos. 6;26 c. wrought in Israel is c.
Jud. 9;57 came c. of Jotham
2 K. 2;8 with a grievous c.
2 K. 22;19 should become a c.
Neh. 10;29 they entered into a c.
Job 31;30 wishing c. to his soul
Prov. 3;33 c. of L. in ho. of wic.
26;2 so c. causeless not come
27;14 he counted a c. to him
28;7 hid. eyes have many a c.
Is. 34;5 therefore c. dev. earth
34;5 down on people of my c.
43;28 given Jacob to the c.
63;15 leave your name for a c.
Jer. 24;9 delivered to be a c.
25;18; 26;6; 44;12; 49;13
26;6 this city a c. to all nations
41;22 therefore is your land a c.
42;18 Dozrah shall become a c.
Lam. 3;65 give thy c. unto them
Dan. 9;11 the c. is poured upon
Zec. 5;3 this is c. that goeth
8;13 ye were c. among heathen
Mat. 2;2 I will send c.
14;7 lest I smite earth with a c.
Acts 23;12 bound under a c. 14
Gal. 3;10 of law, are under c.
13 redeemed us from c. of law
Rev. 22;3 shall be no more c.

CURSE, verb.
Gen. 8;21 I will not c. ground
12;3 will c. him curseth thee
Ex. 22;28 nor c. ruler of thy peo.
Lev. 19;14 shalt not c. the deaf
Num. 22;6 c. me this people, 17
11 now c. me them, 23;7, 13
12 God said, Thou shalt not c.
22;10 I took thee to c. enem. 24;10
17 called c. of all, nor bless
Deut. 23;4 Bal. to c. Neh. 13;2
27;13 shall stand on Ebal to c.
Jos. 24;9 B. called Bal. to c. you
Jud. 5;23 c. Meroz, said angel, c.
2 Sam. 16;9 dead dog c. king ?
10 let him c. L. hath said, c. 11
Job 1;11 c. thee to thy face, 2;5
2;9 said his wife, c. God and die
3;8 let them c. it that c. day
5;7 6;24 but I day, c. inwardly
102;28 let them c. but bless thou
Prov. 11;26 people shall c. him
21;24 him shall the people c.
10;20 c. not king, c. not the rich
Ec. 7;21 c. thy king, and God
Ec. 10;20 c. nor king, c. not the rich
Jer. 15;10 every one doth c. me
Mat. 2;3 I will c. your blessings
Mt. 5;44 M. th. that c. Lu. 6;28
Jam. 4;9 laugh, be turned to m.

CURSED.
Gen. 3;14 serpent c. ; 17 ground
4;11 Cain c. ; 9;25 c. be Canaan
5;29 bec. of ground Lord hath c.
12;3 c. that curseth, Num. 24;9
27;29 c. be he that c. th. Num. 24;9
Lev. 24;9 hath c. his father c.
24;11 t. m of Israelitish woman's son c.
Num. 22;6 whom thou cursest c.
Deut. 27;15 c. be he in city, c. in field
18 c. be the fruit of thy body
19 c. when comest to land, so Jericho
21;23 ye Gibeonites are c.
Jud. 4;9, 27 and c. Abimelech
21;18 c. giveth a wife to Benj.
1 Sam. 14;24 that eateth
15;25 God rid c. David

CUS

1 *Sam.* 26:19 if men, *c.* be they
2 *Sam.* 16:5 Shimei *c.* still, 7, 13
19:21 he *c.* Lord's anointed
1 *K.* 2:8 *c.* me with grievous *c.*
2 *K.* 2:24 *c.* them in name of Lord
9:34 go see now this *c.* woman
Neh. 13:25 I *c.* them
Job 1:5 it may be my sons *c.* G,
3:1 then Job *c.* his day
5:3 suddenly I *c.* his habitation
24:18 portion is *c.* in the earth
Ps. 37:22 *c.* of him shall be cut
119:21 rebuked proud that are *c.*
Ec. 7:22 likewise hast *c.* others
Jer. 11:3 *c.* obeyeth not covenant
17:5 *c.* man that trust. in man
20:14 *c.* be the day I was born
15 *c.* man brought tid. to father
48:10 *c.* doeth Lord's work dec.
c. keepeth back sword
Mal. 1:14 but *c.* be the deceiver
2:2 *c.* your blessings already
3:9 ye are *c.* with a curse for
Mat. 25:41 depart from me ye *c.*
John 7:49 know not law are *c.*
Gal. 3:10 *c.* that continueth not
13 *c.* every one hang, on a tree
2 *Pet.* 2:14 *c.* children, who have
CURSED thing.
Deut. 7:26 lest thou be a *c. thing*,
for it is a *c. thing*.
13:17 cleave naught of *c. thing*
CURSEDST.
Jud. 17:2 silver about which *c.*
Mark 11:21 fig-tree thou *c.* is
CURSES.
Num. 5:23 priest write these *c.*
Deut. 28:15 th. *c.* shall come, 45
29:20 all the *c.* written in this
book, 27; 2 *Chr.* 34:24
21 accord. to all the *c.* of cov.
30:7 put these *c.* on enemies
CURSETH.
Ex. 21:17 he that *c.* his father,
Lev. 20:9; *Prov.* 20:20
Lev. 24:15 whoso *c.* his God
Prov. 30:11 genera. *c.* their father
Mat. 15:4 *c.* his father or mother,
let him die, *Mark* 7:10
CURSING.
Ex. 21:21 charge with oath of *c.*
Deut. 24:20 shall send on thee *c.*
3 x 10 before you blessing and *c.*
2 *Sam.* 16:12 good for his *c.*
Ps. 10:7 full of *c. Rom.* 3:14
59:12 *c.* and lying they speak
109:17 loved *c.* so let it come
18 he clothed himself with *c.*
Prov. 29:24 hear *c.* bewrayeth not
Heb. 6:8 thorns, is nigh to *c.*
Jam. 3:10 out of same mouth *c.*
CURSINGS.
Jos. 8:34 road blessings and *c.*
CURTAIN.
Ps. 104:2 stretchest out the heavens like a *c. Is.* 40:22
CURTAINS.
Ex. 26:1 with ten *c.* 2; 36:9
Num. 4:25 Gershonites bear *c.*
2 *Sam.* 7:2 within *c.* 1 *Chr.* 17:1
Cant. 1:5 comely as *c.* of Solom.
Is. 54:2 stretch forth the *c.*
Jer. 4:20 my *c.* spoiled in a mom.
10:20 none to set up my *c.*
49:29 shall take their *c.*
Hab. 3:7 *c.* of Midian did tremble
CUSH.
Gen. 10:6 Ham, C, 7; 1 *Ch.* 1:8, 9
Is. 11:11 remnant left from C.
CUSHAN. *Hab.* 3:7
CUSHI.
2 *Sam.* 18:21 C. tell the king, 23
Jer. 36:14 princes sent son of C.
Zep. 1:1 Zephaniah, son of C.
CUSTODY.
Num. 3:36 *c.* of sons of Merari
Est. 2:3 virgins to *c.* of Hege, 8
14 to *c.* of Shaashgaz
CUSTOM.
Gen. 31:35 *c.* of women is on me
Jud. 11:39 was a *c.* in Israel
1 *Sam.* 2:13 the priest's *c.* was
Ezr. 3:4 accord. to *c. Jer.* 32:11
4:13 then will they not pay *c.*
20 and *c.* was paid to them
7:24 not impose *c.* on priests
Mat. 9:9 saw Matthew at receipt
of *c. Mark* 2:14; *Luke* 5:27
17:25 whom do kings take *c.?*
Luke 1:9 ac. to *c.* of priest's office
2:27 do for him after *c.* of law
42 Jerusalem after *c.* of feast

CUT

Luke 4:16 as J. *c.* was, he went
John 18:39 *c.* I should release one
Rom. 13:7 *c.* to whom *c.* is due
1 *Cor.* 11:16 we have no such *c.*

CUSTOMS.
Lev. 18:30 these abominable *c.*
Jer. 10:3 *c.* of this people
Acts 6:14 shall change *c.* of M.
16:21 *c.* not lawful to receive
21:21 ought not to walk after *c.*
26:3 thee to be expert in all *c.*
28:17 I com. nothing against *c.*

CUT, Participle.
Lev. 22:24 not offer what is *c.*
Ezek. 16:4 thy navel was not *c.*
Acts 5:33 *c.* to the heart, 7:54

CUT, Verb.
Deut. 14:1 shall not *c.* yourselves
Jud. 9:48 concubine, and *c.* her
1 K. 18:26 *c.* thems. after manner
2 *K.* 24:13 he *c.* all the vessels of
gold, 2 *Chr.* 28:24
1 *Chr.* 20:3 he *c.* peop, with saws
Ps. 58:7 let them be as a
107:16 *c.* bars of iron, *Is.* 45:2
Is. 51:9 art thou not it *c.* Rahab
Jer. 16:6 nor *c.* themselves
36:23 he *c.* roll with penknife
41:8 having *c.* themselves
47:5 how long wilt *c.* thyself
Dan. 2:5 ye will not shall be *c.*
3:29 speak ag. God shall be *c.*
Amos 9:1 *c.* them in the head
Zec. 12:3 bur. them with it be *c.*

CUT asunder.
Ps. 129:4 *c.* a. cords of wicked
Jer. 50:23 hammer of earth *c. a.*
Zec. 11:10 Beauty and *c.* it *a.*
14 I *c. asun.* mine other staff
Mat. 24:51 *c.* him *a. Luke* 12:46

CUT down.
Ex. 34:13 *c. down* their groves,
Deut. 7:5; 2 *K.* 18:4; 23:14
Num. 13:23 *c. down* a branch, 24
Deut. 20:19 tr. for meat not *c. d.*
Job 8:13 in greenness not *c. d.*
14:2 like a flower, and is *c. d.*
7 hope of a tree if it be *c. d.*
23:16 wicked *c. d.* out of time
20 our substance is not *c. d.*
Ps. 37:2 shall soon be *c. down*
80:16 branch is burnt. It is *c. d.*
90:6 in the even. it is *c. down*
Is. 9:10 sycamores are *c. down*
14:12 how art thou *c. d.* to gr.
22:25 the nail shall be *c. down*
Jer. 22:7 *c. d.* thy choice cedars
25:37 habitations *c. down*
48:2 shalt be *c. d.* O Madmen
Nah. 1:14 thus shall be *c. down*
Zep. 1:11 merch. people *c. down*
Mat. 21:8 *c. d.* bra. *Mark* 11:8
Luke 13:7 *c.* it *down*
9 thou shalt *c.* it *down*

CUT off.
Gen. 9:11 nor all flesh be *c. off*
Ex. 12:15 that soul be *c. off*, 19:
31:14; *Num.* 15:30; 19:13
23:23 and I will *c.* them *off*
30:33 he *c. off* from his people,
38; *Lev.* 7:20, 27; 17:4, 9;
19:8; 23:29; *Num.* 9:13
Lev. 17:10 will *c.* him *off*, 18:29;
20:3, 6, 18; *Num.* 15:31
14 cutteth blood shall be *c. off*
20:17 *c. off* in sight of people
Num. 4:18 *c.* not *off* tribe of K.
Deut. 12:29 G. shall *c. off* nations
19:1 God hath *c. off* nations
23:1 hath privy member *c. off*
25:12 *off* her hand pity not
Jos. 3:13 the waters of Jordan
shall be *c. off*, 14, 17
7:9 and shalt *c. off* our name
11:21 Joshua *c. off* Anakim
Jud. 21:6 one tribe *c. off*
Ruth 4:10 dead be not *c. off*
1 *Sam.* 2:31 I will *c. off* thy arm
33 man whom I shall not *c. off*
17:51 David *c. off* Goliath's head
20:15 not *c. off* thy kind. ; 24:21
24:4 David *c. off* the skirt of S.
28:9 how Saul *c. off* wizards
31:9 and they *c. off* Saul's head
2 *Sam.* 4:12 and *c. off* their hands
10:4 II. *c. off* their garments in
the middle, 1 *Chr.* 19:4
20:22 *c. off* the head of Sheba
1 *K.* 9:7 will I *c. off* Is. out of
11:16 *c. off* every male in Edom
14:10 *c. off* from Jeroboam him
18:4 Jezebel *c. off* prophets

CUT

1 *K.* 21:21 *c. off* from Ahab him
that pisseth, 2 *K.* 9:8
1 *Chr.* 17:8 *c. off* all thine enem.
2 *Chr.* 22:7 *c. off* house of Ahab
32:21 angel *c. off* mighty men
Job 4:7 where were right. *c. off?*
6:9 loose his hand, and *c.* me *off*
8:14 whose hope shall be *c. off*
11:10 if he *c. off* who can hinder
18:16 above, his branch be *c. off*
22:16 which were *c. off* out of
24:24 *c. off* as tops of ears of c.
36:20 people *c. off* in their place
Ps. 12:3 *c. off* flattering lips
31:22 *c. off* from bef. thine eyes
34:16 to *c. off* remem. of them
37:9 evil-doers shall be *c. off*
22 they cursed of him be *c. off*
28 seed of wicked sh. be *c. off*
34 wicked are *c. off* shalt see it
38 end of wicked shall be *c. off*
54:5 *c.* them *off* in thy truth
75:10 horns of wick. will I *c. off*
76:12 *c. off* spirit of princes
83:4 said, let us *c.* them *off*
88:5 are *c. off* from thy hand
16 terrors have *c.* me *off*
94:23 *c.* them *off* in their wick.
101:5 slandereth will I *c. off*
8 *c. off* wicked doers from city
103:15 let his posterity be *c. off*
15 Lord may *c. off* memory
143:12 *c. off* enemies
Prov. 2:22 wicked shall be *c. off*
23:18 expect. not be *c. off*, 24:14
Is. 9:14 will *c. off* head and tail
10:7 to *c. off* nations not a few
11:13 adversary of Jud. be *c. off*
14:22 *c. off* from Babylon
15:2 every beard *c. off*
20:2 watch for iniquity *c. off*
38:12 *c.* me *off* with pining
48:9 that I *c.* thee not *off*
19 should not be *c. off*
53:8 he was *c. off* out of land
55:13 that shall not be *c. off*
56:5 as if 'twere a *c. off* a dog's neck
Jer. 7:28 truth is *c. off* fr. mouth
9:21 to *c. off* children fr. without
11:19 let us *c.* him *off* from land
44:7 *c. off* man and woman
11 to *c. off* all Judah
47:4 to *c. off* from Tyrus
5 Ashkelon is *c. off*
48:2 *c.* it *off* from being a nation
25 the horn of Moab is *c. off*
48:26 men of war shall be *c. off*
50:16 *c. off* sower from Babylon
51:6 be not *c. off* in her iniquity
62 this place, to *c.* it *off*
Lam. 3:53 *c. off* my life
Ezek. 14:8 *c.* him *off* from people
13 *c. off* man and beast, 17, 19,
21; 25:13; 26:8
17:9 not *c. off* fruit thereof
17 forts to *c. off* many persons
21:3 *c. off* right. and wicked, 4
23:7 I will *c.* thee *off* from peo.
16 I will *c. off* Cherethim
30:15 *c. off* multitude of No
31:12 ter. of nations *c.* him *off*
35:7 I will *c. off* from Seir him
37:11 we are *c. off* for our parts
Dan. 4:14 *c. off* his branches
9:26 Messiah shall be *c. off*
Hos. 8:4 that they may be *c. off*
10:7 king is *c. off* as foam, 15
Joel 1:5 the new wine is *c. off*, 9
16 meat *c. off* before our eyes?
Amos 1:5 *c. off* inhabitant, 8
2:3 I will *c. off* judge from midst
3:14 horns of altar shall be *c. off*
Ob. 5 how art thou *c. off?*
9 every one of E. may be *c. off*
10 shalt be *c. off* for ever
14 to *c. off* those did escape
Mic. 5:9 I will *c. off* thy horses
10 horses ; 12 witchcrafts
11 *c. off* cities ; *c. off* sooth.
Nah. 1:15 wicked is utterly *c. off*
2:13 *c. off* thy prey from earth
3:15 the sword shall *c.* thee *off*
Hab. 3:17 tho' the flock be *c. off*
Zep. 1:3 *c. off* man from off land
4 *c. off* a remnant of Baal
11 that bear silver *c. off*
3:6 I have *c. off* the nations
7 so dwellings sh. not be *c. off*
Zec. 9:6 *c. off* pride of Philistines
9:6 *c. off* pride of Philistines
10 *c. off* chariot from Ephraim
11:8 three shepherds also I *c. off*
9 to be *c. off*, let it be *c. off*
13:2 I will *c. off* names of idols
8 two parts shall be *c. off*
14:2 residue shall not be *c. off*

DAM

Mal. 2:12 Lord will *c. off* man
Mat. 5:30 if right hand offend *c.*
It *off*, 18:8; *Mark* 9:43, 45
Mark 14:47 *c.* *off* his ear, *Luke* 22:50; *John* 18:10, 26
Rom. 11:22 shalt be *c. off*
1 *Cor.* 11:12 I may *c. off* occasion
Gal. 5:12 I would they were *c. off*

CUT out.
Prov. 10:31 fro. tongue be *c. out*
Dan. 2:34 a stone was *c. out*, 45
Rom. 11:24 *c. out* of olive tree

CUT short.
2 *K.* 10:32 began to *c.* Israel *sh.*
Rom. 9:28 *c.* it *short* in righ.

CUT up.
Job 30:4 who *c. up* mallows
Is. 33:12 as thorns *c. up* shall

CUTTEST, ETH.
Deut. 24:19 when thou *c.* harvest
Job 28:10 he *c.* out rivers
Ps. 46:9 he *c.* the spear in sunder
141:7 as when one *c.* wood
Prov. 26:6 mess, by fool, *c.* off
Jer. 10:3 for one *c.* a tree out of
22:14 and *c.* him out windows

CUTTING.
Ex. 31:5 in *c.* of stones, 35:33
Is. 38:10 I said in *c. off* of days
Hab. 2:10 by *c. off* many people
Mark 5:5 *c.* himself with stones

CUTTINGS.
Lev. 19:28 not make any *c.* 21:5
Jer. 48:37 upon all hands be *c.*

CYMBAL.
1 *Cor.* 13:1 I am as tinkling *c.*

CYMBALS.
2 *Sam.* 6:5 play. one *c.* 1 *Chr.* 13:8
1 *Chr.* 15:16 harps and *c.* 16:42
16:5 Asaph made sound with *c.*
25:6 there were for song with *c.*
2 *Chr.* 5:13 lift up voice with *c.*
29:25 Levites in house with *c.*
Ezr. 3:10 sons of Asaph with *c.*
Ps. 150:5 upon high sounding *c.*

CYPRESS.
Is. 44:14 he taketh the *c.*

CYPRUS.
Acts 4:36 country of C. 11:20
13:4 from Seleucia sailed to C.
15:39 Mark, and sailed to C.
27:4 we sailed under C.

CYRENE.
Mat. 27:32 found a man of C.
Acts 2:10 parts of Libya about C.
11:20 men of Cyprus and C.
13:1 Lucius of C. was in church

CYRENIAN. *Mark* 15:21
CYRENIANS. *Acts* 6:9
CYRENIUS. *Luke* 2:2

CYRUS.
2 *Chr.* 36:22 the first year of C.
Ezr. 1:7 ; 3:7 ; 4:3 ; 5:13
3; 4:28 that saith of C. 45:1
6:28 Dan. prosp. in reign of C.
10:1 in the third year of C.

D.

DABBASHETH. *Jos.* 19:11
DABERATH. *Jos.* 19:12 ; 1 *Ch.* 6:72

DAGGER.
Jud. 3:16 Ehud made him a *d.*
21 took *d.* from right thigh, 22

DAGON. *Jud.* 16:23 ; 1 *Sam.*
5:2, 3, 7 ; 1 *Chr.* 10:10

DAILY. See after DAYS.

DAINTY, IES.
Gen. 49:20 Asher yield royal *d.*
Job 33:20 abhorreth *d.* meat
Ps. 141:4 let me not eat of *d.*
Prov. 23:3 be not desirous of *d.*
6 neither desire his *d.* meats
Rev. 18:14 *d.* are departed

DALE.
Gen. 14:17 valley of S. king's *d.*
2 *Sam.* 18:18 a pillar in king's *d.*

DALMATIA. 2 *Tim.* 4:10
DALMANUTHA. *Mark* 8:10

DAM.
Ex. 22:30 seven days with *d.*
Deut. 22:6 not take *d.* with you.

DAMAGE.
Ezr. 4:22 why should *d.* grow
Est. 7:4 not count. king's *d.*
Prov. 26:6 and drinketh *d.*
Dan. 6:2 should have no *d.*

DAR

DAMARIS.
Acts 27:10 voy. will be with *d*.
2 Cor. 7:9 *d*. by us in nothing
DAMARIS. Acts 17:34
DAMASCUS.
Gen. 15:2 Eliezer of D.
2 Sam. 8:6 put garrisons in D.
2 K. 5:12 Pharpar rivers of D.
8:7 E. came to D. 14:28; 16:9
Is. 7:8; 8:4; 10:9; 17:1, 3
Ezek. 27:18; Amos 1:3; 3:12; 5:27
Acts 9:2 desired letters to D. 10,
  19, 22, 27; 22:6, 10; 26:12
2 Cor. 11:32 in D. the gov. desir.
Gal. 1:17 I returned again to D.
DAMNABLE.
2 Pet. 2:1 who bring in *d*. heres.
DAMNATION.
Mat. 23:14 shall receive greater
  d. Mark 12:40; Luke 20:47
33 can ye escape *d*. of hell
Mark 3:29 in danger of eternal *d*.
John 5:29 to the resurrection of *d*.
Rom. 3:8 whose *d*. is just
13:2 receive to themselves *d*.
1 Cor. 11:29 eateth and drink. *d*.
1 Tim. 5:12 having *d*. because
2 Pet. 2:3 their *d*. slumbereth not
DAMNED.
Mark 16:16 believeth not be *d*.
Rom. 14:23 doubteth is *d*.
2 Thes. 2:12 *d*. who believed not
DAMSEL.
Gen. 24:55 said, Let the *d*. abide
34:3 he loved *d*. spake kindly, 12
Deut. 22:15 tokens of *d*. virginity
21 bring out *d*. and stone her
Jud. 5:30 to ev. man a *d*. or two?
19:4 the *d*. father retained him
Ruth 2:6 It is the Moabitish *d*.
1 K. 1:4 and the *d*. cherished h.
Mat. 14:11 given to *d*. Mark 6:28
26:69 *d*. came to P. John 18:17
Mark 5:39 *d*. is not dead, but
  40 he entereth in where *d*. was
Acts 12:13 n *d*. came to hearken
16:16 *d*. possessed met us
DAMSELS.
Gen. 24:61 Rebekah arose and *d*.
1 Sam. 25:42 Abigail rode with *d*.
Ps. 68:25 among them *d*. playing
DAN, a person
Gen. 30:6; 35:25; 49:16, 17
Deut. 33:22 of D. he said, D. is a
Jud. 5:17 why did D. remain?
DAN, a place.
Gen. 14:14 pursued them unto D.
Deut. 34:1 Moses all Gil. unto D.
Tribe of DAN.
Num. 1:38 num. of D. 13:12; 34:22
Jos. 19:40 came out for D. 21:5
Jud. 18:30 priests to D. till cap.
DANCE, Sub.-tantive.
Ps. 130:3 praise him in *d*. 150:4
Jer. 31:13 virgin rejoice in the *d*.
Lam. 5:15 our *d*. is turned into.
DANCE, Verb.
Jud. 21:21 if dau. of S. come to *d*.
Job 21:11 their children *d*.
Ec. 3:4 and a time to *d*.
Is. 13:21 satyrs shall *d*. there
DANCED.
Jud. 21:23 number that *d*.
2 Sam. 6:14 David *d*. bef. Lord
Mat. 11:17 have not *d*. Luke 7:32
14:6 dau. of Herod. *d*. Mark 6:22
DANCES.
Jud. 11:34 daught. came with *d*.
1 Sam. 21:11 sing of h. in *d*. 29:5
Jer. 31:4 shalt go forth in the *d*.
DANCING.
Ex. 32:19 he saw calf and *d*.
1 Sam. 18:6 women came out *d*.
29:16 spread on all the earth *d*.
2 Sam. 6:16 Dav. *d*. 1 Chr. 15:29
Ps. 30:11 my mourning into *d*.
Luke 15:25 as he came heard *d*.
DANDLED.
Is. 66:12 be *d*. upon her knees
DANGER.
Mat. 5:21 in *d*. of judgment, 22
22 in *d*. of council, of hell-fire
Mark 3:29 in *d*. of eternal dam.
Acts 19:27 not only craft is in *d*.
40 *d*. to be called in question
DANGEROUS.
Acts 27:9 sailing was now *d*.
DANIEL.
Ezek. 14:14 though Noah, D. and
Mat. 24:15 spo. by D. Mark 13:14
DARE.
Job 41:10 none *d*. stir him up

DAR

Rom. 5:7 would even *d*. to die
13:18 *d*. to speak of anything
1 Cor. 6:1 *d*. any of you go to l.
2 Cor. 10:12 *d*. not make ourselv.
DARIUS.
Ezr. 4:5; 5:5; 6:1, 15; Neh. 12:22
Dan. 5:31; 6:9, 25; 9:1
Zec. 7:1 in fourth year of D.
DARK.
Gen. 15:17 when it was *d*.
Lev. 13:6 plague be *d*. 21, 56
Num. 12:8 speak not in *d*. sp.
Jos. 2:5 when *d*. men went out
2 Sam. 22:12 *d*. waters, Ps. 18:11
Neh. 13:19 gates began to be *d*.
Job 3:9 let stars of twilight be *d*.
12:25 they grope in the *d*.
18:6 light be *d*. in his tabernac.
22:13 judge through *d*. cloud?
24:16 in *d*. they dig thro' houses
Ps. 35:6 let their way be *d*.
49:4 open *d*. saying on harp
74:20 *d*. places full of cruelty
78:2 utter *d*. sayings of old
88:12 wonders be known in *d*.?
105:28 sent darkness, made it *d*.
Prov. 7:8 and their *d*. sayings
7:9 in the black and *d*. night
Is. 29:15 their works are in the *d*.
  45:19 not spoken in a *d*. place
Jer. 13:16 feet stumble on *d*. m.
Lam. 3:6 set me in *d*. places
Ezek. 8:12 house of Israel do in *d*.
32:7 make stars thereof *d*.
8 bright lights of heaven *d*.
34:12 in cloudy and *d*. day
Dan. 8:23 understand. *d*. senten.
Joel 2:10 sun and moon be *d*.
Amos 5:8 maketh the day *d*. 20
Mic. 3:6 *d*. to you, day shall be *d*.
Zec. 1:8 light not clear nor *d*.
  14:6 light shall be nor part *d*.
John 6:17 and it was now *d*.
20:1 Mary came when yet *d*.
2 Pet. 1:19 shineth in a *d*. place
DARKEN.
Amos 8:9 *d*. earth in clear day
DARKENED.
Ex. 10:15 so that land was *d*.
Ec. 12:2 moon or stars be not *d*.
3 look out of windows be *d*.
Is. 5:30 light in heav. is *d*.
Is. 13:10 sun, Joel 3:15
Is. 24:11 all joy is *d*. mirth gone
Ezek. 30:18 at Tehaph. day be *d*.
Zec. 11:17 right eye be utterly *d*.
Mat. 24:29 sun be *d*. Mark 13:24
Luke 23:45 and the sun was *d*.
Rom. 1:21 foolish heart was *d*.
Eph. 4:18 the understanding *d*.
Rev. 8:12 so as third part was *d*.
  9:2 sun and the air were *d*.
DARKENETH.
Job 38:2 who is this *d*. counsel
DARKLY.
1 Cor. 13:12 we see thro' a glass *d*.
DARKNESS.
Gen. 1:2 *d*. was upon the deep
5 the *d*. he called Night
18 to divide the light from *d*.
15:12 horror of *d*. fell on Abram
Ex. 10:22 *d*. in all Egypt
  11:20 *d*. to thee, but light
20:21 Moses drew near to *d*.
Deut. 4:11 mount. burnt with *d*.
5:22 words Lord spake out of *d*.
2 Sam. 22:10 foot, and *d*. was
22:29 enlighten my *d*. Ps. 18:28
Job 3:5 let *d*. stain it
  6 for that night, let *d*. seize it
4 meet with *d*. in daytime
10:21 a land of *d*. and *d*. itself
10:4 hath set *d*. in my paths
20:26 all *d*. be hid
22:11 or *d*. that canst not see
23:17 not cut off before *d*. neith.
  hath he covered the *d*.
28:3 an end to *d*. stones of *d*.
31:28 no *d*. where my hide
37:19 not in order speech for *d*.
20 I desired a swallowing-flood
19 as God *d*. whose is the place
Ps. 18:11 *d*. his secret place
  18 made nepanist, him *d*.
97:2 clouds and *d*. about him
104:20 makest *d*. and it is night
105:28 sent *d*. made it dark
112:4 surely *d*. shall cover me
  d. hideth not from thee
Prov. 2:13 to walk in ways of *d*.
4:19 way of the wicked is as *d*.
Ec. 5:4 name be covered with *d*.

DAR

Is. 5:30 look to land, behold *d*.
8:22 shall look, and behold *d*.
45:3 give thee treasures of *d*.
47:5 get thee into *d*. O daughter
60:2 *d*. shall cover the earth, and
  gross *d*. the people
Jer. 13:16 before he cause *d*. and
  make light gross *d*.
Ezek. 32:6 sei *d*. upon thy land
34:12 a day of clouds and *d*.
31 sun be turned to *d*. Acts 2:20
Amos 4:13 maketh morning *d*.
Nah. 1:8 *d*. pursue his enemies
Mat. 6:23 full of *d*. Luke 11:34
8:12 outer *d*. 22:13; 25:30
27:45 sixth hour *d*. Mark 15:33
Acts 13:11 on him mist and *d*.
Eph. 5:11 with works of *d*.
6:12 rulers of *d*. of this world
Col. 1:13 from power of *d*.
1 Thes. 5:5 not of night nor of *d*.
Heb. 12:18 are not come to *d*.
2 Pet. 2:4 deliv. into chains of *d*.
  17 mist of *d*. is reserved
1 John 3:11 *d*. hath blinded
Jude 6 everlast. chains under *d*.
13 is reserved blackness of *d*.
Rev. 16:10 kingd. was full of *d*.

DARKNESS, with day.
Job 3:1 let that day be *d*.
15:23 that day of *d*. is at hand
Ec. 11:8 remember days of *d*.
Is. 58:10 thy *d*. be as noon-day
Joel 2:2 a day of *d*. Zep. 1:15
Amos 5:20 day of Lord be *d*.?

In DARKNESS.
Deut. 28:29 grope as blind at *d*.
1 Sam. 2:9 wicked be silent in *d*.
1 K. 8:12 L. said he would dwell
  in *d*. 2 Chr. 6:1
Job 17:13 made my bed in *d*.
Ps. 82:5 they walk on in *d*.
  88:6 laid me in *d*. in deeps
91:6 pestilence that walketh i. *d*.
107:10 such as sit in *d*.
143:3 made me dwell in *d*.
Prov. 20:20 out in obscure *d*.
Ec. 2:11 fool walketh in *d*.
5:17 eateth in *d*. departeth in *d*.
Is. 42:7 sit in *d*. out of prison
  49:9 to them in *d*. show yoursel.
50:9 light, but we walk in *d*.
Ec. 2:22 knoweth walk in in *d*.
10:35 walketh in *d*. know. not
46 shall not abide in *d*.
1 Thes. 5:4 but ye are not in *d*.
1 John 1:5 and walk in *d*. we lie
2:9 hateth brother, is in *d*. 11

Land of DARKNESS.
Job 10:21 bef. I go to land of *d*.
22 land of *d*. as *d*. itself.
Jer. 2:31 been to Israel *l*. of *d*.

DARKNESS, with light.
Gen. 1:4 G. divided light from *d*.
18 to divide light from *d*.
Job 10:22 where light is as *d*.
12:22 light in short because of *d*.
18:18 driven from light into *d*.
30 by his light I walk, thro' *d*.
Ps. 112:4 ariseth light in *d*.
139:12 *d*. and *l*. are both alike
Ec. 2:13 as light excelleth *d*.
14 no fool. that walk. in *d*.
Is. 5:20 put *d*. for l. and light
42:16 make *d*. light before them
45:7 I form light and create *d*.
50:10 walketh in *d*. hath no *l*.
59:9 we look for *l*. be make it *d*.
Jer. 13:16 look for *l*. he turn. it *d*.
Amos 5:18 day is *d*. not light
Mic. 7:8 I sit in *d*. L. be a light
John 1:5 *l*. sh. in *d*. *d*. comp. not
3:19 men love *d*. rather than *l*.
8:12 walk *d*. have *l*. of life
12:35 while ye have *l*. lest *d*.
46 I come *l*. abide not in *d*.
Acts 26:18 turn from *d*. to light
2 Cor. 4:6 light to shine out of *d*.
  6:14 comm. hath light with *d*.
1 Pet. 2:9 out of *d*. into mary. *l*.
1 John 1:5 in him is no *d*. at all
2:8 *d*. is passed true *l*. shineth

Out of DARKNESS.
Deut. 5:23 heard voice out of *d*.
Job 12:22 deep things out of *d*.

DAU

Job 13:22 he shall return out of *d*.
30 shall not depart out of *d*.
Ps. 107:14 brought them out of *d*.
Is. 29:18 blind see out of *d*.

DARLING.
Ps. 22:20 *d*. from power of dog
35:17 rescue my *d*. from lions

DART, S.
2 Sam. 18:14 Joab took three *d*.
2 Chr. 32:5 Hezekiah made *d*.
Job 41:26 nor the *d*. cannot hold
Prov. 7:23 till *d*. strike thro' liver
Eph. 6:16 to quench fiery *d*. of
Heb. 12:20 thrust thro' with a *d*.

DASH.
2 K. 8:12 wilt *d*. their children
Ps. 2:9 *d*. in pieces like a pot.
91:12 lest thou *d*. foot against a
  stone, Mat. 4:6; Luke 4:11
Is. 13:18 shall *d*. young men
Jer. 13:14 will *d*. one ag. another

DASHED.
Ex. 15:6 thy right hand, O L. *d*.
Is. 13:16 child. be *d*. to pieces.
Jer. 13:14 *d*. Mark 3:10
Hos. 10:14 mo. was *d*. on child.

DASHETH.
Ps. 137:9 *d*. little ones ag. stones
DATHAN, *See* Abiram.

DAUD, ED, ING.
Ex. 2:3 she *d*. ark with either
Ezek. 13:10 *d*. it with untempered
22:28 her prophets *d*. them

DAUGHTER.
Gen. 20:12 *d*. of my father, not *d*.
24:23 whose *d*. art thou, 47
48 master's brother's *d*. to son
34:7 in lying with Jacob's *d*.
8 my son longeth for your *d*.
Ex. 1:16 if a *d*. she shall live
21:31 have gored a son or a *d*.
Lev. 12:6 days fulfilled for a *d*.
18:17 nor take her daughter's *d*.
21:9 if *d*. of priest profane
Num. 27:9 if no *d*. give his inh.
30:8 if. that passes, a *d*. to him.
Deut. 47:24 birth with *d*. of father
26:36 eye he evil toward her *d*.
Jud. 11:40 lament Jephthah's *d*.
1 Sam. 1:16 handmaid a *d*. of B.
18:19 Saul's *d*. should been giv.
2 Sam. 12:3 lamb unto him as a *d*.
1 K. 3:1 Solo. took Pharaoh's *d*.
11:1 many with *d*. of Pharaoh
2 K. 8:18 *d*. of Ahab; *d*. 19
1 Chr. 2:49 *d*. of Caleb Achsa.
Est. 2:7 uncle's *d*. for his own
Ps. 45:10 O *d*. and consider, and
13 king's *d*. glorious within
Cant. 7:1 shoes, O prince's *d*.
Jer. 31:22 backsliding *d*. 49:4
46:19 O *d*. in Egypt, furnish
48:18 *d*. dost inhabit Dibon
Ezek. 14:16 deliv. son nor *d*. 18, 20
16:44 as mother, so is her *d*.
Dan. 11:6 king's *d*. of south come
  17 shall give him *d*. of women
Hos. 1:6 conce. and bare a *d*.
Mic. 5:1 O *d*. of troops
7:6 *d*. riseth up ag. mother, Mat.
10:35; Luke 12:53
Zep. 3:10 *d*. of my dispersed
Mal. 2:11 mar. *d*. of strange god
Mat. 9:22 good comfort.
Mark 5:34; Luke 8:48
10:37 loveth *d*. more than me
14:6 *d*. of Herodias danced
15:28 her *d*. was made whole
Mark 7:26 cast out devil out of *d*.
15:40 Mary mother being a *d*.
Acts 7:21 Pharaoh's *d*. nourished
Heb. 11:24 *d*. of Pharaoh's *d*.

DAUGHTER of Babylon.
Ps. 137:8 O *d*. of B. to be destr.
Is. 47:1 O *d*. of B. on ground
Jer. 50:42 battle ag. thee *d*. of B.
51:33 *d*. of B. like a thre-floor
Zec. 2:7 deliver thyself *d*. of B.

DAUGHTER of the Chaldeans.
Is. 47:1 throne, O *d*. of Chal.
5 into darkness, *d*. of Chal.

DAUGHTER of Edom.
Lam. 4:21 be gl. *d*. of E.
22 thine iniquity, O *d*. of E.

DAUGHTER of Egypt.
Jer. 46:11 up into Gilead, O virg.
24 *d*. of Egypt be confounded

812 CRUDEN'S CONCORDANCE.

DAU

DAUGHTER of Gallim.
Is. 10:33 thy voice d. of Gallim

His DAUGHTER.
Ex. 21:7 sell his d. to be servant
Num. 27:8 to pass to his d.
30:16 statutes bet. fa. and his d.
Deut. 7:3 nor his d. take
18:10 his d. pass, 2 K. 23:10
Jud. 21:1 not give his d. to B.
1 Sam. 17:25 king give him his d.

DAUGHTER of Jerusalem.
2 K. 19:21 d. of J. hath shaken
her head at thee, Is. 37:22
Lam. 2:13 liken to thee, d. of J.
15 wag their head at d. of J.
Mic. 4:8 shall come to d. of J.
Zep. 3:14 rej. with heart, d. of J.
Zec. 9:9 d. of J. thy king cometh

DAUGHTER of Judah,
Lam. 1:15 hath trodden d. of J.
2:2 strong-holds of d. of J.
5 increased d. of J. mourning

DAUGHTER-IN-LAW.
Gen. 38:16 knew not she was d.-in-law
24 Tamar thy d.-in-law played
Lev. 18:15 naked. of thy d.-in-law
20:12 man lie with his d.-in-l.
Ruth 4:15 d.-in-l. which lov. thee
1 Sam. 4:19 d.-in-law with child
Ezek. 22:11 defileth his d.-in-l.
Mic. 7:6 d. aga. mother-in-law,
Mat. 10:35; Luke 12:53

My DAUGHTER.
Deut. 22:17 tokens of my d. virg.
Jos. 15:16 him will I give my d.
Jud. 11:35 my d. hast broh. me
19:24 here is my d. a maiden
Ruth 2:2 she said, Go my d.
3:10 blessed be thou my d.
Mat. 9:18 my d. is even now d.
15:22 my d. is vexed
Mark 5:34 my d. at point of d.

DAUGHTER of my people,
Jer. 22:4 spoiling of d. of p.
Jer. 4:11 wind toward d. of p.
6:14 healed d. of p. 8:11
26 O d. of my p. gird with sack.
8:19 the cry of d. of my p.
21 for hurt of d. of my p.
22 health of d. of p. recovered
9:1 weep for slain of d. of p.
7 shall I do for d. of my p.
14:17 virgin d. of p. is broken
Lam. 2:11 destr. of d. of p. 3:48
4:3 the d. of my p. is bec. cruel
6 iniquity of d. of my p.
10 in destruction of d. of my p.

DAUGHTER of Tarshish.
Is. 23:10 as river, d. of T.

Thy DAUGHTER.
Ex. 20:10 nor thy d. Deut. 5:14
Lev. 18:10 nakedness of thy d. d.
19:29 do not prostitute thy d.
Deut. 7:3 thy d. not give
13:6 if thy d. entice thee
22:17 found not thy d. a maid
2 K. 14:9 give thy d. to my son
Mark 5:35 t. d. is dead, Luke 8:49
7:29 devil is gone out of thy d.

DAUGHTER of Tyre.
Ps. 45:12 d. of T. be there

DAUGHTER of Zidon.
Is. 23:12 O oppressed d. of Z.

DAUGHTER of Zion.
2 K. 19:21 d. of Z. desp. Is. 37:22
Ps. 9:14 in gates of d. of Zion
Is. 1:8 d. of Z. left as a cottage
4:1 washed away filth of d. of Z.
10:32 mount of d. of Z. 16:1
52:2 thyself captive d. of Zion
62:11 d. of Zion thy sal. cometh
Jer. 4:31 voice of d. of Zion
6:2 d. of Z. to a comely woman
23 men of war ag. thee, d. of Z.
Lam. 1:6 d. of Zion beauty dep.
2:1 L. cover d. of Z. with cloud
4 tabernacle of d. of Zion
8 destroy wall of d. of Z.
10 elders of d. of Zion
13 equal to thee, d. of Z.
18 O wall of d. of Zion
4:22 accomplished d. of Z.
Mic. 1:13 sin to d. of Zion
4:8 strong-hold of d. of Zion
10 to bring forth, d. of Zion
13 arise and thresh, O d. of Z.
Zep. 3:14 sing, O d. of Zion
Zec. 2:10 rejoice, d. of Zion, 9:9
Mat. 21:5 d. of Zion king cometh
John 12:15 fear not d. of Zion

DAUGHTERS.
Gen. 6:2 sons of God saw d.

DAU

Gen. 19:36 both d. of Lot with c.
24:3 d. of Can. 37; 28:1, 6
13 d. came out to draw water
27:46 weary of life bec. of d.
30:13 d. will call me blessed
31:26 hast carried away my d.
43 d. my d., 50 if afflict my d.
34:1 Dinah went out to see d.
9 give your d. take our d.
Ex. 2:16 priest of Midian had 7 d.
21:9 deal after the manner of d.
34:16 d. go a whoring after gods
Lev. 26:29 flesh of d. shall ye eat
Num. 26:33 d. of Zeloph. Jos. 17:3
27:7 d. of Zeloph. speak right
36:10 so did d. of Zelophehad
Deut. 23:17 no whore of d. of Is.
28:53 took d. to be wives
41 not give them of our d. 18
Ruth 1:11 turn again my d. 13
1 Sam. 8:13 d. confectionaries
Neh. 5:5 our d. into bondage
7:63 one of d. of B. Ezr. 2:61
10:30 not give d. to p. of land
Job 42:15 none so fair as d. of J.
Ps. 45:9 king's d. am. hon. wom.
144:12 d. be corner-stones
Prov. 31:29 d. done virtuously
Ezek. 23:2 so is my love among d.
9:9 the d. saw and blessed her
Jer. 32:9 ye careless d. give ear
60:4 d. be nursed at thy side
Jer. 9:20 teach your d. wailing
16 call d. to mourning
49:4 her d. be burnt with fire
3 cry, ye d. of Rabbah, gird ye
Lam. 3:51 bec. of d. of my city
Ezek. 13:17 set face ag. d. of peo.
16:46 Samaria and her d. Sod.
49 idlen. was in her, and in d.
55 sister Sodom and d. return
61 give them unto thee for d.
23:2 two wom. d. of one mother
26:6 her d. be slain in field, 8
33:26 her d. go into captivity
34:16 d. of nations lament her
Hos. 4:13 d. shall commit whor.
14 I will not punish your d.
Luke 15:3 his wife of d. of Aaron
Acts 1:14 and four d. virgins
1 Pet. 3:6 whose d. ye are as long

DAUGHTERS of Israel.
Deut. 23:17 no whore of d. of I.
Jud. 11:40 d. of I. yearly to lam.
2 Sam. 1:24 d. of I. weep over S.

DAUGHTERS of Jerusalem.
Cant. 1:5 comely, O d. of J.
2:7 you d. of J. 3:5; 8:4
3:10 paved with love for d. of J.
5:16 my beloved, O d. of J.
Luke 23:28 d. of J. weep not

DAUGHTERS of Judah.
Ps. 48:11 let d. of Judah be glad
97:8 the d. of Judah rejoiced

DAUGHTERS-IN-LAW.
Ruth 1:8 Naomi said d.-in-law

DAUGHTERS of Moab.
Num. 25:1 whore. with d. of M.
Is. 16:2 d. be at fords of Arnon

DAUGHTERS of music.
Ec. 12:4 d. of m. be bro. low

DAUGHTERS of the Philistines.
2 Sam. 1:20 lest the d. of P. rej.
Ezek. 16:27 deliver thee to d. of P.
57 the d. of P. which despise

DAUGHTERS of Shiloh.
Jud. 21:21 if d. of Shiloh come

DAUGHTERS, joined with
Gen. 5:4 begat s. d. 7, 10; 11:11
19:12 thy sons and d. bring out
31:28 not suff. to kiss s. and d.
55 kissed his sons and d.
37:35 sons d. rose to comfort
Ex. 10:9 with s. and d. will we
21:4 have horne him sons or d.
34:16 take of their d. to thy s.
Num. 21:29 sons d. into captiv.
Deut. 12:12 and s. and d. rejoice
31 sons and d. they have burnt,
2 K. 17:17; Jer. 7:31; 32:35
28:32 s. d. given to another peo.
32:19 provoking of his s. and d.
Jos. 7:24 brought Ach. s. and d.
17:6 d. of Manasseh inh. am. s.
Jud. 3:6 gave their d. to their s.
12:9 Ibzan 30 d. for his sons
1 Sam. 30:19 noth. lack. s. nor d.
1 Chr. 23:22 Ele. had no s. but d.
25:5 God gave Heman 14 s. 3 d.

DAY

2 Chr. 11:21 Rehob. had 28 s., 60 d.
13:21 Abijah begat 22 sons 16 d.
Ezr. 9:12 d. to their s. Neh. 13:25
Neh. 4:14 fight for your s. and d.
5:2 our sons and d. are many
10:28 s. and d. clave to brethren
Job 1:2 born to Job 7 s. 3 d. 42:13
Ps. 106:37 sacrificed sons and d.
38 shed blood of their s. and d.
Is. 43:6 bring my s. from far, d.
49:22 bring thy sons in arms, d.
56:5 better than sons and d.
Jer. 3:24 shame dev. sons and d.
16:2 nor shalt have sons nor d.
19:9 cause eat flesh of s. and d.
29:6 wives, beget sons and d.
48:46 s. and d. taken captive
Ezek. 14:16 deliver sons nor d.
16:20 s. and d. and sacrificed
23:4 mine, bare sons and d.
46 shall slay their sons and d.
24:21 s. d. fall by sw. Amos 7:17
25 when I take their s. and d.
Joel 2:28 s. and d. prop. Acts 2:17
3:8 sell sons and d. to Judah
2 Cor. 6:18 be my s. and d. saith L.

Two DAUGHTERS.
Gen. 17:8 I have two d. let me
15 take thy wife and two d.
29:16 Laban had two d. Leah
31:41 I served for thy two d.
Ruth 1:7 N. went out with 1. d.
1 Sam. 2:21 Hannah bare two d.
14:49 Saul's two d. were Merab
Prov. 30:15 horseleech hath t. d.

DAUGHTERS of the uncircumcised.
2 Sam. 1:20 lest d. of u. triumph

DAUGHTERS of Zion.
Cant. 3:11 go forth, O ye d. of Z.
Is. 3:16 d. of Zion are haughty
4:4 filth of d. of Zion

DAVID.

Ruth 4:22 Jesse begat D. Mat.
1:5
1 Sam. 16:13 came upon D.
Sam. 5:1 all tribes of Is. to D.
1 K. 2:10 D. slept, 1 Chr. 29:28
Ps. 72:20 prayers of D. son of J.
Mat. 9:27 son of D. 15:22; 20:30;
Mark 10:47; Luke 18:38
12:3 D. did when hungered,
Mark 2:25; Luke 6:3
21:9 S. of D.; 22:43; Mark 12:35
Rom. 1:3 C. seed of D. 2 Tim. 2:8
Heb. 4:7 saying in D. to-day
Rev. 3:7 key of D.; 5:5 root, 22:16

Hand of DAVID.
1 Sam. 18:16 Lord req. at h. of D.
2 Sam. 3:8 not into hand of D. 18
21:22 fell by h. of D. 1 Chr. 20:8

House of DAVID.
1 K. 12:19 fol. D. but 2 Chr. 10:19
Ps. 122:5 thrones of the h. of D.
Is. 7:2 it was told house of D.
22:22 key of h. of D. I will lay
Zec. 12:7 gl. of h. of D. 8, 10, 12
13:1 fountain opened to h. of D.
Luke 1:27 Joseph, of h. of D. 69
2:4 the house and lineage of D.

DAVID, joined with king.
1 Sam. 21:11 this D. k. of land?
2 Sam. 3:24 anointed D. k. over J.
Jer. 30:9 Lord and D. the king
Hos. 3:5 seek L. and D. their k.
Mat. 1:6 D. the k. and D. the k.
Acts 13:22 raised D. to be their k.

Servant DAVID.
2 Sam. 7:5 my servant D. 8, 26
1 K. 8:25 thy s. D. 2 Chr. 6:16
11:13 for D. s. sake, 132:10;
Is. 37:35
Ps. 78:70 D. his servant, 89:20
Jer. 33:21 brok. with D. my s. 22
Ezek. 34:23 even my servant D.
37:24 D. my ser. shall be king
Luke 1:69 salva. in house of s. D.
Acts 4:25 mouth of thy serv. D.

DAWN, ING.
Jos. 6:15 rose about d. of day
Jud. 19:26 came woman in d.
Job 3:9 nor let it see d. of day
7:4 I am full of tossings to d.
Ps. 119:147 I prevented the d.
2 Pet. 1:19 till the day d. and the

DAY.
Gen. 1:5 God called the light d.
32:26 let me go, d. breaketh
Ex. 13:21 a pillar, night, 40:38
Num. 14:94 each d. for a year
Deut. 4:10 d. thou stoodest bp. L.
9:24 rebellious from d. I knew
24:15 at his d. give him his hire

Jos. 10:13 sun not down ab. a d.
14 was no d. like that
Jud. 19:2 when it is d. kill Sam.
1 Sam. 9:15 told S. a d. before
14:4 d. of which Lord said
26:10 or bls d. shall come to die
2 Sam. 3:35 while yet d. Jer. 13:9
1 K. 2:37 on d. thou goest out
2 K. 4:8 fell on a d. Elisha, 11, 18
Neh. 4:2 make an end in a d.?
Job 1:4 feasted, every one his d.
6 was a d. when sons, 13; 2:1
3:3 d. per. wherein I was born
14:6 till he accomplish his d.
18:20 he astonished at his d.
19:25 stand at latter d. on earth
21:30 reserved to d. of destruction
Ps. 19:2 d. unto d. uttereth
37:13 he seeth his d. is coming
78:42 nor rem. d. he delivered
84:10 a d. in thy courts better
119:164 7 times a d. I praise
Prov. 4:18 and more to perfect d.
7:20 home at the d. appointed
27:1 what a d. may bring forth
Cant. 2:17 till the d. break, 4:6
Is. 7:17 from d. Ephraim dep.
49:13 before d. was, I am he
58:5 a d. to afflict soul? call this
an acceptable d. to Lord?
61:2 d. of vengeance of G. 63:4
Jer. 12:3 prep. for d. of slaughter
17:22 there be till d. I visit
32:31 from the d. they built it
36:2 from the d. I spake to thee
38:28 d. Jerusalem was taken
47:4 of d. that cometh to spoil
50:27 woe, for their d. is come
Ezek. 4:6 each d. for a year
7:10 behold the d. it is come
21:25 prince, whose d. is come
28:15 from d. thou wast created
30:2 woe worth the d.! 3 time
18 at Tehaphne. d. be darken.
Dan. 6:10 petition 3 times a d.
Amos 3:8 maketh d. dark
6:10 end thereof as a bitter d.
Mic. 3:6 d. be dark over them
7:4 the d. of thy watchmen
Zep. 2:2 before d. pass as chaff
Mal. 4:1 d. I rise up to the prey
Zec. 4:10 despi. d. of small things
14:1 d. of L. cometh, 7 a d.
Mat. 7:22 abide d. of his coming?
24:37 d. noeth that shall burn
Mat. 24:36 d. Noe ent. Luke 17:27
50 L. shall come in a d. when
he looketh not, Luke 12:46
25:13 know the d. nor the hour
Mark 1:35 great while before d.
Luke 1:20 d. these be performed
90 d. of his showing to Israel
17:4 trespass seven times in a d.
24 so Son of man be in his d.
John 6:39 raise it up. at last d.
40 raise him at last d. 44, 54
8:56 Abra. rejoiced to see my d.
9:4 work while it is d.
Acts 1:2 until d. he was tak. up
19:21 on a set d. Herod sat
16:35 it was d. 28:12; 27:39
17:31 he hath appointed a d.
27:29 they waited for d.
Rom. 2:5 wrath ag. d. of wrath
13:12 night is far spent, d. at hand, let us
14:6 regardeth d. to the Lord
1 Cor. 3:13 the d. shall declare it
2 Cor. 6:2 now is the d. of salv.
Eph. 4:30 sealed to d. of redem.
Phil. 1:6 perf. it up. the d. of C.
1 Thes. 5:8 children of the d.
5 who are of the d. be sober
Heb. 8:7 he limiteth a certain d.
4 have not spoken of anoth. d.
10:25 see the d. approaching
2 Pet. 1:19 till the d. dawn, and
3:12 to coming of d. of God
Rev. 9:15 were prepared for a d.
See ATONEMENT, BATTLE, CALAMITY, DARKNESS, EVIL, HOLY, LAST.

All the DAY.
Ps. 25:5 do I wait all the d.
71:15 thy salvation all the d.
8; d. rejoice all the d.
102:8 reproach me all the d.
119:97 meditation all the d.
Is. 28:24 ploughman plo. a. d.
65:2 spread out hands all the d.
Lam. 1:13 desolate all the d.
3:3 his hand ag. me all t. d.
14 derision to people all the d.
62 their devices ag. me a. t. d.
Mat. 20:6 stand all the d. idle

CRUDEN'S CONCORDANCE.

DAY

Mat. 6:11 give us *this d.* daily b.
11 23 Sodom remain. to *this d.*
28:15 among Jews to *t. d.*
Luke 2:11 is born *t. d.* a Saviour
4:21 *this d.* scripture fulfilled
19:5 *t. d.* salvation to this house
42 at least in *this thy d.*
Acts 22:3 as ye are all *t. d.*
23:1 good conscience till *t. d.*
24:21 called in question *this d.*
26:22 continue to *t. d.* witness.
29 all that hear me *t. d.*
Rom. 11:8 sh. not hear to *t. d.*

To-DAY.
Gen. 21:26 heard I of it but *to-d.*
Ex. 2:18 come so soon *to-d. ?*
14:13 salvation show you *to-d.*
Lev. 9:4 *to-d.* Lord will appear
1 *Sam.* 11:13 *to-d.* Lord wrought
24:10 how Lord delivered thee
    to-d. into my hand, 26:23
2 *Sam.* 13:4 lean from *d. to-d. ?*
16:3 *to-d.* house of Is. resto. me
1 K. 19:15 will show myself *to-d.*
22:5 inq. at L. *to-d.* 2 *Chr.* 18:4
2 *K.* 4:23 why go to him *to-d. ?*
1 *Chr.* 16:23 show from day to day
    his salvation, *Ps.* 96:2
Job 23:2 *to-d.* my complaint
Ps. 95:7 *to-d.* if ye will hear his
    voice, *Heb.* 3:7, 15; 4:7
Zec. 9:12 *to-d.* do I declare
Mat. 6:30 *to-d.* is, and to-mor.
    is cast into oven. *Luke* 12:28
21:28 work *to-d.* in vineyard
Luke 5:26 strange things *to-d.*
17:32 I do cures *to-d.* and to-mo.
33 must walk *to-d.* and d. fol.
19:5 *to-d.* I abide at thy house
22:43 *to-d.* be with me in para.
24:21 *to-d.* is the third day
Heb. 3:13 while it is called *to-d.*
5:5 *to-d.* have I begotten thee
13:8 the same yesterday, *to-d.*
Jam. 4:13 ye that say *to-d.*, or
2 *Pet.* 2:8 vexed his soul d. *to-d.*

DAY of trouble.
2 *K.* 19:3 this is *d. of t. Is.* 37:3
Ps. 20:1 L. hear thee in *d. of t.*
50:15 call upon me in *d. of t.*
51:16 my refuge in *d. of trou.*
77:2 in *d. of t.* I sought the L.
86:7 in *d. of t.* I will call
Is. 22:5 it is a *d. of trouble*
Jer. 51:2 *d. of t.* shall be ag. her
Ezek. 7:7 time is come, *d. of tr.*
Nah. 1:7 strong-hold in *d. of t.*
Hab. 3:16 I might rest in *d. of t.*
Zep. 1:15 that day is a *d. of t.*

DAYTIME.
Job 8:14 meet with dark. in *d.*
24:16 houses they marked in *d.*
Ps. 22:2 I cry in *d.* hearest not
42:8 his loving kindness in *d.*
78:14 in *d.* led with a cloud
Is. 4:6 a tabor. for shadow in *d.*
21:8 on watch-tower in the *d.*
L uke 21:37 in *d.* he was teaching
2 *Pet.* 2:13 pleasure to riot in *d.*

DAYS.
Gen. 8:3 after 150 *d.* waters ab.
27:41 *d.* of mourning for my *f.*
47:9 *d.* of my pilgrimage
50:4 *d.* of his mourning past
Deut. 4:32 ask now of the *d.* past
10:10 I stayed in mount forty *d.*
1 *Sam.* 13:11 came not within *d.*
1:26 the *d.* were not expired
20:3 been with me these *d.*
1 *Chr.* 13:1 David was full of *d.*
21:15 *d.* as a shadow, *Job* 8:9
23 he died full of *d.* riches, and
2 *Chr.* 24:15 Jehoiada full of *d.*
Ezr. 9:7 since *d.* of fathers
Est. 9:26 they called these *d.*
Job 3:6 not joined to *d.* of year
7:1 his *d.* like *d.* of a hireling ?
12:12 length of *d.* understand.
15:13 spend their *d.* in wealth
32:16 *d.* of afflict. taken hold
37 *d.* of affliction prevent. me
32:7 I said, *d.* should speak
33:25 return to *d.* of his youth
38:11 spend their *d.* in prosper.
42:17 so Job died, full of *d.*
Ps. 21:4 gavest him length of *d.*
31:18 L. knoweth *d.* of upright
44:1 work thou didst in their *d.*
55:23 not live half their *d.*
75:5 considered the *d.* of old
78:33 their *d.* did he consume
89:29 his throne as *d.* of heaven
    45 *d.* of his youth shortened
90:9 all our *d.* are passed away
    10 *d.* of our years threescore

DAY

Ps. 90:12 so ten. us to nu. our *d.*
14 we may be glad all our *d.*
94:13 rest from *d.* of adversity
119:84 many are *d.* of thy ser.
143:5 I remember the *d.* of old
Prov. 3:2 leng. of *d.* add to thee
16 length of *d.* is in right hand
Ec. 3:20 not much rememher *d.*
7:10 that former *d.* were better
8:13 abide with him *d.* of his li.
11:8 remember *d.* of darkness
12:1 while the evil *d.* come not
Is. 23:7 antiquity of ancient *d.*
15 according to *d.* of one king
60:20 *d.* of mourn. shall be end.
65:20 be no more infant of *d.*
22 as *d.* of a tree *d.* of my peo.
Jer. 2:32 *d.* without number
6:11 aged with him full of *d.*
31:33 after those *d.* put my law
36:2 *d.* of Josiah to this day
Lam. 4:18 our *d.* are fulfilled,
Ezek. 12:23 *d.* at hand, effect of
16:22 rem. *d.* of thy youth, 43
Dan. 8:14 unto 2,300 *d.* sanctuary
12:11 set up shall be 1,290 *d.*
12 blessed waiteth to 1,335 *d.*
Hos. 2:13 visit on her *d.* of Baal.
9:7 *d.* of visitation, recompense
10:9 sinned from *d.* of Gibeah
Mic. 7:15 acc. to *d.* of thy com.
Zec. 8:6 ye that hear in these *d.*
11 I will not be as in former *d.*
13 thought in these *d.*
Mal. 3:7 *d.* of fat, ye are gone
Mat. 11:12 *d.* of John Baptist
24:22 those *d.* be shortened, no
    flesh be saved, *Mark* 13:20
37 as *d.* of Noe, so com. of S.
Luke 21:22 these be *d.* of veng.
Acts 3:24 foretold of these *d.*
5:36 bef. these *d.* rose up Theu.
12:3 *d.* of unleav. bread, 20:6
Gal. 4:10 ye observe *d.* months
Eph. 5:16 because the *d.* are evil
Heb. 7:3 beg. *d.* of nor end of life
    10:32 call to remem. former *d.*
1 *Pet.* 3:10 see good *d.* let refrain
Rev. 11:3 shall prophesy 1,260 *d.*
12:6 feed her there 1,260 *d.*
See DAVID, LAST, OLD, JOURNEY.

All the DAYS.
Gen. 3:5 all *t. d.* A. lived 930 *yc.*
8 *d.* of Seth ; 11 of Enos
14 of Cainan ; 23 Enoch
27 Methuselah ; 9:29 Noah
Deut. 4:9 they depart *all the d.*
    10 to fear me *all t. d.* 1 *K.* 8:40
12:1 to possess it *all the d.*
1 *Sam.* 24:31 served L. *all t. d. of J.*
1 *Sam.* 1:11 give him to L. *a. t. d.*
1 *K.* 4:25 safely *all t. d.* of Sol.
Job 14:14 *all d. of* my ap. time
Ps. 23:6 mercy fol. me *all t. d.*
27:4 house of L. *all d.* of my life
15:15 *all t. d.* of the afflicted
31:12 good *all the d.* of her life
Luke 1:75 holi. *all t. d.* of her lif
See His LIFE, Thy LIFE.

DAYS come.
Is. 7:17 *d.* that have not come
Jer. 23:5 behold *d. c.* 7; 31:31
Amos 4:2 *d. c.* he will take you
Mat. 9:15 *d. c.* bridge, shall be
    taken, *Mark* 2:20 ; *Luke* 5:35
Luke 17:22 *d. c.* ye sh. des. to see
21:6 *d. c.* there shall not be left
Heb. 8:8 *d. c.* I will make new c.

Few DAYS.
Gen. 29:20 seemed but a *few d.*
47:9 *f.* and evil *d.* of my pilgr.
Job 14:1 man b. of wo. is *of f. d.*
Ps. 109:8 let his *d.* be *few*
Dan. 11:20 *f. d.* he be destroyed
Heb. 12:10 for a *f. d.* chasten. us

His DAYS.
Gen. 6:3 *his d.* shall be 120 years
10:25 in *h. d.* was earth divided
Deut. 22:19 put her away *all h. d.*
1 *K.* 13:14 A. was perf. *all h. d.*
21:29 not bring the evil in *h. d.*
2 *K.* 8:20 in *his d.* Edom revolted
12:2 Jehoash did right all *h. d.*
1 *Chr.* 22:9 and quietness in *h. d.*
Job 14:5 seeing *h. d.* determined
29:4 travail with pain all *h. d.*
24:1 know him, not see *his d. ?*
Ps. 72:7 in *h. d.* right. flourish
103:15 man, *his d.* are as grass
144:4 *his d.* are as a shadow
Ec. 2:23 all *h. d.* are sorrows
5:17 all *h. d.* eateth in darkness
Is. 65:20 hath not filled *his d.*
Jer. 17:11 in the midst of *his d.*
22:30 a man not prosper in *h. d.*
23:6 in *his d. J.* shall be saved

In the DAYS.

1 *K.* 10:21 silver noth. accounted
    of in *d.* of Sol. 2 *Chr.* 9:20
1 *Chr.* 13:3 inq. not *i. d.* of Saul
2 *Chr.* 26:5 sought G. *in d.* of Z.
32:26 came not *i. d.* of Hezek.
Job 29:2 *i. d.* God preserved me
    4 as I was *in the d.* of my you.
Ps. 37:19 *in d.* of famine satis.
49:5 wherefore fear in *d.* of evil
Ec. 2:16 *in d.* to come be forgot.
11:9 heart cheer thee *in the d.*
12:1 remember thy Creator *in d.*
Lam. 1:7 Jer. remembered *in d.*
Ezek. 16:60 remem. my cov. *in d.*
22:14 hands be strong *in the d.*
Dan. 2:44 *in the d.* of these kings
5:11 *in the d.* of thy father
Hos. 2:15 as *in d.* of her youth
9:9 corrupted as *in d.* of Gibeah
12:9 *in the d.* of solemn feasts
Mat. 2:1 *J.* was born *in d.* of H.
23:30 been *in d.* of our fathers
24:38 for as *in d.* bef. flood
Mark 2:26 *in the d.* of Abiathar
Luke 1:25 L. dealt with me *in d.*
4:25 widows *in d.* of Elias
17:26 *in the d.* of Noe ; 28 Lot
Acts 5:37 Judas *in d.* of taxing
11:28 *in t. d.* of Claudius Cesar
Heb. 5:7 who *in t. d.* of his flesh
1 *Pet.* 3:20 waited *in the d.* of N.
Rev. 10:7 *in d.* of seventh angel

In those DAYS.
1 *Sam.* 3:1 precious *in those d.*
Jer. 3:16 *in those d.* J. be saved
50:4 *in th. d.* Isr. shall seek God
20 *in th. d.* iniquity be sought
Joel 2:29 *in th. d.* I will pour out
    my Spirit, *Acts* 2:18
Luke 1:39 Mary arose *in those d.*
20:1 one of *th. d.* as he taught
Num. 24:14 peo. do to pe. *in t. d.*
Deut. 4:30 *i. d.* If thou turn to L.
31:29 evil befall you *in latter d.*
Jer. 23:23 in *lat. d.* con. it, 30:24
48:47 captivity of Moab *in l. d.*
49:39 captivity of Elam *in l. d.*
Ezek. 38:16 ag. my people *in l. d.*
10:14 befall thy people *in l. d.*
Hos. 3:5 shall fear Lord *in l. d.*

Many DAYS.
Gen. 37:34 J. mourned *many d.*
1 *K.* 17:15 she and *he d.* eat *m. d.*
Ps. 34:12 he that loveth *m. d.*
119:84 *m.* are *d.* of thy serv. ?
Ec. 6:3 *d.* of his years be *many*
11:1 shalt find it after *m. d.*
Is. 24:22 after *many d.* shall they
    be visited, *Ezek.* 38:8
32:10 *m. d.* shall ye be troubled
Jer. 32:14 continue *many d.* 35:7
37:16 Jer. had remained *m. d.*
Ezek. 12:27 vision that he seeth
    is for *m. d. Dan.* 8:26 ; 10:14
Dan. 11:33 fall by captivity *m. d.*
Hos. 3:3 abide for me *many d.*
    4 Is. abide *m. d.* witho. a king
Luke 15:13 *m. d.* after younger
Acts 13:31 *many d.* of them *m. d.*
13:31 he was seen *many d.*
16:18 this did she *many d.*
27:20 nor stars in *m. d.* appear.

My DAYS.
Ex. 20:9 if Tenth be in *my d. ?*
Job 7:6 *my d.* swifter th. shuttle
16 let alone, *my d.* are vanity
9:25 *my d.* swifter than a post
10:20 are not *my d.* few ?
17:1 *my d.* are extinct
11 *my d.* are past, my purposes
29:18 multiply *my d.* as sand
Ps. 39:4 the measure of *my d.*
5 *my d.* as a handbreadth
102:3 *m. d.* consum. like smoke
11 *my d.* are like a shadow
23 he shortened *my d.*
24 not away in midst of *my d.*
Is. 30:26 light of sun as of *s. d.*
Ezek. 3:15 I remained seven. *d.*
Hab. 11:30 compassed *seven d.*

Eight DAYS.
Gen. 17:12 *e. d.* old, be cir. 21:4
Luke 2:21 when *e. d.* where Je.
John 20:26 after *eight d. J.* came

Ten DAYS.
Dan. 1:12 prove thy servant *t. d.*
Rev. 2:10 have tribulat ion *ten d.*

Forty DAYS.
Ex. 24:18 Moses in mount *forty d.* 34:28; *Deut.* 9:9 ; 10:10
Num. 13:25 after *forty d.* 14:34
Deut. 9:25 I fell before L. *f. d.*
Ezek. 4:6 bear iniquity of *J. f. d.*
Jon. 3:4 yet *f. d.* Nine. be over.
Mat. 4:2 he had fasted *forty d.*

CRUDEN'S CONCORDANCE. 815

DEA

Job 27:15 remain be buried in *d.*
28:22 destruction and *d.* say
30:23 thou wilt bring me to *d.*
Ps. 6:5 in *d.* no remem. of thee
7:13 prepared instruments of *d.*
13:8 lest I sleep the sleep of *d.*
22:15 brought me into dust of *d.*
48:14 God be our guide unto *d.*
49:14 *d.* shall feed on them
55:4 terrors of *d.* fallen on me
15 let *d.* seize on them
73:4 no bands in their *d.*
89:48 and shall not see *d.*?
102:20 to loose those ap. to *d.*
116:15 precious is *d.* of saints
118:18 not given me over to *d.*
Prov. 2:18 house inclineth to *d.*
5:5 her feet go down to *d.*
7:27 down to chambers of *d.*
8:36 they that hate me, love *d.*
11:19 pursueth it to his own *d.*
12:28 in pathways there is no *d.*
13:14 from snares of *d.* 14:27
14:12 end, ways of *d.* 16:25
32 right. hath hope in his *d.*
16:14 wrath of king as m. of *d.*
16:31 *d.* life in power of tongue
21:6 vanity tossed of them seek *d.*
24:11 deliver them drawn to *d.*
26:18 madman who casteth *d.*
Ec. 7:26 bitter than *d.*
Cant. 8:6 for love is strong as *d.*
Is. 25:8 swallow up *d.* in victory
28:16 *d.* cannot overflow thee
53:9 with the rich in his *d.*
12 poured out his soul unto *d.*
Jer. 8:3 *d.* chosen rather than life
9:21 *d.* come up to our windows
13:2 as are for *d.* to *d.* 43:11
Lam. 1:20 at home there is as *d.*
Ezek. 18:32 I have no pleasure in *d.* of the wicked, 33:11
31:14 are all delivered unto *d.*
Hos. 13:14 O *d.* I be thy plagues
Jon. 4:9 to be angry unto *d.*
Hab. 2:5 is as *d.* not satisfied
Mat. 2:15 there till *d.* of Herod
10:21 del. bro. to *d. Mark* 13:12
15:4 curseth fath. or moth. let him die the *d. Mark* 7:10
16:28 some here shall not taste
p. to d. Mark 9:1 ; *Luke* 9:27
22:18 con. him to *d. Mark* 10:33
26:38 sorrowf. to *d. Mark* 14:34
66 guilty of *d. Mark* 14:64
Mark 5:23 daugh. at point of *d.*
Luke 2:26 not see *d.* bef. seen C.
22:33 to prison and *d.*
23:22 I found no cause of *d.*
John 4:47 he was at point of *d.*
8:51 he shall never see *d.* 52
11:4 this sickness not unto *d.*
19 Jesus spake of his *d.*
12:33 signifying what *d.* 18:32
21:19 by what *d.* glorify God
Acts 2:24 loosed the pains of *d.*
8:1 consenting to his *d.* 22:20
9 *d.* no cause of *d.* in him
23:4 1 pers. this way to the *d.*
Rom. 5:10 reconciled to God by the *d.* of his Son, *Col.* 1:22
12 and *d.* by sin, so *d.* passed
14 *d.* reigned from Adam to M.
21 as sin hath reigned unto *d.*
6:3 were baptized into his *d.*
4 buried by baptism into *d.*
5 planted in likeness of his *d.*
9 *d.* no more domin. over him
16 whether of sin unto *d.*
21 end of those things is *d.*
23 for the wages of sin is *d.* but
7:5 to bring forth fruit unto *d.*
10 com. to life I found unto *d.*
13 that good made *d.* unto me?
24 from body of this *d.*?
8:2 free from law of sin and *d.*
6 to be carnally minded is *d.*
33 *d.* nor life separ. from love
1 *Cor.* 3:22 life or *d.* all are yours
4:9 were appointed to *d.*
11:26 ye do show the Lord's *d.*
15:21 for since by man came *d.*
26 last enemy be destroy. is *d.*
54 *d.* is swallowed up in vict.
55 O *d.* where is thy sting?
56 the sting of *d.* is sin
2 *Cor.* 1:9 sentence of *d.*
10 deli. us from so great a *d.*
2:16 the savor of *d.* unto *d.*
3:7 ministration of *d.* glorious
4:11 del. to *d.* for Jesus' sake
12 so then *d.* worketh in us
7:10 sorrow of world worketh *d.*
Phil. 1:20 whether by life or *d.*
2:8 obedient to *d.* the *d.* of cross
27 Epaph. sick nigh unto *d.*
30 work of C. he was nigh *d.*
3:10 made conformable to his *d.*

DEA

2 *Tim.* 1:10 hath abolished *d.*
Heb. 2:9 suffering of *d.* crowned, that he taste *d.* for ev. man
14 through *d.* destroy him that had power of *d.*
15 who through fear of *d.*
7:23 to continue, by reason of *d.*
9:15 by means of *d.* for redem.
16 of necessity *d.* of testator
11:5 that he should not see *d.*
Jam. 1:15 sin, bringeth forth *d.*
1 *John* 3:14 not abideth in *d.*
5:16 sin unto *d.* ; 17 not unto *d.*
Rev. 1:18 keys of hell and of *d.*
2:10 be faithful unto *d.*
11 not be hurt of second *d.*
6:8 his name sat on him was *d.*
9:6 shall seek *d. d.* shall flee
12:11 loved not lives to the *d.*
13:3 as it were wounded to *d.*
18:8 her plagues in one day, *d.*
20:6 second *d.* hath no power
13 *d.* and hell deliver. up dead
14 *d.* cast into lake, second *d.*
21:4 there shall be no more *d.*

See DAY.

From DEATH.
Jos. 2:13 deliver our lives *f. d.*
Job 5:20 redeem thee *f. d.*
Ps. 33:19 to del. their soul *f. d.*
56:13 del. my soul *f. d.* 116:8
68:20 to L. belong issues *f. d.*
78:50 spared not their soul *f. d.*
Prov. 10:2 delivereth *f. d.* 11:4
Hos. 13:14 redeem them *f. d.*
John 5:24 *f r. d.* 1 *John* 3:14
Heb. 5:7 able to save *from d.*
Jam. 5:20 shall save a soul *f. d.*

Gates of DEATH.
Job 38:17 *g. of d.* been opened
Ps. 9:13 liftest me from *g. of d.*
107:18 draw near to *gates of d.*

Put to DEATH.
Gen. 26:11 this man *p. to d.*
Ex. 35:2 who. doth work, *p. to d.*
31:21 be *p. to d. Num.* 35:30
Num. 1:51 stranger that cometh nigh *p. to d.* 3:10, 38 ; 18:7
Deut. 13:5 dreamer be *put to d.*
17:6 one witness not be *p. to d.*
24:16 the fathers not be *put to d.* for children, 2 *K.* 14:6
Jos. 1:18 ag. thy com. *p. to d.*
Judg. 6:31 plead. for D. *p. to d.*
Jud. 11:12 may *p. to d.* 1 *Sam.* 11:12
1 *Sam.* 11:13 be *put to d.*
2 *Sam.* 8:2 two lines to *p. to d.*
19:21 shall no Shi. be *put to d.*
1 *K.* 2:8 I will not *put thee to d.*
21 Adonijah shall be *put to d.*
2 *Chr.* 15:13 seek L. be *put to d.*
27:1 cometh into house, *p. to d.*
Est. 4:11 law to *put* him to *d.*
Jer. 26:21 their men be *put to d.*
26:15 knew, if ye *put me to d.*
19 did J. *put* him at all *to d.* ?
38:4 this man be *put to d.*
16 not *put* thee *to d.*
52:27 *put* them *to d.* in Riblah
Mat. 10:21 cause them to be *p. to d. Mark* 13:12; *Luke* 21:16
14:5 have *put* him *to d.*
26:59 son. false wit. ag. J. to *p.* him *to d.* 27:1 ; *Mark* 14:55
Mark 14:1 and *put* him *to d.*
Luke 18:33 shall *put* him *to d.*
23:32 malefact. to be *put to d.*
John 11:53 to *put* him *to d.*
12:10 might *put* Lazarus *to d.*
18:31 not lawful to *p.* any *to d.*
Acts 12:19 keepers to be *put to d.*
26:10 *put to d.* I gave my voice
1 *Pet.* 3:18 *put to d.* in the flesh

See SURELY.

Shadow of DEATH.
Job 3:5 the *shadow of d.* stain it
10:21 land of dark. and *s. of d.*
12:22 bringeth to light *s. of d.*
16:16 eyelids is *shadow of d.*
24:17 is as the *shad. of d.*
28:3 searcheth out *shad. of d.*
34:22 no *s. of d. sinners*
38:17 doors of the *shad. of d.* ?
Ps. 23:4 valley of *shad. of d.*
44:19 cov'ered us with *s. of d.*
107:10 darkness and in *s. of d.*
14 darkness and *shad. of d.*
Is. 9:2 in land of *shad. of d.*
Jer. 2:6 land of the *shad. of d.*
13:16 he turn it to *shad. of d.*
Amos 5:8 *s. of d.* into the morn.
Mat. 4:16 that sat in *s. of d.*
Luke 1:79 light to them in *s. of d.*

DEC

With DEATH.
Is. 28:15 have made cov. *w. d.*
18 cov. *w. d.* be disannulled
Rev. 2:23 kill her children *w. d.*
6:8 power given to kill *w. d.*

Worthy of DEATH.
Deut. 17:6 is *w. of d.*
19:6 he was not *w. of d.*
21:22 have com. sin *w. of d.*
Luke 23:15 nothing *w. of d.*
Acts 23:29 to his charge *w. of d.*
25:11 any thing *wor. of d.*
25 committed nothing *w. of d.*
26:31 doth nothing *w. of d.*
Rom. 1:32 com. such *wor. of d.*

DEATHS.
Jer. 16:4 shall die of grievous *d.*
Ezek. 28:8 die *d. of* them slain
10 die *d. of* uncircumcised
2 *Cor.* 11:23 in *d.* oft

DEBASE.
Is. 57:9 *d.* thyself unto hell

DEBATE, Verb.
Prov. 25:9 *d.* cause with neigh.
Is. 27:8 in measure with *d.*

DEBATE, S.
Is. 58:4 fast for strife and *d.*
Rom. 1:29 full of envy, *d.*
2 *Cor.* 12:20 lest there be *d.*

DEBORAH.
Gen. 35:8 D. died, was buried
Jud. 4:4 and D. judged Israel
5:7 D. a mother in Ier. 12, 15

DEBT, S.
1 *Sam.* 22:2 ev. one in *d. w.* to D.
2 *K.* 4:7 sell oil, pay thy *d.*
Neh. 10:31 exaction of every *d.*
Prov. 22:26 are sureties for *d.*
Mat. 6:12 forgive us our *d.*
18:27 forgave him the *d.*
30 into prison till he pay *d.*
32 I forgave all that *d.*
Rom. 4:4 reward reckoned of *d.*

DEBTOR.
Ezek. 18:7 restored to *d.* pledge
Mat. 23:16 swear by gold, is a *d.*
Rom. 1:14 I am *d.* to the Greeks
Gal. 5:3 a *d.* to do the whole law

DEBTORS.
Mat. 6:12 as we forgive our *d.*
Luke 7:41 a creditor had two *d.*
16:5 he called his lord's *d.*
Rom. 8:12 therefore, we are *d.*
13:27 and their *d.* they are

DECAPOLIS.
Mat. 4:25 followed him from D.
Mark 5:20 to publish in D. 7:31

DECAY, ED, ETH.
Lev. 25:35 if brother fallen in *d.*
Neh. 4:10 strength of bearers *d.*
Job 14:11 and as the flood *d.*
Ec. 10:18 by sloth. building *d.*
Is. 44:26 I will raise up *d.* places
Heb. 8:13 *d.* is ready to vanish

DECEASE.
Luke 9:31 and spake of his *d.*
2 *Pet.* 1:15 after my *d.* in rem.

DECEASED.
Is. 26:14 *d.* they shall not rise
Mat. 22:25 when he married, *d.*

DECEIT, S.
Job 15:35 belly prepareth *d.*
27:4 nor my tongue utter *d.*
31:5 or if my foot hasted to *d.*
Ps. 10:7 his mouth is full of *d.*
35:3 words of his mouth are *d.*
38:12 imagine *d.* all the day
50:19 thy tongue frameth *d.*
55:11 guile depart not
55:14 redeem their soul from *d.*
101:7 worketh *d.* not dwell
119:118 their *d.* is falsehood
Prov. 12:5 coun. of wicked are *d.*
17 false witness showeth *d.*
20 *d. is* in them that imag. ev.
14:8 the folly of fools is *d.*
20:17 bread of *d.* is sweet
26:24 hateth layeth up *d.*
26 hatred is covered by *d.*
Is. 30:10 speak smooth, proph. *d.*
53:9 nor any *d.* in his mouth
Jer. 5:27 their houses full of *d.*
8:5 they hold fast *d.* they refuse
9:6 through *d.* refuse to know
8 their tongue, it speaketh *d.*
14:14 prophecy *d.* of their heart
23:26 are prophets of the *d.*
Hos. 11:12 compasseth me w. *d.*
12:7 balances of *d.* in his hand
Amos 8:5 falsify. balances by *d.*
Zep. 1:9 masters' houses with *d.*
Mark 7:22 out of he. proceed *d.*

DEC

Rom. 1:29 full of debate, *d.*
3:13 with tongues have used *d.*
Col. 2:8 spoil you thro. vain *d.*
1 *Thes.* 2:3 exhortation not of *d.*

DECEITFUL.
Ps. 5:6 Lord will abhor *d.* man
35:20 devise *d.* matters ag. th.
43:1 deliver me from *d.* man.
52:4 O thou *d.* tongue
55:23 *d.* not live half their days
78:57 turned aside like *d.* bow
109:2 mouth of *d.* opened ag. me
120:2 del. my soul fr. *d.* tongue
Prov. 11:18 worketh a *d.* work
14:25 *d.* witness speaketh lies
23:3 his dainties are *d.* meat
27:6 kisses of enemy are *d.*
29:13 poor and *d.* meet together
31:30 favor is *d.* beauty vain
Jer. 17:9 heart is *d.* above all
Hos. 7:16 they are like a *d.* bow
Mic. 6:11 with bag of *d.* weights
12 tongue is *d.* in their mouth
Zep. 3:13 nor *d.* tongue be found
2 *Cor.* 11:13 such are *d.* workers
Eph. 4:22 according to *d.* lusts

DECEITFULLY.
Gen. 31:18 answered Hamor *d.*
Ex. 8:29 let not Pharaoh deal *d.*
Lev. 6:4 or the thing *d.* gotten
Job 6:15 brethren dealt *d.*
13:7 will you talk *d.* for God
Ps. 24:4 nor sworn *d.*
52:2 like a razor, working *d.*
Jer. 48:10 doeth work of Lord *d.*
Dan. 11:23 after league work *d.*
2 *Cor.* 4:2 handling word of G. *d.*

DECEITFULNESS.
Mat. 13:22 the *d.* of rich, choke the word, *Mark* 4:19
Heb. 3:13 hardened thro' *d.* of sin

DECEIVABLENESS.
2 *Thes.* 2:10 all *d.* of unrighte.

DECEIVE.
2 *Sam.* 3:25 Abner came to *d.* th.
2 *K.* 4:28 say, do not *d.* me
18:29 let not Hezekiah *d.* you, 2 *Chr.* 32:15 ; *Is.* 36:14
19:10 let not God *d.* *Is.* 37:10
Prov. 24:28 *d.* not with thy lips
Jer. 9:5 *d.* every one his neigh.
29:8 diviners in midst *d.* you
37:9 saith L. *d.* not yourselves
Zec. 13:4 rough garment to *d.*
Mat. 24:4 no m. *d. Mark* 13:5
24 they shall *d.* the very elect
Rom. 16:18 f. speeches *d.* simple
1 *Cor.* 3:18 let no man *d.* himself
Eph. 4:14 they lie in wait to *d.*
5:6 let no man *d.* you, 2 *Thes.* 2:3 ; 1 *John* 3:7
1 *John* 1:8 have no sin, we *d.*
Rev. 20:3 *d.* the nations no more
8 go to *d.* nations

DECEIVED.
Gen. 31:7 your father hath *d.* me
Lev. 6:2 or if *d.* his neighbor
Deut. 11:16 your heart be not *d.*
1 *Sam.* 19:17 why *d.* me? 28:12
2 *Sam.* 19:26 my servant *d.* me
Job 12:16 *d.* and deceiver are his
15:31 let not *d.* trust in vanity
31:9 if been *d.* by a woman
Is. 19:13 princes of Noph are *d.*
44:20 a *d.* heart turned him
Jer. 4:10 greatly *d.* this people
20:7 O Lord thou hast *d.* me
10 they terribleness *d.* thee
Lam. 1:19 my lovers, they *d.* me
Ezek. 14:9 if prophet be *d.* I h.
Ob. 3 pride of heart *d.* thee
7 men at peace with thee *d.*
Luke 21:8 take heed ye be not *d.*
John 7:47 answ. Are ye also *d.*
Rom. 7:11 for sin *d.* me
1 *Cor.* 6:9 not *d.* 15:33 ; *Gal.* 6:7
1 *Tim.* 2:14 Adam was not *d.* but
Tit. 3:3 deceiv. and being *d.*
Tit. 3:3 were foolish, *d.*
Rev. 18:23 all nations were *d.*
19:20 *d.* them received the mark
20:10 devil that *d.* was cast

DECEIVER.
Gen. 27:12 to my father as a *d.*
Job 12:16 deceived and *d.* are his
Mat. 1:14 cursed *d.* hath a male
Mat. 27:63 we rem. that *d.* said
1 *John* 7 this is a *d.* and antich.

DECEIVERS.
2 *Cor.* 6:8 as *d.* and yet true
Tit. 1:10 many *d.* especially
2 *John* 7 for many *d.* are entered

DECEIVETH.
Prov. 26:19 so is man *d.* neighbor

CRUDEN'S CONCORDANCE. 817

DEC

John 7:12 said, he *d.* the people
Gal. 5:3 nothing, he *d.* himself
Jam. 1:26 but *d.* his own heart
Rev. 12:9 serpent which *d.*
13:14 and *d.* them that dwell

DECEIVING, S.
1 *Tim.* 3:13 *d.* and being deceiv.
Jam. 1:22 not hearers only, *d.*
2 *Pet.* 2:13 sporting with their *d.*

DECENTLY.
1 *Cor.* 14:40 done *d.* and in order

DECIDED.
1 *K.* 20:40 thyself hast *d.* it

DECISION.
Joel 3:14 multi. in valley of *d.*

DECK, ED.
Job 40:10 *d.* thyself with majesty
Prov. 7:16 I have *d.* my bed
Jer. 10:4 they *d.* it with silver
Ezek. 16:11 I *d.* thee with orna.
13 thus wast thou *d.* with gold
Hos. 2:13 she *d.* with ear-rings
Rev. 17:4 wom. was *d.* with gold
18:16 alas, city that was *d.*

DECKEDST.
Ezek. 16:16 *d.* thy high places
23:40 and *d.* with ornaments

DECKEST, ETH.
Is. 61:10 as a bridegroom *d.*
Jer. 4:30 though thou *d.* with g.

DECLARATION.
Job 13:17 hear my *d.* with ears
Luke 1:1 set forth in order a *d.*
2 *Cor.* 8:19 to *d.* of ready mind

DECLARE.
Jos. 20:4 *d.* cause in ears
Jud. 14:12 ye *d.* it in 7 days
1 *K.* 22:13 proph. *d.* good to k.
1 *Chr.* 16:24 *d.* his glory among
the heathen, *Ps.* 96:3
Job 12:8 fishes shall *d.* unto thee
21:31 *d.* his way to his face
26:27 did he see it and *d.* it
31:37 *d.* to him numb. of steps
38:4 *d.* if hast understanding
40:7 *d.* thou to me, 42:4
Ps. 9:11 *d.* among people
19:1 the heavens *d.* glory of G.
22:31 *d.* his right. 50:6; 97:6
50:9 shall dust *d.* thy truth?
40:5 I wo. *d.* and speak of them
50:16 to do to *d.* my statutes?
61:9 all shall *d.* work of God
73:28 I may *d.* all thy works
75:1 thy wondrous works *d.*
78:6 *d.* them to their children
102:21 to *d.* name of Lord in Z.
107:22 *d.* works with rejoicing
118:17 live and *d.* works of L.
118:4 shall *d.* thy mighty acts
Ec. 9:1 considered to *d.* all this
Is. 3:9 *d.* thy sins as Sodom
12:4 *d.* his doings am. people
21:6 let him *d.* what he seeth
41:22 *d.* to us things to come
42:9 new things do I *d.* before
12 *d.* his praise in the islands
43:9 who among them can *d.*
26 *d.* thou mayest be justified
44:7 and who, as I, shall *d.* it
45:19 *r* the Lord *d.* things right
48:6 and will not ye *d.* it ?
58:8 *d.* his garment. ? *Acts* 8:33
66:19 *d.* my glory among Gent.
Jer. 5:20 *d.* this in house of Jac.
9:12 spoken that he may *d.*
31:10 *d.* it in the isles a. far off
38:15 if I *d.* it to thee will thou
42:20 what God say *d.* to us
50:28 *d.* in Z. vengeance of L.
51:10 *d.* in Zion work of Lord
Ezek. 12:16 *d.* their abom. 23:36
40:4 *d.* all thou seest to Israel
Mic. 3:8 *d.* to Jacob his transg.
Zec. 9:12 I *d.* that I will render
Mat. 13:36 *d.* parable of tares
15:15 said Peter, *d.* this parable
Acts 13:32 we *d.* glad tidings
41 though a man *d.* it to you
17:23 worship, him *d.* I to you
25:27 *d.* to you counsel of God
Rom. 3:25 to *d.* his righteous. 26
1 *Chr.* 3:13 the day shall *d.* it
11:17 that I *d.* I praise you not
15:1 I *d.* gospel I preached
Col. 4:7 my unto shall Tych. *d.*
Heb. 11:14 *d.* plainly they seek
1 *John* 1:3 have seen *d.* we to y.
5 message we *d.* unto you.

I will DECLARE.
Job 15:17 I have seen, *d.* I will *d.*
Ps. 2:7 I will *d.* the decree
22:22 *I w. d.* name, *Heb.* 2:12

DED

Ps. 38:18 I *will d.* mine iniquity
66:16 I *will d.* what done
75:9 but *I will d.* forever, I will
145:6 *I will d.* thy greatness
Is. 57:12 *I will d.* thy right.
Jer. 42:4 *I will d.* it
John 17:26 and *will d.* it

DECLARE ye.
Is. 48:20 voice of singing *d.* ye
Jer. 4:5 *d.* ye in Judah, publish
46:14 *d.* ye in Egypt, publish
50:2 *d.* ye among the nations
Mic. 1:10 *d.* ye it not at Gath

DECLARED.
Ez. 9:16 my name may be *d.*
Deut. 4:13 *d.* to you his covenant
Job 26:3 plentifully *d.* the thing
Ps. 40:10 *d.* thy faithfulness
71:17 I *d.* thy wondrous works
77:14 *d.* thy strength am. poop.
88:11 thy loving-kindness be *d.*
119:13 have I *d.* all judgments
26 I have *d.* my ways, and tu.
Is. 21:2 grievous vision is *d.*
10 what I heard of G. have I *d.*
41:26 *d.* from beginning, 45:21
43:12 I have *d.* 41:8; 48:5
48:3 I have *d.* former things
14 which *d.* these things ?
Jer. 36:13 Michaiah *d.* words
42:21 I this day *d.* it to you
Luke 8:47 she *d.* to him before all
John 1:18 seen God; Son *d.* him
17:26 *d.* to them thy name
Acts 9:27 he *d.* how he had seen
10:8 he had *d.* these things
12:17 *d.* how Lord brought him
15:4 *d.* all God hath done
14 Simeon *d.* how God at first
25:14 Festus *d.* Paul's cause to
Rom. 1:4 *d.* to be the Son
9:17 my name might be *d.*
1 *Cor.* 1:11 been *d.* to me of you
3:13 *d.* what is the
Col. 1:8 who *d.* to us your love
Rev. 10:7 was. finished, as he *d.*

DECLARETH, ING.
Is. 41:26 there is none that *d.*
46:10 *d.* the end from beginning
47:13 a voice *d.* from Juan
Hos. 4:12 their staff *d.* unto them
Amos 4:13 *d.* to man his thought
Acts 15:3 *d.* conversion of Gent.
12 *d.* what miracles God wro.
1 *Cor.* 2:1 *d.* to you testimony

DECLINE.
Ex. 23:2 to *d.* after many
Deut. 17:11 nor *d.* from sentence
Ps. 119:157 *d.* from thy testi.
Prov. 4:5 not *d.* from words of my
7:25 let not heart *d.* to her ways

DECLINED, ETH.
2 *Chr.* 34:2 *d.* neither to right
Job 23:11 his way I kept, not *d.*
Ps. 44:18 nor have our steps *d.*
102:11 days as shadow that *d.*
109:23 like shadow when it *d.*
119:51 yet not *d.* from thy law

DECREASE, ED.
Gen. 8:5 waters *d.* continually
Ps. 107:38 not their cattle to *d.*
John 3:30 he must increase, I *d.*

DECREE, ING.
Esth. 5:13 Cyrus made a *d.* 17
6:1 Darius, 12; 7:21 Artaxerxes
Est. 3:15 *d.* in Shushan, 9:11
9:32 the *d.* of Esther confirmed
Job 28:26 made a *d.* for the rain
Ps. 2:7 declare *d.* Lord hath said
148:6 hath made a *d.* not pass
Prov. 8:29 gave to the sea his *d.*
Is. 10:1 decree unrighteous *d.*
Jer. 5:22 bound of sea by per. *d.*
Dan. 2:9 but one *d.* for you
4:17 this is by *d.* of watchers
24 this is *d.* of the Most High
Jon. 3:7 a *d.* of king, establish *d.*
13 Daniel repenteth not the *d.*
26 I make *d.* that in every do.
Jon. 3:7 *d.* of king and nobles
Zep. 2:2 before the *d.* bring forth
Luke 2:1 a *d.* from C. Augustus
Acts 16:4 delivered *d.* to keep
17:7 do contrary to *d.* of Cesar

DECREED.
Est. 2:1 nemesah. what was *d.*
9:31 Esther *d.* and it shall be
1 *Cor.* 7:37 hath so *d.* he will k.

DEDAN.
Gen. 10:7 sons of Raamah, D.

DEE

1 *Chr.* 1:9 Sheba, D. 32
Jer. 25:23 I heard D. drink, 49:8
Ezek. 25:13 D. fall by sw. 37:20

DEDANIM. *Is.* 21:13

DEDICATE.
1 *Chr.* 26:27 spoils did they *d.*
2 *Chr.* 2:4 I build to *d.* it to God

DEDICATED.
Deut. 20:5 a new house, not *d.* it
1 *K.* 7:51 which D. his father had
d. 1 *Chr.* 18:11; 2 *Chr.* 5:1
8:63 *d.* the house, 2 *Chr.* 7:5
15:15 Asa had *d.* in the things his
father had *d.* 2 *Chr.* 15:18
2 *Chr.* 24:7 *d.* things did bestow
31:12 brought *d.* things faith.
Ezek. 44:29 ev. *d.* thing be theirs
Heb. 9:18 nor *d.* without blood

DEDICATION.
Ez. 6:17 at *d.* of this house
John 10:22 at Jerus. feast, of *d.*

DEED.
Gen. 44:15 what *d.* is this
Ez. 9:16 very *d.* for this cause
Jud. 19:30 no such *d.* done
1 *Sam.* 26:4 was come in very *d.*
2 *Sam.* 12:14 by this *d.* given
Est. 1:17 *d.* of queen come
Luke 23:51 not consented to *d.*
24:19 J. who was mighty in *d.*
Acts 4:9 examined of good *d.*
Rom. 15:18 Gentiles obe. by *d.*
1 *Cor.* 5:3 hath done this *d.*
3 hath so done this *d.*
Col. 3:17 ye do in word or *d.*
Jam. 1:25 be blessed in his *d.*
1 *John* 3:18 in word, but in *d.*

DEEDS.
Gen. 20:9 done *d.* ought not to
1 *Chr.* 16:8 make known his *d.*
among the people, *Ps.* 105:1
Ezr. 9:13 all is come for evil *d.*
Neh. 6:19 reported his good *d.*
13:14 wipe not out my good *d.*
Ps. 28:4 give them acc. to their *d.*
Is. 59:18 ac. to *d.* he will repay
Jer. 5:28 overpass *d.* of wicked
25:14 recompense accord. to *d.*
Luke 4:18 a voice *d.* of fathers
23:41 receive reward of our *d.*
John 3:19 their *d.* were evil
20 his *d.* should be reproved
21 *d.* may be made manifest
8:41 ye do *d.* of your father
Acts 7:22 Moses was mighty in *d.*
9:36 Dorcas was full of alms- *d.*
19:18 many showed their *d.*
24:2 worthy *d.* are done
Rom. 3:20 by *d.* of law no flesh just.
28 justified by faith without *d.*
8:13 mortify *d.* of body
2 *Cor.* 12:12 signs and mighty *d.*
Col. 3:9 off old man with his *d.*
1 *Pet.* 2:8 vexed with unlawful *d.*
2 *John* 11 partaker of his evil *d.*
3 *John* 10 I will remember his *d.*
Jude 15 conv. of their ungod. *d.*
Rev. 2:6 hatest *d.* of Nicolaitans
22 except repent of *d.*
16:11 repented not of their *d.*

DEEMED.
Acts 27:27 the shipmen *d.* drew

DEEP, Substantive.
Gen. 1:2 darkness on face of *d.*
7:11 fountains of *d.* were brok.
8:2 fountains of *d.* were stop.
49:25 with blessings of the *d.*
Deut. 33:13 *d.* that coucheth be.
33:19 or me from them rise up
82:3 *d.* the poor and fatherless
Is. 51:10 hath dried Sea of *d.*
Zec. 9:15 Lord shall *d.* them
12:8 in that day L. *d.* inhabit.

DEFENDED, EST, ING.
2 *Sam.* 23:12 Shammah *d.* ground
Ps. 5:11 because thou *d.* them
Is. 31:5 *d.* Jerus. will deliver it
Acts 7:24 he *d.* him, and aveng.

DEFER, RED, ETH.
Prov. 13:12 hope *d.* maketh sick
19:11 discretion *d.* anger
Ec. 5:4 vowest *d.* not to pay it
Is. 49:11 will *d.* mine anger
Dan. 9:19 *d.* not, for own sake
Acts 24:22 Felix *d.* them

DEFY, IED.
Num. 23:7 curse me Jacob, *d.* I;
8 how I *d.* whom L. not *d.* od ?
1 *Sam.* 17:10 I *d.* armies of Israel
25 to *d.* Israel is he come up
26 that he should *d.* the armies
45 against whom thou *d.*
2 *Sam.* 21:21 *d.* Israel, 1 *Chr.* 20:7
23:9 *d.* Philistines gath. there
Job 17:2 *d.* not in their provoc.

DEF

Ps. 69:2 I sink in *d.* mire, *d.* wat.
14 be delivered out of *d.* wat.
80:9 didst cause it take *d.* root
92:5 thy thoughts are very *d.*
95:4 in his hands are *d.* places
135:6 in seas, and all *d.* places
140:10 be cast into *d.* pits
Prov. 18:4 words are as *d.* waters
20:5 counsel like *d.* water
22:14 of strange wom. is a *d.* pit
27:27 for a whore is a *d.* ditch
Ec. 7:24 exceeding *d.* who can
Is. 29:15 seek *d.* to hide counsel
30:33 he hath made Tophet *d.*
Jer. 49:8 dwell *d.* O inhab. of D.
Ezek. 23:32 drink sister's cup *d.*
32:14 make their waters *d.*
34:18 drunk of *d.* waters
Dan. 2:22 revealeth *d.* things
Luke 6:48 and digged *d.*
John 4:11 and the well is *d.*
1 *Cor.* 2:10 search, *d.* things
2 *Cor.* 8:2 *d.* poverty abounded

DEEP, sleep.
Gen. 2:21 a *d. sleep* to fall on A.
15:12 a *d. sleep* fall on Abram
1 *Sam.* 26:12 *d. s.* was on them
Job 4:13 *d. sleep* falleth 33:15
Prov. 19:15 sloth. casteth in *d. s.*
Is. 29:10 spirit of *d. sleep*
Dan. 8:18 I was in a *d. s.* 10:9
Acts 20:9 Eutychus into *d. sleep*

DEEPER.
Job 11:8 it is *d.* than hell, what
Is. 33:19 a people of *d.* speech

DEEPLY.
Is. 31:6 Israel have *d.* revolted
Hos. 9:9 they have *d.* corrupted
Mark 8:12 Jesus sighed *d.*

DEEPNESS.
Mat. 13:5 had no *d.* of earth

DEEPS.
Neh. 9:11 persecutors into *d.*
Ps. 88:6 hast laid me in the *d.*
148:7 praise the Lord, all *d.*
Zec. 10:11 *d.* of river shall dry

DEER.
Deut. 14:5 ye shall eat fallow *d.*
1 *K.* 4:23 Solomon had *d.*

DEFAMED, ING.
1 *Cor.* 4:13 being *d.* we entreat
Jer. 20:10 I heard *d.* of many

DEFEAT.
2 *Sam.* 15:34 *d.* coun. of A. 17:14

DEFENCE.
Num. 14:9 their *d.* is departed
22:25 Almighty be thy *d.*
Ps. 7:10 my *d.* is of God, who
31:2 be thou for house of *d.*
59:9 God is my *d.* 17; 62:2. 6
16 hast been my *d.* in trouble
89:18 L. is our *d.* 94:22 my *d.*
4:6 on glory shall be a *d.*
19:6 brooks of *d.* be emptied
33:16 his *d.* munitions of rocks
Nah. 2:5 *d.* shall be prepared
Acts 19:33 made his *d.*
22:1 hear ye my *d.* I make now
Phil. 1:7 and in *d.* of the gospel
17 I am set for *d.* of gospel

DEFENCED. See city, cities.

DEFEND.
Jud. 10:1 Tola son of Puah arose
to *d.* Israel
2 *K.* 19:34 I will *d.* this city, 20:6;
Is. 37:35; 38:6
Zec. 9:15 Lord of hosts shall *d.*
12:8 Lord shall *d.* Jerusalem

DEL

2 Sam. 21:21 when he d. Is. Jonathan slew him, 1 Chr. 20:7
23:9 when they d. Philistines

DEFILE.
Lev. 11:44 nor d. yours. 18:24
18:28 spue not out when ye d.
Num. 35:34 d. not land ye eh. in.
Cant. 5:3 how shall I d. them?
Is. 30:22 d. covering of images
Ezek. 7:22 robbers shall d. it
9:7 d. the house
20:7 d. not with the idols, 18
28:7 shall d. thy brightness
33:26 d. every man neigh. wife
37:23 d. themselves any more
43:7 my name Israel no more d.
Dan. 1:8 not d. with king's meat
Mat. 15:18 d. the man, Mark 7:15
1 Cor. 3:17 if any d, temple
1 Tim. 1:10 law is for them d.
Jude 8 filthy dreamers d. flesh

DEFILED.
Gen. 34:2 Shechem d. Dinah
Lev. 18:24 in all these, nations d.
1 Chr. 5:1 as he d. his father's b.
Job 16:15 d. my horn in the dust
Ps. 74:7 d. the dwelling-pl. 79:1
106:39 d. with their own works
Is. 43:5 earth is d. under inhab.
59:3 your hands d. with blood
Jer. 2:7 entered ye d. my land
10:18 because they d. my land
Ezek. 4:13 shall Isr. eat d. bread
5:11 because d. my sanctuary
7:24 their holy places shall be d.
18:6 nor d. neighbor's wife, 15
20:43 doings wherein been d.
22:4 d. thyself in idols, 23:7
11 another d. daughter-in-law
23:38 d. my sanctuary same day
28:18 hast d. thy sanctuaries
43:8 d. my holy name
Hos. 5:3 and Israel is d. 8:10
Mic. 4:11 say, let her be d.
Mark 7:2 disc. eat with d. hands
John 18:28 went not in, lest be d.
1 Cor. 8:7 conscience weak, is d.
Tit. 1:15 them that are d. their mind and conscience is d.
Heb. 12:15 thereby many be d.
Rev. 3:4 not d. their garments
14:4 were not d. with women

DEFILEDST, ETH.
Gen. 49:4 father's bed, d. it
Ex. 31:14 d. sab. put to death
Mat. 15:11 goeth into mouth d.
20 with unwashen hand d. not
Mark 7:20 that cometh out d.
Jam. 3:6 tongue, it d. whole bo.
Rev. 21:27 enter anything d.

DEFRAUD, ED.
Lev. 19:13 shalt not d. neighbor
1 Sam. 12:3 whom have I d. ?
Mark 10:19 d. not
1 Cor. 6:7 rather suffer to be d.
8 you d. your brethren
7:5 d. not, except with consent
2 Cor. 7:2 we have d. no man
1 Thes. 4:6 no man d. his brother

DEGENERATE.
Jer. 2:21 turned into d. plant

DEGREE, S.
2 K. 20:9 back, ten d. Is. 38:8
1 Chr. 17:17 a man of high d.
Ps. 62:9 low d. vanity, high d.
Luke 1:52 exalted them of low d.
1 Tim. 3:13 purchase a good d.
Jam. 1:9 brother of low d. rej.

DELAY, ED, ETH.
Ex. 22:29 not d. to offer f.-fruits
32:1 Moses d. to come down
Ps. 119:60 d. not to keep com.
Mat. 24:48 Lord d. Luke 12:45
Acts 9:38 not d. to come to them
25:17 without d. morrow I sat

DELECTABLE.
Is. 44:9 their d. things not profit

DELICACIES.
Rev. 18:3 merc. rich thro' her d.

DELICATE.
Deut. 28:54 the d. man or w. 56
Is. 47:1 no more be called d.
Jer. 6:2 likened Zion to d. wom.
Mic. 1:16 bald for thy d. child.

DELICATES.
Jer. 51:34 filled belly with my d.

DELICATELY.
1 Sam. 15:32 Agag came d.
Prov. 29:21 that d. bringeth up
Lam. 4:5 did feed d. are desolate
Luke 7:25 live d. are in kings'

DELICATENESS.
Deut. 28:56 foot on ground for d.

DEL

DELICIOUSLY.
Rev. 18:7 she lived d. 9

DELIGHT, Substantive.
Deut. 10:15 L. had d. in thy fath.
1 Sam. 15:22 great d. in offering
18:22 the king hath d.
2 Sam. 15:26 I have no d. in thee
Job 22:26 have d. in Almighty
Ps. 1:2 his d. is in law of the L.
16:3 in whom is all my d.
119:24 testimonies are my d.
77 for thy law is my d. 174
Prov. 8:30 I was daily his d.
11:1 just weight is Lord's d.
20 such as upright, are his d.
12:22 deal truly are his d.
15:8 prayer of upright is his d.
16:13 righteous lips d. of kings
18:2 a fool no d. in unders.
19:10 d. not seemly for a fool
24:25 to them that reb. sh. be d.
29:17 he give d. to thy soul
Cant. 2:3 under sha. wi. great d.
Is. 58:2 take d. in app. to God
13 if thou call sabbath a d.
Jer. 6:10 no d. in word of Lord
Mal. 3:1 messenger of cov. ye d.
Rom. 7:22 I d. in law after in. m.

DELIGHT, Verb.
Num. 14:8 if Lord d. in us
2 Sam. 24:3 why should king d.
Job 27:10 put d. in Almighty?
34:9 should d. himself with G.
Ps. 37:4 d. thyself also in Lord
11 d. in abundance of peace
40:8 I d. to do thy will, O God
62:4 d. in lies; 68:30 d. in war
94:19 thy comforts d. my soul
119:16 d. in thy statutes, 35
47 d. in thy com.; 70 d. in law
Prov. 1:22 long will scorners d.,
2:14 d. in frowardness
Is. 1:11 I d. not in blood of bul.
13:17 as for gold, not d. in it
55:2 let your soul d. in fatness
58:2 d. to know my ways
14 shalt d. thyself in the Lord
66:11 in these things I d.

DELIGHTED.
1 Sam. 19:2 Jonath. d. in David
2 Sam. 22:20 d. in me. Ps. 18:19
1 K. 10:9 L. d. in thee, 2 Chr. 9:8
Neh. 9:25 d. in thy great goodn.
Est. 2:14 except king d. in her
22:9 seeing he d. in him
Is. 65:12 did I choose that wherein
I d. not, 66:4
66:11 be d. with her glory

DELIGHTEST, ETH.
Est. 6:6 d. to honor, 7, 9, 11
Ps. 37:23 and he d. in his way
51:16 d. not in burnt-offering
112:1 d. greatly in his command
147:10 d. not in str. of horse
Prov. 3:13 son in whom he d.
Is. 42:1 in whom my soul d.
62:4 for the Lord d. in thee
65:7 soul d. in abominations
Mic. 7:18 because he d. in mercy
Mal. 2:17 G. d. in them do evil

DELIGHTS.
2 Sam. 1:24 clothed you with d.
Ps. 119:92 law been my d.
143 yet thy commar. are my d.
Prov. 8:31 my d. with sons of m.
Ec. 2:8 I gat me the d. of men
Cant. 7:6 how pleasant for d.

DELIGHTSOME.
Mal. 3:12 ye shall be a d. land
DELILAH. Jud. 16:4, 12

DELIVER.
Ex. 23:31 I will d. the inhabit.
Num. 21:2 indeed d. this people
Deut. 7:24 d. kings into thy h.
23:30 neither any that can d. out
of my hand, Is. 43:13
Jos. 2:13 d. our lives from death
Jud. 7:7 by the 300 will I d. M.
1 Sam. 12:21 cannot profit nor d.
24:4 d. enemy into thy hand
26:10 L. will d. Is. to Phil.
1 K. 20:13 I will d. this multi.
22:6 go up king's hand, 12, 15;
2 Chr. 18:5, 11
2 K. 4:18 he will d. Moabites
18:35 should d. Jer. Is. 36:20
2 Chr. 22:15 could not d. own p.
32:13 able to d.; 14 that your God should d. you
Job 10:7 none can d.
29:30 shall d. island of innocent
Ps. 61:4 d. soul from going into pit
115:4; 4 d. my soul, 17:13; 22:20;
116:4; 120:2

DEL

Ps. 7:2 none to d. 50:22
33:17 d. any by his great str.
19 to d. their soul from death
56:13 d. my feet from falling ?
72:12 d. needy when he
74:19 d. not soul of turtle-dove
82:4 d. needy out of the hand
89:48 d. his soul from grave
Prov. 4:9 a crown shalt she d. to
6:3 do this now d. thyself
23:14 shalt d. his soul from hell
Ec. 8:8 wick. d. those given
Is. 5:29 none shall d. prey
29:11 men d. to one learned
31:5 defending also he will d. it
44:20 that he cannot d. his soul
46:2 they could not d. burden
47:14 not d. thems. from flame
50:2 have I no power to d. ?
Jer. 15:9 residue will I d.
21 I d. their children to famine
20:5 d. strength of this city
21:7 d. Zedekiah from sword
22:3 d. spoiled out of hand of
43:11 d. such as are for death
51:6 d. every man his soul, 45
Ezek. 13:21 I will d. my pec. 23
14:14 d. but their own souls
16 shall d. sons nor dan. 18:20
33:5 taketh warning d. his soul
34:10 d. flock from their mouth
Dan. 3:29 no god d. after this
8:4 nor any could d. from ram
Hos. 2:10 none d. her out of hand
Amos 2:14 nor mighty d. himself
6:8 d. city with all therein
Mic. 5:8 teareth, and none can d.
6:14 shalt take hold, but not d.
Zec. 2:7 d. thyself, O Zion
11:6 d. every one into n. hand
Mat. 10:21 bro. d. bro. to death
Acts 25:16 to d. any man to die
1 Cor. 5:5 d. such a one to Satan
2 Cor. 1:10 doeth, and doth d.
2 Pet. 2:9 Lord know. how to d.

DELIVER him.
Gen. 37:22 d. him to his father
1 Sam. 23:20 part be to d. him
2 Sam. 14:7 d. him smote his bro.
20:21 d. him. and I will depart
Job 33:24 d. h. from going to pit
Ps. 22:8 d. him, let him d. him
41:1 L. d. him in time of troub.
2 not d. h. to will of enemies
71:11 for there is none to d. h.
91:14 his love on me, I d. him
15 be with him, I will d. him
Prov. 19:19 d. him must do it
Jer. 21:12 d. him spoiled
Ezek. 33:12 shall not d. him
Mat. 20:19 d. h. to Gen. Mark
10:33; Luke 20:20; Acts 21:11
20:15 and I will d. him
27:43 let him d. him now

DELIVER me.
Gen. 32:11 d. me from Esau
1 Sam. 17:37 d. me from Goliath
23:11 men of Keilah d. me up?
24:15 Lord be judge and d. me
26:24 d. me out of all tribula.
Job 6:23 d. me from enemies, Ps.
31:15; 59:1
Ps. 7:1 save me from them, d. m.
25:20 keep my soul, and d. me
27:12 d. me not to will of enem.
31:2 d. me speedily
39:8 d. me from all my transg.
40:13 be pleased to d. me
43:1 O d. me from the deceitful
51:14 d. me from blood-guilti.
59:2 d. me from workers of iniq.
69:14 d. me out of the mire
70:1 make haste to d. me
71:2 d. me in thy righteous. 31:1
4 d. me out of hand of wicked
109:21 mercy is good, d. thou me
119:134 d. me from op. of man
153 consider affliction, d. me
154 plead my cause, and d. me
170 d. me according to thy w.
140:1 d. me from the evil man
142:6 d. me from my persecutors
143:9 d. me from mine enemies
144:7 d. me out of great waters
11 d. me from strange children
Is. 44:17 d. me, for thou art God
57:13 let thy companies d. me
Jer. 15:21 d. thee from wicked
Dan. 3:17 our God is able d. me
Acts 25:11 no man may d. me
2 Tim. 4:18 d. me from evil work

DELIVER thee.
Deut. 23:14 in camp to d. thee
1 Sam. 17:46 d. thee into
2 K. 20:6 d. t. and city, Is. 38:6
Job 5:19 d. t. in six troubles

DEL

Job 36:18 ransom cannot d. thee
Ps. 50:15 d. t. thou shalt glorify
91:3 d. thee from snare of fowler
Prov. 2:12 d. t. from way of evil
16 d. t. from strange woman
Is. 57:13 thy companies d. thee
Jer. 1:8 with thee to d. t. 15:20
38:20 J. said they shall not d. t.
39:17 I will d. thee in that day
Ezek. 21:31 d. thee to brutish
23:28 d. t. to them thou hatest
25:4 I will d. t. to men of east
7 I will d. thee for spoil
Dan. 6:16 thy G. will d. thee
Hos. 11:8 how shall I d. thee, Is.
Mat. 5:25 judge d. t. Luke 12:58

DELIVER them.
Ex. 3:8 down to d. t. Acts 7:34
Deut. 7:2 Lord shall d. them, 23
Jos. 11:6 d. them up all slain
Jud. 20:28 to-morrow I will d. t.
1 Sam. 14:37 wilt thou d. them.
2 Sam. 5:19; 1 Chr. 14:10
1 K. 8:46 d. t. to ene. 2 K. 21:14
2 Chr. 25:20 came to G. to d. t.
Neh. 9:28 didst d. them
Ps. 34:4 neither any to d. them
Ps. 22:4 didst d. them
37:40 the L. shall d. them
106:43 many times did he d. t.
Prov. 11:6 right. of upr. sha. d. t.
12:6 the mouth of upright d. t.
24:11 forbear to d. them
Jer. 19:20 a Saviour and d. them
Ezek. 7:19 not d. them, Zep. 1:18
34:12 my sheep and d. them
Acts 7:25 God by his hand d. t.
Heb. 2:15 d. t. who through fear

DELIVER us.
Jud. 10:15 d. us only, this day
20:13 d. us children of Belial
1 Sam. 4:8 who shall d. us
12:10 now d. us from enemies
2 K. 18:30 will d. us, Is. 36:15
1 Chr. 16:35 d. us from heathen
2 Chr. 32:11 Lord shall d. us
Ps. 79:9 d. us, purge away sins
Jer. 43:3 to d. us to Chaldeans
Lam. 5:8 none that doth d. us
Dan. 3:17 able and will d. us
Mat. 6:13 d. us fr. evil, Luke 11:4
2 Cor. 1:10 he will yet d. us
Gal. 1:4 d. us from evil world

DELIVER you.
Jud. 10:13 I will d. you no more
14 d. you in tribulation
2 Chr. 32:14 d. you out of hand
Is. 36:14 11. not be able to d. you
46:4 I will carry and d. you
Ezek. 11:9 d. you to strangers
Dan. 3:15 that God sh. d. you
Mat. 10:17 d. you up, Mark 13:9

DELIVERANCE, S.
Gen. 45:7 to save by a great d.
Jud. 15:18 given this great d.
2 K. 5:1 had given d. to Syria
13:17 arrow of Lord's d. and d.
1 Chr. 11:14 saved by a great d.
2 Chr. 12:7 I will grant some d.
Ezr. 9:13 given such d. as this
Est. 4:14 then d. arise to Jews
Ps. 18:50 great d. giveth to king
44:4 command d. for Jacob
Joel 2:32 in Z. and in Jeru. be d.
Ob. 17 upon Zion shall be d.
Luke 4:18 to preach d. to capt.
Heb. 11:35 not accepting d.

DELIVERED.
Gen. 9:2 into your h. are they d.
14:20 blessed be God who d.
25:24 her days to be d. fulfilled
Ex. 1:19 ere midwives come
5:23 nor hast d. thy people
12:27 and d. our houses
18:26 Lord d. all unto me
1 Sam. 4:19 P. wife now to be d.
17:35 d. it of his mouth
30:23 d. company came ag. us
2 K. 19:11 and didst thou be d. ?
Job 22:30 d. by pureness of hands
23:7 he d. for ever from judge
29:12 I d. the poor that cried
Ps. 22:5 they cried and were d.
31:8 not d. me up into hand
55:18 d. my soul in peace
56:13 d. soul, 86:13; 116:8
105:20 beloved may be d. 108:6
69:14 d. from them that hate me
78:61 d. his strength into capt.
Prov. 11:8 is d. out of trouble
9 through knowledge just be d.
21 seed of righteous shall be d.
28:26 walk. wisely, shall be d.

DEL

Ex. 9:15 by wisdom he *d.* city
Is. 36:19 *d.* Samaria out
38:17 *d.* it from pit of corrupt.
49:24 or lawful captive be *d.*
25 prey of terrible shall be *d.*
66:7 was *d.* of a man-child
Jer. 20:13 *d.* soul of the poor
Ezek. 3:19 *d.* thy soul, 33:9
14:16 they only shall be *d.*
17:15 break cov. and be *d.?*
31:14 all *d.* unto death
32:20 she is *d.* to the sword
Dan. 3:28 *d.* serv. that trusted
6:27 who *d.* Daniel from lions
12:1 thy people be *d.*
Joel 2:32 call on L. shall be *d.*
Amos 9:1 shall not be *d.*
Mic. 4:10 go to Bab. there be *d.*
Hab. 2:9 *d.* from power of evil
Mat. 3:15 tempt God are oven *d.*
Mat. 11:27 all things are *d.* to me
of my Father, *Luke* 10:22
27:58 Pilate com. body to be *d.*
Mark 10:33 be *d.* to chief priests
15:15 and *d.* Jesus, *Luke* 23:25
Luke 1:57 she should be *d.* 2:6
4:6 that is *d.* to me
17 *d.* to book of Esaias
9:44 Son be *d.* into hands of m.
12:58 give dilig. mayest be *d.*
18:32 he shall be *d.* to Gentiles
John 16:21 as soon as she is *d.*
18:36 should not be *d.* to Jews
Acts 2:23 *d.* by counsel of God
15:30 Judas and Silas *d.*
27:1 they *d.* Paul to one Julius
28:17 *d.* prisoner from Jerusal.
Rom. 4:25 was *d.* for our offen.
7:6 now we are *d.* from the law
8:21 creature itself shall be *d.*
15:31 *d.* from them not believe
2 *Cor.* 4:11 are always *d.* to dea.
2 *Thes.* 3:2 *d.* from unreas. men
1 *Tim.* 1:20 whom I ha. *d.* to S.
2 *Tim.* 4:17 I was *d.* out of the
mouth of the lion
Heb. 11:11 by faith Sarah was *d.*
2 *Pet.* 2:7 and *d.* just Lot, vexed
22 turned from the com. *d.*
Jude 3 faith once *d.* to the sain.
Rev. 12:2 and pained to be *d.*

See HAND, HANDS.

DELIVERED him.
Gen. 37:21 Reuben *d.* him
Deut. 2:33 God *d.* him before us
1 *K.* 13:26 Lord *d. h.* to the lion
17:23 Elijah *d. h.* to his mother
Ps. 7:4 *d. h.* that is mine enemy
Mat. 18:34 *d. him* to tormentor
27:2 *d. him* to P. Pilate, *Mark*
15:1
18 for envy *d. him, Mark* 15:10
26 *d. h.* to be cruc. *John* 19:16
Luke 7:15 Jesus *d. h.* to his mot.
24:20 how our rulers *d. him*
John 18:30 we not *d. h.* to thee
Acts 7:10 *d. h.* out of afflictions
12:4 *d. h.* to four quaternions

DELIVERED me.
Ex. 18:4 *d. me* fr. swo. of Pha.
Jud. 12:3 I saw ye *d. me* not
2 *Sam.* 22:18 he *d. me* from my
strong enemy, *Ps.* 18:17
20 he *d. me* because he delight-
ed in me, *Ps.* 18:19
49 *d. me* from vio. *Ps.* 18:48
Job 16:11 *d. me* to the ungodly
Ps. 18:43 *d. me* from striv. of pe.
31:4 L. *d. me* from all my foes
54:7 *d. me* out of all my trouble
John 19:11 *d. me* hath great. sin
2 *Tim.* 3:11 out of all L. *d. me*

DELIVERED thee.
1 *Sam.* 24:10 *d. t.* to-d. into m. h.
2 *Sam.* 12:7 I *d. thee* out of the h.
Ps. 81:7 calledst and I *d. thee*
Ezek. 16:27 I *d. t.* to them th. h.
John 18:35 ch. priests *d. t.* to me

DELIVERED them.
Ex. 18:8 Mos. told how L. *d. t.*
Jud. 8:9 *d.* up, deliv. who *d. th.*
2 *K.* 19:12 gods *d. th. Is.* 37:12
Ch. 28:9 *d.* them to trouble
Ps. 78:42 *d. th.* from enemy
107:6 he *d. th.* out of distresses
20 he *d. th.* from destructions
Is. 34:2 hath *d. th.* to slaughter
Mat. 25:14 *d.* to them his goods
Luke 1:2 as they *d. them* un. us
Acts 16:4 *d. t.* decrees for to ke.
1 *Cor.* 11:2 keep ordin. as I *d. t.*
2 *Pet.* 2:4 *d. t.* into chains of d.

DELIVEREDST up.
Num. 21:3 Lord *d. up* the Can.
2 *Sam.* 18:24 *d. up* men that lift
Ob. 14 nor *d. up* those that rem.

DEN

Acts 3:13 glorified Son ye *d.* up
Rom. 2:23 but *d.* him up for us
1 *Cor.* 15:24 have *d.* up kingdom
Rev. 20:13 and hell *d.* up dead

DELIVERED us.
Ex. 2:19 Egyp. *d. us* fr. shep.
Acts 6:14 ch. customs Mos. *d. us*
2 *Cor.* 1:10 *d. us* from so gr. dea.
Col. 1:13 *d. us.* fr. pow. of dark.
1 *Thes.* 1:10 who *d. us* fr. wrath

DELIVERED you.
Rom. 6:17 obeyed doctrine *d. y.*
1 *Cor.* 11:23 that I *d. y.* 15:3

DELIVEREDST, EST.
Ps. 35:10 *d.* poor fr. him spoil.
Mic. 6:14 what *d.* I give to own.

DELIVERER.
Jud. 3:9 L. raised up *d.* to Is. 15
18:28 there was no *d.*
2 *Sam.* 22:2 L. is my *d. Ps.* 18:2
Ps. 40:17 thou art my *d.* 70:5
144:2 my fortress and my *d.*
Acts 7:35 did God send to be a *d.*
Rom. 11:26 come out of Sion *d.*

DELIVERETH.
Job 36:15 *d.* poor in his affliction
Ps. 18:48 *d. me* from enemies
34:7 that fear him, and *d.* them
17 *d.* them out of troubles, 19
97:10 *d.* out of hand of wicked
144:10 who *d.* David from swo.
Prov. 10:2 right. *d.* fr. *d.* 11:4
14:25 a true witness *d.* souls
Dan. 6:27 God *d.* and rescueth

DELIVERING.
Luke 21:12 *d.* you up to synag.
Acts 22:4 *d.* men and women
26:17 *d.* thee from the Gentiles

DELIVERY.
Is. 26:17 near the time of her *d.*

DELUSION, S.
Is. 66:4 I will choose their *d.*
2 *Thes.* 2:11 send them strong *d.*

DEMAND.
Dan. 4:17 *d.* by word of h. ones.

DEMAND, ED.
Job 38:3 *d.* of thee, 40:7; 42:4
Mat. 2:4 *d.* wh. C. sh. be born
Luke 3:14 Soldi. *d.* what shall
17:20 when he was *d.* of Phar.
Acts 21:33 cap. *d.* who he was

DEMAS.
Col. 4:14 ; *Phile.* 34
2 *Tim.* 4:10 D. hath forsaken me

DEMETRIUS.
Acts 19:24 D. a silver, 3 *John* 12

DEMONSTRATION.
1 *Cor.* 2:4 but in *d.* of the Spirit

DEN, S.
Jud. 6:2 Israel made them *d.*
Job 37:8 th. the beasts go into *d.*
38:40 when they couch in *d.*
Ps. 10:9 lieth as a lion in his *d.*
104:22 lay them, down in *d.*
Cant. 4:8 look from the lions' *d.*
Is. 11:8 hand on cockatrice *d.*
32:14 towers be for *d.* forever
Jer. 7:11 house a *d.* of robbers
9:11 Jerusalem a *d.* of dragons
10:22 cit. of Judah a *d.* of drag.
Dan. 6:16 cast him into *d.* of lions
41 cast them into *d.* of lions
Amos 3:4 y. lion cry out of *d.?*
Nah. 2:12 filled *d.* with ravin
Mat. 21:13 a *d.* of th. *Mark* 11:17
Luke 19:46 *d.* wandered in *d.*
Rev. 6:15 bond and free hid in *d.*

DENY.
Jos. 24:27 lest ye *d.* your God
1 *K.* 2:16 *d. me* not, *Prov.* 30:7
Job 8:18 then it shall *d.* him
Prov. 30:9 lest I be full and *d.*
Mat. 10:33 *d. me*, him will I *d.*
16:24 let him *d.* himself, *Mark*
8:34 ; *Luke* 9:23
26:34 *d. me* thrice, 75 ; *Mark*
14:30, 72
Luke 20:27 *d.* any resur.
2 *Tim.* 2:12 if we *d.* he will *d.* us
13 he cannot *d.* himself
Tit. 1:16 in works they *d.* him

DENIED.
1 *K.* 20:7 sent and I *d. him* not
Job 31:28 I sh. have *d.* God above
Mat. 26:70 Peter *d.* bef. all, 72 ;
Mark 14:70 ; *Luke* 22:57 ;
John 18:25, 27
Luke 8:45 all *d. th.* touched him
12:9 he *d.* bef. angels of God
John 1:20 John *d.* not

DEP

Acts 14 but ye *d.* the Holy One
1 *Sam.* 3:8 he hath *d.* the faith
Rev. 3:13 hast not *d.* my faith
3:8 and hast not *d.* my name

DENIETH, ING.
Luke 12:9 that *d. me* before men
2 *Tim.* 3:5 *d.* the power thereof
Tit. 2:12 that *d.* ungodliness
2 *Pet.* 2:1 *d.* L. that bought them
1 *John* 2:22 a liar *d.* Jesus is C.
23 who *d.* Son, hath not Fath.
Jude 4 and *d.* the only Lord God

DENOUNCE.
Deut. 30:18 I *d.* this day

DEPART.
Ex. 33:1 *d.* thou and the peo.
1 *Sam.* 22:5 abide not in hold, *d.*
39:10 as soon as ye be up, *d.*
2 *Sam.* 15:14 speed to *d.* lest he
1 *K.* 12:5 *d.* for three days
Job 20:28 incr. of his house *d.*
Is. 11:9 envy of Ephr. shall *d.*
52:11 *d.* ye, *d.* ye, *Lam.* 4:15
54:10 the mountains shall *d.*
Jer. 50:3 *d.* both man and beast
Ezek. 10:11 sceptre of Eg. shall *d.*
Mat. 8:34 *d.* out of c. *Mark* 5:17
10:14 when ye *d.* out of that ho.
Mark 6:11 ; *Luke* 9:4
Luke 2:29 thy serv. *d.* in peace
13:31 *d.* Herod will kill thee
21:21 let them in midst of, out
John 7:3 said *d.* go into Judea
13:1 Jesus knew he should *d.*
16:7 but if I *d.* I will send him
Acts 16:36 *d.* and go in peace
20 desired them to *d.* out of ci.
22:21 *d.* I will send thee to Gen.
25:4 would *d.* shortly thither
27:12 more part advised to *d.*
1 *Cor.* 7:15 if unb. *d.* let him *d.*
Phil. 1:23 *d.* and to be with Chr.
Jam. 2:16 *d.* in peace, be clothed

DEPART from.
Num. 10:29 *d. f.* tents of these
Deut. 4:9 they *d. fr.* thy heart
Jud. 7:3 fearful *d. from* Gilead
2 *Sam.* 12:10 sw. never *d. from*
2 *K.* 3:3 he *d.* not therefrom, 13:2
10:29 *d. n. f.* sins of Jer. 31:18,
6:11 ; 14:24 ; 15:9, 18 ; 17:22
18:6 Li. *d. n. f.* following Lord
2 *Chr.* 21:38 they *d. n. f.* foll. L.
Ps. 119:102 *n. d. f.* thy judgm.
Luke 2:37 Anna *d.* not *f.* temple

DEPARTED out.
Jud. 6:21 an. *d.* o. of his sight
Mal. 2:8 ye are *d. o.* of the way
Mat. 17:18 rebuked *d.* and he
d. out

DEPARTETH.
Job 27:21 w. car. away and he *d.*
Prov. 14:16 wise man *d. fr.* evil
Ec. 6:4 *d.* in darkness
Is. 59:15 that *d. fr.* evil, a prey
Jer. 3:20 as a with treach. *d.*
17:5 whose heart *d.* from Lord
Nah. 3:1 the prey *d.* not
Luke 9:39 bruis. him hardly *d.*

DEPARTING.
Is. 59:13 in *d.* away from God
Dan. 9:5 *d.* from thy precepts
Hos. 1:2 whoredom, *d.* from Lo.
Mic. 2:0:33 people saw them *d.*
Acts 20:29 aft. my *d.* sh. wolves
Heb. 3:12 in *d.* from living God
11:22 mention of the *d.* of Isra.

DEPARTURE.
Ezek. 26:18 he troubled at thy *d.*
2 *Tim.* 4:6 time of my *d.* is at h.

DEPOSED.
Dan. 5:20 he was *d.* from throne

DEPRIVED.
Gen. 27:45 *d.* of both in one day
Job 39:17 God *d.* her of wisdom
Is. 38:10 *d.* of residue of years

DEPTH.
Job 23:14 saith, It is not in me
38:16 or walked in search of *d.?*
Ps. 33:7 the *d.* in storehouses
Prov. 8:27 compass on face of *d.*
25:3 and the earth for *d.*
Ec. 7:24 is it either in the *d.*
Jos. 2:5 *d.* closed me round ab.
Mat. 18:6 drowned in *d.* of sea.
Mark 4:5 no *d.* of earth wither.
Rom. 8:39 nor *d.* sep. us fr. love
11:33 *d.* of the *d.* of the riches bot.
Eph. 3:18 *d.* of the love of Christ

DEPTHS.
Ex. 15:5 *d.* have covered them
8 *d.* congealed in heart of sea
Deut. 8:7 *d.* springout of valleys
Ps. 68:22 br. peo. from *d.* of sea
71:20 br. me up fr. *d.* of earth
77:16 the *d.* were troubled
95:4 drank. as out of *d.* of God
106:9 led them through *d.*
107:26 they go down to *d.*
130:1 out of the *d.* have I cried
Prov. 3:20 by his knowl. *d.* bro.
8:24 when no *d.* I was brought
the *d.* were set up of fount
Is. 51:10 thou which driedst sea
Mic. 7:19 cast sins into *d.* of sea
Rev. 2:24 have not known the *d.*

DES

Mic. 7:19 cast sins into *d.* of sea
Rev. 2:24 not known *d.* of Satan
DEPUTED.
2 *Sam.* 15:3 no man *d.* of the ki.
DEPUTY.
1 *K.* 22:47 a *d.* was king
Acts 13:8 to turn *d.* fr. the faith
18:12 Gallio was *d.* of Achaia
DEPUTIES.
Acts 19:38 are *d.* let th. implead
DERBE. *Acts* 14:6
DERIDE, ED.
Hab. 1:10 sh. *d.* ev. strong-hold
Luke 16:14 the Pharisees *d.* him
23:35 rulers also with poo. *d.*
DERISION.
Job 30:1 younger, have me in *d.*
Ps. 2:4 L. shall have them in *d.*
44:13 a *d.* to them ab. us, 79:4
59:8 shalt have heathen in *d.*
119:51 proud have had me in *d.*
Jer. 20:7 in *d.* daily ; 8 a *d.* daily
48:26 Moab shall he in *d.* 39
27 was not Israel a *d.* to thee
Lam. 3:14 a *d.* to all my people
Ezek. 23:32 shalt be had in *d.*
36:4 to cities which bec. a *d.*
Hos. 7:16 be their *d.* in Egypt
DESCEND.
Ps. 49:17 glory not *d.* after him
Ezek. 26:20 that *d.* into pit, 31:16
Mark 15:32 let C. *d.* from cross
Acts 11:5 I saw a vision, ves. *d.*
Rom. 10:7 who *d.* into the deep ?
1 *Thes.* 4:16 L. sh. *d.* fr. heaven
DESCENDED.
Ex. 19:18 L. *d.* on Sinai in fire
34:5 L. *d.* in the cloud
Ps. 133:3 as dew that *d.* on Zion
Prov. 30:4 as. to heaven or *d. ?*
Mat. 7:25 rain *d.* floods came, 27
28:2 angel of L. *d.* from heaven
Luke 3:22 H. G. *d.* in bod. shape
Acts 24:1 Ananias high-priest *d.*
Eph. 4:10 he that *d.* is the same
DESCENDETH, ING.
Gen. 28:12 the angels of God ascending and *d. John* 1:51
Mat. 3:16 saw Sp. *d. Mark* 1:10
John 1:32 Spirit *d.* like a dove
33 on whom shalt see spirit *d.*
Acts 10:11 a vessel *d.* as a sheet
Jam. 3:15 this wisdom *d.* not
Rev. 21:10 city *d.* out of heaven
DESCENT.
Luke 19:37 *d.* of mount of Olives
Heb. 7:3 Melchizedek without *d.*
6 *d.* is not counted from them
DESCRIBE, ED, ETH.
Jos. 18:4 go th. land and *d.* it
Jud. 8:14 *d.* to him the princes
Rom. 4:6 as D. *d.* the blessedn.
10:5 Mos. *d.* righteousn. of law
DESERT. *Wilderness.*
Ex. 5:3 three days jour. into *d.*
Num. 27:14 rebelled in *d.* of Zin
Job 24:5 as wild asses in *d.* go
Ps. 78:40 grieve him in *d.*
102:6 I am like an owl of *d.*
106:14 tempted God in the *d.*
Is. 13:21 wild beasts of *d.* shall
lie there, 34:14 ; *Jer.* 50:39
33:1 so it cometh from the *d.*
35:1 the *d.* shall rejoice
6 streams in the *d.*
40:3 straight in *d.* a highway
41:19 I will set in *d.* the fir-tree
42:10 make rivers in the *d.* 20
51:3 her *d.* like garden of Lord
Jer. 17:6 sh. be like heath in *d.*
25:24 poo. dwell in *d.* sh. drink
50:12 Chaldea shall be a *d.*
Ezek. 47:8 these waters go in. *d.*
Mat. 3:16 behold, he is in the *d.*
John 6:31 did e. manna in the *d.*
DESERT land.
Deut. 32:10 found him in a *d. l.*
DESERT place.
Mark 6:31 come ye into a *d. p.*
32 departed into a *d. place,*
Mat. 14:13 ; *Luke* 4:42
Luke 9:10 aside priv. into a *d. p.*
DESERTS.
Is. 48:21 he led them through *d.*
Jer. 2:6 led us thro. a land of *d.*
Ezek. 13:4 proph. like foxes in *d.*
Luke 1:80 J. was in the *d.* till
Heb. 11:38 they wandered in *d.*
DESERT, S.
Ps. 28:4 render to them their *d.*
Ezek. 7:27 ac. to. of. will I judge
DESERVES, ETH, ING.
Jud. 9:16 ac. to *d.* of his hands

DES

Ezr. 9:13 less than our iniq. *d.*
Job 11:6 less than thy iniq. *d.*
DESIRABLE.
Ezek. 23:6 *d.* young men, 12, 23
DESIRE, Substantive.
Gen. 3:16 *d.* shall be to thy hus.
4:7 to thee shall be his *d.*
Deut. 18:6 all *d.* of his mind
1 *Sam.* 9:20 on whom *d.* of Isra.
2 *Sam.* 23:5 salve. and all my *d.*
1 *K.* 10:13 queen of S. all her *d.*
2 *Chr.* 15:15 with their whole *d.*
Job 14:15 *d.* to work of thy han.
31:16 if withheld poor from *d.*
35 *d.* is Almigh. would answer
34:36 *d.* is Job be tried to end
Ps. 10:3 boast. of his heart's *d.*
17 hast heard *d.* of humble
21:2 given him his heart's *d.*
38:9 all my *d.* is before thee
54:7 seen *d.* on enemies, 92:11
59:10 let me see *d.* on enemies
78:29 gave them their own *d.*
92:11 sh. hear my *d.* of wicked
112:8 till he see *d.* on enemies
10 *d.* of wicked shall perish
118:7 shall I see my *d.* on them
145:16 satisfiest *d.* of ev. living
19 fulfil *d.* of them fear him
Prov. 10:24 *d.* of righte. be gr.
11:23 *d.* of righte. is only good
13:12 *d.* cometh, a tree of life
19 *d.* accomplished is sweet
19:22 *d.* of a man is his kindn.
21:25 *d.* of slothful killeth him
Ec. 6:9 then wandering of *d.*
12:5 and *d.* shall fail, because
Cant. 7:10 his *d.* is towards me
Is. 26:8 *d.* of soul to thy name
Jer. 44:14 yc have a *d.* to return
Ezek. 24:16 take *d.* of thine eyes
21 profane *d.* of your eyes, 25
Dan. 11:37 nor reg. *d.* of women
Hos. 10:10 my *d.* I should chas.
Mic. 7:3 uttereth mischievous *d.*
Hab. 2:5 enlargeth his *d.* as hell
Hag. 2:7 *d.* of all nations shall
Luke 22:15 with *d.* I des. to eat
Rom. 10:1 my heart's *d.* for Isr.
15:23 having great *d.* to come
2 *Cor.* 7:7 told me your earnest *d.*
11 what vehement *d.* yea, what
Phil. 1:23 having a *d.* to depart
1 *Thes.* 2:17 see yo. face with *d.*
DESIRE, Verb.
Ex. 10:11 for that ye did *d.*
34:24 nor shall any *d.* thy land
Num. 11:8 *d.* nor *d.* neighbor's wife
7:25 not *d.* the silver or gold
1 *K.* 2:20 I *d.* one small petition
2 *K.* 4:28 *d.* a son of my lord ?
Neh. 1:11 *d.* to fear thy name
Job 13:3 I *d.* to reason with God
21:14 *d.* not knowl. of thy ways
33:32 for I *d.* to justify thee
36:20 *d.* not the night, when
Ps. 40:6 offer. thou didst not *d.*
45:11 greatly *d.* thy beauty
70:2 to confusion *d.* my hurt
73:25 none I *d.* beside thee
Prov. 3:15 canst *d.* not to be co.
23:6 neither *d.* his dainty meats
24:1 nor *d.* to be with him
Is. 53:2 no beauty we sh. *d.* him
Jer. 22:27 land they *d.* to return
Dan. 2:16 *d.* mercies of G. of h,
Amos 5:18 woe to you *d.* day of
Mark 9:35 any *d.* to be first
10:35 for w whatev. we sh. *d.*
11:24 what ye *d.* when ye pray
15:9 *d.* to do as he had done
Acts 28:22 *d.* to hear what think.
1 *Cor.* 14:1 *d.* spiritual gifts
1 *Cor.* 11:12 from them *d.* occas.
Gal. 4:9 *d.* ag. to be in bondage
20 I *d.* to be present with you
21 ye that *d.* to be under law
6:12 as *d.* to make a fair show
13 nor *d.* to keep the law *d.*
Phil. 4:17 not because of *d.* a gift
1 *Tim.* 3:1 *d.* office of a bishop
Heb. 6:11 *d.* ev. one of you do
11:16 they *d.* a better country
Jam. 4:2 ye *d.* to have, not obt.
1 *Pet.* 1:12 angels *d.* to look into
2:2 as babes, *d.* the sincere milk
Rev. 9:6 men shall *d.* to die, and
DESIRED.
Gen. 3:6 tree to be *d.* to m. wise
1 *Sam.* 12:13 behold king ye *d.*
1 *K.* 9:19 Solom. *d.* 2 *Chr.* 8:6
Est. 2:13 what. she *d.* was giv.
Ps. 27:4 one thing I *d.* of Lord
19:10 more to be *d.* th. gold
107:30 bringeth to th., haven

DES

Ps. 132:13 *d.* it for his habitation
14 here dwell for I have *d.* it
Prov. 8:11 *d.* not to be compared
21:20 there is a treasure to be *d.*
Ec. 2:10 what my eyes *d.* I kept
Is. 26:9 with my soul I *d.* thee
Jer. 17:16 neither *d.* woful day
Hos. 6:6 I *d.* mercy, not sacrifice
Zep. 2:1 O nation not *d.*
Mat. 13:17 righte. have *d.* to see
Mark 15:6 one pris. whom th. *d.*
Luke 9:9 and he *d.* to see him
10:24 kings have *d.* to see those
22:31 Satan hath *d.* to sift you
23:25 *d.* from you *d.* of Christ
Acts 12:20 they *d.* peace
13:7 Sergius Paulus *d.* to hear
21 afterward they *d.* a king
25:3 *d.* favor against Paul
1 *Cor.* 16:12 *d.* him to come
1 *John* 5:15 have petitions we *d.*
DESIREDST, EST.
Deut. 18:16 acc. to all thou *d.*
Ps. 51:6 *d.* truth in inw. parts
16 thou *d.* not sacrifice, else
Mat. 18:32 forgave bec. thou *d.*
DESIRES.
Ps. 37:4 give thee *d.* of thy h.
140:8 grant not *d.* of wicked
Eph. 2:3 fulfilling *d.* of the flesh
DESIRETH.
1 *Sam.* 20:4 wh. thy soul *d.* will
2 *Sam.* 3:21 reign over all h. *d.*
Job 7:2 as a serv. *d.* the shadow
23:13 his soul *d.* that he doeth
Ps. 34:12 wh. man is he that *d.*
68:16 hill God *d.* to dwell in
Prov. 12:12 wicked *d.* net of evil
13:4 sluggard *d.* and hath not
21:10 soul of wicked *d.* evil
Ec. 6:2 nothing of all that he *d.*
Luke 5:39 drunk old w. *d.* new
14:32 he *d.* conditions of peace
1 *Tim.* 3:1 bishop, *d.* a good w.
DESIRING.
Mat. 12:46 *d.* to speak with him
20:20 *d.* a certain thing of him
Luke 8:20 breth. *d.* to see thee
2 *Cor.* 5:2 *d.* to be clothed upon
1 *Thes.* 3:6 *d.* greatly to see us
2 *Tim.* 1:4 greatly *d.* to see thee
DESIROUS.
Prov. 23:3 not *d.* of his dainties
Luke 23:8 H. was *d.* to see him
2 *Cor.* 11:32 *d.* to apprehend me
Gal. 5:26 not be *d.* of vain-glory
1 *Thes.* 2:8 affections, *d.* of you
DESOLATE.
2 *Sam.* 13:20 Tamar remained *d.*
Job 15:28 dwelleth in *d.* cities
16:7 made *d.* all my company.
30:3 wildern. in former times *d.*
38:27 to satisfy the *d.* ground
Ps. 25:16 mercy, for I am *d.*
40:15 be *d.* for a reward
69:25 let their habitation be *d.*
143:4 my heart within me is *d.*
Is. 1:7 your country is *d.*
3:26 she *d.* shall sit on ground
7:19 shall rest all in *d.* valleys
13:22 beasts sh. cry in *d.* houses
24:6 that dwell therein are *d.*
48:8 to inherit *d.* heritages
21 lost my children, and am *d.*
54:1 chil. of *d. Gal.* 4:27
3 *d.* cities to be inhabited
Jer. 2:12 be ye very *d.* saith L.
4:9 this is city, *d.* and none
6:8 lest I make thee *d.* a land
9:11 I will make the cities of J.
d. 10:20 ; 32:10 ; 44:6
10:25 made his habitation *d.*
12:11 and being *d.* it mourneth
19:8 this city *d.* and a hissing
32:43 is *d.* without man ; 33:12
49:20 their habitations *d.* 50:45
Lam. 1:13 *d.* all day, 3:11
16 my children are *d.*
4:5 did food delicately are *d.*
5:18 mount. of Zion which is *d.*
Ezek. 6:6 altars may be made *d.*
12:20 ye know their *d.* palaces
22:26 make them *d.* to the end
25:3 Scir, I will make thee *d.*
13 Edom rejoice, bec. it was *d.*
36:3 made you *d.* and swal.
Dan. 9:17 *d.* sanctuary for L.
DESIRED.
Dan. 9:17 sh shine on sanct. *d.*
Hos. 13:16 Sam. shall become *d.*
Joel 1:17 the garners are laid *d.*
18 flocks of sheep are made *d.*
3:19 Egypt shall be a *d.*

DES

Zep. 3:6 their towers are *d.*
2:13 *d.* as *d. Luke* 13:35
Acts 1:20 let his habitation be *d.*
1 *Tim.* 5:5 a wid. indeed, and *d.*
Rev. 17:16 and make her *d.*
18:19 in one hour is she made *d.*
Land DESOLATE.
Lev. 26:34 enjoy sab. as long as
it lieth *d.* 35, 43 ; 2 *Chr.* 36:21
Is. 6:11 until the *land* be ut. *d.*
13:9 of L. cometh to lay *land d.*
62:4 nor thy *l.* more be term. *d.*
Jer. 4:7 gone to make thy *l. d.*
27 Lord said, whole *l.* sh. be *d.*
7:34 cease mirth for *l.* sh. be *d.*
12:11 whole *land* is made *d.*
18:16 their *l. d.* and a hissing
25:38 *l.* is *d.* bec. of his anger
32:43 *l.* whereof ye say, It is *d.*
50:3 nation sh. make her *l. d.*
Ezek. 6:14 the *l. d.* yea more *d,*
12:19 *l.* may be *d.* fr. all therein
15:8 and I will make the *l. d.*
19:7 *land* was *d.* and fulness
29:9 *l.* of E. be *d.* 30:7 ; 32:15
33:28 wh. I have laid *l.* most *d.*
30:34 *d. l.* sh. he tilled, it lay *d.*
35 *l.* that was *d.* is like Eden
Joel 2:20 drive him to a *land d.*
Zec. 7:14 laid the pleas. *land d.*
DESOLATE places.
Job 3:14 built *d. p.* for thems.
Ps. 107:10 seek bread out of *d. p.*
Is. 49:19 thy *d. places* be too nar.
59:10 in *d. p.* as dead men
Ezek. 6:6 high *p.* shall be *d.*
26:20 set thee in *p. d.* of old
36:12 turn thy hand on *d. p.*
Amos 7:9 h. *p.* of Isaac sh. he *d.*
Mal. 1:4 ret. and build the *d. p.*
Shall be, or shall be DESOLATE.
Lev. 26:33 your land *shall be d.*
Job 18:34 cong. of hyp. *sh. be d.*
Ps. 34:21 hate righte. *sh. be d.*
22 none th. trust in him, *s. be d.*
Is. 5:9 many houses *shall be d.*
15:6 waters of Nimrim *sh. be d.*
Jer. 36:9 this city *s. be d.* with.
33:10 which ye say *shall be d.*
49:2 Rabbah *shall be a d.* heap
50:13 Babylon *sh. be* wholly *d.*
51:26 thou *shalt be d.* for ever
Ezek. 6:7 your altars *shall be d.*
29:12 cities of Eg. *shall be d.*
33:28 mountains of Isr. *s. be d.*
35:4 O mount Seir, thou *sh. be d.*
5:9 Eph. *shall be d.* in the
DESOLATE wilderness.
Jer. 12:10 pleas. portion a *d. w.*
Joel 2:3 and behind it is a *d. w.*
3:19 and Edom shall be a *d. w.*
DESOLATION.
Lev. 26:32 will br. land into *d.*
1 *K.* 13:19 should become a *d.*
2 *Chr.* 30:7 up to *d.* as ye see
Job 30:14 in *d.* they rolled
3:25 he not af. of *d.* of wicked
Ps. 73:19 how brought into *d.*
Prov. 1:27 fear cometh as *d.*
3:25 he not af. of *d.* of wicked
Is. 17:9 in that day shall be *d.*
24:12 in the city is left *d.*
47:11 *d.* come on thee sud.
51:19 two things are come, *d.*
64:10 Jerusalem is *d.*
Jer. 2:8 this house sh. bec. a *d.*
25:18 Jerus. and Judah a *d.*
44:2 this day they are a *d.*
22 therefore is your land a *d.*
49:13 Bozra a *d.* ; 17 Edom a *d.*
50:23 how is Bab. become a *d.*
51:43 her cities are a *d.*
Lam. 3:47 fear is come on us, *d.*
Ezek. 7:27 prince clothed with *d.*
23:33 be filled with cup of *d.*
Dan. 8:13 the transgression of *d.*
Hos. 12:1 Eph. daily inc. *d.*
Joel 3:19 Egypt shall be a *d.*
Mic. 6:16 should make thee *d.*
Zep. 1:15 day of wasten. and *d.*
2:4 Ashkelon be a *d.* ; 9 Moab
13 he will make Nineveh a *d.*
14 *d.* shall be in the thresholds
Mat. 12:25 ev. kingd. divided ag.
itself is br. to *d. Luke* 11:17
24:15 abom. of *d. Mark* 13:14
Luke 21:20 thereof is nigh
DESOLATIONS.
Ezr. 9:9 to repair *d.* thereof
Ps. 46:8 what *d.* made in earth
74:3 lift up thy feet to perp. *d.*
Is. 61:4 shall raise up former
d. of many generat.
Jer. 25:9 these nations perp. *d.*
12 Chaldeans' land perp *d.*
Ezek. 35:9 m. Seir perpetual *d.*

CRUDEN'S CONCORDANCE. 821

DES

Dan. 9:2 70 years in d. of Jeru.
18 and behold our d.
26 to end of ward. determined

DESPAIR.
1 Sam. 27:1 Saul sh. d. of me
Ec. 2:20 to cause my heart to d.
2 Cor. 4:8 perplexed, not in d.

DESPAIRED.
2 Cor. 1:8 that we d. even of life

DESPERATE, LY.
Job 6:26 speeches of one that is d.
Is. 17:11 in the day of d. sorrow
Jer. 17:9 the heart is d. wicked

DESPISE.
Lev. 26:15 if ye d. my statutes
1 Sam. 2:30 d. me, be lightly est.
2 Sam. 19:43 why did ye d. us
Est. 1:17 shall d. their husb.
Job 5:17 d. not chast. Almighty.
Prov. 3:11 † Heb. 12:5
6:31 † would d. my life
10:3 sho. d. work of thy hands
31:13 if d. cause of man-servant
Ps. 51:17 contrite h. wilt no d.
73:20 thou shalt d. their image
102:17 will not d. their prayer
Prov. 1:7 but fools d. wisdom
6:30 men do not d. a thief, if
23:9 a fool will d. the wisd. of
· 22 d. not thy mother when old
Is. 33:12 because ye d. this word
Jer. 4:30 thy lovers will d. thee
23:17 say to them that d. me
Lam. 1:8 all that honored, d. her
Ezek. 28:26 plains, on all d. th.
Amos 5:21 I d. your feast-days
Mal. 1:6 O priests, d. my name
Mal. 6:24 d. the other, Luke 16:13
18:10 d. not one of these little
Rom. 14:3 d. him th. eateth not
1 Cor. 11:22 or d. ye church of G.
16:11 let no man there. d. him
1 Thes. 5:20 d. not prophesyings
1 Tim. 4:12 let none d. thy youth
6:2 not d. them bec. brethren
Tit. 2:15 let no man d. thee
2 Pet. 2:10 that d. government
Jude 8 d. dominion

DESPISED.
Gen. 16:4 mistress d. in her eyes
25:34 Esau d. his birthright
Lev. 26:43 they d. my judgm.
Num. 11:20 ye have d. the Lord
14:31 know land ye have d.
15:31 bec. he d. word of Lord
1 Sam. 10:27 they d. him
2 Sam. 6:16 d. him in her heart
2 K. 19:21 daughter of Zion hath d. thee, Is. 37:22
2 Chr. 36:16 mocked, d. his words
Neh. 4:4 hear, O G. for we are d.
Job 12:5 is as a lamp d. of him
19:18 yea, young children d. me
Ps. 22:6 I am d. of peo. Is. 53:3
31 not d. affliction of afflicted
53:5 because God hath d. them
106:21 they d. pleasant land
119:141 I am small and d. yet
Prov. 1:30 they d. all my reproof
5:12 my heart d. reproof
12:8 he of perverse heart be d.
9 he that is d. and hath a serv.
Ec. 9:16 poor man's wisd. is d.
Cant. 8:1 yea, I should not be d.
Is. 5:24 d. word of H. O. of Israel
31:8 he hath d. the cities
53:3 he is d. and re[jected, d.
50:14 that d. thee shall bow
Jer. 22:28 Cun. a d. broken idol?
33:24 they have d. my people
48:15 make thee d. among men
Lam. 2:6 hath d. in indignation
Ezek. 16:59 which hast d. the oath, 17:16, 18, 19
20:13 d. my judgments, 16
22:8 hast d. my holy things
Amos 2:4 bec. they d. law of L.
Ob. 2 thou art greatly d.
Zec. 4:10 d. day of small things
Mat. 1:6 wherein d. we thy n.?
Luke 18:9 rights. and d. others
Acts 19:27 temple of Diana be d.
1 Cor. 1:28 things d. God chosen
4:10 ye honorable, we are d.
Gal. 4:11 my tempta. ye d. not
Heb. 10:28 that d. Moses' law
Jam. 2:6 but ye have d. the poor

DESPISERS.
Acts 13:41 behold, ye d. wonder
2 Tim. 3:3 fierce, d. of those good

DESPISEST, ETH, ING.
Job 36:5 behold, God d. not any
Ps. 69:33 L. d. not his prisoners
Prov. 11:12 void of wisdom d.
13:13 d. word shall be destroyed

DES

Prov. 14:2 perv. in ways, d. him
21 d. his neighbor sinneth
15:5 fool d. father's instruction
20 foolish man d. his mother
32 refuseth instruction d. soul
19:16 that d. his ways shall die
30:17 eye that d. to obey mother
Is. 33:15 d. gain of oppressions
49:7 to him whom man d.
Luke 10:16 d. you d. me ; d. me d.
Rom. 2:4 d. riches of his goodn.
1 Thes. 4:8 that d. d. not man
Heb. 12:2 cross d. the shame

DESPITE.
Ezek. 25:6 † hy d. against Judah
Heb. 10:29 done d. to Sp. of gr.

DESPITEFUL, LY.
Ezek. 25:15 veng. with a d. heart
36:5 with d. minds
Mat. 5:44 d. use you, Luke 6:28
Acts 14:5 assault to use them d.
Rom. 1:30 haters of God d.

DESTITUTE.
Gen. 24:27 not left d. my master
Ps. 102:17 regard prayer of d.
141:8 leave not my soul d.
Prov. 15:21 to him d. of wisdom
Ezek. 32:15 d. of which it was
1 Tim. 6:5 men d. of the truth
Heb. 11:37 being d. afflicted.
Jam. 2:15 if a bro. or sister be d.

DESTROY.
Gen. 18:23 d. right. wi. wicked ?
28 d. all city for lack of five ?
19:13 we will d. this place
Deut. 6:15 lest anger of Lord d.
7:24 d. name from an. heaven
9:14 let me alone, I may d.
31:3 he will d. these nations
32:25 d. young man and virgin
33:27 shall say, d. them
2 Sam. 14:7 we will d. heir also
16 would d. me and my son
20:20 far be it fr. me I should d.
22:41 d. th. hate me, Ps. 18:40
2 K. 10:19 d. worship. of Baal
18:25 go ag. this land and d. it
Ezr. 6:12 d. kings put to hand
Job 8:18 if he d. him fr. his place
10:8 yet thou dost d. me
19:26 worms d. this body
Ps. 5:6 d. them speak leasing
10 d. thou them, O God
21:10 their fruit shalt thou d.
24:5 he shall d. not build up
25:5 likewise d. thee for ever
55:9 d. and divide their tongues
63:10 d. me are mighty
74:8 Let us d. them together
143:12 d. all afflict my soul
144:6 shoot arrows, d. them
145:20 all wicked will he d.
Prov. 1:32 proap. of fools d. th.
11:3 perverseness of transgr. d.
15:25 L. will d. house of proud
21:7 robberies shall d. them
Ec. 5:6 d. work of thy hands ?
7:16 why shouldest d. thyself ?
Is. 3:12 d. way of thy paths
11:9 nor d. in holy mount. 65:25
13:9 shalt d. sinners thereof
25:7 d. in this mount. the face
Jer. 5:10 go upon walls, and d.
6:5 by night d. her palaces,
12:17 I will d. that nation
13:14 I will not spare, but d.
15:6 stretch my hand, and d.
17:18 d. with double destruct.
23:1 pastors that d. the sheep
49:9 if thieves, they will d.
Lam. 3:66 persecute and d. them
Ezek. 9:8 d. all residue of Israel ?
Dan. 8:25 by peace shall he d.
9:26 shall d. city and sanctuary
11:26 food on his dainties d.
Ob. 8 d. wise men out of Edom ?
Mic. 2:10 polluted, it shall d. you
Mat. 2:13 Herod seek child to d.
10:28 fear him, able to d. both
21:41 d. those wicked men
27:20 ask Barab. and d. Jesus
Mark 12:9 d. husband. Lu. 20:16
John 2:19 J. said, d. this temple
Acts 6:14 this Jesus d. this place
1 Cor. 6:13 d. both it and things
Heb. 2:14 d. him had power
1 John 3:8 might d. works of d.
Rev. 11:18 d. th. wh. d. the earth

I will, or will I DESTROY.
Gen. 6:7 I will d. man whom I
Ex. 23:27 I will d. the people
Ps. 18:40 I will utterly d. wicked
118:10 in n. of L. d. them, 11, 12
Is. 42:14 I will d. and dev. at once

DES

Jer. 15:7 I will d. my people
Ezek. 25:7 I will d. thee, 28:16;
Zep. 2:5
30:13 saith Lord I will d. idols
Amos 9:8 I will d. sinf. kingdom
Mark 14:58 I will d. this temple
1 Cor. 1:19 I will d. wisd. of wise

Not DESTROY.
Gen. 18:31 not d. it for 20's sake
Deut. 4:31 not fors. thee, nor d.
9:26 d. not thy people
10:10 Lord would not d. thee
1 Sam. 24:21 not d. my name
2 K. 8:19 n. d. Jud. for Dav. sake
13:23 would not d. them, nor
2 Chr. 12:12 not d. him, altog.
21:7 not d. the house of David
35:21 forbear fr. G. he d. not
Ps. 106:34 did not d. the nations
Is. 65:8 d. it not, bless. is in it
Dan. 2:24 d. n. wise men of Ba.
Rom. 14:20 d. n. work of God

To DESTROY.
Gen. 19:13 hath sent us to d. it
Deut. 9:19 was wroth to d. you
Ps. 40:14 seek soul to d. it. 63:9
119:95 wicked waited to d. me
Is. 10:7 it is in his heart to d.
13:5 they come from far to d.
23:11 Lord given a com. to d.
37:7 wicked devices to d. poor
51:13 as if oppressor ready to d.
54:16 created the waster to d.
Jer. 1:10 set to d. 18:7; 31:28
51:11 device ag. Baby. to d. it
Ezek. 22:27 to d. souls, to get
25:15 despiteful heart to d. it
Dan. 2:12 to d. wise men of Ba.
7:26 to d. his domin. unto end
11:44 go forth with fury to d.
Hos. 11:9 not return to d. Eph.
Mat. 2:13 Herod seek child to d.
5:17 not come to d. but to fulfil
10:28 fear him, able to d. both
26:61 I am able to d. temple
Luke 6:9 to save life or to d. it ?
9:56 not come to d. men's lives
19:47 chief sought to d. him
John 10:10 thief cometh to d.
Jam. 4:12 one lawgiver able to d.

DESTROYED.
Gen. 10:29 d. cities of plain
Deut. 10:7 knowest not E. is d. ?
Deut. 31:4 d. them bef. them, 1:3 ;
2 K. 21:9 ; 2 Chr. 33:9
9:8 Lord angry to have d. you
20:20 until thou ha. d. th. 21, 45
Jud. 20:21 Ben. d. that day, 25
2 Sam. 21:5 devised we sh. d.
14:16 angel that d. 1 Chr. 21:15
2 K. 10:28 thus Jehu d. Baal
15:6 nation was d. of nation
Ezr. 4:15 which cause city d.
Ps. 9:5 thou hast d. the wicked
137:8 O daugh. Bab. to be d.
Prov. 13:23 d. for want of judg.
Is. 14:20 thou hast d. thy land
26:14 theref. hast thou d. them
29:20 many zainters have d.
41:11 from God terror to one
51:55 hath d. out of Babylon the
Ezek. 27:32 like d. in the sea
Hos. 4:6 peo. d. for lack of knowl.
Mat. 22:7 he d. those murderers
Luke 17:27 flood came, and d.
Acts 3:23 d. them that called
13:19 d. seven nations
19:27 her magnificence be d.
Rom. 6:6 body of sin might be d.
1 Cor. 10:9 d. of serpents
Gal. 1:23 preacheth faith he d.
Heb. 11:28 lest he d. firstborn
2 Pet. 2:12 beasts made to be d.
Jude 5 d. them that believed not

Are DESTROYED.
Job 4:20 are d. from morn. to ev.
34:25 so that they are d.

DES

Is. 9:16 they led of them are d.
Jer. 22:20 for thy lovers are d.
Hos. 4:6 a. d. for lack of knowl.
Zep. 3:6 their cities are d.

Not DESTROYED.
2 Chr. 36:10 d. th. n. Ps. 78:38
Dan. 7:11 his kingdom not be d.
2 Cor. 4:9 cast down, but not d.

Shall be DESTROYED.
Gen. 34:30 I shall be d. I and
Est. 4:14 father's house s. be d.
Ps. 37:38 transgressors sh. be d.
93:7 they s. be d. forever
Prov. 13:13 des. word s. be d.
20 companion of fools s. be d.
29:1 hardeneth his neck s. be d.
Is. 10:27 yoke shall be d. bec.
Lam. 48:8 the plain shall be d.
Ezek. 32:8 her helpers s. be d.
Dan. 2:44 sh. never be d. 6:26
11:20 within few days s. be d.
Hos. 10:8 the sin of Is. sh. be d.
Acts 3:23 will not h. sh. be d.
1 Cor. 15:26 last ene. that s. be d.

Utterly DESTROYED.
Deut. 4:26 shall be u. d.
Is. 34:2 L. hath ut. d. all nations

DESTROYER.
Ex. 12:23 d. come into houses
Jud. 16:24 the d. of our country
Job 15:21 in prosperity d. come
Ps. 17:4 kept from paths of d.
Prov. 28:24 is companion of a d.
Jer. 4:7 d. of Gentiles is
Ro. 10:10 were destroyed of d.

DESTROYERS.
Job 33:22 life draweth near to d.
Is. 49:17 g. go forth of thee
Jer. 22:7 prepare d. against thee
50:11 O d. of my heritage

DESTROYEST, ETH.
Deut. 8:20 as nat. which L. d.
Job 9:22 he d. perfect and wick.
14:19 thou d. hope of man
Prov. 6:32 doeth it, d. own soul
11:9 with mouth d. neighbor
31:3 thy ways to that d. kings
Ec. 7:7 and a gift d. the heart
9:18 one sinner d. much good
Mat. 27:40 d. temple, Mark 15:29

DESTROYING.
1 Chr. 21:15 as he was d. L. rep.
Is. 28:2 strong one, as d. storm
Jer. 2:30 sword like a d. lion
51:1 a d. wind ; 25 O d. mount.
Lam. 2:8 not withd. hand fr. d.
Ezek. 9:1 d. weapon in his hand
20:17 eye spared from d. them

See UTTERLY.

DESTRUCTION.
Deut. 7:23 with a mighty d.
32:24 devoured with hunger d.
1 Sam. 5:9 ag. city with great d.
11 was a deadly d. thro. city
Job 5:21 shalt not be afraid of d.
22 at d. and famine shalt laugh
18:12 d. sh. be ready at his side
21:17 how oft cometh d.
20 his eyes shall see his d.
26:6 d. hath no covering
28:22 d. and death say, We
30:12 pu. me upon feet of their d.
24 though they cry to him d.
31:3 is not d. to the wicked ?
12 a fire that consumeth to d.
21 from God terror to me d.
29 if I rejoiced at he d. of him
Ps. 35:8 let d. come unawares,
into that very d. let him fall
86:11 bring to pit of d.
73:18 castedst th. down into d.
88:11 faithulus. declared in d.
90:3 thou turnest man to d.
91:6 d. that wasteth at noond.
103:4 redeemeth thy life fr. d.
Prov. 1:27 your d. as a whirlw.
10:14 mouth of foolish near d.
15 the d. of the poor is poverty
29 d. to workers of iniq. 21:15
13:3 wide his lips shall have d.
14:28 want of people is d. of
15:11 hell and d. are bef. the Lord
16:18 pride goeth before d.
17:19 exalteth gate seeketh d.
18:7 a fool's mouth is his d.
12 before d. heart is haughty

CRUDEN'S CONCORDANCE.

DEV

Prov. 24:2 for their heart sta. *d.*
27:20 hell and *d.* are never full
31:8 such as are appointed to *d.*
Is. 1:28 *d.* of transgr. together
10 25 anger cease in their *d.*
17:6 as *d.* from the Almighty
14:23 Bab. with bosom of *d.*
15:5 shall raise up a cry of *d.*
19:18 shall be called city of *d.*
24:12 gate is smitten with *d.*
49:19 land of thy *d.* too narrow
51:19 desol. and *d.* are come
59:7 wast. and *d.* are in th. paths
60:18 *d.* no more be heard in
Jer. 4:6 from north a gr. *d.* 6:1
20 *d.* upon *d.* is cried, for
17:18 dest. th. with double *d.*
46:20 *d.* cometh out of north
48:3 a voice, spoiling and *d.* 5
50:22 sound of gr. *d.* in land
Lam. 2:11 *d.* of dau. of my p. 3:48
3:17 and *d.* is come upon us
4:10 in *d.* of daugh. of my peo.
Ezek. 7:25 *d.* cometh, seek peace
Hos. 7:13 *d.* to them, transgr.
9:6 are gone, because of *d.*
13:14 O grave, I will be thy *d.*
Joel 1:15 as *d.* from Almighty
Ob. 12 neither rej. in their *d.*
Mic. 2:10 dest. you with sore *d.*
Zec. 11:11 he no more utter *d.*
Mat. 7:13 br. is way lead. to *d.*
Rom. 3:16 *d.* and mis. in ways
9:20 ves. of wrath fitted to *d.*
1 *Cor.* 5:5 Satan for *d.* of flesh
2 *Cor.* 10:8 not for your *d.* 13:10
Phil. 3:19 walk, whose end is *d.*
1 *Thes.* 5:3 then sud. *d.* cometh
2 *Thes.* 1:9 pun. with everlas. *d.*
1 *Tim.* 6:9 drown men in *d.*
2 *Pet.* 3:1 and bring swift *d.*
3:10 unstable wrest to own *d.*

DESTRUCTIONS.
Ps. 9:6 *d.* come to perp. end
35:17 rescue my soul from *d.*
107:20 delivereth from their *d.*

DETAIN, ED.
Jud. 13:16 *d.* me I will not eat
1 *Sam.* 21:7 D. was that day *d.*

DETERMINATE.
Acts 2:23 *d.* counsel of God

DETERMINATION.
Zep. 3:8 *d.* is to gather nations

DETERMINED.
1 *Sam.* 20:7 be sure evil is *d.*
25:17 evil is *d.* ag. our master
2 *Sam.* 13:32 by Absal. been *d.*
2 *Chr.* 25:16 *d.* to destroy thee
Est. 7:7 evil *d.* against him
Dan. 9:24 seventy weeks are *d.*
Lu. 22:22 goeth, as it was *d.*
Acts 3:13 Pil. *d.* to let him go
4:28 what thy counsel *d.* bef.
11:29 ev. man *d.* to send relief
15:2 *d.* Paul and B. to go to Je.
37 Barn. *d.* to take John
17:26 *d.* times to be appointed
19:39 be *d.* in a lawful assembly.
25:25 *d.* to send him to Augustus.
1 *Cor.* 2:2 I *d.* not to know a. J.
2 *Cor.* 2:1 I *d.* this with myself

DETEST.
Deut. 7:26 thou shalt utterly *d.* it

DETESTABLE things.
Ezek. 11:18 shall take away *d. t.*
21 heart walk. after their *d. t.*
37:23 no more defile with *d. t.*

DEVICE.
2 *Chr.* 2:14 to find out every *d.*
Est. 9:25 *d.* return on his head
Ps. 31:11 imag. mischievous *d.*
140:8 further not his wicked *d.*
Ec. 9:10 no work nor *d.*
Jer. 18:11 I devise a *d.* ag. you
51:11 his *d.* is ag. Bab. to dest.
Lam. 3:62 their *d.* ag. me all *d.*
Acts 17:29 graven by man's *d.*

DEVICES.
Job 5:12 disappoint. *d.* of crafty
21:27 *d.* ye wrongfully imagine
Ps. 10:2 let them be taken in *d.*
33:10 *d.* of people of none effect
37:7 bringeth wicked *d.* to pass
Prov. 1:31 be filled with own *d.*
12:2 of wicked *d.* will he cond.
19:21 many *d.* in a man's heart
Is. 32:7 wicked *d.* to dest. poor
Jer. 11:19 had devised *d.* ag. me
18:12 walk after our own *d.*
18 let us devise *d.* ag. Jeremi.
Dan. 11:21 shall forecast his *d.*
2 *Cor.* 2:11 not ignorant of his *d.*

DEV

DEVIL.
Mat. 4:1 to be tempted of the *d.*
9:32 mun poss. w'd a *d.* 12:22
11:18 he hath a *d. Luke* 7:33
13:39 that sowed them is the *d.*
15:22 is vexed with a *d.*
17:18 Jesus rebuked the *d.*
23:41 fire, prepared for the *d.*
Mark 5:15 poss. with *d.* 16, 18
7:29 *d.* is gone out of thy dau.
Luke 4:2 forty days tempt. of *d.*
13 when *d.* had ended tempt.
33 a spirit of an unclean *d.*
35 *d.* had thrown him
8:12 *d.* taketh away the word
29 driven of *d.* into wilderness
9:42 the *d.* threw him down
11:14 when the *d.* was gone out
John 6:70 and one of you is a *d.*
7:20 said, Thou hast a *d.* 8:48
8:44 ye are of your father the *d.*
49 I have not a *d.*; 52 hast a *d.*
10:20 many said, He hath a *d.*
13:2 *d.* having put into Judas
Acts 10:38 heal. all oppr. with *d.*
13:10 thou child of the *d.*
Eph. 4:27 neither give pla. to *d.*
6:11 to stand aga. wiles of *d.*
1 *Tim.* 3:6 fall into cond. of *d.*
7 lest he fall into snare of *d.*
2 *Tim.* 2:26 rec. out of sna. of *d.*
Heb. 2:14 p. of death, that is *d.*
Jam. 4:7 resist *d.* and he will fl.
1 *Pet.* 5:8 your adversary the *d.*
1 *John* 3:8 commit. sin is of *d.*
might destroy works of *d.*
10 children of *d.* are manifest
Jude 9 Mich. contend. with *d.*
Rev. 2:10 *d.* cast some into pris.
12:9 old serpent called the *d.*
12 *d.* is come down
20:2 old serpent which is the *d.*
10 *d.* that deceived, was c. out

DEVILISH.
Jam. 3:15 this wisd. earthly, *d.*

DEVILS.
Lev. 17:7 no more of. sac. to *d.*
2 *Chr.* 11:15 ordained prie. f. *d.*
Ps. 106:37 sacrificed sons to *d.*
Mat. 4:24 poss. with *d.* 8:16, 28,
33; *Mark* 1:32; *Luke* 8:36
8:31 the *d.* besought, *Mark* 5:12
38 saw one casting out *d.* in thy name, *Luke* 9:49
10:17 in my name cast out *d.*
Luke 4:41 *d.* came out of many
8:2 out of whom went seven *d.*
36 by what means he pos. of *d.*
9:1 authority over all *d.*
10:17 even *d.* are subject to us
13:32 tell thut fox, I cast out *d.*
1 *Cor.* 10:20 Gent. sacrifice to *d.* I wo. not ye have fel. with *d.*
21 the cup of *d.* the Lord's table, and of the table of *d.*
1 *Tim.* 4:1 heed to doctr. of *d.*
Jam. 2:19 *d.* believe and tremble
Rev. 9:20 should not worship *d.*
16:14 the spirits of *d.* working
18:2 become habitation of *d.*

See CAST.

DEVISE.
2 *Sam.* 14:14 *d.* means that han.
Ps. 35:4 confusion, *d.* my hurt
41:7 ag. me do they *d.* my hurt
Prov. 3:29 *d.* not evil ag. neigh.
14:22 *d.* evil? but mercy and truth be to them *d.* good
16:30 shutteth eyes to *d.* frow.
Jer. 18:11 *d.* a device against you
18 let us *d.* devices ag. Jerem.
Ezek. 11:2 *d.* mischief in this city
Mic. 2:1 woe to them *d.* iniquity
3 ag. this fam. do I *d.* an evil

DEVISED.
1 *K.* 12:33 month which he *d.*
Est. 8:3 device he had *d.* ag. J.
9:25 *d.* come to own head
Jer. 11:19 *d.* devices against me
51:12 *d.* and done, *Lam.* 2:17
2 *Pet.* 1:16 cunningly *d.* fables

DEVISETH.
Ps. 36:4 *d.* mischief on his bed
52:2 thy tongue *d.* mischiefs
Prov. 6:14 wicked imaginations
16:9 a man's heart *d.* his way
24:8 *d.* evil be called mischievous
Is. 32:7 he *d.* wicked devices to
8 the liberal *d.* liberal things

DEV

DEVOTED.
Lev. 27:29 *d.* thing is most holy
Num. 18:14 every thing *d.*
Ps. 119:38 whose fe *d.* to thy fear

DEVOTIONS.
Acts 17:23 as I beheld your *d.*

DEVOUR.
Gen. 49:27 in morning *d.* prey
Deut. 32:42 sword shall *d.* flesh
2 *Sam.* 2:26 sh. sw. *d.* for ever?
Job 18:13 first-born of death sh. *d.*
Ps. 80:13 wild beast doth *d.* it
Is. 1:7 land, strangers *d.* it
9:12 *d.* Israel with open mouth
18 wickedness sh. *d.* briers
31:8 sword, not of mean man *d.*
42:14 destroy and *d.* at once
56:9 ye beasts of the field, come to *d. Jer.* 12:9; 15:3
Jer. 2:3 all *d.* Israel shall offend
12:12 sw. of L. shall *d.* 46:10, 14
30:16 all that *d.* thee be fer.
Ezek. 36:14 shalt *d.* men no mo.
Dan. 7:5 *d.* much flesh
23 *d.* the whole earth
Hos. 5:7 month *d.* with portions
13:8 will I *d.* them like a lion
Amos 1:4 fire *d.* palaces 7, 10, 12
Ob. 18 kindle in them, and *d.*
Nah. 2:13 sw. *d.* the young lions
Hab. 3:14 rejoic. to *d.* the poor
Zec. 12:6 *d.* all people
Mat. 23:14 ye *d.* widows' houses, *Mark* 12:40; *Luke* 20:47
2 *Cor.* 11:20 if a man *d.* you
Gal. 5:15 if bite and *d.* one ano.
Heb. 10:27 shall *d.* adversaries
1 *Pet.* 5:8 seeking wh. he may *d.*
Rev. 12:4 to *d.* her child as soon

Fire DEVOUR.
Jud. 9:15 let *fire d.* the cedars
20 let *fire d.* the men of Shec.
Ps. 21:9 the *fire* shall *d.* them
50:3 a *fire* shall *d.* before him
Is. 26:11 *f.* of enemies *d.* them
39:11 your breath as *fire d.* you
Ezek. 15:7 another *fire d.* them
23:25 the *fire* shall *d.* thy sons
Amos 5:6 break out like *f. d.* it
Nah. 3:13 *fire* shall *d.* thy bars
Zec. 11:1 *fire* may *d.* thy cedars

It shall DEVOUR.
Job 18:13 *i. s. d.* strength of skin
Is. 10:17 *it shall d.* his thorns
Jer. 5:14 Rev. *it s. d.* them
17:27 and *it shall d.* the palaces of Jerusalem, *Amos* 2:5
Hos. 8:14 *it s. d. Amos* 1:14; 2:2

DEVOURED.
Gen. 37:20 some evil beast *d.* h.
33 *Lev.* 10:2 fire from Lord *d.* them
Num. 26:10 fire *d.* 250 men
Deut. 31:17 hide face shall *d. be*
32:24 be *d.* with burning heat
2 *Sam.* 18:8 wood *d.* more than
22:9 his mouth *d. Ps.* 18:8
Ps. 79:7 for they have *d.* Jacob
Is. 1:20 be *d.* with the sword
24:6 therefore curse *d.* earth
Jer. 2:30 your sword *d.* prophets
3:24 shame hath *d.* the labor
8:16 and have *d.* the land
10:25 eaten up Jacob, *d.* him
30:16 devour thee shall be *d.*
50:7 all that found *d.* them
17 the king of Assyr. hath *d.*
51:34 Nebuchadnezzar *d.* me
Lam. 4:11 hath *d.* found. thereof
Ezek. 15:5 when fire hath *d.* it
16:20 sacrificed sons to be *d.*
19:3 to catch prey, it *d.* men, 6
14 fire hath *d.* her fruit
22:25 a roaring lion, *d.* souls
23:25 the residue be *d.* by fire
35:27 J. will give to be *d. 39:4*
Dan. 7:7 it *d.* and brake, 19
Hos. 7:7 have *d.* their judges
9 strangers have *d.* his streng.
Joel 1:19 fire *d.* pastures, 20
Amos 4:9 palmer worm *d.* trees
7:4 and it *d.* the great deep
Nah. 1:10 shall be *d.* as stubble
Zep. 1:18 be *d.* by jealousy
3:8 earth shall be *d.* with fire
Zec. 9:4 smite *d.* by fire
Mat. 13:4 fowls came *d.* them,
Luke 8:5
Luke 15:30 thy son *d.* living
Rev. 20:9 fire came and *d.* them

DEVOURER.
Mal. 3:11 I will rebuke the *d.*

DEVOUREST, ETH.
Ezek. 36:13 thou land *d.* up men
2 *Sam.* 11:25 sword *d.* one
Prov. 19:28 wicked *d.* iniquity

DID

Prov. 20:25 a snare to man *d.*
Is. 5:24 fire *d.* stubble, *Joel* 2:5
Lam. 2:3 flaming fire, which *d.*
Ezek. 15:4 fire *d.* both ends of it
Joel 2:3 a fire *d.* before them
Hab. 1:13 wicked *d.* more right.
Rev. 11:5 fire *d.* their enemies

DEVOURING.
Ex. 24:17 appearance *d.* fire
Ps. 52:4 lovest all *d.* words
Is. 29:6 visit. with *d.* fire, 30:30
30:27 his tongue as a *d.* fire
33:14 who dwell with *d.* fire?

DEVOUT.
Luke 2:25 Sim. was just and *d.*
Acts 2:5 at Jerusal. Jews *d.* men
8:2 *d.* men car. Steph. to burial
10:2 Cornelius; 7 *d.* soldier
13:50 Jews stirred up *d.* women
17:4 of *d.* Greeks a great mult.
17 P. disputed with *d.* persons
22:12 Ananias a *d.* man

DEW.
Gen. 27:28 G. give thee of the *d.*
39 *Ex.* 16:13 morning the *d.* lay
Num. 11:9 when *d.* fell on camp
Deut. 32:2 my speech distil as *d.*
33:13 blessed be J.'s land for *d.*
28 his heavens shall drop *d.*
Jud. 6:37 if *d.* on fleece only
39 on ground let there be *d.*
2 *Sam.* 1:21 be no *d.* upon you
17:12 light on him as *d.* falleth
1 K. 17:1 there shall not be *d.*
Job 29:19 *d.* lay on my branch
38:28 hath begot. drops of *d.?*
Ps. 110:3 hast *d.* of thy youth
133:3 as the *d.* of Hermon
Prov. 3:20 clouds drop down *d.*
19:12 but his favor is as *d.*
Cant. 5:2 head is filled with *d.*
Is. 18:4 cloud of *d.* in harvest
26:19 thy *d.* as *d.* of herbs
Hos. 6:4 early *d.* it goeth, 13:3
14:5 I will be as the *d.* to Israel
Hag. 1:10 heaven stayed from *d.*
Zec. 8:12 heavens give their *d.*

DIADEM.
Job 29:14 my judgment as a *d.*
Is. 28:5 and for a *d.* of beauty
62:3 a royal *d.* in hand of God
Ezek. 21:26 remove the *d.*

DIAL.
2 *K.* 20:11 down in the *d. Is.* 38:8

DIAMOND.
Ex. 28:18 second row a *d.* 39:11
Jer. 17:1 sin is written with a *d.*

DIANA. *Acts* 19:24, 35
DIBON. *Num.* 21:30; *Jos.* 13:17; *Neh.* 11:25; *Is.* 15:2; *Jer.* 48:18, 22
DIBON-GAD. *Num.* 33:45, 46

DID.
Neh. 9:16 knew not what I *d.*
Mat. 12:3 read what David *d.?*
27:15 wood. things that he *d.*
Mark 3:8 great things he *d.*
6:20 heard *d.* many things; *Acts* 2:22 God *d.* by him
13:24 works none other man *d.*
Acts 3:17 ye *d.* it as *d.* rulers
26:10 which thing I *d.* in Jeru.
2 *Cor.* 8:5 *d.* not as we hoped
1 *Pet.* 2:22 who *d.* no sin, nor

DID, joined with a.
Ex. 7:6 *d.* as L. com. 10, 20;
12:28, 50; 39:32; *Lev.* 8:4;
16:34; 24:23; *Num.* 1:54;
2:34; 20:27; 27:22; 31:31
Jud. 15:11 as they *d.* to me
2 *Sam.* 3:36 as what king *d.*
5:25 David *d.* as L. commanded
1 K. 17:14 as *d.* fathers, so do
1 *Chr.* 14:16 David *d.* as G. com.
Luke 9:54 com. fire as Elias *d.*
Acts 7:51 as your fathers *d.* so do ye
Heb. 4:10 ceased, as God *d.*

DID, joined with evil.
Jud. 2:11 *d.* evil in s. of L. 3:7, 12; 4:1; 6:1; 10:6; 13:1;
1 *K.* 14:22; 15:26, 34; 16:7, 30;
21:20, 25; 2 *K.* 8:18, 24, 27; 21:2, 16, 20;
2 *Chr.* 12:14 Rehob.; 33:22 Amon

CRUDEN'S CONCORDANCE. 823

DIE
Neh. 9:28 had rest, they *d. evil*
Is. 65:12 *d. evil* bef. m. eyce, 66:4
2 *Tim.* 4:14 Alex. *d,* me much a

DID not.
2 *K.* 16:2 Ahaz *d. not* right
Jer. 11:8 but they *d.* them *not*
Mat. 13:58 he *d. not* many works
23:45 *d.* it *not* to one of these
John 8:40 this *d. not* Abraham
2 *Cor.* 7:12 I *d.* it *not* for his cau.

Thus DID.
Job 1:5 thus *d.* Job continually

DIDST.
2 *Sam.* 12:12 thou *d.* it secretly
Ps. 39:9 dumb, because thou *d.*
44:1 work thou *d.* in their days
Is. 64:3 *d.* terrible things

DIDYMUS.
John 11:16 T. cal. D. 20:24; 21:2

DIE.
See on DEAD and DEATH.
Gen. 6:17 every thing shall *d.*
44:22 his father would *d.*
48:30 now let me *d.*
47:29 that Israel must *d.*
Ex. 9:4 nothing *d.* of Israel's
10:28 seest my face, shalt *d.*
11:5 first-born in Egypt shall *d.*
Num. 14:35 in wilder. they sh. *d.*
16:29 if these *d.* common death
20:26 and Aaron shall *d.* there
21:10 let me *d.* death of right.
Deut. 22:5 if one *d.* and have no
children, *Mark* 12:19
31:14 days approach th. must *d.*
32:50 and *d.* in the mount
Jud. 16:30 let me *d.* with Phil.
1 *Sam.* 2:33 increase of house *d.*
31 sons in one day shall *d.*
14:45 said, Shall Jonathan *d.*
2 *Sam.* 18:3 nor if half of us *d.*
1 *K.* 14:12 feet enter child sha. *d.*
2 *K.* 20:1 shall *d.* and not live
2 *Chr.* 25:4 every man shall *d.* for
his own sin, *Jer.* 31:30
Job 2:9 said, Curse God and *d.*
4:21 they *d.* without wisdom
12:2 wisdom shall *d.* with you
14:8 and the stock thereof *d.*
If if man *d.* shall he live ag.
34:20 in a moment shall they *d.*
36:12 shall *d.* without knowl.
14 they *d.* in youth, their life
Ps. 49:10 seeth that wise men *d.*
101:29 sw. their breath, they *d.*
Prov. 10:21 fools *d.* for want of
Ec. 7:17 *d.* before thy time
9:5 living know they shall *d.*
Is. 22:18 large country, there *d.*
51:6 that dwell therein shall *d.*
12 afraid of a man that shall *d.*
65:20 child shall *d.* 100 years old
Jer. 11:22 you, man shall *d.* by
sw. sons and dau. by famine
16:4 shall *d.* of grievous deaths
6 great and the small shall *d.*
24:16 this year thou shalt *d.*
31:6 but thou shalt *d.* in peace
Ezek. 18:4 soul sin. shall *d.* 20
28:8 *d.* deaths of them slain
33:6 that wicked man shall *d.*
27 in caves *d.* of the pestilence
Amos 2:2 Moab shall *d.*
6:9 they shall *d.*
7:17 shalt *d.* in a polluted land
9:10 sinners of my people *d.*
Zec. 11:9 that dieth, let it *d.*
13:8 two parts be cut off and *d.*
Mat. 15:4 curse father or mother
let him *d. Mark* 7:10
22:24 *d.* hav. no s. *Luke* 20:28
Luke 20:36 nei. can *d.* any more
John 4:49 come ere my child *d.*
11:50 one *d.* for the peo. 18:14
51 J. should *d.* for that nation
12:24 except a corn of wheat *d.*
Rom. 5:7 for a r. man will one *d.*
1 *Cor.* 15:22 as in Adam all *d.*
32 not quickened except it *d.*
Heb. 7:8 that *d.* receive tithes
Rev. 14:13 blessed that *d.* in L.

He DIE.
Gen. 38:11 lest *he d.* as bro. did
Num. 35:16 if he smite him that
he d. 20, 21, 23; *Deut.* 13:10;
19:5, 11; 21:21
Deut. 20:5 lest *he d.* in
Jud. 6:30 being son, that *he d.*
2 *Sam.* 11:15 that Uriah may *d.*
1 *K.* 12:2 I wick. in him *he sh. d.*
3:1 David, that he should *d.*
19:4 K. requested he might *d.*
Ps. 41:5 when shall *he d.* and
Prov. 5:23 *he d.* without instruc.
15:10 he that hateth rep. shall *d.*

DIE
Prov. 19:16 *he* do. his ways sh. *d.*
Jer. 22:12 *he d.* whither led cap.
26:10 take up *der.* before *he d.*
Ezek. 3:19 *he* shall *d.* in his iniq.
18:18; 33:9, 13, 18
12:13 not see it, though *he d.*
17:16 in Babylon *he* shall *d.*
John 12:33 death *he* sh. *d.* 18:32

I DIE.
Gen. 26:9 Lest *I d.* for her
27:4 may bless thee before *I d.*
30:1 give me children or *I d.*
45:28 see him before *I d.*
48:21 Israel said to Joseph, *I d.*
50:5 lo, *I d.* ; 24 Jos. said, *I d.*
Deut. 4:22 I must *d.* in this land
Jud. 15:18 shall *I d.* for thirst
Ruth 1:17 where diest will *I d.*
1 *Sam.* 14:43 and lo, *I must d.*
2 *Sam.* 19:37 *I d.* in m. own city
1 *K.* 2:30 nay, *I* will *d.* here
Job 27:5 justify you ; till *I d.*
29:18 *I* shall *d.* in my nest
Prov. 30:7 deny me not for *I d.*
Jer. 37:20 not return, lest *I d.*
Mat. 26:35 *I* sh. *d. Mark* 14:31
1 *Cor.* 15:31 *I d.* daily

Not DIE.
Gen. 42:20 be verified *not d.*
Deut. 18:16 see fire, that I *d. not*
33:6 let Reuben live and *not d.*
Jud. 6:23 shalt *not d.* 1 *Sam.* 20:2;
2 *Sa.* 12:13; 19:23; *Jer.* 38:24
1 *Sam.* 12:19 pray that we *d. not*
20:14 kind. of Lord that I *d. not*
2 *K.* 18:32 ye may live and *not d.*
2 *Chr.* 25:4 fath. n. *d.* for child.
Ps. 118:17 I shall n. *d,* but live
Prov. 23:13 shall n. *d. Ezek.* 18:17,
21, 28; 33:15; *John* 21:23
Is. 51:14 he should *not d.*
66:24 their worm shall *not d.*
Jer. 11:21 *d. not* by our hand
31:4 shall *not d.* by the sword
Ezek. 13:19 souls should *not d.*
Hab. 1:12 we shall *not d.* Lord
John 6:50 eat thereof and *not d.*
21:23 that disciple should *not d.*

Surely DIE.
Gen. 2:17 *s. d.* 20:7 ; 1 *Sam.* 14:44;
22:16 ; 1 *K.* 2:37, 42 ; *Jer.* 26:8;
Ezek. 3:18 ; 33:8, 14
3:4 ye shall *not surely d.*
Num. 26:65 they shall *surely d.*
Jud. 13:29 *s. d.* bec. we ha. seen
1 *Sam.* 14:39 he shall *s. d.* 20:31;
2 *Sam.* 13:5 ; 2 *K.* 8:10 ; *Jer.*
26:18
2 *Sam.* 12:14 child born *shall s. d.*
1 *K.* 1:4 but shalt *surely d.* 6, 16

To DIE.
Gen. 25:32 I am at point to *d.*
Ex. 14:11 to *d.* in wil. *Num.* N. 21:5
Num. 26:10 or his day co. to *d.*
28:9 a snare to cause me to *d.*
Deut. 32:11 give yoursel, to *d.*
Ps. 79:11 that are appointed to *d.*
88:13 and ready to *d.* from youth
Ec. 3:2 born, and a time to *d.*
Jer. 26:11 worthy to *d.* ; 16 not
38:9 he to like to *d.* for hunger
*to to Jonathan's house to *d.*
Jon. 4:9 better for me to *d.*
8 Jonah wished in himself to *d.*
Luke 7:2 centu. serv. ready to *d.*
John 19:7 by law he ought to *d.*
Acts 21:13 I am ready also to *d.*
25:11 I refuse *not to d.*
16 of Romans to del. any to *d.*
Rom. 5:7 some would dare to *d.*
2 *Cor.* 7:3 in our hearts to *d.*
Phil. 1:21 to live is C. to *d.* is
1 *Th.* 8:27 app. to men once to *d.*
Rev. 3:2 that are ready to *d.*
9:6 desire to *d.* and death flee

We DIE.
Gen. 47:15 *we d.* in thy pres. 19
Ex. 14:12 than *we d.* d. in wil.
20:19 speak lest *we d. Deut.* 5:25
Num. 17:12 *we d,* *we* all perish
20:1 that *we* and cattle *d,* there
Num. 14:2 *we* may eat it and *d.*
2 *K.* 7:3 why sit here till *we d.*?
4 if kill us, *we* shall but *d.*
John 11:16 *d.* to-morrow *we* sh. *d.*
1 *Cor.* 15:32

Ye DIE.
Gen. 3:4 nor touch it lest *ye d.*
Ps. 82:7 *ye* shall *d.* like men

DIE
Is. 22:14 not be purged till *ye d.*
Jer. 22:26 there shall *ye d.* 42:16
27:13 why will *ye d. Ezek.* 18:31 ;
33:11
42:22 *ye* shall *d.* by the sword
John 8:21 *ye* sh. *d.* in yo. sins, 24
Rom. 8:13 if live after flesh *ye d.*

DIED.
Gen. 7:21 all flesh *d.* 22
25:8 Sarah *d.* ; 25:8 Abraham
25:17 Ishmael ; 35:8 Deborah
35:19 Rachel, 46:7 ; 35:29 Isaac
50:16 Jacob ; 26 Jos. *Ex.* 1:6
Ex. 2:23 the king of Egypt *d.*
16:3 would to God we had *d.* in
Eg. Num. 14:2 ; 20:3 ; 26:10
Lev. 10:2 Nad. and Ab. *d.* 16:1 ;
Num. 3:4 ; 26:61 ; 1 *Chr.* 24:2
Num. 14:37 searchers of land *d.*
20:28 Aaron *d.* 33:38, 39
16:49 now they that *d.* besides
20:1 Miriam ; 31:8 much peo.
25:9 *d.* in the plague were 24,000
26:11 children of Korah *d.* not
27:3 our father *d.* in the wilder.
ness but *d.* in his own sin
Deut. 34:5 Moses *d.*
Jos. 5:4 all the men of war *d.*
Judg. 9:1 1 *Sam.* 25:1 Sam. ; 37 Nab. heart
31:5 Saul and his armor-bearer
d. 6 ; 1 *Chr.* 10:5, 13
2 *Sam.* 3:33 *d.* Abner as a fool
6:7 there Uzzah *d.* ; 1 *Chr.* 13:10
11:17 Uriah the Hittite *d.*
12:18 on seventh day child *d.*
18:33 I had *d.* for thee, O Ab.
19:6 and all we had *d.* this day
24:15 *d.* of peo. even from Dan
1 *K.* 3:19 this woman's child *d.*
14:17 came to threshold, child *d.*
2 *K.* 4:20 sat on her knees, *d.*
13:14 Elisha, 20 ; 24 Hazael
2 *Chr.* 24:22 he *d.* said. L. look
Job 3:11 why *d.* I not fr. womb?
42:50 so Job *d.* being old
Is. 6:1 Uzziah *d.* ; 14:28 Ahaz *d.*
Ezek. 24:18 at even my wife *d.*
Hos. 13:1 offended in Baal, he *d.*
Mat. 22:27 last of all woman *d.*
Luke 20:32
Luke 16:22 beggar *d.* rich man *d.*
John 11:21 my bro. had not *d.* 32
37 even this man sh. not ha. *d.*
Acts 9:37 Dorcas was sick and *d.*
Rom. 5:6 Christ *d.* for ungodly
8 Christ *d.* for us
14:9 to this end Christ both *d.*
15 for whom C. *d.* 1 *Cor.* 8:11
1 *Cor.* 5:15 if one *d.* for all, then
15 live to him who *d.* for them
1 *Thes.* 4:14 if we believe Jesus *d.*
5:10 *d.* for us, that we sho. live
Heb. 10:28 does. Moses' law *d.*
11:13 these all *d.* in faith, not
32 by faith Joseph when he *d.*
Rev. 8:9 the third part *d.*
11 many men *d.* of wa. bitter
16:3 every living soul *d.* in sea

And he, So he, That he DIED.
Jud. 4:21 nail into tem. so he *d.*
1 *Sam.* 4:18 E. neck bra. *a. he d.*
1:45 reseuced Jon. *h. he d.* not
2 *Sam.* 11:21 sm. Abim. *th. he d.*
2 *K.* 1:17 Ahaziah *d.* according
8:15 eL. on his face, *so th. he d.*
2 *Chr.* 13:20 struck him, *a. he d.*
Luke 20:29 *d. he d.* without chi.
Acts 7:15 *he d.* in Egypt, *he* and
Rom. 6:10 in th *he d.* to sin
2 *Cor.* 5:15 *t. he d.* for all, th. they

DIEST.
Ruth 1:17 wh. thou *d.* I will die

DIET.
Jer. 52:34 for his *d.* continual *d.*

DIETH.
Lev. 22:8 wh. *d.* of itself, not eat
1 *Sam.* 3:33 died A. as a fool *d.*
11:25 in his city may eat *d.*
Job 14:10 man *d.* wasteth away
21:23 one *d.* in his full strength
25 *d.* in bitterness of soul
Ec. 2:16 how *d.* the wise man?
3:19 *d. d.* so *d.* the other
Is. 50:2 their fish *d.* for thirst
66:5 that cutteth off as if *d.*
Ezek. 18:26 iniquity, *d.* in them
32 no pleas. in death of him *d.*
83:7 that that *d.* let it die
Mark 9:44 worm *d.* not, 46, 48

DIL
Rom. 6:9 Christ *d.* no more
14:7 no man *d.* to himself

DYING.
Num. 17:13 be consumed wi. *d.?*
6:27 ye *d.* first *d.* left no seed
Luke 8:42 Jairus' dau. lay a *d.*
2 *Cor.* 4:10 in body the *d.* of Jesus
6:9 as *d.* and behold we live
Heb. 11:21 by faith Jac. when *d.*

DIFFER.
1 *Cor.* 4:7 who maketh thee to *d.*

DIFFERENCE, S.
Ex. 11:7 L. put *d.* b. Eg. and Is.
Lev. 10:10 *d.* bet. holy and unh.
Ezek. 22:26 they have put no *d.*
44:23 teach my people the *d.*
Acts 13:9 no *d.* bet. us and them
Rom. 3:22 that believe, for no *d.*
10:12 no *d.* bet. Jew and Greek
1 *Cor.* 12:5 *d.* of administrations
Jude 22 compassion, making a *d.*

DIFFERETH, ING.
Rom. 12:6 gifts *d,* acc. to grace
1 *Cor.* 15:41 one star *d.* from ano.
Gal. 4:1 the heir when a child *d.*

DIG.
Job 3:21 *d,* for it more than for
6:27 ye *d.* a pit for your friend
11:18 thou shalt *d.* about thee
24:16 in dark *d.* thro' houses
Ezek. 8:8 *d.* now in the wall
12:5 *d.* thro' wall in their sight
Amos 9:2 though they *d.* into hell
Luke 13:8 let it alone till I *d.*
16:3 I cannot *d.*

DIGGED.
Gen. 40:6 in self-will *d.* down
50:5 my grave I have *d.* for me
Num. 21:18 princes *d.* the well
Deut. 6:11 welle *d.* diggedst not
2 *K.* 19:24 I have *d.* and drunk
strange waters. *Is.* 37:25
Ps. 7:15 a pit and *d.* it, 57:6
35:7 they *d.* a pit for my soul
94:13 till pit be *d.* for wicked
119:85 proud *d.* pits for me
Ec. 2:6 not he pruned nor *d.*
7:25 on hills *d.* with mattock
51:1 hole of pit whence ye are *d.*
Jer. 18:20 *d.* pit for my soul, 22
25:18 *d.* and hid lord's money
Luke 6:48 *d.* and laid foundation
Rom. 11:3 *d.* down thine altars
26:27 *d.* pit shall fall, *Ec.* 10:8

DIGGETH.
Prov. 16:27 ungodly *d.* up evil
26:27 *d.* pit shall fall, *Ec.* 10:8

DIGNITY, IES.
Gen. 49:3 Reu. excellency of *d.*
Est. 6:3 what *d.* to Mordecai
Hab. 10:6 folly is set in great *d.*
Ec. 10:6 *d. d.* *Moses'* lord
2 *Pet.* 2:10 sp. evil of *d. Jude* 8

DILIGENCE.
Prov. 4:23 keep heart with all *d.*
Luke 12:58 art in way, give *d.*
Rom. 12:8 that ruleth, with *d.*
2 *Cor.* 8:7 as ye abound in all *d.*
2 *Tim.* 4:9 do thy *d.* to come, 21
Heb. 6:11 cv. one do sh. same *d.*
2 *Pet.* 1:5 giv. all *d.* add to faith
10 *d. d.* to make calling sure
Jude 3 I gave all *d.* to write

DILIGENT.
Deut. 19:18 make *d.* inquisition
Jos. 22:5 take *d.* heed to do com.
Ps. 64:6 accomplish a *d.* search
77:6 my spirit made *d.* research
Prov. 10:4 hand of *d.* mak. rich
12:24 hand of *d.* shall bear rule
27 substance of *d.* is precious
13:4 soul of *d.* sh. be made fat
21:5 thoughts of *d.* tend to ple.
22:29 seest a man *d.* in bus.
27:23 be *d.* to know state of *d.*
2 *Cor.* 8:22 whom we have often
proved *d.* how much more *d.*
2 *Pet.* 3:14 *d.* ye be fo. him in peace

DILIGENTLY.
Ex. 15:26 if wilt *d.* heark. *Deut.*
11:13 ; 28:1 ; *Jer.* 17:24
Deut. 4:9 and keep thy soul *d.*
6:7 teach them *d.* to thy child.
17 *d.* keep commands. 11:22
13:14 ask *d.* and if be truth
19:18 *d.* done for beast of G.
Job 13:17 hear *d.* my sp. 21:2
Ps. 37:10 *d.* consider his place
119: I to keep thy precepts *d.*
Prov. 7:15 *d.* to seek thy face
11:27 he that *d.* seeketh good
23:1 consider *d.* what is before
Jer. 2:10 hearkened *d.*
12:16 *d.* learn the ways of my
Zec. 6:15 if will *d.* obey the voice
Mat. 2:7 inquired *d.* wh. time
8 search *d.* for young child
Luke 15:8 seek *d.* till she find
Acts 18:25 spake and taught *d.*
2 *Tim.* 1:17 he sought me out *d.*
Tit. 3:13 bring Zenas and Ap. *d.*
Heb. 11:6 he is a rewarder of them
that *d.* seek him
12:15 looking *d.* lest any man
1 *Pet.* 1:10 *d.* have inquired and eat

824 CRUDEN'S CONCORDANCE.

DIS

Jer. 2:10 consider d. see if
12:16 d. learn ways of my peo.
Zec. 6:15 if d. obey voice of L.
Mat. 2:8 search d. for yo. child
16 d. inquired of the wise men
Luke 15:8 seek d. till she find it
Acts 18:25 taught d. things of L.
1 Tim. 5:10 she followed d. every
2 Tim. 1:17 in Ro. sought me d.
Heb. 11:6 rew. of them d. seek
12:15 looking d. lest any fail
1 Pet. 1:10 prophets searched d.

DIM.
Gen. 27:1 Is. was old, his eyes d.
48:10 the eyes of Israel were d.
Deut. 34:7 Moses' eye was not d.
1 Sam. 3:2 Eli's eyes wax d. 4:15
Job 17:7 mine eye is d. by sorrow
Is. 32:3 that see, shall not be d.
Lam. 4:1 how is gold become d.
5:17 those things our eyes d.

DIMINISH, ED, ING.
Ex. 5:8 you shall not d. aught
Lev. 25:16 acc. to years shalt d.
Deut. 4:2 nor d. aught, 12:32
Prov. 13:11 w. got. by vanity d.
Is. 21:17 men of Kedar sh. be d.
Jer. 26:2 I com. d. not a word
29:6 may be inc. and not d.
Ezek. 5:11 therefore also d. thee
16:27 I have d. thine ordi. food
29:15 I will d. them
Rom. 11:12 d. of them the riches

DIMNESS.
Is. 8:22 behold, d. of anguish
9:1 d. not be such as in her

DIMON. *Is.* 15:9
DINAH. *Gen.* 30:21; 34:5

DINE, D.
Gen. 43:16 d. with me at noon
Luke 11:37 Pha. bes. him to d.
John 21:12 J. saith, Come and d.
15 had d. Jesus saith to Simon

DINNER.
Prov. 15:17 better is a d. of herbs
Mat. 22:4 I have prepared my d.
Luke 11:38 not washed before d.
14:12 when thou makest a d.

DIONYSIUS. *Acts* 17:34
DIOTREPHES. *3 John* 9

DIP.
Deut. 33:24 Asher d. foot in oil
Ruth 2:14 d. morsel in vinegar
Luke 16:24 that he may d. finger

DIPPED, ETH.
Gen. 37:31 d. coat in the blood
Lev. 9:9 and he d. finger in bl.
Jos. 3:15 priest's feet d. in brim
1 Sam. 14:27 d. rod in honey-co.
2 K. 5:14 Naaman d. in Jordan
Ps. 68:23 thy foot be d. in blood
Mat. 26:23 d. wi. me, Mark 14:20
John 13:26 have d. it, when he d.
Rev. 19:13 with vesture d. in bl.

DIRECT.
Gen. 46:28 d. his face to Goshen
Ps. 5:3 morning d. my prayer
Prov. 3:6 he shall d. thy paths
11:5 righte. of the perf. shall d.
Ex. 10:10 wisd. is profitable to d.
Is. 45:13 I will d. all his ways
61:8 d. their work in truth
Jer. 10:23 to d. his steps
1 Thes. 3:11 L. J. C. d. our way to
2 Thes. 3:5 L. d. hearts into love

DIRECTED, ETH.
Job 32:14 not d. his words aga.
37:3 it under whole heaven
Ps. 119:5 ways were d. to keep
Prov. 16:9 the Lord d. his steps
21:29 upright, he d. his way
Is. 40:13 who hath d. the Spirit

DIRT.
Jud. 3:22 and the d. came out
Ps. 18:42 I cast them out as d.
Is. 57:20 whose waters cast up d.

DISALLOW, ED.
Num. 30:5 father d. her not, 8, 11
1 Pet. 2:4 d. indeed of men, but
7 stone builders d. is made h.

DISANNUL.
Job 40:8 wilt thou d. my judg.?
Is. 14:27 L. purposed, who d. it?
Gal. 3:17 coven. law cannot d.

DISANNULLED, ING.
Is. 28:18 coven. with death be d.
Gal. 3:15 no man d. or addeth
Heb. 7:18 there is a d. of com.

DISAPPOINT, ED, ETH.
Job 5:12 d. devices of crafty
Ps. 17:13 arise, O Lord, d. him
Prov. 15:22 purposes are d.

DIS

DISCERN.
Gen. 31:32 d. thou what is thine
2 Sam. 14:17 so is my Lord to d.
19:35 can I d. bet. good and ev. ?
1 K. 3:9 I may d. betw. good
11 asked unders. to d. judg.
Ezr. 3:13 not d. noise of joy
Job 4:16 not d. form thereof
6:30 taste d. perverse things ?
Ezek. 44:23 cause d. bet. uncl.
Jon. 4:11 d. bet. right and left
Mal. 3:18 d. bet. right. and wick.
Mat. 16:3 can d. sky, Luke 12:56
Heb. 5:14 senses exer. to d. good

DISCERNED, ETH.
1 K. 20:41 king of Israel d. him
Prov. 7:7 I d. among the youths
Ec. 8:5 wise d. time and judg.
1 Cor. 2:14 because spiritually d.

DISCERNER.
Heb. 4:12 is a d. of the thoughts

DISCERNING.
1 Cor. 11:29 not d. the L. body
12:10 to another, d. of spirits

DISCHARGE, D.
Jud. 4:15 the Lord d. Sisera
Ec. 8:8 there is no d. in that war

DISCIPLE.
Mat. 10:24 d. is not above his master, *Luke* 6:40
42 give cup of cold water to d.
27:57 Joseph also was Jesus' d.
John 9:28 art his d. we are Mo.
19:16 went out that other d.
19:26 d. standing by, Jc. loved
38 being a d. but secretly
20:2 d. Jesus loved, 21:7, 20
4 the other d. did outrun Pet.
8 went in also that other d.
21:23 that that d. should not die
24 this is the d. which testif.
Acts 9:10 a certain d. at Damas.
26 believed not that he was d.
36 Joppa a d. named Tabitha
21:16 old d. with whom lodge

My DISCIPLE.
Luke 14:26 be my d.
27 bear cross cannot be my d.
33 fore. not all, not be my d.

DISCIPLES.
Mat. 9:14 then came d. of John
11:1 end of commanding his d.
14:26 when d. saw him on sea
17:6 d. heard it, fell on th. face
19:13 d. rob. them, Mark 10:13
20:17 twelve d. apart in way
22:16 Pharisees sent their d.
26:26 J. took bread, gave to d.
35 likewise also said all the d.
56 d. forsook him and fled
Mark 2:18 why d. of John and of Pharisees fast, *Luke* 5:33
9:14 d. forgotten to take bread
Luke 19:37 d. began to rejoice
John 3:25 betw. John's d. and
4:1 Je. bap. more d. that John
9:28 but we are Moses' d.
13:5 began to wash the d. feet
16:17 art one of this man's d. ?
10:38 told d. she had seen Lord
Acts 9:1 breath. slaughter ag. d.
26 Saul assayed to join the d.
11:26 d. called Christian first
19:1 Ephesus, finding certain d.
30 the d. suffered him not
20:7 d. came to break bread
30 to draw away d. after them

His DISCIPLES.
Mat. 8:23 his d. awoke him
9:19 Jes. followed, so did his d.
28:7 tell his d. he is risen
13 say, ye, h. d. came by night
Luke 5:30 murmur. against h. d.
6:20 lifted up his eyes on his d.
11:1 as John taught his d.
John 9:11 his d. believed on him
4:3 Jes. baptized not but his d.
27 came his d. and marvelled
6:24 his d. were gone away
2:27 will ye also be his d.?
18:1 with his d. over Cedron
2 resorted thither with his d.
20:26 again his d. were within

Of his DISCIPLES.
Mat. 11:2 sent two of his d. Mark 11:1; 14:13; *Luke* 19:29
Mark 6:1 sat with unw. hands
John 6:66 many of his d. went
18:19 high-p. asked J. of his d.
25 art not th. also one of h. d.
21:12 none of his d. durst ask

To his DISCIPLES.
Mat. 14:19 gave loaves to his d.

DIS

Mark 4:34 expounded all to h. d.
Luke 10:23 he turned to his d.
John 21:14 showed hims. to h. d.

My DISCIPLES.
Is. 8:16 seal law among my d.
Mat. 26:18 keep passover with my d. *Mark* 14:14; *Luke* 22:11
John 8:31 my d. indeed, 13:35
15:8 so shall ye be my d.

Thy DISCIPLES.
Mat. 9:14 t. d. fast not, *Mark* 2:18
12:2 thy d. do what is not lawf.
15:2 t. d. transgress tradition ?
17:16 d. they could not cure
Mark 7:5 walk not t. d. accor. to
9:18 t. d. to cast him, *Luke* 9:40
Luke 19:39 Master rebuke thy d.
John 7:3 t. d. see works thou
Job 36:10 openeth their ears to d.

DISCLOSE.
Is. 26:21 earth shall d. her blood

DISCOMFITED.
Jos. 10:10 L. d. them before Is.
Jud. 4:15 the Lord d. Sisera
8:12 Gideon d. all the host
1 Sam. 7:10 thundered on Ph. d.
2 Sam. 22:15 d. them, *Ps.* 18:14
Is. 31:8 young men shall be d.

DISCOMFITURE.
1 Sam. 14:20 was a very great d.

DISCONTENTED.
1 Sam. 22:2 d. gathered to David

DISCONTINUE.
Jer. 17:4 d. from thy heritage

DISCORD.
Prov. 6:14 he soweth d.
19 soweth d. among brethren

DISCOVER.
1 Sam. 14:8 d. ourselves to them
Job 41:13 d. face of his garment ?
Prov. 18:2 his heart may d. itself
25:9 not a secret to another
Is. 3:17 L. will d. th. secret parts
Jer. 13:26 d. thy skirts, *Nah.* 3:5
Lam. 4:22 he will d. thy sins
Ezek. 16:37 I will d. thy nakedn.
Hos. 2:10 will I d. her lewdness
Mic. 1:6 I will d. the foundations

DISCOVERED.
1 Sam. 14:11 d. thems. to garri.
22:6 Saul heard David was d.
Is. 22:8 he d. covering of Judah
57:8 hast d. thyself to another
Jer. 13:22 thy skirts d.
Lam. 2:14 not d. thine iniquity
Ezek. 13:14 foundat. shall be d.
16:36 nakedness d. thro' whor.
57 before thy wickedn. was d.
21:24 that your transgr. are d.
22:10 d. their father's nakedn.
23:10 those d. her nakedness
Hos. 7:1 iniq. of Ephraim was d.

DISCOVERETH, ING.
Hab. 3:13 d. foundation to neck

DISCOURAGE, D.
Num. 21:4 soul of people was d.
32:7 why d. heart of people ? 9
Deut. 1:21 fear not, nor be d.
28 brethren have d. our heart
Is. 42:4 shall not fall nor be d.
Col. 3:21 children, lest they be d.

DISCREET.
Gen. 41:39 none so d. and wise
Tit. 2:5 teach yo. women to be d.

DISCREETLY.
Mark 12:34 Jesus saw he ans. d.

DISCRETION.
Ps. 112:5 guide affairs with d.
Prov. 1:4 to the young man d.
2:11 d. shall preserve thee
3:21 keep wisdom and d.
5:2 fair woman without d.
19:11 d. deferreth his anger
Is. 28:26 God instruct him to d.
Jer. 10:12 stretched heav. by d.

DISDAINED.
1 Sam. 17:42 Goliath d. David
Job 30:1 fathers I would have d.

DISEASE.
2 K. 1:2 I d. recov. of this d.
8:8 shall I recover of this d. ?
2 Chr. 16:12 in his d. he sought
21:15 bowels fall by reason of d.
18 d. smote him with incur. d.
Job 30:18 by d. garment changed

DIS

Ps. 38:7 filled with loathsome d.
41:8 an evil d. say they, cleav.
Ec. 6:2 this is vanity, an evil d.
Mat. 4:23 healing d. 9:35; 10:1
John 5:4 whole of whatsoever d.

DISEASES.
Ex. 15:26 none of these d.
Deut. 28:60 bring on thee d.
29:22 they lay d. of sore d.
24:25 they left him in great d.
Ps. 103:3 who healeth all thy d.
Mat. 4:24 were taken with divers d. *Mark* 1:34; *Luke* 4:40
Luke 9:1 gave power to cure d.
Acts 19:12 d. departed from them
28:9 had d. in island, came

DISEASED.
1 K. 15:23 Asa was d. in his feet
21 because ye have pushed d.
14:35 brought all d. *Mark* 1:32
John 6:2 miracles he did on d.

DISFIGURE.
Mat. 6:16 hypocrites d. faces

DISGRACE.
Jer. 14:21 do not d. the throne

DISGUISE, ED, ETH.
1 Sam. 28:8 and Saul d. himself
1 K. 14:2 Jerob. said, d. thyself
22:30 one of prophets d. himself
22:30 d. myself, 2 Chr. 18:29
2 Chr. 35:22 Josiah d. to fight
Job 24:15 adulterer d. his face

DISH, ES.
Jud. 5:25 butter in a lordly d.
2 K. 21:13 as a man wipeth a d.
Mat. 26:23 dip. in d. *Mark* 14:20

DISHONEST. *See* GAIN.

DISHONESTY.
2 Cor. 4:2 renounced things of d.

DISHONOR.
Ezr. 4:14 to see king's d.
Ps. 35:26 clothed with d. 71:13
69:19 thou hast known my d.
Prov. 6:33 and d. shall he got.
Rom. 9:21 another vessel to d.
1 Cor. 15:43 sown in d. raised in
2 Cor. 6:8 by honor and d.
2 Tim. 2:20 are vess. some to d.

DISHONOR, EST, ETH.
Mic. 7:6 the son d. the father
John 8:49 Father, and ye d. me
Rom. 1:24 to d. their own bodies
2:23 breaking law, d. God
1 Cor. 11:4 man d. head ; 5 wom.

DISINHERIT.
Num. 14:12 I will d. them

DISMAYED.
Deut. 31:8 nor be d. *Jos.* 1:9 ; 8:1 ; 10:25 ; 1 *Chr.* 22:13 ; 28:20 ;
2 Chr. 20:15, 17 ; 32:7
1 Sam. 17:11 they were d. 2 K.
Is. 21:3 I was d. at seeing of it
41:10 not d. for I; 17; 16:2; 23:4;
30:10 ; 46:27; Ezek. 2:6; 3:9
23 that we may be d.
Jer. 8:9 the wise ones are d. 10:2
17:18 let them be d. let not me
46:5 have I seen them d. and
48:1 M. is d.; 49:37 Elam be d.
50:36 mighty of Babylon be d.
Ob. 9 mighty men shall be d.

DISMAYING.
Jer. 48:39 Moab shall be a d.

DISMISSED.
Acts 15:30 d. they came to Anti.
19:41 spoken, he d. assembly

DISOBEDIENCE.
Rom. 5:19 by one man's d.
2 Cor. 10:6 readiness to rev. d.
Eph. 2:2 worketh in child. of d.
5:6 on children of d. *Col.* 3:6
Heb. 2:2 d. received just recom.

DISOBEDIENT.
1 K. 13:26 man of G. who was d.
Neh. 9:26 they were d. rebelled
Luke 1:17 turn d. to wisd. of just
Acts 26:19 not d. to heav. vision
Rom. 1:30 d. to par. 2 *Tim.* 3:2
10:21 forth my hands to d. peo.
1 Tim. 1:9 law was made for d.
Tit. 1:16 deny him, being d.
3:3 we also were sometimes d.
1 Pet. 2:7 to them d. the stone
8 stumble at word, being d.
3:20 which sometime were d.

DISOBEYED.
1 K. 13:21 as hast d. mouth of L.

DISORDERLY.
2 Thes. 3:6 withd. from broth. d.

DIS

2 *Thes.* 3:7 behaved not ours. *d.*
11 some walk among you *d.*
DISPATCH.
***Ezek.* 23:47** *d.* them with swords
DISPENSATION.
1 *Cor.* 9:17 a *d.* of gospel
***Eph.* 1:10** *d.* of fulness of times
3:2 heard of *d.* of grace of God
***Col.* 1:25** minister acc. to *d.* of G.
DISPERSE, ED.
2 *Chr.* 11:23 Rehob. *d.* of child.
***Est.* 3:8** certain people *d.* among
***Ps.* 112:9** he hath *d.* 2 *Cor.* 9:9
***Prov.* 5:16** let thy fountains be *d.*
15:7 lips of wise *d.* knowledge
***Is.* 11:12** gather *d.* of Judah
***Ezek.* 12:15** *d.* them in the coun.
20:23; 22:15; 30:23, 26
29:13 *d.* thee in the countries
36:19 were *d.* through countries
***Zep.* 3:10** my *d.* shall bring
***John* 7:35** will he go to the *d.*
***Acts* 5:37** obeyed him, were *d.*
DISPERSIONS.
***Jer.* 25:34** days of *d.* accomp.
DISPLAYED.
***Ps.* 60:4** ban. that it may be *d.*
DISPLEASE.
***Num.* 22:34** if it *d.* thee
1 *Sam.* 20:7 *d.* not the lords
2 *Sam.* 11:25 Joab, let not this *d.*
***Prov.* 24:18** L. see it, it *d.* him
DISPLEASED.
***Gen.* 48:17** hand on Ephr. it *d.*
***Num.* 11:1** complained, it *d.* L.
10 Moses also was *d.*
1 *Sam.* 8:6 the thing *d.* Samuel
18:8 saying of Saul, and he said
2 *Sam.* 11:27 th. D. had done. *d.*
1 *K.* 1:6 father had not *d.* him
20:43 went to his house *d.* 21:4
1 *Chr.* 21:7 God was *d.* with this
***Ps.* 60:1** thou has been *d.*
15:5 it *d.* him
***Dan.* 6:14** king *d.* with himself
***Jon.* 4:1** it *d.* Jonah exceedingly
***Hab.* 3:8** Lord *d.* against rivers
***Zec.* 1:2** L. been *d.* with fathers
15 sore *d.* with heathen at ease,
for I was but a little *d.*
***Mat.* 21:15** scribes saw, were *d.*
***Mark* 10:14** Jesus saw it, was *d.*
41 *d.* with James and John
***Acts* 12:20** Herod highly *d.* with
DISPLEASURE.
***Deut.* 9:19** I was afraid of hot *d.*
***Jud.* 15:3** though I do them a *d.*
***Ps.* 2:5** vex them in his sore *d.*
6:1 chasten me in hot *d.* 38:1
DISPOSED, ING.
***Job* 34:13** who *d.* whole world?
37:15 know when God *d.* them
***Prov.* 16:33** *d.* thereof is of L.
1 *Cor.* 10:27 feast, ye be *d.* to go
DISPOSITION.
***Acts* 7:53** law by *d.* of angels
DISPOSSESS.
***Num.* 33:53** shall *d.* the inhabi.
***Deut.* 7:17** how can I *d.* them?
***Jud.* 11:23** God hath *d.* the A.
DISPUTATION, S.
***Acts* 15:2** had no small *d.*
***Rom.* 14:1** but not to doubtful *d.*
DISPUTE, ED.
***Job* 23:7** righteous might *d.*
***Mark* 9:34** *d.* who sh. be greatest
***Acts* 9:29 S. *d.* ag. the Grecians
17:17 Paul *d.* in the synagogues
***Jude* 9** Mich. *d.* about body of M.
DISPUTER.
1 *Cor.* 1:20 where is *d.* of world?
DISPUTING, S.
***Acts* 6:9** *d.* with Stephen
15:7 been much *d.* Peter rose
19:8 *d.* and persuading, 9
24:12 they neither found me *d.*
***Phil.* 2:14** all things without *d.*
1 *Tim.* 6:5 perverse *d.*
DISQUIET, ED, NESS.
1 *Sam.* 28:15 why hast thou *d.*
***Ps.* 38:8** roared by reason of *d.*
42:5 surely am *d.* in vain
43:5 O my soul, why art thou *d.*
within me? 11; 42:5
***Prov.* 30:21** earth is *d.*
***Jer.* 50:34** *d.* inhabitants of Bab.
DISSEMBLED, ETH.
***Jos.* 7:11** stolen, and *d.* also
***Prov.* 26:24** he that hateth it, *d.*
***Jer.* 42:20** for ye *d.* when ye sent
***Gal.* 2:13** other Jews *d.* likewise

DIV

DISSEMBLERS.
***Ps.* 26:4** nor will I go in with *d.*
DISSENSION.
***Acts* 15:2** had no small *d.*
23:7 arose a *d.* between Phari.
DISSIMULATION.
***Rom.* 12:9** let love be without *d.*
***Gal.* 2:13** carried away with *d.*
DISSOLVE, ED, EST.
***Job* 30:22** thou *d.* my substance
***Ps.* 75:3** Inhab. thereof are *d.*
***Is.* 14:31** thou Palestina art *d.*
24:19 the earth is clean *d.*
34:4 the host of heaven be *d.*
***Dan.* 5:16** thou canst *d.* doubts
Nah. 2:6 palace shall be *d.*
2 *Cor.* 5:1 house of this taber. *d.*
2 *Pet.* 3:11 all these things be *d.*
12 heavens on fire shall be *d.*
DISTAFF.
***Prov.* 31:19** her hands hold *d.*
DISTIL.
***Deut.* 32:2** my speech *d.* as dew
***Job* 36:28** the clouds *d.* on man
DISTINCTION.
1 *Cor.* 14:7 exc. *d.* in the sounds
DISTINCTLY.
***Neh.* 8:8** in book of the law *d.*
DISTRACTED, ION.
***Ps.* 88:15** I suff. thy ter. I am *d.*
1 *Cor.* 7:35 attend without *d.*
DISTRESS, Substantive.
***Gen.* 35:3** answered me in my *d.*
42:21 therefore is this *d.* come
***Jud.* 11:7** ye come when he *d.*
1 *Sam.* 22:2 in *d.* came to David
2 *Sam.* 24:17 in my *d.* I called on
L. *Ps.* 18:6; 118:5; 120:1
1 *K.* 1:29 redeemed soul out of *d.*
2 *Chr.* 28:22 in *d.* Ahaz trespass.
***Neh.* 2:17** ye see the *d.* we are in
9:37 and we are in great *d.*
***Ps.* 4:1** enlarged me when in *d.*
***Prov.* 1:27** mock when *d.* cometh
***Is.* 25:4** stre. to the needy in *d.*
***Lam.* 1:20** O Lord, for I am in *d.*
***Ob.* 12** nor spoken proudly in *d.*
14 nor deliv. those in day of *d.*
***Zep.* 1:15** that day is a day of *d.*
17 I will bring *d.* upon men
***Luke* 21:23** great *d.* in land
25 on the earth *d.* of nations
***Rom.* 8:35** love of C. *d.* shall *d.*
1 *Cor.* 7:26 good for the present *d.*
1 *Thes.* 3:7 comforted in your *d.*
DISTRESS, ED.
***Gen.* 32:7** Jacob was greatly *d.*
***Deut.* 2:9** *d.* not the Moabites
19 *d.* not the Ammonites
28:53 wherewith *d.* thee, 55, 57
***Jud.* 2:15** Israel *d.* 10:9
1 *Sam.* 13:6 the people were *d.*
14:24 men of Is. *d.* 28:15** Saul
30:6 David *d.* for people rage
2 *Sam.* 1:26 *d.* for thee, Jonathan
1 *Chr.* 28:20 king of Assy. *d.* A.
***Is.* 29:2** yet I will *d.* Ariel
7 that *d.* her be as a dream
***Jer.* 10:18** I have the inhabitants
4 *Cor.* 4:8 troubled yet not *d.*
DISTRESSES.
***Ps.* 25:17** O bring me out of *d.*
107:6 he deliv. them out of *d.*
13 he saved them out of *d.* 19
28 bringeth them out of *d.*
***Ezek.* 30:16** Noph hath daily *d.*
2 *Cor.* 6:4 approve ourselves in *d.*
12:10 I take pleasure in *d.* for
DISTRIBUTE.
***Neh.* 13:13** their office was to *d.*
***Luke* 18:22** sell all and *d.* to poor
1 *Tim.* 6:18 rich to be ready to *d.*
DISTRIBUTED, ETH, ING.
***Job* 21:17** God *d.* sorrows
***John* 6:11 Je. *d.* to the disciples
***Rom.* 12:13** *d.* to neces. of saints
1 *Cor.* 7:17 God hath *d.* to every
2 *Cor.* 10:13 ac. to rule G. hath *d.*
DISTRIBUTION.
***Acts* 4:35** *d.* made to every one
2 *Cor.* 9:13 for your liberal *d.*
DITCH, ES.
2 *K.* 3:16 make valley full of *d.*
***Job* 9:31** plunge me in the *d.*
***Ps.* 7:15** fallen into *d.* he made
***Prov.* 23:27** a whore is a deep *d.*
***Is.* 22:11** *d.* between two walls
***Mat.* 15:14** fall into *d.* *Luke* 6:39
DIVERS, S.
***Deut.* 22:9** not sow with *d.* seed
11 not wear garment of *d.* sorts
25:13 shalt not have *d.* weights

DIV

***Deut.* 25:11** in house *d.* measures
***Jud.* 5:30** to S. a prey of *d.* colors
2 *Sam.* 12:18 gar. of *d.* colors, 19
1 *Chr.* 29:2 stones of *d.* colors
2 *Chr.* 20:11 *d.* of Asher humbled
***Est.* 3:8** their laws *d.* from all
***Ps.* 78:45** sent *d.* sort of flies
105:31 came *d.* sorts of flies
***Prov.* 20:10** *d.* weights, *d.* meas.
23 *d.* weights are abomination
***Ec.* 5:7** there are also *d.* vanities
***Ezek.* 17:3** a great eagle *d.* colors
***Dan.* 7:3** beasts *d.* one from ano.
23 *d.* from all kingdoms
***Mat.* 4:24** sick with *d.* diseases,
Mark 1:34; *Luke* 4:40
24:7 earthquakes in *d.* places,
Mark 13:8; *Luke* 21:11
Mark 8:3 for *d.* came from far
***Acts* 19:9** when *d.* were hardened
1 *Cor.* 12:10 *d.* kinds of tongues
2 *Tim.* 3:6 led away with *d.* lusts
***Tit.* 3:3** serving *d.* lusts and ple.
***Heb.* 1:1** in *d.* manners spake
2:4 witness with *d.* miracles
9:10 *d.* washings; 13:9 *d.* doct.
***Jam.* 1:2** fall into *d.* temptations
DIVERSITIES.
1 *Cor.* 12:4 *d.* of gifts; 6 opera.
28 set in church *d.* of tongues
DIVIDE.
***Gen.* 1:6** let firmament *d.* waters
14 be lights to *d.* the day, 18
49:27 at night he shall *d.* spoil
***Ex.* 14:16** over the sea and *d.*
26:33 veil shall *d.* between holy
***Num.* 31:27** *d.* the prey into two
***Jos.* 1:6** *d.* for inheritance, 13
22:8 *d.* the spoil with brethren
1 *Sam.* 19:29 thou and Z. *d.* land
***2 Sam.* 19:29** *d.* thou living child, 26
***Neh.* 9:11** didst *d.* sea, *Ps.* 74:13
22 didst *d.* them into corners
***Job* 27:17** innocent shall *d.* silver
***Ps.* 55:9** and *d.* their tongues
***Is.* 53:12** will I *d.* him a portion
***Ezek.* 5:1** take balances, and *d.*
45:1 *d.* land by lot, 47:21, 22
48:29 this is land ye shall *d.*
***Dan.* 11:39** he shall *d.* land
***Luke* 12:13** that he *d.* the inheri.
22:17 *d.* it among yourselves
I will DIVIDE.
***Gen.* 49:7** *I will d.* them in Jacob
***Ex.* 15:9** said, *I will d.* spoil
***Is.* 53:12** *will I d.* him a portion
DIVIDED.
***Gen.* 1:4** *d.* light; 7 *d.* waters
10:5 were isles of Gentiles *d.*
25 in his days was the earth *d.*
32 nations *d.* after the flood
14:15 Abram *d.* himself ag. them
15:10 *d.* Abram *d.* them in midst
32:7 Jacob *d.* people
***Ex.* 14:21** the waters were *d.*
***Deut.* 4:19** which God hath *d.*
32:8 Most High *d.* to nations
***Jos.* 14:5** they *d.* land, 18:10
2 *Sam.* 1:23 in death were not *d.*
***1 K.* 3:25** divide living child
16:21 Israel were *d.*
18:6 Ahab and Ob. *d.* the land
***Job* 38:25** hath *d.* a watercourse
***Ps.* 68:12** she that tar. *d.* spoil
78:13 he *d.* the sea, and caused
55 *d.* them an inheritance by
lot, *Acts* 13:19
136:13 to him which *d.* Red sea
***Is.* 33:23** prey of great spoil *d.*
34:17 his hand *d.* it by line
51:15 I am the Lord that *d.* sea
***Lam.* 4:16** anger of Lord *d.* them
***Ezek.* 37:22** nor be *d.* into two k.
***Dan.* 2:41** kingdom shall be *d.*
5:28 kingdom *d.* given to M.
11:4 kingdom *d.* toward four w.
***Hos.* 10:2** heart is *d.* now found
***Amos* 7:17** thy land shall be *d.*
***Mic.* 2:4** he hath *d.* our fields
***Mat.* 12:25** house *d.* not stand,
Mark 3:24; *Luke* 11:17
***Luke* 12:52** *d.* three against two
15:12 father *d.* to them his living
***Acts* 14:4** multi. was *d.* 23:7
***Rev.* 16:19** city was *d.*
DIVIDER.
***Luke* 12:14** made me *d.* over you

DO

DIVIDETH.
***Job* 26:12** *d.* sea with his power
***Ps.* 29:7** voice of L. *d.* flames
***Is.* 34:17** he hath *d.* it to them
***Mat.* 25:32** *d.* his sheep fr. goats
***Luke* 11:22** and *d.* his spoils
DIVIDING.
***Is.* 63:12** *d.* water before them
***Dan.* 7:25** and a *d.* of time
1 *Cor.* 12:11 *d.* to every man
2 *Tim.* 2:15 rightly *d.* the word
***Heb.* 4:12** to *d.* asunder of joints
DIVINATION, S.
***Num.* 22:7** rewards of *d.*
23:23 nor any *d.* against Israel
***Deut.* 18:10** useth *d.* 2 *K.* 17:17
***Jer.* 14:14** they prophesy *d.*
***Ezek.* 12:24** nor flattering *d.* in Is.
13:7 not spoken a lying *d.*
23 see no more divine *d.*
21:21 the king of Babylon stood
to use *d.*
***Acts* 16:16** pos. with spirit of *d.*
DIVINE, Verb.
***Gen.* 44:15** a man as I can *d.*?
1 *Sam.* 28:8 *d.* to me by fam. sp.
***Ezek.* 13:9** prophets that *d.* lies
21:29 while they *d.* a lie
***Mic.* 3:6** that ye shall not *d.*
11 prophets *d.* for money
DIVINE, Adjective.
***Prov.* 16:10** *d.* sentence in lips
***Heb.* 9:1** ordinances of *d.* service
2 *Pet.* 1:3 *d.* power hath given
4 be partakers of *d.* nature
DIVINER, S.
***Deut.* 18:14** hearkened to *d.*
1 *Sam.* 6:2 Phili. called for *d.*
***Is.* 44:25** that maketh *d.* mad
***Jer.* 27:9** hearken not to your *d.*
28:8 let not your *d.* deceive you
***Mic.* 3:7** and the *d.* confounded
***Zec.* 10:2** the *d.* have seen a lie
DIVINETH, ING.
***Gen.* 44:5** this it whereby he *d.*?
***Ezek.* 22:28** and *d.* lies to them
DIVISION, S.
***Ex.* 8:23** put a *d.* between
***Jud.* 5:15** for *d.* of Reuben, 16
***Luke* 12:51** nay but rather *d.*
***John* 7:43** there was a *d.* among
the people, 9:16; 10:19
***Rom.* 16:17** mark them wh. ca. *d.*
1 *Cor.* 1:10 be no *d.* among you
3:3 whereas there is am. you *d.*
11:18 I hear there be *d.* am. you
DIVORCE, ED.
***Jer.* 3:8** given her a bill of *d.*
***Mat.* 5:32** shall marry her *d.*
DIVORCEMENT.
***Deut.* 24:1** write her bill of *d.* 3
***Is.* 50:1** your mother's *d.*?
***Mark* 10:4 M. suffered bill of *d.*
See WRITING.
DO.
***Gen.* 18:25** Judge of all *d.* right?
31:16 what God hath said, *d.*
41:25 what he is to *d.* 28
***Ex.* 1:16** teach you what ye sh. *d.*
19:8 all L. hath spok. we will *d.*
***Lev.* 18:5** if a man *d.* he sh. live,
Neh. 9:29; *Ezek.* 20:11, 13, 21
***Num.* 22:20** word I say shalt *d.*
24:14 this peo. *d.* to thy people
***Deut.* 7:11** command, to *d.* them
10:19 *d.* to him as he thought to
27:26 words of law, to *d.* them
29:9 may hear it and *d.* it 31:12
***Jos.* 7:9** *d.* to thy great name?
22:24 what have ye to *d.* with L.
24:15 *d.* all written in the law,
**1 *Chr.* 16:40; 2 *Chr.* 34:21
***Jud.* 1:14** as *d.* to *d.* in comparison of your
10:15 *d.* to us what seem. good
18:18 the priest, What *d.* ye?
1 *Sam.* 16:3 show thee what *d.*
20:4 what God will *d.* for me
28:15 thou shalt *d.* great things
2 *Sam.* 3:18 now then *d.* it
15:26 *d.* to me as seemeth good
1 *K.* 2:6 acc. to thy wisdom
8:32 and judge thy servants
39 forgive, and *d.* 2 *Chr.* 6:23
11:33 to *d.* right, 38; 14:8
2 *K.* 18:18 to *d.* with peace? 19
17:31 after former manners
1 *Chr.* 4:10 *d.* all thou hast said
**21:8 *d.* away thy ser.
**2 *Chr.* 19:11 do hood what is *d.*
**20:12 nor know we what to *d.*
**33:8 if then will go, *d.* it.

826 CRUDEN'S CONCORDANCE.

DO

Ezr. 4:2 we seek God as ye d.
7:19 to seek law and to d. it
Neh. 2:12 put in my heart to d.
9:24 d. with them as they
Job 7:20 d. to thee? O Preserver
11:8 high as heav. what d.?
13:20 d. not two things to me
Ps. 40:8 I delight to d. thy will
50:16 to d. to dec. my statutes?
109:21 but d. thou for me
119:132 to d. to those
143:10 teach me to d. thy will
Prov. 3:27 power of hand to d.
Ec. 9:10 d. it with thy might
Is. 10:3 d. in day of visitation?
43:7 Lord d. all these things
Jer. 5:31 d. in the end thereof?
11:4 obey my voice and d. them
14:7 d. it for thy name's sake
39:19 d. to him as he shall say
42:3 show thing we may d.
50:15 hath done d. to her, 29
Lam. 1:22 d. to them as done
Ezek. 5:6 resst thou what they d.
24:22 ye shall d. as I have done
36:37 be inquired of, to d. it for
Dan. 9:19 Lord, hearken and d.
11:3 d. accord. to his will, 15, 36
Hos. 10:3 should king d. to us?
Amos 3:7 Lord d. nothing
Jon. 4:9 I d. well to be angry
Mic. 6:8 but to d. justly
Zec. 1:21 what come these to d.?
8:16 these are things ye shall d.
Mat. 5:19 shall d. and teach
47 what d. ye more than oth.?
8:29 wh. have we to d. w. thee?
Mark 1:24; Luke 4:34
12:50 whosoever sh. d. the will
of my Father, Mark 3:35
20:15 d. what I will with own
33 wh. will ye I d. Mark 10:36
21:27 author. I d. these things,
Mark 11:33; Luke 20:8
23:5 works they d.
27:19 to d. with that just man
Mark 7:8 such like ye d. 13
Luke 4:23 d. also in thy country
6:2 why d. that not lawful
11 what they might d. to Jes.
31 as ye would that men sh. d.
8:21 hear word of God and d. it
16:4 I am resolved what to d.
17:10 done what was duty to d.
23:34 know not what they d.
John 2:5 whatsoever he saith d.
4:34 my meat is to d. will
5:30 I can of myself d. nothing
6:6 he knew what he would d.
28 what shall we d.? Acts 2:37
7:17 if any man will d. his will
6:29 I d. those things please
9:33 of G. he could d. nothing
11:47 Pharisees said, What d.?
13:7 what I d. knowest not
15 ye shall d. as I have done
17 happy are ye if ye d. them
14:13 works I d. shall he d. also
14 ask in my name, I will d. it
15:14 if ye d. what I command
21 will they d. unto you, 16:3
17:4 work thou gavest me to d.
21:21 what shall this man d.?
Acts 1:1 d. of all Jesus began to d.
4:28 d. whatsoever thy counsel
9:6 what wilt thou have me d.?
10:6 what thou oughtest to d.
14:15 why d. ye these things?
Rom. 1:32 not only d. the same
4. by nature doing th. in law
7:15 for what I d. I allow not,
but what I hate, that d. I
1 Cor. 7:36 let him d. what he
10:31 ye d. all to glory of God
2 Cor. 8:10 not only to d. but
Gal. 3:10 writ. in law to d. them
5:21 d. such shall not inherit
Eph. 6:21 know and how I d.
Phil. 2:13 G. worketh both to d.
4:9 heard and seen in me, d.
Col. 3:17 whatsoev. ye d. in word
or deed, d. all in n. of J.
23 whats. ye d. d. it heartily
1 Thes. 4:10 d. it, to w. breth.
5:11 edify. even as also ye d.
24 faithful who also will d. it
2 Thes. 3:4 ye both d. and will d.
Phile. 21 wilt d. more than I say
Heb. 4:13 whom we have to d.
10:7 lo, I come to d. thy will, 9
13:6 not fear what man shall d.
21 perfect to d. his will
2 Pet. 1:10 if ye d. these, never
1 John 3:22 and d. those things
Rev. 2:5 and d. the first works

Can, or **canst DO.**
Job 22:17 what can Almighty d.

DO

Job 42:2 thou c. d. every thing
Ps. 11:3 can the righteous d.?
Ezek. 3:3 I will d. to them
36:4 fear what flesh can d. 11
118:6 not fear what man can d.
Mark 9:22 if canst d. anything
Luke 12:4 no more they can d.
John 5:19 Son can d. nothing, 30
15:5 without me ye can d. noth.
Phil. 4:13 I can d. all through C.

See DO COMMANDMENTS.

DO, with evil.
Ez. 23:2 not fol. a mult. to d. e.
Lev. 3:4 soul swear to d. evil
Deut. 31:29 bec. ye will d. evil
2 Sam. 12:9 despised L. to d. e.
2 K. 8:12 evil thou wilt d.
17:17 sold themselves to d. evil
21:9 Man. seduced to d. more e.
Ps. 34:16 face ag. them d. evil
37:8 fret not thyself to d. evil
Prov. 2:14 who rejoice to d. evil
24:8 he that deviseth to d. evil
Ec. 5:1 consider not they d. evil
8:11 fully set in them to d. evil
12 a sinner d. evil 100 times
Is. 1:16 wash ye, cease to d. evil
41:23 d. good or evil that we
Jer. 4:22 people are wise to d. e.
10:5 for they cannot d. evil
13:23 accustomed to d. evil
18:10 if it d. evil in my sight
Ezek. 6:10 I would d. this evil
Mic. 7:3 d. evil with both hands
Zep. 1:12 nor will he d. evil
Mark 3:4 to d. evil? Luke 6:9
Rom. 3:8 d. evil that good come
13:4 if thou d. evil be afraid
2 Cor. 13:7 I pray that ye d. no e.
1 Pet. 3:12 against them that d. e.

DO, joined with good.
Num. 27:46 d. shall my life d.
Num. 24:13 to d. g. or bad
Deut. 8:16 to d. thee good
28:63 Lord rejoice to d. you g.
30:5 and he will d. thee good
Jud. 17:13 Lord will d. me good
1 Sam. 1:23 d. what seemeth g.
14:36, 40; 2 Sam. 19:37, 37
3:18 the Lord d. what seemeth
him good, 2 Sam. 10:12
2 K. 10:5 d. that g. in thine eyes
1 Chr. 19:13 Lord d. what is g.
Neh. 5:9 it is not g. that ye d.
Ps. 34:14 d. g. 37:3, 27; 51:18;
125:4; Mat. 5:44; Luke 6:9, 33
36:3 ho hath left off to d. g.
Prov. 31:12 she will d. him g.
Ec. 3:12 for a man to d. good
4:1:23 you, d. good, or d. evil
Jer. 4:22 to d. good no knowl.
10:5 not, is it in them to d. g.
13:23 then may ye d. good
20:14 d. with me as seemeth g.
29:32 nor behold the g. I will d.
32:40 turn away to d. them g.
41 rejoice over them to d. g.
3:19 hear all the good I d.
Mic. 2:7 words d. g. to upright
Zep. 1:12 the L. will not d. good
Mark 3:4 is it lawful to d. g. on
the sabbath days? Luke 6:9
14:7 poor, ye may d. them g.
Luke 6:33 if ye d. g. to them that
d. good to you
Rom. 7:19 g. that I would, I d.
21 when I would d. g. evil is
13:3 d. good thou shalt have g.
Gal. 6:10 d. good unto all men
1 Tim. 6:18 that they d. good
Heb. 13:16 to d. g. and commun.
Jam. 4:17 knoweth to d. good
1 Pet. 3:11 eschew evil, and d. g.

What have I to DO.
2 Sam. 16:10 to, d. with? 19:22
1 K. 17:18 to. A. I to d. with thee
2 K. 3:13; 2 Chr. 35:21; Mark
5:7; Luke 8:28; John 2:4
Hos. 14:8 to. d. any more
1 Cor. 5:12 what d. to judge

I shall, I will, will I, or shall I DO.
Gen. 27:37 what s. I d. now
Num. 22:17 I will d. what sayest
33:56 I s. d. to you, as I th. to d.
Jos. 3:11 I w. d. a thing in Isr.
20:4 thy soul desireth, I will d.
28:15 known wh. I s. d.
2 Sam. 18:4 best I will d. 19:38
Job 31:14 what d. when G. riseth
34:32 I will d. no more
Prov. 34:29 I will d. so to him
Is. 5:5 I w. d. to my vineyard
46:10 I will d. all my pleasure
11 have purposed, I will al. d.
48:11 for own sake will I d. it

DO

Jer. 29:32 good I will d. for my
Ezek. 3:3 I will d. to thee what I
7:27 d. to them after their way
32:14 spoken, and will d. it
24:14 : 36:36
Hos. 6:4 what shall I d. to thee?
Amos 4:12 thus will I d. to thee
Mic. 19:16 good thing shall I d.
27:22 what shall I d. with J.?
Luke 16:3 what shall I d.? 20:13;
Acts 22:10
John 14:13 ask, that will I d.
14 ask in my name, I will d. it
2 Cor. 11:12 what I do, I will d.

See JUDGMENT.

Must DO.
Num. 23:26 that I must d.
Acts 16:30 wh. m. I d. to be sav.?

DO not.
Ex. 20:10 in it thou shalt not d.
any work, Lev. 23:31
31:24 not d. after their works
Lev. 16:29 d. no work, 23:3, 28;
Deut. 15:19 ; Jer. 17:24
16:3 after their doings, not d.
Num. 32:19 and shall he n. d. it?
Deut. 12:8 n. d. after all we d.
20:13 I d. thee no wrong
23:2 they say and d. not
Mark 6:5 d. no mighty work
Luke 6:46 d. not the things I say
John 8:38 not to d. mine own
10:37 if I d. not works of my F.
Rom. 7:15 that I d. not, 19
8:3 what the law could not d.
2 K. 10:5 yet I d. not cannot d. the things
Rev. 19:10 see thou d. it not, 22:9

Observe, with **DO.**
Deut. 5:32 ob. to d. 31; 11:32;
12:1; 24:8; 2 K. 17:37
6:3 ob. to d. it, 11:32; 28:13, 15,
58; 31:12; 32:46
25 if we ob. to d. these com.
15:5 to ob. to d. all the law
Jos. 1:7 ob. to d. all the law
Ezek. 37:24 observe and d. them
Mat. 23:3 you, that obser. and d.

Will we, or **we will DO.**
Ex. 19:8 said, we w. d. 24:3, 7
Deut. 5:27 w. w. hear it, and d.
Jos. 1:16 command. us, w. w. d.
2 K. 10:5 d. all thou shalt bid
Jer. 42:20 and w. w. d. it
44:17 we will certainly d.
Shall we, or we shall DO.
Jud. 13:8 what we shall d.
2 Sam. 16:20 what we shall d.
1:7:6 sh. we d. after his saying?
2 K. 6:15 alas, how shall we d.?
Est. 1:15 what sh. we d. to V.?
Ps. 60:12 through God w. sh. d.
valiantly, 108:13
Cant. 8:8 what sh. we d.
Jos. 1:11 what shall we d.?
Luke 3:10 what s. we d.? 12, 14
John 6:28 d. th. we might work?
Acts 2:37 what shall we d.?
4:16 what sh. we d. to these m.?

DO, joined with so.
Num. 22:30 wont to d. so to th.?
32:23 not d. so, ye have sinned
Deut. 12:30 so will I d.
1 Sam. 8:8 served oth. gods, no d.
1 K. 11:41 as fathers, so d. they
Prov. 24:29 I will d. so to him
Is. 10:11 so d. to Jerusalem
Jer. 23:6 L. d. so. Mat. 18:35
7:12 sh. d. to you, so d. ye
18:35 so shall Father d. to you
John 14:31 Fa. gave com. so I d.
Acts 7:51 fathers did, so d. ye
Col. 3:13 forgave you, so d. ye
Jam. 2:12 so d. ye, as they that

DO, joined with well.
Gen. 4:7 if d. well; if not well
21:23 with thee In all thou d.
Deut. 12:28 when thou d. good
1 K. 8:3 prosper in all thou d.
10:9 what d. here, Elijah? 13
20:22 mark and see what d.
Job 9:12 say, What d. thou?
35:6 what d. against him?
Ps. 49:18 d. well to thyself
77:14 the God that d. wonders
86:10 and d. wondrous things
119:68 art good, and d. good
Ec. 8:4 what d. thou? Dan. 4:35
Jer. 11:15 d. evil, then rejoicest
15:5 to ask how fare d. thou?
Ezek. 12:9 house said, What d.?
16:30 seeing, d. all these things
John 3:16 thou d. these things?
13:27 that thou d. do quickly
2:15:26 take heed wait th. d.
Rom. 2:1 judg. d. same things, d.
Jam. 2:19 believest, thou d. well
3 John 5 d. faithfully what th. d.

DOETH.
Ex. 31:14 for whosoever d. any
work therein, 15; Lev. 23:30
Job 5:9 great things, 9:10;
37:5; Ps. 72:18; 136:4
33:13 soul desireth, that he d.
Ps. 1:3 what. he d. shall prosper
14:1 none d. 3; 53:1, 3; Ro. 3:12
15:5 d. these never be moved
118:15 hand d. valiantly, 16
26:2 said of mirth, What d. it
3:14 whatsoever God d. it shall
be for ever, and God d. it
7:20 not a man that d. good
8:3 he d. whatso. pleaseth him
Is. 56:2 blessed is man d. this
Dan. 4:35 d. accord. to his will
9:14 L. is righteous in all he d.
Mal. 2:12 L. cut off man d. this
Mat. 6:3 left know what right d.
7:24 sayings and d. them
24 and d. not, Luke 6:49
8:9 and he d. it, Luke 7:8
John 5:19 he d. these d. the Son
7:51 before it know what he d.
9:31 d. his will, and he heareth
15:15 knoweth not what lord d.
Rom. 10:5 that d. these things
Gal. 3:12 shall live by them, Gal. 3:12
Eph. 6:8 good thing any man d.

DOCTOR.
Luke 2:46 J. in midst of the d.
5:17 d. of the law sitting by
Acts 5:34 Gamaliel a d. of law

DOCTRINE.
Dt. 29:9 make to understand d.
32:24 murmured, shall learn d.
10:8 stock is d. of vanities
Mat. 7:38 aston. at his d. 22:33;
Mark 1:22 ; 11:18 ; Luke 4:32
16:12 beware of d. of Pharisees
Mat. 1:27 what new d. is this?
4:2 in his d. 12:38
John 7:17 shall know of the d.
18:19 asked Jesus of his d.
Acts 2:42 contl. in apostles' d.
5:28 filled Jerus. with your d.
13:12 being astonished at the d.
17:19 what this new d. is?

CRUDEN'S CONCORDANCE. 827

DOI
Rom. 6:17 that form of d.
16:17 contrary to the d.
1 Cor. 14:6 except I speak by d.
26 every one of you hath a d.
Eph. 4:14 with every wind of d.
1 Tim. 1:3 teach no other d.
4:13 give attendance to d.
16 heed to thyself to thy d.
5:17 who labor in word and d.
6:1 his d. be not blasphemed
3 the d. according to godliness
2 Tim. 3:16 is profitable for d.
4:2 exhort with long suf. and d.
Tit. 2:7 in d. showing incorrupt.
10 adorn d. of God our Saviour
Heb. 6:1 principles of the d.
2 of the d. of baptisms, and
2 John 9 abideth not in the d. of Christ ; abideth in d.
Rev. 2:14 that hold d. of Balaam
15 that hold d. of Nicolaitans

Good DOCTRINE.
Prov. 4:2 I give you good d.
1 Tim. 4:6 in words of good d.

My DOCTRINE.
Deut. 32:2 my d. drop as rain
Job 11:4 my d. is pure
John 7:16 my d. is not mine
2 Tim. 3:10 fully known my d.

Sound DOCTRINE.
1 Tim. 1:10 contrary to sound d.
2 Tim. 4:3 not endure sound d.
Tit. 1:9 by sound d. to exhort
2:1 speak things become s. d.

This DOCTRINE.
2 John 10 and bring not this d.
Rev. 2:24 as have not this d.

DOCTRINES.
Mat. 15:9 for d. com. Mark 7:7
Col. 2:22 comm. and d. of men
1 Tim. 4:1 heed to d. of devils
Heb. 13:9 not carried with sundr. d.

DOEG. 1 Sam. 22:7 ; 22:18, 22

DOG.
Ex. 11:7 ag. Is. not a d. move
Deut. 23:18 a d. into house
Jud. 7:5 as a d. lappeth
1 Sam. 17:43 am I a d. ? 2 K. 8:13
24:14 wh. dost pursue ? after a d. ?
2 Sam. 3:8 am I a d. head ?
9:8 upon such a dead d. as I am
16:9 this dead d. curse my lord ?
Ps. 22:20 from power of d.
59:6 make a noise like a d. 14
Prov. 26:11 as a d. returneth to his vomit, 2 Pet. 2:22
17 taketh a d. by the ears
Ec. 9:4 a living d. is better than
Is. 66:3 as if he cut off d. neck

DOGS.
Ex. 22:31 cast it to the d. Mat. 15:26 ; Mark 7:27
1 K. 14:11 d. eat, 16:4 ; 21:24
21:19 the place where d. licked
21 d. shall eat J. 2 K. 9:10, 36
22:38 d. licked up his blood
Job 30:1 I disd. to set with d.
Ps. 22:16 d. have compassed me
68:23 and the tongue of thy d.
Is. 56:10 dumb d. ; 11 greedy d.
Jer. 15:3 and the d. to tear
Mat. 7:6 which is holy unto d.
15:27 d. eat of crm. Mark 7:28
Luke 16:21 the d. licked his sores
Phil. 3:2 beware of d.
Rev. 22:15 for without are d.

DOING.
Ex. 15:11 d. wonders
1 K. 20:23 d. right, 2 Chr. 20:32
1 Chr. 22:16 arise and be d.
Job 32:22 in so d. my Maker
Ps. 64:9 wisely consider of his d.
66:5 he is terrible in d.
118:23 the L.'s d. it is marvellous, Mat. 21:42 ; Mark 12:11
Is. 58:2 keepeth hand from ev. d.
Mat. 24:46 find so d. Luke 12:13
Act 10:38 went about d. good
24:20 found any evil d. in me
Rom. 12:20 in so d. shalt heap
2 Cor. 8:11 perform the d. of it
Eph. 6:6 d. the will of God
1 Tim. 4:16 in d.

Well-DOING.
Rom. 2:7 continuance in w.-d.
Gal. 6:9 w. In w.-d. 2 Thes. 3:13
1 Pet. 2:15 with w.-d. ye silence
3:17 better suffer for w.-d.
4:19 com. souls to him in w.-d.

DOINGS.
Lev. 18:5 after d. of Egypt and Canaan, shall ye not do
Deut. 28:20 wickedness of thy d.

DON
Jud. 2:19 ceased not from own d.
2 Chr. 17:4 not after d. of Israel
Ps. 9:11 declare his d. Is. 12:4
77:12 I will also talk of thy d.
Prov. 20:11 known by his d.
Is. 1:16 put away evil of your d.
3:8 their d. are against the L.
10 shall eat the fruit of their d.
Jer. 4:4 because of evil of your d., 21:12 ; 26:3 ; 44:22
18 thy d. have procured these
7:3 am. your d. ; 26:13 ; 35:15
11:18 showedst me their d.
17:10 fruit of his d. 21:14
18:11 and make your d. good
23:2 visit on you evil of your d.
22 evil of d. 25:5 ; Zec. 1:4
32:19 give accord. to fruit of d.
Ezek. 14:22 ye shall see their d.
20:43 shall ye remember d.
44 nor according to corrupt d.
21:24 in all your d. sins do ap.
21:14 thy d. shall judge
36:17 defiled it by their own d.
19 according to d. I judged th.
31 shall remember d. not good
Hos. 4:9 reward them their d.
5:4 not frame d. to turn to God
7:2 their own d. have beset th.
9:15 for wicked. of d. I will dr.
12:2 acc. to d. will he recomp.
Mic. 2:7 are these his d. ?
3:4 have behaved ill in their d.
7:13 be desolate, for fruit of d.
Zep. 3:7 corrupted all their d.
not be ashamed for any d.
Zec. 1:6 accord. to our d. so d.

DOLEFUL.
Is. 13:21 full of d. creatures
Mic. 2:4 with a d. lamentation

DOMINION.
Gen. 1:26 d. over the fish, 28
27:40 thou shalt have the d.
37:8 shalt thou have d. over us ?
Num. 24:19 he that shall have d.
Jud. 5:13 have d. over nobles
1 K. 4:24 Solomon had d.
1 Chr. 18:3 to establish his d.
Neh. 9:37 have d. over our bod.
Job 25:2 d. and fear are with him
38:33 thou set the d. thereof
Ps. 8:6 to have d. over the works
19:13 sins, let them not have d.
49:14 the upright shall have d.
72:8 have d. from sea to sea
103:22 in all places of his d.
114:2 and Israel his d.
119:133 let not any iniq. have d.
145:13 thy d. endureth
Is. 26:13 other lords have had d.
Dan. 4:3 his d. from generation
22 d. reacheth to end of earth
31 d. is an everlasting d. 7:14
6:26 his d. be even unto the end
7:6 d. was given to the beast
12 beasts had d. taken away
14 was given him d. and glory
26 they shall take away his d.
27 d. sh. be given to the saints
11:3 shall rule with great d. 5
Mic. 4:8 to thee, even the first d.
Zec. 9:10 his d. from sea
Mat. 20:25 princes exercise d.
Rom. 6:9 death hath no more d.
7:1 law hath d. over a man
2 Cor. 1:24 d. over your faith
Eph. 1:21 above might and d.
1 Pet. 4:11 to whom be praise and d. for ever, 5:11 ; Rev. 1:6
Jude 8 despise d.
25 to him who is God be d.

DOMINIONS.
Dan. 7:27 all d. shall serve him
Col. 1:16 whether thrones or d.

DONE.
Ex. 18:9 goodness L. had d. to I.
31:15 six days man work be d.
33:2 ; Lev. 23:3
Lev. 8:37 things forbid, to be d.
Num. 23:2 saw all Israel had d.
27:1 name of our father d. aw. ?
32:13 all had d. evil was con.
Deut. 32:27 the vild that hath d.
32:31 where fore hath the L. d.
1 Sam. 1 K. 20:9 ; 2 Chr. 7:21
2 Sam. 13:12 to be d. in Israel
Neh. 9:33 we have d. wickedly,
Ps. 106:6 ; Dan. 9:5, 15
Est. 6:6 shall he d. to the man
Job 21:31 repay what he hath d. ?
Ps. 30:9 he spake, and it was d.
71:19 hast d. gr. things, 106:21
126:3 d. to thee, false tongue?

DON
Ec. 1:9 is d. is what shall be d.
2:12 hath been already d.
Is. 44:4 who hath d. it
44:23 for the Lord hath d. it
Jer. 48:19 him flecth, what is d.
Ezek. 30:8 it is d. saith the Lord
Dan. 11:36 determined sh. be d.
Mat. 6:10 thy will be d. 26:42 ;
Luke 11:2 ; 22:42
8:13 so be it d. to thee
11:21 works d. in you, had been d. in Tyre, Luke 10:13
18:19 it shall be d. for them
23:23 these ought ye to have d.
Luke 11:42
25:21 well d. good servant, 23
40 as ye have d. it to one of
these, ye have d. it to me
27:54 things that were d. 28:11
Mark 5:19 things the L. hath d. for thee, 20 ; Luke 8:39
6:30 told him what they had d.
9:13 d. to him what they listed
13:30 not pass till these be d.
15:8 to do, as he had ever d.
Luke 1:49 hath d. great things
15:9 evils Herod had d.
8:56 tell no man what was d.
9:10 told him all they had d.
14:22 it is d. as thou hast com.
17:10 we have d. that which was our duty to do
John 5:29 they that have d. good
to life ; they that have d. ev.
Acts 4:28 determ. before to be d.
14:27 rch. all G. had d. 15:4
21:14 the will of the Lord be d.
Rom. 9:11 d. any good or evil
1 Cor. 9:15 nor be so d. unto me
13:10 in part shall be d. away
14:26 let all be d. to edifying
40 be d. decently
16:14 be d. with charity
2 Cor. 5:10 things d. in body
Eph. 6:13 having d. all to stand
Phil. 2:3 nothing be d. through strife
Col. 4:9 known all things d.
Rev. 16:17 saying, It is d. 21:6
22:6 which must shortly be d.

Have I DONE.
Num. 22:28 what h. I d. to thee,
1 K. 19:20 ; Mic. 6:3
Jud. 8:2 what have I now d. ?
1 Sam. 17:29
1 Sam. 20:1 what h. I d. ?
26:18 ; 29:8 ; Jer. 8:6
He hath, or hath he DONE.
Lev. 24:19 as h. d. so be done
Jud. 15:10 as he hath d. to us
1 Sam. 6:9 h. h. d. us this gr. ev.
12:24 great things he hath d.
20:32 what hath he d. ?
1 Chr. 16:12 rem. his marvellous works h. d. Ps. 78:4 ; 98:1 ; 105:5
Ps. 66:16 declare wha. he hath d.
115:3 he h. d. what he pleased
Prov. 24:29 as he hath d. to me
Is. 12:5 he hath d. excel. things
Ezek. 24:24 that he hath d. shall ye do
33:16 he hath d. that is lawful
Joel 2:20 he hath d. great things
Mark 7:37 he hath d. all things
2 Cor. 5:10 receive accor. h. h. d.

I have DONE.
Gen. 28:15,till I have d. that I h.
Jud. 1:7 as I h. d. so G. reqt. me
15:11 as th. did to me, so I. d.
2 Sam. 19:29 I have d. this thing
24:10 I h. d. foolishly, 1 Ch. 21:8
2 K. 20:3 how I have d. it ?
Job 31:33 I have d. iniquity
Ps. 39:9 O L. it I have d. this
119:121 I h. d. judgement
Is. 38:15 by wh. of hand I h. d. it
46:10 I have d. all ; 48:5 I h. d.
37:26 heard how I have d. it
Jer. 3:7 after not of, without ca.
8:6 I have d. it
John 13:12 what I have d. to you ?
15 do as I have d. to you

Hast thou DONE.
Gen. 3:13 what h. t. d. ? 31:26 ;
Num. 23:11 ; 1 Sam. 13:11 ;
2 Sam. 3:24 ; John 18:35
20:9 what h. th. d. unto us ?
2 Sam. 7:21 do thy servant know
16:10 wherefore hast thou d. so ?
1 K. 1:6 why h. d. so ?
2 Sam. 7:20 to thy servant, 1 Chr. 17:19
Is. 10:21 those things h. thou d.
Jer. 1:10 why hast thou d. this ?

DOO
Thou hast DONE.
Gen. 3:13 what is this thou h. d. ?
12:18 ; 26:10 ; 29:25 ; Jud. 15:11 ; 2 Sam. 12:21
14 because thou hast d. this, 22:16 ; 2 Chr. 25:16
20:9 t. h. d. deeds on, n. to be d.
27:45 he forget what t. h. d.
31:28 thou h. d. foolish, 1 Sam. 13:13 ; 2 Chr. 16:9
Jos. 7:19 tell me what thou hast d. 1 Sam. 14:43
Ps. 40:5 wonderful works t. h. d.
52:6 praise thee bec. t. h. d. it
109:27 know that thou h. d. it
Jer. 2:23 know what thou hast d.
Lam. 1:21 are glad thou h. d. it
22 as thou hast d. unto me
2:20 consider to whom t. h. d.
Ezek. 16:48 Sod. not d. as t. h. d.
50 deal with these as thou h. d.
Ob. 15 as t. h. d. be done to thee
Jon. 1:14 t. h. d. as it pleaseth

Not DONE.
Gen. 20:9 deeds ought not be d.
Num. 16:28 not d. of mine own
Deut. 32:27 Lord hath not d. all
Is. 5:4 done that I have not d. ?
46:10 declaring things not yet d.
Jer. 3:10 neither shall that ho d.
Ezek. 5:9 that I have not d.
Dan. 9:12 not been d. as on Jer.
11:24 do what his fat. not d.
Amos 3:6 in city, L. not d. it ?
Acts 26:26 was not d. in a corner

DONE, with this.
Gen. 21:26 wot n. who hath d. t.
43:28 what is this God hath d.
Jud. 2:2 not obeyed, why d. t. ?
6:29 Who hath d. this t 15:6
Sam. 28:18 hath Lord d. this
Ps. 7:3 O Lord, if I have d. this
22:31 declare that he hath d. th.
51:4 and d. this evil in my sight
Is. 41:20 hand of Lord hath d. this
Ezek. 23:38 moreover this they have d. unto me
Mark 5:32 her that had d. this
Luke 23:41 t. man d. nothing amiss
Acts 4:7 by what p. ha. ye d. t. ?

DOOR.
Gen. 4:7 sin lieth at the d.
19:9 came near to break the d.
Ex. 12:23 will pass over the d.
Deut. 15:17 thrust it through ear
2 Sam. 13:17 bolt the d. after h.
2 K. 4:15 she stood in the d.
9:3 then open the d. and flee
Est. 2:21 which kept the d. 6:2
Job 31:9 laid wait at neighb. d.
34 I went not out of the d.
Ps. 141:3 keep the d. of my lips
Prov. 26:14 as d. turneth
Cant. 5:4 in hand by hole of d.
8:9 if she be a d. we will inclose
Ezek. 8:8 in wall, behold a d.
10:19 stood at d. of the east gate
11:1 at d. of the gate 25 men
41:3 breadth of d. ten cubits
46:3 peo. shall worship at the d.
Hos. 2:15 valley of A. d. of hope
Amos 9:1 smite the lintel of the d.
Mat. 27:60 rolled great stone to d. of sepul.here, Mark 15:46
28:2 rolled stone from the d.
Mark 1:33 city was gather. at d.
2:2 no room, no not about the d.
16:3 who roll us stone from d. ?
John 10:1 entereth not by the d.
2 that entereth in by the d.
7 I am the d. 9
18:16 but Peter stood at the d.
Acts 5:9 feet at d. to carry thee
12:13 as Peter knocked at the d.
14:27 opened d. of faith to Gen.
1 Cor. 16:9 great d. and effectual
2 Cor. 2:12 a d. was opened to me
Col. 4:3 open a d. of utterance
Jam. 5:9 judge standeth bef. d.
Rev. 3:8 before thee an open d.
20 stand at d. If any man ope.
4:1 a d. was open in heaven

DOOR, with house.
Gen. 19:11 that were at d. of h.
43:19 communed at d. of house
Ex. 12:22 none go out of d. of h.
Jud. 19:26 fell down at d. of h.
1 K. 6:9 Naam. stood at d. of h.
3:31 Mordecai's gate, from d.
Prov. 5:8 not nigh d. of her h.
8:34 waiting at d. of her h.
9:14 she sitteth at d. of her h.
Ezek. 8:14 to d. of Lord's h. 47:1

828 CRUDEN'S CONCORDANCE.

DOU

DOOR, *with* keeper, s.
2 *K*. 25;18 captain of the guard took the three k. of d. *Jer*. 52:24
1 *Chr*. 15;24 Obed. and Jeh. d.-k.
Ezek. 6:2 k. of d. sought to lay
Es. 84:10 I had rather be a d.-k.
Jer. 35:4 Maaseiah *keep*. of the d.

DOOR, *with* posts.
Ex. 12:7 blood on upper d.-p.
21:6 master bring him to d.-p.
Deut. 11:20 write them on d.-p.
Is. 6:4 p. of d. moved at the vo.
Ezek. 41:3 he measured p. of d.
16 measured the d.-p.

DOOR, *with* shut.
Gen. 19:6 L. s. d. ; 10 ang. s. d.
2 *K*. 4:4 shalt *shut* d. upon thee
6:32 *shut* d. hold him fast at d.
Mat. 6:6 hast *shut* thy d. pray
23:10 d. was s. ; *Luke* 11;7 d. is
now s.
Luke 13:25 hath s. to the d.
Jno. 3:8 opcn d. no man can s.

DOOR, *with* tabernacle.
Ex. 28:4 bring to d. of *tab*. 40;12 ;
Lev. 4:4 ; 8:3, 4 ; 12:6 ; *Num*. 6:10
11 by d. of t. 38 ; 40;29 ; *Lev*. 1:5 ; *Num*. 27:2
42 burnt-offering at d. of t. 53:0,
10 ; 38:8 ; 40;28 ; *Lev*. 1:3 ; 3:2 ;
4:7, 18
40:6 d. of *tabcr. Num.* 25;6
Lev. 8:31 at d. of t. 35 ; 14;11 ;
16:7 ; 17:6 ; *Num*. 6:18 ; 10:3 ;
Jos. 19:51
33 shall not go out of d. of t.
10:7 not go out from d. of t.
14;23 d. of t. 13;14, 29 ; 19:21 ;
Num. 6:13 ; 16;19, 50 ; 20;6
17:4 bring, it not to d. of *tab*. 9
Num. 12;5 in d. of *tab*. 16;18
Deut. 31;15 pillar of cloud ov. d.

DOOR, *joined with* tent.
Gen. 18:1 Abra. sat in the *tent* d.
10 Sarah heard it in the *tent* d.
Ex. 33:8 ev. man at his t. d. 10
Num. 11;10 weep. ev. men in d.
16;27 Abiram stood in t. d.
Jud. 4;20 Stand in d. of *tent*

DOORS.
Jos. 2:19 whosoever go out of d.
Jud. 3;25 opened not d. of parlor
11:31 cometh forth of d.
16:3 Samson took d. of the city
1 *Sam*. 3:15 Samuel opened t. d.
21;13 D. scrabbled on d. of gate
Jud. 3:22 opened d. to traveller
38;10 set bars and d. to the sun
17 seen d. of shadow of death?
41:14 who open. d. of his face?
Ps. 24;7 up, ye everlasting d. 9
78:23 though opened d. of heav.
Prov. 8:3 wisdom crieth at the d.
34 waiting at posts of my d.
Is. 57:8 behind d. set up
Ezek. 33;20 talking in the d.
Mic. 7:5 d. of mouth from her
Zec. 11;1 open thy d. O Lebanon
Mal. 24:33 at the d. *Mark* 13;29
Acts 5;19 angel opened prison d.
23 keepers standing before d.
16;26 all the d. were opened
27 keeper seeing prison d. op.

Shut DOORS.
Jud. 3;23 Ehud *shut* d. of parlor
2 *Chr*. 28;24 s. up d. of L.'s ho.
29;7 have *shut* d. of the porch
Neh. 6;10 let us *shut* d. of temple
7;3 *shut* the d. and bar them
Job 3;10 *shut* not up d. of womb
38;8 *shut* up the sea with d. ?
Ec. 12;4 d. be s. in the streets
Is. 26;20 enter, and shut thy d.
Mal. 1;10 *shut* d. for naught
John 20;19 d. *sh. Jesus* came, 26
Acts 21;30 the d. were shut

DOR. *Jud*. 1;27 : 1 *K*. 4;11
DORCAS. *Acts* 9;30, 39

DOTE, ED, ING.
Jer. 50;36 and they shall d.
Ezek. 23;5 Aholah d. on Assyri.
1 *Tim*. 6;4 d. about questions
DOTHAN. *Gen*. 37;17 ; 2 *K*. 6;13

DOUBLE.
Gen. 43;12 and take d. money
Ex. 22;4 found, let him pay d.
7 if found, let him pay d.
Deut. 15;18 worth a d. hired ser.
21;17 giving him a d. portion
2 *K*. 2;9 d. portion of thy spirit
1 *Chr*. 12;33 every m. not d. heart
Job 11;6 d. to that which is

DRA

Job 41;13 to him with d. bridle?
12;2 with s d. heart do speak
Is. 40;2 rec. d. for all her sins
61;7 your shame have d. in their land they shall possess d.
Jer. 16;18 recomp. their sin d.
17;18 with d. destruction
Zec. 9;12 I will render d. to thee
1 *Tim*. 3;8 deacons not d.-tong.
5;17 worthy of d. honor
Rev. 18;6 d. unto her d. in cup d. hath filled, fill to her d.

DOUBLE-MINDED.
Jam. 1;8 a d.-m. man is unstable
4;8 purify your hearts, ye d.-m.

DOUBLED.
Gen. 41;32 dream was d. twice
Ex. 28;16 four-square, being d.
39;9 span was breadth, being d.
Ezek. 21;14 sword be d. third ti.

DOUBT, S.
Deut. 28;66 thy life hang in d.
Dan. 5;16 thou canst dissolve d.
Acts 28;4 no d. this man is a mur.
Gal. 4;20 for I stand in d. of you
1 *John* 2;19 wo. no d. have con.

DOUBT.
Mat. 14;31 wheref. didst thou d. ?
21;21 if ye have faith and d. not
Mark 11;23 not d. in his heart
John 10;24 how long make us d. ?

DOUBTED, ETH.
Mat. 21;17 but some d.
Acts 5;24 d. where, would grow
10;17 Peter d. in himself
25;20 I d. of such questions
Rom. 14;23 d. is damned

DOUBTFUL.
Luke 12;29 nei. be ye of d. mind
Rom. 14;1 not to d. disputations

DOUBTING.
John 13;22 d. of whom he spake
Acts 10;20 go, nothing d. 11;12
1 *Tim*. 2;8 men pray without d.

DOUBTLESS.
Ps. 126;6 d. come again rejoicing
Is. 63;16 d. thou art our father
1 *Cor*. 9;2 yet d. I am to you
Phil. 3;8 d. I count all but loss

DOUGH.
Ex. 12;39 unleavened cakes of d.
Num. 15;20 offer a cake of d. 21
Neh. 10;37 first-fruits of our d.
Jer. 7;18 women knead their d.
Ezek. 44;30 give priest first of d.
Hos. 7;4 after he hath kneaded d.

DOVE.
Gen. 8;8 N. sent forth a d. 10, 12
9 the d. found no rest
Ps. 55;6 tho. I had w. like a d.
68;13 ye shall be as w. of a d.
Cant. 1;15 thou hast d. eyes, 4;1
5;2 my sister, my d.
6;9 my d. my undefiled
Is. 38;14 I did mourn as a d.
Jer. 48;28 and be like the d.
Hos. 7;11 Eph. is like a silly d.
11;11 they shall tremble as a d.
Mat. 3;10 like a d. *Mark* 1;10 ; *Luke* 3;22 ; *John* 1;32

DOVES.
2 *K*. 6;25 of a cab of d. dung
Cant. 5;12 eyes are as eyes of d.
Is. 59;11 we mourn sore like d.
60;8 flee as d. to their windows.
Ezek. 7;16 like d. d. of the valleys
Nah. 2;7 lead as with voice of d.
Mat. 10;16 harmless as d.
21;12 that sold d. *Mark* 11;15
John 2;14 those that sold d.

DOWN, ED.
Job 1;7 walking *up and* d. 2;2
Ps. 30;15 wander *up and* d.
109;23 I am tossed *up and* d.
Ezek. 28;14 *up a. d.* in midst
Zec. 10;12 shall walk *up a. d.*
Acts 27;27 were driven *up and* d.

DOWN-SITTING.
Ps. 139;2 thou knowest my d.

DOWNWARD.
2 *K*. 19;30 take root d. *Is*. 37;31
Ec. 3;21 spirit of beast goeth d.
Ezek. 1;27 appear. of loins d. 8;2

DOWRY.
Gen. 30;20 end. me with good d.
34;12 ask me never so much d.
Ex. 22;17 according to the d.
1 *Sam*. 18;25 king desireth not d.

DRAG.
Hab. 1;15 gather them in their d.
16 burn incense to their d.

DRA

DRAGGING.
John 21;8 d. the net with fishes

DRAGON.
Ps. 91;13 d. shalt thou trample
29, 27;1 slay d. that is in sea
51;9 cut Rahab and wounded d.
Jer. 51;34 swallow. me up like d.
Ezek. 29;3 Pharaoh, the great d.
Rev. 12;3 behold, a great red d.
9 d. was cast out, 13
17 d. was wroth with the wom.
13;2 the d. gave him his power
4 they worshipped the d.
11 he spake as d.
16;13 come out of mouth of d.
20;2 he laid hold on the d.

DRAGON-WELL.
Neh. 2;13 I went out before d.-w.

DRAGONS.
Deut. 32;33 wine is poison of d.
Job 30;29 I am a brother to d.
Ps. 44;19 brok. us in place of d.
74;13 breakest the heads of d.
148;7 praise the Lord, ye d.
Is. 13;22 d. in pleasant palaces
34;13 he habitation for d. 35;7
43;20 d. and owls shall hon. me
Jer. 9;11 Jerusalem a den of d.
10;22 cities of Judah a den of d.
14;6 snuffed up wind like d.
51;37 Babylon a dwelling for d.
Mic. 1;8 make wailing like d.
Mal. 1;3 heritage waste for the d.

DRAMS.
1 *Chr*. 29;7 gave of gold 10,000 d.
Ezr. 2;69 gave 61,000 d. of gold
8;27 20 basons of gold, of 1,000 d.
Neh. 7;70 gave to treas. 1,000 d.
71 gave 20,000 d. of gold, 72

DRANK.
Gen. 9;21 Noah d. of the wine
24;46 I d. made camels drink
27;25 brought wine and he d.
Num. 20;11 the congregation d.
Deut. 32;38 d. wine of drink-of.
1 *Sam*. 30;12 nor d. water
1 *K*. 13;19 eat bread in it d. wa.
17;6 and he d. of brook
Dan. 1;5 king ap. of wine he d.
5;1 d. before the thousand
3 his concubines d. in them
Mark 14;23 and they all d. of it
Luke 17;27 they eat, they d. 28
John 4;12 Jacob d. thereof
1 *Cor*. 10;4 d. of that spirit, rock

DRAUGHT.
Mat. 15;17 out in d. *Mark* 7;19
Luke 5;4 let down nets for a d.
9 astonished at d. of fishes
Jam. 1;14 d. away of his own

DRAUGHT-HOUSE.
2 *K*. 10;27 made Baal's house a d.

DRAVE.
Ex. 14;25 they d. them heavily
Jos. 10;10 d. not out Canaanites
24;12 and d. them out from be-
fore you, *Jud*. 6;9
18 Lord d. out before us
Jud. 1;19 J. d. out inhabitants
2 *Sam*. 6;3 d. the cart, 1 *Chr*. 13;7
2 *K*. 17;21 Jeroboam d. Israel
from following the Lord
Acts 7;45 whom God d. out
18;16 d. them from judgm.-seat

See DROVE.

DRAW.
Gen. 24;44 will d. for thy camels
Ex. 13;9 I will d. my sword
Jud. 4;7 I will d. to thee Sisera
9:54 d. thy sword, and slay me,
1 *Sam*. 31;4 ; 1 *Chr*. 10;4
33;23 d. from city to highways
John 12;32 d. all men unto me
Job 20;28 every man d. after him
Ps. 28;3 d. me not with the w.
Cant. 1;4 d. me, we will run aft.
Is. 5;18 d. iniquity with cords
66;19 nations that d. the bow
Ezek. 21;3 will d. forth my sw.
28;7 strangers d. their swords
30;11 d. their swords ag. Egypt
32;20 d. her and all her multi.
John 4;11 hast nothing to d. w.
6;44 except the Father d. him
12;32 I will d. all men unto me
21;6 were not able to d. it
Acts 20;30 d. away disciples
Jam. 2;6 d. you before judg.-seat
4;8 d. nigh to G. he will d. n.

DRA

DRAW *back*.
Ezek. 21;5 d. not my sword back
89 not of them who d. back

DRAW *near*.
1 *Sam*. 14;36 let us d. near to G.

DRE

1 *Sam*. 14;38 d. ye n. h. all t. ch.
Ps. 73;28 good to d. n. to God
107;18 d. near to gates of death
Is. 29;13 d. *near* with their lips
45;20 d. n. ye that are escaped
57;3 d. *near* ye sons of sorceress
Jer. 30;21 cause him to d. *near*
46;3 and d. *near* to battle
Ezek. 9;1 charge ov. city, to d. n.
22;4 caused thy days to d. *near*
Joel 3;9 let all men of war d. n.
Heb. 10;22 d. n. with true heart

DRAW *nigh*.
Ex. 3;5 said d. not *nigh* hither
Ps. 69;18 d. *nigh* to my soul
91;10 d. *nigh* that fol. misch.
Ec. 12;1 nor years d. *nigh*
Is. 5;19 coun. of Holy One d. n.
Heb. 7;19 by the which we d. n.
Jam. 4;8 d. n. to G. he will d. n.

DRAW *out*.
Ex. 12;21 d. *out* and take a lamb
Lev. 26;33 d. *out* a sword after
Jud. 3;22 not d. dagger out of
Job 41;1 canst d. *out* leviathan ?
Ps. 35;3 d. *out* also the spear
85;5 wilt thou d. o. thine anger
Prov. 20;5 m. of und. will d. it o.
Is. 57;4 do ye d. o. tongue
58;10 d. *out* soul to the hungry
Jer. 49;20 d. them *out*, 50;45
Lam. 4;3 sea-monster d. *out*
Mat. 5;3 I will d. *out* a sword
after them, 12 ; 12;14
Hag. 2;16 to d. *out* fifty vessels
John 2;8 d. *out* now, and bear

DRAW *up*.
Job 40;23 he can d. *up* Jordan

DRAW, *joined with* water.
Gen. 24;13 dau. come to d. wa.
1 *Sam*. 9;11 maid going to d. wa.
Is. 12;3 with joy shall ye d. wa.
Nah. 3;14 d. *waters* for the siege
John 4;7 woman of S. to d. wa.

DRAWN.
Num. 22;23 his sword d. 31 ; *Jos*. 5;13 ; 1 *Chr*. 21;16
Deut. 30;17 d. away, and wo. gods
Jos. 8;6 till d. them from city
Job 20;5 it is d. and cometh out
Ps. 37;14 wicked d. out sword
55;21 than oil, yet d. swords
Prov. 24;11 that are d. to death
Jer. 21;15 fled from d. swords
22;9 that are d. from breasts
31;3 with loving-kindness d.
Lam. 2;3 d. back his right hand
Ezek. 21;5 Lord d. my sword, 28
Acts 11;10 d. up again to heaven
Jam. 1;14 d. away of his own

DRAWER, S.
Deut. 29;11 to d. of water
Jos. 9;21 be d. of water, 23, 27

DRAWETH.
Deut. 25;11 the one d. near
Jud. 19;9 day d. towards even.
Job 24;22 he d. the mighty
33;22 his soul d. near to grave
Ps. 10;8 d. him into his net
88;3 life d. *nigh* to the grave
Luke 21;8 near delivery
Luke 21;28 the time d. near
thy your redemption d. *nigh*
Jam. 5;8 coming of L. d. *nigh*

DRAWING.
Jud. 5;11 in places of d. water
John 6;19 Jesus d. *nigh* to ship

DREAD, Substantive.
Gen. 9;2 d. of you be on ev. beast
Ex. 15;16 d. shall fall upon them
Deut. 2;25 to put d. of thee upon
the nations, 11;25
Job 13;11 his d. fall upon you ?
21 let not thy d. make me afr.
Is. 8;13 and let him be your d.

DREAD, Verb.
Deut. 1;29 I said to you, d. not
1 *Chr*. 22;13 be strong, d. not

DREADFUL.
Gen. 28;17 how d. is this place
Job 15;21 a d. sound is in his ears
Is. 18;7 a d. rings, they were d.
Dan. 7;7 a fourth beast d. 19
9;4 O Lord the great and d. God
Hab. 1;7 the Chaldeans are d.
Mal. 1;14 name d. among heath.
4;5 great and d. day of the Lord

DREAM, Substantive.
Gen. 20;3 to Abimelech in a d.
31;10 Jacob saw in a d. the rams
24 God came to Laban in a d.
37;5 Joseph dreamed a d. 9, 10

DRE

Gen. 40:5 but. and ba. a *d.* both
41:7 it was a *d.* 1 *K.* 3:15
25 *d.* of Pharaoh is one, 36
Num. 12:6 I. will speak in a *d.*
Jud. 7:13 told a *d.* to his fellow
1 *K.* 3:5 to Solomo i in a *d.*
Job 20:8 he shall fly away as a *d.*
33:15 in a *d.* openeth ears
Ps. 73:20 as a *d.* when one awak.
Ec. 5:3 a *d.* com. through busin.
Is. 29:7 fight ag. Ariel be as a *d.*
Jer. 23:28 hath *d.* let him tell *d.*
Dan. 2:4 tell thy servants the *d.*
36 this is the *d.*
4:19 *d.* be to th. that hate thee
7:1 Daniel had a *d.* wrote it.
Mat. 1:20 angel of Lord app. to
   Joseph in a *d.* 2:13, 19
2:12 warned of God in a *d.* 22
27:19 I have suffered in a *d.*

DREAM, Verb.
Ps. 126:1 were like them that *d.*
Joel 2:28 old men *d. Acts* 2:17

DREAMED.
Gen. 28:12 Jac. *d.* ; 37:5 Jos. *d.*
40:5 officers *d.* ; 41:1 Phar. 15
Jer. 23:25 proph. said, I have *d.*
29:8 dreams you cause to be *d.*
Dan. 2:1 Nebuchadnezzar *d.*

DREAMER, S.
Gen. 37:19 said, This *d.* cometh
Deut. 13:3 not hearken to *d.*
5 *d.* shall be put to death
Jer. 27:9 hearken not to your *d.*
Jude 8 filthy *d.* defile the flesh

DREAMS.
Gen. 37:8 hated him for his *d.*
20 what will become of his *d.*
41:12 and he interpreted our *d.*
42:9 Joseph remembered the *d.*
1 *Sam.* 28:6 answer. not by *d.* 15
Job 7:14 thou scarest me with *d.*
Ec. 5:7 in multitude of *d.* are
Jer. 23:27 forget my name by *d.*
32 that prophesy false *d.*
Dan. 1:17 understand. in all *d.*
Zec. 10:2 diviners told false *d.*

DREAMETH.
Is. 29:8 hungry man *d.* a thirsty

DREGS.
Ps. 75:8 *d.* wicked shall drink
Is. 51:17 drunken *d.* of cup, 22

DRESS.
Gen. 2:15 into garden to *d.* it
18:7 young man hasted to *d.* it
Deut. 28:39 plant vincy. *d.* them
2 *Sam.* 12:4 to *d.* for wayfaring
13:5 Tamar *d.* meat in my sight
1 *K.* 18:25 Elijah said, *d.* it first

DRESSED.
2 *Sam.* 12:4 *d.* poor man's lamb
19:24 Mephib. not *d.* his feet
Heb. 6:7 for them by wh. it is *d.*

DRESSER.
Luke 13:7 said to *d.* of vineyard

DREW.
Gen. 24:20 Rebekah *d.* water, 45
37:28 they *d.* up Joseph
38:29 as Zarah *d.* back his hand
Ex. 2:10 I *d.* him out of water
16 Jethro's daughters *d.* water
Jos. 8:26 Jos. *d.* not hand back
Jud. 8:10 fell 120,000 *d.* sword
20 the youth *d.* not his sword
20:2 400,000 that *d.* sword
Ruth 4:8 so he *d.* off his shoe
2 *Sam.* 22:17 he *d.* me out of
   many waters, *Ps.* 18:16
23:16 mighty men *d.* water out
   well Beth. 1 *Chr.* 11:18
24:9 in Israel 800,000 *d.* sword
1 *K.* 22:34 *d.* a bow, 2 *Chr.* 18:33
2 *K.* 9:24 Jehu *d.* bow
1 *Chr.* 19:16 *d.* forth before Syrians
21:5 Israel were 1,100,000 that *d.*
   sword, Judah 470,000
Jer. 38:13 so they *d.* up Jeremiah
Hos. 11:4 *d.* with cords of a man
Mat. 13:48 *d.* to shore, *Mark* 6:53
26:51 Peter *d.* his sword, *Mark*
   14:47; *John* 18:10
Luke 22:54 and the sabbath *d.* on
John 2:9 servants *d.* the water
21:11 *d.* the net full of fishes
Acts 5:37 *d.* away much people
11:10 *d.* Paul out of the city
16:19 *d.* P. and S. into mark..pl.
27 jailer *d.* his sword
17:6 *d.* Jason and certain breth.
19:33 they *d.* Alexander out
21:30 *d.* Paul out of temple
Rev. 12:4 *d.* third part of stars

DREW near, or nigh.
Gen. 47:29 time *d. n.* is. m. die

DRI

1 *Sam.* 17:40 David *d. n.* to Goll.
2 *Sam.* 18:25 Ahimaaz *d. near*
Zep. 3:2 *d.* not *near* to her God
Mat. 21:1 when they *d. n.* to Jer.
   34 time of fruit *d. near*, he sent
Luke 15:25 elder son *d. n.* to ho.
22:47 Judas *d. n.* to kiss
24:15 Jesus himself *d. near*
28 they *d. nigh* to the village
Acts 7:17 time of promise *d. n.*
   31 as Mos. *d. near* to behold it
27:27 *d. near* some country

DREWEST.
Lam. 3:57 *d. near* in day I called

DRIED. See after **DRY.**

DRINK, Substantive.
Gen. 21:19 and gave she had *d.*
24:14 thy camels *d.* also, 46
Lev. 11:34 *d.* drunk in such ves.
Num. 20:8 give congregation *d.*
Jud. 4:19 she gave Sisera *d.*
Est. 1:7 *d.* to vessels of gold
Ps. 78:15 *d.* as out of gr. depths
102:9 mingled my *d.* with weep.
104:11 gave *d.* to every beast
Is. 32:6 cause *d.* of thirsty
43:20 to give *d.* to my people
Hos. 2:5 lovers that gave me *d.*
4:18 their *d.* is sour
Hab. 2:15 giveth his neighbor *d.*
Hag. 1:6 ye are not filled with *d.*
Mat. 25:35 and ye gave me *d.*
   37 g. thee *d.* ; 42 gave me no *d.*
John 4:9 a Jew, askest *d.* of me
   6:55 my blood is *d.* indeed
Rom. 12:20 enemy thirst, give *d.*
14:17 kingdom not meat and *d.*
1 *Cor.* 10:4 drink same spirit. *d.*
Col. 2:16 judge in meat or in *d.*

Strong DRINK.
Lev. 10:9 do not drink *strong d.*
Num. 6:3 Nazarite sep. fr. *s. d.*
Deut. 14:26 money for *str. d.*
29:6 nor drank *s. d.* forty years
Jud. 13:4 wife not drink *s. d.*
1 *Sam.* 1:15 wine nor *str. d.*
Prov. 20:1 *strong d.* is raging
31:4 princes *strong d.*
6 *s. d.* to him ready to perish
Is. 5:11 may follow *strong d.*
22 men of strength min. *s. d.*
24:9 *str. d.* bitter to them
28:7 erred through *st. d.* they
   are out of the way thro' *s. d.*
29:9 stag. but not with *strong d.*
56:12 fill ourselves with *str. d.*
Mic. 2:11 prophecy of *strong d.*
Luke 1:15 shall not drink *s. d.*

DRINK-OFFERING.
Ex. 29:40 a *d. o.* shall be of wine
Lev. 23:13 *d. o.* shall be of wine
18 *d.-o.* hot poured *d.-o.*
65:11 furnish *d.-o.*
Joel 1:9 *d.-o.* cut off
13 the *d.-o.* is withholden
2:14 return, and leave a *d.-o.*

DRINK-OFFERINGS.
Lev. 23:18 with *d.-o.* 37; *Num.*
   6:15; 28:31; 29:11, 18, 19, 21,
   24, 30, 33, 37, 39
Num. 28:14 *d.-o.* half a hin of w.
Deut. 32:38 drank wine of *d.-o.*
Ezr. 7:17 buy speedily *d.-o.*
Ps. 16:4 their *d.-o.* of blood
Jer. 7:18 *d.-o.* to oth. gods, 19:13;
   32:29
44:17 *d.-o.* to qu. of heaven, 18
Ezk. 20:28 there poured out *d.-o.*
45:17 princes part to give *d.-o.*

DRINK, Verb.
Gen. 24:18 *d.* my lord, 46
   with flocks came to *d.*
Ez. 15:21 what shall we *d.?*
   32:20 made children of Israel *d.*
Lev. 10:9 do not *d.* wine nor
Num. 6:3 nor *d.* liquor of grapes
Jud. 7:5 howeth down to *d.*
Ruth 2:9 go to the vessels, and *d.*
1 *Sam.* 30:11 made him *d.* water
   of, 17 ; 1 *Chr.* 11:18, 19
1 *K.* 13:8 shall *d.* at the brook
   22. 3:15 king and Haman to *d.*
Job 21:20 *d.* wrath of Almighty
Ps. 36:8 *d.* of river of thy pleas.
60:3 *d.* wine of astonishment
62:21 gave me vinegar to *d.*
75:8 wicked of earth shall *d.*
78:44 into blood that not *d.*
80:5 givest them tears to *d.*
110:7 *d.* of the brook
Prov. 4:17 they *d.* wine
   31:5 lest they *d.* and forget law
   7 *d.* and forget his poverty
Cant. 5:1 *d.* yea, *d.* abundantly
Is. 24:9 drink bit. to them *d.* it

DRI

Is. 51:22 no more *d.* it again
62:9 *d.* it in courts of holiness
65:13 my servant shall *d.*
Jer. 16:7 cup of consolation to *d.*
23:15 make *d.* water of gall
25:15 cause nations to *d.* it
   16 they shall *d.* and be moved
27 *d.* ye, be drunken, and spue
28 Ye shall certainly *d.*
35:14 to this day they *d.* none
49:12 whose judgm. was not to
   d. of cup, but thou shalt *d.*
Ezk. 4:11 time to time shalt *d.*
23:32 *d.* of thy sister's cup
34:19 *d.* that ye have fouled
Dan. 5:2 concubines might *d.*
Amos 4:1 masters, Let us *d.*
Ob. 16 the heathen *d.* continu-
   ally, yea, they shall *d.*
Hab. 2:16 *d.* and let thy foreskin
Hag. 1:6 ye *d.* but are not filled
Zec. 9:15 *d.* and make a noise
Mat. 10:42 whoso giveth to *d.* to
20:22 are ye able to *d.* of the cup
   I shall *d.* of? *Mark* 10:38
   23 shall *d.* indeed, *Mark* 10:39
29 nor. *d.* till that day I *d.* it,
   Mark 14:25; *Luke* 22:18
42 may not pass, except I *d.* it
27:34 gave him vinegar to *d.*
48 put it on a reed, and gave
   him to *d.* *Mark* 15:36
Mark 16:18 if *d.* any deadly th.
John 4:10 saith, Give me to *d.*
7:37 let him come to me and *d.*
18:11 shall I not *d.?*
1 *Cor.* 10:4 did all *d.* the same
21 *d.* cup of L. and of devils
11:25 this do. as oft as ye *d.* it
12:13 all to *d.* into one Spirit

DRINK water, or waters.
Gen. 24:43 m. of thy pitcher to *d.*
Ex. 7:24 for w. to *d.*
   15:23 could not *d. waters* of M.
17:1 no water for the peo. to *d.*
Num. 5:24 *d.* bitter *water*, 26, 27
20:5 neither any w. to *d.* 33:14
17 nor *d. water* of wells, *Deut.*
   2:6 wa. for money, *d.* 28
Jud. 4:19 us. to *d.* for I am thir.
7:6 rest bowed to *d. water*
1 *Sam.* 30:11 Egyptian *d. w.*
2 *Sam.* 23:15 give me to *d.* of *w.*
   of Bethlehem, 1 *Chr.* 11:17
1 *K.* 13:8 nor will I *d. water*, 9
17:10 a little *w.* that I may *d.*
2 K. 3:17 val. fill. with *w.* may *d.*
18:31 *d.* ev. one *wa. cis. Is.* 36:16
Job 22:7 given *w.* to weary to *d.*
Prov. 5:15 *d.* wa. out of thy cist.
25:21 give *w.* to *d.*
Jer. 2:18 *d. water* of Sihor
8:14 so. of gall to *d.* 9:15
Ezk. 4:11 *d. water* by meas. 16
12:18 *d.* thy *water* with tremb.
19 *d.* their *wa.* with astonish.
31:14 their trees that *d. w.* 16
Dan. 1:12 pulse to eat, *wat.* to *d.*
Amos 9:14 wondered to *d. water*
Jno. 3:7 let not feed nor *d. w.*
Mark 9:41 cup of *w.* to *d.*
John 4:7 Give me to *d.*
1 *Tim.* 5:23 *d.* no longer *water*

DRINK, with wine.
Gen. 19:32 our father *d. wine*
Lev. 10:9 not *d. wine* when go
Num. 6:3 *d.* no vinegar of *w.*
20 Nazarite may *d. w.*
Deut. 29:6 plant vineyards, but
   not *d. of wine, Amos* 5:11
Jud. 13:4 M. wife not *d. w.* 7, 14
2 *Sam.* 16:2 *w.* such as faint m. *d.*
Prov. 4:17 *d. wine* of violence
9:5 *d.* of *wine* I have mingled
31:4 it is not for kings to *d. w.*
Ec. 2:3 if. give mine heart to *d. w.*
9:7 *d.* thy *w.* with a merry
Is. 5:22 are mighty to *d. wine*
22:13 *wine*, Let us eat and *d.*
24:9 shall not *d. wine*
29:9 cause of stagger not *d. w.*
Jer. 35:2 give Rechabites *w.* to *d.*
6 *d.* no *w.* ye shall *d.* no *w.*
Ezk. 44:21 nor any priest *d. w.*
Dan. 1:8 purposed not to *d. w.*
5:1 king *d. w.* before thousand
Amos 2:8 *d. w.* of condemned
6:6 *d. w.* in bowls
9:14 plant vineyards and *d. w.*
Mic. 2:11 not *d.* of *wine* and *str.*
Mark 15:23 gave to *d. w.* mingled
Rom. 14:21 not good to *d. wine*
Rev. 14:8 all nations *d.* of *w.*
   10 *d.* of *wine* of wrath of G.

DRI

DRINKERS.
Joel 1:5 howl, all ye *d.* of wine

DRINKS.
Heb. 9:10 only in meats and *d.*

DRINKETH.
Gen. 44:5 in which my lord *d.?*
Deut. 11:11 land *d.* water of rain
Job 6:4 poison *d.* up my spirit
15:16 *d.* iniquity like water
34:7 like Job who *d.* scorning
40:23 behold, he *d.* up a river
Prov. 26:6 *d.* damage
Is. 29:8 he *d.* but he awaketh
44:12 the smith, he *d.* no water
Mark 2:16 *d.* with publican?
John 4:13 *d.* this wa. shall thirst
14 *d.* of water I shall give him
6:54 *d.* my blood hath eter. life
56 *d.* my blood, dwelleth in me
1 *Cor.* 11:29 *d.* unworth. *d.* dam.
Heb. 6:7 which *d.* in the rain

DRINKING.
Gen. 24:22 camels had done *d.*
Ruth 3:3 till Boaz have done *d.*
1 *Sam.* 30:16 were eating and *d.*
1 *K.* 4:20 Judah and Israel *d.*
10:21 Solomon's *d.* vessels
16:9 E. was *d.* ; 20:12 Benhad.
1 *Chr.* 12:39 with D. three days *d.*
Est. 1:8 *d.* was according to law
Job 1:13 sons and daughters *d.*
18:8 eating flesh, and *d. w.*
Mat. 11:18 John came neither
   eating nor *d. Luke* 7:33
19 eating and *d. Luke* 7:34
24:38 and *d.* till the flood came
Luke 10:7 *d.* such as they give

DRIVE.
Ex. 6:1 with a strong hand *d.* out
23:28 hornets, which shall *d.*
29 I will not *d.* out in one year
30 by little and little I will *d.*
33:2 I will *d.* out the Canaanite
34:11 behold, I *d.* out the Amorite
Num. 22:6 I may *d.* them out
11 able to overcome, and *d.*
33:55 if ye will not *d.* out the
Deut. 4:38 *d.* out nations from
   bef. thee, 9:4, 5 ; *Jos.* 3:10
9:3 so shalt thou *d.* them out
11:23 then will the Lord *d.* out
18:12 Lord doth *d.* them out
33:6 them will I *d.* out
14:12 then I shall be able to *d.*
15:63 Judah could not *d.* out
17:12 Manasseh could not *d.* out
13 not utterly *d.* out, *Jud.* 1:21
18 shalt *d.* out the Canaanites
28:3 *d.* them out of your sight
13 no more *d.* out, *Jud.* 2:3, 21
Jud. 1:19 Judah could not *d.* out
21 Benjamin not *d.* out Jebus.
27 Manasseh ; 29 Ephraim
31 Asher ; 31 Naphtali
11:24 whom Lord shall *d.* out
2 *K.* 4:24 *d.* slack not thy riding
2 *Chr.* 20:7 *d.* out inhabitants
Job 18:11 ter. *d.* him to his feet
24:3 *d.* away ass of fatherless
Ps. 44:2 didst *d.* out heathen
68:2 as smoke, so *d.* them away
Prov. 22:15 rod of correction *d.* it
Is. 22:19 *d.* thee from thy station
Jer. 23:2 bring a curse whither I *d.*
24:9 whither I shall *d.* you
46:15 Lord did *d.* them
Ezk. 4:13 whither I will *d.* them
Dan. 4:25 *d.* thee from men, 32
Hos. 9:15 *d.* th. out of my house
Joel 2:20 *d.* the northern army
Zep. 2:4 out Ashd. at noonday
Acts 27:15 ship, we let her *d.*

DRIVEN.
Gen. 4:14 hast *d.* me out this day
Ex. 10:11 *d.* from Pharaoh's pre.
22:10 the beast be *d.* away
Num. 32:21 *d.* out his enemies
Deut. 4:19 be *d.* to worship them
30:1 whither Lord hath *d.* thee
4:27 *d.* to other gods, *Jer.* 16:15
Jos. 23:9 L. *d.* out great nations
1 *Sam.* 26:19 *d.* me out this day
Job 6:13 is wisdom *d.* from me?
13:25 break leaf *d.* to and fro?
18:18 *d.* from light to darkness
30:5 *d.* forth from among men
Ps. 40:14 let *d.* back backward
68:2 as smoke is *d.* away
114:3 Jordan was *d.* back, 5
Prov. 14:32 wicked is *d.* away
Is. 8:22 shall be *d.* to darkness
19:7 sown by brooks *d.* away
41:2 as *d.* stubble to his bow
Jer. 8:3 in places whither *d.*
23:3 ; 29:14, 18 ; 32:37
46:28 from all lands whither *d.*

DRO

Jer. 23:2 *d.* them away not visit.
12 be *d.* on, and fall therein
40:12 places whither *d.* 43:5
46:28 end of nations, whither *d.*
49:5 shall be *d.* out every man
50:17 lions have *d.* him away
Ezek. 31:11 I have *d.* him out for
34:4 brought that *d.* away, 16
Dan. 4:33 *d.* from men, 5:21
9:7 through all countries *d.*
Hos. 13:3 as chaff *d.* with whirl.
Mic. 4:6 gather her *d.* Zep. 3:19
Luke 8:29 *d.* of devil into wilder.
Acts 27:17 and so were *d.*
27 *d.* up and down in Adria
Jam. 1:6 like wave *d.* with wind
3:4 though *d.* of fierce winds

DRIVER.
Job 39:7 nor regard, crying of *d.*

DRIVETH.
2 *K.* 9:20 for he *d.* furiously
Ps. 1:4 like chaff wind *d.*
Prov. 25:23 wind *d.* away rain
Mark 1:12 *d.* him to wilderness

DRIVING.
..*ng.* 2:23 *d.* them out hastily
2 *K.* 9:20 *d.* is like *d.* of Jehu
1 *Chr.* 17:21 by *d.* out nations

DROMEDARY, IES.
1 *K.* 4:28 brought barley for *d.*
Est. 8:10 sent letters on young *d.*
Is. 60:6 *d.* of Midian cover thee
Jer. 2:23 thou art a swift *d.*

DROP, S.
Job 36:27 maketh small the *o.*
38:28 who begotten *d.* of dew?
Cant. 5:2 locks with *d.* of night
Is. 40:15 nat. are as *d.* of bucket
Luke 22:44 as great *d.* of blood

DROP.
Deut. 32:2 doctrine *d.* as rain
33:28 hoav. *d.* dew, *Prov.* 3:20
Job 36:28 which the clouds do *d.*
Ps. 65:11 thy paths *d.* fatness
12 *d.* on pastures of wilderness
Prov. 5:3 lips of a str. woman *d.*
Cant. 4:11 lips *d.* as honey-comb
Is. 45:8 *d.* down, ye heavens
Ezek. 20:46 *d.* thy word
21:2 *d.* thy word to holy places
Joel 3:18 mountains shall *drop*
down new wine, **Amos** 9:13
Amos 7:16 *d.* not thy word ag. Is.

DROPPED, ETH.
Jud. 5:4 heavens *d.* clouds *d.*
1 *Sam.* 14:26 the honey *d.*
2 *Sam.* 21:10 water *d.* on them
Job 29:22 my speech *d.* on them
Ps. 68:8 heavens *d.* at pres. of G.
Ec. 10:18 thr. idleness house *d.*
Cant. 5:5 hands *d.* with myrrh

DROPPING.
Prov. 19:13 a continual *d.* 27:15
Cant. 5:13 his lips *d.* myrrh

DROPSY.
Luke 14:2 a man wh. had the *d.*

DROSS.
Ps. 119:119 the wicked like *d.*
Prov. 25:4 take *d.* from silver
26:23 covered with silver *d.*
Is. 1:22 thy silver is become *d.*
25 purely purge away thy *d.*
Ezek. 22:18 house of Israel *d.* 19

DROUGHT.
Gen. 31:40 in day *d.* consumed
Deut. 8:15 fiery serpents and *d.*
Job 24:19 *d.* cons. snow-waters
Ps. 32:4 my moisture into the *d.*
Is. 58:11 L. satisfy thy soul in *d.*
Jer. 2:6 through a land of *d.*
17:8 not be careful in year of *d.*
50:38 a *d.* is upon her waters
Hos. 13:5 know thee in land of *d.*
Hag. 1:11 and I called for a *d.*

DROVE.
Gen. 32:16 ev. *d.* by themselves
33:8 what meanest by all this *d.*

DROVE, Verb.
Gen. 3:21 so God *d.* out the man
15:11 Abram *d.* fowls away
Ex. 2:17 shepherds *d.* them
Num. 21:32 *d.* out the Amorites
Hab. 3:6 *d.* asunder the nations
John 2:15 *d.* them out of temple

DROWN.
Cant. 8:7 neither can floods *d.* it
1 *Tim.* 6:9 *d.* men in perdition

DROWNED.
Ex. 15:4 are *d.* in Red sea
Amos 8:9 *d.* as by flood of E. 9:5
Mat. 18:6 better *d.* in the sea
Heb. 11:29 Egyptians were *d.*

DRY

DROWSINESS.
Prov. 23:21 *d.* shall clo. with rags

DRUNK.
Deut. 29:6 nor have you *d.* wine
32:42 my arrows *d.* with blood
Jud. 15:19 *d.* his spirit came ag.
1 *Sam.* 1:15 I have *d.* nei. wine
1:13 Dav. made Uriah *d.*
1 *K.* 13:22 hast eaten and *d.*
16:9 Elah drinking himself *d.*
20:16 Bencha. drinking hims. *d.*
2 *K.* 6:23 eat. and *d.* he sent aw.
19:24 *d.* strange wat. *Is.* 37:25
Cant. 5:1 *d.* my wine
Is. 51:17 hast *d.* cup of his fury
63:6 make them *d.* in my fury
Jer. 46:10 be *d.* with their blood
51:57 I will make *d.* her princes
Ezek. 34:18 *d.* of the deep waters
Dan. 5:4 *d.* praised gods of gold
23 thou and concubines have *d.*
Ob. 16 *d.* on my holy mountain
Luke 5:39 having *d.* old wine
13:26 eaten and *d.* in thy pres.
John 2:10 well *d.* then worse
Eph. 5:18 *d.* wherein is excess
Rev. 17:2 *d.* with wine of fornic.
18:3 all nations *d.* of wine

DRUNKARD.
Deut. 21:20 this our son is a *d.*
Prov. 23:21 *d.* sh. come to pov.
26:9 as a thorn into hand of *d.*
Is. 24:20 the earth reel like a *d.*
1 *Cor.* 5:11 with bro. a *d.* eat not

DRUNKARDS.
Ps. 69:12 I was song of the *d.*
Is. 28:1 woe to *d.* of Ephraim, 3
Joel 1:5 awake, ye *d.* and weep
Nah. 1:10 while drunken as *d.*
1 *Cor.* 6:10 nor *d.* inherit kingd.

DRUNKEN.
Gen. 9:21 Noah was *d.*
1 *Sam.* 1:14 How long be *d.?*
25:36 Nabal was very *d.*
Job 12:25 stag. like *d. Ps.* 107:27
Is. 19:14 as a *d.* man staggereth
29:9 *d.* but not with wine, 51:21
49:26 be *d.* with their own blood
51:17 *d.* dregs of cup of trem.
Jer. 23:9 I am like a *d.* man
25:27 be *d.* and spue, and fall
48:26 *d.* for he magnified hims.
49:12 they have assuredly *d.*
51:7 golden cup made earth *d.*
Lam. 3:15 *d.* with wormwood
4:21 thou shalt be *d. Nah.* 3:11
5:4 *d.* our water for money
Nah. 1:10 while *d.* as drunkards
Hab. 2:15 and makest him *d.* also
Mat. 24:49 begin to eat and drink
with the *d. Luke* 12:45
Luke 17:8 serve me till I have *d.*
Acts 2:15 not *d.* as ye suppose
1 *Cor.* 11:21 and another is *d.*
1 *Thes.* 5:7 be *d.* are *d.* in night
Rev. 17:6 woman *d.* with blood

DRUNKENNESS.
Deut. 29:19 to add *d.* to thirst
Ec. 10:17 not for strength not *d.*
Jer. 13:13 all inhabitants with *d.*
Ezek. 23:33 shalt be filled with *d.*
39:19 amorch. 23:33 shall be filled with *d.*
39:19 and 31 overcharged with *d.*
Rom. 13:13 not in rioting and *d.*
Gal. 5:21 works of flesh are *d.*

DRUSILLA. *Acts* 24:24

DRY.
Lev. 13:30 it is a *d.* scall
Jos. 9:5 broad was *d.* 12
Jud. 6:37 it be *d.* on all the earth
39 let it be *d.* only on fleece
Job 13:25 pursue the *d.* stubble?
Ps. 105:41 they ran in *d.* places
Prov. 17:1 better is a *d.* morsel
Is. 25:5 as the heat in a *d.* place
32:2 be as rivers in a *d.* place
44:27 saith to the deep, Be *d.*
56:3 say, I am a *d.* tree
Jer. 4:11 a *d.* wind, not to fan
Ezek. 17:24 made *d.* tree flourish
20:47 devour every *d.* tree
30:12 I will make the rivers *d.*
37:2 bones *d.* 4 O ye *d.* bones
Hos. 9:14 give them *d.* breasts
13:15 his spring shall become *d.*
Nah. 1:4 rebuk. sea, maketh it *d.*
Zec. 9:11 sav. at stubble fully *d.*
Zep. 2:13 make Nineveh *d.* like
Mat. 12:43 *d.* places, *Luke* 11:24
Luke 23:31 be done in the *d.?*

DRY ground.
Gen. 8:13 face of *ground* was *d.*
Ex. 4:16 on *d. g.* in sea, 22

DUM

Jos. 3:17 the priests stood firm
on *d. ground* in Jordan
2 *K.* 2:8 Elisha went over on *d. g.*
Ps. 107:33 water-spr. into *d. g.*
35 turneth *d. g.* into water-sp.
Is. 44:3 will pour floods on *d. g.*
53:2 as a root out of a *d. g.*
Ezek. 19:13 planted in a *d. g.*

See LAND.

DRY, Verb.
Job 12:15 waters, they *d.* up
15:30 flame *d.* up his branches
Is. 42:15 will *d.* up herbs, pools
44:27 *d.* up thy rivers; 50:2 sea
Jer. 51:36 I will *d.* up her sea
Zec. 10:11 deeps of river shall *d.*

DRIED.
Gen. 8:7 until waters were *d.* up
Lev. 2:14 green ears of corn *d.* by
Num. 6:3 moist grapes or *d.*
11:6 our soul is *d.* away
Jos. 2:10 Lord *d.* up Red sea
4:23 *d.* up waters of Jordan
5:1 heard Lord had *d.* up Jord.
9:5 *d.* and mouldy was their pr.
1 *K.* 13:4 Jeroboam's hand *d.*
17:7 brook *d.* because no rain
2 *K.* 19:24 with sole of foot have
I *d.* the rivers, *Is.* 37:25
Job 18:16 his roots be *d.* beneath
28:4 they are *d.* up
Ps. 22:15 my strength is *d.*
69:3 my throat is *d.* eyes fail
106:9 Red sea, it was *d.* up
Is. 5:13 multi. *d.* up with thirst
19:5 river be wasted and *d.* up
6 brooks of defence be *d.* up
51:10 it which hath *d.* the sea?
Jer. 23:10 places of wilder. *d.* up
50:38 her waters shall be *d.* up
Ezek. 17:24 *d.* up the green tree
19:12 east wind *d.* up her fruit
37:11 they say, Our bones are *d.*
Hos. 9:16 their root is *d.* up
13:15 his fountain is *d.* up
Joel 1:10 the new wine is *d.* up
12 vine is *d.* 20 rivers are *d.*
Zec. 11:17 arm be clean *d.* up
Mark 5:29 fount. of her blood *d.*
11:20 saw the fig-tree *d.* up
Rev. 16:12 Euphrates was *d.* up

DRIEDST, ETH.
Job 14:11 and as the flood *d.* up
Ps. 74:15 *d.* up mighty rivers
Prov. 17:22 broken spirit *d.* bon.
Nah. 1:4 Lord *d.* up all the riv.

DRY-SHOD.
Is. 11:15 make men go over *d.-s.*

DUE.
Lev. 10:13 thy *d.* thy sons' *d.* 14
Deut. 18:3 shall be the priest's *d.*
1 *Chr.* 15:13 sought not after *d.*
16:29 the glory *d.* to his name,
Ps. 29:2; 96:8
Prov. 3:27 with. not to whom *d.*
Mat. 18:34 pay all that was *d.*
Luke 23:41 we receive *d.* reward
Rom. 13:7 to whom tribute is *d.*
1 *Cor.* 7:3 to the wife *d.* benevol.

DUE season.
Lev. 26:4 it *d. s. Deut.* 11:14
Num. 28:2 to offer to me in *d. s.*
Ps. 104:27 meat in *d. s.* 145:15
Prov. 15:23 a word spoken in *d. s.*
Ec. 10:17 princes eat in *d. s.*
Mat. 24:45 in *d. s. Luke* 12:42
Gal. 6:9 in *d. s.* we shall reap

DUE time.
Deut. 32:35 foot slide in *d. time*
19 *d.* thou art, to *d.* shalt ret.
13:16 if number the *d.* of earth
16:27 who sat but *d.* and ashes
Ex. 8:16 say to Aaron, smite *d.*
9:9 it shall become small *d.*
Lev. 14:41 pour out *d.*
17:13 blood, and cover it with *d.*
K. 23:12
Num. 23:10 who can count *d.*
Deut. 9:21 I cast *d.* into brook,
2 *K.* 23:12
28:24 make rain of thy land *d.*
Ps. 7:6 elders put *d.* on heads
3 *Sam.* 16:13 Shimei cast *d.*
1 *K.* 18:38 fire of L. consumed *d.*
20:10 if the *d.* of Samaria suffice
2 *Chr.* 34:4 made *d.* of images
33:12 sprinkled *d.* upon heads
7:9 flesh clothed with clods of *d.*
10:9 bring me into *d.* again?
28:6 earth, it hath *d.* of gold
34:15 shall turn again to *d.*
38:38 *d.* groweth into hardness
40:13 bind and repent in *d.* and ashes
Ps. 22:15 brought me into the *d.*
30:9 shall *d.* praise thee, shall
72:9 enemies shall lick the *d.*
78:27 rained flesh on them as *d.*

DUS

Prov. 31:8 open thy mouth for *d.*
Is. 35:6 tongue of *d.* shall sing
53:7 sheep before shearers is *d.*
56:10 his watchmen all *d.* dogs
Ezek. 3:26 *d.* and not be reproveer
24:27 speak, and be no more *d.*
33:22 and I was no more *d.*
Dan. 10:15 to the grou. I bec. *d.*
Hab. 2:18 to make him *d.* idols
19 saith to *d.* stone, Arise
Mat. 9:32 bro. to him a *d.* man
33 the *d.* spake, *Luke* 11:14
12:22 and *d.* and he healed
15:30 having with them those *d.*
31 saw the *d.* speak, *Mark* 7:37
Mark 9:25 thou *d.* spirit, come
Luke 1:20 shalt be *d.* until the
Acts 8:32 lamb *d.* before shearer
1 *Cor.* 12:2 carried away to *d.*
2 Pet. 2:16 the *d.* ass speaking

DUNG, Substantive.
Ex. 29:14 and *d.* burn, *Lev.* 4:11 ;
8:17; 16:27; *Num.* 19:5
1 *K.* 14:10 as taketh away *d.*
2 *K.* 6:25 cab of dove's *d.*
9:37 carcass of Jezebel be as *d.*
18:27 eat their own *d. Is.* 36:12
Job 20:7 perish like his own *d.*
Ps. 83:10 they became as *d.*
Jer. 8:2 be for *d.* on the earth
9:22 carcasses fall as *d.*
16:4 shall be as *d.* ; 25:33 be *d.*
Ezek. 4:12 shalt bake it with *d.*
15 given cow's *d.* for man's *d.*
Zep. 1:17 their flesh be as the *d.*
Mal. 2:3 spread *d.* on your faces,
even *d.* of solemn feasts
Phil. 3:8 I count all things but *d.*

DUNG, Verb.
Luke 13:8 dig about, and *d.* it

DUNG-GATE.
Neh. 3:13 Ha. rep. to *d.-g.* 12:31

DUNGHILL, S.
1 *Sam.* 2:8 beg. from *d. Ps.* 113:7
Ezr. 6:11 let his house be a *d.*
Ps. 25:10 as straw trodden for *d.*
Lam. 4:5 embrace *d.*
Dan. 2:5 houses be made a *d.*
3:29 their houses be made a *d.*
Luke 14:35 salt not fit for the *d.*

DUNGEON.
Gen. 40:15 should put me into *d.*
41:14 Joseph hastily out of *d.*
Jer. 37:16 to first-born in the *d.*
38:6 cast him into the *d.*
10 take up Jere. out of the *d.*
11 let them put to Jerem.
Lam. 3:53 cut off my life in *d.*
55 called on thy name out of *d.*

DURA. *Dan.* 3:1

DURABLE.
Prov. 8:18 *d.* riches are with me
Is. 26:18 be for *d.* clothing

DURETH.
Mat. 13:21 but *d.* for a while

DURST.
Est. 7:5 that *d.* presume to do so
Job 32:6 *d.* not show my opinion
Mat. 22:46 *d.* not ask more ques.
Mark 12:34 ; *Luke* 20:40
John 21:12 none *d.* ask him
Acts 5:13 *d.* no man join to them
7:32 then Moses *d.* not behold
Jude 9 *d.* not bring a railing ac.

DUST.
Gen. 2:7 God formed man of *d.*
3:14 *d.* shalt eat all the *d.*
19 *d.* thou art, to *d.* shalt ret.
13:16 if number the *d.* of earth
18:27 who am but *d.* and ashes
Ex. 8:16 say to Aaron, smite *d.*
9:9 it shall become small *d.*
Lev. 14:41 pour out *d.*
17:13 blood, and cover it with *d.*
2 *K.* 23:12
Num. 23:10 who can count *d.*
Deut. 9:21 I cast *d.* into brook,
28:24 make rain of thy land *d.*
Ps. 7:6 elders put *d.* on heads
2 *Sam.* 16:13 Shimei cast *d.*
1 *K.* 18:38 fire of L. consumed *d.*
20:10 if the *d.* of Samaria suffice
2 *Chr.* 34:4 made *d.* of images
Job 2:12 sprinkled *d.* upon heads
7:5 flesh clothed with clods of *d.*
10:9 bring me into *d.* again?
28:6 earth, it hath *d.* of gold
34:15 shall turn again to *d.*
38:38 *d.* groweth into hardness
42:6 abhor and repent in *d.* and ashes
Ps. 22:15 brought me into the *d.*
30:9 shall *d.* praise thee, shall
72:9 enemies shall lick the *d.*
78:27 rained flesh on them as *d.*

CRUDEN'S CONCORDANCE. 831

DWE

Ps. 102:14 serve, favor d. thereof
103:14 remembereth we are d.
Ec. 12:7 shall d. return to earth
Is. 34:7 third d. shall be made fat
9 d. be turned into brimstone
40:12 comprehended d. of earth
49:23 lick up the d. of thy feet
52:2 shake thyself from the d.
65:25 d. be the serpent's meat
Lam. 3:16 cast d. on their heads.
Ezek. 27:30
Ezek. 24:7 to cover it with d.
26:4 I will scrape her d. from
10 their d. shall cover thee
Amos 2:7 pant after d. of earth
Mic. 7:17 they shall lick the d.
Nah. 1:3 clouds are d. of his feet
Hab. 1:10 for they shall heap d.
Mat. 10:14 sha. off the d. of your feet, Mark 6:11; Luke 9:5
Luke 10:11 the d. we do wipe off
Acts 13:51 they shook off the d.
22:23 as throw d. into the air
Rev. 18:19 cast d. on their heads

As the DUST.
Gen. 13:16 thy seed as the d. of the earth, 28:14; 2 Chr. 1:9
Deut. 9:21 calf small as the d.
2 Sam. 22:43 I beat them as small as the d. Ps. 18:42
Job 22:24 lay up gold as the d.
27:16 heap up silver as d.
Is. 5:24 their blossom go up as d.
40:15 nations as small d. of bal.
41:2 he gave as d. to his sword
Zep. 1:17 blood be poured out as d.
Zec. 9:3 heaped up silver as d.

In the DUST.
Job 4:19 foundation is in the d.
7:21 now shall I sleep in the d.
16:15 defiled my horn in the d.
17:16 rest together in the d.
20:11 lie down with him in t. d.
21:26 lie down alike in the d.
39:14 warmeth eggs in the d.
40:13 hide them in the d. toget.
Ps. 7:5 lay my honor in the d.
Is. 2:10 hide thee in the d.
26:19 and sing, ye in the d.
47:1 and sit in the d. O virgin
Lam. 3:29 putteth mouth in t. d.
Ezek. 12:3 sleep in d. shall awake
Mic. 1:10 roll thyself in the d.
Nah. 3:18 nobles shall dwell in d.

Like the DUST.
2 K. 13:7 like the d. by thresh.
Is. 29:5 thy strangers be like d.

Of the DUST.
Gen. 2:7 L. formed man of the d.
Num. 5:17 take of d. in the tab.
Deut. 32:24 serpents of d.
1 Sam. 2:8 out of d. Ps. 113:7
Job 5:6 cometh not of the d.
Prov. 8:26 highest part of d.
Ec. 3:20 all are of the d.
Is. 29:4 be low out of d.

To the DUST.
Ps. 22:29 that go down to the d.
44:25 soul is bowed down to d.
104:29 they die and return to d.
119:25 soul cleaveth to the d.
Ec. 3:20 all are d. and turn to d.
Is. 25:12 bring fortress to d.
26:5 bringeth city even to the d.

DUTY.
Ex. 21:10 d. of mar. not dimin.
Deut. 25:5 d. of a husband's bro.
Ec. 12:13 whole d. of man
Luke 17:10 that which was d.
Rom. 15:27 their d. to minister

DWARF.
Lev. 21:20 a d. shall not come

DWELL.
Gen. 9:27 Japhet d. in tents of
Ex. 2:21 content to d. with man
25:45 I will d. amongst Israel
Lev. 13:46 unclean shall d. alone
Num. 23:9 the people sh. d. alone
35:34 L. d. am. child. of Israel
Deut. 12:11 cause his name d.
33:12 d. between his shoulders
Jud. 9:41 Gaal not d. in Shech.
17:10 M. said Levite d. with me
1 Sam. 27:5 that I may d. there
1 K. 6:13 I will d. among Israel
8:12 he would d. in thick dark.
17:9 get to Zarepth. and d. there
2 K. 4:13 d. among mine own p.
Job 3:5 let a cloud d. upon it
11:14 not wickedness d. in tab.
18:15 shall d. in his tabernacle
30:6 d. in clefts of the valleys
Ps. 5:4 nei. sh. evil d. with thee
15:1 who sh. d. in thy holy hill
20:15 his soul shall d. at ease

Ps. 37:27 depart from evil, and d.
65:4 that he may d. in thy cou.
8 that d. in the uttermost pa.
68:16 hill God desireth to d. in
18 Lord might d. among them
72:9 that d. in wilderness
84:10 than d. in tents of wicked.
101:6 faithful, that they may d.
120:5 that I d. in tents of Kedar
132:14 my rest, here will I d.
139:9 I d. in uttermost parts
143:3 made me to d. in darkness
Prov. 1:33 whoso hearken. sh. d.
8:12 I wisdom d. with prudence
21:19 better to d. in wilderness
Is. 6:5 I d. in midst of a people
11:6 wolf shall d. with lamb
13:21 owls shall d. there
26:5 bringeth down them th. d.
19 awake ye that d. in the dust
30:19 the people shall d. in Z.
32:16 judgment shall d. in wil.
18 people d. in a habitation
33:14 d. with devouring fire?
16 he shall d. on high
24 the people that d. therein
34:11 the owl and raven sh. d.
40:22 spread, ent as tent to d. in
49:20 place to me that I may d.
58:12 restorer of paths to d. in
65:9 my servants shall d. there
Jer. 49:8 d. deep, O inhabitants
Ezek. 2:6 dost d. among scorp.
43:7 d. in midst, ♱; Zec. 2:10, 11
Hos. 3:3 I make to d. in taber.
14:7 that d. under his shadow
Joel 3:20 Judah shall d. for ever
Mic. 4:10 shalt d. in the field
7:14 flock which d. solitarily
Nah. 3:18 O Asey, nobles sh. d.
Hag. 1:4 to d. in ceiled houses?
Zec. 9:6 a bastard sh. d. in Ash.
Mat. 12:15 d. there, Luke 11:26
Luke 21:35 that d. on the face of the earth, Acts 17:26
Acts 7:4 land wherein ye now d.
28:16 P. suff. to d. by himself
Rom. 8:9 Sp. of G. d. in you, 11
1 Cor. 7:12 she pleased to d. wit
2 Cor. 6:16 G. hath said I will d.
Eph. 3:17 C. d. in hearts by faith
Col. 1:19 in him sh. all fulness d.
3:16 let word of C. d. in you
1 Pet. 3:7 husbands d. with them
2 Pet. 3:13 wc d. in him
Rev. 7:15 he on throne shall d.
12:12 ye heavens, and ye that d.
13:6 against them that d.
21:3 and he will d. with them

DWELL, with earth.
1 K. 8:27 will God d. on earth?
2 Chr. 6:18
Dan. 4:1 languages that d. in all the earth, 6:25
Rev. 3:10 try them that d.
6:10 blood on them that d. on e.
13:8 all that d. on e. shall wors.
14 deceiveth them that d. on e.
11:6 preach to them th. d. on e.
17:8 they that d. on earth

DWELL, with house.
Deut. 20:20 built house and not d. Amos 5:11
2 Sam. 7:2 I d. in a house of cedar, 1 Chr. 17:1
5 build hou. to d. 1 Chr. 17:4
1 K. 3:30 built A. in fear. and d.
3:17 I and th. wom. d. in one h.
8:13 surely built A. to d. in
Job 4:19 that d. in h. of cl.
19:15 d. in h. count me stranger
Ps. 23:6 d. in A. of Lord for ever
27:4 that I may d. in h. of Lord
84:4 they that d. in thy house
101:7 work deceit not d. my h.
Prov. 21:9 better d. in the corner
Jer. 29:5 build h. d. in them, 28

DWELL, with Jerusalem.
1 Chr. 23:25 that ye may d. in J.
Neh. 11:2 offered them. to d. at J.
Jer. 33:16 J. shall d. safely
Zec. 8:3 I will d. in midst of J.
Acts 2:14 all ye that d. at Jerus.
4:16 manifest to all that d. in J.

DWELL, with land.
Gen. 24:37 Canaan. in wh. I d.
26:2 d. in l. which I shall tell
34:21 let them d. in the land
35:1 arise d. there, 46:3
45:10 Goshen thou mayest d. in
Lev. 25:18 shall d. in l. in safety
Num. 35:34 defile not l. wh. I d.

Deut. 30:20 thou mayest d. in l.
Jos. 17:12 the Canaanites would d. in that land, Jud. 1:27
2 K. 25:24 fear not to d. in land, Jer. 25:5; 40:9
Ps. 37:3 so thou shalt d. in l.
68:6 rebellious d. in a dry land
85:9 that glory may d. in our l.
Is. 9:2 d. in l. of shadow of death
Jer. 50:3 l. desol. none shall d.
Ezek. 28:25 they d. in their land
38:12 the people that d. in land
Hos. 9:3 shall not d. in Lord's l.

DWELL, with place.
Ex. 15:17 in p. th. hast ma. to d.
1 Sam. 12:8 d. in this place
2 K. 6:1 the p. we d. is strait
2 a place where we may d.
1 Chr. 17:9 shall d. in their pla.
Is. 57:15 in high and holy p.

DWELL safely.
Prov. 1:33 to me shall d. safely
Jer. 23:6 Israel shall d. safely
Ezek. 28:26; 34:25, 28; 38:8
32:37 cause them to d. safely
Ezek. 38:11 them that d. safely

DWELL in safety.
Lev. 25:18 ye shall d. in the land in safety, 19; Deut. 12:10
Deut. 33:12 beloved of the Lord in safety
28 Israel shall d. in safety
Ps. 4:8 L. makest me to d. in s.

DWELL therein.
Num. 14:30 to make you d. t.
33:53 shall d. t. Deut. 11:31
Ps. 24:1 and they that d. therein
37:29 the righteous shall d. th.
69:36 love his name shall d. t.
Ps. 33:24 people that d. therein
51:6 that d. therein shall die
Jer. 4:29 and not a man d. th.
12:4 wick. of them, that d. t.
48:9 cities without any to d. t.
50:39 thu owls shall d. therein
Acts 1:20 let no man d. therein

DWELL together.
Ps. 133:1 brethren to d. together

DWELLERS.
Is. 18:3 all ye, and d. on earth
Acts 1:19 was known to all d. at Jer.
1:28 d. in Mesopotamia we be

DWELLEST.
1 Sam. 4:4 who d. bet. cherubim, Ps. 80:1; Is. 37:16
Ps. 123:1 thou that d. in heaven
Jer. 49:16 d. in the clefts, Ob. 3
51:13 thou that d. upon waters
Ezek. 12:2 thou d. in midst
Dan. 1:28 Master, where d. th. ?
John 1:38 Master, where d. thou.

DWELLETH.
Lev. 19:34 stranger that d.
25:29 brother that d. poor, 47
Num. 35:20 God d. as a lion
Jos. 6:25 Rahab d. in Israel
22:19 the Lord's tabernacle d.
1 Sam. 4:4 who d. bet. cherubim, 2 Sam. 6:2; 1 Chr. 13:6
7:2 the ark d. within
Job 15:28 he d. in desolate cities
33:1 that d. in it, 'f
Ps. 9:11 sing to the Lord who d.
26:8 place where thine honor d.
113:5 L. our G. who d. on high
135:21 blessed L. who d. at Jer.
Is. 8:18 L. who d. in mount Z.
33:5 the Lord, for he d. on high
Jer. 44:2 desolation, no man d.
49:31 that d. without care
Lam. 1:3 J. d. among heathen
Ezek. 10:46 sister d. at right ha.
16:44 as is the mother, d.
Hos. 8:3 every idol d. there,
shall mourn, Amos 8:8
Mat. 23:21 sweareth by him d.
Mark 5:3 who had d. in tombs
John 6:56 my flesh d. in me, 66
11:10 Father that d. in you
17 the Spirit, for he d. in you
Acts 7:48 d. not in temples made with hands, 17:24
Rom. 7:17 d. in me, 20
8:11 quicken by Spirit that d.
1 Cor. 3:16 Spirit of G. d. in you
Col. 2:9 d. the fulness of God
2 Tim. 1:14 H. Gh. wh. d. in us
2 Pet. 3:13 earth where. d. right.
1 John 3:17 how d. love of G. ?
24 that keepeth com. d. in him
4:13 d. in love, God d. in us
15 d. in G. God d. in him

DWE

1 John 4:16 he that d. in love, d.
2 John 2 which d. in us
Rev. 2:13 slain am. you, Satan d.

DWELLING, Substantive.
Gen. 27:39 thy d. shall be fatness
2 Chr. 6:2 built place for thy d.
Ps. 49:14 cons. in grave from d.
91:10 no plague come nigh d.
Prov. 21:20 in the d. of the wise
24:15 against d. of the righteous
Dan. 2:11 gods d. not with flesh
4:25 thy d. with beasts, 32; 5:21
Zep. 3:7 d. should not be cut off
Nah. 2:11 wh. is d. of the lions?
Mark 5:3 his d. among tombs

DWELLING.
Gen. 25:27 plain man, d. in tents
Lev. 25:29 if a man sell a d. hou.
Num. 24:21 strong is thy d. place
1 K. 8:30 in heaven thy d. place
39, 43, 49; 2 Chr. 6:21, 30, 30, 39, 49; 2 Chr. 6:21, 30, 30, 30
2 Chr. 30:27 prayer up to holy d.
36:15 compassion on d. place
Job 8:22 d. place of the wicked
21:28 d. places of the wicked?
27 Babylon shall become a d.
52:5 shall pluck thee out of d.
74:7 cast, d. place of thy name
76:2 his d. place in Zion
79:7 laid waste his d. place
90:1 hast been our d. place
Is. 4:5 create on every d. place
18:4 will consider in my d. pla.
Jer. 46:19 daughter d. in Egypt
51:30 have burnt their d. places
Ezek. 38:11 all them d. without
Joel 3:17 Lord your God d. in Z.
Hab. 1:6 possess d. places
Acts 2:5 were d. at Jerusalem
19:17 known to Greeks d. at E.
1 Cor. 4:11 no certain d. place
1 Tim. 6:16 d. in light
Heb. 11:9 d. in taberna. with I.
2 Pet. 2:8 Lot, righteous man d.

DWELLINGS.
Ex. 10:23 child, of Isr. li. in d.
Lev. 3:17 a perpet. statute thro' all d. 23:14; Num. 35:29
7:26 eat no blood in any of d.
23:3 do no work in all your d. 31
Job 18:21 the d. of wicked
30:6 made barren land his d.
Ps. 55:15 wicked, is in their d.
87:2 gates of Z. than all d. of J.
Is. 32:18 people dwell in sure d.
Ezek. 25:4 men of east shall ha d.

DWELT.
Gen. 11:2 and they d. there, 31; 26:17; 2 K. 16:6; 1 Chr. 4:43; 2 Chr. 28:18
Num. 31:10 they d. 2 K. 17:29
1 K. 13:11 old proph. in B. 25
Job 22:25 and I d. as a king
Ps. 74:2 Z. wherein thou hast d.
Is. 23:1 the city where David d.
Jer. 2:6 a land where no man d.
39:14 J. d. among the people
Ezek. 3:15 that d. by river Cheb.
31:6 mul. shadow d. nations, 17
Dan. 4:21 beasts of field d.
Zec. 7:7 rejoicing city that d.
Luke 1:55 fear ca. on all that d.
John 1:14 W. made flesh and d.
39 and saw where he d.
Acts 13:17 they d. as strangers
28:30 Paul d. in hired house
Rev. 11:10 torm. them that d.

DWELT at.
Gen. 22:19 and Abraham d. at B.
Jud. 9:41 Abimelech d. at X.
1 K. 15:18 Benhad. d. at Damas. 2 Chr. 16:2
Je. 17:26 Son, d. at N. Is. 37:37
1 Chr. 2:55 scribes which d. at A.
9:31 Levites d. at Jerusalem
Acts 9:32 S. came down d. at L.
9:35 Paul d. in hired house
28:30 Paul d. in hired house
Re. 11:10 torm. them that d.

DWELT in.
Num. 20:15 we have d. in Egypt
21:31 Is. d. in land of Amorites
Deut. 2:12 d. in their stead, 21, 22; 3:4; 5:22
13:16 of thee that d. in bush
Jud. 8:11 of Nobah d. in tents
2 Sam. 7:6 nor d. in any house
Job 29:25 I d. as a king
Ps. 120:5 woe d. in M. of Kedar
Prov. 8:12 all that d. in Ephes.
Is. 48 Abraham d. 2 years in d.
1 K. 2:38 Shimei d. in Jerusalem
12:2 J. fled from Sol. d. in E.
2 K. 13:5 Israel d. in their tents
15:5 A. d. in house, 2 Chr. 26:21
22:14 H. the prophetess d. in Jer. in college, 2 Chr. 34:22

832   CRUDEN'S CONCORDANCE.

EAR

Ezr. 2:70 Levites, Nethinim, *d.*
 in cities, *Neh.* 3:26; 11:21
Neh. 7:73 Israel *d. is* their cities
Ps. 94:17 almost *d. in* silence
Is. 13:20 shall it be *d. in* from
 generation, *Jer.* 50:39
Jer. 33:10 we have *d. in* tents
Ezek. 30:17 Israel *d. in* own land
 37:26 *d.* safely *in* their land
Dan. 4:12 the fowls *d. in* boughs
Mat. 2:23 Joseph *d. in* city Naz.
 4:13 Jesus *d. in* Capernaum
Luke 13:4 above all that *d. in* J.
Acts 7:2 Abraham *d. in* Charr. 4
 19:10 they who *d. in* Asia heard
2 *Tim.* 1:5 *d. in* grandmother

DWELT therein.

Deut. 2:10 E. *d. t.;* 23 giants *d. t.*
1 *K.* 11:24 went to Dam. and *d. t.*
 12:25 Jerob. built S. and *d. th.*
Neh. 13:16 *d.* men of Tyre *th.*
Ps. 68:10 congregation hath *d. t.*

DWELT with,

Ruth 2:23 and Ruth *d. with* her
1 *Sam.* 22:1 moth. *d. w. k.* of M.
1 *Chr.* 4:23 they *d. with* king
Ps. 120:5 my soul hath long *d. w.*
Jer. 40:6 J. *d. w.* him among peo.

DYED.

Is. 63:1 with *d.* garm. from Boz.
Ezek. 23:15 *d.* attire upon heads

DYING. See after DIE.

E.

EACH.

Gen. 15:10 Abraham laid *e.* piece
 34:25 Sim. and Levi took *e.* man
 40:5 *e.* his dr. 45:22 *e.* changes
Ex. 18:7 asked *e.* other of welf.
Num. 1:44 *e.* one was for house
 7:3 they brought for *e.* one an ox
 16:17 Aaron *e. of* *e.* his censer
Jos. 22:14 of *e.* chief house *e.* one
Jud. 21:22 reserved not to *e.* man
Ruth 1:9 may find rest *e. of* you
1 *K.* 7:*e.* man his mouth
 22:10 kings *e.* sat on his throne
2 *K.* 15:20 of *e.* man fifty shekels
Ps. 85:10 right, and pe. kissed *e.*
Is. 2:20 they made *e.* one
 6:3 seraphim, *e.* had six wings
 35:7 where *e.* lay, shall be grass
 57:2 *e.* one walking in his upr.
Ezek. 4:6 thee *e.* day for a year
Luke 13:15 doth not *e.* on sabbath
Acts 2:3 tongues sat upon *e.* of
Phil. 2:3 let esteem other better
2 *Thes.* 1:3 charity toward *e.* oth.
Rev. 4:8 beasts had *e.* six wings

EAGLE.

Lev. 11:13 *e.* have, *Deut.* 14:12
Deut. 28:49 swift as the *e.* flieth
 32:11 as an *e.* stirreth her nest
Job 9:26 *e.* that hasteth to prey
 39:27 doth the *e.* mount up ?
Prov. 23:5 riches fly away as an *e.*
 30:19 way of an *e.* in the air
Jer. 49:40 shall fly as an *e.*
 14:16 make thy nest high as *e.*
Ezek. 1:10 had face of an *e.* 10:14
 17:3 a great *e.* with gr. wings, 7
Dan. 4:33 hairs gro. fthrs. of *e.*
 7:4 a lion, and had *e.* wings
Hos. 8:1 as an *e.* ags. the house
Mic. 1:16 thy baldness as the *e.*
Hab. 1:8 Chaldeans shall fly as *e.*
Rev. 4:7 fourth beast like fly. *e.*
 12:14 to woman wings of gr. *e.*

EAGLES.

Ex. 19:4 I bare you on *e.* wings
2 *Sam.* 1:23 were swifter than *e.*
Ps. 103:5 thy youth is ren. like *e.*
Prov. 30:17 young *e.* shall eat it
Is. 40:31 mount with wings as *e.*
Jer. 4:13 his horses swifter th. *e.*
Lam. 4:19 pers. swifter than *e.*
Mat. 24:28 *e.* be gath. Luke 17:37

EAR.

Ex. 21:6 bore *e. Deut.* 15:17
1 *Sam.* 9:15 L. hath told S. in *e.*
2 *K.* 19:16 bow down *e. Ps.* 31:2;
 86:1
Neh. 1:6 let thine *e.* be attent. 11
Job 4:12 and mine *e.* received
 12:11 *e.* try words ? 34:3
 13:1 mine *e.* hath heard
 29:11 when the *e.* heard me
 21 to me men gave *e.* waited
 36:10 he openeth also their *e.*
 42:5 I heard by hearing of *e.*
Ps. 10:17 wilt cause thine *e.*
 31:2 bow down thine *e.* to me
 58:4 like adder that stoppeth *e.*
 77:1 and he gave *e.* unto me
 94:9 he that planted the *e.*

EAR

Ps. 116:2 he hath inclined his *e.*
Prov. 5:1 and bow thine *e.* to
 5:13 incline mine *e.* to them
 15:31 the *e.* that heareth
 17:4 and a liar giveth *e.* to
 18:15 the *e.* of the wise seeketh
 20:12 hearing *e.* seeing eye
 22:17 thine *e.* hear the words
 25:12 reprover on obedient *e.*
 28:9 turneth away *e.* from hear.
Ec. 1:8 nor is the *e.* filled with
 Is. 48:8 time thine *e.* was not
 50:4 he wakeneth my *e.* to hear
 5 Lord hath opened mine *e.*
 59:1 *e.* heavy that it cannot h.
 64:4 nor perceived by the *e.*
Jer. 6:10 their *e.* is uncircumc.
 7:24 inclined their *e.* 26; 11:8;
 17:23; 25:4; 34:14; 44:5
 9:20 let your *e.* receive the word
 35:15 ye have not inclined *e.*
Lam. 3:56 hide not *e.*
Amos 3:12 fr. the lion piece of *e.*
Mic. 10:27 what ye hear in the *e.*
 26:51 smote off his *e. Mark* 14:47
Luke 12:3 ye have spoken in *e.*
 22:51 touched his *e.* and healed
John 18:26 servant whose *e.* Pet.
1 *Cor.* 2:9 not seen, nor *e.* heard
 12:16 if the *e.* shall say
Rev. 2:7 he that hath *e.* let hear,
 11, 17, 29 ; 3:6, 13, 22 ; 13:9

Incline EAR.

Ps. 17:6 in. thine *e.* to me, 71:2;
 88:2 ; *Is.* 37:17 ; *Dan.* 9:18
 45:10 O daughter, *incline* th. *e.*
 49:4 I will *incline* mine *e.* to
Prov. 2:2 that thou *in.* thine *e.*
 4:20 *in.* thin. *e.* to my saying
Is. 55:3 *in.* your *e.* and come

Give EAR.

Ex. 15:26 if thou wilt *give e.*
Deut. 1:45 not *g. e.* to your voice,
 2 *Chr.* 24:19 ; *Neh.* 9:30
 32:1 *give e.* O heavens
Jud. 5:3 *give e.* O ye princes
Job 34:2 *give e.* to me
Ps. 5:1 *g. e.* to my words, 54:2
 17:1 *g. e.* to my pra. 55:1 ; 86:6
 39:12 *give e.* to my cry. 143:1
 49:1 *give e.* all ye inhabitants
 78:1 *g. e.* O, p.; 80:1 *g. e.* sheph.
 84:8 *give e.* O God of Jacob
 143:1 *g. e.* to my supplications
Is. 1:2 *give e.* O earth
 10 *g. e.* to the law of our God
 8:9 *give e.* all of far countries
 28:23 *give ye e.* and hear
 42:23 who among you will *g. e.?*
 51:4 hearken and *g. e.* to me
Jer. 13:15 *give e.* be not proud
Hos. 5:1 and *give ye e.* O house
Joel 1:2 *g. e.* all ye inhabitants

Right EAR.

Ex. 29:20 tip of *right e. Lev.* 8:23,
 24 ; 14:14, 17, 25, 28
Luke 22:50 c. off ri. *e. John* 18:10

EAR, of corn.

Ex. 9:31 for barley was in the *e.*
Mark 4:28 the *e.* full corn in *e.*

EAR, Verb.

1 *Sam.* 8:12 set them to *e.* ground
Is. 30:24 oxen that *e.* the ground

EARED, ING.

Gen. 45:6 neither *e.* nor harvest
Ex. 34:21 in *e.* time and harvest
Deut. 21:4 valley neither *e.* sown

EARLY.

Gen. 19:2 ye shall rise *e.* and go
Jud. 7:3 let him depart *e.*
Ps. 46:5 God shall help her
 57:8 I will awake *e.* 108:2
 63:1 my God, *e.* will I seek thee
 78:34 they inquired *e.* after God
 90:14 satisfy us *e.* with mercy
 101:8 *e.* destroy the wicked
Prov. 1:28 they shall seek me *e.*
 8:17 seek me *e.* shall find me
Is. 26:9 will I seek thee *e.*
Hos. 5:15 they will seek me *e.*
 6:4 as *e.* dew it goeth, 13:3
Luke 24:22 woman *e.* at sepulchre.
John 18:28 led J. *e.* unto h.
 20:1 com. Mary Magdalene *e.*
Jam. 5:7 till he receive *e.* rain
 See ARUSE, RISE, RISEN, RISING,
 ROSE, MORNING.

EAR-RING.

Gen. 24:22 took a golden *e.-r.*
 30 when Laban saw *e.-r.*
 47 I put *e.-r.* upon her face
Job 42:11 ev. one gave J. an *e.-r.*
Prov. 25:12 *e.-r.* of gold

EAR

Ps. 34:5 gave J. all their *e.-r.*
Ez. 32:2 break off the gold, *e.-r.*
 35:22 brought *e.-r.* for offering
Num. 31:50 we have broug. *e.-r.*
Jud. 8:24 give ev. man the *e.-r.*
Is. 3:20 L. will take away *e.-r.*
Ezek. 16:12 I put *e.-r.* in th. ears
Hos. 2:13 decked hers. with *e.-r.*

EARS.

Gen. 44:18 speak in my lord's *e.*
 50:4 speak in the *e.* of Pharaoh
Ex. 10:2 mayest tell in *e.* of son
 17:14 rehearse in *e.* of Joshua
Num. 3:9 in *e.* of men of Shech. 3
1 *Sam.* 3:11 the *e.* shall tingle,
 2 *K.* 21:12 ; *Jer.* 19:3
 2 *Sam.* 7:22 we heard with our *e.*
 22:7 my cry did enter into his *e.*
Job 15:21 dreadful sound in his *e.*
 28:22 heard fame with our *e.*
 33:16 he openeth the *e.* of men
Ps. 18:6 cry came into his *e.*
 34:15 his *e.* are open
 44:1 we heard with our *e.*
 115:6 have *e.* hear not, 135:17
Prov. 21:13 whoso stop. his *e.*
 23:9 speak not in the *e.* of a fool
 26:17 taketh a dog by the *e.*
Is. 11:3 the hearing of his *e.*
 33:15 stoppeth *e.* from hearing
 35:5 *e.* of deaf shall be unstop.
 43:8 and deaf that have *e.*
Jer. 2:2 and cry in the *e.* of Jer.
 5:21 O people, which have *e.*
 20:20 Zep. read in the *e.* of Jer.
Mat. 23:15 come to governor's *e.*
Mark 7:33 put fingers into his *e.*
 35 his *e.* were opened
 8:18 having *e.* hear ye not ?
Acts 7:51 uncirc. in heart and *e.*
 17:20 bring. strange things to *e.*
Rom. 15:8 hath given *e.*
2 *Tim.* 4:3 having itchings.
Jam. 5:4 *e.* of Lord of sabaoth
1 *Pet.* 3:12 and his *e.* are open to
Deut. 22:4 L. hath not *g. e.* to *h.*
 29:4 revealed in mine *e.*
Ezek. 8:18 tho' they cry in m. *e.*
 9:1 he cried also in mine *e.*
Luke 1:44 salut. sounded in m. *e.*

EARS of the People.

Ex. 11:2 speak in *e. of* the peo.
Deut. 32:44 M. spake in *e. of* pe.
Jud. 7:3 proclaim in *e. of* the peo.
1 *Sam.* 11:4 told thi. in *e. of* p.
2 *K.* 18:26 not in *e. of* Jer. 26:11
Neh. 8:3 *e. of* p. were attentive

Their EARS.

Gen. 35:4 ear-rings wear in t. *e.*
Ex. 32:3 ear-rings in *their e.*
2 *K.* 19:28 read in *their e.* 2 *Chr.*
 31:20 ; *Jer.* 36:15
Is. 6:10 *t. e.* heavy, lest hear with
 t. e. Mat. 13:15; *Acts* 28:27
Mic. 7:16 *their e.* shall be deaf
Zec. 7:11 stopped *t. e. Acts* 7:57
 2 *Tim.* 4:4 turn th. *e.* from truth

Thine EARS.

Ps. 10:17 cause *thine e.* to hear
Prov. 23:12 apply *thine e.*
Is. 30:21 *t. e.* shall hear a word
 43:20 children say in *thine e.*
Ezek. 3:10 hear w. th. *e.* 40:4 ; 44:5
 16:12 I put ear-rings in *thine e.*
 23:25 shall take away *thine e.*
 24:26 to hear with *thine e.*

Your EARS.

Job 13:17 declaration with *y. e.*
Jer. 26:11 incline *your e.* to words
 26:15 as blood will bring on *y. e.*
 15 Lord sent to speak in *your e.*
Mat. 13:16 but blessed are *your e.*
Luke 4:21 scripture fulfi. in *y. e.*
 9:44 let sayings sink in *your e.*

EARS of Corn.

Gen. 41:5 seven *e. of corn.* 22
Lev. 2:14 meat-offering, green *e.*
 23:14 green *e.* not groen *e. of corn*
Deut. 23:25 mayest pluck the *e.*

EAR

Ruth 2:2 go and glean *e. of*
2 *K.* 4:42 brought full *e. of corn*
Mat. 12:1 discip. began to pluck
 e. of c. Mark 2:23; *Luke* 6:1
See SEVEN.

EARNEST, Substantive.

2 *Cor.* 1:22 *e. of* the Spirit, 5:5
Eph. 1:14 *e. of* our inheritance

EARNEST, Adjective.

Rom. 8:19 *e.* expecta. of creature
2 *Cor.* 7:7 when he told *e.* desire
 8:16 put same *e.* care into Titus
Phil. 1:20 accord. to my *e.* expec.
Heb. 2:1 to give more *e.* heed

EARNESTLY.

Num. 22:37 did I not *e.* send
1 *Sam.* 20:6 D. *e.* asked leave, 28
Job 7:2 serv. *e.* desireth shadow
Jer. 11:7 I *e.* protested to fathers
 31:20 I do *e.* remember him still
Mic. 7:3 evil with both hands *e.*
Luke 22:44 he prayed *e.*
 56 a certain maid *e.* looked
Acts 3:12 why look ye so *e.*
 23:1 Paul *e.* beholding council
1 *Cor.* 12:31 covet *e.* the best gifts
2 *Cor.* 5:2 we groan *e.* desiring
Jam. 5:17 pray. *e.* that it not rain
Jude 3 should *e.* con. for faith

EARNETH.

Hag. 1:6 *e.* wages *e.* to put in bag

EARTH.

Gen. 1:2 the *e.* was without form
 10 God called the dry land *e.*
 11 let *e.* bring forth, 24
 12 *e.* brought forth grass
 28 replenish the *e.* 9:1
 6:11 *e.* was corrupt before God
 7:17 the ark was lifted above *e.*
 8:14 in second mo. was *e.* dried
 22 *e.* rem. seed-time not cease
 10:25 the *e.* divided, 1 *Chr.* 1:19
 18:18 all nations of *e.* blessed in
 him, 22:18 ; 26:4 ; 28:14
 27:28 God give thee fatness of *e.*
 41:47 *e.* brought forth by hand.
Ex. 9:29 *e.* is the Lord's, *Deut.*
 10:14 ; *Ps.* 24:1 ; 1 *Cor.* 10:26
 15:12 the *e.* swallowed them
 20:24 altar of *e.* thou shalt make
Num. 16:30 *e.* open her mouth
 32 *e.* opened mouth and swal-
 lowed, 26:10 ; *Ps.* 106:17
 34 lost *e.* swallow us up
Deut. 28:23 *e.* under thee be iron
 32:1 hear, O *e.* the words
 13 ride on high places of *e.*
 22 a fire shall consume the *e.*
1 *Sam.* 2:8 pil. of the *e.* are L.'s
 4:5 so that the *e.* rang again
 14:15 and the *e.* quaked
 2 *Sam.* 1:2 with *e.* on head, 15:32
 22:8 then the *e.* shook, *Ps.* 18:7
1 *K.* 1:40 so that the *e.* rent
 2 *K.* 5:17 two mules' burden of *e.*
1 *Chr.* 16:31 let *e.* rej. *Ps.* 96:11
 33 cometh to judge the *e. Ps.*
 96:13 ; 98:9
Neh. 9:6 thou made *e. Is.* 45:12
Job 5:25 offspring as grass of *e.*
 9:6 shaketh *e.* out of her place
 24 *e.* given into hand of wicked
 11:9 measure longer than *e.*
 15:19 to whom *e.* was given
 16:18 O *e.* cover not my blood
 24:4 the poor of the *e.* hide
 26:7 hangeth *e.* upon nothing
 30:6 to dwell in caves of the *e.*
 8 were viler than the *e.*
 37:17 when he quieteth the *e.*
 38:4 I laid foundations of the *e.*
 18 the breadth of the *e.?*
Ps. 2:8 uttermost parts of the *e.*
 10 be instr. ye judges of the *e.*
 12:6 silver tried in furnace of *e.*
 33:13 his seed shall inherit the *e.*
 33:5 *e.* is full of goodness of L.
 37:9 wait on L. inherit *e.* 11, 22
 46:2 though the *e.* be removed
 6 uttered voice, the *e.* melted
 47:9 the shields of the *e.*
 48:2 joy of whole *e.* is mount Z.
 60:2 made the *e.* to tremble
 63:9 the lower parts of the *e.*
 66:1 joy. noise unto L. all ye *e.*
 67:6 *e.* yield inc. *Ezek.* 34:27
 68:8 *e.* shook, heavens dropped
 32 sing. kingdoms of *e.*
 71:20 from the depths of the *e.*
 72:6 showers that water the *e.*
 73:9 *e.* and inhabit. *Is.* 24:19
 8 wicked of the *e.* shall wring
 76:8 *e.* feared ; 77:18 *e.* tre. 97:4
 82:8 O God, judge the *e.*
 90:2 or ever thou hadst form. *e.*

CRUDEN'S CONCORDANCE. 833

EAR

Ps. 97:1 let the *e.* rejoice
99:1 let the *e.* be moved
102:25 laid the founds. of the *e.*
104:5; Prov. 8:29; Is. 48:13
148:13 his glory is above the *e.*
Prov. 3:19 L. founded *e. Is.* 24:1
8:23 or over *e.* was
25 not made the *e.* nor fields
25:3 *e.* for depth unsearchable
30:16 the *e.* not filled with wat.
21 for three things *e.* disquiet.
Ec. 1:4 the *e.* abideth for ever
5:9 the profit of the *e.* for all
Is. 4:2 fruit of *e.* excellent
11:4 smite the *e.* with rod
9 *e.* full of knowledge of Lord
24:4 the *e.* mourneth, 33:9
19 *e.* broken, *e.* is dissolved
20 *e.* shall reel; 26:19 cast out
29:2 *e.* shall disclose blood
40:22 sit, on the circle of the *e.*
28 the Creator of ends of the *e.*
45:8 let *e.* open; 12 I m. the *e.*
22 be saved, all ends of the *e.*
51:6 look on *e. e.* shall wax old
66:1 the *e.* is my footstool
Jer. 4:23 I beheld *e.* with. form
24 for this shall the *e.* mourn
6:19 hear, O *e.* I will bring evil
22:29 O *e. e. e.* hear the word of
the Lord, Mic. 1:2
46:8 saith, I will cover the *e.*
49:21 the *e.* is moved, 50:46
Ezek. 7:21 give to wick. of the *e.*
9:9 Lord hath forsaken the *e.*
43:2 *e.* shined with his glory
Hos. 2:23 the *e.* will hear corn
Amos 8:9 I will darken the *e.*
Jon. 2:6 the *e.* with her bars
Mic. 7:17 like worms of the *e.*
Nah. 1:5 the *e.* is burnt up
Hab. 2:14 *e.* filled with knowl.
3:3 *e.* was full of his praise
9 didst cleav. the *e.* with rivers
Zec. 1:10 to and fro thro. *e.* 5:7
4:10 eyes wh. run through the *e.*
Mat. 4:6 I smite *e.* with curse
Mat. 5:5 meek shall inherit *e.*
35 sw. not by *e.* it is footstool
13:5 had not much *e.* Mark 4:5
Mark 4:28 *e.* bringeth forth fruit
John 3:31 of the *e.* is earthly
1 Cor. 15:47 first man of *e.*
2 Tim. 2:20 ves. of wood and *e.*
Heb. 12:26 whose voice shook *e.*
Jam. 3:7 precious fruit of the *e.*
2 Pet. 3:10 *e.* and works therein
Rev. 7:3 hurt not the *e.* nor sea
11:6 have power to smite the *e.*
12:16 the *e.* opened her mouth
13:14 caus. *e.* to worship beast
18:1 and the *e.* was lightened
19:2 whore which did corrupt *e.*
23:11 from whose face tho *e.* fled
See BEASTS, DUST, ENDS, FACE,
KINGS, HEAVEN, PEOPLE, WHOLE.

All the EARTH.
Gen. 1:26 dominion over all the *e.*
7:3 seed on the face of all *t. e.*
11:9 confound lang. of all *t. e.*
18:25 Judge of all *t. e.* do right?
19:31 after manner of all the *e.*
Ex. 19:5 for all the *e.* is mine
31:10 not been done in all the *e.*
Num. 14:21 all *t. e.* filled with gl.
Jos. 23:14 all *t. e.* 1; Zec. 5:3
27:14 way of all the *e.* 1 K. 2:2
1 Chr. 16:14 judgments in all the
e. Ps. 105:7
30 fear *t. e. Ps.* 33:8; 96:9
Ps. 8:1 excellent in all the *e.* 9
47:2 k. over all *e.* 7; Zec. 14:9
57:5 be above all *e.* 11; 108:5
68:4 all the *e.* shall worship
82:8 high over all the *e.* 97:9
Is. 10:14 I gathered all `. *e.*
12:5 this is known in all the *e.*
Jer. 26:6 city a curse to all the *e.*
51:7 made all the *e.* drunken
Lam. 2:15 king. rule over *a. t. e.*
Hab. 2:20 let all the *e.* keep sil.
Zec. 1:11 all the *e.* sitteth still
Luke 23:44 darkn. over all the *e.*
Rom. 10:18 son. went into *a. t. e.*
Rev. 5:6 sp. of G. sent into all *e.*

From the EARTH.
Gen. 2:6 went up a mist *f. the e.*
7:23 destroyed *from the e.*
8:11 waters abated *from the e.*
Ex. 9:15 *from the e. Jos.* 7:9; Ps.
109:15; Prov. 2:22; Nah. 2:13
2 Sam. 12:20 D. arose *from the e.*
Job 18:17 rememb. perish *f. t. e.*
Ps. 106:7 praise Lord *from the e.*
Amos 3:5 a snare *from the e.*
John 12:32 If lifted up *f. the e.*
Acts 8:33 his life is taken *f. the e.*

EAR

Acts 9:8 Saul arose *from the e.*
22:22 away with fellow *f. the e.*
Rev. 6:4 to take peace *f. the e.*
14:3 144,000 redeemed *f. the e.*

In the EARTH.
Gen. 1:22 let fowl mult. *in the e.*
4:12 a vagabond *in the e.* 14
6:5 wickedness great *in the e.*
10:8 Nim. mighty one *in the e.*
19:31 not a man *in t. e.*
45:7 pres. a posterity *in the e.*
2 Sam. 7:9 name like great men
in the *e. 1 Chr.* 17:8
23 what nat. *in t. e.* like Israel?
1 Chr. 17:21
14:20 know all things *in the e.*
1 Chr. 29:11 all *in the e.* is thine
2 Chr. 6:14 no G, like those *in t. e.*
Job 1:7 to and fro *in the e.* 2:2
8 none like Job *in the e.* 2:3
14:8 root wax old *in the e.*
24:18 portion cursed *in the e.*
39:14 ostrich leav. eggs *in the e.*
Ps. 16:3 saints that are *in the e.*
46:8 desolations made *in the e.*
10 I will be exalted *in the e.*
58:11 God that judgeth *in the e.*
72:16 a handful of corn *in the e.*
119:19 I am a stranger *in the e.*
Is. 26:9 thy judgm. are *in the e.*
16 not wrought deliver. *in t. e.*
40:21 stock not take root *in t. e.*
42:4 he set judgment *in the e.*
62:7 Jerusalem a praise *in the e.*
65:16 blesseth himself *in the e.*
sweareth *in the e.*
Jer. 31:22 a new thing *in the e.*
Joel 2:30 show wonders *in the e.*
Mat. 25:18 digged *in the e.*
25 hid thy talent *in the e.*
Mark 4:31 mustard seed sown *in
t. e.* less than all seeds *in t. e.*
1 John 5:8 three that witn. *i. t. e.*

On, or upon the EARTH.
Gen. 6:12 God looked *upon the e.*
7:4 I will cause rain *upon the e.*
8:17 multiply *upon the e.* and
19:23 sun was risen *upon the e.*
28:12 ladder set *upon the e.*
Ex. 10:6 since they were *u. the e.*
Deut. 4:10 live up. *e.* 19:1, 19
30 upon the *e.* showed great fire
12:16 pour it *upon the e.* 24
2 Sam. 12:16 David lay *u. the e.*
1 K. 8:27 will God dwell *on the
e. ? 2 Chr.* 6:18
17:14 L. sends rain *upon the e.*
Job 7:1 time to man *on e.* ?
19:25 stand at latter day *u. t. e.*
20:4 man was placed *on the e.*
37:6 snow, be thou *on the e.*
41:33 *on e.* there is not his like
Ps. 7:5 enemy tread life *on the e.*
67:2 thy way known *upon the e.*
73:25 none *upon e.* I desire bes.
Prov. 30:24 four th. little *u. the e.*
Ec. 7:20 not a just man *u. the e.*
10:7 princes as serv. *upon the e.*
11:3 clouds empty th. *upon t. e.*
Cant. 2:12 flowers appear *on t. e.*
Is. 24:22 consumption *upon the e.*
Jer. 9:3 not valiant for truth *u. e.*
Lam. 2:11 liver poured *u. the e.*
Amos 3:5 fall in snare *u. the e.*
Mat. 9:10 lay not up treas. *on e.*
Luke 2:14 hath power *on e.* to for.
chew. Mark 2:10; Luke 5:24
10:21 come to send peace *on e.*
10:49 thou shalt bind *on e.* 18:18
23:9 call no man father *u. the e.*
Mark 9:3 no fuller *on e.* can wh.
Luke 2:14 glory to God, *on e.*
12:49 come to send fire *o. t. e.*
51 come to give peace *on e.* ?
18:8 shall he find faith *on e.* ?
John 17:4 glorified thee *on the e.*
Rom. 9:28 a short work *on the e.*
Col. 3:2 affec. not on things *on e.*
5 mortify your members *o. t. e.*
Heb. 8:4 on *e.* not be a priest
11:13 strangers *on the e.*
12:25 ref. him that spake *on e.*
Jam. 5:5 lived in pleas. *on the e.*
17 it rained not *on the e.*
Rev. 3:10 that dwell *upon the e.*
11:10 dw. on *e.* 13:8; 14:6; 17:8
5:7 hail and fire cast *upon the e.*
11:10 dw. *on e.* 13:8; 14:6; 17:8
16:2 poured vial *upon the e.*

Out of the EARTH.
1 Sam. 28:13 ascend. *out of the e.*
2 Sam. 23:4 grass *out of the e.*
1 Chr. 22:3 iron is taken *out of the e.*
5 *e.* bring forth *it cometh bread*

EAS

Ps. 85:11 truth sh. spr. *o. of t. e.*
104:35 sinners be cons. *o. of t. e.*
Jam. 7:17 four kings *out of the e.*
Hos. 2:18 battle *out of the e.*
Mic. 7:2 good perish *out of the e.*
Rev. 13:11 beast up *out of the e.*

To, or unto the EARTH.
Gen. 24:52 bow. himself *to the e.*
42:6 they bowed *to the e.* 43:26
Jos. 5:14 Josh. fell *to the e.* 7:6
1 Sam. 5:3 D. on his face *to the e.*
17:49 Goliath his face *to the e.*
24:41 bow. herself *to e.* 1 K. 1:31
26:8 smite him *to the e.*
20 let not my blood fall *to t. e.*
2 Sam. 14:11 not one hair shall
fall *to the e.* 1 K. 1:52
2 K. 10:10 fall *to t. e.* no word
Job 12:8 or speak *to the e.*
17:21 bowing down *to the e.*
41:25 belly cleaveth *unto the e.*
50:4 ho shall call *to the e.*
146:4 he returneth *to his e.*
Ec. 3:21 sp. of beast goeth *to e.*
12:7 dust ret. *to t. e.* spirit to G.
Is. 15:10 contem. *to the* whole *e.*
Hos. 5:3 and former rain *to the e.*
Acts 9:4 and Saul fell *to the e.*
10:11 great sheet down *to the e.*
Rev. 6:13 stars of hea. fell *t. t. e.*
12:13 dragon cast *unto the e.*

EARTHEN.
Lev. 6:28 *e.* ves. wherein sodden
11:33 *e.* vessel wherein falleth
14:5 birds killed in *e.* vessel, 50
Num. 5:17 water in *e.* vessel
Jer. 19:1 a potter's *e.* bottle
32:14 evidences in an *e.* vessel
Lam. 4:2 esteemed as *e.* pitchers
2 Cor. 4:7 treasure in *e.* vessels

EARTHLY.
John 3:12 if I told you *e.* things
31 he that is of the earth is *e.*
2 Cor. 5:1 our *e.* house of tabern.
Phil. 3:19 who mind *e.* things
Jam. 3:15 this wisd. is *e.* sensual

EARTHQUAKE.
1 K. 19:11 an *e.* L. was not in *e.*
12 after the *e.* a fire
Amos 1:1 two years before the *e.*
Zec. 14:5 ye fled before the *e.*
Mat. 27:54 centurion saw the *e.*
28:2 a great *e. Acts* 16:26; Rev.
6:12; 11:13
Rev. 8:5 thunder. and *e.* 11:19
16:18 great *e.* so mighty an *e.*

EARTHQUAKES.
Mat. 24:7 famines and *e. Mark*
13:8; Luke 21:11

EARTHY.
1 Cor. 15:47 first man of earth, *e.*
48 have borne image of *e.*

EASE, Substantive.
Deut. 28:65 shalt thou find no *e.*
Job 12:5 a lamp despised of him *e.*
16:12 at *e.*; 21:23 being at *e.*
Ps. 25:13 soul shall dwell at *e.*
129:4 scorning of those at *e.*
Is. 32:9 rise up, ye women at *e.*
11 tremble, ye women at *e.*
Jer. 46:27 Moab hath been at *e.*
Ezek. 23:42 voice of multi. at *e.*
Amos 6:1 woe to them as at *e.* in Z.
Luke 12:19 take thine *e.* eat

EASE, Verb.
Deut. 23:13 thou wilt *e.* thyself
Is. 1:24 *e.* me of adversaries

EASED.
Job 16:6 I am not *e.*
2 Cor. 8:13 that other men be *e.*

EASIER.
Ex. 18:22 it shall be *e.* for thyself
Mat. 9:5 whether is *e.* to say,
Mark 2:9
19:24, for camel to go thro' eye,
Mark 10:25; Luke 18:25
Luke 16:17 *e.* for heaven

EASILY.
1 Cor. 13:5 is not *e.* provoked
Heb. 12:1 sin which doth *e.* beset

EAST.
Gen. 2:8 *e.* of garden of Eden
13:10 Lot journeyed...
Num. 2:3 *on e. side* of Moses
34:10 east border of your *e.*
Ezek. 48:2 Asher a portion, *e.* side

EAST border.
Num. 34:10 point out your *e. bor.*
Jos. 4:19 encamped in the *e. bor.*
15:5 the *e. border* was salt sea

EASTER.
Acts 12:4 after *e.* to bring him

EAST gate.
Neh. 3:29 Shem. keeper of *e. gate*
Jer. 19:2 entry of the *e. gate*
Ezek. 10:19 stood at door of *e. g.*
11:1 Spirit brought to the *e. g.*

EAST side.
Num. 2:3 on *e. side* shall J. pitch
Jos. 7:2 Ai, on *e. side* of Bethel
Jud. 11:18 came by *e. side* of N.
Ezek. 48:2 fr. the *e. side* even unto,
3, 4, 5, 6, 7, 8, 23, 24, 25, 26, 27
Jon. 4:5 Jonah sat on *e. s.* of city

EASTWARD.
Gen. 13:14 lift. eyes, *Deut.* 3:27
2 K. 13:17 open the window *e.*
1 Chr. 26:17 *e.* were six Levites
Ezek. 47:3 man with line went *e.*

EAST wind.
Gen. 41:6 blasted with *e. w.* 23, 27
Ex. 10:13 brought an *e. w.* 14:21
Job 15:2 fill his belly with *e. w.*
27:21 *e. w.* carrieth him away
38:24 scattereth *e. w. wind*
Ps. 48:7 breakest ship with *e. w.*
78:26 caused *e. wind* to blow
Is. 28:8 rough in day of *e. w.*
Ezek. 17:10 the *e. wind* touch. it
19:12 and the *e. wind* dried up
Jon. 4:8 God prepared *e. wind*
Hab. 1:9 faces sup. up as *e. wind*

EASY.
Prov. 14:6 knowledge is *e.* to b.
Mat. 11:30 my yoke is *e.*
1 Cor. 14:9 *e.* to be understood
Jam. 3:17 wisdom from ab. is *e.*

EAT.

Gen. 2:16 of every tree thou may. *e.*
3:5 day ye *e.* eyes sh. be opened
9 Eve did *e.* ; 12 I did *e.* 13
14 and dust shalt thou *e.*
16 in sorrow shalt thou *e.*
27:4 savory meat that I may *e.*
25 *e.* of my son's ven. may *e.*
49:17 the birds did *e.* them
43:32 Egyptians *e.* by themsel.
Ex. 12:8 they sh. *e.* the flesh, 11
12 beasts may every *e.* meat
12:8 bitter herbs they shall *e.*
43 no str. sh. *e.* 48; Lev. 22:13
44 then shall he *e.*
56 *e.* manna, John 6:31, 49, 58
20:26 Aaron and sons shall *e.*
Lev. 6:16; 8:31
Lev. 6:18 all males shall *e.* 29;
7:6; Num. 18:10
7:6 clean shall *e.* Num. 18:11
10:12 *e.* it without leaven
11:21 ye may *e.* 22; Deut. 14:20
22:11 Aaron and his sons sh. *e.*
22:30 what shall we *e.* say
23:14 ye shall neither *e.* reserve
25:20 your reserve shall *e.*
Num. 11:5 fish we did *e.* freely
13 flesh that we may *e.*
21:3 the peo. *e.* of the sacrifices
Deut. 12:15 *e.* within thy gates
15. mine and clean *e.* 22; 20:11
27 *e.* meat; *s.* 14:11; 16:5; Ezek. 44:3
20 I will *e.* flesh
22:12 give to stra. th. he may *e.*
23:11 thou mayest *e.* grapes

CRUDEN'S CONCORDANCE.

EAT

Deut. 28:39 for worms shall e. th.
58 e. fruit of body, Lam. 2:20
32:38 e. fat of sacrifices
Jos. 5:11 they e. of old corn
Judg. 19:6 they tarried, and did e.
1 Sam. 1:18 Hannah did e.
9:13 they e. that be bidden
14:34 and e. and sin not
30:34 Jonathan did e. no meat
2 Sam. 9:11 e. at table, 1 K. 2:7
1 K. 14:11 him that dieth of J. dogs e. 16:4; 21:23; 2 K. 9:10, 36
17:12 that we may e. and die
19:5 arise e. Acts 10:13; 11:7
2 K. 4:43 they shall e. and
(1 they did e. and left thereof
6:23 give son that we may e.
29 we boiled my son, and did e.
19:31 e. ev. m. of vine, Is. 36:16
2 Chr. 33:18 yet did e. passover
Neh. 5:2 that we may e.
9:15 so they did e. P. 78:29
Job 3:24 sighing cometh before I e.
31:8 and let another e.
Ps. 50:13 the meek shall e.
22 ye on earth shall e.
51:18 will I e. the flesh of bulls
74:23 man did e. angels' food
128:2 thou shalt e. the labor
Prov. 1:31 e. fruit, Is. 3:10
13:21 they that love shall e. fruit
24:13 my son, e. thou honey
33:17 young eagles shall e. it
Ec. 2:25 for who can e. f
5:11 are increased that e. them
12 whether he e. little or much
10:16 princes e. in the morning
17 princes e. in due season
Cant. 4:16 come into gar. and e.
Is. 4:1 we will e. our own bread
7:15 butter and honey sh. he e.
22 butter and honey sh. one e.
9:20 e. on left hand, e. flesh
11:7 lion shall e. straw, 65:25
33:24 oxen and asses shall e.
37:30 plant vineyards, and e. the fruit, 65:21; Jer. 29:5, 28
51:8 worms shall e. them
55:1 come ye, buy and e.
2 hearken to me, and e. good
65:4 peo. which e. swine's flesh
13 my servants shall e.
22 not plant and another e.
Jer. 15:16 found, and I did e.
19:9 shall e. the flesh of friend
Ezek. 2:8 open thy mouth and e.
3:1 e. that thou findest, e. roll
4:10 e. by wei.; 5:10 fath. e. so.
16:13 thou didst e. fine flour
34:3 ye e. the fat
Dan. 4:33 Nebuch. did e. grass
Hos. 4:10 shall e. and not have enough, Mic. 6:14; Hag. 1:6
9:3 shall e. unclean things
4 e. thereof shall be polluted
Amos 6:4 that e. the lambs
Mic. 3:3 who also e. the flesh
Zec. 11:9 let the rest e.
Mat. 12:4 David did e. shew-bre. 14:30 did all e. 13:37; Mark 6:12; 8:8; Luke 9:17
15:27 dogs e. of crm. Mark 7:28
24 they that did e. were 4,000
26:21 as they did e. he said, Mark 14:18
26 take e. this my body, Mark 14:22; 1 Cor. 11:24
Mark 2:16 e. with publicans
6:44 that did e. were above 5,000
11:14 no man e. fruit of thee
14:12 mayest e. the passover, 14; Luke 22:8, 11; John 18:28
Luke 6:1 did e. rubbing them
10:8 e. such things as are set
15:23 let us e. and be merry
14:3 he took it, and did e.
John 4:31 saying, Master, e.
6:26 because ye did e. of loaves
53 exc. ye e. flo. of Son of m.
Acts 2:16 they did e. their meat
11:3 and didst e. with them
23:14 e. nothing till slain Paul
Rom. 14:3 believeth he may e. all
23 doubteth is damned if he e.
1 Cor. 8:8 e. are better, if we e. n.
9:4 we have not power to e.
10:18 who e. of the sacrifices
25 whatl. sold in shamb. that e.
27 e. asking no question
2 Thes. 3:10 work not, neither e.
Jam. 5:17 word will e. as cank.
Jam. 3:3 and shall e. your flesh
Rev. 17:16 shall e. her flesh
19:15 that e. flesh of kings

See BLOOD, BREAD, FAT.

EAT, with drink.

Gen. 24:54 e. and drink, 21:30; 1 Sam. 30:16
Ex. 24:11; Jud. 9:27; 19:4
Ex. 32:6 to e. and d. 1 Cor. 10:7
34:28 e. br. nor d. Deut. 9:9, 18
2 Sam. 11:11 to e. and d. f
12:3 e. of his meat and drink
19:35 taste what I e. or drink f
1 K. 13:8 not e. bread nor drink water, 9, 17, 22
19:41 E. said, e. and drink
K. 6:22 th. they may. e. and d.
18:27 e. th. and d. piss, Is. 36:12
Ezr. 10:6 E. e. no bread nor dr.
Neh. 8:10 e. the fat and d. the s.
Ec. 4:10 nor e. nor d. three days
Job 1:4 called sisters to e. and d.
18:4 nothing better than e.
and drink, 8:13; 5:18; 8:13
Cant. 5:1 e. O friends, you, dri.
Is. 21:5 e. drink, ye princes
22:18 e. and drink, 1 Cor. 15:39
Ezek. 25:4 e. fruit and dr. milk
39:17 e. flesh and drink blood
Dan. 1:12 pulse to e. water to d.
Mat. 6:25 d. or d. 31; Luke 12:29
24:49 e. and d. w. d. Luke 18:45
Luke 5:33 e. and d. with yours
31 thy disciples e. and drink
12:19 take thine ease, e. drink
17:27 they did e. they drank, 28
Acts 9:9 did neither e. nor drink
23:12 e. nor d. till killed P. 21
Rom. 14:21 e. flesh nor d. wine
1 Cor. 9:4 power to e. and to d.
10:31 whether ye e. or drink
11:22 houses to e. and drink in?
26 ye e. bread and drink cup
27 e. and drink unworthily
29 so let him e. and drink

He did EAT.

Gen. 25:28 he did e. of his ven.
27:25 to Isaac, and he did e.
3:36 save the bread He did e.
Num 1:9 John did e. locusts
Luke 4:2 days he did e. nothing
Gal. 2:12 he did e. with Gentiles

EAT not.

Gen. 2:17 shalt not e. 3:1, 3
3:11 I commanded not to e. 17
9:4 blood not e. Lev. 19:26; Deut. 12:16, 23-25; 15:23
32:32 child, of Is. e. not of sinew
43:32 Egyptians might not e.
Ex. 12:9 e. n. of raw nor sodden
43 foreigner shall not e. thereof
Lev. 7:23 ex. they wash e. not, 21
Luke 22:16 I will not e. thereof
1 Cor. 5:11 with such no not to e.
10:28 e. not for his sake

Shall ye EAT.

Ex. 12:11 s. ye e. with loins gird.
15 seven days shall ye e. 20
22:31 shall ye e. any flesh torn
Lev. 10:14 wave-breast shall ye e.
11:3 cheweth the cud, that shall ye e. Deut. 14:4, 6
22 in the fifth year shall ye e.

Ye shall EAT.

Ex. 12:11 ye shall e. it with haste
18 ye shall e. unleavened bread
16:12 at even ye shall e. flesh
Lev. 7:23 ye shall e. no fat. 15
23:14 ye shall e. neither bread
25:12 ye shall e. the increase
19 ye shall e. your fill
21 ye sh. e. of old store, 26:10
Deut. 14:11 clean birds ye sh. e.
K. 19:29 e. this year, Is. 37:30
Is. 1:19 if obedient ye shall e.
61:6 ye sh. e. riches of Gentiles
Joel 2:26 ye shall e. in plenty
Luke 12:22 what ye e.

To EAT.

Gen. 16:8 L. shall give flesh to e.
Deut. 12:20 longeth to e. flesh
2 K. 4:40 pouret out for m. to e.
Neh. 8:10 nor enough to e.
Neh. 8:30 had thou enough to e.
Ps. 78:24 manna on them to e.
Prov. 23:1 sit. to e. with a ruler
25:27 not good to e. much honey
31:15 given power to e.
Ec. 32:18 shall be for them to e.
Jer. 19:9 cause th. to e. the flesh

EAT

Ezek. 3:2 caused me to e. th. roll
3 cause thy belly to e.
Dan. 4:25 to e. grass, 32
Mic. 7:1 there is no cluster to e.
Hab. 1:8 eagle that hasteth to e.
Mat. 12:1 to pluck ears and to e.
4 not lawful to e. Mark 2:26; Luke 6:4
14:16 give them to e. Mark 6:37; Luke 9:13
15:20 to e. with unwash. hands
32 nothing to e. Mark 8:1, 2
20:17 prepare to e. passover?
Mark 5:43 given her to e.
6:31 no leisure to e.
Luke 22:15 to e. this passover
John 4:32 meat for e. ye know not
33 brought him aught to e. f
6:52 man give us his flesh to e. f
1 Cor. 8:10 emboldened toe. things
11:20 not to e. Lord's supper
Rev. 2:7 to e. of the tree of life
14 to e. things sacrificed, 20
17 to e. of hidden manna

EAT up.

Gen. 41:4 did e. up seven fat, 20
Num. 24:8 he shall e. up nations
Ps. 27:2 enemies came to e. up me
105:35 did e. up all the herbs
Is. 50:9 moth shall e. up, 51:8
Jer. 5:17 e. up thy harvest, s. up flocks, e. up vines
22:22 wind e. up all pastures
Hos. 4:8 they e. up the sin of
Nah. 3:15 shall e. up like canker
Rev. 10:9 take it, and e. it up

EATEN.

Gen. 3:11 hast thou e. of tree
14:24 which young men have e.
11:21 when they had e. them
12:8 no leavened br. he e. 7
21:28 his flesh shall not be e.
27:31 not be e. because it is ho.
Lev. 10:16 shall be e. in the holy place, 26; 7:6
23 wholly burnt not be e. 7:19
30 no sin-offering shall be e.
7:15 shall be e. the same day, 16
10:17 why not e. sin offering?
11:13 not be e. 41; Deut. 14:10
19:6 shall be e. same day, 22:30
Num. 28:17 br. be e. Ezek. 45:21
26:14 I have not e. in mourning
22:6 ye have not e. bread
31:20 when they shall have e.
Jos. 5:12 had e. of old coru.
Ruth 8:7 when Boaz had e. and
1 Sam. 28:20 e. no bread all day
30:12 had e. his spirit came
1 K. 13:28 lion not e. the carcass
Neh. 5:14 have not e. the bread
Job 6:6 unsavory e. without salt
31:17 or have e. my morsel
39 if I have e. the fruits
Ps. 69:9 zeal of thy house hath e. me up, John 2:17
102:9 I have e. ashes like bread
Prov. 9:17 bread e. in secret
23:8 morsel e. shalt thou vomit
Cant. 5:1 I have e. my honey-co.
Is. 3:14 ye have e. my vineyard
Jer. 10:25 they have e. up Jacob
24:2 could not be e. 29:17; 29:17
31:29 e. sour grapes, Ezek. 18:2
Hos. 10:13 ye have e. the fruit
Joel 2:26 ye have e. in plenty
Mat. 14:21 and they that had e.
Mark 8:9
Luke 13:26 we have e. and drunk
17:8 I have e. afterward thou e.
Acts 10:10 would have e.
14 I have nev. e. any th. com.
12:23 he was e. of worms
27:38 when they had e. enough
Rev. 10:10 had e. it, belly bitter

EATER, S.

Jud. 14:14 out of e. came forth
Prov. 23:20 not amongst e. of flesh
Is. 55:10 give bread to the e.
Nah. 3:12 fall into mouth of e.

EATEST.

Gen. 2:17 day thou e. thou shalt
1 Sam. 1:8 why e. thou not?

EATETH.

Ex. 12:15 whos. e. leav. bread, 19
Lev. 7:18 that e. 25, 23; 17:10
Num. 13:32 land e. up inhabit.
1 Sam. 14:24 cursed m. that e. 28
Job 5:5 harvest the hungry e. up
21:25 never e. with pleasure
40:15 behemoth e. grass as an ox
Pr. 106:20 an ox that e. grass
Prov. 13:25 righteous e. to satisfy

EDI

Prov. 30:20 she e. and wipeth m.
31:27 she e. not bread of idlen.
Ec. 4:5 fool e. his own flesh
Is. 29:8 he e. but awaketh
44:16 with part he e. flesh
59:5 that e. of their eggs
Mat. 9:11 why e. your master, Mark 2:16; Luke 15:2
John 6:54 whoso e. my flesh
56 that e. my flesh dwelleth in
57 so he that e. me shall live
58 so that e. of this bread
Rom. 14:2 another weak e. herbs
3 let not him that e. despise
6 e. to L. that e. not, to L. e. n.
20 evil for who e. with offence
23 because e. not of faith
1 Cor. 9:7 planteth vineyard and e. not? and e. not of milk?
11:29 that e. unworth. e. damn.

EATING.

Ex. 12:4 ev. man to his e. 16:18
Jud. 14:9 Samson went on e.
1 Sam. 14:34 ev. m. ox, with b.
2 K. 4:40 as they were e. pottage
Job 20:23 upon him while he is e.
Is. 66:17 e. swine's flesh
Amos 7:2 made an end of e. grass
Mat. 26:26 were e. J. took br.
Luke 22:30 e. and drinking
11:21 in e. ev. one tak. own sup.

See DRINKING.

EBAL.

Deut. 11:29 mount E. 27:4, 13
Jos. 8:30 an altar in mount E.

EBED.

Jud. 9:30; Ezr. 8:6

EBED-MELECH.

Jer. 38:8 E. spake to king, 39:16

EDEN-EZER.

1 Sam. 4:1 and pitched beside E.
5:1 bro. the ark from E. 7:12

EBER.

Gen. 10:21, 25; Num. 24:24

ED.

Jos. 22:34

EDEN.

Gen. 2:15 man into garden of E.
Is. 51:3 her wilderness like E.
Ezek. 28:13; 31:9, 16, 18; 36:35
Joel 2:3 is as the garden of E.
Amos 1:5 cut off sceptre from E.

EDGE.

Ex. 13:20 e. of wild. Num. 33:6
20:10 loops in the e. of curtain
Ec. 10:10 do not whet the e.

See TEETH.

EDGE of the sword.

Gen. 34:26 slew I. with e. of s.
Ex. 17:13 Amalek with e. of s.
Jos. 8:24 smote Ai. with e. of s.
Jud. 1:15 Sisera; 20:10 Jabe-gil.
Job 1:15 Job's ser. with e. of s. 17
Ps. 89:43 turned the e. of the s.
Jer. 21:7 smite them with e. of s.
Luke 21:24 Jews fall by e. of sw.
Heb. 11:34 their faith esc. e. of s.

EDGED.

Ps. 149:6 two-e. sword in hand
Prov. 5:1 sharp as a two-e. sword
Heb. 4:12 word of God sharper than two-e. sword
Rev. 1:16 mouth sharp two-e. 6

EDGES.

Jud. 3:16 Eh. a dagger had two e.
Rev. 2:12 sharp sw. with two e.

EDIFICATION.

Rom. 15:2 please neighbor to e.
1 Cor. 14:3 speaketh to men to e.
2 Cor. 10:8 L. hath given us for e.
13:10 Lord hath given me to e.

EDIFIED.

Acts 9:31 churches had rest, e.
1 Cor. 14:17 the other is not e.

EDIFIETH.

1 Cor. 8:1 knowledge puffeth, charity e.
14:4 he that speaketh e. hims. he that prophes. e. the church

EDIFY.

Rom. 14:19 one may e. another
1 Thes. 5:11 e. one another.

EDIFYING.

1 Cor. 14:5 church may receive e.
14 that ye may excel to the e.
14:26 let all things be done to e.
2 Cor. 12:19 all thin. for your e.
Eph. 4:12 e. of body of Christ
16 the body to the e. of itself
29 good to the use of e.
1 Tim. 1:4 quest. rather than e.

CRUDEN'S CONCORDANCE. 835

EGY
EDOM.
Gen. 25:30 was called E. 36:1
Ex. 15:15 dukes of E. amazed
Num. 20:21 E. refused to give Israel passage. 21:18
2 Sam. 8:14 gar. in E, 1 Chr. 18:13
2 K. 8:20 E. revolted, 14:10; 2 Chr. 21:20
Ps. 60:8 over E. cast shoe. 108:9
Is. 63:1 that cometh from E. ?
Jer. 49:7 concerning E. saith Lord, Ezek. 25:12
Amos 2:1 king of E. 9:12
Ob. 8 doct. wise men out of E.

EDOMITE. Deut. 23:7; 2 K. 8:21
EDREI. Deut. 1:4

EFFECT, Substantive.
Num. 30:8 make vow of no e.
Ps. 33:10 devices of peo. of no e.
Is. 32:17 the e. of righteousness
Ezek. 12:23 and e. of every vision
Mat. 15:6 com. of G. e. of none e.
Mark 7:13 word of God of none e.
Rom. 3:3 unbelief make the faith of God without e.
4:14 prom. of none e. Gal. 3:17
9:6 word hath taken none e.
1 Cor. 1:17 cr. of C. be of none e.
Gal. 5:4 Chr. is become of no e.

EFFECT, Verb.
Jer. 48:30 lies shall not so e. it

EFFECTED.
2 Chr. 7:11 Sol. prosperously e.

EFFECTUAL.
1 Cor. 16:9 a great door and e.
2 Cor. 1:6 is e. in enduring suff.
Eph. 3:7 by the e. working of
4:16 according to e. working
Phile. 6 faith may become e.
Jam. 5:16 the e. prayer of right.

EFFECTUALLY.
Gal. 2:8 he that wrought e. in P.
1 Thes. 2:13 the word e. worketh

EFFEMINATE.
1 Cor. 6:9 nor e. shall inherit

EGG.
Job 6:6 any taste in white of e. ?
Luke 11:12 ask e. will offer scor. ?

EGGS.
Deut. 22:6 whet. young ones or e.
Job 39:14 ostr. leaveth e. in earth
Is. 10:14 one gathereth e.
59:5 hatch cockatrice's e.
Jer. 17:11 partridge sitteth on e.

EHUD.
EHI, Gen. 46:21
EGLAH, 2 Sam. 3:5
EGLAIM. Is. 15:8
EGLON. Jud. 3:14, 17

EGYPT.
Gen. 13:10 from the river of E. 45:19 made me lord of all E.
Ex. 3:20 will smite E. 7:4; 10:7
2 K. 18:21 thou trustest on E. 24
Is. 19:16 E. like unto women, 24
Jer. 2:18 in way of E. ? 26
Ezek. 29:2 ag. E. 30:15; 32:12
Joel 3:19 E. a desolat. Zec. 10:11
Nah. 3:9 Ethiopia and E. were
Acts 7:10 governor over E.
Heb. 11:27 by faith he forsook E.
Rev. 11:8 is called Sodom and E.

In, and into EGYPT.
Gen. 46:4 go down with thee i. E.
Ex. 10:2 things I wrought in E.
16:3 carry in E. in L; 18:1, 9
Num. 11:18 well with us in E.
14:3 for us to return into E. 4
22:15 and we have dwelt in E.
Deut. 1:30 did for you in E. 4:31
Jos. 24:14 fathers served in E.
Is. 19:1 Lord shall come into E.
Jer. 25:21 fled and went into E. 41:17 to go into E. 42:15 44:19 Go ye not into E. 43:2
Mat. 2:13 flee into E. 14

Land of EGYPT.
Gen. 13:10; 41:19, 51; 45:18; 47:6
Ps. 78:12 marvel, in, in E. 80:5
Heb. 8:9 out of the land of E.
Jude 5 saved peo. out of L. of E.

Out of EGYPT.
Gen. 13:1 Abraham out of E. 47:30 carry me out of E.
Ex. 3:11; 12:39; 13:9, 16
Num. 11:20 came forth out of E. 22:11 is a people come out of E.
Jud. 2:1 made you go out of E.
Heb. 3:16 all that came out of E.

To EGYPT.
Is. 19:21 L. shall be known to E.
31:1 woe to them that go to E.
Hos. 7:11 they call to E.

EGYPTIAN, S.
Gen. 16:1, 3; 21:9; 39:1, 5; 41:55

ELD
Ex. 2:11 E. smiting Heb. 12, 19
3:22 shall spoil the E. 12:36
14:9 E. pursued after, 10, 13, 25
19:4 seen what I did to the E.
32:12 wherefore should the E. Num. 14:13 M. said, Then the E.
20:15 and E. vexed us and our
1 Sam. 30:11 found an E. in field
Is. 19:2 I will set the E. 4, 21, 23
Acts 21:38 art not thou that E. ?
Heb. 11:29 E. assaying to do

EHUD.
Jud. 3:15 raised up E. 16, 23, 26
1 Chr. 7:10 sons of Bilhan, E. 8:6

EIGHT.
Gen. 17:12 he that is e. days old, 21:4; Luke 2:21
22:23 these e. Milcah did bear
Num. 29:29 e. bullocks, two rams
Jud. 3:8 Israel served e. years
12:14 Abdon judged Is. e. y. e.
1 K. 7:10 of stones of e. cubits
2 K. 22:1 Josiah reigned e. years
22:1 Joel. was e. years old, 2 Chr. 34:1
2 Chr. 29:17 sanct. L. in e. days
Ec. 11:2 to seven, also to e.
Ezek. 40:31 had e. steps, 34; 37
41 e. tables slew sacrifices
Mic. 5:5 seven shepherds, e. men
Luke 9:28 about an e. days after
John 20:26 after e. days
Acts 9:33 E. kept his bed e. years
1 Pet. 3:20 e. souls were saved

EIGHTH.
Lev. 23:22 shall sow e. year
1 K. 6:38 which is e. month
1 Chr. 24:10 the e. to came forth
Zec. 1:1 in e. month word came
2 Pet. 2:5 saved Noah the e. per.
Rev. 17:11 beast that was, is the e.
21:20 e. foundation was a beryl
See DAY, DAYS.

EIGHT hundred.
Gen. 5:4 Adam lived e. h. years

EIGHTEEN.
1 K. 7:15 two pillars of brass e. cubits, 2 K. 25:17; Jer. 52:21
2 Chr. 11:21 Reho. took e. wives
Luke 13:4 e. on whom tower fell
16 Satan hath bound e.

EIGHTEENTH.
1 K. 15:1 e. year of Jer. 2 Chr. 13:1
1 Chr. 24:15 e. lot came forth
25:25 the e. to Hanani
Jer. 32:1 was e. year of Nebuch.

EITHER.
John 19:18 crucifi. on e. side one
Rev. 22:2 e. side river tree of life

EKRON.
1 Sam. 5:10 us ark came to E.
2 K. 1:2 the god of E. 3:6, 16
Amos 1:8 my hand against E.
Zep. 2:4 E. shall be rooted up
Zec. 9:5 very sorrowful, 7

EKRONITES.
Jos. 13:3 the land of the E. not
1 Sam. 5:10 ark on. to Ekron, E.

ELAH.
Gen. 36:41 duke E. 1 K. 4:18
1 Sam. 17:2 by the valley of E.
21:9 Goliath in valley of E.
1 K. 16:8 E. son of Baasha
1 K. 15:30 son of E. 17:1; 18:1, 9
1 Chr. 4:15 son of Caleb, E. 9:8

ELAM.
Gen. 10:22 children of Shem, E.
14:1 Chedorlaomer king of E.
Is. 11:11 recover people from E.
21:2 go up, O E. 22:6 E. bare
Jer. 25:25 kings of E. 49:34, 30, 39
Ezek. 32:24 there is E. and all
Dan. 8:2 in the province of E.

ELAMITES.
Ezr. 4:9 E. wrote letter, Acts 2:9

ELATH. 2 K. 14:22; 16:6
EL-BETHEL. Gen. 35:7
ELDAD. Num. 11:26, 27

ELDER.
Gen. 10:21 S. brother of Ja. the e.
25:23 e. serve young. Rom. 9:12
1 K. 2:29 he is mine e. brother
Job 32:4 waited till Job had sp.
Ezek. 16:16 thy e. sister is Sam.
Luke 15:25 his e. son was in field
1 Tim. 5:2 entreat the e. women
1 Pet. 5:5 younger, submit to e.

ELDER, for ruler.
1 Tim. 5:1 rebuke not an e.
19 against e. receive not acc.
1 Pet. 5:1 who am also an e.
2 John 1 the e. to the elect lady
3 John 1 the e. unto Gaius

ELE
Gen. 50:7 e. of his house went
Ex. 4:15 e. of congr. lay hands
Num. 11:25 L. gave spirit to 70 e.
Deut. 22:10 before the L. your e.
31:28 gather to me all e.
32:7 ask thy father and e.
Jos. 16:4 e. of the town
1 K. 21:11 e. did as Jezebel sent
2 K. 6:32 Elisha and e. sat
10:1 Jehu sent to e. of Jezreel
19:2 Hezekiah sent e. Is. 37:2
Ps. 107:32 in assembly of e.
Prov. 31:23 known among e.
Lam. 1:19 e. gave up the ghost
2:10 e. of Zion sit upon ground
4:16 favored not e. 5:12
Ezek. 8:1 and the e. of Judah sat
Joel 1:14 gather the e. 2:16
Mat. 15:2 tradition of the e. ?
16:21 suffer things of e. 27:12
26:20 e. sought false witness
27:20 e. persuaded the multit.
41 mocking with the e. said
28:12 assembled with the e.
Mark 7:3 tradition of the e.
8:31 rejected of the e. Luke 9:22
15:1 held a consultation with e.
Acts 4:5 e. were gath. together
23 all that the c. had said
6:12 stirred up the peo. and e.
11:30 sent it to the e. by Barn.
14:23 ordained e. in ev. church
15:4 of the church and of the e.
6 the apostles and e. came
22 apostles, e. and brethren
16:4 decrees ordained of the e.
1 Tim. 5:17 e. rule well
Tit. 1:5 ordain e. in every city
Jam. 5:14 call for e. of church
1 Pet. 5:1 e. which are am. you
Rev. 4:4 I saw twenty-four e.
10:14 e. fall, 5:8, 14; 11:16; 19:4
5:5 one one of e. saith
6 in midst of e. stood a Lamb
7:11 angels stood about the e.
13 one of the e. answered

ELDERS, with eity.
Deut. 19:12 e. of city shall fetch
21:3 e. of city shall take heifer
21:19 bring son to e. of his city
Jud. 8:16 he took e. of the city
Ruth 4:2 H. took men of e. of city
Ezr. 10:14 the e. of every city

ELDERS of Israel.
Ex. 3:16 gather the e. of Israel
12:21 M. called for e. of Israel
18:12 e. of Israel came to eat
24:1 seventy city's e. of Is. 11:16
Deut. 27:1 e. of Isr. commanded
31:9 delivered law to e. of Isr.
Jos. 7:6 e. of Isr. put dust on
2 Sam. 5:3 e. of I. came to king at
Hebron, 1 K. 8:3; 1 Chr. 11:3
17:4 pleased all e. of Israel
Ezek. 20:1 c. of I. came to inq.
Acts 4:8 rulers of peo. and e. of I.

ELDERS, with people.
Num. 11:24 M. gathered seventy men of the e. of the people
1 Sam. 15:30 honour before e. of p.
Mat. 21:23 the e. of people came, Luke 22:60
27:1 e. of the peo. took counsel

ELDEST.
1 Sam. 17:13 E. E.'s three eldest
14 David was the e. 14; 4:14
1 K. 16:34 foundation in Abiram his e. son
Mat. 27:56 cried, E. E. lama, Mark 15:34

ELEAD. 1 Chr. 7:21
ELEALEH. Num. 32:37; Is. 15:4; 16:9; Jer. 48:34

ELEASAH.
Ex. 6:25; 28:1; Num. 3:2; 26:60;
Jos. 14:1; 17:4; 19:51; 24:33
Lev. 10:16 M. was angry with E.
Num. 3:1 E. minister, in priest's
26:1 E. and Aaron told sum of
Deut. 10:6 near bef. E. 26:28
Ezr. 7:5 came near bef. E. 34:31
Jos. 14:1 Joshua and E. divided
24:33 Eleazar son of Aaron died

ELECT.
Is. 42:1 mine e. in whom my
45:4 Israel mine e. I have called
65:9 mine e. shall inherit it
22 mine e. shall long enjoy

ELI
Mat. 24:22 for the e. those days shall be short. Mark 13:20
24 dec. the very e. Mark 13:22
31 angels gather e. Mark 13:27
Luke 18:7 G. avenge his own e. ?
Rom. 8:33 to charge of God's e. ?
Col. 3:12 put on as e. of G. how.
1 Tim. 5:21 before the e. angels
2 Tim. 2:10 endure for the e. sake
Tit. 1:1 to the faith of God's e.
1 Pet. 1:2 e. according to foreku.
2:6 chief corner-stone, e. prec.
2 John 1 the elder to the e. lady
13 the children of thy e. sister

ELECTED.
1 Pet. 5:13 church at Bab. e. with

ELECTION.
Rom. 9:11 purpose accord. to e.
11:5 remn. according to the e.
7 the e. hath obtained it
28 the e. they are beloved
1 Thes. 1:4 knowing your e. of G.
2 Pet. 1:10 your calling and e.

EL-ELOHE-Israel. Gen. 33:20

ELEMENTS.
Gal. 4:3 under e. of the world
9 the weak and beggarly e.
2 Pet. 3:10 e. melt with heat, 12

ELEVEN.
Gen. 32:22 Jacob took his e. sons
37:9 sun, moon, and e. stars
Ex. 26:7 e. curtains shalt make
36:14 e. curt. 15 e. of one size
Num. 29:20 e. bullocks, two rams
Deut. 1:2 e. days' journey fr. H.
Jos. 15:51 e. cities with villages
Jud. 16:5 e. hun. pieces of silver
17:2 e. hundred shekels of silv.
2 K. 23:36 Jehoiakim reigned e. years in Joru. 2 Chr. 36:5
24:18 Zedekiah reigned e. years, 2 Chr. 36:11 ; Jer. 52:1
Mat. 28:16 e. disciples went to G.
Mark 16:14 he appeared to the e.
Luke 24:9 told to the e. and rest
33 found the e. gath. together
Acts 1:26 numb. with e. apostles
2:14 P. with the e. said to them

ELEVENTH.
1 K. 6:38 e. year was ho. finished
1 Chr. 24:12 the e. lot came forth
25:18 the e. to Azareel
27:14 e. capt. for the e. month
Jer. 1:3 Jer. proph. e. year of Z.
39:2 in e. year city was bro. up
Ezek. 26:1 word of L. came to e.
Zec. 1:7 e. year, 30:20; 31:1
Mat. 20:6 about e. hour he went
9 were hired about the e. hour
Rev. 21:20 e. foundat. of the city

ELHANAN. 2 Sam. 21:19; 23:24; 1 Chr. 11:26; 20:5

ELI.
1 Sam. 1:25 brou. the child to E.
2:12, 27; 3:5, 6, 8, 12, 14; 4:14
1 K. 2:27 spake concerning E.
Mat. 27:46 cried, E. E. lama, Mark 15:34

ELIAB.
Num. 1:9; 2:7; 7:24, 29; 16:16
Deut. 11:6 he did to sons of E.
1 Sam. 16:6 E. heard, 1 Chr. 2:13
1 Chr. 6:27 E. the son of Nahath
15:18 E. port. 20; 16:5 E. with
2 Chr. 11:18 took daughter of E.

ELIADA.
2 Sam. 5:16; 1 Chr. 3:8; 2 Chr. 17:17

ELIAKIM.
2 K. 18:18 out to Rabshakeh E.
23:34 made E. son, 2 Chr. 36:4
Is. 22:20; 30:1
Mat. 1:13 Abiud begat E. and E.

ELIAS, (i. e. ELIJAH).
Mat. 11:14 this is E. 17:3, 10, 11;
Mark 9:4, 11, 12, 13

ELIASHIB.
1 Chr. 3:24; 24:12; Ezr. 10:6, 24, 27, 36; Neh. 3:1, 20, 21; 12:10, 22, 23; 13:4, 7, 28

ELIEZER.
Gen. 15:2 steward of house is E.
Ex. 18:4 name of Moses' son E.
Num. 3:4; 1 Chr. 7:8; 15:24; 23:15, 17; 26:25; 27:16; 2 Chr. 20:37; Ezr. 8:16; 10:18, 23, 31; Luke 3:29 E. was the son of Jo.

ELIHOREPH. 1 K. 4:3

ELIHU.
1 Chr. 12:20; 20:7; 27:18; Job 32:2
1 K. 17:1 E. the Tishbite, 18, 22
1 K. 19:19 he found the child also
2 K. 1:8 E. went to, 8, 7, 10, 12, 10
1 K. 2:1 had done, 9:30; 21:21

END

Ps. 46:9 wars cease *unto e.*
119:33 I shall keep it *unto the e.*
Is. 68:11 proclaimed *u. e.* of earth
Dan. 6:26 his dominion be *u. e.*
Mat. 28:20 I am with you *u. e.*
John 13:1 loved them *u. the e.*
1 *Cor.* 1:8 confirm you *unto the e.*
Heb. 3:6 hold fast confidence *u. e.*
14 if hold begin. steadfast *u. e.*
6:11 assurance of hope *unto e.*
Rev. 2:26 keepeth my works *u. e.*

ENDAMAGE.
Ezr. 4:13 *e.* the revenue of kings

ENDANGER, ED.
Ec. 10:9 cleav. wood shall be *e.*
Dan. 1:10 *e.* my head to the king

ENDED, ETH, ING.
Gen. 2:2 seventh day G. *e.* work
2 *Sam.* 22:18 so they *e.* the mat.
Job 31:40 the words of Job are *e.*
Ps. 72:20 prayers of David are *e.*
Is. 24:8 noise of them rejoice *e.*
60:20 days of mourn. shall be *e.*
Jer. 8:20 the summer is *e.*
Mat. 7:28 when Jesus *e.* sayings
Luke 4:2 forty days *e.* he hunger.
13 devil had *e.* all temptation
John 13:2 supper being *e.*
Rev. 1:8 the beginning and *e.*

1 *Tim.* 1:4 heed to *e.* genealogies
Heb. 7:16 after power of an *e.* life

ENDEAVOR, ED, ING.
Acts 16:10 *e.* to go into Macedo.
Eph. 4:3 *e.* to keep unity of spir.
1 *Thes.* 2:17 we *e.* to see your f.
2 *Pet.* 1:15 will *e.* ye may be able

ENDEAVORS.
Ps. 28:4 accord. to wicked. of *e.*

EN-DOR.
Jos. 17:11 E. and her t, *Ps.* 83:10
1 *Sam.* 28:7 woman at E. hath *e.*

ENDOW.
Ex. 22:16 *e.* her to be his wife

ENDS.
Deut. 33:17 push peo. to *e.* of *e.*
1 *Sam.* 2:10 shall judge *e.* of *e.*
Job 28:24 looketh to *e.* of the *e.*
37:3 lightning unto *e.* of earth
38:13 take hold of *e.* of earth
Ps. 19:6 his circuit to the *e.* of it
22:27 *e.* of world shall remember
48:10 so is thy praise to the *e.* of
59:13 G. ruleth in Jacob to the *e.*
65:5 confidence of *e.* of the *e.*
67:7 *e.* of the earth sh. fear him
98:3 *e.* of earth seen salvation
135:7 vapors to ascend from the
e. of earth, *Jer.* 10:13; 51:16
Prov. 17:24 eyes of fool are in *e.*
30:4 established *e.* of the earth?
Is. 40:28 Creator of *e.* of earth
41:5 *e.* of the earth were afraid
9 taken from *e.* of the earth
43:6 daughters from *e.* of earth
45:22 be saved, all the *e.*
52:10 all *e.* see salvation of God
Jer. 16:19 shall come from the *e.*
25:31 a noise to *e.* of the earth
Ezek. 15:4 fire devoureth both *e.*
Mic. 5:4 shall he be great to *e.*
Zec. 9:10 his dominion to *e.* of
Acts 13:47 be for salvation to *e.*
Rom. 10:18 words to *e.* of world
1 *Cor.* 10:11 *e.* of world are come

ENDUED.
Gen. 30:20 *e.* me with good dow.
2 *Chr.* 2:12 son *e.* with prudence
13 cunning man *e.* with under.
Luke 24:49 ye be *e.* with power
Jam. 3:13 *e.* with knowledge

ENDURE.
Gen. 33:14 children be able to *e.*
Ex. 18:23 thou shalt be able to *e.*
Est. 8:6 can I *e.* to see the evil
Job 8:15 fast, but it shall not *e.*
31:23 I could not *e.*
Ps. 9:7 the Lord shall *e.* for ever,
102:12, 26; 104:31
30:5 weeping may *e.* for a night
72:5 fear thee as long as sun *e.*
17 his name shall *e.* as the sun
89:29 his seed to *e.* for ever, 36
Ezek. 22:14 can thy heart *e.*
Mat. 24:13 he th. *e.* shall *e.* to the
end, *Mark* 13:13
Mark 4:17 so *e.* but for a time
2 *Thes.* 1:4 tribulations that ye *e.*
2 *Tim.* 2:3 hardness
10 *e.* all things for elect's sake
4:3 will not *e.* sound doctrine
5 but *e.* afflictions
Heb. 12:7 if ye *e.* chastening, God

ENE

Heb. 12:20 not *e.* what was com.
Jam. 5:11 count them hap. w. *e.*
1 *Pet.* 2:19 for conscience *e.* grief

ENDURED.
Ps. 81:15 should have *e.* for ever
Rom. 9:22 God *e.* with long-suff.
2 *Tim.* 3:11 what persecut. I *e.*
Heb. 6:15 after he had patient. *e.*
10:32 *e.* great fight of afflictions
11:27 *e.* as seeing him invisible
12:2 *e.* cross; 3 *e.* such contrad.

ENDURETH.
Ps. 30:5 anger *e.* but a moment
52:1 goodness of G. *e.* contin.
72:7 peace, so long as moon *e.*
100:5 truth *e.* to all generations
145:13 dominion *e.* through all
Mat. 10:22 *e.* to the end be saved
John 6:27 meat which *e.* unto life
1 *Cor.* 13:7 charity *e.* all things
Jam. 1:12 bless. that *e.* tempta.

ENDURETH for ever.
1 *Chr.* 16:34 his mercy *e. for ever*,
41; 2 *Chr.* 5:13; 7:3, 6; 20:21;
Ezr. 3:11; *Ps.* 106:1; 107:1;
118:1-4; 136:1-3, etc.; 136:8;
Jer. 33:11
Ps. 111:3 righte. *e. f. e.* 112:3, 9
117:2 his truth *e. for ever*
119:160 thy judgements *e. for ev.*
135:13 thy name, O L. *e. for e.*
1 *Pet.* 1:25 word of the L. *e. f. e.*

ENDURING.
Ps. 19:9 fear of Lord clean, *e.*
2 *Cor.* 1:6 effectual in *e.* same
Heb. 10:34 in heaven *e.* substance

ENEAS. *Acts* 9:34
EN-EGLAIM. *Ezek.* 47:10

ENEMIES.
Ez. 15:6 right hand dashed the *e.*
9 the *e.* said, I will pursue
23:22 I will be *e.* to thine on,
Num. 10:9 if go to war against *e.*
35:23 and was his *e.*
Deut. 32:27 feared wrath of the *e.*
42 beginning of revenges on *e.*
33:27 he shall thrust out the *e.*
Jud. 10:25 God delivered our *e.*
1 *Sam.* 2:32 *e.* in my habitation
18:25 Saul became David's *e.*
24:19 his *e.* will he let him go?
1 *K.* 8:33 when thy people be
overcome before *e.* 2 *Chr.* 6:24
46 if sin, and thou deliver to *e.*
2 *Chr.* 25:8 make thee fall bef. *e.*
Est. 7:1 *e.* not counterv. damage
6 the *e.* is this wicked Haman
Job 12:10 cometh unto the *e.*
Ps. 7:5 let the *e.* persecute
8:2 mightest still *e.* and avenger
9:6 O thou *e.* destructions are
42:9 mourning bec. of *e.*? 43:2
41:10 makest me to turn from *e.*
55:3 I mourn bec. of voice of *e.*
12 not an *e.* that reproached
61:3 a strong tower from the *e.*
64:1 preserve life from fear of *e.*
71:3 all that *e.* hath done
10 *e.* blasphemed me, *e.*
74:10 remember thy name?
18 remember *e.* hath reproach.
78:42 he delivered from *e.* 61
89:23 the *e.* not exact upon him
138:7 hath persecuted
Prov. 27:6 kisses of *e.* are deceit.
Lam. 1:5 *e.* come in like a flood
63:10 was turned to be their *e.*
Jer. 6:25 sword of *e.* is on ev. side
12:11 came *e.* to entreat thee
19:17 scatter them before *e.*
30:11 with wound of an *e.*
Lam. 1:9 *e.* hath magnified
16 because *e.* prevailed
2:9 drawn back hand bef. the *e.*
4 hath bent his bow like an *e.*
5 the Lord was an *e.*
4:12 *e.* should have entered
Ezek. 36:2 the *e.* had said, Aha
Hos. 8:3 is. *e.* shall pursue him
Mic. 4:10 my people there my *e.*
Nah. 3:11 seek strength bef. of *e.*
Mat. 13:25 his *e.* sowed tares
28 said, An *e.* hath done this
Luke 10:19 all power of the *e.*
Acts 13:10 thou *e.* of all righte.
1 *Cor.* 15:26 the last *e.* is death
Gal. 4:16 am I become your *e.*
2 *Thes.* 3:15 not as an *e.*
Jam. 4:1 friend of world *e.* of G.

Hand of the ENEMY.
Lev. 26:25 shall be delivered into
the hand of the *e. Neh.* 9:27
Ps. 31:8 me up into *h. of e.*
78:61 he deliv. his glory in *e. h.*

ENE

Ps. 106:10 red. from *h. of e.* 107:2
Lam. 1:7 people fell into *h. of e.*

Mine ENEMY.
1 *Sam.* 19:17 sent away mine *e. f.*
2 *Sam.* 22:18 mine *e. Ps.* 18:17
1 *K.* 21:20 found me, O mine *e. f.*
Job 16:9 mine *e.* sharpe. his eyes
27:7 let mine *e.* be as wicked
Ps. 7:4 I deliv. him th. is mine *e.*
13:2 how long mine *e.* be exalt.
4 lest mine *e.* say, I have prev.
41:11 mine *e.* not triumph
Lam. 2:22 I swaddled, mine *e.*
Mic. 7:8 rej. not aga. me, O m. *e.*
10 she that is *m. e.* shall see it

Thine ENEMY.
Deut. 28:57 thine *e.* shall distress
1 *Sam.* 24:4 deliver thine *e.* 26:8
28:16 Lord is become thine *e.*
2 *Sam.* 4:8 the head of thine *e.*
Job 13:24 holdest me for thine *e.*
Prov. 24:17 rej. not when *t. e.* fall
25:21 if *t. e.* hunger, *Rom.* 12:20
Lam. 2:17 thine *e.* to rejoice
Zep. 3:15 the L. cast out thine *e.*
Mat. 5:43 Thou shalt hate *th. e.*
Rom. 12:20 if *th. e.* hung. feed h.

ENEMIES.
1 *Sam.* 18:25 avenged of king's *e.*
20:15 when Lord cut off *e.* of D.
16 rej. it at hand of David's *e.*
2 *Sam.* 12:14 occasion to *e.* to bl.
18:39 *e.* be as that young man
2 *Chr.* 20:29 Lord fought aga. *e.*
Ps. 17:9 hide me from deadly *e.*
27:20 *e.* of L. be as fat of lambs
45:5 arrows sharp in king's *e.*
127:5 shall speak with *e.* in gate
Jer. 12:7 belov. into hand of L. *e.*
48:5 heard cry of destruction
Lam. 1:2 friends are become *e.*
5 her *e.* prosper
Mic. 7:6 *e.* are of own house
Rom. 5:10 when *e.* we were rec.
11:28 as conc. gospel, they are *e.*
1 *Cor.* 15:25 put all *e.* under feet
Phil. 3:18 *e.* of the cross of Chr.
Col. 1:21 *e.* in your mind

His ENEMIES.
Gen. 22:17 seed possess gate of *his e.*
Num. 24:8 the nations *his e.*
32:21 be hath driven out *his e.*
Deut. 33:7 be a help from *his e.*
2 *Sam.* 7:1 rest from *his e.*
18:19 Lord avenged of *his e.*
22:1 out of the hand of all *his e.*
1 *K.* 22:9 give rest fr. all *h. e.*
Ps. 10:5 *his e.* he puffeth at them
41:2 not deliv. h. to will of *h. e.*
68:1 let *his e.* be scattered
21 G. shall wound head of *h. e.*
72:9 and *his e.* shall lick the d.
76:66 smote *his e.* in hinder pa.
89:42 hast made *his e.* to rejoice
97:3 a fire burneth up *his e.*
112:8 till he see des. upon *h. e.*
132:18 *his e.* clothe with shame
Prov. 16:7 *his e.* be at peace
Is. 9:11 shall join also to *our e.*
42:13 he shall prevail ag. *his e.*
59:18 recompense to *his e.*
66:6 rendereth recomp. to *his e.*
14 hand be known tow. *h. e.*
Nah. 1:2 reserveth wrath to *h. e.*
3 darkness shall pursue *his e.*
Heb. 10:13 *h. e.* made footstool

Mine ENEMIES.
Num. 23:11 curse mine *e.* 24:10
Deut. 32:41 vengeance to mine *e.*
1 *Sam.* 2:1 enlarged over *m. e.*
14:24 be avenged on *mine e.*
2 *Sam.* 5:20 L. hath broken forth
upon *mine e.* 1 *Chr.* 14:11
22:4 saved from *m. e. Ps.* 18:3
38 pursued *mine e. Ps.* 18:37
41 heads of *m. e. Ps.* 18:40
49 bringeth me forth fr. *m. e.*
Ps. 3:7 hast smitten all *mine e.*
6:7 waxeth old bec. of *m. e.*
10 let all *mine e.* be ashamed
7:6 because of rage of *mine e.*
9:3 *m. e.* are turned
18:48 he deliv. me from *mine e.*
23:5 in presence of *mine e.*
27:2 let not *m. e.* triumph, 25:19
19 consider *m. e.* they are mn.
27:2 *m. e.* came to eat my flesh
6 head above *mine e.*
11 because of *mine e.*
12 deliv. me n. to will of *m. e.*
31:11 I was a reproach am. *m. e.*
15 from hand of *mine e.*

ENE

Ps. 38:19 but *mine e.* are lively
41:5 *mine e.* speak evil of me
42:10 *m. e.* reproach me, 102:8
54:5 shall reward evil to *m. e.*
7 desire upon *mine e.* 59:10
56:2 *m. e.* would swal. me up
Ps. 59:1 *m. e.* shall turn back
59:1 deliver me from *m. e.* 143:9
69:4 they being mine *e.*
18 deliver me, bec. of *mine e.*
71:10 *mine e.* speak against me
92:11 see desire on *mine e.*
119:98 wiser than *mine e.*
139 *m. e.* have forgotten
137 many are *mine e.*
138:7 forth thy hand ag. *m. e.*
139:22 I count them *mine e.*
143:12 cut off *mine e.*
Is. 1:24 avenge me of *mine e.*
Lam. 1:21 *m. e.* heard of my tro.
3:52 *m. e.* chased me like a bird
Luke 19:27 *m. e.* bring and slay

Our ENEMIES.
Deut. 32:31 *our e.* being judges
1 Sam. 4:3 save us from *our e.*
14:10 but deliver us from *our e.*
2 *Sam.* 19:9 saved us fr. *o. e. Ps.*
44:7
Ps. 44:5 push down *our e.*
60:12 tread *our e.* 108:13
80:6 *our e.* laugh am. themselves
136:24 redeemed us from *our e.*
Lam. 3:46 *o. e.* op. their mouths
Luke 1:71 be saved from *our e.*
74 being delivered from *our e.*

Their ENEMIES.
Lev. 26:36 in land of *their e.*
Jos. 7:8 turn. backs before *t. e.* 12
21:44 stood not a man of *th. e.*
23:1 rest from *t. e. Est.* 9:16
Jud. 2:14 into the hand of *t. e.*
16 deliv. them from *t. e.* 8:34
2 *K.* 17:31 sea overwhelmed *t. e.*
Ps. 78:53 sea overwhelmed *t. e.*
44:14 should scoff subdue *th. e.*
105:24 stronger than *their e.*
106:11 waters covered *their e.*
42 *their e.* oppressed *them*
Jer. 15:9 deliver to sw. bef. *t. e.*
19:7 fall before *their e.* 20:4
20:5 into the hand of *t. e.* 21:7;
34:20, 21; *Ezek.* 39:23
Ezek. 39:27 out of *their e.* hands
Amos 9:4 captivity before *th. e.*
Mic. 11:5 live devoureth *their e.*
12 *their e.* beheld them

Thine ENEMIES.
Gen. 14:20 del. *t. e.* into thy hand
Ex. 23:22 an enemy to *thine e.*
27 make *thine e.* to turn
Num. 10:35 let *thine e.* be scat.
Deut. 6:19 cast out all *thine e.*
20:1 *t. e.* shall distress, 28:53
33:29 *thine e.* be found liars
Jos. 7:13 not stand bef. *t. e.*
Jud. 5:31 so let *t. e.* perish
11:36 veng. for thee of *thine e.*
1 *Sam.* 25:29 souls of *th. e.* sling
2 *Sam.* 7:9 cut off *t. e.* 1 *Chr.* 17:8
24:13 three months before *t. e.*
1 *K.* 3:11 nor asked the life of
thine e. 2 *Chr.* 1:11
Ps. 8:2 because of *thine e.*
21 thy hand find out all *th. e.*
66:6 thy power *thine e.* submit
68:23 dipped in blood of *thine e.*
74:4 *t. e.* roar; 83:2 *t. e.* make t.
23 forget not the voice of *t. e.*
89:10 scattered *t. e.* with thy arm
51 wherewith *th. e.* reproached
92:9 *thine e.* O Lord, shall per.
110:1 *thine e.* thy foot-stool, *Mat.*
22:41; *Mark* 12:36; *Luke*
20:43; *Heb.* 1:13
2 in the midst of *thine e.*
132:20 *th. e.* take thy name in v.
Is. 26:11 fire of *t. e.* devour them
62:8 no in. give corn to *th. e.*
66:14 wrath be known with *t. e.*
Lam. 2:16 *th. e.* have opened th.
Dan. 4:19 interpreta. be to *th. e.*
Mic. 4:10 deli. thee from *thine e.*
5:9 all *thine e.* shall be cut off
Luke 19:43 *t. e.* shall cast trench

Your ENEMIES.
Lev. 26:7 ye shall chase *your e.*
8 *your e.* fall bef. you by sword
16 sow in vain, *y. e.* shall eat it
17 shall be slain bef. *your e.*

ENO

ENO
Lev. 26:37 to stand before your *e.*
Num. 10:9 be saved from your *e.*
11:42 before y. *e. Deut.* 1:42
Deut. 20:4 L. goeth to fight y. *e.*
23:9 ye shall be sold to y. *e.*
Jos. 10:25 shall Lord do to y. *e.*
1 *Sam.* 12:11 L. delivered you out of hand of y. *e.* 2 *K.* 17:39
Mat. 5:44 love y. *e. Luke* 6:27, 35

ENGAGED.
Jer. 30:21 who is this *e.* his heart

EN-GEDI.
Jos. 15:62 wilder. of Judah E.
1 *Sam.* 24:29 D. dwelt at E. 24:1
2 *Chr.* 20:2 Jehoshap. are in E.

ENGINES.
2 *Chr.* 26:15 Uzziah made *e.*
Ezek. 26:9 set *e.* of war ag. walls

ENGRAFTED.
Jam. 1:21 with meekness *e.* wo.

ENGRAVE, EN.
Zec. 3:9 I will *e.* graving thereof
2 *Cor.* 3:7 ministration of dea.

ENGRAVER.
Ex. 28:11 work of an *e.* in stone
33:24 Aholiab, an *e.*

ENJOIN, ED.
Job 36:23 hath *e.* him his way
Phile. 8 to *e.* what is convenient
Heb. 9:20 blood which G. hath *e.*

ENJOY, ED.
Lev. 26:34 land *e.* her sab. 43
Num. 36:8 Is. may *e.* inheritance
Deut. 28:41 beget sons, not *e.* th.
Jos. 1:15 ret. to land, and *e.* it
2 *Chr.* 36:21 till land *e.* sabbaths
Ec. 2:1 *e.* pleasure, this is vanity
24 his soul *e.* good, 3:13; 5:18
6. 6:5:22 elect long *e.* the work
Acts 24:2 we *e.* great quietness
1 *Tim.* 6:17 giv. all things to *e.*
Heb. 11:23 th. *e.* pleasures of sin

ENLARGE.
Gen. 9:27 God shall *e.* Japheth
Ex. 34:24 I will *e.* thy borders
1 *Chr.* 4:10 wouldst *e.* my coast
Ps. 119:32 shalt *e.* my heart
Is. 54:2 *e.* the place of thy tent
Amos 1:13 might *e.* their border
Mic. 1:16 *e.* thy baldness as eagle
Mat. 23:5 *e.* borders of garments

ENLARGED.
1 *Sam.* 2:1 mouth is *e.* over ena.
2 *Sam.* 22:37 *e.* steps, *Ps.* 19:36
Ps. 4:1 *e.* me when in distress
25:17 troubles of my heart are *e.*
Is. 5:14 hell *e.* herself
57:8 thou hast *e.* thy bed
63:5 heart shall fear and be *e.*
2 *Cor.* 6:11 O Cor. our heart is *e.*
13 for recompense, be ye also *e.*
10:15 that we shall be *e.* by you

ENLARGETH, ING.
Deut. 33:20 blessed be he *e.* Gad
Job 12:23 he *e.* the nations, and
Ezek. 41:7 and there was an *e.*
Hab. 2:5 who *e.* his desire as hell

ENLARGEMENT.
Est. 4:14 *e.* from another place

ENLIGHTEN, ED.
Ps. 18:28 L. will *e.* my darkness
1 *Sam.* 14:27 Jon.'s eyes were *e.*
Job 33:30 *e.* with light of living
Ps. 97:4 his lightnings *e.* world
Eph. 1:18 eyes of understand. *e.*
Heb. 6:4 impos. for those once *e.*

ENLIGHTENING.
Ps. 19:8 is pure, *e.* the eyes.

EN-MISHPAT. *Gen.* 14:7

ENMITY.
Gen. 3:15 I will put *e.* betw. thee
Num. 35:22 he thrust without *e.*
Luke 23:12 before they were at *e.*
Rom. 8:7 carnal mind is *e.* ag. G.
Eph. 2:15 abolished in his flesh *e.*
16 having, slain the *e.* thereby
Jam. 4:4 friendship of world is *e.*

ENOCH.
Gen. 4:17 bare E.
5:22 E. walked with God.
Luke 3:37 Mathus, was son of E.
Heb. 11:5 E. was translated
Jude 14 E. also prophesied
ENON. *John* 3:23

ENOS.
Gen. 4:26 call. his son's name E.
Luke 3:38 Cainan was son of E.

ENOUGH.
Gen. 33:9 Esau said, I have *e.*
11 take my blessing, I have *e.*
34:21 land is large *e.* for them

ENT

Gen. 45:28 it is *e. Jos.* is yet alive
Ex. 9:28 entreat Lord, for it is *e.*
36:5 bring much more than *e.*
Jos. 17:16 hill is not *e.* for us
2 *Sam.* 24:16 it is *e.* 1 *K.* 19:4;
1 *Chr.* 21:15; *Mark* 14:41;
Luke 22:38
2 *Chr.* 31:10 we have had *e.* to *e.*
Prov. 30:15 things say not, It is *e.*
16 fire that saith not, It is *e.*
Is. 56:11 can never have *e.*
Jer. 49:9 will destroy till have *e.*
Hos. 4:10 eat, and not have *e.*
Hag. 1:6 ye eat, but have not *e.*
Mal. 3:10 not room *e.* to rec. it
Mat. 10:25 *e.* for disciple to be
25:9 be not *e.* for us and you
Luke 15:17 servants have bread *e.*
ENQUIRE. *See* INQUIRE.

ENRICH, ED, EST.
1 *Sam.* 17:25 king will *e.* him
Ezek. 27:33 didst *e.* kings of earth
Ps. 65:9 *e.* it with river of God
1 *Cor.* 1:5 in everything ye are *e.*
2 *Cor.* 9:11 being *e.* in every th.

EN-ROGEL.
2 *Sam.* 17:17 Ahim. stayed by E.
1 *K.* 1:9 sheep and oxen by E.

ENSAMPLE.
Phil. 3:17 as ye have us for an *e.*
2 *Thes.* 3:9 to make oursel. an *e.*
2 *Pet.* 2:6 Sodom and Gomor. *e.*

ENSAMPLES.
1 *Cor.* 10:11 hap. to them for *e.*
1 *Thes.* 1:7 so that ye w. *e.* to all
1 *Pet.* 5:3 but being *e.* to the flo.

ENSIGN, S.
Ps. 74:4 set up their *e.* for signs
Is. 5:26 he will lift up an *e.*
11:10 stand for an *e.* to people
12 set up an *e.* for the nations
18:3 when he lifteth up an *e.*
30:17 till ye be left as *e.* on hill
31:9 his princes be afraid of *e.*
Zec. 9:16 lifted as an *e.*

ENSNARED.
Job 34:30 lest people be *e.*

ENSUE.
1 *Pet.* 3:11 seek peace, and *e.* it

ENTANGLE, ED, ETH.
Ex. 14:3 they are *e.* in the land
Mat. 22:15 how they might *e.* him
Gal. 5:1 be not *e.* with yoke
2 *Tim.* 2:4 *e.* him affairs of life
2 *Pet.* 2:20 they are again *e.*

ENTER.
Deut. 27:8 children shall *e.* cong.
23:12 stranger shall *e.* into covenant
J. Sam. 23:7 my cry did *e.* his *e.*
2 *K.* 7:4 if *e.* city, then famine
19:23 I will *e.* into the lodgings of his borders, *Is.* 37:24
Job 22:4 will he *e.* into judgm. ?
31:23 *e.* into judgment with God
Ps. 37:15 sword *e.* their heart
45:15 shall *e.* into king's palace
100:4 *e.* into gates with thanks.
118:20 gate into which right. *e.*
Prov. 18:6 fool's lips *e.* content.
Is. 2:10 *e.* into the rock
3:14 *e.* into judg. with ancients
26:2 righteous nation may *e.* in
20 *e.* thou into thy chambers
57:2 he shall *e.* into peace
Jer. 7:2 that *e.* gates, 17:20 ; 22:2
14:18 if I *e.* into the city, famine
17:25 shall *e.* gates, kings, 22:4
21:13 shall *e.* our habitations ?
42:15 if ye set faces toe. Egypt
Ezek. 7:22 robbers shall *e.* it
13:9 nor *e.* into land of Israel
20:10 as men *e.* into a city
37:5 cause breath to *e.* into you
44:2 gate shut, no man *e.* by it
16 shall *e.* into my sanctuary
Dan. 11:7 shall *e.* into fortress
24 he shall *e.* peaceably
40 he shall *e.* into the countries
41 he shall *e.* into glorious land
Joel 2:9 *e.* in at the windows
Amos 5:5 nor *e.* into Gilgal
Mat. 5:20 in no case *e.* into king.
6:6 prayest, *e.* into thy closet
7:13 *e.* in at str. gate, *Luke* 13:24
21 shall *e.* kingd. of God, 18:3;
10:11 city ye *e. Luke* 10:8, 10
12:29 *e.* str. man's *h. Mark* 3:27
45 *e.* in dwell there, *Luke* 11:26
18:8 it is better to *e.* into life halt, 9; *Mark* 9:43, 45, 47
19:17 if thou wilt *e.* into life
24 rich man to *e.* into kingdom, *Mark* 10:25; *Luke* 18:25

ENT

Mat. 23:21 *e.* into joy of thy Lord
Mark 1:45 no more openly *e.* city
5:12 *e.* into swine, *Luke* 8:33
6:10 house ye *e. Luke* 9:4; 10:5
9:25 and *e.* no more into him
14:38 *e.* into tempt. *Luke* 22:46
Luke 8:16 which *e.* in may see
13:24 many will seek to *e.* in
24:26 and fo *e.* into his glory ?
John 3:4 can he *e.* into womb
5 he cannot *e.* into king. of G.
Acts 14:22 through tribulation *e.*
20.29 grievous wolves shall *e.* in
Heb. 4:3 *e.* into rest, if *e.* rest, 5
6 remaineth, some must *e.*
11 let us labor to *e.* that rest
10:19 *e.* holiest by blood of Jes.
Rev. 15:8 no man able to *e.* tem.
21:27 in no wise *e.* that defileth
22:14 *e.* in thro. gates into city

ENTER not.
Ps. 143:2 *e. not* into judgment
Prov. 4:14 *e. not* path of wicked
23:10 *e. not* fields of fatherless
Jer. 16:5 *e. not* house of mourn.
Mat. 10:5 any city of Samar. *e. n.*
26:41 *e. n.* into temp. *Luke* 22:40

Not ENTER.
Num. 20:24 Aaron *not e.* into la.
2 *Chr.* 7:2 priests could *not e.* h.
Ps. 95:11 should *not e.* my rest
Is. 59:14 and equity cannot *e.*
Lam. 1:10 should *not e.* congreg.
Ezek. 20:38 they shall *not e.* land
4:13 nor uncircumcised *e.* sanct.
Rom. 11:9 *not e.* into city
Mat. 18:3 *not e.* king. of heaven
19:23 rich man *not e.* kingdom
Heb. 3:11 *not e.* into my rest, 18
19 *not e.* because of unbelief
See KINGDOM.

ENTERED,
1 *Chr.* 13:12 *e.* into co. to seek L.
27:2 Jotham *e.* not temple of L.
Job 38:16 *e.* into springs of sea ?
22 *e.* into treas. of the snow?
Jer. 2:7 but when ye *e.* ye defiled
9:21 death is *e.* into our palaces
34:10 which had *e.* into coven.
Lam. 1:10 heath. *e.* her sanctuary
4:12 enemy should have *e.* gates
16:8 *e.* into a cove. with thee
34:20 they *e.* unto heathen
44:2 God of Isr. hath *e.* in by it
Ob. 11 foreigners *e.* his gates
Hab. 3:16 rottenness *e.* my bones
Mat. 12:4 he *e.* the house of God
24:38 Noah *e.* ark, *Luke* 17:27
Mark 6:56 whith. he *e.* laid sick
Luke 1:40 Mary *e.* ho. of Zachar.
7:44 I *e.* thy house, thou gavest
9:34 they feared as they *e.* cloud
11:52 lawyers, ye *e.* not, them
22:3 *e.* Satan into J. *John* 13:27
John 4:38 others *e.* into lab.
10 are *e.* city, there shall meet
John 4:38 others *e.* into their labors
18:1 a garden, into which he *e.*
33 then Pilate *e.* judgment-hall
Acts 11:8 nothing uncl. *e.* mouth
Rom. 5:12 sin *e.* ; 20 law *e.*
1 *Cor.* 2:9 nor have *e.* heart of m.
Heb. 4:6 *e.* not bec. of unbelief
10 for he that is *e.* into his rest
6:20 forerunner is for us *e.*
9:12 he *e.* once holy place, 24
Jam. 5:4 *e.* ears of L. of Sabaoth
2 *John* 7 many deceivers are *e.*
Rev. 11:11 S. of life *e.* into them

ENTERETH.
Prov. 2:10 wisdom *e.* heart
17:10 a reproof *e.* more into wise
Mat. 15:17 whatsoever *e.* in at the mouth, *Mark* 7:18
Mark 5:40 *e.* where damsel was
Luke 22:10 fol. into house he *e.*
John 10:1 *e.* not by door into fold
2 *e.* in by door, is the sheph.
Heb. 6:19 *e.* into that within veil
9:25 as high-priest *e.* every year

ENTERING.
Gen. 26:14 Philistines *e.* Isaac
30:11 Rachel *e.* her sister
Jos. 8:35 Joseph's brethren *e.* him
Ps. 105:18 they *e.* Moses also
Mat. 4:4 a man is *e.* of neighbor
Ezek. 31:9 trees in garden *e.* him

ENVIES.
1 *Pet.* 2:1 laying aside malice, *e.*

ENVIEST, ETH.
Num. 11:29 *e.* thou for my sake ?
1 *Cor.* 13:4 charity *e.* not

ENV

ENTERPRISE.
Job 5:12 hands cannot perform *e.*

ENTERTAIN.
Heb. 13:2 not forgetful to *e.* stran.

ENTICE.
Ex. 22:16 if a man *e.* a maid
Deut. 13:6 wife *e.* thee secretly
Jud. 14:15 *e.* thy husband
16:5 said to Delilah, *e.* him
2 *Chr.* 18:19 who shall *e.* Ahab ?
20 I will *e.* him ; 21 sh. *e.* him
Prov. 1:10 if sinners *e.* cons. not

ENTICED, ETH.
Job 31:27 if heart been secretly *e.*
Prov. 16:29 a viol. man *e.* neigh.
Jer. 20:10 peradvent. he will be *e.*
Jam. 1:14 is tempted when *e.*

ENTICING words.
1 *Cor.* 2:4 preaching not w. *e. w.*
Col. 2:4 any beguile with *e. w.*

ENTIRE.
Jam. 1:4 that ye be per. and *e.*

ENTRANCE.
Jud. 1:24 show us *e.* into city
Ps. 119:130 *e.* of word giv. light
1 *Thes.* 2:1 yourself, know our *e.*
2 *Pet.* 1:11 so an *e.* be ministered

ENTREAT.
Ex. 8:8 P. called for Moses, and said *e.* L. 28; 9:28; 10:17
9 when shall I *e.* for thee
29 I will *e.* Lord that swarms
Ruth 1:16 *e.* me not to leave thee
1 *Sam.* 2:25 man sin, who sh. *e.* ?
1 *K.* 13:6 *e.* the face of L. thy G.
Prov. 19:6 many will *e.* favor
Jer. 15:11 cause enemy *e.* thee
Acts 7:6 should *e.* them evil
1 *Cor.* 4:13 being defamed, we *e.*
Phil. 4:3 I *e.* thee also, y.-fellow
1 *Tim.* 5:1 but *e.* him as a father

ENTREATED.
Gen. 12:16 he *e.* Abraham well
23:21 I *e.* for his wife, L. was *e.*
Ex. 5:22 why hast evil *e.* peo. ?
8:30 Moses went and *e.* L. 12:16
Deut. 26:6 Egyptians evil *e.* us
1 *Sam.* 24:25 *e.* L. was *e.* for the la.
Ezr. 8:23 sought G. and was *e.*
Job 19:16 *e.* him with my mouth
17 I *e.* for children's sake
Ps. 119:58 *e.* thy favor
Is. 19:22 he shall be *e.* of them
Mat. 22:6 *e.* spiteful, *Luke* 18:32
Luke 15:28 his father, *e.* him
20:11 *e.* him shamefully
1 *Thes.* 2:2 we were shameful. *e.*
Heb. 12:19 *e.* word not be spoken
Jam. 3:17 wisd. is easy to be *e.*

ENTREATETH.
Job 24:21 he evil *e.* the barren

ENTREATIES.
Prov. 18:23 poor useth *e.* but rich
2 *Cor.* 8:1 pray. us with much *e.*

ENTRY.
Prov. 8:3 wis. crieth at *e.* of city
Ezek. 8:5 behold at the *e.*
40:15 *e.* before little chamber
Jer. 19:2 *e.* of east gate
26:10 sat in *e.* new gate
43:9 hide stones in *e.* P's house

ENVY, Substantive.
Job 5:2 *e.* slayeth the silly one
Prov. 14:30 *e.* is rottenness of bones
27:4 who able to stand bef. *e. ?*
Ec. 9:6 hatred and *e.* is perished
Is. 11:13 *e.* of Ephraim shall dep.
26:11 be ashamed for their *e.*
Mat. 27:18 for *e. Mark* 15:10
Acts 7:9 patriarchs mov. with *e.*
13:45 Jews filled with *e.* spake
17:5 the Jews moved with *e.*
19:30 full of *e.* murder
Phil. 1:15 prea. Christ even of *e.*
1 *Tim.* 6:4 whereof cometh *e.*
Tit. 3:3 living in malice and *e.*
Jam. 4:5 spirit in us lusteth to *e.*

ENVY, Verb.
Prov. 3:31 *e.* not the oppressor
23:17 let not heart *e.* sinners
Is. 11:13 Ephraim sh. not *e.* Jud.

ENVIED.
Gen. 26:14 Philistines *e.* Isaac
30:1 Rachel *e.* her sister
Ps. 106:16 they *e.* Moses also
Ec. 4:4 a man is *e.* of neighbor
Ezek. 31:9 trees in garden *e.* him

ENVIES.
1 *Pet.* 2:1 laying aside malice, *e.*

ENVIEST, ETH.
Num. 11:29 *e.* thou for my sake ?
1 *Cor.* 13:4 charity *e.* not

CRUDEN'S CONCORDANCE. 839

EPI
ENVYING.
Rom. 13:13 lot as walk, not in *e*.
1 Cor. 3:3 for whereas there is *e*.
Gal. 5:26 *e*. one another
Jam. 3:14 but if ye have bitter *e*.
16 where *e*. is, is confusion
ENVYINGS.
2 Cor. 12:20 I fear lest there be *e*.
Gal. 5:21 wor. of the flesh are *e*.
ENVIOUS.
Ps. 37:1 *e*. aga. workers of iniq.
73:3 for I was *e*. at the foolish
Prov. 24:1 be not *e*. ag. evil men
19 neither be *e*. at the wicked
ENVIRON.
Jos. 7:9 Canaanites *e*. us round
EPAPHRAS.
Col. 1:7 as ye learned of E. our
4:12 E. saluteth you, Phile. 23
EPAPHRODITUS.
Phil. 2:25 send to you E. 4:18
EPENETUS. Rom. 16:5
EPHAH.
Lev. 19:36 a just *e*. Ezek. 45:10
Is. 5:10 seed of homer yield an *e*.
Amos 8:5 making the *e*. small
Zec. 5:8 and be cast it into the *e*.
EPHAH. Gen. 25:4; 1 Chr. 1:33; 2:46, 47; Is. 60:6
EPHES-DAMMIM. 1 Sam. 17:1
EPHESIANS. Acts 19:28, 34, 35
EPHESUS.
Acts 18:19 P. came to E. 21; 19:17
1 Cor. 15:32 fought with be. at E.
2 Tim. 1:18 minis. to me at E.
Rev. 1:11 to E.; 2:1 angel at E.
EPHOD.
Ex. 28:4 they shall make an *e*. 6
Lev. 8:7 he put the *e*. upon him
Jud. 8:27 Gideon made an *e*.
17:5 the man Micah made an *e*.
1 Sam. 2:18 Samuel gird. with *e*.
2:19 David said, Bring *e*. 30:7
2 Sam. 6:14 D. was girded with linen *e*. 1 Chr. 15:27
Hos. 3:4 many days without *e*.
EPHPHATHA. Mark 7:34
EPHRAIM, a place,
2 Sam. 13:23 sheepsh. beside E.
2 Chr. 13:19 A. took E. and tow.
John 11:54 into city called E.
Mount EPHRAIM.
Jos. 17:15 if m *e*. E. be too narrow
Jud. 2:9 buried Joshua in m. E.
7:24 through mount E. 17:1, 8
1 Sam. 1:1 of m. E. 2 Sam. 20:21
9:4 Saul passed through mo. E.
2 K. 5:22 two men co. fr. m. E.
Jer. 31:6 upon m. E. 50:19
EPHRAIM, a person or people.
Gen. 41:52 Jos's. son was E.
48:14 right hand on E. head, 20
Num. 1:10 the prince of E. 7:48
2:18 shall be the standard of E.
Deut. 33:17 ten thousands of E.
Jud. 5:14 out of E. was a root
12:4 Jephthah fought with E.
1 Chr. 7:22 E. their fath. mourn.
2 Chr. 17:2 garrisons in E. 25:10
30:18 E. not clea.; 31:1 images
Ps. 60:2 before E. stir up stren.
Is. 7:8, 9, 17; 9:9, 21; 11:13; 28:1
Jer. 7:15 cast out wh. seed of E.
Ezek. 37:16 stick of E. 19; 48:5
Hos. 5:3, 5, 9, 13, 11; 6:10; 7:1, 8
8:9 E. hired lov.; 11 E. is vain,
9:3, 8; 10:6, 11; 11:8, 9, 12
12:8 E. say, Wh. to do with id, ?
Zec. 9:10 chariot from E. 13
EPHRAIM is.
Ps. 60:7; Jer. 31:9, 20; Hos. 4:17
Hos. 7:11 E. silly d. ; 10:11 heifer
EPHRAIM, with tribe.
Num. 1:33 nu. of E. 13:8; 33:24
Jos. 16:8 inheritance of E. 24:5
Ps. 78:67 chose not tribe of E.
EPHRAIMITE, S. Jud. 12:5, 6
EPHRATAH.
Ruth 4:11 worthily in E.
1 Chr. 2:50 first born of E. 4:4
Ps. 132:6 we heard of it at E.
Mic. 5:2 Beth-lehem E. tho' little
EPHRATH. Gen. 35:16, 19; 48:7; 1 Chr. 2:19
EPHRATHITE, S. Ruth 1:2; 1 Sam. 1:1; 17:12; 1 K. 11:26
EPHRON. Gen. 23:8, 16; 25:9; 49:30; 50:13
EPICUREANS. Acts 17:18
EPISTLE.
Acts 15:30 they deliv. *e*. 23:33

ERR
Rom. 16:22 I Tert. who wrote *e*.
1 Cor. 5:9 I wrote to you in an *e*.
2 Cor. 3:2 ye are our *e*. written
3 declared to be *e*. of Christ
7:8 the same *e*. made you sorry
Col. 4:16 wh. this *e*. is read, likewise read *e*. from Laodicea
1 Thes. 5:27 this *e*. be read to all
2 Thes. 2:15 taught by word or *e*.
3:14 if obey not word by this *e*.
17 which is the tok. in every *e*.
2 Pet. 3:1 this sec. *e*. I now write
EPISTLES.
2 Cor. 3:1 or need *e*. of commen.
2 Pet. 3:16 as in all his *e*. speak.
EQUAL.
Ps. 17:2 eyes behold things *e*.
55:13 but it was thou, mine *e*.
Prov. 26:7 legs of lame are not *e*.
Is. 40:25 to wh. sh. I be *e*. ? 46:5
Lam. 2:13 *e*. to thee, O virgin
Ezek. 18:25 The way of the Lord is not *e*. 29; 33:17, 20
29 O Isr. are not my ways *e*. ?
33:17 their way is not *e*.
Mat. 20:12 hast made them *e*.
Luke 20:36 are *e*. unto angels
John 5:18 himself *e*. with God
Col. 4:1 gave servants what is *e*.
Rev. 21:16 breadth and height *e*.
EQUAL, Verb.
Job 28:17 gold and crystal not *e*.
19 topaz of Ethi. shall not *e*. it
EQUALITY.
2 Cor. 8:14 by an *e*. may be an *e*.
EQUALS.
Gal. 1:14 I profited above my *e*.
EQUITY.
Ps. 98:9 he shall judge with *e*.
99:4 thou dost establish *e*.
Prov. 1:3 to rec. instruction of *e*.
2:9 shalt thou understand *e*.
17:26 to strike princes for *e*.
Ec. 2:21 whose labor is in *e*.
Is. 11:4 repr. with *e*. for meek
59:14 and *e*. cannot enter
Mic. 3:9 ye that pervert all *e*.
Mal. 2:6 walked with me in *e*.
ER. Gen. 38:3, 7; 1 Chr. 2:3; 4:21; Luke 3:28
ERASTUS.
Acts 19:22 sent Timoth. and E.
2 Tim. 4:20 E. abode at Corinth
ERRAND.
Gen. 24:33 I have told mine *e*.
Jud. 3:19 I have a secret *e*.
2 K. 9:5 an *e*. to thee, O captain
ERR.
2 Chr. 33:9 M. made Judah to *e*.
Ps. 95:10 do *e*. in their heart
119:21 which do *e*. from thy
118 hast trodden them that *e*.
Prov. 14:22 not *e*. that dev. evil?
19:27 instruc. that causeth to *e*.
Is. 3:12 they wh. lead thee cause thee to *e*. 9:16
19:14 have caused Egypt to *e*.
28:7 they *e*. in vision
30:28 a bridle caus. them to *e*.
35:8 wayfaring men shall not *e*.
63:17 hast thou made us to *e*.
Jer. 23:13 by their prophets caused Israel to *e*. 32; Mic. 3:5
Hos. 4:12 whoredoms caused to *e*.
Amos 2:4 lies have caused to *e*.
Mat. 22:29 ye do *e*. not know. the scriptures; Mark. 12:24, 27
Heb. 3:10 in their hearts
Jam. 1:16 do not *e*. my beloved 5:19 if any *e*. from the truth
ERRED.
Lev. 5:18 ignor. wherein he *e*.
1 Sam. 26:21 have *e*. exceedingly
Job 6:24 wherein I have *e*.
19:4 indeed that I have *e*.
Ps. 119:110 I *e*. not from thy pre.
Is. 28:7 have *e*. thro' wine, priest and prophet have *e*.
27:31 that *e*. in spirit shall come
1 Tim. 6:10 have *e*. from the faith
21 some have *e*. concern. faith
2 Tim. 2:18 concern. tru. have *e*.
ERRETH.
Prov. 10:17 refuseth reproof *e*.
Ezek. 45:20 for every one that *e*.

ESC
Mat. 27:64 last *e*. worse than first
Rom. 1:27 recompense of their *e*.
Jam. 5:20 from the *e*. of his way
2 Pet. 2:18 them who live in *e*.
3:17 led away with *e*. of wicked
1 John 4:6 know we spirit of *e*.
Jude 11 after the *e*. of Balaam
ERRORS.
Ps. 19:12 can understand his *e*. ?
Jer. 10:15 the work of *e*. 51:18
Heb. 9:7 he offer. for *e*. of people
ESAIAS. See ISAIAH.
ESAR-HADDON. 2 K. 19:37; Ezr. 4:2; Is. 37:38
ESAU.
Gen. 25:25 his name E. 27, 29
27:11 E. is a hairy m. 21, 24, 42
32:3 sent messengers to E. 11, 18
33:4 E. ran to meet him, 8; 35:1
36:1 genera. of E.; 43 fa. of E.
Deut. 2:5 mt. S. to E. Jos. 24:4
Jer. 49:10 I have made E. bare
Ob. 6 E. searched out, 18:21
Mal. 1:2 E. J 's br. ? 3; Rom. 9:13
Heb. 11:20 Isaac blessed E.
12:16 profane person as E.
ESCAPE, Substantive.
Ps. 55:8 hasten my *e*. from storm
ESCAPE, Verb.
Gen. 19:17 *e*. to the mountain
20 Oh let me *e*.; 22 *e*. thither
1 Sam. 27:1 *e*. to land of Philist.
2 Sam. 15:14 let us flee, not else *e*.
1 K. 16:40 let none *e*. 2 K. 9:15
2 K. 10:24 if any of the men *e*.
10:31 *e*. out of Zion. Jo. 37:32
Ezr. 9:8 to leave a remnant to *e*.
Est. 4:13 think not thou shalt *e*.
Job 11:20 the wicked shall not *e*.
Ps. 55:7 shall I bring; by iniq. ?
71:2 and cause me to *e*.
141:10 wicked fall, whilst I *e*.
Prov. 19:5 speak. lies, shall not *e*.
Ez. 7:26 pleaseth God shall *e*.
Is. 20:6 and how shall we *e*.
66:19 those that *e*. to the nati.
Jer. 11:11 evil not be able to *e*.
25:35 nor princip. of the flock *e*.
32:4 Zed. not *e*. 34:3; 38:18, 23
Ezek. 6:9 *e*. out Zion. Jo. 37:32
Dan. 11:41 *e*. out of his hand
42 the land of Egypt sh. not *e*.
Joel 2:3 nothing shall *e*. them
Ob. 14 cut off those that did *e*.
Mal. 3:32 *e*. Amalek, in land of hell?
Luke 21:36 account, worthy to *e*.
Acts 27:42 kill prisoners, lest any *e*.
Rom. 2:3 shalt *e*. judg. of God ?
1 Thes. 5:3 and they shall not *e*.
Heb. 2:3 how sh. *e*. if we neglect
12:25 much more shall not we *e*.
ESCAPED.
Gen. 14:13 there came one had *e*.
Num. 21:29 sons that *e*. into cap.
Deut. 23:15 not deliver servant *e*.
Jos. 8:22 not, 1 Sam. 30:17
21:17 inherit. for them that *e*.
2 Sam. 1:3 I *e*. ; 4:10 I am *e*.
19:10 D. fled and *e*. that night
2 Sam. 4:1 *e*. out of the ca. am. 1 e.
4:5 and Barlab and Isaiah *e*.
1 K. 20:20 Ben-hadad the king *e*.
2 K. 19:30 remnant *e*. of Judah shall take root, Is. 37:31
Est. 9:1 did not return to us that I *e*.
Job 1:15 I only am *e*. 16, 17, 19
19:20 with the sk. of my teeth
Ps. 124:7 our soul is *e*. as a bird
Is. 4:2 comely for them *e*.
10:20 and such as are *e*. of Jacob
45:20 draw near, ye that are *e*.
Jer. 51:50 have *e*. rem. l, akir off
Ezek. 17:27 opened to him *e*.
33:21 one that had *e*. came
John 10:39 *e*. out of their hands
Acts 27:44 so they *e*. all safe
28:4 tho' *e*. the sea, yet ven.
2 Cor. 11:33 I was let down and *e*.

EST
Heb. 11:34 through faith *e*.
12:25 if *e*. not who refused him
2 Pet. 1:4 *e*. corruption in world
2:18 those that were risen *e*.
20 *e*. the pollutions of world
ESCAPETH.
1 K. 19:17 that *e*. swo. of Hazael shall Jehu slay; that *e*. Jehu
Job 15:30 bring flame upon him *e*.
Jer. 48:19 ask her *e*. Wh. is done ?
Ezek. 24:26 *e*. sh. come unto thee
Amos 9:1 he that *e*. not be deliv.
ESCAPING.
Ezr. 9:14 there should be no *e*.
ESCHEW.
1 Pet. 3:11 let him *e*. evil, do good
ESCHEWED, ETH.
Job 1:1 feared God, *e*. evil, 8; 2:3
ESEK. Gen. 26:20
ESHCOL.
Gen. 14:13 M. brother of E. 24
Num. 13:24 place called brook E.
32:9 went up unto valley of E.
ESLI. Luke 3:25
ESPECIALLY.
Ps. 31:21 *e*. am. my neighbors
Acts 25:26 *e*. before thee, O king
Gal. 6:10 *e*. the househ. of faith
1 Tim. 4:10 *e*. of tho. that believe
5:8 prov. *e*. for them of his own
17 *e*. they who labor in word
2 Tim. 4:13 but *e*. the parchments
Phile. 16 a brother beloved *e*.
ESPOUSALS.
Cant. 3:11 crowned in day of *e*.
Jer. 2:2 I remem. love of thine *e*.
ESPOUSED.
2 Sam. 3:14 deliv. me Michal I *e*.
Mat. 1:18 when Mary was *e*. to J.
Luke 1:27 to a virgin *e*. to a man
2 Cor. 11:2 *e*. you to one husband
ESPY.
Jos. 14:7 Moses sent me to *e*.
See SPY, SPIED.
ESROM. Mat. 1:3; Luke 3:33
ESTABLISH.
Gen. 6:18 will I *e*. cov. 9:9; 17:7;
Lev. 26:9; Ezek. 16:62
17:19 I will *e*. my covenant, 21
Deut. 8:18 that he may *e*. his cov.
29:9 L. shall *e*. thee a holy peo.
28:15 he may *e*. thee for a peo.
1 Sam. 1:23 L. *e*. 2 Sam. 7:25
2 Sam. 7:13 I *e*. his kingdom, 14; I and to *e*. ; 14:17; 22:16; 56
1 K. 9:5*e*. throne of thy kingdom
15:4 and to *e*. Jerusalem
1 Chr. 17:12 *e*. his throne for ever
22:10 *e*. 18 will I *e*. throne
28:7 God loved Israel to *e*. them
Job 36:7 doth *e*. them for ever
Ps. 7:9 *e*. Just; 48:8 G. will *e*. it
87:5 the Highest shall *e*. her
89:2 faithfulness shalt *e*.
4 thy seed will I *e*. for ever
90:17 *e*. work of our hands, *e*.
99:1 thou dost *e*. equity, thou
119:38 *e*. thy word to thy serv.
Prov. 15:25 *e*. border of the wid.
Is. 49:7 to *e*. it, with judgment
02:7 till he *e*. and make Jerus.
Jer. 33:2 that formed it, to re. *e*.
Ezek. 16:60 will *e*. an everla. cov.
Dan. 6:7 consult, to *e*. royal stat.
11:14 exalt thems. to *e*. vision
Amos 5:15 *e*. judgm. in the gate
Rom. 3:31 yen, we *e*. the law
10:3 going about to *e*. own
10:25 power to *e*. you
1 Thes. 3:2 sent Tim. to *e*. you
13 *e*. your hearts unblame able
2 Thes. 2:17 *e*. you in ev. g. word
3:3 Lord shall *e*. you, and keep
Heb. 10:9 that he may *e*. second
Jam. 5:8 patient, *e*. your hearts
1 Pet. 5:10 the God of all grace *e*.
ESTABLISHED.
Gen. 9:17 token of covenant I *e*.
41:32 because thin. Is *e*. by God
42:20 made and *e*. thee ?
1 Sam. 3:20 S. was *e*. a prophet
13:13 would t. *e*. thy kingdom
20:31 thou shalt not be *e*. nor
2 Sam. 5:12 Lord had *e*. Dav. set
7:26 let the house of thy servant David be *e*. 1 Chr. 17:21
1 K. 2:12 king. was *e*. greatly
1 Chr. 17:24 let thing be *e*.
2 Chr. 1:9 L. let thy promise be *e*.
Job 21:8 seed is *e*. in their sight

CRUDEN'S CONCORDANCE. 841

EVE

Ps. 146:6 L. keepeth truth *f. e.*
10 the Lord shall reign *for e.*
Prov. 27:24 riches are not *for e.*
Ec. 2:16 no rem. of wise *for e.*
3:14 God doeth, shall be *for e.*
9:6 nor any more a portion *f. e.*
Is. 26:4 trust ye in Lord *for e.*
32:17 quietness and assu. *for e.*
34:10 smoke thereof go up *f. e.*
17 they shall possess it *for e.*
42:8 word of O. shall stand *f. e.*
51:6 my salvation shall be *for e.*
8 my righteousness be *for e.*
57:16 I will not contend *for e.*
60:21 my words not depart *f. e.*
60:21 thy peo. inherit land *f. e.*
64:9 nor remember iniquity *f. e.*
65:18 be glad and rejoice *for e.*
Jer. 3:5 he reserve anger *for e.*
12 I will not keep anger *for e.*
17:4 fire which shall burn *for e.*
25 J. and this city remain *f. e.*
31:40 plucked up any more *f. e.*
32:39 they may fear me *for e.*
Lam. 3:31 will not cast off *for e.*
5:19 thou, O L. remainest *for e.*
20 wherefore forget us *for e.?*
Ezek. 37:25 be their prince *for e.*
43:7 in midst of I-rael *for e.* 9
Dan. 2:44 his kingdom stand *f. e.*
4:34 praised him that liveth *f. e.*
6:26 G. of Daniel, steadfast *f. e.*
7:18 saints possess kingdom *f. e.*
12:7 sw. by him that liveth *f. e.*
Joel 3:20 Judah shall dwell *for e.*
Ob. 10 shalt be cut off *for e.*
Mic. 2:9 tak. away my glory *f. e.*
4:7 Lord reign over them *for e.*
7:18 retaineth not anger *for e.*
Mat. 1:1 L. hath indignation *f. e.*
Mat. 6:13 power and glory *for e.*
Luke 1:33 reign over Jacob *for e.*
55 spake to Ab. and seed *f. e.*
John 6:35 serv. abideth not *f. e.*
12:34 that Christ abideth *for e.*
Rom. 1:25 Creator, blessed *for e.*
9:5 over all, God blessed *for e.*
11:36 be glory *for e.* 16:27
2 Cor. 9:9 righte. remaineth *f. e.*
Phile. 15 shouldst rec. him *for e.*
Heb. 10:12 *for e.* sat down
11 perfected *f. e.* them sancti.
13:8 J. C. same to-day and *f. e.*
1 Pet. 1:23 which liveth *for e.*
25 word of Lord endureth *f. e.*
2 John 2 be with us *for e.*

Live for EVER.
Gen. 3:22 tree of life and l. *for e.*
Deut. 32:40 and say, I *live for e.*
1 K. 1:31 let king David *l. for e.*
Ps. 22:26 heart shall *live for e.*
49:9 should still *live for e.*
Dan. 2:4 O king *live for e.* 3:9;
5:10; 6:6, 21
Zec. 1:5 prophets, do they l. *for e.*
John 6:51 if any man eat of this
bread, he shall *l. for e.* 58

For EVER and EVER.
Ex. 15:18 reign *for e. and e.*
1 Chr. 16:36 blessed be God *for e. and e.* 29:10; Dan. 2:20
Neh. 9:5 bless your G. *for e. and e.*
Ps. 9:5 their name *for e. and e.*
10:16 Lord is king *for e. and e.*
21:4 length of days *for e. and e.*
45:6 thy throne, O G. is *for e.*
17 praise thee *for e. and e.*
48:14 this G. is our God *for e. a.*
52:8 I trust in mercy of G. *f. e. a.*
111:8 stand fast *for e. and e.*
119:44 I keep thy law *for e. a. e.*
145:1 bless thy name *for e. a. e.*
2 thy name *for e. and e.* 21
148:6 stablish. them *fore. and e.*
Is. 30:8 be for time to come *for e.*
34:10 none pass thro' it *for e. a.*
Jer. 7:7 land I gave *for e. and e.*
25:5 to you and fathers *for e. a.*
Dan. 7:18 pos. kingdom *f. e. a. e.*
12:3 as the stars *for e. and e.*
Mic. 4:5 in name of God *f. e. a. e.*
Gal. 1:5 glory *for e. and e.* Phil.
4:20; 1 Tim. 1:17; 2 Tim.
4:18; Heb. 13:21
Heb. 1:8 throne O G., is *for e. a. e.*
Rev. 4:9 who liveth *for e. a. e.* 10;
5:14; 10:6; 15:7
5:13 honor be to L. *for e. and e.*
7:12 power be to our G. *f. e. a. e.*
11:15 G. shall reign *for e. and e.*
20:10 be tormented *for e. and e.*
22:5 shall reign *for e. and e.*

EVERLASTING.
Gen. 17:8 an e. possession, 48:4
21:33 the e. God, Is. 40:28; Rom.
16:26

EVE

Gen. 40:26 bound of the e. hills
Ex. 40:15 e. priesth. Num. 25:13
Deut. 33:27 underm. are e. arms
Ps. 24:7 e. doors, 9; 100:5 mercy e.
112:6 righte. in e. remembrance
119:142 thy righteousn. is e. 144
139:24 lead me in the way e.
145:13 kingd. is an e. kingdom,
Dan. 4:3; 7:27; 2 Pet. 1:11
Prov. 10:25 an e. foundation
Is. 26:6 be called, the e. Father
26:4 in L. Jehov. is e. strength
33:14 dwell with e. burnings?
35:10 with e. joy, 51:11; 61:7
45:17 e. salva. ; 54:8 e. kindness
55:13 e. sign; 56:5 e. na. 63:12
60:19 L. be to thee an e. lig. 20
Jer. 10:10 e. king; 20:11 e. confu.
23:40 bring an e. reproach on y.
31:3 loved thee with an e. love
Dan. 4:34 is an e. dominion, 7:14
Hab. 3:6 e. mountains scattered
Mat. 18:8 cast into e. fire, 25:41
25:46 go into e. punishment
Luke 16:9 into e. habitations
2 Thes. 1:9 pun. with e. destruc.
2:16 hath given us e. consolation
1 Tim. 6:16 to honor and pow. e.
Jude 6 the angels res. in e. cha.
Rev. 14:6 the e. gospel to preach
See COVENANT.

From EVERLASTING.
Ps. 14:31 bles. be G. *f. e.* 106:48
90:2 *from e.* to e. thou art God
93:2 throne of God, *from e.*
103:17 mercy of the L. is *f. e.*
Prov. 8:23 I was set up *from e.*
Is. 63:16 O, L. thy name is *f. e.*
Mic. 5:2 whose goings forth *f. e.*
Hab. 1:12 art thou not *f. e.* O L.

EVERLASTING life.
Dan. 12:2 awake, some to e. *life*
Mat. 19:29 shall inherit e. *life*
Luke 18:30 world to come e. *life*
John 3:16 believeth, have e. *l.* 36
4:14 water springing up to e. *l.*
5:24 heareth my words hath e. *l.*
6:27 which endureth to e. *life*
40 the Son, may have e. *life*
47 believeth on me hath e. *life*
12:50 commandment is *life e.*
Acts 13:46 unworthy of e. *life*
Rom. 6:22 ye have the end, e. *l.*
1 Tim. 6:19 hereafter bel. to e. *l.*

EVERMORE.
2 Sam. 22:51 mercy unto Dav. e.
1 Chr. 17:14 throne he estab. e.
Ps. 16:11 are pleasures *for e.*
18:50 mercy to his seed *for e.*
37:27 do good, and dwell *for e.*
77:8 doth his promise fail *for e.?*
86:12 will glorify thy na. *for e.*
89:28 mercy keep *for* him *for e.*
52 blessed be the L. *for e.* am.
92:8 Lord, art most high *for e.*
105:4 seek Lord, seek his face e.
106:31 counted for righte. *for e.*
113:2 blessed be the L. *for e.*
115:18 will bless the Lord *for e.*
114:6 L. preser. thy going out e.
122:12 sit upon thy throne *for e.*
133:3 Lord command. life *for e.*
John 6:34 e. give us this bread
2 Cor. 13:11 Father blessed *for e.*
1 Thes. 5:16 rejoice e.
Heb. 7:28 who is consecra. *for e.*
Rev. 1:18 behold, I am alive *for e.*

EVERY.
Gen. 6:5 e. imagination was evil
Is. 139:16I refrained *for e.* evil
104:I have e. false way, 128
Prov. 15:3 eyes of L. are in e. pl.
30:5 e. word of God is pure
Is. 45:23 e. knee, Rom. 14:11
Mat. 4:4 by e. word that proc.
1 Cor. 4:17 as I teach e. wh. In e.
2 Cor. 10:5 into captiv. e. thong.
Eph. 1:21 abo. e. na. Phil. 2:9
2 Tim. 2:21 prep. to e. good work
Heb. 12:1 lay aside e. weight
Jam. 1:17 e. good and perf. gift
1 John 4:1 believe not e. spirit

See BEAST, CITY, DAY, MAN,
MORNING, WAY, SIDE, THING.

EVERY one.
Num. 16:3 cong. are holy e. one
Ex. 12:3 ye are alive e. one of y.
1 K. 22:28 hearken e. one of you
2 Chr. 36:18 Lord had pardon e. one
Ps. 71:18 thy power to e. one
118:8 e. o. that trusteth, 125:38
Is. 43:7 e. o. called by my name
55:1 ho, e. o. that thirsteth
Jer. 25:5 turn e. o. from evil way

EVI

Dan. 12:1 e. o. found writ. in b.
Mat. 7:8 e. o. that ask. Lu. 11:10
Mark 7:14 hearken to me e. one
Luke 19:26 to e. one which hath
John 3:8 so is e. one born of Sp.
16:37 e. o. that is of truth,
Acts 17:27 not far from e. o.
Rom. 14:12 e. o. sh. give account
2 Tim. 2:19 e. o. that nameth

EVERY where.
1 Chr. 13:2 abroad to breth. e. w.
Mark 16:20 and preached e. w.
Luke 9:6 pre. gosp. e. w. heal. e. 8
Acts 17:30 com. all e. w. to rep.
28:22 e. w. spoken against
1 Cor. 4:17 as I teach e. where in
Phil. 4:12 e. w. in all things
1 Tim. 2:8 that men pray e. w.

EVIDENCE.
Jer. 32:10 I subscribed the e. and
Heb. 11:1 e. of things not seen

EVIDENCES.
Jer. 32:44 buy fields, subscribe e.

EVIDENT.
Job 6:28 for it is e. to you if I lie
Gal. 3:11 justified by the law
Phil. 1:28 e. token of perdition
Heb. 7:14 e. L. sprang out of J.
15 it is yet far more e. for that

EVIDENTLY.
Gal. 3:1 Jesus C. been e. set forth

EVIL.
Gen. 19:19 some e. take me, I die
44:5 ye have done e. in so doing
31 e. that shall come on my fa.
50:20 ye thought e. against me
Ex. 5:23 done e. to this people
10:10 look to it, e. is before you
32:14 the L. repented of the e.
2 Sam. 24:16; 1 Chr. 21:15
Deut. 19:20 com. no more such e.
29:21 Lord sh. sep. him unto e.
30:15 set bef. thee death and e.
31:29 e. befall you in latter days
Jud. 2:15 hand of L. ag. th. *for e.*
20:34 they knew not e. was near
1 Sam. 20:7 e. is determined
21:11 e. nor trang. in my hand
17 whereas I rewarded thee e.
23:17 e. is determ. aga. master
28 e. hath not been found
25:18 what e. is in my hand?
26:6 I have not found e. in thee
2 Sam. 3:39 Lord rev. doer of e.
12:11 I will raise up e. ag. thee
13:7 worse than all e. that befell
1 K. 14:9 e. above all before thee
16:25 Omri wrought e. in eyes of
21:23 the L. hath spoken e. con-
cerning thee, 2 Chr. 18:22
2 K. 21:12 bringing such e. on J.
22:20 eyes not see all the e. I br.
1 Chr. 21:17 that have done e.
2 Chr. 20:9 if when e. cometh
Est. 7:7 he saw e. determined
Job. 2:11 and eschewed e. 8; 2:3
5:19 in seven e. no evil touch
30:26 I looked for good, e. came
42:11 comforted him over all e.
Ps. 5:4 nor sh. e. dwell with thee
7:4 if I rewarded e. to him
15:3 nor doeth e. to his neighbor
21:11 intended e. against thee
23:4 I will fear no e. for thou art
31:21 e. shall slay the wicked
36:4 he abhorreth not e.
40:14 put to shame wish me e.
41:5 mine enemies speak e.
49:5 in days of e.?
52:9 givest thy mouth to e.
54:5 reward e. to my enemies
56:5 thoughts aga. me *for e.*
90:15 years wherein we seen e.
91:10 e. befall thee, Jer. 23:17
97:10 that love the Lord, hate e.
109:20 that speak e. ag. my soul
119:101 e. shall haul the foot e.
Prov. 1:16 feet run to e. Is. 59:7
31 shall be quiet from fear of e.
3:29 devise not e. ag. neighbor
5:14 almost in all e. in midst
11:27 happy to the just
12:13 in them that imagine e.
21 no e. happen to the just
14 e. pursueth sinners
14:22 they err that devise e.?
16:4 wicked *for* day of e.
17 uprightly man bringeth e.
20 seeking him bringeth e.
17:11 an evil man seeketh e.
13 whoso rewardeth e. *for* good
20:8 king scattereth e.
30 stripes the inward parts
21:10 soul of the wicked des. e.
22:3 pru. man foreseeth e. 27:12

Being, brought EVIL.
Jos. 23:15 b. on you e.
2 Sam. 15:14 lest A. b. e. on us
1 K. 14:10 b. e. on house of Jero.
17:20 also b. e. on the widow?
21:29 not b. the e. in his days
2 K. 22:16 I will b. e. upon this
place, 2 Chr. 34:24
2 Chr. 31:26 not call back word
Jer. 4:6 I will b. e. from the north
6:19 I will b. e. upon this people
11:11 I will b. e. upon them
19:14 e. upon this place, 15
23:12 b. e. the year of visitation

EVI

Jer. 23:20 I begin to b. e. on the
33:17 b. on Judah all the e. 39:31
39:16 b. words on this city for e.
45:5 I will b. e. upon all flesh
See DID, DO.

EVIL, *joined with* **good.**
Gen. 2:9 tree of kno. g. and e. 17
3:5 as gods know. g. and e. 22
14:4 whereof, rewarded e. for g. f.
Deut. 1:39 no kno. bet. g. and e.
1 *Sam.* 25:21 requit. me e. for g.
2 *Sam.* 19:35 disc. bet. g. and e. ?
1 *K.* 22:8 prophecy g. but e. 18
2 *Chr.* 18:7 nev. prophe. g. but e.
17 not prophesy *good* but e.
Job 2:10 receive g. and not e. ?
30:26 I looked for *good*, e. came
Ps. 35:12 rew. me e. for g. 109:5
38:20 render e. for g.
52:3 thou lovest e. more than g.
Prov. 15:3 behold. e. and the g.
17:13 rewardeth e. for *good*
31:12 will do him *good*, not e.
Is. 5:20 woe to th. call e. g, g. e.
7:15 refuse e. and choose g. 16
Jer. 18:20 e. be recomp. for g. ?
42:6 whe. g. or e. we will obey
Lam. 3:38 proceed. not e. and g.
Amos 5:14 seek g. and not e. that
9:4 eyes on them for e. not g.
Mic. 3:2 hate *good* and love e.
Rom. 7:21 do g. e. is present
9:11 having done *good* or e.
Heb. 5:14 exerc. to disc. g. and e.
3 *John* 11 follow not e. but *good*
See GREAT.

From EVIL.

Gen. 48:16 redeemed me *f.* all e.
1 *Sam.* 25:30 kept his serv. *f.* e.
1 *Chr.* 4:10 keep me *from* e.
Job 28:28 to depart *f.* e.
1 chap. *f.* e. 37:27; *Prov.* 3:7
13:17 preserve thee *f.* all e.
Prov. 4:27 remove thy foot *f.* e.
13:19 abomination to depart *f.* e.
14:16 a wise man departeth *f.* e.
16:6 men depart *from* e.
17 to depart *from* e.
Is. 59:15 *f.* e. makes himself
Jer. 9:3 they proceed *f.* e. to e.
23:22 should have turned *f.* e.
way, and e. of their doings
51:64 Bab. not rise *from* the e.
Mat. 6:13 del. us *f.* e. *Luke* 11:4
John 17:15 keep them *f.* e.
2 *Thes.* 3:3 and keep you *f.* e.
1 *Pet.* 3:10 refrain his tong. *f.* e.

Put away EVIL.

Deut. 13:5 p. the e. e. from m.
17:7 *put* the e. a. from nm. 19:19;
21:21; 22:21, 24; 24:7
19 *put* e. *away* from Israel,
21:29; *Jud.* 20:13
Ec. 11:10 *put* a. e. from thy flesh
Is. 1:16 wash your. p. *away* e.

EVIL in the sight of *the* **Lord.**
Num. 32:13 e. in *s.* *Jud.* 3:12
Jud. 2:11 Isr. did e. in *s.* of the
Lord, 3:7, 12; 4:1; 6:1; 10:6;
13:1; 1 *K.* 11:6; 14:24; 15:26,
34; 16:7, 30; 22:52; 2 *K.* 8:18,
27; 13:2, 11; 14:24; 15:9, 18,
24, 28; 17:2; 21:2, 20; 2 *Chr.*
22:4; 33:2, 22; 36:5, 9, 12
1 *Sam.* 15:19 didst e. in *s.* of L.
1 *K.* 16:19 in doing e. in *s.* of L.
21:20 sold to work e. in *s.* of L.
2 *K.* 3:2 wrought e. in *s.* of L.
17:17 to do e. in *s.* of Lord
21:16 in doing what was e. in *s.*
of Lord, 23:32, 37; 24:9, 19
1 *Chr.* 2:3 Er was e. in *s.* of L.
2 *Chr.* 33:6 Man. wro. e. in *s.* of L.

This EVIL.

Ex. 32:12 repent of *t.* e.
1 *Sam.* 6:9 hath done us *t.* gr. e.
12:19 added *t.* e. to ask a king
2 *Sam.* 13:16 *t.* e. in send. away
1 *K.* 9:9 L. brought on th. *t.* e.
2 *K.* 6:33 behold *t.* e. is of Lord
2 *Chr.* 7:22 therof. brought *t.* e.
Neh. 13:18 our G. bring *t.* e. on
Job 2:11 A.'s friends heard of *t.* e.
Ps. 51:4 done *t.* e. in thy sight
Jer. 16:10 pronounced *t.* e. ag. us
32:23 hast caused all *t.* e.
42 as I brought *t.* e. on people
40:2 pronoun. *t.* e. ag. them
44:7 whereof. commit *t.* great e.
23 therof. *t.* e. happeneth. to y.
Dan. 9:13 all *t.* e. is come on us
Jon. 1:7 for whose cause *t.* e. 8

EVIL, *Adjective.*
Gen. 6:5 thoughts only e. 8:21

EVI

Gen. 37:20 e. beast dev. him, 33
Ex. 5:19 did see vero in. e. case
33:4 when heard those e. tidings
Num. 14:27 how long bear e. con.
20:5 bring ns unto this e. place
Deut. 1:35 not one of this e. gen.
22:14 on e. name upon her, 19
28:54 his e. toward brother
56 her eye be e. toward husb.
1 *Sam.* 2:23 your e. dealings
K. 5:4 nor e. occurrent
Ezr. 9:13 come for our e. deeds
Ps. 41:8 e. disease cleav. to him
64:5 encourage in an e. matter
78:49 by sending e. angels
112:7 not be afraid of e. tidings
140:11 let not e. speaker be evi.
Prov. 6:24 to keep from e. woman
11:19 the e. bow before the good
Ec. 5:14 perish by e. travel
6:2 end it is an e. disease
9:12 fishes taken in e. net
12:14 secret e. whether good or e.
Jer. 2:19 ti is an e. and bitter
Jer. 8:3 that remain of e. family
12:14 against mine e. neighbors
13:10 e. people refuse to hear
22:10 their course is e.
24:3 e. figs, very e. 8; 20:17
49:23 they have heard e. tidings
Ezek. 5:16 e. arrows of famine
17 will I send on you e. beasts
6:11 for all the e. abominations
34:25 cause e. beasts to cease
38:10 shalt think an e. thought
Hab. 2:9 coveteth an e. covetons.
Mat. 5:45 sun to rise on the e.
7:11 if being e. *Luke* 11:13
18 cannot bring forth e. fruit
12:34 how can ye being e. speak
39 an e. generation, *Luke* 11:20
15:19 out of the heart proceed
e. thoughts, *Mark* 7:21
24:48 if e. servant say to heart
Luke 6:23 cast out name as e.
6:45 bring to unthankful and e.
John 3:19 because deeds were e.
Acts 24:20 found e. doing in me
1 *Cor.* 15:33 e. communications
Gal. 1:4 deliver us from e. world
Eph. 4:31 e. speaking be put aw.
Phil. 3:2 beware of evil workers
Col. 3:5 mortify e. concupiscence
1 *Tim.* 6:4 cometh e. surmisings
Tit. 1:12 Cretians are e. beasts
Heb. 10:22 sprinkled from e.
Jam. 2:4 judges of e. thoughts
4:16 all such rejoicing is e.
1 *Pet.* 3:1 laying aside e. speak.
Rev. 2:2 canst not bear them e.

EVIL day *or* **days.**
Gen. 47:9 few and e. d. of life
Prov. 15:15 d. of afflicted are e.
Ec. 12:1 e. days come not
Amos 6:3 put far away e. d.
Eph. 5:16 because days are e.
6:13 able to withstand in e. day
Day of EVIL. *See* EVIL, *Subst.*

EVIL doer *or* **doers.**
Job 8:20 neither will he help e. d.
Ps. 26:5 hated congrego. of e. d.
37:1 fret not because of e. d.
9 e. d. shall be cut off, but
94:16 will rise up aga. e. do. ?
119:115 depart from me ye e. d,
Is. 1:4 sinful nation seed of e. d.
9:17 every one is an e. d.
14:20 seed of e. d.
31:2 will arise ag. house of e. d.
Jer. 20:13 deliv. poor from e. d.
23:14 strengthen hands of e. d.
2 *Tim.* 2:9 I suffer trou. as e. d.
1 *Pet.* 3:12 speak ag. you as e. d.
14 sent for punishment of e. d.
3:16 speak e. of you as of e. d.
4:15 let none suffer as an e. d.

See DOINGS, EYE.

EVIL heart.
Gen. 8:21 imagination of h. is e.
Jer. 3:17 after imagina. of e. h.
7:24 walked in imagina. of e. h.
11:8 every one in imagi. of e. h.
16:12 after imagination of e. h.
18:12 do imagination of e. h.
Heb. 3:12 be an e. h. of unbelief

EVIL man *or* **men.**
Job 35:12 bec. of pride of e. men
Ps. 10:15 break arm of e. man
140:1 deliver me from e. man
Prov. 2:12 deli. from way of e. m.
4:14 go not in way of e. men
12:12 wicked desir. net of e. m.
17:11 e. man seeketh only rebel.
24:1 be not envious aga. e. men
19 fret not because of e. men
20 shall be no reward to e. m.

EXA

Prov. 28:5 e. m. unders. not judg.
29:6 in transg. of e. m. is snare
Mat. 12:35 e. m. out of e. tren-
sure, bring. e. th. *Luke* 6:45
2 *Tim.* 3:13 e. m. shall wax wor.
See REPORT.

EVIL spirit *or* **spirits.**
Jud. 9:23 e. s. betw. Abimelech
1 *Sam.* 16:14 e. s. troub. him, 15
16 when e. *spirit* is upon thee
23 e. *spirit* departed from him
18:10 e. *spirit* came on S. 19:9
Luke 7:21 cured many of e. s.
8:2 a woman healed of e. *spirits*
Acts 19:12 e. s. went out of them
15 e. s. said, Jesus, I know, Pa.
16 man in whom e. s. was

EVIL thing.
Neh. 13:17 what e. t. is this you
Ps. 141:4 incline not heart to e. t.
Ec. 8:3 stand not in an e. thing
5 keepeth com. sh. feel no e. t.
12:14 secret t. wheth. good or e.
Jer. 2:19 it is an e. t. and bitter
Tit. 2:8 no e. t. to say of you

EVIL things.
Jos. 23:15 bring on you all e. t.
Prov. 15:28 poureth out e. t.
Jer. 3:5 hast done e. t.
Mat. 12:35 e. man br. forth e. t.
Mark 7:23 e. t. come from within
Luke 16:25 likewise Lazarus e. t.
Rom. 1:30 inventors of e. things
1 *Cor.* 10:6 not lust after e. t.

EVIL time.
Ps. 37:19 not be ashamed in e. t.
Ec. 9:12 are snared in an e. t.
Amos 5:13 it is an e. t.
Mic. 2:3 nor go haughtily, *t.* is e.

EVIL way.
1 *K.* 13:33 J. ret. not from e. w.
Ps. 119:101 refrained fr. ev. e. w.
Prov. 8:13 fear of L. to hate e. w.
28:10 to go astray in e. way
Jer. 18:11 return ye from e. w.
25:5; 26:3; 35:15; 36:3, 7
28:8 turn ev. one from e. w.
10 saw they turned from e. w.

EVIL ways.
2 *K.* 17:13 turn from your e. ways.
Ezek. 33:11
Ezek. 36:31 remember your e. w.
Zec. 1:4 turn ye now from e. w.

EVIL work *or* **works.**
Ec. 4:3 hath not seen e. work
8:11 sentence against an e. work
John 7:7 works thereof are e.
Rom. 13:3 terror to good but e. w.
2 *Tim.* 4:18 deliver me from e. w.
1 *John* 3:10 works to no were e

EVIL, *Adverb.*
Ec. 5:22 e. entreated this peo. ?
Deut. 26:6 Egypt e. entreated us
1 *Chr.* 7:23 went e. with his ho.
Job 24:21 e. entreated the barren
John 18:23 spoken e. bear with.
Acts 7:6 entreat e. 400 years
19 same e. entreated our fath.
14:2 e. affected against brethren
19:9 spake of e. that way before
23:5 not speak e. of ruler of peo.
Rom. 14:16 not good be e. spoken
1 *Cor.* 10:30 am I e. spoken of
Jam. 4:11 sp. not e. he that spe.
4 of a brother, speaker. of law
1 *Pet.* 3:10 whereas they speak e.
17 than suffer for e. doing
4:4 speaking e. of you
14 on his part e. spoken of
2 *Pet.* 2:2 way of truth e. spok. of
10 speak e. of dignities. *Jude* 8
12 speak e. of things they un-
derstand not, *Jude* 10
EVIL-MERODACH, 2 *K.* 25:27;
Jer. 52:31

EVILS.
Deut. 31:17 e. and befall them.
will say, Are not these e.
Ps. 40:12 innumer. e. comp. me
Jer. 2:13 have committed two e.
Ezek. 6:9 loathe themselves for e.
Luke 3:19 for all e. H. had done

EWE *or* **EWES.**
Gen. 21:28 Abraham set seven e.
31:38 thy e. not cast their young
Lev. 14:10 take one e. lamb
22:28 nothing save e. lamb
Ps. 78:71 from following the e.

EXACT.
Deut. 15:3 of foreigner may e. ag.
Neh. 5:10 I likewise might e.

EXA

Neh. 5:11 hundredth of mo. ye e.
Ps. 89:22 enemy not e. upon him
Is. 58:3 in fasts you e. all labors
Luke 3:13 e. no more than is app.

EXACTED, ETH.
2 *K.* 15:20 Menahem e. of Israel
23:35 Jehoakim e. the gold
Job 11:6 G. e. less than iniquity

EXACTION, S.
Neh. 10:31 would leave e. of debt
Ezek. 45:9 take away your e.

EXACTORS.
Is. 60:17 make e. righteousness

EXALT.
Ex. 15:2 father's G. I will e.
1 *Sam.* 2:10 e. horn of anointed
Job 17:4 shalt thou nor e. them
Ps. 34:3 let us e. his name
37:34 e. thee to inherit the land
66:7 let not rebellions e. thems.
92:10 my horn e. like the horn
99:5 e. ye the Lord our God, 9
107:32 let e. him in congreation
118:28 art my God, I will e. thee
140:8 lost wicked e. themselves
Prov. 4:8 e. her, she shall prom.
Is. 13:2 e. the voice unto them
14:13 I will e. throne above sta.
23:1 art my God, I will e. thee
Ezek. 21:26 e. him that is low
29:15 nor e. itself above nations
31:14 to the end none of trees e.
Dan. 11:14 robbers of thy peo. e.
36 e. himself above every god
Hos. 11:7 none would e. him
Ob. 4 tho' e. thyself as the eagle
Mat. 23:12 whoso shall e. himself
1 *Cor.* 11:20 if a man e. himself
1 *Pet.* 5:6 may e. you in time

EXALTED.
Num. 24:7 kingdom shall be e.
1 *Sam.* 2:1 said, My horn is e.
2 *Sam.* 5:12 he had e. kingdom
22:47 e. be the God of the rock
of my salvation, *Ps.* 18:46
1 *K.* 1:5 Adonijah e. himself
14:7 1 e. thee from people, 16:2
2 *K.* 19:22 against whom hast
thou e. thy voice ? *Is.* 37:23
1 *Chr.* 29:11 thou art e. as head
Neh. 9:5 is e. above all blessing
Job 5:11 mourn be e. to safety
24:24 are e. for a little while
36:7 establish, and they are e.
Ps. 12:8 when the vilest are e.
13:2 how long ene. e. over me ?
21:13 be e. in thine own streng.
46:10 I will be e. am. heathen,
I will be e. in the earth
47:9 to God, he is greatly e.
57:5 be e. above heavens, 11
75:10 horns of right. shall be e.
89:16 thy right. sh. they be e.
17 in thy favor our horn be e.
19 e. one chosen out of people
24 in my name his horn be e.
97:9 art e. far above all gods
108:5 e. above the heavens
112:9 his horn be e. with honor
138:16 right hand of Lord is e.
Prov. 11:11 by blessing city is e.
Is. 2:2 mount. of Lord's house be
e. above the hills, *Mic.* 4:1
11 L. be e. 17; 5:16
12:4 mention that his name ise.
30:18 be e. that he have mercy
33:5 L. is e. ; 10 now will I be e.
40:4 every valley shall be e.
49:11 my highway shall be e.
52:13 my servant shall be e.
Ezek. 17:24 I the Lord e. low tr.
19:11 her stature was e. 85:13
Hos. 13:1 Ephraim e. himself
Mat. 11:23 e. to heav. *Luke* 10:15
23:12 humble himself shall be e.
e. *Luke* 14:11; 18:14
Luke 1:52 e. them of low degree
Acts 2:33 by right hand of God e.
5:31 him hath God e.
13:17 God of Israel e. the people
2 *Cor.* 11:7 that you might be e.
12:7 be e. above measure, 7
Phile. 2:9 God hath high. e. him
Jam. 1:9 bro. rejoice that he is e.

EXALTEST, ETH.
Ex. 9:17 e. thyself against my
people
Job 36:22 God e. by his power
Ps. 148:14 e. horn of his people
Prov. 14:29 hasty of sp. e. folly
34 righteousness e. a nation
17:19 e. gate, seek. destruction
Luke 14:11 e. him, 18:14
1 *Cor.* 10:5 every thing that e.
2 *Thes.* 2:4 e. him above all

CRUDEN'S CONCORDANCE. 843

EXC

EXAMINATION.
Acts 25:26 after *e.* had, I might

EXAMINE.
Ezr. 10:16 sat down to *e.* matter
Ps. 26:2 *e.* me O Lord
1 *Cor.* 9:3 answer to them that *e.*
11:28 let a man *e.* himself
2 *Cor.* 13:5 *e.* yourselves, prove

EXAMINED, ING.
Luke 23:14 I have *e.* him
Acts 4:9 if we be *e.* of good deed
12:19 Herod *e.* the keepers
22:24 should be *e.* by scourging
29 departed who should *e.* him
24:8 by *e.* of whom thou mayest
28:18 *e.* me, would ha. let me go

EXAMPLE, S.
Mat. 1:19 make her a public *e.*
John 13:15 have given you an *e.*
1 *Cor.* 10:6 were our *e.*
1 *Tim.* 4:12 *e.* of believers
Heb. 4:11 fall after same *e.*
8:5 serve unto *e.* of heavenly
Jam. 5:10 prophets for *e.* suffer.
1 *Pet.* 2:21 C. suff. leav. us an *e.*
Jude 7 for an *e.* suffering
See UNSAMPLE, S.

EXCEED.
Deut. 25:3 forty stripes and not
e. lest if he *e.* brother
Mat. 5:40 right. *e.* the scribes
2 *Cor.* 3:9 ministration *e.*

EXCEEDED.
1 *Sam.* 20:41 wept, till David *e.*
1 *K.* 10:23 Sol. *e.* all for riches

EXCEEDEST, ETH.
1 *K.* 10:7 wisdom *e.* the fame
2 *Chr.* 9:6 *e.* fame that I heard

EXCEEDING.
Gen. 13:1 thy *e.* great reward
17:6 make thee *e.* fruitful
27:34 E. cried with *e.* bitter cry
Ex. 1:7 Israel waxed *e.* mighty
19:16 the trumpet *e.* loud
Num. 14:7 land we passed is *e.*
1 *Sam.* 2:3 no more *e.* proudly
2 *Sam.* 8:8 D. took *e.* much brass
12:2 man had *e.* many flocks
1 *K.* 4:29 G. gave Sol. wisdom *e.*
1 *Chr.* 22:5 brought *e.* much spoil
22:5 must be *e.* magnifical ·
2 *Chr.* 11:12 cities *e.* strong
14:14 was *e.* much spoil in them
16:12 Asa, disease was *e.* great
32:27 Hez. had *e.* much riches
Ps. 21:6 hast made him *e.* glad
43:4 I go unto God, my *e.* joy
119:96 thy command. is *e.* broad
Prov. 30:24 four things are *e.* w.
Ez. 7:21 which is *e.* deep
Ezek. 9:9 Iniq. of Is. Is *e.* great
16:13 and wast *e.* beautiful
37:10 *e.* great army
47:10 fish of great sea *e.* many
Dan. 3:24 the furnace was *e.* hot
7:19 fourth beast was *e.* dreadful
8:9 horn, which waxed *e.* great
Jon. 3:3 was an *e.* great city
4:6 Jonah was *e.* glad
Mat. 2:10 rej. with *e.* great joy
16 Herod mocked, was *e.* wro.
4:8 taketh up into *e.* high moun.
5:12 rejoice and be *e.* glad
8:28 possess. with devils *e.* fier.
26:22 they were *e.* sorrowful
38 *e.* sorrowful, *Mark* 14:34
Mark 6:26 the king was *e.* sorry
9:3 his raiment *e.* white as snow
Acts 7:20 M. born, and was *e.* fa.
Rom. 7:13 sin become *e.* sinful
2 *Cor.* 4:17 work. *e.* weight glory
9:14 for *e.* grace of God in you
Eph. 1:19 *e.* greatness
2:7 might shew *e.* riches of gra.
3:20 is able to do *e.* abundantly
1 *Tim.* 1:14 grace of L. *e.* abund.
1 *Pet.* 4:13 be glad all. with *e.* joy
2 *Pet.* 1:4 *e.* great promises
Jude 24 you faultless with *e.* joy
Rev. 16:21 the pla. was *e.* great

EXCEEDINGLY.
Gen. 7:19 the waters prevailed *e.*
16:10 men of Is. were sinners *e.*
16:10 I will multiply thy seed *e.*
17:2 I will multiply thee *e.*
20 I will multiply Ishmael *e.*
27:33 and Isaac trembled very *e.*
36:11 Jacob increased *e.* 47:27
1 *Sam.* 15:15 Amman hated her *e.*
2 *K.* 10:4 elders Samaria *e.* afraid
1 *Chr.* 22:5 L. magnified Sol. *e.* mon *e.* 2 *Chr.* 1:1
2 *Chr.* 17:12 Jeh. waxed great *e.*
26:8 Uzziah strength. himself *e.*
Neh. 2:10 it grieved them *e.*

EXC

Est. 4:4 queen was *e.* grieved
Job 3:22 rejoice *e.* when they find
Ps. 68:3 the righteous *e.* rejoice
106:11 lusted *e.* in the wilderu.
119:167 testim. I love them *e.*
123:3 *e.* filled with contempt, 4
Is. 24:19 the earth is moved *e.*
Dan. 7:7 a fourth beast strong *e.*
Jon. 1:10 men were *e.* afraid
16 the men feared the Lord *e.*
4:1 it displeased Jonah *e.*
Mat. 19:25 they were *e.* afraid
Mark 4:41 they feared *e.* and said
15:14 cried out the more *e.*
Acts 16:20 these men do *e.* tron.
20:11 being *e.* mad against them
27:18 *e.* tossed with a tempest
2 *Cor.* 7:13 and *e.* the more joyed
Gal. 1:14 *e.* zealous of the tradit.
1 *Thes.* 3:10 praying *e.*
2 *Thes.* 1:3 your faith groweth *e.*
Heb. 12:21 Moses said, I *e.* fear

EXCEL.
Gen. 49:4 unsta. as wa. sh. not *e.*
1 *Chr.* 15:21 with harps on Sh. *e.*
Ps. 103:20 that *e.* in strength
Is. 10:10 images did *e.* them
1 *Cor.* 14:12 seek that ye may *e.*

EXCELLED, EST.
1 *K.* 4:30 Sol's wisdom *e.* Egypt
Prov. 31:29 but thou *e.* them all

EXCELLETH.
Ec. 2:13 wis. *e.* folly, light *e.* da.
3 *Cor.* 3:10 reason of glory that *e.*

EXCELLENCY.
Gen. 49:3 *e.* of dignity, *e.* of pow.
Ex. 15:7 greatness of thine *e.*
Deut. 33:26 who rideth in his *e.*
29 who is the sword of thy *e.*
Job 4:21 their *e.* go away ?
13:11 his *e.* make afraid ?
20:6 *e.* mount up to the heavens
37:4 thunder, with voice of h. *e.*
40:10 deck with majesty and *e.*
Ps. 47:4 the *e.* of Jacob
68:4 cast him down from his *e.*
68:34 his *e.* is over Israel
Ec. 7:12 the *e.* of knowledge is
Is. 12:19 beauty of the Chald. *e.*
35:2 *e.* of Carmel, *e.* of our God
60:15 I make thee an eternal *e.*
Ezek. 24:21 the *e.* of your streng.
Amos 6:8 I abhor the *e.* of Jacob
8:7 L. hath sworn by *e.* of Jacob
Nah. 2:2 *e.* of Jacob, the *e.* of Is.
1 *Cor.* 2:1 not with *e.* of speech
2 *Cor.* 4:7 that *e.* of pow. may be
Phile. 3:8 all things lost for *e.*

EXCELLENT.
Est. 1:4 showed *e.* majesty
Job 37:23 Almighty he *e.* in power
Ps. 8:1 how *e.* thy name ! 9
16:3 *e.* in wh. is all my delight
37:27 bow *e.* is thy loving-kind.
76:4 more *e.* than the mountains
141:5 it shall be an *e.* oil
148:13 Lord, his name alone is *e.*
150:2 accord. to his *e.* greatness
Prov. 8:6 I will speak of *e.* things
12:26 righte. more *e.* th. neigh.
17:7 *e.* speech become. n. a fool
Cant. 5:15 countenance *e.*
Is. 4:2 fruit of earth shall be *e.*
12:5 L. hath done *e.* things
28:29 L. of hosts *e.* in working
Ezek. 16:7 come to *e.* ornaments
Dan. 2:31 whose brightn, was *e.*
4:36 *e.* majesty was added unto
6:19 *e.* spirit found in D. 6:3
11 *e.* wisdom is found in thee
Luke 1:3 most *e.* Theophilus
Acts 23:26 the *e.* governor Felix
Rom. 2:18 approvest things more *e.*
Phile. 1:10
1 *Cor.* 12:31 show I a more *e.* way
Heb. 1:4 obtained a more *e.* name
8:6 obtained a more *e.* ministry
11:4 A. offered more *e.* sacrifice
2 *Pet.* 1:17 voice from the *e.* glo.

EXCEPT.
Gen. 32:26 not go *e.* thou bless
42:15 *e.* young. bro. come, 43:3, 5
Num. 16:13 *e.* make thyself a pr.
Deut. 32:30 *e.* their Rock had sold
Jos. 7:12 *e.* you destroy accursed
1 *Sam.* 25:34 *e.* thou hadst hasted
2 *Sam.* 3:13 *e.* thou first bring Mi.
5:6 *e.* thou take away the blind
2 *K.* 4:24 slack not riding *e.*
Est. 2:14 *e.* king delighted
4:11 hold forth golden sceptre
Ps. 127:1 *e.* L. build, *e.* L. keep
Prov. 4:16 sleep not *e.* done mis.
Is. 1:9 *e.* L. left remu. *Rom.* 9:29
Dan. 3:24 our wors. god, *e.* o. G.

EXE

Dan. 6:5 *e.* find it con. law of
Amos 3:3 two walk *e.* agreed ?
Mat. 5:20 *e.* righteousness exc.
12:29 *e.* bind str. m. *Mark* 3:27
18:3 I say to you *e.* ye be conv.
19:9 put away wife *e.* for forni.
24:22 *e.* day be short, *Mark* 13:20
26:42 may not pass *e.* I drink
Mark 7:3 Phar. *e.* wash oft
Luke 13:3 *e.* ye go and buy meat
13:2 *e.* ye repent, ye shall per. 5
John 3:2 *e.* G. be with him
3 *e.* a man be born again
3:5 *e.* a man be born of water
27 nothing *e.* it be given
4:18 *e.* ye see signs and wonders
6:44 *e.* the Father draw him
65 *e.* it were given him
12:24 *e.* a corn of wheat fall into
15:4 ye cannot bear fruit *e.* ye
19:11 no power *e.* it were given
20:25 *e.* I see print of the nails
Acts 8:1 all sent. *e.* the apostles
31 *e.* some man guide me ?
15:1 *e.* ye be circumcised
24:21 *e.* it be for this one voice
26:29 all as I am, *e.* these bonds
27:31 *e.* these abide in ship
Rom. 7:7 not known lust *e.* law
10:15 how preach *e.* they be sent
1 Cor. 14:5 with tongues *e.* he in.
6 *e.* I shall speak by revelation
7 *e.* they give distinction
9 *e.* ye utter words easy under.
15:36 not quickened *e.* it die
2 Cor. 12:13 *e.* I was not burden.
13:5 *e.* ye be reprobates ?
2 *Thes.* 2:3 *e.* come a falling aw.
2 *Tim.* 2:5 not crowned, *e.* he str.
Rev. 2:5 remove candle *e.* th. rep.
22 tribulation *e.* they repent
1 *Cor.* 15:27 is *e.* who put things

EXCESS.
Mat. 23:25 within are full of *e.*
Eph. 5:18 wine, wherein is *e.*
1 *Pet.* 4:3 lusts, and *e.* of wine
4 ye run not to the same *e.*

EXCHANGE.
Gen. 47:17 Jos. gave bread in *e.*
Lev. 27:10 *e.* thereof shall be
Job 28:17 *e.* of it shall not be
Mat. 16:26 wh. sh. a man give in *e.* for his soul ? *Mark* 8:37

EXCHANGE, Verb.
Ezek. 48:14 nor *e.* first-fruits

EXCHANGERS.
Mat. 25:27 to put money to *e.*

EXCLUDE, D.
Rom. 3:27 boasting ? it is *e.*
Gal. 4:17 they would *e.* you

EXCUSE.
Luke 14:18 began to make *e.*
Rom. 1:20 so they are without *e.*

EXCUSE, Verb.
2 *Cor.* 12:19 think you we *e.* our.

EXCUSED, ING.
Luke 14:18 have me *e.* 19
Rom. 2:15 thoughts accus. or *e.*

EXECRATION.
Jer. 42:18 and ye shall be an *e.*
44:12 shall be an *e.* and reproach

EXECUTE.
Ex. 12:12 will *e.* judgment
Num. 8:11 that they may *e.* service
Ps. 119:84 when wilt thou *e.*
149:7 to *e.* vengeance upon heathen
9 to *e.* the judgment written
Jer. 7:5 *e.* judg. between man and
21:12 *e.* judgment in the morn.
22:3 *e.* ye judg. and righteousness
23:5 branch shall *e.* judg. 33:15
30:24 *e.* intents of his heart
Ezek. 5:8 *e.* judgments in thee, 10
15 when I shall *e.* judg. in thee
11:9 I will *e.* judg. among you
16:41 I will *e.* judg. upon thee
17 I will *e.* vengeance upon them
30:14 and I *e.* judgments in No.
19 thus I will *e.* judg. In Egypt
39:21 *e.* judgment that I have
Mic. 5:15 and I will *e.* vengeance
7:9 *e.* judgment for me
Zec. 7:9 *e.* true judgment
8:16 *e.* judgment of truth
John 5:27 given authority to *e.*
Rom. 13:4 minister of G. *e.* wrath
Jude 15 to *e.* judgment on all

EXECUTED.
Num. 33:4 on gods the L. *e.* judg.
Deut. 33:21 he *e.* justice of the L.

EXE

2 *Sam.* 8:15 D. *e.* ju. 1 *Chr.* 18:14
1 *Chr.* 6:10 *e.* the priest's office
24:2 E. and Ith. *e.* priest's office
Ezr. 7:26 let judg. be *e.* speedily
Ps. 106:30 Phinchas, and *e.* judg.
Ec. 8:11 sentence not *e.* speedily
Jer. 23:20 anger of the L. have *e.*
Ezek. 11:12 sai. *e.* my judg. 20:24
18:8 *e.* true judg. bet. man, 17
23:10 they had *e.* judg. upon her
28:22 I shall have *e.* judg. 30
39:21 shall see judg. I have *e.*
Luke 1:8 wh. Z. *e.* priest's office

EXECUTEDST.
1 *Sam.* 28:18 nor *e.* wrath on A.

EXECUTEST, ETH.
Ps. 9:16 is known by judg. he *e.*
99:4 thou *e.* judgment in Jacob
103:6 Lord *e.* right. and judgm.
146:7 L. *e.* judgm. for the oppr.
Is. 46:11 that *e.* my counsel
Jer. 5:1 if any *e.* judgment
Joel 2:11 he is str. that *e.* word
2 *Chr.* 11:14 Jero. cast off from *e.*
24:8 J. *e.* judg. on Ahab's house

EXECUTION.
Est. 9:1 decree to be put in *e.*
Mark 6:27 king sent an *e.*

EXEMPTED.
1 *K.* 15:22 a procla. none was *e.*

EXERCISE.
1 *Tim.* 4:8 bodily *e.* profit. little

EXERCISE, Verb.
Ps. 131:1 nor do I *e.* things
Jer. 9:24 L. which *e.* loving-kind.
Mat. 20:25 princes of the Gen. *e.* dominion, that are great *e.* authe. *Mark* 10:42; *Lu.* 22:25
Acts 24:16 I *e.* mys. to have cons.
1 *Tim.* 4:7 *e.* thyself to godliness

EXERCISED, ETH.
Ec. 1:13 sore trav. to be *e.* 3:10
Ezek. 22:29 peo. of land *e.* robb.
Heb. 5:11 senses *e.* to discr. good
12:11 fruit of right. to them *e.*
2 *Pet.* 2:14 heart *e.* with covetous
Rev. 13:12 *e.* power of first beast

EXHORT.
Acts 2:40 many words did he *e.*
27:22 I *e.* you to be of good ch.
1 *Thes.* 4:1 brethren, and *e.* you
5:14 now we *e.* you, warn unru.
2 *Thes.* 3:12 comm. and *e.* by C.
1 *Tim.* 2:1 I *e.* that first of all
6:2 these things teach and *e.*
2 *Tim.* 4:2 *e.* with long-suffering
Tit. 1:9 may be able to *e.* and co.
2:6 young men *e.* to be sober
9 *e.* servants to be obedient
15 speak, *e.* and rebuke
Heb. 3:13 *e.* one another daily
1 *Pet.* 5:1 the elders am. you I *e.*
Jude 3 for me to write and *e.*

EXHORTATION.
Luke 3:18 many things in *e.*
Acts 13:15 ye have word of *e.* say
20:2 when P. had given much *e.*
Rom. 12:8 exhort, let wait on *e.*
1 *Cor.* 14:3 speak unto men to *e.*
2 *Cor.* 8:17 he accepted the *e.*
1 *Tim.* 4:13 give attendance to *e.*
Heb. 12:5 ye have forgot, the *e.*
13:22 suffer the word of *e.*

EXHORTED, ING.
Acts 11:23 B. *e.* to cleave to Lord
14:22 *e.* them to con. in fai.
15:32 *e.* brethren with m. words
18:27 breth. wrote *e.* disciples
Heb. 10:25 but *e.* one anoth. and
1 *Pet.* 5:12 by S. I have written *e.*
1 *Thes.* 2:11 you how have we *e.*

EXILE.
2 *Sam.* 15:19 a stranger and an *e.*
Is. 51:14 captive *e.* hasteneth

EXORCISTS.
Acts 19:13 vagabond Jews, *e.*

EXPECTATION.
Ps. 9:18 *e.* of poor shall not per.
62:5 my *e.* is from him
Prov. 10:28 *e.* of wicked, 11:7
11:23 *e.* of the wicked is wrath
23:18 *e.* sh. not be cut off, 24:14
Is. 20:5 be ashamed of *e.* of Ethi.
6 behold, such is our *e.*
Zec. 9:5 her *e.* shall be ashamed
Luke 3:15 as peo. were in *e.*
Acts 12:11 delivered fr. *e.* of J. wa.
Rom. 8:19 *e.* of creature wait. eh
Phil. 1:20 my earnest *e.*

EXPECTED, ING.
Jer. 29:11 to give an *e.* end

CRUDEN'S CONCORDANCE.

FAC

Is. 50:6 I *hid* not my *f.* from sh.
54:8 in wrath I *hid* my *f.*
53:2 sins have *h.* his *f.* from you
64:7 thou hast *hid* thy *f.*
Jer. 10:17 not *hid* from city
33:5 *hid* my *f.* from city
Ezek. 39:23 *h.* I my *f.* fr. them, 24
29 nor will I *hide* my *f.*
Mic. 3:4 he will *h. f.* at that time
Rev. 6:16 *hide* us from *f.* of him
FACE of the house.
Ezek. 41:14 breadth of *f. of* house
FACE of the Lord.
Gen. 19:13 cry before *f. of the L.*
1 *Sam.* 26:20 blood before *f. of L.*
1 *K.* 13:6 entreat *f. of the Lord*
Ps. 34:16 *f. of the Lord* against
them that do evil, 1 *Pet.* 3:12
Lam. 2:19 heart before *f. of L.*
Luke 1:76 go before *f. of Lord*
FACE of the porch.
Ezek. 40:15 *f. of the p.* 50 cubits
41:25 thick planks on *f. of the p.*
FACE, with him, looked, see, saw, seen.
Gen. 32:30 aftsrw. I will *s.* his *f.*
33:10 therefore have I *s.* thy *f.*
43:3 shall not *s.* my *f.* 5; 44:23
45:30 let me die since I have *s. f.*
48:11 not thought to *see* thy *f.*
Ex. 10:28 *see* my *f.* no more
20 Moses said, I will *see* thy *f.*
33:20 thou canst not *see* my *f.*
23 but my *f.* shall not be *seen*
34:35 children of Is. *s. f.* of M.
2 *Sam.* 14:28 two *f. s.* not king's *f.*
2 *K.* 14:8 let us *look* one another
in the *f.* 2 *Chr.* 25:17
11 looked one another in the *f.*
Est. 1:14 7 princes *w. s.* king's *f.*
Acts 6:15 *saw* his *f. as f.* of angel
25:35 sh. *see* my *f.* no more, 38
Col. 2:1 as have not *seen* my *f.*
Rev. 22:4 they shall *see* his *f.*
Seek FACE.
1 *Chr.* 16:11 *seek* his *f. Ps.* 105:4
2 *Chr.* 7:14 if my people *s.* my *f.*
Ps. 24:6 that *seek* thy *f.* O Jacob
27:8 *s.* ye my *f.* thy *f.* L. will I *s.*
Prov. 7:15 I came to *seek* thy *f.*
Hos. 5:15 till they *seek* my *f.*
Set FACE.
Gen. 31:21 J. *set f.* to mount Gil.
Lev. 17:10 *set f.* against soul, 20:6
20:3 *set f.* ag. that m. 5; 24:18
26:17 *set* my *f.* aga. *Jer.* 44:11
Jr. 21:10 *set* my *f.* ag. this city
Ezek. 4:3 *set* my *f.* against it
6:2 *set* thy *f.* tow. mountains
13:17 *set* thy *f.* ag. daughters
15:7 *set* my *f.* against them
20:46 *set* thy *f.* toward the south
21:2 *set* thy *f.* toward Jerusalem
16 whithersoever thy *f.* is *set*
24:21 *f.* ag. Zidon; 29:2 *f.* ag. P.
35:2 *f.* ag. mount s.; 38:2 *f.* A. G.
Dan. 9:3 I *set* my *f.* to Lord God
10:15 *set* my *f.* toward ground
11:17 he shall *set* his *f.* to enter
Luke 9:51 *set f.* to go to Jerusa.
FACE shine.
Num. 6:25 L. *make f.* to *s.* on thee
Ps. 31:16 make thy *f.* to *shine* on
thy servant, 119:135
67:1 cause his *f.* to *shine* on us
80:3 cause thy *f.* to *shine*, 7, 19
104:15 to make his *f.* to *shine*
Ec. 8:1 maketh his *f.* to *shine*
Dan. 9:17 cause thy *f.* to *sh.*
Mat. 17:9 his *f.* did *shine* as sun
FACE of the sky.
Mat. 16:3 disc. the *f. Luke* 12:56
FACE of the waters.
Gen. 1:2 S. of G. mov. *f. of w.*
7:18 ark went upon *f. of the w.*
29 dried that thy *f.*th. *f.* not
FACE of the wilderness.
Ex. 16:14 on *f. of the w.* lay
FACE of the world.
Job 37:12 command. on *f. of w.*
Is. 14:21 nor fill *f. of w.*
27:6 Israel sll *f. of w.* with fruit
FACES.
Gen. 9:23 their *f.* were backward
Ex. 10:7 Moses laid before th. *f.*
20:20 his fear be before your *f.*
25:20 *f.* shall look one to another
37:9 mercy-seat-ward *f.* of cher.
2 *Sam.* 19:5 shamed *f.* of serv.
1 *K.* 8:13 all Israel set *f.* on me
1 *Chr.* 19:8 *f.* were like *f.* of lions
2 *Chr.* 3:13 their *f.* were inward
Job 9:34 he covereth *f.* of judges
40:13 bind their *f.* in secret

FAI

Ps. 34:5 *f.* were not ashamed
Is. 3:15 that ye grind *f.* of poor
13:8 their *f.* shall be as flames
23:8 will wipe tears from all *f.*
53:3 hid as it were our *f.* from
Jer. 1:8 be not afraid of their *f.*
8:3 their *f.* harder than a rock
30:6 all *f.* turned into paleness
42:15 set *f.* to enter, 17; 44:12
50:5 Zion, with *f.* thitherward
Lam. 5:12 *f.* of elders not hon.
Ezek. 1:6 ev. one four *f.* 10, 11, 15
7:18 shame shall be on their *f.*
8:16 with *f.* toward the east
14:6 turn *f.* from abominations
20:47 all *f.* shall be burnt
41:18 every cherub had two *f.*
Dan. 8:7 unto us confusion of *f.*
Joel 2:6 *f.* shall gather blackness
Nah. 2:10 *f.* sup up as east w.
Mal. 2:3 I will spread dung on *f.*
Mat. 6:16 hypocrites disfigure *f.*
Luke 24:5 have bowed *f.* to earth
Rev. 7:11 fell before throne on *f.*
9:7 *f.* of locusts as *f.* of men
See Fell on FACE, or FACES.

FADE.
2 *Sam.* 22:46 strangers shall *f.*
away, *Ps.* 18:45
Is. 64:6 and we all *f.* as a leaf
Jer. 8:13 and the leaf shall *f.*
Ezek. 47:12 who. leaf shall not *f.*
1 *Pet.* 1:11 rich man shall *f.* away
FADETH.
Is. 1:30 as an oak, whose leaf *f.*
24:4 and *f.* the world *f.*
40:7 grass withereth, flower *f.*
24:4 inheritance *f.* not away
5:4 cro. of glory that *f.* not aw.
FADING.
Is. 28:1 glorious beauty *f.* flow.
4 beauty shall be *f.* flower

FAIL, Substantive.
Jos. 3:10 without *f.* drive Can.
Jud. 11:30 without *f.* deliver A.
Ezr. 6:9 day by day without *f.*
FAIL, Verb.
Gen. 47:16 cattle, if money *f.*
Deut. 28:32 eyes *f.* with longing
Jos. 1:5; 1 *Chr.* 28:20
1 *Sam.* 17:32 no man's heart *f.*
2 *K.* 2:4 shall not *f.* man on thro.
of Isr. 8:25; 9:5; 2 *Chr.* 6:16
17:14 neith. sh. cruse of oil *f.* 16
Neh. 4:10 let nothing *f.* of all
9:32 not *f.* keep days of P. 24
Job 11:20 eyes of wicked shall *f.*
14:11 as waters *f.* from the sea
17:5 eyes of his children sh. *f.*
31:16 caused eyes of wid. to *f.*
Ps. 12:1 faithful *f.* fr. am. men
31:9 mine eyes *f.* while I wait
77:8 doth his promise *f.* for ever
119:82 mine eyes *f.* for thy word
123 mine eyes *f.* for thy salva.
Prov. 22:8 rod of his anger sh. *f.*
Ec. 12:5 desire *f.* man goeth
Is. 19:5 wat. *f.* 31:3 he that sh. *f.*
38:14 mine eyes *f.* with looking
44:16 no one of these shall *f.*
58:11 mine eyes *f.* with looking
42:4 not *f.* nor be discouraged
57:16 spirit should *f.* before me
58:11 spring whose waters *f.* not
Jer. 14:6 eyes did *f.* bec. no gra.
15:18 as waters that *f. f.*
48:33 wine to *f. Hos.* 9:2
Lam. 2:11 mine eyes *f.* with tea.
3:22 because compassions *f.* not
Hab. 3:17 labor of olive shall *f.*
Luke 16:9 ye *f.* they may receive
17 one tittle of the law to *f.*
Luke 22:32 prophecies they *f.*
1 *Cor.* 13:8 prophecies they sh. *f.*
Heb. 1:12 thy years shall not *f.*
11:32 time would *f.* me to tell
12:15 any man *f.* of grace of G.

FAILED.
Gen. 42:28 their heart *f.* them
47:15 money *f.* in land of Egypt
Jos. 3:10 waters *f.* were cut off
21:45 *f.* not any good which L.
promised, 23:14; 1 *K.* 8:56
Job 19:14 my kinsfolk have *f.*
Ps. 142:4 refuge *f.* no man cared
Cant. 5:6 soul *f.* when he spake
Lam. 4:17 our eyes as yet *f.*

FAILETH.
Gen. 47:15 who. we die? money *f.*
Job 21:10 gendereth and *f.* not
Ps. 31:10 strength *f.* me, 38:10

FAI

Ps. 40:12 my heart *f.* me, 73:26
71:9 forsake not when strength
102:24 my desh *f.* of fatness
143:7 O Lord, my spirit *f.*
Ec. 10:3 wisdom *f.* him
Is. 15:6 grass *f.* no green thing
41:17 their tongue *f.* for thirst
44:12 hungry and his strength *f.*
Ezek. 12:22 and every vision *f.*
Luke 12:33 treas. in heaven, *f.* not
1 *Cor.* 13:8 charity never *f.* but

FAILING.
Deut. 28:65 L. shall give *f.* of ey.
Luke 21:26 men's heart *f.* for fe.

FAIN.
Job 27:22 *f.* flee out of his hand
Luke 15:16 *f.* filled belly

FAINT, Adjective.
Gen. 25:29 E. and he was *f.* 30
Deut. 25:18 when thon wast *f.*
Jud. 8:4 *f.* yet pursuing them
1 *Sam.* 14:28 peo. were very *f.* 31
30:10 so *f.* could not go over, 21
2 *Sam.* 16:2 such as be *f.*
Is. 1:5 the whole heart is *f.*
13:7 shall all hands be *f.*
29:8 awaketh, behold he is *f.*
40:29 he giveth power to the *f.*
Jer. 8:18 my heart is *f.*
Lam. 3:17 for this our heart is *f.*

FAINT, Verb.
Deut. 20:3 let not your hearts *f.*
8 lest his brethren's heart *f.*
Jos. 2:9 inhabitants of land *f.*
Prov. 24:10 *f.* in day of adversity
Is. 40:30 shall *f.* *Amos* 8:13
31 walk and not *f.*
Jer. 31:16 and lest your hearts *f.*
Lam. 2:19 young children *f.*
Ezek. 21:7 every spirit shall *f.*
15 their heart may *f.*
Mat. 15:32 fasting, lest they *f.*
Mark 8:3 away fasting, will *f.*
Luke 18:1 to pray, not to *f.*
2 *Cor.* 4:1 rec. mercy we *f.* not
16 for which cause we *f.* not
Gal. 6:9 shall reap, if we *f.* not
Eph. 3:13 *f.* not at my tribula.
Heb. 12:3 and *f.* in your minds
5 nor when rebuked of him

FAINTED.
Gen. 45:26 Jacob's heart *f.*
Ps. 27:13 *f.* unl. I had believed
107:5 their soul *f.* in them
Is. 51:20 thy *f. K.* 4:8:3 *f.* in my sighing
Ezek. 31:15 trees of field *f.*
Dan. 8:27 I Daniel *f.*
Jon. 2:7 soul *f.* I remem. Lord
4:8 *f.* and wished in him. to die
Mat. 9:36 comp. on them bec. *f.*
Rev. 2:3 labored, and hast not *f.*

FAINTEST, ETH.
Job 4:5 upon t. ace. and thou *f.*
Ps. 84:2 soul *f.* for courts of L.
119:81 my soul *f.* for salvation
Is. 10:18 a standard-bearer *f.*
40:28 ends of earth *f.* not

FAINTHEARTED.
Deut. 20:8 and *f.* let him return
Is. 7:4 nor be *f.* for the two tails
Jer. 49:23 H. and Arpad are *f.*

FAINTNESS.
Lev. 26:36 send *f.* into hearts

FAIR.
Gen. 6:2 daugh. of men were *f.*
12:11 Sar. *f.* 14; 24:16 R. 29:17
1 *K.* 1:4 Abishag a *f.* damsel
Est. 1:11 Vashti *f.* 2:7 Est. *f.*
2:2 young virgins be sought
Job 2:7 weather cometh out
42:15 so *f.* as Job's daughters
Prov. 7:21 with *f.* speech
11:22 *f.* woman with discretion
26:25 when he speaketh, *f.*
Cant. 1:15 thou art *f.*; 4:1, 7
2:10 my love, my *f.* one, 13
4:10 *f.* is thy love, my sister
6:10 *f.* as moon; 7:6 *f.* art thou
Is. 5:9 many houses great and *f.*
54:11 lay stones with *f.* colors
Jer. 11:16 and olive-tree *f.*
12:6 though they speak *f.* words
46:20 Egypt like a very *f.* heifer
Ezek. 16:17 hast taken *f.* jewels
23:41 satest on *f.* bed
31:3 cedar in L. with *f.* branches
7 *f.* in his greatness
9 made him *f.* by multitude
Dan. 4:12 leaves were *f.* 21
Amos 8:13 *f.* virgins shall faint
Zec. 3:5 let them set a *f.* mitre
Mat. 16:2 it will be *f.* weather
Acts 7:20 Moses was *f.* exceeding *f.*

FAI

Rom. 10:18 *f.* speeches deceive
Gal. 6:12 make *f.* show in flesh
FAIRER, EST.
Jud. 15:2 younger sist. *f.* than
Ps. 45:2 *f.* than child. of men
Cant. 1:8 O *f.* am. wo. 5:9; 6:1
Dan. 1:15 countenances app. *f.*
FAIR-HAVENS.
Acts 27:8 place called the *f.-h.*
FAIRS.
Ezek. 27:12 tra. in *f.* 14, 16, 19, 22
27 thy *f.* shall fall into the seas
FAITH.
Deut. 32:20 in whom is no *f.*
Mat. 6:30 O ye of little *f.* 8:26;
14:31; 16:8; *Luke* 12:28
8:10 great *f.* no not. *Luke* 7:9
9:2 *f.* am. wo. 5:9; 6:1
9:22 *f.* hath made thee whole,
29 according to your *f.*
15:28 great is thy *f.* he it
17:20 because of your unbelief
21:21 if ye have *f.* 22; *Mark* 11:22
23:23 judgment, mercy, and *f.*
Mark 4:40 ye have no *f.*
11:22 Jesus saith, Have *f.* in G.
Luke 17:5 Lord increase our *f.*
6 if ye had *f.* ye might say
18:8 wh. S. of man com. fi. *f.?*
22:32 prayed that *f.* fail not
Acts 6:5 Ste. a man full of *f.* *f.*
7 priests were obedie. to the *f.*
11:24 Barnabas good, full of *f.*
13:8 seek. to turn deputy fr. *f.*
14:9 that he had *f.* to be healed
22 exhorting to continue in *f.*
27 opened door of *f.* to Gentil.
16:5 churches established in *f.*
20:21 *f.* toward our L. Jesus C.
24:24 Felix heard P. concern. *f.*
Rom. 1:3 obedience to *f.*
12 comforted mutual *f.*
17 righte. of G. rev. fr. *f.* to *f.*
3:3 make *f.* of God without ef.
22 excluded by law of *f.*
28 justified by *f.* without deeds
30 circumcis. by *f.* uncircum. *f.*
31 make void the law by *f.*
4:3 *f.* counted for righteous, 9
11 circumc. seal of righte. of *f.*
12 steps of that *f.* of Abraham
13 through righteous of *f.*
14 they of the law be heirs *f.* is v.
16 of *f.* of the *f.* of Abraham
20 righte. which is of G. 10:6
10:8 word of *f.* which we prea.
17 so then *f.* cometh by hear.
12:3 God dealt measure of *f.*
6 according to proportion of *f.*
14:22 hast thou *f.*
23 eat. not of *f.* not of *f.* is sin
16:26 for the obedience of *f.*
1 *Cor.* 12:9 another *f.* by same S.
13:2 though I have all *f.*
13 now abideth *f.* hope, chari.
Gal. 1:23 *f.* which once destroy.
3:2 or by the hearing of *f.* 5
7 they which are of *f.*
12 law is not of *f.* but man
23 before *f.* came; 25 *f.* is co.
5:6 *f.* which worketh by love
22 fruit of Sp. is love, joy, *f.*
6:10 household of *f.*
Eph. 4:5 one L. one *f.* one bapt.
13 come in the unity of the *f.*
6:16 taking the shield of *f.*
Phil. 1:25 further, and joy of *f.*
27 striving tog. for. *f.* of gospel
1 *Thes.* 1:3 rememb. work of *f.*
3:2 for all men have *f.*
1 *Tim.* 3:5 *f.* unfeigned
19 holding *f.* concerning *f.*
3:9 holding the mystery of *f.*
4:1 some sh all depart fr. the *f.*
5:8 he hath denied the *f.* and is
12 have cast off their first *f.*
6:10 have erred from the *f.* 21
11 follow *f.*; 12 fight fight of *f.*
2 *Tim.* 1:5 unfeigned *f.* in thee
2:18 overthrow the *f.* of some
22 follow *f.*; 3:8 reprobate *f.*
3:10 thou hast fully known *f.*
4:7 have kept the *f.* henceforth
Tit. 1:1 the *f. of G.* elect
4 T. mine own son aft. com. *f.*
13 sound in the *f.* 2:2
Phile. 5 hearing of thy *f.*
6 communica. of thy *f.*
Heb. 4:2 not mixed with *f.*
10:1 not laying the foundat. of *f.*
22:22 in full assurance of *f.*
23 hold fast profession of *f.*
11:1 *f.* is substance of things
6 without *f.* impossi. to pl. G.
2 and finisher of our *f.*
13:7 whose *f.* follow, consider.
Jam. 2:1 *f.* with respect of pers.
14 be hath *f.* can *f.* save h.
17 with. works is dead, 20, 26
18 hast *f.* and I have works
22 *f.* wrought with works, and
by works was *f.* made perf.
5:15 prayer of *f.* shall save sick
2 *Pet.* 1:1 obtained like prec. *f.*
1 *John* 5:4 overcome, wor. our *f.*
Jude 3 earnestly contend for *f.*

CRUDEN'S CONCORDANCE.

FAI

Jude 20 building yours. on h. *f.*
Rev. 2:13 hast not denied my *f.*
   13 I know thy works and *f.*
   13:10 patience and *f.* of saints
   14:12 that keep the *f.* of Jesus

By FAITH.

Hab. 2:4 shall live by *f. Rom.*
   1:17; *Gal.* 3:11; *Heb.* 10:38
Acts 13:9 purifying hearts by *f.*
   26:18 sanctified by *f.*
Rom. 3:22 righteous. of G. by *f.*
   28 justi. b. *f.* 5:1; *Gal.* 3:16; 3:24
   30 justify circumcision by *f.*
   5:2 we have access by *f.*
   11:20 standest by *f.* 2 *Cor.* 1:24
   2 *Cor.* 5:7 walk by *f.* not by sight
   Gal. 2:20 I live by *f.* of S. of God
   3:24 promise by *f.* might be giv.
   26 child. of G. by *f.* in *Chr.* J.
   5:5 hope of righteousness by *f.*
Eph. 3:12 we have access by *f.*
   17 C. may dwell in hearts by *f.*
Phil. 3:9 righteousn. of G. by *f.*
Heb. 11:4 by *f.* Abel; 5 by *f.* En.
   7 by *f.* Noah; 8 by *f.* Ara. 9, 17
   20 by *f.* Isaac; 21 Jac.; 22 Jos.
   23 by *f.* Moses, 24:27; 31 Rah.
   29 by *f.* passed through Red s.
   30 by *f.* walls of Jer. fell down
Jam. 2:24 works justi. not by *f.*

In FAITH.

Rom. 4:19 being not weak in *f.*
   20 but was strong in *f.*
   14:1 him weak in *f.* receive you
1 *Cor.* 16:13 stand fast in *f.*
2 *Cor.* 13:5 exam. wh. ye be in *f.*
Col. 1:23 if ye continue in the *f.*
   2:7 and established in the *f.*
1 *Tim.* 1:2 Tim. my own son in *f.*
   4 godly edifying which is in *f.*
   2:7 teacher of the Gentiles in *f.*
   13 saved, if they continue in *f.*
   3:13 they purchase boldn. in *f.*
   4:12 example of believers in *f.*
2 *Tim.* 1:13 hold fast form in *f.*
Heb. 11:13 these all died in *f.*
Jam. 1:6 but let them ask in *f.*
   2:5 poor of this world, rich in *f.*
   1 *Pet.* 5:9 resist, steadfast in *f.*

Their FAITH.

Mat. 9:2 Jesus seeing their *f.*
Mark 2:5; *Luke* 5:20

Through FAITH.

Acts 3:16 through *f.* in his name
Rom. 3:25 propitiation *t. f.*
   31 justify uncircumcision *t. f.*
   do we make void law *t. f.*
Gal. 3:8 God justify heathen *t. f.*
   14 promise of the Spirit *t. f.*
Eph. 2:8 are ye saved *t. f.*
   Phil. 3:9 righteousn. wh. is *t. f.*
   Col. 2:12 risen *t. f.* of ope. of G.
2 *Tim.* 3:15 wise to salvation *t. f.*
Heb. 6:12 *t. f.* inherit promises
   11:3 *t. f.* we und. worlds framed
   11 *t. f.* S. received strength
   24 *thro' f.* he kept the passover
   33 *thro' f.* subdued kingdoms
   39 obtained a good report *t. f.*
1 *Pet.* 1:5 kept *t. f.* to salvation

Thy FAITH.

Mat. 9:22 *t. f.* hath made thee whole, *Mark* 5:34; 10:52;
   Luke 8:48; 17:19
   15:28 O woman, great is *thy f.*
Luke 7:50 *t. f.* h. saved th. 18:43
   22:31 prayed that *thy f.* fail not
Phile. 6 communication of *thy f.*
Jam. 2:18 show *t. f.* without w.

Your FAITH.

Mat. 9:29 according to *y. f.* be it
Luke 8:25 where is *your f.?*
Rom. 1:8 *y. f.* is spoken
1 *Cor.* 2:5 *y. f.* not stand in wis.
   15:14 *your f.* is also vain, 17
2 *Cor.* 1:24 dominion over *y. f.*
   10:15 when *your f.* is increased
Eph. 1:15 after I heard of *y. f.*
Phil. 2:17 offer. on service of *y. f.*
Col. 1:4 since we heard of *y. f.*
   2:5 steadfastness of *y. f.* in Ch.
1 *Thes.* 1:8 *your f.* to God ward
   3:5 I sent to know *your f.*
   7 we were comforted by *y. f.*
   10 what is lacking in *your f.*
2 *Thes.* 1:3 *y. f.* groweth exceed.
Jam. 1:3 trying of *y. f.* worketh
1 *Pet.* 1:7 trial of *y. f.* precious
   9 end of *y. f.* even salvation
   21 that *y. f.* might be in God
2 *Pet.* 1:5 add to *your f.* virtue

FAITHFUL.

Num. 12:7 Mo. *f.* *Heb.* 3:2, 5
Deut. 7:9 *f.* G. who keepeth cov.
1 *Sam.* 2:35 will raise up *f.* pric.

FAL

2 *Sam.* 20:19 *f.* in Israel
Neh. 13:13 *f.* to distribute
Ps. 12:1 the *f.* fail from am. men
   31:23 the Lord preserveth the *f.*
   89:37 as a *f.* witness in heaven
   101:6 mine eyes shall be on *f.*
   119:86 commandments are *f.*
   138 thy testimonies very *f.*
Prov. 11:13 *f.* spirit conc. matter
   13:17 a *f.* ambassador is health
   14:5 a *f.* witness will not lie
   20:6 a *f.* man who can find?
   27:6 *f.* the wounds of a friend
Is. 1:21 how is *f.* city become
   26 shalt be called the *f.* city
   8:2 I took unto me *f.* witness.
Jer. 42:5 L. be *f.* witness bet. us
Dan. 6:4 forasmuch as he was *f.*
Hos. 11:12 Ju. is *f.* with saints
Mat. 24:45 who then is *f.*
   25:21 well done, good and *f.* se.
   23 *f.* in a few th. *Luke* 19:17
Luke 12:42 who is *f.* and wise?
   16:10 *f.* in least is *f.* in much
   12 not *f.* in what is ano. man's
Acts 16:15 ye have judged me *f.*
1 *Cor.* 1:9 God is *f.* 10:13
   4:2 stewards, that a man be *f.*
   17 sent Timothy, *f.* in the L.
   7:25 mercy of the Lord to be *f.*
Gal. 3:9 blessed with *f.* Abraham
Eph. 1:1 to saints and *f.* in C. J.
   6:21 Tychicus a *f.* minister
Col. 1:2 saints and *f.* breth. in C.
   7 Ep. for you *f.* minister, 4:7
   4:9 Onesimus, a *f.* brother
1 *Thes.* 5:24 *f.* is he that calleth
2 *Thes.* 3:3 L. is *f.* who stablish
1 *Tim.* 1:12 Christ he counted *f.*
   15 a *f.* saying, 4:9; *Tit.* 3:8
2 *Tim.* 2:2 same commit to *f.* m.
   11 *f.* saying; 13 he abideth *f.*
Tit. 1:6 having *f.* children
   9 holding fast the *f.* word
Heb. 2:17 he might be *f.*
   3:2 *f.* to him that appointed h.
   10:23 is *f.* that promised, 11:11
1 *Pet.* 4:19 souls as to a *f.* Crea.
1 *John* 1:9 he is *f.* to forgive us
Rev. 1:5 C. the *f.* witness, 3:14
   2:10 be *f.* unto death
   13:11 was called *f.*
   21:5 words are true and *f.* 22:6

FAITHFULLY.

2 *K.* 12:15 for they dealt *f.* 22:7
2 *Chr.* 31:12 brought offerings *f.*
   31:12 men did the work *f.*
Prov. 29:14 *f.* judgeth the poor
Jer. 23:28 speak my word *f.*

FAITHFULNESS.

1 *Sam.* 26:23 render to man his *f.*
Ps. 5:9 no *f.* in their mouth
   36:5 thy *f.* reacheth unto clouds
   40:10 I have declared thy *f.*
   88:1 I will make known thy *f.*
   2 thy *f.* shalt thou establish
   5 thy *f.* also in the congrega.
   8 who is like unto thee in *f.*
   11 *f.* round about thee?
   24 *f.* and my mercy be with him
   92:2 good to show *f.* every night
   119:75 in *f.* hast afflicted me
   90 thy *f.* is unto all genera.
   143:1 in thy *f.* answer me
Is. 11:5 *f.* shall be his girdle
   25:1 thy counsels of old are *f.*
Lam. 3:23 great thy *f.*
Hos. 2:20 I will betroth thee in *f.*

FAITHLESS.

Mat. 17:17 *f.* generation, *Mark* 9:19; *Luke* 9:41
John 20:27 not *f.* but believing

FALL, Substantive.

Prov. 16:18 haughty spirit bef. *f.*
   29:16 righteous shall see their *f.*
Jer. 49:21 moved at noise of *f.*
Mat. 7:27 great was the *f.* of it
Luke 2:34 child set for *f.*
Rom. 11:11 thro' their *f.* salva. tion is come to the Gentiles
   12 if *f.* of them be riches

FALL, Verb.

Gen. 2:21 deep sleep to *f.* on A.
   43:18 we that *by f.* on us by w.
   49:17 his rider shall *f.* backwa.
Lev. 19:29 land *f.* to whoredom
   26:36 sh. *f.* when none pursue
   37 shall *f.* one upon another
   11:32 on *f.* any, *f.* wild. 32
Jud. 15:12 ye will not *f.* on
1 *Sam.* 14:10 hand of us mcom.
Ruth 2:16 let *f.* some handfuls
1 *Sam.* 3:19 none of words *f.* gr.
   14:45 no hair of head *f.* ground,
   2 *Sam.* 14:11; 1 *K.* 1:52; *Acts*
   22:17 would not *f.* on the pric.

FAL

1 *Sam.* 22:18 turn th. and *f.* on pr.
2 *Sam.* 1:15 *f.* on h. 1 *K.* 2:29, 31
   24:14 *f.* in hand of G. not *f.* into hand of man, 1 *Chr.* 21:13
2 *K.* 7:4 let us *f.* unto host of S.
   10:10 *f.* nothing of word of L.
1 *Chr.* 12:19 he will *f.* to master
2 *Chr.* 21:15 till bowels *f.* out
Est. 6:13 thou begun to *f.*
Job 13:11 his dread *f.* on you
   31:22 arm *f.* fr. shoulder-blade
Ps. 5:10 *f.* by own counsels
   9:3 enemies sh. *f.* and perish
   10:10 that the poor may *f.*
   35:8 into destruction let him *f.*
   37:24 he *f.* shall not be utterly
   64:8 make their tongue to *f.* on
   69:7 shall *f.* like one of princes
   91:7 a thousand shall *f.*
   118:13 thrust at me I might *f.*
   140:10 burning coals *f.* on them
   141:10 wicked *f.* into own nets
   145:14 Lord upholdeth all th. *f.*
Prov. 10:8 a prating fool sh. *f.* 10
   11:5 wicked shall *f.*
   14 wh. no counsel is the peo. *f.*
   28 trusteth in his riches sh. *f.*
   22:14 abhor. of L. sh. *f.* therein
   24:16 shall *f.* into mischief
   26:27 whoso diggeth pit shall *f.*
   28:14 that hardeneth heart sh. *f.*
   18 perverse shall *f.* at once
Ec. 4:10 if they *f.* one lift fellow
   11:3 if the tree *f.* tow. the south
   Is. 10:4 they sh. *f.* under slain
   31 Lob. shall *f.* by mighty one
   22:25 nail fast, sure place sh. *f.*
   24:20 earth shall *f.* and not rise
   30:13 inig. as breach ready to *f.*
   40:30 young men sh. utterly *f.*
   47:11 mischiefs sh. *f.* upon thee
Jer. 6:15 *f.* am. them that *f.* 8:12
   21 fathers and sons shall *f.*
   8:4 shall they *f.* and not arise?
   9:22 carcasses of men shall *f.*
   15:8 I have caused him to *f.*
   19:7 whirlwind *f.* on head, 30:23
   23:27 drunken, and spue, and *f.*
   37:14 *f. f.* not away to Chaldeans
   44:12 shall all *f.* in land of Eg.
   46:6 they shall stumble and *f.*
   48:44 that fleeth shall *f.* into pit
   49:26 young men, *f.* 50:30
   50:32 most proud stumble and *f.*
   51:4 slain *f.* in land of C. 47, 49
   44 wall of Babylon shall *f.*
Lam. 1:14 made strength to *f.*
Ezek. 5:12 *f. f.* in the midst
   13:11 it shall *f.* and ye, O great hailstones, shall *f.*
   21:6 piece by piece, let no lot *f.*
   22:20 shall *f.* on open field, 23
   30:6 they that uphold E. sh. *f.*
   22 I will cause the sword to *f.*
   32:12 will I cause multit. to *f.*
   33:12 not *f.* thereby in the day
   35:8 in all thy rivers shalt th. *f.*
   38:20 steep places *f.* ev. wall *f.*
   39:3 arrows of *b. f.* sh. *f.* mo.
   4 *f.* on mountains, 5 op. field
Dan. 11:14 robbers of pe. pl. *f.*
   19 but he shall stumble and *f.*
   34 they shall *f.* by sword
   45 shall come to his end, *f.*
Hos. 4:5 shalt thou *f.* in the day
   14:9 transgressors shall *f.*
   10:2 their altar sh. *f.* to gro.
   8:8 Isr. shall *f.* into grain *f.*
   9:1 some enemy, there I. *f.*
   Mic. 7:8 when I *f.* I shall rise
Zec. 11:2 *f.* into the mouth
   Mat. 10:29 not sparrow *f.*
   12:11 if it *f.* into a pit
   15:14 *f.* into ditch, *Luke* 6:39
   27 crumbs wh. *f.* masters' tab.
   21:44 whoso *f.* on this stone bo
   Luke 20:18
   21:29 stars shall *f.* from heaven,
   Mark 13:25
   Luke 10:18 I beheld S. as lightl. *f.*
   13:4 on whom tower fell
   Acts 27:17 lest they *f.* into quic.
   32 cut ropes and let her *f.* off
   34 shall not a hair *f.* from head
   Rom. 11:11 stumbled that sh. *f.*
   11:11 to *f.* in brother's way
1 *Cor.* 10:12 take heed lest he *f.*
1 *Tim.* 3:6 *f.* into condemnation
   7 lest *f.* into reproach
   6:9 will be rich *f.* into tempta.
Heb. 4:11 lest any *f.* after same
   10:31 fearful to *f.* into hands
Jam. 1:2 ye *f.* into temptations

FAL

Jam. 5:12 swear not, lest ye *f.*
2 *Pet.* 1:10 do th. things, ye n. *f.*
   3:17 lest ye *f.* from steadfastn.
Rev. 6:16 mount. and ro. *f.* on us
   9:1 I saw a star *f.* from heaven

FALL away.

Luke 8:13 in time of tempt. *f. a.*
Heb. 6:6 if they *f. a.* to renew

FALL down.

Deut. 22:4 thy brother's ass *f. d.*
   28:52 wall of city shall *f. d.*
1 *Sam.* 31:13 David let spit. *f. d.*
Ps. 72:11 all kings shall *f. down*
Is. 31:3 that is holp, shall *f. d.*
   34:4 their host shall *f. d.*
   44:19 sh. I *f. d.* to sto. of troe?
   45:14 the Sabeans shall *f. d.*
   46:6 they *f. d.* yea, they worsh.
Ezek. 30:25 arms of Pha. sh. *f. d.*
Dan. 3:5 *f. d.* and worsh. image, 10
   15 if ye *f. d.* and worship im.
   11:26 and many shall *f. down*
Mat. 4:9 *f. d.* and wor. *Luke* 4:7
Rev. 4:10 twenty-four elders *f. d.*

FALL, joined with sword.

Ex. 5:3 he *f.* with pest. or s.
Num. 14:3 to this land to *f.* by s.
   43 and ye shall *f.* by the *sword*
2 *K.* 19:7 Senacherib *f.* by *swo.*
Ps. 63:10 sh. *f.* by *s.* *Ezek.* 6:11
Is. 3:25 thy men shall *f.* by *s.*
   13:15 every one shall *f.* by the *s.*
   31:7 I will cause him to *f.* by the *s.* in h. own la. *Jer.* 19:7
Jer. 20:4 P.'s friends sh. *f.* by *s.*
Ezek. 5:12 third part sh. *f.* by *s.*
   6:11 that is near shall *f.* by *s.*
   17:19 ye shall *f.* by the *s.*
   17:21 fugitives shall *f.* by thes.
   23:25 remnant shall *f.* by tho *s.*
   25:13 they of D. sh. *f.* by the *s.*
   30:5 men in league eh. *f.* by t. *s.*
   22 I will cause the *sword* to *f.*
Dan. 11:33 underst. *f.* by the *s.*
Hos. 7:16 princes sh. *f.* by the *s.*
   13:16 Samaria shall *f.* by the *s.*
Joel 2:8 they *f.* on the *sword*
Luke 21:24 shall *f.* by edge of *s.*

FALLEN.

Gen. 4:6 why is thy conute. *f.?*
Le. 13:41 hair *f.* off from head
   25:35 thy brother be *f.* in decay
Jud. 3:25 their lord was *f.* dead
1 *Sam.* 5:3 Ja. was *f.* upon his fa.
   26:12 a deep sleep *f.* upon them
   31:8 S. and h. sons *f.* 1 *Chr.* 10:8
2 *Sam.* 3:38 a great man *f.* this d.
Is. 14:11 Elisha was *f.* sick
2 *Chr.* 20:24 dead bodies *f.*
   23:9 our fathers have *f.*
Est. 7:8 Ham. was *f.* on the bed
Ps. 30:8 brought down and *f.*
   36:12 the workers of iniquity *f.*
Is. 14:12 thou *f.* fr. heaven, O L.
Ezek. 32:27 nil of them *f.* 23:21
Hos. 14:1 hast *f.* by iniquity
Luke 11:5 an ox *f.* into a pit?
Acts 8:16 H. G. was *f.* on none
   20:9 Eutychus *f.* into deep sl.
   26:14 when we were all *f.*
   27:29 lest they have *f.* on rock
   28:6 looked when D. sh. *f.* dead
Phile. 1:12 *f.* out to fur. of gospel
Rev. 2:5 rem. whence thou art *f.*

Are FALLEN.

2 *Sam.* 1:4 ma. of the peo. are *f.*
   19 how are mighty *f.* 2 *Sa.* 1:27
   22:39 *a. f.* under feet, *Ps.* 18:38
Ps. 16:6 lines are *f.*
   55:4 ter. of death *are f.* on me
   69:9 reproaches of them *are f.*
   72:16 they *are f.* both headl.
Jer. 38:19 Jews that *are f.* to C.
Lam. 2:21 my virgins *are f.*
Ezek. 31:12 his branches *are f.*
Hos. 7:7 all their kings *are f.*
1 *Cor.* 15:6 some *are f.* asleep, 18
   Gal. 5:4 you. every *f.* from grace
Rev. 17:10 seven kings, five a. *f.*

Is FALLEN.

Num. 32:19 lot *is f.* on th. side of
Job 1:16 fire of G. *is f.* fr. heav.
Ps. 7:16 mischief shall *f.*
Is. 3:8 Jer. ruined, and Jud. *is f.*
   21:9 B. *is f. is f. Rev.* 14:8; 18:2
   59:14 truth *is f.* in the streets
Jer. 48:32 spoil. *is f.* on *vint.* 51
51:8 Babylon is suddenly *f.*
Lam. 5:16 crown *is f.* from our heads
Ezek. 13:12 when the wall *is f.*
Amos 5:2 virgin of Israel *is f.*

Is FALLEN.

FAL

Amos 9:11 raise up tab. th. is *f*.
Acts 15:16 labor, of D. wh. is *f*.

FALLEST, ETH.
Ec. 1:10 when *f.* ont any war
2 *Sam.* 3:29 not fall one that *f.*
31 as a man *f.* bef. wick. men
17:12 as dew *f.* on ground
Job 1:13 deep sleep *f.* 33:15
Prov. 13:17 mess. *f.* into misch.
17:20 perv. tongue *f.* into mis.
24:16 just man *f.* seven times
17 rejoice not when enemy *f.*
Ec. 4:10 him alone when *f.*
11:3 wh. tree *f.* there shall it be
Is. 31:4 the leaf *f.* off the vine
44:15 image and *f.* down, 17
Jer. 37:13 thou *f.* away to Chald.
Dan. 3:6 whoso *f.* not down, 11
Mat. 17:15 ofttimes *f.* into fire
Luke 11:17 house div. ag. ho. *f.*
13:12 goods that *f.* to me
Rom. 14:4 master he stand, or *f.*
Jam. 1:11 flower th. *f.* 1 *Pet.* 1:24

FALLING.
Num. 24:4 *f.* into trance, 16
Job 4:4 upholden him that *f.*
14:18 mount *f.* cometh to nau.
Ps. 56:13 del. feet from *f.* 116:8
Prov. 25:26 righte. *f.* bef. wick.
Is. 34:4 as a *f.* fig from fig-tree
Luke 8:47 trembling *f.* down
22:44 drops of blood *f.* down
Acts 1:18 and Judas *f.* headlong
1 *Cor.* 14:25 *f.* he will worsh. G.
2 *Thes.* 2:3 except come a *f.* aw.
Jude 24 is able to keep from *f.*

FALLOW.
Jer. 4:3 *f.* ground, *Hos.* 10:12

FALSE.
Ex. 23:1 shalt not raise *f.* report
7 keep thee far from a *f.* mat.
2 *K.* 9:12 it is *f.* tell us now
Job 33:1 my words shall n. be *f.*
Ps. 119:104 I hate ev. *f.* way, 128
12:3 done thee, *f.* tongue
Prov. 11:1 *f.* balance is abomina-
tion
17:4 giveth heed to *f.* lips
25:23 a *f.* balance is not good
33:14 whoso boasteth of a *f.* gift
Jer. 14:14 prophecy a *f.* vision
23:32 prophesy *f.* dreams
37:14 it is *f.* I fall not away
Lam. 2:14 seen for thee *f.* bur-
dens
Ezek. 21:23 shall be as a *f.* divin.
Zec. 8:17 evil, love no *f.* oath
10:2 divin. have told *f.* dreams
Mat. 24:24 shall arise *f.* Christs
and *f.* prophets, *Mark* 13:22
Luke 19:8 any thing by *f.* accusa.
2 *Cor.* 11:13 such are *f.* apostles
26 in perils among *f.* brethren
Gal. 2:4 because of *f.* brethren
Tit. 2:3 they be not *f.* accusers
2 *Pet.* 2:1 there sh. be *f.* teachers
See PROPHET.

FALSE prophets.
Mat. 7:15 *f. p.* in sheep's cloth.
24:11 many *f. p.* shall rise, 24
Mark 13:22 *f. p.* rise show signs
Luke 6:26 did fathers to the *f. p.*
2 *Pet.* 2:1 there were *f. p.* ani. p.
1 *John* 4:1 *f. p.* gone out

FALSE witness, es.
Ex. 20:16 thou shalt not bear *f.*
wit. *Deut.* 5:20; *Mat.* 19:18
Deut. 19:16 if a *f.* witness rise up
18 if the witness be a *f.* witness
Ps. 27:12 *f.* witnesses are risen
35:11 *f. w.* did rise
Prov. 6:19 a *f. w.* speaketh lies
12:17 a *f. w.* show. deceit, 14:5
19:5 *f. w.* not be unpunished, 9
21:28 *f.* witness shall perish
25:18 that beareth *f. w.*
Mat. 15:19 out of heart pro. *f. w.*
26:59 elders sought *f. w.* ag. Je.
60 many *f.* witnesses came, at
last came two *f.* witnesses
Mark 14:56 bear *f. w.* ag. him, 57
Acts 6:13 and set up *f. w.*
1 *Cor.* 15:15 we are *f.* witness.

FALSEHOOD.
2 *Sam.* 18:13 sh. have wrong. *f.*
Job 21:34 in answers remaineth *f.*
Ps. 7:14 he hath brought forth *f.*
119:118 for deceit is *f.*
144:8 a right hand of *f.* 11
Is. 28:15 under *f.* have we hid
57:4 seed of *f.* ? 59:13 words of *f.*
Jer. 10:14 image is *f.* 51:17
Hos. 7:1 for they commit *f.*
Mic. 2:11 walking in spirit and *f.*

FAM

FALSELY.
Gen. 21:23 thou wilt not deal *f.*
Lev. 6:3 lost, and sweareth *f.*
19:11 neither deal *f.* nor lie
12 not swear by my name *f.*
Deut. 19:18 witn. have testifi. *f.*
Ps. 44:17 nor have we dealt *f.*
Jer. 5:2 L. liveth, they swear *f.*
31 prophets prophesy *f.* 29:9
6:13 every one dealeth *f.* 8:10
7:9 ye steal, mur. and swear *f.*
40:16 for thou speakest *f.* of Is.
43:2 speakest *f.* L. hath not sent
Hos. 10:4 swe. *f.* in making cov.
Zec. 5:4 enter house swear *f.*
Mat. 5:11 say evil against you *f.*
Luke 3:14 nor accuse any *f.*
1 *Tim.* 6:20 opp. of science *f.*
1 *Pet.* 3:16 *f.* accuse good conv.

FALSIFYING.
Amos 8:5 *f.* balances by deceit

FAME.
Gen. 45:16 *f.* was heard in Phar.
Num. 14:15 have heard *f.* of thee
Jos. 6:27 Joshua's *f.* was noised
9:9 we heard the *f.* of God
1 *K.* 4:31 *f.* was in all nations
10:1 heard *f.* of Sol. 2 *Chr.* 9:1
7 wish. exceedeth *f.* 2 *Chr.* 9:6
1 *Chr.* 14:17 *f.* of D. was to all
Est. 9:4 Mordecai's *f.* thro' prov.
Job 28:22 we have heard *f.*
Is. 66:19 that have not heard *f.*
Jer. 6:24 we have heard the *f.*
Zep. 3:19 and I will get them *f.*
Mat. 4:24 *f.* of J. abroad, *Mark*
1:28; *Luke* 4:14, 37; 5:15
9:26 the *f.* thereof went abroad
31 they spread abroad his *f.*
14:1 Herod heard of *f.* of Jesus

FAMILIAR.
Job 19:14 my *f.* friends have for.
Ps. 41:9 my *f.* friend lift up heel

FAMILIAR spirit.
Lev. 20:27 man or wom. of a *f. s.*
1 *Sam.* 28:7 wo. that hath *f. s.* 8
2 *Chr.* 33:6 Man. dealt with *f. s.*
Is. 29:4 as one that hath a *f. s.*

FAMILIAR spirits.
Lev. 19:31 reg. not th. have *f. s.*
20:6 soul that turneth after *f. s.*
Deut. 18:11 nor consulter w. *f. s.*
1 *Sam.* 28:3 S. put away th. *f. s.*
2 *K.* 21:6 with *f. s.* ; 23:24 *f. s.*
Is. 8:19 seek *f. s.* ; 19:3 hath *f. s.*

FAMILIARS.
Jer. 20:10 *f.* watched for halting

FAMILY.
Lev. 20:5 I will set face ag. his *f.*
25:10 return ev. man to his *f.* 41
47 the stock of the strange. *f.*
Num. 36:6 *f.* of father's tribe, 12
Deut. 29:18 lest a *f.* turn from L.
Jos. 7:14 *f.* which Lord taketh
Jud. 1:25 go man and all his *f.*
9:15 my *f.* is poor in Manasseh
21:24 one of a cit. two of a *f.*
Zec. 12:12 *f.* sh. mourn, 13, 14
Eph. 3:15 *f.* in heav. and earth

FAMILIES.
Gen. 10:5 Gentiles divided aft. *f.*
32 aft *f.* of Noah, 28:14
Ex. 12:21 take lamb ac. to yo. *f.*
Num. 4:18 people after their *f.*
Job 31:34 did cont. of *f.* ter. me?
Ps. 68:6 G. setteth solitary in *f.*
107:41 mak. him *f.* like a flock
Jer. 1:15 will call all *f.* of north
10:25 fury on *f.* call not name
33:9 will take all the *f.* of north
31:1 God of all the *f.* of Israel
33:24 *f.* which L. hath chosen
Ezek. 20:32 as *f.* of countries
Amos 3:2 you have I kn. of all *f.*
Nah. 3:4 selleth *f.* thro' witchcr.
Zec. 12:14 *f.* that remain
14:17 will not come of all *f.*

FAMINE.
Gen. 12:10 *f.* was grievous in la.
26:1 *f.* in land, besides first *f.*
41:27 7 empty ears 7 years *f.*
30 *f.* shall consume the land
31 plenty not kn. by rea. of *f.*
56 *f.* was over all face of earth
47:13 fainted by reason of *f.*
Ruth 1:1 ruled there was *f.* in la.
2 *Sam.* 21:1 *f.* in the days of D.
24:13 shall 7 years of *f.* come?
1 *K.* 8:37 in land *f.* 2 *Chr.* 20:9
18:2 *f.* in Samaria, 2 *K.* 6:25
2 *K.* 7:4 enter the city
8:1 the Lord hath call. for a *f.*
25:3 *f.* prevailed in J. no bread
2 *Chr.* 32:11 if. per. you to die *f.*
Job 5:20 in *f.* he shall red. thee *f.*

FAR

Job 5:22 at destruc. *f.* thou sh. la.
33:3 want and *f.* were solitary
Ps. 33:19 keep them alive in *f.*
37:19 in days of *f.*
105:16 he called for a *f.*
Is. 14:30 I will kill root with *f.*
51:19 destruction, *f.* and sword
Jer. 14:15 by *f.* sh. proph. be con.
18 them that are sick with *f.*
15:2 such for the *f.* to the *f.*
18:21 deliver up children to *f.*
21:7 deliver from the *f.* to Neb.
24:10 send *f.* am. them, 29:17
27:8 nation will I pun. with *f.*
34:17 liberty for you to the *f.*
42:16 the *f.* shall follow
52:6 the *f.* was sore in the city
Lam. 5:10 skin black, bec. of *f.*
Ezek. 5:12 part consumed with *f.*
16 evil arrows of *f.*
17 I send on you *f.* 14:13
7:15 *f.* within *f.* and pestilence
12:16 leave a few men from *f.*
36:29 will lay no *f.* upon you
Amos 8:11 I will send *f.*
Luke 4:25 great, *f.* through land
15:14 a mighty *f.* in that land
Rom. 8:35 *f.* sep. fr. love of C.?
Rev. 18:8 in one day, death, *f.*

By the FAMINE.
Jer. 11:22 sons and d. die by *t. f.*
11:12 7 will consume by *t. f.* 13
16:4 be con. by *t. f.* 44:12, 18, 27
21:9 abideth in city die by *t. f.*
38:2 shall die by *t. f. Ezek.* 6:12
17 *they* shall die by *t. f.*
22 fami. to shall die by *t. f.*
44:13 I have punish. J. by *t. f.*
Ezek. 6:11 they shall fall by *t. f.*

FAMINES.
Mat. 24:7 shall be *f.* pestilences,
Mark 13:8 ; *Luke* 21:11

FAMISH, ED.
Gen. 41:55 all land of Egypt *f.*
Prov. 10:3 not suffer right. to *f.*
Is. 5:13 their honor. men are *f.*
Zep. 2:11 will *f.* gods of earth

FAMOUS.
Num. 16:2 *f.* in congrega. 26:9
Ruth 4:11 he thou *f.* in Bethleh.
14 his name may be *f.* in Israel
1 *Chr.* 5:24 *f.* men, 12:30
Ps. 74:5 was *f.* as he lifted a axe
136:18 to him who slew *f.* kings
Ezek. 23:10 became *f.* am. wom.
32:18 daughters of *f.* nations

FAN, Substantive.
Is. 30:24 winnowed with *f.*
Jer. 15:7 I will fan with *f.*
Mat. 3:12 wh. *f.* is in h. *Luke* 3:17

FAN, Verb.
Is. 41:16 sh. *f.* them, winds sh.
Jer. 4:11 a dry wind not to *f.*
15:7 I will *f.* them with a fan
51:2 fanners that shall *f.* her

FAR.
Gen. 18:25 *f.* from thee to slay
Ex. 8:28 ye shall not go very *f.*
23:7 keep *f.* from false matter
Deut. 12:21 *f.* from thee, 14:24
30:22 stranger from a *f.* land
Jos. 9:22 from you
Jud. 9:17 adventured life *f.*
1 *Sam.* 20:9 J. said, *f.* be it from
Sam. 23:17 *f.* be it from me
4:11 *f.* be it from me
6:10 separ. unc. *f.* from an.
Job 5:4 sons from his help, 4
Job 8:4 children *f.* from safety
11:14 iniquity *f.* away, 22:23
34:10 *f.* be it from God
Ps. 10:5 judg. are *f.* out of sight
22:1 why art *f.* from help. me?
38:27 that are *f.* from thee
97:9 L. exalted *f.* above all gods
103:12 as *f.* as east fr. west
109:17 blessing be *f.* from him
119:155 salva. is *f.* from wicked
Prov. 4:24 set away froward *f.*
15:29 Lord is *f.* from the wicked
27:10 for net. is *f.* more, 31:10 better a neighbor *f.*
Ec. 2:13 *f.* as light excel. dark.
Is. 46:13 not turn rivers *f.* away
46:12 hear my heart *f.* from right.
40:1 hear for called me from w.
59:9 is judgment *f.* from us
Jer. 51:64 thus *f.* are words of J.
Ezek. 8:6 that my sanct. *f.* from
11:15 get ye *f.* from the L.
11:16 Lord of hosts *f.* off
Amos 6:3 put *f.* away evil day
Mat. 16:22 he it *f.* from thee, L.
Mark 6:35 day was now *f.* spent
12:34 not *f.* from kingd. of God

FAS

Mark 13:34 man taking a *f.* jour.
Luke 7:6 was not *f.* from house
22:51 Jesus said, Suf, ye thus *f.*
24:29 for the day is *f.* spent
50 out as *f.* as to Bethany
John 21:8 were not *f.* from land
Acts 17:27 not *f.* from every one
22:21 send thee *f.* hence to Gen.
23:15 meet us as *f.* as Ap. foram
Rom. 13:12 the night is *f.* spent
2 *Cor.* 4:17 *f.* more ex. weight
Eph. 1:21 *f.* abo. all principality
4:10 ascended up *f.* above all
Phil. 1:23 with C. wh. is *f.* bet.
Heb. 7:15 it is yet *f.* more evid.
See COUNTRY, COUNTRIES.

FAR from me.
1 *Sam.* 2:30 Be it *f.* from me,
22:15 ; 2 *Sam.* 20:20 ; 23:17
Job 13:21 thy hand *f. from me*
19:13 hath put my bro. *f. f. me*
21:16 wicked is *f. f. m.* 22:18
30:10 they flee *f. from me*
Ps. 22:11 O Lord be not *f. f. me,*
19 ; 35:22 ; 38:21 ; 71:12
27:9 hide not thy face *f. f. me*
88:8 mine acquaintance *f. f. me*
18 lover and friend *f. from me*
Prov. 30:8 remove *f. f. me* vanity
Jer. 7:28 but was *f. from me*
Is. 29:13 their heart *f. from me*
1:16 comfort. is *f. from me*
Ezek. 44:10 Lev. are gone *f. f. me*
Mat. 15:8 is *f. f. me, Mark* 7:6

From FAR.
Deut. 28:49 na. ag. *f. f. Jer.* 5:13
Job 36:3 fetch my know. *f. f.*
Ps. 139:2 understandest *f. f.*
10:3 deceit, which sh. come *f. f.*
22:3 which are fled *f. f.*
30:27 the name of L. com. *f. f.*
43:6 bring my sons *from f.* 60:9
49:1 hearken, ye people *from f.*
12 these shall come *from f.*
60:4 thy sons shall come *from f.*
Jer. 30:10 I will save thee *from f.*
46:27 for men to come *f. f.*
Mark 8:3 div. of them came *f. f.*
See AFAR.

FAR off.
Deut. 13:7 serve the gods *f. off*
20:15 thus do to cities very *f. off*
30:11 nor is com. *f. off*
2 *Sam.* 15:17 king tarried *f. off*
2 *Chr.* 6:36 captives to land *f. off*
Prov. 27:10 than a brother *f. off*
Ec. 7:24 *f. f. off* who find out?
Is. 17:13 they shall flee *f. off*
33:13 ye *f. off,* what I done
17 behold land that is *f. off*
46:13 my right, not be *f. off*
57:19 peace to him *f. off*
60:11 salvation, not it is *f. off*
Ezek. 6:12 *f. off* die of pestilence
8:6 *f. off* from my sanctuary ?
11:16 I have cast them *f. off*
12:27 prophesieth of times *f. off*
22:5 those that be *f. off* sh. mock
Dan. 9:7 confus. to Israel *f. off*
Joel 2:20 rem. *f. off* north, army
3:8 sell them to Sabeans *f. off*
Mic. 4:7 her cast *f. off,* a nation
Zec. 6:25 *f. off* come and build
Eph. 2:13 *f. off* are made nigh
17 preached peace to you *f. off*

FARE.
1 *Sam.* 17:18 look how thy br. *f.*
Jon. 1:3 paid the *f.* thereof
Luke 16:19 rich man *f.* sumptu.

FAREWELL.
Luke 9:61 bid them *f.* at home
Acts 15:29 well *f.* 18:21 ; 23:30
2 *Cor.* 13:11 finally brethren, *f.*

FARTHER. See FURTHER.

FARTHING, S.
Mat. 5:26 paid the uttermost *f.*
10:29 two sparrows sold for *f.?*
Mark 12:42 threw two mites, a *f.*
Luke 12:6 five sparr. for two *f.?*

FASHION.
Gen. 6:15 this is *f.* which make
Ex. 26:30 *f.* of tabernacle
37:19 bowls made after the *f.*
1 *K.* 6:38 built ac. to all the *f.*
2 *K.* 16:10 Ahaz sent *f.* of altar
Job 41:33 hands *f.* inc. *Ps.* 119:73
31:15 not one *f.* us in the wo.?
Ps. 33:15 he *f.* their hearts alike
139:16 in continuance were *f.*
Is. 22:11 nei. respect to him *f.* it
44:12 the smith *f.* it with ham.

CRUDEN'S CONCORDANCE. 849

FAT

Is. 45:9 clay say to him that *f.*
Ezek. 16:7 thy breasts are *f.*
Phil. 3:21 *f.* like to his glo. body
1 *Pet.* 1:14 not *f.* to former lusts

FAST, Adverb.
Jud. 15:13 we will bind thee *f.*
Ps. 65:6 strength set *f.* moun.
Prov. 4:13 *f.* hold of instruction
Jer. 48:16 afflic. of M. hasteth *f.*
50:33 took captiv. held them *f.*
Jon. 1:5 lay in ship, *f.* asleep

FAST, Substantive.
1 *K.* 21:9 pro. a *f.* 2 *Chr.* 20:3;
Ezr. 8:21; *Jer.* 36:9; *Jon.* 3:5
Is. 58:3 in *f.* you find pleasure
5 a *f.* wilt thou call this a *f.*?
if this the *f.* I have chosen?
Joel 1:14 sanc. *f.* call assem. 2:15
Zec. 8:19 *f.* of 4th, 5th, 7th, 10th month
Acts 27:9 *f.* was now already past

FAST, Verb.
2 *Sam.* 12:23 child dead, why *f.*?
Is. 58:4 ye *f.* for strife, sh. not *f.*
Jer. 14:12 when *f.* I will not hear
Zec. 7:5 did ye at all *f.* unto me?
Mat. 6:16 ye *f.* be not of sad counten. that may ap. to *f.*
9:14 disc. *f.* not? *Mark* 2:18
15 then *f.* *Mark* 2:20; *Lu.* 5:35
Mark 2:18 disc. of J. used to *f.*
19 children of bridechamber *f.*
Luke 5:33 discip. of J. *f.* often?
18:12 I *f.* twice in the week

FASTED, EST.
Jud. 20:26 *f.* th. day, 1 *Sam.* 7:6
1 *Sam.* 31:13 *f.* 7 d. 1 *Chr.* 10:12
2 *Sam.* 1:12 *f.* for S. ; 1 *K.* 21:27 A.
Neh. 1:4 Neh. *f.* and pra. *Ez.* 0:23
Is. 58:3 why have we *f.*?
Mat. 4:2 Jesus *f.* forty days
6:17 when thou *f.* anoint head
Acts 13:3 *f.* laid hands on them

FASTING, S.
Neh. 9:1 were assembled with *f.*
Es. 4:3 dec. came there was *f.*
Ps. 35:13 humbled soul with *f.*
69:10 chast. my soul with *f.*
109:24 knees weak through *f.*
Jer. 36:6 the words on *f.* day
Dan. 6:18 passed the night *f.*
9:3 B. set him. to seek by *f.*
Joel 2:12 turn ye with *f.*
Mat. 15:32 send them away *f.*
17:21 but by *f.* *Mark* 9:29
Mat. 3:4 send them away *f.*
Luke 2:37 Anna served G. with *f.*
Acts 10:30 four days ago I was *f.*
14:23 and had prayed with *f.*
27:33 fourteenth day ye cont. *f.*
1 *Cor.* 7:5 give yourselves to *f.*
2 *Cor.* 6:5 approv. ourselves in *f.*
11:27 *f.* often, in cold and nak.

FASTEN, ED, ING.
Judg. 4:21 J. *f.* nail into ground
1 *Chr.* 10:10 *f.* head in temple
Job 38:6 wher. are foundations *f.*
Ec. 12:11 as nails *f.* by masters
Is. 22:23 I will *f.* him as a nail
25 nail *f.* in the sure place
41:7 he *f.* it, it sh. not be moved
Ec. 10:4 they *f.* it with nails
Luke 4:20 eyes of all *f.* on him
Acts 3:4 Peter *f.* his eyes on him
11:6 when I had *f.* my eyes
28:3 a viper *f.* on his hand

FAT.
Gen. 4:4 Abel brought *f.* of flock
Ex. 23:18 take the *f.*, 23; *Lev.* 3:3,
4, 9, 10; 4:8; 7:3, 4
Lev. 3:16 all the *f.* is the Lord's
4:26 burn his *f.* 6:12; 17:6
7:24 *f.* of beast that dieth
23 *f.* from Lord consumed *f.*
Deut. 32:14 *f.* of lambs, *f.* of fat
Jud. 3:22 *f.* closed on the blade
1 *Sam.* 2:16 from *f.* of mighty
2 *Chr.* 35:14 offer *f.* until night
Job 15:27 collops of *f.* on flanks
Ps. 17:10 inclosed in *f.* own *f.*
Is. 1:11 full of *f.* of fed beasts
34:6 *f.*, *f.* of kidneys
43:24 nor filled me with *f.*
Ezek. 44:7 ye offer *f.* and blood

Eat **FAT.**
Gen. 45:18 shall eat *f.* of land
Lev. 3:17 eat no *f.* 7:23
7:25 whoso eateth *f.* be cut off
Num. 22:38 eat *f.* of sacrifices
Neh. 8:10 eat *f.* drink the sweet
Ezek. 34:3 ye eat *f.* and clothe
34:10 ye shall eat *f.* till full
Zec. 11:16 shall eat flesh of *f.*

FAT

FAT, Adjective.
Gen. 41:2 came up seven kine *f.*
49:20 out of A. his bread be *f.*
Num. 13:20 land *f.* or lean
Deut. 31:20 when waxen *f.* then
32:15 Jeshurun waxed *f.* kicked
Jud. 3:17 Egl. was very *f.* man
1 *Sam.* 2:29 to make *f.* with off.
28:24 the woman had a *f.* calf
1 *Chr.* 4:40 they found *f.* pasture
Neh. 9:25 took a *f.* land &c. 25
Ps. 22:29 they *f.* on earth
37:20 enemies as *f.* of lambs
92:14 shall be *f.* and flourish.
119:70 heart is as *f.* as grease
Prov. 11:25 lib. soul be made *f.*
13:4 soul of diligent be made *f.*
15:30 good report mak. bones *f.*
28:25 trusteth in L. be made *f.*
Is. 5:17 of *f.* ones strangers eat
6:10 make the bos. of th. peo. *f.*
10:16 send am. *f.* ones leanness
25:6 feast of *f.* th. full of marr.
28:1 on head of the *f.* valleys, 4
30:23 bread be *f.* and plenteous
34:6 sword of the L. is made *f.*
7 dust shall be *f.* with fatness
58:11 L. shall make *f.* thy bones
Jer. 5:28 waxen *f.* they shine
50:11 ye are grown *f.* as heifer
Ezek. 34:14 in *f.* pasture sh. feed
16 I will destroy *f.* and strong
20 judge bet. *f.* cattle and lean
45:15 lamb out of *f.* pastures
Amos 5:22 nor req. off. of *f.* bea.
Hab. 1:16 by them portion is *f.*

FATHER.
Gen. 17:4 be *f.* of many nations,
5; *Rom.* 4:17, 18
44:19 have ye a *f.*? 20 we have
45:8 made me a *f.* to Pharaoh
Lev. 18:10 *f.* was an Egyptian
Num. 11:12 as nursing *f.*
30:16 statutes betw. *f.* and dau.
Jud. 17:10 be to me a *f.*
18:19 be to us a *f.* and a priest
Est. 3:7 Esther had not *f.* nor
Job 29:16 I was a *f.* to the poor
31:18 with me as with a *f.*
38:28 hath the rain a *f.*?
Ps. 68:5 a *f.* of fatherless is God
103:13 as a *f.* pitieth children
Prov. 3:12 correcteth, as *f.* son
4:1 hear the instruction of a *f.*
10:1 maketh a glad *f.* 15:20
17:21 of a *f.* hath no joy
23:24 *f.* of righteous wis. rejoice
24 *f.* of righteous wis. rejoice
22:9 called everlasting *f.*
22:21 Eliakim be *f.* to inhabit.
38:19 *f.* to child. make kn. truth
Jer. 31:9 for I am a *f.* to Israel
Ezek. 18:4 as soul of *f.* so of son
20 son shall not bear iniq. of *f.*
22:7 in thee they set light by *f.*
Mic. 7:6 son dishonoreth the *f.*
Mal. 1:6 a *f.* where mine honor?
2:10 have we not all one *f.*?
Mat. 10:20 *f.* del. ch. *Mark* 13:12
37 that loveth *f.* more than me
11:25 Jesus said, I th. thee, *F.*
25 so *F., Lu.* 10:21 ; *John* 11:41
27 knoweth the Son but the *F.*
13:4 that cursedeth *f.* *Mark* 7:10
19:5 leave *f.* and cleave to wife
29 that hath forsaken *f.* for my name's sake, *Mark* 10:29
24:36 knoweth no man but *F.*
Mark 9:24 *f.* of child with tears
13:32 knoweth no man but *F.*
14:36 Abba, *F.* all th. possible
Luke 10:22 who the *F.* is, but R.
11:11 if a son ask bread of a *f.*
12:53 *f.* be divided against the son and son against the *f.*
15:21 *f.* I have sinned agn. hea.
16:27 I pray thee *f.* send him
22:42 *F.* if willing, remove cup
23:31 *F.* forgive them, they
46 *F.* into thy hands I com.
John 1:14 only begotten of *F.*
18 Son who is in bosom of *F.*
3:35 *F.* loveth the Son, 5:20
4:23 *f.* seeketh in spirit, worship
5:19 do noth. but what *F.* do
21 as *F.* rais. up dead, so Son
22 the *F.* judgeth no man, but hath committed
26 the *F.* hath life in himself
36 works *F.* hath giv. me bear witness *F.* hath sent me
37 *F.* which hath sent, 8:16;
12:49; 14:24; 1 *John* 4:14
6:45 will be... you to the *F.*
8:27 all the *F.* giveth me, shall
39 *F.* will that I lose nothing
44 Jesus whose *f.* we know?

FAT

John 6:44 exc. the *F.* draw him
45 learned of *F.* cometh to me
46 not any hath seen the *F.* he
57 so, me, and I live by the *F.*
8:16 am not alone, but I and *F.*
18 *F.* beareth witness of me
27 unders. not he spake of *F.*
29 *F.* hath not left me alone
41 we have one *F.* even God
44 devil is liar, and the *f.* of it
10:15 *F.* know. me, so I the *F.*
36 whom the *F.* hath sanctified
38 *F.* is in me, and I in him
12:27 *F.* save me from this hour
28 *F.* glorify thy name, then
50 as *F.* said to me, so I speak
13:1 should depart unto the *F.*
3 that *F.* had given all things
14:6 com. to the *F.* but by me
8 Lord, show us the *F.*
9 seen me, hath seen the *F.*
11 I in *F.* and *F.* in me, 17:21
13 *F.* may be glorified in Son
12:27 *F.* save me from this hour
16 I will pray the *F.* for you, 16:26
23 my *F.* love him, we come to
28 go to the *F.* for *F.* is gr. than
31 I love the *F.* as *F.* gave co.
15:9 as the *F.* hath loved me, so
16 whatsoever ye ask *F.* 16:26
26 I will send Comfor. from *F.*
16:3 not known the *F.* nor me
15 all things *F.* hath, are mine
16 because I go to the *F.* 17
25 show you plainly of the *F.*
27 the *F.* loveth you, because
28 came from *F.* and go to *F.*
32 am not alone, *F.* is with me
17:1 *F.* hour is come, glorify S.
5 O *F.* glorify thou me with
11 holy *F.* keep th. given me
21 as I will they be when *F.* in me
25 O right. *F.* world hath not
Acts 1:4 wait for promise of *F.*
7 *F.* put in his own power
2:33 received of *F.* the promise
Rom. 4:11 he *f.* of them believe
12 *f.* of circumcision to them
16 Abraham, who is *f.* of us all
6:4 as Christ was raised by *F.*
8:15 whereby we cry, Abba, *F.*
11:28 are belov. for the *f.* sakes
15:6 *F.* of our L. J. C. 2 *Cor.* 1:3;
11:31; *Eph.* 1:3 ; 1 *Pet.* 1:3
1 *Cor.* 8:6 is but one God, the *F.*
15:24 deliv. up kingdom to *F.*
2 *Cor.* 1:3 *F.* of mercies
6:18 I will be a *F.* unto you
Gal. 1:3 peace from *F.* 2 *Tim.*
1:2; *Tit.* 1:4
4 ac. to will of God and our *F.*
4:2 until time appointed of *F.*
6 Spirit crying, Abba, *F.*
Eph. 1:17 G. of Jesus *F.* of glory
18 access by one Spirit to *F.*
3:14 bow my knees unto the *F.*
4:6 one God and *F.*
5:20 giving thanks to *F.* Col.
1:3, 12 ; 3:17
6:23 love with faith from *F.*
Phil. 2:11 is Lord, to glory of *F.*
Col. 1:19 it pleas. *F.* that all fuln.
2:2 acknowl. of mystery of *F.*
1 *Tim.* 5:1 church in God the *F.*
2:11 charged you, as a *f.* doth
1 *Tim.* 5:1 entreat him as a *f.*
Heb. 1:5 I will be to him a *F.* he
7:3 Melchizedek without *f.*
12:7 what son *f.* chasten. not?
9 in subjection to *F.* of spirits
Jam. 1:17 com. from *F.* of lights
27 pure religion before *F.*
3:9 bless we God, even the *F.*
1 *Pet.* 1:2 foreknowl. of the *F.*
17 call on *F.* who judgeth
1 *Jn.* 1:2 receiv. from *F.* honor
1 *John* 1:2 life wh. was with *F.*
3 our fellow. is with *F.*
2:1 advocate with the *F.* J.
13 because ye have known *F.*
15 love of the *F.* is not in him
16 pride of life is not of the *F.*
22 antichrist deni. *F.* and Son
23 whoso denieth S. hath not *F.*
24 continue in the S. and in *F.*
3:1 what manner of love the *F.*
5:7 three bear record, the *F.*
2 *John* 3 mercy and peace fr. *F.*
4 as received a com. from *F.*
9 abideth in Christ hath *F.*
Jude 1 sanctified by God the *F.*

FAT

Gen. 2:24 shall a man leave his *f.*
Mark 10:7; *Eph.* 5:31
26:7 Jacob obeyed his *f.* and his
31:53 J. sware by fear of his *f.*
37:1 his *f.* was a stranger
2 to deliver him to his *f.*
44:22 the lad cannot leave his *f.*
46:1 sacrifices to God of his *f.*
29 Joseph went to meet his *f.*
47:12 Joseph nourished his *f.*
Ex. 21:15 smit. *f.* be put to dea.
17 curseth his *f.* *Lev.* 20:9
Lev. 19:3 fear every man his *f.*
Deut. 21:18 will not obey his *f.*
27:16 setteth light by his *f.*
33:9 his *f.* I have not seen him
1 *Sam.* 14:1 Jona. told not his *f.*
19:4 snake good of D. to his *f.*
22:34 A. *f.* had done him shame
2 *Sam.* 7:14 will be his *f.* he son
10:2 as his *f.* showed kindness to me, 1 *Chr.* 19:2
1 *K.* 11:4 not perf. as David h. *f.*
6 as did Dav. his *f.* 15:11; 2 *K.*
18:3 ; 2 *Chr.* 28:1 ; 29:2
33 not as *f.* 2 *K.* 14:3 ; 16:2
15:3 walked in all sins of his *f.*
26 way of *f.* 22:43 ; 2 *K.* 21:20
2 *K.* 3:2 did evil, but not like *f.*
1 *Chr.* 17:13 I will be his *f.* 28:6
2 *Chr.* 8:1 L. appeared to D. his *f.*
17:4 Jehos. sought God of his *f.*
34 in ways of David his *f.* 3
Prov. 13:1 hear. instruction of *f.*
15:5 despiseth h. *f.* instruction
17:25 foolish son a grief to h. *f.*
19:13 is the calamity of his *f.*
26 wasteth his *f.* caus. shame
28:24 curseth h. *f.* I am put out
29:7 com. of riot, shameth his *f.*
24 whoso robbeth his *f.*
29:3 lov. wisdom rejoiceth h. *f.*
30:17 mocketh *f.* ravens pick
Is. 45:10 woe to him saith to *f.*
Ezek. 18:14 son seeth h. *f.* sins
17 nor die for iniquity of his *f.*
Amos 2:7 his *f.* go in to maid
Zec. 13:3 his *f.* shall thrust him
Mal. 1:6 a son honors his *f.*
10:35 at variance ag. his *f.*
15:5 to h. *f.* it is gift, *Mark* 7:11
6 and honor not his *f.* be free
16:27 Son come in glory of h. *F.*
Mark 8:38 ; *Luke* 9:26
21:31 whether did will of h. *f.*?
Luke 1:32 give him thr. of his *f.*
59 called after name of his *f.*
62 they made signs unto his *f.*
9:42 J. delivered him to his *f.*
14:26 and hate not his *f.*
15:12 younger said to his *f.*
20 arose and came to his *f.*
John 5:18 said that G. was his *F.*
Acts 16:1 but his *f.* was a Greek
Heb. 7:10 in the loins of his *f.*
Rev. 1:6 kings and pr. to his *F.*
14:1 his *F.* name in foreheads

See **HOUSE.**

FATHER-IN-LAW

Ex. 18:1 Moses' *f.-in-law*, 8, 11,
17 ; *Jud.* 1:16 ; 4:11
Ex. 18:27 M. let *f.-in-law* depart
Jud. 19:4 *f.-in-law* retained him
John 18:13 *f.-in-law* to Caiaphas

My FATHER

Gen. 19:31 I lay yest. with *my f.*
20:12 the daughter of *my f.*
22:31 R. cried, Bless me, *my f.*
31:5 the God of *my f.* 42 ; 32:9;
Ex. 18:4
44:31 thy servant *my f.* 27:30
32 surety for the lad to *my f.*
45:3 doth *my f.* yet live?
47:1 *my f.* and breth. are come
Deut. 26:5 a Syrian was *my f.*
Jos. 2:13 will save alive *my f.*
Jud. 9:17 *my f.* fought for you
11:36 I have not told it *my f.*
14:16 *my f.* and mother
19:18 what is *my f.* family?
20:2 *my f.* will do nothing
13 L. be with thee as with *my f.*
22:3 let *my f.* be with you
2 *Sam.* 16:3 restore king. of *my f.*
1 *K.* 2:32 beard not before *my f.*
41 walketh in *my f.* way will
3:6 showed to D. *my f.* mercy
7 made king instead of *my f.*
5:3 *my f.* could not build house
8:17 in heart of *f.-in-law* to build
12:10 little finger be thicker th.
my f. loins, 2 *Chr.* 10:10
11 *my f.* lade you, I sh. 10:11
2 *Chr.* chastised, 2 *Chr.* 10:14

FAT

1 K. 15:19 lea. be. my f. 2 Chr. 16:3
19:20 kiss my f. and mother
2 K. 2:12 Elisha cried, my f. my f.
6:21 my f. shall I smite them?
13:14 Joash said, my f. my f.
1 Chr. 28:4 chose me bef. all ho.
of my f. and among sons
2 Chr. 2:3 didst deal with my f.
Job 17:14 I said to corrup. my f.
Ps. 27:10 f. and mother forsake
89:26 thou art my F. my God
Prov. 4:3 for I was my f. son
Is. 8:4 knowledge to cry my f.
Jer. 2:27 stock, thou art my f.
3:4 thou not cry, my F. ? 19
22:15 brought tidings to my f.
Dan. 5:13 my f. brought out of J.
Mat. 7:21 doeth will of F. 12:50
8:21 go bury my f. Luke 9:59
10:32 him confess before my F.
33 him will I deny bef. my F.
11:27 delivered of F. Luke 10:22
15:13 my F. hath not planted
16:17 my F. in heaven revealed
18:10 angels beh. face of my F.
19 it shall be done of my F.
35 heavenly F. also do to you
20:23 it is prepared of my F.
24:36 that day know, but my F.
25:34 come, ye blessed of my F.
26:29 drink it new in F. kingd.
39 O my F. let this cup pass
42 my F. tby will be done
53 I cannot pray to my F. ?
Luke 2:49 about my F. business
15:18 I will arise and go to my f.
16:27 send him to my f. house
22:29 as my F. hath appointed
24:49 the promise of my F.
John 5:17 my F. worketh
30 but the will of my F.
43 I am come in my F. name
6:32 my F. giv. you true bread
65 except it be given of my F.
8:19 nel. know me, nor my F.
28 as my F. hath taught
38 I have seen with my F.
49 I honor my F. ye dishonor
54 it is my F. that honor. me
10:17 doth my F. love me
18 this com. I recel. of my F.
25 works I do in my F. name
29 my F. is greater than all
30 I and my F. are one
32 good works from my F.
37 If I do not works of my F.
12:26 him will my F. honor
14:7 should have known my F.
12 because I go to my F. 16:10
20 shall know I am in my F.
21 shall be loved of my F. 23
23 my F. is greater than I
15:1 my F. is the husbandman
8 herein is my F. glorified
10 I kept my F. commandm.
15 all that I heard of my F.
23 hateth me hateth my F. 24
18:11 cup my F. hath given
20:17 to my F. and your F.
21 as my F. hath sent me, so
Rev. 2:27 as I received of my F.
3:5 confess his name bef. my F.

Our FATHER.
Gen. 19:31 o. F. old; 32 o. f. dri.
43:28 our f. is in good health
44:31 o. f. with sorrow to grave
Num. 27:3 o. f. died in wildern.
4 nnms of our f. done away ?
1 Chr. 29:10 bless. be th. L. o. F.
Is. 63:10 thou art our F.
64:8 art our F. we are the clay
Jer. 35:6 our f. com. drink no w.
Mat. 8:9 our F. Luke 11:2
Mark 11:10 blessed king. of o. f.
Luke 3:8 have Abraham to our f.
John 4:12 greater than o. f. ? 8:53
Acts 7:2 God appeared to our f.
Rom. 1:7 peace fr. G. our F. 1 Cor.
1:3; 2 Cor. 1:2; Eph. 1:2; Phil.
1:2; Col. 1:2; 1 Thes. 1:2; 2 Thes.
1:2; 1 Tim. 1:2; Phile. 3.
9:10 even by our f. Isaac
Gal. 1:4 will of God and our F.
Phil. 4:20 to our F. be glory
1 Thes. 1:3 sight of G. and o. F.
3:11 our F. direct our way
13 stablish in holiness bef. o. F.
2 Thes. 1:1 church in God our F.
2:16 our F. comfort our hearts

Their FATHER.
Gen. 9:23 saw not naked. of t. f.
19:36 with child by their f.
Ex. 40:15 didst anoint their f.
1 Sam. 2:25 heark. not to their f.
10:12 one said, Who is their f.?
1 Chr. 24:2 N. Abihu died bef. t. f.
2 Chr. 21:3 t. f. gave great gifts

FAT

Job 42:15 t. f. gave inheritance
Prov. 30:11 that curseth their f.
Jer. 16:7 con. to drink for t. f.
35:14 Jona. sons obeyed t. f. 16
Ezek. 22:10 disc. t. f. nakedness
Mat. 4:21 with Zebedee their f.
22 left t. f. and followed him

Thy FATHER.
Gen. 12:1 get from thy f. house
46:3 I am the God of thy f.
49:25 by the God of thy f.
26 blessings of thy f. prevailed
50:16 t. f. com. before he died
17 forgive serv. of G. of thy f.
Ex. 20:12 honor t. f. and mother,
Deut. 5:16; Mat. 15:4; 19:19
28:8 A. G. of t. f. promised
32:6 is not he t. f. bought thee ?
7 ask thy f. and he will show
Ruth 2:11 thou hast left thy f.
1 Sam. 20:6 if thy f. miss me
2 Sam. 5:21 chose me before t. f.
10:3 thinkest thou that D. doth
honor thy f. 1 Chr. 19:3
16:19 served in thy f. presence
1 K. 12:10 for David t. f. sake
2 K. 3:13 get to prophets of t. f.
20:5 than saith the G. of D. t. f.
2 Chr. 21:12 ; B. 32:5
1 Chr. 28:9 son, know G. of t. f.
2 Chr. 7:17 if walk bef. me as t. f.
Job 15:10 much elder than thy f.
Prov. 1:8 instruct. of thy f. 23:22
6:20 keep thy f. commandment
23:25 t. f. and mother sh. be gl.
27:10 thy f. friend forsake not
Ez. 43:27 thy first f. hath sinned
58:14 heritage of Jacob thy f.
Jer. 12:6 house of t. f. dealt trea.
22:15 did not thy f. eat, drink
Ezek. 16:3 thy f. was an Amorite
Dan. 5:11 in the days of thy f.
18 God gave thy f. a kingdom
Mat. 6:4 t. F. who seeth in secret
6 pray to t. f. F. who is in secret
Mark 7:10 M. said, Honor thy f.
10:19; Luke 18:20 ; Eph. 6:2
Luke 2:48 thy f. and I sought
15:27 thy f. hath killed calf
John 8:19 Where is thy f. ?

Your FATHER.
Gen. 31:7 your f. hath deceived
43:7 is our f. alive ?
44:17 ant up in peace to your f.
45:10 bring your f. and come
46:2 hearken unto Israel your f.
Jer. 35:18 obeyed Jonadab y. f.
Ezek. 16:45 your f. an Amorite
Mat. 5:16 glorify your F. in hea.
45 may be children of your F.
48 as y. F. in heaven is perfect
6:1 otherwise no reward of y. F.
8 y. F. knoweth what things ye
have need of, 32; Luke 12:30
14 if ye forgive, y. F. will for.
15 nel. will y. F. forgive your
trespasses, Mark 11:25, 26
10:20 sparrow fall without y. F.
18:14 not will of y. F. one perish
23:9 call no man y. f. on earth,
one is your F. in heaven
Luke 6:36 as your F. is merciful
12:32 y. F. pleas. to give kingd.
John 8:38 that seen with your F.
41 ye do the deeds of your f.
42 f. said, if God were your F.
44 ye are of y. f. the devil, and
the lusts of y. f. ye will do
20:17 I asc. to my F. and y. F.

FATHERS.
Ex. 10:6 thy f. nor thy f. f.
20:5 visiting iniquity of f. 34:7;
Num. 14:18 ; Deut. 5:9
Deut. 24:16 f. not be put to death
for children, 2 K. 14:6
Job 30:1 f. I would ha. disdained
Prov. 19:14 inheritance of f.
28:23 kings be thy nursing f.
Jer. 8:2 f. and sons sh. fall, 13:14
7:18 f. kindle the fire
31:29 f. eaten sour grapes, Ezek.
18:2
32:18 recompensest iniq. of f.
47:3 f. not look back to child.
Ezek. 5:10 f. shall eat the sons
Mat. 4:6 turn t. to ch. Luke 1:17
John 7:22 of Moses, but of the f.
12:32 promise made to the f.
22:3 perf. manner of law of f.
Rom. 9:5 whose are the f.
1 Cor. 4:15 have ye not many f.
2 Cor. 6:4 prov. not, Col. 3:21
Heb. 1:1 in times past to f.
12:9 we had f. who corrected
2 Pet. 3:4 since the f. fell asleep

FAT

1 John 2:13 write unto you f. 14
See BURIED, CHIEF.

His FATHERS.
2 K. 15:9 did evil as his f. had
21:22 fors. G. of h. f. 2 Chr. 21:10
2 Chr. 21:19 like burning of h. f.
28:25 A. provoked L. G. of h. f.
32:19 to seek God of his f.
33:12 humbled before G. of h. f.
Ps. 49:19 generation of his f.
109:14 iniquity of his f.
Dan. 11:24 what his f. not done
37 nor regard the God of his f.
38 a god whom his f. knew not
Acts 13:36 Dav. was laid to h. f.

My FATHERS.
Gen. 47:9 not at. years of my f.
30 I will lie with my f.
48:16 name of my f. be named
49:29 bury me with my f.
Ex. 15:2 he is my f. God
1 K. 19:4 no better than my f.
21:3 inheritance of my f. 4.
2 K. 19:12 which my f. destroyed,
2 Chr. 32:14 ; Is. 37:12
2 Chr. 32:13 I and my f. done
Ps. 39:12 so. as my f. were
Dan. 2:23 O God of my f.
28:9 L. A. worship God of my f.
Gal. 1:14 traditions of my f.

Our FATHERS.
Gen. 46:34 we and also o. f. 47:3
Num. 20:15 our f. went down
36 to be sware to our f. 30:3, 15
29:7 cried to the God of our f.
Deut. 6:23 brought o. f. out of E.
Jud. 6:13 mirac. o. f. told us of?
1 K. 8:57 be was with our f. 58
58 statutes he commanded o. f.
Ezr. 33:13 our f. not hearkened
1 Chr. 12:17 G. of o. f. rebuke it
29:15 are sojourners, as our f.
18 O Lord of our f. keep for
ever to the heart, 2 Chr. 30:6
2 Chr. 6:31 gavest o. f. Neh. 9:36
6:25 God of our f. hope it
9 o. f. have fallen by the sword
34:21 our f. have not kept word
Ezr. 5:12 after o. f. provoked G.
7:27 besought be God of our f.
9:7 since o. f. in great trespass
Neh. 9:9 see affliction of our f.
16 our f. dealt proudly
Ps. 22:4 our f. trusted in thee
44:1 o. f. told what didst, 78:3
106:6 we have sinned with o. f.
7 o. f. understood not wonders
Is. 64:11 our f. praised thee
Jer. 3:24 devoured labor of o. f.
25 and our f. not obeyed voice
16:19 our f. have inherited lies
44:17 as we have done, our f.
Lam. 5:7 our f. sinned
Dan. 9:8 confus. of face to our f.
16 our sins and inlq. of our f.
Mic. 7:20 sworn to o. f. from old
Mal. 2:10 profaning cov. of our f.
Mat. 23:30 in days of our f.
Luke 1:55 as he spake to our f.
72 mercy promised to our f.
Acts 3:13 God of our f. wors. in
25 cove. God made with our f.
5:30 G. of o. f. raised up Jesus
7:11 our f. found no sustenance
15 Jacob died, he and our f.
19 and evil entreated our f.
38 he which spake with our f.
39 whom o. f. would not obey
13:17 God of Israel chose our f.
32 15 yoke o. f. not able to bear
promise made to our f.
26:6 well spake by E. to our f.
28:25 well spake by E. to our f.
1 K. 8:40 David slept so, 11:21
43 Sol. slept so. f. 2 Chr. 9:31
2 K. 30:21 M. s. w. f. 2 Chr. 32:33
2 Chr. 26:23 Uzziah slept with f.

Their FATHERS.
Ex. 4:5 G. of t. f. hath appeared
Lev. 26:39 in iniquity of their f.
40:40 confess iniq. of their f.
Num. 11:12 sweerest to t. f. 14:23;
Deut. 10:11; 31:20 ; Jos. 1:6;
Jud. 2:1
Deut. 30:25 foreaken cov. of t. f.
Jos. 4:6 children ask their f. 21
22:14 head of house of their f.
Jud. 2:10 gathered to their f.
17 forsook the God of their f.
19 corrupted more than t. f.
20 covenant I commanded t. f.

FAT

Jud. 2:22 keep way of L. as t. f.
1 K. 8:34 land thou gavest to t.
f. 48; 2 Chr. 6:25, 38
9:9 brought t. f. out of Egypt
14:15 he gave to their f. 2 K.
31:3; Jer. 16:15 ; 24:10
22 provok. above all t. f. done
1 Chr. 5:25 transgr. ag. God of t.
29:20 blessed God of their f.
2 Chr. 7:22 for. G. of t. f. 24:24 ; 28:6
11:16 sacrifice to God of their f.
13:18 relied on God of their f.
14:4 to seek God of t. f. 15:12
19:4 back to the God of their f.
20:33 prepa. hearts to G. of t. f.
30:7 trespassed ag. God of t. f.
22 confession to God of their f.
34:33 following The God of t. f.
36:15 G. of t. f. sent messengers
Job 8:8 prepare to search of t. f.
15:18 wise men told from t. f.
Ps. 78:8 might not be as their f.
12 marv. things in sight of t. f.
57 dealt unfaithfully like t. f.
Prov. 17:6 glory of child. are t. f.
Is. 14:21 slaughter for iniq. of f.
Jer. 7:26 did worse than their f.
9:14 Baalim, which t. f. taught
16 nor t. f. have known, 19:4
23:27 as t. f. forgotten my name
31:32 not accord. to covenant I
made with t. f. 11:10 ; Heb. 8:9
50:7 sinned ag. L. hope of t. f.
Ez. 2:3 have transgressed
5:10 and sons shall eat their f.
20:4 cause know abom. of t. f.
Amos 2:4 after which t. f. walked
Mal. 4:6 heart of children to t. f.
Luke 6:23 in like manner did t. f.
26 so did t. f. to false prophets

Thy FATHERS.
Gen. 15:15 shalt go to thy f.
Ex. 13:5 sware to thy f. 11; Deut.
1:8; 16: 7:13, 13; 8:18; 9:5;
13:17; 19:8; 26:11; 30:30
Deut. 4:31 not forget cov. of t. f.
37 because he loved thy f. 10:15
10:22 thy f. went with 70 persons
12:1 land the G. of thy f. giveth
19:8 land he prom. thy f. 37:8
30:5 multipl. thee above thy f.
9 as he rejoiced over thy f.
3:16 with thy f. 1 Sam. 7:12
1 K. 13:22 not to sepulchre of t. f.
20:17 thy f. laid up
21:20 to thy f. 3 Chr. 34:28
1 Chr. 17:11 go to be with thy f.
Ps. 45:16 instead of thy f.

Your FATHERS.
Gen. 48:21 bring to land of y. f.
Ex. 3:13 God of your f. sent me,
Deut. 1:11; 4:1; Jos. 18:3;
2 Chr. 28:9 ; 29:5
Num. 32:14 risen up in y. f. stead
Jos. 24:2 your f. dwelt other side
6 I brought y. f. out of Egypt
1 Sam. 12:7 acts L. did to y. f.
8 y. f. cried, L. bro. forth y. f.
2 Chr. 13:12 fight L. ag. you as y. f.
30:7 not like y. f. 8; Zec. 1:4
Ezr. 10:11 confes. to G. of y. f.
Ps. 95:9 your f. tempted, Heb. 3:9
Is. 65:7 and iniquities of your f.
Jer. 2:5 iniq. y. f. found in me ?
11:7 I earnestly protested to y. f.
10:11 your f. have forsaken me
12 done worse than your f.
34:14 y. f. heark. not unto me
44:3 knew not, they nor your f.
9 forgotten wickedn. of y. f.
Ezek. 20:18 not in statutes of y. f.
27 in this your f. blasphemed
30 after manner of your f.
36 as I pleaded with your f.
37:25 dwelt in land y. f. dwelt
Hos. 9:10 I saw y. f. as first ripe
Joel 1:2 been in days of your f.
Zec. 1:2 L. displeased with y. f.
4 be not as your f.
5 your f. where are they ?
6 words take hold of your f. ?
8:14 when your f. provoked me
Mal. 3:7 days of y. f. are gone
Mat. 23:32 fill up measure of y. f.
Luke 11:47 your f. killed them
48 ye allow deeds of your f.
John 6:49 your f. did eat manna
58 your f. eat, and are dead
Acts 7:51 resist Holy G. as y. f.
52 have not y. f. persecuted ?
1 Pet. 1:18 by tradition from y. f.

FATHERLESS.
Ex. 22:22 not afflict f. child

CRUDEN'S CONCORDANCE. 851

FAV

Ex. 22:24 your children sh. be f.
Deut. 10:18 execute judgment of f.
   f. Ps. 62:3; Is. 1:17
Job 5:27 ye overwhelm the f.
  22:9 arms of f. been broken
  24:3 drive away ass of the f.
  9 pluck f. from the breast
  22:12 because I delivered the f.
  31:17 the f. not eaten thereof
  21 if I lifted up my hand ag. f.
Ps. 10:14 thou art helper of f.
  18 judge the f. and oppressed
  68:5 a father of the f.
  109:9 let his children be f.
  12 nor any favor his f. children
Prov. 23:10 enter not fields of f.
Is. 1:23 judge not f. Jer. 5:28
  9:17 not have mercy on their f.
Jer. 49:11 leave thy f. children
Lam. 5:3 we are orphans and f.
Ezek. 22:7 in thee have vexed f.
Hos. 14:3 in thee f. findeth mercy
Mal. 3:5 witness ag. those op. f.
Zech. 1:27 pure religion to visit f.

FATHERLESS, with stranger.
Deut. 14:29 stra. and f. shall eat,
  24:19, 20, 21; 26:12, 13
  16:11 s. and f. rejoice with thee
  24:17 not perv. jud. of s. nor f.
  27:19 perv. judg. of s. and f.
Ps. 94:6 slay s. and murder f.
  146:9 Lord preserveth s. and f.
Jer. 7:6 if ye oppress not the st. and f. 22:3; Zech. 7:10

FATHOMS.
Acts 27:28 found it twenty f.

FATLING, S.
1 Sam. 15:9 Saul spared best of f.
Ps. 66:15 burnt sacrifices of f.
Is. 11:6 lion, and the f. together
Ezek. 39:18 all of them f. of B.
Mat. 22:4 oxen and f. are killed

FATNESS.
Gen. 27:28 G. give thee of the f.
  39 dwelling be f. of the earth
Deut. 32:15 art covered with f.
Jud. 9:9 should I leave my f.
Job 15:27 cover. face with his f.
  36:16 thy table sh. be full of f.
Ps. 36:8 satisfied with f.
  63:5 my soul satisfied as with f.
  65:11 all thy paths drop f.
  73:7 eyes stand out with f.
  109:24 my flesh faileth of f.
Is. 17:4 f. of his flesh wax lean
  34:6 sword of Lord is fat with f.
  7 their dust he made fat w. f.
  55:2 let soul delight itself in f.
Jer. 31:14 soul of priests with f.
Rom. 11:17 partak. of f. of olive

FATS.
Joel 2:24 f. shall overflow, 3:13

FATTED.
Jer. 46:21 men like f. bullocks
See CALF.

FATTEST.
Ps. 78:31 wrath of God slew f.
Dan. 11:24 enter on the f. places

FAULT, S.
Gen. 41:9 I remember f. this day
Ex. 5:16 f. is in thine own peo.
Deut. 25:2 beaten accord. to h. f.
1 Sam. 29:3 I found no f. in him
2 Sam. 3:8 charged me with a f.
Ps. 19:12 cleanse from secret f.
59:4 they prepare wi. hout my f.
Dan. 6:4 could find no f. in him
Mat. 18:15 trosp. tell him his f.
Mark 3:1 I find no f. in th. man, 41; John 18:38; 19:4, 6
Rom. 9:19 doth he yet find f. f
1 Cor. 6:7 utterly a f. among you
Gal. 6:1 man be overtaken in f.
Heb. 8:8 finding f. with them
Jam. 5:16 conf. f. one to another
1 Pet. 2:20 if when buffeted for f.
Rev. 14:5 without f. bef. throne

FAULTLESS.
Heb. 8:7 if first cov. had been f.
Jude 24 is able to present you f.

FAULTY.
2 Sam. 14:13 king speak as one f.
Hos. 10:2 shall they be found f.

FAVOR, Substantive.
Gen. 39:21 give Jos. f. in sight of Egyptians, 11:3; 12:36
Deut. 28:50 not show f. to young
33:23 O Napht. sat. fied with f.
Jos. 11:20 they inheri have no f.
1 Sam. 2:26 Samuel in f. with L.

FEA

Job 10:12 granted me life and f.
30:5 in him f. is life.
1 hy f. made mountain to sta.
  44:3 because hadst a f. to them
  45:12 rich shall entreat thy f.
  89:17 in thy f. our horn exalted
  106:4 remember me with f. thou
  112:5 a good man showeth f.
  119:58 I entreated thy f.
Prov. 11:27 seek. good procur. f.
  13:15 good understand. giv. f.
  14:9 among righteous there is f.
  35 king's f. toward wise serv.
  16:15 his f. is as a cloud of rain
  19:6 many entreat f. of prince
  12 king's f. is as dew np. grass
  21:10 his neighbor findeth no f.
  22:1 lov. f. rather to be chosen
  29:26 many seek the ruler's f.
  31:30 f. is deceitful
Ec. 9:11 nor f. to men of skill
Is. 26:10 f. he showed to wicked
  27:11 formed showe them no f.
  60:10 but in my f. I had mercy
Jer. 10:13 I will not show f.
Dan. 1:9 brought Daniel into f.
Luke 2:52 Jesus increased in f.
Acts 2:47 f. with all the people
  7:10 God gave Moses f. in sight
  25:3 high-priest desired f.

Find or found FAVOR.
Gen. 18:3 if I have f. f. 30:27;
  Num. 11:15; 1 Sam. 20:29;
Neh. 3:5; Est. 5:8; 7:3; 8:5
Num. 11:11 why h. I not f. f. f
Deut. 24:1 that, she find no f.
1 Sam. 10:22 David hath f. f.
  25:8 let the young men find f.
2 Sam. 15:25 if I f. f. in ey. of L.
Prov. 3:4 so f. f. in sight of God
  28:23 find mercy, than he flat.
Cant. 8:10 I was as one found f.
Luke 1:30 hast f. f. with God
Acts 7:46 who f. f. before God

Obtain, ed, eth FAVOR.
Ex. 2:15 Esther ob. f. 17; 5:2
Prov. 8:35 findeth me shall ob. f.
  12:2 good man ob. f. of Lord
  18:22 findeth a wife, obtaineth f.

FAVOR, Verb.
1 Sam. 29:6 the lords f. thee not
Ps. 35:27 f. my righteous cause
  102:13 set time to f. her, the time is come
  14 thy servants f. dust thereof
  109:12 to f. fatherless children

FAVORABLE.
Jud. 21:22 be f. for our sakes
Job 33:26 God will be f. unto him
Ps. 77:7 will L. be f. no more?
  85:1 hast been f. to thy land

FAVORED, EST, ETH.
Gen. 29:17 Rachel was well f.
  39:6 Jos. well f.; 41:2 kine, 18
  41:3 ill f. kine, 4, 19, 21, 27
2 Sam. 20:11 f. Joab, go after J.
Ps. 41:11 by this I know thou f.
Lam. 4:16 they f. not the elders
Dan. 1:4 children well f. skilful
Nah. 3:4 wheeed. of well f. har.
Luke 1:28 hail, thou highly f.

FEAR, Substantive.
Gen. 9:2 f. of you be on ev. beast
  31:42 f. of Is. had been with me
  53 Jacob sware by f. of his f.
Ex. 15:16 f. sh. fall upon them
  23:27 send my f. before thee
Deut. 2:25 f. of thee on nations
  11:25 lay f. of you on land
1 Chr. 14:17 f. of him on nations
Ezr. 3:3 f. was on them because
Neh. 6:9 that put me in f. 19
Est. 8:17 f. of Jews fell on them
  9:3 f. of Mordecai fell on them
Job 4:8 is not this thy f.
  11 f. came on me and trmb.
  6:14 forsaketh f. of Almighty
  9:34 let not his f. terrify me
  15:4 yea, thou castest off f. and
  21:9 their houses are safe from f.
  22:10 sudden f. troubleth thee
  25:2 dominion and f. with him
  32:22 no words in f.
Ps. 5:7 in thy f. will I worship
  9:20 put them in f. O Lord
  14:5 there were they in great f.
  31:11 I was a f. to acquaintance
  13 f. was on every side
  48:6 f. took hold upon them
  53:5 were in f.; 55:5 f. is come
  64:1 pres. my life fr. f. of enemy
  90:11 in thy f. so is thy wrath
  105:38 Egypt glad, f. fell on them
  119:88 thy serv. devot. to thy f.
  120 my flesh trembleth for f.
Prov. 1:26 mock when f. cometh
  27 when your f. cometh as d.

FEA

Prov. 1:33 be quiet from f. of evil
  3:25 be not afraid of sudden f.
  10:24 f. of wicked come on him
  20:2 f. of king as roaring of lion
  29:25 f. of man bringeth a snare
Cant. 3:8 sw. bec. of f. in night
Is. 7:25 not come the f. of briers
  8:13 neither fear ye their f.
  13 the Lord, let him be your f.
  14:3 shall give thee rest from f.
  21:4 night of pleasure into f.
  24:17 f. and the pit upon thee
  18 fleeth from f. Jer. 48:44
  29:13 their f. is taught by men
  63:17 hardened heart from thy f.
Jer. 2:19 that my f. is not in thee
  6:25 f. is on ev. side, 20:10
  30:5 we have heard a voice of f.
  32:40 put my f. in their hearts
  48:43 f. shall be on thee, O N.
  49:5 I will bring a f. upon thee
  24 f. hath seized on Damascus
  29 shall cry, f. is on every side
Lam. 3:47 f. and snare is come
Ezek. 30:13 put a f. in land of E.
Mal. 1:6 where is my f. f
Luke 1:12 Z. saw him, f. fell on
  65 f. on all, 7:16; Acts 5:5;
  5:5, 11; 19:17; Rev. 11:11
Rom. 13:7 f. to whom f. is due
1 Cor. 2:3 in weakness and f.
2 Cor. 7:11 what f. the work
Jer. 7:1 not giv. us spirit of f.
Heb. 2:15 through f. of death
  12:28 reverence and godly f.
1 Pet. 1:17 pass time of soj. in f.
  3:15 with meekness and f.
1 John 4:18 no f. in l. cast out f.

For FEAR.
Deut. 28:67 f. the f. thou sh. fear
Jos. 22:24 done it f. f. of thing
1 Sam. 21:10 fled f. f. of S. 23:26
Job 22:4 reprove f. f. of thee f
Is. 31:9 to his strong-hold, f. f.
Jer. 46:5 f. f. was round about
  50:16 f. f. of oppressing sword
Mal. 2:5 f. wherew. he feared
Mat. 14:26 discip. cried out, f. f.
Luke 21:26 hearts failing for f.
  19:38 but secretly f. f. of Jews
  20:19 assembled f. f. of the J.
Rev. 18:10 f. f. of torment, 15

Fear of GOD.
Gen. 20:11 f. of G. not in place
2 Sam. 23:3 ruling in f. of God
Neh. 5:9 to walk in the f. of G. f
  15 so did not I, bec. of f. of G.
Rom. 3:18 no f. of G. bef. th. eyes
2 Cor. 7:1 holiness in f. of God
Eph. 5:21 submitting in f. of G.

Fear of the LORD.
1 Sam. 11:17 f. of L. 2 Chr. 17:10
2 Chr. 14:14 f. of L. on them
  19:7 f. of the L. be upon you
  9 thus do in f. of the Lord
Job 28:24 f. of the L. is wisdom
Ps. 19:9 f. of the Lord is clean
  34:11 I will teach you f. of L.
Prov. 1:7 f. of L. begin. of wisdom
  29 f. of L. they did not choose
  2:5 shall understand f. of the L.
  8:13 f. of L. is to hate evil
  10:27 f. of the L. prolong. days
  14:26 in f. of Lord is str. confid.
  27 f. of L. is a fountain of life
  15:16 better is lit. with f. of L.
  33 f. of L. is instruction
  16:6 by f. of L. men dep. fr. evil
  19:23 f. of the L. tendeth to life
  22:4 by f. of L. are riches and l.
  23:17 be in f. of Lord all day
  24:21 f. of the L. and the king
Is. 2:10 hide in dust, for f. of L.
  19 go into caves, for f. of Lord
  21 go into clefts, for f. of Lord
  11:2 spirit of knowl. f. of Lord
  3 quick understand. in f. of L.
  33:6 f. of L. is treasure
Acts 9:31 walking in f. of the L.

With FEAR.
Mat. 28:8 with f. and great joy
Luke 5:30 with f. all filled with f.
8:37 Gadarenes tak. w. great f.
Phil. 2:12 work out salva. w. f.
Heb. 11:7 N. m. f. prepared ark
1 Pet. 2:18 be subj. to mast. w. f.
Jude 23 and others save with f.

FEA

Without FEAR.
Job 29:16 hor labor in vain w. f.
  41:33 not his like, made w. f.
Luke 1:74 serve him with f.
1 Cor. 16:10 may be with y. w. f.
Phil. 1:14 bold to sp. word w. f.
Jude 12 feeding themselv. w. f.

FEARS.
Ps. 34:4 delivered me fr. all my f.
Ec. 12:5 when f. be in the way
  14 66:4 bring their f. upon them
2 Cor. 7:5 within were f.

FEAR, Verb.
Lev. 19:3 f. every man his moth.
Num. 14:9 nei. f. people of land
  4:10 may learn to f. me
  5:29 O that they would f. me
  28:58 f. glori. name, the Lord
  66 thou shalt f. day and night
  67 fear wherewith thou sha. f.
Jud. 7:10 if thou f. to go down
1 K. 8:40 f. thee, 2 Chr. 6:33
  43 name to f. thee, 2 Chr. 6:33
2 K. 17:38 neither f. other gods
  39 the Lord your G. ye shall f.
1 Chr. 16:30 f. before him all the earth, Ps. 96:9
Neh. 1:11 desire to f. thy name
Job 31:34 did I f. a great multi. ?
Ps. 23:4 no evil
  27:1 whom shall I f. f
  31:19 goodness for them f. thee
  40:3 many shall see it, and f.
  49:5 f. in days of evil ?
  52:6 rights. also shall see and f.
  60:4 a banner to them that f.
  61:5 herit. of those f. thy name
  64:9 shall f. and declare work
  65:7, 8 f. thee as long as sun end.
  86:11 unite my heart to f. name
  102:15 so heath. shall f. thy n.
  119:39 my reproach which I f.
  63 compan. of them that f. th.
  74 they that f. thee will be gl.
  79 let those that f. thee turn
Ec. 3:14 that men f. before him
Is. 8:12 neither f. ye their fear
  19:16 Eg. shall be afraid and f.
  25:3 city of ter. nations f. thee
  44:11 the workmen shall f.
  59:19 so shall they f. name of L.
  60:5 thy heart f. and be enlarg.
Jer. 10:7 who would not f. th. O
  23:4 and they shall f. no more
  32:39 one heart that they f. me
  33:9 shall f. for the goodness
  51:46 and lest ye f. for rumor
Dan. 6:26 f. before G. of Daniel
Hos. 10:5 inhab. of Samaria sh. f.
Mic. 7:17 and f. because of thee
Hag. 1:12 people did f. before L.
Zec. 9:5 Ashk. shall see it, and f.
Mal. 4:2 to you f. my name
Mat. 12:5 whom ye shall f.
Rom. 8:15 spirit of bondage to f.
  11:20 be not high-minded, but f.
2 Cor. 12:20 I f. lest not find you
1 Tim. 5:20 others also may f.
Heb. 4:1 let us f. lest a promise
  12:28 with f. and l. exceedingly f.
Rev. 2:10 f. none of those things
  11:18 rew. to them f. thy name
  14:7 saying f. God and glory

Fear God.
Gen. 42:18 and live, for I f. G.
Ex. 9:30 I know ye will not f. G.
Deut. 6:24 f. thy G. thy G. 23
  25:17 thou sh. f. thy God, 32
Job 1:9 doth J. f. G. for naught ?
Ps. 55:16 all ye that f. God
Ec. 5:7 vanities, but f. thou God
  8:12 well with them that f. G.
  12:13 f. G. and keep his com.
Is. 29:23 they sh. f. G. of Israel
Luke 23:40 dost not thou f. G.
Acts 10:35 f. God, give audience
1 Pet. 2:17 f. God, honor the k.
Rev. 14:7 f. God, and give glory

Hear and FEAR.
Deut. 13:11 h. shall h. a. f. 21:21
  17:13 all the peo. shall h. a. f.
  19:20 who remain sh. hear a. f.

FEAR him.
Deut. 13:4 walk after f. and f. h.
2 K. 17:36 him f. Alm shall yo f.
Job 37:24 men therefore f. him
Ps. 22:23 f. him, glorify him
  25 before them that f. him
  33:8 let all the earth f. h.
  18 eye of L. is on th. f. him
  34:7 encamp. about them f. h.
  9 no want to them that f. h.
  67:7 ends of the earth shall f. h.
  85:9 salva. is nigh them f. him
  103:11 his mercy to them f. h.

852 CRUDEN'S CONCORDANCE.

FEA

Ps. 103:13 L. pit. th. that *f. him*
17 mercy of L. is on them *f. h.*
111:5 meat to them that *f. him*
145:19 desire of them *f. him*
147:11 pleas. in them that *f. h.*
Mal. 10:23 *f. h.* able *Luke* 12:5
Luke 1:50 mercy on them *f. him*
Rev. 19:5 praise G. ye that *f. h.*

Fear the LORD.
Deut. 6:2 mightest *f. t. L.* thy G.
13 shalt *f. L.* 10:20; 2 *K.* 17:39
24 to *f. L.* for our good always
10:12 *f. the L.* walk in his ways
14:23 to *f. L.* 17:19; 31:13, 13
Jos. 4:24 might *f. Lord* your G.
24:14 now therefore *f. the Lord*
1 *Sam.* 12:14 if ye will *f. the L.*
24 *f. L.* serve him in truth
1 *K.* 18:12 but I *f. L.* 2 *K.* 4:1
2 *K.* 17:28 taught them how *f. L.*
Ps. 15:4 h noreth them *f. Lord*
22:23 ye that *f. L.* praise him
33:8 let all the earth *f. the Lord*
34:9 O *f. the L.* ye his saints
115:11 ye that *f. L.* trust in L.
13 he will bless them that *f. L.*
118:4 *f. L.* say, his mercy end.
135:20 ye that *f. L.* bless the L.
Prov. 3:7 *f. L.* depart from evil
24:21 *f. the Lord,* and the king
Jer. 5:24 nor say th. Let us *f. L.*
26:19 did he not *f. the Lord*
Hos. 3:5 afterwards sh. is. *f. L.*
Jon. 1:9 I *f. L.* the G. of heaven

FEAR not.
Gen. 15:1 *f. not* Ab. I am shield
26:24 *f. not,* I am with thee
35:17 midwife said to R. *f. n.*
43:23 Peace be to you, *f. not*
46:3 *f. not* to go down to Egypt
50:19 *f. not,* am I in place of G.?
Ex. 14:13 *f. n.* stand, see salva.
20:20 *f. not* G. is come to prove
Num. 14:9 L. with us, *f.* them *n.*
21:34 L. saith to Mo. *f. him not*
Deut. 20:3 *f. not* your enemies
31 L. doth go before thee. *f.*
not Jos. 8:1; 1 *Chr.* 28:20
Jud. 6:10 *f. not* gods of Amorites
23 peace. *f. not,* thou sh. not d.
1 *Sam.* 4:20 said to her, *f. not*
12:20 Sam. said to people, *f. not*
22:23 abide thou with me, *f. n.*
23:17 Jonathan said to D. *f. not*
2 *Sam.* 13:28 kill Amnon, *f. not*
1 *K.* 17:13 said to widow, *f. not*
2 *K.* 6:16 *f. not,* more with us
17:34 to this day they *f. not* L.
25:24 *f. not* to serve Chaldees
2 *Chr.* 20:17 be with you, *f. n.*
Ps. 55:19 therefore they *f. not* G.
64:4 shoot at him, and *f. not*
Is. 7:4 *f. not* tails of firebrands
35:4 to them of fear. heart, *f. n.*
41:10 *f. n.* I am with thee, 43:5
13 hold thy hand, saying, *f. n.*
41:14 *f. not,* thou worm Jacob
43:1 *f. n.* I have redeemed thee
44:2 *f. not,* O Jacob my servant,
Jer. 30:10; 46:27, 28
8 *f.* ye *not,* ha. not I told th.?
51:7 *f. not* the reproach of men
54:4 *f. n.* thou shalt not be ash.
Jer. 5:22 *f.* ye *not* me?
Lam. 3:57 thou saidst, *f. not*
Dan. 10:12 *f. not,* Daniel, 19
Joel 2:21 *f. not,* be glad
Zep. 3:16 he said to Jer. *f. not*
Hag. 2:5 Sp. rem. am. you, *f. not*
Zec. 8:13 s h. be a blessing, *f. not*
15 do will to Judah, *f.* ye *not*
Mat. 2:5 witness ag. them, *f. not*
Mat. 1:20 *f. n.* to take Mary, but
10:26 *f.* them *not,* nothing cov.
28 *f. not* them who kill body
Luke 1:13 *f. not* Zach.; 30 Mary
2:10 shepherds, *f. n.*; 5:10 Sim.
8:50 *Jairus f. not,* believe only
12:32 *f. not,* little flock
John 6:20 (though I *f. not* God,
John 12:15 *f. not* daughter of S.
Acts 27:24 *f. not,* Paul,
Rev. 1:17 *f. not,* I am the first

Not FEAR.
Ex. 9:30 ye will *n. f.* the L.
2 *K.* 17:35 *not f.* other g ds. 37
Job 9:35 I speak, and *not f.* him
11:15 steadfast, thou shalt *n. f.*
Ps. 27:3 the. host encamp. *not f.*
40:2 *not f.* though earth be rem.
56:4 *n. f.* wh. flesh can do, 118:6
Is. 54:14 from oppression, *n. f.*
Jer. 10:7 who would *not f.* thee
Amos 3:8 who will *not f.*
Luke 23:40 doet *not f.* thou, God?

FEA

Heb. 13:6 *not f.* what man do
Rev. 15:4 who shall *n. f.* thee,

FEARED.
Gen. 26:7 *f.* to say, She is my w.
Ex. 9:20 he that *f.* word of God
Deut. 25:18 Amalek *f.* not God
32:17 to new gods fathers *f. not*
f. were it not I *f.* the wrath of
Jos. 4:14 *f.* Josh. as they did M.
1 *Sam.* 14:26 people *f.* the oath
15:24 because I *f.* the people
1 *K.* 3:28 and of *f.* Israel *f.* king
1 *Chr.* 17:25 they *f. not* the Lord
1 *Chr.* 16:25 to be *f.* above all
gods. *Ps.* 96:4
Ps. 76:7 art to be *f.*; 8 earth *f.*
11 pres. to him ought to be *f.*
78:53 led them safely, so *f. not*
130:4 forgiveness, mayest be *f.*
Is. 41:5 the isles saw it, and *f.*
51:13 hast *f.* continually
57:11 whom hast thou *f.*
Jer. 3:6 treach. sister Jud. *f. not*
42:16 sword ye *f.* overtake you
44:10 nor have they *f.*
Ezek. 11:8 ye have *f.* the sword
Dan. 5:19 nations *f.* before him
Mal. 2:5 wherewith he *f.* me
Mat. 17:15 of Herod *f.* multi. 21:46
Mark 4:41 they *f.* exceedingly
6:20 Herod *f.* John, knowing
11:18 and chief priests *f.* Jesus
32 *f.* the people, 12:12; *Luke*
20:19; 22:2; *Acts* 5:26
Luke 9:34 *f.* as th. entered cloud
45 *f.* to ask him of that saying
18:2 was a judge which *f. not* G.
19:21 I *f.* thee, art austere man
John 9:22 bec. they *f.* the Jews
19:38 *f.* magistrates *f.* whom
Heb. 5:7 *f.* heard, in that he *f.*

FEARED God.
Ex. 1:17 but midwives *f.* God
Neh. 7:2 he *f.* God above many
Job 1:1 Job was one that *f.* G.
Acts 10:2 Cornelius was one *f. G.*

FEARED greatly.
Jos. 10:2 Canaanites *f. greatly*
Num. 12:18 the people *g. f.* L.
1 *K.* 18:3 now Obadiah *f.* Lord *g.*
Job 3:25 thing I *g. f.* is come
Ps. 89:7 God is *g.* to be *f.*
Mat. 27:54 centurion *f. greatly*

FEARED the Lord.
Ex. 14:31 *f. L.* believed Moses
1 *K.* 17:32 so they *f. the L.* 33, 41
Hos. 10:3 no king, bec. not *f. L.*
Jon. 1:16 men *f. L. exceedingly*
Mat. 3:16 that *f.* snake oft, a
book of remem. *f. w.* th. *f. L.*

FEAREST.
Gen. 22:12 I know thou *f.* God
Ps. 57:11 held peace thou *f. not*
Jer. 22:25 hand of them thou *f.*

FEARETH.
Job 1:8 Job one that *f.* God, 2:3
Ps. 25:12 what man is he *f. L.*?
112:1 blessed is the man *f. L.*
is *f.* blessed is every one *f. L.*
Prov. 13:13 *f.* command. be rew.
14:2 walk, in uprightness *f. L.*
16 wise man *f.* and departeth
24:14 hap. is the man *f.* always
31:30 woman *f.* Lord be praised
Ec. 7:18 *f.* God come forth
8:13 because he *f. not* before G.
9:2 as he that *f.* an oath
Is. 50:10 who is am. you *f. L.*?
Acts 10:22 Cornelius one *f.* God
35 he that *f.* him is accepted
13:26 who. among you *f.* God
1 *John* 4:18 *f.* is *not* perf. in love

FEARFUL.
Ex. 15:11 like thee, *f.* in praises
Deut. 20:8 *f.* lot return, *Jud.* 7:3
28:58 mayest fear this *f.* name
Is. 35:4 say to them of *f.* heart
Mat. 8:26 *f.* O ye of little faith?
Mark 4:40 why are ye so *f.*?
Luke 21:11 *f.* sights in div. pla.
Heb. 10:27 *f.* looking for of judg.
31 *f.* to fall into hands of God
12:21 Moses said, I am *f.*
Rev. 21:8 *f.* have part in the lake

FEARFULNESS.
Ps. 55:5 *f.* and trembling come
Is. 21:4 *f.* affrighted me
33:14 *f.* surprised the hypocrites

FEARFULLY.
Ps. 139:14 *f.* and wonderf. made

FEARING.
Jos. 22:25 children cease *f.* Lord
Mark 5:33 the woman *f.* came
Acts 23:10 the captain *f.* lest P.

FEA

Gal. 2:12 *f.* them of circumcision
Col. 3:22 singleness of heart *f.* G.
Heb. 11:27 not *f.* wrath of king

FEAST.
Gen. 19:3 L. made *f.*; 21:8 Abr.
26:30 Isaac; 29:22 Laban
40:20 Pharaoh made a *f.* to all
Ex. 5:1 hold a *f.* to me, 10:9
12:14 keep it a *f. Lev.* 23:39, 41
13:6 seventh day shall be a *f.*
23:14 three times keep *f.* in ye.
32:5 A. said, To-morrow is a *f.*
Num. 29:12 shall keep *f.* to L.
Deut. 16:14 shalt rejoice in thy *f.*
Jud. 14:10 Samson made a *f.*
1 *Sam.* 25:36 N. held *f.* like king
1 *K.* 3:2 all assembled at the *f.*
12:32 Jeroboam ordained a *f.*
like the *f.* that is in Judah
2 *Chr.* 7:8 Sol. kept *f.* 7 days, 9
30:22; *Neh.* 8:18; *Ezek.* 45:23
Est. 1:3 Ahasuerus made *f.* 2:18
9 Vashti made *f.*; 8:17 Jews
Prov. 15:15 merry heart cont. *f.*
Ec. 10:19 *f.* is made for laughter
Is. 25:6 L. make to all peop. a *f.*
Ezek. 45:23 seven days shall a *f.*
Dan. 5:1 Belshazzar made a *f.*
Mat. 27:15 at that *f.* gov. wont to
loose a prisoner, *Mark* 15:6
Luke 2:42 after custom of *f.*
14:13 makest a *f.* call the poor
23:17 must release one at the *f.*
John 2:8 bear to governor of *f.*
4:45 Galileans hav. seen all he
did at *f.* for they went to *f.*
5:1 after this was a *f.* of the J.
6:4 the passover a *f.* of the J.
7:8 go up to this *f.* I go not up
10 went he also up to the *f.*
11 Jews sought him at the *f.*
14 midst of the *f.* Jesus taught
37 that great day of the *f.*
10:22 at Jer. *f.* of dedication
11:56 he will not come to the *f.* ?
12:12 much people come to *f.*
20 Greeks that came to the *f.*
13:29 buy what we need ag. *f.*
Acts 18:21 I must keep this *f.*
1 *Cor.* 5:8 *f.* not with old leaven
10:27 that believe not bid to *f.*

FEAST day or days.
Hos. 2:11 cause her *f. d.* to cease
9:5 what will ye do in day of *f.*
Amos 5:21 I despise your *f. days*
Mat. 26:5 not on *f. d. Mark* 14:2
John 2:23 in *f. d.* many believed

FEAST of the passover.
Mat. 26:2 *f.* of pass. *Mark* 14:1
Luke 2:41 every year at *f. of* pas.
John 13:1 before *f. of* p. J. knew

Solemn FEAST.
Deut. 16:15 seven days keep s. *f.*
Ps. 81:3 blow trumpet on s. *f.*
Lam. 2:7 noise as in day of s. *f.*
Hos. 12:9 dwell as in days of s. *f.*

FEAST of tabernacles.
Lev. 23:34 shall be the *f. of tab.*
Deut. 16:16 in *f.*; 31:10; 2 *Chr.*
8:13
Zec. 14:16 even go up to keep *f.*
18 heathen that come not to *f.*
John 7:2 Jews' *f.* was at hand

FEAST of unleavened bread.
Ex. 12:17 ob. *f.*; 23:15; 34:18
Lev. 23:6 on 15th day is *f.*
Deut. 16:16 in *f.* 2 *Chr.* 8:13
2 *Chr.* 30:13 assemb. to keep *f.*
Mat. 26:17 *f. of un.* discip. came
Mark 14:1 was the *f. Luke* 22:1

FEAST of weeks.
Ex. 34:22 ob. *f.* — *Deut.* 16:10

FEAST, ED.
Job 1:4 sons *f.* in their houses
2 *Pet.* 2:13 sporting while they *f.*
Jude 12 when they *f.* with you

FEASTING.
Est. 9:17 made it a day of *f.* 18
Job 1:5 days of *f.* were gone
Ec. 7:2 go to the house of *f.*
Jer. 16:8 into the house of *f.*

FEASTS.
Lev. 23:2 these are my *f.* 4, 37, 44
Ps. 33:16 hypocr. mockers in *f.*
Is. 1:14 your new moons and *f.*
5:12 pipe and wine in their *f.*
Jer. 9:10 in heat I will make
their *f.*
Ezek. 45:17 to give offerings in *f.*
Amos 8:10 turn your *f.* into mo.
Zec. 8:19 shall be cheerful *f.*
Mat. 23:6 love, uppermost rooms
at *f. Mark* 12:39; *Luke* 20:46
Jude 12 are spots in *f.* of charity

FEE

Appointed FEASTS.
Is. 1:14 ap. *f.* my soul hateth

Set FEASTS.
Num. 29:39 these th. do in set *f.*

Solemn FEASTS.
2 *Chr.* 2:4 build a house for sol. *f.*
8:13 sol. *f.* three times in a y.
Lam. 1:4 bec. none come to s. *f.*
3:6 caused s. *f.* to be forgotten
Ezek. 36:38 flock of Jer. in s. *f.*
46:9 when come be *f. L.* in sol. *f.*
Hos. 2:11 cause to cease her s. *f.*
Nah. 1:15 O Judah, keep thy s. *f.*
Mal. 2:3 even dung of your sol. *f.*

FEATHERED. *See* FOWL.

FEATHERS.
Job 39:13 gavest *f.* to ostrich?
Ps. 68:13 *f.* cov. with yel. gold
91:4 shall cover thee with his *f.*
Ezek. 17:3 an eagle full of *f.*
Dan. 4:33 hairs like eagles' *f.*

FED.
Gen. 48:15 G. who *f.* me all my
Ex. 16:32 bread where. I *f.* you
Deut. 8:3 he *f.* thee with manna
16 *f.* thee in the wilderness
Ps. 37:3 verily thou shalt be *f.*
78:72 *f.* them acc. to his integ.
81:16 *f.* them with finest of wh.
Is. 1:11 full of fat of *f.* beasts
Jer. 5:7 I *f.* them to the full
5:8 as *f.* horses in the morning
Ezek. 16:19 honey-wherew. I *f.*
34:3 ye kill that are *f.*
8 *f.* themselves, *f.* not my flo.
Dan. 4:12 all flesh was *f.* with it
John 21:15 *f.* with grass like ox.
Zec. 11:7 and I *f.* the flock
Mat. 25:37 hunger. and *f.* thee?
Mark 5:14 swine, *Luke* 8:31
Luke 16:21 to be *f.* with crumbs
1 *Cor.* 3:2 have *f.* you with milk

FEEBLE.
Deut. 25:18 Amalekites smote *f.*
1 *Sam.* 2:5 many children *f.*
2 *Sam.* 4:1 Ish-bosheth's han. *f.*
2 *Chr.* 28:15 car. the *f.* on asses
Neh. 4:2 what do these *f.* Jews?
Job 4:4 strengthen. the *f.* knees
Ps. 38:8 I am *f.* and sore broken
105:37 not one *f.* per. am. tribes
Prov. 30:26 conies are *f.* folk
Is. 10:14 remnant shall be *f.*
35:3 weak hands conf. *f.* knees
Jer. 6:24 our hands waxed *f.*
49:24 Damascus is waxed *f.*
50:43 the king's hands waxed *f.*
Ezek. 7:17 all ha. sh. be *f.* 21:7
12:8 he that is *f.* be as the Dav.
1 *Cor.* 12:22 memb. to be more *f.*
1 *Thes.* 5:14 comf. the *f.* minded
Heb. 12:12 lift up the *f.* knees

FEEBLENESS.
Jer. 47:3 fath. h. look back for *f.*

FEEBLER.
Gen. 30:42 the *f.* were Laban's

FEED.
Gen. 37:12 *f.* their father's flock
16 tell me, where they *f.* flocks
46:32 for their trade to *f.* cattle
Ex. 22:5 *f.* in another's field
34:3 nor flocks *f.* nor *f.* that mo.
2 *Sam.* 5:2 shalt *f.* my people *Is.*
7:7 to *f.* Israel, 1 *Chr.* 17:6
1 *K.* 17:4 I com. ravens to *f.* thee
Job 24:2 take away flocks, and *f.*
20 worm sh. *f.* sweetly on him
Ps. 28:9 *f.* them, and lift them
49:14 death shall *f.* on them
78:71 he brought David to *f.* J.
Prov. 10:21 lips of right. *f.* many
Cant. 1:8 roses which *f.* am. lil.
6:2 beloved. gone to *f.* in gardens
Is. 5:17 after their manner
11:7 the cow and the bear sh. *f.*
14:30 first-b. of the poor sh. *f.*
27:10 their calf *f.* and lie down
30:23 thy cattle *f.* in large past.
40:11 *f.* his flock as a shepherd
49:9 they shall *f.* in the ways
61:5 strangers sh. *f.* your flocks
65:25 wolf and lamb shall *f.* to.
Jer. 3:15 sh. *f.* you with knowl.
6:3 sh. *f.* every one in his place
23:2 ag. pastors that *f.* my peo.
4 shepherds shall *f.* them
50:19 Israel shall *f.* on Carmel
Lam. 4:5 *f.* delicately are desol.
Ezek. 34:2 shepherds that *f.* th.
3 but ye *f.* not the flock
10 nor shepherds *f.* thems.
23 servant David shall *f.* them
Dan. 11:26 *f.* of his meat destroy
Hos. 4:16 Lord will *f.* them

CRUDEN'S CONCORDANCE. 853

FEE

Hos. 9:2 wine-press not *f.* them
Jon. 3:7 let them not *f.*
Mic. 5:4 *f.* in strength of Lord
Zep. 3:7 they shall *f.* thereupon
  3:13 shall *f.* none make afraid
Zec. 11:9 I will not *f.*
  16 not *f.* that that standeth
Luke 15:15 sent him to *f.* swine
Acts 20:28 take heed to *f.* church
  1 *Cor.* 13:3 I give all to *f.* poor
Rev. 7:17 L. sh. *f.* and lead them
  12:6 sho. *f.* her there 1,260 days

FEED, imperatively.

Gen. 25:30 *f.* me with red pottage
  27:7 water ye the sheep, *f.* them
  1 *K.* 22:27 *f.* him with bread and water of afflict. 2 *Chr.* 18:26
Prov. 30:8 *f.* me with food conv.
Cant. 1:8 *f.* thy kids beside tents
Mic. 7:14 *f.* thy people
Zec. 11:4 *f.* flock of the slaughter
John 21:15 *f.* my lambs
  16 *f.* my sheep, 17
  1 *Pet.* 5:2 *f.* flock of God

I will FEED.

Gen. 30:31 *I will f.* thy flock
  2 *Sam.* 19:33 *I will f.* thee
Is. 49:26 *I w. f.* them oppr. thee
  58:14 *I w. f.* thee with heritage
Jer. 9:15 *f.* with wormw. 23:15
Ezek. 34:14 *I w. f.* them
  16 *I will f.* the fat with judgm.
Zec. 11:7 *I w. f.* flock of slaught.

FEED, EST, ETH.

Ps. 80:5 *f.* with bread of tears
Prov. 15:14 the mouth of fools *f.*
Cant. 1:7 tell me where thou *f.*
  2:16 *f.* among the lilies, 6:3
Is. 44:20 he *f.* on ashes
Hos. 12:1 Ephraim *f.* on wind
Mat. 6:26 heav. Father *f.* them
Luke 12:24 sow not, God *f.* them
  1 *Cor.* 9:7 who *f.* a flock

FEEDING.

Gen. 37:2 Joseph was *f.* the flock
Job 1:14 ploughing, the asses *f.*
Ezek. 31:10 cause to cease *f.* flock
Nah. 3:11 where *f.* pl. of lions?
Mat. 8:30 swl. *f. Mark* 5:11 ; *Luke* 8:32
Luke 17:7 a servant *f.* cattle
Jude 12 *f.* themsel. without fear

FEEL, ING.

Gen. 27:21 that I may *f.* thee
Jud. 16:26 I may *f.* the pillars
Job 20:20 shall not *f.* quietness
Ps. 58:9 bef. pots can *f.* thorns
Ec. 8:5 keep. comman. *f.* no evil
Acts 17:27 if haply might *f.* after
Eph. 4:19 who being past *f.*
Heb. 4:15 *f.* of our infirmities

FEET.

Gen. 49:10 from between his *f.*
  33 J. gathered up his *f.* in bed
Ex. 3:5 shoes off thy *f. Acts* 7:33
Deut. 2:28 pass thro' on my *f.*
  24:57 young one from hot. *f.*
  33:3 and they sat down at thy *f.*
Jos. 3:15 *f.* of priests in Jordan
  12:24 *f.* on necks of these kings
  11:9 land thy *f.* have trodden
Jud. 3:24 he covereth his *f.*
  4:15 Sisera fled on his *f.* 17
  5:27 at her *f.* he fell down dead
Ruth 3:8 a woman lay at his *f.*
  1 *Sam.* 2:9 keep *f.* of his saints
  24:3 Saul went in to cover his *f.*
  2 *Sam.* 3:34 nor thy *f.* put in fet.
  4:4 lame of his *f.* 9:3, 13
  19 *rat* off th. hands and *f.*
  19:24 Mephib. not dressed his *f.*
  22:34 maketh my *f.* like hind's *f. Ps.* 18:33 ; *Hab.* 3:19
  37 *f.* did not slip, *Ps.* 18:36
  1 *K.* 2:5 bla. *f.* of war in shoes on
  14:6 A. heard the sound of h. *f.*
  12 *f.* enter the city
  15:23 A. diseased *f.* 2 *Chr.* 16:12
  2 *K.* 4:27 she caught by the *f.*
  6:32 sound of master's *f.* beh.
  9:35 found no more than the *f.*
  13:21 dead man stood on his *f.*
  21:8 *f.* of Israel move any more
Neh. 9:21 their *f.* swelled not
Job 12:5 to slip with his *f.*
  13:27 my *f.* in the stocks ; 33:11 a print on heels of my *f.*
  18:8 cast into a net by own *f.*
  11 terrors shall drive him to *f.*
  20:12 was *f.* in hands and *f.*
  30:12 youth push away my *f.*
  Ps. 22:16 pierced hands and *f.*
  25:15 pluck my *f.* out of the net
  31:8 set my *f.* in a large room
  40:2 he set my *f.* on a rock, and

FEE

Ps. 56:13 del. my *f.* fr. falling?
  66:9 suff. not our *f.* to be moved
  73:2 my *f.* were almost gone
  74:3 lift up thy *f.* to desolations
  105:18 whose *f.* hurt with fet.
  115:7 *f.* have they but walk not
  116:8 deliv. my *f.* from falling
  119:59 turned my *f.* to testim.
  101 refr. my *f.* from evil way
  105 thy wo. is a lamp to my *f.*
  122:2 *f.* stand within thy gates
Prov. 1:16 *f.* run to evil, 6:18 ; *Is.* 59:7
  4:26 ponder the path of thy *f.*
  5:5 her *f.* go down to death, her
  6:13 wicked man speak. with *f.*
  28 go on coals, *f.* n. be burnt?
  7:11 her *f.* abide not in house
  19:2 hasteth with his *f.* sinneth
  26:6 cutteth off *f.* and drinketh
  29:5 spreadeth a net for his *f.*
Cant. 5:1 beautiful are thy *f.*
Is. 3:16 a tinkling with their *f.*
  18 ornaments about their *f.*
  6:2 with twain he covered his *f.*
  7:20 lord shall shave hair off *f.*
  23:7 own *f.* shall carry her afar
  26:6 *f.* of poor sh. tread it down
  32:20 send forth the *f.* of Ox
  41:3 he had not gone with *f.*
  49:23 sh. lick up dust of thy *f.*
  52:7 *f.* of him bring. good tid.
  60:13 place of my *f.* glorious
Jer. 13:16 before *f.* stumble on mountain
  14:10 have not refrained their *f.*
  18:22 they hid snares for my *f.*
  38:22 thy *f.* are sunk in mire
Lam. 1:13 spread a net for my *f.*
Ezek. 1:7 their *f.* were straight *f.*
  2:2 Spirit set me on my *f.* 3:24
  16:25 opened thy *f.* to every one
  24:17 put thy shoes upon thy *f.*
  25:6 beca. stamped with the *f.*
  32:2 troubledst wat. with thy *f.*
  34:18 foul residue with your *f.*
  19 what ye have fouled with *f.*
  37:10 and stood upon their *f.*
Dan. 2:33 his *f.* part of iron, 42
  34 smote image upon his *f.*
  7:7 stamped residue with *f.* 19
  10:6 *f.* like br. *Rev.* 1:15 ; 2:18
Nah. 1:3 clouds are dust of his *f.*
  15 *f.* of him bringeth good tid.
Zec. 14:4 *f.* stand on mount of O.
Mat. 10:14 shake off the dust of *f. Mark* 6:11 ; *Luke* 9:5
  15:30 cast the lame at Jesus' *f.*
  18:8 rather than having two *f.*
  28:9 held by *f.* worshipped him
Luke 1:79 *f.* into way of peace
  7:38 kissed his *f.* and anointed
  8:35 found man at *f.* of Jesus
  41 Jai. fell down at Jesus' *f.*
  10:39 M. which sat at Jesus' *f.*
  15:22 put shoes on his *f.*
  21:39 beh. my hands and *f.*
John 11:2 and wiped his *f.* 12:3
  13:12 tho other anged at the *f.*
Acts 3:7 his *f.* received strength
  4:35 laid at apostles' *f.* 37 ; 5:2
  5:9 the *f.* of them which buried
  7:58 clothes at young man's *f.*
  13:25 shoes of His *f.* no worthy
  51 shook off dust of their *f.*
  14:10 Stand upright on *f.*
  16:24 their *f.* fast in the stocks
  21:11 Agabus bound his own *f.*
  22:3 brought up at *f.* of Gamal.
  26:16 rise and stand upon thy *f.*
Rom. 3:15 *f.* swift to shed blood
  10:15 *f.* of them preach gospel
  1 *Cor.* 12:21 to *f.* I have no need
Eph. 6:15 *f.* shod with prepara.
Heb. 12:13 strn. paths for your *f.*
Rev. 3:9 worship before thy *f.*
  10:1 his *f.* as pillars of fire
  11:11 witnesses stood on th. *f.*
  13:2 his *f.* as the *f.* of a bear
  22:8 I fell to worship bef. his *f.*

At his FEET.

Jud. 4:10 with 10,000 of *his f.*
Hab. 3:5 burning coals at *his f.*
  21:41 Again bound *his* own *f.*
Mark 12:31 Syroph. fell at *his f.*
Luke 7:38 she stood at *his f.*
Acts 5:10 Sapphira fell at *his f.*
Rev. 1:17 I fell at *his f.* as dead
  19:10 I fell at *his f.* to worship

FEET, joined with sole, s.

Deut. 11:24 s. of *f.* tread he yours
  1 *K.* 5:3 wars, under s. *f.*
  2 *K.* 19:24 s. of *f.* dried, *Is.* 37:25
Is. 60:14 bow down at s. of *f.*
Ezek. 1:7 s. of *f.* was like a calf's
  43:7 place of s. of my *f.* where
  Mal. 4:3 ashes under s. of your *f.*

FEL

Under FEET.

Ex. 24:10 under his *f.* sapphire
  2 *Sam.* 22:10 dark. u. *f. Ps.* 18:9
  39 they are fallen *under* my *f.*
Ps. 8:6 put all things *under* his *f.* 1 *Cor.* 15:27 ; *Eph.* 1:22
  47:3 subdue nations *u.* our *f.*
  91:13 dragon shalt trample *u. f.*
Is. 14:19 a carcase trodden *u. f.*
  28:3 drunkards be trodden *u. f.*
Lam. 3:34 *u.* his *f.* all prisoners
Mat. 7:6 trample *u.* their *f.*
Rom. 16:20 bruise Sat. *u.* your *f.*
  1 *Cor.* 15:25 all enemies *u.* his *f.*
Heb. 2:8 in subjection *u.* his *f.*
Rev. 12:1 moon *under* her *f.*

FEET, with wash, ed.

Ex. 30:19 A. and his sons shall wash their *f.* 21 ; 40:31
  1 *Sam.* 25:41 *f.* of the disciples' *f.*
John 13:5 wash the disciples' *f.*
  6 Lord, dost thou wash my *f.*?
  10 needeth not save to w. h. *f.*
  14 if I your L. have w. your *f.*
  1 *Tim.* 5:10 she ha. w. saints' *f.*

FEIGN, ED, EST.

  1 *Sam.* 21:13 *f.* himself mad
  2 *Sam.* 14:2 *f.* thyself a mourner
  1 *K.* 14:5 *f.* herself another wom.
Neh. 6:8 thou *f.* them
Ps. 17:1 prayer not out *f.* lips
Luke 20:20 *f.* them. just men
  2 *Pet.* 2:3 with *f.* words

FEIGNEDLY.

Jer. 3:10 turn to me *f.* saith L.

FELIX. *Acts* 23:24 ; 24:3, 25; 25:14

FELL.

  4:8 Cain's countenance *f.*
  44:14 Joseph's breth. *f.* bef. him
  22:30 wrath *f.* on congrega.
Jud. 7:13 smote tent that it *f.*
  8:10 there *f.* 120,000 men
  16:30 the house *f.* on the lords
  1 *Sam.* 4:18 Eli *f.* from seat
  14:7 fear of Lord . . . on people
  11:13 Philistines *f.* before Jon.
  22:18 Doeg *f.* upon the priests
  28:20 Saul *f.* straightway along
  29:3 no fault since he *f.* to me
  31:4 Saul took sw. and . . . on it
  2 *Sam.* 4:4 Mephibosheth *f.*
  20:8 Joab's sword *f.* out, as he
  21:9 they *f.* all seven together
  1 *K.* 2:25 Benaiah *f.* on Adonijah
  20 *f.* on two more men right.
  31 Benaiah *f.* on J. ; 46 Shimei
  20:30 a wall *f.* on 27,000 men
  Ec. 1:13 captain *f.* on his knees
  2:13 mantle that *f.* from Elijah
  4:8 it *f.* on a day, Eli-sha. 11, 18
  5:5 axe head *f.* into the water
  1 *Chr.* 21:15 *f.* bef. 50,000 men
  27:24 *f.* wrath for it against Jer.
  2 *Chr.* 17:10 fear of L. *f.* on all
  20:18 inhabitants *f.* before Lord
  21:19 his bowels *f.* out by reas.
  24 *f.* 25:1 *f.* on my knees, and
  Est. 9:3 fear of Mor. *f.* on them
  Job 1:15 Sabe. *f.* on the asses, 17
  19 house *f.* on the young men
  Ps. 27:2 cut up my foes *f.*
  78:64 their priests *f.* by sword
  105:38 fear of Israel *f.* on Egypt
Jer. 39:9 . . . away *f.* to him, 52:15
  46:16 one *f.* upon another
Lam. 1:7 her people *f.* into hand
  5:13 children *f.* under the wood
Ezek. 8:1 ha. of L. *f.* on me, 11:5
  39:23 so *f.* they all by the sw.
  Dan. 4:31 *f.* a voice from heaven
  10:7 great quaking *f.* on them
  Mat. 7:25 the house *f.* not
  27 house *f. Luke* 6:49
  13:4 seed *f.* by the wayside, *Mark* 4:4 ; *Luke* 8:5
  Mark 9:20 he *f.* on ground and wallowed
  14:35 Jesus *f.* on the ground
  Luke 10:30 *f.* among thieves, 36
  13:4 on whom tower in Silo. *f.*
  15:20 his father *f.* on his neck
  16:21 crumbs wh. *f.* from table
  John 12:24 *f.* into gr. corn of wh.
  Acts 1:25 Jud. by transgress. *f.*
  26 the lot *f.* upon Matthias
  7:60 had said this, he *f.* asleep
  9:4 Saul *f.* and heard a voice
  10:10 Peter *f.* into a trance
  10 Holy Ghost *f.* on all, 11:15
  12:7 chains *f.* off Peter's hands
  13:11 there *f.* on him a mist

FEL

Acts 13:36 D. *f.* on sleep, saw cor.
  19:17 fear *f.* on Jews at Ephesus
  20:10 Paul *f.* on Eutychus
  37 they all *f.* on Paul's neck
  22:7 I *f.* unto the ground, and
  Rom. 11:22 on them wh. *f.* sever.
  15:3 reproached thee, *f.* on me
  1 *Cor.* 10:8 *f.* in one day 23,000
  Heb. 3:17 whose carcases *f.*
  2 *Pet.* 3:4 the fathers *f.* asleep
  Rev. 1:17 I *f.* at his feet as dead
  6:13 and the stars of heaven *f.*
  8:10 *f.* great star from heaven
  11:11 fear *f.* on them which saw
  13 tenth of city *f.* by earthqua.
  16:2 there *f.* a grievous sore
  19 and the cities of nations *f.*
  21 there *f.* on men a great hail
  19:10 I *f.* at his feet to worship

See FACE, FACES.

FELL, down.

Deut. 6:18 I *f. down* before L. 25
Jos. 6:20 shouted, the wall *f. d.*
  8:25 be bowed, he *f. d.*
  12:26 concubine *f. d.* at door
  1 *Sam.* 31:1 *f. d.* in Gil, 1 *Chr.* 10:1
  1 *Sam.* 2:16 so they *f. d.* together
  23 A-sahel *f. d.* there and died
  10:18 Shimei *f. down*
  2 *K.* 1:2 Ahaziah *f. d.* thro' latt.
  2 *Chr.* 13:17 *f. d.* of Is. 500,000 m.
  Job 1:20 Job *f. d.* on the ground
  Ps. 107:12 *f. down* none to help
  Dan. 3:7 all nations *f. d.* and w.
  23 these three *f. d.* in furnace
  Mat. 2:11 wise men *f. d.* and wo.
  18:26 servant *f. d.* saying, 29
  Mark 3:11 unclean spirits *f. d.*
  Luke 5:8 P. *f. d.* at Jesus' knees
  8:28 man which had devils *f. d.*
  Acts 1:20 Janarias *f. d.* 5 ; 17:16 Samar.
  Acts 5:5 Ananias *f. d.* ; 10 Sapp.
  10:25 Cornelius; 16:29 jailer
  19:35 the image which *f. down*
  20:9 Eutychus *f. d.*
  Heb. 11:30 by faith the walls *f. d.*
  Rev. 5:8 elders *f. d.* 14 ; 19:4
  22:8 John *f. d.* before the angel

FELL, on.

  2 *Sam.* 3:34 bef. wick. so *f.* thou
  2 *K.* 3:19 shall *f.* every good tree
  6:5 as one was *f.* a beam

FELLER.

Is. 14:8 no *f.* is come up, ag. us

FELLOW.

Gen. 19:9 this *f.* came in (to so),
Ex. 2:13 why smit. thou thy *f.*?
  Acts 7:27 who made thee a *f.*?
  21:35 shall *f.* every good tree
  1 *Sam.* 21:15 brought this *f.* to
  play the madman, shi. this *f.*
  Luke kept all this *f.* hath
  Luke 2:16 caught ev. one this *f.*
  1 *K.* 22:27 *f.* in pris. 2 *Chr.* 18:26
  2 *K.* 9:11 came this mad *f.*
  Ec. 4:10 fall, one will lift his *f.*
  Is. 34:14 satyr shall cry to his *f.*
  Zec. 13:7 awake, O sword, agai.
  my Sh. and man th. is my *f.*
  Mat. 26:71 *f.* also w. J. *Lu.* 22:59
  Luke 23:2 this *f.* pervert. nation
  John 9:29 for this *f.* we know not
  Acts 18:13 *f.* persu. to worship G.
  22:22 away with such a *f.* from
  24:5 found this man a pestil. *f.*

FELLOW-CITIZENS.

Eph. 2:19 *f.-citizens* with saints

FELLOW-HEIRS.

Rom. 8:17 *f.-heirs* with Christ

FELLOW-HELPER, S.

  2 *Cor.* 8:23 Titus, my *f.-helper*
  3 *John* 8 be *f.-h.* to the truth

FELLOW-LABORER, S.

  1 *Thes.* 3:2 sent Tim. our *f.-lab.*
  Phil. 4:3 with other *f.-labor.s*
  Phile. 1 Paul to Phile. our *f.-l.*
  24 Marcus, Demas, Lucas, *f.-l.*

FELLOW-PRISONER, S.

Rom. 16:7 Aud. and Junia *f.-p.*
Col. 4:10 Aristarch. *f.-p.* saluteth
Phile. 23 Epaphras my *f.-p.* in C.

FELLOW-SERVANT, S.

Mat. 18:28 *f.-serv.* who owed him
  29 *f.-s.* fell down at his feet
  31:36 begin to smite his *f.-s.*
  Col. 1:7 Epaphras our dear *f.-serv.*
  4:7 Tychicus, who is a *f.-serv.*
  Rev. 6:11 *f.-s.* should be fulfilled
  19:10 I am thy *f.-serv.* 22:9

FELLOW-SOLDIER.

Phil. 2:25 Epaphroditus my *f.-s.*
Phile. 2 Paul to Archippus, *f.-s.*

FET

FELLOW-WORKERS.
Col. 4:11 these only are my *f.-w.*

FELLOWS.
Jud. 18:25 angry *f.* run on thee
2 *Sam.* 6:20 as one of vain *f.*
Ps. 45:7 with the oil of gladness above thy *f. Heb.* 1:9
Is. 44:11 his *f.* shall be ashamed
Ezek. 37:19 tribes of Israel his *f.*
Dan. 2:13 D. and his *f.* to be sla.
7:20 look more stout than his *f.*
Zec. 3:8 thou and thy *f.* that sit
Mat. 11:16 calling to their *f.*
Acts 17:5 lewd *f.* of baser sort

FELLOWSHIP.
Lev. 6:2 deliv. to keep, or in *f.*
Ps. 94:20 iniq. have *f.* wi. thee?
Acts 2:42 contin. in apostles' *f.*
1 *Cor.* 1:9 called to *f.* of his Son
10:20 sh. have *f.* with devils
2 *Cor.* 6:14 what *f.* hath righte.
8:4 *f.* of ministering to saints
Gal. 2:9 the right hand of *f.*
Eph. 3:9 is *f.* of the mystery
5:11 no *f.* with works of darkn.
Phil. 1:5 your *f.* in the gospel
2:1 if there be any *f.* of the Sp.
3:10 know *f.* of his sufferings
1 *John* 1:3 have *f.* with us, our *f.* is with the Father
6 if we say we have *f.* with h.
7 walk in light, we have *f.*

FELT.
Gen. 27:22 and Isaac *f.* Jacob
Ex. 10:21 darkn. that may be *f.*
Mark 5:29 she *f.* she was healed
Acts 28:5 off beast and *f.* no harm

FEMALE.
Gen. 1:27 male and *f.* created, 5:2
6:19 two of ev. sort, male and *f.*
7:16 went in male and *f.*
Lev. 4:28 offering, a *f.* 32; 5:6
Num. 5:3 male and *f.* sh. ye put
Deut. 4:16 likeness of male or *f.*
7:14 not be male nor *f.* barren
Mat. 19:4 m. and *f. Mark* 10:6
Gal. 3:28 in Christ male nor *f.*

FENCE.
Ps. 62:3 ye sh. he as a tottering *f.*

FENCED, Verb.
Job 10:11 *f.* me with bones
19:8 he hath *f.* up my way
Is. 5:2 a vineyard, and he *f.* it

FENCED, Adjective.
Deut. 3:5 32 *f.* walls come down
2 *Sam.* 23:7 touch th. must be *f.*
2 *K.* 3:19 shall smite every *f.* city
17:9 from tower to *f.* city, 18:8
Is. 2:15 day of L. on ev. *f.* wall
Jer. 15:20 make thee a *f.* wall
Ezek. 36:35 ruined cities bec. *f.*

FENCED cities.
Num. 32:17 dwell in *f. c.*
Deut. 9:1 pos. *c. f.* up to heaven
Jos. 10:20 rest entered into *f. c.*
14:12 that the *cities* were *f.*
2 *Sam.* 20:6 lest he get *f. c.*
2 *K.* 18:13 should. lay waste *f. c.*
2 *Chr.* 8:5 Solomon built *f. cities*
12:4 Shishak took *f. c.* of Judah
Jer. 5:17 sh. impoverish thy *f. c.*
Dan. 11:15 shall take most *f. c.*
Hos. 8:14 Judah hath multi. *f. c.*
Zep. 1:16 day of alarm ag. *f. c.*

FENS.
Job 40:21 Behemoth in cov. of *f.*

FERRET.
Lev. 11:30 the *f.* unclean

FERRY-BOAT.
2 *Sam.* 19:18 *f.-b.* for king's hou.

FERVENT, LY.
Acts 18:25 Apollos, *f.* in spirit
Rom. 12:11 *f.* in spirit, serv. L.
2 *Cor.* 7:7 your *f.* mind tow. me.
Col. 4:12 laboring *f.* in prayers
Jam. 5:16 *f.* pray. of a righteous
1 *Pet.* 1:22 ye love one another *f.*
4:8 above all th. have *f.* charity
2 *Pet.* 3:10 melt with *f.* heat, 12

FEST'US. *Acts* 24:27; 25:9,14,23; 26:25

FETCH.
Gen. 18:5 will *f.* morsel of bread
27:13 I will *f.* thee from thence
Num. 20:10 *f.* water out of rock?
Deut. 30:4 thence will L. *f.* thee
Jud. 11:5 went to *f.* Jephthah
1 *Sam.* 4:3 *f.* ark of covenant
6:21 come and *f.* ark up to you
16:11 send and *f.* Saul, 20:31
2 *Sam.* 5:23 *f.* a compass behind
14:13 king doth not *f.* banished

FIE

2 *Sam.* 14:20 *f.* ab. this form of
1 *K.* 17:10 *f.* me a little water
2 *K.* 6:13 wh. that I may *f.* him
2 *Chr.* 18:8 *f.* quick. Micaiah son
Job 36:3 *f.* my knowl. from far
Is. 56:12 I will *f.* wine
Acts 16:37 come, and *f.* us out

FETCHED.
1 *Sam.* 7:1 *f.* up ark of the Lord
10:23 they *f.* Saul thence
2 *Sam.* 9:5 and *f.* Mephibosheth
11:27 *f.* Bath-sheba to his house
14:33 *f.* they *f.* from Ophir gold
3 *K.* 11:4 Jehoiada *f.* rulers
Jer. 26:23 *f.* Urijah out of Egypt
Acts 28:13 thence we *f.* compass

FETTERS.
Jud. 16:21 bound Samson with *f.*
2 *Sam.* 3:34 nor thy feet put in *f.*
2 *K.* 25:7 bound Zedeki. with *f.*
2 *Chr.* 33:11 Mana. bound with *f.*
36:6 Jehoiakim bound with *f.*
Ps. 105:18 feet they hurt with *f.*
149:8 to bind nobles with *f.*
Mark 5:4 often with *f. Lu.* 8:29

FEVER.
Deut. 28:22 smite thee with a *f.*
Mat. 8:14 P. wife's mother sick of *f. Mark* 1:30; *Luke* 4:38
John 4:52 at 7th hour *f.* left him
Acts 28:8 father of Pub. sick of *f.*

FEW.
Gen. 34:30 I few *f.* in num. th. will slay
47:9 *f.* and evil have the days
Lev. 26:22 you *f. Deut.* 4:27; 28:62
Num. 13:18 the people wheth. *f.*
20:54 to *f.* give less inher. 33:6
56 divided betw. many and *f.*
Deut. 26:5 sojourned with a *f.*
33:6 let not Reuben's men be *f.*
1 *Sam.* 14:6 to save by many or *f.*
2 *Chr.* 29:34 the prie. were too *f.*
Neh. 7:4 city large, but people *f.*
Job 10:20 are not my days, *f.*?
14:1 man is of *f.* days
16:22 when a *f.* years are come
Ec. 5:2 let thy words be *f.*
9:14 a little c. y. and *f.* men
12:3 grinders cease, because *f.*
Is. 10:19 rest of trees shall be *f.*
24:6 are burned, and *f.* men left
Ezek. 5:3 also leave *f.* men in num.
12:16 leave a *f.* men from sword
Dan. 11:20 *f.* days he destroyed
Mat. 7:14 *f.* there be that find it
7:37 laborers are *f. Luke* 10:2
22:16 call. but *f.* chosen, 24:14
23:21 faithful in *f.* things, 23
Mark 6:5 hands on a *f.* sick folk
Luke 12:48 beaten with *f.* stripes
13:28 *f.* that be saved?
Acts 24:4 wouldst hear *f.* words
Eph. 3:3 wrote afore in *f.* words
Heb. 12:10 for *f.* days chastened
13:22 I have written in *f.* words
1 *Pet.* 3:20 where. *f.* that is eight
Rev. 2:14 a *f.* things ag. thee, 20
3:4 a *f.* names even in Sardis

But a FEW.
Gen. 29:20 seemed but a *f.* days
Lev. 25:52 if remain *b.* a *f.* years
Num. 7:3 men of Ai are *but a f.*
1 *Chr.* 16:19 *but f. Ps.* 105:12
Jer. 42:2 for we are left *but a f.*

Not a FEW.
Is. 10:7 cut off nations *not a f.*
Jer. 30:19 multi. them, *not be a f.*
Acts 17:4 chief women *not a f.*

FEWER, EST.
Num. 33:54 to *f.* give less inher.
Deut. 7:7 ye were *f.* of all people

FEWNESS.
Lev. 25:16 accord. to *f.* of years

FIDELITY.
Tit. 2:10 serv. showing good *f.*

FIELD.
Gen. 23:20 *f.* and cave made sure
27:27 smell of son is as of a *f.*
31:4 Rachel and Leah to the *f.*
49:30 in *f.* Abra. bought, 50:13
Ex. 22:5 cause a *f.* to be eaten
6 so that the *f.* be consumed
Lev. 25:3 six years sh. sow thy *f.*
27:17 if he sanctify his *f.* 19
if he will not redeem the *f.*
Deut. 5:21 neith. sh. covet his *f.*
Jos. 15:18 ask a *f. Jud.* 1:14
Ruth 2:9 go not to *f.* in ano. *f.*
4:5 day thou buyest *f.* of Naomi
2 *Sam.* 14:30 Joab's *f.* is near
21 why serv. set my *f.* on fire
2 *K.* 18:17 in highway of fuller's *f. Is.* 7:3; 36:2

FIE

Neh. 13:10 every one to his *f.*
Ps. 96:12 let the *f.* be joyful
Prov. 24:30 went by *f.* of slothful
27:26 goats are the price of *f.*
31:16 considereth a *f.* and buy.
Ec. 5:9 king is served by the *f.*
Is. 5:8 woe to them lay *f.* to *f.*
16:10 taken out of plentiful *f.*
Jer. 19:4 herbs of ev. *f.* wither ?
26:18 plou. like a *f. Mic.* 3:12
34:7 buy thee my *f.* 8,25
33:9 nol. have we vineyard, *f.*
48:33 gladn. is taken from the *f.*
Joel 1:10 the *f.* is wasted
Mat. 13:24 good seed in his *f.* 31
38 the *f.* is the world, the good
44 is like unto treas. hid in a *f.*
27:7 bought the potter's *f.* 10
8 the *f.* of blood, *Acts* 1:19
Luke 17:7 when come from the *f.*
Acts 1:18 this man parchas. a *f.*

Fruitful FIELD.
Is. 10:18 consume glory of *f. f.*
29:17 Lehan. turned into a *f. f.*
32:15 wilderness be a *fruitful f. fruit. f.* be counted a forest
16 righteous. in the *fruit. f.*
Ezek. 17:5 planted seed in a *f. f.*

In the FIELD.
Gen. 4:8 when they were in t. *f.*
24:63 out to meditate in the *f.*
37:15 Joseph found him *in the f.*
Ex. 9:19 all thou hast *in f.*
25 the hail smote all *in the f.*
16:25 to-day not find it *in the f.*
Deut. 21:1 slain, lying *in the f.*
28:3 bless. sh. thou be *in the f.*
16 cursed sh. thou be *in the f.*
Jud. 13:9 repast came to w. *in f.*
1 *Sam.* 19:3 beside faith. *in the f.*
30:11 found an Egypt. *in the f.*
2 *Sam.* 14:6 two strove *in the f.*
1 *K.* 11:29 two alone *in the f.*
14:11 dieth of Jerob. *in the f.*
21:24 that die. of Ahab *in the f.*
1 *Chr.* 19:9 kings were *in the f.*
Job 24:6 reap ev. one corn *in f.*
Ps. 78:12 marv. things *in f.* 43
Prov. 24:27 fit for thyself *in t. f.*
Jer. 14:18 into the calved *in t. f.*
17:3 O my mountain *in the f.*
41:8 treasures *in the f.* of wheat
Ezek. 7:15 *in the f.* shall die
26:6 slay thy daughters *in t. f.* 8
Mic. 4:10 shalt dwell *in the f.*
Mat. 10:1 to ev. one grass *in t. f.*
Mat. 3:11 vine cast fruit *in the f.*
Mat. 24:18 nor let him *in f.* ret.
Mark 13:16; *Luke* 17:36
40 two be *in f. f., Luke* 17:36
Luke 9:3 sheph. abiding *in t. f.*
12:28 clothe grass to-day *in t. f.*
15:25 his elder son was *in the f.*

Into the FIELD.
Jud. 9:42 people went *into the f.*
1 *Sam.* 6:14 cart came *into the f.*
20:11 D. said, Let us go *into f.*
2 *Sam.* 20:12 removed Am. *into f.*
Cant. 7:11 let us go forth *in. t. f.*
Jer. 6:25 go not forth *into the f.*
14:18 if I go *into f.*

Of the FIELD.
Gen. 2:5 every plant *of the f.*
34:7 some *of t. f.* came out *of t. f.*
47:24 four parts for seed *of t. f.*
Lev. 26:4 trees *of f.* sh. yield frn.
Deut. 30:19 devoted thing *of the f.*
Jud. 5:4 marchedst out *of the f.*
19:16 man from work out *of t. f.*
2 *K.* 9:25 cast in portion *of the f.*
37 carc. as dung on face *of t. f.*
Job 5:23 in league with stones *of f.*
Ps. 103:15 as flower *of f.* he flou.
Cant. 2:7 the roes *of the f.* 3:5
Is. 37:27 inhabit. as grass *of f.*
40:6 and as the flower *of the f.*
43:20 beast *of f.* sh. *f.* me honor
55:12 trees *of the f.* sh. clap hou.
Jer. 4:17 as keepers *of the f.*
18:14 snow from rock *of the f.*
Ezek. 16:7 multiply as bud *of t. f.*
17:24 trees *of the f.* shall know
34:27 tree *of f.* shall fruit
36:30 multiply increase *of the f.*
39:10 no wood out of *f.*
Dan. 4:15 tender grass *of the f.*
Hos. 10:4 as hemlock in the *f.*
12:11 heaps in furrows *of the f.*
Joel 2:11 harv. *of the f.* is perish.
19 I am. *of f.* are devour. of
Mat. 6:28 consider lilies *of the f.*
30 if G. so clothe grass of *t. f.*

See BEAST, BEASTS.

FIF

Open FIELD.
Lev. 14:7 liv. bird loose into *o. f.*
17:5 sacrifices in the *open f.*
Ezek. 16:5 cast out in the *o. f.*
32:4 cast thee on the *open f.*
33:27 that is in *o. f.* give to
39:5 shalt fall upon the *open f.*

FIELDS.
Lev. 25:91 counted as the *f.*
Num. 16:14 hast not given us *f.*
20:17 not pass through *f.* 21:22
Deut. 11:15 send grass into thy *f.*
32:13 eat increase of the *f.*
3t as vine of the *f.* of Gomor.
1 *Sam.* 8:14 he will take your *f.*
22:7 will son of J. give you *f.?*
25:15 a wall to us when in *f.*
1 *K.* 2:26 get thee to thi. own *f.*
1 *Chr.* 16:32 let *f.* rejoice and all
27:25 storehouses in *f.* cities
Neh. 5:10 sendeth waters on *f.*
Ps. 107:37 sow the *f.* and plant
132:6 found it in *f.* of the wood
Prov. 8:26 had not made the *f.*
33:10 enter not to *f.* of fatheri.
Ec. 16:8 *f.* of Heshbon languish
Jer. 32:15 *f.* shall be possessed
43 *f.* bought; 44 mon sh. buy *f.*
Ezek. 29:19 *f.* possess *f.* of Ephraim
Mic. 2:2 they covet *f.* and take
4 he hath divided our *f.*
Hab. 3:17 altho. *f.* yield no meat
Mark 2:23 through *f. Luke* 6:1
Mark 4:35 up eyes, and look on *f.*
Jam. 5:4 which reaped your *f.*

Open FIELDS.
Num. 19:16 slain with s.w. in *o. f.*
2 *Sam.* 11:11 encamped in *o. f.*
Ezek. 29:5 shalt fall upon the *o. f.*

FIERCE.
Gen. 49:7 anger, for it was *f.*
Deut. 28:50 nation of a *f.* count.
Job 4:10 voice of *f.* lion
10:16 huntest me as *f.* lion
28:8 nor hath *f.* lion passed by
41:10 none so *f.* dare stir him
Is. 19:4 a *f.* king shall rule over
33:19 thou shalt not see a *f.* peo.
Dan. 8:23 *f.* countenance shall st.
Hab. 1:8 horses more *f.* than wol.
Mat. 8:28 devils. exceeding *f.*
Luke 23:5 they were more *f.*
2 *Tim.* 3:3 incont., *f.* despisers
Jam. 3:4 ships driven of *f.* winds

FIERCENESS.
Job 39:24 swallo. ground with *f.*
Jer. 25:38 land desolate *f.* of opp.
See ANGER, WRATH.

FIERCER.
2 *Sam.* 19:48 words of J. were *f.*

FIERY.
Num. 21:6 the L. sent *f.* serpents
8 make thee a *f.* serpent
Deut. 8:15 wherein were *f.* serp.
33:2 from right hand went *f.* law
Ps. 21:9 make them as a *f.* oven
Is. 14:29 fruit be *f.* flying serp.
Dan. 3:6 into midst of *f.* furnace
7:9 his throne was like *f.* flame
Eph. 6:16 able to quench *f.* darts
Heb. 10:27 judgment and *f.* indi.
1 *Pet.* 4:12 not stran. con. *f.* trial

FIFTH.
2 *Sam.* 2:23 smote A. under *f.* rib
3:27 Ab. under *f.* 4:6 Ish-bosh.
20:10 J. smote Ama. under *f.* rib
Rev. 6:9 when he opened *f.* seal
9:1 the *f.* angel sounded
10:19 *f.* angel poured out vial

FIFTEEN.
Num. 11:16 Bethany *f.* furl. off J.
Acts 27:28 found it *f.* fathoms
Gal. 1:18 I abode with P. *f.* days

FIFTY.
Num. 4:3 from 30 y. old and upw. even to *f.* 23, 30, 35, 39
8:25 fr. age of *f.* serve no more
1 *K.* 18:4 hid them by *f.* in a cave
2 *K.* 1:9 cap. of *f.* with *f.* 11,13
10 fire consume thee and *f.* 12
Luke 7:41 one 500 pence, other *f.*
John 8:57 art not yet *f.* years old
FIFTY, with six.
Ezr. 2:22 men of Netop. *f.* and s.
FIFTY thousand.
Acts 19:19 price books burnt *f. t.*

FIFTIES.
Mark 6:40 sat d. by *f. Luke* 9:14

CRUDEN'S CONCORDANCE. 855

FIG

FIFTIETH.
Lev. 25:10 shall hallow *f*. year
11 a jubilee shall that *f*. year be

FIG, S.
Gen. 3:7 *f*. leaves for aprons
1 Sam. 25:18 A. took 200 cakes *f*.
30:12 gave Egyptian cake of *f*.
2 K. 20:7 take lump *f*. Is. 38:21
Neh. 13:15 sab. some brought *f*.
Cant. 2:13 fig-t. put. for. green *f*.
Is. 34:4 fall *f*. from fig-tree
Jer. 8:13 shall be no *f*. on fig-tree
24:1 two baskets *f*. one good, 2, 3
8 evil *f*. that cannot be eaten
29:17 make them like vile *f*.
Nah. 3:12 fig-t. with first ripe *f*.
Mat. 7:16 do men gather *f*. of thistles? Luke 6:44
Jam. 3:12 fig bear ber. or vine *f*.
Rev. 6:13 fig-tree casteth unt. *f*.

* **FIG-TREE.**
Jud. 9:10 trees said to *f*.-*t*. 11
1 K. 4:25 dw. under *f*.-*t*. Mic. 4:4
2 K. 18:31 eat ev. one *f*.-*t*. Is. 36:16
Prov. 27:18 keepeth *f*.-*t*.
Hos. 9:10 first ripe in *f*.-*t*. thereof
Joel 1:7 he hath barked my *f*.-*t*.
12 the *f*.-*t*. languisheth
Hab. 3:17 altho' *f*.-*t*. sh. not blo.
Zec. 3:10 call ev. man under *f*.-*t*.
Mat. 21:19 he saw *f*.-*t*. in way, Mark 11:13
20 *f*.-*t*. withered, Mark 11:20, 21
24:32 parable of *f*.-*t*. Mark 13:28
Luke 13:6 man had *f*.-*t*. planted
7 seeking fruit on this *f*.-*t*.
21:29 behold the *f*.-*t*.
John 1:48 und. *f*.-*t*. I saw thee, 50

FIG-TREES.
Deut. 8:8 land of vines, and *f*.-*t*.
Ps. 105:33 smote vines and *f*.-*t*.
Jer. 5:17 eat thy vines and *f*.-*t*.
Hos. 2:12 I will destroy her *f*.-*t*.
Amos 4:9 when *p*. and *f*.-*t*. incr.
Nah. 3:12 strong-ho. be like *f*.-*t*.

FIGHT, Substantive.
1 Sam. 17:20 host was going to *f*.
1 Tim. 6:12 fight the good *f*.
2 Tim. 4:7 I have fought a good *f*.
Heb. 10:32 endured great *f*.
11:34 waxed valiant in *f*.

FIGHT, Verb.
Deut. 1:41 we will go up and *f*.
42 go not up, nor *f*. for I am
1 Sam. 4:9 quit like men, and *f*.
17:10 give man that we may *f*.
2 Sam. 11:20 nigh when ye did *f*.?
1 K. 22:31 *f*. not gr. 2 Chr. 18:30
Ps. 144:1 teach. my fingers to *f*.
Jer. 51:30 men forborne to *f*.
Zec. 10:5 *f*. bec. L. is with them
14:14 Judah shall *f*. at Jerusa.
John 18:36 then would my serv. *f*.
1 Cor. 9:26 *f*. I not as beateth air
Jam. 4:2 ye kill, ye *f*. and war

FIGHT against.
Ex. 1:10 join enemies and *f*. *a*.
Deut. 20:10 nigh to a city to *f*. *a*.
Jos. 19:47 Danites went *f*. *a*. Le.
Jud. 1:1 shall go up first *f*. *a*. ?
11:8 Jephth. to *f*. *a*. Ammon, 9
25 against Israel, or *f*. *a*. them ?
1 Sam. 15:18 *f*. *a*. A. consumed
23:1 Philistines *f*. *a*. Keilah
20:8 I may go *f*. *a*. enemies
1 K. 12:21 not *f*. *a*. 2 Chr. 11:4
20:23 let us *f*. *a*. them, 25
22:32 turned to *f*. *a*. Jehosh.
2 K. 3:21 kings were come to *f*. *a*.
2 Chr. 13:12 *f*. ye not *a*. the Lord
32:2 Neu. purposed to *f*. *a*. Jer.
35:20 Necho came to *f*. *a*. Car.
Neh. 4:8 come and *f*. *a*. Jerusa.
Ps. 35:1 *f*. *a*. them that *f*. *a*. me
56:2 they be many that *f*. *a*. me
Is. 19:2 wh. *f*. every one *a*. brot.
29:7 all nations that *f*. *a*. Ariel
8 nations that *f*. *a*. mount Z.
Jer. 1:19 shall *f*. *a*. thee, 15:20
21:5 I myself will *f*. *against* you
32:24 Ch. *f*. *a*. 29; 34:22; 37:8
Zec. 14:3 *f*. *a*. those nations
Acts 5:39 ye be found *f*. *a*. God
23:9 let us not *f*. *against* God
Rev. 2:16 *f*. *a*. them with sword *f*.

FIGHT for.
Ex. 14:14 L. *f*. *for*, Deut. 1:30; 3:22; 20:4
2 K. 10:3 *f*. *for* master's house
Neh. 4:14 *f*. *for* your brethren
20 our God shall *f*. *for* us
Is. 31:4 L. shall come to *f*. *for* Z.

FIGHT with.
Jud. 9:38 go out and *f*. *with* Ab.

FIL

Jud. 11:6 may *f*. *w*. chil. of Am.
1 Sam. 13:5 Phi. *f*. *w*. Israel, 28:1
17:9 if he be able to *f*. *with* me
32 thy ser. will go and *f*. *w*. P.
2 Chr. 35:22 Jo. disguised to *f*. *w*.
Ec. 30:32 making will he *f*. *w*. on
Jer. 32:5 though ye *f*. *w*. Chald.
Dan. 10:20 return to *f*. *w*. prince
11:11 king of south came *f*. *w*.

FIGHTETH, ING.
Ex. 14:25 L. *f*. for them ag. Eg.
Jos. 23:10 L. God that *f*. for you
1 Sam. 25:28 my lord *f*. battles
Ps. 56:1 O God, he *f*. oppresseth

FIGHTINGS.
2 Cor. 7:5 without *f*. within fears
Jam. 4:1 wh. come wars and *f*. ?

FIGURE.
Deut. 4:16 similitude of any *f*.
Is. 44:13 maketh after *f*. of man
Rom. 5:14 *f*. of him that was
1 Cor. 4:6 these I have in *f*. tra.
Heb. 9:9 which was a *f*. of time
11:19 whence he rec. him in a *f*.
1 Pet. 3:21 like *f*. even baptism

FIGURES.
1 K. 6:29 with carved *f*. of cher.
Acts 7:43 *f*. wh. ye made to wor.
Heb. 9:24 are the *f*. of the true

FILE.
1 Sam. 13:21 a *f*. for mattocks

FILL, Substantive.
Lev. 25:19 ye shall eat your *f*.
Deut. 23:24 may. eat grapes thy *f*.
Prov. 7:18 take our *f*. of love

FILL, Verb.
Gen. 1:22 *f*. waters in the seas
42:25 Jos. com. to *f*. sacks, 44:1
Ex. 10:6 locusts shall *f*. houses
16:32 Mo. said, *f*. a homer of it.
27:21 Jer. shall *f*. face of world
45:19 will *f*. this house with oil
Job 8:21 *f*. mouth with laughing
15:2 sh. wise man *f*. his belly
20:23 when about to *f*. his belly
23:4 would *f*. mouth with argu.
38:39 or *f*. appe. of young lions
41:7 skin with barbed irons ?
Ps. 81:10 mouth wide I will *f*.
83:16 *f*. their faces with shame
110:6 *f*. places with dead bodies
Prov. 1:13 we shall *f*. our houses
8:21 I will *f*. their treasures
Is. 8:8 sh. *f*. breadth of thy land
11:21 nor *f*. the face of world
27:12 will *f*. with strong drink
Jer. 13:13 I will *f*. Ieh. wit. drun.
23:24 I *f*. heaven and earth ?
51:14 I will *f*. thee with men
Ezek. 3:3 *f*. thy bowels
9:7 *f*. the courts with the slain
10:2 *f*. hands and fills the slain
24:4 *f*. it with the choice bones
30:11 shall *f*. land with slain
32:4 *f*. beasts of whole earth
5 I will *f*. val. with thy height
35:8 I will *f*. mount. with slain
Hag. 2:7 will *f*. house with glory
Mat. 9:16 which is put in to *f*. it
15:33 wh. bread to *f*. multitude ?
23:32 *f*. ye up then the measure
John 2:7 *f*. water-pots with water
Rom. 15:13 God of hope *f*. you
Eph. 4:10 he might *f*. all things
Col. 1:24 *f*. up what is behind
1 Thes. 2:16 to *f*. up their sins
Rev. 18:6 cup filled, *f*. double

FILLED.
Gen. 6:13 earth is *f*. with viol.
21:19 and *f*. bottle with water
24:16 Rebekah *f*. her pitcher
26:15 *f*. and *f*. wells with earth
Ex. 2:16 they *f*. troughs to water
16:12 is *f*. *w*. bread, will 35:35
31:3 I have *f*. with S. of G. 35:31
40:34 glory of L. *f*. taberna. 35
Jos. 9:13 bottles of *f*. were new
1 K. 8:10 cloud *f*. house of Lord
11 gl. *f*. house, 2 Chr. 5:14; 7:1,2
18:35 *f*. trench also with water
2 K. 21:16 M. *f*. Jeru. with blood, 24:4
23:14 J. *f*. their places wi. bones
Job 3:15 princes *f*. houses with
16:8 hast *f*. me with wrinkles
22:18 yet he *f*. houses with good
Ps. 38:7 loins *f*. with loath. dis.
71:8 my mouth is *f*. with praise
72:19 let earth be *f*. with glory
80:3 deep rust. in *f*. the land
123:3 hand. are *f*. with contempt
126:2 we *f*. exceedingly *f*. with

FIL

Prov. 5:10 strang. *f*. with wealth
25:16 lest thou be *f*. with honey
30:16 the earth not *f*. with water
22 a fool when *f*. with meat
Ec. 1:8 nor is ear *f*. with hearing
6:3 his soul be not *f*. with good
f. and yet the appetite is not *f*.
Cant. 5:2 my head is *f*. with dew
Is. 6:1 his train *f*. the temple
21:3 are my loins *f*. with pain
33:5 L. hath *f*. Zion with judg.
34:6 sword of L. is *f*. with blood
43:24 *f*. me with fat of sacrifices
Jer. 15:17 hast *f*. me with. indig.
46:12 thy cry hath *f*. the land
51:34 he hath *f*. belly
Lam. 3:15 he hath *f*. with bitter.
30 he is *f*. full with reproach
Ezek. 8:17 *f*. land with violence
10:3 and cloud *f*. the inner court
11:6 ye have *f*. streets with slain
28:16 they *f*. midst with viol.
36:38 waste cities *f*. flocks of
43:5 glory of Lord *f*. house, 44:4
Dan. 2:35 stone cut *f*. whole earth
Nah. 2:12 lion *f*. holes with prey
Hab. 2:16 thou art *f*. with shame
Hag. 1:6 ye are not *f*. with drink
Zec. 9:13 I have *f*. bow with E.
Mat. 27:48 *f*. sponge with vine-
Mark 3:21 new piece that *f*. it up
7:27 let the children first be *f*.
Luke 1:53 he hath *f*. the hungry
2:40 Jesus *f*. with wisdom
5:7 came and *f*. both the ships
14:23 compel that house be *f*.
15:16 would fain have *f*. belly
John 2:7 they *f*. them up to brim
6:13 *f*. twelve baskets with fra.
16:6 sorrow hath *f*. your heart
Acts 2:2 mighty wind *f*. house
4:8 Peter *f*. with the Holy Ghost
5:3 why hath Satan *f*. thy heart
28 have *f*. Jerus. with doctr.
9:17 be *f*. with the Holy Ghost
13:9 Paul *f*. with Holy Ghost
Rom. 1:29 *f*. with all unright.
15:14 *f*. with all knowledge
24 I be somewhat *f*. with
2 Cor. 7:4 I am *f*. with comfort
Eph. 3:19 be *f*. with all fulness
5:18 with wine, but *f*. with Sp.
Phil. 1:11 *f*. with fruits of right.
Col. 1:9 be *f*. with knowledge
2 Tim. 1:4 I may be *f*. with joy
Jam. 2:16 be ye warmed and *f*.
Rev. 8:5 angel *f*. censer with fire
15:1 in them is *f*. up wrath of G.
18:6 cup which she *f*. fill double

Shall be FILLED.
Ex. 16:12 in morning ye *s*. *be f*.
2 K. 3:17 val. *s*. *be f*. with water
Prov. 1:31 *s*. *be f*. with own dev.
8:10 so shall thy barns *be f*.
12:21 wicked *s*. *be f*. with misc.
14:14 backslider shall *be f*. with
20:17 mouth *s*. *be f*. with gravel
hay to know. *s*. chambers *be f*.
17:12 both he *be f*. with misery
Ezek. 23:33 *s*. *be f*. with drunk.
32:20 ye shall be *f*. at my table
Hab. 2:14 earth *s*. *be f*. with the
Mat. 5:6 hunger, they *s*. *be f*.
Luke 1:15 J. *s*. *be f*. with Holy G.
6:21 blessed hunger, ye *sh*. *be f*.

Was FILLED.
Gen. 6:11 *w*. *f*. with violence
K. 7:14 Hiram *was f*. with wis.
A. 3:20 country *was f*. with wa.
2 Chr. 5:13 house *was f*. cloud
16:14 bed *w*. *f*. with sweet odors
Ez. 12:12 mouth *w*. *f*. with laugh.
8:20 ye shall *be f*. at night
Hab. 2:14 earth *w*. *f*. with smoke
Luke 1:41 Elis. *w*. *f*. Holy Ghost
67 Zacharias *was f*. with H. G.
John 12:3 house *was f*. with odor
Acts 13:52 *w*. *f*. with joy and H.G.
Acts 15:58 temple *w*. *f*. with smoke

Were FILLED.
Hos. 13:6 *were f*. and their heart
Mat. 14:20 did eat and *were f*. all *f*. 5:20 *were f*. with fear, saying
6:42 *were f*. with fear, amazing
8:37 they *were f*. with madness
8:23 they *were f*. with water
John 6:11 when they *were f*.
Acts 2:4 all *f*. with H. G. 4:31
3:10 they *were f*. with wonder
5:17 *were f*. with indignation
13:45 Jews *were f*. with envy

FIN

Acts 13:52 disciples *were f*. joy
Rev. 19:21 fowls *w*. *f*. with flesh
See EAT.

FILLEDST.
Deut. 6:11 houses full, thou *f*.

FILLEST.
Ps. 17:14 whose belly thou *f*.

FILLETH.
Job 9:18 he *f*. me with bitterness
Ps. 84:6 rain also *f*. the pools
107:9 he *f*. the hungry soul
129:7 where, mower *f*. not hand
147:14 *f*. thee with finest wheat
Eph. 1:23 fulness of him that *f*.

FILLET, S.
Ex. 27:10 their *f*. shall be of sil-
ver, 11; 36:10, 11, 12, 17, 19
30:36 overlaid chapiters and *f*.
Jer. 52:21 a *f*. of twelve cubits

FILLETED.
Ex. 27:17 be *f*. with silver, 38:17
38:28 overlaid chapiters and *f*.

FILLING.
Acts 14:17 *f*. our hearts with food

FILTH.
Is. 4:4 when L. washed *f*. of Z.
Nah. 3:6 will cast abominable *f*.
1 Cor. 4:13 as the *f*. of the world
1 Pet. 3:21 not put away *f*. of flesh

FILTHINESS.
2 Chr. 29:5 carry *f*. out of holy
Ezr. 6:21 sep. from *f*. of heathen
9:11 unclean with *f*. of people
Prov. 30:12 not washed from *f*.
Is. 28:8 full of vomit and *f*.
Lam. 1:9 her *f*. is in her skirts
Ezek. 22:15 I will consume thy *f*.
24:13 *f*. of it may be notion
13 in thy *f*. is lewdness
36:25 from all *f*. will I cleanse
2 Cor. 7:1 cleanse ours. from all *f*.
Eph. 5:4 nor let *f*. be once named
Jam. 1:21 wherof. lay apart all *f*.
Rev. 17:4 full of abomin. and *f*.

FILTHY.
Job 15:16 much more *f*. is man *f*.
Ps. 14:3 altogeth *f*. be becone *f*. 53:3
Is. 64:6 all our right. as *f*. rags
Zep. 3:1 woe to her that is *f*.
Zec. 3:3 J. clothed with *f*. garm.
4 take away the *f*. garments
Col. 3:8 you put off *f*. communi.
1 Tim. 3:3 not greedy of *f*. lucre, 8
Tit. 1:7 not given to *f*. lucre
1 le tenching for *f*. lu. 1 Pet. 5:2
2 Pet. 2:7 Lot vexed with *f*. con.
Jude 8 *f*. dreamers defile the flesh
Rev. 22:11 *f*. let him be *f*. still

FINALLY.
2 Cor. 13:11 *f*. farewell, Eph. 6:10
Phil. 3:1; 4:8; 2 Thes. 3:1;
1 Pet. 3:8

FIND.
Gen. 19:11 wearied to *f*. the door
Num. 22:23 sin shall *f*. you out
Deut. 22:25 man *f*. damsel, 28
Ruth 1:9 L. grant you may *f*. rest
1 Sam. 20:21 go, *f*. out arrows, 36
24:19 *f*. enemy let him go *f*.
1 K. 18:5 perad. we may *f*. grass
2 Chr. 2:14 to *f*. out every device
Job 23:3 O where I might *f*. him
Ps. 10:15 seek wicked *f*. his wick.
17:11 L. knowest, of God
21:8 hand shall *f*. out those that *f*. thee
K. 7:27 one by one *f*. the account
32:17 seeking find also my words
Cant. 3:8 if I *f*. my beloved
Is. 5:11 receivest shall *f*. plenc.
58:3 in day of fast you *f*. pleas.
Lam. 1:6 like harts that *f*. no
2:9 prophets also *f*. no vision
Dan. 6:4 might to *f*. occasion ag.
5 except we *f*. it con. law of G.
Mat. 7:14 few there be that *f*. it
18:13 and if so he that *f*. it
Mat. 17:13 if happy he might *f*.
13:46 he *f*. one pearl
Luke 6:7 might *f*. accusation
12:38 *f*. them so, blessed are
13:7 seeking fruit and *f*. none
15:4 seek diligently till she *f*. it
John 10:9 in and out, *f*. pasture
Acts 7:46 desired to *f*. tabernacle
17:27 feel after him and *f*. him
23:9 we *f*. no evil in this man
Rom. 8:10 but he yet *f*. but I
2 Cor. 9:4 and *f*. you unprepared
2 Tim. 1:18 *f*. mercy of Lord

See FAVOR.

FIN

Can, or canst FIND.
Gen. 41:38 can f. such one
Ex. 5:11 get straw where c. f. it
Ezr. 7:16 silver and gold can f.
Job 3:22 glad when they can f.
11:7 c. thou by searching f. out
G. c. thou f. out Almighty?
Prov. 20:6 faith. man who c. f. ?
31:10 who c. f. a virtuous wom. ?
Ec. 3:11 c. f. out work G. maketh
7:24 exceed. deep, who c. f. it ?
Jer. 5:1 if ye c. f. man seek. tru.

Cannot FIND.
1 K. 18:12 c. f. thee, will slay
Job 17:10 I c. f. one wise man
37:23 Almighty, we c. f. him
Ec. 8:17 a man c. f. out work

FIND grace.
Gen. 32:5 I may f. grace in thy sight, Ex. 33:13
33:8 to f. g. in sight of my lord
15 let me f. g.; 34:11 l. me f. g.
47:25 let us f. grace in sight of
Ruth 2:2 in wh. sight I shall f. g.
1 Sam. 1:18 let thy handm. f. g.
2 Sam. 16:4 f. grace in thy sight
Heb. 4:16 we may f. g. to help

f. FIND.
Gen. 18:26 I f. in Sod. 50 righte.
28 if I f. 45; 30 if I f. 30 there
Ps. 132:5 I f. out place for L.
Ec. 7:26 I f. more bit. th. death
Cant. 8:1 when I sh. f. thee
Luke 23:4 I f. no fault in this man, John 18:38; 19:4, 6
Rom. 7:18 th. wh. is good I f. not
21 I f. law, that wh. I do good

Not FIND, or FIND not.
Ex. 16:25 to-day ye shall not f.
1 Sam. 17:20 could not f. them
Prov. 1:28 but shall not f. me, Hos. 5:6; John 7:34, 36
Ec. 7:28 soul seeketh, but I f. n.
Cant. 5:6 but I could not f. him
Is. 41:12 sh. not f. them, Hos. 2:7
Hos. 2:6 she shall not f. paths
Luke 5:19 not f. what way they
19:48 not f. what might do to J.
John 7:35 we shall not f. him
Rom. 7:18 how to do good, I f. n.
2 Cor. 12:20 I shall not f. you
Rev. 9:6 death, and shall not f. it

Shall, or shalt FIND.
Deut. 4:29 seek L. thou s. f. him
28:65 s. f. no ease am. nations
Jud. 3:33 as thou s. f. occasion
2 Chr. 20:16 s. f. at end of brook
30:9 children s. f. compassion
Ezr. 4:15 thou s. f. in book
Ps. 17:3 and s. f. nothing
21:8 thy hand s. f. out enemies
Prov. 6:17 they that seek me early s. f. me, Jer. 29:13
Jer. 6:16 s. f. rest Mat. 11:29
Mat. 7:7 and ye s. f. Luke 11:9
10:39 los. life for my sake s. f. it
17:27 thou s. f. a piece of money
21:2 s. f. an ass tied, Mark 11:2
22:9 as many as ye shall f. bid
24:46 when cometh, s. f. so doing, Luke 12:37, 43
Luke 2:12 ye shall f. babe wrapt
18:8 shall he f. faith on earth?
Rev. 18:14 thou s. f. th. no more

FINDETH.
Gen. 4:14 that f. me sh. slay me
Job 33:10 he f. occasions aga. me
Pr. 110:162 I rej. as one f. spoil
Prov. 8:13 happy man f. wisdom
8:35 whoso f. me f. life,
14:6 seeketh wisdom f. it not
18:22 whoso f. wife f. good th.
21:10 his neighbor f. no favor
21 that followeth mercy f. life
Ec. 9:10 whats. thy hand f. to do
Lam. 1:3 am. heathen f. no rest
Hos. 14:8 fathers s. f. mercy
Mat. 7:8 seeketh f. Luke 11:10
10:39 that f. his life shall lose it
12:43 seeking rest f. none
44 f. it empty, Luke 11:25
John 1:41 he first f. own brother
45 Jes. f. Philip; 45 Phi. f. N.

FINDING.
Gen. 4:15 lest any f. Cain
Job 9:10 doeth things past f. out
Is. 58:13 f. thine own pleasure
Luke 11:24 seeking rest f. none
Rom. 11:33 and his ways past f.
Heb. 8:8 for f. fault with them

FINE, Verb.
Job 28:1 place for gold where f.

FINE, Adjective.
Ezr. 8:27 ves. of f. cop. as gold

FIN

Is. 19:9 that work in f. flax
Rev. 1:15 feet like f. brass, 2:18

FINE flour or meal.
Gen. 18:6 three measures of f. m.
Lev. 2:1 offering be of f. fl. 24:5
4 cakes of f. fl. mingled wi. oil
5:7; 7:12; 14:10, 21; 23:13;
Num. 6:15; 7:13, 19, 25, 31,
37, 43, 49, 55, 61; 8:8
1 K. 4:22 30 measures of f. flour
2 K. 7:1 mea. f. f. for she. 16, 18
Ezek. 16:13 thou didst eat f. fl.
19 I gave thee f. flour, and oil
Rev. 18:13 merchandise of f. fl.

FINE gold.
2 Chr. 3:5 overlaid with f. gold
8 most holy overlaid with f. g.
Job 31:24 to f. g. Thou art conf.
Ps. 19:10 desired th. much f. g.
119:127 I love com. above f. g.
Is. 13:12 better than gold, than f. g.
25:12 as ornament of f. g.
Cant. 5:11 head is as most f. g.
15 as pill. set on sock. of f. g.
Is. 13:16 more prec. than gold,
Lam. 4:1 most f. g. changed
2 sons of Z. comparab. to f. g.
Dan. 2:32 Image's head f. gold
10:5 girded with f. g. of Uphaz
Zec. 9:3 T. heaped f. g. as mire

FINE linen.
Ex. 25:4 ye shall take f. linen
26:1 curtains of f. twined linen
31 v. of f. l. 36:35; 2 Chr. 3:14
36 f. twined linen 27:9, 16, 18;
36:37; 38:9, 10, 18
28:5 they sh. take gold and f. l.
6 the ephod of f. linen, 39:2
8 girdle f. l. 39:5, 29; 39:8
35:35 all manner of work and f. linen, 38:23; 2 Chr. 2:14
36:8 curtains of f. linen
39:27 coats of f. l. for Aaron
28 mitre of f. l. bonnets of f. l.
1 Chr. 15:27 clothed wi. robe f. l.
Ezek. 9:15 M. wi. garment of f. l.
Prov. 7:16 decked bed with f. l.
31:24 maketh f. l. and selleth
Ezek. 27:7 f. linen from Egypt
Mark 15:46 Jose. bought f. linen
Luke 16:19 man in pur. and f. l.
Rev. 18:12 merchandise of f. l.
19:8 granted to be arrayed f. l.
14 armies in heav. clot. in f. l.

FINER.
Prov. 25:4 come forth ves. for f.

FINEST.
Ps. 81:16 fed with f. of wheat
147:14 filleth thee with f. of wh.

FINING.
Prov. 17:3 f. pot is for sil. 27:21

FINGER.
Ex. 8:19 mag. said, This f. of G.
29:12 blood on altar with thy f.
31:18 tables written with thy f. of God, Deut. 9:10
Lev. 4:6 sh. dip f. in blood, 17,
25, 30, 34; 8:15; 9:9; 10:14, 19
14:16 priest dip right f. in oil, 27
1 K. 12:10 my little f. thicker,
2 Chr. 10:10
Is. 58:9 putting forth of the f.
Jer. 36:18 wrote with f. of G. cast out
20:25 put my f. into the print
27 reach hither thy f. and beh.
John 8:6 with f. wrote on g.
20:25 put my f. into the print
27 reach hither thy f. and beh.

FINGERS.
2 Sam. 21:20 on every hand six
1 Chr. 20:6
Ps. 8:3 thy heav. work of thy f.
144:1 teacheth my f. to fight
Prov. 6:13 wicked teach, with f.
7:3 bind them on f. write them
Cant. 5:5 my f. wi. sweet myrrh
8:3 which own f. made, 17:8
Jer. 52:21 thickn. of pillar four f.
Mat. 23:4 will not move with one of their f. Luke 11:46
Mark 7:33 he put his f. into ears

FINISH.
Gen. 6:16 in cubit sh. f. it above
Dan. 9:24 f. transgression, make
Luke 14:28 whe. sufficient to f.
29 and is not able to f. it
Zec. 4:9 hands shall f. it work
Acts 20:24 I might f. my course
Rom. 9:28 he will f. the work
2 Cor. 8:6 would also f. in you

FINISHED.
Gen. 2:1 heav. and earth were f.

FIR

Ex. 39:32 all work f. 40:33
1 K. 6:9 Sol. built' house and f.
14, 22, 38; 2 Chr. 5:1; 7:11
7:1 Solomon f. all his house,
9:1, 25; 2 Chr. 8:16
1 Chr. 28:20 till thou hast f.
Ezr. 5:16 build. and yet not f.
6:14 eld. of J. built and f. it, 15
Neh. 6:15 wall f. in 52 days
Dan. 5:26 numbe. kingd. and f.
Mat. 13:53 when Jes. f. parables
19:1 Jesus had f. sayings, 26:1
John 17:4 f. work thou gavest
19:30 said, It is f. bowed head
2 Tim. 4:7 I have f. my course
Heb. 4:3 works f. from foundat.
11:5 sin, wh. f. bring death
Rev. 10:7 mystery of G. sho. be f.
11:7 witnesses ha. f. testimony
20:5 till thousand years were f.

FINISHER.
Heb. 12:2 J. author and f. of faith

FINS.
Lev. 11:9 hath f. eat, Deut. 14:9
10 hath not f. be abomina. 12

FIRE.
Gen. 22:6 Abra. took f. in hand
7 father, behold f. and wood
Ex. 3:2 the bush burned with f.
9:23 Lord sent hail and f. ran
12:8 that night roast with f. 9
19:18 Lord on mount Sinai in f.
22:6 if f. break out, and catch
40:38 f. was on tabernacle by night, Num. 9:16; Deut. 1:33
Lev. 1:7 s. of priest put f. on alt.
8 upon wood in f. 12, 17; 3:5
9:24 came f. out from before L.
10:1 sons of A. put f. in censers
2 out f. from L. and devoured
18:21 any seed pass thr. f. Deut. 18:10; 2 K. 17:17; 23:10
Num. 6:18 and put it in the f.
11:2 M. prayed, f. was quenched
16:46 censer, and put f. thereon
21:28 f. gone out from Heshbon
31:23 cv. thing th. may abide f.
Deut. 4:11 mount. burnt with f.
36 he shewed thee his great f.
5:5 were afraid by reason of f.
Jos. 7:25 Isr. burned A. with f.
Jud. 6:21 rose up f. out of rock
9:15 let f. come out of bramble
16:9 th. of tow when touch. f.
1 K. 18:23 lay wood, put no f. 25
24 God that answereth by f.
38 f. of L. fell, 2 Chr. 7:1, 3
19:12 after earthquake f. but L. not in f. after f. still small
2 K. 1:10 then let f. come down
2:11 a chariot and horses of f.
6:17; mount. full of char. of f.
10:3 A. made son pass thro' f.
19:18 have cast gods into f.
21:6 Manasseh made son pass thro' f. 2 Chr. 33:6
1 Chr. 21:26 ans. fr. heaven by f.
Job 1:16 the f. of God is fallen
18:5 spark of the f. shall not
41:19 and sparks of f. leap out
Ps. 39:3 I was musing f. burned
66:12 went thro' f. and water
68:2 as wax melteth bef. f. so
74:7 have cast f. into sancta.
78:14 with light of f. 105:39
83:14 as the f. burneth the wood
97:3 f. goeth before him,
118:12 quenched as f. of thorns
140:10 let them be cast into f.
148:8 f. and hail, stormy wind
Prov. 6:27 take f. in bosom ?
16:27 in his lips is as burning f.
26:20 no wood is f. goeth out
30:16 and f. saith not enough
Is. 9:5 burning and fuel of f.
18 wickedness burneth as f.
19 people shall be as fuel of f.
10:16 burning like burn. of a f.
30:14 to take f. from hearth
33:11 saith Lord, whose f. is in Z.
37:19 kings of A. cast gods to f.
44:16 burneth part in the f. and
warm. A. I have seen f.
50:11 walk in the light of your f.
64:2 when melti. f. burneth, f.
causeth waters to boil
65:5 f. that burneth all the day
Jer. 4:4 fury come forth like f.
5:14 my words in thy mouth f.
20:9 word as f. shut up in bones
21:12 lest my fury go out like f.

Jer. 22:7 choice cedars in the f.
29:22 king of Baby. roasted in f.
32:35 sons to pass through f. un- to Mol. Ezek. 16:21; 23:20, 31
36:22 there was f. on hearth
23 roll, and cast it into the f.
Lam. 2:3 burned like flaming f.
4 he poured out his fury like f.
Ezek. 1:4 a f. infolding itself
13 f. bright, out of f. lightning
10:6 f. from between wheels
21:31 will blow thee in f. 22:21
22:20 blow f. upon it, to melt
24:9 oven make pile for f. 12
26:3 in the f. of my jeal. 38:19
Dan. 3:27 upon bod. f. had no p.
7:9 wheels like burning f.
10:6 and his eyes as lamps of f.
Hos. 7:6 burneth as a flaming f.
Joel 2:30 f. pillars, Acts 2:19
Amos 5:6 lest he break like f.
7:4 God called to contend by f.
Ob. 18 house of J. shall be a f.
Mic. 1:4 molten as wax before f.
Nah. 1:6 fury poured out like f.
Hab. 2:13 sh. labor in very f.
Zec. 2:5 unto her a wall of f.
3:2 brand plucked out of the f. ?
12:6 hearth of f. like torch of f.
13:9 bring third part thro' f.
Mal. 3:2 he is like a refiner's f.
Mal. 3:10 ev. tree that bringeth
not good fruit is cast into f.
7:19; Luke 3:9; John 15:6
11 baptize with Holy Ghost
and f. Luke 3:16
13:42 cast into furnace of f. 50
17:15 he falleth into f. Mar. 9:22
18:8 be cast into everlasting
f. Mark 9:43, 45
25:41 cursed, into everlasting
Mark 9:44 wh. f. is not quen. 45
14:54 P. warmed himself at f.
Luke 8:54 with thou that wer. f.
17:29 the same day it rained f.
22:55 beh. him as he sat by f.
Acts 3:3 cloven tong. likes as of f.
28:3 when Paul laid sticks on f.
5 he shook off the beast into f.
1 Cor. 3:13 eh. be reveal. by f. 15
2 Thes. 1:8 in flamin. f. taking
Heb. 1:7 ministers a flame of f.
11:34 faith quench. violence f.
12:18 mount that burned with f.
Jam. 3:5 great mat. little f. kin.
f. tongue is a f. a world of ini.
5:3 eat your flesh as it were f.
1 Pet. 1:7 though tried with f.
2 Pet. 3:7 reserved unto f. ag. day
12 heav. being on f. sh. be dis.
Jude 7 the venge. of eternal f.
23 pulling them out of the f.
Rev. 3:18 buy gold tried in f.
4:5 seven lamps of f. burning
8:5 angel filled censer with f.
7 there followed hail and f.
8 great mount. burning with f.
9:17 out of mouths issued f. 11:5
13:13 maketh f. come down
14:18 angel had power over f.
15:2 sea of glass mingled w. f.
16:8 power to scorch men w. f.
20:9 f. came down from God
10 dev. was cast into lake of f.
14 dea. and hell cast lake of f.
21:8 in lake wh. burneth with f.

See BRIMSTONE, BURN OR BURNT, COALS, CONSUME, CONSUMING, DEVOUR, DEVOURED, DEVOURING, FLAME, HELL, MIDST.

Kindle, or kindled FIRE.
Ex. 22:6 that k. f. make restitu.
35:3 ye sh. k. no f. on the sab.
Deut. 32:22 for a f. is k. in my anger, Jer. 15:14; 17:4
2 Sam. 22:13 coals of f. kindled
Ps. 78:21 f. was k. against Jacob
Is. 50:11 beh. all ye that k. a f.
Jer. 7:18 gather. wood, fath. k. f.
11:16 hath k. f. on green olive,
17:4; 43:12; 49:27; 50:32
Lam. 4:11 L. hath k. a f. in Z.
Ezek. 20:47 I will k. f. in forest
24:10 k. f. consume the flesh
Mal. 1:10 nor do ye k. f. on mine
Luke 22:55 f. when it already k. f.
22:55 when had k. a f. in hall
Acts 28:2 barbarious kindled f.

Made by FIRE.
Ex. 29:18 an offering made by f.
23, 41; Lev. 1:9, 13, 17; 3:2, 9,
16; 5:21, 23; 10:12; 22:27; 23:8,
13, 18, 25, 27, 36, 37; 21:7;
Num. 15:3, 10, 13, 14; 18:17;
28:3

CRUDEN'S CONCORDANCE. 857

FIR

Lev. 4:3 offerings of Lord m. by f.
  10; 8:3; 4:35; 5:12; 6:17, 18;
  7:30, 35; 10:12, 15; 21:21; 24:9;
  Deut. 18:1; 1 Sam. 2:28

Pillar of FIRE.
Ex. 14:24 L. looked thro' p. of f.
Rev. 10:1 and his feet as p. of f.

Send, or sent FIRE.
Lam. 1:13 from above he sent f.
Ezek. 39:6 I will s. f. on Magog
Amos 1:4 I will s. f. into h. of H.
  7 I will s. f. on the wall of G.
  10 I will s. f. on wall of Ty. 12
  2:2 I will s. f. on M.; 5 Judah
Luke 12:49 come to s. f. on earth

Set FIRE.
Deut. 32:22 s. on f. foundations
Jos. 8:8 s. city of Ai on f. 19
Jud. 1:8 Judah had s. Jer. on f.
  9:49 the people s. the hold on f.
  15:5 had s. the brands on f.
2 Sam. 14:30 s. J.'s field on f. 31
2 K. 8:12 H. will s. holds on f.
Ps. 57:4 am. th. that are s. on f.
Is. 27:11 women set them on f.
  42:25 he hath set him on f.
Jer. 6:1 s. up a sign of f. in Bet.
  32:29 C. shall s. on f. this city
Ezek. 30:8 s. a f. In Egypt, 14, 16
  39:9 v. on f. burn weapons of f.
Jam. 3:6 tongue s. on f. course
  of nature, is set on f. of hell

Strange FIRE.
Lev. 10:1 N. and Abi. offered s. f.
Num. 3:4 died wh. off. s. f. 26:61

FIREBRAND, S.
Jud. 15:4 S. took f. put f. midst
Prov. 26:18 madman casteth f.
Is. 7:4 two tails of these smok. f.
Amos 4:11 f. plucked out of bur

FIRE-PANS.
Ex. 27:3 make basons and f.-p.
38:3 he made the f.-p. of brass
2 K. 25:15 f.-p. car. Jer. 52:19

FIRES.
Is. 24:15 glorify ye Lord in f.

FIRKINS.
John 2:6 containing two or th. f.

FIRM.
Jos. 8:17 pri. stood f. on gr. 4:3
Job 41:23 are f. in themselves
  24 his heart is as f. as a stone
Ps. 73:4 no bands, but stre. is f.
Dan. 6:7 consulted to make f.
Heb. 3:6 rejoice. of hope f. to end

FIRMAMENT.
Gen. 1:6 f. in midst of waters
  7 G. f. waters under and ab. f.
  8 and God called the f. Heaven
  14 let th. be lights in f. 15, 17
  20 fowl that fly in open f.
Ps. 19:1 f. showeth handiwork
  150:1 praise him in f. power
Ezek. 1:22 likeness of f. as cryst.
  23 a voice from f. over heads
  26 above f. likeness of throne
Dan. 12:3 shine as bright. of f.

FIR.
1 K. 5:8 concerning timber of f.
  6:15 cov. floor with planks of f.
Cant. 1:17 cedar, our rafters of f.

FIR-TREE, S.
1 K. 5:10 H. gave Solo. f.-t. 9:11
  6:34 the two doors were of f.-t.
2 K. 19:23 cut tall f. Is. 37:24
2 Chr. 2:8 send f.-t.; Is. 14:8 f.-t.
  3:5 house he ceiled with f.-t.
Ps. 104:17 for stork f.-t. are house
K. 41:19 I set in the desert f.-t.
  55:13 inst. of th. sh. come f.-t.
  60:13 the f.-t. the pine-tree
Ezek. 27:5 ship-boards, f.-t.
Hos. 14:8 like g. f. t.; Nah. 2:3 f.-t. sh. be terribly sha.

FIR-WOOD.
2 Sam. 6:5 instru. made of f.-w.

FIRST.
Gen. 25:25 f. came out red
  33:28 said, This came out f.
Ex. 34:19 f. of trafts bring to h.
  36:17 f. row sh. be sardius, 39:10
Num. 2:9 f. three sh. f. set forth
  21:20 A malek was f. of nations
Deut. 11:14 save f. rain and lat.
  17:7 hands of witn. shall be f.
1 Sam. 14:35 f. altar S. built L.
2 Sam. 23:19 attained not to f.
  three, 23; 1 Chr. 11:21, 25
Ez. 3:12 glory of the f. house
Job 15:7 art th. the f. man born?
Prov. 18:17 is f. in own cause
Is. 43:27 f. father hath sinned

FIR

Dan. 6:2 Daniel was f. president
  7:4 the f. beast was like a lion
Hag. 2:3 saw house in f. glory
Zec. 12:7 save tents of Judah f.
Mat. 5:24 f. be reconciled to bro.
  6:33 seek ye f. kingdom of God
  7:5 f. cast beam out of own eye,
    Luke 6:42
  8:21 f. to go and bury, Luke 9:59
  12:45 worse than f. Luke 11:26
  17:10 must f. come, Mark 9:12
  27 take up fish that f. cometh
  21:31 of twain? They say, the f.
  36 other servants more than f.
  22:38 this f. com. Mark 12:28, 30
Mark 4:28 f. the blade, then ear
  7:27 let the children f. be filled
  9:35 desire to be f. shall be
  13:10 gospel must f. be publish.
  16:9 appeared f. to Mary Magd.
Luke 6:42 on second esb. after f.
  11:38 that he had not f. washed
  11:38 sit. not down f. and coun.
John 5:4 f. step. in made whole
  8:7 with. sin, let him f. cast st.
Acts 3:26 to you, God sent him
  11:26 called Christ. f. in Antio.
  12:10 passed f. and second ward
  26:23 C. f. that sho. rise fr. dead
Rom. 2:9 of Jew f. also of G. 10
  11:35 who hath f. given to him?
1 Cor. 12:28 f. apostles, sec. pro.
  11:30 let the f. hold his peace
  15:45 f. man A. made liv. soul
  47 f. man is of the earth, eart.
2 Cor. 8:5 f. gave selves to Lord
  12 if there be f. a willing mind
Eph. 1:12 f. trusted in Christ
  6:2 f. command. with promise
1 Thes. 4:16 dead in C. sh. rise f.
2 Thes. 2:3 exc. a falling away f.
1 Tim. 1:16 in me f. C. J. might
  2:13 Ad. was f. formed, then E.
  3:10 let these also f. be proved
  5:12 have cast off their f. faith
2 Tim. 1:5 faith dwelt in gran.
  35 husbandman must f. part.
  4:16 at my f. ans. no man stood
Tit. 3:10 after f. and sec. admo.
Heb. 5:12 which be f. principles
  7:27 offer f. for his own sins
  8:7 f. covenant, 13; 9:1, 15, 18
  9:2 f. tab. where above-bre. 6, 8
  10:9 taketh away f. that he may
Jam. 3:17 wisd. from above is f.
1 John 4:19 love him bec. he f.
Jude 6 angels who kept not f. es.
Rev. 2:4 thou hast left thy f. love
  5 do f. works, else I will come
  13:12 the power of the f. beast
  27:5 this is the f. resurrection
  21:1 f. heaven and f. earth

At the FIRST.
Gen. 13:4 A. made altar at f.
  43:20 came at f. f. to buy food
Deut. 9:18 I fell bef. L. as at f. 25
  1:26 restore judges as at the f.
Ex. 4:22 Is. is my son, my f.-b.
  11:5 all f.-b. in land of E. shall
  12:12 I will smite all f.-b.
  29 smote all f.-b. in Egypt,
    12:15
  13:2 sanctify unto me all f.-b.
  22:29 f.-b. of thy sons shalt
    thou give
  31:20 f.-b. sons red. Num. 18:15
  Num. 3:12 instead of f.-b. 41, 45
  13 bec. all f.-b. be mine
Deut. 21:17 for the right of f.-b.
Jos. 6:26 lay foundation in f.-b.
1 K. 16:34 laid found. in Ab. f.-b.
Job 18:13 f.-b. of death shall dev.
Ps. 78:51 he smote f.-b. in Egypt;
    105:36; 135:8; 136:10
  89:27 my f.-b. higher th. kings
Is. 14:30 the f.-b. of poor sh. feed
Jer. 31:9 and Ephraim is my f.-b.
Mic. 6:7 give f.-b. for transgr.?
Zec. 12:10 in bitterness for f.-b.
Mat. 1:25 bro. forth f.-b. Luke 2:7
Rom. 8:29 f.-b. am. many breth.
Col. 1:15 f.-b. of every creature
  18 beginning, f.-b. from dead
Heb. 1:6 he that destroyed f.-b.
  12:23 are come to church of f.-b.

FIT

FIRST-FRUIT, S.
Ex. 22:29 to offer the f. ripe fr.
  23:16 f. f. of thy labor thou hast
  19 f.-f. of la. 34:26; Deut. 26:2
Lev. 2:12 oblat. of f.-f. ye shall
  14 meat-offer. of f.-f. green ears
  23:10 a sheaf of f.-f. 17:20
Num. 18:12 f.-f. of oil, wine
Deut. 18:4 the f.-f. of thy corn
  26:10 brought f.-f. of G. f.
2 K. 4:42 brought man of G. f.-f.
2 Chr. 31:5 in abundance the f.-f.
Neh. 10:35 f.-f. of our ground
  37 the f.-f. of our dough
  13:44 chambers for f.-f. 13:31
Prov. 3:9 honor L. with f.-f. fruits
Jer. 2:3 Israel f.-f. of his increase
Mic. 7:1 my soul desired f.-fruit
Rom. 8:23 have f.-f. of Spirit
  11:16 if f.-f. be holy
  16:5 f.-f. of Achaia, 1 Cor. 16:15
1 Cor. 15:20 C. f.-f. of them th. 23
Jam. 1:18 kind of f.-fr. of creat.
Rev. 14:4 being the f.-f. unto God

FIRSTLING, S.
Gen. 4:4 Abel brought f. of flock
Ex. 13:12 set apart ev. f. 34:19
  15 f. of ass thou shalt red. 34:20
Lev. 27:26 L. f. of beasts
Num. 18:15 f. of uncl. beasts. 17
Deut. 12:6 ye sh. bring f. of her.
  15:19 f. male sanctify to the L.
  33:17 J.'s glory like f. of bullock

FISH.
Gen. 1:26 dom. over f. of sea, 28
Ex. 7:18 f. in river shall die, 21
Num. 11:22 all f. of sea be gath.
Deut. 4:18 liken. of any f. in wa.
Ps. 8:8 put the f. under his feet
  105:29 waters into blood, slew f.
Is. 19:10 sluices and pools for f.
  50:2 their f. stinketh
Ezek. 29:4 f. to stick to thy scal.
  5 and all the f. of thy rivers
  47:10 f. sh. be as f. of great sea
  17:17 Lord prepared great f.
  2:1 prayed to L. out of f.'s belly
  10 L. spoke to f. it vomited J.
Mat. 7:10 if he ask f. will he give
  17:27 take up f. that first come,
Luke 24:42 gave him piece br. f.
John 21:9 they saw f. laid, 10, 13

FISH, ING.
Jer. 16:16 fishers, and they sh. f.
1 Pet. sailth, I go a f.

FISH-GATE.
2 Chr. 33:14 M. built to ent. f.-g.
Neh. 3:3 f.-g. did sons of H. bull.
  12:39 from above the f.-gate
Zep. 1:10 noise of cry from f.-g.

FISH-HOOKS.
Amos 4:2 will take poster. w. f.

FISH-POOLS.
Cant. 7:4 th. eyes like f.-p. of H.

FISH-SPEARS.
Job 41:7 fill head with f.-s.

FISHERMEN.
Luke 5:2 f. were gone out of th.

FISHES.
Gen. 9:2 fear of you be on all f.
1 K. 4:33 of creeping fist, and f.
Job 12:8 f. of sea shall declare
Ec. 9:12 f. taken in an evil net
Hab. 1:14 sold, mak. as f. of sea
Mat. 14:17 five loaves and two f.
Mar. 6:38 Je. 9:13; John 6:9
  15:34 sev. loaves th. f. Mark 8:7
  Luke 5:6 multi. of f. John 21:6
  9 astonished at draught of f.
John 21:11 P. drew net full gr. f.
1 Cor. 15:39 flesh of be. an. of f.

FIST, S.
Ex. 21:18 one strike ano. with f.
Prov. 30:4 hath gath. wind in f.?
Is. 58:4 smite with f. of wicked.

FIT.
Lev. 16:21 by hand of a f. man
Job 34:18 f. to say to king, Th. wic.?
Luke 9:62 no man put. hand to pl.
  14:35 made f. for neither land
1 Cor. 7:20 Jesus f. for kingdom of G.
  11:13 not f. for him to live
Acts 22:22 not f. that he sh. live
Col. 3:18 wives, submit as f. in L.

PITCHES.
Is. 28:25 doth he not cast f.?

FLA

Is. 28:27 f. not thresh. f. are boa.
Ezek. 4:9 wheat, barley, millet, f.

FITLY.
Prov. 25:11 word f. spok. appl. of
Eph. 2:21 the building f. framed
  4:16 form wh. whole body f. jo.

FITTED, ETH.
1 K. 6:35 gold f. up. carved work
Is. 44:13 carpent. f. it with plan.
Rom. 9:22 ves. of wrath f. to des.

FIVE.
Gen. 14:9 of S. four kings with f.
  18:28 destroy all for lack of f.
Lev. 13:3 f. horde of Ph. Jud. 3:3
Is. 19:18 f. cities speak lang. of C.
  30:17 at rebuke of f. shall ye flee
Mat. 14:17 we have here but f.
  loaves, Mark 6:38; Luke 9:13
  25:2 f. of them wise, f. foolish
Luke 12:6 are not f. spar. sold?
  52:6 father's house f. havo f. b.
John 4:18 hast had f. husbands
2 Cor. 14:19 I rath. speak f. wor.
  11:24 f. times rec. 40 strip.
Rev. 17:10 sev. kings f. are fallen

FIXED.
Ps. 57:7 heart is f. I w. sing, 108:1
  112:7 heart f. trusting in Lord
Luke 16:26 betw. us is a gulf f.

FLAG, S.
Ex. 2:3 she laid the ark in the f.
  5 when she saw ark am. the f.
Job 8:11 can f. grow with. water?
Is. 19:6 reeds and f. shall wither

FLAGON, S.
2 Sam. 6:19 f. of wine, 1 Chr. 16:3
Cant. 2:5 stay me wi. f. com. me
Is. 22:24 even to all vessels of f.
Hos. 3:1 love f. of wine

FLAKES.
Job 41:23 f. of his flesh are join.

FLAME, S.
Gen. 3:24 at gate of Eden f. sw.
Ezek. 20:47 f. flame not be quen.
Num. 21:28 f. fr. city, Jer. 48:45
Jud. 13:20 f. w. up, angel in f.
Job 15:30 f. sh. dry up branches
  41:21 f. goeth out of his mouth
Ps. 29:7 voice of L. div. f. of fire
  106:18 f. burnt up the wicked
Cant. 8:6 coals wh. hath a veh. f.
Is. 5:24 f. consumeth the chaff
  10:17 Holy One shall be for a f.
  13:8 their faces shall be as f.
  29:6 visited with f. of devo. fire
  43:2 nor f. kindle upon thee
Ezek. 20:47 f. sh. not be quench.
Dan. 7:9 throne was like fiery f.
  11 till body given to burning f.
Joel 1:19 f. hath burnt trees
  2:3 behind them a f. burneth
Ob. 18 house of Jos. shall be a f.
Luke 16:24 tormented in this f.
Heb. 1:7 mak. ministers f. of fire
Rev. 1:14 as f. of fire, 2:18; 19:12

FLAMING.
Gen. 3:24 at gard. of Eden f. sw.
Ezek. 20:47 f. flame not be quen.
Nah. 2:3 chariots be w. f. torch.

FLANKS.
Lev. 8:4 the fat which is by the
  f. 10, 15; 4:9; 7:4
Job 15:27 mak. collops of fat on f.

FLASH.
Ezek. 1:14 appear. of f. of lightn.

FLAT.
Lev. 21:18 that hath f. nose
Num. 22:31 Balaam fell f. on face
Jos. 6:5 wall of city sh. fall f. d.

FLATTER, ETH.
Ps. 5:9 they f. with their tongue
  36:2 he f. him. in his own eyes
  78:36 did f. him with mouth
Prov. 2:16 stranger who f. 7:5
  26:19 med. not with him that f.
  28:23 more favor than he that f.
  29:5 man that f. spreadeth a net

FLATTERING.
Job 32:21 not let me accept f. tit. 22
Ps. 12:2 with f. lips
Prov. 7:21 with much f. words
  26:28 a f. mouth worketh ruin
1 Thes. 2:5 neither used f. words

FLATTERY, IES.
Job 17:5 speaketh f. to friends
Prov. 6:24 f. of strange woman
Dan. 11:21 obtain kingdom by f.
  34 many shall cleave with f.

FLAX.
Ex. 9:31 f. was smitten f. boiled

858 CRUDEN'S CONCORDANCE.

FLE

Jos. 2:6 she hid with stalks of f.
Jud. 15:14 cords became as f.
Prov. 31:13 she seeks wool and f.
Is. 19:9 work in fine f. confound.
   42:3 the smoking f. he shall not quench, Mat. 12:20
Hos. 2:5 lovers that give me f.

FLAY, ED.
Mic. 3:3 f. their skins
2 Chr. 35:11 blood, the Levites f.

FLEA.
1 Sam. 24:14 come after f. ! 26:20

FLED.
Gen. 14:10 kings of So. and G. f.
   16:6 H. f. ; 31:22 ; J. f. Hos. 12:12
Ex. 2:15 M. f. fr. P. 4:3 ; Acts 7:29
   14:5 told king of Egypt peop. f.
Ps. 31:11 did see me f. from me
   114:3 the sea saw it and f. Jord.
Is. 22:3 thy rulers are f. tog.
Jer. 4:25 birds of the heavens f.
   9:10 the fowl and beast are f.
Jon. 4:2 therof. I f. to Tarshish
Zec. 14:5 as ye f. before earthqu.
Mat. 8:33 they that kept them f.
   26:56 forsook and f. Mark 14:50
Mark 16:8 f. from the sepulchre
Acts 16:27 supposing prisoners f.
Heb. 6:18 f. for ref. to lay hold
Rev. 12:6 wom. f. ; 10:20 ev. isl. f.
   20:11 face earth and heaven f.

He FLED.
Gen. 35:7 wh. he f. from brother
   39:13 he left ga. and f. 13, 15, 18
Jos. 2:16 fr. whence he f. Num. 35:25
Jon. 1:10 he f. from pres. of L.
Mark 14:52 he left lin. clo. and f.

Is FLED.
Num. 35:32 no sat. for him th. f.
Is. 10:29 Gibeah of Saul is f.

They FLED.
Gen. 14:10 f. th. remained f. to
Jos. 10:11 as f. L. cast gr. ston.
1 Sam. 4:10 f. every man to tent, 1 K. 14:12
Ps. 101:7 at thy rebuke they f.
Is. 21:15 they f. from the swords
Lam. 4:15 when t. f. away
Dan. 10:7 they f. to save themse.
Hos. 7:13 woe for they have f.
Luke 8:34 saw what done t. f.
Acts 19:16 they f. out of house

FLEDDEST.
Gen. 35:1 when f. from face of E.
Ps. 114:5 wh. alled O sea, th. f.

FLEECE.
Deut. 18:4 first of f. give Levites
Jud. 6:37 f. of wool in flo. 38, 39
Job 31:20 warm. with f. of sheep

FLEE.
Gen. 16:8 f. fr. face of mistress
   19:20 this city is near to f. unto
Ex. 21:13 place whither he sh. f.
Lev. 26:17 f. when none pur. 36
Num. 10:35 hate thee f. Ps. 68:1
   35:6 cities, that man-slayer may f. 11, 15 ; Deut. 4:42 ; 19:3, 4, 5 ; Jos. 20:3, 4, 9
Deut. 28:7 and f. seven ways, 25
Jos. 8:5 as at first we will f. 6
   20 had no power to f. this way
Jud. 20:32 let us f. and draw th.
2 Sam. 4:4 nurses haste to f. fell
   24:13 wilt thou f. three months ?
2 K. 9:3 open door and f. ter. not
Neh. 6:11 should such a man f. ?
Job 20:24 he sh. f. from weapon
   27:22 fain f. out of his hand
   41:28 arrow cannot make him f.
Ps. 11:1 how say ye to my soul f.
   68:12 kings of armies f. apace
   139:7 whither sh. I f. fr. pres. ?
   143:9 O Lord, I f. to thee
Prov. 28:1 wick. f. no man purs.
Is. 10:3 will ye f. for help ?
   15:5 fugitives shall f. unto Zoar
   30:16 for we will f. on horses
   17 at rebuke of five sh. ye f.
Jer. 4:29 city f. for noi. of horse.
   6:1 f. save lives, be like Juniper
Amos 5:19 man did f. from lion
Jon. 1:3 Jon. rose up to f. to T.
Mat. 2:13 take young child and f.
   3:7 to f. from wrath ? Luke 3:7
   10:23 when perse. in this city f.
   24:16 let them in Ju. f. to mountains, Mark 13:14 ; Luke 21:21
John 10:5 stranger not follow but f.
1 Cor. 6:18 f. fornl. ; 10:14 f. idol.
1 Tim. 6:11 man of G. f. th. thin.
2 Tim. 2:22 f. also youthful lusts
Jam. 4:7 res. the devil, he will f.
Rev. 9:6 death shall f. from them

FLE

FLEE away.
Gen. 31:27 didst f. a. secretly ?
Job 9:25 days f. a. th. see no good
   20:8 he shall f. away as a dream
Ps. 64:8 all that see them sh. f. a.
Cant. 2:17 shadows f. away, 4:6
Is. 35:10 sighing sh. f. a. 51:11
Jer. 46:8 let not the swift f. away
Amos 7:12 seer, go, f. a. into land
   9:1 that fleeth shall not f. away
Nah. 2:8 Nineveh shall f. away
   3:17 as grasshoppers they f. a.

FLEEING, ETH.
Lev. 26:36 sh. flee as f. from sw.
Deut. 4:42 f. to one of th. cities
   19:11 f. into one of cities
Job 14:2 he f. also as a shadow
   30:3 want and famine f. to wil.
Jer. 48:19 ask him that f.
      of them
John 10:12 a hireling f. 13

FLESH.
Gen. 2:21 G. closed up f. instead 24 and they shall be one f.
   6:3 man, for he is f.
   17:11 circum. f. of foresk. 14, 23
Ex. 4:7 hand turned as other f.
   29:14 f. burn with fire, Lev. 9:11 ; 16:27 ; Num. 19:5
Lev. 6:27 wh. touch f. sh. be holy
   8:31 boil f. at door of tabernacle
   13:10 quick raw f. 14, 15, 16, 24 38 if in skin of f. 39
   15:19 if issue in her f. he blood
   21:5 nor sh. make cuttings in f.
Num. 11:33 f. was betw. teeth
Deut. 32:42 sword shall devour f.
1 Sam. 2:13 f. was in seething
   15 give f. to roast for the prie.
1 K. 17:6 ravens brought bread f.
2 K. 4:34 f. of child waxed warm
2 Chr. 32:8 with him is arm of f.
Neh. 5:5 our f. is as f. of breth.
Job 10:11 hast thou eyes of f. ?
   11 clothed me with skin and f.
Ps. 56:4 not fear what f. can do
   78:20 can he provide f. for peo. ?
   27 he rained f. upon them
   39 remembered th. were but f.
   79:2 f. of saints given to beasts
Prov. 4:22 sayings health to f.
   23:20 not am. riot. eaters of f.
Is. 31:3 horses are f. not spirit
   40:26 feed them with f.
Jer. 17:15 f. is passed from thee
   17:5 cursed be man that mak. f.
Ezek. 4:14 nor came abomina. f.
   11:3 city is caldron, and we f.
   19 I will give heart of f. 36:26
   23:20 whose f. is as f. of asses
   34:10 consume the f. spice it
Dan. 2:11 gods, who. dw. not f.
   7:5 Arise, devour much f.
   10:3 neither f. nor wine
Mic. 3:2 f. sacrifi. f. for sacrifices
Mic. 3:3 pluck f. from off bones
Zep. 1:17 f. shall be poured
Hag. 2:13 bear holy f. in skirt
Zec. 14:12 their f. shall consume
Mat. 16:17 f. and blood not rev.
   19:5 sh. be one f. 6 ; Mark 10:8, 1 Cor. 6:16 ; Eph. 5:31
   24:22 no f. be saved, Mark 13:20
   26:41 sp. will. f. we. Mark 14:38
Luke 24:39 hath not f. and bones
John 1:14 the Word was made f.
   6:63 the f. profiteth nothing
Acts 2:30 seed of David accord. ing to f. Rom. 1:3
Rom. 3:20 shall no f. be justified
   4:1 Abraham as pertaining to f.
   7:25 with f. I serve law of sin
   8:3 law was weak through f.
      G. sent Son in like. of f. s.
   9:3 and kinsmen according to f.
      5 concerning f. Christ came
   13:14 not provision for the f.
1 Cor. 1:29 that no f. should glo.
   15:39 one f. of men, another f.
   50 f. and blood cannot inherit
2 Cor. 4:11 life of J. be manifest f.
   7:5 f. had no rest but troubled
   10:2 as if we walked accord. to f.
Gal. 1:16 confer not with f.
   2:16 shall no f. be justified
   3:3 made perfect by the f. ?
   5:13 liberty for an occasion to f.
   17 f. lusteth ag. Sp. Sp. ag. f.
   24 that are C's crucified f.
Eph. 2:3 conv. in lusts of our f.
   6:5 masters accord. to f. Col. 3:22
   12 wrestle not ag. f. and blood
Heb. 2:14 child, are partak. of f.
   12:9 fathers of f. who corrected
Jude 7 and going after strange f.

FLE

Jude 8 filthy dream. defile the f.
   23 even garments spotted by f.
Rev. 19:18 f. of capt. f. of might.
   21 all fowls were filled with f.

See EAT, EATETH.

After the FLESH.
Rom. 8:1 walk not after the f. 4 5 are a. t. f. mind things of f.
   12 not debtors to live after t. f.
   13 if ye live aft. t. f. ye sh. die
1 Cor. 1:26 not ma. wise m. a. f.
   10:18 behold Israel after the f.
2 Cor. 5:16 we know no man af. the f. have kn. Ch. a. t. f.
   10:3 we do not war after the f.
   11:18 that many glory af. the f.
Gal. 4:23 Ishm. born af. t. f. 29
2 Pet. 2:10 th. that walk af. t. f.

All FLESH.
Gen. 6:12 a. f. had corrupt. way
   13 end of all f. is come bef. me
   6:19 of all f. two of ev. sort. 7:15
   7:21 a. f. died that moved, 8:17 ; 9:11, 15, 16, 17
Lev. 17:14 life of a. f. is the blood
Num. 8:7 let them shave all f.
   16:22 G. of spirits of all f. 27:16
Job 34:15 all f. sh. perish togeth.
Ps. 65:2 to thee shall all f. come
   136:25 who giveth food to all f.
   145:21 let all f. bless holy name
Is. 40:5 all f. sh. see it together
   6 all f. is grass, 1 Pet. 1:24
   49:26 a. f. know I am S. Ez. 21:5
   60:16 will L. plead with all f.
   23 all f. shall come to worship
   24 they sh. be abhorr. to all f.
Jer. 25:31 will plead with all f.
   32:27 I am the Lord God of a. f.
Ezek. 21:4 sword go against a. f.
Dan. 4:12 and all f. was fed of it
Joel 2:28 pour S. on a. f. Acts 2:17
Zec. 2:13 silent all f. before Lord
Luke 3:6 a. f. sh. see salv. of G.
John 17:2 given power over a. f.
1 Cor. 15:39 a. f. is not same f.

His FLESH.
Ex. 29:31 seethe h. f. in holy pl.
Lev. 4:11 burn all h. f. 8:17
   6:10 linen breeches on h. f. 16:4
   15:2 sis. issue of h. f. 4, 13, 19
   14:9 wash h. f. in water, 15:16 ; 16:24, 28 ; Num. 19:7
1 K. 21:27 Ah. put sack on h. f.
2 K. 5:14 his f. came again as
   6:30 for. had sackcloth on his f.
Job 2:5 touch bone and his f.
   31:31 O that we had of his f.
   33:25 f. sh. be fresh. than child's
   41:23 flakes of his f. are joined
Prov. 11:17 that is cruel troub. f.
Ec. 4:5 foldeth hands enfeth. f.
Is. 17:4 fatness of f. wh. wax lean
John 6:52 this man give f. to eat ?
Acts 2:31 nei. his f. did see cor.
Gal. 6:8 that soweth to his f.
Eph. 5:29 no man hated his own f.
   30 memb. of his body, of h. f.
Col. 1:22 reconc. in body of his f.
Heb. 5:7 who in the days of his f.
   10:20 veil, that is to say, his f.

In the FLESH, or In FLESH.
Gen. 17:24 A. circum. in t. f. 25
Ezek. 44:7 uncircum. in the f. 9
Rom. 2:28 circ. outward in the f.
   7:5 in the f. the motions of sins
   8:3 sin condemned sin in the f.
   8 that are in t. f. cannot pl. G.
   9 are not in t. f. but in the Sp.
1 Cor. 7:28 wh. have trouble in f.
2 Cor. 10:3 tho' we walk in the f.
   12:7 was given a thorn in the f.
Gal. 2:20 life wh. I now live in f.
   6:12 to make fair show in the f.
   13 Gentiles in the f.
Phil. 1:22 if I live in the f. this
   24 abide in t. f. more needful
   3:3 have no confidence in t. f.
Col. 2:1 have not seen my face in f.
1 Tim. 3:16 G. was manif. in t. f.
1 Pet. 3:18 put to death in the f.
   2 live rest of his time in the f.
   6 according to men in the f.
   4:2 no more live in t. f.
1 John 4:2 con. C. come in t. f. 3 ; 2 John 7

My FLESH.
Job 4:15 hair of my f. stood up
   6:12 is my f. brass ?
   7:5 my f. is clothed with worms
   13:14 take my f. in my teeth ?
   19:26 yet in my f. shall I see G.

FLO

Ps. 16:9 my f. shall rest in hope, Acts 2:26
   38:3 no soundness in my f. 7
   63:1 my f. longeth for thee
   73:26 my f. faileth
   84:2 my heart and my f. crieth
   109:24 my f. faileth of fatness
   119:120 my f. trembleth for fear
Lam. 3:4 my f. hath he made old
John 6:51 bread I give, is my f.
   54 eat. my f. hath eter. life, 56
   55 my f. is meat indeed
Rom. 7:18 in my f. dwell. no good
   11:14 prov. them wh. are my f.
Gal. 4:14 tem. wh. was in my f.
Col. 1:24 afflict. of Ch. in my f.

See BONE.

Of the FLESH.
Ex. 29:34 aught of t. f. remain
Num. 14:30 sound h. is life of f.
Ec. 12:12 much study is w. of f.
John 1:13 not of will of f. nor
   3:6 which is born of t. f. is flesh
Rom. 8:5 mind the things of t. f.
   9:3 are the children of t. f.
1 Cor. 5:5 to S. for destruc. of f.
2 Cor. 7:1 fr. all filthiness of t. f.
Gal. 4:13 thro' infirmity of t. f.
   5:16 shall not fulfil lusts of t. f.
   19 works of t. f. are manifest
   6:8 soweth to f. sh. of t. f. reap
Eph. 2:3 walked in lusts of the f.
Col. 2:11 the body of sins of t. f.
   23 to the satisfying of the f.
Heb. 9:13 the purifying of the f.
1 Pet. 2:21 put. away filth of t. f.
3 thro' the lusts of t. f.
1 John 2:16 lust of t. f.

Thy FLESH.
Gen. 40:19 birds shall eat thy f.
1 Sam. 17:44 give t. f. unto fowls
2 Sam. 5:1 bo. and t. f. 1 Chr. 11:1
2 K. 5:10 and t. f. shall come
Prov. 5:11 mourn wh. t. f. is con.
Ec. 5:6 to cause t. f. to sin
Is. 58:7 hide not from thy own f.
Ezek. 32:5 will lay t. f. on moun.

Your FLESH.
Lev. 19:28 not make cut. in y. f.
Jud. 8:7 then I will tear y. f.
Ezek. 36:26 heart out of y. f.
Rom. 6:19 infirmity of your f.
Gal. 6:13 they may glory in y. f.
Jam. 5:3 rust shall eat your f.

FLESHED. See FAT, LEAN.

FLESH-HOOK, S.
Ex. 27:3 shalt make his f.-h.
   38:3 the vessels and the f.-h.
Num. 4:14 put on par. cloth f.-h.
1 Sam. 2:13 servant with a f.-h.
   14 all that he f.-h. brought up
2 Chr. 28:17 pure gold for the f.
2 Chr. 4:16 pots and the f.-h.

FLESHLY.
2 Cor. 1:12 not with f. wisdom
   3:3 but in f. tables of the heart
Col. 2:18 puff. up by his f. mind
1 Pet. 2:11 abstain from f. lusts

FLESH-POTS.
Ex. 16:3 when we sat by f.-p.

FLEW.
1 Sam. 14:32 peo. f. upon the sp.
Is. 6:6 then f. one of seraphim

FLIES.
Ex. 8:21 send swarms of f. 31
Ps. 78:45 sent divers sorts of f.
   105:31 divers sorts of f.
Ec. 10:1 dead f. cause ointment

FLIETH.
Deut. 14:19 creeping thing f.
   28:49 as swift as the eagle f.
Ps. 91:5 arrow that f. by day
Nah. 3:16 cank. spoileth and f.

FLIGHT.
Amos 2:14 f. sh. perish from sw.
Mat. 24:20 pray f. be not in winter, Mark 13:18
Heb. 11:34 turned to f. armies

See PUT.

FLINT.
Deut. 8:15 water out of rock of f.
Ps. 114:8 turning f. into fount.
Is. 5:28 hoofs sh. be counted f.
   50:7 have I set my face like f.
Ezek. 3:9 harder than f.

FLINTY.
Deut. 32:13 oil out of f. rock

FLOATS.
1 K. 5:9 I will conv. them by sea in f. 2 Chr. 2:16

CRUDEN'S CONCORDANCE. 859

FLO
FLOCK.
Gen. 4:4 Ab. bro. firstlings of *f.*
37:2 J. was feeding *f.* with bro.
12 brethren went to feed *f.* 13
Ex. 2:16 troughs to wat. filth. *f.*
17 Moses helped, watered *f.* 19
3:1 Moses led *f.* back of desert
Lev. 5:18 a ram without blemish out of *f.*, 6:6; *Ezr.* 10:19;
Ezek. 43:23, 25
27:32 tithe of the herd or of *f.*
Deut. 15:19 first males of *f.*
1 *Sam.* 17:34 took lamb out of *f.*
Job 30:1 set with dogs of my *f.*
Cant. 1:7 makest *f.* to rest
8 by the footsteps of the *f.*
4:1 hair as a *f.* of goats, 6:5
2 teeth like a *f.* of sheep, 6:6
Is. 40:11 he sh. feed *f.* like sheep
Jer. 13:17 L. *f.* is carried captive
20 wh. is *f.* given thee beauti. ?
23:2 ye have scattered my *f.*
3 gather remnant of my *f.*
25:34 principal of the *f.* 35, 36
31:12 the young of the *f.*
49:20 least of *f.* sh. draw, 50:45
51:23 break shepherd and his *f.*
Ezek. 34:5 take the choice of *f.*
34:3 but ye feed not *f.*
6 *f.* scattered on face of earth
8 because my *f.* became a prey
10 I will require my *f.* I will
12 as a sheph. seek. out his *f.*
15 feed my *f.* ; 17 O my *f.*
22 therefore will I save my *f.*
31 *f.* of my pasture are men
Amos 7:15 as I followed *f.*
Jon. 3:7 let not herd nor *f.* taste
Mic. 4:8 thou, O tower of the *f.*
7:14 feed thy people, the *f.* of
Hab. 3:17 the *f.* shall be cut off
Zec. 9:16 save them as *f.* of peo.
11:4 will feed *f.* of slaughter, 7
7 poor of the *f.* that waited, 11
17 idle sheph. that leaveth *f.*
Mal. 1:14 deceiver wh. hath in *f.*
Mat. 26:31 sheep of *f.* sh. be scat.
Luke 2:8 keeping watch over *f.*
12:32 fear not, little *f.*
Acts 20:28 take heed to all the *f.*
29 griev. wolves not sparing *f.*
1 *Cor.* 9:7 who feedeth a *f.*
1 *Pet.* 5:2 feed *f.* of God am, you 3 being examples to the *f.*

Like a FLOCK.
Job 21:11 send little ones l. a. *f.*
Ps. 77:20 leddest people l. a. *f.*
80:1 thou th. leddest Jos. l. a. *f.*
107:41 mak. him families l. a. *f.*
Ezek. 36:37 increase them l. a. *f.*

FLOCKS.
Gen. 29:2 three *f.* of sheep, 3, 8
30:38 J. set rod he pill. bef. *f.* 39
37:14 whether it be well with *f.*
47:4 have no pasture for *f.*
Lev. 1:10 if his offering be of *f.*
Num. 31:9 took spoil of their *f.*
Deut. 7:13 will also bless the *f.*
28:4 blessed be *f.* of thy sheep
18 cursed sh. be *f.* of thy sheep
Jud. 5:16 to hear bleating of *f.*
1 *K.* 20:27 two little *f.* of kids
Job 24:2 violently take away *f.*
Ps. 65:13 past. are clothed wi. *f.*
78:48 he gave *f.* to hot thunder.
Cant. 1:7 turn aside by *f.*
Is. 32:14 palaces sh. be pasture *f.*
60:7 *f.* of Kedar sh. be gathered
61:5 stand and feed *f.*
65:10 Sh. shall be a fold for *f.*
Jer. 31:12 sheph. causing *f.* to flee
13 *f.* sh. pass ag. under the rod
50:8 he as he-goats before the *f.*
Ezek. 34:2 sh. not sheph. feed *f.* ?
Joel 1:14 *f.* of sheep desolate
Mic. 5:8 lion among *f.* of sheep
Zep. 2:14 sea-coast folds for *f.* 11

FLOCKS, with herds.
Gen. 13:5 Lot also had *f.* and *h.*
24:35 L. hath given *h. f.* and *h.*
20:14 Isa. had poss. of *f.* and *h.*
50:8 *f.* and *h.* left in land of G.
Ex. 10:9 will go with *f.* and *h.*
12:32 your *f.* and *h.* and be gone
34:3 let *f.* nor *h.* feed bef. mount
Num. 11:22 sh. *f.* and *h.* be slain
Deut. 12:6 firstlings of *h.* and *f.*
17; 14:23; *Neh.* 10:36
1 *Sam.* 30:20 David *f.* and *h.*
2 *Sam.* 12:2 had many *f.* and *h.*
Prov. 27:23 know *f.* look to *h.*
Jer. 3:24 shame devour *f.* and *h.*
Hos. 5:6 shall go with *f.* and *h.*

FLOOD.
Gen. 6:17 bring a *f.* of water
7:6 *f.* of waters on earth, 7, 10

FLO
Gen. 7:17 *f.* was forty d. on earth
9:11 any more a *f.* to destroy
28 Noah lived after *f.* 350 years
10:1 were sons born after *f.* 32
Jos. 24:2 other side of *f.* 3, 14, 15
Job 14:11 *f.* decayeth and drieth
22:16 foun. overthrown with *f.*
28:4 *f.* breaketh from inhabitant
Ps. 29:10 Lord sitteth upon *f.*
66:6 went through *f.* on foot
69:15 let not water *f.* overflow
90:5 carriest away as with *f.*
Is. 59:19 enemy come in like *f.*
Jer. 46:7 who that cometh as *f.* ?
8 Egypt riseth up like a *f.*
Dan. 9:26 end shall be with a *f.*
11:22 arms of *f.* sh. be overflo.
Amos 8:8 rise up wholly as *f.* 9:5
9:5 drowned as by *f.* of Egypt
Nah. 1:8 an overrunning *f.*
Mat. 24:38 in days before *f.*
39 till *f.* came, *Luke* 17:27
Luke 6:48 *f.* arose stream beat
2 *Pet.* 2:5 bring. in *f.* on world
Rev. 12:15 poured water as *f.* 16

FLOODS.
Ex. 15:8 *f.* stood upright
2 *Sam.* 22:5 *f.* of ungodly made me afraid, *Ps.* 18:4
Job 28:11 bindeth *f.* from overfl.
Ps. 24:2 hath estabil. it upon *f.*
32:6 surely in *f.* of great waters
69:2 waters where *f.* overfl. me
78:44 turned their *f.* into blood
93:3 *f.* have lifted up, O Lord
98:8 let the *f.* clap their hands
Cant. 8:7 neither can *f.* drown
Is. 44:3 pour *f.* on dry ground
Jon. 2:3 *f.* compassed me about
Mat. 7:25 *f.* came, winds bl. 27

FLOOR, Verb.
2 *Chr.* 34:11 timber to *f.* houses

FLOOR, Substantive.
Gen. 50:10 to thresh. *f.* of A. 11
Num. 5:17 pri. sh. take dust in *f.*
15:20 thresh. *f.* 18:27, 30
Deut. 15:14 furnish out of *f.*
Jud. 6:37 a fleece of wool in *f.*
Ruth 3:2 he win. in threshing *f.*
2 *Sam.* 6:6 Nach. th. *f.* 1 *Chr.* 13:9
24:18 rear alt. in thresh. *f.* of A.
21 D. said, to buy threshing *f.*
1 *K.* 6:30 overlaid *f.* of house
2 *K.* 6:27 out of barn *f.*
2 *Chr.* 3:1 threshing *f.* of Ornan
Is. 21:10 and the corn of my *f.*
Jer. 51:33 dau. of B. like thre. *f.*
Dan. 2:35 chaff of sum. thres. *f.*
Hos. 9:1 reward on every corn *f.*
2 *f.* and wine-pa. not feed them
13:3 as chaff driven out of *f.*
Joel 2:24 *f.* shall be full of wheat
Mic. 4:12 gather as sheaves to *f.*
Mat. 3:12 thor. purge *f. Lu.* 3:17

FLOOR.
Ex. 29:2 wheat. *f.* sh. thou make
Lev. 2:2 handful of the *f.* 6:15
Num. 28:5 part of ephah of *f.* for meat-off. 20, 28; 29:3, 9, 14
Jud. 6:19 ephah of *f.* ; 1 *Sam.* 1:24
1 *Sam.* 28:24 took *f.* and kneaded it, 2 *Sam.* 13:8
2 *Sam.* 17:28 bro. *f.* parched corn
See MEAL, FINE.

FLOURISH.
Ps. 72:7 in his days sh. right. *f.*
16 they of city sh. *f.* like grass
92:7 when all workers of iniq. *f.*
12 righteous shall *f.*
13 shall *f.* in courts of our G.
132:18 upon himself sh. crown *f.*
Prov. 11:28 righ. sh. *f.* as bran.
14:11 tabern. of upright shall *f.*
Ec. 12:5 almond-tree shall *f.*
Is. 17:11 thou sh. make seed *f.*
66:11 your bones shall *f.*
Ezek. 17:24 have made dry tree *f.*

FLOURISHED.
Cant. 6:11 went to see vine *f.*
Phil. 4:10 your care of me hath *f.*

FLOURISHETH, ING.
Ps. 90:6 in the morning it *f.*
92:14 they shall be fat and *f.*
102:15 so favour of field, he *f.*
Dan. 4:4 I was at rest, and *f.*

FLOW.
Job 20:28 his goods shall *f.* away
Ps. 147:18 wind blow, waters *f.*
Cant. 4:16 the spices may *f.* out
Is. 2:2 nations shall *f.* unto it
48:21 waters to *f.* out of rock
60:5 shalt see and *f.* together
64:1 mountains mightest *f.* down
Jer. 31:12 *f.* to goodness of L.

FOE
Jer. 51:44 nations sh. not *f.* tog.
Jos. 3:15 hills shall *f.* with milk.
rivers of Jud. *f.* with waters
Mic. 4:1 peo. sh. *f.* to moun. of L.
John 7:38 out of belly sh. *f.* l. w.

FLOWED.
Jos. 4:18 Jordan *f.* over banks
Is. 64:3 mount. *f.* down at pres.
Lam. 3:54 waters *f.* over my head

FLOWETH.
Lev. 20:24 *f.* with milk and hom.
Num. 13:27; 14:8; 16:13, 14;
Deut. 6:3; 11:9; 26:15; 27:3;
31:20; *Jos.* 5:6

FLOWING.
Ex. 3:8 *f.* with milk and honey,
17; 13:5; 33:3; *Jer.* 11:5;
32:22; *Ezek.* 20:6, 15
Prov. 18:4 well-sp. of wis. as *f.*
Is. 66:12 glo. of G. like *f.* stream
Jer. 18:14 cold *f.* waters be fors. ?
49:4 gloriest thou in *f.* valley ?

FLOWER.
Ex. 25:33 *f.* in one branch. 37:19
37:20 almonds, knops, and his *f.*
Lev. 15:24 her *f.* be upon him, 33
1 *K.* 6:18 carved with knops and open *f.* 29, 32, 35 ; 7:26, 49
2 *Chr.* 4:5 cup with *f.* of lilies, 21
Job 14:2 cometh forth as *f.*
15:33 cast off *f.* as olive
Ps. 103:15 as *f.* of field
Is. 18:5 sour grape is rip. in *f.*
28:1 glorious beauty is fad. *f.* 4
40:6 goodliness is as *f.* of field
7 *f.* fadeth, 8; *Neh.* 1:4 ; *Jam.* 1:10, 11; 1 *Pet.* 1:24
1 *Cor.* 7:36 she pass *f.* of her age

FLOWERS.
Ex. 25:31 *f.* of the same, 37:17
Lev. 15:24 her *f.* be upon him, 33
1 *K.* 6:18 carved with knops and open *f.* 29, 32, 35 ; 7:26, 49
2 *Chr.* 4:5 cup with *f.* of lilies, 21
5:13 bed of spices, as sweet *f.*

FLUTE, S.
Dan. 3:5 hear sound of *f.* 7, 10, 15

FLUTTERETH.
Deut. 32:11 as eagle *f.* ov. young

FLUX.
Acts 28:8 lay sick of a *f.*

FLY, Verb.
Is. 7:18 sh. hiss for the *f.* in E.

FLY, Verb.
Gen. 1:20 fowl th. may *f.* earth
1 *Sam.* 15:19 didst *f.* on the spoil
2 *Sam.* 22:11 did *f.* on wings of wind, *Ps.* 18:10
Job 5:7 as spirks *f.* upward
39:26 doth hawk *f.* by thy wis.
Ps. 55:6 then would I *f.* away
90:10 cut off, and we *f.* away
Prov. 23:5 riches *f.* away
Is. 6:2 with two he did *f.*
11:14 *f.* on shoulders of Phillist.
60:8 who are these that *f.*
Jer. 9:21 G. created to *f.* swiftly
Ezek. 13:20 hunt souls to make *f.*
Dan. 9:21 caused to *f.* swiftly
Hos. 9:11 glory shall *f.* away
Hab. 1:8 they shall *f.* as eagle
Rev. 14:6 saw another angel *f.*
19:17 that *f.* midst of heaven

FLYING.
Lev. 11:21 eat of every *f.* thing
Is. 14:29 of cattle and *f.* fowl
Prov. 26:2 as swallow by *f.*
Is. 14:29 shall he fiery *f.* serpent
31:5 birds *f.* so will L. defend J.
Zec. 5:1 and behold a *f.* roll, 2
Rev. 4:7 beast like a *f.* eagle
8:13 angel *f.* thro' midst of hea.

FOAL, S.
Gen. 32:15 ten asses and ten *f.* m.
49:11 binding his *f.* to the vine
Zec. 9:9 colt *f.* of ass, *Mat.* 21:5

FOAM.
Hos. 10:7 king of S. cut off as *f.*

FOAMETH, ING.
Mark 9:18 *f.* and gnasheth with his teeth, *Luke* 9:39
20 on ground and wallowed, *f.*
Jude 13 waves *f.* out own shame

FODDER.
Job 6:5 or loweth ox over his *f.* ?

FOES.
1 *Chr.* 21:12 destroyed before *f.*
Est. 9:16 slew of their *f.* 75,500
Ps. 27:2 mine enemies and *f.*
30:1 not made my *f.* to rejoice
89:23 I will beat down his *f.*
Mic. 7:6 man's *f.* sh. men of own house, *Mat.* 10:36
Acts 2:35 I make *f.* footstool

FOL
FOLD.
Hab. 1:12 as a vesture sh. thou *f.*

FOLD, Substantive.
Is. 13:20 sheph. make their *f.*
65:10 Sharon shall be *f.*
Ezek. 34:14 on mount. shall *f.*
Hab. 3:17 flock sh. be cut from *f.*
Mat. 13:8 bro. forth fruit, some thirty *f.* 23 ; *Mark* 4:8, 20
19:29 forsaken ho. receive 100 *f.*
John 10:16 sheep wh. not of this *f.* one *f.* and one shepherd

FOLDS.
Num. 32:24 build *f.* for sheep, 26
Ps. 50:9 take no he-goats of *f.*
Zep. 2:6 sea-coast be *f.* for flocks

FOLDEN.
Nah. 1:10 wh. they be *f.* together

POLDETH, ING.
Prov. 6:10 *f.* of hands, 24:33
Ezek. 41:24 *f.* doors, 25
Ec. 4:5 *f.* his hands together

FOLK.
Prov. 30:26 conies but feeble *f.*
Jer. 51:58 *f.* shall labor in fire
Mark 6:5 hands on few sick *f.*
John 5:3 multitude of impotent *f.*
Acts 5:16 about, bringing sick *f.*

FOLLOW.
Gen. 24:8 not willing to *f.*
44:4 Jos. said, Up *f.* after men
Ex. 14:4 harden *f.* he shall *f.*
21:22 no mischief *f.* 23
Deut. 16:20 what just sh. thou *f.*
Jud. 9:3 heart's inclined to *f.* A.
1 *K.* 19:20 I will *f.* thee
Ps. 45:14 companions *f.* her
Jer. 17:16 not hasted to *f.* thee
from being pastor *f.* me
Jer. 19:3 prophets from S. that *f.*
Rom. 14:19 *f.* th. make peace
1 *Cor.* 14:1 *f.* after charity, desire
Phil. 3:12 *f.* after, if that I may
1 *Tim.* 5:15 *f.* that which is good
2 *Thes.* 3:9 ensample to you to *f.*
1 *Tim.* 5:24 men they *f.* after
1 *Tim.* 6:11 man of God *f.* 2 *Tim.* 2:22
Heb. 12:14 *f.* peace with all men
that whose faith *f.* considering
1 *Pet.* 3:11 testified glory sh. *f.*
2:21 example, that ye should *f.*
2 *Pet.* 2:2 shall *f.* pernicious ways
3 *John* 11 *f.* not that which is evil
Rev. 14:4 they that *f.* the Lamb
13 and their works do *f.* them

FOLLOW him.
1 *K.* 18:21 if Lord be God, *f. him*
Mark 5:37 suff. no man to *f. him*
Lu. 22:10 *f. h.* into ho. *Mark* 1:13
John 10:4 and the sheep *f. him*

FOLLOW me.
Gen. 24:5 woman not *f. me*, 39
2 *K.* 6:19 *f. me*, I will bring you
Ps. 23:6 goodn. and mercy *f. me*
Mat. 4:19 Jes. saith, *f. me*; 8:22;
9:9; *Mark* 2:14 ; *Luke* 5:27
19:21 take up cross *f. me*, *Mark* 8:34 ; 10:21 ; *Luke* 18:22
Luke 9:59 *f. me*, *John* 1:43 ; 21:22
John 10:27 sheep hear vol. *f. me*
12:26 if man serve, let him *f. me*
13:36 thou canst not *f. me* now
Acts 12:8 garm. about thee *f. me*

FOLLOWED.
Gen. 24:61 R. and damsels *f. m.*
Num. 32:12 *f.* Lord, *Deut.* 1:36
Jud. 2:12 forsook L. *f.* oth. gods
1 *Sam.* 14:22 they *f.* hard after P.
31:2 Philistines *f.* Saul, 1 *Sam.*
2 *Sam.* 2:10 house of Judah *f.* D.
3:31 king David *f.* bier
17:23 Ahith. saw counsel not *f.*
1 *K.* 12:20 half of people *f.* Tibni, half *f.* Omri, 22
2 K. 17:15 vanity, became vain
the *f.* goa plu. on trustworthy *f.*
Ezek. 10:11 head looked they *f.*
Amos 7:15 L. took me as I *f.*
Mat. 27:55 many wom. wh. *f.* J.
Mark 2:9 forth all and *f.* thee,
Luke 18:28

CRUDEN'S CONCORDANCE. 861

FOR

FOOTSTEPS,
Ps. 17:5 that my f. slip not
77:19 thy f. are not known
89:51 reproa. f. of anointed
Cant. 1:8 go by f. of the flock

FOOTSTOOL,
1 Chr. 28:2 house for f. of God
Ps. 99:5 worship at his f. 132:7
110:1 enem. thy f. Mat. 22:44;
Mark 12:36; Luke 20:43; Acts 2:35; Heb. 1:13
Is. 66:1 earth is my f. Acts 7:49
Lam. 2:1 remembered not his f.
Mat. 5:35 by the earth it is his f.
Heb. 10:13 till enemies be f.
Jam. 2:3 sit here under my f.

FORBADE.
Deut. 2:37 nor to whatso. L. f.
Mat. 3:14 John f. him, saying, I
Mark 9:38 we f. him, Luke 9:49
2 Pet. 2:16 ass f. madn. of proph.

FORBARE.
1 Sam. 23:13 Saul f. to go forth
Jer. 41:8 Ishmael f. and slew not

FORBEARANCE,
Rom. 2:4 or despis. riches of f.?
3:25 remission of sins thro' f.

FORBEAR, ING.
Deut. 23:22 f. to vow it
1 K. 22:6 go or f. ? 2 Chr. 18:5
2 Chr. 25:16 f. why be smitten?
35:21 f. thee from meddling
Neh. 9:30 many years didst f.
Job 16:6 I f. what am I eased?
Prov. 24:11 if f. to deliver them
25:15 by long f. prince persuad.
Jer. 20:9 I was weary with f.
40:4 if it seem ill unto thee f.
Ezek. 2:5 will hear, or f. 7; 3:11
3:27 that forbeareth, let him f.
24:17 f. to cry, make no mourn.
Zec. 11:12 give price, if not f.
1 Cor. 9:6 power to f. working?
2 Cor. 12:6 I f. lest any think
Eph. 4:2 f. in love, Col. 3:13
6:9 masters f. threatening
1 Thes. 3:1 could no longer f. 5

FORBID,
Num. 11:28 my lord M. f. them
Mark 9:39 f. him not, Luke 9:50
10:14 suffer little child. and f.
them not, Luke 18:16
Luke 6:29 f. not to take coat also
Acts 10:47 can any man f. water
24:23 f. none of his acquaint.
1 Cor. 14:39 f. not sp. with tong.

God FORBID.
Gen. 44:7 God f. 17; Jos. 22:29;
24:16; 1 Sam. 12:23; 14:45;
20:2; Job 27:5; Luke 20:16;
Rom. 3:4, 6, 31; 6:2, 15; 7:7,
13; 9:14; 11:1, 11; 1 Cor. 6:15;
Gal. 2:17; 3:21; 6:14

FORBIDDEN, ETH, ING,
Lev. 5:17 commit any of things f.
Deut. 4:23 the likeness of what f.
Luke 23:2 f. to give tribute to C.
Acts 16:6 were f. to preach in A.
28:31 preaching no man f. him
1 Thes. 2:16 f. us to speak to G.
1 Tim. 4:3 f. to marry and com.
3 John 10 f. them that would re.

FORBORNE.
Jer. 51:30 mighty men f. to fight

FORCE, Substantive.
Deut. 34:7 his natural f. abated
1 Sam. 2:16 I will take it by f.
Ezr. 4:23 made them cease by f.
Job 30:18 great f. of my disease
40:16 his f. in navel of his belly
Jer. 18:21 out blood by f. of swo.
23:10 is evil, their f. is not right
48:45 shadow because of f.
Ezek. 35:4 with f. ye ruled them
35:5 shed blood by f. of the sw.
Amos 2:14 stro. not strengthen f.
Mat. 11:12 violent take it by f.
Acts 23:10 to take Paul by f.
Heb. 9:17 testament is of f. after

FORCE, ED.
Deut. 22:25 if the man f. her
Jud. 20:5 concubine have they f.
1 Sam. 13:12 I f. myself
2 Sam. 13:12 brother do not f.
14 Amnon f. Tamar, 22, 32
Est. 7:8 will he f. the queen?
Prov. 7:21 with flat. she f. him

FORCES.
Job 36:19 will not esteem the f.
Is. 60:5 f. of Gentiles shall come
11 may bring f. of the Gentiles
Jer. 40:7 captains of the f. 13; 41:11,
13, 16; 42:1, 8; 43:4, 5

FOR

Dan. 11:10 assemble multi. of f.
38 shall he honor the God of f.
Ob. 11 strangers carried away f.

FORCIBLE.
Job 6:25 how f. are right words

FORCING.
Deut. 20:19 f. an axe aga. them
Prov. 30:33 f. of wrath bringeth

FORDS.
Is. 16:2 daughters at f. of Arnon

FORECAST.
Dan. 11:24 sh. f. his devices, 25

FOREFATHERS.
Jer. 11:10 turn. to iniquities of f.
2 Tim. 1:3 whom I served from f.

FOREFRONT.
2 Sam. 11:15 Uriah in f. of battle
2 Chr. 20:27 Jehoshaphat in f.

FOREHEAD.
1 Sam. 17:49 stone sunk in his f.
2 Chr. 26:20 Uzziah leprous in f.
Jer. 3:3 thou hast a whore's f.
Ezek. 3:9 as adamant I made f.
16:12 and I put jewel on thy f.
Rev. 14:9 mark of beast in his f.
17:5 on her f. a name written

FOREHEADS.
Ezek. 3:8 strong against their f.
9:4 on the f. of them that sigh
Rev. 7:3 sealed serv. of God in f.
9:4 not seal of God in their f.
13:16 all to receive a mark in f.
14:1 Father's name in their f.
20:4 nor received his mark on f.
22:4 his name sh. be in their f.

FOREIGNER, S.
Ex. 12:45 a f. not eat thereof
Deut. 15:3 of a f. exact it again
Ob. 11 in the day f. entered gat.
Eph. 2:19 ye are no more f.

FOREKNEW, KNOW.
Rom. 8:29 whom he did f.
11:2 not cast away people he f.

FOREKNOWLEDGE.
Acts 2:23 delivered by f. of God
1 Pet. 1:2 according to f. of God

FOREORDAINED,
1 Pet. 1:20 who verily was f.

FOREPART.
Acts 27:41 f. of ship stuck fast
Heb. 9:30 whither f. is for us

FORESAW.
Acts 2:25 f. Lord always before

FORESEETH, ING.
Prov. 22:3 man f. the evil, 27:12
Gal. 3:8 the scripture f. that God

FORESKIN, S.
Gen. 17:11 circumc. flesh of f. 23
Ex. 4:25 22 ly. cut off f. of son
Lev. 12:3 flesh of his f. sh. be cir.
Deut. 10:16 circumcise f. of heart
Jos. 5:3 circumcised at hill of f.
1 Sam. 18:25 100 f. of Philistines
27 D. brought f. and gave th.
2 Sam. 3:14 espoused for 100 f.
Jer. 4:4 take away the f. of heart
Hab. 2:16 let thy f. be uncovered

FOREST, S.
1 Sam. 22:5 D. came to f. of H.
1 K. 7:2 Solomon built hou. of f.
2 K. 19:23 will enter into f. of his Carmel, Is. 37:34
2 Chr. 27:4 J. built castles in f.
Ps. 29:9 voice of L. discover. f.
50:10 ev. beast of the f. is mine
104:20 beasts of f. do creep forth
Is. 9:18 kindle in thickets of f.
10:18 consume glory of his f.
19 rest of trees of his f. be few
31 cut down the thickets of f.
21:13 in f. of Arab. shall ye lodge
22:8 didst look to armor of f.
29:17 esteemed as a f. 32:15
32:19 hail coming down on f.
44:14 cypress from am. trees f.
23 break forth into singing, O f.
56:9 yea, all ye beasts in the f.
Jer. 5:6 lion out of f. shall slay
10:3 one cutteth a tree out of f.
12:8 heritage, as a lion in f.
21:14 will kindle a fire in his f.
26:18 high places of f. Mic. 3:12
46:23 they shall cut down her f.
Ezek. 15:6 vine-tree am. trees of f.
20:46 prophesy aga. f. of south
47 neither cut my ever. f. of s.
Hos. 2:12 I will make them a f.
Amos 3:4 will lion roar in the f.?
Mic. 5:8 as a lion am. beasts of f.
Zec. 11:2 f. of vintage is come

FOR

FORETELL,
2 Cor. 13:2 I f. you as if present

FORETOLD.
Mark 13:23 I have f. you all
Acts 3:24 proph. f. of these days

FOREWARN, ED.
Luke 12:5 f. whom ye shall fear
1 Thes. 4:6 we also have f. you

FORFEITED.
Ezr. 10:8 substance should be f.

FORGAT.
Gen. 40:23 Joseph, but f. him
Jud. 3:7 children of Israel f. L.
1 Sam. 12:9 when they f. the L.
Ps. 78:11 and they f. his works
106:13 soon f. f. of God th. S.
Lam. 3:17 peace, I f. prosperity
Hos. 2:13 after lovers and f. me

FORGAVE, EST,
Ps. 32:5 f. iniquity of my sin
78:38 he f. their iniquity, and
99:8 wast a God that f. them
Mat. 18:2 and f. him the debt
32 O wicked servant, I f. all
Luke 7:42 he frankly f. them
43 that he to whom he f. most
2 Cor. 3:10 if I f. any thing, for
Col. 3:13 as Christ f. you

FORGED.
Ps. 119:69 proud have f. a lie

FORGERS.
Job 13:4 ye are f. of lies

FORGET.
Gen. 27:45 till thy brother f.
41:51 God made me f. my toil
43 ieast ye f. covenant of Lord
Deut. 4:23 Lord will not f. the cove.
6:12 beware lest f. L. 8:11, 14, 19
9:7 f. not how ye provoked Lord
25:19 blot out Amalek, not f.
1 Sam. 1:11 if not f. handmaid
Job 8:13 so paths of all that f. G.
9:27 I will f. my complaint
11:16 thou shalt f. thy misery
24:20 the womb shall f. him
Ps. 9:17 all nations that f. God
10:12 O Lord f. not the humble
13:1 how long wilt thou f. me?
45:10 f. thine own people, and
50:22 consider this ye that f. G.
59:11 lest my people f.
74:19 f. not congrega. of poor
78:7 might not f. works of God
102:4 that I f. to eat my bread
103:2 f. not all his benefits
119:16 I will not f. thy word
83 do I not f. statutes, 109, 141
93 I will never f. thy precepts
153 for I do not f. thy law
176 for I not f. thy command.
137:5 if I f. thee, O Jerusalem,
let right hand f. cunning
Prov. 3:1 my son f. not my law
4:5 get wisdom, f. it not
31:5 lest they drink and f. law
7 drink and f. his poverty
Is. 49:15 can a woman f. child?
54:4 shalt f. shame of thy youth
65:11 that f. my holy mountain
Jer. 2:32 maid f. her ornaments?
23:27 my people to f. my name
27 as their fathers f. my name
Hos. 4:6 also f. thy children
Amos 8:7 never f. any of works
Heb. 6:10 G. not unrighte. to f.
13:16 to communicate, f. not
Phil. 3:13 those things behind

FORGETFUL, NESS.
Ps. 88:12 known in land of f. ?
Heb. 13:2 not f. to entertain str.
Jam. 1:25 a f. hearer, but a doer

FORGETTEST, ETH, ING.
Job 39:15 f. foot may crush them
Ps. 9:12 f. not cry of humble
44:24 why f. thou our affliction?
Prov. 2:17 f. covenant of her God
Is. 51:13 and f. Lord thy Maker
Phil. 3:13 f. those things behind
Jam. 1:24 he f. what manner of

FORGIVE.
Gen. 50:17 f. trespass of brethren
Ex. 10:17 f. my sin this once
32:32 yet now if wilt f. their sin
Num. 14:19 f. iniquity of people
Jos. 24:19 will not f. your trans.
1 Sam. 25:28 f. trespass of hand.
1 K. 8:30 hear and f. 39, 50; 2
Chr. 6:21, 30, 39

FOR

2 Chr. 7:14 then will I hear and f.
Ps. 25:18 and f. all my sins
86:5 L. art good and ready to f.
Is. 2:9 therefore f. them not
Jer. 18:23 f. not their iniquity
31:34 for I will f. their iniqui.
36:3 I may f. their iniquity al. l
Dan. 9:19 O Lord, hear, O L. f.
Amos 7:2 I said, f. I beseech th.
Mat. 6:12 f. us as we f. Luke 11:4
14 if ye f. men their trespas.
15 ye f. not, neither will you
9:6 hath power on earth to f.
sins, Mark 2:10; Luke 5:24
18:21 how oft sin, and f. him?
35 if ye from your hearts f. not
Mark 2:7 can f. sins, Luke 5:21
11:25 praying, f. that your
26 if ye f. not, will not f.
Luke 6:37 f. ye shall be forgiven
17:3 brother repent, f. him, 4
23:34 Father f. them
2 Cor. 2:7 ye ought rather to f.
10 to whom ye f. any, I f. also
12:13 to you, f. me this wrong
1 John 1:9 to f. us our sins

FORGIVEN.
Lev. 4:20 it sh. be f. 26, 31, 35;
5:10, 13, 16, 18; 6:7; 19:...;
Num. 15:25, 26, 28; Deut. 21:1
Num. 14:19 pardon, as f. from f.
Ps. 32:1 wh. trans. is f. Rom. 4:7
85:3 hast f. iniquity of thy peo.
Is. 33:24 people be f. their iniq.
Mat. 9:2 sins f. thee, 5; Mark
2:5, 9; Luke 5:20, 23; 7:48
12:31 all sin be f. but ag. Ho'y
G. 32; Mark 3:28; Luke 12:10
Mark 4:12 sin should be f. them
Luke 6:37 forgive and ye sh. be f.
7:47 her sins which are entir.
are f. to whom little is f.
Acts 8:22 thought of heart be f.
Eph. 4:32 for Christ's sake f. you
Col. 2:13 having f. all trespasses
Jam. 5:15 com. sins they sh. he f.
1 John 2:12 bec. your sins are f.

FORGIVETH, ING.
Ex. 34:7 f. iniq. Num. 14:18
Ps. 103:3 f. all thine iniquities
Luke 7:49 who is this f. sins?
Eph. 4:32 f. one ano. Col. 3:13

FORGIVENESS, ES.
Ps. 130:4 there is f. with thee
Dan. 9:9 the L. our G. belong f.
Mark 3:29 nev. f. but in danger
Acts 5:31 him G. exalt. to give f.
13:38 through him is preached f.
26:18 they may receive f. of sins
Eph. 1:7 have f. of sins, Col. 1:14

FORGOTTEN.
Gen. 41:30 the plenty shall be f.
Deut. 24:19 and hast f. a sheaf
26:13 neither have I f. them
31:21 this song shall not be f.
32:18 f. God that formed thee
Job 19:14 familiar friends f. me
28:4 even waters f. of the foot
Ps. 9:18 needy not always be f.
10:11 said in heart, God hath f.
31:12 I am f. as dead man
42:9 my rock, why hast f. me?
44:17 yet have we not f. thee
20 if we have f. name of our G.
77:9 hath G. f. to be gracious ?
119:61 but I have not f. thy law
139 mine enemies f. thy words
Ec. 2:16 days to come all be f.
8:10 wicked were f. in the city
9 the memory of them is f.
Is. 17:10 f. God of thy salvation
23:15 Tyre shall be f. 70 years
16 take a harp, thou hast f.
41:3 O Isr. thou shalt not be f.
49:14 Zion said, Lord hath f. me
65:16 the former troubles are f.
Jer. 2:32 pco. f. me, 18:25; 18:15
3:21 have f. the Lord their God
20:11 never be f. 23:40
23:27 forget as fathers have f.
30:14 all thy lovers have f. thee
41:9 f. wickedness of your fath.
50:5 join in cov. shall not be f.
6 have f. their resting place
Lam. 2:6 sabbaths to be f. in Z.
Ezek. 22:12 hast f. me, saith L.
23:35 because thou hast f. me
Hos. 4:6 seeing thou hast f. law
8:14 Israel hath f. his Maker
13:6 therefore have they f. me
Mat. 16:5 f. bread, Mark 8:14
Luke 12:6 not one of them is f.
Ph. 12:5 ye have f. exhortation
1 Pet. 1:9 f. that he was purged

FORKS.
1 Sam. 13:21 they had a file for f.

CRUDEN'S CONCORDANCE. 803

FOU

1 *Sam.* 13:22 no sword *f.* in hand
25:28 evil not been *f.* with thee
29:3 I have *f.* no fault in him
30:11 *f.* an Egyptian in the field
31:8 *f.* S. and three sons fallen
2 *Sam.* 7:27 *f.* in his heart to pray this prayer, 1 *Chr.* 17:25
1 *K.* 7:47 not weight of brass *f.*
11:29 Ahijah *f.* Jerobo. in way
13:28 *f.* his carcass cast in way
18:10 took an oath *f.* thee not
20:36 lion *f.* him and slew him
21:20 *f.* me mine enemy?
2 *K.* 2:17 Elijah, but *f.* him not
9:35 *f.* no more of her than skull
22:8 I *f.* law in house of the L.
23:19 took sixty men *f.* in city
1 *Chr.* 4:40 th. *f.* fat pasture and
2 *Chr.* 19:3 good th. *f.* in thee
Neh. 5:8 *f.* nothing to answer
Job 28:13 nor wisdom *f.* in land
31:29 when evil *f.* mine enemy
32:3 bec. they had *f.* to answer
13 We have *f.* wisdom
33:24 the pit, I have *f.* a ransom
42:15 *f.* so fair as daught. of Job
Ps. 69:20 comforters, but *f.* none
76:5 none have *f.* their hands
84:3 sparrow hath *f.* a house
89:20 I have *f.* Dav. my servant
107:4 and *f.* no city to dwell in
116:3 I *f.* trouble and sorrow
132:6 we *f.* it in the fields
Prov. 7:15 and I have *f.* thee
21:14 so wisdom be when *f.* it
25:16 hast *f.* honey?
Ec. 7:28 I *f.* a woman not *f.*
29 I *f.* God made man upright
Cant. 3:1 but I *f.* him not, 2
3 the watchmen *f.* me, 5:7
4 but I *f.* him my soul loveth
Is. 10:10, *f.* kingdoms of idols
14 my hand *f.* riches of people
22:3 all *f.* in thee are bound
57:10 hast *f.* the life of thy hand
65:1 *f.* of them sought me not
Jer. 2:34 iniquity fath. *f.* in me?
34 in thy skirts is *f.* the blood
5:26 my people are *f.* wicked
15:16 words *f.* I did eat them
23:11 in my house *f.* wickedn.
41:8 *f.* that said, Slay us not
50:7 all that *f.* them dev. them
Lam. 2:16 this is day we have *f.*
Ezek. 22:30 for a man, I *f.* none
Dan. 5:12 ex. spirit *f.* in Daniel
27 art weighed and *f.* wanting
6:4 nor any fault *f.* in Daniel
11 these men *f.* Daniel praying
Hos. 9:10 I *f.* Israel like grapes
12:4 he *f.* him in Beth-el, and
8 I have *f.* me out substance
11:8 from me is thy fruit *f.*
Mic. 1:13 transg. of Is. *f.* in thee
Mat. 2:8 have *f.* him bring word
8:10 not *f.* so gr. faith, *Luke* 7:9
13:14 when a man *f.* he hideth
46 *f.* one pearl of great price
18:28 *f.* one of his fellow serv.
20:6 *f.* others standing idle
24 *f.* nothing thereon,
Mark 11:13; *Luke* 13:6
22:10 gath. as many as they *f.*
26:43 he *f.* them asleep, *Mark* 14:40; *Luke* 22:45
60 *ex.* wit. *f.* none, *Mar.* 14:55
27:32 they *f.* a man of Cyrene
Mark 1:37 when they had *f.* him
7:2 eat with def. hands *f.* fault
30 she *f.* the devil gone out
11:4 *f.* colt tied by door without
Luke 2:16 *f.* babe ly. in a manger
46 after three days *f.* him
4:17 *f.* place where it was writ.
7:10 they *f.* the servant whole
8:35 *f.* the man clothed
15:6 for I have *f.* my sheep
9 when she hath *f.* the piece
17:18 none *f.* that ret. to give gl.
19:32 *f.* even as he said, 22:13
22:2 wo *f.* perverting the nation
44 I have *f.* no fault
24:2 *f.* the stone rolled away
3 *f.* not body of the Lord Jesus
23 when they *f.* not his body
33 *f.* the eleven gath. together
John 1:41 we have *f.* Messias, 45
2:14 Jesus *f.* in the temp. those
Acts 5:10 came in, and *f.* her de.
23 officers *f.* them not in pris.
7:11 our fathers *f.* no sustenan.
9:2 that if he *f.* any of this way
10:27 I *f.* many come together
12:19 when Herod *f.* not Peter
13:6 they *f.* a certain sorcerer
22 I have *f.* David a man after
17:23 I *f.* with inscription
21:5 *f.* this man a pestilent

FOU

Acts 24:20 if they *f.* any evil do
25:25 I *f.* noth. worthy of death
28:14 Puteoli, wh. we *f.* breth.
Rom. 4:1 what Abraham *f.*
7:10 to life I *f.* to be unto death
1 *Cor.* 15:15 we are *f.* false witn.
2 *Cor.* 2:13 bec. I *f.* not Titus
Gal. 2:17 we also are *f.* sinners
Phil. 2:8 *f.* in fashion as a man
3:9 not *f.* having righteousn.
1 *Tim.* 3:10 being *f.* blameless
2 *Tim.* 1:17 Onesiphorus *f.* me
Heb. 12:17 *f.* no place of repent.
1 *Pet.* 1:7 faith be *f.* to praise
2 *John* 4 *f.* of thy children
Rev. 2:2 and hast *f.* them liars
3:2 not *f.* thy works perfect
12:8 nor their place *f.* in heaven
16:20 mountains were not *f.*

Be FOUND.

Gen. 18:29 peradvent. be forty *f.*
Ex. 21:16 a man if he be *f.*
22:2 if that be *f.* breaking up, 7
4 if the theft be certainly *f.*
1 *Sam.* 10:21 Saul could not be *f.*
2 *Sam.* 17:12 come on him where he shall be *f.*
1 *K.* 1:52 if wickedness be *f.*
1 *Chr.* 28:9 seek him he will be *f.* of thee, 2 *Chr.* 15:2
Job 20:8 fly away and not be *f.*
28:12 where shall wisdom be *f.*?
Ps. 32:6 pray when thou be *f.*
36:2 till his iniq. be *f.* hateful
37:36 but he could not be *f.*
Prov. 6:31 if he be *f.* he sh. rest.
16:31 if it be *f.* in way of right.
30:6 and thou be *f.* a liar
Je. 30:14 shall not be *f.* a sherd
35:9 nor any beast be *f.* there
51:3 joy and gladness be *f.*
53:6 seek L. while he may be *f.*
Jer. 29:14 I will be *f.* of you
50:20 sins of J. shall not be *f.*
Ezek. 26:21 shalt never be *f.*
Dan. 11:19 he sh. fall and b. be *f.*
12:1 ev. one that be *f.* written
Hos. 13:9 th. y. be *f.* fruity
Zep. 3:13 nor deceit. tongue be *f.*
Zec. 10:10 place not be *f.*
Acts 5:39 lest *f.*, to fight ag. G.
1 *Cor.* 4:2 a steward be *f.* faithful
2 *Cor.* 5:3 shall not be *f.* naked
11:12 may be *f.* even as we
12:20 be *f.* such as would not
Phil. 3:9 be *f.* in him
2 *Pet.* 3:14 be *f.* of him in peace
Rev. 18:21 Baby. be *f.* no more
22 no craftsman be *f.* in thee
See FAVOR.

FOUND grace.

Gen. 6:8 Noah *f. g.* in eyes of L.
19:19 servant *f. g.* in thy sight
33:10 if I have *f. g.*, 47:29; 50:4
39:4 Joseph *f. grace* in his sight
Ex. 33:12 thou hast also *f. g.*, 17
13 if I have *f. g.*, 16; *Jud.* 6:17; 1 *Sam.* 27:5
16 known that I have *f. g.*?
Num. 32:5 if we have *f. grace*
1 *Sam.* 20:3 father know I *f. g.*
2 *Sam.* 14:22 people *f. g.* in wisdom,

Is FOUND.

Gen. 44:10 with whom cup is *f.*
1 *K.* 14:13 is *f.* some good thing
2 *K.* 22:13 this book that is *f.*
Ezr. 4:19 it is *f.* city been reb.
Job 28:12 root of the matter is *f.*
Prov. 10:13 in lips wisdom is *f.*
Is. 13:15 that is *f.* be thrust
65:8 new wine is *f.* in cluster
Jer. 2:26 the thief when he is *f.*
34 is *f.* the blood of innocents
50:9 a conspiracy is *f.* am. Jud.
Dan. 5:14 excel. wisdom is *f.*, 12
Hos. 14:8 from me is thy fruit *f.*
Luke 15:24 was lost and is *f.*, 32
1 *Cor.* 7:14 boasting is *f.* a truth

Was FOUND.

Gen. 44:12 cup *w. f.* in Benj.
1 *Sam.* 13:22 with S. and J. *w. f.*
2 *Chr.* 15:4 he *was f.* of them, 15
Ezr. 6:2 there *w. f.* at A. a roll
Neh. 7:5 I *f.* a register
13:1 that day *w. f.* written
Esth. 2:23 thing *was f.* out, th.
6:2 *w. f.* written Mordecai
Ezek. 28:15 iniquity *was f.* in thee
Dan. 1:19 among th. was *f.* none
2:35 no place *was f.* for them
5:11 *w. f.* light, underst. *f.* him
6:22 innocency *was f.* in me
23 no manner of hurt *w. f.*
Mal. 2:6 *w. f.* in his lips
Mat. 1:18 *w. f.* with child
Luke 9:36 Jesus *was f.* alone
17:18 no *f.* return, save stranger
Acts 5:10 Philip was *f.* at Azotus
Rom. 4:8 sin *f.* occasion by com.
1 *Pet.* 2:22 nor *w.* guile *f.* in mou.
Rev. 5:4 was *f.* worthy to open

FOU

Rev. 14:5 in th. mo. *w. f.* no guile
18:24 in her *was f.* blood of pro.
20:11 *was f.* no place for them

Was not FOUND.

Mal. 2:6 iniq. *w. n. f.* in his lips
Heb. 11:5 Enoch *was not f.*
Rev. 20:15 *was not f.* written.

FOUNDATION.

Ex. 9:18 not been in Eg. since *f.*
Jos. 6:26 lay *f.* in his first-born
1 *K.* 5:17 hewn stones to lay *f.*
6:37 in fourth year was *f.* laid
7:9 of costly stones from the *f.*
Ezr. 3:11 when *f.* of house was laid
Neh. 3:15 laid *f.* thereof
Job 4:19 whose *f.* is in the dust
22:16 *f.* overflown with a flood
Ps. 87:1 *f.* is in holy mountains
102:25 of old thou hast laid *f.*
137:7 rase it, rase it, even to *f.*
Prov. 10:25 righteous is ever. *f.*
Is. 28:16 I lay in Zion for a *f.*
33:6 wisdom shall be stability
48:13 my hand laid *f.* of earth
Ezek. 13:14 *f.* thereof he discov.
Hab. 3:13 discovering *f.* to neck
Hag. 2:18 day the *f.* was laid
Zec. 4:9 Zerubbabel hath laid *f.*
8:9 prophets when the *f.* was laid
12 I which lay *f.* of the earth
Luke 6:48 laid the *f.* on a rock
49 without a *f.* built a house
14:29 after he hath laid the *f.*
Rom. 15:20 bui. on ano. man's *f.*
1 *Cor.* 3:10 master-build. laid *f.*
11 for other *f.* can no man lay
12 if any build on this *f.* gold
Eph. 2:20 on *f.* of the prophets
1 Tim. 6:19 laying up a good *f.*
2 *Tim.* 2:19 *f.* of G. standeth sure
Heb. 1:10 laid *f.* of the earth
6:1 not laying *f.* of repentance
Rev. 21:19 the first *f.* jasper

FOUNDATION of the world.

Mat. 13:35 secret from *f. of w.*
25:34 kingdom prep. fr. *f. of w.*
Luke 11:50 blood shed fr. *f. of w.*
John 17:24 before *f. of w.*
Eph. 1:4 chosen in we fr. *f. of w.*
Heb. 4:3 works finish. fr. *f. of w.*
9:26 suffered fr. *f. of w.*
1 *Pet.* 1:20 foreord. bef. *f. of w.*
Rev. 13:8 L. slain from *f. of w.*
17:8 names not writ. fr. *f. of w.*

FOUNDATIONS.

Deut. 32:22 set on fire *f.* of moun.
2 *Sam.* 22:8 *f.* of heaven moved
16 *f.* were discov. *Ps.* 18:7, 15
Ezr. 4:12 and joined the *f.*
6:3 let the *f.* be strongly laid
Ps. 11:3 if *f.* be destroyed, what
82:5 all the *f.* are out of course
104:5 who laid *f.* of the earth
Prov. 8:29 appointed *f.* of earth
Is. 58:12 of old-time waste *f.*
21:16 of the earth do shake
40:21 not underst. from the *f.*
51:13 Lord that laid *f.* of earth
16 I may lay *f.* of the earth
58:11 lay *f.* with sapphires
24:2 *f.* rise up, *f.* cannot be searched
50:15 her *f.* are fallen
51:26 not take of thee sto. for *f.*
Lam. 4:11 it hath devour. the *f.*
Ezek. 30:4 Egypt's *f.* brok. down
41:8 the *f.* of the side-chambers
Mic. 1:6 will discover *f.* thereof
6:2 ye strong *f.* of the earth
Acts 16:26 *f.* of prison were shook
Heb. 11:10 for a city that hath *f.*
Rev. 21:14 walls of city had 12 *f.*
19 *f.* garnished with precious stones

FOUNDED.

Ps. 24:2 he hath *f.* it on the seas
89:11 fuln. thereof thou *f.* them
104:8 to place thou *f.* for them
119:152 testimonies, hast *f.* th.
Prov. 3:19 by wisdom hath *f.*
Is. 14:32 the Lord hath *f.* Zion
28:16 in Zion *f.* a stone
Amos 9:6 *f.* his troop in earth
Mat. 7:25 it fell not, *f.* on a rock
Luke 6:48 W was *f.* on a rock

FOUNDER.

Jud. 17:4 gave them to the *f.*
Jer. 6:29 the *f.* melteth in vain
10:9 work of the hands of the *f.*
14 *f.* conf. by graven im. 51:17

FOU

FOUNTAIN.

Gen. 16:7 found Hagar by a *f.*
Lev. 11:36 a *f.* wherein is water
20:18 he discovered her *f.* the *f.*
Deut. 33:28 *f.* of J. be on a land
Prov. 5:16 be dispersed
8:21 no *f.* abounding with wat.
24 he strengthened, *f.* of deep
Ps. 74:15 thou didst cleave the *f.*
114:8 flint into a *f.* of water
Prov. 5:18 let thy *f.* be blessed
13:14 law of wise is a *f.* of life
14:27 fear of Lord is a *f.* of life
25:26 is as a troubled *f.*
Ec. 12:6 pitcher be broken at *f.*
Cant. 4:12 *f.* sealed; 15 *f.* of gar.
15 of living wat. 13 *f.* of life
Is. 41:18 *f.* in the valleys
Jer. 2:13 *f.* of living wat.
6:7 as *f.* casteth out waters
9:1 Oh that mine eyes were a *f.*
Joel 3:18 a *f.* shall come forth
Zec. 13:1 that day a *f.* be opened
Mark 5:29 *f.* of her blo. dried up
Jam. 3:11 *f.* send forth sw. wat.
12 no *f.* can yield salt water
Rev. 21:6 I will give of *f.* of life

FOUNTAINS.

Gen. 7:11 *f.* of deep broken up
8:2 *f.* of the deep were stopped
Deut. 8:7 bringeth into land of *f.*
1 *K.* 18:5 go to all *f.* of water
2 *Chr.* 32:4 much pe. who stop. *f.*
Prov. 5:16 let thy *f.* be dispersed
8:24 brought forth when no *f.*
28 strengthened *f.* of deep
Rev. 7:17 lead them to living *f.*
8:10 star fell on the *f.* of waters
14:7 worship him made the *f.*
16:4 angel poured his vial on *f.*

FOUR.

Gen. 2:10 river became *f.* heads
14:9 *f.* kings joined battle
47:24 *f.* parts be own, for seed
Ex. 22:1 shall restore *f.* sheep
Ezr. 11:20 fowls going on all *f.*
27 go on all *f.* unclean. 42
Job 42:16 son's sons, even *f.*
Prov. 30:15 *f.* say not, It is eno.
18 be *f.* things wh. I know not
21 be *f.* things little on earth
29 *f.* things are comely
Is. 17:6 *f.* or five in out. branch
Jer. 15:3 app. over them *f.* kinds
Ezek. 1:5 *f.* living creatures
14:21 *f.* sore judgments on Jer.
37:9 from *f.* winds, O breath
Dan. 3:25 lo, I see *f.* men loose
7:2 *f.* winds strove on sea
17 these *f.* beasts are *f.* kings
8:8 came *f.* notable horns
22 *f.* kingdoms shall stand
11:4 kingdom towards *f.* winds
Amos 1:3 for *f.* w. not turn away
punish. 6, 9, 11, 13; 2:1, 4, 6
Zec. 1:18 and behold *f.* horns
Mat. 21:31 gather his elect from
the *f.* winds, *Mark* 13:27
John 4:35 yet *f.* months, harvest
11:17 Lazarus in grave *f.* days
19:23 made *f.* parts of his garm.
Acts 10:30 *f.* days ago was fast.
21:9 Philip had *f.* daughters
23 we have *f.* men have a vow
Rev. 4:6 round throne *f.* beasts
5:14 *f.* beasts saith, Amen, 8:6
9:14 *f.* angels wh. are bound
14:3 a new song before *f.* beasts
19:4 and the *f.* beasts fell down
See CORNERS, DAYS.

FOUR times.

Neh. 6:4 sent *f.* *t.* after this sort

FOURFOLD.

2 *Sam.* 12:6 restore the lamb *f.*
Luke 19:8 any thing, I restore *f.*

See FOOTED, TWENTY, HUNDRED, THOUSAND.

FOURSCORE

Gen. 7:7 Moses was *f.* years old, when spake to Pharaoh
Jud. 3:30 land had rest *f.* years
2 *Sam.* 19:32 Barzillai was *f.* yea.
1 *K.* 6:25 as *f.*'s heel for *f.* pieces
Ps. 90:10 and if they be *f.* years
Cant. 6:8 and *f.* concubines
Luke 2:37 wid. *f.* and four years
10 take thy bill and write *f.*

FOURSCORE and five.

Jos. 14:10 I am this day *f.* and *f.*

FOURSQUARE.

Rev. 21:16 the city lieth *f.*

FOURTEEN.

Gen. 31:41 serv. *f.* years for dau.
Mat. 1:17 from Dav. to carrying away *f.* to ch. *f.* generations

CRUDEN'S CONCORDANCE.

FRA
2 Cor. 12:2 man above f. years
Gal. 2:1 f. years after I went up

FOURTEENTH.
Acts 27:27 f. night was come
See DAY.

FOURTH.
Gen. 15:16 in f. gen. come hither
Ex. 20:5 iniq. to f. generation,
34:7; Num. 14:18; Deut. 5:9
Lev. 19:24 in f. year fruit holy
2 K. 10:30 child. of f. gen. 15:12
Dan. 2:10 f. kingdom str. as iron
3:25 f. is like the Son of God
7:23 f. beast, he the f. kingdom
11:2 the f. shall be far richer
Mat. 14:25 J. came in f. watch
Rev. 4:7 f. beast like flying eagle
6:7 when opened the f. seal
8:12 the f. angel sounded
16:8 f. angel poured vial
See DAY, MONTH, PART.

FOWL.
Gen. 1:26 dominion over f. 28
2:19 God formed every f. of air
7:23 f. of heaven was destroyed
8:17 bring forth of f. of cattle
9:2 fear of you be on every f.
10 establish covenant with f.
Deut. 4:17 likeness of winged f.
Job 28:7 a path no f. knoweth
Ps. 8:8 have dominion over f.
148:10 flying f. praise the L.
Jer. 9:10 f. of heavens are fled
Ezek. 17:23 under it sh. dw. all f.
39:17 speak to ev. feathered f.
44:31 not eat torn f. or beast
Dan. 7:6 four wings of a f.

FOWLS.
Gen. 7:3 take of f. also by sevens
15:11 when f. came on carcasses
Lev. 1:14 burnt sacrifice be of f.
11:13 f. have in abomination
Deut. 14:20 of clean f. may eat
28:26 carcases be meat to all f.
1 Sam. 17:44 thy flesh to the f. 46
1 K. 4:33 Solomon spake of f.
14:11 dieth, f. eat, 16:4; 21:24
Neh. 5:18 f. were prepar. for me
Job 12:7 ask f. and they sh. tell
Ps. 50:11 I know all the f.
78:27 rained f. as sand of sea
Is. 18:6 be left to f. of mountains,
f. shall summer upon them
Dan. 4:14 f. get from his branch.
Mat. 6:26 the f. they sow not
13:4 f. dev. Mark 4:4; Lu. 8:5
Mark 4:32 f. m. lodge, Lu. 13:19
Luke 12:24 are ye better than f. ?
Acts 10:12 wherein were f. 11:6
Rev. 19:17 an angel cried to all f.
21 f. were filled with the flesh

FOWLS of heaven.
Job 35:11 wiser than f. of heaven
Ps. 79:2 thy servants meat to f.
104:12 f. of h. have their habit.
Jer. 7:33 carcasses of peo. meat
for f. of h. 16:4; 19:7; 34:20
Ezek. 29:5 Ph. for meat to f. of h.
31:6 f. of h. made nests in bougs.
13 on his ruin sh. f. of h. rem.
38:4 f. of h.aven to remain
33:20 f. of h. shake at my pres.
Dan. 2:38 f. of h. to Nebuchad.
Hos. 2:18 covenant with f. of h.
4:3 shall languish with f. of hea.
7:12 bring them down as f. of h.
Zep. 1:3 I will consume f. of hea.
Luke 13:19 f. of h. lodged in brn.

FOWLER, S.
Ps. 91:3 from the snare of the f.
124:7 soul out of the snare of f.
Prov. 6:5 as a bird from the f.
Hos. 9:8 prophet is a snare of f.

FOX, ES.
Jud. 15:4 Samson caught 300 f.
Neh. 4:3 f. shall break stone-wa.
Ps. 63:10 shall be portion for f.
Cant. 2:15 take f. the little f.
Lam. 5:18 the f. walk upon Zion
Ezek. 13:4 thy proph. are like f.
Mat. 8:20 f. ha. holes, Luke 9:58
Luke 13:32 go tell f. I cast out

FRAGMENTS.
Mat. 14:20 took up the f. Mark
6:43; Luke 9:17; John 6:13
Mark 8:19 many baskets of f.
John 6:12 gather up the f.

FRAIL.
Ps. 39:4 may know how f. I am

FRAME.
Ps. 103:14 he knoweth our f. he
Ezek. 40:2 was as the f. of a city

FRE
FRAME, ED, ETH.
Jud. 12:6 not f. to pronounce it
Ps. 50:19 thy tongue f. deceit
94:20 which f. mischi. by a law
Is. 29:16 f. say to him that f. it?
Jer. 18:11 I f. evil against you
Hos. 5:4 will not f. to turn to G.
Eph. 2:21 in whom the build. f.
Heb. 11:3 worlds f. by word of G.

FRANKINCENSE.
Ex. 30:34 spices with pure f.
Lev. 2:1 put f. 5:11; 24:7; Num. 5:15
16 priest burn oil with f. 6:15
1 Chr. 9:29 appoint. to oversee f.
Neh. 13:5 where they laid the f.
Cant. 3:6 who this perf. with f. ?
4:6 I will get me to the hill of f.
14 calamus with all trees of f.
Mat. 2:11 they present, to him f.
Rev. 18:13 no man buy, their f.

FRANKLY.
Luke 7:42 f. forgave them both

FRAUD.
Ps. 10:7 his mouth is full of f.
Jam. 5:4 hire kept back by f.

FRAY.
Deut. 28:26 f. thom, Jer. 7:33
Zec. 1:21 these are come to f.

FRECKLED.
Lev. 13:39 it is a f. spot groweth

FREE.
Ex. 21:2 in sev. year go out f.
Deut. 15:12; Jer. 34:9, 14
5 if servant say, I will not go out f.
11 she go out f. with. money
26 let him go f. for eye's sake
Lev. 19:20 not put to dea. not f.
Num. 5:19 be f. from bitter wat.
28 if woman not defiled, be f.
Deut. 15:18 not hard wh. sen. f.
21:5 sh. he f. at home one year
24:5 father's house f.
1 Sam. 17:25 father's house f.
2 Chr. 29:31 were of f. heart off.
Job 3:19 servant f. from master
39:5 who sent out wild ass f.
Ps. 51:12 uphold me with f. Sp.
88:5 f. am. the dead, like slain
105:20 the king let him go f.
Is. 58:6 to let the oppressed go f.
Jer. 34:9 each let servant go f.
11 whom they let go f. to ret.
Mat. 15:6 honor not father, be f.
17:26 then are the children f.
Mark 7:11 it is Corb. he sh. be f.
John 8:32 truth sh. make you f.
33 sayest, Ye shall be made f.
36 if Son make you f. f. indeed
Acts 22:28 but I was f. born
Rom. 3:15 not as offence. so f.
16 f. gift is of many offences
17 f. gift came upon all men
6:18 being made f. from sin, 22
20 were f. from righteousness
7:3 husband be dead, she is f.
8:2 He made me f. from death
1 Cor. 7:21 if mayest be made f.
9:1 not an apostle, am I not f. ?
19 though I be f. from all men
12:13 by one Spirit, bond or f.
Gal. 3:28 bond nor f. Col. 3:11
4:26 Jerus. which is above is f.
31 but children of the f.
3:1 liberty wherew. C. made us f.
Eph. 6:8 receive of L. bond or f.
1 Thes. 3:1 word have f. course
1 Pet. 2:16 as f. not using liberty
Rev. 13:16 f. and bond to receive
19:18 flesh of both bond and f.

FREED.
Jos. 9:23 shall none of you be f.
Rom. 6:7 he dead, is f. from sin

FREEDOM.
Lev. 19:20 wom. not f. given her
Acts 22:28 with great sum this f.

FREELY.
Gen. 2:16 of every tree f. eat
Num. 11:5 fish we did eat f.
1 Sam. 14:30 if people eaten f.
Ezr. 2:68 chief fathers offered f.
7:15 king hath offered f. to God
Ps. 54:6 will f. sacrifice to thee
Hos. 14:4 I will love them f.
Mat. 10:8 f. received, f. give
Acts 2:29 breth. let me f. speak
26:26 before whom I speak f.
Rom. 8:32 justified f. by grace
8:32 give us f. all things
1 Cor. 2:12 the things f. given us
11:17 preach. gospel of G. f.
Rev. 21:6 of fountain of life f.
22:17 whosoever will, let him take f.

FRI
FREEMAN.
1 Cor. 7:22 called, is the Lord's f.
Rev. 6:15 bond and f. hid them.

FREE offerings.
Ex. 36:3 f. offerings every morn
Amos 4:5 publish the f. offerings

FREQUENT.
2 Cor. 11:23 in prisons more f.

FREEWILL-OFFERING.
Lev. 22:21 a f.-off. sh. be perfect
Deut. 23:23 f.-off. shalt thou keep
Ezr. 3:5 willingly offered a f.-off.
7:16 silver canst find with f.-off.
8:28 silver and gold f.-offering

FREEWILL-OFFERINGS.
Deut. 12:6 thither bring f.-offer.
Ps. 119:108 accept f.-offerings

FREE-WOMAN.
Gal. 4:22 had two sons by f.-w.
23 but he of f. was by promise
31 not child. of bondw. of f.-w.

FRESH, ER.
Num. 11:8 taste of manna as f.
Job 29:20 my glory was f. in me
33:25 flesh be f. than a child's
Ps. 92:10 anointed with f. oil
Jam. 3:12 yield salt water and f.

FRET.
Lev. 13:55 burn it in fire, it is f.

FRET, TED, ETH, ING.
Lev. 13:51 is a f. leprosy, 14:44
1 Sam. 1:6 to make her f.
Ps. 37:1 f. not, 7, 8; Prov. 24:19
Prov. 19:3 his heart f. against L.
Is. 8:21 when hungry they sh. f.
Ezek. 16:43 f. me in these things

FRIEND.
Ex. 33:11 G. spake as man to f.
Deut. 13:6 if thy f. entice thee
Jud. 14:20 he used as his f.
2 Sam. 13:3 Amnon had a f. Jon.
15:37 Hushai, David's f. 16:16
16:17 is it his thy kindness to f. ?
2 Chr. 20:7 to seed of Abr. thy f.
Job 6:14 pity he showed from f.
27 and you dig a pit for your f.
Ps. 35:14 as though been my f.
41:9 familiar f. lift up his heel
88:18 lover and f. far from me
Prov. 6:1 if be surety for thy f.
3 hand of f. make sure thy f.
17:17 a f. loveth at all times
18 surety in presence of his f.
18:24 a f. closer than a brother
19:6 is a f. to him giveth gifts
22:11 the king shall be his f.
27:6 faithful are wounds of a f.
9 man's f. by hearty counsel
10 own f. father's f. forsa. not
14 bless. f. with loud voice
17 sharpeneth counten. of f.
Cant. 5:16 beloved, this is my f.
Is. 41:8 art seed of Abra. my f.
Jer. 6:21 the neighbor and his f.
19:9 eat every one flesh of his f.
Hos. 3:1 belo. of her f. adulteress
Mic. 7:5 trust ye not in a f.
Mat. 11:19 f. of public. Luke 7:34
20:13 f. I do thee no wrong
22:12 f. how camest in hither ?
26:50 f. why art thou come ?
Luke 11:5 shall have a f. and say, f. lend me three loaves
14:10 may say, f. go up higher
John 3:29 f. of bridegr. rejoiceth
11:11 our f. Lazarus sleepeth
19:12 thou art not Cesar's f.
Acts 12:20 made Blastus their f.
Jam. 2:23 Abraham call. f. of G.
4:4 f. of world, is enemy of G.

FRIENDLY.
Jud. 19:3 to speak f. to her
Ruth 2:13 spoken f. to handm.
Prov. 18:24 show himself f.

FRIENDS.
1 Sam. 30:26 D. sent spoil to f.
2 Sam. 3:8 kindness to Saul's f.
19:6 lovest enemies hatest f.
1 K. 16:11 left not one of his f.
Est. 5:10 Haman called for his f.
14 then said wife and f. to him
6:13 Haman told f. every thing
Job 2:11 when Job's three f. he.
16:20 my f. scorn me
17:5 speaketh flattery to his f.
19:14 my f. have forgotten me
19 my inward f. abhorred me
21 have pity on me, O ye f.
32:3 Elihu's wrath kind. ag. f.
42:7 kindled ag. Eliphaz and f.
10 when he prayed for his f.
Ps. 38:11 f. aloof from my sore
Prov. 14:20 the rich hath many f.
16:28 whisperer separat. chief f.

FRU
Prov. 17:9 repeat. matter, sep. f.
18:24 hath f. show him. friendly
19:4 wealth maketh many f.
7 more do f. go far from him
Cant. 5:1 eat, O f. drink, yea
Jer. 20:4 thee a terror to thy f.
6 buried there, thou and thy f.
38:22 thy f. have set thee on
Lam. 1:2 her f. have dealt treac.
Zec. 13:6 wounded in house of f.
Mark 3:21 when his f. heard of it
5:19 J. saith, Go home to thy f.
Luke 7:6 centurion sent f. to him
12:4 my f. be not afraid of them
14:12 a dinner, call not thy f.
15:6 he calleth together his f.
9 she calleth her f. saying
29 make merry with my f.
16:9 make f. of the mammon
21:16 ye shall be betrayed by f.
23:12 Pilate and Herod made f.
John 15:13 down his life for his f.
14 ye are my f. if ye do what I
15 but I have called you f.
Acts 10:24 Cornelius called his f.
19:31 who were f. sent to him
27:3 liberty to go to his f.
3 John 14 f. salute thee, greet f.

FRIENDSHIP.
Prov. 22:24 no f. with angry man
Jam. 4:4 f. of world is enmity

FRINGE, S.
Num. 15:38 make f. put on f. 39
Deut. 22:12 make thee f.

To and FRO.
Gen. 8:7 a raven, went to and f.
2 K. 4:35 Elisha walked to and f.
Job 1:7 said, F. going to and f.
7:4 I am full of tossings to and f.
13:25 a leaf driven to and f.
Ps. 107:27 they reel to and f.
Prov. 21:6 vanity tossed to and f.
Is. 24:20 earth shall reel to a. f.
53:4 running to and f. of locusts
49:21 and removing to and f.
Ezek. 27:19 Dan going to and f.
Zec. 1:10 L. sent to walk to a. f.
11 we have walked to and f.
6:7 walk to a. f. so they walked to and f. through earth
Eph. 4:14 no more tossed to a. f.
See RUN.

FROGS.
Ex. 8:2 all thy borders with f.
7 the magicians brought up f.
Ps. 78:45 he sent f. which devi.
105:30 the land brought forth f.
Rev. 16:13 unclean spirits like f.

FRONT.
2 Sam. 10:9 f. of battle ag. him

FRONTLETS.
Ex. 13:16 be for f. between eyes
Deut. 6:8 shall be as f. 11:18

FROST.
Gen. 31:40 f. consumed by night
Ex. 16:14 as small as the hoar f.
Job 37:10 by breath of G. f. given
38:29 f. of heaven, who hath
Ps. 78:47 dest. syca. trees with f.
147:16 he scattereth the hoar f.
Jer. 36:30 Jeh. body cast out to f.

FROWARD.
Deut. 32:20 a very f. generation
2 Sam. 22:27 with f. wilt show thyself f. Ps. 18:26
Job 5:13 counsel of f. carried, he.
Ps. 101:4 a f. heart shall depart
Prov. 2:12 man speaketh f. thin.
15 ways crooked, f. in paths
4:24 put away fr. thee f. mouth
6:12 walketh with a f. mouth
8:8 there is nothing f. in them
11:20 of a f. heart doth he hate
10:21 f. tongue shall be cut out
11:20 of a f. heart, 17:20
16:28 a f. man soweth strife
30 shut. eyes to devise f. things
17:20 f. heart, findeth no good
22:5 thorns are in way of the f.
Is. 57:17 the way of a man is f.
1 Pet. 2:18 serv. he subject to f.

FROWARDLY.
Is. 57:17 he went on f. in way

FROWARDNESS.
Prov. 2:14 delight in f. of wicked
6:14 f. is in his heart
10:32 mouth of wicked speak f.

FROZEN.
Job 38:30 face of the deep is f.

FRUIT.
Gen. 1:29 every tree wherein is f.
4:3 Cain brought of the f.

CRUDEN'S CONCORDANCE.

GEN

Mat. 21:23 who *g.* thee authority? *Mark* 11:28; *Luke* 20:2
23:35 ye *g.* me meat, *g.* drink
John 1:12 *g.* he power to bec. so.
3:16 G. so loved w. he *g.* Son
10:29 Fa. who *g.* them me is
14:31 as Father *g.* me command.
Acts 2:4 to speak as Sp. *g.* utter
1 *Cor.* 3:6 watered, but G. *g.* inc.
Gal. 1:4 *g.* him. for sins. *Tit.* 2:14
2:20 loved me, *g.* himself for me
Eph. 1:22 *g.* him to be head over
4:8 captive and *g.* gifts
11 he *g.* some apostles, some
5:25 loved church *g.* hims. for
1 *Tim.* 2:6 *g.* himself ransom
Rev. 13:20 dragon *g.* him power

GAVE up.
Gen. 25:8 Abraham *g. up* ghost
17 Ishmael; 35:29 Isaac *g. up*
Lam. 1:19 my elders *g. up* ghost
Mark 15:37 J. *g. up* ghost, 39;
Luke 23:46; *John* 19:30
Acts 5:5 An. *g. up* gh.; 12:23 He.
Rev. 20:13 the sea *g. up* the dead

GAVEST.
Gen. 3:12 wom. whom thou *g.*
1 *K.* 8:34 land which thou *g.* to fathers, 40, 48; 2 *Cor.* 6:25, 31, 38; *Neh.* 9:35
Neh. 9:20 *g.* Spirit, *g.* water for
g. g. kingdoms; 27 *g.* saviour
Ps. 21:4 he asked life, th. *g.* it
Luke 7:44 *g.* me no water, 45
John 17:4 I finis. work thou *g.*
12 those thou *g.* I have kept
22 the glory thou *g.* I have *g.*
18:9 thou *g.* me ha. I lost none

GAY.
Jam. 2:3 that weareth *g.* cloth.

GAZA.
Jud. 16:1 Samson went to G.
Jer. 47:1 Pharaoh smote G. 5
Amos 1:7 send fire on wall of G.
Zec. 9:5 king sh. perish from G.
Acts 8:26 goeth from Jeru. to G.

GAZE.
Ex. 19:21 break thro' to L. to *g.*

GAZING.
Nah. 3:6 I will set thee *g.* stock
Acts 1:11 why stand ye *g.* to h.?
Heb. 10:33 were made *g.* stock

GEBA.
Jos. 21:17 G. with, 1 *Chr.* 6:60
1 *K.* 15:22 Asa b. G. 2 *Chr.* 16:6
Is. 10:29 taken lodging at G.
Zec. 14:10 be as plain from G.

GEBAL. *Ps.* 83:7; *Ezek.* 27:9
GEBIM. *Is.* 10:31

GEDALIAH.
2 *K.* 25:24 G. sware, *Jer.* 40:9
1 *Chr.* 25:9 G. and Z. *Jer.* 10:19
Jer. 38:1 G. son of Pashur heard
41:2 Ishmael smote G. 43:6
Zep. 1:1 son of Cushi, son of G.

GEHAZI. 2 *K.* 4:12, 27; 5:21, 25; 8:4
GEMARIAH. *Jer.* 29:3; 36:25

GENDER.
Lev. 19:19 sh. not let cat. *g.* wi.
2 *Tim.* 2:23 knowing th. *g.* str.

GENDERED, ETH.
Job 21:10 bull *g.* and faileth not
38:29 hoary frost, who *g.* it?
Gal. 4:24 mount Sin. wh. *g.* to

GENEALOGY.
1 *Chr.* 5:1 *g.* not to be reckoned
Ezr. 2:62 sought *g.* *Neh.* 7:64
8:1 *g.* of them that went up
Neh. 7:5 I found register of *g.*

GENEALOGIES.
1 *Chr.* 9:1 Israel reckoned by *g.*
2 *Chr.* 12:15 book of She. con. *g.*
2:10 portions to all reck. by *g.*
1 *Tim.* 1:4 no heed to endless *g.*
Tit. 3:9 avoid fool. questions *g.*

GENERAL.
1 *Chr.* 27:34 *g.* king's army Joab
Heb. 12:23 *g.* assembly and chu.

GENERALLY.
2 *Sam.* 17:11 Is. be *g.* gathered
Jer. 48:38 laments. *g.* on house-t.

GENERATION.
Gen. 7:1 ha. I seen right. in
Ex. 17:16 war with Amal. fr. *g.*
Deut. 23:2 not enter to tenth *g.*
3 Am. to tenth *g.* not enter
8 Ed. and Eg. in third *g.*
32:5 perverse and crooked *g.* 20
Jud. 2:10 that *g.* gath. to father
Jb. 14:7 preserve them from *g.*

GEN

Ps. 14:5 God is in *g.* of righte.
22:30 accounted to Lord for a *g.*
24:6 this *g.* of them that seek
49:19 he shall go to *g.* of fathers
73:15 I should offend ag. the *g.*
78:4 show. to *g.* praise of Lord
6 that *g.* to come might know
8 a stubborn and rebellious *g.*
95:10 grieved with *g. Heb.* 3:10
109:13 *g.* fol. name be blotted
112:2 *g.* of upright be blessed
145:4 one *g.* praise thy works
Prov. 27:24 crown end. eve. *g.*?
30:11 a *g.* that curseth father
12 there is *g.* pure in own eyes
13 *g.* lofty; 14 *g.* whose teeth
Ec. 1:1 one *g.* passeth, another *g.*
Is. 13:20 not dwell in from *g.* to *g. Jer.* 50:39
34:10 from *g.* to *g.* l' shall lie, 17
51:8 my salvat. be from *g.* to *g.*
53:8 who decl. his *g. Acts* 8:33
Lam. 5:19 throne rem. fr. *g.* to *g.*
Dan. 4:3 his. dom. f. *g.* to *g.* 34
Mat. 1:1 book of *g.* of Jesus Ch.
3:7 O *g.* of vipers, 12:34; 23:33; *Luke* 3:7
11:16 shall liken *g. Luke* 7:31
12:39 adulterous *g.* seeketh sign, 16:4; *Mark* 8:12; *Luke* 11:29
41 in judgm. with *g. Luke* 11:32
42 queen of S. wi. *g. Luke* 11:31
17:17 O perverse *g. Mark* 9:19; *Luke* 9:41
23:36 things come on this *g.*
24:34 this *g.* not pass, *Mark* 13:30; *Luke* 21:32
Mark 8:38 asha. of me in sin. *g.*
Luke 1:50 mercy on them *g.* to *g.*
11:30 so sh. S. of man be to *g.*
50 blood of proph. req. of *g.* hi
16:8 child. of world in *g.* wiser
Acts 2:40 save from untoward *g.*
13:36 David, after served own *g.*
1 *Pet.* 2:9 ye are a chosen *g.*
See **FOURTH.**

GENERATIONS.
Gen. 2:4 these are *g.* of heavens
5:1 *g.* of Ad.; 6:9 *g.* of N. 10:1
8:9 Noah was perfect in his *g.*
9:12 covenant for perpetual *g.*
11:10 *g.* of Shem; 27 *g.* of Te.
17:12 every man-ch. in *g.* circ.
25:12 *g.* of Ish. 13; 1 *Chr.* 1:29
19 *g.* of Isaac; 36:1 *g.* of E. 9
37:2 these are the *g.* of Jacob
Ex. 3:15 memorial to all *g.*
12:14 feast to Lord through. *g.*
42 to night to be observed in *g.*
26:92 homer to be kept for *g.* 33
27:21 a statute forever to their *g.* 30:21; *Lev.* 3:17; 7:36; 10:9; 17:7; 23:14, 21, 31, 41
30:8 incense; 31 oil through. *g.*
31:13 sab. a sign through *g.* 16
40:15 everlasting priest, thro' *g.*
Deut. 7:9 L. keepeth cov. 1,000 *g.*
32:7 consider years of many *g.*
Jud. 3:2 *g.* of Israel might teach
Ruth 4:18 these are *g.* of Pharez
1 *Chr.* 16:15 word which he commanded to a 1,000 *g. Ps.* 105:8
Job 42:16 J. saw son's a, four *g.*
Ps. 33:11 thoughts of h. to all *g.*
45:17 name remember. in all *g.*
61:6 the king's years as many *g.*
72:5 shall fear thee thro' all *g.*
79:13 will show praise to all *g.*
85:5 th. draw anger to all *g.*?
89:4 will build throne to all *g.*
90:1 our dwelling-pla. in all *g.*
100:5 his truth end. to all *g.*
102:12 thy remem. to all *g.*
24 thy years through all *g.*
106:31 counted righte. to all *g.*
119:90 thy faith. Is to all *g.*
135:13 thy mem. through. all *g.*
145:13 thy dom. through. all *g.*
146:10 thy G. O Zion to all *g.*
Is. 41:4 calling *g.* from begin.
51:9 awake, O arm of L. as in *g.*
60:15 make thee joy of *g.*
61:4 repair desolations of *g.*
Mat. 1:17 fr. Abr. to Dav. 14 *g.*
Luke 1:48 *g.* sh. call me blessed
Col. 1:26 mys. hid fr. ages and *g.*

GENNESARET. *Mat.* 14:34; *Mark* 6:53; *Luke* 5:1

GENTILE.
Rom. 2:9 Jew first, also of *g.* 10

GENTILES.
Gen. 10:5 isles of *g.* were divided
Is. 11:10 root of Jes. to it sh. *g.*
42:1 judgm. to *g. Mat.* 12:18

GEN

Is. 42:6 light to *g.* 49:6; *Luke* 2:32; *Acts* 13:47
49:22 I will lift my hand to *g.*
54:3 thy seed shall inherit the *g.*
60:3 *g.* shall come to thy light
5 forces of *g.* shall come, 11
16 shalt suck the milk of *g.*
61:6 ye shall eat the riches of *g.*
9 seed sh. be known am. the *g.*
62:2 *g.* sh. see thy righteousness
66:12 glory of *g.* like flow. stre.
19 declare my glory among *g.*
Jer. 4:7 destroyer of *g.* is on way
14:22 vanities of *g.* cause rain?
Ezek. 2:6 king and princes am. *g.*
Ezek. 4:13 eat defil. bread am. *g.*
Joel 3:9 proclaim ye this am. *g.*
Mic. 5:8 remnant of Jacob am. *g.*
Zec. 1:21 to cast out horns of *g.*
Mat. 1:15 name sh. be *g.* ar. in
4:15 Galilee of the *g.*
6:32 after all th. things *g.* seek
10:5 go not into way of the *g.*
18 testimony ag. them and *g.*
12:21 in his name sh. the *g.* trn.
20:19 shall deliver him to the *g. Mark* 10:33; *Luke* 18:32
25 prin. of *g.* exer. *Luke* 22:25
Luke 21:24 Jerusal. trodden of *g.*
till times of *g.* be fulfilled
John 7:35 to disp. am. *g.* teach *g.*
Acts 7:45 with Je. into pos. of *g.*
9:15 to bear my name before *g.*
10:45 on the *g.* was poured gift
11:1 *g.* received word of God
18 hath G. to *g.* granted rep.?
13:42 *g.* besought words preach.
46 P. and B. said, We turn to *g.*
14:27 opened door of faith to *g.*
15:3 declare the conversion of *g.*
7 *g.* by my mou. sh. hear word
12 wonders G. wrought am. *g.*
14 God first did visit *g.* 17
19 them which from am. the *g.*
23 greeting to breth. of the *g.*
18:6 henceforth I will go to *g.*
21:19 God wrought am. the *g.*
21 teach. J. am. *g.* to forsake
25 touch. the *g.* which believe
22:21 I will send thee far to *g.*
26:20 *g.* that they should repent
23 Ch. sh. show light to the *g.*
28:28 salvation of God sent to *g.*
Rom. 1:13 fruit, as am. other *g.*
2:14 *g.* which have not the law
24 God blasphemed am. the *g.*
3:9 proved Jews and *g.* and *g.*
9:24 not of Jews, but also of *g.*
30 *g.* wh. follo. not after right.
11:11 salvation is come to the *g.*
12 dimin. of them riches of *g.*
13 so you *g.* as the apos. of *g.*
25 till the fulness of *g.* be come
13:9 that *g.* might glorify God;
I will confess among *g.*
10 rejoice, ye *g.* with his peo.
11 praise L. all *g.* and laud
12 over *g.* in him shall *g.* trust
16 minist. of Jesus Christ to *g.*
that offering up of the *g.* 18
27 if *g.* have been made parta.
16:4 all the churches of the *g.*
1 *Cor.* 5:1 not named among *g.*
10:20 thing *g.* sacrifice to devils
32 offence neither to J. nor *g.*
12:2 ye know ye were *g.* carried
13 whether we be Jews or *g.*
Gal. 2:12 he did eat with *g.*
14 man. of *g.* why compel. *g.*?
15 Jews, and not sinners of *g.*
3:14 blessing of Abraham on *g.*
Eph. 2:11 in time past *g.* in flesh
3:1 prisoner of Jesus Ch. for *g.*
6 that *g.* should be fellow-heirs
8 preach am. *g.* unsea. riches
4:17 ye walk not as other *g.*
Col. 1:27 glory of mystery am. *g.*
1 *Thes.* 2:16 forbid. to spe. to *g.*
4:5 in lust of concupis. as the *g.*
1 *Tim.* 2:7 ordained teacher of *g.*
1:11 preached to the *g.*
2 *Tim.* 1:11 teacher of *g.*
4:17 preached fully to *g.*
1 *Pet.* 2:12 convers. honest am. *g.*
4:3 to have wrought will of *g.*
Rev. 11:2 the court is given to *g.*

GENTLE.
1 *Thes.* 2:7 were *g.* among you
2 *Tim.* 2:24 ser. of L. must be *g.*
Tit. 3:2 *g.* showing all meekness
Jam. 3:17 wisd. from ab. pure *g.*
1 *Pet.* 2:18 subject not only to *g.*

GENTLENESS.
2 *Sam.* 22:36 thy *g.* made me great, *Ps.* 18:35

GHO

2 *Cor.* 10:1 I bes. you by *g.* of C.
Gal. 5:22 fruit of the Spirit is *g.*

GENTLY.
2 *Sam.* 18:5 deal *g.* with Absalom
Is. 40:11 *g.* lead those wi. young
GERA. *Jud.* 3:15; 2 *Sam.* 16:5
GERAHS. *Ex.* 30:13; *Lev.* 27:25; *Num.* 3:47; 18:16; *Ezek.* 45:12
GERAR. *Gen.* 20:1, 2; 26:6, 20
GERGESENES. *Mat.* 8:28

GERIZIM.
Deut. 11:29 bles. on mt. G. 27:12
Jos. 8:33 ags. mount G. *Jud.* 9:7

GERSHOM, GERSHON.
Ex. 46:11 G. Kohath and Merari
Ex. 6:16; *Num.* 3:17; 1 *Chr.* 6:1; 23:6
Ex. 2:22 name of Moses' son G.
Num. 3:21 G. family of Libnites
4:28 sons of G. 7:7; 10:17
Jos. 21:6 children of G. had, 27
Ezr. 8:2 sons of Phinehas, G.

GESHUR.
2 *Sam.* 13:37 and went to G. 38
14:23 Joab went to G. 32
15:8 servant vowed a vow at G.

GESHURITES.
Jos. 13:13 G. dw. among, 1 *Sam.* 27:8

GET.
Gen. 34:4 *g.* me damsel to wife
Ex. 14:17 will *g.* honor up. Pha.
Lev. 14:21 poor and cannot *g.* 22
Deut. 8:18 power to *g.* wealth
Jud. 14:2 *g.* her me to wife, 3
1 *K.* 1:2 that king may *g.* heat
Ps. 119:104 precepts I *g.* under.
Prov. 4:5 *g.* wisdom, *g.* underst.
16:16 better *g.* wisd. than gold
17:16 in hand of fool to *g.* wis.
Ec. 3:6 there is a time to *g.*
Lam. 3:7 I cannot *g.* out
Ezek. 22:27 to *g.* dishonest gain
Dan. 4:14 beasts *g.* from under
Zep. 3:19 I will *g.* them praise
Luke 9:12 lodge and *g.* victuals
2 *Cor.* 2:11 lest Sat. *g.* advantage
Jam. 4:13 buy, sell, and *g.* gain

GET thee.
Gen. 12:1 *g. t.* out of co. *Acts* 7:3
10:28 *g. t.* thee from me
19:14 Lord said to Moses, *g. t.* down, 32:7; *Deut.* 9:12
1 *K.* 17:3 *g. t.* hence; 9 to Zarep.
18:41 Elijah said, *g. thee up*
K. 3:13 *g. t.* to prophets of fath.
Is. 49:9 G. *g. t.* to high mount.
47:5 and *g. thee* into darkness
Jer. 13:1 *g. thee* a linen girdle
Mat. 4:10 J. saith, *g. t.* hence. 8.
16:23 said to Peter, *g. t.* behind me, 8. *Mark* 8:33; *Luke* 4:8
Acts 10:20 arise, *g. thee* down
22:18 *g. t.* quickly out of Jerus.

GET ye.
Gen. 19:14 said, Up, *g. ye* out
Ex. 5:4 *g. you* to your burdens
11 *g. you* str. wh. you can find
Num. 16:24 *g. y.* up fr. tab. of K.
Jos. 2:16 *g. you* to the mountain
1 *Sam.* 25:5 *g. you* up to Carmel
Jer. 49:30 flee, *g. you* far off

GETHSEMANE. *Mat.* 26:36 called G. *Mark* 14:32

GETTETH.
2 *Sam.* 5:8 whoso *g.* to gutter
Prov. 3:13 man that *g.* underst.
9:7 reproveth scorner *g.* shame, rebuketh wicked man *g.* blot
15:32 hear. reproof *g.* underst.
18:15 prudent *g.* knowledge
19:8 that *g.* wisdom loveth soul
Jer. 17:11 *g.* riches not by right
48:44 that *g.* out of pit

GETTING.
Gen. 31:18 J. carried cattle of *g.*
Prov. 4:7 with all thy *g.* get und.
21:6 *g.* of treas. by lying tongue

GHOST.
Gen. 49:33 J. yielded up the *g.*
Job 10:18 I had given up *g.*
11:20 hope as giving up of *g.*
14:10 man giveth up *g.*
Jer. 15:9 she hath given up *g.*
Mat. 27:50 J. cried, yielded up *g.*

CRUDEN'S CONCORDANCE. 871

GLO

GLADNESS.
Num. 10:10 in day of g. ye shall
2 Sam. 6:12 Da. br. ark with g.
1 Chr. 16:27 strength and g. in
2 Chr. 29:30 sang praises with g.
30:21 Israel kept feast with g.
23 kept other seven days w. g.
Neh. 8:17 there was great g.
Est. 8:16 had light, and g. 17
9:17 day of feast, and g. 18, 19
Ps. 4:7 thou put g. in my heart
30:11 thou girded me with g.
45:7 anoi. with oil of g. Heb. 1:9
15 with g. shall they be brou.
51:8 make me to hear joy and g.
97:11 g. is sown for the upright
100:2 serve the Lord with g.
105:43 brought chosen with g.
106:5 that I may rejoice in g.
Cant. 3:11 day of g. of his heart
Is. 22:13 joy and g. slay. oxen
30:29 have song and g. of heart
35:10 obtain joy and g. 51:11
51:3 joy and g. found therein
Jer. 7:34 voice of mirth and g.
16:9; 25:10
31:7 sing with g. for Jacob
33:11 heard voice of joy and g.
43:33 joy and g. taken fr. field
Joel 1:16 joy and g. from h. of G.
Zec. 8:19 h. of Jud. joy and g.
Mark 4:16 who receive it with g.
Luke 1:14 shalt have joy and g.
Acts 2:46 eat meat w. g. of heart
12:14 who opened not gate for g.
14:17 fill. hea. with food and g.
Phil. 2:29 receive him with all g.

GLASS, ES.
Is. 3:23 Lord will take away g.
1 Cor. 13:12 we see through a g.
Jam. 1:23 man beholdeth his n. g.
Rev. 4:6 sea of g. like unto crys.
15:2 sea of g. mingled with fire
21:18 city pure gold, like c. g. 21
See LOOKING.

GLEAN, ED.
Lev. 19:10 not g. v. Deut. 24:21
Ruth 2:2 let me go to field and g.
3 she came and g. after reapers
Jer. 6:9 they shall g. the remnant

GLEANING, S.
Jud. 8:2 is not g. of gr. of E. ph.
Jud. 8:2 is not g. of gr. of E.ph.
24:15 as g. grapes when vint.
Jer. 49:9 thieves not leave some g.?
Mic. 7:1 as grape g. of the vint.

GLEDE.
Deut. 14:13 shall not eat the g.

GLISTERING.
1 Chr. 29:2 I have pre. g. stones
Job 20:25 the g. sword cometh
Luke 9:29 his rains, white and g.

GLITTER, ING.
Deut. 32:41 if I whet. g. sword
Job 39:23 the g. spear rattleth
Ezek. 21:10 furb. that it may g.
28 furbished to cons. bec. of g.
Nah. 3:3 horseman lifteth g. sp.
Hab. 3:11 shining of thy g. spear

GLOOMINESS.
Joel 2:2 darkn. g. Zep. 1:15

GLORIFY.
Ps. 22:23 seed of Jacob g. him
53:15 and thou shalt g. me
86:9 nations shall come and g.
12 and I will g. thy name
Is. 24:15 g. ye Lord in the fires
25:3 the strong people g. thee
60:7 I will g. house of my glory
Jer. 30:19 I will also g. them
Mat. 5:16 g. Father in heaven
John 12:28 F. g. thy name
13:32 God sh. g. him in himself
16:14 he shall g. me
17:1 g. thy son, that thy Son g.
5 g. me with thine own self
21:19 what death he sho. g. G.
Rom. 15:6 mind and mouth g. G.
9 that Gentiles might g. God
1 Cor. 6:20 g. God in body and s.
2 Cor. 9:13 g. God for your subj.
1 Pet. 2:12 g. God in the day of visit.
4:16 g. God on this behalf
Rev. 15:4 and g. thy name

GLORIFIED.
Lev. 10:3 bef. all peo. I will be g.
Is. 26:15 increased nation, art g.
44:23 L. hath g. himself in Is.
49:3 O Is. in whom I will be g.
55:5 Holy One of Is. hath g. 60:9
61:21 that I may be g.
61:3 planting of L. that he be g.

GLO

Is. 66:5 said, Let the Lord be g.
Ezek. 28:22 I will be g. in midst
39:13 the day that I shall be g.
Dan. 5:23 God hast thou not g.
Mat. 9:8 marvelled, and g. God,
Mark 2:12; Luke 5:26
15:31 they g. the God of Israel
Luke 4:15 synagogues, being g.
7:16 and they g. God
13:13 made straight, and g. G.
17:15 leper g. G.; 23:47 centur.
John 7:39 because Jes. not yet g.
11:4 Son of God might be g.
12:16 but when Jesus was g.
23 the Son of man should be g.
28 I have g. it, will glorify it
13:31 Son of man g. God is g.
32 if G. be g. in him G. sh. gl.
14:13 Father may be g. in Son
15:8 my Father g. ye bear fruit
17:4 I have g. thee on earth
10 and I am g. in them
Acts 3:13 G. of fathers hath g. S.
4:21 men g. God
11:18 held peace, and g. God
13:48 Gentiles g. word of Lord
21:20 they g. Jerusalem g. Lord
Rom. 1:21 they g. him not as G.
8:17 that we may be also g.
30 wh. he justified, them he g.
2 Thes. 1:10 wh. he come to be g.
12 name of Jesus may be g.
1 Pet. 4:11 G. in all things be g.
Rev. 18:7 how much g. herself

GLORIFIETH, ING.
Ps. 50:23 whoso. offer. praise g.
Luke 2:20 shep. return. g. G.
5:25 departed to own ho. g. God
18:43 blind man followed, g. G.

GLORY, Substantive.
Gen. 31:1 father's gotten this g.
Ex. 28:2 garm. for A. for g. 40
1 Sam. 2:8 inherit throne of g.
4:21 g. is departed from Isr. 22
1 Chr. 22:5 ho. for L. must be g.
29:11 thine is greatness, power
and g. Mat. 6:13
Est. 5:11 H. told g. of riches
Job 29:20 g. of nostrils terrible
Ps. 21:7 King of g. wh. come in, 9
10 who is this King of g.?
29:3 the God of g. thundereth
49:16 g. of house is increased
73:24 afterward receive me to g.
79:9 O God, for g. of name
87:9 that g. may dwell in land
Ps. 73:17 art g. of their strength
108:5 changed g. into similit.
145:11 g. of thy kingdom
149:5 the saints be joyful in g.
Prov. 3:35 wise shall inherit g.
17:6 g. of children are fathers
19:11 g. of young men is strom.
25:27 to search own g. is not g.
28:12 righteous rej. there is g.
Is. 3:10 hide for g. of maj. 10, 21
4:5 the g. shall be a defence
6:3 the land is full of his g.
10:3 where will ye leave g.?
12 punish g. of high looks
16 consume g. of his forest
13:19 Babylon g. of kingdoms
14:18 all lie in g. each in house
16:14 g. of M. sh. be contemn
17:3 as g. of children of Israel
4 g. of Jacob sh. be made thin
21:16 the g. of Kedar shall fail
22:18 this is the g. of father's ho.
24:9 to stain pride of g.
Jer. 2:11 people have changed g.
13:11 might be to me for a g.
16 cr. owns of your g.
Ezek. 26:20 be g. in land of liv.
31:25 from them joy of their g.
39:9 open g. of the country
39:20 g. in land of the living
31:18 art thou thus like to g.?
Dan. 2:37 power and g. 7:14
4:36 g. of kingdom returned
11:39 increase in g.
Ho. 8:7 change g. into shame
10:11 Ephraim, there g. fly away
11:5 priests mour. for g. thereof
Mic. 1:15 Adullam the g. of Isr.
Nah. 2:9 none end of store and g.
Hab. 2:10 filled wh. shame for g.

GLO

Hag. 2:3 saw house in first g.?
7 fill house with g. saith Lord
9 g. of latter house greater
Zec. 2:5 I will be g. in midst
8 after g. sent me to nations
6:13 build temple, he bear g.
11:3 their g. is spoiled
12:7 g. of house of Dav. g. of J.
Mat. 4:8 kingd. and g. of them
6:2 sound trumpet, have g.
10:27 in g. of Fa. Mark 8:38
24:30 S. coming with power and
g. Mark 13:26; Luke 21:27
Luke 2:14 g. to G. in high. 19:38
12 the g. of thy people Israel
4:6 power will I give th. and g.
9:31 in g. spake of his decease
John 17:5 wh. I had with thee
22 g. thou gavest me
Acts 7:2 G. of g. appeared
12:28 because he gave not G. g.
22:11 I could not see g. of light
Rom. 4:20 strong, giving g. to G.
6:4 raised by g. of the Father
8:18 not wor. be com. with g.
9:4 pertaineth g. and covenants
23 had afore prepared unto g.
11:36 g. for ev. Gal. 1:5; 2 Tim.
4:18; Heb. 13:21; 1 Pet. 5:11
16:27 to God be g. 1 Tim. 1:17
1 Cor. 2:7 God ordained to our g.
8 not crucified the Lord of g.
11:7 woman is the g. of the men
15 wo. ha. long hair, is g. to h.
2 Cor. 3:7 g. of countenance
9 if condemnation be g. righte.
10 no g. by reason of g. th. ex.
18 all are changed from g. to g.
4:17 work. eternal weight of g.
8:19 administered g. of Lord
23 messengers, and g. of Christ
Eph. 1:6 praise of g. of his grace
12 believed for g. give you Spirit
18 know what is riches of g.
3:13 tribulations, wh. is your g.
21 c. to the church by Chr. J.
Phil. 1:11 fruits, by Christ to g.
3:19 whose g. is in their shame
4:19 according to his rich. in g.
20 God and our F. be g. for ev.
Col. 1:27 Christ the hope of g.
3:1 ye sh. appear with him in g.
1 Thes. 2:6 nor of men sought g.
12 called you to king. and g.
20 for ye are our g. and joy.
2 Thes. 1:9 pun. from g. of power
2:14 obtaining of g. of our Lord
1 Tim. 3:16 received up into g.
2 Tim. 2:10 Christ, with eter. g.
Heb. 2:10 bring ing sons unto g.
3:3 man counted worthy mo. g.
9:5 cherubim of g. shadowing
1 Pet. 1:8 rej. with joy full of g.
11 testified g. that sho. follow
21 God raised him, gave him g.
4:14 spirit of g. resteth on you
5:1 the g. that shall be revealed
2 Pet. 1:3 that hath called us to g.
17 voice to him from excel. g.
3:18 to him be g. ever. Rev. 1:6
23 only G. our Savior, be g.
Rev. 4:11 worthy to rec. g. 5:19
7:12 blessing and g. to our God
11:13 rem. affrighted, gave g.
See CROWN, HONOR, VAIN.

Give GLORY.
Jos. 7:19 my son, give g. to God
1 Sam. 6:5 shall give g. to God
1 Chr. 16:28 o. to L. g. 29; Ps.
96:7; 08:7, 8; 1 Pet. 14:16
Ps. 84:11 L. will g. grace and g.
115:1 to thy name give g.
Is. 42:12 let them g. g. unto L.
Mal. 2:2 in heart, to give g.
Jer. 13:16 returned to give g.
Rev. 4:9 those beasts give g.
14:7 fear God, give g. to him
16:9 repented not to give g.

GLORY of God.
Ps. 19:1 heavens declare g. of G.
Prov. 25:2 g. of God to conceal
John 11:4 sickness is for g. of G.
40 see g. of G. of God?
Acts 7:55 S. looked, saw g. of G.

GLO

Rom. 3:23 short of g. of God
5:2 rej. in hope of the g. of God
15:7 as C. receiv. us, to g. of G.
1 Cor. 10:31 all to g. of G.
11:7 man is image and g. of God
2 Cor. 4:6 lig. of kno. of g. of G.
15 thanks. redound to g. of G.
Phil. 2:11 to the g. of God
2:11 J. is Lord to the g. of God
Rev. 15:8 filled w. sm. f. g. of G.
21:11 Jerusa. having g. of God
23 the g. of God did lighten it

His GLORY.
Deut. 5:24 L. hath showed his g.
33:17 his g. firstling of bullock
1 Chr. 16:24 declare his g. among
the heathen, Ps. 96:3
Ps. 21:5 his g. is great in salva.
29:9 every one speak of his g.
49:17 his g. shall not descend
72:19 earth be filled with his g.
76:61 deliv. his g. to enemy's h.
89:44 hast made h. g. to cease
97:6 and all the people see h. g.
102:16 build J. appear in his g.
113:4 b. g. above heav. 148:13
Is. 3:8 to provoke eyes of his g.
6:3 whole earth full of his g.
10:16 his g. kindle a burning
58:19 his g. from rising of sun
60:2 his g. shall be seen
Jer. 22:18 Ah L. or Ah his g.
Ezek. 43:2 earth shin. with h. g.
Hab. 3:3 his g. covered heavens
Mat. 6:29 Sol. in h. g. Luke 12:27
19:28 S. of m. sit in h. g. Lv. 9:26
Luke 9:32 wh. awoke, saw his g.
24:26 enter into his g.
John 1:14 beheld h. g. g. of only
2:11 J. manifested forth his g.
12:41 said E. when saw his g.
Rom. 3:7 thru. my lie unto h. g.
9:23 known riches of his g.
Eph. 1:12 the praise of his g. 14
3:16 according to riches of his g.
Heb. 1:3 the brightness of his g.
1 Pet. 4:13 when h. g. be revealed
Jude 24 before presence of h. g.
Rev. 18:1 earth light. with h. g.

My GLORY.
Gen. 45:13 of all my g.
Ex. 29:43 sanctified by my g.
33:22 while m. g. passeth by
Num. 14:22 wh. have seen m. g.
38:19 hath stript me of my g.
29:20 my g. was fresh in me
Ps. 3:3 thou art m. g. and lifter
4:2 long turn m. g. to shame?
16:9 m. g. rej.; 30:12 m. g. sing
57:8 awake, m. g.; 62:7 m. g.
108:1 give praise with m. g.
Is. 42:8 m. g. not give, 48:11
43:7 created him for my g.
46:13 salvation for Israel my g.
60:7 will glorify house of my g.
66:18 shall come and see my g.
19 seen m. g. declare m. g.
Ezek. 39:21 set my g. am. heath.
Mic. 2:9 from chil. taken my g.
John 17:24 that they may behold my g.

GLORY of the Lord.
Ex. 16:7 ye shall see g. of L.
10 g. of L. appear. Lev. 9:6;
Num. 14:10; 16:19, 42; 20:6
24:16 g. of the L. like devour. fire
40:34 g. of the L. filled taber. 35
Lev. 9:6 g. of the L. shall appear
Num. 14:21 filled with g. of L.
1 K. 8:11 the g. of the L. fill t.
the house, 2 Chr. 5:14; 7:1,
2, 3; Ezek. 43:5; 44:4
Ps. 104:31 g. of the L. sh. endure
138:5 for great is the g. of L.
Is. 35:2 they shall see g. of L.
40:5 g. of the L. sh. be reveal
58:8 g. of the L. sh. be thy rewar
60:1 g. of the L. is risen
Ezek. 1:28 likeness of g. of L.
3:12 blessed be g. of the Lord
23 g. of the L. stood there
10:4 g. of the L. went fr. cheru.
18 g. of L. departed from chere
11:23 g. of the L. came into ho.
43:4 g. of L. came into hou.
Hab. 2:14 filled wit. know. g. of L.
Luke 2:9 g. of the L. shone round
2 Cor. 3:18 g. of the L.

Thy GLORY.
Ex. 33:18 said, Show me thy g.
Ps. 8:1 thy g. above the heavens
45:3 sword on thigh, with thy g.
57:5 thy g. ab. earth, 11; 108:5
63:2 see thy power and g.

CRUDEN'S CONCORDANCE.

GNA
Ps. 90:16 let *t. g.* app. unto chil.
102:15 all kings of earth thy *g.*
Is. 22:18 chariots of *t. g.*
  60:19 God *thy g.* ; 62:2 see *thy g.*
  63:15 behold from habit. of *t. g.*
Jer. 14:21 not dis. throne of *t. g.*
  48:18 come down from *thy g.*
Hab. 2:16 spewing sh. be on *t. g.*

GLORIOUS.
Ex. 15:6 right hand, O Lord, *g.*
  11 like Lord. *g.* in holiness
Deut. 28:58 fear this *g.* name
2 *Sam.* 8:20 *g.* was the k. of Isr.
1 *Chr.* 29:13 praise thy *g.* name
Neh. 9:5 blessed be thy *g.* name
Ps. 45:13 king's dau. *g.* within
  66:2 make his praise *g.*
  72:19 blessed be *g.* name
  66:4 more *g.* than mountains
  87:3 *g.* things spoken of thee
  111:3 work honorable and *g.*
  145:5 speak of *g.* honor of maj.
  12 make known *g.* majesty
Is. 4:2 branch of the Lord be *g.*
  11:10 root of Jesse, his rest *g.*
  22:23 for a *g.* throne to house
  28:1 *g.* beauty is fading flower
  4 *g.* beauty on head of valley
  33:21 *g.* L. be a place of streams
  47:5 I shall be *g.* in eyes of L.
  60:13 the place of my feet *g.*
  63:1 who is this, *g.* in apparel?
  12 led them with his *g.* arm
  14 people to make *g.* name
Jer. 17:12 a *g.* high throne from
Ezek. 27:25 *g.* in midst of seas
Dan. 11:16 he sh. stand in *g.* land
  41 he shall enter into *g.* land
  45 between seas, in *g.* holy m.
Luke 13:17 rejoiced for *g.* things
Rom. 8:21 into *g.* liberty of chil.
1 *Cor.* 3:7 ministration of *g.* rather *g.*
  3:8 ministration of Sp. rather *g.*
  4:4 lest light of *g.* gospel shine
Eph. 5:27 present it a *g.* church
Phil. 3:21 fashioned like *g.* body
Col. 1:11 according to his *g.* power
1 *Tim.* 1:11 accord. to *g.* gospel
Tit. 2:13 looking for *g.* appearing

GLORIOUSLY.
Ex. 15:1 he hath triumphed *g.*
Is. 24:23 reign before ancients *g.*

GLORY, Verb.
Ex. 8:9 Moses said, *g.* over me
2 *K.* 14:10 *g.* of this, and tarry
1 *Chr.* 16:10 *g.* ye in his holy name, *Ps.* 105:3
  35 we may *g.* in thy praise
Ps. 63:11 swear, by him shall *g.*
  64:10 be upright in heart sh. *g.*
  106:5 I may *g.* with thy inheri.
Is. 41:16 shalt *g.* in Holy One
  45:25 in L. shall seed of Isr. *g.*
  14:2 and in him shall they *g.*
  9:23 let not wise, rich man *g.*
  24 *g.* in this, that he knoweth
Rom. 4:2 he hath whereof to *g.*
  5:3 we *g.* in tribulations also
  15:17 I have whereof I may *g.*
1 *Cor.* 1:29 no flesh *g.* in his pre.
  31 *glor. g.* in L. 2 *Cor.* 10:17
  3:21 let no man *g.* in men
  4:7 as if hadst not received?
  9:16 nothing to *g.* of
2 *Cor.* 5:12 to *g.* on our behalf, who *g.* in appearance
  11:12 wherein *g.* be found
  18 *g.* after the flesh, I will *g.*
  20 if *g.* I will *g.* of my infirmi.
  12:1 not expedient for me to *g.*
  5 I *g.* of myself I will not *g.*
  6 I desire to *g.* not be a fool
  9 rather *g.* in my infirmities
Gal. 6:13 may *g.* in your flesh
  14 I should *g.* save in the cross
2 *Thes.* 1:4 so that we *g.* in you
Jam. 3:14 if ye have envy, *g.* not

GLORIEST, ETH.
Jer. 9:24 let him that *g.* 1 *Cor.* 1:31; 2 *Cor.* 10:17
  49:4 why *g.* thou in valleys?

GLORYING.
1 *Cor.* 5:6 your *g.* is not good
  9:15 than any sh. make *g.* void
2 *Cor.* 7:4 great is my *g.* of you
  12:11 I am become a fool in *g.*

GLUTTON.
Deut. 21:20 this our son is a *g.*
Prov. 23:21 *g.* sh. come to poverty.

GLUTTONOUS.
Mat. 11:19 a man *g. Luke* 7:34

GNASH, ED, ED, ETH, ING.
Job 16:9 he *g.* on me, *Ps.* 37:12
Ps. 35:16 *g.* on me with teeth

GO
Ps. 112:10 he shall *g.* w. his teeth
Lam. 2:16 hiss and *g.* the teeth
Mat. 8:12 *g.* of t. 13:42, 50; 22:13;
  24:51; 25:30; *Luke* 13:28
Mark 9:18 he foameth and *g.*
Acts 7:54 *g.* on him with teeth

GNAT.
Mat. 23:24 strain at *g.* sw. camel

GNAW, ED.
Zep. 3:3 they *g.* not the bones
Rev. 16:10 *g.* tongues for pain

GO.
Gen. 3:14 on thy belly shalt *g.*
  16:8 whither wilt thou *g.?*
  24:42 prosper my way wh. I *g.*
  58 wilt thou *g.* with this man?
  26:16 Abi. said to Is. *g.* from us
  28:20 if G. keep me in way I *g.*
  32:26 let me *g.* ; I will not let thee *g.* except thou bless me
  37:30 whither shall I *g.?*
  43:8 send the lad, we will *g.*
Ex. 3:19 will not let you *g.* 4:21
  21 when ye *g.* sh. not *g.* empty
  4:23 let my son *g.* if thou refuse, 8:3, 21; 9:2; 10:4
  5:1 let my people *g.* 7:16; 8:1, 20; 9:1, 13; 10:3
  2 nor will I let Israel *g.*
  8:8 I will let people *g.* 28; 9:28
  32 nor would he let people *g.*
  7:14; 9:35; 10:20, 27
  10:9 *g.* with our young and old
  13:21 light to *g., Neh.* 9:12, 19
  14:5 that we have let Israel *g.*
  17:5 *g.* on before the people
  23:23 angel *g.* bef. thee, 32:34
  32:23 to *g.* before us, *Acts* 7:40
  33:14 my pres. sh. *g.* with thee
  34:9 if found grace, *g.* am. us
Num. 22:13 L. refuseth leave to *g.*
  20 if the men called thee, *g.*
  24:14 now I *g.* unto my people
  31:23 make it *g.* through fire
  32:6 *g.* to war, and ye sit here?
  17 but we will *g.* ready armed
Deut. 1:33 way ye should *g.*
  4:5 ye *g.* 6:1; 11:8, 11; 30:18
  40 that it *g.* well, 5:16; 19:13
  11:28 if ye *g.* after gods, 28:14
  31:6 he it is that doth *g.*
  7 must *g.* with this people
  8 he it is that doth *g.* bef. thee
  16 whither they *g.* amongst
  21 know imagine, they *g.* do
Jos. 1:16 whither sendest will *g.*
  3:4 may know way ye must *g.*
Jud. 7:3 let *g.* man and family
  4:8 if thou wilt *g.*, then I will *g.*
  9:14 said, *g.* in this thy might
  7:4 this shall *g.* the same sh. *g.*
  18:6 is way wherein ye *g.*
  9 not slothful to *g.* to possess
  19:25 day began, they let her *g.*
Ruth 1:18 stead., minded to *g.*
1 *Sam.* 5:11 let it *g.* th. its place
  6:8 did they not let people *g.?*
  12:21 *g.* after vain things
  16:2 how can I *g.?* if Saul hear
  17:32 not able to *g.* ag. Philist.
  18:2 let him *g.* no more home
  23:13 D. went whither could *g.*
2 *Sam.* 12:23 I shall *g.* to him
  13:13 whither cause shame to *g.*
  15:20 seeing I *g.* whither I may
  17:11 *g.* to battle in thy person
  20:11 David, let him *g.* after *J.*
1 *K.* 2:3 I *g.* way of all the earth
  11:22 let me *g.* in any wise
  13:17 nor *g.* by way thou camest
  20:42 let *g.* a man appointed
  22:4 with me, 2 *Chr.* 18:3
2 *K.* 3:7 *g.* with me ag. Moab?
  4:23 wilt thou *g.* to him to-day?
  6:22 set bread that he may *g.*
  10:21 he that letteth him *g.*
  18:21 *g.* into hand, *Is.* 36:6
2 *Chr.* 14:11 in thy name we *g.*
  25:7 let not army of Israel *g.*
  8 if thou wilt *g.* do it, be stro.
Job 6:18 they *g.* to nothing
  10:21 before I *g.* whence I shall not return, 16:22
  20:26 it *g.* ill with him
  21:28 not asked th. *g.* by way?
  27:6 righteous, I will not let *g.*
  32:8 teach in way shall *g.?*
  39:15 before I *g.* hence, and be
  42:9 why *g.* I mourning, 43:2
  38:32 canst *g.* to the north paths?
  39:5 canst thou *g.* to the north
  50:6 shepherds caused *g.* a.
  84:7 *g.* fr. strength to strength
  85:13 right. shall *g.* before him
  85:14 mercy and truth *g.* before
  107:7 might *g.* to a city of habi.
  132:7 we will *g.* into his taber.
  139:7 whither *g.* from thy pres.

GO
Prov. 2:19 none that *g.* return
  3:23 *g.* and come ag. to-morrow
  6:26 can one *g.* on hot coals
  9:15 passengers who *g.* right on
  17 *g.* from presence of foolish
  15:12 neither scorner *g.* to wise
  19:7 more do his friends *g.* far
  22:6 train child in way he sh. *g.*
  30:29 three things which *g.* well
Ec. 3:20 all *g.* unto one place
  5:15 naked to *g.* as he came, 16
  6:6 do not all *g.* to one place?
  7:2 to *g.* to house of mourning
  9:3 they *g.* to the dead
  10:15 kn. not how to *g.* to city
  12:5 mourners *g.* about streets
Cant. 3:4 I would not let him *g.*
Is. 3:16 and mincing as they *g.*
  6:8 and who will *g.* for us?
  8:7 L. bri. up people, *Acts* 28:26
  27:4 I would *g.* through them
  28:13 they might *g.* and fall
  45:13 shall let *g.* my captives
  48:17 by way shouldest *g.*
  58:8 righteousn. *g.* before thee
  62:10 *g.* thro' *g.* thro' the gates
Jer. 1:7 shalt *g.* to all I send th.
  9:2 I might *g.* from my people
  31:22 how long *g.* about, O dau.
  34:3 *g.* to Babylon, *Mic.* 4:10
  40:4 good to *g.* there *g.* 5
  42:2 voice shall *g.* like serpent
  50:33 refused to let them *g.*
Ezek. 8:6 *g.* in, *g.* far in fr. sanctu.?
  14:17 sword *g.* through the land
  21:16 *g.* thee one way or other
Hos. 5:6 *g.* with floc. to seek L.
  7:11 they *g.* to Assyria
  12 when they *g.* I will spread
  11:3 I taught Ephr. also to *g.*
Mic. 5:8 if he *g.* through tread.
Zec. 6:7 the bay sought to *g.*
  8 these *g.* towards the north
  8:21 inhab. of one city *g.* to an.
  23 *g.* with you, we have heard
  9:4 *g.* with whirlwinds of south
Mat. 2:22 Joseph was afraid to *g.*
  5:41 *g.* with him twain, *Luke* 7:8
  8:7 and I say *g.* and he goeth
  10:6 *g.* rath. to lost sheep of Is.
  20:10 *g.* f. sir, and went not
  23:9 *g.* rather to them that sell
Mark 6:38 *g.* see ; 11:6 let th. *g.*
  8:31 I kill *g.* before him
Luke 1:17 shall *g.* before him
  9:51 set face to *g.* to Jerusalem
  60 *g.* and preach kingd. of God
  10:37 *g.* thou and do likewise
  22:33 I am ready to *g.* to prison
  68 not ans. me, nor let me *g.*
  23:22 chastise him, let him *g.*
John 6:68 L. to whom sh. we *g.*
  7:33 I *g.* unto him sent me
  8:14 but I know whither I *g.*
  21 I *g.* my way, whither I *g.*
  13:36 whither I *g.* not follow
  14:2 I *g.* to pre. place for you
  4 whither I *g.* ye know
  12 bec. I *g.* to Father, 16:10
  28 I *g.* to Father, 16:17, 28
  19:12 if thou let this man *g.*
Acts 1:25 *g.* to his own place
  4:23 let them *g.* they went to
  8:27 threatened, let them *g.*
  21 being let *g.* went to comp.
  5:40 sh. not speak, let them *g.*
  16:35 saying, Let those men, *g.*
  20:22 bound in spirit to Jer.
  25:12 to Cesar shalt thou *g.*
  28:15 examined me, let me *g.*
Rom. 15:25 now I *g.* to Jerusal.
1 *Cor.* 6:1 *g.* to law before unjust
  10:27 and ye be disposed to *g.*
  16:4 if meet I *g.* also, *Col.* for
2 *Cor.* 9:5 exhort breth., *g.* before
Phil. 2:26 how I will *g.* with me
Jam. 4:13 will *g.* un. such a city

See **FREE**.

GO aside,
Num. 5:12 if any man's wi. *g. a.*
Deut. 28:14 shalt not *g. a.* from
Acts 4:15 commanded th. to *g. a.*

GO astray,
Job 38:41 not see hr.'s ox *g. a.*
Ps. 58:3 *g. a.* as soon as born
  119:176 like sheep goes *g. a.*
  20:5 causeth righteous to *g. a.*
  28:10 whoso causeth right to *g. a.*

GO away,
Ex. 8:28 not *g.* very far away
Deut. 15:16 say, I will not *g. a.*
1 *Sam.* 24:19 he let one. *g. a.?*

GO
Job 4:21 doth not excel. *g. a.?*
  15:30 by breath of mouth *g. a.*
Jer. 51:40 escaped sword *g. a.*

GO back
Is. 3:14 I will roar and *g. a.*
Mat. 33:46 *g. a.* to ever. punish.
John 6:67 will ye also *g. b.?*
  14:28 how I said, I *g. a.* 16:7

GO their way
John 18:8 let these *g. their way*

GO thy way.
Dan. 12:13 *g. t. way* till the end
Acts 24:25 *g. thy w.* for this time

GO your way,
Mark 11:2 *g. your w.* into village
Luke 10:10 rec. you not, *g. y. w.*
Ex. 14:31 caused sea to *g. back*
Jos. 23:12 yc in any wise *g. back*
Jud. 11:35 mouth, I cannot *g. b.*
2 *K.* 20:9 shall the shadow *g. b.*
Ps. 80:18 not *g. back* from thee
Jer. 40:5 *g. back* to Gedaliah, son
Ezek. 24:14 I will not *g. back*

GO down,
Gen. 46:3 fear not to *g. d.* to Eg.
Num. 16:30 *g. d.* into the pit
Deut. 24:15 nor sun *g. d.* on hire
Jos. 10:13 son hasted not to *g. d.*
Jud. 7:10 fear to *g. d. g.* with P.
2 *Sam.* 11:8 *g. d.* to thy house.
2 *K.* 1:15 *g. down* with him
  20:10 shadow to *g. d.* ten deg.
Job 21:13 in moment *g. d.* to gr.
  33:24 all that *g. d.* to dust
  38:1 like th. *g. d.* to pit, 143:7
  55:15 let *g. d.* quick into hold
  107:23 that *g. d.* to sea in ships
  115:17 any that *g. d.* into silence
Prov. 5:4 her feet *g. d.* to death
Is. 5:14 ent out, as those *g. d.*
  8:7 woe to th. *g. d. to* Eg. 31:1
  33:18 *g. d.* into pit cannot hope
  60:20 sun sh. not *g. d.* nor moon
Jer. 50:27 let *g. d.* to slaughter
Ezek. 26:20 them that *g. d.* to the pit, 31:14; 32:18, 24, 25, 29, 30
  47:8 th. waters *g. d.* into desert
Amos 8:9 sun to *g. d.* at noon
Mic. 3:6 sun *g. d.* over prophets
Mark 13:15 him on ho. not *g. d.*
Acts 25:5 able to *g. d.* with me
Eph. 4:26 not let *g. d.* on wrath

GO forth,
Gen. 8:16 *g. f.* of the ark, thou
  42:15 not *g. f.* hence, except
2 *Sam.* 11:1 at time kings *g. f.*
  18:2 I will *g. f.* with you myself
  19:7 if thou *g. not f.* not tarry
1 *K.* 2:36 *g.* not *f.* any whither
  22:22 he said, I will *g. forth*
Is. 2:3 sh. *g. forth* of Zion, *Mic.* 4:2
  28:29 make his people to *g. f.*
  49:9 say to prisoners, *g. f.*
  17 make thee waste thee *g. f.*
  62:1 till righteou. thereof *g. f.*
Jer. 29:25 not *forth* into field
  14:18 If I *g. f.* into the field
  15:2 whither shall we *g. forth?*
  25:32 evil *g. f.* from nation to
  30:23 this shall *g. f.* in dances
  38:17 wilt *g. f.* to king of Baby.
  43:12 he shall *g. f.* in peace
  48:9 *g. f.* to be capt.
  50:8 in that day mossen. sh. *g. f.*
Dan. 11:44 he sh. *g. f.* with fury
Joel 2:16 let bridegr. *g. f.* cham.
Hab. 1:4 judgment never *g. f.*
Zec. 6:5 four spirits wh. *g. f.*
  6 black horses *g. f.* to north
  14:3 then sh. L. *g. f.* and fight
Mal. 4:2 ye sh. *g. f.* and grow
Mat. 24:26 Is in desert, *g.* not
Acts 16:3 would Paul have *g. f.*
Heb. 13:13 let us *g. forth* to him
Rev. 16:14 sp. of devils wh. *g. f.*

GO forward,
Ex. 14:15 speak to Is. they *g. f.*
2 *K.* 20:9 shadow *g. f.* ten deg.
Job 23:8 I *g. forw.* but he is not there

CRUDEN'S CONCORDANCE. 873

GO in, into, or not GO in.
Num. 4:19 A. and sons sh. g. in
8:15 after that sh. Levites g. in
27:17 g. out and g. in before
32:6 should not g. into the land
Deut. 1:36 Josh. sh. g. in thither
4:1 and g. in and possess. 8:1
Ps. 26:4 not g. in with dissem.
118:19 open gates, I will g. in
110:35 g. in path of thy com.
132:7 we will g. into his tabern.
Prov. 27:10 nor g. i. brother's h.
Is. 2:19 g. into holes of rocks
Jer. 4:5 let us g. into def. cities
36:5 I cannot g. into house of L.
42:14 we will g. into land of E.
19 L. said, g. ye not i. Egypt
Ezek. 46:10 when they g. into
Nah. 3:14 g. i. to clay, and tread
Zec. 6:10 g. into house of Josiah
Mat. 2:20 take child, g. into Isr.
7:13 many there be that g. in
20:4 g. into the vineyard, 7
21:2 g. into village, Luke 19:30
31 harlots g. into king. of God
22:9 g. into highways, bid to
23:13 neither g. in, nor suffer
26:18 g. into city, Mark 14:13
Mark 6:36 may g. into country
6:26 nor g. into town, nor tell
16:15 g. into all the world
Luke 13:24 and would not g. i.
John 10:9 he shall g. in and out
Acts 1:11 ye see him g. i. heaven
Rev. 17:8 beast shall g. i. perdi.
See CAPTIVITY.

GO in.
Gen. 16:2 g. in unto my maid
19:34 make drink wine, g. in
30:3 my maid Bilhah, g. in to
38:8 g. in unto brother's wife
Deut. 21:13 thou g. in to her
22:13 take a wife, g. in to her
25:5 husb. shall g. in to her
Jos. 23:12 make marriages, g. in
Jud. 15:1 will g. in to my wife
2 Sam. 16:21 g. in to faith. concu.
1 K. 1:13 ye sh. not g. in to them
Ezek. 23:44 as they g. in to wom.
Amos 2:7 man and father g. in

GO in peace.
Gen. 15:15 g. to thy fathers in p.
Ex. 4:18 g. in p. to thy father in p.
10:23 people g. to place in p.
Jud. 18:6 said to Danites, g. in p.
1 Sam. 1:17 E. said to H. g. in p.
20:42 Jona. said to Dav. g. in p.
25:35 David said to Ab. g. in p.
29:7 Achish said to D. g. in p.
2 Sam. 15:9 said to Abs. g. in p.
1 K. 2:6 let not head g. do. in p.
K. 5:19 Elisha said, g. in peace
Mark 5:31 g. in p. and he whole
Luke 7:50 saved thee, g. in p. 8:48
Acts 15:33 they were let g. in p.

Let us GO.
Gen. 37:17 let us g. to Dothan
Ex. 3:18 now let us g. three days'
journey, 5:3
5:8 they say, let us g. sac. 17
13:15 [h. would hardly l. us g.
Deut. 13:2 l. us g. aft. gods, 6:13
1 Sam. 9:9 let us g. to seer, 10
11:14 let us g. to Gilgal, and
14:1 let us g. to Philistines, 6
2 K. 6:2 let us g. to Jordan
1 Ch. 12:2 let us g. into h. of Lord
Is. 2:5 let us g. to mount. of L.
Jer. 4:5 let us g. into def. cities
35:11 let us g. drawn by palaces
35:11 let us g. to Jeru. for fear
43:16 let us g. to our people
51:9 let us g. one to country
Mark 1:38 let us g. to next towns
14:42 let us g. he that betrayeth
Luke 2:15 let us g. to Bethlehem
John 11:7 let us g. to Judea
15 let us g. to him; 16 that we
11:31 aries. let us g. hence
Acts 15:36 let us g. visit brethren
Heb. 6:1 let us g. to perfection

I will GO.
Gen. 13:9 I w. g. right, I w. g. l.
24:58 wilt g. with man? I w. g.
33:12 I w. g. bef. thee, Is. 45:2
45:28 I w. g. see him bef. I die
Num. 20:19 I will g. on feet
22:3 stand by burnt-off. I w. g.
Deut. 2:27 I will g. along high.
Jud. 1:3 I w. g. with me
4:8 if thou g. with me, I w. g.
9 I will surely g. with thee
10:20 I w. g. as at other times
Ruth 1:16 wh. thou goest, I w. g.
2 K. 3:6 he answered, I will g.
2 Chr. 18:3 said, I w. g. to battle

Ps. 43:4 then w. I g. to altar of
66:13 I will g. into thy house
71:16 I will g. in strength of L.
118:19 open gates, I will g. in
Jer. 2:25 strangers, after I will g.
Ezek. 38:11 I will g. to them.
Hos. 2:5 said, I w. g. after lovers
7 I will g. to my first husband
5:15 I will g. to my place, till
Mic. 1:8 I w. g. stript and naked
Zec. 8:21 seek the Lord, I will g.
Mat. 26:32 I w. g. before into
Galilee, Mark 14:28
Luke 15:18 I w. arise and g. to
Acts 16:5 hence I w. g. to Gent.

GO near.
Deut. 5:27 g. n. hear all L. says
2 Sam. 1:15 g. n. fall upon him
Job 31:37 as a prince wou. I g. n.
Acts 8:29 g. n. join to chariot

GO not, or not GO,
Ex. 33:15 if thy presence g. not
Num. 10:30 Hob. said, I will n. g.
20:20 he said, Thou shalt n. g.
22:12 said to Bal. shalt not g.
18 n. o. bey. word of L. 24:13
Deut. 3:27 shalt n. g. over Jordan
6:14 ye shall n. go after
gods, 1 K. 11:10
24:19 thou sh. n. g. to fetch it
32:52 thou shalt not g. thither
Jos. 8:4 g. n. far from the city
Jud. 20:8 we will n. g. to tents
Ruth 3:17 g. n. to mother
1 Sam. 17:39 D. said, I cannot g.
29:8 I may not g. to fight one.
2 Sam. 13:25 n. all g. would n. g.
2 K. 2:18 did I not say, g. n.?
1 Chr. 21:30 David could n. g.
2 Chr. 25:13 soldiers should n. g.
Prov. 4:13 take instruc. let n. g.
14 g. n. into way of evil men
22:24 with furious man sh. n. g.
Is. 12:12 shall n. g. with haste
Jer. 10:5 be borne, they cann. g.
16:8 sh. n. g. to house of feast
25:6 p. n. after other gods, 35:15
27:18 vessels left g. not to Baby.
42:19 g. not into Egypt, 43:2
40:12 thou shalt not g. unpun.
Lam. 4:18 cannot g. in streets
Ezek. 42:14 priests sh. not g.
Mat. 10:5 g. n. way of Gent.
Luke 10:7 g. n. fr. house to house
17:23 there, g. n. after, 21:8

GO over.
Deut. 3:25 let me g. o. see land
24 Joshua sh. g. o. before, 29
4:14 land whither ye g. over, 26;
31:13; 32:47
22 I must not g. o. Jordan
27:2 shalt not g. o. the heights
30:13 who shall g. o. sea for us
31:3 the Lord will g. o. before
31:3 thou shalt not g. o. thither
Jos. 1:2 arise, g. over this Jordan
Jud. 12:5 Eph. said, Let me g. o.
1 Sam. 14:1 let us g. to Ph. 6
14:6 to faint, could not g. o.
2 Sam. 15:22 to Ittai, g. o. and g.
19:37 Chimham, let him g. o.
Is. 8:7 come and g. over banks
11:15 make men g. o. dry-shod
51:23 bow down, we may g. o.
Jer. 41:10 Ishm. departed to g. o.

GO out.
Gen. 9:10 all that g. out of ark
21:11 women g. o. to draw wat.
43:1 every man g. o. from me
Ex. 6:11 let child. of Isr. g. out
4:26 behold, I g. out from thee
11:8 after that I will g. out
10 not let chil. of Israel g. out
12:22 none shall g. out of door
16:4 people g. o. and gather
23 no man g. o. on sev. day
21:2 in sev. year he sh. g. o.
3 came by himse. g. o. by him.;
4 he shall, g. out by himself
5 if serv. will g. out, I will g. o.
7 maid-serv. not g. o. as men
11 then shall she g. o. free
Lev. 6:13 fire on altar never g. o.
15:16 if a child. of Isr. g. out
21:12 nor g. out of sanctuary
25:28 in Jubilee it sh. g. o. 31
30 nor g. o. in Jub.; 54 sh. g. o.
Deut. 24:5 taken wife, not g. o.
28:25 thou shalt g. out one way
Jos. 2:19 who g. o. blood on head

Jud. 9:38 g. o. and fight them
10:20 will g. o. not aft. them
20:28 sh. I again g. o. to bat. to
1 Sam. 18:8 g. o. stand bes. fath.
20:11 let us g. o. into the field
28:1 Achish said, g. o. with me
2 Sam. 5:24 the L. sh. g. o. befo.
21:17 thou sh. g. no more o.
1 K. 15:17 not suf. any to g. o. or
come in to Asa, 2 Chr. 16:1
20:31 ropes on our heads, g. o.
1 Chr. 14:15 then shalt g. o. to bat
2 Chr. 18:21 g. o. be a lying spirit
20:17 to-morrow g. out against
26:18 g. o. of sanctuary, hast. tr.
30 yea, himself hasted to g. o.
Ps. 60:10 not g. o. with armies
60:10 not g. o. with armies
Prov. 22:10 scorner, contem. g. o.
Ec. 8:3 not hasty to g. o. of sight
Is. 52:11 depart, g. o. fr. thence
12 ye sh. not g. o. with haste
55:12 ye shall g. out with joy
Jer. 13:16 ev. o. of midst of her
Ezek. 15:7 shall g. out from fire
44:3 prince sh. g. o. same way
46:9 enter. by north, g. o. by s.
Amos 4:3 sh. g. out at breaches
Zec. 14:8 waters g. o. fr. J.
Mat. 25:6 bridegr. cometh, g. o.
Luke 9:5 when ye g. o. of that city
14:21 g. o. into streets and lanes
21 g. o. into high. and hedges
1 Cor. 5:10 must g. o. of world
Heb. 11:8 A. when he call. to g. o.
Rev. 3:12 over. g. no more out
20:8 sh. g. o. to deceive nations

GO in.
Gen. 11:3 let us make brick
g. to, let us build; 7
Ec. 2:1 g. to no now, I will prove
Is. 5:5 g. to, I tell what I will
Lam. 4:13 g. to, ye that say
5:1 g. to now, ye rich men

GO up.
Gen. 35:1 arise, g. up to Bethel, 3
41:33 let Isd. g. up with breth.
44:17 g. up in peace
50:6 Phar. said, g. up, bury fa.
Ex. 3:8 frogs g. up into houses
17:12 g. not up into mount
20:26 nor sh. g. up by steps
32:1 neither sh. not g. up Mt.
32:30 sinned a sin, I will g. up
33:1 g. up, thou and the people
3 I will not g. up in midst
34:21 not desire land, g. up
Lev. 19:16 thou shalt not g. up
and down as a tale-bearer
Num. 13:30 let g. up and pos. it
31 not able to g. up ag. people
14:42 g. not up; 44 pres. to g.
22:41 let hra.'s wife g. up
30:12 who sh. g. up to heaven
20:28 ye g. up to Jer. ag. again
Jud. 1:1 who g. up for us to fight
9 L. said, Judah sh. g. up, 20:18
2:1 I made you g. up out of Eg.
11:37 g. up and down on mount.
19:8 we may g. up against than
20:9 up by lot against v.; Gileah
18 which sh. g. up first to bat.
23 shall I g. up? 28 g. up nex.
1 Sam. 1:22 not g. up till child
6:20 to whom sh. h. g. up fr. us?
9:13 find him before he g. up
11 Samuel to g. up to place, 19
14:9 say, Tarry, will not g. up
2 Sam. 2:1 g. up into any of cities of
Jud. 9 L. said, g. up to Heb.
19:3 shall I g. up again, Will
15:20 I make thee g. up with me
23:13 shall I g. up to L. g.
that I should g. up ?
24:18 g. up, rear alt. 1 Chr. 21:18
1 K. 12:4 not g. up, 2 Chr. 11:4
17 people g. up to do sacrifice
27:2 where g. up ? 28 g. up, no
Jud. 17:14 up to land of Jerus.
18:25 g. up, leave it alone
22:6 shall I g. to R. g. up?
1 Chr. 14:10 g. up, ? 2 Chr. 18:14
22:5 when he g. up before
19:11 hope unto me, will g. up
2 Chr. 32:1 g. up to their houses
3:2 up to house of G. of Jacob
4:1 of L. pledges when we g. up
Jud. 5:11 when g. be might
1 Sam. 22:1 Dav. who g. at hai.
32:21 his part is that g. to bat.
18:25 bef. there be g. up to bat.
20 when I g. to battle
19:11 make g. to battle

Ezr. 7:9 to g. up from Babylon
18 minded to g. up, go with me
4:3 fox g. up he break down
Ps. 104:8 g. up by mountains
132:3 I will not g. up into bed
Cant. 6:6 sheep g. up from wash.
7:8 I will g. up to palm-tree
Is. 2:3 let us g. up to mountain
of Lord, Mic. 4:2
7:6 let us g. up against Judah
15:5 with weep. sh. they g. up
21:2 g. up, E.; 34:10 smoke g. up
35:9 nor ravenous beast g. up
52:2 g. up against thine land
Jer. 5:10 g. ye upon her walls
6:4 and let us g. up at noon
21:2 Nebuchadnezzar may g. up
23:30 g. up to Lebanon, and cry
31:6 let us g. up Z. to the L.
46:8 I will g. up and cov. earth
11 g. up to Gilead, take balm
48:5 continual weep. sh. g. up
50:3 g. up to Kedar, spoil
50:2 g. up aga. land of Merath.
Ezek. 38:11 g. up to unwalled v.
40:26 seven steps to g. up to it
Hos. 4:15 nei. g. up to Bethaven
Hag. 1:8 g. up to mount, bring
Zec. 14:16 g. up fr. year to year
Mat. 20:18 we g. up to Jerusal.
Mark 10:33; Luke 18:31
Luke 14:10 Friend, g. up higher
John 7:8 g. up to feast, I g. not
Acts 15:2 g. up to Jer. about qu.
21:4 Paul not g. up to Jerus. 12
25:9 wilt thou g. up to Jeru. ?

GO a whoring.
Ex. 34:15 g. a whor. after gods
16 sons, daughters g. a whor.
Lev. 20:5 cut off all that g. a w.
Num. 15:39 ye use to g. a whor.
Deut. 31:16 people will g. a who.
2 Chr. 21:13 Je. made Ju. g. a w.
Ps. 73:27 destroyed all g. a who.
Ezek. 6:9 g. a whor. after idols

GOEST.
Gen. 28:15 keep thee wh. thou g.
32:17 whi. g. thou ? Jud. 19:17;
Zec. 2:2; John 13:36; 16:5
Ex. 33:16 that thou g. with us.
34:12 no cove. whither thou g.
Num. 14:14 g. bef. them by day
Deut. 7:1 bringeth thee into
12:20 cut off nations whit.g.
20:1 g. to battle, seest, 21:10
23:20 God bless thee whither
thou g. Jos. 1:7
26:2 blessed when thou g. out
6 cursed when thou g. out
21 prestilence whither thou g.
31 plucked land whi. thou g.
32:50 die in mount whither g.
Jos. 1:9 L. with thee whi. th. g.
Jud. 1:3 g. take a wife of Phili.
Ruth 1:16 whi. thou g. I will go
2 Sam. 15:9 where. g. with us ?
1 K. 2:37 day g. over brook, 42
Prov. 4:12 when g. steps not sr.
6:22 when thou g. it shall lead
Ec. 3:1 keep thy foot, g. to ho.
8:10 wisdom in grave whith. g.
9:10 beasts for prey whith. thou g.
Mat. 8:19 I will follow whither-
soever thou g. Luke 9:57
Luke 12:58 thou g. with adver.
John 11:8 g. thou thither again ?
14:5 we know not whi. thou g.

GOETH.
Ex. 7:15 he g. out into water
22:20 dirt, by that sun g. down
28:29 Aaron bear when he g.
30 hold sund heard when he g.
34:22 out that g. on all four
14:16 that g. into house unclean
22:3 seed g. from him, 22:4
16:17 none to his sanct. when g.
23:21 when if g. fr. holy place
27:21 where it g. ag. holy thing
Num. 5:29 when wife g. aside
Deut. 1:30 L. which g. before
20:4 Lord your G. g. with you
23:9 host g. a. keep from evil
23 what g. out of lips, perform
24:13 pledge when sun g. do.
Jud. 5:31 when g. he might
1 Sam. 22:14 Dav. who g. at hai.
32:21 his part is that g. to bat.

CRUDEN'S CONCORDANCE. 875

GOD

Rev. 5:9 redeemed us *to* G. by b.
12:5 child caught up *unto* G.
14:4 first-fr. *unto* G. and Lamb
See TRUE.

With GOD.
Gen. 5:22 En. walked *w.* G. 24
6:9 N. walked *w.* G.; 32:24 Jac.
Ex. 19:17 br. peo. to meet *w.* G.
1 *Sam.* 14:45 wrought *w.* G.
2 *Sam.* 23:5 ho. be not so *w.* G.
2 *Chr.* 33:21 forbear med. *w.* G.
Job 9:2 sh. man be just *with* G.
13:3 I desire to reason *with* G.
16:21 plead for a man *with* G.
25:4 can a man be just *w.* G. ?
27:13 por. of wicked man *w.* G.
34:9 sh. delight himself *w.* G.
23 he enter into judg. *with* G.
37:22 *with* G. is ter. majesty
Ps. 78:8 spirit not stead. *w.* G.
Hos. 11:12 Judah yet ruleth *w.* G.
12:3 Jacob had power *with* G.
Mat. 19:26 *w.* G. all things possi.
Mark 10:27; *Lu.* 1:37; 18:27
Luke 1:30 hast found favor *w.* G.
2:52 increased in favor *with* G.
John 1:1 the Word was *with* G.
5:18 him. equal *w.* G. *Phil.* 2:6
Rom. 2:11 no resp. of pers. *w.* G.
5:1 by faith, we have pe. *w.* G.
9:14 is there unright. *with* G. ?
1 *Cor.* 3:9 we are labourers *w.* G.
19 wisdom of world fool. *w.* G.
7:24 ev. man therein abide *w.* G.
2 *Thes.* 1:6 a right. thing *with* G.
Jam. 4:4 friendsh. enmity *w.* G.
1 *Pet.* 2:20 is acceptable *w.* G.

Would GOD. *See* WOULD.

Your GOD.
Gen. 43:23 y. G. hath given treas.
Ex. 8:25 go ye, sacrifice to y. G.
Lev. 11:45 bringing you out of Egypt: be *your* G. 22:33; 25:38; *Num.* 15:41
26:12 I will be *your* God ye my people, *Jer.* 7:23; 11:4; 30:22; *Ezek.* 36:28
Num. 10:10 a memorial bef. y. G.
15:40 my com. to holy to y. G.
Jos. 24:27 lest ye deny *your* G.
1 *Sam.* 10:19 have rejected y. G.
2 *Chr.* 32:14 that y. G. deliver y.
15 much less sh. y. G. deliver ?
Is. 35:4 y. G. come with veng.
42:1 com. my people, saith y. G.
9 cities of Judah, behold y. G.
59:2 separ. bet. you and y. G.
Joel 2:26 name L. y. G. saith Lord
Deut. 2:47 of a truth it is, y. G. is
Hos. 1:9 I will not be *your* G.
John 8:54 ye say that he is y. G.
20:17 ascend to my God, y. G.
See LORD *your* God.

GODDESS.
1 *K.* 11:5 Sol. went after the g.
37 worshipped Ashtor. the g.
Acts 19:27 temple of gr. g. Diana
35 Ephesians worshippers of g.
37 nor yet blasph. of your g.

GODHEAD,
Acts 17:29 nor think g. like gold
Rom. 1:20 his eter. power and g.
Col. 2:9 in him fulness of the g.

GODLY.
Ps. 4:3 L. set apart him that is g.
12:1 help, for the g. man ceas.
32:6 for this every one g. pray
Mal. 2:15 he might seek g. seed
2 *Cor.* 1:12 in g. sincer. our con.
7:9 sorry after a g. manner, 11
10 for g. sorrow worketh rep.
11:2 jeal. over you with g. jeal.
2 *Tim.* 3:12 all that live g. in C.
Tit. 2:12 that ye should live g.
Heb. 12:28 serve G. with g. fear
2 *Pet.* 2:9 how to deliver the g.
3 *John* 6 bring for. after g. sort

GODLINESS.
1 *Tim.* 2:2 may lead a life in g.
10 becometh women profess. g.
3:16 great is the mystery of g.
4:7 exer. thyself rather unto g.
8 g. is profit. unto all things
6:3 the doctrine according to g.
5 supposing that gain is g.
6 g. with contentment is gain
11 follow righteousness, g. fai.
2 *Tim.* 3:5 having a form of g.
Tit. 1:1 truth which is after g.
2 *Pet.* 1:3 things pertain to g.
6 add to g. brotherly kind. 7.
3:11 persons ought to be in g.

GOD-WARD.
Ex. 18:19 be thou for peo. to G.

GOD

2 *Cor.* 3:4 have we thro. C. to G.
1 *Thes.* 1:8 faith to G. is spread.

GODS.
Gen. 3:5 ye shall be as g.
31:30 where, hast stolen my g. ?
Ex. 12:12 ag. all g. of Egypt
20:23 sh. not make g. of silver
22:28 thou sh. not revile the g.
23:24 shalt not bow to their g.
32 make no cove. with their g.
32:1 these be thy g. O Israel, 8
31 they have made g. of gold
34:15 go a whoring after their g.
17 make no molt. g. *Lev.* 19:4
Num. 25:2 people to sac. of g.
33:4 the Egyptians' g. L. exec. judgme. *Jer.* 43:12, 13; 46:25
Deut. 7:25 im. of their g. burn
10:17 Lord your G. is God of g.
12:3 hew down im. of their g.
30 inquire not after their g.
31 have done abomina. to their g. sons and dau. in fire to g.
13:7 entice thee to g. of people
20:18 not do as they to their g.
32:37 sh. say, Where are th. g. ?
Jos. 22:22 Lord God of g. know.
23:7 nor mention of their g.
Jud. 5:8 they chose new g.
6:10 fear not g. of Amorites
10:14 cry to g. ye have chosen
17:5 Micah had a house of g.
18:24 ye have taken my g.
Ruth 1:15 sister-in-law ba. to g.
1 *Sam.* 4:8 g. smote Egypt.
6:5 his hand from off your g.
17:43 Phil. cursed Da. by his g.
28:13 I saw g. as. out of earth
2 *Sam.* 7:23 redeem. from th. g.
1 *K.* 11:8 turn your heart after g.
8 Solomon sacrificed to their g.
12:28 behold thy g. O Israel
18:24 call name of your g. 25
19:2 let g. do so to me, 20:10
20:23 their g. are g. of hills
1 *K.* 17:29 every nation made g.
33 feared the L. served own g.
18:33 hath g. delivered his land ?
19:12; 2 *Chr.* 32:13, 14; *Is.* 36:18; 37:12
34 wh. are g. of IT. ? *Is.* 36:19
10:18 cast g. in. fire, were no g.
1 *Chr.* 5:25 went a whoring *af.* g.
10:10 armor in house of their g.
14:12 left their g. David burnt
1 *Chr.* 13:8 calv. Jero. ma. for g.
9 a priest to th. that are no g.
23:14 tur. g. of Seir to be his g.
28:23 Ahaz sacrificed to the g.
Ezr. 1:7 vessels in house of g.
Ps. 82:1 he judg. among the g.
6 said, Ye are g. *John* 10:34
136:2 give thanks unto God of g.
Is. 21:9 Bab. fall. her g. broken
41:23 we may know yc are g.
42:17 images, Ye are our g.
Jer. 2:11 changes g. are no g. ?
28 where are thy g. thou made ?
to number of cit. are thy g.
11:12
5:7 sworn by th. that are no g.
10:11 g. have not made heaven
11:12 to g. they offer incense
16:20 man make g. are no g. ?
43:35 that burn. incense to g.
Dan. 2:11 can show it, except g.
47 your God is a God of g.
4:8 in whom is spirit of holy g.
9 sp. of g. is in thee, 18; 5:14
5:4 g. of gold and silver, 23
11 like the wisdom of the g.
14:8 carry into E. g. w. princes
23 speak things ag. God of g.
Hos. 14:3 ne. say, Ye are our g.
Nah. 1:14 out of house of thy g.
John 10:35 if he called them g.
Acts 14:11 the g. are come down
19:26 be no g. made with hands
1 *Cor.* 8:5 called g. there be g.
Gal. 4:8 ser. to th. wh. are no g.
See SERVE.

All GODS.
Ex. 18:11 L. greater than all g.
1 *Chr.* 16:25 ab. all g. *Ps.* 96:4
26 all g. of peo. idols, *Ps.* 96:5
97:7 worship all g. *Ps.* 135:5
Ps. 95:3 L. is a K. above all g.
97:7 worship all g.; 9 ab. all g.
Zep. 2:11 famish all g. of earth

Among the GODS.
Ex. 15:11 am. t. g. who like g. L.
2 *K.* 18:35 who a. t. g. could del. cou. ? 2 *Chr.* 32:14; *Is.* 36:20
Ps. 86:8 a. t. g. none like thee

GOL

Other GODS.
Ex. 20:3 no other g. before me, *Deut.* 5:7
23:13 make no mention of o. g.
Deut. 6:14 ye shall not go after o. g. 11:28; 28:14; 1 *K.* 11:10; *Neh.* 7:70
7:4 turn thy son to serve o. g.
8:19 if thou walk after o. g.
17:3 hath gone and served o. g.
29:26; *Jos.* 23:16; *Jud.* 10:13; 1 *Sam.* 8:8; *Jer.* 11:10
18:20 speak in name of o. g.
30:17 o. g. and serve, *Jer.* 22:9
31:18 that day turned to o. g.
20 will they turn to other g.
Jud. 2:12 forsook L. fol. other g.
17 went a whoring after o. g.
19 follow. other g. to serve th.
1 *Sam.* 26:19 say, Go serve o. g.
1 *K.* 9:9 have taken hold upon other g. 2 *Chr.* 7:22
11:4 wives turned heart af. o. g.
14:9 hast gone and made o. g.
2 *K.* 5:17 not offer sacri. to o. g.
17:7 Is. sinned and feared o. g.
35 ye shall not fear o. g. 37, 38
22:17 and burnt incense to oth. g. 2 *Chr.* 34:25; *Jer.* 1:16; 19:4
2 *Chr.* 28:25 Ahaz bur. in. to o. g.
Jer. 7:6 nor walk after other g.
9 o. g. wh. ye know not, 13; 10
16:11 fur. me, walked after o. g.
44:5 burn. no incense to other g.
8 burning incense to o. g. 15
Hos. 3:1 look to o. g. love wine
See SERVE.

Strange GODS.
Gen. 35:2 put a. s. g. 1 *Sam.* 7:3
4 gave Jacob s. g. *Jos.* 24:23
Deut. 32:16 provoked with s. g.
Jos. 24:20 forsake L. serve s. g.
Jud. 10:16 put away their s. g.
2 *Chr.* 14:3 Asa took altar of s. g.
33:15 Josiah took away s. g.
Jer. 5:19 as ye served strange g.
Acts 17:18 a setter forth of s. g.

GOG

1 *Chr.* 5:4 ; *Ezek.* 38:2, 3, 16, 18; 39:11
Rev. 20:8 G. and Magog, to gath.

GOLD.

Gen. 2:11 land of Havilah, is g.
12 the g. of that land is good
41:42 put chain of g. on Jos.
Ex. 20:23 sh. make gods of g.
25:12 shalt cast four rings of g. for ark, 27; 26:29; 36:33, 26, 37; 37:3, 13
28:5 take g. and blue, and pur.
6:4 g. of offerings they ma. of g.
8 oracle overlaid w. g. *Ps.* 47:6
10:21 ve. of Le. p. g. 2 *Chr.* 4:22
1 *Chr.* 28:17 p. g. for flesh-hooks
Job 28:19 wisd. not val. wi. p. g.
21:2 a crown of p. g. on head
Rev. 21:18 city p. g.; 21 street

GOLD, with silver.
Gen. 24:35 A. abi. rich in s. and g. 24
44:8 steal of lord's hon. s. or g.
Ex. 3:22 jewels of silver and g.
11:2; 12:35
25:3 this offering, take s. and g.
31:4 in g. and brass, 35:32
Num. 22:18 ho. fu. s. and g. 24:13
31:22 only g. and s. abide fire
Deut. 7:25 shalt not des. s. and g.
8:13 s. and g. is multiplied
17:17 sh. he multiply s. and g.
29:17 seen their idols, s. and g.
Jos. 6:19 s. and g. con. to L. 24
22:8 ret. to tents with s. and g.
2 *Sam.* 8:11 silver and g. David dedicated, 1 *K.* 7:51
21:4 will have no s. or g. of Sa.
1 *K.* 15:15 Asa brought into ho. of L. s. and g. 2 *Chr.* 15:18
15 Asa took s. and g. 2 *Chr.* 16:2
19 s. pr. of s. and g. 2 *Chr.* 16:3
20:3 s. and g. is mine; 5 s. and g.
2 overlaid cherub. with g. 2 *Chr.* 3:10
Ezr. 1:4 help with silver and g.
2:69 gave s. and g.; 7:15
8:25 weighed silver and g. 33
Est. 1:6 beds were of g. and s.
Job 22:1 vein for s. a place for g.
28:15 not gotten for g.
Ps. 68:13 with s. feathers w. g.
105:37 br. forth with s. and g.
115:4 idols are s. and g. 135:15
119:72 law better than g. and s.
Prov. 8:10 not silver receive knowledge rather than g.
17:3 fining-pot for s. fur. for g.
25:11
22:1 favor rather than s. or g.
33:41 apples of g. in pict. of s.

GOL

2 *Cor.* 4:7 cand'sticks of g.; 8 ba.
23 snuffers, censers, spoons, g.
9:18 steps to throne, foots. g.
12:9 Shishak carried shield of g.
Ezr. 8:27 copper precious as g.
Neh. 7:70 Tirsh. gave 1,000 dr. g.
71 chief of Ath. gave g.; 72
Job 22:24 lay up as dust g. of O.
23:10 I shall come forth like g.
28:6 earth hath the dust of g.
15 cannot be gotten for g.
16 it cannot be valued with g.
17 g. and crys. cannot equal it
31:24 if I made g. my hope
33:10 he esteem riches? not g.
42:11 gave Job an ear-ring of g.
Ps. 19:10 more to be des. than g.
45:9 stand queen in p. of Ophir
72:15 him be given g. of Sheba
Prov. 11:22 je. of g. in swine's s.
16:16 better to get wis. than g.
20:15 g. and a multi. of rubies
Cant. 1:10 comely g. chains g.
3:14 as g. rings set with beryl
Is. 30:22 ornament of im. of g.
40:19 spreadeth it over with g.
60:17 for brass I will bring g.
Jer. 4:30 deckest with orna. of g.
Lam. 4:1 how is g. become dim
Ezek. 27:22 merchants oc. wi. g.
Dan. 2:38 head of g.; 3:1 im. g.
5:23 hast praised the gods of g.
29 chain of g. about Dan. neck
Zec. 4:2 a candlestick all of g.
13:9 I will try th. as g. is tried
Mat. 2:11 they pres. to him g.
23:16 swear by g. of the temple
17 whe. greater, g. or temple ?
1 *Tim.* 2:9 not adorned with g. or pearls, 1 *Pet.* 3:3
Heb. 9:4 ark over. round with g.
Jam. 2:2 come man with g. ring
1 *Pet.* 1:7 faith more pre. than g.
Rev. 3:18 to buy of me g. tried
4:4 elders on heads crowns of g.
9:7 locusts on heads crowns g.
17:4 woman was decked with g.
18:16 great city decked with g.

See BEATEN, CROWN, FINE.

Pure GOLD.
Ex. 25:11 overlay ark with pure g. 24; 30:3; 37:2, 11, 26
17 a mercy-seat of p. g. 37:6
29 dishes, of pure g. 37:16, 23
31 cand., p. g. 37:17; 1 *K.* 7:49
38 snuff dishes p. g. 2 *Chr.* 4:22
37:4 chains of p. g. 22; 39:15
1 K. 6:20 oracle overlaid w. p. g.
10:21 ve. of Le. p. g. 2 *Chr.* 4:22
1 *Chr.* 28:17 p. g. for flesh-hooks
Job 28:19 wisd. not val. wi. p. g.
21:2 a crown of p. g. on head
Rev. 21:18 city p. g.; 21 street

CRUDEN'S CONCORDANCE. 877

CRUDEN'S CONCORDANCE. 879

GOT

GOSHEN.
Gen. 45:10 dwell in land of G.
46:34; 47:4, 6, 27
Ex. 8:22; 9:26; *Jos.* 10:41; 11:16; 15:51

GOSPEL.
Mark 1:1 beginning of *g.* of J. C.
15 said, Repent and believe *g.*
8:35 lose life for my sake and *g.*
10:29 for my sake and *g.*
13:10 the *g.* must be published
Acts 15:7 by my mouth hear *g.*
20:24 the *g.* of the grace of God
Rom. 1:1 separat. to the *g.* of G.
9 I serve with my spirit in *g.*
16 not ashamed of *g.* of Christ
2:16 judge secrets ac. to my *g.*
10:16 have not all obeyed the *g.*
11:28 concerning *g.* are enemies
15:16 ministering the *g.* of God
29 blessing of the *g.* of Christ
16:25 estab. you according to *g.*
1 *Cor.* 4:15 begotten you thro' *g.*
9:12 lest we hinder *g.* of Christ
17 a dispensation of *g.* is com.
18 I preach *g.* I may make *g.*
of Christ with. charge; that
I abuse not my po. in the *g.*
23 this I do for the *g.* sake
2 *Cor.* 4:3 if *g.* hid, hid to them
4 light of glor. *g.* should shine
8:18 whose praise is in *g.*
9:13 prof. subjection to the *g.*
11:4 receive another *g. Gal.* 1:6
Gal. 1:7 would pervert *g.* of Chr.
2:2 communicated *g.* I preach
5 truth of *g.* might continue
7 *g.* of uncir. committed to me
14 according to truth of the *g.*
Eph. 1:13 *g.* of your salvation
3:6 partake prom. in Chr. by *g.*
6:15 preparation of *g.* of peace
19 make known mystery of *g.*
Phil. 1:5 fellowship in the *g.*
7 def. and confirmation of *g.*
12 fallen out to furthera. of *g.*
27 let your conversation be as
becom. *g.* striv. for faith of *g.*
2:22 hath served with me in *g.*
4:3 help-women with me in *g.*
15 in the beginning of the *g.*
Col. 1:5 heard hef. of truth of *g.*
23 not moved from hope of *g.*
1 *Thes.* 1:5 *g.* came not in word
2:2 bold to speak the *g.* of God
4 to be put in trust with *g.*
8 willing to impart not *g.* only
3:2 Ti. our fellow-laborer in *g.*
2 *Thes.* 1:8 on them that obey
not the *g.*, 1 *Pet.* 4:17
2 *Ti.* 1:10 according to *g.* of G.
2 *Tim.* 1:8 partaker of affli. of *g.*
10 immortality to light thro' *g.*
2:8 J. C. raised according to *g.*
Phile. 13 minist. in bonds of *g.*

GOSPEL, *with* preach, ed, ing.
Mat. 4:23 Jesus went *preaching*
the *g.* 9:35; *Mark* 1:14
11:5 poor have *g. p. Luke* 7:22
24:14 *g.* be *p.* 26:13; *Mark* 14:9
Mark 16:15 *p. g.* to ev. creature
Luke 4:18 anointed me to *p. g.*
9:6 *p.* the *g.* and healing
20:1 he taught and *preached g.*
Acts 8:25 *pre. g.* to Samaritans
10:36 L. hod called us to *p. g.*
Rom. 1:15 I am ready to *p. g.*
15:19 beautiful feet that *p. g.*
15:19 I have fully *pre. g.* of Ch.
20 so have I strived to *prea. g.*
1 *Cor.* 1:17 not to bapt. but *pre. g.*
9:14 that he, *p.* should live of *g.*
16 tho' I *p. g.* nothing to glory
of, woe to me if I *pre.* not *g.*
18 when I *p. g.* I may make *g.*
17 a man have *g.* which I *pre.*
2 *Cor.* 2:12 I came to T. to *pre. g.*
10:14 as far as to you in *p. g.*
11:7 I *pr.* to you freely the *g.*
Gal. 1:8 tho' we *pr.* any other *g.*
11 *p. g.* of me not after man
2:2 *pren.* before the *g.* to Abra.
4:13 infirmity of flesh I *p. g.*
1 *Thes.* 2:9 we *p.* to you *g.* of G.
Heb. 4:2 to us was *g.* preached
1 *Pet.* 1:12 them that *pre.* the *g.*
25 which by *g. b. pr.* to you
4:6 for this cause was the *g. p.*
Rev. 14:6 having everl. *g.* to *p.*

GOT.
Gen. 39:12 Jos. *g.* him out, 13
Ps. 44:3 *g.* not land by own sw.
Ec. 2:7 I *g.* servant, and maidens

GOTTEN.
Gen. 4:1 I have *g.* a man

GRA

Ex. 14:18 when I have *g.* honor
Lev. 6:4 thing he hath deceit. *g.*
Deut. 8:17 hand hath *g.* wealth
2 *Sam.* 17:13 the *g.* into a city
Job 28:15 wisdom not *g.* for gold
31:25 rejoic. bec. hand *g.* much
Ps. 98:1 arm hath *g.* victory
Prov. 13:11 wealth *g.* by vanity
20:21 inheritance *g.* hastily
Ec. 1:16 *g.* more wisdom than all
Is. 15:7 abundance *g.* they carry
Ezek. 28:4 wisdom hast *g.* riches
Dan. 9:15 thou hast *g.* renown
Rev. 15:2 them that *g.* victory

1 *K.* 21:7 dost *g.* kingdom of Is.?
Job 34:17 shall he that hateth *g.*?
Ps. 67:4 thou sh. *g.* the nations

GOVERNMENT, S.
Is. 9:6 *g.* shall be upon shoulder
7 of inc. of his *g. sh.* be no end
22:21 I commit *g.* to his hand
1 *Cor.* 12:28 *g.* diversi. of tongues
2 *Pet.* 2:10 them that despise *g.*

GOVERNOR.
Gen. 42:6 Jos. *g.* over land, 43:26
1 *K.* 18:3 Ob. *g.* over Ahab's ho.
1 *Chr.* 29:22 anointed S. chief *g.*
Ezr. 5:14 C. deliv. vessels to *g.*
Neh. 5:14 not eaten bread of *g.*
18 required not the bread of *g.*
Ps. 22:28 he is *g. am.* the nation
Jer. 30:21 *g.* sh. proceed fr. them
40:5 go back to Gedaliah the *g.*
41:2 Ish. smote Gedaliah the *g.*
Hag. 1:14 L. stirred up Zerub. *g.*
2:2 speak to Zerub. the *g.* 21
Zec. 9:7 eh. be as a *g.* in Judah
Mal. 1:8 offer it now to thy *g.*
Mat. 2:6 out of thee sh. come *g.*
27:11 if this come to *g.'s* ears
John 2:8 bear to *g.* of the feast
Acts 24:1 Informed *g.* against P.
2 *Cor.* 11:32 the *g.* under Aretas
Jam. 3:4 ships turned wh. *g.* list.

GOVERNORS.
Judg. 5:9 my heart low, *g.* of Isr.
11 out of Machir came down *g.*
Ezr. 8:36 delivered com. to *g.*
Neh. 2:7 let letters be given to *g.*
5:15 the *g.* chargeable to people
Dan. 3:48 made Dan. chief of *g.*
Zec. 12:5 *g.* of Judah shall say
6 will make *g.* of J. like hearth
Mat. 7:18 sh. be brought bef. *g.*
Gal. 4:2 under tutors and *g.*
1 *Pet.* 2:14 submit yourself. to *g.*

GOURD, S.
2 *K.* 4:39 one gathered wild *g.*
Jon. 4:6 God prepared *g.* J. glad
7 a worm smote *g.* it withered
10 thou hast had pity on the *g.*
GOZAN. 2 *K.* 17:6; 18:11; 19:12; 1 *Chr.* 5:26; *Is.* 37:12

GRACE.
Ezr. 9:8 little space *g.* showed
from L. 9:11 E. obtained *g.* in sight
Ps. 45:2 *g.* poured into lips
84:11 Lord is a sun, will give *g.*
Prov. 1:9 an ornament of *g.*
3:22 so shall they be life and *g.*
34 giveth *g.* to lowly, *Jam.* 4:6
4:9 to head ornament of *g.*
22:11 for *g.* of lips king his fri.
Zec. 4:7 shoutings, crying, *g. g.*
12:10 will pour the Spirit of *g.*
John 1:17 begotten of F. full of *g.*
16 have all received *g.* for *g.*
17 *g.* and truth came by J. C.
Acts 4:33 great *g.* was on them
14:3 testimony to word of his *g.*
26 which believed thro' *g.*
20:32 com. you to word of *g.*
Rom. 1:5 by wh. we received *g.*
7 *g.* and peace from G. our F.
1 *Cor.* 1:3; *1 Phi.* 1:2; *Col.*
1:2; *Eph.* 1:2; *Phil.* 1:2; *Gal.*
1:3; 1 *Thes.* 1:1; 2 *Thes.* 1:2; *Phile.* 3
3:24 justified freely by his *g.*
4:4 reward is not reckoned of *g.*
16 that it might be by *g.*
5:2 we have access into this *g.*
17 receive abundance of *g.*
20 sin abounded, *g.* much more
21 *g.* reign thro' righteousness
Rom. 6:1 in. in sin, that *g.* abound?
14 under *g.* 15 bec. under *g.*?
11:5 according to election of *g.*
6 if by *g.* no more of works
23 if thou art a *g.* God
12:3 through *g.* given unto me
6 gifts differing according to *g.*
15:15 the *g.* given to me of God
1 *Cor.* 10:30 if I by *g.* be partak.
15:10 *g.* bestowed not in vain

GRA

2 *Cor.* 4:15 *g.* red. to glory of G.
8:6 finish in you the same *g.*
7 see that ye abound in this *g.*
19 travel with us with this *g.*
9:8 G. is able to make *g.* abound
12:9 my *g.* is sufficient for thee
Gal. 1:6 who called you to *g.*
15 G. who called me by his *g.*
2:9 when James perceived *g.*
5:4 justi. by law, fallen from *g.*
Eph. 1:6 praise of the glory of *g.*
7 according to riches of *g.*
2:5 by *g.* saved through faith, 8
7 might show the riches of *g.*
3:8 to me is this *g.* given
4:7 to ev. one of us is given *g.*
29 may minister *g.* to hearers
6:24 *g.* with all that love L. J.
Phil. 1:7 are all partakers of *g.*
Col. 3:16 sing. with *g.* in hearts
4:6 let speech be alway with *g.*
18 *g.* be with you, 2 *Tim.* 4:22;
Tit. 3:15; *Heb.* 13:25
2 *Thes.* 2:16 hope through *g.*
1 *Tim.* 1:2 *g.* mercy, and peace
from G. our Father, 2 *Tim.*
1:2; *Tit.* 1:4; 2 *John* 3
1:14 *g.* of Lord abundant
6:21 *g.* be with thee. Amen
Heb. 1:11 *g.* mercy in sight of
Eut. 2:8 the king *g.* my petition
Job 6:5 G. *g.* the thing I long for
Ps. 20:4 *g.* thee to thine heart
83:7 O Lord, *g.* us salvation
119:29 *g.* me thy law graciously
140:8 *g.* not, O L. de. of wicked
Mat. 20:21 *g.* my two sons may
sit, *Mark* 10:37
Luke 1:74 *g.* to us that we being
Acts 4:29 *g.* with boldness
Rom. 15:5 G. *g.* you to be like-m.
Eph. 3:16 *g.* you to be strength.
2 *Tim.* 1:18 L. *g.* he find mercy
Rev. 3:21 *g.* to sit in my throne

GRANTED.
1 *Chr.* 4:10 God *g.* what he requ.
Ezr. 1:13 and knowl. Is. *g.* thee
Ezr. 7:6 king *g.* all his requests
Neh. 2:8 *g.* accord. to hand of G.
Est. 5:6 petit. sh. be *g.* 7:2; 9:12
9:13 let it be *g.* to Jews in Shu.
Job 10:12 hast *g.* life and favor
Prov. 10:24 desire of right. be *g.*
Acts 11:18 *G.* *g.* Gen. repentance
14:3 *g.* signs to be done by han.
Rev. 19:8 *g.* she sh. be arrayed

GRAPE.
Lev. 19:10 not gather *g.* of wine
Deut. 32:14 drink blood of *g.*
Job 15:33 shake off unripe *g.*
Cant. 2:13 *g.* give good smell
7:12 the tender *g.* appear
Is. 18:5 sour *g.* is ripening
Jer. 31:29 have eaten a sour *g.*
30 ev. man that eateth sour *g.*
Mic. 7:1 as *g.* gleanings of vint.

GRAPE-GATHERER.
Jer. 6:9 turn back hand as *g. g.*
49:9 if *g. g.* come, *Ob.* 5

GRAPES.
Gen. 40:10 clusters bro. ripe *g.*
49:11 washed clothes in bl. of *g.*
Lev. 25:5 nor gather *g.* undressed
11 in jubilee, nor ga. *g.* of vine
Num. 6:3 nor shall eat moist *g.*
13:20 time of the first ripe *g.*
23 cut a branch with clus. of *g.*
Deut. 23:24 mayest eat *g.* thy fill
24:21 wh. thou gatherest the *g.*
28:30 plant vine. not ga. *g.* 39
32:32 their *g.* are *g.* of gall
Judg. 8:2 gleaning of *g.* of Ephr.
9:27 went out, gathered their *g.*
Cant. 2:15 vines have tender *g.*
7:7 breasts are like clust. of *g.*
Is. 5:2 it should bring forth *g.*
4 bring forth *g.* brw. wild *g.*?
17:6 gleaning *g.* shall be left
24:13 e when vintage is done
Jer. 8:13 there sh. be no *g.* on v.
25:30 as they that tread *g.*
49:9 gleaning *g. Ob.* 5
Ezek. 18:2 have eaten sour *g.*
Hos. 9:10 Israel as *g.* in wilderness
Amos 9:13 treader of *g.* ov. sower
Mat. 7:16 men ga. *g.* of thorns?
Luke 6:44 nor of brambles ga. *g.*
Rev. 14:18 ga. *g.* are fully ripe

GRASS.
Gen. 1:11 earth bring forth *g.*
12 the earth brought forth *g.*
Num. 22:4 licketh up *g.* of field
Deut. 11:15 send *g.* for thy cattle
29:23 nor any growth there in
32:2 as small rain upon *g.*
2 *Sam.* 23:4 the *g.* springing out

GRA

Gen. 33:11 G. hath dealt *g.* with
Ps. 119:29 grunt me thy law *g.*
Hos. 14:2 receive us *g.*

GRAFT, ED.
Rom. 11:17 wild olive-t. wert *g.*
13 that I might be *g.* in
23 they sh. be *g. G.* is able to *g.*
24 cut out and *g.* these ho *g.*

GRAIN, S.
Amos 9:9 not least *g.* fall on ear.
Mat. 13:31 kingdom of heaven is
like a *g.* of mustard-seed,
Mark 4:31; *Luke* 13:19
17:20 faith as a *g.* of mustard-s.
ye shall say to this mount.
remove, *Luke* 17:6
1 *Cor.* 15:37 *g.* wheat, or other *g.*

GRANDMOTHER.
2 *Tim.* 1:5 faith dwelt in thy *g.*

GRANT, Substantive.
Ezr. 3:7 accord, to *g.* of Cyrus

GRANT, Verb.
Lev. 25:24 *g.* a redemption
1 *Sam.* 1:17 God *g.* thee petition
1 *Chr.* 21:22 *g.* this threshing-fl.;
thou shall *g.* it me
2 *Chr.* 12:7 I will *g.* them deliv.

GRO

1 *K*. 2:8 Shim. cursed w. *g*. curse
12:4 *g*. service, 2 *Chr*. 10:4
Ps. 10:3 his ways always *g*.
31:18 speak *g*. things ag. right.
Prov. 15:1 *g*. words stir up anger
16 correct, *g*. to him that fors.
Ec. 2:17 work w. under sun *g*.
Is. 15:4 life shall be *g*. unto him
21:2 *g*. vision is declared to me
Jer. 6:28 are all *g*. revolters
10:19 my wound is *g*.
14:17 broken with very *g*. blow
16:4 they shall die of *g*. deaths
23:19 *g*. whirlwind shall fall
30:12 wound is *g*. *Nah*. 3:19
Mat. 23:4 burdens *g*. *Luke* 11:46
Acts 20:29 *g*. wolves enter am. y.
25:7 *g*. complaints against Paul
Phil. 3:1 to me indeed is not *g*.
Heb. 12:11 no chast, joyous but *g*.
1 *John* 5:3 commandments not *g*.
Rev. 16:2 a *g*. sore on men
GRIEVOUSLY.
Is. 9:1 afterward did *g*. afflict
Lam. 1:8 Jerusa. hath *g*. sinned
20 heart is turned, I *g*. rebelled
Ezek. 14:13 sin, by trespassing *g*.
Mat. 8:6 servant, *g*. tormented
15:28 my daughter is *g*. vexed
GRIEVOUSNESS.
Is. 10:1 that write *g*. they presc.
21:15 fled from the *g*. of war
GRIND.
Jud. 16:21 Sam. did *g*. in prison
Job 31:10 let my wife *g*. to anot.
Is. 3:15 mean ye to *g*. faces?
47:2 millstones and *g*. meal
Lam. 5:13 took young men to *g*.
Mat. 21:44 *g*. him to p. *Lu*. 20:18
GRINDERS, ING.
Ec. 12:3 *g*. cease, bec. are few
4 when sound of *g*. is low
Mat. 24:41 two wom. *g*. *Lu*. 17:35
GRIZZLED.
Gen. 31:10 speckled and *g*. 12
Zec. 6:3 in chariot we. *g*. horses
6 the *g*. go forth to, the south
GROAN.
Job 24:12 men *g*. from out of city
Jer. 51:52 thro' land wounded *g*.
Joel 1:18 how do the beasts *g*.
Rom. 8:23 we ourselves *g*. within
2 *Cor*. 5:2 we *g*. des. to be cloth.
4 we in this tabernacle do *g*.
GROANED, ETH.
John 11:33 he *g*. in spirit
Rom. 8:22 the *g*. whole creation *g*.
GROANING, s.
Ex. 2:24 God heard their *g*.
6:5 heard *g*. of Israel, *Acts* 7:34
Job 3:2 stroke is heavier than *g*.
Ps. 6:6 I am weary with *g*.
38:9 my *g*. is not hid from thee
102:5 *g*. bones cleave to skin
20 to hear the *g*. of prisoner
Ezek. 30:24 *g*. of wounded man
John 11:38 Jesus *g*. in himself
Rom. 8:26 *g*. that cannot be ut.
GROPE, ETH.
Deut. 28:29 *g*. at noon as blind *g*.
Job 5:14 *g*. in noonday
12:25 *g*. in dark without light
Is. 59:10 *g*. for wall like blind
GROSS.
Is. 60:2 *g*. darkness cover people
Jer. 13:16 make it *g*. darkness
Mat. 13:15 waxed *g*. *Acts* 28:27
GROVE.
Gen. 21:33 planted *g*. in Beer-sh.
Deut. 16:21 not plant *g*. near alt.
Jud. 6:25 cut down *g*. by it, 26
1 *K*. 14:15 made idol in *g*. 2 *Chr*. 15:16
16:33 A. made *g*. to provoke G.
2 *K*. 13:6 remained *g*. in Samar.
17:16 Israel made *g*. served Baal
21:3 reared up altars, made a *g*.
23:6 brought *g*. from ho. of L.
15 Josiah burnt high place and *g*.
GROVES.
Ex. 34:13 cut down *g*. *Deut*. 7:5
Deut. 12:3 burn their *g*. with fire
Jud. 3:7 served *g*. 2 *Chr*. 24:18
1 *K*. 14:23 built *g*. on every high hill, 2 *K*. 17:10
18:19 prophets of the *g*. 400
2 *K*. 18:4 Hezekiah cut down *g*.
23:14 Jos. cut *g*. 2 *Chr*. 34:3, 4
2 *Chr*. 14:3 brake images, cut *g*.
17:6 Jehos. took away the *g*.
33:3 M. made *g*. ; 19 set up *g*.
34:5 purge Judah from the *g*.
Is. 17:8 neither shall, he respect *g*.

GRO

Jer. 17:2 remember altars and *g*.
Mic. 5:14 I will pluck up thy *g*.
GROUND, Verb.
Ex. 32:20 *g*. to powder, *Deut*. 9:21
Num. 11:8 the people *g*. manna
GROUND corn.
2 *Sam*. 17:19 *g*. c. on well's mou.
GROUND.
Gen. 2:5 not a man to till *g*.
7 God formed man of dust of *g*.
19 of *g*. the Lord formed every
3:17 cursed is *g*. for thy sake
4:2 Cain was a tiller of the *g*.
10 blood crieth to me from *g*.
5:29 the *g*. the L. hath cursed
8:21 not again curse the *g*.
Ex. 3:5 stan. is holy *g*. *Acts* 7:33
Num. 16:31 *g*. clave asunder
Jud. 4:21 fastened nail into *g*.
1 *Sam*. 8:12 set them to ear his *g*.
14:25 wood of the *g*. full of lentiles
2 *K*. 2:19 water naught, *g*. barron
9:26 cast him into the plat of *g*.
2 *Chr*. 4:17 cast them in clay *g*.
Neh. 10:35 first-fruits of our *g*.
Job 5:6 trouble spring out of *g*.
14:8 tho. stock thereof die in *g*.
18:10 snare is laid for him in *g*.
38:27 desolate and waste *g*.
39:24 swal. the *g*. with fierceness.
Ps. 105:35 dev. fruit of their *g*.
107:33 turn. springs into dry *g*.
35 turneth dry *g*. to water-spr.
Is. 28:24 break clods of his *g*.
30:24 shalt break out of the *g*.
30:23 then shalt not sow the *g*.
34 asses that ear the *g*. sh. eat
35:7 parched *g*. shall bec. a pool
51:23 hast laid thy body as *g*.
Jer. 4:3 br. your fal. *g*. *Hos*. 10:12
14:4 because *g*. is chapt
Lam. 2:9 gates are sunk into *g*.
Ezek. 12:6 thou see not the *g*. 12
Dan. 8:5 came, touched not *g*.
12:8 branch of *g*. for things of *g*.
Mal. 3:11 not destroy fruit of *g*.
Mat. 13:8 into good *g*. *Luke* 8:8
23 send into good *g*. *Luke* 8:15
Mark 4:26 sho. cast seed into *g*.
Luke 12:16 *g*. of a certain man
13:7 why cumbereth it the *g*. ?
14:18 have bought a piece of *g*.
19:44 sh. lay thee with the *g*.
23:45 shook off the parcel of *g*. ?
Mark 4:26 seed *g*. kno. not how
Acts 22:7 I fell to the *g*.
Eph. 4:15 may *g*. into him
1 *Pet*. 2:2 milk of word, th. ye *g*.
2 *Pet*. 3:18 *g*. in grace and kno.
GROWETH.
Ex. 10:5 locusts eat ev. tree *g*.
Lev. 13:39 spot that *g*. in skin
25:5 *g*. of its own accord, 11
Deut. 29:23 nor any grass *g*.
Jud. 16:9 the day *g*. to an end
Job 38:38 dust *g*. into hardness
Ps. 90:5 grass which *g*. up, 6
129:6 withereth afore it *g*. up
Is. 37:30 such as *g*. of itself
Mark 4:32 when it is sown it *g*.
Eph. 2:21 *g*. unto holy temple
2 *Thes*. 1:3 faith of *g*. exceedingly
GROWN.
Gen. 38:11 Sh. be *g*. ; 14 was *g*.
Ex. 2:11 when Moses was *g*.
Deut. 32:15 thou art *g*. thick
Ruth 1:13 till they were *g*. ?
1 Sam. 25:36 tarry at Je. till your beards be *g*. 1 *Chr*. 19:5
Ezr. 9:6 tresp. *g*. up to heavens
Ps. 144:12 sons as plants *g*. up
Prov. 24:31 *g*. over with thorns
Jer. 50:11 ye are *g*. fat as heifer
Ezek. 16:7 hrts. fashioned, hair *g*.
Dan. 4:22 *g*. strong, greatness *g*.
33 *g*. like eagles' feathers
Mat. 13:32 when *g*. greatest
GROWTH.
Amos 7:1 shooting up of lat. *g*.
GRUDGE.
Lev. 19:18 nor bear *g*. against pe.
GRUDGE, Verb.
Ps. 55:15 let them *g*. if not satis.
Jam. 5:9 *g*. not one ag. another
GRUDGING, LY.
2 *Cor*. 9:7 let him give, not *g*.
1 *Pet*. 4:9 hospitality without *g*.
GUARD.
Gen. 37:36 sold to capt, of *g*. 39:1
41:12 servant to captain of *g*.

GUA

Neh. 8:6 worship, Lo. faces to *g*.
Ps. 74:7 dwe. of thy name to t. *g*.
89:39 prof. crown, casting to *g*.
41 cast his throne down to t. *g*.
147:6 casteth the wicked to t. *g*.
Is. 14:12 cut down to the *g*. ?
21:9 im. he hath brok. to the *g*.
25:12 bring to the *g*.
26:5 lofty city he layeth to t. *g*.
Jer. 14:2 languish, black to t. *g*.
Lam. 2:2 strom. of Judah, to t. *g*.
10 virgins hang heads to t. *g*.
Ezek. 19:12 mother cast to the *g*.
26:11 thy garrison sh. go to t. *g*.
Dan. 8:7 cast ram down to t. *g*.
10 hosts and stars to the *g*.
12 cast down the truth to t. *g*.
Amos 3:14 h. of altar fall to t. *g*.
Ob. 3 shall bring me to the *g*.
Mat. 10:29 shall not fall to the *g*.
Luke 22:44 dr. of blood fall. to *g*.
22:18 and fell to the *g*.
Acts 22:7 fell to the *g*.
GROUND.
1 *Tim*. 3:15 pillar and *g*. of truth
GROUNDED.
Is. 30:32 *g*. staff shall pass
Eph. 3:17 rooted and *g*. in love
Col. 1:23 in faith, *g*. and settled
GROW.
Gen. 2:9 L. G. ma. ev. tree to *g*.
Num. 6:5 the locks of his hair *g*.
Jud. 16:22 hair of head be. to *g*.
2 *Sam*. 23:5 th. he make it not *g*.
2 *K*. 19:29 out such things as *g*.
Job 8:11 can rush *g*. with. mire?
14:19 things that *g*. out of dust
31:40 thistles *g*. inst. of wheat
39:4 they *g*. up with the corn
Ps. 92:12 *g*. like cedar in Leba.
104:14 grass to *g*. 11. 17:5
Ec. 11:5 how the bones *g*.
Is. 11:1 br. sh. *g*. out of his roots
53:2 sh. *g*. up as a tender plant
Jer. 12:2 they *g*. yea, bring forth
33:15 branch of righte. to *g*. to D.
Ezek. 47:12 nor suffer locks *g*. lo.
Hos. 14:5 he shall *g*. as the lily
7 shall revive, and *g*. as vine
Jon. 4:10 madest *g*. which came
Mal. 4:2 ye shall *g*. up as calves
Mat. 6:28 how they *g*. *Luke* 12:27
13:30 let both *g*. together
21:19 no fruit *g*. on thee hence.
Mark 4:27 seed *g*. kno. not how
Acts 5:24 doubted whereunto this *g*.
Eph. 4:15 may *g*. into him
1 *Pet*. 2:2 milk of word, th. ye *g*.
2 *Pet*. 3:18 *g*. in grace and kno.
GUILE.
Ex. 21:14 if a man slay with *g*.
Ps. 32:2 in whose spirit is no *g*.
34:13 lips from *g*. 1 *Pet*. 3:10
55:11 deceit and *g*. depart not
John 1:47 Israelite in wh. no *g*.
2 *Cor*. 12:16 I caught you with *g*.
1 *Thes*. 2:3 exhortation not in *g*.
1 *Pet*. 2:1 lay aside malice and *g*.
22 nor was *g*. found in his mo.
Rev. 14:5 in mo. was found no *g*.
GUILT.
Deut. 19:13 *g*. of inno. blood, 21:9
GUILTY.
Gen. 42:21 we are verily *g*.
Ex. 34:7 not clear *g*. *Num*. 14:18
Lev. 5:2 he shall be uncl. and *g*.
3 wh. he knoweth not, be *g*. 4
5 when *g*. he shall con. his sin
17 he sinned and is *g*.
6:4 he sinned and is *g*.
Num. 35:27 kill slayer not be *g*.
31 for a murderer *g*. of death
Jud. 21:22 not *g*. that sh. be *g*.
Mat. 26:10 net curse, thou be *g*.
Ezek. 22:4 art become *g*. in blo.
Mat. 23:18 *g*. by gift on it, he *g*.
26:66 he is *g*. of death, *Mark* 14:64
Rom. 3:19 the world may bec. *g*.
1 *Cor*. 11:27 *g*. of body and blood
Jam. 2:10 offend in one, *g*. of all
GUILTINESS.
Gen. 26:10 shouldest have bro. *g*.
Ps. 51:14 del. me from blood-*g*.
GUILTLESS.
Ex. 20:7 hold him *g*. *Deut*. 5:11
Jos. 2:19 blood on him, we be *g*.
1 *Sam*. 26:9 ag. L.'s anointed *g*.
2 *Sam*. 3:28 I and kingdom *g*. of blood
1 *K*. 2:9 hold him not *g*. for thou
Mat. 12:7 not have condemned *g*.

GUI

1 *K*. 14:27 committed shields to chief of *g*. 2 *Chr*. 12:10
2 *K*. 25:8 capt. of *g*. *Jer*. 52:12
10 cap, of *g*. walls, *Jer*. 52:14
11 captain of *g*. carried away
12 captain of *g*. left of poor
Neh. 4:22 in night may be a *g*.
23 nor men of *g*. put off clothes
Jer. 40:5 cap. of *g*. gave him vic.
52:30 cap. of *g*. took capt, 4,600
Ezek. 38:7 be thou a *g*. to them
Dan. 2:14 Dan. ans. capt, of *g*.
Acts 28:16 deli, pris. to cap. of *g*.
GUARD-CHAMBER.
1 *K*. 14:28 guard bare them to *g*.-*c*. 2 *Chr*. 12:11
GUEST.
Luke 19:7 to be *g*. with sinner
GUEST-CHAMBER.
1 *K*. 1:41 Adonijah and *g*. heard
Prov. 9:18 *g*, in depths of hell
Zep. 1:7 L. hath prep. and bid *g*.
Mat. 22:10 wed. furnished wi. *g*.
11 the king came in to see *g*.
GUIDE, s.
Ps. 48:14 our *g*. even to death
55:13 it was thou, a man, my *g*.
Prov. 2:17 forsak. *g*. of her youth
6:7 having no *g*. overseer, ruler
23:4 thou art *g*. of my youth
Mic. 7:5 put not confidence in *g*.
Mat. 23:16 ye blind *g*. 24
Acts 1:16 *g*. to turn that took J.
Rom. 2:19 thou art *g*. of blind
GUIDE.
Job 38:32 canst th. *g*. Arcturus?
Ps. 25:9 meek will *g*. in judgm.
31:3 for thy name's sake *g*. me
32:8 I will teach and *g*. thee
73:24 shalt *g*. me with counsel
112:5 *g*. his affairs with discre.
Prov. 11:3 integrity of upright *g*.
Is. 49:10 by springs shall *g*. th.
51:18 there is none to *g*. her
58:11 L. shall *g*. thee continual.
Luke 1:79 *g*. feet into way of pc.
John 16:13 he will *g*. you
1 *Tim*. 5:14 you. women *g*. house
GUIDED, ING.
Gen. 48:14 *g*. hands wittingly
Ex. 15:13 *g*. them in strength
2 *Chr*. 32:22 Lord *g*. on ev. side
Job 31:18 *g*. her from mother's
Ps. 78:52 *g*. them in wilderness
72 *g*. them by skilful of hands
GUILE.
Ex. 21:14 if a man slay with *g*.
Ps. 32:2 in whose spirit is no *g*.
34:13 lips from *g*. 1 *Pet*. 3:10
55:11 deceit and *g*. depart not
John 1:47 Israelite in wh. no *g*.
2 *Cor*. 12:16 I caught you with *g*.
1 *Thes*. 2:3 exhortation not in *g*.
1 *Pet*. 2:1 lay aside malice and *g*.
22 nor was *g*. found in his mo.
Rev. 14:5 in mo. was found no *g*.
GUILT.
Deut. 19:13 *g*. of inno. blood, 21:9
GUILTY.
Gen. 42:21 we are verily *g*.
Ex. 34:7 not clear *g*. *Num*. 14:18
Lev. 5:2 he shall be uncl. and *g*.
3 wh. he knoweth not, be *g*. 4
5 when *g*. he shall con. his sin
17 he sinned and is *g*.
6:4 he sinned and is *g*.
Num. 35:27 kill slayer not be *g*.
31 for a murderer *g*. of death
Jud. 21:22 not *g*. that sh. be *g*.
Mat. 26:10 net curse, thou be *g*.
Ezek. 22:4 art become *g*. in blo.
Mat. 23:18 *g*. by gift on it, he *g*.
26:66 he is *g*. of death, *Mark* 14:64
Rom. 3:19 the world may bec. *g*.
1 *Cor*. 11:27 *g*. of body and blood
Jam. 2:10 offend in one, *g*. of all

HAD
GULF.
Luke 16:26 bet. us and you a g.
GUR. 2 *K.* 9:27
1 *K.* 18:28 till the blood g. out
Ps. 78:30 en. rock, waters g. out
105:41 open. rock, waters g. out
Is. 48:21 cl. rock, waters g. out
Jer. 9:18 eyelids g. out with wat.
Acts 1:18 burst as. bowels g. out
GUTTER, *s.*
Gen. 30:38 Jacob set rods in g.
41 laid rods bef. cat. in the g.
2 *Sam.* 5:8 getteth up to the g.

H
HA.
Job 39:25 saith am. trump. ..a, *ha*
HADERGEON.
Ex. 28:32 hole of a h. 39:23
Job 41:26 dart, h. cannot hold
HADERGEONS.
2 *Chr.* 26:14 h. Uzziah prepared
Neh. 4:16 half of servants held h.
HABITABLE.
Prov. 8:31 in the h. part of earth
HABITATION.
Ex. 15:2 I will prepare him a h.
Lev. 13:46 with. the camp his h.
1 *Sam.* 2:29 offering com. in h.
28 shall see an enemy in my h.
2 *Sam.* 15:25 show me it and h.
2 *Chr.* 6:2 a house of h. for thee
29:6 turned from the h. of Lord
Ezr. 7:15 G. of Is. whose h. in J.
Job 5:8 but suddenly I cursed h.
24 shall visit h. and sh. not sin
8:6 h. of righteousness prosper.
18:15 brimstone scat. upon h.
Ps. 26:8 loved h. of thy house
33:14 from place of h. looketh
63:25 let their h. be desolate
71:3 he thou my strong h.
89:14 the h. of thy throne, 97:2
91:9 made the Most High thy h.
104:12 fowls of heaven have h.
107:7 might go to a city of h. 36
132:5 find a h. for God of Jacob
13 L. hath desired it for his h.
Prov. 3:33 blesseth the h. of just
Is. 22:16 graveth h. for himself
31:18 peo. dwell in peaceable h.
33:20 shall see Jerus. a quiet h.
31:16 it shall be a h. of dragons
33:7 h. of dragons sh. be grass
63:15 from the h. of thy holiness
Jer. 9:6 thy h. in midst of deceit
10:25 have made his h. desolate
23:30 L. sh. mightily roar on h.
31:23 L. bless, O h. of just, 50:7
41:17 dwelt in the h. of Chim.
49:19 not c. ag. h. of stro. 50:44
50:19 let. Israel again to his h.
45 he sh. make their h. desol.
Ezek. 29:14 cause E. return to h.
Ob. 3 wh. h. high, saith in heart
Hab. 3:11 sun and moon st. in h.
Acts 1:20 let his h. be desolate
17:26 determined bounds of h.
Eph. 2:22 h. of God thro' Spirit
Jude 6 angels wh. left their h.
Rev. 18:2 Baby. become h. of de.
Holy HABITATION.
Ex. 15:13 guided them to h. h.
Deut. 26:15 look down from h. h.
Ps. 68:5 an. of wid. is G. in h. h.
Jer. 25:30 utter voice from h. h.
Zec. 2:13 raised out of *holy h.*
HABITATIONS.
Gen. 49:5 Instru. of cruelty in h.
Ex. 12:20 in h. eat unl. bread
35:3 kindle no fire thro' your h.
Ps. 74:20 dark places full of h.
Is. 54:2 stretch forth curt. of h.
Jer. 9:10 h. of wild. lamentation
21:13 who sh. enter into our h.?
25:37 peaceable h. are cut down
49:20 sh. make their h. desolate
Lam. 2:2 h. swallowed h. of J.
Ezek. 6:14 h. make Lami desolate
Amos 1:2 h. of shepherds mourn
Luke 16:9 receive into everl. h.
HACHILAH.
1 *Sam.* 23:19 D. hid in H. 26:1
HAD.
Job 31:31 O that we h. of his fl.!
42:10 twice as much as he h.
Ps. 81:10 I A. rather be a door-k.
Ec. 7 to h. h. in reverence of all
Mat. 13:16 he said all that he h.
22:28 of sev. for they all h. her
Mark 12:44 did cast in all she h.
John 4:18 hast h. five husbands

HAI
John 12:6 Judas h. the bag. and
15:24 h. not come they h. not h.
17:5 the glory I h. with thee
Acts 2:44 believed h. all common
Heb. 7:6 blessed him h. promises
1 *John* 2:7 com. h. fr. beginning
2 *John* 5 we h. from beginning.
See **ALL, COMPASSION,**
HADST.
Gen. 30:30 little h. bef. I came
Heb. 10:8 offer. for sin h. no pla.
HADADEZER, HADAR-EZER.
2 *Sam.* 8:3, 5, 7, 8, 9, 10, 12; 10:16;
1 *K.* 11:23; 1 *Chr.* 18:3
HADADRIMMON. *Zec.* 12:11
HADASSAH. *Est.* 2:7
HADORAM.
Gen. 10:27; 1 *Chr.* 1:21; 18:10
2 *Chr.* 10:18 Rehoboam sent H.
HADRACH. *Zec.* 9:1
HAFT.
Jud. 3:22 the h. also went in
HAGAR. *Gen.* 16:1, 3, 8, 10;
21:9, 14, 17; 25:12
HAGARENES. *Ps.* 83:6
HAGARITES. 1 *Chr.* 5:10, 19, 20
HAGGAI.
Ezr. 5:1 H. prophesied to J. 6:14
Hag. 1:1 L. by H. 3; 2:1, 10, 20
HAGGITH. 2 *Sam.* 3:4; 1 *K.*
1:5; 2:13; 1 *Chr.* 3:2
HAIL.
Ex. 9:18 cau. to rain grievous h.
23 Lord sent thunder and h.
26 children of Is. were, no h.
29 any more h.; 33 h. ceased
Job 38:22 seen treasures of h. ?
Ps. 78:47 destroyed vines wi. h.
48 gave cattle also to h.
105:32 he gave them h. for rain
148:8 fire, h. snow. and vapor
Is. 28:17 h. shall sweep away
Hag. 2:17 I smote you with h.
Rev. 8:7 there follow. h. and fire
11:19 temple opened, great h.
16:21 th. fell on men a great h.
HAIL, Verb.
Is. 32:19 people dwell, it shall h.
HAIL.
Mat. 26:49 Judas said, h. Master
27:29 h. king of the Jews, *Mark*
15:18; *John* 19:3
Luke 1:28 ang. came to M. said h.
HAILSTONES.
Jos. 10:11 which died with h.
Ps. 18:12 h. and coals of fire, 13
Is. 30:30 L. show indig. with h.
Ezek. 13:11 O grent h. shall fall
13 shall be great h. in my fury
38:22 great h. fire, brimstone
HAIR.
Lev. 13:3 h. in plague tur. white
30 plague yellow h.; 31 bl. h.
37 there is black h. grown
14:8 and shave off all his h. 9
Num. 6:19 h. of separa. shaven
Jud. 20:16 sling stones at h.
2 *Sam.* 14:26 he was heavy
1 *K.* 1:52 not a h. fall to earth
Neh. 13:25 I plucked off their h.
Job 4:15 h. of my flesh stood up
Cant. 4:1 h. as flock of goats, 6:5
Is. 3:24 instead of welhset h.
7:20 h. shave head, and h.
50:6 plucked off h.
Jer. 7:29 cut off thy h. O Jerus.
Ezek. 5:1 div. h.; 16:7 h. grown
Mat. 3:4 camel's h.; *Mark* 1:6
5:36 can make oath by h. wh. or bl.
John 11:2 wiped feet with h. 12:3
1 *Cor.* 11:14 if a man have long h.
15 woman have long h. glory
1 *Tim.* 2:9 not with broid. h. nor
1 *Pet.* 3:3 plaiting h. wear. gold
Rev. 6:12 black as sackel. of h.
9:8 had h. as the h. of women
See **GOATS, HEAD.**
HAIRS.
Gen. 42:38 br. down h. 41:29, 34
Deut. 32:25 h. of grey h.
Ps. 40:12 more than h. of h. 69:4
Is. 46:4 to hoar h. will I carry
Dan. 3:27 h. like eagles' feathers
Hos. 7:9 gray h. here and there
Mat. 10:30 the h. of head num-bered, *Luke* 12:7
Luke 7:38 wipe with h. of h. 44
21:11 h. were white like wool
HAIRY.
Gen. 25:25 all over like h. gour.
27:11 Esau h. man; 23 hands h.

HAM
2 *K.* 1:8 Elijah was a h. man
Ps. 68:21 h. scalp of such a one
HALE, ING.
Luke 12:58 advers. h. thee to ja.
Acts 8:3 Saul h. men and women
HALF.
Ex. 24:6 h. blood, h. sprinkled
Lev. 6:20 h. in morn. h. at night
1 *Sam.* 14:14 with h. acre of land
2 *Sam.* 10:4 shave off h. of beards
19:40 h. of Israel conducted D.
1 *K.* 3:25 h. child to one, h. oth.
10:7 h. was not told, 2 *Chr.* 9:6
13:8 wilt give me h. thy house
16:21 h. followed Tibni, h. Omri
Neh. 13:24 h. in speech of Ashd.
Ev. 5:3 to the h. of the king-
dom, 7:2; *Mark* 6:23
Ps. 55:23 bl. men not liv h. days
Dan. 12:7 and a h. *Rev.* 12:14
Zec. 14:2 h. of city into captivity
h. to. tow. south, h. to. tow. sea
Luke 10:30 leaving him h. dead
19:8 h. of goods I give to poor
Rev. 8:1 silence about h. an hour
11:9 bodies three days and h. 11
See **SHEKEL, HIN, TRIBE.**
HALL.
Mat. 27:27 sold, took Jes. into h.
Mark 15:16 soldiers led him to h.
Luke 22:55 kindled fire in the h.
See **JUDGMENT.**
HALLOW.
Ex. 20:1 h. them to minister
Lev. 22:32 I am the L. who h.
25:10 shall h. the fiftieth year
Num. 3:13 h. all firstborn, I h.
Jer. 17:22 A. ye sabbath-d. 24, 27
Ezek. 20:20 and h. my sabbaths
44:24 keep laws h. my sabbaths
HALLOWED.
Ex. 20:11 bless. sabbath and h. it
29:21 Aaron be h. and his garm.
22:6 L. eh. deliver it into king's
h. 12, 15; 2 *Chr.* 8:95; 28:5
2 *K.* 7:2 who. h. king leaned. 17
Ezr. 7:9 good h. of God on him
9:2 h. of princes chief in tresp.
Job 6:24 given into h. of wicked
12:6 into whose h. G. bringeth
16 in h. is soul of ev. liv. thing
20:22 h. of wicked come on him
21:16 good is not in their h.
23:10 mighty take. away wit. h.
37:7 scaleth up h. of ev. man
Ps. 31:8 not shut into h. of ene.
36:11 let not h. of wicked rem.
71:4 deliver, me out of h. of
wicked, 82:4; 97:10
123:2 serv. look to h. of masters
127:4 in h. of mighty man
146:6 two-edged sword in th. h.
Prov. 6:3 come into h. of friend
10:4 poor dealeth slack h. but
h. of diligent maketh rich
11:21 h. join h. not unpun. 16:5
12:21 h. of diligent bear rule
17:16 in h. of fool get wisdom?
26:9 thorn goeth into h. of drn.
Ec. 10:18 staff in h. my indigna.
Is. 2 shake h. may go into gates
13:1 into h. of cruel lord
26:2 cast down to earth wi. h.
Jer. 12:7 belo. into h. of enemies
18:1 vessel marred in h. of pot.
6 as clay in the potter's h.
21:5 outstretch. h. against you
26:21 h. of Ahikam with Jere.
Lam. 5:6 given h. to Egyptians
12 princes are hanged by h. h.
Ezek. 2:9 a h. was sent to me
3:3 put forth form of h. 1c:8
12:6 not. by h. of any man
13:23 more h. strength. h. of needy
21:10 no goal in h. that sw. sw.
16:49 neither strengthen the h.
37:19 stick in h. of Ephraim
40:5 in man's h. a measur. reed
Dan. 5:5 came forth h. and wrote
24 h. in whose h. thy breath is
8:25 he shall be broken with h.
9:10 beheld, a h. tou hed me
Joel 3:8 sons and dau. to h. Jud.
Zec. 11:17 sword be on his arm
Mark 3:1 man whose h. wither.
1 h. man that h. withered
Luke 9:62 no man having h. to
22:21 h. of him that betrayeth
John 3:35 hath given all things
13:3 Father had given all things
Rev. 10:2 he had in his h. a little
14:9 h. receive mark in foreh.
17:4 golden cup in her h. full
20:1 angel having in h. key

HAN
HANANI.
1 *K.* 16:1 to Jehu son of H. 7
2 *Chr.* 25:4 H. son of Heman, 25
2 *Chr.* 16:7 H. seer, *Neh.* 1:2; 7:2
12:3 Jehu son of H. *2 K.* 20:34
Neh. 12:36 H. with musical inst.
HANANIAH.
1 *Chr.* 3:19 sons of Zerub. H.
Ezr. 10:28 H. Zab. stra. wives
Neh. 3:8 H. repaired, 7:2; 10:23;
12:12
Jer. 28:12 H. had broken J.'s, 17
37:13 son of H. took Jeremiah
Dan. 1:7 to H. name of S. 2:17
HAND.
Gen. 9:2 into h. are they deliv.
41:17 in whose h. cup found
Ex. 6:1 strong h. drive them out
13:3 strength of h. L. brought
14:8 Israel went out with a high
h. *Num.* 33:3
16 stretch out h. over the sea
19:13 there sh. not a h. touch it
21:24 h. for h. *Deut.* 19:21
34:29 tables of testi. in Mos. h.
38:15 on this h. or that h.
Deut. 13:9 h. of all the people
25:12 cut off her h.
Jos. 2:19 blo. on head h. on him
Jud. 1:35 h. of house of Joseph
4:9 sell Sisera into h. of a wom.
15:16 fall into h. of uncircum.
1 *Sam.* 12:8 who. h. rec. bribe?
13:22 nor spear fou. in h. of Is.
17:50 no sword in h. of David
23:19 when business was in h.
22:17 their h. also is with Dav.
2 *Sam.* 13:5 ont it at her h. 6
14:19 the h. of Joab in all this
21:20 had on every h. six fing.
1 *Chr.* 20:6
24:14 into h. of men, 1 *Chr.* 21:13
1 *K.* 2:46 established in h. of Sol.
13:6 king's h. was restored ag.
18:44 ariseth cloud like man's h.
22:6 L. sh. deliver it into king's
h. 12, 15; 2 *Chr.* 8:95; 28:5
2 *K.* 7:2 who. h. king leaned. 17
Ezr. 7:9 good h. of God on him
9:2 h. of princes chief in tresp.
Job 6:24 given into h. of wicked
12:6 into whose h. G. bringeth
16 in h. is soul of ev. liv. thing
20:22 h. of wicked come on him
21:16 good is not in their h.
23:10 mighty take. away wit. h.
37:7 scaleth up h. of ev. man
Ps. 31:8 not shut into h. of ene.
36:11 let not h. of wicked rem.
71:4 deliver, me out of h. of
wicked, 82:4; 97:10
123:2 serv. look to h. of masters
127:4 in h. of mighty man
146:6 two-edged sword in th. h.
Prov. 6:3 come into h. of friend
10:4 poor dealeth slack h. but
h. of diligent maketh rich
11:21 h. join h. not unpun. 16:5
12:21 h. of diligent bear rule
17:16 in h. of fool get wisdom?
26:9 thorn goeth into h. of drn.
Ec. 10:18 staff in h. my indigna.
Is. 2 shake h. may go into gates
13:1 into h. of cruel lord
26:2 cast down to earth wi. h.
Jer. 12:7 belo. into h. of enemies
18:1 vessel marred in h. of pot.
6 as clay in the potter's h.
21:5 outstretch. h. against you
26:21 h. of Ahikam with Jere.
Lam. 5:6 given h. to Egyptians
12 princes are hanged by h. h.
Ezek. 2:9 a h. was sent to me
3:3 put forth form of h. 1c:8
12:6 not. by h. of any man
13:23 more h. strength. h. of needy
21:10 no goal in h. that sw. sw.
16:49 neither strengthen the h.
37:19 stick in h. of Ephraim
40:5 in man's h. a measur. reed
Dan. 5:5 came forth h. and wrote
24 h. in whose h. thy breath is
8:25 he shall be broken with h.
9:10 beheld, a h. tou hed me
Joel 3:8 sons and dau. to h. Jud.
Zec. 11:17 sword be on his arm
Mark 3:1 man whose h. wither.
1 h. man that h. withered
Luke 9:62 no man having h. to
22:21 h. of him that betrayeth
John 3:35 hath given all things
13:3 Father had given all things
Rev. 10:2 he had in his h. a little
14:9 h. receive mark in foreh.
17:4 golden cup in her h. full
20:1 angel having in h. key

HAN

Jer. 20:6 man w. h. h. on loins?
Heb. 2:10 lifted his h. on high
Mat. 19:13 h. h. on th. *Mark* 10:16
27:24 washed h. h. be, multitude
Mark **8:23** his h. on his eyes, 25
Luke **24:40** shew, h. h. *John* 20:20
50 lifted up h. h. blessed them
John **13:9** given all th. into his h.
20:25 see in h. h. print of nails
Acts **9:17** putting his h. on him
12:1 Herod stretched forth his h.
7 his chains fell off from h. h.
* **2 Cor. 11:33** by wall, escap. h. h.
Eph. **4:28** working with h. h.

See LAY, LAID.

My HANDS.

Gen. 20:5 in innocency of my h.
Jud. 12:3 I put my life in my h.
2 Sam. 22:21 according to cleanness of my h. *Ps.* 18:20, 24
33 he teacheth my h. to war,
Ps. **18:34 ; 144:1**
Neh. **6:9** O God, strengthen my h.
Job **9:30** make my h. ne. so clean
14:17 any iniquity in my h.
31:7 any blot cleaved to my h.
Ps. **7:3** if there be iniq. in my h.
22:16 pierced my h. and my feet
26:6 wash my h. in innocency
28:2 lift my h. tow. thy oracle
63:4 lift my h. in thy name
73:13 I have washed my h.
119:48 my h. will I lift
141:2 lifting up my h. as even.
143:6 stretch forth my h.
Is. **10:13** bless. be work of my h.
45:11 concerning work of my h.
12 my h. stretched out heavens
49:16 on palms of my h.
50:21 people the work of my h.
65:2 I have spread out my h.
Dan. **3:15** del. you out of my h.
10:10 on the palms of my h.
Luke **24:39** be. my h. *John* 20:27
John **13:9** also my h. and head
Rom. **10:21** I stretched my h.
2 Tim. 1:6 by putting on of m. h.

Our HANDS.

Gen. 5:29 concerning toil of o. h.
Deut. **21:7** o. h. have not shed h.
Jos. **2:24** delivered into our h.
Jud. **13:23** a meat-off. at our h.
1 Sam. 17:47 give you into o. h.
Pr. **41:20** stretched out our h.
90:17 establish work of our h.
Jer. **6:24** our h. wax feeble
Lam. **3:41** our heart with our h.
Hos. **14:3** work of our h.
1 Cor. 4:12 work, with our own h.
1 John 1:1 our h. hand, word of

Their HANDS.

Ex. **29:10** put t. h. on head
15 put t. h. on head of ram, 19
Num. **8:10** put their h. on Levit.
12 lay their h. on the bullock
Deut. **1:25** brought fruit in t. h.
21:6 wash t. h. over the heifer
2 Sam. 4:12 they cut off their h.
2 K. 11:12 they clapped their h.
22:17 prov. me to anger with works of their h. **2 Chr.** 34:25
Ezr. **1:6** strengthened their h.
5:8 work prospereth in their h.
6:22 strengthen t. h. in work
Neh. **2:18** streng. t. h. for work
6:9 their h. shall be weakened
8:6 t. h. cannot perf. enter.
30:2 whereto stre. t. h. profit?
Ps. **76:5** m. of mi. not found t. h.
91:12 angels bear thee in t. h.
125:3 lest right. put t. h. to in.
Is. **25:11** tog. with spoils of t. h.
59:6 act of violence is in t. h.
65:22 elect enjoy work of t. h.
Jer. **1:16** worshipped works t. h.
32:30 prov. with works of t. h.
Ezk. **10:7** t. h. and wings full
23:37 blood is in their h. 45
Jon. **3:8** turn from viol. in t. h.
Hag. **2:14** ev. work of t. h. uncl.
Mal. **4:6** in their h. they shall bear thee up, *Luke* **4:11**
15:2 wash not t. h. why, they eat
26:67 others smote him with the palms of t. h. *Mark* **14:65**
Mark **5:23** exc. wash t. h. eat not
Luke **6:1** rubbing them in t. h.
John **19:3** smote him with their h.
Acts **14:3** won. to be done by t. h.
Rev. **7:9** wh. robes, palms in t. h.
9:20 repented not of wor. of t. h.
20:4 nor had rec. mark in t. h.

Thy HANDS.

Deut. **16:15** Lord shall bless thee in all works of thy h. 24:19
Jud. **7:11** afterw. thy h. be stren.

HAP

2 Sam. 3:34 t. h. were not bound
Job **10:3** to despise work of h.?
6 thy h. made and fashion, me
14:15 desire to work of thy h.
22:30 deliv. by pureness of t. h.
Ps. **8:6** domin. over work of t. h.
102:25 heavens work of thy h.
119:73 thy h. have made me
128:2 shalt eat labor of thy h.
138:8 forsake not works of t. h.
143:5 I muse on work of thy h.
Jer. **2:37** thy h. on thy head
Lam. **2:19** lift thy h. for thy chil.
Mic. **5:13** no more worship t. h.
Zec. **13:6** wh. are these in t. h.?
Luke **23:46** to thy h. I com. my
John **21:18** shalt stretch thy h.
Heb. **1:10** heavens works of t. h.
2:7 set him over works of thy h.

HANDSTAVES.

Ezk. **39:9** shall burn the h.

HANDWEAPON.

Num. **35:18** smite him with h.

HANDWRITING.

Col. **2:14** blotting out the h.

HANG.

Gen. **40:19** Pharaoh shall h. thee
Num. **25:4** h. them bef. the Lord
Deut. **21:22** if thou h. him
23:66 thy life shall h. in doubt
Est. **6:4** speak to h. Mordecai
7:9 king said, h. him thereon
Is. **22:24** they sh. h. on him glory
Lam. **2:10** virgins h. their heads
Ezk. **15:3** take pin to h. any ves.
Mat. **22:40** on th. two h. all law
Acts **28:4** v. hang, h. down
Heb. **12:12** up hands wh. h. down

HANGED.

Gen. **40:22** h. chief baker. 41:13
Deut. **21:23** that is h. is accursed
2 Sam. 17:23 Ahithoh. h. ; 18:10 A.
21:9 seven sons of Saul h. they
Est. **2:23** chamberlains were h.
7:10 h. Ham. ; 9:14 h. ten sons
Ps. **137:2** h. harps on willows
Lam. **5:12** princes h. by hands
Ezk. **27:10** O. tra. h. shield, 11
Mat. **18:6** bet. millst. were h. ab. his neck, *Mark* **9:42** ; *Lu.* **17:2**
27:5 Judas went and h. himself
Luke **23:39** thieves who were h.
Acts **5:30** and h. on tree, 10:39

HANGETH.

Job **26:7** h. earth upon nothing
Gal. **3:13** cursed ev. one h. on tr.

HANGING, Substantive.

Jos. **10:26** h. on trees till evening

HANGING, Substantive.

Ex. **26:36** make h. for door of tent
37 make for the h. five pillars
27:16 h. for court-gate, 38:18 ;
39:40 ; **40:8, 33**
35:15 h. for door enter. tabernacle, 38:37 ; **39:38 ; 40:5, 28**

HANGINGS.

Ex. **27:9**, 100 cub. 11 ; **38:9**, 11
12 shall be h. of 50 cubits, 38:12
35:17 h. of court, **38:9**, **10**, **15** ;
39:40 ; *Num.* **3:26 ; 4:26**
2 K. 23:7 women wove h. for gr.

HANNAH.

1 Sam. 1:2 ; 2:21

HANOCH.

Gen. **25:4** ; **46:9** ;
Num. **26:5 ; 1 Chr. 1:33 ; 5:3**

HANUN.

2 Sam. 10:1 H. reig. **1 Chr.** 19:4
Neh. **3:13, 30** H. repaired val. gate, 30

HAPLY.

Mark **11:13** if h. he mi. find fruit
Luke **14:29** lest h. after laid fou.
Acts **5:39** lest h. found fight a. G.
17:27 if h. they might feel

HAPPEN.

Prov. **12:21** no evil h. to the just
Is. **41:22** show us what shall h.

HAPPENED.

2 Sam. 1:6 as I h. by chance on
Jer. **44:23** therefore evil is h.
Rom. **11:25** blindness is h. to Is.
1 Cor. 10:11 th. h. for ensamples
Phil. **1:12** things h. me fallen
1 Pet. 4:12 strange thing h. to y.
2 Pet. 2:22 h. according to prov.

HAPPENETH.

Ec. **2:14** one ev. h. to them all
15 as it h. to fool, so it h. to me
9:11 time and chance h. to all

HAPPY.

Deut. **33:29** h. art thou, O Israel
1 K. 10:8 h. men, h. thy servants, **2 Chr. 9:7**
Job **5:17** h. is man. wh. G. correc.

HAR

Ps. **127:5** h. man hath quiver full
137:8 A. he who reward. thee, 9
144:15 h. people in such a case, h. peo. whose God is the L.
146:5 h. is he that hath G. of J.
Prov. **3:13** h. man find. wisdom
14:21 h. he hath mercy on poor
16:20 whoso trust. in L. h. is he
28:14 h. is man that fear. alway
29:18 that keepeth law, h. is he
Jer. **12:1** why A. deal treacher. ?
Mal. **3:15** we call the proud h.
Jon. **13:17** kn. things, h. if do th.
Rom. **14:22** h. is he that condemn.
Jam. **5:11** them h. who endure
1 Pet. 3:14 suffer for righte. h. ye
4:14 reproached for Ch. h. ye

HAPPIER.

1 Cor. 7:40 she is h. if she abide

HARAN, a man.

Gen. **11:26** T. begat H. **27, 28, 31**

HARAN, a place.

Gen. **11:31** Terah came to H. 32
12:4 Abram departed out of H.
27:43 flee to H. **28:10 ; 29:4**
2 K. 19:12 fath. destr. H. *Is.* **37:12**

HARD.

Gen. **18:14** any th. too h. for L. ?
35:16 Rachel had A. labor, 17
Ex. **1:14** lives bit. with h. bond.
18:26 h. cause too h. bro. to Mo.
17:8 matter too h. in judgment
26:5 Egypt laid on h. bondage
2 Sam. 3:39 sons of Zeruiah too h.
1 K. 10:1 to prove with A. questions, **2 Chr. 9:1**
2 K. 2:10 thou hast asked A. th.
Job **41:24** as h. as piece of millst.
Ps. **60:3** showed peo. h. things
94:4 how long wick. spe. h. th.
Prov. **13:15** way of transgr. is h.
Jer. **32:17** nothing too h. 27
Ezk. **3:5** to people of h. lang. 6
Mat. **25:24** I knew thou art h.
Mark **10:24** h. for th. tru. in rich.
John **6:60** this is a h. saying
Acts **9:5** A. to kick ag. pri. 26:14
2 Pet. 3:16 thi. h. to be underst.
Jude **15** convince of h. speeches

HARD, Adjective.

Lev. **3:9** rump off h. backbone
1 Chr. 19:4 cut garm. h. by but.
Ps. **63:8** followeth h. after thee
Jon. **1:13** rowed h. to br. to land
Acts **18:7** joined h. to synagogue

HARDEN.

Ex. **4:21** I will h. Pharaoh's heart, 7:3 ; **14:4**
14:17 h. hearts of Egyptians
Deut. **15:7** shalt not A. thy heart
Jos. **11:20** L. to A. their hearts
Ps. **95:8** h. not your hearts, *Heb.* **3:8**; **4:7**

HARDENED.

Ex. **7:13** L. har. Pha. 'a heart, 9:12;
10:1, 20, 27; **11:10**; **14:8**
8:15 he h. his heart, 32 ; 9:34
14 so Pha.'s heart was h. 22:
9:7; **13:15**
Deut. **2:30** G. h. his spirit
1 Sam. 6:6 why h. your hearts
Neh. **9:16, 17 ; 13:** thelc necks
Job **9:4** who hath h. himself.
39:16 h. against her young ones
Is. **63:17** why hast thou h. heart ?
Jer. **7:26** but h. their neck
Dan. **5:20** his mind h. in pride
Mark **6:52** for their heart was h.
8:17 have ye your heart yet h. ?
John **12:40** blinded eyes, h. heart
Acts **19:9** when divers were h.
Heb. **3:13** lest any of you be h.

HARDENETH.

Prov. **21:29** wicked man h. face
28:14 h. heart fall into mischief
29:1 being reproved h. his neck
Rom. **9:18** whom he will he h.

HARD-HEARTED.

Ezk. **3:7** house of Israel are h.-h.

HARDLY.

Gen. **16:6** when Sarai dealt h.
Ex. **13:15** when Pharaoh would h. let
Is. **8:21** shall pass through it h.
Mat. **19:23** rich m. h. ent. kingd. of G. *Mark* **10:23** ; *Luke* **18:24**
Luke **9:39** h. departeth from him

HARDNESS.

Job **38:38** dust groweth into h.
Mat. **19:8** h. of hearts, *Mark* **10:5**

HAR

Mark **3:5** grieved for h. of heart
Mark **16:14** nph. with h. of heart
Rom. **2:5** h. and impenitent heart
2 Tim. 2:3 h. as soldier of J. C.

HARE.

Lev. **11:6** h. is uncl. *Deut.* **14:7**

HARLOT.

Gen. **34:31** d. wi. sister as wi. h. ?
38:15 he thought her to be a h.
Lev. **21:14** high-priest not take h.
Jos. **2:1** spies came to h.'s house
6:17 only Rahab the h. sh. live
Jud. **16:1** Sam. saw there a h.
Prov. **7:10** woman wi. attire of h.
Is. **1:21** faithful city become h.
23:15 after 70 years T. sing as h.
Jer. **2:20** wanderest, playing h.
3:1 thou hast played the h. 6, 8
Ezk. **16:15** playedst the h.
16 playedst h. ; **28** played h.
41 cease to cease from play. h.
23:5 Aholah played the h.
Hos. **2:5** mother hath played h.
4:15 though Israel play the h.
Joel **3:3** given a boy for a h.
Mic. **1:7** return to the hire of h.
Nah. **3:4** whored. of well fav. h.
1 Cor. 6:15 make th. mem. of h.
16 is joined to a h. is one body
Heb. **11:31** h. Rahab perished not
Jam. **2:25** R. the h. just, by wor.

HARLOTS.

Prov. **29:3** keepeth comp, with h.
Jer. **5:7** assemble troops in h. h.
Hos. **4:14** sacrifice with h.
Mat. **21:31** h. go into king. of G.
32 publicans and h. believed h.
Luke **15:30** devoured liv. with h.
Rev. **17:5** Babylon, mother of h.

HARM.

Lev. **5:16** amends for h. done
2 K. 4:41 was no h. in the pot
1 Chr. 16:22 pro, no h. *Ps.* **105:15**
Prov. **3:30** if he have done no h.
Jer. **39:12** do him no h.
Acts **16:28** no h. ; **27:21** gained h.
28:5 felt no h. ; **6** saw no h. ; **21**
spake any h.

HARM, Verb.

1 Pet. 3:13 h. you, if fol. of good !

HARMLESS.

Mat. **10:16** serp. and h. as doves
Phil. **2:15** may be h. sons of G.
Heb. **7:26** holy, h. and undefiled

HARNESS, Substantive.

2 K. 22:11 girdeth on h. boast
22:34 joints of h. **2 Chr. 18:33**
2 Chr. 9:24 brought every man h.

HARNESS, ED, Verb.

Ex. **40:4** h. horses, and horsemen
Jer. **46:4** h. horses, and horsemen

HAROD.

Jud. **7:1**

HAROSHETH.**

Jud. **4:2**

HARP.

Gen. **4:21** fa. of th. th. handle h.
1 Sam. 10:5 meet proph. with h.
16:16 cunning player on h.
1 Chr. 25:3 prophesied with h.
Job **21:12** th. timbrel and h.
30:31 h. is turned to mourning
Ps. **33:2** praise L. with h. 150:3
43:4 on the h. will I praise thee
49:4 open dark saying upon h.
57:8 psaltery and h. **108:2**
71:22 I will sing with h. **92:3** ;
98:5 ; **147:7** ; **149:3**
81:2 bring hither the pleasant h.
Is. **5:12** A. and viol fol their feasts
16:11 bowels sound like a h.
Dan. **3:5** sound of h. 7, 10, 15
1 Cor. 14:7 whether pipe or h.

HARPS.

2 Sam. 6:5 D. and Is. played h.
1 K. 10:12 made of almug-trees h.
1 Chr. 13:8 hanged h. upon willows
14:2 harp. with h. ; **13:2** h. of G.
See CYMBAL.

HARPED.

1 Cor. 14:7 kn. what piped or h. ?

HARPERS.

Rev. **14:2** I heard the voice of h.
18:22 voice of h. heard no more

HARROW.

Job **39:10** will h. h. valleys.

HARROWS.

2 Sam. 12:31 under h. of iron
1 Chr. 20:3 cut with saws and h.

HART, S.

Deut. **12:15** may eat flesh of the h. **14:5 ; 15:22**
Ps. **42:1** as h. panteth after water
Is. **35:6** lame man leap as a h.

HAS

Lam. 1:6 princes become like h. *A.*
See YOUNG.

HARVEST.
Gen. 8:22 earth rem. *h.* not cease
45:6 shall not, be caring nor *h.*
Ex. 23:10 the feast of *h.* 34:22
Lev. 23:5 accord of *h.* not reap
1 *Sam.* 6:13 men reaping their *h.*
12:17 is it not wheat-*h.* to-day?
Job 5:5 whose *h.* hungry eateth
Prov. 6:8 ant gather food in *h.*
10:5 sleepeth in *h.* caus. shame
26:1 snow in sum. as rain in *h.*
Is. 9:3 according to joy in *h.*
16:9 shouting for *h.* is fallen
17:11 *h.* be heap in day of grief
18:4 cloud of dew in heat of *h.*
5 afore *h.* when bud be perfect
23:3 *h.* of the river is her reven.
Jer. 5:17 they shall eat up thy *h.*
24 reserveth to us weeks of *h.*
8:20 *h.* is past, sum, is ended
Joel 1:11 the *h.* of field perished
3:13 in sickle, for the *h.* is ripe
Amos 4:7 yet three months to *h.*
Mat. 9:37 the *h.* is plenteous
38 pray L. *h.* to send, *Luke* 10:2
13:30 grow together until *h.*
39 the *h.* is end of the world
Mark 4:29 put in sickle, *h.* come
Luke 10:2 said, The *h.* is great
John 4:35 fields are white to *h.*
Rev. 14:15 the *h.* of earth is ripe

HARVEST-MAN.
Is. 17:5 when *h.*-*m.* gather, corn
Jer. 9:22 the handful after *h.*-*m.*

Time of HARVEST.
Jos. 3:15 Jord. overfloweth *t. h.*
Prov. 25:13 cold of snow *t. of h.*
Jer. 50:16 handforth sickle in *h.*-*t.*
51:33 the *t. of her h.* shall come
Mat. 13:30 *t. of h.* say to reapers

HAST.
Mat. 19:21 sell all thou *h.* *Mark*
10:21; *Luke* 18:22
25:25 there thou *h.* that is thine
John 6:68 *h.* words of eternal life
7:20 thou *h.* a devil, 8:48, 52
Rom. 14:22 *h.* thou faith?
1 *Cor.* 4:7 what *h.* thou that did.
Jam. 2:18 thou *h.* faith
Rev. 2:6 but this thou *h.*
3:8 *h.* a little strength, 3:1, 4
11 hold that fast which thou *h.*

HASTE, Substantive.
Ex. 12:11 ye shall eat in *h.*
33 out of land in *h.* *Deut.* 16:3
1 *Sam.* 21:8 king's business re-
quired *h.*
Ps. 31:22 said in *h.* I am cut off
116:11 I said in *h.* All men liars
Is. 52:12 shall not go out with *h.*
Dan. 3:24 king rose in *h.*
6:19 went in *h.* to den of lions
Mark 6:25 came in *h.* to the king
Luke 1:39 went to hill-coun. w. *h.*

HASTE.
Gen. 19:22 *h.* thee, escape thither
1 *Sam.* 23:27 *h.* thee, for Philis.
Ps. 22:19 strength, *h.* to help me
See MAKE HASTE.

HASTED.
Gen. 18:7 and he *h.* to dress it
Jos. 4:10 people *h.* over Jordan
10:13 the sun *h.* not to go down
1 *Sam.* 17:48 David *h.* and ran to
23:26 Abigail saw Da, she *h.* 42
23:21 the witch at Endor *h.*
1 *K.* 20:41 prophet *h.* and took
2 *Chr.* 26:20 himself *h.* to go out
Est. 6:12 Haman *h.* to his house
14 they *h.* to bring Haman
Job 31:5 foot hath *h.* to deceit
Ps. 48:5 and *h.* away, 16:17
Acts 20:16 Paul *h.* to Jerusalem

HASTEN.
Ps. 16:4 *h.* after another god
55:8 I would *h.* my escape
Is. 5:25 who can *h.* more than I?
I 60:22 I, will *h.* in his time
Jer. 1:12 I will *h.* my word

HASTENED, ETH.
Est. 3:15 being *h.* by king, 8:14
Is. 51:11 the exile *h.* to be loosed
Jer. 17:16 not *h. fr.* being pastor

HASTETH.
Job 20:29 as eagle that *h.* to prey
Prov. 7:23 as a bird *h.* to snare
19:2 he that *h.* wi. his feet sin.
28:22 *h.* to be rich, hath evil eye
Ec. 1:5 sun *h.* to where he arose
Hab. 1:8 fly as eagle that *h.*
Zep. 1:14 day of Lord *h.* greatly

HAT

HASTILY.
Jud. 2:23 without driving th. *h.*
Prov. 20:21 inheritance gotten *h.*
25:8 go not forth *h.* to strive
John 11:31 saw Mary she rose *h.*

HASTING.
Is. 16:5 and *h.* righteousness
2 *Pet.* 3:12 *h.* to day of the Lord

HASTY.
Prov. 14:29 *h.* of spirit exal. folly
Ec. 5:2 let not thy heart be *h.*
7:9 be not *h.* in thy spirit
8:3 not too *h.* to go out of sight
Is. 28:4 as *h.* fruit before summer
Dan. 2:15 why is decree so *h.?*
Hab. 1:6 bitter and *h.* nation

HATCH, ETH.
Is. 34:15 owl shall *h.* and gather
59:5 they *h.* cockatrice's eggs
Jer. 17:11 as partridge on eggs *A.*

HATE.
Gen. 24:60 possess of those th. *A.*
Lev. 19:17 shalt not *h.* brother
26:17 th. *h.* you sh. reign over
Num. 10:35 let them that *h.* thee
Deut. 22:13 go unto her and *h.*
24:3 if the latter husband *h.* her
2 *Chr.* 19:2 love them that *h.* L.?
Job 8:22 *h.* thee clothed with *h.*
Ps. 21:8 find those that *h.* thee
34:21 th. *h.* righteous sh. be des.
68:1 that *h.* him flee before him
83:2 *h.* thee have lifted up head
88:23 plague them that *h.* him
97:10 ye that love L. *h.* evil
105:25 turned their heart to *h.*
129:5 let th. he turned that *h.* Z.
Prov. 1:22 fools, will ye *h.* know.
6:16 these six doth the Lord *h.*
8:13 fear of the Lord is to *h.* evil
9:8 rep. not scorner, lest *h.* thee
12:1 all brethren of poor *h.* him
29:10 bloodthirsty *h.* the uprig.
Ec. 3:8 time to *h.* and time to *h.*
Amos 5:10 that *h.* him that reb.
15 *h.* the evil, love the good
21 I *h.*, I. good, and love evil
Mic. 3:43 love neigh. *h.* enemy
44 good to th. *h.* y. *Luke* 6:27
6:24 he will *h.* one, *Luke* 16:13
21:10 betray and *h.* one another
Luke 1:71 saved from hand th. *h.*
6:22 blessed are ye when men *h.*
14:26 *h.* not his father
John 7:7 the world cannot *h.* you
15:18 world *h.* you, 1 *John* 3:13
Rev. 17:16 these shall *h.* whore

I HATE.
1 *K.* 22:8 *I h.* him, 2 *Chr.* 18:7
Ps. 101:3 *I h.* work of them
119:104 *I h.* every false way, 128
113 *I h.* vain th. thy law I love
163 *I h.* and abhor lying
139:21 *I h.* them that hate thee
22 *I h.* them with perfect hate,
Prov. 8:13 froward mouth do *I h.*
Is. 61:8 *I h.* robbery for burnt-off.
Jer. 44:4 do not this thing *I h.*
Amos 5:21 *I h.* your feast-days
Zec. 8:17 these are things *I h.*
Rom. 7:15 what *I h.*, that do I
Rev. 2:6 deeds of Nicolati. *I h.* 15

HATE me.
Ex. 20:5 h. *m.* 5:9
Deut. 5:9; *Ps.* 9:13 unff. of them that *h. me*
Ps. 9:13 let them whink that *h. me*
38:19 *h. me* wrong, many; 69:4
41:7 all that *h. me* whisper log.
69:14 deliv. fr. them that *h. me*
118:7 see deliv on th. that *h. me*
Prov. 8:36 they that *h. me*

HATED.
Gen. 27:11 Esau *h.* Jacob
37:4 *A.* Joseph yet the more, 5, 8
49:23 shot at him and *h.* him
Deut. 1:27 her, Lord *h.* us, 9:28
4:42 *h.* him n. 19:1, 6; *Jos.* 20:5
21:15 *h.* acknowledge son of *h.*
Jud. 15:2 I thought thou *h.* her
2 Sam. 6:8 lame and blind are *h.*
Est. 9:1 rule them that *h.* them
Ec. 2:5 *h.* congreg. of evil-doers
31:6 I *h.* them that regard lying
44:7 put them to shame that *h.*
109:41 they *h.* him could well
129 they *h.* knowledge
Prov. 1:29 they *h.* knowledge
5:12 how have I *h.* instruction!
14:17 man of wicked dev. is *h.*

HAU

Prov. 14:20 poor is *h.* even of nei.
Ec. 2:17 *h.* life; I *h.* labor
Is. 60:15 been forsaken and *h.*
Jer. 12:8 have I *h.* my heritage
Ezek. 16:37 gather them thou *h.*
35:6 since thou hast not *h.* blood
Hos. 9:15 *h.*, them for wicked.
Mal. 1:3 I *h.* Esau, *Rom.* 9:13
Mat. 10:22 ye shall be *h.* *Mark*
13:13; *Luke* 21:17
24:9 ye shall be *h.* of all nations
Luke 19:14 his citizens *h.* him
John 15:18 it *h.* me bef. it *h.* you
24 seen and *h.* both me and F.
25 they *h.* me without a cause
17:14 the world hath *h.* them
Eph. 5:29 no man *h.* own flesh
Heb. 1:9 thou hast *h.* iniquity

HATEFUL, LY.
Ps. 36:2 iniq. be found to be *h.*
Tit. 3:3 *h.* hating one another
Rev. 18:2 cage uncl. and *h.* bird

HATERS.
Ps. 81:15 *h.* of L. should submit
Rom. 1:30 backbiters, *h.* of God

HATEST.
2 *Sam.* 19:6 and *h.* thy friends
Ps. 5:5 *h.* workers of iniquity
45:7 lov. righte. *h.* wickedness
50:17 thou *h.* instruction
Rev. 2:6 *h.* deeds of Nicolaitans

HATETH.
Deut. 7:10 not slack to *h.* him
16:22 nor set up image Lord *h.*
Job 34:17 *h.* he who *h.* right go.?
Ps. 11:5 loveth viol, his soul *h.*
120:6 dwelt him that *h.* peace
Prov. 11:15 *h.* suretyship is sure
12:1 he that *h.* reproof is brutish
13:5 a righteous man *h.* lying
24 he that spareth rod *h.* son
15:10 that *h.* reproof shall die
27 he that *h.* gifts shall live
26:24 *h.* dissem. with lips
28 lying tongue *h.* those afflic.
28:16 *h.* cove. sh. prolong days
29:24 partner with thief *h.* soul
Is. 1:14 appo. feasts my soul *h.*
Mat. 2:16 he *h.* putting away
John 3:20 ev. one doeth evil *h.* l.
7:7 me world *h.* bee. I testify
12:25 *h.* life in world sh. keep it
15:19 not of world, world *h.* you
23 *h.* me, my Father also
1 *John* 2:9 *h.* bro. is in dark. 11
3:15 *h.* his brother is murderer
4:20 I love G. *h.* brother, is liar

HATING.
Ex. 18:21 *h.* covetousness
Tit. 3:3 and *h.* one another
Jude 23 *h.* garm. spotted by flesh

HATH.
Prov. 22:20 who *h.* woe? who *h.*
sorrow? who *h.* wounds?
Is. 45:9 *h.* no ha. 50:10 no light
55:1 *h.*, no money, buy and eat.
Jer. 49:1 *h.* I. no sons? *h.* no heir?
Mal. 3:30 *h.* not, where to lay his
head, *Luke* 9:58
11:15 he that *h.* ears to hear,
12:9, 43; *Mark* 4:9; *Luke* 8:8;
14:35; *Rev.* 2:7
13:12 whoso, *h.* to him shall he
giv, who *h.* not, sh. be taken
that he *h.* 25:29; *Mark* 4:25;
Luke 8:18; 19:26
24 stablisheth *h.* he *h.* layeth hold
1 *John* 3:17 he that *h.* the Son *h.*
life, *h.* not Son, *h.* not life
2 *John* 3 whoso *h.* not in Ch. *h.* not
G. abideth *h.* Father and S.

HATRED.
Num. 35:20 he thrust him of *h.*
Ps. 25:19 hate me w. th cruel *h.*
109:3 camp. me about with *h.*
5 rewarded me *h.* for my love
139:22 hate them with perf. *h.*
Prov. 10:12 *h.* stirreth up strifes
18 hideth *h.* with lying lips
15:17 than stalled ox and *h.*
Ec. 9:1 know. either love or *h.*
6 their *h.* and envy perished
Hos. 9:8 proph. is *h.* in house of G.
Gal. 5:20 witchcraft, *h.*, variance

HATS.
Dan. 3:21 bound in hosen and *h.*

HAUGHTY.
2 *Sam.* 22:28 th. eyes are upon *h.*
Ps. 131:1 my heart is not *h.*
Prov. 16:18 *h.* spirit before a fall
18:12 before destruction heart *h.*
21:24 *h.* scorner is his name

HEA

Is. 3:16 daughters of Zion are *h.*
24:4 the *h.*, people of the earth
Zep. 3:11 no more *h.*

HAUGHTINESS.
Is. 2:11 *h.* of men bowed down
17 *h.* of men shall be made low
13:11 lay low the *h.* of terrible
16:6 heard *h.* of Moab, *Jer.* 48:29

HAUNT, Substantive.
1 *Sam.* 23:22 see where his *h.* is

HAUNT.
1 *Sam.* 30:31 where D. wont to *h.*
Ezek. 26:17 ter. he on all that *h.*

HAVE. See COMPASSION, DO-
MINION, etc.

HAVEN.
Gen. 49:13 Zebulun dwell at *h.*
Ps. 107:30 bringeth to desired *h.*
Acts 27:12 *h.* not commodious

HAVOC.
Acts 8:3 S. made *h.* of the church

HAWK.
Lev. 11:16 *h.* abom. *Deut.* 14:15
Job 39:26 doth A. fly by wisdom?

HAY.
Prov. 27:25 *h.* appear. and grass
Is. 15:6 the *h.* is withered away
1 *Cor.* 3:12 buildeth on found. *h.*

HAZAEL.
1 *K.* 19:15 ano. H. to be king, 17
2 *K.* 8:9 H. went to meet Elisha
10:32 H. smote them, *John* 1:4
12:17 H. set face to go to Jeru.
13:3 Israel into the hand of H.

HAZEL.
Gen. 30:37 Jacob took rods of *h.*

HAZELELPONI.
1 *Chr.* 4:3

HAZEROTH.
Num. 11:35; 12:16; 33:17

HAZON.
Jos. 11:10 Joshua took H.
Jud. 4:2; 1 *K.* 9:15; 2 *K.* 15:29
Jer. 49:30 dwell deep, inh. of H.

HE.
Gen. 3:16 *h.* shall rule over thee
49:8 *h.* whom brot, shall praise
Deut. 32:39 I am A. and there is
the God with me, *Is.* 41:4;
43:10, 13; 46:4; 48:12
Mat. 24:26 *h.* is in desert
Mark 12:32 is none other but *h.*
John 1:15 *h.* of whom I spake, 30
7:11 wh. is *h.* 25 is not this *h.?*
8:28 then shall ye k. th. I am A.
9:9 is *h.* but *h.* said, I am *h.*
36 and said, Who is A. L.? 37
1 *Cor.* 10:22 we stronger than *h.?*

See BLESSED, DID, SAITH.

HEAD.
Gen. 3:15 it shall bruise thy *h.*
40:13 Ph. sh. lift up thy *h.* 19
49:26 blessings on head of Jos.
and on top of *h. Deut.* 33:16
Ex. 29:10 A. and sons put hands
on *h.* of bul. *Lev.* 4:4; 8:11
15 Aar. and sons put hands on
h. of ram, *Ver.* 8:18, 22
1 *Sam.* 1:11 hand on *h.* of offering
4:29 hand on *h.* of offering, 31
13:45 clothes rent, and his *h.* b.
19:22 shalt rile before hoary *h.*
21:5 not make bald, on the *h.*
Num. 5:18 priest uncov. wo. *h.*
6:5 no razor come on Nazar. *h.*
7 consecration of God on his *h.*
9 sh. shave *h.* 18; *Deut.* 21:12
18 burn *h.* of consecration
Jud. 13:5 no razor come on *h.*
1 *Sam.* 17:57 Goliath's *h.* in hand
31:9 and they cut off Saul's *h.*
2:22 make the keeper of my *h.*
17:22 earth upon *h.* 19:22
Ezek. 9:10 and said, Am A dog's *h.?*
16:9 take off his *h.*
2 *K.* 2:3 master from *h.* to day, 5
4:19 said to his fa. My *h.* my *h.*
6:31 *h. of E.* shall stand on him
10:22 dau. of J. hath shaken *h.*
2 *Chr.* 6:23 recompen. way on *h.*
Ezr. 9:6 iniq. increased over *h.*
Neh. 4:4 l turn reproach upon *h.*
Ps. 3:3 lifter of my *h.*
3 my *h.* is lifted up
Est. 7:10 life thou hast gi. *h.*
22:7 about out lip, shake the *h.*
23:5 anointest my *h.* with oil
27:6 now sh. my *h.* be lifted up

CRUDEN'S CONCORDANCE.

HEA

Ps. 38:4 iniq. gone over my *h.*
60:7 Ephr. strength of A. 108:8
28:21 G. shall wound *h.* of one.
110:7 therefore sh. he lift up *h.*
110:9 *h.* of those that comp. me
141:5 which shall not break *h.*
Prov. 10:6 blessings on *h.* of just
11:26 blessing on *h.* selleth corn
25:22 of fire on *h.* Rom. 12:20
Ec. 2:14 wise man's eyes in *h.*
Cant. 2:6 hand under my *h.* 8:3
5:2 my *h.* is filled with dew
11 *h.* as fine gold; 7:5 *h.* as C.
Is. 1:5 the whole *h.* is sick
51:11 everlasting joy on their *h.*
58:5 bow down *h.* as a bulrush?
59:17 helmet of salvation on *h.*
Jer. 2:37 and thy hands on thy *h.*
9:1 O that my *h.* were waters
Ezek. 9:10 recompense way on *h.*
29:18 every *h.* was made bald
Dan. 2:38 thou art this *h.* of gold
Joel 3:4 recompense on your *h.* ?
Amos 2:7 dust on *h.* of the poor
8:10 bring baldness on every *h.*
9:1 he said, Cut them in the *h.*
Zec. 1:21 no man did lift up *h.*
4:7 set crowns on *h.* of Josiua
Mat. 5:36 neither swear by thy *h.*
27:30 sm. him on *h.* Mark 15:19
Mark 6:24 *h.* of John the Baptist
Luke 7:46 *h.* wi. oil didst not an.
John 13:9 also my hands and *h.*
1 Cor. 11:4 *h.* cov. dishonoreth
10 ought to *h.* power on her *h.*
12:21 the *h.* to the foot
Eph. 1:22 gave him *h.* to church,
4:15; Col. 1:8
Col. 2:19 holding *h.* from body
Rev. 19:12 on *h.* many crowns
See BEARD, BALD, BOW, BOWED, COVER, COVERED, CROWN.

Bed's HEAD.
Gen. 47:31 bowed hims. on *h. h.*

HEAD of the corner.
Mat. 21:42 beco. *h.* Mark 12:10;
Lu. 20:17; Acts 4:11; 1 Pet. 2:7

HEAD, for ruler, governor.
Num. 17:3 one rod *h.* of house
Deut. 28:13 L. will make thee A.
44 sh. be *h.* and thou the tail
Jud. 11:9 I your *h.* ƒ 11 him A.
1 Sam. 15:17 when last kept me
to be *h.* Ps. 18:43
Is. 7:8 *h.* of Damascus is Rezin, 9
9:14 cut off from Is. *h.* and tail
15 ancient and honorable is *h.*
Jer. 22:6 Gilead to me, *h.* of Leb.
Hos. 1:11 sp. themselves one *h.*
Hab. 3:13 *h.* out of ho. of wicked
strike through *h.* of villages
1 Cor. 11:3 *h.* of man is Ch. *h.* of
woman man, *h.* of Ch. is G.
Eph. 5:23 husband is *h.* of wife,
even as Christ is *h.* of church
Col. 2:10 who *h.* of principality

HEAD, for top, chief.
Is. 28:1 on *h.* of fat valleys, 4
51:20 lie at the *h.* of all streets
Ezek. 16:25 built places at *h.*
31:21 king stood at *h.* of 2 ways

HEAD, with hair, e.
Lev. 13:40 *h.* is fallen off *h.* 41
14:9 leper shave *hair* off his *h.*
Num. 6:5 locks of *h.* of *h.* grow
18 take *h.* of *h.* of his separat.
Jud. 16:22 *h.* of *h.* began to grow
1 Sam. 14:45 not *h.* of *h.* fall
2 Sam. 14:26 *h.* of *h.* at 200 shek.
Ezr. 9:3 plucked off *h.* of my *h.*
Jer. 40:18 more than *h.* of *h.* Eze.
Cant. 7:5 *h.* of thy *h.* like purple
Dan. 3:27 nor *hair* of *h.* singed
7:9 *h.* of his *h.* like pure wool
Mat. 10:30 *h.* of your *h.* number.
Luke 12:7
Luke 7:38 wipe with *h.* of *h.* 44
21:18 shall not a *h.* of *h.* perish
Acts 27:34 nor a *hair* fall from *h.*
Rev. 1:14 his *h.* and *h.* were white

HEADBANDS.
Is. 3:20 take away *h.*

HEADLONG.
Job 5:13 counsel of frow. car. *h.*
Luke 4:29 cast him down *h.*
Acts 1:18 falling *h.* he burst asu.
Spear's HEAD.
1 Sam. 17:7 *spear's h.* weighed
600 shekels, 2 Sam. 21:16

HEADSTONE.
Ps. 118:22 *h.* of corner
Zec. 4:7 bring *h.* with shoutings

HEADS.
Gen. 40:23 bowed th. A. Ex. 4:31

HEA

Lev. 10:6 uncover not your *h.*
1 K. 20:31 let us put ropes on *h.*
32 put ropes on their *h.*
2 K. 10:6 *h.* of your master's sons
6 brought the *h.* of king's sons
Ps. 24:7 lift your *h.* O ye gates, 9
66:12 men to ride over our *h.*
74:13 breakest the *h.* of dragon
14 brakest the *h.* of leviathan
109:25 shaked their *h.*
Is. 15:2 on their *h.* be baldness
35:10 everlasting joy on their *h.*
Jer. 14:3 they covered their *h.*
Ezek. 7:18 bald. sh. be on their *h.*
11:21 recomp. way on *h.* 22:31
32:27 laid swords under *h.*
44:18 linen bonnets on their *h.*
20 they shall poll their *h.*
Mat. 27:39 wag. *h.* Mark 15:29
Luke 21:28 and lift up your *h.*
Acts 18:6 yo, blood be on your *h.*
Rev. 9:7 their *h.* as it were cro.
13:1 a beast having seven *h.*
3 I saw one of his *h.* wounded
17:9 seven *h.* seven mountains
18:19 they cast dust on their *h.*

HEADS, for governors.
Ex. 18:25 made th. *h.* over peo.
Num. 25:4 take all the *h.* of peo.
Ps. 110:6 wound *h.* over counter.
Mic. 3:1 hear, O *h.* of Jacob. 9
11 *h.* thereof judge for reward
See FATHERS.

HEADY.
2 Tim. 3:4 men be *h.* high-mind.

HEAL.
Deut. 32:39 I kill, I wound, I *h.*
2 K. 20:5 A. thee, add to thy da.
8 Chr. 7:14 forgive sin, *h.* land
Ps. 6:2 *h.* me, for bones are vex.
41:4 *h.* my soul, I have sinned
60:2 *h.* the breaches thereof
Ec. 3:3 time to kill, time to *h.*
Is. 57:18 seen ways, and *h.* 19
Jer. 3:22 I will *h.* your backslid.
17:14 *h.* me, O Lord
30:17 I will *h.* thee of wounds
Lam. 2:13 br. great, who can *h.* ?
Hos. 6:1 ha. torn, and will *h.* us
14:4 I will *h.* their backslidings
Mat. 8:7 I will come and *h.* him
10:8 *h.* the sick, Luke 9:2; 10:9
12:10 *h.* on sab.-day Luke 14:3
13:15 be converted and I sho. *h.*
them, John 12:40; Acts 28:27
Mark 3:2 *h.* on sabbath, Luke 6:7
Luke 4:18 to *h.* broken-hearted
23 Physician, *h.* thyself
John 4:47 come down and *h.*
Acts 4:30 stretching hand to *h.*

HEALED.
Ex. 21:19 sh. cause him to be *h.*
Lev. 13:18 boil *h. ;* 37 scall is *h.*
14:3 plague of leprosy be *h.* 48
2 K. 2:21 *h.* waters ; 22 waters *h.*
8 Chr. 30:20 L. heark. and *h.* pe.
Ps. 30:2 cried to thee, thou *h.*
107:20 sent his word and *h.* th.
Is. 6:10 and convert, and be *h.*
53:5 with his stripes we are *h.*
Jer. 6:14 have *h.* the hurt, 8:11
17:14 and I shall be *h.*
51:9 we would have *h.* Babylon
Ezek. 34:4 neither have *h.* sick
47:8 the waters shall be *h.* 9
11 the marshes shall not be *h.*
Hos. 7:1 when I would have *h.*
11:3 knew not that I *h.* them
Mat. 4:24 palsy, and be *h.* 8:16
8:8 my serv. shall be *h.* Lu. 7:7
12:15 follow. he *h.* them, 14:14
Luke 8:43 nor could be *h.* of any
13:14 therefore come and be *h.*
17:15 saw he was *h.* turned ba.
22:51 touch. his ear and *h.* him
John 5:13 *h.* wist not who it was
Acts 4:14 beh. man who was *h.*
14:9 that he had faith to be *h.*
Heb. 12:13 but let it rather be *h.*
1 Pet. 2:24 wh. stri. ye were *h.*
Rev. 13:3 deadly wo. was *h.* 12

HEALER.
Is. 3:7 saying, I will not be a *h.*

HEALETH.
Ex. 15:26 the L. that *h.* thee
Ps. 103:3 bless Lord who *h.* dis.
147:3 he *h.* the broken in heart
Is. 30:26 *h.* stroke of th. wound

HEALING, Substantive.
Jer. 14:19 there is no *h.* for us
Nah. 3:19 th. is no *h.* thy bruise
Mal. 4:2 with *h.* in his wings
Luke 9:11 healed them need *h.*
Acts 4:22 miracle of *h.* showed

HEA

1 Cor. 12:9 another gift of *h.* 28
30 have all the gifts of *h. ?*
Rev. 22:2 leaves for *h.* of nations

HEALING.
Jer. 30:13 thou hast no *h.* medic.
Mat. 4:23 *h.* all man. of sickness
9:35 preach. gos. *h.* every w.
Acts 10:38 *h.* all oppressed

HEALTH.
Gen. 43:28 our father in good *h.*
2 Sam. 20:9 in *h.* my brother ?
Ps. 42:11 *h.* of my count. 43:5
67:2 saving *h.* may be known
Prov. 3:8 it sh. be *h.* to thy nav.
4:22 they are *h.* to their flesh
12:18 tongue of the wise is *h.*
13:17 a faithful ambassador is *h.*
16:24 sweet to soul, *h.* to bones
Jer. 8:15 looked for *h.* 14:19
15 for *h.* and beh. trouble
30:17 I will restore *h.* unto thee
Acts 27:34 take meat, this is *h.*
3 John 2 mayest be in *h.*

HEAP, Substantive.
Gen. 31:46 a *h.* cat on the *h.*
52 this *h.* be witness
Ex. 15:8 floods stood as *h.* Jos. 3:13, 16 ; Ps. 33:7 ; 78:13
Deut. 13:16 shall be a *h.* for ever
Jos. 7:20 over him *h.* of stones
Ruth 3:7 lie down at *h.* of corn
2 Sam. 18:17 great *h.* on Absal.
Cant. 7:2 belly like *h.* of wheat
Is. 17:11 harvest shall be a *h.*
25:2 hast made of a city a *h.*
Jer. 30:18 city builded on own *h.*
Mic. 1:6 Samaria a *h.* of the field
3:12 walk thro' *h.* of waters
Hag. 2:16 came to a *h.* of 20 meas.

HEAP, Verb.
Deut 32:23 *h.* mischs upon them
Job 16:4 *h.* up words against you
27:16 he *h.* up silver as the dust
36:13 hypocrites in heart *h.* wr.
Prov. 25:22 *h.* coals, Rom. 12:20
Ex. 3:20 to gather and to *h.* up
Hab. 1:10 sh. *h.* dust and take it
2 Tim. 4:3 *h.* to themsel. teach.

HEAPED.
Ps. 39:6 he *h.* up riches
Hab. 2:5 *h.* unto him all people
Jam. 5:3 have *h.* treasure toget.

HEAPS.
Jud. 15:16 jaw of ass, *h.* on *h.*
2 K. 10:8 lay ye them in two *h.*
2 Chr. 31:6 and laid them by *h.*
Job 15:28 bonnes ready to bec. *h.*
Ps. 79:1 laid Jerusalem on *h.*
Jer. 9:11 make Jerusal. *h.* 26:18
31:21 set thee up, make *h.* high
Hos. 12:11 their altars are as *h.*
Mic. 3:12 Jerus. shall become *h.*

HEAR.
Gen. 21:6 all that *h.* laugh
Ex. 32:18 them that sing do I *h.*
Num. 23:18 ri. up, Balak, and *h.*
30:4 her vow and her bond
Deut. 1:16 *h.* causes betw. breth.
4:10 make them *h.* my words
5:1 A. Is. the statutes, 6:3; 9:1;
20:3; Is. 48:1; Mark 12:29
27 *h.* all the L. or G. shall say
12:28 *h.* these words, I am
13:12 shall *h.* say in one of cit.
30:12 bring it that we may *h.*
31:12 *h.* and fear L. 13; Jer. 6:10
Jud. 5:3 *h.* O ye kings, give ear
1 Sam. 2:23 *h.* your evil dealings
15:14 low. of oxen which I *h.*
16:2 if Saul *h.* it, he will kill me
Neh. 2:16 out of city, *h.* *h.*
23:25 soon as *h.* Ps. 18:44
K. 4:31 *h.* wisdom of Solomon,
2 Chr. 9:7, 23 ; Mat. 12:42 ; Luke 11:31
8:30 A. in heaven and forg. 32,
36, 39, 43, 45, 49; 2 Chr. 6:21
18:26 saying, O Baal, *h.* us
2 K. 7:6 A. a noise of chariots
18:28 A. the word of the great
king, Is. 36:13; 37:17
1 Chr. 14:15 wh. thou *h.* sound
Neh. 1:6 *h.* the prayer of servant
4:4 A. O God, we are despised
5:6 *h.* their cry, and understand
Job 5:27, *h.* it, and know thou it
13:17 *h.* dilig. my speech, 21:2
27:9 *h.* his cry ? 31:35 *h.* me
42:4 A. I beseech thee
Ps. 4:1 *h.* my prayer, O G. 39:12;
54:2; 84:8; 102:1; 143:1
20:1 L. *h.* thee in day of troub.

HEA

Ps. 20:9 let the king *h.* us
27:7 *h.* O Lord, when I cry
30:10 A. O L. and have mercy
49:1 A. this all ye people
50:7 *h.* peo. I will speak, 81:8
51:8 make me *h.* joy and gladn.
59:7 who, say they, doth *h. ?*
61:1 A. my cry, O God
66:16 *h.* all ye that fear God
102:20 *h.* groaning of prisoner
138:4 *h.* words of thy mouth
143:8 to *h.* thy loving-kindness
Prov. 1:8 *h.* instruction of father
4:1 *h.* ye children, instruction
10 *h.* and rec. sayings, 19:20
8:6 *h.* I speak of excel. things
33 *h.* instruction, and be wise
19:27 cease to *h.* instruction
22:17 *h.* the words of the wise
23:19 *h.* thou, my son, be wise
Ec. 5:1 more ready to *h.* than
7:5 better to *h.* rebuke of wise
12:13 *h.* conclusion of matter
Cant. 8:13 cause me to *h.*
Is. 1:2 *h.* O heavens, give ear
6:9 *h.* ye indeed, Mark 4:12
18:3 bloweth a trumpet, *h.* ye
33:13 *h.* ye that are afar off
34:1 earth *h.* all that is therein
42:18 *h.* ye deaf; 23 will *h.*
43:9 let them *h.* and say truth
48:14 assemble yourself, and *h.*
55:3 *h.* soul sh. live. John 5:25
Jer. 5:16 *h.* ye nat. 19 O earth
11:2 *h.* words of covenant, 6
10 forefathers ref. to *h.* 13:10
13:15 *h.* ye, give ear, L. spoken
18:2 cause thee to *h.* my words
33:22 cause my peo. to *h.* words
38:25 princes *h.* that I have tal.
49:20 *h.* counsel of Lord, 50:45
Lam. 1:18 A. I pray you, all peo.
Ezek. 2:8 *h.* wh. I say unto thee
3:17 *h.* wo. at my mouth, 33:7
27 he that heareth, let him *h.*
33:31 *h.* words, not do them, 32
Dan. 9:17 *h.* prayer of thy serv.
19 A. O Lord, forgive, hearken
Hos. 5:1 A. ye this, O priests
Joel 1:2 *h.* this, old men
Amos 3:1 *h.* this word L. hath
spoken, 4:1; 5:1; 8:4
Mic. 1:2 *h.* all ye people
3:1 *h.* I pray you, heads of J. 9
6:2 A. O mountains; *h.* ye rod
Nah. 3:19 all that *h.* bruit sh.
Mat. 11:4 show John thi. ye *h.*
5 deaf *h.* Mark 7:37 ; Luke 7:22
13:17 *h.* things ye *h.* Luke 10:24
15:10 he said to multitude, *h.*
17:5 bel. Son, *h.* him, Mark 9:7
18:17 if he neglect to *h.* them
Mark 4:18 are such as *h.* the
word, 20; Luke 8:13, 15
24 heed wh. ye *h.* you that *h.*
Luke 5:1 pressed on him to *h.*
15 multit. came together to *h.*
6:17 came to *h.* him
8:18 take heed there. how ye *h.*
21 wh. *h.* word and do it, 11:23
9:9 who is this of whom I *h. ?*
16:2 how is it I *h.* this of thee ?
Moses and prophets *h.* them
19:48 peop. very attentive to *h.*
21:38 came to temple to *h.* him
John 5:30 I *h.* I ju. 6:60 who *h. ?*
7:51 judge man before it *h.* him
9:27 whereof. wo. ye *h.* it aga. ?
10:3 sheep *h.* voice
12:47 if man *h.* words, bel. not
14:24 word wh. ye *h.* is not mi.
Acts 2:8 *h.* ev. man in own tong.
25 which ye *h.* and see, and *h.*
10:22 and to *h.* words of thee
33 A. all things command. thee
13:7 desired to *h.* word of God
44 whole city came to *h.* word
15:7 Gen. by my mouth *h.* word
17:21 A. some new thing
22:1 A. ye my defence
24:4 *h.* us of thy clemency
25:22 I would *h.* man myself
28:22 to *h.* what thou thinkest
1 Cor. 11:18 I *h.* th. be divisions
Phil. 1:27 may *h.* of your affairs
2 Thes. 3:11 we *h.* that some wo.
1 Tim. 4:16 and them that *h.*
2 Tim. 4:17 all Gentiles mig. *h.*
Jam. 1:19 eve. one be swift to *h.*
1 John 5:15 know that he *h.* us
3 John 4 *h.* children walk in tru.
Rev. 1:3 bles. *h.* words of prop.
9:20 neither see, nor *h.* nor wa.
See EAR, EARS, VOICE.

HEAR me.
1 K. 18:37 *h.* me, O Lord *h.* me

HEA

HEARER, S.
Rom. 2:13 not h. of law are just.
Eph. 4:29 minister grace unto h.
2 Tim. 2:14 subverting of the h.
Jam. 1:22 doers of word, not h.
23 if any be a h. of the word
25 he being not a forgetful h.

HEAREST.
1 Sam. 24:9 h. thou m.'s words?
2 Sam. 5:24 h. sound in mulb...t.
1 K. 8:30 h. forgive, 2 Chr. 6:21
Ps. 22:2 cry in daytime, h. not
65:2 thou that h. prayer
Mat. 21:16 h. thou what th. say?
27:13 h. thou not how many th.
John 3:8 and thou h. the sound
11:42 that thou h. me always

HEARETH.
Deut. 29:19 h. words of curse
1 Sam. 3:9 L. thy servant h. 10
Job 34:28 h. cry of the afflicted
Ps. 34:17 righte. cry, the Lord h.
38:14 as a man that h. not
69:33 L. h. poor, desp. not pris.
Prov. 8:34 blessed is man h. me
13:1 h. his father's instruction
8 but poor h. not rebuke
15:29 he h. prayer of righteous
31 that h. reproof of life, 32
18:13 answ. matter before h. it
21:28 the man that h. speaketh
25:10 that h. it put thee to sha.
29:24 h. cursing, bewrayeth not
Is. 42:20 open ears, but h. not
Ezek. 3:27 he that h. let him hear
Mat. 7:24 h. say. 26; Luke 6:47, 49
13:19 h. word of the kingdom
20 that h. the word, 22, 23
Luke 10:16 he that h. you h. me
John 3:29 standeth and h. him
5:24 h. my word, and believeth
8:47 that s of G. h. G.'s words
9:31 God h. not sinners
18:37 that is of truth, h. voice
2 Cor. 12:6 above th. he h. of me
1 John 4:5 the world h. them
6 he that knoweth God h. us
5:14 ask accord. to will, he h. us
Rev. 22:17 him that h. say, Come
18 to ev. man that h. the words

HEARING.
Deut. 31:11 read this law in th. h.
2 Sam. 18:12 our h. king charged
2 K. 4:31 neither voice nor h.
Job 33:8 hast spoken in my h.
42:5 I have heard of thee by h.
Is. 11:3 nor reprove af. h. of ears
21:3 bowed down at the h. of it
33:15 stoppeth ears fr. h. blood
Ezek. 9:5 said in my h. Go
10:13 cried unto them in my h.
Amos 8:11 h. word of the Lord
Acts 25:21 reserved to h. of Aug.
23 entered into the place of h.
Rom. 10:17 faith cometh by h.
1 Cor. 12:17 where were the h. ?
Gal. 3:2 or by the h. of faith, 5
Heb. 5:11 seeing ye are dull of h.

HEARING, Verb.
Prov. 20:12 h. ear, L. hath made
28:9 away ear from h. the law
Ec. 1:8 nor is ear filled with h.
Mat. 13:13 and h. they hear not
14 by h. ye shall hear
15 dull of h. Acts 28:27; Heb. 5:11
Mark 6:2 many h. were aston.
Luke 2:46 h. them and asking
Acts 5:5 Ananias h. these words
8:6 h. and seeing miracles
9:7 h. a voice, but seeing no m.
18:8 Corinthians h. believed
Phile. 5 h. of thy love and faith
3 John 2:3 Lot is seeing and h.

HEARKEN.
Ex. 6:30 sh. Pharaoh h. to me ?
Deut. 7:12 h. to these judgments
11:13 h. dilig. to my commands
13:3 h. to voice of L. Jer. 17:24
18:15 to him ye shall h.
23:13 if thou h. to commandments, 1 K. 11:38
Jos. 1:17 so will we h. unto thee
1 Sam. 15:22 to h. th. fat of rams
33:24 who will h. to you in this ?
1 K. 8:28 have thou respect to h.
29 h. to prayer, 52; 2 Chr. 6:19, 20
Neh. 13:27 h. then to you ?
Ps. 81:8 if thou wilt h. unto me
Prov. 29:12 if a ruler h. to lies
Is. 32:3 ears of th. that hear h.
42:23 will h. for time to come?
Jer. 26:3 will h. and turn fr. evil
5 h. to prophets whom I sent
29:12 pray to me, and I will h.
35:13 not rec. instruction to h.

HEA

Zec. 7:11 but they refused to h.
Acts 4:19 h. to you
12:13 a damsel came to h.

HEARKEN, imperatively.
Gen. 23:15 h. to me; 49:2 h. to Is.
Num. 23:18 h. to me, son of Zip.
Deut. 4:1 h. O Israel, to statutes
27:9 take heed, and h. O Israel
Jud. 9:7 h. to me, men of Shech.
1 K. 8:30 h. to the supplications, 2 Chr. 6:21
22:28 h. O peo. every one of you
2 Chr. 18:27 he said, h. all peop.
20:15 h. ye, all Judah, and Jer.
Job 13:6 h. to pleadings
32:10 I said h. to me, 33:31
33:1 I pray, h. to my words
34:10 h. unto me, men of under.
34 w. man h. 31:14 h. to this
Ps. 34:11 h. I will teach you
45:10 h. O daughter, and consid.
Prov. 7:24 h. to me, O chil. 8:32
Is. 28:23 h. and hear my speech
34:1 ye nations, h. ye peo. 49:1
46:3 h. unto me, O house of Jacob, 48:12; Hos. 5:1
12 h. to me, stout-hearted
51:1 h. to me, th. fol. righteous.
4 h. unto me, my people
7 h. to me, ye th. know right.
55:2 h. diligently unto me
Dan. 9:19 O Lord, h. and do
Mic. 1:2 h. O earth, and all ther.
Mark 7:14 h. to me every one
Acts 2:14 h. to my words
7:2 brethren, and fathers, h.
13:13 men and brethren, h.
Jam. 2:5 my beloved brethren

See voice.

HEARKEN, with not.
Gen. 34:17 not h. to be circum.
Ex. 7:4 not h. to you, 22; 11:9
Deut. 13:3 n. h. to that dreamer
17:12 will not h. to the priest
18:19 will not h. to my words
21:18 he will not h. to them
23:3 n. h. to Bal. Jos. 24:10
Jos. 1:18 will n. h. to thy words
Jud. 2:17 would not h. to judges
1 K. 20:8 elders said h. n. to him
2 K. 17:40 n. h. but after manner
18:31 h. n. to Hezek. Is. 36:16
2 Chr. 10:16 Rehob. would not h.
35:16 h. spake, they would n. h.
Job 33:31 if n. h. hold thy peace
Ps. 58:5 n. h. to voice of charm.
61:11 would not h. to my voice
Jer. 6:10 uncircumcised cannot h.
17 said, We will not h. 44:16
7:27 they will not h. unto thee
11:11 tho. they cry, I will not h.
16:12 they may not h. to me
17:27 if ye will not h. to me.
26:4 Ezek. 20:39
23:16 h. not to prophets, 27:9, 14, 16, 17; 29:8
29:19 wilt thou not h. to me?
Ezek. 3:7 h. n. h. to me, not to me
20:8 and would not h. unto me
Hos. 9:17 did n. h. Zec. 1:4

HEARKENED.
Gen. 30:17 God h. unto Leah
22 God h. to Rachel and open.
30:10 that Joseph h. not to her
Ex. 6:12 of Isr. have not h. to me
7:13 Phar. h. not, 9:12, 13; 9:13
Deut. 9:19 Lord h. to me, 10:10
18:14 nations h. to obs. of times
34:9 Is. h. to Joshua. Jos. 1:17
1 Sam. 28:21 woun. of En. h. to S.
1 K. 12:15 king h. not to people, 2 Chr. 10:15
24 they h. to word of the Lord
15:20 A. to king, Asa, 2 Chr. 16:4
2 K. 13:4 the Lord h. to Jehoahaz
16:9 king of Assyria h. to Asa
20:13 Hezekiah h. to messengers
21:9 Judah h. not to the law
22:13 our fathers h. not to words
2 Chr. 24:17 J. h. to the princes
25:16 Amaz. h. not to the prop.
33:22 Josiah h. not to Pharaoh
Neh. 9:16 h. not to thy commandments, 29, 34; Jer. 34:11
Est. 3:3 Mordecai h. not to them
Ps. 81:13 O that thou hadst h.
Is. 21:7 and he h. diligently
48:18 O that thou hadst h.
Jer. 6:19 have not h. to my words
26:5 I sent, but ye have not h.
29:19 devices in a man's h.
32:33 counsel in h. like deep wa.
81:1 king's h. is in hand of L.
4 a high look and a proud h.
22:11 pureness of h. king his fr.
15 foolish, bound in h. of child

HEA

Mat. 3:16 the Lord h. Jer. 8.
Acts 27:21 should have h. to me
See voice.

HEARKENEDST.
Deut. 28:15 thou h. not to the L.

HEARKENETH, ING.
Ps. 103:20 angels h. to the voice
Prov. 1:33 h. to me sh. dw. safely
12:15 he that h. to coun. is wise

HEART, Noun.
Gen. 45:26 and Jacob's h. fainted
Ex. 23:9 know h. of a stranger
28:30 they shall be on Aaron's h.
35:35 hath filled with wisd. of h.
Lev. 26:16 and cause sorrow of h.
Num. 32:7 discourage h. of Is. ?
9 they discouraged the h. of Is.
Deut. 5:29 such a h. in them
28:28 smite wi. astonish. of h.
47 serv. not L. with glad. of h.
65 L. sh. give thee trembling h.
29:4 L. hath not given h. to per.
Jos. 14:8 made h. of people melt
Jud. 5:15 great thoughts of h.
18:20 the priest's h. was glad
1 Sam. 1:13 Han. spake in her h.
10:9 God gave him another h.
16:7 the Lord looketh on the h.
17:32 Let no man's h. fail
24:5 and David's h. smote him
25:31 offence of h. to my lord
36 and Nabal's h. was merry
2 Sam. 6:16 she despised him in h.
14:1 king's h. was tow. Absalom
18:14 darts thro. h. of Absalom
14 bowed h. of men of Judah
1 K. 3:9 an understanding h.
12 given thee understanding h.
8:66 glad of h. 2 Chr. 7:10
10:2 com. of all in h. 2 Chr. 9:1
11:4 perfect, as the h. of David
12:27 then wh. the h. of this peo.
2 K. 6:11 h. of king of Ar. troub.
Neh. 2:2 nor h. for any but h.
1 Chr. 12:33 not of double h.
16:10 let the h. rej. Ps. 105:3
29:17 triest h. 18; Jer. 11:20
2 Chr. 7:11 came into Solom.'s h.
22:9 turned h. of king
27 such as this is the king's h.
Neh. 2:2 noth. else but sor. of h.
Est. 1:10 h. of king merry
5:9 H. went forth with glad h.
Job 8:10 wise in h. and mighty
12:24 he taketh away h. of chief
23:13 caused widow's h. to sing
37:24 respecteth not wise of h.
38:36 given understanding to h.
Ps. 12:2 double h. they speak
19:8 sta. of L. right, rejoicing h.
34:18 nigh them of broken h.
41:21 knoweth secrets of the h.
45:5 arrows sharp in h. of enc.
58:2 ye work ; G:6 h. deep
73:7 more than h. could wish
101:4 froward h. shall depart
5 a proud h. will not I suffer
104:15 wine, make glad the h.
bread strengtheneth. man's h.
Prov. 6:18 a h. that deviseth wicked
7:10 a woman subtle of h.
9:5 he of an understanding h.
10:8 wise in h. will co. comma.
12:8 he of perverse h.
20 deceit is in the h. of them
23 heaviness in h. of man
13:12 hope defer. maketh h. sick
14:10 h. knoweth own bitters,
13 in laughter h. is sorrowful
14 backslider in h. be filled
30 a sound h. is life of the flesh
33 wisdom resteth in h. of him
15:7 h. of foolish doeth not so
13 merry h. mak. cheer. coun.
by sorrow of h. sp. is broken
14 h. of him th. understandeth
15 a merry h. hath contin. feast
28 h. of righte. studieth to an.
30 light of eye rejoiceth h. of h.
16:1 preparation of h. from L.
5 proud h. abomination to L.
9 a man's h. deviseth his way
21 wise of h. shall be prudent
23 h. of wise teach. his mouth
17:16 price in hand, hath no h.
20 froward h. find. no good
22 merry h. doeth good
18:12 bef. destruc. h. is haughty
19:21 devices in a man's h.
20:5 counsel in h. like deep wa.
21:1 king's h. is in hand of L.
4 a high look and a proud h.
22:11 pureness of h. king his fr.
15 foolish, bound in h. of child

HEA

Prov. 24:12 pon. the h. cons. it ?
25:3 h. of k. is unsearchable
20 he that singeth to heavy h.
26:23 wicked h. is like potsherd
27:9 ointment and perf. rej. h.
Ec. 7:9 of man answereth man
28:25 proud h. stirreth up strife
31:11 h. of her husb. doth trust
Ec. 7:3 sadn. of count. h. is bet.
4 h. of wise in house of mourn.
h. of fools in house of mirth
8:5 a wise man's h. discerneth
11 h. of men is set to do evil
9:3 the h. of men is full of evil
7 drink thy wine wi. merry h.
10:2 a wise man's h. at ri. hand,
but a fool's h. is at his left
Is. 6:10 make their h. fat, Mat. 13:15; Acts 28:27
12:12 I will punish the stout h.
13:7 every man's h. shall melt
30:29 shall have gladness of h.
32:4 h. of rash shall understand
33:4 say to them of fearful h.
44:20 dec. h. turned him aside
57:1 man layeth to h. Jer. 12:11
15 revive the h. of contrite on.
59:13 uttering from h. words
65:14 my serv. sing for joy of h.
but ye cry for sorrow of h.
Jer. 4:9 the h. of king sh. perish
3:23 people hath a rebellious h.
9:26 Is. are uncircumcised in h.
11:20 that triest reins and h.
17:9 h. is deceitful ab. all things
10 I the Lord search h.
20:12 L. that seest reins and h.
24:7 I will give a h. to know me
Lam. 3:65 give thou sorrow of h.
Ezek. 11:19 stony h. out of flesh
13:22 ye made h. of righte. sad
18:31 make a new h. and new s.
21:7 ev. h. sh. melt, all be feeble
25:15 veng. with despiseful h.
36:26 give you a h. of flesh
44:7 uncir. in h. 9; Acts 7:51
Dan. 4:16 a beast's h. be giv. him
7:4 and a man's h. was given it
Hos. 4:11 new wine take away h.
7:11 Eph. is like dove without h.
Nah. 2:10 h. melt. knees smite
Zec. 12:15 this city said in her h.
Mal. 2:2 ye do not lay it to h.
4:6 the h. of fathers, h. of child.
Mat. 11:29 meek and lowly in h.
12:34 of abund. of h. Luke 6:45
35 treasure of h. Luke 6:45
15:18 from the h. and defile man
19 out of h. evil th. Mark 7:21
Mark 10:14 upbr. with hard h.
Luke 2:19 M. pondered in her h.
51 mother, kept sayings in h.
24:25 fools, slow of h. to believe
John 13:2 devil put into h. of J.
Acts 2:46 eat meat wi. singl. of h.
5:33 were cat to h. 7:54
11:23 purpose of h. they cl. to L.
Rom. 2:5 thy impeni. h. treas. up
29 circumcision of h. in the sp.
6:17 ye obeyed from h. that doc.
10:10 with the h. man believeth
1 Cor. 2:9 nei. enter. in h. of man
7:37 hath so decreed in his h.
2 Cor. 2:4 anguish of h. I wrote
3:3 written in fleshly tables of h.
8:16 earnest care into h. of Tit.
Eph. 6:5 doing will of G. from h.
Col. 3:22 in singl. of h. fear. God
1 Thes. 2:17 in presence, not in h.
Heb. 4:12 is a discerner of the h.
10:22 draw near with a true h.
13:9 good the h. be establ-hed
1 Pet. 3:4 let be hidden man of h.
2 Pet. 2:14 a h. ex. with covetous
Rev. 18:7 she saith in her h. I sit

HEART.
Ex. 15:8 congealed in h. of sea
Is. 19:1 h. of Egypt shall melt
Mat. 12:40 Son of man in h.

HEART, with all.
Deut. 11:13 with all your h. Jos.
22:5 ; Jer. 32:41
13:3 love the Lord with all your h. 30:6; Mat. 22:37;
Mark 12:30, 33; Luke 10:27
26:16 ; do them with all h. ye
30:2 obey the L. with all h. 2:10
Jud. 16:17 h. told all his h. 18
1 K. 2:4 walk before me with all h. 8:23
8:48 return to thee with all th.
2 K. 23:25 ; 2 Chr. 6:33
14:9 David fol. me wi. all his h.
2 K. 23:3 covenant to walk with
all their h. 2 Chr. 34:31
2 Chr. 15:12 G. of fa. with all h.
15 had sworn with all their h.

CRUDEN'S CONCORDANCE.

HEA

Tender-HEARTED.
2 *Chr.* 13:7 Reho. young and *t.-h.*
Eph. 4:32 kind one to ano. *t.-h.*

Wise-HEARTED.
Ex. 28:3 spe. to all th. are *w.-h.*
31:6 hearts of all that are *w.-h.*
35:10 *w.-h.* among you sh. come
25 women that were *w.-h.*
35:1 wro. every *w.-h.* man, 2, 8

HEARTH.
Gen. 18:16 make cakes upon *h.*
Ps. 102:3 bones are burnt as *h.*
Is. 30:14 sherd to take fire fr. *h.*
Jer. 36:22 a fire on the *h.* burnt.
23 roll into fire that was on *h.*
Zec. 12:6 governors of J. like *h.*

HEARTY, ILY.
Prov. 27:9 friend by *h.* counsel
Col. 3:23 do it *h.* as to the Lord

HEARTS.
Jos. 7:5 *h.* of the people melted
1 *Sam.* 10:26 A. G. had touched
2 *Sam.* 15:6 Absal. stole *h.* of Is.
1 *K.* 8:39 thou only knowest the *h.*
A. 2 *Chr.* 6:30
1 *Chr.* 28:9 Lord searcheth all *h.*
Ps. 7:9 God trieth *h. Prov.* 17:3
Prov. 15:11 more then *h.* men
21:2 the Lord pondereth the *h.*
31:8 wine to those of heavy *h.*
Ezek. 32:9 also vex *h.* of people
Dan. 11:27 kings' *h.* to do misc.
Luke 1:17 turn *h.* of the fathers
2:35 thoughts of *h.* be revealed
21:26 men's *h.* failing them
Acts 1:24 know. *h.* of men, 15:9
Rom. 5:27 he that searcheth *h.*
16:18 deceive *h.* of the simple
1 *Cor.* 4:5 manifest counsels of *h.*
Rev. 2:23 I am he searcheth *h.*

Our HEARTS.
Jos. 2:11 heard, *our h.* did melt
1 *K.* 8:58 incline *our h.* to him
Acts 14:17 filling *o. h.* with food
Rom. 5:5 love of G. abr. in *our h.*
2 *Cor.* 1:22 earnest of S. in *our h.*
3:2 *our* epistle written in *o. h.*
4:6 God hath shined in *our h.*
7:3 in *our h.* to die and live
1 *Thes.* 2:4 God, who trieth *o. h.*
H 'b. 10:22 *our h.* fr. evil consci.
1 *John* 3:19 assure *o. h.* bef. him

Their HEARTS.
Lev. 26:36 a faintness into *t. h.*
Jud. 9:3 *t. h.* inclined to foll. A.
19:22 making *their h.* merry
2 *Chr.* 6:14 be. thee with all *t. h.*
11:16 set *their h.* to seek the L.
20:33 not prep. *their h.* to God
Job 1:5 sons cursed G. in *their h.*
Ps. 33:15 fashioneth *their h.* alike
35:25 let them not say in *t. h.*
81:12 gave up to *t.* own *h.* lust
125:4 that are upright in *t. h.*
Is. 44:18 hath shut *their h.* they
Jer. 31:33 law in *t. h. Heb.* 8:10
31:40 I will put my fear in *t. h.*
Ezek. 13:2 prop. out of *t.* own *h.*
Zec. 7:12 *t. h.* as an adamant
Mark 2:6 reasoning in *their h.*
3:5 grieved for hardness of *t. h.*
4:15 word sown in *t. h. Lu.* 8:12
Luke 1:51 imaginations of *t. h.*
66 heard laid them up in *t. h.*
Acts 7:39 *t. h.* turned back to E.
Rom. 1:24 through lust of *th. h.*
2:15 work of law written in *t. h.*
Col. 2:2 *h.* might be comforted
Heb. 3:10 always err in *their h.*
Rev. 17:17 G. hath put it in *t. h.*

Your HEARTS.
Gen. 18:5 comfort ye your *h.*
Deut. 20:3 O Is. let not y. *h.* faint
32:46 set y. *h.* to all the words
Jos. 23:25 incline y. *h.* to the L.
1 *Sam.* 6:6 do ye harden *your h.*?
7:3 return to L. with all your *h.*
and prepa. *your h.* to the L.
Jer. 42:20 dissembled in *your h.*
Zec. 8:17 none ima. evil in *y. h.*
Mal. 2:4 think evil in *your h.*?
18:35 if from y. *h.* forgive not
19:4 hec. of hardness of y. *h.*
Mark 2:8 why reas. *th.* in y. *h.*?
Luke 5:22 reason ye in *your h.*?
15:15 God knoweth *your h.*
21:14 settle in y. *h.* not to me.
24:38 why are ye overcharged
24:38 do thoughts arise in *y. h.*?
Gal. 4:6 sent S. of Son into y. *h.*
Eph. 3:17 Ch. may dwell in y. *h.*
5:19 mel. in y. *h.* to L. *Col.* 3:16
6:23 that he might comfort y. *h.*

HEA

Phil. 4:7 keep y. *h.* and minds
Col. 3:15 peace of G. rule in y. *h.*
4:8 estate and comfort y. *h.*
1 *Thes.* 3:13 may stablish y. *h.*
2 *Thes.* 2:17 comfort *your h.*
3:5 Lord direct *your h.* into love
Jam. 3:14 if ye ha. strife in y. *h.*
4:8 pur. y. *h.* ye double-minded
5:5 ye have nourished y. *h.*
8 be ye patient, stablish y. *h.*
1 *Pet.* 3:15 sanctify Lord in y. *h.*
2 *Pet.* 1:19 day-star arise in y. *h.*

HEAT.
Gen. 8:22 cold and *h.* summer
18:1 tent-door in *h.* of the day
Deut. 29:23 what menneth the *h.*
1 *Sam.* 11:11 slew till *h.* of day
1 *K.* 1:1 gat no *h.* ; 2 Lord get *h.*
Job 24:19 drought and *h.* cons.
30:30 bones are burnt with *h.*
Ps. 19:6 is nothing hid from *h.*
Is. 4:6 shad. in day from *h.* 25:4
18:4 clear *h.* on herbs, and like
cloud of dew in *h.* of harvest
25:5 as *h.* in a dry place, even *h.*
49:10 neither *h.* nor sun smite
Jer. 17:8 not see when *h.* cometh
36:30 dead body cast out to *h.*
Ezek. 3:14 I went in *h.* of spirit
Mat. 20:12 borne burden and *h.*
Luke 12:55 so. wind blow, be *h.*
Acts 28:3 came viper out of the *h.*
Jam. 1:11 sun risen with bur. *h.*
2 *Pet.* 3:10 elements melt with *h.*

HEATED.
Dan. 3:19 more th. wont to be *h.*
Hos. 7:4 as an oven *h.* by baker

HEATH.
Jer. 17:6 like *h.* in desert, 48:6

HEATHEN.
2 *Sam.* 22:44 kept me to be head
of *h. Ps.* 18:43
2 *K.* 16:3 abominat. of *h.* 17:15;
21:2 ; 2 *Chr.* 28:3; 30:14
17:8 Is. walked in statutes of *h.*
1 *Chr.* 16:35 deliver us from *h.*
2 *Chr.* 20:6 ruled over king. of *h.*
33:9 Judah do worse than the *h.*
Ezr. 6:21 fr. filthiness of the *h.*
Neh. 5:3 redeem. Jews sold to *h.*
Ps. 2:1 do *h.* rage ? *Acts* 4:25
8 I give the *h.* for inheritance
9:5 thou hast rebuked the *h.*
15 the *h.* are sunk in the pit
19 let *h.* he judged in thy sight
10:16 the *h.* perish. out his land
33:10 counsel of A. to naught
44:2 how th. didst drive out *h.*
46:6 the *h.* raged, the kingdoms
47:8 God reigneth over the *h.*
59:5 therof, awake to visit all A.
8 have all the A. in derision
78:55 cast out the A. also, 80:8
79:1 A. are come into thine inh.
6 pour wrath on *h. Jer.* 10:25
10 *h.* say, Wh. their G. ? 115:2
94:10 he that chastiseth the *h.*
96:2 openly show. in right of *h.*
102:15 A. shall fear name of L.
106:41 gave them to hand of *h.*
118:10 *h.* compassed me about
149:7 exe. vengeance upon A.
Lam. 1:10 seen that *h.* entered
Ezek. 11:12 after manners of *h.*
20:9 not be polluted be. *h.* 14,22
23 say, we will be as the *h.*
41 sanctified before *h.* 28:25
22:1 made thee a repr. to the *h.*
16 thine inheri. in sight of *h.*
23:30 gone a whoring after *h.*
25:7 deliver, thee for spoil to *h.*
8 house of Jud. is like to all *h.*
34:29 neither hear name of *h.*
36:3 possession to residue of *h.*
4 to the residue of the *h.*
6 ye have borne shame of *h.*
23 *h.* know that I am the Lord,
36; 37:28; 38:16; 39:7
39:21 the *h.* shall see my judg.
Joel 2:17 *h.* sho. rule over them
3:11 come, all ye *h.* gather
12 let the *h.* be wakened
Amos 9:12 possess rem. of all *h.*
Ob. 15 day of L. is near on *h.*
16 so sh. *h.* drink continually
Mic. 5:15 exe. fury upon the *h.*
Hab. 3:12 didst thr. *h.* in anger
Zep. 2:11 isles of *h.* sh. worship
Hag. 2:22 destroy strength of *h.*
Zec. 1:15 displeased with *h.*
9:10 he sh. speak peo. to the A.

HEA

Zec. 14:14 wealth of *h.* shall he
Mat. 6:7 see not repeti. as A. do
18:17 let him be to thee as a *h.*
2 *Cor.* 11:26 in perils by the *h.*
Gal. 2:9 should go unto the *h.*
3:8 God would justify the *h.*

Among the HEATHEN.
Lev. 26:33 I will scat. you *a. t. h.*
Jer. 9:16 ; *Ezek.* 20:23; 22:15
38 ye shall perish am. *the h.*
2 *Sam.* 22:50 I will gi. thanks to
thee, O L. *a. t. h. Ps.* 18:49
1 *Chr.* 16:24 declare his glory
am. the h. Ps. 96:3
Ps. 44:11 thou scatter us *a. t. h.*
14 mak. us a by-word *a. the h.*
46:10 I will be exalted *a. t. h.*
96:10 say *a. t. h.* Lord reigneth
10:35 scatter them *am. the h.*
47 O L. gather us from *a. t. h.*
110:6 he shall judge *am. the h.*
126:2 *a.* A. L. ha. done great
Jer. 49:15 ma. thee small *a. t. h.*
Lam. 4:75 *a.* A. shall no more co.
20 under his shad. live *a. t. h.*
Ezek. 11:16 cast th. far off *a. t. h.*
12:16 declare abomina. *a. t. h.*
16:14 renown went forth *a. t. h.*
36:19 scatter thee *am. the h.*
21 Isr. profaned *a. the h.* 22, 23
24 will take you fr. *a. h.* 37:21
30:21 will set my glory *a. t. h.*
Joel 2:19 no more a repro. *a. t. h.*
Ob. 1, an ambas. is sent *a. t. h.*
2 made thee small *a. the h.*
Hab. 1:3 behold ye *a. the h.*
Zec. 6:13 were a curse *a. t. h.*
Mal. 1:11 name be great *a. h.* 14
Gal. 1:16 preach him *a. t. h.*

HEAVE, D.
Ex. 20:27 *h.* of ram of consecra.
Num. 15:20 offering so sh. ye *h.*
19:30 ye *h.* the best thereof, 32
See OFFERING, SHOULDER.

HEAVEN.
Gen. 1:1 G. created *h.* and earth
8 God called the firmament *h.*
14 lights in firmam. of *h.* 15
20 fowl that fly in firma. of *h.*
28:10 scatter them *am. the h.*
8:2 windows of *h.* were stopped
14:19 pos. *h.* and earth, 22
19:24 rained fire from Lord of *h.*
27:28 G. give thee of d. of *h.* 39
17:7 This is the gate of *h.*
42:25 bless thee w. bless. of *h.*
Ex. 20:11 Lord made *h.* 31:17
24:10 as it were the body of *h.*
Lev. 26:19 make your *h.* as iron
Deut. 4:11 burned to midst of *h.*
29 I call *h.* and earth to wit-
ness, 30:19; 31:28
32 ask from side of *h.* to other
36 out of *h.* made th. hear vol.
10:14 A. and *h.* of *h.* is L.'s
11:17 be shut up *h.* 1 *K.* 8:35;
2 *Chr.* 6:26; 7:13
28:12 open *h.* to give thee rain
23 *h.* over thy head shall be
24 Lord rain, of *h.* dust, *No.* 1:9
33:13 the precious things of *h.*
26 God of J. rid. upon the *h.*
1 *Sam.* 2:10 out of *h.* sh. he thun.
2 *Sam.* 18:9 up bet. *h.* and earth
21:10 water dropped out of *h.*
22:8 the foundations of *h.* mov.
1 *K.* 8:27 *h.* and *h.* of heav. not
contain thee, 2 *Chr.* 2:6; 6:18
35 when *h.* is shut up no rain
2 *K.* 19:15 th. hast made *h.* and
earth, *2 Par.* 2:12; *Neh.* 9:6
1 *Chr.* 21:16 angel betw. *h.* and
Job 14:12 till *h.* is no more, sh. *h.*
Ps. 27:27 A. shall reveal his iniquity
22:12 is nor G. in heri. of *h.*?
14 walketh in the circuit of *h.*
26:11 the pillars of *h.* tremble
38:29 frost of *h.* who ha. ge. it?
33 knowest thou ordin. of *h.*?
37 who can stay bottles of *h.*
Ps. 19:6 going is from end of *h.*
68:34 *h.* and earth praise him
78:23 he opened the doors of *h.*
24 given them of corn of *h.*
89:11 *h.* is thine as days of *h.*
103:11 *h.* is high above earth
105:40 sat. them wi. bread of *h.*
115:15 L. who ma. *h.* and earth,
121:2; 124:8; 134:3; 146:6;
Jer. 37:16; *Acts* 39:17 ; *Acts*
4:24 ; 14:15 ; *Rev.* 10:6
147:8 covereth A. with clouds
148:13 gl. is above earth and *h.*
Prov. 25:3 *h.* for height, earth
Is. 40:12 hath meted out *h.*
66:1 A. is my throne, *Acts* 7:49

HEA

Jer. 7:18 cakes to queen of *h.*
10:2 be not dism. at signs of *h.*
23:21 do not I fill A. and earth ?
31:37 if A. above can be meas.
33:25 not appointed ordin. of *h.*
44:17 Inc. to qu. of A. 18, 19, 25
51:15 hath stretched out the *h.*
Lam. 4:19 swifter th. eagles of *h.*
Ezek. 8:3 lift. me be. earth and *h.*
32:7 I will cover the *h.*
8 lights of *h.* will I make dark
Dan. 4:15 he wet with dew of *h.*
23, 25, 33 ; 5:21
35 doeth will in army of *h.*
5:21 lifted thyself ag. L. of *h.*
7:2 four winds of *h.* strove
13 ame came with clouds of *h.*
8:8 toward four winds of *h.* 11:4
Amos 9:6 build his stories in *h.*
Hag. 1:10 *h.* is stayed from dew
Zec. 2:6 spr. you as winds of *h.*
Mat. 3:10 not open wind. of *h.*
Mat. 3:16 A. and earth pass away,
24 nor swear by *h. Jam.* 5:12
11:25 thee, L. of *h. Luke* 10:21
23:22 swear by *h.* swear by G.
24:30 S. of man com. in clouds
of A. 30:64 ; *Mark* 14:62
31 elect from one end of A.
35 A. and earth sh. pass away,
Mark 13:31 ; *Luke* 21:33
30 not angels of *h.* but my F.
Mark 13:27 elect fr. ut. part of *h.*
Luke 3:21 J. praying, *h.* opened
4:25 when the A. was shut up
15:18 have sinned against *h.* 21
16:17 easier for A. and earth
18:29 powers of A. sh. be shaken
John 1:51 ye shall see A. open
Acts 3:21 wh. the *h.* must receive
10:11 saw *h.* opened, *Rev.* 19:11
6:14 A. departed as a scroll
8:13 angel flying thro' A. 14:6
10:6 created *h.* and the things
11:6 these have power to shut *h.*
16:17 a great voice out of *h.*
21 a great hail out of *h.*
19:20 rejoice over her, thou A.
19:17 to the fowls that fly in *h.*
20:9 fire came from G. out of *h.*
11 I earth and *h.* fled away
21:1 I saw a new A. and earth
10 Jerus. descending out of A.
See FOWL, FOWLS.

From HEAVEN.
Ex. 16:4 rain bread *from h.*
20:22 talked with you *from h.*
Neh. 9:13
Deut. 26:15 look down *from h.*
Is. 63:15; *Lam.* 3:50
28:24 as dust *f.* A. shall it come
Jos. 10:11 L. cast great sto. *f. h.*
Jud. 5:20 fought *f. h.* the stars
2 *Sam.* 22:14 L. thundered *fr. h.*
2 *K.* 1:10 let fire come down *f. h.*
th. came down fi. *f. h.* 12, 14
1 *Chr.* 21:26 answ. *f. h.* by fire
2 *Chr.* 6:21 hear *f. h.* 23, 27, 30
7:1 fire came down *from h.*
14 I will hear *f. h.* and forgive
Neh. 9:15 gav. them bread *f. h.*
Job 1:16 fire of G. fallen *from h.*
Ps. 14:2 L. look. down *f.* A. 53:2
33:13 the Lord looketh *from h.*
73:23 judment to be heard *f. h.*
80:14 O God, look down *f. h.*
85:11 right. shall look *from h.*
102:19 *f.* h. did the L. behold
19 *h.* 13 how art thou fal. *f. h.*
35:10 as snow falleth *from h.*
Lam. 2:1 Lord cast down *f. h.*
Dan. 4:31 a voice *f. h. Mat.* 3:17;
Luke 3:22 ; *John* 12:28
21:33 wh. was it? *f. h.* or of
men? *Mark* 11:30; *Lu.* 20:4
28:2 for the angel descended
f. h. Rev. 10:1 ; 18:1; 20:1
Mark 8:11 sign *f. h. Luke* 11:16
Luke 9:54 com. fire to come *f. h.*
10:18 behe. S. as lightning *f. h.*
17:29 fire and brimstone *f. h.*
21:11 great signs sh. th. be *f. h.*
22:43 angel *f. h.* strengthening
John 1:32 I saw S. descend. *f. h.*
3:13 came down *f. h.* is above
6:31 he gave bread *from h.*
32 M. gave you not bread *f. h.*
38 I came *f. h.* not to do, 42
41 bread came *f.* A. 50, 51, 58
Acts 2:2 there came a sound *f. h.*
9:3 a light *f.* A. sh. 22:6 ; 26:13
11:5 a great sheet let down, *f. h.*

CRUDEN'S CONCORDANCE. 893

HEA

Acts 14:17 and gave us rain *f. h.*
Rom. 1:18 wra. of G. is rev. *f. h.*
1 *Cor.* 15:47 sc. man is Lord *f. h.*
2 *Cor.* 5:2 clothed with ho. *f. h.*
Gal. 1:8 angel *f. h.* preach
1 *Thes.* 1:10 wait for Son *from h.*
4:16 the L. shall descend *fr. h.*
2 *Thes.* 1:7 L. J. be revealed *fr. h.*
Heb. 12:25 him that speak. *f. h.*
1 *Pet.* 1:12 with H. G. sent *f. h.*
Rev. 8:10 fell a great star *f. h.*
9:1 I saw a star fall *from h.*
10:4 I heard a voice *f. h.* saying,
Seal things and write them
not, 8; 11:12; 14:2, 13; 18:4
13:13 fire come down *from h.*

See GOD *of Heaven.*

Host, s of HEAVEN.
Deut. 4:19 *h. of h.* worship him
17:3 hath worship. the *h. of h.*
1 *K.* 22:19 saw L. sit on thr. and *h. of h.* sit by, 2 *Chr.* 18:18
2 *K.* 17:16 Israel worshi. *h. of h.*
21:3 Manasseh worshipped all the *host of h.* 2 *Chr.* 33:3
23:4 bra. vessels for *host of h.* 5
Neh. 9:6 made *h. of h.* with their *h.* and *host of h.* worsh. thou
Is. 34:4 *h. of h.* sh. be dissolved
Jer. 8:2 spread them bef. *h. of h.*
33:22 as *h. of h.* cannot be num.
Dan. 8:10 great, even to *h. of h.*
Zep. 1:5 off them worship *h. of h.*
Acts 7:42 to worship *host of h.*

In HEAVEN.
Ex. 20:4 nor likeness of anything in *h. Deut.* 5:8
Deut. 8:31 what God in *h.* can
4:39 the Lord is G. in *h.* above
Jos. 2:11 he is God in *h.* above
1 *K.* 8:23 is no God like thee *in h.* 2 *Chr.* 6:14
30 hear thou in *h.* 32-49
2 *K.* 7:2 L. make wind. in *h.,* 19
1 *Chr.* 29:11 all in *h.* and earth
Job 16:19 my witness is in *h.*
Ps. 11:4 Lord's throne is in *h.*
73:25 wh. have I in *h.* but thee
77:18 voice of thunder in *h.*
76:26 east wind to blow in *h.*
69:6 who in *h.* can be co. to L. ?
37 as faithful witnesses in *h.*
113:6 hum. him. to things in *h.*
119:80 thy word is settled in *h.*
Ec. 5:2 God in *h.* thou up. earth
Is. 34:5 sw. shall be bathed in *h.*
Dan. 2:28 G. in *h.* reveal. secrets
Amos 9:6 buildeth stories in *h.*
Mat. 5:12 great is your rew. in *h.*
16 glorify your Father is in *h.*
45 chil. of your F. who is in *h.*
48 be perfect as your F. in *h.*
6:9 Our Father in *h. Luke* 11:2
10 on earth as in *h. Luke* 11:2
20 but lay up treasures in *h.*
7:11 F. in *h.* give good things
21 will of my F. in *h.* 12:50
10:32 confess bef. my F. in *h.*
33 him will I deny bef. F. in *h.*
16:17 F. wh. is in *h.* revealed it
19 shall be bound in *h.* 18:18
19:10 deep. not little ones in *h.*
19:21 treasure in *h. Luke* 18:22
22:30 angels in *h. Mark* 12:25
24:3 one is your F. who is in *h.*
24:30 sign of Son of man in *h.*
24:18 all power given me in *h.*
Mark 11:26 nor F. in *h.* forgive
13:27 powers in *h.* sh. be shak.
31 not angels which are in *h.*
Luke 6:23 your re. is great in *h.*
12:30 your names are writ. in *h.*
15:7 joy in *h.* over one sinner
19:38 peace in *h.* glory in high
John 3:13 even Son of man in *h.*
Acts 2:19 wonders in *h.* above
1 *Cor.* 8:5 whe. in *h.* or in earth
Eph. 1:10 gath. in one, *both* in *h.*
3:15 family in *h.* is named
6:9 your Master in *h. Col.* 4:1
Phil. 2:10 of things in *h.*
3:20 our conversation is in *h.*
Col. 1:5 hope wh. is laid up in *h.*
16 things create'd that are in *h.*
20 to reconcile all things in *h.*
Heb. 10:34 have in *h.* better sub.
12:23 first-born written in *h.*
1 *Pet.* 1:4 inherit. reserved in *h.*
1 *John* 5:7 three bear rec. in *h.*
Rev. 4:1 a door was opened in *h.*
2 a throne was set in *h.*
5:3 every creature in *h.* saying
8:1 sil. in *h.*; 11:15 voices in *h.*
11:19 temple of G. opened in *h.*

HEA

Rev. 12:1 ap. great wonder in *h.* 3
7 there was war in *h.*
8 nor place fou. any more in *h.*
13:6 to blaspheme them in *h.*
14:17 came out of temple in *h.*
15:1 I saw another sign in *h.*
5 tabernacle of testimony in *h.*
19:14 the armies in *h.* followed

Into HEAVEN.
2 *K.* 2:1 L. wo. take Elijah *i. h.*
11 Eli. went by a whirlw. *i. h.*
Ps. 139:8 ascend *into h.* art there
Prov. 30:4 ascend. *i. h. Rom.* 10:6
Is. 14:13 I will ascend *into h.*
Mark 16:19 L. was received *i. h.*
Luke 2:15 angels gone away *t. h.*
24:51 he was parted, carried *i. h.*
Acts 1:11 gazing *i. h.* taken *i. h.*
7:55 Stephen looked up *into h.*
10:16 vessel received *i. h.* 11:10
Heb. 9:24 but *into h.* itself
1 *Pet.* 3:22 gone *i. h.* on right h.

See KINGDOM.

HEAVEN, with stars.
Gen. 1:17 G. set *stars* in fir. of *h.*
22:17 will multiply thy seed as *stars* of *h., Deut.* 1; *Ex.* 32:13;
1 *Chr.* 27:23; *Neh.* 9:23
Deut. 1:10 are as *stars* of *h.* 10:22
28:62 were as *s. of h.* for mult.
Is. 13:10 *s. of* sh. not give light
Ezek. 32:7 cover *h.* make *s.* dark
Nah. 3:16 multiplied as *s. of h.*
Mat. 24:29 *s.* fall *fr. h., Mark* 13:25
Rev. 6:13 *stars* of *h.* fell on earth
12:4 his tail drew third of *s. of h.*

To, or unto HEAVEN.
Gen. 11:4 tower may reach *u. h.*
28:12 top of it may reach *to h.*
Deut. 1:28 cities walled *to h.,* 9:1
30:12 who sh. go up for us *to h.*
32:40 for I lift up my hand *to h.*
1 *Sam.* 5:12 cry of city w. up *to h.*
1 *K.* 8:54 with hands spread *to h.*
2 *Chr.* 30:9 s rage th. reach. *u. h.*
Ps. 107:26 they mount up *to h.*
Jer. 51:9 her judg. reacheth *u. h.*
Dan. 4:11 tree reached *to h.* 20
Amos 9:2 tho' they climb up *t. h.*
Mat. 11:23 Cap. art exalted *to h. Luke* 10:15
14:19 look. up *to h.* he blessed,
Mark 6:41; *Luke* 9:16
Mark 7:34 looking *to h.* he sighed
Luke 18:13 not lift his eyes *u. h.*
John 3:13 no man ascen. up *to h.*
17:1 Je. lifted up his eyes *to h.*
2 *Cor.* 12:2 caught up *to* third *h.*
Rev. 10:5 angel lifted hand *to h.*
11:12 ascend. up *to h.* in a cloud
18:5 her sins have reached *u. h.*

Toward HEAVEN.
Gen. 15:5 look now *toward h.*
Ex. 10:22 stretch. his hand *t. h.*
Jud. 13:20 flame went up *t. h.*
1 *K.* 8:22 Solomon spread forth his hands *tow. h.* 2 *Chr.* 6:13
Job 2:12 dust on their heads *t. h.*
Prov. 23:5 fly aw. as eagle *t. h.*
Acts 1:10 looked steadfast. *t. h.*

Under HEAVEN.
Gen. 1:9 waters *under h.* be gat.
6:17 to destroy all flesh fr. *u. h.*
7:19 high hills *u.* the whole *h.*
Deut. 4:19 to all nations *u. h.*
7:24 dest. th. name fr. *u. h.* 9:14
29:20 L. blot out name fr. *u. h.*
2 *K.* 14:27 blot out. of Is. fr. *u. h.*
Job 28:24 G. seeth *u.* the whole *h.*
37:3 directeth it *u.* the whole *h.*
41:11 whatsoever is *u. h.* is mine
Ec. 1:13 search out all th. *u. h.*
2:3 that good they sho. do *u. h.*
3:1 a time to ev. purpose *u. h.*
Luke 17:24 lightn. one part *u. h.*
Acts 2:5 devout of ev. nation *u. h.*
4:12 none oth. name *u. h.* given
Col. 1:23 gospel to ev. creat. *u. h.*

HEAVENLY.
Mat. 6:14 *h.* Father forgive
26 your *h.* Father feedeth them
32 *h.* F. knoweth ye have need
15:13 ev. plant *h.* F. hath not
18:35 so shall my *h.* Father do
Luke 2:13 the *h.* host praising G.
11:13 your F. *h.* gi. H. Spi. to th.
John 3:12 I tell you of *h.* things
Acts 26:19 not disob. to *h.* vision
1 *Cor.* 15:48 as is the *h.* such are *h.* shall bear the image of the *h.*
Eph. 1:3 blessings in *h.* places
3:10 the powers in *h.* places
2 *Tim.* 4:18 Lord pres. to *h.* king.
Heb. 3:1 partakers of *h.* calling;
6:4 have tasted of the *h.* gift

HEA

Heb. 8:5 exa. and sh. of *h.* things
9:23 *h.* things with better sacri.
11:16 *h.* country; 12:22 *h.* Jeru.

HEAVENS.
Gen. 2:1 *h.* and earth finished
4 general. of the *h.* and earth
Deut. 32:1 O *h.* I will sp. *Is.* 1:2
33:26 his *h.* sh. drop down dew
Jud. 5:4 trembled, *h.* dropped
2 *Sam.* 22:10 bow, the *h. Ps.* 18:9
1 *K.* 8:27 *h.* cannot contain thee
1 *Chr.* 16:26 Lord made *h. Neh.* 9:6; *Ps.* 96:5; 102:25; 136:5
31 let the *h.* be glad, earth rej.
2 *Chr.* 6:25 hear fr. the *h.* 33,35,39
Job 14:12 till *h.* be no more
15:15 *h.* not clean in his sight
20:6 excellency mount up to *h.*
26:13 by Sp. he garnished the *h.*
35:5 look to the *h.* and see
Ps. 8:1 thy glory above *h.* 113:4
3 when I consider thy *h.*
19:1 *h.* declare the glory of God
33:6 by word of *L.* were *h.* made
50:4 sh. call to the *h.* from above
6 *h.* shall declare his righteou.
57:5 be thou exalted, O God, above the *h.* 11; 108:5
10 mercy is great to *h.* 108:5
68:4 that rideth upon the *h.* 33
8 *h.* dropped at presence of G.
73:9 set their mouth ag. the *h.*
89:5 *h.* shall praise thy wonders
11 the *h.* are thine, earth also
96:11 the *h.* rejoice, *Rev.* 12:12
97:6 *h.* declare his righteousness
104:2 stretchest out *h. Is.* 40:22
108:4 mercy is great above *h.*
115:16 the *h.* are the Lord's
144:5 bow thy *h.* O L. and come
148:1 praise in the Lord from *h.*
Prov. 3:19 he established the *h.*
8:27 when he prepared the *h.*
Is. 13:13 shake the *h., Hag.* 2:6,21
34:4 the *h.* shall be rolled toget.
44:23 sing, O ye *h.* for L. done it
24 stretch. forth the *h.* 45:12
51:13; *Jer.* 10:12; *Zec.* 12:1
45:8 drop down, ye *h.* above
48:13 my right hand spanned *h.*
49:13 sing, O *h.* be joy. O earth
50:3 I clothe *h.* with blackness
51:6 lift your eyes to *h.*
55:9 as *h.* higher than earth
63:15 look down fr. *h.* and behold
64:1 rend the *h.* and come down
65:17 behold, I crea the new *h.*
66:22 new *h.* which I will make
Jer. 2:12 be astonished, O ye *h.*
4:23 I beh. *h.* they had no light
15 birds of *h.* were fled, 9:10
24 earth mourn, *h.* above black
10:11 gods not made *h.* sh. peri.
14:22 can the *h.* give showers ?
Ezek. 1:1 *h.* were open. *Mat.* 3:16
Dan. 4:26 known tha. *h.* do rule
Hos. 2:21 I will hear the *h.*
Joel 2:10 the *h.* shall tremble
3:16 *h.* shall shake, *Amos* 9:5
Zec. 8:6 four spirits of the *h.*
8:12 the *h.* shall give their dew
Mat. 24:29 powers of *h.* shaken
Mark 1:10 he saw the *h.* opened
10:1 not ascended to *h.*
7:56 behold, I see the *h.* opened
Acts 1:10 *h.* work of thy hands
4:14 High-p. is passed into *h.*
7:26 H.-p. made higher than *h.*
2 *Pet.* 3:5 word of G. *h.* were of old
10 *h.* sh. pass away with gr. no.
12 *h.* being on fire shall be dis.

In the HEAVENS.
Ps. 2:4 he that sitteth in the *h.*
18:13 L. also thundered in the *h.*
36:5 thy mercy, O L. is in the *h.*
89:2 faithfulness estab. in the *h.*
103:19 L. prep. his throne in *h.*
123:1 God is in the *h.*
Mat. 5:12 O thou that dwell. in *t. h.*
123:1 O waters in the *h.* 5:10
Lam. 3:41 lift hearts to G. in *h.*
Mat. 3:30 show wonders in the *h.*
2 *Cor.* 5:1 not made w. hands, in *h.*
Heb. 8:1 Mi. of sanctuary in the *h.*
9:23 patterns of things in the *h.*

HEAVY.
Ex. 17:12 Moses' hands were *h.*

HED

1 *K.* 14:6 sent to thee with *h.* tid.
Neh. 3:13 bondage *h.* on people
Job 33:7 neither shall hand be *h.*
38:4 *h.* burden, they are too *h.*
Ps. 25:20 songs to a *h.* heart
27:3 stone is *h.* sand weighty
31:8 wine to those of *h.* hearts
Is. 6:10 and make their ears *h.*
24:20 transgression shall be *h.*
30:27 the burden thereof is *h.*
46:1 carriages were *h.* loaden
58:6 to undo the *h.* burdens ?
58:1 nei. his ear *h.* that it cannot
Lam. 3:7 made chain *h.*
Mat. 11:28 ye that are *h.* laden
23:4 for they bind *h.* burdens
26:37 he sorrowful, and very *h.*
43 eyes were *h. Mark* 14:33, 40
Luke 9:32 were *h.* with sleep

HEAVIER.
Job 6:3 *h.* than sand of the sea
23:2 my stroke is *h.* than groan.
Prov. 27:3 a fool's wrath is *h.*

HEAVILY.
Ex. 14:25 that drave them *h.*
Ps. 35:14 bowed *h.* as one mour.
Is. 47:6 on ancient *h.* laid yoke?

HEAVINESS.
Ezr. 9:5 I rose from *h.*
Job 9:27 I will leave off my *h.*
Ps. 69:20 broken heart full of *h.*
119:28 my soul melteth for *h.*
Prov. 10:1 foul, son *h.* of mother
12:25 *h.* in heart mak. it stoop
14:13 end of that mirth is *h.*
Is. 61:3 garm. of praise for *h.*
Rom. 9:2 great *h.* and sorrow
2 *Cor.* 2:1 wou. not come ag. in *h.*
Phil. 2:26 brother was full of *h.*
Jam. 4:9 your joy be turned to *h.*
1 *Pet.* 1:6 if need be ye are in *h.*

HEBER.
Gen. 46:17 Beriah, H. 1 *Chr.* 7:31
Jud. 4:11 H. the Kenite, 17; 5:24
Luke 3:35 Phalec, was son of H.

HEBREW.
Gen. 14:13 Abra, the H. 39:14
41:12 a young man, a H.
Ex. 2:11 Egyptian smiting a H.
Jer. 34:9 should let a H. go free
John 19:13 Pilate spake in H.
Acts 21:40 spake in H. 22:2; 26:14
Rev. 9:11 in H. Abaddon, 16:16

HEBREW man.
Deut. 15:12 if brother, a H. man

HEBREW servant.
Gen. 39:17 H. s. came, *Ex.* 21:2

HEBREW woman, women.
Ex. 1:16 midwife to H. w. 19
2:7 a nurse of the H. women ?
Deut. 15:12 if any H. w. be sold

HEBREWESS. *Jer.* 34:9

HEBRON, place.
Gen. 23:2 Sarah died in H. 35:27;
Jos. 14:15; *Jud.* 1:10
Num. 13:22 H. built before Zoan
2 *Sam.* 2:11 Dav. was king in H.
5:5; 1 *K.* 2:11; 1 *Chr.* 29:27
3:32 buried Abner in H.
1 *Chr.* 6:55; 11:1; 12:38
15:7 Abraham vowed in H. 10
2 *Chr.* 28 perfect heart to H.

HEBRON, person.
Ex. 6:18 Kohath, H. *Num.* 3:19
1 *Chr.* 6:25, 43; 66:2, 18; 15:9; 23:12, 19; 24:27

HEDGE, s.
Job 1:10 not made a *h.* ab. him ?
Ps. 80:12 broken her *h.* ? 89:40
Prov. 15:19 way of sloth *h.* of th.
Ec. 10:8 breaketh *h.* serpent bite
Is. 5:5 take away the *h.* thereof
Jer. 49:3 run to and fro by the *h.*
Ezek. 13:5 not able, ber. his *h.* 22:30
Mic. 7:4 sharper than a thorn *h.*
Nah. 3:17 ye grass-hoppers in *h.*
Mark 12:1 he set a *h.* about it
Luke 14:23 go to highway and *h.*

894   CRUDEN'S CONCORDANCE.

HEI

HEDGE, D.
Job 3:23 way is hid, whom G. h.
Lam. 3:7 he hath h. me about
Hos. 2:6 h. up thy way with tho.
Mat. 21:33 vineyard, h. it round

HEED.
2 K. 10:31 Jehu took no h.
Ps. 119:9 tak. h. ac. to thy word
Prov. 17:4 giveth h. to false lips
Ec. 12:9 preacher gave good h.
Jer. 18:18 not gi. h. to any words
19 give h. to me, O Lord
Acts 3:5 he gave h. unto them
8:6 people of Sam. gave h. to P.
10 gave h. to Simon least to
1 Tim. 1:4 h. to fables, Tit. 1:14
4:1 giving h. to seducing spirits
Heb. 2:1 we ought to give more h.
See TAKE.

HEEL, S.
Gen. 3:15 thou sh. bruise his h.
25:26 hold on E. h. Hos. 12:3
49:17 an adder biteth horse h.
Job 13:27 print on h. of my feet
18:9 gin shall take him by h.
Ps. 41:9 h. ag. me, John 13:18
49:5 iniq. of my h. compass me
Jer. 13:22 iniq. thy h. made bare

HEGE. Est. 2:3

HEIFER.
Num. 19:2 red h.; 5 burn the h.
Deut. 21:3 the elders sh. take a h.
4 strike off the h. neck
6 shall wash hands over the h.
Jud. 14:18 if ye had not plow. h.
Is. 15:5 cry out for Moab as h.
Jer. 46:20 Egypt is like a fair h.
48:34 uttered their voice as a h.
50:11 grown fat as h. at grass
Hos. 4:16 Is. as a backsliding h.
10:11 Ephraim is as h. taught
Heb. 9:13 ashes of h. sp. unclean

HEIGHT, S.
Gen. 6:15 h. of ark sh. be 80 cu.
Ex. 25:10 ark of Shittim-wood, a cu. and half h. 23; 37:1, 10
27:1 h. of altar, three cu. 38:1
18 h. of court, five cubits, 38:18
33:2 h. of altar of incense, 37:25
1 Sam. 16:7 look not on h. of sta.
17:4 Goliath's h. 6 cu. and a sp.
1 K. 6:2 h. of house of G. 30 cu.
20 oracle twenty cubits in h.
26 h. of cherub was ten cubits
7:2 h. of house 30 cubits
10 h. of one chapiter 5 cubits
23 h. of molten sea five cubits
27 h. of one base three cubits
Ezr. 6:3 h. of God's house 60 cu.
Job 22:12 God in h. of heaven?
Ps. 102:19 looked fr. h. of sanct.
148:1 praise the Lord in the h.
Prov. 25:3 the heaven for h.
Is. 7:11 ask it in the h. above
14:14 I will ascend above the h.
Jer. 49:16 O thou that holdest h.
51:53 formify h. of her strength
Ezek. 17:23 in h. of Israel, 20:40
19:11 she appeared in her h.
31:5 therefore his h. was exalted
14 none of the trees exalt for h.
32:5 fill the valleys with thy h.
Dan. 3:1 image wh. h. was 60 cu.
4:11 h. reached unto heaven, 20
Amos 2:9 h. was like h. of cedars
Rom. 8:39 nor h. nor depth
Eph. 3:18 the h. of love of Ch. ?
Rev. 21:16 breadth and h. equal

HEINOUS.
Job 31:11 for this is a h. crime

HEIR, S.
Gen. 15:3 born in my house is h.
4 This shall not be thine h.
21:10 Ishmael shall not be h.
2 Sam. 14:7 we will destroy h.
Prov. 30:23 handmaid h. to mis.
Jer. 49:1 hath Is. no sons? no h. ?
2 Is. h. to them that were his h.
Mic. 1:15 I will bring h. to thee
Mat. 21:38 this is the h. Mark 12:7; Luke 20:14
12:3 should be h. of world
14 if they wh. are of law be h.
8:17 h. of G. joint h. with Ch.
Gal. 3:29 h. according to promise
4:1 h. as long as he is a child
7 an h. of God through Christ
30 son of bond-w. sh. not be h.
Eph. 3:6 Gent. sh. be fellow h.
Tit. 3:7 h. according to the hope
Heb. 1:2 whom he appointed h.
11 wh shall be h. of salvation
6:17 God willing to show to h.
11:7 became h. of righteousness
Jam. 2:5 h. of the kingdom

HEL

1 Pet. 3:7 as h. together of grace
HELAM. 2 Sam. 10:16
HELBON. Ezek. 27:18

HELD.
Ex. 17:11 wh. Moses h. up hand
Jud. 7:20 h. lamps in left hands
2 Chr. 4:5 sea h. 3,000 baths
Neh. 4:16 half h. both spears
17 other hand he h. a weapon
Est. 5:2 king h. out golden scep.
Job 23:11 my foot h. his steps
Ps. 32:9 wh. mouth must be h.
94:18 thy mercy, O L. h. me up
Cant. 3:4 I h. him, and wo. not
7:5 king is h. in the galleries
Jer. 50:33 took captives, h. them
Dan. 12:7 h. up his right hand
Mat. 12:14 h. a coun. Mark 15:1
Luke 22:63 men that h. Jesus
Acts 3:11 man was healed, h. P.
14:4 part h. with J. part apostles
Rom. 7:6 whereto we were h.
Rev. 6:9 slain for testim. they h.

HELD peace.
Gen. 24:21 wondering h. his p.
Lev. 10:3 Aaron h. his peace
Num. 30:7 husband h. p. 11, 14
Neh. 5:8 h. th. p. found nothing
Job 29:10 nobles h. their peace
Is. 36:21 I h. my p. from good
Is. 57:11 have not I h. my peace?
Mat. 26:63 Jesus h. his peace
Luke 14:4 h. p. 20:26; Acts 11:18
Acts 15:13 h. their p. Ja. answer
HELDAI. Zec. 6:10
HELI. Luke 3:23
HELKATH-HAZZURIM. 2 Sam. 2:16

HELL.
Deut. 32:22 fire burn unto low. h.
2 Sam. 22:6 sorrows of h. com-passed me, Ps. 18:5; 66:13
Job 11:8 deeper than h.
26:6 h. is naked before him
Ps. 9:17 wicked turned into h.
16:10 not le. soul in h. Acts 2:27
55:15 go down quick to h.
116:3 pains of h. gat hold on me
139:8 bed in h. thou art there
Prov. 5:5 steps take hold on h.
7:27 house way to h. going do.
9:18 guests are in depths of h.
15:11 h. and destruction bef. L.
24 he may depart from h.
23:14 deliver his soul from h.
27:20 h. and destruction ne. full
Is. 5:14 h. hath enlarged herself
14:9 h. from beneath is moved
15 shalt be brought down to h.
28:15 with h. are we at agreem.
18 agreem. with h. not stand
57:9 debase thyself even to h.
Ezek. 31:16 I cast him down to h.
17 went down to h. with him
32:21 speak to him out of h.
27 down to h. with weapons
31 h. I believe, h. thine anhol.
Luke 5:7 they sh. come and h.
10:40 bid her therefore h. me
Acts 16:9 co. to Macedonia, h. us
21:28 crying out, Men of Israel, h.
Phil. 4:3 h. women wh. labored
Heb. 4:16 to h. in time of need

HELPED.
Ex. 12:27 Moses stood up and h.
1 Sam. 7:12 hitherto the L. h. us
1 K. 1:7 follow. Adonijah h. him
1 Chr. 15:26 God h. the Levites
2 Chr. 26:13 ev. one h. to destroy
15 marvellously h.
Job 26:2 how hast thou h. him
Ps. 28:7 I am h. ; 118:13 L. h. me
116:6 brought Hou, he h. me
Is. 41:6 h. ev. one his neighbor
49:8 in day of salvation h. thee
Zec. 1:15 h. forw. the affliction
Acts 18:27 he h. them much
Rev. 12:16 earth h. the woman

HELMET, S.
2 K. 14:26 nor any h. for Israel
Job 38:13 mar my path, no h.
Ps. 10:14 art h. of hutherless
Ps. 10:1 my h.; 54:4 G. my h.
72:12 deliver him hath no h.
Jer. 47:4 Tyrus and Zidon ev. h.
Rom. 16:9 Urbane our h. in Ch.
Heb. 13:6 Lord is my h.

HELPERS.
1 Chr. 12:18 peace he to thy h.
Job 9:13 proud h. do stoop under
Ezek. 30:8 her h. sh. be destroyed
Nah. 3:9 Put and Lubim were h.
Rom. 16:3 Prisca and Aq. my h.
2 Cor. 1:24 but are h. of your joy
3 John 8 be fellow-h. to the truth

HER

HELPETH.
1 Chr. 12:18 for thy God h. thee
Is. 31:3 both he that h. shall fall
Rom. 8:26 Sp. also h. infirmities
1 Cor. 16:16 sub. to ev. one h. us

HELPING.
Ezr. 5:2 were prophets of G. h.
Ps. 22:1 why art so far from h.
2 Cor. 1:11 h. together by prayer

HELPS.
Acts 27:17 used h. undergi. ship
1 Cor. 12:28 healings, h. govern.

HELVE.
Deut. 19:5 head slippeth from h.

HEM, S.
Ex. 28:33 on h. thou shalt make pomegra. 34; 39:24, 25, 26
Mat. 9:20 touch. h. of gar. 14:36

HEMAN.
1 K. 4:31 Sol. was wiser than H.
1 Chr. 2:6; 6:33; 15:17, 19; 16:42; 25:5; 2 Chr. 5:12; 29:14; 35:15

HEMLOCK.
Hos. 10:4 judgment spr. up as h.
Amos 6:12 fruit of righte. to h.
HEN. Zec. 6:14

HEN.
Mat. 23:37 h. gath. ch. Lu. 13:34

HENCE.
Gen. 37:17 carry us not up h.
Ex. 33:15 be no more
Mat. 17:20 remove h. to yon. pla.
Luke 4:9 cast thyself down fr. h.
13:31 get thee h. ; 16:26 from h.
John 2:16 take these things h.
14:31 let us go h. ; 18:36 not h.
Acts 22:21 send thee h. to Gen.

HENCEFORTH.
Ps. 125:2 L. about people from h.
131:3 hope in the Lord from h.
52:1 h. there sh. no more come
59:21 thy seed's seed h.
Mic. 4:7 L. reign in Zion from h.
Mat. 23:39 ye shall not see me h.
Luke 5:10 fear not, from h. thou
12:52 h. sh. be five in one house
Acts 18:6 h. I will go to Gentiles
2 Cor. 5:15 not h. live to themsel.
Eph. 4:17 h. walk not as other
2 Tim. 4:8 h. laid up a crown
Rev. 14:13 blessed die in L. fr. h.

HENCEFORWARD.
Num. 15:23 h. am. generations
Mat. 21:19 no fruit gr. on thee h.

HEPHZI-BAH.
2 K. 21:1 Manasseh's mother, H.
Is. 62:4 thou shalt be called H.

HERALD.
Dan. 3:4 then a h. cried aloud

HERB.
Gen. 1:11 bring forth the h. 12
29 every h. bearing seed
2:5 made every h. ; 3:18 eat h.
9:3 h. I have given all things
Ex. 9:22 hall smote ev. h. 25
10:12 locusts eat every h. 15
Deut. 32:2 rain on tender-h.
2 K. 19:26 as green h. Is. 37:27
Job 8:12 withered bef. other h.
38:27 bud of tender h. to spring
Ps. 37:2 shall wither as green h.
104:14 causeth h. to grow
Is. 66:14 bones flourish like h.

HERBS.
Ex. 12:8 with bitter h. Num. 9:11
Deut. 11:10 as a garden of h.
1 K. 21:2 have it for gard. of h.
Prov. 15:17 better a dinner of h.
27:25 h. of mountains gathered
Is. 18:4 dew as dew of h.
26:19 I will dry up all their h.
Jer. 12:4 h. of every field wither
Mat. 13:32 is greatest among all h. Mark 4:32
Luke 11:42 all manner of h.
Heb. 6:7 and bringeth forth h.

HERD, S.
Lev. 19:9 with flocks and h.
Deut. 12:21 shalt kill of thy h.
2 Sam. 12:4 spared to take of h.
1 Chr. 27:29 over the h. in Shar.
Ec. 6:3:10 a place for h. to lie
Jer. 31:12 toge. for young of h.
Joel 1:18 h. of cattle perplexed
Jon. 3:7 let not h. taste any thing
Hab. 3:17 shall be no h. in stalls

CRUDEN'S CONCORDANCE. 895

HER

Mat. 8:30 a *h.* of swine feeding
  Mark 3:11; *Luke* 8:32
See FLOCKS.

HERDMAN, MEN.
Gen. 13:7 strife betw. *h.* 26:20
1 *Sam.* 21:7 Doeg chiefest of *h.*
Amos 1:1 who was am. *h.* of Te.
7:14 I was o prophet, but a *h.*

HERE,
Deut. 5:3 who are all of us *h.*
Ps. 132:14 my rest, *h.* I dwell
Is. 28:10 *h.* a little, th. a little, 13
Hos. 7:9 gray hairs *h.* and there
Mat. 12:41 a greater than Jonas
  is *h.* 42; *Luke* 11:31, 32
16:28 standing *h. Luke* 9:27
17:4 L. it is good for us to be *h.*
24:23 lo, *h.* is Ch. *Mark* 13:21
28:6 he is not *h.* he is risen,
  Mark 16:6; *Luke* 24:6
Mark 13:1 what buildings are *h.*
John 11:21 if th. hadst been *h.* 32
Acts 9:10 behold, I am A. Lord
  10:33 we are all *h.* before God
Heb. 13:14 *h.* have we no city
See STAND.

HEREAFTER.
Is. 41:23 things that come *h.*
Dan. 2:29 come to pass *h.* 45
Mat. 26:64 *h.* sh. ye see S. of m.
Mark 11:14 no man eat of thee *h.*
Luke 22:69 *h.* sh. Son of man sit
John 1:51 *h.* ye sh. see heaven
13:7 thou shalt know *h.*
14:30 *h.* I will not talk with you
1 *Tim.* 1:16 to them wh. *h.* bell.
Rev. 1:19 things which sh. be *h.*
4:1 show things wh. must be *h.*
9:12 come two woes more *h.*

HEREBY.
Jos. 3:10 *h.* know G. is am. you
1 *John* 2:3 *h.* we do know him
  5 *h.* know that we are in him
  3:16 *h.* perceive we love of God
  19 *h.* know we are of the truth
  24 *h.* we know he abideth in us
  4:2 *h.* know ye Spirit of God
  6 *h.* know we the Sp. of truth
  13 *h.* know that we dw. in him

HEREIN.
1 *John* 4:10 *h.* is love, not that
Acts 24:14 the way they call *h.*
1 *Cor.* 11:19 there be *h.* am. you
Gal. 5:20 works of flesh wrath, *h.*
2 *Pet.* 3:1 bring in damnable *h.*

HERETIC.
Tit. 3:10 *h.* after sec. admonition

HERETOFORE.
1 *Sam.* 4:7 been such a thing *h.*
2 *Cor.* 13:2 them which *h.* sinned

HEREUNTO.
1 *Pet.* 2:21 even *h.* were ye called

HEREWITH.
Mal. 3:10 and prove me now *h.*

HERITAGE, s.
Ex. 6:8 I will give it you for *h.*
Job 20:29 *h.* appointed by God
  27:13 *h.* of oppressors they rec.
Ps. 16:6 yea, I have a goodly *h.*
61:5 *h.* of those fear thy name
94:5 break thy peo. afflict thy *h.*
111:6 give them *h.* of heathen
119:111 testimonies taken as *h.*
127:3 children are a *h.* of the L.
135:12 gave their land for a *h.*
  136:21, 22
Is. 49:8 inherit the desolate *h.*
54:17 *h.* of servants of the Lord
58:14 feed thee with *h.* of Jacob
Jer. 2:7 my *h.* an abomination
3:19 sh. I give thee goodly *h.*
12:7 left *h.* ; 8 my *h.* is as lion
9 my *h.* is as speckled bird
15 bring ag. every man to his *h.*
17:4 thou shalt discont. from *h.*
50:11 O destroyers of my *h.*
Joel 2:17 give not thy *h.* to reproach
3:2 I will plead wi. them for *h.*
Mic. 2:2 oppress a man and *h.*
7:14 feed the flock of thy *h.*
18 passeth transgression of *h.*
Mal. 1:3 I laid Esau's *h.* waste
1 *Pet.* 5:3 being lords over G.'s *h.*

HERMAS, HERMES, *Ro.* 16:14
HERMOGENES. 2 *Tim.* 1:15

HERMON.
Jos. 13:11 all ut. H. Reuben had
Ps. 89:12 H. shall rejoice in thy
133:3 dew of H. that descended
Cant. 4:8 look from the top of H.

HERMONITES. *Ps.* 42:6

HID

HEROD.
Mat. 2:12 not return to H. 15, 16
14:3 for H. had laid hold. 6
Mark 8:15 leaven of H. 6:17, 21
Luke 8:1 H. tetrarch of Galil. 19
9:7 H. heard of Jesus, 13:31
23:7 sent J. to H. 8, 11, 12, 15
Acts 4:27 H. and Pontius Pilate
12:1 H. vexed the chu. 6, 11, 21

HERODIANS.
Mat. 22:16 they sent th. disciples
  with the H. *Mark* 12:13
Mark 3:6 P. took coun. with H.

HERODIAS.
Mat. 14:3 John in prison for H. 6
Mark 6:19 H. had quarrel, 17, 22
Luke 3:19 H. reprov. by J. for H.

HERODION. *Rom.* 16:11

HERON.
Lev. 11:19 *h.* uncl. *Deut.* 14:18
HERSELF. *See* SELF.

HESHBON.
Num. 21:28 fire go. out of H. 30
Jud. 11:26 Is. dw. in H. *Neh.* 9:22
Cant. 7:4 like fish-pools of H.
Is. 15:4 H. shall cry. *Jer.* 48:2
16:8 for field of H. languish, 9
Jer. 48:2 in H. they have evil, 45

HETH, *Gen.* 10:15; 23:7; 25:10;
  27:46; 49:32; 1 *Chr.* 1:13

HEW, ED.
Ex. 34:1 *h.* 2 tables, *Deut.* 10:1
  4 *h.* two tables, *Deut.* 10:3
Deut. 12:3 *h.* down grav. images
19:5 goeth with his neigh. to *h.*
1 *Sam.* 11:7 S. *h.* oxen in pieces
15:33 Samuel *h.* Agag in pieces
2 *Chr.* 2:3 Solo. told 80,000 to *h.*
Jer. 2:13 my peo. *h.* them cist.
Dan. 4:14 *h.* down the tree, 23
Hos. 6:5 I *h.* them by the proph.
Deut. 29:11 from *h.* of wood
Jos. 9:21 be *h.* of wood, 23
27 Jos. made them *h.* of wood
1 *K.* 5:15 80,000 *h.* in mountains,
  2 *Chr.* 2:18
Jer. 46:22 ag. Eg. as *h.* of wood

HEWETH.
Is. 10:15 boast aga. him that *h.*
22:16 *h.* him out a sepulchre

HEWN.
Prov. 9:1 *h.* out seven pillars
Is. 10:33 high ones shall be *h.*
33:9 Leb. is asha. and *h.* down
51:1 rock whence ye are *h.*
Mat. 3:10 *h.* down and cast into
  fire, 7:19; *Luke* 3:9
27:60 *h.* out of a rock, *Mark*
  15:46; *Luke* 23:53

HEZEKIAH, *called* EZEKIAS.
2 *K.* 16:20 H. reign. in his stead,
18:13 H. gave all silver, 22, 31
19:1 H. hea. it, 15; 20:1, 3, 12, 21
2 *Chr.* 29:27 H. com. burnt-offerings, 30:18; 32:8, 17, 33
30:20 the Lord hearkened to H.
31:2 H. appoin. 32:6, 17, 24
Is. 36:7, 14, 16; 37:1, 15; 38:1, 3;
  39:1, 2, 8

HEZRON.
Gen. 46:9 Reuben, H. *Ex.* 6:14
Ruth 4:18 H. begat Ham
1 *Chr.* 2:9 sons of H. 18, 21, 25

HID.
Gen. 3:8 Adam and his wife *h.*
10 I was naked, and I *h.* myself
Ex. 2:2 *h.* Moses three months
12 *h.* *h.* the Egyptian in sand
3:6 and Moses *h.* his face
Jos. 2:4 Rahab *h.* the spies, 6
6:17 she *h.* the messengers, 25
1 *K.* 18:4 Obadiah *h.* prophets, 13
2 *K.* 4:27 the Lord *h.* it from me
11:2 they *h.* him and his nurse,
  2 *Chr.* 22:11
Job 17:4 *h.* heart fr. understand.
Ps. 9:15 in net which they *h.*
22:24 nei. *h.* his face from him
35:7 they *h.* for me their net
8 net he hath *h.* catch himself
119:11 word I *h.* in my heart
140:5 proud *h.* a snare for me
Is. 42:2 he quiver he *h.* me
Jer. 13:5 I *h.* my face fr. shame
38:3 we *h.* not faces from him
Mat. 5:14 city set on hill *h.*
13:33 he *h.* meal, *Luke* 13:21
44 treasure *h.* in field
25:18 digged and *h.* his talent
25:25 I *h.* thy talent in earth
Luke 1:24 Elizabeth *h.* herself
John 8:59 but Jesus *h.* himself
Rev. 6:15 bondm. and freem. *h.*

HID.
2 *Sam.* 18:13 no mat. *h.* fr. king,
  1 *K.* 10:3; 2 *Chr.* 9:2
Job 3:21 mor men that *h.* treas.
28:11 thing *h.* bringeth forth
21 *h.* from eyes of all living
38:30 wat. are *h.* as with a stone
Pr. 17:14 belly filled wi. *h.* treas.
19:6 nothing *h.* from the heat
Prov. 2:4 as for *h.* treasure
Is. 40:27 my way is *h.* from L.
42:22 are *h.* in prison-houses
Jer. 16:17 iniq. *h.* fr. mine eyes
Hos. 13:12 sin of Ephraim is *h.*
Mat. 10:26 noth. *h.* th. sh. not be
  kn. *Mark* 4:22; *Lu.* 8:17; 12:2
Luke 8:45 saying who *h.* 18:34
19:42 are *h.* from thine eyes
Ep. 3:9, begin. been *h.* in G.
Col. 1:26 been *h.* from ages
2:3 *h.* all the treas. of wisdom
3:3 your life is *h.* with Ch. in G.
Heb. 11:23 by faith Moses was *h.*

Be HID.
Gen. 4:14 from thy face sh. I be *h.*
Lev. 4:13 be *h.* fr. assembly, 5:3, 4
Num. 20:20 sh. be *h.* in secret plac.
Jer. 29:14 under. of pru. men be *h.*
Hos. 13:14 repentance shall be *h.*
Amos 9:3 they be *h.* fr. my sight
Nah. 3:11 thou shalt be *h.*
Zep. 2:3 ye shall be *h.*
2 *Cor.* 4:3 if our gospel be *h.*

Not be HID.
Mat. 5:14 city on hill not be *h.*
Mark 7:24 but he could not be *h.*
1 *Tim.* 5:25 otherwise not be *h.*

Not HID.
Ps. 32:5 mine iniq. have I not *h.*
38:9 my groaning is not *h.*
69:5 my sins are not *h.* fr. thee
119:15 my substance was not *h.*
Jer. 16:17 are not *h.* fr. my face,
  nor their ini. *h.* fr. mine eyes

HIDDEKEL.
Gen. 2:14 river is H. *Dan.* 10:4

HIDDEN.
Lev. 5:2 *h.* from him
Deut. 30:11 it is not *h.* from thee
Job 24:1 are not *h.* from thee
Ps. 51:6 in *h.* part make know
83:3 consulted ag. thy *h.* ones
Prov. 28:12 wicked rise, man *h.*
Is. 45:3 give thee *h.* riches
48:6 showed thee things, *h.* th.
Ob. 6 *h.* things sought up
Acts 26:26 none of these *h.*
1 *Cor.* 2:7 *h.* wisdom G. ordained
4:5 bring to light *h.* things
2 *Cor.* 4:2 renounced *h.* things
1 *Pet.* 3:4 the *h.* man of heart
Rev. 2:17 give to eat of *h.* manna

HIDE, *Substantive,*
Lev. 8:17 *h.* flesh he burnt, 9:11

HIDE, *Verb.*
Gen. 18:17 shall I *h.* from Abra.
1 *Sam.* 3:17 *h.* it not from me, If
  thou *h.* 2 *Sam.* 14:18
Job 13:20 not *h.* myself from thee
14:13 wouldest *h.* me in grave
20:12 he *h.* it under his tongue
33:17 and *h.* pride from man
40:13 *h.* them in dust together
Ps. 17:8 *h.* me under thy wings
27:5 in time of tro. he sh. *h.* me
31:20 sh. *h.* them in thy pres.
51:9 *h.* thy face from my sins
64:2 *h.* me from secret counsel
Prov. 2:1 *h.* my com. with thee
Is. 1:15 I will *h.* mine eyes
2:10 and *h.* thee in the dust
16:3 *h.* outcasts
26:20 *h.* thyself a little moment
58:7 *h.* not fr. thine own flesh
Jer. 36:19 *h.* thee and Jeremiah
Lam. 3:56 *h.* not ear at my brea.

HID

Ezek. 28:3 no secret they can *h.*
31:8 cedars could not *h.* him
39:29 neither will I *h.* my face
Jam. 5:20 *h.* a multitude of sins
Rev. 6:16 *h.* us from him that
See FACE.

HIDE himself.
Jer. 23:24 *h. h.* in secret places
John 12:36 J. did *h. h.* them

HIDE themselves.
2 *K.* 7:12 gone out to *h. t.* in fle.
Job 24:4 poor of the earth *h. t.*
34:22 where work. of iniq. *h. t.*
Amos 9:3 *h. t.* in top of Carmel

HIDEST.
Job 13:24 why *h.* thy face? *Ps.*
  44:24; 88:14
Ps. 10:1 why *h.* thy, in trouble?
104:29 thou *h.* thy face
Is. 45:15 thou art G. th. *h.* thys.

HIDETH.
Job 23:9 *h.* himself on right hand
34:29 when he *h.* his face
42:3 who is he that *h.* counsel?
Ps. 10:11 he *h.* face will nev. see
139:12 darkn. *h.* not from thee
Prov. 10:18 *h.* hated with lying
19:24 sloth. *h.* his hand, 26:15
22:3 pru. man *h.* himself, 27:12
27:16 whosoever *h.* her, *h.* wind
28:27 that *h.* eyes sh. ha. curse
Is. 8:17 *h.* face from house of J.
Mat. 13:44 man hath found, he *h.*

HIDING.
Job 31:33 *h.* iniq. in my bosom
Ps. 32:7 art my *h.* place, 119:114
Is. 28:17 waters overflow *h.* pla.
32:2 as *h.* place from the wind
Hab. 3:4 was *h.* of his power

HIEL, 1 *K.* 16:34
HIGGAION. *Ps.* 9:16

HIGH.

Gen. 29:7 Lo, it is yet *h.* day
Deut. 12:2 served gods on *h.* mo.
28:52 up above the very *h.*
1 *Chr.* 17:17 state of man *h.* deg.
Job 11:8 *h.* as heaven
22:12 stars, how *h.* they are!
38:15 the *h.* arm sh. be broken
41:34 he beholdeth all *h.* things
Ps. 18:27 bring down *h.* looks
49:2 give ear, both low and *h.*
62:9 men of *h.* degree are a lie
71:19 thy righteous. O G. is *h.*
89:13 and *h.* is thy right hand
97:9 thou L. art *h.* above earth,
  113:4; 138:6
101:5 him that hath a *h.* look
103:11 heaven is *h.* above earth
131:1 things too *h.* for me
136:6 L. be *h.* he hath respect
139:6 is *h.* I cannot attain
149:6 let *h.* praises of God be
150:5 praise him on *h.* sounding
Prov. 18:11 as *h.* wall in conceit
21:4 *h.* look, and proud heart
24:7 wisdom is too *h.* for a fool
Ec. 12:5 afraid of that wh. is *h.*
Is. 2:12 L. on cedars that *h.*
6:1 Lord on a throne, *h.* and
10:14 I will punish his *h.* looks
22:16 as a breach in a *h.* wall
52:13 my servant sh. be very *h.*
57:15 the *h.* and lofty One
Jer. 17:12 a glorious *h.* throne
Ezek. 21:26 abase him is *h.*
21:3 habitation is *h.* that saith
John 13:1 sabbath was a *h.* day
Acts 13:17 with a *h.* arm bro. he
Rom. 12:16 mind not *h.* things
13:11 it is *h.* time now to awake
19:15 cast. down ev. *h.* th.
Phil. 3:14 prize of the *h.* calling
Rev. 21:12 Jerusal. had a wall *h.*

See GATE, GOD, HILL, HILLS.

Most HIGH.
Num. 24:16 knowledge of M. H.
2 *Sam.* 22:14 M. H. ut. his voice
Ps. 7:17 sing praise to name of
  the Lord M. H. 9:2; 92:1
46:4 tabernacle of the M. H.
47:2 the Lord M. H. is terrible
50:14 pay thy vows to the M. H.
56:2 fight me, O thou M. H.
57:2 I will cry unto God M. H.
73:11 is there knowl. in M. H.
77:10 right hand of M. H.
78:17 provoking the M. H. 56
82:6 ye are children of M. H.
83:18 art M. H. over all earth

CRUDEN'S CONCORDANCE.

HIL

Ps. 91:1 dwelleth in pl. of M. H.
9 made M. H. thy habitation
92:8 but thou, Lord, art *m.* h,
107:11 contem. counsel of M. H.
Is. 14:14 will be like the M. H.
Lam. 3:35 before face of M. H.
38 out of M. H. proc. not evil
Dan. 4:17 M. H. ruleth in kingd.
24 the decree of the M. H.
25 M. H. rules kingdom. 32
34 and I blessed the M. H.
7:18 saints of M. H. take king.
22 judg. given saints of M. H.
25 speak words against M. H.
27 saints of the M. H.
Hos. 7:16 return not to M. H.
11:7 called them to the M. H.
Acts 7:48 M. H. dwelleth not
See MOUNTAIN.

On HIGH.

Deut. 28:1 G. will set thee on *h.*
Job 5:11 set on *h.* th. that be low
16:19 and my record is on *h.*
31:18 she lifteth up herself on *h.*
27 eagle make her nest on *h.*
Ps. 7:7 for the. sakes return on *h.*
68:18 thou hast ascended on *h.*
93:29 O God, set me up on *h.*
91:14 I will set him on *h.*
93:4 L. on *h.* is mightier than
107:41 setteth he the poor on *h.*
Is. 26:5 bring. down them on *h.*
32:15 Sp. poured on us fr. on *h.*
40:26 lift up your eyes on *h.*
58:4 your voice heard on *h.*
Luke 1:78 day-spring from on *h.*
Eph. 4:8 he ascended up on *h.*
See PLACE, PLACES, PRIEST, TOWER.

HIGHER.

1 *Sam.* 9:2 S. *h.* than any of pe.
Job 35:5 clouds. which are *h.*
Ps. 61:2 lead to Rock that is *h.*
89:27 make him *h.* than kings
Ec. 5:8 there be *h.* than they
Is. 55:9 as hea. are *h.* than earth, so my ways *h.* th. your ways
Jer. 36:10 Bar. read in *h.* court
Dan. 6:3 one horn *h.* than other
Luke 14:10 may say, Go up *h.*
Rom. 13:1 subject to *h.* powers
Heb. 7:26 high-p. made *h.* than

HIGHEST.

Ps. 18:13 the H. gave his voice
87:5 H. himself shall establish
Prov. 8:26 nor *h.* part of dust
9:3 crieth on *h.* places of city
Ec. 5:8 higher than *h.* regard.
Ezek. 17:3 *h.* branch of cedar
Mat. 21:9 hosan. in *h. Mark* 11:10
Luke 1:32 called Son of the H.
35 power of H. overshad. thee
76 be called prophet of the H.
2:14 glory to G. in H. 19:38
6:35 ye shall be chil. of the H.
14:8 sit not down in *h.* room
20:46 love *h.* seats in synagog.

HIGHLY.

Luke 1:28 Thou art *h.* favored
16 *h.* esteemed among men
Rom. 12:3 think of him. more *h.*
Phil. 2:9 G. hath *h.* exalted him
1 *Thes.* 5:13 to est. them very *h.*

HIGH-MINDED.

Rom. 11:20 not *h. m.* 1 *Tim.* 6:1
2 *Tim.* 3:4 traitors, heady, *h. m.*

HIGHNESS.

Job 31:23 his *h.* I could not en.
Is. 13:3 that rejoice in my *h.*

HIGHWAY, S.

Jud. 5:6 days Jael *h.* unoccupied
Prov. 16:17 *h.* of upright
Is. 11:16 *h.* for his people
19:23, a *h.* out of Eg. to Assyria
33:8 *h.* lie waste, way-faring
35:8 and a *h.* shall be there
40:3 make *h.* desert a *h.* for G.
49:11 my *h.* shall be exalted
62:10 cast up *h.* gather stones
Jer. 31:21 thy heart towards *h.*
Amos 5:16 shall say in all *h.*
Mat. 22:9 go into *h. Luke* 14:23
Mark 10:46 Bartimeus sat by *h.*

HILKIAH.

2 *K.* 18:18 Eliak. son of H. 22:12
Is. 8:4 II. on E.'s right. 12:7
Is. 22:20 s. of H. 2 *Chr.* 34:20, 22

HILL.

Jos. 24:33 Eleazar buried in *h.*
1 *Sam.* 10:5 come to *h.* of G. 10
Ps. 3:4:3 shall accend to *h.* of L.
4:26 remember thee from *h.* M.
68:15 *h.* of L. is as *h.* of Bashan
16 *h.* G. desireth to dwell in

HIN

Cant. 4:6 get to *h.* of frankinc.
Is. 5:1 viney. in very fruitful *h.*
10:32 shake hand ag. *h.* of Jeru.
30:17 as an ensign on a *h.*
31:4 Lord shall fight for *h.*
40:4 mount. and *h.* be made low
Jer. 16:18 hunt them from ev. *h.*
31:39 measuring line on *h.* G.
49:16 holdest height of the *h.*
50:6 gone from mountain to *h.*
Mat. 5:14 city that is set on a *h.*
Luke 3:5 ev. *h.* be brought low
4:29 led him to brow of the *h.*
9:37 were come down from *h.*
Acts 17:22 Paul stood in Mars *h.*

HILL-COUNTRY.

Jos. 13:6 inh. of *h.-c.* drive out
Luke 1:39 Mary went to *h.-c.*
65 noise. through all *h.-c.* of J.

High HILL, S,

Gen. 7:19 *h. h.* under heaven
1 *K.* 14:23 groves on every *high h.,* 2 *K.* 17:10
Ps. 68:15 *high h.* as hill of B.
16 ye *high h.,* ? this is the *h.*
Is. 30:25 on *high h.* rivers of wa.
Jer. 2:20 on *h. h.* thou wand. 23
17:2 remember groves on *h. h.*
Ezek. 6:13 sla. sm. idols on *h. h.*
34:6 sheep wand. on every *h. h.*

Holy HILL.

Ps. 2:6 set my king on *h. h.* of
3:4 Lord heard me out of *h. h.*
15:1 who sh. dwell in thy *h. h.*
43:3 bring me to thy *h. h.?*
99:9 worship at his *h. h.*

HILL, with top.

Ex. 17:9 will stand on top of *h.*
Num. 14:44 pres. to go to *h. t.*
Jud. 10:8 S. carried to *top* of *h.*
1 *K.* 1:9 Elijah sat on *top* of *h.*

HILLS.

Gen. 49:26 eh. bound of everl. *h.*
Num. 23:9 fr. the *h.* I behold him
Deut. 8:7 spring out val. and *h.*
11:11 a land of *h.* and valleys
33:15 precious things of last. *h.*
1 K. 20:23 gods are gods of *h.,* 28
22:17 saw all *h.* scattered on *h.*
2 *K.* 10:4 burnt incense on the *h.*
2 *Chr.* 2:3:4
Job 15:7 wast thou made be. *h. ?*
Ps. 18:7 foundations of *h.* moved
50:10 cattle on thousand *h.*
65:12 little *h.* rejoice on ev. side
72:3 the little *h.* by righteousn.
80:10 *h.* covered with shadow
93:1 strength of *h.* is his also
97:5 *h.* melted like wax
98:8 the *h.* be joyful together
104:10 springs. which run am. *h.*
13 watereth *h.* from chambers
32 he touch. *h.* and they smo.
114:4 little *h.* skip. like lam. 6
121:1 will lift mine eyes to *h.*
148:9 mount. and *h.* praise Lord
Prov. 8:25 *h.* I brought forth
Cant. 2:8 he cometh skip. on *h.*
Is. 2:2 shall be exalted above *h.*
14 day of L. shall be on all *h.*
7:25 on all *h.* shall not come fear
40:12 weighed *h.* in balance ?
41:15 shalt make *h.* as chaff
42:15 make waste mount. and *h.*
54:10 mount. depart, *h.* remov.
55:12 *h.* break forth into sing.
65:7 blasphemed me up. the *h.*
Jer. 3:23 salva. hoped for from *h.*
13:27 thy abominations on *h.*
Ezek. 6:3 thus saith L. to *h.* 36:4
36:6 to *h.* to rivers and valleys
Joel 3:18 *h.* shall flow with milk
Mic. 4:1 be exalted above *h.*
6:1 let the *h.* hear thy voice
Nah. 1:5 *h.* melt, earth is burnt
Hab. 3:6 perpetual *h.* did bow
Luke 23:30 say to *h.* Cover us

HIM.

Rom. 11:36 of *h.* through *h.* and to *h.* are all things

HIN.

Ex. 29:40 fourth part of *h.* of oil
30:24 of oil-olive a *h.*
Lev. 19:36 a just *h.* shall ye have
23:13 the fourth part of a *h.* of oil, *Num.* 15:4; 28:14
Num. 15:5 fourth part of a *h.* of wine
6 the third part of a *h.* of wine
9 mingled with half a *h.* of oil
Ezek. 4:11 sixth part of a *h.* of wa.
45:24 *h.* of oil for ep. 46:5, 7, 11
46:11 a *h.* of oil to temper with
14 *h.* of oil third part of epnah

HIND, S.

Gen. 49:21 Naph. is a *h.* let loose

HIR

2 *Sam.* 22:34 my feet like *h.* feet,
Ps. 18:33; *Hab.* 3:19
Job 39:1 mark when *h.* calve ?
Ps. 29:9 voice of L. mak. *h.* calve
Prov. 5:19 as loving *h.* and roe
Cant. 2:7 by *h.* of field, 3:5
Jer. 14:5 h. calved in the field

HINDER, Verb.

Gen. 24:56 *h.* me not, seeing L.
Neh. 4:8 and *h.* the building
Job 9:12 taketh away, who *h. ?*
11:10 shut up, who *h.* him ?
Acts 8:36 what A. me to be bap.
1 *Cor.* 9:12 lest we sho. *h.* gospel
Gal. 5:7 who did *h.* you ?

HINDERED, ETH.

Ezr. 6:8 exp. given, be not *h.*
Is. 14:6 is persecuted, none *h.*
Luke 11:52 entering in, ye *h.*
1 *Thes.* 2:18 wo. ha. come, S. *h.*
1 *Pet.* 3:7 your prayers be not *h.*

HINDER end, sea.

2 *Sam.* 2:23 smote with *h. e.* of
Zec. 14:8 half toward the *h. sea*

HINDERMOST, or HIND-MOST.

Gen. 33:2 put Rachel and Jos. *h.*
Num. 2:31 go *h.* with standards
Deut. 25:18 and smote *h.* of those
Jos. 10:19 and smite *h.* of them
Jer. 50:12 *h.* of nations wildern.

HINDER part, s.

1 *K.* 7:25 their *h. parts* were inward. 2 *Chr.* 4:4
Ps. 78:66 smote enemies in *h. p.*
Joel 2:20 *h. part* tow. utmost sea
Mark 4:38 J. was in *h. p.* of ship
Acts 27:41 *h. p.* broken with wa.

HINGES.

1 *K.* 7:50 the *h.* of gold for doors
Prov. 26:14 door turneth upon *h.*

HINNOM.

Jos. 15:8 border by valley of H.
2 *K.* 23:10 Tophet, in val. of H.
2 *Chr.* 28:3 incense in val. of H.
33:6 to pass through fire in H.
Jer. 19:2 valley of the son of H.
32:35 high places in valley of H.
See COME.

HIP.

Jud. 15:8 sm. them *h.* and thigh

HIRAM.

2 *Sam.* 5:11 H. king, 1 *Chr.* 14:1
1 *K.* 5:1 H. sent his servants, 8
7:13 Sol. sent and fetched H.
9:12 H. came to see. 27 ; 10:11

HIRE, Substantive.

Gen. 31:8 ring-stra. sh. be thy A.
Ex. 22:15 hired thing ca. for *h.*
Deut. 23:18 not fr. *h.* of a whore
1 *K.* 5:6 to thee will I give *h.*
Mic. 1:7 gather. it of *h.* of whore,
1 *Sam.* 11:6 Saul T'rish the H
Ezek. 16:41 thy mother a H. 43

HITTITES.

Gen. 15:20 band of H. *Jos.* 1:4
Ex. 3:8, 17; 13:5 ; 23:28 ; *Deut.* 7:1 ; 20:17 ; *Jos.* 3:10
Jud. 3:5 ; 1 *K.* 9:20 ; *Neh.* 9:8

DIVITES, much in HITTITES.

HO.

Ruth 4:1 *h.* such a one. sit down
Is. 55:1 *h.* ev. one that thirsteth
Zec. 2:6 A. *h.* come forth

HOAR, HOARY. *See* FROST, HAIRS, HEAD.

Job 41:32 would think deep *h.*
Num. 10:20 sa. to H. *Jud.* 4:11

HOBAD.

HOSED.

Acts 27:40 they A. up mainsail
HOLD, Substantive.
Jud. 9:46 entered *h.* of god Ber.
49 put them to *h.* set *h.* on fire
1 *Sam.* 22:4 David in *h.* 24:22 ;
2 *Sam.* 5:17 ; 23:14
Jer. 31:30 remained in their *h.*
Ezek. 19:9 brought him into *h.*
Acts 4:3 in *h.* to next day
18:2 the *h.* of ev. foul spirit
See STRONG.

HOLD.

Gen. 21:18 *h.* him in thy hand
Ex. 9:2 if thou *h.* them still !
9:2 and wilt *h.* them still)
10:9 we must *h.* a feast unto L.
20:7 L. not *h.* guilt, *Deut.* 5:11
1 *Sam.* 2:9 sh. *h.* peace to deub
6:6 Uzziah. put *h.* to ark of G.
and took *h.* of it. 1 *Chr.* 13:9
1 *K.* 2:9 now *h.* him not guiltless

CRUDEN'S CONCORDANCE. 897

HOL

Ex. 4:11 *h.* out golden sceptre
Job 6:24 and I will *h.* my tongue
9:28 wilt not *h.* me innocent
13:19 if I *h.* my tongue
17:9 right, shall *h.* on his way
Ps. 17:5 *h.* my goings in thy pa.
119:53 hor. hath taken *h.* on me
117 *h.* thou me up, I sh. be safe
139:10 thy right hand sh. *h.* me
Prov. 31:19 her hands *h.* distaff
Cant. 3:8 they all *h.* a sword
Is. 41:13 L, *h.* thy right hand
42:6 and I will *h.* thy hand
Jer. 2:13 broken cist. *h.* no wat.
50:42 anguish took *h.* of him
Amos 6:10 he say, *h.* thy tongue
Zec. 11:5 *h.* themsel. not guilty
Mat. 6:24 *h.* to one, *Luke* 16:13
21:26 for all *h.* J. as a prophet
Mark 7:4 they received to *h.*
Rom. 1:18 *h.* truth in unrighte.
Phil. 2:29 *h.* such in reputation
2 *Thes.* 2:15 *h.* traditions ye have
Heb. 3:14 If we *h.* our confidence
Rev. 2:14 *h.* doctrine of Balaam
15 *h.* doctrine of Nicolaitans
See CAUGHT.

HOLD fast.
Job 8:15 he sh. *h.* it *f.* but not en.
27:6 my righteousness I *h. fast.*
Jer. 8:5 they *h. f.* deceit
1 *Thes.* 5:21 *h. fast* that is good
2 *Tim.* 1:13 *h. f.* form of so. wor.
Heb. 3:6 we *h. f.* the confidence
4:14 *h. f.* our profession, 10:23
Rev. 2:25 *h. f.* till I come
3:3 and *h. fast* and repent
11 *h.* that *f.* which thou hast

HOLD peace.
Ex. 14:14 ye shall *h.* your peace
Num. 30:4 if her father *h.* his *p.*
14 if her husband *h.* his *p.*
Jud. 18:19 *h. p.* lay hand on m.
2 *Kings* 18:20 *h.* thy *p.* my master
2 *K.* 2:3 *h.* you your peace, 5
Neh. 8:11 *h.* your *p.* day is holy
Job 11:3 lies make men *h. p. f*
13:13 *h.* your *p.* let me alone
13:21 *h.* thy *p.* and I will speak
33 *h.* thy *p.* I will teach thee
Ps. 83:1 O. G, *h.* not thy *p.* 109:1
Is. 62:1 for Z.'s sake not *h.* my *p.*
6 *h.* their *p.* day nor night
64:12 *h.* peace and afflict us?
Jer. 4:19 cannot *h.* peace
Zep. 1:7 *h.* thy *p.* at pres. of L.
Mat. 20:31 reb. them bec. they
sh. *h. p. Mark* 10:48; *Luke*
18:39
Mark 1:25 *h.* thy *p. Luke* 4:35
Luke 19:40 if they *h. p.* the sto.
Acts 12:17 beckoning to *h.* th. *p.*
18:9 be not afraid, *h.* not thy *p.*
1 *Cor.* 14:30 let the first *h.* his *p.*
See TAKE.

HOLDEN.
2 *K.* 23:22 not *h.* such a pass. 23
Job 36:8 *h.* in cords of affliction
Ps. 18:35 right hand hath *h.* me
71:6 by thee have I been *h.* up
73:23 *h.* me up by right hand
Prov. 5:22 *h.* with cords
Is. 45:1 wh. right hand I have *h.*
Luke 24:16 their eyes were *h.*
Acts 2:24 not possi. he sho. be *h.*
Rom. 14:4 yea, he shall be *h.* up

HOLDEST.
Est. 4:14 *h.* thy peace this time
Job 13:24 wherefore *h.* thou me
Ps. 77:4 thou *h.* my eyes waking
Jer. 49:16 O thou that *h.* height
Rev. 2:13 thou *h.* fast my name

HOLDETH.
Job 2:3 he *h.* fast his integrity
26:9 *h.* back face of his throne
Ps. 66:9 bless God who *h.* soul
Prov. 11:12 man of und. *h.* peace
17:28 a fool when he *h.* peace
Dan. 10:21 none *h.* w. me but M.
Rev. 2:1 *h.* stars in right hand

HOLDING.
Is. 33:15 shak. hands fr. *h.* bribes
Jer. 6:11 I am weary with *h.* in
Mark 7:3 *h.* tradition of elders
Phil. 2:16 *h.* forth word of life
2:29 and not *h.* the head
1 *Tim.* 1:19 *h.* faith
3:9 *h.* the mystery of faith
Tit. 1:9 *h.* fast faithful word
Rev. 7:1 four angels *h.* four win.

HOLES.
Ex. 28:32 a *h.* in the top of it
1 *Sam.* 14:11 Heb. come out of *h.*
2 *K.* 12:9 cheninda bored a *h.*
Cant. 5:4 in hand by *h.* of door

HOL

Is. 2:19 go into *h.* of rocks, 7:19
11:8 child sh. play on *h.* of asp.
42:22 they are all snared in *h.*
51:1 look to the *h.* of the pit
Jer. 16:16 hunt them out of *h.*
Ezek. 8:7 behold a *h.* in the wall
Nah. 2:12 filled his *h.* with prey
Hag. 1:6 put it in a bag with *h.*
Zec. 14:12 eyes consume in th. *h.*
Mat. 8:20 foxes ha. *h. Luke* 9:58

HOLIER, EST.
Is. 65:5 for I am *h.* than thou
Heb. 9:3 tabern. is called the *h.*
8 way to *h.* not yet manifest
10:19 to enter *h.* by blood of J.

HOLLY.
1 *Thes.* 2:10 how *h.* we behaved

HOLINESS.
Ex. 15:11 who like thee, in *h. f*
28:36 *h.* to Lord, 32:30; *Zec.*
14:20, 21
1 *Chr.* 16:29 worship L. in beauty
of *h. Ps.* 29:2; 96:9
2 *Chr.* 20:21 praise beauty of *h.*
31:18 sanctified themselv. in *h.*
Ps. 30:4 remem. of his *h.* 97:12
47:8 God sitteth on throne of *h.*
48:1 praised in mount. of his *h.*
60:6 G. hath spoken in his *h.* 108:7
89:35 sw. by my *h.* I will not lie
93:5 *h.* becom. thy house, O L.
110:3 willing, in beauties of *h.*
Is. 23:18 her hire sh. be *h.* to
35:8 sh. be called the way of *h.*
62:9 drink it in courts of my *h.*
63:15 from habitation of thy *h.*
18 peo. of thy *h.* have posse. it
Jer. 2:3 Israel was *h.* to the Lord
31:23 O mountain of *h.*
Amos 4:2 hath sworn by his *h.*
Ob. 17 on mount Z. shall be *h.*
Mal. 2:11 Ju. hath prof. *h.* of L.
Luke 1:75 might serve him in *h.*
Acts 3:12 *h.* we had made him walk
Rom. 1:4 according to spirit of *h.*
6:19 servants to righte. unto *h.*
22 ye have your fruit unto *h.*
2 *Cor.* 7:1 perfect. *h.* in fear of G.
Eph. 4:24 new man created in *h.*
1 *Thes.* 3:13 stablish hearts in *h.*
4:7 not to uncleanness, but to *h.*
1 *Tim.* 2:15 conti. in faith and *h.*
Heb. 12:10 be partakers of his *h.*
14 peace with men, and *h.*

HOLLOW.
Gen. 32:25 *h.* of thigh, 32
Ex. 27:8 altar *h.* boards, 38:7
Jud. 15:19 God clave a *h.* place
Is. 40:12 waters in *h.* of hand

HOL

Ps. 105:42 remembered *h.* prom.
11:9 *h.* is *h.* in all his works
Prov. 9:10 knowl. of *h.* is under
30:3 nor have I knowl. of the *h.*
Is. 4:3 Jerus. shall be called *h.*
6:3 *h. h. h.* is the Lord of Hosts
13 *h.* seed substance thereof
27:13 worship in *h.* mountain
52:10 L. made bare his *h.* arm
58:13 call sabbath, *h.* of the L.
64:10 *h.* cities are a wilderness
11 *h.* and beaut. house is burnt
Jer. 11:15 *h.* flesh passed fr. thee
23:9 because of L. and *h.* words
Ezek. 22:26 no difference betw.
h. and profane
36:38 incr. them as the *h.* flock
42:13 *h.* chambers where priests
14 their garments, they are *h.*
44:19 lay them in *h.* chambers
23 differ. betw. *h.* and profane
45:1 offer *h.* portion of land, 4
46:19 *h.* chambers of priests
48:10 for priests be *h.* oblation
20 shall offer *h.* oblation, 21
Dan. 4:8 D. before me, in whom
is spirit of *h.* gods, 9, 18; 5:11
11:28 heart against *h.* covenant
30 indignation ag. *h.* covenant
intel. with forsakers of *h. c.*
Hag. 2:13 if one bear *h.* flesh,
skirt touch br. sh. It be *h. f*
Zec. 2:13 L. raised up *h.* habita.
Mat. 7:6 gi. not th. is *h.* to dogs
25:31 and *h.* angels with him
Mark 6:20 he was just and *h.*
8:38 with *h.* angels, *Luke* 9:26
Luke 1:70 by the mouth of *h.*
prophets, *Acts* 3:21
72 remember his *h.* covenant
2:23 every male called *h.* to L.
John 17:11 *h.* Father keep those
Acts 4:27 against thy *h.* child J.
30 won. done by name of *h.* ch.
7:33 place thou standest is *h.*
10:22 warned from G. by *h.* ang.
Rom. 1:2 prom. by *h.* scriptures
7:12 commandment is *h.* just
11:16 fir. fruit be *h.* if root be *h.*
12:1 bodies *h.* sacrifice to G.
16:16 salute with *h.* kiss, 1 *Cor.*
16:20; 1 *Cor.* 13:12; 1 *Thes.*
5:26; 1 *Pet.* 5:14
1 *Cor.* 3:17 temple of God is *h.*
7:14 else chil. but now are *h.*
34 may be *h.* in body and spi.
Eph. 1:4 be *h.* with. blame, 5:27
Col. 1:22 present *h.* and unblam.
3:12 elect of G. *h.* and beloved
1 *Thes.* 5:27 to all *h.* brethren
1 *Tim.* 3:5 *h.* hands
2 *Tim.* 1:9 called us with *h.* call.
3:15 hast known *h.* scriptures
Tit. 1:8 bishop be sober, *h.* tem.
Heb. 3:1 *h.* brethren, partakers
7:26 high-pr. hea. us who is *h.*
1 *Pet.* 1:15 *h.* in conversation, 16
2:5 *h.* priesth. offer up sacrifices
9 *h.* nation, a peculiar people
3:5 *h.* women who trusted in G.
1 *Pet.* 1:18 with him in *h.* mount
2:21 moved me *h.* Jerusalem
22:11 he that is *h.* be *h.* still
See CONVOCATION.

HOLY day.
Ex. 35:2 seventh shall be *h.* day
Neh. 8:9 if *h.* unto L. 10, 11
10:31 not buy it on sab. *h. d.*
13:10 pleas. on my *h. d.*
Ps. 42:4 multitude that kept *h. d.*
Is. 58:13 doing plea. on my *h. d.*
Col. 2:16 no man judge of *h. d.*
See GARMENTS.

HOLY Ghost.
Mat. 1:18 with child of H. G.
20 conceived in her is of H. G.
3:11 with H. G. *Mark* 1:8; *Luke*
3:16; *John* 1:33; *Acts* 1:5
12:31 blasph. ag. H. G. not forgiven,
Mark 3:29; *Luke* 12:10
28:19 baptize in name of H. G.
Mark 12:36 David said by the H.
Ghost, *Acts* 1:16
Luke 1:15 filled with H. G. 41, 67
2 Zacharias filled with H. G. 67

HOL

Luke 2:25 Sim. H. G. upon him
26 revealed unto him by H. G.
3:22 H. G. desc. in bodily shape
4:1 Jesus being full of H. G.
12:12 H. G. shall teach you
John 7:39 H. G. not yet given
14:26 Comforter, who is H. G.
20:22 receive ye H. G. *Acts* 2:38
Acts 1:2 he thro. H. G. had given
8 the H. G. is come on you
2:4 all filled with H. G. 4:31
33 promise of the H. G.
4:8 filled with the H. Ghost
5:3 S. filled he. to lie to H. G. ?
32 are witnesses, so is H. G.
6:3 men full of the H. Ghost
5 Stephen, man full of H. G.
7:51 stiff-n. alw. resist H. G.
55 Stephen full of H. Ghost
8:15 prayed th. might re. H. G.
17 hands on th. received H. G.
18 when S. saw H. G. was giv.
19 hands, they receive H. G.
9:17 might. be filled with H. G.
31 walking in comfort of H. G.
10:38 G. anoint. J. with H. G.
44 H. G. fell on all who heard
45 on Gentiles was pou. H. G.
47 received H. G. as well as we
11:15 H. G. fell on them
16 shall be baptized with H. G.
24 Barnabas, full of H. G.
13:4 being sent forth by H. G.
9 filled with H. Ghost
52 disciples filled with H. G.
15:8 giving H. G. as he did
28 it seemed good to the H. G.
16:6 forbidden of H. G. to prea.
19:2 received H. G. ? we have
not heard there be H. G.
6 hands on them, H. G. came
20:23 save that the H. G. witn.
28 H. G. made you overseers
21:11 thus saith the H. G.
28:25 spake H. G. by Esaias
Rom. 5:5 shed in hearts by H. G.
9:1 consc. bear. wit. in H. G.
14:17 kingd. of G. joy in H. G.
15:13 through power of H. G.
16 being sancti. by the H. G.
1 *Cor.* 2:13 words w. h. H. G. tea.
6:19 body is temple of H. G.
12:3 Jesus is Lord, but by H. G.
2 *Cor.* 6:6 by the H. G. by love
13:14 communion of H. G.
1 *Thes.* 1:5 gospel came in H. G.
6 rec. word with joy of H. G.
2 *Tim.* 1:14 good th. k. by H. G.
Tit. 3:5 renewing of H. G.
Heb. 2:4 with gifts of H. G.
3:7 H. G. saith, To-day if ye h.
6:4 made partakers of H. G.
9:8 H. Ghost this signifying
10:15 whereof H. G. is a witness
1 *Pet.* 1:12 H. G. sent fr. heaven
2 *Pet.* 1:21 as moved by H. G.
1 *John* 5:7 Fat. Word, and H. G.
Jude 20 beloved, pray. in H. G.
See GOD, HABITATION, HILL.

Most HOLY.
Ex. 26:33 betw. holy and *m. h.*
28:37 an altar *m. h.* 40:10
Le. 2:3 remnant be Aaron's, *h.*
is *m. h.* 10; 6:17; 10:12
6:25 sin-offering *m. h.* 29; 10:17
7:1 tresp.-offering is *m. h.* 6; 14:13
21:22 both of *m. h.* and holy
24:9 cakes of flour *m. h.* to him
Num. 4:4 about an *h.* things
18:9 approach *m. h.* things
18:10 *m. h.* place sh. thou eat it
1 *K.* 6:16 built th. for *m. h.* place
7:50 made rev. for *m. h.* place
both brought the ark unto *most*
h. place, 2 *Chr.* 5:7
1 *Chr.* 23:13 A. to sanctify *m. h.*
2 *Chr.* 3:8 holi. *h.* house
10 in *m. h.* house made cheru.
31:14 distri. of *m. h.* things
Ezr. 2:63 not eat of *most h.*
things, *Neh.* 7:65
Ezek. 43:12 whole limit *h.* shall be *m. h.*
44:13 not come near *m. h.* place
45:3 sanctuary and *m. h.* place
Dan. 9:24 to anoint *most h.*
23 building on *m. h.* faith
Jude 20 building on *m. h.* faith

Holy mountain.
Ps. 87:1 foundation is in *h. m.*
Is. 11:9 nor destr. in all my *h. m.*
56:7 will I bring to my *h. m.*
57:13 shall inherit my *h. m.*
65:11 y are th. forget my *h. m.*
Ezek. 28:14 in *h. m.* of God
Dan. 9:16 anger turned fr. *h. m.*

HOL

Dan. 9:20 pres. suppli. for *h. m.*
11:45 plant tabernacles in *h. m.*
Joel 2:1 so, an alarm in my *h. m.*
3:17 L. dwelling in Z. my *h. m.*
Ob. 16 drunk on my *h. m.*
Zec. 8:3 mount. of L. called A. *m.*

HOLY name.
Lev. 20:3 Molech, prof. my *h. n.*
22:2 profane not my *h. n.* 32
1 **Chr.** 16:10 glory ye in his *h. name, Ps.* 105:3
35 thanks to A. *n. Ps.* 106:47
29:16 build a house for thy *h.*
Ps. 33:21 trusted in his *h. name*
99:3 praise terrible *n.* it is *h.*
103:1 L. bless his *h. n.* 145:21
111:9 *h.* and rev. his *n. Lu.* 1:49
Is. 57:15 lofty One, wh. *n.* is *h.*
Ezek. 20:39 pollute you my *h. n.*
36:20 profaned my *h. n.*
22 your sakes, for *h. n.'s sake*
39:7 make known *h. n.* in Isr.
25 be jealous for my *h. n.*
43:7 my *h. n.* is. no more defile
8 defiled my *h. n.* by aborni.
Amos 2:7 to profane my *h. n.*

HOLY oil.
Ex. 30:25 *h.* anolnt. *o.* 31; 37:29
Ps. 89:20 with *h. oil* I anoi. him

HOLY One.
Deut. 33:8 Thummim and Urim
be with thy H. One.
Job 6:10 not con. words of H. O.
Ps. 16:10 nor suffer H. O. to see
corruption, **Acts** 2:27; 13:35
89:19 in vision to my H. O.
Is. 10:17 H. O. *eh.* be for a flame
29:23 sanctify H. O. of Jacob
40:25 *eh.* I be equal? saith H. O.
43:15 I am the Lord, your H. O.
49:7 Redeemer of Is. his H. O.
Dan. 4:13 H. O. down fr. heaven
Hos. 11:9 H. O. in midst of thee
Hab. 1:12 from everl. my H. O.
3:3 H. O. came from mount F.
Mark 1:24 I know th. who th. a.
the H. O. of G. **Luke** 4:34
Acts 3:14 ye denied the H. One
1 **John** 2:20 unction from H. One

HOLY One of Israel.
2 *K.* 19:22 lifted thy eyes against
the H. O. of *Israel, Is.* 37:23
Ps. 71:22 O thou H. O. of *Israel*
78:41 limited the H. O. of *Israel*
89:18 the H. O. of *Is.* is our ki.
Is. 1:4 provoked the H. O. of *Is.*
5:19 coun of H. O. of *Israel*
24 despised word of H. O. of *I.*
12:6 great is H. O. of *Is.* in mid.
17:7 have respect to H. O. of *I.*
29:19 rejoice in H. O. of *Israel*
30:11 cause H. O. of *Is.* to cease
12 saith the H. O. of *Is.* 15
31:1 look not to the H. O. of *Is.*
41:14 saith thy Red. H. O. of *I.*
16 shalt glory in H. O. of *Is.*
20 H. O. of *Is.* hath created it
43:3 I am the L. the H. O. of *I.*
15 I am the Lord, H. O. of *Is.*
47:4 L. is his name, H. O. of *Is.*
48:17 Red. H. O. of *Israel,* 54:5
49:7 Red. of *I.* and *h.* O. of *I.*
55:5 nat. run to thee, H. O. of *I.*
60:9 bring th. gold to H. O. of *I.*
14 the Z. of the H. O. of *Is.*
Jer. 50:29 proud aga. H. O. of *I.*
51:5 filled w. sin ag. H. O. of *I.*
Ezek. 39:7 I am the L. H. O. in *I.*

HOLY ones.
Dan. 4:7 dem. by word of *h. o.*

HOLY people.
Deut. 7:6 *h. p.* to the L. 14:2, 21
26:19 thou may be *h. p.* to Lord
28:9 L. shall estabi. thee a *h. p.*
Is. 62:12 shall call them *h. p.*
Dan. 8:24 and destroy *h. p.*

HOLY place.
Ex. 26:23 goeth in unto *h. p.* 35
43 to minister in *h. place,* 29:30
29:31 scethe his flesh in the *h. p.*
31:11 sweet incense for *h. p.*
35:19 do service in *h.* 39:1, 41
38:24 gold in all work of a *h. p.*
Lev. 6:16 unlea. bread sh. be eat.
in *h. p.* 26; 7:6; 10:13; 24:9
27 shalt wash that in the *h. p.*
10:17 eaten sin-offer. in *h. p.* 18
14 blood not bro. within *h. p.*
11:13 any burnt-offering in *h. p.*
16:2 come not at all tim. to *h. p.*
16 atonement for *h. p.* 17, 27
23 end of reconciling the *h. p.*
31 shall wash his flesh in a *h. p.*
Jos. 5:15 *p.* wh. thou stand is *h.*
1 *K.* 8:8 staves were seen in *h. p.*

HOM

2 **Chr.** 29:3 carry filth. out of *h. p.*
30:27 prayer came to his *h. p.*
Ezr. 9:8 to give us a nail in *h. p.*
Ps. 24:3 *eh.* stand in his *h. p.*
46:4 streams make glad the *h. p.*
68:17 Lord is on. them in *h. p.*
Ec. 8:10 had gone from *p.* of *h.*
Is. 57:15 I dw. in high and *h. p.*
Ezek. 41:4 this is the most *h. p.*
42:13 *p.* is *h.*; 14 out of *h. p.*
Mat. 24:15 abomination in *h. p.*
Acts 6:13 blasph. words ag. *h. p.*
21:28 this man polluted *h. p.*
Heb. 9:12 Christ entered *h. p.*
25 priest entered ev. year *h. p.*

HOLY places.
2 **Chr.** 8:11 bee. the *places* are *h.*
33:20 they *shall be h.* to the L.
Ezek. 41:4 *h. be h.* unto you, 87
27:9 man giveth to L. *s. be h.*
10 exchange thereof *s. be h.* 33
21 the Jublee, it *s. be h.* to L.
34 the tenth *s. be h.* unto the L.
Num. 6:5 Nazarite *s. be h.* to L.
Deut. 23:14 theref. *s.* camp be *h.*
Ezek. 45:1 portions *s. be h.*
Joel 3:17 then *J.* Jerusalem be *h.*
Ps. 51:11 take not H. S. fr. me
Is. 63:10 rebel. and vexed H. S.
Mat. 12:31 *h.* S. within him?
Luke 11:13 heav. Fa. give H. S.
Eph. 1:13 sealed wi. H. S. of pro.
4:30 grieve not the H. S. of God
1 **Thes.** 4:8 given us his H. S.

HOLY temple.
Ps. 5:7 worship tow. A. *t.* 138:2
11:4 the Lord is in his *h. temple*
65:4 satis. with goodness of *h. t.*
79:1 *h. temple* have they defiled
Jon. 2:4 look again tow. thy *h. t.*
7 my prayer came to thy *h. t.*
Mic. 1:2 L. from *h. t.* be witness
Hab. 2:20 the Lord is in his *h. t.*
Eph. 2:21 groweth to *h. t.*

HOLY thing.
Lev. 22:10 no stranger eat of *h. t.*
Num. 4:15 *eh.* not touch any *h. t.*
Ezek. 48:12 obtain. to them. a *t. h.*
Luke 1:35 that *h. th.* born of thee

HOLY things.
Ex. 28:38 bear iniq. of *h. t.*
Lev. 5:15 thro. ignorance in *h. t.*
22:2 sep. from the *h. t.* of *Is.*
4 not eat of *h. t.* till clean. 6, 12
7 shall afterward eat of *h. t.*
15 shall not profane A. *t.* of *Is.*
16 to bear iniq. when eat *h. t.*
Num. 4:20 not see. *h. t.* are cov.
18:32 neither sh. ye pollute *h. t.*
Deut. 12:26 thy *h. t.* take and go
1 **Chr.** 23:28 office purifying *h. t.*
2 **Chr.** 31:6 bro. in tithe of *h. t.*
Neh. 10:33 ordinances for *h. t.*
12:47 sanctified *h. t.* to Levites
Ezek. 22:8 thou despised my *h. t.*
26 priests have profaned *h. t.*
44:8 not kept charge of my *h. t.*
Zep. 9:13 minister about *h. t.*

HOME.

Gen. 43:16 bring these men *h.*
Ex. 9:19 not brought *h.* sh. die
Deut. 21:12 br. her A. to thy hou.
24:5 shall be free at *h.* one year
Ruth 1:21 L. hath brought me *h.*
1 **Sam.** 6:7 bring their calves *h.*
10 men shut up th. calves at *h.*
18:2 go no more A. to fath.'s ho.
31:11 word not fetch A. banish.
17:23 Ahithophel gat him *h.*
1 *K.* 5:14 a month *h.* L. two at *h.*
13:7 come A. with me, 15
1 **Chr.** 13:12 bring ark of G. 13
2 **Chr.** 25:10 go *h.* they return A.
Est. 5:10 when Haman came *h.*
Job 39:12 wilt believe *h.* thy seed
Ps. 68:12 she that tarried at *h.*
Prov. 7:19 good man is not at *h.*
20 come *h.* at day appointed
Ec. 12:5 man goeth to his long *h.*
Lam. 1:20 at *h.* there is as death
Hab. 2:5 neither keepeth at *h.*
Hag. 1:9 when ye brought it *h.*

HON

Mat. 8:6 my serv. lieth at A. sick
Mark 5:19 go A. to thy friends
Luke 9:61 bid th. farewell at A.
John 19:27 took her to his own *h.*
20:10 disc. went to their own *h.*
1 *Cor.* 11:34 hunger, eat at *h.*
14:35 ask husbands at *h.*
2 **Cor.** 5:6 we are at *h.* in body
1 **Tim.** 5:4 to show piety at *h.*
Tit. 2:5 be discreet, keepers at *h.*

HOME-BORN.
Ex. 12:49 to him that is A.-*b.*
Lev. 18:9 whe. *b.* at A. or abroad
Jer. 2:14 is Israel a A.-*o.* slave?

HOMER.
Lev. 27:16 a A. of barley-seed
Ez. 5:10 seed of a A. yield ephah
Ezek. 45:14 for ten baths are a *h.*
Hos. 3:2 hou. for *h.* and half *h.*

HONEST.
Luke 8:15 an A. and good heart
Acts 6:3 seven of *h.* report
Rom. 12:17 A. in sight of all
2 *Cor.* 8:21 A. in sight of L.
13:7 do that which is A.
Phil. 4:8 whatso. things are A.
1 *Pet.* 2:12 having conversat. A.

HONESTLY.
Rom. 13:13 walk A. as in the day
1 **Thes.** 4:12 walk A. toward them
Heb. 13:18 in all things to live A.

HONESTY.
1 **Tim.** 2:2 lead life god. and A.

HONOR, S.
Gen. 49:6 A. be not thou united
Ex. 14:17 get me A. on Phar. 18
Num. 22:17 promote thee to A. 37
24:11 L. hath kept thee from A.
Jud. 4:9 journey not be for th. A.
13:17 what is thy name that
2 *Sam.* 6:22 shall I be had in A.
1 **Chr.** 17:18 canst thou add to A.
29:12 riches and A. come of thee
28 D. died, full of riches and A.
2 **Chr.** 1:11 not asked riches or A.
17:5 Jehosh. had riches and A.
18:1 had riches and A. in abund.
26:18 not for thy A. Uzziah
32:27 Hezek. had riches and A.
33 sons of David did him A.
Est. 1:4 riches of glo. A. majesty
20 wives shall give to husb. A.
6:3 wh. A. has been done for th.?
6 do the *Jews* had for own A.
Job 14:21 his sons come to A.
Ps. 7:5 see. lay mine A. in dust
8:5 crowned with A. *Heb.* 2:7, 9
21:5 A. and maj. thou laid on him
26:8 where riches A. dwelleth
49:12 man being in A. abid. not
56:2 sing forth A. of his name
71:8 mouth filled with thy A.
66:2 A. and majesty in his sanc.
104:1 thou art clothed with A.
112:9 horn eh. be exalt. with A.
145:5 speak of A. of thy majesty
145:9 thine A. have all his saints
Prov. 3:16 left hand riches and A.
4:8 she shall bring thee to A.
5:9 lest thou give th. A. to oth.
6:18 riches and A. are with me
11:16 gracious woman retain. A.
14:28 the people is the king's A.
15:33 bef. A. is humility, 18:12
20:3 an A. to cease from strife
21:21 follow, mercy, findeth A.
22:4 fear of L. are riches and A.
25:2 A. of kings to search
26:1 A. is not seemly for a fool
8 so is he that giv. A. to a fool
25:23 A. shall uphold humble
31:25 and A. are her clothing
Ec. 6:2 to wh. G. hath given A.
10:1 that is in reputation for A.
Jer. 33:9 an A. before all nations
Dan. 2:6 receive rewards and A.
4:30 built for A. of my majesty
36 A. and helpfulness returned
5:18 G. gave father glory and A.
11:21 shall not give A. of king.
Mal. 1:6 where is mine A.
1:6 wh. is mine A. saith L. wh.
John 5:41 I rec. not A. from men
44 receive A. one of another
8:54 honor myself, A. is nothing
Rom. 2:7 seek glory and A.
10 A. to ev. man worketh good
9:21 of same lump ma. ves. to A.
12:10 in A. prefer. one another
1 Cor. 12:23 bestow abund. A. 24
2 *Cor.* 6:8 by A. and dishonor

HON

Col. 2:23 not in A. to satis. flesh
1 **Thes.** 4:4 to possess vessel in A.
1 **Tim.** 1:17 to G. be A. and glory
5:17 elders worthy of double A.
6:1 count masters worthy of A.
16 to whom be A. and power
2 **Tim.** 2:20 some to A. 21
Heb. 3:3 more A. than house
5:4 no man taketh A. to himself
1 *Pet.* 1:7 to praise, A. glory
3:7 A. to wife as weaker vessel
2 *Pet.* 1:17 from G. the Father A.
Rev. 4:9 beasts give glory and A.
11 to receive glory and A. 5:12
5:13 A. power, and might, be to
him, 7:12; 19:1
19:7 let us rejoice, give A.
21:24 glory and A. to it, 26

HONOR, Verb.
Ex. 20:12 A. thy father and thy
mother, *Deut.* 5:16; *Mat.*
15:4; 19:19; *Mark* 7:10; 10:19;
Luke 18:20; *Eph.* 6:2
Lev. 19:15 not A. per. of mighty
32 shalt A. the face of old man
Jud. 9:9 by me they A. God
1 *Sam.* 2:30 th. th. A. me I will A.
15:30 yet A. me now bef. elders
Est. 6:6 delighteth to A. 7, 9, 11
Ps. 91:15 deliver him and A. him
Prov. 3:9 A. L. with thy substa.
Is. 29:13 with lips do A. me
43:20 beast of field shall A. me
58:13 A. him, not doing own
Dan. 4:37 and A. King of heaven
11:38 A. God of forces. a god
whom fa. knew not sh. he A.
Mat. 13:6 A. not fath. or mother
John 5:23 all men A. Son as A. F.
8:49 I A. Father, ye dishonor me
12:26 him will Father A.
1 **Tim.** 5:3 A. wid. that are wid.
1 *Pet.* 2:17 A. all men. A. the king

HONORABLE.
Num. 22:15 sent princes more A.
1 *Sam.* 9:6 th. is in the city a man
of God, and he is an A. man
2 *Sam.* 23:19 was he not most A.
of three? 1 *Chr.* 11:21
23 was more A. than the thirty
1 *Chr.* 4:9 more A. than brethren
Job 22:8 the A. man dwelt in it
Ps. 45:9 daughters am. A. women
111:3 his work is A. and glori.
149:8 bind their kings with ch.
Is. 3:3 doth take away A. man
5 base behave proudly ag. A.
5:13 their A. men are famished
23:8 traffickers are A. of earth
9 into contempt all A. of earth
42:21 magnify law. make it A.
43:4 been A.; 58:13 holy of L. A.
Mark 15:43 Jos. A. counsellor
Luke 14:8 lest more A. man be
Acts 13:50 J. stirred up A. wom.
17:12 A. women not few believ.
1 *Cor.* 4:10 ye are stro. ye are A.
12:23 members we think less A.
Heb. 13:4 marriage A. bed unde.

HONORED.
Ex. 14:4 I will be A. on Pharaoh
Prov. 13:18 regard, reproof be A.
27:18 wait. on master sh. be A.
Lam. 1:8 all that A. her despise
5:12 faces of elders were not A.
1 *Cor.* 12:20 or one member be A.

HONOREST, ETH.
1 *Sam.* 2:29 A. thy sons above me
Ps. 15:4 A. them that fear Lord
Prov. 12:9 he that A. himself
14:31 that A. him hath mercy
Mat. 1:6 son A. father
Mat. 15:8 A. me w. lips, *Mark* 7:6
John 5:23 A. not Son, A. not Fa.
6:54 It is my Father that A. me

HONEY.
Gen. 43:11 carry a little A. spices
Ex. 10:31 wafers made with A.
Lev. 2:11 burn no leaven, nor A.
Deut. 8:8 a land of oil-olive and
A. 2 *K.* 18:32
32:13 he made him to suck A.
Jud. 14:8 A. in carcase of lion, 9
18 what is sweeter than A. ?
1 *Sam.* 14:25 was A. upon ground
26 A. dropped; 29 I tasted A. 43
2 *Sam.* 17:29 bro. A. and butter
1 *K.* 14:3 take a cruse of A.
Job 20:17 sh. not see brooks of A.
Ps. 19:10 judgment sweeter than
A. 119:103

CRUDEN'S CONCORDANCE. 899

HOP

Ps. 61:16 h. out of rock sati. thee
Prov. 24:13 eat h. is good, 25:16
25:27 not good to eat much h.
Cant. 4:11 h. and milk und. ton.
5:1 honey-comb with my h.
Is. 7:15 butter and h. sh. he eat
22 butter and h. sh. ev. one eat
Jer. 41:8 treasures of h. in field
Ezek. 3:3 in my mouth as h.
27:17 Ju. traded in h. and balm
Mat. 3:4 J. Baptist's meat locus.
and wild h. Mark 1:6
Rev. 10:9 thy mouth sweet as h.
10 in my mouth sweet as h.
See FLOWETH, FLOWING.

HONEY-COMB.
1 Sam. 14:27 and dip. it in h.-c.
Ps. 19:10 sweeter than h.-c.
Prov. 5:3 lips of str. wo. as h.-c.
16:24 pleasant words are as h.-c.
24:13 eat h.-c. sweet to thy taste
27:7 full soul loatheth a h.-c.
Cant. 4:11 thy lips drop as a h.-c.
5:1 eaten my h.-c. with honey
Luke 24:42 gave piece of h.-c.

HOODS.
Is. 3:23 I will take away the h.

HOOF, S.
Ex. 10:26 shall not a h. be left
Lev. 11:3 whatever parteth h.
4 of them that divide the h.
5 divideth not h. 6; Deut. 14:7
7 swine, tho' div. h. Deut. 14:8
Jud. 5:22 were horse h. broken
Ps. 69:31 better than ox with h.
Is. 5:28 horses' h. shall be coun,
Jer. 47:3 noise of stamping of h.
Mic. 4:13 will make thy h. brass.

HOOK, S.
Ex. 26:32 h. of gold, 37; 36:36
2 K. 19:28 h. in nose, Is. 37:29
Job 41:1 dr. leviathan wi. h. ? 2
Is. 2:4 sp. into prun. h., Mic. 4:3
Ezek. 29:4 put h. in thy jaw, 38:4
40:43 with. were h. hand broad
Joel 3:10 pruning h. into spears
Mat. 17:27 cast a h. take up fish

HOPE.
Ezr. 10:2 there is h. in Israel
Job 4:6 this thy fear, thy h. ?
5:16 poor hath h. iniq. stoppeth
7:6 my days spent without h.
8:13 hypocrite's h. sh. peri. 14
11:18 because there is h.
20 h. be as giving up of ghost
14:7 h. of tree if it be cut down
19 thou destroyest h. of man
27:8 what is h. of hypocrite ?
Ps. 78:7 might set their h. in G.
146:5 happy he whose h. is in L.
Prov. 10:28 h. of right. gladness
11:7 h. of unjust men perisheth
13:12 h. defer. mak. heart sick
14:32 the right, hath h. in death
19:18 chast. son wh. there is h.
26:12 h. of fool than him, 29:20
Ec. 9:4 joined to liv. there is h.
Is. 57:10 no h. Jer. 2:25; 18:12
Jer. 14:8 O the h. of Israel, 17:13
17:7 blessed man whose h. L. is
31:17 there is h. in end, saith L.
50:7 the Lord, h. of their fath.
Lam. 3:21 therefore have I h.
Ezek. 37:11 our bones are h. lost
Hos. 2:15 val. of Achor door of h.
Joel 3:16 L. will be h. of his peo.
Zec. 9:12 turn, ye prisoners of h.
Acts 16:19 h. of gains was gone
23:6 h. and resurrection of dead
24:15 h. tow. G. which th. allow
26:6 judged for h. of the prom.
27:20 nei h. we should be saved
28:20 for h. of Israel I am bound
Rom. 3d patience, experien. h.
5 h. maketh not ashamed
8:24 we, by h. but h. seen is noth.
15:4 thro'. patien. might have h.
13 that ye may abound in h.
1 Cor. 9:10 he partaker of his h.
13:13 faith, h. charity, th. three
15:19 in this life only we ho. h.
2 Cor. 1:7 our h. of you is stead.
8:12 seeing that we have such h.
10:15 when faith is increased
Gal. 5:5 the Spirit wait for h.
Eph. 1:18 h. of his calling
2:12 no h. with. G. in world
4:4 as ye are called in one h.
Col. 1:5 h. laid up for you in hea.
23 not moved from h. of gospel
27 Christ in you, h. of glory
1 Thes. 1:3 patience of h. in Jes.
2:19 for what is our h. or joy ?
4:13 as others who have no h.
5:8 helmet the h. of salvation

HOR

2 Thes. 2:16 given us good h.
1 Tim. 1:1 Lord Jesus, is our h.
Tit. 2:13 for that blessed h.
3:7 accord. to h. of eternal life
Heb. 3:6 rejoic. of h. firm to end
6:11 full assurance of h. to end
18 to lay hold on h. before us
19 wh. h. we have as an anch.
7:19 bringing in of a better h.
1 Pet. 1:3 begot. us to a lively h.
21 faith and h. might be in G.
3:15 reason of h. that is in you
1 John 3:3 man that hath this h.

In HOPE.
Ps. 16:9 rest in h. Acts 2:26
Rom. 4:18 ag. hope believ. in h.
5:2 rejoice in h. of glory of God
8:20 subjected the same in h.
12:12 rejoicing in h. patient
15:13 that ye may abound in h.
1 Cor. 9:10 plougheth in h. thres.
Tit. 1:2 in h. of eternal life

My HOPE.
Job 17:15 where is now my h.?
19:10 my h. hath he removed
31:24 if I have made gold my h.
Ps. 39:7 my h. is in thee
71:5 thou art my h. Jer. 17:17
119:116 asha. of my h. Phil. 1:20
Lam. 3:18 my h. perished

HOPE, Verb.
Job 6:11 stren. that I should h.
Ps. 22:9 didst make me h.
31:24 all that h. in the L.
33:18 h. in his mercy, 147:11
22 as we h. in thee
38:15 L. do I h. thou wilt hear
42:5 h. thou in God, 11; 43:5
71:14 but I will h. continually
119:49 hast caused me to h.
81 h. in thy word, 114; 130:5
130:7 let Israel h. in L. 131:3
Lam. 3:24 there. will I h. in him
26 that man both h. and wait
Luke 6:34 them of whom ye h.
Acts 26:7 our tribes h. to come
Rom. 8:24 why doth he h. for ?
25 if we h. for that we see not
Phil. 2:23 him I h. to send pres.
1 Pet. 1:13 be sober, and h. to end

HOPED.
Job 6:20 con. bec. they had h.
Ps. 119:43 have h. in thy judgm.
74 I have h. in thy word, 147
166 L. I have h. for thy salva.
Jer. 3:23 vain is salvation h. for
Luke 23:8 h. to have seen mirac.
Acts 24:26 h. money sho. be giv.
Heb. 11:1 substance of th. h. for

HOPETH.
Luke 6:35 lend, h. for nothing ag.
1 Cor. 13:7 charity h. all things

HOPHNI. 1 Sa. 1:3; 2:34; 4:11, 17

HOR.
Ex. 3:1 come to H. 1 K. 10:8
Deut. 1:6 spake to us in H. 4:15
Ps. 106:19 made a calf in H.
Mal. 4:4 commanded M. in H.

HOR-HAGIDGAD. Num. 33:32

HORMAH.
Num. 14:45 discomfi. to H. 21:3
1 Sam. 30:30 pre. to H. 1 Chr. 4:30

HORN.
Ex. 21:29 if ox push with h.
1 Sam. 2:1 my h. is exalted in L.
10 sh. exalt h. of his anointed
16:1 fill thy h. with oil, 13
Sam. 22:3 h. of my sal, Ps. 18:2
1 K. 1:39 Zadok took a h. of oil
Job 16:15 defiled my h. in dust
Ps. 75:4 wicked, lift not up h. 5
89:17 our h. shall be exalted
21 in my name oh. h. be exalted
92:10 my h. shalt thou exalt
112:9 his h. shall be exalted
132:17 make h. of David to bud
Lam. 2:3 cut off all the h. of Is.
Ezek. 29:21 cause h. of h. to bud
Dan. 7:8 am. them a little h. 20
21 great words which h. spake
21 h. made war with saints
8:5 he goat had a notable h.
8 great h. was broken
9 came forth little h.
21 great h. that is betw. eyes
Mic. 4:13 I will make thy h. iron
Zec. 1:21 lift up h. over the land
Luke 1:69 raised up h. of salvat.

HORNS.
Gen. 22:13 caught in thic. by h.
Ex. 27:2 make h. of it on four
corners, his h. be of the
same, 30:2; 37:25; 38:2

HOR

Ex. 29:12 put off the bl. on h. of
the altar, Lev. 4:7, 18, 25, 30,
34; 8:15; 9:9; 16:18
30:3 pure gold overlay h. 37:26
Deut. 33:17 h. like h. of unicorns
1 K. 22:11 Zedekiah made h.
of iron, 2 Chr. 18:10
Ps. 22:21 from h. of unicorns
69:31 bullock that hath h.
75:10 h. of wicked will I cut off,
but h. of righ. sh. be exalted
118:27 bind sacrifice to h. of alt.
Ezek. 27:15 present h. of ivory
34:21 pushed all diseased wi. h.
Dan. 7:7 fou. beast had ten h. 20
8 I consid. h. three h. pluc. up
24 ten h. ten kings
8:3 ram two h. two h. were high
6 he-goat ca. to ram had two h.
7 smote ram, brake his two h.
20 two h. kings of Me. and P.
Amos 6:13 not taken h. by sirc. ?
Mic. 4:13 A. coming out of hand
Zec. 1:18 and behold, four h.
19 h. have scattered Judah, 21
Rev. 5:6 in midst L. having 7 h.
12:3 a red dragon, having ten h.
13:1 beast ten h. stra. h. ten cro.
11 beast had two h. like a lamb
17:3 scarlet-colored beast, ten h.
7 beast seven heads and ten h.
12 ten h. thou saw. ten kin. 16

See RAMS.

HORNET, S.
Ex. 23:28 will send h. bef. thee
Deut. 7:20 L. send h. am. them
Jos. 24:12 I sent the h. bef. you

HORONAIM. Jer. 48:3, 5, 34

HORRIBLE.
Ps. 11:6 on wicked rain h. temp.
40:2 brought me out of h. pit
Jer. 5:30 h. thing committed
18:13 virgin of Is. done h. thing
23:14 seen in proph. a h. thing
Hos. 6:10 seen h. thing in Israel

HORRIBLY.
Jer. 2:12 be h. afraid, O ye heav.
Ezek. 32:10 kings sh. be h. afraid

HORROR.
Gen. 15:12 a h. of great darkness
Ps. 55:5 h. hath overwhelmed
119:53 h. hath taken hold on me

HORSE.
Gen. 49:17 adder biteth h. heels
Ex. 15:21 h. and rider thr. in sea
Jud. 5:22 were h. hoofs broken
1 K. 10:29 a h. for 150 shekels,
2 Chr. 1:17
Est. 6:8 h. king rideth on, 9, 10
Job 39:18 scorneth h. and rider
19 hast thou giv. h. strength?
Ps. 32:9 be ye not as h. or mule
33:17 a h. vain thing for safety
76:6 char. and h. cast into sleep
147:10 del. not in strength of h.
Prov. 21:31 h. prep. ag. battle
26:3 a whip for h. a bridle for
Ec. 13:18 led thro' deep, as a h.
Is. 43:17 rusheth into the battle
Amos 2:15 he th. rideth h. deliv.
Zec. 1:8 riding upon a red h.
9:10 cut off the h. from Jerus.
10:3 made them as goodly h.
12:1 smite every h. with blind.
14:15 shall be plague of the h.
Rev. 6:2 behold white h. 19:11
4 red h. ; 5 black h. ; 8 a pale h.
14:20 blood came to h. bridles
19:19 war ag. him that sat on h.
21 slain wi. sw. of him sat on h.

HORSEBACK.
2 K. 9:18 on h. to meet Jehu, 19
Est. 6:9 on h. through city, 11
8:10 sent letters by posts on h.

HORSE-GATE.
2 Chr. 23:15 entering bt h.-g.
Neh. 3:28 from h. repaired the
Jer. 31:40 corner of the h.-g.

HORSE-LEECH.
Prov. 30:15 h. had two daugh.

HORSEMAN, MEN.
Gen. 50:9 with Jos. chariots, h.
Ex. 14:9 h. of Pharaoh pursued
17 honor on Pharaoh and his h.
15:19 Pharaoh and h. went into
the sea, Jos. 24:6
1 Sam. 8:11 your sons to be h.
2 Sam. 1:6 h. followed after him
1 K. 4:26 Sol. had 12,000 h. 10:26
9:19 Solomon had cities for h.
22 ; 2 Chr. 8:6, 9
2 K. 2:12 chariot of Is. h. thereof
13:14 O my father, the h. of Is.
18:24 put thy trust in Eg. for h.
2 Chr. 16:8 host with many h.
Ezr. 8:22 ashamed to ask h.
Neh. 2:9 sent captains and h.
Is. 21:7 saw a chariot with h. 9
22:7 h. shall set themselves
31:1 trust in h. bec. they strong
Jer. 4:29 shall flee for noise of h.
46:4 get up ye h. and stand
Ezek. 23:6 h. riding on horses, 12
26:10 walls shake at noise of h.
38:4 bring forth horses and h.
Dan. 11:40 the king of the north
shall come with h.
Hos. 1:7 not save by horses nor h.
Joel 2:4 as h. so shall they run
Nah. 3:3 h. lifteth up bright sw.
Hab. 1:8 h. shall spread the mes.
and th. h. sh. come from far
Acts 23:23 ready h. threescore
Rev. 9:16 number of army of h.

HOSANNA.
Mat. 21:9 h. to the Son of D. 15
Mark 11:9 h. bles. is he that come.
h. in highest, 10; John 12:13

HOSEN.
Dan. 3:21 men bound in their h.

HOSEA, HOSHEA.
See ROSHEA.

HOS

Is. 2:7 (h. land is also full of h.
3:24 their h. hoofs sh. be coun.
27:16 for we will flee upon h.
31:1 stay on h. trust in chariots
Jer. 4:13 h. are swifter than eag.
6:9 were as fed h. in the morn.
8:16 snorting of his h. was heard
12:5 canst thou contend wi. h. ?
46:4 harness the h. and get up
47:3 stamping of hoof of his h.
51:27 cause h. come up as cater.
Ezek. 17:15 give him h. and peo.
23:6 horsemen riding on h. 12
20 whose issue is like les. of h.
23 all of th. riding on h. 38:15
27:14 traded in thy fairs with h.
Hos. 1:7 save th. by battle nor h.
14:3 we will not ride on h.
Joel 2:4 app. of h. as horsemen
Amos 6:12 sh. h. run upon rock ?
Mic. 5:10 cut off thy h. out of thy
3:8 thou didst ride on thy h.
13 didst walk thro' sea with h.
Hag. 2:22 overthrow h. and rid.
Zec. 1:8 behind him were red h.
6:2 first chariot red h. sec. black
3 third white h. in fou. bay h.
10:5 riders on h. be confounded
14:20 that day upon bells of the
h. Holiness to the Lord
Jam. 3:3 we put bits in h. mou.
5:7 the h. that the locusts were like h.
17 I saw the h. the heads of h.
18:13 buyeth merchandise of h.
19:14 armies follow. on white h.
18 eat flesh of kings and h.

See CHARIOTS.

HORSELEECH.
Prov. 30:15 h. had two daugh.

HOSEN.
Dan. 3:21 men bound in their h.

HOSHEA.
Deut. 32:44; H. spake to people
2 K. 15:30 H. made, 17:1, 3; 18:10
1 Chr. 27:20 ruler of Ephraim, H.
Neh. 10:23 H. and Han. seal. co.

HOSPITALITY.
Rom. 12:13 given to h. 1 Tim. 3:2
Tit. 1:8 but a lover of h.
1 Pet. 4:9 use h. one to another

HOST.
Luke 10:35 and gave them to h.
Rom. 16:23 Gaius my h.

HOST.
Gen. 2:1 earth finish. all h. of th.
32:2 he said, This is God's h.
Ex. 14:4 honored on him h. ; 17
24 L. look to h. of Egyptians
28 waters covered h. of Pha.
16:13 dew lay round about h.
Num. 31:14 wroth with offi. of h.
Deut. 2:14 men of war we. fo. h.
23:9 when h. goeth forth ag.
Jos. 1:11 pass thro' h. and com.

HOU

Jos. 3:2 officers went thro' the *h*.
 8:14 as capt. of the *h*. of the L.
Jud. 4:2 captain of the *h*. was Sisera
 7:8 *h*. of Midian was beneath
 9 get thee down unto the *h*. 10
 13 cake of bro. tumbled into *h*.
 8:11 Gideon smote the *h*. 12
1 Sam. 11:11 S. came into the *h*.
 14:15 there was trembling in *h*.
 19 the noise of the *h*. went on
 17:20 D. came as *h*. was going
 28:5 S. saw the *h*. of Philistines
 29:6 coming with me in *h*.
2 Sam. 20:23 Joab was over all *h*.
1 Chr. 18:15
 23:16 brake thro' *h*. 1 Chr. 11:18
1 K. 2:32 Abner captain of the *h*.
 22:34 carry me out of the *h*.
2 K. 3:9 no water for the *h*.
 4:13 be spoken to capt. of *h*. ?
 6:14 horses and *h*. to Dothan
 7:4 let us fall to *h*. of the Syri.
 6 L. made *h*. to he. noise of *h*.
 9:5 captains of A. were sitting
 25:19 prin. scribe of *h*. Jer. 52:25
1 Chr. 9:19 fathers over *h*. of L.
 12:22 a great *h*. like the *h*. of G.
2 Chr. 18:31 carry me out of *h*.
 24:24 the L. delivered a great *h*.
Ps. 27:3 tho' a *h*. should encamp
 33:6 all *h*. made by thy mouth
 16 no king saved by mul. of *h*.
Is. 13:4 L. muster. *h*. of battle
 21:21 L. sh. pun. *h*. of high ones
 40:26 bring. out *h*. by number
Jer. 51:3 destroy utterly all her *h*.
Ezek. 1:24 speech, as noise of *h*.
Dan. 8:10 cast down some of *h*.
 11 magni. hims. to prince of *h*.
 12 *h*. given him ag. daily sacr.
 13 *h*. to be trodden under foot
Ob. 20 the captivity of this *h*.
Luke 2:13 heavenly *h*. prais. G.

See HEAVEN.

HOSTAGES.
2 K. 14:14 Jehoash took A. and returned to Sam. 2 Chr. 25:24

HOSTS.
Ex. 12:41 *h*. of L. went out of E.
Ps. 103:21 bless L. all ye *h*.
 103:11 O G. go forth with our *h*.?
 148:2 praise ye him, all his *h*.
Jer. 3:19 heritage of *h*. of nations

See GOD, LORD.

HOT.
Ex. 16:21 when *h*. waxed *h*.
Lev. 13:24 there is a *h*. burning
Deut. 9:19 anger and *h*. displeas.
 19:6 while his heart is *h*.
Jos. 9:12 our bread we took *h*.
Jud. 3:14 L. was *h*. against Isr. 20; 3:8; 10:7
 6:39 let not thine anger be *h*.
1 Sam. 11:9 by the time sun be *h*.
 21:6 put *h*. bread when laten
Neh. 7:3 not open, till sun be *h*.
Job 6:17 when *h*. they are cons.
Ps. 6:1 neither chasten in thy *h*. displeasure, 38:1
 39:3 my *h*. was *h*. within me
 78:48 flocks to *h*. thunderbolts
Prov. 6:28 one go upon *h*. coals?
Ezek. 24:11 brass of it may be *h*.
Dan. 3:22 furnace was exceed. *h*.
1 Tim. 4:2 seared with *h*. iron
Rev. 3:15 neither cold nor *h*. I would thou wert cold or *h*. 16

See WAX, Verb.

HOTLY.
Gen. 31:36 th. hast so *h*. pursued

HOTTEST.
2 Sam. 11:15 front of the *h*. bat.

HOUGH, ED.
Jos. 11:6 shall *h*. their horses
 9 *h*. horses, burnt chariots
2 Sam. 8:4 Da. *h*. chariot horses

HOUR.
Dan. 4:19 D. astonish, for one *h*.
M'r. 3:33 whole from that *h*.
 17:18 ch. was cured from that *h*.
 22:3 went out about the third *h*.
 5 sixth and ninth *h*.; 6 elev. *h*.
 12 these have wro. but one *h*.
 25:13 that *h*. knoweth no man, 13; *Mark* 13:32
 41 such an *h*. as ye think not, 50; *Luke* 12:40, 46
 23:15 know neither day nor *h*.
 26:40 is at hand, S. of man
 27:45 from sixth *h*. was darkness over the land to ninth *h*. *Mark* 15:33; *Luke* 23:44

HOU

Mat. 27:46 ninth *h*. Jesus cried, *Mark* 15:34
Mark 13:11 given you in that *h*.
 14:35 if pos. the *h*. might pass
 15:25 third *h*. they cruci. him
Luke 10:21 in that *h*. J. rejoiced
 12:39 what *h*. thief would come
 22:53 your *h*. and power of dar.
 59 about the space of one *h*.
John 2:4 mine *h*. is not yet come
 4:6 it was about sixth *h*. 19:14
 21 believe me, *h*. cometh, 23
 53 then inq. he the *h*. he began to amend, at sev. *h*. fev. left
 5:25 the *h*. is coming, 28; 16:32
 7:30 *h*. was not yet come, 8:20
 12:23 *h*. is come, Son be gl. 17:1
 27 Fa. save me from this *h*. for this cause came I to this *h*.
 13:1 Jes. knew his *h*. was come
 16:21 because her *h*. is come
 19:27 from that *h*. disciple took
Acts 2:15 it is third *h*. of day
 3:1 *h*. of prayer being ninth *h*.
 10:3 about ninth *h*. angel com.
 9 P. went to pray about 6th *h*.
 23:23 make ready at the third *h*.
1 Cor. 4:11 to this present *h*.
 15:30 in jeopardy every *h*. ?
Gal. 2:5 gave place, not for an *h*.
Rev. 3:3 not know what *h*. I will
 10 from *h*. of temptation
 8:1 was silence about half an *h*.
 9:15 prepare, for an *h*. and a day
 14:7 *h*. of his judgment is come
 17:12 rec. power as kings one *h*.
 18:10 in one *h*. is thy jud. come
 17 in one *h*. great riches is co.
 19 city in one *h*. made desolate

Same HOUR.
Dan. 3:6 *h*. S. cast into furn. 15
 4:33 same *h*. was thing fulfilled
 5:5 in s. *h*. came forth fingers
Mat. 8:13 serv. was healed s. *h*.
 10:19 given you s. *h*. *Luke* 12:12
Luke 7:21 same *h*. cured many
 20:19 s. *h*. son. to lay ha. on him
John 4:33 knew it was at s. *h*.
Acts 16:18 he came out same *h*.
 33 took them s. *h*. of the night
Rev. 11:13 s. *h*. was earthquake

HOURS.
John 11:9 twelve *h*. in day?
Acts 5:7 about three *h*. after
 19:34 all cried about two *h*.

HOUSE.
Gen. 19:4 men compassed the *h*.
 21:31 I have prepared *h*. room
 39:5 L. blessed Egyptian's *h*.
 43:2 the *h*. of Pharoah heard
Ex. 8:3 frogs shall come into *h*.
 12:3 a lamb according to the *h*.
 30 not A. wh. was not one dead
 46 not carry flesh out of the *h*.
 13:3 out of the *h*. of bond. 14;
Deut. 5:6; 6:12
 20:17 shalt not covet neighbor's *h*. *Deut.* 5:21
Lev. 14:36 priest sh. empty the *h*.
 38 priest shall go out of the *h*.
 and shut up *h*. 45, 46, 49
 25:30 *h*. sold in walled city
Deut. 7:8 red. out of *h*. of bond.
 8:14 brought you out of land of *h*. 5. from *h*. of bondage, 13:5, 10; *Jos.* 24:17; *Jud.* 6:8; *Jer.* 31:32; *Mic.* 6:4
 25:10 *h*. of him hath shoe loosed
Jos. 2:15 *h*. was on town wall
Jud. 16:26 pillars whon *h*. stand.
 27 *h*. full of men and women
 30 the *h*. fell upon the lords
 17:5 Micah had a *h*. of gods
 16:18 no man received me to *h*.
 24 sons of Belial beset *h*. 20:5
1 *Sam.* 3:14 I have sw. to *h*. of E.
 5:2 brought ark into *h*. of Dag.
 7:1 bro. ark to *h*. of Abinadab
 9:18 tell me where acer's *h*. is
 25:36 L. make my Lord sure *h*.
2 *Sam.* 3:1 war betw. *h*. of Saul
 8 shew kindness to *h*. of Saul
 5:8 lame and blind not co. to *h*.
 6:11 L. blessed *h*. of Obed-edom,
 David brought ark from his *h*. 12; 1 *Cor.* 13:14
 7:6 not dw. in any *h*. 1 *Chr.* 17:5
 11 he will make thee a *h*.
 20 bless *h*. of serv. 1 *Chr.* 17:27
 12:8 I gave thee thy master's *h*.
1 *K.* 2:31 who made me a *h*.
 6:22 whole *h*. overlaid with gold
 9:25 so Solomon finished the *h*.
 12:21 and Jeroboam made a *h*.
 15:15 bee *h*. did eat many days
 21:24 thy *h*. like *h*. of Jeroboam
2 *K.* 8:3 cry to the king for her *h*.

HOU

2 *K.* 8:18 as did the A. of Ahab,
 27; 1 *Chr.* 21:6; 22:1
 9:8 A. of Ahab shall perish
 10:3 fight for your master's *h*.
 21 and the A. of Baal was full
 27 the A. of Baal a draught *h*.
 20:13 Hez. showed A. of precio. things, A. of arm. *Is.* 39:2
 23:27 A. of wh. my name sh. be
 25:9 ov. great man's *h*. he burnt
2 *Chr.* 7:1 glory of the Lord filled the A. *Ezek.* 43:4, 5
 12 chosen this place for *h*.
Ezr. 5:8 went to *h*. of great God
 6:3 in Jer. let the *h*. be builded
Est. 2:3 gather all virgins to *h*.
 20:19 A. which he builded not
Job 1:13 drink. in brother's *h*. 18
 19 wind came smote cor. of *h*.
 20:19 A. which he builded not
 21:28 where is *h*. of the prince?
 30:23 to *h*. appointed for all liv.
 38:20 know paths to the *h*.
 39:6 whose *h*. I made wilderm.
Ps. 31:2 rock be *h*. of defence
 61:3 sparrow hath found a *h*.
 105:17 stork, fir-trees are her *h*.
Prov. 2:18 A. inclineth to death
 7:8 go. nian went way to her *h*.
 11 her feet abide not in her *h*.
 27 her *h*. is the way to hell
 9:1 wisdom hath builded her *h*.
 12:7 A. of righteous shall stand
 14:11 *h*. of wicked overthrown
 15:25 L. will destroy A. of proud
 17:1 A. full of sacrifices
 19:14 A. and riches are inherit.
 21:9 dwell in *h*.-top, 25:24
 12 right. consider, A. of wicked
 24:3 through wisdom is *h*. built
 25:17 withdraw fr. neighbor's *h*.
 27:10 foot *h*. day of calamity
Ec. 7:2 to go to *h*. of mourning, than *h*. of feasting
 10:18 thro' idleness *h*. droppeth
 12:3 keepers of *h*. shall tremble
Cant. 1:17 beams of our *h*. cedar
 2:4 brought me to banquet *h*.
 3:4 bro. him into my mother's *h*.
 8:2 br. thee into my mother's *h*.
Is. 5:8 woe to them join *h*. to *h*.
 6:4 A. was filled with smoke
 11:17 open, not *h*. of prisoners
 13:22 cry in their desolate *h*.
 31:2 against *h*. of evil-doers
 50:7 I will glo. *h*. of my glory
 64:11 holy and beaut. *h*. burnt
Jer. 10:5 enter not *h*. of mourn.
 6 sh. not go into *h*. of feasting
 22:29 nor return to A. of f. 38:28
Ezek. 2:5 they are a rebellious *h*. 3:9, 26, 27; 12:3
 8 be not rebellious like that *h*.
 12:2 devilled in midst of reb. A.
 17:12 say now to rebellious *h*.
 24:3 utter parable to rebel. *h*.
 48:11 show them the form of *h*.
 42 law of *h*. on top of mount.
Amos 1:5 sceptre from *h*. of E.
 3:15 winter *h*. with summer *h*.
 6:11 smite great *h*. and little *h*.
 7:16 not word ag. *h*. of Isaac
Ob. 18 A. of Es. be for stubble
Mic. 3:12 mountain of the *h*. shall be as high places
 4:2 let us go up to *h*. of God
Nah. 1:14 out of *h*. of thy gods
Zec. 5:4 enter into *h*. of thief
 6:10 of him that swearth falsely
Mat. 7:25 and beat upon that *h*. 27; *Luke* 6:18
 10:12 come into a *h*. salute it
 13 if *h*. be worthy, let your peace come, *Luke* 10:5
 12:29 every *h*. divided ag. itself
 29 strong man's *h*. *Mark* 3:27
 20:11 murmured ag. man of *h*.
 23:38 your *h*. is left to you desolate, *Luke* 13:35
 24:43 man of *h*. known, *Luke* 12:39
Mark 3:25 A. divided ag. itself
 10:29 hath left A. or brethren
 14:14 good man of A. *Lu.* 22:11
 13:30 hath left A. or brethren
Luke 10:7 into that A. remain
 13:6 light candle and sweep *h*.
 19:9 is salvation come to *h*.
Acts 2:2 sound fr. heaven fill. *h*.
 46 breaking bread from A. to *h*.
 5:42 they ceased not to teach
 10:6 lodged with S. *h*. by seasi.
 17:5 Jews assaulted *h*. of Jason
 18:7 fled out of that *h*. naked
 20:20 tau. publicly, from *h*. to *h*.
Rom. 16:5 great church in th. *h*.
1 *Cor.* 1:11 are of the *h*. of Chloe

HOU

1 *Cor.* 16:15 the A. of Stephan. 19
2 *Cor.* 5:1 earthly A. be dissolved
 2 clothed with *h*. from heaven
1 *Tim.* 5:13 wander. from *h*. to *h*.
 14 younger women guide *h*.
2 *Tim.* 1:16 mercy to *h*. of Ones.
 2:20 in a great *h*. vessels of gold
Heb. 3:3 built *h*. more h. than A.
 4 every *h*. is built by some m.
 6 wh. A. are we, if we hold fast
2 *John* 10 receive him not into *h*.

See AARON, BORN, BUILD or BUILT, CHIEF, DAVID, DOOR, DWELL.

HOUSE, with Father.
Gen. 12:1 get thee fr. *father's h*.
 24:7 G. took me from *father's h*.
 38 then sh. go to my *fa.'s h*.
 40 wife for my son of *f.'s h*.
 31:14 portion for us in *fa.'s h*.
 38:11 remain widow at *f.'s h*.
 41:51 God made me forget *f.'s h*.
 46:31 breth. and *f.'s h*. are come
 50:22 in Egypt, he and *f.'s h*.
Ex. 12:3 accord. to h. of *fathers*
Num. 1:2 sum of Israel by *h*. of their *f*. 18, 22, 24, 33
 4 every one head of A. of his *f*. 44; *Jos.* 22:14
 2:2 pitch with ensign of *f.'s h*.
 3:15 children of Levi after *h*. of their *fathers*, 20; 4:46
 17:2 accord. to *h*. of their *f.'s*, 3
 18:1 thou and *f.'s h*. bear. iniq.
 30:3 being in her *father's h*.
 16; *Deut.* 22:21 play woman in *f.'s h*.
Jos. 2:12 show kindn. to *f.'s h*.
Jud. 6:15 least in my *f.'s h*.
 9:18 risen against my *f.'s h*.
 11:2 shalt not inherit in *f.'s h*.
 14:15 we burn thee so *f.'s h*.
 16:31 the *h*. of his *f*. buried him
1 *Sam.* 2:27 appear to *h*. of thy *f*.
 30 A. of thy *f*. should walk
 17:25 will make his *f.'s h*. free
 18:2 go no more home to *f.'s h*.
 22:16 thou and all *f.'s h*. sh. die
 24:21 not destr. name out *f.'s h*.
2 *Sam.* 3:29 rest on Joab and his *father's h*.
 14:9 iniq. be on me, and *f.'s h*.
 19:28 all of *f.'s h*. dead men
1 *K.* 2:31 innoc. blood fr. *f.'s h*.
 18:18 thou and *f.'s h*. trou.
1 *Chr.* 28:4 God chose me bef. *father's h*.
Ezr. 2:59 their *f.'s h*. *Neh.* 1:6
 10:16 chief of the *h*. of *f*.
Neh. 1:6 I and *f.'s h*. have sinned
Est. 4:14 and *f.'s h*. be destroyed
Ps. 45:10 forget peo. and *f.'s h*.
Is. 3:6 hold of brother of *h*. of *f*.
 7:17 bring on thy *f.'s h*. days
 22:23 glorious throne to *f.'s h*.
 24 hang on him glory of *f.'s h*.
Jer. 12:6 th. of *f*. dealt treacher.
Luke 16:27 send him to *f.'s h*.
John 2:16 make not my *F.'s h*. a house of merchandise
 14:2 in *F.'s h*. are many mans.
Acts 7:20 M. nourished in *f.'s h*.

HOUSE of God.
Gen. 28:17 none oth. but A. of *G*.
 22 this sto. I set sh. be *G.'s h*.
Jos. 9:23 draw. water for *h*. of *G*.
Jud. 18:31 A. of *G*. was in Shiloh
 20:18 to the *h*. of *G*.
 31 high. goeth up to *h*. of *G*.
2 *Chr.* 5:14 gl. of L. fill. A. of *G*.
 22:12 he was hid in A. of *G*.
 23:3 sct A. of *G*. in his state
 33:7 Man. set image in *h*. of *G*.
 36:19 they burnt the *h*. of *G*.
Ezr. 5:8 went to *h*. of great *God*
 15 let *h*. of G. be builded. 6:7
 7:23 let it be done for *h*. of *G*.
 8:36 let A. to me met in *h*. of *G*.
 13:11 why A. of *G*. forsaken?
Ps. 42:4 went to *h*. of *G*. 55:14
 52:8 an olive-tree in *h*. of *G*.
 81:10 door-keeper in *h*. of *G*.
 84:10 come, let us go up to *h*. *of G*. *Mic.* 4:2
Hos. 9:8 proph. hated in *h*. of *G*.
Joel 1:13 drink-offering with-holden from *h*. of *G*.
 16 gladness cut off fr. *h*. of *G*.
Zec. 7:2 sent to *h*. of *G*. men eat showbread, *Mark* 2:26
Mat. 12:4 entered *h*. of *G*. did eat showbread, *Mark* 2:26

HOUSE.
1 *Tim.* 3:15 beh. thy. in *h*. of *G*.
Heb. 10:21 High-p. over. *h*. of *G*.
1 *Pet.* 4:17 judg. begin at *h*. of *G*.

It's HOUSE.
Gen. 12:17 L. plagu. P. and A. A.

HUN

Two HUNDRED.
John 6:7 *t. h.* penny, not suffi.

Three HUNDRED.
Jud. 7:6 number lap. *t. h.* men
15:4 Samson caught *t. h.* foxes
2 *Sam.* 21:16 sp. weigh. *t. h.* sh.
1 *K.* 11:3 S. had *t. h.* concubines
John 12:5 ointm. for *t. h.* pence

Four HUNDRED.
Gen. 15:13 afflict *f. h. yo. Acts* 7:6
1 *Sam.* 30:17 *f. h.* young men
1 *K.* 18:19 prop. of groves, *f. h.*
Acts 5:36 *f. h.* joined themselves

Four HUNDRED and thirty.
Ex. 12:40 in *E. f. h. t.* years
Gal. 3:17 law, wh. was *f. h. t.*

Four HUNDRED and fifty.
1 *K.* 18:19 pro. of Baal *f. h. f.* 22
Acts 13:20 judges about *f. h. f.*

Four HUNDRED and eighty.
1 *K.* 6:1 in *f. h. e.* years Solom.

Four HUNDRED thousand.
Jud. 20:2 Benjamin *f. h. t.* 17
2 *Chr.* 13:3 array wi. *f. h. t.* men

Four HUNDRED and seventy thousand.
1 *Chr.* 21:5 *f. h. s. t.* drew sword

Five HUNDRED.
Num. 31:28 one soul *f. h.* for L.
Luke 7:41 one owned *f. h.* pence
1 *Cor.* 15:6 *f. h.* brethren at once

Six HUNDRED.
Gen. 7:6 *N. s. h.* yo. flood ca. 11
Jud. 3:31 Shamgar slew *si. h.*
1 *Sam.* 17:7 spear weigh. *s. h.* sh.
1 *K.* 10:16 six *h.* shekels of gold to one target, 2 *Chr.* 9:15

Six HUNDRED and sixty-six.
Rev. 13:18 num. bo *six h. s. s.*

Six HUNDRED thousand.
Num. 1:46 all numb. were *s. h. t.*

Seven HUNDRED.
1 *K.* 11:3 Sol. had *seven h.* wives

Nine HUNDRED and thirty.
Gen. 5:5 Adam lived *nine h. t. y.*

Nine HUNDRED sixty-nine.
Gen. 5:27 Methus. *n. h. s-n.* yo.

HUNDREDS.
Ex. 18:21 rul. of *h.* 25; *Deut.* 1:15
N. um. 31:14 wr. with capt. ov. *h.*
1 *Sam.* 22:7 J. make captn. of *h.*
2 *Sam.* 18:1 D. set captains of *h.*
4 all the people came out by *h.*
2 *K.* 11:4 Jehoi. set rul. over *h.*
10 to captains over *h.* did pri.
give spears, 2 *Chr.* 23:9
1 *Chr.* 13:1 consu. wi. capt. of *h.*
24:1 D. assembled capt. over *h.*
23:6 captains of *h.* off. willingly
Chr. 23:1 Jeh. took capt. of *h.*
Mark 6:40 sat do. in ranks by *h.*

HUNGER, Substantive.
Ex. 16:3 kill this assembly wi. *h.*
Deut. 28:48 serve thine ene. in *h.*
32:24 shall be burnt with *h.*
Neh. 9:15 bread fr. heaven for *h.*
Ps. 34:10 do luck and suffer *h.*
Prov. 19:15 idle soul sh. suffer *h.*
Jer. 38:9 he is like to die for *h.*
42:14 see no war nor have *h.*
Lam. 2:19 him for *h.*
4:9 they that be slain with *h.*
Ezek. 34:29 no more con. with *h.*
Luke 15:17 and I perish with *h.*
2 *Cor.* 11:27 I have been in *h.*
Rev. 6:8 to kill with *h.*

HUNGER, Verb.
Deut. 8:3 he suffered thee to *h.*
Is. 49:10 shall not *h.* nor thirst
Mat. 5:6 blessed are they that *h.*
after righteous. *Luke* 6:21
Luke 6:25 woe to full, ye shall *h.*
John 6:35 com. to me sh. never *h.*
Rom. 12:20 if enemy *h.* feed him
1 *Cor.* 4:11 we both *h.* and thirst
11:31 if any man *h.* let him eat
Rev. 7:16 they shall *h.* no more

HUNGER-BITTEN.
Job 18:12 his stren. sh. be *h.-b.*

HUNGERED.
Mat. 4:2 aftwards *h. Luke* 4:2
12:1 his disciples were *a. h.*
3 what David did when he was *a. h. Mark* 2:25; *Luke* 6:3
21:18 as he returned to city ho *h.*
25:35 I *h.* and ye gave me meat
37 when saw we thee *a. h.* 44
44 I *h.* and ye gave me no meat

HUNGRY.
2 *Sam.* 17:29 the people be *h.*
2 *K.* 7:12 they kn. that we be *h.*

HUR

Job 5:5 whose harv. the *h.* eateth
22:7 withholden bread from *h.*
24:10 take the sheaf fr. the *h.*
Ps. 50:12 if I *h.* I would not tell
107:5 *h.* and thirsty
9 filleth *h.* soul with goodness
36 there he maketh *h.* to dwell
146:7 Lord giveth food to the *h.*
Prov. 6:30 to satis. soul when *h.*
25:21 if enemy be *h.* give bread
27:7 to *h.* soul bitter th. is sw.
Is. 8:21 hardly bestead and *h.*
when *h.* shall fret themselv.
9:20 snatch on right hand, be *h.*
29:8 when a *h.* man dreameth
32:6 to make empty soul of *h.*
44:12 is *h.* and strength faileth
58:7 not deal thy bread to *h. h.*
10 draw out thy soul to the *h.*
65:13 serv. eat. but ye sh. be *h.*
Ezek. 18:7 giv. his bread to *h.* 16
Mark 11:12 from Beth. he was *h.*
Luke 1:53 filled *h.* with good th.
Acts 10:10 Peter became very *h.*
1 *Cor.* 11:21 one *h.* another drun.
Phil. 4:12 to be full and be *h.*

HUNT.
Gen. 27:5 Es. went to *h.* venison
1 *Sam.* 26:20 as wh. one doth *h.*
Job 38:39 wilt *h.* prey for lion ?
Ps. 140:11 evil sh. *h.* violent man
Prov. 6:26 adulteress will *h.*
Jer. 16:16 *h.* them from ev. mou.
Ezek. 13:18 will yo *h.* souls ?
20 wherewith ye there *h.* souls
Mic. 7:2 *h.* every man his broth.

HUNTED.
Ezek. 13:21 no more in y. hand *h.*

HUNTER, S.
Gen. 10:9 he was a mighty *h.* be.
I. even as N. the mighty *h.*
27:27 Esau was a cunning *h.*
Prov. 6:5 as a roe fro. hand of *h.*
Jer. 16:16 and after I send for *h.*

HUNTEST, ETI.
Lev. 17:13 *h.* and catcheth beast
1 *Sam.* 24:11 yet thou *h.* my soul
Job 10:16 *h.* me as a fierce lion

HUNTING.
Gen. 27:30 E. brother came fr. *h.*
Prov. 12:27 roast. not took in *h.*

HUR.
Ex. 17:10 H. wre. up, 12; 24:14
1 *Chr.* 2:19 which bare H. 20, 50

HURL, ETH, ING.
Num. 35:20 *h.* at him by lying
1 *Chr.* 12:2 ri. hand and left in *h.*
Job 27:21 as a stone *h.* him out

HURT, Substantive.
Gen. 4:23 slain yo. man to my *h.*
26:29 that thou wilt do no *h.*
31:29 in power of hand to do *h.*
1 *Sam.* 20:21 peace to thee, no *h.*
24:9 behold, David seek. thy *h.*
2 *Sam.* 18:32 all that rise to do *h.*
2 *K.* 14:10 why slanderst thou med. to thy *h.* ? 2 *Chr.* 25:19
Ezr. 4:22 damage to *h.* of kings ?
Ps. 15:4 that sweareth to his *h.*
35:4 that devise my *h.* 70:2
26 ashamed that rej. at my *h.*
38:12 seek my *h.* speak mlsch.
41:7 aga. me do they devise *h.*
71:13 cov. with reproach seek *h.*
al brought to sha. seek my *h.*
Ec. 5:13 riches for owners to *h.*
8:9 ruleth over another to his *h.*
Jer. 6:14 healed *h.* of peo. 8:11
7:6 neith. walk after gods to *h.*
8:21 for *h.* of my people am I *h.*
10:19 woe is me for my *h.*
23:6 and I will do you no *h.*
7 ye provo. me to your own *h.*
34:1 not welfare of peo. but *h.*
Dan. 3:25 ha. no *h. ... h.* in him
6:22 no manner of *h.* found
Acts 27:10 of this voyage be with *h.*

HURT, Participle.
Ex. 22:10 if a beast be *h.* 14
1 *Sam.* 25:15 and we not *h.*
Ec. 10:9 remov. stones sh. be *h.*
Jer. 8:21 for *h.* of my peo. am I *h.*
Rev. 2:11 not be *h.* of sec. death

HURT, Verb.
Gen. 31:7 G. suff. hi. not to *h.* me
Ex. 21:22 *h.* woman with child
35 if one man's ox *h.* another's
1 *Sam.* 25:7 shepherds we *h.* not
2 *K.* 8:29 wh. Syrians *h.* him
Ps. 105:18 feet *h.* with fett.
Is. 11:9 shall not *h.* nor destroy in my holy mountain, 65:25
27:3 lest any *h.* it, I will keep it

HUS

Dan. 6:22 lions have not *h.* me
Mark 16:18 it shall not *h.* them
Luke 4:35 out of him, *h.* him not
Acts 18:10 set on thee to *h.*
Rev. 6:6 see thou *h.* not the oil
7:2 given to *h.* earth and sea
9:4 should not *h.* grass of earth
10 their power was to *h.* men
19 heads, with them they *h.*
11:5 if any *h.* them, fire proceed.

HURTFUL.
Ps. 144:10 deli. David fr. *h.* swo.
1 *Tim.* 6:9 rich fall into *h.* lusts

HURTING.
1 *Sam.* 25:34 Lord kept me fr. *h.*

HUSBAND.
Ex. 4:25 bloody *h.* art thou, 26
Lev. 19:20 lieth with woman be-trothed to a *h. Deut.* 22:23
21:3 may be defiled for sister who had no *h. Ezek.* 44:25
Num. 30:6 if she had at all a *h.*
Deut. 22:23 woman married to a *h.*
24:3 if the latter *h.* hate her
4 former *h.* may not take her
25:5 duty of a *h.* brother to her
28:56 eye sh. be evil to. *h.*
Ruth 1:12 I am too old to have *h.*
Jer. 3:11 *h.* with wife sh. be tak.
31:32 altho' I was a *h.* to them
Joel 1:8 girded with sackcl. for *h.*
Mat. 1:16 Joseph *h.* of Mary
Mark 10:12 if a woman put away *h.*
John 4:17 have no *h.* 18
Rom. 7:2 dead she is loosed, 3
1 *Cor.* 7:2 *h.* render to wife due benevolence, like. wife to *h.*
4 *h.* hath not power of own
11 let not *h.* put away his wife
14 unbeliev. *h.* is sanctified by wife, and wife sancti. by *h.*
2 *Cor.* 11:2 espoused to one *h.*
Gal. 4:27 more chil. than hath *h.*
Eph. 5:23 the *h.* is head of wife
1 *Tim.* 3:2 *h.* of one wi. *Tit.* 1:6

Her HUSBAND.
Gen. 3:6 eat fruit, gave to *h. h.*
Lev. 22:7 wo. put away *fr. h. h.*
Num. 5:20 to anoth. inst. of *h. h.*
30:7 on day *h. h.* heard, 11, 12, 13, 14
Deut. 25:5 *h. h.* brot. go in unto
Ruth 1:9 in house of *h. h.*
1 *Sam.* 1:22 sa. unto *h. h.* let me
2:19 she came up with *her h.*
Mat. 1:19 Joseph *h. h.* being just
Luke 16:18 mar. her aw. fr. *h. h.*
Rom. 7:2 bound by law to *h. h.*
3 *her h.* dead she be free
1 *Cor.* 7:3 woman have *h.* own *h.*
10 let not wife depart fr. *her h.*
11 be reconciled to *her h.*
34 how wife may please *h. h.*
39 bound as long as *her h.*
Eph. 5:33 wife reverence *her h.*
Rev. 21:2 bride adorned for *her h.*

My HUSBAND.
Gen. 29:32 *my h.* will love me
31 will *my h.* be joined to me
30:18 given maiden to *my h.*
20 now will *my h.* dw. wi. me
Deut. 25:7 *my h.* brother refuseth
2 *Sam.* 14:5 I am a widow, *my h.* dead, 2 *K.* 4:1
Hos. 2:7 and return to *my* first *h.*

Our HUSBAND.
Gen. 3:16 desire shall be to *t. h.*
Num. 5:13 anoth. inst. of *t. h.* 20
2 *K.* 4:26 is it well with *thy h.*
Is. 54:5 maker thy *h.* Lord of h.
Jer. 7:16 thou shalt save *thy h.*

HUSBANDMAN.
Gen. 9:20 Noah began to be a *h.*
Amos 5:16 call *h.* to mourning
Zec. 13:5 a prophet, am a *h.*
John 15:1 Fath. is *h.*
2 *Tim.* 2:6 the *h.* that laboureth
Jam. 5:7 *h.* waiteth for fruit of earth

I AM

HUSBANDMEN.
2 *K.* 25:12 he left of the poor to be *h. Jer.* 52:16
Jer. 31:24 shall dwell in Judah *h.*
Joel 1:11 be ashamed ye *h.* howl
Mat. 21:33 he let it out to *h. Mark* 12:2 ; *Luke* 20:9
34 sent his servants to *h. Mark* 12:2 ; *Luke* 20:10
38 when *h.* saw the son, *Mark* 12:7 ; *Luke* 20:14
40 what will he do to those *h.* ?
41 let out vineyard to other *h.*
Luke 20:16
Mark 12:2 might receive fr. *h.* 9

HUSBANDRY.
2 *Chr.* 26:10 Uzziah loved *h.*
1 *Cor.* 3:9 ye are God's *h.* ye are

HUSBANDS.
Ruth 1:11 they may be your *h.* ?
13 stay for them fr. having *h.*
Est. 1:17 despise *h.* in their eyes
20 wives give to *h.* honour
Ezek. 16:45 loathed *h.* and child.
John 4:18 thou hast had five *h.*
1 *Cor.* 14:35 ask their *h.* at home
Eph. 5:22 wives submit to *h.* 24
25 *h.* love your wives, *Col.* 3:19
Col. 3:18 wives, submit to own *h.*
1 *Tim.* 3:12 deac. *h.* of one wife
Tit. 2:4 teach women to love *h.*
5 be obedient to their own *h.*
1 *Pet.* 3:1 in subjection to own *h.*
7 yo *h.* dwell with them accor.

HUSHAI.
2 *Sam.* 15:32 H. to meet D. 17:5
1 *Chr.* 27:33 H. king's companl.

HUSK, S.
Num. 6:4 kernel even to the *h.*
2 *K.* 4:42 full ears of corn in *h.*
Luke 15:16 filled belly with *h.*

HUZZAB.
Nah. 2:7

HYMENEUS.
1 *Tim.* 1:20 wh. is H. 2 *Tim.* 2:17

HYMN, S.
Mat. 26:30 when they had sung a *h. Mark* 14:26
Eph. 5:19 spea. in psalms and *h.*
Col. 3:16 admo. in psalms and *h.*

HYPOCRISY, IES.
Is. 32:6 iniquity, to practise *h.*
Mat. 23:28 within you are full of *h.*
Mark 12:15 he knowing the ir *h.*
Luke 12:1 leaven of Pharisees *h.*
1 *Tim.* 4:2 speaking lies in *h.*
1 *Pet.* 2:1 aside all malice and *h.*
Jam. 3:17 wisdom pure witho. *h.*

HYPOCRITE.
Job 8:13 the *h.* hope shall perish
13:16 *h.* shall not come bef. him
17:8 innocent stir up against *h.*
20:5 joy of *h.* but for a moment
27:8 what is the hope of the *h.* ?
34:30 that the *h.* reign not, lest
Prov. 11:9 *h.* with mouth destroy
Is. 9:17 for every one is a *h.*
Mat. 7:5 *h.* first cast out beam
12:35 *h.* doth not each house ox?

HYPOCRITES.
Job 15:34 congrega. of *h.* desolate
36:13 *h.* in heart heap up wrath
Is. 33:14 fearfulness surprised *h.*
Mat. 6:2 not sound trump. as *h.*
5 thou shalt not be as *h.*
16 when ye fast, be not as *h.*
15:7 ye *h.* well did Esaias prophesy, *Mark* 7:6
16:3 O *h.* ye discern face of sky, 22:18 Why tempt ye me, ye *h.*
23:13 Phari. *h.* ye shut kingd. ag. men, 14, 15, 23, 25, 27, 29
24:51 appoint *h.* his portion
Luke 11:44 scribes and Phari. *h.*

HYPOCRITICAL.
Ps. 35:16 *h.* mockers in feasts
Is. 10:6 send him ag. *h.* nation

HYSSOP.
Ex. 12:22 bunch of *h.* and dip it
Lev. 14:4 cedar, and *h.* 6, 49, 51, 52
Num. 19:6 and *h.* into midst of
18 take *h.* dip it in water
1 *K.* 4:33 cedar-tree, even unto *h.*
Ps. 51:7 purge with *h.* be clean
John 19:29 sponge and put it on *h.*
Heb. 9:19 blood with *h.* sprinkl.

I

Ex. 3:14 I AM, THAT I AM.
Deut. 32:39 I, even I, am he
Ps. 31:1 I the Lord, the first, I am
Mic. 43:11, 25
10 am with thee, I am thy G.

CRUDEN'S CONCORDANCE.

IDO

Mat. 26:22 be. to say, L. is it I?
IBIIAR. 2 *Sa.* 5:15 ; 1 *Ch.* 3:6 ; 14:5

ICE.
Job 6:16 blackish by reason of *i.*
38:29 out of wh. womb came *i.?*
Ps. 147:17 he casteth forth his *i.*
ICHABOD. 1 *Sam.* 4:21; 14:3

ICONIUM.
Acts 13:51 Barnab. came unto I.
14:1 in I. went into synago. 19
2 *Tim.* 3:11 afflictions came at I.

IDDO.
2 *Chr.* 9:29 I. seer, 12:15 ; 13:22
Ezr. 5:1 I. prophesied, *Zec.* 1:1, 7
Neh. 12:4 I. with priests went up

IDLE.
Ex. 5:8 be *i.* therefore they cry
17 he said, Ye are *i.*, ye are *i.*
Prov. 19:15 *i.* soul suffer hunger
Mat. 12:36 ev. *i.* word men speak
20:3 standing *i.* in market-pl. 6
Luke 24:11 seemed as *i.* tales
1 *Tim.* 5:13 they learn to be *i.*

IDLENESS.
Prov. 31:27 eateth not bread of *i.*
Ec. 10:18 thro' *i.* house droppeth
Ezek. 16:49 abundan. of *i.* in her

IDOLATER, S.
1 *Cor.* 5:10 with the covet. or *i.*
11 any called a brother be an *i.*
6:9 *i.* not inherit kingdom of G.
10:7 neither be *i.* as some were
Eph. 5:5 who is *i.* hath any inh.
Rev. 21:8 *i.* have part in the lake
22:15 murderers and *i.* and liars

IDOLATROUS.
2 *K.* 23:5 Jos. put down *i.* priests

IDOLATRY, IES.
1 *Sam.* 15:23 is as iniquity and *i.*
Acts 17:16 city wholly given to *i.*
1 *Cor.* 10:14 beloved, flee from *i.*
Gal. 5:20 the works of the flesh *i.*
Col. 3:5 covetousness, which is *i.*
1 *Pet.* 4:3 walked in abomina. *i.*

IDOL, Adjective.
Zec. 11:17 woe to *i.* shepherd

IDOL.
1 *K.* 15:13 she made an *i.* in grove, 2 *Chr.* 15:16
2 *Chr.* 33:7 set *i.* in house of God
Is. 48:5 lest say, Mine *i.* hath
66:3 inc. as if he blessed an *i.*
Jer. 22:28 is this C. a broken *i.*
Acts 7:41 offered sacrifice to *i.*
1 *Cor.* 8:4 *i.* noth. in world, 10:19
7 some with conscience of *i.*

IDOLS.
Lev. 19:4 turn not to *i.* ; 26 no *i.*
26:30 cast your carcasses on *i.*
Deut. 29:17 ye have seen their *i.*
1 *Sam.* 31:9 publ. *i.* in house of *i.*
1 *K.* 15:12 Asa removed the *i.*
21:26 A. did abomi. in follow. *i.*
2 *K.* 17:12 th. serv. *i.* 2 *Chr.* 24:18
21:11 made Judah to sin with *i.*
23:24 *i.* that were spied in land
1 *Chr.* 10:9 carry tidin. to their *i.*
16:26 all gods of the peo. are *i.*
2 *Chr.* 13:8 Asa put *i.* out of Jud.
34:7 Josiah cut down all *i.* in Is.
Ps. 96:5 all gods of nations are *i.*
97:7 that boast themselves of *i.*
106:36 and they served their *i.*
115:4 *i.* are silv. and g. 135:15
Is. 2:8 land is full of *i.* worship
18 *i.* he shall utterly abolish
20 shall cast away his *i.* 31:7
10:11 as I done to Samaria and her *i.*, so do to Jer. and her *i.*
19:1 *i.* of Egypt shall be moved
3 seek to *i.* and to charmers
45:16 mak. of *i.* go to confusion
46:1 their *i.* were on the beasts
57:5 inflam. yourselves with *i.*
Jer. 50:2 her *i.* are confounded
38 they are mad upon their *i.*
Ezek. 6:6 your *i.* may be broken
9 go a whoring after their *i.*
13 did offer savor to their *i.*
8:10 I saw all the *i.* of Israel
14:3 set up their *i.* in heart, 4, 7
6 turn yourselves from your *i.*
18:20 wi. *i.* of thy abomination
18:6 nor lift eyes to *i.* 12, 15
20:7 defile not yourse. with *i.* 18
16 heart after *i.* ; 24 eyes af. *i.*
31 ye pollute yourselves with your *i.* 22:4 ; 23:7, 30, 37
39 pol. my name no more wi. *i.*
22:3 the city maketh *i.*
23:30 slain their chil. to their *i.*
49 bear the sins of your *i.*
30:13 I will destroy *i.*

IMA

Ezek. 36:25 fr. *i.* clea. yon, 37:23
44:10 went astray after *i.*
12 ministered before their *i.*
Hos. 4:17 Ephr. is joined to *i.*
8:4 of silver and gold made *i.*
14:8 what have I to do with *i.*
Mic. 1:7 the *i.* will I lay desolate
Hab. 2:18 trust. to make dumb *i.*
Zec. 10:2 *i.* have spoken vanity
13:2 I will cut off names of *i.*
Acts 15:20 abst. fr. polluti. of *i.*
29 abst. fr. meats offer. *i.* 21:25
Rom. 2:22 thou that abhorrest *i.*
1 *Cor.* 8:1 touching th. offered to *i.* 4, 10 ; 10:19, 28 ; *Rev.* 2:14, 20
12:2 Gentiles carried to dumb *i.*
2 *Cor.* 6:16 agree. of G. with *i.?*
1 *Thes.* 1:9 turned to God from *i.*
1 *John* 5:21 keep yourself. from *i.*
Rev. 9:20 not wor. devils and *i.*

IDUMEA.
Is. 34:5 sword sh. come on I. 6
Ezek. 35:15 all I. shall be, 36:5
Mark 3:8 multi. followed from I.

IGNOMINY.
Prov. 18:3 and with *i.* reproach

IGNORANCE.
Lev. 4:2 if a soul sh. sin thro' *i.*
5:15 ; *Num.* 15:24, 27, 28, 29
13 congre. sin thro' *i.* ; 22 ruler
27 if the people sin through *i.*
Num. 15:25 forgiv. them, it is *i.*
Acts 3:17 through *i.* ye did it
17:30 times of *i.* God winked at
Eph. 4:18 alienated through *i.*
1 *Pet.* 1:14 according to lusts in *i.*
2:15 put to silen. *i.* of fool. men

IGNORANT.
Ps. 73:22 and *i.* I was as a beast
Is. 56:10 all *i.* they are all dumb
63:16 though Abram be *i.* of us
Acts 4:13 perceived they were *i.*
Rom. 1:13 I would not have you *i.* brethren, 1 *Cor.* 10:1 ; 12:1 ; 2 *Cor.* 1:8 ; 1 *Thes.* 4:13
10:3 being *i.* of God's righteous,
11:25 sh. be *i.* of this mystery
1 *Cor.* 14:38 ignor. let him be *i.*
2 *Cor.* 2:11 not *i.* of Satan's devi.
Heb. 5:2 have compassion on *i.*
2 *Pet.* 3:5 they willingly are *i.*
8 be not *i.* of this one thing

IGNORANTLY.
Num. 15:28 soul sinneth *i.*
Deut. 19:4 wh. killeth neighbor *i.*
Acts 17:23 ye *i.* worship I declare
1 *Tim.* 1:13 because I did it *i.*

ILL.
Gen. 41:3 kine *i.*-fav. 4, 19, 20, 21
4:6 why dealt so *i.* with me?
Deut. 13:21 hath any *i.* blemish
Ps. 106:32 it went *i.* with Moses
Is. 3:11 woe to wicked, sh. be *i.*
Joel 2:20 *i.* savor shall come up
Rom. 13:10 love worketh no *i.*

ILL, or evil-favoredness.
Deut. 17:1 not sac. sheep wherein is blemish or *e.-f.*

ILLUMINATED.
Heb. 10:32 after ye *i.* endur. fight

ILLYRICUM.
Rom. 15:19 round about unto I.

IMAGE.
Gen. 1:26 let us make man in our *i.* 27 ; 9:6
5:3 in his own *i.* after his *i.*
Lev. 26:1 nor rear up a standing *i. Deut.* 16:22
1 *Sam.* 19:13 Michal took an *i.*
2 *Chr.* 33:7 set car. *i.* in ho. of G.
Job 4:16 *i.* was before mine eyes
Ps. 73:20 shalt despise their *i.*
Ezek. 8:3 there was seat of *i.* 5
Dan. 2:31 great *i.* stood bef. thee
35 stone smote *i.* bec. moanet.
3:1 Nebuchad. made *i.* of gold
6 worship the golden *i.* 10, 15
Hos. 3:4 sh. abide without an *i.*
Mat. 22:20 whose is this *i.* ; *Mark* 12:16 ; *Luke* 20:24
Acts 19:35 *i.* which fell from Ju.
Rom. 1:23 changed gl. of G. to *i.*
8:29 be conformed to *i.* of Son
11:4 bowed the knee to *i.* of B.
1 *Cor.* 11:7 he is *i.* and gl. of G.
15:49 we have borne *i.* of earthy
2 *Cor.* 3:18 changed into *i.* from gl.
4:4 Christ is *i.* of God, *Col.* 1:15
Col. 3:10 *i.* of him that created
Heb. 1:3 express *i.* of his person
10:1 not the very *i.* of things
Rev. 13:14 make *i.* to the beast
15 give life to the *i.* of beast
14:9 if any man worship *i.*
11 have no rest, who worsh. *i.*

IMP

Rev. 15:2 vic. ov. beast and his *i.*
16:2 sore fell on them wors. *i.*
19:20 he deceived them wors. *i.*
20:4 not worshipped bea. nor *i.*
See GRAVEN.

IMAGE-WORK.
2 *Chr.* 3:10 two cherubim L.-*w.*

Molten IMAGE.
Deut. 9:12 made them a m. *i.*
Ps. 106:19 worshipped molten *i.*
Is. 10:14 his m. *i.* falseh. 51:17
Hab. 2:18 what profit. the m. *i.*

IMAGES.
Gen. 31:19 stolen fath.'s *i.* 34, 35
Ex. 23:24 eb. break their *i.* 34:13 ;
Deut. 7:5 ; *Num.* 33:52
Lev. 26:30 will cut down your *i.*
1 *Sam.* 6:5 *i.* of emerods, 11
K. 14:9 hast made *i.* to pro. me
23 high places, *i.* and groves
2 *K.* 10:36 they brought *i.* out
11:18 *i.* brake, 18:4 ; 23:14
17:10 set up *i.* ; 16 they made *i.*
23:24 Josiah put away *i.* in land
Is. 17:8 not look to groves or *i.*
27:9 groves and *i.* not stand up
30:22 ye shall defile orna. of *i.*
41:29 their molten *i.* are wind
Jer. 43:13 break *i.* of B.-shemesh
50:2 her *i.* are broken in pieces
Ezek. 6:4 your *i.* shall be broken
6 that your *i.* may be cut down
7:20 made *i.* of abominations
16:17 mad. to thyself *i.* of men
21:21 king of Bab. consulted *i.*
23:14 *i.* of Chaldeans portrayed
30:13 will cause their *i.* to cease
Hos. 10:1 have made goodly *i.*
2 break their alt. spoil their *i.*
13:2 they have made *i.* of silver
Amos 5:26 borne tab. of your *i.*
Mic. 5:13 standing *i.* will I cut off

IMAGERY.
Ezek. 8:12 in chamber of *i.*

IMAGINATION, S.
Gen. 6:5 *i.* of his heart was evil
8:21 *i.* of man's heart is evil
Deut. 29:19 though I walk in *i.*
31:21 for I know their *i.*
1 *Chr.* 28:9 understands all the *i.*
29:18 keep this in *i.* of heart
Prov. 6:18 heart rh. devis. wic. *i.*
Jer. 23:17 ev. one walketh after *i.*
Lam. 3:60 hast seen *i.* ag. me
61 hast heard their *i.* ag. me
Luke 1:51 scattered proud in *i.*
Rom. 1:21 became vain in th. *i.*
2 *Cor.* 10:5 casting down *i.*
See HEART.

IMAGINE.
Job 6:26 ye *i.* to reprove words?
21:27 devices wrong. *i.* ag. me
Ps. 2:1 do peo. *i.* vain thing?
38:12 and *i.* deceits all day long
62:3 how long will ye *i.* mischief?
140:2 *i.* mischiefs in their heart
Prov. 12:20 deceit in them *i.* evil
Hos. 7:15 yet do they *i.* mischief
Nah. 1:9 what do ye *i.* ag. L?
Zec. 7:10 let none *i.* evil, 8:17
Acts 4:25 do peo. *i.* vain things?

IMAGINED, ETH.
Gen. 11:6 nothing rest. they *i.*
Ps. 10:2 taken in devices they *i.*
21:11 they *i.* mischievous device
Nah. 1:11 one *i.* evil ag. the L.

IMMEDIATELY.
Mat. 26:74 *i.* the cock crew, *Luke* 22:60 ; *John* 18:27
Mark 1:31 *i.* the fever left her
4:13 Satan cometh *i.* and taketh
Lu. 6:49 *i.* fell ; 8:44 *i.* stanched
19:11 kingdom of God *i.* appear
Acts 12:23 *i.* angel of L. smote
16:26 *i.* all doors were opened
Rev. 4:2 and *i.* was in the Spirit

IMMORTAL.
1 *Tim.* 1:17 K. eternal, *i.* invis.

IMMORTALITY.
Rom. 2:7 to them who seek for *i.*
1 *Cor.* 15:53 mortal must put on *i.*
54 this mortal shall have put on *i.*
1 *Tim.* 6:16 *i.* dwelling in light
2 *Tim.* 1:10 brought *i.* to light

IMMUTABLE.
Heb. 6:18 that by two *i.* things

IMMUTABILITY.
Heb. 6:17 the *i.* of his counsel

IMPART, ED.
Job 39:17 nor *i.* to her underst.
Luke 3:11 him *i.* to him ha. none

INC

Rom. 1:11 *i.* some spiritual gift
1 *Thes.* 4:8 unwilling to ha. *i.* souls

IMPEDIMENT.
Mark 7:32 had *i.* in his speech

IMPENITENT.
Rom. 2:5 thou, after thy *i.* heart

IMPERIOUS.
Ezek. 16:30 work of an *i.* woman

IMPLACABLE.
Rom. 1:31 without affection, *i.*

IMPLEAD.
Acts 19:38 let them *i.* one anoth.

IMPORTUNITY.
Luke 11:8 because of his *i.*

IMPOSE, ED.
Ezr. 7:24 not be lawful to *i.* toll
Heb. 9:10 carnal ordinances *i.* ou

IMPOSSIBLE.
Mat. 17:20 nothing *i.* unto you
19:26 with men is *i.*, *Mark* 10:27 ;
Luke 1:37 with G. noth. *i.* 18:27
17:1 *i.* but offences will come
Heb. 6:4 *i.* for those enlightened
18 it was *i.* for G. to lie
11:0 without faith *i.* to please G.

IMPOTENT.
John 5:3 a multitude of *i.* folk
Acts 4:9 good deed done *i.* man
14:8 man at Lystra, *i.* in feet

IMPOVERISH, ED.
Jud. 6:6 Israel was greatly *i.*
Is. 40:20 he that is so *i.*
Jer. 5:17 shall *i.* fenced cities
Mal. 1:4 Edom saith, We are *i.*

IMPRISONED.
Acts 22:19 I *i.* and beat them

IMPRISONMENT, S.
Ezr. 7:26 banishment or *i.*
2 *Cor.* 6:5 approv. in stripes, in *i.*
Heb. 11:36 mockings, bonds, *i.*

IMPUDENT.
Prov. 7:13 with *i.* face she said
Ezek. 2:4 for they are *i.* children
3:7 house of Is. *i.* hard-hearted

IMPUTE, D.
Lev. 7:18 nor sh. it be *i.* to him
17:4 blood sh. be *i.* to that man
1 *Sam.* 22:15 let not king *i.* any t.
2 *Sam.* 19:19 not my lord *i.* iniq.
Rom. 4:8 Lord will not *i.* sin
11 righteous. mi. be *i.* to them
22 therefore it was *i.* to him for righteousness, 23 ; *Jam.* 2:23
24 to whom it shall be *i.*
5:13 sin not *i.* wh. th. is no law

IMPUTETH, ING.
Ps. 32:2 whom Lord *i.* not iniq.
Hab. 1:11 *i.* his power to his god
Rom. 4:6 to whom G. *i.* righte.
2 *Cor.* 5:19 not *i.* tresp. to them

INASMUCH.
Mat. 25:40 *i.* as ye have done it
45 *i.* as ye did it not to one

INCENSE.
Ex. 30:8 shall burn perpetual *i.*
9 ye shall offer no strange *i.*
37:29 pure *i.* of sweet spices
40:5 altar of gold for b. bef. ark
Lev. 10:1 took censer, put *i.*
16:13 put *i.* on fire before Lord
Num. 7:14 spoon full of *i.* 26
16:35 fire cons. 250 men offer. *i.*
40 Mo. said to Aar. Put on *i.*
47 put on *i.* and made atonem.
Deut. 33:10 shall put *i.* bef. thee
2 *Chr.* 30:14 altars of *i.*
34:25 burned *i.* to other gods
Ps. 66:15 offer to thee *i.*
141:2 prayer set bef. thee as *i.*
Is. 1:13 *i.* is an abomination
43:23 not wearied thee with *i.*
60:6 shall bring gold and *i.*
66:3 burneth *i.* as if he blessed
Jer. 6:20 why cometh *i.* from S. ?
11:17 prov. to anger, offering *i.*
41:5 offerings and *i.* in the hand
48:35 him that burneth *i.*
Ezek. 8:11 thick cloud of *i.* went
16:18 mine oil and *i.* before them
Mal. 1:11 ev. place *i.* be offered
Luke 1:10 without *i.* at time of *i.*
Rev. 8:3 given to him much *i.*
4 smoke of *i.* ascended bef. G.

See ALTAR, BURN, BURNT.

Sweet INCENSE.
Ex. 25:6 spices for sweet *i.* 35:8, 28 ; *Num.* 4:16
31:11 oil and s. *i.* for holy place
39:38 brought oil and s. *i.* to M.
Lev. 16:12 hands full of sweet *i.*

INC

INCENSED.
Is. 41;11 *i.* ag. thee be ashamed
43:24 *i.* against him be ashamed

INCLINE.
Jos. 24:23 *i.* your heart to the L.
1 *K.* 8:58 he may *i.* our hearts
Ps. 78:1 *i.* your ears to words
119:36 *i.* my heart to thy testi.
141:1 *i.* not my heart to evil
See EAR.

INCLINED, ETH.
Jud. 9:3 hearts *i.* to follow A.
Ps. 40:1 Lord *i.* unto me, 116:2
119:112 *i.* my heart to thy stat.
Prov. 2:18 her house *i.* to death
5:13 nor *i.* mine ear to them
Jer. 7:24 nor *i.* ear, 26; 11:8;
17:23; 34:14
25:4 not *i.* y. ear, 35:15; 44:5

INCONTINENCY.
1 *Cor.* 7:5 tempt you not for y. *i.*

INCONTINENT.
2 *Tim.* 3:3 without affection, *i.*

INCORRUPTIBLE.
Rom. 1.23 changed glory of *i.* G.
1 *Cor.* 9:25 to obtain an *i.* crown
15:52 the dead shall be raised *i.*
1 *Pet.* 1:4 an inheri, *i.* undefiled
23 born of *i.* seed by word of G.

INCORRUPTION.
1 *Cor.* 15:42 cor. it is raised in *i.*
50 nei. doth corruption inh. *i.*
53 corruptible must put on *i.*
54 corrup. shall have put on *i.*

INCREASE, Substantive.
Lev. 25:36 no usury of him or *i.*
37 lend him victuals for *i.*
26:4 the land shall yield her *i.*
20 land shall not yield her *i.*
Num. 18:30 *i.* of threshing-floor
32:14 an *i.* of sinful men
Deut. 14:22 tithe of *i.* of seed
28 bring forth tithe of *i.*
32:13 cursed be *i.* of kine, 51
1 *Sam.* 2:33 *i.* of thy household. die
Job 20:28 *i.* of house shall depart
31:12 root out all mine *i.*
Ps. 67:6 earth shall yield her *i.*
73:12 gave their *i.* to caterpillar
85:12 our land shall yield her *i.*
Prov. 14:4 much *i.* by stre. of ox
18:20 with *i.* of lips sh. be filled
Ez. 5:10 not be satisfied with *i.*
Is. 9:7 *i.* of his gov. he no end
Jer. 2:3 *i.* was holiness to Lord
Ezek. 18:8 nor hath taken *i.* 17
13 on usury, taken *i.* 22:12
31:37 earth shall yield her *i.*
Zec. 8:12 ground sh. give her *i.*
1 *Cor.* 3:6 I planted, G. gave *i.* 7
Eph. 4:16 maketh *i.* of the body
Col. 2:19 body incr. wi. *i.* of G.

INCREASE, Verb.
Lev. 25:16 by years thou *i.* price
Deut. 6:3 ye may *i.* mightily
7:22 beasts of field *i.* on thee
1 *Chr.* 27:23 would L. Is. like ours
Job 8:7 thy latter end greatly *i.*
Ps. 44:12 dost not *i.* thy wealth
62:10 riches *i.* set not heart
71:12 in world, *i.* in riches
115:14 the L. shall *i.* you more
Prov. 1:5 wise man *i.* learn. 9:9
22:16 oppresseth poor to *i.* rich.
24:28 they perish, righteous *i.*
Ec. 5:11 goods *i.* increased eat
6:11 be many things that *i.*
Is. 29:19 meek *i.* their joy in L.
Ezek. 5:16 I will *i.* famine on you
36:29 *i.* it, lay no famine on you
37 *i.* them with men like a flock
Dan. 11:39 he shall *i.* with glory
Hos. 4:10 commit whoredo. not *i.*
Luke 17:5 said, Lord, *i.* our faith
John 3:30 must *i.* I must decrease.
2 *Cor.* 9:10 *i.* fruits of righteous.
1 *Thes.* 3:12 L. make y. *i.* in love
4:10 that ye *i.* more and more
2 *Tim.* 2:16 *i.* to more ungodli.

INCREASED.
Gen. 7:17 wat. *i.* bare up ark, 18
30:30 little hadst, it is now *i.*
43 *Jacob i. ; Ex.* 1:7 Israel *i.*
1 *Sam.* 14:19 noise went on and *i.*
2 *Sam.* 15:12 conspir. of fa. *i.* greatly
Ezr. 9:6 iniq. *i.* over our head
Ps. 3:1 they *i.* that trouble me
4:7 their corn and wine *i.*
49:16 glory of his house is *i.*
62:10 if riches of life sh. be *i.*
Ec. 2:9 I *i.* more than all bef. me
5:11 they are *i.* that eat them
Is. 9:3 multip. nation, not *i.* joy
26:15 thou hast *i.* nation, O L.

INF

Jer. 5:6 their backslidings are *i.*
15:8 widows *i.* ab. sands of sea
30:14 bec. thy sins were *i.* 15
Ezek. 16:26 *i.* thy whored. 23:14
28:5 by wisdom hast thou *i.*
Dan. 12:4 knowledge shall be *i.*
Hos. 4:7 as they *i.* so th. sinned
10:1 accord. to fruit, he *i.* altars
Mark 4:8 that sprang up and *i.*
Luke 2:52 Jesus *i.* in wisdom
Acts 6:7 and the word of God *i.*
16:5 churches *i.* in number daily
2 *Cor.* 10:15 hope when faith is *i.*
Rev. 3:17 rich, and *i.* with goods

INCREASEST, ETH.
Job 10:16 afflic. *i. ;* 12:23 *i.* nati.
17 *i.* thine indig. upon me
Ps. 74:23 the tumult of those *i.*
Prov. 11:24 scattereth and yet *i.*
23:28 *i.* transgressors am. men
24:5 man of know. *i.* strength
28:8 unjust gain, *i.* substance
Ec. 1:18 knowledge, *i.* sorrow
Is. 40:29 no *i.* strength
Hos. 12:1 *i.* lies and desolation
Hab. 2:6 woe to him that *i.* that
Col. 2:19 body *i.* with inc. of G.

INCREASING.
Col. 1:10 *i.* in knowledge of God

INCREDIBLE.
Acts 26:8 L. sho'uld raise dead ?

INCURABLE.
2 *Chr.* 21:18 smote him wi. *i.* di.
Job 34:6 my wound is *i.* without
Jer. 15:18 why is my wound *i. ?*
30:12 bruise is *i. ;* sorrow is *i.*
Mic. 1:9 wound *i.* it is come to J.

INDEBTED.
Luke 11:4 forgive every one *i.*

INDEED.
Gen. 37:8 sh. thou *i.* reign ov. us?
10 mother and breth. *i.* come?
1 *K.* 8:27 but will God *i.* dwell on
earth ? 2 *Chr.* 6:18
1 *Chr.* 4:10 wouldest bless me *i.*
Job 19:4 be it *i.* that I have erred
Jer. 6:9 hour ye *i.* see ye *i.* but
Mat. 3:11 I *i.* baptize, *Mark* 1:8 ;
Luke 3:16
Mark 11:32 he was a prophet *i.*
Luke 24:34 *i.* just. ; 24:34 risen *i.*
John 1:47 behold an Israelite *i.*
4:42 that this is *i.* the Christ
6:55 flesh meat *i.* blood drink *i.*
7:26 do rulers know *i.* this is C. ?
8:36 Son make free, ye be free *i.*
Rom. 8:7 law, neither *i.* can be
1 *Tim.* 5:3 hon. widows are wi. *i.*
5 that is widow *i.* desolate, 16
See ENDEAVOR.

INDIGNATION.
2 *K.* 3:27 great *i.* against Israel
Deut. 29:28 Lord rooted *i.* upon me
Ps. 69:24 poor out thy wrath, *i.*
102:10 bec. of thine *i.* and wrath
Is. 10:5 staff in hand is mine *i.*
25 yet a little, the *i.* sh. cease
13:5 weapons of *i.* 34:2; 50:25
26:20 till *i.* be overpast
30:27 his lips are full of *i.*
34:3 *i.* of Lord is on all nations
66:14 *i.* kno. towards enemies
Jer. 10:10 not able to abide *i.*
15:17 thou hast filled me with *i.*
Lam. 2:6 despised in *i.* of anger
Ezek. 21:31 pour mi. *i.* upon thee
22:31 not rained on day of his *i.*
31 poured out mine *i.* on them
Dan. 11:30 *i.* against holy coven.
Mic. 7:9 I will bear *i.* of Lord
Nah. 1:6 who can stand bef. *i. ?*
Hab. 3:12 march thro' land in *i.*
Zec. 1:12 had *i.* seventy years
Mat. 20:24 moved wi. *i.* ag. two
Mark 14:4 saying, To what
Luke 13:14 ruler answer. with *i.*
Acts 5:17 ye were filled with *i.*
Rom. 2:8 obey unright. *i.* wrath
2 *Cor.* 7:11 yea, what *i. !*
Heb. 10:27 looking for of fiery *i.*
Rev. 14:10 poured out cup of *i.*

INDITING.
Ps. 45:1 heart is *i.* good matter

INDUSTRIOUS.
1 *K.* 11:28 young man was *i.*

INEXCUSABLE.
Rom. 2:1 therefore thou art *i.*

INFALLIBLE.
Acts 1:3 showed him. by *i.* proo.

INF

INFAMOUS.
Ezek. 22:5 mock thee wh. art *i.*

INFAMY.
Prov. 25:10 th. *i.* turn not away
Ezek. 36:3 are an *i.* of the people

INFANT, S.
1 *Sam.* 15:3 slay man, wo. and *i.*
Job 3:16 as *i.* wh. never saw light
Is. 65:20 no more an *i.* of days
Hos. 13:16 *i.* be dashed in pieces
Luke 18:15 they bro. *i.* to him

INFERIOR.
Job 12:3 understand. not *i.* 13:2
Dan. 2:39 another kingdom *i.*
2 *Cor.* 12:13 *i.* to other churches

INFIDEL.
2 *Cor.* 6:15 that believ. with *i. ?*
1 *Tim.* 5:8 is worse than an *i.*

INFINITE.
Job 22:5 are not th. iniquities *i. ?*
Ps. 147:5 his understanding is *i.*
Nah. 3:9 her strength, it was *i.*

INFIRMITY.
Lev. 12:2 days of separation for *i.*
Ps. 77:10 this is mine *i.*
Prov. 18:14 sp. of man sustain *i.*
Luke 13:11 woman which had *i.*
12 thou art loosed fr. thine *i.*
John 5:5 an *i.* thirty-eight years
Rom. 6:19 bec. of *i.* of your flesh
Gal. 4:13 through *i.* I preached
Heb. 5:2 himself comp. with *i.*
7:28 high-priests which have *i.*

INFIRMITIES.
Mat. 8:17 himself took our *i.*
Luke 5:15 to be healed of *i.*
7:21 cured many of their *i.* 8:2
Rom. 8:26 Sp. also helpeth our *i.*
15:1 strong bear *i.* of the weak
2 *Cor.* 11:30 things conc. mine *i.*
12:5 *i.* gl. not, but in mine *i.* 9
10 I take pleasure in mine *i.*
1 *Tim.* 5:23 use wine for thine *i.*
Heb. 4:15 touched with feel. of *i.*

INFLAME, ING.
Is. 5:11 conti. till wine *i.* them
57:5 *i.* yourselves with idols

INFLAMMATION.
Lev. 13:28 an *i.* of the burning
Deut. 28:22 L. smite thee with *i.*

INFLICTED.
2 *Cor.* 2:6 punishm. which was *i.*

INFLUENCES.
Job 38:31 bind *i.* of Pleiades ?

INFOLDING.
Ezek. 1:4 *i.* itself, and a brightn.

INFORM, ED.
Deut. 17:10 accord. to all they *i.*
Dan. 9:22 *i.* me, talked with me
Acts 21:21 are *i.* thou teachest, 24
24:1 *i.* against Paul, 25:2, 15

INGATHERING.
Ex. 23:16 feast of *i.* end of year

INGRAFTED.
Jam. 1:21 rec. with meek. *i.* word

INHABIT.
Num. 35:34 defile not land wh. *i.*
20:19 not for *i.* earth
Prov. 4:21:11 village Kedar doth *i.*
65:21 sh. build houses and *i.* th.
22 sh. not build, and anoth. *i.*
Jer. 17:6 shall *i.* parched places
Jer. 32:24 that *i.* wastes of her.
Amos 9:14 waste cities *i.* them
Zep. 1:13 build houses, not *i.*

INHABITANT.
Is. 5:9 houses great without *i.*
6:11 cities be wasted without *i.*
12:6 cry out and shout, *i.* of Zi.
24 *i.* of this isle shall say
47:11 snare on thee, O *i.* of earth
Jer. 2:15 cities burned witho. *i.*
4:7 cities laid waste without *i.*
9:11 I will make Jerusalem a d.
10:17 gather wares, O *i.* of fort.
21:13 I am against thee, O *i.*
26:9 desolate, witho. *i.* 34:22, 87
Amos 1:5 will cut off *i.* from A.
8 I will cut off *i.* from Ashdod
Mic. 1:12 the *i.* of Maroth
13 to thee, O *i.* of Lachish
15 bring heir, O *i.* of Mareshah
Zep. 2:5 destroy, th. sh. be no *i.*
3:6 cities destroyed, is none *i.*

INHABITANTS.
Gen. 19:25 overthrow *i.* of cities
Ex. 15:15 *i.* of Canaan melt
23:31 deliver *i.* of land int. h.
Num. 13:32 land eateth up *i.*
14:14 they heard thou Lord art
32:17 before *i.* of the land
33:52 drive out all the *i.*
55 let not *i.* of *i.* of land remain
Deut. 13:15 surely smite *i.* of city

INH

Jos. 2:24 *i.* of country do faint
11:19 peace, save *i.* of Gibeon
17:12 could not drive out the *i.*
Jud. 1:19, 27
Jud. 5:7 *i.* of the villages ceased
23 curse ye bitterly *i.* thereof
Ruth 4:4 buy it before the *i.*
2 *K.* 19:26 *i.* were of small power
2 *Chr.* 20:23 ags. *i.* of mount Seir
Job 26:5 are formed from und. *i.*
Ps. 33:8 *i.* of world stand in awe
14 he looketh on all *i.* of earth
49:1 give ear, all ye *i.* of world
75:3 earth and *i.* thereof dissolv.
Is. 10:13 put down *i.* like a man
18:3 ye *i.* of the world, see ye
23:2 be still, ye *i.* of the isle, 6
24:1 and scattere. abroad the *i.*
5 earth defiled under *i.* thereof
6 the *i.* of the earth are burned
26:9 *i.* of world learn righteous.
18 nor have *i.* of the world fal.
38:11 no more with *i.* of world
40:22 *i.* thereof as grasshoppers
42:10 *i.* sing to Lord a new song
11 let *i.* of rock sing
49:19 land nar. by reason of *i.*
Jer. 13:13 fill *i.* wi. drunkenness
21:6 I will smite *i.* of this city
25:14 as bondmen, and *i.* thereof
25:29 ev. upon *i.* thereof, 50:35
26:15 bring innocent blood on *i.*
46:8 dwell deep, O *i.* of D. 30
51:12 stir against *i.* of Babylon
35 blood upon *i.* of Chaldea
Lam. 4:12 *i.* of world not believ.
Dan. 4:35 *i.* of earth are nothing
Mic. 6:12 *i.* thereof spoken lies
16 *i.* should make *i.* a hissing
Zec. 8:20 come *i.* of many cities
21 *i.* of one city go to another
Rev. 17:2 *i.* of earth made drunk
See JERUSALEM.

INHABITANTS of the land.
Gen. 34:30 stink among *i.* of *l.*
Ex. 23:12 let me, con. *i.* of *l.* 15
Num. 33:17 because of *i.* of *l.*
Jos. 2:9 all the *i.* of the *l.* faint
7:9 *i.* of *l.* land shall hear of *i.*
9:24 to destroy all *i.* of the land
Jer. 1:14 evil sh. break on *i.* of *l.*
10:18 I will sling out *i.* of *land*
47:2 all the *i.* of *l.* shall howl
Hos. 4:1 hath controv. wi. *i.* of *l.*
Joel 2:1 let the *i.* of the *l.* tremble
Zec. 11:6 no more pity *i.* of *l*and

INHABITED.
Ex. 16:35 till *i.* came to land *i.*
Lev. 16:22 iniqu. to a land not *i.*
Is. 13:20 it shall never be *i.*
44:26 saith to J. Thou shalt be *i.*
45:18 he formed earth to be *i.*
54:3 make desola. cities to be *i.*
Jer. 6:8 lest I make land not *i.*
17:6 in a salt land and not *i.*
22:6 make thee cities not *i.*
46:26 sh. be *i.* as in days of old
50:13 not be *i.* 39 no more *i.*
Ezek. 12:10 cities *i.* be laid waste
26:17 cm *i.* of seafaring men
36:10 cities *i.* and wastes build.
33:25 desolate places now *i.*
35 *i.* of Jerusal. be *i.* as town
12:6 Jerusalem shall be *i.* again
14:10 lifted up, *i.* in her place
11 Jerusalem shall be safely *i.*

INHABITERS.
Rev. 8:13 woe, woe, to *i.* of earth
12:12 woe to *i.* of earth and sea

INHABITEST, ETH.
Job 15:28 in houses no man *i.*
Ps. 22:3 thou that *i.* prais. of Is.
Is. 57:15 lofty One that *i.* eternity

INHABITING.
Ps. 74:14 meat to peo. *i.* wilder.

INHERIT.
Gen. 15:8 wh. I kn. *i.* I sh. *i.* it ?
Ex. 32:13 they sh. *i.* it for ever
Num. 18:24 given it to Lev. to *i.*
26:55 names of tr. of father sh. *i.*
32:19 not *i.* on yonder side Jor.
Deut. 1:38 shall cause he. to *i.* it
21:16 maketh his sons *i.* *i.* hath
Jud. 11:2 not *i.* in fa.'s house
1 *Sam.* 2:8 *i.* the throne of glory
Ps. 25:13 his seed sh. *i.* the earth
37:9 wait on Lord *i.* the earth
11 meek sh. *i.* earth, *Mat.* 5:5
82 blessed of him shall *i.* earth
29 righteous shall *i.* the land
69:36 seed of servants sh. *i.* it
82:8 thou sh. *i.* all nations
Prov. 3:35 wise shall *i.* glory
8:21 maketh his sons *i.* substa.
11:29 troubl. own house, *i.* wi.
14:18 the simple *i.* folly
Is. 49:8 to *i.* desolate heritages

CRUDEN'S CONCORDANCE.

INH

Is. 54:3 thy *seed* shall *i.* Gentiles
65:9 and mine elect shall *i.* it
Jer. 49:1 why doth M. *i.* G. & Gad?
Zec. 2:12 the L. shall *i.* Judah
Mat. 19:29 sh. *i.* everlasting life
25:34 come *i.* the kingdom pre.
Mark 10:17 that I may *i.* eternal
life, *Luke* 10:25; 18:18
1 *Cor.* 6:9 unrigh. not *i.* king. G.
10 nei. extortion. *i. Gal.* 5:21
15:50 flesh and blood cannot *i.*
kingd. of G. nor cor. *i.* inc.
Heb. 6:12 thro' faith *i.* promises
1 *Pet.* 3:9 ye should *i.* blessing
Rev. 21:7 he overcom. *i.* things

INHERIT land.
Gen. 28:4 thou mayest *i. land*
Num. 34:13 this is *land* ye sh. *i.*
Deut. 2:31 thou mayest *i.* his *l.*
16:20 *i.* t. L. giveth thee, 19:3
Ps. 37:29 righteous shall *i.* the *l.*
34 he sh. exalt thee to *i.* the *l.*
Is. 60:21 shall *i.* the *l.* for ever

INHERITANCE.
Gen. 31:14 is there any *i.* ?
Ex. 15:17 plant th. in thine *i.*
Lev. 25:46 take them as *i.*
Num. 18:20 have no *i.* thine *i.*
27:8 cause his *i.* to pass
9 *i.* broth. 10 father's brethren
32:19 our *i.* is fallen on this
side, 32; 34:15
34:18 to divide the land by *i.*
36:3 put to the *i.* of the tribe, 4
9 nor *i.* remove from one tribe
Deut. 4:20 people of *i.* as ye are
9:26 destroy not *i.* 29 thy *i.*
32:9 Jacob is the lot of his *i.*
Jos. 13:14 sac. of L. their *i.* 18:7
33 the L. G. of Is. was their *i.*
24:28 people depart, every man
to his *i. Jud.* 2:6 ; 21:24
Ruth 4:6 not red. *i.* mar mine *i.*
1 *Sam.* 10:1 anointed thee over *i.*
26:19 from abiding in *i.* of Lord
2 *Sam.* 20:1 neither have we *i.*
in son of Jesse, 1 *K.* 12:16
21:3 ye may bless *i.* of the Lord
1 *K.* 8:51 be thy peo. and t. *i.* 53
Neh. 11:20 every one in his *i.*
Job 31:2 what *i.* of Almighty ?
Ps. 16:5 the portion of mine *i.*
28:9 thine *i.* 33:12 cho. for *i.*
37:18 their *i.* shall be for ever
47:4 shall choose our *i.* for us
68:9 thou didst confirm thine *i.*
74:2 thine *i.* th. hast redeemed
78:62 was wroth with his *i.*
71 broug. him to feed Is. his *i.*
79:1 heathen come into thine *i.*
94:14 neither will he forsake *i.*
105:11 Canaan, lot of your *i.*
106:5 may glory with thine *i.*
40 that he abhorred his own *i.*
Prov. 13:22 good man leaveth *i.*
17:2 part of *i.* among brethren
19:14 hou. and riches *i.* of fath.
20:21 *i.* may be gotten hastily
Ec. 7:11 wisdom good with an *i.*
Is. 19:25 blessed be Is. mine *i.*
47:6 I have polluted mine *i.*
63:17 for serv. sake, tribes of *i.*
Jer. 10:16 is. rod of his *i.* 51:19
32:8 for right of Is. is thine
Lam. 5:2 *i.* turned to strangers
Ezek. 44:28 to them for *i.* I am *i.*
46:16 *i.* shall be his son's, 17
18 not take people's *i.*
Mat. 21:38 let us seize on his *i.*
Mark 12:7 l. be ours, *Luke* 20:14
Luke 12:13 he divide *i.* with me
Acts 20:32 *i.* among sanctified
20:16 *i.* an. them sancti. by fa.
Gal. 3:18 if the *i.* be of the law
Eph. 1:11 in whom obtained *i.*
14 the earnest of our *i.*
18 riches of the glory of his *i.*
5:5 hath any *i.* in kingd. of Ch.
Col. 1:12 partakers of *i.* of saints
3:24 ye shall rec. the rew. of *i.*
Heb. 1:4 he hath by *i.* obtained
9:15 promise of eternal *i.*
1 *Pet.* 1:4 begot. *i.* incorruptible

For INHERITANCE.
Ex. 34:9 take us *for* thine *i.*
Num. 18:21 tenth in Is. *f. i.* 26
26:53 land sh. be divided *f.* an *i.*
33:54; 34:2; 36:2; *Jud.* 4:21;
26; 15:4; 19:10; *Jos.* 13:6, 7,
23; 14:1; 19:49, 51; *Ezek.* 45:1;
47:22; 48:29
Deut. 20:16 the Lord doth give
thee *for* an *i.* 21:23; 24:4;
25:19; *Jos.* 11:21; 13:6;
J 14:3; 1 *K.* 8:36; 1 *Chr.* 6:27;
Jer. 3:18

INI

Ps. 2:8 give thee heathen *f. i.*
Ezek. 33:24 land is given us *f. i.*
47:14 land sh. fall to you *f.* an *i.*
Heb. 11:8 a place he sho. rec. *f. i.*

No, or None INHERITANCE.
Num. 18:20 sh. have no *i.* 21,
24 ; 26:62; *Deut.* 10:9 ; 14:27,
29; 18:1, 2; *Jos.* 13:14, 33; 14:3
2 *Chr.* 10:16 we have no *i.* in son
Acts 7:5 he gave him *none i.*

INHERITANCES.
Jos. 19:51 the *i.* Joshua divided

INHERITED, ETH.
Num. 32:18 not return till Is. *i.*
35:8 his inheriting which he *i.*
Ps. 105:44 *i.* labor of the people
Jer. 16:19 our fathers *i.* lies
Ezek. 33:24 Abraham *i.* the land
Heb. 12:17 would have *i.* blessing

INHERITOR.
Is. 65:9 out of Jud. *i.* of mount
See ENJOY, ENJOIN.

INIQUITY.
Gen. 15:16 *i.* of the Amorites
19:15 lest he consumed in *i.*
44:16 G. ha. found out *i.* of ser.
Ex. 20:5 visiting the *i.* of fathers
upon the children, 34:7;
Num. 14:18; *Deut.* 5:9
Ex. 28:38; *Lev.* 16:22; 18:25
34:7 forgiving *i. Num.* 14:18
Lev. 18:25 therefore do I visit *i.*
Num. 5:15 bringing *i.* to rem.
31 the man be guiltless from *i.*
23:21 not beheld *i.* in Jacob
Num. 22:4 God of truth with. *i.*
Jos. 22:17 is *i.* of P. too little ?
1 *Sam.* 3:14 *i.* of Eli's not purged
15:23 and stubbornness is as *i.*
20:8 if th. be in me *i.* slay me
25:24 let *i.* be, 2 *Sam.* 14:9
3 *Sam.* 14:32 if there be *i.* in me
19:19 let not L. impute *i.* to me
24:10 to take away *i.* of thy ser-
vant, 1 *Chr.* 21:8
2 *Chr.* 19:7 there is no *i.* with L.
Job 4:8 they that plough *i.*
5:16 and *i.* stoppeth her mouth
6:29 I pray you, let it not be *i.*
30 is there *i.* in my tongue?
11:6 exact. less th. *i.* deserv.
14 if *i.* be in thy hand
13:5 thy mouth uttereth thine *i.*
16 filthy is man wh. drink. *i.*
22:23 put away *i.* from thy tab.
3 *Sam.* 23:24 I may see mine *i.* ?
33:9 nor is there *i.* in me
34:32 if I have done *i.*
36:21 take heed, regard not *i.*
23 who can say, Thou wro. *i.* ?
Ps. 7:3 if be *i.* in my hands
14 behold, he travaileth with *i.*
32:2 to whom L. imputeth not *i.*
17:42 *i.* shall stop her mouth
106:14 let *i.* of his fa.'s be rem.
119:3 do no *i.* walk in his ways
138 let not *i.* have dominion
125:3 let not *i.* put forth hands to *i.*
Prov. 16:6 by truth *i.* is purged
19:28 mouth of wicked devou. *i.*
22:8 soweth *i.* shall reap vanity
Ec. 3:16 place of right. *i.* there
Is. 1:4 a people laden with *i.*
31 even the solemn meeting
5:18 woe to them that draw *i.*
6:7 thine *i.* is taken away
14:21 prepare for *i.* of fathers
22:14 *i.* not be purged from you
27:9 work for *i.* is rem. to rem.
30:13 *i.* shall be as a breach
40:2 her *i.* is pardoned
53:6 L. laid on him *i.* of us all
57:17 for *i.* of covetousness
59:2 your fingers defiled with *i.*
4 bring forth *i.* 6 works of *i.*
64:9 nor remember *i.* for ever
Jer. 2:5 what *i.* have fa. fo. in me
22 thine *i.* is marked before me
3:13 only acknowledge thine *i.*
13:22 greatn. of *i.* are thy skirts
14:20 acknowledge *i.* of fathers
16:10 our *i.* 17 *i.* hid from eyes
18 recompense *i.* 15 *i. Lam.* 5:7
32:18 recompensest *i.* of fathers
Lam. 2:14 not discovered thine *i.*

INI

Lam. 4:22 punishm. of *i.* accom.
will visit *i.* O daug. of Edom
Ezek. 4:4 lay *i.* of house of Is. on
7:13 nor strength, himself in *i.*
18:17 not die for *i.* of his father
30 so *i.* shall not be your ruin
21:23 call to remembrance *i.* 24
25 *i.* sh. have an end, 29; 35:5
28:15 till *i.* found in thee
18 defiled sanctu. by *i.* of traf.
41:12 houses of Israel fall into *i.*
Dan. 9:24 reconciliation for *i.*
Hos. 7:1 *i.* of Ephraim discovered
10:9 children of *i.* 13 reaped *i.*
12:8 they shall find no *i.* in me
11 is there *i.* in Gilead ?
13:12 *i.* of Ephraim bound up
14:1 thou hast fallen by thine *i.*
2 take away *i.* rec. graciously
Mic. 2:1 woe to them devise *i.*
3:10 build up Jerusalem with *i.*
Hab. 2:12 like thee, pardoneth *i. ?*
Hab. 1:13 canst not look on *i.*
2:12 woe to him estab. city by *i.*
Zep. 3:5 just Lord, will not do *i.*
13 remnant of Israel not do *i.*
Zec. 3:4 caused *i.* pass from thee
9 remove *i.* of land in one day
Mal. 2:6 *i.* not found in his lips
Mat. 13:41 gather them wh. do *i.*
23:28 are full of hypocrisy and *i.*
24:12 because *i.* shall abound
Acts 1:18 field with reward of *i.*
8:23 thou art in bond of *i.*
Rom. 6:19 servants to *i.* unto *i.*
1 *Cor.* 13:6 rejoiceth not in *i.* but
2 *Thes.* 2:7 mystery of *i.* doth w.
2 *Tim.* 2:19 nameth C. dep. fr. *i.*
Tit. 2:14 might redeem us fr. *i.*
Heb. 1:9 and thou hast hated *i.*
Jam. 3:6 tong. is fire, world of *i.*
See BEAR, COMMIT, COMMITTED.

His INIQUITY.
Num. 15:31 *his i.* be upon him
Job 20:27 heavens revealed *his i.*
21:19 G. layeth up *i.* for chil.
Ps. 36:2 *his i.* be found hateful
Jer. 31:30 die for *his i. Ezek.*
3:18, 19 ; 7:16 ; 18:26
Ezek. 1:17 stum.-block of *h. i.* 17
14:18 sh. die in *h. i.* 33:8, 9
33:6 he is taken away in *his i.*
2 *Pet.* 2:16 Bal. rebuked for *h. i.*

Mine INIQUITY.
1 *Sam.* 20:1 what is *mine i. ?*
2 *Sam.* 22:24 I kept *myself* from *mine i. Ps.* 38:27
Job 7:21 not take away *m. i. ?*
10:6 thou inquirest after *m. i.*
11 not acquit me from *mine i.*
31:33 hiding *m. i.* in my bosom
Ps. 32:11 pardon *m. i.* it is great
51:10 sire, faileth beca. of *m. i.*
32:5 *mine i.* have I not hid
38:18 for I will declare *mine i.*
51:2 wash me thoro. fr. *m. i.*

Their INIQUITY.
Lev. 26:39 pine away in *their i.*
40 if they confess *th. i.* 41, 43
Num. 4:5 and cover not *their i.*
Neh. 4:5 cover not *their i.*
Ps. 69:27 add *i.* unto *t. i.*
94:23 bring upon them *their i.*
106:43 were bro. low for *their i.*
Jer. 13:11 punish wicked for *t. i.*
16:18 I will recompense *th. i.*
18:23 know counsel to slay us
25:12 I will punish them for *th. i.*
32:18 thou recompensest *t. i.*
Lam. 4:13 for *i.* of her priests
Ezek. 28:18 by multi. of thine *i.*
Dan. 4:27 break off thine *i.*
9:13 we might turn from our *i.*
Mic. 7:19 he will subdue our *i.*
Acts 3:26 turn. ev. one fr. his *i.*
Rom. 4:7 blessed they wh. *i.* for.
Rev. 18:3 God hath renewab. *i.*

Their INIQUITIES.
Lev. 16:22 goat bear on him *t. i.*
Ps. 107:17 fools bec. of *their i.*
Is. 53:11 he shall bear *their i.*
Jer. 33:8 I will pardon all *their i.*
Lam. 5:7 we have borne *t. i.*
Ezek. 32:27 *t. i.* be on their bones
Heb. 8:12 *t. i.* rem. no more, 10:17

Your INIQUITIES.
Num. 14:34 forty ye. ye bear *y. i.*
Is. 50:1 for y. *i.* ye sold yourself
53:2 y. *i.* separated you and G.
65:7 *your i.* I will recompense
Jer. 5:25 y. *i.* turned away thin.
Ezek. 24:23 ye pine away for *y. i.*
36:31 lothe yourselves for *y. i.*
Amos 3:2 punish you for *y. i.*

INJURED.
Gal. 4:12 ye have not *i.* me at all

INJURIOUS.
1 *Tim.* 1:13 a persecutor and *i.*

INJUSTICE.
Job 16:17 not for *i.* in my hands

INK.
Jer. 36:18 wrote them with *i.*
2 *Cor.* 3:3 not with *i.* but the S.
2 *John* 12 not wr. wi. *i.* 3 *John* 13

INKHORN.
Ezek. 9:2 writer's *i.* by side, 3, 11

INN.
Gen. 42:27 ass proven, in the *i.*
43:21 came to *i.* opened sacks
Ex. 4:24 in the *i.* met him
Luke 2:7 no room for them in *i.*
10:34 brought him to an *i.*

INNER.
1 *K.* 6:27 cherubim in *i.* house
1 *Chr.* 28:11 patterns of *i.* parlors
Est. 4:11 to king into *i.* court
5:1 Esther stood in the *i.* court
Ezek. 10:3 cloud filled the *i.* cou.
42:15 end of measuring *i.* house
46:1 gate of *i.* court sh. six da.
Acts 16:24 thrust th. into *i.* pris.
Eph. 3:16 strengthened in *i.* man
See CHAMBER.

INNERMOST.
Prov. 18:8 *i.* parts of belly, 26:22

INNOCENCY.
Gen. 20:5 in the *i.* of my hands
Ps. 26:6 wash my hands in *i.*
73:13 I washed hands in *i.*
Dan. 6:22 *i.* was found in me
Hos. 8:5 how long ere attain
to *i. ?*

INN

Ps. 14:4 *w. of i.* no knowl. ? 53:4
28:3 draw not away wi. *w. of i.*
36:12 the *w. of i.* fallen
37:1 nor be envious ag. *w. of i.*
59:2 deliver me from *w. of i.*
64:2 insurrection of the *w. of i.*
92:7 all the *w. of i.* do flourish
9 the *w. of i.* shall be scattered
94:4 *w. of i.* boast themselves
16 stand up for me ags. *w. of i.*
125:5 lead th. forth with *w. of i.*
141:9 keep me fr. gins of *w. of i.*
Prov. 10:29 dest. to *w. of i.* 21:15

INIQUITIES.
Lev. 16:21 confess over goat all *i.*
26:39 in *i.* of fa. sh. they pine
Ezr. 9:6 *i.* Increased over head
13 punished beca. *i.* deserved
Neh. 9:2 Is. confessed *i.* of fath.
Job 13:23 how many are mine *i.*
26 makest me to poss. *i.* of yo.
22:5 wicked. great, *i.* infinite
Ps. 38:4 *i.* gone over my head
40:12 *i.* have taken hold upon me
51:9 hide fa. fr. sins, blot out *i.*
61:6 search out *i.* 65:3 *i.* preva.
79:8 remember not ag. us *i.*
90:8 hast set our *i.* before
103:3 L. who forgiveth all *i.*
10 nor rewarded us accord. to *i.*
130:3 shou. mark *i.* who stand ?
8 redeem Israel from all his *i.*
Prov. 5:22 own *i.* take wicked
Is. 43:24 wearied me with th. *i.*
53:5 he was bruised for our *i.*
59:12 our *i.* we know them
61:8 *i.* like wind taken us away
7 consum. us because of our *i.*
Jer. 11:10 to *i.* of forefathers
14:7 though our *i.* testify ag. us
Lam. 4:13 for *i.* of her priests
Ezek. 28:18 by multi. of thine *i.*
Dan. 4:27 break off thine *i.*
9:13 we might turn from our *i.*
Mic. 7:19 he will subdue our *i.*
Acts 3:26 turn. ev. one fr. his *i.*
Rom. 4:7 blessed they wh. *i.* for.
Rev. 18:5 God hath rememb. *i.*

Work INIQUITY.
Ps. 141:4 with men that w. *i.*
Hos. 6:8 city of them that w. *i.*
Mat. 7:23 depart fr. me, ye w. *i.*

Workers of INIQUITY.
Job 31:3 punishment to *w. of i.*
34:8 go in comp. with *w. of i.*
22 *w. of i.* hide themselves
Ps. 5:5 hatest all *workers of i.*
6:8 all you ye *w. of i. Luke* 13:27

CRUDEN'S CONCORDANCE.

ISL

Jo?. 17:18 they have *i*. chariots
Job 19:24 graven with *i*. pen
20:24 shaft *i*. shaft *i*es from *i*. weapon
Is. 48:4 thy neck is an *i*. sinew
Jer. 1:18 thee this day *i*. pillar
Ezek. 4:3 take unto thee *i*. pan
Dan. 7:7 it had great *i*. teeth
Acts 12:10 came to the *i*. gate

IRONS.
Job 41:7 fill skin with barbed *i*. ?

IS.
Rev. 1:4 which *i*. was, and *i*. to come, 8 ; 4:8
17:8 that was, *i*. not, yet *i*.
10 one *i*. the other *i*. not come

IS not.
Gen. 37:30 said, The child *i*. not
44:13 youn. with fa. one *i*. n. 32
42:36 Joseph *i*. not, Simeon *i*. n.
Rev. 17:8 beast was, and *i*. n. 11

ISAAC.
Gen. 17:19 his name I. 21:3, 12
21:10 heir with my son, even I.
22:2 take thine only son I. 9
23:1 take a wife for I. 14
25:5 had unto I. 9, 11, 23, 26
26:1 I. went to Abimelech
23:1 I. called Jacob, blessed h.
31:42 fear of I. had been with
35:27 Jacob came to I. 29
44:15 God before wh. I. walked
Ex. 3:6 the God of I. 15, 16; 4:5;
Gen. 26:2 ; 1 K. 18:36 ; 1 *Chr*.
29:18; 2 *Chr*. 30:6; *Mat*. 22:32;
Mark 12:26; *Luke* 20:37;
Acts 3:13
Jos. 24:3 and gave him I.
1 *Chr*. 16:16 unto I. *Ps*. 105:9
Amos 7:9 high places of I.
Mat. 1:2 Abraham begat I. and I. begat J. *Luke* 3:34; *Acts* 7:8
8:11 many shall sit down with I.
Luke 13:28 see I. in kingd. of G.
Rom. 9:10 conceived by father I.
Gal. 4:28 we, as I. was, are of pro.
Heb. 11:9 in tabernacles with I.
17 Abraham offered up I.
33 I. blessed Jacob, *Jam*. 2:21

ISAIAH, or ESAIAS.
2 *K*. 19:2 Eliakim to I. 20; 2 *Chr*.
26:1 I. came to him, *Is*. 38:1
2 *Chr*. 26:22 acts did I. wr. 32:32
Is. 20:3 my serv. I. hath walked
Mat. 3:3 pro. E. 4:14 ; 8:17 ; 12:17 ;
13:14 ; *Luke* 3:4 ; *John* 1:23
15:7 E. proph. of you, *Mark* 7:6
Luke 4:17 book of prophet E.
John 12:39 bec. that E. said, 41
Acts 8:28 the eunuch read E. 30
23:25 spake the H. Ghost by E.
Rom. 9:27 E. crieth conc. Israel
10:16 E. saith, L. who hath ? 20
13:12 E. saith, There shall be

ISCARIOT. *See* JUDAS.
ISII-BOSHETH. 2 *Sam*. 2:6;
3:8, 14; 4:8, 12

ISHMAEL.
Gen. 16:11 call name I. 15, 16
17:18 O that I. mi. live, 20, 25
25:17 these are the years of I.
28:9 then went Esau unto I.
2 *K*. 25:23 I. came to, *Jer*. 40:8
Jer. 40:14 Ammon, sent I. 15, 16
41:6 I. went to meet the, 10, 15

ISHMAELITES.
Gen. 37:27 let us sell him to I.
39:1 Potiphar bought him of I.
Jud. 8:24 because they were I.
Ps. 83:6 I. confederate ag. thee

ISLAND.
Job 22:30 deliver *i*. of innocent
Is. 34:14 most wild beasts of *i*.
Acts 27:16 running under cert. *i*.
26 must he cast on certain *i*.
24:1 knew *i*. was called Melita
i. possess. of chief man of *i*.
28:9 who had diseases in *i*.
Rev. 6:14 every *i*. was moved out
16:20 every *i*. fled away

ISLANDS.
Is. 11;11 recover people from *i*.
13:22 wild beasts of *i*. shall cry
41:1 keep silence bef. me, O *i*.
42:12 declare Lord's praise in *i*.
15 make rivers *i*. dry up pools
59:18 the *i*. he will pay recomp.
Jer. 50:39 wild beasts of *i*. dwell

ISLE.
Is. 20:6 the inhabitant of the *i*.
23:2 be still, inhabitants of *i*.
6 howl, ye inhabitants of the *i*.
Acts 13:6 through *i*. to Paphos
28:11 ship which wintered in *i*.
Rev. 1:9 was in *i*. called Patmos

ISS

ISLES.
Gen. 10:5 th. were *i*. of Gentiles
Est. 10:1 A. laid a tribute on *i*.
Ps. 72:10 kings of *i*. bring pres.
97;1 let multitudes of *i*. be glad
Is. 24:15 glorify Lord in the *i*.
40:15 tak. up *i*. as a little thing
41:5 the *i*. saw it and feared
42:4 the *i*. shall wait for his law
49:1 listen, O *i*. unto me
51:5 *i*. shall wait upon me and trust. 60:9
60:19 *i*. afar off not heard fame
Jer. 2:10 pass over *i*. of Chittim
23:22 kings of *i*. drink after th.
Ezek. 26:15 sh. not *i*. sh. at sou, ?
18 *i*. tremble, *i*. shall be troub.
27:3 merch. of peo. for many *i*.
6 brought out of *i*. of Chittim
7 blue and purple from *i*. of E.
15 many *i*. were merchandise
35 inhabit. of *i*. be astonished
39:6 devil carelessly in the *i*.
Dan. 11:18 siu. turn his face to *i*.
Zep. 2:11 *i*. of heathen worship

ISRAEL.
Gen. 32:28 na. no more J. but I.
35:10 I. sh. he name, 1 *K*. 18:31
47:31 I. bowed him. on bed's h.
48:20 in thee sh. I. bless, 49:21
8:2 voice to let I. go, 14:5,30
Num. 10:29 good concerning I.
36 return to I. 20:14 ; 21:2, 17
23:7 deiy I. ; 24:17 out of I.
Deut. 33:2,1 dwell, 1 *K*. 4:25
1 *Chr*. 22:13 O. of I. 1 *K*. 18:26 ;
1 *Chr*. 6:16 ; 30:6 ; *Mat*. 15:31
Ps. 14:7 I. shall be glad. 53:6
25:22 redeem I. out of all troub.
131:4 that keepeth I. not. slum.
123:5 peace sh. be upon I. 128:6
Jer. 14:8 O Lord, hope of I. 17:13
50:20 iniquity of I. sought, 51:5
Hos. 11:1 I. a child, I loved him
8 how deliver thee, I. ? 12:14
Acts 28:20 for hope of I. bought
Rom. 9:6 not all I. of I. 27, 31
10:1 prayer for I. they be saved
19 did not I. know?
11:2 intercession ap. I. 7, 21
1 *Cor*. 10:18 behold I. after flesh
Gal. 6:16 peace upon the I. of G.

O ISRAEL.
Jer. 32:4 these be thy gods, O I.
Num. 24:5 thy tabernacles, O I.
Deut. 4:1 hearken, O I. 5:1; 6:3;
5:1 O I. 6:3, 4; 9:1 ; 20:3 ; *Ps*.
50:7; *Is*. 44:1 ; 48:12
33:29 happy th. O I. *Mark* 12:29
2 *Sam*. 20:1 cv. man to his tents, O I. ; 1 *K*. 12:16 ; 2 *Chr*. 10:16
1 *K*. 12:28 behold thy gods, O I.
Jabok. 22:20 for hope of I. *Deut*. 2:37;
3:16 ; *Jos*. 14:8
43:1 O I. fear not, 22 ; *Jer*. 30:10
4:22 remember these, O I. 40:3
Jer. 4:1 return, O I. *Hos*. 14:1
8:3 O I. thy prophets
Hos. 9:1 rejoice not, O I. for joy
10:9 O I. thou hast sinned from
13:9 O I. thou hast destr. thys.
Amos 4:12 to meet thy God, O I.
Zep. 9:14 shout O I. be glad

ISRAELITE.
Num. 23:14 the I. that was slain
2 *Sam*. 17:25 son of Ithra, an I.
John 1:47 behold an I. indeed
Rom. 11:1 I also am an I.

ISRAELITES.
Ex. 9:7 not one of cattle of I.
Lev. 23:42 I. shall dwell in booths
Jos. 3:17 I. passed on dry ground
1 *Chr*. 9:2 first inhabit. were I.
Rom. 9:4 I. to whom pertaineth
2 *Cor*. 11:22 are they I.? so am I.

ISRAELITISH. *Lev*. 24:10, 11

ISSACHAR.
Gen. 30:18 L. called his name I.
49:14 I. is a strong ass
Num. 26:25 called by name I.
4:17 sh. come a Star out of J.
26:21 I. shall be for my people
Jos. 19:1 God of J. 46:7 ; 75:9 ; 76:6
81:1 ; 84:8 ; 94:7 ; 114:7 ; 132:3 ; 146:5
57:2 Z. more than dwell. of J.
103:23 J. sojourned in land of H.
135:4 L. chos. J. 21 ; 148:14 ; 149:1
2 *Chr*. 30:18 I. had not cleansed
Ezek. 48:25 border of Simeon, I.

Tribe of ISSACHAR.
Num. 1:29 numbered of *t*. of I.
2:5 next Judah shall be *t*. of I.
31:26 prince of *t*. of I.? Pallied
Jos. 19:23 inheritance of *t*. of I.
21:6 families of *tribe of* I. and
Ezek. 48:26 ; 1 *Chr*. 6:62, 72
Rev. 7:7 *t*. of J., were seal, 12,000

JAC

ISSUE, Substantive.
Gen. 48:6 *i*. which th. begettest
Lev. 12:7 *i*. of blood, 15:25 ; *Mat*.
9:20; *Mark* 5:25; *Luke* 8:43, 44
15:2 hath running of *i*. 3 ° 32:4
3 he that hath *i*. spit upon, 28
Is. 22:24 the offspring and *i*.
Ezek. 23:20 *i*. like the *i*. of horses
Mat. 22:25 having no *i*. left wife

ISSUE.
2 *K*. 20:18 sons that *i*. *Is*. 39:7
Ezek. 47:8 waters *i*. toward east

ISSUED.
Job 38:8 break forth as if it *i*.
Ezek. 47:1 waters *i*. from under
12 waters *i*. out of sanctuary
Dan. 7:10 fiery str. *i*. came forth
Mic. 9:17 out of mouth *i*. fire 18

ISSUES.
Ps. 08:20 to God belong the *i*.
Prov. 4:23 out of heart are *i*.

ITALY. *Acts* 18:2
27:1 that we should sail into I.
Heb. 13:24 they of I. salute you

ITCH, ING.
Deut. 28:27 L. smite thee with *i*.
2 *Tim*. 4:3 teachers having *i*. ears

ITHAMAR.
Ex. 6:23 Abihu and I, 1 *Chr*. 6:3
Num. 4:28 under hand of I.
1 *Chr*. 24:3 Ahimel. of sons of I.
Ezr. 8:2 of the sons of I. Daniel

ITHIEL.
Neh. 11:7 I. son of Jes. *Prov*. 30:1

ITUREA. *Luke* 3:1

IVAH.
2 *K*. 18:34 gods of Hena and I. ?
19:13 wh. king of I. ? *Is*. 37:13

IVORY.
1 *K*. 10:18 throne of *i*. 2 *Chr*. 9:17
22 silver and *i*. 2 *Chr*. 9:21
22:29 *i*. house wh. Ahab made
Ps. 45:8 out of the *i*. palaces
Cant. 5:14 his belly as bright *i*.
7:4 thy neck is as a tower of *i*.
Amos 3:15 houses of *i*. sh. perish
6:4 that lie upon beds of *i*.
Rev. 18:12 no man buy. ves. of *i*.

J.

JAAZANIAH.
2 *K*. 25:23 J. came to Gedaliah
Jer. 35:3 J. of Hechab, *Ezek*. 8:11

JABAL. *Gen*. 4:20

JABBOK. *Gen*. 32:22; *Deut*. 2:37;
3:16; *Jos*. 12:2

JABESH.
1 *Sam*. 11:5 S. of men of J. 31:12
2 *K*. 15:10 the son of J. conspired

J ; DESH-GILEAD.
Jud. 21:8 none fr. J.-G. 10, 12, 14
1 *Sam*. 11:1 Naha. enc. ag. J.-G.
31:11 J.-G. heard Phi. had done,
1 *Chr*. 10:11
2 *Sam*. 2:4 men of J.-G. 21:12

JABIN.
Jos. 11:1 when J. king of Hazor
Jud. 4:2 sold into hand of J. 24
Ps. 83:9 do to them as unto J.

JABNEH.
2 *Chr*. 26:6

JACHIN.
1 *K*. 7:21 right h. J. 2 *Chr*. 3:17

JACINTH.
Rev. 9:17 breastplates of fire, J.
21:20 eleventh found. was a J.

JACOB.
Gen. 25:26 he was called J. 27
Num. 23:7 curse me, J. and defy
24:17 wh. come a Star out of J.
Est. 33:29 of J. on land of corn
Ps. 20:1 God of J. 40:7; 75:9; 76:6
81:1 ; 84:8 ; 94:7 ; 114:7 ; 132:3 ;
146:5
57:2 Z. more than dwell. of J.
103:23 J. sojourned in land of H.
135:4 L. chos. J. 21 ; 148:14 ; 149:1
Is. 2:5 of J. 41:21 ; *Mic*. 4:2 ; *Mal*.
2:2,12; *Mat*. 22:32 ; *Mark* 12:26 ; *Luke* 20:37;
Acts 3:13 ; 7:32, 46
27:9 iniq. of J. purged, 48:20
41:14 thou worm J. *Jer*. 30:10
41:5 call himself by name J. 23
58:14 feed with heritage of J.
Amos 7:2 by whom sh. J. arise ? 5
Jer. 2:3 J. yet I loved J. *Ro*. 9:13
3:6 sons of J. not consumed

JEA

Mat. 1:2 I. begat J. ; 15 Matthan
8:11 J. in king. of G. *Luke* 13:28
John 4:6 J.'s well was there
Rom. 11:26 turn ungodl. from J.
Heb. 11:20 by faith Is. bles. J. 21

JAEL.
Jud. 4:17 fled to tent of J. 5:6
JAIL. *Pr*. 68:4

JAHAZ.
Num. 21:23 fou. at J. *Deut*. 2:32
Is. 15:4 heard to J. *Jud*. 11:20

JAHAZAH.
Jos. 21:36 J. to Lev. *Jer*. 48:21

JAILER.
Acts 16:23 charging J. to keep

JAIR.
Num. 32:41 J. took to. *Deut*. 3:14
Jud. 10:3 J. judged Is. 22 years
5 J. died ; 1 *Chr*. 2:22 begat J.

JAIRUS.
Mark 5:22 J. a ruler, *Luke* 8:41
JAMBRES. 2 *Tim*. 3:8

JAMES.
Mat. 4:21 J. and John, *Mark* 1:19
10:3 J. son of Zeb. *Mark* 3:17
3 J. son, *Mark* 3:18; *Acts* 1:13
13:55 J. and Joses, *Mark* 6:3 ;
15:40 ; 16:1 ; *Luke* 24:10
17:1 Peter, J. and John, *Mark*
5:37; 9:2 ; 13:3 ; 14:33 ; *Luke*
8:51 ; *Acts* 1:13
Mark 16:41 disci. w'. J. *Lu*. 5:10
Acts 12:2 Herod killed J. wi. sw.
Gal. 1:19 save J. Lord's brother
2:12 certain came from J. 9

JANGLING.
1 *Tim*. 1:6 turned aside to vain *j*.

JANNA. *Luke* 3:24
JANNES. 2 *Tim*. 3:9

JAPHETH.
Gen. 5:32 J. son of N. 6:10; 7:13
9:23 Shem and J. took garm. 18
27 God en. enlarge J. 1 *Ch*. 1:4
10:1 unto J. sons born, 21

JAREB. *Hos*. 5:13 ; 10:6
JARED. *Gen*. 5:15; *Luke* 8:37
JASHER. *Jos*. 10:13 ; 2 *Sam*. 1:18

JASON.
Acts 17:5 house of J. *Rom*. 16:21

JASPER.
Ex. 28:20 onyx and *j*. 39:13
Ezek. 28:13 diamond and *j*. cov.
Rev. 4:3 to look upon like to *j*.
21:11 light was like to *j*. stone
18 build. of wall of city was *j*.
19 the first foundation was *j*.

JAVAN.
Gen. 10:2 sons of Jap. J. 1 *Chr*. 1:5
Is. 66:19 those that escape to J.
Ezek. 27:13 J. and Tubal thy, 19

JAVELIN.
Num. 25:7 took a *j*. in his hand
1 *Sam*. 18:10 J. in S. hand, 19:9
20:33 he smote the *j*. into wall

JAW.
Jud. 15:19 God clave place in *j*.
Ps. 22:15 tongue cleaveth to *j*.
Is. 30:28 a bridle in *j*. of people
Hos. 11:4 take off yoke on their *j*.

JAWBONE.
Jud. 15:15 Samson found *j*. of ass
16 with *j*. of ass have I slain
17 cast away *j*. out of his hand

JAW-TEETH.
Prov. 30:14 their *j*. *d*. as knives

JAZER.
Num. 32:1 land of J. 3 ; *Is*. 16:9

JEALOUS.
Ex. 20:5 the Lord thy G. am a J. God. 34:14 ; *Deut*. 4:24 ;
5:9; 6:15 ; 24:19
1 *K*. 19:10 have been *j*. for L. 14
Ezek. 36:25 ; for my holy name
Joel 2:18 then will the L. be *j*.
Nah. 1:2 God is *j*. and L. reven.
Zec. 1:14, *j*. for Jer. ; 8:2, *j*. for Z.
2 *Cor*. 11:2 I am *j*. over you

JEALOUSY.
Num. 5:14 sp. of *j*. come on him
15 it is an offering of *j*. 18, 25
29 this is the law of *j*.
25:11 consumed not Is. in my *j*.
32:16 prov. him to *j*. 1 *K*. 14:22
21 moved me to *j*. *Rom*. 10:19

CRUDEN'S CONCORDANCE.

JOU

1 *Chr.* 20:25 Levites J. over tre.
2 *Chr.* 22:7 destr. by com. to J.

JORDAN.

Gen. 13:11 Lot chose plain of J.
Jos. 3:15 J. overfloweth banks
4:3 stones out of midst of J.
22:25 made J. a border betw. us
Jud. 3:28 fords of J. 7:24; 12:5
2 *Sam.* 19:15 king returned to J.
2 *K.* 2:13 Elisha stood by J.
5:10 saying, Wash in J. seven
Job 40:23 trust, can draw up J.
Ps. 42:6 remember fr. land of J.
114:3 J. was driven back, 5
Jer. 12:5 do in swelling of J. ?
49:19 from swelling of J. 50:44
Zec. 11:3 pride of J. is spoiled
Mat. 3:6 in J. *Mark* 1:5, 9

Beyond JORDAN.

Gen. 50:10 floor of Atad bey. J, 11
Deut. 3:25 good land beyond J.
Jos. 13:8 inherit. beyond J. 18:7
Is. 9:1 bey. J. in Galil. *Mat.* 4:15
John 1:28 Bethabara bey. J. 3:26

Over JORDAN.

Gen. 32:10 I passed over J.
Num. 32:5 br. us not o. J. 33:51
Deut. 3:27 not go o. J. 4:21; 31:2
9:1 to pass o. J. this day, 11:31
Jos. 1:2 go over J. 11
4:22 Israel came over J. 24:11
2 *Sam.* 2:29 passed o. J. 17:22;
19:15; 1 *Chr.* 12:15; 19:17

JORIM, JOSE. *Luke* 3:29

JOSEPH.

Gen. 30:24 she called his name J.
37:5 J. dreamed a dream
32:5 Egypt, 's house for J.'s sake
42:6 butler told his dream to J.
43:32 J. is a fruitful bough, 26
50:7 J. went up to bury father
Deut. 33:13 J. blessed be his land
1 *Chr.* 5:2 the birthright was J.
Ps. 81:1 leadest J. like a flock
105:17 J. who was sold for a ser.
Ezek. 37:16 for J. stick of Ephr.
47:13 J. shall have two portions
48:32 one gate of J. gate of D.
Amos 6:6 grieved for afflict. of J.
Acts 7:9 patriarchs sold J. 13, 14
Heb. 11:21 J. blessed sons of J. 22

JOSEPH, *husband of Mary.*
Mat. 1:16; 2:13; *Luke* 2:4; 3:23;
4:22; *John* 1:45; 6:42

JOSEPH, *name of divers men.*
Num. 13:7 of Igal, son of J.
Mat. 27:57 J. of Arim. 59; *Mark*
15:43, 45; *Lu.* 23:50; *Jo.* 19:38
Luke 3:24 was son of J. 26, 30
Acts 1:23 two, J. called Barsabas

JOSES.

Mat. 13:55 Ja. and J. *Mark* 6:3
27:55 moth. of J. *Mark* 15:40, 47
Acts 4:35 J. surnamed Barnabas

JOSHUA, JEHOSHUA, OSHEA.
Ex. 17:13 J. discomfited Amalek
24:13 Moses and his minister J.
Jos. 1:10 J. commanded officers,
9:1 to 24:31
1 *Sam.* 6:14 into field of J. 18
1 *K.* 16:34 wh. he spake by J.
Hag. 1:1 J. son of Josed. 12, 14
Zec. 3:1 showed me J. h.-priest
6:11 set crowns on head of J.

JOSIAH.

1 *K.* 13:2 child born, J. by name
2 *K.* 21:24 J. king, 2 *Chr.* 33:25
22:1 J. was eight years old
23:29 J. ag. Phar. 2 *Chr.* 35:22
2 *Chr.* 35:1 J. kept passo. 18–25
Jer. 1:2 in days of J. 3:6
22:11 word came in days of J.
Mat. 1:10 Amon begat J. 11

JOT.

Mat. 5:18 one J. or tittle

JOTHAM.

Jud. 9:5 J. son of Jerubbaal, 21
2 *K.* 15:5 J. judged, 2 *Chr.* 26:21
1 *Chr.* 2:47 sons of Jahdai, J. 5:17
2 *Chr.* 27:6 J. became mighty
Is. 1:1; *Ho.* 1:1; *Mic.* 1:1; *Mat.* 1:9

JOURNEY.

Gen. 24:21 L. made J. prosperous
31:23 La. pursued him 7 days' J.
Ex. 13:20 took J. from Succoth
16:1 Israelites took J. from Elim
Num. 9:10 be in J. yet keep pass.
13 not in J. forbear. keep pass.
Deut. 10:11 take thy J. before people
Jos. 9:11 take victuals for your J.
Jud. 4:9 J. thou takest not

JOY

1 *Sam.* 18:18 L. sent thee on a J.
1 *K.* 18:27 or he is in a J.
19:7 the J. is too great for thee
2 *K.* 3:9 compa. of seven days' J.
Neh. 2:6 how long sh. thy J. be?
Prov. 7:19 man gone a long J.
Mat. 10:10 nor scrip for your J.
Mark 6:8 nothing for J. *Luke* 9:3
Luke 11:6 a friend of mine in J.
15:13 took J. into a far country
John 4:6 Jesus wearied with J.
Rom. 1:10 have prosperous J.
15:24 I trust to see you in my J.
1 *Cor.* 16:6 bring me on my J.
Tit. 3:13 Zenas and Apollos on J.
3 *John* 6 whom bring forw. on J.

Day's JOURNEY.

Num. 11:31 quails fall a day's J.
1 *K.* 19:4 went day's J. to wild.
Jon. 3:4 to enter city d.'s J.
Luke 2:44 a d.'s J. am. acquaint.
Acts 1:12 from Jerusal. a day's J.

See Three DAYS.

JOURNEYED.

Gen. 12:9 Ab. J. going south, 20:1
13:11 Lot J. east; 33:17 Jacob J.
33:8 Israel J. toward Beth-el
Ex. 40:37 th. J. not, *Num.* 9:21
Num. 9:17 children of Israel J. 18
19 kept charge of L. and J. not
Acts 9:3 as S., J. he came near Da.
7 men J. with him stood, 26:13

JOURNEYING.

Num. 10:28 J. of Israel's armies
29 we are J. to the place
Luke 13:22 as he was J. toward J.
2 *Cor.* 11:26 in J. often, in perils

JOURNEYS.

Gen. 13:3 Abram went on his J.
Ex. 17:1 J. according to comma.
40:36 went on in J. *Num.* 10:12
38 cloud on taber. thro' their J.
Num. 10:6 an alarm for their J.
33:1 these are the J. of Israel, 2

JOY, Substantive.

1 *Chr.* 12:40 there was J. in Israel
15:16 lift. up the voice with J.
25 went to bring the ark wi. J.
29:17 seen with J. the peo. offer
Ezr. 3:12 hol discern shout of J.
6:16 ded. of hou. of God with J.
Neh. 8:10 J. of L. is your strength
12:43 J. of Jern. heard afar off
8:12 8:16 light, J. and honor
9:22 turned from sorrow to J.
make days of feasting and J.
Job 8:19 this is the J. of his way
20:5 J. of hypocrite but a mom.
29:13 caus. widow's hea. sing J.
33:26 will see his face with J.
41:22 sorrow turned to J.
Ps. 16:11 presence fulness of J.
27:6 offer in taber. sacrifi. of J.
30:5 J. cometh in the morning
42:4 I went with the voice of J.
43:4 I go to G. my exceeding J.
48:2 J. of the earth is mount Z.
51:12 restore to me J. of salva.
67:4 be glad and sing for J.
105:43 bro. forth people with J.
126:5 sow in tears sh. reap in J.
137:6 prefer not Jer. to chief J.
Prov. 12:20 counsel of peace is J.
14:10 stranger not intermed. J.
15:21 folly is J. desti. of wisdom
23 man hath J. by ans. of moth.
17:21 father of a fool hath no J.
21:15 J. to the just to do judg.
Ec. 2:10 with. not heart from J.
26 God giveth knowled. and J.
5:20 God ans. him in J. of heart
9:7 go thy way, eat bread wi. J.
Is. 9:3 increased J. accord. to J.
12 L. sh. have no J. in yo. mee.
12:3 with J. shall ye draw water
16:10 J. taken out plentiful field
24:8 J. harp ceas.; 11 J. is dark.
32:13 houses of J. 14 J. w. asses
35:2 rej. even with J. and sing.
51:3 J. and gladness shall be
52:9 my soul be J. in the Lord
61:3 J. for mourn. 7 J. shall be
Jer. 15:16 word was J. of my hea.
31:13 turn th. mourning into J.
33:9 it sh. be to me a name of J.
48:27 whom skippedst for J.

JOY

Jer. 48:33 J. is tak. fr. plen. field
49:25 city of my J.
Lam. 5:15 the J. of our heart
5:15 the J. of our heart is ceased
Ezek. 24:25 take fr. them J. of gl.
36:5 with in. J. of all th. heart
Dan. 0:1 rejoiced not, O Is. for J.
Joel 1:12 J. is withered from men
Zep. 3:17 rejo. over thee with J.
Mat. 13:20 anon with J. receiveth
it, *Luke* 8:13
44 for J. thereof goeth and sell.
25:21 enter into J. of thy L. 23
Lu. 1:44 babe leaped in wo. for J.
6:23 rej. in that day, leap for J.
10:17 seventy returned with J.
15:7 J. in heav. over one sinner
10 there is J. in pres. of angels
24:41 they yet believed not for J.
John 3:29 my J. therefo. is fulfil.
15:11 that my J. might remain in
you, th. your J. might be full
16:20 sorrow be turned to J.
21 for J. that a man is born
22 your J. no man tak. fr. you
24 that your J. be full
17:13 J. fulfilled in themselves
22:28 make me full of J.
Rom. 14:17 kingdom of God is J.
15:13 God filled you with J.
32 co. to you wi. J. by will of G.
2 *Cor.* 1:24 are helpers of your J.
2:3 that my J. is J. of you all
7:13 more joyed we for J. of T.
8:2 their J. abounded to riches
Gal. 5:22 Spirit is love, J. peace
Phil. 1:4 making request with J.
25 furtherance and J. of faith
2:2 my J. 4:1 J. and crown
1 *Thes.* 1:6 received word with J.
2:19 what is our hope or J. ?
20 for ye are our glory and J.
2 *Tim.* 1:4 I may be filled with J.
Philem. 20 let me have J. of thee
Heb. 12:2 for J. that was bef. him
12:17 do it with J. not with grief
Jam. 1:2 count J. when ye fall
4:9 J. be turned into heaviness
1 *Pet.* 1:8 rej. with J. unspeakab.
4:13 glad also with exceeding J.
1 *John* 1:4 J. be full, 2 *John* 12
3 *John* 4 no greater J. than to h.
Jude 24 faultless with exceed. J.

See GLADNESS.

Great JOY.

1 *K.* 1:40 peo. rejoiced with g. J.
1 *Chr.* 29:9 rejoiced, in Jerusalem
Neh. 12:43 rejoice with great J.
Mat. 2:10 rejoiced with great J.
28:8 from sep. wi. fear and g. J.
Luke 2:10 br. tidings of great J.
24:52 returned to Jer. with g. J.
Acts 8:8 there was g. J. in th. city
15:3 caused g. J. to the brethren
Phile. 7 we have g. J. in thy love

Shout, or Shouted for JOY.

Ezr. 3:12 shouted aloud for J.
Job 38:7 sons of God shouted f. J.
Ps. 5:11 let th. shout for J. 35:27
32:11 s. for J. 132:9, 16 let up.
63:13 the valleys shout for J.
132:9 let thy saints s. for J. 16

JOY, Verb.

Ps. 21:1 shall J. in thy strength
Is. 9:3 bef. thee rejoice and J.
65:19 I rejoice and J. in my peo.
Hab. 3:18 I will J. in G. of salva.
Zep. 3:17 J. over thee with sing.
Rom. 5:11 but we also J. in God
Phil. 2:17 J. and rejoice wi. you
1 *Thes.* 3:9 joy wherewith we J.

JOYED.

2 *Cor.* 7:13 more joy for joy of T.

JOYFUL.

Ezr. 6:22 L. hath made them J.
Job 3:7 lo. that night be solitary
Ps. 5:11 th. love thy name be J.
35:9 my soul be J. in the Lord
63:5 praise thee with J. lips
66:1 make a J. noise to God
81:1 sing aloud, make a J. noise

JOY

Is. 61:10 soul shall be J. in my G.
2 *Cor.* 7:4 J. in all our tribulat.

JOYFULLY.

Ec. 9:9 live J. wi. wife th. lovest
Luke 19:6 Zacch. received him J.
Heb. 10:34 took J. spoil. of goods

JOYFULNESS.

Deut. 28:47 servedst not L. w. J.
Col. 1:11 to long-suffering with J.

JOYING.

Col. 2:5 with you in the spirit, J.

JOYOUS.

Is. 22:2 art full of stirs, a J. city
23:7 is this your J. city, whose
32:13 all houses of joy in J. city
Heb. 12:11 no chastening seem. J.

JUBAL. *Gen.* 4:21

JUBILEE.

Lev. 25:9 trumpet of the J. 10:54
27:17 his field from year of J. 18
Num. 36:4 J. then th. inheritance

JUDAH.

Gen. 29:35 she called his name J.
35:23 the sons of Leah, J.
38:15 J. thought Tamar a harlot
46:12 sons of J. 28; *Num.* 26:19
49:8 J. he whom thy brethren
9 J. is a lion's whelp
10 sceptre not depart from J.
Ex. 1:2 sons of Israel. Levi, J.
Num. 2:3 camp of J. shall pitch
Deut. 33:7 blessing of J. 27:12
Jos. 7:17 bro. family of J. 18:5
Jud. 1:2 J. go first, 19; 20:9
1 *Sam.* 18:16 all J. loved David
2 *Sam.* 5:5 David reigned, 19:15
1 *K.* 14:22 J. did evil, 1 *K.* 17:19
2 *K.* 8:19 L. not destroy J. 14:10
21:11 ma. J. sin, 16; 2 *Chr.* 28:9
23:27 remove J. out of my sight
2 *Chr.* 12:12 in J. things w. well
Ps. 60:7 J. my lawgiver, 108:8
76:1 in J. God known, 114:2
Is. 1:1 vision conc. J. 3:1; 7:6
11:12 together dispersed of J. 13
22:8 discovered covering of J.
Jer. 17:1 sin of J. with. with iron
33:7 captiv. of J. return. 42:18
50:20 sins of J. not found; 51:5
Joel 3:20 J. dw. for ever, *Am.* 2:4
Mic. 5:2 among thousands of J.
Zec. 2:12 L. inh. J. 12:7; 14:14
Mat. 2:11 J. dealt treacherously
3 covering of J. pleasant
Mat. 1:2 Ja. begat J. J. J. begat
Rev. 7:14 our L. sprang of J.

Land of JUDAH.

Deut. 34:2 showed him land of J.
Ruth 1:7 to return in land of J.
Is. 19:17 l. of J. a terror, 26:1
Mat. 2:6 Bethlehem, in l. of J.

Men of JUDAH.

Jud. 15:10 m. of J. why come
2 *Sam.* 2:4 m. of J. anointed D.
19:14 heart of J. 41; 22:2
24:9 men of J. 500,000
Ezr. 10:9 m. of J. gathered toget.
Is. 5:7 m. of J. his pleas. plant
Jer. 36:31 upon the men of J. all
43:9 in sight of men of J.
44:27 all m. of J. be consumed
Dan. 9:7 confusion to men of J.

Tribe of JUDAH.

Num. 1:27 numb. of tribe of J.
7:12 Nahson, prince of t. of J.
1 *K.* 12:20 t. of J. followed Dav.
2 *K.* 17:18 none left but t. of J.
Ps. 78:68 but he chose t. of J.
Rev. 5:5 L. of t. of J. prevailed
7:5 of tribe of J. sealed 12,000

JUDAS.

Mat. 13:55 brethren Sim. and J.
26:47 J. one of twelve, *Mark*
14:43; *Lu.* 22:47; *John* 18:3, 5
27:3 J. repented, bro. 30 pieces
Luke 6:16; *John* 6:71
John 13:29 because J. had bag
14:22 J. saith, How is it
Acts 1:16 D. spake concern. J. 25
5:37 after this man rose up J.
9:11 inquire in the house of J.
15:22 J. surnamed Barsabas, 27

JUDAS Iscariot.

Mat. 10:4 J. I. who betra. *Mark*
3:19; *Luke* 6:16; *John* 6:71;
13:2
26:14 J. I. to chief p. *Mark* 14:10
Luke 22:3 enter. Satan into J. I.
John 13:26 he gave sop to J. I.

JUDEA.

Ezr. 5:8 went into prov. of J.
Mat. 24:16 them wh. be in J. flee,
Mark 13:14; *Luke* 21:21

CRUDEN'S CONCORDANCE. 911

912 CRUDEN'S CONCORDANCE.

JUD

Rev. 18:10 in one hour thy j. co.
20:4 and j. was given to them
See DEAR, DAY.

Do JUDGMENT.
Gen. 18:19 do justice and j. 1 K.
10:9; Prov. 21:3; Jer. 22:15
1 K. 3:28 wisdom of G. to do j.
2 Chr. 9:8 set over them to do j.
Prov. 21:7 they refuse to do j.
15 it is joy to the just to do j.
Jer. 51:47 do j. on gr. images, 52

JUDGMENT-HALL.
John 18:28 led Jesus to h. of j.
themselves we. not into j.-h.
33 Pilate entered j.-h. again
19:9 went into the j.-h.
Acts 23:35 kept in Herod's j.-h.

In JUDGMENT.
Lev. 19:15 no unright. in j. 35
Num. 35:12 bef. congrega. in j.
Deut. 1:17 not respect per. in j.
Jud. 5:10 ye that sit in j.
Job 9:32 come together in j.
37:23 excel. in power and in j.
Ps. 1:5 shall not stand in j.
23:9 meek will he guide in j.
Prov. 16:10 transgress. not in j.
18:5 overthrow righteous in j.
21:23 not good res. persons in j.
Is. 5:16 L. of hosts exalted in j.
28:6 sitteth in j. T stumble in j.
32:1 princes shall rule in j.
54:17 tongue rise ag. thee in j.
Jer. 4:2 in righteouss. and in j.
Ezek. 44:24 in contro. stand in j.
Hos. 2:19 betroth thee to me in j.
Mal. 3:5 come near to you in j.
Mat. 12:41 men of Nin. rise in j.
42 queen of south shall rise in
j. Luke 11:31, 32
Phil. 1:9 love may abound in j.

Into JUDGMENT.
Job 14:3 and bringest me into j.
22:4 enter with thee into j.
34:23 enter into j. with God
Ps. 143:2 enter not j. wi. serv.
Ec. 11:9 will bring thee into j.
12:14 God bring ev. work into j.
Is. 3:14 Lord will enter into j.

My JUDGMENT.
Job 27:2 taken away my j. 34:5
29:14 my j. was as a robe
40:8 wilt thou disannul my j. ?
Ps. 35:23 awake to my j.
Is. 40:27 my j. is passed over
49:4 my j. is with the Lord
51:4 make my j. to rest
Ezek. 39:21 heathen sh. see my j.
John 5:30 my j. just; 8:16 my j.
1 Cor. 7:25 yet I give my j.
40 happier if she abi. in my j.

JUDGMENT-SEAT.
Mat. 27:19 set on j.-s. John 19:13
Ac's 18:12 J. brought him to j.-s.
16 he drave them from this j.-s.
17 beat Sosthenes before j.-s.
25:10 I stand at Caesar's j.-s.
17 on morrow I sat on j.-s.
Rom. 14:10 sh. all stand before
j.-s of Christ, 2 Cor. 5:10
Jam. 2:6 draw you before j.-s.

JUDGMENTS.
Ex. 6:6 redeem you with j. 7:4
21:1 j. thou sh. set before them
Num. 33:4 on gods L. executed j.
33:24 judge according to th. j.
Deut. 33:10 sh. teach Jac. thy j.
2 Sam. 22:23 his j. were before
me, Ps. 18:22
1 Chr. 16:14 j. of mouth, Ps. 105:7
14 his j. in all earth, Ps. 105:7
Neh. 9:29 sinned against thy j.
Ps. 10:5 thy j. are out of sight
19:9 the j. of the Lord are true
31:3 thy j. are a great deep
48:11 let Judah be glad of thy j.
72:1 give the king thy j. O God
97:8 because of thy j. O Lord
119:7 I learned thy righteouss. j.
13 lips declared j. of thy mo.
20 longing it hath unto thy j.
30 thy j. have I laid before me
39 reproach, for thy j. are good
41 for I have hoped in thy j.
52 I remember thy j. of old
62 because of thy right. j. 164
75 I know that thy j. are right
102 have not departed from j.
106 I will keep righteous j.
108 teach me j. j. 120 afraid of j.
137 right. upright are thy j.
156 quicken me accor. to thy j.
160 ev. one of thy righteous.
175 and let thy j. help me
147:20 his j. they have not kno.

JUS

Prov. 19:29 J. prep. for scorners
Is. 9:8 in way of thy j.
9 when thy j. are in the earth
Jer. 12:1 talk with thee of thy j.
Ezek. 5:7 accord. to j. of nations
8 execute j. in midst of thee,
10, 15; 11:9
16:41 exe. j. in sight of women
23:24 judge thee accord. to j.
28:26 executed j. on all those
34:16 I will feed them with j.
39:5 departing from thy j.
Hos. 6:5 thy j. are as the light
Zep. 3:15 L. taken away thy j.
Rom. 11:33 unsearch. are his j.
1 Cor. 6:4 have j. of things of life
Rev. 15:4 j. are made manifest
16:7 righteous are thy j. 19:2

My JUDGMENTS.
Lev. 18:4 ye shall do my j.
5 ye shall keep my j. 25:18
26:15 if your soul abhor my j.
43 because they despised my j.
1 Chr. 28:7 constant to do my j.
Ps. 89:30 chil. walk not in my j.
Jer. 1:16 utter my j. ag. them
Ezek. 5:6 changed my j. to wick.
7 neither have kept my j.
14:21 send my four sore j. on J.
44:24 judge it accord to my j.

Statutes and JUDGMENTS.
Lev. 18:5 keep my stat. and my
j. 26; 20:22; Deut. 7:11; 11:1;
26:16, 17; 30:16; 1 K. 2:3;
8:58; 9:4; 11:33
19:37 ye sh. observe all my
statutes a. my j. Deut. 11:32;
12:1; 2 Chr. 7:17
Deut. 4:1 I hearken to s. a. j. 5:1
8 I have taught you sta. and j.
8 hath sta. and j. so righteous
14 te. st. and j. 6:1; Ezr. 7:10
5:31 st. and j. them shalt teach
6:20 what mean statutes and j.
8:11 keeping s. and j. Neh. 1:7
1 K. 2:12 walk in s. execute j.
2 Chr. 19:10 between s. and j.
Neh. 9:13 gav. them right. s. a. j.
10:29 to do all his sta. and j.
Ps. 147:19 showeth his s. and j.
Ezek. 5:6 rol. my j. and my sta.
11:12 not walked in my j. nor
executed my j. 20:13, 16, 21
18:9 walked in my statutes and
j. 17; 20:19; 37:24
20:11 gave them s. and sho. j.
18 not in s. of fath. nor th. j.
25 gave th. s'a. not good, a. j.
Mal. 4:4 law of M. with s. and j.

JUICE.
Cant. 8:2 wine of j. of pomegra.

JULIA.
JULIA. Rom. 16:15
JULIUS. Acts 27:1

JUMPING.
Nah. 3:2 noise of the j. chariots

JUNIA. Rom. 16:7

JUNIPER.
1 K. 19:4 Elijah sat under j. 5
Job 30:4 cut j. roots for meat
Ps. 120:4 arrows, coals of j.

JUPITER.
Acts 14:12 called Barnabas J.
19:35 which fell down from J.

JURISDICTION.
Luke 23:7 belong to Herod's j.

JUST.
Gen. 6:9 Noah was j. man
Lev. 19:36 j. balance, j. weights,
a j. ephah, and a j. hin, Deut.
25:15; Ezek. 45:10
Deut. 16:18 judge with j. judgm.
32:4 a God, j. and right is he
2 Sam. 23:3 rul. men must be j.
Neh. 9:33 j. in all brought on us
Job 4:17 man be more j. than G.
9:2 should man he j. with God
12:4 j. man is laughed to scorn
27:17 but the j. shall put it on
34:17 right. and j. condemn ?
Ps. 7:9 wicked, end. establish j.
37:12 wicked plotteth against j.
Prov. 3:33 bless. habitation of j.
4:18 path of j. as shining light
9:9 teach a j. man, he will incr.
10:6 blessing upon he. of the j.
7 memory of the j. is blessed
20 tongue of j. is as choice sil.
31 mouth of j. bringeth word.
11:1 a j. weight is his delight
9 thro' knowledge j. delivered
12:13 j. sh. come out of trouble
21 sh. no evil happen to the j.
13:22 weal. of sin. laid up for j.
16:11 j. wt. and balance Lord's
17:15 condemneth j. is abomi.

JUS

Prov. 17:26 to punish the j. is
18:17 first in own cause seem. j.
20:7 j. man walketh in integrity
21:15 joy to j. to do judgment
21:16 j. man falleth seven times
29:10 hate upright, j. seek soul
Ec. 7:15 a j. man that perisheth
20 not a j. man on earth
8:14 j. men to wh. it happeneth
Is. 26:7 way of j. is uprightness,
dost weigh path of j.
29:21 j. for thing of naught
45:21 a j. God, and a Saviour
Lam. 4:13 shed blood of j. in her
Ezek. 18:5 man be j. and do right
9 he is j. he shall surely live
Hos. 14:9 j. shall walk in them
Amos 5:12 they afflict the j.
Hab. 2:4 j. sh. live by faith, Rom.
1:17; Gal. 3:11; Heb. 10:38
Zep. 3:5 the j. Lord is in midst
Zec. 9:9 he is j. and hav. salva.
Mat. 1:19 Joseph, being a j. man
5:45 send. rain on j. and unjust
13:49 sever wicked from am. j.
27:19 nothing to do with j. man
24 innocent of blood of j. per.
Mark 6:20 knew he was j. man
Luke 1:17 disobed. to wisd. of j.
2:25 Simeon was j. and devout
14:14 at the resurrec. of the j.
15:7 ninety and nine j. persons
20:20 spies feign themselves j.
23:50 Jos. was good man and j.
John 5:30 and my judgment is j.
Acts 10:22 Cornelius, a j. man
24:15 resurrection of j. and unj.
Rom. 2:13 not hear. of law are j.
3:8 damnation j. 26 might be j.
7:12 the commandment holy. j.
Phil. 4:8 whatsoev. things are j.
Col. 4:1 give servants what is j.
Tit. 1:8 bishop must be j. holy
Heb. 2:2 received j. recompense
12:23 sp. of j. men made perfect
Jam. 5:6 condemned and kill. j.
1 Pet. 3:18 the j. for the unjust
2 Pet. 2:7 delivered j. Lot
1 John 1:9 he is j. to forgive sins
Rev. 15:3 j. and tr. are thy ways

Most JUST.
Job 34:17 condemn him is m. j. ?

JUST One.
Acts 3:14 ye denied the J. O.
7:52 show. bef. coming of J. O.
22:14 his will, and see that J. O.

JUSTICE.
Gen. 18:19 keep w. of L. to do j.
Deut. 33:21 execute, the j. of L.
2 Sam. 8:15 David executed j.
1 Chr. 18:14
13:4 made judge I would do j.
Job 8:3 doth Almigh. pervert j. ?
36:17 and j. take hold on thee
37:23 excellent in plenty of j.
Ps. 89:3 do j. to afflicted
89:14 j. and judgm. are habita.
119:121 have done judg. and j.
Prov. 1:3 to rec. instruction of j.
8:15 kings reign, princes dec. j.
Ec. 5:8 seest perverting of j.
Is. 9:7 to estab. his thro. with j.
56:1 and do j. for my salvation
59:2 ask of me ordinances of j.
59:4 none calleth for j. nor pio.
11 j. standeth afar of
Jer. 23:5 execute judgm. and j.
31:23 L. bless thee, habita. of j.
Ezek. 45:9 O princes, execute j.
See DO JUDGMENT, before.

JUSTIFICATION.
Rom. 4:25 raised again for our j.
5:16 gift of many offences to j.
18 free gift ca. on all men to j.

JUSTIFY.
Ex. 23:7 I will not j. the wicked
Deut. 25:1 they sh. j. righteous
Job 9:20 if I j. myself
27:5 God forbid I should j. you
33:32 for I desire to j. thee
Ps. 82:3 j. the wicked for reward
Is. 5:23 j. the wicked for reward
53:11 by right. servant j. many
Luke 10:29 willing to j. himself
16:15 j. yourselves before men
Rom. 3:30 God sh. j. circumcis.
Gal. 3:8 foreseeing God j. heath.

JUSTIFIED.
Job 11:2 man full of talk he j. ?
12:16 behold, I know I sh. be j.
25:4 can man be j. with God ?
32:2 j. himself rather than God
Ps. 51:4 that thou mightest be j.
143:2 no man living be j.
Is. 43:9 may be j. 26 thou be

KEE

Is. 43:25 L. all seed of Isr. be j.
Jer. 3:11 backsliding Is. j. hers.
Ezek. 16:51 j. sisters in abom. 52
Mat. 11:19 wisdom is j. of her
children, Luke 7:35
12:37 by thy words th. sh. be j.
Luke 7:29 and publicans j. G.
18:14 this man went down j.
Acts 13:39 all that believe are j.
from wh. ye could not be j.
Rom. 2:13 doers of law sh. be j.
3:4 might. be j. in thy sayings
20 no flesh be j. in his sight
24 j. freely by his gra. Tit. 3:7
28 a man is j. by faith, 5:1;
Gal. 2:16; 3:24
4:2 if Abraham we. j. by works
5:1 j. by faith we have peace
9 j. by his blood, we shall be
6:30 whom he j. he also glorifi.
1 Cor. 4:4 yet am I not hereby j.
6:11 ye are j. in name of L. J.
Gal. 2:16 not j. by law, 3:11
5:4 whosoever are j. by law
1 Tim. 3:16 j. in spirit
Jam. 2:21 was not Abraham j. ?
24 see how by works was j.
25 was not Rahab j. by works ?

JUSTIFIER.
Rom. 3:26 j. of him who believ.

JUSTIFYING, ETH.
1 K. 8:32 and j. the righteous,
2 Chr. 6:23
Prov. 17:15 he that j. the wicked
Is. 50:8 he is near that j.
Rom. 5:3 him that j. ungodly
8:33 God's elect ? is G. that j.

JUSTLE.
Nah. 2:4 the chariots shall j.

JUSTLY.
Mic. 6:8 L. require but to do j.
Luke 23:41 indeed j. we receive
1 Thes. 2:10 holily and j. behav.

JUSTUS.
Acts 1:23 who was surnamed J.
18:7 one. man's house named J.
Col. 4:11 Jesus who is called J.

K

KAB.
2 K. 6:25 k. of doves' dung sold

KABZEEL. Jos. 15:21

KADESH.
Gen. 14:3 to Emish. which is K.
Num. 13:26 wilder. of Par. to K.
Num. 20:1 ye abode in K. many
Ps. 29:8 shak. wilderness of K.

KADESH-BARNEA.
Num. 32:8 I sent them from K.
Deut. 1:2 eleven days to K.
Jos. 10:41 smote from K. to Gaza

KAREAH, or CAREAH. 2 K.
25:23; Jer. 40:8, 13; 41:11;
43:4

KEDEMAH. Gen. 25:15
KEDEMOTH. Deut. 2:25

KEDAR.
Gen. 25:13 of Ish. K. 1 Chr. 1:29
Ps. 120:5 I dwell in tents of K.
Cant. 1:5 comely as tents of K.
Is. 21:16 glory of K. sh. fail, 17
42:11 vil. that K. doth inhabit
60:7 flocks of K. sh. be gather.
Jer. 2:10 see and behold isl. K.
49:28 concerning K. thus saith
Ezek. 27:21 princes of K. occu.

KEEP.
Gen. 2:15 L. put him in E. to k.
18:19 shall k. the way of Lord
28:15 am with thee to k. thee, 20
41:35 let them k. food in cities
Ex. 12:6 k. it till fourteenth day
14 ye sh. k. it a feast to L. 20;
23:15; 34:18; Lev. 23:41
47 congregation of Is. sh. k. it
20:6 remember sab.-day to k. it,
31:13, 14, 16; Deut. 5:12, 15
22:7 man deliver money to k.
23:7 k. thee from false matter
14 three times k. a feast
20 I send an angel to k. thee
25 k. the sabbaths, 20;
26:2; Is. 56:4
23:32 k. a feast ev. 2 Chr. 30:13
25:18 k. my judg. and do them
Num. 6:24 L. bless thee and k.
9:3 in fourteenth day ye shall k.
29:12, L. feast to the L. sev. days
30:7 k. himself to inheritance, 9
Deut. 7:8 k. the oath
12 the L. sh. k. the covenant

KIL

Is. 34:6 with fat of *k.* of rams
KIDRON. 2 *Sam.* 15:23
KIDS.
Gen. 27:9 fetch me from th., 2 *k.*
16 put skins of *k.* on his hands
Lev. 16:5 two *k.* of the goats
1 *K.* 20:27 like two bt. floc. of *k.*
Cant. 1:8 feed thy *k.* bes. shep.'s

KILL.
Gen. 4:15 lest any find. C. *k.* him
12:12 th. wi. *k.* me, but save th.
27:42 purposing to *k.* thee
37:21 said, Let us not *k.* him
Ex. 1:16 if it be son, ye *k.* hi u
2:14 intend. to *k.* me? *Acts* 7. 28
16:3 *k.* this assembly
17:3 *k.* us an l chil. with thirst
22:18 thou shalt not *k.* *Deut.*
5:17; *Mat.* 5:21; *Rom.* 13:9
22.1 if man steal ox, and *k.* it
23:11 *k.* bullock before the L.
Lev. 1:5; 4:4
Lev. 1:11 *k.* it on side altar, 15:15
3:2 *k.* it at door of tabernacle
4:24 *k.* it in place where they *k.*
11:30 he shall *k.* one of the birds
20:4 seed to Moloch, *k.* him not
16 shalt *k.* woman and beast
Num. 11:15 if deal thus, *k.* me
14:15 if thou *k.* all this people
16:13 bro. us to *k.* us in wilder.
22:33 for now would I *k.* thee
31:17 *k.* ev. woman known man
Deut. 4:42 who *k.* his neighbour
12:15 mayest *k.* and eat flesh
13:9 thou shalt surely *k.* him
32:39 I *k.* and I make alive
Jud. 13:23 L. were plea. to *k.* us
16:2 wh. it is day, we sh. *k.* him
20:31 began to *k.* 39
1 *Sam.* 17:9 be able to *k.* me
19:2 Saul seeketh to *k.* thee, 17
25:15 a your thou wilt not *k.* me
2 *Sam.* 14:7 that we may *k.* him
32 let him *k.* me
21:4 nor for us sh. th. *k.* any m.
2 *K.* 5:7 a m I G d, to *k.* ?
7:4 if they *k.* us, we sh. but die
11:15 follow, her *k.* with sword
2 *Chr.* 35:6 *k.* the passover
Est. 3:13 let. by posts to *k.* Jews
Est. 3:3 time to *k.* time to heal
Ec. 11:33 *k.* thy rest with famine
20:1 let them *k.* sacrifices
Ezek. 34:3 *k.* them that are fed
Mat. 2:13 *k.* sh. he in daug.
10:28 fear not them which *k.*
the body, *Luke* 12:4
21:38 heir, come let us *k.* him,
Mark 12:7; *Luke* 20:14
23:34 some of them ye shall *k.*
26:4 take J. by subtl. to *k.* him
Mark 3:4 to save life, or to *k.* ?
10:19 do not *k. Lu.* 18:20; *Jr.* 2:11
Luke 15:23 Herod will *k.* thee
15:23 bring fatted calf and *k.* it
John 5:18 J. sought to *k.* him, 7:1
7:19 why go ye about to *k.* me?
25 is this he wh. th. seek to *k.* ?
8:22 *k.* himself; 37 to *k.* 40
13:10 thief com. to steal and *k.*
Acts 9:23 counsel to *k. P.* 22:21
10:13 rise, Peter, *k.* and eat
24:15 are ready to *k.* him
25:3 lay, wait in way to *k.* him
27:42 counsel to *k.* prisoner
Jam. 2:11 yet if thou *k.*
4:2 ye *k.* and desire to have
Rev. 2:23 I will *k.* her children
6:4 that they sho. *k.* one anoth.
8 power was given them to *k.*
9:5 that they should not *k.* th.
11:7 beast overco. and *k.* them

KILLED.
Gen. 37:31 Joseph's coat, *k.* kid
Ex. 21:29 the ox hath *k.* a man
Lev. 6:25 place wh. burnt-offer.
is *k.* sin-off. be *k.* bef. the L.
8:19 ram he *k.* 14:5 bird he *k.*
14:6 dip them in blo. of bird *k.*
Num. 16:41 ye *k.* peo. of the L.
31:19 whoso. hath *k.* any person
1 *Sam.* 24:11 cut skirt, *k.* not
25:11 take my flesh I have *k.*
2 *Sam.* 12:9 thou hast *k.* Uriah
1 *K.* 21:19 *k.* and tak. possession?
2 *Chr.* 25:3 slew th. that *k.* king
30:15 *k.* the passover, 35:1, 11;
Ezr. 6:20
Ps. 44:22 for thy sake are we *k.*
Prov. 9:2 she hath *k.* her beasts
Lym. 2:21 thou ha. *k.* not pitied
Mat. 10:21 *k.* and raised again.
Mark 6:19 wo. have *k.* him
21:35 be. one, and *k. Mark* 12:5

Mat. 22:4 oxen and fatlin. are *k.*
23:31 chil. of them *k.* prophets
Mark 12:8 *k.* him cast him out
14:12 wh. they *k.* the passover
12:8 after he hath *k.* ha. power
Luke 11:47 fathers *k.* them, 48
12:5 after he hath *k.* ha. power
Luke 15:27 hath *k.* fatted calf, 30
23:7 day when pass. must be *k.*
Acts 3:15 *k.* the Prince of life
4:12 *k.* James, brother of John
16:27 would have *k.* himself
23:12 nor drink till they *k.* Paul
Rom. 8:36 for thy sake we are *k.*
11:3 L. they have *k.* thy proph.
2 *Cor.* 6:9 chastened and not *k.*
1 *Thes.* 2:15 *k.* the Lord Jesus
Jam. 5:6 condemned and *k.* just
Rev. 6:11 sh. be *k.* as they were
9:18 the third part of man *k.*
20 the rest which were not *k.*
11:5 if hurt him he must be *k.*
13:10 must he be *k.* with sword
15 image of beast, should be *k.*

KILLEDST, EST.
Ex. 2:14 as thou *k.* Egyptian
1 *Sam.* 23:37 *k.* prophets, *Luke*13:34

KILLETH.
Lev. 24:17 he that *k.* any man sh.
be put to dea. *Num.* 35:30
18 that *k.* a beast, 21
Num. 35:11 *k.* any unawares, 15;
Deut. 19:4; *Jos.* 20:3, 9
1 *Sam.* 2:6 L. *k.* and maketh alive
Job 5:2 wrath *k.* the foolish man
24:14 the murderer *k.* the poor
Prov. 21:25 dos. of slothful *k.* him
Ec. 6:5 he that *k.* an ox
John 10:2 who *k.* you do. G. ser.
Is. 54:8 letter *k.* Sp. giveth life
Rev. 13:10 he that *k.* with sword
must be killed

KILLING.
2 *Chr.* 30:17 charge of *k.* passover
Is. 22:13 slaying oxen, *k.* sheep
Hos. 4:2 swearing, lying, and *k.*
Mark 12:5 beating some, *k.* some

KIN.
Lev. 18:6 none appro. to near *k.*
20:19 he uncovereth his near *k.*
25:25 *k.* come to redeem it, 49
Ruth 2:20 man is near *k.* to us
2 *Sam.* 19:42 king near *k.* to us

KIND.
2 *Chr.* 10:7 if thou be *k.* to people
Luke 6:35 G. is *k.* to unthankful
1 *Cor.* 13:4 charity suff. and is *k.*
Eph. 4:32 be *k.* one to another

KIND, Substantive.
Gen. 1:11 yield. fruit after *k.* 12
21 waters brought forth after *k.*
25 God made beast after his *k.*
6:20 fowls after *k.* cattle aft.
k. ev. creeping thing after *k.*
Lev. 11:14 hawk after his *k.* 16,
19; *Deut.* 14:14
19:19 not let cattle with div. *k.*
Neh. 13:20 sellers of all *k.* ware
Mat. 3:5 I planted trees of all *k.*
Mat. 13:47 gathered of every *k.*
17:21 *k.* go. not out, *Mark* 9:29
1 *Cor.* 15:39 th. is one *k.* of flesh
Jam. 1:18 be a *k.* of first-fruits
3:7 every *k.* of beast and birds

KINDS.
Gen. 8:19 creepeth after their *k.*
2 *Chr.* 16:14 with divers *k.* spices
Jer. 15:3 appoint over th. four *k.*
1 *Cor.* 12:10 divers *k.* of tongues
14:10 are so many *k.* of voices

KINDLE.
Prov. 26:21 con. man to *k.* strife
Is. 9:18 shall *k.* in the thickets
10:16 *k.* a burning like a fire
30:83 breath of Lord doth *k.* it
Jer. 83:4 *k.* fire in the forest
k. 21:14 I will *k.* a fire, *Lam.*
Ob. 18 fire and flame *k.* in them

KINDLED.
Gen. 10:6 bewall burn. L. hath *k.*
Num. 11:33 wrath of the Lord
was *k. Deut.* 11:17; 2 *K.*
22:13, 17; *Ps.* 106:40
1 *Sam.* 20:3 coals *k. Ps.* 18:8
Num. 11:10 he hath *k.* his wrath
32:3 then was *k.* wrath of Elihu
42:7 wrath is *k.* against thee
Ps. 2:12 wrath is *k.* but a little
124:3 their wrath is *k.* against us
Jer. 50:11 sparks that ye have *k.*
Ezek. 20:48 I the Lord have *k.* it
Hos. 11:8 my repentings are *k.*
Luke 12:49 will I, if it be *k.* ?

See ANGER, FIRE.

KIN

KINDLETH.
Job 41:21 his breath *k.* coals
Is. 44:15 L. and baketh bread
Jam. 3:5 how great, a little fire *k.*

KINDLY.
Gen. 24:49 if you deal *k.* 47:29
31:3 Shech. spake *k.* to damsel
50:21 Joseph spake *k.* to breth.
Jos. 2:14 deal *k.* and truly
Ruth 1:8 the L. deal *k.* with you
1 *Sam.* 20:8 deal *k.* with thy ser.
Rom. 12:10 be *k.* one to another

KINDNESS.
Gen. 20:13 *k.* thou shalt show
21:23 the *k.* I have done to thee
24:12 O L. show *k.* to my master
43:14 and show *k.* I pray thee
Jos. 2:12 *k.* to my fa.'s house
Jud. 8:35 nor showed *k.* to Ger.
Ruth 2:20 not left off *k.* to living
3:10 show. more *k.* in latter end
1 *Sam.* 15:6 ye showed *k.* to Isr.
20:14 show me the *k.* of the L.
2 *Sam.* 2:5 showed *k.* to your lord
6 I also will require you this *k.*
9:3 that I may show *k.* to him
10:2 I will show *k.* to Hanun
1 *K.* 2:7 *k.* to sons of Barzillai
3:6 kept for David this great *k.*
2 *Chr.* 24:23 J. remember. not *k.*
Neh. 9:17 G. gracious, of great *k.*
Est. 2:9 maiden obt. *k.* of him
Ps. 31:21 showed me marvel. *k.*
117:2 for his merciful *k.* is great
119:76 merciful *k.* be my comf.
141:5 right. smite, it sh. be a *k.*
Prov. 19:22 desire of man is his *k.*
31:26 in her tongue is law of *k.*
Is. 54:8 with *k.* will I have mercy
10 *k.* shall not depart from thee
Joel 2:13 he is of gr. *k. Jon.* 4:2
Acts 28:2 showed us no little *k.*
2 *Cor.* 6:6 by long-suffering by *k.*
Eph. 2:7 in his *k.* toward us
Col. 3:12 on *k.* humbleness of mind
Tit. 3:4 after the *k.* of G. our
2 *Pet.* 1:7 brotherly *k.* to *k.* char.

Loving-KINDNESS.
Ps. 17:7 show thy *l.-k.* 92:2
26:3 thy *l.-k.* is before mine eyes
36:7 how excellent is thy *l.-k.*
10 O continue thy *l.-k.* to them
40:10 not concealed thy *l.-k.*
11 let thy *l.-k.* preserve me
42:8 Lord will command *l.-k.*
48:9 we thought of thy *l.-k.* O G
51:1 have mercy accord. to *l.-k.*
63:3 thy *l.-k.* is better than life
69:16 for thy *l.-k.* is good
88:11 sh. *l.-k.* be dec. in grave?
89:33 *l.-k.* will I not take fr. him
92:2 to show forth *l.-k.* in morn.
103:4 crowneth thee with *l.-k.*
107:43 understand *l.-k.* of the L.
119:56 quicken me after *l.-k.* 159
138:2 praise thy name for *l.-k.*
143:8 cause me to hear thy *l.-k.*
Jer. 9:24 L. which exercise *l.-k.*
16:5 tak. away peace, even *l.-k.*
31:3 with *l.-k.* have I drawn thee
32:18 show *l.-k.* unto thousands
Hos. 2:19 betro. th. to me in *l.-k.*

Loving-KINDNESSES.
Ps. 25:6 remem. mercies and *l.-k.*
89:49 where are thy former *l.-k.*
Is. 63:7 mention *l.-k.* of the Lord

KINDRED.
Gen. 12:1 get thee fr. *k. Acts* 7:3
24:4 go to *k.* and take wife, 38:40
31:3 return to thy *k.* 13; 32:9
43:7 asked us strictly of our *k.*
Num. 10:30 dep. to own la. and *k.*
Jos. 6:23 brought out all her *k.*
Ruth 2:3 of *k.* of Elimelech, 3:2
Est. 2:10 show. not peo. or *k.* 20
8:6 end. to see destruction of *k.*
Ezek. 11:15 men of thy *k.* said
Luke 1:61 none of *k.* called
Acts 4:6 were of *k.* of high-priest
7:13 Joseph's *k.* known to Pha.
14 sent, called to him his *k.*
Rev. 5:9 redeemed us out of ev. *k.*
14:6 gospel to preach to ev. *k.*

KINDREDS.
1 *Chr.* 16:28 give to the Lord, you
Ps. 22:27 *k.* of nations worship
Acts 3:25 all *k.* of earth blessed
Rev. 1:7 all *k.* of earth shall wail
7:9 multitude of *k.* before throne
11:9 *k.* see dead bodies thr. days
13:7 pow. given him over all *k.*

KINE.
Gen. 32:15 forty *k.* ten bulls to E.

KIN

Gen. 41:2 seven well-favored *k.* 18
3 seven *k.* out of river, 4, 19, 20
26 seven good *k.* are sev. years
27 sev. ill-favored *k.* sev. years
Deut. 7:13 bless increa. of thy *k.*
28:4 blessed be incr. of thy *k.*
51 cursed be incr. of thy *k.*
22:14 butter of *k.* milk of sheep
1 *Sam.* 6:7 ta. two milch *k.* tie *k.*
10 took two *k.* 12 *k.* took way
2 *Sam.* 17:29 and cheese of *k.*
Amos 4:1 hear this, ye *k.* of Bas.

KING.
Gen. 14:18 M. *k.* of Sal. *Heb.* 7:1
17 arose new *k.* over Egypt
Num. 23:21 shout of a *k.* am. th.
24:7 his *k.* be higher than Agag
Deut. 17:14 I will set *k.* over me
15 him *k.* he was *k.* in Jeshurun
Jud. 8:18 resem. child. of a *k.*
9:8 trees went to anoint a *k.*
17:6 in those days no *k.* in Isr.
18:1; 19:1; 21:25
1 *Sam.* 2:10 L. give strength to *k.*
8:5 go make us a *k.* to judge us
6 pl. a *k.* 9 show man. of *k.* 11
10 have a *k.* 22 make th. a *k.*
20 that our *k.* may judge us
10:19 nay, but set a *k.* over us
24 said, G. save the *k.* 2 *Sam.*
16:16; 2 *K.* 11:12; 2 *Chr.* 28:11
12:1 I have made a *k.* over you
2 the *k.* walketh before you
12 said, Nay, a *k.* sh. reign ov.
us, when God was your *k.*
17 wicked. great in asking a *k.*
19 this evil, to ask a *k.*
25 cons. both you and your *k.*
15:1 I have provided me a *k.*
16:1 have provided me a *k.*
22:15 let not *k.* imp. any thing
24:20 I know that thou sh. be *k.*
25:36 Nabal held feast like a *k.*
2 *Sam.* 3:12 estab. him *k.* over I.
11:8 a mess of meat from *k.*
12:7 I anointed thee *k.* over Is.
14:9 *k.* and his throne be guiltl.
17 as an angel of God, so is my
lord the *k.* 19:27
14:14 controversy, ca. to *k.*
15:2 none deputed of *k.* to hear
16:9 sh. this dead dog curse *k.* ?
17:2 I will smite the *k.* only
18:12 is no matter hid from *k.*
19:9 *k.* saved us out of hand
11 speech of Israel come to *k.*
22 I know that I am *k.* over Is.
43 we have ten parts in the *k.*
22:51 tower of salv. for his *k.*
1 *K.* 1:35 Solomon *k.* in my stead
3:7 servant *k.* instead of David
28 heard judg. the *k.* judged
8:66 *k.* and all Is. offer. sacrifice
10:3 not any thing hid from *k.*
11:37 thou shalt be *k.* over Isr.
21:10 didst blaspheme G. and *k.*
12:13 prophets declare good to
the *k.* 2 *Chr.* 18:12
k. 4:17 M. in E. a deputy was *k.*
4:13 wouldest be spok. for to *k.*
7:2 lord on whose hand *k.* lean.
9 go to cry to the *k.* for her hou.
12 *k.* showed thou shalt be *k.*
20 E. made *k.* over themselves
11:8 be with *k.* as he goeth out
Chr. 4:23 they dwelt wi. the *k.*
28:29 worshipped Lord and *k.*
2 *Chr.* 2:11 he made thee *k.* 9:8
10:15 *k.* hearkened not to peop.
11:22 he thought to make him *k.*
22:11 stoned him at com. of *k.*
23:16 thou madest of *k.* counsel?
Ezr. 4:12 be it kn. to *k.* 13; 5:8
6:10 pray for life of *k.* and sons
7:27 put in *k.* heart to beautify
8:22 req. of *k.* band of soldiers
Neh. 1:11 I was the *k.* cup-bearer
2:5 said to *k.* delighteth to honor
6 *k.* word went out of *k.* month
Job 15:24 as a *k.* ready to battle
18:14 bring him to *k.* of terrors
29:25 dwelt as a *k.* in the army
34:18 say to a *k.* thou art wick.
41:34 a *k.* over children of pride
Ps. 2:6 set my *k.* upon holy hill
5:2 harken, my *k.* and my God, 84:3
10:16 Lord is *k.* for ever, 29:10
72:10 deliverance giveth he to *k.*
20:9 let *k.* hear us when we call

KIN

Ps. 21:1 k. shall joy in thy stren.
7 the k. trusted in the Lord
24:7 k. of glory shall come in, 9
8 who is k. of glory? the Lord
10 L. of hosts, he is k. of glory
5:2:16 so k. saved by multitude
45:1 things I made touc. the k.
11 so shall the k. greatly desi.
14 brought to the k. in raim.
47:6 praises to k. 7 God is k.
61:6 prolong k. life and years
68:11 the k. shall rejoice in God
72:1 give the k. thy judgments
74:12 God is my k. of old
89:18 H. One of Israel is our k.
98:6 make a noise bef. L. the k.
99:4 k. also loveth judgment
149:2 children of Z. joyful in k.
Prov. 14:28 people is the k. hon.
35 k. favor toward wise serv.
20:28 mercy and truth pres. k.
22:11 the k. shall be his friend
24:21 fear the Lord and the k.
25:5 take wicked from bef. k.
30:27 the locusts have no k.
31 k. against wh. no rising up
Ec. 2:12 man do cometh after k.
5:9 k. hims. served by the field
8:4 where word of a k. is power
10:16 woe to thee, wh. k. is ch.
17 bles. wh. k. is son of noble
20 curse not the k. In thought
Cant. 1:4 k. bro. me to chamber
12 while the k. sitteth at table
3:11 S. Solomon with the crown
Is. 6:5 mine eyes ha. seen the k.
8:21 curse their k. and their G.
32:1 k. according to days of one k.
30:33 for the k. it is prepared
32:1 k. shall reign in righteous.
33:17 thine eyes shall see the k.
22 L. is our k. he will save us
43:15 Creator of Israel your k.
57:9 wentest to k. with ointm.
Jer. 4:9 heart of k. shall perish
8:19 is not her k. in her?
10:10 true God, everlasting k.
23:5 a k. shall reign and prosper
5:22:25 wh. said to k. the k. to th.
46:18 k. whose name is the Lord
**of hosts, 4:13:5; 51:57
49:38 I will des. k. and princes
Lam. 2:6 L. despised k. and pri.
Ezek. 17:13 hath tak. of k. seed
16 k. dwell. that made him k.
22:7 I will bring a k. of kings
26 br. k. to them all, 31
Dan. 2:26 bring me in before the k. and I will show the k.
4:31 while word was in k. mou.
37 I honor k. of heaven
5:5 k. saw part of hand, wro.
8:23 a k. of fierce countenance
11:3 a mighty k. shall stand u
36 k. sh. do accord. to his wil
Hos. 3:4 Is. sh. abide without k.
5 k. seek L. and Dav. their k.
13:10 a k. g lad while wicked.
5 In day of our k. princes made
10:3 what then should a k. do?
7 her k. is cut off, as the foam
13:10 will be thy k. give me k.
11 gave thee k. in mine ang.r
Amos 7:13 k. chapel, the k. court
Mic. 4:9 why cry, is there no k.?
Zec. 9:9 k. cometh, Mat. 21:5
14:9 L. shall be k. over all earth
16 go up to worship k. 17
Mat. 1:22, hewed to cert. k. 22:2
22:11 when the k. came in
Mark 6:25 came with haste to k.
Luke 14:31 what k. goeth to war
19:38 blessed be k. that cometh
23:2 that he himself is Ch. a k.
John 6:15 to make him k.
12:15 behold thy k. cor., on ass
18:37 Pil. said, Art thou a k.?
13:15 whoso maketh himself k.
11 Pilate saith, Behold your k.
15 shall I crucify your k.?
Ac's 7:18 till another k. arose
12:1 afterward they desir. a k.
17:7 do another k. one Jesus
1 Tim. 1:17 now to the k. eternal
6:15 K. of kings, and L. of lords
Heb. 11:23 not afraid of k. com.
1 Pet. 2:13 who. to k. as supreme
17 fear God, honor the k.
Rev. 9:11 they had a k. over th.
15:3 just are thy ways, K. of sal.
17:14 L. of lords, K. of ki., 19:16

KING of the *Amorites*. See SIHON.

KING of Assyria.

2 K. 15:19 Pul k. of A. ag. land
20 exac. money to give k. of A.
17:6 Hosea k. of A. took Sama.

KIN

2 K. 18:11 k. of A. did car. I. to A.
33 deliv. out of hand of k. of A.
Ezr. 6:22 turned heart of k. of A.
Is. 7:17 L. bring upon k. of Ass.
20 shave by k. of Assyr. head
Jer. 50:17 k. of A. devoured him
Nah. 3:18 slumber, O k. of Assy.

See BAStLAN, BABYLON, DAVID.

KING of Egypt.

Ex. 3:19 k. of Egypt not let you
2 K. 24:7 k. of Egypt came not
2 Chr. 12:2 k. of E. came ag. Jer.
33:6 k. of E. put him down at J.
**4 k. of E. made Eliakim king
Is. 30:6 so is k. of Egypt to all

See PHARAOH, GREAT, HOUSE, JEWS.

KING of Israel.

1 Sam. 26:20 k. of Israel is come
2 Sam. 6:20 glorious was k. of Is.
1 K. 22:31 fight only wi. k. of Is.
32 it is k. of Is. 2 Chr. 18:31
2 K. 6:11 which of us for k. of Is.
16:7 out of hand of k. of Israel
2 Chr. 18:30 fight not, sa. wi. k. of
Hos. 10:15 k. of Israel be cut off
Zep. 3:15 L. of Israel in midst
Mat. 27:49 if he be k. of Israel let him descend, Mark 15:32
John 1:49 thou art k. of Israel
12:13 blessed is the k. of Israel

KING of Judah.

2 K. 22:18 k. of J. wh. sent you
2 Chr. 33:21 what have I to do with thee, thou k. of Judah
Jer. 37:7 k. of J. who sent you?

KING of Moab.

Num. 23:7 k. of M. brought h. A.
Jos. 21:9 k. of M. warred ag. Is.
Jud. 3:14 k. ser. k. of M. 18 yrs.
11:25 art thou bet. th. k. of M.?
2 K. 3:4 k. of M. a sheep-master
26 k. of Moab saw hail le
Jer. 27:9 send yokes to k. of M.

O KING.

1 Sam. 17:55 O k. I cannot tell
22:17 I sal. O k. 2 Sam. 14:9, 2:1
16:4; 19:26; 1 K. 1:18, 25, 24:
20:4; 2 K. 6:12, 26; 8:3
Dan. 2:4 O k. live forever, 3:9
4:22 I the k. thou, O k. that art gr.
27 O k. let counsel be accept.
6:7 ask peti. save of thee, O k.
8 now, O k. establish decree
22 O k. I have done no hurt
Acts 23:13 O k. I saw in way
19 O K. I was not disobedient

KING of Persia.

Ezr. 4:3 k. of Per is commanded
5 releas of Darius k. of P. 20
7 Bish, wrote unto k. of P. 6:14

See CYRUS.

KING of Syria.

1 K. 8:29 k. of S. ere. on horse
2 K. 5:1 capt. of host of k. of S.
7 k. of N. sick; 9 k. of N. sent
13 bow. k. of S. oppress. them
17:1 out of mind of k. of Syria
16:7 relied on k. of Syria
13:24 whoso maketh himself, it Bet-HADAD, HAZAEL, REZIN.

KING of Tyre.

2 Sam. 5:11 H. k. of T. 1 Chr. 14:1
1 K. 5:1 k. of T. s lit servants
2 Chr. 2:11 k. of T. ans. in writ.

KINGS.

Gen. 17:6 k. shall come out of thee, 16; 35:11
26:31 k. that reigned in Edom
Jos. 10:5 five k. of Amorites fied.
24 put feet on necks of those k.
12:21 all these k. thirty and one
Jud. 1:7 seventy k. thu. cut off
Sam. 11:1 when k. go to battle
1 K. 3:13 not any k. like thee,
10:23; 2 Chr. 1:12; 9:22
4:24 Solomon over all the k.
2 K. 3:10 called three k. together
21 the k. are surely slain
10:4 two k. stood not bef, him

KIN

1 Chr. 16:21 reprov, k. Ps. 105:14
2 Chr. 9:23 k. sought presence S.
21:20 the sepulchres of k. 21:25
26:23 field of burial belong. to k.
Ezr. 4:15 city being hurtful to k.
6:12 G. dest. k. alter this home
7:12 Artaxerxes king of k. to E
Neh. 9:32 tron. little to us and k.
34 nor have our k. kept thy law
Job 3:14 had I been at rest wi. k.
12:18 he looseth the bond of k.
36:7 k. are they on the throne
Ps. 2:2 the k. of the ear, Acts 4:26
10 therefore, O k. be instruct.
45:9 k. daughters among women
48:4 lo, the k. were assembled
68:12 k. of armies did flee apace
14 the Almighty scat. k. in it
29 sh. k. bring presents to thee
72:11 k. shall fall down be. him
76:12 terrible to k. of the earth
89:27 higher than k. of the ear.
102:15 k. of earth sh. fear thy g.
110:5 strike k. in day of wrath
119:46 speak of testim. befo. k.
135:10 smote nations, and sl. k.
138:1 which smote great k. 18
138:4 k. of earth praise th. 148:11
144:10 he that giveth salva. to k.
149:8 bind their k. with chains
Prov. 8:15 by me k. reign
16:12 abom. for k. commit wick.
19 right. lips are delight of k.
22:20 dilig. shall stand before k.
27:3 honor of k. to search mat.
3 heart of k. is unsearchable
30:28 the spider is in k. palaces
31:3 ways to that wh. destroy k.
4 it is not for k. to drink
Ec. 2:8 peculiar treasure of k.
Is. 7:16 land forsaken of both k.
10:8 are not princes altoge. k.?
14:18 k. of nations lie in glory
20:1 I am the son of ancient k.
24:21 L. punish k. of the earth
41:2 who made him ruler over k.
45:1 I will loose the loins of k.
49:7 k. shall see and arise
23 k. sh. be thy nursing fathers
60:3 k. to brighin. of thy rising
10 k. shall minister to thee
11 that their k. may be broug.
16 thou shalt suck breast of k.
62:2 all k. shall see thy glory
Jer. 2:26 k. and princes ashamed
13:13 k. that sit on David's thr.
22:4 k. sitting upon throne of D.
25:18 made Judah and k. drink
49:30 with burnings of former k.
44:17 k. and princes bu. incense
46:25 punish their k. and gods
42:3 their k. shall go to captivi.
50:41 many k. shall be raised up
51:7 I will lay thee before k.
57:2 as more deflie my name
Dan. 2:21 remoxeth k. set. up k.
4:4 in the days of these k.
47 that your G. is a Lord of k.
7:17 four great beasts are four k.
24 the ten horns are ten k.
9:6 spake to thy name to our k.
8 to k. and princes belong con.
11:2 three k. 27 these k. hearts
Hos. 7:7 all their k. are fallen
8:4 they set up k. but not by me
Pr.6, 14:28 shall seoff at k.
Mat. 10:18 bronc. before k. for my sake, Mark 13:9; Luke 21:12
17:25 wh. of earth, of whom do
Luke 10:24 have desired to see
22:25 k. of Gentiles exercise
1 Cor. 4:8 ye have reigned as k.
1 Tim. 2:2 pray. for k. and for L.
6:15 King of k. and Lord of lords, Rev. 17:14; 19:16
Heb. 7:1 returned from slaugh. k.
Rev. 1:5 J. Christ prince of k.
6 made us k. and priests to G.
10:11 must prophesy before k.
16:12 way of k. of east prepared
17 spirits which go forth to k.
16 ten k. r. one hour with bea
17:2 with whom k. of earth com.
10 seven k. receive pow. as k.
18:3 k. of earth com. fornic. 0
14 of earth have committed
15:3 k. of earth who shall bewail
19:10 eat the flesh of k. and cap.
21:24 of the earth bring glory

KINGS of the *Amorites*.

Deut. 4:47 two k. of the A. 31:4;
Jos. 2:10; 9:10; 24:12

KIN

Jos. 10:5 five k. of A. together, 6

See BOOK, GREAT.

KINGS of Israel.

1 K. 14:19 book of the Chronicles of the k. of Is. 15:31;
16:5, 14, 20, 27; 22:39; 2 K.
10:5, 14; 10:34; 13:8, 12; 14:15, 28; 15:11, 15, 21, 26, 31
16:33 prov. more th. all k. of I.
20:31 k. of I. are merciful kings
2 K. 17:2 evil but not as k. of I.
23:19 away houses k. of I. made
**2 a passo. in days of k. of I.
1 Chr. 9:1 written k. of I.
2 Chr. 16:11; 25:26;
27:7; 28:26; 32:32; 33:18
2 Chr. 20:34 in book of Jehu who is mentioned in book of the k. of I. 35:27; 32:8
28:27 not into sepul. of k. of I.
Mic. 1:14 shall be a lie to k. of I.

KINGS of Judah.

1 K. 14:29 the book of the Chronicles of the k. of Jud. 15:7, 23; 22:45; 2 K. 8:23; 15:6, 30; 16:19; 20:20; 21:17, 25; 23:28; 24:5
2 K. 12:19 written in the book of the Chronicles of the k. of J. 2 Chr. 25:26; 28:26; 32:32; 35:27; 36:8
23:11 horses k. of J. had given
12 down altars k. of J. made
22 not pass. in days of k. of J.
2 Chr. 32:11 houses k. of J. des.
Jer. 1:18 made pillar ag. k. of J.
8:1 bring out bones of k. of J.
19:4 gods k. of J. ha. not known
20:5 treas. of k. of J. to enemies
44:9 forgot. wickedn. of k. of J.

See KINGS of *Israel*.

KINGDOM.

Ex. 19:6 ye sh. be a k. of priests
Deut. 3:4 took k. of Og in Bash.
1 Sam. 10:16 mat. of k. he told
25 Sam. told manner of the k.
11:14 renew k. th. 14:47 took k.
15:28 Lord rent of k. to-day
18:8 w. can he have, more but k.?
2 Sam. 3:10 translate k. from S.
16:3 restore me k. of my father
1 K. 2:22 ask k. he is elder bro.
11:11 will rend k. from th. 31:35
13 will not rend away all k. 31
12:21 to bring k. again to Rehoboam, 2 Chr. 11:1
14:8 rent k. from house of Dav.
2 K. 14:5 as soon as k. confirmed
2 Chr. 16:20 fr. one k. to another people, Ps. 105:13
20:11 thine is the K. O Lord,
**Ps. 22:28; Mat. 6:13
2 Chr. 13:8 withstand k. of Lord
2:9 no power to keep still k.
Neh. 9:35 not serv. thee in th. k.
Est. 1:14 pri. wh. sat first in k.
2 such a time as this k.
5:3 be given to half of k. 6; 7:2
4:2 shall fight k. ag. k., Mat.
**21:7; Mark 13:8; Luke 21:10
60:14 k. not serve thee, Jer. 27:8
**Pr. 22:28; Mat. 6:13
Eccl. 4:14 sh. r. poor, born in k.
Jer. 18:7 I speak concerning a k.
Lam. 2:2 he hath polluted the k.
Ezek. 16:13 didst prosper into k.
17:14 the k. might be base
20:14 shall be there a base k.
Dan. 2:37 hath given thee k.
41 wh. G. of heaven set up a k.
4:17 rulieth in k. of men, 25, 32
31 the k. is departed from thee
36 against him, concerning k.
5:11 the spirit of holy gods in k.
28 thy k. is divided
28 thy came salute upon passes. k.
27 whose k. is an everlasting k.
21:21 not give the honor of k.
Hos. 1:4 cause to cease k. of Isr.
Amos 9:8 k. of Lord's
Mat. 4:23 gosp. of k. 9:35; 21:14
8:12 child. of k. shall be cast
12:25 k. divided k. bro. to dese.
26 Satan casteth out Sat.
13:38 good seed are child. of k.
43 shine as sun in k. of Father
23:31 inherit k. prepared for you
24:14 gospel of k. preached
26:29 drink it new in Fath. k.
Luke 11:2 blessed be k. of fath.
19:14 nobleman went to rec. k.
22:29 I appoint unto you a k.
Acts 1:6 restore k. again to Isr.?
1 Cor. 15:24 delivered up k.
Heb. 12:28 th. cannot be mo
Jam. 2:5 heirs of k. he promised

CRUDEN'S CONCORDANCE.

KIN

2 *Pet.* 1:11 entrance into everl. *k.*
Rev. 1:9 companion in *k.*
17:12 which have received no *k.*
17 and give their *k.* to tae bea.

k. THRONE, ESTABLISH, ESTABLISHED.
Mat. 6:33 but seek ye first the *k.* of God, *Luke* 12:31
12:25 *k. of God* is come unto you, *Luke* 10:9, 11:20
19:24 than for a rich man to enter into *k. of G. Mark* 10:23; *Luke* 18:24
21:31 harlots go into *k. of God*
43 *k. of G.* be taken from you
Mark 1:14 preaching *k. of God*, *Acts* 8:12; 28:23, 28:31
15 the *k. of God* is at hand
4:11 to know the mystery of *k. of God*, *Luke* 8:10
9:1 till they have seen *k. of G.*
47 better to enter into *k. of G.*
10:14 each in *k. of G. Luke* 18:16
15 whoso not receive *k. of G.*
21 hard for th. trust in riches to enter *k. of G.* 25; *Lu.* 18:25
12:31 art not far from *k. of God*
14:25 I drink it new in *k. of G.*
15:43 which waited for the *k. of God*, *Luke* 23:51
Luke 4:43 I must preach *k. of G.*
6:20 for yours is the *k. of God*
7:28 least in *k. of G.* greater th.
9:2 sent th. to preach *k. of G.* 60
27 not taste de. till see *k. of G.*
62 ha. back, not fit for *k. of G.*
13:28 see prophets in *k. of God*
14:15 he eat bread in *k. of God*
16:16 lives *k. of God* preached
17:20 *k. of God* cometh not
21 *k. of God* is within you
18:29 left chil. for *k. of G.* appear
19:11 tho. *k. of G.* sho. appear
21:31 that *k. of G.* is at hand
22:16 no fulfilled in *k. of God*
18 not drink until *k. of G.* co.
John 3:3 bo. ag. can see *k. of G.*
5 cannot enter into *k. of God*
Acts 1:3 things pertaining to *k. of God*, 8:12; 19:8
14:22 tnro' tribul. enter *k. of G.*
28:23 expou. and testi. *k. of G.*
Rom. 14:17 *k. of G.* is not meat
1 *Cor.* 4:20 *k. of God* is not in w.
6:9 unright. not inherit *k. of G.* 10 nor extortioners inhe. *k. of God*, *Gal.* 5:21; *Eph.* 5:5
15:50 flesh can. in. *k. of G.*
2 *Thes.* 1:5 worthy *k. of God*
Rev. 12:10 is come *k. of* our *God*

KINGDOM of heaven.
Mat. 3:2 repent, for *k. of heaven* is at hand, 4:17; 10:7
5:3 theirs is *k. of heaven*, 10
19 least in *k. of h.* g. in *k.*
20 in no case ent. *k of h.* 18:3
7:21 with, Lord, sh. ent. *k. of h.*
8:11 sit with Abrah. in *k. of h.*
11:11 least in *k. of h.* gre. th. he
12 *k. of heaven* suffer. violence
13:11 know mysteries of *k. of h.*
19:19 give thee keys of *k. of h.*
18:1 who is great. in *k. of h.* / 4
23:13 shut up *k. of h.* aga. men

His KINGDOM.
Gen. 10:10 begin. of *his k.* was B.
Num. 24:7 *his k.* shall be exalted
Deut. 17:18 sit. on throne of *h. k.*
1 *Chr.* 11:10 strengthened in *h. k.*
2 *Chr.* 1:1 S. strengthen. in *h. k.*
Ps. 103:19 *h. k.* ruleth over all
145:12 glorious majesty of *h. k.*
Is. 9:7 *h. k.* to order and establi.
Dan. 4:3 *his k.* is an everl. king.
34 *h. k.* fr. generat. 6:26; 7:14
11:4 *h. k.* broken and pluck. up
Mat. 12:26 *h. k.* stand? *Lu.* 11:18
13:41 gather out of *his k.* all th.
15:24 S. of man coming in *h. k.*
Luke 1:33 of *h. k.* sh. be. no end
1 *Tim.* 2:12 called yon to *h. k.*
2 *Tim.* 4:1 appearing and *his k.*
Rev. 16:10 *his k.* full of darkness

My KINGDOM.
Gen. 20:9 brou. on me and *m. k.*
2 *Sam.* 3:28 I and *m. k.* are guilt.
4:36 glo. of my *k.* in *my k.*
6:8a in every dominion of *my k.*
Mark 6:23 to half of *my k.*
Luke 22:30 drink at my table in *my k.*
John 18:36 *my k.* not of th. world

Thy KINGDOM.
1 *Sam.* 13:11 *t. k.* sh. not contin.

KIS

Ps. 45:6 *t. k.* ri. sceptre, *Heb.* 1:3
113:11 speak of glory of *thy k.*
13 *thy k.* is everlasting kingd.
Dan. 4:26 *t. k.* shall be sure
5:11 man in *t. k.* 26 numb. *t. k.*
28 *t. k.* divided to Med. and P.
Mat. 6:10 *t. k.* come, *Luke* 11:2
22:31 the other do left in *t. k.*
Luke 23:42 thou comest to *t. k.*

KINGDOMS.
1 *Sam.* 10:18 out of hand of all *k.*
1 *K.* 4:21 Sol. reigned over all *k.*
2 *K.* 19:15 God of all *k.* of earth
2 *Chr.* 12:8 may know serv. of *k.*
20:6 then rulest over all the *k.*
36:23 all *k.* hath the Lord given me, *Ezr.* 1:2
Ps. 46:6 heath. raged, *k.* moved
79:6 wrath on *k.* have not called
102:22 *k.* gathered to serve Lord
Is. 10:10 hand found *k.* of idols
13:4 noise of *k.* of nations gath.
14:16 is this man did shake *k.*
23:11 shook *k.* *Jer.* 1:10 over *k.* I have set thee
15:4 rem. to all *k.* 24:9; 34:17
25:26 all *k.* of world shall drink
29:18 make th. a terror to all *k.*
34:1 *k.* fought against Jerusal.
Ezek. 17:13 be the bas. of the *k.*
37:22 nor be divided into two *k.*
Dan. 2:14 shall cons. all these *k.*
7:23 shall be diverse from all *k.*
8:22 four *k.* arise out of nation
Nah. 3:5 will show *k.* thy shame
Zep. 3:8 assemble the *k.* to pour
Hag. 2:22 overthrow throne of *k.*
Mat. 4:8 all *k.* of world, *Luke* 4:5
Heb. 11:33 thro' faith subdued *k.*
Rev. 11:15 *k.* of world are *k.* of L.

KINGLY.
Dan. 5:20 deposed from *k.* thro.

KINSFOLK, S.
1 *K.* 16:11 none of Baasha's *k.*
2 *K.* 10:11 Jehu slew Ahab's *k.*
Job 19:14 *k.* failed and forgot, me
Luke 2:44 sought Jesus among *k.*
21:16 betrayed by *k.* and friends

KINSMAN.
Num. 5:8 if the man have no *k.*
27:11 give his inheritance to *k.*
Ruth 3:9 near *k.* 12 *k.* neurer
13 perform to thee part of a *k.*
4:1 behold, *k.* of whom B. spake
14 not left thee without a *k.*
John 18:26 *k.* whose ear P. cut off
Rom. 10:11 salute Herodi. my *k.*

KINSMEN.
Ruth 2:20 is one of our next *k.*
Ps. 35:11 lovers and *k.* stood off
Luke 14:12 call not breth. nor *k.*
Acts 10:24 Cornelius called his *k.*
Rom. 9:3 my *k.* according to flesh
10:7 salute *k.* 21 *k.* salute you

KINSWOMAN, MEN.
Lev. 18:12 is my father's near *k.*
13 she is thy mother's near *k.*
17 for they are her near *k.*
Prov. 7:4 call understand. thy *k.*

KIR.
2 *K.* 16:9 people captive to K.
Is. 15:1 K. of M. is laid waste
Amos 9:7 bro. Assyrians from K.

KIR-HARASETH.
2 *K.* 3:25 in K. left they stones
Is. 16:7 foundations of K. shall

KIRIATHAIM.
Gen. 14:5 smote Z. in Shav. K.
Jer. 48:1 K. is confounded, 23

KIRJATH-ARBA.
Gen. 23:2 Sar, died in K. *Jos.* 14:15; 20:7; *Jud.* 1:10

KIRJATH-JEARIM.
Jos. 9:17 K. a city of Hivites
1 *Sam.* 7:1 men of K. fetched ark
1 *Chr.* 13:6 the ark of God fr. K.
2 *Chr.* 1:4 broug. the ark fr. K.

KIRJATH-SEPHER. *Jos.* 15:15, 40

KISH.
1 *Sam.* 9:1 man wh. na. K. 14:51
10:11 wh. is come to son of K.
2 *Sam.* 21:14 Sa. in sepulchre K.
Acts 13:21 G. gave the son of K.

KISS, ES.
Prov. 27:6 *k.* of an enemy deceit.
Cant. 1:2 *k.* me with *k.* of mouth
Luke 7:45 thou gavest me no *k.*
22:48 betra. Son of man wi. *k.*?
Rom. 16:16 salute with a holy *k.*
1 *Cor.* 16:20 gr. wi. *k.* 2 *Cor.* 13:12
1 *Thes.* 5:26 greet breth. w. h. *k.*
1 *Pet.* 5:14 greet with *k.* of chari.

KNE

KISS, Verb.
Gen. 27:26 come near and *k.* me
31:28 not suffered to *k.* my sons
1 *Sam.* 10:9 Ama. by heard to *k.*
1 *K.* 19:20 *k.* my father and mot.
Ps. 2:12 *k.* Son, lest he be angry
Prov. 24:26 every man *k.* his lips
Cant. 1:2 *k.* me with kisses of m.
8:1 I would *k.* thee, yet I should
13:2 men sacrif. *k.* the calv.
Mat. 26:48 whomsoever I *k.* hold him fast, *Mark* 14:44
Luke 7:45 not ceased *k.* my feet
22:47 Judas drew near to J. to *k.*

KISSED.
Gen. 27:27 Ja. came and *k.* him
29:11 Jacob *k.* Rachel and wept
31:55 La. *k.* sons and daughters
45:15 J. *k.* all his brethren
48:10 J. *k.* Joseph's sons
50:1 Jos. fell on fa.'s face *k.* him
Ex. 4:27 met Moses and *k.* him
18:7 met father-in-law *k.* him
Ruth 1:9 Na. *k.* daughters-in-law
1 *Sam.* 10:1 poured oil and *k.* S.
20:41 Jonathan and David *k.*
2 *Sam.* 14:33 king *k.* Absalom
19:5 Absa. *k.* any man came ni.
1 *K.* 19:18 mouth hath not *k.*
Job 31:27 month hath *k.* hand
Ps. 85:10 and peace *k.* each other
Prov. 7:13 caught him *k.* him
Mat. 26:49 said, Hail, Master, and *k.* him, *Mark* 14:45
Luke 7:38 M. *k.* feet and anointed
13:20 fell on his neck and *k.* him
Acts 20:37 fell on P.'s neck *k.* h.

KITE.
Lev. 11:14 *k.* uncl. *Deut.* 14:13

KITTIM. *Gen.* 10:4; 1 *Chr.* 1:7

KNEAD, ED
Gen. 18:6 *k.* it and make cakes
1 *Sam.* 28:24 took flour and *k.* it
2 *Sam.* 13:8 Tamar took flour *k.*
Jer. 7:18 women *k.* their dough
Hos. 7:4 the baker *k.* the dough

KNEADING.
Ex. 8:3 frogs co. into *k.*-troughs
12:34 *k.*-troughs bound to cloth.

KNEE.
Gen. 41:43 they cried, Bow the *k.*
Is. 45:23 unto me every *k.* sh. bow, *Rom.* 14:11; *Phil.* 2:10
Mat. 27:29 bowed the *k.* bef. him
Rom. 11:4 bowed the *k.* to Baal

KNEEL, ED.
Gen. 24:11 ma. his camels *k.* do.
2 *Chr.* 6:13 Solomon *k.* on knees
Dan. 6:10 D. *k.* three times a day
Luke 22:41 and Jesus *k.* down
Acts 7:60 Stephen *k.* and cried
9:40 Peter *k.* prayed; 20:36 P.
21:5 we *k.* down on the shore

KNEELING.
1 K. 8:54 Solomon rose from *k.*
Mat. 17:14 came to him *k.*-ing, *Mark* 10:17
Mark 1:40 came a leper *k.*

KNEES.
Gen. 30:3 maid sh. hear on my *k.*
48:12 bron. them fr. between *k.*
50:23 brought up on Joseph's *k.*
Deut. 28:35 Lord smite thee in *k.*
Jud. 7:5 bowed down *k.* 6
16:19 made Sam. sleep on his *k.*
1 *K.* 8:54 arose fr. kneeling on *k.*
19:18 *k.* have not bowed to Baal
2 *K.* 1:13 fell on *k.* before Elijah
4:20 sat on mother's *k.* till noon
2 *Chr.* 6:13 Sol. kneeled on his *k.*
Ezr. 9:5 I fell on my *k.*
Job 3:12 why did *k.* prevent me
4:4 strengthened the feeble *k.*
Ps. 109:24 *k.* weak thro' fasting
Is. 35:3 confirm the feeble *k.*
66:12 and be dandled on her *k.*
Ezek. 7:17 *k.* weak as water, 21:7
47:4 the waters were to the *k.*
Dan. 5:6 *k.* smote one ag. another
6:10 kneeled on *k.* three times
10:10 a hand set me upon my *k.*
Nah. 2:10 the *k.* smite together
Mark 15:19 bowing *k.* worship.
Luke 5:8 Peter fell at Jesus' *k.*
Eph. 3:14 bow my *k.* to Father
22:12 hands hang do. fe. *k.*

KNEW.
Gen. 4:1 Adam *k.* E. his wife, 25
17 Cain *k.* wife, she conceived
28:16 Jud. *k.* her again no more
Jud. 19:25 *k.* her abused her
19:25 *k.* her abused her

KNE
1 *K.* 1:4 but the king *k.* her not
Mat. 1:25 Joseph *k.* her not

KNEW.
Gen. 3:7 Adam and Eve *k.* that
9:24 Noah *k.* what son had done
38:9 O. *k.* seed should not be h.
42:7 Joseph saw and *k.* breth. 8
Num. 34:16 *k.* knowl. of M. H.
Deut. 34:10 wh. L. *k.* face to face
18:32 Saul F. L. was with David
20:39 D. and Jonathan *k.* mat.
22:17 bec. they *k.* when he fled
28:17 Saul *k.* David's voice
2 *Sam.* 11:16 *k.* that valiant men
2 *Chr.* 33:13 Manas. *k.* L. was G.
Est. 1:13 that *k.* law and judgm.
Job 23:3 *k.* where I might find
Is. 48:4 I *k.* thou art obstinate
7 should. say, Behold, I *k.* th.
Jer. 1:5 I formed thee, I *k.* thee
38:8 I *k.* this was word of Lord
41:4 slain Gedaliah, no man *k.*
44:15 *k.* wives burnt incense
Dan. 5:21 he *k.* Most High ruled
6:10 Daniel *k.* wri. was signed
Jon. 4:2 *k.* thou art a graci. God
Zec. 11:11 *k.* it was word of L.
Mat. 7:23 profess I never *k.* you
12:25 J. *k.* thoughts, *Luke* 6:8
25:24 I *k.* thee, thou art hard m.
Mark 1:34 because they *k.* him
Luke 4:41 they *k.* he was Christ
12:47 servant *k.* his lord's will
24:31 eyes opened, they *k.* him
John 2:24 because he *k.* all men
25 for he *k.* what was in man
6:6 himself *k.* what he would do
64 Jesus *k.* from the beginning
11:42 I *k.* that thou hearest me
57 if any man *k.* where he was
13:1 Jesus *k.* his hour was co.
11 he *k.* who should betray h.
28 no man at the table *k.* for
18:2 Judas *k.* the place
19:28 Jesus *k.* all thi. accompl.
21:12 none *k.* it was Peter's voi.
Acts 3:10 they *k.* that it was the L.
1 *Sam.* 3:19 sons of Eli *k.* n. L.
20:39 the lad *k.* not any thing
2 *Sam.* 11:20 *k.* ye a. th. would
18:29 but I *k.* not what it was
22:44 peop. I *k.* n. sh. serve me
Job 29:12 Job's friends *k.* him *n.*
29:16 cause I *k.* n. I search. out
42:3 th. I *k.* n. wonder. for me
Ps. 35:11 charge things I *k.* not
Prov. 24:12 behold, we *k.* it not
Is. 42:16 blind by ways they *k.* n.
55:5 nations that *k.* not thee
Jer. 2:8 that handle law, *k.* me n.
11:19 I *k.* not they had devised
44:3 serve gods whom they *k.* n.
Dan. 11:38 whom fathers *k.* not
Hos. 8:4 made prin. and I *k.* it n.
11:3 they *k.* not till I've flood came
Luke 2:43 Jos. and mother *k.* n.
12:48 *k.* not and did commit th.
John 1:10 the world *k.* him not
31 and I *k.* him not, 33
20:9 they *k.* not the scriptures
14 *k.* not that it was J. 21:4
Acts 12:27 because they *k.* him n.
19:32 *k.* n. wherefore they came
27:39 when day, they *k.* n. land
1 *Cor.* 1:21 by wisdom *k.* not G.
Gal. 4:8 then when ye *k.* not God
1 *John* 3:1 because it *k.* him not

KNEWEST.
Deut. 8:3 fed with manna, *k.* not
Ruth 2:11 to people thou *k.* not
Neh. 9:10 *k.* that they dealt proud
Job 38:5 declare it if thou *k.* *not*
Mat. 25:26 thou *k.* I reaped where
I sowed not, *Luke* 19:22
Luke 19:44 *k.* not time of visit.
John 4:10 if thou *k.* gift of God

KNO

KNIFE.
Gen. 22:6 Abraham took *k.* 10
Jud. 19:29 took *k.* and laid hold
Prov. 23:2 put a *k.* to thy throat
Ezek. 5:1 take the ·a sharp *k.* 2

KNIVES.
Jos. 5:2 make sharp *k.*
3 Joshua made him sharp *k.*
1 K. 18:28 cut themselves with *k.*
Ezr. 1:9 nine and twenty *k.*
Prov. 32:14 teeth as *k.* dev. poor

KNIT.
Jud. 20:11 *k.* were *k.* together
1 Sam. 18:1 Jonathan *k.* to Da.
1 Chr. 12:17 my heart be *k.* to y.
Acts 10:11 sheet *k.* at four corne.
Col. 2:2 hearts *k.* together in lo.
19 body *k.* together increaseth

KNOCK, ED.
Mat. 7:7 *k.* it sh. be op. Lu. 11:9
Luke 13:25 begin to *k.* at door
Acts 12:13 as Peter *k.* at the door
Ibid. 16 *k.* stand at door and *k.*

KNOCKETH, ING.
Cant. 5:2 voice of beloved that *k.*
Mat. 7:8 him that *k.* shall be
opened, Luke 11:10
Luke 12:36 when he *k.* they may
Acts 12:16 Peter continued *k.*

KNOP, S.
Ex. 25:31 his *k.* and his flowers,
31, 34, 35; 37:17, 19, 20, 24
1 K. 6:18 cedar carved with *k.*
7:24 *k.* compass. it. *k.* cast into

KNOW.
Gen. 3:5 God doth *k.* your eyes
24 one of us, to *k.* good and e.
19:21 I will go and see, I will *k.*
Ex. 18:16 *k.* the statutes of God
Num. 11:21 they shall *k.* the la.
Deut. 4:39 *k.* this day, 11:2
8:2 *k.* what was in thy heart
13:3 *k.* whether ye love the Lo.
Jos. 4:22 let your children *k.*
23:13 and Israel he shall *k.*
II · A 3:41 city of my peo. doth *k.*
11 before one could *k.* another
1 Sam. 17:47 assembly shall *k.* L.
21:2 let no man *k.* any thing
24:11 *k.* there is no evil in me
28:3 *k.* what thy servant can do
2 Sam. 3:25 thy going out, *k.* all
19:20 serv. *k.* that I have sinned
1 K. 8:31 *k.* every man the
plague, 2 Chr. 6:29
2 K. 5:8 b. *k.* there is a prophet
10:10 *k.* there shall fall nothing
1 Chr. 28:9 *k.* thou G. of thy fat.
2 Chr. 13:5 to *k.* that the L. gave
Ed. 4:5 *k.* what it was, and why
Job 5:24 *k.* thy tabernacle
25 *k.* that thy seed sh. be great
27 and *k.* thou it for thy good
7:10 nor shall his place *k.* him
8:9 but of yesterday, *k.* nothing
11:6 *k.* that God exacteth less
8 what canst thou *k.*?
13:23 make me *k.* my transgres.
15:8 *k.* that G. hath overthrown
21:29 G. reward. him, he sh. *k.*
22:13 sayest, How doth God *k.*?
23:1 they *k.* that *k.* him not see 1
17 If one *k.* them, thy are in
31:6 *k.* am. oursel. what is good
37:15 dost *k.* when God dispos.
38:20 *k.* the paths to the house
42:3 *L.* hath set apart godly
9:10 that *k.* thy nu. trust in thee
33:4 L. make me to *k.* mine end
40:10 still, and *k.* that I am G.
51:6 in hid. part make me to *k.*
53:21 let them *k.* that G. ruleth
73:11 doth *k.* 16 thought to *k.*
89:15 blessed are they that *k.*
103:16 place shall *k.* it no more
139:23 *k.* my heart, *k.* my thou.
142:1 no man would *k.* me
143:3 *k.* way wherein I should
Prov. 1:2 *k.* wisd. and instruct
4:1 attend to *k.* understanding
10:32 righteous *k.* wh. is accept.
27:23 dilig. to *k.* state of flocks
Ec. 1:17 gave heart to *k.* wisdom
8:17 tho. a wise man think to *k.*
9:5 the living *k.* they shall die
11:9 *k.* that G. will bring in ju.
Is. 7:16 before the child *k.* to ref.
19:21 Egyptians shall *k.* the L.
41:20 that they may see and *k.*
43:10 all flesh shall *k.* I am
50:4 *k.* how to speak in season
52:6 my people sh. *k.* my name
58:2 and delight to *k.* my ways
65:16 *k.* that I the L. am thy *k.*
Jer. 2:19 *k.* it is evil to forsake

Jer. 9:6 thro' deceit refuse to *k.*
15:15 *k.* that for thy sake I suf.
16:21 cause them to *k.* my hand,
and they sh. *k.* my name is
17:9 heart deceit. who can *k.* it?
21:7 give them a heart to *k.* me
31:34 *k.* the Lord, for they shall
all *k.* me, Heb. 8:11
26:19 let no man *k.* where ye be
Ezek. 2:5 *k.* ha. been a pro. 33:33
8:13 *k.* I the Lord have spoken
25:14 they sh. *k.* my vengeance
38:16 all that *k.* thee he aston.
39:30 they *k.* I am with them
37:28 heathen shall *k.* 39:23
Dan. 2:21 know. to them who *k.*
4:25 *k.* that M. High ruleth, 32
7:16 made me *k.* interpretation
11:32 peo. that *k.* God be strong
Hos. 2:20 thou shalt *k.* the Lord
9:7 Israel shall *k.* it
13:4 thou sh. *k.* no God but me
14:9 prudent, and he sh. *k.* th.
Mic. 3:1 for you to *k.* judgment
Zec. 2:9 I the L. sent me, 4:9
Mal. 2:4 ye sh. *k.* I have sent th.
4:5 *k.* not thy left hand *k.*
7:11 *k.* how to give, Luke 11:13
9:30 see no man *k.* it. Mark
5:43; 7:24; 9:30
12:11 it is given to you to *k.*
Mark 4:11; Luke 8:10
24:33 *k.* desolation is near,
Mark 13:23; Luke 21:20
John 4:42 we *k.* that this is Chr.
7:17 he shall *k.* of the doctrine
10:4 sheep fol. they *k.* his voice
14 am good Shep. *k.* my sheep
13:7 thou shalt *k.* hereafter
35 men *k.* ye are my disciples
13:31 behold, they *k.* what I ea.
Ac's 1:7 not for you to *k.* times
22:14 *k.* his will and see J. One
26:4 from my youth *k.* all Jews
Rom. 7:1 speak to them that *k.*
10:19 I say, Did not Israel *k.*?
1 Cor. 2:11 neither can he *k.* th.
8:2 know. noth. as ought to *k.*
Eph. 3:19 *k.* the love of Christ
1 Thes. 3:5 I se. to *k.* your faith
4:4 ev. one sho. *k.* how to pos.
5:12 *k.* them who labour among
1 Tim. 4:3 believe and *k.* truth
2 Tim. 3:1 *k.* also that *k.* last d.
Tit. 1:16 profess that they *k.* G.
Jam. 4:20 with thou *k.* O vain
Jude 10 what they *k.* naturally
Rev. 2:23 churches sh. *k.* I am he
3:9 make them *k.* I have loved

See CERTAIN, CERTAINLY, CERTAINTY.

I KNOW.
Gen. 12:11 *I k.* thou art fair wo.
15:8 *I k.* that I shall inherit?
18:19 *I k.* he will com. his chil.
22:12 *I k.* that thou fearest God
48:19 *I k.* it, my son, *I k.*
Ex. 3:7 said, *I k.* their sorrows
4:14 brother? *I k.* he can speak
18:11 *I k.* L. grea. than all gods
33:12 *I k.* thee by thy name, 17
Deut. 31:21 *I k.* th. imagination
29 *I k.* that after my death
Jos. 2:9 *I k.* L. hath given you
Jud. 17:13 *I k.* L. will do good
1 Sam. 20:30 *I k.* cho. son of J.
21:20 *I k.* thou shalt surely be
29:9 *I k.* thou art good
2 K. 2:3 *I k.* it, hold peace, 5
5:15 *I k.* there is no G. in earth
19:27 *I k.* thy abode, Is. 37:28
1 Chr. 29:17 *I k.* thou triest heart
21:8 *I k.* my G. hath deliverance
Job 9:28 *I k.* thou wilt not hold
Ibid. 19:25 *I k.* my Redeemer liveth
21:27 *I k.* your thoughts
30:23 *I k.* thou wilt bring me to death
42:2 *I k.* thou canst do every th.
Ps. 20:6 *I k.* L. saveth anointed
41:11 *I k.* thou favorest me
50:11 *I k.* all fowls of mountain
119:75 *I k.* O L. thy judg. right.
135:5 *I k.* L. is greater above all
140:12 *I k.* L. will maint. cause
Ec. 3:12 *I k.* no good in them
14 *I k.* whatsoever God doeth
8:12 *I k.* it shall be well with
Is. 48:4 *I k.* that thou art obsti.
66:18 *I k.* works and thoughts
Jer. 10:23 *I k.* the way of man
11:18 L. given me knowl. *I k.* it
23:11 *I k.* abomin. *I k.* thou
23 *I k.* am not witness, sai. L.
48:30 *I k.* his wrath, saith L.
Ezek. 11:5 *I k.* things that come
Hos. 13:5 *I k.* thee in wilder

Jon. 1:12 *I k.* for my sake temp.
Mat. 25:5 *I k.* that ye seek Jesus
Mark 1:34 *I k.* who thou art.
Luke 4:34
Luke 1:18 whereby sh. *I k.* this
John 4:25 *I k.* that Messias com.
8:37 *I k.* ye are Abraham's seed
55 *I k.* him; 9:25 one thi. *I k.*
10:15 knoweth me, *I k.* Father
11:22 *I k.* that what thou ask G.
24 *I k.* that he shall rise again
13:18 *I k.* whom I have chosen
Acts 12:11 *I k.* for a surety Lord
19:15 Jesus *I k.* and Paul *I k.*
10:35 *I k.* ye see my fa. no more
Rom. 7:18 *I k.* in me dw. no good
1 Cor. 4:4 *I k.* nothing by myself
13:12 *I k.* in part, then shall *I k.*
Phil. 1:19 *I k.* this shall turn
25 *I k.* I shall abide with you
4:12 *I k.* how to be abased, *I k.*
2 Tim. 1:12 *I k.* whom I believed
1 Jo. 2:4 he that saith, *I k.* him
Rev. 2:2 *I k.* thy works, 13; 3:8

KNOW not, or not KNOW.
Gen. 4:9 where is Abel? *I k. not*
27:2 *I k. not* day of my death
1 Sam. 3:7 Sam. did *not* yet *k.* L.
1 K. 18:12 Sp. carry thee *I k. not*
Ezr. 7:23 *k. not*, manner of God
Job 9:21 would *I not k.* my soul
15:9 know. thou that we *k. n.?*
21:29 do ye *not k.* their tokens?
24:13 *k. not* the ways thereof
16 dig in dark. they *k. n.* light
20 God *not* to give flatter. titles
36:26 God great. *we k.* him *not*
Ps. 71:15 *k. n.* numbers thereof
82:5 *k. not* neither understand
94:10 teach men, shall *not* he
k.?
101:4 *I* will *n. k.* wicked person
121:3 doth *not* he *k.* it, mall th.
30:18 four things which *I k. not*
Ec. 9:5 dead *k. not* anything
Is. 1:3 but Israel doth *not k.*
43:19 ye *n. k.* it? 41:8 *I k. not*
47:11 *not k.* from wh. it ariseth
56:8 way of peace they *k. not*
Jer. 5:4 they *k. not* way of Lord
7:9 after gods, whom ye *k. n.?*
8:7 my people *k. not* judgments
9:3 they *k. not* me, saith Lord
12:25 furr on heathen *k.* thee *n.*
Ezek. 28:19 shalt *k. not* me *k. n.*
Hos. 2:8 did *n. k.* I gave her corn
Amos 3:10 th. *k. not* to do rightly
Mic. 4:12 *k. not* thoughts of Lo.
Mat. 25:12 I say, *I k.* you *not*
26:70 I *k. not* what thou sayest
74 saying, *I k. not* the man, 74;
Mark 14:68, 71
Mark 20:28 ye *k. not* what ye ask
12:24 because ye *k. not* scriptures
Luke 7:31 seeing *I k. not* a man
13:25 *I k. n.* whence you are, 27
22:57 say, Woman, *I k.* him *not*
60 I *k. not* what thou sayest
21:34 they *k. not* what they do
John 8:19 ye *k.* neither me nor F.
9:29 we *k. not* from wh. he is
John 5:11 we speak th. we do *k.*
6:70 wh. they worship
k. not; we *k.* what we worship
7:27 we *k.* whence this man is
8:14 ye *k. not* whence I came
9:30 we *k.* that God spake to
Moses
31 we *k.* God heareth not sin.
11:51 we *k. not* will, th. preser.
13:35 we *k.* his testim. is true
Rom. 7:14 we *k.* law is spiritual
8:28 we *k.* things work for good
to them who lo. G. wh. il no.
Mark 12:14 Luke 20:21
Mat. 22:16 we *k.* thou art true,
6:22 ye *n. k.*, our fathers
Phil. 3:10 that I my y. *k.* him
Col. 4:6 ye *n. k.* how to answer
1 Tim. 3:15 *n. k.* how thou oug.
20 we *n. k.* him that is true

We KNOW, or KNOW we.
Gen. 20:5 they said, we *k.* him
Deut. 18:21 how shall we *k.* wo.
2 Chr. 20:12 nor *k.* we what to do
Job 36:26 G. is gr. we *k.* not him
Is. 26:14 our iniqui. we *k.* them
Rom. 6:3 then wh. we *k.* if we fol.
we cry to me, My G. we *k.* Thee
Mat. 22:16 we *k.*, thou art true,
Mark 12:14; Luke 20:21
John 3:11 we speak th. we do *k.*
4:22 wh. *k.* not what ye worship
we *k.* what we worship
6:19 we *k.* that is our devil
9:20 we *k.* that his is our son
9:24 we *k.* that God spake to
Moses
31 we *k.* God heareth not sin.
11:51 we *k. not* will, th. preser.
13:35 we *k.* his testim. is true
Rom. 7:14 we *k.* law is spiritual
8:28 we *k.* things work for good
1 Cor. 8:1 we *k.* have knowl.
4 we *k.* an idol is noth. in w.
13:9 for we *k.* in part, and prop.
2 Cor. 5:1 we *k.* if our earthly h.
10 *k.* we no man after the flesh
1 Tim. 1:8 we *k.* that law is good
Heb. 10:30 we *k.* him hath said
1 John 2:3 we *k.* that we know
5 *k.* that we are in him
18 we *k.* that it is the last time
29 we *k.* that wh. he sh. appear
3:2 we *k.* we are of the truth
3:19 *k.* we are of the truth
21 we *k.* that he abideth in us
4:6 we are of truth and error
13 *k.* we that we dwell in him
16 we *k.* and believed love
5:16 we *k.* we heareth us, we
k. we have petitions
19 we *k.* we are of God
20 *k.* we may *k.* him that
is true

KNOW that I am the Lord.
Ex. 6:7 ye shall *k.* that *I am* the
L. 16:12; 1 K 20:28; Ezek.
16:62; 20:20, 42, 44; 24:24;
28:24; 29:6, 9, 21; 30:8;
33:29; 34:27; 35:15; 36:33;
38:23; 39:6, 28
7:5 Egyptians *k.* that *I am the L.*
Ezek. 20:26 I am the Lord

CRUDEN'S CONCORDANCE.

CRUDEN'S CONCORDANCE. 919

KOR
Acts 22:30 k. the certainty, 23:28
Rom. 1:19 wh. may be k. of God
11:34 who hath k. the mind of Lord, 1 Cor. 2:16
1 Cor. 13:12 even as I also am k.
14:7 k. what is piped or harped
2 Cor. 3:2 epistle known and read
5:16 have k. Christ after flesh
6:9 unknown, and yet well k.
Gal. 4:9 k. God or are k. of God
Eph. 3:10 might he k. by church
Phil. 4:5 moderation k. to all m.
2 Tim. 3:10 fully k. my doctrine
15 fr. a child k. holy scriptures
1 John 2:13 bec. ye ha. k. him, 14
2 John 1 them that have k. truth

Made, or madest KNOWN.
Gen. 45:1 Joseph m. himself k.
Neh. 9:14 m. k. thy holy sabbath
Ps. 98:2 Lord m. k. his salvation
103:7 m. k. his ways to Moses
Dan. 2:23 m. k. to us king's m.
Hos. 5:9 m. k. that which sh. be
Luke 2:17 m. k. abroad saying
John 15:15 all I heard, I m. k.
Acts 2:28 m. k. to me ways of life
7:13 Joseph m. k. to brethren
Rom. 16:26 m. k. to all nations
Eph. 1:9 m. k. to us mystery
3:3 he m. k. to me mystery
Phil. 4:6 requests be m. k. to G.
2 Pet. 1:16 m. k. coming of our L.

Make KNOWN.
Num. 12:6 I will m. myself k.
1 Chr. 16:8 m. k. his deeds amo. people, Ps. 105:1
Ps. 89:1 m. k. thy faithfulness
106:8 m. k. his mighty power
145:12 to m. k. to sons of men
Prov. 1:23 make k. my words
Is. 38:19 father sh. m. k. truth
61:2 m. thy name k. to adverse.
Ezek. 39:11 ma. myself k. among them
39:7 m. my holy name k. in Isr.
Dan. 2:25 man will m. k. to king
Lord m. k. to the king, 29
Hab. 3:2 in midst of years m. k.
Rom. 9:22 God will. to m. po. k.
23 m. k. riches of his glory
Eph. 6:19 m. k. mystery of gosp.
Col. 1:27 to whom G. will m. k.

Not KNOWN.
Gen. 19:3 two dau. have not k. man, Num. 31:18, 35; Jud. 21:12
41:21 it. be k. they had eaten
31 plenty shall it. be k. in land
Ex. 6:3 by name Jehovah I n. k.
Deut. 11:2 chil. have n. k. 31:13
24 after gods ye k. n. 13:6, 13
Jud. 3:1 ind not k. wars of Can.
16:9 so his strength was not k.
Ruth 3:14 not be k. wo. came in
Ps. 1:12 a. k. to be wife of Cor.
Ps. 16:3 peo. whom I have n. k.
77:19 thy footsteps are not k.
78:6 wn. on heather ha. n. k.
95:10 n. k. my ways, Heb. 3:10
147:20 judgm. they have n. k.
Pr. 6:5 not seen nun n. k. any th.
Is. 42:16 paths they have not k.
41:18 have n. k. nor understood
45:4 tho' thou hast n. k. me, 5
Jer. 4:31 they have not k. me
Ezek. 32:9 count. thou hast n. k.
Dan. 3:5 will n. make k. drea. 9
4:7 n. make k. interpreta. 5:8
Hos. 5:3 they have not k. the L.
Nah. 3:17 place n. k. w. they are
Mal. 12:27 is nothing hid that shall n. be k. Luke 8:17; 12:2
John 8:55 ye have not k. him
1:29 yet hast thou not k. me
18:3 h.ve not k. the Father nor
17:25 Fa. world hath n. k. thee
Rom. 3:17 way of pe. they not k.
7:7 I had n. k. sin but by law
2 Pet. 2:21 not k. way of right.
1 John 3:6 sinner not n. seen not k.
Rev. 2:21 not k. the depths of S.

KORAH.
Gen. 36:11; Ex. 6:16; Num. 14, 16; 17:1; 1 Chr. 6:3, 22, 51
1 Chr. 15:5 of sons of K. Uriel

KOHATHITES. Num. 3:31; Jos. 21:3; 2 Chr. 20:19.

KORAH.
Gen. 35:5 Aholibamah bare K. 16
Ex. 6:21 sons of Iz. K. Num. 10:1
16:5 told censers, K. 19, 49
27:9 Dathan sir. in comp. of K.
27:3 father not in comp. of K.
1 Chr. 1:35 the sons of Keau, K.
Jude 11 perished in gains. of K.

LAB

L.

LADAN.
Gen. 24:29 Reb. had a brother L.
36:36 Jac. fed rest of L.'s flocks
31:3 countenance of L. 13, 55
32:4 I have sojourned with L.

LABOR, Substantive.
Gen. 31:42 G. seen l. of my hands
35:16 Rachel had hard l. 17
Deut. 26:7 L. heard, looked on l.
Neh. 5:13 God sha. ev. man fr. l.
Job 39:11 will th. leave l. to him
Ps. 90:10 their strength l. sorrow
104:23 man gooth to l. till even.
105:44 inherited l. of the people
107:14 bro. down heart with l.
109:11 let stranger spoil his l.
128:2 sh. eat the l. of thy hands
Prov. 10:16 l. tendeth to life
13:11 galnareth by l. shall incr.
11:23 in all l. there is profit
Ec. 1:3 wh. profit hath man of l.
8 all things are full of l. man
2:10 rejoiced in my portion of l.
18 I hated all l. wh. I had tak.
19 shall he rule over all my l.
21 man whose l. is in wisdom
22 what hath man of all his l.?
24 enjoy good in l. 3:13; 5:18
4:8 yet is th. no end of all his l.
9 they have a good rewa. for l.
5:15 nothing of l. he may carry
19 rejoice in l. this is gift of G.
6:7 l. of man is for his mouth
9:9 portion in thy l. under sun
10:15 l. of foolish wearieth
Is. 45:14 l. of Egypt come to thee
55:2 why spend your l. for that
Jer. 3:24 devoured l. of fathers
20:18 came l out of wo. to see l. ?
Ezek. 23:29 giv. land of Eg. for l.
Hab. 3:17 though l. of olive fail
Hag. 1:11 drought on l. of hands
John 4:38 reap wh. bestow. no l.
Rom. 16:6 bestow. much l. on us
1 Cor. 3:8 man rec. accord. to l.
15:58 know your l. is not in vain
Gal. 4:11 lest I bestow. l. in vain
Phil. 1:22 this is fruit of my l.
1 Thes. 1:3 remember. l. of love
2:9 remember our l. and travail
3:5 and our l. be in vain
2 Thes. 3:8 but wrought with l.
Heb. 6:10 not forget your l. of lo.
Rev. 2:2 I kn. thy l. and patience

LABOR, Verb.
Ex. 5:9 dayes l. 20:9; Deut. 5:13
Jos. 24:13 for wh. ye did not l.
Neh. 4:22 guard us, and l. on day
Job 9:29 why then l. l in vain?
Ps. 127:1 exc. L. build l. in vain
144:14 oxen may be strong to l.
Prov. 23:3 his hands refuse to l.
23:4 l. not to be rich, cease from
Ec. 4:8 saith, For whom do I l.?
8:17 tho' a man l. to seek to ent.
Is. 22:4 weep, l. not to comfort
65:23 they shall not l. in vain
Jer. 51:58 the prop. sh. l. in vain
Lam. 5:5 under persecution we l.
Mic. 4:10 l. to bring forth, O Zi.
Hab. 2:13 people should l. in fire
Jud. 11:38 to. to me all ye th. l.
John 6:27 l. not for meat th. per.
Rom. 16:9 Tryphon, who l.
1 Cor. 4:12 l. with our own hands
2 Cor. 5:9 wh. wh. therefore l. to be accepted
Eph. 4:28 let h. l. to the best
Col. 1:29 whereunto I l. striving
1 Thes. 5:12 know them which l.
1 Tim. 4:10 l. and suffer reproach
5:17 that l. in word and doctrine
Heb. 4:11 l. to enter into that rest

LABORED.
Neh. 4:21 so we l. in the work
Job 20:18 he l. for, sh. he restore
Ec. 2:11 looked on labor I. l. to do
19 rule over my labor I have l.
21 there is wh. l. prof. ha. he lt.
22 what hath a man for all he l.?
5:16 what prof. hath he that l.?
49:4 I said, I have l. in vain
62:8 not drink, for which thou l.
Dan. 6:14 king l. to deliv. Daniel
Jon. 4:10 l. and ye are entered
Luke 5:5 have toiled all night
John 4:38 other men l. ye entered
Rom. 16:12 Persis l. much in L.
1 Cor. 15:10 l. more abundantly
Phil. 2:16 I have not l. in vain
4:3 help those that l. with me
Rev. 2:3 for my name's sake

LABORER, S.
Mat. 9:37 harvest plenteous, but
few, 38; Luke 10:2
20:1 went out early to hire l.
Luke 10:7 l. is worthy of his hire
1 Cor. 3:9 together with God

LAD

1 Tim. 5:18 l. is worthy of rewa.
Jam. 5:4 behold the hire of the l.

LABORETH.
Prov. 16:26 he that l. l. for him.
Ec. 3:9 wh. profit in that he l.?
1 Cor. 16:16 sub. to ev. one that l.
2 Tim. 3:6 the husbandm. that l.

LABORING.
Ec. 5:12 sleep of l. man sweet
Acts 20:35 l. ye ou. to sup. weak
Col. 4:12 l. for you in prayer
1 Thes. 2:9 l. night and day

LABORS.
Ex. 23:16 first-fruits of thy l.
Deut. 28:33 thy l. sh. a nation eat
Prov. 5:10 l. be in ho. of stranger
Is. 58:3 in day of fast ye ex. all l.
Jer. 20:5 I will deliver all their l.
Hos. 12:8 in my l. sh. find no ini.
Hag. 2:17 smote you in all the l.
John 4:38 are entered in their l.
2 Cor. 6:5 in l. in watchings
10:15 boasting of other men's l.
11:23 l. more abund. in stripes
Rev. 14:13 may rest from their l.

LACE.
Ex. 28:28 sh. bind the breastpla. with l. 37; 39:31

LACHISH.
Jos. 10:32 the Lord delivered L.
2 Ki. 14:19 and he fled to L.
18:14 Hezek. sent to king to L.
2 Chr. 11:9 Rehoboam built L.
32:9 king sent to L. after him
Mic. 1:13 O inhabitant of L. bind

LACK, Substantive.
Gen. 18:28 wilt des. all for l. five?
Ex. 16:18 that gathered little had no l. 2 Cor. 8:15
Job 4:11 lion perish. for l. of prey
38:41 young wand. for l. of meat
4:6 peo. destroyed for l. ka.
Phil. 2:30 life to supply l. of ser.
1 Thes. 4:12 that ye l. of nothing

LACK, Verb.
Gen. 18:28 if there shall l. five
Deut. 8:9 shall not l. anything
Ps. 34:10 the young lions do l.
Ec. 9:8 let thy head l. no oint.
Mat. 19:20 I kept, wh. l. I yet?
Jam. 1:5 any l. wisd. ask of God

LACKED.
Deut. 2:7 thou hast l. nothing
1 K. 4:27 provid. victual, l. noth.
Neh. 9:21 sustain th. th. l. noth.
Luke 22:35 l. ye any thing?
Acts 4:31 any amo. them that l.
1 Cor. 12:24 honor to which l.
Phil. 4:10 careful, l. opportunity

LACKEST.
Mark 10:21 but one thing thou l. Luke 18:22

LACKETH.
Num. 31:49 there l. not one man
2 Sam. 3:29 not fall one l. bread
Prov. 6:32 adult. l. understand.
12:9 honor. himself and l. bread
2 Pet. 1:9 th. l. th. things is blind

LACKING.
Lev. 2:13 th. sha. be one th. l.
Jud. 21:3 sh. be one tribe l.
Jer. 23:4 no more, nor sh. be l.
1 Cor. 16:17 wh. was l. they sup.
2 Cor. 11:9 l. to me breth. sup.
1 Thes. 3:10 might perf. what is l.

LAD.
Gen. 21:17 God heard voice of l.
18 lift up l. 19 gave l. drink
24:14 was with l. and he grew
22:5 I and the l. will go yonder
12 lay not thy hand upon the l.
43:22 l. cannot leave father, 30
38 abide·fast. of l. let the l. go
21 his life is bound up in the l.
44:16 I. redeemed me, bless l.
1 Sam. 20:36 shoot, and l. Run
2 l. l. his the barley loaves

LADDER.
Gen. 28:12 behold a l. set up

LADE, ED.
Gen. 45:17 l. beasts, go to Canaan
Neh. 4:17 l. bessets, go to Chaman
Phil. 4:16 l. wrought to work
Luke 11:46 l. men with burdens
Acts 28:10 l. us wi. th. necessary

LADEN.
Gen. 45:23 l. with good things
Is. 1:4 a people l. with iniquity
Mat. 11:28 l. are heavy l.
2 Tim. 3:6 women, l. with sins

LAM

LADETH, ING.
Neh. 13:15 some on sab. l. asses
Hab. 2:6 woe to him that l. him.
Acts 27:10 damage not only of l.

LADY.
Is. 47:5 no more be called a l.
7 saidst, I shall be a l. for ever
2 John 1 the elder to the elect l.
5 l. that we love one another

LADIES.
Jud. 5:29 wise l. answered her
Est. 1:18 likew. shall l. of Persia

LAID. See after LAY.
LAISH. Jud. 18:14; 1 Sam. 25:44;
2 Sam. 3:15; Is. 10:30

LAKE.
Luke 5:1 Jesus stood by l. of G.
2 two ships standing by the l.
8:23 a storm of wind on the l.
33 herd ran violently into l.
Rev. 19:20 both cast in l. fire
20:10 devil cast into l. of fire
14 death and hell cast in l.
15 not in bo. of life, cast into l.
21:8 murderers have part in l.

LAMB.
Gen. 22:7 l. for a burnt offering?
8 God will provide himself a l.
Ex. 12:3 they shall take a l. 21
5 l. shall be without blemish
12:13 sh. redeem with a l. 34:20
29:39 one l. th. sh. offer in morn. other l. at even. 41; Nu. 28:4
40 a l. a tenth deal of flour, Num. 28:21, 29; 29:4, 10, 15
Lev. 9:3 take a l. of first year, 14:10; Nu. 6:12; 7:15, 21
14:12 the priest shall take l.
23:12 sh. offer a l. with. blemish
Num. 6:14 ewe l. of first year
15:5 with the sacrifice for one l.
1 Sam. 7:9 Samuel off. sucking l.
2 Sam. 12:4 took poor man's l.
Is. 11:6 wolf shall dwell with l.
10:1 send ye l. to ruler of land
53:7 he was brought as a l. to the slaughter, Jer. 11:19
65:25 wolf and l. sh. feed toget.
66:3 sacrificeth a l. as if he cut
Ezek. 45:15 one l. out of a flock
Hos. 4:16 L. will feed them as l.
John 1:29 behold the L. of G. 36
Acts 8:32 a l. dumb bef. shearer
1 Pet. 1:19 as a l. without blem.
Rev. 5:6 midst of old, stood a L.
12 worthy the L. that was slain
6:16 hide us from wrath of L.
7:10 salvation to our G. and L.
14 made white in blood of L.
17 L. shall feed and lead
12:11 overc. him by blood of L.
13:8 L. sl. from found. of world
11 he had two horns like a l.
14:1 L. stood on the mount Si.
4 these are they that follow L.
10 tormented in presence of L.
15:3 song of M. and song of L.
17:14 war with L. L. overc.
19:7 for marriage of L. is come
9 called to marriage of L. wife
14 twelve apostles of L.
22 God Alm. and L. are temple
23 the L. is the light thereof
27 writ. in the L. book of life
22:1 out of thr. of God and L. 3

LAMBS.
Gen. 30:10 J. did separate the l.
Num. 7:87 l. of first year twelve
Deut. 32:14 with fat of l.
1 Sam. 15:9 R. spared the best l.
2 K. 3:4 Moab rendered 100,000 l.
1 Chr. 29:21 David offered 1,000 l.
2 Chr. 29:22 priests killed l. 32
Ezr. 7:17 thou mayest buy l.
Ps. 37:20 wick. fat, as the fat of l.
114:4 little hills skip, like l. 6
Prov. 27:26 l. for thy clothing
Is. 1:11 I deli. not in blood of l.
40:11 feed and their number
34:6 sword of L. with blood of l.
51:40 gather for l. with his sins
Jer. 51:40 like l. to slaughter
Ezek. 39:18 shall drink blo. of l.
Amos 6:4 eat l. out of flock
Luke 10:3 Jes. with. l. among wolves
John 21:15 Jes. saith, Feed my l.

Seven LAMBS.
Gen. 21:28 offer with bread a l. 1
Num. 28:11 ye shall offer s. l.
first year, 19, 27; 29:2, 8, 36
2 Chr. 29:21 brought s. l. for off. fering

LAN

Two LAMBS.
Ex. 29:38 two l. of the first year offer, Num. 28:3
Lev. 14:10 on 8th day take two l.
Num. 28:9 and on sabbath two l.

LAME.
Lev. 21:18 l. man sh. not appro.
Deut. 15:21 if l. shalt not sacrif.
2 Sam. 4:4 Jon. had son, l. 9:3. 13
5:6 exc. take away blind and l.
19:26 because thy servant is l.
Job 29:15 eyes to blind, feet to l.
Prov. 26:7 legs of l. are not equal
Is. 33:23 the l. take the prey
35:6 l. man leap as a hart
Jer. 31:8 bring with them the l.
Mal. 1:8 ye offer l. for sacrifice?
Mat. 11:5 the l. walk, 15:31; 21:14;
 Luke 7:22
Luke 14:13 call poor, l. and blind
Acts 3:2 a man, l. fr. womb, car.
8:7 many th. were l. we. healed
Heb. 12:13 l. be turn. out of way

LAMECH. Gen. 4:18, 19; 5:25;
1 Chr. 1:3; Luke 3:36

LAMENT.
Jud. 11:40 dau. of Is. went to l.
Is. 19:8 fishers also mourn and l.
32:12 they shall l. for the teats
Jer. 16:5 neither go to l. them, 6
22:18 they shall not l. for him
34:5 l. thee, saying, Ah, L.
Ezek. 32:16 daugh. of nations l.
Joel 1:8 l. like virgin with sacke.
13 gird yourselves, l. ye priests
Mic. 2:4 l. with doleful lamenta.
John 16:20 Ye shall weep and l.
Rev. 18:9 kings of earth shall l.

LAMENTED.
1 Sam. 6:19 people l. because L.
25:1 Israelites l. Samuel, 28:3
2 Sam. 1:17 David l. over Saul
3:33 the king l. over Abner
2 Chr. 35:25 Jeremiah l. for Joel.
Jer. 16:4 die and not be l. 25:33
Mat. 11:17 but ye have not l.
Luke 23:27 a great company l.

LAMENTABLE.
Dan. 6:20 king cried wi. l. voice

LAMENTATION.
Gen. 50:10 mourned with sore l.
2 Sam. 1:17 D. lamented with l.
Ps. 78:64 widows made no l.
Jer. 7:29 l. on high places
9:10 habitations of wildern. a l.
31:15 in Ramah l. Mat. 2:18
48:38 there shall be l. generally
Lam. 2:5 Lord hath increased l.
Ez. k. 19:1 take up a l. for prince.
14 this is a l. and sh. be for a l.
26:17 take up l. on king of Tyr.
32:2 take up a l. for Pharaoh, 16
Amos 5:16 such as are skilf. of l.
8:10 turn all your songs into l.
Acts 8:2 great l. over Stephen

LAMENTATIONS.
2 Chr. 35:25 of Josiah in their l.
Ezek. 2:10 was written therein l.

LAMP.
Gen. 15:17 burning l. that passed
Ex. 27:20 cause the l. to burn
1 Sam. 3:3 ere l. went out
2 Sam. 22:29 thou art my l. O L.
1 K. 15:4 G. gave him a l. 2 Chr.
 Job 12:5 as a l. despised in him
Ps. 119:105 thy word is l. to feet
132:17 ordained l. for mine ano.
Prov. 6:23 commandment is a l.
13:9 l. of wicked sh. be put out
20:20 curs. father, l. be put out
Is. 62:1 salva. as l. that burneth
Rev. 8:10 burning as it were a l.

LAMPS.
Ex. 25:37 light l. thereof, 40:4
30:7 dress. l. burn incense on it
35:14 his l. with oil for the light
40:25 lighted the l. before the Lord, Num. 8:2, 3
Lev. 24:2 l. to burn 2 Chr. 13:11
Jud. 7:16 put l. within pitchers
 20 hold the l. in their left hand
1 K. 7:49 l. of gold, 2 Chr. 4:20
Job 41:19 out of mon. go burn. l.
Ezek. 1:13 like appearance of l.
Dan. 10:6 his eyes as l. of fire
Mat. 25:1 ten virgins took l. 3, 4
 7 virgins arose, trimmed th. l.
 8 give us oil, our l. are go. out
Seven LAMPS.
Ex. 37:23 s. l. of pure gold
Zec. 4:2 candlestick and seven l.
Rev. 4:5 seven l. of fire burning

LANCE.
Jer. 50:42 they that hold l. cruel

LAN

LANCETS.
1 K. 18:28 cut themselves with l.

LAND.
Gen. 2:12 gold of that l. is good
10:11 out of that l. went Ashur
12:1 into l. I show thee, Acts 7:3
13:6 l. not able to bear them
17:8 I will give unto thee and thy seed the l. 28:13; 35:12
20:15 behold, my l. is before th.
24:37 Canaanite, in wh. l. I dw.
47:20 brought l. so l. beca. Ph.
22 l. of priests he bought not
10:13 the l. was darkened
20:13 days may be long upon l.
Lev. 16:26 goat bear iniquit. to l.
18:26 l. spue not you out, 20:22
25:2 l. keep a sabbath, 26:34
23 l. not be sold, the l. is mine
27:4 l. sh. yield increase, 25:19
 28 l. of your enem. eat you up
Num. 13:18 l. is a l. eateth inhab.
14:24 serv. Cal. I will bring to l.
15:2 wh. come into l. of habita.
 19; Deut. 17:14; 18:9; 26:1
32:4 country l. am l. for cattle
33:53 for blood defileth the l.
Deut. 2:20 counted l. of gi. 3:13
8:9 l. whose stones are iron
11:12 a l. which L. careth for
 29:23 wh. l. brimstone and salt
32:10 found him in a desert l.
 49 he will be merciful to his l.
33:13 blessed of the L. be his l.
34:1 Lord showed him all the l.
Jos. 2:1 sent men, sav. View l.
11:16 Joshua took all that l. 23
14:15 the l. had rest from war
15:19 a l. for wh. ye did not lab.
Jud. 3:11 l. rest forty years, 30
 had rest fourscore years
12:10 ye shall come to a large l.
1 Sam. 14:29 father troubled l.
2 Sam. 3:12 say, Whose is the l. ?
9:7 I restore thee all the l. of S.
17:26 manner of G. of the l. 27
17:33 delivered his l. Is. 36:18
21:3 move any more out of the l.
 1 Chr. 35:9
23:13 left poor of l. Jer. 52:16
1 Chr. 4:40 and the l. was wide
 3:6 when he had purged the l.
Ezr. 9:13 out good of l. Is. 1:19
Neh. 5:10 let us leave up any l.
Job 31:38 my l. cry against me
37:13 correct. or his l. or mercy
39:6 the barren l. his dwellings
Ps. 10:16 O l. who hearken peri. out of l.
42:6 remember thee fr. l. of Jor.
44:3 got not l. in possession
52:5 root thee out of l. of living
80:9 deep root, and it filled l.
101:6 mine eyes on faithful of l.
104:1 make dry l. springs
Jer. 50:12 hindermost shall be a dry l.
51:43 cities are a l. and wilder.
Hos. 2:3 lest I set her as a d. l.
Ion. 1:9 who made sea and d. l.
Hag. 2:6 shake sea and dry l.
Heb. 11:20 pass. R. sea as by d. l.
See DWELL, EGYPT, GOOD.

In the LAND.
Gen. 13:7 Canaanite dw. in the l.
41:31 plenty not be ka. in the l.
47:4 to sojourn in the l. in the l.
27 Is. gat sacrifice to G. in the l.
26 L. wh. do this thing in the l.
Lev. 26:6 I will give peace in the l.
Deut. 5:16 go well wi. thee in l.
11:9 that you may prolong your days in the l. 21; 25:15
25:19 given thee rest in the l.
32:47 as long as live in the l.
Jud. 18:7 no magistr. in the l.
2 Sam. 13:4 that I ye. judge in l.
2 Chr. 6:31 fear in. so long as in l.
32:31 that was done in the l.
Job 28:13 nor is it found in the l.
Ps. 27:13 good, of the L. in the l.
116:9 walk before L. in the l.
142:5 thou art my port. in the l.
Is. 7:22 sh. every one eat in l. l.
33:11 not see Lord in the l.
Ezek. 26:20 set glory in the l.
32:23 terror in the l. 24:25
37:22 make them one nat. in l.
Mat. 2:6 the l. sh. be his posses.
Ios. 4:1 there is no truth in the l.
Luke 21:23 great distress in the l.
Heb. 11:9 by faith he soj. in the l.
See INHABITANTS, INHERIT, ISRAEL, JUDAH.

LAN

Jer. 22:27 l. whereu. they desire
23:15 profaneness, gone forth to l.
46:12 thy cry hath filled the l.
50:18 punish king of Bab. and l.
 38 it is the l. of graven images
51:43 l. wherein no man dwell.
Ezek. 7:23 l. full of bloody crimes
8:17 have filled l. with violence
9:9 and the land is full of blood
14:17 sword on l. 19 pestilence
17:5 he took also of seed of the l.
13 hath taken mighty of the l.
22:24 the l. is not cleansed
30 stand in gap before me for l.
32:4 then I leave thee up, the l.
33:2 when I bring sw. upon l.
24 l. given us for inheritance
36:5 appointed l. into possess.
13 thou l. devourest up men
38:9 a cloud to cover the l. 16
11 to l. of unwalled villages
39:12 they may cleanse the l.
Dan. 11:16 stand in glorious l. 41
Hos. 4:3 therefore shall l. mourn
Joel 1:6 a nation come up upon l.
2:3 the l. is as garden of Eden
4 of l. be glad; 3 parted l.
Amos 8:2 forsaken upon her l.
7:10 l. not able to bear words
8:4 make poor of the l. to fail
8 shall not l. tremble for this?
Zep. 3:19 and fame in every l.
Zec. 3:9 remove iniq. of that l.
12:12 l. shall mourn, ev. family
13:2 unclean spirit pass out of l.
Mat. 9:26 fame went abr. into l.
10:15 tolerable for l. of S. 11:24
27:45 was darku. over all the l.
Mark 15:33
Mark 6:47 and he alone on the l.
Luke 14:35 neither fit for the l.
21:23 be great wrath on this l.
John 6:21 immed. ship was at l.
Acts 4:37 Barn. having l. sold it
5:8 tell me whether ye sold l.
27:39 was day, they knew not l.
43 into the sea, and get to l. 44
See BENJAMIN, CHALDEANS, CANAAN, DARKNESS, DESOLATE, DIVIDE, DIVIDED.

Dry LAND.
Gen. 1:9 and let the d. l. appear
10 God called the dry l. earth
7:22 all that was in dry l. died
Ex. 4:9 water made thee on dry l.
14:21 Lord made the sea dry l.
29 Israel walked on dry l.
15:19 on d. of. of. Neh. 9:11
Jos. 4:18 priests lifted on d. l.
22 Is. came over Jord. on d. l.
Ps. 63:1 long. for thee in a d. l.
66:6 turned the sea into dry l.
68:6 rebellions dwell in dry l.
95:5 his hands formed the d. l.
Is. 41:18 make dry l. springs
Jer. 50:12 hindermost shall be a dry l.
51:43 cities are a l. and wilder.
Hos. 2:3 lest I set her as a d. l.
Ion. 1:9 who made sea and d. l.
Hag. 2:6 shake sea and dry l.
Heb. 11:20 pass. R. sea as by d. l.

Thy LAND.
Ex. 23:10 six years sh. sow t. l.
 26 noth. sh. cast young in t. l.
34:24 nor sh. any man desire t. l.
Deut. 7:13 will bless fruit of t. l.
21:23 that t. by be not defiled
28:12 to give the rain to thy l.
 18 cursed be fruit of thy l. 42
2 Sam. 24:13 sh. fam. come to t. l.
Ps. 85:1 been favorable to thy l.
Is. 8:8 wings fill breadth of t. l.
60:18 viol, no more heard in t. l.
62:4 nor sh. l. l. be termed des.
 L. delight. in thee, and t. l.
Ezek. 32:8 set darkness on thy l.
Amos 7:17 thy l. shall be divided
Nah. 3:13 gates of t. l. sh. be wi.

Your LAND.
Gen. 47:23 I bought you and y. l.
Lev. 9:9 harvest of y. l. 23:22
25:25 and dwell in y. l. safely
 l. nor shall sw. go through y. l.
 20 y. l. sh. not yield her inc.
Deut. 11:14 give you rain of y. l.
1 Sam. 6:5 light. hand fr. off y. l.
Jer. 5:19 serv. strun. gods in y. l.
Is. 7:20 remove you fa. fr. y. l.
44:22 theref. is y. l. a desolation

LANDED, ING.
Acts 18:22 when who l. at Cesarea
21:3 sailed to Syria and l. at T.
28:12 at Syracuse three days

LANDMARK, S.
Deut. 19:14 not remo. thy neighbor's l. Prov. 22:28; 23:10
27:17 cursed that removeth l.
Job 24:2 some remove the l.

CRUDEN'S CONCORDANCE.

LANDS.
Gen. 41:54 dearth in all l. 57
47:18 not left but bodies and l.
Jud. 11:13 restore those l. again
1 Chr. 14:17 fame of D. went all l.
2 Chr. 17:10 fear fell on all the l.
32:17 gods of other l. have not
Exr. 9:1 not separ. fr. peo. of l.
Neh. 5:3 have mortgaged our l.
5 for other men have our l.
11 restore, I pray you, their l.
Ps. 49:11 th. l. after own names
56:1 make noise all ye l. 100:1
105:44 give them l. of heathen
106:27 to scatter them in l.
107:3 gathered them out of l.
Jer. 27:6 these l. to Nebuchadn.
Ezek. 20:6 wh. is glory of all l. 15
39:27 gather out of enemies' l.
Mal. 1:29 hath forsaken houses,
l. Mark 10:29
Mark 10:30 rec. hundred-fold, l.
Acts 4:34 were possessors of l.

LANES.
Luke 14:21 go quickly into the l.

LANGUAGE, S.
Gen. 11:1 wh. earth was of one l.
6 people is one, have all one l.
7 and there confound their l. 9
2 K. 18:26 speak in the Syrian l.
19 Neh. 13:24 chil. not speak Jews' l. but accord. to l. of people
Ps. 19:3 no l. wh. voice is heard
81:5 heard a l. I understood not
114:1 from a people of strange l.
Is. 19:18 five cities speak l. Can.
Jer. 5:15 wh. l. thou know. not
Ezek. 3:5 to a people of hard l. 6
Dan. 3:4 people, nations and l.
7 all l. fell down and worship.
29 every l. that speaketh amiss
4:1 Neb. nil l. 6:25 D. to all l.
5:19 all l. trembled and feared
7:14 nations, and l. who. serve
Zep. 3:9 turn to people a pure l.
Zec. 8:23 ten men out of all l.
Acts 2:6 heard th. speak in all l.

LANGUISH.
Is. 16:8 the fields of Heshbon l.
19:8 spread nets on wat. sh. l.
24:4 haughty people of earth l.
Jer. 14:2 the gates of Judah l.
Hos. 4:3 every one therein sh. l.

LANGUISHED, ETH.
Is. 24:4 world l. and fad. away
7 the vine l. 33:9 the earth l.
Jer. 15:9 that hath borne seven l.
Lam. 2:8 wall lament, l. together
Joel 1:10 tho oil l. 12 fig-tree l.
Nah. 1:4 Bashan l. and Carmel l.

LANGUISHING.
Ps. 41:3 L. strength, on bed of l.

LANTERNS.
John 18:3 Judas cometh with l.

LAODICEA.
Col. 2:1 for them at L. 4:13,15,16

LAODICEANS.
Col. 4:16 in church of L. Rev. 3:14

LAP.
2 K. 4:39 gathered gourds, l. full
Neh. 5:13 I shook my l. and said
Prov. 16:33 lot is cast into the l.

LAPPED, ETH.
Jud. 7:5 that l. water as a dog
6 number l. were three hund.
7 by them th. l. I will save you

LAPWING. See BAT.

LARGE.
Ex. 3:8 into a good and l. land
2 Sam. 22:20 he brought me into
- a l. place, Ps. 18:19
Neh. 4:19 the work is gre. and l.
9:35 not served thee in l. land
Ps. 31:8 set my feet in a l. room
118:5 Lord set me in a l. place
Is. 22:18 toss thee in a l. country
30:33 rattle feed in l. past. 33
Jer. 22:14 I will build l. chamb.
Ezek. 23:32 sist. cup deep and l.
Hos. 4:16 L. feed thee in a l. pl.
Mat. 28:12 gave l. money to sol.
Mark 14:15 and he will show you
a l. upper room, Luke 22:12
Gal. 6:11 l. letter I have written
Rev. 21:16 length and l. as breadth

LARGENESS.
1 K. 4:29 God gave S. l. of heart

LASCIVIOUSNESS.
Mark 7:23 out of heart proceed l.
2 Cor. 12:21 not repented of the l.
Gal. 5:19 works of the l. manif. l.
Eph. 4:19 given themselves to l.

1 Pet. 4:3 when we walked in l.
Jude 4 turning grace of G. into l.

LAST.
Gen. 49:19 Gad sh. overcome at l.
Num. 23:10 my l. end be like his
2 Sam. 23:1 l. words of David
1 Chr. 23:27 by l. words of David
Neh. 8:18 from first day to the l.
Prov. 5:11 thou mourn at the l.
Is. 41:4 I Lord, first and l. 44:6;
48:12; Rev. 1:11, 17; 2:8;
22:13
Lam. 1:9 remembereth not l. end
Dan. 8:3 the higher came up l.
Amos 9:1 will slay the l. of them
Mat. 12:45 l. state of that man is
worse than first, Luke 11:26
19:30 first shall be l. and l. first,
20:16; Mark 10:31; Luke 13:30
20:12 l. have wrought one hour
14 give to l. even as unto thee
27:64 l. error worse than the fi.
Mark 9:35 first, same sh. be l.
Luke 12:59 till th. hast paid l. m.
1 Cor. 4:9 set forth us apostles l.
15:8 l. of all he was seen of me
26 l. enemy is death; 45 l. Ad.
Rev. 2:19 l. works be more tli. fi.

LAST day, s.
Gen. 49:1 befall you in l. days
John 6:39 should raise it up ag.
at the l. d. 40, 44, 54
7:37 in l. d. great day of feast
11:24 he shall rise again at l. d.
2 Tim. 3:1 l. day perilous times
Heb. 1:2 spoken in l. d. by his S.
Jam. 5:3 heaped treasure for l. d.
2 Pet. 3:3 come in l. d. scoffers

LAST time, s.
1 Pet. 1:5 to be revealed in l. t.
20 manifest in these l. times
1 John 2:18 children, it is the l. t.
Jude 18 should be mockers in l. t.

LASTED.
Deut. 32:15 provokes th. of l. hills
Jud. 14:17 wept whilst feast l.

LATCHET.
Is. 5:27 l. of their shoes broken
Mark 1:7 l. of wh. shoes, Lu. 3:16

LATE, LY.
Ps. 127:2 vain for you to sit up l.
Mic. 2:8 of l. my people risen up
Acts 18:2 Aquila l. come from I.

LATIN.
Luke 23:38 writ. in L. John 19:20

LATTER.
Deut. 11:14 give first and l. rain
Job 19:25 Redeemer, at l. day
29:23 open. mouth, as for l. rain
Prov. 16:15 as cloud of l. rain
19:20 mayest be wise in l. end
Jer. 8:3 there ha. been no l. rain
5:24 form, and l. rain in season
Dan. 8:23 l. time of their kingd.
Hos. 6:3 as l. and former rain
Joel 2:23 l. rain in first month
Amos 7:1 in beginning of l. grow
Hag. 2:9 glory of l. house greater
Zec. 10:1 rain in time of l. rain
1 Tim. 4:1 in l. times some dep.

See DAYS, END.

LATTICE.
Jud. 5:28 cried through the l.
2 K. 1:2 Ahaziah fell through l.
Cant. 2:9 show. himself thro' l.

LAUD.
Rom. 15:11 praise L. and l. him

LAUGH.
Gen. 18:13 wheref. did Sarah l.?
21:6 G. made me to l. all will l.
Job 5:22 at famine thou shalt l.
9:23 will l. at trial of innocent
22:19 innocent l. them to scorn
Ps. 2:4 sitteth in heavens sh. l.
22:7 that see me l. me to scorn
37:13 the Lord shall l. at him
52:6 righteous also sh. l. at him
59:8 thou, O L. shalt l. at them
80:6 enemies l. among themselves
Prov. 1:26 l. at your calamity
29:9 rage or l. there is no rest
Ec. 3:4 time to weep, time to l.
Luke 6:21 that weep, ye sh. l.
25 woe unto you that l. now

LAUGHED.
Gen. 17:17 Abra. l. 18:12 Sarah
18:15 S. denied, saying, I l. not
2 K. 19:21 daughter of Zion hath
l. Is. 37:22
Job 29:24 if I l. them to sco.
Neh. 2:19 they l. us to scorn
Job 41:2 upright man l. to scorn
Mat. 9:24 they l. him to scorn,
Mark 5:40; Luke 8:53

LAUGHETH, ING.
Job 8:21 he fill thy mouth with l.
41:29 ha. l. at shaking of a spear

LAUGHTER.
Ps. 126:2 mouth filled with l.
Prov. 14:13 in l. heart sorrowful
Ec. 2:2 I said of l. It is mad
7:3 sorrow is better than l.
6 thorns, so is the l. of fool
Jam. 4:9 l. turned to mourning

LAUNCH, ED.
Luke 5:4 Sim. l. out into deep
8:22 go over, and they l. forth
Acts 21:1 after had L. 27:2, 4

LAVER, S.
Ex. 30:18 make a l. of brass
28 l. and fo. 31:9; 35:16; 39:39
38:8 he made the l. of brass
40:7 thou shalt set the l. 30
Lev. 8:11 anoint, both l. and foot
1 K. 7:30 under l. were unders.
38 made ten l. of brass; one l.
40 bathe; and ev. l. 4 cubits
40 and H. made the l.
43 and the ten l. on the bases,
1 Chr. 4:6, 14
2 K. 16:17 king A. removed l.

LAW.
Is. 40:6 they l. gold out of bag

LAW.
Gen. 47:26 made it a l. over land
Ex. 12:49 1 l. Num. 15:16, 29
Deut. 17:11 to sentence of the l.
33:2 fr. right hand went fiery l.
4 Moses commanded us a l.
Jos. 8:32 wrote copy of l. to R.
22:5 take heed to the l. 2 K.
17:37; Jer. 31:8
2 K. 17:34 nor do after the l.
1 Chr. 22:12 mayest keep l. of G.
2 Chr. 19:10 between l. and com.
30:16 place according to l. of M.
Ezr. 7:6 scribe in l. 12, 21
14 according to l. of thy God
26 not do l. of G. and l. of king
Neh. 8:7 cause people understa. l.
9 wh. they heard the wo. of l.
13:29 made oath to walk in it, l.
12:44 gather them portions of l.
Est. 1:8 drinking according to l.
4:11 l. of his to put to death
16 which is not according to l.
Job 22:22 rec. l. from his mouth
Ps. 1:2 in his l. he meditates
37:31 l. of his G. is in his heart
78:5 for he appointed a l. in Is.
10 refused to walk in his l.
81:4 was a l. of the G. of Jacob
105:10 confirm. same to J. for l.
119:72 l. of mouth bet. than gold
Prov. 1:8 forsake not the l. of thy
mother, 6:20
6:23 commandm. lamp, l. is light
13:14 l. of wise is fount. of life
28:4 forsake l. praise wick. such
as keep l. contend with them
29:18 keep. l. is a happy is he
31:5 lest drink and forget the l.
26 in her tongue is l. of kindn.
Is. 2:3 out of Zion shall go forth
the l. Mic. 4:2
8:16 seal l. 10 to l. and testimony
42:4 the isles sh. wait for his l.
21 Lord will magnify the l.
51:4 a l. shall proceed from me
52:8 they that handle the l.
Jer. 2:8 perish from priest
44:23 not obey, nor walk in l.
Lam. 2:9 the l. is no more
Ezek. 7:26 l. perish from priests
Dan. 6:5 concerning l. of his G.
8 according to l. of Medes, 15
Hos. 4:6 has forgotten l. of God
Hob. 1:4 theref. the l. is slacked
Zep. 3:4 priests have viol. the l.
Hag. 2:11 ask now the priests
Mal. 2:6 l. of truth was in mouth
7 for they should seek the l.
8 work the l. at his mouth
9 have been partial in the l.
Mat. 5:17 not to come to dest. l.
7:12 for this is l. and the Proph.
11:13 l. pro. till Jo. Luke 16:16
22:36 great commandment in l.
40 on two command. hang l.
23:23 omitted weightier mat. l.
Luke 2:27 after custom of the l.
10:26 what is written in the l.
16:17 easier heaven and earth
pass than one tittle of l. fail
24:44 written in l. of Moses
John 1:17 l. was given by Moses
7:19 did not Moses give you l.
24 l. of Moses should not be

LAW of the Lord.
Ex. 13:9 L.'s l. be in thy mouth
2 K. 10:31 no heed to wa. in l. L.

CRUDEN'S CONCORDANCE.

LAW

2 *Chr.* 12:1 R. forsook *l. of t. L.*
31:4 encouraged in *l. of the L.*
Ezr. 7:10 heart to seek *l. of L.*
Ps. 1:2 delight is in *l. of the L.*
19:7 the *l. of the L.* is perfect
119:1 blessed th. walk in *l. of L.*
Is. 5:24 cast away the *l. of L.*
30:9 children not hear *l. of L.*
Amos 2:4 they have des. *l. of L.*

My LAW.
Ex. 16:4 whether walk in *my l.*
2 *Chr.* 6:16 childr. walk in *my l.*
Ps. 78:1 my peo. to *my l.* incline
Prov. 3:1 my son, forg. not *my l.*
4:2 fors. not *my l.* 7:2 keep *my l.*
Is. 51:7 peo. in wh. heart is *my l.*
Jer. 6:19 not hearken, unto *my l.*
16:11 fors. me, not kept *my l.*
31:33 put *my l.* in their parts
44:10 nor walked in *my l.*
Ezek. 22:26 priests ha. vio. *my l.*
Hos. 8:1 they trespass ag. *my l.*
12 writ. to him things of *my l.*

This LAW.
Num. 5:30 priests shall exe. *t. l.*
Deut. 1:5 Moses to declare *this l.*
17:18 write him a copy of *t. l.*
28:58 If th. wilt not observe *t. l.*
31:9 M. wrote *t. l.* 11 read *t. l.*
24 wri. words of *t. l.* in a book

This is the LAW,
Ezek. 43:12 *this is the t. of* house
Mat. 7:12 *this is the l.* and prop.

Thy LAW.
Deut. 33:10 shall teach Isr. *thy l.*
Neh. 9:26 cast *t. l.* behind backs
34 nor our princes kept *thy l.*
Ps. 40:8 *t. l.* is within my heart
94:12 teachest him out of *thy l.*
119:18 wondr. things art of *t. l.*
29 and grant *t. l.* graciously
34 and I shall keep *thy l.*
41 so shall keep *t. l.* continu.
51 have I not declined fr. *t. l.*
53 I rememb. and kept *thy l.*
61 I have not forgotten *thy l.*
70 but I delight in *thy l.*
77 for *t. l.* is my delight, 92, 174
85 pits, wh. are not after *t. l.*
97 love *t. l.* 109 not forget *t. l.*
113 *t. l.* I love, 163; 126 ma. vo.
136 because they keep not *t. l.*
142 *t. l.* is truth; 150 far fr. *t. l.*
165 peace have they love *t. l.*
Jer. 32:23 nor walk in *t. l.*
Dan. 9:11 have transgressed *t. l.*

Under the LAW.
Rom. 6:14 ye are not *under t. l.*
15 sho. we sin bec. not *u. t. l.*
1 *Cor.* 9:20 as *u. t. l.* that I might
gain them th. that are *u. t. l.*
21 not without law to G. *u. l.*
Gal. 3:23 kept *u. l.* 4:4 made *u. l.*
4:5 sent Son to red. them *un. l.*
5:18 led by Sp. are not *u. t. l.*

Without LAW.
2 *Chr.* 15:3 Is. hath been *with. l.*
Rom. 2:12 many as sinned *w. l.*
3:21 righteousness of God *w. l.*
7:8 *w. l.* sin dead; 9 I was alive
1 *Cor.* 9:21 *w. l.* not *w. l.* to God

Written in the LAW.
1 *K.* 2:3 as it is *written in the l.*
of Moses, 2 *Chr.* 23:18 ; 35:4;
31:3; *Ezr.* 3:2; *Neh.* 10:34,
36; *Dan.* 9:13; *Luke* 2:23
Dan. 9:11 oath is *w. in t. l. of*
Moses
Luke 10:26 what is *writ. in t. l.?*
24:44 all must be ful. *w. in t. l.*
Acts 24:14 hello. things *w. in t. l.*

LAWS.

Gen. 26:5 Abraham kept *my l.*
Ex. 16:28 how long re! *my l.?*
18:16 make them know *l.* of G.
20 teach th. ordinances and *l.*
Neh. 9:13 thou gavest th. true *l.*
Est. 1:19 among *l.* of Persians
3:8 their *l.* are div. from all peo.
nei. keep they the king's *l.*
Is. 24:5 ha. have transgressed *l.*
Dan. 7:25 to change times and *l.*
9:10 nor obeyed to walk in *l.*
Heb. 8:10 put *my l.* in mind
10:16 put *my l.* in their hearts

LAWFUL.

Is. 49:24 sh. *l.* captive be deliv. ?
Ezek. 18:5 do that which is *l.* 21, 27 ; 33:14, 19
19 *son* ha. done that is *l.* 33:16
Mat. 12:2 do what is not *l. Mark*
2:24; *Luke* 6:2
4 was not *l.* for him to eat,
Mark 2:26; *Luke* 6:4

LAY

Mat. 12:10 is it *l.* to heal on sab. ?
12; *Mark* 3:4; 6:9; 14:3
14:4 it is not *l.* for thee to have
her, *Mark* 6:18
19:3 *l.* to put aw. wife? *Mar.* 10:2
John 5:10 not *l.* to carry thy bed
18:31 not *l.* to put man to death
Acts 19:39 determ. in *l.* assembly
22:25 is it *l.* to scourge a Rom. ?
1 *Cor.* 6:12 all things *l.* 10:23
2 *Cor.* 12:4 not *l.* for man to utter

LAWFULLY.
1 *Tim.* 1:8 go. if a man use it *l.*
2 *Tim.* 2:5 not crown, except *l.*

LAWGIVER.

Gen. 49:10 *l.* from betw. his feet
Num. 21:18 digged by direc. of *l.*
Deut. 33:21 in a portion of the *l.*
Ps. 60:7 Judah is *my l.* 108:8
Is. 33:22 L. is our *l.* and king
Jam. 4:12 one *l.* is able to save

LAWLESS.

1 *Tim.* 1:9 law for *l.* disobedient

LAWYER, L.

Mat. 22:35 a *l.* asked, *Luke* 10:25
Luke 7:30 *l.* reject, counsel of G.
11:46 woe to you *l.* 52; 14:3 J.

LAY,

Ex. 5:8 tale of bricks ye shall *l.*
16:13 *l.* round about host, 14
22:25 neither sh. thou *l.* on him
Lev. 1:7 *l.* the wood on the fire
8 priests sh. *l.* parts in ord. 12
Num. 12:11 L. *l.* not sin upon us
Deut. 7:15 *l.* on them that hate
11:25 *l.* fear of you upon land
21:8 *l.* not innoc. blood to peop.
Jud. 16:3 Sam. *l.* till midnight
Ruth 3:8 a woman *l.* at his feet
1 *Sam.* 3:15 Samuel *l.* till morn.
26:5 Saul *l.* in the trench, 7
2 *Sam.* 4:5 who *l.* on bed at noon
12:3 ewe-lamb *l.* in his bosom
16 D. *l.* all night on earth, 13:31
1 *K.* 13:31 *l.* my bones beside his
18:23 *l.* it on wood put no fire
2 *K.* 4:34 went and *l.* on the chi.
2 *Chr.* 36:21 long as she *l.* desol.
Est. 4:3 *l.* in sackcloth and ashes
Job 29:19 dew *l.* all ni. on branch
34:23 not *l.* on man more than
Ps. 7:5 *l.* mine honor in the dust
38:12 seek life, *l.* snares for me
84:3 a nest, where she *l.* young
Ec. 7:2 living will *l.* it to heart
Is. 3:8 woe to them that *l.* field
13:9 *l.* land desolate, *Ezek.* 35:28
11 will *l.* low hau. of terrible
22:22 house of D. *l.* on shoulder
25:12 the fortress shall be *l.* low
28:16 I will *l.* in Z. a tried stone
17 judgment will I *l.* to the li.
29:3 *l.* a snare for him that re.
34:15 there sh. the great owl *l.*
Jer. 6:21 will *l.* stones with colors
51:11 *l.* their quiver be desolate
Ezek. 4:1 take a tile and *l.* it be.
4 *l.* iniquity of house of Israel
25:14 *l.* vengeance on Edom, 17
32:5 will *l.* thy flesh on mount
36:29 I will *l.* no famine upon
34 land be tilled, it *l.* desolate
37:6 I will *l.* sinews upon you
Jon. 1:14 *l.* not on us inno. blood
Mic. 1:7 idols with I *l.* desolate
Mal. 2:2 if ye will not *l.* it to he.
Mat. 8:20 hath not where to *l.*
his head, *Luke* 5:58
6:6 place where the Lord *l.*
Mark 2:4 bed wh. sick of palsy *l.*
Luke 19:44 *l.* thee with gro und
Acts 7:60 L. *l.* not this sin to th.
13:23 *l.* on you no grea. burden
Rom. 9:33 *l.* any thing to God's
9:33 *l. l.* in Zion a stumbling-st
1 *Cor.* 16:2 every one *l.* by him
Heb. 12:1 let us *l.* aside ev. weig.
Jam. 1:21 *l.* apart all filthiness
1 *Pet.* 2:6 *l.* in Zion a chief cor.

See FOUNDATION.

LAY down.

Gen. 19:33 L. per. not she *l. d.* 35
28:11 Jacob *l. d.* in place to sl.
Num. 23:24 not *l. d.* as a lion
Jud. 5:27 he *l. down* at her feet
Ruth 3:4 uncov. feet, *l.* thee *d.*
1 *Sam.* 19:24 Saul *l. down* naked
Job 17:3 *l. d.* put me in surety
Ps. 3:5 I will *l.* me *d.* in peace
104:22 young lions *l. d.* in dens
Ezek. 19:2 mother *l. d.* am. lions
Amos 2:8 *l.* thems. *d.* on clothes
John 10:15 *l. d.* life for sheep, 17

LAI

John 10:18 *l.* it *down* of myself
18:37 *l. d.* my li. for thy sake, 38
15:13 *l. d.* his life for his friends
1 *John* 3:16 *l. d.* lives for breth.

LAY hand.
Gen. 22:12 *l.* n. thy *h.* on the lad
37:22 no blood, *l.* no *h.* on Jos.
Ex. 7:4 I may *l.* my *h.* on Egypt
Lev. 3:2 *l. h.* on head of offer. 8
4:4 sh. *l. h.* on bullock's he. 15
20 sh. *l. h.* on siu-offering, 33
Num. 27:18 L. said, *l. h.* on Jos.
Jud. 18:19 *l. h.* on thy mouth
Job 9:33 any days-man to *l. h.*
21:5 mark me, *l. h.* on mouth
40:4 will *l.* my *h.* on my mouth
41:8 *l. h.* on him, remem. battle
Prov. 30:32 tho' evil, *l. h.* mouth
Is. 11:14 eb. *l.* their *h.* on Edom
Mic. 7:16 sh. *l. h.* on their mou.
Mat. 9:18 come, *l.* thy *h.* on her

LAY hands.
Lev. 16:21 *l.* b. *l. h.* bo. *h.* on goat
Num. 8:12 Lev. *l. h.* on bullocks
Neh. 13:21 again, *l. h.* on you
Mat. 21:46 they sought to *l. h.*
on him, *Luke* 20:19
Mark 5:23 come *l.* thy *h.* on her
16:18 *l. h.* on sick, they recover
Luke 21:12 they shall *l. h.* on you
1 *Tim.* 5:22 *l. h.* suddenly on no

LAY hold.
Prov. 3:18 tree of life to th. *l. h.*
Ec. 2:3 I sought to *l. h.* on folly
Is. 5:29 roar, and *l. h.* on prey
Jer. 6:23 *l. h.* on bow and spear
Zec. 14:13 ev, one *l. h.* on neigh.
Mat. 22:21 friends went to *l. h.*
12:12 sought to *l. hold* on him
1 *Tim.* 6:12 *l. h.* on eter. life, 19
Heb. 6:13 *l. h.* on hope sat be. us

LAY up.
Ex. 16:23 *l. up* manna till morn.
33 *l. up* a pot of manna
Num. 17:4 sh. *l.* them *up* in tab.
Deut. 11:18 *l. up* my words
Job 22:22 *l. up* his words in heart
24 then shalt *l. up* gold as dust
Prov. 7:1 *l. up* my commandm.
10:14 wise men *l. up* knowledge
Mat. 6:19 *l.* not *up* for your treas.
20 *l. up* treasures in heaven
2 *Cor.* 12:14 children not to *l. up*

LAY wait.
Ezr. 8:31 del. fr. such as *l.* in w.
Ps. 71:10 *l.* wait for my soul
Prov. 1:11 let us *l.* w. *l.* for blood
18 they *l.* w. for their own bl.
24:15 *l.* not w. against righte.
Jer. 5:26 *l.* w. as he that setteth

LAY waste.
Is. 5:6 I will *l.* it *w.* it sh. not
3 *Ci*

LAY with.
Gen. 10:33 *l.* w. her father, 34, 35
16:30 Jacob *l. w.* L. that night
34:2 Shechem *l. with* Dinah
35:22 Reuben *l. with* Bilhah
Deut. 22:22 man that *l. w.* wom.
25 man that *l. w.* her shall die
29 that *l. w.* her give 50 shek.
1 *Sam.* 2:22 Eli's sons *l.* w. wom.
2 *Sam.* 12:14 A. forc. T. and *l.* w.
Ezek. 23:8 in her youth *l. w.* her

LAY wait.
Job 31:9 *l.* w. at neighbor's door
Lam. 4:19 *l.* w. for us in wait.
Acts 23:3 Jews *l. w.* for hi. 23:30

LAID down.
Ps. 7:5 *l.* w. his dwelling-place
Is. 13:1 Kir *l.* w. 23; 7. L. w.
23:14 ships, your strength *l.* w.
37:16 kings of Assy. *l.* w. nat.
64:11 pleasant things are *l.* w.
Jer. 4:7 thy cities sh. bo *l.* w.
without an inhabita. *Ezek.*
6:6; 12:20; 19:7; 26:12
Ezek. 26:2 sh. be repl. now *l.* w.
Amos 7:9 sanctuaries of Is. *l.* w.
Nah. 3:7 and say, Ninev. is *l.* w.

LAI

Is. 47:6 thou hast heavily *l.* yoke
58:5 L. *l.* on him iniq. of us all
Jer. 50:24 *l.* a snare for thee
Ezek. 32:19 *l.* wi. the uncircum.
38:12 saying, They are *l.* de-ol.
Hos. 11:4 I *l.* meat unto them
Ob. 7 *l.* a wound under thee
Mic. 5:1 hath *l.* siege against us
Hab. 2:19 it is *l.* over with gold
Hag. 2:15 before a stone was *l.*
Zec. 3:9 behold stone I have *l.*
Mat. 3:10 axe *l.* to root, *Luke* 3:9
27:60 *l.* it in his own new tomb
Mark 7:30 her daughter *l.* on bed
15:47 M. beheld where he was *l.*
16:6 behold where they *l.* him
Luke 2:7 first-born *l.* in manger
16:20 Lazarus was *l.* at his gate
23:53 wherein never man before
was *l. John* 19:41
John 11:34 wh. have ye *l.* him?
20:2 know not wh. th. *l.* him, 13
Acts 3:2 *l.* at gate of temple
4:37 *l.* money at apostles' f. 5:2
9:37 *l.* her in an upper chamber
13:36 David *l.* to his fathers
25:7 *l.* compla. could not prove
1 *Cor.* 9:16 necessity *l.* upon me
2 *Tim.* 4:16 *l.* not to their charge

See FOUNDATION.

LAID down.
Jos. 2:8 bef. they were *l. down*
1 *Sam.* 3:2 Eli *l. d.* in his place
2 and Samuel was *l. d.* to sleep
2 *Sam.* 13:8 Amnon was *l. down*
1 *K.* 19:6 and *l.* him *down* again
21:4 Ahab came and *l.* him *d.*
Ps. 3:5 I me *d.* and slept
Luke 19:22 tak. up th. I *l.* not *d.*
Acts 4:35 *l.* th. *d.* at apostles' fe.
7:58 *l. d.* their clothes at young
Rom. 16:4 for my life *l. d.* necks
1 *John* 3:16 he *l. d.* his life for us

LAID hand.
Ex. 24:11 on the nobles *l.* not *h.*
1 *Sam.* 18:19 Tamar *l. h.* on head
Est. 9:10 *l.* not *h.* on sp. 15, 16
Job 29:9 *l.* up their *h.* on mouth
Ps. 139:5 hast *l.* thy *h.* upon me
Rev. 1:17 *l.* his right *h.* upon me

LAID hands.
Lev. 6:14 A. a. h. sons *l. h.* 18, 22
Num. 27:23 and Moses *l. h.* ha.
on Joshua, *Deut.* 34:9
Ob. 13 nor *l. h.* on th. substance
Mat. 21:31 *l. h.* took him by the
Mark 6:5 *l.* on a few sick folk
Luke 4:40 *l. h.* on ev. one of th.
13:13 he *l.* his *h.* on her
John 7:30 but no man *l.* hands
on him, 44; 8:20
Acts 4:3 *l. h.* on apostles, 5:18
6:6 they *l. h.* on the deacons
13:3 *l. h.* on Paul and Barnabas
19:6 Paul *l.* his *h.* on them

LAID hold.
Gen. 19:16 *l. h.* on Lot's hand
1 *Sam.* 15:27 S. *l. h.* on Saul,
2 *Chr.* 7:22 *l. hold* on other gods
Mat. 14:3 *l. h.* on J. *Mark* 6:17
Luke 23:26 *l. h.* on one Simon
Rev. 20:2 *l. hold* on the dragon

LAID up.
Gen. 41:48 Jos. *l. up* food in cit.
Ex. 16:34 A. *l.* pot of manna up,
Num. 17:7 M. *l.* up rods befo. L.
1 *Sam.* 10:25 S. *l.* it up before L.
21:12 David *l. up* words in he.
Ezr. 6:1 treasures *l. up* in Baby.
Ps. 31:19 hast *l. up* for them
Prov. 13:22 wealth of sin. *l. up*
Cant. 7:13 fruits I have *l. up*
Is. 15:7 that *l. up* sh. they carry
32:18 hire not treasured or *l. up*
Luke 1:66 all *l.* them *up* in hearts
12:19 thou hast mu. goods *l. up*
Col. 1:5 hope wh. is *l. up* for you
2 *Tim.* 4:8 is *l. up* for me a crown

LAI.
Ex. 10:19 *l.* locusts into Red sea
Num. 11:25 came *l.* up. 70 elders
Ps. 66:9 our God holdeth soul *l.*
Ezek. 43:14 *l.* upon earth *l.*
17 *l.* shall be fourteen cubits
Luke 19:44 *l.* thee even with ground

CRUDEN'S CONCORDANCE. 923

LEA

LAIDEST.
Ps. 66:11 *l.* affliction on loins
Luke 19:21 th. takest up th. th. *l.*

LAIN.
Gen. 26:10 have *l.* with thy wife
Jud. 21:11 destroy wom. th. *l.*
Job 3:13 now should I have *l.* +t.
Ps. 68:13 ye have *l.* am. the pots
John 20:12 where body of Jes. *l.*

LAYEST, ETH.
Num. 11:11 *l.* burden of people
1 *Sam.* 28:9 *l.* a snare for my life
Job 21:19 G. *l.* up his iniquity
24:12 God *l.* not folly to them
41:26 sword of him that *l.* at h.
Ps. 104:3 *l.* beams of chambers
Prov. 2:7 *l.* up wisd. for righte.
26:24 *l.* up deceit within him
Is. 26:5 the lofty city he *l.* low
56:2 blessed is man that *l.* hold
57:1 and no man *l.* it to heart
Jer. 9:8 *l.* wait ; 12:11 *l.* to heart
Ezek. 12:21 that *l.* up treasure
15:5 he *l.* it on his shoulders

LAYING.
Num. 35:20 *l.* wait, th. he die, 22
Ps. 64:5 commune of *l.* snares
Mark 7:8 *l.* aside commandment
Luke 11:54 *l.* wait for him
Acts 8:18 *l.* on of apostles' hands
9:24 *l.* wait was known of Saul
23:16 Ishmael heard of th. *l.* w.
23:3 *l.* wait in the way to kill
1 *Tim.* 4:14 with *l.* on of hands
6:19 *l.* up in store good founda.
Heb. 6:1 not *l.* again foundation
2 and of *l.* on of hands
1 *Pet.* 2:1 *l.* aside all malice

LAZARUS.
Luke 16:20 beggar named L.
John 11:2 Mary whose broth. L.
12:2 L. one that sat at table, 17

LEAD.
Ex. 15:10 sank as *l.* in waters
Num. 31:22 *l.* that may abide fire
Job 19:24 graven with iron and *l.*
Jer. 6:29 *l.* is consumed of the fi.
Ezek. 22:18 *l.* in midst of furnace
20 as th. gather *l.* I gather you
27:12 and *l.* Tarshish traded
Zec. 5:7 lifted up a talent of *l.*
8 weight of *l.* on mouth there.

LEAD.
Gen. 33:14 *l.* on softly as cattle
Ex. 13:21 pillar of cloud *l.* them
32:34 *l.* the people to the place
Deut. 32:12 Lord alone did *l.* hi.
Jud. 5:12 *l.* thy captivity captive
Neh. 9:19 pil. of cloud to *l.* them
Ps. 5:8 *l.* me in thy righteousne.
25:5 *l.* in truth; 27:11 *l.* in plain
31:3 for thy name's sake *l.* me
43:3 light and truth, let them *l.*
60:9 *l.* me into Edom ? 108:10
61:2 *l.* to rock higher than I
125:5 *l.* th. with workers of ini.
139:10 there sh. thy hand *l.* me
24 *l.* me in the way of everlas.
143:10 *l.* me in land of upright.
Prov. 8:20 *l.* in way of righteous.
Cant. 8:2 *l.* thee to mother's ho.
Is. 3:12 that *l.* thee cause to err
11:6 a little child shall *l.* them
42:11 gently *l.* those with young
42:16 *l.* th. in paths not known
49:10 hath mercy on them, *l.* th.
57:18 I will *l.* him and restore
63:14 so didst thou *l.* thy people
Jer. 31:9 with supplica. I *l.* them
Nah. 2:7 her maids *l.* her
Mat. 6:13 *l.* us not into temptat.
Luke 11:4
15:14 If blind *l.* blind, *Lu.* 6:39
Luke 13:15 and *l.* him to water,
Acts 13:11 seeking some to *l.* hi.
1 *Cor.* 9:5 not power to *l.* sister
1 *Tim.* 2:2 we may *l.* a quiet life
Heb. 8:9 *l.* them out of Egypt
Rev. 8:17 Lamb feed and *l.* them

LEADER, S.
1 *Chr.* 12:27 Jehoi. *l.* of Aaroni.
13:1 David consulted with ev. *l.*
1 *Chr.* 32:21 saugth wid. can off *l.*
Is. 9:16 *l.* of people cause to err
55:4 given him a *l.* to the peop.
Mat. 15:14 bo blind *l.* of the blin.

LEADEST.
Ps. 80:1 *l.* Joseph like a flock

LEADETH.
Job 12:17 he *l.* counsellors away
19 he *l.* princes away spoiled
Ps. 23:2 *l.* me beside still waters
3 *l.* me in paths of righteousn.
Prov. 16:29 *l.* him into way

LEA

Is. 48:17 thy God which *l.* thee
Rev. 14:3 no man could *l.* song
14 narrow is way that *l.* to life
John 10:3 calleth sheep and *l.* th.
Rom. 2:4 goodn. of God *l.* to rep.
Rev. 13:10 *l.* sh. go into captivity

LEAF.
Gen. 8:11 in her mou. was oli. *l.*
Lev. 26:36 sound of a shaken *l.*
Job 13:25 break *l.* dr. to and fro?
Ps. 1:3 his *l.* shall not wither
Is. 1:30 be as oak whose *l.* fadeth
34:4 host fall as *l.* 64:6 fade as *l.*
Jer. 17:8 but her *l.* shall be green
Ezek. 47:12 the *l.* shall not fade

LEAVES.
Gen. 3:7 sew. fig *l.* made aprons
Jer. 36:23 when Je. read 3 or 4 *l.*
Mat. 21:19 nothing thereon but *l.*
Mark 11:13
24:32 put. forth *l. Mark* 13:28
Rev. 22:2 *l.* for healing of nations

LEAVES, *for doors.*
1 *K.* 6:34 two *l.* of the one door
Ezek. 41:24 doors had two *l.* apl.

LEAGUE.
Jos. 9:15 made *l.* wi. Gibeon, 16
Jud. 2:2 make no *l.* wi. Inhabit.
1 *Sam.* 22:8 made *l.* with David
3 *Sam.* 5:3 David made *l.* wt. th.
1 *K.* 5:12 Hiram and Sol. made *l.*
15:19 a *l.* between me and thee
2 *Chr.* 16:3 break *l.* with Baasha
Job 5:23 in *l.* with stones of field
Ezek. 30:5 men that is in *l.* sh. f.
Dan. 11:23 after *l.* he work dece.

LEAH.
Gen. 29:16 daughter was L., 30:19
Ruth 4:11 L. make wom. like L.

LEAN, ED.
Jud. 16:26 I may *l.* on pillars
2 *K.* 18:21 on which if a man *l.*
go into hand, *Is.* 36:6
Job 8:15 *l.* on house, it not stand
Prov. 3:5 *l.* not to own underst.
Mic. 3:11 *l.* his hand on the Lord
John 21:20 *l.* on the breast at su.

LEANETH, ING.
2 *Sam.* 3:29 one *l.* on a staff
2 *K.* 5:18 *l.* on my hand in house
Cant. 8:5 cometh up *l.* on belov.
John 13:23 was *l.* on Jesus' bos.
Heb. 11:21 Jacob *l.* on top of sta.

LEAN, NESS.
Gen. 41:3 out of river *l.* flesh, 19
4 *l.* fleshed eat up sev. fat, 30
2 *Sam.* 13:4 being king's son *l.*
Ps. 106:15 sent *l.* into their soul
Is. 10:16 L. send am. fat ones *l.*
17:4 fatness of flesh sh, wax *l.*
24:16 I said, My *l.* my *l.* I woe
24:30 judge betw. fat and *l.*

LEAP.
Gen. 31:12 rams wh. *l.* on cattle
Lev. 11:21 have legs to *l.* withal
Deut. 33:22 Dan sh. *l.* from Bash
Job 41:19 sparks of fire *l.* out
Ps. 68:16 why *l.* ye, ye high hills
Is. 35:6 then shall lame man *l.*
Joel 2:5 like chariots sh. they *l.*
Luke 6:23 rejoice ye, *l.* for joy

LEAPED.
Gen. 31:10 rams wh. *l.* upon cat.
2 *Sam.* 22:30 *l.* over wa. *Ps.* 18:29
Luke 1:41 babe *l.* in womb, 44
Acts 14:10 and he *l.* and walked
19:16 evil spirit was, *l.* on them

LEAPING.
2 *Sam.* 6:16 Michal saw David *l.*
Cant. 2:8 behold, he cometh *l.*
Acts 3:8 and he *l.* up and walked

LEARN.
Deut. 4:10 may *l.* to fear, 14:23
5:1 may *l.* and keep, and do th.
17:19 read that he may *l.* to fear
31:12 hear, and *l.* and fear the L.
13 children may *l.* to fe. the L.
Ps. 18:37 teigh *l.* statutes, 73
Prov. 22:25 lest thou *l.* his ways
Is. 1:17 *l.* to do well, seek judg.
2:4 war any more, *Mic.* 4:3
26:9 inhabitants *l.* righteousne.
10 will not wicked *l.* righteous.
28:21 that murmured *l.* doctrine
Jer. 10:2 *l.* not way of heathen
12:16 diligently *l.* ways of peop.
Mat. 9:13 *l.* what th. meaneth
11:20 *l.* of me, for I am meek
24:32 *l.* parable of *l. Mark* 13:28
1 *Cor.* 14:35 *l.* any thi. let th. ask
1 *Tim.* 2:11 let wom. *l.* in silence
5:4 *l.* first to sh. piety at home

LEA

Tit. 3:14 *l.* to maint. good works
Rev. 14:3 no man could *l.* song

LEARNED.
Gen. 30:27 have *l.* by experience
Ps. 106:35 heathen, and *l.* works
119:7 I have *l.* righteous judg.
Prov. 30:3 I neith. *l.* wisdom nor
Is. 29:11 deliver to one that is *l.*
50:4 God given me tongue of *l.*
he waken. ear to hear as *l.*
John 6:45 man that hath *l.* of F.
7:15 man letters, hav. never *l.*
Acts 7:22 Moses *l.* wisdom of E.
Eph. 4:20 ye have not so *l.* Chr.
Phil. 4:11 *l.* in ev. state to be co.
2 *Tim.* 3:14 contin. in thing thou
l. knowing of wh. th. *l.* th.
Heb. 5:8 yet *l.* he obedience

LEARNING.
Prov. 1:5 wise man will incre. *l.*
9:9 just man, he will incre. in *l.*
16:21 sweetn. of lips increas. *l.*
23 he. of wise addeth *l.* to lips
Dan. 1:17 G. gave them skill in *l.*
Acts 26:24 *l.* doth make thee mad
Rom. 15:4 things writ. for our *l.*
2 *Tim.* 3:7 ever *l.* and never able

LEASING.
Ps. 4:2 how long seek after *l.*?
5:6 shalt destroy them speak *l.*

LEAST.
Gen. 32:10 not worthy *l.* of merc.
Jud. 6:15 *l.* in my father's house
Mat. 2:6 not *l.* among the prince.
11:11 *l.* in kingdom of heaven
greater than he, *Luke* 7:28
1 *Cor.* 15:9 I am least of the apo.
Eph. 3:8 less than *l.* of all saints
See **GREATEST.**

At LEAST.
1 *Sam.* 21:4 kept at *l.* from wom.
Luke 19:42 know, at *l.* in thy day

LEATHER.
2 *K.* 1:8 girt with a girdle of *l.*

LEATHERN.
Mat. 3:4 John had *l.* girdle about

LEAVE, *Substantive.*
Num. 22:13 L. refuseth to give *l.*
1 *Sam.* 20:6 Da. asked *l.* of me, 28
Neh. 13:6 obtained I *l.* of king
Mark 5:13 Jesus gave them *l.*
John 19:38 *l.* to take away body
Acts 18:18 Paul took *l.* of breth.
21:6 taken our *l.* of one of another
2 *Cor.* 2:13 taking *l.* I went to M.

LEAVE.
Gen. 2:24 *l.* father and mother,
Mat. 19:5 ; *Mark* 10:7 ; *Eph.* 5:31
33:15 L. wt. thee some of the fo.
41:22 the lad cannot *l.* his fath.
Ex. 16:19 let no man *l.* manna
23:11 *l.* beasts of field shall eat
Lev. 7:15 eat *l.* peace-offer. 22:30
19:28 off garn. and *l.* them tho.
19:10 *l.* them for the poor, 23:22
Num. 9:12 *l.* none of the passov.
32:15 again *l.* them in wilderne.
Deut. 28:51 shall not *l.* thee corn
l. remnant of chil. he shall *l.*
Jud. 16:9 should I *l.* my fatness
13 said, Should I *l.* my wine
Ruth 1:16 entreat me not to *l.*
1 *Sam.* 9:5 lest my father for asses
2 *Sam.* 14:7 not *l.* husb. a name
2 *K.* 4:43 shall eat and *l.* thereof
19:7 nor did he *l.* of the people
Ezr. 9:8 *l.* us remnant to escape
12 *l.* it for inheritance to chil.
Neh. 5:10 work cease whi. I *l.* it
10:31 would *l.* the seventh year
Job 39:11 wilt *l.* labour to him?
14 she *l.* eggs in earth, 39:22
39:26 left with thee and thy *l.*
17:11 *l.* substance to their babes
27:9 my herit. *l.* me not, 119:121
39:10 *l.* their wealth to others
141:8 *l.* not my soul dest.
Prov. 13:22 *l.* paths of uprightne.
Ec. 2:18 *l.* it to man after me
10:4 enter sp. *l.* not, *l.* not place
Jer. 9:2 I might *l.* my people
14:9 call, by thy name, *l.* us not
17:11 *l.* th. in midst of his days
48:24 *l.* cities and dwell in rocks
49:9 not *l.* some glean. grapes?
11 *l.* child. I will preserve them
Ezek. 16:39 *l.* thee naked, 23:29
Dan. 2:44 *l.* blessing behind him
Amos 5:3 *l.* ten to Israel
7 *l.* off righteousness in earth

LED

Mal. 4:1 *l.* neit. root nor branch
Mal. 3:21 *l.* thy gift bef. the alt.
18:12 *l.* ninety and nine, *Luke* 15:4
23:23 and not to *l.* other undone
Luke 19:44 not *l.* in th. one stone
John 11:27 my peace I *l.* wi. you
16:28 I *l.* world and go to Fath.
32 *l.* me alone, yet I am not *l.*
1 *Cor.* 7:13 let her not *l.* him.

I will, *or* **will I LEAVE.**
Job 9:27 I will *l.* off my heavine.
10:1 I will *l.* complaint on mys.
Ezek. 6:8 I will *l.* a remnant
12:16 but I will *l.* a few men
29:5 I w. *l.* thee into wilderness
32:4 I will *l.* thee in midst of Zion

I will not LEAVE.
2 *K.* 2:2 I will not *l.* thee, 4:30
John 14:18 I w. n. *l.* you comfort.

LEAVED.
Is. 45:1 open him two *l.* gates

LEAVETH.
Prov. 13:22 good man *l.* inherit.
28:3 sweeping rain wh. *l.* no fo.
Mat. 4:11 thee the devil *l.* him

LEAVEN.
Ex. 12:15 away *l.* seven days, 19
13:25 not offer the blood with *l.*
Lev. 2:11 no meat-off. made wi. *l.*
10:12 eat meat-offeri. without *l.*
Amos 4:5 offer a sacrifice with *l.*
Mat. 13:33 kingdom of heaven is like *l. Luke* 13:21
16:6 beware of *l.* Phar. and Sad. 11 ; *Mark* 8:15 ; *Luke* 12:1
12 th. not beware of *l.* of bread
1 *Cor.* 5:6 little *l. wh.* lump, *Gal.* 5:9
7 purge out therefore the old *l.*
8 keep the feast, not wi. old *l.*

LEAVENED.
Ex. 12:15 wh. eateth *l.* bread, 19
20 eat nothing *l.* in habitations
Mat. 13:33 till whole was *l. Luke* 13:21
See **BREAD.**

LEAVENETH.
1 *Cor.* 5:6 little leaven *l.* lump, *Gal.* 5:9

LEAVING.
Rom. 1:27 *l.* natural use of wom.
Heb. 6:1 *l.* principles of Christ
1 *Pet.* 2:21 suffered, *l.* an examp.

LEBANON.
Deut. 3:25 goodly mount, and L.
Jud. 3:3 Hiv. dwell in mount L.
1 *K.* 5:14 ten tho. a month to L.
2 *K.* 19:23 sides of L. *Is.* 37:24
Ps. 29:5 L. like young unicorn
72:16 fruit shake like L. 92:12
Cant. 4:8 L. my spou. 11, 15 ; 5:15
34 thy navel is as tower of L.
Is. 10:34 L. shall fall, 33:9
29:17 L. turned into fruit. field
35:2 glory of L. be given unto it
40:16 L. not sufficient to burn
60:13 glory of L. sh. come to th.
Jer. 18:14 leave the snow of L.?
22:6 thou art head of L. to me
Lam. 4:9 child. better *l.* to mourn
Hos. 14:5 forth roots as L. 6, 7
Nah. 1:4 flower of L. languisheth
Hab. 2:17 violence of L. sh. cov.
Zec. 10:10 them into land of L.
11:1 open thy doors, O L.

LIBBES, *Mat.* 19:3

LED.
Gen. 24:27 being in way, L. *l.* me
24 am hath *l.* me to thy right.
Ex. 3:1 Moses *l.* flock to back of
13:17 God *l.* them through wilde.
15:13 in mercy *l.* forth the peo.
Deut. 8:2 L. *l.* thee forty years
29:5 I have *l.* you forty yea. in wilde.
2 *K.* 6:19 L. *l.* them away captives
Ps. 55:14 I came of L. to mourn
Is. 9:16 *l.* of th. are destroyed
48:21 thirsted not wh. he *l.* them
53:7 *l.* as lamb, *Acts* 8:32
55:12 for ye sh. be *l.* forth with peace
63:12 *l.* them by th. right way
13 led through deep
Jer. 2:6 L. *l.* us thro' wilderness
2:8 L. *l.* them by the way
Ezek. 39:28 which *l.* house of Israel

CRUDEN'S CONCORDANCE. 925

LIA

Luke 10:32 likewise a L. came
Acts 4:36 Barnabas a L. hav. land

LEVITES.

Ex. 38:21 counted for serv. of L.
Lev. 25:33 cit. of L. may L. rede.
Num. 1:50 sh. appoint L. ov. tab.
51 the L. shall take it down
53 the L. shall pitch round abo.
3:9 shall give L. unto Aaron
12 I have taken L. the L. mine
41 take the L. for me, 45; 8:14
7:5 thou sh. give wago. unto L.
8:6 take L. fr. I. and cleanse
11 Aaron sh. offer L. bef. the L.
13:6 taken L. to do service, 24
24 tithes I have given to the L.
35:2 give unto the L. cities, 8
Jos. 14:3 to L. he gave none inh.
21:3 Is. gave these cities to L. 8
41 cities of L. were forty-eight
1 *Sam.* 6:15 L. took down ark
1 *Chr.* 15:15 child. of L. bare ark
26 G. helped L. that bare ark
2 *Chr.* 5:12 L. were singers, 7:6
19:11 also the L. shall be officers
23:6 L. shall comp. the king, 7
29:5 ye L. sanctify yourselves
31:13 of the L. there were scrib.
35:14 L. prep. for themselves, 15
Ezr. 6:18 set L. in their courses
Neh. 8:7 L. caused peo. to under.
11 the L. stilled the people
12:27 at dedica. th. sought L.
13:10 L. were fled every one
29 defiled priesthood of the L.
Ezr. 31:22 I will multiply the L.
Ezek. 44:10 L. are gone bear ini.
48:11 not astray wh. L. went

Priests and LEVITES.

Deut. 17:9 come to priest, and L.
Jos. 3:3 see p. a. L. bearing ark
1 *K.* 8:4 p. a. L. brought ark
2 *Chr.* 23:4 p. a. L. sh. be porters
29:34 pri. and L. more upright
30:15 pri. and L. were ashamed
21 L. and priest, praised the L.
27 p. and L. blessed the peop.
31:9 Hez. questioned wi. p. a. L.
35:8 princes gave to pr. and L.
Ezr. 6:20 pr. and L. were purif.
9:1 p. a. L. have not separated
10:5 Ezra made pr. a. L. to sw.
N. A. 9:38 our princes, L. and p.
12:34 we cast lots amo. p. a. L.
13:30 p. a. L. purified themsely.
Is. 03:21 take of th. for p. and L.
Jer. 33:18 p. a. L. not want a man
21 the L. the p. my ministers
John 1:19 Jews sent p. and L.

LEVITICAL.

Heb. 7:11 were by L. priesthood

LEVY, Substantive.

1 *K.* 5:13 Sol. raised L. of 30,000
9:15 reason of L. Solomon raised
11 Adoniram was over the L.

LEVY, Verb.

Num. 31:28 L. a tribute to the L.
1 *K.* 9:21 on those did Solom. L.

LEWD, LY.

Ezek. 16:27 asham. of thy L. way
22:11 L. defiled thy daughter
23:44 went in, unto the L. wom.
Acts 17:5 Jews took f. fellows

LEWDNESS.

Jud. 20:6 th. have committed L.
Jer. 11:15 wrought L. with many
13:27 seen L. of thy whoredom
Ezek. 16:43 sh. not commit this L.
58 thou hast borne L. and abo.
22:9 midst of thee th. commit L.
22:21 remember. L. of thy youth
27 I make thy L. to cease, 48
35 hear thou also thy L.
49 sh. all recompense your L.
24:13 in thy filthiness is L.
Hos. 2:10 will I discover her L.
6:9 priests murder, commit L.
Acts 18:14 matter of wrong or L.

LIAR.

Job 24:21 who will make me a L. ?
Prov. 17:4 L. giv. ear to naughty
19:22 poor man better than a L.
30:6 and thou be found L.
Jer. 15:18 wilt th. be to me as L.?
John 8:44 L. and the father of it
55 say, I know him not, be L.
Rom. 3:4 God true, ev. man a L.
1 *John* 1:10 slandered, make him L.
2:4 keepeth not com. is L. 4:20
22 is a L. but he that denieth
5:10 believ. not G. made him L.

LIARS.

Deut. 33:29 enemies found L.
Ps. 116:11 ha.ste, all men are L.

LIE

Is. 44:25 frustrateth tokens of L.
Jer. 50:36 a sword is upon the L.
1 *Tim.* 1:10 law is made for L.
Tit. 1:12 Cretians are always L.
Rev. 2:2 and hast found them L.
21:8 all L. have th. part in lake

LIBERAL, LY.

Deut. 15:14 shalt furnish him L.
Prov. 11:25 L. soul sh. be made fat
Is. 32:5 vile sh. not be called L.
8 the L. deviseth L. things
2 *Cor.* 9:13 your L. distribution
Jam. 1:5 God giveth all men L.

LIBERALITY.

1 *Cor.* 16:3 bring your L. to Jeru.
2 *Cor.* 8:2 the riches of their L.

LIBERTINES.

Acts 6:9 called a synagogue of L.

LIBERTY.

Lev. 25:10 proclaim L. thro' land
Ps. 119:45 and I will walk at L.
Is. 61:1 proclaim L. to captives
Jer. 34:8 covenant to proclaim L.
15 done right, in proclaim. L.
17 not heark. to me proclaim-
ing L. I proclaim a L. for you
Ezek. 46:17 his to the year of L.
Luke 4:18 set at L. them bruised
Acts 24:23 keep P. let him have L.
26:32 man might been set at L.
27:3 gave L. to go to his friends
Rom. 8:21 from bondage into L.
1 *Cor.* 7:39 she is at L. to marry
8:9 take heed lest th. L. of yours
10:29 my L. judged of another
2 *Cor.* 3:17 Sp. of L. is, there is L.
Gal. 2:4 came priv. to spy our L.
5:1 stand fast in the L. wherew.
13 ye have been called to L. bre.
Heb. 13:23 brother Tim. set at L.
Jam. 1:25 whoso look. to law of L.
2:12 be judged by the law of L.
1 *Pet.* 2:16 not using L. for a cloak
2 *Pet.* 2:19 they promise them L.

LIBNAH.

Num. 33:20 pitched in L. 21
Jos. 10:29 passed to L. 21:13
2 *K.* 8:22 L. revolted, 2 *Chr.* 21:10

LIBYA.

Ezek. 30:5; *Acts* 2:10

LIDYANS.

Jer. 46:9; *Dan.* 11:43

LICE.

Ex. 8:16 dust became L. 17, 18
Ps. 105:31 L. in all their coasts
Acts 21:40 whom he had giv. P. L.
23:16 accused have L. to answer

LICK.

Num. 22:4 this company L. up all
1 *K.* 21:19 shall dogs L. thy blood
Ps. 72:9 enemies sh. L. the dust
Is. 49:23 L. up dust of thy feet
Mic. 7:17 sh. L. dust like a serp.

LICKED, ETH.

Num. 22:4 L. up all, as ox L. grass
1 *K.* 18:38 L. up water in trench
21:19 dogs L. blood of Naboth
22:28 the dogs L. up his blood
Luke 16:21 dogs ca. and L. sores

LID.

2 *K.* 12:9 bored a hole in the L.

LIE, falsehood.

Ps. 62:9 men of hi. degree are a L.
119:69 proud forged a L. ag. me
Is. 44:20 is not a L. in rig. hand ?
Jer. 27:10 prophesy a L. to you to
Ezek. 16:13 sh. not commit this L.
24:15 mak. peo. to trust in a L.
23:31 caused you to trust in a L.
Ezek. 21:29 divine a L. to thee
Mic. 1:14 whose houses are a L.
John 8:44 speaketh L. he speak.
Rom. 1:25 changed truth into L.
3:7 through my L. to his glory
2 *Thes.* 2:11 that they L. believe a L.
1 *John* 2:21 no L. is of the truth
27 of all things, and is no L.
Rev. 21:27 whoso. maketh a L.
22:15 whoso. lov. and maketh L.

LIES.

Jud. 16:10 th. hast told me L. 13
Job 11:3 L. maketh men hold peace ?
Ps. 40:4 such as turn aside to L.
58:3 wicked go astray, speak. L.
62:4 delight in L. curse inwardly
63:11 mouth speak. L. be stopp.
101:7 tell. L. not tarry in my sight
Prov. 6:19 him w. whose speak. L.
11:5 a false witness will utter L.
25 deceitful witness speak. L.
19:5 speaketh L. shall not escape
9 he that speaketh L. p.

LIE

Prov. 29:12 if a ruler heark. to L.
30:8 remove fr. me vanity and L.
Is. 9:15 prophet that teacheth L.
28:15 have made L. our refuge
17 sweep away the refuge of L.
55:3 your lips have spoken L.
4 trust in vanity, and speak L.
Jer. 9:3 bend like th. bow for L.
5 tau. their tongue to speak L.
14:14 proph. prophe. L. 23:25, 26
16:19 our fathers have inher. L.
20:6 hast prophesied L.
23:14 commit adult. walk in L.
32 cause peo. to err by their L.
48:30 his L. shall not so effect it
Ezek. 13:8 spoken vanity, seen L.
9 upon prophets that divine L.
22 whil. L. ye made right. sad
23:28 divining L. unto them
24:12 she wearied herself with L.
Dan. 11:27 speak L. at one table
Hos. 7:3 princes glad with L.
13 have spoken L. against me
10:13 ye have eaten fruit of L.
11:12 Ephr. comp. about wi. L.
12:1 he increaseth L. and desol.
Amos 2:4 L. caused them to err
Mic. 6:12 inhabi. have spoken L.
Nah. 3:1 city, it is full of L.
Hab. 2:18 and a teacher of L.
Zep. 3:13 Israel sh. not speak L.
1 *Tim.* 4:2 speak. L. in hypocrisy

LIE, Verb.

Lev. 6:2 if a soul L. to his neigh.
19:11 steal, nor L. one to another
20:19 man, that he sho. L.
1 *Sam.* 15:29 Str. of Is. will not L.
2 *K.* 4:16 do not L. to handmaid
Job 6:28 is evident to yo uif I L.
34:6 should I L. against my right
Ps. 89:35 I will not L. to David
Prov. 14:5 faith. witn. will not L.
Is. 63:8 my peo. that will not L.
12:11 walk. in falsehood do L.
Hab. 2:3 it shall speak and not L.
Acts 5:3 hath h. filled heart to L.
Rom. 9:1 I say truth in Christ, I
L. not. 1 *Tim.* 2:7
Cor. 11:31 L. knoweth, I L. not
Gal. 1:20 I wrote, behold I L. not
Col. 3:9 L. not one to another
Tit. 1:2 life, God that cannot L.
promised, *Heb.* 6:18
Jam. 3:14 L. not against the truth
1 *John* 1:6 w. L. and do not truth
Rev. 3:9 they are Jews, but do L.

LIED, ETH.

Lev. 6:3 lost, and L. concerning
1 *K.* 13:18 but he L. unto him
Ps. 78:36 L. unto him w. tongues
Is. 57:11 been afraid, thou hast L.
Acts 5:4 h. not L. unto men

LIE, to recline.

Gen. 47:30 I will L. with my fat.
Ex. 23:11 let the ground L. still
Deut. 22:20 curses in hook L. on h.
Jud. 19:20 thy wants L. on me
1 *Sam.* 3:5 L. down again
1 *K.* 1:2 let her L. in thy bosom
Ps. 57:4 I L. even among lions
88:5 like slain that L. in grave
Ez. 4:11 two L. together ha. heat
Is. 11:6 will beasts sh. L. There
11:18 kings of nations L. inglory
51:20 sons L. at head of streets
Ezek. 4:4 L. also upon thy left side
6 L. again on thy right side
9 thou sh. lie on thy side 390 d.
31:18 L. in midst of uncircume.
32:21 they L. uncircumcised, 30
28 thou sh. L. in midst of uncir.
31:18 shall thy L. in a good fold
John 5:6 when Jesus saw him L.

LIE, ETH down.

Lev. 18:23 to L. thereto, 20:16
26:6 L. d. and none make afraid
Num. 23:24 not L. d. till he eat
Deut. 23:2 cause him to L. down
Job 7:4 sh. L. d. but I say, Sh. I ri.
11:18 yea, thou shalt L. d. safely
20:11 L. d. with him in the dust
21:26 shall L. d. alike in the dust
27:19 rich man shall L. down
33:14 L. in green pastures
Is. 14:8 in the midst of a rock
Is. 14:30 shall L. d. in safety
Ezek. 34:14 shall L. in a good fold
15 I will cause flock L. d.
Hos. 2:18 make them L. d. safely
Zep. 2:7 sh. L. d. in the evening
14 flocks sh. L. d. 15 beasts L. d.
3:13 remnant of Israel shall L. d.

LIE, ETH in wait.

Ex. 21:13 if a man L. not in wait
Deut. 19:11 hate neighbor, L. w.
Jos. 8:4 sh. L. in w. against city
Jud. 9:32 L. in wait in the field
Ps. 10:9 L. in w. secretly as a lion
59:3 they L. in w. for my soul
Prov. 7:12 L. in w. at ev. corner
12:6 wicked are to L. in wait
23:28 she L. in w. as for a prey
Mic. 7:2 they all L. in w. for bl.
Acts 23:21 L. in wait for him
Eph. 4:14 L. in w. to deceive me

LIE, ETH waste.

Neh. 2:3 fathers' sepulchres L. w.
17 see how Jerusalem L. waste
Is. 33:8 the highways L. waste
Hag. 1:4 and this house L. waste

LIE, ETH with.

Gen. 19:32 and we will L. w. him
30:15 he shall L. w. thee to-night
39:7 L. w. me, 12; 2 *Sam.* 13:11
Ex. 22:16 if a man L. w. a maid
19 whoso L. with beast
Lev. 15:18 w. whom man shall L.
15:24 if any man L. with her at
18:20 not L. carnally w. neigh.
22 shalt not L. with mankind
23 neither sh. thou L. w. beast
19:20 L. carnally with bondmaid
20:11 man L. w. his father's wife
12 if a man L. with daugh.-in-l.
13 mankind as he L. w. woman
15 if a man L. with a beast
18 if man L. w. wom. ha. sick.
Num. 5:13 if a man L. with her
Deut. 22:23 find her, and L. with
25 man force her, and L. w. her
27:20 that L. with father's wife
21 L. w. beast; 22 sist. 23 mot.
28:30 betroth a wife, sho. L. w.
2 *Sam.* 11:11 go to L. w. my wife?
Cant. 1:13 sh. L. all night betwixt
Mic. 7:5 mouth from her that L.

LIERS in wait.

Jos. 8:14 wist not th. were L. i. w.
Jud. 9:25 men of Sh. set L. in w.
16:12 L. in w. abid. in chamber
20:33 the L. in wait came forth
37 L. in w. hasted and rushed

LIEST.

Gen. 28:13 land whereon thou L.
Deut. 6:7 wh. thou L. down, 11:19
Jos. 7:10 wheref. L. on thy face?
Prov. 3:24 L. down sh. not be afr.

LIETH.

Gen. 4:7 not well, sin L. at door
49:25 blessings of deep L. under
Lev. 14:47 that L. in house
15:4 bed whereon he L. is uncl.
20 th. sh. L. on is unclean, 26
24 bed whereon he L. be unc. 33
Num. 19:16 one that L. in grave
24:9 L. as lion, as a great lion
Ps. 41:8 evil dis. L. sh. rise no more
88:7 thy wrath L. hard on me
Mat. 8:6 servant L. at home sick
Mark 5:23 L. at point of death
Rom. 12:18 as much as L. in you
1 *John* 5:19 w. world L. in wickedn.

LIEUTENANTS.

Ezr. 8:36 king's commis. to L.
Est. 3:12 commanded king's L.
8:9 Mord. had commanded it to
9 rulers and L. helped Jews

LIFE.

Gen. 1:20 done, creature hath L.
2:7 G. breathed the breath of L.
9 tree of L. in garden, 3:22
3:14 keep the way of tr. of L.
6:17 dest. all wherein is L. 7:22
9:4 flesh with L. thereof shall ye not
eat, *Lev.* 17:14
18:10 when I will I ret. L. of time
18:10 return ac co. to ti. of L.
42:15 by the L. of Pharaoh, 16
44:30 with me to go down to him
49:30 he shall bow down
Ex. 21:23 L. for L. *Deut.* 19:21
Lev. 17:11 L. of flesh is in blood
18 L. is toofa be had L. L. for it
21 it shall be L. L. for L.

CRUDEN'S CONCORDANCE.

CRUDEN'S CONCORDANCE. 927

LIG

LIGHT.
Num. 21:5 soul loatheth *l.* bread
Deut. 27:16 cursed set. *l.* by faith.
Jud. 9:4 vain and *l.* persons
2 *Sam.* 2:18 A=hel was *l.* of foot
Ezek. 22:7 set *l.* by fath. and mo.
Zep. 3:4 prophets *l.* and treach.
Mat. 11:30 yoke easy, burden *l.*
22:5 *l.* of it and went their ways
2 *Cor.* 4:17 *l.* affliction worketh

LIGHT thing.
1 *Sam.* 18:23 seemeth it a *l. th.?*
2 *K.* 20:10 *l.* shadow go down
Is. 49:6 *l.* that should, be serv.

LIGHT, Substantive.
Gen. 1:3 God said, Let there be *l.*
4 God saw *l.* 5 G, called *l.* day
16 the lesser *l.* to rule the nig.
Ex. 10:23 Is. had *l.* in dwellings
14:20 the pillar gave *l.* by night
Num. 4:16 pertaineth oil for *l.*
1 *Sam.* 14:27 quench not *l.* of Is.
23:4 shall be as *l.* of morning
1 *K.* 7:4 *l.* was against *l.*
11:36 David my serv. may ha. *l.*
Neh. 9:19 pillar of fire to shew *l.*
Est. 8:16 *J.* had *l.* and gladness
Job 3:4 nelt. let *l.* shine upon it
9 let it look for *l.* but have no.
3:20 *l.* given him in misery, 23
10:22 where the *l.* is as darkness
12:22 bring, to *l.* shadow of de.
18:5 *l.* of wicked sh. be put out
6 *l.* shall be dark in his tabor.
22:28 *l.* shalt shine on thy ways
24:13 those that rebel ag. the *l.*
14 murderer rising with *l.*
16 they know not the *l.*
25:3 upon wh. doth not *l.* arise?
28:11 thing hid bringeth to *l.*
33:28 his life shall see the *l.*
30 enlightened with *l.* of living
36:30 spreadeth his *l.* upon it
32 with clouds he covereth *l.*
37:15 caused *l.* of cloud to shine
21 see not bright *l.* in clouds
38:15 fr. wicked *l.* is withholden
19 wh. is way where *l.* dwell. ?
24 by what way is *l.* parted ?
Ps. 4:6 lift up *l.* of countenance
27:1 Lord is my *l.* and salvation
37:6 bring forth righteous, as *l.*
38:10 *l.* of mine eyes, it is gone
49:19 they shall never see *l.*
74:16 prepared the *l.* and sun
78:14 all the night with a *l.*
97:11 *l.* is sown for the righte.
104:2 who coverest thyself with *l.*
118:27 L. who hath showed us *l.*
119:105 and a *l.* to my path
130 entra. of thy words giv. *l.*
139:12 darkn. and *l.* alike to thee
Prov. 4:18 path of just as shin. *l.*
6:23 commandm. lamp, law is *l.*
13:9 *l.* of righteous rejoiceth
15:30 *l.* of eyes rejoiceth heart
Ec. 2:17 *l.* is sweet and pleasant
12:2 or the *l.* be not darkened
Is. 3:20 darkness for *l. l.* darkn.
30 *l.* is darkened in heavens
8:20 because there is no *l.* in th.
9:2 great *l.* on th. hath *l.* shined
10:17 *l.* of Is. shall be for a fire
13:10 moon sh. not cause his *l.*
to shine, *Mat.* 21:29; *Mark* 13:24
30:26 *l.* of moon as *l.* of sun, *l.*
of sun as the *l.* of seven days
51:4 judgment rest for *l.* to peo.
59:9 wait for *l.* but behold obs.
60:19 L. be to thee everlast. *l.*
Jer. 4:23 beheld heav. had no *l.*
13:16 value from them *l.* of cand.
31:35 L. giv. sun for *l.* by day,
moon and stars for *l.* by nig.
Dan. 2:22 *l.* dwelleth with him
Am. 5:3 judgm. as *l.* goeth forth
Mic. 7:9 L. bring me forth to *l.*
Hab. 3:3 his brightness was as *l.*
11 at *l.* of thine arrows
Zep. 3:5 morn. bring judgm. to *l.*
Zec. 14:6 in that day *l.* not be cl.
Mat. 4:16 in death, *l.* sprung up
6:22 *l.* of world; 15 if giveth *l.*
16 let your *l.* so shine be. men
6:22 the *l.* of the body is the
eye, *Luke* 11:31, 36
17:2 his raiment white as the *l.*
Luke 2:32 *l.* to lighten Gentiles
8:16 enter in may see *l.*, 11:33
16:8 wiser than children of *l.*
John 1:9 life was the *l.* of men
7 come to bear witness of *l.* 8
9 true *l.* wh. lighteth every m.
3:19 *l.* is come into the world
20 ev. one doeth evil hateth *l.*
21 that doeth truth com. to *l.*

LIG

John 5:35 was a burn. and shi. *l.*
8:12 I am *l.* of world, he that
fol. me sh. have *l.* of life, 9:5
11:9 because he seeth the *l.*
10 because th. is no *l.* in him
12:35 a little wh. is *l.* with you
36 wh. ye have *l.* believe in *l.*
46 am come a *l.* into world
Acts 9:3 shined about him a *l.*
12:7 a *l.* shined in the prison
13:47 to be a *l.* to the Gentiles
16:29 called for a *l.* and sprang
22:6 there shone a great *l.* round
9 they with me saw indeed *l.*
26:13 midday I saw in way a *l.*
23 *l.* to people and to Gentiles
Rom. 2:19 *l.* of them are in dark.
13:12 put on the armor of *l.*
14:5 bring to *l.* hid. things
2 *Cor.* 4:4 lest *l.* of gospel shine
6 commanded *l.* to shine out
11:14 transf. into an angel of *l.*
Eph. 5:8 are *l.* walk as chil. of *l.*
13 all things made man. by *l.*
whatso. doth manifest is *l.*
Col. 1:12 inherit. of saints in *l.*
1 *Thes.* 5:5 are all children of *l.*
1 *Tim.* 6:16 dwelling in *l.* no man
2 *Tim.* 1:10 who brought life to *l.*
1 *Pet.* 2:9 called you to marvel. *l.*
2 *Pet.* 1:19 *l.* that shin. in dark place
1 *John* 1:5 G. is *l.* in him no da.
Rev. 18:23 *l.* of candle sh. no mo.
21:11 *l.* like a stone most prec.
23 the Lamb is the *l.* thereof
22:5 they need no *l.* of the sun

See **COUNTENANCE, DARKNESS.**

Give LIGHT.
Gen. 1:15 let them be to *g. l.*
Ex. 13:21 pillar of fire to *give l.*
2 *K.* 8:19 *give* him a 2 *Chr.* 21:7
Neh. 9:12 *g.* them *l.* in the way
Ps. 105:39 fire to *g. l.* in night
Is. 13:10 stars of heaven not *g. l.*
42:5 *g.* for a *l.* to Gentiles, 49:6
69:19 moon *g. l. Mat.* 24:29
Mat. 5:15 *g. l.* to all, *Luke* 11:36
2 *Cor.* 4:6 *g. l.* of knowle. of G.
Eph. 5:14 Christ shall *g. thee l.*

In the LIGHT.
Ps. 56:13 may walk *in the l.*
Is. 2:5 let us walk *in the l.* of L.
50:11 walk *in the l.* of your fire
John 12:35 light, believe *in l. l.*
1 *John* 1:7 *in l. l.* as he is in *l.*
2:9 he that saith he is *in the l.*
10 lov. brother, abideth *in t. l.*
Rev. 21:24 nations sh. walk *i. t. l.*

Thy LIGHT.
Ps. 36:9 in *thy l.* we see light
43:3 send out *t. l.* and thy truth
Is. 58:8 then sh. *t. l.* break forth
10 then sh. *t. l.* rise in obscuri.
60:1 shine, for *thy l.* is come
2 Gentiles shall come to *thy l.*
19 the sun sh. be no more *t. l.*
20 L. shall be *t. l.* everlasting *l.*

LIGHT, ED.
Ex. 25:37 wh. *l.* the lamps, 40:4
Ps. 18:28 thou will *l.* my candle
Mat. 5:15 nor put a candle
Luke 8:16 hath *l.* candle, 11:33
15:8 doth not *l.* a candle
Rev. 7:16 nor sh. sun *l.* on them

LIGHT on.
Ruth 2:3 to *l. on* part of B.'s fie.
2 *Sam.* 17:12 will *l. on* him

LIGHTED.
Gen. 21:64 saw *l.* she *l. off* camel
Jos. 15:8 *l. off* ass, *Jud.* 1:14
Jud. 4:15 Sisera *l. off* his chariot
1 *Sam.* 25:23 Abigail *l. off* those
2 *K.* 5:21 Naaman *l.* from chari.

LIGHTEDST, ETH.
Gen. 30:11 a *l.* on certain place
Deut. 19:5 slip, and *l. on* neigh.
Is. 9:8 word to Jacob it *l. on* Isr.
Jer. 9:4 on whomsoever it *l. on*
Nah. 2:22 fourth is *l.* Son of God
Jon. 1:6 that waver, is *l.* a wave
Mat. 3:16 a man beholding his face
5:17 F. was subject to *l.* passio.
John 1:9 *l.* obtain. *l.* precious faith
1 *John* 1:11 *l.* the wh. shall be *l.* him
14:14 in day *l.* 14:14
Luke 22:1 R. light of glory of did. *l.*

LIGHTEN, ETH.
Ps. 34:5 looked in him and we. *l.*
77:18 the lightnings *l.* the world
Luke 2:32 *l.* both their eyes
17:24 lightn. *l.* out of one part
28:1 it earth *l.* with his glory

See **ENLIGHTENED.**

LIK

LIGHTER.
1 *K.* 12:4 make thou our yoke *l.*
9, 10; 2 *Chr.* 10:10
Ps. 62:9 altogether *l.* than vanity

LIGHTEST, ETH.
Ex. 30:8 Aaron *l.* lamps at even
Num. 8:2 when thou *l.* lamps
John 1:9 true light *l.* every man

LIGHTING.
Is. 30:30 L. show *l.* down of arm
Mat. 3:16 a dove, and *l.* on him

LIGHTLY.
Gen. 26:10 might *l.* have lain
Is. 9:1 he *l.* afflicted the land
Jer. 4:24 all the hills moved *l.*
Mark 9:39 *l.* speak evil of me

See **ESTEEMED.**

LIGHTNESS.
Jer. 3:9 thro' *l.* of her whoredo.
23:32 cause peo. to err by the *l.*
2 *Cor.* 1:17 minded, did I use *l.?*

LIGHTNING.
Job 28:26 made way for *l.* of thu.
37:3 directeth *l.* to ends of earth
38:25 divided a way for the *l.*
Ezek. 1:14 ran as appearance of *l.*
Dan. 10:6 face as appearance *l.*
Mat. 24:27 as *l.* cometh out of
the east, *Luke* 17:24
28:3 his countenance was as *l.*
Luke 10:18 as *l.* fall from heaven

LIGHTNINGS.
Ex. 19:16 thunders, *l.* and cloud
21:18 all the people saw the *l.*
Job 38:35 send *l. th.* th. may go ?
Ps. 18:14 *l.* and discomfited th.
77:18 *l.* lighted the world, 97:4
135:7 he maketh *l.* for the rain
Jer. 10:13 mak. *l.* w. rain, 51:16
Nah. 2:4 chariots shall run like *l.*
Rev. 4:5 out of throne proceed. *l.*
8:5 thunderings and *l.* 16:18
16:18 *l.* and a great earthquake

LIGHTS.
Gen. 1:14 let there be *l.* in firm.
16 God make two great *l.*
1 *K.* 6:4 windows of narrow *l.*
Ex. 19:7 made great *l.*
Ezek. 32:8 bri. *l.* will I make d.
Luke 12:35 loins girded, *l.* burn.
Acts 20:8 *l.* in upper chamber
Phil. 2:15 ye shine as *l.* in world
Jam. 1:17 down from Father of *l.*

LIGN-ALOES.
Num. 24:6 trees of *L-a.* L. plant.

LIGURE.
Ex. 28:19 third row a *l.* 39:12

LIKE.
Ex. 15:11 who is *l. thee?*
Deut. 33:29; 1 *K.* 8:23; *Ps.* 35:10
Mic. 7:18
Is. 57:20 wicked *l.* troubled sea
66:6 iniquities *l.* wind bear his
Jer. 11:19 *l.* a lamb bro. to slau.
22:29 is not my word *l.* fire?
Ezek. 18:10 doe'n *l.* any of these
Dan. 3:25 fourth is *l.* Son of God
7:13 one *l.* the Son of man came
Hos. 4:9 sh. be *l.* people, *l.* priest
Mat. 13:31 *l.* to a grain of mus-
tard-seed, *Mark* 4:31; *Luke* 13:19
41 *l.* a treasure; 45 *l.* a merch.
47 *l.* a net; 52 *l.* a household, 20:1
22:2 heav. is *l.* to a certain king
Acts 14:15 are men of *l.* passions
Heb. 2:17 made *l.* his brethren
7:3 made *l.* to the Son of God
Jam. 5:17 Elias was a man of *l.*
pas. *1 Pet.* 3:21

See **MANNER.**

No LIKE.
Ex. 8:10 there is *no l. l.* Lord
Jer. 30:7 *l.* *l.* 33:22 ; 2 *Sa.*
7:22 ; 1 *Chr.* 17:20
46:6 *n. l.* cry of Lord of Egypt

LIN

1 *Sam.* 10:24 *n. l.* S. among peo.
1 *K.* 3:12 there was *n. l.* Solomon
21:25 there was *n. l.* to Ahab.
2 *K.* 18:5 there was *n. l.* Hezeki.
Ps. 86:8 among the gods *n. l.* to
thee, *Jer.* 10:6, 7
Jer. am G. there is *n. l.* me
Jer. 30:7 day is great, *n. l. it*
Dan. 1:19 among all *n. l.* Daniel

Such LIKE.
Mark 7:8 *s. l.* things ye do, 13
Gal. 5:21 drunkenness, and *s. l.*

LIKE, ED.
Deut. 25:7 *l.* not to take her, 8
1 *Chr.* 28:4 sons of my fat. *l.* me
Rom. 1:28 did not *l.* to retain G.

LIKEN.
Is. 40:18 to whom *l.* G.? 25; 46:5
Lam. 2:13 what sh. I *l.* to thee?
Mat. 7:24 I will *l.* him to a man
11:16 whereunto *l.* this genera-
tion ? *Luke* 7:31
Mark 4:30 *l.* kingd. ? *Luke* 13:20

LIKENED.
Ps. 89:6 who am, sons *l.* to L. ?
Jer. 6:2 *l.* the daughter of Zion
Mat. 7:26 sh. he *l.* to foolish m.
13:24 heaven is *l.* 18:23 ; 25:1

LIKENESS.
Gen. 1:26 make man after *l.* 5:1
5:3 A. begat a son in his own *l.*
Ex. 20:4 not make *l.* of anythi'g
Deut. 4:16 the *l.* of male or fe-
male, 17, 18, 23, 25 ; 5:8
Ps. 17:15 wh. awake with thy *l.*
Is. 40:18 what *l.* comp. to him ?
Ezek. 1:5 *l.* of four liv. creatures
26 *l.* of the glory of the Lord
10:21 *l.* of the hands of men
Rom. 6:5 in *l.* of his death, we
shall be in *l.* of resurrection
8:3 G. sending Son in *l.* of flesh
Phil. 2:7 was made in *l.* of men

LIKETH.
Deut. 23:16 dwell where it *l.* him
Amos 4:5 this *l.* you, O child. of

LIKING.
Job 39:4 young on. are in good *l.*
Dan. 1:10 why see faces worse *l.*

LIKEWISE.
Ps. 49:10 *l.* brut. person perish
52:5 God shall *l.* destroy thee
Jer. 7:22 *l.* have I not cursed others
Mat. 20:5 also, sixth hour, did *l.*
21:36 and they did unto them *l.*
Luke 6:31 do ye also to them *l.*
13:5 ye shall all *l.* perish, 5
12:54 *l.* Laz. received evil thin.
22:20 *l.* also cup after supper
John 5:19 there doeth the Son *l.*
1 *Cor.* 7:3 *l.* the wife to husband
11:25 *l.* he himself *l.* took part
Heb. 2:14 are yourselves *l.*
Jude 8 *l.* these filthy dreamers
Rev. 8:12 day shone not, night *l.*

LILY.
Cant. 2:1 I am the *l.* of the val.
I am, a thorn, so my love
Hos. 14:5 Is. shall grow as the *l.*

LILIES.
Cant. 2:16 below, feed. am. *l.* 6:3
4:5 like two roses among the *l.*
5:13 lips like *l.* dropping myrrh
7:2 belly like wheat set with *l.*
Mat. 6:28 consider the *l.* how
they grow. *Luke* 12:27

LILY-WORK.
1 *K.* 7:19 chapiters were of *L-w.*
22 on top of pillars was *L-w.*

LIME.
Is. 33:12 peo. be as burnings of *l.*
Amos 2:1 bur. of king of E. to *l.*

LIMIT, ED, ETH.
Ps. 78:41 Holy One of Israel
Ezek. 43:12 *l.* thereof shall be ho.
Heb. 4:7 he *l.* a certain day

LINE, S.
2 *K.* 21:13 over J. *l.* of Samaria
Job 38:5 stretched *l.* on earth
Ps. 16:6 fallen in places
19:4 their *l.* is gone thro' earth
78:55 divided inheritance by *l.*
Is. 28:10 *l.* must be upon *l.* 13
17 judgm. also w. to the *l.*
34:11 stretch on it *l.* of confus.
Amos 7:17 land be divided by *l.*
Zec. 1:16 be stretched on Jeru.
2 *Cor.* 10:16 in another man's *l.*

LINEAGE.
Luke 2:4 he was of *l.* of David

LINEN.
Ex. 28:42 make them *l.* breeches

CRUDEN'S CONCORDANCE.

LIO

Lev. 6:10 put on *l.* garment, 16:4
1 *Sam.* 2:18 minis. with *l.* ephod
22:18 slew 85 that did we. *l.* ep.
2 *Sam.* 6:14 D. girded wi. *l.* eph.
1 *K.* 10:28 Solomon had *l.* yarn brought, 2 *Chr.* 1:16
Jer. 13:1 get thee a *l.* girdle
Mat. 27:28 he wrapped it in a clean *l.* cloth, *John* 19:40
Mark 14:51 *l.* cloth about his bo.
52 left *l.* cloth and fled naked
Luke 24:12 P. beheld *l.* clothes la. by themselves, *John* 20:6
John 20:5 John saw the *l.* clothes

LINEN.
Lev. 19:19 nor shall a garment mingled of *l.* and woollen co. upon thee. *Deut.* 22:11
1 *Chr.* 15:27 D. had ou eph. of *l.*
Mark 13:46 wrap. in *l. Luke* 23:53
Rev. 15:6 angels clothed in *l.*

See FINE.

LINGERED, ETH.
Gen. 19:16 Lot *l.* men laid hold
43:10 except *l.* we had returned
2 *Pet.* 2:3 judg. of a long time *l.*

LINTEL, S.
Ex. 12:22 strike *l.* and two posts
1 *K.* 6:31 *l.* and posts a fifth part
Amos 9:1 smite *l.* posts shake
Zep. 2:14 bittern lodge in upper *l.*

LINUS. 2 *Tim.* 4:21

LION.
Gen. 49:9 Judah couched as a *l.*
Num. 23:9 Israel lay down as a *l.*
Deut. 33:20 Gad dwelleth as a *l.*
Jud. 14:8 turned to see carc. of *l.*
bees and honey in carc. of *l.*
1 *Sam.* 17:34 ca. a *l.* and took la.
2 *Sam.* 17:10 heart as hea. of a *l.*
23:20 slew *l.* in pit, 1 *Chr.* 11:22
1 *K.* 13:24 a *l.* met him by way and slew him. *l.* also stood
20:36 a *l.* sh. slay thee; a *l.* fou.
Job 4:10 roaring of *l.* voice of *l.*
13:16 huntest me as a fierce *l.*
28:8 nor the fierce *l.* passed by
38:39 wilt th. hunt prey for *l.?*
Ps. 7:2 lest tear my soul like *l.*
10:9 lieth in wait secretly as a *l.*
17:12 like a *l.* greedy of his prey
22:13 they gaped on me as a *l.*
91:13 thou shalt tread on the *l.*
Prov. 19:13 king's wra. is as a *l.*
22:2 fear of king is as roar. of *l.*
22:13 saith, There is a *l.* in way
26:13 *l.* in way, a *l.* in the street
28:1 righteous are bold as a *l.*
30:30 a *l.* strongest am. beasts
Ec. 9:4 liv. dog better th. dead *l.*
Is. 5:29 th. roaring sh. be like *l.*
11:7 *l.* sh. eat str. like ox, 65:25
21:8 he cried, A *l.* my lord
35:9 no *l.* there, nor ravenous
38:13 as *l.* so will he bre. bones
Jer. 2:30 devour, prophet's like *l.*
4:7 *l.* is come from his thicket
5:6 a *l.* out of forest sh. slay th.
12:8 my heritage is to me as a *l.*
25:38 forsak. his covert as the *l.*
49:19 shall come up like *l.* 50:44
Lam. 3:10 he was to me as a *l.*
Ezek. 1:10 face of *l.* on right side
19:1 third was the face of a *l.*
22:25 a conspir. like a roaring *l.*
Dan. 7:4 first like a *l.* had wings
Hos. 5:14 I will be to Ephr. a *l.*
11:10 he shall roar like a *l.*
13:7 to them as *l.* 8 will devour
Joel 1:6 teeth of a *l.* cheek-teeth
Amos 3:4 *l.* roar bath no prey?
8 *l.* roared, who will not fear?
it taketh out of mouth of *l.*
Mic. 5:8 rem. of Jac. sh. be as *l.*
Nah. 2:11 *l.* tare in pieces
2 *Tim.* 4:17 de. out of mouth of *l.*
1 *Pet.* 5:8 devil as a *l.* walk. abo.
Rev. 4:7 first beast was like a *l.*
5:5 the *l.* of the tribe of Judah
10:3 a loud voice as a *l.* roareth
13:2 his mouth was as mo. of *l.*

See BEAR.

LION-LIKE.
2 *Sam.* 23:20 slew two *l.-l.* men of Moab 1 *Chr.* 11:22

Old LION.
Is. 30:6 whence come the old *l.?*
Nah. 2:11 even the old *l.* walked

Young LION.
Jr. 11:6 calf and a *l.* lie down
31:4 like as the *young l.* roaring
Ezek. 19:3 it became a *young l.* 6
32:2 like a *y. l.* of the nations
41:19 face of *y. l.* towards tree

LIP

LIONESS, ES.
Ezek. 19:2 wh. is thy moth. ? a *l.*
Nah. 2:12 lion strangled for his *l.*

LIONS.
2 *Sam.* 1:23 S. and Jon. strong. *l.*
1 *K.* 10:19 two *l.* stood beside the stays, 2 *Chr.* 9:18
2 *K.* 17:25 L. sent *l.* among them
1 *Chr.* 12:8 faces like faces of *l.*
Ps. 22:21 save me from *l.* mouth
35:17 rescue my darling from *l.*
57:4 my soul is among *l.* I lie
Cant. 4:8 top of Am. from *l.* dens
Is. 15:9 *l.* upon him that escap.
Jer. 50:17 *l.* driven Israel away
51:38 shall roar together like *l.*
Ezek. 19:2 she lay down amo. *l.*
Dan. 6:27 D. from power of *l.*
Nah. 2:11 wh. is dwelling of *l.?*
Zep. 3:3 princes are roaring *l.*
Heb. 11:33 faith sto. mouths of *l.*
Rev. 9:8 teeth as the teeth of *l.*
17 heads of horses as hea. of *l.*

See DEN.

LION'S whelp, s.
Gen. 49:9 Judah is *l.'s w.* from
Deut. 33:22 Dan is a *l.'s whelp*
Job 4:11 *l.'s w.* scattered abroad
28:8 *l.'s w.* have not trodden it
Jer. 51:38 sh. yell as *l.'s whelps*

Young LIONS.
Ps. 34:10 *y. l.* suffer hunger
58:6 break out gr. teeth of *y. l.*
104:21 *y. l.* roar after their prey
Is. 5:29 *y. l.* roared upon him
Ezek. 19:6 nourished among *y. l.*
38:13 the *y. l.* shall say to t'ee
Zec. 11:3 voice of roaring of *y. l.*

LIP.
Lev. 13:45 a covering on his *l.*
Ps. 22:7 they shoot out the *l.*
Prov. 12:19 *l.* of truth establish,
12 words of other *l.* be taken
63:5 praise thee with joyful *l.*
120:2 deli. my soul from lying *l.*
140:3 poison is under their *l.*
8 wet a lacivet of own *l.* cover
Prov. 4:24 perverse *l.* put fr. th.
5:3 *l.* of a strange woman drop
7:21 flatter. of *l.* she forced him
10:13 in *l.* of him that hath un.
21 *l.* of righteous feed many
32 *l.* of righteous know
12:22 lying *l.* abomination to L.
14:3 *l.* of wise sh. preserve them
7 not in him *l.* of knowledge
23 talk of *l.* tendeth to penury
15:7 *l.* of wise disperse knowl.
16:13 rich *t. l.* delight of kings
21 sweet. of *l.* increaseth learn.
17:4 wicked giv. heed to false *l.*
7 less do lying *l.* bec. a prince
18:6 fools *l.* enter into conten.
20:15 *l.* of knowl. are a jewel
24:2 their *l.* talk of mischief
26:23 burning *l.* like a potsherd
24 *l.* of *l.* of wisd. himself
Cant. 7:9 an opening *l.* of sleep
Is. 6:5 a man of unclean *l.* I dwell in midst of people of uncl. *l.*
28:11 stammer. *l.* will he speak
29:13 peo. with *l.* do honor me
57:19 I create the fruit of the *l.*
59:3 your *l.* have spoken lies
Ezek. 36:3 tak. up in *l.* of talkers
24:17 cover not *l.* of lips, 22
Mic. 3:7 they shall cover their *l.*
Mal. 2:7 priest's *l.* keep knowl.
Mat. 15:8 that honoureth me with their *l. Mark* 7:6
Rom. 3:13 poison is under the *l.*
1 *Cor.* 14:21 other *l.* I speak to
Heb. 13:15 fruit of *l.* giv. thanks

His LIPS.
Job 2:10 did not J. sin with his *l.*
11:5 G. open his *l.* against thee
23:12 back fr. comman. of his *l.*
Ps. 21:2 withholden req. of his *l.*
Prov. 10:19 refrain his *l.* is wise
19:27 his *l.* as a burning fire
30 his *l.* bringeth evil to pass
17:28 shutteth his *l.* is a man of
18:7 his *l.* are snare of his soul
19:1 that is perverse in his *l.*
20:19 that flattereth with his *l.*

LIT

Prov. 22:11 for grace of his *l.* the
22:26 kiss his *l.* gives ri. answer
Cant. 5:13 his *l.* like lilies drop.
Is. 11:4 breath of *l.* *l.* slay wick.
30:27 his *l.* full of indignation
Mal. 2:6 iniq. not found in his *l.*
1 *Pet.* 3:10 his *l.* speak no guile

My LIPS.
Ps. 16:4 their names into my *l.*
40:9 not refrained my *l.* O Lord
51:15 O Lord, open thou my *l.*
63:3 my *l.* shall praise thee
66:14 vows, which my *l.* uttered
89:34 thing gone out of my *l.*
119:13 wi. my *l.* have I declared
171 my *l.* shall utter thy praise
141:3 Lord, keep door of my *l.*
Prov. 8:6 the opening of my *l.* 7
Jer. 17:16 came out of my *l.* was
Dan. 10:16 sons of men tou. my *l.*

Thy LIPS.
2 *K.* 19:28 I will put my bridle in thy *l. Is.* 37:29
Job 8:21 fill thy *l.* with rejoicing
13:6 *l.* own *l.* testify aga. thee
Ps. 17:4 word of *l.* I have kept
34:13 keep *t. l.* from spea. guile
45:2 grace is poured into thy *l.*
Prov. 5:2 thy *l.* may keep know.
22:18 they shall be fitted in *t. l.*
23:16 when thy *l.* speak right
24:28 deceive not with thy *l.*
27:2 praise thee, not *l.* own *l.*
Cant. 4:3 thy *l.* are like scarlet
11 thy *l.* drop as honey-comb
Is. 6:7 this hath touched thy *l.*
Ezek. 24:17 cover not thy *l.*

LIQUOR, S.
Ex. 22:29 offer the first of thy *l.*
Num. 6:3 nor drink an. *l.* of gr.
Cant. 7:2 goblet wh. want. not *l.*

LISTED.
Mat. 17:12 done to him whatsoever they *l. Mark* 9:13

LISTEN.
Is. 49:1 *l.* O isles, unto me

LISTETH.
John 3:8 wind bloweth, where *l.*
Jam. 3:4 whithersoever goverr. *l.*

LITTERS.
Is. 66:20 bring your breth. in *l.*

LITTLE.
Gen. 30:30 but *l.* thou hadst
Ex. 12:4 househ. too *l.* for lamb
16:18 that gathered *l.* had no lack, 2 *Cor.* 8:15
22:30 by *l.* and *l.* drive them out, *Deut.* 7:22
Num. 22:38 and gather hat *l.* in
Jos. 22:17 is iniq. of Peor too *l.*
1 *Sam.* 15:17 *l.* in th. own sight
1 *K.* 12:10 my *l.* finger thicker than, 2 *Chr.* 10:10
17:12 *l.* oil in cruse; 13 *l.* cake
18:44 *l.* cloud like a man's hand
20:27 Is. pitch. like two *l.* flocks
2 *K.* 5:2 brought captive *l.* maid
Ezr. 9:8 give us a *l.* reviving
Neh. 9:32 let not trouble seem *l.*
Job 4:12 ear received a *l.* thereof
10:20 not my days *l.* cease
15:11 conso. of God sm. with thee
36:2 suffer me a *l.* I will sh. thee
Ps. 2:12 anger be kindled but a *l.*
8:5 made him a *l.* lower than the angels, *Heb.* 2:7
37:16 *l.* that a right. man hath
42:6 therefore rem. *l.* that seek G.
72:16 shall *l.* 118:37 not dir. *L.*
119:114 understand, and I sh. *l.*
119:111 let not soul. it sh. praise *L.*
146:2 while I *l.* will I praise L.
Prov. 4:4 keep my com. 7:2
9:5 forsake foolish and *l.*
15:27 he that hateth gifts sh. *l.*
Ec. 6:3 *l.* many years sh: 11:9
8:9 *l.* joyfully wi. wife th. lovest
22:33 hearts sh. *l.* that seek G.
25:16 *l.* by these things men *l.*
55:3 hear, and your soul shall *l.*
Jer. 28:20 and thy soul shall *l.*
Lam. 4:20 under shad. we sh. *l.*
Ezek. 3:27 he shall surely *l.* 18:9,
17; 33:13, 15, 16
16:6 when thou wast in blood *l.*
18:19 kept my statutes shall *l.*
21, 24; 20:11, 25
24 wicked man doeth sh. he *l.*
24 turn yourselves and *l.* 33:11
33:10 sins on us, how sh. we *l.?*
19 do that wh. is law. he sh. *l.*
37:3 can these bones *l.?*
47:9 ev. thing liveth and moveth whither riv. cometh shall *l.*
Hos. 6:2 he will rev. us, we sh. *l.*
Amos 5:4 seek me, and ye sh. *l.* 6
Jon. 4:3 bet. to die than to *l.* 8

LIV

Mat. 26:39 he went a *l.* further,
Mark 1:19; 14:35
Mark 5:23 my *l.* daughter lieth
Luke 7:47 to whom *l.* is forgiven
12:32 *l.* flock; 19:3 *l.* of stature
19:17 been fulfilled in a very *l.*
John 6:7 every one may take a *l.*
Acts 5:34 apostles forth a *l.* space
26:2 showed us *l.* kindness
1 *Cor.* 5:8 *l.* leaven leav. *Gal.* 5:9
2 *Cor.* 11:1 bear with me a *l.*
16 that I may boast myself a *l.*
1 *Tim.* 4:8 bodily ex. profiteth *l.*
5:23 use *l.* wine for stomach's
Heb. 2:9 a *l.* lower than angels
Jam. 3:5 tongue is a *l.* member
4:14 vapor appeareth for *l.* time
Rev. 3:8 thou hast a *l.* strength
6:11 should rest for a *l.* season
20:3 be loosed a *l.* season

See BOOK, CHAMBERS, CHILD, CHILDREN.

LITTLE one, s.
Gen. 19:20 Lot said, It is a *l.* one
44:20 have a *l.* one, broth. dead
Ex. 10:10 go and your *l.* ones. 24
Num. 8:35 before women and *l.* o.
2 *Chr.* 20:13 before Lord and *l. o.*
Ezr. 8:21 seek right way for *l. o.*
Ps. 137:9 dasheth *l. l. o. w.* stones
Is. 60:22 *l. one* bec. a thousand
Zec. 13:7 turn my hand on *l. o.*
Mat. 10:42 dri. to one of th. *l. o.*
18:6 offend one of these *l. ones,*
Mark 9:42; *Luke* 17:2
10 despise not one of th. *l. o.*
14 one of these *l. o.* sho. perish

LITTLE while.
Job 24:24 exalted for a *l.* while
Ps. 37:10 a *l. w.* and the wicked
Is. 10:25 *l. w.* indignation cease
63:18 possessed it but a *l. w.*
Jer. 51:33 a *l. w.* harvest sh. co.
Hos. 1:4 a *l. while* I will avenge
Hag. 2:6 a *l. w.* I will sh. heaven
John 7:33 *l. w.* I am with, 13:33
12:35 a *l. w.* is light with you
14:19 *l. w.* world seeth me no
16:16 *l. w.* ye sh. see me, 17, 19
18 a *l. while* we cannot tell
Heb. 10:37 *l. w.* he that sh. come

LIVE.
Is. 6:5 hav. a *l.* coal in his hand

See GOAT.

LIVE.
Gen. 3:22 tree of life *l.* for ever
19:20 and my soul shall *l.*
20:7 pray for thee, thou shalt *l.*
27:40 by the sword shalt thou *l.*
31:32 fo. thy go. let him not *l.*
42:18 this do, and *l.* for I fear G.
Ex. 33:20 no man see me and *l.*
Lev. 18:5 he shall *l.* in them,
Neh. 9:29; *Ezek.* 20:11, 13, 21
Num. 21:8 looketh on ser. sh. *l.*
24:23 shall *l.* when G. doeth
Deut. 4:10 fear me all days sh. *l.*
33 hear, as thou hast, and *l.?*
8:3 by ev. wo. of L. doth man *l.*
19:5 flee to one of th. cit. and *l.*
33:6 let Reuben *l.* and not die
Job 14:14 man die, sh. he *l.* eg. 7
21:7 do wicked *l.* become old ?
Ps. 22:26 your heart *l.* for ever
49:9 *l.* and not see corruption
63:4 will I bless thee while I *l.*
69:32 hearts sh. *l.* that seek G.
72:15 shall *l.* 118:17 not die. *L.*
119:144 understand, and I sh. *l.*
175 let soul *l.* it sh. praise thee
146:2 while I *l.* will I praise L.
Prov. 4:4 keep my com. 7:2
9:5 forsake foolish and *l.*
15:27 he that hateth gifts sh. *l.*
Ec. 6:3 *l.* many years sh: 11:9
8:9 *l.* joyfully wi. wife th. lovest
Is. 26:14 dead, deceased, sh. not *l.*
19 thy dead *l.* with dead body
38:16 by these things men *l.*
55:3 hear, and your soul shall *l.*
Jer. 28:20 and thy soul shall *l.*
Lam. 4:20 under shad. we sh. *l.*
Ezek. 3:27 he shall surely *l.* 18:9,
17; 33:13, 15, 16
16:6 when thou wast in blood *l.*
18:19 kept my statutes shall *l.*
21, 24; 20:11, 25
24 wicked man doeth sh. he *l.*
32 turn yourselves and *l.* 33:11
33:10 sins on us, how sh. we *l.?*
19 do that wh. is law. he sh. *l.*
37:3 can these bones *l.?*
47:9 ev. thing liveth and moveth whither riv. cometh shall *l.*
Hos. 6:2 he will rev. us, we sh. *l.*
Amos 5:4 seek me, and ye sh. *l.* 6
Jon. 4:3 bet. to die than to *l.* 8

CRUDEN'S CONCORDANCE. 929

LIV

Hab. 2:4 just sh. *l*. by his faith,
Rom. 1:17
Mat. 4:4 not *l*. by bread, *Lu.* 4:4
0:18 she shall *l. Mark* 5:23
Luke 10:28 this do, and th. sh. *l*.
20:38 not G. of dead, all *l*. unto
John 3:35 hear voice of S. and *l*.
6:57 I *l*. by F. so he that eateth me, even he shall *l*. by me
11:25 tho' he were de. yet sh. *l*.
14:19 because I *l*. ye sh. *l*, also
Acts 17:28 in him we *l*. and move
22:22 it is not fit that he sho. *l*.
Rom. 6:2 *l*. any longer therein ?
8 we believe wesh. *l*. with him
8:12 debtors not to *l*. after flesh
13 if yo *l*. after flesh, ye sh. die, if thro' Sp. mortify bo. ye *l*.
10:5 doeth these things shall *l*. by them, *Gal.* 3:12
12:18 *l*. peaceably with all men
14:8 whether we *l*. we *l*. to Lo. whe. we *l*. or die we are L.'s
1 *Cor.* 9:13 *l*. of things of temple
14 preach gospel sho. *l*. of gos.
2 *Cor.* 4:11 *l*. are deliv. to death
6:9 behold, we *l*. as chastened
7:3 to die and *l*. with you
13:4 *l*. with him by power of G.
Gal. 2:14 Gentiles to *l*. as Jews
19 that I might *l*. unto God
20 I *l*. yet not I, life I now *l*. in flesh, I *l*. by faith of S. of G.
3:11 just *l*. by faith, *Heb.* 10:38
5:25 if we *l*. in the Spirit
Phil. 1:21 for me to *l*. is Christ
24 if I *l*. in the flesh
1 *Thes.* 3:8 we *l*. if sta. fast in L.
5:10 died that we sh. *l*. wi. him
2 *Tim.* 2:11 we sh. also *l*. with
3:12 all *l*. godly suf. persecution
Tit. 2:12 we should *l*. soberly
Heb. 12:9 to F. of spirits and *l*.
13:18 willing to *l*. honestly
Jam. 4:15 if Lord will we sh. *l*.
1 *Pet.* 2:24 we *l*. to righteousness
4:2 no longer should I *l*. in flesh
6 *l*. according to God in Spirit
2 *Pet.* 2:6 to those that *l*. ungodly
18 escaped from them *l*. in err.
1 *John* 4:9 we might *l*. thro' him
Rev. 13:14 beast had wound did *l*.

See FOR EVER.

As I LIVE,
Num. 14:21 as I *l*. earth bo fill. 28
Job 27:6 so long as I *l. Ps.* 104:33 ;
116:2
Is. 49:18 as I *l*. saith the Lord ;
Jer. 22:24 ; *Ezek.* 5:11 ; 14:16, 18, 20 ; 16:48 ; 17:16, 19 ; 18:3 ; 20:3, 33 ; 33:11, 27 ; 31:8 ; 33:6, 11 ; *Zep.* 2:9 ; *Rom.* 14:11
Jer. 46:18 as I *l*. saith the king

May, might, or mayest LIVE,
Deut. 4:1 do to them, ye m. *l*.
5:33 ; 8:1 ; 30:6, 16
42 flee, to one of th. citi. *m. l*.
10:20 what is just fol. that *m. l*.
30:19 thou and they *m*. seed *m. l*.
Ps. 119:17 bountif. that I *m. l*.
77 mer. come to me, that I *m. l*.
116 uphold me, that I *may l*.
Jer. 35:7 that ye *m. l*. many days
Ezek. 37:9 slain, that they *m. l*.
Amos 5:14 seek good, th. ye *m. l*.
Eph. 6:3 *mayest l*. long on earth

Not LIVE,
Ex. 19:13 touch mountain not *l*.
Deut. 8:3 man doth *n. l*. by bread only, *Mat.* 4:4 ; *Luke* 4:4
2 *K.* 10:19 wanting he shall *not l*.
20:1 thou shalt *not l. Is.* 38:1
Job 7:16 I would *not l*. always
Ps. 55:23 wicked. *n. l*. half th. days
Is. 26:14 are dead, they sh. *not l*.
Ezek. 13:19 souls that should *n. l*.
18:13 ho shall *not l*.
Zec. 13:3 say, Thou shalt *not l*.
Acts 7:19 to the end they *m. n. l*.
25:24 ought *not to l*. any longer
28:4 vengeance suffereth *n. to l*.
2 *Chr.* 5:15 *shu. n. l*. to themsel.

LIVED,
Gen. 25:6 from Isaac, while he *l*.
Num. 11:30 Joshua and C. *l*. still
21:9 beheld serp. of bras *l*.
Deut. 5:26 heu. voice of G. and *l*.
2 *Sam.* 19:6 if Absalom had *l*.
Ps. 49:18 while he *l*. blessed soul
Ezek. 37:10 into them, and th. *l*.
47:9 divers come thither, *l*.
Jon. 5:5 *l*. in pleasure on earth
Rev. 18:7 hath *l*. deliciously, 9
20:4 *l*. with Christ ; 5 *l*. not ag.

LIV

LIVELY.
Ex. 1:19 Hebrew women are *l*.
Ps. 38:19 but my enemies are *l*.
Acts 7:38 who received *l*. oracles
1 *Pet.* 1:3 begot. us ag. to *l*. hope
2:5 ye, as *l*. stones, are built

LIVER,
Ex. 29:13 the caul above the *l*.
22 ; *Lev.* 3:4, 10, 15 ; 4:9 ; 7:4 ; 8:16, 25 ; 9:10, 19
Prov. 7:23 dart strike through *l*.
Lam. 2:11 *l*. poured upon earth
Ezek. 21:21 he looked in the *l*.

See CAUL.

LIVES,
Ex. 1:14 they made th. *l*. bitter
Jos. 2:13 deliver our *l. fr*. death
2 *Sam.* 1:23 were lovely in th. *l*.
23:17 that went in jeopardy of their *l*, 1 *Chr.* 11:19
Prov. 1:18 lurk privily for own *l*.
6:26 seek their *l*. sh. strait. them
Lam. 5:9 get bread wi. peril of *l*.
Dan. 7:12 *l*. prolon. for a season
Luke 9:56 to destroy men's *l*.
Acts 15:26 men have hazarded *l*.
27:10 voy. be with damage of *l*.
1 *John* 3:16 lay down *l*. for breth.
Rev. 12:11 they loved not their *l*.

LIVEST,
Gal. 2:14 a Jew *l*. after manner
Rev. 3:1 that thou *l*. and art dead

LIVETH,
Gen. 9:3 every thing *l*. be meat
Lev. 14:5 G. talk with man, that *l*.
1 *Sam.* 1:28 to L. as long as he *l*.
20:31 as son of Jesse *l*. on grou.
2 *Sam.* 2:27 as God *l*. unless th.
22:47 the Lord *l*. blessed be my rock, *Ps.* 18:46
1 *K.* 17:28 Elijah said, Thy son *l*.
Job 19:25 I know my Redeemer *l*.
27:2 as G. *l*. who ha. taken away
Ps. 89:48 what man *l*. not see de.?
Jer. 4:2 the Lord *l*. in truth
5:2 Lord *l*. they swear falsely
12:16 my name, the Lord *l*.
Ezek. 7:13 the Lord *l*. 15 ; 23:7, 8
44:26 Egypt, saying, The L. *l*.
Hos. 4:15 nor swear, the Lord *l*.
Amos 8:14 say, Thy G. O Dan, *l*. and the manner of Boersh. *l*.
John 4:50 thy way, son *l*. 51, 53
11:26 whosoever *l*. and believ.
Rom. 6:10 in that he *l. l*. to G.
7:1 over man as long as he *l*. 2
3 while husb. *l*. she be married
14:7 *l*. or dieth to himself
1 *Cor.* 7:39 as long as her husb, *l*.
2 *Chr.* 12:4 *l*. by the power of G.
Gal. 2:20 I live, but Ch. *l*. in me
1 *Tim.* 5:6 *l*. in pleasure is dead
Heb. 7:8 it is witnessed that he *l*.
25 ever *l*. to make intercession
9:17 no strength while testa. *l*.
Rev. 1:18 he that *l*. and was dead

See FOR EVER.

As the Lord LIVETH,
Jud. 8:19 as the L. *l*. if ye have
1 *Sam.* 14:39 as the L. *l*. 45 ; 19:6 ;
20:21 ; 25:26 ; 26:10, 16 ; 28:10 ;
29:6 ; 2 *Sam.* 4:9 ; 12:5 ; 14:11 ;
1 *K.* 1:29
20:3 as *L. l*. there is but a step
23:31 God of Is. *l*. whi. kept me
25:34 as I. *l*. as my lord
1 *K.* 2:24 as the Lord *l*. 2 *K.* 5:20 ;
2 *Chr.* 18:13 ; *Jer.* 38:16
17:1 as Lord God of Is. *l*. 18:15
12 as the Lord thy God *l*. 18:10
2 *K.* 3:14 as Lord of hosts *l*. 5:16

As thy soul LIVETH,
1 *Sam.* 1:20 as s. *l*. I am the wom.
17:55 Abner said, *As thy soul l*.
25:26 *as soul l*. seeing Lord hath
2 *Sam.* 11:11 as *t. s. l*. will not do

LIVING,
Gen. 1:28 dominion over *l*. thing
2:7 and man became a *l*. soul
3:20 she was mother of all *l*.
6:19 every *l*. thing of all flesh
7:4 ev. *l*. substance will I destr.
8:1 Noah and every *l*. thing
9:3, 10, 12, 16 every *l*. thing in water
16:14 ; 11:10 any *l*. thing in water
1 *K.* 3:22 the *l*. is my son, 21
25 divide the *l*. child into two
28 *l*. child to her, be is mother
Job 12:10 in his hand ev. *l*. thing
28:13 *nor* found in land of the *l*.
21 it is hid from eyes of all *l*.
30:23 house appointed for all *l*.

LOA

Job 33:30 enlight. wi. light of *l*.
Ps. 27:13 good. of L. in land of *l*.
38:5 root thee out of land of *l*.
56:13 walk in the light of the *l*.
58:9 sh. take th. away, both *l*.
69:28 blotted out of book of *l*.
142:5 my portion in land of *l*.
142:5 my portion in land of *l*.
143:16 satisfied every *l*. thing
Ec. 4:2 more than *l*. are alive
15 I considered all *l*. wh. walk
6:8 knoweth to walk before *l*.
7:2 the *l*. will lay it to heart
9:4 that is joined to all the *l*.
5 the *l*. know that they sh. die
Cant. 4:15 a well of *l*. water
Is. 4:3 written among *l*. in Jer.
8:19 seek to their God for the *l*.
38:11 not see L. in land of the *l*.
19 the *l*. the *l*. he sh. prai. thee
53:8 cut off out of the land of *l*.
Jer. 2:13 forsaken *l*. waters, 17:13
11:19 cut him off fr. land of *l*.
Lam. 3:39 whereof. doth *l*. comp.
Ezek. 26:20 set glory in land of *l*.
32:23 terror in land of *l*. 24-32
Dan. 4:17 that the *l*. may know
Zec. 14:8 *l*. waters shall go out
Mat. 22:32 God is the God of *l*.
Mark 12:27 ; *Luke* 20:38
Mark 12:44 cast in even all her *l*.
Luke 8:43 spent *l*. on physicians
15:12 he divided to them his *l*.
13 wasted subs. with riot. *l*. 30
24:5 why seek ye *l*. among dead
John 4:10 given thee *l*. water
11 fr. whence hast thou *l*. wat.
6:51 I am the *l*. bread wh. came
57 the *l*. Father hath sent me
7:38 sh. flow rivers of *l*. water
Rom. 12:1 bodies a *l*. sacrifice
14:9 Lord both of dead and *l*.
1 *Cor.* 15:45 A. was made *l*. soul
Col. 2:20 L. in world are subject
Heb. 10:20 by a new and *l*. way
1 *Pet.* 2:4 coming as to a *l*. stone
Rev. 7:17 Lamb lead to *l*. fount.
16:3 every *l*. soul died in the sea

See BIRD, CREATURE, GOD.

LIZARD,
Lev. 11:30 *l*. snail, mole, unclean

LO.
Job 8:19 strength, *l*. he is strong
Ps. 37:36 pas. away, *l*. he was not
40:7 L. I come ; 182:6 *l*. heard
52:7 *l*. the man that made not G.
73:27 *l*. they *l*. are far sh. peri.
92:9 *l*. thine enemies sh. perish
Cant. 2:11 *l*. the winter is past
Is. 25:9 *l*. this is our God
Jer. 4:23 *l*. it was without form
23 and *l*. there was no man
Hos. 1:9 and *l*. is came to little
Mat. 24:23 *l*. here is Chr. *l*. there
28:20 *l*. I am with you always
Acts 13:46 *l*. we turn to Gentiles
Heb. 10:7 I. *l*. I co. to do thy will, 9

LOADEN,
Is. 46:1 carriages were heavy *l*.

LOADETH,
Ps. 68:19 daily *l*. us wi. benefits

LOAF,
Ex. 29:23 one *l*. of bread
1 *Chr.* 16:3 D. dealt to ev. one a *l*.
Mark 8:14 nei. had more th. one *l*.

LO-AMMI, *Hos.* 1:9

LOAN,
1 *Sam.* 2:20 *l*. which is lent to L.

LOATHE,
Ex. 7:18 Egypt, shall *l*. to drink
Job 7:16 I *l*. it, I would not live
Ezek. 6:9 *l*. themselves for evils
20:43 *l*. yourselves in own sight
36:31 *l*. yourselves for iniquities

LOATHED,
Jer. 14:19 hath thy soul *l*. Zion ?
Zec. 11:8 my soul also *l*. them

LOATHETH,
Num. 21:5 our soul *l*. this light bread
Prov. 27:7 full soul *l*. honey-co.
Ezek. 16:45 *l*. husb. and children

LOATHSOME,
Num. 21:30 till it be *l*. to you
Ps. 38:7 loins filled with a *l*. dis.
Prov. 13:5 a wicked man is *l*.

LOATHING,
Ezek. 16:5 thou wast cast out to *l*.

LOF

2 *K.* 4:42 brought men of G. 20 *l*.
Mat. 14:17 we have here but 5 *l*.
19 and he took five *l. Mark* 6:38 ; *Luke* 9:13
15:34 how many *l*. have ye?
36 took the seven *l. Mark* 8:6
16:9 nor remem. five *l*. of 5,000
10 nor the seven *l*. of the 4,000
Mark 6:44 eat of *l*. were 5,000
52 consider. not miracles of *l*.
Luke 11:5 say, Fri. lend me 3 *l*.
John 6:9 lad here hath 5 barley *l*.
11 Jesus took *l*. and distribut.
13 fragments of five barley *l*.
26 because ye did eat of the *l*.

See BREAD.

LOCK, S.
Num. 6:5 let *l*. of the hair grow
19 on *l*. of his separation
Jud. 16:13 weavest the seven *l*.
Neh. 3:3 set up doors, and *l*. thereof, 6, 13, 14, 15
Cant. 4:1 doves' eyes with. thy *l*.
5:2 my *l*. are filled with drops
5 myrrh on handles of the *l*.
11 his *l*. are bushy, and black
6:7 thy temples within thy *l*.
7:5 47:2 uncov. thy *l*. make bare
Ezek. 8:3 he took me by *l*. of he.
44:20 nor suffer *l*. to grow long

See BARS.

LOCUST,
Lev. 11:22 *l*. aft. his kind, bald *l*.
Ps. 78:46 gave th. labor to the *l*.
109:23 tossed up and down as *l*.
Joel 1:4 hath *l*. eaten, wh. *l*. left
2:25 restore years *l*. hath eaten

LOCUSTS,
Ex. 10:4 to-morrow I will bri. *l*.
Deut. 28:38 *l*. shall consume it
Ps. 105:34 he spake, and *l*. came
Prov. 30:27 the *l*. have no king
Is. 33:4 running to and fro of *l*.
Nah. 3:15 make thyself ma. as *l*.
Mat. 3:4 his meat was *l*. and wild honey, *Mark* 1:6
Rev. 9:3 th. came out of smoke *l*.
7 shapes of *l*. we. like to hors.

LODGE,
Is. 1:8 daughter of Z. left as a *l*.

LODGE, Verb.
Gen. 24:23 is th. room for us to *l*.?
Num. 22:8 *l*. here this night
Jos. 4:3 place where ye shall *l*.
Jud. 19:9 *l*. here, that thy heart
20 *l*. 4:22 let every one *l*. in Jer.
13:21 why *l*. ye about the wall?
Job 24:7 naked *l*. without cloth.
31:32 stran. did not *l*. in street
Cant. 7:11 let us *l*. in the villages
Is. 21:13 forest in Ara. sh. ye *l*.
65:4 and *l*. in monuments
Jer. 4:14 how long vain thong. *l*.
Zep. 2:14 beasts sh. *l*. in lintels
Mat. 13:32 birds *l*. in branches, *Mark* 4:32 ; *Luke* 13:19
Acts 21:16 with wh. we should *l*.

LODGED,
Gen. 32:13 J. *l*. there that night
21 *l*. that night in company
Jos. 2:1 a harlot's house, and *l*.
3:1 came to Jordan and *l*. there
4:8 carried them, where they *l*.
6:11 ark of the L. *l*. in camp
1 *K.* 19:9 came into a cave and *l*.
1 *Chr.* 9:27 *l*. round house of God
Neh. 13:20 *l*. without Jerusalem
Is. 1:21 righteousness *l*. in it
Mat. 21:17 went to Betha, and *l*.
Acts 10:18 whether Simon *l*. th.
23 he then three days courteous.
1 *Tim.* 5:10 if she have *l*. strang.

LODGEST,
Ruth 1:16 wh. th. *l*. I will lodge

LODGETH,
Acts 10:6 *l*. with one Si. a tanner

LODGING,
Jos. 4:3 leave them in the *l*.
2 *K.* 19:23 enter *l*. of his borders
Is. 10:29 taken up their *l*. at G.
Acts 28:23 came to him into *l*.
Philc. 22 withal prepare me a *l*.

LOFT,
Acts 20:9 Euty. fell from third *l*.

LOFTY,
Ps. 73:8 corrupt, they speak *l*.
Is. 2:11 *l*. looks of man shall be bowed

LOFTINESS,
Is. 2:17 *l*. of man shall be bowed

930 CRUDEN'S CONCORDANCE.

LON

Jer. 48:29 the pride of Moab, his *l.*

LOG.

Lev. 14:10 priest take a *l.* 12, 24

LOINS.

Gen. 35:11 kings co. out of thy *l.*
37:34 J. put sackcloth on his *l.*
46:26 souls out of his *l. Ex.* 1:5
Ex. 12:11 eat it, with *l.* girded
28:42 breeches reach from the *l.*
Deut. 33:11 smite thro' *l.* of them
1 *K.* 2:5 blood in girdle about *l.*
8:19 son shall come forth of thy *l.* 2 *Chr.* 6:9
12:10 thicker than my father's *l.* 2 *Chr.* 10:10
20:31 put sackcloth on our *l.*
2 *K.* 1:8 girdle of leather about his *l. Mat.* 3:4; *Mark* 1:6
4:29 gird up thy *l.* 9:1; *Job* 38:3; 40:7; *Jer.* 1:17
Job 31:20 if his *l.* ha. not blessed
43:16 lo, his strength is in his *l.*
Ps. 38:7 my *l.* filled wi. disease
69:1 laid. affliction upon our *l.*
63:23 their *l.* continually shake
Is. 5:27 neither girdle of *l.* loosed
11:5 righteousn. girdle of his *l.*
20:2 loose sackcloth from thy *l.*
21:3 are my *l.* filled with pain
32:11 gird sackcl. upon your *l.*
Jer. 13:1 a linen girdle put on *l.*
30:6 ev. man with hands on *l.*
48:37 upon *l.* shall be sackcloth
Ezek. 1:27 fr. appearance of his *l.*
8:2 from his *l.* downward, fire
21:6 with the breaking of thy *l.*
23:15 with girdles upon their *l.*
44:18 have linen breeches on *l.*
47:4 the waters were to the *l.*
5:5 joints of *l.* were loosed
10:5 i. were gird. with fine gold
Amos 8:10 bring sack. on your *l.*
Nah. 2:1 make thy *l.* strong
10 and much pain is in all *l.*
Luke 12:35 let your *l.* be girded
Acts 2:30 of his *l.* he wo. raise C.
Eph. 6:14 hav. your *l.* girt about
Il. b. 7:5 came out of *l.* of Abrah.
10 he was yet in *l.* of his father
1 *Pet.* 1:13 wheref. gird *l.* of mind

LOIS. 2 *Tim.* 1:5

LONG.

Ex. 19:13 trumpet sound. *l.* 19
34:12 that thy days may be *l.*
Num. 9:19 the cloud tarried *l.*
Deut. 1:6 ye dwelt *l.* enough, 2:3
10:6 overtake him, way is *l.*
Jos. 6:5 they make a *l.* blast
1 *K.* 3:11 not asked *l.* 2 *Chr.* 1:11
2 *Chr.* 15:3 for a *l.* season Israel
Iv. 91:16 wi. *l.* life will I satisfy
93:10 forty years *l.* was I grieved
120:6 my soul hath *l.* dwelt
129:3 ploughers made *l.* furrows
141:3 that have been *l.* dead
Prov. 3:2 *l.* life sh. th. add to thee
7:19 good man is gone a *l.* jour.
23:30 they that tarry *l.* at wine
35:15 *l.* forbearing is a prince
Ec. 12:5 man go. to his *l.* home
l.. 65:22 elect *l.* enjoy the work
Jer. 37:26 this my captivity is *l.*
Lam. 2:20 wo. eat child span *l.* ?
Ezek. 17:3 great eagle *l.* winged
41:20 nor suffer locks to grow *l.*
Dan. 10:1 time appointed was *l.*
Hos. 13:13 not stay *l.* in the place
Mat. 11:21 repented *l.* ago
23:14 for pretence make *l.* pray. *Mark* 12:40; *Luke* 20:47
Mark 12:38 who go in *l.* clothing, *Luke* 20:46
16:5 clothed in a *l.* white garm.
Luke 18:7 tho' he bear *l.* with th.
23:8 to see him *l.* of a season
Acts 20:9 Paul was *l.* preaching
1 *Cor.* 11:14 if a man have *l.* hair
15 wom. have *l.* hair, it is glo.
Eph. 5:3 mayest live *l.* on earth
1 *Tim.* 3:15 if I tarry *l.* that thou
Jam. 5:7 husbandm. ha. *l.* pati.
See AGO.

As LONG as.

Lev. 26:34 as *l.* as it lieth des. 35
Num. 9:18 as *l.* as cloud abode
Deut. 31:13 as *l.* as ye live
1 *Sam.* 1:28 lent *l.* as he liveth
20:31 as *l.* as son of Jesse liveth
2 *Chr.* 26:5 as *l.* as he sought L.
36:21 as *l.* as she lay desolate
Ps. 72:5 as sun and m. endure
17 name continued as *l.* as sun
104:33 sing to L. as *l.* as I live
112:2 call up, him as *l.* as I live

LOO

Ezek. 42:11 as *l.* as they, as broad
Mat. 9:15 as *l.* as bridegroom is with them, *Mark* 2:19
John 9:5 as *l.* as I am in world
Rom. 7:1 over man as *l.* as he liv.
1 *Cor.* 7:39 bound as *l.* as husb.
Gal. 4:1 heir as *l.* as he is a child
1 *Pet.* 3:6 daught. as *l.* as do well
2 *Pet.* 1:13 as *l.* as I am in taber.
See CUBITS, DAY, HOUR.

So LONG.

Jud. 6:28 chariot so *l.* in coming
2 *Chr.* 3:31 fear thee so *l.* as live
Est. 5:13 so *l.* as I see Mordecai
Job 27:6 not repro. so *l.* as I live
Ps. 72:7 so *l.* as moon endureth
12:1 marvel. he tarried so *l.*
Rom. 7:2 her husb. so *l.* as liveth
Heb. 4:7 after so *l.* a time

LONG time.

Gen. 26:8 had been there a *l. t.*
35:15 dwelt in Egypt *l. t.*
Deut. 20:19 besiege a city a *l. t.*
28:11 a *l. t.* after Josh. wax. old
1 *Sam.* 7:2 wh. ark abode *l.* was *l.*
Ec. 43:14 have a *l.* holden peace
Lam. 5:20 forsake us so *l. time*
Luke 8:37 man had devils a *l. t.*
20:9 went to far country for *l. t.*
John 5:6 a *l. time* in that case
14:9 have I been so *l. t.* with you
Acts 14:3 *l. time* abode with disciples, 28
2 *Pet.* 2:3 judgm. of *l. t.* lingereth

LONG while.

Acts 20:11 a *l.* w. till bre. of day

LONG, Verb.

Job 3:21 *l.* for death, but com, not
6:8 grant me thing that I *l.* for
Rom. 1:11 for I *l.* to see you
2 *Cor.* 9:14 prayer wh. *l.* after you
Phil. 1:8 greatly I *l.* after you all

LONGED.

2 *Sam.* 13:39 David *l.* to go forth
23:15 David *l.* and said, O that one, 1 *Chr.* 11:17
Ps. 119:40 I *l.* after thy precepts
131 I *l.* for thy commandments
174 I have *l.* for thy salvation
Phil. 2:26 for he *l.* after you all
4:1 dearly beloved and *l.* for

LONGEDST.

Gen. 31:30 *l.* after father's house

LONGER.

Ex. 9:28 and ye shall stay no *l.*
Jud. 2:14 could not any *l.* stand
2 *K.* 6:33 should I wait for L. *l.* ?
Job 11:9 measure is *l.* than earth
Jer. 44:22 the L. could no *l.* bear
Luke 16:2 may. be no *l.* steward
Acts 18:20 desired him to tarry *l.*
25:24 he ought not to live any *l.*
Rom. 6:2 how live any *l.* therein
2 *Thes.* 3:1 we could no *l.* forb. 5
1 *Pet.* 4:2 *l.* live rest of his time
Heb. 10:6 there sho. be time no *l.*

LONGETH.

Gen. 34:8 my son *l.* for your dau.
Deut. 12:20 thy soul *l.* to eat flesh
Ps. 63:1 flesh *l.* for thee
64:2 my soul *l.* for courts of L.

LONGING.

Deut. 28:32 eyes sh. fail *l.* for th.
Ps. 107:9 he satisfieth the *l.* soul
119:20 soul break. for *l.* it hath

LONG-SUFFERING.

Ex. 34:6 Lo. G. *l.-s. Num.* 14:18;
Ps. 86:15; 2 *Pet.* 3:9
Jer. 15:15 me not aw. in thy *l.-s.*
Rom. 2:4 despi. riches of his *l.-s.*
9:22 endured with much *l.-s.*
2 *Cor.* 6:6 by *l.-s.* by kindness
Gal. 5:22 fruit of Sp. is love, *l.-s.*
Eph. 4:2 with *l.-s.* forbearing
Col. 1:11 strengthened to all *l.-s.*
3:12 elect of G. meekness, *l.-s.*
1 *Tim.* 1:16 Ch. might show *l.-s.*
2 *Tim.* 3:10 kno. my faith, *l.-s.*
4:2 with all *l.-s.* and doctrine
1 *Pet.* 3:20 *l.-s.* of God waited
2 *Pet.* 3:15 *l.-s.* of L. is salvation

LOOK, Verb.

Ps. 18:27 bring down high *l.*
101:5 a high *l.* I will not suffer
Prov. 6:17 Lord hateth a proud *l.*
21:4 high *l.* and proud heart
Is. 2:11 lofty *l.* of man humbled
10:12 punish glory of his high *l.*
Ezek. 2:6 nor dismayed at *l.* 3:9
Dan. 7:20 *l.* more stout than fel.

LOO

LOOK.

Gen. 15:5 *l.* now towards heaven
19:17 for life, *l.* not behind thee
41:33 let Pharaoh *l.* out a man
42:1 why *l.* one upon another ?
Ex. 25:20 faces *l.* one to another
Deut. 9:27 *l.* not to stubbornness
28:32 thine eyes shall *l.* and fail
1 *Sam.* 16:12 Dav. goodly to *l.* to
K. 1:6 *l.* one another in face
1 *Cor.* 12:17 G. of fat. *l.* thereon
Job 3:9 *l.* for light, have none
20:21 sh. no man *l.* for his goods
35:5 *l.* to the heavens and see
Ps. 5:3 prayer to thee and *l.* up
40:12 that I am not able to *l.* up
123:2 eyes of serv. *l.* to masters
Prov. 27:23 and *l.* well to herds
Ec. 12:3 that *l.* out at windows
Cant. 4:8 *l.* from top of Amana
Is. 5:30 if one *l.* unto the land
8:21 curse king, and *l.* upward
22 they shall *l.* unto the earth
17:7 shall a man *l.* to his maker
22:4 *l.* away fr. me, I will weep
31:1 they *l.* not to H. One of Is.
42:18 *l.* ye blind, th. ye may see
45:22 *l.* unto me, and be saved
51:1 *l.* to rock whence are hewn
50:11 all *l.* to their own way
60:11 *l.* for judgment, but none
66:2 but to this man will I *l.*
Jer. 13:16 while ye *l.* for light
39:12 take and *l.* well to him
40:4 and I will *l.* well to thee
46:5 mighty fled, and *l.* not back
47:3 fathers not *l.* back to child
Hos. 3:1 who *l.* to other gods
Jon. 2:4 *l.* toward holy temple
Mic. 7:7 therefore I *l.* to the Lord
Nah. 2:8 but none shall *l.* back
Mat. 11:3 *l.* for ano. ? *Luke* 7:19,20
Mark 8:33 and make him *l.* up
Luke 21:28 thi. begin, then *l.* up
John 7:52 *l.* for out of Galilee
Acts 6:3 *l.* ye out seven men
7:55 quest. of words, *l.* ye to it
2 *Cor.* 3:13 steadfastly *l.* to end
4:18 we *l.* at things wh. are seen
Phil. 3:20 we *l.* for the Saviour
Heb. 9:28 to them th. *l.* he ap.
1 *Pet.* 1:12 angels desire to *l.* in.
2 *Pet.* 3:13 we *l.* for new heav.
14 seeing ye *l.* for such things
2 *John* 8 *l.* to yourselves
Rev. 5:3 no man able to *l.* there.
4 to read book out *l.* thereon

LOOK down.

Deut. 26:15 *l.* d. from holy habi.
Ps. 80:14 *l. d.* and behold this vine
85:11 right. *l. d.* from heaven
Is. 63:15 *l. down* from heaven
Lam. 3:50 till L. *l. d.* and behold

LOOK on, or upon.

Gen. 12:11 a fair woman to *l.* on
24:16 Rebekah fair to *l.* on, 26:7
Ex. 3:6 Moses afraid to *l. u.* G.
39:43 Moses did *l. upon* all work
Lev. 13:3 priest *l.* w. the plague
Num. 15:39 that ye may *l.* w. it
2 *Sam.* 9:8 *l.* w. such a dead dog
16:12 L. will *l.* w. my affliction
2 *Chr.* 24:22 L. *l.* w. and require
Job 6:28 be content, *l.* w. me
40:12 *l.* w. ev. one that is proud
Ps. 22:17 bones stare and *l. upon*
25:18 *l. upon* mine affliction
35:17 how long wilt thou *l.* on ?
84:9 *l.* w. face of thine anointed
119:132 *l.* w. me, and be merciful
Prov. 4:25 let eyes *l.* right on
23:31 *l.* not on wine wh. it is red
Cant. 1:6 *l.* not on me
6:13 that we may *l. upon* thee
Is. 33:20 *l. upon* Zion, the city
51:6 *l. upon* the earth beneath
Mic. 4:11 let our eye *l.* w. Zion
Mat. 37 that *l.* w. thee, shall flee
Hab. 1:13 purer eye *l.* w. iniq.
2:15 mayest *l.* w. their nakedn.
Zec. 12:10 *l.* w. me they pierced
Jon. 6:26 Y. *l. upon* the morrow
John 4:35 lift eyes, *l. upon* fields
19:37 *l.* w. him whom they pierced
Acts 3:4 P. and J. said, *l.* w. us, 12
Phil. 2:4 *l.* not on his own things
Rev. 4:3 was to *l.* w. like a jasper

LOOKED.

Gen. 6:12 God *l.* on the earth
19:26 his wife *l.* back fr. behind
26:8 *l.* out at a window
Ex. 2:12 this way and th. way
4:31 *l.* on their afflic. *Deut.* 26:7
14:24 the Lord *l.* on the host
32:8 the people *l.* after Moses
Num. 24:20 when he *l.* on Amal.

LOO

Jud. 5:28 *l.* out at window
6:14 the Lord *l.* upon him
1 *Sam.* 6:19 they had *l.* into ark
2 *Sam.* 6:16 Michal *l.* thro' win.
22:17 f. but th. was none to save
1 *K.* 18:43 serv. went up and *l.*
2 *K.* 2:24 El. turned back and *l.*
9:30 Jezebel *l.* out at a window
14:11 *l.* one another in the face
Ps. 14:2 L. *l.* if any did underst.
34:5 *l.* to him, and were light.
53:2 G. *l.* down on chil. of men
102:19 *l.* down fr. his sanctuary
100:25 when they *l.* they shaked their heads
Cant. 1:6 bec. son hath *l.* on me
Is. 5:7 *l.* it sho. br. forth grapes
7 *l.* for judg. behold oppress.
22:11 ye have not *l.* to maker
Jer. 8:15 we *l.* for peace, 14:19
46:5 *l.* 10:11 whither the houd *l.*
21:21 consulted, he *l.* in liver
Hag. 1:9 *l.* for much, came to lit.
Mark 6:41 he *l.* up to heaven
8:24 he *l.* and said, I see men
Luke 1:25 *l.* on me to take away
2:38 all that *l.* for redemption
10:22 a Lev. came and *l.* on him
22:61 Lord turn, *l.* upon Peter
John 13:22 disc. *l.* one on anoth.
Acts 1:10 *l.* steadfastly to heaven
28:6 after they *l.* a great while
11:6; 11:10 *l.* for city hath found.
1 *John* 1:1 which we have *l.* upon

I LOOKED.

Job 30:26 *I l.* for good, evil came
Ps. 69:20 *I l.* for some to take
12:4 I l. on my right hand
Prov. 7:6 *I l.* thro' my casement
24:32 *I l.* on it, received instr.
Ec. 2:11 *I l.* on works my hands
Is. 5:4 *I l.* it sho. br. forth grapes
68:3 *I l.* there was none to help
Acts 22:13 same hour *I l.* upon
Rev. 4:1 *I l.* and beh. a door was opened, 6:8; 14:1, 14; 15:5

LOOKEST.

Job 13:27 *l.* narrowly to paths
Hab. 1:13 *l.* on them deal treach.

LOOKETH.

Num. 21:8 when he *l.* on it
20 *l.* toward Jeshimon, 23:28
1 *Sam.* 16:7 *l.* on outw. appear.
Job 7:2 a hireling *l.* for reward
28:24 he *l.* to ends of the earth
33:27 he *l.* on men, and if any
Ps. 33:13 Lord *l.* from heaven
104:32 *l.* on earth, it trembleth
Prov. 31:27 *l.* well to household
Cant. 6:10 who is she th. *l.* forth
l. 28:4 when he that *l.* upon it
Mat. 5:28 who *l.* on wom. to lust
24:50 lord shall come when he *l.* not for him, *Luke* 12:46
Jam. 1:25 whoso *l.* into perf. law

LOOKING.

1 *Chr.* 15:29 Michal *l.* out window
Is. 38:14 mine eyes fail with *l.*
Mat. 14:19 *l.* up to hea. *Luke* 9:16
Mark 7:34 and *l.* up to heaven
13:40 there were also women *l.*
Luke 6:10 *l.* round about th. all
9:62 *l.* back, fit for king. of G.
21:26 hearts failing for *l.* after
Acts 6:15 *l.* steadfastly on him
23:21 *l.* for a promise from thee
Tit. 2:13 *l.* for that blessed hope
Heb. 10:27 fearful *l.* for of judgm.
12:2 *l.* unto Jesus the author
15 *l.* diligently, lest any fail
2 *Pet.* 3:12 *l.* for the coming of G.
Jude 21 *l.* for mercy of our L. J.

LOOKING-GLASS, ES.

Ex. 38:8 laver and foot of *l.-g.*
Job 37:18 spre. out sky as *l.-g.*

LOOPS.

Ex. 26:4 make *l.* of blue, 5
36:11 made *l.* of blue on curtain

LOOSE.

Gen. 49:21 Naph. is a hind let *l.*
Lev. 14:7 let the living bird *l.*
Deut. 25:9 he would let *l.* his hand
30:11 they have let *l.* the bridle
Dan. 3:25 lo, I see four men *l.*

LOOSE, Verb.

Jos. 5:15 *l.* thy shoe fr. off foot
Job 38:31 canst thou *l.* the bands
Ps. 102:20 *l.* th. appoin. to death
Is. 20:2 *l.* sackcloth fr. thy loins
45:1 I will *l.* the loins of kings
52 O. J. *l.* thyself from bands
58:6 *l.* the bands of wickedness
Jer. 40:4 behold, I *l.* thee this day
Mat. 16:19 ye *l.* on earth, 18:18

CRUDEN'S CONCORDANCE.

LOR

Ps. 37:4 delight thyself in the L.
Ls. 58:14
7 rest in the L. and wait
56:10 in t. L. will I praise his
64:10 the righteous shall be gl.
in the L. 104:34
Prov. 3:5 trust in the L. wi. hea.
Is. 26:4 in t. L. Jehovah is ever.
45:24 in the L. have I righteous.
25 in the L. seed of Is. justifi.
Zep. 3:2 trusted not in the L.
Acts 9:42 many believed in t. L.
14:3 speaking boldly in the L.
Rom. 16:2 ye receive her in t. L.
8 Amplias, my belov. in t. L.
12 who labored much in t. L.
13 Rufus chosen in the L.
22 Tertius, salute you in t. L.
1 Cor. 1:31 glorieth, let him glo.
in the L. 2 Cor. 10:17
4:17 faith. in L. 7:22 call. in L.
7:39 be married, only in the L.
9:1 my work in the L.?
2 apostleship are ye in t. L.
11:11 nor woman wi. man in L.
15:58 labor not in vain in t. L.
Eph. 2:21 a holy temple in t. L.
4:17 therefore, testify in the L.
5:8 now are ye light in the L.
6:1 obey your parents in the L.
10 brethren, be strong in t. L.
21 a faithful minister in the L.
Phil. 1:14 brethren in the L.
2:29 receive him theref. in t. L.
4:1 stn. fast in t. L. 1 Thes. 3:8
2 be of the same mind in t. L.
10 I rejoiced in the L. greatly
Col. 3:18 submit to husb. in t. L.
4:7 Tychicus fellow-ser. in t. L.
17 minist. th. received in t. L.
1 Thes. 5:12 th. over you in t. L.
2 Thes. 3:4 have confidence in L.
Phile. 16 the flesh and in t. L.
20 let me have joy of thee in
t. L. refr. my bowels in t. L.
Rev. 14:13 bless. are dead in t. L.

See REJOICE, TRUST.

LORD is.
Gen. 28:16 the L. is in this place
Ex. 9:27 the L. is righteous, I
wicked, 2 Chr. 12:6
15:2 the L. is my strength
3 L. is man of war, L. is name
Num. 14:9 the L. is long-suffering, of
18 the L. is long-suffering, of
great, Nah. 1:3
42 for the L. is not among you
1 K. 8:60 know that the L. is G.
2 Chr. 13:10 the L. is our God
15:2 L. is wi. you wh. ye for h.
Ps. 10:16 the L. is king for ever
34:8 O taste and see L. is good
59:18 L. is our defence and king
92:15 show that L. is upright
99:1 L. is clothed with strength
94:22 L. is my defence and rock
95:3 the L. is a great G. 96:4;
99:2; 135:5
100:3 L. is gr. 118:9; 145:9; Jer.
33:11; Lam. 3:25; Nah. 1:7
103:8 L. is merciful and gra-
cious, 111:4; 145:9
113:4 L. is high ab. all nations
118:6 the L. is on my side
121:5 L. is keeper. L. is shade
125:3 the L. is round about
129:4 L. is righteous, 145:17;
Lam. 1:18; Dan. 9:14
145:18 L. is nigh to all that call
Prov. 15:29 L. is far from wicked
Is. 30:18 L. is God of judgment
Jer. 10:10 the L. is the true God
17:7 trust in L. who. hope L. is
35:11 L. is with me as terri. one
Lam. 3:24 the L. is my portion
Ezek. 35:35 name of city, L. is t.
Amos 5:8 the L. is his name, 9:6
Zep. 3:5 just L. is in midst, 15
Luke 24:34 the L. is risen indeed
2 Cor. 3:17 the L. is that Spirit
Phil. 4:5 the L. is at hand
Heb. 13:6 the L. is my helper
1 Pet. 2:3 tasted the L. is graci.

See MADE.

My LORD.
Gen. 19:18 said, not so, my L.
Jud. 6:13 my L. if L. be wi. us
15:9 my L. shall I save Israel
Ps. 16:2 said, Thou art my L.
35:23 stir up thyself, my God
and my L. Zech 20:28
110:1 Lord said to my L. Mat.
22:44; Mark 12:36; Luke
20:42; Acts 2:34
Is. 21:8 my L. I stand on tower
Dan. 10:17 serv. of my L. talk?

LOR

Zec. 1:9 O my L. wh. are these?
4:4; 6:4; 4:5 no, my L. 13
Mal. 24:48 my L. delayeth his
coming, Luke 12:45
Luke 1:43 mother of my L. come
John 20:13 taken away my L.
Phil. 3:8 knowledge of Ch. Jes.
my L.

Name of the LORD.
Gen. 12:8 A. called on n. of t. L.
26:25 Isaac called on n. of t. L.
Ex. 20:7 shalt not take name of
the L. in vain, Deut. 5:11
33:19 proclaim n. of the L.
34:5 L. proclaimed n. of the L.
Lev. 24:11 blasphe. n. of the L. 16
Deut. 18:5 minister in n. of L. 7
21 prophet speak. in n. of t. L.
28:10 called by the n. of the L.
32:3 I will publish n. of the L.
Jos. 9:9 serv. come of n. of t. L.
1 Sam. 17:45 come in n. of t. L.
20:42 sw. both of us in n. of L.
2 Sam. 6:2 called by n. of the L.
1 K. 22:16 that which is true in
name of the L. 2 Chr. 18:15
Job 1:21 blessed be the name of
the L. Ps. 113:2
Ps. 20:7 will remember n. of t. L.
102:15 heathen fear n. of the L.
21 to declare n. of L. in Zion
113:1 praise the name of t. L.
118:10 ; 118:5, 19 ; Joel 2:26
118:4 then called I on n. of t. L.
118:26 cometh in n. of the L.
124:8 give thanks to n. of t. L.
124:8 our help is in n. of t. L.
129:8 we bless you in n. of t. L.
Prov. 18:10 n. of L. strong tower
Is. 18:7 to place of n. of the L.
24:15 glorify the n. of the L.
50:27 n. of L. cometh fr. far
56:6 and to love the n. of the L.
59:19 so sh; they fear n. of t. L.
Jer. 3:17 nations gath. to n. of L.
Mic. 4:5 walk in name of the L.
5:4 in majesty of n. of the L.
Zep. 3:9 th. trust in n. of t. L.
Mat. 21:9 cometh in n. of the L.
23:39; Mark 11:9, 10; Luke
13:35; 19:38; John 12:13
Acts 9:29 spake boldly in n. of L.
10:48 baptized in n. of the L.
19:13 call over them n. of t. L.
21:13 ready to die for n. of t. L.

O LORD.
Ex. 15:11 who like thee. O L.?
2 Sam. 23:17 far from thee, O L.
1 Chr. 17:20 O L. none like thee
Ps. 6:3 but then, O L. how long
9:1 O L. our Lord, how excel.
22:19 not far fr. me O L. 35:22
113:1 not unto us. O L.
Rev. 6:10 how long, O L. holy

Of the LORD.
Ps. 6:35 hath. this evil is of L.
Prov. 20:24 man's goings of t. L.
21:31 battle, safety is of t. L.
Acts 22:14 will of t. L. be done
1 Cor. 11:23 received of the L.
Jam. 5:11 seen the end of the L.

See ANGER, ANGEL, COMMAND-
MENT, CONGREGATION, COUN-
SEL, DAY, EYES, FACE, FEAR,
FEAST, GLORY, HAND, HOUSE,
KNOWLEDGE, LAW, OFFER-
INGS, PRAISE.

Saith the LORD.
Num. 14:13 what the L. s.
1 K. 22:14 L. s. that will I speak

See LIVE, SAVED.

LORD, with seek.
1 Chr. 16:10 heart rejoice that s.
L. Ps. 105:3, 4
11 seek the L. and his strength
22:19 set your heart to seek the
L. 2 Chr. 14:4 not heart to s. L.
14:4 commanded Jud. to s. L.
15:13 whoso. would not seek L.
20:3 Jehosh. set himself to s. L.
Ezr. 6:21 were come to seek L.
Ps. 22:26 praise L. that s. him
34:10 that s. L. shall not want
Prov. 28:5 th. s. L. understand
Is. 9:19 neither do they seek the
L. 31:1; Hos. 7:10
51:1 ye that seek the L.
55:6 s. L. wh. he may be found
Jer. 50:4 go and s. the L. God
Hos. 3:5 return and seek the L.
5:6 go with herds to s. the L.
10:12 it is time to seek the L.
Amos 5:6 s. L. and ye shall live

LOR

Zep. 2:3 s. the L. meek of earth
Zec. 8:21 let us go and s. the L.
22 many people come and s. L.
Mal. 3:1 L. wh. ye s. sud. come
Acts 15:17 residue might r. the L.
17:27 they should s. the L.

LORD, with sent.
Ex. 7:16 L. of Hebrews s. me
Jer. 26:9 L. hath truly sent him
15 Hanamiah, L. hath not s.
Acts 9:17 L. Jesus s. me to thee
12:11 know L. hath sent angel

Serve the LORD.
Ex. 10:7 that they may s. t. L.
22:25 ye shall s. t. L. your God
Deut. 10:12 to s. t. L. thy God
Jos. 24:14 fear and s. ye the L.
15 seem evil an. you to s. t. L.
18 therefore will we s. L. 21, 24
1 Sam. 12:20 s. L. with your hea.
2 Sam. 15:8 then I will s. L.
2 Chr. 30:8 s. L. your God, 35:3
33:16 cons. Judah to s. L. 34:33
Ps. 2:11 s. L. wi. fear, rejoice
100:2 serve t. L. with gladness
102:22 kingdoms gather. to s. L.
Col. 3:24 ye serve t. L. Christ

Servant, s. of the LORD.
Deut. 34:5 Moses, the s. of t. L.
Jos. 1:1 death of Moses s. of L.
13 Moses the servant of the L.
commanded, 8:31, 33; 11:12;
22:2, 5; 2 K. 18:12
15 Moses, s. of the L. gave you,
12:6; 13:8; 18:7; 22:4
24:29 Joshua, son of Nun, s. of
the L. died, Jud. 2:8
Ps. 113:1 praise the L. praise, O
ye servants of the L. 134:1
134:1 O ye servants of the L.
Is. 42:19 blind or deaf as L.'s s.
54:17 heritage of s. of the L.
2 Tim. 2:24 s. of the L. not strive

See SHOWED.

Sight of the LORD.
Gen. 38:7 Er wicked is s. of L.
Ezr. 10:19 accepted in s. of L.
Deut. 6:18 good in s. of L. 12:28
21:9 do what is right in s. of
the L. 21:9; 2 K. 12:2; 14:3;
15:3, 34; 18:3; 22:2; 2 Chr.
20:32; 24:2; 25:2; 29:4; 27:2;
26:4; 81:8
1 Sam. 12:17 wicked, ha. done
in s. of L. 1 K. 21:25; 2 K.
21:6
2 K. 3:18 light thing in s. of L.
10:3 did not what was right in
s. of the L. 2 Chr. 26:1
Ps. 116:15 precious in s. of L.
Mal. 2:17 good in s. of the L.
Luke 1:15 be great in s. of L.
2 Cor. 8:21 not only in s. of L.
Jam. 4:10 humble in s. of the L.

See EVIL, SMITE.

Spirit of the LORD.
Jud. 3:10 S. of the L. came on O.
6:34 S. of the L. came on Gid.
11:29 S. of the L. came on Jep.
13:25 S. of the L. began to move
Samson, 14:6, 19; 15:14
1 Sam. 10:6 S. of the L. ca. on S.
16:13 S. of the L. came on Dav.
14 S. of the L. depart. from D.
2 Sam. 23:2 S. of the L. spake
1 K. 18:12 S. of L. wh. carry thee
22:24 which way went S. of the
L. 2 Chr. 18:23
2 K. 2:16 lest S. of L. taken him
2 Chr. 20:14 on Ja. came S. of L.
Is. 11:2 S. of t. L. rest upon him
40:7 bec. S. of L. bloweth on it
13 hath directed S. of the L.
59:19 S. of t. L. lift up stand.
61:1 S. of the L. God on me
63:14 S. of L. caused him rest
Ezek. 11:5 S. of L. fell upon me
37:1 carried me in S. of the L.
Mic. 2:7 is the S. of L. straitened
3:8 full of power by S. of the L.
Acts 5:9 tempt S. of the L.
8:39 S. of L. caught away Philip
2 Cor. 3:17 wh. S. of t. L. liberty
18 even as by S. of the L.

LORD, with spoken.
Ex. 4:30 L. hath s. will ye do
34:32 in command. all L. had s.
Num. 10:29 the L. hath s. good
14:2 hath L. indeed s. by Moses
Jos. 21:45 failed not L. had s.
1 Sam. 25:30 L. done good ha. s.
2 Sam. 3:18 do it, the L. hath s.
1 K. 13:3 sign which L. hath s.
Ps. 50:1 hath s. and called

LOR

Jer. 23:35 what hath the L. s. 37
48:8 destroyed, as the L. hath s.
Ezek. 22:28 when L. hath not s.
26:5 for I have s. it, saith the
L. 28:10; 39:5
Amos 3:8 L. God hath spoken
Mat. 1:22 wh. was s. of L. 2:15
Mark 16:19 after L. had spoken
Acts 9:27 seen L. and he had s.
Heb. 2:3 began to be s. by the L.

Temple of the LORD.
2 Chr. 26:16 U. went in. t. of L.
Jer. 7:4 t. of the L. are these
Ezek. 8:16 at door of t. of L. 25
men, with backs to, t. of L.
Hag. 2:15 bef. sto. laid in t. of L.
Zec. 6:12 build t. of L. 13:15
14 for memorial in t. of the L.
Luke 1:9 Z. went into t. of t. L.

Voice of the LORD.
Ps. 29:3 v. of L. is upon waters
29:5 hearh. not to v. of t. L.
Is. 6:8 I heard v. of the L.
Acts 7:31 v. of the L. came to M.

Way of the LORD.
Gen. 18:19 house. keep w. of L.
Jud. 2:22 will keep way of t. L.
Ps. 119:1 blessed walk w. of L.
Prov. 10:29 way of L. is streng.
Is. 40:3 prepare ye w. of the L.
Mat. 3:4; Mark 1:3; Lu. 3:4
Jer. 5:4 know not w. of the L.
John 1:23 make stra. w. of the L.
Acts 18:25 Apollos in. in w. of L.

Ways of the LORD.
2 Sam. 22:22 for I have kept the
w. of the L. Ps. 18:21
2 Chr. 17:6 lifted up in w. of L.
Ps. 138:5 sing in the w. of L.
Hos. 14:9 the w. of L. are right
Acts 13:10 cease perv. w. of L.

Word of the LORD.
Num. 22:18 can. go bey. w. of L.
Deut. 5:5 show you w. of the L.
2 Sam. 22:31 w. tried, Ps. 18:30
1 K. 13:1 came man by w. of L.
2 cried ag. altar in word of L.
17:24 w. of L. in my mouth
2 K. 10:10 earth noth. of w. of L.
20:19 good is w. of L. Is. 39:8
Ps. 33:4 the word of L. is right
6 by w. of L. heavens made
103:19 w. of L. tried him
Is. 2:3 the word of the L. from
Jerusalem, Mic. 4:2
Amos 8:12 to seek w. of L.
Zep. 2:5 w. of L. against you
Zec. 4:6 w. of L. to Zerubbabel
1 Thes. 1:8 sounded out w. of L.
4:15 say unto you by w. of L.
2 Thes. 3:1 w. of L. have free co.
1 Pet. 1:25 w. of L. endu. for. ev.

Words of the LORD.
Ex. 24:3 M. told people all w. of
the L. Num. 11:24
4 Moses wrote all w. of the L.
2 Chr. 29:15 came by w. of the L.
Jer. 12:6 w. of L. pure words
Jer. 36:4 Bar. wrote all w. of L.
Amos 8:11 fam. of hear. w. of L.

See CAME, HEAR.

Works of the LORD.
Jos. 24:31 known all w. of L.
Jud. 2:7 seen all great w. of L.
Ps. 28:5 regard not w. of the L.
46:8 behold great w. of the L.
77:11 I will remember w. of L.
107:24 these see the w. of the L.
111:2 the works of the L. are great
118:17 declare the w. of the L.

Wrath of the LORD.
Num. 11:33 w. of the L. kindled
Deut. 11:17 w. of L. kindle aga.
2 K. 22:13 for great is the wrath
of the L. 2 Chr. 34:21
2 Chr. 12:12 wrath of L. turned
29:8 w. of the L. upon Judah
32:26 w. of L. came not on them
36:16 until wrath of L. arose
Ps. 106:40 w. of L. kindled
Is. 9:19 thro' w. of L. land dark.
13:13 earth rem. in w. of L.
Jer. 50:13 because of w. of the L.
Ezek. 7:19 gold not deliver them
in day of w. of t. L. Zep. 1:18

CRUDEN'S CONCORDANCE. 933

CRUDEN'S CONCORDANCE.

LOV

Eph. 5:25 husb. *l.* your wives as
C. loved ch. 28, 33; *Col.* 3:19
6:24 grace be with th. *l.* our L.
1 *Thes.* 4:9 taught to *l.* one ano.
2 *Tim.* 4:8 them that *l.* his ap.
Tit. 2:4 young women to *l.* hus.
3:15 greet them that *l.* us in fa.
Jam. 1:12 them that *l.* him. 2:5
1 *Pet.* 1:8 whom not seen, ye *l.*
23 *l.* one ano. with pure heart
2:17 honor men, *l.* brotherhood
3:8 as *l.* brethren; 19 that *l.* life
1 *John* 2:15 *l.* not the world
3:11 fr. begin. that we should *l.*
14 because we *l.* the brethren
23 *l.* one another, as he gave
4:12 if we *l.* one another
19 *l.* him bec. he first loved us
20 can he *l.* G. hath not seen
21 loveth God *l.* his brother al.
5:2 we *l.* the children of God

I LOVE.

Ex. 21:5 eh. say, *I l.* my master
Jud. 16:15 cau't thou say, *I l.*
2 *Sam.* 13:4 *I l.* Tamar, my broth.
Ps. 116:1 *I L.* bec. he heard
119:97 O how *I l.* thy law
113 but thy law do *I l.* 163
119 therof. *I l.* thy testimonies
127 *I l.* thy commands ab. gold
159 consi. how *I l.* thy precepts
167 thy testimonies *I l.* exce.
Prov. 8:17 *I l.* them that *l.* me
John 14:31 know th. *I l.* the Fa.
21:15 L. knowest *I l.* thee, 16, 17
2 *Cor.* 12:15 tho' the more *I l.* you
1 *John* 4:20 if a man say, *I l.* God
2 *John* 1 *l.* in the truth, 3 *John* 1
Rev. 3:19 as many as *I l.* I rebuke

LOVE me.

Gen. 29:32 my husb. will *l. me*
Ex. 20:6 showing mercy to them
that *l. me*, *Deut.* 5:10
Prov. 8:17 I love them that *l. me*
31 that *l. me* to imb. substance
John 8:42 G. your F. ye wo. *l. me*
10:17 therof. doth Father *l. me*
14:15 if ye *l. me*, keep my com.
23 man *l. me*, keep my words

LOVE not.

Prov. 20:13 *l. not* sleep
1 *Cor.* 16:22 if any man *l. not* L.
2 *Cor.* 11:11 because *I l. you not*?
1 *John* 2:15 *l. not* the world
3:18 *n. l.* in word nor tongue

LOVED.

Gen. 24:67 took Rebe. and *l.* her
27:28 *l.* Esau, Rebekah *l.* Jacob
37:14 made such as his father *l.*
29:18 Jacob *l.* Rachel more, 30
34:3 Shechem *l.* Dinah
37:3 Israel *l.* Joseph more, 4
Deut. 4:37 bec. he *l.* thy fathers
7:8 because L. *l.* you, 23:5; 33:3
Jud. 16:4 Samson *l.* a woman
1 *Sam.* 1:5 Elkanah *l.* Hannah
16:21 and Saul *l.* David
18:1 Jonathan *l.* David, 3; 20:17
16 Israel and Judah *l.* David
20 Michal Saul's daughter, *l.* D.
2 *Sam.* 12:24 the L. *l.* Solomon
13:1 Amnon son of David *l.* Ta.
15 love wherewith he *l.* her
1 *K.* 3:3 Solomon *l.* the Lord
10:9 the Lord *l.* Israel, 2 *Chr.* 9:8
11:1 Solomon *l.* many women
2 *Chr.* 2:11 and the Lord *l.* his
people, *Is.* 48:14
11:21 Rehoboam *l.* Maachah
Neh. 13:26 Uzziah *l.* husbandry
Est. 2:17 king *l.* Esther abo. all
Job 19:19 they whom I *l.* turned
Ps. 47:4 excellency of Jacob he *l.*
78:68 mount of Zion which he *l.*
109:17 *l.* cursing, so let it come
Jer. 8:2 host of heaven they *l.*
11:10 thus ha. they *l.* to wander
Ezek. 16:37 gather th. thou ha. *l.*
Hos. 9:1 thou hast *l.* a reward
10 abomina. according as *l.*
11:1 when Is. was child, I *l.* him
Mal. 1:2 whereln hast th. *l.* us?
4:11 profaned holin. of L. he *l.*
Mark 10:21 J. beholding *l.* him
Luke 7:47 sins forgiven, *l.* much
John 3:16 God so *l.* the world
19 *l.* darkness rather th. light
11:5 Jesus *l.* Martha, and sister
36 said Jews, Behold how he *l.*
12:43 they *l.* the praise of men
13:1 hav. *l.* his own, he *l.* them
23 discip. whom Jesus *l.* 19:26;
20:2; 21:7, 20
14:21 he that lov. me shall be *l.*
22 if ye *l. me*, you would rejoice

LOV

John 15:9 as F. *l.* me, so I *l.* you
10:27 Father lov. you, ye *l. me*
17:23 hast *l.* them, as thou *l. me*
26 love wh. thou hast *l.*
Rom. 8:37 conquer. thro' him *l.*
2 *Cor.* 12:15 love you, less I be *l.*
Gal. 2:20 who *l.* me, gave hims.
Eph. 3:2 love wherewith he *l.* us
5:2 as Christ also hath *l.* us
25 even as Christ *l.* the church
2 *Thes.* 4:10 Demas *l.* this world
2 *Tim.* 4:10 Demas *l.* this world
Heb. 1:9 thou hast *l.* righteousn.
2 *Pet.* 2:15 Balaam *l.* the wages
1 *John* 4:10 not that we *l.* God
11 if God so *l.* us
19 love him, bec. he first *l.* us
Rev. 1:5 to him that *l.* us
12:11 *l.* not their lives to death

I have LOVED.

Ps. 26:8 *I have l.* thy house
119:47 commands wh. *I h. l.* 48
Is. 48:1 *I have l.* thee, therefore
Jer. 2:25 *I have l.* strangers
31:3 *I h. l.* with everlasting love
Mal. 1:2 *I have l.* you, yet ye say
John 13:34 as *I ha. l.* you, 15:12
15:9 Father *l.* me so *I h. l.* you
Rom. 9:13 Jacob *I have l.* but E.
Rev. 3:9 make them know *I h. l.*

LOVEDST.

Is. 57:8 thou *l.* their bed where
John 17:24 *l.* me bef. foundation

LOVELY.

2 *Sam.* 1:23 S., and Jo. *l.* in lives
Cant. 5:16 he is altogether *l.*
Ezek. 33:32 art to them as *l.* song
Phil. 4:8 whatsoev. things are *l.*

LOVER.

1 *K.* 5:1 Hiram was *l.* of David
Ps. 88:18 *l.* and friend hast put
Tit. 1:8 *l.* of hospitali. *l.* of men

LOVERS.

Ps. 38:11 *l.* and friends stand
Jer. 8:1 played hard with ma. *l.*
4:30 thy *l.* will despise thee
22:20 for all thy *l.* are destroyed
22 thy *l.* shall go into captiv.
30:14 all thy *l.* have forgot. thee
Lam. 1:2 all her *l.* none to comf.
is called for *l.* they decelv. me
Ezek. 16:33 giv. gifts to all thy *l.*
36 nakedn. discover. wt. thy *l.*
23:22 raise up thy *l.* again. thee
Hos. 2:5 go after *l.* I follow *l.*
10 discover lewd. in sight of *l.*
12 rewards my *l.* ha. given me
8:9 Ephraim hath hired *l.*
2 *Tim.* 3:2 men be *l.* of own selves
4 *l.* of pleas. more than *l.* of G.

LOVES.

Prov. 7:18 solace ourselves wi. *l.*
Cant. 7:12 there I give thee my *l.*

LOVEST.

Jud. 14:16 hate me, and *l.* not
2 *Sam.* 19:6 thou *l.* thine enemies
Ps. 45:7 thou *l.* righteousness
52:3 thou *l.* evil more than good
4 thou *l.* all devouring words
Ec. 9:9 live with wife thou *l.*
John 11:3 he whom th. *l.* is sick
21:15 son of Jo. *l.* th. me? 16, 17

LOVETH.

Gen. 41:30 and his father *l.* him
Deut. 10:18 Lord *l.* the stranger
Ps. 11:5 him that *l.* violence
7 Lord *l.* righteousness, 33:5
34:12 man that *l.* many days?
37:28 Lord *l.* judgment, 99:4
87:2 the Lord *l.* gates of Zion
119:140 word is pure, thy ser. *l.*
146:8 the Lord *l.* the righteous
Prov. 3:12 whom L. *l.* he correct.
12:1 *l.* instruction, *l.* knowledge
13:24 that *l.* him, chasten. him
15:9 *l.* him followeth aft. right.
12 scorner *l.* not one th. repro.
17:17 a friend *l.* at all times
19 *l.* transgres. that *l.* strife
19:8 getteth wisdom *l.* own soul
21:17 he that *l.* wine and oil
22:11 that *l.* pureness of heart
29:3 *l.* wisdom rejoiceth father
Ec. 5:10 *l. l.* of silver, th. *l.* abun.
Cant. 1:7 O thou wh. my soul *l.*
3:2 seek him my soul *l.* 3, 4
Is. 1:23 every one *l.* gifts
Mal. 10:37 that *l.* fath. or mother
Luke 7:5 for he *l.* our nation
7:47 to whom little is forgiven. *l.* little
John 3:35 Father *l.* Son, 5:20
12:25 that *l.* his life sh. lose it
14:21 hath com. he is *l.* me.
he that *l.* me be loved of Fa.
24 *l.* me not, keep. not sayings

LUR

John 16:27 the Fath. hims. *l.* you
Rom. 13:8 that *l.* another
Eph. 5:28 that *l.* wife *l.* himself
Heb. 12:6 whom L. *l.* he chasten.
1 *John* 2:10 he that *l.* his brother
3:10 be that *l.* not his brother
14 *l.* not broth. abideth 4:8, 20
4:7 ev. one that *l.* is born of G.
21 he who *l.* God, *l.* his brother
5:1 L. him begat, *l.* him begot.
Rev. 22:15 *l.* and maketh a lie

LOVING.

Prov. 5:19 let her be as *l.* hind
22:1 *l.* favor rather than silver
Is. 56:10 sleeping, *l.* to slumber
See KINDNESS, KINDNESSES.

LOW.

Deut. 28:43 sh. co. down very *l.*
1 *Sam.* 2:7 the Lord bringeth *l.*
2 *Chr.* 26:10 cattle in *l.* country
28:18 invaded cities of *l.* count.
Job 5:11 set on high th. that be *l.*
40:12 look on proud bring him *l.*
Ps. 49:2 high and *l.* rich and poor
62:9 men of *l.* degree are vanity
136:23 remember. us in *l.* estate
Prov. 29:23 man's pride be him *l.*
Ec. 10:6 the rich sit in *l.* place
Is. 25:12 high walls sh. he lay *l.*
26:5 lofty city he layeth it *l.*
29:4 speech *l.* out of the dust
32:19 city sh. be *l.* in a *l.* place
Lam. 3:55 name out of *l.* dunge.
Ezek. 17:6 vine of *l.* stature
21 know I have exalted *l.* tree
21:26 exalt him that is *l.*
26:20 set in *l.* parts of earth
Luke 1:48 he regarded *l.* estate
52 exalted them of *l.* degree
Rom. 12:16 to men of *l.* estate
1 *Tim.* 2:9 brother of *l.* degree
10 rich in that he is made *l.*

See BROUGHT.

LOWER.

Lev. 13:20 *l. l.* be in sight *l.* than
Neh. 4:13 set in *l.* places the peo.
Ps. 8:5 thou hast made him *l.*
than the angels, *Heb.* 2:7, 9
63:9 go into *l.* parts of the earth
Prov. 25:7 *l.* in presen. of prince
Is. 24:5 gave heed, wat. of *l.* pool
44:23 shout ye *l.* parts of earth
Eph. 4:9 descended into *l.* parts

LOWERING.

Mat. 16:3 the sky is red and *l.*

LOWEST.

Deut. 32:22 shall burn to *l.* hell
1 *K.* 12:31 made priests of *l.* of
people, 13:33; 2 *K.* 17:32
Ps. 86:13 deliv. soul from *l.* hell
88:6 thou hast laid me in *l.* pit
Luke 14:9 begin to take *l.* room
10 and sit down in the *l.* room

LOWETH, ING.

1 *Sam.* 6:12 kine went along *l.*
15:14 what meaneth *l.* of oxen?
Job 6:5 *l.* the ox over his fodder?

LOWLY.

Ps. 138:6 hath he respect to *l.*
Prov. 3:34 he giveth grace to *l.*
11:2 but with *l.* is wisdom
16:19 be of humble spirit wi. *l.*
Zec. 9:9 *l.* and riding on an ass
Mat. 11:29 for I am meek and *l.*

LOWLINESS.

Eph. 4:2 walk with *l.* and meek.
Phil. 2:3 in *l.* of mind, esteem

LUCAS. *Phile.* 24

LUCIFER. *Is.* 14:12

LUCIUS. *Acts* 13:1; *Rom.* 16:2

LUCRE.

1 *Sam.* 8:3 S. sons turned after *l.*
1 *Tim.* 3:3 bishop not greedy of
l. 8
Tit. 1:7 not given to filthy *l.*
11 teach. things not for filthy *l.*
1 *Pet.* 5:2 flock not for filthy *l.*

LUKE. *Col.* 4:14; 2 *Tim.* 4:11

LUKEWARM.

Rev. 3:16 because thou art *l.*

LUMP.

2 *K.* 20:7 take *l.* of figs, *Is.* 38:21
Rom. 9:21 of same *l.* one vessel
11:16 first-fruit holy *l.* is holy
1 *Cor.* 5:6 leav. whole *l. Gal.* 5:9
7 old leav. that ye be a new *l.*

LUNATIC.

Mat. 4:24 those were *l.* he healed
17:15 mercy on my son, he *l.*

LURK.

Prov. 1:11 come, let us *l.* privily
13 they *l.* privily for own lives

LYI

LURKING.

1 *Sam.* 23:23 knowl. of *l.* places
Ps. 10:8 in *l.* places of villages
17:12 yo. lion *l.* in secret places

LUST.

Ex. 15:9 my *l.* shall be satisfied
Ps. 78:18 asking meat for th. *l.*
30 not estranged from their *l.*
81:12 up to their own hearts' *l.*
Rom. 1:27 burned in their *l.* one
7:7 had not known *l.* except law
Gal. 5:16 not fulfi *l.* of flesh
Jam. 1:14 when drawn of his *l.*
15 when *l.* hath conceived
2 *Pet.* 1:4 corrup. in world thro' *l.*
2:10 after flesh in *l.* of unclean.
1 *John* 2:16 *l.* of flesh, *l.* of eye
17 passeth away, and *l.* thereof

LUST, Verb.

Prov. 6:25 *l.* not after beauty
Mat. 5:28 look. on woman to *l.*
1 *Cor.* 10:6 not *l.* after evil things
Jam. 4:2 ye *l.* and have not

LUSTED, ETH.

Num. 11:34 buried people that *l.*
Deut. 12:15 what thy soul *l.* after,
20, 21; 14:26
Ps. 106:14 they *l.* exceedingly
1 *Cor.* 10:6 not lust as th. also *l.*
Gal. 5:17 flesh *l.* against the Sp.
Jam. 4:5 spirit in us *l.* to envy
Rev. 18:14 fruits thy soul *l.* after

LUSTING.

Num. 11:4 mixed multit. fell a *l.*

LUSTS.

Mark 4:19 *l.* of things cho. word
John 8:44 *l.* of father ye will do
Rom. 6:12 sho. obey th. *l.* thereof
13:14 no provision. to fulfil *l.*
Gal. 5:24 crucified flesh with *l.*
Eph. 2:3 conversa. in *l.* of flesh
4:22 corrupt accord. to deceit. *l.*
1 *Tim.* 6:9 foolish and hurtful *l.*
2 *Tim.* 2:22 flee youthful *l.*
4:3 after own *l.* heap teachers
Tit. 2:12 that denying worldly *l.*
3:3 divers *l.* and pleasures
Jam. 4:1 hence, even of your *l.* ?
3 may consume it on your *l.*
1 *Pet.* 1:14 according to former *l.*
2:11 you abstain fr. fleshly *l.*
4:2 no longer live to *l.* of men
4:3 walked in *l.* excess of wine
2 *Pet.* 2:18 allure thro' *l.* of flesh
Jude 16 complain. walk. after *l.*
18 walk after their ungodly *l.*

LUSTY.

Jud. 3:29 slew 10,000 men, all *l.*

LUZ. *Gen.* 28:19; 48:3; *Jud.* 1:23

LYCAONIA. *Acts* 14:6, 11

LYDDA. *Acts* 9:32, 35, 38

LYDIA. *Ezek.* 30:5; *Acts* 10:14,40

LYING.

Ps. 31:6 I have hated them that
regard *l.* vanities
18 let *l.* lips be put to silence
52:3 lovest *l.* rather than right.
59:12 cursing and *l.* they speak
109:2 spoken with *l.* tongue
119:29 remove fr. me way of *l.*
163 I hate and abhor *l.* but
120:2 deliver my soul fr. *l.* lips
Prov. 6:17 proud look, a *l.* tong.
10:18 hatred with *l.* lips is fool
12:19 *l.* tongue is for a moment
22 *l.* lips abomination to the L.
13:5 righteous man hateth *l.*
17:7 do *l.* lips become a prince
21:6 treas. by *l.* tongue vanity
26:28 *l.* tongue hat. those afflict.
Is. 32:9 rebellious peo. *l.* child.
32:7 wicked devices, *l.* words
59:13 in *l.* against the Lord
Jer. 7:4 trust ye not in *l.* words
8 behold, ye trust in *l.* words
29:23 spo. *l.* words in my name
Ezek. 13:6 vanity and *l.* divina.
19 *l.* to my peo. that hear lies
Dan. 2:9 ye have prep. *l.* words
Hos. 4:2 swearing, *l.* and killing
Jon. 2:8 observe *l.* vanities forsa.
Eph. 4:25 put. away *l.* sp. truth
2 *Thes.* 2:9 wonders with *l.* wl.

LYING.

Ex. 23:5 ass of him hateth th. *l.*
Deut. 22:6 bird's nest bef. thee *l.*
Is. 56:10 *l.* down, lov. to slumber
Luke 2:12 babe *l.* in manger, 16
John 13:25 *l.* on Jesus' breast
20:5 he saw the linen clothes *l.*
7 napkin not *l.* wi. lin. clothes

LYING spirit.

1 *K.* 22:22 a *l. spl.* in the mouth
of prophets, 2 *Chr.* 18:21
23 Lord hath put a *l. spirit* in
prophets, 2 *Chr.* 18:22

CRUDEN'S CONCORDANCE. 935

MAD

LYING in wait.
Jud. 16:9 th. were men l. in w.
Lam. 3:10 as a bear l. in wait
Acts 20:19 by l. in wait of Jews
23:16 heard of their l. in wait

LYING with.
Gen. 34:7 l. with Jacob's daugh.
Num. 31:17 known man by l. w.
18 not kn. l. 35; Jud. 21:12
Deut. 22:22 man found l. w. wom.

LYSANIAS. Luke 3:1
LYSIAS. Acts 23:26
LYSTRA. Acts 14:6, 8; 16:1, 2;
2 Tim. 3:11

M.

MAACHAH, Gen. 22:24; 2 Sam.
3:8; 1 Chr. 3:2
MAASEIAH,
2 Chr. 26:7 Zic. slew M. Jer. 21:1
MAATH. Luke 3:26

MACEDONIA.
Acts 16:9 into M. 18:5; 19:21
Rom. 15:26 pleased them of M.
2 Cor. 7:5 were come into M.
8:1 grace of God churches of M.
9:2 I boast of you to them of M.
11:9 brethren from M. supplied
1 Thes. 1:7 that believe in M. 8
4:10 brethren that are in M.

MACHIR. Gen. 50:23; Nu. 26:29;
27:1; 32:39; 36:1; Jos.
17:1; Jud. 5:14; 2 Sam. 9:4; 17:27
MACHPELAH. Gen. 23:9, 17, 19,
25:9; 49:30; 50:13

MAD,
Deut. 28:34 m. for sight of eyes
1 Sam. 21:13 feigned himself m.
2 K. 9:11 this m. fellow to thee
Ps. 102:8 they th. are m. ag. me
Ec. 2:2 it is m. of mirth
7:7 oppres, maketh wise man m.
Is. 44:25 maketh diviners m.
Jer. 25:16 be moved and be m.
23:26 man is m. put in prison
50:38 they are m. upon idols
51:7 therof. the nations are m.
Hos. 9:7 the spiritual man is m.
John 10:20 he hath devil, is m.
Acts 12:15 said to Rh. Th. art m.
13:11 being exceed. m. ag. th.
24 much learn. make thee m.
25 I am not m. most noble F.
1 Cor. 14:23 not say ye are m. f

MADE, meant of God, Lord,
Christ.
Gen. 1:31 G. saw ev. thing he m.
5:1 in liken. of G. m. he him, 9:6
6:6 repent. he had m. man, 7
I have MADE.
Gen. 7:4 destroy liv. sub. I h. m.

MADE haste.
Gen. 24:46 Rebekah m. haste
Jud. 13:10 Manoah's wife m. h.
2 Sam. 4:4 Mephib.'s nurse m. h.
Ps. 119:60 I m. h. delayed not
Luke 19:6 Zaccheus m. h.

See ISRAEL, SIN, KNOWN.

MADE manifest.
Luke 8:17 shall not be m. m.
John 1:31 that he sho. be m. m.
3:21 his deeds may be m. m.
9:3 works of God sho. be m. m.
Rom. 10:20 I was m. m. to those
16:26 now is m. m. to nations
1 Cor. 3:13 work shall be m. m.
11:19 approved may be m. m.
14:25 secrets of his heart m. m.
2 Cor. 4:10 J. should be m. m. 11
11:6 we have been thoro. m. m.
Eph. 5:13 approved are m. m.
Col. 1:26 m. m. to his saints
2 Tim. 1:10 now m. m. by Christ
Heb. 9:8 holiest not yet m. m.
1 John 2:19 they might ho m. m.
Rev. 15:4 thy judgm. are m. m.

MADE peace.
Jos. 9:15 Joshua m. p. 10:1, 4
11:19 not a city m. p. with Is'r.
2 Sam. 10:19 when the servants
of Hadarezer were smit. th.
m. p. with Isr. 1 Chr. 19:19
1 K. 22:44 Jehoshaphat m. peace

MADE ready.
Gen. 43:25 they m. r. present
43:26 Joseph m. ready chariot
Jud. 6:19 G. went and m. r. kid
1 Chr. 28:2 had m. r. for building
Ps. 7:12 bent his bow and m. r.
Hos. 7:6 have m. ready their
heart

MAH

Mat. 26:19 discip. m. r. passov.
Mark 14:16; Luke 22:13
2 Cor. 10:16 boast of things m. r.
Rev. 19:7 wife hath m. herself r.

MADE void.
Num. 30:12 her husb. hath m. v.
Ps. 89:39 hast m. v. covenant
119:126 they have m. v. thy law
Rom. 4:14 law heirs, faith m. v.

MADE, passively.
John 1:3 all things m. by him,
without him not any th. m.
10 the world was m. by him
14 the Word was m. flesh
3:6 bo m. whole † 14 m. whole
8:33 bo m. free; 9:39 m. blind

MADEST.
Jon. 4:10 neither m. it grow
Heb. 2:7 m. him low. th. angels

MAD man, men,
1 Sam. 21:15 ha. I need of m. m.
Prov. 26:18 m. m. casteth firebr.
Jer. 48:3 O m. m. sw. sh. pursue
26:71 another m. saw him, Mark
14:69; Luke 22:50

MADMANNAH, MADMENAH,
MADMEN, Jos. 15:31; Is.
10:31; Jer. 48:2

MADNESS.
Deut. 28:28 smite thee with m.
Ec. 1:17 to know wisd. and m.
2:12 I turned myself to beh. m.
7:25 wickedness of folly and m.
9:3 m. is in heart, wh. they live
10:13 his talk is mischievous m.
Ec. 12:4 m. horse and rider m.
Luke 6:11 they were filled w. m.
2 Pet. 2:16 dumb as forbade m.

MAGDALA. Mat. 15:30

MAGICIAN, S.
Gen. 41:8 Pharaoh called for m.
Ex. 7:11 the m. of Egypt did so
in like manner, 22; 8:7, 18
9:11 m. could not stand bef. M.
Dan. 1:20 ten times bet. than m.
2:2 king commanded to call m.
10 asked such things at any m.
4:7 then came in the m.
G 0 Belteshazzar, master of m.
5:11 father made master of m.

MAGISTRATE, S.
Jud. 18:7 no m. in the land
Ezr. 7:25 Ezra set m. and judges
Luke 12:11 they bring you to m.
58 when thou goest to the m.
Acts 16:20 Paul and Silas to m.
22 m. commanded to beat them
35 the m. sent the serjeants, 36
Tit. 3:1 put th. in mi. to obey m.

MAGNIFICAL.
1 Chr. 22:5 the house must be m.

MAGNIFICENCE.
Acts 19:27 her m. sh. be destro.

MAGNIFY.
Jos. 3:7 will I begin to m.
Job 7:17 what is man that thou
shouldest m. him?
19:5 if ye will m. yourselves
36:21 remember thou m. work
Ps. 34:3 O m. the Lord with me
35:26 cloth. with shame that m.
38:16 th. m. themselves ag. me
55:12 did m. himself against me
69:20 did m. him with thanksg.
Is. 10:15 saw m. itself ag. him?
42:21 he will m. the law
Ezek. 38:23 thus will I m. myself
Dan. 8:25 m. himself in his heart
11:36 the king shall m. himself
37 he shall m. himself above
Luke 1:46 my soul doth m. the L.
Acts 10:46 sp, wt. tongues, m. G.
Rom. 11:13 apostle, I m. office

MAGNIFIED.
Gen. 19:19 hast m. thy mercy
2 Sam. 7:26 and let thy name be
m. 1 Chr. 17:24
1 Chr. 29:25 L. m. Solo. 2 Chr. 1:1
Ps. 33:27 let the Lord be m.
40:16 say contin. L. bo m. 70:4
138:2 thou hast m. thy word
Jer. 48:26 m. hims. 42; Dan. 8:11
Lam. 1:9 enemy hath m. hims.
Zep. 2:8 m. against their border
Mal. 1:5 L. will be m. from Isr.
Acts 5:13 the people m. them
19:17 name of the L. Jesus m.
Phil. 1:20 Ch. be m. in my body

MAGOG.
Gen. 10:2; 1 Chr. 1:5; Ezek. 38:2
Rev. 30:8 gather G. and M. battle

MAHALATH, 2 Chr. 11:18

MAHANAIM.
Gen. 32:2 J. called the place M.
1 K. 2:8 when I went to M.

MAJ

MAHER-SHALAL-HASH-
BAZ.
Is. 8:1 write concerning M.

MAHLAH. Num. 26:33
MAHLON. Ruth 1:2, 5; 4:9,10

MAID.
Gen. 16:2 go in to my m.
6 behold, thy m. is in thy hand
30:3 behold, my m. Bilhah
Ex. 2:5 she sent her m.
8 m. went and called mother
21:20 if a man smite his m.
22:16 if man entice m. not betr.
Deut. 22:14 fou. her not a m. 17
2 K. 5:2 bro. captive little m.
Est. 2:7 m. fair and beautiful
Job 31:1 why sho. I think on m. ?
Prov. 30:19 way of man with m.
Is. 24:2 be as with m. with mist.
Jer. 2:32 can m. forget ornam. ?
51:22 break young man and m.
Amos 2:7 and fa. go to same m.
Mat. 9:24 m. is not dead
26:71 another m. saw him, Mark
14:69; Luke 22:56
Luke 8:54 called, saying, m. arise

MAID-CHILD.
Lev. 12:5 if she bear a m.-c. unc.

MAIDEN.
Gen. 30:18 given m. to my husb.
Jud. 19:24 my daughter, a m.
2 Chr. 36:17 comp. on young m.
Luke 8:51 father and moth. of m.

MAIDENS.
Ex. 2:5 m. walk. along by river
Ruth 2:8 abide fast by my m.
1 Sam. 9:11 m. going to dr. wat.
Est. 4:16 I and my m. will fast
Job 41:5 bind him for thy m. ?
Ps. 78:63 m. not giv. to marri.
148:12 y. men and m. praise L.
Prov. 9:3 hath sent forth her m.
31:15 she giveth a portion to m.
27:27 I got me serv. and m.
Ezek. 44:22 take m. of seed of Is.
Luke 12:45 ser. begin to beat m.

MAIDS.
Est. 2:9 preferred her and m.
Job 19:15 m. count me stranger
Lam. 5:11 ravished m. in cities
Ezek. 9:6 slay both m. and chil.
Nah. 2:7 her m. shall lead her
Zec. 9:17 cheerful, new wine m.

MAID-SERVANT.
Ex. 11:5 first-born of m.-s.
20:10 thy m.-s. sh. do no work
17 not covet neighbor's m.-s.
21:7 sell daughter to be m.-s.
27 if he smite out m.-s.'s tooth
Deut. 5:14 that thy m.-s. rest
21 nor desire neighbor's m.-s.
15:17 to thy m.-s. do likewise
Jud. 9:18 Abimel. son of m.-s.
Job 31:13 if I did despise m.-s.
Jer. 34:9 man-s. and m.-s. go, 10

MAID-SERVANTS.
Gen. 20:17 Ab. wife and m.-s.
81:33 I. entered two m.-s. tents
Deut. 12:12 rejoice, ye and m.-s.
1 Sam. 8:16 sh. take your m.-s.
2 Sam. 6:22 of tho m.-s. sh. I be
2 K. 5:26 time to receive m.-s. ?

MAIL.
1 Sam. 17:5 with coat of m. 38

MAIMED.
Lev. 22:22 blind or m. shall not
Mat. 15:30 those that were m.
31 when they saw m. to walk
18:8 rather to enter into life m.
Luke 14:13 make feast, call m.
21

MAINSAIL.
Acts 27:40 hoised up m. to wind

MAINTAIN.
1 K. 8:45 then m. and m. their
cause, 49, 59; 2 Chr. 6:35, 39
Job 13:15 I will m. mine own
Ps. 140:12 L. will m. afflicted
Tit. 3:8 to m. good works, 14

MAINTAINED, ST.
Ps. 9:4 thou hast m. my right
16:5 L. is my portion, m. my lot

MAINTENANCE.
Ezr. 4:14 we have m. from king
Prov. 27:27 m. for thy maidens

MAJESTY.
1 Chr. 29:11 thine, O Lord, is m.
25 bestowed on him royal m.
Est. 1:4 showed honor of his m.
Job 87:22 with G. is terrible m.
40:10 deck thyself now with m.

MAK

Ps. 21:5 honor and m. hast thou
29:4 voice of the L. is full of m.
45:3 glory and m. 4 in m. ride
93:1 Lord is clothed with m.
96:6 honor and m. are bef. him
104:1 thou art clothed with m.
145:5 speak of honor of thy m.
12 glorious m. of his kingdom
Is. 2:10 glory of his m. 19, 21
24:14 shall sing for m. of the L.
26:10 not behold the m. of Lord
Ezek. 7:20 ornament, he set in m.
Dan. 4:30 built for honor of m.
36 excellent m. added to me
5:18 G. gave Nebuchadnez. m.
Mic. 5:4 feed in m. of name of L.
Heb. 1:3 on right hand of m. 8:1
2 Pet. 1:16 eye-witness. of his m.
Jude 25 to God be glory and m.

MAKE.
Gen. 1:26 m. man: 2:18 m. him
3:6 tree desired to m. one wise
12:2 will m. thee a great nation,
21:18; 46:3; Ex. 32:10
2 Sam. 7:11 will m. thee a house
Ps. 39:4 L. m. me to kn. mi. end
90:15 m. us glad accord. to days
86:5 to wh. will ye m. equal
Ec. 12:2 m. Jerusalem a cup
Mal. 2:15 did not he m. one ?
Mat. 27:65 m. it sure as ye can
Mark 5:39 why m. ye this ado ?
John 10:24 long m. us to doubt ?
Eph. 2:15 to m. in himself of tw.
Rev. 21:5 I m. all things new
See AFRAID, ATONEMENT, COVE-
NANT, DESOLATE, DESOLA-
TION, END, FIRE, GOOD.

MAKE haste.
Deut. 32:35 come on them m. h.
1 Chr. 35:21 G. comman. to m. h.
Est. 5:5 cause Haman m. h. 6:10
Job 20:2 for this I m. haste
Ps. 38:22 m. haste to help me, O
Lord, 40:13; 70:1; 71:12
70:5 needy, m. h. to me, 141:1
Prov. 1:16 m. h. shed b. Is. 59:7
Cant. 8:14 m. haste, my beloved
Is. 28:16 believeth sh., not m. h.
49:17 thy children sh. m. haste
Jer. 9:18 m. h. take up wailing
Nah. 2:5 m. haste to wall thereof
Acts 22:18 m. h. out of Jerusalem
See KNOWN.

MAKE manifest.
1 Cor. 4:5 m. m. counsels of hea.
Eph. 5:13 wh. doth m. m. is light
Col. 4:4 may m. it m. as I ought
See MENTION, NOISE.

MAKE ready.
1 K. 12:3 they m. r. their arrow
21:12 when shall m. r. thine ar.
Ezek. 7:14 blown trump. to m. r.
Mat. 14:15 m. r. Luke 22:12
Luke 1:17 m. r. a peo. prepared
17:8 rather say, m. r. wherew.

MAKE speed.
2 Sam. 15:14 m. speed to depart
Is. 5:19 let him m. s. and hasten

MAKE waste.
Lev. 26:31 I will m. your cit. w.
Is. 42:15 I will m. w. mountains
Ezek. 5:14 I will m. Jerusa. w.
29:10 m. land of Egypt w. 30:12

MAKER.
Job 4:17 more pure than his M.?
32:22 my M. will soon take me
35:10 where is God my M. ?
36:3 ascribe righteous. to my M.
Ps. 95:6 kneel before L. our M.
Prov. 14:31 reproacheth his M.
17:5 mock. poor, reproach. M.
22:2 rich and poor, L. M. of all
Is. 1:31 the m. of it as a spark
17:7 shall man look to to the m.
22:11 have not looked to the m.
45:9 woe to him striv. with M.
16 go to confusion m. of idols
51:13 forgettest the L. thy M.
54:5 thy M. is thy husband
Jer. 33:9 rises with Is. the M.
Hos. 8:14 Is. hath forget. his M.
Hab. 2:18 what profiteth graven
image that m. thy trusteth ?
Heb. 11:10 builder and m. is God

MAKEST.
Is. 45:9 shall the clay say to him
that fash. it, What m. thou ?
John 8:53 whom m. thou thys. ?
10:33 being a man, m. thyself G.

MAKETH.
Deut. 27:15 with which the L. m.
1 Sam. 2:6 L. killeth and m. alive
7 the L. m. poor and rich, m. rich

MAN

Is. 44:24 I am L. th. m, all thin.
Acts 0:34 Jesus C. m. thee whosoever
1 Cor. 4:7 who m. thee to differ?
2 Cor. 2:2 who is he th. m. glad?
Rev. 21:27 what. m. a lie, 22:15

MAKETH haste.
Prov. 28:20 m. haste to be rich

MAKING.
Ps. 19:7 the testimony of the L. is sure, m. wise simple
Ez. 12:13 of m. books no end
Mark 7:13 m. word of G. none eff.
John 5:18 m. hims. equal wi. G.
2 Cor. 6:10 yet m. many rich
Eph. 1:16 m. mention of you,
1 Thes. 1:2; Phile. 4
Phil. 1:4 prayer for you, m. req.
Jude 22 have compassion, m. dif.

MAKING, Noun.
Ezek. 27:16 wares of thy m. 18
MAKKEDAH. Jos. 10:10, 16, 20, 28
MALCHAM. Zep. 1:5
MALCHUS. John 18:10

MALE.
Gen. 17:23 cv. m. circ. 34:15, 22, 24
Ex. 13:12 tha m. shall be Lord's, 34:19; Luke 2:23
Lev. 1:3 a m. without blemish, 10; 4:23; 22:19
7:6 every m. am. priests sh. eat
Num. 1:2 every m. by their polls
3:15 every m. from a month old
31:17 kill ev. m. little ones
Deut. 20:13 shalt smite every m.
Jud. 21:11 ye sh. destroy ev. m.
1 K. 11:15 smitten every m. 16
Mal. 1:14 wh. hath in flock a m.
See **FEMALE.**

MALE-CHILDREN.
Jos. 17:2 were m.-c. of Manas.

MALEFACTOR, S.
Luke 23:32 two m. led with him
33 they crucified him, and m.
John 18:30 if he were not a m.

MALES.
Gen. 34:25 Si. and Levi slew m.
Ex. 12:48 m. be circumcised
13:15 sacri. to L. all being m.
23:17 thy m. shall appear before the Lord God, Deut. 16:16
Num. 31:7 Midianites, slew m.
Deut. 15:19 firstling m. sanctify
Jos. 5:4 m. came out of Egypt
2 Chr. 31:19 gi. portions to all m.

MALICE.
1 Cor. 5:8 not with leaven of m.
14:20 howbeit in m. be ye chil.
Eph. 4:31 put away fr. you all m.
Col. 3:8 also put off all these, m.
Tit. 3:3 sometimes living in m.
1 Pet. 2:1 laying aside all m.

MALICIOUS.
3 John 10 og. us with m. words

MALICIOUSNESS.
Rom. 1:29 with unrighteous. m.
1 Pet. 2:16 for a cloak of m.

MALIGNITY.
Rom. 1:29 full of envy, mur. m.

MALLOWS.
Job 30:4 cut up m. by bushes
MAMMON.
Mat. 6:24 G. and m. Luke 16:13
Luke 16:9 friends of m. of unr. 11

MAMRE.
Gen. 13:18 A. dwelt in M. 14:13
15:24 Eshcol, M. let th. portion
23:17 bef. M. 19; 49:30; 50:13

MAN.
Gen. 1:26 God said, Let us make m. in our image, 27; 9:6
2:7 L. G. formed m. of the dust
18 is not good m. sho. be alone
25 both naked, m. and his wife
3:22 the m. is bec. as one of us
6:3 Sp. shall not strive with m.
19:8 I have two daughters wh. have not kn. m. Num. 31:35
24:65 what m. is this walketh?
Deut. 4:32 since day G. creat. m.
5:24 God doth talk with m.
8:3 m. doth not live by bread only, Mat. 4:4; Luke 1:4
20:19 tree of the field is m. life
Jos. 7:14 come m. M. 17, 18
Jud. 8:21 as m. is, so strength
9:13 wine cheereth G. and m.
16:7 weak as another m. 11, 17
1 Sam. 9:6 m. of G. honorable m.
16:7 Lord seeth not as m. seeth
2 Sam. 12:7 said, Th. art the m.
16:7 power out, thou bloody m. 8
2 K. 9:11 ye know tho m.

MAN

2 Chr. 19:6 ye judge not for m.
Job 4:17 sh. m. be mo. just th. G.
7:17 what is m. that thou sho. ?
magnify him? 15:14; Ps. 8:4;
144:3; Heb. 2:6
9:2 how sh. m. be just wi. G. ?
10:4 or seest thou as m. seeth?
5 are thy days as days of m.?
11:12 vain m. would be wise
13:7 art thou first m. born?
14 wh. is m. th. he sh. be cle.?
25:6 much less m. that is worm
32:13 G. thrusteth down, not m.
33:12 God is greater than m.
Ps. 56:11 not afr. wh. m. can do
78:25 m. did eat angels' food
80:17 thy hand be on the m.
104:23 m. goeth forth to work
118:6 not fear wh. m. can do
Prov. 20:24 m.'s goings are of L.
Ec. 6:11 what is m. the better?
12 kno. what is good for m.?
Isa. 11:9 I am God, and not m.
Mic. 6:8 show. O m. wh. is good
Zec. 13:7 ag. m. that is my fellow
Mat. 19:6 what G. ha. joined, let not m. put asun. Mark 10:9
26:72 I do not know the m. 74
Mark 2:27 sab. was made for m.
Luke 5:20 m. thy sins forgiven
18:4 fear not G. nor regard m.
22:58 Peter said, m. I am not
60 m. I kn. not what thou say.
23:53 laid in sepulchre whereon nev. m. was laid, John 19:41
John 2:25 knew what was in m.
19:5 Pilate said, Behold the m.
1 Cor. 8:11 whom he knoweth the things of a m. ?
11:3 head of the woman is m.
8 the m. is not of the woman
9 but the woman for the m.
11 nor is the m. with. the wo. nor woman without the m.
12 even so is m. by woman
15:21 by m. came death, by m.
45 first m. Adam was made
47 first m. is of the earth; the second m. is the L. fr. hea.
2 Cor. 4:16 tho' our outward m. perish. inward m. is renew.
Gal. 1:1 not of men, nei. by m.
11 I preached not after m.
Eph. 2:15 ma. of tw. one new m.
3:16 by his Sp. In the inner m.
4:24 ye have put on new m.
Col. 3:10 put on new m. renewed
1 Tim. 4:8 despi. not m. but G.
1 Tim. 2:5 one Mediator bet. G. and men, the m. Chr. Jesus
1 Pet. 3:4 hidden m. of the heart

A MAN.

Gen. 4:23 for I have slain a m.
19:31 not a m. to come in unto
41:38 a m. in whom Sp. of G. is
42:11 in their anger slew a m.
1 Sam. 13:14 L. sought him a m.
14:36 let us not leave a m.
16:17 provide me a m. can play
17:8 choose you a m. for you
10 give me a m. we may fight
25:17 a m. cannot speak to him
30:17 there escaped not a m.
2 Sam. 3:34 as a m. falleth before
20:1 there happened to be a m.
1 K. 2:2 and show thyself a m.
4 not fail a m. on throne, 8:25
20:39 behold, a m. turned aside
2 K. 10:21 th. was not a m. left
1 Chr. 22:9 shall be a m. of rest
2 Chr. 6:16 not fail th. a m. 7:18
Job 9:11 sho. such a m. flee?
32:3 a m. a light given to a m.
4:17 a m. be more pure th. God
9:32 he is not a m. as I am
12:14 behold, he shut. up a m.
14:14 if a m. die, sh. he live?
16:21 O that one mi. plead for a m. with G. as a m. pleadeth
21:3 can a m. be profit. to God?
31:26 what. a m. pr. G. find a m.
33:8 thy wicked. may hurt a m.
37:20 if a m. speak
Ps. 43:1 gird loins like a m. 40:7
Pr. 58:14 as a m. heareth not
55:13 it was thou, a m. equal
88:4 a m. th. hath no strength
102:17 he sent a m. before them
147:10 not pleas. in legs of a m.
Prov. 3:30 striven not with a m.
14:12 seem. right to a m. 16:25
16:2 all ways of a m. are clean
7 when a m.'s ways please L.
27:21 so is a m. to his praise
28:12 wicked rise a m. hidden

MAN

Prov. 28:23 he that rebuketh a m.
29:20 seest th. a m. th. is hasty?
Ec. 2:26 God giv. to a m. good
4:4 a m. is envied of neighbor
6:2 a m. wh. G. ha. given rich.
12 who tell a m. what sh. he?
10:14 a m. cannot tell wh. sh.
Cant. 8:7 if a m. would give all
Is. 5:6 a m. of unclean lips
13:12 make a m. more prec.
17:7 at that day shall a m. look
24:20 a m. can stretch himself
29:21 make a m. an offender
32:2 a m. shall be a hiding pl.
47:3 I will not meet th. as a m.
53:3 he is a m. of sorrows
58:5 day for a m. to afflict soul?
Jer. 4:29 not a m. dwell therein
5:1 seek if ye can find a m.
15:10 borne me a m. of strife
16:20 shall a m. make gods?
22:30 a m. that shall not prosp.
23:9 a m. wine hath overcome
30:6 whether a m. doth travail?
31:22 woman sh. compass a m.
33:17 D. shall never want a m.
18 nor shall priest want a m.
35:19 Jon. shall not want a m.
36:43 away like a m. to battle
Lam. 3:36 it is good for a m.
27 good for a m. he bear yoke
39 a m. for punishment of sins
Ezek. 22:30 I sought for a m.
28:2 thou art a m. and not G. 9
32:2 if people of land take a m.
Dan. 2:10 not a m. on earth can
7:4 st. as a m. and a m.'s heart
10:11 O Daniel, a m. beloved
Hos. 9:12 shall not be a m. left
11:4 drew th. wi. cords of a m.
Amos 2:7 a m. and fa. go to maid
5:19 as if a m. did flee fr. lion
Mic. 2:2 oppress a m. and house
7:6 a m.'s enemies the men of his own house, Mat. 10:36
Mal. 3:17 as a m. spareth his own
Mat. 8:9 am a m. und. au. Lu. 7:8
10:35 to set a m. at variance
12:12 is a m. better than sheep?
15:11 out of mouth defileth a m.
19:3 is it lawful for a m. to put away wife? Mark 10:2
22:24 if a m. die, having no ch.
26:18 go into city, to such a m.
Mark 14:13; Luke 22:10
Luke 1:34 seeing I kn. not a m.
5:8 for I am a sinful m. O Lord
John 3:6 a m. sent from God
30 a m. who is a m. sent from God
Acts 4:9 a m. ha. bel. of G. of C.
1 Cor. 3:12 if a m. build on fou.
14 a m. work; 15 work burn.
18 if a m. am. you seem. wise
8:2 if a m. love God, 11:34 hunger
10:28 if a m. say this is offered
10:29 if a m. not used to it
2 Cor. 5:17 if any m. be in Chr.
10:7 if any m. trust to himself
12:6 lest a m. sho. think of me
Gal. 1:9 if a m. pre. other gosp.
Eph. 2:9 lest any m. should boa.
1 Thes. 5:15 for evil to any m.
2 Thes. 3:8 nor eat a m.'s bread
Heb. 4:11 a m. fall after same
10:38 if any m. draw back
13:16 a m. full of grace of God
Jam. 1:13 nor tempteth any m.
1 Pet. 4:11 if any m. speak
1 John 2:1 if a m. sin, ha. advo.
15 love not the world
4:1 believe not any m. teach
Rev. 3:20 if a m. hear my voice
22:18 if a m. add to these thin.
19 if any m. take away words

See **BEAST, BLESSED, CURSED.**

MAN-CHILD.

Gen. 17:10 m.-c. be circumc. 12
14 uncircumc. m.-c. be cut of
Lev. 12:2 if wom. bo. borne m.-c.
1 Sam. 1:11 give to handm. m.-c.
Job 3:3 it was said, There is a m.-c. conceived, Jer. 20:15
Is. 66:7 deliv. of m.-c. Rev. 12:5
Rev. 12:13 wom. bro. forth m.-c.
See **EACH.**

Every MAN.

Gen. 16:12 his hand he ag. e. m.
45:1 cause e. m. to go out
Ex. 10:17 e. m. give as able
2 Sam. 13:9 they went out e. m.
Phil. 2:4 look not e. m. on his
See **EVIL, FOOLISH.**

MAN of God.

Deut. 33:1 M. m. of G. Jos. 14:6
Jud. 13:6 m. of G. came to me
1 Sam. 2:27 a m. of G. to Eli
9:6 there is in city a m. of G.

MAN

Ex. 24:14, if a. m. have matters
34:3 nor let a. m. be seen thro'
24 nor shall any m. desire land
Num. 6:9 if any m. die suddenly
21:9 if serpent had bitten a. m.
Deut. 19:11 if any m. hate neigh.
22:8 if any m. fall from thence
Jos. 1:5 not a. m. be able to sta.
Jud. 4:20 if any m. inquire, Is there any m. here?
16:17 and be like a. other m.
18:7 no business with a. m. 28
1 Sam. 2:16 a. m. said, Fall not
1 Sam. 13:5 wh. a. m. came nigh
19:22 eh. a. m. be put to death
21:4 nor for as eh. th. kill a. m.
2 K. 4:29 meet a. m. salute h. n.
2 Chr. 6:5 nor chose I any m.
Neh. 2:12 nor told I a. m. wh. G.
32:21 not accept any m.
Prov. 30:2 more brutish th. a. m.
Is. 52:14 more marred th. a. m.
Jer. 44:26 in month of any m.
Ezek. 9:6 come not near any m.
Dan. 6:7 ask petition of a. m. 12
10:7, 5:40 if any m. see thee
11:27 nor know. a. m. the Fat.
12:19 nor sh. a. m. hear voice
16:24 if any m. will come after me, Luke 9:23
21:3 if a. m. say aught to you
Mark 11:3; Luke 19:31
22:16 nor carest thou for a. m.
46 nor durst any m. fr. th. day
24:23 if any m. say, Lo here is Christ, Mark 13:21
Mark 1:44 say nothing to a. m.
4:23 if a. m. hath ears to hear,
7:16; Rev. 13:9
5:4 neit. could a. m. tame him
9:30 not that a. m. she. knew it
Luke 14:26 if a. m. come to me
19:8 taken any thing from a. m.
John 4:33 hath a. m. bro. aught
6:46 not th. a. m. hath seen F.
51 if any m. eat of this bread
7:17 if a. m. do his will know
37 a. m. thirst, let him come
10:9 by me if any m. enter in
11:57 if a. m. knew where he were
12:26 if any m. serve me
47 if any m. hear my words
18:31 be no loss of a. m. 8. 22
27:22 be no loss of a. m. 8. of C.
Rom. 8:9 if a. m. ha. not 8. of C.
14 a. m. work; 15 work burn.
18 if a. m. am. you seem. wise
8:2 if a. m. love God, 11:34 hunger
10:28 if a. m. say this is offered
10:29 if a. m. not used to it
2 Cor. 5:17 if any m. be in Chr.
10:7 if any m. trust to himself
12:6 lest a. m. sho. think of me
Gal. 1:9 if a. m. pre. other gosp.
Eph. 2:9 lest any m. should boa.
1 Thes. 5:15 for evil to any m.
2 Thes. 3:8 nor eat a. m.'s bread
Heb. 4:11 a. m. fall after same
10:38 if any m. draw back
13:16 a. m. full of grace of God
Jam. 1:13 nor tempteth any m.
1 Pet. 4:11 if any m. speak
1 John 2:1 if a. m. sin, ha. advo.
15 love not the world
4:1 believe not any m. teach
Rev. 3:20 if a. m. hear my voice
22:18 if a. m. add to these thin.
19 if any m. take away words

Any MAN.

Gen. 34:15 nor shall a. m. kn. her

CRUDEN'S CONCORDANCE.

MAN
Deut. 22:22 *m.* found lying with w. both *m.* th. lay with the w. and w.
1 *Sam.* 15:3 slay both *m.* and w.
27:9 left neither *m.* nor w. alive
1 *Chr.* 10:3 dealt to *m.* and w.
2 *Chr.* 15:13 not seek L. *m.* or w.
Jer. 44:7 cut off *m.* w. and child.
51:22 break in pieces *m.* and w.
1 *Cor.* 11:3 head of the w. is *m.*
7 *woman* is the glory of the *m.*
8 *m.* is not of w, but w. of *m.*
11 nor is *m.* without w. in L.
12 as w. is of *m.* so is *m.* by w.
1 *Tim.* 5:16 any *m.* or w. ha. wi.

Young MAN.
Gen. 4:23 slain y. *m.* to my hurt
18:7 Abraham gave it to a y. *m.*
41:12 there was with us a y. *m.*
Num. 11:27 ran y. *m.* and to. M.
Deut. 22:25 des. y. *m.* and virgin
Jud. 17:12 y. *m.* bec. his priest
1 *Sam.* 9:2 S. was a choice y. *m.*
17:58 whose son art thou, y. *m.*
30:13 I am *young m.* of Egypt
2 *Sam.* 1:5 said to *young m.* 13
14:21 bring y. *m.* Absal. again
18:5 deal gently with the y. *m.*
29 is y. *m.* Absalom safe? 32
32 enemies of lord be as y. *m.*
1 *K.* 11:28 Solomon seeing y. *m.*
2 *K.* 6:17 L. opened eyes of y. *m.*
9:4 the y. *m.* went to Ramoth
1 *Chr.* 12:28 Zadok, a *young m.*
2 *Chr.* 36:17 no compas. on y. *m.*
Ps. 119:9 sh. y. *m.* cleanse way?
Prov. 1:4 to y. *m.* knowledge
7:7 y. *m.* void of understanding
Ec. 11:9 rej. O y. *m.* in youth
Is. 62:5 as y. *m.* marrieth virgin
Jer. 51:22 break y. *m.* and maid
Mat. 19:20 *young m.* said
Mark 14:51 follow, certain y. *m.*
16:5 y. *m.* sitting on right side
Luke 7:14 y. *m.* I say to thee
Acts 7:58 clothes at y. *m.*'s feet
20:9 there sat in window a y. *m.*
23:17 bring y. *m.* to captain, 18
22 captain let the y. *m.* depart

MANAEN. *Acts* 13:1

MANASSEH.
Gen. 41:51 called first-born M.
48:5 two sons M. and Eph. 20
2 *K.* 20:21 M. reign. 2 *Chr.* 33:33
21:9 M. seduced th. to do ev. 16
24:3 sins of M. took came upon
2 *Chr.* 32:11 M. among thorns
19 M. knew that Lord was G.
Ps. 60:7 M. mine, 80:2; 108:8
Is. 9:21 M. shall eat Ephraim

Tribe of MANASSEH.
Num. 1:35 of *tribe of* M. 32,200
Jos. 4:12 the half *t. of* M. passed
13:7 and half *tribe of* M.
17:1 lot for M. 20:8; 22:10
1 *Chr.* 5:18 half *t.* M. 6:70; 12:31
26:32 G. half *tribe of* M. 27:21
Rev. 7:6 *t. of* M. sealed 12,000

MANDRAKES.
Gen. 30:14 Reuben found *m.*
15 wouldest take my son's *m.* ?
he sh. lie wi. thee for s.'s *m.*
16 hired thee with my son's *m.*
Cant. 7:13 *m.* give a smell

MANEH. *Ezek.* 45:12

MANGER.
Luke 2:7 and laid him in a *m.*
12 shall find him lying in *m.*
16 found the babe lying in. *m.*

MANIFEST.
Ec. 3:18 with that God might *m.* them
John 14:21 *m.* myself to him
22 *m.* thyself to us
Acts 4:16 miracle. *m.* to all at J.
Rom. 1:19 kn. of G. is *m.* in th.
1 *Cor.* 3:13 *m.* counsels of hearts
15:27 It is *m.* he is excepted
2 *Cor.* 2:14 makes *m.* the savor
Gal. 5:19 works of flesh are *m.*
Phil. 1:13 bonds in Christ are *m.*
Col. 4:4 that I may make it *m.*
2 *Thes.* 1:5 a *m.* token of righte.
1 *Tim.* 3:16 God was *m.* in flesh
5:25 good works of some are *m.*
2 *Tim.* 3:9 body be *m.* to all *m.*
Heb. 4:13 no creat. that is not *m.*
1 *Pet.* 1:20 was *m.* in these times
1 *John* 3:10 children of G. are *m.*

See MADE.

MANIFESTATION.
Rom. 8:19 for *m.* of sons of God
1 *Cor.* 12:7 *m.* of S. giv. to man
2 *Cor.* 4:2 *m.* of truth commend.

MANIFESTED.
Mark 4:22 hid wh. sh. not be *m.*
John 2:11 and *m.* forth his glory
17:6 *m.* thy name unto men
Rom. 3:21 righteous. of G. is *m.*
Tit. 1:3 in due time *m.* his word
1 *John* 3:5 *m.* to take away our sins
4:9 in this was *m.* love of God

MANIFESTLY.
2 *Cor.* 3:3 *m.* declared to be epi.

MANIFOLD.
Neh. 9:19 *m.* mercies forsook.
27 *m.* mercies gavest them.
Ps. 104:24 how *m.* are works
Amos 5:12 I kn. your *m.* transg.
Luke 18:30 not receive *m.* more
Eph. 3:10 known *m.* wisd. of G.
1 *Pet.* 1:6 through *m.* temptatio.
4:10 stewards of *m.* grace of G.

MANKIND.
Lev. 18:22 shall not lie with *m.*
20:13 man lie with *m.* as wom.
Job 12:10 in hand breath of *m.*
1 *Tim.* 1:10 law of them defile *m.*
Jam. 3:7 hath been tamed of *m.*

MANNA.
Ex. 16:15 they said, It is *m.*
35 Israel did eat *m.* 40 years
Num. 11:6 noth. besides this *m.*
7 *m.* was as coriander-seed
9 fell on camp, *m.* fell on it
Deut. 8:3 fed thee with *m.* 16;
Neh. 9:20; *Ps.* 78:24
Jos. 5:12 *m.* ceased, no more
John 6:31 fathers did eat *m.* 49
58 not as fathers did eat *m.*
Rev. 2:17 to eat of hidden *m.*

MANNER.
Gen. 25:23 two *m.* of peo. sepa.
Ex. 1:14 bitter in *m.* of service
12:16 no *m.* of work done in th.
21:9 *m.* of trespass, to. of lost
31:3 *m.* of workmansh. 5; 35:31,
33, 35; 36:1; 1 *Chr.* 28:21
Lev. 5:10 offer, ac. to *m.* *Nu.* 9:14
23:31 ye shall do no *m.* of work
24:22 one *m.* of law *Num.* 15:6
Num. 5:13 she be taken with *m.*
28:18 do no *m.* of servile work
Deut. 4:15 no *m.* of similitude
15:2 this is *m.* of the release
27:21 lieth wi. any *m.* of beast
Ruth 4:7 this *m.* in former time
1 *Sam.* 8:9 show *m.* of king. 11
10:25 Samuel told *m.* of kingd.
21:5 bread is in a *m.* common
2 Sam. 7:19 is this *m.* of man?
2 *K.* 1:7 what *m.* of man?
11:14 stood by pillar, as *m.* was
17:26 know not *m.* of G. of land
1 *Chr.* 23:29 for all *m.* of meas.
Est. 1:13 king's *m.* towards all
Ps. 107:18 abhor. all *m.* of meat
Cant. 7:13 all *m.* of pleas. fruits
Is. 5:17 lambs feed after their *m.*
Jer. 22:21 this hath been thy *m.*
Dan. 6:23 no *m.* of hurt found
Mat. 4:23 heal. all *m.* sickn. 10:1
5:11 say all *m.* of evil ag. you
8:27 what *m.* of man is this,
Mark 4:41; *Luke* 8:25
12:31 all *m.* of sin forg. to men
Mark 13:1 see what *m.* of ton.
Luke 1:29 what *m.* of salutation
66 what *m.* of child sh. th, be?
7:39 what *m.* of woman this
9:55 know not what *m.* of spirit
24:17 what *m.* of communicat. ?
John 19:40 as *m.* of J. is to bury
Acts 17:2 Paul, as his *m.* was
20:18 know wh. *m.* I have been
23:16 it is not *m.* of Romans
25:4 my *m.* of life from youth
2 *Cor.* 7:9 sorry after godly *m.*
1 *Thes.* 1:5 ye kn. what *m.* of *m.*
9 what *m.* of entering in we
Heb. 10:25 as the *m.* of some is
Jam. 1:24 forge, what *m.* of man
1 *Pet.* 1:11 wh, what *m.* of time
15 holy in all *m.* of conversa.
2 *Pet.* 3:11 what *m.* of persons
1 *John* 3:1 behold what *m.* of love
Rev. 11:5 in this *m.* be killed
22:2 which bare 12 *m.* of fruits

After the MANNER.
Gen. 18:11 with S. *m.* *m.* of wom.
19:31 come in unto us *a. t. m.*
Jud. 18:7 *a. t. m.* of Zidonians
Ez. 10:21 *a. t. m.* of E. 26; *Am.* 4:10
23:15 *a. t. m.* of Babylonians

MAN
Ezek. 23:45 *a. the m.* of adulter.
Mich 2:6 *a. the m.* of mriying J.
Acts 15:1 circumcised *a. t. m.* M.
Rom. 6:19 I speak *a. the m.* of men, 1 *Cor.* 15:32; *Gal.* 3:15
1 *Cor.* 11:25 *a.* same *m.* he took
Gal. 2:14 *a. the m.* of Gentiles

After this MANNER.
Mat. 6:9 *after this m.* pray ye
1 *Cor.* 7:7 one *a. this m.* and an.

See LIKE.

Lev. 20:23 not walk in *m.* of nat.
2 *K.* 17:34 do after former *m.*
Ezek. 11:12 after *m.* of heathens
Acts 13:18 40 years suff. their *m.*
1 *Cor.* 15:33 ev. com. co. good *m.*
Heb. 1:1 God in divers *m.* spake

MANOAH. *Jud.* 13:8, 21; 16:31

MANSIONS.
John 14:2 in Fa.'s ho. many *m.*

MANTLE, S.
Jud. 4:18 Jael cov. Sis, with *m.*
1 *Sam.* 28:14 covered with a *m.*
1 *K.* 19:13 Elijah wrapped in *m.*
19 *E.* cast his *m.* upon Elisha
2 *K.* 2:8 Elijah took *m.* smote
13 Elisha took Elijah's *m.* 14
Ezr. 9:3 I he. th. I rent my *m.* 5
Job 1:20 Job arose and rent *m.*
2:12 they rent every one his *m.*
Ps. 109:29 confusion, as with *m.*
Is. 3:22 I will take away the *m.*

MANY.
Gen. 17:4 thou sh. be a father of *m.* nations, 5; *Rom.* 4:17, 18
37:3 a coat of *m.* colors, 23, 32
32:10 pass, and *m.* perish
Num. 13:18 which, he few or *m.*
26:56 pos. divided between *m.*
35:8 from them have *m.* cities
Deut. 15:6 lend to *m.* nations, 28:12
31:17 *m.* evils shall befall, 21
1 Sam. 14:6 save by *m.* or few
1 *K.* 4:30 Judah and Is. were *m.*
7:47 they were exceeding *m.*
2 *Chr.* 14:11 no. to help with *m.*
Neh. 7:2 he feared God above *m.*
13:26 among *m.* nations no king
Ps. 3:1 *m.* are they that rise up
2 be *m.* that say of my soul, 4:6
25:19 mine enemies are *m.* 56:2
32:10 *m.* sor. shall be to wicked
31:19 *m.* are afflictions of right.
40:3 *m.* sh. see it and fear
55:18 for there were *m.* with me
Prov. 4:10 years of thy life be *m.*
10:21 lips of righteous feed *m.*
14:20 the rich hath *m.* friends
19:4 wealth maketh *m.* friends
Ec. 11:8 days of darkness be *m.*
Is. 5:3,12 he bare the sin of *m.*
Jer. 42:3 are left but few of *m.*
46:16 he made *m.* to fall
Lam. 1:22 for my sighs are *m.*
Ezek. 33:24 we are *m.* land given
Dan. 12:4 *m.* sh. run to and fro
Mat. 7:13 *m.* there be that go
24 *m.* will say to that day, L.
8:11 *m.* sh. come from east and
13:58 did not *m.* mighty works
19:30 *m.* first be last, *Mark* 10:31
20:16 *m.* called, few chos. 22:14
24:5 *m.* sh. co. in my name and
sh. dec. *m.* *Mark* 13:6; *Luke* 21:8
12 love of *m.* shall wax cold
26:28 my blood shed for *m.*
28:28 *m.* sh. he turn to Lord
Mark 5:1 fell and ri. eth. of Is. Israel
4:33 *m.* widows; 27 *m.* lepers
7:47 her sins *m.* are forgiven
John 6:9 are they among so *m.* ?
60 *m.* of his disciples said, 60
21:11 for all so *m.* net not brok.
Acts 9:13 I have heard by *m.*
19:19 *m.* bro. books and burnt
26:10 *m.* of saints did I shut up
Rom. 5:15 off. of *m.* many men *m.* offen.
12:5 be. *m.* are one body in Ch.
1 *Cor.* 1:26 not *m.* wise, not *m.*
4:15 yet have ye not *m.* fathers
Ruth at feet I *m.* own rebuked.
1 *Cor.* 6:5 mine that *m.* the bed
2 *K.* 3:19 *m.* good piece of land
Job 30:13 they *m.* my path, they
Jer. 13:9 thus I *m.* pride of Jud.

MARRED.
Is. 52:14 his visage was so *m.*
Jer. 13:7 girdle *m.* 12 s. *m.*
Nah. 2:2 and *m.* vine branches
Mark 2:22 the bottles will be *m.*

MAR
Heb. 7:23 they truly were *m.* pr.
9:28 Christ once bear sins of *m.*
11:12 spring of one so *m.* stars
Jam. 3:1 my brethren, be not *m.*

After MANY.
Ez. 23:2 speak in a cause to decline *after m.*

As MANY as.
Jud. 3:1 as *m.* as had not known
2 *Sam.* 2:23 as *m.* as came to pl.
2 *Chr.* 29:31 as *m.* as of free hea.
Mat. 22:9 as *m.* as ye find bid
Mark 6:56 as *m.* as touched him
Luke 11:8 as *m.* as he needeth
John 1:12 as *m.* as received him
Acts 2:39 to you as *m.* as L. shall call
36 as *m.* as ha. spoken foreto.
5:11 fear ca. on as *m.* as heard
36 as *m.* as obeyed him, 37
13:48 as *m.* as ordained to life
Rom. 2:12 as *m.* as have sinned
8:14 as *m.* as are led by Sp. of
Gal. 3:10 as *m.* as are of works
6:12 as *m.* as desire to make
16 as *m.* as walk to this rule
Phil. 3:15 let as *m.* as be perfect
Col. 2:1 as *m.* as not seen my fa.
1 *Tim.* 6:1 as *m.* servants as are
Rev. 2:24 as *m.* as have not this
3:19 as *m.* as I love I rebuke
13:15 as *m.* as are no. not worship

See DELIVERED, DAYS, NOW.

MANY people.
Deut. 2:21 p. great and *m.*
Jud. 7:2 p. too *m.* for; 4 too *m.*
2 *Sam.* 1:4 *m.* of the p. are fallen
Ezr. 10:13 p. are *m.* time of rain
Est. 8:17 *m.* p. of land bec. Jews
Ec. 2:3 *m.* *people* shall go
17:12 woe to multitude of *m.* p.
Ezek. 3:6 not to *m.* p. of strange
17:9 wither with. *m.* p. to pluck
32:9 I will vex hearts of *m.* p.
10 I will make *m.* p. amazed
38:9 and *m.* p. with thee, 15
Mic. 4:3 be shall judge am. *m.* p.
13 shalt beat in pieces *m.* p.
5:7 remnant of J. amidst *m.* p.
Zec. 8:22 *m.* p. come and seek L.
Rev. 10:11 must prop. bef. *m.* p.

MANY things.
Job 23:14 *m.* such *t.* are wi. him
Ec. 6:11 *m.* t. that incr. vanity
Is. 42:20 seeing *m.* t. but observ.
Mat. 13:3 spake *m.* t. in parables
16:21 and suffer *m.* *things*, *Mark* 8:31; 9:12; *Luke* 9:22; 17:25
25:21 ruler over *m.* *things*
27:19 I have suffered *m.* *things*
Mark 6:20 he did *m.* t. and heard
Luke 10:41 troubled about *m.* t.
John 8:26 have *m.* t. to say, 16:12
21:25 *m.* other t. wh. Jesus did
Acts 25:9 that I ought to do *m.* t.
26:9 I ver. thought to do *m.* t.
1 *Tim.* 3:4 suffer. so *m.* t. in vai.
Heb. 5:11 we have *m.* t. to say
2 *John* 12 *m.* t. to write to you, 3 *John* 13

MANY a time, s.
1 *K.* 22:16 how *m.* t. I adj. thee?
Neh. 9:28 *m.* times didst thou deliver them, *Ps.* 106:43
Ps. 78:39 *m.* a t. turned anger
129:1 *m.* a *t.* they afflicted me, 2

See WATERS.

MANY years.
Lev. 25:51 if th. be *m.* y. behind
Ezr. 5:11 house builded *m.* y.
Neh. 9:30 *m.* years didst forbear
Ec. 6:3 if a man live *m.* years
11:8 if a man live *m.* y. and rej.
Ez. 38:10 *m.* days and y. troubled
Ezek. 38:17 wh. prophesied *m.* y.
Zec. 7:3 weep as I done th. *m.* y.
Luke 12:19 goods laid up *m.* y.
15:29 these *m.* y. do I serve
Acts 24:10 been *m.* y. a judge
17 after *m.* y. I came to bring
Rom. 15:23 desire *m.* y. to come.

MAR.
Lev. 19:27 nor *m.* corn. of beard
1 *Sam.* 6:5 mice that *m.* the land
Rev. 13:9 thus I *m.* pride of Jud.

MARA. *Ruth* 1:20

CRUDEN'S CONCORDANCE. 939

MAR

MARAH.
Ex. 15:23 drink of wat. of M.
Num. 33:8 3 days, pitched in M.

MARAN-ATHA.
1 Cor. 16:22 him ho anath. m.

MARBLE.
1 Chr. 29:2 prepared m. in abun.
Est. 1:6 silver rings, pill. of m.
Cant. 5:15 his legs as pill. of m.
Rev. 18:12 ves. of m. no man buy.

MARCH.
Ps. 68:7 didst m. thro' wildern.
Jer. 46:22 shall m. with army
Joel 2:7 shall m. ev. one his ways
Hab. 1:6 m. thro' breadth of land
3:12 thou didst m. through land

MARCHED, ST.
Ex. 14:10 Egypt. m. after them
Jud. 5:4 thou m. earth trembled

MARCUS.
Col. 4:10 M. sister's son to Barn.
Phile. 24 M. saluteth, 1 Pet. 5:13

MARK.
Acts 12:12 John, surnam. M. 25
15:39 took M. sailed to Cyprus
2 Tim. 4:11 take M. bring him

MARK, Substantive.
Gen. 4:15 L. set a m. upon Cain
1 Sam. 20:20 as tho' I shot at m.
Job 7:20 why set me as a m. ag.
(thee? 16:12; Lam. 3:12
Ezek. 9:4 a m. on men that sigh
Phil. 3:14 press tow. m. for prize
Rev. 13:16 caused all to rec. a m.
17 none buy, save that had m.
14:9 any man rec. m. in foreh.
11 whosoever receiveth his m.
15:2 overimage, and over his m.
16:2 on them had m. of beast
19:20 deceived them that rec. m.
20:4 nor his m. they liv. wi. Ch.

MARK, Verb.
Ruth 3:4 thou shalt m. the place
1 K. 20:7 m. how this man seek.
22 m. and see what thou doest
Job 18:2 m. and we will speak
21:5 m. me and be astonished
33:31 m. well, O J. heark. to me
Ps. 37:37 m. the perfect man
48:13 m. well her bulwarks
56:6 they m. my steps
130:3 if thou shouldest m. iniq.
Ezek. 44:5 m. entering of house
Rom. 16:17 m. th. who cause div.
Phil. 3:17 m. them who walk so

MARKED.
1 Sam. 1:12 Eli m. her mouth
Job 22:15 hast thou m. old way ?
24:16 they had m. in daytime
Jer. 2:22 Iniquity is m. bef. me
23:18 m. his word and heard it
Luke 14:7 m. how they ch. rooms

MARKS.
Lev. 19:28 not print any m.
Gal. 6:17 I bear in body m. of L.

MARKEST.
Job 10:14 if I sin, thou m.
33:11 stocks, he m. all my paths
Is. 44:13 m. it out with compass

MARKET, S.
Ezek. 27:13 traded in m. 17, 19, 25
Mat. 11:16 children sitting in m.
20:3 others standing idle in m.
23:7 love greetings in the m.
Luke 11:43; 20:46
Mark 7:4 when they come fr. m.
12:38 love salutations in m.
Luke 7:32 child. sitting in m.-pl.
John 5:2 a pool by the sheep-m.
Acts 16:19 drew them into m.-p.
17:17 disputed in the m. daily.

MARRIAGE.
Ex. 21:10 duty of m. sh. he not
Ps. 78:63 maid, not given to m.
Mat. 22:2 king made m. for son
4 ready, come unto the m.
9 all ye find, bid to the m.
30 in resurrection not given in
m. Mark 12:25; Luke 20:35
21:38 given bi m. until day N.
25:10 ready went wi. him to m.
Luke 17:27 given in m. 20:34
John 2:1 a m. in Cana of Galilee
1 Cor. 7:38 giveth her in m.
Heb. 13:4 m. is honourable in all
Rev. 19:7 m. of Lamb is come
9 called to m. supper of Lamb

MARRIAGES.
Gen. 34:9 make ye m. with us
Deut. 7:3 nei. shalt thou make m.
Jos. 23:12 if ye make m.

MARRY.
Gen. 38:8 go to bro. wife, m. her

MAR

Num. 30:6 only to family of th.
father's tribe shall they m.
Deut. 25:5 wife of dead sh. not m.
Is. 62:5 so shall thy sons m.
Mat. 5:32 m. her that is divorced
19:9; Mark 10:11
19:10 be so, it is not good to m.
22:24 brother shall m. his wife
30 nei. m. nor given in marri.
Mark 12:25; Luke 20:35
1 Cor. 7:9 cannot cont. let them
m. better to m. than to burn
36 he sinneth not, let them m.
1 Tim. 4:3 forbidding to m. and
5:11 wax wanton, they will m.
14 younger wom. m. bear chil.

MARRIED.
Gen. 19:14 to them th. m. daugh.
Ex. 21:3 m. wife go out wi. him
Lev. 22:12 if m. to a stranger
Num. 12:1 E. woman he had m.
36:3 if m. to sons of other tribes
Deut. 22:22 lying with wom. m.
1 Chr. 2:21 m. wh. sixty years old
Neh. 13:23 m. wives of Ashdod
Prov. 30:23 odious wh. she is m.
Is. 54:1 more of desolate than m.
62:4 thy land shall be m.
Jer. 3:14 turn, for I am m. to you
Mal. 2:11 m. dau. of strange god
Mat. 22:25 first when he had m.
Mark 6:17 for he had m. her
10:12 m. another com. adultery
Luke 14:20 m. a wife, can, come
17:27 they drank, they m. wives
Rom. 7:3 husband liv. she be m.
1 Cor. 7:10 to the m. I command
33 but he that is m. careth for
34 she that is m. car. for thin.
39 to be m. to whom she will

MARRIETH.
Is. 62:5 as young man m. virgin
Mat. 12:9 m. her is put away,
doth com. adult. Luke 16:18

MARRYING.
Neh. 13:27 in m. strange wives
Mat. 24:38 m. giving in marriage

MARINERS.
Ezek. 27:8 inha. of Zidon thy m.
9 ships of sea with their m.
27 m. fall into midst of seas
29 m. come down fr. th. ships
Jon. 1:5 the m. were afraid

MARROW.
Job 21:24 bones moisten. with m.
Ps. 63:5 soul satisfied as wi. m.
Prov. 3:8 health and m. to bones
Is. 25:6 feast of things full of m.
Heb. 4:12 divi. asund. of j. and m.

MARSHES.
Ezek. 47:11 miry places and m.

MARS-HILL. Acts 17:22

MART.
Is. 23:3 she is a m. of nations

MARTHA.
Luke 10:38 a woman named M.
40 M. was cumbered, 41
John 11:1 town of M. 11:5, 19, 20

MARTYR, S.
Acts 22:20 blood of thy m. Step.
Rev. 2:13 Anti. was faithful m.
17:6 drunken with blood of m.

MARVEL, S.
Ex. 34:10 m. as have not been
1 Chr. 11:14 so m. Satan transf.

MARVEL.
Ec. 5:8 m. not at the matter
Mark 5:20 and all men did m.
John 5:20 that ye may m.
28 m. not at this, hour is com.
7:21 done one work, and ye m.
Acts 3:12 Is. why m. ye at this ?
Gal. 1:6 I m. that ye are so soon
1 John 3:13 m. not if world hate
Rev. 17:7 where'f. didst thou m. ?

MARVELLED.
Gen. 43:33 men m. one at anoth.
Ps. 48:5 saw it, and so they m.
Mat. 8:10 Jesus heard it, he m.
27 but the men m. saying
9:8 m. and glorified God, 33
22:22 they m. at him, Mark
12:17 ; Luke 20:26
27:14 govern. m. Mark 15:5, 44
Mark 6:6 m. because of unbelief
Luke 1:21 m. he tarried so long
63 name is John, they m. all
2:33 Joseph and his mother m.
7:9 when J. heard, he m. at him
John 4:27 m. he talked wi. wom.
7:15 Jews m. how knoweth thi
Acts 2:7 m. are not th. Gallileans
4:13 m. took knowled. of them

MAS

MARVELLOUS.
Job 5:9 who doeth m. things
10:16 thou showest thyself m.
Ps. 17:7 show m. loving-kinds.
31:21 showed me m. kindness
78:12 m. things did he in sight
98:1 he hath done m. things
118:23 it is m. in our eyes, Mat.
21:42; Mark 12:11
Dan. 11:36 speak m. things
Mic. 7:15 show unto him m. thi.
Zec. 8:6 he m. in mine eyes ?
John 9:30 herein is a m. thing
1 Pet. 2:9 called you into m. light
Rev. 15:1 ano. sign great and m.

MARVELLOUS work, **s.**
1 Chr. 16:12 remo. his m. works,
Ps. 105:5
24 declare m. w. amo. nations
139:14 great and m. are thy w.
Is. 29:14 m. w. and a wonder,
Rev. 15:3

MARVELLOUSLY.
2 Chr. 26:15 he was m. helped
Job 10:6 greet M. beste. labor
Hab. 1:5 beh. regard, wonder m.

MARY.
Mat. 1:16 Joseph husband of M.
13:55 called M. Mark 6:3; 16:1
Luke 1:27 virgin's name was M.
2:5 with M. his wife, 16, 19
10:42 M. hath cho. John 11:1, 20
John 12:3 M. took pound of oint.
19:25 M. stood by cross, 20:16
Acts 1:14 conti. in prayer, wi. M.
12:12 Peter came to house of M.
Rom. 16:6 greet M. beste. labor

MARY Magdalene.
Mat. 27:56 amo. wh. were M. M.
61; Mark 15:40; John 19:25
28:1 came M. M. John 20:1
Mark 16:1 M. M. brought spices,
Luke 24:10
John 20:18 M. M. told disciples

MASONS.
2 Sam. 5:11 Hiram sent to David
m. 1 Chr. 14:1
2 K. 12:12 gave money to m.
1 Chr. 22:2 set m. to hew stones
2 Chr. 24:12 hired m. to rep. hou.

MASSAH.
Ex. 17:7 place M. Deut. 33:8
Deut. 6:16 tempted in M. 9:22

MAST, S.
Prov. 23:34 lieth on top of a m.
Is. 33:23 could not strength. m.
Ezek. 27:5 cedars to make m.

MASTER.
Gen. 39:20 m. put Jos. in prison
Ex. 21:8 she pleased not her m.
22:8 m. of the house be brought
Jud. 19:22 spake to m. of house
1 Sam. 25:17 determined ag. m.
26:16 ye have not kept your m.
2 Sam. 2:7 your m. Saul is dead
1 K. 22:17 The Lord said, These
have no m. 2 Chr. 18:16
2 K. 2:3 alas m. it was borrowed
2:3 drink, and go to their m.
10:2 seeing your m. sons
6 take heads of your m. sons
19:6 say to your m. Is. 37:6
1 Chr. 15:27 Chenan. m. of song
Dan. 1:3 king spake to the m.
Mal. 1:6 if I be m. wh. fear ?
2:12 the Lord will cut off m.
Mat. 8:19 m. I will follow thee
9:11 why eat. your m. wi. pub. ?
10:25 if they have called m. Be.
12:38 m. we would see a sign
17:24 doth not your m. pay tri. ?
22:16 m. we know that thou art
true, Mark 12:14
24:45 whom his m. made ruler
26:18 m. saith, Time is at hand
25 Judas said, m. Is it I ?
49 hail m. kissed, Mark 14:45
Mark 5:35 why troubl. thou m. ?
9:17 good m. I brought my son
10:17 good m. what shall I do ?
Luke 10:25
12:35 ye know not wh. m. com.
Luke 7:40 m. say ; 8:24 perish
8:49 thy daughter is dead, trou.
13:25 when m. of house is risen
John 8:4 m. this woman was
11:28 m. is come and call. for th.
13:13 ye call me m. ye say well
14 I your m. washed your feet

MAT

Acts 27:11 centurion believed m.
Eph. 6:9 m. is in heaven, Col. 4:1

His MASTER.
Gen. 24:9 hand un. thigh of h. m.
39:2 Jos. was in house of his m.
Ex. 21:4 if h. m. given him wife
Deut. 23:15 thou sh. not deliv. to
his m. serv. escaped fr. h. m.
Jud. 19:11 servant said to h. m.
1 Sam. 25:10 serv. break fr. h. m.
29:4 reconcile himself to his m.
2 K. 5:1 Naaman great wi. h. m.
6:32 sound of h. m. feet behind ?
9:31 had Zi. peace, slew h. m. ?
19:4 his m. hath sent to re-
proach God. Is. 37:4
1 Chr. 12:19 he will fall to h. m.
Job 3:19 servant free from h. m.
Prov. 27:18 that waiteth on h. m.
30:10 accuse not a serv. to h. m.
Is. 1:3 ass knoweth his m. crib
Mal. 1:6 a serv. honoreth his m.
Mat. 10:24 disciple is not above
his m. Luke 6:40
25 that disciple be as h. m.
Luke 6:40 ev. one perf. as h. m.
Rom. 14:4 to h. m. he standeth

My MASTER.
Gen. 24:12 my m. Abrah. 14:65
39:8 my m. wotteth not what is
Ex. 21:5 scr. say, I love my m.
1 Sam. 24:6 God forbid I do this
to my m. 10
30:13 my m. left me bec. I fell
2 K. 5:18 my m. goeth into house
20 my m. hath spared Naaman
6:15 my m. how shall we do ?
10:9 I conspired against my m.
Mat. my m. sent me to thy
master ? Is. 36:12
Is. 36:8 give pledges to my m.

Thy MASTER.
Gen. 24:51 be thy m. son's wife
1 Sam. 29:10 rise early wi. t. m.
2 Sam. 9:9 I give t. m. all that S.
12:8 t. m. house, t. m. wives
16:3 where is thy m. son ?
2 K. 2:3 will take away t. m. 5
9:7 shalt smite house of t. m.
18:27 master sent me to thy m.

MASTER-BUILDER.
1 Cor. 3:10 as wise m.-b. I have

MASTERS.
Ex. 21:4 children sh. be her m.
Ps. 123:2 eyes of serv. look to m.
Prov. 25:13 refresheth soul of m.
Amos 4:1 say to m. let us drink
Zep. 1:9 fill m. houses with vnl.
Mat. 6:24 no man can serve two
m. Luke 16:13
23:10 neither be ye called m.
Acts 16:16 brought m. much gain
Eph. 6:5 be obedient to m. Col.
3:22; Tit. 2:9; 1 Pet. 2:18
9 ye, m. do the same things
unto them, Col. 4:1
1 Tim. 6:1 count their m. worthy
2 they that have m. not despise
Jam. 3:1 not many m. knowing

MASTERY, IES.
Ex. 32:18 them that shout for m.
Dan. 6:24 lions had m. of them
1 Cor. 9:25 strive. for the m.
2 Tim. 2:5 if a man strive for m.

MATE.
Is. 34:15 every vult. with her m.
16 none shall want her m.

MATRIX.
Ex. 13:12 all that open m. 15
34:19 all that open m. is mine
Num. 3:12 inst. of first-b. op. m.
18:15 ev. thing th. open m. thi.

MATTAN. 2 K. 11:18 ; 2 Chr.
23:17

MATTATHIAS. Luke 3:25

MATTER.
Gen. 24:9 aware concerning m.
30:15 Is it small m. th. hu. tak.
Ex. 18:16 have m. come to me
22 ev. great m. they shall bring
26 ev. small m. judged thems.
23:7 keep thee far fr. false m.
Num. 16:49 died about m. of C.
25:18 beguiled you in m. of 1.
31:16 caus. trespass to m. of P.
Deut. 3:26 sp. no more to me of
this m. 17:8 hard m. 19:15
22:26 thou sh. do nothing to m.
Ruth 3:18 know how m. will fall
1 Sam. 10:16 of the m. of kingd.
20:23 m. thou and I spoken of
2 Sam. 1:4 how went the m. ?
18:13 i un. in. fald wrought
20:18 ended m. 21 m. not so
1 K. 8:59 let m. of his servant
15:5 save only in the m. require
2 Chr. 30:22 every co. pert. to m.

MEA

1 *Chr.* 27:1 served king in any *m.*
2 *Chr.* 8:15 departed not from any *m.*
24:5 the *m.* they hastened not
Ezr. 5:5 till *m.* came to Darius
Neh. 6:13 have *m,* for evil report
Est. 2:23 inquisition made of *m.*
Job 19:28 seeing root of the *m.*
32:18 answer, I am full of *m.*
Ps. 45:1 heart inditing good *m.*
64:5 encourage them. In evil *m.*
Prov. 11:13 spirit concealeth *m.*
16:20 that handleth a *m.* wisely
17:9 repeat. *m.* separateth frien.
18:13 answereth *m.* bef. heareth
25:2 honor of kings to search *m.*
Ec. 10:20 hath wings tell *m.*
12:13 hear conclusion of *m.*
Jer. 38:27 *m.* was not perceived
Dan. 2:10 not a man can sh. *m.*
7:28 hitherto is the end of *m,*
9:23 understand *m,* and consid.
Mark 10:10 discl. asked same *m.*
Acts 13:6 elders consider this *m.*
18:14 said, If it were *m.* of wro.
19:38 if Demetrius have a *m.*
24:22 I will know uttenn. of *m.*
1 *Cor.* 6:1 dare any having a *m.*
2 *Cor.* 9:5 as a *m.* of bounty
Gal. 2:6 maketh no *m.* to me
Jam. 3:5 how gr. a *m.* little fire

This MATTER.
Deut. 3:26 speak no more of *t. m.*
32:26 stay, neighbour so is *th. m.*
1 *Sam.* 30:24 hearken in *this m.*
2 *Sam.* 19:42 angry for *this m.* ?
Ezr. 5:5 concerning *this m.*
10:4 *this m.* belongeth to thee
9 people trembling bec. of *t. m.*
Est. 9:26 concerning *this m.*
Dan. 1:14 M. consented in *t. m.*
3:16 not careful to ans. in *t. m.*
Acts 8:21 nei, part nor lot in *t. m.*
17:32 hear thee again of *this m.*
2 *Cor.* 7:11 yoursel. clear in *t. m.*

MATTERS.
Ex. 24:14 if any have *m.*
1 *Sam.* 16:18 prudent in *m.*
2 *Sam.* 11:19 end of telling *m.*
15:3 see *m.* are good and right
19:29 speakest any more of *m.* ?
2 *Chr.* 19:11 Ama. over you in *m.*
Neh. 11:24 all *m.* concerning peo.
Est. 3:4 Mord.'s *m.* would stand
9:31 the *m.* of the fastings, 32
Job 33:13 giv. not account of *m.*
Ps. 35:20 deceitful *m.* ag. them
131:1 nor exercise myself in *m.*
Dan. 1:20 in *m.* of wisd. he found
7:1 and told the sum of the *m.*
Mat. 23:23 omitted weightier *m.*
Acts 16:15 no judge of such *m.*
19:39 any thing come. other *m.*
25:20 he judged of these *m.*
1 *Cor.* 6:3 judge the smallest *m.*
1 *Pet.* 4:15 busybody in men's *m.*
MATTHEW. *Mat.* 9:9; 10:3;
Mark 3:18; *Luke* 6:15; *Acts* 1:13
MATTHIAS. *Acts* 1:23, 26
MATTOCK, S.
1 *Sam.* 13:20 sharpen axe and *m.*
21 they had a file for the *m.*
2 *Chr.* 34:6 did Josiah with th. *m.*
Is. 7:25 hills be digged with *m.*
MAUL.
Prov. 25:18 false witness, is a *m.*
MAW.
Deut. 18:3 to priest 2 ch. and *m.*
MAZZAROTH. *Job* 38:32
MEADOW, S.
Gen. 41:2 and they fed in a *m.*
Jud. 20:33 out of *m.* of Gibeah
MEAL.
Num. 5:15 ephah of barley *m.*
2 *K.* 4:41 *m.* cast it into pot
1 *Chr.* 12:40 nigh brought *m.*
Is. 47:2 millstones, grind *m.*
Hos. 8:7 bud shall yield no *m.*
See BARREL, MEASURES.
MEAL-TIME.
Ruth 2:14 at *m.-t.* come hither
MEAN, Verb.
Ex. 12:26 *m.* ye by this service ?
Deut. 6:20 what *m.* testimonies ?
Jos. 4:6 what *m.* th. stones ? 21
Is. 3:15 what *m.* ye that ye beat
Ezek. 17:12 what this, *m.* ye ?
18:2 what *m.* ye that use prov. ?
Mark 9:10 wh. ris. fr. dead *m.* ?
Acts 10:17 what vision sho. *m.*
17:20 know what th. things *m.*
21:13 what *m.* ye to weep and
2 *Cor.* 8:13 I *m.* not that oth. men

MEA

MEAN, Adjective.
Prov. 22:29 not stand bef. *m.* men
Is. 2:9 *m.* man boweth down
5:15 *m.* man shall be bro. down
31:8 sw. not of *m.* man devour
MEAN time.
Luke 12:1 *m. t.* gath. multitude
MEAN while.
1 *K.* 18:45 *m. w.* heaven black
John 4:31 *m. w.* disciples prayed
Rom. 2:15 thoughts *m. w.* accus.
MEANEST, ETH.
Gen. 33:8 what *m.* thou by this ?
Deut. 29:24 what *m.* this anger ?
1 *Sam.* 4:6 wh. *m.* this shout ? 14
15:14 what *m.* this bleating ?
2 *Sam.* 16:2 what *m.* thou by these ? *Ezek.* 37:18
Jon. 1:6 wh. *m.* thou, O sleep. ?
Mat. 9:13 learn what that *m.*
18:7 if ye had kn. what this *m.*
Acts 2:12 saying, What *m.* this ?
MEANING, Substantive.
Dan. 8:15 D. had sought for *m.*
1 *Cor.* 14:11 if I know not the *m.*
MEANING.
Acts 27:2 *m.* to sail by coa. of A.
MEANS.
Ex. 34:7 will by no means clear the guilty, *Num.* 14:18.
Jud. 5:22 broken by *m.* of pran.
16:5 by what *m.* may prevail
2 *Sam.* 14:14 doth he devise *m.*
1 *K.* 20:39 if by any *m.* be miss.
Jer. 5:31 priests bear rule by *m.*
Mat. 1:19 hath been by your *m.*
Mat. 5:36 by no *m.* come out
Luke 5:18 sought *m.* to bring
10:19 nothing by any *m.* hurt
John 9:21 by what *m.* he seeth
Acts 4:9 by what *m.* he is whole
18:21 must by all *m.* keep feast
Rom. 1:10 any *m.* I mi. journey
11:14 if by any *m.* this flesh)
9:22 I might by all *m.* save
27 by any *m.* when I preached
2 *Cor.* 1:11 by *m.* of many
11:3 lest by any *m.* as serpent
Gal. 2:2 lest by any *m.* I sho. run
1 *Thes.* 3:5 lest by some *m.*
2 *Thes.* 2:3 no man dec. by any *m.*
3:16 peace always by all *m.*
Heb. 9:15 by *m.* of death called
MEANT.
Gen. 50:20 God *m.* it unto good
Luke 15:26 asked what these *m.*
18:36 passed, asked what it *m.*
MEASURE.
Ex. 26:2 curtains sh. ha. one *m.* 8
Lev. 19:35 do not unright. in *m.*
Deut. 25:15 just *m.* sh. th. have
1 *K.* 6:25 cub. one *m.* 7:37 bases
K. 7:1 a *m.* of fine flour, 16, 18
Job 11:9 the *m.* thereof is longer
28:25 weigheth the waters by *m.*
Ps. 39:4 to know *m.* of my days
80:5 tears to drink in great *m.*
Is. 5:14 hell opened without *m.*
27:8 in *m.* when it shoot. forth
40:12 com. dust of earth in *m.*
Jer. 30:11 I cor. thee in *m.* 46:28
51:13 *m.* of thy covetousness
Ezek. 4:11 drink water by *m.* 16
Mic. 6:10 scant *m.* abominable
Mat. 7:2 with what *m.* you mete
Mark 4:24; *Luke* 6:38
23:32 fill ye up *m.* of your fath.
Mark 6:51 amazed beyond *m.*
Luke 6:36 good *m.* pressed down
John 3:34 G. giveth not Sp. by *m.*
Rom. 12:3 dealt to every man *m.*
2 *Cor.* 1:8 were pressed out of *m.*
10:13 not boast of things with. our *m.* but acco. to *m.* 14, 15
11:23 in stripes above *m.*
12:7 lest I be exalted above *m.*
Gal. 1:13 beyond *m.* I persecuted
Eph. 4:7 according to *m.* of Ch.
13 to the *m.* of the stature
16 working in *m.* of every part
Rev. 6:6 *m.* of wheat for penny
21:17 according to *m.* of a man
MEASURE, Verb.
Num. 35:5 *m.* from without city
Deut. 21:2 they shall *m.* to cities
Is. 65:7 I will *m.* their for. work
Ezek. 43:10 let them *m.* pattern
Rev. 11:1 and *m.* temple of God
21:15 a golden reed to *m.* city
MEASURED.
Ruth 3:15 *m.* six meas. of barley
2 *Sam.* 8:2 *m.* with a line
Is. 40:12 who *m.* wat. in hand ?

MEA

Jer. 31:37 heaven ab. can be *m.*
33:22 sand of sea cannot be *m.*
Ezek. 40:5 he *m.* the breadth of building, 6, 8, 9, 11, 13, 24
41:5 he *m.* wall ; 13 *m.* house
15 *m.* the length of building
42:16 he *m.* east with a measu.
17 *m.* north ; 18 south ; 19 west
Hos. 1:10 sand of sea not be *m.*
Hab. 3:6 he stood and *m.* earth
Rev. 21:16 *m.* city ; 17 *m.* wall
MEASURES.
Gen. 18:6 three *m.* of fine meal
Deut. 25:14 not have divers *m.*
1 *K.* 4:22 Solo.'s provision 30 *m.* of flour, and 60 *m.* of meal
5:11 gave Hir. 20,000 *m.* wheat.
20 *m.* of pure oil, 2 *Chr.* 2:10
18:32 would contain 2 *m.* seed
2 *Chr.* 23:26 for all manner of *m.*
Ezr. 7:22 hundred *m.* of wheat
Job 38:5 hath laid *m.* thereof ?
Prov. 20:10 divers *m.* abo. to L.
Jer. 13:25 is portion of thy *m.*
Ezek. 40:24 accord. to these *m.* 29
28 gate according to th. *m.* 32
Hag. 2:16 a heap of twenty *m.*
Mat. 13:33 like unto leaven hid in three *m.* meal, *Luke* 13:21
Luke 16:6 a hundred *m.* of oil
7 he said, A hundred *m.* wheat
See BARLEY.
MEASURING.
Jer. 31:39 *m.* line shall go forth
Ezek. 40:3 man with *m.* reed, 5
42:16 with *m.* reed, 17, 18, 19
Zec. 2:1 with *m.* line in hand
2 *Cor.* 10:12 *m.* thems. by them.
MEAT.
Gen. 1:29 to you it sh. be for *m.*
30 I have given ev. herb for *m.*
9:3 ev. moving thing sh. be *m.*
27:31 E. also made savory *m.*
Lev. 22:11 he that is born in his house shall eat of his *m.*
25:6 land shall be *m.* for you, 7
Deut. 3:6 ye sh. buy *m.* of them
28 shalt sell me *m.* for money
20:20 destroy trees not for *m.*
Jud. 1:7 kings gathered their *m.*
14:14 of eater came forth *m.*
1 *Sam.* 20:5 not fall to sit at *m.*
2 *Sam.* 11:8 follow, a mess of *m.*
12:3 it did eat of his own *m.*
1 *K.* 10:5 she saw the *m.* of his table, 2 *Chr.* 9:4
19:8 he went in strength of *m.*
1 *Chr.* 12:40 were nigh bro. *m.*
Ezr. 3:7 gave *m.* and drink
Job 6:7 ref. are as sorrowful *m.*
12:11 doth not mouth taste *m.* ?
20:14 *m.* in bowels is turned
33:20 soul abhorreth dainty *m.*
34:3 as the mouth tasteth *m.*
36:31 giveth *m.* in abundance
38:41 wander for lack of *m.*
Ps. 42:3 tears have been my *m.*
44:11 given us like sheep for *m.*
59:15 wand. up and down for *m.*
69:21 gave me gall for my *m.*
74:14 gavest him to be *m.* to p.
78:18 tempted G. by asking *m.*
25 he sent them *m.* to the full
30 while *m.* was in mouths
104:21 yo. lions seek *m.* fr. God
27 mayest give them their *m.*
107:18 soul abhorreth all *m.*
145:15 givest them *m.* in season
Prov. 6:8 ant provideth her *m.*
30:22 a fool when filled with *m.*
31:15 giveth *m.* to household
Is. 62:8 no more gi. *m.* to enem.
65:25 be bread and dust his *m.*
Lam. 1:11 pleasant things for *m.*
19 elders died wh. they sou. *m.*
Ezek. 4:10 *m.* shall be by weight
16:19 my *m.* which I gave thee
29:5 I have given thee for *m.* to beasts, 34:5, 8
34:10 may not be *m.* for them
47:12 trees for *m.* fruit for *m.*
Dan. 1:8 not defile hims. with *m.*
4:12 in it was *m.* for all, 21
11:26 th. feed of *m.* sh. destroy
Hos. 11:4 I laid *m.* unto them
Joel 1:16 is not the *m.* cut off ?
Hab. 1:16 portion is fat, *m.* plen.
3:17 the fields shall yield no *m.*
Mat. 3:4 and his *m.* was locusts
6:25 life more th. ? *Lu.* 12:23
9:10 as Jesus sat at *m.* in house, 26:7 ; *Mark* 2:15 ; 14:3 ; 16:14 ; *Luke* 24:30

MED

Mat. 10:10 wor. worthy of his *m.*
15:37 the broken *m. Mark* 8:8
24:45 *m.* in due seas. *Luke* 12:42
25:35 hungered, ye gave me *m.*
42 hungered, gave me no *m.*
Luke 3:11 he that hath *m.*
8:55 commanded to give her *m.*
14:10 worship in presence of th. that sit at *m.*
17:7 will say, Sit down to *m.*
22:27 greater, he that sit. at *m.*
24:41 here any *m.* ? *John* 21:5
John 4:8 discl. gone to buy *m.*
32 I have *m.* to eat ye know
34 my *m.* is to do will of him
6:27 labor not for the *m.* which perisheth, but for that *m.*
55 for my flesh is *m.* indeed
Acts 2:46 eat their *m.* with glad.
9:19 when he had received *m.*
27:33 besou. them to take *m.* 34
Rom. 14:15 grie. wi. thy *m.* dest. not with *m.* for wh. C. died
17 kingdom of God not *m.*
20 for *m.* dest. not work of G.
1 *Cor.* 3:2 with milk, not wi. *m.*
8:8 *m.* commend. us not to G.
10 if any man see thee sit at *m.*
13 if *m.* make brother offend
10:3 did eat same spiritual *m.*
Col. 2:16 no man judge you in *m.*
Heb. 5:12 milk, not strong *m.*
12:16 for *m.* sold his birthright
See FATTED.
MEAT-OFFERING.
Ex. 29:41 according to *m.-o.*
Lev. 2:1 offer a *m.-o.* 4, 5, 7, 14
6:14 this is law of *m.-o.* 7:37
Num. 4:16 to Eleazar daily *m.-o.*
15:6 for *m.-o.* two tenth deals of flour, 28:9, 13
Jer. 22:25 altar to offer *m.-o.*
Jud. 13:19 took kid with *m.-o.*
1 *Chr.* 21:23 wheat for the *m.-o.*
Ezek. 42:13 there they lay *m.-o.*
44:20 they shall eat the *m.-o.*
46:5 *m.-o.* he an ephah for ram
7 *m.-o.* an eph. for bullock, 11
Joel 1:9 the *m.-o.* is cut off
13 the *m.-o.* is withholden
2:14 over a *m.-o.* to our God
MEAT-OFFERINGS.
Jos. 22:29 build altar for *m.-o.*
1 *K.* 8:64 Solomon offered *m.-o.*
Neh. 13:5 where they laid *m.-o.*
Jer. 33:18 nor want kindle *m.-o.*
Ezek. 45:17 priu. part give *m.-o.*
Amos 5:22 though ye offer *m.-o.*
MEATS.
Prov. 23:6 nei. desire dainty *m.*
Acts 15:29 abstain fr. *m.* offered
1 *Cor.* 6:13 *m.* for belly, belly *m.*
1 *Tim.* 4:3 to abstain from *m.*
Heb. 9:10 which stood only in *m.*
13:9 estab. with grace, not *m.*
MEDAD. *Num.* 11:26
MEDAN. *Gen.* 25:2
MEDDLE.
Deut. 2:5 *m.* not that of mount S.
19 *m.* not with child. of Am.
K. 14:10 why *m.* to thy hurt ?
2 *Chr.* 25:19
Prov. 20:19 *m.* not with him
24:21 *m.* not fr. given to change
MEDDLED, ETH.
Prov. 17:14 contention bef. it *m.*
26:17 *m.* strife bef not belonging
MEDDLING.
2 *Chr.* 35:21 forbear fr. *m.* with G.
Prov. 20:3 every fool will be *m.*
MEDE, S.
2 *K.* 17:6 in cities of M. 18:11
Ezr. 6:2 in province of M.
Est. 1:19 among laws of M.
Is. 13:17 will stir M. *Jer.* 51:11
Dan. 5:28 king. is given to M.
6:8 law of M. 12 ; 9:1 ; 11:1
MEDIA.
Est. 1:3 of Persia and M. 14, 18
10:2 book of kings of M.
Dan. 8:20 two horns kings of M.
MEDIATOR.
Gal. 3:19 angels in hand of *m.*
20 a *m.* is not a *m.* of one
1 *Tim.* 2:5 is but one *m.* Jesus
Heb. 8:6 of a better covenant
9:15 he is *m.* of New Testament
12:24 J. *m.* of the new covenant
MEDICINE, S.
Prov. 17:22 doeth good like a *m.*

MEE

Jer. 30:13 thou hast no heal. *m.*
46:11 in vain thou use many *m.*
Ezek. 47:12 the leaf sh. be for *m.*

MEDITATE.
Gen. 24:63 Isaac went out to *m.*
Jos. 1:8 *m.* therein day and nig.
Ps. 1:2 doth *m.* day and night
63:6 *m.* on th. in night watches
77:12 I will *m.* of all thy work
119:15 I *m.* in thy precepts, 78
23 serv. *m.* in thy statutes, 48
148 I might *m.* in thy word
143:5 I *m.* on all thy works
Is. 33:18 thy heart sh. *m.* terror
Luke 21:14 settle it not to *m.*
1 *Tim.* 4:15 *m.* upon these things

MEDITATION.
Ps. 5:1 give ear, consider my *m.*
19:14 let *m.* of heart be accept.
49:3 *m.* of heart sh. be of under.
104:34 *m.* of him shall be sweet
119:97 love thy law, it is my *m.*
99 thy testimonies are my *m.*

MEEK.
Num. 12:3 Moses was very *m.*
Ps. 22:26 *m.* sh. eat and be satis.
25:9 *m.* will he guide in judgm.
37:11 *m.* shall inherit the earth
76:9 God arose to save all *m.*
147:6 the Lord lifted up the *m.*
149:4 beautify *m.* with salvation
Is. 11:4 for the *m.* of earth
29:19 *m.* shall increase their joy
61:1 good tidings to the *m.*
Amos 2:7 turn aside way of *m.*
Zep. 2:3 seek L, ye *m.* of earth
Mat. 5:5 blessed are the *m.*
11:29 for I am *m.* and lowly
21:5 thy king cometh to thee *m.*
1 *Pet.* 3:4 ornament of a *m.* spirit

MEEKNESS.
Ps. 45:4 because of truth and *m.*
Zep. 2:3 seek *m.* ye shall be hid
1 *Cor.* 4:21 sh. I come in sp. of *m.*?
2 *Cor.* 10:1 beseech by *m.* of Chr.
Gal. 5:23 fruit of the Spirit is *m.*
6:1 restore in the spirit of *m.*
Eph. 4:2 with lowliness and *m.*
Col. 3:12 put on *m.* long-suffer.
1 *Tim.* 6:11 love, patience, *m.*
2 *Tim.* 2:25 in *m.* instruct. those
Tit. 3:2 showing *m.* to all men
Jam. 1:21 receive with *m.* word
3:13 works with *m.* of wisdom
1 *Pet.* 3:15 reason of hope wi. *m.*

MEET, Adjective.
Gen. 2:18 make a help *m.* for him
20 not found help *m.* for Adam
Ex. 8:26 it is not *m.* so to do
Deut. 3:18 all that are *m.* for war
Jud. 5:30 *m.* for necks of them
Job 34:31 it is *m.* to be said to G.
Prov. 11:24 withhol. more th. *m.*
Jer. 26:14 do wi. *m.* as seem. *m.*
27:5 to whom it seemed *m.*
Ezek. 15:4 is it *m.* for any work
5 less shall it be *m.* for work
Mat. 3:8 fruits *m.* for repentance
15:26 not *m.* to take children's
bread, *Mark* 7:27
Acts 26:20 works *m.* for repent.
Rom. 1:27 recomp. wh. was *m.*
1 *Cor.* 15:9 not *m.* to be called
15:4 if it be *m.* that I go also
Col. 1:12 made us *m.* to be part.
2 *Thes.* 1:3 thank God, as it is *m.*
Heb. 6:7 herbs *m.* for them
2 *Pet.* 1:13 think *m.* to stir you

MEETEST.
2 *K.* 10:3 look out the *m.* of

MEET, Verb.
Gen. 24:65 walketh to *m.* us?
32:6 *E.* cometh to *m.* thee, 33:4
46:29 Joseph went up to *m.* Is.
Ex. 4:14 Aaron com. to *m.* thee
27 go into wilderu. to *m.* Mos.
18:7 M. went to *m.* faith.-in-law
19:17 bro. people to *m.* with G.
25:22 there I will *m.* with thee,
29:42, 43; 30:6, 36; *Num.* 17:4
Num. 23:15 while I *m.* Lord
Jos. 2:16 lest pursuers *m.* you
9:11 take victuals, go *m.* them
Jud. 11:31 out doors to *m.* me
31 daughter came to *m.* him
14:5 lion roared *m.* against him
2 4:18 *m.* company of proph.
18:6 women came to *m.* Saul
23:22 Lord sent thee to *m.* me
2 *Sam.* 6:20 Michal came to *m.* D.
1 *K.* 2:8 Shimei came down to *m.*
18:16 Obadiah went to meet A.
21:18 go down to *m.* Ahab
2 *K.* 1:3 go up to *m.* messengers
7 man came up to *m.* you?

MEM

2 *K.* 2:15 sons of prop. came to *m.*
4:26 run, I pray thee, to *m.* her
29 if *m.* any man, sal. him not
8:8 and go, *m.* the man of God
9 so Hazael went to *m.* him
9:17 take horseman, send to *m.*
Neh. 6:2 let us *m.* together, 10
Job 5:14 *m.* darkness in daytime
39:21 goeth to *m.* armed men
Prov. 7:15 came I forth to *m.*
17:12 bear robbed of whelps *m.*
22:2 rich and poor *m.* together
29:13 the poor and deceit. man
m. together
Is. 7:3 go forth to *m.* Ahaz
14:9 hell is moved to *m.* thee
34:14 beasts of desert shall *m.*
47:3 I will not *m.* him
Jer. 51:31 one post run to *m.* an.
Amos 4:12 prepare to *m.* thy G.
Zec. 2:3 angel went out to *m.*
Mat. 8:34 city came out to *m.* J.
25:1 went forth to *m.* bridegro.
6 bridegro. com. go to *m.* him
Mark 14:13 there shall *m.* you a
man, *Luke* 22:10
Luke 14:31 ten thou. to *m.* him
Acts 28:15 came to *m.* us as far
1 *Thes.* 4:17 in clouds to *m.* Lord

MEETEST, ETH, ING.
Gen. 32:17 E. my brother *m.* thee
Num. 35:19 when he *m.* him, 21
1 *Sam.* 21:1 afraid at *m.* of Dav.
Is. 1:13 iniq. even solemn *m.*
64:5 thou *m.* him that rejoiceth

MEGIDDO.
Jud. 5:19 fought by wat. of M.
1 *K.* 9:15 raised a levy build M.
2 *K.* 9:27; 23:30; 2 *Chr.* 35:22
MEGIDDON, *Zec.* 12:11
MEHETABEL, *Gen.* 36:39
MEHUJAEL, *Gen.* 4:18
MELCHI, *Luke* 3:24

MELCHISEDEK.
Gen. 14:18 M. bro. forth bread
Ps. 110:4 order of M, *Heb.* 5:10
Heb. 7:1 M. priest of God, 10, 21
MELITA, *Acts* 28:1

MELODY.
Is. 23:16 make sweet *m.* sing
51:3 found therein, voice of *m.*
Amos 5:23 not hear *m.* of viols
Eph. 5:19 making *m.* to Lord

MELONS.
Num. 11:5 we remember the *m.*

MELT.
Ex. 15:15 inhabit. of Canaan *m.*
Jos. 2:11 our hearts did *m.*
14:8 bret. made heart of peo. *m.*
1 *Sam.* 17:16 heart of Him, ul. *m.*
Ps. 58:7 let them *m.* away
Is. 13:7 every man's heart shall
m. Ezek. 21:7
10:1 heart of Egypt shall *m.*
Jer. 9:7 behold, I will *m.* them
Ezek. 22:20 to *m.* it, I will leave
13 the hills shall *m. Nah.* 1:5
2 *Pet.* 3:10 elem. *m.* with heat, 12

MELTED.
Ex. 16:21 sun waxed hot it *m.*
Jos. 5:1 heard that th. hearts *m.*
7:5 the hearts of the people *m.*
Jud. 15:5 mountains *m.* bef. Lord
1 *Sam.* 14:16 multitude *m.* away
Ps. 22:14 heart in the midst of
me is *m.*
46:6 uttered voice, the earth *m.*
97:5 the hills *m.* like wax
107:26 soul *m.* bec. of trouble
Is. 34:3 mountains *m.* wi. blood
Ezek. 22:21 ye in the midst thereof
22 as silver is *m.* in furnace

MELTETH.
Ps. 58:8 as a snail which *m.* let
68:2 wax *m.* so let wicked peri.
119:28 my soul *m.* for heaviness
147:18 sendeth out word *m.* th.
Jer. 6:29 the founder *m.* in vain
Nah. 2:10 heart of Nineveh *m.*

MELTING.
Jam. 64:2 as when *m.* fire burns

MEMBER.
Deut. 23:1 his privy *m.* cut off
1 *Cor.* 12:14 body is not one *m.*
19 all one *m.* where were hu.?
26 one *m.* suffer, one *m.* honor.
Jam. 3:5 the tongue is a little *m.*

MEMBERS.
Job 17:7 my *m.* are as a shadow
Ps. 138:16 in book all *m.* written
Mat. 5:29 one of *m.* sh. perish, 30
Rom. 6:13 let. your *m.* instrum.
7:5 sins did work in our *m.*

MEN

Rom. 7:23 see ano. law in *m.* wa.
12:4 many *m.* in one body
5 every one *m.* one of another
1 *Cor.* 6:15 your bodies *m.* of C.
12:12 the body hath many *m.*
18 but now hath G. set the *m.*
20 but now are they many *m.*
26 all the *m.* suffer with it
27 are the body of Ch. and *m.*
Eph. 4:25 are *m.* one of another
5:30 we are *m.* of his body
Col. 3:5 mortify your *m.* on ear.
Jam. 3:6 tongue one of our *m.*
4:1 lusts that war in your *m.*

MEMORIAL.
Ex. 3:15 *m.* unto all generations
17:14 wri. this for a *m.* in book
28:12 for stones of *m.* to Israel
39 be for a *m.* before the L. 30:7
30:16 money may be for a *m.*
Lev. 23:24 a *m.* of blowing trumpets, *Num.* 10:10
24:7 frankinc. on bread for *m.*
Num. 5:15 it is an offering of *m.*
16 offering of *m.* in her hands
16:40 brazen censers a *m.* to Is.
31:54 gold of captains for *m.*
Jos. 4:7 th. stones sh. be for *m.*
Neh. 2:20 have no portion nor *m.*
Est. 9:28 nor *m.* of them perish
Ps. 9:6 th. *m.* perished with th.
135:13 *m.* through. all generat.
Hos. 12:5 L. of hosts; L. is his *m.*
Zec. 6:14 the crowns be for a *m.*
Mat. 26:13 this be told for a *m.*
of her, *Mark* 14:9
Acts 10:4 prayers come up for *m.*

MEMORY.
Ps. 109:15 cut off *m.* of them
145:7 utter *m.* of thy goodness
Prov. 10:7 *m.* of the just blessed
Ec. 9:5 *m.* of them is forgotten
Is. 26:11 made their *m.* to perish
1 *Cor.* 15:2 keep in *m.* I preach.

MEMUCAN, *Est.* 1:14, 16, 21
MEMPHIS, *Hos.* 9:6

MEN.
Gen. 4:26 began *m.* to call on L.
6:1 when *m.* began to multiply
18:2 lo, three *m.* by him
19:4 *m.* of the city, *m.* of Sodom
32:28 power with God and *m.*
34:21 these *m.* are peaceable
42:11 true *m.* 31; 43:16 bring
46:32 *m.* are shepherds
Ex. 1:17 saved *m.* children, 18
10:11 ye th. *m.* serve the Lord
31:23 thrice in year *m.* children
Num. 13:32 *m.* of great stature
14:14 put out eyes of these *m.*
20 these *m.* die the death of all
Deut. 1:35 not one of these *m.*
shall see good land
33:6 let R. liv. not his *m.* he few
Jud. 6:27 he feared *m.* of city
1 *Sam.* 2:33 and *m.* of *m.* a woman
1 *Sam.* 2:26 favor with L. and *m.*
10:12 play the *m.* for our people
19:26 dead *m.* before the king
23:3 raiseth over *m.* must be just
30 slew two lion-like *m.* of
Moab, 1 *Chr.* 11:22
2 *Chr.* 6:18 will God dw. wi. *m.*?
Ps. 9:20 kn. thems. to be but *m.*
17:14 from *m.* wh. are thy hand
82:7 but ye shall die like *m.*
Is. 7:13 *m.* thing to weary *m.*?
31:3 now the Egyptians are *m.*
38:16 O L. by th. things *m.* live
Jer. 5:1 any *m.* that exec. judgm.
Lam. 3:39 these *m.* sons of Bel.
Mic. 7:6 man's enemies are *m.*
Heb. 1:14 naked *m.* as fishes
Mat. 7:12 whatsoe. ye would *m.*
should do to you, *Luke* 6:31
10:32 conf. me bef. *m. Luke* 12:8
13:25 *m.* slept, enemy came
16:13 *m.* say I am? *Mark* 8:27
Mark 8:24 *m.* as trees walking
Luke 20:6 stone split, with *m.* it is
impossible, *Luke* 18:27
Luke 2:14 good will toward *m.*
6:26 when all *m.* speak of you
12:8 so wh. *m.* have committed,
18:11 I am not as other *m.* are
22:58 thou art one of them
Acts 1 thou hast not lied unto *m.*
20 to obey God rather than *m.*
5:4 thou hast not lied unto *m.*
29 we ought to obey God rather than *m.*
10:28 cometh upon you, ye *m.*
14:11 *m.* are come down to us in
15 we are *m.* of like passions
21:16 void of offe. tow. G. and *m.*
27:10 hurt with damage of *m.*
Rom. 1:27 *m.* with *m.* working
1 Cor. 4:3 ape. to angels and *m.*
14:2 for he speaketh not to *m.*

1 *Cor.* 14:21 with *m.* of other to.
2 *Cor.* 8:13 not that other *m.* be
Gal. 6:7 L. not to *m.* Col. 3:23
1 *Thes.* 2:4 speak not as plea. *m.*
Heb. 6:16 for *m.* verily swear
7:8 *m.* that die receive tithes
9:27 is appointed to *m.* once to
12:23 spir. of just *m.* made perf.
Jam. 3:9 therewith curse we *m.*
1 *Pet.* 4:6 judged according to *m.*
2 *Pet.* 1:21 holy *m.* of G. spake
Rev. 9:4 only those *m.* wh. have
21:3 tabernacle of G. is with *m.*

All MEN.
Ps. 89:47 made all *m.* in vain
116:11 I sa, in haste, a. *m.* liars
Ez. 7:2 that is the end of all *m.*
Zec. 8:10 set a. *m.* ag. neighbor
Luke 6:26 woe wh. a. *m.* speak
John 5:23 all *m.* sh. honor the S.
12:32 will draw all *m.* unto me
Rom. 5:12 death pas. upon a. *m.*
18 judgment came on all *m.* to
condemnation, the free gift
came on all *m.* to justificat.
12:17 honest in sight of all *m.*
18 live peaceably with all *m.*
1 *Cor.* 7:7 I would all *m.* were as
9:19 for tho' I be free fr. all *m.*
15:19 we are of all *m.* most mis.
2 *Cor.* 3:2 kn. and read of all *m.*
Gal. 6:10 let us do good to all *m.*
1 *Thes.* 2:15 contrary to all *m.*
5:15 follow wh. is good to all *m.*
2 *Thes.* 3:2 all *m.* have not faith
1 *Tim.* 2:1 giving tha. for a. *m.*
4 will have all *m.* to be saved
4:10 trust in God, Sa. of all *m.*
2 *Tim.* 2:24 be gentle to all *m.*
4:16 no man stood, all *m.* forso.
Tit. 2:11 grace of G. ap. to all *m.*
Heb. 12:14 peace with all *m.*
Jam. 1:5 ask of G. th. giv. all *m.*
1 *Pet.* 2:17 honor all *m.* love bro.
3 *John* 12 D. good rep. of all *m.*
See BRETHREN, CHIEF, CHILDREN, CHOSEN, EVIL, GREAT.

In MEN.
1 *Cor.* 3:21 no man glory in *m.*
See ISRAEL, JUDAH.

Like MEN.
1 *Sam.* 4:9 your. l. *m.* 1 *Cor.* 16:13
Ps. 82:7 ye shall die like *m.*
Hos. 6:7 they *l. m.* trans. cove.
Luke 12:36 *l. m.* that wait for L.

Mighty MEN.
Gen. 6:4 *m.* wh. were of old
Jos. 1:14 *m. m.* of valor sh. pass
8:3 Joshua ch. out 30,000 *m. m.*
1 *Sam.* 2:4 bows of *m. m.* broken
2 *Sam.* 16:6 *m. m.* on his right
17:8 *m. m.* that they may be *m.*
23:8 these be names of *m. m.*
16 *mighty m.* brake host, 17
1 *K.* 1:8 *m. m.* not with Adonij.
10 *m. m.* and Sol. he called not
K. 15:20 exact. of *m. m.* of valor
24:14 carri. away *m. m.* of valor
1 *Chr.* 5:24 and were *m. m.* of
valor, 7:7, 9, 11, 40
12:1 they were among the *m. m.*
21 *m. m.* submitted to Dav.
2 *Chr.* 13:3 *m.* set battle against
Abijah, being *mighty m.* of
valor, 14:8; 17:13, 14, 16
25:6 Amaz. hired 100,000 *m. m.*
32:3 Il. took counsel with *m. m.*
21 angel cut off all the *m. m.*
Neh. 11:14 their brethren *m. m.*
Job 34:24 break in pieces *m. m.*
Ec. 7:19 wisdom strength. *m. m.*
Is. 21:17 *m. m.* shall be diminish.
Jer. 5:16 they are all *mighty m.*
49:9 *m. m.* come; 48:14 we are
48:41 the hearts of *m. m.* of M.
49:2 heart of *mighty m.* of Ed.
50:36 a sword is upon her *m. m.*
51:30 *m. m.* of Babylon forbear.
56 her *m. m.* are taken
57 drunk captains and *m. m.*
Lam. 1:15 L. hath trodden *m. m.*
Ezek. 39:20 at table with *m. m.*
Dan. 3:20 commanded *m. m.*
19 prepare war, wake up *m. m.*
Ob. 9 thy *m. m.* O Teman
Nah. 2:3 shield of his *mighty m.*
Zec. 10:5 they shall be as *m. m.*
Rev. 6:15 *m. m.* hid themselves
19:18 ye may eat flesh of *m. m.*

MEN-PLEASERS.
Eph. 6:6 eye-servants as *m.-p.*
Col. 3:22

CRUDEN'S CONCORDANCE. 943

MER

Zec. 7:9 execute judgm. s. m.
Luke 1:58 L. s. great m. on her
10:37 that showed m. on him
Rom. 9:16 but of God that s. m.
Jam. 2:13 that hath s. no m.

Thy MERCY.

Gen. 19:19 hast magnified t. m.
Ex. 15:13 in t. m. led forth peo.
Num. 14:19 greatness of thy m.
Neh. 13:22 according to thy m.
Ps. 3:7 in multitude of thy m.
6:4 return, O Lord, save me for thy m.'s sake, 31:16
13:5 I have trusted in thy m.
25:7 accor. to thy m. remem. me
31:7 I will rejoice in thy m.
33:22 let thy m. O L. be upon us
36:5 t. m. O L. is in the heavens
44:26 redeem us for t. m.'s sake
57:10 thy m. is great to heavens
59:16 I will sing aloud of thy m.
69:13 in multitude of thy m.
85:7 show us t. m. 86:13 great
90:14 O satisfy us with thy m.
94:18 t. m. O Lord, held me up
108:4 thy m. is great above hea.
109:21 because thy m. is good
26 according to thy m.
115:1 for t. m. and truth's sake
119:64 earth is full of thy m.
124 deal wi. servant ac. to t. m.
138:8 thy m. endureth for ever
143:12 of t. m. cut off mine ene.

MERCIES.

Gen. 32:10 not worthy of thy m.
2 Sam. 24:14 for his m. are great,
1 Chr. 21:13
2 Chr. 6:42 remember m. of Dav.
Neh. 9:19 in m. forsook. th. not
27 according. to thy m. thou gav.
31 m. didst not consume them
Ps. 51:1 thy m. blot out transg.
63:13 in multitude of thy m.
16 according to thy tender m.
89:1 I will sing of the m. of L.
106:7 remembered not thy m.
45 repented accord. to his m.
119:41 let thy m. also come
Is. 54:7 with m. will I gather
55:3 sure m. D. of. Acts 13:31
63:15 where is thy m. tow. me?
Jer. 16:5 taken away my m.
42:12 I will show m. unto you
Lam. 3:22 of L.'s m. we are not
32 compassion according to m.
Dan. 2:18 m. concerning this
9:9 to the L. our God belong m.
18 not for righteous. but m.
Zec. 1:16 I am returned with m.
Rom. 12:1 I bes. you by m. of G.
2 Cor. 1:3 Father of m. and God
Phil. 2:1 if there be any fellow-ship, any bowels of m.
Col. 3:12 put on bowels of m.

Tender MERCIES.

Ps. 25:6 remem. thy t. m. 51:1
40:11 withhold not thy ten. m.
77:9 in anger shut up his t. m.
79:8 thy tender m. prevent us
103:4 L. crown. thee with t. m.
119:77 thy t. m. come unto me
156 great are thy ten. m. O L.
145:9 t. m. over all his works
Prov. 12:10 t. m. of wicked cruel

MERCIFUL.

Gen. 19:16 Lord being m. to Lot
Ex. 34:6 L. G. m. and gracious
Deut. 4:31 the L. G. is m. 7:9
32:43 and will be m. to his land
2 Sam. 22:26 with m. thou wilt show thyself m. Ps. 18:25
1 K. 20:31 kings of Is. m. kings
2 Chr. 30:9 L. G. gracious and m.
Neh. 9:17 ready to pardon and m.
Ps. 26:11 redeem me, and be m. to me, 41:4, 10; 56:1; 57:1; 86:3; 119:58, 132
37:26 He righteous is ever m.
59:5 be not m. to any wicked
67:1 G. be m. to us, and bl. us
103:8 Lord is m. and gracious
117:2 his m. kindness is great
119:76 m. kindness for my com.
Prov. 11:17 m. man doeth good
Is. 57:1 m. men are taken away
Jer. 3:12 I am m. saith the Lord
Joel 2:13 he is gracious and m.
Mat. 5:7 m. shall obtain mercy
Luke 6:36 be m. as your F. is m.
18:13 God be m. to me a sinner
Heb. 2:17 be a m. high-priest.
8:13 be m. to their unright.

MERCIAH.

Zec. 17:7 called name of place M.

MES

Num. 20:13, 24 ; Deut. 32:51 ; 33:8
Ps. 81:7 proved thee at wat. M.

MERODACH. Jer. 50:2
MERODACH-BALADAN. Is. 39:1
MEROM. Jos. 11:5, 7
MEROZ. Jud. 5:23

MERRY.

Gen. 43:34 drank and were m.
Jud. 9:27 trode grapes, made m.
16:25 their hearts were m.
19:6 and let thy heart be m.
Ruth 3:7 Boaz's heart was m.
1 Sam. 25:36 Nabal's heart m.
2 Sam. 13:28 when Amnon is m.
1 K. 4:20 Judah and Isr. were m.
21:7 and let thy heart be m.
2 Chr. 7:10 sent people away m.
Est. 1:10 heart of king was m.
Prov. 15:13 m. heart ma. cheerf.
15 m. heart ha. continual feast
17:22 a m. heart doeth good
Ec. 8:15 better to eat and be m.
9:7 drink wine with m. heart
10:19 laughter, wine maketh m.
Is. 24:7 the m. hearted do sigh
Jer. 30:19 voi. of th. th. make m.
31:4 dances of th. that make m.
Luke 12:19 cat, and be m.
15:23 and be m. 24 ; 29 I might
32 it was meet we should be m.
Jam. 5:13 is any m. ? sing paul
Rev. 11:10 rejoice and make m.

MERRILY.

Est. 5:14 go in m. with king

MESCHECH.

Gen. 10:2 M. son of Japheth,
1 Chr. 1:5, 17
Ps. 120:5 I sojourn in M.
Ezek. 38:1 ag. chief prince of M.

MESOPOTAMIA.

Gen. 24:10 Eliezer went to M.
Deut. 23:4 hired M. ag. M. Jud. 3:8
1 Chr. 19:6 hire chari. out of M.
Acts 2:9 dwellers in M. we hear
7:2 G. appeared to Abra. in M.

MESS, ES.

Gen. 43:34 sent m. to them, Benjamin's m.
2 Sam. 11:8 Uriah a m. from king

MESSAGE.

Jud. 3:20 I have m. from God
1 K. 20:12 Benhad. heard this m.
Prov. 26:6 sendeth m. by fool
Hag. 1:13 spake Hag. in L.'s m.
Luke 19:14 citiz. sent m. aft. him
1 John 1:5 m. we ha. heard, 3:11

MESSENGER.

Gen. 50:16 sent a m. to Joseph
1 K. 19:2 Jezebel sent m. to Elij.
22:13 the m. went to call Micaiah, 2 Chr. 18:12
2 K. 5:32 ere the m. came to him
6:32 see, came to take m. but
Job 1:14 there came a m. to Job
33:23 if there be m. interpreter
Prov. 13:17 m. fall. into mischief
17:11 cruel m. shall be sent
25:13 faithful m. to them that
Is. 42:19 so my m. that I sent ?
Jer. 51:31 one m. run to meet
Ezek. 23:40 to wh. a m. was sent
Hag. 1:13 Haggai, the Lord's m.
Mal. 2:7 he is m. of L. of hosts
3:1 send my m. of covenant, Mat. 11:10 ; Mark 1:2 ; Luke 7:27
2 Cor. 12:7 m. of Satan to buffet
Phil. 2:25 companion, your m.

MESSENGERS.

Gen. 32:3 Jacob sent m. to Esau
Num. 22:5 Balak sent m. to Bal.
Jos. 2:1 Rahab hid the m. 3:5
1 Sam. 19:11 Saul sent m. 20
25:14 David sent m. to salute
2 Sam. 3:26 sent m. to D. on his behalf
8:12 sent m. to D. on his behalf
5:11 11. sent m. to D. (Chr. 14:1
11:4 Dav. sent m. to Bathsheba
12:27 Joab sent m. to David
2 K. 1:3 meet the m. of Ahaziah
17:4 Hoshea had sent m. to So
19:23 m. th. hast reproached L.
1 Chr. 19:2 m. to comfort Hanun
2 Chr. 36:15 L. sent them by m.
16 they mocked the m. of God
Prov. 16:14 wrath of king as m.
Is. 14:32 answer m. of nation ?
18:2 go ye swift m. to a nation
37:14 letter from m. and read it
41:26 performeth counsel of m.
57:9 didst send thy m. afar off
Jer. 27:3 send by hand of the m.
Ezek. 23:16 sent m. into Chaldea

MID

Ezek. 30:9 m. go forth from me
Nah. 2:13 voice of m. no more
Luke 7:24 m. of John were gone
9:52 and sent m. before his face
2 Cor. 8:23 m. of the churches
Jam. 2:25 Rahab had receiv. m.

MESSIAH.

Dan. 9:25 from commandment to build Jerus. unto the M.
26 after 62 weeks M. be cut off
John 1:41 found M. wh. is Christ
4:25 I know that M. cometh

MET.

Gen. 32:1 angel of God m. him
33:8 by this drove I m. ?
Ex. 3:18 God of the Hebrews m. with us, 5:3
4:24 L. m. him, sought to kill
27 Aaron went and m. Moses
5:20 they m. Moses and Aaron
Num. 23:4 God m. Balaam, 16
1 Sam. 10:10 prophets m. Saul
1 K. 13:24 was gone, lion m. him
Ps. 85:10 mercy and tru. m. tog.
Prov. 7:10 m. him a woman
Amos 5:19 and a bear m. him
Mat. 8:28 m. him two devils
Mark 11:4 place wh. two ways m.
Luke 9:37 much people m. him.
John 12:18
17:12 m. him ten men lepers
John 11:20 Martha m. him, 30
27:41 a place where two seas m.
Heb. 7:1 m. Abraham returning

In the MIDST.

Gen. 2:9 tr. of life in t. m. 3:3
15:10 A. divided them in t. m.
Ex. 8:22 I am L. in t. m. of earth
14:20 dry land in m. 15:19
33:3 I will not go up in m.
Num. 2:17 tabern. in va. of camp
35:5 shall be in m. Ezek. 48:15
Deut. 11:3 acts he did in m. of E.
23:11 God walketh in t. m.
Jos. 3:17 in m. of Jordan, 4:10
7:21 hid in the m. of my tent
2 Sam. 18:14 in the m. of oak
4 K. 6:20 were in m. of Samaria
1 Chr. 12:4 garments in the m.
Neh. 4:11 till we come in the m.
Ps. 22:14 in the m. of bowels
22 I m. t. m. of the congregation will I praise thee, Heb. 2:12
40:8 God is in the m. of me
102:24 take not away in m. of d.
110:2 rule in m. of enemies
138:7 I walk in m. of trouble
Prov. 4:21 keep th. in m. heart
5:14 all evil in m. of congrega.
8:20 in the m. of paths of judg.
14:33 is in m. of fools is folly
23:34 lieth down in the m.
Ec. 6:5 in th' m. of a people
7:6 set a king in the m. of it
12:6 great is the Holy One in the m. of thee, Jer. 11:9
10:23 blessing in t. m. of land
17:11 in m. of his days
Lam. 4:13 blood of just in m.
Ezek. 5:5 set in m. of nations
6:7 shall fall in m. of you, 11:7
17:16 in m. of Babylon shall die
22:20 in the m. of my house
43:7 I will dw. in t. m. of Is. 9
Dan. 3:25 walking in m. of fire
Joel 2:27 I am in the m. of Israel
Mic. 6:14 cast. down shall be m.
Nah. 3:13 in m. of thee are wo.
Hab. 3:2 in the m. of the years
Zep. 3:5 L. is in the m. righteous
12 leave in the m. a poor people
15 Lord is in the m. of thee
Zec. 2:5 glory in the m. of her
10 will dwell in m. of thee, 11
8:3 dwell in the m. of Jerus. M
Mat. 18:2 sheep in m. of wolves
14:31 ship was in the m. of sea
Mark 3:3 stand forth in the m.
18:2 little child in m. Mark 9:36
Luke 2:40 a temple was rent in m.
21:21 Jesus himself stood in m.
24:36 Jesus himself stood in m.
John 19:18 and Jesus in the m.
Rev. 1:13 in m. of th. four beasts
5:6 in m. of throne Lamb, 7:17

Into the MIDST.

Ex. 14:16 ch. Is. shall go into t. m.
33:5 I will come into t. m. of
Ps. 57:6 t. m. whereof they are
Jer. 21:4 assemble th. t. m. of cl.
51:63 cast it into th. m. of river
Ezek. 8:1 cast them i. m. of fire
15:4 will gather you into m.
of Jerusalem

CRUDEN'S CONCORDANCE.

MIDST.
Out of the MIDST.
Ex. 3:4 o. of m. of bush, 24:16
Deut. 4:12 L. spake out of the m.
   of fire, 15:33, 36; 5:4, 22, 24
34 take nation out of m. of an.
Jos. 4:3 out of m. of Jordan, 8
Is. 21:16 cometh out of m. of pit
52:11 depart, go out of the m. of
   her, Jer. 50:8; 51:6, 45
Ezek. 11:7 forth out of m. of it
29:4 br. thee out of m. of rivers
32:21 sp. to him o. of m. of hell
Zep. 3:11 away out of m. of thee

MIDWIFE, VES.
Gen. 35:17 m. said unto Rachel
38:28 m. bound on hand a thread
Ex. 1:16 when ye do the office of
   a m. 17, 19, 20, 21

MIGHT, Substantive.
Gen. 49:3 lte. first-born, my m.
Num. 14:13 this people in thy m.
Deut. 3:24 do according to thy m.
6:5 love thy God with all thy m.
8:17 m. of my hand gotten weal.
28:32 be no m. in thy hand
Jud. 5:31 sun goeth forth in m.
6:14 go in thy m. 16:30 bowed
1 Sam. 6:14 D. danced with all m.
2 K. 23:25 J. turned to L. wi. m.
24:16 king bro. cap. men of m.
1 Chr. 12:8 men of m. came to D.
29:2 I prepared house with m.
12 in thy hand is power and m.
2 Chr. 20:6
2 Chr. 20:12 have no m. ag. this
Est. 10:2 Ahasue. power and m.
Ps. 76:5 none of the men of m.
145:6 speak of m. of thy acts
Ec. 9:10 find. do it with thy m.
Is. 11:2 m. shall rest on him
33:13 ye that acknow. my m.
40:26 call. them by great. of m.
29 to them that have no m.
Jer. 9:23 nor let man glory in m.
10:6 thy name is great in m.
16:21 cause th. to know my m.
49:35 break chief of their m.
51:30 their m. hath failed
Ezek. 32:30 ashamed of their m.
Dan. 2:20 wisdom and m. are his
23 O G. who hast given me m.
4:30 built by m. of my power
Mic. 3:8 full of judgment and m.
7:16 nations confound. at th. m.
Zec. 4:6 not by m. nor by power
Eph. 1:21 far above all m. power
3:16 to be strengthened with m.
Col. 1:11
6:10 L. and in power of his m.
2 Pet. 2:11 angels greater in m.
Rev. 7:12 glo. and m. be unto G.
See FULFILLED.

MIGHTY.
Gen. 10:9 m. hunter before L.
18:18 Abraham bec. a m. nation
23:6 thou art a m. prince
Ex. 1:7 children of Israel, m. 20
9:28 be no more m. thunderings
10:19 L. turned a m. west wind
15:10 sank as lead in m. water
Lev. 19:15 nor honor person of m.
Num. 22:6 this people are too m.
Deut. 4:37 he bro. thee out with
   m. power, 9:29
26:5 a nation, m. and populous
Jud. 5:13 have dominion over m.
23 came not to help L. ag. m.
1 Sam. 4:8 out of hand of m. gods
2 Sam. 1:19 how are m. fallen! 25
21 shield of the m. is cast aw.
1 K. 4:1:15 m. of the land captive
1 Chr. 1:10 Nim. m. 12:28 Zadok
2 Chr. 26:13 made war with m.
27:6 so Jotham became m.
Ezr. 4:20 been m. king over Jer.
7:28 mercy to the bef. m. princes
Neh. 3:16 N. repaired to thee m.
9:11 threw. stone in m. waters
Job 5:15 he saveth poor from m.
   0:23 redeem me fr. hand of m. ?
9:4 wise in heart, is. in streng.
19:1 hp to overthroweth him m.
21 weakeneth strength of m.
21:7 wherefore are wicked m. ?
24:22 draweth m. wi. his power
34:20 shall be taken away
35:9 by reason of arm of m.
41:25 raiseth himself, m. afraid
Ps. 24:8 strong and m. in battle
29:1 give to the L. O m.
45:3 gird thy sword, O most m.
68:3 m. a. gathered against me
69:33 send out voice. m. voice
74:15 thou driedst up m. rivers
89:1 God in congrega. of the m.
89:6 who am. sons m. like to L.?

MIL
Ps. 89:13 thon hast a m. arm
19 I have laid help upon one m.
93:4 L. mightier than m. waves
106:8 make m. power known
112:2 seed shall be m. on earth
135:10 smote nat. slew m. kings
Prov. 16:32 better than the m.
18:18 lot parteth betwe. the m.
23:11 their Redeemer is m.
Is. 3:25 thy m. sh. fall in war
5:22 woe to them that are m.
11:15 wi. m. wind sh. his hand
22:17 carry thee aw. wi. m. cap.
42:31 shall prey be taken fr. m.?
63:1 in righteousness, m. to save
Jer. 5:15 m. and ancient nation
32:19 gr. in counsel, m. in work
33:3 I will show thee m. things
Ezek. 17:13 hath taken m. of land
32:12 swords of m. make th. fall
21 strong among m. sh. speak
27 not lie wi. m. that are fallen
38:15 come with a m. army
39:18 ye shall eat flesh of m.
Dan. 4:3 m. are his wonders !
8:24 his power shall be m.
11:3 a m. king shall stand up
Amos 2:14 nei. shall m. deliver
16 courageous am. m. sh. flee
5:12 m. king, for m. in stream
Jon. 1:4 there was a m. tempest
Zec. 11:2 howl, m. are spoiled
Mat. 11:20 most of m. works
21 if m. works which were, 23
13:54 hath this man m. works?
58 he did not many m. works
   there, Mark 6:5
14:2 John the Bap. therefore m.
   works do show, Mark 6:14
Mark 6:2 m. works by his hand
Luke 1:49 m. hath done great th.
52 he hath put down the m.
9:43 amazed at m. power of G.
19:37 praised God for m. works
24:19 was a prophet m. in deed
Acts 7:22 Moses was m. in words
18:24 Apol. was m. in script.
Rom. 15:19 obed. thro' m. signs
16:21 not many m.
27 choo. weak, to confound m.
2 Cor. 10:4 warfare m. thro' God
13:3 is not weak, but m. in you
Gal. 2:8 the same was m. in me
Eph. 1:19 working of m. power
1 Thes. 1:7 J. with his m. angels
Rev. 6:13 when shak. of m. wind
10:1 I saw ano. m. angel, 18:21
18:10 m. city ; 19:6 m. thunder.
See ACTS, GOD, HAND, MAN, MEN.

MIGHTY one.
Gen. 10:8 N. began to be a m. o.
Is. 1:24 Lord of hosts, the m. O.
   of Is. 30:29 ; 49:26 ; 60:16
10:34 Leb. shall fall by a m. o.
28:2 L. hath a m. and strong o.
Jer. 20:11 L. is wi. me as a m. o.
Ezek. 31:11 deliver. him to m. o.

MIGHTY ones.
Jud. 5:22 broken by their m. o.
Is. 13:3 have called my m. ones
Jer. 46:5 their m. o. are beaten
Joel 3:11 cause m. o. to come

MIGHTIER.
Gen. 26:16 thou art m. than we
Ex. 1:9 child. of Is. m. than we
Num. 14:12 and m. than they
Deut. 4:38 ; 7:1 ; 9:1, 14 ; 11:23
Ps. 93:4 L. is m. than many m.
Ec. 6:10 not. contend with m.
Mat. 3:11 that com. aft. mo is m.
   than I, Mark 1:7 ; Luke 3:16

MIGHTIES.
1 Chr. 11:12 Ele. was one of 3 m.
19 these thi. did these three m.
24 D. had a name am. three m.

MIGHTILY.
Deut. 6:3 ye may increase m.
Jud. 4:3 Jabin m. oppressed Is.
14:6 Sp. of the L. came m. 15:14
Jer. 25:30 the Lord shall m. roar
Jon. 3:8 man and beast cry m.
Nah. 2:1 fortify thy power m.
Acts 18:28 m. convinced Jews
19:20 so m. grew word of God
Col. 1:29 worketh in me m.
Rev. 18:2 cried m. saying, Bab.

MILCAH.
Gen. 11:29 M. daught. of Haran,
   24:20 ; 34:15 ; Num. 26:33

MILCH.
Gen. 32:15 thirty m. camels
1 Sam. 6:7 take two m. kine, 10

MILCOM.
1 K. 11:5, 33 ; 2 K. 23:13

MILDEW. See BLASTING.

MIN
Mat. 5:41 compel thee to go a m.
MILETUM. 2 Tim. 4:20
MILETUS. Acts 20:15, 17

MILK, Substantive.
Gen. 18:8 A. took butter and m.
49:12 his teeth be white wi. m.
Deut. 32:14 kine, m. of sheep
Jud. 4:19 J. opened bottle of m.
5:25 asked water, she gave m.
Job 10:10 not pou. me out as m. ?
21:24 his breasts are full of m.
Prov. 27:27 shalt have goats' m.
30:33 churning m. bring. butter
Cant. 4:11 m. under thy tongue
5:1 drunk wine with my m.
12 his eyes washed with m.
Is. 7:22 abund. of m. shall give
28:9 that are weaned from m.
55:1 wi. and m. without honey
60:16 thou sh. suck m. of Gent.
Lam. 4:7 Nazar. whiter than m.
Ezek. 25:4 eat fruit, and drink m.
Joel 3:18 hills shall flow with m.
1 Cor. 3:2 I have fed you with m.
9:7 who eateth not of the m. ?
Heb. 5:12 as have need of m. ?
18 ev. one useth m. is a babe
1 Pet. 2:2 new-born babes des. m.
See FLOWING.

MILK.
Is. 66:11 that ye may m. out

MILL, S.
Ex. 11:5 m. servant behind m.
Num. 11:8 ground manna in m.
Mat. 24:41 two wom. grind. at m.

MILLET.
Ezek. 4:9 take m. m. and make bre.

MILLIONS.
Gen. 24:60 mother of thous. m.

MILLO.
Jud. 9:6 house of M. gather. 20
2 Sam. 5:9 round about from M.
1 K. 9:24 Solo. build M. 11:27
2 K. 12:20 slew Joash in M.

MILLSTONE, S.
Deut. 24:6 no man take m. pled.
Jud. 9:53 a woman cast a piece
   of m. 2 Sam. 11:21
Job 41:24 heart as hard as a m.
Is. 47:2 take m. and grind meal
Jer. 25:10 take away sound of m.
Mat. 18:6 a m. hanged about his
   neck, Mark 9:42 ; Luke 17:2
Rev. 18:21 an angel took up a
   stone like a great m.

MINCING.
Is. 3:16 walk. and m. as they go

MIND, Substantive.
Gen. 26:35 a grief of m. to Isaac
Lev. 24:12 m. of L. showed them
Deut. 18:6 come wi. desire of m.
28:65 L. sh. give thee sor. of m.
30:1 call th. to m. am. the nat.
1 Chr. 28:9 serve forth willing m.
Neh. 4:6 peo. had a m. to work
Job 23:13 one m. who turn him?
Ps. 31:12 a dead man out of m.
Prov. 21:27 bring. it wi. wic. m.
29:11 a fool uttereth all his m.
Is. 26:3 wh. m. is stayed on thee
46:8 again to m. O transgress.
65:17 former sh. not come to m.
Jer. 3:16 ark not come to m.
44:21 came it not into his m. ?
Dan. 5:20 m. hardened in pride
Hab. 1:11 then sh. his m. change
14:13 P. called t.w. works of J.
Luke 12:29 nei. be of doubtful m.
Acts 17:11 all readiness of m.
20:19 serv. L. with humi. of m.
Rom. 1:28 ga. up to reprobate m.
7:25 with m. I serve law of God
8:7 carnal m. enmity against G.
27 knoweth what is m. of Sp.
11:34 who hath kno. m. of L. ?
12:16 same m. one tow. another
14:5 persuaded in his own m.
15:6 may with one m. glori. G.
1 Cor. 1:10 joined in the same m.
2:16 known m. of L. to instruct
2 Cor. 7:7 fervent m. toward me
8:12 if a willing m. it is accept.
13:11 brethr. be of one m. Phil.
   1:27 ; 2:2
Eph. 2:3 desires of flesh and m.
4:17 Gent. walk in vanity of m.
Phil. 2:3 in lowli. of m. let each
4:2 be of the same m. in the L.
Col. 2:18 puffed up by fleshly m.
3:12 humbleness of m. meekn.

MIN
2 Thes. 2:2 not soun shaken in m.
2 Tim. 1:7 spirit of sound m.
Tit. 1:15 m. and conscience defi.
3:1 put them in m. to be subj.
Heb. 8:10 my laws into th. m.
1 Pet. 3:8 be ye all of same m.
4:1 arm yours, like. wi. one m.
5:2 filthy lucre, but of ready m.
Rev. 17:9 m. which hath wisdom
13 these have one m. and shall
See ALIENATED.

Mine, or my MIND.
Num. 16:28 done th. of m. own m.
24:13 good or bad of m. own m.
1 Sam. 2:35 that wh. is in m. m.
Jer. 15:1 my m. could not be
19:5 nei. came it to my m. 32:35
Lam. 3:21 this I recall to my m.
Rom. 7:23 war. ag. law of my m.

Thy MIND.
1 Sam. 9:20 set not t. m. on asses
Job 34:33 should it be according
Ezek. 38:10 thi. came into t. m.
Dan. 2:29 thou. came into t. m.
Mat. 22:37 love L. the G. wi. all
t. m. Mark 12:30 ; Luke 10:27
Phile. 14 without thy m.

Your MIND.
Rom. 12:8 if y. m. I should bury
Jer. 51:50 Jer. come into your m.
Ezek. 11:5 things come into y. m.
20:32 that wh. cometh into y. m.
Rom. 12:2 by renewing of y. m.
2 Cor. 8:19 declar. of y. ready m.
9:2 I know forwardness of y. m.
Eph. 4:23 renewed in sp. of y. m.
Col. 1:21 enemies in your m.
1 Pet. 1:13 loins of y. m. be sober

MIND, Verb.
Rom. 8:5 m. things of the flesh
12:16 m. not high things, but
Phil. 3:16 let us m. same thing
19 who m. earthly things

MINDED.
Ruth 1:18 she was steadfastly m.
2 Chr. 24:4 m. to repair house
Ezr. 7:13 m. of th. own free will
Mat. 1:19 m. to put her away
Rom. 8:6 to be carn. m. is death,
   to be spiritually m. is life
11:20 be not high-m. but fear
15:5 grant you to be like-m.
2 Cor. 1:15 I was m. to come
17 thus m. did I use lightness
Gal. 5:10 be no otherwise m.
Phil. 2:2 that ye be like-m.
20 no man like-m. will care
3:15 as many as be perf. be thus
m. if ye be otherwise m.
1 Thes. 3:4 consi. the double-m.
1 Tim. 6:17 rich be not high-m.
2 Tim. 3:4 men heady, high-m.
Tit. 2:6 exhort to be sober-m.
Jam. 1:8 double-m. man unstab.
4:8 purify hearts ye double-m.

MINDFUL.
1 Chr. 16:15 be m. of covenant
Neh. 9:17 fathers were not m.
Ps. 8:4 what is man, that thou
   art m. of him? Heb. 2:6
111:5 ever be m. of covenant
115:12 L. hath been m. of us
17:10 not born m. of rock
2 Tim. 1:4 being m. of thy tears
Heb. 11:15 been m. of that coun.
2 Pet. 3:2 be m. of words spoken

MINDING.
Acts 20:13 P. m. himself to go

MINDS.
Jud. 19:30 consider, speak yo. m.
1 Sam. 17:8 he chafed in their m.
2 K. 9:15 if it be your m.
Ezek. 24:25 they set their m.
36:5 with despiteful m. to cast
Acts 14:2 their m. evil affected
28:6 they changed their m. and
   said he was a god
2 Cor. 3:14 their m. were blind
4:4 god of th. world ha. blin. m.
5:13 or sob. m. it is for yo. ca.
Phil. 4:7 peace of G. keep yo. m.
1 Tim. 6:5 corrupt m. 2 Tim. 3:8
Heb. 10:16 in m. will I write
12:3 wear. and faint in your m.
1 Pet. 3:1 I stir up your pure m.

MINE.
Gen. 31:43 all that thou seest m.
48:5 m. as Reuben and S. be m.
Ex. 19:5 for all the earth is m.
Ps. 50:12
Ps. 60:7 Gilead m. Man. m. 108:8
Ezek. 23:4 were m. 5 she was

CRUDEN'S CONCORDANCE. 945

MIN

Ex. 20:9 river m. 35:10 count. m.
Hag. 2:8 silver is m. gold is m.
Mal. 3:17 they sh. be m. saith L.
Mat. 22:23 not m. Mark 10:40
John 17:10 m. are thine, thine m.

MINGLE.

Is. 5:22 men m. strong drink
Dan. 2:43 m. with seed of men

MINGLED.

Ex. 9:24 fire m. with the hail
Lev. 19:19 not s. field wi. m. seed
Ezr. 9:2 holy seed m. themsel,
Ps. 102:9 m. drink wi. weeping
106:35 were m. among heathen
Prov. 9:2 she hath m. her wine
5 drink of wine wh. I have m.
Is. 19:14 L. m. a perverse spirit
Jer. 25:20 cup to all m. peo. 24
50:37 sw. of m. peo. Ezek. 30:5
Luke 13:1 blood Pilat had m.
Rev. 8:7 hail and fire m. with bl.

MINISH, ED.

Ex. 5:19 not m. aught of task
Ps. 107:39 again they are m.

MINISTER.

Ex. 24:13 Moses and his m. Jos.
Jos. 1:1 spake to Joshua, M. m.
Mat. 20:26 your m. Mark 10:43
Luke 4:20 gave book again to m.
Acts 13:5 had also J. to their m.
20:16 make th. a m. and win.
Rom. 13:4 is m. of G. to thee, 6
15:8 Ch. was m. of circumcision
16 be m. of Jesus to Gentiles
Gal. 2:17 is Ch. the m. of sin?
Eph. 3:7 whereof I was made a
m. Col. 1:23, 25
6:21 Ty. a faithful m. Col. 4:7
Col. 1:7 Epaphras, a faithful m.
1 Thes. 3:2 brother and m. of G.
1 Tim. 4:6 a good m. of Christ
Heb. 8:2 a m. of the sanctuary

MINISTER, Verb.

Ex. 28:1 that he may m. to me in
the priest's office. 3, 4, 41;
29:1, 44; 30:30; 31:10; 35:19;
32:41; 40:13, 15
35 it shall be upon Aar. to m.
29:44 sanctify Aar. to m. to me
Lev. 7:35 presented them to m.
Num. 8:26 m. wi. their brethren
Deut. 10:8 tribe of L. to m. to h.
21:5 God hath chos. them to m.
1 Sam. 2:11 child did m. to Lord
1 K. 8:11 priest could not stand
to m. 2 Chr. 5:14
1 Chr. 15:2 chosen to m. bef. hi.
23:13 to m. to the Lord and to
give thanks, 2 Chr. 31:2
2 Chr. 13:10 pries. m. sons of A.
Ps. 9:8 m. judgment to people
Is. 60:7 rams of Nebaioth m.
10 their kings shall m. to thee
Jer. 33:22 multi. Levites that m.
Ezek. 40:46 near to m. 44:15, 16
44:11 stand before them to m.
Mat. 20:28 to be unministered to,
but to m. Mark 10:45
25:44 and did not m. to thee?
Acts 24:23 acquaint. to m. to him
Rom. 15:25 I go to m. to saints
27 m. to them in carnal things
1 Cor. 9:13 m. about holy things
2 Cor. 9:10 m. bread for your fo.
Eph. 4:29 m. grace to hearers
1 Tim. 1:4 which m. questions
Heb. 1:14 m. to heirs of salvation
6:10 minis. to saints, and do m.
1 Pet. 1:12 but to us they did m.
4:10 m. the same one to another
11 if any man m. let him do it

MINISTERED.

Num. 3:4 E. and I. m. Deut. 10:6
1 Sam. 2:18 Samuel m. bef. L. 3:1
3 Sam. 19:17 his servant that m.
1 K. 1:4 Abishag m. to David, 15
19:21 Elijah, and m. to him
Ezek. 44:12 m. before their idols
Dan. 7:10 thousands m. unto him
Mat. 4:11 angels came and m. to
him, Mark 1:13
8:15 she rose and m. Mark 1:31
Luke 8:3 m. to him of substance
Acts 13:2 as they m. and fasted
20:34 have m. to my necessities
2 Cor. 3:3 epistle of Ch. m. by us
Phil. 2:25 that m. to my wants
Col. 2:19 having nourishment m.
2 Tim. 1:18 many h. m. at Ephe
Phile. 13 he might have m.
Heb. 6:10 have m. to the saints
2 Pet. 1:11 entrance be m. to you

MINISTERETH.

2 Cor. 9:10 m. seed to the sower
Gal. 3:5 that m. to you the Spi.

MIR

MINISTERING.

1 Chr. 9:28 charge of m. vessels
28:13 courses of m. 14 m. vessels
Ezek. 44:11 house, m. to house
Mat. 27:55 followed J. m. to him
Rom. 12:7 w. on m. 15:16 m. gos.
2 Cor. 8:4 and take on us the m.
9:1 for as touching m. to saints
Heb. 1:14 are they not m. spirits
10:11 every priest standeth m.

MINISTERS.

1 K. 10:5 atten.of his m. 2 Chr. 9:4
Ezr. 7:24 not lawful, toll on m.
8:17 they sho. bring un. us m.
Ps. 103:21 m. that do his pleas.
104:4 m. a flaming fire, Heb. 1:7
Is. 61:6 shall call you m. of God
Jer. 33:21 covenant be broken
with David and my m.
Ezek. 45:4 holy port. for the m.
Joel 1:9 m. weep between the porch
Luke 1:2 from beginn. were m.
Rom. 13:6 m. attend. continually
1 Cor. 3:5 m. by whom ye belie.
4:1 so account of us as of the m.
2 Cor. 3:6 who made us able m.
6:4 approv. ourselv. as m. of G
11:15 his m. also be transformed
as the m. of righteousness
23 are they m. of Christ? I am

MINISTRATION.

Luke 1:23 days of m. were ended
Acts 6:1 widows neglected in m.
2 Cor. 3:7 if m. of death glorious
8 m. of Spirit be glorious? 9
9:13 the experiment of this m.

MINISTRY.

Num. 4:12 instruments of m.
2 Chr. 7:6 D. praised by their m.
Hos. 12:10 used similitud. by m.
Acts 1:17 had obtain. part of m.
25 that he may take part of m.
6:4 will give ourselves to m.
12:25 when they fulfilled th. m.
20:24 finish my course, and m.
21:19 things G. wro. by his m.
1 Cor. 16:15 addicted to m. of sa.
2 Cor. 4:1 seeing we have this m.
5:18 giv. us m. of reconciliation
6:3 that the m. be not blamed
Eph. 4:12 work of m. for edify.
Col. 4:17 take heed to the m.
1 Tim. 1:12 putting me into m.
2 Tim. 4:5 full proof of thy m.
11 profitable to me for the m.
Heb. 8:6 obtained a more ex. m.
9:21 sprinkled the vessels of m.

MINNI.
Jer. 51:27

MINNITH.
Jud. 11:33

MINSTREL.

2 K. 3:15 but now bring me a m.
Mat. 9:23 when Jesus saw the m.

MINT.

Mat. 23:23 ye pay tithe of m.
Luke 11:42 ye tithe m. all herbs

MIRACLE.

Ex. 7:9 P. sh. speak. Show a m.
Mark 6:52 consid. not m. of loa.
9:39 no man which shall do m.
John 4:54 second m. Jesus did
10:41 many said, Jo. did no m.
Acts 4:16 a notable m. been done
22 on wh. this m. was wrong.

MIRACLES.

Num. 14:22 which have seen m.
Deut. 11:3 have not seen his m.
29:3 th. eyes have not seen those m.
Hos. 7:15 do they imagine m.
Acts 13:10 full of m. and mischief
23 many bell. wh. they saw m.
3:2 no man can do th. m. ex. G.
6:30 not because ye saw the m.
7:31 will he do more m. his m.?
11:47 this man doeth many m.
12:37 he had done so many m.
Acts 2:22 approved of God by m.
6:8 Stephen did great m.
8:6 hearing and seeing the m.
13 wondered, beholding the m.
10:11 G. wrought spec. m. by P.
1 Cor. 12:10 in the working of m.
28 teachers; after that m.
29 are all workers of m.?
Heb. 2:1 G. bearing with. wi. m.
Rev. 13:14 deceiv. by means of m.
16:14 spirits of devils work. m.
19:20 false prophet th. wro. m.

MIRE.

2 Sam. 22:43 stamp them as m.
of street, Is. 10:6; Mic. 7:10

MIS

Job 8:11 can rush grow wit. m.?
30:19 he hath cast me into m.
41:30 spread. things on the m.
Ps. 69:2 I sink in deep m. where
14 deliver me out of the m.
Jer. 38:6 in dung, no wat. but m.
22 thy feet are sunk in the m.
Zec. 9:3 gold as m. of streets
10:5 tread th. enemies in the m.
2 Pet. 2:22 sow wallowing in m.

MIRY.

Ps. 40:2 bro. me out of m. clay
Ezek. 47:11 m. pla. not be healed
Dan. 2:41 iron mixed with m. 43

MIRIAM.

Ex. 15:20 M. took a timbrel in
Num. 12:1 M. and Aaron, 10, 15
Deut. 24:9 what God did to M.
Mic. 6:4 I sent before thee M.

MIRTH.

Gen. 31:27 sent th. away wi. m.
Neh. 8:12 peo. went to make m.
Ps. 137:3 that wasted us dem. m.
Prov. 14:13 end of m. heaviness
Ec. 2:1 I will prove th. with m.
2 I said of m. what doeth it?
7:4 heart of fools is in ho. of m.
8:15 then I commended m.
Is. 24:8 m. of tabrets
11 the m. of the land is gone
Jer. 7:34 I will cause to cease
the voice of m. from Judah,
16:9; 25:10; Hos. 2:11
Ezek. 21:10 sh. we th. make m.?

MISCARRYING.

Hos. 9:14 give them a m. womb

MISCHIEF.

Gen. 42:4 lest some m. bef. him
38 if m. befall him, 44:29
Ex. 21:22 and yet no m. follow
23 if for m. did he bring them
32 knowest peo. that are on m.
1 Sam. 23:9 Saul practised m.
2 Sam. 16:8 art taken in thy m.
1 K. 11:25 the m. that Hadad did
20:7 this man seeketh m.
1 Cor. 7:9 some m. will befall us
Neh. 6:2 thought to do me m.
Est. 8:3 E. sou. to put away m.
Job 15:35 conceive m. and vanity
Ps. 7:14 tra. forth falsehood
16 hath m. shall ret. on his head
10:7 under his tongue is m.
14 thou beholdest m. and spite
26:10 in whose hands is m.
28:3 but m. is in their hearts
36:4 wicked dev. m. on his bed
52:1 why boast, thyself in m.?
55:10 m. and sorrow in midst
62:3 how long will ye ima. m.?
94:20 frameth m. by a law
119:150 draw nigh that fol. m.
140:9 m. of own lips cover them
Prov. 4:16 ex. they ha. done m.
6:14 he deviseth m. continually
18 feet swift in running to m.
10:23 is sport to a fool to do m.
11:27 that seek. m. it shall co.
12:21 wicked be filled with m.
13:17 wicked mes. falleth in m.
17:20 a perv. tongue fall. in m.
24:2 their heart studieth m.
Ezek. 7:26 m. sh. come upon m.
11:2 men that devise m.
Dan. 11:27 king's hearts to do m.
Hos. 7:15 do they imagine m.
Acts 13:10 full of m. and mischief

MISCHIEFS.

Deut. 32:23 heap m. upon them
Ps. 52:2 thy tongue deviseth m.
140:2 imagine m. in their heart

MISCHIEVOUS.

Ps. 21:11 imagined a m. device
38:12 seek my hurt, speak m. t.
Prov. 24:8 be called m. person
Ec. 10:13 end of his talk is m.
Mic. 7:3 man utter. his m. desire

MISERABLE, LY.

Job 16:2 Job said, m. comforters
Mat. 21:41 m. destroy wicked m.
1 Cor. 15:19 are of all men most m.
Rev. 3:17 know. not thou art m.

MISERY.

Jud. 10:16 soul grieved for m.
Job 3:20 is light giv. to him in m.
11:16 thou shalt forget thy m.
Prov. 31:7 rem. his m. no more
Ec. 8:6 the m. of a man is great
Lam. 1:7 Jerusal. in days of m.
3:19 re. mine affliction and m.

MOA

Rom. 3:16 m. are in their ways
Jam. 5:1 howl for your m.

MISHAEL.

Ex. 6:22; Lev. 10:4; Neh. 8:4
Dan. 1:6 of childr. of Judah, M.

MISS.

Jud. 20:16 sling at, and not m.
1 Sam. 20:6 if thy fath. at all m.

MISSED, ING.

1 Sam. 20:18 thou shalt be m.
25:7 neither was there aught m.
15 neith. m. any thing as long
21 nothing was m. of all
1 K. 20:39 any means be be m.

MIST.

Gen. 2:6 th. went a m. fr. earth
Acts 13:11 there fell on him a m.
2 Pet. 2:17 m. of darkn. reserved

MISTRESS.

Gen. 16:4 Sarah her m. despised
8 flee fr. my m. 8, 9 return to
1 K. 17:17 son of m. fell sick
2 K. 5:3 said to her m. would G.
Ps. 123:2 eyes of maiden to m.
Prov. 30:23 that is heir to her m.
Is. 24:2 as with maid so with m.
Nah. 3:4 the m. of witchcrafts

MISUSED.

2 Chr. 36:16 they m. his prophe.

MITE, S.

Mark 12:42 a certain poor widow
threw in two m. Luke 21:2
Luke 12:59 thou hast paid last m.

MITRE.

Ex. 28:4 make a m. 39; 29:28
39:6 put the m. upon his head
16:4 wi. lin. m. sh. he be attired
Zec. 3:5 set fair m. on his head

MIXED.

Ex. 12:38 m. multitude went up
Num. 11:4 m. multi. fell a lust,
Neh. 13:3 separated fr. m. multi.
Prov. 23:30 go to seek m. wine
Is. 1:22 thy wine m. with water
Dan. 2:41 iron saw. the iron m.
Hos. 7:8 Ephraim is, am. people
Heb. 4:2 not being m. with faith

MIXTURE.

Ps. 75:8 there is a cup full of m.
John 19:39 Nicodemus, and bro.
a m. of myrrh and aloes
Rev. 14:10 poured out without m.

MIZAR.
Ps. 42:6

MIZPAH.

Gen. 31:49 na. of heap called M.
1 K. 15:22 Ge. and M. 2 Chr. 16:6
2 K. 25:23 to Ged. to M. Jer. 41:1
Jer. 40:8 men of Gibeon und M.
41:3 slew all J. that were at M.
Hos. 5:1 have been a snare on M.

MIZPEH.

Jos. 15:38 Dilean and M,
Jud. 10:17 in M. 11:11; 21:5
20:1 Israel was gathered in M.
1 Sam. 7:5 all Is. to M. 6; 22:3
10:17 Samuel called peo. to M.

MIZRAIM.
Gen. 10:6
MNASON. Acts 21:16

MOAB.

Gen. 19:37 daugh.'s son was M.
Ex. 15:15 trembl. on men of M.
Num. 21:29; 22:3; 24:17; 25:1
Deut. 2:18 pass thro' coast of M.
34:5 Moses died in land of M.
Jud. 3:29 they slew of M. about
10:6 Israel serv. the gods of M.
11:15 took not away land of M.
Ruth 1:2 co. into country of M.
1 Sam. 14:47 Saul fought ag. M.
2 Sam. 8:2 David smote M. 23:20
1 K. 11:7 the abomination of M.
2 K. 1:1 then M. rebelled, 3:7, 23
1 Chr. 4:22 dominion in M. 18:11
2 Chr. 20:1 chil. of M. came ag. Jeh. 10
Neh. 13:23 J. married wiv. of M.
Ps. 60:8 M. my washpot, 108:9
Is. 15:1 be confederate ag. thee
Is. 11:14 lay the hand upon M.
15:1 burden of M. 16:13; 25:10
46:1; Ezek. 25:8; Amos 2:2
16:6 heard of pride of M. 11,
14; Jer. 48:29
25:10 M. shall be trodden down
Jer. 9:26; Egypt, Judah, and M.
25:21 made M. to drink of cup
27:3 send a fire upon M.
Zep. 2:9 M. shall be as Sodom

MOABITE.

Deut. 23:3 M. sh. not, Neh. 13:1
1 Chr. 11:46 Ithma the M. a val.

MOM

MOABITES.
Gen. 19:37 the father of the M.
Deut. 2:9 said, Distress not M.
Jud. 3:28 L. hath delivered M.
2 Sam. 8:2 M. beca. 1 Chr. 18:2
1 K. 11:1 loved women of the M.
2 K. 3:18 he will deli. the M. 24
13:20 bands of M. invaded, 24:2
Ezr. 9:1 to abominations of M.

MOCK, Substantive.
Prov. 14:9 fools make a m. at sin

MOCK.
Gen. 39:14 bro. Heb. to m. us, 17
Job 13:9 mocketh, do ye m. him
21:3 after I have spoken, m. on
Prov. 1:26 m. wh. your fear com.
Jer. 38:19 and they m. me
Lam. 1:7 did m. at her sabbaths
Ezek. 22:5 shall m. thee who art
Mat. 20:19 deliver to G. to m. h.
Mark 10:34 m. him and scourge
Luke 14:29 begin to m. him

MOCKED.
Gen. 19:14 one that m. to sons
Num. 22:29 hec. thou hast m. me
Jud. 16:10 m. me, 13, 15
1 K. 18:27 at noon, Elijah m. th.
2 K. 2:23 little child. m. Elisha
2 Chr. 30:10 lau. to scorn and m.
36:16 m. the messengers of God
Neh. 4:1 Sanballat m. the Jews
Job 12:4 one m. of his neighbor
Mat. 2:16 H. saw that he was m.
27:29 they bowed the knee and
m. 31; Mark 15:20
Luke 18:32 m. spitef. entreated
22:63 men that held J. m. him
23:11 Herod m. 36 soldiers m.
Acts 17:32 resurrection, some m.
Gal. 6:7 not deceiv. G. is not m.

MOCKER, S.
Job 17:2 are th. not m. with me?
Ps. 35:16 hypocrit. m. in feasts
Prov. 20:1 wine is a m. st. drink
Is. 28:22 be not m. lest bands be
Jer. 15:17 sat not in assem. of m.
Jude 18 sh. be m. latter times

MOCKEST, ETH.
Job 11:3 when thou m. sh. no m.
13:9 as one m. anoth. do ye so
39:22 m. at fear, not affrighted
Prov. 17:5 m. poor repro. Maker
30:17 that m. at his father
Jer. 20:7 derision, ev. one m. me

MOCKING.
Gen. 21:9 saw son of Hagar m.
Mat. 27:41 priests m. Mark 15:31
Acts 2:13 oth. m. said, These m.

MOCKING, S.
Ezek. 22:4 made thee a m. to all
Heb. 11:36 had trial of cruel m.

MODERATION.
Phil. 4:5 let your m. be known

MODERATELY.
Joel 2:23 gi. you former rain m.

MODEST.
1 Tim. 2:9 adorn in m. apparel

MOIST.
Num. 6:3 nor shall he eat m. gr.

MOISTENED.
Job 21:24 bones m. with marrow

MOISTURE.
Ps. 32:4 m. turned to drought
Luke 8:6 because it lacked m.

MOLADAH. Jos. 15:26

MOLE.
Lev. 11:30 snail and m. are uncl.

MOLES. See BATS.

MOLECH.
Lev. 18:21 pass thro. fire to M.
20:2 of his seed to M. Jer. 32:35
1 K. 11:7 a high place for M.
2 K. 23:10 son pass thro' to M.

MOLLIFIED.
Is. 1:6 nor m. with ointment

MOLOCH. Amos 5:26; Acts 7:43

MOLTEN.
Ex. 32:4 he had made a m. calf,
8; Deut. 9:12, 16; Neh. 9:18
34:17 no m. gods, Lev. 19:4
1 K. 7:16 chapiters of m. brass
23 a m. sea; 30 undersct. m.
Job 28:2 brass is m. out of stone
37:18 sky as a m. looking-glass
Ezek. 24:11 filthiness be m. in it
Mic. 1:4 mountains shall be m.
See IMAGE.

MOMENT.
Ex. 33:5 midst of thee in a m.
Num. 16:21 consume th. in a m.

MON

Job 7:18 shouldest try him e. m.
20:5 joy of hypoc. but for a m.
21:13 in a m. go down to grave
34:20 in a m. shall they die
Ps. 30:5 his anger end. but a m.
73:19 into desolation as in a m.
Prov. 12:19 ly. tong. but for a m.
Is. 26:20 as it were for a m.
27:3 I will water it every m.
47:9 things shall come in a m.
54:7 for a small m. have I forsa.
8 I hid my face fr. th. for a m.
Jer. 4:20 my curtains in a m.
Lam. 4:6 Sodom overth. in a m.
Ezek. 26:16 tremble ev. m. 32:10
Luke 4:5 king. of world in a m.
1 Cor. 15:52 be changed in a m.
2 Cor. 4:17 which is but for a m.

MONEY.
Gen. 23:9 as much m. as worth
13 I will give thee m. for field
31:15 quite devoured our m.
42:25 to restore every man's m.
27 espied m. 28 m. restored
43:12 double m. in hand. 18
44:1 ev. man's m. in sack's mo.
47:14 gathered all m. in Egypt
15 m. faileth ; 18 our m. spent
Ex. 21:11 go out free without m.
21 he is his m. 35 divide m.
30 be laid on him a sum of m.
22:7 man deliver m. to neighbor
25 lend m. to any of my people
30:16 take atonement m. of Isr.
Lev. 22:37 not give him m. on
usury, Deut. 23:19
Num. 3:49 Mos. took redemp. m.
Deut. 2:6 and water for m. 28
14:25 turn into m. 26 bestow m.
23:14 not sell her at all for m.
Jud. 5:19 took no gain of m.
16:18 lords bro. m. to Delilah
17:4 restored m. to his mother
1 K. 21:2 give worth of it in m.
2 K. 5:26 is it a time to rec. m. ?
12:4 the m. of dedicated things
7 now receive no more m. 8
10 m. in chest, 2 Chr. 24:11
16 and sin m. was not brought
15:20 exacted the m. of Israel
22:33 Jehoiakim gave m. to Ph.
Ezr. 3:7 gave m. also to masons
7:17 buy speedily with this m.
Neh. 5:4 borrowed m. for king
10 my servants exact of th. m.
Est. 4:7 sum of m. H. promised
Job 31:39 eaten fruits without m.
42:11 ev. man also gave him m.
Ps. 15:5 putteth not m. to usury
Prov. 7:20 taken bag of m.
Ec. 7:12 wisd. and m. is a defen.
10:19 but m. answers all things
Is. 52:3 be redeemed without m.
55:1 he that hath no m. come
2 wheref. spend ye m. for that
Jer. 32:9 weigh. m. 17 shekels 10
44 men shall buy fields for m.
Lam. 5:4 drunk. our wa. for m.
Mic. 3:11 prophets divine for m.
Mat. 17:24 received trib. m. ca.
27 thou shalt find a piece of m.
25:18 earth, hid his lord's m.
27 m. to exchange. Luke 19:23
28:12 large m. to soldiers, 15
Mark 6:8 they took no m. in
their purse, Luke 9:3
12:41 people cast m. into treas.
14:11 and promised to give him
m. Luke 22:5
Acts 4:37 brought m. and laid it
8:18 Simon offered them m.
20 P. said, m. perish with thee
24:26 hoped m. sho. been given
1 Tim. 6:10 love of m. root of all
See BOUGHT.

MONEY-CHANGERS.
Mat. 21:12 Jesus overthrew ta-
bles of m. -c. Mark 11:15
John 2:14 found in temple m.-c.

MONSTERS.
Lam. 4:3 sea m. draw out breast

MONTH.
Gen. 29:14 J. tarried with Ja.
Ex. 13:4 came ye out in m. Ab.
23:15 keep feast in the m. Abib
34:18 in m. Abib thou ca. fr. E.
Deut. 16:1; Jos. 5:10
Lev. 27:6 from a m. old to 5 years
Num. 3:15 ev. male fr. a m. old,
22, 28, 34, 39, 40, 43; 26:69
9:22 m. or year cloud tarried
11:20 eat flesh, even a wh. m. 21
18:16 from a m. old shalt thou
28:14 burnt-offer. every m. 29:6
Deut. 21:13 in house full m.

MOO

1 K. 4:7 his m. made provis. 27
5:14 m. they were in Lebanon
Ezr. 9:29 m. turned fr. sorrow
Est. 3:24 her m. they shall find
Hos. 5:7 m. devour th. with por.
Zec. 11:8 I cut off in one m.
Rev. 9:15 prep. for a day and m.
22:2 yielded her fruit every m.
See FIRST.

Second MONTH.
Gen. 7:11 s. m. fouar. broken up
8:14 in s. m. was earth dried
Ex. 16:1 came to ein in sec. m.
Num. 1:1 in s. m. take sum of
9:11 on s. m. shall keep pass-
over, 2 Chr. 30:2
10:11 on s. m. cloud was taken

Third MONTH.
Ex. 19:1 in t. m. came into Sin.
Ezek. 31:1 in t. m. hegan to lay b.
Ezek. 31:1 in t. m. word of Lord

Fourth MONTH.
2 K. 25:3 f. m. famine prevailed
Jer. 39:2 f. m. city broken up
52:6 f. m. famine sore in city
Zec. 8:19 fast of f. m. be joy
See FIFTH.

Sixth MONTH.
Hag. 1:1 in s. m. word of L. ca.
15 in s. m. did work in hou. of
Luke 1:26 in s. m. angel sent
36 s. m. with her called barren
See SEVENTH.

Eighth MONTH.
Zec. 1:1 e. m. came word to Ze.

Ninth MONTH.
Ezr. 10:9 m. poo. sat tremb.
Jer. 36:22 sat in house in n. m.
Hag. 2:10 n. m. came word of L.
Zec. 7:1 word came to Z. in n. m.

Tenth MONTH.
Gen. 8:5 decreased until tenth m.
Ezr. 10:16 sat down in tenth m.
Est. 2:16 taken to king in t. m.

Eleventh MONTH.
Deut. 1:3 e. m. Moses spake to
Zec. 1:7 e. m. came word to Zec.

Twelfth MONTH.
Est. 3:7 cast lots to twelfth m.
Ezek. 32:1 t. m. word of L. came

This MONTH.
Ex. 12:2 t. m. sh. be beginning
3 t. m. take every man a lamb
Neh. 9:1 t. m. Israel assembled

MONTHLY.
Is. 47:13 the m. prognosticators

MONTHS.
Num. 10:10 in begin. of your m.
28:11 in beginnings of m. offer
Jud. 11:37 let me alone two m.
1 Sam. 6:1 ark in country 7 m.
2 Sam. 2:11 D. reign. seven years
and six m. 5:5; 1 Chr. 3:4
6:11 ark was with O.-edom 3 m.
1 K. 5:14 two m. were at home
1 Chr. 27:1 thro' the m. ol year
Est. 2:12 after she had been 12
m. purified, six m. with odors
of myrrh, six m. with odors
Job 3:6 not come to numb. of m.
7:3 made to possess m. of vani.
14:5 number of his m. wi. thee
21:21 number of his m. cut off
29:2 O that I were as in m. past
39:2 canst thou number the m. ?
Ezek. 39:14 after end of seven m.
47:12 new fruit according to m.
Dan. 4:29 at th. end of twel. m.
Luke 1:24 and hid herself five m.
4:25 when heaven was shut up
3 yc. and 6 m. Jam. 5:17
John 4:35 yet four m. then harv.
Acts 18:11 P. abode year and m.
19:8 three m. disputed with th.
20:3 continued three m. 28:11
Rev. 9:5 be tormented five m. 10
11:2 tread under foot 42 m.
13:5 power given to con. 42 m.
See THREE.

MONUMENTS.
Is. 65:4 pco. which lodge in m.

MOON.
Deut. 33:14 precious thin. by m.
Jos. 10:12 m. in valley of Ajalon
Job 25:5 behold m. it shine, not
31:26 when I considered the m.
72:7 so long as m. endureth
89:37 establi. forever as the m.
104:19 appointed m. for seasons
Ec. 12:2 while sun, m. or stars
Cant. 6:10 fair as m. clear as sun
Is. 3:18 round tires like the m.
See SUN.

MOR

New MOON,
1 Sam. 20:5 to-mor. is new m. 18
2 K. 4:23 neither new m. nor sa.
Ps. 81:3 blow trumpet in n. m.
Is. 66:23 fr. one new m. to anoth.
Ezek. 46:1 in n. m. sh. be opened
6 in n. m. offer young bullock
Amos 8:5 will n. m. be gone?
Col. 2:16 judge you of the n. m.

New MOONS,
1 Chr. 23:31 offer burnt sacri. in
n. m. 2 Chr. 2:4; 31:3; Ezr.
3:5; Neh. 10:33; Ezek. 46:3
Is. 1:13 new m. and sabbaths
14 n. m. and feasts my soul ha.
Ezek. 45:17 drink-off. to new m.
Hos. 2:11 cause new m. to cease

MORDECAI.
Ezr. 2:2 M. came up, Neh. 7:7
Est. 2:5 a Jew, name was M.
10:3 M. was next to Ahasuerus

MORE.
Ex. 1:12 the m. they afflicted
them, the m. they grew.
16:17 gath. some m. some less
30:15 the rich shall not give m.
1 Sam. 3:17 G. do so to th. a. m.
Ps. 19:10 m. to be des. than gold
Ts:14 I will praise th. m. and m.
Mat. 18:16 take with th, 1 or 2 m.
John 21:15 lovest thou me m. ?
Heb. 12:26 once m. I shake, 27
See ABUNDANTLY.

Any MORE,
Gen. 8:12 dove ret. not any m.
21 not curse ground a. m. 9:11
17:5 nor name A. m. be call. Ab.
35:10 nor a. m. be called Jacob
Ex. 8:29 not deal deceitful. a. m.
11:6 nor a cry be like it any m.
Lev. 7:13 nei. be with you a. m.
Mat. 5:9 I will not do any m.
Ezek. 5:9 I will not do any m.
Hos. 14:8 what have I any m. ?
Luke 22:16 I will not eat any m.

Much MORE.
Ex. 36:5 the people bring m. m.
Mat. 6:30 sh. he not m. m. clo. ?
Luke 7:26 m. m. than a prophet
Rom. 5:9 m. m. be. now justified
10 much m. being reconciled
17 m. m. they that receive
20 when sin abound. gra. m. m.
2 Cor. 3:11 m. m. wh. remaineth

No MORE.
Ex. 2:14 came no m. to king
Job 7:8 see me no m. 9 come up
10 shall return no m. to house
Rev. 3:12 no m. 4 death;
22:3 curse

MOREOVER.
Ps. 19:11 m. by th. serv. warned
Is. 39:8 m. there shall be peace
Heb. 11:36 m. of bonds and imp.

MORIAH.
Gen. 22:2 get th. into land of M.
2 Chr. 3:1 Sol. built house in M.

MORNING.
Gen. 19:15 when the m. arose
24:54 Abra. rose up in the m.
28:31 rose betimes in the m.
29:25 in the m. behold it was L.
40:6 Jos. came into them in m.
49:27 in m. he sh. devour prey
Ex. 7:15 get thee to Phar. in m.
8:20 in m. east wind bro. locusts
14:27 sea returned to stre. in m.
16:7 in m. ye sh. see glory of L.
8 give you in the m. bread, 12
13 in the m. the dew lay round
23:26 one lamb in m. Num. 28:4
34:2 be ready in the m.
25 nor shall pass. be left to m.
Lev. 6:9 burning all night to m.
Num. 9:21 cloud taken sp in m.
Deut. 28:67 in m. would it were
Jud. 6:31 put to death whilst m.
16:2 in the m. when it is day
19:27 rose in m. opened doors
20:19 chil. of Israel rose in m.
2 Sam. 23:4 he shall be as
the m. when the sun riseth,
even a m. without clouds
24:11 when D. was up in the m.
1 K. 3:21 when I arose in the m.
Job 7:21 now shall I sleep in m.
Neh. 4:21 some labored from m.
8:3 read from m. until mid-day
Job 7:21 thou shalt seek me in m.
39:27 certali. forever at the m.
24:17 m. is to th. as shad. of de.
38:12 hast thou commanded m.
41:18 his eyes like eyelids of m.
Ps. 5:3 my voice shalt thou hear
in the m. O Lord, in the m.

CRUDEN'S CONCORDANCE. 947

MOR

Ps. 30:5 but joy cometh in the *m.*
49:14 dominion over them in *m.*
59:16 will sing thy mercy in *m.*
88:13 in the *m.* shall my prayer
90:5 the *m.* they are like grass
6 in the *m.* it flourisheth up
119:147 I prevented dawn. of *m.*
130:6 they that watch for *m.*
139:9 if I take wings of the *m.*
143:8 thy lovingkindness in the *m.*
Ec. 10:16 princes eat in the *m.*
11:6 in the *m.* sow thy seed
Cant. 6:10 she looketh like *m.*
Is. 14:12 O Lucifer, son of *m.*
17:14 before the *m.* he is not
21:12 watchman said, *m.* com.
· 38:19 *m.* by *m.* sh. it pass over
58:8 he wakeneth *m.* by *m.*
58:8 thy light break forth as *m.*
Jer. 5:8 were as fed horses in *m.*
20:16 hear the cry in the *m.*
21:12 execute judgm. in the *m.*
Ezek. 7:7 the *m.* is come on thee
10 the *m.* is gone forth, the rod
12:8 in the *m.* came word of L.
24:18 I spake to the peo. in the *m.* at even my wife died, I did in the *m.* as commanded
33:22 it came to me in the *m.*
Hos. 6:3 his going forth is as *m.*
4 your goodness is as *m.* cloud
7:6 in the *m.* it burneth as fire
10:15 in a *m.* sh. king be cut off
Joel 2:2 as *m.* spread on mount.
Amos 4:13 maketh the *m.* dark.
5:8 turn shad. of death into *m.*
Jon. 4:7 God prepared a worm
Mic. 2:1 when the *m.* is light
Mat. 16:3 in the *m.* it will be fo.
27:1 when the *m.* was come
Mark 11:20 in *m.* as they passed
13:35 at cock-crowing, or in *m.*

Early in the MORNING.
Gen. 19:27 Abraham gat up *e.* in the *m.* 21:14; 22:3
28:18 Jacob rose up *e.* in the *m.*
31:55 Laban rose *e.* in the *m.*
Ex. 8:20 said, Rise *e.* in *m.* 9:13
24:4 Moses rose *early* in *m.* 34:4
Jos. 3:1 Joshua rose *early* in the *m.* 6:12; 7:16; 8:10
Jud. 6:38 men of city *r.* e. in *m.*
1 *Sam.* 1:19 they rose up *e.* in *l.* *m.* 29:11; 2 *K.* 3:22; 19:35; 2 *Chr.* 20:20; *Is.* 37:36
15:12 Sa. rose *e.* in *m.* 17:20 D
2:10 wherefore rise *e.* in the *m.*
Job 1:5 Job rose up *e.* in the *m.*
Prov. 27:14 rising *early* in the *m.*
Is. 5:11 woe to th. th. rise *e.* in *m.*
37:36 arose *e.* in *t.* m. all dead
Dan. 6:19 Darius rose *e.* in *t.* m.
Mat. 20:1 went *early* in the *m.*
Mark 16:2 *early* in the *m.* came to sepulchre, *Luke* 24:1
Luke 21:38 came *e.* i. m. *John* 8:2
Acts 5:21 entered temple *e.* i. m.

See EVENING.

Every MORNING.
Ex. 16:21 gath. manna *every m.*
36:7 burn sweet incense *e. m.*
Lev. 6:12 priest burn wood *e. m.*
1 *Chr.* 9:27 *e. m.* pertain. to por.
a *Chr.* 13:11 burn to Lord *e. m.*
Job 7:18 shouldest visit him *e. m.*
Ps. 73:14 have been chaste. *e. m.*
Is. 33:2 be thou our arm *e. m.*
Lam. 3:23 L.'s mercies new *e. m.*
Ezek. 46:13 prepare a lamb *e. m.*
Amos 4:1 bring sacrifices *e. m.*
Zep. 3:5 *e. m.* doth bring judgm.

MORNING light.
1 *Sam.* 14:36 spoil th. until *m. l.*
25:22 pertain to him by *m. l.*
36 Abi. told nothing until *m. l.*
2 *Sam.* 17:22 passed *J.* by *m. l.*
2 *K.* 7:9 if we tarry until *m. li.*

See CLOUD.

MORNING star.
Job 38:7 wh. *m. s.* sang together
Rev. 2:28 I will give him *m. s.*
22:16 I, Jesus, am bright *m. s.*

Until the MORNING.
Ex. 12:10 let noth. of it remain *u. the m.* 16:19; 23:18; 29:34
Lev. 7:15; *Num.* 9:12
16:23 some of th. left *u. t. m.*
23 lay up for you *until the m.*
Lev. 19:13 not abide *u. t. m.*
Deut. 16:4 any flesh rem. *u. m.*
Jud. 19:25 abused her *u. t. m.*
Ruth 3:13 down *u. t. m.* 14 lay
1 *Sam.* 3:15 Samuel lay *u. t. m.*
19:2 take heed to thyself *u. t. m.*

MOS

2 *K.* 19:8 heads of kings *u. t. m.*
Prov. 7:18 our fill of love *u. m.*
Is. 38:13 I reckoned *until the m.*

MORNING watch.
Ex. 14:24 in *m. w.* L. said to M.
1 *Sam.* 11:11 mi. of host in *m. w.*

MORROW.
Ex. 8:23 to-*m.* shall this sign be
9:5 to-*m.* the L. sh. do this thi.
6 L. did thing, on *m.* cattle di.
16:23 to-*m.* is rest of holy sab.
19:10 sanc. them to-day and *m.*
32:5 to-*m.* is a feast to the Lord
Lev. 7:16 on *m.* remain. eat. 19:6
22:30 leave none of it till *m.*
23:15 ye shall count from *m.*
Num. 11:18 sanctify yourselves against to-*m. Jos.* 7:13
16:16 they and A. to-*m.* bef. L.
41 on *m.* congreg. murmured
Jos. 3:5 to-*m.* L. will do wond.
5:12 manna ceased on the *m.*
22:18 to-*m.* wroth wi. congreg.
Jud. 19:9 to-*m.* get early on way
20:28 to-*m.* I will deliver them
Jude 9 dispute, about body of M.
1 *Sam.* 11:9 to-*m.* by th. sun hot
20:5 to-*m.* is the new moon, 18
28:19 to-*m.* shalt thou and sons
1 *K.* 20:6 send ser. to thee to-*m.*
2 *K.* 6:28 will eat my son, to-*m.*
8:15 on *m.* he took a thick cloth
2 *Chr.* 20:16 to-*m.* go ye down, 17
Est. 5:8 to-*m.* as king hath said
12 to-*m.* am I invited to her
Prov. 3:28 to-*m.* I will give
27:1 boast not thyself to-*m.*
Is. 22:13 let us eat, for to-*m.* we die, 1 *Cor.* 15:32
56:12 to-*m.* shall be as this day
Zep. 3:3 gu. not bones till to-*m.*
Mat. 6:30 to-*m.* is cast into oven, *Luke* 12:28
34 take no thought for *m.* for *m.* sh. take thought for itself
Luke 12:19 to-day, and to-*m.*
31 walk to-day and to-*m.*
Acts 20:7 P. rea. to depart on *m.*
23:20 to-*m.* thou shalt hear him
Jam. 4:13 to-day or to-*m.* will go
14 know not what sh. be on *m.*

MORSEL.
Gen. 18:5 fetch a *m.* of bread
Jud. 19:5 comf. heart with *m.*
Ruth 2:14 dip thy *m.* in vinegar
Job 31:17 eaten my *m.* myself
Ps. 147:17 bef. dry *m.* and quiet
23:8 *m.* hast eaten shalt vomit
Heb. 12:16 E. for *m.* sold birthri.

See DREAD.

MORSELS.
Ps. 147:17 cast. forth ice like *m.*

MORTAL.
Job 4:17 *m.* man mo. just th. G. ?
Rom. 6:12 sin reign in *m.* body
8:11 quicken yo. bodies by Spi.
1 *Cor.* 15:53 *m.* on immortal, 54
2 *Cor.* 4:11 J. manifest. in yo. fle.

MORTALITY.
2 *Cor.* 5:1 *m.* swallow. up of life

MORTALLY.
Deut. 19:11 smite neighbor *m.*

MORTAR.
Gen. 11:3 slime had they for *m.*
Ex. 1:14 serve in *m.* and brick
Lev. 14:42 take *m.* and plast. ho.
45 break down *m.* of the house
Is. 41:25 upon princes as up. *m.*
Ezek. 13:10 daubed it with untempered *m.* 11, 14, 15; 22:28
Nah. 3:14 clay, and tread the *m.*

MORTAR.
Prov. 27:22 bray fool in *m.*

MORTGAGED.
Neh. 5:3 we have *m.* our lands

MORTIFY.
Rom. 8:13 ye *m.* deeds of body
Col. 3:5 *m.* your members

MOSEROTH. *Num.* 33:30

MOSES.
Ex. 2:10 called his name M.
Num. 1:3 so I was with M. 3:7
Ps. 105:26 he sent M. and Aaron
106:16 envied M. in the camp
Is. 63:12 by right hand of M.
Jer. 15:1 though M. stood be. me
Mal. 4:4 remember ye law of M.
Mat. 17:3 there appeared M. and Elias, *Mark* 9:4; *Luke* 9:30
19:7 why did M. command. ?
23:2 Pharisees sit in M.' seat
Mark 10:3 what did M. com. ?

MOT

Mark 12:19 M. wrote, *Luke* 20:28
Luke 16:29 M. and prophets
20:37 M. showed at the bush
24:27 beginning at M. and pro.
John 1:17 law given by M. 45
3:14 as M. lifted serpent
5:45 M. accuseth ; 46 believed M.
6:32 M. ga. you not that bread
7:19 M. give you law ? 22, 23
9:28 M. disciples ; 29 G. spake
Acts 3:22 M. said, A prophet
6:11 blas. words against M. 14
7:20 M. born, 22, 25, 37
13:39 not justified by law of M.
15:1 circumcised after M. 5
21 M. hath in every city them
21:21 teachest to forsake M.
26:22 things M. did say, 28:23
2 *Cor.* 3:13 not as M. who, 15
2 *Tim.* 3:8 as Jan. withstood M.
Heb. 3:2 M. faithful, 3, 5, 16
9:19 M. spoken every precept
10:28 despised M. law
11:23 by faith M. was hid three
12:21 M. said, I fear and quake
Jude 9 dispute, about body of M.
Rev. 15:3 sing the song of M.

MOST.
Prov. 20:6 *m.* men proclaim
Luke 7:42 wh. will love him *m.* ?
43 he to whom he forgave *m.*
Acts 20:38 sorrowing *m.* of all for
1 *Cor.* 14:27 two, or at *m.* three

MOTE.
Mat. 7:3 *m.* in brother's eye, *Luke* 6:41
4 let me pull *m.* out of th. eye
5 then th. see clear. to cast *m.* out of broth.'s eye, *Luke* 6:42

MOTH.
Job 4:19 crushed before the *m.*
27:18 buildeth his house as *m.*
Ps. 39:11 beauty consu. like *m.*
Is. 50:9 shall eat them, 51:8
Hos. 5:12 I be to Ephr. as a *m.*
Mat. 6:19 *m.* and rust corrupt, 20
Luke 12:33 where no *m.* corrupt.

MOTH-EATEN.
Jam. 5:2 your garments are *m.-e.*

MOTHER.
Gen. 3:20 was *m.* of all living
17:16 shall be a *m.* of nations
21:60 *m.* thousands of millions
32:11 lest he come and sm. *m.*
Lev. 20:14 her *m.* is wickedness
Jud. 5:7 Deb. arose a *m.* in Isr.
24 *m.* of Sisera looked out
Ruth 1:8 ret. each to her *m.*'s house
1 *Sam.* 17:25 Zeruiah, Joab's *m.*
20:19 to destroy a *m.* in Israel
1 *K.* 2:19 a seat for the king's *m.*
3:27 child, she is the *m.* thereof
2 *K.* 21:5 carried away king'e *m.*
Ps. 113:9 to a joyful *m.* of child.
Prov. 30:11 generat. not bless *m.*
Cant. 6:9 only one of her *m.*
Is. 50:1 who. bill of *m.* divorce ?
Jer. 50:12 *m.* be sore confound.
Ezek. 16:44 as is *m.* so is daugh.
45 your *m.* was a Hittite
5 to. wh. hath played the harlot
19:2 *m.* was dashed in pieces
Hos. 7:6 daughter riseth up ag.
Mat. 8:14 P.'s wife's *m.* 10. 4:38
11:8 before instructed of her *m.*
19:12 so born from *m.*'s womb
20:20 *m.* of Zebedee's children
Luke 8:19 of L. unto *m.* and breth.
John 2:1 *m.* of J. there, *Acts* 1:14
19:25 *m.*'s sister, *m.* of J.
27 dis. took her unto his *m.*
Acts 7:20 nourished *m.* of all
Rom. 16:13 salute R. and his *m.*

MOTHER-IN-LAW.
Deut. 27:23 curs. lieth wi. *m.-i.-l.*
Ruth 1:14 Or. kissed her *m.-i.-l.*
2:23 R. dwelt with her *m.-i.-l.*
3:17 go not empty to thy *m.-i.-l.*
Mic. 7:6 dau.-in-law ag. *m.-i.-l.*
Mat. 10:35 ; *Luke* 12:53

My MOTHER.
Gen. 20:12 not daughter of *m. m.*
Jud. 8:19 the sons of *my m.*
16:17 Nazar. from *my m.*'s wo.
1 *K.* 2:20 to her, Ask on, *my m.*
Job 1:21 naked out of *m. m.*'s w.
3:10 sh. not doors of *my m.*'s w.
17:14 to worm, Thou art *m. m.*
31:18 guid. her fr. *m. m.*'s wo.
Ps. 22:9 wh. on *m. m.*'s breasts
10 my God from *m. m.*'s belly
51:5 in sin did *m. m.* conc. me
63:8 allow to us *m.*'s children
71:6 out of *m. m.*'s bowels
139:13 cov. me in *m m.*'s womb
Prov. 4:3 bel. in sight of *my m.*
Cant. 1:6 *my m.*'s children ang.
3:4 brou. him to *my m.*'s house
8:1 sucked the breasts of *m m.*
2 bring th. into *my m.*'s house
Is. 49:1 from bowels of *my m.*
Jer. 15:10 woe to me, *my m.*
20:14 day wherein *my m.* bare
17 my *m.* might be my grave
Mat. 12:48 Jesus said, Who is *my m.* ? *Mark* 3:33
49 behold *my m.* and brethren, *Mark* 3:34 ; *Luke* 8:21
Gal. 1:15 separat. fr. *m m.*'s w.

Thy MOTHER.
Gen. 27:29 let *thy m.*'s sons bow
37:10 I and *thy m.* bow to thee ?
Lev. 18:7 nakedness of *thy m.*
1 *Sam.* 15:33 *thy m.* be childless
Prov. 1:8 law of *t. m.* 6:20
23:22 and despise not *thy m.*
25 *thy m.* that bare thee
Jer. 22:26 *thy m.* that bare thee
Ezek. 16:3 fa. Amorite, *t. m.* Hit.
45 thou art *t. m.*'s daughter
Hos. 4:5 I will destroy *thy m.*
10 *thy m.* is like a vine
Mat. 12:47 beh. *t. m.* and breth.
Mark 8:32 ; *Luke* 8:20 ; *John* 19:27
2 *Tim.* 1:5 which dwelt in *t. m.*

MOTHERS.
Is. 49:23 queens be thy nurs. *m.*
Jer. 16:3 saith the L. concern. *m.*
Lam. 2:12 say to to the *m.* where is corn and wine ? swel was in
poured out their *m.* bosom
5:3 fatherless, our *m.* as widows
Mark 10:30 hun. fold, sisters, *m.*
1 *Tim.* 1:9 law for murder. of *m.*
5:2 entreat elder women as *m.*

MOTIONS.
Rom. 7:5 the *m.* of sinful work

MOU

MOULDY.
Jos. 9:5 bread dry and *m.* 12

MOULTING.

Job 20:6 excel. *m.* to heavens
20:27 die, ought a. it, thy com. ?
Ps. 107:26 they to up to heaven
Is. 40:31 wait up. L. up. *m.*wings
155:12 ye *m.* up of Lilith they go

1 *Chr.* 4:9 A. *m.* called name Ja.
2 *Chr.* 22:3 his *m.* was his coun.
Ps. 35:14 as one mourn. for *h. m.*
109:14 not sin of *h* is *m.* blotted
131:2 child weaned of *his m.*
Prov. 10:1 son is heavi. of *h. m.*
15:20 foolish man despis. *h. m.*
28:15 hath bringeth *h. m.* to sh.
31:1 prophecy *h. m.* taught him
K. 5:15 came forth of *h. m.*'s *w.*
Cant. 3:11 *his m.* crowned him
6:9 113 wh. *h. m.* comforteth
Mat. 1:18 *A. m.* was espoused
2:13 young child and *h. m.* 20
12:46 *h. m.* stood with, *Mark* 3:31 ; *Luke* 8:19
13:55 is not *h. m.* called Mary ?
Luke 1:15 Holy G. fr. *h. m.*'s wo.
60 *h. m.* said, He sh. be call. J.
2:51 *h. m.* kept these sayings
7:12 only son of *h. m.* a widow
15 he delivered him to *h. m.*
John 8:4 sec. time into *h. m.*'s w.
19:25 *h. m.* stood by cross of J.
26 when J. saw *h. m.*
Acts 3:2 lame fr. *h. m.* wo. 11:8
Rom. 16:13 salute R. and *his m.*

MOTHERS-IN-LAW.
1 *Chr.* 4:9 A. *m.* called name Ja.

MOU

Is. 40:31 shall *m.* up with wings
Jer. 51:33 tho. Babylon aho. *m.*
Ezek. 10:16 cherub. lift to *m.* 19

MOUNT.

Gen. 31:54 J. offered sacri. on *m.*
Ex. 18:5 encamped at *m.* of G.
19:12 whoso toucheth the *m.*
14 Moses went down from the *m.* 32:15; 34:29
16 thick cloud upon *m.* 24:15
18 *m.* Si. was altoget. on smo.
23 set bounds about the *m.*
24:16 glory of Lord upon *m.* Si.
17 devouring fire on top of *m.*
31:18 L. gave Mos. on *m.* Sinai
32:19 M. brake them beneath *m.*
34:2 and come up to *m.* Sinai
3 nor let man be seen thro' *m.*
Num. 13:23 they departed fr. *m.*
20:28 Aaron died in *m.* Hor
Deut. 1:6 dw. long enough in *m.*
7 turn you, go to *m.* of Amor.
9:15 the *m.* burned with fire
27:13 these shall stand on *m.* E.
33:2 L. shined forth from *m.* P.
Jud. 4:6 draw towards *m.* Tabor
2 *Sam.* 15:30 D. went by the *m.*
32 *m.* where he worshipped G.
1 *K.* 19:8 Elijah went to *m.* of G.
11 stand on the *m.* bef. the L.
2 *K.* 23:13 the *m.* of corruption
Neh. 9:13 thou camest on *m.* Si.
Cant. 4:1 flock of goats fr. *m.* G.
Is. 10:32 *m.* of dau. of Zion. 16:1
14:13 I will sit on *m.* of congre.
27:13 worship in holy *m.* at J.
30:8 siege ag. thee with a *m.*
Jer. 6:6 cast a *m.* against Jerusa.
Ezek. 4:2; 21:22; 26:8
Dan. 11:15 k. of north cast np *m.*
Ob. 8 destroy unders. out *m.* E.
21 saviors sh. come to judgo *m.*
Hab. 3:3 H. One from *m.* Paran
Acts 7:30 in wildernes of *m.* S.
Gal. 4:24 one from the *m.* Sinai
25 Agar is *m.* Sinai in Arabia
Heb. 12:18 not come to the *m.*

See CARMEL, GERIZIM.

Before the MOUNT.

Ex. 19:2 Israel camped *b.t.m.*
34:3 nei. let flocks feed *b.t.m.*

See EPHRAIM.

In, or into the MOUNT.

Gen. 22:14 *in t. m.* of L. be seen
31:54 tarried all night *in t. m.*
Ex. 4:27 met him *in t. m.* of God
10:12 take heed, go not up *t. m.*
24:12 come *i. t. m. Deut.* 10:1
13 went *in t. m.* of G. 15, 18
18 M. was *in t. m.* 40 days and 40 nights, *Deut.* 9:9; 10:10
25:40 after pat. showed thee *in t. m.* 26:30; 27:8; *Heb.* 8:5
Num. 27:12 get thee *into m.* A.
Deut. 32:50 die *in m.* as A. died
Jos. 8:30 altar to L. *in m.* Ebal
1 *K.* 28:16 spied sepulchres *in m.*
2 *Chr.* 8:1 house of L. *in m.* Mo.
Is. 23:21 L. rise up as *in m.* P.
Acts 7:38 angel spake *in m.* Sin.
2 *Pet.* 1:18 we were *in* holy *m.*

See OLIVES.

MOUNT of Olives.

Zec. 14:4 his feet shall stand on *m.* of O. *m.* of O. shall clea.
Mat. 21:1 they were come to the *m.* of *Olives, Luke* 19:29
21:9 upon *m. of O. Mark* 13:3
16:30 they went out into *m.* of *O. Mark* 14:26; *Luke* 22:39
Luke 19:37 at descent of *m. of O.*
21:37 and abode in *m. of O.*
Acts 1:12 returned fr. *m. of O.*

See SEIR, ZION.

MOUNTS.

Jer. 32:24 *m.* are come to city
33:4 houses thrown down by *m.*
Ezek. 17:17 for him, by cast. *m.*

MOUNTAIN.

Gen. 14:10 they th. re. fled to *m.*
19:17 escape to *m.* 19 not escape
Ex. 3:1 came to the *m.* of G.
12 peo. sh. serve God on th. *m.*
19:3 L. called to him out of *m.*
20:18 people saw *m.* smoking
Num. 14:40 gat th. into top of *m.*
Deut. 2:3 ye have compassed *m.*
3:25 let me see that goodly *m.*
4:11 *m.* burnt with fire, 5:23
Jos. 2:16 get ye to *m.* and hide
11:16 Jos. took the plain and *m.*
14:12 give me *m.* 17:18 *m.* thine
Jud. 1:19 drave out inhabitants of *m.*

MOU

1 *Sam.* 17:3 Philistines stood on a *m.* on one side, and Israel stood on a *m.* on the oth. si.
23:26 Saul went on this side of the *m.* and David on th. si.
2 *K.* 2:16 S. cast him on some *m.*
6:17 *m.* full of horses and char.
Job 14:18 *m.* fall. com. to naught
Ps. 11:1 flee as bird to your *m.* ?
30:7 hast made my *m.* to stand
78:54 bro. to *m.* his right hand
Is. 2:2 *m.* of L.'s house. *Mic.* 4:1
3 let us go to *m. of L. Mic.* 4:2
30:17 as a beacon on top of *m.*
29 one goeth with pipe to *m.*
40:4 every *m.* and hill sh. be made low, *Luke* 3:5
Jer. 16:16 hunt them fr. every *m.*
17:3 O my *m.* in the field
20:18 *m.* of the house as high places of forest, *Mic.* 3:12
5*t*6 people gone fr. *m.* to hill
51:25 O destroying *m.* saith L. I will make thee a burnt *m.*
Lam. 5:18 because of *m.* of Zion
Ezek. 11:23 gl. of L. stood on *m.*
28:16 cast thee out of *m.* of God
43:12 law of house on top of *m.*
Dan. 2:35 stone became great *m.*
45 the stone was cut out of *m.*
Mic. 7:12 co. to thee fr. *m.* to *m.*
Hag. 1:8 go up to *m.* bring wood
Zec. 4:7 who art th. O great *m.*
8:3 be called the *m.* of the Lord
14:4 half of the *m.* shall remove
Mat. 5:1 he went up into a *m.*
14:23; 15:29; *Mark* 3:13; 6:46; *Luke* 6:12; 9:28; *John* 6:3, 15
17:1 bringeth them into a high *m.* 9 and as they came down from the *m. Mark* 9:9
20 have faith, say to this *m.* Remove, 21:21; *Mark* 11:23
28:16 *m.* where Jesus appointed
Mark 5:32 swine feeding on *m.*
Heb. 12:20 much as beast tou. *m.*
Rev. 6:14 every *m.* and isl. not
8:8 a great *m.* burning with fire

High MOUNTAIN.

Is. 13:2 lift up banner up. *h. m.*
30:25 shall be upon every *h. m.*
40:9 get thee up kilo the *h. m.*
57:7 on *h. m.* hast th. set thy b.
Jer. 3:6 gone np npon ev. *h. m.*
Ezek. 17:22 plant it on a *high m.*
40:2 set me on a very high *m.*
Mat. 4:8 devil taken him up into an exceeding *h. m. Luke* 4:5
17:1 Jesus taketh P., James and *Ro.* 31:20 ear. on in Sp. to *h. m.*

See HOLY.

In the, or in this MOUNTAIN.

Gen. 19:30 went and dwelt *in m.*
Ex. 13:17 plant them *in the m.*
Num. 13:17 said, Go up *in. t. m.*
Deut. 32:49 get thee up *in t. m.*
Ps. 48:1 G. praised *in m.* of holi.
Is. 25:6 *in this m.* L. make feast
7 destroy *in t. m.* face of cov.
10 *in this m.* hand of L. rest
Ezek. 17:23 *in the m.* of Israel
Amos 4:1 *in the m.* of Samaria
6:1 trust to the. trust *in m.* of S.
John 4:20 fath. worship, *in t. m.*
21 nei. *in this m.* nor Jerusal.

MOUNTAINS.

Gen. 7:20 the *m.* were covered
8:4 the ark rested upon the *m.*
5 tenth month tops of *m.* seen
Num. 23:46 departed from the *m.*
Deut. 12:2 destroy pla. on hi. *m.*
Num. 11:21 cut off Anakim fr. *m.*
Jud. 5:5 *m.* melted from bef. L.
11:37 go up and down on *m.*
1 *Sam.* 1:21 *m.* of Gilboa
I K. 19:11 a strong wind rent *m.*
1 *Chr.* 12:8 swift as roes on *m.*
2 *Chr.* 18:16 Israel scatter. on *m.*
Job 9:5 which removeth the *m.*
24:8 overturneth *m.* by roots
40:20 *m.* bring him forth food
Ps. 36:6 thy right. like great *m.*
46:2 though the *m.* be carried
48:1 Zion sides of *m.* on north
50:10 cattle upon 1000 *m.*
65:6 his strength setteth fast *m.*
72:3 *m.* bring peace to the peo.
76:4 more glori. than *m.* of prey
83:14 flame setteth *m.* on fire
87:1 foundation in the holy *m.*
104:6 waters stood above *m.*
8 up by the *m.* down by valle.
114:4 *m.* skipped like rams, 6
125:2 as *m.* round about Jerusa.
133:3 dew that descended on *m.*
144:5 touch *m.* they shall smoke

MOU

Ps. 147:8 mak. gr. to grow on *m.*
138:9 *m.* and hills praise the L.
Prov. 8:25 before *m.* were settled
Cant. 2:8 cometh leaping on *m.*
17 be like a roe on the *m.* 8:14
4:8 look from *m.* of the leopards
Is. 2:14 day of L. be on high *m.*
14:25 *m.* tread him under foot.
18:3 lifteth up ensign on the *m.*
31:3 *m.* melted with their blood
40:12 hath weighed *m.* in scales
41:15 thou shalt thresh the *m.*
42:15 make waste *m.* and hills
44:23 into singing, ye *m.* 49:13
49:11 make all my *m.* a way
52:7 how beautiful on the *m.* are the feet, *Nah.* 1:15
54:10 for the *m.* shall depart
55:12 *m.* shall break forth befo.
64:1 *m.* flow down at presen. 3
65:7 have burned incense on *m.*
Jer. 4:24 boh. *m.* and th. tromb.
9:10 for *m.* will I take up weep.
13:16 feet stumble on dark *m.*
17:26 from *m.* bringing offerin.
31:5 plant vines on *m.* of Sama.
46:18 as Tabor among the *m.*
50:6 turned them away on *m.*
Lam. 4:19 pursued us on the *m.*
Ezek. 6:2 set face toward *m.* of I.
7:16 sh. be on the *m.* like doves
18:6 not eaten upon *m.* 11, 15
19:9 voice no more heard on *m.*
22:9 thay eat upon the *m.*
31:12 upon *m.* branches fallen
32:5 I will lay thy flesh on *m.*
33:28 *m.* of Is. shall be desolate
34:6 sheep wander. through *m.*
13 feed them on *m.* of Israel, 14
35:8 fill his *m.* with slain men
36:1 prophesy unto *m.* Is. 4
8 *m.* of Is. shoot forth branch.
37:22 one nation on *m.* of Israel
38:8 gathered ag. *m.* of Is.
20 *m.* shall be thrown down
21 sw. against him thro' all *m.*
39:2 bring thee on *m.* of Israel
4 shall fall on the *m.* of Israel
17 great sacrifice on *m.* of Isr.
Joel 2:2 morn. spread upon *m.*
3:18 *m.* sh. drop down new wine
Amos 3:9 assemble on *m.* of Sa.
4:13 formeth M. L. is his name
9:13 *m.* shall drop sweet wine
Obad. 1:4 the *m.* shall be molten
6:1 contend thou before the *m.*
2 O ye *m.* the L.'s controversy
Nah. 1:5 the *m.* quake at him
3:18 people scattered on the *m.*
Hab. 3:6 everlasting *m.* scattered
10 *m.* saw thee, and trembled
Hag. 1:11 for a drought on *m.*
Zec. 6:1 chariots bet. *m.* of brass
Mat. 18:12 leaveth ninety-nine
Mark 5:5 in *m.* crying
13:14 let them in Jud. flee to *m.*
1 *Cor.* 13:2 that I could remo. *m.*
Rev. 16:20 *m.* were not found
17:9 seven heads are seven *m.*

In the MOUNTAINS.

Ex. 32:12 to slay them *in t. m.*
Num. 33:47 pitched *in t. m.* of A.
Deut. 2:37 cam. not to cit. *in m.*
Jos. 10:6 kings that dw. *in t. m.*
Jud. 5:2 Is. made dens *in t. m.*
1 *K.* 5:15 80,000 hewers *in t. m.*
2 *Chr.* 21:11 high places *in t. m.*
Jer. 13:16 noise of multi. *in t. m.*
Hob. 11:38 wandered *in the m.*

Of the MOUNTAINS.

Gen. 8:5 tops *of t. m.* were seen
22:2 offer him on one *of the m.*
Num. 23:7 out *of the m.* of east
Deut. 32:22 foundations *of t. m.*
33:15 chief thin. *of t. anci* ent *m.*
Jud. 9:25 for him in top *of t. m.*
36 peo. down from top *of t. m.* sees! shadow *of the m.*
1 *K.* 19:33 to hei. *of t. m. Is.* 37:24
31:6 all showers *of the m.*
39:8 range *of t. m.* is pasture
Ps. 50:11 all fowl *of the m.*
72:16 handful corn on top *of m.*
Prov. 27:25 herbs *of t. m.* gath.
Is. 14:25 upon *m.* tread him
42:11 shout from top *of the m.*
Jer. 3:23 fr. multitude *of the m.*
4:24 witness. *in cities of t. m.*
8:13 in cities *of the m.*
Ezek. 6:13 slain in passes *of t. m.*
7:16 sounding sc. *of the m.*
Hos. 4:13 sacri. on tops *of the m.*
Joel 2:5 char. on tops *of the m.*
Jon. 2:6 down to bot. *of the m.*
Mic. 1:4 *m.* sh. be molt. under h.
4:1 estab. in the top *of the m.*
Nah. 1:5 flee to valley *of the m.*
Rev. 6:15 hid in rocks *of the m.*

MOU

To the MOUNTAINS.

Cant. 4:6 *to the m.* of myrrh
Is. 22:5 trouble and crying *to t. m.*
Ezek. 6:3 saith L. *to the m.* 36:4
32:6 water with blood *to the m.*
36:1 prophesy *to the m.* of Is. 6
Hos. 10:8 sh. say *to the m.* Cover
Mark 13:14 that he in Judea flee *to the m. Luke* 21:21
Luke 23:30 *to m.* Fall, *Rev.* 6:16

MOURN.

Gen. 23:2 Ab. came to *m.* Sarah
1 *Sam.* 16:1 how long *m.* for S. ?
3:31 and *m.* before Abner
1 *K.* 13:29 old proph. came to *m.*
14:13 all Israel sh. *m.* for him
Job 2:11 this day is holy, *m.* not
Job 2:11 appointm. to *m.* wl. hi.
5:11 those wh. *m.* may be exal.
14:22 soul within him shall *m.*
Ps. 55:2 I *m.* in my complaint
Prov. 5:11 and th. *m.* at the last
9:2 wicked rule, the people *m.*
Ec. 3:4 time to *m.* time to dance
Is. 3:26 gates sh. lament and *m.*
10:7 for Kir-haraseth shall ye *m.*
19:8 fishers *m.* 38:14 I did *m.*
59:11 we *m.* sore like doves
61:2 sent me to comf. all that *m.*
3 to appoint them that *m.* in Z.
66:10 rejoice all ye that *m.*
Jer. 4:28 for this earth shall *m.*
12:4 how long sh. the laud *m.* ?
48:31 *m.* for the men of Kir-her.
Lam. 1:4 the ways of Zion do *m.*
Ezek. 7:12 let not the seller *m.*
27 king shall *m.* and the prin.
21:16 nei. sh. thou *m.* nor weep
33 shall pine away and *m.*
31:15 caused Leb. to *m.* for him
Hos. 4:3 theref. sh. the land *m.* ?
10:5 peo. shall *m.* over Samaria
Joel 1:9 the Lord's ministers *m.*
Amos 1:2 habita. of shepher. *m.*
8:8 every one *m.* therein. 9:5
Zec. 12:10 and shall *m.* for him
12 land *m.* every family apart
Mat. 5:4 blessed are they that *m.*
6:16 child, of bride-cham. *m.* ?
24:30 all the tribes of earth *m.*
Luke 6:25 laugh, for ye sh. *m.*
Jam. 4:9 afflicted, *m.* and weep
Rev. 18:11 merch. weep and *m.*

MOURNED.

Gen. 37:34 Jacob *m.* for his son
50:3 Egyptians *m.* for Jacob, 10
Ex. 33:4 heard th. evil tidings, they *m. Num.* 14:39
Num. 20:29 congreg. *m.* for A.
1 *Sam.* 1:35 Samuel *m.* for Saul
2 *Sam.* 1:12 *m.* for Saul and Jon.
11:26 Bath-sheba *m.* for Uriah
13:37 David *m.* for his son Ab.
14:2 one that had *m.* for dead
1 *K.* 13:30 they *m.* over man of G.
14:18 Is. *m.* for Jeroboam's son
1 *Chr.* 7:22 Ephr. their father *m.*
2 *Chr.* 35:24 Judah *m.* for Josiah
Ezr. 10:6 *m.* for transgression
Neh. 1:4 sat and *m.* certain days
Jer. 16:6 nor shall *m.* for them
Mat. 11:17 we have *m.* unto you, *Luke* 7:32
Mark 16:10 as they *m.* and wept
1 *Cor.* 5:2 and have not rather *m.*

MOURNER, S.

2 *Sam.* 14:2 feign thyself a *m.*
Job 29:25 one that comforteth *m.*
Ec. 12:5 *m.* go about the streets
Is. 57:18 restore comf. to his *m.*
Hos. 9:4 sacrif. be as bread of *m.*

MOURNETH.

2 *Sam.* 19:1 king *m.* for Absalom
Ps. 35:14 I bowed as one that *m.*
88:9 mine eye *m.* by reason of *Is.* 24:4 earth *m.* and fad. 33:9
7 new wine *m.* vine languish.
Jer. 12:11 viney. being desol. *m.*
14:2 Jud. *m.* and gates languish
23:10 bec. of swearing land *m.*
Joel 1:10 land *m.* corn is wasted
Zec. 12:10 one that *m.* first-born

MOURNFULLY.

Mal. 3:14 we have walked *m.*

MOURNING.

Gen. 27:41 days of *m.* at hand
50:10 made a *m.* for his father
11 saw *m.* this is a grievous *m.*
Deut. 26:14 not eaten in *m.*
34:8 days of *m.* for Mo. ended
2 *Sam.* 11:27 when *m.* was past
19:2 victory was turned to *m.*
Est. 4:3 there was *m.* am. Jews
9:22 was turned to them fr. *m.*
Job 3:8 ready to raise their *m.*

CRUDEN'S CONCORDANCE. 949

MOU

Job 30:31 harp also is turn. to m.
Ps. 30:11 turned m. to dancing
Ec. 7:2 better go to house of m.
    4 heart of wise in house of m.
Is. 22:12 Lord did call to m.
    51:11 sor. and m. shall flee away
    60:20 days of m. shall be ended
    61:3 give them oil of joy for m.
Jer. 6:26 m. as for an only son
    16:5 enter not into house of m.
    31:13 turn their m. into joy
Lam. 2:5 daughter of Judah m.
    5:15 our dance is turned into m.
Ezek. 2:10 lamentations, m. woe
    24:17 no m. for dead; 31:15 I cau.
Joel 2:12 with weeping and m.
Amos 5:16 call husbandm. to m.
    8:10 feasts into m. I will make
    it as the m. of an only son
Mic. 1:11 came not forth in m.
Zec. 12:11 m. in Jerusalem as m.
    of Hadadrimmon
Mat. 2:18 great m. Rachel weep.
2 Cor. 7:7 he told us your m.
Jam. 4:9 laugh. be turned to m.
Rev. 18:8 one day death and m.

MOURNING.
Gen. 37:35 go down to grave m.
2 Sam. 14:2 put on m. apparel
Est. 6:12 H. hasted to house m.
Job 30:28 I went m. without sun
Ps. 38:6 I go m. all day long
    42:9 why go I m. because of oppression of enemy? 43:2
Jer. 9:17 call for the m. women
    16:7 m. to conf. them for dead
Ezek. 7:16 m. for their iniquities
Dan. 10:2 D. was m. three weeks
Mic. 1:8 will make a m. as owls

MOUSE.
Lev. 11:29 weasel and m. be unc.
Is. 66:17 eating abomin. and m.

MOUTH.
Gen. 8:11 in her m. was olive lo.
    24:57 damsel, inquire at her m.
    29:2 great stone on well's m.
    3 rolled stone fr. well's m. 10
    42:27 his money was in sack's
    m. 43:12, 21
Ex. 4:11 who made man's m.?
    16 he shall be to thee in. of m.
Num. 12:8 him speak m. to m.
    16:30 earth open her m. and r.
    22:5 L. put a word in Bal.'s m.
    33:50 put to death by m. of witnesses, Deut. 17:6; 19:15
Jos. 10:18 sto. to m. of cave, 27
    22 open m. of cave, bring out
1 Sam. 1:12 Eli marked her m.
2 Sam. 14:3 J. put words in w.
    17:19 a covering over well's m.
1 K. 19:18 every n. not kissed
    22:13 the prophets declare good
    to the king with one m.
    22 lying spirit in m. of his
    prophets; 23; 2 Chr. 18:21, 22
2 Chr. 35:22 ken. not to m. of G.
    36:21 fulfil word of Lord by m.
    of Jeremiah, 24; Ezr. 1:1
Est. 7:8 word we out king's m.
Job 5:16 iniquity stop. her m.
    12:11 doth m. taste meat? 34:3
    32:5 there was no answer in m.
Ps. 8:2 out of m. of babes
    22:21 save me from the lion's m.
    32:9 m. must be held with brid.
    37:30 m. of right. speak. wisd.
    38:14 in wh. m. are no reproofs
    62:11 but m. that speaketh lies
    63:15 let not the pit shut her m.
    107:42 iniquity shall stop her m.
    109:2 m. of wick. m. of deceitf.
    126:2 m. filled with laughter
    141:7 bones scat. at grave's m.
Prov. 4:24 put away froward m.
    5:3 her m. is smoother than oil
    6:12 walketh wi. frow. m. 10:32
    8:13 the froward m. do I hate
    10:6 violence cov. m. of wicked
    11 m. of fool. near destruction
    31 m. of just bringeth wisdom
    11:11 city over, by m. of wicked
    12:6 m. of upright deliver them
    1:13 in m. of fool. is rod of pride
    15:2 m. of fools poureth foolish.
    14 m. of fools feed. on foolish.
    28 m. of wicked pour. out evil
    16:1 words of a man's m. deep
    7 a fool's m. is his destruction
    19:28 m. of wicked devour iniq.
    24:14 m. of a strange woman
    26:7 parable in m. of fools, 9
    28 flattering m. worketh ruin
    30:20 eateth and wipeth her m.
Ec. 10:12 words of a w. man's m.

MOU

Is. 9:12 devour Is. with open m.
    17 and every m. speaketh folly
    57:4 ag. wh. make ye wide m.?
    59:21 Sp. not depart out of m.
Jer. 32:4 speak m. to m. 34:3
    36:4 Baruch wrote from m. of
    Jeremiah, 27, 32; 45:1
    44:17 goeth forth out of m.
    26 no more named in m.
Lam. 3:38 out of m. of Most H.
Ezek. 21:22 open m. in slaughter
    16:31 of the heart m. speaketh
Dan. 4:31 word was in king's m.
    6:17 stone laid on m. of the den
    7:5 it had three ribs in m. of it
    8 a m. speaking gr. things, 20
Hos. 2:17 names of B. out her m.
Amos 3:12 a shep. tak. out of m.
Nah. 3:12 fall into m. of eater
Zec. 5:8 weight of lead on m.
Mat. 4:1 proceed. out of m. of G.
    12:34 of the heart m. speaketh
    13:11 what go. in m. defil. not
    18:16 in m. of two or three witness, every word, 2 Cor. 13:1
    21:16 out m. of babes ha. praise
Luke 1:70 spake by m. of proph.
    21:15 I will give you a m.
Acts 1:16 the Holy Ghost spake
    by m. of David, 4:25
    3:18 showed by m. of proph. 21
    13:27 tell you same things by m.
    23:2 commanded to smit on m.
Rom. 3:14 wh. m. is full of curs.
    10 every m. may be stopped
    10:10 with m. confes. is made
1 Cor. 9:9 not muzzle m. of ox
2 Tim. 4:17 deliv. out m. of lion
Jam. 3:10 out of m. proceed bles.
Rev. 1:16 a m. speaking blasph.
    16:13 spirits out of m. of dragon

His MOUTH.
Ex. 4:15 and put words in his m.
    and I will be with his m.
Num. 22:16 G. put word in his m.
Deut. 18:18 put words in h. m.
1 Sam. 14:26 put hand to h. m. 27
    17:35 delivered it out of his m.
2 Sam. 18:25 there is tid. in h. m.
    22:9 fire out of his m. Ps. 18:8
1 K. 8:15 wi. h. m. to D. 2 Chr. 6:4
1 K. 4:34 he put his m. on his m.
Job 15:30 by breath of his m.
    21:5 wicked, he went m. h. 20:15
    41 write all th. words h. m.
    13 keep it still within h. m.
    22:22 receive law from his m.
    23:12 esteemed words of his m.
    37:2 sound goeth out of his m.
    40:23 draw up Jord. into his m.
    41:19 out of his m. go bu. lamps
    21 a flame goeth out of his m.
Ps. 10:7 h. m. is full of cursing
    33:6 made by breath of h. m.
    36:3 words of his m. are iniq.
    38:13 dumb man open. not h. m.
    55:21 words of his m. smoother
    105:5 rem. judgments of h. m.
Prov. 2:6 out of h. m. knowledge
    11:9 his m. destroyeth neighb.
    13:2 eat good by fruit of his m.
    3 keepeth his m. keep. his life
    15:23 hath joy by ans. of h. m.
    15:7 of his m. thunegers, not judg.
    16:10 divine sentence is in h. m.
    23 heart of wise teacheth h. m.
    26 for his m. craveth it of him
    18:6 his m. calleth for strokes
    20 satisfied with fruit of his m.
    19:21 not bring it to h. m. 26:15
    20:17 his m. filled with gravel
    21:23 keepeth h. m. keep. soul
    22:7 labor of man is for h. m.
    10:13 words of his m. is foolish.
    6:16 h. m. is sweet, m. lovely
Is. 11:4 earth with rod of h. m.
Jer. 9:8 speak. peace, with h. m.
    28 writeth all th. words h. m.
    51:44 bring out of h. m. that wh.
Lam. 3:29 putteth his m. in dust
    41 long. cleav. to roof of h. m.
Ezek. 3:2 seek the law of h. m.
Luke 1:64 and his m. was opened
    4:22 gracious words out of h. m.
    6:45 abund. of heart h. m. speak
    19:22 out of thine own m. will I
    22:71 have heard of his own m.
John 19:29 and put it to his m.
1 Thes. 2:8 consume with sp. of his m.
1 Pet. 2:22 neither guile in h. m.

MOU

Rev. 1:16 out of his m. went, a
    sharp sword, 19:15, 21
    12:15 cast out of his m. water
    13:2 his m. was as mou. of lion
See LORD.

My MOUTH.
Gen. 45:12 my m. speak to you
Num. 22:38 put. in my m. 23:12
Deut. 32:1 hear words of my m.
1 Sam. 2:1 my m. is enlarg. over
Job 9:11 I will not refrain my m.
    9:20 my own m. shall cond. me
    16:5 strengthen you with my m.
    19:16 entreated serv. wi. my m.
    23:4 fill my m. with arguments
    31:27 my m. kissed my hand
    30 neither suffer. my m. to sin
    33:2 tongue ha. spok. in my m.
    40:4 I lay my hand upon my m.
Ps. 17:3 my m. shall not transgr.
    19:14 words of my m. be accept.
    34:1 praise continual. be my m.
    39:1 keep my m. with a bridle
    40:3 put a new song in my m.
    49:3 my m. shall speak of wisd.
    51:15 my m. sh. forth thy praise
    54:2 give ear to words of my m.
    63:5 my m. shall praise thee
    66:14 my m. hath spoken when I
    17 I cried to him with my m.
    71:8 my m. be filled with praise
    15 my m. show forth righteou.
    78:1 incl. ears to wor. of my m.
    2 I will open my m. in a para.
    89:1 with my m. will I make kn.
    103:20 praise the L. with my m.
    119:43 word of tr. out of my m.
    103 sweet. th. honey to my m.
    108 freewill-offerings of my m.
    137:6 tongue cl. to roof of my m.
    141:3 set a watch before my m.
    143:9 my m. sh. speak praise
Prov. 4:5 fr. words of my m. 5:7
    7:24 attend to words of my m.
    8:7 for my m. shall speak truth
    8 words of my m. in righteous.
Is. 6:7 he laid the coal on my m.
    30:2 have not asked at my m.
    31:16 my m. it hath commanded
    48:3 things forth out of my m.
    49:2 made my m. like sharp
    55:11 word that go. out my m.
Jer. 1:9 Lord touched my m.
    15:19 thou shalt be as my m.
Ezek. 3:3 in my m. like honey
    17 hear word at my m. 33:7
    4:14 abomin. flesh into my m.
Dan. 10:3 flo. nor wine in my m.
    16 one of G. sons touched my m.
Mat. 13:35 open my m. in parab.
Acts 11:8 any time enter, my m.
    15:7 Gentiles by my m. sh. hear
Eph. 6:19 open my m. boldly
Rev. 3:16 spit thee out of my m.
    10:10 hook in my m. sweet

MOUTH, with opened.
Num. 4:11 earth opened her m.
Num. 16:32 open. m. 26:10; Deut. 11:6
    22:28 Lord opened m. of the ass
Jud. 11:35 o. my m. to Lord, 36
Job 3:1 op. Job his m. and curs.
    32:24 opened their m. Ps. 22:13
Ps. 39:9 I o. not my m. because
    109:2 m. of deceitful o. ag. me
    119:131 I o. my m. and panted
Ps. 8:13 hell hath opened her m.
    10:14 there was none that o. m.
    63:7 yet he opened not his m.
Ezek. 3:2 I o. my m. he caused
    24:27 thy m. be opened, 33:22
Dan. 10:16 o. my m. and spake
    17:27 when thou hast o. his m.
Luke 1:64 his m. was o. immediately
Acts 8:32 he open. not his m.
    35 Philip o. his m. preached
    10:34 P. o. his m. and said
2 Cor. 6:11 our m. is ope. to you
Rev. 12:16 earth ope her m.
    13:6 he o. his m. in blasphemy

MOUTH, with openeth.
Prov. 24:7 dumb man o. not his m.
    31:26 she o. her m. with wisdom

Their MOUTH.
Jud. 7:6 put their m. to l. m.
Neh. 9:20 not thy manna fr. t. m.
Ps. 5:9 for in t. m. is no faithful.
    17:10 enclos. in own fat, with t. m.
    22:9 gaped upon me with t. m.
    33:9 princes laid hand on t. m.
    49:13 tongue cle. to roof of t. m.
    59:7 faithfulness in t. m.

MOV

Ps. 17:10 with their m. they spe. proudly
    58:6 bre. teeth, O God, in t. m.
    59:7 they belch out with t. m.
    12 sin of t. m. and words of li.
    62:4 bless with t. m. curse inw.
    73:9 set t. m. aga. the heavens
    78:36 did flatter him with t. m.
    149:6 praises of God be in t. m.
Is. 29:13 peo. draw near wi. t. m.
Jer. 7:28 truth cut off from t. m.
    12:2 thou art near in their m.
Lam. 2:16 enemies opened t. m.
Ezek. 33:31 with t. m. they show
    34:10 deliver my flock from t. m.
Mic. 6:12 tongue deceitf. in t. m.
    7:16 sh. lay their hand on t. m.
Zep. 3:13 deceit. tongue in t. m.
Zec. 14:12 tongue cons. in t. m.
Mal. 15:8 draweth nigh wi. t. m.
Jude 16 t. m. speak. great words
Rev. 9:19 power is in t. m.
    11:5 fire proceedeth out of t. m.
    14:5 in t. m. was found no guile

Thy MOUTH.
Ex. 4:12 I will be with thy m. 15
    13:9 Lord's law may be in t. m.
    23:13 of other gods out of t. m.
Deut. 23:23 promised with t. m.
    30:14 word is nigh thee, in thy m. Rom. 10:8
Jos. 1:8 not depart out of t. m.
Jud. 9:38 where is now thy m.?
    11:36 opened thy m. to the Lord
    18:19 b. upon t. m. Prov. 30:32
2 Sam. 1:16 t. m. testif. ag. thee
1 K. 8:24 spa. wi. t. m. 2 Ch. 6:15
    17:24 word of L. in t. m. truth
Job 8:2 words of t. m. like wind
    21 fill thy m. with laughing
    15:5 thy m. uttereth thine iniq.
    6 th. own m. condemneth thee
    13 let. such words go out t. m.
Ps. 50:16 take my coven. in t. m.
    19 thou givest thy m. to evil
    81:10 open t. m. wide I will fill
    103:5 satisfi. t. m. wi. good th.
    119:13 the judgments of thy m.
    72 law of thy m. is better to me
    88 keep testimony of thy m.
    138:4 hear the words of thy m.
Prov. 6:2 with t. m. of thy words
    27:2 praise th. not thine own m.
    31:8 open thy m. for the dumb
    9 open t. m. judge righteously
Ec. 5:2 not rash with thy m.
    6 suffer not t. m. cause fle. to sin
Cant. 7:9 roof of t. m. like wine
Is. 51:16 words in t. m. Jer. 1:9
    59:21 which I put in thy m.
Jer. 5:14 make words in t. m. fire
Ezek. 3:3 open thy m. and eat
    3:26 tongue cle. to roof of t. m.
    21 I will open t. m. and th. sh.
    16:56 S. not mentioned by t. m.
Hos. 8:1 set trumpet to thy m.
Mic. 7:5 keep doors of thy m.
Luke 19:22 out of thine own m.
Rom. 10:9 in t. m. confess with thy m.
Rev. 10:9 in t. m. sweet as honey

Your MOUTH.
Num. 32:21 proceed. out of y. m.
1 Sam. 2:3 come out of your m.
Job 21:5 lay your hand on y. m.
Ezek. 35:13 with y. m. boasted
Joel 1:5 wine is cut off from y. m.
Eph. 4:29 no corrupt communication out of your m. Col. 3:8

MOUTHS.
Num. 21 forgotten out of m. of seed
Ps. 22:41 gap. on me with th. m.
    78:30 meat was yet in their m.
    115:5 have m. speak not, 135:16
    135:17 not. is nor breath in m.
Jer. 14:15 wine not in their m.
Dan. 6:22 G. hath shut m. of lions
Acts 44:25 spoken with your m.
Tit. 1:11 wh. m. must be stopped
Heb. 11:33 stop. the m. of lions
Jam. 3:3 put bits in horses' m.
Rev. 9:17 out of their m. issued fire

MOVE.
Lev. 11:17 not a dog m. tongue
Deut. 32:21 m. th. to jealousy
2 Sam. 7:10 plant Is. m. no more
Neh. 4:8 us. not to m. a sickle
Mat. 23:4 not them to jealousy
Rom. 11:14 m. to emul. my flesh
Mic. 7:17 m. out of their holes
Acts 17:28 in him we live, m.
    20:24 none of these things m.
    24:25 fasten th t. m. not

MOVEABLE.
Prov. 5:6 her ways are m.

MOVED.
Gen. 1:2 Spirit of G. m. on waters
    7:21 all flesh died that m.
Deut. 32:21 m. me to jealousy
Jos. 10:21 none m. tongue ag. Is.
Ruth 1:19 the city was m. about
1 Sam. 1:13 her lips m. but voice
2 Sam. 18:33 king m. at this
2 K. 23:18 let no man m. his bones
Est. 5:9 he stood up, nor m. for
Job 37:1 m. out of their place
Mat. 23:4 they will not m. them

950 CRUDEN'S CONCORDANCE.

MUL

MUL.
Acts 17:28 live, *m.* ha. our being
 20:24 none of th. things *m.* me
MOVEABLE.
Prov. 5:6 her ways are *m.*
MOVED.
Gen. 1:2 Sp. of God *m.* on waters
 7:21 all flesh died that *m.*
Deut. 32:21 *m.* me to jealousy
Jos. 10:21 none *m.* his tongue
 15:18 that she *m.* him to ask of father a field, *Jud.* 1:14
Ruth 1:19 city was *m.* ab. them
 1 *Sam.* 1:13 only her lips *m.*
 2 *Sam.* 18:33 king was much *m.*
 22:8 foundations of heaven *m.*
 24:1 he *m.* David against them
 1 *Chr.* 16:30 world stable, that it be not *m. Ps.* 93:1; 96:10
 17:9 and shall he *m.* no more
 2 *Chr.* 18:31 G. *m.* them to depart
Ezr. 4:15 they have *m.* sedition
Job 37:1 at this my heart is *m.*
 41:23 they cannot be *m.*
Ps. 10:6 I shall not be *m.* 16:8;
 30:6; 62:2, 6.
 13:4 those rejoice when I am *m.*
 13:5 doeth these sh. never be *m.*
 18:7 foundations of the hills *m.*
 21:7 trusteth in L. sh. not be *m.*
 46:5 sh. not be *m.* God sh. help
 6 heathen raged, kingdoms *m.*
 55:22 never suff. right. to be *m.*
 66:9 suffer. not our feet to be *m.*
 68:8 S. was *m.* at presence of G.
 78:58 they *m.* him to jealousy
 99:1 L. reigneth, let earth be *m.*
 112:6 surely he shall not be *m.*
 121:3 not suffer thy foot to be *m.*
Prov. 12:3 root of the righteous shall not be *m.*
Cant. 5:4 my bowels *m.* for him
Is. 6:4 the posts of the door *m.*
 7:2 heart was *m.* as trees are *m.*
 10:14 there was none *m.*
 14:9 hell fr. ben. is *m.* for thee
 19:1 idols of Egypt shall be *m.*
 24:19 earth brok. down and *m.*
 40:20 im. that sh. not be *m.* 41:7
Jer. 4:24 all the hills *m.* lightly
 25:16 they sh. drink and be *m.*
 40;7 whose waters *m.* 8
 49:21 the earth is *m.* at noise
 50:46 at taking of Bab. earth *m.*
Dan. 8:7 he was *m.* with choler
 11:11 king of south shall be *m.*
Mat. 9:36 he was *m.* with compassion on them, 14:14; 16:27;
 Mark 1:41; 6:34
 20:24 were *m.* with indignation
 21:10 all the city was *m.* saying
Mark 15:11 chief priests *m.* peo.
Acts 2:25 that I sho. not be *m.*
 17:5 but the Jews *m.* with envy
 21:30 city was *m.* and peo. ran
Col. 1:23 be not *m.* from gospel
 1 *Thes.* 3:3 no man be *m.* by
Heb. 11:7 Noah, *m.* with fear
 11:28 kinged. wh. cannot be *m.*
 2 *Pet.* 1:21 as *m.* by the H. Ghost
Rev. 6:14 mount, and island *m.*

MOVEDST, ETH.
Gen. 1:21 created ev. crea. th. *m.*
 9:2 fear sh. be upon all that *m.*
Lev. 11:46 every creature that *m.*
Job 2:3 thou *m.* against him
Ps. 69:34 every thing that *m.*
Prov. 23:31 not on wi, wh. it *m.*
Ezek. 47:9 that *m.* whithersoever

MOVER.
Acts 24:5 this fel. *m.* of sedition

MOVING.
Gen. 1:20 wat. bring forth *m.* cre.
 9:3 every *m.* thing sh. be meat
Prov. 16:30 *m.* his lips

MOVING, Substantive.
Job 16:5 *m.* of my lips, assn. gri.
John 5:3 waiting for *m.* of water

MOWER.
Ps. 129:7 *m.* filleth not his hand

MOWINGS.
Amos 7:1 growth after king's *m.*

MOWN.
Ps. 72:6 like rain upon *m.* grass

MUCH.
Luke 12:48 to whom *m.* is given, of him shall *m.* be required

MUFFLERS.
Is. 3:19 I will take away the *m.*

MULBERRY-TREES.
2 *Sam.* 5:23 come upon th. over against the *m.-t.* 1 *Chr.* 14:14
 24 sound in the tops of *m.-t.*

MUL

MULE.
2 *Sam.* 13:29 every man upon *m.*
 18:9 Absalom rode upon a *m.*
 1 *K.* 1:33 to ride on my *m.* 38;44
Ps. 32:9 be not as horse or *m.*
Zec. 14:15 plague of horse, of *m.*

MULES.
Gen. 36:24 found *m.* in wildern.
 1 *K.* 10:25 brought *m.* a rate year by year, 2 *Chr.* 9:24
 18:5 grass to save the *m.* alive
 2 *K.* 5:17 given to serv. two *m.*
 1 *Chr.* 12:40 on camels and *m.*
Ezr. 2:66 their *m.* were 245, *Neh.* 7:68
Est. 8:10 sent letters by *m.* 14
Is. 66:20 bring your breth. ou *m.*

MULTIPLY.
Gen. 1:22 be fruitful and *m.* 28;
 8:17; 9:7; 35:11
 6:1 men began to *m.* on earth
 16:10 I will *m.* Hag. seed, 17:20
 17:2 *m.* thee exceedingly, 48:4
 22:17 in multiplying I will *m.* thy seed, 26:4, 24; *Heb.* 6:14
 28:3 G. Almighty bless and *m.*
Ex. 1:10 deal wisely, lest th. *m.*
 7:3 I will *m.* my signs in Egypt
 23:29 lest beast of the field *m.*
 32:13 thou saidst, I will *m.* your seed, *Lev.* 26:9; *Deut.* 7:13;
 13;17; 28:63; 30:5
Deut. 17:16 shall not *m.* horses
 17 neither shall he *m.* wives
 1 *Chr.* 4:27 neither did family *m.*
Job 29:18 I shall *m.* my days
Jer. 30:19 I will *m.* them
 33:22 so will I *m.* seed of David
Ezek. 16:7 I have caused th. to *m.*
 36:10 will *m.* men; 11 *m.* man
 30 I will *m.* fruit of the tree
 37:26 I will place and *m.* them
Amos 4:4 at G. *m.* transgression
2 *Cor.* 9:10 *m.* your seed sown

MULTIPLIED.
Gen. 47:27 Israel *m. Ex.* 1:7, 20
Ex. 1:12 afflicted *m.* and grew
 11:9 my wonders may be *m.*
Deut. 1:10 L. your G. ha. *m.* you
 8:13 gold is *m.* all thou hast *m.*
 11:21 that your days be *m.*
Jos. 24:3 I *m.* his seed
Job 27:14 children be *m.* for sw.
 35:6 if thy transgress. be *m.* ?
Ps. 16:4 their sorrows sh. be *m.*
 38:19 they that hate me are *m.*
 107:38 bless. them, they are *m.*
Prov. 9:11 thy days shall be *m.*
 29:16 when wicked are *m.*
Is. 9:3 thou hast *m.* the nation
 59:12 our transgressions are *m.*
Jer. 3:16 when ye be *m.*
Ezek. 5:7 ye *m.* more than nati.
 11:6 *m.* your slain in this city
 16:25 hast *m.* whoredoms, 29:10
 26 *m.* fornications; 51 *m.* abo.
 21:15 hast may faint, ruins *m.*
 31:5 boughs *m.* 33:13 *m.* words
Dan. 4:1 peace be *m.* 6:25; 1 *Pet.* 1:2; 2 *Pet.* 1:2; *Jude* 2
Hos. 2:8 not know I ye. her silver
 12:10 I have *m.* visions
Nah. 3:16 hast *m.* merchants
Acts 6:1 number of disciples *m.* 7
 7:17 people grew and *m.* in Eg.
 9:31 walk. in fear of L. were *m.*
 12:24 word of G. grew and *m.*

MULTIPLIEDST.
Neh. 9:23 their children also *m.*

MULTIPLIETH.
Job 9:17 he *m.* my wounds
 34:37 he *m.* his words ag. God
 35:16 *m.* words without knowl.

MULTIPLYING.
Gen. 22:17 in *m. Heb.* 6:14

MULTITUDE.
Gen. 16:10 it shall not be numb. for *m.* 32:12; 1 *K.* 3:8
 28:3 G. Alm. make thee a *m.*
 30:30 it is now incre. unto a *m.*
 48:4 make of thee a *m.* 16, 19
Ex. 12:38 a mixed *m.* went up
 23:2 not follow a *m.* to do evil
Num. 11:4 mixed *m.* fell lusting
Deut. 1:10 are as the stars for *m.*
 10:22; 28:62; *Heb.* 11:12
Jos. 11:4 sand on sea-shore for *m. Jud.* 7:12 ; 1 *Sam.* 13:5;
 2 *Sam.* 17:11; 1 *K.* 4:20
 1 *Sam.* 1:16 the *m.* melted away
 2:13 ye shall in *m.* of the tr.
Jud. 4:7 *m.* of Sisera
Jos. 5:3 great *m.* 7:13 they are as all the *m.*
 19:23 with *m.* of my chariots to sides of Lebanon, *Is.* 37:24

MUR

2 *Chr.* 1:9 a peo. like dust for *m.*
 14:11 in thy name go aga. *m.*
 20:24 the *m.* were dead bodies
 32:18 a *m.* not cleansed thous.
 33:7 he not afraid of all the *m.*
Neh. 13:3 separated fr. mixed *m.*
Est. 5:11 Haman told of the *m.*
 10:3 Mordecai accepted of *m.*
Job 11:2 sh. *m.* of words be ans. ?
 32:7 *m.* of years sh. teach wisd.
 35:9 by reason of *m.* of oppres.
 39:7 he scorneth *m.* of the city
Ps. 5:7 come in *m.* of thy mercy
 10 cast out in *m.* of transgres.
 33:16 th. is no king saved by *m.*
 42:4 gone with *m.* to hou. of G.
 49:6 boast in *m.* of their riches
 51:1 accord. to *m.* of thy merci.
 68:30 rebuke the *m.* of bulls
 69:13 O God, in *m.* of mercy
 16 accor. to *m.* of thy mercies
 74:19 deliver me not to the *m.*
 94:19 *m.* of my thoughts within
 104:7 rem. not *m.* of thy merc.
 45 accor. to *m.* of his mercies
 105:30 I will praise am. the *m.*
Prov. 10:19 in the *m.* of words
 11:14 *m.* of counsellors, 24;6
 15:22 *m.* of counsellors establ.
 20:15 gold, and a *m.* of rubies
 Ec. 5:3 through *m.* of business, fool's voice by *m.* of words
 7 *m.* of dreams div. vanities
 Is. 1:11 wh. purpose *m.* of sacri.
 5:13 *m.* dried up with thirst
 14 *m.* descend into hell
 17:12 woe to *m.* of many people
 22:5 *m.* of terrors the Lord G.
 31:4 when *m.* of shepherds
 47:12 stand your with the *m.* 0
 13 wearied in *m.* of counsels
 60:6 *m.* of camels shall cover
 63:7 *m.* of his loving-kindness.
Jer. 10:13 *m.* of waters, 51:16
 12:6 called a *m.* after thee
 30:14 wounded for *m.* of iniq.
 46:23 I will punish the *m.*
Lam. 1:5 for *m.* of transgres.
 3:32 accord. to *m.* of mercies
Ezek. 7:12 wrath is on the *m.* 14
 13 vision touching whole *m.*
 14:4 accor. to *m.* of his idols
 27:12 by *m.* of riches, 18, 33
 16 by the *m.* of the wares. 18
 31:18 Phar. and all his *m.* 32:32
 32:24 Elam and *m.* 26 Tubal
 39:11 bury Gog, and all his *m.*
Dan. 10:6 like voice of a *m.*
 11:13 k. of north set forth a *m.*
 Ho. 9:7 recomp. for *m.* of iniq.
 10:13 thou didst trust in *m.*
Nah. 3:3 there is a *m.* of slain
Mat. 14:5 he feared the *m.* 21;46
 15:32 compas. on *m. Mark* 8:2
Mark 5:31 *m.* throng. *Luke* 8:45
Luke 2:13 th. was wi. angel a *m.*
 12:1 guth. an innumerable *m.*
 6:2 betr. him in absence of *m.*
 47 while he yet sp. behold *m.*
 23:1 whole *m.* of them arose
John 5:13 a *m.* being in that pl.
 21:6 not able for *m.* of fishes
Acts 4:32 the *m.* that believed
 6:5 saying pleased whole *m.*
 16:22 *m.* rose against them
 21:22 *m.* must come together
Jam. 5:20 sh. save a soul fr. dea. and shall hide a *m.* of sins
 1 *Pet.* 4:8 charity cov. *m.* of sins
See **GREAT.**

MULTITUDES.
Ezek. 32:20 draw her and her *m.*
Joel 3:14 *m. m.* in val. of decis.
Mat. 9:33 and the *m.* marvelled
 36 when he saw *m.* was mov.
 21:9 *m.* cried, saying, Hosanna
Acts 5:14 *m.* of men and women
 13:45 J. saw the *m.* were filled
Rev. 17:15 the waters are *m.*
See **GREAT.**

MUNITION, S.
Is. 29:7 fight ag. her and her *m.*
 33:16 defence sh. be *m.* of rocks
Nah. 2:1 keep *m.* watch the way

MURDER.
Ps. 10;8 in secret doth *m.* inno.
 94:6 slay widow, *m.* fatherless
Jer. 7:9 *m.* and com. adultery ?
Hos. 6:9 priests *m.* in the way

MURDER, S.
Mat. 15:19 out of the heart proceed *m. Mark* 7:21
 19:18 said, Thou shalt do no *m.*
 27:1 Barab., committed *m.*
Luke 23:19 for cer. made *m.* pri. 25

MUS

Rom. 1:29 envy, *m.* debate
Gal. 5:21 flesh are envyings, *m.*
Rev. 9:21 nor repented of th. *m.*

MURDERER.
Num. 35:16 *m.* the *m.* sh. surely be put to death, 17, 18, 21, 30
 19 revenger of blood slay *m.* 21
 31 no satisfac. for life of a *m.*
 2 *K.* 6:32 see how th. son a *m.*
Job 24:14 *m.* rising with light
Hos. 9:13 Eph. bring chil. to *m.*
John 8:44 a *m.* from beginning
Acts 3:14 *m.* be granted to you
 28:4 no doubt this man is a *m.*
 1 *Pet.* 4:15 let none suffer as *m.*
 1 *John* 3:15 whoso hateth broth. is a *m.* ye know that no *m.*

MURDERERS.
2 *K.* 14:6 child. of *m.* he slew
Is. 1:21 lodged in it, but now *m.*
Jer. 4:31 wearied, because of *m.*
Mat. 22:7 sent and destroyed *m.*
Acts 7:52 have been now the *m.*
 21:38 4,000 men that were *m.*
 1 *Tim.* 1:9 law made for *m.*
Rev. 21:8 *m.* shall have part
 22:15 with. are whoremongers. *m.*

MURMUR.
Ex. 16:7 that ye *m.* against us ?
 8 hear. your *m. Num.* 14:27
Num. 14:36 made congrega. *m.*
 16:11 what is Aa. that ye *m.* ?
 17:5 whereby they *m.* ag. you
John 6:43 *m.* not am. yourselves
 1 *Cor.* 10:10 neither *m.* as some

MURMURED.
Ex. 15:24 *m.* against Moses, 17:3
 16:2 whole congregation of Isr. *m. Num.* 14:2; 16;41
Num. 14:29 20 y. old, wh. ha. *m.*
Deut. 1:27 ye *m.* in your tents
Jos. 9:18 congre. *m.* ag. princes
Ps. 106:25 but *m.* in their tents
Is. 29:24 that *m.* sh. learn doctr.
Mark 14:5 they *m.* against her
Luke 5:30 scribes and Phari. *m.*
 15:2 they *m.* saying, This man
 19:7 *m.* that he was going to be
John 6:41 the Jews *m.* at him
 61 he knew his disciples *m.*
 7:32 Pharisees heard people *m.*
 1 *Cor.* 10:10 as some of them *m.*

MURMURERS.
Jude 16 these are *m.* complainers

MURMURING, S.
Ex. 16:7 he heareth your *m.* 8, 9,
 12 ; *Num.* 14:27
 9 your *m.* are not against us
Num. 17:5 make to cease *m.* of I.
 10 take away their *m.* fr. me
John 7:12 much *m.* among peo.
Acts 6:1 a *m.* against Hebrews
Phil. 2:14 do all thi. without *m.*

MURRAIN.
Ex. 9:3 be a very grievous *m.*

MUSE, ED, ING.
Ps. 39:3 I was *m.* the fire burned
 143:5 I *m.* on works of thy han.
Luke 3:15 all men *m.* in th. hear.

MUSHI. *Ex.* 6:13

MUSIC.
 1 *Sam.* 18:6 meet Saul with *m.*
 1 *Chr.* 15:16 instruments of *m.*
 2 *Chr.* 5:13 ; 23:13 ; 34:12
 Ezr. 7:6 wi. instruments of *m.*
Ec. 12:4 dau. of *m.* bro. low
Lam. 3:63 rising ; I am their *m.*
Dan. 3:5 kinds of *m.* 7;10, 15
 6:18 instruments of *m.* brought
Amos 6:5 inv. instruments of *m.*
Luke 15:25 elder son heard *m.*

MUSICAL.
 1 *Chr.* 16:42 *m.* instrum. of God
Neh. 12:36 *m.* instru. of David
Ec. 2:8 as *m.* instruments.

MUSICIANS.
Rev. 18:22 vo. of *m.* heard no *m.*

MUST.
Gen. 29:26 it *m.* not be so done
 30:16 thou *m.* come in to me
 43:11 if it *m.* be so now, do this
Num. 23:12 *m.* I not take heed
 36 Lord speaketh that I *m.* do
Deut. 4:22 I *m.* die in this land
 1 *Sam.* 14:43 and Jo. *m.* die
 2 *Sam.* 2:23 rul. men *m.* be just
Ezr. 10:12 said, so *m.* we do
Mark 8:31 S. of man ev. suff. 9:12 he accomplished, 14:4
 24:7 Son of man *m.* be delivered
John 3:7 ye *m.* be born again
Acts 4:12 whereby we *m.* be sav.

NAI

Acts 9:6 told th. what th. *m.* do
Rom. 13:5 *m.* needs be subject
1 Cor. 5:10 then *m.* ye needs go

MUSTARD-SEED. *See* GRAIN.

MUSTERED, ETH.
2 *K.* 25:19 scribe *m. Jer.* 52:25
Is. 13:4 Lord *m.* host of battle

MUTTER, ED.
Is. 8:19 wizards th. peep and *m.*
59:3 tongue hath *m.* perversed.

MUTUAL.
Rom. 1:12 comforted by *m.* faith

MUZZLE.
Deut. 25:4 not *m.* ox, 1 *Cor.* 9:9; 1 *Tim.* 5:18

MYRA. *Acts* 27:5

MYRRH.
Gen. 37:25 bearing balm and *m.*
43:11 carry man a pres. *m.* nuts
Ex. 30:23 pure *m.* 500 shekels
Est. 2:12 6 months wi. oil of *m.*
Ps. 45:8 *m.* aloes and cassia
Prov. 7:17 perf. my bed with *m.*
Cant. 1:13 bundle of *m.* is belov.
3:6 perf. with *m.* and frankinc.
4:6 get to moun. of *m.* and aloes
14 *m.* and aloes with chief spi.
5:1 gath. my *m.* with my spice
5 my hands dropped with *m.*
13 dropping sweet-smelling *m.*
Mat. 2:11 presented gold and *m.*
Mark 15:23 mingled with *m.*
John 19:39 bro. a mixture of *m.*

MYRTLE.
Neh. 8:15 go forth and fetch *m.*
Is. 41:19 plant in wildern, the *m.*
55:13 inst. of brier come up *m.*

MYRTLE-TREES.
Zec. 1:8 stood am. *m.-t.* 10, 11

MYSIA. *Acts* 16:7, 8

MYSTERY.
Mark 4:11 given to know *m.*
Rom. 11:25 that ye be ign. of *m.*
16:25 according to revela. of *m.*
1 *Cor.* 2:7 speak wis. of G. in *m.*
15:51 I show you a *m.*
Eph. 1:9 made known to us *m.*
3:3 made known to me the *m.*
4 knowledge in the *m.* of Ch.
9 all see fellowship of *m.*
5:32 this is a great *m.*
6:19 to make known *m.* of the gospel, *Col.* 1:26, 27; 4:3
Col. 2:2 *m.*'acknowledgment of *m.*
2 *Thes.* 2:7 *m.* of iniq. doth work
1 *Tim.* 3:9 holding *m.* of faith
16 great is the *m.* of godliness
Rev. 1:20 *m.* of the seven stars
10:7 *m.* of God, sho. he finished
17:5 *m.* Babylon ; 7 *m.* of wom.

MYSTERIES.
Mat. 13:11 *m.* of the kingdom, to them not given, *Luke* 8:10
1 *Cor.* 4:1 stewards of *m.* of God
13:2 tho' I understand all *m.*
14:2 in the Sp. he speaketh *m.*

N.

NAAMAN.
2 *K.* 5:1 N. was leper, 11, 20, 27
Luke 4:27 none cleansed, sav. N.

NAASSON, *or* **NAHSHON.**
Num. 1:7 pri. was N, 2:3; 10:14
7:12 he that off, first day was N,
Ruth 4:20 Amminadab begat N.
1 *Chr.* 2:10, 11; *Mat.* 1:4
Luke 3:32 Salmon was son of N.

NABAL.
1 *Sam.* 25:3 was N. 4, 25, 38, 39
27:3 A. N. wife, 30:5; 2 *Sam.* 2:2

NABOTH.
1 *K.* 21:1 N. had vineyard, 7:19
2 *K.* 9:21 in portion of N. 25, 26

NADAB.
Ex. 6:23 Aaron, N. *Lev.* 10:1
24:1 come up, N. and Abihu, 9
Num. 3:4 N. died before I*s.* 26:61
1 *K.* 15:29 N. reigned, 15:25

NAGGE. *Luke* 3:25

NAHASH.
1 *Sam.* 11:1 N. came up, 12:12
2 *Sam.* 10:2 son of N. 1 *Chr.* 19:2

NAHOR.
Gen. 11:22 Se, begat N. 24, 26, 29
22:20 brother N. 23 ; 24:15, 24
24:10 servant went to city of N.
31:53 God of Abraham and N.

NAIL.
Jud. 4:21 Jael took a *n.* of tent
22 the *n.* was in his temples

NAM

Jud. 5:26 she put her *h.* to the *n.*
Ezr. 9:8 give us a *n.* in holy pl.
Is. 22:23 a *n.* in a sure place, 25
Zec. 10:4 out of him came the *n.*

NAILS.
Deut. 21:12 sh. head, pare her *n.*
1 *Chr.* 22:3 iron in abund. for *n.*
2 *Chr.* 3:9 weight of *n.* fifty she.
Ec. 12:11 *n.* fastened by masters
Is. 41:7 his idol with *n. Jer.* 10:4
Dan. 4:33 his *n.* like bird's claws
7:19 beast, wh. *n.* were of brass
John 20:25 finger into print of *n.*

NAIL.
Col. 2:14 he *n.* it to his cross

NAIN. *Luke* 7:11

NAIOTH.
1 *Sam.* 19:18 Da. dwelt at N. 20:1

NAKED.
Gen. 2:25 were *n.* not ashamed
3:7 knew they were *n.* 10, 11
Ex. 32:25 Moses saw peo. were *n.* for Aa. had made them *n.*
1 *Sam.* 19:24 Saul lay down *n.*
2 *Chr.* 28:15 with spoil clothed *n.*
Job 1:21 *n.* came I out of womb, and *n.* shall I return thither
22:6 stripped *n.* of their clothi.
24:7 cause *n.* to lodge with. 10
26:6 hell is *n.* before him
Ec. 5:15 *n.* shall he return
*I*s.* 58:7 when thou seest the *n.*
Lam. 4:21 shalt make thyself *n.*
Ezek. 16:7 hi. covered the *n.* 16
Hos. 2:3 lest I strip her *n.*
Amos 2:16 flee away *n.*
Mic. 1:8 I will go stripped and *n.*
11 having thy shame *n.*
Hab. 3:9 bow was made quite *n.*
Mat. 25:36 *n.* and ye clothed me
38 when saw we thee *n.* ? 44
Mark 14:51 cloth ab. his *n.* body
52 and fled from them *n.*
John 21:7 Peter was *n.* and cast
Acts 19:16 fled out o. house *n.*
1 *Cor.* 4:11 to this hour we are *n.*
2 *Cor.* 5:3 shall not be found *n.*
Heb. 4:13 but all things are *n.* to
Jam. 2:15 if brother or sis. be *n.*
Rev. 3:17 poor, and blind, and *n.*
16:15 garments, lest he walk *n.*
17:16 make her desolate and *n.*

See BARE.

NAKEDNESS.
Gen. 9:22 H. saw *n.* of father, 23
42:9 see the *n.* of the land, 12
Ex. 20:26 thy *n.* not discovered
28:42 breeches to cover *n.*
Lev. 18:6 none sh. uncover th. *n.*
7 the *n.* of father or mother, 8, 11, 15; 20:11
9 *n.* of sister ; 10 of son's daus.
17 *n.* of father's wife's daugh.
12 not uncover *n.* of f.'s sister
13 *n.* of mother's sister, 20:19
14 not uncover *n.* of f.'s broth.
15 *n.* of daughter-in-law
16 *n.* of thy brother's wife
17 *n.* of a woman and daught.
19 *n.* of wo. put apart. 20:18
20:17 sister's *n.* she see his *n.*
21 hath uncovered brother's *n.*
Deut. 28:48 serve thine ene. in *n.*
1 *Sam.* 20:30 confu. of moth.'s *n.*
Is. 47:8 thy *n.* sh. be uncovered
Lam. 1:8 they have seen her *n.*
Ezek. 16:8 I covered thy *n.* yea
36 thy *n.* discovered, 23:18
16:37 discover thy *n.* to them
22:10 discovered th. father's *n.*
23:10 discovered her *n.* slew her
Hos. 2:9 wool and flax to cov. *n.*
Nah. 3:5 show the nations thy *n.*
Hab. 2:15 mayest look on th. *n.*
Rom. 8:35 shall *n.* separate us ?
2 *Cor.* 12:7 in cold and *n.*
Rev. 3:18 shame of *n.* not appear

NAME.
Gen. 2:19 that was *n.* thereof
6:4 and called their *n.* Adam
11:4 us a *n.* lest we be scattered
n. called after *n.* of breth.
Ex. 3:13 I L, whose *n.* is Jealous
Lev. 18:21 nei. profane the *n.* of
Num. 17:2 write every man's *n.*
27:4 why should *n.* of our father
Deut. 7:24 destroy *n.* under heav.
9:14 blot out *n.* fr. under heav.
22:14 bring up an evil *n.* on her
19 br. up an evil *n.* on virgin
25:6 succeed hi. *n.* of his broth.
7 raise his brother a *n.* in Isr.
26:19 high in *n.* and honor

NAM

Deut. 28:58 fear this g], and fe. *n.*
Jos. 23:7 nor make mention of *n.*
Ruth 4:5 raise up *n.* of dead, 10
17 her neighbors gave it a *n.*
2 *Sam.* 6:2 *n.* called by *n.* of Lord
7:9 I made th. great *n.* like *n.*
of gre. men in earth, 1 *Chr.* 17:8
23 God redeemed to make him a *n.* 1 *Chr.* 17:21
8:13 David gat him a *n.* when
14:7 not leave to my husb. a *n.*
22:19 Abishai had *n.* amo. three
22 the *n.* among three mighty men, 1 *Chr.* 11:20, 24
1 *K.* 1:47 G. make *n.* of Solomon better than thy *n.*
14:21 Lord did choose to put his *n.* there, 2 *Chr.* 12:13
18:24 call on *n.* of your gods, 25
21:8 Jezebel wrote in Ahab's *n.*
2 *K.* 14:27 not blot out *n.* of Isr.
Ezr. 2:61 and was called after their *n. Neh.* 7:63
5:1 prophesied in *n.* of G. of Is.
Neh. 9:10 didst thou get th. a *n.*
6:8 write for J. in king's *n.*
10 18:17 he shall have no *n.*
Ps. 9:5 put out their *n.* for ever
20:1 the *n.* of the God of Jacob
5 in *n.* of G, set up our banne.
41:20 if we forgot, *n.* of our G.
68:30 I will praise the *n.* of God
83:4 the *n.* of Israel be no more
18 whose *n.* alone is Jehovah
69:3 let th. praise thy great *n.*
109:13 let th. *n.* be blotted out
113:3 the L.'s *n.* is to be praised
Prov. 10:7 *n.* of wicked shall rot
18:10 *n.* of Lord is strong tower
22:1 good *n.* rather than riches
Ec. 6:4 cometh with vanity, *n.*
6 his *n.* shall be covered
7:1 good *n.* bet. than oint.
Cant. 1:3 thy *n.* is as oint. pour.
Is. 14:22 cut off *n.* of Bab.
26:8 desire of soul is to thy *n.*
13 *sh.* make mention of thy *n.*
55:5 give a *n.* an everlasting *n.*
62:2 called by a new *n.*
63:12 make himself everlast. *n.*
14 to make thyself a glori. *n.*
65:15 ye shall leave your *n.* for a curse to my chosen, and call his servants his chosen *n.*
Jer. 13:11 might be for *n.* 33:9
33:16 the *n.* she shall be called
46:18 King, whose *n.* is the Lord of hosts, 48:15; 51:57
Ezek. 20:9 *n.* is called Barnah
21:2 son of man, write *n.*
24:35 the *n.* of the city shall be
26:1 according to then. of my G.
Hos. 2:17 no more remem. by *n.*
Amos 5:27 whose *n.* is G. of hos.
Mic. 4:5 in the *n.* of his god, we will walk in the *n.* of the L.
Zep. 3:20 I will cut off *n.* of Ch.
3:20 I will make you a *n.*
Zec. 6:12 whose *n.* is Branch
Mat. 10:41 receiv. a prophet in the *n.* of a prophet, a righteous
4:41 cup of wat. in *n.* of disciple
28:19 baptizing them in *n.* of F.
Luke 1:61 none of kl. call. by *n.*
63 saying, His *n.* is John
John 1:6 f. God, who. *n.* was J.
3:18 not believed in *n.* of only
5:43 am come in my Father's *n.*
10:25 I do in my Father's *n.*
12:28 baptized in *n.* of L. *P.* J.
Acts 4:7 by what power, *n.* done this ?
12 neither other *n.* under heav.
17 sp. to no man in this *n.*
18 no man teach in this *n.* 40
30 wonders done by *n.* of child.
5:28 sh. not teach in this *n.* 40
8:12 concerning the *n.* of Jesus
9:15 bear my *n.* bef. Gentiles
10:43 whoso believeth in him
15:26 hazarded lives for *n.* of L.
19:5 baptized in *n.* of Lord J.
13 *n.* of the Lord J.
17 *n.* of the Lord Jesus
Rom. 1:5 obedience to faith am. all nations for his *n.*
2:24 *n.* of God is blasphemed
15:9 confess to thee among the Gentiles, and sing to thy *n.*
1 *Cor.* 1:2 call upon *n.* of Je. C.
10 speak same thing by *n.*
13 or were ye baptized in *n.*?
15 lest any had baptized in *n.*
6:11 *n.* of Lord J. Sp. of our G.
Eph. 1:21 above every *n.* that is
5:20 thanks in *n.* of L. Jesus

NAM

1 *John* 3:23 be. on *n.* of Son, 5:13
Rev. 2:17 a *n.* no man knoweth
3:1 hast a *n.* that thou livest
13 I will write on him *n.* of G.
13:1 on his heads *n.* of blasph.
14:1 Father's *n.* in their forehe.
16:9 men blasph. the *n.* of God
17:5 on her forehead was a *n.*
19:12 a *n.* written no man knew
16 on his thigh a *n.* written

See CALLED.

By, *or* **by the NAME.**
Ex. 6:3 I appeared by *t. n.* of G.
33:12 I know thee by *n.* 17
Num. 4:32 by *n.* ye shall reckon
Jos. 21:9 th. cities menti. by *n.*
14:11 2 *Chr.* 28:15; 31:19
Est. 2:14 exc. were called by *n.*
Is. 43:5 sh. call himself by the *n.* of Jacob, and surname him self by the *n.* of Israel, 48:1
45:3 I the Lord call thee by *n.*
John 10:3 calleth his sheep by *n.*
Acts 4:10 by the *n.* of J. this man
1 *Cor.* 1:10 I bes. you by *n.* of L.
3 *John* 14 greet friends by *n.*

See EXPRESSED.

His NAME.
Ex. 3:13 shall say, What is *his n.*? *Prov.* 30:4
15:3 the Lord is his *n. Jer.* 32:2; *Amos* 5:8; 9:6
20:7 not guiltless that taketh his *n.* in vain, *Deut.* 5:11
28:21 w1. *h. n.* sh. they be, 29:14
Deut. 6:13 shalt swear by *h. n.*
10:8 bless in his *n.* 1 *Chr.* 23:13
12:5 choose to put *his n.* there, 21; 1 *K.* 14:21; 2 *Chr.* 12:13
14 *sh.* cause *his n.* to dw. there, 16:6, 11; 26:2
26:6 *his n.* he not put out of Isr.
19 *his n.* sh. be called a new *n.*
29:20 Lord shall blot out *his n.*
Jud. 13:6 uelt. told he me *h. n.*
17 what is *his n.* ? 18
1 *Sam.* 12:22 for *his n.*'s sake, *Ps.* 23:3; 106:8; 1 *John* 2:12; 3 *John* 7
18:30 *his n.* was much set by
25:25 as *his n.* is, Nabal is *his n.*
1 *Chr.* 16:8 call up *h. n.* make known his deeds, *Ps.* 105:1
Ps. 12:4
29 gl. due to *h. n. Ps.* 29:2 ; 96:8
Ezr. 6:12 G. caused *his n.* dwell
Neh. 1:9 ex. exalt *his n.* 113:2
41:5 shall he die 6. *n.* perish ?
69:4 rideth on heav. by *h. n.* J.
69:36 that love *his n.* dw. there.
72:17 *his n.* shall endure for ever
19 and blessed be *h.* is glori. *n.*
78:5 *his n.* is great in Israel
89:2 unto L. bless *his n.* 100:4
96:6 Samuel that call on *his n.*
111:9 holy and reverend is *h. n.*
148:13 praises to *h. n.* it is pleas.
149:3 praise *his n.* in the dance
Prov. 21:24 haug. scorner is *h. n.*
Is. 9:6 *his n.* cw. with darkness
Ec. 7:14 *his n.* Imman. *Mat.* 1:23
9:6 *his n.* be called Wonderful
12:4 that *his n.* is exalted
47:4 the Lord of hosts is *his n.* 48:2; 51:15; 54:5; *Jer.* 10:16; 48:2; 31:35; 50:34; *Amos* 4:13
Jer. 11:19 *h. n.* no more remem.
cut off, says any more fr. *h. n.*
23:6 this is *h. n.* he shall be ca.
33:16 Lord God of hosts is *h. n.*
Zec. 10:12 up and down in *h. n.*
14:9 shall be one L. and *h. n. o.*
Mal. 3:16 them th. tho. on *h. n.*
Mat. 1:23 sh. call *h. n.* Emman.
1:21 sh. call *h. n.* Jesus, *Luke* 1:31
12:21 *his n.* shall Gentiles trust
Mark 6:14 *h. n.* was spread abr.
Luke 1:13 thou sh. call *h. n.* J.
2:21 circu. *h. n.* was called J.
6:22 east out your *n.* as evil
24:47 remission of sins in *h. n.*
John 1:12 that believe on *h. n.*
2:23 many believed in *h. n.*
5:43 if come. in *his own n.*
20:31 might have life thro' *h. n.*
Acts 3:16 *h. n.* thro' faith in *h. n.*
4:1 worthy to suffer for *h. n.*
10:43 thro' *his n.* whoso, believ.
15:14 take out a peo. for *h. n.*
Rom. 1:5 am. all nations for *h. n.*
Heb. 6:10 love ye show. to *h. n.*
13:15 giving thanks to *h. n.*
Rev. 3:5 not blot out *his n.*

CRUDEN'S CONCORDANCE.

NAM

Rev. 6:8 A. n. sat on him was de.
13:6 ag. God to blaspheme h. n.
17 the number of his n. 13:2
14:11 receiveth mark of h. n.
22:4 his n. sh. be in th. forehea.
See HOLY, LORD.

My NAME.
Gen. 32:29 why ask after my n. *f*
46:16 let my n. be named
Ex. 3:15 this is my n. for ever
9:16 that my n. may be declared
20:24 where I record my n.
23:21 prov. not. my n. is in him
Lev. 19:12 not swear by my n.
20:3 M. to profane my holy n.
Num. 6:27 put my n. on Israel
Deut. 18:19 speak in my n. 20
Jud. 13:18 why ask, after my n. *f*
1 *Sam.* 24:21 not destroy my n.
2 *Sam.* 7:13 house for my n. 1 K.
5:5; 8:18, 19; 1 *Chr.* 22:10
12:28 city be called after my n.
18:18 no son to keep my n.
1 K. 8:16 my n. might be there.
29; 11:36; 2 K. 21:4, 7; 2 *Chr.*
6:5, 6; 7:16; 33:4, 7
9:7 house I hallowed for my n.
1 *Chr.* 22:8 house to my n. 28:3
2 *Chr.* 6:8 build house for my n.
7:20 house I ha. sanct. for my n.
Neh. 1:9 to set my n. *Jer.* 7:12
Ps. 89:24 in my n. sh. horn be
91:14 bec. he hath known my n.
Is. 29:23 shall sanctify my n.
41:25 ri. of sun call on my n.
42:8 I am the L. that is my n.
48:9 for my n.'s sake I defer
11 how abo. my n. be pollut. *f*
49:1 he made mention of my n.
52:5 my n. ev. day is blasphem.
6 my people shall know my n.
56:5 cast out for my n.'s sake
Jer. 14:14 in my n. 15; 23:25
10:21 they sh. know my n. L.
23:27 they lie. to cause peo. for-
get my n. as fa. forgot my n.
27:15 lie in my n. 29:9, 21, 23
34:16 turned and polluted my n.
44:26 sworn by my great n. my
n. no more named.
Ezek. 20:9 wro. for my n. 22:44
38:23 will sanctify my great n.
Zec. 13:9 call on my n.
Mal. 1:6 priests th. despise my n.
11 my n. sh. be great am. Geu.
in ev. place incen. off. my n.
14 my n. dreadful am. heathen
2:2 to give glory unto my n.
5 and was afraid before my n.
4:2 you that fear my n. the sun
Mat. 10:22 hat. for my n.'s sake,
24:9; *Mark* 13:13 *Luke* 21:17
18:5 receive a child in my n.
Mark 9:37; *Luke* 9:48
20 two or three gath. in my n.
19:29 fors. houses for my n.'s sa.
24:5 many shall come in my n.
Mark 13:6; *Luke* 21:8
Mark 5:9 say. My n. is Legion
9:39 no man do miracle in my n.
41 give water to drink in my n.
16:17 in my n. sh. cast out dev.
Luke 21:12 rulers for my n.'s sa.
John 14:13 what. ye ask in my n.
14; 15:16; 16:23, 24, 26
26 Comf. he will send in my n.
15:21 these thi. do for my n.'s
Acts 9:15 cho. ves. to bear my n.
16 must suffer for my n.'s sake
15:17 on whom my n. is called
Rom. 9:17 that my n. be declared
1 *Cor.* 1:15 I bapt. in mi. own n.
Rev. 2:3 for my n.'s sake laboured
13 holdest fast my n.
3:8 and hast not denied my n.
See CALLED.

Thy NAME.
Gen. 12:2 make thy n. great
17:5 t. n. Abram, but t. n. be A.
32:27 said, What is thy n. *f* 29;
Jud. 13:17
28 thy n. be no more Jacob
but Israel, 35:10; 1 K. 18:31
Ex. 5:29 to P. to speak in thy n.
Jos. 7:9 what do to t. great n. *f*
Jud. 7:2 lest t. n. be magnifi.
24:36 sing praise to t. n. *Ps.* 9:2;
18:49; 61:8; 66:4; 92:1
1 K. 1:47 Solom. better than t. n.
8:33 turn and confess thy n. and
pray, 2 *Chr.* 6:24, 26,33
41 but cometh for thy n.'s sake
42 they shall hear of t. great n.
43 that all peo. may know thy
n. this house is called by
thy n. 2 *Chr.* 6:33, 34, 43

NAM

1 K. 8:44, house I built for thy
n. 48
1 *Chr.* 17:24 thy n. may be mag.
29:13 and praise t. n. *Ps.* 44:8
2 *Chr.* 6:20 wouldest put thy n.
14:11 in thy n. we go ag. multi.
20:8 built thee a sanctu. for t. n.
9 for thy n. is in this house
Neh. 1:11 servants who fear t. n.
9:5 blessed be t. glorious n.
Ps. 5:11 th. love t. n. be joyful
how excel. is t. n. in earth
8:1 how excel. is t. n. in earth
9:10 they that know t. n. trust
22:22 will declare t. n. *Heb* 2:12
23:11 for t. n.'s sake pardon
31:3 for t. n.'s sake lead me
44:5 thro' thy n. tread them
45:17 I will make thy n. be rem.
48:10 accor. to t. n. so is praise
52:9 wait on t. n. 54:1 save me
61:5 heritage of those fear t. n.
63:4 lift my hands in thy n.
74:7 defiled dwelling-pla. of t. n.
10 sh. enemy bla. t. n. for ev. *f*
18 fool. peo. blasphemed t. n.
21 poor and needy praise t. n.
75:1 t. n. is near works declare
79:6 not call. on t. n. *Jer.* 10:25
9 help us, O God, for g. of t. n.
purge our sins for t. n.'s s.
80:18 we will call upon thy n.
83:16 that they may seek thy n.
O Lord
86:9 all nations glorify t. n. 12
11 unite my heart to fear t. n.
89:12 Hermon sh. rej. in t. n. 16
109:21 O Lord, for t. n.'s sake
116:4 to call on t. n. but to t. n.
119:55 I remembr. t. n. in night
132 to do to those love thy n.
138:2 praise t. n. for lov.-kindu.
magnified word above t. n.
139:20 enemies take t. n. in vain
140:13 righ. give thanks to t. n.
142:7 out of pris. I praise t. n.
143:11 qui. me for t. n.'s sake
145:1 I will bless thy n. 2
21 I will praise t. n. *Is.* 25:1
Cant. 1:3 t. n. is as ointment
Is. 26:8 des. of our soul to thy n.
13 make mention of thy n.
63:16 O L. t. n. is from everlas.
64:2 make t. n. kn. to adversar.
7 there is none calleth on t. n.
Jer. 10:6 thy n. is great in might
11:16 L. called thy n. olive-tree
14:7 do thou it for thy n.'s sake
9 not abhor us for t. n.'s sake
21 thy n. set letters in thy n. to J.
Lam. 3:55 called on thy n.
Mic. 6:9 man of wisd. see thy n.
Nah. 1:14 no more of thy n. to
Mal. 1:6 ha. we despised thy n. *f*
Mat. 6:9 hal. be t. n. *Luke* 11:2
7:22 in t. n. have we cast out
Mark 9:9 wh. is t. n. *f* *Luke* 8:30
9:38 out dev. in t. n. *Luke* 9:49
Luke 10:17 devils subj. thro' t. n.
John 12:28 Father, glorify t. n.
17:6 manifested t. n. to men, 26
11 F. keep thro' thi. own n. 12
Acts 9:14 all that call on thy n.
Rom. 15:9 conf. and sing to t. n.
Rev. 11:18 rew. th. that fear t. n.
15:4 who not fear and glo. t. n. *f*
See CALLED.

NAME, Verb.
1 *Sam.* 16:3 anoi. to me him I n.
28:8 bring him up wh. I shall n.
Is. 62:2 mouth of Lord shall n.

NAMED, ETH.
Gen. 23:19 A. weigh. silver he n.
27:36 is he not rightly n. Jac. *f*
48:16 let my name be n. on the.
2 K. 17:34 chil. of Jacob he n. I.
Ec. 6:10 what hath been, is n.
Is. 61:6 shall be n. priests of L.
Jer. 44:26 shall no more be n.
Amos 6:1 n. chief of the nations
Mic. 2:7 O thou that art n. of J.
Luke 2:21 J. was n. of the angel
Rom. 15:20 not where Ch. was n.
1 *Cor.* 5:1 forni. not n. am. Gen.
Eph. 1:21 ab. ev. name that is n.
3:15 fam. in heav. and earth n.
5:3 covetouss. let it not be n.
1 *Tim.* 2:19 every one that n. C.

NAMELY.
Ec. 5:13 evil, n. riches kept
Is. 7:20 L. shave, n. by Assyria
Mark 12:31 n. this, shalt love

NAMES.
Gen. 2:20 Adam gave n. to cattle
26:18 called n. after n. f. called

NAT

Ex. 23:13 make no mention of n.
of other gods, *Deut.* 12:3
28:9 grave n. of child. of Isr. 21
12 Aaron bear n. before L. 29
Num. 1:2 numb. of n. by th. poll
Ezr. 5:4 what n. make building
Ps. 16:4 nor take th. n. in my lips
49:11 call lands after own n.
147:4 stars call. by n. *Is.* 40:26
Hos. 2:17 take away n. of Baalim
Zec. 13:2 cut off the n. of idols
Luke 10:20 n. written in heaven
Acts 1:15 number of n. were 120
18:15 if it be question of n.
Phil. 4:3 wh. n. are in book of li.
Rev. 3:4 hast a few n. in Sardis
13:8 whose n. not written, 17:8
17:3 woman full of n. of blasph.
21:12 n. written, n. of 12 tribes
14 in them the n. of 12 apostl.

NAOMI.
Ruth 1:2 Elimelech's wife, N. 20
2:1 N. had a kinsman of husb.
4:5 buy. field of hand of N. 9, 17

NAPKIN.
Luke 19:20 I have kept in a.
John 11:44 face bound with a n.
20:7 n. that was about his head

NAPHTALI.
Gen. 30:8 Rachel called name N.
35:25 Rachel's handmaid, N.
46:24 s. of N. *Nu.* 1:42; 1 *Ch.* 7:13
49:21 N. is a hind let loose
Deut. 27:13 E. to curse; Dan, N.
33:23 said, O N. satisfied with
Jos. 19:32 sixth lot came to N.
Jud. 1:33 nor did N. drive out
4:10 Barak called Z. to Kedesh
5:18 Zebulun and N. jeoparded
6:35 Gid. sent messengers to N.
7:23 themselves tog. out of N.
1 K. 15:20 smote N. 2 *Chr.* 16:4
Is. 9:1 he afflicted the land of N.
Ezek. 48:3 a portion for N. 34
Mat. 4:13 dw. in borders of N. 15

Tribe of NAPHTALI.
Num. 1:43 of t. of N. 53,400
Jos. 19:39 inheritance of t. of N.
1 K. 7:14 widow's son of t. of N.
Rev. 7:6 of t. of N. sealed 12,000

NARROW.
Num. 22:26 angel of L. sto. in n.
Jos. 17:15 if Ephraim be too n.
1 K. 6:4 windows of n. lights
Prov. 23:27 strs. woman is n. pit
Is. 49:19 land of destruct. too n.
Mat. 7:14 n. is way lead. to life

NARROWED, ER.
1 K. 6:6 in wall made n. rests
Is. 28:20 n. than he can wrap

NARROWLY.
Job 13:27 lookest n. to my paths
Is. 14:16 shall n. look upon thee

NATHAN.
2 *Sam.* 5:14 son of David, N. 7:2
7:17 so did N. speak, 12:1, 25
1 K. 1:10 N. called not, 22, 34
4:5 son of N. was over officers
1 *Chr.* 29:29 writt. in book of N.
Zec. 12:12 family of house of N.
Luke 3:31 Matthata, son of N.

NATHANAEL.
John 1:45 Philip findeth N. 21:2

NATION.
Gen. 15:14 n. serve will I judg.
20:4 wilt slay a righteous n. *f*
21:13 bondwoman I make n.
35:11 a n. kings come of thee
Ex. 9:24 in I. since it became n.
19:6 shall be a holy n. 1 *Pet.* 2:9
21:8 to sell her to a strange n.
33:13 this n. is thy people
Lev. 18:26 nor n. commit abomi.
20:23 not walk in manners of n.
Num. 14:12 I will make of thee a
great n. *Deut.* 9:14
Deut. 4:34 L. assayed to take
a n. fr. midst of another n. *f*
7:7 for fewest of land shall n. eat
36 bring thee and king to a n.
49 bring n. ag. thee from far
50 a n. of fierce countenance
32:28 are a n. void of counsel
2 *Sam.* 7:23 what n. like thy
people *f* 1 *Chr.* 17:21
1 K. 18:10 no n. my lord ha. not
so. to seek th. took oath of n.
Ezr. 17:29 every n. made gods
1 *Chr.* 16:20 went from n. to n.
2 *Chr.* 15:6 n. was destroyed of n.

NAT

2 *Chr.* 32:15 god of any n. was able
Job 34:29 done ag. a n. or man
Ps. 33:12 bless. is n. wh. G. is L.
43:1 O G. plead ag. ungodly n.
83:4 cut off from being a n.
105:13 went from one n. to ano.
106:5 rejoice in gladness of n.
147:20 not dealt so with any n.
Prov. 14:34 righteous. exalt. n.
Is. 1:4 sinful n. laden with iniq.
2:4 n. sh. not lift sword against
n. *Mic.* 4:3
9:3 thou hast multiplied the n.
10:6 send him aga. hypocrit. n.
14:32 what ans. messeng. of n. *f*
18:2 messengers to a n. scatter.
and peeled, a n. meted, 7
26:2 open that righ. n. may en.
15 thou increas. n. O L. the n.
49:7 sai. L. to him n. abhorreth
55:5 shalt call n. thou know. not
58:2 seek me as a n. that did ri.
60:12 n. not serve thee perish
22 small one beco. a strong n.
65:1 a n. not called by my name
66:8 or shall n. be born at once *f*
5:9 my soul be avenged on such
a n. 29; 9:9
15 I will bring a n. on you fr.
afar, a mighty n. ancient n.
7:28 a n. that obey. not the L.
12:17 I will ext. destroy that n.
18:7 concern. n. pluck 'it up, 9
8 n. ag. whom I pronounced
25:12 punish n. for iniq. 27:8
32 evil sh. go forth fr. n. to n.
31:36 Israel cease being n. 33:24
46:31 put you up to wealthy n.
50:3 no n. white L. sh. not come
50:3 out of north cometh n. ag.
Lam. 4:17 have watched for a n.
Ezek. 2:3 send thee to Is. rebe. n.
37:22 I will make them one n.
Dan. 8:22 four kingd. out of n.
12:1 trou. nev. was since was n.
Joel 1:6 a n. come upon my land
Amos 6:14 will raise ag. you a n.
Mic. 4:7 will make her strong n.
Hab. 1:6 Ch. bitter and hasty n.
Zep. 2:1 gather together, O n.
5 woe to the n. of Cherethites
Hag. 2:14 this peo. and n. before
Mal. 3:9 this n. have robbed me
Mat. 21:43 king. of G. given to n.
24:7 n. sh. rise against n. *Mark*
13:8; *Luke* 21:10
Luke 7:5 loveth our n. built us
John 11:48 R. shall take our n.
50 one man die, n. perish not
51 prophesied, Jesus die for n.
52 not for that n. only, but th.
18:35 thine own n. hath deliver.
Acts 2:5 devout men out of ev. n.
7:7 n. to whom they be in bond
10:22 good rep. am. n. of Jews
21:2 worthy deeds done to th. n.
10 thou hast been judge to n.
26:4 life was at first am. own n.
28:19 aught to accuse my n.
Gal. 1:14 profit. abi. equals in n.
Phil. 2:15 midst of perverse n.
Rev. 5:9 redee. us out of every n.
14:6 gospel to preach to ev. n.
See FOOLISH.

NATIONS.
Gen. 10:32 by th. were n. divided
14:1 TI. king of n. made war, 9
17:4 shalt be a father of many
n. 5; 48:19; *Rom.* 4:17, 18
6 I will make n. of thee, 35:11
16 Sarah sh. be a mother of n.
25:23 L. said, Two n. in thy wo.
27:29 let n. bow down to thee
Ex. 34:24 I will cast out the n.
before thee, *Deut.* 4:38; 7:22
Lev. 18:24 the n. are defiled
28 as it spued out the n.
Num. 23:9 not be reckon. am. n.
24:8 Israel shall eat up the n.
20 Amalek was first of the n.
Deut. 2:25 I will put fear on n.
4:27 L. shall scatter you among
the n. *Neh.* 1:8
7:1 Lord hath cast out many n.
9:1 n. great. than thyself, 11:23
12:29 God shall cut off n. 19:1
15:6 shalt lend to many n. 28:12
29:1 L. will set thee abo. all n.
32:8 Most High divid. to the n.
43 rejoice, O ye n. with his pe.
Jud. 2:23 the Lord left those n.
1 K. 11:2 of n. which the L. said
1 *Chr.* 17:23 ser. gods aft. man. of n.

CRUDEN'S CONCORDANCE. 953

NAT

2 *K*. 18:33 gods of *n*. deli. 19:12; 2 *Chr*. 32:13, 14; *Is*. 36:18
1 *Chr*. 16:31 say am. *n*. L. reign.
1.:21 driving out *n*. bef. people
Neh. 13:26 am. many *n*. no king
Job 12:23 the *n*. he enlargeth *n*.
Ps. 9:20 *n*. know themselves
22:27 kindreds of *n*. worsh. thee
*Lord is governor am. the *n*.
47:3 shall subdue *n*. tinder foot
57:9 sing to thee am. *n*. 108:3
68:7 his eyes behold the *n*.
67:4 let the *n*. be glad
96:3 all gods of the *n*. are idols
106:27 overthrow seed among *n*.
34 did not destroy *n*. L. com.
Prov. 24:24 *n*. shall abhor him
Is. 2:4 he sh. judge amo. the *n*.
5:26 will lift up an ensign to *n*.
10:7 in his heart to cut off *n*.
11:12 shall set up ensign for *n*.
14:6 ruled the *n*. in anger
12 wh. didst weak, the *n*. 23:3
18 kings of the *n*. lie in glory
33:3 at lifting up *n*. were scat.
34:1 come near, ye *n*. *Jer*. 31:10
40:15 *n*. are as a drop of bucket
52:15 so sh. he sprinkle many *n*.
55:5 *n*. that knew not thee, run
60:12 those *n*. shall be wasted
64:2 *n*. tremble at thy presence
66:19 send th. that escape to *n*.
Jer. 1:5 ordai. thee prophet to *n*.
10 I have set thee over the *n*.
4:2 *n*. shall bless themselves
10:7 not fear thee, King of *n*. ?
10 *n*. not able to abide his ind.
22:8 many *n*. sh. pass this city
25:14 *n*. shall serve, 27:7
31 L. had a controver. with *n*.
46:12 *n*. heard of thy shame
50:12 hindermost of *n*. a wilder.
46 cry is heard among the *n*.
51:7 *n*. have drunken, *n*. mad
20 wi. thee will I break *n*.
27 prepare the *n*. against her
41 Bab. an astonishm. am. *n*.
44 *n*. shall not flow together
Lam. 1:1 city that was gr. am. *n*.
Ezek. 5:6 wickedn. more than *n*.
14 make thee a reproach am. *n*.
6:8 remnant shall escape am. *n*.
9 remember me among *n*.
12:15 I shall scatter th. am. *n*.
19:4 the *n*. also heard of him
8 *n*. set ag. him on every side
25:8 many *n*. come against thee
5 it shall become a spoil to *n*.
28:7 bring upon thee the terri-
ble of the *n*. 30:11; 31:12
32:12 scatter Egypt am. *n*. 30:23
15 sh. no more rule over the *n*.
31:16 I made *n*. shake at sound
32:9 men art like lion of the *n*.
10 daughters of *n*. lament, 18
35:10 these two *n*. shall be mine
36:13 land hast bereaved thy *n*.
37:22 shall be no more two *n*.
38:8 brought forth out of *n*. 12
23 be known in eyes of *n*.
39:27 sancti. in sight of many *n*.
Hos. 8:10 have hired among *n*.
9:1‡ shall be wanderers amo. *n*.
Joel 3:2 they scattered among *n*.
Amos 6:1 woe to th. chief of *n*.
Mic. 4:2 *n*. shall say, Let us go
3 he shall rebuke strong *n*.
11 many *n*. gathered ag. thee
Nah. 3:4 selleth *n*. thro' whored.
5 I will show *n*. thy nakedness
Hab. 1:17 sh. not spare to slay *n*.
2:8 thou hast spoiled many *n*.
13 he drove asunder the *n*.
Zep. 3:8 I have cast off the *n*.
8 my determin. is to gather *n*.
Zec. 2:11 many *n*. joined to Lord
8:22 strong *n*. come to seek L.
22 out of all languages of *n*.
Luke 12:30 these do *n*. seek after
21:25 upon earth distress of *n*.
Acts 13:19 he dest. seven *n*. in C.
Rev. 2:26 I give power over *n*.
10:11 must prophesy before *n*.
11:9 *n*. shall see dead bodies
18 *n*. were angry, thy wrath
13:7 power given him over all *n*.
10:10 the cities of the *n*. fell
17:15 waters are *n*. and tongues
20:3 should deceive *n*. no more
21:24 *n*. wh. are saved sh. walk
26 shall bring honor of *n*. to it
22:2 leaves were for heal. of *n*.

See GREAT.

All NATIONS.
Deut. 4:19 hath divided to all *n*.
23:37 become thy word am. all *n*.

NAT

1 *K*. 4:31 his fame was in all *n*,
1 *Chr*. 16:24 decl. works am. *a*. *n*.
2 *Chr*. 32:23 mag. in sight of *a*. *n*.
Ps. 67:2 saving health am. all *n*.
72:11 all *n*. shall serve him
17 all *n*. shall call him blessed
82:8 for thou shalt inherit all *n*.
86:9 all *n*. shall worsh. bef. thee
113:4 L. is high above all *n*.
117:1 praise Lord all ye *n*.
118:10 all *n*. compassed me ab.
Is. 2:2 all *n*. shall flow unto it
25:7 destroy tho vail over all *n*.
34:2 indignation of L. on all *n*.
40:17 all *n*. before him as noth.
66:18 gather all *n*. *Joel* 3:2
20 br. your breth. out of all *n*.
Jer. 27:7 all *n*. serve, *Dan*. 7:14
Amos 9:9 house of Is. am. all *n*.
Hab. 2:5 gathereth to him all *n*.
Hag. 2:7 I will shake all *n*. and
desire of all *n*. shall come
Zec. 14:2 I will gather a. *n*. ag. J.
19 punish, of all *n*. come not
Mat. 3:19 all *n*. call you blessed
to all *n*. *Mark* 13:10; *Luke* 24:47; *Rom*. 16:26
25:32 bef. him sh. be gath. all *n*.
28:19 go ye, and teach all *n*.
Mark 11:17 called of all *n*.
Luke 21:24 led captive into all *n*.
Acts 14:16 suffered all *n*. to walk
17:26 made of one blood all *n*.
Rom. 1:5 obed. to faith am. all *n*.
Gal. 3:8 shall all *n*. be blessed
Rev. 7:9 a multitude of all *n*.
12:5 to rule all *n*. with a rod
14:8 she made all *n*. drink, 18:3
15:4 all *n*. sh. come and worsh.
18:23 by thy sor. all *n*. deceived

All the NATIONS.
Gen. 18:18 all the *n*. of the earth
be blessed, 22:18; 20:4
Deut. 14:2 ab. all the *n*. of earth
17:14 set a king over me, as all
the *n*. 1 *Sam*. 8:5, 20
30:1 call them to mind am. all *n*.
3 L. gather thee from all *t*. *n*.
Ps. 9:17 all *t*. *n*. that forget G.
Is. 14:26 hand stretch, on *a*. *t*. *n*.
76:7 multitude of all the *n*. 8
37:18 laid waste all the *n*.
43:9 let all the *n*. be gathered
52:10 bare arm in eyes of all *n*.
61:11 spring forth bef. all the *n*.
Jer. 3:17 all the *n*. shall be gath.
25:15 e. *n*. drink; 17 made *a*. *n*.
26:6 this city a curse to all *n*.
28:14 gather you from all *t*. *n*.
16 a reproach am. all *t*. *n*. 4:6
33:9 joy and honor bef. all *t*. *n*.
46:28 make full end of all the *n*.
Zec. 7:14 scat. them am. all *t*. *n*.
12:9 destroy all the *n*. that came
14:16 left of all the *n*. that came

These NATIONS.
Deut. 7:17 th. *n*. are more than I
9:4 for wickedness of these *n*. 5
11:23 the Lord drive out all *t*. *n*.
12:30 did *t*. *n*. serve th. gods?
18:14 *t*. *n*. heark. to observers
28:65 am. *t*. *n*. shalt find no rest
Jud. 2:21 what L. done these *n*.
4 divided to you by lot *th*. *n*.
12 If ye cleave to rem. of *t*. *n*.
13 will no more drive out *t*. *n*.
Jud. 3:1 *t*. *n*. L. left to prove Is.
2 *K*. 17:41 so these *n*. feared Lord
Jer. 25:9 bring them against *t*. *n*.
28:11 I put yoke of iron on *t*. *n*.

NATIVE.
Jer. 22:10 no more see *n*. country

NATIVITY.
Gen. 11:28 Ha. died in land of *n*.
Ruth 2:11 hast left land of *n*.
Ezek. 16:16 let us go to land of *n*.
4 thy *n*. in day th. wast born
21:30 judge thee in land of *n*.
23:15 Chaldea, land of their *n*.

NATURE
Rom. 1:26 change th. against *n*.
2:14 do by *n*. things in the law
27 uncircu. by *n*. judge thee?
11:21 olive tree, wh. is wild by *n*.
24 grafted contrary to *n*.
1 *Cor*. 11:14 doth not *n*. itself
Gal. 2:5 Jews by *n*. not sinners
4:8 which by *n*. are no gods
Eph. 2:3 by *n*. children of wrath
Heb. 2:16 took not *n*. of angels

NAZ

Jam. 3:6 set. on fire course of *n*.
2 *Pet*. 1:4 partakers of divine *n*.

NATURAL.
Deut. 34:7 nor his *n*. force abat.
Rom. 1:26 women change *n*. use
27 men leaving *n*. use of wom.
31 without *n*. affec. 2 *Tim*. 3:3
11:21 G. spared not *n*. bran, 23
1 *Cor*. 2:14 *n*. man rece. not Sp.
15:44 sown *n*. body, is *n*. body
46 that which is *n*. was first
Jam. 1:23 a man behold. *n*. face
2 *Pet*. 2:13 th. as *n*. brute beasts

NATURALLY.
Phil. 2:20 *n*. care for your state
Jude 10 but what they know *n*.

Gen. 20:15 sho. serve me for *n*. ?
Deut. 15:17 clo. *n*. cursed thing
15:9 brother, thou givest him *n*.
28:63 L. rej. to bring you to *n*.
2 *K*. 2:19 city pleasant, water *n*.
Neh. 4:15 God bro. counsel to *n*.
Job 1:9 doth Job fear G. for *n*. ?
8:22 place of wick. come to *n*.
14:18 mount. fall. cometh to *n*.
22:6 pledge fr. thy broth. for *n*.
Ps. 33:10 counsel of heath. to *n*.
41:12 sellest thy people for *n*.
Prov. 1:25 set at *n*. all counsel
20:14 it is *n*. it is *n*. saith buyer
Is. 8:10 take counsel, come to *n*.
29:20 terrible one is brok. to *n*.
21 turn aside just for th. of *n*.
41:12 nothing, as a thing of *n*.
24 nothing, and your work *n*.
49:4 spent my strength for *n*.
52:3 sold yourselves for *n*.
5 people is taken away for *n*.
Jer. 14:14 vision, a thing of *n*.
Amos 5:5 Beth-el sh. come to *n*.
6:13 which rejoice in thing of *n*.
Mat. 1:20 shut doors for *n*. ? nei.
kindle fire on mi. altar for *n*.
Mark 9:12 set at *n*. *Luke* 23:11
Acts 4:11 this is stone set at *n*.
5:30 scattered and brought to *n*.
38 if work of men, come to *n*.
19:27 craft in danger set at *n*.
Rom. 14:10 set at *n*. thy broth. ?
1 *Cor*. 1:28 to bring to *n*. things
2:6 wisd. of th. world com. to *n*.
2 *Thes*. 3:8 man's bread for *n*.
Rev. 18:17 riches come to *n*.

NAUGHTY.
Prov. 6:12 a *n*. person walketh
17:1 liar giveth ear to *n*. tongue
Jer. 24:2 basket had very *n*. figs

NAUGHTINESS.
1 *Sam*. 17:28 the *n*. of thy heart
Prov. 11:6 taken in their own *n*.
Jam. 1:21 all superfluity of *n*.

NAUM. *Luke* 3:25

NAVEL.
Job 40:16 force is in *n*. of belly
Prov. 3:8 sh. be health to thy *n*.
Cant. 7:2 thy *n*. is like a goblet
Ezek. 16:4 thy *n*. was not cut

NAVES.
1 *K*. 7:33 *n*. and spokes molten

NAVY.
1 *K*. 9:26 Solo. made *n*. of ships
27 Hir. sent in *n*. his servants
10:11 the *n*. of Hiram bro. gold
22 Solomon had at sea a *n*.

NAY.
1 *K*. 2:17 he will not say thee *n*.
20 say not *n*. will not say th. *n*.
Mat. 5:37 let your communicati.
be yea, yea, *n*. *n*. *Jam*. 5:12
Luke 13:3 *n*. except ye repent, 5
16:30 he said, *n*. fath. Abraham
Acts 16:37 *n*. verily, but let th.
Rom. 3:27 *n*. but by law of faith
9:20 *n*. but O man
2 *Cor*. 1:17 be yea, yea, *n*. *n*.
19 Jesus Christ was not yea
and *n*.
Jam. 5:12 let your *n*. be *n*.

NAZARENE. *Mat*. 2:23
NAZARENES. *Acts* 24:5

NAZARETH.
Mat. 2:23 dw. in a city called N.
21:11 Jesus of N. *Mark* 1:24; 10:17; *Luke* 4:31; 18:37; 24:19
Luke 1:26 Gabriel was sent to N.
2:4 Joseph came to N.
51 Jesus returned to N.
4:16 come to N.
John 1:45 J. of N. *Acts* 10:38
Acts 2:22; 4:10; 6:14; 22:8
10:38 God anointed Jesus of N.
20:9 contra. to name of Jesus of N.

NEC

Num. 6:2 a vow of a N. to sepa-
rate themselves, 18, 19, 21
Jud. 13:5 shall be a N. 7; 16:17

NAZARITES.
Lam. 4:7 her N. purer than snow
Amos 2:11 raised yo. men for N.
12 ye gave N. wine to drink
NEAPOLIS. *Acts* 16:11

NEAR.
Gen. 19:20 city is *n*. to flee to
45:10 thou shalt be *n*. to me
48:10 bro. them *n*. and kissed
Lev. 18:6 not appr. any *n*. of kin
Num. 16:9 br. you *n*. to him. 10
Deut. 5:27 go th. *n*. and hear G.
Jud. 20:34 knew not evil was *n*.
2 *Sam*. 19:42 the king is *n*. of kin
Job 41:16 one is so *n*. another
Ps. 22:11 trou. is *n*. 75:1 name is
119:151 thou art *n*. O Lord
Is. 43:21 and bring them *n*.
55:6 call upon L. while he is *n*.
57:19 peace be to him that is *n*.
Ezek. 22:5 those that be *n*. mock
Ob. 15 day of L. is *n*. *Zec*. 1:14
Mat. 24:33 it is *n*. even at doors

See CAME, COME, DRAW, DREW.

NEARER.
Ruth 3:12 is a kinsman *n*. than I
Rom. 13:11 our salvation *n*. than

NEBAIOTH.
Gen. 25:13 Ish. N. 1 *Chr*. 1:29
Is. 60:7 rams of N. sh. minister

NEBO.
Num. 32:3 N. is a land for cattle
Deut. 32:49 unto mount N. 34:1
1 *Chr*. 5:8 even unto N. *Ezr*. 2:29; 10:43
Neh. 7:33 of the other N. fifty-t.
Is. 15:2 Moab shall howl over N.
46:1 N. stoopeth, *Jer*. 48:1
Jer. 48:22 Judgm. come upon N.

**NEBUCHADNEZZAR, NE-
BUCHADREZZAR.**
1 *K*. 24:1 N. came against Jerus.
25:1; 2 *Chr*. 36:6; *Jer*. 39:1
25:22 peo. N. left, 1 *Chr*. 6:15; *Jer*. 24:1; 29:1; 52:28
Ezr. 1:7 vess. N. taken, 5:14, 6:5
Jer. 27:8 not serve N. 28:11, 14
29:21 them into the hand of N.
28:28 this city by hand of N.
Dan. 26:7 I will br. on N. 7jus N.
Dan. 2:1 N. dreamed 4:37
3 N. ma. image of gold, 19, 24
4 this came upon king N. 33
5:18 high G. gave N. a kingdom

NEBUZAR-ADAN.
2 *K*. 4:253 N. came to Jerusalem
Jer. 39:10 N. left of poor of tho

NECESSARY.
Job 23:12 his words more th. *n*.
Acts 13:46 *n*. the word be spoken
15:28 no burden than th. *n*. thi.
28:10 laded us with things *n*.
2 *Cor*. 9:5 thought it *n*. to exhort
Phil. 2:25 supposed it *n*. to send
Tit. 3:14 good works for *n*. uses
Heb. 9:23 *n*. patterns sh. be purf.

NECESSITY.
Luke 23:17 of *n*. he must release
Rom. 12:13 distr. to *n*. of saints
1 *Cor*. 7:37 having no *n*. and *no*.
9:16 for *n*. is laid upon me
2 *Cor*. 9:7 give not grud. or of *n*.
Phil. 4:16 once and unig. to my *n*.
Heb. 7:12 there is of *n*. a change
8:3 it is of *n*. this man have
9:16 there must of *n*. be death

NECESSITIES.
Acts 20:34 hands minis. to my *n*.
2 *Cor*. 6:4 as ministers of ti. in *n*.
12:10 I take pleasure in *n*.

NECHO. 2 *K*. 23:29

NECK.
Gen. 27:16 skins on smooth of *n*.
40 break yoke from off thy *n*.
41 *K*. fell on his *n*. and kissed
41:42 gold chain ab. Joseph's *n*.
Ezek. 16:11; *Dan*. 5:7, 16, 29
45:14 Jos. fell on Benjamin's *n*.
46:29 he fell on Jacob's *n*.
49:8 thy hand be on *n*. of enemies
Lev. 13:12 if font. be, blu a. 31:30
38:58 if wind. be upon thy *n*.
Jos. 10:24 strike of heifer's *n*.
Jos. 10:24 put feet on *n*. of kings
Jud. 6:26 he hath not word by *n*. an.
Jud. 8:21 ornam. on camel's *n*.
Neh. 9:29 they hardened their *n*.

954 — CRUDEN'S CONCORDANCE.

NEE

Job 15:26 on him, even on his n.
16:12 hath taken me by the n.
39:19 clothed n. with thunder?
41:22 in his n. remain. strength
Ps. 75:5 speak not with a stiff n.
Prov. 1:9 sh. be chains ab. thy n.
3:3 bind them about thy n., 6:21
22 life and grace to thy n.
Cant. 1:10 thy s. is comely
4:4 thy n. is like the tow. of D.
9 ravi. wi. one chain of thy n.
7:4 thy n. is a tower of ivory
Is. 8:8 sh. reach even to the n.
10:27 yoke be taken from thy n.
30:28 reach to midst of the n.
48:4 thy n. is an iron sinew
52:2 loose thyself fr. bands of n.
66:3 as if he cut off a dog's n.
Jer. 17:23 they made their n. stiff
27:2 yok, and put th. on thy n.
8 put n. under yoke of king, 11
28:10 took yoke from Jer. n. 12
14 put a yoke on n. of nations
30:8 break his yoke from off n.
Lam. 1:14 transgr. are on my n.
Hos. 10:11 passed over on her n.
Hab. 3:13 foundation to the n.
Mat. 18:6 a millstone hanged ab.
his n., Mark 9:42; Luke 17:2
Luke 15:20 father fell on his n.
Acts 15:10 yoke on n. of disciples
20:37 fell on P.'s n., kissed him
See HARDEN.

NECKS.

Jos. 10:24 feet on n. of th. kings
Jud. 5:30 n. of them take spoil
8:21 ornaments on camels' n. 26
2 Sam. 22:41 given me n. of enemies, Ps. 18:40
Neh. 3:5 put not n. to the work
9:16 with stretched-forth n.
Jer. 27:11 br. your n. under yoke
Lam. 5:5 n. under persecution
Ezek. 21:29 br. thee on n. of slain
Mic. 2:3 shall not remove your n.
Rom. 16:4 laid down th. own n.

NECROMANCER.

Deut. 19:11 not be an. yon a n.

NEED.

Deut. 15:8 sufficient for his n.
1 Sam. 21:15 ha, I n. of madmen
2 Chr. 2:16 as much as thou n.
20:17 shall not n. to fight in bat.
Ezr. 6:9 let wh. they n. be given
Prov. 31:11 sh. have no n. of sp.
Mat. 3:14 I have n. to be baptiz.
6:8 your F. knoweth what thin. ye have n. of, 32; Lu. 12:30
9:12 that be whole n. not a physician, Mark 2:17; Luke 5:31
14:16 they n. not depart, give
21:3 the L. hath n. of th. Mark 11:3; Luke 19:31, 34
26:65 what further n. have we?
Mark 14:63; Luke 22:71
Mark 2:25 D. did when he had n.
Luke 9:11 healed th. that had n.
15:7 just persons n. no repent.
John 13:29 things we have n. of
Acts 2:45 as ev. man had n. 4:35
Rom. 16:2 assist in what she n.
1 Cor. 7:36 n. so require, let him
12:21 not say, I have no n.
24 our comely parts have no n.
2 Cor. 3:1 or n. we epistles?
Phil. 4:12 I kn. how to suffer n.
19 God sh. supply all your n.
1 Thes. 1:8 that we n. not speak
4:9 brotherly love, n. not write
5:1 of the times ye have n. to.
Heb. 4:16 to help in time of n.
5:12 n. one teach you; n. milk
7:11 what n. th. another priest
10:36 ye have n. of patience
17; 1:6 n. be, ye are in heavi.
1 John 2:27 n. not any man teach
3:17 see his brother have n.
Rev. 3:17 I have n. of nothing
21:23 city no n., of sun or moon
22:5 n. no candle, nor light

NEEDED.

John 2:25 n. not any who testify
Acts 17:25 tho' he n. anything

NEEDEST, ETH.

Gen. 33:15 Jacob said, What n.
Luke 11:8 as many as he n.
John 13:10 n. not save to wash
16:30 and n. not that any man
Eph. 4:28 to give him that n.
2 Tim. 2:15 workm. n. not to be
Heb. 7:27 who n. not offer sacrif.

NEEDFUL.

Ezr. 7:20 n. for house of thy G.
Luke 10:42 but one thing is n.
Acts 15:5 n. to circumcise them

NEI

Phil. 1:24 abide in flesh more n.
Jam. 2:16 things n. for the body
Jude 3 it was n. for me to write

NEEDLE.

Mat. 19:24 to go thro' eye of a n.
Mark 10:25; Luke 18:25

NEEDLE-WORK.

Ex. 26:36 hanging wrought with
n.-w. 27:16; 36:37; 38:18
28:39 ma. girdle of n.-w. 39:29
Jud. 5:30 divers colors of n.-w.
Ps. 45:14 bro. raiment of n.-w.

NEEDS.

Gen. 17:13 must n. be circumci.
19:9 this fel. will n. be a judge
24:5 must I n. bri. thy son ag.?
2 Sam. 14:14 for we must n. die
Jer. 10:5 must n. be born, beca.
Mat. 18:7 n. be that offen. come
Mark 13:7 such things must n.
Luke 14:18 I must n. go and see
John 4:4 must n. go thro' Sama.
17:23 Christ must n. have
21:29 multitude must n. come
Rom. 13:5 ye must n. be subject
1 Cor. 5:10 must ye n. go out
2 Cor. 11:30 if I must n. glory

NEEDY.

Deut. 15:11 open thy hand to n.
24:14 servant that is poor and n.
Job 24:14 thy turn n. out of way
14 murderer kill. poor and n.
Ps. 9:18 n., not alway he forgot.
12:5 the sighing of n. will arise
35:10 del. poor and n. 72:4, 13
37:14 bent bow to cast down n.
40:17 I am poor and n. 70:5
72:12 he sh. deliver the n. 82:4
13 he sh. spare the poor and n.
74:21 poor and n. praise thy na.
82:3 justice to afflicted and n.
4 del. poor and n. from wicked
86:1 I am poor and n. 109:22
109:16 persecuted poor and n.
113:7 lifteth n. out of dunghill
Prov. 30:14 de. n. from am. men
31:9 plead cause of poor and n.
20 reacheth forth hands to n.
Is. 10:2 turn aside n. fr. judgm.
14:30 n. shall lie down in safety
25:4 been a strength to the n.
26:6 steps of n. shall tread it do.
32:7 even when the n. speaketh
41:17 poor and n. seek water
Ps. 5:28 right of n. do they not
22:16 judg. cause of poor and n.
Ezek. 16:49 strength. hands of n.
18:12 oppressed the poor and n.
22:29 people vexed poor and n.
Amos 4:1 kine of Bash. crush n.
8:4 O ye that swallow up the n.
6 buy the n. for a pair of shoes

NEESINGS.

Job 41:18 by his n. light doth sh.

NEGLECT.

Mat. 18:17 if he shall n. to hear
them; n. to hear the church
1 Tim. 4:14 n. not gift in thee
Heb. 2:3 how escape, if n. salv.?

NEGLECTED, ING.

Acts 6:1 widows n. in ministra.
Col. 2:23 n. body, not in honor

NEGLIGENT.

2 Chr. 29:11 be not n. for the L.
2 Pet. 1:12 not b s n. to put you

NEHEMIAH.

Ezr. 2:2 N. came with them, N.
Neh. 1:1 the words of N. son of
3:16 N. son of Azbuk, repaired
8:9 N. wh. is the Tirsha, 10:1
12:47 Israel in days of N. gave

NEHUSHTAN. 2 K. 18:4

NEIGHBOR.

Ex. 3:22 wom. borrow of n. 11:2
1 Sam. 15:28 hath given it to a n.
Prov. 27:10 better is a n. that is
Jer. 6:21 n. and friends sh. peri.
9:20 and teach every one her n.
Luke 10:36 n. to him ans. thieves

NEIGHBOR, Adjective.

Jer. 49:18 overthrow of Sod. and
the n. cities thereof, 50:40

His NEIGHBOR.

Ex. 12:4 him and h. n. take lamb
22:8 put his n. h.'s goods, 9, 11
14 borrow ought of his n.
32:27 go slay every man his n.
Lev. 20:10 with his n.'s wife sh.
be put to death, Deut. 22:24
24:19 man cause blemish in h. n.
Deut. 4:42 kill his n. unaw. 19:4
15:2 creditor that lent to his n.
19:11 if any hate his n.

NEP

Deut. 22:26 a man ris. ag. his n.
27:24 curs. he th. smiteth h. n.
Ruth 4:7 his shoe, gave to his n.
1 K. 8:31 if man trespa. ag. h. n.
2 Chr. 6:22 if a man sin ag. h. n.
Job 12:4 as one mocked of h. n.
16:21 a man pleadeth for h. n.
Ps. 12:2 sp. vanity each wi. h. n.
15:3 nor doeth evil to his n.
101:5 whoso slandereth his n.
Prov. 6:29 goeth to h. n.'s wife
11:9 a hypocrite destroy. h. n.
12 void of wis. desp. h. n. 14:21
12:26 right, more ex. than h. n.
14:20 poor is hated even of h. n.
16:29 a vio. man enticeth his n.
18:17 his n. cometh and search.
19:4 poor is separated fr. his n.
21:10 his n. findeth no favor
25:18 bear false witn. ag. his n.
26:19 man that deceiveth his n.
29:5 flattereth h. n. spreadeth
Ec. 4:4 a man envied of his n.
9:8 oppressed ev. one by h. n.
Is. 3:5 every one against h. n.
41:6 helped every one his n.
Jer. 5:8 neighed after h. n.'s wife
7:5 judgm. bet. man and his n.
9:4 take ye heed ev. one of h. n.
5 th. will deceive ev. one h. n.
8 speak peaceably to his n.
13 neeth his n.'s service
22:13 useth his n.'s service
22:27 and n. wh. ye please for n.
23:27 dreams tell ev. one to h. n.
30:5 speak unto his n. in pea.
31:34 teach no more every man
his n., Heb. 8:11
34:15 proclaiming li. to h. n. 17
Ezek. 18:6 not. defi. h. n.'s wi. 15
11 defiled h. n. 22:11; 33:26
Hab. 2:15 giveth h. n. drink
Zec. 3:10 call every man his n.
8:10 I set men ev. one ag. h. n.
16 speak ev. man truth to h. n.
17 let none ima. evil ag. h. n.
Mark 12:33 love h. n. as himself
Acts 7:27 he that did his n. wro.
Rom. 13:10 work, no evil to h. n.
15:2 let every one please his n.
Eph. 4:25 speak truth with h. n.

My NEIGHBOR.

Job 31:9 I laid wait at my n.'s d.
Luke 10:29 to Je. Who is my n.?

Thy NEIGHBOR.

Ex. 20:16 thou sh. not bear false
witness ag. thy n. Deut. 5:20
Lev. 18:20 not lie wi. t. n.'s wife
19:13 thou sh. not defraud t. n.
15 in righte. shalt judge thy n.
16 nor stand ag. blood of t. n.
17 in any wise rebuke thy n.
18 thou sh. love t. n. as thyself
Deut. 5:21 nor desire t. n.'s wife
19:14 not rem. t. n.'s landmark
Prov. 3:28 say not to thy n. Go
29 devise not evil against t. n.
24:28 be not witness ag. thy n.
25:9 debate thy cause with t. n.
17 with. foot fr. t. n.'s house
Mat. 5:43 shalt love thy n. 19:19;
19:21; Mark 12:31; Luke
10:27; Rom. 13:9; Gal. 5:14;
Jam. 2:8

NEIGHBORS.

Jos. 9:16 heard th. were their n.
Ruth 4:17 her n. gave it a name
2 K. 4:3 borrow vessels of thy n.
Ps. 28:3 speak peace to their n.
31:11 I was reproach am. my n.
44:13 makest us repro. to our n.
79:4 are become reproach to n.
12 render to our n. sevenfold
80:6 makest us a strife to our n.
89:41 he is a reproach to his n.
Jer. 12:14 saith L. ag. all evil n.
Ezek. 16:26 com. forni. with n.
22:12 gained of n. by exto.
23:5 she doted on her n. Assyr.
14:12 make sup. call not rich n.
called together his n.
John 9:8 n. who had seen him

NEIGHED.

Jer. 5:8 one n. after neigh. wife

NEIGHING, S.

Jer. 8:16 treadeth at n. of strong
13:27 I have seen adult. and n.

NEPHEW, S.

Jud. 12:14 A. had 40 sons, 30 n.
Job 18:19 neither have son nor n.
Is. 14:22 I will cut off son and n.
1 Tim. 5:4 if widow have children

NER. 1 Chr. 8:33; 9:36, 39

NEREUS. Rom. 16:15

NERGAL. 2 K. 17:30

NEST.

Num. 24:21 pat. thy n. in a rock
Deut. 22:6 if a n. be before thee
32:11 eagle stirreth up her n.
Job 29:18 I shall die in my n.
30:27 eagle make n. on high
Ps. 84:3 swal. found n. for herse.
Prov. 27:8 bird that wand. fr. n.
Is. 10:14 ha. found as n. riches
16:2 wander. bird cast out of n.
34:15 great owl make n.
Jer. 22:23 make. thy n. in cedars
48:28 dove makes n. in holes
49:16 make n. as high as eagle
Ob. 4 set thy n. among stars
Hab. 2:9 he may set n. on high.

NESTS.

Ps. 104:17 wh. birds make th. n.
Ezek. 31:6 all fowls made their n.
Mat. 8:20 birds of air n. Lu. 9:58

NET.

Job 18:8 cast into n. by own feet
19:6 God comp. me with his n.
Ps. 9:15 in n. they hid
25:15 pin. my feet out of n. 31:4
35:7 hid for me their n. in a pit
5 his n. he hid catch himself
57:6 prepared n. for my steps
66:11 thou broughtest us into n.
140:5 spread a n. by wayside
Prov. 1:17 in vain n. is spread
12:12 wick. desir. n. of evil men
29:5 man that flatter. spreadth n.
Ec. 9:12 fishes taken in evil n.
Is. 51:20 as a wild bull in a n.
Lam. 1:13 spr. a n. for my feet
Ezek. 12:13 n. will I spread. 17:20
19:8 nations shall spread n.
32:3 spread my n. over thee
Hos. 5:1 ye have been n. on Ta.
7:12 spread my n. on them
Mic. 7:2 hunt brother with a n.
Ps. 1:15 catch them in their n.
16 therefore sacrifice to their n.
17 shall they empty their n. ?
Mat. 4:18 cast n. into, Mark 1:16
13:47 kingd. of heaven is like n.
Luke 5:5 I will let down the n.
6 multitude of fishes, n. broke
John 21:6 cast n. on right side
11 n. to land; not n. broken

NETS.

1 K. 7:17 n. of checker work
Ps. 140:10 wick. fall into own n.
Ec. 7:26 wom. whose heart is n.
Is. 19:8 they that sp. n. hawaiish
Ezek. 26:5 spreading of n. in sea
14 place to spread n. of, 47:10
Mat. 4:21 James and J. mending
their n., Mark 1:19; Lu. 5:2
Mark 1:18 forsook n. follow. him
Luke 5:4 down n. for a draught

NETHANEEL.

Num. 1:8 N. the son of Zuar
2:5 N. the son of Zuar, shall be
captain, 7:18, 23; 10:15
1 Chr. 2:14 N. fourth son of Jes.
15:24 N. and Amasai blew with
24:6 the son of N. the scribe
26:4 sons of Obed-e. J. and N.
2 Chr. 17:7 Jehoshaphat sent N.
Ezr. 10:22 N. prie. Neh. 12:21, 36

NETHANIAH.

2 K. 25:23 son of N. 23; Jer. 40:8
1 Chr. 25:2 son of Asaph, N. 12
2 Chr. 17:8 Le. to teach, even N.
Jer. 36:14 princes sent son of N.
41:2 Ishmael, son of N. 15

NETHER.

Ezr. 19:17 they stood at n. part
Deut. 24:6 no man take n. millst.
Jos. 15:19 gave her upper springs
and n. springs, Jud. 1:15
Ezek. 31:14 deli. to death n. parts
16 comf. in n. parts of earth
18 down to n. parts of ear.
32:18 cast do. to n. parts of ear.
24 gone down to n. pa. of e.

NETHERMOST.

1 K. 6:6 n. chamb. 5 cub. broad

NETHINIM.

1 Chr. 9:2 first inhabitants N.
Ezr. 2:43 N. went with Zerub.
58 the N. were 392, Neh. 7:60
7:7 some of N. went up to Jer.
24 shall not be lawful to im. N.
8:17 Iddo and broth. the N. 20
20:22 N. dwelt in Oph. 11:21
10:28 N. separated from people
11:21 Zi. and Gispa over the N.

NETTLES.

Job 30:7 under n. th. were gath.
Prov. 24:31 n. had covered face
Is. 34:13 n. and bram. in fortres

CRUDEN'S CONCORDANCE. 955

NEW
Hos. 9:6 *n.* possess pleas. places
Zep. 2:9 M. shall be breeding *n.*

NETWORK, s.
Ex. 27:4 grate of *n.* brass, 38:4
1 *K.* 7:18 two rows round *n.* 42
41 two *n.* upon the chapiters
42 400 pomegranates for two *n.*
Is. 19:9 weave *n.* be confounded
Jer. 52:22 with *n.* on chapiters
23 pomegranates on *n.* wa. 100

NEVER.
Mat. 9:33 it was *n.* so seen in Is.
27:14 answered him to *n.* a word

NEW.
Ex. 1:8 arose a *n.* king over Eg.
Lev. 26:10 br. forth old, bec. of *n.*
Num. 16:30 Lord make a. thing
Deut. 20:5 built *n.* house, 22:8
24:5 taken a *n.* wife, not go
32:17 sacri. to devils, to *n.* gods
Jud. 5:8 they chose *n.* gods
1 *Sam.* 6:7 make a *n.* cart
2 *Sam.* 6:3 on *n.* cart, 1 *Chr.* 13:7
21:16 being girded with *n.* sw.
1 *K.* 11:29 J. clad with *n.* gar. 30
Job 32:19 to burst like *n.* bottles
Ps. 33:3 sing *n.* song, 96:1; 98:1;
144:9; 149:1; *Is.* 42:10
40:3 put *n.* song in my mouth
Ec. 1:9 no *n.* thing under sun
10 may be said, This is *n. ?*
Cant. 7:13 pleas. fruit *n.* and old
Is. 42:9 *n.* things I declare, 48:6
43:19 I will do a *n.* thing
62:2 be called by a *n.* name
65:17 *n.* heavens, *n.* earth, 66:22
Jer. 26:10 *n.* gate of L.'s ho. 36:10
31:22 Lord hath creat. *n.* thing
Lam. 3:23 Lord's mercies are *n.*
Ezek. 11:19 I will put *n.* spirit, 36:26
18:31 make *n.* heart and *n.* spi.
47:12 trees bring forth *n.* fruit
Mat. 9:16 *n.* cloth to an old gar.
Mark 2:21; *Luke* 5:36
17 put *n.* wine into *n.* bottles,
Mark 2:22; *Luke* 5:38
13:52 bring. out things *n.* and o.
26:28 is my blood of *n.* testament, *Mark* 14:24; *Lu.* 22:20;
1 *Cor.* 11:25
28 drink it *n.* with, *Mark* 14:25
27:60 Jos. laid body in *n.* tomb
Mark 1:27 what *n.* doct. is this?
16:17 speak with *n.* tongues
John 13:34 *n.* com. I give you
Acts 17:19 what this *n.* doct. is?
21 tell or hear some *n.* thing
1 *Cor.* 5:7 ye may be a *n.* lump
2 *Cor.* 3:6 able minist. of *n.* test.
5:17 in Ch. he is a *n.* creature;
all things are become *n.*
Gal. 6:15 but a *n.* creature
Eph. 2:15 of twain, one *n.* man
4:24 ye put on *n.* man, *Col.* 3:10
Heb. 9:15 Media. of *n.* testament
10:20 by *n.* and living way
1 *Pet.* 2:2 as *n.* born babes desi.
2 *Pet.* 3:13 *n.* heavens, *n.* earth
1 *John* 2:7 write no *n.* comman.
8 *n.* commandment I write
2 *John* 5 not as though I wrote *n.* commandment
Rev. 2:17 *n.* name written
8:12 name is *n.* Jerusalem; I will
write my *n.* name, 21:2
5:9 they sung a *n.* song, 14:3
21:1 I saw *n.* heaven and *n.* ear.
5 behold, I make all things *n.*
See COVENANT, MOON.

NEW wine.
Neh. 10:39 bring off. of *n.* wine
13:5 chamber where a. *w.* laid
12 bro. tithe of *n. w.* to treas.
Prov. 3:10 presses burst wi. *n. w.*
Is. 24:7 the *n. w.* mourneth
65:8 as *n. w.* is found in cluster
Hos. 4:11 *n. w.* take away heart
9:2 the *n. w.* shall fail in her
Joel 1:5 *n. w.* cut off; ld dried up
2:19 mountains shall drop *n. w.*
Hag. 1:11 call. for drou. on *n. w.*
Zec. 9:17 *n. w.* ma. maids cheer.
Mat. 9:17 *n. w.* into old bottles,
but *n. wine* into new, *Mark* 2:22; *Luke* 5:37
Acts 2:13 these men full of *n. w.*

NEWLY.
Deut. 32:17 to gods *n.* came up
Jud. 7:19 they had *n.* set watch

NEWNESS.
Rom. 6:4 shall walk in *n.* of life
7:6 should serve in *n.* of spirit

NEWS.
Prov. 25:25 so good *n.* from a far

NEXT.
Gen. 17:21 bear at set time *n.* ye.
Ex. 12:4 let him *n.* take lamb
Deut. 21:3 city whi. is *n.* slain
6 elders of city *n.* to slain man
1 *Sam.* 23:17 I shall be *n.* to th.
30:17 Dav. smote to ev. of *n.* day
Ezd. 10:3 Mordecai was *n.* to A.
Mat. 27:62 *n.* day that followed
Mark 1:38 go into *n.* towns
John 1:29 *n.* day John see, Jes.
Acts 4:3 put th. in hold to *n.* day
13:42 words preached *n.* sab. 44

NICANOR. *Acts* 6:5

NICODEMUS.
John 3:1 N. a ruler of the Jews
7:50 N. came to Jesus, 19:39

NICOLAITANS. *Rev.* 2:6, 15
NICOPOLIS. *Tit.* 3:12
NIGER. *Acts* 13:1

Len. 21:3 virgin that is *n.* to him
Num. 24:17 beh. him, not *n.* star
Deut. 4:7 hath G. so *n.* them?
22:2 if bro. be not *n.* unto thee
30:14 *n.* unto thee, *Rom.* 10:8
2 *Sam.* 11:20 wh. appr. so *n. ?* 21
1 *K.* 8:59 let my words be *n.*
Ps. 34:18 is *n.* them of bro. hea.
85:9 salva. *n.* them that fear him
145:18 L. is *n.* to all that call
Joel 3:1 day of L. is *n.* at hand
Mat. 24:33 sum. is *n. Luke* 21:30
Mark 13:29 know that it is *n.*
Luke 21:20 kn. that desola. is *n.*
31 know that king. of G. is *n.*
John 6:4 and the passover was *n.*
11:55 the Jews' passover was *n.*
Eph. 2:13 made *n.* by blood of C.
17 preach. to th. that were *n.*
Phil. 2:27 sick, *n.* unto death, 30
Heb. 6:8 is rejected, *n.* to cursing
See CAME, DRAW.

NIGHT.
Gen. 1:5 the darkness he call. *n.*
14 lights, to divide day from *n.*
1:16 lesser light to rule *n.*
19:2 tarry all *n. Num.* 22:19;
Jud. 19:6, 9
33 drink wine that *n.* 34, 35
34:54 tarried all *n.* 28:11; 31:54;
32:13, 21
30:15 shall lie with thee to *n.* 16
40:5 spake to *n.* in visi. of *n.*
42:27 at *n.* he shall divide spoil
Ex. 12:8 eat the flesh in that *n.*
42 is a *n.* to be observed to L.
14:20 not near other all *n.*
Lev. 6:9 burning on altar all *n.*
19:13 not abide with thee all *n.*
Num. 14:1 people wept that *n.*
22:8 said, Lodge here this *n.* 19
21:25 body not remain all *n.*
Jud. 6:40 God did *n.* to that *n.*
25 angel ashamed her all tim *n.*
Ruth 1:12 if I have a husb. to *n.*
1 *Sam.* 15:11 S. cried to L. all *n.*
19:11 if thou save not life to *n.*
28:25 Saul went away that *n.*
2 *Sam.* 2:29 Abner walked all *n.*
32 J. and his men went all *n.*
12:16 David lay all *n.* on earth
17:1 will pursue after D. this *n.*
16 lodge not this *n.* in plain
2 *K.* 19:35 th. *n.* the angel smote
1 *Chr.* 1:7 that *n.* did G. ap. to S.
9:33 charge over them *n.* and d.
Job 3:3 let *n.* perish in which
it was said, *n.* be maidtiful
4:13 the visions of *n.*
7:4 when shall the *n.* be gone ?
20:19 dew lay all *n.* on my bra.
30:26 desire not *n.* peo. cut off
35:10 G. giveth songs in the *n.*
36:20 desire not the *n.*
Ps. 1:2 law medita. day and *n.*
6:6 all the *n.* I make my bed
16:7 my reins instr. me in *n.*
17:3 hast visited me in the *n.*
22:2 I cry in *n.* *n.* seasons
42:8 in *n.* *n.* his song sh. be wi.
77:2 sore ran in *n.* *n.* ceased not
6 call to rem. my song in *n.* *n.*
90:4 1,000 years as watch in *n.* *n.*
105:39 a fire to give light *n. n.*
119:55 remem. thy name in *n.*
Ec. 2:23 taketh not rest in the *n.*
Cant. 3:8 we. his sword be. *n.*
Is. 15:1 in *n.* *n.* M. is laid waste
29:7 noiseth desired thee in the *n.*
21:11 watchman what of the *n.*
12 watchman, what of the *n.* ?
10 morning cometh, also the *n.*
Jer. 36:30 *n.* shall be out to *n.* *n.*
14:17 let my eyes run down *n.*
Lam. 1:2 weepeth sore in the *n.*
2:19 arise, cry out in the *n.*
Dan. 2:19 secret revealed in *n.*
5:30 that *n.* was Belshaz. slain
6:18 king passed the *n.* fasting
Hos. 7:6 their baker sleep. all *n.*

NIG
Joel 1:13 lie all *n.* in sackcloth
Amos 5:8 mak. day dark with *n.*
Jon. 4:10 ca. up in *n.* perish, in *n.*
Mic. 3:6 *n.* shall be to you
Mat. 26:31 sh. be offended beca.
of me this *n. Mark* 14:27
34 this *n.* thou shalt deny me
Luke 5:5 tolled all *n.* taking not.
6:12 he continued all *n.* in pray.
12:20 this *n.* thy soul be requi.
17:34 that *n.* two sh. be in one
John 9:4 *n.* com. no man work
13:30 he went out, it was *n.*
21:3 that *n.* they caught noth.
Acts 12:6 same *n.* Pe. was sleep.
16:9 took them same hour of *n.*
23:11 *n.* follow. Lord stood by
27:23 stood by me this *n.* angel
Rom. 13:12 *n.* is spent
1 *Cor.* 11:23 *n.* he was betrayed
1 *Thes.* 5:5 we are not of the *n.*
Rev. 21:25 be no *n.* there, 22:5

By NIGHT.
Gen. 20:3 to Ab. in dream by *n.*
31:24 G. ca. to La. in dre. by *n.*
39 whot. stolen by day or by *n.*
40 drou. consu. me, frost by *n.*
Ex. 12:31 called M. and A. by *n.*
13:21 by *n.* in pillar of fire, 22;
14:20; 40:38; *Neh.* 9:12
Num. 9:16 appear. of fire by *n.*
21 taken up by day or by *n.*
Josh. 1:33 fire by *n.* to show way
28:10 uncleanness by *n.*
1 *Sam.* 14:36 go after Phili. by *n.*
22:8 Saul came to woman by *n.*
2 *Sam.* 21:10 nor the beasts by *n.*
1 *K.* 3:5 Lord appeared to Solomon by *n.* 1 *Chr.* 7:12
2 *K.* 6:14 came by *n.* compassed
25:4 fled by *n. Jer.* 52:7
Ps. 91:5 sh. not be afraid by *n.*
121:6 nor moon smite thee by *n.*
134:1 by *n.* stand in house of L.
136:9 moon rule by *n. Jer.* 31:35
Prov. 31:18 goeth not out by *n.*
Cant. 3:1 by *n.* I sought him
Is. 4:5 shining of a fire by *n.*
Jer. 9:5 let us go by *n.* destroy
39:4 went forth out of city by *n.*
49:9 if thieves by *n.* will desir.
Dan. 7:2 I saw in my vision by *n.*
Ob. 5 if thieves, if robbers by *n.*
Mat. 2:14 took young ch. by *n.*
27:64 disciples come by *n.* 28:13
Luke 2:8 watch over flock by *n.*
John 3:2 Nicod. came by *n.* 19:39
Acts 5:19 angel by *n.* open. pris.
9:25 took P. by *n.* let him down
See DAY.

In the NIGHT.
1 *K.* 3:19 wom. child died *i. t. n.*
Neh. 2:12 arose *i. t. n.* 15 I went
4:22 *in t. n.* they may guard us
6:10 *in t. n.* will they slay thee
Job 5:14 in noonday as *in the n.*
27:20 tempest stealeth *in t. n.*
34:25 overturneth them *in the n.*
35:10 who giv. songs *in the n. ?*
Ps. 16:7 my reins inst. me *i. t. n.*
17:3 hast visited me *in the n.*
22:2 cry *in the n.*, season
42:8 *in t. n.* his song sh. be wi.
77:6 I call to remem. my song *in the n.*
Is. 26:9 with my soul desir. *in t. n.*
30:29 a song as when a holy solemnity is kept *in the n.*
59:10 stumble at noonday as *in the n.*
Jer. 6:5 arise, let us go *in the n.*
14:17 let my eyes run down *in the n.*
36:30 dead bo. be cast out *in t. n.*
Lam. 1:2 weepeth sore *in the n.*
2:19 arise, cry out *in the n.*
Mic. 3:6 *n.* shall be to you

NIGHTS.
Gen. 7:4 rain 40 days, 40 *n.* 12
Job 7:3 wearisome *n.* appointed
Is. 21:8 set in ward whole *n.*
See DAYS.

NIGHTHAWK.
Lev. 11:16 *n.* not eat, *Deut.* 14:15

NIGHT-WATCHES.
Ps. 63:6 I medit. on thee in *n.-w.*
119:148 prevent *n.-w.* to medit.

NIMRIM. *Is.* 15:6

NOB
NIMROD.
Gen. 10:8 C. begat N. 1 *Chr.* 1:10
Mic. 5:6 land of Assyria and N.

NINE.
Deut. 3:11 Og's bedst. *n.* cubits
Neh. 11:1 *n.* parts dw. in oth. cit.
Luke 17:17 where are the *n. ?*
See HUNDRED.

NINETEEN.
2 *Sam.* 2:30 lacked of D. serv. *n.*

NINETEENTH.
2 *K.* 25:8 in the *n.* year of Nebuchadnezzar the house of the Lord was burnt, *Jer.* 52:12

NINETY.
Gen. 5:9 Enos lived *n.* years
17:17 Sa. that is *n.* y. old. bear?

NINETY-SIX.
Ezr. 8:35 offer. for Is. *n.-s.* rams

NINETY-EIGHT.
1 *Sam.* 4:15 Eli was *n.-e.* ye. old

NINETY-NINE.
Gen. 17:1 Ab. was *n.-n.* years old
24 *n.-n.* years old when circu.
Mat. 18:12 do. he not le. the *n.-n.* and seek. ? 13; *Luke* 15:4, 7

NINEVEH.
Gen. 10:11 Asher builded N.
1 *K.* 19:36 Sen. at N. *Is.* 37:37
Nah. 1:1 the burden of N. 2:8
3:7 N. is waste, who will bem. ?
Zep. 2:13 make N. a desolation
Mat. 12:41 men of N. *Luke* 11:32

NINEVITES. *Luke* 11:30

NINTH.
Lev. 25:22 eat old fruit till *n.* ye.
1 *Chr.* 12:12 Elzabad, *n.* captain
27:12 *n.* captain for *n.* month
Mat. 20:5 went out ab. *n.* hour
27:45 darkness over all the land
unto *n.* hour, *Mark* 15:33
46 *n.* hour Jesus gave up ghost
Acts 3:1 hour of prayer, being *n.*
10:3 C. saw. vis. ab. *n.* hour, 30
Rev. 21:20 *n.* founda. was topaz
See DAY, MONTH.

NISAN.
Neh. 2:1 in the month N.
Est. 3:7 first month N.

NISROCH. 2 *K.* 19:37; *Is.* 37:38

NITRE.
Prov. 25:20 as vinegar upon *n.*
Jer. 2:22 tho' thou wash with *n.*

NO.
Jer. 46:25 pun. N. *Ezk.* 30:14, 16
Nah. 3:8 better th., populous N.

NOADIAH.
Ezr. 8:33 N. the son of Binnui
Neh. 6:14 think on prophet. N.

NOAH, NOE.
Gen. 5:29 called his name N. 30
6:8 N. found grace in eyes of L.
9 gen. of N. 10; 32; 1 *Cor.* 1:4
7:23 N. only remained alive
8:1 God remembered N. 9:26
9:21 N. awoke fr. his wine, 29
Is. 54:9 this is as waters of N.
Ezek. 14:14 N. Daniel, Job, 20
Mat. 24:37 days of N. *Luke* 17:26
Heb. 11:7 by faith N. be. warned
1 *Pet.* 3:20 waited in days of N.
2 *Pet.* 2:5 old world, but saved N.

NOAH, *Num.* 26:33; 27:1; 30:11;
Jos. 17:3

NOB.
1 *Sam.* 21:1 David came to N. to
Ahi. 22:9, 11; 19
Neh. 11:32 chil. of Ben. dw. at N.
Is. 10:32 shall he remain at N.

NOBLE.
Ezr. 4:10 *n.* Asnapper brought
Est. 6:9 one of king's *n.* princes
Jer. 2:21 I planted thee a *n.* vine
John 4:46 a *n.* man whose son
Acts 16:9 vision to P. in *i. n.* 169
1 *Thes.* 5:3 day cometh as thief
in t. n. a 2 *Pet.* 3:10
See DAY, MONTH.

NOBLES.
1 *K.* 21:8 *n.* were in city
Neh. 2:16 *n.* knew not whit. I
Job 29:10 *n.* held peace, tongue
Ps. 83:11 make their *n.* like Or.
149:8 bind their *n.* with fetters
Ec. 10:17 *n.* king is son of *n.*
Jer. 14:3 *n.* have sent little ones
27:20 with *n.* of Judah sent letters

CRUDEN'S CONCORDANCE.

NOO

Neh. 7:5 G. put in hea. to gath. n.
10:29 they clave to brethren, n.
13:17 I contended with n. of J
Job 29:10 the n. held their peace
Ps. 83:11 make their n. like Oreb
149:8 bind n. with fet. of iron
Prov. 6:16 princes rule, n. judg
Ec. 10:17 wh. king is son of n.
Is. 13:2 go into gates of the n.
34:12 shall call n. to kingdom
43:14 brought down all their n.
Jer. 14:3 n. sent their little ones
27:20 Nebuc. carried captive n.
30:21 n. shall be of themselves
39:6 king slew all n. of Judah
Jon. 3:7 decree of king and n.
Nah. 3:18 thy n. dwell in dust
NOD. Gen. 4:16

NOISE.
Ex. 20:18 heard n. of trumpet
32:17 th. is a n. of war in camp
18 n. of them that sing I hear
Jos. 6:10 not shout nor make n.
Jud. 5:11 deliv. fr. n. of archers
1 Sam. 4:6 what meaneth n. ? 14
  14 this is the n. ye have heard
2 K. 7:6 n. of char. n. of horses
11:13 Athali. heard n. of peop.
  Chr. 23:12
1 Chr. 15:28 making n. with psal.
Ezr. 3:13 n. of joy fr. n. of weep.
Job 36:29 understand n. of taber.
  33 n. thereof showeth concern.
37:2 hear attentive. n. of voice
Ps. 33:3 play skill. with loud n.
42:7 call. at n. of water-spouts
55:2 I mourn and make a n.
59:6 make a n. like a dog, 14
65:7 stilleth the n. of the seas
66:1 make a joyful n. to God,
    all ye lands, 81:1; 95:1, 2;
    98:4, 6; 100:1
93:4 L. mightier than n. of wat.
Is. 9:5 ev. battle is w. confu. n.
13:4 n. of a multitude in moun-
    tains, a tumult, n. of kingd.
14:11 n. of thy viols is down
17:12 a n. like n. of the seas
24:8 n. of them that rej. cudeth
18 he who fleeth from the n.
25:5 shalt bring n. of strangers
29:6 visited of L. with great n.
31:4 nor abase himself for n.
33:3 at n. of tumult people fled
66:6 a voice of n. from the city
Jer. 4:19 my heart maketh n.
  29 the city shall flee for the n.
10:22 the n. of the bruit is come
11:16 n. of gr. tumult he kindl.
25:31 n. sh. co. to ends of earth
46:17 F. king of Egypt is but n.
47:3 at n. of stamping of horses
49:21 earth is moved at the n.
    of their fall, at the cry the n.
50:46 at n. of taking of Babylon
51:55 n. of th. voice is uttered
Lam. 2:7 made n. in house of L.
Ezek. 1:24 n. of their wings, like
    the n. of great waters, 43:2
3:13 n. of wheels, n. of rushing
19:7 land was desolate by n.
26:10 thy walls sh. shake at n.
    13 cause n. of songs to cease
37:7 as I prophesied, th. was n.
Joel 2:5 like n. of char. n. of fires
Amos 5:23 take fr. me n. of songs
Mic. 2:12 they sh. make great n.
Nah. 3:2 n. of whip, n. of wheels
Zep. 1:10 n. of cry fr. fish-gate
Zec. 9:15 drink and make n.
Mat. 9:23 saw peo. making a n.
2 Pet. 3:10 hea. past away wi. n.
Rev. 6:1 I heard the n. of thund.

NOISED.
Jos. 6:27 Joshua, fame was n.
Mark 2:1 n. he was in the house
Luke 1:65 th. sayings n. abroad
Acts 2:6 when this was n. abroad

NOISOME.
Ps. 91:3 deli. thee fr. n. pestilen.
Ezek. 14:21 send sw. and n. bea.
Rev. 16:2 fell a n. grievous sore

There was NONE.
Num. 21:35 t. w. n. left him alive
2 Sam. 22:42 they looked, but th.
    was n. to save, Ps. 18:41
Ps. 139:16 yet t. w. n. of them

NOON.
Gen. 43:16 sh. dine with me at n.
    25 present ag. Jos. came at n.
Jud. 19:8 tarried until after n.
2 Sam. 4:5 who lay on bed at n.
1 K. 18:26 called on Ba. until n.
    27 at n. Elijah mocked them
20:16 and they went out at n.

NOR

2 K. 4:29 sat on her knees till n.
25:17 at n. will I pray
Cant. 1:7 mak. flock to rest at n.
Jer. 6:4 arise, let us go up at n.
Amos 8:9 can. sun go down at n.
Acts 22:6 about n. th. shone lig.

NOONDAY.
Deut. 28:29 thou sh. grope at n.
Job 5:14 they grope in the n.
11:17 th. age be clearer than n.
Ps. 37:6 bring forth judgm. as n.
91:6 destruction that wast. at n.
Is. 16:3 as night, in midst of n.
58:10 thy darkness sh. be as n.
59:10 we stumble at n. as night
Jer. 15:8 I have a spoiler at n.
Zep. 2:4 drive out Ashdod at n.

NOONTIDE.
Jer. 20:16 hear the shouting at n.

NOPH.
Is. 19:13 princes of N. deceived
Jer. 2:16 the children of N. have
46:14 publish in N. 19 N. shall
Ezek. 30:13 ima. cease out N. 16

NORTH.
Gen. 28:14 thou sh. spread to n.
1 K. 7:25 three oxen looking
    toward n. 2 Chr. 4:4
1 Chr. 9:24 porters were tow. n.
Job 26:7 he stretched out the n.
37:9 cold cometh out of the n.
    22 fair weather com. out of n.
Ps. 48:2 on sides of n. the city
89:12 n. and south, thou created
Ec. 1:6 wind turneth about to n.
11:3 if the tree fall toward the n.
Is. 14:13 I will sit in sides of n.
43:6 I will say to the n. G. up
Jer. 1:13 pot's face toward the n.
    14 out of the n. an evil break
    forth, 4:6; 46:20
    15 families of kingdoms of n.
3:11 proclaim th. words tow. n.
    18 come together out of th. n.
6:1 evil appeareth out of the n.
23:8 which led Is. out of n. 31:8
25:9 take all the families of n.
    26 the kings of n. far and near
46:6 they shall fall toward n.
    10 L. hath a sacrifice in the n.
    24 delivered to people of the n.
47:2 waters rise up out of the n.
50:3 out of n. cometh a nation
    9 a whirlw. came out of n.
    41 lifted mine eyes toward n.
50:47 all faces from south to n.
21:4 all flesh from south to n.
39:30 princes of n. all of th.
40:44 prospect toward the n. 40
41:11 one door toward n. 42:4
42:1 and building toward n.
    4 doors n. 11 chambers n. 13
46:19 holy chamb. looked to n.
48:10 holy oblation toward n.
Dan. 11:6 come to king of the n.
    8 more years than king of n.
    11 fight wi. the king of the n.
    13 the king of n. shall return
    15 k. of the n. cast up a m. 40
    44 tidings of n. sh. trouble hi.
Zec. 2:6 black horses go into n.
    6 have quieted my spirit in n.
14:4 mount. sh. remove tow. n.
Rev. 21:13 on n. were three gates

NORTH border.
Num. 34:7 this sh. be your n. b. 9
From the NORTH.
Ps. 107:3 gathered from the n.
    and the south, Is. 43:6; Jer.
    16:15; 23:8
Is. 14:31 come f. t. n. a smoke
41:25 I raised up one from t. n.
Jer. 4:6 I will bring evil f. the n.
6:22; 10:22; 50:9, 41; 51:48
25:9 f. t. n. king of kings, f. t. n.
39:8 will cause ch. to come f. n.
Amos 8:12 wander f. t. n. to east
Zec. 2:6 fled f. the land of f. n.
Luke 13:29 come f. t. n. sit down
NORTH quarter.
Jos. 15:5 Judah's border is n. q.
NORTH side.
Ex. 26:20 tabernacle on n. s.
    35 thou shalt put table on n. s.
Num. 2:25 camp of Dan on n. s.
Jud. 21:19 feast n. s. Beth-el
3 K. 16:14 brazen altar on n. s.
Ezek. 42:17 he measured the n. s.
48:30 goings out of city on n. s.

NORTHERN.
Jer. 15:12 break n. iron, and ste.
Joel 2:20 I will remove n. army

NORTHWARD.
Gen. 13:14 look n. Deut. 3:27

NOT

Ex. 40:22 tabernacle n. without
Lev. 1:11 on side of altar n.
Ezek. 3:3 ye mount. turn you n.
1 Sam. 14:3 front of one rock n.
1 Chr. 26:14 Zechar.'s lot ca. n.
17 n. were four Levites a day

NOSE.
Lev. 21:18 a flat n. sh. not offer
Is. 11:28 hook in thy n. 2 K. 19:28
Job 40:24 his n. pierceth through
41:2 canst thou put hook in n. ?
Prov. 30:33 wringing of the n.
Cant. 7:4 thy n. is as tower of L.
8 smell of thy n. like apples
Is. 65:5 th. are a smoke in my n.
Ezek. 8:17 put branch to their n.
23:25 take away thy n. and ears

NOSES.
Ps. 115:6 n. have they, smell not
Ezek. 39:11 stop n. of passengers

NOSE-JEWELS.
Is. 3:21 L. take away their n. j.

NOSTRILS.
Gen. 2:7 G. breath. into m.'s n.
7:22 in wh. n. was breath of life
Ex. 15:8 wi. blast of thy n. wat.
Num. 11:20 eat till it come out n.
2 Sam. 22:9 went a smoke out of
    his n. Ps. 18:8. 15
16 blast of the breath of his n.
Job 4:9 breath of n. consumed
27:3 Spirit of God is in my n.
39:20 glory of his n. is terrible
41:20 out of his n. goeth smoke
Is. 2:22 whose breath is in his n.
Lam. 4:20 brea. of n. was taken
Amos 4:10 sti. of camps unto n.

NOTABLE.
Dan. 8:5 the goat had a n. horn
    8 for it came up four n. ones
Mat. 27:16 had then n. prisoner
Acts 2:20 before n. day of L. co.
4:16 n. miracle hath been done

NOTE, ED.
Is. 30:8 write it, n. it in book
Dan. 10:21 n. in scripture of tru.
2 Thes. 3:14 n. that man

NOTE.
Rom. 16:7 are of n. am. apostles

NOTHING.
Gen. 11:6 n. will be restrained
19:8 only unto these men do n.
Ex. 12:10 let n. of it remain
16:18 had n. over, 2 Cor. 8:15
22:3 have n. then he sh. be sold
Deut. 22:26 damsel thou sh. do n.
28:55 he had n. in his hand
2 Sam. 24:24 wh. doth cost me n.
1 K. 8:9 there was n. in the ark
11:22 answered n. Luke 23:35
Job 6:18 they go to n. and perish
21 for now ye are n. ye see
8:9 of yesterday, and know n.
24:25 make speech n. worth
26:7 hangeth the earth upon n.
34:9 it profiteth a man n.
Ps. 17:3 tried me and sh. find n.
39:5 mine age is as n. bef. thee
49:17 he shall carry n. away
119:165 and n. sh. offend them
Prov. 9:13 and knoweth n.
13:4 desir. and hath n. 20:4
7 mak. himself rich, yet ha. n.
22:27 if thou hast n. to pay
Ec. 3:14 n. can be put to it
5:15 he sh. take n. of his labor
9:2 he wanteth n. for his soul
7:14 should find n. after him
Is. 34:12 her princes shall be n.
40:17 nations bef. him are as n.
    are to him less than n. 41:29
23 bring. princes to n. 41:11, 12
Jer. 10:24 lost th. bring me to n.
33:14 ask a thing, hide n. fr. me
39:10 left of poor which had n.
50:26 let n. of her be left
Lam. 1:12 is it n. to you ?
Ezek. 13:3 prop. that ha. seen n.
Dan. 4:35 Inhabit. of earth as n.
Amos 3:4 lion cry if taken n.
5 taken up snare, and taken n.
7 surely Lord God will do n.
Hag. 2:3 in comp. of it as n.
Mal. 1:12 ft. altar, it is contemptible
    to you, Luke 13:7
26:69 answered thou n.
27:12 he answer. n. Mark 14:60,
    61; 15:3, 4, 5
10 ha. n. to do with just man
Mark 5:26 and was n. bettered
9:29 forth by n. but by prayer
Luke 5:5 have toiled all night
    and taken n. John 21:3
7:42 they had n. to pay
10:19 n. sh. by any means hurt

NOU

Luke 11:6 I ha. n. to set bef. him
22:41 this man hath done n.
John 3:27 man can receive n.
5:19 S. can do n. of himself, 30
6:12 gather, that n. be lost
39 given me, I should lose n.
63 the flesh profiteth n.
7:26 they say n. 8:23 I do n.
9:33 could do n. 11:49 know n.
12:19 perc. how ye prevail n. ?
14:30 prince of world hath n.
15:5 without me ye can do n.
16:23 that day ye sh. ask me n.
24 ye asked n. in my name
18:20 in secret have I said n.
Acts 10:20 doubting n. 11:12
19:36 quiet. and do n. rashly
20:20 kept back n. profitable
23:14 eat n. until we ha. slain P.
27:33 fasting, having taken n.
1 Cor. 1:19 bring to n. understa.
4:4 I know n. by myself
5 judge n. before the time
8:2 knoweth n. yet as he ought
9:16 I have n. to glory of
13:2 charity, am n. 2 Cor. 12:11
3 not charity, it profit. me n.
2 Cor. 6:10 having n. yet possess
12:6 can do n. against the truth
Gal. 5:2 Ch. shall profit you n.
Phil. 2:3 let n. be done thro' str.
1 Tim. 4:4 good, n. to be refused
5:21 doing n. by partiality
6:4 he is proud, knowing n.
7 we brought n. carry n. out
Tit. 3:13 that n. be wanting
Phile. 14 thy mind woo. I do n.
Heb. 2:8 left n. that is not put
7:19 for the law made n. perfect
Jam. 1:4 and entire, wanting n.
6 him ask in faith, n. wavering
3 John 7 taking n. of the Gentiles.
For NOTHING.
Ex. 21:2 seventh go free for n.
Luke 6:35 lend, hoping for n. ag.
Phil. 4:6 be careful for n. but
In NOTHING.
Acts 17:21 A. spent time in n.
2 Cor. 12:11 in n. am I behind
Phil. 1:20 in n. I shall be asha.
28 in n. terrified by adversary.
Is NOTHING.
Num. 11:6 is n. besides manna
Jud. 7:14 is n. else save sword
1 Sam. 27:1 there is n. bet. than
1 K. 18:43 and said, There is n.
2 K. 20:15 there is n. among my
    treasure. Is. 39:4
2 Cor. 14:11 is n. with th. to help
Neh. 2:2 is n. else but sorrow
Est. 6:3 th. is n. done for him
Ps. 19:6 th. is n. k. beat thereof
Prov. 8:8 there is n. froward or
Jer. 32:17 is n. too hard for thee
Mat. 10:26 is n. that sh. not be
    reveal. Mark 4:22; Luke 13:2
23:16 swear by temple, it is n.
18 shall swear by altar, it is n.
Mark 7:15 th. is n. from without
John 8:54 my honor n.
Rom. 14:14 there is n. unclean
1 Cor. 7:19 circumcision is n.
8:4 an idol is n. in the world
Gal. 6:3 is n. he deceiv. himself
Tit. 1:15 that are defiled is n.
Of NOTHING.
Is. 41:24 behold, ye are of n.
1 Thes. 4:12 may have lack of n.
Rev. 3:17 increa. have need of n.
NOTWITHSTANDING.
Luke 10:11 n. be sure of this
20 n. in this rejoice not
1 Tim. 2:15 n. she shall be saved

NOUGHT. See NAUGHT.

NOURISH.
Gen. 45:11 will n. thee, 50:21
Is. 7:21 man sh. n. young cow
23:4 nor do I n. up young men
44:14 an ash, the rein doth n. it

NOURISHED.
Gen. 47:12 Joseph n. his father
2 Sam. 12:3 lamb he bought n.
Is. 1:2 n. and brought up child.
Ezek. 19:2 she n. her whelps
Acts 7:20 n. in father's house
21 Pharaoh's daughter n. him
12:20 n. by the king's country
Jain. 5:5 have n. your hearts as
Rev. 12:14 n. for a time, times

NOURISHER, MENT.
Ruth 4:15 shall be n. of old age
Col. 2:19 and bands having n.

CRUDEN'S CONCORDANCE. 957

NUM
NOURISHETH, ING.
Dan. 1:5 so *n.* them three years
Eph. 5:29 but *n.* his flesh.
NOVICE.
1 *Tim.* 3:6 not *n.* lest lifted
NOWADAYS.
1 *Sam.* 25:10 many servants *n.*
NUMBER, Substantive.
Gen. 34:30 I being few in *n.*
41:49 for it was without *n.*
Ex. 12:4 according to *n.* of souls
16:16 according to *n.* of pers.
23:26 *n.* of thy days I will fulfil
Lev. 25:15 *n.* of years after jubil.
n. of years of fruit, 16, 50
26:22 shall make you few in *n.*
Num. 1:2 *n.* of names, 18, 22
3:22 *n.* of males a nu. old, 28-43
46 odd *n.* to be redeemed
14:29 *n.* from twenty years old
15:12 according to *n.* prep. do to
ev. one according to their *n.*
23:10 who can count *n.* of Isr. ?
31:36 half of portion was in *n.*
Deut. 4:27 *n.* am. heathen, 28:62
7:7 more in *n.* than any people
25:2 to be beaten by a certa. *n.*
32:8 according to the *n.* of Isra.
Jos. 4:5 a stone according to *n.* 8
Jud. 6:5 camels without *n.* 7:12
7:6 *n.* that lapped were 300 men
1 *Sam.* 6:4 *n.* of lords of Philist.
18 *n.* of cities of the Philistine
2 *Sam.* 2:15 and went over by *n.*
24:2 may know *n.* of the peo.
9 gave up sum of *n.* of people
1 *K.* 18:31 12 stones accord. to *n.*
1 *Chr.* 7:2 *n.* was in days of Dav.
9 *n.* of th. after genealogy, 40
11:11 *n.* of mighty men D. had
22:16 gold and silver th. is no *n.*
23:3 their *n.* by their polls
23:7 the *n.* that were instruct.
27:23 David took not *n.* of them
2 *Chr.* 12:3 people were with, *n.*
29:12 *n.* of chief of the fathers
35:24 *n.* of priests sanctified th.
Ezr. 1:9 this is *n.* of the vessels
2:2 the *n.* of the people of Isra.
3:4 daily burnt-offerings by *n.*
6:17 according to the *n.* of tith.
8:34 by *n.* and by weight ev. o.
Neh. 7:7 according to *n.* of them
3:6 not come into *n.* of months
5:9 things without *n.* 9:10
14:5 *n.* of months are with thee
15:20 *n.* of years hid, to oppres.
25:3 is th. any *n.* of his armies?
31:37 dec. to him *n.* of my steps
31:24 mighty men without *n.*
36:26 *n.* of his years he search.
38:21 tho *n.* of thy days is great
Ps. 105:12 but a few men in *n.*
24 caterpillars, and without *n.*
139:18 more in *n.* than the sand
147:4 he telleth *n.* of the stars
Cant. 6:8 and virgins without *n.*
Is. 21:17 residue of *n.* of archers
40:26 bring. out their host by *n.*
65:11 drink-offering to that *n.*
Jer. 2:28 *n.* of cities are thy gods
32 forgotten me days with. *n.*
11:13 accord. to *n.* of thy cities
41:28 small *n.* that escape sword
Ezek. 5:3 shalt take a few in *n.*
Dan. 8:2 I understood *n.* of years
Hos. 1:10 *n.* of Israel, *Rom.* 9:27
Nah. 3:3 there is great *n.* of car.
Luke 22:3 Judas, being of the *n.*
John 6:10 sat, *n.* 5,000, *Acts* 4:4
Acts 1:15 *n.* of names were 120
5:36 to Theu. a *n.* of men joined
6:1 *n.* of discip. was multipl. 7
11:21 great *n.* bel. and turned
16:5 churches were incre. in *n.*
2 *Cor.* 10:12 not make ours. of *n.*
1 *Tim.* 5:9 let not wid. be ta. *n.*
Rev. 5:11 *n.* was 10,000 x 10,000
7:4 I heard the *n.* of them which
9:16 *n.* the army of horsemen
13:17 *n.* of name ; 18 count *n.*
18 *n.* of a man, his *n.* is 606
15:2 had victory over *n.* of bea.
20:8 *n.* of Gog is as sand of sea

NUMBER, Verb.
Gen. 13:16 if a man can *n.* dust
15:5 stars, if able to *n.* them
Lev. 15:13 *n.* 7 days for cleansing
28 shall *n.* to herself 7 days
23:15 after 7th sab. sh. *n.* 50 days
25:8 sh. *n.* 7 sabbaths of years
Num. 1:3 Aaron shall *n.* them
49 thou shalt not *n.* tribe of L.
3:40 *n.* all first-born males of I.
4:23 until fifty years old *n.* th. 30

OAK
Deut. 16:9 seven weeks shalt
thou *n.* begin to *n.*
1 *Sam.* 14:17 *n.* see who is gone
2 *Sam.* 24:1 go *n.* Is. and Judah
2 go *n.* people, 4 ; 1 *Chr.* 21:2
1 *K.* 20:25 *n.* thee an army like
1 *Chr.* 21:1 provok. Dav. to *n.* I.
27:24 J. began to *n.* finished *n.*
Job 38:37 who can *n.* the clouds?
39:2 canst thou *n.* the months?
Ps. 90:12 teach us to *n.* our days
Is. 65:12 will I *n.* yon to the sw.
Rev. 7:9 multi. no man could *n.*
NUMBERED.
Gen. 13:16 shall thy seed be *n.*
16:10 not be *n.* for multi. 32:12
Ex. 38:25 *n.* of congregation, 26
Num. 1:21 those th. were *n.* of
them, 23, 44, 46 ; 2:4, 13, 15,
19, 21, 23, 26, 28, 30
47 Levites were not *n.* 2:33
2:9 were *n.* in camp of Judah
16 were *n.* in camp of Reuben
24 *n.* of Ephraim ; 31 *n.* of Dan
3:16 and Moses *n.* them, 42
39 *n.* of Levites were 22,000
4:34 *n.* sons of Kohathites, 37
38 were *n.* of Gershonites, 41
42 *n.* *n.* of sons of Merari, 45
7:2 princes over th. that we. *n.*
11:20 wildern. all that were *n.*
26:51 these were *n.* of chil. of I.
Jos. 8:10 Joshua *n.* the people
1 *Sam.* 13:4 S. *n.* peo. in Telaim
2 *Sam.* 18:1 David *n.* the people
24:10 heart sm. him after he *n.*
1 *K.* 3:8 people that cannot be *n.*
8:5 sheep and oxen that could
not be *n.* 2 *Chr.* 5:6
20:15 *n.* princes of provinces
27 Is. were *n.* like two flocks
2 *K.* 3:6 Jehoram *n.* all Israel
1 *Chr.* 21:17 com. people to be *n.*
23:3 Lev. were *n.* fr. 30 years, 27
24:1 Solo. *n.* all strangers
25:5 *n.* them from 30 years old
Ezr. 1:8 Cyrus *n.* the vessels to
Ps. 40:5 more than can be *n.*
Ec. 1:15 wanting cannot be *n.*
2. 22:10 ye have *n.* the houses
53:12 *n.* with trans. *Mark* 15:28
Jer. 33:22 host of hea. can. be *n.*
Dan. 5:26 God hath *n.* thy king.
Hos. 1:10 sand of sea *n.* can. be *n.*
Mat. 10:30 hairs of your head are
all *n.* *Luke* 12:7
Acts 1:17 for he was *n.* with us
26 Matthias *n.* wi. 11 apostles
NUMBEREST.
Ex. 30:12 a ransom, wh. thou *n.*
Job 14:16 now thou *n.* my steps
NUMBERING.
Gen. 41:49 corn until he left *n.*
2 *Chr.* 2:17 Solom *n.* wherewith D.
NUMBERS.
1 *Chr.* 12:23 these are *n.* of bands
2 *Chr.* 17:14 these are *n.* of them
Ps. 71:15 I know not *n.* thereof
NURSE.
Gen. 24:59 sent away Re. and *n.*
35:8 Deborah, Rebek.'s *n.* died
Ex. 2:7 sh. I call to thee a *n.* ?
Ruth 4:16 Naomi became *n.*
2 *K.* 11:2 took him up
2 *Chr.* 22:11
1 *Thes.* 2:7 as *n.* cherish. her ch.
NURSE, ED.
Ex. 2:7 she may *n.* the child
9 take this child and *n.* it, and
the wo. took the ch. and *n.*
Is. 60:4 dau. sh. be *n.* at thy side
NURSING.
Num. 11:12 carry th. as *n.* father
Is. 49:23 kings be *n.* fathers, and
queens thy *n.* mothers
NURTURE.
Eph. 6:4 bring th. up in *n.* of L.
NUTS.
Gen. 43:11 pres. *n.* and almonds
Cant. 6:11 down into gard. of *n.*
NYMPHAS. *Col.* 4:15

O.
OAK.
Gen. 35:4 Jacob hid gods und. *o.*
8 nurse was buried und. an *o.*
Jos. 24:26 set it up under an *o.*
Jud. 6:11 angel of J. sat und. *o.*
2 *Sam.* 18:9 went under an *o.*
10 Absalom hanged in an *o.*
14 was alive in midst of the *o.*

OBE
1 *K.* 13:14 found man of G. un. *o.*
1 *Chr.* 10:12 buried bones un. *o.*
Is. 1:30 be as *o.* whose leaf. fad.
6:13 as tell-tree, or *o.* whose
44:14 cyp. and *o.* to make *n.* god
Ezek. 6:13 idols under every *o.*
OAKS.
Is. 1:29 shall be asham. of the *o.*
2:13 day of Lord on all the *o.*
Ezek. 27:6 of *o.* they made oars
Hos. 4:13 burn incense under *o.*
Amos 2:9 Amorite strong as *o.*
Zec. 11:2 O ye *o.* of Bashan
OAR, S.
Is. 33:21 sh. go no galley with *o.*
Ezek. 27:6 of *o.* of Ba. made *o.*
29 all that handle *o.* shall cry
OATH.
Gen. 24:8 be clear from my *o.* 41
26:3 I will perform the *o.* which
I sware to Abraham, *Deut.*
7:8 ; *Ps.* 105:9 ; *Jer.* 11:5
28 let there be an *o.* betw. us
50:25 J. took *o.* of childr. of Is.
Ex. 22:11 *o.* of Lord be betw. us
Lev. 5:4 pronounce with an *o.*
Num. 5:19 priest char. her by *o.*
21 L. make thee *o.* am. *o.* thea
30:2 if a man swear an *o.* 10
13 ev. binding *o.* to afflict soul
Deut. 29:12 his *o.* wh. L. maketh
14 you only do I make this *o.*
Jud. 21:5 Israel made a great *o.*
1 *Sam.* 14:26 people feared the *o.*
27 S. charged them with *o.* 28
Jos. 9:11 and *o.* w'e'l be. bi him
1 *K.* 8:43 why hast not kept *o.* ?
8:31 *o.* be laid on him, *o.* come
before thine alt. 2 *Chr.* 6:22
19:10 he took an *o.* of kingdom
Eccl. 8:2 in regard to *o.* of God
1 *Chr.* 16:16 mindful *o.* to Isa.
Neh. 18:15 Judah rejoiced at *o.*
10:29 an *o.* to walk in God's law
Ps. 89:3 have sworn
Ec. 8:2 as he that feareth an *o.*
9:2 sweareth an *o.* feareth *o.*
Ezek. 16:59 despised *o.* 17:18, 19
17:13 hath taken an *o.* of him
16 king, whose *o.* he despised
21:23 *o.* in sight of them for *o.*
Zec. 8:17 love no false *o.*
Mat. 14:7 promised with *o.*
9 for the *o.'s* sake, *Mark* 6:26
26:72 deni. with *o.* I do not kn.
Luke 1:73 the *o.* which he sware
Acts 2:30 God hath swo. with *o.*
23:21 bound themselves with *o.*
Heb. 6:16 an *o.* for confirmation
17 God confirmed it by an *o.*
28 *o.* which was since the law
Jam. 5:12 sw. not by any oth. *o.*

OATHS.
Ezek. 21:23 that have sworn *o.*
Hab. 3:9 naked, according to *o.*
Mat. 5:33 perform to L. thine *o.*

OBADIAH.
1 *K.* 18:3 Ahab called O. 4, 7, 16
2 *Chr.* 17:7 sent to O. 33:12
Ezr. 8:9 O. son of Jeh. went up
Neh. 10:5 O. seal, 12:25 O. was
Ob. 1 vision of O. thus saith

ODED.
Ruth 4:17 called his name O.
21 Boaz begat O. 1 *Chr.* 2:12 ;
Mat. 1:5
1 *Chr.* 11:47 O. one of D.'s val. m.
2 *Chr.* 28:1 son of O. into coven.
Luke 3:32 Jes. wh. was son of O.

OBED-EDOM.
2 *Sam.* 6:10 carried the ark into
the house of O. 11, 12 ; 1 *Chr.*
13:13, 14 ; 15:25
1 *Chr.* 15:18 O. a porter, 21, 24

OBEDIENCE.
Rom. 1:5 *o.* to faith among all
6:16 by *o.* of one many be made
16:19 your *o.* is come abroad
26 made known for *o.* to faith
1 *Cor.* 14:34 women to be und. *o.*
2 *Cor.* 7:15 remembereth *o.* of all
10:5 captivity to *o.* of Christ
6 disobed. when *o.* is fulfilled
Phile. 21 confidence in thy *o.*
Heb. 5:8 learned *o.* by things suf.
1 *Pet.* 1:2 sanctificat. of Sp. to *o.*

OBEDIENT.
Ex. 24:7 Lord hath said, be *o.*
Num. 27:20 Israel may be *o.*
Deut. 4:30 be *o.* to his voice

OBE
Deut. 8:20 bec. ye wo. not be *o.*
2 *Sam.* 22:45 strangers shall be *o.*
Prov. 25:12 reprover on *o.* ear
Is. 1:19 if *o.* ye shall eat good
42:24 nei. were th. *o.* to his law
Acts 6:7 priests were *o.* to faith
Rom. 15:18 make Ge. *o.* by word
2 *Cor.* 2:9 know whether ye be *o.*
Eph. 6:5 servants be *o.* *Tit.* 2:9
Phil. 2:8 Ch. became *o.* to death
Tit. 2:5 wives, be *o.* to husbands
1 *Pet.* 1:14 be as *o.* children

OBEY.
Gen. 27:8 son, *o.* my voice, 13, 43
Ex. 5:2 who is Lord that I *o.*
19:5 now if ye will *o.* my voice
23:21 *o.* his voice ; 22 indeed *o.*
Deut. 11:27 a blessing if ye *o.* L.
13:4 *o.* his voice, 27:10 ; 30:2, 8 ;
1 *Sam.* 12:14
30:20 thou mayest *o.* his voice
Jos. 24:24 L.'s voice will we *o.*
1 *Sam.* 8:19 peo. refused to *o.* S.
13:22 to *o.* n. bet. than sacrifice
Neh. 9:17 and refused to *o.*
Job 36:11 if they *o.* and serve
Pr. 18:44 as th. hear, they sh. *o.*
Prov. 30:17 despis. to *o.* mother
Jer. 7:23 *o.* my voice, 11:4, 7
26:13 amend your ways, *o.* voice
of the Lord your God, 38:20 ;
Zec. 6:15
35:14 Rechab. *o.* their father's
42:6 we will *o.* the voice of the
L. our God, that it may be
well with us wh. we *o.* the L.
Dan. 7:27 shall serve and *o.* him
Mal. 8:27 winds and sea *o.* him ?
Mark 4:11 ; *Luke* 8:25
Acts 5:29 *o.* G. rather than men
32 God hath given to them *o.*
Rom. 2:8 them that *o.* unright.
6:12 that ye sho. *o.* it in lusts
16 servants to *o.* his servants
ye are to whom ye *o.*
Eph. 6:1 *o.* parents. *Col.* 3:20
Col. 3:22 servants *o.* masters
Tit. 3:1 put them in mind to *o.*
Heb. 5:9 salvation to all that *o.*
13:17 *o.* them that have the rule
Jam. 3:3 put bits in horses' mou.

Not OBEY.
Deut. 11:28 curse, if ye will not
o. 28:62 ; 1 *Sam.* 12:12 ; *Job*
36:12 ; *Jer.* 12:17 ; 18:10
21:18 *not o.* voice of his father
1 *Sam.* 15:19 wh. didst then *n. o.*?
Jer. 42:13 we will *not o.* the L.
Dan. 9:11 might *n. o.* thy voice
Acts 7:39 our fathers would *n. o.*
Rom. 2:8 and do *not o.* the truth
Gal. 3:1 who bewitched you, th.
you should *not o.* ?
2 *Thes.* 1:8 ven. on th. that *o. n.*
3:14 if any man *o. n.* our word
1 *Pet.* 3:1 if any man *o. not* word
4:17 them that *o. not* gospel ?

OBEYED.
Gen. 22:18 bec. thou hast *o.* 26:5
28:7 Ja. *o.* his father and moth.
Jos. 22:2 have *o.* my voice
1 *Sam.* 15:20 I have *o.* voice of L.
24 I feared peo. and *o.* th. voice
28:21 handmaid *o.* thy voice
1 *Chr.* 29:23 Israel *o.* Solomon
2 *Chr.* 11:4 they *o.* and let th. go
Ps. 99:8 wast tho. God of Jonadah, 10
18 *o.* the comm. of your father
Jer. 3:13 not, have we *o.* the L.
Hag. 1:12 people *o.* voice of L.
Acts 5:36 many as *o.* Theud. 37
Rom. 6:17 *o.* from heart th. doc.
Phil. 2:12 ye *o.* not in my pres.
Heb. 11:8 by faith Abraham *o.*
1 *Pet.* 3:6 Sarah *o.* Abraham

Not OBEYED.
Jos. 5:6 consumed, they *o. n.*
Jud. 2:2 *n. o.* my voice, 6:10
1 *K.* 20:36 hast *n. o.* voice of L.
2 *K.* 18:12 they *n. o.* voice of L.
Prov. 5:13 *not o.* voice of teach.
Jer. 3:13 ye have *n. o.* my voice,
25 ; 42:21 ; 43:4, 7 ; 44:23
9:13 *n. o.* my voice, 32:23 ; 40:3 ; *Dan.* 9:10, 14
Zep. 3:2 she *n. o.* the voice
Rom. 10:16 have *n.* all *o.* gospel

OBEYEDST, ETH.
1 *Sam.* 28:18 *o.* not voice of L.
Is. 50:10 who *o.* voice of serv. ?
Jer. 7:28 a nation that *o.* not
the Lord

CRUDEN'S CONCORDANCE.

OBT

Jer. 11:3 cur. be man that o. not
22:21 that thou o. not my voice

OBEYING
Jud. 2:17 fa. o. they did not so
1 Sam. 15:22 as in o. voice of L.
1 Pet. 1:22 puri. souls in o. truth

OBEISANCE.
Gen. 37:7 your sheaves made o.
9 aga. moon, 11 stars made o.
43:28 they made o. to Joseph
Ex. 18:7 Moses did o. to father
2 Sam. 1:2 Amalek. did o. to D.
14:4 woman of Tekoah did o.
15:5 when any man ca. to do o.
1 K. 1:16 Bath-sheba did o. to D.
2 Chr. 24:17 princes of J. made o.

OBJECT.
Acts 24:19 o. if th. had aught ag.

OBLATION.
Lev. 2:4 o. of a meat-off. 5, 7, 13
12 as for o. of first-fruits offer
3:1 if his o. be a sacri. of peace
8:13 offer his o. for his vows
Num. 18:9 o. of theirs be holy
31:50 we have bro. an o. for L.
Is. 19:21 Egypt, sh. do o. to L.
40:20 impoverish, he hath no o.
60:3 offereth o. as swine's flesh
Jer. 14:12 when they offer an o.
Ezek. 44:30 ov. o. sh. be priest's
45:1 when ye divide land, off. o.
13 o. ye shall offer, 46:9, 20, 21
16 give this o. for prince in Is.
Dan. 2:46 sho. offer an o. to Da.
9:21 time of o. 27 o. to cease

OBLATIONS.
Lev. 7:36 com. Israel to offer o.
2 Chr. 31:14 distribute o. of Lord
Is. 1:13 bring no more vain o.
Ezek. 20:40 require first-fru. of o.

OBSCURE.
Prov. 20:20 lamp put in o. dark.

OBSCURITY.
Is. 29:18 blind see out of o.
53:10 shall thy light rise in o.
59:9 wait for light, but beho. o.

OBSERVATION.
Luke 17:20 king. of G. not wi. o.

OBSERVE.
Ex. 12:17 ye shall o. feast of un-
leav. bread, 24; Deut. 16:1
31:16 o. sabbath ; 34:22 o. feast
34:11 o. that wh. I comm. thee
Lev. 19:26 nor enchant. o. times
37 ye sh. o. all my statutes,
2 Chr. 7:17; Neh. 1:5; Ps.
105:45; Ezek. 37:24
Num. 28:2 sacrifice shall ye o.
Deut. 16:13 o. feast of tabernac.
1 K. 20:33 men did diligently o.
Ps. 107:43 will o. these things
119:34 o. with my whole heart
Prov. 23:26 let thine eyes o. ways
Jer. 8:7 the crane and swallow o.
Ezek. 20:18 neither o. judgments
Hos. 13:7 as a leop. will I o. th.
Jon. 2:8 that o. lying vanities
Mat. 28:20 teaching them to o.
Acts 16:21 custo. not lawful to o.
21:25 Gentiles o. no such thing
Gal. 4:10 ye o. days, and months
1 Tim. 5:21 thou o. these things
See DO.

OBSERVED.
Gen. 37:11 his father o. saying
Ex. 12:42 it is a night to be o.
Num. 15:22 not o. commandm.
Deut. 33:9 for Levi o. thy word
2 Sam. 11:16 when J. o. the city
2 K. 21:6 Manasseh o. the times,
2 Chr. 33:6
Hos. 14:8 I heard him, o. him
Mark 6:20 He. feared and o. him
10:20 these I o. from my youth

OBSERVER, S.
Deut. 18:10 th. shall not be an o.
14 these nations hearken. to o.

OBSERVEST, ETH.
Ec. 11:4 he that o. the wind
Is. 42:20 seeing things, o. not

OBSTINATE.
Deut. 2:30 L. G. made his hea. o.
Is. 48:4 I knew that thou art o.

OBTAIN.
Gen. 16:2 may be I may o. chil.
Prov. 8:35 o. favor of the Lord.
Is. 35:10 they shall o. joy, 51:11
Dan. 11:21 shall o. the kingdom
Luke 20:35 worthy too. th. world
Rom. 11:31 thro' mercy they may o.
1 Cor. 9:24 so run, that ye may o.

OFF

1 Cor. 9:25 do it to o. corrupt. cro.
1 Thes. 5:9 to o. salvation by L.
2 Tim. 2:10 o. salvation in C. L.
Heb. 4:16 that we may o. mercy
11:35 might o. bet. resurrection
Jam. 4:2 ye kill and cannot o.

OBTAINED.
Neh. 13:6 I o. leave of the king
Est. 2:9 Esth. o. kindn. 17 she o.
Hos. 2:23 that had not o. mercy
Acts 1:17 had o. part of ministry
22:28 great sum o. I freedom
26:22 having o. the help of God
27:13 suppos. they o. th. purpo.
Rom. 11:7 Is. not o. what he seek,
for, but the elect. hath o. it
30 o. mercy thro' their unbelief
1 Cor. 7:25 one that hath o. mer.
Eph. 1:11 we have o. inheritance
1 Tim. 1:13 I o. mercy, bec. ig. 16
Heb. 1:4 o. more excellent name
6:15 endured, he o. the promis.
8:6 he o. a more excel. ministry
9:12 hav. o. eternal redemption
11:2 the elders o. good report, 39
4 Abel o. witness he was righ.
33 o. promises, stop. mouths
1 Pet. 2:10 o. mercy, now have o.
2 Pet. 1:1 o. like precious faith
See FAVOR.

OBTAINING.
2 Thes. 2:14 o. the glory of our L.

OCCASION.
Gen. 43:18 he may seek o. ag. us
Jud. 9:33 as find o. 1 Sam. 10:7
14:4 Samson sought o. ag. Phil.
2 Sam. 12:14 given o. to enemies
Ezr. 7:20 find o. against us
Jer. 2:24 in her o. who can turn?
Ezek. 18:3 not have o. any more
Dan. 6:4 sought to find o. could
find none o.
Rom. 7:8 o. by commandment, 11
14:13 put not o. to fall in way
2 Cor. 5:12 we give you o. to glo.
8:8 I speak by o. of forwardnes.
11:12 that I may cut off o. them
which desire o.
Gal. 5:13 use not liberty for an o.
1 Tim. 5:14 younger give none o.
1 John 2:10 none o. of stumbling

OCCASIONED.
1 Sam. 22:22 have o. death of all

OCCASIONS
Deut. 22:14 o. of speech agn. 17
Job 33:10 findeth o. against me

OCCUPATION.
Gen. 46:33 wh. o. ? 47:3; Jon. 1:8
Acts 18:3 by o. were tent-makers
19:25 workmen of like o.

OCCUPY.
Ezek. 27:9 marin. o. merchandise
Luke 19:13 servan. o. till I come

OCCUPIED, ETH.
Ex. 38:24 gold was o. for work
Jud. 16:11 ropes th. never we. o.
Ezek. 27:16 Syria o. 19 Javan o.
21 Arabia o. 22 Sh. o. in fairs
1 Cor. 14:16 o. room of unlearned
Heb. 13:9 profited th. that ha. o.

OCCUPIERS.
Ezek. 27:27 o. of merchandi. fall

OCCURRENT.
1 K. 5:4 adversary nor evil o.

ODD.
Num. 3:48 o. num. to be redeem.

ODED.
2 Chr. 15:1 on Azariah son of O.
28:9 prophet was th. called O.

ODIOUS.
1 Chr. 19:6 made themselves o.
Prov. 30:23 for an o. woman

ODOR, S.
Lev. 26:31 not smell sav. of yo. o.
2 Chr. 16:14 in bed of sweet o.
Est. 2:12 oil of myrrh sweet o.
Jer. 34:5 th. they burn o. for thee
Dan. 2:46 after sweet o. to Daniel
John 12:3 filled with o. of ointm.
Phil. 4:18 an o. of a sweet smell
Rev. 5:8 golden vials full of o.
18:13 no man buyeth their o.

OFFENCE.
1 Sam. 25:31 this shall be no o.
Is. 8:14 o. to both houses of Is.
Hos. 5:15 they acknowl, their o.
Mat. 16:23 Sa. thou art o. to me
18:7 woe to man by wh. o. com.
Acts 24:16 conscience void of o.
Rom. 5:15 not as o. so is free gift,
17 by one man's o. death reig.
18 by the o. of one m. dead. 18

OFF

Rom. 5:20 that the o. might abo.
9:33 stumbling-stone, rock of o.
14:20 man who eateth with o.
1 Cor. 10:32 give no. o. 2 Cor. 6:3
2 Cor. 11:7 have I committed o.
Gal. 5:11 o. of cross ceased
Phil. 1:10 with. o. till day of Ch.
1 Pet. 2:8 o. to them wh. stumble

OFFENCES.
Ec. 10:4 yielding pacifi. great o.
Mat. 18:7 beca. of o. for it must
needs be that o. Luke 17:1
Rom. 4:25 was deliver. for our o.
5:16 the free gift of many o.
16:17 mark them which cause o.

OFFEND.
Job 34:31 I will not o. any more
Ps. 73:15 I sho. o. ag. generation
119:165 nothing shall o. them
Jer. 2:3 that devour him shall o.
50:7 adversaries said, We o. not
Hos. 4:15 let not Judah o.
Heb. 1:11 shall pass over and o.
Mat. 5:29 if thy right eye o. thee
30 if thy right hand o. thee,
18:8, 9; Mark 9:43, 45, 47
13:41 gather all things that o.
17:27 lest we should o. them
18:6 whoso o. one of these,
Mark 9:42, Luke 17:2
John 6:61 said, Doth this o. yon?
1 Cor. 8:13 brother o. lest he o.
Jam. 2:10 yet o. in one point
3:2 in many things we o. all

OFFENDED.
Gen. 20:9 ha. I o. thee? Jer. 37:18
40:1 butler and baker had o.
2 K. 18:14 have o. return fr. me
2 Chr. 28:13 have o. against L.
Prov. 18:19 a brother o. is harder
Jer. 2:3 all that devour him o.
Ezek. 25:12 Edom hath greatly o.
Hos. 13:1 when Ephraim o. in B.
Mat. 11:6 blessed is he who shall
not be o. Luke 7:23
13:21 when persecution aris. by
and by he is o. Mark 4:17
57 were o. in him, Mark 6:3
15:12 Pharis. o. after they heard
24:10 then shall many be o.
26:31 o. becau. of me this night
33 tho' all men shall be o. yet
will I never be o. Mark 14:29
Acts 25:8 nor ag. Cæsar ha. I o.
Rom. 14:21 whereby brother is o.
2 Cor. 11:29 is o. and I burn not?

OFFENDER, S.
1 K. 1:21 I and my son counted o.
Acts 25:11 if I be an o. or have

OFFER.
Ex. 22:29 to o. the first-fruits
23:18 shalt not o. blood, 34:25
29:36 one lamb o. in morning,
either at even, 41; Nu. 28:4, 8
30:9 o. no strange inc. thereon
Lev. 1:3 o. male without blemish,
3:6; 22:19, 20
2:13 with offerings thou shalto.
3:1 if he o. peace-offering, o. it
without blem. 6; 9:2; 19:5
12 goat he shall o. before Lord
5:8 o. for sin-offering first, 9:7
6:14 sons of A. o. before L. 26;
14:19; 15:15, 30; Num. 6:11
7:3 o. of it all the fat thereof
12 o. it for a thanksgiv. 22:29
14 ho o. an heave-off. 19 o.
17:7 no more o. sacri. to devils
9 to the door to o. it to Lord
21:6 eaten same day ye o. it
21:6 bread of their G. they doo.
21 hath blemish, not come noo.
Num. 7:11 they o. their offerings
8:11 Aaron o. Levites, 13, 15
9:7 that we may not o.
13:7 o. th. part of a bin of wine
19 shall o. a heave-offer. 18:24,
26, 28, 29
16:40 no stranger come to o. in.
28:24 ye shall o. daily the meat
Deut. 12:14 L. sh. choose, there o.
18:3 priest's due fr. them th. o.
33:19 shall o. sacrifices of right-
eousness, Ps. 4:5
Jud. 3:18 made an end to o. pre.
1 Sam. 1:21 went up to o. to L.
2:19 with her hush. to o. sacri.
28 him my priest, to o. on alt.
2 Sam. 24:12 o. thee three things,
1 Chr. 21:10
1 K. 13:2 o. priests of high places
2 Chr. 30:14 too. so willingly, 17
2 Chr. 23:14 made vessels to o.
Ezr. 6:10 o. sacrifices to God
Ps. 16:4 of blood will I not o.

OFF

Ps. 27:6 therefore I o. in tabern.
50:14 o. to God thanksgiving
51:19 then sh. they o. bullocks
66:15 will o. to thee burnt sacr.
72:10 kings of Sheba sh. o. gifts
116:17 o. sacrifice of thanksgiv.
Is. 57:7 wentest up to o. sacrifice
Jer. 11:12 gods to wh. th. o. inc.
Ezek. 20:31 when ye o. your gifts
44:7 when ye o. my bread
15 they shall o. to me the fat
45:1 ye shall o. an oblation to
the Lord, 13; 48:9
Dan. 2:36 o. an oblation to Dan.
Hos. 9:4 not o. wine-off. to Lord
Amos 4:5 o. sacrifice of thanksg.
Hag. 2:14 th. o. there is unclean
Mal. 1:7 ye o. polluted bread
8 o. it now to thy governor
3:3 o. to the Lord an offering in
Mat. 5:24 then come and o. gift
8:4 o. gift Moses commanded,
Mark 1:44; Luke 5:14
Luke 6:29 check, o. also other
11:12 will he o. him scorpion ?
Heb. 5:1 o. gifts and sacrifices
3 ought for hims. to o. for sins
7:27 needeth not to o. sacrifice
8:3 h.-priest ordained to o. this
man ha. somewhat also to o.
9:25 he should o. himself often
13:15 by him let us o. sacrifice
1 Pet. 2:5 by J. C. to o. sacrifice
Rev. 8:3 should o. with prayers
See BURNT-OFFERINGS.

OFFERED.
Gen. 31:54 Ja. o. sacrifice. 46:1
Ex. 33:22 every man o. offering
Lev. 9:15 elevr. goat, o. it for sin
10:1 Nadab and Abi. o. strange
fire, 16:1; Num. 3:4; 26:61
Num. 7:2 o. for the dedicat. 10
8:21 Aaron o. them as offering
22:40 Balak o. oxen and sheep,
23:2, 4, 14, 30
Jud. 5:2 willingly o. themselv. 9
13:19 took a kid and o. it
1 Sam. 1:4 time that Elkanah o.
2 Sam. 6:17 o. peace-offer, 24:25
2 K. 8:62 Solomon and Is. o. 63
12:32 Jeroboam o. in Beth-el, 33
22:43 peo. o. yet in high places
Ac. 3:20 meat-offering was o.
16:12 A. approached altar and o.
16:15 Zedekiah willingly o.
2 Chr. 15:11 Asa o. to the Lord
17:16 Amaziah willingly o.
Ezr. 1:6 that was willingly o.
2:68 some of fathers o. freely
6:17 o. at dedic. of house of God
7:15 freely o. to the G. of Israel
10:19 they o. a ram of the flock
Neh. 11:2 willingly o. themselves
12:43 that day th. o. great sacri.
Job 3:76 hast o. a meat-offering
66:3 as if he o. swine's blood
Jer. 32:29 have o. incense to Ba.
Ezek. 20:28 o. there th. sacrifices
Dan. 11:18 reproach o. to cease
Amos 5:25 have ye o. me sacri. ?
Jon. 1:16 and o. sacrifice to Lord
Mal. 1:11 inc. be o. to my name
Acts 8:18 Simon o. them money
15:29 meats o. to idols, 21:25
21:26 an offering should be o.
1 Cor. 8:1 things o. to idols, 4, 7,
10; 10:19, 28
Phil. 2:17 if I be o. on the service
2 Tim. 4:6 I am ready to be o.
Heb. 5:7 he had o. up prayers
7:27 who he o. up himself
9:7 blood, wh. he o. for himself
9 o. gifts; 14 o. himself to G.
28 C. o. to bear sins of many
11:4 by faith Abel o. to God
17 Ab. when tried, o. up Isaac
Jam. 2:21 A. justified when he o.

OFFERETH.
Lev. 6:26 priest that o. it for sin
7:18 imputed to him that o. it
21:8 he o. the bread of thy God
Ps. 50:23 o. praise glorifieth me
Is. 66:3 he that o. oblation as if

OFFERING, Substantive.
Gen. 4:3 Cain brought o. unto L.
4 L. had respect to Abel and o.
Ex. 25:2 bring me o. of ev. man
30:13 half shekel be o. of Lord
15 o. to Lord make atonement
Lev. 1:2 bring your o. of cattle
14 o. of fowls; 2:1 fine flour
2:11 no meat-o. made with leav.
3:2 lay his hand on head of o. 8
6:20 o. of Aaron and sons
7:16 if o. be vow. or volunt. o.
Num. 5:15 o. of jeal. o. of mem.

CRUDEN'S CONCORDANCE. 959

OFF

Num. 7:10 princes off. *o.* bef. all.
8:11 offer Levites for an *o.* 21
9:13 *o.* of L. in appointed seas.
10:15 said, Respect not their *o.*
1 *Sam.* 2:29 wher. kick at mi. *o.* *f*
3:14 shall not be purged with a.
26:19 if Lord have stirred thee up ag. me, let him accept *o.*
1 *K.* 18:29 prophesied till *o.* of evening sacrifice
1 *Chr.* 16:29 *o.* come, *Ps.* 96:8
Neh. 10:39 Is. sh. bring *o.* of corn
Is. 43:23 nor caus. th. serv. wi. *o.*
53:10 make his soul *o.* for sin
66:20 bring your breath, for an *o.*
Ezek. 20:28 provocat. of their *o.*
Zep. 3:10 daughter bring my *o.*
Mal. 1:10 nor accept *o.* at hand
13 bro. *o.* should I accept this *f*
2:13 regardeth not *o.* any more
3:3 offer to Lord an *o.* in right.
Rom. 15:16 *o.* of Gent. be accept.
Eph. 5:2 an *o.* to God for us
Heb. 10:5 *o.* thou wouldest not. 8
10 through *o.* of body of Jesus
14 by one *o.* he hath perfected
18 there is no more *o.* for sin

See BURNT, DRINK, FIRE.

OFFERING, Participle.
1 *Sam.* 7:10 as S. was *o.* burnt-*o.*
2 *Chr.* 8:12 *o.* according to com.
29:29 made end of *o.* th. king
30:22 seven days, *o.* peace-off.
35:14 sons of Aa. were busied *o.*
Ezr. 7:16 priests *o.* willingly for
Jer. 11:17 provoke me *o.* to Baal
Luke 23:36 and *o.* him vinegar
Heb. 10:11 ev. priest *o.* sacrifices

Heave-OFFERING,
Ex. 29:27 sanctify the *h.-o.*
Lev. 7:14 oblation for a *heave-o.*
Num. 15:19 sh. offer up *h.-o.* 20
21 of first dough gi. *h.-o.* to L.
18:24 tithes they offer as a *h.-o.*
28 give the Lord's *h.-o.* to Aa.
31:29 give to Eleazar for *h.-o.*
41 tribute wh. was the L. *h.-o.*

See MEAT, MAKE, FIRE, BURNT-offering.

Peace-OFFERING,
Lev. 3:1 sacrifice of *p.-o.* 3, 6, 9

Sin-OFFERING,
Ex. 29:14 the flesh of bullock sh. thou burn, it is a *s.-o. Lev.* 4:21, 21; 6:30, 11, 13
30:10 bl. of *s.-o.* of atonements
Lev. 4:3 let him bring a young bullock without blemish, for a *s.-o.* 16:3, 27; *Num.* 8:8
25 priest take blood of *s.-o.* 5:9
29 lay hand on head of *s.-o.* 34
30 bri. lamb for *s.-o. Num.* 6:14
5:6 lamb or kid of goats for *s.-o.* 9:3; 10:5, 15, 27; 23:19
8 priest shall offer the *s.-o.* fir.
6:25 this is the law of *s.-o.* 7:37
1:7 as *s.-o.* so is trespass, 14:13
9:2 take a young calf for a *s.-o.*
10:16 Moses sought goat of *s.-o.*
17 why have ye not eaten *s.-o.*
12:6 bring turtle-dove for a *s.-o.*
16:25 fat of *s.-o.* shall he burnt
Num. 7:16 kid of goats for *s.-o.* 22, 28; 15:24; 28:15; 29:5
2 *Chr.* 29:24 *s.-o.* made for Israel
Ezr. 8:35 12 he-goats for *s.-o.*
Ps. 40:6 *s.-o.* hast not required
Ezek. 43:19 priest bull. for *s.-o.*
25 every day a goat for a *s.-o.*
44:27 sanctuary, shall offer *s.-o.*
29 they shall eat the *sin-o.*
46:20 place wh. priests boil *s.-o.*

Trespass-OFFERING.
Lev. 5:6 he sh. bring *t.-o.* to L.
15 lamb without ble. for *t.-o.*
6:5 shall give it in day of *t.-o.*
14:12 take one he-lamb for *t.-o.* 21, 24, 25; *Num.* 6:12
1 *Sam.* 6:3 any wise return *t.-o.* 4 what shall be the *t.-o.* ? 8, 17
Ezek. 40:39 to slay *t.-o.* 42:13
41:29 eat *t.-o.* and ev. dedicated
46:20 where priests sh. boil *t.-o.*

Wave-OFFERING,
Ex. 29:24 for a *w.-o.* 26; *Lev.* 7:30; 8:27, 29; 9:21; 10:15; 14:12, 21; 23:20; *Num.* 18:11
27 sanctify breast of *w.-o.*
Lev. 23:15 bro. sheaf of *wave-o.*

Wood-OFFERING,
Neh. 10:34 cast lots for *wood-o.*
13:31 *w.-o.* at times appointed

OFFERINGS.
Lev. 1:10 if his *o.* be of the flocks

OFF

Lev. 2:13 with all thy *o.* shalt offer salt
1 *Sam.* 2:29 fat with chief of *o.*
2 *Sam.* 1:21 let th. be no fic. of *o.*
2 *Chr.* 31:12 people brought in *o.*
35:8 gave priests for passo. *o.* 9
13 holy *o.* sod they in pots
Neh. 10:37 first-fruits of *o.* 12:44
Ps. 20:3 L. remember all thy *o.*
Jer. 41:5 *o.* and incense in hands
Ezek. 20:40 there will I requi. *o.*
Hos. 8:13 sacrifice flesh for *o.*
Amos 5:25 ye off. me *o.* 40 yrs. *f*
Mal. 3:4 *o.* of Judah be pleasant
8 robbed thee? in tithes and *o.*
Luke 21:4 of abund. cast in to *o.*
Acts 24:17 to bring alms and *o.*

See BURNT, DRINK, FREE.

Made by FIRE.

Heave-OFFERINGS.
Num. 18:8 given charge of *h.-o.*
Deut. 12:6 ye shall bring *heave-o.*

OFFERINGS of the Lord.
1 *Sam.* 2:17 men abhor. *o.* *of* *l.* L.

See MEAT.

Peace-OFFERINGS.
Ex. 24:5 sacrifice *p.-o.* of oxen
20:28 a heave-offering of *p.-o.*
32:6 people brought *peace-o.*
Lev. 4:26 shall burn as fat of *p.-o.* 31, 35; 6:12
7:11 law of sacri. of *p.-o.* 18, 37
17:5 offer them for *p.-o.* 23:19
Num. 6:14 lamb *p.-o.* 17 a ram
7:17 sacri. of *p.-o.* two oxen, five lambs, 23, 29, 35, 41; 28:39
10:10 blow over sacrifice of *p.-o.*
Jos. 8:31 Joshua sacrificed *p.-o.*
22:23 if offer *p.-o.* let L. req. it
Jud. 20:26 Is. offered *p.-o.* 21:4
1 *Sam.* 10:8 offer *pence-o.* 11:15
2 *Sam.* 6:17 D. offered *p.-o.* 24:25; 1 *Chr.* 21:26
1 *K.* 3:15 Sol. offered *p.-o.* 8:63
9:25 thrice a year D. offered *p.-o.*
1 *Chr.* 31:2 appo. priests for *p.-o.*
33:16 Manasseh offered *p.-o.*
Prov. 7:14 I have *p.-o.* with me
Ezek. 40:15 *p.-o.* to make rec. 17
46:2 priest prepare his *p.-o.* and 12 prince prep. voluntary *p.-o.*
Amos 5:22 not regard *p.-o.* of fat

Sin-OFFERINGS.
Neh. 10:33 *sin-o.* to make atone.

Thank-OFFERINGS.
2 *Chr.* 29:31 bring *t.-o.* to house
33:16 altar, and sacrificed *t.-o.*

Wave-OFFERINGS.
Num. 18:11 *w.-o.* I have given

Wine-OFFERINGS.
Hos. 9:4 not off. *w.-o.* plea. to G.

OFFICE.
Gen. 41:13 me he restored to *o.*
Ex. 1:16 wh. ye do *o.* of midwife
1 *Chr.* 6:32 they waited on th. *o.*
9:22 David did ordain in set *o.*
2 *Chr.* 24:11 chest hro. to king's-*o.*
31:18 in th. set *o.* they sancti.
Neh. 13:13 their *o.* was to distri.
Ps. 109:8 let another take his *o.*
Ezek. 44:13 sh. not do *o.* of priest
Rom. 11:13 I magnify my *o.*
2 *Cor.* 8:22 have *o.* proved thing
Heb. 10:11 *o.* off. same sacrifices

Priest's OFFICE.
Ex. 28:1 minister to me in the *p.'s-o.* 3, 4, 41; 29:1, 44; 30:30; 35:19; 40:13, 15; *Lev.* 7:35; *Num.* 3:3
29:9 *p.'s o.* shall be theirs
31:10 minister in *p.'s o.* 39:41
Num. 3:4 Itha. minis. in *p.'s o.*
18:7 thou and sons keep *p.'s o.*
Deut. 10:6 Elea. min. in *p.'s o.*
1 *Chr.* 6:10 Aza. executed *p.'s o.*
2 *Chr.* 11:14 cast th. off fr. *p.'s o.*
Luke 1:8 Zacharias exec. *p.'s o.*

OFFICER.
Gen. 37:36 *f* off. *o.* of Phar. 39:1
Jud. 9:24 Is and Zebul his *o.* *f*
1 *K.* 4:5 Zabud was principal *o.*
19 Geber was only *o.* in land
22:9 Ahab called an *o.* and said
2 *K.* 8:6 king appointed *o.*
25:19 Nebuzaradan took *o.*
Mat. 5:25 delly. thee to *o.* and *o.* cast into prison, *Luke* 12:58

OFFICERS.
Gen. 40:2 Pha. wroth with two *o.*
41:34 let him ap. *o.* over land
Ex. 5:15 *o.* of Israel cried to Ph.

OIL

Ex. 5:19 *o.* did see th. we. in ev.
Num. 11:10 gather unto me the *o. Deut.* 31:28
Deut. 1:15 made it. *o.* am. tribes
16:18 judges and *o.* sh. th. make
20:5 *o.* shall speak to people, 8
1 *Sam.* 8:15 viney. give to his *o.*
1 *K.* 4:5 Azariah over the *o.*
7 Solomon had 12 *o.* over Isr.
2 *K.* 11:15 Jehoiada comman. *o.*
18 appointed *o.* over the house,
2 *Chr.* 23:18
24:13 Jehoia. went out with *o.*
15 *o.* and mighty car. he away
1 *Chr.* 23:4 6,000 were *o.* and jud.
29:29 Chenaniah and sons for *o.*
Est. 9:3 *o.* of kings helped Jews
Jer. 29:26 be *o.* in house of Lord
John 7:32 priests and *o.* to take
45 *o.* answ. Never man spake
18:3 Judas having received *o.*
12 *o.* took Je. 22 *o.* struck Jes.
Acts 5:22 the *o.* found them not

OFFICES.
1 *Sam.* 2:36 put me into prie. *o.*
1 *Chr.* 24:3 dis. priests acc. to *o.*
2 *Chr.* 7:6 priests waited on th. *o.*
Neh. 13:14 not good deeds for *o.*

OFFSCOURING.
Lam. 3:45 hast made us as *o.*
1 *Cor.* 4:13 *o.* of all things

OFFSPRING.
Job 5:25 thy *o.* as grass of earth
21:8 *o.* is estab. bef. their eyes
27:14 *o.* not satisfied with bread
31:8 let my *o.* be rooted out
Is. 22:24 sh. hang on him, the *o.*
44:3 poor blessing on thine *o.*
48:19 *o.* of bowels like gravel
61:9 their *o.* shall be known
65:23 seed of the blessed, and *o.*
Acts 17:28 we are also his *o.* 29
Rev. 22:16 I am the *o.* of David

OFT.
2 *K.* 4:8 as *o.* as he passed by
Mat. 9:14 *f* how *o.* we and P. fast *o. f*
17:15 ofttimes he fall. into fire, and *o.* into water, *Mark* 9:22
18:21 how *o.* sh. my broth. sin *f*
Mark 7:3 exc. th. wash *o.* eat not
1 *Cor.* 11:25 as *o.* as ye dr. cup
11:23 prisons, in deaths *o.*

OFTEN, ER.
Prov. 29:1 that being *o.* reproved
Mal. 3:16 feared the L. spake *o.*
Mark 3:4 *o.* bound with fetters
23:38 why do dis. of J. f. *o.* *f*
Acts 24:26 Felix sent for him *o.*
1 *Cor.* 11:26 as *o.* as ye eat bread
2 *Cor.* 11:26 in journeyings *o.*
27 I have been in watchings *o.*
1 *Tim.* 5:23 use wine for *o.* infir.
Heb. 9:25 nor yet offer himself *o.*
26 he must *o.* have suffered
Rev. 11:6 smite earth as *o.* as wi.

OFTENTIMES.
Job 33:29 th. things work. G. *o.*
Ec. 7:22 *o.* thy heart knoweth
Luke 8:29 *o.* it had caught him
John 18:2 Je. *o.* resorted thither
Rom. 1:13 *o.* I purposed to come

OG.
Deut. 31:4 as he did to *O.*
Jos. 2:10 you did to *O.* 13:31
1 *K.* 4:19 was in the count. of *O.*

OIL.
Gen. 28:18 Jacob poured *o.* on the top of it, 35:14
Ex. 25:6 take *o.* for the light, 35:11; 37:29
29:2 cakes tempered with *o.* 40
30:25 anoin. with *o.* of holy ointm.
Lev. 2:1 shall pour *o.* upon it, 6
4 cakes of fine flour mingled with *o.* 11:5b; 21; 23:13; *Num.* 6:15; 7:13, 19, 25, 31, 37, 43, 49, 55, 61, 67, 73, 79; 8:8; 28:13; 29:3, 9, 14
15 thy meat offering, put *o.*
upon it, 5:12
16 priest shall burn part of *o.*
5:11 he shall put no *o.* upon it,
Num. 5:15

OIN

Deut. 28:40 sh. not anoint thys. wi. *o.* 2 *Sam.* 14:2; *Mic.* 6:15
32:13 suck *o.* out of rock
33:24 let Asher dip his foot in *o.*
1 *Sam.* 10:1 Sa. took a vial of *o.*
16:1 fill thy horn with *o.* 13
1 *K.* 1:39 Z. took horn of *o.*
5:11 gave Hir. 20 measures of *o.*
17:12 *o.* in cr. 14 nor cr. of *o.* 16
2 *K.* 4:2 nothing in house save *o.*
6 *o.* stayed ; 7 go sell the *o.*
9:1 take this box of *o.* to tha. 3
6 he poured the *o.* on his head
1 *Chr.* 27:28 over the cellars of *o.*
Ezr. 3:7 *o.* to them of Zidon
Est. 2:12 with *o.* of myrrh
Job 24:11 *o.* within their walls
29:6 poured me out rivers of *o.*
Ps. 23:5 anoint my head with *o.*
45:7 anointed with *o.* of gladness
55:21 words were softer than *o.*
104:15 *o.* to make face to shine
109:18 comm like *o.* into bones
141:5 be a kindness, an excel. *o.*
Prov. 5:3 mouth smoother th. *o.*
21:20 *o.* in dwelling of the wise
Is. 61:3 give *o.* of joy for mourn.
Jer. 41:8 we have treasures of *o.*
Ezek. 16:13 thou didst eat *o.* 19
18 set mine *o.* and incense
27:17 Ju. traded in honey and *o.*
32:14 cause rivers to run like *o.*
45:14 ordinance of *o.* bath of *o.*
24 a hin of *o.* for an ephah
Hos. 2:5 lovers that give me *o.*
12:1 *o.* is carried into Egypt
Mic. 6:7 with 10,000 rivers of *o.* *f*
Mat. 25:3 virg. took no *o.*
4 wise took *o.* 8 give us yo. *o.*
Luke 7:46 with *o.* didst not ano.
10:34 a hundred measures of *o.*

See ANOINTED, ANOINTING, BEATEN, LOG.

OIL, with wine.
Num. 18:12 best of *o.* and *w.* off.
Deut. 7:13 L. will bless *w.* and *o.*
12:17 not eat the tithe of thy *w.* and *o.* 14:23
18:4 first-fr. *w.* and *o.* 2 *Chr.* 31:5
28:51 leave th. th. *w.* or *o.*
1 *Chr.* 9:29 overseers the *w.* and *o.*
12:40 were nigh bro. *w.* and *o.*
2 *Chr.* 2:10 baths *w.* and *o.* 15
41:51 Reboh. put in *o.* and *w.*
35:28 H. storehou. for *w.* and *o.*
Ezr. 6:9 give *w.* *o.* according
7:22 100 baths *w.* 100 baths *o.*
Neh. 5:11 restore *w.* and *o.*
10:37 first-fruits of *w.* and *o.*
39 offer. of corn, new *w.* and *o.*
13:5 tithes of corn, *w.* and *o.* 12
Prov. 21:17 loveth wine and *o.*
Jer. 31:12 flow to L. for *w.* and *o.*
40:10 gather ye *w.* fruits and *o.*
Hag. 1:11 drought on *w.* and *o.*
2:12 *w.* or *o.* shall it be holy ?
Luke 10:34 pouring in *o.* and *w.*
Rev. 6:6 nor hurt not *w.* and *o.*
18:13 no man buy th. *w.* and *o.*

OILED.
Ex. 29:23 one cake of *o.* bread,
Lev. 8:26

OIL-OLIVE.
Ex. 27:20 *o.-o.* beaten for light
30:24 take thou of *o.-o.* a hin
Lev. 24:2 br. unto thee pure *o.-o.*
Deut. 8:8 land of *o.* 2 *K.* 18:32

OIL-TREE.
Is. 41:19 plant in wild. the *o.-t.*

OINTMENT.
Ex. 30:25 make of it holy *o.*
2 *K.* 20:13 Hezek. showed them precious *o. Is.* 39:2
Job 41:31 maketh sea boil like *o.*
Ps. 133:2 it is like precious *o.*
Prov. 27:9 *o.* and perfu. rej. hea.
16 right hand bewrayeth *o.*
Ec. 7:1 good name bet. than *o.*
9:8 and let thy head lack no *o.*
10:1 dead flies cause *o.* to stink
Cant. 1:3 name is as *o.* poured
his *o.* modified with *o.*
Is. 57:9 wentest to king with *o.*
Mat. 26:7 box of precious *o. Mark* 14:3 ; *Luke* 7:37
9 *o.* might been sold, *John* 12:5
12 she poured *o.* on my body
Mark 14:4 why this waste of *o.* ?
Luke 7:38 anoin. feet with *o.* 46
John 11:2 anoi. the L. wi. *o.*
12:3 Mary took pound of *o.*
house was filled with odor of the *o.*

CRUDEN'S CONCORDANCE.

ORE

ORDER, Substantive.
2 K. 23:4 comp. priests of sec. o.
1 Chr. 6:32 waited accord. to o.
15:13 sought him not aft. due o.
23:31 o. commanded them be, L.
25:2 acc. to o. of D. 6; 2 Ch. 8:14
Job 10:22 land of dark. without o.
Ps. 110:4 prl. after o. of M. Heb.
5:6, 10; 6:20; 7:11, 17, 21
1 Cor. 16:1 have gi. o. to church.
Col. 2:5 beholding your o.
Heb. 7:11 not called after o. of A.

In ORDER.
Gen. 22:9 Abr. laid wood in o.
Ex. 40:4 thou sh. set in o. thin.
that are to be set in o. Lev.
17, 8, 12; 6:12; 24:8
24 he set bread in o. upon it
2 Sam. 17:23 put his house in o.
1 K. 18:33 Elijah put wood in o.
2 K. 20:1 set house in o. Is. 38:1
2 Chr. 13:11 show-bread set in o.
29:35 service of house of L. in o.
Job 33:5 set words in o. bef. me
Ps. 50:21 th. in o. bef. thine eyes
Ec. 12:9 the preacher set in o.
Is. 44:7 set it in o. before me?
Ezek. 41:6 chambers were 30 in o.
Luke 1:1 hand to set forth in o. a
Acts 18:23 country of Phry. in o.
1 Cor. 11:31 rest will I set in o.
15:23 ev. man shall rise in his o.
Tit. 1:5 I left thee to set in o.

ORDER, Verb.
Ex. 27:21 Aa. o. it, Lev. 24:3, 4
Jud. 13:12 how sh. we o. child?
1 K. 20:14 who shall o. battle?
Job 23:4 o. my cause before him
37:19 we cannot o. our speech
Ps. 119:133 o. steps in thy word
Is. 41 upon his kingdom to o. it
Jer. 46:3 o. ye buckler and shield

ORDERED, ETH.
Jud. 6:26 build altar in o. place
2 Sam. 23:5 covenant o. and sure
Job 13:18 I have o. my cause, I
Ps. 37:23 steps of good man are o.
50:23 who o. conversation arig.

ORDERINGS.
1 Chr. 24:19 these were their o.

ORDERLY.
Acts 21:21 walkest o. keepest law

ORDINANCE.
Ex. 12:14 feast of passover for an
o. forever, 24, 43; 13:10
15:25 made a statute and an o.
Num. 9:14 according to o. of passover, 2 Chr. 35:13
10:8 to be to you for an o. for e.
18:8 and to thy sons by au o.
for ever, 2 Chr. 2:4
19:2 o. of L. commanded, 31:21
Jos. 24:25 set them o. in Shech.
1 Sam. 30:25 made it o. for ever
2 Chr. 35:25 made them o. in Is.
Ezr. 8:10 after the o. of David
Is. 24:5 the law changed the o.
58:2 forsook not o. of their God
Ezek. 46:14 offering by perpet. o.
Mal. 3:14 what prof. we kept o. ?
Rom. 13:2 power resists o. of G.
1 Pet. 2:13 submit to every o. of

ORDINANCES.
Ex. 18:20 shalt teach them o.
Lev. 18:3 neither walk in their o.
4 ye sh. keep mine o. 30; 22:9;
2 Chr. 33:8; Ezek. 11:20;
43:11; 1 Cor. 11:2
Num. 9:12 to o. of passover, 14
2 K. 17:37 o. he wrote for you
Neh. 10:32 made o. made for us
Job 38:33 knowest thou the o. of
heaven? Jer. 31:35; 33:25
Ps. 99:7 kept o. he gave them
119:91 continue according to o.
Is. 58:2 ask of me o. of justice
Jer. 31:36 if o. depart before me
Ezek. 43:18 these are o. of altar
44:5 o. of the house of the Lord
Mal. 3:7 gone away fr. mine o.
Luke 1:6 commandments and o.
of Lord
Eph. 2:15 commandment contained in o.
Col. 2:14 out handwriting of o.
20 are ye subject to o./
Heb. 9:1 had o. of divine service
10 carnal o. imposed on them

ORDINARY.
Ezek. 16:27 diminished o. food

ORED.
Jud. 7:25 of Mid. Zeeb, O. 8:3
Ps. 83:11 their nobles like O.
Is. 10:26 of Midian at rock of O.

OUG

ORGAN, S.
Gen. 4:21 of such as handle o.
Job 21:12 rejoice at sound of o.
30:31 my o. turned into voice
Ps. 150:4 praised him with o.

ORION.
Job 9:9 maketh O. Amos 5:8
38:31 loose the bands of O.?

ORNAMENT.
Prov. 1:9 o. of grace to thy head
4:9 give to head an o. of grace
25:12 as an o. of fine gold, so is
Is. 30:22 defile o. of molten ima.
49:18 clothe thee as with an o.
Ezek. 7:20 the beauty of his o.
1 Pet. 3:4 o. of meek, quiet spirit

ORNAMENTS.
Ex. 33:4 no man put on him o.
5 put off thy o. from thee, 6
Jud. 8:21 o. on camels' neck
2 Sam. 1:24 S. who put o. on you
Is. 3:18 tinkling o. about feet
61:10 decketh himself with o.
Jer. 2:32 can a maid forget her o.
4:30 deckest thee wi. o. of gold
Ezek. 16:7 come to excellent o.
11 decked thee with o. put
23:40 deckedst thyself with o.
1 Chr. 21:15 floor of O. 18, 28
20 O. turned back, saw angel
25 Da. gave to O. 600 shekels

ORPAH.
Ruth 1:4 name of one O. other R.
14 O. kissed Naomi, but Ruth

ORPHANS.
Lam. 5:3 are o. our mothers wid.

OSPREY, OSSIFRAGE.
Lev. 11:13 o. and o. Deut. 14:12

OSTRICH, ES.
Job 39:13 wings and feath. to o.?
Lam. 4:3 like o. in the wildern.

OTHER.
Gen. 28:17 none o. but ho. of G.
Jud. 13:10 came to me o. day
16:17 and be like any o. man
30 go out, as at o. times before
2 Sam. 3:10 b. called as are o. th.
24:3 S. sat on seat as at o. tim.
1 Chr. 6:10 there is no o. save th. here
28:5 K. of Is. restored whole o. to
Mark 3:5; Luke 6:10
Mark 7:4 many o. thin. th. be, 8
12:32 and there is none o. but he
Luke 14:32 o. is yet a gr. way off
18:11 that I am not as o. men
John 15:24 works no o. man did
21:25 there are many o. things
Acts 4:12 nei. is salva. in any o.
8:34 himself, or of some o. man?
See GOD, GODS, ONE, SIDE.

OTHERS.
Mat. 5:47 wh. do ye more the o.?
Mark 15:31 saved o. Luke 23:35
Phil. 2:4 also on the things of o.
1 Thes. 2:6 not yet of o. sought
Ezek. 30:18 they eat passover o.
Ps. 38:16 o. should rej. over me
Rom. 11:6 o. grace be no. grace;
o. work is no more work
Gal. 5:10 will be none o. minded
Phil. 3:15 any thing you be o.
1 Tim. 5:3 if any mau teach o.
Jos. 15:17 O. took it, Jud. 1:13
Jud. 3:9 raised deliverer, O. 11

OTHNIEL.
Ex. 28:11 o. of gold, 30:6, 13
13 thou shalt make o. of gold
14 fasten chains to the o. 39:18
25 thou shalt fasten in two o.

OUGHT, or rather AUGHT,
Gen. 39:6 he knew not o. he had
47:18 there is not o. left
Mat. 12:46 not car. forth o. flesh
Lev. 11:25 whoso beareth o. car.
19:6 if o. remain unto third day
25:14 sellest o. or buyest o.
Num. 15:24 if o. be committed
30:6 or uttered o. out of her lips
Deut. 4:2 not add or diminish o.
30:14 nei. have I taken o. in my mourn. nor given o. for dout
Jos. 21:45 there failed not o.
Ruth 1:17 if o. but death part
1 Sam. 12:4 nor hast th. taken o.
5 have not found o. in my ha.
25:7 neither was th. o. missing
30:22 he will not give them o.
2 Sam. 3:35 if I taste bread or o.
14:10 whoso saith o. to thee

OVE

2 Sam. 14:19 can turn fr. o. my lo.
Mat. 5:23 brother hath o. ag. th.
21:3 if any man say o. to you
Mark 7:12 suf. him no more do o.
8:23 and asked him if he saw o.
11:25 forgive, if ye have o. ag.
Acts 4:33 brought him o. to eat?
Acts 4:32 bef. said o. was his own
24:19 if they had o. against me
28:19 had o. to ac. my nation of
Phile. 18 if he oweth thee o.

OUGHT.
Gen. 20:9 o. not be done, 34:7;
Lev. 4:2, 27
2 Sam. 13:12 no such th. o. to be
1 Chr. 12:32 kn. what Is. o. to do
Mat. 23:23 o. ha. done, Lu. 11:42
Acts 24:19 who o. to have been
Rom. 8:26 to pray for as we o.
1 Tim. 5:13 speak. th. they o. not
Tit. 1:11 teach. thi. they o. not
Jam. 3:10 these thi. o. not to be
4:15 that ye o. to say, If the L.
2 Pet. 3:11 what pers. o. ye to be
3 John 8 we therefore o. to rec.

OURS.
Gen. 31:16 hath taken that is o.
34:23 shall not ev. beast be o.?
Mark 12:7 the inheritance shall
be o. Luke 20:14
1 Cor. 1:2 Jesus, both th. and o.
2 Cor. 1:14 ye are o. day of L.

OURSELF, S.
Ps. 147:2 gathereth o. of Israel
Is. 11:12 shall assemble o. 56:8
16:3 hide o. 4 let my o. dwell
27:13 o. in land of Eg. worship
Jer. 30:17 bec. they called thee o.
49:36 o. of Elam shall not come

OUTER.
Ezek. 46:21 brong. me to o. court
Mat. 8:12 o. darkn. 22:13; 25:30

OUTGOINGS.
Jos. 17:9 o. of it at sea, 19:29
18:19 o. of the border at north
19:14 o. thereof are in the valley
22 o. of border at the Jord. 33
Ps. 65:8 makest o. of morning

OUTLANDISH.
Neh. 13:26 o. women caused Sol.

OUTLIVED.
Jud. 2:7 elders that o. Joshua

OUTRAGEOUS.
Prov. 27:4 wrath is cruel, ang. o.

OUTRUN.
John 20:4 other disciple o. Peter

OUTSIDE.
Jud. 7:11 Gideon went to the o.
1 K. 7:9 o. towards great court
Ezek. 40:5 beho. a wall on the o.
Mat. 23:25 o. and platte. Lu. 11:39
26 that o. of them be clean also

OUTSTRETCHED.
Deut. 26:8 us out with an o. arm
Jer. 21:5 fight you with o. arm
27:5 made earth by my o. arm

OUTWARD.
1 Sam. 16:7 looketh on o. appear.
1 Chr. 26:29 for the o. business
Neh. 11:16 Levites for o. business
Est. 6:4 Ham. come to o. court
Mat. 23:27 appear beautiful o.
Rom. 2:28 which is o. in flesh
2 Cor. 4:16 tho' our o. man perish
10:7 things after o. appearance?
1 Pet. 3:3 not that o. adorning

OUTWARDLY.
Mat. 23:28 o. appear righteous
Rom. 2:28 not a Jew wh. is one o.

OVEN.
Lev. 2:4 offering baken in o. 7:9
11:35 whether it be o. or ranges
26:26 bake your bread in one o.
Lam. 5:10 skin was black like o.
Hos. 7:4 as an o. heated by baker
6 made ready heart like an o. ?
Mal. 4:1 that shall burn as an o.
Mat. 6:30 cast into o. Luke 12:28

OVENS.
Ex. 8:3 frogs come into thine o.

OVE

OVER.
Num. 27:16 set man o. congrega.
Cant. 2:11 winter past, rain is o.

OVER against.
Num. 8:2 lamp g. light o. a. 3
2 Sam. 5:23 come on them o. ag.
mulberry-trees, 1 Chr. 14:14
1 K. 20:29 pitched one o. a. other
Neh. 7:3 ev. one to he o. a. house
Ez. 7:14 God set one o. a. o:her
Jer. 31:39 line go forth o. ag. it
See ALL, HIM, JORDAN, ISRAEL,
ME, THEE, THEM, US, YOU.

OVERCAME.
Acts 10:16 evil spi. was, o. them
Rev. 3:21 even as I also o.
12:11 o. him by blood of Lamb

OVERCHARGE, D.
Luke 21:34 lest your hearts be o.
2 Cor. 2:5 that I may not o. you

OVERCOME.
Gen. 49:19 troop shall o. him
Num. 13:30 are well able to o. it
22:11 peradventure I sh. o. them
2 K. 16:5 Ahaz, could not o. him
Cant. 6:5 eyes, they have o. me
Is. 28:1 head of them that are o.
Jer. 23:9 man whom wine hath o.
23:11 stronger shall o. him
John 16:33 I have o. the world
Rom. 3:4 o. wh. thou art jud'ed
12:21 be not o. of evil, o. evil
2 Pet. 2:19 of whom man is o.
20 ag. entangled therein and o.
1 John 2:13 o. wicked one, 14
4:4 are of God, have o. them
Rev. 11:7 beast wh. o. witnesses
13:7 war with saints, o. them
17:14 and Lamb shall o. them

OVERCOMETH.
1 John 5:4 born of God o. world.
victory o. world, 5
Rev. 2:7 o. will I give tree of life
11 he that o. shall not be hu't
17 him that o. will I gi. to eat
26 him that o. will I grant to sit
3:5 he that o. shall be clothed
12 him that o. will I make pil.
21 that o. will I grant to sit
21:7 that o. shall inh, all things

OVERDRIVE.
Gen. 33:13 if men she. o. them

OVERFLOW.
Deut. 11:4 water of Red sea o.
Ps. 69:2 come where floods o.
15 let not waterfloods o. me
Is. 8:8 thro' Jud. o. and go over
10:22 consumpti. decreed sh. o.
28:17 waters o. the hiding-place
43:2 rivers they sh. not o. thee
Jer. 47:2 waters of north o. land
Dan. 11:10 certai. come, o. 26, 40
Joel 2:24 fats o. with wine, 3:13

OVERFLOWED, ETH.
Jos. 3:15 in harvest Jor. o. hanks
Ps. 78:20 smote rock, streams o.
2 Pet. 3:6 world o. with water

OVERFLOWING.
Job 28:11 bindeth floods from o.
38:25 watercourse for o. of wat.
Is. 28:2 flood of mighty wat. o.
15 when o. scourge pass, 18
30:28 his breath as o. stream
Jer. 47:2 north sh. be an o. flood
Ezek. 13:11 be an o. shower, 13
38:22 min o. rain and hailstones
Hab. 3:10 the o. of the water

OVERFLOWN.
1 Chr. 12:15 Jor. when it had o.
Job 22:16 wh. foundation was o.
Dan. 11:22 with flood they be o.

OVERLAY.
Ex. 25:11 o. ark, 24; 3 :3
37:2 o. altar with brass, 38:2

OVERLAID.
Ex. 26:32 pillars o. with gold
36:6 o. staves of shittim-wood
1 K. 3:19 died, because she o. it
2 Chr. 4:9 he o. doors with brass
Cant. 5:14 belly as bri. ivory o.
See GOLD.

OVERLAYING.
Ex. 38:17 the o. of chapiters, 19

OVERLIVED.
Jos. 24:31 days of elders the o. J.

OVERMUCH.
Ec. 7:16 righte. o. 17 be not o.
2 Cor. 2:7 swallow. with o. sor.

OVERPASS.
Jer. 5:28 they o. deeds of wicked

OVE

OVERPAST.
Ps. 57:1 refuge until calam. be *o.*
Is. 26:20 hide until judgm. be *o.*

OVERPLUS.
Lev. 25:27 let him restore the *o.*

OVERRAN, RUNNING.
2 *Sam.* 18:23 Ahimaaz *o.* Cushi
Nah. 1:8 an *o.* flood will he make

OVERSEE.
1 *Chr.* 9:29 appointed to *o.* vess.
2 *Chr.* 2:2 3,600 to *o.* them

OVERSEER.
Gen. 39:4 made *o.* over house, 5
39:5; 41:3 Joel th. *o.* 14 Zabd. *o.*
2:2 *o.* of Levites; 12:42 Jez. *o.*
Prov. 6:7 the ant having no *o.*

OVERSEERS.
Gen. 41:34 let Pharaoh appoint *o.*
2 *Chr.* 2:18 Solomon set 3,600 *o.*
31:13 *o.* under hand of Cononiah
34:12 *o.* of all that wrought, 13
17 deliv. mon. into hand of *o.*
Acts 20:28 H. Ghost made you *o.*

OVERSHADOW, ED.
Mat. 17:5 bright cloud *o.* them,
Mark 9:7; *Luke* 9:34
Luke 1:35 power of High. *o.* thee
Acts 5:15 shadow of P. *o.* them

OVERSIGHT.
Gen. 43:12 peradv. it was an *o.*
Num. 3:32 *o.* of them that keep
4:16 the *o.* of all the tabernacle
2 *K.* 12:11 that had *o.* of house of
L. 2:5, 9; 2 *Chr.* 34:10
1 *Chr.* 9:23 had thee *o.* of the gates
Neh. 11:16 had the *o.* of business
13:4 the *o.* of the house of God
1 *Pet.* 5:2 taking *o.* not by const,

OVERSPREAD, ED.
Gen. 9:19 of th. the earth was *o.*
Dan. 9:27 the *o.* of abominations

OVERTAKE.
Gen. 44:4 when thou dost *o.* th.
Ex. 15:9 I will pursue, I will *o.*
Deut. 19:6 her avenger *o.* slayer
28:2 blessings come and *o.* thee
15 these curses shall *o.* thee, 45
2 *K.* 25 for ye shall *o.* them
1 *Sam.* 30:8 thou sh. surely *o.* th.
2 *Sam.* 15:14 lest Absalom *o.* us
Is. 59:9 nei. doth justice *o.* us
Jer. 42:16 sw. ye feared sh. *o.* you
Hos. 2:7 shall not *o.* her lovers
10:9 the battle did not *o.* them
Amos 9:10 evil shall not *o.* us
13 ploughman sh. *o.* the reaper
1 *Thes.* 5:4 should *o.* you as thief

OVERTAKEN, ETH.
1 *Chr.* 21:12 flee till sword *o.* th.
Ps. 18:37 pursu. enemies *o.* them
Gal. 6:1 if a man be *o.* in a fault

OVERTHREW.
Gen. 19:25 God *o.* those cities, 29
Ex. 14:27 L. *o.* Eg. *Ps.* 136:15
Deut. 29:23 which L. *o.* in anger
Is. 13:19 when G. *o.* Sodom and
Gomo. *Jer.* 50:40; *Amos* 4:11
Jer. 20:16 be as cities the Lord *o.*
Mat. 21:12 J. *o.* tables of money-
chang. *Mark* 11:15; *John* 2:15

OVERTHROW, Substantive.
Gen. 19:29 O. sent Lot out of *o.*
Deut. 29:23 *o.* of Sod. *Jer.* 49:18
2 *Pet.* 2:6 condemn. cities with *o.*

OVERTHROW, Verb.
Gen. 19:21 I will not *o.* this city
Ex. 23:24 thou sh. *o.* their gods
Deut. 12:3 ye shall *o.* their altars
2 *Sam.* 10:3 D. sent to spy and *o.*
11:25 make battle strong, *o.* it
1 *Chr.* 19:3 David sent *to o.* land
Ps. 106:26 to *o.* them in wildern.
27 to *o.* their seed am. nations
140:4 have pur. to *o.* my goings
11 evil hunt vio. man to *o.* him
Prov. 18:5 not good to *o.* righte.
Hag. 2:22 I will *o.* the throne of
kingd. I will *o.* the chariots
Acts 5:39 if it be of G. ye can. *o.*
2 *Tim.* 2:18 *o.* the faith of some

OVERTHROWETH.
Job 12:19 lead. princes, *o.* mighty
Prov. 13:6 wickedness *o.* sinner
21:12 G. *o.* wicked for wickedn.
22:12 *o.* words of transgressor
29:4 he that receiv. gifts *o.* land

OVERTHROWN.
Ex. 15:7 hast *o.* them that rose
Jud. 9:40 and many were *o.*
2 *Sam.* 17:9 some of them be *o.*
2 *Chr.* 14:13 Ethiopians were *o.*
Job 19:6 know th. G. hath *o.* me

OX

Ps. 141:6 their judges are *o.*
Prov. 11:11 city is *o.* by wicked
12:7 wicked *o.* 14:11 ho. of wic.
Is. 1:7 your land is desolate as *o.*
Jer. 18:23 let them be *o.* bef. th.
Lam. 4:6 S. was *o.* as in moment
Dan. 11:41 many countries be *o.*
Amos 4:11 I have *o.* some of you
Jon. 3:4 40 days Ninev. sh. be *o.*
1 *Cor.* 10:5 were *o.* in wilderness

OVERTOOK.
Gen. 31:23 *o.* Jacob in mount
25 Lab. *o.* Jacob; 44:6 steward
Jud. 18:22 Micah *o.* chil. of Dan
20:42 battle *o.* men of Benjamin
2 *K.* 25:5 army of Chaldeans *o.*
Zedekiah, *Jer.* 39:5; 52:8
Lam. 1:3 her persecutors *o.* her

OVERTURN.
Job 12:15 waters, they *o.* earth
Ezek. 21:27 I will *o.* *o.* *o.* it

OVERTURNED, ETH.
Jud. 7:13 the tent fell and *o.* it
Job 9:5 which *o.* the mountains
28:9 *o.* mountains by the roots
34:25 know th. works and *o.* th.

OVERWHELM, ED.
Job 6:27 you, *o.* fatherless
Ps. 55:5 and horror hath *o.* me
61:2 when my heart is *o.*
77:3 my spirit *o.* 142:3; 143:4
78:53 the sea *o.* their enemies
124:4 then the waters had *o.* us

OVERWISE.
Ec. 7:16 nor make thyself *o.*

OWE

Rom. 13:8 *o.* no man any thing

OWED.
Mat. 18:24 one *o.* him 10,000 tal.
28 one which *o.* him a 100 pen.
Luke 7:41 the one *o.* 500 pence

OWEST, ETH.
Mat. 18:28 pay me that thou *o.*
Luke 16:5 how much *o.* thou? 7
Phile. 18 thee, or *o.* thee aught
19 *o.* to me even thine own

OWL.
Lev. 11:16 *o.* and cuckoo, *Deut.*
14:15, 16; *Is.* 34:11, 15
17 the little *o.* and cormorant
Ps. 102:6 I am like *o.* of desert

OWLS.
Job 30:29 I am companion to *o.*
Is. 13:21 *o.* shall dwell there,
34:13; *Jer.* 50:39
43:20 dragons and *o.* honor me
Mic. 1:8 make a mourning as *o.*

OWN.

1 *Chr.* 29:14 *o.* have we giv. thee
16 we prepared, is all thine *o.*
Mat. 20:15 do wi. I will wi. *o.*?
Luke 16:12 you that which is *o.*?
John 1:11 came to his *o.* *o.* rece.
13:1 loved his *o.* that were
15:19 would would love his *o.*
Acts 5:4 was it not in th. *o.* pow.?
1 *Cor.* 6:19 ye are not your *o.*
10:24 let no man seek his *o.*
20 cons. not th. *o.* but of oth.
13:5 charity seeketh not her *o.*
Phil. 2:21 seek their *o.* things
1 *Tim.* 5:8 provide not for his *o.*

See COUNSEL, COUNTRY, EYES,
HEART, HOUSE, LAND,
PEOPLE, SELF, SELVES, SOUL,
WAY, WAYS, WILL.

OWNER.
Ex. 21:28 *o.* of ox shall be quit
34 *o.* of pit sh. make it good
36 his *o.* hath not kept him in
22:11 *o.* of it th. accept thereof
12 make restitution to *o.*
15 but if *o.* thereof be with it
1 *K.* 16:24 Shemer, *o.* of the hill
Is. 1:3 the ox knoweth his *o.*
Acts 27:11 believed *o.* of the ship

OWNERS.
Job 31:39 caused *o.* to lose lives
Prov. 1:19 taketh away life of *o.*
Ec. 5:11 what good is there to *o.*
13 riches kept for *o.* to th. hurt
Luke 19:33 *o.* said, Why loose ye

OWNETH.
Lev. 14:35 he that *o.* the house
Acts 21:11 bind man *o.* th. girdle

OX

Ex. 20:17 not covet, *o. Deut.* 5:21
21:28 if *o.* gore, he stoned, 29 30
32:1 if man steal *o.* or sheep
4 whether it be *o.* or ass, he
22:4 if thou meet th. enemy's *o.*
12 thine *o.* and thine ass rest

PAD

Ezr. 34:19 firstl. of *o.* or sheep mi.
Lev. 7:23 eat no fat *o.* or sh.
Num. 7:3 for each of princes *o.*
22:4 as the *o.* licketh up grass
Deut. 5:14 *o.* do no work on sab.
14:4 *o.* sheep, and goat may eat
22:1 not see bro.'s *o.* go astray
10 not plough with *o.* and ass
25:4 not muzzle *o.* treadeth out
corn, 1 *Cor.* 9:9; 1 *Tim.* 5:18
Jos. 6:21 they destroy *o.* and
sheep, 1 *Sam.* 15:15
Jud. 3:31 slew 600 with *o.*-goad
6:4 left neither sheep nor *o.*
1 *Sam.* 12:3 wh. *o.* have I taken?
14:34 bring ev. man *o.* and sheep
Neh. 5:18 for me daily one *o.*
Job 6:5 loweth *o.* over fodder?
24:3 take widow's *o.* for pledge
40:15 Behemoth eat. grass as *o.*
Ps. 69:31 please L. better than *o.*
106:20 glory into similitu. of *o.*
Prov. 7:22 *o.* goeth to slaughter
14:4 incre. by strength of the *o.*
15:17 better than a stalled *o.*
Is. 1:3 the *o.* knoweth his owner
11:7 lion shall eat straw like *o.*
32:20 send for. the feet of the *o.*
65:2 killeth *o.* as if he slew man
25 lion and *o.* shall eat straw
Ezek. 1:10 four had face of an *o.*
Luke 13:15 each loose *o.* on sab.
14:5 an *o.* or ass fallen into a pit

Wild OX.
Deut. 14:5 wild *o.* ye may eat

OXEN.
Gen. 12:16 Ab. had *o.* and asses
32:5 J. said, I have *o.* and asses
34:28 sons of J. took Shech. *o.*
Abr. 9:3 hand of Lord is upon *o.*
22:1 restore five *o.* for one ox
Num. 7:3 princes bro. twelve *o.*
22:40 Balak offered *o.* and sheep
28:1 prepare me here seven *o.*
Deut. 14:26 bestow money for *o.*
Jud. 3:31 slew *o.* with ox-goad
1 *Sam.* 11:7 hewed yoke of *o.*
14:14 yoke of *o.* might plough
32 took sheep and *o.* and slew
15:9 Agag and the best of the *o.*
14 what meaneth lowing of *o.*?
22 greater best of sheep and *o.*
27:9 David took away the *o.*
2 *Sam.* 6:6 hold of it, *o.* shook it
13 Da. sacrificed *o.* and fatlings
24:22 bought thres.-floor and *o.*
Is. 17 Adonijah slew *o. 19, 25*
4:23 daily provision, ten fat *o.*
7:25 one sea, twelve *o.* under it,
44; 2 *Chr.* 4:4, 15
8:63 S. off. sacrifice to L. 22,000
o. 120,000 sheep. 2 *Chr.* 7:5
19:20 E. was ploughing with *o.*
20 Elisha left *o.* ran after Elij.
21 took yoke of *o.* slew them
2 *K.* 5:26 is it a time to rec. *o.* ?
2 *Chr.* 15:11 offered of spoil 700 *o.*
18:2 Ahab killed sheep and *o.*
29:33 consecrated things 600 *o.*
31:6 they brought in tithes of *o.*
35:8 for passo. three hundred *o.*
Job 1:3 his substance was 500 *o.*
14 *o.* ploughing, asses feeding
42:12 gave him 1,000 yoke of *o.*
Ps. 8:7 to have dominion over *o.*
144:14 that our *o.* may be strong
Prov. 14:4 wh. no *o.* crib is clean
Is. 7:25 for treading forth of *o.*
22:13 joy and gladn. slaying *o.*
30:24 *o.* and asses ea. cl. prov.
Jer. 51:23 I break in sun. and *o.*
Dan. 4:25 eat gr. as *o.* 32; 5:21
Amos 6:12 plough there with *o.*
Mat. 22:4 *o.* and fatlings killed
Luke 14:19 bought 5 yoke of *o.*
John 2:14 those in temple sold *o.*
15 had of cords drove *o.* out of
1 *Cor.* 9:9 doth G. ta. care for *o.*?

OZIAS. *Mat.* 1:8, 9

P.

PAARAI. 2 *Sam.* 23:35

PACES.
2 *Sam.* 6:13 when gone six *p.* he

PACIFY, ED, ETH.
Est. 7:10 then king's wrath *p.*
Prov. 16:14 a gift in secret *p.* anger
Ec. 10:4 yielding *p.* gr. offences
Ezek. 16:63 when I am *p.* toward

PADAN-ARAM.
Gen. 25:20 dau. of Bethuel of P.
28:6 Isa. sent Jacob away to P.
7 his father, and was gone to P.
31:18 and gotten in P.

PAL

Gen. 35:9 J. when he came fr. P.
26 sons born to him in P. 46:15

PADDLE.
Deut. 23:13 have *p.* on weapon

PAGIEL.
Num. 1:13 P. son of Ocran, 7:72
PAID. *See after* PAY.

PAIN.
Job 14:22 flesh on him sh. have *p.*
15:20 wicked travaileth with *p.*
33:19 is chastened also with *p.*
Ps. 25:18 mine affliction and *p.*
48:6 *p.* as a woman in travail,
Is. 13:8; 26:17
Is. 21:3 my loins filled with *p.*
26:18 child, we have been in *p.*
66:7 bef. her *p.* came, she was
Jer. 6:24 *p.* as wo. in trav. 22:23
12:13 put themselves to *p.* but
15:18 why is my *p.* perpetual
30:23 with *p.* on head of wicked
51:8 Babylon, take balm for *p.*
Ezek. 30:4 great *p.* in Ethiopia, 9
16 Sin shall have great *p.*
Mic. 4:10 *p.* and labor to bring
Nah. 2:10 much *p.* is in all loins
Rom. 8:22 creation travail. in *p.*
Rev. 16:10 gnawed tongues for *p.*
21:4 nor shall th. be any more *p.*

See PANGS.

PAINED.
Ps. 55:4 my heart is sore *p.*
Is. 23:5 they shall be sorely *p.*
Jer. 4:19 I am *p.* at very heart
Joel 2:6 people shall be much *p.*
Rev. 12:2 and *p.* to be delivered

PAINS.
1 *Sam.* 4:19 *p.* came upon her
Ps. 116:3 *p.* of hell gat hold
Acts 2:24 hav. loosed *p.* of death
Rev. 16:11 blasphem. bec. of *p.*

PAINFUL, NESS.
Ps. 73:16 it was too *p.* for me
2 *Cor.* 11:27 and *p.* in watchings

PAINTED, ST.
2 *K.* 9:30 Jezebel *p.* her face
Jer. 22:14 and *p.* with vermilion
Ezek. 23:40 thou *p.* thy eyes

PAINTING.
Jer. 4:30 thou rentest face wi. *p.*

PAIR.
Luke 2:24 offer *p.* of turtle-doves
Rev. 6:5 a *p.* of balances in hand

PALACE.
1 *K.* 16:18 Zimri burnt king's *p.*
21:1 Naboth had viney. by *p.*
2 *K.* 15:25 smote Pekaniah in *p.*
16:18 eunuchs in *p.* of king
1 *Chr.* 29:1 the *p.* is not for man
19 perfect heart to build the *p.*
Ezr. 4:14 maintenance fr. the *p.*
Neh. 1:1 was in Shushan the *p.*
7:2 ruler of *p.* charge over Jer.
Est. 3:15 in Shushan the *p.* 8:14
9:12 destroyed 500 men in the *p.*
Ps. 45:15 enter into king's *p.*
144:12 after similitude of a *p.*
Cant. 8:9 build a *p.* of silver
Is. 25:2 made a *p.* of strangers
Dan. 4:4 flourishing in my *p.*
6:18 king went to *p.* pa. night
11:45 he shall plant *p.* between
seas
Amos 4:3 shall cast them into *p.*
Nah. 2:6 opened, *p.* dissolved
Mat. 26:58 Pe. followed Jesus to
high-priest's *p. Mark* 14:54
Luke 11:21 a strong man keep. *p.*
Phil. 1:13 bonds manifest in *p.*

PALACES.
2 *Chr.* 36:19 burnt all the *p.*
Ps. 45:8 myrrh, out of ivory *p.*
48:3 G. is known in *p.* for refu.
13 mark bulwarks, consider *p.*
78:69 sanctuary like high *p.*
122:7 prosperity within thy *p.*
Prov. 30:28 spider is in king's *p.*
Is. 13:22 dragons sh. cry in thy *p.*
32:14 the *p.* shall be forsaken
34:13 thorns come up in her *p.*
Jer. 6:5 let us destroy her *p.*
9:21 death is entered into our *p.*
17:27 fire shall devour *p.* of J.
49:27 consume *p.* of Benhadad
Lam. 2:5 hath swallowed his *p.*
7 hath given *p.* into hand of e.
Amos 3:9 publish in *p.* of Ash.
lod. in *p.* of Egypt
10 store up robbery in their *p.*
11 he shall spoil thy *p.*
Mic. 5:5 he tread tread in our *p.*

See DEVOUR.

PAR

PALE, NESS.
Is. 29:22 ncl. shall face wax p.
Jer. 30:6 all faces turned into p.
Rev. 6:8 looked, behold p. horse

PALESTINA.
Ex. 15:14 hold on men of P.
Is. 14:29 rej. not, thou, whole P.
31 cry, O city, thou, whole P.

PALM.
Lev. 14:15 pour into p. 26
John 18:22 struck Jesus with p.
   PALM branches.
Neh. 8:15 to mount and fet. p. b.
   PALMER-WORM.
Joel 1:4 what p.-w. left, loc. eat.
2:25 restore years p.-w. eaten
Amos 4:9 fig-trees, the p.-w. dev.
   PALMS.
1 Sam. 5:4 p. of hands cut off
2 K. 9:35 they found skull and p.
Is. 49:16 grav. thee on p. of hand.
Dan. 10:10 set me on p. of hands
Mat. 26:67 others smote him wi.
p. of their hands, Mark 14:65
Rev. 7:9 white robes, p. in han.
   PALM-TREE.
Jud. 4:5 dwelt under p.-t. of D.
Ps. 92:12 right. flour like p.-t.
Cant. 7:7 stature is like to a p.-t.
8 I will go up to the p.-t.
Jer. 10:5 are upright as the p.-t.
Ezek. 41:19 face of man tow. p.-t.
Joel 1:12 p.-t. and apple-tree
   PALM-TREES.
Ex. 15:27 El. wh. were 70 p.-t.
Lev. 23:40 take branches of p.-t.
Deut. 34:3 show. him city of p.-t.
Jud. 1:16 out of city of p.-t.
3:13 M. possessed city of p.-t.
1 K. 6:29 wi. figures of p.-t. 32,35;
7:36; 2 Chr. 3:5; Ezek. 40:16
2 Chr. 28:15 bro. th. to to. of p.-t.
John 12:13 took branches of p.-t.
   PALSY, IES.
Mat. 4:24 had p. he healed them,
Mark 2:3; Luke 5:18
8:6 ser. lieth at home sick of p.
9:2 Je. said to sick of p. S. thy
sins be forgiven, Mark 2:5
Mark 2:10 sick of p. Luke 5:24
Acts 8:7 many taken with p. and
9:33 Eneas, who was sick of p.
   PAMPHYLIA.
Acts 13:13 P. came to Perga in P.
15:38 departed from them fr. P.
27:5 had sailed over sea of P.
   PAN.
Lev. 2:5 meat-offer. baken in p.
6:21 in a p. it shall be made
7:9 dressed in p. it shall be pries.
1 Sam. 2:14 serv. stuck it into p.
2 Sam. 13:9 Tam. took p. poured
Ezek. 4:3 take unto thee iron p.
   PANS.
Ex. 27:3 make p. to rec. ashes
Num. 11:8 baked manna in p.
1 Chr. 9:31 thi. made in p. 23:29
2 Chr. 35:13 offer. sod they in p.
   PANGS.
Is. 13:8 p. sh. take hold of them
21:3 p. take hold me as p. of w.
26:17 wom. crieth out in her p.
Jer. 22:23 gracious when p. come
48:41 heart of wom. in p. 49:22
50:43 p. as of a wom. Mic. 4:9
   PANNAG.
Ezek. 27:17 traded in market, P.
   PANT, ED, ETH.
Ps. 38:10 my heart p. stren. fail.
42:1 as hart p. so p. my soul
119:131 open. my mouth and p.
Is. 21:4 at the vision my heart p.
Amos 2:7 that p. after the dust
   PAPER.
Is. 19:7 reeds shall wither
2 John 12 would not write wi. p.
   PAPHOS. Acts 13:6
   PAPS.
Ezek. 23:21 for the p. of thy you.
Luke 11:27 bles. are p. th. suck,
23:29 blessed p. never gave suck
Rev. 1:13 girt p. with gold, gird.
   PARABLE.
Num. 23:7 Balaam took up p. and
said, 24:3, 15, 20, 21, 23
Job 27:1 J. continued his p. 29:1
Ps. 49:4 I will incline ear to a p.
78:2 mouth, in a p. will I utter
Prov. 26:7 p. in mouth of fools, 9
Ezek. 17:2 speak a p. to Israel.
24:3 utter p. to rebellious house
Mic. 2:4 take up a p. against you
Hab. 2:6 these take up p. ag. you

PAR

Mat. 13:18 hear p. of the sower
24 ano. p. put ho. 31, 33; 21:33
34 with. p. sp. not, Mark 4:34
34:32 learn a p. of the fig-tree,
   Mark 13:28; Luke 21:29
Mark 4:10 asked him of p. 7:17;
   Luke 8:9
12:12 spoken p. ag. th. Lu. 20:19
Luke 5:36 he spake a p. to them,
   6:39; 8:4; 12:16; 13:6; 14:7;
   15:3; 18:1, 9; 19:11; 20:9;
   21:29; John 10:6
12:41 L. spak. thou this p. to us?
   PARABLES.
Ezek. 20:49 doth he not speak p. ?
Mat. 13:3 spake many things to
them in p. 13:34; 22:1; Mark
3:23; 4:2, 13, 33; 12:1
Mark 4:13 how will ye kn. all p. ?
Luke 8:10 p. seeing might not see
   PARADISE.
Luke 23:43 to-day with me in p.
2 Cor. 12:4 was caught up into p.
Rev. 2:7 in the midst of p. of G.
   PARAMOURS.
Ezek. 23:20 doted upon their p.
   PARAN.
Gen. 21:21 wil. of P. Num. 10:12;
   12:16; 13:3, 26; 1 Sam. 25:1
Deut. 33:2 forth from mount P.
Hab. 3:3 Holy One came from P.
   PARBAR. 1 Chr. 26:18
   PARCEL.
Gen. 33:19 J. bought p. of a field,
   Jos. 24:32; John 4:5
Ruth 4:3 Na. selleth a p. of land
1 Chr. 11:13 p. of gr. full of bar. 14
   PARCHED.
Is. 35:7 p. ground become pool
Jer. 17:6 shall inhabit p. places
   See corn.
   PARCHMENTS.
2 Tim. 4:13 bri. especially the p.
   PARDON.
Ex. 23:21 not p. your trangres.
34:9 p. our iniq. Num. 14:19
1 Sam. 15:25 p. my sins
2 K. 5:18 Lord, p. thy servant
24:4 which Lord would not p.
2 Chr. 30:18 good L. p. ev. one
Neh. 9:17 G. ready to p. gracious
Job 7:21 why not p. my transg. ?
Is. 55:7 he will abundantly p.
Jer. 5:1 I will p. it; 7 shall I p.
33:8 I will p. all their iniquities
50:20 I will p. whom I reserve
   PARDONED, ETH.
Num. 14:20 I have p. ac. to word
Is. 40:2 tell her that iniq. is p.
Lam. 3:42 thou hast not p.
Mic. 7:18 G. like thee, p. iniq. ?
   PARE.
Deut. 21:12 shave head, p. nails
   PARENTS.
Mat. 10:21 children shall rise up
against their p. Mark 13:12
Luke 2:27 p. brought in child Je.
8:56 her p. were astonished, but
18:29 is no man that hath left p.
21:16 ye shall be betrayed by p.
John 9:2 who did sin, man or p. ?
22 these words spake p. 23
Rom. 1:30 diso. to p. 2 Tim. 3:2
2 Cor. 12:14 chi. not lay up for p.
Eph. 6:1 chil. obey p. Col. 3:20
1 Tim. 5:4 learn to requite th. p.
Heb. 11:23 Mo. was hid of his p.
   PARLOR, S.
Jud. 3:20 Eg. was sitting in p.
23 Ehud shut doors of the p.
1 Sam. 9:22 S. bro. them to p.
1 Chr. 28:11 gave S. pattern of p.
   PARMENAS. Acts 6:5
   PART.
Ex. 16:17 at nether p. of mount
Lev. 2:16 p. of beaten corn, p. oil
Num. 18:20 nei. have p. am. th.
Deut. 10:9; 12:12; 14:27, 29;
   18:1; Jos. 14:4; 18:7; 1 am
thy p. and inherit. in Israel
22:41 utmost p. of people, 33:12
Jos. 22:25 ye have no p. in L. 27
Ruth 3:3 to light on p. of field
3:13 perf. p. of kinsman
1 Sam. 23:20 our p. sh. be to del.
30:24 his p. is that goeth to bat.
2 Sam. 20:1 we have no p. in D.
2 K. 18:24 if able on thy p. to set
Neh. 2:20 have no p. in Jerusal.
1 Chr. 12:29 greatest p. kept ho.
2 Chr. 29:16 prie. we. to inner p.

PAR

Neh. 1:9 cast out to uttermost p.
5:11 rest, hundredth p. of mon.
Job 32:17 I will answer my p.
Ps. 5:9 inward p. is wickedness
51:6 in hidden p. know wisdom
118:7 L. takes my p. with them
Prov. 8:26 nor highest p. of dust
13:9 rejoic. in habitable p. of ear.
17:2 p. of inherit. amo. breth.
Is. 7:18 hiss for fly in utmost p.
24:16 fr. utmost p. heard songs
44:16 he burneth p. in fire, 19
Ezek. 45:17 prince's p. to give
Dan. 2:33 p. iron, p. clay, 41, 42
5:5 king saw p. of the hand, 24
11:31 arms shall stand on his p.
Amos 7:4 it dev. deep, eat up p.
Mark 4:38 in hinder p. of ship
9:40 not against us, is on our p.
Luke 10:42 M. hath chos. good p.
17:24 lightning lighteneth one
p. shining to other p.
John 13:8 wash th. not, ha. no p.
10:23 four parts, ev. soldier a p.
Acts 1:17 obtained p. of ministry
25 may take p. of this minist.
5:2 Ananias kept p. of price. 3
8:21 thou hast neith p. nor lot
14:4 p. wi. Jews, p. wi. apostles
19:32 p. knew not whereof, came
23:6 the one p. were Sadducees
27:14 more p. advised to depart
1 Cor. 12:24 honor to that p.
13:5 greater p. rem. to this day
10:17 was lacking on your p.
1 Cor. 6:15 p. believ. wi. infidel?
7:14 Thr. 8:8 that he of the contr. p.
Heb. 2:14 himself took p. of same
1 Pet. 4:14 on th. p. he is evil spo.
of, on your p. glorified
Rev. 20:6 th. 2d resurrection
21:8 liars sh. have p. in lake
22:19 G. shall take away his p.
   PART, Verb.
Lev. 2:6 shalt p. meat-offering
Ruth 1:17 if aught but death p.
2 Sam. 14:6 th. was none to p.
Job 41:6 shall they p. him among
   the merchants?
Ps. 22:18 they p. my garments
   In PART.
Rom. 11:25 blindness in p. to Is.
1 Cor. 13:9 know in p. proph. p.
10 that is p. sh. be done away
12 I know in p. but then sh. I
   Third PART.
2 K. 11:5 a t. p. enter on Sabba.
   t. p. of you be port.
Neh. 10:32 charge ours. wi. t. p.
Ezek. 5:2 burn with fire a t. p. of
   t. p. smite about it, a third
p. scatter in the wind, 12
Zec. 13:8 a third p. shall be left
9 I will bring the t. p. thro' fire
Rev. 8:7 t. p. of trees was burnt
t. p. sea became blood
9 t. p. of creat. died. t. p. ships
11 t. p. of wat. bec. wormwood
12 t. p. of sun, moon, and stars
9:15 prep. to slay t. p. of men
12:4 his tail drew t. p. of stars
   Fourth PART.
1 Sam. 9:8 have f. part of shek.
1 K. 6:33 posts of olive-tree f. p.
2 K. 6:25 f. p. cab of doves' dung
Neh. 9:3 read one f. p. ano. f. p.
Rev. 6:8 power given over f. p.
   Fifth PART.
Gen. 41:34 take up f. p. of land
47:24 give f. p. to Pharaoh, 26
Lev. 5:16 add f. p. thereto, 6:5;
   22:14; 27:13,27,31; Num.5:7
   Tenth PART.
Ex. 16:36 homer is the tenth p.
Lev. 5:11 tenth p. of an ephah of
   Num. 5:15 t. p. of ephah of meal
   18:26 ye shall offer even t. p.
Ezek. 45:11 ephah may cont. t. p.
Heb. 7:2 Abra. gave a t. p. of all
Heb. 7:4 this t. p. of city fell
   PARTS.
Gen. 47:24 four p. sh. be yo. own
Num. 24:25 pay thing lack. in p.
Jos. 18:5 divide into seven p. 6, 9
   18:9 divided land into 7 p.
Jud. 9:43 dividing into three p.
2 Sam. 19:43 have ten p. in king
1 K. 16:21 Is. divided into two p.
2 K. 11:7 two p. watch ab. king

PAR

Neh. 11:1 9 p. div. in other cities
Job 26:14 th. are p. of his ways
41:12 I will not conceal his p.
Ps. 2:8 uttermost p. of earth
63:9 go into lower p. of earth
65:8 dwell in utmost p. afraid
139:9 dwell in utmost p. of sea
Prov. 18:8 go to innerm. p. 26:22
Is. 3:17 Lord will disc. secret p.
44:23 shout, ye lower p. of earth
Jer. 34:18 between p. thereof, 19
Ezek. 26:20 in the low p. of earth
31:14 to nether p. of earth, 18
16 comforted in the nether p.
of earth, 32:18, 24
37:11 we are cut off for our p.
38:15 place out of north p. 39:2
Mat. 12:42 she came from utter-
most p. Luke 11:31
John 19:23 garments made 4 p.
Rom. 15:23 no more place in p.
1 Cor. 12:24 comely p. no need
Eph. 4:9 descended into low. p.
Rev. 16:19 city divided into 3 p.
   See BACK, HINDER, INWARD.
   PARTED.
Gen. 2:10 river p. into four heads
2 K. 2:11 chariot p. both asunder
14 waters p. hither and thither
Job 38:24 what way is light p. ?
Joel 3:2 scatter. and p. my land
Mat. 27:35 p. his garments. Mark
   5:24; Luke 23:34; John 19:24
Luke 24:51 blessed them, was p.
Acts 2:45 p. them to all men
   PARTETH.
Lev. 11:3 p. hoof, Deut. 14:6
Prov. 18:18 lot p. betw. mighty
   PARTAKER.
Ps. 50:18 been p. with adulterers
1 Cor. 9:10 who. he p. of his hope
23 I be p. thereof with you
10:30 p. why am I evil spok. of?
1 Tim. 5:22 p. of oth. men's sins
2 Tim. 1:8 be thou p. of afflicti.
2:6 husbandman be p. of fruits
1 Pet. 5:1 I am also p. of the gl.
2 John 11 biddeth G. speed is p.
   PARTAKERS.
Mat. 23:30 not been p. in blood
Rom. 15:27 if Gentiles have been
p. of their spiritual things
1 Cor. 9:13 are p. with the altar
10:17 we are all p. of that bread
18 are not they which eat p.?
21 cannot be p. of Lord's table
2 Cor. 1:7 you are p. of sufferings
Eph. 3:6 p. of his promise in Ch.
5:7 be not ye there. p. wi. them
Phil. 1:7 all are p. of my grace
Col. 1:12 to be p. of inheritance
1 Tim. 6:2 they are p. of benefit
Heb. 2:14 children p. of flesh
and blood
3:1 p. of the heavenly calling
14 we are made p. of Christ
6:4 made p. of the Holy Ghost
12:8 chastise. whereof all are p.
10 that we be p. of his holiness
1 Pet. 4:13 p. of Christ's suffer.
2 Pet. 1:4 p. of the divine nature
Rev. 18:4 that ye be not p. of her
   PARTAKEST.
Rom. 11:17 with them p. of root
   PARTHIANS. Acts 2:9
   PARTIAL, ITY.
Mal. 2:9 but have been p. in law
1 Tim. 5:21 doing nothing by p.
Jam. 2:4 are ye not p. yourself. ?
3:17 without p. and hypocrisy
   PARTICULAR, LY.
Acts 21:19 P. declared p. things
1 Cor. 12:27 of C. members in p.
Eph. 5:33 ev. one in p. love wife
Heb. 9:5 we cannot now speak p.
   PARTIES.
Ex. 22:9 both p. come bef. judg.
   PARTING.
Ezek. 21:21 king of B. stood at p.
   PARTITION.
1 K. 6:21 he made a p. of gold
Eph. 2:14 bro. middle wall of p.
   PARTLY.
Dan. 2:42 be p. strong, p. broken
1 Cor. 11:18 divisions, I p. belie.
Heb. 10:33 p. gaz.-stock, p. com.
   PARTNER, S.
Prov. 29:24 whoso is p. with a
   thief
2 Cor. 8:23 Titus, he is my p.
Phil. 17 if count me a p. receive
Luke 5:7 they beckoned to th. p.
10 James and John were p.

CRUDEN'S CONCORDANCE. 965

PAS

PARTRIDGE.
1 Sam. 26:20 when one hunt a p.
Jer. 17:11 as p. sitteth on eggs

PASHUR.
Neh. 10:3 P. sealed, Jer. 20:6
Jer. 20:1 P. son of Im. smote, 2
3 L. call, not thy name P.
21:1 Zedekiah sent unto him P.
38:1 Gedal. the son of P. and P.

PASS.
Gen. 18:5 after that ye shall p.
41:32 will shortly bring it to p.
Ex. 33:19 will make my good p.
Num. 27:7 inherit, of fa. to p. 8
Jos. 1:14 ye shall p. before breth.
1 Sam. 16:10 Jesse made 7 sons p.
Neh. 2:14 no place for beast to p.
Job 6:15 as stream they p. away
11:16 rem. it as waters that p.
14:20 pre. he troubled, p. away
Prov. 16:30 he bringeth evil to p.
22:3 and the simple p. on, 27:12
Is. 30:32 grounded staff shall p.
33:21 no gallant ship shall p.
37:26 have I brought it to p.
Jer. 6:19 tb. I have given shall p.
15:14 make th. p. with enemies
33:13 flocks sh. p. under hands
51:43 nor doth son of man p.
Ezek. 20:37 I will cause you to p.
32:19 wh. dost th. p. in beauty?
Amos 6:2 p. ye unto Calneh
Mic. 1:11 p. ye away, inhabit. of
2:13 their king shall p. before
Zep. 2:2 decree br. forth, day p.
Zec. 3:4 have caused Iniqs. to p.
Mat. 5:18 heav. and earth sh. p.
26:39 cup p. fr. me, Mark 14:35
Luke 16:26 wh. would p. fr. hen.
nor can they p. fr. us to you
19:4 he was to p. that way
1 Cor. 7:36 if she p. flower of age
2 Pet. 3:10 heavens sh. p. away

PASS by.
Ex. 33:22 cover thee whi. I p. by
Ps. 80:12 all they that p. by
89:41 all that p. by way spoil
Jer. 22:8 many nations sh. p. by
Lam. 1:12 ye that p. by behold
3:15 all that p. by clap th. hands
Ezek. 5:14 sight of all that p. by
37:2 caused me to p. by them
Amos 7:8 I will not p. by th. 8:2
Mic. 2:8 garm. of them that p. by
Mat. 8:28 no man might p. by
Luke 18:36 hearing multit. p. by

See CAME, COME.

Not PASS.
Num. 20:17 will n. p. thro fields
18 Edom said, Thou shalt n. p.
Job 14:5 his bounds he cannot p.
19:8 fenced my way, cannot p.
Ps. 148:6 a decree wh. shall n. p.
Prov. 8:29 waters cannot p. n.
Jer. 5:22 decree that it cannot p.
Mat. 24:34 this gene. shall not p.
away, Mark 13:30; Luke
21:32
35 heaven and earth shall pass
away, but my word sh. n. p.
away, Mark 13:31; Lu. 21:33

PASS not.
Gen. 18:3 p. not away from serv.
2 K. 6:9 thou p. not such a place
Prov. 4:15 avoid it, p. not by it
Amos 5:5 we p. not to Beer-sheba

PASS over.
Gen. 8:1 God made wind p. o.
31:52 I will not p. o. this heap
32:16 p. o. bef. me, put a space
33:14 Lord p. o. bef. thy servant
Ex. 12:13 I will p. over you, 23
15:16 till thy people p. over
Num. 32:27 serv. will p. o. 29:32
30 not p. o. with you armed
Deut. 2:18 p. o. thro' Ar this day
3:18 shall p. over armed before
9:1 p. o. Jord un, 11:31; 27:2;
Jos. 1:11; 3:6, 14; 4:5
Jos. 22:19 p. o. into the land
Jud. 3:28 p. not suffer man p. o.
1 Sam. 14:8 will p. o. to th. men
Ps. 104:9 that they may not p. o.
Prov. 12:11 to p. o. a transgres.
Is. 25:6 p. over to Tarshish
31:9 p. over to his stronghold
Jer. 5:22 yet can they not p. o.
Ezek. 47:5 river I could not p. o.
Dan. 4:16 seven times p. o. 25
11:40 king of north shall p. o.
Hab. 1:11 chance, he shall p. o.
Luke 11:42 p. over judgment

PAS

PASS through.
Gen. 30:32 p. f. thy flock to-day
Ex. 12:12 p. t. Eg. this night
Lev. 18:21 any of thy seed p. t.
fire, Deut. 18:10; 2 K. 17:17
Num. 20:17 p. t. thy country
21:23 Sihon would not suffer Is.
to p. thro' Jud. 11:20
Deut. 2:4 p. thr. coasts of Edom
28 I will p. thro' on my feet
Jos. 1:11 p. t. host and command
2 Sam. 12:31 p. t. brick kiln
1 K. 18:6 divided land to p. t. it
2 K. 16:3 to p. t. the fire, 21:6;
23:10; 2 Chr. 33:6; Jer.
32:35; Ezek. 20:26, 31
Ps. 78:13 caused to p. t. 136:14
Is. 8:8 shall p. through Judah
28:19 p. thro' thy land as a river
34:10 none sh. p. t. it for ever
Jer. 9:10 so that none can p. t.
Lam. 3:44 prayers sho. not p. t.
4:21 cup shall also p. t. to thee
Ezek. 14:15 nol. beasts p. t. land
no man p. t. 29:11; 33:28
39:15 passengers that p. t. land
Dan. 11:10 p. t. and overflow
Joel 3:17 shall p. t. her any more
Amos 5:17 I will p. thro' thee
Nah. 1:12 cut down, wh. be p. t.
15 wicked no more p. t. thee
Zec. 9:8 no oppressor p. t. them
1 Cor. 16:5 shall p. t. Macedonia

PASSAGE, S.
Num. 20:21 Edom refused Is. p.
Jos. 22:11 an altar at p. of Israel
Jud. 12:6 and slew him at p.
1 Sam. 13:23 Ph. went out to p.
14:4 betw. p. were sharp rocks
Is. 10:29 are gone over the p.
Jer. 22:20 lift thy voice, cry fr. p.
51:32 show Bab. p. are stopped

PASSED.
Gen. 15:17 a lamp that p. betw.
Num. 20:17 have p. thr. border
Jos. 3:4 have not p. this way
1 Sam. 15:12 gone about and p.
29:2 Philist. p. on by hundreds
2 Sam. 15:18 servants p. on
2 K. 4:8 Elisha p. to Shunem
6:26 2d Solomon p. all kings
Job 4:15 spirit p. before my face
9:26 my days are p. away
15:19 no stranger p. am. them
Ps. 18:19 his thick clouds p.
37:36 yet he p. away, and lo
90:9 all our days are p. away
Cant. 3:4 little that I p. fr. them
Is. 41:3 pursued, and p. safely
Jer. 11:15 holy flesh p. from thee
46:17 hath p. time appointed
Dan. 3:27 smell of fire p. on th.
6:18 went and p. night fasting
Nah. 3:19 wicked p. continually
Mark 6:35 now the time is far p.
John 5:24 but is p. from death to
life, 1 John 3:14
Rom. 5:12 death p. on all men
Heb. 4:14 High-pri. p. into heav.
Rev. 21:1 first earth were p. aw.
4 former things are p. away

PASSED by.
Ex. 34:6 Lord p. by before him
1 K. 19:19 p. by and saw the lion
19:11 Lord p. by; 2 K. 4:8 p. by
1 K. 20:39 servant as he p. by
Job 28:8 nor hath fierce lion p. b.
Ps. 48:4 the kings p. by together
Ezek. 16:6 I p. by and saw thee, 8
36:34 in sight of all that p. by
Hab. 3:10 o'erfl. of waters p. by
Mat. 20:30 heard that Jesus p. by
Mark 6:48 would have p. by them
Luke 10:31 p. by on other side, 32
John 8:59 midst of them, so p. by
Acts 17:23 as I p. by and beheld

PASSED over.
Gen. 31:21 and p. over the river
32:10 with staff I p. over Jordan
Ex. 12:27 p. over houses of Isr.
Jos. 3:17 all priests p. over, 4:11
4:10 people hasted and p. over
11 the ark of the Lord p. o. r r
1 Sam. 15:32 p. o. to Bethuron
2 Sam. 15:22 king and peo. p. o.
Is. 40:27 judgment p. o. from G.
Ezek. 47:5 river could not be p. o.
Hos. 10:11 p. o. upon her neck
Jon. 2:3 billows and waves p. o.

PASSED through.
Gen. 12:6 Abram p. t. land
Num. 14:7 land which we p. t.
2 Chr. 30:6 posts p. t. country
Ezek. 9:4 angel p. t. city
Mic. 2:13 they p. t. gate and
Zec. 7:14 that no man p. t.

PAS

Acts 12:10 and p. thro' one street
1 Cor. 10:1 our fathers p. t. sea
Heb. 11:29 they p. thro' Red sea

PASSEDST.
Jud. 12:1 why p. thou over

PASSENGERS.
Prov. 9:15 she standeth to call p.
Ezek. 39:11 will give G. val. of p.
14 bury with p. those that re.
15 when p. see a man's bone

PASSEST.
Deut. 30:18 on land whi. thou p.
2 Sam. 15:33 if p. on, thou sh. be
1 K. 2:37 day thou p. over brook
Is. 43:2 when p. through waters

PASSETH.
Ex. 30:13 every one that p. 14
33:22 while my glory p. by
Jos. 3:11 Lord p. over before you
2 K. 4:9 man of G. wh. p. by us
12:4 money of every one that p.
Job 9:11 he p. on also, but I
14:20 againist him, and he p.
37:21 wind p. and clean, them
Ps. 8:8 whatever p. thro' the sea
78:39 arc a wind thai p. away
103:16 for the wind p. over it
144:4 as a shadow that p. away
Prov. 10:25 as whirlwind p. so is
26:17 he th. p. by and meddleth
Ec. 1:4 one generation p. away
Is. 29:5 as chaff that p. away
Jer. 2:6 no man p. through, 9:12
18:16 every one that p. 19:8
Ezek. 35:7 from it him that p.
Hos. 13:3 early dew that p. away
Zep. 7:18 G. that p. by transgr.
Zec. 9:6 on. one that p. by her
3:6 streets waste, none p. by
Lam. 1:6 like haris find no p.
Ezek. 34:14 feed in good p. fat p.
18 small th. to ha. eat. good p.
31 flock of my p. are men, I G.
Hos. 13:6 ac. to their p. so filled
Joel 1:18 beasts groan, ha. no p.
John 10:9 go in and out, find p.

PASTURES.
1 K. 4:23 b. had 20 ox. out of p.
Ps. 23:2 maketh me lie green p.
65:12 drop upon p. of wilderu.
13 p. are clothed with flocks
Is. 30:23 cnt. sh. feed in large p.
49:9 p. shall be in high places
Jer. 23:10 pleas. places of wil. p.
Lam. 1:6 her young rams p.
Joel 1:19 fire hath devour. p. 20
2:22 p. of wilderness do spring

PATARA.
Acts 21:1 from thence unto P.

PATE.
Ps. 7:16 viol. come do. on own p.

PATH.
Gen. 49:17 D. be an adder in p.
Num. 22:24 angel of L. st. in p.
Job 28:7 p. which no fowl know.
30:13 mar my p. set forward
41:32 he maketh a p. to shine
Ps. 16:11 show me the p. of life
27:11 lead me in a plain p.
77:19 way in sea, p. in great wa.
119:35 make me to go in p.
105 thy word a light to my p.
139:3 thou compassest my p.
142:3 them thou knewest my p.
Prov. 1:15 refrain foot fr. their p.
2:9 sh. understand every good p.
4:15 enter not into p. of wicked
18 p. of just is as shining light
26 ponder the p. of thy feet
5:6 lest thou ponder p. of life
Is. 26:7 dost weigh p. of just
30:11 out of way, turn out of p.
43:16 maketh p. in mighty wat.
Joel 2:8 walk, every one in his p.

PATHROS. Is. 11:11; Ezek. 29:14; 30:14

PATHWAY.
Prov. 12:28 in p. thereof no dea.

PATHS.
Job 6:18 p. of way turned aside
8:13 p. of all that forget God
13:27 lookest narrowly to my p.
19:8 hath set darkness in my p.
24:13 neh. abide in p. thereof
33:11 feet in stocks, mar. my p.
38:20 thou sh. know p. of house
Ps. 8:8 passeth thro' p. of seas
17:4 kept me fr. p. of destroyer
5 hold up my goings in p. thy p.
23:3 leadeth me in p. of righte.
25:4 O Lord, teach me thy p.
10 p. of L. mer. and truth
65:11 p. drop fatness on pasture
Prov. 2:8 keep. p. of judgment

CRUDEN'S CONCORDANCE.

PAV

Prov. 2:13 leave *p.* of uprightn.
15 and they froward in their *p.*
18 her *p.* incline unto the dead
19 nei. take hold of *p.* of life
20 keep *p.* of the righteous
3:6 direct *p.* 17 *p.* are peace
4:11 I have led thee in right *p.*
7:25 go not astray in her *p.*
8:2 standeth in places of *p.*
20 I lead in *p.* of judgment
Is. 2:3 walk in his *p. Mic.* 4:2
3:12 they destroy way of thy *p.*
42:16 lead th. in *p.* not known
58:12 called, the restorer of *p.*
59:7 destruction are in their *p.*
8 have made them crooked *p.*
Jer. 6:16 in way, ask for old *p.*
18:15 ancient *p.* to walk in *p.*
Lam. 3:9 he made my *p.* crooked
Hos. 2:6 she shall not find *p.*
Mat. 3:3 make his *p.* straight.
Mark 1:3; *Luke* 3:4
Heb. 12:13 made strai. *p.* for feet

PATIENCE.

Mat. 18:26 have *p.* with me, and I will pay thee all. 29
Luke 8:15 br. forth fruit with *p.*
21:19 in *p.* possess ye your souls
Rom. 5:3 tribulation worketh *p.*
4 *p.* experience, experi. hope
8:25 do we with *p.* wait for it
15:4 we thro' *p.* might ha. hope
5 G. *p.* grant you to be like-min.
2 *Cor.* 6:4 ministers of God in *p.*
12:12 signs we. am. you in all *p.*
Col. 1:11 strengthened to all *p.*
1 *Thes.* 1:3 remem. your *p.* in *J.*
2 *Thes.* 3:4 gl. in you for your *p.*
1 *Tim.* 6:11 follow after love, *p.*
2 *Tim.* 3:10 hast known my *p.*
Tit. 2:2 be found in faith. *p.*
Heb. 6:12 thro' *p.* inh. promises
10:36 ye have need of *p.*
12:1 run with *p.* race before us
Jam. 1:3 trying of faith work. *p.*
4 let *p.* have her perfect work
5:7 husbandman hath long *p.*
10 an example of *p.* 11 *p.* of *J.*
2 *Pet.* 1:6 add to temper. *p.* to *p.*
Rev. 1:9 compan. in *p.* of Jesus
2:2 I know thy *p.* 19; 3 hast *p.*
3:10 hast kept word of my *p.*
13:10 here is *p.* of saints, 14:12

PATIENT.

Ec. 7:8 *p.* in sp. better than pro.
Rom. 2:7 *p.* continu. in well-do.
12:12 in hope, *p.* in tribulation
1 *Thes.* 5:14 be *p.* toward all men
2 *Thes.* 3:5 *p.* waiting for Christ
1 *Tim.* 3:3 lac. but *p.* 2 *Tim.* 2:24
Jam. 5:7 be *p.* breth. 8 ye also *p.*

PATIENTLY.

Ps. 37:7 rest in *L.* and wait *p.*
40:1 I waited *p.* for the Lord
Acts 26:3 I bes. thee hear me *p.*
Heb. 6:15 after he had *p.* endured
1 *Pet.* 2:20 if ye be buff. take it *p.*
if ye do well and su. ta. it *p.*

PATMOS.

Rev. 1:9 in the isle called P.

PATRIARCH, S.

Acts 2:29 freely speak of *p.* Dav.
7:8 *Jacob* begat the twelve *p.*
9, sold Joseph into Egypt
Heb. 7:4 *p.* Abraham paid tithes

PATRIMONY.

Deut. 18:8 cometh of sale of *p.*

PATROBAS.** *Rom.* 16:14

PATTERN, S.

Ex. 25:9 *p.* of all instruments
40 make them after their *p.*
Jos. 22:28 the *p.* of altar of Lord
2 *K.* 16:10 Ahaz sent *p.* of altar
1 *Chr.* 28:11 D. g. S. *p.* 12, 18, 19
Ezek. 43:10 let them measure *p.*
1 *Tim.* 1:16 in me C. mig. sh. *p.*
Tit. 2:7 show. thyself *p.* of good
Heb. 8:5 accord. to *p.* I showed
9:23 necessary that *p.* of things

PAUL.

Acts 13:9 then Saul, called P.
23:16 but P. was suffered to
(*Vide Acts passim.*)
1 *Cor.* 1:13 whether P. or Apollos, or
3:22 whether P. or Apollos, or
1:21 saluta. of me P. *Col.* 4:18
1 *Thes.* 2:18 ev. I P. 2 *Thes.* 3:17
Phile. 9 such a one as P.
2 *Pet.* 3:15 as our belov. P. wrote

PAUL'S.

Acts 13:7 the deputy Sergius P.

PAVED.

Ex. 24:10 under feet *p.* work
Cant. 3:10 being *p.* with love

PEA

PAVEMENT.

2 *K.* 16:17 put sea on *p.* of stones
2 *Chr.* 7:3 all Isr. bowed upon *p.*
Est. 1:6 beds were on *p.* of red
Ezek. 40:17 chambers and a *p.*
18 *p.* by side of gates lower *p.*
42:3 over against *p.* was gallery
John 19:13 Pil. sat in pla. call. P.

PAVILION, S.

2 *Sam.* 22:12 ma. dar. *p. Ps.* 18:11
1 *K.* 20:12 Ben. drinking in *p.* 16
Ps. 27:5 he shall hide me in *p.*
31:20 keep them secretly in a *p.*
Jer. 43:10 Nebuch. spread his *p.*

PAW, S.

Lev. 11:27 goeth on *p.* unclean
1 *Sam.* 17:37 de. me out of *p.* of

PAWETH.

Job 39:21 horse *p.* in the valley

PAY.

Ex. 21:19 sh. *p.* for loss of time
36 he shall surely *p.* ox for ox
22:7 If he be found, *p.* double, 9
Num. 20:19 if I drink I will *p.*
Deut. 23:21 shall not slack to *p.*
2 *Sam.* 15:7 let me go *p.* my vow
1 *K.* 20:39 thou shalt *p.* a talent
2 *K.* 4:7 sell oil, and *p.* thy debt
2 *Chr.* 8:8 them did S. make to *p.*
Ps. 22:25 *p.* my vows, 66:13; 116:14, 18
Job 22:27 and shalt pay thy vows
Pr. 22:25 *p.* vows, 66:13; 116:14, 18
50:14 *p.* thy vows to Most High
70:11 vow, and *p.* to the Lord
Prov. 19:17 giv. will he *p.* again
22:27 if hast nothing to *p.*
Ec. 5:4 defer not to *p.* it, *p.* that
5 not vow, than vow and not *p.*
Lam. 3:17 rem. my soul from *p.*
Ezek. 7:25 seek *p.* th. shall be in.
12:19 *p.* and there was no *p.* 16
34:25 make a covena. of *p.* 37:26
Dan. 8:25 by *p.* he shall destroy
Ob. 7 men at *p.* deceived thee
Mic. 3:5 bite with teeth, cry *p.*
5:5 this man sh. be *p.* when A.
Hag. 2:9 this place I will give *p.*
Zec. 6:13 counsel of *p.* betw. th.
8:10 nor was th. any *p.* to him
16 execute judgment and *p.*
10 therefore love truth and *p.*
Mal. 2:5 covenant of life and *p.*
Mat. 10:13 worthy, let *p.* come
34 not I am come to send *p.*
Mark 9:50 have *p.* one with ano.
Luke 1:79 guide feet to way of *p.*
2:14 on earth *p.* good will tow.
10:5 if son of *p.* th. your *p.* rest
12:51 I am come to give *p.*
19:38 *p.* in heaven, gl. in highe.
42 things belong to thy *p.*
John 14:27 *p.* I lea. you. *p.* I give
16:33 in me you might have *p.*
Acts 10:36 preaching *p.* by Jesus
12:20 *p.* to their country, brought
1 Cor. 1:3; *Eph.* 1:2; *Phil.* 1:2
2:10 *p.* to every man work good
6:1 to be spiritually mind. is *p.*
8:6 to be spiritually mind. is *p.*
10:15 that preach gospel of *p.*
14:17 the kingdom of God is *p.*
19 fol. things that make for *p.*
15:13 fill you with all joy and *p.*
1 *Cor.* 7:15 G. hath call. us to *p.*
14:33 author of *p.* as in church.
Gal. 5:22 Spirit is love, joy, *p.*
Eph. 2:14 is our *p.* 15 making *p.*
17 Christ came and preach. *p.*
4:3 unity of Spirit in bond of *p.*
6:15 preparation of gospel of *p.*
Phil. 4:7 *p.* of God passeth und.
Col. 1:2 grace and *p.* from G. our
Father, 1 *Pet.* 1:1; 2 *Thes.* 1:2; 1 *Tim.* 1:2; 2 *Tim.* 1:2;
Tit. 1:4; *Phile.* 3; 2 *John* 3
3:15 *p.* of God rule in your hea.
1 *Thes.* 5:3 when they sh. say *p.*
2 *Thes.* 3:16 L. of *p.* give you *p.*
2 *Tim.* 2:22 follow *p. Heb.* 12:14
Heb. 7:2 king of Salem is k. of *p.*
11:31 Rahab received spies in *p.*
Jam. 3:18 *p.* of them, to make *p.*
Rev. 1:4 *p.* from him that is, was
6:4 power giv. to him to take *p.*

PEACE be.
Jud. 6:23 L. said, *p.* to thee
1 *Sam.* 25:6 *p.* be to thee — house
1 *Chr.* 12:18 *p.* be to thee, *p.* be to
Ps. 122:7 *p.* be within thy walls
8 now say, *p.* be within thee
Dan. 4:1 *p.* be multiplied, 6:25;
1 *Pet.* 1:2; 2 *Pet.* 1:2; *Jude* 2;

PEA

Ps. 120:7 I am for *p.* they for war
122:6 pray for *p.* of Jerusalem
125:5 but *p.* sh. be upon Israel
128:6 thou shalt see *p.* upon Is.
147:14 maketh *p.* in thy borders
Prov. 3:17 pleasantness, paths *p.*
12:20 to counsellors of *p.* is joy
16:7 maketh enemies to be at *p.*
Ec. 3:8 time of war, time of *p.*
Is. 9:6 Prince of *p.* 7 increase *p.*
26:12 Lord thou wilt ordain *p.*
27:5 *p.* with me, he shall ma. *p.*
32:17 work of righteo. sh. be *p.*
33:7 ambassadors of *p.* sh. weep
38:17 or *p.* I had great bittern.
48:7 make *p.* and create evil
22 th. is no *p.* to wicked. 57:21
52:7 publisheth *p. Nah.* 1:15
53:5 chastisem. of our *p.* on him
54:10 nor coven. of *p.* be remov.
13 great shall be *p.* of thy chil.
55:12 with joy, led forth with *p.*
57:2 enter into *p.* rest in beds
19 fruit of lips, *p. p.* to him
59:8 way of *p.* kn. *Rom.* 3:17
66:12 I will extend *p.* to her
Jer. 4:10 ye sh. have *p.* whereas
6:14 *p. p.* when th. is no *p.* 8:11
14:13 for no good, a time of *p.*
12:5 if in land of *p.* they weari.
Jer. 29:7 in *p.* sh. ye have peace
34:5 but thou shalt die in *p.*
Mal. 2:6 walked with me in *p.*
28:9 ent. serv. depart in *p.*
1 *Cor.* 16:11 cond. him forth in *p.*
2 *Cor.* 13:11 one mind, live in *p.*
Jam. 2:16 depart in *p.* be warm.
3:18 righteousness is sown in *p.*
2 *Pet.* 3:14 be found of him in *p.*

See GO, MADE, OFFERINGS.

PEACEABLE.
Gen. 34:21 these men *p.* with us
Sam. 20:19 one of them th. *p.*
1 *Chr.* 4:40 land was wi. and *p.*
Is. 32:18 peo. dwell in *p.* habita.
Jer. 25:37 *p.* habitations are cut
1 *Tim.* 2:2 lead a quiet and *p.* li.
Heb. 12:11 yieldeth the *p.* fruit
Jam. 3:17 wisd. is pure, *p.* gent.

PEACEABLY.
Gen. 37:4 could not speak *p.*
Jud. 11:13 restore those lands *p.*
21:13 send some *p.* to Benjam.
1 *Sam.* 16:4 said, Comest thou *p.*
5 *p.* I am come, 1 *K.* 2:13
1 *Chr.* 12:17 if ye be come *p.*
Dan. 11:21 shall come in *p.* 24
Rom. 12:18 live *p.* with all men

PEACEMAKERS.
Mat. 5:9 blessed are the *p.*

PEACOCKS.
1 *K.* 10:22 the navy came, bringing *p.* 2 *Chr.* 9:21
Job 39:13 gav. goodly win. to *p.* *?*

PEARL.
Mat. 13:46 found *p.* of great price
Rev. 21:21 ev. gate was of one *p.*

PEARLS.
Job 28:18 no menti. of coral or *p.*
Mat. 7:6 neither cast *p.* bef. sw.
13:45 like merchant seeking *p.*
1 Tim. 2:9 not with *p.* or costly
Rev. 17:4 woman decked with *p.*
18:12 no man buy. merchandi. *p.*
21:21 twelve gates were twe. *p.*

PECULIAR.
Ex. 19:5 sh. be *p.* treasure to me
Deut. 14:2 *p.* people unto himself, 26:18; 1 *Pet.* 2:9
Ps. 135:4 chosen is. for *p.* treas.
Ec. 2:8 *p.* treas. of kings
Tit. 2:14 purify to himself *p.* people

PEDIGREES.
Num. 1:18 they declared their *p.*

PEELED.
Is. 18:2 nation scatter. and *p.* 7
Ezek. 29:18 every shoulder was *p.*

PEEP, ED.
Is. 8:19 wizards that *p.* and mut.
10:14 none opened mouth or *p.*

PEKAH.
2 *K.* 15:25 P. conspired again. 29
30 conspiracy against P. 16:5
2 *Chr.* 28:6 P. slew in Judah
Is. 7:1 Rezin and P. went towa.

PEKAHIAH. 2 *K.* 15:22, 23

PELATIAH.
1 *Chr.* 3:21 son of Hananiah P.
4:43; *Neh.* 10:22; *Ezek.* 11:13

PEL

Dan. 10:19 *p. be* to thee, he stro.
Luke 10:5 *p. be* to this house
24:36 he saith unto them, *p. be* to you, *John* 20:19, 21, 26
Gal. 6:16 *p. be* on them
Eph. 6:23 *p. be* to brethren, love
1 *Pet.* 5:14 *p. be* with all in Chr.
3 *John* 14 *p. be* to thee, our frie.

God of PEACE.
Rom. 15:33 *God of p.* be wi. you
16:20 *God of p.* sh. bruise Satan
2 *Cor.* 13:11 the *God of p.* shall be with you, *Phil.* 4:9
1 *Thes.* 5:23 *God of p.* sanctify
Heb. 13:20 *God of p.* make you perfect

See HELD, HOLD.

In PEACE.
Gen. 26:29 sent thee away *in p.*
28:21 I come to fa.'s house *in p.*
Jud. 11:31 when I return *in p.*
2 *Sam.* 15:27 return to city *in p.*
19:30 king is come again *in p.*
1 *K.* 2:5 Joab shed blood *in p.*
22:17 man *in p.* 2 *Chr.* 18:16, 26
27 *in* prison. until I come *in p.*
2 *Chr.* 19:1 Jehosh. return. *in p.*
30:24 thy taber. shall be *in p.*
Ps. 4:8 I will lay me down *in p.*
55:18 be delivered my sent *in p.*
Is. 26:3 wilt keep him in perf. *p.*
Jer. 29:7 in *p.* sh. ye have peace
34:5 but thou shalt die *in p.*
Mal. 2:6 walked with me *in p.*
28:9 ent. serv. depart *in p.*
1 *Cor.* 16:11 cond. him forth *in p.*
2 *Cor.* 13:11 one mind, live *in p.*
Jam. 2:16 depart *in p.* be warm.
3:18 righteousness is sown *in p.*
2 *Pet.* 3:14 be found of him *in p.*

CRUDEN'S CONCORDANCE.

PEO

2 *Cor.* 6:16 they shall be *my p.*
See DAUGHTER.

Of the PEOPLE.

Gen. 23:23 manner *of p.* be sep.
49:10 to him sh. gather. *of p.* be
Num. 26:4 take sum *of t. p.* fr. 20
Jos. 4:2 take 12 men *of the p.*
1 *Sam.* 9:2 higher than any *of the p.* 10:23
14:24 none *of the p.* tasted food
26:15 ca. one *of t. p.* destr. king
2 *K.* 13:7 nor did he leave *of t. p.*
Ezr. 2:3 *of the p.* of th. countries
Neh. 5:1 th. was a gre. cry *of t. p.*
7:73 some *of the p.* dw. in cities
Ps. 72:4 sh. judge poor *of thy p.*
89:19 exalted one out *of the p.*
Is. 51:4 judg. for a light *of t. p.*
63:3 *of the p.* there was none
John 7:31 many *of t. p.* believed
11:42 bec. *of t. p.* that stand by
Acts 4:21 punish, beca. *of the p.*
Heb. 9:7 hims. and errors *of t. p.*
Rev. 11:9 they *of p.* see dead bod.
See EARS, ELDERS.

One PEOPLE.

Gen. 23:23 one *p.* sh. be stronger
34:16 dwell wi. you, bec. *one p.*
22 dwell with us, to be *one p.*

Own PEOPLE.

Ex. 5:16 the fault is in thi. *o. p.*
1 *Chr.* 17:21 went to redeem *o. p.*
2 *Chr.* 25:15 could not deli. *o. p.*
Ps. 45:10 forget also thy *own p.*
7,052 made his *o. p.* to go forth
Is. 13:14 ev. man turn to his *o. p.*
Jer. 46:16 let us go ag. to our *o. p.*

The PEOPLE.

Gen. 11:6 L. said, Behold *the p.*
Ex. 3:4 why *let t. p.* from work?
5 *the p.* of land now are many
12:27 and *t. p.* bowed the head
13:31 *the p.* feared L. believed
13:14 *the p.* sh. hear and be afr.
16 *the p.* pass over wh. th. hast
24 *the p.* murmured, saying
16:30 *the p.* rest. on seventh day
17:1 th. was no water for *the p.*
2 *t. p.* did chide Mo. *Num.* 20:3
6 water out of it, *the p.* drink
18:19 be th. for *the p.* God-ward
19:9 *t. p.* may hear when I spe.
17 Moses brought forth *the p.*
20 down wh. *the p.* saw it afar; 21
24:8 Moses sprinkled it on *t. p.*
Lev. 9:7 ato. for thyself and *t. p.*
15 sin-offer. for *the p.* 16; 16:15
Num. 11:2 *the p.* cried to Moses
13:18 see *the p.* that dwelleth
14:1 *the p.* wept; 39 *t. p.* mour.
21:5 *the p.* spake against God
23:9 lo, *the p.* shall dwell alone
24 *the p.* rise up as a great lion
Deut. 4:10 said, Gather me *the p.*
13 *the* priest's due from *t. p.*
33:3 loved *the p.* *t* push *the p.*
19 they shall call *t. p.* to moun.
Jos. 4:10 and *the p.* hasted over
6:20 *t. p.* shout. 24:28 *t. p.* dep.
Jud. 7:2 *t. p.* are with thee. 4
1 *Sam.* 2:13 priest's cust, wi. *t. p.*
4:4 *t. p.* sent to Sh. to bring ark
8:19 *the p.* ref. to obey Samuel
14:45 *the p.* said, Sh. Jonathan
die? so *the p.* rescued Jona.
15:15 *the p.* spared best of sheep
21 *the p.* took of the spoil oxen
30:6 *t. p.* spake of stoning him
2 *Sam.* 1:4 *t. p.* fled from battle
15:18 *the p.* there. with Absalom
1 *K.* 1:40 *the p.* piped with pipes
10:22 *the p.* that followed Omri
prevailed against *the p.*
2 *K.* 4:41 pour out for *the p.*
43 give *t. p.* that they may eat
11:17 coven. bet. king and *t. p.*
18:36 but *the p.* held their peace
24:13 inquire of Lord for *the p.*
2 *Chr.* 12:3 *the p.* without numb.
23:33 *the p.* had not prepa. 30:3
37:2 and *the p.* did yet corruptly
30:20 and the Lord healed *the p.*
34:3 *the p.* rest. on words of H.
Ezr. 10:13 but *the p.* are many
Neh. 4:6 *t. p.* had mind to work
5:13 *the p.* did accord. to prom.
7:4 but *the p.* were few therein
8:16 *the p.* bow. palm branches
11:2 *t. p.* blessed all that offered
Est. 3:6 showed him *t. p.* of Mo.
4:11 *the p.* of king's provinces
Job 12:2 no doubt but ye are *t. p.*
34:30 lest *the p.* be ensnared
Ps. 2:1 why do *t. p.* im. vain th.?

PEO

Ps. 33:12 bles. *t. p.* he hath cho.
44:2 bow thou didst afflict *t. p.*
45:17 *the p.* praise thee for ever
56:7 in th. anger cast down *t. p.*
67:3 let *the p.* praise thee, O G. 5
85:15 blessed is *t. p.* that know
92:7 we are *t. p.* of his pasture
99:13 he sh. judge *t. p.* with tru.
99:9 he sh. judge *t. p.* with eq.
9:1 L. reign, let *the p.* tremble
105:1 make kno. deeds am. *t. p.*
Prov. 11:14 no coun. is, *t. p.* fall
29:2 *the p.* rejoiced, *t. p.* mourn
Is. wh. is no vision, *t. p.* perish
Is. 9:2 *t. p.* that walked in dark.
13 *t. p.* turneth not to him em.
14:9 and *the p.* shall take them
24:2 be with *t. p.* so with priest
30:19 *the p.* shall dwell in Zion
33:24 *t. p.* be forgiven th. iniq.
34:5 my sword sh. come on *t. p.*
40:7 *t. p.* is grass, grass wither.
51:7 *the p.* in wh. heart is my law
63:6 wilt tread *t. p.* in mi. anger
18 *t. p.* of thy holi. possess. it
Jer. 31:2 *t. p.* left of sw. found gr.
37:4 Jeremiah went amo. *the p.*
39:14 so he dwelt among *the p.*
40:5 go back and dw. with *t. p.* 6
51:58 *the p.* shall labor in vain
Ezek. 11:17 gather you from *t. p.*
20:34 br. you out from *t. p.* 34:13
32:7 I will cut thee off fr. *the p.*
36:30 bring thee down with *t. p.*
33:31 come to thee as *t. p.* con.
36:20 these are *the p.* of Lord
38:4 thou shalt fall, and *the p.*
42:14 approa. th. things for *t. p.*
44:19 shall not sanctify *the p.*
Dan. 9:26 *the p.* of the prince
11:32 *the p.* that know th. G.
Hos. 4:14 *t. p.* doth not underst.
10:5 *the p.* thereof shall mourn
10 *t. p.* sh. be gath. aga. them
Joel 2:6 *the p.* sh. be much pain.
Amos 3:6 sh. *t. p.* not be afraid?
Jon. 3:5 *t. p.* of Nin. believ. God
Hab. 2:13 *the p.* shall labor in fire,
the p. shall weary themselv.
Zep. 2:10 magnif, ag. *t. p.* of L.
Hag. 1:12 *t. p.* did fear the Lord
Mal. 1:4 *the p.* against whom L.
Mat. 4:16 *t. p.* saw great light
21:26 we fear *t. p.* *Mark* 11:32
Luke 1:21 *t. p.* waited for Zacha.
3:15 as *the p.* were in expecta.
4:42 *the p.* sou. 5:1 *t. p.* pressed
6:40 *the p.* gladly received him
9:13 whom say *t. p.* that I am?
20:19 feared *t. p.* 22:2 ; 23:5 str.
23:14 one that perverteth *t. p.*
John 7:12 he deceiveth *the p.*
11:50 man sho. die for *t. p.* 18:14
Acts 5:13 *the p.* magnified them
8:6 *t. p.* wi. one accord ga. heed
14:11 *t. p.* saw wh. P. had done
19 persuaded *t. p.* and ston. P.
20:17 delivering thee from *t. p.*
Heb. 5:3 as for *t. p.* so for hims. 7:27
7:11 under it *t. p.* received law
13:12 he might sanctify *the p.*
Jude 5 Lord having saved *the p.*

This PEOPLE.

Ex. 3:21 I will give *t. p.* favor
5:22 why hast evil entrea. *t. p.?*
17:4 cried, Wh. sh. I do to *t. p.?*
18:18 wear away. thou and *t. p.*
34:9 seem *t. p.* If what did *t. p.*
31 *t. p.* have sinned a great sin
33:12 sayest, Bring up *this p.*
Num. 11:11 burden of all *t. p.*
14 I am not able to bear all *t. p.*
14:11 how long will *t. p.* prov. ?
13 tf thou kill *t. p.* as one man
16 not able to br. *t. p.* into land
19 pardon *t. p.* bast forg. *t. p.*
22:6 I pray thee, curse *t. p.* 17
24:14 *th. p.* shall do to thy peo.
Deut. 5:28 heard voice of *this p.*
9:13 saying, I have seen *this p.*
27 look not to stubborn. of *t. p.*
31:7 for thou must go with *t. p.*
16 *t. p.* will go whor. after gods
Jud. 2:20 *t. p.* have transgressed
9:29 would to G. *t. p.* were und.
38 is not *this the p.* thou des.?
1 K. 14:8 wh. L. and *t. p.* ch.
14 *K.* 12:6 that I may answ. *t. p.*
9 *p.* 2 *Chr.* 10:9, 9
27 if *t. p.* do sacrifice at Jeru-
salem
14:2 I should be king over *t. p.*
18:37 that *this p.* may know
2 *K.* 6:18 smite *t. p.* wi. blindn.
2 *Chr.* 1:10 come in before *th. p.*
Neh. 5:10 all I have done for *t. p.*
Is. 4:9 go and tell *t. p.* hear ye

PEO

Is. 6:10 make the heart of *t. p.*
fat, *Mat.* 13:15; *Acts* 28:26, 27
9:16 leaders of *t. p.* cause th. err
23:13 *t. p.* was not till A. founded
28:14 scornful men that rule *t. p.*
29:13 *t. p.* dr. near me wi. mou.
14 a marv. work among *t. p.*
43:21 *t. p.* ha. I form. for myself
Jer. 4:10 thou hast deceived *t. p.*
5:14 my words fire, *t. p.* wood
6:19 I will bring evil on *this p.*
21 stumbling-blo. bef. *this p.*
7:16 therefore pray not thou for *this p.* 11:14; 14:11
8:5 why is *this p.* slidden back?
13:10 *t.* evil *p.* who ref. to hear
15:1 my mind co. not be to. *t. p.*
19:5 tak. away my peace fr. *t. p.*
19:11 even so will I break *t. p.*
23:32 they shall not profit *t. p.*
26:15 makest *t. p.* trust in a lie
29:32 a man to dwell amo. *t. p.*
32:42 bro. great evil upon *t. p.*
33:24 not what *t. p.* have spok.
33:16 *t. p.* have not hearkened
36:7 anger pronounced ag. *t. p.*
37:18 what have I offend. *t. p. ?*
Mic. 2:11 sh. be prophet of *t. p.*
Hag. 2:14 so is *this p.* before me
Zec. 8:6 in eyes of remn. of *t. p.*
11 I will not be to *this p.*
12 cause rem. of *t. p.* possess
Mark 7:6 *t. p.* hon. me with lips
Luke 9:13 sho. buy meat for *t. p.*
21:23 th. sh. be wrath upon *t. p.*
John 7:49 *t. p.* knoweth not law
Acts 13:17 G. of *t. p.* chose our
1 *Cor.* 14:21 I will speak to *t. p.*

Thy PEOPLE.

Ex. 5:23 neither delivered *t. p.*
15:16 till *t. p.* pass over, O Lord
22:28 ca. ruler of *t. p.* *Acts* 23:5
33:11 poor of *t. p.* *thy p.* may eat
33:13 consider this nation *t. p.*
16 I and *t. p.* have found grace
27:1 make thee a curse and oath among *thy p.*
27:15 shalt be gathered to *t. p.*
31:19 *Deut.* 32:50
Deut. 9:12 *t. p.* corrupted thems.
20 O Lord, destroy not *thy p.*
29 yet are they *t. p.* *Neh.* 1:10
Ruth 1:10 return wi. thee to *t. p.*
16 *thy p.* shall be my people
2 *Sam.* 7:23 and what nation is like *thy p.* ? 1 *Chr.* 17:21
23 bef. *t. p.* wh. thou redeeme.
1 *K.* 8:2 serv. is in midst of *t. p.*
8:44 if *thy p.* go out to battle
50 forgive *t. p.* 2 *Chr.* 6:24, 39
51 they be *t. p.* 20:42 *thy p.* his
22:4 my people as *t. p.* 2 *Chr.* 18:3
1 *Chr.* 21:17 not hand be on *t. p.*
29:18 thoughts of heart of *t. p.*
Ezr. 8:26 blessing is upon *thy p.*
26 showed *thy p.* hard things
Jer. 29:16 *p.* he will be enticed
Rom. 3:17 for good news so. dio
2 *Tim.* 2:25 *p.* G. give them rep.

PERCEIVE.

Deut. 29:4 not given heart to *p.*
Jos. 22:31 *p.* Lord is am. us
1 *Sam.* 12:17 *p.* your wickedness
2 *Sam.* 19:6 I *p.* if A. had lived
1 *K.* 14:9 I *p.* this is a holy man
Job 8:11 *p.* not ; 23:3 cannot *p.*
14:21 *p.* it not ; 38:15 deeper not
33:19 deeper speech th. canst *p.*
Mat. 13:14 shall see, and sh. not
p. *Mark* 4:12 ; *Acts* 28:26
Mark 7:18 do ye not *p.* whatsoe.
p. 8:17 *p.* ye not, neither unders.
Luke 8:46 I *p.* virtue out of me
John 4:19 I *p.* thou art a prophet
12:19 *p.* ye how pre. nothing?
Acts 8:23 *p.* art in gall of bitter.
10:34 *p.* G. is no respect. of per.
17:22 I *p.* ye are too superstitio.
2 *Cor.* 7:8 I *p.* ep. made you sor.
1 *John* 3:16 here, *p.* we love of G.

PERCEIVED.

Gen. 19:33 *p.* not wh. she lay, 35
1 *Sam.* 3:8 L. had called Samuel
28:14 Saul *p.* it was Samuel
2 *Sam.* 5:12 D. *p.* Lord establish.
him king over Is. 1 *Chr.* 14:2
1 *K.* 22:33 when captains *p.* it
was not king. 2 *Chr.* 18:32
Neh. 6:12 *p.* G. had not sent him
16 *p.* this work was wrou. of G.
13:10 *p.* portion of L. not given
Job 38:18 *p.* breadth of earth?
Ec. 1:17 I *p.* this also is vexat.
2:14 I *p.* one event happeneth
Is. 64:4 nor *p.* what God prep.
Jer. 33:16 who hath *p.* his word

PER

Ez. 19:10 go to *t. p.* 12 bounds to n.
Deut. 30:2 priest speak to *the p.*
5 officers shall speak *to the p.*
Jud. 8:5 loaves of bread to *the p.*
Ruth 2:11 to *t. p.* th. knowest not
1 *Sam.* 20:7 Abishai came to *t. p.*
2 *Sam.* 24:3 L. thy G. add to *t. p.*
1 *K.* 12:15 king heark. not to *p.*
1 *Chr.* 4:42 give *to p.* they may eat
1 *Chr.* 10:9 carry tidings *to t. p.*
2 *Chr.* 32:6 said I *to the p.* lodge
Neh. 4:22 said I *to the p.* lodge
5:15 govern. chargeable *to t. p.*
Ps. 0:8 minister judgm. *to the p.*
72:3 shall bring peace *to the p.*
Is. 42:5 giveth breath *to the p.*
49:22 set up my standard *to t. p.*
55:4 given him for witness *to t. p.*
a leader and com. *to t. p.*
Ezek. 24:18 spake *to t. p.* in mor.
Dan. 7:27 kingdom given *to t. p.*
Joel 3:9 sell them *to t. p.* aft. off
Mic. 3:3 cometh *to t. p.* will he.
Zep. 3:9 turn *to t. p.* pure langu.
Mat. 12:46 yet talked *to the p.*
Acts 5:20 speak in temple *to t. p.*
10:2 which gave alms *to the p.*
42 comma. us to preach *to t. p.*
13:31 seen of witnesses *to the p.*
17:5 J. sought to bring *to the p.*
19:33 made his defence *to the p.*
21:39 suffer me to speak *to the p.*
25:2 chiefs show fight *to the p.*

PEOPLES,

Rev. 10:11 prophesy bef. many *p.*
17:15 waters thou sawest are *p.*
PEOR. *Num.* 23:28 ; 25:18 ; *Jos.* 22:17

PERADVENTURE.

Gen. 18:24 *p.* there be 50 righte.
28 *p.* there lack five of the fifty
29 *p.* forty ; 30 *p.* thirty ; 31 *p.* twenty
32 this once, *p.* ten shall be
24:5 *p.* wom. not be willing. 39
27:12 my father *p.* will feel me
31:31 *p.* take by force thy daug.
32:20 *p.* he will accept of me
42:4 lest *p.* mischief befall him
43:12 *p.* it was an oversight
44:34 *p.* evil come on my father
50:15 Joseph will *p.* hate us
Ex. 13:17 lest *p.* people repent
32:30 *p.* I shall make atonement
Num. 22:6 *p.* I shall prevail, 11
23:3 *p.* L. will come to meet me
27 *p.* it please God thou curse
Jos. 9:7 *p.* ye dwell among us
1 *Sam.* 6:5 *p.* he will lighten ha.
9:6 *p.* he can show us our way
1 *K.* 18:5 *p.* we may find grass
27 *p.* sleep, must be awaked
20:31 *p.* he will save thy life
Ezr. 2:10 *p.* Spirit hath cast him
Jer. 20:10 *p.* he will be enticed
Rom. 5:7 for good man so. die
2 *Tim.* 2:25 *p.* G. give them rep.

CRUDEN'S CONCORDANCE. 969

PER

Jer. 38:27 for matter was not p.
Mat. 21:46 p. he spa. *Luke* 20:19
22:18 Jesus p. their wickedness
Mark 2:8 Jesus p. they reasoned
Luke 1:22 p. he had seen vision
5:22 when Jesus p. the thoughts
9:45 saying hid, they p. it not
20:23 but he p. their craftiness
John 6:15 J. p. would make him
Acts 4:13 p. they were unlearned
2:16 Paul p. part were Pharise.
Gal. 2:9 James p. grace giv. me

PERCEIVEST, ETH.
Job 14:21 low, but he p. it not
33:14 G. speaketh, man p. it not
Prov. 14:7 p. not in him knowl.
31:18 p. her merchandi. is good
Luke 6:41 p. not beam in own eye

PERCEIVING.
Mark 12:28 p. he answered well
Luke 9:47 Jesus p. the thought
Acts 14:9 p. he had faith to be

PERDITION.
John 17:12 no. lost but son of p.
Phil. 1:28 to them a token of p.
2 *Thes.* 2:3 be revealed, son of p.
1 *Tim.* 6:9 wh. drown men in p.
Heb. 10:39 who draw back to p.
2 *Pet.* 3:7 and p. of ungodly men
Rev. 17:8 beast goeth into p.
11 beast is eighth, goeth in. p.

PERFECT, Adjective.
Gen. 6:9 N. p. 17:1 be thou p.
Lev. 22:21 freewill-offering be p.
Deut. 18:13 thou shalt be p. with
25:15 have p. weight, p. measu.
1 *Sam.* 14:41 S. said, Give p. lot
2 *Sam.* 22:33 he girdeth me p. w.
Ps. 18:32
1er. 7:12 Ariax. to E. p. pence
Job 1:1 that man was p. 8; 2:3
8:20 G. not cast away a p. man
9:20 I am p. 21 tho' I were p.
22 he destroyeth p. and wicked
22:3 thou makest thy ways p. f
Ps. 37:37 p. man, end is peace
64:4 may shoot in secret at p.
101:2 behave myself in a p. way
6 he that walketh in a p. way
139:22 I hate th. with p. hatred
Prov. 2:21 p. shall remain in it
4:18 path of just shin. to p. day
11:5 righteousn. of p. sh. direct
Is. 26:3 keep him in p. peace
Ezek. 16:14 p. thro' my comelin.
27:3 thou said, I am of p. beauty
11 made thy beauty p. 28:12
28:15 thou wast p. in thy ways
Mat. 5:48 be p. even as Fa. is p.
19:21 if thou wilt be p. go sell
Luke 1:3 hav. had p. understan.
John 17:23 be made p. in one
Acts 3:16 given him p. soundn.
24:2 taught accor. to p. manner
21:22 having more p. knowledge
Rom. 12:2 what is p. will of God
1 *Cor.* 2:6 among th. that are p.
2 *Cor.* 12:9 strength p. in weakn.
13:11 be p. be of good comfort
Col. 3:5 are ye made p. by flesh?
Eph. 4:13 till we come to p. man
Phil. 3:12 not as tho' already p.
15 as many as be p.
Col. 1:28 present every man p.
4:12 stand p. in will of God
1 *Thes.* 3:10 p. which is lacking
2 *Tim.* 3:17 man of G. may be p.
Heb. 2:10 Captain of salvation p.
6:3 being made p. heca. Author
7:19 for law made nothing p.
9:9 not make him did service p.
11 greater and more p. tabern.
10:1 law never make comers p.
11:40 without us not made p.
12:23 spirits of just men made p.
13:21 G. make you in every
Jam. 1:4 let patience have her p.
work, that ye may be p.
17 every p. gift is from above
25 looketh into p. law of liber.
2:22 by works was faith ma. p.
3:2 offend not, same is p. man
1 *Pet.* 5:10 after suffer. make p.
1 *John* 4:17 herein is love made p.
18 no love casteth out fear, he
that feareth is not p. in love

See HEART.

I PERFECT.
Deut. 32:4 his work is p.
2 *Sam.* 22:31 way to p. *Ps.* 18:30
Job 36:1 he that is p. in kn. 37:16
Ps. 19:7 law of L. is p. convert.
Is. 38:3 have I walked in p. w.
42:19 blind us he that is p.
Mat. 5:48 as Father is in heaven
is p.

PER

Luke 6:40 every one that is p.
1 *Cor.* 13:10 that wh. is p. is co.

PERFECT, Verb.
Ps. 138:8 L. will p. wh. concern.

PERFECTED.
2 *Chr.* 8:16 so house of G. was p.
24:13 and work was p. by them
Ezek. 27:4 builders have p. bea.
Mat. 21:16 thou hast p. praise
Luke 13:32 third day I shall be p.
Heb. 10:14 by one offer ho ha. p.
1 *John* 2:5 in him is love of G. p.
4:12 love one ano. his love is p.

PERFECTING.
2 *Cor.* 7:1 p. holin. in fear of G.
Eph. 4:12 for p. of the saints

PERFECTION.
Job 11:7 find Almighty to p. f
15:29 nor shall he prolong p.
28:3 he searcheth out all p.
Ps. 50:2 out of Zion, p. of beauty
119:96 I have seen an end of p.
Is. 47:9 come upon thee in th. p.
Lam. 2:15 men call p. of beauty
Luke 8:14 bring no fruit to p.
2 *Cor.* 13:9 wish. even your p.
Heb. 6:1 let us go on to p.
7:11 if p. were by Levit. priest.

PERFECTLY, NESS.
Jer. 23:20 lat. days consider it p.
Mat. 14:36 touch. made p. whole
Acts 18:26 expound. way of G. p.
23:15 Inq., something more p.
1 *Cor.* 1:10 be p. joined together
Col. 3:14 charity is the bond of p.
1 *Thes.* 5:2 know p. that day of

PERFORMANCE.
Luke 1:45 shall he p. of th. thin.
2 *Cor.* 8:11 p. out of that ye have

PERFORM.
Gen. 26:3 I will p. oath, I sware
to Ab. *Deut.* 9:5; *Luke* 1:72
Ex. 18:18 not able to p. it thys.
Num. 4:23 that enter to p. serv.
Deut. 4:13 commanded you to p.
23:23 gone out of thy lips sh. p.
25:7 nor p. duty of husband's
brother
Ruth 3:13 p. part of kinsman
1 *Sam.* 3:12 I will p. against Eli
2 *Sam.* 14:15 king will p. requ.
1 *K.* 6:12 then I will p. my word
2 *K.* 23:3 to p. the words of this
covenant, 24; 2 *Chr.* 34:31
Est. 5:8 if please king to p. req.
Job 5:12 cannot p. enterprise
Ps. 21:11 a device not able to p.
61:8 that I may daily p. vows
119:106 have sworn, I will p. it
Is. 9:7 zeal of Lord will p. this
19:21 pay a vow to L. and p. it
Jer. 1:12 for I will hasten to p. it
11:5 p. oath which I have sworn
28:6 L. p. words thou hast pro.
29:10 I will p. good word, 33:14
11:25 will verity p. your vows
Ezek. 12:25 word, and will p. it
Mic. 7:20 wilt p. truth to Jacob
Nah. 1:15 keep feasts, p. vows
Mat. 5:33 p. to Lord thine oaths
Is. 10 any spoken, abic also to p.
7:18 how to p. that wh. is good
2 *Cor.* 8:11 now p. the doing of
Phil. 1:6 p. it until day of J. Ch.

PERFORMED.
1 *Sam.* 15:11 S. hath not p. com.
13 I have p. commandm. of L.
1 *K.* 8:20 Lord hath p. his word,
2 *Chr.* 6:10 ; *Neh.* 9:8
Est. 1:15 Vashti not p. comma.
5:6 half of kingdom he p. 7:2
Ps. 65:1 unto thee vo. vow be p.
Is. 10:12 Lord h. p. his w. on Zi.
Jer. 23:20 till p. thoughts, 30:24
31:18 not p. words of covenant
35:14 words of Jonad. are p. 16
51:29 purpose of Lord sh. be p.
Ezek. 37:14 spo. and p. it, saith
Lord
Luke 1:20 these things be p.
2:39 wh. they had p. all things
Rom. 12:28 wh. I have p. all this

PERFORMETH, ING.
Num. 15:3 offering to p. vow, 8
Neb. 5:31 man p. not th. promise
Job 23:14 he p. thing appointed
Ps. 57:2 cry to G. that p. all thi.
Is. 41:26 p. counsel of messeng.

PERFUME, S.
Ex. 30:35 shalt make it a p. 37
Prov. 27:9 p. rejoice the heart
Is. 57:9 didst increase thy p.

PER

PERFUMED.
Prov. 7:17 p. bed with myrrh
Cant. 3:6 who is this cometh p. f

PERGA. *Acts* 13:13 ; 14:25
PERGAMOS. *Rev.* 1:11 ; 2:12

PERHAPS.
Phile. 15 p. he depart. for season

PERIL, S.
Lam. 5:9 get our bread with p.
Rom. 8:35 shall p. separate us?
2 *Cor.* 11:26 p. of waters, of rob.

PERILOUS.
2 *Tim.* 3:1 p. times shall come

PERISH.
Gen. 41:36 p. not thro' famine
Ex. 19:21 and many of them p.
Num. 17:12 die, we p. we all p.
24:20 latter end be that p.
Deut. 11:17 lest ye p. quickly
26:5 ready to p. was my father
28:20 thou p. quick. 22; *Jo.* 23:13
Jud. 5:31 let enemies p. O Lord
1 *Sam.* 26:10 into battle and p.
Est. 3:13 cause to p. all J. 7:4
4:16 if I p. I p. 8:11 p. power
9:28 nor memorial p. fr. th. seed
Job 3:3 let the day p. I was born
4:9 by the blast of God they p.
20 p. for ever, without any
6:18 paths go to nothing and p.
8:13 bless. of hypo. ready to p.
31:19 p. for want of clothing
Ps. 2:12 lest he be angry, ye p.
9:18 expectation of poor not p.
49:10 fool and brutish person p.
12 like beasts that p. 20
68:2 let wicked p. 83:17
80:16 p. at the rebuke of thy
146:4 very day his thoughts p.
Prov. 11:10 wh. wicked p. 28:28
29:18 there is no vision, peo. p.
31:6 drink to him ready to p.
Is. 26:14 those riches p. by evil
Is. 26:14 made th. memory to p.
27:13 which were ready to p.
Jer. 18;18 the law shall not p.
27:10 drive you out, ye p. 15
48:15 remnant in Ashdod p.
Ezek. 25:7 I will cause thee to p.
Dan. 2:18 that D. should not p.
Jon. 1:6 that we p. not. 3:9
14 not p. for this man's life
8:23 L. save us, we p. *Luke* 8:24
9:17 wine runneth out, bot. p.
18:14 one of little ones sho. p.
Mark 4:38 carest th. not we p. f
Luke 13:33 prophet p. out of Je.
15:17 bread eno. I p. wi. hunger
21:18 not a hair of your head p.
John 3:15 whoso belie. not, p. 16
11:50 that whole nation p. not
Acts 8:20 thy money p. with th.
13:41 despisers, wonder and p.
2 *Cor.* 2:15 savor of C. in them p.
4:16 tho' outward man p. inwa.
Col. 2:22 which all are to p.
2 *Thes.* 2:10 unrig. in th. that p.
2 *Pet.* 3:9 not willing any sho. p.

Shall PERISH.
Deut. 4:26 ye s. among heath.
26 ye s. soon utterly p.
8:19 *Mat.* 26:13 ; *Jos.* 23:16
1 *Sam.* 27:1 I s. one day p. by S.
1 *K.* 2:8 whole house of A. s. p.
Job 3:13 by hypocrite's hope s. p.
18:17 rememn. s. p. 20:7 ; 36:12
31:15 all flesh shall p., together
Ps. 1:6 way of ungodly shall p.
2:12 ye shall all likewise p. 5
10:16 heathen s. p. out of his
112:10 desire of wicked shall p.
Prov. 10:28 ex. of wick. s. p. 11:7
19:9 false witness shall p.
21:28 a false witness shall p.
Ec. 29:11 wisd. of wise men s. p.
Is. 41:11 that strive with thee s. p.
50:12 king, not serve thee s. p.
11:23 heart of the king s. p.
10:11 the gods s. p. 15 ; 51:18
28:49 valley also s. p. and pain
Ezek. 7:25 lau. s. p. from priest
25:7 remnant of Phil. s. p. 5
Zec. 1:3 therefore the flight s. p.
3:15 honors of ivory shall p.
Mat. 20:52 s. p. with sword
Luke 5:37 bottles s. p. 12 ; 13:3, 5
John 10:28 the sheep s. never p.
Rom. 2:12 as have s. without law
s. p. also without law
1 *Cor.* 1:18 the crucified s. p.
8:11 weak brother s. p.
2 *Pet.* 2:12 shall utterly p.

PER

PERISHED.
Num. 16:83 they p. fr. congreg.
Jos. 22:20 that man p. not alone
2 *Sam.* 1:27 weapons of war p. f
Job 4:7 who ev. p. being innoc.
30:2 in whom old age was p.
Ps. 9:6 memorial is p. with them
10:16 heathen are p. out of land
119:92 I sho. have p. in afflict.
Ec. 9:6 envy is p. *Jer.* 7:28 truth
Jer. 48:36 riches he hath got. p.
49:7 is counsel p. from prudent
Lam. 3:18 strength and hope p.
Joel 1:11 the harvest of field is p.
Jon. 4:10 which came up and p.
Mic. 4:9 why cry? is couns. p. f
7:2 good man p. out of earth
Mat. 8:32 h. of swine ran and p.
Lu. 11:51 p. bet. altar and temp.
Acts 5:37 he also p. and as many
1 *Cor.* 15:18 fallen asleep in C. p.
Heb. 11:31 harlot Rahab p. not
2 *Pet.* 3:6 overflo. with water, p.
Jude 11 p. in gainsaying of C.

PERISHETH.
Job 4:11 lion p. for lack of prey
Prov. 11:7 hope of unjust men p.
Ec. 7:15 th. is a just man that p.
Is. 57:1 righteous p. and no man
Jer. 9:12 land p. and is burnt up
John 6:27 labor not for meat p.
Jam. 1:11 grace of fashion of it p.
1 *Pet.* 1:7 more prec. than gold p.

PERISHING.
Job 33:18 his life fr. p. by sword

PERIZZITE. *Gen.* 13:7; *Ex.* 33:2; 34:11; *Jos.* 9:1; 11:3
PERIZZITES. *Gen.* 15:20; *Ex.* 3:8, 17; 23:23; *Jud.* 1:5; 3:5; 2 *Chr.* 8:7; *Ezr.* 9:1

PERJURED.
1 *Tim.* 1:10 for liars p. persons

PERMISSION.
1 *Cor.* 7:6 I speak this by p.

PERMIT.
1 *Cor.* 16:7 tarry awhile, if L. p.
Heb. 6:3 this will we do, if G. p.

PERMITTED.
Acts 26:1 thou art p. to speak
1 *Cor.* 14:34 not p. wo. to speak

PERNICIOUS.
2 *Pet.* 2:2 shall fol. their p. ways

PERPETUAL.
Gen. 9:12 cov. for p. generations
Ex. 28:9 priest's office be for p.
31:16 keep sab. for p. covenant
Lev. 3:17 a p. stat. not to eat fat
24:9 be Aaron's by a p. statute
25:34 it is their p. possession
Num. 19:21 a p. statute
Ps. 9:6 destruc. come to p. end
7:13 lift up feet to p. desolation
78:66 put them to a p. reproach
Jer. 5:22 by p. decree, it cannot
8:5 slid. back by p. backsliding?
15:18 why is my pain p. and my
18:16 land desolate, p. hissing
23:40 bring upon you p. shame
25:9 make them p. desolations, 12
49:13 cities thereof be p. wastes
50:5 join Lord in a p. covenant
51:39 may sleep a p. sleep, 57
Ezek. 35:5 hast had a p. hatred
9 I will make thee p. desolat.
46:14 p. ordinance to the Lord
Hab. 3:6 and the p. hills did bow

PERPETUALLY.
1 *K.* 9:3 be there p. 2 *Chr.* 7:16
Amos 1:11 his anger did tear p.

PERPLEXED.
Est. 3:15 city Shushan was p.
Joel 1:18 herds of cattle are p.
Luke 9:7 H. was p. 24:4 they were
2 *Cor.* 4:8 but not in despair

PERPLEXITY.
Is. 22:5 it is a day of p. by Lord
Mic. 7:4 now shall be their p.
Luke 21:25 distress of nation, p.

PERSECUTE.
Job 19:22 why p. me as G.?
28 p. him, seeing root is fo.
Ps. 7:5 nor see p. them thr. p.
10:2 wicked in his pride doth p.
31:15 deli. me from them that p.
33:0 they p. him thou hast sm.
71:11 p. and take him
83:15 so p. them with thy tem.
119:61 hol. me on, bec. I p.
Jer. 17:18 confoun. that p. me

CRUDEN'S CONCORDANCE.

PER

Jer. 20:18 I will *p.* them wt. sw.
Lam. 3:66 *p.* and destroy them
Mal. 5:11 bles. when men *p.* you
 44 pray for them which *p.* you
 10:23 when they *p.* you in one
 23:34 *p.* them from city to city
Luke 11:49 they shall *p.* 21:12
John 5:16 the Jews *p.* Jesus
 15:20 they will also *p.* you
Rom. 12:14 bless them which *p.*

PERSECUTED.
Deut. 30:7 curses on them th. *p.*
Ps. 109:16 because he *p.* the poor
 119:161 princes *p.* me wi. cause
 143:3 enemy hath *p.* my soul
Is. 14:6 ral. nations in anger *p.*
Lam. 3:43 with anger, and *p.* us
Mat. 5:10 blessed which are *p.*
 12 so *p.* they prophets bef. you
John 15:20 if they have *p.* me
Acts 7:52 have not your fath. *p.*
 22:4 I *p.* this way unto death
 26:11 I *p.* them to strange cities
1 *Cor.* 4:12 being *p.* we suffer it
 15:9 I *p.* church of G. *Gal.* 1:13
3 *Cor.* 4:9 we are *p.* not forsaken
Gal. 1:23 *p.* as in times past
 4:29 born after flesh *p.* him
1 *Thes.* 2:15 killed L. and *p.* us
Rev. 12:13 dragon *p.* woman that

PERSECUTEST, ING.
Acts 9:4 Saul, Saul, why *p.* thou
 me? 22:7; 26:14
 5 I am Jesus, whom thon *p.*
 22:8; 26:15
Phil. 3:6 concern. zeal, *p.* church

PERSECUTION.
Lam. 5:5 under *p.* have no rest
Mat. 13:21 wh. *p.* ar. *Mark* 4:17
Acts 8:1 great *p.* against church
 11:19 were scatter. abroad on *p.*
 13:50 and raised *p.* against Pa.
Rom. 8:35 sh. *p.* sep. us fr. C. ?
Gal. 5:11 why do I yet suffer *p.* ?
 6:12 lest they should suffer *p.*
2 *Tim.* 3:12 godly shall suffer *p.*

PERSECUTIONS.
Mark 10:30 have lands with *p.*
2 *Tim.* 12:20 I take pleasure in *p.*
2 *Thes.* 1:4 faith in all your *p.*
2 *Tim.* 3:11 kn. my *p.* at Antioch

PERSECUTOR, S.
Neh. 9:11 their *p.* thou threwest
Ps. 7:13 ordaineth arrows ag. *p.*
 119:157 revenge me of my *p.*
Jer. 15:15 revenge me of my *p.*
 20:11 therof. my *p.* sh. stumble
Lam. 1:3 all her *p.* overtook her
 4:19 *p.* are swifter than eagles
1 *Tim.* 1:13 who was before a *p.*

PERSEVERANCE.
Eph. 6:18 watching with all *p.*

PERSIA.
2 *Chr.* 36:20 reign of king. of P.
Est. 1:3 to power of P. 14, 18
Ezek. 27:10 P. and Lud, 38:5
Dan. 8:20; 10:13, 20; 11:2

PERSIS. *Rom.* 16:12

PERSON.
Lev. 19:15 nor honor *p.* of mighty
Num. 35:30 one witness sh. not
 testify against any *p.*
Deut. 18:26 inn. and clean *p.* eat
 27:25 reward to slay innocent *p.*
 28:50 shall not regard *p.* of old
1 *Sam.* 16:18 David a comely *p.*
 25:35 and have accepted thy *p.*
2 *Sam.* 4:11 have slain a righ. *p.*
 14:14 nei. doth G. respect any *p.*
 17:11 to battle in thine own *p.*
Job 22:29 shall save humble *p.*
Ps. 15:4 a vile *p.* is contemned
 49:10 fool and brutish *p.* perish
 101:4 I will not kn. a wicked *p.*
 105:37 feeble *p.* am. their tribes
Prov. 28:17 to the blood of any *p.*
Is. 32:5 vile *p.* shall be no more
 6 the vile *p.* will speak villany
Jer. 44:6 Johanan took ev. *p.* left
 52:25 took seven near king's *p.*
Ezek. 16:5 to loathing of thy *p.*
 33:6 if the sword take any *p.*
 44:25 priests come at no dead *p.*
Dan. 11:21 sh. stand up. a vi. *p.*
Mat. 22:16 regardest not *p.* of
 men, *Mark* 12:14
 27:24 inno. of blood of this *p.*
1 *Cor.* 5:13 put away wicked *p.*
2 *Cor.* 2:10 forgave I it in *p.* of C.
Heb. 1:3 express image of his *p.*
 12:16 or profane *p.* as Esau
2 *Pet.* 2:5 saved Noah, eighth *p.*

PERSONS.
Gen. 14:21 give me *p.* take goods

PER

Lev. 27:2 *p.* shall be for the L.
Num. 19:18 sh. sprinkle it up. *p.*
Deut. 10:17 regardeth not *p.*
 22 fat. went into Eg. wi. 70 *p.*
Jud. 9:2 sons of J. were 70 *p.*
 5 slew threescore and ten *p.* 18
1 *Sam.* 9:22 wh. were about 30 *p.*
 22:18 Doeg slew eighty-five *p.*
 22 occasion, death of all the *p.*
2 *K.* 10:6 king's sons being 70 *p.*
 7 took king's sons, slew 70 *p.*
Ps. 26:4 ha. not sat with vain *p.*
Prov. 12:11 follow. vain *p.* 28:19
Jer. 52:29 carried from J. 832 *p.*
 30 carried away of Jews 745 *p.*
Ezek. 17:17 to cut off many *p.*
 27:13 traded the *p.* of men
Jon. 4:11 more than 120,000 *p.*
Zep. 3:4 her prophets treach. *p.*
Luke 15:7 ninety-nine just *p.*
Acts 17:17 disp. with devout *p.*
1 *Tim.* 1:10 law made for *p.* of
2 *Pet.* 3:11 what *p.* oug. ye to be
Jude 16 hav. men's *p.* in admir.

See RESPECT.

PERSUADE.
1 *K.* 22:20 who shall *p.* Ahab
 21 I will *p.* him; 22 thou *p.*
2 *Chr.* 32:11 doth not Hezek. *p.*
Is. 36:18 hew. lest Hezc. *p.* yon
Mat. 28:14 we will *p.* him, and
2 *Cor.* 5:11 terrors of L. *p.* men
Gal. 1:10 do I now *p.* men?

PERSUADED.
2 *Chr.* 18:2 Ahab *p.* Jehosaphat
Prov. 25:15 forbea. is a prince *p.*
Mat. 27:20 priests *p.* the multi.
Luke 16:31 will not be *p.* of one
 20:6 be *p.* John was a prophet
Acts 13:43 *p.* them to continue
 14:19 who *p.* the people
 18:4 Paul *p.* Jews and Greeks
 19:26 Paul hath *p.* much people
 21:14 when he would not be *p.*
 26:26 I am *p.* none of th. things
Rom. 4:21 *p.* that what he had
 8:38 I am *p.* that nothing can
 14:5 let every man be fully *p.*
 14 I know and am *p.*
 15:14 I myself also am *p.* of you
2 *Tim.* 1:5 I am *p.* that in thee
 12 I am *p.* he is able to keep
Heb. 6:9 are *p.* bet. things of you
 11:13 hav. seen afar off, were *p.*

PERSUADETH, EST.
2 *K.* 18:39 when Hezekiah *p.* you
Acts 18:13 P. *p.* men to worship
 26:28 almost thou *p.* me to be

PERSUADING.
Acts 19:8 *p.* things concerning
 28:23 *p.* them concerning Jesus

PERSUASION.
Gal. 5:8 *p.* cometh not of him

PERTAIN.
Lev. 7:20 peace-offerings *p.* to L.
1 *Sam.* 25:22 all that *p.* to him
Rom. 12:17 things which *p.* to G.
1 *Cor.* 6:3 things *p.* to this life
2 *Pet.* 1:3 all things that *p.* to life

PERTAINED.
Num. 31:43 half that *p.* to the
Jud. 6:11 under oak that *p.* to J.
1 *Sam.* 25:21 of all that *p.* to N.
2 *Sam.* 2:15 which *p.* to Ish-bos.
 6:12 G. blessed all that *p.* to O
 9:9 given all that *p.* to Saul
 16:4 thine are all that *p.* to M.
1 *K.* 4:8 S. made vessels that *p.*
 7:41 that *p.* to king of E.
1 *Chr.* 9:27 opening ev. morn. *p.*
2 *Chr.* 12:4 took the cities wh. *p.*
 34:33 Josiah took away abo. *p.*

PERTAINETH.
Lev. 14:32 that wh. *p.* to cleans.
Num. 4:16 office of Eleaz. *p.* of
Deut. 22:5 wo. not wear what *p.*
2 *Chr.* 26:16 it *p.* not to Uzziah
Rom. 4:4 to whom *p.* adoption
Heb. 7:13 he *p.* to another tribe

PERTAINING.
1 *Chr.* 26:33 rulers *p.* to God
Acts 1:3 things *p.* to kingd. of G.
1 *Cor.* 6:4 judgm. of thi. *p.* to life
Heb. 2:17 H.-priest in thi. *p.* to G.
 5:1 ordained in things *p.* to G.
 9:9 not perf. as *p.* to conscience

PERVERSE.
Num. 22:32 thy way is *p.* bef. me
Deut. 32:5 they are a *p.* generat.
1 *Sam.* 20:30 son of *p.* woman
Job 6:30 cannot disc. *p.* things?
 9:20 my mouth sh. prove me *p.*
Prov. 4:24 *p.* lips put from thee

PET

Prov. 8:8 noth. fro. or *p.* in them
 12:8 he of a *p.* heart sh. be desp.
 14:2 he that is *p.* despiseth him
 17:20 hath a *p.* tongue falleth
 19:1 he that is *p.* in his lips
 23:33 heart shall utter *p.* things
 28:6 he that is *p.* in his ways
 18 he that is *p.* in ways sh. fall
Is. 19:14 L. mingled a *p.* spirit
Mat. 17:17 O *p.* genera. *Luke* 9:41
Acts 20:30 men arise speaking *p.*
Phil. 2:15 blameless in *p.* nation
1 *Tim.* 6:5 *p.* disputings of men

PERVERSELY.
2 *Sam.* 19:19 what servant did *p.*
1 *K.* 8:47 have sin. and done *p.*
Ps. 119:78 they dealt *p.* with me

PERVERSENESS.
Num. 23:21 neither seen *p.* in Is.
Prov. 11:3 *p.* of trans. shall des.
 15:4 *p.* therein as a breach in
Is. 30:12 ye trust in *p.* and stay
 59:3 your tongues muttered *p.*
Ezek. 9:9 and the ci. is full of *p.*

PERVERT.
Deut. 16:19 a gift doth *p.* words
 24:17 thou shalt not *p.* judgm.
Job 8:3 doth God *p.* judgment or
 34:12 nor will the Al. *p.* judgm.
Prov. 17:23 to *p.* ways of judgm.
 31:5 and *p.* the judgment of any
Mic. 3:9 hear this, ye that *p.* eq.
Acts 13:10 not cease to *p.* right
Gal. 1:7 would *p.* the gos. of C.

PERVERTED.
1 *Sam.* 8:3 Sa.'s sons *p.* judgm.
Job 33:27 have *p.* what was right
Is. 47:10 thy wisdom, it hath *p.*
Jer. 3:21 they have *p.* their way
 23:36 ye have *p.* the words of G.

PERVERTETH.
Ex. 23:8 gift *p.* the righteous
Deut. 27:19 cursed be he that *p.*
Prov. 10:9 he that *p.* his ways
 19:3 foolishness of a man *p.* way
Luke 23:14 man that *p.* people

PERVERTING.
Ex. 5:8 violent *p.* of judgment
Luke 23:2 this fellow *p.* nation

PESTILENCE.
Ex. 5:3 lest he fall on us wi. *p.*
 9:15 I may smite thee with *p.*
 Num. 14:12 will sm. th. with *p.*
Deut. 28:21 L. sh. make *p.* cleave
2 *Sam.* 24:13 3 days' *p.* 1 *Chr.* 21:12
1 *Chr.* 21:14
1 *K.* 8:37 if there be famine, *p.*
 2 *Chr.* 6:28; 7:13; 20:9
Ps. 78:50 gave li. life over to *p.*
 91:3 deli. thee from noisome *p.*
 6 nor *p.* that walketh in dark.
Jer. 14:12 I will consume them
 by *p.* 24:10; 27:8
 21:6 inhabitants shall die by *p.*
 9 abideth in city die by *p.* 38:2
 27:13 why will ye die by *p.* ?
 28:8 prophets of old prop. of *p.*
 29:17 I will send upon th. *p.* 18
 32:24 city is given bec. of *p.* 36
 34:17 liberty for you to the *p.*
 42:17 go to D. shall die by *p.* 22
 44:13 as I punished Jeru. by *p.*
Ezek. 5:12 a third *p.* die with *p.*
 17 *p.* and blood pass thro' thee
 6:11 by sword, famine, and *p.* 12
 7:15 sword without, *p.* within
 12:16 I will leave a few from *p.*
 33:27 be in caves shall die of *p.*
 38:22 I will plead eq. him wi. *p.*
Amos 4:10 I have sent am. you *p.*
Hab. 3:5 before him went *p.* and

PESTILENCES.
Mat. 24:7 shall be *p. Luke* 21:11

PESTILENT.
Acts 24:5 found this man a *p.* fel.

PESTLE.
Prov. 27:22 bray a fool with a *p.*

PETER.
Mat. 14:29 when P. was come
 16:18 I say to thee thou art P.
 23 said to P. get th. *Mark* 8:33
 17:1 taketh P. James and John,
 26:37; *Mark* 5:37; 9:2; 14:33;
 Luke 8:51; 9:28
 24 they rec. tribute, came to P.
 26:58 P. follow. to H. P. *Mark*
 14:54; *Luke* 22:54; *John* 18:15
 75 P. re. *Mark* 14:72; *Lu.* 22:61
 Mark 16:7 disci. and P. *John* 1:44
 John 18:26 our P. cut off, 21:17
 Acts 1:15 in those days P. stood

PHE

Acts 3:3 sec. P. and John, 4:8, 19
 5:15 shadow of P. 8:14; 9:40
 10:13 P. kill and eat, 44; 11:7
 12:3 to take P. also, 6, 7, 11, 18
Gal. 1:18 went to see P. 2:7, 8, 14

Simon PETER.
Mat. 4:18 S. sus saw S. called P.
 10:2 the first S. who is called P.
 16:16 he surnamed P.
Luke 5:8 S. P. fell at Jes. knees
 6:14 Simon whom he named P.
John 13:6 cometh to S. P. 20:2
 21:15 Jesus saith to Simon P.
Acts 10:5 call for one S. whose
 surname is P. 32; 11:13

PETITION, S.
1 *Sam.* 1:17 G. gr. thee thy *p.* 27
1 *K.* 2:16 ask one *p.* deny me not
 20 I desire one small *p.* of thee
2 *K.* 3:6 what is *p.*? 7:6; 9:12
 8 if it please king to grant *p.*
 7:3 let my life be given at my *p.*
Ps. 20:5 Lord fulfil all thy *p.*
Dan. 6:7 whoso. ask *p.* of any, 12
 13 maketh *p.* three times a day
1 *John* 5:15 we have *p.* we desired

PHALEC.
Luke 3:35 Ragan was son of P.

PHARAOH.
Gen. 19:17 the Lord plagued P.
 40:2 P. wroth against, 13, 14
 41:1 P. dream. 4, 7, 16, 84, 55
 Ex. 5:2 P. said. who is the Lo.?
 14:4 will be honored upon P. 17
 1 *K.* 3:1 made affinity with P.
 7:8 Solo. made a house for P.
 2 *K.* 17:7 br. th. out fr. under P.
 18:21 P. to that trust, *Is.* 36:6
 23:33 accor. to command. of P.
 Neh. 9:10 wond. on P. *Ps.* 135:9
 Ps. 136:15 overthrew P. in R. sea
 Is. 19:11 say ye to P. 30:2, 3
 Jer. 46:17 made P. drink, 37:11
 46:17 P. a noise; 47:1 smote G.
 Ezek. 29:2 face ag. P. 3; 30:22
 30:21 break. arm of P. 25; 31:18
 Acts 7:13 kindred known to P. 21
 Rom. 9:17 scripture saith to P.
 Heb. 11:24 to be called son of P.

PHARAOH-HOPHRA. *Jer.*

PHARAOH-NECHO.
2 *K.* 23:29 P.-N. went up, 33-35
Jer. 46:2 word came ag. P.-N.

PHAREZ.
Gen. 38:29 name was called P.
 46:12 sons of Ju. P. 1 *Chr.* 2:4;
 Num. 1:3; *Luke* 3:33; the
 sons of P. *Num.* 20:20, 21;
 Ruth 4:18; 1 *Chr.* 2:5; 9:4
 Ruth 4:12 be like the house of P.

PHARISEE.
Mat. 23:26 thou blind P. cleanse
Luke 11:37 P. beso. him to dine
 18:10 went to pray. one a P.
 Acts 23:6 I am a P. son of a P.
 26:5 after strict. sect I lived a P.
Phil. 3:5 touching the law a P.

PHARISEES.
Mat. 5:20 exceed righteous. of P.
 9:14 why do F. fast? 1 *Mark* 2:18
 34 P. said, He cast. out devils
 15:12 thou P. were offended
 16:6 beware of leaven of the P.
 11; *Mark* 8:15; *Luke* 12:1
 19:3 P. also came to him
 23:2 scribes and P. sit in M. seat
 23 woe to scr. and P. 14, 15, 23,
 25, 27, 29; *Luke* 11:42, 43, 44
Luke 5:30 P. murmured, 15:2
 16:14 scribes and P. watched him
 7:30 P. rejected counsel of God
 11:39 P. make cl. outside of cup
 16:14 P. who were covet. heard
John 1:24 were sent were of P.
 3:1 a man of the P. named Nic.
 7:32 P. sent officers to take him
 48 any P. believed on him?
 11:47 then P. gathered a council
 57 P. had given a commandm.
Acts 15:5 rose certain sect of P.
 23:7 dissension bet. P. and Sad.
 8 no resur. P. but confess both

PHARPAR.
2 *K.* 5:12 Abana and P. better

PHEBE.
Rom. 16:1 I com. unto you P.

PHENICE.
Acts 11:19 travelled as far as P.
 15:3 Paul and Barnabas passed
 through P.
 21:2 and, ship sailing over to P.
 27:12 they might attain to P.

PIE

PHILADELPHIA.
Rev. 1:11 write and send it to P.
3:7 angel of the church in P.

PHILIP.
Mat. 10:3 P. and Barthol. *Mark* 3:18; *Luke* 6:14; *Acts* 1:13
14:3 for his brother P. wife, *Mark* 6:17; *Luke* 3:19
Luke 3:1 his brother P. tetrarch
John 1:43 Jesus findeth P. 44, 45
12:21 the same came to P. 22
14:9 hast thou not kn. me, P. ?
Acts 6:5 P. the deacon, 8:29
8:5 P. preached, 6, 12, 13, 30, 35
21:8 ye enter. into house of P.

PHILIPPI.
Acts 16:12 Neapo. we came to P.
20:6 we sailed away from P.
1 *Thes.* 2:2 shamef. entreat at P.

PHILISTIA.
Ps. 60:8 P. triumph thou
87:4 Behold P. and Tyre, this
108:9 over P. will I triumph

PHILISTIM.
Gen. 10:14 came P. 1 *Chr.* 1:12

PHILISTINE.
1 *Sam.* 17:8 not I a P. 32, 43, 49
21:9 sw. of Goliath the P. 22:10
2 *Sam.* 21:17 Abishai smo. the P

PHILISTINES.
Gen. 21:34 Abraham in P. land
26:14 Isaac had flocks, P. env.
15 P. stopped wells Abrah. 18
Ex. 13:17 led th. not through P.
Ps. 83:7 the P. with the
Is. 2:6 soothsayers like the P.
9:12 before, and the P. behind
11:14 fly on shoulders of the P.
Zep. 2:5 land of P. I will destroy
Zec. 9:6 will cut off pride of P.

PHILOLOGUS.
Rom. 16:15 salute P. Julia, and

PHILOSOPHY.
Col. 2:8 lest any spoil you th. p.

PHILOSOPHERS.
Acts 17:18 cor. p. encounte. him

PHINEHAS.
Ex. 6:25 Eleazer's wife bare P.
Num. 25:11 P. hath turned wra.
Jos. 22:13 Israel sent P. 24:33
Jud. 20:28 P. stood before the
1 *Sam.* 1:3 Hophni and P. the
2:34 Hophni and P. sh. both die
4:17 Hophni and P. are dead, 19
14:3 the son of P. the Lord's
Ezr. 7:5 Abishua son of P. the
8:2 of the sons of P. Gershom, 33
Ps. 106:30 then stood up P.

PHLEGON.
Rom. 16:14 salute Asyncritus, P.

PHRYGIA.
Acts 16:6 had gone throughe. P.
18:23 went over all count. of P.

PHUVAH.
Jud. 7:11 he went down with P.

PHYLACTERIES.
Mat. 23:5 th. make broad th. p.

PHYSICIAN.
Jer. 8:22 is there no p. there?
Mat. 9:13 th. that have no ne, not a p. *Mark* 2:17; *Luke* 5:31
Luke 4:23 proverb, p. heal thys.
Col. 4:14 Luke, the beloved p.

PHYSICIANS.
Gen. 50:2 Joseph com. p. to embalm father; p. embalm. Is.
2 *Chr.* 16:12 Asa sou. not t. b. p.
Job 13:4 ye are all p. of no value
Mark 5:26 suffer many things of p. *Luke* 8:43

PICK.
Prov. 30:17 ravens shall p. It out

PICTURES.
Num. 33:52 shall destroy all p.
Prov. 25:11 apples of gold in p.
Is. 2:16 day of L. on pleasant p.

PIECE.
Gen. 15:10 one p. ag. another
Num. 10:2 trumpets of whole p.
1 *Sam.* 2:36 crouch to him for p.
2 *Sam.* 6:19 to every one a good p. of flesh, 1 *Chr.* 16:3
23:11 p. of grou. full of lentiles
2 *K.* 3:19 mar good p. of land, 25
Job 41:24 hard as p. of millstone
42:11 ev. man gave p. of money
Prov. 6:26 bro. to a p. of bread
28:21 for p. bread man transgr.
Cant. 4:3 tem. p. of pomeg. 6:7
Jer. 37:21 give him daily p. bre.

PIL

Ezek. 24:4 every good p. the thi.
6 bring it out p. by p. let no
Amos 3:12 mouth of lion p. of e.
4:7 one p. was rained on, and p.
Mat. 9:16 no man putt. p. of new cloth, *Mark* 2:21; *Luke* 5:36
17:27 thou sh. find p. of money
Luke 14:18 I bought p. of grou.
15:8 lose one p. doth li. p cand.
24:42 ga. him p. of broiled fish

PIECES.
Gen. 15:17 lamp passed betw. p.
21:10 given bro. 1,000 p. of silv.
33:19 bou. for 100 p. *Jos.* 24:32
37:28 sold Jos. for 20 p. of silver
33 Joseph is rent in p. 44:28
45:22 gave to Benjamin thirty p.
Ex. 22:13 if it be torn in p.
Lev. 2:6 part meat-offering in p.
9:13 presented burnt-of. with p.
Jud. 9:4 gave A. 70 p. of silver
16:5 give thee 1,100 p. of silver
19:29 div. concubine into 12 p.
1 *Sam.* 11:7 S. hewed oxen in p.
15:33 Samuel hewed Agag in p.
K. 11:30 Ahij. rent garm. in p.
19:11 wind brake in p. the rocks
2 *K.* 2:12 Eli. rent clothes in p.
5:5 Nam. took 6,000 p. of gold
6:25 ass's head sold for eigh. p.
18:4 brake in p. brazen serpent
2 *Chr.* 23:17 brake the images in
p. 34:4; *Mic.* 1:7
Job 16:12 brake bones are as p. of brass
Ps. 7:2 reading in p. none deliv.
50:22 be it I tear you in p.
68:30 till ev. one submit with p.
74:14 breakest heads of L. in p.
Cant. 8:11 for fruit bring 1,000 p.
Is. 3:15 beat my people to p. ?
Jer. 5:6 goeth out be torn in p. ?
23:29 hammer break, rock in p.
Lam. 3:11 he hath pull. me in p.
Ezek. 4:14 not est. th. torn in p.
13:19 reliable me for p. of bread
24:4 gather p. thereof into pot
Dan. 2:34 brake image in p. 45
6:24 lions brake in p.
7:7 lion teeth, and bra. in. p. 19
Hos. 8:6 bought her for fifteen p.
Mic. 3:3 chop my people in p.
4:13 sh. beat in p. many people
5:8 as a lion teareth in p.
Nah. 2:12 lion did tear in p.
Zec. 11:12 th. weighed thirty p.
13 cast them to 30 p. *Mat.* 27:6, 9
Luke 15:8 woman having ten p.
19:19 found price 50,000 p.
Mat. 15:37 sh. fo. basket fu. p. *Mark* 8:8
22:44 and some on p. of the ship

See BREAK, BROKEN, CUT, DASH, DASHED.

PIERCE.
Num. 24:8 th. them with arrows
2 *K.* 18:21 hand, p. It. *Is.* 36:6
Luke 2:35 sword sh. p. thro' soul

PIERCED.
Job 30:17 my bones are p.
Ps. 22:16 p. my hands and feet
Zec. 12:10 they sh. look on me wh. they have p. *John* 19:37
John 19:34 one of soldiers p. side
1 *Tim.* 6:10 p. th. with sorrows
Rev. 1:7 they also which p. him

PIERCETH, ING.
Job 40:24 Behemoth's nose p.
Is. 27:1 l. shall punish p. serp.
Heb. 4:12 word of G. quick p.

PIERCINGS.
Prov. 12:18 speaketh like p. of a

PIETY.
1 *Tim.* 5:4 learn to show p.

PIGEON. *See* YOUNG.

PILATE.
Mat. 27:2 they delivered him to Pontius P. 24; *Mark* 15:1
Mark 15:5 so that P. marvel. 44
Luke 3:1 Pon. P. being governor
23:12 same day P. and Her. fd
John 18:33 P. entered lodg. hall
19:8 when P. heard, 12, 19, 38
Acts 3:13 pres. of P. 1 *Tim.* 6:13

PILE.
Is. 30:33 p. of it fire and wood
Ezek. 24:9 make p. for fire great

PIS

PILGRIMS.
Heb. 11:13 we. strangers and p.
1 *Pet.* 2:11 as p. abs. from lusts

PILLAR.
Gen. 10:26 became a p. of salt
28:18 J. set it for p. 24; 35:14
31:13 where thou anointedst p.
51 behold this p. 52 p. witn.
35:20 Jacob set p. on R.'s grave
Ex. 33:9 cloudy p. descended 10
Jud. 9:6 A. king by plain of p.
20:40 flame arose with p.
2 *Sam.* 18:18 Absa. reared up a p.
1 *K.* 7:21 set up right p. left p.
2 *K.* 11:14 the king stood by a p. 23:3; 2 *Chr.* 23:13
Neh. 9:12 led. them by cloudy p.
Ps. 99:7 spake to th. in cloud. p.
Is. 19:19 and a p. at the border
Jer. 1:18 have made thee iron p.
52:21 p. was eighteen cubits
1 *Tim.* 3:15 p. and groun. of truth
Rev. 3:12 overcom. I make a p.

See CLOUD, FIRE.

PILLARS.
Ex. 24:4 M. built alt. and 12 p.
26:32 hang veil upon four p.
27:10 p. thereof brass hooks of p. 11; 38:10, 11, 12, 17
10 p. four; 36:17 sockets for p.
Jud. 16:25 Samson between p.
1 *Sam.* 2:8 p. of earth are Lord's
1 *K.* 7:15 he cast two p. of brass
10:12 made of almug-trees p.
2 *K.* 18:16 Hez. cut gold from p.
25:13 Chaldees brake in pieces p. 16; *Jer.* 52:17, 20
Est. 1:6 fast. to rings and p
Job 9:6 shaketh earth out of pl.
26:11 p. of heaven tremble, 26:11
Ps. 75:3 I hear up the p. of it
Prov. 9:1 hath hewn her sev. p.
Cant. 3:6 com. like p. of smo.
10 make p. thereof of silver
5:15 p. of marble set on gold of
Joel 2:30 I will show p. of smoke
Gal. 2:9 J. and Cephas to be p.
Rev. 10:1 feet were as p. of fire

PILLED.
Gen. 30:37 J. p. whi. strakes, 38

PILLOW, S.
Gen. 28:11 Jac. put stones for p.
18 Jacob took stone his p.
1 *Sam.* 19:13 p. of goat's hair, 16
Ezek. 13:18 woe to women sew. p.
20 behold, I am against. your p.
Mark 4:38 J. was asleep on a p.

PILOTS.
Ezek. 27:8 wise men were thy p.
29 shake at the sound of thy p.

PIN.
Jud. 16:14 Delil. fast. with a p.
Ezek. 15:3 take p. of vine-tree?

PINE, ETH, ING.
Lev. 26:39 shall p. away. in iniq. of their fathers shall they p.
Is. 38:12 cut me off with p.
Lam. 4:9 bleep. p. away, stricken
Ezek. 24:23 p. away for iniqu.
33:10 sins on us, we p. away
Mark 9:18 gnash. teeth, p. away

PINE.
Neh. 8:15 olive and p. branches

PINE-TREE.
Is. 41:19 plant p. *t.* and box
60:13 p.-*t.* and box-trees sh. co.

PINNACLE.
Mat. 4:5 p. of temple, *Luke* 4:9

PINS.
Ex. 27:19 make p. of tabernacle, 35:18; 38:20, 31; 39:40
Num. 3:37 under Merari, p. 4:32

PIPE.
1 *Sam.* 10:5 com. of proph. wi. p.
Is. 1:49 the people played w. p.
Is. 5:12 the p. are in their feasts
30:29 when one goeth with a p.
Ezek. 28:13 workmanship of p.

PIPED.
1 *K.* 1:40 people p. with pipes
1 *Cor.* 14:7 how kno. wh. is p. ?

PIPERS.
Rev. 18:22 voice of p. be. no mo.

PISGAH.
Num. 21:14 Bamoth to top of P.
23:14 up into top of P. 34:1
34:1 under the springs of P.

PIT

PISIDIA.
Acts 13:14 came to Antioch in P.
14:24 had passed throughout P.

PISS.
2 *K.* 18:27 drink own p. *Is.* 36:12

PISSETH. *See* WALL.

PIT, S.
Gen. 14:10 Siddim full of slime p.
37:20 cast him into some p. 21
Ex. 21:34 owner of p. ma. good
Lev. 11:36 a p. wherein is water
Num. 16:30 go down into p. 33
1 *Sam.* 13:6 Israelites hide in p.
2 *Sam.* 17:9 is now hid in so. p.
18:17 cast Absalom in great p.
28:20 s l. lion in p. 1 *Chr.* 11:22
2 *K.* 10:14 Jehu slew them at p.
Job 17:16 go down to bars of p.
33:18 keep. back soul from p. 30
24 deliver him from the p. 28
Ps. 9:15 heathen sunk into p.
28:1 like them that go into p.
30:3 I should not go down to p.
9 what profit in my blood, when I go down to the p. ?
32:7 hid for me their net in p. /
40:2 br. me out of horrible p.
55:23 br. them to p. of destruct.
69:15 let not p. shut her mouth
88:4 counted wi. th. go to p.
6 thou laid me in the lowest p.
119:85 proud digged p. for me
140:10 let th. be cast in. deep p.
143:7 go down to p. *Prov.* 1:12
Prov. 22:14 mouth of wo. deep p.
23:27 strange wo. is narrow p.
28:10 fall himself into own p.
17 he shall flee to the p.
Is. 14:15 brought to sides of p.
19 that go down to stones of p.
24:17 p. and snare are on thee
18 he that cometh out of midst of p. *Jer.* 46:43, 44
22 prisoners are gathered in p.
30:14 water withal out of the p.
51:1 hole, from p. of corruption
38:17 go down to p. cannot hope
57:9 he should not die in the p.
Jer. 2:6 L. led us thro' a. p. of p.
14:3 came to p. found no water
41:7 cast them into midst of p.
9 p. which Asa made for fear
Lam. 4:20 anoi. of L. taken in p.
Ezek. 19:4 he was taken in p. 8
26:20 descend into p. 28:8
31:14, 16; 32:18, 24, 25, 29, 30
32:23 graves set in the side of p.
Zec. 9:11 sent prisoners out of p.
Mat. 12:11 if it fall into a p. on the sabbath, *Luke* 14:5

See BOTTOMLESS, DIG, DIGGED.

PITCH, Substantive.
Gen. 6:14 pitch it within with p.
Ex. 2:3 she daubed it with p.
Is. 34:9 streams be turned to p. and the land bec. burning p.

PITCH, Verb.
Num. 1:52 Is. sh. p. by his camp
3:1 L. shall p. round tabernacle
2:2 ev. man shall p. by standard
Jud. 1:31 search out place to p.
Jos. 4:20 Joshua did p. 12 stones
Is. 13:20 neither sh. Arabian p.
Jer. 6:3 shepherds shall p. tents

PITCHED.
Gen. 12:8 Abram p. his tent, and
12:12 Lot p. his tent toward S.
31:17 I. p. in valley of Gerar, 25
31:25 Jacob p. tent in mount, Laban p. in Gilead
35:21 Israel p. his tent before
Jos. 4:19 Israel p. in Wilderness
Jud. 7:1 Isr. and p. beside well
Heb. 8:2 tabernacle which L. p.

PITCHER, S.
Gen. 24:14 let down p. I pray th.
45 Rebekah came with p. 48
17 ran, 16 empty p. lamps in p.
19 brake p. that were in, 20
Ec. 12:6 or the p. be broken at

972 CRUDEN'S CONCORDANCE.

CRUDEN'S CONCORDANCE. 973

PLA

1 K. 15:14 A. *p.* were not remov.
22:43; 2 K. 12:3; 14:4; 15:4, 35
2 K. 17:20 gods in houses of A. *p.*
18:4 Hezekiah removed A. *p.* 22
23:8 defiled A. *p.* brake A. *p.* 13;
2 Chr. 31:1; 32:12; *Is.* 36:7
20 slew all the priests of A. *p.*
2 Chr. 11:15 ord. priests for A. *p.*
14:3 Asa took away *high p.* 5
15:17 A. *p.* not ta. away, 20:33
17:6 Jehosha. took away A. *p.*
21:11 J. made A. *p.* 28:25 Ahaz
34:3 purge Jerusalem from A. *p.*
Job 23:2 he maketh peace in A. *p.*
Ps. 78:58 provok. him with A. *p.*
Prov. 8:2 stand. on top of A. *p.*
9:14 sitteth on a seat in the A. *p.*
Is. 15:2 he is gone up to A. *p.*
41:18 I will open rivers in A. *p.*
49:9 pastures shall be in A. *p.*
58:14 cause thee to ride on A. *p.*
Jer. 3:2 lift up thine eyes to A. *p.*
21 a voice heard on *high p.*
4:11 dry wind in A. *p.* of wilder.
7:29 take up a lamenta. in A. *p.*
12:12 spoilers come on all A. *p.*
14:6 wild asses did stand in A. *p.*
17:3 I will give thy A. *p.* for sin
26:18 mountain shall become as
A. *p.* of the forest, *Mic.* 3:12
48:35 him that offereth in A. *p.*
Ezek. 6:3 I will destroy your A. *p.*
16:16 deckedst A. *p.* divers colo.
39 shall break down thy A. *p.*
36:2 ancient *high p.* are ours
Hos. 10:8 A. *p.* of Aven destroyed
Amos 4:13 and treadeth upon the
A. *p.* of the earth, *Mic.* 1:3
7:9 A. *p.* of Isaac sh. be desolate
Mic. 1:5 what are A. *p.* of Judah ?
Hab. 3:19 make me walk on A. *p.*
Eph. 6:12 spiritual wick. in A. *p.*
See BUILT.

Waste PLACES.
Is. 5:17 *waste p.* of fat ones
51:3 I. will comfort her *w. p.*
52:9 ye *waste p.* of Jerusalem
58:12 shall build the old *w. p.*

PLAGUE, Substantive.
Ex. 11:1 bri. one *p.* on Pharaoh
12:13 the *p.* shall not be on you
Lev. 13:3 hair in *p.* turned wh. 17
5 if *p.* spr. not in skin, 6, 7, 14, 28
30 if man or wo. ha'h *p.* lest
see *p.* 31, 32, 50, 51, 55; 14:37
44 lepr. man, *p.* is in his head
50 shut up it that hath the *p.*
58 if *p.* be departed from them
14:35 there is as it were a *p.* in
Num. 8:19 he no *p.* among Israel
11:33 L. smote people with a *p.*
16:46 wrath is out, *p.* begun. 47
48 the *p.* was stayed, 50; 25:8
Deut. 28:61 every *p.* not written
Jos. 22:17 although there was *p.*
4 *Sam.* 6:4 one *p.* was on you all
2 *Sam.* 24:21 that the *p.* may be
stayed, 1 *Chr.* 21:22
1 K. 8:38 kn. ev. man *p.* of heart
2 Chr. 21:14 wi. *p.* will I. smite
Ps. 91:10 nor any *p.* come nigh
106:29 the *p.* brake upon them
30 judgm. so the *p.* was stayed
Zec. 14:12 be *p.* L. will smite, 18
Mark 5:29 she was healed of *p.*
34 and be whole of *p.*
Rev. 16:21 blasphemed *p.* of hail

PLAGUE, Verb.
Ps. 89:23 *p.* them that hate him

PLAGUED.
Gen. 12:17 the Lord *p.* Pharaoh
Ex. 32:35 the Lord *p.* the people
Jos. 24:5 and I *p.* Egypt
1 *Chr.* 21:17 that th. should be *p.*
Ps. 73:5 nor are *p.* like oth. men
14 all the day have I been *p.*
Gen. 12:17 L. plagued Ph. wi. *p.*
Ex. 11:1 will send all my *p.*
Lev. 26:21 bring 7 times more *p.*
Deut. 28:59 L. will make thy *p.*
1 *Sam.* 4:8 gods smote Eg. wi. *p.*
Jer. 18:6 leem. of *p.* 49:17; 50:13
Hos. 13:14 I will be thy *p.*
Mark 3:10 as many as had *p.*
Luke 7:21 cured many of their *p.*
Rev. 9:20 rest not killed by the *p.*
11:6 to smite earth with *p.*
18:9 O. hath power over th. *p.*
18:4 that ye recei. not of her *p.*
8 therefo. shall her *p.* come in
22:18 God sh. add to him the *p.*
See SEVEN.

PLAIN, Adjective.
Gen. 25:27 Jacob was a *p.* man

PLA

Ps. 27:11 lead me in a *p.* path
Prov. 8:9 th. are *p.* to him that
15:19 the way of righteous is *p.*
Is. 26:25 he made *p.* the face
40:4 and rough places made *p.*
Jer. 48:21 judgment come on *p.*
Hab. 2:2 make it *p.* upon tables
Mark 7:35 loosed, he spake *p.*

PLAIN, Substantive.
Gen. 11:2 *p.* in land of Shinar
13:10 Lot beheld all the *p.* 11
12 Lot dwelled in cities of *p.*
19:17 nor stay thou in all the *p.*
25 he overthr. cities in the *p.*
Jos. 11:16 Jos. took valley and *p.*
Jud. 9:6 made Ab. king by *p.*
1 *Sam.* 10:3 come to *p.* of Tabor
3 *Sam.* 2:29 Abner walked ther *p.*
15:28 I will tarry in the *p.* until
18:23 Ahimaaz ran by the *p.*
1 K. 7:46 in *p.* of Jord. did king
cast them, 2 Chr. 4:17
2 K. 25:4 went to *p.* Jer. 52:7
Neh. 3:22 after him priests of *p.*
Jer. 17:26 shall come from the *p.*
21:13 against thee, O rock of *p.*
48:8 *p.* shall be destroyed
Ezek. 3:22 go forth in the *p.* 23
8:4 the vision that I saw in *p.*

PLAINS.
Gen. 18:1 L. appeared in the *p.*
Num. 22:1 Is. pitched in *p.* 33:49
26:63 numbered Israel in the *p.*
31:12 spoil to camp in the *p.*
35:1 L. commanded in the *p.*
Deut. 34:1 Mo. went from the *p.*
2 *Sam.* 17:16 lodge not in the *p.*
2 K. 25:5 Chaldees overtook him
in the *p.* *Jer.* 39:5; 52:8
1 *Chr.* 27:28 over trees in low *p.*
2 *Chr.* 9:27 cedar in lower *p.*
26:10 Uzziah had cattle in *p.*

PLAINLY.
Ex. 21:5 if the servant *p.* say
Deut. 27:8 write this law very *p.*
1 *Sam.* 2:27 *p.* appear to house
10:16 told us *p.* that the asses
Ezr. 4:18 let. hath been *p.* read
Is. 32:4 stammerer sh. speak *p.*
John 10:24 if thou be C. tell us *p.*
11:14 Jesus said to them *p.*
16:25 now speakest thou *p.* and
29 now speakest thou *p.* and
Heb. 11:14 such things declare *p.*

PLAINNESS.
2 Cor. 3:12 we use gr. *p.* of speech

PLAITING.
1 Pet. 3:3 let it not be *p.* of hair

PLANES.
Is. 44:13 fitteth image with *p.*

PLANETS.
2 K. 23:5 burnt incen. to sun, *p.*

PLANKS.
1 K. 6:15 covered floor with *p.*
Ezek. 41:25 were thick *p.* on face
26 side of house, and thick *p.*

PLANT, Substantive.
Gen. 2:5 Lord made every *p.*
Job 14:9 bring forth like Ja. *p.*
Is. 5:7 *p.* of his pleasant
17:11 shalt make thy *p.* grow
53:2 shall grow as *p.* out
Jer. 2:21 turned into degener. *p.*
23:29 raise for them a *p.*
Mat. 15:13 every *p.* my Father

PLANTS.
1 *Chr.* 4:23 that dwell among *p.*
Ps. 128:3 thy children like *p.*
144:12 our sons may be as *p.*
Cant. 4:13 thy *p.* are an orchard
16:8 have broken down *p.*
Jer. 48:32 thy *p.* are gone over

PLANT, Verb.
Ex. 15:17 *p.* them in mount of
Deut. 16:21 shalt not *p.*
28:30 thou shalt *p.* a vineyard, 39
2 *Sam.* 7:10 I will *p.* 1 *Chr.* 17:9
1 *K.* 19:29 *p.* vineyards, *Is.* 37:30
Ps. 107:37 thou shalt *p.* plea.
31:10 I will *p.* in wilderness
41:19 I will *p.* in wilderness
51:16 that I may *p.* heavens
65:21 they shall *p.* vineyards
Jer. 1:10 to build and to *p.*
18:9 a kingdom, to build to *p.*
24:6 and not pluck, 42:10
25:5 *p.* gardens, and eat fruit
31:5 shalt *p.* vines on mount.
28 I watch thee to bu. and *p.*
32:41 I will *p.* them in this land
35:7 nor shall you sow, nor *p.*

PLA

Ezek. 17:22 *p.* it on a high, 23
28:26 they shall *p.* vineyards
36:36 I., build and *p.* that
Dan. 11:45 he sh. *p.* tabernacles
Amos 9:14 they sh. *p.* vineyards
15 I will *p.* them upon th. land
Zep. 1:13 they sh. *p.* vineyards

PLANTATION.
Ezek. 17:7 water it by fur. of *p.*

PLANTED.
Gen. 2:8 God *p.* a garden eastw.
9:20 Noah *p.* vine; 21:33 A. *p.*
Num. 24:6 trees which L. hath *p.*
Ps. 1:3 like a tree *p. Jer.* 17:8
80:8 cast out heathen, and *p.*
92:13 those that be *p.* in house
94:9 *p.* ear shall he not hear?
104:16 cedars which he hath *p.*
Ec. 3:2 t *p.* time, 5 t *p.* trees
3:2 pluck up that which is *p.*
Is. 5:2 *p.* it with the choicest
40:24 yea, they shall not be *p.*
Jer. 2:21 I had *p.* thee a noble
11:17 Lord of hosts that *p.* thee
12:2 thou hast *p.* them, they
45:1 what I have *p. I will pluck
Ezek. 17:5 *p.* it in a fruitful, 8
10 being *p.* shall it prosper?
19:10 *p.* by the waters, she was
Amos 9:13 Ephr. is *p.* in a place
5:11 ye have *p.* vineyards
Mat. 15:13 heavenly Fath. not *p.*
21:33 householder *p. Mark* 12:1
Luke 20:9
Luke 17:6 and be thou *p.* in sea
17:28 they sold, they *p.* builded
Rom. 6:5 have been *p.* together
1 Cor. 3:6 have *p.* Apollos water.

PLANTEDST, ETH.
Deut. 6:11 trees which thou *p.*
Prov. 31:16 fruit she *p.* vineyard
Is. 44:14 he *p.* ash, and the rain
1 *Cor.* 3:7 neither is he that *p.*
8 he that *p.* and he that wat.
9:7 who *p.* a vineyard, and eateth

PLANTERS.
Jer. 31:5 *p.* shall plant and eat

PLANTING, S.
Is. 60:21 branch of my *p.*
61:3 called the *p.* of the Lord
Mic. 1:6 make Samaria as *p.*

PLANTS.
Is. 38:21 lay it for a *p.* on boil

PLASTER, ED.
Lev. 14:42 and shall *p.* the house
48 plague, after house was *p.*
Deut. 27:2 *p.* them with *p.* 4
Dan. 5:5 wrote on *p.* of palace

PLAT.
2 K. 9:26 requite thee in this *p.*
cast him into the *p.* of

PLATE.
Ex. 28:36 sh. make a *p.* of pure
39:30 they made the *p.* of holy
Lev. 8:9 on his forefront put *p.*

PLATES.
Ex. 39:3 beat gold into thin *p.*
Num. 16:38 sin. of censers *p.* 39
1 K. 7:30 every base had *p.* of
Jer. 10:9 silver spread into *p.* is

PLATTED.
Mat. 27:29 *p.* crown of thorns,
Mark 15:17; *John* 19:2

PLATTER.
Mat. 23:25 cl. outsi. *Lu.* 11:39

PLAY.
Ex. 32:6 rose to *p.* 1 Cor. 10:7
Deut. 22:21 *p.* whore in fa. house
1 *Sam.* 16:16 that he may *p.* wi.
17 now a man that can *p.* well
2 *Sam.* 2:14 *p.* men arise and *p.*
6:21 therefore will I *p.* bef. L.
10:12 and let us *p.* the men for
40:20 where beasts of field *p.*
Job 41:5 wilt th. *p.* with him as
Ps. 33:3 skilfully with a loud
Ps. 104:26 whom thou made to *p.*
Is. 11:8 sucking child shall *p.*

PLAYED.
Jud. 19:2 concubine *p.* whore
1 *Sam.* 16:23 Da. *p.* with his hand
26:21 I have *p.* fool, and have
2 *Sam.* 6:5 wi. all is. *p.* 1 *Chr.* 13:8
2 K. 3:15 when the minstrel *p.*
See HARLOT.

PLAYER, S.
1 *Sam.* 16:16 who be a cunning *p.*
Ps. 68:25 the *p.* on instruments
87:7 as well the singers as *p.* on

PLE

PLAYETH, ING.
1 *Sam.* 16:18 Jesse, cunning in *p.*
1 *Chr.* 15:29 Da. dancing and *p.*
Ps. 68:25 am. them damsels *p.*
Ezek. 23:44 as to woman that *p.*
Zec. 8:5 boys and girls *p.* in the

PLEA.
Deut. 17:8 hard betw. *p.* and *p.*

PLEAD.
Jud. 6:31 will ye *p.* for Baal?
Job 9:19 shall set me a time to *p.*
13:19 who is he that will *p.* wi.
16:21 O that one might *p.* for a
19:5 if ye will *p.* against me my
23:6 will he *p.* against me pow.
Is. 1:17 judgment. *p.* for widow
3:13 Lord stand up to *p.* and
43:26 let us *p.* together, declare
66:16 by fire will the Lord *p.*
Jer. 2:9 will yet *p.* with you, 35
29 wherof. will ye *p.* with me?
12:1 righteous, when I *p.* with
25:31 Lord will *p.* with all flesh
Ezek. 17:20 I will *p.* with him
35 and will I *p.* with you
38:22 I will *p.* against him with
Hos. 2:2 *p.* with your mother, *p.*
Joel 3:2 and I will *p.* with them
Mic. 6:2 and the Lord will *p.*
See CAUSE.

PLEADED, ETH.
1 *Sam.* 25:39 blessed be L. th. *p.*
Job 16:21 as a man *p.* for neigh.
Is. 51:22 saith thy God that *p.*
59:4 justice, nor any *p.* for tru.
Lam. 3:58 O Lord, thou hast *p.*
Ezek. 20:36 as I *p.* with fathers

PLEADING.
Job 13:6 hearken to the *p.* of my

PLEASANT.
Gen. 2:9 ev. tree grow that is *p.*
3:6 *p.* to the eyes and a tree
49:15 Issachar saw that it was *p.*
2 *Sam.* 1:23 S. and Jon. were *p.*
26 *p.* hast thou been to me
1 K. 20:6 whatever is *p.* they
2 K. 2:19 situation of city is *p.*
Ps. 16:6 lines fallen in *p.* places
106:24 they despised *p.* land
133:1 how *p.* for breth. to dwell
135:3 sing praises, it is *p.* 147:1
Prov. 2:10 knowledge is *p.*
19:9 in loving kind and *p.* toe
5:17 words of the pure are *p.*
9:17 bread eaten in secret is *p.*
16:24 words are honey-comb
22:18 for it is *p.* if thou keep
24:4 chambers filled with all *p.*
Ec. 11:7 *p.* it is for the eye to
Cant. 1:16 thou art fair, yea, *p.*
7:6 how fair and *p.* art thou, O
13 at our gates are all *p.* fruits
Is. 5:7 men of Ju. his *p.* plant
13:22 dragons shall cry in th. *p.*
17:10 shalt thou plant *p.* plants
32:12 they lament for *p.* fields
54:12 thy borders of *p.* stones
64:11 and all our *p.* things are
Jer. 3:19 sh. I give th. a *p.* land?
12:10 made my *p.* portion a des.
23:10 *p.* places of wilderness
25:34 shall fall like *p.* vessel
31:20 Ephr. is he a *p.* child?
Lam. 1:7 remembered all her *p.*
10 spread his hand over her *p.*
11 have given their *p.* things
2:4 slew all that were *p.* to eye
Ezek. 26:12 shall destroy thy *p.*
33:32 song of one that hath *p.*
Hos. 8:9 grant toward al. land
18:8 I ate me *p.* bread
13:29 honour *p.* and *p.* in *p.*
Joel 2:18 Ephr. is in a *p.* place
3:5 ta. my *p.* things into tempi.
Amos 5:11 planted *p.* vineyards
Mic. 2:9 cast out from *p.* houses
Nah. 2:9 gl. out of *p.* furniture
Zec. 7:14 laid *p.* land desolate
Mal. 3:4 offering of Ju. be *p.*

PLEASANTNESS.
Prov. 3:17 her ways are w. of *p.*

PLEASE.
Ex. 21:8 if she *p.* not master
Num. 23:27 peradvent. it will *p.*
2 *Sam.* 7:29 let it *p.* 1 *Chr.* 17:27
Job 6:9 even *p.* G. to destroy me
20:10 his children shall seek to *p.* the poor
Ps. 69:31 this also shall *p.* Lord
Prov. 16:7 man's ways *p.* Lord
Cant. 2:7 love till he *p.* 3:5; 8:1
Is. 2:6 th. themselves in children
55:11 accomplish that which I *p.*
56:4 choose things that *p.* me
John 8:29 I do th. things that *p.*

PLE

Rom. 6:8 they in flesh cannot *p.*
15:1 bear and not *p.* ourselves
2 let every one *p.* his neighbour
Cor. 7:32 car. how he may *p.* L.
33 *p.* his wife; 34 she may *p.*
10:33 even as I *p.* all men
Gal. 1:10 do I seek to *p.* men?
1 *Thes.* 2:15 they *p.* not G.
4:1 ought to walk and to *p.* G.
2 *Tim.* 2:4 that ye may *p.* him
Tit. 2:9 to *p.* them well in all
Heb. 11:6 with. faith impos. *p.* G.

PLEASED.
Gen. 28:8 daugh. of Ca. *p.* not I.
45:16 it *p.* Pharaoh well
Num. 24:1 Balaam saw it *p.* L.
Jud. 13:23 if the Lord were *p.*
14:7 and she *p.* Samson well
1 *Sam.* 12:22 it *p.* L. to make you
18:26 it *p.* D. to be the king's
2 *Sam.* 3:36 what the king did *p.*
19:6 if we had died, it had *p.*
1 *K.* 3:10 Solomon's speech *p.* L.
2 *Chr.* 30:4 thing *p.* the king,
Neh. 2:6; *Est.* 1:21; 2:4
Est. 2:9 the maiden *p.* the king
5:14 the thing *p.* Haman, he
Ps. 40:13 be *p.* O Lord, to deliver
51:19 then shalt thou be *p.* with
1*K.*3 G. hath done whatsoever
he *p.* 135:6; *Jon.* 1:14
Is. 53:10 it *p.* the Lord to bruise
Mic. 6:7 will the Lord be *p.* with
Mal. 1:8 will he be *p.* with thee?
Acts 6:5 saying *p.* the multitude
12:3 bec. Herod saw it *p.* Jews
Rom. 15:3 for even Christ *p.* not
26 for it hath *p.* them of, 27
1 *Cor.* 1:21 it *p.* G. by foolishness
7:12 she *p.* to dwell with him
1:2:18 God set members as it *p.*
15:38 G. giveth it a body as it *p.*
Gal. 1:10 for if I yet *p.* men, I
15 it *p.* God to reveal his Son
Col. 1:19 *p.* Father that in him
Heb. 11:5 had testimony he *p.* G.

Well PLEASED.
Is. 42:21 Lord is *well p.* for his
Mat. 3:17 in whom I am *well p.*
12:18; 17:5; *Mark* 1:11; *Luke*
3:22; 2 *Pet.* 1:17
1 *Cor.* 10:5 God was not *well p.*
Heb. 13:16 such sacri. G. is *w. p.*

Men-PLEASERS.
Eph. 6:6 eye-s. as *m.-p. Col.* 3:22

PLEASETH.
Gen. 16:6 do to her as it *p.* thee
Jud. 14:3 get her for me, she *p.*
Est. 2:4 maiden which *p.* king
Ec. 7:26 whoso *p.* G. sh. escape
8:3 he doeth whatsoever *p.* him

PLEASING.
Est. 8:5 if I be *p.* in his eyes
Hos. 9:4 neither shall they be *p.*
Col. 1:10 worthy of L. to all *p.*
1 *Thes.* 2:4 so we speak, not as *p.*
1 *John* 3:22 do things that are *p.*

Well-PLEASING.
Phil. 4:18 acceptable, *well-p.* to
God
Col. 3:20 for this is *well-p.* to L.
Heb. 13:21 work. what is *well-p.*

PLEASURE.
Gen. 18:12 old, shall I have *p.*?
1 *Chr.* 29:17 I know thou hast *p.*
Ezr. 5:17 let king send his *p.*
Neh. 9:37 dom. over cattle at *p.*
Est. 1:8 drink to every man's *p.*
Job 21:21 what *p.* hath he in he. ?
25 and never eateth with *p.*
22:3 is it any *p.* to Almighty
Ps. 5:4 not a God that hath *p.*
35:27 which hath *p.* in prosper.
51:18 do good in good *p.* to Z.
102:14 servants take *p.* in her
103:21 bless L. ye that do his *p.*
105:22 bind his princes at his *p.*
111:2 sou. out of all that have *p.*
147:10 taketh not *p.* in the legs
11 the Lord taketh *p.* in them
149:4 the Lord taketh *p.* in his
Prov. 21:17 he that loveth *p.*
Ec. 2:1 enjoy *p.* 5; I no *p.* in fools
12:1 say, I have no *p.* in them
Is. 1:11 what purp. of my *p.* turned
44:28 Cyrus shall perform my *p.*
46:10 stand, I will do all my *p.*
48:14 will do his *p.* on Babylon
53:10 and *p.* of the Lord shall
58:3 in day of your fast find *p.*
13 doing thy *p.* not finding *p.*
Jer. 2:24 snuffeth wind at her *p.*
34:16 set at liberty at their *p.*
48:38 a vessel wherein is no *p.*
Ezek. 16:37 wh. thou hast tak. *p.*

PLO

Ezek. 18:23 have I any *p.* that
wicked should die, 32; 33:11
Hos. 8:8 Is. vessel wherein no *p.*
9:4 like and I will take *p.* in it
Mal. 1:10 I have no *p.* in you
Luke 12:32 Father's good *p.* to
Acts 24:27 to do the Jews a *p.*
25:9 Festus to do the Jews a *p.*
Rom. 1:32 but have *p.* in them
2 *Cor.* 12:10 therefore I take *p.* in
Eph. 1:5 according to good *p.* 9
Phil. 2:13 to will and do his *p.*
2 *Thes.* 1:11 fulfil good *p.* of his
2:12 had *p.* in unrighteousness
1 *Tim.* 5:6 that liv. in *p.* is dead
Heb. 10:6 in sac. thou ha. no *p.* 8
38 my soul shall have no *p.* in
12:10 chastened us after own *p.*
Jam. 5:5 ye have lived in *p.* on
2 *Pet.* 2:13 as th. that count it *p.*
Rev. 4:11 for thy *p.* they are and

PLEASURES.
Job 36:11 spend their years in *p.*
Ps. 16:11 at thy right hand *p.*
36:8 drink of the river of thy *p.*
Is. 47:8 thou that art given to *p.*
Luke 8:14 are choked with the *p.*
Tit. 3:3 serv. divers lusts and *p.*
Heb. 11:25 enjoy the *p.* of sin

PLEDGE.
Gen. 38:17 wilt thou give a *p.?*
18 what *p.?* 20 sent to rec. *p.*
Ex. 22:26 take raiment to *p.*
Deut. 24:6 no man take millst. to
p. he taketh a man's life to *p.*
12 shalt not sleep with *p.* 13
17 not take widow's raim. to *p.*
1 *Sam.* 17:18 fare, take their *p.*
Job 22:6 tak. *p.* from thy broth.
24:3 take a widow's ox for a *p.*
9 and they take a *p.* of the poor
Prov. 20:16 take a *p.* of him for
a strange woman, 27:13
Ezek. 18:7 to debtor his *p.* 12, 16
33:15 if wicked restore the *p.* he
Amos 2:8 on clothes laid to *p.* by
2 *K.* 18:23 give *p.* to, *Is.* 36:8

PLEIADES.
Ps. 9:9 wh. maketh Orion and *P.*
33:31 bind the influences of *P.?*

PLENTEOUS.
Gen. 41:34 fifth part in *p.* year
Deut. 28:11 L. make thee *p.* 30:9
2 *Chr.* 1:15 solo. made gold *p.*
Ps. 86:5 art *p.* in mercy, 15
103:8 Lord is merciful, and *p.* in
130:7 with him is *p.* redemption
Is. 30:23 bread shall be fat and *p.*
Hab. 1:16 fat, and their meat *p.*
Mat. 9:37 the harvest truly is *p.*

PLENTEOUSNESS.
Gen. 41:53 seven years *p.* ended
Prov. 21:5 of diligent tend to *p.*

PLENTIFUL.
Ps. 68:9 thou didst send *p.* rain
Is. 16:10 joy is taken out of *p.*
Jer. 2:7 and I brought you to *p.*
48:33 gladness is taken from *p.*

PLENTIFULLY.
Ps. 31:23 *p.* rewardeth the proud
Job 26:3 hast *p.* declared thing
Luke 12:16 ground bro. forth *p.*

PLENTY.
Gen. 27:28 God give thee *p.* of
41:29 seven years of great *p.*
31 *p.* shall not be kno. in land
Lev. 11:36 wherein there is *p.*
2 *Chr.* 31:10 to eat have left *p.*
Job 22:25 shalt have *p.* of silver
37:23 in power and *p.* of justice
Prov. 3:10 barns be filled with *p.*
28:19 he that tilleth shall ha. *p.*
Jer. 44:17 then had we *p.* of vict.
Joel 2:26 sh. eat in *p.* and praise

PLOTTETH.
Ps. 37:12 wicked *p.* against just

PLOUGH.
Luke 9:62 having put hand to *p.*

PLOUGH.
Deut. 22:10 shalt not *p.* with ox
1 *Sam.* 14:14 yoke oxen might *p.*
Job 4:8 they that *p.* iniquity
Prov. 20:4 sluggard will not *p.*
Is. 28:24 doth the ploughman *p.*
Hos. 10:11 Judah sh. *p.* Jacob
Amos 6:12 will one *p.* there with
1 *Cor.* 9:10 he plougheth sho. *p.*

PLOUGHED, ETH.
Jud. 14:18 If ye had not *p.*
Ps. 129:3 ploughers *p.* on back
Jer. 26:18 shall be *p.* *Mic.* 3:12

POL

Hos. 10:13 have *p.* wickedness
1 *Cor.* 9:10 that *p.* sh. pl. in hope

PLOUGHING.
1 *K.* 19:19 Elisha, who was *p.*
Job 1:14 oxen were *p.* and the
Prov. 21:4 the *p.* of the wicked
Luke 17:7 having a servant *p.*

PLOUGHMAN, MEN.
Is. 28:24 doth *p.* plough all day
61:5 sons of alien sh. be your *p.*
Jer. 14:4 the *p.* were ashamed
Amos 9:13 the *p.* shall overtake

PLOUGHSHARES.
Is. 2:4 beat sw. into *p. Mic.* 4:3
Joel 3:10 beat your *p.* into swo.

PLUCK.
Lev. 1:16 shall *p.* away his crop
Num. 33:52 *p.* down their high
2 *Chr.* 7:20 then will I *p.* them up
Job 24:9 they *p.* fatherless from
Ps. 25:15 shall *p.* my feet out
52:5 *p.* thee our of thy place
74:11 thy right hand, *p.* it out
80:12 thou which pass by *p.*
Ec. 3:2 and a time to *p.* up
Jer. 12:14 *p.* the house of Judah
17 utterly *p.* up and destroy
18:7 a kingdom, *p.* it up
22:24 would I *p.* thee thence
24:6 plant, and not *p.* 42:10
31:28 watched over th. to *p.* up
45:4 wh. I planted I will *p.* up
Ezek. 17:9 people, *p.* up by roots
23:34 thou sh. *p.* off thine own
Mic. 3:2 *p.* off the skin from
3:14 I will *p.* up thy groves
Mat. 5:29 if right eye offend thee
p. it out, 18:9; *Mark* 9:47
12:1 beg. to *p.* corn, *Mark* 2:23
John 10:28 nor sh. any *p.* them
29 no man is able to *p.* them

PLUCKED.
Gen. 8:11 was an olive leaf *p.* off
Ex. 4:7 and he *p.* his hand out
Deut. 23:25 shall be *p.* from land
Ruth 4:7 a man *p.* off his shoe
2 *Sam.* 23:21 *p.* the spear out of
Egyptian's hand, 1 *Chr.* 11:23
Ezr. 9:3 *p.* off hair of my head
Neh. 13:25 and *p.* off their hair
Job 29:17 *p.* spoil out of his teeth
Is. 50:6 them that *p.* off hair
Jer. 6:29 wicked are not *p.* away
12:15 after I have *p.* them out
Ezek. 19:12 she was *p.* up in fury
Dan. 7:4 I beh. till wings we. *p.*
8 three of the first horns *p.* up
11:4 his kingdom sh. be *p.* up
Amos 4:11 as a firebrand *p.* out
Zec. 3:2 not this *p.* out of fire ?
Mark 5:4 chains *p.* asunder
Luke 6:1 disciples *p.* ears of corn
17:6 be thou *p.* up by the root
Gal. 4:15 *p.* out your own eyes
Jude 12 twice dead, *p.* up by ro.

PLUCKETH.
Prov. 14:1 the foolish *p.* it down

PLUMB-LINE.
Amos 7:7 L. stood on wall made
by a *p.-l.* wi. *p.-l.* in hand, 8
2 *K.* 21:13 stretch over Jerus. *p.*
Is. 28:17 lay righteousness to *p.*
Zec. 4:10 shall see *p.* in hand

PLUNGE.
Job 9:31 sh. thou *p.* me in ditch

POETS.
Acts 17:28 certain of your own *P.*

POINT, S.
Gen. 25:32 I am at the *p.* to die
Ec. 5:16 in all *p.* as he came
Jer. 17:1 with a *p.* of diamo.
Mark 5:23 daughter at *p.* of death
John 4:47 was at the *p.* of death
Heb. 4:15 was in all *p.* tempted
Jam. 2:10 offend in one *p.* is gu.

POINT.
Num. 34:7 *p.* out for you mount
Job 41:30 sharp *p.* upon mire

POISON.
Deut. 32:24 with *p.* of serpents
33 their wine is *p.* of dragons
Job 6:4 *p.* drinketh up my spirit
20:16 he shall suck *p.* of asps
Ps. 58:4 their *p.* like *p.* of serp.
140:3 adders' *p.* under their lips
Rom. 3:13 *p.* of asps under lips
Jam. 3:8 tongue is evil, full of *p.*

POLE.
Num. 21:9 set on *p.* 9 M. put it

POO

POLICY,
Dan. 8:25 *p.* cause craft to pros.

POLISHED,
Ps. 144:12 *p.* after sim. of palace
Is. 49:2 hath made me *p.* shaft
Dan. 10:6 his feet like to *p.* brass

POLISHING.
Lam. 4:7 their *p.* was of sapph.

POLL, S.
Num. 1:2 every male by their *p.*
18:20, 22; 1 *Chr.* 23:3, 24
Hos. 7:9 stra. hast devo. his str.

POLL, ED.
1 *Sam.* 14:26 *p.* head, ye. end *p.*
Ezek. 44:20 they sh. *p.* th. heads
Mic. 1:16 and *p.* thee for children

POLLUTE.
Num. 18:32 neither *p.* holy thin.
35:33 so shall ye not *p.* the land
Jer. 7:30 in the house to *p.* it
Ezek. 7:21 *p.* my secret place, 22
13:19 will ye *p.* am. my people
20:31 ye *p.* yourselves with your
idols, 32:30; 36:18
39 *p.* holy name no more, 39:7
44:7 in my sanctuary to *p.* it
Dan. 11:31 they sh. *p.* sanctuary

POLLUTED.
Ex. 20:25 lift tool, thou hast *p.*
2 *K.* 23:10 Josiah *p.* the altar
Ps. 106:38 land *p.* with blood
Is. 47:6 I have *p.* mine inherit.
48:11 how sho. my name be *p.*
Jer. 2:23 canst say, I am not *p.*?
3:1 not land be greatly *p.*? 2
34:16 ye turned and *p.* my name
Ezek. 5:11 as I live hast thou *p.*
my sanctuary, *p.* hath been
Ezek. 14:11 they be *p.* with my
16:6 I saw thee *p.* in own bl. 22
20:9 it should not be *p.* 14, 22
13 sabbaths greatly *p.* 16, 21, 24
26 I *p.* them in their own gifts
30 are ye *p.* after your fath. ?
36:17 way *p.* with Babylonians
Hos. 6:8 Gilead a city that is *p.*
9:4 all that eat thereof sh. be *p.*
Amos 7:17 thou sh. die in *p.* land
Mic. 2:10 not rest, because it is *p.*
Zep. 3:1 woe to her that is *p.*
Mal. 1:7 her priests have *p.* sanctuary
1:7 offered *p.* bread on altar
12 say. The ta. of the L. is *p.*
Acts 21:28 hath *p.* this holy place

POLLUTING.
Is. 56:2 keepeth sab. fr. *p.* it, 6

POLLUTION, S.
Ezek. 22:10 that was spart for *p.*
Acts 15:20 that they abs. from *p.*
2 *Pet.* 2:20 after having escap. *p.*

POLLUX. *Acts* 28:11

POMEGRANATE.
Ex. 28:34 gold. bell and *p.* 39:26
1 *Sam.* 14:2 S. tarried under a *p.*
Cant. 4:3 temp. like piece *p.* 6:7
8:2 cause th. to drink juice of *p.*
Joel 1:12 the *p.* trees are wither.
Hag. 2:19 *p.* hath not bro. forth

POMEGRANATES.
Ex. 28:33 make *p.* 30:24, 25
Num. 13:23 they brought of *p.*
20:5 no pla. of seed, vines, or *p.*
Deut. 8:8 into land of *p.* oil-olive
1 *K.* 7:18 chapiters with *p.* 2 *K.*
25:17; 2 *Chr.* 3:16; *Jer.* 52:22
Cant. 4:13 orch. of *p.* with fruits
6:11 see wheth. *p.* budded, 7:12

POMMELS.
2 *Chr.* 4:12 *p.* of the chapiters

POMP.
Is. 5:14 *p.* shall descend to hell
14:11 *p.* is brought to the grave
Ezek. 7:24 make *p.* of strong ce.
30:18 *p.* of strength cease, 32:12
32:12 shall spoil the *p.* of Egypt
Acts 25:23 A. and B. come wi. *p.*

PONDER, ED, ETH.
Prov. 4:26 *p.* the path of thy feet
5:6 lest thou *p.* the path of life
21 the L. *p.* all his goings
21:2 L. *p.* heart; 24:12 he that
Luke 2:19 Mary *p.* them in her
heart

PONDS.
Ps. 7:19 stretch hand on *p.* 8:5
Is. 19:10 purposes, that make *p.*

PONTUS. *Acts* 2:9; 18:2;
1 *Pet.* 1:1

POOL.
2 *Sam.* 2:13 on one side of the *p.*
4:12 they hanged them over *p.*

CRUDEN'S CONCORDANCE. 975

POO

2 K. 18:17 by the conduit of the upper p. *Is.* 7:3; 36:2
Neh. 2:14 I went to the king's p.
Is. 22:9 waters of the lower p.
11 a ditch for wa. of the old p.
35:7 parched ground bec. a p.
41:18 I will make wilderness p.
Nah. 2:8 Nin. of old is like a p.
John 5:3 there is at Jerusal. a p.
7 no man to put me into a p.
9:7 wash in p. of Siloam, 11

POOLS.

Ex. 7:19 stretch thy hand on p.
Ps. 84:6 rain also filleth the p.
Ec. 2:6 I made me p. of water
Is. 14:23 I will make it for p.
42:15 I will dry up p. and herbs

POOR.

Ex. 23:11 p. of thy people eat
30:15 the p. shall not give less
Lev. 14:21 if he be p. and cannot
19:10 shalt leave them for the p.
15 shalt not resp. person of p.
25:25 if brother be p. 35, 39, 47
Deut. 15:4 when there he no p.
11 the p. shall never cease out
Ruth 3:10 young men, p. or rich
1 *Sam.* 2:7 L. make. p. and rich
8 raiseth up the p. *Ps.* 113:7
2 *Sam.* 12:1 one rich, the oth. p.
2 *K.* 25:12 captain of guard left
Jer. 39:10; 40:7; 52:15, 16
Job 5:15 he saveth p. from sword
16 p. hath hope. iniq. stoppeth
20:10 chil. sh. seek to please p.
19 because he oppressed the p.
24:4 p. of earth hide themselves
9 they take a pledge of the p.
14 murderer kill. p. and needy
29:12 because I delivered the p.
32:25 my soul grieved for p. ?
31:16 if I withheld p. fr. desire
19 have seen p. without cover.
34:19 nor reg. rich more than p.
28 they cause cry of p. to come
36:15 deliver p. *Ps.* 72:13
Ps. 9:18 expecta. of p. not perish
10:2 wicked in pride do pers. p.
8 his eyes are set against p.
9 he lieth in wait to catch p.
10 p. may fall by strong ones
14 p. commit, himself to thee
19:5 for the oppression of the p.
14:6 shamed the counsel of p.
35:10 deliverest the p. from him
37:14 bent bow to cast down p.
40:17 but I am p. (69:29); 70:5;
86:1; 109:22
41:1 he that considereth p.
49:2 low and high, rich and p.
68:10 prepared goodness for p.
69:33 L. heareth p. and despis.
72:4 he shall judge p. of people
13 spare the p. 82:3 defend p.
74:21 let the p. praise thy name
88:1 deliver the p. and needy
107:41 yet setteth he p. on high
103:31 stand at right hand of p.
132:15 satisfy her p. with bread
140:12 maintain right of the p.
Prov. 10:4 becometh p. dealeth
15 destruction of p. is poverty
13:7 mak. himself p. hath riches
8 the p. heareth not rebuke
23 much food is in tillage of p.
14:20 p. is hated of neighbor
21 hath mercy on p. happy
31 oppres. p. reproach. Maker
17:5 mock. p. reproach. Maker
18:23 the p. useth entreaties
19:4 p. is separ. from neighbor
7 brethren of p. do hate him
21:13 stoppeth ears at cry of p.
22:2 rich and p. meet together
7 the rich ruleth over the p.
16 he that oppresseth the p.
28:8 for him that will pity p.
11 p. that hath understanding
15 so is wicked ruler over p.
29:7 considereth cause of p. 13
14 king faithfully judgeth p.
30:9 lest I be p. and steal
14 teeth as swords, to devo. p.
31:9 plead the cause of the p.
Ec. 4:14 his kingdom becom. p.
5:8 seest oppression of the p.
what hath the p. that know.
Is. 3:14 the spoil of the p. is in
15 grind the faces of the p. ?
10:2 take the right from the p.
30 to Laish, O p. Anathoth
11:4 with righ. sh. he judge p.
14:30 the first-born of the p.
32 p. of his people shall trust
26:6 feet of the p. shall tread
29:19 even p. among men shall
32:7 destroy the p. with lying

POR

Is. 41:17 the p. and needy seek
58:7 that thou bring the p.
Jer. 2:34 blood of p. innocents
5:4 I said. Surely these are p.
20:13 delivered soul of the p.
22:16 judge the cause of the p.
Ezek. 16:49 strength. hand of p.
18:12 oppressed p. and needy
22:29 they have vexed the p.
Amos 2:6 sold the p. for shoes
7 dust on the head of the p.
4:1 oppress the p. and crush
5:11 your treading is on the p.
12 turn aside the p. in gate
8:4 make p. of the land to fail
6 we may buy p. for silver
Hab. 3:14 rejoicing to devour p.
Zep. 3:12 the p. shall trust in L.
Zec. 7:10 oppress not the p.
11:7 I will feed even you, O p.
11 p. of the flock waited on me
Mat. 5:3 blessed are p. in spirit
11:5 the p. have gospel preach.
26:11 ye have the p. always,
Mark 14:7; *John* 12:8
Mark 12:43 p. widow, *Luke* 21:3
Luke 6:20 blessed be ye p. yours
14:13 call the p. the malmed, 21
John 12:6 not that he car. for p.
Rom. 15:26 make contribu. for p.
2 *Cor.* 6:10 as p. yet making rich
8:9 for your sakes he became p.
Gal. 2:10 should remem. the p.
Jam. 2:3 hath not G. chos. the p.
6 but ye have despised the p.
Rev. 3:17 knowest not th. art p.
13:16 he causeth rich and p. to

Is POOR.

Ex. 22:25 of my peo. that is p.
Deut. 24:14 op. servant that is p.
15 for he is p. and setteth his
Jud. 6:15 my family is p.
Prov. 19:1 better is the p. 28:6
22:22 rob not poor bec. he is p.
Ec. 4:13 better is a p. and wise
Is. 66:2 to him that is p.

POOR man.

Ex. 23:3 nor countenance p. m.
Deut. 15:7 is a p. m. harden not
24:12 if a p. man, sleep not wi.
1 *Sam.* 18:23 seeing I am a p. m.
2 *Sam.* 12:3 p. man had nothing
Ps. 34:6 this p. m. cried, and the
109:16 persecu. p. and needy m.
Prov. 19:22 a p. man is better
21:17 loveth pleas. sh. be a m.
28:3 a p. man that oppresseth
29:13 p. and deceitful m. meet
Ec. 9:15 found in it p. wise man
16 p. man's wisdom is despis.
Jam. 2:2 there come in a p. man

To the POOR.

Lev. 23:22 leave them to the p.
Est. 9:22 sending gifts to the p.
Job 29:16 I was a father to the p.
36:6 he giveth right to the p.
Ps. 112:9 giv. to t. p. 2 *Cor.* 9:9
Prov. 22:9 giveth bread to the p.
28:27 he that giveth to the p.
31:20 stretcheth hand to the p.
Is. 23:4 been a strength to the p.
Dan. 4:27 show. mercy to the p.
Mat. 19:21 gi. to t. p. *Mark* 10:21
Luke 4:18 preach to the p. 7:22
19:8 half of goods I give to t. p.
John 13:29 give somet. to the p.
1 *Cor.* 13:3 my goods to feed t. p.
Jam. 2:5 and rich to the p. Stand

Thy POOR.

Ex. 23:6 wrest judgment of t. p.
Deut. 15:7 hand fr. thy p. brother
11 open thy hand wide to t. p.
Ps. 74:19 forget not thy p. forever

PROCURE, EST.

Lev. 27:8 if he be p. than thy
2 *K.* 24:14 none remained save p.

POPLAR, S.

Gen. 30:37 Jacob took rods of p.
Hos. 4:13 burn incense under p.

POPULOUS.

Deut. 26:5 bec. a nation great, p.
Nah. 3:8 art thou better than p.

PORCH.

Jud. 3:23 Ehud went through p.
1 *Chr.* 28:11 D. gave Sa. patt. p.
2 *Chr.* 29:7 shut doors of the p.
Mat. 26:71 was gone out into p.
Mark 14:68 into the p. the cock
John 10:23 Je. walked in S.'s p.
Acts 3:11 togeth. in Solomon's p.
5:12 with one accord in S.'s p.

POS

PORCHES.

Ezek. 41:15 with temple and p.
John 5:2 Bethesda, having 5. p.

PORCUS.

Acts 24:27 P. Festus came into

PORTER, S.

2 *Sam.* 18:26 watch. called to p.
2 *K.* 7:10 lepers called to the p.
1 *Chr.* 9:17 the p. were Shallum
23:5 four thousand were p.
2 *Chr.* 8:14 p. by their courses
35:15 the p. waited at ev. gate
Ezr. 7:7 p. and Nethinim went
Neh. 7:73 Levites and p. dwelt
Mark 13:34 commanded the p. to
John 10:3 to him the p. openeth

PORTION.

Gen. 14:24 let them take their p.
31:14 is there yet any p. for us?
48:22 given thee p. above breth.
Num. 31:47 It. took one p. of 50
Deut. 21:17 giv. him double p.
32:9 the Lord's p. is his people
33:21 in a p. of the lawgiver
Jos. 17:14 given me but one p.
1 *Sam.* 1:5 to Hannah he gave p.
1 *K.* 12:16 what p. have we in
David? 2 *Chr.* 10:16
2 *K.* 2:9 let a double p. of thy
9:10 eat Jez. in p. of Jez. 36, 37
2 Joram met him in p. of Na.
25 cast him in p. of Na.'s field
2 *Chr.* 28:21 Ahaz took p. out of
31:4 to give p. of the priests, 16
Ezr. 4:16 shalt have no p.
Neh. 2:20 no p. nor right in Jer.
11:23 a certain p. should be
Job 20:29 this is p. of a wicked
21:16 their p. is cursed in earth
26:14 lit. a p. is heard ? 27:13
31:2 what p. of G. is fr. above?
Ps. 11:6 this shall be the p. of
125 L. is the p. of mine Inher.
17:14 who have p. in this life
63:10 shall be a p. for foxes
73:26 God is my p. for ever
119:57 thou art my p. 119:5
Prov. 31:15 giv. a p. to maidens
Ec. 2:10 and this was my p.
21 shall he leave it for his p.
3:22 for that is his p. 5:18; 9:9
5:19 G. given power to take p.
9:9 nor have they any more p.
11:2 give a p. to seven, and also
Is. 17:14 this is the p. of them
17:12 I will divide him a p.
57:6 stones of stream is thy p.
61:7 they sh. rejoice in their p.
Jer. 10:16 the p. of Jacob, 51:19
12:10 they have tro. my p. made
my p. a desolate wilderness
13:25 this is p. of thy measures
52:34 every day a p. until death
Lam. 3:24 the Lord is my p.
Ezek. 45:1 shall offer a holy p. 4
6 the residue of the p. of h.m east
Dan. 1:8 with p. of king's meat
4:15 let his p. be with beasts, 23
11:26 feed of the p. of his meat
Mic. 2:4 changed p. of my people
Hab. 1:16 by them their p. is fat
Zec. 2:12 Lord inherit Ju. his p.
12:10 they have tro. my p. made
my p. a desolate wilderness
13:25 this is p. of thy measures
52:34 every day a p. until death
Mat. 24:51 appoint him his p. w.
Luke 12:42 give them their p.
15:12 father, give me p. of goods

PORTIONS.

Deut. 18:8 they shall have like p.
Jos. 17:5 fell ten p. to Manasseh
1 *Sam.* 1:4 gave her daughters p.
Neh. 8:10 send p. to them, 12
12:44 p. priests; 47 p. of sing.
13:10 p. of Levites not given
Est. 9:19 a day of sending p. 22
Ezek. 47:13 div. sh.'l ha. two p.
48:29 this shall divide. their p.
Hos. 5:7 month shall devo. their p.

PORTRAY, ED.

Ezek. 4:1 p. upon it city Jerusal.
8:10 all the idols of Israel p.
23:14 images of Chaldeans p.

POSSESS.

Gen. 22:17 seed p. gate, 24:60
24 130 and p. the gate of hose
27 next kinsman shall p. it
2 *Chr.* 9:11 cost us out of thy p.
Job 7:3 made p. me of vanity
13:26 mak. me to p. iniquities
Is. 34:11 bittern, p. it; owl p.
17 possess it; dwell gene. to g.
57:13 putteth trust in me, shall p. l.
63:18 people of thy holiness
Ezek. 7:24 they shall p. houses

POS

Ezek. 35:10 be mine, we will p.
36:12 I will cause Is. to p. thee
Dan. 7:18 the saints shall p. the
Hos. 9:6 silver, nettle shall p.
Amos 9:12 they may p. Edom
Ob. 17 house of Jacob shall p.
19 sh. p. Esau, and Benj. p. G.
Hab. 1:6 Chaldeans to p. that is
Zep. 2:9 remnant shall p. them
Zec. 8:12 I will cause rem. to p.
Luke 18:12 give tithe of all I p.
21:19 in patience p. your souls
1 *Thes.* 4:4 know how to p. ves.

POSSESS, with land.

Lev. 20:24 give I. to p. *Nu.* 33:53;
Deut. 3:18; 5:31; 17:14
Num. 14:24 thy seed shall p. it, 1
I will bring them into this l.
Deut. 1:8 go in and p. the land,
4:1; 6:18; 8:1; 9:5, 23; 10:11;
11:31; *Jos.* 1:11
4:5 land whither ye go to p. it,
14, 26; 5:31; 6:1; 7:1; 11:10,
11, 29; 23:20
9:4 Lord brought me to p. th. l.
6 gives not this l. to p. for thy
11:8 be strong, and p. the land
28:21 consum. off l.n. goest to p.
63 plucked off the l. goest to p.
Jos. 23:5 ye shall p. their land
24:8 that ye might p. their land
Jud. 18:9 enter to p. the land
1 *Chr.* 28:8 ye may p. this good l.
Ezr. 9:11 ye go to p. an uncl. l.
Neh. 9:15 they should p. the l.
Is. 14:2 Is. sh. p. them in l. of L.
57:13 put. trust in me, shall p. l.
61:7 their l. sh. they p. double
Ezek. 33:25 shall ye p. t. l.? 26
Amos 2:10 1 bro. you to p. land

POSSESSED.

Num. 21:24 Is. p. Sihon's land
Deut. 30:5 to land thy fathers p.
Jos. 13:1 much land to be p.
21:43 p. it and dw. therein, 22:9
Jud. 3:13 Ez. king of M. p. city
11:21 Is. p. land of Amorites. 22
2 *K.* 17:24 men of Ava p. Sam.
Ps. 139:13 thou hast p. my reins
Prov. 8:22 L. p. me in beginning
Is. 63:18 peo. of holiness hath p.
Jer. 32:15 vineyards shall be p.
23 and they came in and p. it
Dan. 7:22 saints p. the kingdom
Luke 8:36 he that was p. of dev.
Acts 4:32 none sold aught he p.
10:16 a damsel p. with a spirit
1 *Cor.* 1:30 buy as tho' th. p. not
See DEVILS.

POSSESSEST, ETH, ING.

Deut. 26:1 come into land and p.
Num. 36:8 ev. daughter that p.
Luke 12:15 a man's life consists
not in things which he p.
2 *Cor.* 6:10 noth. yet p. all th.

POSSESSION.

Gen. 17:8 I will give land of Can.
for everlasting p. 48:4
26:14 Isaac had p. of flocks
47:11 gave them p. in land of E.
Lev. 14:34 wh. I give to you for p.
25:25 if bro. sold some of his p.
33 the Levites' p. shall go out
45 strangers sh. be your p. 46
27:16 if man sanc. some of his p.
21 return to wh. p. did belong
Num. 24:18 Edom be p. S. be a p.
27:7 give u. a p. among breth.
32:5 given to thy serv. for p.
22 the land shall be your p.
32:5 slayer shall return to his p.
Deut. 2:5 mount Seir to E. for p.
9 not give Moab Ar to Is, for p. 19
11:6 earth swallow. all as th. p.
32:49 which I gave Israel for p.
Jos. 12:6 Moses gave I. for a p.
22:4 get you unto land of your p.
19 if p. be unclean, take you p.
K. 21:15 take p. of vineyard
19 hast thou killed. taken p. ?
2 *Chr.* 20:11 cast us out of thy p.
11:3 Ju. dwelt ev. one of p.
Ps. 2:8 uttermo. parts for thy p.
44:3 got not land by p. by sword
69:35 dwell and have it in p.
83:12 take houses of God in p.
Prov. 28:10 upri. have good in p.
Ezek. 11:15 get you far from L.
25:4 I will deliver thee for p.
36:2 high places are ours to p.
44:28 give them no p. in Israel
45:8 inherit. of his own p.

PRA

Rev. 6:8 *p.* giv. th. over 4th part
7:12 *p.* and might be giv. to G.
9:3 to them was given *p.*
10 their *p.* was to hurt men
19 their *p.* is in their mouth
11:3 give *p.* to my 2 witnesses
6 *p.* to shut heav. *p.* over wat.
12:10 now is *p.* of his Ch. come
13:2 the dragon gave him *p.* 4
5 *p.* was given to continue, 7
12 he exercis. *p.* of first beast
15 *p.* give life; 14:18 *p.* ov. fire
15:8 filled with smoke from *p.*
16:9 *p.* giv. him to scorch men
9 blasphemed G. who hath *p.*
17:12 receive *p.* as kings
13 give their *p.* and strength
19:1 glory, honor, and *p.* to L.
POWER of God.
Mat. 22:29 not know. scriptures
nor *p. of God, Mark* 12:24
Luke 9:43 amazed at *p. of God*
22:69 sit on right of *p. of God*
Acts 8:10 man is great *p. of God*
Rom. 1:16 gospel is the *p. of God*
1 *Cor.* 1:18 saved, it is *p. of God*
24 Christ the *p. of God*
2:5 not stand but by *p. of God*
2 *Cor.* 6:7 of truth, by *p. of God*
13:4 he liveth by *p. of God,* we
eh. live with him by *p. of G.*
2 *Tim.* 1:8 according to *p. of G.*
1 *Pet.* 1:5 by *p. of G.* thro' faith
See GREAT.
In POWER.
Gen. 31:29 in *p.* of my hand
Ex. 15:6 ri. hand glorious in *p.*
Job 31:7 why are wick. mi. in *p.*
37:23 excellent in *p.* and judg.
Prov. 3:27 it is in *p.* of thine
18:21 and life in *p.* of tongue
Is. 40:26 that he is strong in *p.*
Nah. 1:3 slow to anger, *gr.* in *p.*
Luke 1:17 go before him in *p.*
4:14 Jesus returned in *p.* of Sp.
1 *Cor.* 4:20 not in word, but in *p.*
12:43 sown in weakn. rei. in *p.*
Eph. 6:10 strong in Lord and *p.*
1 *Thes.* 1:5 in word and in *p.*
2 *Pet.* 2:11 angels greater in *p.*
My POWER.
Gen. 31:6 wi. all my *p.* I served
Ex. 9:16 to show in thee my *p.*
Deut. 8:17 my *p.* got. me wealth
Dan. 4:30 Babyl. build by my *p.*
Rom. 9:17 I might show my *p.*
1 *Cor.* 9:18 I abuse not my *p.*
No POWER.
Ez. 21:8 he shall have no *p.*
Lev. 26:37 have no *p.* to stand
1 *Sam.* 30:4 had no *p.* to weep
2 *Chr.* 14:11 help them ha. no *p.*
22:9 house of Ahaziah had no *p.*
Is. 50:2 have I no *p.* to deliver?
Dan. 3:27 on bodi. fire had no *p.*
8:7 there was no *p.* in the ram
John 19:11 ha. no *p.* against me
Rom. 13:1 th. is no *p.* but of God
Rev. 20:6 second death hath no *p.*
Thy POWER. ·
Deut. 9:29 brought. out by thy *p.*
Job 1:12 all th. he hath is in *t. p.*
Ps. 21:13 sing, and praise thy *p.*
59:11 scat. by *t. p.*; 16 sing *t. p.*
63:2 to see *t. p.* and thy glory
66:3 through greatness of thy *p.*
71:18 *t. p.* to ev. one is to come
79:11 accord. to greatn. of *t. p.*
110:3 be willing in day of *t. p.*
145:11 they shall talk of thy *p.*
Nah. 2:1 fortify thy *p.* mightily
POWERFUL.
Ps. 29:4 the voice of the L. is *p.*
2 *Cor.* 10:10 for his letters are *p.*
Heb. 4:12 word of G. is quick, *p.*
POWERS.
Mat. 24:29 *p.* of heaven shall be
sh. *Mark* 13:25; *Luke* 21:26
Luke 12:11 when brought bef. *p.*
Rom. 8:38 nor *p.* can separ. fr. G.
13:1 *p.* that be ordained of God
Eph. 3:10 *p.* in heavenly places
6:12 against principalit. and *p.*
Col. 1:16 *p.* were created by him
2:15 hav. spoiled *p.* made show
Tit. 3:1 to be subject to *p.*
Heb. 6:5 tasted *p.* of the world
1 *Pet.* 3:22 right hand of God *p.*
PRACTICES.
2 *Pet.* 2:14 exercised with cov. *p.*
PRACTISE.
Ps. 141:4 not to *p.* wicked works
Is. 32:6 the vile *p. p.* hypocrisy
Dan. 8:24 shall destroy, and *p.*
Mic. 2:1 morning is light they *p.*

PRA

PRACTISED.
1 *Sam.* 23:9 S. secretly *p.* misc.
Dan. 8:12 lit. horn *p.* and prosp.
PRAISE, Substantive.
Deut. 10:21 thy *p.* and thy God
26:19 to make thee high in *p.*
Jud. 5:3 I will sing *p.* to the L.
God of Israel, *Ps.* 7:17; 9:2;
57:7; 61:8; 104:33
1 *Chr.* 16:35 may glory in thy *p.*
2 *Chr.* 23:13 taught to sing *p.*
Neh. 9:5 who is exalted above *p.*
12:46 days of D. we. songs of *p.*
Ps. 9:14 I may show all thy *p.*
22:25 my *p.* shall be of thee
30:12 glory may sing *p.* to thee
33:1 for *p.* is comely for upright
34:1 his *p.* shall be in my mou.
35:28 shall speak of thy *p.*
40:3 *p.* to God, 42:4 voice of *p.*
48:10 thy *p.* to ends of earth
50:23 whoso offereth *p.* glorifie.
51:15 my mouth sh. show thy *p.*
65:1 *p.* waiteth for thee, O God
66:2 and make his *p.* glorious
8 make voice of his *p.* be hea.
71:6 my *p.* shall be continually
8 mouth be filled with thy *p.*
78:13 show thy *p.* 98:4 sing *p.*
100:4 enter his courts with *p.*
102:21 dec. his *p.* in Jerusalem
106:2 who can utter all his *p.*?
12 sang *p.* 47 triumph in *p.*
108:1 I will sing, and give *p.*
109:1 O. of my *p.* 111:10 *p.* end.
119:171 my lips shall utter *p.*
138:1 before gods will I sing *p.*
145:21 mouth sh. speak *p.* of L.
147:1 *p.* is comely; 7 sing *p.* on
148:14 exalteth the *p.* of saints
149:1 sing his *p.* in congregati.
Prov. 27:21 so is man to *p.*
Is. 42:8 not give *p.* to images
10 sing his *p.* from end of ear.
12 declare his *p.* in the islands
43:21 they sh. show forth my *p.*
48:9 and for my *p.* will I refrain
60:18 thou shalt call thy gat. P.
61:3 garment of *p.* for heaviness
11 L. will cause *p.* to spr. forth
62:7 make Jerusa. a *p.* in earth
Jer. 13:11 might be to me a *p.*
17:14 O Lord, thou art my *p.*
26 bring. sacrifices of *p.* 33:11
33:9 shall be to me a joy a *p.*
48:2 shall be no more *p.* of Mo.
51:41 how is *p.* of earth surpr.!
Hab. 3:3 earth was full of his *p.*
Zep. 3:19 get them *p.* and fame
20 make you a *p.* am. all peo.
Mat. 21:16 thou hast perfect. *p.*
Luke 18:43 they saw it, gave *p.*
John 9:21 give G. the *p.*
12:43 *p.* of men more than *p.* G.
Rom. 2:29 whose *p.* is not of m.
13:3 thou shalt have *p.* of the
1 *Cor.* 4:5 ev. man have *p.* of G.
2 *Cor.* 8:18 whose *p.* is in gospel
Eph. 1:6 predestinat. to *p.* of gl.
12 *p.* of gl. who trusted in C. 14
Phil. 1:11 of C. to *p.* and gl. of G.
4:8 if any *p.* think on th. things
Heb. 2:12 in church will I sing *p.*
13:15 let us offer sacrifice of *p.*
1 *Pet.* 1:7 might be found to *p.*
2:14 for *p.* of them that do well
4:11 to whom be *p.* for ever
PRAISE, Verb.
Gen. 49:8 he whom breth, sh. *p.*
Lev. 19:24 fruit holy to *p.* Lord
1 *Chr.* 29:13 thy glorious name
2 *Chr.* 8:14 Lev. to *p.* bef. prie.
20:21 sho. *p.* beauty of holiness
31:2 in *p.* gates of tents of L.
Ps. 21:13 so will we sing and *p.*
22:23 ye that fear Lord *p.* him
shall the dust *p.* thee?
42:5 I shall yet *p.* him, 11 43:5
4:2 in G. we boast, *p.* name
45:17 there. shall people *p.* thee
49:18 men *p.* thee, wh. doest w.
53:19 sh. *p.* thee; 5 mon. *p.*
67:3 let peop. praise th. 5 let. *p.*
68:31 heaven and earth *p.* him
74:14 I will yet *p.* thee more
76:10 wrath of man sh. *p.* thee
88:10 sh. dead arise and *p.* th.
89:5 heavens sh. *p.* thy wonders
102:8 let them *p.* thy great name
107:32 *p.* him in cong. of elders
113:1 *p.* him, O serv. of L. 135:1
117:1 *p.* him, all ye nations
135:3 seven ti. a day I *p.* thee
175 let my soul live, it sh. *p.*
139:2 I will *p.* thy name for thy
4 kings of earth shall *p.* thee

PRA

Ps. 142:7 br. out of pris. that I *p.*
145:4 genera. sh. *p.* thy works
10 thy works shall *p.* thee, O
147:12 *p.* L. Jeru. *p.* G. O Zion
148:1 *p.* ye L. *p.* him in heights
2 *p.* him, angels, *p.* him, host
3 *p.* sun and moon, *p.* ye stars
4 *p.* him, ye heaven of heavens
149:3 let them *p.* his name in dance
150:1 *p.* G. in sancta. *p.* him in
2 *p.* him for his acts, *p.* him
3 *p.* with trump; 4 *p.* timbrel
5 *p.* him on sounding cymbals
Prov. 27:2 let anot. man *p.* thee
28:4 forsake the law *p.* wicked
31:31 let her own works *p.* her
Is. 24:15 grave cannot *p.* thee
19 the living he shall *p.* thee
Jer. 31:7 *p.* ye and say, O Lord
Dan. 2:23 I thank and *p.* thee
4:37 I *p.* and extol K. of heaven
Joel 2:26 *p.* the name of the Lord
Luke 19:37 discl. began to *p.* G.
1 *Cor.* 11:2 *p.* you, that ye reme.
17 in this I *p.* you not, 22
Rev. 19:5 saying, *p.* our God
I will, or will I PRAISE.
Gen. 29:35 Leah said, *I will p.*
Ps. 7:17 *I will p.* the Lord
9:1 *I w. p.* thee, 111:1; 138:1
28:22 in congrega. w. *I p.* thee
28:7 with my song wi. *I p.* him
35:18 *I w. p.* om. much people,
57:9; 108:3; 109:30
43:4 on harp will *I p.* thee, O G.
52:9 *I will p.* thee for ever,
54:6 *I w. p.* thy name, O Lord
56:4 in G. *w. I p.* his word, 10
69:30 *I w. p.* the name of God
71:22 *I w. p.* thee with psaltery
86:12 *I w. p.* thee, O Lord, God
118:19 *I w. p.* into them, *p.* L.
21 *I w. p.* thee, thou heard me
28 thou art my God, *I w. p.* th.
119:7 *I w. p.* thee with upright.
135:1 *I w. p.* L. *I w.* name
145:2 *I w. p.* thy name for ever
Is. 12:1 *I w. p.* thee, though thou
25:1 *I w. p.* thy name
PRAISE ye the Lord, or PRAISE the Lord.
Jud. 5:2 *p.* ye *t. L.* for aven. Isr.
1 *Chr.* 16:25 dally shall he *p. t. L.*
25:3 with a harp to *p. the L.*
2 *Chr.* 20:21 *p. t. L.* for his bea.
Ezr. 3:10 cymbals to *p. t. L.*
Ps. 22:26 sh. *p. t. L.* seek him
32:2 *p. t. L.* with harp
102:18 peo. created shall *p. t. L.*
104:35 *p.* ye the *L.* Mic.1, 48;
105:1; 112:1; 113:1, 9; 115:18;
110:19; 117:2; 135:1; 146:1,
10; 147:20; 149:1, 14; 149:1,
0; 150:1, 6; *Jer.* 20:13
107:8 O that men would *p. t. L.*
15, 21, 31
109:30 I will greatly *p. t. Lord*
116:19 I will *p. t. L.,* 135:3 *p. Lord*
102:2 while I live will *p. t. L.*
117:1 *p.* ye *t. L.* for H is good
12 *p. t. L.* for I lived, praise God
148:7 *p. t. L.* from the earth
12 *p. t. L.* call upon name
62:9 shall eat it, and *p. t. L.*
Jer. 33:11 *p. t. Lord* of hosts
Rom. 15:11 *p. t. L.* all ye Gentil.
PRAISED.
Jud. 16:24 people *p.* Dagon
2 *Sam.* 14:25 none to be so m. *p.*
1 *Chr.* 16:25 L. worthy to be *p.*
Ps. 48:1; 96:4; 145:3
48:1 of the people *p.* the Lord
21:5 four thousand *p.* the Lord
2 *Chr.* 7:3; *Neh.* 5:13
2 *Chr.* 5:13 with instrum. *p.* L.
7:6 David *p.* by their ministry
29:30 Levites and priests *p.* L.
Ezr. 3:11 shouted when th. *p. L.*
Dan. 4:34 I *p.* the most High
5:4 drank, *p.* the gods of gold, 23
Luke 1:64 mouth opened, *p.* G.
PRAISES.
Ex. 15:11 who is like th. in *p.*?
2 *Sam.* 22:50 sing *p.* to thy name,
Ps. 18:49; 92:1; 135:3
2 *Chr.* 29:30 commanded to
sing *p.* to Lord, they sang *p.*
Ps. 9:11 sing *p.* to the Lord 7
Ps. 22:3 O thou that inhabitest *p.*

PRA

Ps. 27:6 yea, I will sing *p.* to G.
47:6; 68:32; 75:9; 108:3
47:7 sing *p.* with understanding
56:12 render *p.* to thee, 144:9
68:4 sing to G. *p.* to his name
78:4 to genera. to come *p.* of L.
146:2 I will sing *p.* to my God
147:1 good to sing *p.* to our G.
148:3 sing *p.* to him with tim.
61 let *p.* of God be in mouths
Is. 60:6 show forth *p.* of the L.
63:7 I will mention *p.* of Lord
Acts 16:25 Paul and Silas sang *p.*
1 *Pet.* 2:9 show forth *p.* of him
PRAISETH.
Prov. 31:28 her husb. also, *p.* her
PRAISING.
2 *Chr.* 5:13 sound heard in *p.* L.
23:12 Athaliah heard people *p.*
Ezr. 3:11 they sang in *p.* Lord
Ps. 84:4 will be still *p.* thee
Luke 2:13 heavenly host *p.* God
20 shepherds returned *p.* God
24:53 contin. in temple *p.* God
Acts 2:47 eat with gladn. *p.* G.
3:8 and leaping, and *p.* God, 9
PRANCING, S.
Jud. 5:22 broken by means of *p.*
Nah. 3:2 the noise of *p.* horses
PRATING.
Prov. 10:8 a *p.* fool shall fall, 10
3 *John* 10 *p.* ag. us with malicio.
PRAY.
Gen. 20:7 he shall *p.* for thee
1 *Sam.* 7:5 S. said, I will *p.* for y.
12:19 *p.* for thy servants to L.
23 I should sin in ceasing to *p.*
2 *Sam.* 7:27 in his heart to *p.*
1 *K.* 8:30 when they *p.* 35, 42, 44,
48; 2 *Chr.* 6:26, 34, 38
Luke 6:12 th. my hand he restored
2 *Chr.* 6:34 *p.* make supplica. 32
37 *p.* in land of their captivity
7:14 if my people shall *p.*
Ezr. 6:10 *p.* for life of the king
Neh. 1:6 hear prayer which I *p.*
Ps. 5:2 in morn. will I *p.*, to him ?
32:6 *p.* to G. he will be favor.
42:8 serv. *Job* shall *p.* for you
Ps. 5:2 my God, to thee will I *p.*
55:17 morn. and noon will I *p.*
122:6 *p.* for peace of Jerusalem
Is. 16:12 come to sanctuary to *p.*
44:20 *p.* to a god cannot save
Jer. 7:16 therefore *p.* not thou
29:7 peace of city, *p.* to Lord
12 go to, me, and I will hearken
37:3 *p.* now to the L. 42:2, 20
42:4 *p.* to the L. your God
Zec. 7:2 sent men to *p.* b. Lord
8:21 speedily *p.* before Lord, 22
Mat. 5:44 *p.* for them which de-
spitefully use, *Luke* 16:27
6:5 for they love to *p.* standing
6 *p.* to Father which is in sec.
9 after this manner *p.* ye
9:38 *p.* L. of harvest, *Luke* 10:2
14:23 he went to a mount. to *p.*
Mark 6:46; *Luke* 6:12; 9:28
19:13 put hands on them and *p.*
26:36 go *p.* yonder, *Mark* 14:32
41 watch and *p.* *Mark* 14:38,
Luke 21:36; 22:40, 46
53 think. thou that I cannot *p.*
Mark 5:17 and they began to *p.*
11:24 what ye desire when ye *p.*
Luke 11:1 Lord, teach us to *p.*
2 he said to them, When ye *p.*
18:1 men ought always to *p.*
10 two men went to tem. to *p.*
John 14:16 I will *p.* Fath. 16:26
17:9 I *p.* for th. *p.* not for world
15 *I p.* not that thou take them
20 nor *p.* I for these alone
Acts 8:22 of G. if perh. thought
24 Simon said, *p.* ye to the L.
10:9 Peter went up house-top to *p.*
Rom. 8:26 kn. not what we *p.* for
1 *Cor.* 11:13 wom. *p.* uncovered ?
14:13 let him *p.* that he interpr.
14 if I *p.* in unknown tongue
15 *p.* with sp. *p.* with underst.
2 *Cor.* 5:20 *p.* you, be rec. to God
13:7 I *p.* to G. that ye do no ev.
Phil. 1:9 this I *p.* that your love
Col. 1:9 we do not cease to *p.*
1 *Thes.* 5:17 *p.* without ceasing
25 brethren, *p.* for us, 2 *Thes.*
3:1; *Heb.* 13:18
2 *Thes.* 1:11 we *p.* always for you
1 *Tim.* 2:8 I will that men *p.*
2 *Tim.* 4:16 *I p.* God it be not l.

CRUDEN'S CONCORDANCE.

PRA

Jam. 5:13 any afflicted? let hi. *p.*
14 and let them *p.* over him
16 confess your faults, and *p.*
1 *John* 5:16 I do not say he sh. *p.*

PRAYED.
Gen. 20:17 Abraham *p.* God
Num. 11:2 Mo. *p.* fire queuched
21:7 M. *p.* for people, *Deut.* 9:26
Deut. 9:20 I *p.* for Aa. same time
1 *Sam.* 1:10 Hannah *p.* to L. 21
27 for this child I *p.* 8:6 Sam.
2 *K.* 4:33 Elisha *p.* L. 6:17, 18
19:15 Hezekiah *p.* before Lord
20:2; 2 *Chr.* 30:18; 32:24
2 *Chr.* 32:20 Isaiah *p.* 33:13 Ma.
Job 42:10 captivity when Job *p.*
Jer. 32:16 Jeremiah *p.* unto L.
Dan. 6:10 D. *p.* 3 ti. a day, 9:4
Jon. 2:1 Jonah *p.* to L. 4:2
Mat. 26:39 Je. fell and *p.* 42:44;
Mark 14:35, 39; *Luke* 22:41
Mark 1:35 solitary place and *p.*
Luke 5:3 Jesus *p.* him he would
16 withdrew into wilde. and *p.*
9:29 as he *p.* countenance altar.
18:11 the Pharisee stood and *p.*
22:32 I *p.* that thy faith fail not
44 agony he *p.* more earnestly
John 4:31 his disciples *p.* him
Acts 1:24 the disciples *p.* and sa.
4:31 when they had *p.* the place
8:15 Peter and John *p.* for them
9:40 Peter *p.* 10:2 Cornel. *p.* 30
10:48 they they *p.* him to tarry
13:3 had fasted and *p.* 14:23
16:9 *p.* him, saying, Come to M.
25 at midnight Paul and S. *p.*
20:36 Paul kneeled down and *p.*
21:5 we kneeled on shore and *p.*
22:17 while I *p.* in the temple
28:8 to whom P. entered and *p.*
Jam. 5:17 E. *p.* it mi. not rain, 18

PRAYER.
2 *Sam.* 7:27 pray this *p.* to thee
1 *K.* 8:28 respect *p.* of thy serv.
45 hear thou in heaven their *p.*
49; 2 *Chr.* 6:35, 39, 40
54 made end of praying this *p.*
2 *K.* 19:4 *p.* for remnant, *Is.* 37:4
2 *Chr.* 7:15 ears be attent to *p.*
20:27 their *p.* came to dwelling
33:18 Manasseh's *p.* how *G.* 19
Neh. 1:6 thou mayest hear the *p.*
4:9 nevertheless we made our *p.*
Job 15:4 yea, thou restrainest *p.*
22:27 shalt make thy *p.* to him
Acts 9:11 beh. he *p.* 11:5 I was *p.*
Ps. 65:2 O thou that hearest *p.*
72:15 *p.* shall be made for him
80:4 how long be angry ag. *p. ?*
102:17 he will regard *p.* of desti.
109:4 but I gave myself unto *p.*
7 and let his *p.* become sin
Prov. 15:8 *p.* of upri. is delight
29 heareth the *p.* of righteous
28:9 his *p.* shall be abomination
Is. 26:16 poured out as *p.*
56:7 joyfully in my house of *p.*
for my house shall be called
a house of *p. Mat.* 21:13;
Mark 11:17; *Luke* 19:46
Jer. 7:16 lift up cry nor *p.* 11:14
Lam. 3:8 *p.* should not pass
Dan. 9:3 set face to L. seek by *p.*
17 God, hear *p.* of thy servant
Hab. 3:1 a *p.* of Ha. the prophet
Mat. 17:21 not out but by *p.* and
fasting, *Mark* 9:29
Luke 1:13 Zacharias, thy *p.* hea.
Acts 3:1 temple at hour of *p.*
6:4 we will give ourselves to *p.*
10:31 Cornelius, thy *p.* is heard
12:5 *p.* made without ceasing
16:13 *p.* was wont be made
1 *Cor.* 7:5 give yourselves to *p.*
2 *Cor.* 1:11 helping by *p.* for us
9:14 by their *p.* for you, which
Eph. 1:18 praying with all *p.*
Phil. 1:4 in every *p.* of mine
19 turn to my salvat. thro' *p.*
4:6 by *p.* let requests be known
1 *Tim.* 4:5 it is sanctified by *p.*
Jam. 5:15 *p.* of faith shall save
16 *p.* of a righteous man avail.
1 *Pet.* 4:7 be sober, watch un. *v.*
See HEARD.

In **PRAYER.**
Neh. 11:17 Mattan. began in *p.*
Dan. 9:21 I was speaking in *p.*
Mat. 21:22 whatso. ye ask in *p.*
Luke 6:12 contin. all night in *p.*
Acts 1:14 they continued in *p.*
Rom. 12:12 contin. instant in *p.*
Col. 4:2 continue in *p.* watch

My **PRAYER.**
Job 16:17 in mine hands; also
my *p.* is pure

PRE

Ps. 4:1 I have mercy, hear my *p.*
17:1; 39:12; 54:2
5:3 in morn. will I direct my *p.*
6:9 the Lord will receive my *p.*
33:13 my *p.* returned to bosom
42:8 my *p.* to God of my life
55:1 give ear unto my *p.* O God
61:1 attend to my *p.* 64:1; 84:8;
86:6; 102:1; 143:1
66:19 attended to voice of my *p.*
20 God hath not turned my *p.*
69:13 my *p.* is to thee
88:2 let my *p.* come before th.
13 in morn. sh. my *p.* prev. th.
141:2 let my *p.* be set bef. thee
5 my *p.* shall be in their calam.
Lam. 3:8 be shutteth out my *p.*
Jon. 2:7 my *p.* came to thee
Rom. 10:1 my *p.* to G. for Is. is

PRAYERS.
Ps. 72:20 *p.* of David are ended
Is. 1:15 when ye make many *p.*
Mat. 23:14 for pretence making
long *p. Mark* 12:40; *Luke*
20:47
Luke 2:37 Anna continued in *p.*
5:33 disciples of John make *p. ?*
Acts 2:42 breaking bread, and *p.*
10:4 thy *p.* are come up bef. G.
Rom. 1:9 I make mention of you
in my *p. Eph.* 1:16; 1 *Thes.*
1:2; 1 *Tim.* 1:3; *Phile.* 4.
15:30 strive with me in your *p.*
Col. 4:12 Epaphras labor. in *p.*
1 *Tim.* 2:1 exh. that *p.* be made
5:5 widow indeed contin. in *p.*
Phile. 22 thro' your *p.* be given
Heb. 5:7 when he had offered *p.*
1 *Pet.* 3:7 that your *p.* be not
12 his ear is open to their *p.*
Rev. 5:8 which are *p.* of saints
8:3 offer it with *p.* of saints, 4

PRAYEST.
Mat. 6:5 when thou *p.* not be

PRAYETH, ING.
1 *Sam.* 1:12 as Hannah contin. *p.*
1 *K.* 8:28 hearken to prayer wh.
thy servant *p.* 2 *Chr.* 6:19, 20
Is. 44:17 he worshippeth it, *p.*
Dan. 6:11 three found Daniel *p.*
9:20 I was speaking, and *p.*
Mark 11:25 when ye stand *p.*
Luke 1:10 people were *p.* with.
3:21 Jes. *p.* the heaven opened
9:18 as he was alone *p.*
11:1 he was *p.* be said, Lord, te.
12:12 many were together *p.*
1 *Cor.* 11:4 every man *p.* with his
14:14 my spirit *p.* but my und.
2 *Cor.* 8:4 *p.* us to rec. the gift
Eph. 6:18 *p.* always in the Spirit
Col. 1:3 *p.* for you; 4:3 *p.* for us
1 *Thes.* 3:10 night and day *p.*
Jude 20 ye *p.* in the Holy Ghost

PREACH.
Neh. 6:7 appoint. prophets to *p.*
Is. 61:1 hath anointed me to *p.*
Jon. 3:2 *p.* to it preaching I bid
Mat. 4:17 fr. that J. s. began to *p.*
10:7 as ye go *p.* saying, The k.
11:1 he departed thence to *p.*
Mark 1:4 John did *p.* baptism
3:14 send fo. forth to *p. Luke* 9:2
Luke 4:18 to *p.* deliverance, 19
9:60 go and *p.* kingdom of God
Acts 5:42 ceased not to *p.* J. C.
16 be commanded to *p.*
5:21 in every city there that *p.*
10:5 forbidden by H. Ghost to *p.*
17:3 Je. whom I *p.* to you is C.
Rom. 10:8 word of faith wh. we *p.*
15 how shall they *p.* exc. sent ?
1 *Cor.* 1:23 we *p.* Christ crucified
9:16 tho' I *p.* the gospel, I have
noth. to glory, woe if I *p.* not
15:11 so we *p.* so ye believed
2 *Cor.* 4:5 we *p.* not ourselves
Gal. 8:8 the gospel which I *p.*
5:11 breth. if I yet *p.* circumci.
Eph. 3:8 I should *p.* am. Gent,
Phil. 1:15 some indeed *p.* Christ
16 one *p.* Christ of contention
Col. 1:28 we *p.* warning every
2 *Tim.* 4:2 *p.* the word, be inst.

PREACHED.
Ps. 40:9 I have *p.* righteousness
Mat. 11:5 poor have the gospel *p.*
Mark 1:7 John *p.* saying, There
2:2 he *p.* the word to them
3:14 with them into synagogues
6:12 *p.* that men should repent
16:20 went and *p.* every where
Luke 3:18 many others thi. *p.* he
16:16 the kingdom of God is *p.*
24:47 remission of sin sho. be *p.*

PRE

Acts 3:20 J. C. who before was *p.*
4:2 *p.* thro' J. the resurrection
8:5 *p.* C. to Samaria; 35 *p.* Jes.
25 *p.* the word of L. *p.* gospel
40 Philip *p.* in all cities till he
9:20 Saul *p.* C. in synagogues
10:37 baptism which John *p.*
13:5 they *p.* the word of God
24 when John had first *p.* bef.
38 *p.* to you forgiveness of sins
42 that th. words might be *p.*
13:36 let us visit wh. we ha. *p.*
17:13 word of G. was *p.* of Paul
18 he *p.* J. and the resurrect.
20:7 Paul *p.* ready to depart
1 *Cor.* 9:27 lest wh. I *p.* to others
15:1 keep in memory what I *p.*
12 if C. be *p.* that he rose
Cor. 1:19 J. who was *p.* am. you
11:4 Jes. whom we have not *p.*
Gal. 1:8 oth. gospel th. we ha. *p.*
Eph. 2:17 and *p.* peace to you
1:18 Christ *p.* and I rejoice
Col. 1:23 was *p.* to every creature
1 *Tim.* 3:1 *p.* unto the Gentiles
Heb. 4:2 word *p.* did not profit
6 they to whom it was first *p.*
1 *Pet.* 3:19 *p.* to spirits in prison
See GOSPEL.

PREACHER.
Ec. 1:1 words of *p.* son of David
12 I the *p.* was king over Isr.
12:9 because *p.* was wise
10 the *p.* sought to find words
Rom. 10:14 hear without a *p.* ?
1 *Tim.* 2:7 ord. a *p.* 2 *Tim.* 1:11
2 *Pet.* 2:5 Noah, *p.* of righteous.

PREACHEST, ETH, ING.
Jon. 3:2 preach to it the *p.* I bid
Mat. 3:1 came John *p. Luke* 3:3
12:41 at *p.* of Jonas, *Luke* 11:32
Luke 8:1 and showing tidings
p. through towns *p.* the gospel
Acts 8:4 went every where *p.*
19 *p.* concern. kingdom of G.
10:36 *p.* peace by Jesus Christ
11:19 *p.* word to none but Jews
19:13 *p.* Jesus, whom Paul *p.*
20:9 as P. was long *p.* Eutychus
25 among wh. I have gone *p.*
28:31 *p.* the kingdom of God
Rom. 2:21 *p.* a man sho. not steal
16:25 according to *p.* of Jesus
1 *Cor.* 1:18 *p.* of cross is foolish.
21 by foolishness of *p.* to save
2:4 my *p.* was not with enticing
15:14 if C. not risen, our *p.* vain
Gal. 2:2 com. to you *p.* goa.
Gal. 1:23 he *p.* faith he destroyed
2 *Tim.* 4:17 by me *p.* might be
Tit. 1:3 manif. his word thro' *p.*

PRECEPT, S.
Neh. 9:14 commandedst them *p.*
Ps. 119:4 com. us to keep thy *p.*
15 I will meditate in thy *p.* 78
27 make me to understand *p.*
40 I have longed after thy *p.*
45 seek *p.* 87 forsook not thy *p.*
56 bec. I kept thy *p.* 100, 168
68 I will keep thy *p.* 69, 134
93 I will never forget thy *p.*
94 have sought thy *p.*
104 thro' thy *p.* I get underst.
110 yet I erred not from thy *p.*
128 thereof, I esteem all thy *p.*
141 yet do not I forget thy *p.*
159 consider how I love thy *p.*
173 I have chosen thy *p.*
Is. 28:10 *p.* upon *p.* *p.* on *p.* 13
29:13 fear taught by *p.* of men
Jer. 33:18 ye kept all Jonad. *p.*
Dan. 9:5 rebelled. dep. fr. thy *p.*
Mark 10:5 he wrote you this *p.*
Heb. 9:19 Moses had spok. ev. *p.*

PRECIOUS.
Gen. 24:53 to R.'s mother *p.* thi.
Deut. 33:13 for *p.* things of heav,
14 for *p.* fruits brought forth
15 for the *p.* things of the hills
16 for *p.* things of the earth
1 *Sam.* 3:1 word of Lord was *p.*
26:21 my soul *p.* in thine eyes
2 *K.* 1:13 let my life be *p.* 14
20:13 Hezekiah shewed them *p.*
things, *Is.* 39:2
2 *Chr.* 20:25 and *p.* jewels, which
Ezr. 1:6 streng. with *p.* things
Job 28:10 seeth every *p.* thing
16 cannot be val. with *p.* onyx
Ps. 49:8 redemption of soul is *p.*
72:14 *p.* sh. their blood in sight
116:15 *p.* in sight of L. is death
133:2 it is like the *p.* ointment

PRE

Ps. 139:17 how *p.* thy thoughts
Prov. 1:13 sh. find *p.* substance
3:15 wis. is more *p.* than rubies
6:26 adulteress hunt for *p.* life
12:27 subst. of a dili. man is *p.*
20:15 lips of knowl. a *p.* jewel
24:4 cham. filled with *p.* riches
Ec. 7:1 a *p.* name bet. th. *p.* oin.
Is. 13:12 man more *p.* than gold
28:16 I lay in Zion a *p.* corner-
stone, 1 *Pet.* 2:6
43:4 thou wast *p.* in my sight
Jer. 15:19 take *p.* from the vile
20:5 I will deliver the *p.* things
Lam. 4:2 the *p.* sons of Zion
Ezek. 22:25 ha. taken *p.* things
27:20 merchant in *p.* clothes
Dan. 11:8 carry away th. *p.* ves.
43 power over all *p.* things
1 *Pet.* 1:7 more *p.* than gold
19 but with *p.* blood of Christ
2:4 stone chosen of God, and *p.*
7 to you which believe he is *p.*
2 *Pet.* 1:1 obtained like *p.* fruit
4 exceed. great and *p.* prom.
Rev. 18:12 no man buyeth *p.* ves.
21:11 light was like a stone, *p.*

PREDESTINATE, ED.
Rom. 8:29 did foreknow, did *p.*
30 wh. he did *p.* them he call.
Eph. 1:5 hav. *p.* us to adoption
11 *p.* according to purpose

PRE-EMINENCE.
Ec. 3:19 man hath no *p.* above
Col. 1:18 that he might have *p.*
3 *John* 9 Diot. loveth to have *p.*

PREFER, ED, ING.
Est. 2:9 *p.* her and her maidens
Ps. 137:6 if I *p.* not J. above joy
Dan. 6:3 Daniel was *p.* ab. prea.
John 1:15 com. after me is *p.* 27
30 who is *p.* before me
Rom. 12:10 in honor *p.* one ano.
1 *Tim.* 5:21 without *p.* one bef.

PREMEDITATE.
Mark 13:11 neither *p.* whatsoev.

PREPARATION, S.
1 *Chr.* 22:5 I will make *p.* for it
Prov. 16:1 *p.* of heart of man
Nah. 2:3 torches in day of *p.*
Mat. 27:62 day that followed the
day of *p. Mark* 15:42; *Luke*
23:54; *John* 19:14, 31, 42
Eph. 6:15 shod with *p.* of gospel

PREPARE.
Ex. 15:2 I will *p.* him a habitat.
Num. 15:5 a drink-offering *p.*
12 seven; to number ye sh. *p.*
23:1 B. said, *p.* me seven oxen
29 build altars, *p.* me seven
Deut. 19:3 shalt *p.* thee a way
Jos. 1:11 your *p.* your victuals
22:26 let us *p.* to build altar
1 *Sam.* 7:3 *p.* your hearts to L.
1 *Chr.* 9:32 to *p.* shewbread
29:18 O L. God *p.* their heart
2 *Chr.* 2:9 *p.* timber in abund.
35:6 sanctify yourselves, and *p.*
Job 8:8 *p.* thyself to the search
11:13 *p.* thy heart toward him
27:16 *p.* raiment; 17 may *p.* it
Ps. 10:17 thou wilt *p.* their heart
59:4 *p.* themselves with. fault
61:7 O *p.* mercy and truth
107:36 that they may *p.* a city
Prov. 24:27 *p.* thy work without
30:25 *p.* their meat in summer
Is. 14:21 *p.* slaugh. for children
21:5 *p.* table, watch in tower
40:3 *p.* ye the way of the Lord,
Mal. 3:1; *Mat.* 3:3; *Mark*
1:2, 3; *Luke* 1:76
20 workmen to *p.* grav. image
57:14 say, Cast ye up, *p.* way
62:10 *p.* ye way of the people
65:11 *p.* a table for that troop
Jer. 6:4 *p.* ye war against her
12:3 *p.* them for day of slaugh.
22:7 I will *p.* destroyers
46:14 say ye, Stand fast and *p.*
51:12 set watchm. *p.* ambushes
Ezek. 4:15 th. shalt *p.* thy bread
38:7 be thou prepared, *p.* for th.
45:17 he shall *p.* sin-offering
46:13 *p.* lamb and meat-offering
Joel 3:9 *p.* war; *Amos* 4:19 *p.* meet
Mic. 3:5 they *p.* war against him
Mat. 11:10 shall *p.* way bef. thee
26:17 where wilt thou th. we *p.*
Mark 14:12; *Luke* 22:9
Luke 3:4 *p.* ye way of L. 7:27
John 14:3 I go to *p.* place, 3

CRUDEN'S CONCORDANCE. 979

PRE

1 *Cor.* 14:8 who shall *p.* to bat, ?
Phile. 22 *p.* me also a lodging
PREPARED.
Gen. 24:31 I *p.* house and room
Ex. 12:39 neither *p.* any victual
23:20 br. thee to place I have *p.*
Num. 23:4 I have *p.* seven altars
2 *Sam.* 15:1 Absalom *p.* chariots
1 *K.* 6:19 the oracle he *p.* in he,
1 *Chr.* 15:1 Da. *p.* a place for ark
of God, 3, 12; 2 *Chr.* 1:4; 3:1
22:3 David *p.* iron in abundance
5 Dav, *p.* abund. bef. 14; 29:2
2 *Cor.* 8:16 work of Solo. was *p.*
12:14 Rehe. *p.* not his heart
19:3 Jehoshaphat *p.* his heart
20:33 peo. had not *p.* th. heart
26:14 Uz. *p.* shields and spears
27:5 Jotham *p.* his ways bef. L.
29:19 vessels A. cast away we *p.*
36 rejoiced G. had *p.* the peo.
31:11 *p.* chamb. in house of L.
35:20 when Josiah had *p.* tem.
Ezr. 7:10 Ezra had *p.* his heart
Neh. 5:18 which was *p.* for me
8:10 them for wh. nothing is *p.*
Est. 5:4 banq. I have *p.* 12; 6:14
6:4 Mordecai on gallows *p.* 7:10
Job 28:27 he *p.* it and searched it
29:7 when I *p.* my seat in street
Ps. 7:13 he *p.* instrum. of death
9:7 hath *p.* his throne for judg.
57:6 they *p.* a net for my steps
68:10 thou hast *p.* good. for poor
74:16 thou hast *p.* light and sun
103:19 the L. hath *p.* his throne
Prov. 8:27 when he *p.* heavens
19:29 judg. are *p.* for scorners
21:31 horse *p.* ag. day of battle
Is. 30:33 Tophet, for king it is *p.*
64:4 neit. eye seen what he *p.*
Ezek. 23:41 a table *p.* before it
28:13 workmanship of pipes *p.*
38:7 he thou *p.* and pre. thyself
Dan. 2:9 ye have *p.* lying words
Hos. 2:8 silver and gold they *p.*
6:3 going forth *p.* as morning
Jon. 1:17 the L. *p.* great fish
4:6 God *p.* a gourd; 7 *p.* worm
8 God *p.* a vehement east wind
Nah. 2:5 the defence shall be *p.*
Zep. 1:7 Lord hath *p.* a sacrifice
Mat. 20:23 it sh. he given to th.
for whom it is *p.* *Mark* 10:40
22:4 I have *p.* my dinner
25:34 kingdom *p.* 41 into fire *p.*
Mark 14:15 a large upp. room *p.*
Luke 1:17 people *p.* for the Lord
2:31 *p.* before face of all people
12:47 knew L.'s will, but *p.* not
23:56 they *p.* spices, 24:1
Rom. 9:23 ves. of mercy afore *p.*
1 *Cor.* 2:9 things God *p.* for them
2 *Tim.* 2:21 *p.* to ev. good work
Heb. 10:5 a body hast thou *p.* me
11:7 Noah *p.* ark to the saving
16 he hath *p.* for them a city
Rev. 8:6 seven angels *p.* to sound
9:7 locusts like hors. *p.* for bat.
15 which were *p.* for an hour
12:6 the woman hath a place *p.*
16:12 kings of east may be *p.*
21:2 holy city *p.* as a bride
PREPAREDST.
Ps. 80:9 thou *p.* room before it
PREPARED, ETH.
Num. 15:8 wh. thou *p.* a bullock
2 *Chr.* 30:19 *p.* heart to seek G.
Job 15:35 their belly *p.* deceit
Ps. 21:5 *p.* a table before me
65:9 thou *p.* them corn for it
147:8 who *p.* rain for the earth
PREPARING.
Neh. 13:7 *p.* him a chamber
1 *Pet.* 3:20 Noah, wh. ark was *p.*
PRESBYTERY.
2 *Tim.* 4:14 laying on hands of *p.*
PRESCRIBED, ING.
Ezr. 7:22 salt without *p.*
Is. 10:1 grievous, they have *p.*
PRESENCE.
Gen. 3:8 hid from *p.* of the Lord
4:16 Cain went from *p.* of Lord
27:30 Jacob was scarce from *p.*
45:3 Joseph's breth. troub. at *p.*
47:15 why shu. we die in thy *p.*
Ex. 10:11 driven from Phar. *p.*
14:1 my *p.* sh. go with thee, 15
23:20 Israel depart. fr. *p.* of M.
Lev. 22:3 shall be cut off fr. my *p.*
Num. 20:6 Moses went from *p.*
1 *Sam.* 18:11 David avoided *p.*
19:10 he slipped out of Saul's *p.*
2 *Sam.* 16:19 in thy father's *p.* so
will I be in thy *p.*

PRE

1 *K.* 12:2 Jer. fled fr. *p.* of Solo.
K. 5:14 regard *p.* of Jehoshap.
5:27 and he went out fr. his *p.*
13:23 nei. cast he them fr. his *p.*
24:20 cast them out from his *p.*
1 *Chr.* 16:27 glory and honor in *p.*
33 shall trees sing at *p.* of G.
2 *Chr.* 9:23 kings sought *p.* of S.
20:9 stand bef. house in thy *p.*
Est. 1:10 been sed in his *p.*
7:6 Haman was afraid at *p.*
Job 1:12 Sa. went fr. *p.* of L. 2:7
23:15 I am troubled at his *p.*
Ps. 9:3 shall perish at thy *p.*
16:11 in thy *p.* fulness of joy
17:2 sentence come from thy *p.*
31:20 hide th. in secret of thy *p.*
31:11 can me not away fr. thy *p.*
68:8 wicked perish at *p.* of G.
8 Sinai moved at the *p.* of G.
95:2 come bef. *p.* with thanks.
97:5 hills melted at the *p.* of G.
100:2 come bef. *p.* with singing
114:7 tremble at *p.* of the Lord
139:7 whither flee from thy *p.*?
140:13 upright sh. dw. in thy *p.*
Prov. 14:7 go fr. *p.* of a fool. man
Is. 1:7 strangers dev. land be. *p.*
19:1 idols of Eg. be moved at *p.*
63:9 angel of his *p.* saved them
64:1 moun. might flow at thy *p.*
Jer. 4:26 cities broken at *p.* of L.
5:22 will ye not tremble at *p.*
23:39 cast out of my *p.* 52:3
Ezek. 38:20 shall shake at my *p.*
Jon. 1:3 Jonah rose to flee fr. *p.*
10 men knew he fled fr. *p.* of L.
Nah. 1:5 earth is burnt at his *p.*
Zep. 1:7 hold peace at *p.* of Lord
Luke 13:26 eat, and drunk in *p.*
Acts 3:19 refreshing come fr. *p.*
5:41 departed from *p.* of council
1 *Chr.* 1:29 no flesh sho. gl. in *p.*
2 *Cor.* 10:1 who in *p.* am base
10 but his bodily *p.* is weak
Phil. 2:12 not as in my *p.* only
1 *Thes.* 2:17 taken from you in *p.*
2 *Thes.* 1:9 destruct. fr. *p.* of L.
Jude 24 faultless before *p.*

In the PRESENCE.
Gen. 16:12 dwell in *t.* *p.* of bret.
23:11 in the *p.* of my people
25:18 Ish. died in *t.* *p.* of breth.
2 *Sam.* 16:19 I not serve in *t.* *p.*
1 *K.* 8:22 Solomon stood in *t.* *p.*
1 *Chr.* 24:31 cast lots in *t.* *p.* of D.
Ps. 23:5 a table in *t.* *p.* of his peo.
116:14 in *t.* *p.* of all his peo. 13
Prov. 17:18 in *t.* *p.* of friend
25:6 put not thyself in *t. p.*
Jer. 28:1 Hanan. spake in *the p.*
Luke 1:19 stand in *t. p.* of God
14:10 worship in *t. p.* of them
15:10 joy in *t. p.* of ang. of G.
John 20:30 signs did J. in *the p.*
Acts 3:13 deni. him in *t. p.* of P.
16 given him soundness in *p.*
27:35 gave thanks to G. in *t. p.*
1 *Thes.* 2:19 are not ye in *t. p.*
Heb. 9:21 appear in *the p.* of G.
Rev. 14:10 in *p.* of ang. in *t.* of L.
PRESENT.
Gen. 32:13 he took a *p.* for E. 18
32:20 receive my *p.* at my hand
43:11 said, Carry the man a *p.*
26 brought him the *p.* in hand
Jud. 3:15 Is. sent a *p.* to Eglon
18 depart not till I bring *p.*
1 *Sam.* 9:7 th. is not *p.* for man
30:26 a *p.* of spoil of enemies
1 *K.* 9:16 for *p.* to his daughter
10:25 bro. ev. man *p.* 2 *Chr.* 9:21
15:19 I have sent thee a *p.*
2 *K.* 8:8 the king said, Take a *p.*
17:4 bro. no *p.* to king of Assyr.
18:31 agreem. by *p.* *Is.* 36:16
20:12 sent a *p.* to Hez. *Is.* 39:1
Is. 16:7 a *p.* brought to the Lord
Ezek. 27:15 brought *p.* horns

PRESENT, Adjective.
1 *Sam.* 13:15 S. numb. people *p.*
2 *Sam.* 20:4 and be thou here *p.*
1 *K.* 20:27 Israel numbered all *p.*
1 *Chr.* 29:17 seen thy people *p.*
2 *Chr.* 34:32 Josiah Israel *p.* at Jerusal.
31:1 Israel *p.* went and all. them
1 *Esd.* 8:25 caused all *p.* to stand to it
Ezr. 8:25 all *p.* help in trouble
Est. 4:16 gather all the Jews *p.*
Ps. 46:1 G. is *p.* help in trouble
Luke 13:1 *p.* power of the L. was *p.*
18:30 rec. more in this *p.* life

PRE

John 14:25 I have spok. being *p.*
Acts 10:33 are we all *p.* bef. God
21:18 all the elders were *p.*
Rom. 7:18 to will is *p.* with me
21 do good, evil is *p.* with me
8:18 sufferings of this *p.* time
38 nor things *p.* able to separ.
11:5 even at this *p.* time
1 *Cor.* 3:22 things *p.* or to come
4:11 to this *p.* hour we thirst
5:3 *p.* in spirit, as tho' I were *p.*
7:26 this is good for *p.* distress
15:6 greater part rem. to this *p.*
2 *Cor.* 5:8 willing to be *p.* wi. L.
9 that whether *p.* or absent
10:2 I may not be bold when *p.*
11:9 when I was *p.* with you
13:2 if I were *p.* second time
10 I write, bei. being *p.*
Gal. 1:4 deliver us fr. *p.* world
4:18 not only when I am *p.*
20 I desire to be *p.* with you
1 *Tim.* 4:10 hav. loved *p.* world
Tit. 2:12 live godly in *p.* world
Heb. 9:9 figure for time then *p.*
12:11 no chastening for the *p.*
2 *Pet.* 1:12 establish. in *p.* truth

PRESENT, ED.
Gen. 46:29 Jos. *p.* himself to fa.
47:2 *p.* 5 brethren to Pharaoh
Ex. 34:2 and *p.* thyself there
Lev. 2:8 when it is *p.* to priest
9:12 Aaron's sons *p.* blood, 18
14:11 priest shall *p.* the man
16:10 the scapegoat shall be *p.*
27:8 bef. priest shall *p.* himself
Num. 3:6 and *p.* the tribe of Le.
Deut. 31:14 *p.* yours. before tab.
32:44 *p.* themselves bef. God
Jud. 6:19 Gid. brought and *p.* it
20:2 tribes of Is. *p.* themselves
1 *Sam.* 10:19 *p.* yourselves be. L.
17:16 Goliath the Phil. *p.* hims.
Job 1:6 sons of G. ca. to *p.* them.
2:1 Satan came to *p.* himself
Jer. 36:7 will *p.* their supplicat.
38:26 I *p.* supplication bef. king
42:9 ye sent to *p.* your supplic.
Ezek. 20:28 they *p.* provocation
Dan. 9:18 we do not *p.* supplica.
Mat. 2:11 they *p.* to him gifts
Luke 2:22 to *p.* him to the Lord
Acts 9:41 cull. saints, *p.* her alive
23:33 *p.* Paul before him
2 *Cor.* 4:14 raise by Jesus, *p.* us
11:2 that I may *p.* you to Christ
Eph. 5:27 might *p.* it to himself
Col. 1:22 *p.* you holy unblamable
28 ev. may *p.* ev. man perfect
Jude 24 him that is able to *p.* y.
2 *Cor.* 11:8 every *p.* above measure
Phil. 3:11 I *p.* toward the mark
PRESENTING.
Dan. 9:20 *p.* my supplica. be. L.
PRESENTLY.
1 *Sam.* 2:16 not fa. to burn fat *p.*
Prov. 12:16 fool's wrath *p.* kno.
Mat. 21:19 *p.* fig-tree withered
26:53 *p.* give more than 12 legi.
Phil. 2:23 him I hope to send *p.*
PRESENTS.
1 *Sam.* 10:27 brought him no *p.*
1 *K.* 4:21 they brought *p.* and
2 *K.* 17:3 Hos. gave Shalman. *p.*
Ps. 68:29 kings shall bring *p.*
72:10 and the isles shall bri. *p.*
76:11 let all bring *p.* to him
Mic. 1:14 give *p.* to Moreshethg.
PRESERVE.
Gen. 19:32 we were *p.* seed, 34
45:5 send me before you to *p.*
7 G. sent to *p.* you a posterity
Deut. 6:24 he might *p.* us alive
Ps. 12:7 thou shalt *p.* them O L.
16:1 *p.* me, O G. in thee I trust
25:21 let uprightness *p.* me
32:7 shalt *p.* me from trouble
40:11 let thy lovingkind. *p.* me
41:2 L. will *p.* and keep alive
2 prayer truth without *p.* him
64:1 hear me, *p.* my life fr. fear
79:11 *p.* th. those tb. are to die
86:2 *p.* my soul, for I am holy
121:7 L. *p.* thee, he sh. *p.* soul
8 Lord shall *p.* thy going out
140:1 *p.* fr. vio. man, 4
Prov. 2:11 discretion shall *p.* th.
4:6 forsake her not, shall *p.* th.
11:3 lips of wise shall *p.* them
22:28 mercy and truth *p.* king
Is. 31:5 he will *p.* Jerusalem
49:8 I will *p.* thee and gi. thee
Jer. 49:11 child. I will *p.* alive
Luke 17:33 will *p.* to life king
PRESERVED, ETH.
Gen. 32:30 God and my life is *p.*

PRE

Jos. 24:17 and *p.* us in the way
1 *Sam.* 30:23 Lord who hath *p.*
2 *Sam.* 8:6 L., *p.* D. 1 *Ch.* 18:6, 13
Job 10:12 visitation *p.* my spirit
20:2 in days when God *p.* me
36:6 he *p.* not the life of wicked
Ps. 31:23 the Lord *p.* the faithful
37:28 his saints are *p.* forever
97:10 he *p.* the soul of his saints
116:6 the Lord *p.* the simple
145:20 L. *p.* them that love him
146:9 the Lord *p.* the strangers
Prov. 2:8 he *p.* way of his saints
16:17 keep. his way *p.* his soul
Is. 49:6 to restore the *p.* of Israel
Hos. 12:13 by a proph. was he *p.*
Am. 4:17 both are *p.* *Luke* 5:38
1 *Thes.* 5:23 *p.* soul, and body
Jude 1 sanctified, and *p.* in J. C.
PRESERVER.
Job 7:20 O thou P. of men?
PRESERVEST.
Neh. 9:6 L. made and *p.* them all
Ps. 36:6 O L. *p.* man and beast
PRESIDENTS.
Dan. 6:2 over three *p.* Dan. first
3 Daniel was prefer. above *p.*
6 *p.* and princes assembled, 7
PRESS.
Mark 2:4 could not come nigh
for the *p.* *Luke* 8:19
5:27 came in the *p.* behind him
30 Jesus turn. about in the *p.*
Luke 19:3 Zacch. not so J. for *p.*
PRESS, ES.
Prov. 3:10 *p.* burst with wine
Is. 16:10 tread no wine in th. *p.*
Joel 3:13 for the *p.* is full
Hag. 2:16 fifty vessels out of *p.*
See WINE.
PRESS-FAT.
Hag. 2:16 came to *p.* to draw
PRESS, ED, ETH.
Gen. 19:3 Lot *p.* on two angels
9 they *p.* sore on Lot, near do.
40:11 I took grapes and *p.* them
Jud. 16:16 Delilah *p.* wi. words
1 *Sam.* 13:25 Absalom *p.* him, 27
Est. 8:14 posts *p.* on by com.
Ps. 38:2 thy hand *p.* me sore
Ezek. 23:3 their breasts *p.* bruis.
Amos 2:13 I am *p.* as a cart is *p.*
Mark 3:10 *p.* on to touch him
Luke 5:1 as the people *p.* to hear
6:38 good measure *p.* down
8:45 multit. throng and *p.* thee
16:16 every man *p.* into it
Acts 18:5 Paul was *p.* in spirit
2 *Cor.* 1:8 were *p.* above measure
Phil. 3:14 I *p.* toward the mark
PRESUME, ED.
Deut. 18:20 prophet who shall *p.*
Ecc. 7:5 is he that durst *p.*
Num. 14:44 but they *p.* to go up
PRESUMPTUOUS.
Ps. 19:13 keep. serv. fr. *p.* sins
2 *Pet.* 2:10 *p.* are they, self-will.
PRESUMPTUOUSLY.
Ex. 21:14 if a man come *p.*
Num. 15:30 aught *p.* *Deut.* 17:12
Deut. 1:43 went *p.* up into hill
17:13 hear and do no more *p.*
18:22 prophet hath spoken it *p.*
PRETENCE.
Mat. 23:14 for a *p.* make long
prayers, *Mark* 12:40
Phil. 1:18 whether in *p.* or truth
PREVAIL.
Gen. 7:20 15 cubits did waters *p.*
Num. 22:6 peradventure I sh. *p.*
Jud. 16:5 by what means we *p.*
1 *Sam.* 2:9 by str. sh. no man *p.*
17:9 if I *p.* against him
26:25 great things and still *p.*
2 *Chr.* 14:11 O L. let not man *p.*
Est. 6:13 shalt not *p.* ag. him
Job 15:24 trouble shall *p.* ag. him
18:9 robber shall *p.* against him
Ps. 9:19 L. let not man *p.*
12:4 wi. our tongue will we *p.*
65:3 iniquities *p.* against me
Ec. 4:12 if one *p.* against him
Is. 7:1 could not *p.* against it
16:12 M. shall come, but no *p.*
42:13 *p.* shall *p.* against enemies
47:12 if so thou mayest *p.*
Jer. 1:19 they sh. not *p.* ag. thee,
saith the Lord, 15:20; 20:11
5:22 waves roar, can they not *p.*
20:10 we shall *p.* against him
Dan. 11:7 deal. ag. him and *p.*
Mat. 16:18 gates of hell sh. not *p.*

CRUDEN'S CONCORDANCE.

PRE

Mat. 27:24 Pi. saw he could *p.*
John 12:19 perceive ye how ye *p.*

PREVAILED.

Gen. 7:18 waters *p.* and inc. 19
24 waters *p.* on earth 150 days
30:8 I have wrestled and *p.*
32:25 when he saw he *p.* not
24 po. wi. G. and men, hast *p.*
47:20 the famine *p.* over them
49:26 bless. of thy fath. hath *p.*
Ex. 17:11 Israel *p.* Amalek *p.*
Jud. 1:35 hand of house of J. *p.*
2 *Sam.* 11:23 men *p.* against us
24:4 king's word *p.* against J.
2 *K.* 25:3 the famine *p.* in the ci.
1 *Chr.* 5:2 Judah *p.* above breth.
2 *Chr.* 13:18 J. *p.* bec. th. relied
Ps. 13:4 I have *p.* against thee
129:2 have not *p.* against me
Jer. 20:7 stronger than I, and *p.*
38:22 friends *p.* against thee
Lam. 1:16 weep bec. enemy *p.*
Dan. 7:21 sa. horn *p.* ag. saints
Hos. 12:4 power over angel *p.*
Ob. 7 men deceived thee and *p.*
Luke 23:23 voices of chief pr. *p.*
Acts 19:16 in whom evil spirit *p.*
20 mig. grew word of G. and *p.*
Rev. 5:5 root of David hath *p.*
12:8 dragon and his angels *p.*

PREVAILEST, ETH.

Job 14:20 *p.* for ever against him
Lam. 1:13 fire in bones, and it *p.*

PREVENT.

Job 3:12 why did knees *p.* me?
Ps. 59:10 G. of mercy shall *p.* me
79:8 let thy tender mercies *p.*
88:13 in morn. sh. my prayer *p.*
119:148 mine eyes *p.* ni.-watches
Amos 9:10 evil shall not *p.* us
1 *Thes.* 4:15 shall not *p.* them

PREVENTED, EST.

2 *Sam.* 22:6 the snares of death
p. me. *Ps.* 18:5
19 *p.* me in day of ca. *Ps.* 18:18
Job 30:27 days of afflict. *p.* me
41:11 who *p.* that I sho. repay?
Ps. 21:3 *p.* him with blessings
119:147 I *p.* dawning of morn.
Is. 21:14 they *p.* with. th. bread
Mat. 17:25 Jesus *p.* him, saying,
Simon

PREY.

Gen. 46:9 from the *p.* my son
27 in morning he shall dev. *p.*
Num. 14:3 our wives and childr.
sh. be a *p.* ? 31; *Deut.* 1:39
23:24 not lie down till eat of *p.*
31:12 captives and *p.* to Moses
27 divide the *p.* in two parts
Deut. 2:35 cattle we took for a *p.*
3:7; *Jos.* 8:2, 27; 11:14
Jud. 5:30 div. *p.* a *p.* of divers
8:24 give me the car-rings of
his *p.*
2 *K.* 21:14 Judah sh. become a *p.*
Neh. 4:4 give them for a *p.*
Est. 3:13 spoil of th. for *p. B.* 11
9:15 on *p.* laid not hand, 16
Job 4:11 lion peris. for lack of *p.*
9:26 as eagle that hasteth to *p.*
24:5 as wild asses rising for *p.*
39:29 wilt th. hunt *p.* for lion?
30:29 from thence sho seek. *p.*
Ps. 17:12 a lion greedy of *p.*
76:4 more ex. than mount. of *p.*
104:21 young lions roar after *p.*
124:6 hath not given us for *p.*
Prov. 23:28 lieth in wait as for *p.*
Is. 5:29 roar and lay hold of *p.*
10:2 widows may be their *p.*
6 take *p.* of a hypocrite, nation
31:4 young lion roaring on *p.*
33:23 the *p.* of a great spoil
42:22 for a *p.* none delivereth
49:24 sh. *p.* be taken fr. mighty?
59:15 from evil mak. hims. a *p.*
Jer. 21:9 his life shall be to him
for a *p.* 38:2; 39:18; 45:5
30:16 and all that *p.* on thee will
I give for a *p.*
Ezek. 7:21 give to stran. for a *p.*
13:3 yo. lion, hunted to catch *p.*
22:27 princes like wol. raven, *p.*
26:12 make a *p.* of merchandise
29:19 shall take her spoil and *p.*
34:8 bec. my flock became a *p.*
22 flock sh. no more be a *p.* 28
31 to the cities that bec. a *p.*
36:12 go take spoil and *p.* 13
Dan. 11:24 scatter am. them *p.*
Amos 3:4 lion roar hath no *p.* ?
Nah. 2:12 lions filled holes wi. *p.*
13 I will cut off thy *p.* fr. earth
3:1 bloody city, *p.* departeth not
Zep. 3:3 till day I rise up to *p.*

PRI

PRICE, S.

Lev. 25:16 according to years fn.
n. to fewness, diminish *p.* 50
52 shall give him again the *p.*
53:8 not bring *p.* of a d.
2 *Sam.* 24:24 I will buy it of thee
at a *p.* 1 *Chr.* 21:22, 24
Job 28:13 man knoweth not *p.* 15
18 *p.* of wisdom is above rubi.
Prov. 17:16 *p.* in hand of fool?
27:26 goats are the *p.* of field
31:10 her *p.* is far above rubies
Is. 45:13 shall let go not for *p.*
55:1 wine and milk without *p.*
Jer. 15:13 give to spoil witho. *p.*
Zec. 11:12 give me *p.* weighed
13 a goodly *p.* I was prized at
Mat. 13:46 found one pearl of *p.*
27:6 beca. it is the *p.* of blood
Acts 4:34 brought *p.* of the thin.
5:2 kept back part of the *p.* 3
19:19 counted *p.* of books burnt
1 *Cor.* 6:20 bought with a *p.* 7:23
1 *Pet.* 3:4 meek spirit of great *p.*

PRICKED, ING.

Num. 33:55 th. that remain be *p.*
Acts 9:5 kick against the *p.* 26:14

PRIDE.

Lev. 26:19 break *p.* of your pow.
1 *Sam.* 17:28 *p.* and naughtiness
2 *Chr.* 32:26 Hez. humbled for *p.*
Job 33:17 he may hide *p.* fr. man
35:12 because of *p.* of evil men
41:15 scales are his *p.* shut up
Ps. 10:2 wicked in *p.* doth perse.
4 throu' *p.* of his countenance
31:20 hide them from *p.* of man
36:11 let not the foot of *p.* come
59:12 taken in their *p.*
73:6 theref. *p.* compasseth them
Prov. 8:13 *p.* I hate; 11:2 *p.* com.
13:10 by *p.* cometh contention
14:3 mouth of fool. is rod of *p.*
16:18 *p.* goeth before destructi.
29:23 a man's *p.* bring him low
Is. 9:9 say in *p.* of their hearts
16:6 have heard *p.* of M. his
haughtiness and *p. Jer.* 48:29
23:9 to stain *p.* of glory
25:11 shall bring down their *p.*
28:1 woe to the crown of *p.* 3
Jer. 13:9 I will mar *p.* of Judah
17 shall weep for your *p.*
49:16 thy *p.* of thy heart received
Ezek. 7:10 rod blos. *p.* budded
16:49 iniqu. of thy sister Sod. *p.*
56 not mentioned in day of *p.*
30:6 *p.* of power sh. come down
Dan. 4:37 those that walk in *p.*
5:20 mind was hardened in *p.*
Hos. 5:5 *p.* of Israel testify, 7:10
Ob. 3 *p.* of thy heart deceived
Zep. 2:10 shall they have for *p.*
3:11 take away th. rejoice in *p.*
Zec. 9:6 cut off *p.* of Philistines
10:11 *p.* of Assyria bro. down
11:3 the *p.* of Jordan is spoiled
Mark 7:22 out of heart pride, *p.*
1 *Tim.* 3:6 being lifted up wi. *p.*
1 *John* 2:16 *p.* of life, not of Fa.

PRIEST.

Gen. 14:18 *p.* of M. H'igh, *Heb.* 7:1
Ex. 2:16 *p.* of M. had seven dau.
Lev. 1:9 *p.* sh. burn it all on the
altar, 13, 17; 4:24, 6, 10; 3:11,
16; 4:10; 31:35; 7:5, 31
4:6 the *p.* shall dip his finger, 17
20 *p.* shall make atonement for
them, 26; 5:6; 6:7; 14:18,
13:15, 30; 16:6; 19:22
7:8 *p.* shall have skin of offering
13:3 *p.* sh. look on plague, 5, 6,
17, 20, 21, 25, 26, 37, 30, 31, 32
22:10 and all this right paper in
14:36 *p.* dip his hand all on the *p.*
21:9 if daughter of a *p.* profane
22:11 if *p.* buy any soul
26:11 *p.* shall wave it before L.
27:8 *p.* shall value him, accord.
Num. 3:32 Eleazar *p.* chief of Le.
5:15 then *p.* shall execute on her
25 *p.* shall take her spoil and *p.*
30 *p.* execute on her this law
35:25 nol dw. till death of h. *p.*
Deut. 20:2 the *p.* shall approach
26:4 *p.* shall take offering out
Jud. 17:5 one of sons became *p.*
13 I have Levite to *p.*
18:4 Micah hired me, am his *p.*
1 *Sam.* 2:14 the *p.* took himself
28 did I choose him to be *p.* ?
35 raise me up a faithful *p.*
14:36 then said *p.* Draw to God
21:2 the *p.* answered, no bread

PRI

1 *Sam.* 21:6 *p.* gave him h. bread
1 *K.* 2:27 Abiathar from being *p.*
2 *Chr.* 13:9 the same may be a *p.*
13:3 Israel without teaching *p.*
Ezr. 2:63 stood up a *p.* *Neh.* 7:65
Ps. 110:4 a *p.* for ever after order
of Melch. *Heb.* 5:6; 7:17, 21
Is. 8:2 I took witnesses, Uriah *p.*
24:2 as with people, so with *p.*
28:7 the *p.* and prophet erred
Jer. 6:13 to the *p.* every one
dealeth falsely, 8:10
14:18 *p.* go to a land they k. not
18:18 lav wh. not perish from *p.*
23:11 prophet and *p.* are profa.
33 when a *p.* sh. ask thee, 34
29:26 Lord made thee *p.*
Lam. 2:6 despis. the king and *p.*
20 the *p.* and prophet be slain
Ezek. 7:26 law shall perish fr. *p.*
44:21 nor sh. any *p.* drink wine
31 *p.* sh. not eat any thing to.
Hos. 4:4 they that strive with *p.*
6 thou shalt be no *p.* to me
9 shall be like people like *p.*
Amos 7:10 the *p.* of Bethel sent
Zec. 6:13 shall be *p.* on throne
Mal. 2:7 *p.* lips sho. keep knowl.
Mat. 8:4 go, show thyself to the
p. Mark 1:44: *Luke* 5:14
Luke 1:5 a certain *p.* Zacharias
10:31 came down a certain *p.*
Heb. 7:3 abideth a *p.* continually
11 what need another *p.* rise
15 after Melchizedek aris. a *p.*
20 without an oath was ma. *p.*
8:4 he should not be a *p.*
10:11 ev. *p.* standeth minister,

See CHIEF.

High-PRIEST.

Lev. 21:10 *h.-p.* not uncover head
Num. 35:25 in city of refuge till
death of *h.-p. Jos.* 20:6
2 *K.* 12:10 money in chest, *h.-p.*
put it in boxes, 2 *Chr.* 24:11
Zec. 3:1 Joshua *h.-p.* 8; 6:11
Mat. 26:3 pal. of *h.-p. Luke* 22:54
57 led him to Caiaphas, *the*
h.-p. John 18:24
26:63 *h.-p.* rent clothes, *Mark*
14:53
Mark 2:26 days of Abinthar, *h.-p.*
John 11:49 Caia. *h.-p.* 51; 18:13
18:15 disciple was kn. to *h.-p.*
19:1 Saul went to the *h.-p.*
22:5 also the *h.-p.* doth witness
23:4 revilest thou God's *h.-p.* ?
Heb. 2:17 be a faithful *h.-p.*
3:1 consider apostle *h.-p.*
4:14 have great *h.-p.* in heaven
15 *h.-p.* wh. cannot be touched
5:1 *h.-p.* taken from amo. men
5 C, glo. not himself to be *h.-p.*
10 called a *h.-p.* after Mc. 6:20
7:26 such a *h.-p.* became to us
8:1 we have such a *h.-p.* on the.
3 every *h.-p.* ordained to offer
9:7 second, went *h.-p.* alone
11 a *h.-p.* of good things
25 the *h.-p.* entereth holy place
10:21 having a *h.-p.* over house
13:11 bro. into sanctu. by *h.-p.*

See OFFICE.

PRIESTS.

Gen. 47:22 land of *p.* bought not
26 except land of the *p.* only
Ex. 19:6 to me a kingdom of *p.*
22:10 a sojourner of the *p.*
23:30 holy to the Lord for the *p.*
Deut. 18:3 this shall be *p.* due
Jos. 3:17 *p.* that bare the ark
6:4 *p.* bare seven trumpets, 13
Jud. 18:30 he and sons were *p.*
1 *Sam.* 5:5 nor the *p.* of Dagon
6:2 Philistines called for the *p.*
22:17 turn and slay *p.* of Lord
1 *K.* 8:3 and *p.* took up the ark
12:31 Jeroboam made *p.* 13:33
13:2 on thee sh. he offer the *p.*
2 *K.* 10:11 John slew Ahab's *p.*
19 call me all Baal's *p.*
17:6 *p.* had not repaired breach
21:5 he put down idolatrous *p.*
Jer. 4:h the son was for the *p.*
5:12 120 *p.* sounding trumpets
6:41 let *p.* be clothed with salv.
8:14 appointed courses of the *p.*
13:9 not cast out *p.* of Lord ?
12 *p.* with trump. to cry alarm
23:6 came to house of L. have *p.*
20:19 Uzziah was wroth with *p.*

PRI

2 *Chr.* 29:34 but the *p.* were too
30:3 *p.* had not sancti. themsel.
34:5 Josiah burnt bones of *p.*
35:8 gave it to *p.* for offerings
Ezr. 6:18 set *p.* in divisions
20 *p.* killed the passover for *p.*
8:7 *p.* been delivered to kings
Neh. 9:16 nor had I told it to *p.*
3:28 after him repaired the *p.*
9:32 trouble that come on *p.*
34 we nor our *p.* kept thy law
Ps. 78:64 their *p.* fell by sword
99:6 Moses and Aaron among *p.*
132:9 let thy *p.* be clothed with
16 clothe her *p.* with salvation
Is. 37:2 he sent elders of *p.*
61:6 named thou *p.* of the Lord
Jer. 1:18 against the *p.* thereof
2:8 *p.* said not, Where is Lord?
26 *p.* ashamed; 4:9 *p.* aston.
5:31 *p.* bare rule by th. means
8:1 bones of *p.* they shall bring
13:13 fill *p.* with drunkenness
31:14 satiate souls of *p.*
32:32 provoke to anger, their *p.*
48:7 into captivity with *p.* 49:3
Lam. 1:4 her *p.* sigh, her virgins
19 my *p.* gave up the ghost
4:13 iniq. of her *p.* shed blood
16 they respected not the *p.*
Ezek. 22:26 her *p.* viola. my law
40:45 this chamber is for *p.*
Hos. 5:1 hear this. O *p.* hearken
6:9 comp. of *p.* murder in way
Joel 1:9 the *p.* mourn, 13; 2:17
Mic. 3:11 the *p.* teach for hire
Zep. 1:4 cut off names of the *p.*
3:4 *p.* polluted the sanctuary
Mag. 2:11 as *p.* concerning law
Mal. 1:6 yon, O *p.* that despise
2:1 *p.* this command. is for you
happy sabbath, *Mark*
2:26; *Luke* 6:4
Mark 2:26 is not lawful but for *p.*
Luke 17:14 show yourselves to *p.*
Acts 4:1 the *p.* came upon them
6:7 a comp. of *p.* were obedient
Heb. 7:21 *p.* made without oath
p. not suffered to continue
8:4 seeing there are *p.* that offer
Re. 1:6 made us *p.* to God, 5:10
20:6 sh. be *p.* of God and Christ

See CHIEF, LEVITES, OFFICE.

High-PRIESTS.

Luke 3:2 An. and Ca. were *h.-p.*
Heb. 7:27 not daily as *h.-p.*
28 the law maketh men *h.-p.*

PRIESTHOOD.

Ex. 40:15 everl. *p.* throughout
generations, *Num.* 25:13
Num. 16:10 and seek ye the *p.*
18:1 shall bear iniquity of *p.*
Jos. 18:7 *p.* of L. is their inherit.
Ezr. 2:62 polu. fr. *p. Neh.* 7:64
Neh. 13:29 defiled *p.* cove. of *p.*
Heb. 7:5 Levi, who receive the *p.*
11 If perfection were by Le. *p.*
12 for the *p.* being changed
14 M. spake nothing conc. *p.*
24 hath an unchangeable *p.*
1 *Pet.* 2:5 a holy *p.* 9 a royal *p.*

PRINCE.

Gen. 23:6 thou art a mighty *p.*
32:28 as *p.* hast thou po. wi. G.
34:2 wh. Shechem *p.* of country
17:6 for each *p.* a rod, twelve
34:18 take one *p.* of every tribe
Jos. 22:14 each chief house a *p.*
Jud. 3:28 kn. ye not a *p.* is fallen
1 *K.* 11:34 his days make him *p.*
14:7 made thee *p.* over peo. 16:2
Job 31:37 where is house of a *p.*
31:37 as a *p.* I go near him
Prov. 14:28 want is dest. of a *p.*
17:7 lower in presence of the *p.*
19 forbearing is a *p.* persuaded
25:15 that want. understand.
Cant. 7:1 beautif. thy feet, O *p.*
Is. 9:6 called the *P.* of peace
Jer. 51:59 Seraiah was a quiet *p.*
Ezek. 7:27 the *p.* shall be clothed
12 *p.* must bear reproach in Jerusal.
21:25 profane, wicked *p.* of Is.
28:2 say to the *p.* of Tyrus
30:13 be no more a *p.* of Egypt
34:24 my servant David, a *p.*
37:25 David sh. be th. *p.* for ev.
38:2 the *p.* of Meshech, 3; 39:1
44:3 gate for *p.* shall sit in it
45:17 it sh. be the *p.* part to give

PRI

Ezek. 40:2 the *p.* sh. enter by por.
4 offering that the *p.* shall offer
12 when *p.* prepareth an offeri.
16 if *p.* give a gift to any sons
18 *p.* shall not take people's hi.
43:21 residue shall be for the *p.*
Dan. 1:7 to whom *p.* gave names
8 he requested of *p.* of eunuchs
9 Daniel in favor with the *p.*
8:11 magnifi. himself even to *p.*
25 shall stand up against the *p.*
9:25 build unto Messiah the P.
26 people of *p.* that shall come
10:13 the *p.* of Persia withstood
20 *p.* of Persia, *p.* of Gre. come
21 none hold. but Michael *p.*
11:18 but a *p.* for his own beha.
22 also the *p.* of the covenant
12:1 Michael stand up, great *p.*
Hos. 8:4 shall abide without a *p.*
Mic. 7:3 *p.* and judge ask reward
Mat. 9:34 casteth out dev. by *p.*
of devils, 12:24; *Mark* 3:22
John 12:31 the *p.* of this world
14:30 for the *p.* of world cometh
16:11 *p.* of this world is judged
Acts 3:15 killed the P. of life
5:31 him God exalted to be a P.
Eph. 2:2 according to *p.* of air
Rev. 1:5 Jesus Christ P. of kings

PRINCES.
Gen. 12:15 *p.* also of Pharaoh
17:20 *p.* shall beh. begat, 25:16
Num. 7:3 for two *p.* 10 *p.* offer.
1:2 rose up 250 *p.* 21:18 *p.* dig.
22:8 and *p.* abode with Balaam
35 Ba. sent *p.* more honorable
Jos. 9:15 *p.* of congreg. sware
13:21 M. smote with *p.* of Mid.
22:14 P. ten *p.* sent to Reuben
Jud. 5:3 give ear, O ye *p.*
15 *p.* of Issachar were with D.
7:25 two *p.* of the Midianites
1 *Sam.* 2:8 to set them among *p.*
29:4 *p.* of Philisti. were wroth
1 *K.* 20:14 by young men of *p.*
1 *Chr.* 4:38 these *p.* in families
28:21 *p.* will be at thy command
2 *Chr.* 28:14 left spoil before *p.*
30:12 do commandments of *p.*
Ezra 9:2 gave willingly to people
32:18 trans. of his *p.* to Babylon
Ezr. 7:28 bef. king's mighty *p.*
9:2 hand of *p.* hath been chief
10:8 according to counsel of *p.*
Neh. 9:34 nei. have *p.* kept law
Est. 1:3 feast to all his *p.* 2:18
6:9 of one of the king's noble *p.*
Job 3:15 had been at rest with *p.*
4:19 leadeth *p.* away spoiled
21 he poureth contempt on *p.*
29:9 the *p.* refrained talking
34:18 say to *p.* ye are ungodly?
19 him that accepteth not *p.*
Ps. 45:16 *p.* in all the earth
47:9 *p.* of people are gathered
68:27 *p.* of Zebulun, *p.* of Nap.
31 *p.* shall come out of Egypt
76:12 he shall cut off spirit of *p.*
82:7 and fall like one of the *p.*
105:22 bind his *p.* at his pleas.
107:40 poureth contempt on *p.*
113:8 set him wi. *p.* even wi. *p.*
118:9 tru. in L. than conf. in *p.*
119:23 *p.* also did speak ag. me
161 *p.* perse. me without cause
148:3 put not your trust in *p.*
148:11 *p.* and judges of earth
Prov. 8:15 *p.* decree; 16 *p.* rule
17:26 it is not good to strike *p.*
19:10 much less a ser. to rule *p.*
28:2 many are the *p.* thereof
31:4 not for *p.* to drink strong
Ec. 10:7 *p.* walking as servants
16 when thy *p.* eat in the mor.
17 blessed art thou, wh. *p.* eat
Is. 1:23 thy *p.* are rebellious
8:4 I will give children to th. *p.*
14 L. enter into judgm. wi. *p.*
10:8 are not my *p.* alto. kings?
19:11 *p.* of Zoan, *p.* of Noph, 13
21:5 ye *p.* anoint the shield
23:8 whose merchants are *p.*
30:4 his *p.* were at Zoan, amba.
31:9 *p.* shall be afraid of ensign
34:12 all her *p.* shall be nothing
40:23 that bringeth *p.* to nothi.
41:25 and he shall come upon *p.*
43:28 I profaned *p.* of sanctuary
49:7 *p.* shall worship; her. of L.
Jer. 1:18 brazen walls ag. the *p.*
2:26 Is. kings and *p.* ashamed
4:9 heart of *p.* sh. be astonish.
8:1 shall bring out bones of *p.*
17:25 *p.* sitting on throne of D.
25:18 said, This man is not

PRI

Jer. 32:32 kings and *p.* pro. me
34:21 *p.* I will give to enemies
38:17 if thou go to k. of B. *p.*
48:7 Ch. and *p.* go to capt. 49:3
49:38 I will destroy from the *p.*
50:35 sword on *p.* and wise men
51:57 I will make drunk her *p.*
Lam. 1:6 *p.* become like harts
2:9 kings and *p.* am. Gentiles
5:12 *p.* are hanged by th. hand
Ezek. 22:27 *p.* like wolves raven.
23:15 dyed attire, all of them *p.*
32:29 Edom and her *p.*
30 the *p.* of the north
39:18 ye shall drink blood of *p.*
45:8 my *p.* no more oppr. people
Dan. 3:2 king sent to gather *p.*
6:1 to set over kingdom, 120 *p.*
4 *p.* sought occasion ag. Dani.
8:25 stand ag. the Prince of *p.*
9:8 confusion of face to our *p.*
10:13 Michael one of *p.* came
11:5 one of his *p.* sh. be strong
Hos. 7:3 they make *p.* glad
5 the *p.* have made him sick
16 their *p.* shall fall by sword
8:4 made *p.* and I knew it not
10 shall sorrow for king of *p.*
9:15 all their *p.* are revolters
13:10 Give me a king and *p.*
Amos 1:15 into captiv. he and *p.*
Mic. 3:1 hear, *p.* of house of Is.
Hab. 1:10 the *p.* shall be a scorn
Zep. 1:8 I will punish the *p.*
3:3 *p.* within her are roar. lions
Mat. 20:25 *p.* of Gent. exercise
1 *Cor.* 2:6 nor wisdom of the *p.*
8 none of *p.* of this world

See PRINCES.
2 *K.* 24:14 carried away all the *p.*
1 *Chr.* 29:24 all *p.* submit. them.
2 *Chr.* 24:23 destroyed all the *p.*
Est. 1:16 done wro. to all the *p.*
3:1 set his seat above all the *p.*
Is. 33:11 all th. *p.* as Zebah said
Jer. 36:21 it in ears of all the *p.*
Ezek. 26:16 all the *p.* of the sea
Amos 2:3 will slay all the *p.*
See ISRAEL.

PRINCES of Judah.
Neh. 12:31 I brought up *p.* of Ju.
Ps. 68:27 there is *p.* of Judah
Jer. 52:10 slew all the *p.* of Jud.
Mat. 2:6 not least am. *p.* of Jud.

PRINCESS, ES.
1 *K.* 11:3 Solom. had 700 wiv. *p.*
Lam. 1:1 *p.* among provinces

PRINCIPAL.
Ex. 30:23 take th. also *p.* spices
Lev. 6:5 shall restore it in the *p.*
Num. 5:7 recomp. tresp. with *p.*
1 *K.* 4:5 son of Nathan *p.* officer
2 *K.* 25:19 the *p.* scribe of the host, *Jer.* 52:25
1 *Chr.* 24:31 even *p.* household
31 even *p.* fathers cast lots
Neh. 11:17 Mattaniah *p.* to begin
Prov. 4:7 wisdom is the *p.* thing
Is. 16:8 broken down *p.* plants
28:25 cast in *p.* wheat and barl.
Jer. 25:34 ho to ashes, *p.* of flock
35 nor the *p.* of the flock escape
Mic. 5:5 raise ag. him 8 *p.* me.
Acts 25:23 *p.* of the city entered

PRINCIPALITY, IES.
Jer. 13:18 your *p.* sh. come down
Rom. 8:38 *p.* nor powers able
Eph. 1:21 far above all *p.* power
3:10 to *p.* might be kn. wisdom
6:12 wrestle ag. *p.* and power
Col. 2:10 *p.* were created by him
2:10 head of all *p.* and power
15 having spoiled *p.* he made
Tit. 3:1 mind to be subject to *p.*

PRINCIPLES.
Heb. 5:12 one teach you first *p.*
6:1 *p.* of the doctrine of Christ

PRINT, ED.
Lev. 19:28 shall not *p.* any mar.
Job 19:23 O that my words were *p.* in a book

PRINT.
Job 13:27 settest a *p.* on heels
John 20:25 exc. I see in *p.* of nails, and put my finger into *p.*

PRISCA, 2 *Tim.* 4:19
PRISCILLA, *Acts* 18:2, 26; *Rom.* 16:3; 1 *Cor.* 16:19

PRISON.
Gen. 39:20 Potiph. put Jos. in *p.*
40:3 put butler and baker in *p.*
42:19 bound in house of your *p.*
1 *K.* 22:27 put this fellow in *p.* 2 *Chr.* 18:26

PRI

2 *K.* 17:4 bound Hoshea in *p.*
25:29 changed his *p.* garment, *Jer.* 52:31, 33
Neh. 3:25 Palal repaired by *p.*
Ps. 142:7 bring my soul out of *p.*
Ec. 4:14 for out of *p.* he cometh
Is. 24:22 they sh. be shut up in *p.*
42:7 bring out prisoners from *p.*
22 all of them hid in *p.*
53:9 he was taken from *p.*
61:1 proclaim opening of the *p.*
Jer. 32:2 Jeremiah was shut in *p.*
12 before Jews in court of *p.*
33:1 word came to Jerem. while in *p.* 37:21; 38:6, 28; 39:15
37:4 had not put him into *p.*
15 put him in *p.* in Jon. house
37:18 took Jeremiah out of *p.*
52:11 put Zedekiah in *p.*
Mat. 4:12 John was cast into *p.*
5:25 be cast into *p.* *Luke* 12:58
11:2 J. heard in *p.* works of C.
14:3 Herod put him in *p.*
18:30 he cast him into *p.*
25:36 I was in *p.* ye came to me
39 when saw we thee in *p.* ? 44
Mark 1:14 after J. was put in *p.*
6:17 Her. had bound John in *p.*
Luke 3:20 he shut up John in *p.*
22:33 go with thee both into *p.*
23:19 for murder cast in *p.* 25
John 3:24 John not yet cast in *p.*
Acts 5:18 put apostles in com. *p.*
19 angel by night op. *p.* doors
8:3 men and women, com. to *p.*
12:4 Peter in *p.* 5 kept in *p.*
7 light in *p.* 17 L. br. out of *p.*
16:23 Paul and Silas cast in *p.*
24 inner *p.* 27 *p.* doors open
26:10 saints did I shut in *p.*
1 *Pet.* 3:19 preach, to spirits in *p.*
Rev. 2:10 shall cast some into *p.*
20:7 S. shall be loosed out his *p.*
See CAVE.

PRISON-HOUSE.
Jud. 16:21 S. did grind in *p.-h.*
1 *K.* 22:27 *p.-h.* 2 *Chr.* 18:26
Is. 42:7 in darkness out of *p.-h.*

PRISONER.
Ps. 79:11 let sighing of *p.* come
102:20 hear groaning of the *p.*
Mat. 27:15 release to people a *p.*
Acts 23:18 P. *p.* called me to him
25:27 unreasonable to send a *p.*
28:17 yet was I delivered *p.*
Eph. 3:1 I P. the *p.* of Christ, 4:1; *Phile.* 1:9
2 *Tim.* 1:8 not ashamed of his *p.*
See FELLOW.

PRISONERS.
Gen. 39:20 where king's *p.* were
22 keeper committed to *p.*
Num. 21:1 took some of Israel *p.*
Job 3:18 there the *p.* rest toge.
Ps. 68:6 L. despiseth not his *p.*
146:7 the Lord looseth the *p.*
Is. 10:4 bow down under tier *p.*
14:17 opened not house of *p.*
20:4 Assyria shall lead Egyp. *p.*
24:22 *p.* gathered together as *p.*
49:9 mayest say to *p.* Go forth
Lam. 3:34 crush under feet the *p.*
Zec. 9:11 I have sent forth thy *p.*
12 turn to str.-hold, *p.* of hope
Acts 16:25 prayed, *p.* heard them
27 supposing *p.* had been fled
Acts 27:1 delivered Paul and other *p.*
42 soldiers' couns. was to kill *p.*

PRISONS.
Luke 21:12 delivering you in *p.*
Acts 22:4 in *p.* men and wom.
2 *Cor.* 11:23 in *p.* more frequent

PRIVATE, LY.
Mat. 24:3 disciples came to C. *p.*
Mark 6:32 Jesus went *p.* into a ship *p. Luke* 9:10
9:28 J. and J. ask him *p.* 13:3
Luke 10:23 turned to disciples *p.*
Acts 23:19 with Paul's kinsm. *p.*
Gal. 2:2 to them of reputation *p.*
2 *Pet.* 1:20 any *p.* interpretation

PRIVILY.
Jud. 9:31 he sent messengers *p.*
1 *Sam.* 24:4 Da. cut Saul's skirt *p.*
Ps. 10:8 eyes *p.* set against poor
11:2 may *p.* shoot at upright
31:4 of the net laid *p.* 142:3
64:5 commune of lay. snares *p.*
101:5 whoso *p.* slandereth neigh.
Prov. 1:11 lurk *p.* for innocent, 18 lurk *p.* for their own lives
Mat. 1:19 to put her away *p.*
2:7 Her. when he had *p.* called
Acts 16:37 now do they thrust us out *p.* ?

PRO

Gen. 2:1 I came in *p.* to spy out
2 *Ki.* 2:1 *p.* bring damna. here.

PRIVY.
Deut. 23:1 *p.* number cut off
1 *K.* 2:44 wickedness heart *p.* to
Ezek. 21:14 enters *p.* chamber
Acts 5:2 wife also being *p.* to it

PRIZE.
1 *Cor.* 9:24 but one receiveth *p.*
Phil. 3:14 I press toward the *p.*

PRIZED.
Zec. 11:13 price that I was *p.* at

PROCEED.
Jos. 6:10 word *p.* out of mouth
2 *Sam.* 7:12 seed wh. shall *p.*
Job 40:5 but I will *p.* no further
Is. 29:14 I *p.* to do marvel. work
51:4 for a law shall *p.* from me
Jer. 9:3 they *p.* from evil to evil
30:21 governor shall *p.* fr. midst
Hab. 1:7 judgm. and dign. sh. *p.*
Mat. 15:18 *p.* out of mouth defile
Rom. 7:3 murders, *Mark* 7:21
Eph. 4:29 no corrupt commu. *p.*
2 *Tim.* 3:9 they shall *p.* no furt.

PROCEEDED.
Num. 30:12 whats. *p.* out of lips
Jud. 11:36 do that which *p.* out
Job 36:1 Elihu also *p.* and said
Luke 4:22 gracious words wh. *p.*
John 8:42 for I *p.* forth from God
Acts 12:3 he *p.* to take Peter also
Rev. 19:21 sword *p.* out of mouth

PROCEEDETH, ING.
Gen. 24:50 thing *p.* from the L.
Num. 30:2 according to all th. *p.*
Deut. 8:3 by every word that *p.* out of mouth of G. *Mat.* 4:4
1 *Sam.* 24:13 wick. *p.* fr. wicked
Ez. 10:5 error which *p.* fr. ruler
Lam. 3:38 out of M. High *p.* not
Hab. 1:4 wrong judgment *p.*
John 13:26 Spi. of truth *p.* fr. F.
Jam. 3:10 out of the same mo. *p.*
Rev. 11:5 fire *p.* out of th. mouth
22:1 water of life *p.* out of thr

PROCESS.
Gen. 4:3 in *p.* of time Cain bro.
38:12 in *p.* of time Shuah died
Ex. 2:23 in *p.* of time k. of Eg.
Jud. 11:4 in *p.* chil. of Ammon
2 *Chr.* 21:19 in *p.* Jehor.'s howe.

PROCHORUS, *Acts* 6:5

PROCLAIM.
Ex. 33:19 I will n. name of Lord
Lev. 23:2 feast of L. 4, 21, 37
25:10 *p.* lib. *Deut.* 20:10 *p.* peace
Jud. 7:3 *p.* in ears of people
1 *K.* 21:9 *p.* a fast, set Naboth on
4 *K.* 10:20 John said, *p.* solemn
Neh. 8:15 *p.* they fetch branches
Prov. 20:6 men *p.* own goodness
Is. 61:1 he sent me to *p.* liberty
1 *p.* the acceptable year of L.
Jer. 3:12 p. th. words, 11:6; 19:2
7:2 stand in gate of L. *p.* there
34:8 made a coven. to *p.* liberty
17 I *p.* a liberty for you to sw.
Joel 3:9 *p.* this among the Gent.
Amos 4:5 *p.* the freeofferings

PROCLAIMED.
Ex. 34:5 *p.* name of Lord, 6
36:6 they caused it to be *p.*
1 *K.* 21:12 they *p.* a fast, set
2 *K.* 10:20 solemn asse ni. and *p.*
23:16 man of G. *p.* who *p.* it
2 *Chr.* 34:8 Jehoshaphat *p.* a fast
Ezr. 8:21 I *p.* a fast at Ahava
Est. 6:11 Haman *p.* before him
Is. 62:11 hath *p.* to end of world
Jer. 36:9 they *p.* a fast before L.
Jon. 3:5 *p.* a fast, put on sacke.
7 caused it to be *p.* thro' Nine.
Luke 12:3 he *p.* on houseten

PROCLAIMETH, ING.
Prov. 12:23 heart of fools *p.*
Is. 61:2 *p.* liberty ac. unto, 17
Jer. 34:17 a *p.* of liberty
Rev. 5:2 I saw a strong angel *p.*

PROCLAMATION.
Ex. 32:5 Aaron made *p.*
1 *K.* 15:22 king Asa made a *p.*
22:36 went *p.* throughout host
2 *Chr.* 24:9 made a *p.* through
30:5 estab. a *p.* throughout Is.
36:22 out of not laid *p.* 1:4:2
Ezr. 10:7 they made *p.* in Judah
Dan. 5:29 Belshaz car made *p.*

PROCTOR, ED, ETH.
Prov. 11:27 seek. good *p.* favor
Jer. 2:17 hast thou not *p.* this
4:18 thy doings *p.* th. things
26:19 might we a great evil
Jer. 33:9 for all prosperity I *p.* to it

PRODUCE.
Is. 41:21 *p.* your cause, saith L.
PROFANE, Adjective.
Lev. 21:7 not tn. wife th. is *p.* 14
Jer. 23:11 proph. and priests *p.*
Ezek. 21:25 thus *p.* prince of I
28:18 cast as *p.* out of mount.
42:20 sanctuary and *p.* place
44:23 differc. betw. holy and *p.*
48:15 sh. be a *p.* place for city
1 *Tim.* 1:9 law is made for *p.*
4:7 ref. *p.* and old wives' fables
6:20 avoid *p.* babbl. 2 *Tim.* 2:16
Heb. 12:16 lest Eh. he any *p.* per.
PROFANE, Verb.
Lev. 18:21 neit. shalt thou *p.* G.
19:12; 20:3; 21:6; 22:2, 32
21:12 shall not *p.* sanctuary, 23
15 nor shall *p.* his seed among
23:9 if they *p.* my ordinance
15 shall not *p.* holy things
Neh. 13:17 evil do, *p.* sabbath
Ezek. 22:39 came to sanctu. to *p.*
24:21 I will *p.* my sanctuary
Amos 2:7 to *p.* my holy name
Mat. 12:5 priests in temple *p.*
Acts 24:6 gone about to *p.* temp.
PROFANED.
Lev. 19:8 he *p.* hallowed thing
Ps. 89:39 thou hast *p.* his crown
Is. 43:28 I have *p.* the princes of
Ezek. 22:8 thou *p.* my sab. 23:38
26 *p.* my holy things, I am *p.*
25:3 sanctuary when it was *p*
36:20 they *p.* my holy name
21 my name Is. had *p.* 23
Mal. 1:12 ye have *p.* it, ye say
2:11 Jud. hath *p.* holiness of L.
PROFANENESS.
Jer. 23:15 prophets of Jeru. is *p.*
PROFANETH, ING.
Lev. 21:9 she *p.* her father, she
Neh. 13:18 bring wrath by *p.* sab.
Mal. 2:10 by *p.* covenant of fath.
PROFESS.
Deut. 26:3 I *p.* this day to the L.
Mat. 7:23 I *p.* I never knew you
Tit. 1:16 they *p.* they know God
PROFESSED, ING.
Rom. 1:22 *p.* themsel. to be wise
2 *Cor.* 9:13 glori. God for your *p.*
1 *Tim.* 2:10 becometh women *p.*
6:12 hast *p.* a good profession
21 some *p.* have erred
PROFESSION.
2 *Tim.* 6:12 professed a good *p*
Heb. 3:1 the High-priest of our *p.*
4:14 let us hold fast our *p.* 10:23
PROFIT, Substantive.
Gen. 25:32 what *p.* sh. birthright
37:26 what *p.* if we slay broth.?
Est. 3:8 it is not for king's *p.*
Job 21:15 what *p.* if we pray
30:2 whereto strength *p.* me?
35:3 what *p.* if I be cleansed
Pr. 30:9 what *p.* is in my blood?
Prov. 14:23 in all labor th. is *p.*
Ec. 1:3 what *p.* hath a man of all his labor? 3:9; 5:16
2:11 there was no *p.* under sun
5:9 the *p.* of the earth is for all
7:11 by wisdom there is *p.* to
Is. 30:5 help nor *p.* but shame
Jer. 16:19 things where. is no *p.*
Rom. 3:1 what *p.* of circumcis.?
1 *Cor.* 7:35 I sp. for your own *p.*
10:33 not seeking mine own *p.*
2 *Tim.* 2:14 words to no *p.*
Heb. 12:10 chasteneth us for *p.*
PROFIT, Verb.
1 *Sam.* 12:21 thi. wh. cannot *p.*
Job 35:8 thy righteousn. may *p.*
Prov. 10:2 wickedness *p.* nothing
, 11:4 riches *p.* not in day of wra.
Is. 30:5 peo. that could not *p.* 6
44:9 delectable things eh. not *p.*
47:12 thou shalt be able to *p.*
57:12 works, shall not *p.* thee
Jer. 2:8 things that do not *p.*
11 for that which doth not *p.*
7:8 lying words that cannot *p.*
12:13 put to pain, but sh. not *p.*
23:32 they sh. not *p.* this peop.
Mark 8:36 what *p.* if gain world
1 *Cor.* 4:7 ev. man to *p.* 12:7
14:6 what shall I *p.* you ?
Gal. 5:2 Ch. shall *p.* you nothing
Heb. 4:2 word preach. did not *p.*
Jam. 2:14 what doth it *p.* breth.
16 give not thi. needf. wh. *p.* ?
PROFITABLE.
Job 22:2 can a man be *p.* to God ?
Ec. 10:10 wisdom is *p.* to direct

PRO
Is. 44:10 image is *p.* for nothing
Jer. 13:7 girdle was *p.* for noth.
Mat. 5:29 *p.* members perish, 30
Acts 20:20 I kept noth. *p.* to you
1 *Tim.* 4:8 godliness is *p.* to all
2 *Tim.* 3:16 all Scripture is *p.*
4:11 M. is *p.* to me for ministry
Tit. 3:8 th. things are *p.* to men
Phile. 11 but now *p.* to thee
PROFITED, ETH.
Job 33:27 I have sinned, it *p.* not
34:9 it *p.* noth. to delight in G.
Hab. 2:18 what *p.* graven image
Mat. 15:5 it is a gift whatever thou might. be *p.* *Mark* 7:11
16:26 what is man *p.* if he gain
John 6:93 quicken. flesh *p.* noth.
Rom. 2:25 circumcision *p.* if th.
1 Cor. 13:3 not char. it *p.* noth.
Gal. 1:14 I *p.* in Jews' religion
1 *Tim.* 4:8 bodily exerci. *p.* little
Heb. 13:9 not *p.* them that occu.
PROFITING.
1 *Tim.* 4:15 thy *p.* may appear
PROFOUND.
Hos. 5:2 the revolters are *p.*
PROGENITORS.
Gen. 49:26 above bless. of my *p.*
PROGNOSTICATORS.
Is. 47:13 let monthly *p.* stand up
PROLONG, ED
Deut. 4:26 not *p.* your days, 30:18
40 that thou mayest *p.* days on earth, 5:16, 33 ; 6:2 ; 11:9 ;
17:20 ; 22:7
32:47 ye shall *p.* your days
Job 6:11 that I should *p.* life ?
15:29 wicked sh. not *p.* perfect.
Ps. 61:6 thou will *p.* king's life
Prov. 28:2 by knowl. shall be *p.*
16 he that hateth covet. sh. *p.*
Ec. 8:12 a sinner's days be *p.*
13 neit. shall wicked *p.* his days
Is. 13:22 her days shall not be *p.*
53:10 seed, he shall *p.* his days
Ezek. 12:22 the days are *p.* and
25 to pass, it sh. be no more *p.*
28 none of my words be *p.* more
Dan. 7:12 their lives were *p.* for
PROLONGETH.
Prov. 10:27 fear of Lord *p.* days
PROMISE, Substantive.
Num. 14:34 kn. my breach of *p.*
1 *K.* 8:56 not failed of good *p.*
2 *Chr.* 1:9 let *p.* to David be esta.
Neh. 5:12 do according to this *p.*
13 perform. not *p.* accor. to *p.*
Ps. 77:8 doth *p.* fail evermore?
105:42 remembered his holy *p.*
Luke 24:49 send *p.* of my Fath
Acts 1:4 wait for *p.* of the Father
2:33 received *p.* of Holy Ghost
39 the *p.* is to you and children
7:17 time of the *p.* drew nigh
13:23 his *p.* ha. raised a Saviour
32 *p.* made to fathers
23:21 looking for a *p.* from thee
26:6 hope of the *p.* made of G, 7
Rom. 4:13 *p.* that he sh. be heir
14 the *p.* is made of none effect
16 the *p.* might be sure to seed
20 he staggered not at the *p.*
9:8 chil. of *p.* counted for seed
9 this is word of *p.* I will come
Gal. 3:14 receive *p.* of the Spirit
17 who. make *p.* of none effect
18 it is no more of *p.* but God gave it to Abraham by *p.*
19 to whom the *p.* was made
22 that the *p.* by faith of J. C.
29 ye are heirs according to *p.*
4:23 he of free woman was by *p.*
28 we, as Isaac, children of *p.*
Eph. 1:13 with Holy Spirit of *p.*
2:12 strangers from coven. of *p.*
3:6 partakers of his *p.* in Christ
6:2 first commandment with *p.*
1 *Tim.* 4:8 hav. the *p.* of the life
2 *Tim.* 1:1 according to *p.* of life
Heb. 4:1 fear, lest a *p.* being left
6:13 God made *p.* to Abraham
15 after he endured he obtai. *p.*
17 will. to show to heirs of *p.*
9:15 *p.* of eternal life, 10:36
11:9 sojourned in land of *p.*
13 these all received not the *p.*
33 obtained promi. 39 not *p.*
9 Lord not slack concer. his *p.*
13 according to his *p.* we look
1 *John* 2:25 this is the *p.* he hath
PROMISE, Verb.
2 *Pet.* 2:19 while they *p.* liberty, they servants of corruption

PRO
PROMISED.
Ex. 12:25 give according as he *p.*
Num. 14:40 go to place Lord *p.*
Deut. 1:11 L. bless as he *p.* 15:6
6:3 increase as the Lord *p.* thee
10:9 L. is his inherit. as he *p.*
12:20 L. enlarge border, as he *p.*
19:8 give thee land he *p.* 27:3
26:18 to be his people as he *p.*
Jos. 23:5 possess th. land as L. *p.*
2 *Sam.* 7:28 *p.* goodness to serv.
1 *K.* 2:24 made me house he *p.*
5:12 L. gave S. wisdom as he *p.*
8:20 I sit on thro. of Is. as L. *p.*
56 given rest to peopleas he *p.*
9:5 as I *p.* to David, thy father
1 K. 8:19 *p.* to gi. light, 2 *Chr.* 21:7
1 *Chr.* 17:26 th. hast *p.* goodness
2 Chr. 6:10 set on throne as L. *p.*
Neh. 9:23 concern. whi. thou *p.*
Jer. 32:43 all good I *p.* 33:14
Mat. 14:7 Herod *p.* with oath
Mark 14:11 *p.* to give money
Luke 1:72 mercy *p.* to our fath.
22:6 he *p.* to betray him
Acts 7:5 he *p.* to give it to him
Rom. 1:2 gospel wh. he had *p.*
4:21 what he *p.* he was able
Tit. 1:2 *p.* before world began
Heb. 10:23 he is faithful that *p.*
11:11 him faithful that had *p.*
12:26 hath *p.* saying, Yet once
Jam. 1:12 L. *p.* them love, 2:5
1 *John* 2:25 hath *p.* us eter. life
PROMISEDST.
1 *K.* 8:24 David that thou *p.* 25
Neh. 9:15 *p.* they sho. go to land
PROMISES.
Rom. 9:4 to whom pertain *p.*
15:8 to confirm *p.* made to fath.
2 *Cor.* 1:20 all *p.* of God in him
7:1 having therefore these *p.*
Gal. 3:16 to Abra. were *p.* made
18 law against *p.* of God?
Heb. 6:12 thro' faith inherit *p.*
7:6 M. blessed him that had *p.*
8:6 established upon better *p.*
11:13 not having received *p.*
17 he that received *p.* off. son
33 through faith obtained *p.*
2 *Pet.* 1:4 given to us exceeding

PROMISING.
Ezek. 13:22 wick. way by *p.* life
PROMOTE, ED.
Num. 22:17 *p.* to honor, 24:11
37 am I not able to *p.* thee to
Jud. 9:9 go to be *p.* over, 11, 13
Prov. 4:8 exalt her, sh e sh. *p.* th.
Dan. 3:30 the king *p.* Shadrach
PROMOTION.
Ps. 75:6 *p.* cometh not from east
Prov. 3:35 shame be *p.* of fools
PRONOUNCE.
Lev. 5:4 man sh. *p.* with an oath
Jud. 12:6 not frame to *p.* right
Jer. 11:17 the Lord hath *p.* evil
16:10 *p.* this great evil agai. us?
19:15; 35:17; 40:2
26:13 Lord will rep. of evil he *p.*
19 Lord repented of evil he *p.*
34:5 for I have *p.* the word
36:7 L. hath *p.* ag. this people
PRONOUNCING.
Lev. 5:4 if a soul sware, *p.* to do
PROOF, S.
Acts 1:3 hims. alive by many *p.*
2 *Cor.* 2:9 might know the *p.*
13:3 since ye seek a *p.* of Christ
Phil. 2:22 ye know the *p.* of him
2 *Tim.* 4:5 *p.* of thy ministry
PROPER.
1 *Chr.* 29:3 mine own *p.* good
Acts 1:19 in *p.* tongue, Aceldama
1 *Cor.* 7:7 every man hath *p.* gift
Heb. 11:23 saw he was a *p.* child
PROPHECY.
2 *Chr.* 9:29 Nol.'s acts in *p.* of A.
15:8 when Asa heard *p.* of Oded
Neh. 6:12 he pronounced this *p.*
Prov. 30:1 *p.* man spake to Ithiel
31:1 *p.* that his mother tau. him
Mat. 13:14 fulfilled *p.* of Esaias
20 no *p.* of script. is of private
21 *p.* came not by will of man
Rev. 1:3 bless. they that hear *p.*

PRO
Rev. 11:6 rain not in da. of th. *p.*
19:10 testimony of J. is sp. of *p.*
22:7 blessed that keepeth th. *p.*
10 seal not the say. of the *p.*
19 if any man take from this *p.*
PROPHECIES.
1 *Cor.* 13:8 whether *p.* they cease
1 *Tim.* 1:18 according to *p.* befo.
PROPHESY, Verb.
Num. 11:27 Eldad and Me. do *p.*
1 *K.* 22:8 he doth not *p.* good
18 not *p.* good, 2 *Chr.* 18:17
1 *Chr.* 25:1 should *p.* with harps
Is. 30:10 *p.* not right, *p.* deceits
Jer. 5:31 the prophets *p.* falsely
11:21 *p.* not in name of the L.
14:14 prophets *p.* lies, *p.* false
16 people to whom they *p.* cast
23:16 heark. not to proph. th. *p.*
25 *p.* lies in my name, 26, 32 ;
27:10, 14, 15, 16 ; 29:9, 21
25:30 *p.* against inhab. of earth
26:12 Lord sent me to *p.* against
Ezek. 4:7 *p.* against Jerusalem
6:2 *p.* ag. mount. of Israel; 36:1
11:4 *p.* against Jaza. and Pel, *p.*
13:2 *p.* against proph. that *p.* 17
20:46 *p.* aga. the forest of south
21:2 *p.* against Israel ; 9 Israel,
14 Son of man *p.* smite hands
28 *p.* concerning Ammon. 25:2
28:21 Son of man *p.* against Zid.
29:2 *p.* ag. Pharaoh, king Eg.
30:2 *p.* against Egypt and say
34:2 *p.* against shepherds of Is.
35:2 *p.* against mount Seir
36:6 *p.* concerning land of Israel
37:4 *p.* on th. bones; 9 *p.* wind
38:2 *p.* against Gog, 14 ; 39:1
Joel 2:28 sons sh. *p.* *Acts* 2:17, 18
Amos 2:12 say. *p.* not, *Mic.* 2:6
3:8 L. spoken, who can but *p.* ?
7:12 eat bread, and *p.* there
13 *p.* not any more to Beth-el
15 L. said, Go, *p.* to my pe. Is.
16 *p.* not against house of Isa.
Mic. 2:11 I will *p.* to thee of wine
Zec. 13:3 when any sh. *p.* then
Mat. 13:7 well did Es. *p.* of you
26:68 *p.* unto us, thou Ch. *Mark* 14:65 ; *Luke* 22:64
Acts 2:17 dau. sh. *p.* your young
Acts 21:9 had virgins wh. did *p.*
1 *Cor.* 13:9 part, and *p.* in part
14:1 rather *p.* 39 covet to *p.*
24 if all *p.* 31 we may all *p.*
Rev. 10:11 thou must *p.* before
11:3 witnesses sh. *p.* 1,260 days
PROPHESIED.
1 *Sam.* 10:10 Spirit of God came on Saul, and he *p.* 11 ;
18:10 ; 19:23, 24
1 *K.* 18:29 they *p.* until evening
22:10 prophets *p.* 12 ; 2 *Chr.* 18:9
1 *Chr.* 25:2 the sons of Asaph *p.*
2 *Chr.* 20:37 Eliezer *p.* against J.
Ezr. 5:1 Zechariah *p.* to the J.
Jer. 2:8 the prophets *p.* by Baal
20:1 Pashur heard that Jere. *p.*
23:13 the prophets of Samar. *p.*
21 I have not spok. yet they *p.*
26:9 why hast thou *p.* in name
18 Micah *p.* in days of Hezek.
20 Urijah *p.* 28:8 *p.* against
29:31 Shem. hath *p.* to you a lie
37:19 where prophets which *p.?*
Ezek. 11:13 when I *p.* Pelat. died
37:7 I *p.* as I was comm. I *p.* 10
38:17 who *p.* I would bring thee
Zec. 13:4 proph. asha. when *p.*
Mat. 7:22 Lord, have we not *p.*
11:13 the proph. *p.* until John
Mark 7:6 well hath Es. *p.* of you
Luke 1:67 his father Zacharias *p.*
John 11:51 Caiaphas *p.* that Jes.
Acts 19:6 wi. tongues and *p.*
1 *Cor.* 14:5 I would rather ye *p.*
Jude 14 Enoch *p.* of these things
PROPHESIETH.
Jer. 28:9 prophet wh. *p.* of peace
Ezek. 12:27 ho. *p.* of times far off
Zec. 13:3 thrust him when he *p.*
1 *Cor.* 11:4 with head uncov.
14:3 he that *p.* speak. unto men
4 he that *p.* edifieth church
5 greater he that *p.* than tong.
PROPHESYING, S.
1 *Sam.* 10:13 made an end of *p.*
19:20 saw comp. of prophets *p.*
Ezr. 6:14 they prospered thro' *p.*
1 *Cor.* 11:4 having head cover.
14:6 exce. I speak to you by *p.*
22 but *p.* serveth not for them
1 *Thes.* 5:20 despi. not *p.* prove all

CRUDEN'S CONCORDANCE.

PUT

Job 41:2 can. p. hook in. his no.?
Ps. 4:7 p. gladness in my heart
8:6 thou hast p. all things un-
 der his feet, 1 Cor. 15:25, 27;
 Eph. 1:22; Heb. 2:8
9:20 p. in fear, O L. that nation
31:18 let lying lips be p. to sile.
43:3 p. new song in my mouth
 14 let them be p. to shame that
 wish me evil, 44:7; 53:5
44:9 thou hast p. us to shame
78:66 p. them to perp. reproach
88:18 lover and friend p. fr. me
118:8 tr. L. than p. con. in man
 9 tr. L. than put confi. in prin.
119:31 O L. p. me not to shame
Prov. 25:8 nei. p. thee to shame
 10 heareth it p. thee to shame
Ec. 10:10 p. to more strength
Cant. 5:3 p. off coat, how p. on?
Is. 5:20 that p. darkn. for light
10:13 I ha. p. down inhabitants
42:1 I have p. my Spirit upon
 him, Mat. 12:18
47:11 not be able to p. it off
51:16 p. words in mou. Jer. 1:9
 23 p. into hand that afflict th.
53:10 he hath p. him to grief
59:21 words I p. in thy mouth
63:11 where is he that p. his H.
 Spirit within him?
Jer. 3:19 how shall I p. thee am.
8:14 Lord our G. p. us to silence
12:13 they p. themselves to pain
31:33 p. my law in inward parts
32:40 will p. my fear in hearts
Ezek. 8:17 p. branch to th. nose
11:19 I will put a new spirit
 within you, 36:26, 27; 37:14
16:14 comel. I had p. upon thee
29:4 p. hooks in thy jaws, 38:4
30:12 p. s fear in land of Egypt
37:6 p. breath in you, ye shall
Dan. 5:19 and whom he p. down
Mic. 3:12 I will p. them together
7:5 p. not confidence in a guide
Zep. 3:19 ha. been p. to shame
Mat. 5:15 candle p. under bushel
19:6 so man p. asun. Mark 10:9
25:52 p. up thy swo. John 18:11
Mark 10:16 p. his hands on them
Luke 1:52 hath p. down mighty
15:22 p. it on him and p. a ring
John 5:7 none to p. me into pool
Acts 1:7 Fa. p. in his own power
4:3 they p. the apostles in hold
5:25 men whom ye p. in prison
13:46 p. word of God from you
13:9 p. no difference between us
1 Cor. 15:24 p. down authority
 25 p. his enemies under his fe.
2 Cor. 8:16 G. p. same care in T.
Eph. 4:22 p. off old man, Col. 3:9
Col. 3:8 ye also p. off these, ang.
1 Tim. 1:12 p. thee in remembr.
Tit. 3:1 p. them in mind to be
 subject
Phile. 18 p. that on my account
Heb. 2:5 hath he not p. in subj.
6:6 p. him to an open shame
8:10 I will p. my laws in mind
10:16 p. my laws into th. hearts
Jam. 3:3 p. bits in horses' mou.
1 Pet. 3:15 p. to silence ignoran.
2 Pet. 1:14 I must p. off this tab.
Jude 5 will p. you in remembr.
Rev. 2:24 p. on you none other
17:17 God hath p. in th. hearts

PUT away

Gen. 35:2 p. away strange gods
Lev. 21:7 nor take a woman p. a.
Deut. 19:13 p. a. guilt of it. 21:9
22:19 he may not p. her a. 29
Jos. 24:14 p. a. strange gods,
 23; Jud. 10:16; 1 Sam. 7:3
1 Sam. 1:14 Eli said, p. a. wine
2 Sam. 7:15 Saul whom I p. a.
12:13 Lord hath p. a. thy sin
2 Chr. 15:8 Asa p. a. abom. idols
Rev. 10:3 a cove. to p. a. wives
 19 gave hands to p. a. wives
Ps. 18:22 I did not p. away his
 statutes
27:9 p. not thy serv. a. in anger
Prov. 4:24 p. a. a froward mou.
Is. 50:1 whom I have p. away
Jer. 3:1 if a man p. a. his wife
 8:2 if a man a given her a bill of div.
Ezek. 45:22 put p. take her a.
Hos. 2:2 let her p. a. whoredoms
Amos 6:3 that p. far a. evil day
Mat. 1:19 J. minded to p. her a.
Mark 10:2 lawful to p. a. wife?
 13 if a woman p. a. her husb.
1 Cor. 5:13 p. a. wicked person
7:11 let not hush. p. a. wife, 12
Eph. 4:31 evil speaking be p. a.

PUT

1 Tim. 1:19 some having p. aw.
Heb. 9:26 p. a. sin by sacrifice
 See DEATH, EVIL.

PUT forth.

Gen. 3:22 lest he p. f. take tree
8:9 N. p. f. his hand and took
19:10 men p. forth their hand
22. 6:4 p. f. thy hand and take
Deut. 33:14 precious things p. f.
Jud. 15:15 Samson p. f. took
1 Sam. 14:27 Jonathan p. f. rod
22:17 servants not p. f. to slay
24:10 not p. f. my hand ag. L.
2 Sam. 6:6 Uzziah p. forth his
 hand to ark, 1 Chr. 13:9
13:12 not p. f. my hand against
1 K. 13:4 Jeroboam p. f. his ha.
Job 1:11 p. f. hand and tou. 2:5
 12 on himself p. not f. hand
Ps. 55:20 p. f. his hands ag. him
123:3 lest righteous p. f. hands
Prov. 8:1 understan. p. f. voice?
25:6 p. not f. thyself in presen.
Jer. 1:9 Lord p. f. his hand
Ezek. 8:3 he p. f. form of a hand
 Mat. 9:25 when peop. were p. f.
13:24 para. p. he f. 31; Lu. 14:7
Acts 5:34 to p. the apostles forth
9:40 but Peter p. them all forth

PUT on,

Gen. 28:20 raiment to p. on
Lev. 6:10 priest sh. p. on linen
11 he sh. p. on other garments
16:4 shall p. on holy linen coat
Deut. 22:5 nor man p. on wom.'s
2 Sam. 1:24 S. p. on ornaments
14:2 p. on mourning apparel
1 K. 22:30 but p. thou on thy
 robes, 2 Chr. 18:29
Job 3:21 all able to p. on armor
Job 27:17 the just shall p. it on
Cant. 5:3 how shall I p. it on?
Is. 51:9 p. on strength, 52:1
Jer. 13:1 take girdle, p. it on, 2
Ezek. 24:17 and p. on thy shoes
Mat. 6:25 nor what ye shall p. on,
 Luke 12:22
21:7 p. on the ass their clothes
Mark 6:9 not p. on two coats
Luke 15:22 p. on him best robe
Rom. 13:14 p. ye on the L. J. C.
Gal. 3:27 baptized, have p. on C.
Eph. 4:24 p. on new m. Col. 3:10
Col. 3:12 p. on bowels of mercies
 14 p. on charity, which is bo.

PUT out.

Gen. 38:28 one p. out his hand
Lev. 6:12 fire of altar not be p. o.
Num. 5:2 p. out of camp leper, 4
 3 male and fem. shall p. o. p.
10:14 wilt thou p. out the eyes?
Deut. 7:22 L. will p. o. tho. nati.
25:6 that his name be not p. o.
Jud. 16:21 Philis. p. o. S.'s eyes
2 Sam. 13:17 p. this woman out
2 Chr. 29:7 have p. o. lamps
Job 18:5 light of wicked be p. o.
 6 his candle be p. out, 21:17;
  Prov. 13:9; 20:20; 24:20
Ps. 9:5 p. o. their name for ever
Ezek. 32:7 when I p. thee out
Mark 5:40 when he had p. them
 all out, Luke 8:54
John 9:22 be p. o. of synagogues
10:2 p. you out of synagogues
Jud. 9:15 p. t. in my shadow
2 K. 19:24 p. t. on Eg. R. 36:9
1 Chr. 5:20 they p. th. t. in him
Ps. 4:5 p. your trust in the Lord
5:11 all that p. t. in thee rejoice
7:1 O L. God in thee I p. trust,
 10:1; 25:20; 71:1
9:10 know thy name, p. trust
 in them
11:1 in L. p. I my t. 31:1; 71:1
17:7 which p. their t. in thee
36:7 p. their t. under thy wings
56:4 in God I have p. my trust
73:28 I have p. my t. in the L.
143:8 p. not your t. in princes
Jer. 39:18 thy t. in me
Jer. 39:18 hast p. the t. in thee
1 Thes. 2:4 p. in t. with gospel
Heb. 2:13 I will p. my t. in him

PUT, Participle.

Lev. 11:38 if water be p. on seed
19:19 shall be p. apart sev. days
Num. 19:19 not as long as she is p.
1 K. 22:10 kings p. on their rob.
2 K. 14:12 Judah was p. to worse
1 Chr. 19:16 Syri. p. to worse, 19
2 Chr. 2:14 cv. device shall be p.
6:24 if Israel be p. to the worse
25:22 Jud. was p. to the worse

QUE

Ps. 35:4 be p. to shame, 83:17
71:1 let me never be p. to con.
Prov. 25:7 shouldest be p. lower
Ec. 3:14 nothing can be p. to it
Ec. 5:4:4 shalt not be p. to shame
Jer. 50:42 every one p. in array
Zep. 3:19 have been p. to shame
Mar. 9:16 for that p. in to fill up
Luke 1:14 on I who was p. in prison
John 19:2 deity had p. on him
Heb. 2:8 noth. not p. under him
Rev. 11:9 not be. be p. in graves

PUTEOLI.

Acts 28:13 came next day to P.

PUTIEL. Ex. 6:25

PUTTEST.

Deut. 12:18 p. thy hands, 15:10
2 K. 18:14 that thou p. on me
Ps. 119:119 thou p. away wicked

PUTTETH.

Ex. 30:33 p. any on a stranger
Num. 22:38 God p. in my mouth
Deut. 25:11 woman p. forth hand
Job 15:15 he p. no trust in saints
38:8 p. for. his hand upon rock
33:11 he p. my feet in the stoc.
Ps. 15:5 he that p. not his money
75:7 p. down one and set. up
Prov. 25:25 p. his trust in Lord
80:25 p. his trust in L. be safe
Is. 57:13 p. trust in me pos. land
Lam. 3:29 p. his mouth in dust
Mic. 3:5 p. not into their mouths
Mat. 9:16 p. new cloth, Lu. 5:36
Lu. 8:16 no man p. ligh. candle
16:18 whoso p. away his wife
John 10:4 p. forth his own sheep

PUTTING.

Lev. 16:21 p. them upon head
Jud. 7:6 p. their hand to mouth
Is. 58:9 p. forth of the finger
Mal. 2:16 God hateth p. away
Acts 9:12 Ananias p. his hand, 17
19:33 Alex. J. p. him forward
Rom. 15:15 sort. as p. in mind
Col. 2:11 in p. off body of sins
1 Tim. 1:12 p. me into ministry
2 Tim. 1:6 by p. on my hands
1 Pet. 3:21 not p. a. filth of flesh

PUTREFYING.

Is. 1:6 wounds, bruises, p. sores

Q.

QUAILS.

Ex. 16:13 at even q. came up.
Num. 11:31 a wind fr. L. brot. q.
32 the people stood, gather. q.
Ps. 105:40 asked, he brought q.

QUAKE, ED.

Ex. 19:18 the mount q. greatly
1 Sam. 14:15 trembled, earth q.
Joel 2:10 earth shall q. bef. them
Nah. 1:5 the mountains q. at hi.
Mat. 27:51 earth q. the rocks re.
Heb. 12:21 M. said, I fear and q.

QUAKING.

Ezek. 12:18 eat thy bread with q.
Dan. 10:7 great q. fell on them

QUANTITY.

Is. 22:24 hang vessels of small q.

QUARREL.

Lev. 26:25 a sword sh. avenge q.
2 K. 5:7 see how he seeketh a q.
Mark 6:19 Her. had q. ag. John
Col. 3:13 if any have q. ag. any

QUARRIES.

Jud. 3:19 Ehud turned from q.
 26 Ehud escaped beyond the q.

QUARTER.

Gen. 19:4 peo. from ev. q. to Lo.
Jos. 18:14 Kirjath-jearim, w. q.
Is. 47:15 merchants wander to q.
56:11 every one fur. gain from q.
Mark 1:45 came to him fr. ev. q.
 See SOUTH.

QUARTERS.

Ex. 13:7 no leav. seen in thy q.
Deut. 22:12 fringes on four q.
1 Chr. 9:24 in four q. were port.
Is. 49:20 from four q. of heaven
Acts 9:32 Peter passed thr. all q.
16:3 Jews which were in th. q.
28:7 in the same q. were posse-
Rev. 20:8 nations in q. of earth

QUATERNIONS.

Acts 12:4 deliv. Peter to four q.

QUARTS.

Rom. 16:23 Q. a brother, salute.

QUEEN.

1 K. 10:1 q. of Sheba heard of
 fame of Solomon, 2 Chr. 9:1

QUI

1 K. 10:4 wh. q. saw Solom.'s w.
 10 spices q. of She. gave to S.
 13 Solomon gave q. of Sheba
  all her desire, 2 Chr. 9:3, 12
 11:19 gave Hadad sister of q.
15:13 Asa removed Maachah
 from being q. 2 Chr. 15:16
2 K. 10:13 salute children of q.
Neh. 2:6 king said, q. sitting by
Est. 1:9 Vashti q. made feast
 11 bring the q. 12 q. refused
 15 wh. sh. we do to q. Vashti?
 16 the q. hath not done wrong
 17 deed of q. sh. come abroad
 2:4 maiden that pleaseth be q.
 17 made Esther q. ins. of Vas.
4:4 q. grieved; 5:3 will. q. Est.
5:12 q. let no man to banquet
7:2 what is thy petition, q. Es.?
7 Haman made request to q.
 8 will he force the q. befo. me
8:1 house of Haman to Esth. q.
9:31 Mordecai and Esth. the q.
Ps. 45:9 the q. in gold of Ophir
Jer. 13:18 say to king and q.
44:17 burn inc. to q. of heaven
 25 vowed to burn incense to q.
Dan. 5:10 q. came to banq. house
 11 man q. of south shall rise
 up in judgment, Luke 11:31
Acts 8:27 Candace, q. of Ethiop.
Rev. 18:7 I sit q. am no widow

QUEENS.

Cant. 6:8 there are threesc. q. 9
Is. 49:23 their q. nursing moth.

QUENCH.

2 Sam. 14:7 they shall q. my coal
21:17 thou q. not light of Israel
Ps. 104:11 wild asses q. thirst
Cant. 8:7 waters cannot q. love
Is. 1:31 both burn, none q. them
42:3 shall he not q. Mat. 12:20
Jer. 4:4 burn, none q. it, 21:12
Amos 5:6 none to q. it in Beth-el
Eph. 6:16 to q. darts of wicked
1 Thes. 5:19 q. not the Spirit

QUENCHED.

Num. 11:2 fire q. 2 Chr. 34:25
2 K. 22:17 wrath shall not be q.
Ps. 118:12 they are q. as thorns
Is. 34:10 not be q. night nor day
43:17 they are q. as tow
66:24 nor shall their fire be q.
 Mar. 9:44, 46, 48
Ezek. 20:47 fla. sh. not be q. 48
Mark 9:43 fire never be q. 45
 44 where fire is not q. 46, 48
Heb. 11:34 q. the violence of fire

QUESTION, Substantive.

Mat. 22:35 lawyer asked him q.
Mark 11:29 I ask one q. ans. me
 12:34 durst ask q. Luke 20:40
John 3:25 arose q. bet disciples
Acts 15:2 came to apos. about q.
18:15 if it be q. of words
19:40 danger to be called in q.
23:6 of resur. called in q. 24:21
1 Cor. 10:25 asking no q. for, 27

QUESTION, Verb.

Mark 8:11 Phar. began to q. him
9:16 What q. ye with them?

QUESTIONED, ING.

2 Chr. 31:9 Heze. q. with priests
Mark 1:27 q. among themselves
9:10 q. what rising from dead
14 and scribes q. with them
Luke 23:9 Pilate q. with him

QUESTIONS.

1 K. 10:1 queen came to prove q.
 3 Sol. told her q. 2 Chr. 9:1, 2
Mat. 22:46 nei. ask him more q.
Luke 2:46 hearing and asking q.
Acts 23:29 accused of q. of law.
25:19 certain q. against him
20 doubted such manner of q.
26:3 thee to be expert in q.
1 Tim. 1:4 minister q. than edi.
6:4 doting about q. and strifes
2 Tim. 2:23 unlearned q. Tit. 3:9

QUICK.

Lev. 13:10 there be q. raw flesh
24 the q. flesh that burneth
Num. 16:30 go down q. into pit
Ps. 55:15 go down q. into hell
124:3 swallowed us up q.
Is. 11:3 make him of q. undert.
Acts 10:42 orda. to be judge of q.
1 Tim. 4:1 sh. judge q. and dead
Heb. 4:12 the word of God is q.
1 Pet. 4:5 to judge q. and dead

QUICKEN.

Ps. 71:20 thou shalt q. me again
80:18 q. us, we will call on name
119:25 q. me according, 107, 154
37 q. me in thy way

CRUDEN'S CONCORDANCE. 987

QUI

Ps. 119:40 *q.* me in thy righteen.
98 *q.* me after thy kindn. 159
149 *q.* me accord. to judgment
143:11 *q.* me, L. for name's sake
Rom. 8:11 shall *q.* mortal bodies

QUICKENED.

Ps. 119:50 thy word hath *q.* me
68 with precepts th. hast *q.* me
1 *Cor.* 15:36 thou sowest is not *q.*
Eph. 2:1 you he *q.* who were de.
5 *q.* us toge. with C. *Col.* 2:13
1 *Pet.* 3:18 death in flesh, *q.* by S.

QUICKENETH.

John 5:21 Father *q.* them, Son *q.*
6:63 Sp. *q.* flesh profit. nothing
Rom. 4:17 God, who *q.* dead
1 *Tim.* 6:13 God, who *q.* all thi.

QUICKENING.

1 *Cor.* 15:45 Adam made *q.* spir.

QUICKLY.

Gen. 18:6 make ready *q.* meas.
27:20 hast thou found it so *q.*
Ex. 32:8 turned *q.* out of way,
Deut. 9:12, 16; *Jud.* 2:17
Num. 16:46 go *q.* to congregation
Deut. 9:3 down *q.* 11:17 per. *q.*
28:20 perish *q.* because of doin.
Jos. 2:5 pursue *q.* overtake them
10:6 come up to us *q.* save us
23:16 ye shall perish *q.* off land
1 *Sam.* 20:19 thou sh. go down *q.*
2 *Sam.* 17:16 send *q.* and tell D.
18 went both of them away *q.*
21 arise, pass *q.* over the wat.
2 *K.* 1:11 said, Come down *q.*
Ec. 4:12 threef. cord not *q.* bro.
Mat. 5:25 agree with adversa. *q.*
28:7 go *q.* tell discip. he is risen
8 they departed *q.* *Mark* 16:8
Luke 14:21 sit down *q.* write fifty
John 11:29 M. arose *q.* came to J.
13:27 J. That thou doest do *q.*
Acts 12:7 saying, Arise and *q.*
22:18 get thee *q.* out of Jerusal.
Rev. 2:5 repent, else I come *q.* 16
3:11 behold, I come *q.* 22:7, 12
11:14 third woe cometh *q.*
22:20 I come *q.* even so come

QUICKSANDS.

Acts 27:17 they should fall into *q.*

QUIET.

Jud. 16:2 Phil. laid wait were *q.*
18:7 after Zidonians, *q.* secure
2 *K.* 11:20 city *q.* 2 *Chr.* 23:21
1 *Chr.* 4:40 land was wide and *q.*
2 *Chr.* 14:1 in his days land *q.*
5 the kingdom was *q.* 20:30
Job 3:13 now who. I have been *q.*
26 nelt. was I *q.* trouble came
21:23 dieth, being at ease, *q.*
Ps. 35:20 devise ag. *q.* in land
107:30 glad, because they be *q.*
Prov. 1:33 whoso hearken. be *q.*
Ec. 9:17 wor. of wise heard in *q.*
Is. 7:4 take heed, and be *q.* fear
14:7 the earth is at rest, and *q.*
32:18 my peo. shall dwell in *q.*
33:20 see Jerusal. *q.* habitation
Jer. 30:10 Jacob return, be in *q.*
47:6 how long ere thou be *q.* ?
7 he *q.* seeing L. given charge
49:23 sorrow on sea, can. be *q.*
51:59 Seraiah was a *q.* prince
Ezek. 16:42 fury rest, I will be *q.*
Nah. 1:12 though *q.* be cut down
Acts 19:36 ye ought to he *q.*
1 *Thes.* 4:11 that ye stu. to be *q.*
1 *Tim.* 2:2 we may lead a *q.* life
1 *Pet.* 3:4 ornament of a *q.* spirit

QUIETED, ETI.

Job 37:17 *q.* earth by south wind
Ps. 131:2 *q.* myself as a child
Zec. 6:8 *q.* my spirit in north

QUIETLY.

2 *Sam.* 3:27 Joab took Abner *q.*
Lam. 3:26 *q.* wait for salva. of L.

QUIETNESS.

Jud. 8:28 the country was in *q.*
1 *Chr.* 22:9 I will give *q.* to Isr.
Job 20:20 sh. not feel *q.* in belly
34:29 *q.* who can make trouble?
Prov. 17:1 bet. dry morsel and *q.*
Ec. 4:6 better is handful with *q.*
Is. 30:15 in *q.* and assurance
32:17 righte. *q.* and assurance
Acts 24:2 we enjoy great *q.*
2 *Thes.* 3:12 we eat, that with *q.*

QUIT.

Ex. 21:19 smote him he *q.*
Jos. 2:20 we will be *q.* of oath
1 *Sam.* 4:9 *q.* like men, 1 *Cor.* 16:13

QUITE.

Gen. 31:15 *q.* devoured our mon.

RAH

Ez. 23:34 *q.* break down images
Num. 17:10 *q.* take away murm.
33:52 *q.* pluck down high places
2 *Sam.* 3:24 Abner away, *q.* gone
Job 6:13 is wisdom *q.* from me ?
Hab. 3:9 thy bow made *q.* naked

QUIVER.

Gen. 27:3 take thy *q.* and bow
Job 39:23 *q.* rattleth against him
Ps. 127:5 man that hath *q.* full
Is. 22:6 E. bare *q.* with chariots
49:2 polished shaft in his *q.*
Jer. 5:16 *q.* is as open sepulchre
Lam. 3:13 arrows of *q.* ent. reins

QUIVERED.

Hab. 3:16 my lips *q.* at the voice

R.

RABBAH, or RABBATH.

Deut. 3:11 is it not in R. of chil.
2 *Sam.* 11:1 J. besieged R. 12:26
17:27 Shobi of R. brought beds
1 *Chr.* 20:1 Joab smote R. and
Jer. 49:2 alarm heard in R. 3
Ezek. 21:20 sw. may come to R.
25:5 I will make R. a stable
Amos 1:14 a fire in wall of R.

RABBI.

Mat. 23:7 called of men, *r. r.*
8 be not ye called *r.* for one is
John 1:38 li. wh. dwellest thou *r.*
49 R. thou art the Son of God
3:2 R. we know thou art teach.
26 R. he that was with thee
6:25 R. when cam. thou hither ?

RABBONI.

John 20:16 M. turn. and saith, R.

RAB-SHAKEH.

2 *K.* 18:17 Assy. sent, *Is.* 36:2
37 told words of R. *Is.* 36:22
19:4 hear words of R. 37:4

RACE.

Ps. 19:5 strong man to run a *r.*
Ec. 9:11 *r.* is not to the swift
1 *Cor.* 9:24 they wh. run in a *r.*
Heb. 12:1 run with patience *r.*

RACHEL.

Gen. 29:12 Jacob told R. that he
30:1 R. bare no chil. R. 22
2 anger was kindled ag. R. 22
31:19 R. had stolen imag. 34
35:19 R. died, 24 ; 46:22 ; 48:7
Ruth 4:11 make woman like R.
1 *Sam.* 10:2 men by R. sepulch.
Jer. 31:15 R. weeping, *Mat.* 2:18

RAFTERS.

Cant. 1:17 beams cedar *r.* of fir

RAGAU.

Luke 3:35 Saruch, the son of R.

RAGE.

2 *K.* 5:12 Naaman turned in a *r.*
19:27 I know thy *r. Is.* 37:28
2 *Chr.* 16:10 A. in a wrath *r.* cor
28:9 ye have slain them in a *r.*
Job 39:24 swalloweth. ground wi. *r.*
40:11 cast abroad *r.* of wrath
Ps. 7:6 lift up thyself bec. of *r.*
Prov. 6:34 jeal. is *r.* of a man
Dan. 3:13 Neb. commanded in *r.*
Hos. 7:16 fall for *r.* of th. tongue

RAGE, Verb.

Ps. 2:1 heathen *r. ? Acts* 4:25
Prov. 29:9 whefh. he *r.* or laugh
Jer. 46:9 come up *r.* ye chariots
Nah. 2:4 chariots sh. *r.* in street.

RAGED, ETH.

Ps. 46:6 heath. *r.* kingd. moved
Prov. 14:16 fool *r.* is confident

RAGING.

Ps. 89:9 thou ruiest *r.* of sea
Prov. 20:1 strong drink *r.*
Jon. 1:15 sea ceased from *r.*
Luke 8:24 rebuked *r.* of water
Jude 13 *r.* waves of sea foam.

RAGS.

Prov. 23:21 clothe man with *r.*
Is. 64:6 righte. are as filthy *r.*
Jer. 38:11 Ebed. took rotten *r.*
12 *r.* under thine armholes

RAHAB.

Jos. 2:1 house of R. 6:17, 25
Ps. 87:4 I make mention of R.
89:10 thou hast broken R. in
Is. 51:9 not it that hath cut R.
Mat. 1:5 Salmon begat R. of R
Heb. 11:31 by faith harlot R.
Jam. 2:25 was not R. justified ?

RAI

RAIL, ED.

1 *Sam.* 25:14 Nabal *r.* on David's
2 *Chr.* 32:17 Sen. wrote let. to *r.*
Mark. 15:29 that passed *r.* on J.
Luke 23:39 one of malefactors *r.*

RAILER.

1 *Cor.* 5:11 keep not com. wi. *r.*

RAILING.

1 *Tim.* 6:4 whereof co. strife, *r.*
1 *Pet.* 3:9 not rendering *r.* for *r.*
2 *Pet.* 2:11 angels br. not *r.* accu.
Jude 9 durst not bring *r.* accus.

RAIMENT.

Gen. 24:53 serv. gave *r.* to Reb.
27:15 Rebekah took goodly *r.*
28:20 if L. give me *r.* to put on
41:14 Joseph shaved, changed *r.*
45:22 each man changes of *r.*
Ex. 3:22 borrow of Eg. *r.* 12:35
21:10 her *r.* sh. he not diminish
22:9 trespass for sheep, for *r.*
26 thou take neighbor's *r.* 27
Lev. 11:32 uncl. beasts fall on *r.*
Num. 31:20 purify all your *r.*
Deut. 8:4 thy *r.* waxed not old
10:18 L. loveth stranger, giv. *r.*
21:13 put *r.* of captivity fr. her
22:3 lost *r.* restore
24:13 he may sleep in his *r.*
17 shalt not take a widow's *r.*
Jos. 22:8 return with much *r.*
Jud. 3:16 E. a dagger under *r.*
8:26 purple *r.* that was on kings
Ruth 3:3 and put thy *r.* on thee
1 *Sam.* 28:8 Saul disg. put on *r.*
2 *K.* 5:5 Naam. took chang. of *r.*
7 *Chr.* 9:24 Solomon, gold, and *r.*
Est. 4:4 sent *r.* to clothe Morde.
Job 27:16 tho' he prep. *r.* as clay
29, 45:11 brought to king in *r.*
Is. 14:19 cast out as *r.* of slain
63:3 and I will stain all my *r.*
Ezek. 16:13 *r.* was of fine linen
Zec. 3:4 clothe him with *r.*
Mat. 3:4 J. had *r.* of camel's hair
6:25 body more th. *r. Luke* 12:23
28 why take ye thought for *r.*?
11:8 clothed in soft *r. Lu.* 7:25
17:2 his *r.* white as light, *Mark* 9:3 ; *Luke* 9:29
27:31 put his own *r.* on him
28:3 and his *r.* white as snow
Luke 19:30 thieves strl. him of *r.*
23:34 parted his *r. John* 19:24
Acts 18:6 Paul shook his *r.*
22:20 I kept *r.* of them that sle.
1 Tim. 6:8 having food and *r.*
Jam. 2:2 a poor man in vile *r.*
Rev. 3:5 be clothed in white *r.*
18 buy white *r.* that thou ma.
4:4 I saw 24 elders in white *r.*

RAIN, Substantive.

Gen. 7:12 *r.* was upon earth
8:2 *r.* from heaven was restrain.
Ex. 9:33 the *r.* was not poured
34 Pharaoh saw the *r.* ceased
Lev. 26:4 will give you *r.* in due
season, *Deut.* 11:14 ; 28:12
Deut. 11 drink. of *r.* of heaven
17 shut up heaven that th. be no *r.*
2 *K.* 8:35 ; 2 *Chr.* 6:26 ; 7:13
28:21 Lord shall make *r.* of land
32:2 my doctrine sh. drop as *r.*
Jud. 12:17 call on L. send thun.
18 Lord sent thunder and *r.*
2 *Sam.* 1:21 let there be no *r.*
23:4 as clear shining after *r.*
1 *K.* 8:36 hear, give *r.* 2 *Chr.* 6:27
17:1 th. shall be no *r.* nor dew
14 Lord shall send *r.* upon earth
18:1 I will send *r.* upon earth
41 abun. of *r.* 44 a great *r.*
45 there was a great *r.*
Job 5:10 giveth *r.* upon the earth
28:26 made a decree for *r.*
29:23 waited for me as for *r.*
37:6 to small *r.* and to great *r.*
38:28 hath *r.* a father ?
Ps. 68:9 didst send plentiful *r.*
72:6 he shall come down *r.*
84:6 *r.* filleth the pools
105:32 he gave them hail for *r.*
135:7 he caus. lightnings for *r.*
147:8 L. prepareth *r.* for earth
Prov. 25:14 like clouds without *r.*
23 north wind driveth away *r.*
26:1 snow in summer, and *r.* in
28:3 oppresseth poor is like a *r.*
Ec. 11:3 if clouds be full of *r.*
12:2 nor clouds return after *r.*
Cant. 2:11 the *r.* is over and go.

RAI

Is. 4:6 covert from storm and *r.*
5:6 com. clouds they rain no *r.*
30:23 thou shalt he give tho *r.*
44:14 an ash, *r.* doth nourish it
55:10 as *r.* cometh from heaven
Jer. 5:24 let us fear L. giveth *r.*
10:13 maketh lightn. wi. *r.* 51:16
14:4 ground chapt, no *r.* was
22 vanities of G. can cause *r. ?*
Ezek. 1:28 as bow in cloud in *r.*
38:22 I will *r.* an overflowing *r.*
Hos. 6:3 shall make us as the *r.*
Joel 2:23 cause to come down *r.*
Amos 4:7 I have withholden *r.*
Zec. 14:17 upon th. be no *r.*
Mat. 5:45 he sendeth *r.* on just
7:25 and the *r.* descended, 27
Acts 14:17 did good, and gave *r.*
28:2 because of the present *r.*
Heb. 6:7 earth drinketh in the *r.*
Jam. 5:18 and the heav. gave *r.*
See LATTER.

RAIN, Verb.

Gen. 2:5 L. not caused it to *r.*
7:4 cause to *r.* 40 days a. nights
Ex. 9:18 to-morrow cause it to *r.*
16:4 I will *r.* bread from heaven
Job 20:23 G. shall *r.* his fury
38:26 cause it to *r.* on the earth
Ps. 11:6 on wicked he shall *r.*
Is. 5:6 that they *r.* no rain on it
Ezek. 38:22 I will *r.* overflow. ra.
Hos. 10:12 come and *r.* righteou.
Amos 4:7 I caused it to *r.* on city
Jam. 5:17 E. pray it might. not *r.*
Rev. 11:6 *r.* not in days of prop.

RAINBOW.

Rev. 4:3 th. was a *r.* round about
10:1 and a *r.* was upon his head

RAINED.

Gen. 19:24 L. *r.* upon S. and G.
Ex. 9:23 the L. *r.* hail on Egypt
Ps. 78:24 *r.* down manna, 27
Ezek. 22:24 the land not *r.* upon
Amos 4:7 one piece was *r.* upon
Luke 17:29 it *r.* fire from heaven

RAINY.

Prov. 27:15 dropping in a *r.* day

RAISE.

Gen. 38:8 *r.* seed to brother ?
Ex. 23:1 shalt not *r.* false report
Deut. 18:15 L. thy God *r.* up a
prophet, 18 ; *Acts* 3:22 ; 7:37
25:7 refuseth to *r.* up to brother
Jos. 8:29 *r.* ther. a heap of stones
Ruth 4:5 *r.* up name of dead, 10
1 *Sam.* 2:35 *r.* faithful priest
2 *Sam.* 12:11 *r.* evil against thee
17 went to *r.* him from earth
1 *K.* 14:14 L. shall *r.* king in Is.
1 *Chr.* 17:11 I will *r.* up thy seed
Job 3:8 ready to *r.* up mourning
19:12 his troops *r.* up ag. me
30:12 *r.* ways of destruction
Ps. 41:10 L. be merciful, *r.* me
Is. 15:5 *r.* cry of destruction
29:3 I will *r.* forts against thee
41:25 will *r.* up decayed places
49:6 servant to *r.* tribes of Jacob
Jer. 6:22 *r.* foundations of genera.
49:14 *r.* no former desolations
Jer. 23:5 will *r.* to Dav. a branch
50:9 *r.* ag. Babylon assembly
32 none *r.* him ; 51:1 *r.* wind
Ezek. 23:22 will *r.* lovers ag. th.
34:29 *r.* up plant of renown
Hos. 6:2 in third day he will *r.*
Joel 3:7 *r.* them whither ye driv.
Amos 5:2 virgin of Is. none to *r.*
6:14 I will *r.* a nation ag. you
9:11 I will *r.* tabernacle of Dav.
Mic. 5:5 *r.* against him 7 sheph.
Hab. 1:3 th. are that *r.* up strife
6 I will *r.* up Chaldeans
2:7 *r.* up that shall vex thee
Mal. 2:9 *r.* children to J. *Lu.* 3:8
22:71 *r.* up seed to his brother,
Mark 12:19 ; *Luke* 20:28
John 2:19 three days I will *r.* it
6:39 nothing lost, *r.* it up, 54
Acts 3:6 to *r.* on fire,
26:8 why incredible G. *r.* dead ?
1 *Cor.* 6:14 th. *r.* up us by power
2 Cor. 4:14 sh. *r.* up us by Jesus
Heb. 11:19 God able to *r.* him up
Jam. 5:15 L. shall *r.* him up

RAISED.

Ex. 9:16 f. *r.* thee up to show my
power, *Rom.* 9:17
Jos. 8:7 chil. he *r.* up in stead
7:26 *r.* over him heap of stones
Jud. 2:16 L. *r.* up judges, 18
3:9 *r.* a deliverer to Israel, 15

CRUDEN'S CONCORDANCE.

RAM

2 *Sam.* 23:1 who was r. on high
1 *K.* 5:13 Sol. r. a levy of Is. 9:15
Ex. 1:5 all whose spirit God r.
Job 14:13 nor r. out of their sleep
Cant. 6:5 r. th. under apple-tree
Is. 14:9 it r. up kings of nations
23:13 Assyrians r. palaces of C.
41:2 r. righteous man from eat
25 I r. up one from the north
45:13 I r. him up in righteous.
Jer. 6:22 great nation r. fr. earth
20:15 L. r. proph. in Babylon
50:41 kings shall be r. fr. earth
51:11 L. r. spirit of kings of M
Dan. 7:5 bear r. up on one side
Amos 2:11 I r. up sons for prop.
Zec. 2:13 r. out of holy habitati.
9:13 when I r. thy sons, O Zion
Mat. 11:5 dead r. up, *Luke* 7:22
16:21 r. again, 17:23; *Luke* 9:22
Luke 1:69 r. up horn of salvation
20:37 dead are r, Moses showed
John 12:1 Laz. whom he r. 9, 17
Acts 2:24 whom God hath r. up
32; 3:15, 26; 4:10; 5:30; 10:40;
13:30, 33, 34; 17:31; *Rom.*
10:9; 1 *Cor.* 6:14; *Gal.*
4:14; *Gal.* 1:1; *Eph.* 1:20
12:7 angel r. Peter; 13:22 r. Da.
13:23 G. r. Israel a Saviour J.
Rom. 4:24 bel. on him that r. J.
25 r. again for our justification
6:4 C. was r. fr. dead by Father
9 Ch. r. fr. dead, dieth no mo.
7:4 to him who is r. from dead
8:11 if Sp. of him that r. Jesus
1 *Cor.* 15:15 r. up C, wh. he r. n.
16 dead rise not, C. is not r.
17 if C. be not r. faith r. is vain
35 bed say, How are dead r.?
42 sown in cor. r. in incorru, 52
43 is is r. in glory, r. in power
44 sown natu. body, r. spirit.
Eph. 2:6 r. us together in Ch. J
2 *Cor.* 2:12 through G. who r. him
1 *Thes.* 1:10 Son, he r. from dea.
2 *Tim.* 2:8 Je. seed of Da. was r.
Heb. 11:35 wom. received dead r.
1 *Pet.* 1:21 bel. in G. that r. him

RAISER.
Dan. 11:20 stand up r. of taxes

RAISETH.
1 *Sam.* 2:8 he r. poor, *Ps.* 113:7
Job 41:25 r. himself, mighty
Ps. 107:25 commands, r. winds
145:14 he r. those bowed, 146:8
John 5:21 the Father r. up dead
2 *Cor.* 1:9 trust in G. wh. r. dead

RAISING.
Hos. 7:4 baker who coaseth fr. r.
Acts 24:12 found me r. up people

RAISINS.
1 *Sam.* 25:18 Ab. took 100 clus. r.
30:12 gave Egyp. two clusters r.
2 *Sam.* 16:1 met D. 100 bunch. r.
1 *Chr.* 12:40 brought bunch. of r.

RAM.
Ruth 4:19 : 1 *Chr.* 2:9, 10, 25, 27
Job 32:2 Elihu of kindred of R.

RAM.
Gen. 15:9 take a r. 3 years old
22:13 a r. caught in a thicket
Ex. 29:15 take one r. 16 slay r.
22 r. of conse. 27, 31 ; *Lev.* 8:22
Lev. 9:2 take r. for burnt-offer.
4 r. peace-offer. 19:21 trespass
Num. 5:8 besi. r. for atonement
Ezr. 10:19 they offered r.
Ezek. 43:23 they sh. offer a r. 25
34:24 ephah for a r. 45:5, 7, 11
46:6 in day of new moon a r.
Dan. 8:3 I saw r. had two horns
4 I saw r. pushing westward
6 goat ran to r. had two horns
7 no power in r. to deliver r.

RAMS.
Gen. 31:10 r. leaped ring-stre. 12
38 r. of flock have I not eaten
32:14 Jacob sent Esau twenty r.
Deut. 32:14 with r. breed of Bas.
1 Sam. 15:22 hearken fa. fat of r.
2 *K.* 3:4 Moah rendered 100,000 r.
1 *Chr.* 29:21 sacrifi. to L. 1,000 r.
2 *Chr.* 17:11 offl. at dedication 300 r.
Ezr. 6:17 off. at dedication 200 r.
7:17 buy with this money r.
8:35 offered ninety-six r. for sin
Ps. 66:15 with fat of r. *Is.* 34:6
114:4 mount, skipped like r. 6
Is. 1:11 full of burnt-offeri. of r.
31:6 filled with fat of kids, of r.
60:7 r. of Nebaioth sh. minister
Jer. 51:40 br. to slaughter like r.
Ezek. 27:21 Kedar occupied in r.
34:17 I judge betw. r. and goats

RAN

Ezek. 30:18 ye sh. dr. blood of r.
Mic. 6:7 L. be pleased with r. ?
See **BATTERING, SEVEN.**

RAMS' horns.
Jos. 6:4 seven priests shall bear
before ark r. *horns,* 5, 6, 8, 13

RAMS' skins.
Ex. 25:5 r. *sk.* dyed red, 26:14;
35:7 ; 36:19; 39:34

RAMAH, RAMA.
Jos. 18:25 R. a city of tribe of
Jud. 4:5 Deborah dwelt betw. R.
1 *Sam.* 1:19 his house in R. 2:11
7:17 return to R. 15:34; 16:13
8:4 elders came to S. unto R.
19:18 Dav. came to Sa. to R. 22
23:1 buried in house at R. 28:3
1 *K.* 15:17 builit R. 2 *Chr.* 16:1
2 *K.* 8:29 wonn. at R. 2 *Chr.* 22:6
Neh. 11:33 chil. of B. dwell at R.
Is. 10:29 R. is afraid, Gibeah of
Jer. 31:15 heard in R. *Mat.* 2:18
Ezek. 27:22 the merchants of R.
Hos. 5:8 blow ye trumpet in R.

RAMOTH-GILEAD.
Deut. 4:43 ; *Jos.* 20:8 ; 21:38
1 *K.* 4:13 Geber officer in R.
22:3 that R. is ours, 4, 6, 12, 15
2 *K.* 8:28 against Hazael in R.
9:1 take box of oil, go to R. 14
2 *Chr.* 18:3, 11, 14; 22:5

RAMPART.
Lam. 2:8 he made r. to lament
Nah. 3:8 whose r. was the sea

RAN.
Gen. 18:2 Abr. r. from tent-door
7 r. to herd; 24:17 r. meet R.
24:20 Rebek. r. to well to draw
28:11 Rachel r. and told father
13 Laban r. to meet Jacob and
33:4 Esau r. and embraced him
Ex. 9:23 fire r. along the ground
Num. 11:27 r. one and told Mo.
16:47 Aaron r. into congregat.
Jud. 7:21 host of Midian r. fled
13:10 Manoah's wife r. showed
1 *Sam.* 3:5 Samuel r. to Eli, said
10:23 they r. and fetched Saul
17:22 D. r. and saluted brethren
51 D. r. stood upon Philistine
20:36 as lad r. he shot an arrow
2 *Sam.* 18:23 Ahimaaz r. by plain
1 *K.* 2:30 serv. of Shimel r. away
18:33 water r. about the altar
46 Elijah r. before Ahab to Je.
19:20 Elisha r. after Elijah
22:35 blood r. in midst of char.
Ps. 77:2 my sore r. in the night
105:41 waters r. in dry places
133:2 ointment r. down on bea.
Jer. 23:21 I have not sent, they r.
Ezek. 1:14 the living creatures r.
41:2 in. r. out waters on ri. side
Dan. 8:6 the goat r. to the ram
Mat. 8:32 herd of swine r. into
sea, *Mark* 5:13 ; *Luke* 8:33
Mark 6:33 and r. afoot thither
Luke 15:20 father r. fell on neck
19:4 Zacch. r. and climbed tree
John 20:4 they r. both together
Acts 8:11 the people r. unto th.
7:57 they r. upon Stephen with
8:30 Philip r. to the chariot and
12:14 knew Peter's voice she r.
14:14 Paul and Barnabas r. in
21:30 people r. and took Paul
32 captain took soldiers and r.
27:41 they r. the ship aground
Jude 11 r. after error of Balaam

RANG.
1 *Sam.* 4:5 shouted, the earth r.
1 *K.* 1:45 Is. shouted, the city r.

RANGE.
Job 39:8 r. of mountains pasture

RANGES.
Lev. 11:35 r. for pots, be broken
2 *K.* 11:8 cometh in r. be slain
15 ha. her forth, r. 2 *Chr.* 23:14

RANGING.
Prov. 28:15 roar. lion and r. bear

RANK.
Gen. 41:5 on one stock, r. good
7 seven thin ears dev. r. ears
Num. 2:16 set forth in second r.
24 shall go forward in third r.
1 *Chr.* 12:33 of Ze. 50,000 keep r.
38 men that keep r. came to H.

RANKS.
1 *K.* 7:4 against light three r. 5
Joel 2:7 shall not break their r.
Mark 6:40 sat down in r. by
hundreds,

REA

RANSOM, Substantive.
Ex. 21:30 shall give for r. of life
30:12 give ev. man r. for his so.
Job 33:24 del. from pit, I found r.
36:18 great r. cannot deliv. thee
Ps. 49:7 nor can they give G. a r.
Prov. 6:35 will not regard any r.
13:8 r. of man's life are riches
21:18 wicked be r. for righteous
Is. 43:3 I gave Egypt for thy r.
Mat. 20:28 even us the Son of
man ga. life a r. *Mark* 10:45
1 *Tim.* 2:6 who gave himself r.

RANSOM.
Hos. 13:14 will r. them fr. grave

RANSOMED.
Is. 35:10 r. of the L. shall return
51:10 made sea a way for the r.
Jer. 31:11 L. redeemed J. and r.

RAPHA and RAPHU.
Num. 13:9 Benj. Palti, son of R.
1 *Chr.* 8:37 R. Eleasah, Azel

RARE.
Dan. 2:11 r. thing king requireth

RASE.
Ps. 137:7 r. it. r. it to foundat.

RASH, LY.
Ec. 5:2 be not r. with mouth
Acts 19:36 be quiet, do nothi. r.

RATE.
Ex. 16:4 peo. gather certain r.
1 *K.* 10:25 mules at r. 2 *Chr.* 9:24
Ex. 23:30 daily r. for every day
2 *Chr.* 8:13 even after a certain r.

RATHER.
Jos. 22:24 we have not r. done
2 *K.* 5:13 r. when he saith to th.
Mat. 25:9 go ye r. to th. th. sell
Mark. 5:26 but r. grew worse
Rom. 8:34 yea, r. that is risen a.
1 *Cor.* 7:21 be made free, use it r.
Gal. 4:9 or r. known of God
Heb. 13:19 I beseech you r. do

RATTLETH.
Job 39:23 quiver r. against him

RATTLING.
Nah. 3:2 noise of r. of wheels

RAVEN.
Gen. 8:7 Noah sent forth a r.
Lev. 11:15 r. unclean, *Deut.* 14:14
Job 38:41 prov. r. food, *Ps.* 147:9
Prov. 30:17 r. of val. shall pick
Cant. 5:11 bushy, black as r.

RAVENS.
1 *K.* 17:4 commanded r. to feed
6 the r. brought Elijah bread
Luke 12:24 consider r. nei. sow

RAVENING.
Ps. 22:13 gaped as r. lion
Ezek. 22:25 like a roaring lion r.
27 princes are like wolves r.
Mat. 7:15 they are r. wolves
Luke 11:39 inw. part is full of r.

RAVENOUS.
Is. 35:9 nor any r. beast sh. go
46:11 calling a r. bird from east
Ezek. 39:4 give thee to r. birds

RAVIN, Verb.
Gen. 49:27 Benjamin r. as wolf

RAVIN.
Nah. 2:12 lion filled dens with r.

RAVISHED.
Prov. 5:19 be thou r. with love
20 why be r. with st. woman ?
Cant. 4:9 thou hast r. my heart
Is. 13:16 wives of Bab. sh. be r.
Lam. 5:11 r. the women in Zion
Zec. 14:2 women in Jerus. be r.

RAW.
Ex. 12:9 eat not it r. nor sodden
Lev. 13:10 if th. be quick r. flesh
15 priest see r. flesh, r. flesh
1 *Sam.* 2:15 not sod. flesh, but r.

RAZOR.
Num. 6:5 nor r. upon head, *Jud.*
13:5 ; 16:17 ; 1 *Sam.* 1:11
Ps. 52:2 tongue like a sharp r.
Is. 7:20 Lord shave with a r.
Ezek. 5:1 take thee a barber's r.

REACH.
Gen. 11:4 tower r. to heaven
Ex. 28:42 breeches r. to thighs
Lev. 26:5 threshing r. to vintage
Num. 34:11 border shall r. to sea
Job 20:6 his head r. unto clouds
28:4 sh. r. even to neck
Zec. 14:5 mountains sh. r. to A.
John 20:27 r. hither thy finger
2 *Cor.* 10:13 meas. r. to you

REA

REACHED.
Gen. 28:12 ladder's top r. to hea.
Ruth 2:14 he r. her parched corn
Dan. 4:11 height r. to heaven, 20
2 *Cor.* 10:14 tho' we r. not to you
Rev. 18:5 Babyl.'s sins r. heaven

REACHETH.
2 *Chr.* 28:9 rage that r. to heav.
Ps. 36:5 faithfulness r. clouds
108:4 thy truth r. to the clouds
Prov. 31:20 r. hands to needy
Jer. 4:10 the sword r. to the soul
18 because it r. to thy heart
51:9 Bab.'s judgm. r. to heaven
Dan. 4:22 thy greatness r. heav.

REACHING.
Phil. 3:13 r. forth to th. things

READ (*short e*).
Jos. 8:34 r. in audience of people
2 *K.* 5:7 king of Isr. r. the letter
22:8 Shaphan r. book of law, 10
23:2 Josiah r. in their ears book
of the covenant, 2 *Chr.* 34:30
1 *Chr.* 34:24 Jeri. all the curses r.
Ezr. 4:18 letter been plainly r.
Neh. 8:3 he r. before all the book
of the law, 8; 13:1
9:3 stood in their place and r.
Est. 6:1 book of records was r.
Is. 37:14 received let. and r. it
Jer. 29:29 Zephani. the priest r.
36:10 then r. Bar. words of Jer.
21 Jehudi r. it in ears of king
23 he r. three or four leaves
Mat. 12:3 have ye not r. ? 19:4;
21:16 ; 22:31 ; *Mark* 2:25 ;
12:10, 26 ; *Luke* 6:3
John 19:20 this r. many of Jews
Acts 8:28 eunuch r. Esaias prop.
32 place of scripture wh. he r.
13:27 prophets r. ev. sab. 15:21
23:34 Governor had r. the letter
2 *Cor.* 3:2 epistle known and r.
15 when M. is r. the veil is on
Col. 4:10 when this epistle is r.
1 *Thes.* 5:27 that this epistle be r.

READ (*long e*).
Deut. 17:19 shy, night, therein
31:11 thou sh. r. this law before
Is. 30:11 th. r. I pray thee, 12
34:16 seek out book of L. and r.
Jer. 36:6 go and r. in the roll
15 sit do. and r. it in our ears
51:61 cometh to Babylon and r.
Dan. 5:7 whosoever shall r. this
17 gifts be to thyself, I will r.
Mat. 21:42 did ye never r. in sc. ?
Luke 4:16 Jesus went in for to r.
Acts 8:30 Philip heard him r. E.
2 *Cor.* 1:13 we write none other
things than what ye r.
Eph. 3:4 wh. ye r. ye may und.
Col. 4:16 r. epistle fr. Laodicea.
Rev. 5:4 none worthy to r. book

READEST.
Luke 10:26 in law, how r. thou?
Acts 8:30 un. thou what thou r. ?

READETH.
Hab. 2:2 he may run that r. it
Mat. 24:15 whoso r. let him un-
derstand, *Mark* 13:14
Rev. 1:3 blessed is he that r.

READING.
Neh. 8:8 caused to understand r.
Jer. 36:8 r. in the book of the L.
51:63 wh. hast ma. an end of r.
Acts 13:15 after the r. of the law
23:21 an unknown away in r.
1 *Tim.* 4:13 give attendance to r.

READINESS.
Acts 17:11 received word in r.
2 *Cor.* 8:11 as there was a r.
10:6 r. to revenge disobedience

READY.
Ex. 17:4 people r. to stone me
19:11 r. against third day, 15
34:2 r. in morning, and come
Num. 16:17 we will go r. armed
32:17 be r. armed bef. Is. of Is.
1 *Sam.* 13:15 thy servants are r.
16:22 hast no tidings r. ?
Ezr. 7:6 Ezra was a r. scribe
Neh. 9:17 art a God r. to pardon
Est. 3:14 they should be r. 8:13
Job 3:8 r. to raise their mourning
15:23 day of darkn. is r. at hand
24 prevail as a king r. to battle
28 in houses r. to become hea.
18:12 destruction r. at his side
29:13 blessing of him r. to perl.
Ps. 88:17 for I am r. to halt
45:1 tongue pen of a r. writer
86:5 Lord art good, r. to forgive
88:15 r. to die from my youth

CRUDEN'S CONCORDANCE. 989

REA

Prov. 24:11 those *r.* to be slain
31:6 stro. drink to him *r.* to pe.
Ec. 5:1 *r.* to hear th. give sacrif.
Is. 27:13 who were *r.* to perish
30:13 iniq. as breach *r.* to fall
32:4 tongue of stam. *r.* to speak
38:20 the L. was *r.* to save me
51:13 as if he were *r.* to destroy
Dan. 3:15 if ye be *r.* to worship
Mat. 22:4 fatlings killed, all *r.*
8 the wedding is *r. Luke* 14:17
24:44 be ye also *r. Luke* 12:40
25:10 they that were *r.* went in
Mark 14:38 spirit is *r.* flesh weak
Luke 7:2 servant sick, *r.* to die
22:33 L. I am *r.* to go with thee
John 7:6 your time is always *r.*
Acts 21:13 I am *r.* not to be boa.
23:21 are *r.* looking for promise
Rom. 1:15 I am *r.* to preach gos.
2 *Cor.* 8:19 declaration of *r.* mind
9:2 Achaia was *r.* a year ago
3 that, as I said, ye might be *r.*
5 that the same might be *r.*
12:14 third time I am *r.* to come
1 *Tim.* 6:18 ye be *r.* to distribute
2 *Tim.* 4:6 now *r.* to be offered
Tit. 3:1 be *r.* to every good work
Heb. 8:13 is *r.* to vanish away
1 *Pet.* 1:5 *r.* to be revealed
3:15 be *r.* always to give answer
4:5 give account to him th. is *r.*
5:2 not for lucre, of a *r.* mind
Rev. 3:2 things that are *r.* to die
12:4 wo. was *r.* to be delivered

See MADE, MAKE.

REALM.
2 *Chr.* 20:30 the *r.* of Jehosaph.
Ezr. 7:13 they of my *r.* who go
23 why he wrath against *r.?*
Dan. 1:20 better th. all in his *r.*
6:3 king tho. to set him over *r.*
9:1 Darius, king over *r.* of Chal.
11:2 stir np all ng. *r.* of Grecia

REAP.
Lev. 19:9 when ye *r.* 23:10, 22
25:5 groweth of itself sh. not *r.*
11 ye shall neither sow nor *r.*
Ruth 2:9 eyes be on field they *r.*
1 *Sam.* 8:12 set your serva. to *r.*
2 *K.* 19:29 in the third year sow and *r. Is.* 37:30
Job 4:8 sow wickedness *r.* same
24:6 they *r.* every one his corn
Ps. 126:5 sow in tears *r.* in joy
Prov. 22:8 soweth iniq. *r.* vanity
Ec. 11:4 regard clouds sh. not *r.*
Jer. 12:13 sown wheat, *r.* thorns
Hos. 8:7 sown wind, *r.* whirlwind
10:12 sow in rightco. *r.* in mercy
Mic. 6:15 th. sh. sow, but not *r.*
Mat. 6:26 fowls of the air *r.* not
25:26 I *r.* where I sowed not
John 4:38 to *r.* whereon no labor
1 *Cor.* 9:11 if we *r.* carnal things
2 *Cor.* 9:6 sow, sparingly *r.* spar.
Gal. 6:7 man sow. that sh. he *r.*
8 soweth to flesh shall *r.* cor.
9 we shall *r.* if faint not
Rev. 14:15 thrust in sickle and *r.*

REAPED.
Hos. 10:13 wickedness *r.* iniquity
Jam. 5:4 laborers which *r.* fields
Rev. 4:16 his sickle, ear. was *r.*

REAPER, S.
Ruth 2:3 Ruth gleaned after *r.*
7 I pray, let me glean after *r.*
3 *K.* 4:18 he went out to the *r.*
Amos 9:13 ploughm. overtake *r.*
Mat. 13:30 say to *r.* gather tares
39 enemy is devil, *r.* are angels

REAPEST.
Lev. 23:22 not cl. riddance wh. *r.*
Luke 19:21 thou *r.* didst not sow

REAPETH.
Is. 17:5 the harvest-man *r.* ears
John 4:36 he that *r.* recei. wages
37 one soweth, another *r.*

REAPING.
1 *Sam.* 6:13 Beth-shem. were *r.*
Mat. 25:24 man, *r. Luke* 19:22

REARWARD. *See* REREWARD.

REASON, Substantive.
1 *K.* 9:15 this is *r.* of the levy
Prov. 26:10 seven men render *r.*
Ec. 7:25 I applied to search *r.*
Dan. 4:36 at time my *r.* returned
Acts 6:2 not *r.* we leave word
18:14 O J. *r.* would I who. bear
1 *Pet.* 3:15 ask. you a *r.* of hope

By REASON.
Gen. 41:31 plenty not kno. by *r.*
Ex. 2:23 Isr. sighed by *r.* bonda.
3:7 cry by *r.* of their taskmast.

REB
Num. 9:10 uncl. *by r.* dead body
18:6 things given *by r.* of anoi.
Deut. 5:5 afraid *by r.* of the fire
1 *K.* 14:4 Abijah's eyes *by r.* age
2 *Chr.* 5:14 not minister *by r.*
20:15 not afraid *by r.* of multit.
Job 17:7 eye dim *by r.* of sorrow
31:23 *by r.* of highness not end.
37:19 speech *by r.* of darkness
41:25 *by r.* of break. they purify
Ps. 78:65 man shout. *by r.* wine
90:10 if *by r.* of str. be fourscore
Jer. 49:19 too nar. *by r.* of inhabi.
Ezek. 19:10 branches *by r.* of wa.
Dan. 8:12 given *by r.* of transgr.
Jon. 2:2 I cried *by r.* of affliction
John 12:11 *by r.* many beli. on J.
Rom. 8:20 *by r.* of him who subj.
Heb. 5:3 *by r.* hereof, oil. for sins
7:23 not continue *by r.* death
2 *Pet.* 2:2 *by r.* of whom truth

REASON, Verb.
1 *Sam.* 12:7 I may *r.* with you
Job 9:14 cho. words to *r.* with you
13:3 and desire to *r.* with God
15:3 sh. he *r.* with unpro. talk?
1:18 now, let us *r.* together
Mat. 16:8 J. said, Why *r.* among yourselves, *Mark* 2:8 ; 8:17
Luke 5:21 scr. and Pha. began *r.*
22 what *r.* ye in your hearts *r.*

REASONABLE.
Rom. 12:1 sacrifice, your *r.* serv.

REASONED.
Mat. 16:7 r. am. themselv. 21:15;
Mark 9:10 ; 11:31 ; *Luke* 20:5
Mark 2:8 J. perceived they so *r.*
Luke 20:14 the husbandmen *r.*
24:15 while they *r. J.* drew near
Acts 17:2 three sabbaths Paul *r.*
18:4 he *r.* in synagogue ev. sab.
19 Paul *r.* with J. at Ephesus
24:25 as he *r.* of righteousness

REASONING.
Job 13:6 hear my *r.* and hearken
Mark 2:6 scribes *r.* in th. hearts
12:28 having heard them *r.* tog.
Luke 9:46 arose *r.* among them
Acts 28:29 J. departed, and had *r.*

REASONS.
Job 32:11 gave ear to your *r.*
Is. 41:21 br. *r.* saith king of Jac.

REBEKAH.
Gen. 22:23 Bethuel begat R.
24:15 R. came out, 51, 59, 60, 67
25:28 R. loved Jacob, 20
27:42 words of Esau were told R.
29:12 that he was R. son, 35:8
49:31 they buried Isaac and R.
Rom. 9:10 when R. conceived

REBEL.
Num. 14:9 only *r.* not aga. Lord
Jos. 1:18 whosoever *r.* shall die
22:16 builded altar ye might *r.*
19 *r.* not agai. L. *r.* not ag. us
29 God forbid we *r.* against L.
1 *Sam.* 12:14 ye obey and not *r.*
15 if ye will not obey L. but *r.*
Neh. 2:19 will ye *r.* aga. king ?
6:6 thon and Jews think to *r.*
Job 24:13 those that *r.* aga. light
Is. 1:20 if ye *r.* ye sh. be devour.
Hos. 7:14 assemble for corn, *r.*

REBELLED.
Gen. 14:4 thirteenth year they *r.*
Num. 20:24 because yo *r.* ag. my word at Meribah, 27:14 ;
Deut. 1:26, 43 ; 9:23
1 *K.* 12:19 Rehobo. fled, so Is. *r.*
ng. house of Da. 2 *Chr.* 10:19
2 *K.* 1:1 Moab *r.* ag. Israel, 3, 5, 7
18:7 Hezek. *r.* ng. Assyria
24:1 Jehoiakim *r.* against Neb.
20 *Ne.* *r.* 2 *Chr.* 36:13 ; *Jer.* 52:3
Ezr. 4:36 ho that *r.* recei. wages
Neh. 9:26 dwelt, dhowho. and *r.* ag. thee
Ps. 5:10 for they *r.* against thee
105:28 they *r.* not against word
107:11 they *r.* ag. words of God
Is. 1:2 nourish. children, they *r.*
63:10 *r.* and vexed Holy Spirit
Lam. 1:18 have *r.* 20 *grievo. r.*
3:42 we have *r.* has not pardon.
Ezek. 2:3 send ih. to nation th. *r.*
17:15 he *r.* in sending to Egypt
Dan. 9:5 *r.* by departing fr. thee
9 to God mercy, though we have *r.*
Hos. 13:16 Samaria *r.* against G.

REBELLEST.
2 *K.* 18:20 what is this wh. thou trust, that thon *r.? Is.* 36:5

REB

Deut. 31:27 know thy *r.* and still
Jos. 22:22 sh. know if it be in *r.*
1 *Sam.* 15:23 *r.* is as witchcraft
Ezr. 4:19 that *r.* made therein
Neh. 9:17 in *r.* appointed a capt.
Job 34:37 addeth *r.* unto his sin
Prov. 17:11 evil man seeketh *r.*
Jer. 28:16 hast taught *r.* 29:34

REBELLIOUS.
Deut. 9:7 *r.* against L. 24 ; 31:27
21:18 a stubborn and *r.* son
1 *Sam.* 20:30 son of the *r.* woman
Ps. 66:7 let not *r.* exalt themsel.
68:6 the *r.* dwell in a dry land
18 for *r.* 78:8 *r.* generation
Is. 1:23 princes *r.* companions
30:1 woe to *r.* chil. saith Lord
9 a *r.* people ; 50:5 I was not *r.*
65:2 spread hands to a *r.* people
Jer. 4:17 she ha. been *r.* saith L.
5:23 this' people hath a *r.* heart
Ezek. 2:3 send thee to a *r.* nation
5 they are a *r.* house, 6, 7 ; 3:9, 26, 27 ; 12:2, 3
6 be not *r.* like that *r.* house
12:2 dwell. in midst of *r.* house
17:12 *r.y* to *r.* house, 44:6
24:3 utter parable to *r.* house

REBELS.
Num. 17:10 A. rod token ag. *r.*
20:10 M. and A. said, Hear, *r.*
Ezek. 20:38 I will purge out *r.*

REBUKE, Substantive.
Deut. 28:20 Lord send on thee *r.*
2 *K.* 19:3 this is day of *r. Is.* 37:3
Ps. 18:15 at thy *r.* blast of nost.
76:6 at *r.* horse cast into sleep
80:16 per. at *r.* of thy countenance
104:7 at thy *r.* they fled away
Prov. 13:1 a scorner hear. not *r.*
8 but the poor hearcth not *r.*
27:5 opener *r.* bet. than secret love
Ec. 7:5 better to hear *r.* of wise
Is. 25:8 *r.* of his peo. take away
30:17 thousand flee at *r.* of one
at the *r.* of five shall ye flee
50:2 at thy *r.* I dry up the sea
51:20 thy sons lie full of *r.* of G.
66:15 render his *r.* with flames
Jer. 15:15 for thy sake I suff. *r.*
Hos. 5:9 Ep. sh. be des. day of *r.*
Phil. 2:15 without *r.* in per. nat.

REBUKE, Verb.
Lev. 19:17 in any wise *r.* neigh.
Ruth 2:16 glean them, *r.* her not
1 *Chr.* 12:17 God look thereon, *r.*
Ps. 6:1 O Lord, *r.* me not, 38:1
68:30 *r.* the spearmen, the bulls
Prov. 9:8 *r.* wise man
24:25 them that *r.* him
Is. 2:4 shall *r.* nations, *Mic.* 4:3
17:13 nations rush, G. *r.* them
54:9 I vow. not be wroth, nor *r.*
Zec. 3:2 Lord *r.* thee, even Lord
that hath chosen Jer. *r.* thee
Mal. 2:11 *r.* devo. for your sakes
3:11 *r.* devourer for your sakes
Mat. 16:22 P. *r.* him, *Mark* 8:32
Luke 17:3 if broti. trespass *r.* him
19:39 said, Master, *r.* thy disc.
1 *Tim.* 5:1 *r.* not elder, entreat
20 them that sin, *r.* before all
2 *Tim.* 4:2 *r.* with long-suffering
Tit. 1:13 wherefi. *r.* sharply, 2:15
Jude 9 Mich. said, The L. *r.* thee
Rev. 3:19 as many as I love I *r.*

REBUKED.
Gen. 31:42 lath seen and *r.* thee
37:10 his father *r.* him, and said
Neh. 5:7 I *r.* the nobles and rul.
Ps. 9:5 hast *r.* the heathen, hast
108:9 he *r.* Red sea, it was dry
119:21 thou hast *r.* the proud
Mat. 8:26 he *r.* the wind and the sea, *Mark* 4:39 ; *Luke* 8:24
17:18 J. *r.* devil, and he depart.
19:13 his disci. *r.* them, *Mark* 10:13 ; *Luke* 18:15
20:31 multitude *r.* blind men
Mark 1:25 he *r.* the devil, 9:25 ; *Luke* 4:35 ; 9:42
8:33 Jesus *r.* Peter, Get behind
Luke 4:39 stood, and *r.* the fever
41 devils came out of many, *r.*
23:40 thief answering, *r.* him
Heb. 12:5 nor faint when *r.*
2 *Pet.* 2:16 Balaam was *r.* for ini.

REBUKER.
Hos. 5:2 I have been a *r.* of all

REBUKES.
Ps. 39:11 with *r.* dost cor. man
Ezek. 5:15 execute judgment in *r.* 25:17

REC

REBUKETH, ING.
2 *Sam.* 22:16 discover, at *r.* of L.
Prov. 9:7 he that *r.* wicked man
24:25 to that *r.* shall find favor
Amos 5:10 hate him that *r.* in
Nah. 1:4 he *r.* sea, and maketh
Luke 4:41 be *r.* th. suffered not

RECALL.
Lam. 3:21 this I *r.* to mind

RECEIPT.
Mat. 9:9 Mat. sitting at the *r.* of custom, *Mark* 2:14 ; *Lu.* 5:27

RECEIVE.
Deut. 33:3 ev. one *r.* thy words
1 *Sam.* 10:4 thou *r.* of their han.
Job 2:10 *r.* good at hand of G. ?
27:13 shall *r.* of the Almighty
Ps. 6:9 Lord will *r.* my prayer
24:5 he shall *r.* blessing from L.
49:15 G. red. soul, he sh. *r.* me
73:24 afterward *r.* me to glory
75:2 when I *r.* congregation
Prov. 2:1 if th. wilt *r.* my words
10:8 wise will *r.* commandm.
Ec. 57:6 sho. I *r.* comfort in these
Ezek. 16:61 asha. when *r.* sisters
Jan. 2:6 ye shall *r.* of me gifts
Mic. 1:11 shall *r.* of you standing
Zep. 3:7 thou wilt *r.* instruction
Mat. 10:41 pr. a prophet's reward
11:5 the blind *r.* their sight
14:15 it is, this is E. *r.* come
19:11 all men cannot *r.* saying
20:7 whatsoever ye right that *r.*
21:22 believing, ye shall *r.*
34 that they might *r.* fruits
Mark 4:16 *r.* the word with gladness, *Luke* 8:13
20 hear the word, and *r.* it
10:51 Lord, that I might *r.* my sight, *Luke* 18:41
11:24 wh. ye pray, believe ye *r.*
Luke 10:8 city ye enter, they *r.*
16:9 into everlasting habita.
23:41 we *r.* reward of our deeds
John 5:43 own name, him ye *r.*
44 can ye believe, wh. *r.* honor
7:39 they that believe, *r.* H. G.
14:3 come again, and *r.* you
16:14 he shall *r.* of mine
24 ask and ye shall *r.*
Acts 1:8 but ye shall *r.* power
2:38 ye shall *r.* gift of Holy G.
8:15 pray. they might *r.* H. G.
10 on who. I lay hands may *r.*
9:12 that he might *r.* his sight
17 J. sent me, thou *r.* thy sig.
10:43 believeth *r.* remis. of sins
26:18 may *r.* forgiveness of sins
Rom. 5:17 *r.* abundance of grace
15:7 *r.* ye one anot. as C. *r.* us
1 *Cor.* 3:8 ev. man *r.* his reward
14 work abide, he *r.* reward
4:7 didst *r.* it, why glory ?
2 *Cor.* 5:10 every one *r.* things
6:17 unclean thing, I will *r.* you
8:4 praying, we would *r.* gift
11:4 or if ye *r.* another spirit
Gal. 3:14 might *r.* promise of S.
Eph. 6:8 same shall he *r.* of L.
Col. 3:24 shall *r.* reward of inh.
25 he shall *r.* for wrong done
Phile. 15 should. *r.* him for ever
17 if thou *r.* me then did *r.* tithes
Heb. 7:8 men that die *r.* tithes
9:15 might *r.* promise, 10:36
Jam. 1:7 think he *r.* any thing
3:1 sh. *r.* greater condemnation
5:7 he *r.* early and latter rain
1 *Jn.* 5:4 might *r.* crown of glory
1 *John* 3:22 whatso. we ask we *r.*
2 John 8 that we *r.* a full reward
10 *r.* him not into your house
Rev. 4:11 if any man *r.* mark
17:12 *r.* powers as kings

RECEIVE, *imperatively*.
Gen. 33:10 *r.* I pray, my present
Job 22:22 *r.* law from his mouth
Prov. 4:10 and *r.* my sayings
Ec. 8:20 *r.* not of thy lips, the word
Ezek. 3:10 *r.* all my words
Luke 18:42 *r.* sight, be grac. shall
John 20:22 he saith, *r.* Ho. Ghost
Acts 7:59 L. Jes. *r.* my spirit
22:18 *r.* my testimony conc. me
Rom. 14:1 him weak in faith *r.*
15:7 *r.* one ano. as Ch. received
2 Cor. 7:2 *r.* us, we have wron.
Phil. 2:29 *r.* him in L. with glad.
4:10 Mar. if he come, *r.* him
Phile. 12 *r.* him th. is mine ow.
17 count me partner, *r.* him

RECEIVE, *neutrely*.
2 K. 5:16 I will rec. none, 20
Job 2:10 we *r.* good, not *r.* evil ?

CRUDEN'S CONCORDANCE.

REC

Jer. 35:13 will ye not r. instruc.
Ezek. 36:30 ye shall r. no more
Mark 10:15 whosoever sh. not r. kingdom of G. **Luke** 18:17
Luke 9:53 they did not r. him
10:10 they r. you not, go into
18:30 who shall not r. manifold
John 3:11 ye r. not our witness
27 a man can r. noth. except
5:41 I r. not honor from men
43 come in F.'s na. ye r. me not
14:17 Sp. whom world cannot r.
Acts 22:18 will not r. testimony
1 **Cor.** 4:7 wh. hast thou, not r. ?
2 **Cor.** 6:1 r. not grace of G. in v.
Jam. 4:3 ye ask and r. not
2 **John** 10 r. him not into house
3 **John** 10 ref. doth he r. breth.

RECEIVE, *infinitively.*
Gen. 4:11 earth op. mouth to r.
Deut. 9:9 gone up to r. tables
1 **K.** 8:64 brnz. altar was too little to r. burnt-offer. 2 **Chr.** 7:7
2 **K.** 5:26 time to r. money, to r.
12:8 priest to r. no more money
Prov. 1:3 r. instruction of wisd.
Jer. 5:3 refused to r. correction
Mal. 3:10 not room enough to r.
Mat. 19:12 to r. it, let him r. it
Mark 2:2 no room to r. them
Luke 6:34 of whom ye hope to r.
Acts 8:27 ex. disciples to r. him
22:35 more bles. to give than r.
3 **John** 8 we ought to r. such
Rev. 4:11 thou worthy to r. glo.
5:12 worthy is L. to r. power
13:16 causeth to r. mark in ha.

RECEIVED.
Gen. 26:12 Isaac r. hundred-fold
Ex. 32:4 Aaron r. at th. hand
Num. 12:14 let Miriam be r. in
23:20 I r. commandm. to bless
Jos. 13:8 Gadites r. inheritance
1 **Sam.** 12:3 of wh. hand ha. I r.
2 **K.** 19:14 Hezekiah r. the letter, **Is.** 37:14
1 **Chr.** 7:15 David r. them
Job 4:12 mine ear r. little thereof
Ps. 68:18 hast r. gifts for men
Prov. 24:32 I looked and r. inst.
Ec. 4:2:3 she hath r. of L.'s hand
Ezek. 18:7 hath not r. usury nor
Zep. 3:2 she r. not correction
Mat. 10:8 freely ye r. freely give
13:20 r. into stony gr. 22 thorns
23 r. seed into good ground
20:9 r. every man a penny, 10
34 immedi. their eyes r. sight
Mark 7:4 many things they r.
10:52 he immediately r. sight, **Luke** 18:43; **Acts** 9:18
Lu. 19 was r. into heav. **Acts** 1:9
Luke 6:24 ye have r. consolation
8:40 the people gladly r. him
9:11 r. them, spake of kingdom
51 time come he who. he f. up
10:38 Martha r. him into house
15:27 r. him safe and sound
19:6 Zaccheus r. him joyfully
15 returned, having r. kingd.
John 1:11 on. to his own, own r.
12 as many as r. him he gave
16 of fulness r. grace for grace
3:33 he that hath r. testimony
4:15 when come, Galii. r. him
6:21 willingly r. him in ship
9:11 washed, and I r. sight
15 Pharis. asked how r. sight
10:18 comman. r. of my Father
17:8 given thy words, r. them
18:3 Ju. having r. band of men
Acts 1:9 cloud r. him out of sig.
3:33 hav. r. of Father promise
41 they r. word were baptized
7:53 who have r. law by angels
8:14 Samaria r. word of God
17 hands on them r. Holy Gh.
9:19 r. meat was strengthened
10:47 which have r. Holy Gh.
11:1 heard Genti. r. word of G.
15:4 they were r. of the church
17:7 whom Jason hath r.
11 Bereans r. word with readi.
19:2 have r. the Holy Ghost ?
20:24 ministry which I r. of L.
21:17 the brethren r. us gladly
28:5 from whom I r. letters
28:7 Publius r. us: Paul r. all
21 nei. r. letters out of Judea
Rom. 1:15 by whom we r. grace
5:11 by whom we r. atonement
8:15 have not r. spirit of bond.
14:3 him that eateth, G. r. him
15:7 rec. one another as C. r. us
1 **Cor.** 2:12 r. not spirit of world
4:7 glory, as if thou hadst not r.
11:23 I r. of Lord that which

REC

1 **Cor.** 15:1 which ye r. 3 wh. I r.
2 **Cor.** 4:1 as we r. mercy
11:4 spirit which ye have not r.
Gal. 1:9 anoi. gospel than ye r.
12 I r. it not of man, neither
3:2 r. ye Sp. by works of law ?
4:14 r. me as an angel of God
Phil. 4:9 thi. ye have r. and seen
Col. 2:6 as ye r. Christ, so walk
4:10 whom ye r. commandm.
17 take heed to minis. thou r.
1 **Thes.** 1:6 r. word in affliction
2:13 when ye r. the word, ye r.
4:1 as ye r. of us how to walk
2 **Thes.** 2:10 they r. not the truth
1 **Tim.** 3:16 believed, r. into gl.
4:3 meats God created to be r.
4 crea. good, if r. with thanks.
Heb. 2:11 under it people r. law
10:26 if sin after r. knowledge
11:13 not having r. promises
17 r. promises offered only one
19 whence he r. him in a figure
33 woman r. dead raised to life
39 these r. not the promise
1 **Pet.** 4:10 every one hath r. gift
2 **Pet.** 1:17 he r. from God honor
John 4 we have r. a command
Rev. 2:27 power, as r. of Father
3:3 remember how thou hast r.
19:20 that had r. mark of beast
20:4 nor r. mark reigned wi. C.

RECEIVEDST.
Luke 16:25 in lifetime r. good th.

RECEIVER.
Is. 33:18 scribe ? where is r. ?

RECEIVETH.
Jud. 19:18 no man r. to house
Job 35:7 what r. he of thy hand ?
Prov. 21:11 when wise r. know.
29:4 he that r. gifts, overthr.
Jer. 7:28 nation r. not correction
Mal. 3:13 r. offer. with good-will
Mat. 7:8 that asketh r. **Luke** 11:10
10:40 that r. you, r. me ; r. me, 41 he that r. a prophet, right,
13:20 heareth word, anon r. it
18:5 one such little child, r. me
Mark 9:37 r. not me, but him that sent me, **Luke** 9:48
Luke 15:2 this man r. sinners
John 3:32 no man r. his testim.
12:48 he that r. not my words
1 **Cor.** 9:24 run all, one r. prize
Heb. 6:7 earth r. blessing fr. God
7:9 L. who r. tithes, paid tithes
Rev. 2:17 know. saving he r. it
14:11 whoso. r. mark of name
RECEIVETH not,
1 **Cor.** 2:14 r. not things of God
3 **John** 9 but Diotrephes r. us n.

RECEIVING.
2 **K.** 5:20 in not r. at his hands
Rom. 5:10 when enem. r. to God
1 **Cor.** 7:11 let her he r. to hush.
2 **Cor.** 8:18 hath r. so to himself
10 in Ch. stand, be ye r. to God
Col. 1:21 were enemies, yet he r.

RECONCILIATION.

Lev. 8:15 to make a r. upon it
2 **Chr.** 29:24 made r. with blood
Ezek. 45:15 make r. for them, 17
Dan. 9:24 to make r. for iniquity
2 **Cor.** 5:18 given us ministry of r.
19 committed to us word of r.
Heb. 2:17 r. for the sins of people

RECONCILING.

Lev. 16:20 he made end of r.
Rom. 4:22 by nature r. Instrum.
2 **Cor.** 5:19 God in Chr. r. world

RECORD, Substantive.
Ezr. 6:2 therein was r. written
Job 16:19 behold, r. is on high
John 1:19 this is the r. of John
33 John bare r. saying, 34
8:13 thou nearest r. of thyself,
thy r. is not true, 14
12:17 the peo. with him, bare r.
19:35 he saw bare r. his r. true
Rom. 10:2 bear r. they have zeal
2 **Cor.** 1:23 I call God for a r.
8:3 to their power I bear r.
Gal. 4:15 I bear you r.
Phil. 1:8 God is my r.
Col. 4:13 I bear r. he hath zeal
1 **John** 5:7 th. are 3 that bear r.
10 G. gave of his Son, 11
3 John 12 we bear r. our r. is true
Rev. 1:2 who bare r. of word of G.

RECKONING.

2 **K.** 22:7 there was no r. made
1 **Chr.** 23:11 they were in one r.

RECOMMENDED.

Acts 14:26 who. they had been r.
15:40 being r. to grace of God

REC

RECOMPENSE.
Deut. 32:35 belong. veng. and r.
Job 15:31 vanity shall be his r.
Prov. 12:14 r. shall be rendered
Is. 35:4 God will come with a r.
59:18 repay r. to his enemies
66:6 voice of L. that render. r.
Jer. 51:6 will render to her a r.
Lam. 3:64 render to them a r.
Hos. 9:7 the days of r. are come
Joel 3:4 will ye render me r. ?
7 I will return r. on your head
Luke 14:12 a r. be made thee
Rom. 1:27 rec. r. of their error
11:9 let their table be made a r.
2 **Cor.** 6:13 for a r. in the same
Heb. 2:2 transgr. received a r.
10:35 hath great r. of reward
11:26 he had respect to the r.

RECOMPENSES.
Is. 34:8 a year of r. for Zion
Jer. 51:56 L. God of r. sh. requ.

RECOMPENSE, Verb.
Num. 5:7 he shall r. his trespass
8 if he have no kinsman to r.
Ruth 2:12 the Lord r. thy work
2 **Sam.** 19:36 sho. king r. me ?
Job 34:33 r. it whe. thou refuse
Prov. 20:22 say not, I will r. evil
Is. 55:6 I will r. into th. bosom
Jer. 16:18 I will r. their iniquity
25:14 I will r. them, **Hos.** 12:2
50:29 r. her according to work
Hos. 2:9 and I will r. my wool
Mark 16:18 hands on sick, th. r.
1 **Tim.** 2:26 may r. themselves

RECOMPENSED.
1 **Sam.** 30:18 r. all Am. took, 19
2 **Sam.** 22:21 r. according to
not give aught of spoil we r.
2 **K.** 13:25 and r. cities of Israel
14:28 warred, and r. Damascus
10:6 Rez. king of Syria r. Elath
20:7 laid it on the boil. he r.
Ez. 38:8 Hezekiah sick, r. 20:1
Jer. 8:22 why is not my peo. r. ?
41:16 Johanan took people he r.

RECOVERING.
Luke 4:18 r. of sight to the blind

RED.
Gen. 25:25 came out r. all over
30 feed me with that r. pottage
40:12 eyes shall be r. with wine
Ex. 25:5 rams' skins dyed r.
26:14 ; 35:7 ; 36:19 ; 39:34
35:23 vi. wh. was found r. skins
Num. 19:2 bring thee a r. heifer
Ezr. 8:22 Modiice saw water r.
Est. 1:6 a pavement of r. blue
Ps. 75:8 wine is r. full of mixtu.
Prov. 23:31 look not on wine r.
Is. 1:18 though your sins be r.
27:2 sing, a vineyard of r. wine
63:2 art thou r. in apparel ?
Nah. 2:3 shield of mighty men r.
Zec. 1:8 a man on a r. horse
6:2 in first chariot we. r. horses
Mat. 16:2 fair weather, sky r. 3
Rev. 6:4 anot. horse that was r.
12:3 great r. dragon, sev. heads

RED sea.
Ex. 10:19 east locusts into R. s.
13:18 G. led them by the R. sea
15:4 captains drowned in R. s.
22 Moses bro. Israel from R. s.
23:31 sea thy bounds from R. s.
Num. 14:25 into wilder. by R. s.
21:14 what he did in the R. s. ?
Deut. 1:40 take journey by R. s.
11:4 he made R. sea overflow
Jos. 2:10 the L. dried up R. sea
4:23 as L. your L. did to R. sea
24:6 Egypt. purs. after to R. s.
Neh. 9:9 heard. their cry by R. s.
Ps. 106:7 provoked him at R. s.
9 rebuked R. s. it was dried up
22 done terrible things by R. s.
136:13 him who divided R. sea
15 overthrew Pharaoh in R. s.
Jer. 49:21 noise was heard in R. s.
Acts 7:36 showed wond. in R. sea
Heb. 11:29 by faith passed R. s.

REDDISH.
Lev. 13:19 somewhat r. 24, 43
42 a white r. sore, a leprosy
49 if plague be r. in garment
13:3 to their power I bear r.
14:37 if plag. be with streaks, r.

REDEEM.
Ex. 6:6 I will r. you with arm
13:13 firstl. of ass shalt r. 34:20
15 first-b. of my chil. r. 34:20
Lev. 25:25 if any of his kin r. it
32 the cities usq the Levit. r.
40 or any of kin may r. him
27:15 house will r. it, 19, 20, 31
Num. 18:15 first-born sh. thou r.
17 firstling of a goat sh. not r.
Ruth 4:4 r. it, if not, I will r. it
6 I cannot r. it for mys. r. th.

CRUDEN'S CONCORDANCE. 991

RED
2 *Sam.* 7:23 wh. nation is like Is. God went to r.? 1 *Chr.* 17:21
Neh. 5:5 is it in our power to r.
Job 5:20 in famine he sh. r. thee
6:23 r. me from hand of mighty
Ps. 25:22 r. Is. O G. out of troub.
26:11 r. me and be merciful
44:26 r. us for thy mercies' sake
49:7 none of th. can r. his brot.
15 G. will r. my soul fr. grave
69:18 draw ni. to my soul, r. it
72:14 r. their soul from deceit
130:8 r. Isr. from all iniquities
Is. 50:2 short. that it cannot r.?
Jer. 15:21 I will r. thee
Hos. 13:14 I will r. them fr. death
Mic. 4:10 L. sh. r. thee fr. Baby.
Gal. 4:5 r. them were under law
Tit. 2:14 he might r. us fr. iniq.

REDEEMED.
Gen. 48:16 the angel which r. me
Ex. 15:13 people whom thou r.
21:8 then shall he let her be r.
Lev. 19:20 with bondmaid not r.
25:30 if house in city be not r.
48 broth. sold may he r. again
54 if he be not r. then go out
27:20 sold field, it sh. not be r.
27 an uncl. beast not r. be sold
28 no devot. thing sh. be r. 29
33 tithe and change not be r.
Num. 3:46 those r. more th. Lev.
Deut. 7:8 L. hath r. you fr. king of Egypt, 15:15; 24:18
9:26 thy people thou hast r.
13:5 L. r. you out of bondage
21:8 merciful to Is. thou hast r.
2 *Sam.* 4:9 L. r. soul, 1 *K.* 1:29
1 *Chr.* 17:21 whom thou r. out of Egypt, *Neh.* 1:10; *Ps.* 77:15
Neh. 5:8 we have r. the Jews
Ps. 31:5 thou hast r. me, O L. G.
71:23 my soul rejo. thou hast r.
74:2 thine inherit. thou hast r.
106:10 he r. them from enemy
107:2 let r. of the Lord say so
130:21 Isra'l r. us from enemies
Is. 1:27 Zion be r. with judgm.
29:22 saith L. who r. Abraham
35:9 but the r. shall walk there
43:1 fear not, I have r. thee
44:22 ret. to me, I have r. thee
23 Lord r. J. 48:20; *Jer.* 31:11
51:11 r. of the L. shall return
52:3 ye sh. be r. without money
9 r. Jer. 62:12 holy people r.
62:2 he is come; 9 he r. the
Lam. 3:58 thou hast r. my life
Hos. 7:13 tho' I r. them, yet they
Mic. 6:4 I r. thee out of house
Zec. 10:8 hiss, I have r. them
Luke 1:68 visited and r. his peo.
24:21 who should have r. Israel
Gal. 3:13 Christ r. us from curse
1 *Pet.* 1:18 not r. with corruptl.
Rev. 5:9 thou hast r. us to God
14:3 the 144,000 which were r.
4 these were r. from am. men

REDEEMEDST.
2 *Sam.* 7:23 r. to thee from Egy.

REDEEMER.
Job 19:25 I know that my R. liv.
Ps. 19:14 O L. my stren. and R.
78:35 the high G. was their R.
Prov. 23:11 their R. is mighty
Is. 41:14 thy R. Holy One, 54:5
43:14 saith L. your R. H. One
44:6 saith L. his R. L. of hosts
24 sai. thy R. 48:17; 49:7; 54:8
47:4 as for our R. Lord of hosts
49:26 I the L. am thy R. 60:16
59:20 the R. shall come to Zion
63:16 art our Father, our R.
Jer. 50:34 their R. is strong

REDEEMETH.
Ps. 34:22 L. r. souls of his serv.
103:4 who r. life fr. destruction

REDEEMING.
Ruth 4:7 manner in Isr. conc. r.
Eph. 5:16 r. the time, *Col.* 4:5

REDEMPTION.
Lev. 25:24 ye shall grant a r.
51 he sh. give price of his r. 52
Num. 3:49 Moses took r. money
Ps. 49:8 r. of their soul is prec.
111:9 he sent r. to his people
130:7 with L. th. is plenteo. r.
Jer. 32:7 right of r. is thine, 8
Luke 2:38 that looked for r.
21:28 your r. draweth nigh
Rom. 3:24 justified thro' r. in C.
8:23 for adoption, r. of our body
1 *Cor.* 1:30 Chr. is made to us r.
Eph. 1:7 in whom we have r. thro' his blood, *Col.* 1:14

REF
Eph. 1:14 r. of purchased poss.
4:30 sealed unto the day of r.
Heb. 9:12 obtai. eternal r. for us
15 the r. of the transgressions

REDNESS.
Prov. 23:29 who hath r. of eyes?

REDOUND.
2 *Cor.* 4:15 grace r. to glo. of G.

REED.
1 *K.* 14:15 L. sh. smite Isr. as r.
2 *K.* 18:21 thou trustest upon the staff of bruised r, *Is.* 36:6
Is. 42:3 a bruised r. shall he not break, *Mat.* 12:20
Ezek. 29:6 been staff of a r. to Is.
40:3 a man with a measuring r.
Mat. 11:7 a r. shaken, *Luke* 7:24
27:29 put a r. in his right hand
30 sm. him with r. *Mark* 15:19
48 sponge on a r. *Mark* 15:36
Rev. 11:1 there was giv. me a r.
21:15 golden r. to meas. city, 16

REEDS.
Job 40:21 lieth in the covert of r.
Is. 19:6 r. and flags sh. wither, 7
35:7 in habita. of dragons be r.
Jer. 51:32 the r. they have burnt
Ezek. 42:16 measured east side, five hundred r. 17, 18, 19
45:1 shall be length of 25,000 r.

REEL.
Ps. 107:27 r. to and fro, and stag.
Is. 24:20 earth shall r. to and fro

REFINE.
Zec. 13:9 I will r. them as silver

REFINED.
1 *Chr.* 28:18 for the altar r. gold
26:4 7,000 talents of r. silver
Is. 25:6 wines on lees wellr.
48:10 I have r. th. not with silv.
Zec. 13:9 refine th. as silver is r.

REFINER.
Mal. 3:2 for he is like a r.'s fire
3 he sh. sit as a r. and purifier

REFORMATION.
Heb. 9:10 on th. until time of r.

REFORMED.
Lev. 26:23 if ye will not be r.

REFRAIN.
Gen. 45:1 J. could not r. himself
Job 7:11 I will not r. my mouth
Prov. 1:15 r. thy foot from path
Ec. 3:5 a time to r. fr. embracing
Is. 48:9 for my praise I will r.
64:12 wilt thou r. thyself, O L.?
Jer. 31:15 r. voice from weeping
Acts 5:38 I say, r. from th. men
1 *Pet.* 3:10 r. his tong. from evil

REFRAINED.
Gen. 43:31 and Joseph r. himself
Est. 5:10 Haman r. himself
Job 29:9 the princes r. talking
Ps. 40:9 I have not r. my lips
119:101 I have r. my feet fr. evil
Is. 42:14 been still, r. myself
Jer. 14:10 have not r. their feet

REFRAINETH.
Prov. 10:19 that r. lips is wise

REFRESH.
1 *K.* 13:7 come house r. thyself
Acts 27:3 J. suffered P. to r. him.
Phile. 20 r. my bowels in the L.

REFRESHED, ETH.
Ex. 23:12 stranger may be r.
31:17 sev. day rested and was r.
1 *Sam.* 16:23 so Saul was r.
2 *Sam.* 16:14 David and people r.
Job 32:20 speak that I may be r.
Prov. 25:13 to r. soul of masters
Rom. 15:32 may sat. and yours
1 *Cor.* 16:18 r. my spi. and yours
2 *Cor.* 7:13 Titus, his spir. was r.
2 *Tim.* 1:16 for he often r. me
Phile. 7 bow. of saints r. by th.

REFRESHING.
Is. 28:12 r. yet they wo. not hear
Acts 3:19 times of r. shall come

REFUGE.
Num. 35:13 six cit. for r. 15
Deut. 33:27 eternal God is thy r.
Jos. 20:3 r. from aveng. of blood
2 *Sam.* 22:3 my high tower and r.
Ps. 9:9 L. be a r. for oppressed
14:6 because the Lord is his r.
46:1 L. r. and str. 7; 48:3 G. known
57:1 thy wings will make my r.
59:16 my r. in day of my trouble
62:7 my r. is God; 8 God is r.
71:7 thou art strong r. 142:5
91:2 he is my r. my fortress, 9
94:22 nor r. till rock of my r.
104:18 hills r. for wild goats
142:1 r. failed; 5 thou art my r.

REG
Prov. 14:26 chil. have place of r.
Is. 4:6 place of r. 25:4 needy r.
28:15 we have made lies our r.
17 hail shall sweep away r.
Jer. 16:19 O L. my r. in affliction
Heb. 6:16 who have fled for r.

REFUSE.
Ex. 4:23 If thou r. to let him go
Lam. 3:45 hast made us as r.
Amos 8:6 may sell r. of wheat

REFUSE, Verb.
Ex. 4:23 If thou r. to let them go, 8:2; 9:2; 10:4
10:3 how long r. to humble thy.
16:28 r. ye to keep my com. ?
22:17 if her father utterly r.
Job 34:33 he will r. or choose
Prov. 8:33 he wise, and r. it not
21:7 because they r. to do judg.
25 his hands r. to labor
Is. 1:20 if ye r. sh. be devoured
7:15 he may know to r. evil, 16
Jer. 8:5 r. to return; 9:6 r. to kn.
13:10 peo. r. to hear my words
25:28 if they r. to take the cup
38:21 if thou r. to go forth
Acts 25:11 if often, I r. not to die
1 *Tim.* 4:7 but r. profane fables
5:11 but the younger widows r.
Heb. 12:25 r. not him that speak.

REFUSED.
Gen. 37:35 Ja. r. to be comforted
39:8 J. r. to lie wi. master's wi.
48:19 Jacob r. to remove hand
Num. 20:21 Edom r. Is. passage
1 *Sam.* 8:10 people r. to obey S.
16:7 look not on him, I r. him
28:23 Saul r. said, I will not eat
2 *Sam.* 2:23 Asa, r. to turn aside
13:9 she poured, Amn. r. to eat
K. 20:35 man r. to smite him
21:15 vineyard he r. to give th.
2 *K.* 5:16 Naaman urged, he r.
Job 6:7 things that my soul r.
Ps. 77:2 soul r. to be comforted
78:10 they r. to walk in his law
67 he the tabernacle of Joseph
118:22 stone which builders r.
Prov. 1:24 I have called, ye r.
Jer. 5:3 r. to receive correction
11:10 fath. r. to hear my words
15:18 my wound r. to be healed
50:33 took them r. to let h. go
Hos. 11:5 because they r. to ret.
Zec. 7:11 but they r. to hearken
Acts 7:35 Moses whom they r.
1 *Tim.* 4:4 and nothing to be r.
Heb. 11:24 Mo. r. to be called son
12:25 r. him th. spake on earth

REFUSEDST.
Jer. 3:3 thou r. to be ashamed

REFUSETH.
Num. 22:13 L. r. to give me lea.
Deut. 25:7 bro. r. to raise mine
Prov. 10:17 he that r. reproof
15:32 that r. instruction despis.
Is. 8:6 people r. the waters of Shiloah
Jer. 15:18 wound r. to be healed

REGARD.
Gen. 45:20 r. not your stuff, for
Ex. 5:9 let not r. vain words
Lev. 19:31 r. not familiar spirits
Num. 28:50 nor r. person of aged
1 *Sam.* 25:25 r. not man of Belial
Is. 13:20 r. not, he is broth.
2 *Chr.* 9:7 L. r. not, he is broth.
Job 3:4 let not G. r. it fr. above
35:13 nor will Almighty r. it
36:21 r. not iniquity
Ps. 28:5 they r. not works of L.
66:18 If I r. iniq. in my heart
81:2 sell. shall ri. of Jacob r. it
102:17 will r. prayer of destitu.
Prov. 5:2 mayest r. discretion
6:35 he will not r. any ransom
Is. 5:12 they r. not work of L.
13:17 M. who sh. til not r. silver
Lam. 4:16 L. will no more r. th.
Dan. 11:37 r. God, nor r. any god
Am. 5:22 nor r. peace-offerings
Hab. 1:5 wonder marvellously
Mal. 1:9 will he r. yo. persons?
Luke 18:4 fear not God nor r.
  man
Rom. 14:6 Lord he doth not r.

REI
REGARDED.
Ex. 9:21 r. not the word of Lord
1 *K.* 18:29 no voice, nor any r.
1 *Chr.* 17:17 thou hast r. me
Ps. 106:44 he r. their affliction
Prov. 1:24 stret. hand. no man r.
Dan. 3:12 O king, have not r.
Luke 1:48 he r. his handmaid
18:2 feared not G. sel. r. man
Heb. 8:9 I r. them not, saith L.

REGARDEST.
2 *Sam.* 19:6 thou r. not princes
Job 30:20 I stand up, r. me not
Mat. 22:16 thou r. not the persons of men, *Mark* 12:14

REGARDETH.
Deut. 10:17 r. not persons
Job 34:19 nor r. rich mo. th. poor
39:7 neither r. crying of driver
Prov. 12:10 right. r. life of beast
16:18 that r. reproof be honored
15:5 that r. reproof is prudent
29:7 wicked r. not cause of poor
Ec. 5:8 higher than highest r.
11:4 he that r. clouds not reap
Dan. 6:13 Daniel r. not thee
Mal. 2:13 r. not offer. any more
Rom. 14:6 that r. day, r. it to L.

REGARDING.
Job 4:20 perish without any r. it
Phil. 2:30 not r. life to sup. lack

REGEM-MELECH. *Zec.* 7:2

REGENERATION.
Mat. 19:28 wh. followed me in r.
Tit. 3:5 saved us by wash. of r.

REGION.
Deut. 3:4 all the r. of Argob, 13
1 *K.* 4:24 dominion over all the r.
Mat. 3:5 went to him r. round J.
4:16 which sat in r. of death
Mark 1:28 fame spread throughout r. of G. *Luke* 4:14; 7:17
6:55 ran thro' whole r. round
Acts 13:49 word of L. pub. thro' r.
14:6 they fled to r. round about
16:6 gone thro' the r. of Galatia

REGIONS.
Acts 8:1 scattered thro' r. of Ju.
2 *Cor.* 10:16 preach in r. beyond
11:10 stop me in r. of Achaia
Gal. 1:21 I came into r. of Syria

REGISTER.
Ezr. 2:62 sought r. *Neh.* 7:64
Neh. 7:5 found a r. of genealogy
REHABIAH. 1 *Chr.* 23:17

REHEARSE, ED.
Ex. 17:14 r. in ears of Joshua
Jud. 5:11 r. righteous acts of L.
1 *Sam.* 8:21 he r. in ear of Lord
17:31 r. David's words bef. Saul
Acts 11:4 Peter r. the matter
14:27 r. all G. done with them

REHOBOAM.
1 *K.* 11:43 R. son of Solo. 14:21
12:6 R. consulted men, 17, 21, 27
14:30 was war between R. 15:6
2 *Chr.* 9:31; 10:6, 17; 11:1
11:17 made R. strong, 21, 22
13:7 against R. when R. was

REHOBOTH.
Gen. 10:11 builded Nin. and R.
26:22 Isaac called the well R.
36:37 S. of R. reigned, 1 *Chr.* 1:48

REHUM.
Ezr. 2:2 R. came with, *Neh.* 12:3
4:8 R. the chancellor, 17, 23
Neh. 3:17 R. the son of Bani
10:25 R. of chief of the people

REIGN, Substantive.
1 *K.* 6:1 Solomon's r. over Israel
1 *Chr.* 4:31 cities to r. of David
29:30 David's acts with r. writ.
2 *Chr.* 36:20 r. of king. Persia
Luke 3:1 year of r. of Tiberius

REIGN, Verb.
Gen. 37:8 shalt thou r. over us?
Ex. 15:18 the Lord shall r. for ever, *Ps.* 146:10
Lev. 26:17 that hate shall r.
Deut. 15:6 r. over many nations
Jud. 9:2 whether r. rei. us, 10, 12, 14
9:8 trees went out to r. 10, 12, 14
1 *Sam.* 8:9 how king shall r. 11
9:17 this same, he shall r. over
11:12 said, Shall S. r. over us?
12:12 a king shall r. over us
1 *K.* 1:11 hast thou not heard
1 *Sam.* 2:11 after me, 17, 30
2:15 set faces on me, I shall r.
16:15 Zimri r. 7 days in Tirzah

CRUDEN'S CONCORDANCE.

REM

Jer. 42:17 no, of th. r. 44:14; 51:62
44:7 com. evil, leave none to r.
Ezek. 7:11 violence risen, no. r.
17:21 they that r. shall be scat.
39:14 men to bury those that r.
Amos 6:9 if there r. ten men
Ob. 14 delivered those that r.
Zec. 12:14 families that r.
Luke 10:7 in same house r. eat.
John 6:12 gather fragm, that r.
15:11 my joy might r. in you
16 chosen that your fruit eh. r.
12:31 bodies sho. not r. on cross
1 Cor. 15:6 of wh. greater part r.
1 Thes. 4:15 r. till coming of L.
17 we which are alive and r.
Heb. 12:27 cannot be shaken r.
1 John 3:24 that ye have heard r.
Rev. 3:2 strengthen things wh. r.

REMAINDER.
Ex. 29:34 thou shalt burn the r.
Lev. 6:16 the r. shall Aaron eat
7:17 r. on third day sh. be bur.
2 Sam. 14:7 leave nei. name, r.
Ps. 76:10 r. of wrath sh. restrain

REMAINED.
Gen. 7:23 Noah only r. alive
14:10 they that r. fled to moun.
Ex. 14:28 th. r. not one chariot
Num. 11:26 there r. two men
33:28 he should r. in city of ref.
36:12 Inh. r. in house of father
Deut. 3:11 king of Bas. r. giants
Jos. 10:20 rest r. entered cities
11:22 in Ashdod there r. Anak.
18:2 there r. of Is. seven tribes
Jud. 7:3 there r. with G. 10,000
1 Sam. 11:11 they which r. scat.
2 K. 10:11 Jehu slew all that r. 17
25:22 people r. set G. over them
1 Chr. 13:14 ark r. in faml. of O.
Ec. 2:9 my wisdom r. with me
Jer. 37:10 there r. wounded men
21 r. in court of prison, 38:13
41:10 Ishm. carried capt. that r.
43:11 his taste r. in him
51:30 mighty men r. in th. holds
Lam. 2:21 L.'s anger none r.
Dan. 10:8 r. no stren. in me, 17
13 I r. there with kings of Pe.
Mat. 11:23 done in S. it would r.
14:20 took up fragments that r.
Luke 9:17; John 6:13
Acts 5:4 wh. it r. was it not thi.

REMAINEST.
Lam. 5:19 thou O L. r. Heb. 1:11

REMAINETH.
Gen. 8:22 while earth r. seed-ti.
and harvest shall not cease
Ex. 12:10 which r. ye shall burn
Lev. 8:32 r. of flesh and bread
16:16 so do for tabernac. that r.
Num. 24:19 destroy him that r.
Jos. 8:29 heap of stones that r.
13:1 there r. land to be possess.
Jud. 5:13 him that r. have dom.
1 Sam. 5:18 stone r. to this day
16:11 J. said, Thero r. youngest
Job 19:4 my error r. with myself
21:34 his nock r. strength
Is. 4:3 ho that r. in J. call. holy
Jer. 38:9 he that r. in city sh, die
Ezek. 6:12 he that r. besieged die
Hag. 2:5 so my Sp. r. am. them
Zec. 9:7 ho that r. shall be for G.
John 9:11 therefore your sin r.
1 Cor. 7:29 it r. they that ha. wi.
2 Cor. 3:11 that which r. glorio.
9:9 his righteousness r. for ev.
Heb. 4:6 it r. some must enter in
9 there r. a rest to peop. of G.
10:26 there r. no sacrifice for sin
1 John 3:9 for seed r. in him

REMAINING.
Num. 9:22 cloud r. on tabernacle
Deut. 3:3 till none was left r.
Jos. 12:33 and he left none r. 37, 39, 40; 11:8
2 Sam. 21:5 dest, fr. r. in coasts
2 K. 10:11 Jehu left Ahab no. r.
1 Chr. 9:33 who r. in chambers
Job 18:19 nor any r. in dwelling
Ob. 18 shall not be any r. of Esau
John 1:33 on wh. shall see Sp. r.

REMALIAH.
Is. 7:1 anger of son of R. 5, 9
8:6 rejoice in Rezin and R. son

REMEDY.
2 Chr. 36:16 wrath arose, no r.
Prov. 6:15 be broken without r.
29:1 be destroyed, without r.

REMEMBER.
Gen. 40:23 did not butler r. Jos.
Ex. 13:3 Moses said to people r.

REM

Ex. 20:8 r. sab.-day to keep holy
Num. 11:5 we r. fish eat in Egypt
15:39 r. all commandm. of Lord
Deut. 5:15 r. thou wast a serv. in
Eg. 15:15; 16:12; 24:18, 22
7:18 r. what L. did to Pharaoh
8:18 r. L. gi. pow. to get wealth
9:7 r. thou provokest L. thy G.
16:3 r. day camest out of Egypt
24:9 r. what Lord did to Miriam
25:17 r. what Amal. did to thee
32:7 r. days of old, consider
Jos. 1:13 r. word wh. Moses com.
Jud. 9:2 r. I am your bone
1 Sam. 25:31 Ab. said, r. handm.
2 Sam. 14:11 let the king r. Lord
2 K. 9:25 r. when I rode after A.
20:3 r. I walk. bef. thee, Is. 38:3
1 Chr. 16:12 r. works, Ps. 105:5
2 Chr. 6:42 r. mercies of David
Neh. 1:8 r. word thou com. Mos.
4:14 r. L. wh. is great and terri
13:29 r. th. that defiled priests.
Job 4:7 r. who perished
7:7 O r. my life is wind
10:9 r. thou hast made me
11:16 r. it as waters that pass
36:24 r. thou magnify his work
41:8 hand upon him, r. battle
Ps. 20:3 r. thy offerings, accept
7 we will r. name of the Lord
22:27 ends of world r. turn to L.
25:6 r. thy mercies ever of old
7 r. not sins of my you. r. me
74:2 r. congreg. thou purchased
18 r. this, enemy reproached
22 r. how foolish man reproa.
78:8 O r. not former iniquities
89:47 r. how short my time is
50 r. L. reproach of thy serv.
103:18 th. that r. his command.
119:49 r. word unto thy servant
132:1 L. r. D. and his afflictions
137:7 r. O Lord, child. of Edom
Prov. 31:7 r. misery no more
Ec. 5:20 he sh. r. not days of life
11:8 let him r. days of darkness
12:1 r. Creator in days of youth
Cant. 1:4 r. love more than wine
Is. 43:18 r. not former th. ? 46:9
64:9 I will not r. sins
64:9 r. L. those, O Jacob, and Is.
46:8 r. this, show yoursel. men
47:7 neither didst r. latter end
54:4 not r. reproach of widow.
64:5 molest not those that r. thee
9 neither r. iniquity for ever
Jer. 3:16 neither shall they r. it
11:10 he will now r. their iniq.
21 r. break not thy covenant
17:2 their children r. their altars
18:20 r. I stood to speak good
31:20 I do earnestly r. him still
41:21 did not the Lord r. them?
51:50 ye that have escaped, r. L.
Lam. 5:1 O L. what is come
Ezek. 16:61 then sh. r. thy ways, 20:43; 36:31
23:27 thou shalt not r. Egypt
Hos. 8:13 now will her r. iniq.
9:9 therefore will r. iniquity
Mic. 6:5 r. now what Ba. counsel.
Hab. 3:2 O L. in wrath r. mercy
Mal. 4:4 r. the law of Moses
Mat. 16:9 r. loaves, Mark 8:18
Luke 1:72 r. his holy covenant
17:32 r. Lot's wife; 24:6 r. how
John 15:20 r. word that I said
16:4 time shall come, ye may r.
Acts 20:31 r. that by three years r. words of the Lord Jesus
Gal. 2:10 we should r. the poor
Eph. 2:11 r. that in time past
Col. 4:18 r. my bonds
1 Thes. 2:9 ye r. breth. our labor
2 Thes. 2:5 r. ye not I told you ?
2 Tim. 2:8 r. that J. Ch. raised
Heb. 13:3 r. them are in bonds
7 r. them which have the rule
Jude 17 r. words spoken of apo.
Rev. 2:5 r. fr. wh. thou art fallen
3:3 r. how thou hast received

I REMEMBER.
Gen. 41:9 I do r. my faults
1 Sam. 15:2 I r. that which Am.
Job 21:6 where I r. I am afraid
Ps. 42:1 when I r. these, I pour
6:16 wh. I r. thee upon my bed
137:6 if I do not r. thee, let my
143:5 I r. the days of old
Jer. 2:2 I r. thee, the kindness
Hos. 7:2 consider not that I r. all

I will REMEMBER.
Gen. 9:15 I r. my coven. 16
Lev. 26:42 I r. r. coven. with A.
45 I r. r. for their sakes r. cove.

REM

Ps. 42:6 therefore will I r. thee
77:10 I will r. the years of, 11
Jer. 31:34 I will r. their sin no more, Heb. 8:12; 10:17
Ezek. 16:60 I will r. my covenant
3 John 10 I will r. deeds he doeth

REMEMBER me.
Jud. 16:28 r. me that I may be
1 Sam. 1:11 look on hand. r. me
Neh. 13:14 r. me, O God, 22, 31
Job 14:13 appoint me, and r. me
Ps. 25:7 r. me, for thy sake, O L.
106:4 r. me with the favor that
Jer. 15:15 O L. thou know. r. me
Ezek. 6:9 escape of you sh. r. me
Zec. 10:9 sh. r. me in far countr.
Luke 23:42 L. r. me when comest
1 Cor. 11:2 ye r. me in all things

REMEMBERED.
Gen. 8:1 G. r. Noah; 19:29 Abr.
30:22 G. r. Rachel; 42:2 Joso. r.
Ex. 2:24 God r. his covenant, 6:5
Num. 10:9 ye shall be r. bef. L.
Jud. 8:34 child. of Isr. r. not L.
1 Sam. 1:19 the Lord r. Hannah
Est. 9:28 days of Pur. sho. be r.
Job 24:20 sin, shall he no more r.
Ps. 45:17 make thy name be r.
77:3 I r. God and was troubled
78:35 they r. G. was their Sav.
39 r. that they were but flesh
42 they r. not his hand, when
98:3 he r. his mercy tow. house
105:8 r. his covenant for ever
42 for he r. his holy promise
106:7 they r. not the multitude
45 he r. for them his covenant
109:14 iniq. of his fathers be r.
16 he r. not to show mercy
111:4 wonderful works to be r.
119:52 I r. thy judgments of old
137:1 we wept, when we r. Zion
Ez. 9:15 no man r. poor man
Is. 23:16 thou mayest be r.
65:17 former bo r. nor come
Jer. 11:19 may to no more r.
Lam. 1:7 Jerusalem r. in days
7 r. not his footstool in anger
Ezek. 3:30 his righteousness sh. not be r. 18:13
16:22 not r. days of youth, 43
21:24 made your iniq. to be r.
25:10 Ammonites may not be r.
Hos. 2:17 no more r. Zec. 13:2
Amos 1:9 not the covenant
Jon. 2:7 soul fainted, I r. Lord
Mat. 26:75 Peter r. the words of Jesus, Luke 22:61
Luke 24:8 they r. his words
22 when ho was risen they r.
John 2:17 disciples r. it was wr.
22 when ho was risen they r. 12:16 wh. J. was glorified th. r.
Acts 11:16 then r. I word of L.
Rev. 18:5 God hath r. her iniqui.

REMEMBEREST, ETH.
Ps. 9:12 mak. inquisition, he r.
88:5 like whom thou r. no more
103:14 he r. we are but dust
Lam. 1:9 she r. not her last end
3:19 r. mine affliction and
1 Cor. 7:15 will. he r. obedience

REMEMBERING.
Lam. 3:19 r. mine affliction and
1 Thes. 1:3 r. your work of faith

REMEMBRANCE.
Ex. 17:14 put out r. of Amalek
Num. 5:15 bring iniquity to r.
Deut. 25:19 blot out r. of Amalek
32:26 make r. of them cease
2 Sam. 18:18 no son to keep r.
1 K. 17:18 to call my sin in r.
Job 18:17 his r. perish fr. earth
Ps. 6:5 in death there is no r.
30:4 thanks at r. of holi. 97:12
34:16 to cut off the r. of them
38:1 r. Lord; 70:1 title
77:6 call to r. my song to night
83:4 heard be no more in r.
102:12 r. unto all generations
112:6 righteous shall be in r.
Ec. 1:11 there is no r. of things
2:16 there is no r. of the wise
Is. 23:18 color of soul, of thee
43:26 put me in r. let us plead
57:8 behind doors set up the r.
Lam. 3:20 soul hath them still in r.
Mal. 3:16 book of r. was written

REM

Mark 11:21 Peter calling to r.
Luke 1:54 hath holpen Is. in r.
22:19 do in r. of me, 1 Cor. 11:24
John 14:26 bring things to yo. r.
Acts 10:31 thine alms had in r.
1 Cor. 4:17 sh. bring you into r.
11:25 as ye drl. of it, in r. of me
Phil. 1:3 I thank God upon ev. r.
1 Thes. 3:6 that ye have good r.
1 Tim. 4:6 if thou put breth. in r.
2 Tim. 1:3 that I have r. of thee
Call to r. unfeigned faith
6 wherefore I put thee in r.
2:14 of th. things put them in r.
Heb. 10:3 there is a r. of sins
32 call to r. the former days
2 Pet. 1:12 always in r. Jude 5
13 putting you in r.
15 have th. things always in r.
3:1 pure minds by way of r.
Rev. 16:19 Babylon came in r.

REMEMBRANCES.
Job 13:12 your r. like to ashes

REMISSION.
Mat. 26:28 blo. shed for r. of sins
Mark 1:4 baptism of repentance for r. Luke 3:3
Luke 1:77 salvation by r. of sins
24:47 that r. should be preached
Acts 2:38 baptized for r. of sins
10:43 whoso belie. sh. receive r.
Rom. 3:25 r. of sins th. are past
Heb. 9:22 without shed bl. no r.
10:18 where r. is, th. is no offe.

REMIT, TED.
John 20:23 sins ye r. they are r.

REMNANT.
Lev. 2:3 the r. of meat-offering
5:13 r. sh. be priest's as offering
14:18 r. of oil in priest's hand
Deut. 28:54 eye evil toward the r.
Jos. 23:12 if ye cleave to the r.
2 Sam. 21:2 Gibeonites r. of Am.
1 K. 14:10 I will take away the r.
2 K. 19:4 lift up thy prayer for the r. Is. 37:4, 31, 32
80 r. escaped shall take root
31 out of Je. shall go forth a r.
21:14 fors. r. of mine inherit.
25:11 r. did Nebuzar-adan carry
2 Chr. 30:6 retu. to the r. of you
Ezr. 3:8 the r. of their brethren
9:8 grace fr. L. to leave us a r.
14 so that there should he no r.
Neh. 1:7 r. left of the captivity
11:11 to recover r. of his people
16 there sh. be highway for r.
11:22 cut off fr. Babylon the r.
30 kill thy root, he sh. sl. thy r.
15:9 I will bring lions on the r.
16:14 the r. shall be very small
17:3 kingdom shall cease from r.
46:3 hearken r. of house of Isr.
Jer. 6:9 they sh. glean r. of Isr.
11:23 there sh. be no r. of them
15:11 it shall be well with thy r.
22:3 I will gather r. of my flock
25:20 the r. of Ashdod did drink
31:7 O L. save thy peo. r. of Is.
40:11 king of Babylon left a r.
15 Jews scatt. r. of Judah perl.
41:16 Joha. took r. of peo. 42:5
42:15 hear the Lord, ye r. of J.
19 O ye r. of Judah, go ye not
41:12 I will take the r. of Judah
28 r. sh. kn. wh. words stand
47:1 Lord will spoil r. of count.
4:3 Lord will spoil Philistines
the r. of the country of Caph.
11:23 L. will make end of r. J.
11:22 behold, therein sh. be a r.
25:25 r. shall fall by the sword
28 destroy the r. of the sea-c.
Joel 2:32 r. whom the L. sh. call
Amos 1:8 r. of Philist. sh. perish
5:15 God will be gracious to r.
9:12 that they may possess r.
Mic. 2:12 I will gather r. of Isra.
4:7 make her that halted, a r.
5:3 r. of brethren return to Isr.
7 r. of Ja. in midst of people, 8
7:18 th. regress. of r. of herit.
Zep. 1:4 I will cut off r. of Baal
2:7 coast for r. of house of Jud.
9 r. of people possess the r.
3:13 r. of Is. sh. not do iniq.
Hag. 1:12 r. obeyed vo. of Lord
14 Lord stirred up spirit of r.
2:2 speak to r. saying
Zec. 8:6 marvellous in eyes of r.
11 will be unto r. of peo. to pr.
12 seed prosper, r. to possess
Mat. 22:6 the r. took his servants
Rom. 9:27 Is. only, r. be saved

CRUDEN'S CONCORDANCE.

REM

Rom. 11:5 at present time there is a r.
Rev. 11:13 the r. were affrighted
12:17 dragon we. to war with r.
19:21 r. were slain with sword

REMOVE.
Gen. 48:17 father's hand to r. it
Num. 36:7 inheritance of Is. r. 9
Deut. 19:14 not r. neigh.'s land.
Jos. 3:3 ye sh. r. from your place
2 *Sam.* 6:10 Da. would not r. ark
2 *K.* 23:27 L. said, I will r. Judah
24:3 Ju. to r. them out of sight
2 *Chr.* 33:8 neither will I r. Isr.
Job 24:2 some r. landmarks, they
27:5 I will not r. mine integrity
Ps. 36:11 let not wicked r. me
39:10 r. thy stroke away fr. me
119:22 r. from me reproach and 29 r. from me the way of lying
Prov. 4:27 r. thy foot from evil
5:8 r. thy way far from her
22:28 r. not the landmarks, 23:10
30:8 r. from me vanity and lies
Ec. 11:10 r. sorrow from heart
Is. 13:13 earth r. out of her place
46:7 from his place sh. he not r.
Jer. 4:1 return, thou shalt not r.
27:10 prophesy lie, r. from land
50:3 they shall r. shall depart
8 r. out of the midst of Babyl.
Ezek. 12:3 r. by day, thou sh. r.
45:9 O princes, r. violence and
Hos. 5:10 like them that r. bound
Joel 2:20 I will r. northern army
3:6 ye might r. them from hoe.
Mic. 2:3 fr. wh. sh. not r. necks
Zec. 3:9 I will r. iniquity of land
14:4 mountain r. toward north
Mal. 17:20 say, r. hence, sh. he r.
Luke 22:42 if willing, r. this cup
1 *Cor.* 13:2 that I could r. mount.
Rev. 2:5 else I will r. candlestick

REMOVED.
Gen. 8:13 Noah r. covering of ark
47:21 Joseph r. people to cities
Ex. 14:19 angel of God r. and
20:18 people saw it and r. afar
Num. 21:12 r. pitched, 33:7-31
Deut. 26:25 r. into all kingdoms
Jos. 3:1 they r. from Shittim
1 *Sam.* 6:3 why his ha. is not r.
2 *Sam.* 20:12 he r. Amasa out of
1 *K.* 15:12 Asa r. the idols
13 r. fr. bei. queen, 2 *Chr.* 15:16
14 high pla. not r. 2 *K.* 15:4, 35
2 *K.* 17:18 the Lord r. Israel out
of his sight, 23 ; 23:27
20 nations wh. th. r. know 18:4 Hezekiah r. the high places
2 *Chr.* 33:19 th. r. burnt-offerings
Job 14:18 rock is r. out of place
18:4 sh. rock be r. out of place?
19:10 hope hath he r. like a tree
36:16 would have r. out of stra.
Ps. 46:2 not fear tho' earth be r.
81:6 r. his shoulder from burden
103:12 so far her. transgressions
104:5 earth, it should not be r.
125:1 as Zion which cannot be r.
Prov. 10:30 righteous never be r.
Is. 6:12 till L. hath r. men away
10:13 I have r. bounds of people
31 Madmenah is r. inhabitants
22:25 the sure place shall be r.
24:20 earth sh. be r. like cottage
26:15 hast r. it to ends of earth
29:13 r. their heart from me
30:20 yet sh. not teachers be r.
33:20 not one of stakes be r.
38:12 mine age r. fr. me as tent
54:10 the hills shall be r. cov.
of my peace shall not be r.
Jer. 15:4 cause to be r. to kingd.
24:9 deliv. to be r. 29:18; 34:17
Lam. 1:8 Jerusalem sinned, is r.
3:17 thou hast r. my soul
Ezek. 7:19 their gold shall be r.
23:46 I will give them to be r.
36:17 way uncl. of a r. woman
Amos 6:7 hang. of them sh. be r.
Mic. 2:4 how hath he r. it fr. me
7:11 in that day sh. decree be r.
Mat. 21:21 Be r. Mark 11:23
Acts 7:4 he r. Abraham into land
13:22 he r. Saul, raised David
Gal. 1:6 marvel ye are so soon r.

REMOVETH.
Deut. 27:17 cursed, th. r. neigh.
Job 9:5 wh. r. the mountains
12:20 he r. speech of the trusty
Ec. 10:9 whoso r. stones be hurt
Dan. 2:21 chan. seasons, r. kings

REMOVING.
Gen. 30:32 r. from flock speckled
Is. 49:21 I am a captive r. to and

REN

Ezek. 12:3 prepare stuff for r. 4
Heb. 12:27 signifieth r. of things

REMPHAN.
Acts 7:43 the star of your god R.

REND.
Ex. 39:23 ephod should not r.
Lev. 10:6 neither r. your clothes
13:56 priest r. plague out of gar.
1 *K.* 11:11 I will r. kingd. 12, 31
13 I will not r. away kingdom
2 *Chr.* 24:27 didst r. clothes, we.
Ec. 3:7 a time to r. time to sew
Is. 64:1 thou wouldest r. heavens
Ezek. 13:11 stormy wind r. it, 13
20:7 and r. all their shoulder
Hos. 13:8 I will r. caul of heart
Joel 2:13 r. your heart, not gar.
Mat. 7:6 lest they turn and r.
John 19:24 not r. it, but cast lots

RENDER.
Num. 18:9 offering they r. holy
Deut. 32:41 I will r. vengeance
43 r. vengeance to adversaries
Jud. 9:57 evil of men of S. G. r.
1 *Sam.* 26:23 L. r. to man faithf.
2 *Chr.* 6:30 r. to ev. man accord.
Job 33:26 will r. to man rightc.
34:11 work of a man shall he r.
Ps. 28:34 r. to them their desert
38:20 they that r. evil for good
56:12 O God, I will r. praises to
79:12 r. to neighbor sevenfold
94:2 r. a word to the proud
116:12 what shall I r. to the L.
Prov. 24:12 shall not he r. to ev.
29 I will r. to the man so?
Rom. 2:6
29 r. to man according to wo.
96:16 seven men can r. reason
Is. 66:15 Lord come to r. anger
Jer. 51:6 r. to Bab. recompen. 24
Lam. 3:64 r. to them recompense
Joel 3:4 ye r. me a recompense?
Zec. 9:12 r. double to thee
Mat. 21:41 r. him fruits in season
22:21 r. unto Cesar things are
C. 's, *Mark* 12:17; *Luke* 20:25
Rom. 13:7 r. to all their dues
1 *Cor.* 7:3 husb. r. to wife bene.
1 *Thes.* 3:9 what thanks can we r.
5:15 see that none r. evil for ev.

RENDERED.
Jud. 9:56 G. r. wickedness of A.
2 *K.* 3:4 king of M. r. king of Is.
2 *Chr.* 32:25 Heze. r. not accord.
Prov. 12:14 rec. of man's ha. r.
Ps. 68:19 r. to man acc. to work
18:4 Hezekiah r. the high places
2 *Chr.* 33:19 th. r. burnt-offerings
Job 14:18 rock is r. out of place

RENDEREST, ING.
Ps. 7:2 my soul r. it in pieces
Jer. 4:30 r. face with painting

RENEW.
1 *Sam.* 11:14 go to G. r. kingd.
Ps. 51:10 r. right sp. within me
Is. 40:31 wait on L. r. strength
41:1 let people r. their stren.
Lam. 5:21 turn us, O L. r. days
Heb. 6:6 if fall, r. to repentance

RENEWED, EST.
2 *Chr.* 15:8 Asa r. the altar of Lord
Job 10:17 r. witnesses ag. me
29:20 my bow was r. in my ha.
Ps. 103:5 youth is r. like eagle's
104:30 thou r. face of the earth
2 *Cor.* 4:16 inw. man r. day by d.
Eph. 4:23 be r. in spirit of mind
Col. 3:10 man wh. is r. in know.

RENEWING.
Rom. 12:2 transform. by r. mind
Tit. 3:5 he sav. us by r. of H. G.

RENOUNCED.
2 *Cor.* 4:2 have r. hidden things

RENOWN.
Gen. 6:4 giants of old, men of r.
Num. 16:2 In. in cong. men of r.
Ezek. 16:14 r. went forth among 15 playedst harlot bec. of thy r.
34:29 raise for them a plant of r.
39:13 shall be to them r. sai. L.
Dan. 9:15 gotten thee r.

RENOWNED.
Num. 1:16 these r. of congrega.
Is. 14:20 evil-doers never r.
Ezek. 23:23 captai. lords, and r.
26:17 r. city was strong in sea

RENT, Substantive.
Is. 3:24 instead of girdle he a r.
Mat. 9:16 r. ma. worse, *Mar.* 2:21
Luke 5:36 then new maketh a r.

RENT, Participle.
Gen. 37:33 Joseph is r. in pieces

REP

Jos. 9:4 wine bot. old and r. 13
2 *Sam.* 15:32 H. with his coat r.
1 *K.* 13:3 altar be r. 5 altar r.
Ezr. 9:5 having r. my garment
Mat. 27:51 veil of temple r. in
tw. *Mark* 15:38; *Luke* 23:45

See **CLOTHES.**

RENT, Verb.
Jud. 14:6 Samson r. lion as he r.
1 *Sam.* 15:27 Saul r. Sam. man.
28 L. hath r. kingdom, 28:17
1 *K.* 11:30 Ahijah r. Jerob. garment
19:11 strong wind r. mountains
2 *K.* 17:21 he r. Israel from Dav.
22:11 king of Jud. r. his clothes
Ezr. 9:3 when I heard I r. garm.
Job 1:20 Job arose, and r. mantle
2:12 Job's fr. r. ev. one mantle
26:8 cloud is not r. under them
Jer. 36:24 nor r. their garments
Ezek. 30:16 Sin have pain, No r.
Mat. 27:51 veil was r. rocks r.
Mark 9:26 spi. cried, and r. him

REPAID.
Prov. 13:21 to right. good be r.

REPAIR.
2 *K.* 12:5 let priests r. breaches
of the house of God, 22:5, 6;
2 *Chr.* 24:4; 34:8, 10
7 why r. ye not house? 22:5, 6
2 *Chr.* 24:5 money to r. house
12 carpenters to r. house of L.
Ezr. 9:9 give reviv. to r. house
Is. 61:4 they shall r. waste cities

REPAIRED.
Jud. 21:23 Benjamin r. cities
1 *K.* 11:27 Solomon r. breaches
18:30 Elijah r. altar of the Lord
2 *K.* 12:6 the priests had not r.
14 and r. the house of the L.
1 *Chr.* 11:8 Joab r. rest of the ci.
2 *Chr.* 29:3 Hezek. r. the doors
32:5 Hezekiah r. Millo in city
33:16 Manasseh r. altar of Lord
Neh. 3:4 next to them r. 5-19
6 and after him r. 17-24

REPAIRER, ING.
2 *Chr.* 24:27 fr. r. of the house
Is. 58:12 shalt be called the r.

REPAY.
Deut. 7:10 will r. him to his face
Job 21:31 r. him what ha. done?
41:11 that I should r. him?
Is. 59:18 accord. to their deeds r.
fury, to islands r. recomp.
Luke 10:35 come again I will r.
Rom. 12:19 I will r. saith the L.
Phile. 19 I Paul, will r. it

REPAYETH.
Deut. 7:10 r. them that hate him

REPEATETH.
Prov. 17:9 but he that r. a mat.

REPENT.
Ex. 13:17 lest peradv. people r.
32:12 turn from thy wrath, r.
Num. 23:19 not son of man, r.
Deut. 32:36 Lord r. for his serv.
1 *Sam.* 15:29 Strength of Is. not r.
1 *K.* 8:47 if they r. in the land
Job 42:6 and r. in dust and ashes
Ps. 90:13 let it r. thee concern.
110:4 Lord will not r. *Heb.* 7:21
Jer. 4:28 I purp. it, will not r.
18:8 nation turn, r. of ev. 26:13
10 that I may r. 42:10 for I r.
Ezek. 14:6; and turn yourselves,
18:30
24:14 neither spare, nei. will r.
Jon. 3:9
Mat. 3:2 preach. saying r. 4:17
Mark 1:15; r. and believe
6:12 preach. that men should r.
Luke 13:3 except ye r. perish, 5
16:30 if one we. fr. dead will r.
17:3 if thy brother r. forgive, 4
Acts 2:38 r. and be baptized ev.
3:19 r. ye therof. be converted
8:22 r. of this thy wickedness
17:30 commandeth all men to r.
26:20 they should r. turn to G.
2 *Cor.* 7:8 I do not r. tho' I did r.
Rev. 2:5 r. or else I will come unto thee
21 I gave her space to r. of her
3:3 how thou hast rec. and r.
19 be zealous therefore and r.

REPENTANCE.
Hos. 13:14 r. sh. be hid fr. eyes
Mat. 3:8 fru. meet for r. *Luke* 3:8
11 I indeed bapti. you unto r.
Mark 1:4 John did pren. bap. of
r. *Luke* 3:3; *Acts* 13:24; 19:4
Luke 13:7 ninety-nine need no r.
24:47 r. and remission of sins
Acts 5:31 God exalted to give r.
11:18 to Gentiles granted r.
20:21 testifying to Greeks r.
26:20 works meet for r.
Rom. 2:4 good. of God lead. to r.
11:29 gifts of God without r.
2 *Cor.* 7:9 I rej. ye sorrowed to r.
10 godly sorrow worketh r.
2 *Tim.* 2:25 if G. will give th. r.
Heb. 6:1 laying again foun. of r.
6 to renew them again to r.
12:17 he found no place of r.
2 *Pet.* 3:9 perish, all come to r.

REPENTED.
Gen. 6:6 it r. Lord he made man
Ex. 32:14 r. of evil, 2 *Sam.* 24:16;
1 *Chr.* 21:15; *Jer.* 26:19
Jud. 2:18 it r. L. because of th.
21:6 the children of Israel, r. 15
1 *Sam.* 15:35 L. r. he made Saul
Ps. 106:45 L. r. acc. to mercies
Jer. 8:6 no man r. him of wick.
20:16 cities L. overthrew r. not
31:19 after I was turned, I r.
Amos 7:3 the Lord r. for this, 6
Jon. 3:10 God r. of the evil
Mat. 11:20 cities bec. they r. not
21 would have r. *Luke* 10:13
12:41 men of Nin. r. *Luke* 11:32
21:29 afterward he r. and went
32 when yo had seen it, r. not
2 *Cor.* 7:10 repent. not to be r.
12:21 many that have not r.
Rev. 2:21 to repent. she r. not
9:20 were not killed, yet r. not
16:9 blasphemed G. r. not, 11

REPENTEST, ETH.
Gen. 6:6 it r. me I made them
1 *Sam.* 15:11 it r. me I set up S.
Jon. 4:2 gracious God r. of evil
Joel 2:13 slow to anger, r. him
Luke 15:7 one sinner r. 10

REPENTING, S.
Jer. 15:6 I am weary with r.
Hos. 11:8 r. are kindled together

REPETITIONS.
Mat. 6:7 use not vain r. as hea.

REPHAIM.
Gen. 14:5 smote R. in Ashteroth
15:20 have I given land of R.
2 *Sam.* 5:18 in valley of R. 22;
23:13; 1 *Chr.* 11:15; 14:9
Is. 17:5 gather. ears in val. of R.

REPHIDIM.
Ex. 17:1 pitch. in R. *Num.* 33:14
8 and fought with Israel in R.
19:2 dep. from R. *Num.* 33:15

REPLENISH, ED.
Gen. 1:28 mult. and r. earth, 9:1
Is. 2:6 bec. they be r. from east
23:2 merchants of Zidon have r.
Jer. 31:25 and I have r. every
Ezek. 26:2 I sh. be r. I am waste pl.
27:25 thou wast r. made glori.
Rom. 9:20 thou that r. ag. God?

REPORT, Substantive.
Gen. 37:2 Jos. brought their r.
Ex. 23:1 shalt not raise false r.
Num. 13:32 brought up evil r.
14:37 men that bring up evil r.
Deut. 2:25 nations shall hear r.
1 *Sam.* 2:24 no good r. I hear
Neh. 6:13 matter for an evil r.
Prov. 15:30 a good r. maketh fat
Is. 23:5 at r. concerning Egypt,
so at the r. of Tyre
28:19 vexation only to under. r.
53:1 who hath believed our r.?
John 12:38; *Rom.* 10:16
Jer. 50:43 Babylon heard the r.
Acts 6:3 seven men of honest r.
10:22 Cornelius was of good r.
22:12 Ananias having a good r.
2 *Cor.* 6:8 by evil r. and good r.
Phil. 4:8 what. things of good r.
1 *Tim.* 3:7 bishop have good r.
Heb. 11:2 elders obt. a good r.
39 having obtained a good r.
2 *John* 12 Demetrius ha. good r.

REPORT, Verb.
Jer. 20:10 r. say they, will r. it
1 *Cor.* 14:25 will r. that God is in

REPORTED.
Neh. 6:6 it is r. among heathen

CRUDEN'S CONCORDANCE.

RES

Num. 16:13 Moses said, r. not
Deut. 1:17 not r. persons, 16:19
2 Sam. 14:14 neither doth God r.
Is. 17:8 nor shall r. that which
RESPECTED, ETH.
Job 37:24 he r. not wise of heart
Ps. 40:4 blessed is man that r.
Lam. 4:16 r. not pers. of priest
RESPECTER.
Acts 10:34 God is no r. of persons
RESPITE.
Ex. 8:15 Phar. saw there was r.
1 Sam. 11:3 said, Give 7 days r.

REST, Substantive.
Gen. 49:15 Issa. saw r. was good
Ex. 16:23 to-morrow r. of sath.
31:15 sev. is sabbath of r. 35:2;
Lev. 16:31; 23:3, 32; 25:4
33:14 and I will give thee r.
Lev. 25:5 a year of r. to land
Deut. 3:20 L. given r. Jos. 1:13
12:9 ye are not yet come to r.
23:19 God hath given thee r.
28:65 neither sh. sole of foot r.
Jos. 1:15 L. hath given breth. r.
14:15 land had r. fr. war, Jud.
3:11; 5:31
21:41 the Lord gave them r.
22:4 God given r. 23:1 L. giv. r.
Jud. 3:30 land had r. 80 years
Ruth 1:9 L. grant you may find r.
3:18 the man will not be in r.
2 Sam. 7:1 L. had giv. him r. 1 K.
5:4; 8:56; 2 Chr. 14:6, 7
1 Chr. 6:31 after that ark had r.
22:9 man of r. I will gi. him r.
23:25 God hath given r. to peo.
28:2 I had to build house of r.
2 Chr. 13:15 L. gave them r.
20:30 G. grave him r., round ab.
Neh. 9:28 after they had r.
Est. 9:16 J. had r. from enemies
Job 3:13 slept, had been at r.
17 there the weary be at r.
26 not in safety, nei. had I r.
11:18 shalt take thy r. in safety
17:16 our r. together is in dust
Ps. 38:3 neither is there any r.
55:6 then we, I fly and be at r.
9:13 thou mayest give him r.
116:7 ret. to thy r. O my soul
132:8 arise, O Lord, into thy r.
14 this is my r. for ever
Prov. 29:17 cor. son, he giv. r.
Ec. 2:23 his heart taketh not r.
6:5 this hath more r. than other
Is. 11:10 Gent. seek, r. be glor.
14:3 the Lord shall give thee r.
7 the earth is at r. Zec. 1:11
18:4 L. said, I will take my r.
28:12 this is r. wherew. weary r.
30:15 retur. and r. sh. ye be sav.
34:14 find for herself a pla. of r.
66:1 where is place of my r. ?
Jer. 6:16 ye shall find r. for souls
30:10 Jacob shall be in r. 46:27
Ezek. 38:11 to them that are at r.
Dan. 4:1 I Nebuchad. was at r.
Mic. 2:10 this is not your r.
Zec. 9:1 Damascus shall be r.
Mat. 11:28 co. unto me, I give r.
29 sh. find r. to your souls
12:43 seek r. Luke 11:24
26:45 take your r. Mark 14:41
John 11:13 had spoken of tak. r.
Acts 7:49 what is place of my r.?
9:31 then had the churches r.
2 Thes. 1:7 are troub. r. with us
Heb. 3:11 not enter into r. 18
4:1 prom. left us of ent. into r.
3 wh. believed do enter into r.
8 if Jesus had given them r.
9 th. remaineth r. to peo. of G.
11 labour therefore to enter r.
See NO.
RESTS.
1 K. 6:6 he made narrowed r.
REST, Adjective.
Ex. 28:10 names of r. on stone
Num. 31:8 r. of them were slain
Deut. 3:11 for of Og king of B.
Jud. 7:6 the r. bowed to drink
2 K. 4:7 live and child. r. of th. r.
1 Chr. 1:16 Joash repair, r. of city
1 Chr. 11:14 brought r. of honey
Neh. 2:1 r. of enem. heard 1 built
11:1 r. of people also cast lots
4:12 wh. done in r. of prov.?
Ps. 17:14 leave r. to their babes
Is. 10:19 the r. of tree be few
Dan. 2:18 D. sh. not per. with r.
Zec. 11:9 r. eat flesh of another
Luke 12:26 why take tho. for r.?
24:9 told eleven and all the r.
Acts 5:13 to Pet. and r. of apost.

RES

Acts 27:44 the r. esc. safe to land
1 Cor. 7:12 to the r. speak I
11:34 the r. will I set in order
1 Pet. 4:2 not live r. of his time
Rev. 2:24 to the r. in Thyatira
20:5 r. of dead lived not again
See ACTS.

REST, Verb.
Gen. 18:4 wash feet, r. und. tree
Ex. 5:5 make th. r. fr. burdens
23:11 in seventh year let it r.
12 seventh day shalt r. 34:21
34:21 in harvest thou shalt r.
Lev. 26:33 not r. in sabbaths
Deut. 5:14 maid-serv. r. as thou
Jos. 3:13 feet of priests shall r.
2 Sam. 3:29 let it r. on head of J.
21:10 birds r. on them by day
2 K. 2:15 sp. of Elijah r. on Elis.
2 Chr. 14:11 we r. on thee
Job 3:18 the prisoners r. togeth.
14:6 may r. till he accomplish
Ps. 16:9 r. in hope, Acts 2:26
37:7 r. in the Lord, wait for him
125:3 rod of wick. not r. on rig.
Prov. 6:35 nor will he r. content
Cant. 1:7 makest flock r. at noon
Is. 7:19 shall r. in deso. valleys
11:2 Sp. of the Lord r. upon him
25:10 in moun. sh. hand of L. r.
28:12 ye cause the w-ary to r.
34:14 I will make judgement to r.
57:2 they shall r. in their beds
20 are like the sea, it cannot r.
62:1 for Jer.'s sake I will not r.
63:14 Sp. of L. caused him to r.
Jer. 31:2 to cause him to r.
Ezek. 5:13 my fury to r. upon th.
16:42; 21:17; 24:13
44:30 may cause blessing to r.
Dan. 12:13 th. shalt r. and stand
Hab. 3:16 I mi. r. day of trouble
Zep. 3:17 he will r. in love
Mark 6:31 come to desert and r.
Luke 10:6 your peace shall r.
Acts 9:4 God did r. seventh day
Rev. 4:8 r. not day and night
6:11 they should r. for a season
14:13 they may r. from labors

RESTED.
Gen. 2:2 he r. on seventh day,
3; Ex. 20:11; 31:17
8:4 the ark r. in seventh month
Ex. 10:14 locusts r. in Egypt
16:30 people r. on seventh day
Num. 9:18 as cloud ab. they r. 23
10:12 cloud r. in wild. of Paran
36 when it r. he said, Ret. O L.
11:25 Spirit r. upon them, 26
Jos. 11:23 the land r. from war
1 K. 6:10 chambers r. on house
2 Chr. 32:8 r. on words of Hez.
Est. 9:17 on 14th day r. 18
Job 30:27 bow. boiled and r.
Luke 23:56 they r. sabbath-day
RESTEST, ETH.
Job 24:23 in safety, where, he r.
Prov. 14:33 wisdom r. in heart
Ec. 7:9 anger r. in bos. of fools
Rom. 2:17 thou art a J. r. in law
1 Pet. 4:14 Sp. of G. r. upon you

RESTING-PLACE, S.
Num. 10:33 to search out a r-pl.
2 Chr. 6:41 O Lord, into thy r-p.
Prov. 24:15 spoil not his r-place
Is. 32:18 dwell in r-p. Jer.
Jer. 50:6 forgotten their r-place

RESTITUTION.
Ex. 22:3 make full r. 5, 6, 12
Job 20:18 according to subs., r. be
Acts 3:21 until the times of r.

RESTORE.
Gen. 20:7 r. the man his wife
40:13 Ph. will r. thee thy place
42:25 to r. every man's money
Ex. 22:1 r. five oxen for an ox
4 theft be found, he shall r.
Lev. 6:5 shall r. it in principal
24:21 killeth a beast, he sh. r.
25:27 r. overpl. to wh. he sold it
Num. 35:25 congregation r. him
Deut. 22:2 things strayed r. aga.
Jud. 11:13 therof. r. those lands
17:3 I will r. it unto thee, 1 Sam.
12:3; 1 K. 20:34
2 Sam. 9:7 r. thee all land of Sa.
12:6 he shall r. lamb fourfold
16:3 to-day house of Isr. r. me
1 K. 20:5 thou shalt deliver me
Neh. 5:11 r. I pray you, 12 will r.
Job 20:10 his ha. r. their goods
18 which he laboured for, sh. r.
Ps. 51:12 r. to me joy of salvati.
Prov. 6:31 he shall r. sevenfould

RET

Is. 1:26 I will r. thy judges
42:22 for spoil. and none sai. r.
49:6 to r. the preserved of Isr.
57:18 will r. comforts unto him
Jer. 27:22 r. them to this place
30:17 r. health to thee
Ezek. 33:15 if wicked r. pledge
Dan. 9:25 command to r. Jerus.
Joel 2:25 I will r. you the years
Mal. 17:11 Elias sh. r. all things
Luke 19:8 I r. him fourfold
Acts 1:6 Lord, wilt thou r. king-
dom ?
Gal. 6:1 r. such a one in meek.

RESTORED.
Gen. 20:14 Abimelech r. Sarah
40:21 r. butler to his butlership
41:13 me he r. to mine office
42:28 money is r. in my sack
Deut. 28:31 thine ass sh. not be r.
Jud. 17:3 r. the 1,100 shekels. 4
1 Sam. 7:14 cities taken were r.
1 K. 13:6 the king's hand was r.
2 K. 8:1 whose son he r. 5
14:22 r. Elath to Jud. 5 Chr. 26:2
2 Chr. 8:2 the citi. Huram had r.
Ezr. 6:5 the vessels brought be r.
Ps. 69:4 I r. that which I took
Ezek. 18:7 r. to debtor his pledge
12 hath not r. pledge
Mat. 12:13 r. whole like as the
other, Mark 3:5 ; Luke 8:10
Mark 8:25 sight r. saw clearly
Heb. 13:19 that I may be r.

RESTORER.
Ruth 4:15 shall be to thee a r.
Is. 58:12 sh. be called r. of paths

RESTORETH.
Ps. 23:3 he r. my soul
Mat. 9:12 El. cometh first and r.

RESTRAIN.
Job 15:8 dost thou r. wisdom ?
Ps. 76:10 the wrath shalt thou r.

RESTRAINED.
Gen. 8:3 rain from heaven was r.
11:6 nothing will be r. fr. them
16:2 Lord r. me from bearing
Ex. 36:6 peo. were r. fr. bring.
1 Sam. 3:13 Eli's sons vile, r. not
Is. 63:15 mercies, are they r. ?
Ezek. 31:15 I r. the floods there.
Acts 14:18 sayings scarce r. peo.

RESTRAINEST.
Job 15:4 thou r. prayer before G.

RESTRAINT.
1 Sam. 14:6 there is no r. to L.

RESURRECTION.
Mat. 22:23 th. is no r. Mark 12:18
28 in r. whose wife sh. she be ?
Mark 12:23 ; Luke 20:33
30 in r. they neither marry, 31
27:53 came out of graves aft. r.
Mark 12:18 no r. Luke 20:27
Luke 14:14 be recompensed at r.
20:27 deny any r. 36 child. of r.
John 5:29 done good r. of life,
done evil, to r. of damnati.
11:25 J. said, I am the r. and life
9:11 David spake of r. of Christ
4:2 they preached thro' Jesus r.
33 witness of r. of Lord Jesus
17:18 preached Jesus and the r.
32 when they heard of r. of dd.
24:15 there shall be a r. of dead
21 touching r. of the dead
Rom. 1:4 by r. from the dead
6:5 shall be in likeness of his r.
1 Cor. 15:13 but if there be no r.
21 by man came r. of the dead
Phil. 3:10 know power of his r.
11 might attain to r. of dead
2 Tim. 2:18 r. is past already
Heb. 11:35 might obtain a better r.
1 Pet. 1:3 by r. of Jesus fr. dead
3:21 save us, by r. of J. Christ
Rev. 20:5 this is the first r.
6 hath part in first r.

RETAIN.
Job 2:9 dost still r. integrity ?
Prov. 4:4 thy heart r. my words
11:16 strong men r. riches
Ec. 8:8 no man power to r.
Dan. 11:6 she sh. not r. power
John 20:23 wh. soever sins ye r.
Rom. 1:28 did not like to r. God
Cant. 6:13 r. r. O Shulami. r. r.
Philem. 13 whom I would have r.

RET

RETAINETH.
Prov. 3:18 happy ev. one r. her
11:16 a graci. woman r. honor
Mic. 7:18 r. not anger for ever

RETIRE.
2 Sam. 11:15 set in battle, and r.
Jer. 4:6 set up stand, r. stay not

RETIRED.
Jud. 20:39 when men of Israel r.
2 Sam. 20:22 they r. from city

RETURN, Substantive.
Gen. 14:17 meet Abrah after r.
1 Sam. 7:17 Sam.'s r. was to Ra.
1 K. 20:22 at r. of the year the
king of Syria will come, 26

RETURN, Verb.
Gen. 3:19 dust th. art, to dust r.
16:9 r. to mistress and submit
18:10 I will cert. r. to thee. 14
31:3 r. to land of kindred, 13
32:9 Lord which saidst to me, r.
Ex. 4:18 let me r. to breth. 19
13:17 people repent, r. to Egypt
Lev. 25:10 r. to posses. 13, 27, 28
41 shall r. unto his own family
27:24 the field shall r. unto him
Num. 10:36 r. L. to many of Is.
14:4 let us make a capt. and r.
35:5 L. said, r. unto Balak
32:29 sh. r. shall r. No. 30:6
Deut. 3:20 then shall r. every
man to his posses. Jos. 1:15
20:5 and r. to his house, 6, 7, 8
30:3 the Lord thy God will r.
8 thou shalt r. and obey the L.
Jos. 22:8 r. with much riches
Jud. 7:3 whos. afraid, let him r.
11:31 when I r. from children
Ruth 1:6 that she might r. fr. M.
8 go r. to her mother's house
15 r. thou after sister-in-law
1 Sam. 6:3 in any wise r. him
6:5 Saul said, Come, let us r.
26:21 then said Saul, I sinned, r.
29:4 said. Make this follow r. 7
2 Sam. 2:26 ere thou bid peo. r. ?
3:16 then said A. to him, Go, r.
10:5 beards grown, r. 1 Chr. 19:5
15:19 goest thou with us ? r.
20 I go whither I may, r. thou
24:13 see what answer I sh. r.
1 K. 2:32 L. shall r. his blood, 33
41 Lord sh. r. thy wickedness
8:48 r. to thee with all th. heart
12:24 r. every man to his house
26 now shall kingd. r. to Dav.
19:15 r. on thy way to wildern.
22:17 r. every man to his house
in peace, 2 Chr. 18:4; 18:16
28 if r. in peace, 2 Chr. 18:27
2 K. 18:14 I offended, r. from me
19:7 king of Assyria sh. r. to his
own land, 33; Is. 37:7, 34
20:10 let shadow r. backward
2 Chr. 6:24 r. confess thy name
10:9 may r. answer to this peo.
18:26 fellow in prison until I r.
30:6 r. to you, he r. unto you
Neh. 2:6 said. When wilt th. r. ?
4:12 whence ye shall r. to us
Est. 9:25 device of Haman sh. r.
Job 1:21 naked shall I r. thither
6:29 r. yea, r. ag. my righteous.
7:10 sh. r. no more to his house
15:22 believeth not he shall r.
17:10 but as for you all, do ye r.
22:23 if thou r. to Almighty
33:25 shall r. to days of youth
36:10 that they r. from iniquity
Ps. 6:4 r. O L. deliver my soul
10 let mine enemies r. asham.
7:7 for their sakes therefore r.
16 mischief r. upon own head
59:6 r. at even. 14 let them r.
73:10 therof. his people r. hith.
74:21 let not oppress. r. asham.
80:14 r. we beseech thee, O G.
90:3 sayest, r. ye child. of men
13 r. O Lord ! how long ?
85:15 judgment r. to righteous.
104:29 they die, r. to their dust
116:7 r. to thy rest, O my soul
Prov. 2:19 no. th. go unto her r.
26:27 rolleth a stone, it will r.
Ec. 1:7 riv. come, thither they r.
5:15 naked sh. r. to go as he ca.
12:2 nor clouds r. after the rain
14:7 r. to him, O God
Cant. 6:13 r. r. O Shulami. r. r.
Is. 6:13 yet in it a tenth shall r.
10:21 remnant of Jacob sh. r. 22
21:12 if ye will, inqu. ye. r. co.
35:10 ransomed of L. sh. r. 51:11
44:22 r. unto me, I redeem. thee
63:17 r. for thy servant's sake

CRUDEN'S CONCORDANCE. 997

RET

Jer. 3:1 shall he r. ag. ? yet r. to
22 r. ye backsliding children
4:1 if thou r. saith L. r. unto
12:15 I will r. and have compa.
15:19 if thou wilt r. let them r.
  unto thee, r. not unto them
18:11 r. ev. one fr. evil way, 35:15
21:7 shall r. with whole heart
30:10 Jacob shall r. 46:27
31:8 great comp. shall r. thither
36:3 r. every man from evil
 7 will r. ev. one from evil way
44:14 should r. into land of Ju.
50:9 none shall r. in vain
Ezek. 16:55 they desire to r. th.
  then and thy daugh. shall r.
18:23 wicked r. fr. ways and live
Dan. 10:20 will r. to fight Persia
11:9 r. into his own land, 10, 28
13 the king of the north sh. r.
29 time appointed he shall r.
30 he shall be grieved, and r
Hos. 2:7 and r. to first husband
 9 I will r. take corn and wine
3:5 afterward chil. of Israel r.
7:16 they r. but not to M. High
8:13 they shall r. to Egypt, 9:3
12:14 reproach shall L. r. to hi.
14:7 they under shadow shall r.
Joel 2:14 know, he will r. repent
3:4 will r. recomp. on head, 7
Ob. 15 reward r. upon thy head
Mic. 5:3 remn. of brethren sh. r.
Mal. 1:4 Edom saith, We will r.
3:7 r. to me, and I will r. to y.
18 r. and discern between rig.
Mat. 10:13 let your peace r.
12:44 r. into house, *Luke* 11:24
24:16 nor let him in field r.
Luke 8:39 r. to thine own house
Acts 15:16 I will r. and build
18:21 I will r. to you, if G. will

To RETURN.

Num. 14:3 not better *to* r. to Eg.
Deut. 17:16 cause peo. *to* r. to E.
Ruth 1:16 not *to* leave th. or *to* r.
1 *Sam.* 29:11 David rose car. *to* r.
2 *Chr.* 10:6 coun. give ye *to* r. T
Neh. 9:17 captain *to* r. to bondage
Jer. 5:3 they have refused *to* r.
 8:5; *Hos.* 11:5
22:27 thy desire *to* r. 44:14
24:10 in causing you *to* r. to th.
  place, 30:3; 32:44; 33:7, 11,
  26; 34:22; 42:12
34:11 caused servants *to* r. 16
Ezek. 21:30 cause *to* r. to sheath ?
47:6 caused me *to* r. to the river
Hos. 11:5 hec. they refused *to* r.
Luke 19:12 rec. kingd. and *to* r.
Acts 13:34 no more *to* r. to corr.
20:3 pur. *to* r. thro' Macedonia

RETURN to, or unto *t.* Lord.

1 *Sam.* 7:3 ye r. *u. t. L.* wi. hea.
Is. 19:22 they shall r. *unto t. L.*
55:7 let him r. *u. t. L.* mercy
Hos. 6:1 let us r. *unto the Lord*
7:10 they do not r. *unto the L.*
14:1 O Is. r. *u. t. L.* hast fallen

Not RETURN.

Num. 32:18 will *not* r. to houses
1 *Sam.* 15:26 S. said, I will *not* r.
2 *Sam.* 12:23 go, he sh. *n.* r. to
1 *K.* 13:16 I may *not* r. with thee
 17 *not* r. *n*. nor wi *not* r. 10:22
32:4 and r. *not* unto them
Is. 45:23 word gone out, sh. *n.* r.
55:11 it shall *not* r. to me void
Jer. 8:4 turn away, and *not* r. ?
15:7 destroy, since they r. *not*
22:11 shall *not* r. any more, 27
23:20 anger of L. sh. *not* r. 30:24
Ezek. 7:13 for seller shall *not* r.
13:22 sho. n. r. fr. wicked ways
21:5 sw. shall *not* r. into sheath
35:9 thy cities shall *not* r.
46:9 he sh. *not* r. by way he re.
Hos. 7:10 they do *not* r. to Lord
11:5 he sh. *not* r. to land of Eg.
 9 I will *not* r. to destroy Ephr.
Mal. 2:14 warned sh. *not* r. to H.
Luke 16:31 hi his. likewise *n. r.*

RETURNED.

Gen. 8:3 waters r. from off earth
 9 dove r. to him; 12 r. not ag.
43:18 because money r. in sacks
Ex. 14:27 sea r. to strength, 28
10:8 M. r. words of people to L.
Lev. 13:16 if she is r. to father's
Num. 24:25 Bal. rose, r. to place
Jos. 2:16 hide till pursu. be r. 22
4:18 waters of Jor. r. to th. pla.
Jud. 2:19 judge was dead, they r.
5:20 she r. answer to herself
11:39 Gid.'s daugh. r. to father
Ruth 1:22 so Naomi and Ruth r.

REV

1 *Sam.* 17:57 D. r. from slaughter
25:39 Lord r. wickedness of Na.
2 *Sam.* 1:22 sw. of S. r. not emp.
3:16 said Ab. Return, and he r.
6:20 Da. r. to bless his househ.
16:8 L. r. on thee blood of home
19:15 king r. and came to Jord.
23:10 peo. r. after him to spoil
1 *K.* 13:10 r. not by way he came
33 after this Jer. r. not fr. evil
2 *K.* 4:35 Elisha r. and walked
2 *Chr.* 25:10 r. home in anger
32:21 Senn. r. with shame face
Neh. 9:28 when they r. and cried
Ps. 35:13 prayer r. into bosom
78:34 they r. inquired after G.
Is. 38:8 the sun r. ten degrees
Jer. 3:7 turn to me, she r. not
14:3 they r. wi. vessels empty
40:12 the Jews r. out of place
Ezek. 1:14 living creatures ran, r.
8:17 r. to provoke me to anger
47:7 I r. lo, at bank of river
Dan. 4:34 understanding, r. 36
Hos. 6:11 r. captivity of people
Amos 4:6 yet not r. to me. 8, 11
Zec. 1:6 they r. and said, As L.
 16 I am r. to Jer. with mercies
7:14 no man passed thro' nor r.
8:3 I am r. to Zion, will dwell
Mat. 21:18 as he r. into city
Mark 14:40 r. found them asleep
Luke 2:20 sheph. r. glorifying G.
4:14 Jesus r. in power of Spirit
8:37 went into ship, and r. back
17:18 that r. to give glory to G.
19:15 r. having received kingd.
23:49 smote breasts, and r.
24:9 r. fr. sepulchre and told all
Acts 8:25 apostles r. to Jerusal.
13:13 and John r. to Jerusalem
21:6 took ship, they r. home
Gal. 1:17 I r. ag. unto Damascus
Heb. 11:15 opportunity to have r.
1 *Pet.* 2:25 r. to Sheph. of souls

RETURNETH.

Ps. 146:4 breath goeth, r. to car.
Prov. 26:11 as dog r. so a fool r.
Ec. 1:6 wind r. accord. to circu.
Is. 55:10 rain r. not thither, but
Ezek. 35:7 that r. I will cut off
Zec. 9:8 encamp bec. of him r.

RETURNING.

Is. 30:15 in r. rest ye be saved
Luke 7:10 r. found servant whole
Acts 8:28 r. sitting in chariot
Heb. 7:1 Abra. r. from slaughter

REUBEN.

Gen. 29:32 called his name R.
30:14 R. went in the days of
35:22 R. went and lay with Bil.
 23 sons of Leah, R. Ja.'s 46:8;
  49:3; *Num.* 2:15; 1 *Chr.* 5:1
37:22 R. said, Shed no blood, 27
42:22 spake not I? 44:37; *Num.*
  16:1; 32:1, 37; *Deut.* 11:6;
Jos. 4:12; 1 *Chr.* 5:3, 18
Num. 2:10 of camp of R. 10:18
7:30 prince of children of R.
32:33 childr. of R. *Jos.* 12:23
Deut. 27:13 mount E. to curse, R.
33:6 let R. live, and let not his
Jos. 15:6 Boh. son of R. 18:17
22:13 R. went to children of R.
Jud. 5:15 divisions of R. 16
Ezek. 48:6 a portion for R. 31

Tribe of REUBEN.

Num. 1:5 of *t. of* R. Elizur, 21
13:4 of *tribe of* R. Shammua
34:14 *tribe of* R. have received
Jos. 20:8; 21:36; 1 *Chr.* 6:63, 78
Rev. 7:5 *tribe of* R. sealed 12,000

REUBENITES.

Num. 26:7 are the families of R.
Deut. 3:12, 16; 29:8; *Jos.* 12:6;
  13:8
Jos. 1:12 Josh. spake to R. 22:1
2 *K.* 10:33 Hazael smote the R.

REUEL.

Job 36:27 heaven sh. r. iniquity
Jer. 33:6 r. them abund. of peace
Dan. 2:47 couldest r. this secret
Mat. 11:27 he *to* whomsoever
Mat. 11:25 hast r. them to babes
Gal. 1:16 pleased G. to r. his son
Phil. 3:15 God sh. r. this unto y.

REVEALED.

Deut. 29:29 things r. to us
1 *Sam.* 3:7 word of Lord r. to S.
 21 L. r. himself to Sam. in Sh.
2 *Sam.* 7:27 hast r. to thy servant
Is. 22:14 r. in mine ears, saith L.
23:1 fr. Chittim it is r. to them
40:5 glory of the Lord sh. be r.

REV

Is. 53:1 arm of L. r. *f John* 12:38
56:1 righteousness near to be r.
Jer. 11:20 unto thee I r. my cau.
Dan. 2:19 th. was secret r. to D.
10:1 a thing was r. to Daniel
Mat. 10:26 nothing covered that
  shall not be r. *Luke* 12:2
11:25 r. th. to babes, *Luke* 10:21
16:17 flesh and blood hath not r.
Luke 2:26 r. to Simeon by H. G.
35 thoughts of many hearts r.
17:30 day when Son of man is r.
Rom. 1:17 therein right. of G. r.
18 wrath of God is r. fr. heav.
8:18 glory which sh. be r. in us
1 Cor. 2:10 God r. them to us
3:13 bec. it shall be r. by fire
14:30 if any thing be r. to ano.
Gal. 3:23 faith whi. should be r.
Eph. 3:5 now r. to holy apostles
2 *Thes.* 1:7 when L. J. shall be r.
2:3 and that man of sin be r.
 6 he might be r. in his time
 8 wick. one r. whom L. cons.
1 *Pet.* 1:5 to be r. in last time
12 unto whom it was r.
4:13 when his glory shall be r.
5:1 partaker of g. that sh. be r.

REVEALER.

Dan. 2:47 G. of gods, r. of secrets

REVEALETH.

Prov. 11:13 talebear. r. sec. 20:19
Dan. 2:22 r. deep and secret th.
 28 G. in heaven that r. secrets
 29 r. secrets maketh known
Amos 3:7 r. secrets to prophets

REVELATION.

Rom. 2:5 r. of judgment of God
16:25 according to r. of mystery
1 *Cor.* 14:6 sh. speak to you by r.
26 every one of you hath a r.
Gal. 1:12 by r. of Jesus Christ
2:2 went up by r. and commu.
Eph. 1:17 may give you sp. of r.
3:3 by r. he made known to me
1 *Pet.* 1:13 grace br. at r. of J. C.
Rev. 1:1 r. of J. C. wh. God gave

REVELATIONS.

2 *Cor.* 12:1 come to visions and r.
7 exalted thro. abundance of r.

REVELLINGS.

Gal. 5:21 works of the fle. are r.
1 *Pet.* 4:3 ye walked in r.

REVENGE, ED, ETH.

Jer. 15:15 know and r. me of
20:10 said we shall take r. on h.
Ezek. 25:12 Edom r. himself on th.
15 Philistines have dealt by r.
2 *Cor.* 7:11 what r. is wr. in you

REVENGER, S.

Num. 35:19 r. sh. slay murde. 21
21 judge between slayer and r.
27 if r. find him and r. kill
2 *Sam.* 14:11 wouldest not suf. r.
Rom. 13:4 minister of God, a r.

REVENGING.

Ps. 79:10 by the r. of the blood

REVENUE.

Ezr. 4:13 thou sh. endamage r.
Is. 23:3 harvest of river is her r.

REVENUES.

Prov. 15:6 in r. of wick. is trou.
16:8 a little is better than gr. r.
Jer. 12:13 be ashamed of your r.

REVERENCE, Verb.

Lev. 19:30 r. sanct. 1 am L. 26:2
Est. 3:2 king's serv. r. Haman
Mat. 21:37 they will r. *Luke* 20:13
Mark 12:6; *Luke* 20:13
Eph. 5:33 wife that fear r. husb.

REVERENCE.

2 *Sam.* 9:6 Mephibosh. did r. Da.
1 *K.* 1:31 Bathsheba did r. king
2 *Sam.* 18:21 Mord. did him not r. 5
Est. 3:2 bowed not nor did him r.
Heb. 12:9 serve God with r.
 28 we may serve God with r.

REVEREND.

Ps. 111:9 holy and r. is his name

REVERSE.

Num. 23:20 he blessed, I can. r.
Est. 8:5 let it be written to r.
8 writing in king's no man r.

REVILE.

Ex. 22:28 thou shalt not r. gods
Mat. 5:11 blessed when men r.

REVILED.

Mat. 27:39 that passed by r. him
Mark 15:32 crucified r. him
John 9:28 they r. him and said
1 *Cor.* 4:12 being r. we bless

REVILERS.

1 *Cor.* 6:10 nor r. inh. king. of G.

REVILEST.

Acts 23:4 r. God's high-priest

REVILINGS.

Is. 51:7 neither afraid of their r.
Zep. 2:8 r. of child. of Ammon

REVIVE.

Neh. 4:2 will they r. the stones?
Ps. 85:6 wilt th. not r. us again
138:7 thou wilt r. me, th. shalt
Is. 57:15 r. spirit and to r. heart
  of contrite ones
Hos. 6:2 after days will he r. us
14:7 they shall r. as corn
Hab. 3:2 O Lord, r. thy work in

REVIVED.

Gen. 45:27 the spirit of Jacob r.
Jud. 15:19 spirit came ag. he r.
1 *K.* 17:22 soul of child ca. he r.
2 *K.* 13:21 touch. bones of Eli. r.
Rom. 7:9 command, came, sin r.
14:9 Ch. both died, rose, and r.

REVIVING.

Ezr. 9:8 to give us a little r. 9

REVOLT.

Is. 59:13 speaking oppres. and r.

REVOLT, Verb.

2 *Chr.* 21:10 same time did Li. r.
Is. 1:5 ye will r. more and more

REVOLTED.

2 *K.* 8:20 Edom r. 22; 2 *Chr.* 21:8
 22 Libnah r. at the same time
Is. 31:6 Israel have deeply r.
Jer. 5:23 people are r. and gone

REVOLTERS.

Jer. 6:28 all grievous r. walking
Hos. 5:2 r. are profound to make
9:15 love no more, princes r.

REVOLTING.

Jer. 5:23 this peo. hath a r. hea.

REWARD, Substantive.

Gen. 15:1 Ab. I am thy great r.
Num. 18:31 it is your r. for serv.
Deut. 10:17 G. who taketh not r.
27:25 cursed that tak. r. to slay
Ruth 2:12 a full r. be given of L.
2 *Sam.* 4:10 wd. have giv. him r.
19:36 king recompense such a r.
1 *K.* 13:7 I will give thee a r.
Job 6:22 Bring me or give a r.
Ps. 15:5 nor taketh r. ag. innoc.
19:11 keeping of them is gre. r.
40:15 let them be desolate for r.
58:11 there is a r. for righteous
70:3 let th. be turned back for r.
91:8 shalt see the r. of wicked
91:2 render a r. to the proud
Prov. 11:18 righteous. a sure r.
21:14 a r. in bosom st. wrath
24:14 there shall be a r.
20 shall be no r. to evil man
Ec. 4:9 they have a good r.
9:5 nei. have they any more r.
Is. 3:11 the r. of hands be given
5:23 which justify wicked for r.
40:10 his r. is with him, 62:11
45:13 go my captives, not for r.
Jer. 40:5 capt. gave Jeremiah r.
Ezek. 16:34 givest r. no r. given
91:8 shall not tho. hast loved a r.
Ob. 15 thy r. shall return upon
Mic. 3:11 judge for r. priests
7:3 and judge asketh for a r.
Mat. 5:12 r. in heaven, *Luke* 6:23
46 if ye love no r. of your Fa.
 if they have their r. 5, 16
10:41 sh. receive a prophet's r.
 42 no wise lose r. *Mark* 9:41
Luke 6:35 your r. shall be great
23:41 we receive due r. of deeds
Acts 1:18 he purch. fi. of iniquit.
Rom. 4:1 to him that work. is r.
1 *Cor.* 3:8 man sh. receive his r.
14 abide, he shall receive a r.
9:17 if willingly, I have a r. 18
Col. 2:18 no man beg. you of r.
3:21 ye sh. receive r. of inherit.
Heb. 2:2 received just recomp. r.
10:35 great recompense of r.
11:26 he had respect to the r.
2 *Pet.* 2:13 shall receive the r. of
  2 *John* 8 that we receive full r.
Jude 11 ran greedily after r. of
Rev. 11:18 time shouldest give r.
22:12 I come quickly, my r. is

REWARD, Verb.

Deut. 32:41 and I will r. them

RIC

1 *Sam.* 24:19 Lord *r.* thee good
2 *Sam.* 3:39 L. sh. *r.* doer of evil
2 *Chr.* 20:11 behold how th. *r.* us
Ps. 54:5 shall *r.* evil to enemies
Prov. 25:22 the L. shall *r.* thee
Hos. 4:9 and I will *r.* them their
Mat. 6:4 Father sh. *r.* thee, 6:18
16:27 he shall *r.* every man
1 *Tim.* 4:14 Lord *r.* him accord.
Rev. 18:6 *r.* her, even as she *rew.*

REWARDED.

Gen. 44:4 whereof, have ye *r.* evil
1 *Sam.* 24:17 th. *r.* good, I *r.* evil
2 *Sam.* 22:21 L. *r.* me acc. *Ps.* 18:20
2 *Chr.* 15:7 your work shall be *r.*
Ps. 7:4 if I have *r.* evil to him
35:12 th. *r.* evil for good, 109:5
103:10 nor *r.* us accord. to iniq.
Prov. 13:13 feareth com. be *r.*
Is. 3:9 they have *r.* evil to them.
Jer. 31:16 work sh. be *r.* saith L.
Rev. 18:6 even as she *r.* you

REWARDER.

Heb. 11:6 a *r.* of them that seek

REWARDETH.

Job 21:19 he *r.* him, sh. know it
Ps. 31:23 plentifully *r.* proud
137:8 happy he that *r.* thee, as
Prov. 17:13 whoso *r.* evil for go.
6:10 both *r.* fool and *r.* transgr.

REWARDS.

Num. 22:7 with *r.* divination
Is. 1:23 every one followeth *r.*
5:17 said, give thy *r.* to another
Hos. 2:12 these are my *r.*

REZIN.

2 *K.* 15:37 R. the king, 16:5;
Is. 7:1
16:6 R. recovered Elath to, 9
Ezr. 9:8 children. of R. *Neh.* 7:50
Is. 7:4 the fierce anger of R. 8
8:6 as this people rejoice in R.
9:11 set up the adversaries of R.

RHEGIUM.

Acts 28:13 comp. and came to R.

RHESA.

Luke 3:27 who was the son of R.

RHODA.

Acts 12:13 to hearken named R.

RHODES.

Acts 21:1 we came unto R.

RIB, S.

Gen. 2:21 God took one of his *r.*
22 the *r.* which God had taken
2 *Sam.* 3:33 sm. *r.* under fifth *r.*
3:27 J. smote Ab. under fifth *r.*
4:6 smote Ishbosh. under fifth *r.*
20:10 J. smote Ama. un. fifth *r.*
Dan. 7:5 beast had *r.* in mouth

RIBBAND.

Num. 15:38 on fring. of bord. a *r.*

RICH.

Gen. 13:2 Abram was *r.* in cattle
14:23 lest say, I ha. made A. *r.*
Ex. 30:15 *r.* shall not give more
Lev. 25:47 if a stranger was *r.*
Ruth 3:10 fol. not men poor or *r.*
1 *Sam.* 2:7 L. maketh poor and *r.*
2 *Sam.* 12:1 two men in city, 1 *r.*
Job 15:29 he shall not be *r.* nei.
34:19 nor regardeth the *r.* more
Ps. 45:12 *r.* shall entreat favor
49:2 hear this, both *r.* and poor
16 be not afraid when one is *r.*
Prov. 10:4 hand of dilig. mak. *r.*
22 blessing of Lord, maketh *r.*
13:7 there is that mak. hims. *r.*
11:20 the *r.* hath many friends
18:24 the *r.* answereth roughly
21:17 lov. wine and oil not *r.*
22:2 *r.* and poor meet together
7 *r.* ruleth over the poor
16 giveth to *r.* shall come to
23:4 labor not to be *r.* cease
28:6 perverse, though he be *r.*
20 he maketh haste to be *r.* 22
Ec. 5:12 abund. of *r.* not suffer
10:6 and the *r.* sit in low place
20 curse not *r.* in thy bedcham.
Is. 53:9 and with *r.* in his death
Jer. 5:27 are great and waxen *r.*
Hos. 12:8 Ephraim said, I am *r.*
Mic. 6:12 *r.* men thereof are full
Mark 12:41 many that were *r.*
Luke 1:53 the *r.* he sent away
6:24 woe unto you that are *r.*
12:21 that is not *r.* toward God
14:12 call not thy *r.* neighbors
16:1 certain *r.* man, 19:2
21 sorrowful, he was very *r.*
Rom. 10:12 same Lord is *r.* to all
1 *Cor.* 4:8 are full, now ye are *r.*
2 *Cor.* 6:10 yet making many *r.*
8:9 *r.* yet poor, ye might be *r.*

RICH man, or men.

2 *Sam.* 12:2 *r.* man had many fl.
Job 27:19 *r.* man shall lie down
Prov. 10:15 *r.* man's wealth is his strong city, 18:11
28:11 *r.* man is wise in his own
Jer. 9:23 let not the *r.* man glory
Mic. 6:12 *r.* men thereof are full
Mat. 19:23 *r.* m. sh. hardly enter
24 than a *r.* m. to enter kingd.
of God, *Mark* 10:25; *Lu.* 18:25
27:57 a *r.* man of Arimathea
Luke 12:16 ground of *r.* man bro.
16:1 a certain *r.* m. had a stew.
19 a *r.* man was clo. in purple
21:1 and saw the *r.* man casting
Jam. 1:11 so shall the *r.* m. fade
2:6 do not *r.* men oppress you?
5:1 ye *r.* men, weep and howl
Rev. 6:15 *r.* men hid themselves

RICHER.

Dan. 11:2 the fourth sh. be far *r.*

RICHES.

Gen. 31:16 the *r.* G. hath taken
36:7 *r.* more than they might
Jos. 22:8 return with much *r.*
1 *Sam.* 17:25 enrich with great *r.*
2 *K.* 5:11 neither hast asked *r.*
2 *Chr.* 1:11
12 giv. thee both *r.* and honor
10:23 Solom. exceeded all kings
of earth for *r.* 2 *Chr.* 9:22
1 *Chr.* 29:12 *r.* and honor come
28 David died full of days, *r.*
Est. 1:4 showed *r.* of kingdom
5:11 Haman told them of his *r.*
Job 20:15 he swallowed down *r.*
36:19 will he esteem thy *r.*?
Ps. 37:16 but. than *r.* of wicked
39:6 heapeth up *r.* knoweth not
49:6 boast themselves in th.
52:7 trusted in abund. of his *r.*
62:10 if *r.* increase, set not heart
73:12 ungodly prosper, incr. *r.*
104:24 O Lord, earth is full of *r.*
112:3 wealth and *r.* in his house
119:14 rejo. as much as in all *r.*
Prov. 3:16 in her left hand *r.*
8:18 *r.* and honor are with me
11:4 *r.* profit not in day of wra.
16 women, honor, strong men *r.*
28 he that trust. in *r.* shall fall
13:7 himself poor, hath great *r.*
8 ransom of man's life his *r.*
14:24 crown of wise is their *r.*
19:14 *r.* are inheritance of fath.
22:1 good name rather than *r.*
4 by the fear of the Lord are *r.*
16 oppress. poor to increase *r.*
23:5 for *r.* make themselves wi.
24:4 cham. be filled with all *r.*
27:24 for *r.* are not for ever
30:8 gi. me net. poverty nor *r.*
Ec. 4:8 nor his eyes sati. with *r.*
5:13 even *r.* kept for owners
19 man whom G. given *r.* 6:2
9:11 nor yet *r.* to men of under.
Is. 8:4 *r.* of Damasc. taken away
10:14 hand found as a nest *r.*
30:6 carry their *r.* on yo. asses
45:3 I will give thee hidden *r.*
61:6 ye shall eat *r.* of Gentiles
Jer. 9:23 let not rich man gl. in *r.*
17:11 he that get. *r.* not by rig.
48:36 *r.* he hath gotten perished
Ezek. 26:12 make a spoil of thy *r.*
28:4 by thy wisd. gotten thee *r.*
5 by thy traffic increased *r.*
Dan. 11:2 thro' his *r.* sh. stir up
24 scat. am. prey, spoil and *r.*
28 thee shall he return with *r.*
Mat. 13:22 deceitful. of *r.* choke
word, *Mark* 4:19; *Luke* 8:14
Mark 10:23 hardly th. that ha. *r.*
enter, *Luke* 18:24
Luke 16:11 who will commit *r.*?
Rom. 2:4 or despiseth thou *r.*?
9:23 make kn. *r.* of his glory
11:12 if fall of them be the *r.*
33 O the *r.* of the wisd. of God
2 *Cor.* 8:2 of *r.* of their liberality
Eph. 1:7 redemption accor. to *r.*

RIC

Eph. 2:4 God who is *r.* in mercy
1 *Tim.* 6:9 they th. will be *r.* fall
17 charge th. that are *r.* in this
18 and be *r.* in good works
Jam. 1:10 let the *r.* rejoice in th.
2:5 G. chosen poor, *r.* in faith?
Rev. 2:9 I know pov. thou art *r.*
3:17 bec. thou sayest I am *r.* and
13:16 he causeth the *r.* and poor
18:19 made *r.* all that had ships

RICH man, or men.

2 *Sam.* 12:2 *r.* man had many fl.
Job 27:19 *r.* man shall lie down
Prov. 10:15 *r.* man's wealth is his strong city, 18:11
28:11 *r.* man is wise in his own
Mic. 6:12 *r.* men thereof are full
Mat. 19:23 *r.* m. sh. hardly enter
24 than a *r.* m. to enter kingd.
of God, *Mark* 10:25; *Lu.* 18:25
27:57 a *r.* man of Arimathea
Luke 12:16 ground of *r.* man bro.
16:1 a certain *r.* m. had a stew.
19 a *r.* man was clo. in purple
21:1 and saw the *r.* man casting
Jam. 1:11 so shall the *r.* m. fade
2:6 do not *r.* men oppress you?
5:1 ye *r.* men, weep and howl
Rev. 6:15 *r.* men hid themselves

RIDE.

Gen. 41:43 made him *r.* in char.
Deut. 32:13 made him *r.* on high
Jud. 5:10 that *r.* on white asses
2 *Sam.* 16:2 king's hous. to *r.* on
10:26 saddle ass that I may *r.*
1 *K.* 1:33 cause Solo. to *r.* 38, 44
2 *K.* 10:16 so th. made him to *r.*
Job 30:22 thou causest me to *r.*
Ps. 45:4 and in thy majesty *r.*
66:12 thou hast caused me to *r.*
Is. 30:16 we will *r.* upon swift
58:14 I will cause thee to *r.*
Jer. 6:23 *r.* on horses, 50:42
Hos. 10:11 will make Eph. to *r.*
Hab. 3:8 didst *r.* upon thy horses
Hag. 2:22 overthrow those th. *r.*

RIDER.

Gen. 49:17 so that *r.* shall fall
Ex. 15:1 horse and *r.* thrown, 21
Job 30:18 scorneth horse and *r.*
Jer. 51:21 *r.* break in pieces cha.
Zec. 12:4 smite *r.* with madness

RIDERS.

2 *K.* 19:23 if thou be able to set *r.* on them, *Is.* 36:8
Hag. 2:22 horses and *r.* co. down
Zec. 10:5 *r.* shall be confounded

RIDETH.

Deut. 33:26 who *r.* upon heaven
Est. 6:8 horse king *r.* upon
Ps. 68:4 extol him that *r.* 33
Is. 19:1 the L. *r.* on a swift cloud
Amos 2:15 neither shall he that *r.*

RIDING.

2 *K.* 4:24 slack not thy *r.* for me
Jer. 17:25 kings enter *r.* 22:4
Ezek. 23:6 horsem. *r.* on hors. 12
23 all of them *r.* upon horses
38:15 thou and many people *r.*
Zec. 1:8 a man *r.* on a red horse
9:9 thy king com. unto thee *r.*

RIDGES.

Ps. 65:10 thou waterest *r.* thereof

RIFLED.

Zec. 14:2 houses *r.* wom. ravish.

RIGHT, Substantive.

Gen. 18:25 shall not the Judge of all the earth do *r.*?
Deut. 21:17 *r.* of first-born is his
Ruth 4:6 redeem thou my *r.*
Jam. 19:43 we ha. also more *r.*
2 *Sam.* 19:28 what *r.* have I?
Ezr. 23:7 innocent and *r.* not
Neh. 2:20 no *r.* in Jerusalem
Deut. 4:8 nation ha. judg. so *r.*
32:4 shall justify *r.* 2 *Chr.* 6:23
Jud. 5:11 *r.* acts. 1 *Sam.* 12:7
1 *Sam.* 24:17 than more *r.* than I
2 *Sam.* 41:1 wick. slain *r.* person
2 *K.* 3:22 fell on two men *r.* morn.
Job 34:17 justifying *r.* to give him
2 *K.* 10:30 Jehu said to peo. Be
Ezr. 9:15 G. of Israel *r. Neh.* 9:3
Job 4:7 where were *r.* cut off
9:15 tho' I we. *r.* would not an.
10:15 if I be *r.* not lift up head
15:14 what is man, he be *r.*?
17:9 *r.* also sh. hold on his w.
22:3 is it pleas. to A. th. art *r.*?
19 *r.* see it, glad, *Ps.* 107:42
Ezr. 37: might dispute with him
33:7 he was *r.* in his own eyes

RIG

Eph. 1:18 *r.* of glory of inherita.
2:7 exceeding *r.* of his grace
3:8 I should preach unsearch. *r.*
16 grant you accord. to the *r.*
Phil. 4:19 accord. to *r.* in glory
Col. 1:27 what *r.* of the glory
1 *Tim.* 6:17 nor trust in uncer. *r.*
Heb. 11:26 reproa. of C. greater *r.*
Jam. 5:2 your *r.* are corrupted
Rev. 5:12 worthy Lamb to rec. *r.*
18:17 great *r.* come to naught

RICHLY.

Col. 3:16 let word of C. dwell *r.*
1 *Tim.* 6:17 God who giveth *r.*

RID.

Gen. 37:22 that he might *r.* him
Ex. 6:6 *r.* you out of bondage
Lev. 26:6 *r.* evil beasts out land
Ps. 82:4 *r.* them out of wicked
144:7 *r.* me, and deliver me, 11

RIDDANCE.

Lev. 23:22 th. shalt not make *r.*
Zep. 1:18 shall make speedy *r.*

RIDDEN.

Num. 22:30 ass, wh. thou ha. *r.*?

RIDDLE.

Jud. 14:12 Sam. said, I will now put forth a *r.* to you, 13-19
Ezek. 17:2 put forth a *r.* speak.

RIDE.

Gen. 41:43 made him *r.* in char.
Deut. 32:13 made him *r.* on high
Jud. 5:10 that *r.* on white asses
2 *Sam.* 16:2 king's hous. to *r.* on
10:26 saddle ass that I may *r.*
1 *K.* 1:33 cause Solo. to *r.* 38, 44
2 *K.* 10:16 so th. made him to *r.*
Job 30:22 thou causest me to *r.*
Ps. 45:4 and in thy majesty *r.*
66:12 thou hast caused me to *r.*
Is. 30:16 we will *r.* upon swift
58:14 I will cause thee to *r.*
Jer. 6:23 *r.* on horses, 50:42
Hos. 10:11 will make Eph. to *r.*
Hab. 3:8 didst *r.* upon thy horses
Hag. 2:22 overthrow those th. *r.*

Is RIGHT.

Ex. 15:26 do that which is *r.*
Deut. 6:18 thou shalt do that is *r.* 12:25; 21:9
12:8 what is *r.* in own eyes
1 *K.* 11:33 walked to do that *r.* 38
22:43 Jehos. did *r.* 2 *Chr.* 20:32
2 *K.* 12:2 Jeh. did *r.* 2 *Chr.* 24:2
14:3 Amaziah did *r.* 2 *Chr.* 25:2
15:3 Azariah did *r.* 2 *Chr.* 26:4
34 Jotham did *r.* 2 *Chr.* 27:2
16:2 A. did not *r.* in sight of L.
18:3 Hezekiah did *r.* 2 *Chr.* 29:2
20:3 Josiah did *r.* 2 *Chr.* 34:2
1 *Chr.* 13:4 was *r.* in eyes of peo.
Job 33:27 pervert. that wh. w. *r.*
Ps. 78:37 heart was not *r.*
Jer. 17:16 came out of lips w. *r.*

RIGHT.

Jos. 3:16 people passed *r.* ag. J.

RIGHT corner.

2 *K.* 11:11 guard stood roo. *r. c.*

See FOOT, HAND.

RIGHT forth.

Jer. 49:5 be driven eve. man *r. f.*

RIGHT well.

Ps. 139:14 soul knoweth *r.* well

RIGHTEOUS.

Gen. 7:1 thee ha. I seen *r.* be. me
18:23 wilt destroy *r.* with wic.?
24 if th. be 50 *r.* wilt thou? 26
25 be far from thee to slay *r.*
20:4 L. wilt thou slay a *r.* nati.
38:26 said, She more *r.* than I
Ex. 23:7 innocent and *r.* sl. not
Num. 23:10 let me die death of *r.*
Deut. 4:8 nation ha. judg. so *r.*
32:4 shall justify *r.* 2 *Chr.* 6:23
Jud. 5:11 *r.* acts. 1 *Sam.* 12:7
1 *Sam.* 24:17 than more *r.* than I
2 *Sam.* 4:11 wick. slain *r.* person
2 *K.* 3:22 fell on two men *r.* morn.
Job 34:17 justifying *r.* to give him
2 *K.* 10:30 Jehu said to peo. Be
Ezr. 9:15 G. of Israel *r. Neh.* 9:3
Job 4:7 where were *r.* cut off
9:15 tho' I we. *r.* would not an.
10:15 if I be *r.* not lift up head
15:14 what is man, he be *r.*?
17:9 *r.* also sh. hold on his w.
22:3 is it pleas. to A. th. art *r.*?
19 *r.* see it, glad, *Ps.* 107:42
Ezr. 37: might dispute with him
33:7 he was *r.* in his own eyes

CRUDEN'S CONCORDANCE. 1001

ROC

RODDERY.
Ps. 62:10 become not vain in *r.*
Prov. 21:7 *r.* of wick. dest. them
Is. 61:8 I hate *r.* for burnt-offer.
Ezek. 22:29 exerc. *r.* vexed poor
Amos 3:10 store *r.* in palaces
Nah. 3:1 city full of lies, *r.*
Phil. 2:6 thou. no *r.* to be equal

ROBE.
Ex. 28:4 make an ephod and *r.*
29:5 put on Aa. coat, *r. Lev.* 8:7
1 *Sam.* 18:4 Jona. stripped of *r.*
24:11 skirt of thy *r.* in my hand
1 *Chr.* 15:27 David clothed wi. *r.*
Job 29:14 my judgment was a *r.*
Is. 22:21 will clothe him with *r.*
61:10 cov. me with *r.* of righte.
Jon. 3:6 arose and laid *r.* fr. him
Mic. 2:8 ye pull off *r.* with garm.
Mat. 27:28 put on J. a scarlet *r.*
Luke 15:22 bri. best *r.* put it on
23:11 arrayed him in gorgeo. *r.*
John 19:2 put on Jes. a purple *r.*

ROBES.
2 *Sam.* 13:18 such *r.* we. virgins
1 *K.* 22:30 put thou on thy *r.*
Ezek. 26:16 princes lay away *r.*
Luke 20:46 seri. walk in long *r.*
Rev. 6:11 white *r.* given them
7:9 Lamb, clothed wi. white *r.*
13 in white *r.?* 14 washed th. *r.*

ROCK.
Ex. 17:6 will stand bef. thee on *r.*
33:21 L. Thou stand upon a *r.*
Num. 20:8 sp. to *r.* bef. th. eyes
11 Mo. with rod smote *r.* twice
21:21 puttest thy nest in a *r.*
Deut. 8:15 brought wat. out of *r.*
32:4 he is *r.* his work is perfect
15 lightly esteemed *r.* of salv.
18 *r.* begat thee art unmindful
30 except the *r.* had sold them
31 their *r.* is not as our *r.*
37 where *r.* wh. they trusted ?
Jud. 6:21 fire of *r.* consu. flesh
7:25 slew Oreb on the *r.* Oreb
15:8 Sams. dwelt in top of *r.* E.
20:45 Benj. turned to *r.* of Rim.
1 *Sam.* 2:2 nei. any *r.* like our G.
14:4 sharp *r.* one side, sharp *r.*
2 *Sam.* 22:2 he said, Lord is my *r.*
Ps. 18:2; 94:15
3 G. of my *r.* in wh. I will tru.
32 a *r.* save our G. ? *Ps.* 18:31
47 blessed be my *r.* exalted be
G. of *r.* of salvati. *Ps.* 18:46
23:3 God of Israel said, R. of Is.
1 *Chr.* 11:15 captains went to *r.*
2 *Chr.* 25:12 cas. down fr. top of *r.*
Neh. 9:15 wat. out of *r.* for their
thirst, *Ps.* 78:16; 105:41
Job 14:18 *r.* is remo. out of place
18:4 sh. *r.* be remo. out of pla. ?
19:24 were graven in *r.* for ever
24:8 cmbr. *r.* for want of shelter
28:9 putteth forth hand upon *r.*
29:6 *r.* poured out rivers of oil
39:1 wild goats of *r.* bri. forth ?
24 dwelleth on *r.* on crag of *r.*
Ps. 27:5 shall set me on *r.* 40:2
28:1 unto thee I cry, O L. my *r.*
31:2 be thou my strong *r.*
3 thou art my *r.* and fort. 71:3
42:9 my *r.* why ha. thou forg. ?
61:2 lead me to *r.* higher than I
62:2 God is my *r.* 6; 7 *r.* of str.
78:16 smote *r.* waters gushed
89:26 *r.* of salva. 91:22 *r.* of ref.
92:1 joyful noise to *r.* of salva.
114:8 turned *r.* into stand. wat.
Cant. 2:14 art in clefts of the *r.*
Is. 2:10 enter *r.* hide th. in dust
8:14 *r.* of offence to both houses
10:26 slaughter at *r.* of Oreb
17:10 not mindful of *r.* of stren.
22:16 habita. for himself in a *r.*
32:2 man be as shad. of great *r.*
42:11 let inhabitants of *r.* sing
48:21 caus. wat. to flow out of *r.*
Jer. 5:3 made faces harder th. *r.*
18:14 snow which cometh fr. *r.*
21:13 I am ag. thee, inhab. of *r.*
23:29 hammer that breaketh *r.*
49:16 thou dwell in clefts of *r.*
Ezek. 24:7 set it upon top of *r.*
8 set her blood upon top of *r.*
26:4 make her like top of *r.* 14
Amos 6:12 sh. hors. run upon *r.?*
Ob. 3 thou dwell. in clefts of *r.*
Mat. 7:24 built house upon *r.*
16:18 upon thi. *r.* I build church
27:60 new tomb wh. he had
hewn out in the *r. Mar.* 15:46
Luke 8:6 some fell on *r.* 13 on *r.*

ROE

Rom. 9:33 I lay in Si. a stumb.-
stone, *r.* of offence, 1 *Pet.* 2:8
1 *Cor.* 10:4 drank of spiritual *r.*

ROCKS.
Num. 23:9 top of *r.* I see him
1 *Sam.* 13:6 hid themselves in *r.*
1 *K.* 19:11 strong wind break *r.*
Job 28:10 cutteth rivers amo. *r.*
30:6 dwell in caves of earth, *r.*
Ps. 78:15 he clave *r.* in wilderu.
104:18 *r.* are a refuge for conies
Prov. 30:26 make th. houses in *r.*
Is. 2:19 shall go into holes of *r.*
7:19 they sh. rest in holes of *r.*
57:5 slaying children under *r.*
Jer. 4:29 whole city climb on *r.*
16:16 hunt th. out of holes of *r.*
51:25 I will roll thee from tho *r.*
Nah. 1:6 the *r.* are thrown down
Mat. 27:51 earth quake, *r.* rent
Acts 27:29 lest they sho. fal. on *r.*
Rev. 6:16 said to *r.* Fall on us

ROD.
Ex. 4:4 became a *r.* in his hand
20 Moses took *r.* of God, 17:9
7:9 say to Aa. Take th. *r.* 19
20 lifted up *r.* and smote, 14:16
21:20 man smite servant with *r.*
Lev. 27:32 whatso. pass. und. *r.*
Num. 17:2 wri. man's name on *r.*
8 *r.* of Aaron budded, *Heb.* 9:4
20:11 with his *r.* he smote rock
1 *Sam.* 14:27 Jona. put end of *r.*
2 *Sam.* 7:14 I will chasten with *r.*
Job 9:34 let him take his *r.* away
21:9 neither is *r.* of God upon
Ps. 2:9 shalt break them with *r.*
23:4 thy *r.* and staff comfort me
74:2 redem. *r.* of thine inheri.
89:32 I will visit transg. with *r.*
110:2 the Lord shall send the *r.*
125:3 *r.* of wicked shall not re-
Prov. 10:13 a *r.* for back of fools,
26:3
13:24 he that spar. *r.* hateth son
14:3 mouth of foolish is a *r.* of
22:8 *r.* of his anger shall fail
15 *r.* of correction shall drive
23:13 thou sh. beat them with *r.*
22:15 *r.* and reproof give wisd.
Is. 9:4 hast broken *r.* of oppres.
10:5 O Assyr. *r.* of mine anger
15 as if the *r.* sho. shake itself
24 he shall smite with a *r.* and
26 as his *r.* was on the sea, so
11:1 *r.* out of the stem of Jesse
4 shall smite earth with the *r.*
14:29 *r.* that smote is broken
30:31 Assyr. beat. smote with *r.*
Jer. 10:16 Is. the *r.* of his, 51:19
48:17 how is heuati. *r.* broken !
Lam. 3:1 affliction by *r.* of wra.
Ezek. 7:11 viol. is risen into a *r.*
19:14 fire is gone out of a *r.*
20:37 ca. ice to pass under the *r.*
21:10 contemn. *r.* of my son, 13
Mic. 5:1 smite judge of Is. wi. *r.*
6:9 hear the *r.* who appoint. it
7:14 feed thy people with thy *r.*
1 *Cor.* 4:21 sh. I come with a *r.*?
Rev. 2:27 rule with *r.* of ir. 19:15
12:5 rule nations with *r.* of iron

RODE.
Gen. 24:61 Rebe. and damsels *r.*
Jud. 10:4 he had 30 sons that *r.*
1 *Sam.* 25:20 Abig. *r.* on ass. 42
30:17 400 which *r.* on camels
2 *Sam.* 22:11 he *r.* on a cherub,
and did fly, *Ps.* 18:10
1 *K.* 13:13 old prophet *r.* on ass
2 *K.* 9:16 Jehu *r.* in a chariot
25 when I and thou *r.* togeth.
Est. 8:14 posts that *r.* on mules

RODS.
Gen. 30:37 Jac. took *r.* of poplar
Ex. 7:12 Aaron's rod swall. th. *r.*
Num. 17:6 princes ga. him 12 *r.*
Ezek. 19:11 she had strong *r.* for
12 her strong *r.* were broken
2 *Cor.* 11:25 thrice beaten wi. *r.*

ROE, 8,
1 *Chr.* 12:8 swift as *r.* on mount.
Prov. 5:19 hind and pleasant *r.*
6:5 deli. thyself as *r.* fr. hunter
Cant. 2:7 I charge you by *r.* 3:5
9 my beloved is like a *r.* or a
17 he thou like *r.* or hart, 8:14
Is. 13:14 shall be as chased *r.*

See young.

WILD ROE.
2 *Sam.* 2:18 Asahel was as a *r.*

ROEBUCK, 8,
Deut. 12:15 eat of the *r.* 22; 14:5;
15:22

ROO

1 *K.* 4:23 besides harts and *r.*

ROLL, 8, Substantive.
Ezr. 6:1 sea. made in house of *r.*
Is. 8:1 take thee a great *r.* and
Jer. 36:2 take thee a *r.* of a book
23 till all the *r.* was consumed
28 saith L. Tb. hast burnt th. *r.*
Ezek. 2:9 hand sent, and lo, a *r.*
3:1 cat this *r.* 3 caused me eat
Zec. 5:1 behold, a flying *r.* 2

ROLL, Verb.
Gen. 29:8 till they *r.* away
Jos. 10:18 Joshua said, *r.* stones
1 *Sam.* 14:33 *r.* a great stone
Jer. 51:25 I will *r.* thee down
Mic. 1:10 Aph. *r.* thyself in dust
Mark 16:3 who *r.* us away stone?

ROLLED.
Gen. 29:3 *r.* stone from well, 10
Jos. 5:9 I ha. *r.* away reproach
Job 30:14 *r.* themselves on me
Is. 9:5 garments *r.* in blood
34:4 heavens *r.* toget. *Rev.* 6:14
Mat. 27:60 he *r.* a great stone to
door of sepulch. *Mark* 15:46
28:2 angel came *r.* back stone
Mark 16:4 stone was *r.* away
Luke 24:2 found stone *r.* away

ROLLER.
Ezek. 30:21 to put a *r.* to bind it

ROLLETH.
Prov. 26:27 he that *r.* a stone

ROLLING.
Is. 17:13 nations flee like *r.* thi.

ROMAN.
Acts 22:25 is a Jt. 26, 27, 29
23:27 unders, that he was a R.

ROMANS.
John 11:48 the R. shall come
Acts 16:21 obser. being R. 37, 38
25:17 prison, into hands of R.

ROME.
Acts 2:10 strangers of R. we do
18:2 Jews to depart from R.
19:21 there, I must also see R.
23:11 bear witness also at R.
28:16 when we came to R.
Rom. 1:7 all that be in R. 15
2 *Tim.* 1:17 who was in R.

ROOF, 8.
Gen. 19:8 under shadow of *r.*
Deut. 22:8 a battlement for *r.*
Jos. 2:6 brought them to the *r.*
Jud. 16:27 on *r.* were 3000 men
1 *Sam.* 9:25 Sam. commun. wi. S.
on *r.* 26 David walked on *r.*
2 *Sam.* 11:2 watchman went up to *r.*
Jer. 19:13 on wh. *r.* they, 32:29
Mat. 8:8 not worthy th. should.
come under my *r. Luke* 7:6
Mark 2:4 they uncovered the *r.*

ROOF, with mouth.
Job 29:10 tongue clea. to *r.* of m.
Ps. 137:6 tong. cleave to *r.* of m.
Cant. 7:9 *r.* of m. like best wine
Lam. 4:4 cleaveth to *r.* of his m.
Ezek. 3:26 tong. clea. to *r.* of m.

ROOM.
Gen. 24:23 *r.* in father's house ?
25 have straw, and *r.* to lodge
31 I have prepa. *r.* for camels
26:22 L. made *r.* for us, shall be
1 *K.* 22:35 king put Benlah in
r. Jer. *ay.* *Ezek.* 11:5
8:20 I am risen in *r.* of David,
2 *Chr.* 6:10
19:24 Elis. shalt thou amo. in *r.*
Ps. 31:8 set my feet in large *r.*
80:9 thou preparedst a *r.* before
Prov. 18:16 a man's gift mak. *r.*
Mal. 3:10 shall not be *r.* enough
Mark 2:2 no *r.* to receive them
14:15 a large up. *r. Luke* 22:12
Luke 2:7 because the. was no *r.*
12:17 I have no *r.* to bestow
14:8 sit not down in highest *r.*
10 sit down in the lowest *r.*
22 it is done, and yet th. is *r.*
Acts 1:13 went up to an upper *r.*
21:27 Festus came in Fell's *r.*
1 *Cor.* 14:16 he that occupieth *r.*

ROOMS.
Gen. 6:14 *r.* sh. thou make in ark
1 *Chr.* 4:41 and dwelt in their *r.*
Mat. 23:6 uppermost *r.* at feasts,
Mark 12:39; *Luke* 20:46
Luke 14:7 forth chose chief *r.*

ROOT, substantive.
Deut. 29:18 among you a *r.* that
Jud. 5:14 out of Eph. was a *r.*

ROT

2 *K.* 19:30 Judah shall take *r.*
Job 5:3 I have seen foolish ta. *r.*
14:8 though the *r.* thereof wax
19:28 seeing the *r.* of the matter
28:19 my *r.* spread out by wato.
Ps. 80:9 didst cause vine take *r.*
Prov. 14:3 *r.* of the righteous
12 *r.* of the righteous yieldeth
Is. 5:24 their *r.* shall be rotten.
11:10 a *r.* of Jesse, *Rom.* 15:12
14:30 I will kill thy *r.* with fam.
27:6 come of Jacob take *r.* 37:31
40:24 their stock sh. not take *r.*
53:2 he shall grow up as a *r.* out
Jer. 12:2 they have taken *r.* they
Ezek. 31:7 his *r.* was by waters
Dan. 11:7 out of branch of her *r.*
Hos. 9:16 Eph. is smit. their *r.*
Mal. 4:1 sh. leave neither *r.* nor
Mat. 3:10 axe laid to *r. Luke* 3:9
13:6 because they had not *r.* 21;
Mark 4:6, 17; *Luke* 8:13
Luke 17:6 plucked up by the *r.*
Rom. 11:16 if the *r.* be holy
18 bearest not the *r.* hui *r.* th.
1 *Tim.* 6:10 money is *r.* of all ev.
Heb. 12:15 lest any *r.* of bittern.
Rev. 5:5 *r.* of Da. hath prevailed
22:16 I am the *r.* of David

ROOT, Verb.
1 *K.* 14:15 he shall *r.* up Israel
30:31:12 would *r.* all mine incr.
Ps. 52:5 and *r.* thee out of land
Jer. 1:10 I have set thee to *r.* out
Jer. 12:20 lest ye *r.* up wheat

ROOTED.
Deut. 29:28 the Lord *r.* them out
Job 18:14 confidence sh. be *r.* out
31:8 let my offspring be *r.* out
Ps. 9:28 transgressors sh. be *r.*
Zep. 2:4 Ekron shall be *r.* up
Mat. 15:13 Fa. not planted, *r.* up
Eph. 3:17 being *r.* and grounded
Col. 2:7 *r.* and built up in him

ROOTS.
2 *Chr.* 7:20 pluck them up by *r.*
Job 8:17 his *r.* are wrapped about
18:16 his *r.* shall be dried up
28:9 overturn. mountains by *r.*
30:4 cut juniper *r.* for meat
Jer. 1:11 him. shall grow out of *r.*
Jer. 17:8 spreadeth out her *r.*
Ezek. 17:7 vine did bend her *r.*
Dan. 4:15 stump of his *r.* 23, 26
7:8 horns plucked up by the *r.*
Hos. 14:5 Israel cast forth his *r.*
Amos 2:9 I destroyed his *r.* from
Mark 11:20 fig-tree dried from *r.*
Jude 12 trees, plucked up by *r.*

ROPES.
Jud. 16:11 bi. me wi. new *r.* 12
2 *Sam.* 17:13 Isr. bring *r.* to city
1 *K.* 20:31 and 32 put *r.* on heads.
Acts 27:32 soldiers cut off the *r.*

ROSE, Substantive.
Cant. 2:1 I am *r.* of Sharon
Is. 35:1 desert sh. blossom as *r.*

ROSE, Verb.
Gen. 4:8 Cain *r.* up against Abel
22:3 Abrah. *r.* upon him
Ex. 10:23 nor *r.* any from place
12:30 Pharaoh *r.* up in night
33:10 and all the people *r.* up
Num. 25:7 Phinehas *r.* up from
Jud. 3:15 woman *r.* and stood
Jud. 5:7 inhabit. ceased *r.* up I
20:5 lying in wait of Si. *r. Theud.*
10:11 drink with him after he *r.*
Rom. 14:9 Christ bo. died and *r.*
1 *Cor.* 10:7 eat, and *r.* up to play
15:4 he was buried and *r.* again
2 *Cor.* 8:15 him who died and *r.*
1 *Thes.* 4:11 J. died and *r.* again

See MORNING.

ROT.
Num. 5:21 Lord mn. thigh *r.*
22, 27
Prov. 10:7 name of wicked sh. *r.*
Is. 40:20 choos. a tree will not *r.*

ROTTEN.
Job 13:28 and he, as a *r.* thing
41:27 esteemeth brass as *r.* wo.
Jer. 38:11 put these *r.* rags und.
12 put *r.* rags under thine
Joel 1:17 seed is *r.* under their clods.

CRUDEN'S CONCORDANCE.

CRUDEN'S CONCORDANCE. 1003

S.

SABAOTH.
Rom. 9:29 except L. of s. had left
Jam. 5:4 into ears of the L. of s.

SABBATH.
Ex. 16:23 to-morrow is holy s.
23 to-day is a s. to the Lord
20:10 sev. day is s. of L. 31:15;
35:2; Lev. 23:3; Deut. 5:14
31:14 ye shall keep the s. 16
Lev. 16:31 s. of rest, 23:3, 32
23:11 after s. priest sh. wave it
16 after sev. s. shall ye number
32 first of month sh. ye have s.
32 from even to even your s.
39 first day a s. on eighth a s.
25:2 then sh. land keep a s. 4, 6
Num. 28:10 burnt-offering of s.
2 K. 4:23 neith. new moon nor s.
16:18 covert for s. turned Ahaz
1 Chr. 9:32 prep. show-br. ev. s.
2 Chr. 36:21 desolate she kept s.
Neh. 9:14 madest kn. thy holy s.
10:31 would not buy on the s.
13:15 tread wine-presses on s.
16 men of Tyre sold on the s.
21 came they no more on the s.
Is. 56:2 bles. man that keeps s. 6
58:13 turn foot from s. call s.
66:23 from one s. to another
Ezek. 46:1 on s. it shall be open.
Amos 8:5 when will s. be gone?
Mat. 28:1 in end of s. came Mary
Mark 2:27 s. for m. not m. for s.
28 Son of m. is L. of s. Lu. 6:5
16:1 when s. was past M. Mag.
Luke 6:1 on second s. after first
13:15 doth not each on s. loose?
23:54 preparation, s. drew on
John 5:18 he not only had bro. s.
Acts 13:42 preached to th. next s.
16:13 'n s. we went out of city
13:4 reasoned in syna. every s.
See DAY, DAYS.

SABBATHS.
Ex. 31:13 my s. ye shall keep,
Lev. 19:3, 30; 26:2
Lev. 23:15 seven s. sh. be compl.
25:8 thou shalt number seven s.
26:34 then shall land enjoy s. 35,
43; 2 Chr. 36:21
1 Chr. 23:31 burnt-sa. in s. 2 Chr.
2:4; 8:13; 31:3; Neh. 10:33
Is. 1:13 new moons and s. I can.
56:4 eunuchs that keep my s.
Lam. 1:7 advers. did mock at s.
2:6 L. caused s. to be forgotten
Ezek. 20:12 I gave s. to be sign
13 my s. they polluted, 16, 21
22:8 hast profaned my s. 23:38
26 priests hid eyes from my s.
44:24 keep my laws, hallow s.
46:3 worship at this gate his s.
Hos. 2:11 make to cease her s.

SABEANS.
Job 1:15 the S. fell on the oxen
Is. 45:14 merchandise of the S.
Ezek. 23:12 common sort were S.
Joel 3:8 shall sell them to the S.

SACK.
Gen. 42:25 every man's money
into s. 35; 44:21; 41:1
44:2 silver cup in s. mouth
12 cup was found in Benj.'s s.
Lev. 11:32 s. of uncle. put in wa.

SACKBUT.
Dan. 3:5 sound of s. 7, 10, 15

SACKCLOTH.
Gen. 37:34 Jac. put s. upon loins
2 Sam. 3:31 gird you with s.
21:10 Rizpah took s. and spread
1 K. 20:31 put s. on loins, 31
21:27 A. put s. on flesh, lay in s.
2 K. 6:30 looked, had s. within
19:1 H. cover. him wi. s. Is. 37:1
2 sid. of priests with s. Is. 37:2
1 Chr. 21:16 D. and elders clo. s.
Est. 4:2 none enter cloth. with s.
Job 16:15 sewed s. upon my skin
Ps. 30:11 put off s. girded with
35:13 sick, my clothing was s.
69:11 I made s. also my garm.
Is. 3:24 stomacher, girding of s.
15:3 in street gir. them. with s.
20:2 loose s. from off thy loins
21:12 day did L. call to girding s.
32:11 gird s. on loins, Jer. 4:8;
6:26; 49:3; 3
50:3 I make s. covering of hea.
Lam. 2:10 they girded themsel.
with s. Ezek. 7:18; 27:31
Dan. 9:3 seek L. with fast. and s.
Joel 1:8 lament like virgin wi. s.
13 lie all night in s.

Amos 8:10 I will bring s. on loins
Jon. 3:5 people of Nin. put on s.
6 king covered him with s.
8 man and beast be co. with s.
Rev. 6:12 sun became black as s.
11:3 proph. 1260 days, clo. in s.

SACKCLOTHES.
Neh. 9:1 Is. assembled with s. on

SACKS.
Gen. 42:25 fill s. with corn, 44:1
43:12 money brought again in s.
24 tell who put money in s.
Jos. 9:4 Gibeonites took old s.

SACRIFICE.
Gen. 31:54 J. offer. s. on mount
Ex. 5:17 let us do s. to Lord, 8:8
12:27 it is s. of Lord's passover
34:15 and thou eat of his s.
25 nor s. of passover be left
Lev. 7:12 shall offer s. of thanks.
16 if s. be vow, eaten same day
27:11 beast which they do not s.
Num. 15:3 s. in performing, vow, 8
23:6 s. made by fire unto Lord,
6, 13, 18, 24; 29:6, 13, 36
Deut. 18:3 from them th. offer s.
Jud. 13:21 will offer priest s. to Dagon
1 Sam. 1:21 to offer yearly s. 2:19
2:29 kick ye at my s. and offer. ?
3:14 E.'s house not purged wi. s.
9:12 s. of my people to-day
13:23 to obey is better than s.
16:3 call Jesse to the s. and 3, 5
20:6 is a yearly s. for family, 29
1 K. 12:27 people do s. at Jorus.
18:29 prophesied till evening s.
36 at evening s. E. drew near
2 K. 5:17 not offer s. to other go.
10:19 I have great s. to do to B.
17:36 him sh. ye fear, and do s.
2 Chr. 7:5 S. offered s. 21,000 ox.
12 chosen place for house of s.
Ezr. 8:4 set forth all ill evening s.
5 at even. s. I arose fr. heav'n.
Ps. 40:6 s. oldest not desire, 51:16
50:5 made coven. with me by s.
110:17 I offer s. of thanksgiving.
118:27 bind s. to horns of altar
141:2 lifting up hands as eve. s.
Prov. 15:8 s. of wicked abomina.
21:3 justice more accep. than s.
Ec. 5:1 than give s. of fools
Is. 19:21 Eg. sh. do s. and oblat.
34:6 L. hath a s. in Boz. and Id.
57:7 thi. wentest thou to offer s.
Jer. 33:11 that bring s. of praise
18 nor want man to do s.
46:10 God a s. in north country
Ezek. 39:17 gath. to my s. gro. s.
19 drink blood till drunk of s.
41:21 they shall slay s. for peo.
46:24 ministers boil s. of people
Dan. 8:11 daily s. 9:21; 11:31
12 host given him ag. daily s.
19:11 daily s. sh. he taken away
Hos. 3:4 Is. sh. abide witho. a s.
6:6 I desired mercy and not s.
Mal. 2:13; 18:7
Amos 4:5 offer a s. of thanksgiv.
Jon. 1:16 men offered a s. to L.
Zep. 1:7 L. hath prepared a s. 8
Mal. 1:8 if ye offer blind for s.
Mark 9:49 every s. sh. he salted
Luke 2:24 offer a s. accor. to law
Acts 7:41 in those days off. s. to
14:13 would have done s. with
Rom. 12:1 present your bodies s.
1 Cor. 8:4 off. in s. idols, 10:19, 28
Eph. 5:2 s. to G. for sweet smell
Phil. 2:17 off. on s. of your faith
4:18 s. accep. well-pleas. to God
Heb. 7:27 daily as those to offer s.
9:26 put away sin by s. of him
10:5 s. and off. thou woul. not, 8
12 had offered one s. for sins
13:15 let us offer s. of praise
See BURNT, PEACE-OFFERING.

SACRIFICE, Verb.
Ex. 3:18 go. s. to L. 5:3, 8; 8:27;
10:25; 8:25 go ye s.
8:26 s. abomina. of Egyptians?
13:15 L. s. to L. openeth matrix
20:24 s. thereon peace-offer.
Deut. 15:21 bul. sh. not s. it, 17:1
1 Sam. 1:3 Elkan. went up to s.
15:15 peo. spared best to s. to L.
16:2 I am come to s. to Lord, 5
2 K. 14:4 as yet the people did s.
2 Chr. 28:23
17:35 nor shall s. to other gods
2 Chr. 11:16 came to J. to s. to L.
Ezr. 4:2 seek your God and do s.
Ps. 4:5 will they s.?
Ps. 54:6 I will freely s. to thee,

Ps. 107:22 s. sacrifices of thanks.
Ezek. 39:17 gath. to my s. I do s.
Hos. 4:13 s. on tops of mountains
14 they s. with harlots, there.
8:13 th. s. but L. accepteth not
12:11 they s. bullocks in Gilgal
13:2 let men that s. kiss calves
Jon. 2:9 I will s. with thanksgi.
Hab. 1:16 they s. unto their net
Zec. 14:21 they that s. sh. seethe
1 Cor. 10:20 Gentiles s. to devils

SACRIFICED.
Ex. 32:8 made calf, s. thereunto
Deut. 32:17 s. to devils, not to G.
Jos. 8:31 s. thereon peace-offer.
Jud. 2:5 they s. there unto Lord
1 Sam. 11:15 pe. went to G. to s.
2 Sam. 6:13 Dav. s. ox. and fatl.
1 K. 3:2 only the people s. in the
high places, 3; 2 K. 12:3;
13:4, 35; 16:4; 2 Chr. 28:4
11:8 strange wives, s. to th. go.
2 K. 17:32 lowest priests wh. s.
1 Chr. 21:28 L. answ. thee Isra.
2 Chr. 5:6 assem. be. ark, s. sheep
28:23 A. s. to gods of Damascus
33:16 Manasseh s. on altar of L.
34:4 on graves of th. that had s.
Ps. 106:37 they s. sons to devils
38 they s. to idols of Canaan
Ezek. 39:19 sacri. which I have s.
Hos. 11:2 they s. to Baalim
1 Cor. 5:7 Ch. our Pass. is s. for
Rev. 3:14 things s. to idols, 20

SACRIFICEDST.
Deut. 16:4 flesh s. rem. all night

SACRIFICES.
Gen. 46:1 Is. at Beer-sheba off. s.
Ex. 10:25 thou must give us s.
18:12 Jethro took s. for God
Lev. 10:13 s. of L. made by fire
17:7 sh. no more offer s. to dev.
Num. 25:2 called people to s.
28:2 s. observe to offer in season
Deut. 12:6 thither bring your s.
33:19 offer s. of righteousness
Jos. 13:14 s. of L. their inherita.
22:28 altar not for s. 29
1 Sam. 6:15 sacrificed s. to the L.
15:22 hath L. as great del. in s.
2 Chr. 7:1 fire came and cons. s.
29:31 bring s. they brought in s.
Ezr. 6:3 place where he offer. s.
10 may offer s. to G. of heaven
Neh. 12:43 that day th. off. gr. s.
Ps. 4:5 offer s. of righteousness
27:6 therefore will I offer s. of j.
50:8 not reprove thee for thy s.
51:17 s. of God are a broken sp.
19 pleased with s. of righteous.
106:28 joined to Baal-peor eat s.
107:22 sacrifice s. of thanksgivi.
Prov. 17:1 house full of s.
Is. 1:11 to what purpose your s.?
29:1 year to year, let th. kill s.
43:23 nor honor. me with thy s.
24 nor made me with fat of thy s.
56:7 their s. shall be accepted
Jer. 6:20 nor are your s. sweet
7:21 burnt offerings to your s.
17:26 bringing s. of praise in L.
Hos. 4:19 be ashamed, bec. of s.
9:4 s. be as bread of mourners
Amos 4:4 bring your s. ev. morn.
5:25 have ye offer. unto me s.?
Mark 12:33 love L. is more tl. s.
Luke 13:1 blood Pi. mingl. wi. s.
Acts 7:42 offered s. forty years?
1 Cor. 10:18 eat s. partak. of altar
Heb. 5:1 offer gifts s. for sins
8:3 high-pri. ordained to offer s.
9:9 were offered both gif. and s.
23 heavy. things with better s.
10:3 in th. s. a remembrance
10:11 offering oftentimes s.
13:16 wi. such s. G. is well ple.
1 Pet. 2:5 priesthood to off. up s.
See BURNT.

SACRIFICETH.
Ec. 9:2 he that s. to any good
Is. 65:3 peo. that s. in gardens
Mal. 1:14 and s. a corrupt thing

SACRIFICING.
1 K. 8:5 bef. ark, s. sheep
12:32 s. to calves he had made

SACRILEGE.
Rom. 2:22 dost thou commit s.?

SAD.
Gen. 40:6 J. looked, they were s.
1 Sam. 1:18 countenance no more s.
1 K. 21:5 why is thy spirit so s.?

SADDUCEES.
Mat. 3:7 wh. he saw the S. come
16:1 S. came tempting Jesus
6 beware of leaven of S. 11, 12
22:23 the same day came the S.
34 he had put the S. to silence
Acts 4:1 the priests and S. came
5:17 S. laid hands on apostles
23:6 P. perceiv. one part were S.
8 S. say, There is no resurrect.

SADLY.
Gen. 40:7 why look ye so s.?

SADNESS.
Ec. 7:3 by s. of countenance

SAFE.
1 Sam. 19:11 and ye dwelled s.
Job 21:9 their houses s. from fear
Ps. 119:117 hold me up, I sh. be s.
Prov. 18:10 right. run in, are s.
29:25 whoso trusteth in L. be s.
Ezek. 34:27 sh. be s. in th. land
Luke 15:27 had received him s.
Acts 23:24 may bring him s. to F.
27:44 they escaped all s. to land
Phil. 3:1 to write, for you it is s.
2 Sam. 22:3 thou shalt be in s.

SAFELY.
Ps. 78:53 he led them on s.
Ps. 119:8 heark. to me sh. dw. s.
3:23 shalt thou walk in thy s.
11:15 husb. doth s. trust in her
Is. 41:3 pursued them, passed s.
14:31 Jerusalem shall be s.
Hos. 2:18 will make them lie s.
Mark 14:44 and lead him away s.
Acts 16:23 jailer to keep them s.
See DWELL.

SAFETY.
Job 3:26 not in s. nor had I rest
5:4 his children are far from s.
11 low, thy he exalted to s.
11:18 shalt take thy rest in s.
24:23 given him to be in s.
Ps. 12:5 I will set him in s.
33:17 horse is vain thing for s.
Prov. 11:14 in counsel. is s. 24:6
21:31 horse for battle, s. is of L.
1 Thes. 5:3 sh. say, Peace and s.

SAFFRON.
Cant. 4:14 calamus and cinna.

SAIL, Substantive.
Is. 33:23 could not spread the s.
Ezek. 27:7 spreadedst to be thy s.
Acts 27:17 strake s. so were driv.
40 hoised up main s. to wind

SAIL.
Acts 20:3 he he was about to s.
16 Paul had determined to s.
27:1 when we shou. s. into Italy
21 O, hath given they O. th. s.
Phil. 4:21 salute every s. in C. J.

SAILED.
Luke 8:23 as he s. he fell asleep
Acts 27:7 when we had s. slowly

SAILING.
Acts 21:2 finding a ship s. over
27:9 when s. was now dangerous
9 when s. was now dangerous

SAILORS.
Rev. 18:17 and s. stood afar off

SAINT.
Ps. 106:16 they envied Aa. the s.
Dan. 8:13 I heard one s. speak.
ing, another s. said to that s. which

CRUDEN'S CONCORDANCE. 1005

SAM

1 *Pet.* 1:5 kept thro' faith unto *s.*
9 your faith *s.* of your souls
10 of wh. *s.* prophets have inq.
2 *Pet.* 3:15 long-suffer, of L. is *s.*
Jude 3 to write to you of com. *s.*
Rev. 7:10 *s.* to G. 19:1 *s.* to Lord
12:10 now is come *s.* and stron.

My SALVATION.
Ex. 15:2 L. my song, bec. my *s.*
2 *Sam.* 22:3 shield, horn of my *s.*
47 he rock of my *s. Ps.* 18:46
22:5 all my *s.* all my desire
Job 13:16 he also shall be my *s.*
Ps. 25:5 thou art God of my *s.*
27:1 the Lord is my light and
my *s.* 62:6; *Is.* 12:2
9 O God of my *s.* 51:14; 88:1
38:22 O L. my *s.* 62:2 is my *s.* 6
62:1 God, from him com. my *s.*
7 G. my *s.* 88:26 rock of my *s.*
91:16 and show him my *s.*
118:14 L. bec. my *s.* 21; *Is.* 12:2
140:7 Lord the strength of my *s.*
Is. 12:2 G. is my *s.* is bec. my *s.*
46:13 my *s.* shall not tarry
49:6 my *s.* to end of the earth
51:5 my *s.* gone for. 6 for ever
8 my *s.* it. generation to gene.
56:1 my *s.* is near to come
Mic. 7:7 wait for God of my *s.*
Heb. 3:18 joy in God of my *s.*
Phil. 1:19 I kn. this turn to my *s.*

Thy SALVATION.
Gen. 49:18 I waited for thy *s.*
1 *Sam.* 2:1 bec. I rejoice in *s.*
2 *Sam.* 22:36 hast also given me
the shield of thy *s. Ps.* 18:35
Ps. 9:14 I will rejoice in thy *s.*
13:5 my heart shall rej. in thy *s.*
20:5 we will rejoice in thy *s.*
21:1 in *s.* how shall he rej.
5 his glory is great in thy *s.*
35:3 say unto soul, I am thy *s.*
40:10 declared faithful. and *l. s.*
16 let such as love thy *s.* say
51:12 rest. to me joy of *t. s.* 70:4
69:13 hear me in truth of thy *s.*
29 let thy *s.* set me up on high
71:15 mouth sh. show forth L. *s.*
85:7 O Lord, grant us thy *s.*
106:4 remember me with thy *s.*
119:41 let *t. s.* come ac. to word
81 my soul fainteth for thy *s.*
123 mine eyes fail for thy *s.*
166 Lord, I have hoped for *t. s.*
174 I have longed for *t. s.* O L.
Is. 17:10 hast forgot. God of *t. s.*
62:11 say to Zion, *t. s.* cometh
Luke 2:30 mine eyes ha. seen *t. s.*

SAMARIA.
1 *K.* 16:24 Omri bought hill S.
Mic. 1:6 will make S. as a heap
Luke 17:11 through midst of S.
John 4:4 must needs go thro' S.
Acts 8:1 thro' regions of S. 5, 14

In SAMARIA.
1 *K.* 16:28 O. buried in S. 22:37
20 Ahab reigned in S. 22:51
Amos 3:12 taken that dwell in S.
Acts 1:8 to me in Judea and in S.

SAMARITAN.
Luke 10:31 a certain S. came
17:16 giv. him thanks, was a S.
John 8:48 art a S. hast a devil

SAMARITANS.
2 *K.* 17:29 Ll. places S. had made
Mat. 10:5 city of S. enter not
Luke 9:52 ent. into village of S.
John 4:9 J. have no deal. wi. S.
39 many of S. of that city bel.
40 the S. besought him to tarry
Acts 8:25 preached in vil. of S.

SAME.
Jud. 7:4 *s.* shall go, *s.* sh. not go
Ps. 102:27 but thou art the *s.*
113:3 to going do. of *s. Mal.* 1:11
Mat. 3:11 *s.* is he that *s.* baptize with
Mark 3:35 *s.* is my bro. sis. moth.
Luke 6:33 *s.* thing do *s.*
9:48 least am. all you, *s.* sh. be gr.
13:8 J. *Ch. s.* yesterday, to-day

See DAY, HOUR.

S*MO'. *A. ts* 20:15
SAMOTHRA'CIA. *Acts* 16:11

SAMSON.
Jud. 13:21 bis name M. 16:29
Heb. 11:32 would fail to tell of S.

SAMUEL.
1 *Sam.* 1:20 son, called him S.
2:18 S. ministered bef. 21; 4:1
3:15 and S. feared to show 10:1
10:1 S. took a vial of oil, 15, 16
15:11 it grieved S. 27, 31
10:13 S. took the horn of oil
19:18 Da. fled and came to S.

SAN

1 *Sam.* 28:11 wom. Bring me S.
2 *Chr.* 35:18 like that from S.
Ps. 99:6 S. among them that
Jer. 15:1 though Moses and S.
Acts 3:24 the prophets from S.
13:20 450 years till S. prophet
Heb. 11:32 would fail to tell of S.

SANBALLAT.
Neh. 2:10 when S. heard of it, 19
4:1 when S. heard we builded
6:2 S. and Gos. sent to me, 14
12 for Tobiah and S. had hired
13:28 Joiada son-in-law to S.

SANCTIFICATION.
1 *Cor.* 1:30 of G. is made to us *s.*
1 *Thes.* 4:3 will of G. even your *s.*
4 kn. how to possess ves. in *s.*
2 *Thes.* 2:13 *s.* of Sp. 1 *Pet.* 1:2

SANCTIFY.
Ex. 13:2 *s.* unto me first-born
19:10 go and *s.* them to-day
22 let the priests *s.* themselves
23 set bounds ab. mount, *s.* it
28:41 ano. and *s.* Aa. and sons,
29:33; 40:13; *Lev.* 8:12; 21:8
29:36 shalt *s.* altar, 37; 40:10
44 I will *s.* taberna. and altar
30:29 thou shalt *s.* the taberna.
40:10, 11; *Lev.* 8:11
31:13 I am L. that doth *s.* you,
Lev. 20:8; 21:8; *Ezek.* 20:12
Lev. 11:44 ye shall *s.* yourselves,
20:7; *Num.* 11:18; *Jos.* 3:5;
7:13; 1 *Sam.* 16:5
21:15 seed, I the Lord do *s.* him
23 I the L. do *s.* them, 22:9, 16
27:14 when a man shi. *s.* house
Num. 20:12 believed me not, to
s. me, 27:14
Deut. 5:12 keep the sabbath, to
s. it, *Neh.* 13:22
15:19 firstling males thou sh. *s.*
Jos. 7:13 *s.* people, *s.* yourselves
1 *Chr.* 15:12 said, *s.* yourselves,
2 *Chr.* 29:5; 35:6
23:13 that he sho. *s.* holy things
2 *Chr.* 29:17 apriz. in heart to *s.*
30:17 every one not clean to *s.*
Is. 8:13 *s.* Lord of hosts himself
29:23 they sh. *s.* H. O. of Jacob
66:17 *s.* themselves in gardens
Ezek. 36:23 I will *s.* my gr. name
37:28 I the Lord do *s.* Israel
38:23 I magnify myself, *s.* mys.
44:19 *s.* peo. with garm. 46:20
Joel 1:14 *s.* ye a fast, 2:15
2:16 *s.* congregation, assemble
John 17:17 *s.* them thro' thy tru.
19 for their sakes I *s.* myself
Eph. 5:26 *s.* and cleanse church
1 *Thes.* 5:23 God of peace *s.* you
Heb. 13:12 that he might *s.* peo.
1 *Pet.* 3:15 but *s.* the Lord God

SANCTIFIED.
Gen. 2:3 G. blessed sev. day *s.* it
Ex. 19:14 Moses *s.* the people
29:43 the tabernacle shall be *s.*
Lev. 8:10 *s.* the tabernacl-
15 *s.* the altar; 30 *s.* Aaron
10:3 I will be *s.* in th. that come
27:15 if he that *s.* it will redeem
19 if he that *s.* the field will
Num. 7:1 *s.* tabernacle Instrum.
8:17 I *s.* the first-born of Isr.
Deut. 32:51 because ye *s.* me not
1 *Sam.* 7:1 and *s.* Eleazar his son
16:5 ho *s.* Jesse and his sons
21:5 though it were *s.* this day
1 *Chr.* 15:14 priests and Levit. *s.*
2 *Chr.* 5:11 all the priests were *s.*
7:16 now I have *s.* this hou. 20
29:15 gather, and *s.* themselves
17 *s.* house of L. in eight days
19 all the vessels have we *s.*
30:3 priests had not *s.* themsel.
15 Lev. ashamed, *s.* themselv.
17 many in congregation had
31:18 set office they *s.* themsel.
Job 1:5 Job *s.* sons and daught.
Is. 5:16 holy God shall be *s.*
13:3 I have commanded *s.* ones
Jer. 1:5 I *s.* thee, ordained prop.
12:3 fu. in *s.* day, 96:21
24:21 when I shall be *s.* in her
25 *s.* in sight of heathen, 38:27
Ezek. 20:41 I will be *s.* in you
28:25 when I shall be *s.* in thee
John 10:36 him, whom the Fa. *s.*
17:19 that they also might be *s.*
Acts 20:32 hath inheritance among
them which are *s.* 26:18
Rom. 15:16 offer. being *s.* by H. Ghost
1 *Cor.* 1:2 them th. are *s.* in C. J.
6:11 ye are *s.* in name of Lord

SAN

1 *Cor.* 7:14 husband is *s.* wife is *s.*
1 *Tim.* 4:5 it is *s.* by word of G.
2 *Tim.* 2:21 vessel *s.* for Master's
2:11 they who are *s.* are all
10:10 by which will we are *s.*
14 he perfect. them that are *s.*
29 coven. wherewith he was *s.*
Jude 1 to them that are *s.* by G.

SANCTIFIETH.
Mat. 23:17 temple that *s.* gold?
19 or the altar that *s.* the gift?
Heb. 2:11 he that *s.* and they
9:13 if blood of bulls *s.* to puri.

SANCTUARY.
Ex. 15:17 plant them in the *s.*
25:8 and let them make me a *s.*
30:13 give every one after the *s.*
36:1 all man. of work for *s.* 3, 4
38:24 shek. after sh. of *s.* 25, 26;
Lev. 5:15; 27:3, 25; *Num.*
3:47, 50; 7:13, 19, 25, 31, 37;
18:16
Lev. 4:6 sprinkle blood before *s.*
10:4 carry brethren fr. before *s.*
12:4 nor come into *s.* till her
16:33 make atonem. for holy *s.*
19:30 ye shall rever. my *s.* 26:2
21:12 nei. shall he go out of the
s. nor prof. the *s.* of his God
Num. 3:38 morning stars *s.* fourth.
4:12 wherewith minister in *s.*
10:21 set forward, bearing the *s.*
18:1 bear the iniquity of the *s.*
3 not come nigh vessels of *s.*
5 ye shall keep charge of the *s.*
19:20 he hath defiled *s.* of the L.
Num. 24:26 set up a stone by *s.*
1 *Chr.* 9:29 oversee instrum. of *s.*
22:19 build ye the *s.* of the Lord
31:5 divided for governors of *s.*
28:10 to build a house for the *s.*
2 *Chr.* 20:8 built thee a *s.* therein
26:18 go out of *s.* for thou hast
29:21 for a sin-offering for the *s.*
30:8 yield to L. enter into his *s.*
19 accord. to purification of *s.*
36:17 king of Bab. sl. men in *s.*
Neh. 10:39 where are vessels of *s.*
Ps. 20:2 L. send thee help fr. *s.*
63:2 I have seen thee in the *s.*
68:24 they go into *s.*
73:17 till I went into *s.* of God
74:3 enemy done wickedly in *s.*
7 they have cast fire into thy *s.*
77:13 thy way, O G. is in the *s.*
78:54 brou. them to border of *s.*
69 built his *s.* like high palaces
96:6 stren. and beauty in his *s.*
102:19 looked fr. height of his *s.*
114:2 Jud. his *s.* Is. his domin.
134:2 lift up your hands in *s.*
150:1 praise L. praise God in *s.*
Is. 8:14 L. of hosts, sh. he for *s.*
16:12 he shall come to his *s.*
43:28 I have prof. princes of *s.*
60:13 beautify the place of my *s.*
63:18 our adversaries trodden *s.*
Jer. 17:12 from begin. is our *s.*
Lam. 1:10 heathen enter. her *s.*
2:7 the Lord hath abhor. his *s.*
20 shall prophet be slain in *s.*?
4:1 stones of *s.* are poured out
Ezek. 5:11 thou hast defil. my *s.*
11:16 ho to them as a little *s.*
23:38 defiled my *s.* in same day
22:30 between *s.* and prof. deep
24:21 will profane *s.* your excell.
25:3 heathen, *s.* was profaned
27 when he goeth into *s.*
41:23 the *s.* and most holy place
47:12 their wat. Issued out of *s.*
48:8 *s.* shall be in midst, 10, 21
Dan. 8:11 place of *s.* cast down
13 give *s.* to be trod. und. foot
14 then shall the *s.* be cleansed
9:17 cause favo to shine on *s.*
26 peo. shall destr. city and *s.*
11:31 sh. pollute *s.* of strength
Zep. 3:4 her priests polluted *s.*
9:1 first coven. a tabern.
2 tabernacle which is called *s.*
13:11 whose blood I have bro.
Lev. 21:23 that he prof. not my *s.*
Is. 11:3 a sanctuary my *s.* to desolat.
Jer. 51:51 stran. are come into *s.*
Amos 7:9 *s.* of Is. shall be laid wa.

SAND.
Gen. 22:17 multi. seed as *s.* 32:12
41:49 Joseph gathered corn as *s.*
Ex. 2:12 hid the Egyptian in *s.*
Deut. 33:19 suck of treasures hid in *s.*
Jos. 11:4 went much people as *s.*
Jud. 7:12 their camels were as *s.*
1 *Sam.* 13:5 P. gath. to fight as *s.*

SAT

2 *Sam.* 17:11 all Is. be gath. as *s.*
1 *K.* 4:20 J. and Isr. are mu. as *s.*
29 G. gave S. larg. of he. as *s.*
Job 6:3 it would be heavier th. *s.*
29:18 I shall mul. my days as *s.*
Ps. 78:27 feath. fowls like as *s.*
139:18 more in number than *s.*
Prov. 27:3 sto. heavy, *s.* weighty
Is. 10:22 tho' thy peo. Is. be as *s.*
48:19 seed also had been as *s.*
Jer. 5:22 plac. *s.* for bound of sea
15:8 widows increased above *s.*
33:22 *s.* of sea cannot be meas.
Hos. 1:10 Is. as *s.* *Rom.* 9:27
Hab. 1:9 gather captivity as *s.*
Mat. 7:26 man built house on *s.*
Heb. 11:12 spr. of one many as *s.*
Rev. 13:1 I stood upon *s.* of sea
20:8 number of whom is as *s.*

SANDALS.
Mark 6:9 but be shod with *s.* put
Acts 12:8 gird thyself, bind thy *s.*

SANG.
Ex. 15:1 then *s.* Moses this song
Num. 21:17 Isr. *s.* Spring O well
Jud. 5:1 then *s.* Debor. and Bar.
1 *Sam.* 29:5 not D. of wh. th. *s.*?
2 *Chr.* 29:28 singers *s.* trumpet.
30 they *s.* praises with gladn.
Neh. 12:42 the singers *s.* aloud
Job 38:7 morning stars *s.* togeth.
Ps. 106:12 belie. words *s.* praise
Acts 16:25 Pa. and Sil. *s.* praises

SANK.
Ex. 15:5 *s.* into the bottom
10 *s.* as lead in mighty waters

SAP.
Ps. 104:16 trees of L. full of *s.*

SAPHIR.
Mic. 1:11 thou inhabitant of S.

SAPPHIRA.
Acts 5:1 Ananias, with S. wife

SAPPHIRE.
Ex. 24:10 paved work of *s.* stone
28:18 second row *s. s.* 39:11
Job 28:16 cannot be val. with *s.*
Lam. 4:7 th. polishing was of *s.*
Ezek. 1:26 firm. appearance of *s.*
10:1 over them as it were a *s.*
28:13 *s.* and emerald thy cover.
Rev. 21:19 foundat. of wall was *s.*

SAPPHIRES.
Job 28:6 stones of it place of *s.*
Cant. 5:14 ivory, overlaid with *s.*
Is. 54:11 lay foundations with *s.*

SARAH.
Gen. 17:15 not Sar. but S. shall
18:9 where is S. 11, 13, 14
20:2 Abraham said of S. She is
14 Abimelech restored S.
21:1 the Lord did unto S. as he
23:2 S. died in Kirjath-arba, 19
24:67 brought her into S. tent
25:10 Abra. buried and S. 49:31
Num. 26:46 daugh. of Asher S.
Is. 51:2 look to S. that bare you
Rom. 4:19 deadness of S. womb
9:9 will come, S. sh. have a son
Heb. 11:11 thro' faith S. receiv.
1 *Pet.* 3:6 as S. obeyed Abraham

SARAI.
Gen. 11:29 Ab.'s wife S. 30; 16:1
17:17 plague, Pharaoh bec. of S.
16:6 S. dealt hardly with Ha. 8

SARAL.

SARDINE.
Rev. 4:3 to look upon like *s.* sto.

SARDIS.
Rev. 1:11 write and send it to S.
3:1 to the angel in S. write, 4

SARDIUS.
Ex. 28:17 first row he *s.* 39:10
Ezek. 28:13 *s.* and diam. thy cov.
Rev. 21:20 sixth founda. was *s.*

SARDONYX.
Rev. 21:20 fifth foundat. was *s.*

SAREPTA.
Luke 4:26 S. a city of, 1 *K.* 17:9

SARGON. *Is.* 20:1

SARON.
Acts 9:35 all in S. saw him

SARUCH.
Luke 3:35 which was son of S.

SAT.
Gen. 31:34 Ra. *s.* upon images
Ex. 12:29 Pha. that *s.* on throne
18:13 Moses *s.* to judge people
Jud. 20:26 wept, and *s.* before L.
1 *Sam.* 1:9 E. *s.* by post of temp.
4:13 Eli *s.* by wayside
1 *K.* 16:11 as soon as *s.* on thro.
21:13 chil. of Belial *s.* before N.

CRUDEN'S CONCORDANCE.

SCI

Hab. 3:14 came as whirlw. to *s.*
Zec. 1:21 lift horn over Ju. *s.* it

SCATTERED.
Gen. 11:4 lest he *s.* upon earth
Ex. 5:12 peo. *s.* to gath. stubble
Num. 10:35 let all thine enemies be *s. Ps.* 68:1
Deut. 30:3 whither L. hath *s.* th.
1 *Sam.* 11:11 Ammonites were *s.*
13:8 people were *s.* from Saul
2 *Sam.* 18:8 bat. *s.* over country
22:15 and *s.* them, *Ps.* 18:14
1 *K.* 22:17 saw Is. *s.* 2 *Chr.* 18:16
2 *K.* 25:5 his army *s. Jer.* 52:8
Est. 3:8 certain people *s.* abroad
Job 4:11 stout lions' whe. are *s.*
18:15 brimstone be *s.* on habit.
Ps. 44:11 *s.* us am. heathen, 60:1
53:5 G. *s.* bones of him th. enc.
68:14 when Almighty *s.* kings
89:10 thou hast *s.* thine enemies
92:9 workers of iniqu. sh. be *s.*
141:7 bones *s.* at grave's mouth
Is. 13:2 go ye to a nation *s.*
† present be brought of peo. *s.*
33:3 lifting thy. nations were *s.*
Jer. 3:13 *s.* ways to strangers
10:21 all their flocks shall be *s.*
23:2 ye have *s.* my flock, away
30:11 end of nations wh. I *s.* th.
31:10 he that *s.* Is. will gather
40:15 that Jews should be *s.*
50:17 Israel is a *s.* sheep, driven
Ezek. 6:8 ye be *s.* thro' countries
11:16 though I *s.* them
17:21 th. that remain shall be *s.*
20:13 Egyptians gath. whith. *s.*
31:5 flock *s.* because no shoph.
6 flock was *s.* on face of earth
12 have been *s.* in cloudy day
21 push. diseased till ye *s.* th.
36:19 I *s.* them among heathen
46:18 that my people be not *s.*
Joel 3:2 plead for pe. wh. they *s.*
Nah. 3:18 people is *s.* on mount.
Hab. 3:6 everlast. mountains *s.*
Zec. 1:19 horns wh. ha. *s.* Ju. 21
7:14 I *s.* them with whirlwind
13:7 smite Shepherd, the sheep be *s. Mat.* 26:31; *Mark* 14:27
Mat. 9:36 *s.* as sheep hav. no sh.
Luke 1:51 *s.* proud in imaginat.
John 11:52 gath. children were *s.*
16:32 hour cometh ye sh. be *s.*
Acts 5:36 obey. Theudas were *s.*
8:1 were *s.* thro' regions of Ju.
4 were *s.* went preaching, 11:19
Jam. 1:1 twelve tribes that are *s.*
1 *Pet.* 1:1 strangers *s.* thro' Pon.

SCATTERETH.
Job 37:11 the thick cloud he *s.*
38:24 wh. *s.* east wind on earth
Ps. 147:16 he *s.* the hoarfrost
Prov. 11:24 that *s.* yet increaseth
20:8 king *s.* away evil with eyes
26 a wise king *s.* the wicked
Mat. 12:30 he that gath. not. wi. me, *s.* abroad, *Luke* 11:23
John 10:12 wolf catcheth. *s.* sheep

SCATTERING.
Is. 30:30 L. sh. show anger wi. *s.*

SCENT.
Job 14:9 through *s.* of water
Jer. 48:11 his *s.* is not changed
Hos. 14:7 *s.* thereof as wine of L.

SCEPTRE.
Gen. 49:10 *s.* not depart from Ju.
Num. 24:17 *s.* shall rise out of Is.
Est. 4:11 king shall hold out *s.*
5:2 held out to *s.* Es. golden *s.*
Ps. 45:6 *s.* of kingdom is right *s.*
Is. 14:5 Lord hath broken *s.*
Ezek. 19:11 had strong rods for *s.*
† hath no strong rod to be *s.*
Amos 1:5 cut off him that holdi. *s.*
8 him that holdeth *s.* from A.
Zec. 10:11 the *s.* of Egypt shall
Heb. 1:8 *s.* of righteous. is the *s.*

SCEVA.
Acts 19:14 seven sons of one S.

SCHISM.
1 *Cor.* 12:25 there should be no *s.*

SCHOLAR.
1 *Chr.* 25:8 the teacher as the *s.*
Mat. 2:12 L. cut off master and *s.*

SCHOOL.
Acts 19:9 disputing in *s.* of one

SCHOOLMASTER.
Gal. 3:24 the law was our *s.*
25 we are no longer under a *s.*

SCIENCE.
Dan. 1:4 in wisd. understand, *s.*
1 *Tim.* 6:20 avoi. oppos. of *s.*

SCR

Hab. 1:10 they sh. *s.* at kings

SCOFFERS.
2 *Pet.* 3:3 in last days *s.* walking

SCORCH, ED.
Mat. 13:6 they were *s. Mark* 4:6
Rev. 16:8 power was given to *s.*
9 men were *s.* with great heat

SCORN, Substantive.
Est. 3:6 *s.* to lay hands on Mord.
Ps. 44:13 makest us a *s.* 79:4
Hab. 1:10 princes shall be a *s.*

See LAUGHED.

SCORN, Verb.
Job 16:20 my friends *s.* me
Prov. 9:7 that reproveth a *s.*
8 reprove not a *s.* lest he hate
13:1 but a *s.* heareth not rebuke
14:6 *s.* seeketh wis. findeth not
15:12 *s.* loveth not that reprov.
19:25 smite *s.* the simple will
21:11 when *s.* is punish. simple
24 *s.* is his name, deal. in wra.
22:10 cast out *s.* and contention
24:9 *s.* is abomination to men
Is. 29:20 the *s.* is consumed

SCORNER.
Prov. 1:22 how long will *s.* dell.
3:34 surely he scorneth the *s.*
19:29 judgm. are prepared for *s.*
7:8 stretched hand with *s.*
Ezek. 6:8 ye be *s.* thro' countries

SCORNEST, ETH.
Job 39:7 he *s.* multitude of city
18 she *s.* horse and his rider
Prov. 3:34 surely he *s.* scorner
9:12 if *s.* thou alone sh. bear it
19:28 ungodly witness *s.* judg.
Ezek. 16:31 harlot, in th. thou *s.*

SCORNFUL.
Ps. 1:1 nor sitteth in seat of *s.*
Prov. 29:8 *s.* brit. city into snare
Is. 28:14 hear word of Lord, ye *s.*

SCORNING.
Job 34:7 drinks *s.* like water?
Ps. 123:4 filled wi. *s.* of those at
Prov. 1:22 scorners delight in *s.*

SCORPION.
Luke 11:12 will he off. him a *s.?*
Rev. 9:5 torment was as of a *s.*

SCORPIONS.
Deut. 8:15 thro' wilder. where *s.*
1 *K.* 12:11 I will chastise you with *s.* 14; 2 *Chr.* 10:11, 14
Ezek. 2:6 among *s.* be not afraid
Luke 10:19 power to tread on *s.*
Rev. 9:3 power, as *s.* have power
10 had tails like *s.* and stings

SCORNED.
Lev. 6:28 brazen pot, it sh. be *s.*

SCOURGE, S.
Job 5:21 hid from *s.* of tongue
Job 9:23 if *s.* slay suddenly
Is. 10:26 Lord shall stir up a *s.*
28:15 overflow. *s.* shall pass, 18
John 2:15 made *s.* of small cords

SCOURGE, Verb.
Mat. 10:17 they will *s.* in th. syn.
20:19 shall *s.* him, *Mark* 10:34
23:34 some of them ye shall *s.*
Acts 22:25 is it lawful to *s.* Ro.?

SCOURGED, ETH.
Lev. 19:20 maid, she shall be *s.*
Mat. 27:26 wh. he had *s.* Jesus, *Mark* 15:15; *John* 19:1
Heb. 12:6 the Lord *s.* every son

SCOURGING, S.
Acts 22:24 sh. be examined by *s.*
Heb. 11:36 others had trial of *s.*

SCRABBLED.
1 *Sam.* 21:13 Da. feigned mad, *s.*

SCRAPE, D.
Lev. 14:41 cause house to be *s.*
sh. pour out dust they *s.* off
43 if plague came after he *s.*
Job 2:8 Job took *s.* pot sherd to *s.*
Ezek. 26:4 I will also *s.* her dust

SCREECH-OWL.
Is. 34:14 *s.* also shall rest there

SCRIBE.
2 *Sam.* 8:17 Seraiah was the *s.*
20:25 Sheva was *s.* and Zadok
2 *K.* 18:18 Shebna the *s.* 37; 19:2; *Is.* 36:3, 22; 37:2
22:3 Sha. the *s.* 8, 9, 10, 12; 2 *Ch.* 34:15, 18, 20; *Jer.* 36:10
25:19 princ. *s.* of host, *Jer.* 52:25
1 *Chr.* 24:8 Shemaiah *s.* wrote
27:32 Jona. a wise man and a *s.*

SCY

Ezr. 4:8 Shimshai the *s.* wrote a letter, 9, 17, 23
7:6 Ezra, a ready *s.* 11, 12; *Neh.* 8:4, 9, 13; 12:26, 36
Neh. 8:4 Ezra, *s.* stood on pulpit
Is. 33:18 where is the *s.?*
Jer. 36:12 Elishama the *s.* 20, 21
26 take Baruch the *s.* and Jer.
37:15 house of Jonath. the *s.* 20
Mat. 8:19 a *s.* said, Master, I will
13:52 *s.* instructed unto kingd.
Mark 12:32 *s.* said unto him
1 *Cor.* 1:20 where is the *s.?*

SCRIBES.
1 *Chr.* 2:55 the families of the *s.*
2 *Chr.* 34:13 of Lev. there were *s.*
Est. 3:12 king's *s.* called, 8:9
Jer. 8:8 pen of the *s.* is in vain
Mat. 5:20 ex. righteousness of *s.*
7:29 not as the *s. Mark* 1:22
16:21 suffer many things of *s.*
17:10 say *s.* E. must, *Mark* 9:11
20:18 betrayed to *s. Mark* 10:33
21:15 when the *s.* saw, they we.
23:2 *s.* and Phari. sit in M. seat
13 woe to y. *s.* 14:29; *Lu.* 11:44
Mark 2:6 went certain *s.* reason.
16 when the *s.* saw him cast wi.
8:31 be rejected of *s. Luke* 9:22
9:14 *s.* questioning with discip.
11:18 *s.* and c.-priests, *Lu.* 19:47
12:35 *s.* say Christ is son of D. 1
38 said, Bew. of *s. Luke* 20:46
Luke 5:30 *s.* and Pharisees, 15:2
6:7 *s.* and Pharis. watched him
11:53 *s.* began to urge vehem.
20:1 *s.* came upon him, elders
19 priests and *s.* sought to lay
23:10 *s.* stood and accused him
John 8:3 the *s.* brought a woman
Acts 4:5 *s.* gathered ag. apostles
6:12 *s.* brou. Stephen to council
23:9 *s.* of Pharisees' part arose

SCRIP.
1 *Sam.* 17:40 D. put stones in *s.*
Mat. 10:10 nor *s.* for your journ.
Mark 6:8; *Luke* 9:3; 10:4
Luke 22:35 I sent you without *s.*
36 let him take his purse and *s.*

SCRIPTURE.
Dan. 10:21 what is noted in *s.*
Mark 12:10 ha. ye not read this *s.*
15:28 *s.* was fulfilled which saith
Luke 4:21 this day is *s.* fulfilled
John 2:22 they believed the *s.*
7:42 hath not *s.* said, Ch. com. ?
10:35 the *s.* cannot be broken
19:35 another *s.* saith, They sh.
Acts 1:16 this *s.* must needs have
8:32 place of *s.* which he read
33 Philip began at the same *s.*
Rom. 4:3 what *s.?* 11; *Gal.* 4:30
9:17 *s.* saith, 10:11; 1 *Tim.* 5:18
Gal. 3:8 the *s.* foreseeing that G.
22 the *s.* hath concluded all
2 *Tim.* 3:16 *s.* is by inspi. of G.
Jam. 4:5 think *s.* saith in vain ?
1 *Pet.* 2:6 it is contained in *s.*
2 *Pet.* 1:20 no *s.* is of priv. inter.

SCRIPTURES.
Mat. 21:42 ha. ye nev. read in *s.*
22:29 not know *s. Mark* 12:24
26:54 how shall *s.* be fulfilled ?
Mark 14:49 *s.* must be fulfilled
Luke 24:27 he expounded in all *s.*
32 while he opened to us the *s.*
45 that they mi. understand *s.*
John 5:39 search *s.* for in them
Acts 17:2 he reasoned out of *s.*
11 they searched the *s.* daily
18:24 Apollos, mighty in the *s.*
28 showing by *s.* Jesus was C.
Rom. 1:2 afore by proph. in *s.*
15:4 thro' comf. of *s.* have hope
16:26 by the *s.* made known
1 *Cor.* 15:3 Christ died acc. to *s.*
4 Christ rose according to the *s.*
2 *Tim.* 3:15 from child hast kn. *s.*
2 *Pet.* 3:16 as they do also oth. *s.*

SCROLL.
Is. 34:4 heav. sh. he rolled as *s.*
Rev. 6:14 heaven departed as a *s.*

SCUM.
Ezek. 24:6 woe to the pot wh. *s.*
12 her *s.* went out, her *s.*

SCURVY.
Lev. 21:20 none eh. ap. that is *s.*
22:22 *s.* or scabbed sh. not offer

SCYTHIAN.
Col. 3:11 is neither barbarian, S.

SEA

SEA.
Ex. 14:16 stretch hand over *s.* 27
21 Lord caused the *s.* to go back, made the *s.* dry
15:10 blow, the *s.* covered them
20:11 L. made the *s. Ps.* 95:5;
Jon. 1:9; *Acts* 4:24; 14:15
Deut. 30:13 nor is it beyond *s.*
Jos. 24:7 brought *s.* upon them
1 *K.* 7:23 a molten *s.* 2 *Chr.* 4:2
39 set *s.* on right side of house
10:22 king had at *s.* a navy
18:43 go up, look toward the *s.*
2 *K.* 14:25 he restored coast to *s.*
16:17 Ahaz took down the *s.*
25:13 *s.* did Chaldees break, 16 *Jer.* 52:17
Job 6:11; 38:7
2 *Chr.* 4:15 *s.* for priests to wash
20:2 multi↑. against beyond *s.*
Neh. 9:11 didst divi. *s.* went thro' the *s. Job* 26:12; *Ps.* 74:13; 78:13; *Jer.* 31:35
Job 7:12 am I a *s.?* 38:8 shut *s.?*
11:9 measure is broader than *s.*
14:11 as the waters fail from *s.*
28:14 *s.* saith, It is not with me
41:31 maketh the *s.* like a pot
Ps. 66:6 he turned *s.* to dry land
72:8 have dominion from *s.* to *s.*
78:53 *s.* overwhelmed th. enem.
104:25 this great and wide *s.*
107:23 go down to *s.* in ships
114:3 the *s.* saw it; 5 O thou *s.*
Prov. 8:29 gave to *s.* his decree
Is. 11:9 wat. cover *s. Hab.* 9:14
16:8 branches stretched over *s.*
19:5 waters shall fail from *s.*
23:2 merch. of Zid. pass over *s.*
4 be ashamed, *s.* hath spoken
11 he stretched his hand ov. *s.*
24:14 they shall cry cloud fr. *s.*
42:10 sing to L. ye that go to *s.*
50:2 at my rebuke I dry up *s.*
51:10 art thou w. hath dried *s.?*
57:20 wicked are like troubled *s.*
Jer. 6:23 their voice roar. like *s.*
27:19 saith L. the pillars and *s.*
48:32 plants are gone over *s.*
50:42 their voice sh. roar like *s.*
51:36 I will dry up her *s.*
42 *s.* is come up upon Babylon
Lam. 2:13 breach is great like *s.*
Ezek. 26:3 *s.* causeth his waves
Dan. 7:3 great beasts came fr. *s.*
Amos 8:12 wander from *s.* to *s.*
Jon. 1:11 that *s.* may be calm?
Mic. 7:12 shall come from *s.* to *s.*
Nah. 1:4 he rebuketh the *s.* and
Hab. 3:8 wrath ag. *s.* that didst
15 thou didst walk through *s.*
Hag. 2:6 I shake heav. earth, *s.*
Zec. 9:10 his domin. from *s.* to *s.*
10:11 he shall pass through *s.*
Mat. 8:26 he arose and rebuk. *s.*
27 *s.* obey him, *Mark* 4:39, 41
13:1 Je. went out of ho. sat by *s.*
Luke 21:25 *s.* and waves roaring
Acts 27:30 commit. themsel. to *s.*
28:4 tho' he hath escaped the *s.*
1 *Cor.* 10:1 fathers passed thro' *s.*
Rev. 4:6 before throne was *s.* of
7:2 given to hurt earth and *s.*
10:6 created *s.* things therein
14:7 worship him that made *s.*
15:2 I saw as *s.* of glass, mingled
20:13 the *s.* gave up the dead.
21:1 and there was no more *s.*

By the SEA.
Ex. 14:9 them encamp. by *s. s.*
2 *Sam.* 17:11 Is. as sand by the *s.*
1 *K.* 5:9 I will convey them by the *s.* 2 *Chr.* 2:16
Is. 18:2 sendeth ambassad. by *s.*
Mark 4:1 multitude was by the *s.*
Rev. 18:17 many as trade by *s. s.*

See COAST, GREAT.

In, and into the SEA.
Ex. 15:1 horse and rider *into* *s. s.*
4 Pha.'s host he cast *into* the *s.*
Ps. 77:19 thy way *in* the *s.*
89:25 I will set his hand *in* *s. s.*
Is. 1:7 all rivers run *into* the *s.*
Ezek. 43:16 nath. way *in* the *s.*
Ezek. 20:37 city strong *in* the *s.*
18 isles that are *in* the *s.*
47:8 waters go *into* the *s.* which brought forth *into* the *s.*
Zec. 9:4 mighty tempest *in* the *s.*
12 and cast me *into* the *s.* 15
Mat. 8:24 arose a tempe. *in* the *s.*
10:11 smite hor. power *in* the *s.*
13:47 kingdom of heaven is like a net cast *into* the *s.*

CRUDEN'S CONCORDANCE.   1009

SEA
Mat. 21:21 cast *into* the *s*. *Mark* 11:23
Mark 9:42 we. cast *i. s. Lu.* 17:2
Luke 17:6 be thou plant. *in t. s.*
John 21:7 Pe. cast himself *i. t. s.*
Acts 27:38 cast out wheat *i. t. s.*
48 cast themselves *into the s.*
2 *Cor.* 11:26 in perils *in the s.*
Jam. 3:7 beasts and thi. *in the s.*
Rev. 5:13 ev. creature *in the s.*
16:3 ev. living soul died *in t. s.*
18:19 all that had ships *in t. s.*

Of the SEA.
Gen. 1:26 have dominion over the fish *of the s.* 28; *Ps.* 8:8
9:2 fear upon fishes *of the s.*
32:12 seed as sand *of the s.*
49:13 Z. dwell at haven *of t. s.*
Ex. 15:19 bro. ag. waters *of t. s.*
Num. 11:22 shall fish *of the s.* be
2 *Sam.* 22:16 channels *of t. s.* ap.
4 *K.* 18:14 aris. cloud out *of t. s.*
Job 6:3 heavier than sand *of t. s.*
9:8 tread. upon waves *of the s.*
12:8 fishes *of the s.* sh. declare
36:30 he covereth bot. *of the s.*
38:16 enter into springs *of t. s.*
Ps. 33:7 gathereth waters *of t. s.*
68:22 people fr. depths *of the s.*
89:9 rulest the raging *of the s.*
93:4 mightier th. waves *of t. s.*
135:6 dwell in utte. parts *of t. s.*
Is. 5:30 like roaring *of the s.*
9:1 afflict her by way *of the s.*
10:22 Is. he as sand *of t. s. Hos.* 1:10; *Rom.* 9:27
23:4 even strength *of the s*
51:10 made depths *of the s.*
60:5 abundance *of the s.* sh. be
63:11 bro. them up out *of the s.*
Jer. 5:22 sand for bound *of the s.*
33:22 nei. sand *of t. s.* be meas.
Ezek. 26:16 princes *of the s.*
27:3 Tyrus, at entry *of the s.*
9 ships *of the s.* were in thee
38:20 fishes *of the s.* sh. shake
Hos. 4:3 fishes *of the s.* be taken
Amos 5:8 call waters *of t. s.* 9:6
9:3 hid from sight in bot. *of t. s.*
Mal. 7:19 cast sins in. dep. *of t. s.*
Hab. 1:14 men as fishes *of the s.*
Zep. 1:3 I will con. fishes *of s.*
Mat. 4:15 by way *of the s.* bey. J.
18:6 drowned in depth *of the s.*
Jam. 1:6 wav. is like wave *of s.*
Jude 13 raging waves *of the s.*
Rev. 8:8 third part *of the s.* bec.
13:1 beast rise out *of the s.*
20:8 number is as sand *of the s.*

See NINETH.

On, or upon the SEA.
Ps. 65:5 afar off *upon the s.*
Mat. 40:25 faint-hearted, sor. *on s.*
the s. Mark 6:48; *John* 6:19
Rep. 7:1 wind sho. not blow *o. s.*
16:2 set his right foot *upon t. s.*
15:2 saw th. stand *o. t. s.* of gla.
16:3 poured out vial *upon t. s.*

SEAFARING.
Ezek. 26:17 was inhab. *of s.* men

SEA-MONSTERS.
Lam. 4:3 even the *s.-m.* draw out

See MEN, SALT, SAND.

SEA-SHORE.
Gen. 22:17 seed as sand on *s.-s.*
Ex. 14:30 Egyp. dead upon *s.-s.*
Jos. 11:4 as sand upon *s.-s.*
Jud. 5:17 Asher contin. on *s.-s.*
1 *Sam.* 13:5 Phil. as sand on *s.-s.*
1 *K.* 4:29 heart as sand on *s.-s.*
Jer. 47:7 a charge against *s.-s.*
Heb. 11:12 sand by *s.-s.*

SEASIDE.
Deut. 1:7 turn ye, and go by *s.*
Jud. 7:12 Midi. lay as sand by *s.*
2 *Chr.* 8:17 Solomon went to *s.*
Mat. 13:1 Jesus sat by the *s.*
Mark 2:13 he went again by *s.*
4:1 he began to teach by the *s.*
Acts 10:6 Sim. house is by *s.* 32

SEAS.
Gen. 1:10 gath. of wat. called *s.*
22 and fill the waters in the *s.*
Deut. 33:19 suck of abund. of *s.*
Neh. 9:6 thou hast made the *s.*
Ps. 8:8 passeth thro' paths of *s.*
24:2 he founded it upon the *s.*
65:7 stilleth the noise of the *s.*
69:34 let the *s.* praise him
135:6 Lord pleased. did he in *s.*
Is. 17:12 noise like noise of *s.*
Jer. 15:8 wid. are mo. sand of *s.*
Ezek. 27:1 bor. are in midst of *s.*
25 made glorious in midst of *s.*

G 4

SEA
Ezek. 27:26 in the midst of *s.* 34
28:2 in seat of G. in midst of *s.*
8 slain in the midst of the *s.*
Dan. 11:45 taber. of palace bet. *s.*
Jon. 2:3 cast me into midst of *s.*
Acts 27:41 place wh. two *s.* met

SEAL, Substantive.
1 *K.* 21:8 Jez. sealed wi. Ah. *s.*
Job 38:14 turned as clay to the *s.*
41:15 scales shut with a close *s.*
Cant. 8:6 *s.* on heart, *s.* on arm
John 3:33 his *s.* that God is true
Rom. 4:11 circum. as *s.* of right.
1 *Cor.* 9:2 *s.* of mine apostleship
2 *Tim.* 2:19 hav. this *s.* the Lord
Rev. 6:3 the sec. *s.* 5 the third *s.*
7 the fourth *s.* 9 the fifth *s.*
12 when he opened the sixth *s.*
7:2 having *s.* of the living God
8:1 when he opened seventh *s.*
9:4 hurt those that have not *s.*
20:3 shut him up, set a *s.* upon

SEALS.
Rev. 5:1 book sealed with 7 *s.*
5 lion of J. prevail. to loose *s.*
9 thou art worthy to open *s.*
6:1 the Lamb opened one of *s.*

SEAL, Verb.
Neh. 9:38 prin. and priests *s.* 10:1
Is. 8:16 *s.* law am. my disciples
Dan. 9:24 to *s.* up vision
12:4 D. shut up words, *s.* book
Rev. 10:4 *s.* th. things 7 thunders
22:10 *s.* not sayings of prophecy

SEALED.
Deut. 32:34 is not this *s.* among?
1 *K.* 21:8 letters were *s.* wi. Ah.
Est. 8:12 *s.* wi. king's ring, 8:8
Job 14:17 transgress. *s.* in a bag
Cant. 4:12 my spouse is foun. *s.*
Is. 29:11 vis. as words of book *s.*
Jer. 32:10 I subscri. and *s.* evid.
Dan. 6:17 king *s.* it with *s.* sign.
12:9 words are closed up, and *s.*
John 6:27 him hath *s.*
Rom. 15:28 when I have *s.* to th.
2 *Cor.* 1:22 who hath *s.* and giv.
Eph. 1:13 ye were *s.* with H. Sp.
4:30 whereby ye are *s.* to-day
Rev. 5:1 book *s.* with sev. seals
7:3 hurt not earth, till *s.* serv.
4 I heard number of them *s.*
5 of Jud. were *s.* 12,000, 6, 7, 8

SEALEST, ETH, ING.
Job 9:7 sun, and *s.* up the stars
33:16 and *s.* their instruction
37:7 he *s.* up hand of ev. man
Ezek. 28:12 thou *s.* sum of wisd.
Mat. 27:66 *s.* stone and setting

SEAM.
John 19:23 coat was without *s.*

SEARCH, Substantive.
Ezr. 4:15 that *s.* be made, 6:1
19 *s.* hath been ma. found, 6:1
Job 8:8 prepare thyself to the *s.*
38:16 hast th. walked in the *s.*
Ps. 64:6 accomplish a diligent *s.*
77:6 my spirit made diligent *s.*
Jer. 2:34 not found it by secret *s.*

See APPOINTED, DUE.

SEARCH, Verb.
Num. 13:2 that they may *s.* the land
14:7 land we passed to *s.* is good
Jos. 2:2 men of Is. to *s.* country, *s.*
Jud. 18:2 Danites sent men to *s.*
1 *Sam.* 23:23 I will *s.* him out
2 *Sam.* 10:3 not *s.* the city, 1 *Chr.* 19:3
2 *K.* 10:23 take, and *s.*
Job 13:9 good that he should *s.*
Ps. 44:21 sh. not G. *s.* this out?
139:23 *s.* me, O G. kn. my heart
Prov. 25:2 honor of kings *s.* mat.
27 men to *s.* their own glory
Ec. 1:13 heart to *s.* by wisd. 7:25
Jer. 17:10 I the Lord *s.* heart
29:13 shall *s.* for me with heart
Lam. 3:40 let us *s.* our ways
Ezek. 34:6 none did *s.* nor seek
8 neither did my shepherds *s.*
11 will both *s.* my sheep
39:14 end of 7 months th. they *s.*
Amos 9:3 J. down, thence will *s.*
Zep. 1:12 *s.* Jerus. with candles
Mat. 2:8 *s.* dilig. for young child
John 5:39 *s.* scrip. they testify
7:52 *s.* out of L. ariseth no proph.

SEARCHED.
Gen. 31:31 Lab. *s.* found not, 35
34 bro. evil report of land, *s.*

SEA
Num. 14:34 after number of days *s.* land
Deut. 1:24 came to Eshcol, *s.* it
Job 5:27 *s.* it, know it for good
28:27 he prepared it, *s.* it out
29:16 cause I knew not I *s.* out
32:11 wh. ye *s.* out what to say
36:26 number of his years *s.* out
Ps. 139:1 O L. thou hast *s.* me
Jer. 31:37 founda. of earth *s.* out
46:23 forest, tho' it cannot be *s.*
Ob. 6 how things of Esau *s.* out
Acts 17:11 Bereans *s.* scriptures
1 *Pet.* 1:10 prophets *s.* diligently

SEARCHEST, ETH.
1 *Chr.* 28:9 the Lord *s.* all hearts
Job 10:6 th. thou *s.* after my sin
28:3 and he *s.* out all perfection
39:8 he *s.* after ev. green thing
Prov. 2:4 if thou *s.* as for treas.
18:17 neighbor cometh, *s.* him
28:11 poor th. hath under. *s.* out
Rom. 8:27 *s.* knows mind of Spi.
1 *Cor.* 2:10 Spirit *s.* all things
Rev. 2:23 I am he wh. *s.* reins

SEARCHING, S.
Num. 13:25 ret. from *s.* of land
Jud. 5:16 divisions of Reuben *s.*
Job 11:7 canst thou by *s.* find G.
Prov. 20:27 *s.* inw. parts of belly
Is. 40:28 no *s.* of his understand.
1 *Pet.* 1:11 *s.* what time Sp. of C.

SEARED.
1 *Tim.* 4:2 consc. *s.* wi. hot iron

SEASON, Substantive.
Gen. 40:4 continued a *s.* in ward
Ex. 13:10 keep ordin. in this *s.*
Num. 9:2 Is. comest out of E.
28:12 give rain unto land in *s.*
Jos. 24:7 dw. in wildern. long *s.*
2 *K.* 4:16 this *s.* embrace a son
1 *Chr.* 21:29 altar an *s.* at G.
2 *Chr.* 15:3 for *s.* been with. God
Job 5:26 as corn cometh in his *s.*
38:32 bri. forth Mazzaroth in *s.*
Ps. 1:3 bringeth fruit in his *s.*
22:2 cry in night *s.* not silent
Prov. 15:23 word in *s.* how good?
Ec. 3:1 to every thing th. is a *s.*
Is. 50:4 to speak a word in *s.*
Jer. 5:24 former and lat. rain in *s.*
33:20 not be day and ni. in th. *s.*
Dan. 7:13 lives prolong. for a *s.*
Hos. 2:9 take away wine in *s.*
Mark 12:2 at *s.* he sent to hush.
Luke 1:20 words fulfilled in *s.*
4:13 devil dep. from him for *s.*
13:1 present at that *s. some*
20:10 at the *s.* he sent servant
23:8 desir. to see him a long *s.*
John 5:4 angel went down at *s.*
35 willing for a *s.* to rejoice
Acts 13:11 not seeing sun for *s.*
19:22 himself stayed in A. a *s.*
24:25 convenient *s.* I will call
2 *Cor.* 7:8 though but for a *s.*
2 *Tim.* 4:2 Instant by *s.* out of *s.*
Phile. 15 therefore departed a *s.*
Heb. 11:25 pleas. of sin for a *s.*
1 *Pet.* 1:6 for *s.* if need be
Rev. 6:11 sho. rest yet a little *s.*
20:3 after that loosed a little *s.*

SEASONS.
Gen. 1:14 lights be for signs, *s.*
Ex. 18:22 judge peo. at all *s.* 26
Lev. 23:4 feasts proc. in their *s.*
Ps. 16:7 reins instr. in night *s.*
104:19 appointeth moon for *s.*
Dan. 2:21 changeth times and *s.*
Mat. 21:41 render fruits in th. *s.*
Acts 1:7 not for you to know *s.*
14:17 gave us rain and fruitful *s.*
20:18 I been with you at all *s.*
1 *Thes.* 5:1 of *s.* have no need

SEASON, ED.
Lev. 2:13 shalt thou *s.* with salt
Mark 9:50 wherew. will *s.* it?
Luke 14:31 wherew. sh. it be *s.*?
Col. 4:6 speech be with grace, *s.*

SEAT.
Jud. 3:20 Egl. rose off of his *s.*
1 *Sam.* 1:9 Eli *s.* upon a *s.* 4:13
4:18 he fell from off *s.* backw.
20:18 bec. th. *s.* will be empty
25 sat on *s.* on *s.* by wall
1 *K.* 2:19 a *s.* for king's mother
10:19 stays on each side of *s.*
Est. 3:1 H.'s *s.* above princes
Job 23:3 that I mi. come to *s.*
29:7 I prepared my *s.* in street
Ps. 1:1 sitteth in *s.* of scornful
Prov. 9:14 woman sitteth on *s.*
Ezek. 8:3 *s.* of image of jealousy
Amos 6:3 ye cause *s.* of violence
Mat. 23:2 scribes sit in Moses' *s.*
Rev. 2:13 dwell. where Satan's *s.*

See JUDGMENT, MERCY.

SEATED.
Deut. 33:21 lawgiver was he *s.*

SEATS.
Mat. 21:12 *s.* of them that sold doves, *Mark* 11:15
23:6 chief *s.* in syr. *Mark* 12:39
Luke 1:52 put mighty fr. their *s.*
11:43 ye love uppermost *s.* 20:46
Rev. 4:4 four and twenty *s.* upon th. twenty-four elders
11:16 elders sat before G. on *s.*

SEC
Amos 6:3 cause *s.* of viol. come
Mat. 23:2 Phar. sit in Moses' *s.*
Rev. 2:13 dwel. where Satan's *s.*

See JUDGMENT, MERCY.

SEATED.
Deut. 33:21 lawgiver was he *s.*

SEATS.
Mat. 21:12 *s.* of them that sold doves, *Mark* 11:15

SEBA.
Gen. 10:7 sons of Cush, S. and
Ps. 72:10 kings of Sheba and S.
Is. 43:3 I gave Ethiopia and S.

SEBAT. *Zec.* 1:7

SECOND.
Ex. 26:4 the coupling of the *s.* 5:10; 36:11, 12, 17
28:18 *s.* row he emerald, 39:11
Lev. 5:10 offer *s.* for burnt offer.
Num. 2:16 set forth in *s.* rank
2 *K.* 9:19 he sent *s.* on horseback
1 *Chr.* 15:18 brethren of *s.* degree
Ez. 4:8 one alone, th. is not a *s.*
15 *s.* child stand up in *s.* and
Ezek. 10:14 *s.* face was face of m.
Dan. 7:5 beast, *s.* like to a bear
Mat. 21:30 to *s.* said likewise
22:26 likewise the *s.* had the *s.*
Mark 12:21 ; *Luke* 20:30
John 8:17 *s.* came saying. I and
John 4:54 *s.* miracle Jesus did
Acts 12:10 were past *s.* ward
1 *Cor.* 15:47 *s.* man L. fr. heaven
Heb. 10:9 aw. first, may estab. *s.*
2 *Pet.* 3:1 epistle I write you
Rev. 2:11 not hurt of *s.* dea. 20:6
20:14 hell, this is *s.* death, 21:8

See DAY, MONTH.

SECOND time.
Gen. 43:10 had returned *s.* time
Lev. 13:56 washed the *s. time*
1 *Sam.* 26:8 I will not smite *s. t.*
1 *K.* 18:34 do it *s. t.* did it *s. t.*
2 *K.* 10:6 John wrote letter *s. t.*
Is. 11:11 L. set his hand *s. time*
Jer. 1:13 word of Lord came to me *s. t.*; 13:3; 33:1
42:9 he went L. *t.* prayed
Mat. 14:72 *s. t.* the cock crew
John 3:4 enter *s. time* into womb
21:16 Jesus saith to Pe. *s. time*
Acts 10:15 voice spake to P. *s. t.*
1 *Cor.* 12:2 if I write you a *s. t.*
Heb. 9:28 he shall appear *s. time*

SECOND year.
Gen. 47:18 they came the *s. y.* to Joseph, and said, *Num.* 1:1
Num. 9:1 first month of *s. y.* L.
10:11 *s. y.* cloud was taken up
2 *K.* 19:29 *s. y.* that wh. springeth of same, *Is.* 37:30

SECONDARILY.
1 *Cor.* 12:28 God set *s.* prophets

SECRET, Substantive.
Gen. 49:6 come not into their *s.*
Job 15:8 hast th. heard *s.* of G. ?
29:4 wh. *s.* of G. was upon tab.
40:13 and bind their face in *s.*
Ps. 25:14 *s.* of Lord with them
27:5 in *s.* of tabernacle, 31:20
64:2 may shoot in *s.* at perfect
91:1 dwelleth in *s.* place of most
Prov. 3:32 *s.* is with righteous
9:17 bread eaten in *s.* pleasant
21:14 a gift in *s.* pacifieth anger
23:9 discover not *s.* to another
25:9 not spoken in *s.* 48:16
Dan. 2:18 mercies of G. conc. *s.*
19 then was *s.* revealed to D.
30 *s.* not revealed to me
Amos 3:7 reveals. *s.* to his ser.
Mat. 6:4 alms may be in *s.*
Fath. wh. seeth in *s.* 6, 18
6 pray to Father wh. is in *s.*
18 appear to fast to Fath. in *s.*
John 7:4 doeth any thing in *s.*
no man that doeth in *s.*
18:20 openly, in *s.* said noth.
Eph. 5:12 thi. done of them in *s.*

SECRET, Adjective.
Deut. 27:15 put. idol in *s.* place
29:29 *s.* things belong unto L.
Jud. 3:19 I have *s.* errand
13:18 askest my name, it is *s.* ?
1 *Sam.* 5:9 emerods in *s.* parts

CRUDEN'S CONCORDANCE.

SEE

1 *Sam.* 19:3 abide in *s.* place
Job 14:13 th. thou keep me in *s.*
15:11 is any *s.* thing with thee?
20:26 darkness be hid in *s.* pla.
Ps. 10:9 in *s.* places doth murder
17:12 lion lurking in *s.* places
18:11 made darkn. his *s.* place
19:12 cle. thou me from *s.* faults
64:2 hide me fr. *s.* counsel of wic.
81:7 I answered thee to *s.*
95:2 *s.* sins in light of countena.
91:1 dwel. in *s.* place of Most H.
Prov. 27:5 rebuke bet. th. *s.* love
Ec. 12:14 to judgment ev. *s.* thi.
Cant. 2:14 that art in *s.* places
Is. 3:17 L. will discover *s.* parts
45:3 riches of *s.* places
Jer. 2:34 not found by *s.* search
13:17 soul sh. weep in *s.* places
23:24 hide himself in *s.* places
49:10 I have uncovered *s.* places
Lam. 3:10 as lion in *s.* places
Ezek. 7:22 pollute my *s.* place
Dan. 2:22 reveal. deep *s.* things
Mat. 13:35 kept *s.* from foundation of world, *Rom.* 16:25
24:26 behold, he is in *s.* chamb.
Mark 4:22 nor was any thi. kept *s. Luke* 8:17
Luke 11:33 put. candle in *s.* place

SECRETS.

Deut. 25:11 wife tak. him by *s.*
Job 11:6 shew thee *s.* of wisdom
Ps. 44:21 he knoweth *s.* of heart
Prov. 11:13 talebearer reveal. *s.*
20:19 as a talebearer, reveal. *s.*
Dan. 2:28 a God that revealeth *s.*
29 that revealeth *s.* make. kn.
47 your God is a revealer of *s.*
Rom. 2:16 God shall judge the *s.*
1 *Cor.* 14:25 thus are *s.* of heart

SECRETLY.

Gen. 31:27 wheref. didst flee *s.?*
Deut. 13:6 if bro. entice thee *s.*
27:24 smiteth his neighbour *s.*
28:57 eat for want of things *s.*
Job 2:1 sent two men to spy *s.*
1 *Sam.* 18:22 comm. with Dav. *s.*
21:9 Saul *s.* practised mischief
2 *K.* 17:9 did *s.* things not right
Job 4:12 a thing was *s.* bro. me
13:10 reprove, if you *s.* accept
31:27 heart hath been *s.* enticed
Ps. 10:9 lieth in wait *s.* as a lion
31:20 keep them *s.* in pavilion
Jer. 37:17 Zedekiah asked him *s.*
Hab. 3:14 to devour the poor *s.*
John 11:28 called M. her sister *s.*
19:38 Joseph was a disciple, *s.*

SECT.

Acts 5:17 wh. is *s.* of Sadducees
15:5 the *s.* of Pharisees believed
24:5 of the *s.* of the Nazarenes
26:5 straitest *s.* of our religion
28:22 *s.* everywhere spo. against

SECURE.

Jud. 8:11 smote host, it was *s.*
18:7 after manner of Zidoni. *s.*
Job 11:18 thou shalt be *s.*
12:6 they that provoke G. are *s.*
Mat. 28:14 persuade him, *s.* you

SECURELY.

Prov. 3:29 seeing he dwelleth *s.*
Mic. 2:8 them that pass by *s.*

SECURITY.

Acts 17:9 when they had taken *s.*

SEDITION,

Ezr. 4:15 moved *s.* in city, 19
Luke 23:19 for *s.* in prison, 25
Acts 21:5 this man mover of *s.*
Gal. 5:20 works of flesh are *s.*

SEDUCE, ED.

2 *K.* 21:9 Manasseh *s.* them to do
Is. 19:13 they have also *s.* Egypt
Ezek. 13:10 they have *s.* my peo.
Mark 13:22 signs and wonders *s.*
1 *John* 2:26 concern. them that *s.*
Rev. 2:20 Jezebel to *s.* my serv.

SEDUCERS.

2 *Tim.* 3:13 *s.* shall wax worse

SEDUCETH, ING.

Prov. 12:26 way of wicked *s.*
1 *Tim.* 4:1 giving heed to *s.* spi.

SEE.

Gen. 2:19 to *s.* what he won, call
11:5 Lord came down to *s.* city
41:33 and *s.* if my face no more
43:3 ye *s.* my face no more
43:12 your eyes *s.* the eyes of
s. will go and *s.* Joseph bef.
48:11 I had not tho. to *s.* face
Ex. 3:3 *s.* this great sight, 4
5:19 officers *s.* th. were in evil
6:1 shalt *s.* what I will do to P.

Ex. 10:5 cannot be able to *s.* ear.
28 ta. heed, *s.* my face no mo.
12:13 when I *s.* blood
33:20 no man *s.* me and live
23 thou shalt *s.* my back parts
34:10 people shall *s.* work of L.
Lev. 13:10 priest shall *s.* him, 17
Num. 22:41 thence he might *s.*
23:9 from top of rocks I *s.* him
13 who, mayest *s.* them, sh. *s.*
24:17 I sh. *s.* him, but not now
32:11 none that came out of Eg.
shall *s.* the land, *Deut.* 1:35
Deut. 1:36 save C. he sh. *s.* land
3:25 I pray thee, let me *s.* land
28:34 eyes wh. thou shalt *s.* 67
68 thou shalt *s.* it no more
29:4 hath not given eyes to *s.*
32:20 *s.* what their end will be
39 *s.* now, I, even I, am he
33 thou shalt *s.* land bef. thee
34:4 I have caused thee to *s.*
Jos. 23:10 built great altar to *s.*
1 *Sam.* 13:35 came no more to *s.*
19:3 what I *s.* that I will tell
3 *Sam.* 13:5 when faith, com. to *s.*
14:32 let me *s.* the king's face
1 *K.* 12:16 now *s.* to thine own house, David, 2 *Chr.* 10:16
22:25 *s.* that day, 2 *Chr.* 18:24
2 *K.* 2:10 *s.* when I am taken
6:17 open his eyes th. he may *s.*
20 open eyes that they may *s.*
7:2 shalt *s.* it with thi. eyes, 19
18 send and *s.* 14 go and *s.*
10:16 *s.* my zeal for the Lord
19:16 open, Lord, thine eyes, and *s. Is.* 37:17
22:17 what title is that that I *s.*
2 *Chr.* 25:17 let us *s.* one another
Job 9:17 mine eye no more *s.* good
8 eye th. ha. seen me, *s.* no m.
9:25 days flee away, *s.* no good
17:15 my hope, who shall *s.* it?
19:26 in my flesh shall I *s.* God
27 whom I shall *s.* for myself
20:9 eye shall *s.* him no more
24:1 why do th. not *s.* his days?
15 adulterer sai. No eye sh. *s.*
33:28 his life shall *s.* the light
36:25 every man may *s.* it
Ps. 10:11 God will never *s.* it
14:2 G. looked to *s.* if any, 53:2
31:11 they that did *s.* me
34:8 O taste and *s.* Lord is good
12 many days, he may *s.* good
37:34 wicked cut off, sh. *s.* it
40:3 shall *s.* it and trust in Lord
41:6 *s.* me, he speaketh vanity
49:19 they shall never *s.* light
64:8 say, Who shall *s.* them ?
8 all that *s.* th. shall flee away
66:5 come and *s.* works of God
86:17 they wh. hate me may *s.*
113:8 *s.* his desire upon enemi.
10 wicked *s.* it and be grieved
119:74 be glad when they *s.* me
128:5 shalt *s.* the good of Jerus.
Ec. 1:10 be said, *s.* this is new
2:3 till I might *s.* wh. was good
3:22 to *s.* what sh. be after him
Ec. 6:10 lest *s.* with their eyes
26:11 they shall *s.* and be ashe.
30:20 thine eyes shall *s.* teachers
33:17 thine eyes sh. *s.* the king
41:20 that th. may *s.* and know
48:6 *s.* this; 49:7 kings shall *s.*
52:8 for they shall *s.* eye to eye
15 not been told them wh. th. *s.*
53:2 when we shall *s.* him
10 he shall *s.* his seed
60:5 thou sh. *s.* and flow toget.
61:9 all that *s.* them acknowl.
64:9 behold, *s.* we beseech
Jer. 1:11 I *s.* rod; 13 *s.* seeth. pot
3:10 *s.* if there be such a thing
10 *s.* that it is an evil thing
23 *s.* thy way in the valley
3:3 *s.* where thou hast not been
5:1 *s.* now and know, and seek
6:16 stand ye in the ways and *s.*
7:12 go and *s.* what I did to it
51:61 and shalt *s.* and shalt read
Ezek. 32:31 all the heath. shall *s.*
Dan. 3:25 lo, I *s.* four men loose
Joel 2:28 your young men sh. *s.* visions, *Acts* 2:17
Amos 5:2 pass ye to Cal. and *s.*
Mic. 7:10 mine enemy shall *s.* it
Hab. 2:1 *s.* what he will say
Zec. 5:2 answer, I *s.* flying roll
5 lift your eyes, *s.* what is this
9:5 Ashkelon sh. *s.* and fear
Mal. 1:5 your eyes shall *s.*
3:18 discern, and *s.* your res.

Mat. 8:4 *s.* thou tell no man,
9:30; *Mark* 1:44; *Acts* 23:22
11:4 tell John th. ye hear and *s.*
12:38 would *s.* a sign from thee
24:6 ware, *s.* ye be not troubled
27:4 *s.* thou to that; 24 *s.* to it
28:6 come *s.* place where L. lay
10 Galilee, there shall *s.* me
Mark 3:14 to *s.* what was done
32 *s.* her had done this thing
6:38 go and *s.* 8:24 *s.* men
Luke 2:15 go to Bethleh. and *s.*
3:6 all flesh sh. *s.* salv. of God
6:10 who enter may *s.* 11:33
9:9 he desired to *s.* him, 23:8
27 not taste of death till th. *s.*
14:18 press, I must go and *s.* it
17:22 when ye shall desire to *s.*
23 *s.* here, or *s.* there
19:3 Zaccheus sought to *s.* Jes.
John 1:39 come and *s.* 40; 11:34;
Rev. 6:1, 5, 7
50 thou shalt *s.* greater things
8:51 sayings, sh. never *s.* death
56 Abra. rejoiced to *s.* my day
9:15 do *s.* 25 blind, now I *s.*
39 th. who *s.* not might *s.* and
tho. who *s.* mi. be blind
12:21 saying, Sir, we would *s.* J.
16:22 but I will *s.* you again
Acts 20:25 *s.* my face no more, 38
22:14 know and *s.* that Just One
28:20 I called you, to *s.* you
Rom. 15:21 not sp. of, they sh. *s.*
1 *Cor.* 6:10 if any man *s.* thee
Phil. 1:27 whether I come and *s.*
2:23 soon as I *s.* how it will go
1 *Thes.* 3:17 to *s.* your face with
3:6 desir. to *s.* us, we to *s.* you
1 *Tim.* 6:16 hath seen, nor can *s.*
Heb. 12:14 without, holi. no man *s.*
12:25 come shortly, will *s.* you
1 *Pet.* 3:10 that will *s.* good days
1 *John* 5:16 if any man *s.* brother
3 *John* 14 I shall shortly *s.* thee
Rev. 1:7 every eye shall *s.* him
16:15 naked, they *s.* his shame
18:10 *s.* thou do it not, 22:9
22:4 and they shall *s.* his face

SEE not, or not SEE.

Gen. 21:16 not *s.* death of child
27:1 is, old, that he could *not s.*
43:3 ye shall *not s.* my face, 5
44:26 we may *not s.* man's face
48:10 eyes of Is. dim, could *n. s.*
Ex. 33:20 canst *not s.* my face
Num. 14:23 they shall *not s.*
23:13 ntmost part, shall *not s.*
1 *Sam.* 3:2 Eli could *not s.* 4:15
2 Sam. 3:13 *not s.* my face, exc.
14:24 let *not* Absal. *s.* my face
1 *K.* 14:4 Abijah could *not s.*
2 *K.* 3:17 n. *s.* wind, nor sh. ye *s.*
22:20 thine eyes shall *n. s.* evil
Job 9:11 goeth by, *s.* him *n.*
20:17 *n.* rivers of honey and
23:9 hideth that I cannot *s.* him
34:32 wh. I *s.* not teach thou me
35:14 thou shalt *not s.* him
37:21 men *s.* not bright light
Ps. 58:8 pass away, *not s.* sun
74:9 we *s. not* our signs, there is
89:48 liveth, that *not s.* death
94:7 say, The Lord shall *not s.*
9 formed eye, shall he *not s.?*
115:5 eyes, they *s. not*, 135:16
Is. 26:11 is lifted up, will *not s.*
33:19 th. shalt *not s.* a fierce peo.
38:11 I shall *not s.* the Lord
44:9 they *s. not*, they be asha.
18 shut eyes, that th. cannot *s.*
Jer. 5:21 eyes, *s. not*, *Ezek.* 12:12
12:4 he shall *not s.* our last end
14:13 ye shall *not s.* the sword
17:6 shall *not s.* when good com.
Ezek. 12:6 thou *s. not* ground, 12
-13 shall he *not s.* it, tho' he die
Dan. 3:25 gods of gold, wh. *s. not*
Jon. 3:10 thou shalt *not s.* evil
Mat. 13:13 seeing, *s. not*
23:39 shall *not s.* me, *Lu.* 13:35
24:2 *s.* ye *not* all these things?
Jer. 5:21 eyes, *s.* ye *not?*
Luke 8:10 s., dea. hef. *see* C.
8:10 seeing, they might *not s.*

Luke 17:22 desi. to *s.* ye sh. *not s.*
John 3:3 cannot *s.* kingd. of G.
36 shall *not s.* life, wrath ahid.
9:39 they who *s. not* might *s.*
12:40 that they should *not s.*
16:16 ye shall *not s.* me, 17, 19
18:26 did I *not s.* thee in gard. ?
Acts 22:11 I could *not s.* for glory
Rom. 11:8 th. they should *not s.*
10 darkened that may *not s.*
1 *Cor.* 16:7 for I will *not s.* you
Heb. 9:8 we *s. not* yet all things
11:5 that he should *not s.* death
1 *Pet.* 1:8 tho' now ye *s.* him *not*
2 *Pet.* 1:9 blind, can *not s.* a far

We SEE.

Ps. 36:9 in thy light shall *we s.*
Mark 15:32 *we* may *s. John* 6:30
John 9:41 *we s.* your sin remain.
1 *Cor.* 13:12 *we s.* thro' a glass
1 *Thes.* 3:10 pray. *we* might *s.*
Heb. 2:9 *we do s.* Jesus crowned

Ye SEE, or SEE ye.

Ex. 14:13 *ye s. s.* them no more
16:7 *ye* shall *s.* glory of Lord
Jos. 3:3 when *ye s.* ark of coven.
1 *Sam.* 10:24 *s.* ye him L. chos. ?
Cant. 6:13 what will *ye s.* in Sh.
Is. 6:9 *s.* ye indeed, perceive
Jer. 2:31 O generati. *s.* ye word
42:18 *ye* sh. *s.* this place no more
Ezek. 13:23 *ye* sh. *s.* no more va.
14:22 *ye* shall *s.* their way
Dan. 2:8 *ye s.* thing is gone
Mat. 13:17 have desired to *s.*
th. things *ye s. Luke* 10:23
24:33 when *ye* shall *s.* these th.
Mark 13:29; *Luke* 21:31
28:64 hereafter shall *ye s.* Son of man, *Mark* 14:62
27:24 *s.* ye to it, *Mark* 15:36
28:7 in Ga. shall *ye s. Mark* 16:7
John 14:19 but *ye* sh. *s.* 16:10 *ye s.*
16:16 a lit. *ye* shall *s.* me, 17, 19
Acts 2:33 wh. *ye* now *s.* and hear
25:24 *ye s.* this man, about wh.
1 *Pet.* 1:8 tho' now *ye s.* him *not*

SEEING,

Ex. 4:11 mak. dumb *s.* or blind?
22:10 driven away, no man *s.*
Num. 35:23 *s.* him not
Prov. 20:12 Lord maketh *s.* eye
Ec. 1:8 eye not satisfied with *s.*
Is. 21:3 dismayed at the *s.* of it
33:15 shut. his eyes from *s.* evil
42:20 *s.* many things, but
Mat. 13:13 beca. they *s. s.* not
14 *s.* ye shall see and shall *not*
perc. *Mark* 4:12; *Acts* 28:26
John 9:7 washed and came *s.*
Acts 13:11 not *s.* sun for a season
2 *Pet.* 2:8 *s.* and hearing, vexed

SEED.

Gen. 1:11 herbs yield. *s.* 12, 29
47:19 give *us s.* 23 here is *s.*
24 four parts sh. be own for *s.*
26:16 shall sow your *s.* in vain
27:16 estima. shall he acc. to *s.*
30 tithe of *s.* of land is Lord's
Num. 20:5 it is no place of *s.*
Deut. 11:10 Eg. where sowedst *s.*
28:38 carry much *s.* into field
39:39 shalt take tenth of *s.*
1 *K.* 18:32 conta. 2 measures of *s.*
Ps. 126:6 bearing precious *s.*
Ec. 3:10 *s.* of homer sh. yield ep.
17:11 make thy *s.* to flourish
55:10 it may give *s.* to sower
Jer. 35:7 sow *s.* nor plant viney.
Ezek. 17:5 he took of *s.* of land
Joel 1:17 *s.* is rotten under clods
Hag. 2:19 *s.* yet in barn?
Zec. 8:12 *s.* shall be prosperous
Mal. 2:3 I will corrupt your *s.*
Mat. 13:19 *s.* by way-side, 20
22 *s.* among thorns, 23
23 *s.* into good ground
24 man sowed good *s.* in field
27 soweth good *s.* in thy field
38 good *s.* are the children of
Mark 4:26 cast *s.* into ground
Luke 8:11 *s.* is the word of God
1 *Cor.* 15:38 ev. *s.* his own body
2 *Cor.* 9:10 minister. *s.* to sower
1 *Jn.* 1:23 born, not of corrup. *s.*
1 *John* 3:9 his *s.* remain. in him

See COPULATION.

SEED, for posterity.

Gen. 4:25 G. appoint. me ano. *s.*
7:3 keep *s.* alive on fa. of earth
13:15 Ab. said, To me giv. no *s.*

SEE

Luke 24:23 had s. vision of ang.
37 supposed they had s. a spirit
John 1:18 no man hath s. God at any time, 1 *John* 4:12
3:11 we testify that we have s.
32 what he hath s. and heard
4:45 Galileans had s. all he did
5:37 not at any time s. shape
6:46 not that any man s. Father
8:57 hast thou s. Abraham?
9:8 neighbors which had s. him
37 hast s. it is he that talketh
11:45 had seen what J. did, bel.
14:9 s. me hath s. the Father
15:24 s. and hated both me
20:18 she had s. L. 25 s. Lord
29 bec. thou hast s. believed
Acts 4:20 speak things we ha, s.
9:27 declared how he had s. L.
10:17 vision he had s. sho, mean
11:23 he had s. grace of God
16:10 after he had s. vision
40 s. brethren, comforted them
1 *Cor.* 2:9 eye hath not s. nor ear
9:1 have I not s. Je. Ch. our L.?
Phil. 4:9 things ye heard and s.
Col. 2:1 many as have not s. face
1 *Tim.* 6:16 wh. no man hath s.
1 *John* 1:1 we have s. with eyes
3 have s. declare we unto you
3:6 whoso. sin. hath not s. him
4:14 we have s. and do testify
20 brot. whom he hath s. how can he love G. he ha. not s.?
3 *John* 11 do. evil, hath not s. G.
Rev. 1:19 write thi. thou hast s.
22:8 heard and s. I fell down

HAVE I seen,
Gen. 7:1 thee h. I s. righteous
1 *Chr.* 23:17 now A. I s. people
Ez. 8:6 this h. I s. and applied
Jer. 46:5 whereof, h. I s. dismayed
Zec. 9:8 A. I s. with mine eyes

I have SEEN,
Gen. 32:30 I h. s. G. face to face
33:10 I have s. thy face, 46:30
Ex. 3:3 I h. s. oppression, 16
32:9 I h. s. people, *Deut.* 9:13
Jud. 6:22 bec. I h. s. an angel
2 *K.* 20:5 thus saith the Lord, I h. s. thy tears, *Is.* 38:5
Job 13:17 that wh. I h. s. I decl.
31:19 if I have s. any perish
Ps. 37:35 I h. s. wicked in power
Ec. 1:14 I h. s. works under sun
5:18 evil wh. I h. s. under sun
18 that wh. I h. s. good to eat
8:1 evil which I have s. 10:5
Is. 57:18 I have s. his ways
Jer. 7:11 behold, I h. s. it, sai. L.
Dan. 2:26 make kn. dream I h. s.
John 8:38 I speak that I have s.
Acts 7:34 I h. s. affliction of peo.

Ye have SEEN,
Ex. 14:13 Egypt. wh. ye have s.
19:4 ye h. s. what I did to Egy.
22:22 ye have s. that I talked
Deut. 2:2 ye have s. all, *Jos.* 23:3
Jud. 9:48 ye have s. what he have s. me do
1 *Sam.* 17:25 have ye s. this man
Job 27:12 ye yourselves h. s. it
Luke 7:22 tell J. what ye have s.
John 6:36 ye have s. believe not
8:38 ye do that ye h. s. with fa.
14:7 ye know him, have s. him
Acts 1:11 come as ye h. s. him go
Jam. 5:11 ye have s. end of Lord

SEEN, passively.
Gen. 22:14 mount of L. sh. be s.
Ex. 23:22 my face sh. not be s.
34:3 any man h. thro' mount
Num. 14:14 Lord s. face to face
Jud. 19:30 no deed done nor s.
2 *Sam.* 17:17 might not be s.
Is. 60:2 gl. shall be s. upon thee
Zec. 9:14 L. sh. be s. over them
Mat. 9:33 it was never so s. in I.
23:5 works do to be s. of men
Mark 16:11 he had been s. of her
Acts 1:9 s. of them go, 13:31
Rom. 1:20 invis. things clearly s.
8:24 hope that is s. is not hope
1 *Cor.* 15:5 he was s. of Cephas
6 was s. of above 500 brethren
7 s. of James; 8 was s. of me
2 *Cor.* 4:18 look not at things s.
Heb. 11:1 evid. of things not s.
3 things which are s. not made
7 N. warned of G. things not s.
13 hav. s. them were persuad.
1 *Pet.* 1:8 having not s. ye love

SEER.
1 *Sam.* 9:9 let us go to s. proph. was beforetime called s.
11 is s. here? 18 where s. hou.
19 Samuel answer. I am the s.

SEI

2 *Sam.* 15:27 Art thou not a s.?
2 *Chr.* 16:7 Hanani the s. came
18 did not Iddo the s. did ord.
25:5 Heman, king's s. in word
20:28 Samuel the s. had dedica.
29:29 acts of Da. writ. in book of Sam. s. in book of God, s.
2 *Chr.* 9:29 in visions of Iddo s.
12:15 Reheb. in book of Iddo. s.
16:7 Hanani the s. came to Asa
10 then Asa was wroth with s.
19:2 Jo. son of s. went to meet
29:25 commandment of Gad, s.
30 words of Da. and Asaph, s.
33:15 command. of Jeduthun, s.
Amos 7:12 O thou s. flee away

SEERS.
2 *K.* 17:13 against Is. and J. by s.
Is. 33:18 words of s. th. spake
19 written am. the sayings of s.
Is. 29:10 the s. hath he covered
30:10 who say to the s. see not
Mic. 3:7 then sh. s. be ashamed

SEEST.
Gen. 16:13 spake, Thou G. s. me
31:43 La. said, All thou s. is mi.
Ex. 10:28 day thou s. my face
Deut. 12:13 cv. place that thou s.
Jud. 9:36 s. shadow of mount.
1 *K.* 21:29 s. how Ahab humbleth
Job 10:4 s. thou as man seeth?
Is. 58:3 we fast, thou s. not?
7 when s. naked, cover him
Jer. 1:11 word came to Jeremi. What s. thou ? 13; 24:3; *Amos* 7:8; 8:2; *Zec.* 4:2; 5:2
7:17 s. th. not what th. do in J.
32:24 come to pass, beh. th. s. it
Ezek. 8:6 s. thou what they do?
40:4 declare all thou s. to Israel
Dan. 1:13 as thou s. deal wi. ser.
Luke 7:44 Simon s. thou wom.?
Jam. 2:22 s. thou how faith wro.
Rev. 1:11 what s. write in a book

SEETH.
Gen. 16:13 looked after him s.?
Ex. 4:14 wh. he s. thee, be glad
1 *Sam.* 16:7 L. s. not as man s.
2 *K.* 2:19 city pleasant, as lord s.
Job 28:10 eye s. precious thing
21 he s. under whole heaven
34:21 eyes on man, s. all goings
14:18 because it s. him not, her
28:1 that looked upon it, s. it
Ps. 37:13 b. s. his day is coming
46:10 he s. that wise men die
4:8 day nor night s. sleep
49:10 for he s. wise men die
10 wordel s. me no more
Eccl. 8:17 the Lord s. us not, 7:10
12:27 vision he s. for many days
18:14 son that s. father's sins
Mat. 6:4 Fa. who s. in sec. 6, 18
John 1:29 next day John s. Jesus
5:10 him what he s. Father do
6:40 who s. Son, and believeth
9:21 wh. means he s. we kn. not
12:45 s. me s. him sent me
14:18 because it s. him not, her
10 world s. me no more
Rom. 8:24 what a man s.
2 *Cor.* 12:6 above what he s. me
1 *John* 3:17 s. brother have need

SEETHE.
Ex. 16:23 to-day s. that ye will s.
23:19 sh. not s. a kid in mother's milk, 34:26; *Deut.* 14:21
29:31 s. his flesh in holy place
2 *K.* 4:38 s. pottage for sons of
Ezek. 24:5 let them s. bones
Zec. 14:21 come and s. therein

SEETHING.
1 *Sam.* 2:13 while flesh was s.
Job 41:20 smoke as out of s. pot
Jer. 1:13 what seest thou ? s. pot

SEGUB. 1 *K.* 16:34

SEIR.
Gen. 32:3 to the land of S. the
33:14 I come to my Lord to S.
36:30 sons of S. 21 ; 1 *Chr.* 1:38
Num. 24:18 S. sh. be a possessi.
Deut. 1:44 destroyed you in S.
33:2 Sinai and rose up from S.
Jud. 5:4 thou wentest out of S.
1 *Chr.* 4:42 500 went to mount S.
2 *Chr.* 20:10 children of mount S.

SEL

2 *Chr.* 20:22 ambushm. ag. m. S.
23 stood up against mount S.
Ezek. 25:8 ; 35:2 I am against S.
3 say to it, Behold, O mount S.
7 thus will I make mount S.

SEIZE, ED.
Jos. 8:7 rise up and s. upon city
Job 3:6 let darkness s. upon it
Ps. 55:15 let death s. upon them
Jer. 49:24 Damas, fear s. on her
Mat. 21:38 kill him, s. inherit.

SELAH.
Ps. 3:2 no help for him in God, s.
4 L. heard out of holy hill, s.
8 thy blessing upon people, s.
32:5 forgavest iniq. of my sin, s. *See Ps.* 4:2, 4; 7:5; 9:16, 20; 20:3; 21:2; 24:6, 10; 32:4, 7; 39:5, 11; 44:8; 46:3, 7, 11; 47:4; 48:8; 49:13, 15; 50:6; 52:3, 5; 54:3; 55:7, 19; 57:3, 6; 59:5, 13; 60:4; 61:4; 62:4, 8; 66:4, 7, 15; 67:1, 4; 68:7, 19, 32; 75:3; 76:3, 9; 77:3, 9, 15; 81:7; 82:2; 83:8; 84:4, 8; 85:2; 87:3, 6; 88:7, 10; 89:4, 37, 45, 48; 140:3, 5, 8; 143:6; *Hab.* 3:3, 9, 13

SELEUCIA.
Acts 13:4 they departed unto S.

Own SELF.
Ex. 32:13 swarest by thine o. s.
John 5:30 can of o. s. do nothing
17:5 glorify me with thine o. s.
1 *Cor.* 4:3 I judge not mine o. s.
Phile. 19 even thine own s.
1 *Pet.* 2:24 his o. s. bare our sins

SELFSAME.
Mat. 8:13 servant healed s. hour
1 *Cor.* 12:11 worketh one s. Spirit
2 *Cor.* 5:5 wrought us for s. thing
7:11 s. thing, ye sorrowed after
See Same DAY.

SELF-WILL.
Gen. 49:6 in s.-w. dig. down wall
See FRET, HIDE.

SELF-WILLED.
Tit. 1:7 bishop must not be s.-w.
2 *Pet.* 2:10 presumptuous, s.-w.

SELL.
Gen. 25:31 s. me thy birthright
37:27 let us s. him to Ishmael
25 s. live ox, and divide money
22:1 if man steal ox, kill, or s.
Lev. 25:14 if thou s. to neighbor
29 if a man s. dwelling-house
44 s. s. himself to stranger
Deut. 2:28 sh. s. meat for money
14:21 s. that wh. dieth to alien
21:14 sh. not s. her for money
Jud. 4:9 s. Sisera into hand of w.
57:5 didst s. thy people
Jer. 1:7 go to all that I shall s.
2:10 s. to Kedar; 9:17 s. women
20:31 s. to all them of captivity
Ezek. 30:12 s. land into the hand
48:14 not s. first-fruits of land
Joel 3:8 I will s. your sons and daugh. s. them to Sabeans
Amos 8:5 that we m. s. wheat
6 and s. refuse of the wheat
Zec. 11:5 that s. say, I am rich
Mat. 19:21 and s. that hast, *Mark* 10:21 ; *Luke* 12:33 ; 18:22
25:9 go rather to s. and buy
Luke 22:36 s. garm. buy sword
Jam. 4:13 we will buy and s.
Rev. 13:17 no man mi. buy or s.

SELLER, S.
Is. 24:2 with buyer, so with s.
Ezek. 7:12 rejoice, nor s. mourn
13 s. not return to that sold
Neh. 13:20 s. lodged without Je.
Acts 16:14 Lydia, a s. of purple

SELLEST, ETH.
Ex. 21:16 he that stealeth a man and s. him, *Deut.* 24:7
Ruth 4:3 Naomi s. part of land
Ps. 44:12 s. thy peo. for naught
Prov. 11:26 blessing on him s.
31:24 maketh fine linen, s. it
Nah. 3:4 s. nations thro' whore.
Mat. 13:44 he s. all, buyeth field

SELVEDGE.
Ex. 26:4 s. s. in. coupling, 36:11

Own SELVES.
Acts 20:30 of o. s. shall men rise
2 *Cor.* 8:5 gave their own s. to L.
2 *Tim.* 3:2 lovers of their own s.
1:22 deceiving your own s.
See ASSEMBLE, ED.

SEN

SEMEI.
Luke 3:26 Mattathias son of S.

SENATE.
Acts 5:21 called s. of Is. together

SENATORS.
Ps. 105:22 teach his s. wisdom

SEND,
Gen. 24:7 G. shall s. angel bef. 40
12 s. me good speed this day
54 s. me away unto master, 56
43:4 if thou wilt s. our brother
45:5 God did s. me to prev. life
Ex. 4:13 s. by him thou wilt s.
7:2 s. children of Is. out of land
12:33 s. them out in haste
33:12 know whom thou wilt s.
Num. 16:21 s. hire away
Num. 12:9 men to search land
31:4 every tribe s. thous. to war
Deut. 1:22 s. men bef. to search
19:12 elders s. fetch him thence
28:20 L. sh. s. upon thee cursing
48 enemies L. shall s. ag. thee
Jud. 13:8 man of God didst s.
1 *Sam.* 5:11 s. away ark, 6:8
6:3 s. ark, s. not empty.
9:26 that I may s. thee away
11:3 that we may s. messengers
16:11 said to Jesse, s. fetch Da.
19 Saul said, s. me D. thy son
25:25 saw not men thou didst s.
2 *Sam.* 15:36 me U. the Hittite
14:32 that I may s. thee to king
15:36 ye sh. s. me every thing
17:16 how therefore s. quickly
Mat. 20:9 thou didst s. for serva.
2 *K.* 6:13 shall s. 17 sai s.
6:13 I may s. and fetch him
7:13 let us s. 9:17 s. meet John
15:37 L. began to s. ag. Judah
1 *Chr.* 13:2 s. abroad unto breth.
2 *Chr.* 6:27 s. rain upon land
28:16 A. did s. to king of Assy.
32:9 Sennacherib did s. to Hez.
Ezr. 5:17 s. his pleasure to us
Neh. 2:5 wouldest s. me to Jud.
6:4 s. Sanballat s. me 4 times
8:10 s. portions unto them, 12
Job 21:11 they s. forth little ones
38:35 canst thou s. lightnings?
Ps. 43:3 s. out thy light
57:3 he sh. s. from heaven, and ser. s. reproach ; God s. s.
68:8 he doth s. out his voice
110:2 s. rod of strength out of Z.
118:25 Lord, s. now prosperity
144:7 s. thy hand from above
Prov. 22:21 truth to them that s.
Is. 6:8 wh. shall I s.? I said, s.
10:16 Lord shall s. am. fat ones
16:1 s. ye lamb to ruler of land
19:20 shall s. them a Saviour
32:20 s. the feet of ox and ass
57:5 didst s. thy messengers
Jer. 1:7 go to all that I shall s.
2:10 s. to Kedar; 9:17 s. women
20:31 s. to all them of captivity
Ezek. 30:12 s. fire into Egypt
Joel 2:19 I s. you corn and wine
3:11 s. down your mighty ones
Amos 8:11 I will s. famine on l.
Obad. 1 rumor s. among heathen
Mic. 1:14 shalt s. presents to M.
Hag. 1:11 called for a drought
Mal. 2:2 s. a curse upon you, 3
4:5 I will s. you Elijah prophet
Mat. 9:38 pray ye the Lord will s. forth laborers, *Luke* 10:2
10:34 th. not I come to s. peace
13:41 Son of man shall s. his angels, 24:31 ; *Mark* 13:27
15:23 s. her away, crieth after
21:3 he will s. them, *Mark* 11:3
Mark 3:14 s. to preach, 6:7
5:10 would not s. them away
12 saying, s. us into swine
Luke 15:24 s. Laz. 27 s. to house
John 14:26 Fa. will s. in name
17:8 belie. that thou didst s. me
20:21 as Father hath sent me, s.
Acts 7:35 same did G. s. to be ruler
10:5 s. men to Joppa, 32 ; 11:13
13:22 s. men of their compa. 23
25:3 would s. for him to Jerus.
Phil. 2:19 I trust to s. Timoth.
25 necessary to s. Epaphrodit.
2 *Thes.* 2:11 G. shall s. delusions
Tit. 3:12 I shall s. Artemas unto
Jam. 3:11 fount. s. sweet water?
Rev. 1:11 and s. it to 7 churches
11:10 s. gifts to one another

I SEND.
Ex. 23:20 behold, I s. an angel
Num. 22:37 did I not name s.?
1 *Sam.* 20:12 and I s. not the lad
Is. 6:8 saying, Whom shall I s.?
Jer. 25:15 cu. to whom I s. thee
Ezek. 2:3 I s. thee to Israel, 4
14:21 I s. my four sore judging.
Mat. 10:16 I s. you as sheep
11:10 behold, I s. my messenger, *Mark* 1:2 ; *Luke* 7:27
23:34 behold I s. you prophets

SER

Neh. 3:16 rep. to place over ag. *s.*
Mal. 2:3; 27 are like to whited *s.*
23 because ye garnish the *s.*
Luke 11:47 *s.* of the prophets, 48

SERAIAH.

2 *Sam.* 8:17 S. was the scribe
2 *K.* 25:18 took S. *Jer.* 52:24
23 to Gedaliah, S. *Jer.* 40:8
1 *Chr.* 4:14 S. begat Joab, 35
6:14 Azariah begat S. and S.
Ezr. 7:1 E. son of S. *Neh.* 10:2
Neh. 11:11 S. was ruler of house
12:1 S. the priest went up
12 chief of the fathers of S.
Jer. 36:26 king commanded S.
51:59 S. was a quiet prince
61 Jeremiah said to S. when

SERAPHIM.

Is. 6:2 above it stood the *s.* each
6 one of the *s.* hav. a live coal

SERGEANTS.

Acts 16:35 sent the *s.* saying
38 *s.* told these words to mag.

SERGIUS PAULUS.

Acts 13:7 S. Paulus, a prudent

SERPENT.

Gen. 3:1 the *s.* was more subtile
13 *s.* beguiled me, 2 *Cor.* 11:3
49:17 Dan shall be a *s.* by way
Ex. 4:3 rod bec. a *s.* 7:9, 10, 15
Num. 21:8 said, Make thee a *s.*
9 Moses made a *s.* of brass
2 *K.* 18:4 Hezek. brake brazen *s.*
Job 26:13 hand formed crooked *s.*
Ps. 58:4 th. poison like pois. of *s.*
140:3 sharpen. tongues like a *s.*
Prov. 23:32 at last it bit. like a *s.*
30:19 way of a *s.* upon a rock
Ec. 10:8 whoso break. a hedge *s.*
shall bite him
11 *s.* bite without enchantme.
Is. 14:29 of *s.* root come cockatrice; fruit be as fiery fly. *s.*
27:1 L. sh. punish *s.* crooked *s.*
30:6 viper and fiery flying *s.*
65:25 dust shall be the *s.* meat
Jer. 46:22 voice sh. go like a *s.*
Amos 5:19 and a *s.* bite him
Mic. 7:17 lick the dust like a *s.*
Mat. 10:16 wise as *s.* harmless
John 3:14 as Moses lifted up *s.*
Rev. 12:9 old *s.* called devil, 20:2
14 nourished fr. face of the *s.*
15 the *s.* cast out of his mouth

SERPENTS.

Ex. 7:12 rods, they became *s.*
Num. 21:6 L. sent *s.* amo. them
7 pray to L. he take away *s.*
Deut. 8:15 wherein were fiery *s.*
Jer. 8:17 I will send *s.* among *y.*
Mat. 10:16 be therefore wise as *s.*
23:33 ye *s.* how can ye escape?
Mark 16:18 they shall take up *s.*
Luke 10:19 power to tread on *s.*
1 *Cor.* 10:9 were destroyed of *s.*
Jam. 3:7 beasts and *s.* is tamed
Jas. 3:10 tails were like to *s.*

SERUG. *Gen.* 11:20–23

SERVANT.

Gen. 9:25 Canaan, a *s.* of servan.
24:34 said, I am Abraham's *s.*
49:15 Issa. bowed and bec. a *s.*
51:19 if the *s.* plainly say
Deut. 5:15 remem. thou wast a *s.*
23:15 thou shalt not deliver *s.*
1 *Sam.* 2:13 priest's *s.* came, 15
9:27 bid the *s.* pass on before us
25:41 let thy handmaid be a *s.*
27:3 is not David the *s.* of Saul?
30:13 I am, to an Amalekite
2 *Sam.* 9:2 *s.* named Ziba, 10:17
16:1 Ziba *s.* of Mephibosheth
19:17 wi. Joab sent sent K.'s *s.*
1 *K.* 11:26 Jeroboam Solom.'s *s.*
12:7 if thou wilt be a *s.* to peop.
Neh. 9:10 Tobi. *s.* Am. heard, 19
Job 3:19 there, and the *s.* is free
7:2 as a *s.* earne. desireth shad.
41:4 wilt take Leviathan for a *s.*
Ps. 105:17 Joseph, sold for a *s.*
Prov. 11:29 fool wh. he *s.* to wise
12:9 that is despi. and hath a *s.*
14:35 king's favor tow. a wise *s.*
17:2 wise *s.* shall rule over a son
19:10 much less a *s.* rule princes
22:7 the borrower is *s.* to lender
29:19 a *s.* not correct. with wor.
30:10 accuse not a *s.* to master
22 not bear *s.* when reigneth
Is. 24:2 as *s.* so with his master
42:7 saith Lord to a *s.* of rulers
Jer. 2:14 is Israel a *s.* a slave?
Dan. 6:20 O Daniel, *s.* of liv. G.

Dan. 10:17 can *s.* talk wi. my l.?
Mal. 1:6 *s.* honoreth his master
Mat. 10:24 nor *s.* above his lord
25 enough for *s.* to be as his lo.
18:27 lord of that *s.* was moved
32 O thou wicked *s.* I forg. th.
20:27 be chief, let him be your *s.*
s. 23:11; *Mark* 10:44
24:45 is a faithful and wise *s.*
46 blessed is that *s.* *Luke* 12:43
48 evil *s.* shall say, *Luke* 12:45
50 lord of *s.* sh. come, *Lu.* 12:46
25:21 well done, th. good and
faithful *s.* 23; *Luke* 19:17
26 thou wicked and slothful *s.*
Luke 19:22
30 cast unprofit. *s.* into darkn.
26:51 P. struck *s.* of high-priest,
Mark 14:47; *John* 18:10
Mark 12:2 sent to husband. a *s.*
Luke 12:47 *s.* knew lord's will
14:21 so that *s.* showed his lord
17:7 which having a *s.* plowing
9 doth thank th. *s.*? I trow not
20:10 at season he sent a *s.* 11
John 8:34 commit. sin, *s.* of sin
35 the *s.* abideth not in house
13:16 *s.* is not greater, 15:20
15:15 *s.* knoweth not what lord
Rom. 1:1 Paul a *s.* of Je. Christ
14:4 who judgest ano. man's *s.*?
16:1 Phebe. a *s.* of the church
1 *Cor.* 7:21 art called being a *s.*
21 being a *s.* is L.'s freeman
9:19 I made myself a *s.*
Gal. 1:10 I sho. not be *s.* of Chr.
4:1 child differeth noth. from *s.*
7 art no more a *s.* but a son
Phil. 2:7 he took the form of a *s.*
Col. 4:12 Epaphras, a *s.* of Christ
2 *Tim.* 2:24 *s.* of Lord not strive
Phile. 16 not as a *s.* above a *s.*
Heb. 3:5 Mo. was faithful as a *s.*
1 *Pet.* 2:1 Peter. a *s.* of J. Christ
Jude 1 Jude the *s.* of Jesus Chr.

See DAVID.

SERVANT, S. of God.

Gen. 50:17 forgive *s.* of God
1 *Chr.* 6:49 Moses the *s.* of God
2 *Chr.* 24:9 Moses *s.* of God laid
Neh. 10:29 by hand of Moses *s.* of God
Dan. 6:20 O Daniel *s.* of liv. God
9:11 in law of Mo. the *s.* of God
Tit. 1:1 P. a *s.* of God, an apost.
Jam. 1:1 Ja. a *s.* of G. and of L.
1 *Pet.* 2:16 liberty, as a *s.* of G.
25 sealed the *s.* of our God
12:3 song of Moses the *s.* of G.

See MOSES.

His SERVANT.

Gen. 9:26 Can. shall be his *s.* 27
Ex. 14:31 believed L. and his *s.*
21:20 if a man smite his *s.*
26 if *s.* smite eye of his *s.*
Jos. 5:14 what saith L. to h. *s.*?
9:24 God commanded his *s.* Mo.
Jud. 7:11 Gi. went wi. Ph. his *s.*
19:3 Levite went, having his *s.*
1 *Sam.* 19:4 let not the king sin
against his *s.*
19:15 let not king imp. to his *s.*
25:39 L. hath kept h. *s.* fr. evil
26:18 why doth my lo. pu. h. *s.*?
19 let lord hear words of h. *s.*
2 *Sam.* 9:11 my lord comm. h. *s.*
14:22 king fulfilled req. of h. *s.*
24:21 is my lord come to h. *s.*?
1 *K.* 1:51 that will not slay h. *s.*
6:56 prom. by hand of Mo. h. *s.*
59 maintain cause of h. *s.* Isr.
14:18 spake by h. *s.* Ahi. 15:29
19:3 Eli. left h. *s.* at Beer-sheba
2 *K.* 9:36 word he spake by h. *s.*
14:25 word he spake by h. *s.* Jo.
17:23 Hoshea bec. his *s.* and gave
24:1 Jehoiakim became his *s.*
1 *Chr.* 16:13 O ye seed of Is. h. *s.*
2 *Chr.* 32:16 spake ag. his *s.* Hez
Neh. 4:22 let ev. one with h. *s.*
Ps. 35:27 L. hath pleas. of his *s.*
105:6 O ye seed of Abra. his *s.*
26 he sent Moses his *s.* and A.
42 remembered Abraham his *s.*
136:22 a heritage unto Is. his *s.*
Prov. 29:21 delicately bring. h. *s.*
Is. 42:19 blind, as my *s.*? hear
44:26 confirm. word of his *s.*
48:20 Lord redeemed h. *s.* Jacob
49:5 from the womb to be his *s.*
50:10 obeyeth voice of his *s.*?
Jer. 34:16 ev. man *s.* to ret. ret.
Mat. 8:13 his *s.* was healed
Luke 1:54 hath holpen his *s.* Isr.
7:3 beseeching him wo. heal h. *s.*
14:17 sent h. *s.* at supper-time
Rev. 1:1 by his angel unto h. *s.* J.

See LORD, MAID.

Man-SERVANT.

Ex. 20:10 th. nor *m.-s. Deut.* 5:14
17 not cov. nc. *m.-s. Deut.* 5:21
21:27 smite out his *m.-s.* tooth
32 if the ox shall push a *m.-s.*
Deut. 12:18 eat. thou, and *m.-s.*
16:11 rejoice, th. and thy *m.-s.*
Job 31:13 if desp. cause of *m.-s.*
Jer. 34:9 let ev. man go free, 10

My SERVANT.

Gen. 26:24 multi. seed for my *s.*
44:10 found he sin, be my *s.* 17
Num. 12:7 my *s.* Moses is not so
14:24 my *s.* Caleb had another
Jos. 1:2 Moses my *s.* is dead
1 *Sam.* 22:8 son stirred up my *s.*
27:12 he shall be my *s.* for ever
2 *Sam.* 19:26 O king, my *s.* decei.
2 K. 5:6 have sent Naaman my *s.*
21:8 according to law my *s.* M.
Job 1:8 consider. my *s.* Job? 2:3
19:16 I called my *s.* he gave me
42:7 not spok. right. as my *s.* J.
8 go to my *s.* J. he shall pray
Is. 22:3 like as my *s.* Isa. hath
41:8 Israel, my *s.* Jacob whom
41:9 thou shouldest be my *s.*
52:13 my *s.* deal prudently
65:9 so will I do for my *s.* sake
Jer. 25:9 Nebuchadnezzar my *s.*
27:6; 43:10
30:10 O my *s.* Jacob, 40:27, 28
Ezek. 28:25 given my *s.* J. 37:25
Hag. 2:23 O Zerubbabel my *s.*
Zec. 3:8 my *s.* the BRANCH
Mal. 4:4 law of Moses, my *s.*
Mat. 8:8 my *s.* be healed, *Lu.* 7:7
9 to my *s.* do this, *Luke* 7:8
12:18 my *s.* whom I ha. chosen
John 12:26 th. shall also my *s.* b3

Thy SERVANT.

Gen. 18:3 pass. I pray, fr. thy *s.*
19:19 thy *s.* found gra. *Neh.* 2:5
32:10 mercies showed to thy *s.*
18 say, They be thy *s.* Jacob's
Deut. 32:36 L. sh. repent for h. *s.*
43 he will avenge blood of h. *s.*
1 *Sam.* 3:14 best, give to h. *s.* 15
19:1 S. spake to h. *s.* to kill Da.
22:6 h. *s.* nothing about him
2 *K.* 5:18 h. *s.* came near, spake
1 *Chr.* 19:3 h. *s.* come to search?
2 *Chr.* 35:16 his *s.* spake ag. h.
Neh. 2:20 h.s. will arise
Job 4:18 he put no trust in his *s.*
Ps. 69:36 seed of his *s.* inherit
135:14 repent himself conc. h. *s.*
Prov. 29:19 all his *s.* are wicked
Is. 56:6 love na. of L. to be h. *s.*
65:15 L. call h. *s.* by ano. name
Os. 14 L. be known toward his *s.*
Jer. 22:4 on horses, and his *s.*
36:31 punish him. seed. his *s.*
Ezek. 46:17 if p. give gift to h. *s.*
Dan. 3:30 deliver h. *s.* trusted
Mal. 19:33 king take arc. of h. *s.*
21:34 sent h. *s.* to husbandmen
Luke 19:13 he called his *s.* 3
Rom. 6:16 h. *s.* ye are wh. ye ob.
Rev. 1:1 h. *s.* things must come,
22:6
19:2 hath avenged blood of h. *s.*
5 praise God, ye h. *s.* fear him
22:3 and his *s.* shall serve him

See LORD, MEN.

My SERVANTS.

Lev. 25:12 my *s.* whom I bro. 55
1 *Sam.* 21:2 appoint, my *s.* a pl.
1 *K.* 5:6 my *s.* shall be with thy
servants, 2 *Chr.* 2:8
22:49 let my *s.* go with thy serv,
2 *K.* 9:7 aven. the blood of my *s.*
Neh. 4:23 nor my *s.* put off clo.
5:10 I and my *s.* mig. exact mo.
16 my *s.* were gather. to work
13:19 my *s.* let I at Jerusalem
Is. 65:9 my *s.* shall dwell there
13 my *s.* eat; 14 my *s.* sing
Jer. 7:25 sent to you my *s.* 44:4
John 18:36 then wo. my *s.* fight
12:8 on my *s.* I w'll pour S.
Rev. 2:20 prophe. to seduce my *s.*

See PROPHETS.

Thy SERVANTS.

Gen. 44:16 G. found iniq. of t. *s.*
47:3 they *s.* are shepherds
50:18 said, Behold, we be thy *s.*
Ex. 5:15 dealest thus with thy *s.*
11:9 these thy *s.* how down

CRUDEN'S CONCORDANCE.

SET

Ezr. 5:11 house king of Is. *s. up*
Neh. 6:1 I had not *s. up* doors
Job 5:11 *s. up* those that he low
16:12 and *s. me up* for his mark
Ps. 27:5 and *s. me up* upon rock
69:29 let thy salvation *s. me up*
89:42 *s., up* right hand of adver.
Prov. 8:23 was *s. up* everlasting
Jer. 11:18 *s. up* altars to thine ?
Ezek. 14:3 men *s. up* their idols
31:4 the deep *s.* him *up* on high
Dan. 2:44 God sh. *s. up* a kingd.
5:19 whom he would he *s. up*
Hos. 8:4 they have *s. up* kings
Mal. 3:15 work wickedness *s. up*
Acts 6:13 *s. up* false witnesses
15:16 build ruins, and *s. it up*

SET, *passive.*
Gen. 31:33 th. was *s.* meat before
Ex. 32:22 th. are *s.* on mischief
1 *Sam.* 18:30 his name was *s.* by
20:34 thy life was much *s.* by
1 *K.* 14:8 for his eyes were *s.*
2 *K.* 12:4 money every man *s.* at
Chr. 12:10 *J.* saw battle was *s.*
2 *Chr.* 6:10 I am *s.* on thr. of Is.
29:33 house of Lord *s.* in order
31:15 in their *s.* office to give
Job 36:16 what sh. be *s.* on table
20:5 privily *s.* against poor
41:9 let my prayer be *s.* forth
Ex. 8:11 heart is *s.* to do evil
10:6 folly is *s.* in great dignity
Is. 3:24 instead of well *s.* hair
Jer. 6:23 *s.* in array, *Joel* 2:5
31:29 tooth *s.* on edge, *Ezek.* 18:2
Dan. 7:10 judgment was *s.*
Mat. 5:14 a city *s.* on a hill
27:19 he was *s.* on judgm.-seat
Mark 1:33 when sun was *s.* brought
9:12 things, he *s.* at naught
Luke 2:34 this child is *s.* for fall
7:8 a man *s.* under authority
10:8 eat such as are *s.* bef. you
Acts 4:11 the stone *s.* at naught
19:27 craft in danger to be *s.* at
26:32 man might ha. been *s.* at
1 *Cor.* 10:27 whatever is *s.* before you
Gal. 3:1 Ch. had been *s.* forth
Heb. 6:18 lay hold on hope *s.* bef.
8:1 is *s.* on right hand, 12:2
12:1 run the race *s.* before us
2 joy that was *s.* before him
12:28 brother Tim. *s.* at liberty
Jude 7 cities *s.* forth for example
Rev. 3:21 *s.* down with Father
4:2 a throne was *s.* in heaven

SET day,
Acts 12:21 ou *s. day* He. arrayed

See FACE, FACES, FEASTS.

SET time.
Gen. 17:21 Sa. shall bear at *s. t.*
Ex. 9:5 Lord appointed a *s. t.*
Job 14:13 wouldest appoint a *s. t.*
Ps. 102:13 *s. t.* to favor is come

SETH.
Gen. 5:9 and called him S.
6 S. begat Enos, 1 *Chr.* 1:1 ;
Luke 3:38

SETTER.
Acts 17:18 a *s.* forth of stra. gods

SETTEST.
Deut. 23:20 *s.* hand to, 28:8, 20
Job 7:12 that *s.* a watch over me ?
Ps. 41:12 thou *s.* me before face

SETTETH.
Deut. 24:15 *s.* his heart on it
27:16 cursed that *s.* light by fa.
2 *Sam.* 22:34 *s.* me on hi. places,
Ps. 18:33
Job 28:3 he *s.* an end to darkness
Ps. 36:4 he *s.* himself in a way
65:6 by strength *s.* fast mount.
75:7 put. down one, *s. up* ano.
107:41 *s.* poor on high
Jer. 5:26 as he that *s.* snares
43:3 Baruch *s.* thee on ag. us
Ezek. 14:4 that *s.* idols in heart, 7
Dan. 2:21 remov. kings and *s. up*
4:17 *s. up* over it basest of men

SETTING, S.
Ex. 28:17 set in it *s.* of stones
Ezek. 43:8 in *s.* of their threshold
Mat. 27:66 seal, stone, *s.* a watch
Luke 4:40 when sun was *s.* they

SETTLE.
Ezek. 43:14 fr. ground to lower *s.*
17 *s.* shall be 14 cubits long
20 blood on corners of *s.* 45:19

SETTLE, D, ST.
1 *Chr.* 17:14 will *s.* him in house
Ps. 65:10 thou *s.* furrows thereof
Ezek. 36:11 I will *s.* you af. your

SEV

Luke 21:14 *s.* it in your hearts
1 *Pet.* 5:10 G. strengthen, *s.* you

SETTLED.
1 *K.* 8:13 built a *s.* place for thee
2 *K.* 8:11 he *s.* his countenance
Ps. 119:89 word is *s.* in heaven
Prov. 8:25 before mount. were *s.*
Jer. 48:11 he hath *s.* on lees
Zep. 1:12 are *s.* on their lees
Col. 1:23 faith, grounded and *s.*

SEVEN.
Gen. 46:25 Bil. all souls were *s.*
Ex. 2:16 priest of N. had *s.* dau.
Lev. 23:15 *s.* sab. shall be com.
25:8 number *s.* sabbaths of yrs.
Num. 3:1 bnild here *s.* altars,
prep. *s.* oxen and *s.* rams, 29
Deut. 7:1 *s.* nations greater
16:9 *s.* weeks thou sh. number
28:7 L. cause one. flee *s.* ways
25 shalt flee *s.* ways bef. them
Jos. 6:4 *s.* priests bearing *s.* trumpets, 8, 6, 13
18:2 remained of Is. *s.* tribes
1 *Sam.* 2:5 barren hath born *s.*
16:10 Jesse made *s.* of his sons
2 *Sam.* 21:9 they fell all *s.* toge.
Ezr. 7:14 king and his *s.* couns.
Est. 1:14 the *s.* princes wh. saw
Job 5:19 in *s.* troubles no evil
Prov. 9:1 wisd. hath hewn *s.* pil.
26:25 th. are *s.* abominations
Ezek. 11:3 portion to *s.* also to 8
Is. 4:1 *s.* women take hold of 1
11:15 L. shall smite in *s.* stre.
Ezek. 39:12 *s.* months he burying
Dan. 9:25 Mes. sh. be *s.* weeks
Mic. 5:5 against him *s.* sheph.
Zec. 3:9 upon one stone *s.* eyes
Mark 12:20 and *s.* had her, 23 ;
Luke 20:31, 33
Rev. 1:4 John to *s.* churches in A.
10:3 when he cried, *s.* thunders
12:3 dragon, having *s.* heads and *s.* crowns, 13:1 ; 17:3, 7
15:1 I saw *s.* angels having the *s.* last plagues,
7 to *s.* angels *s.* golden vials
17:1 one of the *s.* angels which had the *s.* vials, 21:9
9 *s.* heads are *s.* mountains
11 beast is of the *s.* and goeth

See DAYS, HUNDRED.

SEVEN bullocks, *or* rams.
Num. 23:29 prepare *s. bul.* &. r.
23:32 seventh day *s. b.* two *r.*
1 *Chr.* 15:26 Lev. offered *s. b.* s. r.
Job 42:8 take you now *s. b.* s. r.
Ezek. 45:23 a burnt-offer. of *s. bul.*

SEVENFOLD.
Gen. 4:15 venge. sh. be taken *s.*
24 If Cain shall be avenged *s.*
Ps. 79:12 render *s.* into bosom
Prov. 6:31 he shall restore *s.*
Is. 30:26 light of sun shall be *s.*

See LAMBS, LAMPS.

SEVEN men.
2 *Sam.* 21:6 let *s. men* of his sons
Prov. 26:16 that *s. m.* that can
Jer. 52:25 *s. m.* that were near
Acts 6:3 look out *s. m.* of honest

SEVEN rams. *See* SEVEN *bul.*

See SEALS.

SEVEN sons.
Ruth 4:15 dau. better than *s. s.*
Job 1:2 were born unto him *s. s.*
42:13 had *s. s.* and three daugh.
Acts 19:14 *s. s.* of Sceva a Jew

SEVEN spirits.
Mat. 12:45 then *s.* other sp. and taketh *s. s. Luke* 11:26
Rev. 1:4 *s. s.* bef. throne of God
3:1 he that hath the *s. s.* of God
4:5 lamps, wh. are *s. s.* of God
5:6 seven eyes, are *s. s.* of God

SEVEN stars.
Amos 5:8 him that maketh *s. s.*
Rev. 1:16 hand *s. s.* 3:1 ; 2:1 ; 3:1
20 myst. of *s. s.* thou sawest ;
s. s. are angels of *s.* churches
SEVEN and *Thirty.* See UNITY.
See THOUSAND.

SEVEN times.
Gen. 33:3 J.a. bowed bef. Es. *s. t.*
Lev. 4:6 priests shall *s.* sprinkle of the blood *s. t.* 17 ; 8:11 ; 14:7 ; 16:14, 19 ; *Num.* 19:4
14:16 sprink. oil wt. fin. *s. t.* 27
51 sprinkle house *s. t.*
25:8 number *s. t.* seven years

SHA

Lev. 26:18 pu. *s. t.* more, 21, 24, 29
Ps. 119:164 *s. t.* a day do I praise
Prov. 24:16 a just man fall, *s. t.*
Dan. 3:19 heat *s. t.* hotter, *s. t.*
4:16 pass, 23, 25, 32
Mat. 18:21 sh. I forgive? till *s. t.*
Luke 17:4 if brother tresp. *s. t.* a day, and *s.* times a day turn

SEVEN and *Twenty. See* TWENTY.

SEVEN years.
Gen. 29:18 serve *s. y.* for Rachel
20 Jac. served *s. y.* for Rachel
27 shalt serve me other *s. y.* 30
41:26 seven good kine are *s. y.* the seven good ears are *s. y.* 47, 48, 53
the *s. y.* of plenty, 34, 47, 48
53 the *s. y.* of plenteousness

SEVENS.
Gen. 7:2 clean beast sh. take by *s.*

SEVENTEEN.
Gen. 37:2 Jos. being *s.* years old
Jer. 32:9 Jer. weighed *s.* shekels

SEVENTEENTH.
Gen. 7:11 on *s.* day the fountains
8:4 ark rested on *s.* day in the

SEVENTH.
Ex. 21:2 in *s.* he sh. go out free
31:15 the *s.* is sabbath of rest
Lev. 23:16 morrow after *s.* sab.

See DAY.

SEVENTH month.
Lev. 16:29 in *s. mon.* afflict your souls, 23:27 ; 25:9
Num. 29:1 in *s. m.* holy conv. 12
1 *K.* 8:2 Isr. assembled at *s. m.*
Hag. 2:1 in *s. m.* the word came
Zec. 8:19 the fast of the *s. month*

See DEATH.

SEVENTH year.
Ex. 23:11 *s. y.* thou sh. let it rest
Lev. 25:4 in *s. y.* shall be a sab.
Deut. 15:12 *s. y.* shalt let him go
2 *K.* 11:4 in *s. y.* Jehoiada sent rulers and capt. 1 *Chr.* 23:1
Est. 2:16 Esther taken in *s. year*
Jer. 52:28 carried captive in *s. y.*
Ezek. 20:1 in tha *s. y.* eld. came

SEVENTY.
Ex. 4:24 ruly Lam. *s.* and sev.
Num. 1:5 of loins of Jacob were *s.*
24:1 and *s.* elders of Israel, 9
Num. 11:16 ga. to me *s.* men, 24
25 gave of spirit unto *s.* elders
Jud. 9:56 wrig. his *s.* brethren
2 *K.* 10:1 Ahab had *s.* sons in, 6
Is. 23:15 Tyre shall be forgot. *s.*
17 after end of *s.* years, the L.
Jer. 25:11 serve Babylon *s.* years
29:10 *s.* years be accomp. at B.
Dan. 9:24 *s.* weeks are determin.
Zec. 7:5 even th. *s.* years did yo
Mat. 18:22 times, but until *s.* ti.
Luke 10:1 L. appointed other *s.*
17 the *s.* returned ag. with joy

SEVER, ED.
Ex. 8:22 I will *s.* in that day
9:4 L. shall *s.* bet. cattle of Isr.
Lev. 20:26 I s. you fr. other peo.
Deut. 4:41 Moses *s.* three cities
Ezek. 39:14 *s.* out men of employ
Mat. 13:49 *s.* wicked fr. the just

SEVERAL, LY.
Num. 28:13 and a *s.* tenth deal, 21, 29 ; 29:10, 15
2 *K.* 15:5 Azariah dwelt in *s.*
Chr. 26:32
2 *Chr.* 31:19 sons of Aa. in *s.* city
Mat. 25:15 according to *s.* ability
1 *Cor.* 12:11 to every man *s.*
Rev. 21:21 cv. *s.* gate was of pearl

SEVERITY.
Rom. 11:22 behold goods. and *s.*

SEW.
Ec. 3:7 time to rend, time to *s.*
Ezek. 13:18 woe to women, *s.* pil.

SEWED, EST, ETH.
Gen. 3:7 *s.* fig-leaves together
Job 14:17 thou *s. up* mine iniq.
16:15 I have *s.* sackloth upon
Mark 2:21 no man *s.* new cloth
SHAALBIM. *Jud.* 1:35
SHAASHGAZ. *Est.* 2:14

SHADE.
Ps. 121:5 L. is thy *s.* upon right

SHADOW.
Gen. 19:8 under *s.* of my roof
Jud. 9:15 put ye. trust in my *s.*
20 thou seest the *s.* of mount.
36 thou seest *s.* of the mountains
Job 20:9 shall thee, go forward ?
10 light thing fore, to go down

SHA

1 *Chr.* 29:15 days as a *s. Job* 8:9
Job 7:2 as a serv. desireth the *s.*
14:2 he fleeth also as a *s.*
17:7 all my members are as a *s.*
40:22 trees cover him with th. *s.*
Ps. 17:8 hide me un. *s.* of wings
36:7 under *s.* of wings, 57:1
63:7 in *s.* of wings will I rejoice
80:10 hills were covered with *s.*
91:1 abide under *s.* of Almighty
102:11 my days are like a *s.*
109:23 I am gone like a *s.*
144:4 days are as a *s. Ec.* 8:13
Ec. 6:12 life be spendeth as a *s.*
Cant. 2:3 I sat under *s.* with del.
Is. 4:6 tabernacle for a *s.* in day
16:3 make thy *s.* as the night
25:4 hast been a *s.* from heat
5 bring heat with *s.* of a cloud
30:2 and trust in *s.* of Egypt
3 and the trust in *s.* of Egypt
32:2 as *s.* of a great rock
38:8 I will bring again *s.* of deg.
49:2 in *s.* of hand hid me, 51:16
Jer. 48:45 under *s.* of Heshbon
Lam. 4:20 und. his *s.* we sh. live
Ezek. 17:23 in *s.* thereof sh. they
31:6 und. his *s.* dw. all nations
12 peo. are gone down from *s.*
17 *s.* of it was under his *s.*
Hos. 4:13 bec. *s.* thereof is good
14:7 dwell under his *s.* sh. retu.
Jon. 4:5 and sat under in *s.*
6 it might be *s.* over his head
Mark 4:32 fowls lodge under *s.*
Acts 5:15 th. *s.* of P. might over.
Col. 2:17 a *s.* of things to come
Heb. 8:5 serve unto *s.* of heaven
10:1 having a *s.* of good things
Jam. 1:17 with whom no *s.* of tu.

See DEATH.

SHADOWS.
Cant. 2:17 *s.* flee away, 4:6
Jer. 6:4 for *s.* of the evening are

SHADOWING.
Is. 18:1 to land *s.* with wings
Ezek. 31:3 a cedar with *s.* shroud
Heb. 9:5 cherubim of gl. *s.* mer.
SHADRACH. *Dan.* 1:7 ; 2:49 ;
3:23-30

SHADY.
Job 40:21 he lieth under *s.* trees
22 the *s.* trees cover him with

SHAFT.
Ex. 25:31 his *s.* and branches,
his bowls, 37:17 ; *Num.* 8:4
Is. 49:2 made me a polished *s.*

SHAKE.
Jud. 16:20 I will go and *s.* mys.
Neh. 5:13 and said, So God *s.*
Job 4:14 made my bones to *s.*
15:33 shall *s.* off unripe grape
16:4 and *s.* my head at you
Ps. 46:3 tho' the mountains *s.*
68:28 make loins contlnu. to *s.*
72:16 fruit shall *s.* like Lebanon
Is. 2:19 he ariseth to *s.* earth, 21
10:15 as if rod should *s.* itself
32 he shall *s.* hand ag. mount
11:15 the Lord shall *s.* his hand
13:2 exalt the voice, *s.* the hand
13 I will *s.* heavens, *Joel* 3:16;
Hag. 2:6, 21
24:18 foundations of earth do *s.*
33:9 Bashan and Carmel *s.* off
52:2 *s.* thyself from dust, O Jer.
Jer. 23:9 broken, all my bones *s.*
Ezek. 26:10 walls sh. *s.* at noise
15 shall not isles *s.* at sound ?
27:28 suburbs shall *s.* at sound
31:16 I made nations *s.*
38:20 men shall *s.* at my pres.
Dan. 4:14 *s.* off his leaves
Amos 9:1 that the posts may *s.*
Hag. 2:7 I will *s.* all nations
Zec. 2:9 I will *s.* my hand on th.
Mat. 10:14 *s.* off dust of your feet,
Mark 6:11 ; *Luke* 9:5
Luke 6:48 beat house, co. not *s.*
Heb. 12:26 I *s.* not earth only

SHAKED.
Ps. 109:25 look. on me, *s.* heads

SHAKEN.
Lev. 26:36 sound of a *s.* leaf shall
1 *K.* 14:15 as a reed is *s.* in wat.
2 *K.* 19:21 daugh. of Jerus. hath *s.* her head at thee, *Is.* 37:22
Job 16:12 neck, *s.* me to pieces
38:13 wicked mi. be *s.* out of it
Ps. 18:7 founda. of hills were *s.*
Nah. 2:3 fir-trees shall be ter. *s.*
3:12 if *s.* they fall into mouth

SHE

Ezek. 34:11 I will search my *s.* 12
Hos. 12:12 for a wife he kept *s.*
Joel 1:18 flocks of *s.* made desol.
Mic. 5:8 a young lion among *s.*
Zec. 13:7 smite shepherd. and *s.*
seat. Mat. 26:31; *Mark* 14:27
Mat. 7:15 false proph. in *s.* cloth.
10:6 go to lost *s.* of house of Is.
12:12 how much man bet. th. *s. ?*
15:24 sent but to lost *s.* of Israel
18:12 man ha. 100 *s.* one be gone
13 he rejoiceth more of that *s.*
Luke 15:4, 6
23:33 shall set *s.* on right hand
John 2:14 in tem. th. that sold *s.*
15 drove out of temple, and *s.*
10:3 entereth door sheph. of *s.*
3 *s.* hear voice, 27; 4 *s.* follow
7 said Jes. I am door of the *s.*
11 shepherd giv. life for his *s.*
12 a hireling leaveth the *s.* 13
14 I know *s.* 16 other *s.* I have
15 I lay down my life for the *s.*
26 ye are not of my *s.* as I said
2:16 saith to Peter, Feed my *s.* 17
Heb. 13:20 L. Jes Shepherd of *s.*
Rev. 18:13 none buyeth *s.* horses

As SHEEP.

Num. 27:17 as *s.* wh. ha. no shep.
1 *K.* 22:17 Israel as *s.* that have
no shepherd, 2 *Chr.* 18:16
Ps. 44:22 we are counted as *s.* for
the slaughter, *Rom.* 8:36
Is. 13:14 as *s.* that no man taketh
53:7 as a *s.* bef. shearers dumb
Mic. 2:12 put together as *s.* of B.
Mat. 9:36 scattered as *s.* having
no shepherd, *Mark* 6:34
10:16 send as *s.* midst of wolves
Acts 8:32 led as *s.* to slaughter
1 *Pet.* 2:25 as *s.* going astray

SHEEPCOTE, S.

1 *Sam.* 24:3 Saul came to *s.*
2 *Sam.* 7:8 took fr. *s.* 1 *Chr.* 17:7

SHEEPFOLD, S.

Num. 32:16 we will build *s.*
Jud. 5:16 why abodest amo. *s. ?*
Ps. 78:70 Dav. took him from *s.*
John 10:1 entereth not *s.* by

SHEEP-GATE.

Neh. 3:1 Eliashib built the *s.-g.*
32 going up of corner to *s.-g.*
12:39 they went on to the *s.-g.*

SHEEP-MARKET.

John 5:2 at Jerusalem by *s.-m.*

SHEEP-MASTER.

2 *K.* 3:4 Mesha was a *s.-m.*
See SHEARERS.

SHEEPSKINS.

Heb. 11:37 they wandered in *s.*

SHEET.

Acts 10:11 descending as *s.* 11:5

SHEETS.

Jud. 14:12 I will give you 30 *s.*

SHEKEL.

Ex. 30:13 *s.* after the *s.* of the
sanctu. a *s.* is twenty gerahs.
Num. 3:47; *Ezek.* 45:12
15 not give less than half *s.*
1 *Sam.* 9:8 ha. fourth part of a *s.*
2 *K.* 7:1 mea. of flour for *s.* 16, 18
Neh. 10:32 charged wi. third of *s.*
Amos 8:5 ephah small, *s.* great

SHEKELS.

Gen. 23:15 land worth 400 *s.* 16
Ex. 21:32 give her master 30 *s.*
Lev. 5:15 estima. by *s.* 27:3–16
Deut. 22:29 damsel's father 50 *s.*
Jos. 7:21 spoils, 200 *s.* silver
Jud. 8:26 weight of rings 1,700 *s.*
17:2 1,100 *s.* I took; 3 resto. *s.*
10 give thee ten *s.* silver
2 *Sam.* 14:26 Ab. wei. hair 200 *s.*
2 *K.* 15:20 exacted of each fifty *s.*
1 *Chr.* 21:25 David gave Ornan
600 *s.*
Neh. 5:15 gover. had taken 40 *s.*
Jer. 32:9 bou. field for 17 *s.* silver
Ezek. 4:10 by weight 20 *s.*
See SANCTUARY.

SHELAH.

Gen. 38:5 Ju.'s son S. 11 till S.
25 I gave her not to S. my son
46:12 J. Er, Onan, and S. *Num.*
26:20; 1 *Chr.* 2:3; 4:21
1 *Chr.* 1:18 begat S. and S. E. 24

SHELEMIAH.

1 *Chr.* 26:14 lot eastw. fell to S.
Ezra 10:39 S. and Nathan had
Neh. 13:13 I made S. treasurer
Jer. 36:14 S. son of Cushi, 26

SHE

SHELTER.

Job 24:8 emb. rock for want of *s.*
Ps. 61:3 hast been *s.* for me

SHELUMIEL.

Num. 1:6 S. son of Zurishaddai,
2:12; 7:36; 10:19

SHEM.

Gen. 5:32 Noah begat S. 6:10;
10:1; 1 *Chr.* 1:4
9:23 S. took a garm. and went
26 blessed be Lord God of S.
27 shall dwell in tents of S.
10:21 the children of S. 22, 31;
11:10; 1 *Chr.* 1:17
Luke 3:36 wh. was the son of S.

SHEMAIAH.

1 *K.* 12:22 word of the Lord came
to S. 2 *Chr.* 11:2; 12:7
2 *Chr.* 4:37 Shimri the son of S.
5:4 Reuben, S. the son of Joel
9:14 of the Levit. S. 16; 15:8, 11;
24:6; 26:4, 6, 7; 2 *Chr.* 17:8;
29:14; 31:15; 35:9; *Ezr.* 8:16;
10:21, 31
Ezr. 8:13 S. son of Adonikam
Neh. 3:29 S. keeper of the east
6:10 I came to the house of S.
10:8 S. a priest, 12:34, 42
11:15 of Lev. S. 12:6, 18, 35, 36
Jer. 29:20 Urijah the son of S.
29:24 S. the Nehelamite, 31, 32
36:12 Delaiah son of S. prince

SHEMINITH.

1 *Chr.* 15:21 with harps on the S.

SHENIR.

Deut. 3:9 the Amorites call S.
Cant. 4:8 look from the top of S.

SHEPHATIAH.

2 *Sam.* 3:4 S. son of D. 1 *Chr.* 3:3
1 *Chr.* 9:8 Meshullam son of S.
12:5 S. the Haruphite came to
27:16 ruler of Simeonit. was S.
Ezr. 2:4 child. of S. *Neh.* 7:9
Jer. 38:1 S. heard the words of

SHEPHERD.

Gen. 46:34 *s.* is abomina. to Eg.
49:24 thence is *s.* stone of Israel
1 *Sam.* 17:40 stones into *s.* bag
Ps. 23:1 the Lord is my *s.*
80:1 give ear, O *s.* of Israel
Ec. 12:11 words given fr. one *s.*
Is. 38:12 age departed as *s.* tent
40:11 feed his flock like a *s.*
44:28 L. saith of Cy. he is my *s.*
63:11 bro. up with *s.* of his flock
Jer. 33:10 keep him as *s.* flock
43:12 array himself as a *s.*
49:19 who is *s.* will stand, 50:44
51:23 I will break *s.* his flock
Ezek. 34:5 scatter, because no *s.*
8 becau. prey bec. th. was no *s.*
12 *s.* seek. out flock am. sheep
23 I will set up one *s.* over th.
Da. feed them, he *s.* 37:24
Amos 3:12 as *s.* takes out mouth
Zec. 10:2 troubled, because no *s.*
11:15 instruments of a foolish *s.*
16 I will raise up a *s.* in land
17 woe to idle *s.* that leav. flo.
13:7 awake, O sword, ag. my *s.*
John 10:2 he is *s.* of sheep
14 a good *s.* know my sheep
16 shall be one fold, and one *s.*
Heb. 13:20 L. J. great *s.* of sheep
1 *Pet.* 2:25 now returned unto *s.*
5:4 when chief *s.* shall appear
See SHEEP.

SHEPHERDS.

Gen. 46:32 the men are *s.*
47:3 serv. are *s.* also our fathers
Ex. 2:17 *s.* came, dro. th. away
19 Eg. deliv. out of hand of *s.*
1 *Sam.* 25:7 now thy *s.* with us
Cant. 1:8 feed kids besi. *s.* tents
Is. 13:20 nor *s.* make folds there
31:4 multi. of *s.* called agn. him
56:11 *s.* that cannot understand
Jer. 6:3 *s.* shall come unto her
33:12 habitation of *s.* causing
Ezek. 34:2 prophecy against *s.* of
Is. should not *s.* feed flocks?
8 nor did *s.* search for flock,
10 I am against *s.* neither shall
s. feed themselves any more
Amos 1:2 habitations of *s.* mourn
Mic. 5:5 raise agai. him seven *s.*
Nah. 3:18 thy *s.* slumber, O king
Zep. 2:6 coasts be cottages for *s.*
Zec. 10:3 anger kindled again. *s.*
11:3 a voice of the howling of *s.*

SHI

Zec. 11:5 th. own *s.* pity th. not
8 3 *s.* I cut off in one month
Luke 2:8 in same country *s.*
20 *s.* returned, glorifying God

SHERD, S.

Is. 30:14 th. sh. not be found a *s.*
Ezek. 23:34 thou sh. break the *s.*

SHERIFFS.

Dan. 3:2 Nebuchadnezzar sent
to gather the *s.* together, 3

SHESHACH.

Jer. 25:26 the king of S. shall
51:41 how is S. taken! how is

SHESHBAZZAR.

Ezr. 1:8 numbered them to S.
5:14 delivered to S. wh. he had
16 S. laid foundation of the

SHEW, see SHOW.

SHIBBOLETH.

Jud. 12:6 say now S. he said

SHIELD.

Gen. 15:1 thy *s.* and reward
Deut. 33:29 Lord, the *s.* of help
Jud. 5:8 *s.* or spear amo. 40,000
1 *Sam.* 17:7 one bearing a *s.* 41
2 *Sam.* 1:21 the *s.* of mighty, *s.* of
Saul as though not anoint.
22:3 he is my *s. Ps.* 3:3; 28:7;
119:114; 144:2
36 given me the *s.* of salva-
tion, *Ps.* 18:35
1 *Chr.* 12:17 3 poun. of gold to 1 *s.*
2 *K.* 19:32 not come wi. *s. Is.* 37:33
1 *Chr.* 12:8 Gadites con. handle *s.*
24 Jud. that bare *s.* and spear
34 Naph. wi. *s.* and spe. 37,000
Job 39:23 spear and *s.* rattleth
41:15 his scales his pride are *s.*
Ps. 5:12 compass him as with *s.*
33:20 Lord is our *s.* 59:11; 84:9
35:2 take hold of *s.* and buckler
76:3 brake arrows of the bow, *s.*
84:11 Lord God is sun and *s.*
91:4 his truth shall be thy *s.*
115:9 he is th. help and *s.* 10, 11
Prov. 30:5 *s.* to them that trust
Is. 21:5 arise, princes, anoint *s.*
22:6 Kir uncovered the *s.*
Jer. 46:3 order buckler and *s.*
9 come forth, that handle *s.*
Ezek. 23:24 ag. th. buckler and *s.*
26:8 hanged *s.* and helmet, 11
Nah. 2:3 *s.* of mighty made red
Eph. 6:16 taking *s.* of faith

SHIELDS.

2 *Sam.* 8:7 David took *s.* of gold,
1 *Chr.* 18:7
1 *K.* 10:17 Solomon made 300 *s.*
of beaten gold, 2 *Chr.* 9:16
14:26 Shishak took away all *s.*
of gold, S. made, 2 *Chr.* 12:9
27 Rehoboam made in their
stead brazen *s.* 2 *Chr.* 12:10
2 *K.* 11:10 gave Da. *s.* 2 *Chr.* 23:9
2 *Chr.* 11:12 in city put a. and *s.*
14:8 of Benja. that bare *s.* 17:17
26:14 Uzziah pre. *s.* and spears
32:5 Hez. made darts and *s.* 27
Neh. 4:16 half held spears and *s.*
Ps. 47:9 *s.* of earth belong to G.
Jer. 51:11 bright arrows, gath. *s.*
Ezek. 38:4 with bucklers and *s.* 5
39:9 shall burn *s.* and weapons

SHIGGAION. See PSALM VII.

SHIGIONOTH.

Hab. 3:1 prayer of prophet on S.

SHILOH.

Gen. 49:10 nor scep. dep. till S.

SHILOH.

Jos. 18:1 assemb. together at S.
8 cast lots for you in S. 10
22:9 departed from Isr. out of S.
Jud. 18:31 house of G. was in S.
21:12 bro. young virgins to S.
19 is a feast of the Lord in S.
21 if the daughters of S. dance
1 *Sam.* 1:3 up to worship in S.
24 Samuel to house of L. in S.
2:14 so did priests in S. to all
3:21 Lord appeared again in S.
4:3 the ark of the Lord out of S.
12 a man came to S. with his
14:3 Ahitub, Lord's priest in S.
1 *K.* 2:27 acu. house of Eli in S.
11:2 out thee to S. to Ahijah
14:4 Jeroboam's wife went to S.
Ps. 78:60 forsook tabeena. of S.
Jer. 7:12 place which was in S.
14 th. house as I ha. done to S.
26:6 I make this house like S.
9 this house came certain fro. S.

SHILOAH.

Is. 8:6 refuseth the waters of S.

SHI

SHIMEAH.

2 *Sam.* 13:3 Jonadab son of S.
32; 21:21; 1 *Chr.* 20:7
1 *Chr.* 3:5 S. was born to David
6:39 Berachiah, the son of S.

SHIMEI.

2 *Sam.* 16:5 S. son of Gera. 19:16
13 S. went along on hill's side
1 *K.* 2:8 thou hast with thee S.
36 two of the servants of S.
4:18 S. the son of Elah
1 *Chr.* 3:19 S. son of Pedaiah. 5:4
4:26 Mish. Hamuel, Zaccur. S.
27 S. had sixteen sons and six
6:17 S. son of Ge. 42; 23:7, 29
23:9 *s.* of S. 10; 25:17 tenth to S.
27:27 over vineyards was S.
2 *Chr.* 29:14 Heman. Jeh. and S.
31:12 over dedicated thi. S. 13
Ezr. 10:23 S. taken strange wife
Est. 2:5 son of Jair, son of S.
Zec. 12:13 family of S. shall

SHIMSHAI.

Ezr. 4:8 S. the scribe wrote, 9
17 king sent an answer to S.

SHINAR.

Gen. 10:10 Calneh in land of S.
11:2 found a plain in land of S.
14:1 Amraphel king of S.
Is. 11:11 recover remna. from S.
Dan. 1:2 carried into land of S.
Zec. 5:11 a house in land of S.

SHINE.

Num. 6:25 L. make his face *s.*
Job 3:4 neither let light *s.* on it
10:3 thou should. *s.* on counsel
11:17 thou shalt *s.* forth
18:5 spark of his fire sh. not *s.*
22:28 light sh. *s.* upon thy ways
36:32 commandeth it not to *s.*
37:15 caused light of cloud to *s.*
41:32 mak. path to *s.* after him
Ps. 31:16 make thy face *s.*
67:1 cause face to *s.* 80:3, 7, 19
80:1 dwellest betw. cherubim *s.*
104:15 oil to make his face to *s.*
119:135 make face *s.* upon serv.
Ec. 8:1 man's wisd. mak. face *s.*
Is. 13:10 not cause light to *s.*
60:1 arise, *s.* thy light is come
Jer. 5:28 are waxen fat, they *s.*
Dan. 9:17 cause thy face to *s.*
12:3 that be wise, sh. *s.* as stars
Mat. 5:16 let your light *s.*
13:43 righteous. *s.* forth as sun
17:2 his face did *s.* as sun
2 *Cor.* 4:4 lest light of Ch. sho. *s.*
6 G. commanded light to *s.*
Phil. 2:15 among whom ye *s.* as
Rev. 18:23 candle sh. *s.* no more
21:23 no need of sun or moon *s.*

SHINED.

Deut. 33:2 the L. *s.* forth fr. Par,
Job 29:3 candle *s.* upon my head
Ps. 50:2 perfect. of beauty G. *s.*
Is. 9:2 upon them hath light *s.*
Ezek. 43:2 the earth *s.* with glory
Acts 9:3 suddenly there *s.* about
12:7 and a light *s.* in the prison
2 *Cor.* 4:6 G. hath *s.* in our hearts

SHINETH.

Job 25:5 to the moon, it *s.* not
Ps. 139:12 night *s.* as the day
Prov. 4:18 shining light that *s.*
Mat. 24:27 lightning *s.* to west
John 1:5 the light *s.* in darkness
2 *Pet.* 1:19 light that *s.* in a dark
1 *John* 2:8 the true light now *s.*
Rev. 1:16 countenance as sun *s.*

SHINING.

2 *Sam.* 23:4 grass springing by *s.*
Prov. 4:18 the just's is a *s.* light
Is. 4:5 upon all assem. a *s.* fire
Joel 2:10 stars sh. withd. *s.* 3:15
Hab. 3:11 his raiment became *s.*
Luke 11:36 *s.* of a candle giveth
John 5:35 burning and a *s.* light
Acts 26:13 above bright. of sun *s.*

SHIP.

Prov. 30:19 way of a *s.* in the sea
Is. 33:21 no gallant *s.* shall pass
Jonah 1:3 found a *s.* going
Mat. 4:21 in a *s.* with Zebedee
8:24 *s.* was covered with waves
14:24 *s.* was tossed, *Mark* 4:37
Mark 1:19 in *s.* mending nets
6:51 into the *s.* but no fear
8:14 had in the *s.* but one loaf
John 6:21 immediately the *s.* was
21:6 cast net on right side of *s.*
8 other disciples came in a *s.*
27:2 entering a *s.* of Adramyt.

SHIPS.

Gen. 49:13 Zebul. a haven for *s.*

SHO

1 *Tim.* 6:15 in his times he *sh. s.*
2 *Tim.* 2:15 *s.* thyself appr. to G.
Heb. 6:11 that every one *s.* dilig.
Jam. 2:18 *s.* me thy faith witho.
3:13 *s.* works out of good conv.
1 *Pet.* 2:9 *s.* forth praises of him
1 *John* 1:2 *s.* unto you etern. life
Rev. 1:1 angel to *s.* servants, 22:6

I will SHOW.
Gen. 12:1 land that *I w. s.* thee
Ex. 33:19 *I w. s.* mercy on whom
I will s. mercy
Judg. 4:22 *I will s.* thee the man
1 *Sam.* 16:3 *I w. s.* what shalt do
22:18 then *I will s.* it thee
1 *K.* 18:15 *I w.* surely *s.* myself
2 *K.* 7:12 *I w. s.* you what Syria.
Job 13:17 *I w. s.* thee that which
Ps. 50:23 *I will s.* the salvation
of God, 91:16
Jer. 18:17 *I will s.* them the back
33:3 *I w. s.* thee mighty things
42:12 *I w. s.* mercies unto you
Dan. 11:2 *I w. s.* thee the truth
Joel 2:30 *I will s.* wonders in
heaven, *Acts* 2:19
Mic. 7:15 *I will s.* marvel. things
Zec. 1:9 *I will s.* thee what these
Luke 6:17 *I will s.* wh. he is like
Acts 9:16 *I will s.* how great evl.
Jam. 2:18 *I will s.* thee my faith
Rev. 4:1 *I will s.* thee things wh.
See KINDNESS.

SHOWED.
Num. 13:26 *s.* them fruit of land
Deut. 34:12 Mo. *s.* in sight of Is.
Jud. 1:25 he *s.* them entrance
13:10 woman *s.* her husband
16:18 he hath *s.* me his heart
Ruth 2:11 *s.* me all th. hast done
2 Sam. 11:9 *s.* it to men of Jab.
2 Sam. 11:22 messenger *s.* David
1 *K.* 1:27 not *s.* it to thy servant
16:27 his might that he *s.* 22:45
2 *K.* 6:6 he *s.* him the place
22:15 there is nothing I have
not *s.* them, *Is.* 39:4
Est. 1:4 *s.* riches of his kingdom
2:6 *s.* him the people of Mordc.
Job 6:14 to afflicted pity *sh.* be *s.*
Ps. 71:18 until I have *s.* thy stren.
Prov. 26:26 wickedness *sh.* be *s.*
Ec. 2:19 I have *s.* myself wise
Is. 40:14 *s.* him way of understa.
Mat. 28:11 *s.* to chief priests
Luke 4:5 devil *s.* him all kingdo.
7:18 disciples of John *s.* him
14:21 serv. came and *s.* him lord
John 10:32 good works have I *s.*
Tit. 3:4 love of Sav. *s.* toward
disciples, 14; *Acts* 1:3
Acts 7:26 Mo. *s.* himself to them
52 which *s.* bef. of the coming
20:20 *s.* taught you publicly
23:22 tell no man hast *s.* these
28:20 P. *s.* to them of Damascus
1 *Cor.* 10:28 for his sake that *s.*
Heb. 6:10 love which ye have *s.*

God, or Lord SHOWED.
Gen. 19:19 thy mercy *s.* to me
32:10 not worthy of mercies *s.*
39:21 the Lord *s.* Joseph mercy
41:25 *God s.* P. what he is about
39 foras. *as God hath s.* thee
48:11 *G.* ha. *s.* me also thy seed
Ex. 24:12 mind of *L.* might be *s.*
Num. 14:11 all signs I have *s.*
among them, *Deut.* 6:22
Deut. 4:36 upon earth he *s.* thee
5:24 *L. our God s.* us his glory
34:1 *Lord s.* him the land of Ca.
Jud. 13:23 hor would he have *s.*
2 *K.* 8:10 *L.* hath *s.* me, he shall
13 the *L. s.* me thou sh. be ki.
Ezr. 9:8 grace *s.* fr. *L.* our God
Ps. 60:3 thou hast *s.* thy people
77:10 hast *s.* me great troubles
111:6 *s.* the power of his works
118:27 *God the L. s.* us light
Is. 26:10 let favor be *s.* to wick.
43:12 *s.* when no strange *God*
48:3 I *s.* th. I did them sudden.
5 bef. it came to pass I *s.* them
Jer. 38:21 word *Lord* hath *s.* me
Ezek. 11:25 thi. *Lord* hath *s.* me
Amos 7:1 *Lord s.* me, 4, 7; 8:1
Mic. 6:8 he hath *s.* thee, O man
Luke 1:58 *Lord* hath *s.* mercy
Acts 3:18 things which *G.* had *s.*
10:40 *G.* raised him and *s.* him
Rom. 1:19 *G.* hath *s.* it to them
2 *Pet.* 1:14 *L.* Jesus hath *s.* me

SHOWEDST, EST.
Neh. 9:10 *s.* signs upon Pharaoh
Jer. 11:18 thou *s.* me their doin.

SHU

Jer. 32:18 that *s.* loving-kind. to
John 2:18 what sign *s.* thou ? 6:30

SHOWETH.
Gen. 41:28 God is about to do, *s.*
Num. 23:3 whatsoever he *s.* me
Job 36:9 he *s.* them their work
33 the noise *s.* concerning it
Ps. 19:2 night unto night *s.*
112:5 good man *s.* favor
147:19 he *s.* his word unto Jac.
Prov. 12:17 speaks tru. *s.* right,
Is. 41:26 no. that *s.* your words
Mat. 4:8 *s.* him all kingdoms
John 5:20 Father *s.* Son all thin.

SHOWING.
Ex. 20:6 and *s.* mercy unto thou-
sands, *Deut.* 5:10
Dan. 5:12 *s.* of hard sentences
Luke 1:80 in deserts till his *s.*
8:1 *s.* glad tidings of kingdom
2 *Thes.* 2:4 as *G. s.* himself
Tit. 2:7 in all things *s.* a pattern

SHOWER.
Ezek. 13:11 be overflowing *s.* 13
34:26 cause *s.* to come in season
Luke 12:54 say. There cometh *s.*

SHOWERS.
Deut. 32:2 my speech distil as *s.*
Job 24:8 the poor are wet with *s.*
Ps. 65:10 mak. earth soft with *s.*
72:6 king shall come like *s.*
Jer. 3:3 *s.* have been withholden
14:22 can the heavens give *s.*?
Ezek. 34:26 his season *s.* of bles.
Mic. 5:7 Jac. shall be as *s.* on gr.
Zec. 10:1 Lord shall give them *s.*

SHRANK.
Gen. 32:32 Is. not eat of sinew *s.*

SHRED.
2 *K.* 4:39 came and *s.* wild gour.

SHRINES.
Acts 19:24 Demet. made silver *s.*

SHRUB.
Gen. 21:15 Ha. cast child und. *s.*

SHRUBS.
Gen. 21:15 Ha. cast child und. *s.*

SHUAH.
Gen. 25:2 Ishbak, S. 1 *Chr.* 1:32
38:2 married daugh. of a Cana-
anite, nam. S. 12; 1 *Chr.* 2:3

SHUAL.
1 *Sam.* 13:17 turned to land of S.

SHULAMITE.
Cant. 6:13 O S. what see in S. ?

SHUN, NED.
Acts 20:27 not *s.* to decl. counsel
2 *Tim.* 2:16 *s.* profane babblings

SHUNAMMITE.
1 *K.* 1:3 they found Abishag a S.
2:17 he gave me Abishag the S.
4:12 why doest ask Abishag S.
2 *K.* 4:12 call this S. 36 ; 25

SHUNEM. 1 *Sam.* 28:4
SHUR. *Gen.* 16:7

SHUSHAN.
Neh. 1:1 I was in S. the palace
Est. 2:8 maidens gathered to S.
3:15 the city S. was perplexed
4:16 gather all the Jews in S.
8:15 the city of S. rejoiced and
9:11 number slain in S. was
15 Jews slew in S. three hund.

SHUT.
Gen. 7:16 the Lord *s.* him in
14:3 wilderness *s.* them in
Num. 12:14 let her be *s.* out
15 Miriam was *s.* out 7 days
Deut. 15:7 nor *s.* hand from poor
Jos. 2:7 they *s.* gate of Jericho
Jud. 9:51 they *s.* tower to them
1 *Sam.* 23:7 he is *s.* in, by enter.
Ps. 69:15 let not pit *s.* mouth
Ec. 6:10 *s.* eyes lest they see
12:22 open and none shall *s.* he
shall *s.* none open
44:18 he hath *s.* their eyes
52:15 kings sh. *s.* their mouths
60:11 gates shall not be *s.* day
Jer. 20:9 is in *s.* up, I could not
36 strengthen that in *s.* up
John 4:46 a nobleman's son *s.*
11:1 Laz. of Bethany was *s.* 2
Mat. 1:8 offer *s.* is it not evil ?
Mal. 4:24 bron. to him *s.* people
6 he healed all th. were *s.* 14:14
9:12 but they that are *s. Mark*
2:17 ; *Luke* 5:31
10:8 heal the *s.* cleanse the lep-
ers, *Luke* 9:2 ; 10:9
23:26 I was *s.* and ye visited me
Mark 2:5 laid hands on a few *s.*
6:13 anoint. many that were *s.*
56 laid *s.* in streets, *Acts* 5:15
16:18 lay hands on the *s.*
Luke 7:2 centurion's serv. was *s.*
10 serv. whole that had been *s.*
John 11:1 Laz. of Bethany was *s.*
Acts 9:37 Dorcas was *s.* and died
19:12 bron. the *s.* handkerchiefs
28:8 father of Publius lay *s.*
Phil. 2:26 heard he had been *s.*
2 *Tim.* 4:20 Tro. I left at Mil. *s.*
Jam. 5:14 *s.* let him call elders
See PALSY.

SHUT up.
Deut. 16:9 beg. to put *s.* to corn
23:25 not move *s.* unto neigh.'s

SIC

Deut. 11:17 and he *s. up* heaven
32:30 the Lord had *s.* them *up*
36 seeth there is none *s. up*
1 *Sam.* 1:5 L. *s. up* Ilag.'s womb
6 the Lord had *s. up* her womb
6:10 *s. up* their calves at home
1 *K.* 8:35 when heaven is *s. up,*
2 *Chr.* 6:26 ; 7:13
14:10 from Jeroboam him that
is *s. up,* 21:21 ; 2 *K.* 9:8
2 *K.* 14:26 th. was not any *s. up*
17:4 king of Assyria *s.* him *up*
2 *Chr.* 28:24 A. *s. up* doors, 29:7
Neh. 6:10 house of Sh. was *s. up*
Job 3:10 because it *s.* not *up*
11:10 *s. up,* who can hinder ?
38:8 who hath *s. up* the sea ?
Ps. 31:8 hast not *s. me up* into
77:9 ha. he *s. up* tender merc. ?
88:8 I am *s. up,* I cannot come
Is. 24:10 every house is *s. up*
22 they shall be *s. s. up* in prison
Jer. 13:19 cities of south be *s. up*
32:2 prophet was *s. up* by Z. 3
33:1 while he was *s. up,* 39:15
36:5 I am *s. up,* I cannot go
Dan. 8:26 *s.* thou *up* the vision
12:4 O Daniel, *s. up* the words
Mat. 23:13 *s. up* kingd. of heav.
Luke 3:20 *s. up* John in prison
4:25 heaven was *s. up* three yrs.
Acts 10:29 many did I *s. up*
Gal. 3:23 *s. up*
Rev. 20:3 *s. up* devil, set a seal

SHUTTETH.
Job 12:14 he *s. up* a man
Prov. 17:28 that *s.* lips is a man
Is. 33:15 *s.* eyes from seeing
Lam. 3:8 when I cry he *s.* out
1 *John* 3:17 *s.* bp bow. of compa.
Rev. 3:7 no m. *s.* and *s.* no m. op.

SHUTTING.
Jos. 2:5 about time of *s.* gate
Job 7:6 swifter than a weaver's *s.*

SICK.
Gen. 48:1 behold, thy father is *s.*
Lev. 15:33 is *s.* of her flowers
1 *Sam.* 19:14 she said, He is *s.*
30:13 three days ago I fell *s.*
2 *Sam.* 12:15 L. struck ch. was *s.*
13:2 Amnon was vexed, fell *s.*
5 Jonadab said, Make thys. *s.*
6 Am. lay down made hims. *s.*
1 *K.* 14:1 the son of Jeroh. fell *s.*
5 cometh to ask for son, he is *s.*
17:17 son of the woman fell *s.*
2 *K.* 1:2 Ahaz. fell down, was *s.*
8:7 Benha. king of Syria was *s.*
29 Joram son of Ahab, bec. he
was *s.* 9:15
Dan. 7:5 rais. up itself on one *s.*
11:17 she is *s.* on my *s.* who I
1 *Chr.* 12:15 Ju. and Benj. on *s.*
Ps. 91:7 thousand shall fall at *s.*
118:6 the Lord is on my *s.* I will
122:1 if it had not be. L. on *s.* 2
Cant. 4:16 fell by the *s.* of gate
30:25 and Abner sat by Saul's *s.*
2 *Sam.* 2:16 thrust w. into his *s.*
13:34 king's sons came by hill *s.*
16:13 Shimei went on hill's *s.*
1 *K.* 9:22 who is on my *s.* who I
2 *Chr.* 12:16 David, and on thy *s.*
1 *Chr.* 12:18 David, and on thy *s.*

SICKLY.
1 *Cor.* 11:30 for this cause ma. *s.*

SICKNESS.
Ex. 23:25 I will take *s.* away
Lev. 20:18 if lie wi. wom. hav. *s.*
Deut. 7:15 L. will take fr. thee *s.*
28:61 ev. *s.* not written in law
1 *K.* 8:37 whatsoever *s.* there be,
2 *Chr.* 6:28
17:17 his *s.* was so sore
2 *K.* 13:14 Elisha was sick of *s.*
2 *Chr.* 21:15 shalt have great *s.*
19 bow. fell out by reas. of *s.*
Ps. 41:3 will make his bed in *s.*
Ec. 5:17 sor. and wrath with *s.*
Is. 38:9 Hez. recovered of his *s.*
12 pining *s.* from day to night
Hos. 5:13 when Ephr. saw his *s.*
Mat. 4:23 Je. went healing all *s.*
9:35 Jesus went about healt. *s.*
10:1 to heal, *s. Mark* 3:15
John 11:4 *s.* is not unto death

SICKNESSES.
Deut. 28:59 sore *s.* of long conti.
21:22 when they see *s.* L. laid
Mat. 8:17 ss. Himself bare our *s.*

SID

Jer. 50:16 cut off (that handfl. *s.*
Joel 3:13 put ye in *s.* harv. ripe
Mark 4:29 immedi. he put. in *s.*
Rev. 14:14 in his hand sharp *s.*
15 thrust in thy *s.* 16, 18, 19

SICKLY.
1 *Cor.* 11:30 for this cause ma. *s.*

SICKNESS.
Ex. 23:25 I will take *s.* away
Lev. 20:18 if lie wi. wom. hav. *s.*
Deut. 7:15 L. will take fr. thee *s.*
28:61 ev. *s.* not written in law
1 *K.* 8:37 whatsoever *s.* there be,
2 *Chr.* 6:28
17:17 his *s.* was so sore
2 *K.* 13:14 Elisha was sick of *s.*
2 *Chr.* 21:15 shalt have great *s.*
19 bow. fell out by reas. of *s.*
Ps. 41:3 will make his bed in *s.*
Ec. 5:17 sor. and wrath with *s.*
Is. 38:9 Hez. recovered of his *s.*
12 pining *s.* from day to night
Hos. 5:13 when Ephr. saw his *s.*
Mat. 4:23 Je. went healing all *s.*
9:35 Jesus went about healt. *s.*
10:1 to heal, *s. Mark* 3:15
John 11:4 *s.* is not unto death

SIDE.
Gen. 6:16 do. of the ark in the *s.*
Ex. 12:7 strl. blood on *s.* posts
17:12 stayed Moses' hands, one
on *s.* the other on oth. *s.*
32:26 who is on the Lord's *s.* let
27 put ev. man his sword by *s.*
Num. 22:24 on this and that *s.*
32:19 not inh. yonder *s.* Jordan
Deut. 4:32 ask from one *s.* heav.
31:26 book of law in *s.* of ark
Jos. 12:9 king on the other *s.* of
Jud. 7:1 Midianites on north *s.*
1 Sam. 6:8 put ark in coffer by *s.*
14:1 with him that bare armor
14:4 passages bet. Jon. sought
20:25 and Abner sat by Saul's *s.*
2 *Sam.* 2:16 thrust w. into his *s.*
13:34 king's sons came by hill *s.*
16:13 Shimei went on hill's *s.*
1 *K.* 9:22 who is on my *s.* who I
1 *Chr.* 12:18 David, and on thy *s.*
2 *Chr.* 14:7 hath giv. rest on ev. *s.*
Ps. 12:8 the wicked walk on ev. *s.*
31:13 fear was on every *s.*
Ps. 6:25 fear *s.* 20:10 ; 49:29
Ezek. 16:33 come to thee on ev. *s.*
19:8 nations set ag. him on ev. *s.*
23:22 bring fu. ag. thee on ev. *s.*
32:21 I will gather them on ev. *s.*
Cor. 4:8 are troubled on ev. *s.* 7:5

Farther **SIDE.**
Mark 10:1 J. came by *f. s.* Jord.
See LEFT.

On this SIDE.
1 *Sam.* 8:33 L. and Jud. stood on *t. s.*
1 *Sam.* 23:26 Saul went on *this s.*
Ezr. 4:16 no portion on this *s.*
Ezek. 1:23 had two wings on *this s.*
40:39 were two tables on *this s.*
Dan. 12:5 stood two. one on *t. s.*

On other SIDE.
Num. 24:2 fathers dwelt on o. *s.*
1 *Sam.* 14:40 I and Jona. on o. *s.*
John 6:25 found him on o. *s.*

Right SIDE.
Ezek. 4:6 he again on thy r. *s.*
47:1 from and, r. *s.* of house, 2
See SEA, SOUTH, WAY, WEST.

SIDES.
1 *Sam.* 24:3 David in *s.* of cave

CRUDEN'S CONCORDANCE. 1023

1024 CRUDEN'S CONCORDANCE.

SIS

Acts 22:16 wash away thy *s*.
Rom. 7:3 *s*. did work in members
Eph. 2:1 who were dead in *s*. 5
5 *Col.* 3:11 putti. off the body of *s*.
1 *Tim.* 5:22 partakers of men's *s*.
24 men's *s*. opened beforehand
Heb. 2:17 reconcilia. for *s*. of pe.
5:1 gifts and sacrifices for *s*.
7:27 for his own *s*. for people's
9:28 Ch. off. to bear *s*. of many
10:4 blood of goats take away *s*.
12 offered one sacrifice for *s*.
Jam. 5:20 and hide multit. of *s*.
1 *Pet.* 2:24 dead to *s*. live to righ.
3:18 Christ once suffered for *s*.
4:8 charity cover multitude of *s*.
2 *Pet.* 1:9 was purged from his *s*.
1 John 2:2 the *s*. of whole world
Rev. 18:4 be not partak. of her *s*.
5 her *s*. have reach. unto heav.
See FORGIVE, FORGIVEN.

My SINS.

Ps. 51:9 hide thy face from my *s*.
69:5 O G. my *s*. not hid fr. thee
Is. 38:17 cast my *s*. behind back

Our SINS.

1 *Sam.* 12:19 added to *our s*.
2 *Chr.* 28:13 int. to add to *our s*.
Neh. 9:37 ki. over us bec. of *o. s*.
Ps. 79:9 purge away *our s*.
90:8 *o. s*. in light of countenance
103:10 not dealt accord. to *o. s*.
Is. 59:12 *our s*. testify against us
Ezek. 33:10 if *our s*. be on us
Dan. 9:16 bec. of *o. s*. peo. beco.
1 *Cor.* 15:3 Christ died for *our s*.
Gal. 1:4 gave himself for *our s*.
Heb. 1:3 himself purged *our s*.
1 *Pet.* 2:24 his own self bare *o. s*.
1 *John* 1:9 if we confess *our s*.
Rev. 1:5 washed us from *our s*.

Their SINS.

Lev. 16:16 transgression in *th. s*.
Num. 16:26 consumed in all *t. s*.
1 *K.* 14:22 provoked with *their s*.
16:2 prov. me to anger with *t. s*.
Neh. 9:2 Israel confessed *their s*.
Is. 58:1 show house of Jacob *t. s*.
Jer. 14:10 vis. *t. s. Hos.* 8:13; 9:9
Mic. 7:19 cast all *t. s*. into sea
Mat. 1:21 save his peo. from *t. s*.
Mark 4:12 *t. s*. should be forgiv.
Luke 1:77 salva. by remis. of *t. s*.
Rom. 11:27 shall take away *t. s*.
1 *Thes.* 2:16 to fill up *t. s*. alway
Heb. 8:12 I w. be merciful to *t. s*.
10:17 *th. s*. remember no more

Your SINS.

Lev. 16:30 may be clean fr. *y. s*.
26:18 punish you for *y. s*. 24, 28
Deut. 9:18 nor drink, bec. of *y. s*.
Jos. 24:19 G. will not forgi. *y. s*.
Is. 1:18 tho' *your s*. be as scarlet
59:2 *your s*. have hid his face
Jer. 5:25 *y. s*. withholden good
Ezek. 21:24 in doings *y. s*. appe.
Amos 5:12 know *y.* trans. and *s*.
John 8:21 seek me. die in *y. s*. 24
Acts 3:19 repeat, that *y. s*. may
1 *Cor.* 15:17 raised, ye are in *y. s*.
Col. 2:13 you being dead in *y. s*.
1 *John* 2:12 *y. s*. are forgiven you

SION, *Deut.* 4:48
See ZION.

SIR.

Gen. 43:20 *s*. we ca. to buy food
Mat. 21:30 I go *s*. and went not
John 4:11 *s*. thou hast nothi. to
49 *s*. come ere my child die
5:7 *s*. I ha. no man to put me in
12:21 saying, *s*. we would see J.
Acts 7:36 *s*. ye are brethren, why
16:30 *s*. wh. mu. I do to be sa.
21:23 where, *s*. he of good cheer
Rev. 7:14 said to him, *s*. th. kno.

SIRION.

Deut. 3:9 which Sidonians call S.
Ps. 29:6 Lebanon and S. like *a*

SISERA.

Jud. 4:2 captain of host was S.
17 S. fled away on his feet. 22
5:20 the stars fought against S.
26 with hammer she smote S.
28 the mother of S. looked out
1 *Sam.* 1:26 sold into hand of S.
Ezr. 2:53 children of S. Nethinim went up, *Neh.* 7:55
Ps. 83:9 do unto them as to S.

SISTER.

Gen. 24:60 our *s*. be thou mother
34:13 defiled Dinah their *s*. 27
31 deal with our *s*. as a harlot?

Ex. 2:4 his *s*. stood afar off
Lev. 13:9 shalt not uncover *s*.
18 thy *s*. 18 a wife to her *s*.
20:17 if a man take *s*. see nake.
21:3 his *s*. *r*. a virgin, be defiled
Num. 8:7 not defiled for his *s*.
Deut. 27:22 curs. that lieth wt. *s*.
Jud. 15:2 youn. *s*. fairer th. she?
2 *Sam.* 13:1 Ab. had fair *s*. Tamar
22 had forced his *s*. Tamar, 32
Cant. 8:8 lit. *s*. hath no breasts
Jer. 3:7 treacherous *s*. Ju. saw it
8 *s*. feared not; 10 *s*. not turn.
22:18 lament, saying, Ah, my *s*.
Ezek. 16:45 thou art *s*. of sisters
46 elder *s*. Samaria, youn. *s*. S.
48 So. thy *s*. not done as thou
22:11 ano. hath humbled his *s*.
23:4 Ah. elder, Aholibah her *s*.
18 mind was alienated from *s*.
31 thou walk. in way of thy *s*.
32 drink of thy *s*. cup deep. 33
41:25 *s*. that hath no hus. defile
Mar. 12:50 same is brother, *s*.
Luke 10:39 had a *s*. *John* 11:1, 5
John 19:25 stood by cross m.'s *s*.
Acts 23:16 Paul's *s*. son heard of
Rom. 16:1 Phebe our *s*. servant
1 *Cor.* 7:15 *s*. is not under bond,
9:5 not power to lead a *s*. *f*
Col. 4:10 Marcus *s*. son to Barna.
Jam. 2:15 if a bro. or *s*. be naked
6 *John* 13 children of thy elect *s*.

SISTER-IN-LAW.

Ruth 1:15 *r.-i.-l*. is gone back

My SISTER.

Gen. 12:13 say, thou art my *s*.
19 why saidst thou, She is my
s. 20:2, 5, 12; 26:7, 9
30:8 I have wrestled with *my s*.
2 *Sam.* 13:5 let *my s*. Tu. come, 6
20 hold thou thy peace, *my s*.
Job 17:14 said to worm, art *my s*.
Prov. 7:4 thou art *my s*.
Cant. 4:9 rav'. *my* heart, *my s*.
10 how fair is thy love, *my s*.
5:1 am come into my gar. *my s*.
2 open to me, *my s*. my love
Mark 3:35 same my bro. *my s*.
Luke 10:40 do. th. not care *my s*.?

SISTERS.

Jos. 2:13 swe. ye will save my *s*.
Job 1:4 called for three *s*. to eat
42:11 came his brethren and *s*.
Ezek. 16:45 th. art sister of thy *s*.
Hos. 2:1 say unto your *s*. Ruha.
Mat. 13:56 *s*. with us? *Mark* 6:3
1 *Tim.* 5:2 int. as *s*. with purity

SIT.

Num. 32:6 go to war ye *s*. here
Jud. 5:10 ye that *s*. in judgment
Ruth 4:1 ho, *s*. down here. 2
1 *Sam.* 9:22 *s*. in chiefest place
16:11 will not *s*. down till he co.
20:5 not fall to *s*. with king
2 *Sam.* 19:8 king doth *s*. in gate
1 *K.* 1:13 Solomon shall *s*. 17
9 shall not man to *s*. on thr. of
Is, 2 *Chr.* 6:16; *Jer.* 33:17
2 *K.* 7:3 *s*. here till we die? 4
10:30 sons *s*. on throne, 15:12
13:27 to men who *s*. *Is.* 36:12
Ps. 26:5 will not *s*. with wicked
69:12 *s*. in gate speak aga. me
110:1 *s*. thou at my right hand
119:23 princes also did *s*.
127:2 vain for you to *s*. up late
Ec. 10:6 rich *s*. in low place
Is. 3:26 desolate *s*. on ground
16:5 *s*. upon the throne in truth
30:7 their strength is to *s*. still
42:7 bring them that *s*. in dark.
47:1 *s*. in dust, *s*. on grou. *s*. 5
5 *s*. thou silent, O daughter
14 not be a fire to *s*. before it
Jer. 8:14 why do we *s*. still?
13:13 I will fill them that *s*.
15:17 I sat not in assembly
16:8 not go to hou. of feas. to *s*.
36:30 none to *s*. on throne of D.
48:18 come fr. glory, *s*. in thirst
Lam. 2:10 elders of Z. *s*. on gro.
Ezek. 26:16 *s*. upon the ground
28:2 said, I *s*. in seat of God
44:3 prince shall *s*. in it to eat
Dan. 7:26 the judgment shall *s*.
Joel 3:12 *s*. to judge the heathen
Zec. 3:8 thou and thy fellows *s*.
6:13 *s*. and rule upon his throne
Mat. 8:11 many sh. *s*. with Abr.
20:21 sons *s*. one on thy ri. hand,
23 but to *s*. on my right hand,
Mark 10:37, 40

Mat. 23:2 Phar. *s*. in Moses' seat
26:36 *s*. ye here, *Mark* 14:32
Luke 9:14 *s*. by fifties in a comp.
12:37 make them to *s*. down,
13:29 shall *s*. in kingdom of G.
14:8 *s*. not down in high. room
12:7 go, and *s*. down in lowest
John 6:10 Jo. said, Make men *s*.
Acts 2:30 Ch. to *s*. on his throne
8:31 come up and *s*. with him
1 *Cor.* 8:10 to see thee *s*. at meat
Jam. 2:3 *s*. th. here in good pla.
Rev. 3:21 *s*. with me in my thro.
18:7 for she saith, I *s*. a queen

SITTETH.

Ex. 18:14 why *s*. thou thyself?
Deut. 0:7 talk of th. when thou *s*.
Ps. 10:29 thou *s*. and speakest
Ps. 1:1 nor *s*. in seat of scornful
10:8 he *s*. in the lurking places
29:10 *s*. on flood; Lord *s*. king
47:8 G. *s*. on throne of holiness
82:1 *s*. betw. the cherubim
Prov. 9:14 for she *s*. at the door
20:8 king *s*. in throne of judgm.
Is. 28:6 to him that *s*. in judgm.
40:22 he that *s*. on the heavens
Jer. 29:16 saith of king that *s*.
Lam. 3:28 *s*. and keepeth silence
Zec. 1:11 behold, earth *s*. still
5:7 woman *s*. in midst of epha.
8:33 *s*. sword by him that *s*.
Luke 14:28 *s*. not down first, 31
22:27 Is not he that *s*. at meat?
1 *Cor.* 14:30 if any thing be revealed to another that *s*. by
Col. 3:1 C. *s*. on right hand of G.
2 *Thes.* 2:4 G. *s*. in temp. of God
Rev. 5:13 power to him that *s*.
6:16 from face of him that *s*.
7:10 salva. to our God which *s*.

SITTING.

1 *K.* 10:5 *s*. of serv. 2 *Chr.* 9:4
13:11 man of God *s*. under oak
22:19 I saw L. *s*. upon his thro.
2 *Chr.* 18:18; *Is.* 6:1
2 *K.* 4:38 sons of proph. were *s*.
9:5 captains of the host were *s*.
Neh. 2:6 queen also *s*. by him
Est. 5:13 Mordecai the Jew *s*.
Jer. 17:25 king *s*. on thr. 22:4, 30
83:7 king *s*. in gate of Benjamin
Lam. 3:63 behold their *s*. down
Mat. 9:9 Matthew *s*. at recei. of
20:54 Son of man *s*. on right
hand of God, *Mark* 14:62
27:36 *s*. down, watched him
Mark 5:15 him that was poss. *s*.
16:5 they saw a young man *s*.
Luke 2:40 found him in midst of doctors
8:35 and found him *s*. clothed
19:15 changers of money *s*.
Acts 2:2 house where th. were *s*.
Rev. 4:4 I saw twenty-four elders *s*.

SITTING-PLACE.

2 *Chr.* 9:18 stays of each side *s*.-*p*.

SITUATE.

Ezek. 27:3 art *s*. at entry of sea
Nah. 3:8 populous No th. was *s*.

SITUATION.

2 *K.* 2:19 *s*. of the city is pleasa.
Ps. 48:2 beauti. for *s*. joy of earth

SIVAN,
Est. 8:9 3d month, month of S.

SIX. *See* BRANCHES.

SIX cities.

Num. 35:6 be *c*. of ref. 13, 15

SIX cubits.

1 *Sam.* 17:4 Goliath's height *s. c*.
Ezek. 40:5 measuring-reed of *s. c*.
41:1 measured posts *s. c*. broad
8 foundations were *s. c*. great
Dan. 3:1 breadth of image *s. c*.

SIX months.

Luke 4:25 heav. was shut three
years and *s. m*. *Jam.* 5:17

SIX sheep.

Neh. 5:18 prep. daily *s*. choice *s*.

SIX sons.

Gen. 30:20 I have borne *s. s*.
1 *Chr.* 3:22 Azel had *s. s*. 9:44

SIX things.

Prov. 6:16 *s. t*. doth Lord hate

SKI.

SIX times.

2 *K.* 13:19 ha. smitten five or *s. t*.

SIX troubles.

Job 5:19 sh. deliver thee in *s. tr*.

SIX water-pots.

John 2:6 were set there *s. wa.-p*.

SIX wings.

Is. 6:2 seraphim, each had *s. w*.
Rev. 4:8 4 beasts had each *s. w*.

SIX years.

Ex. 21:2 *s. y*. shall serve, seventh go fr. *Deut.* 15:12; *Jer.* 34:14
Lev. 25:21 bless. on yon *s*. year
Ezr. 6:15 house finish. in *s*. year
Ex. 4:11 drink water, *s*. part of
39:2 leave but the *s*. part of th.
Mat. 27:45 darkn. over land fr. *s*. to ninth hour, *Mark* 15:33; *Luke* 23:44
John 19:44 crucified about *s*. ho.
Rev. 21:20 *s*. foundn. was sardius

SIXTY.

Gen. 5:15 Mahalal. lived *s*. years
21 Enoch lived *s*. five years
Ler. 27:3 estimation fr. 20 to *s*.
Mat. 13:8 brought forth *s*. fold, 23; *Mark* 4:8, 20

SIZE.

Ex. 36:9 curtains were one *s*. 15
1 *K.* 7:37 bases of one meas. and *s*.
1 *Chr.* 23:29 all manner of *s*. Da.

SKILL.

1 *K.* 5:6 *s*. to hew tim. 2 *Chr.* 2:8
2 *Chr.* 2:7 m. that can *s*. to grave
34:12 all that could *s*. of music

SKILL.

Ec. 9:11 nor favor to men of *s*.
Dan. 1:17 God gave them *s*.
9:22 come to give thee *s*. under.

SKILFUL.

1 *Chr.* 5:18 sons of Re. *s*. in war
15:22 instructed, bec. he was *s*.
26:31 be with thee every *s*. man
2 *Chr.* 2:14 a cunning man, *s*.
Ez. 21:31 gi. you into ha. of *s*.
Dan. 1:4 children *s*. in all wisd.
Amos 5:16 *s*. of lamentation

SKILFULLY, NESS.

Ps. 33:3 sing new song, play *s*.
78:72 guided them by *s*. of hand

SKIN.

Ex. 22:27 his raiment for *s*.
29:14 bullock's flesh, *s. Lev.* 4:11
34:29 wist not that *s*. sho. 30, 35
Lev. 7:8 priest that offer. have *s*.
13:2 in *s*. a rising like plague
4 bright spot, white in the *s*.
10 old leprosy in *s*. of his flesh
38 sh. rend it out of gar. or *s*.
15:17 every *s*. whereon is seed
Num. 19:5 burn heifer, *s*. flesh
Job 2:4 *s*. for *s*. all a man hath
7:5 broken, and loathsome
10:11 clo. me with *s*. and flesh
16:15 sewed sackcl. on *s*. defiled
18:13 it shall dev. strength of *s*.
19:20 bone cleaveth to my *s*. I am esca. with *s*. of my teeth
26 after my *s*. worms des. body
30:30 *s*. black, bones are burnt
41:7 canst fill his *s*. with irons?
Ps. 102:5 my bones cleave to *s*.
Jer. 13:23 can Ethiop. change *s*.?
Lam. 3:4 flesh and *s*. made old
4:8 *s*. cleaveth to their bones
5:10 our *s*. was black like oven
Ezek. 37:6 cover you with *s*. 8
Mic. 3:2 pluck off their *s*.
3 flay their *s*. from off them
Mark 1:6 John had a girdle of *s*.

SKINS.

Gen. 3:21 Lord made coats of *s*.
27:16 put *s*. of goats on hands
Ex. 25:5 *s*. of rams, badgers' *s*.
Lev. 13:59 law of plague of *s*.
16:27 burn in fire their *s*.
Num. 31:20 purify, rai. man, of *s*.
Heb. 11:37 wandered in sheep *s*.

SKIP, PED, EDST.

Ps. 29:6 maketh calves to *s*.
114:4 mountains *s*. like rams, 6
Jer. 48:27 spakest, thou *s*. for joy

SKIPPING.

Cant. 2:8 cometh *s*. upon hills

SKIRT.

Deut. 22:30 not uncov. father's *s*.
Ruth 3:9 spread *s*. over handma.
1 *Sam.* 15:27 he laid hold on *s*.
24:4 Da. cut off *s*. of Saul's robe
11 *s*. of thy robe in my hand
Ezek. 16:8 I sp. my *s*. over thee

CRUDEN'S CONCORDANCE. 1025

SLA

Hag. 2:12 if one bear holy flesh in *s.* and with *s.* touch bread
Zec. 8:23 10 men take hold of *s.*

SKIRTS.

Ps. 133:2 down to *s.* of garments
Jer. 2:34 in *s.* is found blood of
13:22 are thy *s.* discov. *Nah.* 3:5
Lam. 1:9 filthiness is in her *s.*
Ezek. 5:3 bind a few hairs in *s.*

SKULL.

Jud. 9:53 millsto. to break his *s.*
2 *K.* 9:35 no more of Jez. than *s.*
Mat. 27:33 Golgotha, place of *s.*
s. Mark 15:22; *John* 19:17

SKY.

Deut. 33:26 rideth in excell. on *s.*
Job 37:18 hast th. spread out *s.?*
Mat. 16:2 fair weather, *s.* red, 3
Luke 12:56 can discern face of *s.*
Heb. 11:12 many as stars of *s.*

SKIES.

2 *Sam.* 22:12 clou. of *s. Ps.* 18:11
Ps. 77:17 *s.* sent out a sound
Is. 45:8 let *s.* pour down righte.
Jer. 51:9 her judgm. lifted to *s.*

SLACK.

Deut. 7:10 he will be *s.* to him
Jos. 18:3 how long are ye *s.*
Prov. 10:4 poor deal, with *s.* ha.
Zep. 3:16 Z. let not hands be *s.*
2 *Pet.* 3:9 L. not *s.* concer. prom.

SLACK, ED.

Deut. 23:21 vow th. shalt not *s.*
Jos. 10:6 *s.* not hand from serva.
2 *K.* 4:24 *s.* not riding for me
Hab. 1:4 law *s.* judgm. never go.

SLACKNESS.

2 *Pet.* 3:9 as some men count *s.*

SLAIN, active.

Gen. 4:23 *s.* a man to my wound.
Num. 14:16 hath *s.* them in wil.
22:33 surely now I had *s.* thee
Deut. 21:1 not kno. who hath *s.*
Jud. 9:18 ha. *s.* sons upon stones
15:16 bone of an ass *s.* 1,000
1 *Sam.* 18:7 Saul *s.* thous. 21:11
22:21 Saul had *s.* Lord's priests
2 *Sam.* 1:16 I have *s.* Lord's ano.
4:11 wicked men have *s.* righte
13:30 A. hath *s.* all king's sons
21:12 Phillist. had *s.* Saul in Gil.
1 *K.* 13:26 lion ha. to. and *s.* him
16:16 say, Zimri hath *s.* king
19:1 Ah. told he had *s.* prophets
10 *Is.* have *s.* thy prophets, 14
2 *K.* 14:5 servants who had *s.* ki.
2 *Chr.* 21:13 hast *s.* thy brethren
22:1 band of men had *s.* eldest
Est. 9:12 Jews have *s.* 500 men
Job 1:15 Sabeans have *s.* serv. 17
Prov. 7:26 strong men have *s.*
Is. 14:20 destroyed and *s.* people
Jer. 33:5 bod. of men *s.* in anger
41:4 had *s.* Gedaliah, 9, 16, 18
Lam. 2:21 *s.* th. in anger, 3:43
Ezek. 16:21 hast *s.* my children
23:39 *s.* their children to idols
Hos. 6:5 *s.* th. by words of mouth
Amos 4:10 young men have *s.*
Acts 2:23 by wick, hands have *s.*
7:52 *s.* them th. showed coming
23:14 eat noth. till we have *s.* P.

SLAIN, passive.

Gen. 34:27 sons of Ja. came on *s.*
Lev. 26:17 be *s.* before your ene.
Num. 11:22 and the herds be *s.?*
23:24 eat prey, drink blood of *s.*
25:14 Israelite that was *s.* Zimri
Deut. 21:1 if one be found *s.*
28:31 thine ox *s.* bef. thine eyes
Jos. 11:6 dell. them *s.* before Is.
13:22 Balaam also was among *s.*
Jud. 20:4 husband of the woman that was *s.*
1 *Sam.* 19:6 as I. liv. not be *s.*
20:32 wherefore shall he be *s.*
31:1 fell *s.* in Gilboa, 1 *Chr.* 10:1
2 *Sam.* 1:19 beauty of Israel is *s.*
23 bl. of *s.* from fat of mighty
25 O Jonathan, thou wast *s.* in
1 *K.* 11:15 Joab gone to bury *s.*
2 *K.* 3:23 the kings are surely *s.*
11:2 remeth with. ranges, he *s.*
1 *Chr.* 5:22 fell down many *s.*
2 *Chr.* 13:17 fell *s.* of Isr. 500,000
Est. 7:4 for we are sold to be *s.*
Job 39:30 where *s.* are, th. is she
Ps. 62:3 ye shall be *s.* all of you
88:5 like *s.* that lie in the grave
89:10 hast broken Rah. as one *s.*
Pron. 22:13 sloth. sai, I sh. be *s.*
24:11 deliv. them ready to be *s.*
Is. 10:4 they shall fall under *s.*
22:2 thy *s.* men not *s.* with sw.

SLA

Is. 26:21 earth no more cov. her *s.*
27:7 *s.* accord. to slaughter of *s.*
31:3 their *s.* also sh. he cast out
66:16 *s.* of Lord shall be many
Jer. 9:1 night weep for *s.* of peo.
14:18 go into field, beho. *s.* with
18:21 let their young men be *s.*
25:33 *s.* of L. be fr. end of earth
41:9 Ishmael filled the pit wi. *s.*
51:47 her *s.* shall fall in midst
49 Bab. caused *s.* of Is. to fall
Lam. 2:20 priest and proph. be *s.*
4:9 *s.* wi. sw. better than *s.* with
Ezek. 6:7 *s.* shall fall in midst
9:7 fill courts with *s.*
21:14 sw. of *s.* is of great men *s.*
29 bring thee upon necks of *s.*
26:6 her daugh. in field sh. be *s.*
28:8 die deaths of th. that are *s.*
30:11 shall fill land with the *s.*
31:18 sh. lie with them *s.* 32:20
32:20 fall in midst of the *s.* 25
21 lie *s.* by sword, 22, 23, 24
32:8 fill his mount. with *s.* men
37:9 O breath. breathe on th. *s.*
Dan. 2:13 wise men should be *s.*
5:30 in that night was Belsh. *s.*
11:26 many shall fall down *s.*
Zep. 2:12 ye Ethiopi. shall be *s.*
Luke 9:22 Son of man must be *s.*
Acts 5:36 Theud. *s.* and as many
7:42 ye offered to me *s.* beasts?
Eph. 2:16 cross, having *s.* enmity
23:27 sh. *s.* sons and daughters
Res. 2:13 Antipas who was *s.*
5:6 stood Lamb, as had been *s.*
9 wast *s.* 12 Lamb *s.* 13:8
6:9 souls of them that were *s.*

SLANDER, S.

Num. 14:36 by bring. a *s.* on land
Ps. 31:13 I ha. heard *s.* of many
Prov. 10:18 uttereth *s.* is a fool
Jer. 6:28 revolt. walking with *s.*
9:4 every neighbour walk with *s.*

SLANDERED, EST, ETH.

2 *Sam.* 19:27 he hath *s.* thy serv.
Ps. 50:20 thou *s.* mother's son
101:5 *s.* neighbour, him cut off

SLANDERERS.

1 *Tim.* 3:11 wives be grave, not *s.*

SLANDEROUSLY.

Rom. 3:8 not rather, as *s.* report.

SLANG.

1 *Sam.* 17:49 D. took sto. and *s.*

SLAUGHTER.

1 *Sam.* 14:14 first *s.* Jona. made
30 had there not been great. *s.*
17:57 D. returned fr. *s.* of Phill.
Ps. 44:22 counted as sheep for *s.*
Prov. 7:22 after her, as ox to *s.*
Is. 10:26 accord. to *s.* of Midian
14:21 prepare *s.* for his children
27:7 accord. to *s.* of them slain
30:25 day of great *s.* when tow.
34:2 deliv. them to *s.* 6
53:7 bro. as lamb to *s. Jer.* 11:19
65:12 ye shall bow down to *s.*
Jer. 7:32 Toph. but val. of *s.* 19:6
12:3 like sheep for *s.* prep. for *s.*
25:34 days of *s.* are accomplish.
48:15 young men are gone to *s.*
50:27 let them go down to the *s.*
51:40 bri. down like lambs to *s.*
Ezek. 9:2 ev. one had weapon *s.*
21:10 sharpened is to make *s.*
28 sw. is drawn, for *s.* furbish.
26:15 when *s.* is made in midst
Hos. 5:2 revolters profound to *s.*
Ob. 9 nor thou may be cut off by *s.*
Zec. 11:4 feed flock of *s.*
7 I will feed flock of *s.*
Acts 8:32 was led as a sheep to *s.*
9:1 Saul yet breathing out *s.*
Rom. 8:36 accounted as sheep for *s.*
Heb. 7:1 Abra. returning from *s.*
Jam. 5:5 hearts as in days of *s.*

See GREAT.

SLAVE, S.

Jer. 2:14 is Israel a *s.* is he home
Rev. 18:13 buy, merchandise of *s.*

SLAY.

Gen. 4:14 every one shall *s.* me
20:4 wilt thou *s.* a righteous na.
27:41 then will I *s.* brother Ja.
31:39 gather ag. me and *s.* me
34:30 two sons if I bring
37:20 come let us *s.* him, 26
43:16 bring them unto *s.* them
Lev. 4:29 *s.* the sin off. by *s.*
Num. 25:5 *s.* ye ev. one his men
Deut. 13:9 surely *s.* him, 13:13
Jos. 13:22 Israel did *s.* Balaam

SLE

Jud. 8:20 said to J. Up, *s.* them
9:54 *s.* me, that men say not
1 *Sam.* 2:25 bec. L. would *s.* them
14:34 bring ev. man ox, *s.* here
19:15 bri. him that I may *s.* him
20:8 if in me iniq. *s.* me thyself
22:17 said, Turn and *s.* priests
2 *Sam.* 1:9 Sa. said, Stand and *s.*
1 *K.* 1:51 swear he will not *s.*
18:12 cannot find thee, sh. *s.* me
20:36 departed, lion *s.* thee
2 *K.* 8:12 young men will thou *s.*
10:25 go in and *s.* them
17:26 God sent lion, they *s.*
2 *Chr.* 23:14 *s.* her not in ho. of L.
Neh. 4:11 we will *s.* them, cause
50:21 If scourge *s.* suddenly
13:15 though he *s.* me yet will I
Ps. 34:21 evil shall *s.* wicked
50:21 *s.* them not, lest my peop.
94:6 they *s.* widow and stranger
139:19 th. wilt *s.* wick. O God
Prov. 1:32 turn. of simple sh. *s.*
Is. 11:4 with breath shall he *s.*
14:30 he shall *s.* thy remnant
27:1 Lord shall *s.* the dragon
65:15 for Lord God shall *s.* thee
Jer. 5:6 lion of forest sh. *s.* them
20:4 carry Judah capti. *s.* them
29:21 shall *s.* Aluah and Zedek.
41:8 men fo. that said, *s.* us not
Ezek. 9:6 *s.* utter. old and young
23:47 sh. *s.* sons and daughters
26:8 shall *s.* thy daughters
Hos. 2:3 *s.* her with thirst
9:16 yet will I *s.* the fruit
Amos 2:3 I will *s.* all princes
9:1 I will *s.* the last of them
4 comm. sword, it sh. *s.* them
Zec. 11:5 whose possess. *s.* them
Luke 11:49 some they shall *s.*
19:27 bring hither, and *s.* them

To SLAY.

Gen. 18:25 far fr. thee to *s.* right.
22:10 Abra. stretched hand to *s.*
37:18 they conspired to *s.* him
Ex. 2:15 Ph. sought to *s.* Moses
21:14 if come on neighbour to *s.*
Deut. 9:28 bron. the ark to *s.* us
27:25 taketh reward to *s.* inno.
1 *Sam.* 5:10 brou. the ark to *s.* us
19:5 why then sin, to *s.* David?
2 *Sam.* 3:37 not of king to *s.* Ab.
21:2 Saul sought to *s.* them
1 *K.* 17:18 art come to *s.* my son?
18:9 deliv. me to Ahab to *s.* me
Neh. 6:10 to *s.* th. in night to *s.*
Ps. 37:14 to *s.* such as be upright
37 watcheth righte. seeik. to *s.*
Jer. 15:3 appoint sw. to *s.* dogs
Ezek. 13:19 to *s.* souls th. should
John 5:16 Jews, sou. to *s.* him
Acts 5:33 took counsel to *s.* apos.
9:29 they went about to *s.* him

SLAYER.

Num. 35:11 cities of refuge th. *s.*
Deut. 4:42; 19:3, 4; *Jos.* 20:3
28 after death of high-priest *s.* shall return, *Jos.* 20:6
Deut. 19:6 lest avenger pursue *s.*
Jos. 20:5 shall not de-liver the *s.*
21:13 Hebron city of ref. for *s.*
27 Shech. 27 Golan a ref. for *s.*
32 Kedesh in Galilee for the *s.*
38 Ramoth in Gil. refuge for *s.*

SLAYETH.

Gen. 4:15 Lord said, Whoso. *s.* C.
Deut. 22:26 unto damsel, and *s.* him
Job 5:2 wrath killeth, envy *s.*
Ezek. 28:9 tell him that *s.* thee, I am (?, *s.* in hand of him th. *s.*

SLAYING.

Jud. 9:56 rend. wicked. of A. in *s.*
1 *K.* 17:20 evil on widow by *s.*
2 *Chr.* children in the valleys
Is. 22:13 *s.* oxen and killing
28:8 while th. were *s.* them
Ezek. 9:8 *s.* them, I fell on my f.

SLEEP, Substantive.

Gen. 2:21 God caused deep *s.* to fall on Ad.
15:12 deep *s.* fell on Abram
28:16 Jacob awaked out of *s.*
31 departed fr. mine eyes
Jud. 16:14 awaked out of *s.* 20
Job 4:13 in deep *s.* falleth on men
14:12 nor raised out of their *s.*
33:15 lost lest L. de. in deep *s.*
Ps. 13:3 light mine eyes, sleep *s.* of death
76:6 both chariot and horse cast into *s.*
78:65 L. awaked like one out of *s.*
90:5 as *s.* in morning they are as grass
127:2 so he giveth his belov. *s.*
132:4 I will not give *s.* to eyes
Prov. 3:24 lie down, *s.* be sweet
4:16 their *s.* is taken away
6:4 give not *s.* to thine eyes
9 wh. wilt thou arise out of *s.?*
10 a little more *s.* 24:33
19:15 slothfuln. casteth into *s.*
20:13 love not *s.* lest co. to pov.
Ec. 5:12 the *s.* of laboring man
8:16 nei. day nor night seeth *s.*
Is. 29:10 L. pour. on you deep *s.*
Jer. 31:26 my *s.* was sweet to me
51:39 may *s.* a perpet. *s.* 57
Dan. 2:1 his *s.* brake from him
6:18 passed night his *s.* went fr.
8:18 I was in deep *s.* 10:9
Zec. 4:1 man wakened out of *s.*
Mat. 1:24 J. being raised from *s.*
Luke 9:32 were heavy with *s.*
13:11 awake him out of *s.*
9 spoken of taking rest in *s.*
Acts 16:27 keeper awak, out of *s.*
20:9 Euty. being fallen into *s.*
Rom. 13:11 to awake out of *s.*

SLEEP, Verb.

Gen. 28:11 Jacob lay down to *s.*
Deut. 24:12 not *s.* with his pledge
31:16 *s.* with fath. 2 *Sam.* 7:12
Jud. 16:19 ma. him *s.* on her kn.
1 *Sam.* 3:3 Sam. laid down to *s.*
1 *K.* 1:21 lord the king shall *s.*
Est. 6:1 night could not king *s.*
Job 7:21 now sh. I *s.* in the dust
Ps. 4:8 will I lay me down and *s.*
121:4 shall nei. slumber nor *s.*
Prov. 4:16 they *s.* not except
6:9 how long wilt th. O slug.?
10 folding of hands to *s.* 24:33
Ec. 5:12 *s.* of lab. man is sweet, abund. of rich not suffer *s.*
Cant. 5:2 I *s.* but my heart wak.
Is. 5:27 none sh. slumber nor *s.*
Jer. 51:39 may *s.* perp. sleep, 57
Ezek. 34:25 they shall *s.* in woods
Dan. 12:2 many that *s.* in dust
Mat. 26:45 *s.* on now. *Mark* 14:41
Mark 4:27 rise, *s.* and seed spri.
Luke 22:46 why *s.* ye ? rise
John 11:12 if he *s.* he sh. do well
1 *Cor.* 11:30 for th. cause many *s.*
15:51 we shall not all *s.*
1 *Thes.* 4:14 who *s.* in Je. will G.
5:6 let us not *s.* as do others
7 they that *s.* *s.* in the night
10 that whether we wake or *s.*

Jon. 1:6 what mean. thou, O *s.?*

SLEEPEST.

Ps. 44:23 why *s.* thou, O Lord
Prov. 6:22 wh. thou *s.* it sh. keep
Mark 14:37 Simon, *s.* thou?
Eph. 5:14 awake, thou that *s.*

SLEEPETH.

1 *K.* 18:27 said, Peradvent. he *s.*
Prov. 10:5 he that *s.* in harvest.
Hos. 7:6 their baker *s.* all night
Mat. 9:24 maid *s.* not dead but *s. Mark* 5:39; *Luke* 8:52
John 11:11 our friend Lazarus *s.*

SLEEPING.

1 *Sam.* 26:7 S. lay *s.* with. trench
Is. 56:10 I shall not do living slumber
Mark 13:36 lest com. find you *s.*
14:37 cometh and findeth them *s.*
Acts 12:6 Peter was *s.* betw. two

SLEIGHT.

Eph. 4:14 carried by *s.* of men

SLEW.

Gen. 4:8 Cain rose and *s.* Abel
Sam. 34:26 Simeon and Levi *s.*
1 *K.* 3:20 wife of thy handmaid *s.*
Job 1:15 ha. and *s.* the young and *s.* an angel *Jos.* 5:14 we brought not into *s.*
Ps. 3:5 I laid me down and *s.*
Mat. 13:25 while men *s.* his ene.
2:5 hidegreen tarried, they *s.*
27:52 bod. of saints wh *s.* arose
Luke 8:23 while they sailed he *s.*
20:9 lord gave fruits of that *s.*

See FATHERS.

SLEW.

Gen. 34:25 *s.* males; 26 *s.* Hamor
38 in their anger th. *s.* a man
Ex. 2:12 Moses *s.* the Egyptian
32:28 Levi's sons *s.* 3,000 men
Num. 31:7 *s.* kings of Mid. Bala. *s.* they *s.* in Bereb. 10,9 of *Jud.* 1:19 *s.* y. *s.* of Moab 10,000 men
of Shungar *s.* of Phil. 600 men with an ox-goad

1026 CRUDEN'S CONCORDANCE.

SLI

Jud. 9:5 Abim. s. breth. 70 pers.
14:19 Samson s. 30 men of I s.
15:15 jaw-bone Samson s. 1,000
16:30 aloud which he s. at death
1 Sam. 14:31 bron. his ox and s.
17:36 thy servant s. both lion
19:5 life in hand and s. Philist.
22:18 Doeg s. 85 persons that
29:5 sang. Saul s. thousands
2 Sam. 4:12 Da. s. them and cut
8:5 David s. of Syrians 22,000
21:1 because he s. Gibeonites
21:20 s. two lion-like men of
M. he s. a lion, 1 Chr. 11:22
1 K. 18:13 Jeze. s. prophets of L.
40 Elijah s. prophets of Baal
2 K. 9:31 peace, who s. master?
10:9 I s. him, but who s. these?
11:18 people s. Mat. priest of B.
14:5 chil. he s. not, 2 Chr. 25:4
7 he s. of Edom, 1 Chr. 18:12
17:25 L. sent lions wh. s. some
23:20 Jos. s. all the priests of
1 Chr. 7:21 men of Ga. in land s.
2 Chr. 21:4 Jehoram s. his breth.
Neh. 9:26 they s. thy prophets
Est. 9:16 Jews s. of foes 75,000
Ps. 78:34 God s. fattest of them
34 when he s. them, then they
105:29 into blood s. their fish
135:10 s. great; 136:18 s. kings
Is. 66:3 an ox as if he s. a man
Jer. 26:17 because he s. me not
41:2 Ishmael s. all the Jews
8 s. them not among brethren
Lam. 2:4 s. all that were pleas.
Dan. 3:22 fire s. men that took
5:19 whom he would he s.
Mat. 2:16 Herod sent, s. children
22:6 took his serv. and s. them
23:35 whom ye s. betw. temple
Luke 13:4 tower in Sil. fell and s.
Acts 5:30 J. s. whom s. and hang.
10:39 Je. whom they s. and han.
Rom. 7:11 commandment s. me
1 John 3:12 C. who s. his brother

SLEW him.
Gen. 4:8 C. rose ag. Abel and s. h.
23:7 Er was wicked, Lord s. h.
Ex. 2:14 say not, A wom. s. him
12:6 took and s. h. at passover
1 Sam. 17:35 I can. him and s. h.
2 Sam. 1:10 stood upon and s. h.
4:7 smote Ish-bosheth and s. h.
18:15 compassed Absalom s. h.
1 K. 13:24 lion met and s. h. 20:36
2 K. 10:9 I conspired and s. him
15:10 Shall. conspired and s. h.
1 Chr. 10:14 therefore s. he him
1 Chr. 22:11 Athaliah s. him not
24:25 his own servants s. him
33:21 came of his bowels s. h.
33:34 his serv. s. him in house
Jer. 41:2 Ishm. s. h. whom king
Mat. 21:39 cast out of vine. s. h.
Acts 22:20 ratm. of th. that s. h.

SLEWEST.
1 Sam. 21:9 sword of Goli. th. s.

SLIDE, ETH.
Deut. 32:35 foot sh. s. in due time
Ps. 26:1 trusted in L. I sh. not s.
37:31 none of his steps shall s.
Hos. 4:16 Is. s. as backslid. heifer

SLIDDEN.
Jer. 8:5 why peo. of Jer. s. back

SLIGHTLY.
Jer. 6:14 healed my peo. s. 8:11

SLIME.
Gen. 11:3 brick for s. s. for mor.
Ex. 2:3 she daubed ark with s.

SLIME-PITS.
Gen. 14:10 Sid. was full of s.-p.

SLING, Verb.
Jud. 20:16 ev. one could s. stones
1 Sam. 25:29 them shall he s. out
Jer. 10:18 s. out inhabit. at once

SLING, s.
1 Sam. 17:40 Da. had s. in hand
David prevailed with a s.
25:29 sling enem. as out of a s.
2 Chr. 26:14 Uzziah prepared s.
Prov. 26:8 bindeth stone in a s.

SLINGERS.
2 K. 3:25 s. went about it, smote

SLING-STONES.
Job 41:28 s. turned into stubble

SLIP, PETH.
Deut. 19:5 head s. from helve
2 Sam. 22:37 feet not s. Ps. 18:36
Job 12:5 he that is ready to s.
Ps. 17:5 that my footst. s. nor
38:16 wh. foot s. they magnify
94:18 foot s. mercy held me up
Heb. 2:1 lest we sho. let them s.

SME

SLIPPED.
1 Sam. 19:10 D. s. out of S.'s pre.
Ps. 73:2 steps had well nigh s.

SLIPPERY.
Ps. 35:6 let their way be dark, s.
73:18 didst set them in s. places
Jer. 23:12 th. way be to them s.

SLIPS.
Is. 17:10 thou shalt set it with s.

SLOTHFUL.
Jud. 18:9 be not s. to poss. land
Prov. 12:24 s. shall be under tri.
27 s. roast. not he took huint.
15:19 way of s. is as a hedge
18:9 s. is broth. to great waster
19:24 s. hid. hand in bos. 26:15
21:25 desire of s. killeth him
22:13 s. saith, Th. is a lion, 26:13
24:30 went by field of s. viney.
Mat. 25:26 wicked and s. servant
Rom. 12:11 not s. in business
Heb. 6:12 ye be not s. but follow.

SLOTHFULNESS.
Prov. 19:15 s. cast. into deep sle.
Ec. 10:18 by s. building decayeth

SLOW.
Ex. 4:10 s. of speech, of s. tong.
Neh. 9:17 thou art G. s. to anger
Prov. 14:29 s. to wrath, of great
Luke 24:25 O fools, s. of heart
Tit. 1:12 Cretians liars, s. bellies
Jam. 1:19 s. to speak, s. to wrath
See ANGER.

SLOWLY.
Acts 27:7 had sailed s. many days

SLUGGARD.
Prov. 6:6 go to the ant, thou s.
9 how long wilt th. sleep, O s.
10:26 smoke to eyes, so s. to th.
13:4 the soul of s. desireth
20:4 the s. will not plough
26:16 s. wiser in own conceit

SLUICES.
Is. 19:10 th. make s. and ponds

SLUMBER, Substantive.
Ps. 132:4 not give s. to eyelids
Prov. 6:4 eye, nor s. to eyelids
10 a little sleep, little s. 24:33
Rom. 11:8 G. hath given them s.

SLUMBER, ED, ETH.
Ps. 121:3 that keep. will not s. 4
Is. 5:27 none shall s. nor sleep
56:10 watchm. lying, lov. to s.
Nah. 3:18 thy shepherds s. O king
Mat. 25:5 bridegroom tar. th. s.
2 Pet. 2:3 their damnation s. not

SLUMBERINGS.
Job 33:15 God speak. in s. on bed

SMALL.
Gen. 30:15 is it s. matter that th.
Ex. 16:14 s. thi. s. as hoarfrost
Num. 16:13 is it s. thing th. hast
2 Sam. 7:19 a s. thing in thy sight, O Lord, 1 Chr. 17:17
22:43 beat. s. as dust, Ps. 18:42
1 K. 19:12 after fire, still s. voice
Is. 7:13 is it s. th. to weary men?
60:22 a s. one sh. bec. a nation
Jer. 30:19 and they sh. not be s.
49:15 make take s. am. heathen
Amos 7:2 Ja. arise ? for he is s. 5
8:5 pass s. and ephah
Zec. 4:10 desp. day of s. things?
See GREAT.

SMALLEST.
1 Sam. 9:21 Benja. of s. tribes?

SMART.
Prov. 11:15 surety for str. sh. s.

SMELL, Substantive.
Gen. 27:27 Is. smelled s. of rahn.
s. of my son is as s. of a field
Cant. 2:13 tender grape give s.
4:10 s. of oint. better th. spices
11 s. of garm. like s. of Leban.
7:8 s. of thy nose like apples
8 s. of thy nose like grapes, 13
Is. 3:24 instead of sweet s. stink
Dan. 3:27 nor s. of fire passed on
Hos. 14:6 his s. as Lebanon
Phil. 4:18 sent an od. of sweet s.

SMELL, Verb.
Ex. 30:38 make like to that to s.
Deut. 4:28 gods wh. neither see nor s.
Ps. 45:8 garments s. of myrrh
115:6 noses have they, s. not
Amos 5:21 not s. in your assem.

SMELLED, ETH.
Gen. 8:21 Lord s. a sweet savor
27:27 Isaac s. rahn. blessed him
Job 39:25 he s. the battle afar off

SMI

SMELLING.
Cant. 5:5 fing. with s. myrrh, 13
Eph. 5:2 sacrifi. to G. for s. sav.

SMELLING, Substantive
1 Cor. 12:17 hear. where were s. ?

SMITE.
Gen. 32:8 to one comp. and s. it
Ex. 7:17 I will s. upon waters
12:23 not suffer destroyer to s.
17:6 thou shalt s. rock in Horeb
21:18 if men strive, one s. ano.
26 if a man s. eye of servant
Num. 22:6 prev. that we s. them
24:17 sceptre out of Is. s. Moab
25:17 vex Midianites, s. them
35:16 if he s. him with instrum.
18 if he s. him wi. hand-weap.
Deut. 7:2 shalt s. Canaanites
13:15 shalt surely s. inhabitants
20:13 thou shalt s. every male
28:7 thou sh. s. Midianites
22:24 then Benj. began to s. 39
1 Sam. 17:46 I will s. thee
18:11 Saul said, I will s. David
20:33 Saul cast javelin to s. him
23:2 s. Philistines? Go, s. Phil.
26:8 let me s. him to earth
2 Sam. 2:22 why sho. I s. thee?
13:28 when I say, s. Amnon
15:14 lest he s. city with sword
17:2 and I will s. the king only
18:11 said, Why not s. him th.?
1 K. 20:35 in word of the L. s. me
2 K. 3:19 shall s. ev. fenced city
6:21 sh. I s. them? sh. I s. th.?
9:7 thou shalt s. house of Ahab
27 John said, s. him in the
13:17 sh. s. Syri. till consumed
18 said to king, s. upon ground
Ps. 121:6 sun not s. thee by day
141:5 let righte. s. it be kindn.
Prov. 19:25 s. a scorner
Is. 10:24 shall s. thee with rod
40:10 nei. heat nor sun s. them
58:4 fast to s. with fist of wick.
Ezek. 5:2 part of hair, s. about
6:11 s. wi. hand. stamp wi. foot
21:12 son of man, s. on thy thi.
14 prophesy, s. hands together
Amos 9:1 he said, s. lintel of do.
Mic. 5:1 they shall s. judge of Is.
Nah. 2:10 the knees s. together
Zec. 10:11 s. the waves in sea
11:6 s. ev. one into neigh. hand
Mal. 5:39 wh. sh. s. th. on cheek
24:49 begin to s. his fellow-serv.
Luke 22:49 Lord, shall we s. with the sword?
Acts 22:2 commanded to s. Paul
2 Cor. 11:20 suffer s. you on face
Rev. 11:6 wtne. hav. pow. to s.

SMITE, referred to God.
Gen. 8:21 nor will I s. any more
Ex. 3:20 stretch hand, and s. E.
9:15 I may s. thee and people
12:12 I will s. first-born in Eg.
Num. 14:12 s. them with pestil.
Deut. 28:35 L. s. thee in knees
33:11 s. through loins
1 Sam. 26:10 Da. said, L. shall s.
2 Sam. 5:24 shalt Lord go bef. s.
1 K. 14:15 L. shall s. Is. as a reed
2 K. 6:18 s. this people wi. bind.
2 Chr. 21:14 wi. plague will L. s.
Is. 11:15 s. earth with rod of mou.
15 the Lord shall s. Egypt in the seven streams, 19:22
Jer. 21:6 I will s. inhabit. of City
Ezek. 21:17 I will s. hands toge.
39:3 s. thy bow out of hand
Amos 3:15 I will s. winter-house
6:11 Lord will s. great house
Zec. 9:4 L. will s. her power
12:4 I will s. ev. horse and rider
13:7 awake, O sword, s. Sheph.
Mat. 26:31; Mark 14:27
14:12 plague wherewith L. s. 18
Mal. 4:6 lest I s. earth wi. a cur.
Rev. 19:15 with it sho. s. nations

SMITERS.
Is. 50:6 I gave my back to the s.

SMITEST, ETH.
Ex. 2:13 wheref. s. thy fellow?
21:12 s. man so he die
15 s. fath. or moth. put to des.
Deut. 25:11 wife to deliver husb.
out of hand of him th. s. him
27:24 cursed that s. his neighb.
Job 26:12 by understanding he s.
Is. 9:13 turn not to him that s.
Lam. 3:30 cheek to him that s.
Ezek. 7:9 kn. that I am L. that s.

SMO

Luke 6:29 s. thee on one cheek
John 18:23 why s. thou me?

SMITH.
1 Sam. 13:19 no s. found in Isra.
Is. 44:12 s. with tongs worketh
54:16 I created s. bloweth coals

SMITHS.
2 K. 24:14 Nebuchadnez. carried away s. 16; Jer. 24:1
Jer. 29:2 s. were departed fr. Jer.

SMITING.
Ex. 2:11 Egyptian s. a Hebrew
1 K. 20:37 so th s. wounded him
2 K. 3:24 went forward s. Moab
Mic. 6:13 make thee sick in s.

SMITTEN.
Ex. 7:25 after Lord had s. river
22:2 if thief be found, and be s.
Num. 14:42 go not up that ye be not s. Deut. 1:42
22:32 wherefore hast th. s. ass
33:4 buried first-born L. had s.
1 Sam. 4:2 Is. s. bef. Philist. 10
3 why hath L. s. us bef. Phil. ?
5:19 lamented bec. L. s. many
30:1 Amalek had s. Ziklag
2 Sam. 2:31 had s. of Ab.'s men
11:15 that ye may be s.
1 K. 8:33 when people of Is. be s.
11:15 after he had s. ev. male
2 K. 2:14 when he had s. waters
3:23 kings have s. one another
14:10 hast s. Ed. 2 Chr. 25:19
2 Chr. 20:22 M. and Seir were s.
25:16 why should. thou be s. ?
26:20 because L. had s. him
Job 16:10 have s. me on cheek
Ps. 3:7 hast s. mine enemies
69:26 becrue. him thou hast s.
102:4 my heart is s. withered
143:3 hath s. my life to ground
Is. 5:25 the L. hath s. his people
24:12 gate is s. with destruction
27:7 hath he s. him, as smo. th.
53:4 est. him stricken, s. of God
Jer. 2:30 in vain ha. I s. children
14:19 why hast thou s. us
Eze. 22:13 I have s. my hand at
33:21 came, saying, City is s.
9:16 Ephraim is s. root dried
Amos 4:9 s. you, blast. not return.
Acts 23:3 commanded me to be s.
Rev. 8:12 third part of sun was s.

SMOKE, Substantive.
Gen. 19:28 s. of country went up s.
Ex. 19:18 mount Si. was on a s.
Deut. 29:20 of A's ascended up, 21
Jud. 20:38 ms. s. rise out of city
2 Sam. 22:9 there went up a s.
out of his nostrils, Ps. 18:8
Job 41:20 out of his noster. go. s.
Ps. 37:20 wicked consu. into s.
68:2 as s. is driven away
102:3 my days are consu. like s.
119:83 I am bec. like bottle in s.
Prov. 10:26 as s. to eyes, so slug.
Cant. 3:6 com. like pillars of s.
Is. 4:5 on her assemb. s. by day
6:4 the house was filled with s.
9:18 mount like lifting up of s.
14:31 shall come from north s.
34:10 thereof shall go up
51:6 heavens eh. vanish like s.
65:5 th. are as s. in my nose
Hos. 13:3 as s. out of chimney
Joel 2:30 fire, and pillars of s.
Nah. 2:13 burn her chariots in s.
Acts 2:19 firu, and vapor of s.
Rev. 8:4 s. of incense ascended
9:2 arose s. out of bottoml. pit
3 came out of s. locu. on earth
17 out of mouth iss. fire and s.
18 3d part of men killed by s.
14:11 s. of their torment ascend.
15:8 temple was filled with s.
18:9 lament for her when see s.
18 they saw s. of her burning
19:3 and her s. rose up for ever

SMOKE.
Deut. 29:20 anger of Lord sh. s.
Ps. 74:1 G. why thine anger s. ?
104:32 toucheth hills, they s.
144:5 touch mountains, they s.

SMOKING.
Gen. 15:17 behold, a s. furnace
Ex. 20:18 peo. saw mountain s.
Is. 7:4 tails of th. s. firebrands
42:3 s. flax not que. Mat. 12:20

SMOOTH.
Gen. 27:11 E. hairy, I am a man
16 skins of kids on s. of neck

CRUDEN'S CONCORDANCE.

SOL

Lam. 5:4 our wood is *s*. unto us
Ezek. 7:18 seller not retu. that *s*.
Joel 3:3 have *s*. a girl for wine
6 children of Judah have ye *s*.
7 out of place whit. ye *s*. them
Amos 2:6 they *s*. right. for silver
Mat. 10.29 not two sparrows *s*.
13:46 and *s*. all that he had
18:25 commanded him to be *s*.
21:12 cast out th. that *s*. of them
s. Mark 11:15; *Luke* 19:45
26:9 this ointm. might ha. been
s. Mark 14:5; *John* 12:5
Luke 12.6 five sparrows *s*.
17:28 they *s*. they planted
John 2:14 in temple that *s*. oxen
18 said to them thut *s*. doves
Acts 2:45 *s*. their possessi. 4:34
4:37 Joses having land *s*. it
5:1 Ananias *s*. 8 ye *s*. land for
4 after it was *s*. was it not in
Rom. 7:14 carnal, *s*. under sin
1 *Cor.* 10:25 whats. is *s*. in sham.
Heb. 12:16 for one morsel *s*. birt.

SOLDERING.
Is. 41:7 ready for *s*. he fastened

SOLDIER.
John 19:23 to every *s*. a part
Acts 10:7 Cornelius called a *s*.
28:16 suff. Paul to dwell with *s*.
2 *Tim.* 2:3 end. as a good *s*. of C.
4 hath chosen him to be a *s*.

SOLDIERS.
2 *Chr.* 25:13 *s*. fell upon cities
Ezr. 8:22 I ashamed to requ. *s*.
Is. 15:4 armed *s*. of Moab cry
Mat. 8:9 having *s*. und, *Luke* 7:8
27:27 the *s*. took J. and gathered to him *s*.
28:12 they gave money to *s*.
Luke 3:14 *s*. demanded, saying
John 19:23 the *s*. took his garm.
24 these things theref. *s*. did
32 then came *s*. and bra. legs
34 one of the *s*. with a spear
Acts 12:4 delivered Peter to *s*.
6 Pe. was sleeping bet. two *s*.
18 no small stir among the *s*.
21:35 he was borne of the *s*.
23;23 make ready 200 *s*.
27:31 P. said to the *s*. Except
32 then the *s*. cut off the ropes
42 *s*. counsel was to kill pris.

SOLE.
Gen. 8:9 dove found no rest for *s*.
Deut. 28:35 wi. botch from *s*. of
56 not set *s*. of foot upon gro.
65 nei. shall *s*. of thy foot tread
Jos. 1:3 place *s*. of foot tread
1 *Sam.* 14:25 from *s*. of foot to cr.
Job 2:7 Satan smote Job fr. *s*. of
Is. 1:6 from *s*. of foot to head
Ezek. 1:7 *s*. of feet li. *s*. of calf's
See FEET.

SOLEMN.
Num. 10:10 in your *s*. days ye sh.
Ps. 92:3 praise with *s*. sound
Is. 1:13 iniq. even the *s*. meet.
Lam. 2:22 called as in a *s*. day
Hos. 9:5 will ye do in *s*. day?
See ASSEMBLY, FEAST, FEASTS.

SOLEMNITY, IES.
Deut. 31:10 in the *s*. of the year
Is. 30:29 as wh. a holy *s*. is kept
33:20 upon Z. the city of our *s*.
Ezek. 45:17 burnt-offerings in *s*.
46:11 in *s*. meat-offering shall

SOLEMNLY.
Gen. 43:3 the man did *s*. protest
1 *Sam.* 8:9 yet protest *s*. to them

SOLITARY.
Job 3:7 let that night be *s*.
30:3 for famine they were *s*.
Ps. 68:6 G. setteth *s*. in families
107:4 wandered in a *s*. way
Is. 35:1 wilderness and *s*. place
Lam. 1:1 how doth city sit *s*.
Mark 1:35 Je. departed to *s*. pl.

SOLITARILY.
Mic. 7:14 feed peo. which dw. *s*.

SOLOMON.
2 *Sam.* 5:14 there was born to David S, 1 *Chr.* 3:5; 14:4
12:24 he called his name S. and
1 *K.* 1:10 S. his brother, 19, 26
13, sh. reign after me, 17, 30
21 I and my son S. shall be
34 God save king S. 39, 43
37 wi. D. even so he be wi. S.
47 God make name of S. better
51 S. swear to me that he will
2:1 David charged S. his son, 43
3:1 S. made affinity with Phar.
3 S. loved Lord; 10 S. asked

SON

1 *K.* 3:5 Lord appear to S. 9:2; 2 *Chr.* 1:7; 7:12
4:22 S. provision for one day
29 God gave S. wisdom, 5:12
34 hear wis. of S. from all the kings, *Mat.* 12:42; *Luke* 11:31
5:1 Hiram sent servants to S.
13 king S. raised a levy out of
6:14 S. built house and finished it, 2 *Chr.* 7:11; *Acts* 7:47
7:51 so ended the work S. made
8:1 S. assemb. elders, 2 *Chr.* 5:2
22 S. spread forth his hands to
54 S. made an end, 2 *Chr.* 7:1
65 S. held a feast; 9:26 S. ma.
10:1 when queen of Sheba heard of fame of S. 2 *Chr.* 9:1
24 all sought to S. 2 *Chr.* 9:23
Neh. 13:26 did not S. sin by th.?
Prov. 1:1 prov. of S. 10:1; 25;1
Cant. 1:1 Song of songs wh. is S.
3:7 behold, his bed which is S.
8:11 S. had vineyard at Baal-h.
12 *Jer.* 52:20 sea S. made, *Jer.* 27:19
Mat. 1:6 Da. begat S. 7 S. begat
6:29 S. in all his gl. *Luke* 12:27
12:42 greater than S. *Luke* 11:31
John 10:23 Je. walked in S. por.
Acts 3:11 ran to them in S. porch
5:12 with one accord in S. por.

SOMEBODY.
Luke 8:46 Jesus said, *s*. touched
Acts 5:36 Then, boasting to be *s*.

SOMETHING.
Mark 5:43 that *s*. should be giv.
Luke 11:54 seeking to catch *s*.
John 13:29 he sth. give *s*. to poor
Acts 3:5 expecting to receive *s*.
23:15 would inquire *s*. more per.
18 young man hath *s*. to say
Gal. 6:3 man think him. to be *s*.

SOMETIMES.
Eph. 2:13 ye who were *s*. afar off
Col. 3:7 in which ye walked *s*.

SOMEWHAT.
Lev. 4:22 when *s*. ruler hath done *s*.
1 *K.* 2:14 he said, I have *s*. to say
2 *K.* 5:20 I will run and take *s*.
Luke 7:40 have *s*. to say unto th.
Acts 23:20 inq. *s*. more perfectly
25:26 I might have *s*. to write
Rom. 15:24 if first I be *s*. filled
2 *Cor.* 5:12 may have *s*. to answer
10:8 tho' I should boast *s*. more
Gal. 2:6 th. who seemed to be *s*.
Heb. 8:3 this man have *s*. to offer
Rev. 2:4 I have *s*. against thee

SON.

Gen. 17:16 I will give thee a *s*. of Sarah, 19; 18:10, 14
21:2 Sarah bare Abraham a *s*. 7
24:36 my master's wife bare a *s*.
51 let her be master's *s*. wife
25:33 he hath given ma this *s*.
30:6 G. heard me, given me *s*.
24 Lord shall add to me ano. *s*.
35:17 thou shalt have this *s*.
37:3 bec. he was *s*. of old age
Ex. 1:16 if *s*. then ye kill him
22 every *s*. born cast into river
2:10 child grew, and bec. her *s*.
4:22 Israel is my *s*. even my
23 If my *s*. go, and if thou re.
Num. 23:18 hearken, *s*. of Zippor
27:4 hath no *s*. 8 and have no *s*.

SON

Deut. 13:6 if *s*. of mo. ent. thee.
21:16 not make *s*. of belov. first-born before *s*. of hated, 17
20 our *s*. is stubborn, rebellious
28:56 eye sh. be evil tow. her *s*.
Jos. 6:26 in young. *s*. set up gat.
Jud. 5:12 lead captive *s*. of Ab.
9:18 made *s*. of his servant king
11:2 thou art *s*. of strange wo.
34 he had nei. *s*. nor daughter
13:3 conceive and bear a *s*. 5, 7
1 *Sam.* 1:23 Hannah gave *s*. suck
4:20 fear not, th. hast borne a *s*.
10:11 wh. is come to *s*. of Kish ?
16:18 I have seen a *s*. of Jesse
17:55 whose *s*. ? 58 whose *s*. art
20:27 wheref. com. not *s*. of J. ?
31 as long as *s*. of Jesse liveth
22:7 will *s*. of Jesse give fields ?
9 I saw *s*. of Jesse com. to N.
13 hear, now, thou *s*. of Ahit.
25:10 who is the *s*. of Jesse ?
17 he is such a *s*. of Belial
2 *Sam.* 1:13 I am *s*. of a stranger
9:9 give *s*. all that pertain. to S.
10:2 show kindness to *s*. of Na.
16:3 where is thy master's *s*.
18:12 put forth ha. ag. king's *s*.
18 have no *s*. to keep my name
20 because the king's *s*. is dead
1 *K.* 3:6 thou hast given him a *s*.
5:7 hath given David a wise *s*.
12:16 no inheritance in *s*. of Jesse, 2 *Chr.* 10:16
14:5 cometh to ask of thee for *s*.
22:26 Joa. king's *s*. 2 *Chr.* 18:25
2 *K.* 1:17 because he had no *s*.
4:16 season th. sh. embrace *s*.
28 did I desire a *s*. 37 took *s*.
6:29 give *s*. to eat him, hid *s*.
32 *s*. of a murderer hath sent
8:1 whose *s*. he restored to life
11:1 *s*. was dead, 2 *Chr.* 22:9
4 Jehoiada sho, them king's *s*.
2 *Chr.* 12:18 side, thon *s*. of Jesse
22:9 behold, a *s*. shall be born
Ezr. 7:17 never a *s*. left him
33:3 behold, king's *s*. shall rei.
Job 18:19 nei. have *s*. nor neph.
Ps. 2:12 kiss *s*. lest he be angry
72:1 righteousn. unto king's *s*.
86:16 give strength to thy hand-maid, *s*. of thy handmaid
116:16 I am *s*. of thy hand-ma.
Prov. 3:12 *s*. in whom he delight.
4:3 I was my father's *s*. belov.
7:1 wines *s*. mak. glad fa. 15:20
5 gath. in wine *s*. sleep, in har.
s. caus. shame, 17:2; 19:26
2 *Chr.* 21:17 never a *s*. left him
29:1 dost thou bell. on *s*. of G. ?
10:36 I said, I am the S. of God
11:4 that S. of G. might be glo.
19:7 he made himself S. of God
20:31 beli. Je. is S. of God
Acts 8:37 J. Christ is the S. of G.
9:20 Christ, that he is S. of G.
Rom. 1:4 declared to be S. of G.
2 *Cor.* 1:19 the S. of G. was not
Gal. 2:20 by faith of S. of God
Eph. 4:13 knowledge of S. of G.
Heb. 4:14 high-pr. J. the S. of G.
6:6 crucify to themsel. S. of G.
7:3 made like to the S. of G.
10:29 trod. under foot S. of God
John 3:8 for this purp. S. of G.
4:15 shall confess Je. is S. of G.
5:5 believeth Jesus is S. of God
10 that believeth on S. of God
13 believe on name of S. of G.
20 know that S. of G. is come
19:20 write, saith S. of God

His SON.
Gen. 22:13 bu. off. in stead of h. *s*.
25:11 Abraham, G. blessed h. *s*.
27:31 Jacob mourned for his *s*.
Ex. 22:29 every man give his *s*.
Lev. 21:2 for his *s*. he may be
Num. 20:26 put on Elea. h. *s*. 28
Deut. 1:31 man doth bear his *s*.
7:3 thy daugh. not give to his *s*.
8:5 as a man chasteneth his *s*.
18:10 not any man's *s*. pass
1 *Sam.* 16:19 serve in pres. of h. *s*.
1 *K.* 11:36 and *s*. a light give his *s*.
2 *K.* 3:27 Moab took his eldest *s*.
16:3 made his *s*. to pass thro'
21:6 Manas. made his *s*. to pass
23:10 no man mi. make h. *s*. pass
2 *Chr.* 24:29 Jo. the ki. slew h. *s*.
Prov. 13:24 spareth rod, hat. h. *s*.
29:21 shall have him bec. his *s*.
30:4 what is his *s*. name, if
Jer. 27:7 his *s*. and his son's *s*.
Mal. 3:17 as a man spareth his *s*.
Mat. 21:37 last of all sent his *s*.

SON

Luke 15:13 younger *s*. gathered
16:25 *s*. remember, in thy life.
19:9 forasmuch as he is *s*. of A.
John 1:18 only S. in bosom of F.
3:35 Father loveth the S. 5:20
36 beli. on S. believeth not S.
5:19 S. can do noth. of himself
19 forewh. he will
22 committed all judgm. to S.
23 men should honor S. he th.
honor, not S. honor. not F.
26 given to S. to have life
6:40 ev. one who seeth the S.
46 is not this Jes. *s*. of Joseph
6:33 *s*. abideth; 9:19 is this *s*. ?
36 if S. shall make you free
9:20 we kn. that this is our *s*.
14:13 Fa. may be glorified in S.
17:12 none lost but *s*. of perdit.
Acts 4:36 Barnabas, *s*. of consol.
23:6 Pharisee, *s*. of a Pharisee
16 Paul's sister's *s*. heard of
Rom. 9:9 Sarah shall have a *s*.
1 *Cor.* 15:28 then S. himself sub.
Gal. 4:7 no more serv. but a *s*.
Phil. 2:22 as *s*. he serv. in gospel
Col. 4:10 Marcus sister's *s*. to S.
2 *Thes.* 2:3 man of sin, *s*. of per.
1 *Tim.* 1:18 commit to thee *s*. T.
Heb. 1:5 he shall be to me a S.
8 to S. he saith, Thy throne
3:6 Christ as a *s*. over his own
5:8 tho' he were a *s*. yet learned
7:28 word of the oath maketh *s*.
11:24 refu. to be called *s*. of Ph.
12:6 scourg. every *s*. he receiv.
1 *John* 2:22 antic. deni. F. and S.
23 whosoever denieth the S.
the same hath not the Fath.
24 continue in S. and in Fath.
4:14 Father sent S. to be Savi.
5:12 he that hath S. hath life
2 *John* 3 L. Je. Ch. S. of Father
9 hath both the Father and S.

See DAVID.

SON of God.
Dan. 3:25 fourth is like *s*. of G.
Mat. 8:29 thou S. of G. *Luke* 8:28
14:33 of a truth th. art S. of G.
26:63 whether be Ch. S. of G.
27:43 he said, I am the S. of G.
54 was S. of G. *Mark* 15:39
Mark 3:11 art S. of G. *John* 1:49
Luke 1:35 sh. be called S. of G.
3:38 *s*. of Adam, was *s*. of G.
4:41 crying, Thou art Christ the S. of G. 8:28; 12:17
22:70 art th. then the S. of G.?
John 1:34 this is the S. of God
3:18 the only begotten S. of G.
3:35 dost thou beli. on S. of G.?
10:36 I said, I am the S. of God
11:4 that S. of G. might be glo.
19:7 he made himself S. of God
20:31 beli. Je. is S. of God
Acts 8:37 J. Christ is the S. of G.
9:20 Christ, that he is S. of G.
Rom. 1:4 declared to be S. of G.
2 *Cor.* 1:19 the S. of G. was not
Gal. 2:20 by faith of S. of God
Eph. 4:13 knowledge of S. of G.
Heb. 4:14 high-pr. J. the S. of G.
6:6 crucify to themsel. S. of G.
7:3 made like to the S. of G.
10:29 trod. under foot S. of God
John 3:8 for this purp. S. of G.
4:15 shall confess Je. is S. of G.
5:5 believeth Jesus is S. of God
10 that believeth on S. of God
13 believe on name of S. of G.
20 know that S. of G. is come
19:20 write, saith S. of God

CRUDEN'S CONCORDANCE. 1029

SON

Mat. 22:2 made a marr. for his *s.*
43 how is he then h. *s.? Mark* 12:37; *Luke* 20:44
John 3:16 gave *h.* only begot. *S.*
17 God sent not *his S.* to con.
*Ac'*s 3:13 God hath glori. *h. S. J.*
26 God having raised up *h. S.*
Rom. 1:9 serve in gospel of *h. S.*
8:3 God sending *his own S.* in
32 that spared not *his own S.*
Gal. 1:16 it pleas. G. to rev. *h. S.*
4:4 God sent forth *his S.*
1 *Thes.* 1:10 to wait for *his S.*
Heb. 1:2 spoken to us by *his S.*
Jam. 2:21 had offered Isaac *his s.*
1 *John* 1:3 fel. is with F. and *h. S.*
7 blood of Jes. Ch. *h. S,* clea.
2:22 believe on name of *h. S.*
5:9 he hath testified of *h. S.*
10 bell. not rec. G. gave of *h. S.*
11 this life is in *his S.*
20 we are in him, even *his S.*

SON-IN-LAW.

Gen. 19:12 hast thou any *s.-i.-l.?*
Jud. 15:6 Samson the *s.-i.-l.* of
19:5 damsel's fa. said to *s.-i.-l.*
1 *Sam.* 18:18 should he *s.-i.-l.* 23
22:14 faithful as king's *s.-i.-l.?*
2 *K.* 8:27 Johoram was *s.-i.-l.*
Neh. 6:18 Tobiah was *s.-i.-l.* to
13:28 was *s.-i.-l.* to Sanballat

See BELOVED.

My SON.

Gen. 21:23 not deal fal. wi. *my s.*
22:7 he said, Here am I, *my s.*
24:3 not take wife to *my s.* 37
6 bring not *my s.* thither ag. 8
37:8 now theref., *my s.* obey, 43
18 am I, who art thou, *my s.?*
21 wilt. thou be *my* very *s.* 24
37 what shall I do now, *my s.?*
37:33 and said, It is *my s.* coat
35 will go into grave to *my s.*
42:38 he said, *my s.* shall not go
43:28 Joseph *my s.* is yet alive
Ex. 4:22 Is. is *my s.* even *my*
Jud. 8:23 neith. shall *my s.* rule
1 *Sam.* 3:6 I called not *my s.* lie
4:16 what is there done, *my s.?*
10:2 what shall I do for *my s.?*
24:16 voice, *my s.?* David? 26:17
26:21 sinned, return, *my s.* Dav.
2 *Sam.* 7:14 he shall be *my s.*
13:25 *my s.* let us not all go
14:16 dest. me and *my s.* out of
16:11 *my s.* who came forth
18:33 king said, O *my s.* Absal.
my s. my s. Absalom, 19:4
1 *K.* 3:20 took *my s.* from, 23, 23
17:12 dress it for me and *my s.*
2 *K.* 6:29 we boiled *my s.* and eat
14:9 dau. to *my s.* 2 *Chr.* 25:18
1 *Chr.* 17:13 shall he *my s.* 22:10
22:11 *my s.* Lord will be with
23:6 ha. chosen him to be *my s.*
29:1 Sol. *my s.* whom God hath
Ps. 2:7 thou art *my s. Acts* 13:33
Heb. 1:5; 5:5
Prov. 6:3 do this now, *my s.*
23:26 *my s.* give me thy heart
24:21 *my s.* fear thou the Lord
27:11 *my s.* be wise and make
31:2 what, *my s.* and what, son
Jer. 31:20 is Ephra. *my* dear *s.?*
Hos. 11:1 called *my s. Mat.* 2:15
Mat. 3:17 *my* beloved *S.* 17:5
Mark 9:17 I have brought *my s.*
Luke 9:38 Mast. look upon *my s.*
15:24 for this *my s.* was dead
1 *Tim.* 1:2 to Timothy *my* own *s.*
2 *Tim.* 2:1 *my s.* be stro. in grace
Tit. 1:4 to Titus *mine* own *s.*
Philr. 10 I beseech th. for *my s.*
Heb. 12:5 chid, hold, *my s.* be *my s.*

Thy SON.

Gen. 22:2 take *t. s.* thine only *s.*
21:5 must I needs bring *thy s.?*
37:32 know whe. it be *t. s.* coat
4:2:2 behold, *thy s.* Jos. cometh
Ex. 10:2 tell in the ears of *thy s.*
13:8 thou shalt show *thy s.*
14 wh. *t. s.* asketh, *Deut.* 6:20
Deut. 6:21 shalt say unto *thy s.*
7:3 nor daughter take unto *t. s.*
4 they will turn away *thy s.*
Jud. 6:30 bring out *t. s.* that he
8:22 rule over us, thou, *thy s.*
1 *Sam.* 16:19 send me David *t. s.*
1 *K.* 1:12 save life of *thy s.* Solo.
17:19 whom I will so journ
11:12 rend it out of hand of *t. s.*
for then and for *thy s.*
19 give me *t. s.* 23 *t. s.* liveth
2 *K.* 4:36 he said, Take up *thy s.*
6:28 gi. *t. s.* that we may eat, 29

SON

1 *K.* 16:7 I am thy ser. and *thy s.*
Prov. 19:18 chasten *thy s.* while
29:17 correct *thy s.* and he shall
Luke 9:41 Je. said, Bring *thy s.*
15:19 no more wor. to be *t. s.* 21
30 soon as this *t. s.* was come
John 4:50 *thy s.* liveth, 51, 53
17:1 glorify *t. S.* that *t. S.* may
19:26 saith, Woman, beh. *thy s.*

SON of man,
Ezekiel—above ninety times.

SONG.

Ex. 15:1 then sang Moses this *s.*
unto the Lord, *Num.* 21:17
2 the Lord is my strength and
s. Ps. 118:14; *Is.* 12:2
Deut. 31:19 wri. this *s,* th. th. *s.*
21 this *s.* sh. testify aga. them
22 Moses theref. wrote this *s.*
30 Mo. spake words of *s.* 32:44
Jud. 5:12 awake, Debor. utter *s.*
2 *Sam.* 22:1 Da. spa. words of *s.*
1 *Chr.* 6:31 D. set over serv. of *s.*
15:22 chief of Lev. was for *s.* 27
25:6 under their father for *s.*
2 *Chr.* 29:27 *s.* of the Lord began
Job 30:9 I am their *s.* by-word
Ps. 28:7 with my *s.* will I praise
33:3 sing a new *s. Is.* 42:10
40:3 put a new *s.* in my mouth
42:8 in night his *s.* sh. be wi. me
69:12 I was *s.* of the drunkards
30 I will praise God with a *s.*
77:6 I call to remembra. my *s.*
96:1 O sing to the Lord a new *s.*
98:1; 149:1
137:3 they required of us a *s.*
4 how sh. we sing Lord's *s.?*
144:9 I will sing a new *s.*
Ec. 7:5 man to hear *s.* of fools
Cant. 1:1 *s.* of songs which is S.
Is. 5:1 now will I sing to *s.*
23:9 sh. not drink wine wi. a *s.*
26:1 in th. day sh. th. *s.* be sung
30:29 shall have a *s.* as in night
Lam. 3:14 I was their *s.*
Ezek. 33:32 to them as a lovely *s.*
Rev. 5:9 they sung a new *s.* 14:3
14:3 no man could learn that *s.*
15:3 the *s.* of Moses and *s.* of L.

SONGS.

Gen. 31:27 sent thee away wi. *s.*
1 *K.* 4:32 a thousand and five
Chr. 25:7 were instructed in *s.*
Neh. 12:46 in days of D. were *s.*
Job 35:10 G. who giv. *s.* in night
Ps. 32:7 comp. wi. *s.* of deliver
119:54 have been my *s.* in house
137:3 sing us one of the *s.* of Z.
Prov. 25:20 singeth *s.* to heavy
Cant. 1:1 song of *s.* which is Sol.
Is. 24:16 melody, sing many *s.*
Ezek. 26:13 part of earth we heard *s.*
25:10 tumu. of *thy s.* with *s.*
38:20 we will sing my *s.*
Ezek. 26:13 noise of *s.* to cease
Amos 5:23 take away noise of *s.*
8:3 *s.* of temple shall be howl.
10 turn your *s.* into lamentati.
Col. 3:16 hymns, and spiritual *s.*

SONS.

Gen. 9:10 the three *s.* of Noah
10:1 and to them were *s.* born
27:49 let mother's *s.* bow down
42:5 *s.* of Is. came to buy corn
11 we are all one man's *s.* 32
46:5 *s.* of Israel carried Jacob
Lev. 25:22 cut flesh of your *s.*
Is. 45:11 to come concern. *my s.*
Cant. 4:11 but as *my* beloved *s.*

See SEVEN.

Thy SONS.

50 (*Moses* had 70 *s.* kill a fat
12:14 Aholab had 40 s. 30 neph.
19:22 cert. *s.* of Bel. beset house
Ruth 1:11 are there any more *s.*
1 *Sam.* 1:8 am not I but. th. 10 *s.?*
2:12 *s.* of Eli were *s.* of Belial
11 I have given unto *thee* to *thy s.*
2 *Sam.* 2:18 three *s.* of Zeruiah
3:39 *s.* of Zeruiah be too hard
9:11 eat as one of king's *s.*
12 they will turn away *thy s.*
Jud. 6:30 bring out *t. s.* that he
Abs. had 3 *s.* 10:30 bring king's *s.*
16:10 what is pa. of *Z.?* 1927
23:8 *s.* of Bel. shall be as thorns
Isr. 20:35 the *s.* of the prophets
21:10 set two men, *s.* of Belial
2 *Chr.* 22:2 of Eli were forty-
four
Chr. 27:32 and *his* four *s.*
28:8 among the *s.* of my fathers
2 *Chr.* 23:3 Lord said of *s.* of Da.
21:25 blood of the *s.* of Jehoiada
24:23 Huz. a ton *s.* he hanged, 11

SON

Ps. 80:6 who amo. *s.* of mighty?
144:12 our *s.* may be as plants
Is. 51:18 no. to guide her amo. *s.*
56:6 *s.* of strang. that join Lord
60:10 *s.* of stranger build walls
14 *s.* of them th. afflicted thee
Jer. 6:21 *s.* shall fall upon them
13:14 fathers and *s.* together
23:6 beget *s.* ta. wives for yo. *s.*
35:6 drink no wine, ye, nor *s.*
49:1 bath Israel no *s.?* no heir?
Lam. 4:2 precious *s.* of Zion
Ezek. 5:10 fathers eat *s. s.* fathers
23:31 your *s.* pass thro' the fire
33:37 caused *s.* to pass thro' fire
Hos. 1:10 ye are *s.* of living God
Mat. 3:3 he shall purify *s.* of Le.
Mark 3:17 Boanerges, *s.* of thun.
Luke 11:19 your *s.* cast th. out?
1 *Cor.* 4:14 but as my beloved *s.*
4:15 receive the adopt. of *s.*
6 bec. ye are *s.* God hath sent
Heb. 3:10 bring. many *s.* to glory
11:21 Jacob blessed *s.* of Joseph
12:7 G. deal. with you as wi. *s.*

See AARON, DAUGHTER.

SONS of God.

Gen. 6:2 *s. of G.* saw daughters
Job 1:6 *s. of G.* came to pres. 2:1
38:7 *s. of G.* shouted for joy
Hos. 1:10 ye are *s. of* living God
John 1:12 power to bec. *s. of G.*
Rom. 8:14 8p. of God, are *s. of G.*
19 manifestation of *s. of God*
Phil. 2:15 be harmless, *s. of God*
1 *John* 3:1 we be called *s. of G.*
2 beloved, now are we *s. of G.*

His SONS.

Gen. 9:1 God blessed N. and h. *s.*
30:35 gave th. into hands of *h. s.*
Lev. 8:13 sons of Aa. and *h. s.*
18:5 *Jethro* came with *h. s.*
Sam. 8:1 take Aa. and *h. s.* to mini.
Lev. 6:22 priest of *his s.* is anoi.
Deut. 18:5 chosen him and *h. s.*
21:16 he maketh *h. s.* inherit
Sam. 9:18 slain *h. s.* 70 persons
17:11 *Levite* was as one of *h. s.*
1 *Sam.* 8:22 heard all *his s.* did
Sam. 8:11 *s.* when old made *h. s.* Jud.
3 *his s.* walk. not in his ways
16:1 provided a king am. *his s.*
20:6 grieved, ev. man for *his s.*
2 *Sam.* 21:6 let 7 of *h. s.* be deli.
1 *K.* 13:11 *h. s.* came and to him
12 *h. s.* seen my man of God
2 *K.* 10:37 *his s.* smote him with sword, *Is.* 37:38
17:14 Jeroboam and *his s.*
21:7 give light to him and *h. s.*
Jer. 17 carried away *his s.* save the
youngest of *his s.*
36:30 serv. to him and *his s.*
Est. 6:10 life of king and *his s.*
9:26 and *his s.* he hanged
Job 1:4 *his s.* went and feasted
14:21 *his s.* came to honour
Heb. 12:1 canst guide A. with *h. s.?*
Jud. 3, 4 *saw h. s.* and *h. s.* come
Ezek. 46:16 a gift to any of *h. s.*
Dan. 11:10 *h. s.* sh. be stirred up

See MAN.

My SONS.

Gen. 48:9 J. said, They are *my s.*
1 *Sam.* 2:24 *my s.* it is no good
12:2 S. said, *my s.* are with you
1 *Chr.* 28:5 of all *my s.* chosen S.
Job 1:5 it may be *my s.* have sin.
Is. 43:6 bring *my s.* from far
Is. 43:11 but as my beloved *s.*

See SEVEN.

Thy SONS.

Gen. 6:18 the *s.* of my mother
50 (Moses had 70 *s.* kill a fat
12:14 Aholab had 40 *s.* 30 neph.
22:29 first-born of *thy s.* give
Lev. 10:14 *thy* due, and *t. s.* due
Num. 18:1 *t. s.* sh. bear iniquity
11 I have given it to thee to *thy s.*
Deut. 4:9 teach *t. s.* and *t. s.* sons
8:5 *thy s.* walk not in thy ways
26:10 to mine *s.* to her to th.
1 *Sam.* 2:29 *thy s.* be with *me*
Sam. 10:41 people wept very *s.*
28:19 to-mor. shalt thou and *t. s.*
be with me
K. 20:3 thy hand saved we *s.*
39:4 thy house shall bring *thy s.*
51:20 *thy s.* have fainted
Is. 49:25 will contend for *thy s.*
Is. 49:22 they shall bring *thy s.*
60:4 *thy s.* come from far, *s.*
62:5 so shall *thy s.* marry thee
Jer. 5:7 *t. s.* forsaken me
Ezek. 23:25 take *thy s.* and dau.
Mat. 20:21 grant that th. *my* t. *s.*
21:28 a man had *t. s. Lu.* 15:11
26:37 Peter and *t. s.* of Zebedee
Acts 7:29 in Midi. he begat *t. s.*
Gal. 4:22 Abraham had *two s.*

SOON.

Deut. 4:26 ye shall *s.* utt. perish
22:22 Maker *s.* take me away
Ps. 90:10 for it is *s.* cut off
106:13 they *s.* forgat his works
Tit. 1:7 not self-wil. not *s.* angry

SOONER.

Heb. 13:19 restored to you the *s.*
Jam. 1:11 the sun is no *s.* risen

SOOTHSAYER, S.

Jos. 13:22 Balaam son of Beor *s.*
Is. 2:6 pea. because they are *s.*
Dan. 2:27 secret cannot *s.* show
5:7 king cried aloud to bring *s.*
11 whom king made mas. of *s.*
Mic. 5:12 shalt have no more *s.*

SOOTHSAYING.

Acts 16:16 mast. much gain by *s.*

SOP.

John 13:26 to wh. I shall give *a s.*
27 after the *s.* Satan enter. 30

SOPATER, *Acts* 20:4

SORCERER, ESS.

Is. 57:3 draw hither, sons of *s.*
Acts 13:6 certain *s.* a false proph.
8 Elym. the *s.* withstood them

SORCERERS.

Ex. 7:11 called wise men and *s.*
Jer. 27:9 hearken not to your *s.*
Dan. 2:2 N. command, to call *s.*
Mal. 3:5 be a witn. against the *s.*
Rev. 21:8 *s.* sh. have part in lake
22:15 without are dogs and *s.*

SORCERY.

Acts 8:9 who beforetime used *s.*

SORCERIES.

Is. 47:9 come on thee for thy *s.*
12 stand with multi. of thy *s.*
Acts 8:11 long ti. bewitchi. wi. *s.*
Rev. 9:21 nei. repented of th. *s.*
18:23 by *s.* were nations deceiv.

SORE, Adj. or Adv.

Gen. 19:9 pressed *s.* upon man
31:20 bec. thou *s.* longedst after
31:35 day, when they were *s.*
41:56 famine waxed *s.* in land
57 famine was so *s.* in all lands
43:1 famine *s.* in land, 47:4, 13
Deut. 6:22 Lord showed signs *s.*
28:35 Lord shall smite with *s.*
59 make thy plagues wonderful
and thy seed with plagues *s.*
Jud. 10:9 Israel was *s.* distress.
14:17 bec. she lay *s.* upon him
20:34 battle *s.* upon him
33 battle was *s.* ag. 2 *K.* 8:26
21:2 lifted their voices, wept *s.*
1 *Sam.* 1:10 Han. prayed, wept *s.*
5:7 his hand is *s.* on us, and on
us *s.* was against Philistines
2 *Sam.* 12:15 *smel* and servant wept *s.*
1 *K.* 17:17 sickn. so *s.* no breath
2 *K.* 6:11 king of Syria *s.* troub.
20:3 Hezekiah wept *s. Is.* 38:3
21:19 Jeho. died of *s.* dis.
29:19 Ahaz *transgressed s.*
Ezr. 10:1 people wept very *s.*
Neh. 8:8 maketh *s.* bindeth up
Ps. 6:3 my soul is *s.* vexed
38:2 thy hand presseth me *s.*
44:19 thou hast *s.* broken us
55:4 my heart is *s.* pained
118:13 thou hast thrust *s.* at me
127:1 with *s.* and great sword
Is. 9:13 to see book wrath very *s. 0.L*o,
12 wilt thou afflict us very *s.?*
Lam. 1:2 she weepeth *s.* in night
Ezek. 14:21 my four *s.* judgm.
Dan. 6:14 was *s.* displeased
Mat. 21:15 th. were *s.* displeased
Mark 9:26 sp. cried, rent him *s.*
Acts 20:37 wept *s.* and kissed P.

See AFRAID.

SORE, Substantive.

Lev. 13:42 if a white reddish *s.*
2 *Chr.* 6:29 know his own *s.* gri.
Ps. 38:11 friends stood aloof fr. *s.*

1030   CRUDEN'S CONCORDANCE

SOR

Ps. 77:2 my s. ran in the night
Rev. 1v:2 there fell a grievous s.

SOREK.
Jud. 16:4 a woman in vall. of S.

SORES.
Is. 1:6 bruises and putrefying s.
Luke 16:20 Lazarus full of s, of1
Rev. 16:11 blasphemed bec. of s.

SORELY.
Is. 23:5 s. pained at report of T.

SORER.
Heb. 10:29 how much s. punish.

SORROW.
Gen. 3:16 greatly multi. thy s. in
  s. thou shalt bring forth ch.
  17 in s. shalt thou eat of it
  42:38 bring my gray hairs with
    s. to the grave, 44:29, 31
Ex. 15:14 s. take hold of inhab.
Num. 3:10 terror cause s. of heart
Deut. 28:65 L. sh. give s. of mind
1 Chr. 4:9 bec. I bare him wi. s.
Neh. 2:2 noth. else but s. of hea.
Est. 9:22 turned from s. to joy
Job 3:10 hid not s. fr. mine eyes
  6:10 I would harden myself in s.
  17:7 eye dim by reason of s.
  41:22 s. is turned into joy
Ps. 13:2 having s. in my heart
  35:17 my s. continually bef. me
  39:2 holp peace, my s. stirred
  55:10 and s. in the midst of it
  90:10 their strength labor and s.
  107:39 brought low through s.
  116:3 I found trouble and s.
Prov. 10:10 that winketh caus. s.
  23 L. mak. rich, addeth no s.
  15:13 by s. of heart spirit is bro.
  17:21 begetteth fool. doeth to s.
  25:20 who ha. woe? who hath s.
  Ec. 1:18 knowledge, increaseth s.
  5:17 hath much s. and wrath
  7:3 s. is better than laughter
  11:10 remove s. from thy heart
Is. 5:30 look to land, behold s.
  14:3 L. shall give thee rest fr. s.
  17:11 heap in day of desperate s.
  29:2 distress Ariel, th. sh. be s.
  35:10 s. and sighing shall flee
  50:11 ye shall lie down in s.
  51:11 s. and mourning flee away
  65:14 sing, but ye sh. cry for s.
Jer. 8:18 comf. myself against s.
  20:18 womb, see labor and s. ?
  30:15 why criest thou ? s. incu.
  31:13 make them rej. fr. their s.
  45:3 L. hath add. grief to my s.
  49:23 there is s. on the sea
Lam. 1:12 any s., like unto my s.
  18 behold s. 3:65 give them s.
Ezek. 23:33 fill. wi. drunk. and s.
Luke 22:45 found th. sleep. for s.
John 16:6 s. ha. fill. your hearts
  20 your s. shall be turn. to joy
  21 vo. when in travail hath s.
  22 and ye now therefore ha. s.
Rom. 9:2 I have s. in my heart
  2 Cor. 2:3 I sho. have s. from th.
  7 swallo. up with overmuch s.
  7:10 godly s. work. repentance,
    but s. of world worke. death
Phil. 2:27 lest I have s. upon s.
Rev. 18:7 s. give her. see no s.
  21:4 be no more death, neith. s.

SORROW, Verb.
Jer. 31:12 shall not s. any more
  51:29 land shall tremble and s.
Hos. 8:10 they shall s. for burden
1 Thes. 4:13 s. not as others

SORROWS.
Ex. 3:7 cry, for I know their s.
2 Sam. 22:6 s. of hell compassed
  me about. Ps. 18:4, 5 ; 116:3
Job 9:28 I afraid of s.
  21:17 God distribut. s. in anger
  30:3 how themselves, cast out s.
Ps. 16:4 s. shall be multiplied
  32:10 many s. shall be to wick.
  127:2 rise up, to eat bread of s.
Ec. 2:23 his days s. travail grief
Is. 13:8 and s. take hold of them
  53:3 man of s. acquainted with
  4 borne our griefs carri. our s.
Jer. 13:21 shall not s. take as wo.
  Ch.21 s. taken her as a woman
Dan. 10:16 by visions s. turned
Hos. 13:13 s. of travailing woma.
Mic. 4:9 ? 49:24 ? to, or Mark 13:8
1 Tim. 6:10 pierced with many s.

SORROWED, ETC.
1 Sam. 10:2 thy father s. for you
2 Cor. 7:9 I rejoice ye s. to repe.
  11 that ye s. after a godly sort

SORROWFUL.
1 Sam. 1:15 woman of a s. spirit

SOU

Job 6:7 refus. are as my s. meat
Ps. 69:29 I am poor and s. let
Prov. 14:13 in laugh. heart is s.
Jer. 31:25 replenis. every s. soul
Zep. 3:18 gather them that are s.
Zec. 9:5 Gaza see it, be very s.
Mat. 19:22 that, saying, he went
  away s. Luke 18:23, 24
  26:22 were exc. s. Mark 14:19
  37 began to be s. very heavy
  38 soul exceed. s. Mark 14:34
John 16:20 shall be s. but sorrow
2 Cor. 6:10 s. yet always rejoici.
Phil. 2:28 I may be the less s.

SORROWING.
Luke 2:48 father and I so. thee s.
Acts 20:38 s. th. see face no more

SORRY.
1 Sam. 22:8 none of you that is s.
Neh. 8:10 holy to L. nei. be ye s.
Ps. 38:18 I will be s. for my sin
Is. 51:19 who shall be s. for thee
Mat. 14:9 king was s. Mark 6:26
  17:23 and they were exceedi. s.
2 Cor. 2:2 if I ma. yon s. s., is s.
  7:8 s. same epistle made you s.
  9 rejoice not ye wo. s. for ye s.

SORT.
Gen. 6:19 two of cv. s. in ark. 20
1 Chr. 24:5 divid. one s. wi. ano.
  29:14 able to offer after this s.
Ezr. 4:8 wrote to Ar. after th. s.
Neh. 6:4 sent 4 times after this s.
Ezek. 23:42 men of the comm. s.
Dan. 1:10 worse th. chil. of yo. s.
  3:29 no god can def. after this s.
Acts 17:5 lewd fellows of baser s.
Rom. 15:15 writ. boldly in some s.
1 Cor. 3:13 man's work of wh. s.
2 Cor. 7:11 sorrow. after godly s.
2 Tim. 3:6 of this s. who creep
3 John 6 journey after a godly s.

Deut. 22:11 garment of divers s.
Neh. 5:18 store of all s. of wine
Ps. 78:45 divers s. of flies. 105:31
Ezek. 27:24 merch. in all s. of th.
33:4 clothed with all s. of armor

SOSIPATER.
Rom. 16:21 Ja. and S. my kins.

SOSTHENES.
Acts 18:17 the Greeks took S.
1 Cor. 1:1 Paul and S. to church

SOTTISH.
Jer. 4:22 foolish. th. are s. child.

SOUGHT.
Ex. 4:19 men dead wh. s. life
  24 L. met him, s. to kill him
  33:7 that s. L. went to taberna.
Num. 35:23 see, nor s. his harm
Jud. 14:4 Samson s. occasion
1 Sam. 27:1 S. no more for him
  2 Sam. 3:17 s. for Da. to be king
  4:8 head of one. that s. thy life
  21 Saul s. to slay them in zeal
1 K. 10:24 earth s. to Sol. to hear
  K. 2:17 s. three days for Elijah
1 Chr. 26:31 among Heb. were s.
  Chr. 14:7 because we have s. L.
  17:4 s. to Lord God of his father
  22:15 s. after gods of Ed. ? 20
  28:5 s. G. in days of Zachariah,
    as long as he s. the Lord
Neh. 12:27 they s. the Levit. out
Est. 9:2 hand on such as s. hurt
Ps. 34:4 I s. Lord, he heard, 77:2
  111:2 s. out of all that have plo.
  119:10 with wh. heart I s. thee
  94 I have s. thy precepts
Ec. 7:29 s. many inventions
  12:9 preacher s. out many prov.
  16. 62:12 shalt be called s. out
  65:1 s. of them asked not. found
Jer. 8:2 moon, whom they ha. s.
  10:21 the pastors have not s. L.
  26:21 s. to put him to death
  50:20 iniquity of Israel sh. be s.
Lam. 1:19 they s. meat to relieve
Ezek. 22:30 I s. a man am. them
  26:21 tho' s. yet never be found
  34:6 that which was lost
  8 my flock, neither did shepher.
Ob. 6 Esau's hidden things s. up
Zec. 12:9 those that have not s.
Mat. 2:20 dead wh. s. child's life
  21:46 s. to lay hands on him
  Mark 12:12 ; Luke 20:19
Luke 2:48 I s. thee sorrowing
  49 how is it that ye s. me ?
  11:16 others s. a sign fr. heaven
  13:6 s. fr. thereon, found none
  19:3 Zaccheus s. to see Jesus

SOU

John 7:11 J. s. him at feast, 11:56
  30 they s. to take him. 10:39
Acts 12:19 when Herod s. for Pe.
  17:5 they s. to bring them out
Rom. 9:32 bec. s. it not by faith
1 Thes. 2:6 nor of men s. we glo.
2 Tim. 1:17 in Rome he s. me
Heb. 8:7 place shou. have been s.
  12:17 he s. carefully with tears

SOUGHT him.
1 Sam. 10:21 s. h. could not be f.
  13:14 L. s. h. a man to be capt.
  23:14 Saul s. him every day
1 Chr. 15:13 s. not after order
2 Chr. 14:7 s. h. he hath giv. rest
  15:4 when th. s. h. he was found
  15 they s. h. with their desire
Ps. 37:36 I s. h. could not be fou.
  78:34 slew them, then they s. h.
Cant. 3:1 by night I s. h. I s. h.
  but I found him not. 2 ; 5:6
Luke 2:44 they s. h. among kins.
  4:42 people s. h. came to him

SOUL.
Gen. 2:7 man became a living s.
  34:3 s. of son longeth for daugh.
  35:18 as her s. was in departing
Lev. 4:2 if a s. sin thro' ignoran.
  5:1 if a s. sin, and hear swe iri.
  4 if a s. swear, 17:12 no s. eat blood
  17:11 blood not atonem. for s.
  22:11 if priest buy s.
  23:30 whatso. s. doeth any work
Num. 21:4 s. of peo. discouraged
  30:4 every bond she hath bound
    her s. 5, 6, 7, 8, 9, 10, 11, 12, 13
  31:28 one s. of five hund. for L.
Deut. 11:13 serve him with yo. s.
  18 lay up th. words in your s.
  13:3 wheth. you love L. with all
    your s. Jos. 22:5 ; 1 K. 2:4
1 Sam. 18:1 s. of Jonathan knit
  to s. of David
  30:6 s. of the people was griev.
2 Sam. 5:8 blind hated of D.'s s.
  13:39 s. of D. longed to go to A.
1 K. 8:48 return to thee with s.
  17:21 let this child's s. come
2 K. 4:27 let alone, her s. is vex.
1 Chr. 22:19 set yo. s. to seek L.
2 Chr. 6:38 if they return with s.
  15:12 seek the L. with their s.
Job 3:20 life giv. to bitter in s. ?
  14:22 s. within him hath mour.
  16:4 if yo. s. were in my soul's
  24:12 s. of the wounded crieth
Ps. 10:7 law perfect converting s.
  33:19 deliver their s. from death
  31:22 L. redeem. s. of his serve.
  72:14 he shall redeem their s.
  78:50 spared not th. s. fr. death
  86:4 rejoice s. of thy serv. O L.
  94:21 gather against s. of right.
  106:15 sent leanness to their s.
  107:18 their s. abhorreth all me.
  26 th. s. melted bec. of trouble
Prov. 10:3 not suff. s. of righteo.
  11:25 liberal s. shall be made fat
  13:2 s. of transgressors sh. eat
  19 desire accom. is sweet to s.
  16:24 pleasant words sweet to s.
  19:2 s. without knowl. not good
  15 idle s. shall suffer hunger
  21:10 s. of wicked desireth evil
  22:23 Lord will spoil s. of those
  25:13 so refresheth s. of masters
  27:7 full s. loathe, honey-comb,
    to hungry s. bitter is sweet
  Is. 29 woe to them, have empty s.
  32:6 make empty s. of hungry
  55:3 let yo. s. delight in fatness
  58:10 if thou satisfy afflicted s.
  11 sh. s. in drought, make fat
Jer. 4:19 the wo. s. delivered
  20:13 he delivered s. of poor
  31:12 their s. shall be as a gard.
  38:16 L. liveth, made us this s.
Lam. 3:11 for meat to relieve s.
  25 wh. their s. was poured out
  3:25 the Lord is good to the s.
Ezek. 18:4 s. of father, so s. of
    son, the s. that sinneth, 20
  34:31 what your s. pitieth shall
Hos. 9:4 s. shall not come into
  Mic. 7:2 hunt. ev. man his bro.
  Hab. 2:4 s. lifted up is not upri.
  Zec. 11:8 L. was abhorred by s.
Mat. 10:28 fear not them wh. kill
    body, not able to kill the s.
  12:18 my beloved, in wh. my s.
Mark 8:36 if he gain wh. world
    loss own s. ? 37 what shall
    man give in exchange for s. ?
  14:34 my s. sorrowful Mat. 28:3
Luke 1:46 my s. doth magnify L.
  12:20 night thy s. shall be req.
Acts 2:31 his s. not left in hell

My SOUL.
Gen. 12:13 my s. sh. live because
  19:20 let me escape. my s. shall
  27:4 my s. may bless thee. 25
  49:6 O my s. come not into their
Lev. 26:11 my s. sh. not abh. 30
Num. 23:10 my s. die death of
  24:4 if yo. s. were in my soul's
Jud. 10:16 my s. was grieved
  16:16 so that his s. was vexed
  2 K. 23:25 Josiah turned to Lord
    with all his s. 2 Chr. 34:31
Job 14:22 his s. within him
  21:25 dieth in bitterness of h. s.
  23:13 what his s. desireth, even
  27:2 when God tak. away his s.
  31:30 sin. by wish. curse to h. s.
  33:18 keepeth back h. s. fr. pit
  22 his s. draw. near unto grave
  28 will deliver his s. from, 30
Ps. 11:5 violence, his s. hateth
  21:4 who had not lifted up his s.
  25:13 his s. shall dwell at ease
  49:18 wh. he lived he bless. h. s.
  89:48 sh. he deliver his s. from ?
  109:31 save fr. th. condemn h. s.
Prov. 6:30 if steal to satisfy h. s.
  16:17 his way. preserveth h. s.
  21:23 his mouth, keepeth his s.
  22:5 that doth keep his s. shall
  23:14 shalt deliver his s. fr. hell
  29:10 but the just hate h. s.
  29:24 shun. make his s. enjoy
  6:2 wanteth nothing for his s.
  3 his s. be not filled with good
Is. 29:8 awak. and his s. empty
  41:30 be cannot deliver his s.
  53:10 ma. his s. an offer. for sin
  11 see of travail of his s.
  12 poured out h. s. unto death
Jer. 50:19 his s. shall be satisfied
  51:6 deliver every man his s. 45
Ezek. 18:27 right. he sh. sa. h. s.
  33:5 warning, shall deliver h. s.
Hab. 2:4 his s. that is lifted up
Mat. 16:26 lose h. s. own s. give in
    exchange for h. s. ? Mark 8:37
Acts 2:31 his s. not left in hell

My SOUL.
Gen. 12:13 my s. sh. live because
  19:20 let me escape, my s. shall
  27:4 my s. may bless thee. 25
  49:6 O my s. come not into their
Lev. 26:11 my s. shall not abh. 30
Num. 23:10 my s. die death of
Jud. 16:16 my s. vexed, 21:2
  26:21 bece. my s. was precious
2 Sam. 4:9 Lord who hath re-
    deemed my s. 1 K. 1:29
Job 3:1 the things my s. refused
  7:15 that my s. chooseth stran.
  10:1 my s. is weary of life, I will
    speak bitterness of my s.
  19:2 how lo. will ye vex my s. ?
  27:2 Alm. who hath vexed my s.
  30:15 they pursue my s. as wind
  16 my s. is poured out upon
  23 was not my s. gri. for poor ?
Ps. 3:2 who say of my s. There is
  6:3 my s. is sore vex. but, O L.
  4 deliver my s. 17:13 ; 22:20 ;
    116:4 ; 120:2
  13:2 sh. I take couns. in my s. ?
  16:10 not leave my s. Act. 2:27
  23:3 he restoreth my s. he lead.
  25:1 unto th. O L. do I lift my s.
  20 O keep my s. and deliver me
  26:9 gather not my s. with sin.
  30:3 brought my s. from grave
  31:7 hast known my s. in adver.
  9 my s. sh. make boast in L.
  35:3 say unto my s. I am thy s.
  4 put to shame that seek my s.
  7 have digged a pit for my s.
  9 my s. shall be joyful in Lord
  13 I humbled my s. with fast.
  41:4 heal my s. I have sinned
  42:1 I pour out my s. in me
  5 cast down O my s. ? 43 :5
  6 O my s. my s. is cast down
  54:4 L. is with that upho. my s.
  55:18 delivered my s. in peace
  56:6 when they wait for my s.
  13 thou hast delivered my s.
  57:1 be merciful, my s. trusteth
  4 my s. is amo. lions and I lie
  6 my s. is bowed down
  59:3 they lie in wait for my s.
  6:1 my s. waiteth upon God
  5 my s. wait thou only upon G.
  3:1 my s. followeth hard after
  6:16 what G. ha. done for my s.
  7:1 we. are come in unto my s.
  2 draw nigh to my s.
  11:23 my s. shall rejoice
  73:2 my sore ran, my s. refused

CRUDEN'S CONCORDANCE. 1031

SOU

Ps. 84:2 my *s.* longeth for the L.
86:2 preserve my *s.* I am holy
4 O Lord, do I lift my *s.* 143:8
13 thou hast deliv. my *s.* from
84:3 my *s.* is full of troubles
11 why castest thou off my *s.* ?
91:17 my *s.* had dwelt in silence
103:1 bless the Lord, O my *s.* 2,
22; 104:1, 35
109:20 them ih. speak ag. my *s.*
116:7 ret. unto thy rest, O my *s.*
8 thou hast delivered my *s.*
119:20 my *s.* break. for longing
109 my *s.* is continu. in hand
120 therefore doth my *s.* keep,
175 let my *s.* live and it shall
130:2 deliver my *s.* O Lord
6 my *s.* dw. wi. him that hate.
130:5 wait for the Lord, my *s.* 6
138:3 strengthen me in my *s.*
139:14 that my *s.* knoweth well
142:4 no man cared for my *s.*
7 bring my *s.* out of prison
143:11 bring my *s.* out of troub.
146:1 praise the Lord, O my *s.*
Ec. 7:28 which yet my *s.* seeketh
Cant. 1:7 wh. my *s.* lo. 3:1, 2, 3, 4
3:6 my *s.* failed when he spake
Is. 1:14 new moons my *s.* hateth
26:9 with my *s.* have I desired
38:17 in love to my *s.* deliv. it
61:10 my *s.* sh. be joyful in God
Jer. 4:19 hast heard, O my *s.*
5:9 my *s.* be avenged? 29; 9:9
6:8 instructed, lest my *s.* depart
12:7 beloved of my *s.* into hand
13:20 they dig. a pit for my *s.*
32:41 rej. over them my whole *s.*
Lam. 3:24 L. my por. saith my *s.*
58 pleaded the causes of my *s.*
Mic. 6:7 body for sin of my *s.* ?
7:1 my *s.* desired first ripe fruit
Mat. 12:18 in wh. my *s.* is pleas.
20:28 my *s.* is sor. *Mark* 14:34
Luke 1:46 my *s.* doth magnify L.
12:19 I will say to my *s.*
John 12:27 is my *s.* troubled
2 *Cor.* 1:23 for record upon my *s.*
Heb. 10:38 my *s.* sh. have no ple.

Our SOUL.

Num. 11:6 our *s.* is dried away
Ps. 33:20 our *s.* waiteth for Lord
44:25 our *s.* is bowed down
66:9 God who holdeth our *s.*
124:4 stre. had gone over our *s.*
Is. 26:8 the desire of our *s.* is

Own SOUL.

Deut. 13:6 friend as thine *o. s.*
Ps. 22:29 none can keep his *o. s.*
Prov. 6:32 destroyeth his own *s.*
8:36 sinneth, wrongeth his *o. s.*
19:16 commandm. keep. his *o. s.*
20:2 king, sinneth aga. his *o. s.*
22:24 partner with thief ha. *o. s.*
Mat. 16:26 if he shall gain whole world and lose his *o. s.* ? *Mark* 8:36
Luke 2:35 sword pierce thy *o. s.*

That SOUL.

Lev. 17:10 set face ag. *t. s.* 20:6
22:3 that *s.* shall be cut off from
23:30 that *s.* will I destroy from
Num. 15:31 *t. s.* sh. utter. be cut

Thy SOUL.

Gen. 26:19 *thy s.* may bless, 31
Deut. 4:9 keep *thy s.* diligently
29 if seek him with all *thy s.*
6:5 L. thy G. with all *t. s.* 30:6
10:12 serve Lord with all *thy s.*
12:15 whatsoev. *t. s.* lusteth, 11:26
26:16 do with *t. s.* 31:3 obey with *thy s.*
30:2 obey wi. thy heart and *t. s.*
10 turn to Lord with all *thy s.*
1 *Sam.* 2:16 as much as *t. s.* desi.
2:21 whatsoever *t. s.* desireth
2:29 according to desire of *t. s.*
23:20 man riven to pursue *t. s.*
1 *Ki.* 1:237 reign according *t. s.*
Ps. 121:7 L. shall preserve *thy s.*
Prov. 2:10 know. is pleas. to *t. s.*
3:22 shall be life to *thy s.*
19:18 let not *thy s.* spare
22:25 and get a snare to *thy s.*
24:12 he that keepeth *t. s.* doth
14 knowl. of wisdom be to *t. s.*
29:17 be sh. give delight to *t. s.*
Is. 51:23 have said to *t. s.* bow
58:10 draw out *thy s.* to hungry
11 Lord shall satisfy *thy s.*
Jer. 11:9 hurteth *s.* instilled *t. s.*
38:17 forth, *thy s.* shall live, 20
Ezek. 3:19 deliv. *thy s.* 21; 33:9
Hab. 2:10 hast sinned ag. *thy s.*
Mat. 22:37 love L. with all *thy s.*
Mark 12:30; *Luke* 10:27
Luke 12:20 *thy s.* be requi. of thee

SOU

1 *John* 2 even as *thy s.* prosperé.
Rev. 18:14 fruits *t. s.* lust. after
See LIVETH.

SOULS.

Gen. 12:5 A. took *s.* th. had got
46:26 *s.* that came into Egypt
27 sons of Joseph in Egy. were two *s.* all the *s.* of the house of Jacob were 70 *s. Ex.* 1:5
Ex. 12:4 a num according to *s.*
30:15 atonement for your *s.* 16;
Lev. 17:11; *Num.* 31:50
Lev. 18:29 *s.* that commit them
20:25 not make your *s.* abomin.
Num. 16:38 sin. ag. their own *s.*
30:9 wherewith he bound. *s.*
Jos. 23:14 know in all your *s.*
1 *Sam.* 25:29 *s.* of one. shall sling
Ps. 72:13 shall save *s.* of needy
97:10 preserveth *s.* of his saints
Prov. 1:30 that win. *s.* is wise
14:25 a true witness delivers. *s.*
Is. 57:16 spi. should fail, and *s.*
Jer. 2:34 in thy skirts is bl. of *s.*
6:16 rest for your *s. Mat.* 11:29
26:19 procure evil ag. your *s.*
44:7 why com. evil ag. your *s.* ?
Lam. 1:19 sought meat to th. *s.*
Ezek. 7:19 sh. not satisfy their *s.*
13:18 hunt *s.* hunt *s.* of peo. 20
19 slay *s.* that should not die
14:14 should deliver their own *s.*
18:4 *s.* are mine; 22:25 devou. *s.*
Acts 2:41 added to them 3,000 *s.*
7:14 Jacob and his kindred 75 *s.*
14:22 confirming *s.* of disciples
15:24 troubled your, subvert. *s.*
27:37 we. in all in the ship 276 *s.*
1 *Thes.* 2:8 imparted our *s.* to you
Heb. 13:17 they watch for your *s.*
Jam. 1:21 word able to save yo. *s.*
1 *Pet.* 1:22 have purified your *s.*
3:20 that is. eight *s.* were saved
4:19 commit keep. of *s.* to him
Rev. 6:9 I saw *s.* of them slain
18:13 no man buyeth *s.* of men
20:4 I saw *s.* of them beheaded
See AFFLICT.

SOUND, Substantive.

Ex. 28:35 his *s.* shall be heard
Lev. 26:36 *s.* of a shaken leaf
Jos. 6:5 hear *s.* of trumpet, 20
2 *Sam.* 5:24 *s.* of going in the tops of mulberry-trees, 1 *Chr.* 14:15
1 *Ki.* 1:40 earth rent with the *s.*
14:6 Ahijah heard *s.* of her feet
18:41 *s.* of abundance of rain
2 *Ki.* 6:32 is not *s.* of mas. *s. ?*
1 *Chr.* 16:42 with trum. make *s.*
2 *Chr.* 5:13 one *s.* to be heard
Neh. 4:20 in wh. place ye hear *s.*
Job 15:21 dreadful *s.* in his ears
21:12 rejoice at *s.* of the organ
37:2 *s.* that go. out of his mouth
39:24 not believ. he it is the *s.*
Ps. 47:5 gone up with *s.* of trum.
77:17 water, skies sent out a *s.*
89:15 people that know joyful *s.*
92:3 sing upon harp with sol. *s.*
150:3 praise him wi. *s.* of trum.
Ez. 12:4 *s.* of grinding is low
Jer. 4:19 hast heard *s.* of trum.
6:17 hearken to *s.* of trumpet, 19
10:22 *s.* of battle is in the land
50:22 *s.* of battle, 46 *s.* cry is h.
Ezek. 10:5 *s.* of cherubim's wings
26:13 *s.* of thy harps be no more
15 sh. not the isles sha. at *s. ?*
27:28 suburbs shall shake at *s.*
31:16 made nati. to shake at *s.*
Dan. 3:5 ye hear the *s.* 7, 10, 15
Amos 2:2 Moab shall die with *s.*
Mat. 24:31 angels with great *s.*
John 3:8 hearest *s.* canst not tell
Acts 2:2 there came *s.* from hea.
Rom. 10:18 *s.* went into all earth
1 *Cor.* 14:7 thin. with. lifegiv. *s.*
Heb. 12:19 wd. came to *s.* of trum.
Rev. 1:15 *s.* of many waters
9:9 *s.* of wings as *s.* of chariots

SOUND, Adjective.

Ps. 119:80 let my heart be *s.*
Prov. 2:7 he layeth up *s.* wisdom
8:14 counsel is mine and *s.* wis.
14:30 a *s.* heart is life of flesh
Luke 15:27 rec. him safe and *s.*
1 *Tim.* 1:10 contrary to *s.* doctri.
6:3 consent not to *s.* words
2 *Tim.* 1:7 spirit of *s.* mind
13 hold fast form of *s.* words
4:3 will not endure *s.* doctrine
Tit. 1:9 be able by *s.* doctrine
13 that they may be *s.* in faith
2:1 things which become *s.* doctrine

SOU

Tit. 2:2 th. aged men be *s.* in fa.
8 *s.* speech cannot be conden.

SOUND, Verb.

Num. 10:7 shall call *s.* an alarm
1 *Chr.* 15:19 were appointed to *s.*
Is. 16:11 my bowels sh. *s.* for M.
Jer. 48:36 my heart sh. *s.* for M.
Joel 2:1 *s.* alarm in holy mount.
Mat. 6:2 do not *s.* trumpet bef.
1 *Cor.* 15:52 the trumpet shall *s.*
Rev. 8:6 prep. themselves to *s.*
10:7 sev. angel shall begin to *s.*

SOUNDED.

Ex. 19:19 the trumpet *s.* long
1 *Sam.* 20:12 wh. I have *s.* father
Neh. 4:18 he that *s.* the trumpet
Luke 1:44 saluta. *s.* in my ears
Acts 27:28 *s.* found 20 fathoms
1 *Thes.* 1:8 fr. you *s.* word of L.
Rev. 8:7 first angel *s.* and there
8 second *s.* 10 third; 12 fourth
9:1 fifth *s.* 13 sixth; 11:15 sev.

SOUNDETH.

Ex. 19:13 when trumpet *s.* long

SOUNDING.

1 *Chr.* 15:16 singers with *s.* trum.
Is. 63:15 wh. is thy zeal and *s. ?*
Ezek. 7:7 not the *s.* of mountains
1 *Cor.* 13:1 not charity, as *s.* brass

SOUNDNESS.

Ps. 38:3 th. is no *s.* in my flesh, 7
Is. 1:6 no *s.* in it, but wounds
Acts 3:16 given him this perf. *s.*

SOUNDS.

1 *Cor.* 14:7 give a distinct. in *s.*

SOUR.

Jer. 31:29 when *s.* grape, they ha. eaten a *s.* grape, *Ezek.* 18:2
30 ev. man that eateth *s.* grape
Hos. 4:18 their drink is *s.*

SOUTH.

Gen. 12:9 Abr. journeyed tow. *s.*
13:1 A. went into A. 3 went fr. *s.*
28:14 spr. abroad to north and *s.*
Num. 13:29 Amalekites dw. in *s.*
Deut. 33:23 pos. thou west and *s.*
1 *Sam.* 20:41 Dav. arose out of *s.*
1 *Ki.* 7:25 looking towards the *s.* 2 *Chr.* 4:1
Job 37:9 whirlwind cometh of the *s.*
39:26 stretch wings toward *s.*
Ps. 75:6 com. not fr. east nor *s.*
89:12 north and *s.* thou created
107:3 gathered fr. north and *s.*
Ec. 1:6 wind goeth toward *s.*
11:3 if the tree falleth toward *s.*
Cant. 4:16 south wind blow on *s.*
Jer. 13:19 cit. of *s.* shall be shut
Ezek. 21:4 sword ag. fl. fr. *s.* to n.
20:46 face toward *s.* drop *s.* to *s.*
21:4 shall flocks *s.* to *s.*
Dan. 11:5 and the king of the *s.*
Ob. 19 they of *s.* sh. pos. mount
20 captivity sh. pos. cit. of *s.*
Zec. 7:7 when men inhabited *s.*
14:4 mountain remove toward *s.*
Mat. 12:42 queen of *s. Luke* 11:31
Acts 8:26 arise, and go toward *s.*
27:13 wind blew soft, *s.*
Rev. 21:13 on the *s.* three gates

SOUTH border.

Num. 34:3 *s. b.* the outmost coa.
Jos. 15:2 the *s. b.* of Judah

SOUTH country.

Gen. 20:1 Abrah. sojourned *s. c.*
24:62 for Isaac dwelt in the *s. c.*

SOUTH land.

Jos. 15:19 given me *s. l. Jud.* 1:15

SOUTH quarter.

Num. 34:3 *s. q.* be fr. Zin far coast
Jos. 18:15 *s. q.* fr. end of Kirjath.

SOUTH side.

1 *Sam.* 33:27 which were in *s. b.*
Ex. 26:18 boards on *s. s.* 36:23
27:9 south *s.* 13 *s.* 38:9
Num. 2:10 the *s. s.* shall be stan.
Ezek. 48:16 *s. s.* 4,500 meas. 33

SOUTH wind.

Job 37:17 garments warm *s. w.*
Ps. 78:26 he brought in *s. w.*
Cant. 4:16 blow on my gar. *s. w.*
Luke 12:55 see *s. w.* blow, shall
Acts 27:13 *s. w.* blew softly

SPA

SOW, Substantive.

2 *Pet.* 2:22 the *s.* washed, to her

SOW, Verb.

Gen. 47:23 ye shall *s.* the land
Ex. 23:10 *s.* the land, *Lev.* 25:3
Lev. 19:19 sh. not *s.* wi. mingled
25:4 in sev. year shalt not *s.* 11
20 we shall not *s.* nor gather
26:16 shall *s.* your seed in vain
2 *Ki.* 19:29 in the third year *s.* ye,
Is. 37:30
Job 4:8 *s.* wickedness reap same
31:8 let me *s.* let another eat
Ps. 107:37 *s.* fields and viney ards
126:5 *s.* in tears sh. reap in joy
Ez. 11:4 observ. wind, sh. not *s.*
6 in the morning *s.* thy seed
Is. 28:24 ploughman pl. to *s. ?*
30:23 rain of seed thou shalt *s.*
32:20 blessed that *s.* beside wat.
Jer. 4:3 *s.* not among thorns
31:27 I will *s.* the house of Isr.
35:7 net. build house nor *s.* seed
Hos. 2:23 I will *s.* her unto me
10:12 *s.* to yourselves in right.
Mic. 6:15 thou shalt *s.* not reap
Zec. 10:9 *s.* them among people
Mat. 6:26 fowls of the air *s.* not
13:3 a sower went forth to *s.*
Mark 4:3; *Luke* 8:5
27 didst thou *s.* good seed
Luke 12:24 ravens nei. *s.* nor reap
19:21 reap. thou didst not *s.* 22

SOWED, EDST.

Gen. 26:12 Isa. *s.* in land and yea.
Deut. 11:10 wh. thou *s.* thy seed
Jud. 9:45 Abimelech *s.* it
Mat. 13:24 man which *s.* good seed; 25 *s.* tares, 39

SOWER.

Is. 55:10 it may give seed to *s.*
Jer. 50:16 cut off *s.* from Baby.
Mat. 13:18 hear ye parable of *s.*
Mark 4:14 *s.* soweth word
2 *Cor.* 9:10 minister. seed to *s.*

SOWEST.

1 *Cor.* 15:36 thou *s.* not quicken.
37 *s.* not body that shall be

SOWETH.

Prov. 6:14 *s.* discord; 19 *s.* disc.
11:18 that *s.* righteousn. *s.* rew.
16:28 a froward man *s.* strife
22:8 *s.* iniquity, reap vanity
Amos 9:13 overtake him that *s.*
Mat. 13:37 he that *s.* good seed is S.
Mark 4:14 *s.* soweth word
John 4:36 he that *s.* and reapeth
37 true, one *s.* another reapeth
2 *Cor.* 9:6 *s.* sparingly, *s.* bounti.
Gal. 6:7 whatsoever a man *s.*
8 that *s.* to flesh, reap. corrup.

SOWING.

Jer. 11:37 if care, fall on any *s.*
26:5 vint. shall reach to *s.* time

SOWN.

Deut. 21:4 val. nei. eared nor *s.*
22:9 lest fruit of seed *s.* be defi.
29:23 generation see land not *s.*
Jud. 6:3 Israel had *s.* Midi. came
Ps. 97:11 light is *s.* for righteous
Is. 19:7 thing *s.* by brook wither
40:24 plant. yea, shall not be *s.*
61:11 can. things *s.* to spring
Jer. 2:2 after me in a land not *s.*
12:11 they have *s.* wheat, thorns
Ezek. 36:9 ye sh. be tilled and *s.*
Hos. 8:7 *s.* wind, reap whirlwind
Nah. 1:14 no grave of thy name *s.*
Hag. 1:6 *s.* much, bring little
Mat. 13:19 catcheth away that which was *s. Mark* 4:15
19 *s.* by way side, *s.* stony gro.
18 *s.* am. thorns; 20 *s.* on gro.
31 wh. *s.* is less than all seeds
1 *Cor.* 9:11 *s.* to you spar things
Cor. 9:11 *s.* unto you spiritual
15:42 it is *s.* a natural body; raised
2 *Cor.* 9:10 multiply your seed *s.*
Jam. 3:18 righteousn. *s.* in peace

SPA

SPACE.

Gen. 32:16 put *s.* bet. drove and
Lev. 25:8 *s.* of 7 sabbaths of years
Num. 35:4 a between yonr and cit.
1 *Sam.* 36:13 a betw. till D. comp.
Ezr. 9:8 grace sh. be showed
Luke 22:59 about *s.* of one hour
Acts 5:7 *s.* of 3 hours
19:8 spake boldly *s.* of 3 months
34 cried out *s.* of 2 hours
19:10 continued by *s.* of 2 years
Gal. 2:1 after *s.* of 14 years I went
Rev. 2:21 I gave her *s.* to repent
8:1 silence about *s.* of half hour

CRUDEN'S CONCORDANCE.

SPA

Rev. 14:20 blood by *s.* of 1,600 fur.
17:10 must continue a short *s.*

SPAIN.
Rom. 15:24 whenso. I jour. to S.
28 I will come by you into S.

SPAKE.
Gen. 20:9 wh. he *s.* Rachel came
Deut. 1:43 I *s.* ye would not hear
28:68 L. br. thee by whereof I *s.*
1 *Sam.* 1:18 Han. *s.* in her heart
2 *K.* 9:12 and thus *s.* he to him
2 *Chr.* 13:19 one *s.* after manner
33:19 they *s.* ag. God of Jerusa.
Neh. 13:24 *s.* half in speech of A.
Job 2:13 sat down, none *s.* a word
19:16 I arose, they *s.* against me
29:22 after my words they *s.* not
38:16 they *s.* not, but stood still
Ps. 78:19 they *s.* against God
Prov. 30:1 the man *s.* unto Ithiel and Ucal
Jer. 20:8 for since I *s.* I cried out
Ezek. 24:18 so I *s.* to the people
Mat. 3:16 feared L. *s.* one to ano.
Mat. 9:33 devil cast out dumb *s.*
12:22; *Luke* 11:14
21:45 perceived he *s.* of them
Luke 1:55 as he *s.* to our fathers
2:50 understood not say. he *s.*
24:6 remember how he *s.* to you
25 as they thus *s.* Jesus stood
John 1:15 this was he of wh. I *s.*
7:13 no man *s.* openly of him
46 Never man *s.* like this man
8:27 understood not that he *s.*
10:6 wh. things they were he *s.*
41 things John *s.* of this man
12:29 saying fulfil. he *s.* 18:9, 32
13:22 look. doubt. of who. he *s.*
24 who it *sho.* be of who. he *s.*
Acts 13:45 Jews *s.* ag. things sp.
22:9 heard not voice of him *s.*
28:24 as he *s.* for himself, *Fest.*
1 *Cor.* 13:11 wh. child *s.* as child
14:5 I would yo *s.* with tongues
Heb. 12:25 refus. him *s.* on earth
2 *Pet.* 1:21 men of G. *s.* as moved
Rev. 1:12 turn. to see voice th. *s.*

God SPAKE.
Gen. 35:15 place where God *s.*
Deut. 1:6 L. God *s.* to us in Hor.
Jos. 23:14 of good things Go *l s.*
John 9:29 we know G. *s.* to Mo.
Acts 7:6 and God *s.* on this wise
17:5. 14 God who *s.* in time past
See LORD, expressly.

Lord or God SPAKE, implicitly.
1 *Sam.* 9:17 which I *s.* to thee of
28:17 Lord hath done as he *s.*
1 *K.* 6:12 word I *s.* unto David
2 *Chr.* 6:4 who fulfilled that he *s.*
Ps. 33:9 he *s.* and it was done
Jer. 7:13 I *s.* to you, rising up
51 ont to fathers, I broug.
14:14 I sent them not, neither *s.*
31:20 since I *s.* ag. him I rem.
Lam. 1:26 heard one that *s.* 9:2
Luke 24:44 these are words I *s.*
Heb. 4:4 he *s.* in a certain place

SPAKEST.
Jud. 13:11 man *s.* to woman ?
Neh. 0:13 *s.* with them fr. heaven
Jer. 48:27 since thou *s.* skippedst

SPAN.
Ex. 28:16 *s.* length, *s.* brea. 39:9
1 *Sam.* 17:4 G. height. 6 cu. *s.* *s.*
Is. 40:12 meted heaven with *s.*?
Lam. 2:20 wom, eat chil. *s.* long
Ezek. 43:13 bord, of altar be a *s.*

SPANNED.
Is. 48:13 right hand *s.* heavens

SPARE.
Gen. 18:24 not *s.* pl. for 50 right.
Deut. 13:8 sh. not *s.* nor conceal
29:20 Lord will not *s.* him
1 *Sam.* 15:3 destroy Amal. *s.* not
Neh. 13:22 *s.* me accor. to mercy
Job 6:10 let him not, I have not
20:13 he *s.* and forsake it not
27:22 sh. cast upon him, not
30:10 *s.* not to spit in my face
Ps. 39:13 O *s.* that I may recover
72:13 he shall *s.* poor and needy
Prov. 6:34 not *s.* in day of veng.
19:18 let not soul *s.* for crying
Is. 9:19 no man shall *s.* brother
13:18 their eye shall not *s.* chil.
30:14 shall break it, shall not *s.*
54:2 *s.* lengthen cords
58:1 *s.* not, lift voice like trum.
Jer. 13:14 will not *s.* *Ezek.* 24:14
21:7 not *s.* th. 50:11 *s.* no arro.
51:3 *s.* ye not her young men

SPE

Ezek. 5:11 nor mine eyes *s.* 7:4, 9; 8:18; 9:10
9:5 let not your eyes *s.*
Joel 2:17 say. *s.* thy people, O L.
Jon. 4:11 should not I *s.* Nine. ?
Hab. 1:17 not *s.* to slay nations
Mal. 3:17 *s.* th. as man spar. son
Luke 15:17 bread enough to *s.*
Rom. 11:21 lest he also *s.* not
1 *Cor.* 7:28 have trouble, I *s.* you
1 *Cor.* 1:23 to *s.* you I came not
13:2 if I come again, will not *s.*

1 *Sam.* 15:9 Saul and people *s.*
24:10 kill thee, but mine eye *s.*
2 *Sam.* 12:4 to take of his flock
21:7 the king *s.* Mephibosheth
2 *K.* 5:20 master hath *s.* Naaman
Pr. 78:50 he *s.* not soul fr. death
Ezek. 20:17 ml. eye *s.* them from
Rom. 8:32 he that *s.* not his Son
11:21 if God *s.* not nat. branches
Pr. 2:4 if God *s.* not angels
5 *s.* not old world, saved Noah

SPARETH, ING.
Prov. 13:24 that *s.* rod, hat. son
17:27 hath knowledge *s.* words
21:26 righteous giveth, *s.* not
Mal. 3:17 as a man *s.* his son
Acts 20:29 wolves enter, not *s.*

SPARINGLY.
2 *Cor.* 9:6 he who sow. *s.* reap *s.*

SPARK.
Job 18:5 *s.* of his fire not shine
Is. 1:31 maker of it be as a *s.*

SPARKS.
Job 5:7 trouble as *s.* fly upward
41:19 burning lamps, *s.* of fire
Is. 50:11 comp. yourselves wi. *s.*

SPARKLED.
Ezek. 1:7 *s.* like color of brass

SPARROW.
Ps. 84:3 *s.* hath found a house
102:7 as a *s.* upon house-top

SPARROWS.
Mat. 10:29 two *s.* sold for farth. ?
31 more value th. *s.* *Luke* 12:7
Luke 12:6 5 *s.* sold for 2 farth. ?

SPAT.
John 9:6 spok. he *s.* on ground

SPAKE.
Gen. 18:27 ta. on me to *s.* to G. 31
34:30 what shall we *s.* ?
Ex. 6:14 I kn. that he can. *s.* well
99:42 wh. I will meet you to *s.*
31:35 be went in to *s.* with Lord
Num. 12:6 not afraid to *s.* ag. M.
22:35 word I *s.* that thou shalt *s.*
23:12 must I not *s.* which He ?
Deut. 18:19 words *s.* in my name
20 presume to *s.* that *s.* to you
Jos. 19:10 *s.* ye not a word
1 *K.* 12:7 *s.* good words, 2 *Chr.* 10:7
22:24 spirit from mo to *s.* to th.
2 *Chr.* 18:23
Job 8:2 how long *s.* these thi. ?
11:5 oh that G. would *s.* ag. th.
13:7 will ye *s.* wickedly for G. ?
18:2 afterward we will *s.*
36:2 ha. yet to *s.* on G.'s behalf
41:3 will he *s.* soft words ?
Ps. 2:5 them sh. he *s.* in wrath
28:3 which *s.* peace to neigh.
40:5 if I would declare and *s.* of
69:12 that sit in gate *s.* ag. me
71:10 mine enemies *s.* ag. me
85:8 I will hear what L. will *s.*
94:4 how long they *s.* hard thi. ?
119:172 my tongue shall *s.* of
139:20 *s.* against thee wickedly
145:6 shall *s.* of might of thy
21 my mouth sh. *s.* praise of L.
Ec. 3:7 to be silent, time to *s.*
Is. 8:10 if they *s.* not accord. to
28:11 with ano. tongue sh. he *s.*
29:4 thou shalt *s.* out of ground
52:6 I am he tha *t* doth *s.*
Jer. 5:14 saith L. Bec. ye *s.* this
7:27 thou sh. *s.* all these words
13:12 thou shalt *s.* this word to
6:7 I shall *s.* about a nation, 9
20:0 I will not *s.* any more
26:2 word I command to *s.* 8
32:4 shall *s.* with him mouth to mouth
34:3 he shall *s.* with thee
Ezek. 3:7 thou shalt *s.* my words
21:27 shalt *s.* he no more dumb
Hos. 2:3 *s.* at the end it shall *s.*
Mat. 10:19 ye shall *s.* *Mark* 13:11
20 not ye that *s.* *Mark* 13:11
12:34 can ye being evil *s.* good ?

SPE

Mark 14:71 kn. not of wh. ye *s.*
Luke 1:19 I am sent to *s.* to thee
20 not able to *s.* till th. sh. be
22 wh. he came he could not *s.*
6:26 when men *s.* well of you
12:10 whosoever shall *s.* a word
John 3:11 verily we *s.* th. we kn.
9:21 of age, he shall *s.* for himse.
16:13 *s.* of himself, that shall he
Acts 2:11 hear them *s.* in tongue.
26:1 P. thou art permitted to *s.*
Rom. 15:18 I will not dare to *s.*
1 *Cor.* 3:1 I could not *s.* to you as
12:30 do all *s.* with ? 14:23 all *s.*
14:35 sha. for women to *s.* in ch.
2 *Cor.* 2:17 in sight of God *s.* we
4:13 we believe and therefore *s.*
12:19 we *s.* before God in Christ
Col. 4:4 manifest, as I ought to *s.*
1 *Thes.* 1:8 so that we need not *s.*
2:4 so we *s.* not as pleasing men
Til. 3:2 put th. in mind to *s.* evil
Heb. 6:9 we thus *s.* 8:5 cannot *s.*
Jam. 1:19 let ev. man be sl. to *s.*
1 *John* 4:5 thereof. *s.* they of world

SPEAK, imperatively.
Ex. 20:19 *s.* thou, we will hear
Deut. 3:26 Lord said, *s.* no more
5:27 *s.* to us that L. sh. *s.* to th.
1 *Sam.* 3:9 *s.* L. servant hear. 10
2 *Sam.* 17:6 his say. ? if not *s.*
1 *K.* 22:13 *s.* that which is good,
2 *Chr.* 18:12
Est. 5:14 to-morrow *s.* to king
Job 13:22 let me *s.* and answer
33:32 *s.* for I desire to justify th.
33:33 thereof. *s.* what thou know.
Prov. 23:9 *s.* not in ears of a fool
Is. 8:10 *s.* word, it sh. not stand
30:10 who say, *s.* to us smooth
41:1 come near, then let them *s.*
Jer. 1:17 *s.* to them that I comm.
Dan. 10:19 I said, Let my lord *s.*
Zec. 8:16 *s.* the truth, *Eph.* 4:25
Mark 13:11 given to *s.* in that hour, *s.*
Acts 18:9 *s.* hold not thy peace
1 *Cor.* 1:10 let him *s.* to himself
20 let prophets *s.* two or three
3. *s.* ye, and do, as th.

I SPEAK.
Ex. 19:9 peo. may hear, wh. I *s.*
Num. 12:8 I *s.* not wi. your chil.
1 *K.* 22:14 L. saith, that will I *s.*
Job 9:35 then I would I *s.* and not
13:3 I would *s.* to Almighty
19:2 I also could *s.* as ye do
37:20 shall it be told him ?
Ps. 45:1 I *s.* of things that I have
120:7 when I *s.* they are for war
Jer. 1:6 L. I cannot *s.* I am a ch.
6:10 eh. I *s.* and give warning ?
23:7 hear this word that I *s.* is
28:20 voice of the L. which I *s.*
Ezek. 3:27 when I *s.* with thee, I
John 4:26 Jesus saith, I that *s.*
6:63 the words that I *s.* to you
7:17 or whether I *s.* of myself
8:25 as Father taught me, I *s.*
38 I *s.* that which I have *s.*
12:49 gave com. what I should *s.*
50 I *s.* as Father said, so I *s.*
13:18 I *s.* not of all, I know
14:10 words I *s.* I *s.* not of mys.
17:13 these things I *s.* in world
Acts 21:37 P. said, May I *s.* to th.
26:26 bef. whom I also *s.* freely
Rom. 3:5 God unrighte. ? I *s.* as
6:19 I *s.* after manner. *Gal.* 3:15
1 *Cor.* 14:18 I *s.* with tongues mo.
19 I had rather *s.* five words
2 *Cor.* 11:17 that wh. I *s.* I *s.* not
Eph. 6:20 that therein I may *s.*

I will SPEAK, or will I.
Gen. 18:30 L. angry, *I* will *s.* 32
Num. 12:8 with him will I *s.*
24:13 what L. saith, that will I *s.*
1 *K.* 22:14; 2 *Chr.* 18:13
Deut. 32:1 give ear, and I will *s.*
Jud. 6:39 Gideon said, I will *s.*
2 *K.* 9:18 wolf, I will *s.* for thee
Job 32:20 I *w. s.* th. I be refresh.
33:31 hold thy peace, I will *s.*
42:4 hear I will *s.* I will demand
Ps. 50:7 hear, my peo. I will *s.*
78:15 if I say, I will *s.* thus
145:5 I w. *s.* of the honor of thy
Jer. 5:5 to great men, and I *w. s.*
Ezek. 2:1 stand on feet and I *w. s.*
12:25 I will *s.* and word I speak
1 *Cor.* 14:21 wi. other lips no. I *s.*

SPEAKER.
Ps. 140:11 let not evil *s.* be estab.
Acts 14:12 henceforth he was chi. *s.*

SPEAKEST.
1 *Sam.* 9:21 whereof. then *s.* th. ?
Job 2:10 *s.* as one of foolish wom.

SPE

Is. 40:27 why *s.* thou, O Israel
Jer. 43:2 thou *s.* falsely, the Lord
Zec. 13:3 *s.* lies in name of Lord
John 16:29 now *s.* thou plainly
19:10 Pi. saith, *s.* thou not unto
Acts 17:19 know whereof th. *s.* ?

SPEAKETH.
Gen. 45:12 it is my mouth that *s.*
Ex. 33:11 spa. to M. as man *s.*
Num. 23:26 all that Lord *s.*
Job 33:14 G. *s.* once, yea, twice
26:25 wh. he *s.* fair, believe not
Jer. 10:1 word which L. *s.* to you
28:2 thus *s.* L. G. 29:25; 30:2;
Hag. 1:2; *Zec.* 6:12; 7:9
Ezek. 10:5 voice of G. when he *s.*
Mat. 10:20 S. of Father *s.* in you
Joh. 3:31 of earth, *s.* of the earth
34 wh. God sent, *s.* words of G.
7:18 he that *s.* of himself, seek.
26 but lo, he *s.* boldly, they *s.*
8:44 wh. he *s.* a lie, he *s.* of own
Acts 8:34 of wh. *s.* the pro. this ?
Heb. 11:4 he being dead yet *s.*
12:24 that *s.* better things than
25 th. ye refuse not him that *s.*

SPEAKING.
Gen. 24:15 before he had done *s.*
45 before I had done *s.* in her.
Deut. 11:19 *s.* of them when thou
Est. 10:3 *s.* peace to his seed
Job 1:16 wh. he was yet *s.* 17, 18
4:2 who can withhold from *s.* ?
32:15 no more, they left off *s.*
Is. 58:13 nor *s.* thine own words
65:24 while they are yet *s.* I
Jer. 7:13 early, *s.* 25:3; 34:14
Dan. 8:13 I heard one saint *s.*
Acts 14:3 they abode *s.* boldly in
2 *Cor.* 13:3 a proof of Ch. *s.* in me
See END.

SPEAKING, S.
Mat. 6:7 th. be heard for much *s.*
Eph. 4:31 let evil *s.* be put away
1 *Pet.* 2:1 laying aside all evil *s.*

SPEAR.
Jos. 8:18 stretch out thy *s.* 26
Jud. 5:8 a *s.* seen among 40,000 ?
1 *Sam.* 13:22 *s.* with any but wi.
17:7 staff of *s.* like weaver's bea.
2 *Sam.* 21:19; 1 *Chr.* 20:5
45 comest with a sword and *s.*
21:8 under thy hand a *s.*
26:7 S.'s *s.* stuck at bolster, 11
16 now see where king's *s.* is
2 *Sam.* 1:6 Saul lean. upon his *s.*
2:23 Abner with *s.* smote Asahel
23:7 with iron and staff of a *s.*
8 he lifted up his *s.* against 800
18 lifted up his *s.* against 300,
1 *Chr.* 11:11, 20
21 he slew the Egyptian with his own *s.* 1 *Chr.* 11:23
Job 39:23 qui. rattleth, glitter. *s.*
41:26 *s.* of him that lay. at him
39 Leviathan laugheth at a *s.*
Ps. 35:3 draw out *s.* stop my
46:9 breake. bow and cutteth *s.*
Jer. 6:23 lay hold on bow and *s.*
Nah. 3:3 lifteth up sword and *s.*
Hab. 3:11 at shining of glitter. *s.*
John 19:34 one of the soldiers with a *s.* pierced his side

SPEARS.
1 *Sam.* 13:19 Heb. make sw. or *s.*
2 *K.* 11:10 king David's *s.* that were in temple, 2 *Chr.* 23:9
1 *Chr.* 11:12 in ev. city he put *s.*
2 *Chr.* 14:8 Uzziah prep. for them *s.*
Neh. 4:13 I set the people with *s.*
16 the other half held the *s.* 21
Ps. 57:4 whose teeth are *s.* and
Is. 2:4 into hooks, *Mic.* 4:3
Jer. 40:4 furbish *s.* and put on
Ezek. 30:9 shall burn *s.* with fire
Joel 3:10 pruning-hooks into *s.*

SPEARMEN.
Ps. 68:30 rebuke company of *s.*
Acts 23:23 make ready 200 *s.*

SPECIAL.
Deut. 7:6 L. chosen thee, a *s.* pe.
Acts 19:11 *s.* miracles done by P.
See ESPECIALLY.

SPECKLED.
Gen. 30:32 remove cattle *s.* 33, 35, 39
31:8 *s.* thy wages, cattle bare *s.*
Jer. 12:9 heritage is as *s.* bird
Zec. 1:8 red horses, *s.* and white

SPECTACLE.
1 *Cor.* 4:9 made a *s.* to the world

SPED.
Jud. 5:30 have they not *s.* ?

SPI

SPIRIT of error.
1 John 4:6 kn. we s. of tru. and e.
See EVIL.

Faithful SPIRIT.
Prov. 11:13 he that is of faith. s.
See FAMILIAR.

SPIRIT of fear.
2 Tim. 1:7 ha. not giv. us s. of f.

Foul SPIRIT.
Mark 9:25 he rebuked the foul s.
Rev. 18:2 become hold of ev. f. s.

Fruit of the SPIRIT.
Gal. 5:22 f. of the S. is love, joy
Eph. 5:9 f. of s. S. is in all good.

Good SPIRIT.
Neh. 9:20 th. gavest thy good S.
Ps. 143:10 thy S. is g. lead me

SPIRIT of God.
Gen. 1:2 S. of G. moved on wat.
41:38 a man in wh. S. of God is
Ex. 31:3 Boz. wi. S. of G. 35:31
Num. 24:2 S. of G. came on Bal.
1 Sam. 10:10 the S. of God came
on Saul, 11:6 ; 19:23
19:20 S. of G. came on messen.
2 Chr. 15:1 S. of G. came on Aza.
Job 27:3 S. of G. is in my nost,
33:4 S. of God hath made me
Ezek. 11:24 in vision by S. of G.
Mat. 3:16 saw S. of G. descend.
12:28 cast out devils by S. of G.
Rom. 8:9 S. of God dwell in you
14 many as are led by S. of G.
15:19 by the power of S. of G.
1 Cor. 2:11 no man, but S. of G.
14 recei. not things of S. of G.
3:16 S. of God dwelleth in you
6:11 sanctified by the S. of God
7:40 I think I have S. of God
12:3 no man speak, by S. of G.
2 Cor. 3:3 written with S. of G.
Eph. 4:30 grie. not holy S. of G.
1 Pet. 4:14 S. of God rest. on you
1 John 4:2 hereby kn. ye S. of G.

SPIRIT of glory.
1 Pet. 4:14 S. of g. resteth on you

SPIRIT of grace.
Zec. 12:10 house of Da. S. of g.
Heb. 10:29 done desp. to S. of g.
See HOLY.

Humble SPIRIT.
Prov. 16:19 bet. to be of an h. s.
29:23 honor sh. uphold the h. s.
Is. 57:15 with him that is of h. s.

SPIRIT of jealousy.
Num. 5:14 s. of j. co. on him, 30

SPIRIT of judgment.
Is. 4:4 purged Jerusa. by s. of j.
28:6 L. shall be for a s. of jud.

SPIRIT of knowledge.
Is. 11:2 s. of k. sh. rest upon him
See LORD, LYING.

SPIRIT of meekness.
1 Cor. 4:21 come in s. of m. ?
Gal. 6:1 such a one in s. of m.

My SPIRIT.
Gen. 6:3 my S. sh. not always
Job 6:4 poison drinketh up my s.
7:11 spunk in anguish of my s.
10:12 visita. hath preserv. m. s.
21:4 who. not my s. be troubled
Ps. 31:5 into hand I com. my s.
77:3 I my s. was overwhelmed
6 my s. made diligent search
143:4 my s. overwhelmed in me
7 hear me, O L. my s. faileth
Prov. 1:23 I will pour out my s.
Is. 26:9 with my s. will I seek
30:1 covering, but not of my s.
38:16 in th. things is life of m. s.
42:1 I ha. put my S. upon him
44:3 pour my S. upon thy seed
59:21 my S. that is upon thee
Ezek. 3:14 went in heat of my s.
36:27 my S. within you, 37:14
39:29 pour. my S. on house of I.
Dan. 2:3 and my s. was troubled
7:15 I Dan. was griev. in my s.
Hag. 2:5 my S. remain. am. you
Zec. 4:6 by power, but by my S.
6:8 quiet. my s. in north count.
Mat. 12:18 I will put my S. on
Luke 1:47 my s. hath rejoi. in G.
23:46 in thy hands I com. my S.
Acts 7:59 Lord Je. receive my s.
Rom. 1:9 wh. I serve with my s.
1 Cor. 5:4 when gath. and my s.
14:14 my s. prayeth, but my
16:18 they have refresh. my s.

SPI

2 Cor. 2:13 had no rest in my s.

New SPIRIT.
Ezek. 11:19 a n. s. in you, 36:26
18:31 a new heart and new s.

Newness of SPIRIT.
Rom. 7:6 we sho. serve in n. of s.

Patient SPIRIT.
Ec. 7:8 p. in s. bet. than proud

Perverse SPIRIT.
Is. 19:14 L. hath mingled a p. s.

Poor SPIRIT.
Mat. 5:3 blessed are poor in s.

SPIRIT of promise.
Eph. 1:13 sealed with H. S. of p.

SPIRIT of prophecy.
Rev. 19:10 testimo. of J. is s. of p.

SPIRIT of slumber.
Rom. 11:8 G. given them s. of s.

Sorrowful SPIRIT.
1 Sam. 1:15 a woman of a s. s.

SPIRIT of truth.
John 14:17 S. of t. whom world
15:26 S. of t. which proceedeth
16:13 when S. of truth is come
1 John 4:6 hereby kn. we S. of t.
See VEXATION.

Unclean SPIRIT.
Zec. 13:2 cause uncl. s. to pass
Mat. 12:43 when the u. s. is gone
out of a man, Luke 11:24
Mark 1:23 synag. a man wi. u. s.
26 when u. s. had torn him
3:30 they said, He hath an u. s.
5:2 met him a man with u. s.
8 come out, th. u. s. Luke 8:29
7:25 whose daugh. had an u. s.
Luke 9:42 Jesus rebuked u. s.

SPIRIT of understanding.
Is. 11:2 the s. of u. sh. rest upon

SPIRIT of whoredoms.
Hos. 4:12 s. of w. caused to err
5:4 s. of w. is in midst of them

SPIRIT of wisdom.
Ex. 28:3 wh. I filled wi. s. of w.
Deut. 34:9 Joshua full of s. of w.
Is. 11:2 s. of w. sh. rest up, him
Eph. 1:17 G. may give s. of w.

Wounded SPIRIT.
Prov. 16:14 w. s. who can bear ?

SPIRITS.

Num. 16:22 O God, the God of s.
27:16
Ps. 104:4 mak. angels s. Heb. 1:7
Prov. 16:2 Lord weigheth the s.
Ec. 6:5 th. are four s. of heaven
Mat. 8:16 cast out s. with word
10:1 power ag. uncl. s. Mark 6:7
Mark 1:27 commandeth he the
unclean s. Luke 4:36
3:11 uncl. s. fell down bef. him
5:13 unclean s. entered swine
Luke 10:20 rejoice not that s. are
Acts 5:16 vexed with unclean s.
8:7 s. crying, came out of many
1 Cor. 12:10 to ano. discern. of s.
14:32 s. of proph. are subject to
1 Tim. 4:1 giv. heed to seduc. s.
Heb. 1:14 mi. all ministering s.
12:9 in subjection to Fath. of s.
23 to s. of just men made per.
1 Pet. 3:19 preach. to s. in prison
1 John 4:1 try s. wheth. they are
Rev. 16:13 I saw 3 unclean s. like
14 they are the s. of devils
See EVIL, FAMILIAR, SEVEN.

SPIRITUAL.

Hos. 9:7 the s. man is mad
Rom. 1:11 impart to you s. gift
7:14 we know that the law is s.
15:27 partak. of their s. things
1 Cor. 2:13 comparing s. things
with s. t.
15 he that is s. judgeth all thi.
3:1 could not spe. to you as to s.
9:11 have sown unto you s.
10:3 did all eat same s. meat
4 same s. dri. drunk of s. rock
12:1 concern. s. gifts, brethren
14:1 desire s. gifts ; 12 zeal. of s.
37 if any man think himself s.
15:44 s. body, there is s. body
46 that was not first whi. is s.
afterwards that which is s.
Gal. 6:1 ye which are s. restore
Eph. 1:3 blessed us with s. bless.
5:19 speak. to yours. in s. songs
6:12 wrestle against s. wickedn.
Col. 1:9 filled with s. understand.
3:16 admon. in psa. and s. songs
1 Pet. 2:5 built up a s. house, to offer s. sacrifices

SPO

Is. 17:14 portion of th. that s. us
33:1 when shalt cease to s. thou
Jer. 5:6 wolf of even. sh. s. them
20:5 I will give Jerusal. to s. it.
30:16 they that s. thee sh. be a s.
47:4 day cometh to s. Philistines
49:28 Kedar, s. men of the east
50:10 all that s. shall be satisfied
Ezek. 14:15 they s. it so that it be
32:12 they shall s. pomp of Egy.
39:10 they shall s. those that
Hos. 10:2 break altars s. images
13:15 he shall s. treasure of all
Hab. 2:8 remn. of peo. sh. s. thee
Zep. 2:9 residue of people shall s.
Mat. 12:29 s. goods ? Mark 3:27
Col. 2:8 lest any man s. you

SPOILED.

Gen. 34:27 sons of Jacob s. city
Ex. 12:36 they s. the Egyptians
Deut. 28:29 sh. be oppress. and s.
Jud. 2:14 band of spoilers that s.
1 Sam. 14:48 Is. fr. them that s.
2 K. 7:16 Is. s. tents of Syrians
2 Chr. 14:14 A. s. cities of Gerar
Job 12:17 leadeth coun. away s.
19 leads princes away s.
Prov. 22:23 spoil soul of th. that s.
Is. 13:16 their houses shall be s.
18:2 whose land rivers have s. 7
24:3 land shall be utterly s.
33:1 spoilest. and wast not s.
48:23 this is s people rob. and s.
Jer. 2:14 a serv. why is he s. ?
4:13 woe unto us s. for we are s.
20 whole land is s. tents are s.
30 wh. thou art s. wh. wilt do ?
9:19 are we s. ! 10:20 taber. is s.
21:12 deliver him that is s. 22:3
25:36 L. hath s. their pasture
48:1 Nebo is s. 15 Moab is s. 20
49:3 Ai is s. 10 E. his seed is s.
51:55 Lord hath s. Babylon
Ezek. 18:7 s. none by violence, 16
12 hath oppressed, hath s. 18
23:46 I will give them to be s.
39:10 shall spoil those that s.
Hos. 10:14 fortresses shall be s.
Amos 3:11 thy palaces shall be s.
5:9 strengtheneth s. ag. strong
Mic. 2:4 say, We be utterly s.
Hab. 2:8 hast s. many nations
Ec. 2:8 sent to nations wh. s.
11:3 because mighty are s.
Zec. 2:8 glory s. for pride of Jor. is s.
Col. 2:15 having s. principalities

SPOILER.

Is. 16:4 fr. face of s. the s. cease
21:2 s. spoileth, go up, O Elam
Jer. 6:26 s. suddenly come on us
15:8 I brought upon them a s.
48:8 s. sh. come upon every city
18 s. of M. shall come on thee
32 s. is fallen upon thy fruits
51:56 bec. s. is come on Babylon

SPOILERS.

Jud. 2:14 be delivered them into hand of s. 2 K. 17:20
1 Sam. 13:17 s. out of camp of P.
14:15 the s. they also trembled
Jer. 12:12 s. are come upon high
51:48 s. come to her from north
53 from me sh. s. come to her

SPOILEST, ETH.

Ps. 35:10 deliveri. poor from him s.
Is. 21:2 spoiler s. Hos. 7:1 rob. s.
33:1 woe to thee that s.
Nah. 3:16 canker-worm s. fleeth

SPOILING.

Ps. 35:12 good. to s. of my soul
Is. 22:4 c. of daught. of my peo.
Jer. 48:3 voice from Horonaim s.
Heb. 1:3 s. and violence bef. me
10:34 joyf. s. of your goods

SPOILS.

Jos. 7:21 saw among s. a garment
1 Cor. 26:27 out of s. did dedic.
Is. 25:11 bri. down pride with s.
Luke 11:22 and divideth his s.
Heb. 7:4 Abrah. gave tenth of s.

SPOKEN.

Gen. 18:19 L. br. what he hath s.
Num. 14:28 as ye have s. so will
23:17 we have s. ag. L. and thee
32:19 he is. not make it good ?
Deut. 18:17 well s. that th. ha. s.
1 Sam. 25:30 L. done all he hath s.
27:1 people had gone up
1 K. 18:24 peo. said, It is well s.
2 K. 4:13 thou be s. for to king ?
87:23 glorious things are s. of
Ec. 7:21 ta. heed to all words s.
Cant. 8:8 in the day wh. she be s.
Jer. 26:15 s. to us in name of L.

SPO

Mal. 3:13 wh. ha. we *s.* ag. thee?
Luke 18:34 nor kn. they things *s.*
John 15:22 if I had not co. and *s.*
Acts 8:34 none of things *s.* come
13:46 word *who.* first ha. been *s.*
19:36 these things cannot be *s.*
Rom. 15:21 to wh. he was not *s.*
1 **Cor.** 10:30 why am I evil *s.* of
14:9 shall it be kno. what is *s.?*
1 **Pet.** 4:14 on their part evil *s.* of
2 **Pet.** 2:2 way of truth evil *s.* of

SPOKEN, *with* **God.**
Gen. 21:2 time of wh. God had *s.*
Ps. 62:11 *G.* hath *s.* once, twice
Mat. 22:31 that wh. was *s.* by *G.*

See LORD.

I have, or **have I SPOKEN.**
Gen. 28:15 done what *I* h. *s.*
Ex. 32:13 land *I have s.* of
1 **Sam.** 20:23 matter wh. *I h. s.* of
Job 40:5 once h. *I s.* will not ans.
Ps. 116:10 therefore have *I s.* 2
Cor. 4:13
Is. 45:19 *I h.* not *s.* in sec. 48:16
46:11 *I h. s.* it, bring it to pass
48:15 *I,* even *I h. s.* I called
Jer. 35:17 *I h. s.* have not heard
Ezek. 12:28 word *I h. s.* be done
13:7 L. saith, Albeit *I h.* not *s.*
26:5 *I h. s.* it, saith Lord, 28:10
38:17 art thou he of wh. *I h. s.*
John 12:49 *I h.* not *s.* of myself
14:25 *have I s.* 15:11; 16:1, 25, 33

SPOKEN, *with* **prophet.**
Mat. 2:23 fulfilled whic *i* was *s.*
by the *prophet,* 13:35; 27:35
3:3 that was *s.* of by thu *p.* Es.
4:14 *s.* by E*s.* p. 8:17; 12:17; 21;4

Thou hast SPOKEN.
Ex. 4:10 nor since *thou h. s.*
10:29 Moses said, *T. h. s.* well
33:17 I will do this thing *t. h. s.*
Deut. 1:14 thing which *t. h. s.*
2 **K.** 20:19 good is word of Lord
which *thou hast s. Is.* 39:8
Est. 6:10 let nothing fail *t. h. s.*
Jer. 3:5 *t. h. s.* done evil things
32:24 that *t. h. s.* is come to pass
44:16 as for word *t. h. s.* unto us
51:62 O **L.** *t. h. s.* ag. this place

SPOKES.
1 **K.** 7:33 follocs and *s.* all molten

SPOKESMAN.
Ex. 4:16 be sh. be thy *s.* to peo.

SPONGE.
Mat. 27:48 one of them took a *s.*
Mark 15:36; **John** 19:29

SPOON.
Num. 7:14 one *s.* of ten shekels,
20, 26, 32, 38, 44, 50, 56, 62

SPOONS.
Ex. 25:29 make dishes and *s.*
Num. 4:7 put there. dishes and *s.*
7:84 silver bowls, twelve *s.* 80
1 **K.** 7:50 *s.* wo. gold, 2 **Chr.** 4:22
2 **K.** 25:14 *s.* took, **Jer.** 52:18, 19
2 **Chr.** 24:14 rest of money *s.* ma.

SPORT, Substantive.
Jud. 16:25 Sam. make *s.* made *s.*
27 behold while Sams. made *s.*
Prov. 10:23 *s.* to fool to do misc.
26:19 saith, Am not I in *s.?*

SPOUT, ING.
Gen. 26:8 Isa. was *s.* wi. Rebek.
Is. 57:4 ag. whom *s.* yourselves?
2 **Pet.** 2:13 *s.* themsel. with dec.

SPIT.
Num. 12:2 hr. father without *s.*
28:3 two lambs without *s.* 9, 11;
29:17, 26
Deut. 32:5 *s.* is not *s.* of his chill.
Job 11:15 thy face without *s.*
Cant. 4:7 there is no *s.* in thee
Eph. 5:27 glori. church, not ha. *s.*
1 **Tim.** 6:14 keep com. without *s.*
Heb. 9:14 off. himself without *s.*
1 **Pet.** 1:19 as a lamb without *s.*
2 **Pet.** 3:14 be found without *s.*

See SIGHT.

SPOTS.
Jer. 13:23 can leopard change *s.?*
2 **Pet.** 2:13 *s.* they are and blem.
Jude 12 the. are *s.* in your feasts

SPOTTED.
Gen. 30:32 removing *s.* cattle
33 brou. cattle, speckled and *s.*
Jude 23 hating garm. *s.* by flesh

SPOUSE, *S.*
Cant. 4:8 come from Leb. my *s.*
9 ravi. my heart, my sister, *s.*
10 fair thy love, my sister, *s.* 11
11 lips, O my *s.* drop as honey

SPR

Cant. 4:12 garden inc. is my sis. *s.*
5:1 into my garden, my sister, *s.*
Hos. 4:13 your *s.* commit adult.
14 I will not punish your *s.*

SPOUTS. *See* WATER-SPOUTS.

SPRANG.
Mark 4:8 fruit th. *s.* up, **Luke** 8:8
Acts 16:29 call. for light and *s.* in
Heb. 7:14 evident **L.** *s.* out of *J.*
11:12 there *s.* of one many

See SPRUNG.

SPREAD.
Gen. 33:19 wh. *J. s.* tent, 35:21
Num. 4:7 on table *s.* cloth, 11
Deut. 22:17 *s.* cloth before elders
Jud. 8:25 they *s.* a garment
15:9 Philistines *s.* thems. in **L.**
2Sam. 5:18 Philist. also came and *s.* thems. 22; 1 **Chr.** 14:9, 13
16:22 they *s.* Absal. tent on roof
17:19 wom. *s.* covering on well
21:10 Rizpah *s.* sackclo. for her
1 **K.** 8:54 with hands *s.* to heaven
2 **K.** 8:15 Hazael *s.* cloth on face
19:14 *s.* letter bef. **L.** *Is.* 37:14
Ps. 105:39 he *s.* a cloud for cov.
140:5 *s.* a net by the way-side
Prov. 1:17 net *s.* in sight of bird
Is. 14:11 worm is *s.* under thee
19:8 *s.* nets on water languish
33:23 they could not *s.* the sail
Jer. 8:2 they sh. *s.* them bef. sun
10:9 silv. *s.* into plates brought
Lam. 1:13 hath *s.* net for my feet
Eze. 2:10 he *s.* the roll before me
12:13 my net also will *I s.* 17:20
32:14 be a place to *s.* nets upon
Hos. 5:1 have been a net *s.* on **T.**
7:12 when they go, I will *s.* net
14:6 branches sh. *s.* his beauty
Joel 2:2 as morn. *s.* upon mount
Mal. 2:3 I will *s.* dung on your fa.
Mark 1:28 *s.* abroad his fame, *s.*
11:8; **Luke** 19:36
Acts 4:17 but that it *s.* no further

SPREAD *abroad.*
Gen. 10:18 Canaanites were *s. a.*
28:14 thou shalt *s. a.* to west
Ex. 9:29 I will *s. a.* hand to **L.**
Ps. 1 **Rom.** 30:16 th. were *s. a.* earth
2 **Sam.** 22:43 *s. a.* mine enemies
2 **Chr.** 26:8 Uzziah's name *s. a.* 15
Mat. 9:31 they *s. a.* his fame
Mark 6:14 name of Jesus was *s. a.*
1 **Thes.** 1:8 faith to God-w. is *s. a.*

SPREAD *forth.*
Num. 24:6 as valleys are th. *s. f.*
1 **K.** 8:7 cherubim *s. f.* 2 wings
22 **S.** *s. f.* hands, 2 **Chr.** 6:12, 13
Ps. 1:15 wh. ye *s. f.* your hands
44:20 **S.** I shall *s. f.* hands, swim.
42:5 saith **J.** he that *s. f.* earth
Ezek. 47:10 a place to *s. f.* nets

SPREAD *over.*
Num. 4:6 shall *s.* a cloth of blue
Is. 25:7 that is *s.* o. all nations
Jer. 48:40 shall *s.* wings o. Moab
49:22 he sh. *s.* his wings o. Boz.
Ezek. 16:8 I *s.* my *skirt over* thee
19:8 nations *s.* their net o. him
Ezek. 37:9 cherubim *s. o.* wings,
1 **Chr.** 28:18

Ezr. 9:5 *s. out* my hands to **L.**
Job 29:19 my root *s.* o. by water
37:18 hast th. wi. him *s. o.* sky?
Is. 65:2 *s. o.* hands to a rebel.
Lam. 1:10 advers. *s. o.* his hand
Ezek. 32:3 will *s. o.* net over thee

SPREADEST, ETH.
Lev. 13:8 if priest see that scab *s.*
Deut. 32:11 as eagle *s.* her wings
Job 9:8 wh. alone *s.* out heavn.
26:9 and he *s.* his cloud upon it
36:30 he *s.* his light upon it
Prov. 29:5 flatter. neighb. *s.* a net
Is. 25:11 he that shall *s.* hands
44:24 that *s.* the heavens as a tent
42:1 the **L.** that *s.* abroad
Jer. 4:31 daughter of **Z.** *s.* hands
17:8 a tree that *s.* out her roots
Ezek. 27:7 which *s.* for thy sail
Lam. 1:17 **Z.** *s.* forth her hands

SPREADING.
Ps. 37:35 I have seen wicked *s.*
Ezek. 17:6 and became a *s.* vine

SPREADING, S.
Job 36:29 underst. *s.* of clouds?
Ezek. 26:5 a place *s.* of nets

SPRIGS.
Is. 18:5 before harvest cut off *s.*
Ezek. 17:6 a vine, shot forth *s.*

SPI

SPRING, Substantive.
2 **K.** 2:21 he went forth to the *s.*
Prov. 25:26 troub. and corrupt *s.*
Cant. 4:12 spouse, is *s.* shut up
Is. 58:11 sh. be like *s.* of water
Hos. 13:15 his *s.* sh. become dry

SPRINGS.
Deut. 4:49 under *s.* of Pisgah
Jos. 10:40 smote country of *s.*
12:8 kings in plains and in *s.*
15:19 give me *s.* of water, gave upper *s. Jud.* 1:15
Job 38:16 hast entered into *s.?*
Ps. 87:7 all my *s.* are in thee
104:10 he sendeth *s.* into valleys
107:33 turn. water *s.* into dry
35 turn. dry ground to water *s.*
Is. 35:7 land become *s.* of water
41:18 I will make dry land *s.*
49:10 by *s.* of water guide them
Jer. 51:36 I will make her *s.* dry
1 **Sam.** 9:26 about *s.* of day **Sam.**

See DAYSPRING.

SPRING.
Ezek. 17:9 in all leaves of her *s.*

SPRING, Verb.
Num. 21:17 Is. sang, *s.* up, O w.
Deut. 8:7 and depths that *s.* out
Jud. 19:25 when day began to *s.*
Job 5:6 nei. doth trouble *s.* out
38:27 bud of tender herb to *s.*
Ps. 65:11 truth sh. *s.* out of earth
92:7 wh. wicked *s.* as the grass
Is. 42:9 bef. they *s.* forth I tell
43:19 now it shall *s.* forth
44:4 they sh. *s.* np as am. grass
45:8 righteousness *s.* up togeth.
58:8 thy health shall *s.* forth
61:11 gard. causeth things to *s.*
Ezek. 2:22 for the pastures do *s.*
Mark 4:27 seed *s.* he kn. not how

SPRINGETH.
2 **K.** 19:29 eat in second year that
which *s.* of same, *Is.* 37:30
Hos. 10:4 thus judgment *s.* up

SPRINGING.
Gen. 26:19 found well of *s.* water
2 **Sam.** 23:4 as tender grass *s.* out
Ps. 65:10 thou blessest the *s.*
John 4:14 a well of water *s.* up
Heb. 12:15 any root *s.* trouble you

SPRINKLE.
Ex. 9:8 let Moses *s.* the ashes
Lev. 14:7 *s.* on him to be cleansed
51 *s.* the house seven times
16:14 shall *s.* it upon the seat
19 the clean person shall *s.* it
Num. 8:7 *s.* water of purifying
19:18 shall *s.* it upon the tent
19 the clean person shall *s.* it
Is. 52:15 sh. he *s.* many nations
Ezek. 36:25 clean wa. upon you

SPRINKLED, ETH.
Lev. 7:14 priest's that *s.* blood
Num. 19:13 wa. not *s.* on him, 20
Num. 19:21 a dust on their heads
Heb. 9:19 he *s.* the book and peo.
10:22 hearts *s.* from evil consc.

See BLOOD.

SPRINKLING.
Heb. 11:28 their faith kept *s.* of blood
12:24 we are come to blood of *s.*
1 **Pet.** 1:2 *s.* of blood of **Jesus Ch.**

SPROUT.
Job 14:7 tree that it will *s.* again

SPRUNG.
Mat. 4:16 shad. of death, light *s.*
13:5 and they *s.* up, *Mark* 4:5
26 but when blade was. up
Luke 8:6 as soon as it was *s.* up

SPUE.
Lev. 18:28 th. land *s.* you, 20:22
Jer. 25:27 *s.* fall, rise no more
Rev. 3:16 I will *s.* thee out

SPEWING.
Hab. 2:16 *s.* shall be on thy glory

SPUN.
Ex. 35:25 th. which they had *s.*

SPY.
Num. 13:16 M. sent to *s.* land, 17
21:32 M. sent 2 men to *s.* 32:8
Jud. 18:2 Danit. sent serv. to *s.* out the city, 1 **Chr.** 19:3
2 **K.** 6:13 go *s.* where he is
Gal. 2:4 came in privily to *s.*

STA

2 **K.** 9:17 a watchman *s.* company
13:21 they *s.* a band of men
23:16 he *s.* sepulchres that were

See ESPY, ESPIED.

SPIES.
Gen. 42:9 said, Ye are *s.* 14, 16
31 then *sh.* I know ye are no *s.*
Num. 21:1 **I.** came by way of *s.*
Jos. 6:23 young men that were *s.*
1 **Sam.** 26:4 David sent out *s.*
Luke 20:20 they sent forth *s.*
Heb. 11:31 Rahab had received *s.*

SQUARE.
1 **K.** 7:5 doors and posts were *s.*
Ezek. 43:2 *s.* round about, 50 cub.

See FOUR-SQUARE.

SQUARED.
Ezek. 41:21 posts of temp. were *s.*

SQUARES.
Ezek. 43:16 *square* in 4 *s.* thereof

STABLE, Substantive.
Ezek. 25:5 I will make Rab. a *s.*

STABLE.
1 **Chr.** 16:30 world also sh. be *s.*

STABILITY.
Is. 33:6 knowl. *s.* of thy times

STABLISH. *See* ESTABLISH.

STACHYS.
Rom. 16:9 salute Urbane and **S.**

STACKS.
Ex. 22:6 *s.* of corn be consumed

STACTE.
Ex. 30:34 take to th. *s.* onycha

STAFF.
Gen. 32:10 with my *s.* I passed
38:18 give me thy sig. and *s.* 25
Ex. 12:11 with *s.* in your hand
21:19 and walk abroad on his *s.*
Num. 13:23 between two on a *s.*
22:27 Balaam sm. ass with a *s.*
Jud. 6:21 put forth end of *s.*
1 **Sam.** 17:7 *s.* of his spear like weav.'s beam, 2 **Sam.** 21:19
40 Dav. took his *s.* in his hand
2 **Sam.** 3:29 one that leaneth on a *s.*
23:7 fenced with *s.* of a spear
21 he went down to him with *s.*
18:21 thou trust. on *s. Is.* 36:6
Ps. 23:4 thy rod and *s.* comf. me
Is. 3 **L.** will take fr. **Ju.** the *s.*
9:4 hast brok. *s.* of his shoulder
10:5 and the *s.* in their hand is
15 or as if *s.* should lift itself
24 lift up his *s.* against thee
14:5 **L.** hath broken *s.* of wicked
28:27 fitches beaten out wi. a *s.*
30:32 wh. grounded *s.* shall pass
Jer. 48:17 how is strong *s.* broken
Ezek. 29:6 have been a *s.* to Is.
Hos. 4:12 their *s.* declar. to them
Zec. 8:4 every man with his *s.*
11:10 I took my *s.* even beauty
14 cut asunder my other *s.*
Mark 6:8 take nothing, save a *s.*
Heb. 11:21 lean. on top of his *s.*

See BREAD.

STAGGER.
Job 12:25 *s.* like a drunken man,
Ps. 107:27

STAGGERED, ETH.
Is. 19:14 as a drunken man *s.*
Rom. 4:20 *s.* not at promise of **G.**

STAIN.
Job 3:5 and shadow of death *s.* it
Is. 23:9 **L.** purposed to *s.* pride
63:3 sprinkled, I will *s.* my rai.

STAIRS.
1 **K.** 6:8 went up with winding *s.*
2 **K.** 9:13 under him on *s.*
Neh. 9:4 then stood on *s. Je.* dda
Cant. 2:14 in secret places of *s.*
Ezek. 43:17 *s.* look towards east
Acts 21:40 Paul stood on the *s.*

STAKES.
Is. 33:20 not one of *s.* removed
54:2 bind and strengthen thy *s.*

STALK.
Gen. 41:5 seven ears on one *s.* 22
24 hid them with *s.* of flax
Hos. 8:7 no *s.* bud yield no meal

STALL.
Amos 6:4 out of midst of the *s.*
Mal. 4:2 grow up as calves of *s.*
Luke 13:15 his ox or his ass fro. *s.*

CRUDEN'S CONCORDANCE.

STA

STALLS.
1 *K.* 4:26 Solomon had forty thousand *s.*
2 *Chr.* 32:28 Hezek. had *s.* for all
Hab. 3:17 there be no herd in *s.*

STALLED.
Prov. 15:17 th. a *s.* ox. and hatr.

STAMMERERS.
Is. 32:4 tongue of *s.* shall speak

STAMMERING.
Is. 28:11 *s.* lips and anoth. tongue
33:19 not see a peo. of *s.* tongue

STAMP.
2 *Sam.* 22:43 did *s.* them as mire
Ezek. 6:11 smite *s.* with thy foot

STAMPED.
Deut. 9:21 I *s.* calf and ground
2 *K.* 23:6 Josiah *s.* the grove
15 *s.* high pla. small to powder
2 *Chr.* 15:16 A. cut her idol and *s.*
Ezek. 23:6 thou hast *s.* with feet
Dan. 7:7 a fourth beast *s.* 19
8:7 he-goat cast down and *s.* 10

STAMPING.
Jer. 47:3 at noise of *s.* of hoofs

STANCHED.
Luke 8:44 wo.'s issue of o.ood *s.*

STAND,
Ezek. 29:7 their loins to be at a *s.*

STAND, Verb.
Lev. 27:14 priest, so shall it *s.* 17
Deut. 25:8 if he *s.* to it and say
Jos. 20:4 *s.* at enter. gate of city
1 *Sam.* 12:16 *s.* see this thing
13:3 *s.* beside my father in field
1 *K.* 17:1 as L. liveth bef. whom
1 *s.* 18:15; 2 *K.* 3:14; 5:16
2 *K.* 5:11 I thought he will *s.*
10:4 not, how then shall we *s.*?
1 *Chr.* 23:30 to *s.* every morning
2 *Chr.* 34:32 caused all pres. to *s.*
Ezr. 10:14 let rulers of congreg. *s.*
Esd. 8:11 and to *s.* for their life
Job 8:15 loan on house, sh. not *s.*
19:25 *s.* at latter day on earth
Ps. 38:11 my kinsm. *s.* afar off
43:9 on right hand did *s.* queen
78:13 made waters to *s.* as heap
109:6 let Sa. *s.* at his right hand
31 shall *s.* at right hand of poor
122:2 our feet *s.* with. thy gates
130:3 mark'iniqui. O L. who *s.* ?
Prov. 19:21 counsel of L. shall *s.*
25:6 *s.* not in pl. of great men
Ec. 8:3 *s.* not in an evil thing
Is. 7:7 saith L. It sh. not *s.* 8:10
14:24 I purposed, so it sh. *s.*
40:8 word of our G. sh. *s.* for ever
46:10 counsel shall *s.* I do pleas.
61:5 strangers *s.* and feed flocks
Jer. 6:16 *s.* ye in the ways
4:28 know whose word shall *s.*
46:21 did not *s.* bec. day came
Ezek. 17:14 keeping cov. might *s.*
Dan. 2:44 kingd. shall *s.* for ever
11:6 king of the north sh. not *s.*
Mic. 5:4 and feed in strength
Nah. 2:8 *s. s.* shall they cry
Mat. 3:2 who *s.* when he appear.
Mark 11:25 when ye *s.* praying
Acts 1:11 why *s.* gaz. to heaven?
5:20 go, *s.* and speak in temple
26:6 I *s.* and judged for hope
Rom. 14:4 G. able to ma. him. *s.*
2 *Cor.* 1:24 joy. for by faith ye *s.*
Eph. 6:13 having done all to *s.*
Pet. 5:12 grace of G. wherein a *s.*
Rev. 3:20 I *s.* at door and knock
6:17 who shall be able to *s.* ?
18:15 merchants *s.* afar off

STAND abroad,
Deut. 24:11 *s. a.* man br. pledge

STAND against,
Lev. 19:16 nor *s. a.* blood of thy neighbour
Jer. 44:29 my words sh. *s. a.* you

STAND aloof.
Ps. 38:11 my friends *s. aloof*

STAND back,
Gen. 19:9 *s. b.* this fellow came

STAND before,
Ex. 8:20 *s. before* Pharaoh, 9:13
17:6 I will *s. before* thee on rock
Lev. 26:37 power to *s.* enemies
Num. 27:21 he sh. *s. b.* Eleazar
35:12 till *s. b.* congre. *Jos.* 20:6
Deut. 7:24 no man able to *s. b.*
11:25; *Jos.* 1:5 ; *Job* 41:10
9:2 who *s. b.* children of Anak?
19:17 both men shall *s. b.* Lord
20:10 *s.* this day all of you b. L.
1 *Sam.* 6:20 who able to *s. b.* L. ?

STA

1 *Sam.* 16:22 let David, I pray, *s. b.* me
1 *K.* 10:8 happy are thy servants who *s. b.* thee, 2 *Chr.* 9:7
2 *Chr.* 20:9 we *s. b.* house
Ezr. 9:15 we cannot *s. b.* thee
Job 41:10 who is able to *s. b.* me?
Prov. 22:29 a man diligent sh. *s.*
Neh. 12:9 a man, shall not *s. b.* mean
27:4 who is able to *s. b.* envy?
Jer. 7:10 *s. b.* me in this house
15:19 if th. ret. th. shalt *s. b.* me
35:19 do, not want man to *s. b.*
49:19 shepherd *s. b.* me? 50:44
Dan. 1:5 at end might *s. b.* king
8:4 no beast night *s. b.* him
11:16 none shall *s. b.* him
Nah. 1:6 who can *s. b.* his indi. ?
Luke 21:36 worthy to *s. b.* Son
Rom. 14:10 all *s. b.* judgm.-seat
Rev. 20:12 small and gr. *s. b. G.*

STAND by,
Ex. 18:14 peo. *s. by* thee to even
7: 15 *s. b. by,* I am ho. th. thou
Jer. 48:19 *s. by,* ask, What done
Zec. 3:7 walk am. th. that *s. by*
4:14 anointed ones that *s. by* L.
John 11:42 bec. of peo. wh. *s. by*

STAND fast.
Jer. 46:14 say ye, *s. f.* and prep.
1 *Cor.* 16:13 wat. yo, *s. f.* in faith
Gal. 5:1 *s. f.* in liberty Ch. made
Phil. 1:27 *s. f.* in sp. 4:1 *s. f.* in L.
1 *Thes.* 3:8 live, if ye *s. f.* in L.
2 *Thes.* 2:15 *s. f.* and hold trad.

STAND forth.
Mark 3:3 sa. to man, *s. f. Lu.* 6:8

STAND here,
Deut. 5:31 *s.* thou *here* by me
2 *Sam.* 18:30 turn aside, and *s. h.*
Mat. 20:6 why *s.* ye *h.* all day?
Acts 4:10 doth this man *s. here*

STAND in,
Ps. 4:4 *s. in* awe, and sin not
5:5 foolish sh. not *s. in* thy sig.
24:3 who sh. *s. in* his holy pl. ?
76:7 *s. in* thy sight wh. angry?
89:43 not made him to *s. in* bat.
134:1 by night *s. in* house, 135:2
Jer. 26:2 *s. in* court of L.'s house
Ezek. 13:5 not gone to *s. in* bat.
Dan. 12:13 *s. in* lot end of days
Zec. 14:4 feet *s. in* that day
Mat. 24:15 abomin. *s. in* holy pl.
Gal. 4:20 for I *s. in* doubt of you

STAND on.
Ex. 17:9 to-morrow I *s. on* hill
1 *K.* 6:31 if head of Eli. *s. on* him
Dan. 11:17 sh. not *s. on* his side

STAND out.
Ps. 73:7 eyes *s. out* with fatness

STAND perfect.
Col. 4:12 may *s. p.* and complete

STAND still,
Ex. 14:13 fear ye not, *s. s.* and see salv. of L. 2 *Chr.* 20:17
Num. 9:8 *s. s.* I will hear wh. L.
Jos. 3:8 ye shall *s. s.* in Jordan
10:12 sun *s. s.* upon Gibeon
1 *Sam.* 9:27 I pray, *s.* thou *s.*
12:7 *s. s.* that I may reason
14:9 we will *s. s.* in our place
Job 37:14 *s. s.* consi. works of G.
Jer. 51:50 escaped sword *s.* not *s.*

STAND strong.
Ps. 30:7 made mountain to *s. s.*

STAND there.
Num. 11:16 may *s. t.* with thee
Deut. 18:7 Levites who *s.* there
Jam. 2:3 say to the poor, *s. th. t.*

STAND together.
Is. 50:8 let us *s. t.* who plea.

STAND up,
Neh. 5:9 *s. up,* bless L. your G.
Job 30:20 I *s. up,* thou regar. not
33:5 set words in order, *s. up*
Ps. 35:2 shield, *s. up* for my help
94:16 who will *s. up* for me ag.
Is. 27:9 images shall not *s. up*
41:1 let them *s. up,* let them
48:13 call to th. they *s. up* tog.
51:17 awake, *s. up,* O Jerusa.
Dan. 8:22 4 kingd. *s. up* of nati.
11:2 sh. *s. up* 3 kings in Persia
3 a mighty king shall *s. up,* 4
14 many *s. up* ag. king of sou.
12:1 that time *s.* Michael *s. up*
Acts 10:26 Peter said, *s. up,* I am

STAND upon.
2 *Chr.* 33:21 thou *s.* rock
Deut. 27:12 shall *s. u.* mount Ge.

STA

Jos. 3:13 shall *s. upon* a heap
2 *Sam.* 1:9 Saul said, *s. upon* me
Is. 19:11 *s. u.* mount before L.
Ezek. 2:1 *s. u.* thy feet. *Acts* 26:16
33:26 *s. u.* sword, work abomi.
Dan. 7:4 made *s. upon* foot
Hab. 2:1 I will *s. u.* my watch
Zec. 14:12 while they *s. u.* feet

STAND upright.
Ps. 20:8 we are risen, and *s. u.*
Dan. 10:11 underst. words, *s. u.*
Acts 14:10 he said to cripple, *s. u.*

STAND with.
Num. 1:5 men that sh. *s. w.* you

STAND without.
Ezr. 10:13 are not able to *s. w.*
Mat. 12:47 *s. w.* to sp. *Luke* 8:20

STANDARD.
Num. 2:3 on east side sh. *s.* of J.
10 on south side be *s.* of Reu.
18 on west side be *s.* of Ephr.
25 on north side be tho *s.* of D.
10:14 in first place went *s.* of J.
Is. 49:22 I will set up *s.* to peo.
59:19 L. sh. lift up a *s.* ag. him
62:10 lift up a *s.* for the people
Jer. 4:6 set up *s.* toward Zion
21 how long see *s.* hear trum.
50:2 set ye up *s.* 51:12, 27

STANDARD-BEARER.
Is. 10:18 as when *s. b.* fainteth

STANDARDS.
Num. 2:31 Dan go hindm. wi. *s.*

STANDEST
Gen. 24:31 whoref. *s.* thou with, ?
Ex. 3:5 place wher. th. *s.* is holy ground, *Jos.* 5:15; *Acts* 7:33
Ps. 10:1 why *s.* afar off, O Lord ?
Rom. 11:20 bec. thou *s.* by faith

STANDETH.
Deut. 1:38 Jos. who *s.* bef. thee
29:15 with him that *s.* with us
Jud. 16:26 pillars wher. house *s.*
Ps. 1:1 nor *s.* in way of sinners
26:12 my feet *s.* in even place
33:11 counsel of Lord *s.* for ever
119:161 my heart *s.* in awe
Cant. 2:9 beheld, he *s.* beh. wall
Is. 3:13 *s.* to plead, *s.* to judge
46:7 set him in his place, he *s.*
Zec. 11:16 for feed that that *s.*
John 1:26 *s.* one among you
Rom. 14:4 to his own mas. he *s.*
1 *Cor.* 7:37 that *s.* steadf. in heart
8:13 eat no flesh while world *s.*
10:12 that thinketh he *s.* take
Heb. 10:11 every priest *s.* daily
Jam. 5:9 Judge *s.* before door
Rev. 10:8 angel who *s.* on sea

STANDING, Substantive.
Ps. 69:2 sink in mire whe. no *s.*
Mic. 1:11 shall rec. of you his *s.*

STANDING.
Lev. 26:1 nor rear yo up a *s.* im.
1 *Sam.* 19:20 S. *s.* appointed over
22:6 servants were *s.* about him
1 *K.* 22:19 h. of hea. *s.* 2 *Chr.* 18:18
Ps. 107:35 wildern. into *s.* water
114:8 flint into a *s.* upon altar
Mic. 5:13 I will cut off thy *s.* im.
Zec. 3:1 Sa. *s.* at his right hand
6:3 go forth from *s.* before Lord
Mat. 6:5 love to pray *s.* in syna.
20:3 saw others *s.* in the mark.
Luke 1:11 angel *s.* on side of alt.
John 8:9 and woman *s.* in midst
Acts 2:14 Peter *s. up* with eleven
5:25 men are *s.* in temple
7:55 J. *s.* on right hand of G. 56
22:20 I was *s.* by, and consent.
Heb. 9:8 while tabor. was yet *s.*
2 *Pet.* 3:5 earth *s.* out of water
See **CORN.**

STANK.
Ex. 7:21 the fish in the river *s.*
8:14 th. gathered frogs, land *s.*
16:20 manna bred worms and *s.*
2 *Sam.* 10:6 Ammon saw they *s.*

STAR.
Ps. 20:17 bones, Luoid and *s.*
Num. 24:17 sh. co. a *s.* out of J.
Amos 5:26 ye have borne *s.*
Mat. 2:2 have seen his *s.* in east
9 lo, *s.* which they saw in east

STA

Mat. 2:10 wh. they saw *s.* th. rej.
Acts 7:43 took up *s.* of your god
1 *Cor.* 15:41 *s.* differ. from ano. *s.*
Rev. 8:10 there fell a great *s.* 11
9:1 a *s.* fell from heaven to ear,
DAYSTAR. *See* DAT.

Morning STAR.
Rev. 2:28 I will give him *m. s.*
22:16 I am the bright and *m. s.*

STAR-GAZERS.
Is. 47:13 let the *s.-g.* stand up

STARS.
Gen. 1:16 G. made lights, ma. *s.*
1:15 tell the *s.* if thou be able
37:9 sun, moon, and eleven *s.*
Deut. 4:19 when seest *s.* sho. be
Jud. 5:20 *s.* in their courses
Neh. 4:21 fr. morn. till *s.* appear.
Job 3:9 let *s.* of twilight be dark
9:7 sun, and sealeth up the *s.*
22:12 behold height of *s.*
25:5 *s.* are not pure in his sight
33:7 morning *s.* sang together
Ps. 8:3 moon and *s.* which thou
136:9 moon and *s.* to rule by ni.
147:4 telloth number of the *s.*
148:3 praise him, ye *s.* of light
Ec. 12:2 while sun or *s.* be not
Is. 14:13 *s.* my throne above *s.*
Jer. 31:35 giveth *s.* for a light
Ezek. 32:7 I will make *s.* dark
Dan. 8:10 cast down some of *s.*
12:3 shall shine as *s.* for ever
Joel 2:10 *s.* withdraw shin. 3:15
Ob. 4 tho' set thy nest among *s.*
Luke 21:25 th. sh. be signs in *s.*
Acts 27:20 nei. sun nor *s.* appear
1 *Cor.* 15:41 another glory of *s.*
Heb. 11:12 so many as *s.* of sky
Jude 13 rag. waves, wandering *s.*
Rev. 8:12 third part of *s.* was
12:1 upon head a crown of 12 *s.*

See **HEAVEN, SEVEN.**

STATE.
Ps. 39:5 man at best *s.* is vanity
Mat. 12:45 last *s.* is worse than the first, *Luke* 11:26

See **ESTATE.**

STATELY.
Ezek. 23:41 sattest upon a *s.* bed

STATION.
Is. 22:19 I will drive thee from *s.*

STATURE.
Num. 13:32 saw, men of great *s.*
1 *Sam.* 16:7 look not on hei. of *s.*
2 *Sam.* 21:20 a man of great *s.*
1 *Chr.* 11:23; 20:6
Cant. 7:7 thy *s.* is like a pa.-tree
Is. 10:33 high one of *s.* be hewn
45:14 men of *s.* shall come over
Ezek. 13:18 kerchi. on head of *s.*
17:6 it became a vine of low *s.*
19:11 her *s.* was exalted among
31:3 Assy. was cedar of high *s.*
Mat. 6:27 not add one cubit to his *s. Luke* 12:25
Luke 2:52 Jesus increased in *s.*
19:3 Zaccheus little of *s.* climb.
Eph. 4:13 measure of *s.* of Christ

STATUTE.
Ex. 15:25 he made a *s.* and ordi.
29:9 priests' office for perpet. *s.*
Lev. 3:17 a perpetual *s.* 10:34;
24:9 ; *Num.* 19:21
6:18 shall be a *s.* upon altar
7:84 it shall be a *s.* for ever
Num. 27:11 sh. be for a *s.* 35:29
Jos. 24:25 ho set a *s.* in Shechem
1 *Sam.* 30:25 David made it a *s.*
Ps. 81:4 this was a *s.* for Israel
Dan. 6:7 consulted to estab. a *s.*
15 that no *s.* king establisheth

STATUTE for ever.
Ex. 27:21 it shall be a *s. for ever,* 28:43 ; 29:28 ; *Lev.* 6:18 ; 7:91 ; 10:9 ; 16:31 ; 23:41; *Num.* 18:23
Lev. 6:22 it is an *s. for e.* to the L.
Num. 19:10 to stran, for a *s. f. e.*

STATUTES.
Ex. 18:16 them know *s.*
Lev. 10:11 teach Israel all the *s.*
Num. 30:16 these are *s.* the L.
Deut. 4:6 which shall hear th. *s.*
16:12 shall observe and do th. *s.*
17:19 may learn to keep these *s.*
2 *K.* 17:8 walking in the *s.* of Da.
17:34 neither do they after th. *s.*
37 *s.* he wrote, ye shall do
2 *Chr.* 33:8 take heed to do the *s.*
Neh. 9:14 commandedst them *s.*
Ps. 19:8 *s.* of Lord are right
Ezek. 20:25 I gave th. *s.* not good
33:15 if wicked walk in *s.* of life
Mic. 6:16 for *s.* of Omri are kept

CRUDEN'S CONCORDANCE.

STA

His STATUTES,
Ex. 15:26 if thou wilt keep his s.
  Deut. 6:17; 10:13; 11:1
Deut. 27:10 thou shalt do his s.
2 Sam. 22:23 A. s, I did not dep.
1 K. 8:61 perfect, to walk in A. s.
2 K. 17:15 they rejected h. s. and
  23:3 made a covenant to keep
  his s, 2 Chr. 34:31
Ezr. 7:11 Ezra a scribe of his s.
Ps. 18:22 did not put away his s.
  105:45 they might observe h. s.
Jer. 44:23 in his law, nor in A. s.
See JUDGMENTS.

My STATUTES,
Gen. 26:5 Abraham kept my s.
Lev. 18:5 keep my s. 26; 19:19
  25:18 wherefore yo sh. do my s.
  26:3 if walk in my s. and keep
  15 and if ye despise my s. or if
  43 their soul abhorred my s.
1 K. 3:14 if thou wilt keep my s.
  11:34 because he kept my s.
2 K. 17:13 keep my com. my s.
2 Chr. 7:19 if ye forsake my s.
Ps. 50:16 hast thou to decl. my s.
  89:31 if they break my s.
Jer. 44:10 neither walk. in my s.
Ezek. 5:6 hath changed my s.
  7 ye have not walked in my s.
  11:20 they may walk in my s.
  18:19 when son hath kept my s.
  36:27 cau. you to walk in my s.
Zec. 1:6 my s. did take hold of

Thy STATUTES,
1 Chr. 29:19 heart to keep thy s.
Ps. 119:12 O Lord, teach me t. s.
  26, 33, 61, 68, 124, 135
  16 I will delight my. in thy s.
  23 thy servant did med. in t. s.
  48 and I will meditate in thy s.
  54 thy s. have been my songs
  71 that I might learn thy s.
  80 let my heart be sou, in t. s.
  83 yet do I not forget thy s.
  112 inclined my heart to t. s.
  117 I will have respect to t. s.
  118 hast trod. that err fr. t. s.
  155 the wicked seek not t. s.
  171 thou hast taught thy s.

STAVES,
Ex. 25:13 makes s. of shittim-w.
  28; 27:6; 30:5; 37:4
  14 put s. into rings, 15; 27:7;
  37:5; 38:7
  40:20 he set s. on arrk and
Num. 4:6 put in s. ther. 8, 11, 14
  21:18 nobles digged with their s.
1 Sam. 17:43 com. to me wi. s.?
1 Chr. 13:15 L. carried ark wi. s.
Hab. 3:14 didst strike with his s.
Zec. 11:7 I took unto me two s.
Mat. 10:10 coats nor s. Luke 9:3
  26:47 Judas, with him a multitude with s. Mark 14:43

STAY, Substantive.
Lev. 13:5 if plague in st. ho at s.
2 Sam. 22:19 L. my s. Ps. 18:18
Is. 3:1 L. doth take away the s.
  19:13 they that are s. of tribes

STAYS,
1 K. 10:19 s. on either side thro.
  2 Chr. 9:18

STAY, Verb.
Gen. 19:17 nel. s. thou in plain
Ex. 9:28 ye shall s. no longer
Jos. 10:19 s. not, pursue after
Ruth 1:13 would ye s. for them?
1 Sam. 15:16 s. I will tell thee
  20:38 make speed, haste, s. not
2 Sam. 21:10 s. hand, 1 Chr. 21:15
Job 37:4 he will not s. them
  38:37 can s. bottles of heaven
Prov. 28:17 let no man s. him
Cant. 2:5 s. me with flagons
Is. 10:20 sh. no more s. on him
  29:9 s. yourselves and wonder
  30:12 and s. on oppression
  31:1 woe to th. that s. on hors.
  48:2 s. themselves on God of I.
  50:10 trust in L. s. on his God
Jer. 4:6 not flee I will bel. evil
  20:9 I was weary, I could not s.
Dan. 4:35 none can s. his hand
Hos. 13:13 not s. in place

STAYED,
Gen. 8:10 Noah s. seven days, 12
  32:4 I have s. there until now
Ex. 10:24 flocks and herds be s.
  17:12 An. and Hur s. up Moses'
Num. 16:18 plague s. 50; 25:8;
  2 Sam. 24:25; Ps. 106:30
Jos. 10:13 stood still, moon s.
  24:7 Da. s. servants with waters

STE

1 Sam. 30:9 those that were left
  behind s.
2 Sam. 17:17 Jon. s. by En-rogel
  24:21 that plague may be s. fr.
  people, 1 Chr. 21:22
1 K. 22:35 king was s. in chariot,
  2 Chr. 18:34
2 K. 4:6 not a vessel more, oil s.
  13:18 he smote thrice, and s.
  15:20 king of Assyria s. not
Job 38:11 shall thy waves be s.
Is. 26:3 keep him wh. mind. is s.
Lam. 4:6 overthro. no hands s.
Ezek. 31:15 great waters were s.
Hag. 1:10 heav. is s. earth is s.
Luke 4:42 peo. came and s. him
Acts 19:22 he himself s. in Asia

STAYETH,
Is. 27:8 he s. his rough wind

STEAD,
Gen. 30:2 Ja. said, Am I in G. s.?
  44:33 let serv. abide in s. of lad
Ex. 29:30 priest in s. Lev. 16:32
Num. 10:31 to us in s. of eyes
  32:14 risen in your fathers' s.
Ex. 5:7 wh. he raised in their s.
Job 16:4 in my soul's s.
  33:6 acc. to thy wish in G.'s s.
  34:24 sh. set others in their s.
2 Cor. 5:20 pray you in Ch.'s s.
See REIGNED.

STEADFAST,
Job 11:15 yea, thou shalt be s.
Ps. 78:8 spirit was not s. with G.
  37 neither were s. in his covenant
Dan. 6:26 living God s. for ever
1 Cor. 7:37 stand. in his heart s.
  15:58 beloved brethren, be s.
2 Cor. 1:7 our hope of you is s.
Heb. 2:2 spok. by angels was s.
  3:14 if we hold our confid. s.
  6:19 an anchor sure and s.
1 Pet. 5:9 whom resist s. in faith

STEADFASTLY,
2 K. 8:11 settled countenance s.
Luke 9:51 he s. set fa. to go to J.
Acts 1:10 while they looked s.
  2:42 s. in the apostles' doctrine
  6:15 they all looking s. on him
  7:55 Step. looked s. into heav.
  14:9 who s. beholding him, and
2 Cor. 3:7 Is. could not s. behold
  13 could not s. look to the end

STEADFASTNESS,
Col. 2:5 s. of your faith in Christ
2 Pet. 3:17 lest ye fall fr. your s.

STEADS,
1 Chr. 5:22 they dwelt in their s.

STEADY,
Ex. 17:12 Moses' hands were s.

STEAL,
Gen. 31:27 wheref. didst s. away
  44:8 how should we s. silver?
Ex. 20:15 shalt not s. Lev. 19:11;
  Deut. 5:19; Mat. 19:18; Rom.
  13:9
22:1 if a man s. an ox, he shall
1 Sam. 19:3 as people s. away
Prov. 6:30 if he s. to satisfy soul
  30:9 or lest I be poor and s.
Jer. 7:9 will ye s. murder, and
  23:30 I am ag. prophets that s.
Mat. 6:19 thi. break thro' and s.
  20 thieves do not break nor s.
Mark 10:19 do not s. Luke 18:20
John 10:10 thief com. but to s.
Rom. 2:21 wh. dost, dost thou s.
Eph. 4:28 that stole s. no more
STEALERS. See MENSTEALERS.

STEALETH,
Ex. 21:16 he that s. a man
Job 27:20 waters s. him away
  29:8 but for every one that s.

STEALING,
Deut. 24:7 if it man be found s.
Hos. 4:2 by swearing and s.

STEALTH,
2 Sam. 19:3 peo. gat them by s.

STEEL,
2 Sam. 22:35 s. is brok., Ps. 18:34
Job 20:24 how of s. strike him
Jer. 15:12 shall iron break the s?

STEEP,
Ezek. 38:20 s. places shall fall
Mic. 1:4 poured down s. place
Mat. 8:32 the swine ran violently
  down s. place, Mark 5:13;
  Luke 8:33

STEM,
Is. 11:1 a rod out of s. of Jesse

STI

1 Sam. 20:3 th. is but s. between
Job 31:7 if my s. hath turned out

STEPHANAS,
1 Cor. 1:16 baptis. house. of S.
  16:15 house of N. the first-fruits
  17 I am glad of coming of S.

STEPHEN,
Acts 6:5 chose S. a man full, 8
  7:59 they stoned S. calling on
  8:2 devout men carried S. to his
  11:19 abroad on perse. about S.
  22:20 blood of thy martyr S.

STEPPED, ETH.
John 5:4 whosoev. first s. in was
  7 another s. down before me

STEPS,
Ex. 20:26 neither go up by s.
2 Sam. 22:37 thou hast enlarged
  my s. Ps. 18:36
1 K. 10:19 the throne had six s.
  20 twelve lions on s. 2 Chr. 9:19
Job 14:16 thou numberest my s.
  18:7 s. of his strength be strait.
  23:11 my foot hath held his s.
  29:6 I washed my s. with butter
  31:4 see my ways and count s.
  37 I would declare my s.
Ps. 17:11 compassed us in our s.
  37:23 s. of a good man ordered
  31 none of his s. shall slide
  44:18 nor have our s. declined
  56:6 mark my s. when th. wait
  57:6 prepared a net for my s.
  73:2 my s. had well nigh slipped
  85:13 set us in the way of his s.
  119:133 order my s. in thy word
Prov. 4:12 thy s. take hold not
  5:5 her s. take hold on hell
  16:9 the Lord directeth his s.
  20; 16:9 of the needy sh. trod.
Jer. 10:23 not in man to dir. his s.
Lam. 4:18 they hunt our s. we
Ezek. 40:22 went to it by 7 s. 26
  49 brought me by s. whereby
Dan. 11:43 Ethiopi. be at his s.
Rom. 4:12 walk in s. of that faith
2 Cor. 12:18 walked we not in s.?
1 Pet. 2:21 that ye sho. fol. his s.

STERN,
Acts 27:29 cast 4 ancho. out of s.

STEWARD,
Gen. 15:2 s. of my house
  43:19 they came near to the s.
  44:1 Joseph said to s. of house
Mat. 20:8 L. of vineyi. saith to s.
Luke 8:3 whose sn. Is that faithful s.
  16:1 rich man who had a s.
  2 thou mayest be no longer s.
  8 L. commended the unjust s.
Tit. 1:7 bishop blameless s. of G.
1 Cor. 28:1 David assembled s.
1 Cor. 4:1 s. of mysteries of God
  2 required in a s. that a man
1 Pet. 4:10 good s. of grace of G.

STEWARDSHIP,
Luke 16:2 give account of thy s.
  3 my lord taketh fr. me the s. 4

STICK, Verb,
Job 33:21 bones not seen, s. out
  41:17 scales are joined, they s.
Ps. 38:2 arrows s. fast in me
Ezek. 29:4 cau. fish to s. to scales

STICK,
2 K. 6:6 cut down a s. and cast it
Lam. 4:8 withered like a s.
Ezek. 37:16 one s. another s. 17

STICKS,
Num. 15:32 gath. s. on sabbath
1 K. 17:10 woman was gather. s.
  12 behold, I am gathering 2 s.
Ezek. 37:20 s. whereon thou writ.
Acts 28:3 Paul gath. bundle of s.

STICKETH,
Prov. 18:24 friend s. closer than

STIFF,
Deut. 31:27 I know thy s. neck
Ps. 75:5 speak not with a s. neck

STIFF-NECKED,
Ex. 32:9 this peo., it is s.-n. peo.
  33:3 not s. n. am. people, Deut. 9:6
  5 say to Is. Ye are a s. n. peo.
  34:9 go am. us, for it is s. n. p.
Deut. 9:13 this people, it is s. n.
  10:16 be no more s. n.
2 Chr. 30:8 ye resist n. not your fath.
Acts 7:51 s. n. ye resist H. Ghost

STI

2 Chr. 36:13 s. his neck and har.

STILL, Adverb,
Ex. 9:2 and wilt hold them s.
Num. 14:38 Josh. and C. lived s.
2 Sam. 14:32 to have been th. s.
2 K. 7:4 and if we sit s. here
Job 2:9 dost s. retain th. integ. ?
  3:13 now should I have lain s.
  20:13 tho' he keep it s. within
Ps. 49:9 that he should s. live
Jer. 8:14 why do we sit s.?
Rev. 22:11 unj. s. filthy s. holy s.
See STAND, STOOD.

STILL, Adjective and Verb.
Ex. 15:16 sh. be as s. as a stone
Jud. 18:9 land good, are ye s.?
1 K. 19:12 after fire, s. small voice
  22:3 Ram. is ours, and we be s.
Ps. 4:4 commun. with heart, be s.
  8:2 thou mightest s. the enemy
  23:2 leadeth me besides. waters
  40:10 be s. and kn. that I am G.
  76:8 the earth feared, and was s.
  83:1 hold not, and be not s. O G.
  107:29 so that waves ther. are s.
Is. 23:2 be s. ye inhabit. of isle
  30:7 their strength is to sit s.
  42:14 been s. and refrai. myself
Jer. 47:6 sw. of L. rest and be s.
Mark 4:39 to pea. Peace, be s.

STILLED,
Num. 13:30 Caleb s. the people
Neh. 8:11 the Levites s. the peo.

STILLEST, ETH,
Ps. 65:7 who s. noise of the seas
  89:9 when waves n. i. thou s. th.

STING,
1 Cor. 15:55 where is s. ? 56 s. of
Rev. 9:10 were s. in their tails

STINGETH,
Prov. 23:32 it s. like an adder

STINK, Substantive,
Is. 3:24 instead smell, shall be s.
  5:13 s. come out of their carcas.
Joel 2:20 his s. shall come up
Amos 4:10 made s. of your camps

STINK, Verb,
Gen. 31:30 ye have made me to s.
  16:24 manna laid up, did not s.
Ps. 38:5 wounds s. and corrupt

STINKETH, ING,
Ec. 10:1 send forth a s. savor
Is. 50:2 fish s. there is no water
John 11:39 L. by this time he s.

STIR,
Num. 24:9 who shall s. him up ?
Job 17:8 innocent s. himself ag.
  41:10 no. is so fierce th. dare s.
Ps. 35:23 s. up thyself, and
  78:38 did not s. up all his wrath
Prov. 15:1 griev. words s. anger
Cant. 2:7 that ye s. not up my
  love, 3:5; 8:4
  10:26 L. shall s. up a scourge
  13:17 behold, I will s. up Medes
  42:13 he shall s. up jealousy
Dan. 11:2 shall s. up agst. realm
  25 s. up his power agai. king
2 Tim. 1:6 thou s. up gift of God
Hag. 1:14 L. s. up spirit of Z.; 3:1

STIR,
Ac. 12:18 s. among the soldiers
  19:23 no small s. about way

STIRRED,
Ex. 35:21 s. him up, 26; 30:2
  36:10 I. ha. s. thee up agai. me
1 K. 11:11 L. s. up an adversary
  23 G. s. him up, 24 up adver.
  21:25 Jez. s. up, Ahab, his wife
2 Chr. 21:16 s. up Phillistines
  36:22 the Lord s. up the spirit
  of Cyrus, Ezr. 1:1
Ps. 39:2 and my sorrow was s.
Dan. 11:10 his sons shall be s.
  25 king of south be s. up
Hag. 1:14 L. s. spirit of Zerubb.
Acts 6:12 the s. up the people,
  17:13; 21:27
  13:50 Jews s. up devout women
  17:16 P. his spirit was s. in him

STIRRETH,
Deut. 32:11 as eagle s. her nest
Prov. 10:12 hatred s. up strife
  15:18 wrath. man s. strife, 29:22
  26:20 tell. wood s. fire, so stri.
  28:25 proud heart s. up strife
Is. 14:9 hell s. up dead for thee
  64:7 none s. up himself to

CRUDEN'S CONCORDANCE.

STO

Is. 64:7 none *s.* up hims. to take
Luke 43:5 he *s.* up peo. touching

STOCK.
Lev. 25:47 to the *s.* of stranger's
Job 14:8 though *s.* thereof die
Is. 40:24 their *s.* not take root
44:19 sh. I fall down to the *s.?*
Jer. 2:27 saying to a *s.* Thou art
10:8 *s.* is a doctrine of vanities
Acts 13:26 chil. of *s.* of Abraham
Phil. 3:5 of the *s.* of Is. a Hebr.

STOCKS.
Job 13:27 puttest my feet in *s.*
33:11 he putteth my feet in *s.*
Prov. 7:22 as fool to correct. of *s.*
Jer. 3:9 committed adul. with *s.*
20:2 Pashur put Jerem. in *s.* 3
29:26 put him in prison and *s.*
Hos. 4:12 peo. ask counsel at *s.*
Acts 16:24 their feet fast in *s.*

Gazing-**STOCK.**
Nah. 3:6 I will set th. as a g.-s.
Heb. 10:33 ye were made a g.-s.

STOICS.
Acts 17:18 cer. philosophers of *s.*

STOLE.
Gen. 31:20 Ja. *s.* away unawares
2 *Sam.* 15:6 Abs. *s.* hearts of Is.
2 *K.* 11:2 Jehosheba *s.* Joash fr.
   king's sons, 2 *Chr.* 22:11
Mat. 28:13 disciples *s.* him while
Eph. 4:28 let him th. *s.* steal no

STOLEN.
Gen. 30:33 shall be counted *s.*
31:19 Rachel has *s.* images, 32
   30 wherefore hast *s.* my gods?
40:15 ind. I was *s.* away out of
Ex. 22:7 if the stuff be *s.* out of
   12 if it be *s.* from him, he shall
Jos. 7:11 they have *s.* and dissem.
2 *Sam.* 19:41 have men of Jud. *s.*
   41:12 men of Jab. had *s.* bones
Prov. 9:17 *s.* waters are sweet
Ob. 5 would they not have *s.?*

STOMACH.
1 *Tim.* 5:23 use wine for *s.* sake

STOMACHER.
Is. 3:24 inst. of *s.* gird. of sack.

STONE.
Gen. 11:3 they had brick for *s.*
28:18 Jacob set up a *s.* 22; 31:45
29:3 rolled *s.* from well's, 8, 10
35:14 Jacob set up a pillar of *s.*
49:24 the sheph. the *s.* of Israel
Ex. 4:25 Zippor. took a sharp *s.*
15:5 they sank to bottom as a *s.*
16 they shall be still as a *s.*
17:12 they took a *s.* and put it
21:18 if one smite ano. with a *s.*
28:10 six on *s.* six on other *s.*
Lev. 26:1 nor set up image of *s.*
Num. 35:17 if smite with a *s.* 23
Jos. 4:5 take ave. man of you *s.*
15:6 border went to *s.* of Bohan
16:17 border descend. to *s.* of B.
24:27 this *s.* shall be a witness
Jud. 9:5 slew 70 persons on a. 1 *S.*
1 *Sam.* 14:18 *s.* remain. to this day
7:12 Samuel set up a *s.*
17:49 Da. took from his bag a *s.*
50 David prevailed with a *s.*
20:19 remain by the *s.* Ezel
23:37 Nah.'s hen. died, bec. as *s.*
2 *Sam.* 17:13 not one *s.* found
1 *K.* 5:17 house was built of *s.*
   18 cedar, there was no *s.* seen
2 *K.* 8:25 on land east ov. man *s.*
1 *Chr.* 22:15 there are hew. of *s.*
2 *Chr.* 2:14 skilful to work in *s.*
Neh. 9:11 thou throwest as a *s.*
Job 28:2 brass is molten out of *s.*
   38:30 waters are hid as with a *s.*
   41:24 his heart is as firm as a *s.*
Ps. 91:12 lest thou dash foot ag.
   a. *s. Mat.* 4:6; *Luke* 4:11
118:22 *s.* wh. build. ref. is head
   s. Mat. 21:42; *Mark* 12:10
Prov. 20:8 as he that rolleth a *s.* it will
27 as he that rolleth a *s.* it will
27:3 a *s.* is heavy, a fool's wrath
Jer. 2:27 to a *s.* Thou hast brought
51:26 shall not take of thee a *s.*
Lam. 3:58 they cast a *s.* upon me
Dan. 2:34 a *s.* was cut out of, 45
6:17 a *s.* laid on mouth of den
Hab. 2:11 *s.* shall cry out of wall
   19 wo to him saith to dumb *s.*
Hag. 2:15 *s.* was laid upon a *s.*
Zec. 3:9 upon one *s.* seven eyes
4:7 wh. bri. forth head. *s.* thereof
7:12 made hearts as adamant *s.*
Mat. 7:9 will give *s.? Luke* 11:11
   21:44 whoso. shall fall on this
     s. shall be brok. *Luke* 20:18

STO

Mat. 24:2 not be left one *s. Mark*
   13:2; *Luke* 19:44; 21:6
27:66 sealing *s.* setting a watch
28:2 angel came and rol. back *s.*
Mark 4:4 command this *s.* th. It
20:17 *s.* which builders reject.
Acts 4:11; 1 *Pet.* 2:7
22:41 withdr. fr. them a *s.* cast
24:2 fou. *s.* rolled away, *Mark*
   16:4; *John* 20:1
John 1:42 Cephas, by inter, a *s.*
2:6 were set six water-pots of *s.*
8:7 let him first cast *s.* at her
11:38 a cave, a *s.* lay upon it
   39 take away *s.* 41 they took *s.*
Acts 17:29 Godhead is like *s.* gra.
Rev. 16:21 hail fell ev. *s.* wei. of
18:21 angel took up *s.*

Burdensome **STONE.**
Zec. 12:3 I will make Jer. a b. *s.*

See CORNER, GREAT, HEWED.

Hewn **STONE.**
Ex. 20:25 not build altar of h. *s.*
2 *K.* 22:6 timber and h. *s.* to re-
   pair house, 2 *Chr.* 34:11
Lam. 3:9 encl. my ways wi. h. *s.*
Ezek. 40:42 four tables of h. *s.*
Amos 5:11 built houses of h. *s.*
Luke 23:53 sepulchre was h. in *s.*

Living **STONE.**
1 *Pet.* 2:4 coming as to l. *s.* chos.

Precious **STONE.**
Prov. 17:8 a gift is a p. *s.* in his
19, 28:16 in Zion a p. *s.* 1 *Pet.* 2:6
Ezek. 28:13 p. *s.* was thy cover.
Rev. 17:4 with gold and p. *s.*
21:11 was like a p. *s.* most p.

See STUMBLING.

STONE-SQUARERS.
1 *K.* 5:18 builders and *s.-s.* did

Tables of **STONE.**
Ex. 24:12 I give th. t. of *s.* 31:18
34:1 hew two t. of *s. Deut.* 10:1
4 Moses hewed two t. of *s.* 5:22
9:9 I was up to receive t. of *s.*
10 L. deliv. to me two t. of *s.*
1 *K.* 8:9 in ark save two t. of *s.*
2 *Cor.* 3:3 not in t. of *s.* in fleshly

Tried **STONE.**
Is. 28:16 I lay in Zion a tried *s.*

White **STONE.**
Rev. 2:17 I will give him a wh. *s.*

STONE, joined with wood.
Ex. 7:19 in vessels of w. and *s.*
Deut. 4:28 work of men's han. w.
   and *s.* 28:36, 64; 29:17; 2 *K.*
   19:18; *Is.* 37:19; *Ezek.* 20:39
Dan. 5:4 gods of wood and *s.* 23
Rev. 9:20 wor. idols of w. and *s.*

STONE of Zoheleth.
1 *K.* 1:9 Adonij. slew sheep by *s.*

See WALL.

STONE, Verb.
Ex. 8:26 will they not *s.* us?
17:4 almost ready to *s.* me
Lev. 20:2 people shall *s.* him
27 shall *s.* wizards with stones
24:14 let congreg. *s.* him, 16, 23
   23 *s.* adulterers with stones
Deut. 13:10 *s.* with stones entic.
17:5 *s.* idolat. 21:21 *s.* rebellious
22:21 *s.* her that playeth whore
24 *s.* her that playeth with stones
1 *K.* 21:10 car. Nah. out, *s.* him
Ezek. 16:40 shall *s.* thee with *s.*
23:47 company shall *s.* them
Luke 20:6 the people will *s.* us
John 10:31 Jews took ston. to *s.*
32 for wh. of works do *s.* me?
11:8 Jews of late son. to *s.* thee
Acts 14:5 assault made to *s.* th.

STONED.
Ex. 19:13 he shall be *s.* or shot
21:28 ox shall be surely *s.* 29, 32
32 sh. all Israel *s.* Achan
1 *K.* 12:18 all Israel *s.* Adoram,
   2 *Chr.* 10:18
21:13 they *s.* Naboth, 14, 15
2 *Chr.* 24:21 they *s.* Zechariah in
Mat. 21:35 beat one, *s.*
John 8:5 Moses com. such he *s.*
Acts 5:26 lest should have been *s.*
7:58 they *s.* Stephen, calling, 59
14:19 having *s.* Paul, drew him
2 *Cor.* 11:25 beaten, once was I *s.*
Heb. 11:37 they were *s.* sawn as.
12:20 touch mount it shall be *s.*

STONES.
Gen. 31:46 Jacob said, Gather *s.*
Ex. 28:11 engrave two *s.* 12
17 of *s.* even four rows of *s.*

STO

Ex. 28:21 *s.* sh. be wi. names of Is.
33:7 that ch. he *s.* for memorial
Lev. 14:42 *s.* in place of those *s.*
45 break down house, *s.* of it
21:20 or hath his *s.* broken
Deut. 8:9 a land wh. *s.* are iron
22:1 wound. in *s.* sh. not enter
27:4 set up these *s.* in mount E.
5 altar of *s.* 8 write on *s.*
Jos. 4:6 what mean these *s.?* 21
8 took twelve *s.* out of Jordan
8:32 wrote on *s.* a copy of law
Jud. 20:16 sli. *s.* at hair-breadth
1 *Sam.* 17:40 David chose five *s.*
2 *Sam.* 16:6 Shimei cast *s.* 13
1 *K.* 5:18 prepared timber and *s.*
10:27 king made silver to be as
   s. 2 *Chr.* 1:15; 9:27
15:22 took away *s.* 2 *Chr.* 16:6
18:31 Elijah took twelve *s.*
2 *K.* 3:19 good piece land with *s.*
25 Kir-haraseth left th. the *s.*
1 *Chr.* 12:2 hurling *s.* shooting
2 *Chr.* 26:14 pre. slings to cast *s.*
Neh. 4:2 will they revive the *s.?*
Job 5:23 in league with *s.* of field
6:12 is strength the stren. of *s.?*
8:17 wrapped, seeth place of *s.*
14:19 the waters wear the *s.*
22:24 gold of O. as *s.* of brooks
28:6 the *s.* of it are place of
40:17 sinews of his *s.* are wrp.
Ps. 102:14 serv. take pleas. in *s.*
137:9 dasheth little ones aga. *s.*
Ec. 3:2 cast *s.* time to gather *s.*
10:9 whoso removeth *s.* be hurt
Is. 5:2 gathered out *s.* thereof
14:19 that go down to *s.* of pit
27:9 the *s.* of altar as chalk *s.*
54:11 I will lay *s.* with fair col.
12 I make bord. of pleasant *s.*
57:6 amo. smooth *s.* of stream
60:17 for *s.* iron; 62:10 gather *s.*
Jer. 3:9 commit. adultery with *s.*
43:10 I will set his throne on *s.*
Lam. 4:1 *s.* of sanct. poured out
Ezek. 26:12 lay thy *s.* in the mid.
28:14 walked in midst of *s.*
Mic. 1:6 pour down *s.* in valley
Zec. 5:4 consu. it with *s.* thereof
9:16 shall be as *s.* of a crown
Mat. 3:9 of these *s.* to raise up
   children, *Luke* 3:8
4:3 command h. he made bread
Mark 12:4 at him they cast *s.*
13:1 see what manner of *s.* here
Luke 19:40 *s.* would immedi. cry
John 8:59 took *s.* to cast, 10:31
Acts 7:59 called to God, 8:7 *s.* by him
27:23 there *s.* by me angel of G.

Corner **STONES.**
Ps. 144:12 daughters be as c. *s.*

STONES of costly.
See COSTLY.

STONES of darkness.
Job 28:3 searcheth out *s.* of *d.*

STONES of emptiness.
Is. 34:11 stret. out upon *s.* of *e.*

Glistering **STONES.**
1 *Chr.* 29:2 I have prepared g. *s.*

Gravel **STONES.**
Lam. 3:16 bro. my teeth wi. g. *s.*

See GREAT.

Heap of **STONES.**
Jos. 7:26 raised a h. of *s.* on Ac.
8:29 a h. of *s.* on king of Ai
2 *Sam.* 18:17 laid h. of *s.* on Abs.

Hewed **STONES.**
1 *K.* 5:17 brought h. *s.* foundati.
7:9 according to meas. of h. *s.* 11

Hewn **STONES.**
Deut. 31:15 pillar of cloud *s.* o,
Jos. 5:13 a man *s.* o. against him
Ezek. 10:4 glory of L. *s.* o. three.
Luke 4:39 *s.* o. her, rebuked fever

Marble **STONES.**
1 *Chr.* 29:2 marble *s.* in abund.

Precious **STONES.**
2 *Sam.* 12:30 tal. of gold wi. p. *s.*
1 *K.* 10:2 queen of S. came wi. p. *s.*
11 navy brou. p. *s.* 2 *Chr.* 9:10
2 *Chr.* 9:2 I prepared all p. *s.*
8 with whosoev. p. *s.* were found
Chr. 29:8 garnis. house wi. p. *s.*
32:27 made treasuries for p. *s.*
Ezek. 27:22 occupied in fairs p. *s.*
28:13 covering of p. *s.*
27:22 build on founda. p. *s.*
Job 4:16 spirit *s.* I could not discern.

STO

STONY.
Ps. 141:6 overthrown in *s.* places
11:19 I take *s.* heart, 26:26
Mat. 13:5 some fell on *s.* places,
   20; *Mark* 4:5, 16

STOOD.
Gen. 18:22 Abraham *s.* before L.
Num. 16:48 *s.* bet. dead and liv.
Jos. 3:16 waters *s.* and rose up
Ex. 9:15 other Jews *s.* for lives
Ps. 33:9 command, and it *s.* fast
Jer. 46:15 they *s.* not because L.
Ezek. 1:21 those *s.* these *s.* 10:17
24 when they *s.* let down win.
Dan. 12:5 behold. there *s.* other
Mat. 12:46 brethren *s.* without
Acts 10:9 there *s.* man of Maced.
27:21 Paul *s.* forth in the midst

STOOD above.
Gen. 28:13 Lord *s.* a. the ladder
2 *Chr.* 24:20 Zechariah *s.* a. peo.
Ps. 104:6 waters *s.* a. mountains

STOOD afar.
Ex. 20:18 people *s.* afar off, 21
Luke 17:12 led lepers, *s.* a. off
Rev. 18:17 trade by sea *s.* a. off

STOOD before.
Gen. 19:27 place where he *s.* b. L.
43:15 went to Ezy. *s.* b. Joseph
Lev. 9:5 congregation *s.* b. Lord
Jos. 20:9 until he *s.* b. congrega.
Num. 10:28 Phinehas *s.* b. ark
1 *K.* 12:6 old men *s.* b. b. Solo-
   mon, 2 *Chr.* 10:6
8 young men *s.* b. L. 2 *Chr.* 10:6
22:21 spirit *s.* b. L. 2 *Chr.* 18:20
2 *K.* 10:4 two kings *s.* not b. him
Ps. 106:23 had not Mo. *s.* b. him
Jer. 18:20 I *s.* b. th. to spe. good
Ezek. 8:11 th. *s.* b. them 70 men
Dan. 1:19 th. *s.* b. the king, 2:2
Zec. 3:4 spake to those *s.* b. him.

STOOD by.
Ex. 18:13 the people *s.* by Moses
Jud. 3:10 that *s.* by went fr. him
18:16 men *s.* by entering of gate
1 *Sam.* 1:26 wom. *s.* by thee, O L.
1 *K.* 13:1 Jeroboam *s.* by altar
2 *K.* 2:7 they two *s.* by Jord. 15
Ezek. 43:6 man *s.* by me, and sa.
Dan. 7:16 near to one that *s.* by
12:5 an angel of Lord *s.* b.
Mark 14:47 one th. *s.* by drew sw.
15:35 some that *s.* by, wh. they
Luke 19:24 said to them th. *s.* by
Acts 23:11 night fol. L. *s.* by him
27:23 there *s.* by me angel of G.

STOOD in.
Ps. 5:20 Mo. and Aa. *s.* in way
Num. 1:5 L. *s.* in door of taber.
10:27 Dath. and Abir. *s.* in door
22:22 angel of L. *s.* in way, 24
Sam. 23:12 *s.* in midst ground
2 *Chr.* 20:6 *s.* in his place, 35:10
34:31 king *s.* in his place
Neh. 8:7 people *s.* in their place
Jer. 23:18 who *s.* in counsel of L.
Ob. 14 nor *s.* in cross-way
Luke 24:36 Jesus *s.* in the midst
   of them, *John* 20:19, 26
Rev. 5:6 in midst of elders *s.* a L.

STOOD on.
1 *Sam.* 17:3 Philist. *s.* on moun-
   tain, Israel *s.* on a mountain
26:13 David *s.* on top of a hill
1 *Chr.* 6:39 Asaph *s.* on rt. hand
Rev. 14:1 a Lamb *s.* on mount S.

STOOD over.
Deut. 31:15 pillar of cloud *s.* o,
Jos. 5:13 a man *s.* o. against him
Ezek. 10:4 glory of L. *s.* o. three.
Luke 4:39 *s.* o. her, rebuked fever

STOOD round.
Acts 14:20 disciples *s.* round him
Rev. 7:11 angels *s.* r. about thro.

STOOD still.
Jos. 10:13 sun *s.* st. moon stayed
13:13 cities that *s.* st. in strength
2 *Sam.* 2:23 as many as came *s.* s.
20:12 when man saw people *s.* s.
Job 4:16 spirit *s.* s. I could not discern.
32:16 they spake not, but *s.* s.
Hab. 3:11 sun and moon *s.* still
Mat. 20:32 Jesus *s.* s. called them
Mark 10:49 Je. *s.* s. commanded
Luke 7:14 th. that bare him *s.* s.

STOOD there.
Ex. 34:5 L. descended, and *s.* t.
Ezek. 3:23 behold, glo. of L. *s.* t.
Mat. 27:47 some *s.* t. *Mark* 11:5

STO

STOOD up.
Gen. 23:3 Abr. s. up fr. bef. dead
Ex. 2:17 M. s. up, helped them
Num. 11:32 peo. s. up all night
1 Chr. 21:1 Sat. s. up against Is.
2 Chr. 13:4 Abijah s. up and said
20:19 Levites s. up to praise Lo.
Neh. 8:5 opened book, peo. s. up
9:3 they s. up in their place
Job 4:15 hair of my flesh s. up
2°8 yo. men saw me, aged s. up
30:28 I s. up and cried in cong.
Acts 4:26 kings of earth s. up ag.

STOOD upon.
Gen. 41:17 I s. u. bank of river
1 Sam. 17:51 David s. u. Philist.
2 Sam. 1:10 so I s. u. S. slew him
2 K. 13:21 and s. upon his feet
Amos 7:7 s. u. wall made by line
Rev. 11:11 two proph. s. u. feet

STOOD with.
Gen. 45:1 th. s. with him no man
Lam. 2:4 s. with right hand
Luke 9:32 two men th. s. w. him
John 18:18 Peter s. with them
2 Tim. 4:16 no man s. with me
17 L. s. w. me, strengthen. me

STOODEST.
Num. 22:34 kn. not thou s. in w.
Deut. 4:10 day that thou s. be. L.
Ob. 11 day thou s. on other side

STOOL, s.
Ex. 1:16 wh. ye see them on s.
2 K. 4:10 set for him bed, and s.

STOOP.
Job 9:13 proud hel. s. under him
Prov. 12:25 mak. heart of man s.
Is. 46:2 they s. they bow down
Mark 1:7 I am not worthy to s.

STOOPED.
Gen. 49:9 Jud. s. down, couched
1 Sam. 24:8 David s. 28:14 Saul s.
2 Chr. 36:17 no co. on him th. s.
John 8:6 Jesus s. down, wrote, 8
20:11 she s. down, and looked

STOOPETH, ING.
Is. 46:1 Nebo s. their idols
Luke 24:12 s. down, John 20:5

STOP.
1 K. 18:44 that rain s. thee not
2 K. 3:19 s. all wells of water, 25
2 Chr. 32:3 took coun. to s. wat.
Ps. 35:12 s. way ag. that persec.
107:42 iniquity sh. s. her mouth
Ezek. 39:11 s. noses of passenge.
2 Cor. 11:10 no man s. me

STOPPED.
Gen. 8:2 wind. of heaven were s.
26:15 Philistin. had s. wells, 18
Lev. 15:3 flesh be s. fr. his issue
2 Chr. 32:4 who s. all fountains
30 Hezekiah s. water-course
Neh. 4:7 breaches began to be s.
Ps. 63:11 that speake. lies, be s.
Jer. 51:32 passages are s. reeds
Zec. 7:11 refused, s. their ears
Acts 7:57 they s. their ears, ran
Rom. 3:19 ev. mouth may be s.
Tit. 1:11 wh. mouths must be s.
Heb. 11:33 s. mouths of lions

STOPPETH.
Job 5:16 iniquity s. her mouth
Ps. 58:4 like adder that s. ears
Prov. 21:13 whoso s. his ears
Is. 33:15 s. ears fr. hearing blood

STORE, Verb.
Amos 3:10 who s. up violence

STORE, Substantive.
Gen. 26:14 Isaac had s. of serva.
41:36 that food shall be for s.
Lev. 25:22 eat of old s. 26:10
Deut. 28:5 bles. be basket and s.
17 cursed sh. be basket and s.
32:34 is not this laid up in s.
1 K. 10:10 gave of spices great s.
2 K. 20:17 fathers laid up in s. to
1 Chr. 29:16 this s. com. of thine
2 Chr. 11:11 he put s. of victuals
31:10 that is left is this great s.
Neh. 5:18 s. of all sorts of wine
Ps. 144:13 our garners afford. s.
Is. 39:6 fathers laid up in s.
Nah. 2:9 there is none end of s.
1 Cor. 16:2 let ev. one lay by in s.
1 Tim. 6:19 laying in s. a good
2 Pet. 3:7 by word are kept in s.

STORE CITIES.
1 K. 9:19 cities of S. Solomon had
2 Chr. 8:4 s. c. which he built, 6
16:4 th. smote s. c. of Naphtali
17:12 Jehosha. built s. c. in Ju.

STOREHOUSE.
Mal. 3:10 bring tithes into the s.

STR

Luke 12:24 the ravens have no s. nor barn

STOREHOUSES.
Gen. 41:56 Joseph opened the s.
Deut. 28:8 command bless. on s.
1 Chr. 27:25 over s. was Jehona.
2 Chr. 32:28 Hezekiah made s.
Ps. 33:7 layeth up depth in s.
Jer. 50:26 open her s. cast her

STORK.
Lev. 11:19 s. not eat, Deut. 14:18
Ps. 104:17 for s. the fir-trees
Jer. 8:7 s. knoweth her times
Zec. 5:9 had wings like a s.

STORM.
Job 21:18 as chaff that s. carrieth
27:21 s. hurl. him out of place
Ps. 55:8 I hasten my escape fr. s.
83:15 make them af. with thy s.
107:29 he maketh the s. a calm
Is. 4:6 and for a covert from s.
25:4 hast been a refuge from s.
28:2 wh. as destroying s. shall
29:6 shalt be visited with s.
Ezek. 38:9 shall come like a s.
Nah. 1:3 Lord hath his way in s.
Mark 4:37 there arose a great s.
Luke 8:23 there came down a s.

STORMY.
Ps. 107:25 raiseth the s. wind
148:8 s. wind fulfilling his word
Ezek. 13:11 s. wind shall rend, 13

STORY.
2 Chr. 13:22 acts of Abijah in s.
24:27 in the s. of book of kings

STORIES.
Gen. 6:16 with sec. and third s.
Ezek. 41:16 galleries three s. over
42:3 against gallery in three s. 5
Amos 9:6 build. his s. in heaven

STOUT.
Job 4:11 s. lion's whelps are sca.
Is. 10:12 I punish fruit of s. heart
Dan. 7:20 who. look was more s.
Mal. 3:13 your words ha. been s.

STOUT HEARTED.
Ps. 76:5 s.-h. are spoiled, they
Is. 46:12 heark. unto me, ye s.-h.

STOUTNESS.
Is. 9:9 they say in the s. of heart

STRAIGHT.
Gen. 6:5 second s. before him, 20
Ps. 5:8 make thy way s. before
Ec. 1:15 crooked can. be made s.
7:13 for who can make that s. ?
Is. 40:3 make s. in desert a high.
4 the crooked shall be made s.
42:16; 45:2; Luke 3:5
Jer. 31:9 cause to walk in s. way
Ezek. 1:7 their feet were s. feet
9 they went s. forw. 12; 10:22
Mat. 3:3 make his paths s. Mark
1:3; Luke 3:4; John 1:23
Luke 13:13 she was made s. and
Acts 9:11 go into street called S.
Heb. 12:13 made s. paths for feet

STRAIGHTWAY.
1 Sam. 9:13 ye shall s. find him
28:20 Saul fell s. along on earth
Prov. 7:22 goeth after her s.
Mat. 4:20 s. left nets, Mark 1:18
21:3 s. will send hi. Mark 11:3
Mark 5:31 s. and s. they knew him
Luke 5:39 no man s. desire. new
John 13:32 God shall s. glorify
Acts 5:10 then fell she down s. at
22:29 then s. they departed from
23:30 when told me, I sent s. to

STRAIN.
Mat. 23:24 guides s. at a gnat

STRAIT, s.
1 Sam. 13:6 saw they were in s.
2 Sam. 24:14 in a s. 1 Chr. 21:13
Job 36:22 sufficiency sh. he in s.
36:16 removed thee out of s.
Lam. 1:3 overtook her betwe. s.
Phil. 1:23 I am in a s. betwixt two

STRAIT.
2 K. 6:1 place we dwell is two s.
Is. 49:20 place is too s. for me
Mat. 7:13 enter ye in at s. gate
14 bec. s. is gate, Luke 13:24
Job 18:24 in s. place inclose
Jer. 19:9 seek lives shall s. them

STRAITENED.
Job 18:7 steps of stre. shall be s.
87:10 breadth of the waters is s.
Prov. 4:12 thy steps sh. not be s.
Ezek. 42:6 building was s. more
Mic. 2:7 is Spirit of Lord s.?
Luke 12:50 how am I s. till it be
2 Cor. 6:12 not s. in us, s. in your

STR

STRAITEST.
Acts 26:5 after most s. sect

STRAITLY.
Gen. 43:7 asked s. of our state
Gen. 6:1 Jericho was s. shut up.
Mark 1:43 he s. charged him and
Acts 4:17 let us s. threaten them
5:28 did not we s. comma. you ?

STRAITNESS.
Deut. 28:53 eat child. in s. 55, 57
Job 36:16 place wh. there is no s.
Jer. 19:9 eat flesh of friend in s.

STRAKE.
Acts 27:17 they fearing s. sail
See STRUCK.
STRAKES. See STREAKS.

STRANGE.
Gen. 42:7 Joseph made himself s.
Ex. 2:22 stranger in s. land, 18:3
21:8 sell her to a s. nation
30:9 ye shall offer no s. incense
Lev. 10:1 Nadab and Abihu offer-
ed s. fire, Num. 3:4; 26:61
2 K. 19:24 I have drunk s. waters
Job 19:3 not asha. make your. s.
17 my breath is s. to my wife
31:3 a s. punishment to workers
Ps. 114:1 went fr. peo. of s. lang.
137:4 sing L.'s song in s. land
Prov. 21:8 the way of man is s.
Is. 17:10 shalt set it with s. lips
28:21 he may do his s. work,
bring to pass his s. act
Jer. 2:21 how turned into s. vine
8:19 provoked with s. vanities
Ezek. 3:5 sent to peo. of s. spee.
Mal. 2:5 that turn aside s. from
Zep. 1:8 clothed with s. apparel
Luke 5:26 have seen s. things
Acts 7:6 sojourn in a s. land
17:20 bringest s. things to ears
26:11 I persecuted to s. cities
Heb. 11:9 sojourn. as in s. country
13:9 be not carried with s. doct.
1 Pet. 4:4 they think it s. ye run
12 think it not s. concerning
trial, as though s. thing
Jude 7 as So. going after s. flesh
See CHILDREN, GOD, GODS.

STRANGE woman.
Jud. 11:2 likewi. did he for s. w.
20:2 of s. that give seed to Mol.
23:45 children of s. w. Ps. 144:7
Jos. 8:35 s. that were conversing
2 Sam. 22:45 s. sh. submit them.
46 s. sh. fade away, Ps. 18:44, 45
1 Chr. 16:19 ye were s. Ps. 105:12
22:2 David commanded to ga.
29:15 we are s. as were our fath.
2 Chr. 2:17 Solomon numbered s.
32:32 s. of Is. and Judah rejoic.
Neh. 9:2 seeds of Is. sepa. from s.
13:30 cleansed I them from all s.
Ps. 54:3 s. are risen up agn. me
109:9 the Lord preserveth the s.
Prov. 5:10 s. be filled wi. wealth
17 let be only thine own, not s.
Is. 1:7 your land s. devour it in
2:6 they please themselves in s.
5:17 place of fat ones eat s. eat
11:14 s. be joined with them
25:2 made a palace of s. no city
5 shalt bring down noise of s.
29:5 multitude of thy s. shall be
60:10 sons of s. sh. build walls
61:5 s. shall feed your flocks
Jer. 2:25 I have loved s. after th.
3:13 hast scatter. thy ways to s.
5:19 so sh. ye serve s. in a land
35:7 live in land where ye bo. s.
51:51 s. are come into sanctuar.
Lam. 5:2 inherit. is turn. s. houses
Ezek. 7:21 I give it in hand of s.
16:32 wife taketh s. inst. of hus.
28:10 die deaths by hands of s.
30:12 make land waste by s.
47:22 s. that sojourn with you
Hos. 7:9 devoured his strength
8:7 the s. shall swallow it up
Joel 3:17 th. shall no s. pass thro'
Ob. 11 in the day that s. carried
Mat. 17:25 tribute? of child. or s.
Acts 2:10 and s. of Rome, Jews
See FATHERLESS.

STRANGERS.
Gen. 31:15 are we not count. s. ?
36:7 land where. were s. Ex. 6:4
Ex. 22:21 s. in Egypt, 23:9; Lev.
19:34; 23:23; Deut. 10:19
Lev. 17:10 whatsoever of s. that
20:2 of s. that give seed to Mol.

STRANGE women.
Jud. 7:4 Solomon loved many s. w.
Prov. 22:14 mouth of s. is pit
23:33 th. eyes shall behold s. w.

STRANGELY.
Deut. 32:27 lest adver. behave s.

STRANGER.
Gen. 15:13 thy seed shall be a s.
17:8 I will give thee land where
in thou art a s. 28:4 ; 37:1
27 bought with money of the s.
23:4 I am s. Ps. 39:12 ; 119:19
Ex. 2:22 I ha. been s. in str. land
12:19 cut off, whether a s. Lev.
16:29 ; 17:15 ; Num. 15:30
43 th. no s. eat thereof, 29:33
49 homeborn and s. Lev. 24:22
Num. 9:14 ; 15:15, 16, 29
20:10 nor s. that is within thy
gates, Deut. 5:14
22:21 thou shalt not oppress a s.
23:9 ye know heart of a s. see'g
12 that the s. may be refreshed
30:33 whoso. putteth it upon s.
Lev. 17:12 neither sh. any s. eat
22:10 no s. eat, 25:22 ; 53:8
25:17 s. sojourn in thy land
22:10 no s. of band
21:16 as well s. when blasphem.
22:13 then' her fa. s. ha. no inh.
47 if a s. wax rich by thee
Num. 1:51 s. th. cometh nigh sh.
be put to death, 3:10, 38
16:14 if a s. sojo. and will offer
16:40 that no s. offer incense
18:7 the s. that cometh nigh
19:10 to Israel and s. a statute
35:15 cit. of ref. for s. Jos. 20:9
Deut. 14:21 giveth it to s.
10:18 loveth the s. in giving s.

CRUDEN'S CONCORDANCE.

STR

1 *Pet.* 2:11 beseech you as *s.* pll.
3 *John* 5 whatso. thou doest to *s.*

STRANGLED.
Nah. 2:12 the lion did tear and *s.*
Acts 15:20 abst. from *s.* 29; 21:25

STRANGLING.
Job 7:15 my soul chooseth *s.* and

STRAW.
Gen. 24:25 we have *s.* and prove.
32 he gave *s.* and provender for
Ex. 5:7 no more give *s.* 10, 16, 18
11 get *s.* where you can find it
Jud. 19:19 there is *s.* and proven.
1 *K.* 4:28 barley. and *s.* for horses
Job 41:27 esteem. iron as *s.* brass
Is. 11:7 lion eat *s.* like ox, 65:25
25:10 Moab sh. be trodden as *s.*

STREAKS.
Gen. 30:37 Jacob pilled white *s.*
Lev. 14:37 if plague be wi. holl. *s.*

STREAM.
Num. 21:15 what he did at the *s.*
Job 6:15 as *s.* of brooks they pass
Ps. 124:4 the *s.* had gone over
Is. 27:12 L. shall beat off to the *s.*
30:28 breath as an overflowing *s.*
33 like as *s.* of brimstone
57:6 among smooth stones of *s.*
66:12 glory of G. like flowing *s.*
Dan. 7:10 fiery *s.* issu. and came
Amos 5:24 righteo. as mighty *s.*
Luke 6:48 *s.* beat vehemently, 49

STREAMS.
Ex. 7:19 stretch hand on *s.* 8:5
Ps. 46:4 *s.* make glad city of God
78:16 he brought *s.* out of rock
20 waters gushed, *s.* overflow.
126:4 turn our capt. captivi. as *s.*
Cant. 4:15 living waters, *s.* fr. L.
Is. 11:15 L. shall smite in sev. *s.*
30:25 on ev. high hill *s.* of wat.
33:21 place of broad rivers and *s.*
34:9 *s.* shall be turned into pitch
35:6 waters break out *s.* in desert

STREET.
Gen. 19:2 abide in *s.* all night
Deut. 13:16 gather spoil into *s.*
Jos. 2:19 go out of house into *s.*
Jud. 19:15 he sat down in *s.* 17
2 *Sam.* 21:12 had stolen fr. the *s.*
22:43 stamp them as mire of *s.*
2 *Chr.* 29:4 gather, in east *s.* 32:6
Ezr. 10:9 peo. sat in *s.* of house
Neh. 8:1 people gathered into *s.*
5:3 he read therein before *s.*
Est. 4:6 ran on horseback thro. *s.* 11
Job 18:17 sh. have no name in *s.*
29:7 I prepared my seat in the *s.*
31:32 strang. did not lodge in *s.*
Prov. 7:8 pas. thro' the *s.* near
Is. 42:2 not hea. in *s. Mat.* 12:19
51:23 hast laid thy body as *s.*
59:14 truth is fallen in the *s.*
Jer. 37:21 bread out of bakers' *s.*
Lam. 2:19 faint for hun. is ev. *s.*
4:1 stones poured out in ev. *s.*
Ezek. 16:24 high place in *s.* 31
Dan. 9:25 the *s.* shall be built ag.
Acts 9:11 go into *s.* call. Straight
12:10 Peter pass. through one *s.*
Rev. 11:8 dead bodies sh. lie in *s.*
21:21 *s.* of city was pure gold
22:2 in midst of *s.* tree of life

STREETS.
2 *Sam.* 1:20 publish it not in *s.* of
1 *K.* 20:34 shalt make *s.* in Dam.
Ps. 18:42 I cast them as dirt in *s.*
55:11 guile depart not fr. her *s.*
144:13 sheep br. forth 10,000 in *s.*
14 be no complaining in our *s.*
Prov. 1:20 wisd. utter. voice in *s.*
5:16 rivers of waters in the *s.*
7:12 now is she in the *s.* lieth
22:13 lion, I shall be slain in *s.*
26:13 violent sl. A lion lie in *s.*
Ec. 12:4 doors shall be shut in *s.*
5 the mourners go about the *s.*
Cant. 3:2 I will go about in the *s.*
Is. 5:25 carcasses were torn in *s.*
10:6 tread them like mire of *s.*
15:3 in th. *s.* they sh. gird them
24:11 a crying for wine in the *s.*
51:20 thy sons lie at head of *s.*
Jer. 5:1 run through *s.* of Jerus.
7:17 seest th. what they do in *s.*
11 cause to cease from *s.* of Je.
9:21 cut off young men from *s.*
11:6 proclaim words in *s.* of Je.
13 accord. to number of *s.* of J.
14:16 people be cast out in the *s.*
33:10 mirth shall be heard in *s.*
44:6 anger was kind. in *s.* of J.
9 wickedness they commi. in *s.*
44:38 shall be lamentation in *s.*
49:26 men shall fall in *s.* 50:30

STR

Jer. 51:4 are thrust through in *s.*
Lam. 2:11 suckli, swoon in *s.*
21 young and old lie in the *s.*
4:5 delicately, are desolate in *s.*
8 Nazarit. are not known in *s.*
14 wandered as blind men in *s.*
18 th. hunt onr steps in one *s.*
Ezek. 7:19 sh. cast silver in the *s.*
11:6 ye have filled *s.* with slain
26:11 hoofs of horses tread thy *s.*
28:23 will send blood into her *s.*
Amos 5:16 wailing in all *s.*
Mic. 7:10 trodden as mire of *s.*
Nah. 2:4 chariots shall rage in *s.*
3:10 dashed in pieces at top of *s.*
Zep. 3:6 I made their *s.* waste
Zec. 8:4 old women sh. dw. in *s.*
5 *s.* sh. be full of boys and gir.
9:3 heaped up gold as mire in *s.*
Mat. 6:2 not sound a trum. in *s.*
5 pray standing in corners of *s.*
Mark 6:56 sick in *s. Acts* 5:15
Luke 10:10 go into the *s.* of same
13:26 thou hast taught in our *s.*
14:21 go into *s.* and lanes of city

STRENGTH.
Gen. 4:12 ground sh. not yield *s.*
49:3 Reuben, L. brought, 14, 16
Num. 23:22 *s.* of unicorn, 24:8
1 *Sam.* 2:4 stumbl. are girt wi. *s.*
9 for by *s.* shall no man prevail
10 he shall give *s.* un. his king
15:29 the *S.* of Israel will not lie
28:22 that thou mayest have *s.*
2 *Sam.* 22:40 thou hast girded me
with *s. Ps.* 18:39, 39
2 *K.* 18:20 and *s.* for war, *Is.* 36:5
19:3 and there is no *s. Is.* 37:3
1 *Chr.* 16:27 *s.* and gladn. are in
28 give to the Lord glory and
Ps. 96:7
16:11 seek the Lord and
his s. Ps. 105:4
Job 18:7 steps of *h. s.* sh. be stra.
12 *his s.* shall he hunger-bitten
13 first-born of death de. *his s.*
21:23 one dieth in *his* full *s.*
37:6 saith to great rain of *his s.*
39:11 trust bec. *h. s.* is great *s.*
21 rejoice, in *h. s.* 40:16 *h. s.* is
Ps. 33:17 nor deli. by *h.* great *s.*
52:7 this man made not G. *h. s.*
59:9 because of *h. s.* will I wait
63:6 by *h. s.* setteth fast mount.
68:34 ascribe *s.* to G. *his s.* is in
78:4 showing to generation *h. s.*
61 delive. *his s.* into captivity
P. 44:12 be is hungry, *h. s.* fail.
60:8 the L. ha. sw. by arm of *h. s.*
63:1 travel, in greatness of *h. s.*
Mic. 11:3 by *h. s.* sh. stand
Hos. 7:9 strangers devoured *h. s.*
12:3 by *h. s.* he had power wi. G.
Rev. 1:16 count. as sun in *his s.*

In STRENGTH.
Gen. 49:24 his bow abode in *s.*
1 *K.* 19:8 went *in s.* of meat
Job 9:4 and mighty *in s.* 36:5
Ps. 71:16 I will go *in* the *s.* of L.
103:20 bless L. ye that excel *in s.*
147:10 delight not *in s.* of horse
Dan. 2:37 strengthen *in s.* of Phar.
Acts 9:22 S. he shall feed *in s.* of L.
19 increased more *in s.*

My STRENGTH.
Gen. 49:3 R. beginning of *my s.*
Ex. 15:2 the Lord is *my s.* 2 *Sam.*
22:33; *Ps.* 18:2; 28:7; 118:14;
Is. 12:2
Jos. 14:11 as *my s.* was then, so
is *my s.* now
Jud. 16:17 if I be shav. *my s.* will
19 is *my s.* of stones?
Ps. 18:1 I love thee, O L. *my s.*
19:14 O L. *my s.* 22:15 *my s.* dr.
31:4 the net. for thou art *my s.*
10 *my s.* fails bec. 38:10; 71:9
43:2 thou art the God of *my s.*
59:17 to th. O *my s.* will I sing
62:7 art *my s.* 102:23 *my s.*
144:1 blessed be Lord, *my s.*
Is. 27:5 take hold of *my s.*
49:4 I have spent *my s.* for nan.
5 glorious, my G. sh. be *my s.*
Jer. 16:19 O L. *my s.* and fortress
Lam. 1:14 he made *my s.* to fall
3:18 I said, *my s.* and hope
Hab. 3:19 the Lord God is *my s.*
Zec. 12:5 be *my s.* in L. of hosts
2 *Cor.* 12:9 *my s.* is made perfect

Their STRENGTH.
Jos. 11:13 cit. that stood in *t. s.*
Ps. 37:39 he is *their s.* in trouble
78:4 no lie in death, *t. s.* is firm
90:10 he smote *their s.* 12:3:4
99:17 thou art the glory of *t. s.*
Prov. 20:29 glory of men is *t. s.*
Is. 30:7 Egy. help in vain, *t. s.*
41:1 let people renew *their s.*
40:1 I will bring forth *their s.*
Jer. 21:25 I take from them *t. s.*
Jol. 2:22 G. and vine yield *t. s.*

Thy STRENGTH.
Ex. 13:11 hast guid. them in *t. s.*
Deut. 33:25 as days, so sh. *t. s.* be
Jud. 10:6 tell wher. *t. s.* lieth, 15
2 *Chr.* 6:41 ark of *t. s. Ps.* 132:8
Ps. 21:1 king sha. joy in *thy s.*

STR

Ps. 21:13 be ex. O L. in . own *s.*
54:1 name, judge me by *thy s.*
68:28 G. hath commanded *thy s.*
71:18 until I have showed *thy s.*
74:13 didst divide sea by *thy s.*
77:14 hast declared *t. s.* am. pe.
80:2 stir up *thy s.* and save us
86:16 give *thy s.* to thy servant
110:2 L. shall send rod of *t. s.*
Prov. 24:10 faint, *thy s.* is small
31:3 give not *t. s.* unto women
Is. 17:10 not mind. of rock of *t. s.*
52:1 awake, put on *t. s.* O Zion
63:15 wh. is thy zeal and *thy s.*
Amos 3:11 bro sh. bring down *t. s.*
Mark 12:30 love the Lord with all
thy s. 33; *Luke* 10:27

Your STRENGTH.
Lev. 26:20 *y. s.* be spent in vain
Neh. 8:10 joy of the Lord is *y. s.*
Is. 23:14 ships, *your s.* is waste
30:15 in confidence shall be *y. s.*
Ezek. 24:21 my sanct. ex. of *y. s.*

STRENGTHEN.
Deut. 3:28 charge Joshua, *s.* him
Jud. 10:28 *s.* me, I pray thee—
1 *K.* 22:22 *s.* thys, mark and see
Ezr. 6:22 O God, *s.* my hands
Job 16:5 I would *s.* you with month
16:10 Lord *s.* thee out of Zion
27:14 L. shall *s.* thy heart, 31:24
41:3 Lord will *s.* him on the bed
68:28 *s.* wh. thou hast wrought
89:21 mine arm also shall *s.* him
119:28 *s.* me accord. to thy word
Is. 22:21 I will *s.* him wi. girdle
30:2 to *s.* themselves in strength
33:23 they could not *s.* th. mast
35:3 *s.* we. hands; 41:10 I will *s.*
42 I chosen, *s.* th. length
Jer. 23:14 *s.* hands of evil doers
Ezek. 7:13 nor sh. any *s.* himself
16:49 neither did she *s.* hand of
30:24 I will *s.* arms of king, 25
34:16 I will *s.* that wh. was sick
Dan. 11:1 stood to confirm and *s.*
Amos 2:14 strong sh. not *s.* force
12 I will *s.* house of Judah
Luke 22:32 when convert. *s.* bre.
1 *Pet.* 5:10 God stablish, *s.* you
Rev. 3:2 be watchful and *s.* thi.

STRENGTHENED.
Gen. 48:2 Israel *s.* himself
Jud. 3:12 Lord *s.* Eglon against
7:11 afterwards shall hands be *s.*
1 *Sam.* 23:16 Jona. *s.* hand in G.
2 *Sam.* 2:7 let your hands be *s.*
1 *Chr.* 11:10 who *s.* themselves
21:1 Solom. was *s.* in king.
11:17 they *s.* kingdom of Judah
12:1 when Reho. had *s.* himself
24:13 set house of God and *s.* it
25:11 Amaziah *s.* himself
32:5 distressed Ahaz. but *s.* not
32:5 Hezek. *s.* himself, and built
Neh. 6:9 they *s.* their hands for
Job 4:3 thou hast *s.* weak hands
4 thou hast *s.* the feeble knees
Ps. 52:7 *s.* himself in wickedness
147:13 hath *s.* bars of thy gates
Prov. 8:28 when he *s.* fountains
Ezek. 13:22 ye *s.* hands of wicked
34:4 the diseased have ye not *s.*
Dan. 10:18 touched and *s.* me, 19
11:5 he that began her arm *s.* he
12 cast down many, not be *s.*
Hos. 7:15 bo. bound and *s.* arms
Acts 9:19 received meat, S. was *s.*
Eph. 3:16 to be *s.* with might
Col. 1:11 *s.* with all might accor.
2 *Tim.* 4:17 Lord stood and *s.* me

STRENGTHENEDST, ETH.
Job 12:23 he *s.* himself again. All
Ps. 104:15 which *s.* man's heart
138:3 and *s.* me with strength
Prov. 31:17 gird. loins, *s.* arms
Is. 7:19 wisdom *s.* the wise
Is. 44:14 cypress and oak he *s.*
Amos 5:9 *s.* spoiled ag. strong
Phil. 4:13 all thro' C. who *s.* me

STRENGTHENING.
Luke 22:43 appe. an angel *s.* him
Acts 18:23 Paul *s.* all the discipl.

STRETCH.
Ex. 7:19 *s.* out hand over streams
8:5:6 cherub. *s.* *s.* their wings
9:22 *s.* forth *s.* out the finger to At
2 *K.* 21:13 I will *s.* over Jerusal.
Job 11:13 if thou *s.* out tour, him
39:26 doth hawk *s.* her wings?

CRUDEN'S CONCORDANCE. 1041

STR

Ps. 68:31 soon *s.* her hands to G.
Is. 28:20 shorter th. a man can *s.*
34:11 *s.* upon it hue of confusion
54:2 *s.* curtains of thy habitation
Jer. 10:20 none to *s.* forth tent
Ezek. 30:25 king of Bab. *s.* sword
Amos 6:4 *s.* themsel. on couches
Mat. 12:13 Je. said, *s.* thy hand
John 21:18 shalt *s.* forth hands
2 *Cor.* 10:14 *s.* not beyond meas.

STRETCHED.
Gen. 22:10 A. *s.* hand to slay son
48:14 Israel *s.* out right hand
Ex. 8:6 Aa. *s.* out his hand, 17
9:23 Mo. *s.* forth his rod, 10:13
Jos. 8:18 Joshua *s.* out spear, 26
19 ran as he *s.* out his hand
1 *K.* 6:27 cherub. *s.* forth wings
17:21 and he *s.* himself on the child, 2 *K.* 4:34, 35
1 *Chr.* 21:16 angel with a swo. *s.*
Job 38:5 who hath *s.* line up. it ?
Ps. 44:20 or *s.* to a strange god
88:9 I have *s.* my hands unto th.
136:6 to him that *s.* out earth
Prov. 1:24 bec. I *s.* out my hand
Is. 3:16 walk with *s.* forth necks
5:25 he *s.* forth hand ag. them, *s.* out still, 9:12, 17, 21 ; 10:4
14:26 this is hand that is *s.* out
27 hand *s.* who sh. turn it back?
16:8 her branches are *s.* out
23:11 *s.* out his hand over sea
42:5 *s.* out heavens, 45:12 ; 51:13
Jer. 6:4 shadows of even. *s.* out
10:12 *s.* out heavens by discreti.
51:15 he *s.* heaven by understa.
Lam. 2:8 Lord hath *s.* out a line
Ezek. 1:11 wings were *s.* upward
10:7 cherub *s.* forth his hand
16:27 I have *s.* my hand over th.
Hos. 7:5 *s.* hand with scorners
Amos 8:7 that *s.* sh. be removed
Zec. 1:16 line be *s.* forth on Jer.
Mat. 12:13 *s.* hand, *Mark* 3:5
Luke 22:53 *s.* no hands aga. me
Acts 12:1 Her. *s.* hand to vex chu.
Rom. 10:21 all day I *s.* my hands

See ARM.

STRETCHEDST.
Ex. 15:12 thou *s.* thy right hand

STRETCHEST, ETH.
Job 15:25 *s.* his hand against God
26:7 *s.* north over empty place
Ps. 104:2 who *s.* out the heavens
Prov. 31:20 *s.* her hand to poor
Is. 40:22 that *s.* out the heavens
44:13 the carpen. *s.* out his rule
24 *s.* forth heavens, *Zec.* 12:1

STRETCHING.
Is. 8:8 *s.* of his wings fill land
Acts 4:30 by *s.* forth hand to heal

STREWED.
Ex. 32:20 he ground calf. *s.* it
2 *Chr.* 34:4 he *s.* upon the graves
Mat. 21:8 cut do. branches and *s.*
25:24 gath. where hast not *s.* 26

STRICKEN.
Gen. 18:11 well *s.* in age, 24:1
Jos. 13:1 J. was *s.* in yrs. 23:1, 2
Jud. 5:26 Jael had *s.* his temples
1 *K.* 1:1 David was *s.* in years
Prov. 6:1 *s.* thy hand with stran.
23:35 they have *s.* me, I was
Is. 1:5 sho. ye be *s.* any more ?
16:7 they are *s.* 53:4 est. him *s.*
53:8 for transgression was he *s.*
Jer. 5:3 thou hast *s.* them, they
Lam. 4:9 *s.* for want of fruits
Luke 1:7 Elizab. *s.* in years, 18

STRIFE.
Gen. 13:7 a *s.* bet. the herdmen
s Abra. said, Let there be no *s.*
Num. 27:14 rebell. in *s.* of cong.
Deut. 1:12 can I bear your *s.* ?
Jud. 12:2 I and peo. were at *s.*
2 *Sam.* 19:9 people were at *s.*
Ps. 31:20 keep fr. *s.* of tongues
55:9 have seen *s.* in the city
80:6 makest us a *s.* to neighbours
106:32 ang. him at waters of *s.*
Prov. 15:18 a wrathful man stir.
s. slow to anger app. *s.* 28:22
16:28 a froward man soweth *s.*
17:1 house full of sacrifi. with *s.*
11 begin. of *s.* one letteth out
19 loveth transg. that loveth *s.*
20:3 honor for man to cease fr. *s.*
22:10 cast out scorner, *s.* ceaseth
26:17 he that meddleth with *s.*
20 no talebearer, the *s.* ceaseth
21 so is contentious to kindle *s.*
28:25 proud heart stirreth up *s.*
30:33 forcing of wrath bring. *s.*
Is. 58:4 ye fast for *s.* and debate

STR

Jer. 15:10 borne me a man of *s.*
Ezek. 47:19 to waters of *s.* 48:28
Hab. 1:3 there are th. raise up *s.*
Luke 22:24 a *s.* among disciples
Rom. 13:13 honestly, not in *s.*
1 *Cor.* 3:3 there is among you *s.*
Gal. 5:20 works of the flesh are *s.*
Phil. 1:15 some preach Chr. of *s.*
2:3 let nothing be done thro' *s.*
1 *Tim.* 6:4 wher. cometh envy, *s.*
Heb. 6:16 an oath is end of all *s.*
Jam. 3:14 bitter envying and *s.*
16 where *s.* is, there is confus.

STRIFES.
Prov. 10:12 hatred stirreth up *s.*
2 *Cor.* 12:20 envyings, wraths, *s.*
2 *Tim.* 2:23 knowing that they gender *s.*

STRIKE.
Deut. 21:4 *s.* off heifer's neck
2 *K.* 5:11 come and *s.* his hands
Job 17:3 who will *s.* ha. wi. me ?
20:24 bow of steel *s.* him thro'
Ps. 110:5 *s.* thro' kings in wrath
Prov. 7:23 till a dart *s.* thro' liver
17:26 it is not good to *s.* princes
22:26 be not th. one th. *s.* hands
Hab. 3:14 *s.* thro' with his staves
Mark 14:65 did *s.* Je. with hands

STRIKER.
1 *Tim.* 3:3 bishop no *s.* *Tit.* 1:7

STRIKETH.
Job 34:26 he *s.* th. as wicked men
Prov. 17:18 void of undrstand. *s.*
Rev. 9:5 scorp. when he *s.* a man

STRING, S.
Ps. 11:2 make ready arrow on *s.*
21:12 make thine arrows on *s.*
33:2 Return of 10 *s.* 92:3 ; 144:9
Mark 7:35 *s.* of tongue loosed

STRINGED.
Ps. 150:4 praise him wi. *s.* instr.
Is. 38:20 sing songs to *s.* instru.
Hab. 3:19 singer on *s.* instrume.

STRIPE.
Ex. 21:25 for wound, *s.* for *s.*

STRIPES.
Deut. 25:3 forty *s.* he may give
2 *Sam.* 7:14 with *s.* of children
Ps. 89:32 visit iniquity with *s.*
Prov. 17:10 hundred *s.* into a fool
19:29 *s.* are prepared for fools
20:30 so do *s.* the inward parts
Is. 53:5 with his *s.* we are healed.
1 *Pet.* 2:24
Luke 12:47 beaten with many *s.*
48 knew not, beaten wi. few *s.*
Acts 16:23 laid many *s.* upon th.
33 same hour, washed their *s.*
2 *Cor.* 6:5 in *s.* in imprisonments
11:23 in *s.* above measure
24 of Jews received I forty *s.*

STRIP.
Num. 20:26 *s.* Aaron of garments
1 *Sam.* 31:8 Philistines came to *s.*
Is. 32:11 *s.* ye, make ye bare
Ezek. 16:39 they sh. *s.* thee, 23:26
Hos. 2:3 I *s.* her naked, set her

STRIPPED.
Gen. 37:23 they *s.* Joseph of coat
Ex. 33:6 Israel *s.* themselves
Num. 20:28 Moses *s.* An. of gar.
1 *Sam.* 18:4 Jonathan *s.* himself
19:24 Saul *s.* off his clothes also
31:9 Philist. *s.* Saul of his armour
2 *Chr.* 20:25 jewels wh. th. *s.* off
Job 19:9 *s.* me of glory and honour
22:6 for thou hast *s.* of clothing
Mic. 1:8 therefore I will go,
Mat. 27:28 they *s.* Jesus, put on
Luke 10:30 wh. both *s.* him of rai.

STRIPLING.
1 *Sam.* 17:56 inq. whose son *s.* is

STRIVE.
Gen. 6:3 Spi. not always *s.* with
Ex. 21:18 if men *s.* together
22 *s.* and hurt wo. *Deut.* 25:11
Jud. 8:35 with wh. thou didst *s.*
Jud. 11:25 did he ever *s.* aga. Is.
Job 33:13 why *s.* against him ?
Ps. 35:1 plead with them that *s.*
Prov. 3:30 *s.* not without cause
25:8 go not forth hastily to *s.*
Is. 41:11 they that *s.* shall perish
45:9 let potsherd *s.* wi. potsherd
Hos. 4:4 let no man *s.* thy peo.
ple are *s.* as they that *s.*
Mat. 12:19 he shall not *s.*
Luke 13:21 *s.* to enter strait gate
Rom. 15:30 *s.* wi. me in prayers
2 *Tim.* 2:5 if a man *s.* for mastery

STR

2 *Tim.* 2:14 th. th. *s.* not ab. wor.
24 servant of Lord must not *s.*

STRIVED, ETH.
Is. 45:9 woe to him that *s.* wi. M.
Rom. 15:20 I *s.* to preach gospel
1 *Cor.* 9:25 *s.* for mastery is tem.

STRIVEN.
Jer. 50:24 bec. th. hast *s.* ag. L.

STRIVING.
Phil. 1:27 with mind *s.* for gospel
Col. 1:29 *s.* according to working
Heb. 12:4 not resisted, *s.* aga. sin

STRIVINGS.
2 *Sam.* 22:44 hast deliv. me from
s. of the people, *Ps.* 18:43
Tit. 3:9 avoid contentions and *s.*

STROKE, S.
Deut. 17:8 hard betwe. *s.* and *s.*
19:5 hand fetcheth *s.* wi. axe
21:5 by word every *s.* be tried
Est. 9:5 J. smote enem. with *s.*
Job 23:2 my *s.* is heavier th. my
36:18 lest he take th. with his *s.*
Ps. 39:10 remove thy *s.* from me
Prov. 18:6 fool's mouth call. for *s.*
Is. 14:6 smote with a contin. *s.*
30:26 the Lord healeth the *s.* of
Jer. 14:17 daughter smitten with
Jer. 14:17 daughter of people, *Ps.* 18:43
Ezek. 24:16 deci. of eyes with a *s.*

STRONG.
Gen. 49:14 Issachar is a *s.* ass
24 arms of hands were made *s.*
Ex. 6:1 with a *s.* hand shall, 13:9
Num. 20:20 Ed. came wi. *s.* hand
21:24 border of Ammon was *s.*
22:7 *s.* wine poured out to Lord
Deut. 2:36 not one city too *s.* for
Jos. 14:11 I am as *s.* this day
17:13 Is. were wax. *s.* *Jud.* 1:28
23:9 great nations and *s.*
Jud. 1:14 out of *s.* came sweet.
18:26 Mic. saw they were too *s.*
1 *Sam.* 14:52 when S. saw *s.* man
2 *Sam.* 3:6 Abner made him *s.*
10:11 if Syri. be too *s.* for me, if
Arm. bo too *s.* 1 *Chr.* 19:12
1 *K.* 8:42 wh. hear of thy *s.* hand
2 *Chr.* 11:12 he made the cities *s.*
17 made Rehoboam *s.* 3 years
16:9 eyes run to show himself *s.*
19:11 Izziah was *s.* even in heart
Neh. 9:25 they took *s.* cities
Job 8:2 words be like a *s.* wind
9:19 if I speak of *s.* he is *s.*
37:18 spread out sky that is *s.*
19:25 rejoiceth as a *s.* man
21:8 Lord *s.* and mighty
30:7 made my mount. stand *s.*
31:2 be thou my *s.* rock
35:10 from him that is too *s.* for
38:19 enemies are lively and *s.*
60:9 who br. into a *s.* city ? 108:10
71:3 my *s.* habita. 7 my *s.* refuge
80:15 branch thou madest. *s.* 17
89:8 who is a *s.* Lord like thee ?
89:13 *s.* is thy hand, high is thy
136:12 *s.* hand, *Jer.* 32:21
Prov. 7:26 *s.* men have been
11:16 wom. retai. honor, *s.* men
18:10 harder to be won th. *s.* ci.
19 brother offended is har. *s.* cit.
Ez. 9:11 battle is not to the *s.*
12:3 *s.* men shall bow thems.
Cant. 8:6 for love is *s.* as death
Is. 8:7 L. bringeth waters, *s.* and
17:9 *s.* cities sh. be as forsaken
25:3 theref. shall *s.* glorify thee
26:1 he sung, we have a *s.* city
28:2 hath a mighty and *s.* one
40:10 will come with a *s.* hand
41:21 bring forth *s.* reasons
43:16 maketh a way in *s.* waters
53:12 shall divide spoil with *s.*
60:22 one shall bec. a *s.* nation
Jer. 21:5 will fight wi. a *s.* arm
48:14 mighty, *s.* men of war ?
50:34 th. Redeemer's *s.* the L.
41 *s.* come against Baby. fr. n.
Ezek. 3:14 hand of the L. was *s.*
26:17 city which was *s.* in sea
32:21 spake to *s.* out of hell
Dan. 2:40 kingdom sh. be *s.* as
4:11 tree grew and was *s.*
7:7 a fourth beast terrible, *s.* exc.
11:25 he shall her. *s.* wi. magnif
Joel 1:6 nation is come up, *s.* 2:2
2:11 he is *s.* that executeth word
3:10 let the weak say, I am *s.*
Amos 2:14 *s.* sh. not strengthen
5:9 strengtheneth spoiled ag. *s.*
Mic. 4:3 shall rebuke *s.* nations
7:11 will make her a *s.* nation
Nah. 2:1 make thy loins *s.*

STR

Zec. 8:22 *s.* nations sh. seek L.
Mat. 12:29 how cut. *s.* man's ho.
ezc. bind *s.* man ? *Mark* 3:27
Luke 1:80 child waxed *s.* 2:40
11:21 a *s.* man armed keepeth
Acts 3:16 thro' faith made man *s.*
Rom. 4:20 was *s.* in faith
15:1 we th. are *s.* ought to bear
1 *Cor.* 4:10 are weak, ye are *s.*
1 *Cor.* 13:10 weak, then are I *s.*
Heb. 5:12 milk, not *s.* meat
11:34 out of weak. were made *s.*
1 *John* 2:14 ye are *s.* word of God
Rev. 5:2 I saw a *s.* angel proclai.
18:2 he cried with a *s.* voice
8 *s.* is the Lord God who judg.

De STRONG.
Num. 13:18 see wheth. they be *s.*
28 people be *s.* that dwell in
Deut. 11:18 keep co. that ye be *s.*
Jos. 17:18 drive Canaan, tho' be *s.*
1 *Sam.* 4:9 be *s.* quit yourselves
2 *Sam.* 16:21 hand of all shall be *s.*
1 *K.* 2:2 be thou *s.* show thyself a
1 *Chr.* 28:10 L. chosen thee, be *s.*
2 *Chr.* 15:7 be *s.* work sh. be re.
25:8 do it, be *s.* for the battle
Ezr. 9:12 that ye may be *s.*
Ps. 144:14 that oxen be *s.* to lab.
Is. 35:4 th. of fearful heart, be *s.*
Ezek. 22:14 can thy hands be *s.*
Dan. 2:42 kingd. sh. be partly *s.*
10:19 peace O th. be *s.* yea, be *s.*
11:5 king of the south shall be *s.*
and he *sh.* be *s.* above him
32 pe. that know G. shall be *s.*
Hag. 2:4 be *s.* O Zerubbabel, be
s. O Joshua, let *s.* ye people
Zec. 8:9 let hands be *s.* *s.* that
13 but let your hands be *s.*
Eph. 6:10 brethr. be *s.* in the L.
2 *Tim.* 2:1 my son, be *s.* in grace

See COURAGE, DRINK.

STRONG ones.
Ps. 10:10 may fall by his *s.* ones
Jer. 8:16 sound of neigh. of *s.* on.

STRONGER.
Gen. 25:23 one people shall be *s.*
30:42 feebler were L's *s.* Jac.'s
Num. 13:31 not able, they are *s.*
Jud. 14:18 what is *s.* th. a lion ?
2 *Sam.* 3:1 David waxed *s.* and *s.*
13:14 Amnon being *s.* than she
1 *K.* 20:23 *s.* we shall be *s.* 25
Job 17:9 cl. hands wh. be *s.* and *s.*
Ps. 105:24 he made them *s.* than
112:6 deli. me, they are *s.* th. I
Jer. 20:7 thou art *s.* than I, and
Luke 11:22 wh. a *s.* th. he come
1 *Cor.* 1:25 weak. of G. is *s.* than
10:22 do we pro. L. ? are we *s.* ?

STRONGEST.
Prov. 30:30 wh. is *s.* am. beasts

STRONG-HOLD, S.
Num. 13:19 whe. in tents or *s.* h.
Jud. 6:2 Is. ma. caves and *s.* h.
1 *Sam.* 23:14 David abode in *s.* h.
29 D. dwelt in *s.* h. at En-gedi
2 *Sam.* 5:7 David took *s.* h. of Zion
24:7 came to the *s.* h. of Tyre
2 *K.* 8:12 their *s.* h. set on fire
Is. 23:11 Heb. fortified *s.* h.
Ps. 89:40 broug. his *s.* h. to ruin
Is. 23:11 destroy *s.* h. thereof
23:14 pass over to him *s.* h.
Jer. 48:18 spoiler sh. destroy *s.* h.
41 the *s.* holds are surprised
Lam. 2:2 he hath thr. down *s.* h.
5 Lord destroyed his *s.* holds
Mic. 4:8 unto *s.* h. be gu. in mast *s.* h.
Nah. 1:7 L. a *s.* h. in day of trou.
3:12 thy *s.* h. shall be like fig *s.*
14 draw waters, forti. thy *s.* h.
Hab. 1:10 shall deride every *s.* h.
Zec. 9:3 Tyrus did build a *s.* h.
12 turn to *s.* h. ye prisone.
2 *Cor.* 10:4 bulg. to pull. do. *s.* h.

STRONGLY.
Ezr. 6:3 let foundation be *s.* laid

STROVE.
Gen. 26:20 they *s.* with him, 21
22 another well, and *s.* not
Ex. 2:13 two men of Hebrews *s.*
Lev. 24:10 man of Is. *s.* with h.
Num. 20:13 water, whe. chil. of Is. *s.*
27:3 Dathan, who *s.* against M.
2 *Sam.* 14:6 two of them *s.*
Dan. 7:2 four winds *s.* upon sea
John 6:52 the Jews *s.* am. them.
Acts 7:26 M. show him, as th. *s.*
23:9 scribes , We find no evil

GG

CRUDEN'S CONCORDANCE.

STU

STRUCK.
1 Sam. 2:11 he s. it into the pan
2 Sam. 12:15 the Lord s. the ch.
20:10 Jo. s. him not again, and
2 Chr. 13:20 the Lord s. Jeroboa.
Mat. 26:51 one of them s. a serv.
Luke 22:64 they s. Jesus, John 18:22

STRUGGLED.
Gen. 25:22 children s. together

STUDDLE.
Ex. 5:12 gath. s. instead of straw
15:7 wrath consumed them as s.
Job 13:25 wilt th. pursue dry s. ?
21:18 they are as s. before wind
41:28 stones are turned into s.
29 darts are counted as s. he
Ps. 83:13 make them as s. before
Is. 5:24 as fire devoureth the s.
33:11 conceive chaff br. forth s.
40:24 whirlwind take away as s.
41:2 he gave them as driven s.
47:14 they shall be as s. the fire
Jer. 13:24 I will scatter th. as s.
Joel 2:5 flame, that devou. the s.
Ob. 18 house of E. sh. be for s.
Nah. 1:10 they sh. be devo. as s.
Mal. 4:1 wicked, and proud be s.
1 Cor. 3:12 on the found. hay, s.

STUBBORN.
Deut. 21:18 if a man ha. a s. son
20 say to old. This our son is s.
Jud. 2:19 ceased not from s. way
Ps. 78:8 not as faith. s. a gener.
Prov. 7:11 she is loud and s. her

STUBBORNNESS.
Deut. 9:27 look not to s. of peop.
1 Sam. 15:23 and s. is as iniquity

STUCK.
1 Sam. 26:7 spear s. in ground
Ps. 119:31 I ha. s. unto testimo.
Acts 27:41 part of the ship s. fast

STUDS.
Cant. 1:11 borders of gold wi. s.

STUDY.
Ec. 12:12 much s. is a weariness
1 Thes. 4:11 s. to be quiet
2 Tim. 2:15 s. to show thys. app.

STUDIETH.
Prov. 15:28 heart of righteous s.
24:2 their heart s. destruction

STUFF.
Gen. 31:37 th. hast search. my s.
45:20 regard not your s.
Ex. 22:7 if man deliv. s. to keep
36:7 the s. they had was sufficl.
Jos. 7:11 they put it amo. their s.
1 Sam. 10:22 he hath hid amo. s.
25:13 two hund. abode by the s.
30:24 his part be that tarr. by s.
Ezek. 12:3 prepare s. for removi.
4 bring forth thy s. by day, 7
Luke 17:31 house-top, s. in hou.

STUMBLE.
Prov. 3:23 walk, foot not s. 4:12
4:19 know not at what they s.
Is. 5:27 none sh. be weary nor s.
8:15 many among them shall s.
28:7 err in vision, s. in judgme.
59:10 we s. at noonday as night
63:13 led th. that th. sho. not s.
Jer. 13:16 before your feet s. on
18:15 caused them to s. in ways
20:11 therefore persecuto. sh. s.
31:9 in a way they shall not s.
46:6 they shall s. and fall
50:32 proud shall s. and fall
Dan. 11:19 he shall s. and fall
Nah. 2:3 shall s. in their walk
3:3 they shall s. on corpses
Mal. 2:8 have caused many to s.
1 Pet. 2:8 offence to them that s.

STUMBLED.
1 Sam. 2:4 that s. girt with stre.
1 Chr. 13:9 hold ark. for oxen s.
Ps. 27:2 came to eat flesh, th. s.
Jer. 46:12 mighty s. ag. mighty
Rom. 9:32 th. s. at stumb.-stone
11:11 have s. that they sho. fall

STUMBLETH.
Prov. 24:17 heart glad wh. he s.
John 11:9 walk in day, s. not
10 if man walk in night he s.
Rom. 14:21 whereby thy bro. s.

STUMBLING.
John 2:10 is none occasion of s.

STUMBLING-BLOCK.
Lev. 19:14 nor put a s.-b. bef. blind
Is. 57:14 take s.-b. out of way
Ezek. 3:20 I lay s.-b. before him
7:19 bec. it is s.-b. of their iniq.
14:3 they put s.-b. of iniqui. 4, 7
Zeph. 1:9 made a trap, a s.-b.

SUB

Rom. 14:13 put s.-b. in br. way
1 Cor. 1:23 C. cruci. to Jews s.-b.
8:9 lest liber. of yours bec. s.-b.
Rev. 2:14 Bal. to cast s.-b. bef. Is.

STUMBLING-BLOCKS.
Jer. 6:21 I will lay s.-b. bof. peo.
Zep. 1:3 I will consume s.-b.

STUMBLING, with stone.
Is. 8:14 be for a s. of s. to Israel
Rom. 9:32 stumbled at th. s.-st.
33 behold, I lay in Sion a s.-st.
1 Pet. 2:8 s. of s. to th. that stum.

STUMP.
1 Sam. 5:4 only s. of Da. was left
Dan. 4:15 leave s. in earth, 23, 26

SUBDUE.
Gen. 1:28 replenish earth, s. it
1 Chr. 17:10 I will s. thi. enemi.
Ps. 47:3 he shall s. peo. under
65:1 to s. nations before him
Dan. 7:24 he shall s. three kings
Mic. 7:19 will s. our iniquities
Zec. 9:15 s. with sling-stones
Phil. 3:21 he is able to s. all thi.

SUBDUED, EST.
Num. 32:22 land be s. before L.
29 land shall be s. before you
Deut. 20:20 bulwarks, until be s.
Jos. 18:1 land was s. before th.
1 Sam. 7:13 Philli. were s. 2 Sam.
8:1; 1 Chr. 18:1; 20:4
2 Sam. 8:11 gold of nations he s.
22:40 th. s. under me, Ps. 18:39
1 Chr. 22:18 land is s. before Lord
Neh. 9:24 thou s. inhabi. of land
Ps. 81:14 soon have s. enemies
1 Cor. 15:28 all be s. unto him
Heb. 11:33 thro' faith s. kingdo.

SUBDUETH.
Ps. 18:47 it is G. s. peo. 144:2
Dan. 2:40 iron breaks and s. all

SUBJECT.
Luke 2:51 Jesus was s. to them
10:17 L. even devils are s. to us
20 rejo. not spirits are s. to you
Rom. 8:7 it is not s. to law of G.
20 creature was s. to vanity
13:1 let eve. soul be s. to powers
5 wherefo. ye must needs be s.
1 Cor. 14:32 spirits of prophets
15:28 men sh. Son him. be s.
Eph. 5:24 as church is s. to Chr.
Col. 2:20 are ye s. to ordinances
Tit. 3:1 put in mind to s. to pow.
Jas. 2:15 lifetime s. to bondage
Jam. 5:17 Elias was s. to passio.
1 Pet. 2:18 serv. be s. to masters
3:22 pow. being made s. to him
5:5 all of you be s. one to ano.

SUBJECTED.
Rom. 8:20 who s. same in hope

SUBJECTION.
Ps. 106:42 enemies brou. into s.
Jer. 34:11 brought th. into s. 16
1 Cor. 9:27 br. my body into s.
2 Cor. 9:13 glorify G. for your s.
Gal. 2:5 we gave place by s. not
1 Tim. 2:11 wom. learn with all s.
3:4 having his children in s.
Heb. 2:5 put in s. world to come
8 put all things in s. under foot
12:9 rather be in s. to Father
1 Pet. 3:1 be in s. to husbands, 5

SUBMIT.
Gen. 16:9 s. thyself under her ha.
2 Sam. 22:45 strang. sh. s. them-
selves to me, Ps. 18:44
Ps. 66:3 enemies shall s. to thee
68:30 till every one s. with silv.
1 Cor. 16:16 that ye s. yourselves
Eph. 5:22 s. to husb. Col. 3:18
Heb. 13:17 s. th. watch for souls
Jas. 4:7 s. yourselves theref. to G.
1 Pet. 2:18 s. to every ordinance
5:5 younger s. yourselve, to older

SUBMITTED, ING.
1 Chr. 29:24 ons of Da. s. to Sol.
Ps. 81:15 haters of L. s. to him
Rom. 10:3 not s. to righteousness
Eph. 5:21 s. yours. one to anoth.

SUBORNED.
Acts 6:11 then they s. men who

SUBSCRIBE, D.
Is. 44:5 another shall s. unto L.
Jer. 32:10 I s. evidence, sealed it
12 in pres. of witnesses that s.
44 men shall s. evidences

SUBSTANCE.
Gen. 7:4 I will destroy ev. liv. s.
23 every living s. was destroyed
12:5 Abraham took s. they gath.
13:6 their s. was great, so they
15:14 shall come with great s.

SUC

Gen. 34:23 sh. not th. s. be ours?
36:6 E. took his cattle and his s.
Deut. 11:6 swallow. them and s.
33:11 bless, L. his s. accept work
Jos. 14:4 gave Lev. cities for s.
1 Chr. 27:31 th. were rulers of s.
28:1 stewards over all s. of king
2 Chr. 21:17 carried away all s.
31:3 appoint. king's portion of s.
32:29 God had given Hez. s.
35:7 bullocks, th. were king's s.
Ezr. 8:21 seek ri. way for our s.
10:8 come. s. should be forfeited
Job 1:3 Job's s. was 7,000 sheep
10 his s. increased in the land
5:5 robber swallow. up their s.
6:22 Give a reward of your s. ?
15:29 nor shall his s. continue
20:18 according to s. restitution
22:20 whereas our s. is not cut
30:22 liftest, and dissolv. my s.
Ps. 17:14 leave their s. to babes
105:21 made Joseph ruler over s.
139:15 my s. was not hid fr. thee
16 thine eyes did see my s.
Prov. 1:13 sh. find all precious s.
3:9 honour L. with s. first fruits
6:31 he shall give s. of house
8:21 cause th. love me inherit s.
10:3 he casteth away s. of wick.
12:27 s. of a diligent man preci.
28:8 he that by usury increas. s.
28:8 with harlots, spend. his s.
Cant. 8:7 if a man give s. for love
Jer. 15:13 s. give to spoil, 17:3
Hos. 12:8 I have found me out s.
Ob. 13 nor laid hands on their s.
Mic. 4:13 I will consecrate th. s.
Luke 8:3 minister. to him th. s.
15:13 prodigal wasted hir s.
Heb. 10:34 ye have in heaven a s.
11:1 faith is s. of thi. hoped for

SUCTILE.
Gen. 3:1 serpent more s. than any
2 Sam. 13:3 Jonadab was a s. man
Prov. 7:10 harlot, and s. of heart

SUBTILELY.
1 Sam. 23:22 told me, he deal. s.
Ps. 105:25 to deal s. with serv.
Acts 7:19 dealt s. with our kindr.

SUBTILTY.
Gen. 27:35 thy bro. came with s.
2 K. 10:19 Jehu did it in s. that
Prov. 1:4 to give to s. the simple
Mat. 26:4 might take Jesus by s.
Acts 13:10 O full of s. and mischi.
2 Cor. 11:3 beguiled Eve thro' s.

SUBURBS.
Lev. 25:34 field of s. not be sold
Num. 35:3 s. sh. be for th. cattle
7, 48 cit. six. ye give wi. th. s.
Jos. 14:4 save cities wi. s. 21:2
2 K. 23:11 took by chamber in s.
1 Chr. 11:14 Levites left their s.
2 Chr. 31:19 sh. stakes at sound
48:15 place for dwelli. and for s.
See cities.

SUBVERT, ED, ING.
Lam. 3:36 to s. a man L. approv.
Acts 15:24 troubled you, s. souls
2 Tim. 2:14 to the s. of hearers
Tit. 1:11 who s. whole houses
3:11 th. is such is s. and sinneth

SUCCEED, EST.
Deut. 12:29 when thou s. 19:1
25:6 first-born s. his broth. dead

SUCCEEDED.
Deut. 2:12 children of Es. s. 22
21 Ammonites s. them

SUCCESS.
Jos. 1:8 prosper and have good s.

SUCCOTH.
Gen. 33:17 Jacob journeyed to S.
therefore it is called S.
Ex. 12:37 jour. fr. Rameses to S.
13:20 journ. fr. S. Num. 33:5, 6
Jos. 13:27 God had in valley S.
Jud. 8:5 Gid. said to men of S.
6 Penuel answ. as men of S.
16 he taught men of S.
1 K. 7:46 clay-ground between S.
and Zarthan, 2 Chr. 4:17
Ps. 60:6 mete valley of S. 108:7

SUCCOTH-BENOTH.
2 K. 17:30 men of Bab. made S.

SUCCOR, ED.
2 Sam. 8:5 Syri. came to s. Had.
18:3 better thou s. us out of city
21:17 Abishai s. him, smote Phi.
2 Cor. 6:2 day of salva. I s. thee

SUF

SUCCORER.
Rom. 16:2 she hath been s.

SUCH.
Ex. 34:10 s. as ha. not been done
Rev. 20:6 on s. death ha. no pow.

SUCH a one.
Gen. 41:38 can we find s. a one
Ruth 4:1 ho, s. a one, turn aside

SUCH things.
Neh. 6:8 no s. t. done as thou say.

SUCH, Substantive.
Gen. 21:7 Sarah given children s.
1 Sam. 1:23 Hau. gave her son s.
1 K. 3:21 I rose to give child s.
Lam. 4:3 sea-monsters give s.
Mat. 21:16 them that gave s.
Mark 13:17; Luke 21:23
Luke 23:29 paps that never go. s.

SUCK, Verb.
Deut. 32:13 made him to s. honey
33:19 they shall s. of abund. of
Job 3:12 or breast I should s. ?
20:16 he shall s. poison of asps
39:30 young ones s. up blood
Is. 60:16 thou shalt s. milk of G.
and shalt s. breast of kings
66:11 that ye may s. and be satis.
12 then shall ye s. sh. be borne
Ezek. 23:34 them sh. even s. it out
Joel 2:16 gath. th. that s. breasts

SUCKED.
Cant. 8:1 s. breasts of mother
Luke 11:27 blessed are paps tho. s.

SUCKING.
Num. 11:12 as fa. beareth s. child
1 Sam. 7:9 Samuel took a s. lamb
Is. 11:8 s. ch. play on hole of asp
43:15 can a wom. forget s. child
Lam. 4:4 tongue of s. child cleav.

SUCKLING, S.
Deut. 32:25 s. wi. man of gr. hairs
1 Sam. 15:3 slay man, inf. and s.
22:19 Doeg smo. children and s.
Ps. 8:2 out of mouth of babes
and s. Mat. 21:16
Jer. 44:7 cut off fr. you ch. and s.
Lam. 2:11 s. swoon in streets

SUDDEN.
Job 22:10 s. fear troubleth thee
Prov. 3:25 nor afraid of s. fear
1 Thes. 5:3 then s. destruction

SUDDENLY.
Num. 6:9 if any man die s.
12:4 the Lord spake s. unto Mo.
Jos. 10:9 Joshua came s. 11:7
2 Sam. 15:14 lest he come, s.
Job 5:3 s. I cursed his habitat.
9:23 if scourge by day slay s.
Ps. 6:10 let them be ashamed s.
64:4 s. do they shoot at him
Prov. 6:15 he shall be broken s.
24:22 their calamity sh. rise s.
29:1 shall s. be destroyed.
Ec. 9:12 it falleth s. upon them
Is. 29:5 it shall be at an inst. s.
47:11 desolation shall come s.
48:3 I did them s. they came
Jer. 6:26 spoiler shall s. come
15:8 have caused him to fall s.
49:19 will s. ma. him run, 50:44
51:8 Babylon is s. destroyed
Hab. 2:7 sh. they not rise up s.
Mal. 3:1 the Lord shall s. come
Luke 9:39 and he s. crieth out
Acts 28:6 fallen down dead s.
1 Tim. 3:22 lay hands s. on no m.

SUE.
Mat. 5:40 if any man s. thee

SUFFER.
Ex. 22:18 sh. not s. witch to live
Lev. 19:17 not s. sin upon him
22:16 or s. th. to bear iniquity
Num. 21:23 sih. would not s. Is.
Jos. 10:19 s. not to enter cities
Jud. 15:7 that might not s. me
Est. 3:8 not king's profit to s.
Job 9:18 not s. me to take breath
21:3 s. me that I may speak
80:8 s. me a little, I will show
Ps. 9:13 consider trouble I s. of
55:22 nev. s. right. to be moved
89:38 while I s. terrors, I am
89:33 nor will I s. faithful. fail
101:5 proud heart, will not I s.
121:3 not s. foot to be moved
Prov. 10:3 L. not s. righte. fam.
19:15 idle soul shall s. hunger
Mat. 3:15 s. it to be so, for thus
7:9 ask of wrath sh. s. punish.
Ec. 5:6 s. not mouth to cause
12 abund. of rich not s. to sleep

CRUDEN'S CONCORDANCE. 1043

SUF

Ezek. 44:20 nor *s.* locks to grow
Mal. 3:15 Jesus said, *s.* it to be
8:21 *s.* me to bury, *Luke* 9:59
10:21 he must *s.* many things
17:12; *Mark* 8:31; *Lu.*
9:22; 17:25
17:17 how long shall I *s.* you?
Mark 9:19; *Luke* 9:41
19:14 *s.* little children, *Mark*
10:14; *Luke* 18:16
23:13 neither *s.* ye them th. are
Mark 7:12 *s.* him no more to do
11:16 Je. would not *s.* any man
Luke 22:51 *s.* ye this far,
24:46 it behooved Christ to *s.*
Acts 3:18; 26:23
Acts 3:18 G. showed Ch. should *s.*
5:41 counted worthy to *s.* shame
7:24 seeing one *s.* wrong
9:16 must *s.* for my name's sake
21:39 *s.* me to speak to people
Rom. 8:17 if so be we *s.* wi. him
1 *Cor.* 3:15 if work be burnt sh. *s.*
9:12 used power but *s.* all thi.
10:13 will not *s.* to be tempted
12:26 if one mem. *s.* all mem. *s.*
2 *Cor.* 1:6 same suffer, wh. we *s.*
11:20 ye *s.* if a man bring you
Gal. 6:12 lest they sh. *s.* persec.
Phil. 1:29 given to believe and *s.*
1 *Thes.* 3:4 told you, we should *s.*
2 *Thes.* 1:5 kingd. of G. for wh. *s.*
1 *Tim.* 4:10 we both labor and *s.*
2 *Tim.* 1:12 for wh. cause I also *s.*
2:9 wherein I *s.* as an evil doer
12 if we *s.* we shall also reign
Heb. 11:25 choosing to *s.* afflicti.
13:22 *s.* the word of exhortation
1 *Pet.* 3:17 if ye do well, and *s.*
3:14 if ye *s.* for righteousn. sake
17 it is bet. ye *s.* for well-doing
4:15 let none *s.* as a murderer
16 if any man *s.* as a Christian
19 let them that *s.* according to
Rev. 2:10 those things thou sh. *s.*
11:9 not *s.* dead bodies to be put

SUFFERED.
Gen. 20:6 therefore *s.* I thee not
31:7 God *s.* him not to hurt me
Deut. 8:3 he *s.* thee to hunger.
Jud. 3:28 *s.* not a man to pass
1 *Sam.* 21:7 D. *s.* them not to rise
1 *Chr.* 16:21 he *s.* no man to do
them wrong, *Ps.* 105:14
Job 31:30 neither have I *s.* mouth
Jer. 15:15 for thy sake I *s.* rebuke
Mat. 8:15 *s.* not. it to be so,
3:43 nor *s.* his hou. *Lu.* 12:39
27:19 I have *s.* many things this
Mark 1:34 he *s.* not dev. *Lu.* 4:41
9:10 Jesus *s.* him not, but said
20 8. many things of physici.
Luke 8:32 *s.* them to enter swine
51 he *s.* no man to go in,
13:2 because they *s.* such things
13:26 ought not Ch. to have *s.?*
Acts 13:18 about 40 years *s.* he
14:16 who *s.* all nations to walk
16:7 but the Spirit *s.* them not
19:30 discip. *s.* him not to enter
28:16 P. was *s.* to dwell by hims.
2 *Cor.* 7:12 not for his cau. th. *s.*
Gal. 3:4 have ye *s.* th. in vain ?
Phil. 3:8 for whom I *s.* loss of all
1 *Thes.* 2:2 after that we had *s.*
14 have *s.* like things of your
Heb. 2:18 in that *s.* being tempted
5:8 learn. obed. by things he *s.*
7:23 they were not *s.* to continue
9:26 then must he often have *s.*
13:12 Jesus *s.* without the gate
1 *Pet.* 2:21 Christ *s.* for us, leav.
23 when he *s.* he threatened
3:18 Christ hath once *s.* for sins
4:1 Christ hath *s.* for us in flesh,
he that hath *s.* in the flesh
6:10 after ye have *s.* a while

SUFFEREST.
Rev. 2:20 bec. thou *s.* that wom.

SUFFERETH.
Ps. 66:9 bless G. who *s.* not our
107:38 *s.* not cattle to decrease
Acts 28:4 vengeance *s.* him not
1 *Cor.* 13:4 charity *s.* long, is kind

SUFFERING.
Heb. 2:9 for *s.* of death, crown.

SUFFERINGS.
Rom. 8:18 I reckon that the *s* of
2 *Cor.* 1:5 for as the *s.* of Christ

SUN

2 *Cor.* 1:6 endur, same *s.* wh. we
7 ye are partakers of the *s.*
Phil. 3:10 fellowship of his *s.*
Col. 1:24 who now rejo. in my *s.*
Heb. 2:10 Captain perfect thro' *s.*
1 *Pet.* 1:11 it testified the *s.* of Ch.
4:13 ye are partakers of Ch.'s *s.*
5:1 I am a witn. of the *s.* of Ch.

SUFFICE.
Num. 11:22 sh. herds be *s.* to *s. ?*
Deut. 3:26 let it *s.* thee, speak no
1 *K.* 20:10 if dust of Samar. sh. *s.*
Ezek. 44:6 let it *s.* you of all, 45:9
1 *Pet.* 4:3 for the time past may *s.*

SUFFICED, ETH.
Jud. 21:14 wives, so they *s.* not
Ruth 2:14 she did eat, and was *s.*
18 gave her, after she was *s.*
John 14:8 L. show Fath. it *s.* us

SUFFICIENCY.
Ex. 36:7 the stuff th. had was *s.*
Deut. 13:8 then shalt lend him *s.*
33:7 let his hand be *s.* for him
Prov. 25:16 so much honey as *s.*
Is. 40:16 Leban. is not *s.* to burn
Mat. 6:34 *s.* to the day is the evil
Luke 14:28 whether he have *s.*
John 6:7 200 pennyworth is not *s.*
2 *Cor.* 2:6 *s.* to such a man is this
16 who is *s.* for these things ?
3:5 not that we *s.* of ourselves.
12:9 he said, My grace is *s.*

SUFFICIENTLY.
Is. 23:18 bef. the Lord to eat *s.*

SUIT, S.
Jud. 17:10 I will give thee a *s.*
2 *Sam.* 15:4 man who ha. any *s.*
Job 11:19 many sh. make *s.* unto
Is. 3:22 changeable *s.* of apparel

SUM, Substantive.
Ex. 30:12 if laid on him a *s.* of
38:21 this is the *s.* of tabernacle
Num. 1:2 take *s.* of congre. 26:2
26:4 take the *s.* of the people
31:26 take the *s.* of the prey
2 *Sam.* 24:9 Joab gave up *s.* to
king, 1 *Chr.* 21:5
Est. 4:7 the *s.* of money Haman
Ps. 139:17 great is the *s.* of th.
Ezek. 28:12 thou sealest up the *s.*
Dan. 7:1 Daniel told *s.* of dream
Acts 7:16 Abraham bought for *s.*
22:28 with a great *s.* obtained I
Heb. 8:1 of the things th. is the *s.*

SUM.
2 *K.* 22:4 that he may *s.* the silver

SUMMER.
Gen. 8:22 *s.* and winter, day and
Ps. 32:4 turned into drought of *s.*
74:17 thou hast made *s.* and
Prov. 6:8 provid. meat in *s.* 30:25
10:5 gathereth in *s.* is wise son
26:1 snow in *s.* rain in harvest
Is. 28:4 as hasty fruit before *s.*
Jer. 8:20 harv. is past, *s.* is end.
Dan. 2:35 chaff of *s.* threshing-fl.
Zec. 14:8 in *s.* and in winter it
Mat. 24:32 ye know *s.* is nigh,
Mark 13:28; *Luke* 21:30

SUMMER chamber.
Jud. 3:24 he cov. his feet in *s. c.*

SUMMER fruit.
2 *Sam.* 16:2 *s. f.* for young men
Amos 8:1 a basket of *s. fruit,* 2

SUMMER fruits.
2 *Sam.* 16:1 bro. 100 bun. of *s. f.*
Is. 16:9 shouting for *s. f.*
Jer. 40:10 en. wine and *s. f.* 12
48:32 spoiler is fallen on *s. f.*
Mic. 7:1 as wh. they gather *s. f.*

SUMMER-HOUSE.
Amos 3:15 smite winter-ho. *s.-h.*

SUMMER parlor.
Jud. 3:20 Eg. was sitting in *s. p.*

SUMMER.
Is. 18:6 fowls sh. *s.* upon them

SUMPTUOUSLY.
Luke 16:19 rich man fared *s.*

SUN.
Gen. 15:17 when *s.* went down
19:23 *s.* risen when Lot entered
32:31 Jacob harried, bec. *s.* was
32:31 sun passed Pen. *s.* rose
37:9. moon, stars, made obeis.
Ex. 22:3 when *s.* is risen on him
22:26 raiment to pledge, *s.* gocth
Lev. 22:7 when *s.* is down, he
shall be clean, *Deut.* 23:11

SUN

Num. 25:4 hang them ag. the *s.*
Deut. 4:19 lest wh. thou seest *s.*
17:3 hath worshipped either *s.*
24:15 nor sh. *s.* go down upon it
33:14 precious fruits brou. by *s.*
Jos. 1:4 tow. going down of *s.*
10:12 *s.* stand still upon Gibeon
13 *s.* stood still, moon stayed
Jud. 5:31 that love him be as *s.*
8:13 G. return, before *s.* was up
9:33 soon as *s.* is up, rise early
14:18 said, before *s.* went down
19:14 *s.* went down, they were
2 *Sam.* 11:9 *s.* be hot have help
2 *Sam.* 3:35 aught till *s.* be down
12:11 lie with wives in si. of *s.*
1 will do this bef. Is. and *s.*
23:4 light of morn. when *s.* ris.
2 *K.* 3:22 and *s.* shone on water
23:5 them that burn ince. to *s.*
11 burnt chari. of *s.* with fire
Neh. 7:3 gates be ope. till *s.* hot
Job 8:16 hypocrite green bef. *s.*
9:7 commandeth *s.* riseth not
30:28 I went mourn. without *s.*
31:26 if I beheld *s.* when it shi.
37:21 men see not bright *s.*
58:8 pass aw. th. they see not *s.*
72:5 fear thee as long as *s.*
17 name contin. as long as *s.*
74:16 prepared light and *s.*
84:11 G. is a *s.* and shield
89:36 his throne sh. endure as *s.*
104:22 *s.* ariseth, they gather th.
121:6 *s.* shall not smite by day
136:8 him that made *s.* to rule
148:3 praise him, *s.* and moon
Ec. 1:5 *s.* riseth, *s.* goeth down
6:5 moreo. he hath not seen *s.*
11:7 pleas. for eyes to behold *s.*
12:2 wh. *s.* or stars be not dark.
Cant. 1:6 bec. *s.* looked on me
6:10 fair as moon, clear as *s.*
Is. 24:23 then *s.* sh. be ashamed
30:26 light of moon as *s.* light
49:10 nor heat nor *s.* smite th.
60:19 *s.* be no more li. by day
20 *s.* shall no more go down
Jer. 15:9 her *s.* is gone down
31:35 wh. giveth the *s.* for light
32:7 I will cover *s.* with cloud
Joel 2:10 *s.* be dark. 3:15; *Mat.*
24:29; *Mark* 13:24
31 *s.* sh. be turned to darkness
Amos 8:9 cause *s.* to go down
Jon. 4:8 wh. *s.* did arise, *s.* beat
Mic. 3:6 *s.* go down over proph.
Nah. 3:17 *s.* ariseth, they flee
Mat. 5:45 maketh his *s.* to rise
13:43 then sit. right. shine as *s.*
17:2 his face did shine as the *s.*
Mark 1:16; 10:1
Mark 1:32 *s.* set, they bro. sick
4:6 when *s.* was setting
Acts 2:20 the *s.* into darkness
26:13 light above brightn. of *s.*
27:20 nei. *s.* nor stars appeared
1 *Cor.* 15:41 th. is one glory of *s.*
Eph. 4:26 let not *s.* go down
Jam. 1:11 *s.* is no sooner risen
Rev. 6:12 *s.* became as sackcloth
7:16 nor shall *s.* light on them
9:12 third part of *s.* was smit.
10:2 *s.* and the air were darken.
16:8 angel poured out vial on *s.*
19:17 I saw angel standing in *s.*
21:23 city had no need of *s.* 22:5

See GOETH, GOING, LIGHT.

Under the SUN.
Ec. 1:9 no new thing *und. the s.?*
2:18, 19, 20, 22; 5:18; 9:9
9 there is no new thing *u. t. s.*
14 I have seen all works done
2:11, 17; 4:3, 4; 8:17; 9:3
2:11 there was labor to do *u. s.*
3:16 I saw *u. t. s.* place of judg.
4:7 returned, I saw vanity *u. s.*
7 I beheld I *went u. t. s.* 6:1; 10:5
5:13 evil which I seen *u. t. s.* 6:1
6:1 an evil I have seen *u. t. s.* 10:5
8:9 up. heart in every work *u. s.*
15 hath no better thing *u. t. s.*
9:6 portion in any thing *u. t. s.*
9 days he hath given th. *u. t. s.*
11 I saw *u. t. s.* race not to swi.
13 wisdom have I seen *u. t. s.*

SUNDER.
Ps. 46:9 cutteth the spear in *s.*
107:14 he brake their bonds in *s.*
16 he hath cut bars of iron in *s.*
Is. 27:9 chalk stones bunten in *s.*

SUP

Ps. 45:2 I will cut in *s.* bars of ir.
Nah. 1:13 I will burst bonds in *s.*
Luke 12:46 and cut him in *s.*

SUNDERED.
Job 41:17 stick, they cannot be *s.*

SUNDRY.
Heb. 1:1 God who at *s.* times

SUNG.
Is. 26:1 this song be *s.* in Judah
Mat. 26:30 *s.* hymn, *Mark* 14:26
Rev. 5:9 they *s.* a new song
14:3 *s.* as it were a new song

SUNK.
1 *Sam.* 17:49 stone *s.* into foreh.
2 *K.* 9:24 Jehoram *s.* in chariot
Ps. 9:15 heath. are *s.* in the pit
Jer. 38:6 down, so Jer. *s.* in mire
22 thy feet are *s.* in the mire
Lam. 2:9 her gates are *s.* in the
Acts 20:9 Eutychus *s.* down with

SUP, PED.
Hab. 1:9 their faces shall *s.* up
Luke 17:8 make ready, I may *s.*
1 *Cor.* 11:25 took cup, when he *s.*
Rev. 3:20 I will *s.* with him, he

SUPERFLUITY.
Jam. 1:21 filthiness *s.* of naugh.

SUPERFLUOUS.
Lev. 21:18 man hath any thing *s.*
22:23 lamb, th. hath any thi. *s.*
2 *Cor.* 9:1 it is *s.* to write to you

SUPERSCRIPTION.
Mat. 22:20 wh. is image and *s. ?*
Mark 12:16; *Luke* 20:24
Mark 15:26 *s.* of accu. *Luke* 23:38

SUPERSTITION.
Acts 25:19 questi. ag. him of *s.*

SUPERSTITIOUS.
Acts 17:22 in all thi. ye are too *s.*

SUPPER.
Mark 6:21 Herod made *s.* to lords
Luke 14:12 makest a dinner or *s.*
16 a cert. man made a great *s.*
24 none bid. shall taste of my *s.*
22:20 likewise also cup after *s.*
John 12:2 ther. they made Je. *s.*
13:2 *s.* ended; 4 Je. ris. from *s.*
21:20 disc. lean. on breast at *s.*
1 *Cor.* 11:20 not to eat Lord's *s.*
21 taketh bef. other his own *s.*
Rev. 19:9 that are called to the *s.*
17 come to *s.* of the great God

SUPPLANT, ED.
Gen. 27:36 hath *s.* me two times
Jer. 9:4 every bro. will utterly *s.*

SUPPLE.
Ezek. 16:4 nei. washed to *s.* thee

SUPPLIANTS.
Zep. 3:10 my *s.* shall bring offer.

SUPPLICATION.
1 *Sam.* 13:12 I have not made *s.*
1 *K.* 8:28 respect to *s.* 2 *Chr.* 6:19
30 hearken thou to *s.* 45, 49
52 eyes open to *s.* of thy serv.
54 made end of praying and *s.*
59 words wherewith I made *s.*
9:3 I heard thy *s.* th. hast made
2 *Chr.* 6:29 what *s.* shall be made
32:12 Lord heard Manasseh's *s.*
Job 8:5 wouldest make *s.* to Al.
9:15 I w. make my *s.* to judge
Ps. 6:9 Lo. I hath heard my *s.*
30:8 to L. I made my *s.* 142:1
55:1 hide not thyself from my *s.*
119:170 let my *s.* come bef. thee
Jer. 36:7 th. will present their *s.*
37:20 present. my *s.* bef. king
42:2 let our *s.* be accepted bef.
9 ye sent me to present your *s.*
Dan. 6:11 was present. *s.* bef. G.
9:20 I was present. *s.* before G.
Hos. 12:4 made *s.* to angel and
Acts 1:14 these contin. in pr. *s.*
Eph. 6:18 praying with all *s.* and
Phil. 4:6 by prayer and *s.* let req.

SUPPLICATIONS.
2 *Chr.* 6:21 hearken to *s.* of serv.
39 hear thou *s.* prayer and *s.*
Job 41:3 will Levi. make m. *s. ?*
Ps. 28:6 voice of my *s.* 140:6
31:22 heard my *s.* 31:17; 116:1
Jer. 3:21 weeping and *s.* of Isra.
31:9 with *s.* will I lead them
Dan. 9:3 I set face to seek by *s.*
17 hear prayer of serv. and *s.*
18 we do not pres. *s.* for right.

1044 CRUDEN'S CONCORDANCE.

SUR

Dan. 9:23 begin. of *s.* com. came
Zec. 12:10 pour out Spirit of *s.*
1 Tim. 2:1 *s.* be made for all men
3:5 continueth in *s.* and prayer
Heb. 5:7 be offered prayers and *s.*

SUPPLY, Substantive.
2 Cor. 8:14 abund. may be a *s.*
Phil. 1:19 through prayer and *s.*

SUPPLY, Verb.
Phil. 2:30 not regard. to *s.* lack
4:19 God shall *s.* all your need

SUPPLIED, ETH.
1 Cor. 16:17 what lack. they *s.*
2 Cor. 9:12 not only *s.* want of
11:9 what lacking, brethren *s.*
Eph. 4:16 that wh. every joint *s.*

SUPPORT.
Acts 20:35 ought to *s.* the weak,
1 Thes. 5:14

SUPPOSE.
2 Sam. 13:32 let not my lord *s.*
Luke 7:43 I *s.* that he to whom
12:51 *s.* I am co. to give peace
13:2 *s.* ye these Galileans were
John 21:25 I *s.* world could not
1 Cor. 7:26 I *s.* that this is good
2 Cor. 11:5 I *s.* I was not behind
1 Pet. 5:12 a faithful bro. as I *s.*

SUPPOSED.
Mat. 20:10 they *s.* they sho. have
Mark 6:49 *s.* it had been a spirit
Luke 3:23 Je. as was *s.* son of J.
Acts 7:25 *s.* his brethren would
25:18 none accus. of thi. as I *s.*
Phil. 2:25 I *s.* it neces. to send

SUPPOSING.
Luke 2:44 *s.* him to have been
Acts 14:19 drew P. out, *s.* he had
16:27 jailor *s.* prisoners had fled
27:13 *s.* they had obt. purpose
Phil. 1:16 *s.* to add affliction
1 Tim. 6:5 corrupt minds *s.* gain

SUPREME.
1 Pet. 2:13 whether to king as *s.*

SURE.
Ex. 3:19 I am *s.* king will not
Num. 32:23 be *s.* sin will find
1 Sam. 2:35 build a *s.* house
2 Sam. 23:5 cove. ordered and *s.*
1 K. 11:38 I build thee a *s.* house
Job 24:24 no man is *s.* of life
Ps. 111:7 his commandm. are *s.*
Prov. 6:3 make *s.* thy friend
Is. 33:16 bread given, waters *s.*
55:3 *s.* mercies of D. **Acts** 13:34
John 6:69 are *s.* thou art Christ
16:30 are we *s.* thou knowest
Rom. 15:29 I am *s.* when I come

SURELY.
Ez. 8:12 *s.* it sh. be well with th.
Is. 45:14 *s.* G. is in th. and there
Mat. 26:73 *s.* thou art one of th.
Mark 14:70
Rev. 22:20 *s.* I come quickly
See **DIE.**

SURELY be put to death.
Gen. 2:17 man, *s.* be put to d.
Ex. 19:12 tou. mount, *s.* p. to d.
21:12 killeth, sh. *s.* be put to d.
15 smiteth fa. sh. *s.* be put to d.
16 steal. a man, sh. *s.* be p. to d.
17 curseth his father, shall *s.*
be put to death, **Lev.** 20:9
22:19 lieth with beast, sh. *s.* be
put to death, **Lev.** 20:15, 16
31:14 defileth sab. *s.* p. to d. 15
Lev. 20:2 giveth to M. *s.* p. to d.
10 adulterous sh. *s.* be put to d.
11 lieth wi. fa. wife, bo. *s.* p. d.
12 daughter-in-l. both *s.* p. to d.
13 lie wi. mank. bo. *s.* p. to d.
24:16 blasphem. sh. *s.* be p. to d.
17 killeth mau, sh. *s.* be put to
d. **Num.** 35:16, 17, 18, 21, 31
27:29 but shall *s.* be put to death
Jud. 21:5 ca. not, *s.* be put to d.
Jer. 38:15 w. not *s.* p. me to d.?

SURETY.
Gen. 43:9 I will be *s.* for him
44:32 thy serv. bec. *s.* for lad
Job 17:3 put me in a *s.* with th.
Ps. 119:122 be *s.* for thy serv.
Prov. 6:1 if thou be *s.* for friend
11:15 he that is *s.* for stranger
17:18 becometh *s.* in presence
20:16 *s.* for stranger, 27:13
Heb. 7:22 Je. made *s.* of a better

SURETIES.
Prov. 22:26 not of th. that are *s.*

Of a SURETY.
Gen. 15:13 know of a *s.* thy seed
18:13 sh. I of a *s.* bear a child?

SWA

Gen. 26:9 of a *s.* she is thy wife
Acts 12:11 of a *s.* Lord sent ang.

SURETYSHIP.
Prov. 11:15 he that hateth *s.*

SURFEITING.
Luke 21:34 overcharged with *s.*

SURMISINGS.
1 Tim. 6:4 whereof com. evil *s.*

SURNAME, Substantive.
Mat. 10:3 Lebbeus, *s.* was Thad.
Acts 10:5 Sim. *s.* is P. 32; 11:13
12:12 John, *s.* was M. 25; 15:37

SURNAME, Verb.
Is. 44:5 *s.* hims. by name of Isr.

SURNAMED.
Is. 45:4 *s.* thee, tho' not kn. me
Mark 3:16 Si. he *s.* P. **Acts** 10:18
17 he *s.* th. Boanerges, sons of
Acts 1:23 Barsabas, who was *s.* J.
4:36 by apostles was *s.* Barnab.

SURPRISED.
Is. 33:14 fearfuln. *s.* hypocrites
Jer. 48:41 the strong-holds are *s.*
51:41 how is praise of earth *s.*!

SUSANNA.
Luke 8:3 Joanna and S. minist.

SUSTAIN, ED.
Gen. 27:37 wi. corn and wi. I
1 K. 17:9 comman. a widow to *s.*
Neh. 9:21 forty years didst *s.* th.
Ps. 3:5 I awaked, the Lord *s.* me
55:22 burden on L, he sh. *s.* th.
Prov. 18:14 spirit of man will *s.*
Is. 59:16 his righteous. it *s.* him

SUSTENANCE.
Jud. 6:4 Midian. left no *s.* for Is.
2 Sam. 19:32 Barzillai provid. *s.*
Acts 7:11 our fathers found no *s.*

SWADDLED.
Lam. 2:22 tho. I *s.* hath my ene.
Ezek. 16:4 not salt. not *s.* at all

SWADDLING.
Ez. 38:13 to whom I made *s.* band
Luke 2:7 wrap. him in *s.* clo. 12

SWALLOW.
Ps. 8:3 like *s.* hath found a nest
Prov. 26:2 as *s.* by flying, so the
Is. 38:14 like a crane or a *s.* did I
Jer. 8:7 crane and *s.* observe ti.

SWALLOW, Verb.
Num. 16:30 if earth open and *s.*
34 lest the earth *s.* us up also
2 Sam. 20:19 why wilt thou *s.* up
20 that I should *s.* up or destr.
Job 7:19 nor wilt thou let *s.* dow.
20:18 shall restore, and not *s.* it
Ps. 21:9 the L. shall *s.* them up
56:1 O G. man would *s.* me up
2 mine ene. would *s.* me up
57:3 repr. of him that would *s.*
69:15 nei. let the deep *s.* me up
Prov. 1:12 let us *s.* them up alive
Ec. 10:12 lips of fool *s.* up hims.
Is. 25:8 will *s.* up death in vict.
Hos. 8:7 strangers shall *s.* it up
Amos 8:4 ye that *s.* needy
Ob. 16 and they shall *s.* down•
Jon. 1:17 Lord prep. a fish to *s.*
Mat. 23:24 stra. at gnat, *s.* camel

SWALLOWED.
Ex. 7:12 Aaron's rod *s.* th. rods
15:12 stretch. thy hand, earth *s.*
Num. 16:32 earth opened and *s.*
26:10; **Deut.** 11:6
2 **Sam.** 17:16 lest king be *s.* up
Job 6:3 theref. my words are *s.*
20:15 he hath *s.* down riches
37:20 if speak, he sh. be *s.* up
Ps. 35:25 not say, we *s.* him up
106:17 the earth *s.* up Dathan
124:3 they had *s.* us up quick
Is. 28:7 priest and prophet are *s.*
49:19 they that *s.* thee up, shall
Jer. 51:34 *s.* me up like a dragon
44 br. out mouth that he ha. *s.*
Lam. 2:2 Lord hath *s.* up inhab.
5 he hath *s.* up Israel, hath *s.*
16 they say, We have her up
Ezek. 36:3 they have *s.* you up
Hos. 8:8 Israel is *s.* up. now
1 Cor. 15:54 death is *s.* up in vic.
2 Cor. 2:7 lest such a one be *s.* up
5:4 that mortal. might be *s.* up
Rev. 12:16 earth *s.* up the flood

SWALLOWETH.
Job 5:5 robber *s.* their substance
39:24 he *s.* ground with fierceu.

SWAN.
Lev. 11:18 *s.* unc. **Deut.** 14:16

SWARE.
Gen. 21:31 because th. *s.* both of
24:7 L. God of heaven *s.* to me

SWE

Gen. 24:9 servant *s.* to him conc.
25:33 Ja. said, Sw. to me, he *s.*
26:3 oath which I *s.* to Abrah.
31 Abimel. and Isaac *s.* to one
31:53 Jacob *s.* by fear of Isaac
47:31 Jos. *s.* to Jacob his father
50:24 G. will br. to land he *s.* to
Ex. 13:5 land the Lord *s.* to thy
fathers, 11; 33:1; **Num.** 14:16
30; 32:11; **Deut.** 1:8, 35; 6:10,
18, 23; 7:13; 8:1; 11:9, 21;
26:3; 28:11; 30:20; 31:21, 23;
34:4; **Jos.** 1:6; 5:6; 21:43
Num. 32:10 L. 's anger was kind.
and he *s.* **Deut.** 1:34
Deut. 2:14 were wasted, as L. *s.*
4:21 Lord *s.* that I should not
31 not forget the coven. he *s.*
7:12 wh. he *s.* to thy salvation
8:18 covenant which he *s.* 9:5
Jos. 6:22 br. out Rahab as ye *s.*
9:15 princes *s.* to Gibeonites
20 because of oath we *s.* to th.
14:9 M. *s.* on that day, saying
21:44 according to all that he *s.*
Jud. 2:1 bro. to land which I *s.*
1 Sam. 19:6 Saul *s.* Da. shall not
24:22 David *s.* to Saul
2 Sam. 3:35 Da. *s.* he would not
19:23 D. *s.* to Shimei, **1 K.** 2:8
1 K. 2:23 S. *s.* to A. he sho. die
2 **K.** 25:24 Gedaliah *s.* **Jer.** 40:9
1 Chr. 15:14 they *s.* to the Lord
Ezr. 10:5 they *s.* to put away
Ps. 95:11 I *s.* in wrath, **Heb.** 3:11
132:2 how he *s.* to L. and vowed
Jer. 38:16 king *s.* secretly to Jer.
Ezek. 16:8 I *s.* and entered cove.
Dan. 12:7 *s.* by him, **Rev.** 10:6
Mark 6:23 Herod *s.* to daughter
Luke 1:73 oath which he *s.* to A.
Heb. 3:18 to whom *s.* he that th.
6:13 no greater, he *s.* by himself
7:21 Lord *s.* and will not repent
See **Their Fathers.**

SWAREST.
Ex. 32:13 to whom thou *s.* by
Num. 11:12 carry them to land *s.*
Deut. 26:15 as thou *s.* to our fat.
1 K. 1:17 thou *s.* that Solomon
Ps. 89:49 kindnesses th. *s.* to D.

SWARM.
Ex. 8:21 I will send *s.* of flies
22 no *s.* of flies shall be in Go.
24 there came a grie. *s.* of flies
29 that *s.* of flies may depart
Jud. 14:8 a *s.* of bees and honey

SWEAR.
Gen. 21:23 Abim. said to Abr. *s.*
24 and Abraham said, I will *s.*
24:3 I will make thee *s.* by L.
37 my master made me *s.*
25:33 Jacob said, *s.* to me
47:31 Jacob said to Joseph, *s.*
50:5 father made me *s.* saying
Ez. 6:8 Lord concerning wife, I *s.*
Lev. 5:4 if a soul *s.* pronouncing
19:12 ye shall not *s.* by name
Num. 30:2 if a man *s.* to bind
Deut. 6:13 *s.* by his name, 10:20
Jos. 2:12 Rahab said to spies, *s.*
23:7 nor cause to *s.* by th. gods
Jud. 15:12 *s.* ye will not fall
1 Sam. 20:17 Jon. caused D. to *s.*
24:21 *s.* th. wilt not cut off seed
30:15 *s.* thou wilt nei. kill me
2 **Sam.** 19:7 *s.* by L. if th. go not
1 K. 1:13 didst th. *s.* sh. **Solo.** reign
51 let Solo. *s.* unto me to-day
2:8 he sent to me, he *s.* by L.
8:31 oath laid on him to cause
him to *s.* **2 Chr.** 6:22
2 **Chr.** 36:13 Nebuc. made him *s.*
Ezr. 10:5 Ezra, Lev. and Isr. *s.*
Neh. 13:25 them I *s.* not take
Is. 19:18 five cities in Egypt sh. *s.*
45:23 to me ev. tongue shall *s.*
48:1 wh. *s.* by L. not in truth.
65:16 that swear. shall *s.* by G.
Jer. 4:2 thou shalt *s.* Lord liveth
5:2 Lord liveth, they *s.* falsely
7:9 murder, commit adultery, *s.*
12:16 *s.* by my name, as pers. *s.*
22:5 I *s.* saith Lord, this house
32:22 giv. them land th. didst *s.*
Hos. 4:15 not go to Beth-a. nor *s.*
Amos 8:14 *s.* by sin of Samaria
Zep. 1:5 that *s.* by L. *s.* by Mal.
Mat. 5:34 *s.* not; 36 *s.* not by h.
23:16 *s.* by temple, *s.* by gold
18 whoso shall *s.* by altar
20 whoso theref. sh. *s.* by altar
21 *s.* by temple; 22 *s.* by heav.
26:74 to curse, *s.* **Mark** 14:71
Heb. 6:13 *s.* by no greater, he *s.*

SWE

Heb. 6:16 men verily *s.* by the gr.
Jam. 5:12 my brethren *s.* not

SWEARERS.
Mal. 3:5 a swift witness ag. *s.*

SWEARETH.
Lev. 6:3 was lost, and *s.* falsely
Ps. 15:4 that *s.* to his hurt
63:11 every one that *s.* by him
Ec. 9:2 he that *s.* as he feareth
Is. 65:16 he that *s.* swear by G.
Zec. 5:3 every one that *s.* cut off
4 enter house of him that *s.*
Mat. 23:18 whosoever *s.* by gift
20 *s.* by altar; 21 *s.* by temple
22 *s.* by throne of God

SWEARING.
Lev. 5:1 soul sin, hear voice of *s.*
Jer. 23:10 bec. of *s.* land mourn.
Hos. 4:2 by *s.* lying, and steal.
10:4 *s.* falsely in making coven.

SWEAT.
Gen. 3:19 in *s.* of face eat bread
Ezek. 44:18 any thing causeth *s.*
Luke 22:44 *s.* as drops of blood

SWEEP.
Is. 14:23 *s.* it wi. besom of dest.
28:17 hail sh. *s.* refuge of lies
Luke 15:8 doth not *s.* house

SWEEPING.
Prov. 28:3 is like *s.* rain which

SWEET.
Ex. 15:25 tree into wat. made *s.*
30:23 *s.* cinna. and *s.* calamus
2 **Sam.** 23:1 D. *s.* psalmist of Isr.
Neh. 8:10 eat fat, drink the *s.*
Job 20:12 wickedness *s.* in mouth
21:33 clods of valley shall be *s.*
38:31 bind *s.* influ. of Pleiades?
Ps. 55:14 we took *s.* counsel
104:34 medita. of him sh. be *s.*
119:103 *s.* thy words to taste
141:6 hear my words, they are *s.*
Prov. 3:24 thy sleep shall be *s.*
9:17 stolen waters are *s.* bread
13:19 desire accomplished is *s.*
16:24 pleasant words are *s.*
20:17 bread of dec. *s.* to a man
23:8 and lose thy *s.* words
24:13 eat honey-comb wh. is *s.*
27:7 to han. soul bitter thing *s.*
Ec. 5:12 sleep of laboring man *s.*
11:7 truly light is *s.* pl. thing
Cant. 2:3 fruit *s.* 14; *s.* is voice
5:5 fingers drop. with *s.* myrrh
13 as *s.* flowers, drops. *s.* myrrh
16 his mouth is most *s.* lovely
Is. 3:24 inst. of *s.* smell, stink
5:20 that put bitter for *s.* and *s.*
23:16 make *s.* melody, si. songs
Jer. 6:20 nor your sacri. *s.* to me
31:26 my sleep was *s.* to me
Jam. 3:11 pl. *s.* water and bitter?
Rev. 10:9 in mouth *s.* as hon. 10
See **Incense, Odors, Savor.**

SWEET cane.
Is. 43:24 thou brou. me no *s. s.*
Jer. 6:20 *s. s.* came fr. a far coun.

SWEET spices.
Ex. 30:34 take *s. s.* frankincense
37:29 he made pure inc. of *s. s.*
Mark 16:1 brou. *s. s.* anoint him

SWEET wine.
Is. 49:26 drun. wi. blood as *s. w.*
Amos 9:13 moun. shall drop *s. w.*
Mic. 6:15 *s. w.* but not drink wine

SWEETER.
Jud. 14:18 what is *s.* th. honey?
Ps. 19:12 thy word *s.* th. honey
119:103 words *s.* than honey

SWEETLY.
Job 24:20 worms shall feed *s.*
Cant. 7:9 best wi. goeth down *s.*

SWEETNESS.
Jud. 9:11 sho. I forsake my *s.*?
14:14 out of strong came forth *s.*
Prov. 16:21 *s.* of lips incr. learn.
27:9 so doth *s.* of a man's friend
Ezek. 3:3 his mouth as hon. for *s.*

SWELL, ED.
Num. 5:21 th. rot, belly to *s.* 22
27 belly shall *s.* thigh shall rot
Deut. 8:4 nor thy foot *s.* 40 years
Neh. 9:21 forty years forti. *s.* not

SWELLING, S.
Ps. 46:3 tho' mount. shake wi. *s.*
Is. 30:13 as *s.* breach *s.* in a wall
Jer. 12:5 how do in *s.* of Jordan?
49:19 lion from *s.* of Jord. 50:44
2 **Cor.** 12:20 lest there be *s.* tum.
2 Pet. 2:18 speak *s.* words of van.
Jude 16 their mouth speaketh *s.* words

CRUDEN'S CONCORDANCE. 1045

SWO
SWEPT.
Jud. 5:21 riv. of Kishon s. them
Jer. 46:15 why valiant s. away?
Mat. 12:44 find. it s. Luke 11:25

SWERVED.
1 Tim. 1:6 having s. turned aside

SWIFT.
Deut. 28:49 nation s. as eagle
1 Chr. 12:8 s. as roes on mount.
Job 9:26 passed away as s. ships
21:13 he is s. as waters, behold.
Prov. 6:18 feet s. run. to mischi.
Ec. 9:11 the race is not to s.
Is. 18:2 go, ye s. messengers
19:1 behold, L. rid. on s. cloud
30:16 ride on s. th. pursue he s.
66:20 bring brethr. on s. beasts
Jer. 46:6 let not s. flee away, nor
Amos 2:14 flight sh. perish fr. s.
15 s. of foot sh. not deli. hims.
Mic. 1:13 bind chariot to s. beast
Mal. 3:5 s. s. with. ag. sorcerers
Rom. 3:15 feet s. to shed blood
Jam. 1:19 let every man be s.
2 Pet. 2:1 sh. bring s. destruction

SWIFTER.
2 Sam. 1:23 were s. than eagles
Job 7:6 days are s. than shuttle
9:25 my days are s. than a post
Jer. 4:13 his horses s. than eagles
Lam. 4:19 persecut. s. th. eagles
Hab. 1:8 horses s. than leopards

SWIFTLY.
Ps. 147:15 his word runneth s.
Is. 5:26 behold, they sh. come s.
Dan. 9:21 Gabriel caused to fly s.
Joel 3:4 if ye recompense me s.

SWIM.
2 K. 6:6 and the iron did s.
Ps. 6:6 night ma. I my bed to s.
Is. 25:11 spread. forth hands to s.
Ezek. 47:5 risen, waters to s. in
Acts 27:42 lest any should s. out
43 comman. they that could s.

SWIMMEST, ETH.
Is. 25:11 as he that s. spreadeth
Ezek. 32:6 water land wher. th. s.

SWINE.
Lev. 11:7 s. is unclean, Deut. 14:8
Prov. 11:22 a jewel in a s. snout
Is. 65:4 which s. flesh and broth
66:3 as if he offered s. blood
17 eating s. flesh and abomin.
Mat. 7:6 nei. cast pearls befo. s.
8:30 herd of s. feeding, Mark 5:11; Luke 8:32
31 go into herd of s. Mark 5:12
32 went into s. the herd of s. ran, Mark 5:13; Luke 8:33
Mark 5:14 that went out to s. and
Luke 15:15 he sent him to feed s.
16 filled belly with husks s. eat

SWOLLEN.
Acts 28:6 look. he should have s.

SWOON, ED.
Lam. 2:11 children s. in street
12 wh. they s. as the wounded

SWORD.
Gen. 3:24 cherubim and flam. s.
27:40 by thy s. shalt thou live
34:26 took each man his s.
Ex. 5:21 put a s. in their hand
32:27 put cv. man his s. by side
Lev. 26:6 nor s. go through land
25 br. s. upon yon, Ezek. 5:17; 6:3; 14:17; 29:8; 33:2
33 I will draw out s. after you
37 they sh. fall as were bef. s.
Num. 22:23 angel's s. drawn, 31
29 there was a s. in my hand
Deut. 13:25 s. without. terror
32:25 s. s. of thy excellency
Jos. 5:13 stood with his s. drawn
24:12 not with thy s. nor bow
Jud. 7:18 s. of L. and Gideon, 20
8:20 youth drew not his s.
9:54 draw thy s. and slay me
20:25 drew s. 25,000 that drew s.
46 fell were 25,000 that drew s.
1 Sam. 13:22 neither s. nor spear
15:33 s. as made wom. children
17:39 David girded s. on, 25:11
50 Is. was no s. in hand of Da.
51 D. took his s. and slew him
21:8 not und. hand spear or s.
9 s. of Goli. is wrapt in a cloth
22:10 he gave him s. of Goliath
13 given him bread and s.
25:13 gird ye on cv. man his s.
31:4 Saul took s. s. fell upon it
5 armour-bearer fell upon his s.
2 Sam. 1:22 s. of S. returned not
2:16 thrust s. into fellow's side
26 shall, Sh. s. devour for ever?
3:29 not fail one that fall. on s.

SWO
2 Sam. 11:25 s. devo. one as ano.
12:10 s. sh. never dep. fr. house
18:8 wood devour. more than s.
20:10 Amasa took no heed to s.
23:10 his hand clave unto s.
24:9 in Is. 800,000 men drew s.
1 K. 3:24 bring s. they brough. s.
19:17 that escapeth s. of Hazael
1 Chr. 5:18 men able to bear s.
10:4 Saul took s. s. fell upon it
5 his armor-bear. fell on the s.
21:5 s. 100,000 that drew s.
12 or 3 days s. s. of the Lord
16 the angel having a s. drawn
27 he put up his s. again
30 he was afraid of s. of angel
2 Chr. 20:9 wh. s. of judgm. com.
32:21 kings are delivered to s.
Neh. 4:18 ev. one had his s. gird.
Est. 9:5 Jews smote ene. with s.
Job 5:20 deliver from power of s.
15:22 he is waited for of the s.
19:29 s. for wrath, punish. of s.
20:25 glittering s. cometh out
27:14 if be multiplied it is for s.
40:19 make his s. to approach
41:26 s. of him that layeth at
Ps. 7:12 if turn not will whet s.
17:13 deliv. from wicked, thy s.
22:20 my darling from pow. s.
37:14 wicked have drawn s.
15 s. shall enter their heart
45:3 gird thy s. on thy thigh
57:4 their tongue is a sharp s.
64:3 whet th. tongue like a s.
76:3 brake he the shield and s.
78:62 he gave his people to s.
149:6 a two-edged s. in th. hand
Prov. 5:4 her end as a two-edg. s.
12:18 speaketh like pierc. of s.
25:18 bear. false witness is a s.
Cant. 3:8 every man hath his s.
Is. 2:4 nation not lift. s. ag. nati.
31:8 the s. not of a mean man
34:6 s. of L. is filled with blood
41:2 he gave th. as dust to his s.
49:2 made mouth like sharp s.
51:19 famine and s. are come
65:12 I will number you to s.
66:16 by his s. will Lord plead
Jer. 2:30 your s. devoured proph.
4:10 s. reacheth unto the soul
5:12 neith. shall we see s. nor
6:25 s. of enemy is on ev. side
9:16 I will send s. after them,
24:10; 25:27; 29:17; 49:37
12:12 s. of the L. shall devour
14:13 poo. say, Ye sh. not see s.
15 say s. and famine shall not
18 go forth into field, bef. s. of s.
2 I will appoint the s. to slay
9 residue will I deliver to s.
18:21 pour out th. blood by s.
25:16 they sh. be mad bec. of s.
29 call for a s. Ezek. 38:21
31 he will give wicked to s.
31:2 peo. left of s. found grace
32:24 city given because of s.
34:17 I proclaim a liberty to s.
46:16 s. ye feared s. I will bring
47:6 O thou s. of the Lord, how
48:2 O Madmen, s. shall pursue
10 curs. that keep. back his s.
50:16 fear of the oppressing s.
35 s. L. on Chaldea. and L.
36 s. s. on liars, s. on mighty
37 s. s. on horses, s. on treasu.
51:50 ye that have escaped s.
Lam. 5:9 brc. by peril bec. of s.
Ezek. 5:2 I will draw out s. 12
17 I will bri. s. upon thee, 6:3
bef. some that shall escape s.
7:15 s. is without, pestilence
11:8 ye feared s. I will bring a s.
14:17 if I bring a s. and say, s.
21 my four sore judgm. the s.
21:9 s. s. s. is sharpened, 11
12 terrors, by reason of the s.
13 what if s. contemn the rod
14 let s. be doubled, s. of great
15 set point of the s. against s.
16 appoint s ways, that s. may
19 appoint a way that s.
20 appoint the way for the s.
21:50 r. shall come upon the s.
22 to make it s. strong to hold s.
23 to make it s. strong, it is s.
28 s. s. is drawn for the
30 return s. to his scabbard
30:4 s. shall come upon Egypt
11 to make it s. strong, to hold s.
21 bound up, to hold a s.
22 I will cause the s. to fall out
32:11 s. of the king of Babylon
33:3 when he seeth s. come on
4 if s. come and take him, 6
6 if watchmen see the s. come
26 ye stand upon your s.
35:5 thou hast shed blood by s.
Hos. 2:18 I will break bow and s.
11:6 s. shall abide on his cities
Amos 9:1 thwart will I com. s.
Mic. 4:3 nation not lift s. ag. na.
6:14 deliverest, will I give to s.

SWO
Nah. 2:13 s. shall devour lions
3:3 horseman lift. up bright s.
15 there the s. sh. cut thee off
Zec. 9:13 made thee as s. of mi.
11:17 s. shall be upon his arm
13:7 awake, O s. ag. my sheph.
Mat. 10:34 not send peace, but s.
26:51 drew his s. struck serv.
Mark 14:47; John 18:10
52 put up ag. thy s. John 18:11
Luke 2:35 s. s. sh. pierce thy soul
22:36 he that hath no s. let him
Acts 16:27 he drew his s. and wo.
Rom. 8:35 shall s. separate us
from the love of Christ?
13:4 he beareth not s. in vain
Eph. 6:17 s. of Sp. which is word
Heb. 4:12 sharp. th. two-edged s.
Rev. 1:16 out of mouth went a s.
2:12 the sharp s. with two edges
6:4 was given to him a great s.
19:15 out of his mou. goeth s. 21

By the SWORD.
Gen. 27:40 by thy s. thou sh. live
Lev. 26:7 they ch. fall by the s. 8
2 Chr. 29:9 fath. ha. fallen b. t. s.
Job 33:18 from perish. by the s.
36:12 they shall perish by the s.
Ps. 44:3 got not land by their s.
78:64 their priests fell by the s.
Jer. 11:22 young men shall die by the s. 18:21; 38:2
14:12 I will consu. them by l. s.
15 by s. and famine shall pro.
16:4 shall be consumed by the s. 44:12, 18, 27
19:7 cause them to fall by the s.
21:9 abideth, shall die by the s.
38:2; 42:17, 22
27:13 why will ye die by the s.?
32:36 city sh. be deliver. by t. s.
33:4 houses thro. down by the s.
34:4 Zedek. sh. not die by the s.
44:13 I punished Jerusal. by t. s.
Ezek. 26:6 daugh. be slain by t. s.
11 be sh. slay thy peo. by t. s.
28:23 be judged in her by the s.
31:18 th. that be slain by the s.
32:20, 21, 22, 25, 30; 31:27
39:23 so they fell all by the s.
Amos 7:11 Jerobo. sh. die by t. s.
9:10 my people sh. die by the s.
Hag. 2:22 ev. one by the s. of his
Rev. 13:14 had the wound by a s.

See EDGE, FALL.

From the SWORD.
Gen. 48:22 I took fr. A. wi. m. s.
Ex. 15:9 I will draw my s. my
Deut. 32:41 whet my gilt. s. s. 2
1 Sam. 20:8 neith. brought my s.
Ps. 44:6 neither shall my s. save
Is. 31:5 my s. shall be bathed in
Ezek. 21:3 I will draw my s.
Zeph. 2:12 ye shall be slain by my s.

With the SWORD.
Gen. 48:22 I took fr. A. wi. m. s.
Ex. 5:3 lest he fall on us w. t. s.
22:24 I will kill you w. the s.
Num. 19:16 toucb. slain w. t. s.
20:18 lest I come out w. the s.
21:24 Israel smote him w. the s.
Deut. 13:15 sm. smi. th. w. t. s.
28:22 Lord shall sm. w. t. s.
1 Sam. 17:45 comest w. a s.
17:47 L. saveth not w. s.
51 David drew G.'s s. slew h. w. it.
2 Sam. 12:9 hast slain Uriah w. s.
1 K. 19:1 Elijah slain proph. w. s.
2 K. 8:12 wilt thou slay w. t. s.
11:20 they slew Athaliah with the s.
1 Chr. 21:4 s. vexed young men w. the s.
Ps. 42:10 as w. a s. in my bones
Jer. 4:26 his s. be devoured w. the s.

SYN
Is. 14:19 slain, thr. thro' w. a s.
22:2 thy men not slain w. the s.
27:1 Lord w. his strong s. shall
Jer. 5:17 impover. cities w. t. s.
14:18 behold the lads w. the s.
20:4 he sb. slay Judah w. the s.
27:8 nati. will I punish w. t. s.
29:18 I will persecute w. the s.
Lam. 4:9 that be slain w. the s.
Ezek. 7:15 in field sh. die w. t. s.
26:8 wh. slay daughters w. the s.
31:17 to hell with them that be
Amos 1:11 did remove bro. w. t. s.
9:1 I will slay last of th. w. t. s.
Mic. 5:6 waste Assyria w. the s.
Mat. 26:52 that take the s. shall
perish with the s.
Luke 22:49 wit. we smite w. t. s.?
Acts 12:2 Her. killed Jas. w. t. s.
1 Th. 11:37 tempt. slain w. the s.
Rev. 2:16 I will fight th. w. the s.
6:8 and power to kill w. s. and
13:10 killeth w. s. be kill. w. s.
19:21 remnant were slain with the s.

SWORDS.
1 Sam. 13:19 lest Hebr. make s.
2 K. 3:26 took 700 men drew s.
Neh. 4:13 I set the people w. s.
Ps. 55:21 words were drawn s.
59:7 belch out, s. are in th. lips
Prov. 30:14 gener. tooth are as s.
Cant. 3:8 hold s. expert in war
Is. 2:4 beat their s. into plough-shares, Mic. 4:3
21:15 they fled from the s.
Ezek. 16:40 thrust through w. s.
28:7 strangers sh. draw their s.
30:11 they shall draw their s.
32:12 by s. of the mighty will I
27 they have laid their s. und.
Joel 2:10 best ploughshl. into s.
Mat. 26:47 with Ju. great multi-tude with s. Mark 14:43
Luke 22:38 beho. here are two s.

SWORN.
Gen. 22:16 by myself have I s.
saith L. Is. 45:23; Jer. 49:13;
51:14; Amos 6:8
Ex. 13:19 Joseph had straitly s.
17:16 Lord hath s. that he will
Lev. 6:5 about wh. had s. falsely
Deut. 7:8 keep oath s. Jer. 11:5
13:17 as he hath s. to thy fath.
28:9 estab. th. as he hath s. Jer. 31:7 bri. to land I, s. Neh. 9:15
Jos. 9:18 because princes had s.
19 we have s. to th. 2 Sam. 21:2
Jud. 21:1 men of Is. had s. to M.
5 have s. not to give wives, 18
1 Sam. 3:14 I ha. s. to hou. of E.
2 Sam. 21:2 Is. had s. to Gibeon.
2 Chr. 15:15 had s. with hearts
Neh. 9:15 land in. hadst s. to give
Ps. 24:4 hath not s. deceitfully
89:3 I have s. to David my serv.
35 s. by my holiness, Amos 4:2
102:8 mad ag. me, are s. ag. me
110:4 L. hath s. will not repent
119:106 I have s. will perform
132:11 L. hath in. in truth to D.
Is. 11:24 Lord of hosts hath s.
45:23 I have s. by myself, word
54:9 I have s. wat. no more go
over earth, I have s.
62:8 L. hath s. by his r. hand
Jer. 5:7 s. by th. if ar no gods
44:26 I have s. by my great name
Amos 8:7 Lord hath s. by Jacob
Mic. 7:20 perf. mercy to A. swor.
Acts 2:30 know, God hath s. oath
7:17 pro. drew nigh God had s.
Heb. 4:3 I have s. in my wrath

SYCAMINE.
Luke 17:6 to s. tr. Be plucked

SYCAMORE.
Amos 7:14 and gather of s. fruit

SYCAMORE-TREE.
Luke 19:4 Zaccheus climbed s. t.

SYCAMORE-TREES.
1 K. 10:27 Solomon made cedars as s. trees, 2 Chr. 1:15; 9:27
1 Chr. 27:28 over s. f. Baal hanan
Ps. 78:47 he destroyed their s. t.

SYCAMORES.
Is. 9:10 the s. are cut down

SYCHAR.
John 4:5

SYENE.
Ezek. 29:10

SYNAGOGUE.
Mat. 12:9 he went into their s.
13:54 tau. in their s. Mark 6:2

CRUDEN'S CONCORDANCE.

SYR

Mark 5:22 Jairus, one of the rul. of the s. 36, 38; *Luke* 8:41, 49
Luke 4:16 custom, went into s.
20 eyes of all in s. fast. on him
7:5 loveth nation, built us a s.
John 9:22 he sho. be put out of s.
12:42 lest they be put out of s.
18:20 I ever taught in s. temple
Acts 6:9 then arose cert. of tho s. called s. of the Libertines
13:14 they went into s. on sab.
14:1 P. and Barna. went into s.
17:1 Thessalonica, wh. was a s.
17 he disputed in s. with Jews
18:4 reasoned in s. ev. sabbath
7 Justus, whose house join. s.
8 Crispus, chief ruler of s.
17 Sosthenes, chief ruler of s.
26 Apollos began to speak in s.
22:19 beat in s. such heli. 26:11
Rev. 2:9 but are the s. of Satan
3:9 I will make them of s. of Sa.

SYNAGOGUES.
Ps. 74:8 they burned all s. of G.
Mat. 4:23 Je. went teaching in s. 9:35; *Mark* 1:30; *Luke* 13:10
6:2 as hypocrites do in s.
5 love to pray standing in s.
10:17 scourge you in s. 23:34
23:6 love chief seats in s. *Mark* 12:39; *Luke* 11:43; 20:46
Mark 13:9 in s. ye sh. be beaten
Luke 4:15 taught in s. glorified
44 he preached in s. of Galilee
13:10 they bring you unto s.
21:12 delivering you up to the s.
John 18:2 shall put you out s.
Acts 9:2 Saul desired letters to s.
20 he preached Christ in the s.
13:5 P. and Barn. preached in s.
15:21 being read in s. every sa.
24:12 neither raising people in s.

SYNTYCHE.
Phil. 4:2 I beseech Euod. and S.

SYRACUSE.
Acts 28:12 landing at S. tarried three days

SYRIA.
Jud. 10:6 Is. served gods of S.
2 *Sam.* 8:6 David put garrisons in S. 1 *Chr.* 18:6
15:8 I abode at Geshur in S.
1 *K.* 10:29 kings of S. did th. br.
11:25 Rezon reigned over S.
19:15 Haz. king of S. 2 *K.* 13:3
22:1 without war betw. S. and
2 *K.* 5:1 deliverance given to S.
6:23 bands of S. came no more
7:5 no man in the camp of S.
8:13 that thou sh. be king of S.
13:7 for the king of S. destroy.
17 arrow of deliveran. from S.
19 thou sh. smite S. but thrice
16:6 king of S. recove. El. to S.
2 *Chr.* 18:10 thou shalt push S.
24:23 host of S. came against
28:23 gods of kings of S. help
Is. 7:2 saying, S. is confederate
8 for head of S. is Damascus
Ezek. 16:57 of the daughter of S.
27:16 S. was thy merchant
Hos. 12:12 fled into country of S.
Amos 1:5 S. shall go into captiv.
Mat. 4:24 went throughout all S.
Luke 2:2 Cyrenius governor of S.
Acts 18:18 to the brethren in S.
41 he went through S. and
18:18 sailed thence into S. 21:3; *Gal.* 1:21

SYRIAC.
Dan. 2:4 spake to the king in S.

SYRIAN.
Gen. 25:20 daugh. of Bethnel S. Lab. the S. 28:5; 31:20, 21
Deut. 26:5 a S. ready to perish
2 *K.* 5:20 spared Naaman this S.
18:26 speak in the S. *Is.* 36:11
Ezr. 4:7 written in S. tongue and interpreted in S. tongue
Luke 4:27 saving Naaman the S.

SYRIANS.
2 *Sam.* 8:5 when S. of Da. came, David slew of S. 22,000
6 the S. became David's servants, 1 *Chr.* 18:5, 6
13 returned from smiting of S.
10:6 Ammonites hired the S.
11 if S. be too stro. 1 *Chr.* 19:12
19 the S. feared to help children of Ammon, 1 *Chr.* 19:19
1 *K.* 20:20 the S. fled, and Israel
21 flocks, but S. filled country
29 Israel slew of the S. 100,000
22:11 in. Ahab's ch. S. washed
2 *K.* 5:2 the S. had taken a maid

TAB

2 *K.* 6:9 thith. S. are come down
7:4 let us fall unto host of S.
6 Lord made the host of the S.
10 we came to camp of the S.
6:28 S. wounded Joram, 9:15; 2 *Chr.* 22:5
13:5 from under the hand of S.
17 for thou shalt smite the S.
16:6 the S. came to Elath and
Is. 9:12 S. bef. and Philistines
Jer. 35:11 for fear of army of S.
Amos 9:7 brou. the S. from Kir ?

SYROPHENICIAN.
Mark 7:26 a Greek, a S. by. nat.

T.

TABEAL.
Is. 7:6 a king, even the son of T.

TABERAH.
Num. 11:3 he called the place T.
Deut. 9:22 at T. he provoked L.

TABERING.
Nah. 2:7 vo. of doves t. on brea.

TABERNACLE.
Ex. 25:9 make after pattern of t.
27:9 thou shalt make court of t.
19 vessels of t. of brass, 39:40
26:12 he sanctif. by my glory
33:7 Mo. pitch. t. without camp
11 Josh. departed not out of t.
36:8 them that work, work of t.
39:32 th. was work of t. finished
33 they brought the t. to Mo.
40:2 set up the t. 9 anoint t.
17 on first day the t. was reared
18, 19; *Num.* 7:1
35 reared court round about t.
34 glory of Lord filled the t. 35
36 cloud was taken from over t. *Num.* 9:17; 10:11; 12:10
38 the cloud of Lord was on the t. *Num.* 9:18, 19, 22
Lev. 8:10 Mo. anointed t. and all
15:31 die not when they defile t.
17:4 bringeth not offering bef. t.
26:11 will set my t. among you
Num. 1:50 appoint Levites over t. bear t. sh. encamp ro. t. 53
51 when t. setteth forward, and when t. is to be pitched
53 Levites sh. keep charge of t.
3:7, 25; 18:3; 31:30, 47
4:16 oversi. of t. pertain to E.
5:17 briest eh. take of dust of t.
7:3 they brou. offering before t.
9:15 on day that t. was reared, cloud cov. t. tent of testimo.
10:21 Kohathites did set up t.
11:24 Mos. set 70 elders round t.
24 they went not out unto t.
16:9 seem, small to do ser. of t.
24 get from about t. of Ko. 27
17:13 whoso. com. near t. sh. die
Deut. 31:15 appeared in t. in clo.
Jos. 22:19 wherein L.'s t. dwell.
2 *Sam.* 6:17 set ark in midst t.
7:6 ha. walked in tent and in t.
10:21 Kohathites did set up t.
11:24 Mos. set 70 elders round t.
26 they went not out unto t.
1 *K.* 2:28 Joab fled to t. of Lord
6:4 vessels hi t. bro. 2 *Chr.* 5:5
1 *Chr.* 6:48 Levites for serv. of t.
9:23 they had oversight of the t.
16:39 priests before t. of Lord
17:5 ha. gone from one t. to ano.
21:20 L. M. made in wilderness
29:29 they sh. no more carry t.
2 *Chr.* 1:5 put brazen altar bef. t.
Job 3:24 ho. thy t. sh. be in pea.
13:6 light shall be dark in his t.
14 confidence be rooted out t.
15 destruc. shall dwell in his t.
19:12 his troops encamp rou. t.
20:26 ill with him th. is left in t.
29:4 wh. secret of G. was on t.
31:31 if men of my t. said not
36:28 can any and. noise of t. ?
Ps. 15:1 L. who sh. abide in t. ?
19:4 in them he set a t. for sun
27:5 in secret of his t. hide me
6 I will offer in his t. sacrifices
61:4 I will abide in thy t.
76:2 in Salem is his t. dwell.-pl.
78:60 so he forsook t. of Shiloh
132:3 I will not come into t. ?
Prov. 14:11 t. of upright flourish
Is. 4:6 t. for shadow from heat
16:5 he sh. sit on it in t. of Da.
33:20 t. th. sh. not be ta. down
Lam. 2:4 slew all pleasant in t.
6 he hath violently ta. away t.
Ezek. 37:27 my t. sh. be with th.
41:1 which was breadth of t.
Amos 5:26 have borne t. of Mol.

TAB

Amos 9:11 will I raise up t. of D.
Acts 7:43 ye took up t. of Moloch
46 desired to find a t. for God
15:16 will build again t. of Dav.
2 *Cor.* 5:1 if house of t. he disso.
4 we th. are in th. t. do groan
Heb. 8:2 true t. which L. pitched
5 when Moses was to make t.
9:2 there was a t. made, sanctu.
3 t. which is called holiest
6 priests went alw. into first t.
8 while as first t. was yet stan.
11 priest by greater and per. t.
21 sprinkled with blood the t.
13:10 no right to eat wh. ser. t.
2 *Pet.* 1:13 as long as I am in t.
14 shortly I must put off my t.
Rev. 13:6 blasp. his name and t.
15:5 behold temple of t. opened

See CONGREGATION, DOOR.

TABERNACLE of witness.
Num. 17:7 M. la. rods in t. of w.
8 on mor. M. went into t. of w.
2 *Chr.* 24:6 hr. colle. for t. of w.
Acts 7:44 our fathers had t. of w.

TABERNACLES.
Num. 24:5 how goodly thy t.
Job 11:14 let not wic. dwell in t.
12:6 t. of robbers prosper, they
15:34 fire sh. cons. t. of bribery
22:23 put away iniq. from thy t.
Ps. 43:3 let them bring me to t.
46:4 make glad holy place of t.
78:51 smote their strength in t.
83:6 t. of E. consulted together
84:1 how amiable are thy t.
118:15 salvation is in t. of righte.
132:7 we will go into t. worship
Dan. 11:45 he sh. plant t. of pal.
Hos. 9:6 thorns sh. be in their t.
12:9 make thee to dwell in t.
Mal. 2:12 L. cut off man out of t.
Mat. 17:4 let us make here three t. *Mark* 9:5; *Luke* 9:33
Heb. 11:9 Abrah. dwelling in t.

See FEAST.

TABITHA.
Acts 9:36 a disciple named T.
40 turn. to body said, T. arise

TABLE.
Ex. 25:23 thou sh. also make a t.
27 staves to bear t. 28; 37:14
31:8 Beza. sh. make t. and altar
37:10 made t. 16, vessels on t.
40:22 put t. in tent of congreg.
Lev. 24:6 six on a row on pure t.
Num. 3:31 Kohathites' charge t.
Jud. 1:7 gath. meat under my t.
1 *Sam.* 20:29 co. not to king's t.
34 Jona. arose from t. in fierce
2 *Sam.* 9:7 Mephibosheth sh. eat at my t. 10, 11, 13; 19:28
1 *K.* 2:7 be th. that eat at my t.
4:27 all that came to Solo.'s t.
13:20 sat at t. word of L. came
18:19 proph. eat at Jezebel's t.
2 *K.* 4:10 let us set for him a t.
Neh. 5:17 we. at my t. 150 Jews
Job 36:16 wh. should be set on t.
Ps. 23:5 thou preparest t. be. me
69:22 let th. t. become a snare
78:19 can G. furn. t. in wildern.
128:3 child, like plants about t.
Prov. 3:3 wri. on t. of heart, 7:3
9:2 wisd. hath furnished her t.
Cant. 1:12 wh. king sitteth at t.
Is. 21:5 prepare the t. eat
30:8 write before them in t.
65:11 prepare t. for that troop
Jer. 17:1 it is graven on t. of he.
Ezek. 23:41 prepar. a t. before t.
39:20 ye shall be filled at my t.
41:22 this is t. that is bef. Lord
44:16 shall come near to my t.
Dan. 11:27 shall speak lies at t.
Mal. 1:7 t. of L. is contemptible
12 ye say, t. of Lord is pollut.
Mat. 15:27 dogs eat crumbs from their master's t. *Mark* 7:28
Luke 16:21 cru. fr. rich man's t.
22:21 betrayeth, is wi. me on t.
30 may eat and drink at my t.
John 13:2 L. was one th. sat at t.
13:28 no man at t. knew wh. in.
Rom. 11:9 let their t. be a snare
1 *Cor.* 10:21 ye cannot be partakers of Lord's t. and t. of dev.

See SHOW-BREAD.

Writing TABLE.
Luke 1:63 Zacha. asked for w. t.

TABLES.
Ex. 22:15 t. were writ. on sides
16 t. were work of G. gra. on t.

TAK

Ex. 32:19 cast the t. out of his h.
34:1 write on t. words in first t.
Deut. 10:4 he wr. on t. acco. to t.
5 put t. in the ark, *Heb.* 9:4
1 *Chr.* 28:16 David ga. gold for t.
2 *Chr.* 4:9 Solo. also made ten t.
Is. 28:8 all t. are full of vomit
Ezek. 40:41 8 t. whereon slew sa.
42 four t. were of hewn stone
Hab. 2:2 write vision, plain on t.
Mat. 21:12 he overthrew t. of the money-changers, *Mark* 11:15
Mark 7:4 wash. of cups, pots, t.
John 2:15 dro. out, overthrew t.
Acts 6:2 leave word of G. serve t.
2 *Chr.* 3:3 not in t. of st. fleshly t.

See STONE, TWO.

TABLETS.
Ex. 35:22 brought t. of jewels
Num. 31:50 brought t. atonement
Is. 3:20 I will take away the t.

TABOR.
Jud. 4:6 draw toward mount T.
12 Barak was gone to mount T.
8:18 they whom ye slew at T.?
1 *Sam.* 10:3 come to plain of T.
Ps. 89:12 T. and Hermon shall
Jer. 46:18 surely, as T. is among
Hos. 5:1 a net spread upon T.

TABRET.
Gen. 31:27 have sent thee with t.
1 *Sam.* 10:5 fr. high place with t.
Job 17:6 aforetime I was as a t.
Is. 5:12 t. and wine are in feasts

TABRETS.
1 *Sam.* 18:6 ca. to meet S. wi. t.
Is. 24:8 mirth of t. ceaseth, joy
30:32 it sh. be with t. and harps
Jer. 31:4 again be adorn. with t.
Ezek. 28:13 workmansh. of thy t.

TACHES.
Ex. 26:6 thou shalt make fifty t.
11 thou sh. make fifty t. 33:11
36:13 he made fifty t. of gold. 18
39:33 they brought his t. boards

TACKLING, S.
Is. 33:23 thy t. are loosed, could
Acts 27:19 third day cast out t.

TADMOR.
2 *Chr.* 8:4 Solomon built T.

TAHAPANES, or TEHAPHNEHES.
Jer. 2:16 the children of T. have
43:7 thus came they even to T.
46:14 punish in Noph and T.
Ezek. 30:18 at T. also too shall day

TAHPENES.
1 *K.* 11:19 gave him sister of T.

TAIL.
Ex. 4:4 put out hand, ta. it by t.
Deut. 28:13 make head, not t. 44
Jud. 15:4 foxes, turned t. to t.
Job 40:17 behemoth mov. his t.
Is. 9:14 cut off fr. Is. head and t.
15 prophet teaches. lies, he is t.
19:15 wo. wh. head or t. may do
Rev. 12:4 his t. dr. third of stars

TAILS.
Jud. 15:4 firebrand betw. two t.
Is. 7:4 two t. of these firebrands
Rev. 9:10 t. like scor. stings in t.
19 power in t. their t. like ser.

TAKE.
Gen. 13:9 if thou t. left hand
14:21 give me persons, t. goods
24:3 shalt not t. wife to son, 37
31:32 discern what is thine, t. it
38:23 let her t. it to her, lest we
Ex. 6:7 I will t. you for a people
10:26 thereof must we t. serve L.
17:5 and thy rod t. in thy hand
20:7 not t. na. L. in vain, *Deut.* 5:11
21:14 t. him from mine altar
23:8 sh. t. no gift, *Deut.* 16:19
34:9 t. us for inheritance
Num. 3:6 t. Levites from am. Is.
11:17 I will t. of spirit on thee
16:3 ye t. too much upon you, 7
18:1 t. 1:13 t. ye wise men
4:34 t. him a nation in nation
25:8 if say, I like not to t. her
Ps. 10:42 their land fill Josh. t.
20:4 they shall t. him into city
Jud. 14:15 called to t. th. we ha.
Ruth 3:10 endeth t. the younger
1 *Sam.* 6:8 then t. as out their
17:46 and t. thy head from thee
19:14 S. sent messengers to t. D.
21:9 if thou wilt t. that, t. it
23:11 sh. I bwr t. bread and w.
2 *Sam.* 12:4 spared to t. his flock

TAL

Ec. 2:23 heart *t.* not rest in ni:.
Is. 40:15 he *t.* up Isle· as a little
51:18 nor is there that *t.* hor by
Ezek. 16:32 wh. *t.* strangers inst.
33:4 *t.* not warning; 5 *t.* warn.
Mat. 4:3 devil *t.* him up into ho.
10:38 that *t.* not his criss. and
12:45 *t.* sev. spirits, *Luke* 11:26
Mark 4:15 Satan cometh, and *t.*
away word, *Luke* 8:12
5:19 he *t.* father and mother of
9:18 wher. he *t.* him, he teareth
Luke 6:30 that *t.* goods, ask not
9:33 a spirit *t.* him, he suddenly
John 1:29 Lamb of G. *t.* away sin
10:18 no man *t.* it from me
16:22 your joy no man *t.* fr. you
21:13 Je. then cometh, *t.* bread
1 *Cor.* 11:21 every one *t.* bef. an.
Heb. 10:9 he *t.* away the first

TAKETH hold.
Job 21:6 tremb. *t.* h. on my flesh
Prov. 30:28 spider *t.* h. wi. hands
Is. 56:6 that *t.* h. of my covenant

TAKING.
2 *Chr.* 19:7 with God ne *t.* of gift
Job 5:3 I have seen foolish *t.* root
Ps. 119:9 by *t.* heed thereto
Jer. 50:46 at noise of *t.* of Babyl.
Hos. 11:3 I taught Ephraim also
to go, *t.* them by their arms
Mat. 6:27 by *t.* tho. *Luke* 12:25
Luke 19:22 *t.* up I laid not down
John 11:13 he had spok. of *t.* rest
2 *Cor.* 2:13 *t.* my leave of them, 1
3 *John* 7 th. went forth *t.* nothi.

TALE, S.
Ps. 90:9 we spend years as a *t.*
Ezek. 22:9 carry *t.* to shed blood
Luke 24:11 th. words seemed as *t.*

TALEBEARER.
Lev. 19:16 shalt not go as a *t.*
Prov. 11:13 *t.* rev. secrets, 20:19
18:8 words *t.* are wounds, 26:22
26:20 where is no *t.* strife

TALE, reckoning.
Ex. 5:8 the *t.* of bricks which
18 yet shall he deliver the *t.* of
1 *Sam.* 18:27 foreskl. in *t.* to king
1 *Chr.* 9:28 bring vessels in by *t.*

TALENT.
Ex. 25:39 *t.* of pure gold, 37:24
38:27 sockets, a *t.* for a socket
2 *Sam.* 12:30 weight of crown a *t.*
1 *K.* 20:39 shalt pay a *t.* of silver
2 *K.* 5:22 give them a *t.* of silver
23:33 of *t.* of gold. 2 *Chr.* 36:3
Zec. 5:7 th. was lifted a *t.* of lead
Mat. 25:25 I went and hid thy *t.*
24 take therefore the *t.* fr. him
Rev. 16:21 sto. about weight of *t.*

TALENTS.
Ex. 38:24 gold of off. was 29 *t.*
27 100 *t.* of silver were cast
1 *K.* 16:24 bought hill for two *t.*
2 *K.* 5:5 Naaman took ten *t.*
23 said, Be content, take two *t.*
15:19 Menahem gave P. 1,000 *t.*
18:14 appointed to Hezeki. 300 *t.*
23:33 trib. of 100 *t.* 2 *Chr.* 36:3
1 *Chr.* 19:6 Ammon. sent 1,000 *t.*
29:4 David gave 3,000 *t.* of gold
7 gold 5,000 *t.* of silver 10,000 *t.*
2 *Chr.* 25:9 what do for 100 *t.* ?
27:5 child. of Ammon gave 100 *t.*
Mat. 18:24 one ow. him 10,000 *t.*
25:15 to one he gave five *t.*
See GOLD, SILVER.

TALITHA cumi.
Mark 5:41 he said unto her, *t. c.*

TALK, Substantive.
Job 11:2 man full of *t.* be justi. ?
15:3 reason wi. unprofitable *t.* ?
Prov. 14:23 *t.* of lips tendeth to
Ec. 10:13 end of *t.* is mischievo.
Mat. 22:15 mi. entangle him in *t.*

TALK, Verb.
Num. 11:17 I will com a and com *t.*
Deut. 5:24 seen that God doth *t.*
6:7 shalt *t.* of them when thou
1 *Sam.* 2:3 no more so proudly
2 *K.* 18:26 *t.* not with us in the
1 *Chr.* 16:9 *t.* ye of all his won-
drous works, *Ps.* 105:2
Job 13:7 will ye *t.* deceitfully ?
Ps. 69:26 they *t.* to the grief of
71:24 my tongue shall *t.* of thy
77:12 I will *t.* of thy doings
119:27 so shall I *t.* of thy works
145:11 speak of thy king, and *t.*
Prov. 6:22 when th. awa. it sh. *t.*
24:2 and their lips *t.* of mischi.
Jer. 12:1 let me *t.* with thee
Ezek. 3:22 arise, I will *t.* wi. thee

TAR

Dan. 10:17 how can thy serv. *t.*
John 14:30 I will not *t.* much

TALKED.
Gen. 45:15 his breth. *t.* with him
Ex. 20:22 I *t.* with you, *Deut.* 5:4
32:9 and the Lord *t.* with Moses
34:29 his face shone while he *t.*
1 *Sam.* 14:19 Saul *t.* unto priest
2 *Chr.* 25:16 it ca. to pass as he *t.*
Jer. 38:25 if princes hear I ha. *t.*
Luke 9:30 *t.* with him two men
24:32 heart burn while he *t.*
John 4:27 marvelled that he *t.*
Acts 10:27 as P. *t.* with Cornelius
20:11 *t.* long, till break of day
26:31 th. *t.* between themselves
Rev. 21:15 he th. *t.* with me had

TALKERS.
Ezek. 36:3 taken up in lips of *t.*
Tit. 1:10 there are many vain *t.*

TALKEST.
Jud. 6:17 show me a sign thou *t.*
2 *K.* 2:14 while thou *t.* with king
20:5 he *t.* longer than set time
John 4:27 why *t.* thou with ho?
9:37 it is he that *t.* with thee

TALKING.
Gen. 17:22 he left off *t.* with him
17:22 he is *t.* or pursuing
Est. 6:14 while they were *t.* wi.
Ezek. 33:30 people are *t.* ag. thee
Mat. 17:3 Mo. and Elias *t.* with
him, *Mark* 9:4
Rev. 4:1 voice of a trumpet *t.*

TALKING.
Job 29:9 the princes refrained *t.*
Eph. 5:4 filthiness, nor foolish *t.*

TALL.
Deut. 2:10 *t.* as Anak. 21 ; 9:2
1 *K.* 19:23 cut down *t.* cedar-
trees, *Is.* 37:24

TALLER.
Deut. 1:28 people is *t.* than we

TAMAH.
Gen. 38:6 a wife, wh. na. was T.
24 was told Judah, T. hath
Ruth 4:12 Pharez, wh. T. bare to
Judah, 1 *Chr.* 2:4; *Mat.* 1:3
2 *Sam.* 13:1 a fair sister, na. T.
2 Amn. fell sick for T. 39, 32
14:27 daugh. wh. name was T.
Ezek. 47:19 side southward fr. T.

TAME, ED.
Mark 5:4 neith. could man *t.* him
Jam. 3:7 of sea is *t.* hath been *t.*
8 the tongue can no man *t.*

TAMMUZ.
Ezek. 8:14 wom. weeping for T.

TANNER.
Acts 9:43 Pe. tarried wi. Si. a *t.*
10:6 lodged with Simon a *t.* 32

TAPESTRY. *See* COVERINGS.

TARE.
Gen. 19:2 *t.* all night, and wash
2 Sam. 13:31 king *t.* his garmen.
2 *K.* 2:24 two she-bears *t.* 42 chil.
Mark 9:20 spi. *t.* him, *Luke* 9:42

TARES.
Mat. 13:25 his enemy sowed *t.*
26 then appeared the *t.* also
25 lest while you gather up *t.*

TARGET, S.
1 *Sam.* 17:6 Goli. had a *t.* of brass
1 *K.* 10:16 Solom. made 200 *t.* 600
shekels to one *t.* 2 *Chr.* 9:15
2 *Chr.* 14:8 army that bare *t.*

TARRY.
Gen. 19:2 *t.* all night, and wash
27:44 *t.* with Laban a few days
30:27 if I found favor in eyes *t.*
45:9 come down to me, *t.* not
Ex. 12:39 thrust out, not. *t.* 24:14
Num. 22:19 *t.* ye here till we come
Num. 22:19 I pray you, *t.* here
Jud. 5:28 why *t.* wheels of ch. ?
6:18 I will *t.* until thou come
Ruth 1:13 would ye *t.* for them
1 *Sam.* 1:23 *t.* until th. ha. was.
10:8 seven days shalt thou *t.*
2 *Sam.* 10:5 at Jeri. till beards
be grown, 1 *Chr.* 19:5
11:12 *t.* to-day ; 15:28 I will *t.*
18:14 Joab said, I may not *t.*
19:7 th. will not *t.* one with th.
2 *K.* 2:2 *t.* here, L. sent me, 4, 6
7:9 if we *t.* till morning light
14:10 pl. of this. and *t.* at home
Ps. 101:7 liar not *t.* in my sight
Prov. 23:30 that *t.* long at wine
Is. 46:13 my salvation sh. not *t.*
Jer. 14:8 turneth to *t.* for night
Hab. 2:3 though it *t.* wait for it,
for it will not *t.*

TAS

Mat. 26:38 *t.* and wa. *Mark* 14:34
Luke 24:29 he went to *t.* with th.
49 *t.* ye in city of Jerusalem
John 4:40 besought that he w. *t.*
21:22 if I will that he *t.* 23
Acts 10:48 th. prayed Peter to *t.*
18:20 they desired Paul to *t.*
28:14 were desired to *t.* 7 days
1 *Cor.* 11:33 whereof. *t.* one for a.
16:7 I tr. to *t.* a while with you
8 I will *t.* at Ephesus until P.
Heb. 10:37 will come, and not *t.*

TARRIED.
Gen. 24:54 Abraham's servant *t.*
28:11 Jacob *t.* there all night
31:54 J. and Leb. *t.* all night
Num. 9:19 wh. cloud *t.* long, 22
Jud. 3:25 *t.* they were ashamed
12:8 they *t.* till the afternoon
Ruth 2:7 save that she *t.* a little
1 *Sam.* 13:8 he *t.* 7 days accord.
2 *Sam.* 15:17 king *t.* in place
20:5 he *t.* longer than set time
Ps. 68:12 that *t.* at home divid. spoil
Mat. 25:5 bridegroom *t.* lb. Slept
Luke 1:21 people marvelled he *t.*
2:43 child Jesus *t.* in Jerusalem
John 3:22 he *t.* and baptized
Acts 9:43 P. *t.* many days in Jop.
18:18 Paul *t.* a good while at C.
20:5 going befo. *t.* for us at Tr.
21:4 finding disci. we *t.* 7 days
10 as we *t.* many days at Cesa.
25:6 Festus *t.* at Jerus. ten days
27:33 fourteenth day ye *t.* fast.
28:12 at Syracuse, we *t.* 3 days

TARRIEST, ETH.
1 *Sam.* 30:24 part that *t.* by stuff
Mic. 5:7 that *t.* not for a man,
Acts 22:16 and now why *t.* thou ?

TARRYING.
Ps. 40:17 make no *t.* O G. 70:5

TARSHISH.
Gen. 10:4 Elisha, T. 1 *Chr.* 1:7
1 *K.* 10:22 for the king had at sea
a navy of T. 2 *Chr.* 9:21
2 *Chr.* 20:36 make ships go to T.
37 broken, not able to go to T.
Ps. 48:7 th. breakest ships of T.
72:10 the kings of T. shall bring
Is. 2:16 Lord on all ships of T.
23:1 howl, ye ships of T. 14
6 pass over to T. howl, ye
10 pass as a river, O T. daugh.
60:9 the ships of T. shall wait
66:19 those that escape to T.
Jer. 10:9 silver is brought fr. T.
Ezek. 27:12 T. was thy merchant
25 ships of T. did sing of thee
38:13 the merchants of T. shall
Jon. 1:3 rose up to flee unto T.
4:2 I fled before unto T. for I

TARSUS.
Acts 9:11 inq. for one Saul of T.
30 the brethren sent him to T.
11:25 Barnabas departed to T.
21:39 who am a Jew of T. 22:3

TARTAN.
2 *K.* 17:31 made T. their god
TARTAN. 2 *K.* 18:17

TASK, S.
Ex. 5:13 fulfil works, daily *t.*
14 why not fulfilled *t.* in mak.
19 not minish fr. your daily *t.*

TASKMASTERS.
Ex. 1:11 they set over them *t.*
3:7 cry by reason of their *t.*
5:10 *t.* told people ; 13 *t.* hasted

TASTE, Substantive.
Ex. 16:31 *t.* of manna like wafers
Num. 11:8 *t.* was as *t.* of fresh oil
Job 6:6 any *t.* in white of an egg ?
30 my *t.* disc. perverse things
Ps. 119:103 sw. thy word to *t.* !
Prov. 24:13 honey-co. sweet to *t.*
Cant. 2:3 fruit sweet to my *t.*
Jer. 48:11 his *t.* remained in him

TASTE, Verb.
1 *Sam.* 14:43 but *t.* a little honey
2 *Sam.* 3:35 if T *t.* bread or aught
19:35 can servant *t.* what I eat ?
Job 12:11 doth not mouth *t.* meat
Ps. 34:8 O *t.* and see L. is good
Jon. 3:7 nor flock *t.* any thing
Mat. 16:28 sh. not *t.* death, *Mark* 9:1; *Lu.* 9:27
Luke 14:24 none bidden *t.* of sup.
John 8:52 keep say. nev. *t.* death
Col. 2:21 touch not, *t.* not,
Heb. 2:9 sho. *t.* death for ev. man

TASTED, ETH.
1 *Sam.* 14:24 none *t.* 29 I *t.* hon.

TEA

Job 34:3 words as mouth *t.* meat
Deut. 5:2 Beholaz. while he *t.* wi.
Mat. 27:34 wh. he had *t.* thereof
John 2:9 ruler *t.* wat. made wine
Heb. 6:4 have *t.* of heavenly gift
1 *Pet.* 2:3 *t.* that L. is gracious

TATTLERS.
1 *Tim.* 5:13 not only idle, but *t.*

TATNAI. *Ezr.* 5:3, 6

TAUGHT.
Deut. 4:5 I have *t.* you statutes
31:22 Moses *t.* the children of Is.
Jud. 8:16 he *t.* men of Succoth
2 *Chr.* 6:27 ha. *t.* them good way
17:9 Levites *t.* people in Judah
23:13 rejoiced, *t.* to sing praise
30:22 that *t.* knowledge of L.
35:3 Josiah said to L. that *t.* Is.
Neh. 8:9 Levites that *t.* people
Ps. 71:17 hast *t.* me, 119:102
119:171 hast *t.* me thy statutes
Prov. 4:4 he *t.* me also, and said
11:1 *t.* thee in way of wisdom
31:1 prophecy his moth. *t.* him
Ec. 12:9 he *t.* people knowledge
Is. 29:13 fear *t.* by prec. of men
40:13 being counsel. *t.* him, 14
54:13 thy child. shall be *t.* of G.
Jer. 2:33 therof. hast th. *t.* wick.
9:5 they *t.* tongue to speak lies
14 after Baalim, whi. fathers *t.*
12:16 *t.* my peo. to swear by B.
13:21 *t.* them to be captains
28:16 *t.* them rebellion ag. Lord
29:33 tho' I *t.* them, rising early
Ezek. 23:48 women *t.* not lewdn.
Hos. 10:11 Ephr. is as a heifer *t.*
11:3 I *t.* Ephraim to go, taking
Zec. 13:5 *t.* me to keep cattle
Mat. 7:29 he *t.* them as one hav-
ing authority, *Mark* 1:22
10:1 as he went he *t.* th. again
Luke 11:1 as John *t.* his disciples
13:26 thou hast *t.* in our streets
John 9:43 they sh. be all *t.* of G.
7:14 Je. went into temple. *t.* 28;
Mark 12:35; *Lu.* 19:47; 20:1
8:2 peo. came, he sat *t.* them.
28 as my Father hath *t.* me. I
18:20 I ever *t.* in the synagogue
Acts 4:2 grieved that they *t.* peo.
5:21 entered temple early and *t.*
11:26 P. and Barn. *t.* peo. 14:21
15:1 certain men *t.* the brethren
18:25 Apollos *t.* dilig. tht. of L.
20:20 I showed you and *t.* you
22:3 *t.* accord. to manner of law
Gal. 1:12 nor *t.* but by revelation
6:6 let him that is *t.* communi.
Eph. 4:21 if ye have been *t.*
Col. 2:7 faith, as ye have been *t.*
1 *Thes.* 4:9 ye are *t.* of G. to love
2 *Thes.* 2:15 hold tradi. ye have *t.*
Tit. 1:9 word. as he hath been *t.*
1 *John* 2:27 as anoint. ha. *t.* you
Rev. 2:14 *t.* Bal. to cast stum.-bl.

TAUNT, ING.
Jer. 24:9 I deliver them to be a *t.*
Ezek. 5:13 so it be reproach
Hab. 2:6 these take up a *t.* prov.

TAXATION.
2 *K.* 23:35 exacted of every one *t.*

TAXED.
2 *K.* 23:35 Jehoiakim *t.* the land
Luke 2:1 a decree world sho. be *t.*
3 all went to be *t.* 5 *t.* to be *t.*

TAXES, ING.
Dan. 11:20 stand up a raiser of *t.*
Luke 2:2 *t.* first made when Cy.
Acts 5:37 rose up J. in days of *t.*

TEACH.
Ex. 4:15 I will *t.* wh. ye sh. do
35:34 G. put in his heart he *t.*
Lev. 10:11 may *t.* Is. all statutes
14:57 to *t.* when uncl. and clean
Deut. 4:1 hearken to judgm. *t.*
10 that they may *t.* their child.
14 L. commanded me to *t.* 6:1
31:19 write and *t.* child. of Is.
33:10 they sh. *t.* Ja. judgments
Jud. 13:8 *t.* us what we shall do
1 *Sam.* 12:23 wi. *t.* you good way
2 *Sam.* 1:18 bade th. *t.* use of bow
1 *Chr.* 17:7 *t.* in cities of Judah.
Ezr. 7:10 to *t.* in Israel statutes
40:12 sho. *t.* all say. I. G. knowl.
27:11 will *t.* you by hand of G.
32:7 multitude of years *t.* wisd.
37:19 *t.* us what we shall say
Ps. 25:8 he will *t.* sinners
9 meek will he guide and *t.*

CRUDEN'S CONCORDANCE.

TEM

Is. 44:26 to *t.* thy founds. be laid
66:6 a voice from *t.* voice of L.
Jer. 50:26 decl. veng. of *t.* 51:11
Ezek. 41:1 afterw. brou. me to *t.*
Dan. 5:2 vessels taken out of *t.* 3
Amos 8:3 songs of *t.* be howlings
Zec. 8:9 strong, that *t.* be built
Mal. 3:1 L. come sudd. to his *t.*
Mat. 4:5 set him on a pinnacle
  of *t. Luke* 4:9
12:6 place is one greater than *t.*
23:16 sw. by *t.* or gold of *t.* 17, 21
  35 wh. ye swer bet, *t.* and altar
24:1 show build. of *t. Luke* 21:5
26:61 I am able to dest. *t.* of G.
27:40 destroyest *t. Mark* 15:29
51 veil of *t.* rent in twain, *Mark*
  15:38 ; *Luke* 23:45
Mark 11:16 carry vessels thro' *t.*
14:58 destroy *t.* ma. with hands
Luke 2:37 Au. departed not fr. *t.*
John 2:15 he drove them out of *t.*
  19 destroy *t.* 21 spake of *t.* of
  20 forty and six years *t.* build.
Acts 3:2 laid daily at gate of *t.* to
  ask alms of them ent. *t.* 10
19:27 *t.* of Diana sho. be despis.
21:30 took Paul, drew him out *t.*
24:6 hath gone about to prof. *t.*
25:8 neither against *t.* nor Cesar
1 *Cor.* 3:16 that ye are *t.* of God
17 if any man defile *t.* of G. him
  G. de-*t. t.*, holy, wh. *t.* ye are
6:19 your body is *t.* of H. Ghost
8:10 these sit at meat in idol's *t.*
9:13 they who minister live of *t.*
2 *Cor.* 6:16 hath *t.* of G. wi. idols
Rev. 7:15 serve day and ni. in *t.*
11:1 rise and measure *t.* of God
  2 *t.* of G. was open. in heaven
11:18 ana. angel came out of *t.*
15:5 *t.* of tabernacle was opened
  8 *t.* was filled with smoke from
16:1 I heard a voice out of *t.* 17
21:22 no *t.*, Almig. and Lamb *t.*

See HOLY, LORD.

In, or into the TEMPLE.
1 *Chr.* 6:10 priest's office in the *t.*
Ezr. 5:15 carry these ves. *t. i. t.*
Neh. 6:11 go *i.* the *t.* to save life
Mat. 12:5 priests in *t.* prof. sabb.
21:12 went *into* the *t.* to cast out
  them that sold in *t. Mark*
  11:15; *Luke* 19:45
  14 and lame came to him *i. t. t.*
  15 child. crying in *t.* Hosanna
23:35 teaching *in t. Luke* 21:37
27:5 cast down pieces of sil. *i. t.*
Mark 14:49 I was daily teaching
  in the *t. Luke* 22:53
Luke 1:21 tarried so long in *t. t.*
  2:27 he came by Spirit *into t. t.*
  46 found him *in* the *t.* sitting
18:10 two men went *into* the *t.*
24:53 continu. in *t.* praising G.
Acts 2:46 with one accord *in t. t.*
3:1 Peter and John went *i. the t.*
  3 as go *into t.* 2:20 speak *in t.*
3:23 men are standing *in t.*
21:26 P. entered *t.* 27 saw *in t.*
  28 brought Greeks *i. the t.* 29
24:12 neither found me *in the t.*
  18 *t.* found me purified *in t. t.*
26:21 cause J. caught me *in t.*
2 *Thes.* 2:4 as G. sitteth *t. t.* of G.
Rev. 3:12 I make a pillar *in t.*
15:8 no man able to enter *i. t. t.*

TEMPLES, *of the head.*
Jud. 4:21 sm. nail into kis *t.* 22
5:26 she had stricken thro' his *t.*
Cant. 4:3 thy *t.* like pomegr. 6:7

TEMPLES.
Hos. 8:14 forgat Maker, build. *t.*
Joel 3:5 into *t.* my goodly things
Acts 7:48 the M. H. dwelleth not
  in *t.* made with hands, 17:24

TEMPORAL.
2 *Cor.* 4:18 for things seen are *t.*

TEMPT.
Gen. 22:1 God did *t.* Abraham
Ex. 17:2 wheref. do ye *t.* Lord?
Deut. 6:16 ye shall not *t.* the L.
Is. 7:12 not ask, nor will *t.* L.
Mat. 3:15 that *t.* God are delive.
Mal. 4:7 shalt not *t.* L. *Luke* 4:12
22:18 why *t.* ye me? *Mark* 12:15;
  Luke 20:23
Acts 5:9 ye have agreed to *t.* Sp.
15:10 therefore why *t.* ye God?
1 *Cor.* 7:5 Sa. *t.* you not for your
10:9 neither let us *t.* Christ

TEMPTATION.
Ps. 95:8 as in *t.* in wild. *Heb.* 3:8
Mat. 6:13 and lead us not into *t.*
  Luke 11:4

TEN

Mat. 26:41 that ye enter not into
  t. Mark 14:38 ; *Luke* 22:40, 46
Luke 4:13 wh. devil ended his *t.*
  8:13 in a time of *t.* fall away
22:28 continued with me in *t.*
Acts 20:19 serv. G. with many *t.*
Jam. 1:12 joy when ye fall into *t.*
1 *Pet.* 1:6 are in heaviness thro' *t.*
2 *Pet.* 2:9 L. deli. godly out of *t.*

TEMPTED.
Ex. 17:7 because they *t.* Lord
Num. 14:22 ha. *t.* me ten times
Deut. 6:16 tempt G. ye *t.* in Ma.
Ps. 78:18 they *t.* G. in heart, 41
  56 *t.* and provo. most high God
Ezek. 17:22 I will crop off *t.* one
106:14 lusted, *t.* God in desert
  14:15 on earth, in the *t.* grass, 33
  devil, *Mark* 1:13; *Luke* 4:2
10:9 Jes a lawyer *t.* him
1 *Cor.* 10:9 some *t.* were destroy.
  13 not suffer you to be *t.* above
Gal. 6:1 lest thou also be *t.*
1 *Thes.* 3:5 by means *t.* tempted
Jam. 1:13 tempt. neither *t.* any
  14 ev. man *t.* wh. drawn of lust

TEMPTER.
Mat. 4:3 when *t.* came to him
1 *Thes.* 3:5 by means *t.* tempted

TEMPTETH.
Jam. 1:13 tempt. neither *t.* any

TEMPTING.
Mat. 16:1 the Pharisees *t.* Christ,
  Mark 8:11 ; *Luke* 11:16
19:3 Pharis. came to him *t.* him
22:35 lawyer asked quest. *t.* him
Mark 10:2 put away wife, *t.* him
John 8:6 this they said, *t.* him

TEN.

Gen. 16:3 A.br. w. *t.* years in C.
18:32 I will not dest. for *t.* sake
42:3 Jos.'s *t.* breth. went to buy
Ex. 18:7 M. and Ad. came to *t.*
83:8 stood every man at *t.* door
  10 they worshipped him *t.* door
39:33 they brought the *t.* to Mo.
40:19 he spread *t.* over the tab.
Lev. 14:8 tarry out of *t.* sev. days
Num. 9:15 cloud cov. *t.* of testi.
11:10 heard people weep in *t.*
19:14 when a man dieth in a *t.*
  18 a clean person sh. sprinkle *t.*
25:6 went aft. man of Is. into *t.*
Jos. 7:21 hid it midst of my *t.*
  23 took them out of midst of *t.*
  24 Israel burnt his *t.* and all he
Jud. 4:17 Sisera fled to *t.* of Jael
20 said, Stand in door of the *t.*
21 Jael took a nail of the *t.* and
5:24 blessed above women in *t.*
7:8 he sent rest of Israel to his *t.*
20:8 not any of us go to *t.*
Cant. 4:10 fled every man into
  his *t.* 2 *Sam.* 18:17; 19:8
19:2 fear of people he sent to *t.*
20:1 pur. Goliath's armor in *t.*
Acts 17:8 wife. in a 1 *Chr.* 17:5
16:22 they spread Absalom a *t.*
20:22 retired every man to his *t.*
2 *K.* 7:8 lepers went into one *t.*
1 *Chr.* 15:1 D. pitched a *t.* for ark
2 *Chr.* 25:22 fled ev. man to his *t.*
Is. 13:20 nor Arabian pitch *t.* th.
38:12 age removed as a shep.'s *t.*
40:22 spreadeth them out as a *t.*
54:3 enlarge the place of thy *t.*
Jer. 10:20 none to stretch forth *t.*
37:10 rise up every man in his *t.*

TENT-MAKERS.
Acts 18:3 by occupation *t. -m.*

TENTS.
Gen. 4:20 such as dwell in *t.*
9:27 Japheth shall dwell in *t.*
13:5 Lot also had herds and *t.*
25:27 a plain man, dwelling in *t.*
31:33 L. went into maid-serv. *t.*
Num. 16:16 gather for them to *t.*
Is. 6:13 yet in *t.* shall be a *t.*
John 1:39 it was about *t.* hour
See DAY, DEAL, MONTH, PART.

TEND.
Prov. 21:5 diligent *t.* to plento.

TEN

TENDETH.
Prov. 10:16 labor of righteous *t.*
11:19 as righteousness *t.* to life
  21 withholdeth, it *t.* to poverty
14:23 talk of lips *t.* to penury
19:23 fear of the Lord *t.* to life

TENDER.
Gen. 18:7 Abra. fetched a calf *t.*
33:13 lord know. children are *t.*
Deut. 28:54 men that is *t.* among
  56 the *t.* and delicate woman
33:2 small rain on the *t.* herb
2 *Sam.* 23:4 as *t.* grass springing
2 *K.* 22:19 heart *t.* 2 *Chr.* 34:27
1 *Chr.* 22:5 Sol. young and *t.* 29:1
Job 14:7 *t.* branch will not cease
38:27 cause the *t.* herb to spring
Prov. 4:3 *t.* and belov. in sight of
27:25 the *t.* grass showeth itself
Cant. 2:13 the vines with *t.* grape
  7:12 see whether *t.* grape appear
Is. 47:1 no more be called *t.* and
53:2 shall grow up as a *t.* plant
Ezek. 17:22 I will crop off a *t.* one
Dan. 1:9 G. brought Dan. into *t.*
4:15 in earth, in the *t.* grass, 23
Mat. 24:32 bra. is *t. Mark* 13:28
Luke 1:78 thro' *t.* mercy of God
Jam. 5:11 L. is pitiful, of *t.* mercy

TENDER-HEARTED.
2 *Chr.* 13:7 Reh. young and *t.-h.*
Eph. 4:32 be kind and *t.-h.*

See MERCIES.

TENDERNESS.
Deut. 28:56 set foot ou gro. for *t.*

TENONS.
Ex. 28:17 two *t.* in one board, 19;
  36:22, 24

TENOR.
Gen. 43:7 according to *t.* of words
Ex. 34:27 after *t.* of these words

TENTH.
Gen. 8:5 waters dec. to *t.* month
28:22 *t.* of all give unto the
Ex. 16:36 omer is *t.* part of ephah
29:40 *t.* deal of flour, *Num.* 28:5
Lev. 5:11 *t.* part of ephah, 6:20;
  Num. 5:15
6:20 *t.* part of ep. for meat-off.
16:29 *t.* day of seven. month, 23:27; 25:9
23:13 *t.* deals, 24:5; *Num.* 15:6;
  28:12, 20, 28; 29:3, 9, 14
27:32 *t.* shall be holy to the L.
Num. 18:21 given child. of L. *t.*
28:5 *t.* deal of flour for meat-off.
Deut. 23:2 *t.* genera. not enter
1 *Sam.* 8:15 take *t.* of seed and *t.*
  17 he will take *t.* of sheep
2 *K.* 25:1 *t.* day of the *t.* month,
  Jer. 52:4; *Ezek.* 24:1
Neh. 10:38 *t.* part of *t.* to house
Is. 6:13 but in it shall be a *t.*
Ezek. 45:11 *t.* part of homer, 14
Amos 5:3 leave *t.* to house of Is.
Luke 18:12 give *t.* of all I possess
Heb. 7:2 Abra. gave *t.* of spoils
  4 consider how gr. this man
    was, to wh. Abra. gave *t.*
Rev. 11:13 the *t.* part of city fell

TEN *times.*
Gen. 31:7 changed wages *t. t.* 41
Num. 14:22 have tempt. me *t. t.*
Neh. 4:12 J. came, said to us *t. t.*
Job 19:3 *t. t.* ye reproached me
Dan. 1:20 found them *t. t.* better

TENS.
Ex. 18:21 over them rul. of *t.* 25
Deut. 1:15 heads, captains over *t.*

TER

Num. 24:2 Bal. saw Is. abid. in *t.*
  5 how goodly are thy *t.*, O Jac.
Deut. 1:27 ye murmur. in your *t.*
33 search a pla. to pitch your *t.*
5:30 get you into your *t.* again
11:6 earth swallowed up their *t.*
33:18 rejoice, Issachar, in thy *t.*
Jos. 22:4 get you unto your *t.* 6
  8 return wi. riches unto your *t.*
Jud. 6:5 Midianites came with *t.*
8:11 way of them th. dwelt in *t.*
1 *Sam.* 17:53 spoil. Philistines' *t.*
2 *Sam.* 11:11 Is. and J. abide in *t.*
20:1 every man to his *t.* 1 *K.*
  12:16 ; 2 *Chr.* 10:16
1 *K.* 8:66 I. we. to th. *t.* 2 *Chr.* 7:10
2 *K.* 7:7 Syrians left their *t.* 10
8:21 peo. fled into their *t.* 14:12
13:5 children of Israel dwelt in *t.*
1 *Chr.* 4:41 they smote *t.* of Ham
  8:10 they dwelt in Hagarites' *t.*
2 *Chr.* 14:15 smote *t.* of cattle
31:2 to praise in *t.* of the Lord
Ezr. 8:15 we abode in *t.* 3 days
Ps. 69:25 let none dw. in their *t.*
78:55 made Israel to dwell in *t.*
84:10 th. dwell in *t.* of wickedn.
106:25 murmured in their *t.* and
120:5 I dwell in the *t.* of Kedar
Cant. 1:5 comely as *t.* of Kedar
Jer. 4:20 suddn. are my *t.* spoiled
  6:3 they shall pitch their *t.*
30:18 bring captiv. of Jacob's *t.*
35:7 days ye shall dwell in *t.*
10 but we have dwelt in *t.*
49:29 th. *t.* and flocks shall they
Hab. 3:7 I saw the *t.* of Cushan
Zec. 12:7 L. shall save *t.* of Jud.
14:15 plague of all in these *t.*

TERAH.
Gen. 11:24 begat T. 1 *Chr.* 1:26
  26 T. begat Abr. 27 ; *Jos.* 24:2
31 T. took Abram his son, and

TERAPHIM.
Jud. 17:5 made an ephod and *t.*
18:14 in these houses is *t.* 20
Hos. 3:4 many days without *t.*

TERMED.
Is. 62:4 sh. no more be *t.* forsak.

TERRACES.
2 *Chr.* 9:11 me. of algum-trees *t.*

TERRESTRIAL.
1 *Cor.* 15:40 bodies *t.* glory of *t.*

TERRIBLE.
Ex. 34:10 for it is a *t.* thing
Deut. 1:19 went thro' *t.* wild. 8:15
7:21 Lord is a mighty God and *t.*
10:17 ; *Neh.* 1:5 ; 4:14 ; 9:32
10:21 done *t.* thi. 2 *Sam.* 7:23
Jud. 13:6 angel of God, very *t.*
Job 37:22 with God is *t.* majesty
39:20 glory of his nostrils is *t.*
41:14 teeth are *t.* round about
Ps. 45:4 hand sh. teach *t.* things
47:2 the Lord most high is *t.* he
65:5 by *t.* things in righteous.
66:3 *t.* art thou in thy works
  5 f. is his doing towards men
68:35 thou art *t.* out of thy holy
76:12 he is *t.* to the kings of
99:3 prai. thy great and *t.* name
106:22 done *t.* things by R. sea
145:6 shall speak of thy *t.* acts
Cant. 6:4 art *t.* as an army, 10
Is. 13:11 lay low haughtin. of *t.*
18:2 to a peo. *t.* 7 fr. a people *t.*
21:1 from desert, from a *t.* land
25:3 the city of the *t.* nations
  4 blast of *t.*, ones is as a storm
  5 branch of *t.* shall be bro. low
29:5 mult. of *t.* ones be as chaff
  20 *t.* one is brought to naught
49:25 prey of *t.* sh. be delivered
64:3 when thou didst *t.* things
Jer. 15:21 red. out of hand of *t.*
20:11 L. is as a mighty *t.* one
Ezek. 1:22 colour of the *t.* crystal
28:7 will bring the *t.* of nations
upon thee, 30:11; 31:12
32:12 cause to fall *t.* of nations
  39:1 form of image was *t.*
7:7 fourth beast dreadf. and *t.*
Joel 2:11 L. is great and very *t.*
31 before the great and *t.* day
Hab. 1:7 Chaldeans are *t.* and
Heb. 12:21 so *t.* was sight of it

TERRIBLENESS.
Deut. 26:8 L. brought us with *t.*
1 *Chr.* 17:21 make thee a name *t.*
Jer. 49:16 thy *t.* hath deceived th.

TERRIBLY.
Is. 2:19 to shake *t.* the earth, 21
Nah. 2:3 fir-trees sh. be *t.* shak.

CRUDEN'S CONCORDANCE. 1051

TES
TERRIFY.
Job 3:5 let blackness of day *t.* it
9:31 his rod, let not his fear *t.*
31:34 did contempt of famil. *t.*?
2 *Cor.* 10:9 seem as if I wo. *t.* you
TERRIFIED, EST.
Deut. 20:3 fear not nor be *t.*
Job 7:14 thou *t.* me thro' visions
Luke 21:9 hear of wars, be not *t.*
24:37 they were *t.* and affrighted
Phil. 1:28 in nothing *t.* by adv.
TERROR.
Gen. 35:5 the *t.* of God was upon
Lev. 26:16 will ap. over you *t.*
Deut. 32:25 sw. without, *t.* with,
34:12 in the *t.* which M. shewed
Jos. 2:9 *t.* is fallen upon us
Job 31:23 destruc. fr. G. was a *t.*
33:7 my *t.* not make thee afraid
Ps. 10:5 not afr. for *t.* by night
Is. 10:33 L. will lop bough wi. *t.*
19:17 Ju. shall be a *t.* to Egypt
33:18 thy heart shall meditate *t.*
54:14 thou shalt be far from *t.*
Jer. 17:17 not a *t.* 20:4 *t.* to thys.
32:21 brought forth Isr. with *t.*
Ezek. 26:17 cause *t.* to be on all
21 I make th. a *t.* 27:36; 28:19
32:23 wh. caused *t.* 24, 25, 26, 27
30 with their *t.* they are asha.
32 I have caused my *t.* in land
Rom. 13:3 rulers not *t.* to good
2 *Cor.* 5:11 knowing the *t.* of L.
1 *Pet.* 3:14 be not afraid of th. *t.*
TERRORS.
Deut. 4:34 essa. to take nat. by *t.*
Job 6:4 *t.* of God set themselves
18:11 *t.* shall make him afraid
14 sh. bring him to king of *t.*
20:25 sword cometh, *t.* are upon
24:17 they are in the *t.* of death
27:20 *t.* take hold on him
30:15 *t.* are turned upon me
Ps. 55:4 *t.* of death are fallen on
73:19 utterly consumed with *t.*
88:15 while I suff. *t.* I am distr.
th. *t.* have cut me off
Jer. 15:8 caused *t.* to fall on city
Lam. 2:22 hast called my *t.*
Ezek. 21:12 *t.* by reason of sword
TERTIUS.
Rom. 16:22 I T. who wrote this
TERTULLUS.
Acts 24:1 certain orator nam. T.
2 T. began to accuse Paul
TESTAMENT.
Mat. 26:28 this is my blood in
new *t. Mark* 14:24
Luke 22:20 this cup is the new *t.*
1 *Cor.* 11:25
2 *Cor.* 3:6 made minis. of new *t.*
14 remains veil, in read. old *t.*
Heb. 7:22 surety of a better *t.*
9:15 he is mediator of new *t.* for
redemption under that *t.*
16 where a *t.* is, th. must death
17 *t.* is of force after men dead
20 this is blood of *t.* G. enjoin.
Rev. 11:19 in temple ark of *t.*
TESTATOR.
Heb. 9:16 of neces. be death of *t.*
17 no strength while *t.* liveth
TESTIFY.
Num. 35:30 one witness not *t.*
Deut. 8:19 I *t.* that ye sh. perish
19:16 if a false wit. *t.* against
31:21 song *t.* ag. them as witn.
32:46 set yo. hearts to wor. I *t.*
Neh. 9:31 wherew. thou didst *t.*
Job 15:6 thine own lips *t.* ag. th.
Ps. 50:7 O Is. I *t.* ag. thee, 81:8
Is. 59:12 our sins *t.* against us
Jer. 14:7 our iniquities *t.* ag. us
Hos. 5:5 pride of Israel doth *t.*
Amos 3:13 *t.* in house of Jacob
Mic. 6:3 what have I done? *t.* ag.
Luke 16:28 send Lazn. that he *t.*
John 2:25 that any sho. *t.* of man
3:11 *t.* have seen; 5:39 *t.* of me
7:7 bec. I *t.* of it; 15:26 *t.* of me
Acts 2:40 wi. oth. words did he *t.*
10:42 *t.* it is he was ordained of G.
23:11 to *t.* gospel of grace of G.
26:5 know they, if th. would *t.*
Gal. 5:3 I *t.* to ev. man circum.
Eph. 4:17 this I say, and *t.* in L.
1 *John* 4:14 we ha. seen and *t.*
Rev. 22:16 I Jesus sent ang. to *t.*
18 I *t.* to ev. man that heareth
TESTIFIED.
Ex. 21:29 it hu. been *t.* to owner
Deut. 19:18 *t.* falsely ag. brother
Ruth 1:21 sec. L. hath *t.* ag. me
2 *K.* 17:13 yet L. *t.* against Israel

TES
2 *K.* 17:15 testim. he *t.* ag. them
2 *Chr.* 24:19 prophets *t.* against
them, *Neh.* 9:26
Neh. 13:15 I *t.* against them, 21
John 4:39 for saying wh. wo. *t.*
44 Je. himself *t.* a proph. 13:21
Acts 8:25 wh. they *t.* and preach
18:5 P. *t.* to Jews that J. was C.
23:11 us thou hast *t.* of me at J.
28:23 to whom he *t.* king. of G.
1 *Cor.* 15:15 bec. we ha. *t.* of G.
1 *Thes.* 4:6 we forewarned you, I
1 *Tim.* 2:6 gave himself to be *t.*
Heb. 2:6 one in a certain place *t.*
1 *Pet.* 1:11 *t.* beforeh. sufferings
1 *John* 3:9 witness G. *t.* of his S.
3 *John* 3 *t.* of truth that is in th.
TESTIFIEDST, ETH.
Neh. 9:34 *t.* ag. them by Sp. 30
Hos. 7:10 pride of Is. *t.* his face
John 3:32 wh. he ha. seen, he *t.*
21:24 disciple wh. *t.* for those thi.
Heb. 7:17 he *t.* thou art a priest
Rev. 22:20 which *t.* these things
TESTIFYING.
Acts 20:21 *t.* both to Jews and G.
Heb. 11:4 witn. G. *t.* of his gifts
1 *Pet.* 5:12 *t.* this is grace of God
TESTIMONY.
Ex. 16:34 pot of manna bef. *t.*
25:16 sh. put into ark the *t.* 21
27:21 without vail before *t.*
30:6 mercy-s. over *t. Lev.* 16:13
31:18 gave M. two tables of *t.*
32:15 tables of *t.* in hand, 34:29
38:21 this is sum of tabern. of *t.*
Num. 1:50 Lev. over taber. of *t.*
53 Lev. pitch about taber. of *t.*
9:15 cloud covered the tent of *t.*
10:11 cloud taken off taber. of *t.*
17:4 thou sh. lay up rods bef. *t.*
10 bring Aa. rod again bef. *t.*
Ruth 4:7 and this was a *t.* in Is.
2 *K.* 11:12 gave the king the *t.*
2 *Chr.* 23:11
Ps. 78:5 he established a *t.* in J.
81:5 this he orda. in Jos. for *t.*
119:88 so sh. I keep *t.* of mouth
122:4 tribes go up to the *t.* of Is.
132:12 if thy children keep my *t.*
Is. 8:16 bind up *t.* 20 law and *t.*
Mat. 8:4 off. M. commanded for
a *t. Mark* 1:44; *Luke* 5:14
10:18 *t.* against them, *Mark* 13:9
Mark 6:11 sh. dust for *t. Luke* 9:5
Luke 21:13 ah. turn to you for *t.*
John 3:32 no man receiv. his *t.*
33 he that receiv. *t.* set to seal
8:17 wit. *t.* of two men is true
21:24 know that his *t.* is true
Acts 13:22 to wh. also he gave *t.*
14:3 gave *t.* to word of his grace
22:18 they will not recei. thy *t.*
2 *Cor.* 1:12 *t.* of our conscience
2:1 declaring unto you *t.* of God
2 *Thes.* 1:10 bec. our *t.* was beli.
2 *Tim.* 1:8 not asham. of *t.* of L.
Heb. 3:5 for a *t.* of things which were
11:5 Enoch had *t.* he pleased G.
Rev. 1:2 bare record of *t.* of J. C.
9 I was in Patmos for *t.* of J.
6:9 souls of th. were slain for *t.*
11:7 when they have finished *t.*
12:11 overca. by word of th. *t.*
17 war with them wh. have *t.*
15:5 tabernacle of *t.* in heaven
19:10 *t.* of J. is spirit of proph.
See ARK.
TESTIMONIES.
Deut. 4:45 these are *t.* M. spake
6:17 sh. diligently keep *t.* of G.
20 wh. mean *t.* G. commanded
1 K. 2:3 to keep his statutes and
his *t.* 2 *K.* 23:3 ; 1 *Chr.* 29:19 ;
2 *Chr.* 34:31
Jer. 44:23 nor walked in his *t.*
Neh. 9:34 nor kings hearkened *t.*
Ps. 25:10 keep coven. and his *t.*
78:56 tempted G. kept not his *t.*
93:5 thy *t.* are very sure
99:7 kept *t.* and ordinances
119:2 bles. are they th. keep *t.*
14 rejoiced in way of thy *t.*
22 I have kept thy *t.* 167, 168
24 thy *t.* deli. 31 stuck to thy *t.*
36 incline my heart to thy *t.*
46 I will speak of *t.* bef. kings
59 I turned my feet to thy *t.*
79 have known *t.* turn to me
95 wait, will consider *t.*
99 more than meditation
111 thy *t.* have I taken
119 I love thy *t.* 125 know *t.*
129 thy *t.* are wonderful
138 thy *t.* are righte. faithful
144 righteous. of *t.* everlasting

THE
Ps. 119:146 save me, and I shall
keep *t.*
152 concerning *t.* I have kno.
157 yet do I not decline fr. *t.*
168 *t.* 24:23 have not walked in *t.*
THADDEUS. *Mark* 3:18
THANK.
Luke 6:32 those that love you
what *t.* have ye? 33:34
THANK, Verb.
1 *Chr.* 16:4 appoint, Lev. to *t.* L.
7 Da. delivered psalm to *t.* L.
23:30 stand ev. morning to *t.* L.
29:13 we *t.* thee, praise name
Dan. 2:23 I *t.* thee, praise thee
Mat. 11:25 Je. said, I *t.* thee, O
Fa. L. of heaven, *Luke* 10:21
Luke 17:9 doth he *t.* that serv.?
18:11 G. I *t.* thee, not as oth. men
John 11:41 Father, I *t.* thee
1 *Cor.* 1:4 I *t.* G. on your behalf
14 I *t.* G. I bapt. none of you
14:18 I *t.* G. I speak with tong.
Phil. 1:3 I *t.* G. on rem. of you
1 *Tim.* 2:15 for this wh. I *t.* God
2 *Tim.* 1:3 *t.* G. whom I serve
Phile. 4 I *t.* God, mak. mention
See OFFERING.
THANKED.
2 *Sam.* 14:22 J. bowed, *t.* king
Acts 28:15 P. *t.* G. took courage
Rom. 6:17 G. be *t.* ye were serv.
THANKFUL.
Ps. 100:4 *t.* to him *Col.* 3:15
Rom. 1:21 glori. not, nor we. *t.*
THANKFULNESS.
Acts 24:3 we accept it with all *t.*
THANKING.
2 *Chr.* 5:13 singers were one *t.*
THANKWORTHY.
1 *Pet.* 2:19 *t.* if man endure grief
THANKS.
Neh. 12:31 companies th. gave *t.*
Dan. 6:10 he prayed, and gave *t.*
Mat. 26:27 he took the cup, and
gave *t. Luke* 22:17
Mark 8:6 seven loaves and ga. *t.*
14:23 when he had given *t.* he
Luke 2:38 Anna gave *t.* to Lord
22:19 and gave *t.* and brake it
Acts 27:35 broken it, and ga. *t.* to G.
Rom. 14:6 for he giveth G. *t.* he
cateth not, and giveth G. *t.*
1 *Cor.* 11:24 had given *t.* he bra.
14:17 thou verily givest *t.* well
2 *Cor.* 1:11 *t.* may be given
2:14 to G. who caus. triumph
8:16 *t.* to G. who put care in N.
9:15 *t.* to G. for unspeak. gift
Eph. 5:20 giving *t.* always for all
1 *Thes.* 3:9 what *t.* can we render
Heb. 13:15 offer praise, giving *t.*
Rev. 4:9 give *t.* to him on throne
See GIVE, GIVING.
THANKSGIVING.
Lev. 7:12 if he offer it for a *t.*
Neh. 11:17 to begin *t.* in prayer
12:8 which was over the *t.*
Ps. 26:7 publish with voice of *t.*
50:14 offer unto God *t.* pay vows
69:30 I will mag. him with *t.*
95:2 come before his face wi. *t.*
100: I enter into his gates wi. *t.*
107:22 let sacrifice sacri. of *t.*
147:7 sing to the L. with *t.* sing
Is. 51:3 *t.* and melo. found therein
Jer. 30:19 out of them shall proceed *t.*
Amos 4:5 offer a sacrifice of *t.*
Jon. 2:9 sacrifice with voice of *t.*
2 *Cor.* 4:15 redound thro' us *t.* to God
Phil. 4:6 wi. *t.* let your requests
Col. 2:7 abounding therein wi. *t.*
4:2 watch in the same with *t.*
1 *Tim.* 4:3 to be recei. wi. *t.*
4 creature good if recei. with *t.*
Rev. 7:12 *t.* and hon. be to our G.
THANKSGIVINGS.
Neh. 12:27 keep dedication wi. *t.*
2 *Cor.* 9:12 abundant by many *t.*
THEATRE.
Acts 19:29 they rush. into the *t.*
31 would not adventure into *t.*

THI
THEBEZ.
Jud. 9:50 went Abimelech to T.
1 *Sam.* 11:21 that he died in T.
THEFT, S.
Ex. 22:3 he sh. be sold for his *t.*
4 if the *t.* be found in his hand
Mat. 15:19 out of the heart proceed *t. Mark* 7:22
Rev. 9:21 nei. repented they of *t.*
THELASAR. 2 *K.* 19:12
THENCE.
Num. 23:13 curse me th. fr. *t.* 27
Deut. 4:29 if from *t.* thou seek L.
15 the Lord brought thee out
t. 6:23 ; 24:18
t. 8:23 shall not be from *t.* any
Ezr. 6:6 thereof. be ye far from *t.*
Is. 65:20 no more from *t.* an infant of
Jer. 5:6 every one that goes *t.*
46:14 he shall go forth from *t.*
Luke 16:26 that would come fr. *t.*
THEOPHILUS.
Acts 1:1 treatise have I ma. O T.
THERE.
John 12:26 where I am. *t.* sh. my
14:3 where I am, *t.* ye may be
THEREAT.
Ex. 30:19 wash th. feet *t.* 40:31
Mat. 7:13 many th. be wh. go in *t.*
THEREBY.
Gen. 24:14 *t.* shall I know thou
Job 22:21 with G. *t.* good will co.
Mat. 21:7 they set him *t. Luke* 19:35 ; *John* 12:14
19 found nothing *t.* but leaves,
Mark 11:13 ; *Luke* 13:6
THERETO.
Ps. 119:9 by taking heed *t.*
THEREUNTO.
1 *Pet.* 3:9 knowing ye are *t.* call.
THESSALONICA.
Acts 17:1 at T. was a synagogue
11 more noble than those of T.
27:2 one Aristarchus of T. being
Phil. 4:16 in T. ye sent once and
2 *Tim.* 4:10 Demas depart. to T.
THEUDAS.
Acts 5:36 bef. th. days rose up T.
THICK.
Deut. 32:15 waxen fat, grown *t.*
2 *Sam.* 18:9 under *t.* boughs
1 *K.* 8:15 he took a *t.* cloth, and
Neh. 8:15 branches of *t.* trees
Job 15:26 runneth on *t.* bosses
Ps. 74:5 lift. up axes on *t.* trees
Ezek. 6:13 slain under ev. *t.* tree
19:11 among *t.* branches
31:3 among *t.* boughs, 10, 14
Hab. 2:6 lad. himself with *t.* clay
Luke 11:29 peo. gathered *t.* tog.
See CLOUDS, DARKNESS.
THICKET.
Gen. 22:13 a ram caught in a *t.*
1 *Sam.* 13:6 Israel did hide in *t.*
Is. 9:18 wickedn. sh. kindle in *t.*
10:34 cut down *t.* of the forest
Jer. 4:7 lion is come up fr. his *t.*
29 city sh. flee and go into *t.*
THICKNESS.
2 *Chr.* 4:5 *t.* of wa. a handbreadth
Jer. 52:21 pillar four fingers
Ezek. 41:9 *t.* of wall five cubits
42:10 chamb. were in *t.* of wall
THIEF.
Ex. 22:2 if *t.* be found break. 7
Deut. 24:7 stealing, th. *t.* sh. die
Job 24:14 the murderer is as a *t.*
30:5 cried after them as after *t.*
Ps. 50:18 when thou sawest a *t.*
Prov. 29:24 *t.* hateth his own soul
6:30 not despi. *t.* if he stead
Jer. 2:26 as *t.* ashamed when fo.
Hos. 7:1 *t.* cometh in, robbers
Joel 2:9 shall enter house of *t.*
Zec. 5:4 shall enter house of *t.*
Mat. 24:43 known what hour *t.*
would come he wo. *Luke* 12:39
John 10:1 climbeth up some o. *t.*
10 *t.* cometh not but to steal
12:6 bec. he was a *t.* and had
1 *Thes.* 5:2 day of L. *t.* cometh
4 that day should overtake *t.*
2 *Pet.* 3:10 day of L. will co. as *t.*
Rev. 3:3 I will come as *t.* 16:15
THIEVES.
Is. 1:23 princes rebel. comp. of *t.*
Jer. 48:27 Is. a derision? am. *t.*
49:9 if *t.* by night will destroy
Obad. 5 if *t.* came, would th. not
Mat. 6:19 *t.* break thro. and steal
20 where *t.* do not break thro.
21:13 made it den of *t. Mark* 11:17 ; *Luke* 19:46
27:38 two *t.* crucified with him
44 *t.* cast same in his teeth
Luke 10:30 certain man fell am. *t.*
36 neighbour to him fell am. *t.*
John 10:8 came before me are *t.*
1 *Cor.* 6:10 nor *t.* inherit king. G.
THIGH.
Gen. 24:2 put hand under *t.* 9
32:25 touched hollow of Jacob's *t.*
31 halted upon his *t.* 32
46:26 souls came out of his *t.*
Ex. 28:42 breeches reach to *t.*
Num. 5:21 L. make *t.* to rot, 22, 27
Jud. 3:16 Ehud gird dagger on *t.*
21 put hand, took dag. from *t.*
8:30 G. had 70 sons of his *t.*
15:8 sm. them hip and *t.* slau.
Ps. 45:3 gird sw. on *t.* O Most M.
Cant. 3:8 every man hath sw. *t.*
Jer. 31:19 instruc. I smote on *t.*
Ezek. 21:12 cry, smite upon *t.*
24:4 every good piece *t.* should.
Rev. 19:16 on *t.* name written
THIGHS.
Ex. 28:42 breeches reach to *t.*
Cant. 7:1 joints of thy *t.* are like
Dan. 2:32 belly and *t.* of brass
THINE.
Gen. 14:23 I will not take any *t.*
31:32 look wh. is *t.* with me, ta.
33:9 keep that thou hast unto *t.*
48:6 thy issue *t.* aft. shall be *t.*
Num. 18:9 shall be *t.* of holy
Deut. 15:3 with *t.* ha. let it go
4 day, overtake you as a *t.*

CRUDEN'S CONCORDANCE. 1055

THR

Mic. 5:2 tho' little among *t.* of J.
6:7 will L. be plea. wi. *t.* rams?
Acts 21:23 *t.* of Jews which belie.
Rev. 5:11 number of them, *t.* of *t.*
See CAPTAINS.

THREAD.
Gen. 14:23 not take fr. *t.* to latch.
38:28 bound on hand scarl. *t.* 30
Jos. 2:18 bind scar. *t.* in window
Jud. 16:9 bra. withs as *t.* of tow
12 he brake ropes fr. arms as *t.*
Cant. 4:3 lips like *t.* of scarlet

THREATEN, ED.
Acts 4:17 let us straitly *t.* th. 21
1 *Pet.* 2:23 wh. he suff. he *t.* not

THREATENING, S.
Acts 4:29 Lord, behold their *t.*
9:1 Saul yet breathing out *t.*
Eph. 6:9 same to th. forbearing *t.*

THREE.
Gen. 18:2 and lo, *t.* men stood by
Ex. 21:11 do not th. *t.* unto her
Deut. 4:41 Moses served *t.* cities,
19:2, 3, 7, 9
17:6 mouth of *t.* witnes. 19:15
2 *Sam.* 24:12 I offer thee *t.* things,
1 *Chr.* 21:10
Prov. 30:15 *t.* things never satis.
18 *t.* thi. too wonderf. for me
21 for *t.* thi. earth is disquieted
29 *t.* things which go well,
Ezek. 14:14 *t.* men were in, 16, 18
Acts 10:19 *t.* men seek thee, 11:11
1 *Cor.* 13:13 now abideth these *t.*
14:27 by two, or at most by *t.*
29 let prophets speak two or *t.*
1 *Tim.* 5:19 before two or *t.* wit.
1 *John* 5:7 *t.* bear record in heaven, and these *t.* agree
See DAYS.

THREE months.
Gen. 38:24 about *t. m.* after it
Ex. 2:2 child, she hid him *t. m.*
2 *Sam.* 6:11 ark of L. continued in ho. of O. *t. m.* 1 *Chr.* 13:14
24:13 wilt thou flee *t. m.* before thine enemies? 1 *Chr.* 21:12
Amos 4:7 were yet *t. m.* to harv.
Acts 7:20 M. was nourished *t. m.*
10:8 P. spake the space of *t. m.*
24 Paul abode in Greece *t. m.*
Heb. 11:23 Mo. was hid *t. m. mths*
THREE-TAVERNS. *Act.* 28:15

THREE times.
Ex. 23:14 *t. t.* keep a feast to me
17 *t. t.* in year all males shall appear bef. L. *Deut.* 16:16
Num. 22:28 smitten me *t. t.* 32, 33
1 *K.* 17:21 stretched on child *t. t.*
2 *K.* 13:25 *t. t.* did Joash beat 11.
1 *Chr.* 8:13 offering *t. t.* in year
Dan. 6:10 he kneeled *t. t.* a day
13 D. maketh his petition *t. t.*
Acts 11:10 this was done *t. times*

THREE years.
Gen. 15:9 take heifer *t. y.* old
Lev. 25:21 br. forth fruits for *t. y.*
Deut. 14:28 end of *t. y.* br. tithe
1 K. 2:39 end of *t. y.* S.'s servant
10:22 once in *t. years* came navy
of Tarshish, 2 *Chr.* 9:21
2 *K.* 17:5 Assyr. besieged S. *t. y.*
18:10 at end of *t. y.* th. took it
1 *Chr.* 21:12 tho, either *t. y.* fam.
2 *Chr.* 11:17 made R. strong *t. y.*
t. y. th. walked in way of D.
31:16 fr. *t. y.* old and upwards
Is. 16:14 within *t. y.* as of *t.* hired.
20:3 so Isa. walked barefoot *t. y.*
Jer. 48:34 as a heifer of *t. y.* old
Dan. 1:5 nourishing them *t. y.*
Amos 4:4 br. your tithes aft. *t. y.*
Luke 4:25 shut *t. y. Jam.* 5:17
12:7 th. *t. y.* I come seek, fruit
Acts 20:31 *t. y.* I ceased not to
Gal. 1:18 after *t. y.* I went to J.
See HUNDRED.

THREEFOLD.
Ec. 4:12 *t.* cord not quic. brok.

THREESCORE.
Gen. 25:26 Isaac *t.* wh. she bare
Deut. 3:4 took fr. them *t.* cities,
Jos. 13:30
2 *Sam.* 2:31 Abr. hand, and *t.* died
1 *K.* 4:13 to him pertain, *t.* cities
6:2 length of L.'s house *t.* cub.
2 *K.* 25:19 he took *t.* men of peo.
Jer. 52:25 *Hezron* married *t.* old
2 *Chr.* 11:21 Rehob. took *t.* concu.
Ezr. 6:3 height of temple *t.* cub.
Cant. 3:7 *t.* valli. men are about
6:8 *t.* queens, fourscore concu.

THR

Jer. 52:25 put to death *t.* men
Dan. 3:1 wh. height was *t.* cubits
Luke 24:13 fr. Jerus. *t.* furlongs
1 *Tim.* 5:9 widow be tak. und. *t.*
See SIXTY.

THREESCORE and one.
Num. 31:39 trib. of asses *t. a. o.*

THREESCORE and two.
Dan. 5:31 Dar. *t. a. t.* years old
9:25 in *t. a. t.* weeks street built
26 after *t. a. t.* weeks Messiah

THREESCORE and five.
Is. 7:8 within *t. a. f.* years Eph.

THREESCORE and six.
Gen. 46:26 came with Ja. *t. a. s.*

THREESCORE and ten.
Gen. 46:27 house of Ja. which ca. into E. *t. a. t. Deut.* 10:22
50:3 mourned for Is. *t. a. t.* days
Ex. 15:27 *t. a. t.* palm trees, *Num.* 33:9
Jud. 1:7 *t. a. t.* kings, thum. cut
9:5 slew *t. and t.* persons, 18, 24
12:14 that rode on *t. and t.* asses
2 *Chr.* 29:32 bro. *t. a. t.* bullocks
36:21 to fulfil *t. and ten* years
Ps. 90:10 days of our *t. y. t. a. t.*
Acts 23:23 ready *t. a. t.* horsem.
See SEVENTY.

THREESCORE and twelve.
Num. 31:38 trib. *t. and t.* beeves

THREESCORE and fifteen.
Acts 7:14 Jos.'s kindr. *t. and f.*

THRESH.
Is. 41:15 th. sh. *t.* mountains
Jer. 51:33 floor it is time to *t.* her
Mic. 4:13 and *t.* O daughter of Zi.
Hab. 3:12 didst *t.* heath. in anger

THRESHED, ETH.
Jud. 6:11 Gid. *t.* wheat by the
Is. 28:27 fitches not *t.* with inst.
Amos 1:3 because they *t.* Gilead
1 *Cor.* 9:10 *t.* in hope, be partaker

THRESHING.
Lev. 26:5 *t.* reach to vintage
2 *Sam.* 24:22 here be *t.* instruments, 1 *Cor.* 21:23
2 *K.* 13:7 made th. like dust by *t.*
1 *Chr.* 21:20 Ornan was *t.* wheat
Is. 21:10 my *t.* and corn of floor
28:28 he will not ever be *t.* it
41:15 make sharp *t.* instrument
See FLOOR, FLOORS.

THRESHOLD.
Jud. 10:27 her hands were on *t.*
1 *Sam.* 5:4 hands cut off on the *t.*
5 tread not on *t.* of Dagon
1 *K.* 14:17 came to *t.* child died
Ezek. 9:3 glory of G. on *t.* 10:4
10:18 glory of G. departed fr. *t.*
43:8 in their setting of their *t.*
46:2 prince shall worship at *t.*
47:1 waters issued from under *t.*
Zep. 1:9 pun. all that leap on *t.*

THRESHOLDS.
Neh. 12:25 keeping ward at the *t.*
Ezek. 43:8 setting threshold by *t.*
Zep. 2:14 desolation shall be *t.*

THREW.
2 *Sam.* 16:13 Shi. *t.* stones at Da.
2 *K.* 9:33 they *t.* down high places
Mark 12:42 she *t.* in two mites
Luke 9:42 the devil *t.* him down
Acts 22:23 cried, *t.* dust in air

THREWEST.
Neh. 9:11 persecu. *t.* into deeps

THRICE.
Ex. 34:23 *t.* in year ap. app. 24
2 *K.* 13:18 Joash smote *t.* stayed
19 shalt smite Syria but *t.*
Mat. 26:34 thou shalt deny me *t.*
75; *Mark* 14:30, 72; *Luke* 22:34; *John* 13:38
Acts 10:16 this was done *t.* vessel
2 *Cor.* 11:25 *t.* was I beaten with rods, *t.* I suffered shipwreck
for *t.* this I besought the L. *t.*

THROAT.
Ps. 5:9 *t.* is an open sep. *Rom.* 3:13
69:3 weary of crying, *t.* is dried
115:7 neither speak thro' their *t.*
Prov. 23:2 put a knife to *t.* if glu.
Jer. 2:25 withh. thy *t.* fr. thirst
Mat. 18:28 servant took him by *t.*

THRONE.
Gen. 41:40 in *t.* will I be greater
Deut. 17:18 sitteth on *t.* of king.
1 *Sam.* 2:8 make them inherit *t.*
2 *Sam.* 3:10 to set up *t.* of David
7:13 'stablish *t.* of kingdom, 16

THR

1 *K.* 1:13 Solomon shall sit on my *t.* 17, 24, 30, 35
48 given one to sit on my *t.*
2:4 not fail thee a man on the *t.* of Israel, 8:25; 9:5; 2 *Chr.* 6:16; *Jer.* 33:17
12 Sol. sat on *t.* of David, 24; 8:20; 10:9; 1 *Chr.* 29:23; 2 *Chr.* 6:10
10:18 king made a *t.* 2 *Chr.* 9:17
2 *K.* 10:3 set him on his fath.'s *t.*
30 fourth gener. sit on *t.* 15:12
11:19 Joa. sat on *t.* 2 *Chr.* 23:20
Neh. 3:7 repair. to *t.* of governor
Job 36:7 with kings are th. on *t.*
Ps. 9:4 thou satest in *t.* judging
11:4 the Lord's *t.* is in heaven
45:6 thy *t.* O God, is for ever, *Lam.* 5:19; *Heb.* 1:8
47:8 G. sitteth on *t.* of his holi.
89:4 will build thy *t.* to all gen.
14 jus. and judgm. are of thy *t.*
94:20 sh. *t.* of iniq. ha. fellow.?
132:11 fr. of body will I set on *t.*
12 children shall sit on *t.* for ever
Prov. 20:8 king that sit. in *t.* of
Ec. 5:1 I saw L. sitting upon a *t.*
9:7 on *t.* of Da. and his kingdom
14:13 I will exalt my *t.* ab. stars
22:23 I fasten him as nail in *t.*
47:1 there is no *t.* O daughter of
66:1 heaven is my *t. Acts* 7:49
Jer. 3:17 call Jerusalem *t.* of L.
13:13 kings th. sit on David's *t.*
14:21 do not disgrace *t.* of glory
17:12 a glori. high *t.* from begin.
25 sitting on *t.* of Da. 22:4, 30
22:2 sittest upon the *t.* 29:16
38:30 none to sit on *t.* of David
49:38 I will set my *t.* in Elam
Ezek. 1:26 likeness of a *t.* 10:1
43:7 place of my *t.* shall Is. no
Hag. 2:22 I will overthrow the *t.*
Zech. 6:13 shall sit in *t.* 28:31
29:30 Son shall sit in *t.* 28:31
Luke 1:32 L. sh. give him *t.* of D.
Heb. 4:16 come boldly to *t.* of gr.
8:1 on rt. hand of *t.* of God, 12:2
12:2 sat down at right hand of *t.*
4:2 a *t.* was set, one sat on the *t.*
3 was a rainbow round about *t.*
5 out of *t.* proceed. lightnings. were seven lamps before *t.*
6 before *t.* was a sea of glass, in midst of *t.* and about *t.* were 4 beasts
10 bef. him that sat on *t.* 7:11
5:1 in hand of him that sat on *t.*
6 in the midst of the *t.* a Lamb
7 out of hand of him sat on *t.*
13 glory to him that sit. on *t.*
6:16 hide fr. him that sit. on *t.*
7:9 a multitude stood before *t.*
10 our God which sitteth on *t.*
15 they are bef. *t.* of God, that sitteth on *t.* shall dwell
17 the Lamb in midst of *t.* shall
12:5 without fault before *t.* of G.
19:4 worshipped G. that sat on *t.*
20:11 I saw a great white *t.* and
21:5 he that sat on *t.* said, Beh.
22:1 a river proceeding out of *t.*
3 *t.* of God and Lamb shall be

His THRONE.
Ex. 11:5 that sits on *h. t.* 12:29
1 *Sam.* 14:9 king and *h. t.* guilt.
1 *K.* 1:37 L. make *h. t.* greater, 47
2:19 he bowed, and set on *h. t.*
33 and on *h. t.* shall be peace
16:11 as so. as *h. t.* sat on *h. t.*
22:10 king sit *h. t.* and Jehoshaphat, king of Judah, sat each on *h. t.* 2 *Chr.* 18:9
19 L. sit. on *h. t. 2 Chr.* 18:18
Neh. 13:13 Jeroh. sat upon *h. t.*
25:28 set *h. t.* above the throne
Est. 5:1 queen stood over ag. *h. t.*
Job 26:9 hold, back face of *h. t.*
Ps. 9:7 prepared *h. t.* for judgm.
89:29 *h. t.* to endure as days
36 *h. t.* shall endure as sun
97:2 judgment habita. of *h. t.*
103:19 L. prep. *h. t.* in heaven
Prov. 20:28 *h. t.* is upholden
25:5 wi. earth *h. t.* at gates
29:14 *h. t.* shall be establ.
Jer. 1:15 sh. set every one *h. t.*
13:13 was deposed from *h. t.*
Jon. 3:6 king of N. rose fr. *h. t.*
Zech. 6:13 sit he shall rule *h. t.*
Mat. 19:28 Son of man sit on *h. t.* 25:31
Acts 2:30 raise up Chr. to sit *h. t.*
Rev. 1:4 from seven spi. bef. *h. t.*
3:21 set down wi. my *t.* in *h. t.*

THR

Rev. 12:5 child was cau. up to *h. t.*
See ESTABLISH, E-TABLISHED.

THRONES.
Ps. 122:5 are set *t.* of judgment
Is. 14:9 raised up from their *t.*
Ezek. 26:16 princes sh. come fr. *t.*
Dan. 7:9 till *t.* were cast down
Mat. 19:28 sh. sit on 12 *t. Lu.* 22:30
Col. 1:16 whether they be *t.*
Rev. 20:4 I saw *t.* and they sat

THRONG, ED, ING.
Mark 3:9 lest they should *t.* him
5:24 much peo. *t.* him, *Luke* 8:42
31 thou seest multitude *t.* thee
Luke 8:45 the multitude *t.* thee

THROUGH.
Rom. 11:36 *t.* him, to him, *t.* him 4:16 one God who is *t.* all

THROUGHLY.
Job 6:2 my grief were *t.* weighed
Ps. 51:2 wash me *t.* from iniq.
Jer. 7:5 if ye *t.* amend yo. ways
Ezek. 16:9 I *t.* wash. away blood
Mat. 3:12 *t.* purge, *Luke* 3:17

THROUGHOUT.
Mark 14:9 gosp. preach. *t.* world
John 19:23 woven from the top *t.*
Rom. 1:8 faith is spo. of *t.* world
See GENERATIONS.

THROW.
Jud. 2:2 sh. *t.* down their altars
6:25 *t.* down the altar of Baal
2 *K.* 9:33 *t.* her down, so they
Jer. 1:10 over nations *t.* down
31:28 I watched over them, to *t.*
Ezek. 16:39 th. sh. *t.* down thine
Mic. 5:11 I will *t.* down thy stro.
Mal. 1:4 build, I will *t.* down

THROWING.
Num. 35:17 smite with *t.* stone

THROWN.
Ex. 15:1 horse and rider *t.* 21
Jud. 6:32 he hath *t.* down altar
2 *Sam.* 20:21 his head shall be *t.*
1 *K.* 19:10 Isr. have *t.* down, 14
Jer. 31:40 it shall not be *t.* down
50:15 her walls are *t.* down
Lam. 2:2 L. ha. *t.* down in wrath
17 hath *t.* down, not pitied
Ezek. 29:5 I will have th. *t.* into
19:20 mount. shall be *t.* down
Nah. 1:6 the rocks are *t.* down
Mat. 24:2 stone th. shall not be *t.* down, *Mark* 13:2; *Lu.* 21:6
Luke 4:35 when devil had *t.* him
Rev. 18:21 Babyl. sh. be *t.* down

THRUST.
Ex. 11:1 sh. surely *t.* you out
12:39 they were *t.* out of Egypt
Num. 22:25 Bala.'s ass *t.* herself
25:8 Phinehas *t.* them through
35:20 hate with hatred *t.* him
22 if he *t.* him suddenly with
Deut. 13:5 *so t.* thee out of way
10 he sought to *t.* thee from L.
15:17 *t.* thu awl through his ear
Jud. 3:21 Eb. *t.* dagger into his
6:9 I *t.* fierce together, and
9:54 Zeb. *t.* out Gaal and breth.
11 young man *t.* Ah. through
11:2 and they *t.* out Jephthah
1 *Sam.* 11:2 I may *t.* out yo. eyes
31:4 s. with, *t.* me through, *t.* me th. uncircumcised *t.*, 1 *Chr.* 10:4
2 *Sam.* 2:16 *t.* sw. in his fellow's
18:14 Joab *t.* 3 darts thro' Abs.
23:6 Belial shall be as thorns *t.*
1 *K.* 2:27 Solom. *t.* out Abiathar
2 *K.* 4:27 *t.* Gehazi came to *t.* her
2 *Chr.* 26:20 they *t.* Uzziah out fr.
Ps. 118:13 thou hast *t.* at me
Is. 13:15 every one wh. is *t.* thro'
14:19 raiment of those th. are *t.*
Jer. 51:4 they that are *t.* through
Ezek. 16:40 they shall *t.* thee thro'
31:21 have *t.* wi. side and shoul.
46:18 *t.* them out of possessions
Joel 2:8 neither shall *t.* ano. th.
Zech. 13:3 shall *t.* him through
Luke 4:29 rose and *t.* him out of
5:3 prayed he would *t.* out a lit.
10:15 shalt be *t.* down to hell
13:28 and you yourselves *t.* out
John 20:25, 27 my ha. into his, 27
Acts 7:27 did *t.* him from them
16:24 them into inner prison
37 now do they *t.* us out privily
39 were bound to, and *t.* them
Heb. 12:20 touched mo. *t.* through
Rev. 14:15 *t.* in thy sickle, harv.
16 *t.* in his sickle on the earth
18 *t.* in thy sharp sickle

TID

THRUSTETH.
Job 32:13 God *t*. him down

THUMB, S.
Ex. 29:20 put it on *t*. of right hand. Lev. 8:23; 14:14-28
Jud. 1:6 ran, him and cut off *t*.
7 seventy kings hav. *t*. cut off

THUMMIM.
Ex. 28:30 put on breastplate, the urim and the *t*. Lev. 8:8
Deut. 33:8 let thy *t*. and urim be
Ezr. 2:63 priest with urim and *t*.
Neh. 7:65

THUNDER.
Ex. 9:23 the L. sent *t*. and hail
26 the *t*. shall cease, nor shall
1 Sam. 7:10 L. thundered with *t*.
12:17 send *t*. 18 the Lord sent *t*.
Job 26:14 *t*. of power who und. ?
28:26 way for light, of *t*. 38:25
39:19 clothed neck with *t*. ?
25 smelleth *t*. of captains afar
Ps. 77:18 voice of thy *t*. in heav.
81:7 I answ. thee in place of *t*.
104:7 at voice of thy *t*. th. hasted
Is. 29:6 sh. be visited of L. wi. *t*.
Mark 3:17 Boanerges, is sons of *t*.
Rev. 6:1 as it were the noise of *t*.
14:2 as the voice of a great *t*.

THUNDER, Verb.
1 Sam. 2:10 out of heav. sh. he *t*.
Job 40:9 canst thou *t*. like him ?

THUNDERS.
Ex. 9:33 *t*. and hail ceased, 34
19:16 *t*. and lightning. Rev. 16:18
See SEVEN.

THUNDERBOLTS.
Ps. 78:48 gave their flocks to *t*.

THUNDERED, ETH.
1 Sam. 7:10 Lord *t*. with thunder
2 Sam. 22:14 the L. *t*. Ps. 18:13
Job 37:4 he *t*. with his excellency
5 G. *t*. marvellously with voice
Ps. 29:3 God of glory *t*. the Lord
John 12:29 heard it, said that it *t*.

THUNDERINGS.
Ex. 9:28 be no more mighty *t*.
20:18 all the people saw the *t*.
Rev. 4:5 out throne proc. *t*. 19:6
8:5 th. were voices and *t*. 11:19

THUS and THUS.
Jos. 7:20 *t*. and *t*. have I done
Jud. 18:4 *t*. and *t*. dealeth Micah
2 Sam. 17:15 *t*. *t*. did Ahithop, counsel A. and *t*. a. *t*. have I
1 K. 14:5 *t*. and *t*. say to Jero.'s
2 K. 5:4 *t*. and *t*. said maid of Is.
9:12 *t*. and *t*. spake he to me

THYATIRA.
Acts 16:14 of city of T. worship,
Rev. 1:11 wh. is, send send to T.
2:18 to angel of church in T.
24 to you and to the rest in T.

THYSELF.
Gen. 13:9 separate *t*. I pray thee
14:21 give persons, take goods *t*.
33:9 keep that thou hast unto *t*.
Ex. 10:3 refuse to humble *t*.
28 take heed to *t*. see my face no more, 34:12; Deut. 4:9;
12:13, 19:33; 1 Sam. 19:2
18:22 shall it be easier for *t*.
Est. 4:13 think not with *t*. thou
Ps. 40:18 thou doest well to *t*.
John 1:22 what sayest thou of *t*. ?
18:34 sayest thou this of *t*. ?
Rom. 14:22 hast faith ? have to *t*.

THYINE.
Rev. 18:12 merchant of *t*. wood

TIBERIAS.
John 6:1 Galilee, wh. is sea of T.
23 came other boats from T.

TIBNI.
1 K. 16:21 half people followed T.
22 ag. those that followed T.

TIDAL. Gen. 14:1, 9

TIDINGS.
Ex. 33:4 when peo. heard evil *t*.
1 Sam. 4:19 Phine. wife heard *t*.
11:4 told *t*. of men of Jabesh, 5
27:11 none alive to bring *t*. to G.
2 Sam. 4:4 when *t*. came of Saul
13:30 *t*. came, Absa. hath slain
18:19 run and bear king *t*.
20 thou sh. not bear *t*. this day
22 why run ? hast no *t*. ready
25 C. said, *t*. my lord the king
1 K. 2:28 then *t*. came to Joab
14:5 I am sent to thee with *t*.
1 Chr. 10:9 to carry *t*. to idols
Ps. 112:7 not be afraid of evil *t*.
Jer. 20:15 cursed that brought *t*.
49:23 for they have heard evil *t*.

TIM

Ezek. 21:7 thou shalt answ. for *t*.
Dan. 11:44 *t*. out of east trouble
Luke 1:19 show thee glad *t*. 2:10
8:1 showing glad *t*. kingd. of G.
Acts 11:22 *t*. of th. things came
13:32 declare unto you glad *t*.
21:31 *t*. came to chief captain
Rom. 10:15 bring glad *t*. of good
See GOOD.

TIE.
1 Sam. 6:7 *t*. kine to the cart, 10
Prov. 6:21 and *t*. about thy neck

TIED.
Ex. 39:31 *t*. to it a lace of blue
2 K. 7:10 horses *t*. and asses *t*.
Mat. 21:2 ye shall find an ass *t*.
Mark 11:2, 4; Luke 19:30

TIGLATH-PILESER.
2 K. 15:29 T. took I]. and Kedesh
16:7 Ah. sent messengers to T.
1 Chr. 5:6 T. carried Bee. captive
26 God stirred up spirit of T.
2 Chr. 28:20 T. distressed Ahaz

TILE, ING.
Ezek. 4:1 son of man, take th. a *t*.
Luke 5:19 let him down thro' *t*.

TILL, Conjunctive.
Dan. 4:23 *t*. sev. times pass over
19:13 go thy way *t*. the end be
John 21:22 he tarry *t*. I come, 23
See CONSUMED, MORNING.

TILL, ED, EST, ETH.
Gen. 2:5 not a man to *t*. 3:23
4:12 when thou *t*. ground, it
2 Sam. 9:10 servants shall *t*. land
Prov. 12:11 that *t*. sh. be satisfied
28:19 th. *t*. land sh. have plenty
Jer. 27:11 they that *t*. it, and dw.
Ezek. 36:9 ye sh. be *t*. and sown
34 desolate land shall be *t*.

TILLAGE.
1 Chr. 27:26 them that were for *t*.
Neh. 10:37 Lev. have tithes of *t*.
Prov. 13:23 much food in *t*.

TILLER.
Gen. 4:2 Cain was *t*. of ground

TIMBER.
Lev. 14:45 sh. break down the *t*.
1 K. 5:18 so they prepared *t*.
1 Chr. 22:14; 2 Chr. 2:9
15:22 they took away *t*. of Ra.
Ezr. 5:8 *t*. is laid in walls
6:11 let *t*. be pulled fr. his house
Neh. 2:8 give me *t*. to ma. beams
Ezek. 2:3 lay thy *t*. in water
Hab. 2:11 beam out of *t*. answer
Zec. 5:4 shall consume it with *t*.

TIMBREL.
Ex. 15:20 wom. went out with *t*.
Job 21:12 take psalm, bring *t*.
Ps. 81:2 take psalm, bring *t*.
149:3 sing praises to him with *t*.
150:4 praise him with *t*.

TIMBRELS.
Ex. 15:20 wom. went out with *t*.
Jud. 11:34 daught. came with *t*.
2 Sam. 6:5 house of Is. played before Lord on *t*. 1 Chr. 13:8
Ps. 68:25 damsels play. with *t*.

TIME.
Gen. 18:10 accord. to *t*. of life, 14
24:11 *t*. women go to draw wat.
27:20 *t*. he make him overseer
47:29 *t*. drew nigh Is. must die
Ex. 2:33 old shall pay for loss of *t*.
Lev. 15:25 beyond *t*. of separa.
18:18 besides other in her life-*t*.
Num. 23:20 *t*. was *t*. of ripe gra.
26:10 wh. *t*. fire devou. 250 men
Deut. 16:9 *t*. thou put sickle
Jos. 10:27 at *t*. of going down of sun, 2 Chr. 18:31
42 land did Josh. take at one *t*.
Jud. 18:31 *t*. house of G. in Shi.
2 Sam. 7:11 since *t*. I command.
11:1 *t*. when kings go to battle
23:8 eight hand. slew at one *t*.
1 K. 8:65 to come from *t*. to *t*.
Ezr. 4:10 at such a *t*. 17 ; 7:12
10:13 and it is a *t*. of rain.
Neh. 2:6 return ? I set him a *t*.
Est. 4:14 *t*. they wax warm
9:19 who shall set me a *t*.
15:32 accomplished before his *t*.
22:16 were cut down out of *t*.
38:23 preserved ag. *t*. of trouble
39:1 knoweth. th. *t*. br. forth ?
Ps. 32:6 *t*. thou mayest be found
37:19 not be ashamed in evil *t*.
41:1 L. deli. him in *t*. of trouble
56:3 I am afraid, I trust in th.
69:13 prayer to thee in accept. *t*.

TIM

Ps. 81:15 their *t*. should have endured
89:47 remember how short I. is
103:19 until *t*. his word came
Ec. 3:1 *t*. to ev. purpose, 17 ; 8:6
2 a *t*. to be born, a *t*. to die, a *t*. to plant
7:17 why should thou die before thy *t*. ?
8:5 wise man's heart discern. *t*.
9:11 *t*. and chance happen. to all
12 so are men snared in evil *t*.
Is. 26:17 near *t*. of her delivery
28:19 from *t*. it goeth forth
43:21 decla. this from ancient *t*.
48:16 from *t*. it was, there am I
40:8 in an acceptable *t*. I heard
60:22 L. will hasten it in his *t*.
Jer. 6:15 at *t*. I visit, cast down
8:7 swallow observe *t*. of com.
13 looked for *t*. of health
14:8 Saviour tho. in *t*. of trouble
19 *t*. of healing, behold trouble
30:7 it is *t*. of Jacob's trouble
46:21 *t*. of their visitation 50:27
49:8 *t*. I will vi-it him, 50:31
19 who will app. me *t*. ? 50:44
51:33 floor, it is *t*. to thresh her
Ezek. 4:10 fr. *t*. to *t*. sh. thou eat
16:8 thy *t*. was the *t*. of love
57 as *t*. of thy reproach of dau.
30:3 it shall be the *t*. of heathen
Dan. 2:8 I know ye would gain *t*.
9 speak, till the *t*. be changed
16 desired he would give him *t*.
3:5 at wh. *t*. ye hear cornet, 15
7:12 lives were prolong. for a *t*.
22 *t*. came saints posses. kingd.
25 until *t*. and divid. of *t*. 12:7
9:17 at *t*. of end shall be vision
9:21 touched *t*. of evening obla.
11:24 forecast his devices for a *t*.
35 to make th. white, *t*. of end
40 at *t*. of end king of south
12:1 there shall be a *t*. of trouble
a seal book, even to *t*. of end, 9
11 fr. *t*. sacrifice be taken away
Hos. 10:12 is it *t*. to seek the L.
Mic. 5:3 till *t*. she which travail
Hag. 1:4 is it *t*. for you, O ye
Zec. 14:7 evening *t*. it sh. be light
Mal. 3:11 cast her fruit before *t*.
Mat. 3:11 *t*. they were car. away
2:7 H. inquired *t*. star appeared
8:29 come to torment us bef. *t*.
21:31 when *t*. of fruit drew near
26:18 master saith, *t*. is at hand
Mark 1:15 *t*. is fulfilled, repent
4:17 and so endure but for a *t*.
6:35 and now the *t*. is far passed
11:13 for *t*. of figs was not yet
13:33 ye know not wh. *t*. is
Luke 1:57 Elisabeth's full *t*.
4:5 showed kingd. in mom. of *t*.
7:45 this woman, since *t*. I came
8:13 in *t*. of tempta. fall away
13:35 not see me till I. come
19:44 knew. not *t*. of visitation
John 7:6 my *t*. is not co. your *t*.
16:2 *t*. cometh, whoever killeth
25 *t*. com. I wh. no more speak
7:17 when *t*. of prom. drew nigh
20 in what *t*. Moses was born
17:21 spent their *t*. in no. else
Rom. 13:11 it is high *t*. to awake
5:6 in due *t*. Christ died
8:18 judge nothing before *t*.
7:5 except with consent for a *t*.
29 say, brethren, *t*. is short
Gal. 3:10 redeeming *t*. Col. 4:5
1 Thes. 3:17 taken fr. you short *t*.
2 Thes. 2:6 might be revealed in *t*.
2 Tim. 4:3 *t*. come, will not end.
6 *t*. of my departure is at hand
Heb. 4:16 to help in *t*. of need
5:12 for *t*. ye ought to be teach.
9:9 figure for the *t*. then present
10 impos. till *t*. of reformation
11:32 *t*. would fail to tell of G.
Jam. 4:14 that appeareth little *t*.
1 Pet. 1:17 pass *t*. of sojourning in fear
17 pass *t*. of sojourn[in]g in fear
4:2 no longer live rest of his *t*.
Rev. 1:3 for *t*. is at hand, 22:10
10:3 there should be *t*. no longer
12:12 devil, hav. but short *t*.
12:12 knoweth he hath a short *t*.
14 she is nourished for a *t*.

Any TIME.
Lev. 25:32 Lev. redeem at any *t*.
Num. 22:30 was I ever wont at any *t*.
John 1:18 no man seen G. at any *t*.
5:37 nor heard his voice at a. *t*.
Heb. 2:1 lest at any *t*. we should
1 John 4:12 no man see G. at a. *t*.
See APPOINTED, BEFORE, COME, DAY, DUE.

TIM

In the TIME.
Gen. 38:27 came to pass in the *t*.
1 K. 15:23 in the *t*. of old age he
2 Chr. 28:22 in the *t*. of distress
Neh. 9:27 in the *t*. of trouble thou
Ps. 4:7 in *t*. *t*. when corn increa.
27:5 in the *t*. of trouble sh. hide
71:9 cast not off in the *t*. of age
Jer. 2:27 in the *t*. of trouble they
28 save thee in *t*. *t*. of trouble
11:12 not save th. in *t*. *t*. of tro.
14 not hear th. in *t*. *t*. they cry
18:23 deal thus with th. in *t*. *t*.
Ezek. 27:34 in *t*. *t*. when thou sh.
Hos. 2:9 take corn in the *t*. thor.
Zec. 10:1 rain in the *t*. of rain
Mat. 13:30 in the *t*. of harvest
See LAST, LONG, MANY, OLD, PAST, PROCESS, SET.

That TIME.
Neh. 4:16 from *t*. *t*. forth, 13:21
Is. 16:13 concern. M. since *t*. *t*.
18:7 in that *t*. shall the pres. be
45:21 who hath told it fr. *t*. *t*. ?
Mat. 4:17 from *t*. *t*. Je. began to
16:21 from that *t*. began to show
26:16 from *t*. *t*. J. sought oppor.

At that TIME.
Deut. 5:5 I stood between the Lord and you at that *t*.
9:19 L. hearkened at *t*. *t*. 10:10
Jos. 5:2 Josh. at *t*. *t*. circ.
Jud. 3:29 slew of Moab at *t*. *t*.
21:14 then came Ben. ag. *t*. *t*.
2 Chr. 30:3 not keep passo. at *t*. *t*.
32:17 Je. kept passover at *t*. *t*.
Zep. 3:20 at that *t*. will I br. you
Eph. 2:12 at *t*. *t*. we without Ch.
See THAN.

This TIME.
Ex. 9:14 *t*. *t*. send my plagues
18 to-morrow about *t*. *t*. I will
Num. 23:23 according to *t*. *t*.
Jud. 13:23 nor would at *t*. *t*. ha.
1 Sam. 9:13 ab. *t*. *t*. ye shall find
2 Sam. 17:7 coun. not good at *t*. *t*.
1 K. 2:26 not at *t*. *t*. put to death
19:2 to-morrow L. *t*. 20:6; 2 K.
7:1, 18; 10:6
Neh. 13:6 all *t*. *t*. was not I at J.
Est. 4:14 hold, thy peace at *t*. *t*.
Ps. 113:2 blessed be L. from *t*. *t*.
115:18 we will bless L. from *t*. *t*.
121:8 he will pres. thee from *t*. *t*.
Is. 48:6 showed new thi. fr. *t*. *t*.
Jer. 3:4 wilt thou not fr. *t*. *t*. cry ?
Acts 1:6 wilt thou at *t*. *t*. restore ?
24:25 answ. Go thy way for *t*. *t*.
Rom. 3:26 deci. at *t*. *t*. his right.
9:9 at *t*. *t*. will I come, S. shall
11:5 so at *t*. *t*. present *t*. there is a
1 Cor. 16:12 not to come at *t*. *t*.

TIMES.
Gen. 27:36 supplanted me two *t*.
Lev. 19:26 ye shall not observe *t*.
Deut. 18:10, 14
Jud. 13:25 S. began to move at *t*.
16:20 I will go out as at other *t*.
20:31 began to kill as at other *t*.
1 Sam. 3:10 L. call. as at other *t*.
20:25 sat on seat as at other *t*.
2 K. 21:6 Manasseh observed *t*.
2 Chr. 33:6
1 Chr. 12:32 had understand. of *t*.
29:30 the *t*. that went over him
1 Chr. 15:5 in these *t*. no peace
Ezr. 1:13 men which knew the *t*.
Job 24:1 *t*. are not hid. fr. Almi.
Ps. 9:9 L. a ref. in *t*. of trouble
10:1 why hid. in *t*. of trouble ?
31:15 my *t*. are in thy hand
44:1 works th. didst in *t*. of old
77:5 considered. years of ancient *t*.
Is. 33:6 knowledge stability of *t*.
46:10 from ancient *t*. things not
Ezek. 12:27 he prophesied of *t*.
Dan. 2:21 he changeth *t*. and laws
7:25 think to change *t*. and laws
9:25 streets sh. he built in tro. *t*.
11:14 in th. *t*. shall many stand
12:7 for a time, *t*. Rev. 12:14
Mat. 16:3 not discern signs of *t*. ?
Luke 21:24 till *t*. of the Gentiles
Acts 1:7 not for you to kn. the *t*.
3:19 *t*. of refreshing shall come
21 the *t*. of restitution of all
17:26 math determined the *t*.
30 *t*. of Ignorance God winked
Rom. 11:30 ye in *t*. past have not
2 Cor. 11:24 five *t*. rec. I stripes
Gal. 1:23 persecuted in *t*. past
4:10 days and months, *t*. years
Eph. 1:10 dispense. of fuln. of *t*.
1 Thes. 5:1 of *t*. ye have no need
1 Tim. 4:1 in latter *t*. some shall
6:15 in his *t*. he sh. show who is

CRUDEN'S CONCORDANCE. 1057

TIT

2 *Tim.* 3:1 in last days perilous *t.*
Tit. 1:3 in *t.* manifest. his word
Heb. 1:1 God who at sundry *t.*

All TIMES.
Lev. 16:2 come not at all *t.*
Ps. 34:1 I will bless Lord at all *t.*
62:8 trust in him at all *t.* ye peo.
119:20 to thy judgments at all *t.*
Prov. 5:19 breasts satisfy at a. *t.*
17:17 a friend loveth at all *t.*

See APPOINTED, MANY, SEVEN, TEN, THREE.

TIMNATH.
Gen. 38:12 to his shearers in T.
Jud. 14:1 Samson went to T.

TIMON. *Acts* 6:5

TIMOTHEUS.
Acts 16:1 cert. disciple named T.
Rom. 16:21 T. my work-fellow
1 *Cor.* 16:10 if T. come, see that
2 *Cor.* 1:19 was preach. ev. by T.
Phil. 2:19 trust in L. to send T.
1 *Thes.* 3:2 we sent T. to comfort

TIMOTHY.
2 *Cor.* 1:1 and T. our brother
1 *Tim.* 1:2 T. my son, 2 *Tim.* 1:2
Heb. 13:23 bro. T. set at liberty

TIN.
Num. 31:22 *t.* that may abide fire
Is. 1:25 will take away all thy *t.*
Ezek. 22:18 they are brass, and *t.*
20 as they gather lead and *t.*
27:12 Tarshish was merch. in *t.*

TINGLE.
1 *Sam.* 3:11 ears of ev. one shall
t. 2 *K.* 21:12; *Jer.* 19:3

TINKLING.
Is. 3:16 mi..cing and making a *t.*
18 take away their *t.* ornam.
1 *Cor.* 13:1 I am bec. *t.* cymbal

TIP.
Luke 16:24 may dip *t.* of finger
See RIGHT EAR.

TIPHSAH. 1 *K.* 4:24

TIRE, ED.
2 *K.* 9:30 Jezebel *t.* her head and
Ezek. 24:17 bind *t.* of thy head

TIRES.
Is. 3:18 L. will take away their *t.*
Ezek. 24:23 your *t.* sh. be on hea.

TIRHAKAH. 2 *K.* 19:9

TIRSHATHA.
Ezr. 2:63 T. said th. *Neh.* 7:65
Neh. 7:70 T. gave gold to the
10:1 sealed were Nehem. the T.

TIRZAH.
Num. 26:33 and T. daughters of
Zeloph. 36:11; *Jos.* 17:3
27:1 Hoglah, and Melc. and T.
Jos. 12:24 Joshua sm. king of T.
1 *K.* 14:17 Jeroboam's wife to T.
15:21 Baasha reigned in T. 33
16:8 Elah reigned in T. 15 23,
17 O, besieged in T. 23 reigned
2 *K.* 15:16 smote coasts from T.
Cant. 6:4 th. art beautiful as T.

TITHE.
Lev. 27:30 the *t.* of land is L.'s
Num. 18:26 off. a tenth part of *t.*
Deut. 12:17 not eat the *t.* of corn
14:23 at end of three years bring *t.*
2 *Chr.* 31:5 they brought the *t.*
of all thin. 6, 12; *Neh.* 13:12
Neh. 10:38 Levites shall bring *t.*
Mat. 23:23 pay *t.* of mint, anise

TITHE, Verb.
Deut. 14:22 thou sh. *t.* increase.
Luke 11:42 ye *t.* mint and rue

TITHES.
Gen. 14:20 Abr. gave Melchi. *t.*
Lev. 27:31 man redeem of his *t.*
Num. 18:24 *t.* I have given to L.
24 heave-off. to Lord of your *t.*
Deut. 12:6 ye sh. bring your *t.* 11
. 26:12 made end of tithing the *t.*
14:28, 14:37 Levites might have *t.*
12:5 come were appointed for *t.*
13:5 aforetime they laid *t.* of
Amos 4:4 bring your *t. Mal.* 3:10
Mal. 3:8 ye have robbed me of *t.*
Luke 18:12 I give *t.* of all I poss.
Heb. 7:5 have command. to re. *t.*
6 he received *t.* of Abraham
8 here men that die receive *t.*
9 Levi who received *t.* paid *t.*

TITHING.
Deut. 26:12 end of *t.* 3 1 year is *t.*

TITLE.
2 *K.* 23:17 wh. *t.* is that that I s.

TOL

John 19:19 P. wrote a *t.* and put
20 this *t.* read many of the Je.

TITLES.
Job 32:21 nor give flat. *t.* to man
22 I kn. not to give flattering *t.*

TITTLE.
Mat. 5:18 one *t.* shall in no wise
Luke 16:17 one *t.* of law to fail

TO.
2 *Cor.* 2:13 bec. I found not T.
7:6 comforted us by com. of T.
13 more joyed we for joy of T.
14 which I made before T.
8:6 desired T. *Gal.* 2:1 took T.
16 earnest care into heart of T.
23 whether any inquire of T.
12:18 T. made a gain of you?
Gal. 2:3 nor was T. comp. to be
3 *Tim.* 4:10 T. is departed to D.

TO AND FRO. *See* FRO.

TOB. *Jud.* 11:3, 5

TOBIAH.
Ezr. 2:60 children of T. not also.
Neh. 2:10 T. heard, 19; 4:7; 6:1
6:12 T. hired him; 11:14, of T.
19 T. sent let. put me in fear
13:4 Eliashib was allied to T.
8 cast forth house. stuff of T.

TOI.
Ex. 29:20 upon great *t.* of their
right toe, *Lev.* 8:23, 24;
14:14, 17, 25, 28

TOES.
Jud. 1:6 cut off thumbs and *t.*
7 seventy kings hav. *t.* cut off
1 *Chr.* 20:6 fingers and *t.* were 24
Dan. 2:41 thou sawest the *t.* 42

TOGARMAH.
Gen. 10:3 Riphath, T. 1 *Chr.* 1:6
Ezek. 27:14 of house of T. traded

TOGETHER.
Ezr. 4:3 ourselves *t.* will build
Prov. 22:2 rich and poor meet *t.*
Ec. 4:11 if two lie *t.* then they
Is. 65:25 wolf and lamb sh. feed *t.*
Mat. 18:20 two or three gath. *t.*
19:6 what God hath joined *t.* let
not man put, *Mark* 10:9

See DWELL.

TOI. 2 *Sam.* 8:9, 10
Gen. 5:29 conc. our work and *t.*
41:51 God made me forget my *t.*

TOIL, ED, ING.
Mat. 6:28 they *t.* not, neither do
they spin, *Luke* 12:27
Mark 6:48 saw them *t.* in rowing
Luke 5:5 Mast. we ha. *t.* all nig.

TOKEN.
Gen. 9:12 this is the *t.* of, 13, 17
Ex. 3:12 shall be a *t.* I sent thee
12:13 the blood shall be for a *t.*
13:9 it shall be for a *t.* upon thy hand
Num. 17:10 kept for *t.* Ag. rebels
Jos. 2:12 and give me a true *t.*
Ps. 86:17 show me a *t.* for good
Phil. 1:28 evident *t.* of perdition
2 *Thes.* 1:5 *t.* of righteous judg.
3:17 which is the *t.* in ev. epist.

TOKENS.
Deut. 22:15 br. *t.* of virgin. 17, 20
Job 21:29 do ye not know th. *t.*
Ps. 65:8 they that are afraid at *t.*
135:9 sent *t.* in midst of thee
Is. 44:25 frustrateth *t.* of liars

TOLA.
Gen. 46:13 T. son of I, 1 *Chr.* 7:1
Jud. 10:1 T. son of Puah, arose

TOLD.
Gen. 37:10 he *t.* it to his father
Num. 23:26 *t.* not I thee, all that
Deut. 17:11 he *t.* thee, behold
Jud. 6:13 his miracles fathers *t.*
13:6 neither *t.* he me his name
23 not would have *t. such thi.*
14:2 he come up *t.* his father
16 not forth it, 16; 1 *Sam.* 14:1
1 *K.* 10:7 he *t.* all his friend, 18
13:11 they *t.* to their father
16:13 was it not *t.* my lord
2 *K.* 12:11 gave money, being *t.*
18:37 Rabs. had *t.* what he was
Job 15:18 which wise men have *t.*
Ps. 69:9 spent years as a tale *t.*
Is. 43:8 have not *t.* thee from?
52:15 who ha. *t.* it Dn. that hath
Dan. 8:26 vision which is *t.* true
Jon. 1:10 because he had *t.* them
Mat. 8:33 they went and *t.* every

TON

Mat. 14:12 took the bo. and *t.* J.
Luke 1:45 performance of tain. *t.*
2:18 wondered at things *t.* by
Luke 9:15 man *t.* Jews it was J.
Acts 9:6 be *t.* thee what do, 22:10

TOLD him.
Gen. 29:3 place of wh. G. *t. h.* 9
1 *Sam.* 3:13 *t. h.* I will jud. hou.
t. h. 33:36 so *t. h.* of family rein
2 K. 6:10 place man of God *t. h.*
Job 37:20 it be *t. h.* that I speak
Mark 5:33 woman *t. h.* all truth

TOLD me.
2 *Sam.* 4:10 when one *t. me*
1 *K.* 10:7 the half was not *t. me,*
2 *Chr.* 9:6
14:2 *t. me* I should be king over
2 *K.* 4:27 hid, and hath not *t. me*
8:11 he *t.* wh. should. recover
John 4:29 which *t. me* all thi. 39
Acts 27:25 sh. be as it was *t. me*

TOLD you.
Is. 40:21 *t. y.* from beginning?
Hab. 1:5 not beli. tho' it be *t. y.*
Mat. 24:25 behold, I *t. y.* before
28:7 ye shall see him, lo, I *t. y.*
John 3:12 if I *t. y.* earthly things
8:40 a man that hath *t. y.* truth
9:27 I have *t. y.* already, and *ye*
did not hear, 10:25
14:2 not so, I would have *t. y.*
29 I have *t. y.* before it come
16:4 have I *t. you,* that wh. time
come, ye may remem. I *t. y.*
18:8 said, I have *t. you* I am he
Gal. 5:21 have *t. y.* in time past
Phil. 3:18 walk of whom I *t. you*
1 *Thes.* 3:4 we *t.* you we sh. suff.
2 *Thes.* 2:5 I *t. you* these things

TOLERABLE.
Mat. 10:15 more *t.* for Sodo. and
Gomorrah, 11:24; *Mark* 6:11
Luke 10:12
11:22 more *t.* for Tyre, *Lu.* 10:14

TOLL.
Ezr. 4:13 th. will th. not pay *t.*
20 *t.* trib. and custom was paid
7:24 not be lawful to impose *t.*

TOMB.
Job 21:32 he shall remain in *t.*
Mat. 27:60 Joseph laid body in *t.*
Mark 6:29 laid John's corpse in *t.*

TOMBS.
Mat. 8:28 with devils com. out *t.*
Mark 5:5 he would build *t.* of the prophets

TONGS.
Ex. 25:38 *t.* thereof of gold
Num. 4:9 cov. *t.* wi. cloth of blue
1 *K.* 7:49 *t.* of gold, 2 *Chr.* 4:21
Is. 6:6 coal he had taken with *t.*
44:12 smith with *t.* work. coals

TONGUE.
Ex. 11:7 not a dog move his *t.* Isr.
Jud. 7:5 lappeth of water wi. *t.*
Job 5:21 hid from scourge of *t.*
15:5 thou choosest *t.* of crafty
20:12 hide wickedn. under his *t.*
16 the viper's *t.* sh. slay him
29:10 cl. cleav. to roof of mouth
Ps. 5:9 they flatter with their *t.*
10:7 under his *t.* is mischief
12:3 cut off *t.* speak. proud thi,
4 with our *t.* will we prevail
15:3 backbiteth not with his *t.*
34:13 keep *t.* fr. evil, 1 *Pet.* 3:10
37:30 his *t.* talketh of judgment
50:19 and thy *t.* frameth deceit
52:2 thy *t.* deviseth mischiefs
57:4 their *t.* is a sharp sword
61:3 whet their *t.* like sword
8 make *t.* fall on themselves
68:23 of thy dogs may be dip.
73:9 their *t.* walketh thro' earth
109:2 spo. ag. me with *t.* of ly.
13:3 done to th. thou false *t.* ?
12:2 nor *t.* filled with singing
Prov. 6:17 hateth proud, lying *t.*
24 flattery of *t.* of stra. woman
10:20 *t.* of just are choice silver
31 froward *t.* shall be cut out
12:18 *t.* of the wise is health
19 a lying *t.* is but for a mom.
15:2 *t.* of wise useth knowledge
4 wholes. *t.* is a tree of life
16:1 answer of *t.* is from the L.
17:4 liar giv. ear to naughty *t.*
20 perv. *t.* falls into mischief
18:21 den. and life in pow. of *t.*
21:6 by a lying *t.* is vanity
23 whoso keepeth *t.* keep. soul
25:15 soft *t.* breaketh the bone
23 angry counten. a backbit. *t.*
26:28 lying *t.* hateth th. afflicted

TOO

Prov. 23:32 he that flat. with *t.*
31:26 in her *t.* is law of kindne.
Cant. 4:11 milk are under thy *t.*
Is. 3:8 because their *t.* is ag. L.
11:15 destroy *t.* of Egyptian sea
30:27 his *t.* is as a devour. fire
32:4 *t.* of stammer. speak plain.
33:19 not see peo. of stammer. *t.*
35:6 then shall *t.* of dumb sing
41:17 when th. *t.* faili. for thirst
45:23 unto me ev. *t.* shall swear
50:4 L. ha. giv. me *t.* of learned
54:17 every *t.* that shall rise
55:14 ag. whom draw ye out *t.* ?
53:3 your *t.* muttered perverse.
Jer. 9:3 bend their *t.* like bow
6 taught their *t.* to speak lies
8 *t.* is an arrow shot out
18:18 let us smite him with *t.*
Ezek. 4:4 *t.* of sucking child cle.
Ezek. 3:26 make *t.* cleave to mo.
Hos. 7:16 princes fall for ra. of *t.*
Hab. 1:13 holdest *t.* when wicked
Zec. 14:12 *t.* consume in mouth
Mark 7:33 spit, and touch. his *t.*
35 his *t.* was loosed, *Luke* 1:64
Jam. 1:26 and bridleth not his *t.*
3:5 so the *t.* is a little member
6 the *t.* is fire; *t.* no man tame
8 *t.* can no man tame
John 3:18 nor love in *t.* in tru.

See DECEITFUL, HOLD.

My TONGUE.
2 *Sam.* 23:2 his wo. was in *my t.*
Est. 7:4 if sold, I had held *my t.*
Job 6:30 is there iniqui. in *my t.*
27:4 nor shall *my t.* utter deceit
33:2 *my t.* hath spok. in mouth
Ps. 22:15 *my t.* cleaveth to jaws
35:28 *my t.* shall speak of thy
righteousness, 51:14; 71:24
30:1 heed th. I sin not wi. *my t.*
30:3 hot, then spake I with *my t.*
45:1 *my t.* is pen of ready wri.
66:17 G. was extolled with *my t.*
119:172 *my t.* speak of thy word
137:6 let *my t.* cleave to mouth
139:4 not a word in *my t.*
Luke 16:24 dip finger, cool *my t.*
Acts 2:26 heart rejoice, *my t.* gl.

TONGUE, *for* language, speech.
Gen. 10:5 every one after his *t.*
Deut. 28:49 whose *t.* not unders.
Ezr. 4:7 letter written in syr. *t.*
Is. 28:11 anoth. *t.* will he speak
Dan. 1:4 might teach *t.* of Chal.
John 5:2 call. in Hebrew *t.* Beth.
Acts 1:19 in proper *t.* Aceldama
21:40 how hear we in our own *t.* ?
26:14 saying in Hebrew *t.* Saul
1 *Cor.* 14:2 speak in unkn. *t.* 4 27
9 by *t.* words easy understood
26 every one hath a psalm, a *t.*

Phil. 2:11 ev. *t.* confess., *J.* is L.
Rev. 5:9 redeemed out of every *t.*
9:11 in Hebrew *t.* is Abaddon
11:9 gospel to preach unto ev. *t.*
16:16 in Hebrew *t.* Armageddon

TONGUES.
1 *Tim.* 3:8 be gra. not doubl- *t.*

TONGUES.
Gen. 10:20 sons of N. after th. *t.*
31 sons of Shem, after their *t.*
Ps. 31:20 keep th. fr. strife of *t.*
55:9 O Lord, and divide their *t.*
78:36 lied to him with their *t.*
140:3 sharpened *t.* like a serpe.
Is. 66:18 gath. all nations and *t.*
Jer. 23:31 use their *t.* and say
Mark 16:17 sh. speak w. new *t.*
Acts 2:3 appeared cloven *t.* 4
11 hear in our *t.* works of God
10:46 heard them speak with *t.*
19:6 spake with *t.* prophesied
Rom. 3:13 with *t.* th. used dece.
1 *Cor.* 12:10 divers kinds of *t.* 28
12:1 tho' I speak with *t.* of men
13 they shall cen *t.*
14:5 I would ye all spake wi. *t.*
Rev. 7:9 stood before throne
10:11 prophesy before natio. *t.*
11:9 *t.* and natio. see dead bod.
13:7 power given him over *t.*
16:10 gnawed their *t.* for pain
17:15 thou sawe. are nations, *t.*

TOOK

Gen. 6:21 Dr. was not, G. *t.* him
Num. 11:25 L. *t.* of Spirit on hi.
23:28 L. *t.* not Saul *t.* the kingdom

CRUDEN'S CONCORDANCE.

TOP

2 *Sam.* 7:15 depart, as I *t.* fr. S.
Ps. 22:9 *t.* me out of womb. 71:6
  48:6 fear *t.* hold on them there
  55:14 *t.* sweet counsel together
Amos 7:15 L. *t.* me as I followed
Mat. 8:17 himself *t.* our infirmit.
  25:43 stranger, ye *t.* me not in
Mark 12:20 the first *t.* a wife
  21 second *t.* her, *Luke* 20:29, 30
  14:49 teaching, and ye *t.* me not
John 19:27 *t.* her to his home
Acts 1:16 guide to th. who *t.* Je.
Phil. 2:7 *t.* on him form of servu.
Col. 2:14 *t.* it out of way

TOOK away.

Ps. 69:4 that which I *t.* not aw.
Cant. 5:7 keepers *t.* aw. my veil
Ezek. 16:50 I *t.* them a. as I saw
Hos. 13:11 *t.* king a. in my wra.
Mat. 24:39 flood came, *t.* them a.
John 11:41 they *t.* aw. the stone

He TOOK.

Gen. 34:2 Sh. saw her, *he t.* her
Ex. 4:6 when *he t.* it out, hand
2 *Sam.* 13:11 *he t.* hold of her
  22:17 above *he t.* me, *Ps.* 18:16
1 *K.* 17:19 *he t.* her son out bos.
2 *K.* 5:24 *he t.* them fr. their ha.
Acts 16:33 *he t.* them same hour
  21:11 *he t.* Paul's girdle, bound
Heb. 9:16 *he t.* not hat. of angels

They TOOK.

Gen. 6:2 *t. t.* wives they chose
  14:11 *they t.* all goods of Sodom
  12 *t. t.* Lot, Abram's brother's
Deut. 1:25 *t. t.* of the fruit of land
Jos. 6:20 peo. went, and *t. t.* city
  11:19 all other *they t.* in battle
Jud. 3:6 *t. t.* their daught. to be
2 *K.* 10:14 *t. t.* them alive, and
Ezek. 23:13 I saw *th. t.* one way
Dan. 5:20 *t. t.* his glory from him
Mat. 21:46 *t. t.* him for a prophet
  28:15 *t. t.* the money, and did as
Mark 12:8 *t. t.* him, killed him
Luke 22:54 *t. t.* him, *John* 19:16
Acts 13:29 *t. t.* him down fr. tree

TOOK up.

Num. 23:7 Balaam *t. up* his par.
  able, 18; 24:3, 15, 20, 21, 23
Jos. 3:6 the priests *t. up* the ark,
  6:12; 1 *K.* 2:3
2 *K.* 2:13 *he t. up* mantle of Elij.
  10:15 *t.* him *up* into the chariot
Neh. 5:1 I *t. up* wine and gave
Ezek. 3:12 then the Spirit *t.* me
  up, 11:24; 43:5
Mat. 14:12 they *t. up* body of
  John, *Mark* 6:29
  16:9 many baskets ye *t. up*, 10
Mark 10:16 *he t.* them *up* in arms
Luke 2:28 *t.* him *up* in his arms
Acts 10:26 Pet. *t.* him *up*, saying
Rev. 18:21 mig. angel *t. up* stone

TOOKEST.

Ps. 99:8 tho. thou *t.* vengeance
Ezek. 16:18 *t.* thy broid. garmen.

TOOL.

Ex. 20:25 if lift up thy *t.* thou
  32:4 fashioned it with a grav. *t.*
Deut. 27:5 sh. not lift any iron *t.*
1 *K.* 6:7 nor any *t.* of iron heard

TOOTH.

Ex. 21:24 give *t.* for *t.* *Lev.* 24:20;
  Deut. 19:21; *Mat.* 5:38
  27 if he smite man-servant's *t.*
  he shall go free for *t.* sake
Prov. 25:19 a broken *t.* a foot out

TOP.

Gen. 11:4 tower wh. *t.* may reach
  28:12 *t.* of ladder reached heav.
  18 Ja. poured oil on *t.* of stone
Ex. 19:20 L. came on *t.* of Sinai
  24:17 like fire on *t.* of mount
  28:32 there shall be a hole in *t.*
  30:3 overlay *t.* with gold, 37:26
Num. 14:40 gat into *t.* of mount.
  20:28 Aaron died on *t.* of mount
  23:9 from *t.* of rocks I see him
Deut. 3:27 get into *t.* of Pis. 34:1
  28:35 fr. foot to *t.* of thy head
  33:16 on *t.* of him that was sep.
Jud. 6:26 build alt. on *t.* of rock
  9:51 peo. gat up to *t.* of tower
  15:8 Samson dwelt on *t.* of R.
1 *Sam.* 9:25 commun. on *t.* of, 26
2 *Sam.* 16:22 tent on *t.* of house
1 *K.* 10:19 the *t.* of throne round
2 *K.* 9:13 under him on *t.* of sta.
2 *Chr.* 25:12 cast from *t.* of rock
Esth. 5:2 *t.* of sceptre
Ps. 72:16 corn on *t.* of mountains
  102.7 a sparrow on the house-*t.*
Prov. 8:2 she stand. in *t.* of high
  21:9 in corner of house-*t.* 25:24

TOR

Prov. 23:34 lie. on the *t.* of a ma.
Cant. 4:8 the *t.* of Amana, fr. *t.*
Is. 2:2 L.'s house sh. be establis.
  15 *t. t.* of mountains, *Mic.* 4:1
  17:6 berries in *t.* of the bough
  30:17 a beacon on *t.* of mount.
  42:11 shout fr. the *t.* of mount.
Lam. 2:19 faint for hunger in *t.*
  4:1 stones poured in *t.* of streets
Ezek. 17:4 he cropt off *t.* of twigs
  22 crop off *t.* of young twigs
  24:7 she set it on *t.* of rock
  8 I set her blood on *t.* of rock
  26:4 ma. her like *t.* of rock, 14
  31:3 *t.* was am. boughs, 10, 14
  43:12 house on *t.* of mountains
Nah. 3:10 dashed at *t.* of streets
Mat. 24:17 on house-*t.* *Mark*
  13:15; *Luke* 17:31
  27:51 veil rent fr. *t.* to bottom,
  Mark 15:38
Luke 5:19 they went on house-*t.*
John 19:23 woven fr. *t.* through.
Heb. 11:21 leaning on *t.* of staff

See BILL.

TOPS.

Gen. 8:5 *t.* of mounta. were seen
2 *Sam.* 5:24 when hearest so, on
  t. of trees, 1 *Chr.* 14:15
2 *K.* 19:26 as grass upon house-*t.*
Ps. 129:6; *Is.* 37:27
Job 24:24 cut off as the *t.* of ears
Is. 2:21 into *t.* of ragged rocks
  15:3 on *t.* of houses every one
  22:1 wholly gone up to house-*t.*
Jer. 48:38 lamenta. on house-*t.*
Ezek. 6:13 slain in *t.* of mounta.
Hos. 4:13 sacrifi. on *t.* of mount.
Zep. 1:5 worsh. host on house-*t.*
Mat. 10:27 preach upon house-*t.*
Luke 12:3 proclaim, on house-*t.*

TOPAZ.

Ex. 28:17 a sardius, a *t.* 39:10
Job 28:19 the *t.* of Ethiopia shall
Ezek. 28:13 *t.* was thy covering
Rev. 21:20 beryl, the ninth a *t.*

TOPHET.

2 *K.* 23:10 Josiah defiled T. in v.
Is. 30:33 for T. is ordained of old
Jer. 7:31 built high places of T.
  32 no more be called T. 19:6
  19:11 they shall bury in T.
  12 even make this city as T.
  13 Jerusa. shall be defiled as T.
  14 then came Jeremiah from T.

TORCH.

Zec. 12:6 make govern. like a *t.*

TORCHES.

Nah. 2:3 chariots sh. be with *t.*
  4 chariots shall seem like *t.*
John 18:3 Judas cometh with *t.*

TORMENT, S.

Mat. 4:24 tak. wi. disease and *t.*
Luke 16:23 lift up eyes bel. in *t.*
  28 lest th. come into place of *t.*
1 *John* 4:18 because fear hath *t.*
Rev. 9:5 *t.* was *t.* of a scorpion
  14:11 smoke of their *t.* ascend.
  18:7 so much *t.* and sorrow give
  10 afar off for fear of her *t.* 15

TORMENT, Verb.

Mat. 8:29 art thou come to *t.* us?
Mark 5:7 *t.* me not, *Luke* 8:28

TORMENTED.

Mat. 8:6 serv. lieth grievously *t.*
Luke 16:24 I am *t.* in this flame
  25 he is comforted, thou art *t.*
Heb. 11:37 destitute, afflicted, *t.*
  38 whom the world was not wo.
Rev. 9:5 *t.* five months
  11:10 two prophets *t.* them
  14:10 he sh. be *t.* with fire
  20:10 shall be *t.* day and night

TORMENTORS.

Mat. 18:34 lord deliver. him to *t.*

TORN.

Gen. 31:39 which was *t.* of beasts
  44:28 surely he is *t.* in pieces
Ex. 22:13 not make good what *t.*
  31 nor shall eat any flesh *t.* of
Lev. 7:24 fat of *t.* may be used
  17:15 if any eat that wh. was *t.*
  22:8 dieth itself, or *t.* of beasts
1 *K.* 13:26 lion, which hath *t.* him
  28 rent carcase nor *t.* the ass
Jer. 5:6 that goeth out shall be *t.*
Ezek. 4:14 not eaten of that is *t.*
  44:31 priests eh. not eat th. is *t.*
Hos. 6:1 he hath *t.* he will heal
Mal. 1:13 bro. that which was *t.*
Mark 1:26 uncl. spirit had *t.* him

TORTOISE.

Lev. 11:29 the *t.* shall be unclean

TOU

TORTURED.

Heb. 11:35 oth. were *t.* not acce.

TOSS.

Is. 22:18 he will turn and *t.* thee
Jer. 5:22 tho' waves *t.* themselv.

TOSSED.

Ps. 109:23 I am *t.* up and down
Prov. 21:6 a vanity, *t.* to and fro
Is. 54:11 O thou afflicted, *t.* with
Mat. 14:24 ship was *t.* wi. waves
Acts 27:17 exceedi. *t.* with tem.
Eph. 4:14 children *t.* to and fro
Jam. 1:6 waver. is like wave *t.*

TOSSINGS.

Job 7:4 I am full of *t.* till dawn.

TOTTERING.

Ps. 62:3 ye shall be as a *t.* fence

TOUCH.

Gen. 3:3 nor shall ye *t.* lt lest die
  20:6 suffered I thee not to *t.* her
Ex. 19:12 that ye *t.* not border
  13 shall not a hand *t.* it
Lev. 5:2 if a soul *t.* unclean thi.
  0:27 whatsoever sh. *t.* the flesh
  11:8 carcases sh. not *t.* *Deut.* 14:8
  31 whosoe. doth *t.* them when
  12:4 he sh. *t.* no hallowed thing
Num. 4:15 sh. not *t.* any holy th.
  16:26 and *t.* nothing of theirs
Jos. 9:19 therof. we may not *t.*
Ruth 2:9 they should not *t.* thee
2 *Sam.* 14:10 he shall not *t.* thee
  18:12 none *t.* the young man
  23:7 that shall *t.* them must be
1 *Chr.* 16:22 *t.* not mine anointed,
  Ps. 105:15
Job 1:11 *t.* all he hath, and he
  2:5 *t.* his bone and his flesh, he
  5:19 in seven eh. no evil *t.* thee
  6:7 that my soul refused to *t.*
Ps. 144:5 *t.* the mountains, and
Is. 52:11 *t.* no uncl. 2 *Cor.* 6:17
Jer. 12:14 that *t.* the inheritance
Lam. 4:14 men could not *t.* gar.
  15 it is unclean, depart, *t.* not
Hag. 2:12 if one with hallow *t.* br.
  13 if one that is unclean *t.*
Mat. 9:21 if I but *t.* *Mark* 5:28
  14:36 that they might *t.* the
  hem, *Mark* 6:56; 8:22
Mark 3:10 to *t.* him, *Luke* 6:19
  8:22 besou. him to *t.* blind man
Luke 11:46 ye *t.* not the burdens
  18:15 infants, that he would *t.*
John 20:17 Jesus saith, *t.* me not
1 *Cor.* 7:1 good not for a man *t.*
Col. 2:21 *t.* not, taste not, handle
Heb. 11:28 first-born, sho. *t.* th.
  12:20 if so much as beast *t.* mo.

TOUCHED.

Gen. 20:29 as we have not *t.* thee
  32:25 he *t.* Jacob's thigh, 32
  30:6 fr. *t.* of Syene etc. they fall
Num. 31:19 whose, hath *t.* any
Jud. 6:21 angel of L. *t.* the flesh
1 *Sam.* 10:26 wh. hearts G. ha. *t.*
1 *K.* 6:27 wings of cherubim *t.*
  19:5 an angel *t.* him, and said, 7
2 *K.* 13:21 when the man *t.* bon.
Est. 5:2 Esther *t.* top of sceptre
Job 19:21 hand of G. hath *t.* me
Is. 6:7 in thy L. *t.* my mouth
Jer. 1:9 the Lord *t.* my mouth
Dan. 8:5 he-goat *t.* not ground
  18 *t.* me, and set me upright,
  9:21; 10:10, 16, 18
Mat. 8:3 J. *t.* and Jesus *t.* him, *Mark*
  1:41; *Luke* 5:13
  15 he *t.* her hand, the fever left
  9:20 diseased with an issue *t.*
  garm. *Mark* 5:27; *Luke* 8:13
  29 then *t.* he their eyes, 20:34
  14:36 many as *t.* him were made
  whole, *Mark* 6:56
Mark 5:30 *t.* clothes, *Lu.* 8:45, 47
  7:33 he spit, and *t.* his tongue
Luke 7:14 he came and *t.* the bier
  8:47 declared cause she *t.* him
  22:51 *t.* his ear, healed him
Acts 27:3 next day we *t.* at Zid.
Heb. 4:15 not priest wh. can. be *t.*
  12:18 to mount that might be *t.*

TOUCHETH.

Gen. 26:11 this man shall die
  29:37 whatsoever *t.* altar be holy
Lev. 7:19 flesh that *t.* uncl. thing
  11:26 every one that *t.* be uncl.
  15:5 whoso *t.* his bed, 10, 22, 27
  11 whomsoever he *t.* hath ues.
  12 vessel of earth he *t.* broken
  23 if on her bed wh. he *t.* it, be
  uncl. 27; 22:4, 5; *Num.* 19:22
Num. 19:11 *t.* dead body, 13, 16

TOW

Num. 19:18 *t.* a bone; 21 *t.* water
  of separation
Jud. 16:9 broken when it *t.* fire
Job 4:5 it *t.* thee, th. art troubl.
  Ps. 104:32 he *t.* hills, th. smoke
Prov. 6:29 whoso *t.* her, not inn.
Ezek. 17:10 when east wind *t.* it
Hos. 4:2 break, blood *t.* blood
Amos 9:5 L. of hosts that *t.* land
Zec. 2:8 *t.* you *t.* apple of eye
Luke 7:39 what wom. that *t.* him
1 *John* 5:18 wick. one *t.* him not

TOUCHING.

Lev. 5:13 as *t.* his sin he sinned
2 *K.* 22:18 *t.* words thou heard
Job 37:23 *t.* Almig. not find out
Ps. 45:1 things I made *t.* king
Mat. 7:13 vision is *t.* multitude
  18:19 *t.* any thing they ask
Rom. 11:28 as *t.* elect, they are
1 *Cor.* 8:1 as *t.* things offer. idols
  16:12 *t.* our brother Apollos
Col. 4:10 *t.* whom ye received
2 *Thes.* 3:4 confidence in L. *t.* you

TOW.

Jud. 16:9 as a thread of *t.* brok.
Is. 1:31 the strong shall be as *t.*
  43:17 extinct, are quenched as *t.*

TOWARD, or TOWARDS.

Deut. 28:54 eye evil *t.* his broth.
  56 shall be evil *t.* her husband
2 *Chr.* 24:16 bec. Jeho. had done
  good in Is. L. G. *t.* his house
Ezr. 3:11 his mercy endur. *t.* Is.
  9:9 God to give us reviv. *t.* tem.
  33:7 worship *t.* temple, 138:2
  35:15 mine eyes are ever *t.* L.
  29:3 I lift hands *t.* thy oracle
  Is. 63:7 goodness *t.* house of Is.
Jer. 15:1 mind not be *t.* this peo.
Jon. 2:4 look *t.* thy holy temple
Luke 2:14 pea. good will *t.* men

See HEAVEN.

TOWEL.

John 13:4 he riseth, and took a *t.*

TOWER.

Gen. 11:4 let us build city and *t.*
  5 Lord came to see city and *t.*
  35:21 spread tent beyo. *t.* of E.
Jud. 8:9 I will break this *t.* 17
  9:46 men of *t.* of Shech. entered
  51 there was a strong *t.* in city
  t. men fled to *t.* of salvation
2 *K.* 5:24 came to *t.* he took th.
Prov. 18:10 name of L. strong *t.*
  9:4 thy neck like *t.* of Da.
  7:4 thy neck is as a *t.* of ivory
  Ps. 5:2 built *t.* in midst of viney.
Jer. 6:27 I have set thee for a *t.*
Ezek. 29:10 desolate fr. *t.* of Sy.
Hab. 2:1 I will set me upon *t.*
Mic. 4:8 O *t.* of flock
Mat. 21:33 built a *t.* *Mark* 12:1
Luke 13:4 on whom *t.* of Si. fell
  14:28 you intending to build a *t.*

High TOWER.

2 *Sam.* 22:3 God is my *high t.* *Ps.*
  18:2; 144:2
Is. 3:15 day of L. on every *h. t.*

TOWERS.

2 *Chr.* 14:7 build cit. and make *t.*
  26:9 Uzziah built *t.* in Jerusa.
  10 he built *t.* in desert
  27:4 Jotham built castles and *t.*
  32:5 Hezek. raised up wall to *t.*
  Ps. 48:12 Zion. and tell her *t.*
Cant. 8:10 my breasts like *t.*
Is. 23:13 Assy. set up *t.* thereof
  30:25 high hill riv. when *t.* fall
  32:14 forts and *t.* be for dens
  33:18 wh. is he that counted *t.*?
Ezek. 26:4 sh. break do. her *t.* 9
  27:11 Gammad. were in thy *t.*
Zep. 3:6 their *t.* are desolate

TOWN.

Jos. 2:15 Ra.'s house on *t.* wall
1 *Sam.* 16:4 elders of *t.* trembled
  23:7 by entering into a *t.* that
  27:5 give me a place in some *t.*
Mat. 10:11 whatso. *t.* ye enter
Mark 8:23 led bli. man out of *t.*
  26 neither go into *t.* nor tell
  any in *t.*
John 7:42 C. com. out of *t.* of B.
  11:1 *t.* of Mary and sis. Martha
  30 J. was not yet come into *t.*

TOWNS.

Est. 9:19 J. dwelt in unwalled *t.*
Jer. 19:15 bring on her *t.* the evil

CRUDEN'S CONCORDANCE. 1059

TRA

Zec. 2:4 inhab. as *t.* with. walls
Luke 9:6 and went thro' the *t.*
12 that th. go into *t.* and lodge

TOWN-CLERK.
Acts 19:35 when *t.-c.* appeas. peo.

TRADE.
Gen. 46:32 *t.* about cattle, 34

TRADE, Verb.
Gen. 34:10 and *t.* you therein, 21
Rev. 18:17 as *t.* by sea stood afar

TRADED.
Ezek. 27:12 Tarsh. *t.* in thy fairs
13 Meshech *t.* persons of men
14 they of Togar. *t.* wi. horses
17 Ju. and Is. *t.* in thy market
Mat. 25:16 five tal. went and *t.*

TRADING.
Luke 19:15 ev. man gained by *t.*

TRADITION.
Mat. 15:2 why do disci. transgr.
t. of the elders? Mark 7:5
3 why do you transgr. comma.
of God by *t.?* Mark 7:9
6 made commandment of G. of
none effect by *t.* Mark 7:13
Mark 7:3 hold. *t.* of elders, 8, 9
Col. 2:8 spoil you after *t.* of men
2 Thes. 3:6 *t.* wh. he recei. of us
1 Pet. 1:18 received by *t.* fr. fa.

TRADITIONS.
Gal. 1:14 zealous of *t.* of my fa.
2 Thes. 2:15 hold *t.* ye been tau.

TRAFFIC.
Gen. 42:34 and ye shall *t.* in land

TRAFFIC, Substantive.
1 K. 10:15 had of *t.* of merchants
Ezek. 17:4 carri. it into land of *t.*
28:5 by *t.* hast thou increased
18 defiled sanct. by iniq. of *t.*

TRAFFICKERS.
Is. 23:8 whose *t.* are honorable

TRAIN.
1 K. 10:2 to Jerus. with great *t.*
Is. 6:1 his *t.* filled the temple

TRAIN, Verb.
Prov. 22:6 *t.* ch. in way he sh. go

TRAINED.
Gen. 14:14 Abram armed *t.* serv.

TRAITOR, S.
Luke 6:16 Iscariot which was *t.*
2 Tim. 3:4 in last days men be *t.*

TRAMPLE.
Ps. 91:13 dragon *t.* under foot
Is. 63:3 I will *t.* them in my fury
Mat. 7:6 lest th. *t.* th. and. foot

TRANCE.
Num. 24:4 falling into *t.* 16
Acts 10:10 he fell into a *t.*
11:5 and in a *t.* I saw a vision
22:17 in temple I was in a *t.*

TRANQUILLITY.
Dan. 4:27 be a length. of thy *t.*

TRANSFERRED.
1 Cor. 4:6 I ha. in figure *t.* to my

TRANSFIGURED.
Mat. 17:2 *t.* bef. them, Mark 9:2

TRANSFORMED, ING.
Rom. 12:2 be ye *t.* by renewing
2 Cor. 11:13 *t.* thems. into apost.
14 Sat. is *t.* into angel of light
15 no great thing if min. be *t.*

TRANSGRESS.
Num. 14:41 where. do ye *t.* comm.
mandm. of L.? 2 Chr. 21:19
1 Sam. 2:24 make L.'s peo. to *t.*
Neh. 1:8 if ye *t.* I will scat. you
13:27 heark. to our God by *t.*
Ps. 17:3 purp. mouth sh. not *t.*
25:3 ashe. who *t.* without cause
Prov. 28:21 for bread that man
Jer. 2:20 thou saidst, I will not *t.*
Ezek. 20:38 purge out them fr. *t.*
Amos 4:4 come to Bethel and *t.*
Mat. 15:2 do disciple *t.* tradit.?
3 why do ye *t.* comm. of God?
Rom. 2:27 by circumcis. *t.* law

TRANSGRESSED.
Deut. 26:13 I have not *t.* com.
Jos. 7:11 they *t.* my covenant, 15
23:16 when ye have *t.* covenant
Jud. 2:20 have I *t.* my covenant
1 Sam. 14:33 have *t.* roll a stone
15:24 I have *t.* commad. of the L.
1 K. 8:50 wherein they have *t.*
1 Chr. 2:7 *t.* in thing accursed
5:25 they *t.* ag. G. of their faith,
2 Chr. 12:2 because they *t.* ag. L.
26:16 Uzziah *t.* against the L.
28:19 Ahaz *t.* sore against Lord
36:14 priests and peo. *t.* much
Ezr. 10:10 ye hu. *t.* taken wives

TRA

Ezr. 10:13 many th. *t.* in this th.
Is. 24:5 bec. they have *t.* laws
43:27 thy teachers ha. *t.* ag. me
66:24 look at men's care. that *t.*
Jer. 2:8 the pastors *t.* against me
29 ye all have *t.* against me
3:13 acknowledge thou hast *t.*
33:8 iniquities whereby they *t.*
34:18 give men that *t.* covenant
Lam. 3:42 we ha. *t.* and rebelled
Ezek. 2:3 they and fath. *t.* ag. me
18:31 trangres. whereby ye *t.*
Dan. 9:11 all Is. have *t.* thy law
Hos. 7:13 destruction, bec. they *t.*
Zep. 3:11 doings wherein thou *t.*
Luke 15:29 nor I. thy command.

See COVENANT.

TRANSGRESSEST, ETH.
Est. 3:3 why *t.* king's com. ?
Prov. 16:10 mouth *t.* not in judg.
Hab. 2:5 because he *t.* by wine
1 John 3:4 committeth sin, *t.* law
2 John 9 whoso *t.* and abid. not

TRANSGRESSING.
Deut. 17:2 wickedn. in *t.* coven.
Is. 59:13 in *t.* and lying ag. Lord

TRANSGRESSION.
Ex. 34:7 forgiving *t.* Num. 14:18
Jos. 22:22 if it be in *t.* ag. Lord
1 Sam. 24:11 no *t.* in my hand
1 Chr. 9:1 carried to Babyl. for *t.*
10:13 Saul died for *t.* committed
2 Chr. 29:19 Ahaz cast away in *t.*
Ezr. 9:4 bec. of *t.* of those car.
10:6 he mourned bec. of their *t.*
13:23 make me to know my *t.*
Ps. 17:3 but *t.* is sealed up in a bag
33:9 I am without *t.* I am innoc.
31:6 wound is incurable with. *t.*
Ps. 19:13 innocent from great *t.*
32:1 blessed he wh. *t.* is forgiven
36:1 *t.* of wicked saith within
59:3 wait for sacri. not for *t.* O L.
89:32 them will I visit their *t.*
107:17 fools bec. of *t.* are afflict.
Prov. 12:13 wick. is snared by *t.*
17:9 covereth *t.* seeketh love
19 loveth *t.* that loveth strife
19:11 his glory to pass over *t.*
28:2 for *t.* of land many princes
24 robbeth. sailth, it is no *t.*
29:6 in *t.* of evil man is a snare
16 wicked multiplied, *t.* increa.
22 a furious man aboun. in *t.*
Is. 24:20 *t.* thereof be heavy
53:8 for *t.* of peo. was he strick.
57:4 are ye not children of *t.* ?
58:1 show my people their *t.*
59:20 to them that turn from *t.*
Ezek. 33:12 deliver in day of his *t.*
Dan. 8:12 ag. sacri. by reas. of *t.*
13 sacrifice, and *t.* of desolat.
9:24 seventy weeks to finish *t.*
Amos 4:4 at Gilgal multiply *t.*
Mic. 1:5 for *t.* of Jacob is all this;
what is the *t.* of Jacob ?
3:8 full of power to dec. to J. *t.*
6:7 first-born for my *t.* and fruit
7:18 pass. by *t.* of remnant
Acts 1:25 from which J. by *t.* fell
Rom. 4:15 wh. no law is, is no *t.*
5:11 after similit. of Adam's *t.*
1 Tim. 2:14 being decei. was in *t.*
Heb. 2:2 every *t.* receiv. recomp.
1 John 3:4 for sin is *t.* of the law

TRANSGRESSIONS.
Ex. 23:21 will not pard. your *t.*
Lev. 16:16 atonement bec. of *t.*
21 Aa. confess over goat th. *t.*
Jos. 24:19 will not forg. your *t.*
1 K. 8:50 forgive people their *t.*
Job 13:23 I covered my *t.* an Ad.
35:6 if thy *t.* be multiplied
36:9 sheweth their work and *t.*
Ps. 5:10 cast them out in their *t.*
25:7 sins of my youth, my *t.*
32:5 I will confess my *t.* unto L.
39:8 deliver me from all my *t.*
51:1 mercy, blot out all my *t.*
3 for I acknowl. my *t.* my sin
65:3 as for our *t.* purge th. away
103:12 so far hath he removed *t.*
Is. 43:25 he that blotteth out *t.*
44:22 blot. as a thi. cloud thy *t.*
50:1 for your *t.* is your mother
53:5 he was wounded for our *t.*
59:12 our *t.* are multiplied bef.
bee, for our *t.* are with us
Jer. 5:6 because th. *t.* are many
Lam. 1:5 multita. of her *t.* gone
14 yoke of my *t.* bound by his
24 do to th. as to me for my *t.*
Ezek. 14:11 nor polluted wi. th. *t.*
18:22 his *t.* not be mentioned

TRA

Ezek. 18:28 he turn. away from
all his *t.*
30 turn yourselves fr. your *t.*
31 cast away all your *t.*
21:24 your *t.* are discovered
33:10 If our *t.* be upon us
37:23 nor defile thems. with *t.*
39:24 according to their *t.* have
Amos 1:3 for three *t.* of Damas.
6 *t.* of Gaza, 9 Tyrus; 11 Ed.
13 *t.* of Am. 2:1 Moab; 4 Ju.
2:6 Isr. 3:14 visit *t.* of Israel
5:12 I know your manifold *t.*
Mic. 1:13 *t.* of Is. found in thee
Gal. 3:19 law was add. bec. of *t.*
Heb. 9:15 for redemption of *t.*

TRANSGRESSOR.
Prov. 21:18 *t.* be ransom for upr.
22:12 he overthrow. words of *t.*
Is. 48:8 called a *t.* from womb
Gal. 2:18 I make myself a *t.*
Jam. 2:11 kill, th. art become *t.*

TRANSGRESSORS.
Ps. 37:38 *t.* be destroyed togeth.
51:13 will I teach *t.* thy ways
59:5 be not merciful to wick. *t.*
Prov. 2:22 *t.* shall be rooted out
11:3 perversen. of *t.* destr. them
6 be taken to their naughti.
13:2 soul of *t.* shall eat violence
15 favor, but way of *t.* is hard
23:28 she increaseth *t.* am. men
26:10 God rewardeth fool and *t.*
Is. 1:28 destruction of *t.* together
46:8 bring it ag. to mind, ye *t.*
53:12 he was numbered with *t.*
and made intercession for *t.*
Hos. 8:23 when *t.* are come
Hos. 14:9 but *t.* sh. fall therein
Mark 15:28 he was numbered
with *t.* Luke 22:37
Jam. 2:9 are convin. of law as *t.*

TRANSLATE, D.
2 Sam. 3:10 *t.* kingdom fr. Saul
Col. 1:13 *t.* us into kingd. of Son
Heb. 11:5 Enoch was *t.* that he
by faith En. was *t.* not testim.

TRANSLATION.
Heb. 11:5 bef. *t.* he had testim.

TRANSPARENT.
Rev. 21:21 str. of city was *t.* glass

TRAP, S.
Jos. 23:13 *t.* and snares
Job 18:10 and a *t.* is laid for him
Ps. 69:22 welfare, let become *t.*
Jer. 5:26 well, set a *t.* catch men
Rom. 11:9 let their table be made
a snare, a *t.*

TRAVAIL.
Gen. 38:27 in time of her *t.*
Ex. 18:8 told Jethro *t.* by way
Num. 20:14 know. *t.* ha. befallen
Ps. 48:6 pain as woman in *t.*
Jer. 6:24; 13:21; 22:23; 49:24;
50:43; Mic. 4:9, 10
Ec. 1:13 more *t.* G. given to men
2:23 days are sorrows, *t.* grief
3:10 seen *t.* G. hath giv. to men
4:4 I considered all *t.* ev. work
6 than both hands full with *t.*
8 is vanity, yea, it is a sore *t.*
5:14 riches perish by evil *t.*
Is. 23:4 *t.* not, 53:11 *t.* of soul
Jer. 3:21 voice and *t.* of woman in *t.*
30:6 see whether man doth *t.*
Lam. 3:5 compas. wi. gall and *t.*
John 16:21 woman in *t.* hath sor.
Gal. 4:19 my little *t.* of whom *t.*
1 Thes. 2:9 for ye remembe. our *t.*
5:3 destruction cometh as *t.*
2 Thes. 3:8 wrought with *t.* night

TRAVAILED.
Gen. 35:16 Rach. *t.* 38:27 Tam. *t.*
1 Sam. 4:19 Phinehas' wife *t.*
Ps. 68:7 bef. chr. I brought forth
8 as soon as Zion *t.* brou. forth

TRAVAILEST, ETH.
Job 15:20 wick. man *t.* wi. pain
Ps. 7:14 behold, he *t.* with iniq.
Is. 13:8 in pain as a woman *t.*
21:3 pangs of a woman that *t.*
Jer. 31:8 her that *t.* with child
Mic. 5:3 till she who *t.* br. forth
Rom. 8:22 creation *t.* in pain
Gal. 4:27 break forth thou th. *t.*

TRAVAILING.
Is. 42:14 I cry like woman in *t.*
Hos. 13:13 sorrows of *t.* woman
Rev. 12:2 *t.* in birth, and pained

TRAVEL.
Acts 19:29 Paul's companion in *t.*
2 Cor. 8:19 chosen *t.* of churches
to *t.*

TRE

TRAVELLED, ETH.
Prov. 6:11 as one that *t.* 24:34
Acts 11:19 *t.* as far as Phenice

TRAVELLER, S.
2 Sam. 12:4 came *t.* to rich man
Jud. 5:6 *t.* walk. thro' by-ways
Job 31:32 I open. my doors to *t.*

TRAVELLING.
Is. 21:13 O ye *t.* companies
63:1 who is this *t.* in his stren. ?
Mat. 25:14 heaven is as a man *t.*

TRAVERSING.
Jer. 2:23 dromedary *t.* her ways

TREACHEROUS.
Jer. 3:7 her *t.* sister Jud. saw it
8 her *t.* sister Jud. fear. not, 10
11 justi. herself more than *t.* J.
9:2 an assembly of *t.* men
Zep. 3:4 proph. are light and *t.*

TREACHEROUSLY.
Jud. 9:23 dealt *t.* with Abimel.
Is. 33:1 deal. *t.* they dealt not *t.*
48:8 thou wouldest deal very *t.*
Jer. 3:20 as a wife *t.* departeth
5:11 of Judah dealt *t.* Mal. 2:11
12:1 why hap. th. deal very *t.* ?
6 they have dealt *t.* with thee
Jer. 12:6 her friends ha. dealt *t.*
Hos. 5:7 they dealt *t.* against L.
6:7 there they dealt *t.* agai. me
Mal. 2:10 why do we deal *t.* ev.
14 wife aga. whom th. dealt *t.*
15 let none deal *t.* against wife
16 take heed, th. ye deal not *t.*

TREACHERY.
2 K. 9:23 there is *t.* O Ahaziah

TREAD.
Deut. 11:24 whereon your feet *t.*
25 dre. of you on all land ye *t.*
32:29 thou sh. *t.* on high places
1 Sam. 5:5 none *t.* on thresho. of
Job 24:11 *t.* their wine-presses
40:12 *t.* down wick. in. th. place
Ps. 7:5 let him *t.* down my life
44:5 thro' thy name *t.* them
60:12 *t.* down our enemi. 108:13
91:13 thou shalt *t.* upon the lion
Is. 1:12 require. to *t.* my courts ?
10:6 to *t.* them down like mire
14:25 mountains *t.* him under
16:10 tread, shall *t.* out no wine
26:6 the foot shall *t.* it down
63:3 I will *t.* them in anger, 6
Jer. 25:30 as they that *t.* grapes
48:33 wine fail, none *t.* shout.
Ezek. 26:11 with horses sh. he *t.*
34:18 must *t.* residue with feet
Dan. 7:23 fourth beast *t.* it down
Hos. 10:11 Eph. loveth to *t.* corn
Mic. 1:3 L. will *t.* on high places
5:5 wh. Assyrian *t.* our palaces
6:15 thou shalt *t.* olives
Nah. 3:14 *t.* mortar, make brick.
Zec. 10:5 which *t.* their enemies
Mal. 4:3 ye shall *t.* down wicked
Luke 10:19 power to *t.* on scorp.
Rev. 11:2 city they *t.* under foot

TREADER, S.
Is. 16:10 *t.* shall tread no wine
Amos 9:13 *t.* of grapes sh. over.

TREADETH.
Deut. 25:4 not muz. ox wh. he *t.*
corn, 1 Cor. 9:9 ; 1 Tim. 5:18
Job 9:8 *t.* upon waves of the sea
Is. 41:25 come as potter *t.* clay
63:2 garme. like him th. *t.* wine
Amos 4:13 that *t.* on high places
Mic. 5:6 wh. he *t.* within borders
Rev. 19:15 he *t.* wine-press of w.

TREADING.
Neh. 13:15 some *t.* wine-presses
Is. 7:25 be for *t.* of lesser cattle
22:5 a day of tro. and *t.* down
Amos 5:11 forasmuch as your *t.*

TREASON.
1 K. 16:20 acts of Zim. and his *t.*
2 K. 11:14 cried *t.* *t.* 2 Chr. 23:13

TREASURE.
Gen. 43:23 God hath given you *t.*
Ex. 19:5 a peculiar *t.* Ps. 135:4
Deut. 28:12 L. shall open good *t.*
Jos. 6:19 the *t.* of house of the L.
1 Chr. 29:8 wi. whom was *t.* gave it to *t.* of work
Ps. 17:14 belly th. fillest with *t.*
135:4 chosen Is. for his *t.*
Prov. 15:6 in house of right. is *t.*
in thou great *t.* and trouble
21:20 there is *t.* to be desired
Ezr. 2:8 1 gathered *t.* of kings

TRE

Is. 33:6 fear of the Lord is his *t.*
Ezek. 22:25 taken *t.* and precious
Hos. 13:15 spoil *t.* of pleas. ves.
Mal. 6:21 where *t.* is, *Lu.* 12:34
12:35 a good man out of good *t.*
evil man of evil *t. Luke* 6:45
18:41 kingd. of heav. is like a *t.*
52 bring, out of *t.* new and old
19:21 thou sh. have *t.* in heaven,
Mark 10:21; *Luke* 18:22
Luke 12:21 so is he that lay. up *t.*
33 provide *t.* in the heavens
Acts 8:27 eunu. had charge of *t.*
2 *Cor.* 4:7 *t.* in earthen vessels
Jam. 5:3 heaped *t.* for last days

TREASURE-CITIES.
Ex. 1:11 built for Pharaoh *t.-c.*

TREASURE-HOUSE.
Ezr. 5:17 search be made in *t.-h.*
7:20 bestow it out of king's *t.-h.*
Neh. 10:38 L. bring tithe to *t.-h.*
Dan. 1:2 brou. vessels into *t.-h.*

TREASURED.
Is. 23:18 sh. not be *t.* nor laid up
Rom. 2:5 *t.* up wrath ag. day of

TREASURER, s.
Ezr. 1:8 Cyr. brou. vessels by *t.*
7:21 I Artax. make decree to *t.*
Neh. 13:13 I made *t.* over treas.
Is. 22:15 get thee unto this *t.*
Dan. 3:2 Nebuch. gathered *t.* 3

TREASURES.
Deut. 32:34 sealed up am. my *t.*
33:19 sh. suck of *t.* hid in wand
1 *K.* 7:51 put dedicated among *t.*
14:26 Shishak took away the *t.*
15:18 Asa took gold left in the *t.* 2 *Chr.* 16:2
2 *K.* 12:18 Jehoa. took gold fou.
in *t.* 14:14; 16:8 Ahaz took
18:15 Hez. gave silv. found in *t.*
20:13 Hezek. showed silver and
gold in his *t.* 15; *Is.* 39:2, 4
24:13 Nebuchad. carried out the
t. of house of Lord and *t.* of
king's house, 2 *Chr.* 36:18
1 *Chr.* 26:26 breth. were over *t.*
27:25 over king's *t.* was Azmav.
2 *Chr.* 8:15 command. concer. *t.*
Neh. 12:44 some appointed for *t.*
Job 3:21 dig more than for hid *t.*
38:22 *t.* of snow? *t.* of hail?
Prov. 2:4 if search, as for hid *t.*
8:21 I will fill *t.* of those that
10:2 *t.* of wickedn. profit noth.
21:6 got. of *t.* by lying tongue
Is. 2:7 neith. any end of their *t.*
10:13 I have robbed their *t.*
30:6 carry *t.* on bunches of cam.
45:3 I will give thee *t.* of dark.
Jer. 10:13 wind out of *t.* 51:16
15:13 *t.* to spoil, 17:3; 20:5
41:8 for we have *t.* in the field
48:7 bec. thou trusted in thy *t.*
49:4 daughter, trusted in her *t.*
50:37 a sword is on her *t.*
51:13 dwe. on waters abun. in *t.*
Ezek. 28:4 silver and gold in *t.*
Dan. 11:43 have power over *t.*
Mic. 6:10 are yet *t.* of wickedn. ?
Mat. 2:11 wh. th. had opened *t.*
6:19 lay not up for yourselves *t.*
20 lay up for yourself, *t.* in hea.
Col. 2:3 in wh. are hid *t.* of wis.
Heb. 11:26 greater riches than *t.*

TREASURY.
Jos. 6:19 sil. sh. come into *t.* 24
Jer. 38:11 went into hou. und. *t.*
Mat. 27:6 not lawful to put in *t.*
Mark 12:41 Je. sat against *t.* and
beheld peo. cast mon. into *t. Luke* xli:1 rich cast. gifts into *t.*
John 8:20 words spake Je. in *t.*

TREASURIES.
1 *Chr.* 9:26 Levites were over *t.*
28:11 gave Sol. pattern of *t.* 12
2 *Chr.* 32:27 Hez. made *t.* for sil.
Neh. 13:13 brought tithe into *t.*
Est. 3:9 bring it into king's *t.*
4:7 H. prom. to pay to king's *t.*
Ps. 135:7 bringeth wind out of *t.*

TREATISE.
Acts 1:1 former *t.* have I made

TREE.
Gen. 1:29 I have given you ev. *t.*
2:9 G. made ev. *t.* to grow, the *t.*
of life and *t.* of knowledge
16 of every *t.* of the garden
2:17 of *t.* of knowl. not eat, 3:3
3:6 woman saw the *t.* was good
11 hast thou eaten of *t.* ? 17
12 woman gave me of the *t.*
24 lest he take also of *t.* of life
24 to keep the way of *t.* of life

TRE

Gen. 18:4 rest yoursel. under *t.*
8 he stood by them und. the *t.*
40:19 Phara. sh. hang thee on *t.*
Ex. 9:25 the hail brake every *t.*
15:25 the Lord showed him a *t.*
Deut. 19:5 fetch. stroke to cut *t.*
20:19 *t.* of the field is man's life
21:23 body sh. not remain on *t.*
Jos. 8:29 take king of Ai from *t.*
1 *Sam.* 22:6 Saul abode under *t.*
31:13 they buried th. under a *t.*
2 *K.* 3:19 and shall fell ev. good *t.*
23:23 were hanged on a *t.*
Est. 2:23 were hanged on a *t.*
Job 14:7 hope of a *t.* if cut down
19:10 hope hath he remo. like *t.*
24:20 wicked. sh. be brok. as *t.*
Ps. 1:3 like a *t.* plant by rivers
Prov. 3:18 she is a *t.* of life to th.
11:30 fr. of righte. is a *t.* of life
13:12 desire com. it is a *t.* of life
15:4 a wholes. tongue is a *t.* of
Is. 40:20 chooseth a *t.* that will
44:19 sh. I fall d. to stock of *t.* ?
56:3 nei. eunu. say, I am dry *t.*
65:22 as days of a *t.* are days of
66:17 purify themsel. behind *t.*
Jer. 10:8 one cutteth a *t.*
11:19 let us destroy the *t.*
17:8 as a *t.* planted by waters
Ezek. 15:2 vine *t.* more th. any *t.*
17:24 brought down high *t.* exalted
low *t.* dried up green *t.*
made dry *t.* to flourish
21:10 contemneth rod, as ev. *t.*
31:8 nor any *t.* in garden of G.
34:27 *t.* of field shall yield fruit
36:30 I will multiply fruit of *t.*
Dan. 4:10 beh. a *t.* 11, 14, 20, 23
Joel 2:22 fear not *t.* beareth fruit
Mat. 3:10 ev. *t.* that bringeth not
good fruit, 7:19; *Luke* 3:9
7:17 good *t.* bring. good fruit,
cor. *t.* evil fruit, *Luke* 6:43
18 good *t.* cannot bri. evil fruit
12:33 make *t.* good and fr. good,
t. kno. by fruit, *Luke* 6:44
Luke 17:6 mi. say to sycamine *t.*
Acts 5:30 wh. ye hanged on a *t.*
10:39 Je. wh. they hanged on *t.*
Gal. 3:13 cursed is th. hang. on *t.*
1 *Pet.* 2:24 bare sins in body on *t.*
Rev. 2:7 I will give to eat of *t.*
7:1 wind sh. not blow on any *t.*
9:4 not hurt green thing, nor *t.*
22:2 in midst was the *t.* of life
14 may have right to *t.* of life

See GREEN.

TREES.
Gen. 3:8 hid amongst *t.* of gard.
23:17 *t.* were made sure to Abr.
Ex. 10:15 locusts did eat fr. of *t.*
Lev. 19:23 planted all man. of *t.*
23:40 take boughs of goodly *t.*
26:4 *t.* of the field shall yield
Num. 24:6 as *t.* of lign-aloes wh.
t. planted, and as cedar *t.*
Deut. 16:21 not plant grove of *t.*
20:19 sh. not destroy *t.* thereof
20 *t.* th. know. not *t.* for meat
Jos. 10:26 J. hang. them on 5 *t.*
Jud. 9:8 *t.* went to anoint king
9 to be promoted over *t.* 11, 13
10 *t.* said to the fig-tree reign
1 *K.* 4:33 he spake of *t.* fr. cedar
2 *K.* 3:25 they felled the good *t.*
1 *Chr.* 16:33 th. shall *t.* of wood
sing, *Ps.* 96:12
Neh. 10:35 bring first-fr. of *t.* 37
Ec. 2:5 planted *t.* of all kinds
Cant. 2:3 as apple-tree am. the *t.*
4:14 all *t.* of frankincense
Is. 7:2 moved as the *t.* of wood
Ezek. 20:28 glorious *t.* of the forest
41:19 palm-tr. betw. cheru. and *t.*
Dan. 4:14 and cut off his branches
Mat. 3:10 axe is laid to root of *t.*
Mark 8:24 I see men as *t.* walk.
Luke 21:29 behold fig-tree and all *t.*
Jude 12 *t.* whose fruit withereth
Rev. 7:3 hurt not *t.* till we have
8:7 third part of *t.* was burnt up

See PALM.

TREMBLE.
Deut. 2:25 nations sh. *t.* because
20:3 do not *t.* because of them
Ezr. 10:3 that *t.* at commandm.
Job 9:6 the pillars thereof *t.*
26:11 the pillars of heaven *t.*
Ps. 60:2 hast made earth to *t.*
99:1 L. reigneth, let the peo. *t.*
114:7 *t.* earth, at presence of L.
Ec. 12:3 keepers of house sh. *t.*
Is. 5:25 hills did *t.* th. carcasses
14:16 man that made earth *t.*
32:11 *t.* ye wom. be at ease, *t.*
64:2 nati. may *t.* at thy presence
66:5 hear word of L. ye that *t.*
Jer. 5:22 will ye not *t.* at my pre.
10:10 at his wrath earth shall *t.*
33:9 they sh. fear for the goodness
51:29 land of Babylon shall *t.*
Ezek. 26:16 *t.* at ev. mom. 32:10
18 now shall the isles *t.* in day
Dan. 6:26 men *t.* bef. G. of Dan.
11 th. sh. *t.* as a bird out of E.
Joel 2:1 let inhabitants of land *t.*
10 quake, the heavens shall *t.*
Amos 8:8 sh. not land *t.* for this ?
Heb. 3:7 captains of Midi. did *t.*
Jam. 2:19 the devils beli. and *t.*

TREMBLED.
Gen. 27:33 I. *t.* very exceedingly
Ex. 19:16 peo. th. was in camp *t.*
Jud. 5:4 earth *t.* heavens dropped,
5 *Sam.* 7:10 *t.*
1 *Sam.* 4:13 Eli's heart *t.* for ark
14:15 spoilers *t.* 16:4 elders *t.*
28:5 Saul was afraid, heart *t.*
2 *Sam.* 22:8 mountains *t.* *Ps.* 18:7;
77:18; 97:4
Ezr. 9:4 assemb. ev. one *t.* that *t.*
Dan. 5:19 all peo. and nations *t.*
Hab. 3:16 my belly *t.* and I *t.* in
Mark 16:8 fled fr. sepulch. th. *t.*
Luke 8:47 woman *t.* came
Acts 7:32 Moses *t.* 16:25 Philippi *t.*

TREMBLETH.
Job 37:1 at this also my heart *t.*
Ps. 104:32 looketh on earth it *t.*
119:120 my flesh *t.* for fear
Is. 66:2 I will look to him that *t.*

TREMBLING.
Ex. 15:15 *t.* take hold on mighty
Deut. 28:65 L. sh. give *t.* heart
1 *Sam.* 13:7 people followed *t.*
14:15 in the host was a great *t.*
Ezr. 10:9 peo. sat *t.* because of
Job 4:14 fear ca. upon me and *t.*
21:6 *t.* taketh hold on my flesh
Ps. 2:11 serve L. rejoice with *t.*
55:5 fearfulness and *t.* are come
Is. 51:17 dregs of the cup of *t.* 22
Jer. 30:5 voice of *t.* we heard
Ezek. 12:18 drink thy wat. wi. *t.*
26:16 clothe themselves with *t.*
Dan. 10:11 had spoken, I stood *t.*
Hos. 13:1 Eph. spake *t.* he exalt.
Zec. 12:2 make Jeru. a cup of *t.*
Mark 5:33 woman *t. Luke* 8:47
Acts 9:6 he *t.* said, What wilt th. ?
16:29 keeper came *t.* fell down
1 *Cor.* 2:3 with you in much *t.*
2 *Cor.* 7:15 how with fear and *t.*
Eph. 6:5 serv. be obed. with *t.*
Phil. 2:12 work out sal. with *t.*

TRENCH.
1 *Sam.* 17:20 Dav. came to the *t.*
26:5, 7 Saul slopping in the *t.*
2 *K.* 18:32 Elijah made a *t.* about
35 filled the *t.* with water, 38
Luke 19:43 enemies sh. cast a *t.*

TRESPASS, Substantive.
Gen. 31:36 wh. is my *t.* that thou
50:17 forgive *t.* of thy servants
Ex. 22:9 manner of *t.* whether
Lev. 5:15 for his *t.* to L. a ram
26:40 conf. their *t.* th. trespass
Num. 5:6 when any do *t.* ag. L.
7 he shall recompense his *t.*
27 if she *t.* against husband
1 *Sam.* 25:28 forg. *t.* of handm.
1 *K.* 8:31 be cause of *t.* be la.
9 *Chr.* 21:18 ev. come on *t.* for *t.*
28:13 ye intend to add to our *t.*
29:19 Manasseh's prayer and *t.*
Ezr. 9:2 rul. been chief in this *t.*
6 our *t.* is grown unto heavens
7 in great *t.* to this day, 13

TRE

Mat. 21:8 others cut down bran.
of *t.* and strewed. *Mark* 11:8
Mark 8:24 I see men as *t.* walk.
Luke 21:29 behold fig-tree and all *t.*
Jude 12 *t.* whose fruit withereth
Rev. 7:3 hurt not *t.* till we have
8:7 third part of *t.* was burnt up

See PALM.

TREMBLE.
Deut. 2:25 nations sh. *t.* because
20:3 do not *t.* because of them
Ezr. 10:3 that *t.* at commandm.
Job 9:6 the pillars thereof *t.*
26:11 the pillars of heaven *t.*
Ps. 60:2 hast made earth to *t.*
99:1 L. reigneth, let the peo. *t.*
114:7 *t.* earth, at presence of L.
Ec. 12:3 keepers of house sh. *t.*
Is. 5:25 hills did *t.* th. carcasses

TRI

Ezr. 10:10 wives, to iner. *t.* of Is.
19 th. offered a ram for their *t.*
Ezek. 17:20 I will plead for his *t.*
18:24 in his *t.* he hath trespass.
Dan. 9:7 bec. of *t.* they trespass.

TRESPASSES.
Ezr. 9:15 before thee in our *t.*
Ps. 68:21 one as goeth on in *t.*
Ezek. 39:26 they have borne th. *t.*
Mat. 6:14 if ye forg. men their *t.*
15 if forgive not *t.* neither will
your Fa. forgive yo. *t.* 18:35
Mark 11:25 Fath. may forgive *t.*
26 nei. will F. forgive your *t.*
2 *Cor.* 5:19 not imputing their *t.*
Eph. 2:1 who were dead in *t.*
Col. 2:13 having forg. you all *t.*

See COMMIT, COMMITTED, OFFERING.

TRESPASS-MONEY.
2 *K.* 12:16 *t.-m.* was not brought

TRESPASS, Verb.
1 *K.* 8:31 man *t.* ag. his neighb.
2 *Chr.* 19:10 lest *t.* they *t.* not
26:22 Ahaz did *t.* yet more
Mat. 18:15 if brother *t.* tell fault
Luke 17:3 if bro. *t.* rebuke him
4 if he *t.* ag. thee seven times

TRESPASSED.
Lev. 5:19 he hath *t.* against L.
26:40 if confess trespass they *t.*
Num. 5:7 recompensed ag. wh. *t.*
Deut. 32:51 bec. ye *t.* against me
2 *Chr.* 26:16 sanct. for th. host *t.*
29:6 our fathers have *t.*
30:7 not like fath. who *t.* ag. L.
33:23 Amon *t.* more and more
Ezr. 10:2 we have *t.* ag. our God
Ezek. 17:20 trespass that he *t.*
Dan. 9:7 trespass that they *t.*
Hos. 8:1 they *t.* against my law

TRESPASSING.
Lev. 6:7 any *t.* he hath done in *t.*
Ezek. 14:13 land sinneth by *t.*

TRIAL.
Job 9:23 laugh at *t.* of innocent
Ezek. 21:13 it is a *t.* what if swo.
2 *Cor.* 8:2 how in *t.* of affliction
Heb. 11:36 others had *t.* of mock.
1 *Pet.* 1:7 *t.* of your faith might
4:12 not strange concerning *t.*

TRIBE.
Num. 1:4 man of every *t.* 13:2;
34:18
4:18 cut not off *t.* of Kohathites
18:2 *t.* of thy father bring thou
31:4 of every *t.* a thousand, 5, 6
36:6 marry to the family of *t.* 8
t. inherit. from once *t.* to ano. *t.*
Deut. 1:23 I took twelve, one of
a *t. Jos.* 3:12; 4:2, 4
20:18 *t.* whose heart turneth
Jos. 7:14 *t.* which Lord taketh
18:4 give out 3 men for each *t.*
Jud. 21:3 one *t.* lacking in Is. 6
1 *K.* 11:13 one *t.* to son, 32, 36
1 *Chr.* 6:61 of family of that *t.*
6:71 *t.* 47:28 in what *t.* the stran.
Heb. 7:13 he pertain. to anoth. *t.*
14 of wh. *t.* Mo. spake nothing

See REUBEN, SIMEON, and the rest.

TRIBES.
Ex. 28:21 according to 12 *t.* 39:14
Num. 24:2 in tents accord. to *t.*
33:54 according to *t. of fathers
34:13 give to the nine *t. Jos.*
13:7 ; 14:2
15 two *t.* and the half have received
inheritance, *Jos.* 14:3
Deut. 1:13 wise men, am. your *t.*
18:5 G. hath cho. him out of *t.*
Jos. 7:14 brought according to *t.*
1 *Sam.* 10:19 present your. by L.
K. 11:31 I will give ten *t.* to
18:31 according to number of *t.*
Ps. 105:37 not one feeble amo. *t.*
122:4 the *t.* go up, *t.* of the Lord
Is. 19:13 that are stay of *t.*
63:17 for *t.* of thine inheritance
Ezek. 45:8 to Isr. according to *t.*
Hab. 3:9 according to oaths of *t.*
Mat. 24:30 th. *t.* of earth mourn
Acts 26:7 promise our 12 *t.* hope
Jam. 1:1 the twelve *t.* scattered
Rev. 7:4 sealed 144,000 of all *t.*

See ISRAEL.

TRIBULATION.
Deut. 4:30 wh. in *t.* if thou turn
Jud. 10:14 let th. deliv. you in *t.*
1 *Sam.* 26:24 deli. me out of all *t.*
Mat. 13:21 when *t.* ariseth, he is

CRUDEN'S CONCORDANCE.

TRO

Mat. 24:21 then shall be great *t.*
29 immed. after *t. Mark* 13:24
John 16:33 ye shall have *t.*
Acts 14:22 we must thro' *t.* enter
Rom. 2:9 *t.* and ang. on eve. soul
5:3 know. *t.* worketh patience
8:35 shall *t.* separate us fr. Ch. *t*
12:12 rejo. in hope, patient in *t.*
2 *Cor.* 1:4 who comforte. us in *t.*
7:4 I am exceeding joyful in *t.*
1 *Thes.* 3:4 we should suffer *t.*
2 *Thes.* 1:6 recompense *t.* to th.
Rev. 1:9 John your compan. in *t.*
2:9 I know thy works, and *t.*
10 ye shall have *t.* ten days
22 I will cast th. into great *t.*
7:14 they which came of great *t.*

TRIBULATIONS.

1 *Sam.* 10:19 saved you out of *t.*
Rom. 5:3 but we glory in *t.* also
Eph. 3:13 faint not at *t.*
2 *Thes.* 1:4 for your faith in all *t.*

TRIBUTARY.

Lam. 1:1 how is she become *t.*

TRIBUTARIES.

Deut. 20:11 the people shall be *t.*
Jud. 1:30 Canaani. bec. *t.* 33, 35

TRIBUTE.

Gen. 49:15 Issa. bec. servant to *t.*
Num. 31:28 levy a *t.* to the Lord
37 Lord's *t.* of sheep was 675
38 L.'s *t.* of the beeves was 72
39 Lord's *t.* threescore and one
40 16,000 the Lord's *t.* 32 pers.
Deut. 16:10 with *t.* of a freewill
Jos. 16:10 Canaan. under *t.* 17:13
2 *Sam.* 20:24 Ad. was over *t.* 1 *K.*
4:6; 12:18; 2 *Chr.* 10:18
1 *K.* 9:21 on these did Sol. levy *t.*
2 *K.* 23:33 Pharaoh put land to *t.*
2 *Chr.* 8:8 did Solo. make pay *t.*
17:11 Philistines brou. *t.* silver
Ezr. 4:13 will they not pay *t.*
20 *t.* and custom paid to them
6:8 *t.* expenses be given to men
7:24 not lawful to imp. *t.* on Le.
Neh. 5:4 bor. money for king's *t.*
Prov. 12:24 slothful be under *t.*
Mat. 17:24 doth not mas. pay *t.?*
25 of whom do kings take *t.?*
22:17 is it lawf. to give *t.* to Ce.?
Mark 12:14; *Luke* 20:22
Luke 23:2 forbidding *t.* to Cesar
Rom. 13:6 for this can. pay ye *t.*
7 render *t.* to whom *t.* is due

TRICKLETH.

Lam. 3:49 mine eye *t.* down, and

TRIMMED, EST.

2 *Sam.* 19:24 M. had not *t.* beard
Jer. 2:33 *t.* way to seek love *t*
Mat. 25:7 arose, *t.* their lamps

TRIUMPH, ED, ING.

Ex. 15:1 he hath *t.* gloriously, 21
2 *Sam.* 1:20 lest uncircumcised *t.*
Ps. 25:2 let not enemies *t.* over
41:11 mine enemy doth not *t.*
60:8 Philistia, *t.* th. bec. of me
92:4 *t.* in works of thy hands
94:3 L. how long sh. wicked *t.?*
106:47 gi. thanks, *t.* in thy pra.
108:9 over Philistia will I *t.?*
2 *Cor.* 2:14 causeth us to *t.* in C.
Col. 2:15 show of them *t.* over

TRIUMPH, ING.

Job 20:5 that *t.* of wicked is short
Ps. 47:1 shout unto God with *t.*

TROAS.

Acts 16:8 by M. they came to T.
11 loosing from T. 20:5 at T.
2 *Cor.* 2:12 when I came to T. to
2 *Tim.* 4:13 the cloak I left at T.

TRODE.

Jud. 9:27 *t.* grapes, cursed Abi.
2:8:43 I. *t.* Benjamites wi. ease
2 *K.* 7:17 people *t.* upon him, 20
9:33 Jehu *t.* Jezebel under foot
14:9 beast *t.* thist. 2 *Chr.* 25:18
Luke 12:1 they *t.* one on another

TRODDEN.

Deut. 1:36 land *t.* on, *Jos.* 14:9
Jud. 5:21 hast *t.* down strength
Job 22:15 old way wicked have *t.*
28:8 lion's whelps have not *t.* it
Ps. 119:118 th. hast *t.* all that err
Is. 5:5 vineyard shall be *t.* down
11:10 as a carcase *t.* under foot
18:2 in nation meted, *t.* down
25:10 M. *t.* under as straw is *t.*
28:3 drunkards of Eph. sh. be *t.*
18 scourge pass, then be *t.* do.
63:3 I have *t.* wine-press alone
18 adversaries have *t.* sanctu.
Jer. 12:10 th. have *t.* my portion

TRO

Lam. 1:15 L. hath *t.* under foot
mighty men, hath *t.* virgin
Ezek. 34:19 flock eat ye have *t.*
Dan. 8:13 sanctu. and host be *t.*
Mic. 7:10 now shall she be *t.*
Mat. 5:13 salt unsavory to be *t.*
Luke. 6:5 fell by way-side. was *t.*
21:24 Jerus. sh. be *t.* of Gentil.
Heb. 10:29 *t.* under foot Son of G.
Rev. 14:20 wine-p. *t.* witho. city

TROGYLLIUM. *Acts* 20:15

TROOP,

Gen. 30:11 a *t.* cometh; 49:19 a *t.*
shall overcome him
1 *Sam.* 30:8 sh. I pursue this *t.?*
2 *Sam.* 2:25 Benjamin bec. one *t.*
3:22 Joab came from pursu. a *t.*
22:30 I run through *t. Ps.* 18:29
23:11 Phil. were gath. into a *t.*
13 *t.* pitched in valley of Rep.
Is. 65:11 prep. a table for that *t.*
Jer. 18:22 sh. bring a *t.* suddenly
Hos. 7:1 *t.* of rob. spoileth with.
Amos 9:6 founded his *t.* in earth

TROOPS.

Job 6:19 the *t.* of Tema looked
19:12 his *t.* come together, and
Jer. 5:7 they assembled by *t.* in
Hos. 6:9 as *t.* of robbers wait for
Mic. 5:1 gath. in *t.* O daug. of *t.*
Hab. 3:16 invade them wi. his *t.*

TROUBLE, Substantive,

1 *Chr.* 22:14 in my *t.* I prepared
2 *Chr.* 15:4 when they in *t.* did
turn and sought L. *Neh.* 9:27
Job 3:26 nol. quiet, yet *t.* came
5:6 neither doth *t.* spring out of
7 man born to *t.* as sparks fly
14:1 is of few days, full of *t.*
15:24 *t.* shall make him afraid
27:9 will G. hear wh. *t.* cometh?
30:25 I weep for him in *t.*
31:29 quietn. who can make *t.?*
38:23 I reserved aga. time of *t.*
Ps. 9:9 L. will be a refuge in *t.*
13 consider my *t.* wh. I suffer
10:1 why hid. th. thyself in *t.?*
22:11 be not far fr. me, *t.* is near
27:5 in time of *t.* he sh. hide me
31:7 thou hast considered my *t.*
9 mercy, O Lord, for I am in *t.*
32:7 thou shalt pres. me from *t.*
37:39 strength in time of *t.*
41:1 L. will deli. him in ti. of *t.*
46:1 God is our ref. a help in *t.*
54:7 he hath deliv. me out of *t.*
59:11 give us help from *t.*
60:11 my mouth hath spo. in *t.*
69:17 hide not face, I am in *t.*
73:5 they are not in *t.* as other
78:33 years did he consu. in *t.*
49 cast on them indign. and *t.*
81:7 calledst in *t.* I deliv. thee
91:15 I will be with him in *t.*
102:2 hide not face fr. me in *t.*
107:6 cried to Lord in *t.* 13, 19
26 soul is melted because of *t.*
28 they cry to Lord in their *t.*
116:3 pains gat hold, I found *t.*
119:143 *t.* and angu. have taken
138:7 tho' I walk in midst of *t.*
142:2 I showed before him my *t.*
143:11 bring my soul out of *t.*
Prov. 11:8 right. del. out *t.* 12:13
15:6 in revenues of wicked is *t.*
16 than treas. and *t.* therewith
25:19 unfaithful man in *t.*
Is. 1:14 new-moons, they are a *t.*
8:22 look to earth and behold *t.*
17:14 behold at evening tide *t.*
26:16 L. in *t.* they visited thee
30:6 into land of *t.* carry riches
33:2 be our salvat. in the time of *t.*
46:7 not, save him out of *t.*
65:23 shall not bring forth for *t.*
Jer. 2:27 in *t.* will say, Save us
28 if they can save th. in thy *t.*
8:15 looked for health, behold *t.*
11:12 shall not save them in *t.*
14 in them th. cried for their *t.*
11:8 Saviour of *t.* in time of *t.*
19 looked for healing, behold *t.*
30:7 it is time of Jacob's *t.*
Lam. 1:21 enem. heard of my *t.*
Dan. 12:1 there sh. be time of *t.*
1 *Cor.* 7:28 shall have *t.* in flesh
2 *Cor.* 1:4 able to com. them in *t.*
8 that have yon ignor. of our *t.*
2 *Tim.* 2:9 I suffer *t.* as evil-doer

See DAY.

TROUBLES,

Deut. 31:17 *t.* sh. befall them, 21
Job 5:19 he sh. del. thee in six *t.*
Ps. 25:17 *t.* of heart are enlarged
22 redeem Is. O God, out of *t.*

TRO

Ps. 34:6 L. saved him out of *t.* 17
71:20 wh. hast show. me sure *t.*
88:3 our. for my soul is full of *t.*
Prov. 21:23 he keepeth soul fr. *t.*
Is. 65:16 former *t.* are forgotten
Mark 13:8 shall be famine and *t.*

TROUBLE, Verb.

Jos. 6:18 lest ye *t.* camp of Israel
7:25 Lord shall *t.* thee this day
Jud. 11:35 one of th. that *t.* me
2 *Chr.* 32:18 they cried to *t.* th.
Ps. 3:1 how increas. that *t.* me?
13:4 those that *t.* me rejoice
Ezek. 32:13 nei. foot of man *t.* th.
nor hoofs of beasts *t.* them
Dan. 4:19 let not interpr. *t.* thee
5:10 let not thy thoughts *t.* thee
11:44 tidings out of north *t.* him
Mat. 26:10 why *t.* ye the woman?
Mark 14:6
Luke 7:6 Lord, *t.* not thyself
11:7 say, *t.* me not, door is shut
Acts 15:19 *t.* not G. turned to G.
16:20 th. do exceedingly *t.* city
20:10 *t.* not yoursel. his life is
2 *Cor.* 1:7 there be some th. *t.* you
5:12 th. were cut off who *t.* you
6:17 henceofor. let no man *t.* me
2 *Thes.* 1:6 trib. to th. that *t.* you
Heb. 12:15 lest bitterness *t.* you

TROUBLED.

Gen. 34:30 ye ha. *t.* me, *t.* make
41:8 in morn. Ph.'s spirit was *t.*
45:3 his brethren *t.* at his pres.
Ex. 14:24 L. *t.* host of Egyptians
Jos. 7:25 why hast thou *t.* us?
1 *Sam.* 14:29 father hath *t.* land
16:14 evil spirit fr. Lord *t.* him
28:21 woman saw that S. was *t.*
2 *Sam.* 4:1 Abner dead, all Is. *t.*
1 *K.* 18:18 I have not *t.* Israel
2 *K.* 6:11 king of Syria was *t.*
Ezr. 4:4 peo. *t.* them in building
Job 4:5 toucheth thee, thou art *t.*
21:4 why shou. not spirit be *t.?*
23:15 theref. am I *t.* at his pres.
Ps. 30:7 hide thy face, I was *t.*
38:6 I am *t.* 77:4 I am so *t.*
46:3 tho' waters roar and be *t.*
48:5 kings were *t.* hasted away
77:3 I remember. God and was *t.*
16 the depths also were *t.*
83:17 let them be confou. and *t.*
90:7 by thy wrath are we *t.*
104:29 hidest thy face, th. are *t.*
Prov. 25:26 is as a *t.* fountain
Is. 32:10 and *t.* years shall ye be *t.*
11 wom. be *t.* ye careless ones
57:20 wicked are like the *t.* sea
Lam. 1:20 my bowels are *t.* 2:11
Ezek. 7:27 hands of peo. sh. be *t.*
26:18 isles in sea shall be *t.*
32:35 their kings be *t.* in count.
Dan. 2:1 Neb.'s spirit was *t.* 3
4:5 visions of my head *t.* 7:15
19 his thoughts *t.* him
5:6 Belshaz.'s thoughts *t.* him, 9
7:28 my cogitations much *t.* me
Zec. 10:2 *t.* because no shepherd
Mat. 2:3 Herod was *t.* and Jerus.
14:26 they were *t. Mark* 6:50
24:6 not *t.* thi. must co. to pass,
Mark 13:7; *John* 14:1, 27
Luke 1:29 troubled way of *t.*
10:41 Martha *t.* about many thi.
24:38 why are *t.* and why do
John 5:4 angel went down and *t.*
7 no man wh. water is *t.* to put
11:33 and went *t.* 12:27; 13:21
Acts 15:24 some fr. us have *t.* ye
17:8 they *t.* people and rulers
17:13 they *t.* the people
2 *Thes.* 1:7 you that are *t.* rest
4 that ye be not *t.* nei. by spi.
1 *Pet.* 3:14 not of. of terror, nor *t.*

TROUBLEDST.

Ezek. 32:2 thou *t.* waters wi. feet

TROUBLER.

1 *Chr.* 2:7 Achar, the *t.* of Israel

TROUBLEST, ETH.

1 *Sam.* 16:15 an evil spirit *t.* thee
1 *K.* 18:17 art thou he that *t.* Is.?
Job 23:16 sudden fear *t.* thou
31:23 heart soft, Almighty *t.* me
Prov. 11:17 that is cruel *t.* flesh
15:27 greedy of gain, *t.* his own
17:17 that *t.* his house, inh. wind
Mark 5:35 why *t.* the Master?
Luke 8:49 thy *t.* not Master?
18:5 because this widow *t.* me
Gal. 5:10 he *t.* you shall bear

TROUBLING.

Job 3:17 there wicked cease fr. *t.*
John 5:4 sten. in after *t.* of water

TRU

TROUBLOUS.

Dan. 9:25 sh. be built in *t.* times

TROUGH, S.

Gen. 24:20 empt. pitcher into *t.*
30:38 J. set rods in watering *t.*
Ex. 8:3 they filled *t.* to water
8:3 frogs sh. go into kneading *t.*
12:34 th. kneading *t.* bound up

TROW.

Luke 17:9 thank serva.? I *t.* not

TRUCE-BREAKERS.

1 *Tim.* 3:3 last days shall be *t.-b.*

TRUE.

Gen. 42:11 we are *t.* men, 31
19 if ye be *t.* men let one of y.
Deut. 17:4 if ye be *t.* and, 22:20
2 *Sam.* 7:28 God, thy words be *t.*
1 *K.* 10:6 it was a *t.* report I
heard, 2 *Chr.* 9:5
22:16 tell me noth. but that is *t.*
Neh. 9:13 gavest them *t.* laws
Ps. 19:9 judgments of Lord are *t.*
119:160 thy word is *t.* fr. begin.
Dan. 3:14 is it *t.* O Shadrach, do
3:4 O king; 6:12 thing is *t.*
10:1 revealed and thing was *t.*
Mat. 22:16 thou art *t. Mark* 12:14
Luke 16:11 com. to trust *t.* riches
John 1:9 that was the *t.* light
4:37 herein is saying *t.* inasmuch
5:31 of myself, my wit. is not *t.*
32 Father giveth the *t.* bread
7:18 same is *t.* 8:13 reco. not *t.*
28 he that sent me is *t.* 8:26
8:14 record is *t.* 16 judgme. is *t.*
17 testimony of two men is *t.*
10:41 all things J. spake were *t.*
9:35 and his record is *t.* 21:21
Acts 12:9 wist not that it was *t.*
2 *Cor.* 1:18 as God is *t.* our word
6:8 as deceivers, and yet *t.*
Phil. 4:8 whatsoev. things are *t.*
1 *Tim.* 3:1 this is a *t.* saying
Tit. 1:13 this witness is *t.* wher.
Heb. 8:2 t.. tabernacle which L.
9:24 which are figures of the *t.*
10:22 draw near with a *t.* heart
1 *Pet.* 5:12 this is *t.* grace of God
2 *Pet.* 2:22 accordi. to *t.* proverb
1 *John* 2:8 which thing is *t.*
5:20 may kn. him that is *t.* and
we are in him that is *t.*
3 *John* 12 ye know our rec. is *t.*
Rev. 3:7 saith holy, he that is *t.*
14 saith faithful and *t.* witness
6:10 long, O Lord, holy and *t.?*
15:3 just and *t.* are thy ways
16:7; are thy judgments, 19:2
19:9 these are *t.* say. of G. 22:6
11 he th. ent was Faith. and *T.*
21:5 write, for these words are *t.*

TRUE God.

2 *Chr.* 15:3 Is. ha. been wi. *t. G.*
Jer. 10:10 Lord is the *t. God*
John 17:3 eternal life to kn. *t. G.*
1 *Thes.* 1:9 from idols to *t. G.*
1 *John* 5:20 this is the *t. God*

TRULY.

Num. 14:21 *t.* as I live, saith L.
Ps. 116:16 *t.* I am thy servant
Prov. 12:22 deal *t.* are his delight
Mat. 9:37 *t.* the harvest is plent.
Luke 20:21 teachest way of G. *t.*
John 4:18 no husb. saidst thou *t.*

TRUMP.

1 *Cor.* 15:52 at last *t.* dead shall
1 *Thes.* 4:16 L. shall des. with *t.*

TRUMPET.

Ex. 19:16 voice of *t.* excee. loud
20:18 people heard noise of *t.*
Num. 10:4 if th. blow wi. one *t.*
Jud. 7:16 put a *t.* in every man's
Ps. 81:3 blow *t.* in new moon
Is. 18:3 when he bloweth *t.* hear
27:13 great *t.* shall be blown
58:1 lift up thy voice like a *t.*
Jer. 4:5 blow ye the *t.* in land
6:1 blow the *t.* in Tekoah
51:27 blow *t.* among nations
Ezek. 7:14 they have blown the *t.*
33:3 if ye blow *t.* and warn, 6
Hos. 5:8 blow ye the *t.* in Ramah
8:1 set the *t.* to thy mouth
Joel 2:1 blow the *t.* in Zion, 15
Amos 3:6 sh. *t.* be blo. not trou.
Zep. 1:16 day of *t.* ag. fenced cit.
Zec. 9:14 blow *t.* shall blow *t.*
1 *Cor.* 14:8 *t.* give an uncertain
15:52 at sixth angel which had *t.*

See BLEW, SOUND, SOUNDED.

TRUMPETS.

Lev. 23:24 a memorial of blow. *t.*
Num. 10:2 make two *t.* of silver

CRUDEN'S CONCORDANCE.

TRU

Num. 10:8 sons of Aa. bl. with *t.*
10 blow with *t.* over burnt-off.
22:1 day of blowing *t.* unto you
31:6 wt. *t.* to blow to his hand
Jos. 6:4 priests sh. blow with *t.*
8 bearing seven *t.* of rams'
Jud. 7:8 300 men took *t.* 16
19 they blow the *t.* 20, 22
2 *K.* 9:13 they blew with *t.* sayi.
11:14 trumpeters blew with *t.*
1 *Chr.* 13:8 with cymbals and *t.*
15:24 the priests did blow wt. *t.*
before ark of God, 16:6, 42;
2 *Chr.* 5:12; 7:6; 13:12, 14
29 Israel brought up ark wi. *t.*
2 *Chr.* 5:13 they lift voice with *t.*
23:27 song of L. began with *t.*
Job 39:25 horse say. am. *t.* Ha, ha
Ps. 98:6 wi. *t.* make joyful noise
See SEVEN.

TRUMPETERS.
2 *K.* 11:14 and *t.* stood by king
2 *Chr.* 5:13 *t.* and singers were
23:28 singers sang, and *t.* sound.
Rev. 18:22 vol. of *t.* heard no mo.

TRUST.
Job 8:14 wh. *t.* sh. be a spider's
13:15 putteth no *t.* in his saints
Ps. 40:4 that maketh Lord his *t.*
71:5 O Lord GOD, thou art my *t.*
141:8 in thee is my *t.* leave not
Prov. 22:19 thy *t.* may be in Lord
28:25 that puts his *t.* in Lord
29:25 who putteth his *t.* in Lord
Is. 30:3 *t.* in Egypt shall be conf.
57:13 that putteth *t.* in me shall
Luke 16:11 com. to *t.* true riches
2 *Cor.* 3:4 such *t.* ha. we thro' C.
1 *Tim.* 1:11 gospel, com. to my *t.*
1:20 keep that commi. to thy *t.*
See PUT.

TRUST, Verb.
Ruth 2:12 thou art come to *t.*
2 *Sam.* 22:3 in him will I *t. Ps.*
18:2; 91:2
31 a buckler to all that *t.* in
him, *Ps.* 18:30
1 *K.* 18:20 on whom dost thou *t.?*
2 *Chr.* 32:10; *Is.* 36:5,
21 so is Pharaoh to all that *t.*
in him, *Is.* 36:6
22 we *t.* in L. our God, *Is.* 36:7
30 neither let Hezekiah make
you *t.* in the Lord, *Is.* 36:15
Job 13:15 yet will I *t.* in him
13:31 let not him *t.* in deceit. *t.*
32:1 judg. bef. him, *t.* in him
39:11 wilt *t.* him bec. strong?
Ps. 20:7 some *t.* in chariots
25:2 I *t.* in thee, 31:6; 55:23;
56:3; 143:8
31:19 hast wrou. for them th. *t.*
34:22 none th. *t.* in him sh. be
37:3 *t.* in the Lord, and do good,
5; 40:3; 62:8; 115:9, 10, 11;
Prov. 3:5; *Is.* 26:4
40 he sh. save, because they *t.*
44:6 I will not *t.* in my bow
49:6 they that *t.* in their wealth
52:8 I *t.* in the mercy of God
61:4 I will *t.* in cov. of thy wings
62:10 *t.* not in oppression
64:10 rejoice, shall be glad, and *t.*
91:4 under his wings sh. thou *t.*
118:8 it is better to *t.* in Lord, 9
115:42 answer, I *t.* in thy word
125:1 that *t.* in the Lord, *Is.* 26:3
144:2 shield, and he in wh. I *t.*
Prov. 31:11 her husband doth *t.*
Is. 12:2 I will *t.* not be afraid
14:32 poor of his people shall *t.*
30:2 to *t.* in shadow of Egypt
12 because ye *t.* in oppression
31:1 and *t.* in chariots because
42:17 ashamed th. *t.* in images
50:10 let him *t.* in name of L.
51:5 on mine arm shall they *t.*
59:4 they *t.* in vanity and speak
Jer. 7:4 *t.* ye not in lying words
8 ye *t.* in lying words
14 by name, wherein ye *t.*
9:4 and *t.* ye not in any brother
28:15 makest peo. to *t.* in, 29:31
44:25 punish Ph. and all that *t.*
49:11 let thy widows *t.* in me
Ezek. 16:15 th. didst *t.* in beauty
39:13 if he *t.* to his own righte.
Hos. 10:13 thou didst *t.* in way
Amos 6:1 that *t.* in mount. of Sa.
Mic. 7:5 *t.* ye not in a friend
Nah. 1:7 L. knoweth them th. *t.*
Zep. 3:12 I shall *t.* in name of L.
Mat. 12:21 in his name shall Gentiles *t. Rom.* 15:12
Mark 10:24 them that *t.* in riches
John 5:45 Moses in whom ye *t.*

TRU

Rom. 15:24 I *t.* to see you in my
1 *Cor.* 16:7 I *t.* to tarry a while
2 *Cor.* 1:9 sho. not *t.* in ourselves
10 in whom we *t.* that he will
13:7 if any man *t.* to himself
Phil. 3:4 if any think. hath to *t.*
1 *Tim.* 4:10 we *t.* in living God
6:17 they *t.* not in uncertain
3 *John* 14 I *t.* I shall shortly see thee

TRUSTED.
Deut. 32:37 rock in wh. they *t.?*
Jud. 11:20 Sih. *t.* not Is. to pass
20:36 they *t.* to the liers in wait
2 *K.* 18:5 he *t.* in the Lord God
22:4 our fathers *t.* th. have *t.* 5
8 he *t.* on Lord that he would
22:1 I have *t.* in L. 26:7; 31:14;
52:8
52:7 I have *t.* in the abund. of his riches
1 Chr. 5:20 because they *t.* in him
41:9 familiar friend in wh. I *t.*
52:7 *t.* in abund. of his riches
78:22 *t.* not in his salvation
Is. 47:10 th. hast *t.* in thy wick.
Jer. 13:25 thou hast *t.* in falseh.
48:7 thou hast *t.* in thy works
49:4 daugh. that *t.* in her treas.
Dan. 3:28 God delivereth that *t.*
Zep. 3:2 she *t.* not in the Lord
Mat. 27:43 he *t.* in God, let him
Luke 11:22 armor wherein he *t.*
18:9 cer. which *t.* in themselves
24:21 we *t.* it had been he that
Eph. 1:12 who first *t.* in Christ
13 in whom ye also *t.* after ye
1 *Pet.* 3:5 holy wom. who *t.* in G.

TRUSTEDST.
Deut. 28:52 walls down thou *t.*
Jer. 5:17 cities wherein thou *t.*
12:5 land of peace wher. thou *t.*

TRUSTEST.
2 *K.* 18:19 what confidence is this
wherein thou *t.? Is.* 36:4
21 *t.* on bruised reed, *Is.* 36:6
19:10 G. in wh. thou *t. Is.* 37:10

TRUSTETH.
Job 40:23 he *t.* that he can draw
Ps. 21:7 the king *t.* in the Lord
32:10 that *t.* in L. mercy shall
34:8 blessed is man th. *t.* 84:12;
Prov. 16:20; *Jer.* 17:7
57:1 be merci. my soul *t.* in thee
82:3 save thy serv. that *t.* in thee
112:8 so is ev. one that *t.* 135:18
Prov. 11:28 he that *t.* in riches
28:26 that *t.* his heart is a fool
31:29 peace bec. he *t.* in thee
Jer. 17:5 cursed be man *t.* man
Hab. 2:18 maker thereof *t.* in it
1 *Tim.* 5:5 th. is a widow, *t.* in G.

TRUSTING.
Ps. 112:7 heart is fixed, *t.* in L.

TRUSTY.
Job 12:20 removeth speech of *t.*

TRUTH.
Gen. 24:27 not left dest. mas. of *t.*
32:10 not worthy of least of *t.*
42:16 be proved, whether any *t.*
Ex. 18:21 men of *t.* hating cov.
34:6 abundant in goodness and *t.*
Deut. 13:14 if it be *t.* 22:4 G. of *t.*
2 *Sam.* 2:6 L. show kindn. and *t.*
15:20 mercy and *t.* be with thee
1 *K.* 17:24 word of the Lord is *t.*
2 *K.* 20:19 if *t.* be in my, *Is.* 39:8
2 *Chr.* 18:15 any nothing but *t.*
31:20 Hez. wrought that was *t.*
Est. 9:30 letters with words of *t.*
Ps. 15:2 speaketh *t.* in heart
22:10 paws that *t.* are promised
31:5 redeemed me, O L. G. of *t.*
43:4 ride prosperously bec. of *t.*
51:6 thou desirest *t.* in inward
57:3 God shall send forth his *t.*
60:4 ban. be displayed bec. of *t.*
61:7 O prepare mercy and *t.*
85:10 mercy and *t.* met togeth.
11 *t.* shall spring out of earth
86:15 plenteous in mercy and *t.*
89:14 mercy and *t.* sh. go before
91:4 his *t.* shall be thy shield
96:13 he shall judge peo. with *t.*
98:3 he hath remembered his *t.*
100:5 his *t.* endur. to all, 117:2
119:30 I have chosen way of *t.*
142 and thy law is the *t.* 151
146:6 L. is God who keepeth *t.*
Prov. 8:3 let not *t.* forsake thee
8:7 for my mouth shall speak *t.*
12:17 he that speaks *t.* showeth
17 lip of *t.* shall be established
14:22 mercy and *t.* be to them
16:6 by mercy and *t.* iniquity is
20:28 mercy and *t.* preserve king

TRU

Prov. 23:23 kn. certain. of words
of *t.* answer the words of *t.*
23:23 buy the *t.* and sell it not
Ec. 12:10 writ. were words of *t.*
Is. 25:1 coun. are faithf. and *t.*
26:2 nation which keepeth *t.*
42:3 bring forth judgm. unto *t.*
43:9 let th. hear, and say, It is *t.*
59:4 nor any pleadeth for *t.*
14 for *t.* is fallen in the street
15 yea, *t.* falleth, and he
Jer. 5:1 if th. be that seeketh *t.*
3 O L. are not th. eyes upon *t.?*
7:28 *t.* is perished and cut off
9:3 they are not valiant for *t.*
5 deceive and will not speak *t.*
33:6 revealed aboundance of *t.*
Dan. 4:37 all whose works are *t.*
7:16 I asked him *t.* of this, 19
8:12 it cast down *t.* to ground
10:21 is noted in scriptures of *t.*
11:2 now will I show thee the *t.*
Hos. 4:1 no *t.* nor mercy in land
Zec. 7:20 will perform *t.* to Jac.
Zec. 8:3 Jer. be called city of *t.*
16 speak ye every man *t.* execute judgment of *t. Eph.* 4:25
19 thoref. love the *t.* and peace
Mal. 2:6 law of *t.* in his mouth
Mat. 15:27 she said, *t.* Lord, yet
Mark 5:33 woman told him *t.*
12:32 Master, thou hast said *t.*
Luke 1:14 full of grace and *t.*
17 grace and *t.* came by J. C.
8:31 *t.* bare witness unto the *t.*
6:32 Ka. *t.* and *t.* make you free
8:40 seek to kill me, that told *t.*
44 abode not in *t.* because no
t. in him
45 I tell *t.* ye believe me not
46 if I say *t.* why not believe?
14:6 I am the way, *t.* the life
16:7 I tell you *t.* it is expedient
18 Sp. of *t.* guide you into all *t.*
17:19 be sanctified through *t.*
13:37 th. I should bear witness
to *t.* every one that is of *t.*
38 Pil. saith to him, what is *t.?*
Acts 26:25 I spe. forth words of *t.*
Rom. 1:18 hold *t.* in unrighteous.
25 changed *t.* of God into a lie
2:2 judgm. of G. according to *t.*
8 to them that do not obey *t.*
20 hast form of knowl. and *t.*
3:7 if *t.* of G. ha. more abound.
9:1 I say *t.* in Christ, I lie not
15:8 minister of circumci. for *t.*
1 *Cor.* 5:8 unleavened bread of *t.*
2 *Cor.* 4:2 by manifestation of *t.*
7:14 boast. I made is found a *t.*
11:10 as *t.* of Ch. is in me none
12:6 for I will say the *t.*
13:8 we can do nothing ag. *t.*
Gal. 2:5 *t.* of gospel might conti.
14 walked not according to *t.*
3:1 ye should not obey *t.* 5:7
4:16 enemy bec. I tell you *t.?*
Eph. 4:15 speak. the *t.* in love
21 taught by him as *t.* is in J.
5:9 fruit of Spirit is in all *t.*
6:14 hav. your loins girt with *t.*
2 *Thes.* 2:10 recei. not love of *t.*
12 damned who believe not *t.*
13 salvation thro' belief of *t.*
1 *Tim.* 2:4 come to knowl. of *t.*
7 I speak *t.* in Christ, lie not
3:15 the pillar and ground of *t.*
4:3 received of them wh. kn. *t.*
6:5 corrupt minds, destitu. of *t.*
2 *Tim.* 2:15 rightly dividing *t.*
25 repent. to acknowledg. of *t.*
3:7 to come to knowledge of *t.*
8 Jambres, so do these resist *t.*
4:4 turn away their ears from *t.*
Tit. 1:1 to acknowledging of *t.*
14 commandm. that turn fr. *t.*
Heb. 10:26 received knowl. of *t.*
Jam. 3:14 lie not against the *t.*
5:19 if any of you err fr. the *t.*
1 *Pet.* 1:22 purified in obeying *t.*
2 *Pet.* 2:2 way of *t.* evil spok. of
1 *John* 1:6 we lie, do not the *t.*
8 dece. ourselves, *t.* is not in us
2:4 *t.* not in him; 27 *t.* is no lie
21 because ye know not *t.* and
no lie is of the *t.*
3:19 we know that we are of *t.*
8:6 witness, because Spirit is *t.*
2 *John* 1 they that have known *t.*
2 for *t.* sake that dwell. in us
3 *John* 3 test. of *t.* that is in thee
8 might be fellow-helpers to *t.*
12 good report of men and of *t.*

In TRUTH.
Jos. 24:14 serve Lord in *t.* 1 *Sam.* 12:24
Jud. 9:15 if in *t.* ye anoint me

TRI

1 *K.* 2:4 if my children walk in *t.*
3:6 as Da. walked bef. thee in *t.*
2 *K.* 20:3 I have walked in *t.*
Ps. 3:4 works done in *t.* 111:8
132:11 L. hath sworn in *t.* to D.
145:18 L. nigh to all call in *t.*
Is. 10:20 stay on Holy One in *t.*
16:5 he shall sit upon it in *t.*
48:1 mention of G. but not in *t.*
61:8 I will direct th. work in *t.*
Jer. 4:2 swear, the L. liveth in *t.*
Zec. 8:8 I will be their God in *t.*
Mat. 22:16 teachest the way of
God in *t. Mark* 12:14
John 4:23 in spirit and in *t.* 24
2 *Cor.* 7:14 speak all things in *t.*
Col. 1:6 ye knew grace of G. in *t.*
1 *Thes.* 2:13 it is in *t.* word of G.
1 *John* 3:18 love in tongue, in *t.*
2 *John* 3 Son of the Father in *t.*
4 I found of thy children walking in *t.* 3 *John* 4

In the TRUTH.
Ps. 69:13 hear in *t. t.* of salva.
John 8:44 mur. abode not in *t. t.*
1 *Cor.* 13:6 charity rejoic. in *t. t.*
2 *Pet.* 1:12 be established in *t. t.*
2 *John* 1 I love in *t. t.* 3 *John* 1
3 *John* 3 as thou walkest in *t. t.*

Of a TRUTH.
Jer. 26:15 of a L. Lord sent me
Dan. 2:47 of *a t.* it is, your G. is
Mat. 14:33 of *a t.* thou art Son
Luke 4:25 I tell you of *a t.* 9:27
12:44 of *a t.* I say unto, 21:3
John 6:14 of *a t.* th. proph. 7:40
Acts 4:27 of *a t.* ag. holy child J.
1 *Cor.* 14:25 God is in you of *a t.*
See SPIRIT.

Thy TRUTH.
Ps. 25:5 lead me in *thy t.* teach
26:3 and I have walked in *thy t.*
30:9 shall dust declare *thy t.?*
40:10 *thy t.* from great congreg.
11 *thy t.* continu. preserve me
43:3 send out *thy light* and *t. t.*
54:5 enemies, cut th. off in *t. t.*
57:10 *thy t.* unto clouds, 108:4
71:22 praise *thy t.* 89:11 in *t. t.*
89:49 swarest to David in *thy t.*
115:1 glory for *t. t.* sake, 138:2
Is. 38:18 cannot hope for *thy t.*
19 chil. shall make known *t. t.*
Dan. 9:13 might understand *t. t.*
John 17:17 sanctify th. thro' *t. t.*

Word of TRUTH.
Ps. 119:43 take not *w. of t.* out
2 Cor. 6:7 appr. ours. by *w. of t.*
Eph. 1:13 that ye heard *w. of t.*
Col. 1:5 ye heard bef. in *w. of t.*
2 *Tim.* 2:15 dividing *word of t.*
Jam. 1:18 begat he us by *w. of t.*

TRY.
Jud. 7:4 I will *t.* them for thee
Job 7:18 that thou should. *t.* him
12:11 doth not the ear *t.* words
Ps. 11:4 eyelids *t.* chil. of men
26:2 exam. me, O L. *t.* my reins
Ec. 3:18 that God might *t.* them
9:7 melt and *t.* them, *Zec.* 13:9
17:10 Lord search heart, *t.* reins
Lam. 3:40 let us search and *t.*
Dan. 11:35 some fall to *t.* them
Pet. 4:12 trial wh. is to *t.* you
1 *John* 4:1 *t.* spirits whether of G.
Rev. 3:10 temptation to *t.* them

TRIED.
Deut. 21:5 by Lev. ev. stroke be *t.*
2 *Sam.* 22:31 the word of the
Lord is *t. Ps.* 18:30
Job 23:10 when he hath *t.* me
34:36 desire is that J. may be *t.*
Ps. 12:6 as silver is *t.* in furnace
17:3 th. hast *t.* me, find nothing
66:10 hast *t.* us as silver is *t.*
105:19 word of the Lord *t.* him
Is. 28:16 I lay in Z. a *t.* stone
Jer. 12:3 thou hast *t.* my heart
Dan. 12:10 many be puri. and *t.*
Zec. 13:9 try them as g. is *t.*
Heb. 11:17 Abra. when he was *t.*
Jam. 1:12 when *t.* receive crown
1 *Pet.* 1:7 tho' it be *t.* with fire
Rev. 2:2 hast *t.* them which say
10 into prison, ye may be *t.*
3:18 buy of me gold *t.* in the fire

TRIEST, ETH.
1 *Chr.* 29:17 I know thou *t.* heart
Job 34:3 ear *t.* words as mouth
Ps. 7:9 righteous God *t.* hearts
11:5 the Lord *t.* the righteous

CRUDEN'S CONCORDANCE. 1063

TUR

Prov. 17:3 but Lord *t.* the hearts
Jer. 11:20 O L. that *t.* the reins
23:12 L. of hosts that *t.* righto.
1 Thes. 2:4 but God who *t.* hearts

TRYING.
Jam. 1:3 *t.* of faith work, patien.

TRYPHENA, TRYPHOSA.
Rom. 16:12 salute T. and T. who

TUBAL.
Gen. 10:2 Ja. Javan, T. 1 Ch. 1:5
Is. 66:19 those that escape to T.
Ezek. 27:13 Javan T. thy merch.
32:26 Meshech, T. and multit.
38:2 of Meshech and T. 3; 39:1

TUMBLED.
Jud. 7:13 a cake *t.* into the host

TUMULT.
1 Sam. 4:14 wh. noise of this *t.* ?
2 K. 19:28 thy *t.* come unto mine ears, Is. 37:29
Ps. 65:7 stilleth *t.* of the people
74:23 *t.* of th. that rise ag. thee
83:2 lo, thine enemies make a *t.*
Is. 33:3 at noise of *t.* people fled
Jer. 11:16 with noise of a great *t.*
Hos. 10:14 *t.* rise among people
Amos 2:2 Moab shall die with *t.*
Zec. 14:13 a *t.* fr. Lord am. them
Mat. 27:24 rather a *t.* was made
Mark 5:38 he seeth *t.* and them
Acts 21:34 could not know for *t.*
24:18 with multitude, nor wi. *t.*

TUMULTS.
Amos 3:9 behold gre. *t.* in midst
2 Cor. 6:5 ourselves as min. in *t.*
12:20 whisperings, swellings, *t.*

TUMULTUOUS.
Is. 13:4 a *t.* noise of kingdoms
22:2 thou that art a *t.* city
Jer. 48:45 devour head of *t.* ones

TURN.
Est. 2:11 ev. maid's *t.* was come
15 when *t.* of Esther was come

TURN, Verb.
Gen. 24:49 that I may *t.* to right
Ex. 3:3 I will now *t.* aside, and see
23:27 make thine enemies *t.*
34:12 from thy fierce wrath
Num. 14:25 to-morrow *t.* you
20:17 will not *t.* to right hand
22:23 he smote the ass to *t.* her
26 wh. was no way to *t.* right
Deut. 1:40 *t.* ye, take journey
30:3 Lord will *t.* their captivity
31:20 th. will th. *t.* to oth. gods
34:20 then he will *t.* and do
Jud. 20:8 nor any *t.* into house
1 Sam. 14:7 *t.* I am with thee
22:17 *t.* and slay priests of L. 18
2 Sam. 14:19 none can *t.* to ri. or
2:l said, Let him *t.* to house
1 K. 8:35 *t.* from their sin, 2 Chr. 6:26, 37; 7:14
9:6 if you *t.* from following me
17:3 *t.* eastward, hide thyself
22:34 thy hand, 2 Chr. 18:33
2 K. 9:18 *t.* thee behind me, 19
17:13 *t.* ye from your evil ways, Jer. 18:8; 26:3; Zec. 1:3, 4
1 Chr. 12:23 to *t.* kingd. of Saul
2 Chr. 35:22 *t.* would not *t.* face
Neh. 1:9 *t.* and keep com. Ezek. 3:20; 18:21; 33:11, 14, 19
9:26 testified to *t.* them to thee
Job 5:1 wh. of saints wilt th. *t.* ?
14:6 *t.* fr. him that he may rest
23:13 who can *t.* him?
24:4 they *t.* needy out of way
Ps. 4:2 how long will ye *t.* glory ?
7:12 if he *t.* not, will whet sw.
21:12 make them *t.* their back
25:16 *t.* unto me, 69:16; 86:16
85:4 *t.* us, O God of our salva.
119:79 let those th. fear thee *t.*
132:11 sworn to D. he will not *t.*
Prov. 1:23 *t.* you at my reproof
4:15 *t.* from it and pass away
27 *t.* not to right hand nor left
Ec. 2:20 and all *t.* to dust again
Cant. 2:17 *t.* my beloved, and
Is. 13:14 ev. one *t.* to his people
19:6 shall *t.* rivers far away
23:16 he will *t.* and tow thee
28:6 *t.* shall *t.* to her lute
28:6 strength to them *t.* battle
31:6 *t.* ye *t.* to right and left
31:6 *t.* ye to him fr. whom Is.
59:20 to them that *t.* fr. transg.
Jer. 2:35 his anger shall *t.* fr. me
3:7 and I said, *t.* unto me, 14
13:16 before ho *t.* it Into death

TUR

Jer. 31:18 *t.* th. me, I sh. bo turn.
44:5 hearken, not to *t.* fr. wick.
50:16 *t.* every one to his people
Lam. 5:21 *t.* us unto thee, O L.
Ezek. 3:19 he *t.* not fr. wick. 33:9
4:8 sh. not *t.* from one side to
7:22 my face will I *t.* fr. them
14:6 *t.* fr. idols, 18:30, 32 ; 33:9, 11 ; Hos. 12:6 ; Joel 2:12
30:9 I will *t.* unto you, and ye
36:12 to *t.* hand on desol. places
Dan. 9:13 might *t.* fr. iniquities
11:18 shall he *t.* face unto isles
19 shall *t.* his face toward fort
12:3 that *t.* many to righteous.
Hos. 5:4 frame their doings to *t.*
12:6 therefore *t.* thou to thy G.
Amos 1:8 *t.* my hand ag. Ekron
8:10 I will *t.* feasts into mourn.
Jon. 3:8 *t.* cv. one from evil way
Zep. 3:9 *t.* to people pure langu.
13:7 *t.* my hand upon little ones
Mal. 4:6 he sh. *t.* heart of fathers
Mat. 5:39 check, *t.* to him other
Luke 1:17 to *t.* hearts of fathers
21:13 sh. *t.* to you for a testim.
Acts 13:46 wo *t.* to the Gentiles
14:15 sho. *t.* from these vanities
26:18 to *t.* them from darkn. to
20 should repent and *t.* to God
Phil. 1:19 this sh. *t.* to my salva.
Tit. 1:14 comm. that *t.* fr. truth
Jam. 3:3 wo *t.* about their body
2 Pet. 2:21 to *t.* from command.
Rev. 11:6 to *t.* waters to blood

TURN again.
Jud. 11:8 we *t. a.* to thee now
Ruth 1:11 *t. a.* my daughters, 12
1 Sam. 15:25 *t. a.* with me, 30
1 K. 8:33 when Israel shall *t. a.*
12:27 heart of people *t.* again
13:9 nor *t. a.* by same way, 17
2 K. 1:6 go *t.* again to the king
2 Chr. 30:6 *t. a.* to L. 9 if ye *t. a.*
Job 34:15 man sh. *t. a.* to dust
Ps. 18:37 nor did I *t. a.* till they
60:1 displeas. O *t.* thys. to us *a.*
80:3 *t.* us *a.* O L. of hosts, 7, 19
85:8 let them not *t. a.* to folly
104:9 th. *t.* not *a.* to cover earth
126:4 *t.* again our captivity
Jer. 25:5 *t.* yo *a.* from evil way
31:21 *t. a.* O virgin, *t. a.* to cit.
Lam. 3:40 try our ways, *t.* again
Ezek. 8:6 *t. a.* thou sh. see, 13, 15
Mic. 7:19 will *t. a.* have compas.
Zec. 10:9 live with child. *t.* again
Mal. 7:6 lest they *t. a.* and rend
Luke 10:6 it shall *t.* to you again
17:4 seven times in a day *t. a.*
Gal. 4:9 *t. a.* to weak elements

TURN aside.
Ex. 9:3 I will *t. a.* and see this
Deut. 5:39 not *t. a.* to right hand
17:20 *t.* not *a.* from command.
31:29 after my death ye will *t. a.*
Jos. 23:6 that ye *t.* not *a.* there-
from, 1 Sam. 12:20, 21
Ruth 3:1 ho, such a one, *t. aside*
2 Sam. 2:21 *t. a.* and take armor
2 he refused to *t. aside*
18:30 king said, *t. a.* stand here
Ps. 40:4 respect, not such as *t. a.*
125:5 far such as *t. a.* to crooked
Is. 10:2 *t. a.* needy from judgm.
29:21 *t. a.* just for thing of nau.
30:11 *t. aside* out of the way
Amos 2:7 that *t. a.* way of meek
5:12 they *t. a.* poor in the gate
Mal. 3:5 *t. a.* stranger from right

TURN away.
Gen. 27:44 till brother's fury *t. a.*
45 till thy broth.'s anger *t. a.*
Num. 32:15 if ye *t. a.* from after
him, Deut. 30:17; Jos. 22:16;
2 Chr. 7:19
Deut. 7:4 they will *t.* away my son
13 he hath spoken to *t.* you *a.*
1 K. 11:2 sh. will *t. a.* your heart
2 Chr. 14:11 go not, *t. a.* fr. thence
2 Chr. 25:27 Amaziah did *t. a.*
25:10 that wrath may *t. a.* fr.
Ps. 106:23; Prov. 24:18
30:9 L. will *t. a.* his face
Ps. 119:37 *t. a.* mine eyes from
39 *t. a.* my reproach wh. I fear
Prov. 28:9 wise men *t. a.* wrath
Cant. 6:5 *t. a.* thine eyes from me
Is. 58:13 if *t. a.* foot from sabbath
Jer. 8:10 thou sh. *t. a.* face fr. L.
8:4 sh. ho *t. a.* and not return?
18:20 I stood to *t. a.* thy wrath
32:40 I will not *t. a.* from them

TUR

Ezek. 14:6 *t. a.* faces from abom.
Jon. 3:9 God will *t. a.* fr. fierce
Mal. 2:6 did *t.* many *a.* from ini.
2 Tim. 3:5 traitors, fr. such *t. a.*
4:4 sh. *t. a.* their ears fr. truth
Heb. 12:25 how esca. if we *t. a.* ?

TURN back.
Deut. 23:13 *t. b.* and cover that
1 K. 2:22 then sh. mine enemies *t. b.*
Is. 14:27 hand stretc. who *t. b.* ?
Jer. 4:28 nei. will I *t. b.* from it
21:4 I will *t. b.* weapons of war
46:5 flee yea, *t. back*, dwell deep
Ezek. 38:4 I will *t.* thee *b.* 39:2
Mark 13:16 not *t. b.* to take gar.

TURN in.
Gen. 19:2 lords, *t. in*, I pray you
Jud. 4:18 *t. in*, my lord, *t. in*
12:11 let us *t. in* to this city of
2 K. 4:10 the man of God sh. *t. in*
Prov. 9:4 wh. is simple, *t. in*, 16

TURN to the Lord.
Deut. 4:30 if th. *t. to the L.* 30:10
2 Sam. 15:4 in iron. did *t. to t. L.*
Ps. 22:27 world shall *t. to the L.*
Lam. 3:40 try ways, *t. to the L.*
Hos. 14:2 take words, *t. to the L.*
Joel 2:13 rend heart, *t. to the L.*
Luke 1:16 many sh. ho *t. to the L.*
2 Cor. 3:16 when it sh. *t. to the L.*

TURNED.
Gen. 3:24 a flaming sword wh. *t.*
42:24 Joseph *t.* about from them
Ex. 7:15 rod was *t.* to a serpent
Num. 21:33 *t.* and went by B.
Deut. 23:5 *t.* the curse, Neh. 13:2
31:18 are *t.* unto other gods
Jud. 2:17 they *t.* out of the way
15:4 *t.* took firebra. and *t.* tail
1 Sam. 10:6 sh. be *t.* to ano. man
14:21 they also *t.* to be with Is.
47 whithersoever he *t.* himself
2 Sam. 2:19 Asahel *t.* not fr. fol.
1 K. 2:15 the kingdom is *t.* about
28 Joab *t.* after Adonijah
11:9 his heart was *t.* fr. the L.
2 K. 3:12 Naaman *t.* went away
20:2 *t.* his face to wall, Is. 38:2
23:25 no king *t.* to L. like him
1 Chr. 10:14 *t.* kingd. unto David
12:23 *t.* kingd. of L. fr. him
20:10 *t.* her, then destroyed not
29:6 fathers have *t.* their backs
Est. 2:1 tho' *t.* to the contrary
Job 16:11 G. *t.* me into hands of
19:19 wh. I loved are *t.* ag. me
28:5 it is *t.* up as it were fire
30:15 terrors are *t.* upon me
31:7 if my step *t.* out of the way
38:14 it is *t.* as clay to the seal
41:22 the captivity of Job
Ps. 9:17 wick. sh. be *t.* into hell
30:11 thou hast *t.* my mourning
81:14 *t.* my hand ag. adversar.
105:25 he *t.* their heart to hate
119:59 I *t.* my feet unto testim.
Ec. 2:12 I *t.* myself to behold wis.
2:12 I pleasure he *t.* into fear
5:15 we have *t.* every one to his
63:10 was *t.* to be their enemy
Jer. 2:21 how *t.* into degenerate ?
27 *t.* back, not face
3:10 Judah hath not *t.* to me
6:11 their houses sh. be *t.* unto
8:6 every one *t.* to his course
23:22 they should have *t.* fr. evil
31:18 I shall be *t.* 19 I was *t.*
32:33 they *t.* unto me the back
31:15 ye have *t.* and polluted
16 ye *t.* and polluted my name
46:21 how hath M. *t.* their back
Lam. 1:20 heart *t.* within me
3:3 surely against me is he *t.*
4:11 our colors *t.* to strangers
5:21 turn us, O L. we sh. be *t.*
Ezek. 1:9 they *t.* not, 12 ; 10:11
17:6 a vine, whose branches *t.*
Dan. 10:16 my sorrows *t.* upon
Hos. 7:8 Ephraim is a cake not *t.*
11:8 my heart is *t.* within me
Joel 2:31 sun shall be *t.* Acts 2:20
Amos 6:12 ye have *t.* judg. into
Jon. 3:10 they *t.* from their evil
Mic. 2:16 cup of L.'s hand he *t.*
Zec. 14:10 land be *t.* into plain
Mark 5:30 Jes. *t.* about in press
Luke 22:61 L. *t.* looked upon Pe.
John 16:20 sor. shall *t.* into joy

TUR

Acts 7:42 God *t.* gave them up
9:35 all at Lyd. saw and *t.* to L.
11:21 a great number *t.* to Lord
15:19 the Gentiles are *t.* to God
17:6 ho. *t.* the world upside do.
1 Thes. 1:9 show how ye *t.* to G.
Heb. 11:34 *t.* to flight armies of
12:13 lest lame ho *t.* out of way
Jam. 2:4 *t.* with a very em. iuda
2 Pet. 2:22 dog is *t.* to his vomit

TURNED again.
Jud. 20:41 Is. *t. a.* Benjamites
1 Sam. 15:31 Samuel *t. a.* after S.
2 Sam. 22:38 I *t.* not *a.* till I had
Ps. 126:1 L. *t. a.* captivity of Zi.

TURNED aside.
Ex. 3:4 Lord saw that he *t. a.*
32:8 have *t. a.* Deut. 9:12, 16
1 K. 15:5 David *t.* not *aside* from
20:39 a man *t. a.* brought man
2 K. 22:2 Josiah *t.* not *a.* to right
Job 6:18 paths of their way *t. a.*
Cant. 6:1 w thy beloved *t. a.* ?
Ps. 44:20 deceived heart *t.* him *a.*
Lam. 3:11 hath *t.* aside my ways
1 Tim. 5:15 some already *t. aside*

TURNED away.
Num. 14:43 ye are *t. a.* from L.
20:21 Israel *t. away* from him
25:4 anger of Lord may be *t. a.*
1 Phine. hath *t. a.* my wrath *a.*
1 K. 11:3 wives *t. a.* his heart, 4
2 Chr. 29:6 our fathers *t. a.* faces
Ps. 66:20 not *t. away* my prayer
78:38 many time *t.* he anger *a.*
Is. 5:25 for all this his anger is not *t. a.* 9:12, 17, 21 ; 10:4
12:1 anger *t. a.* 50:5 nor *t. t. a.*
Jer. 5:25 your iniq. have *t. away*
46:5 have I seen th. *t. a.* back ?
50:6 shepherds have *t.* them *a.*
Dan. 9:16 let thy fury be *t. a.*
Hos. 14:4 mine anger is *t. away*
Nah. 2:2 L. hath *t. a.* excellency
Acts 19:26 P. ha. *t. a.* much peo.
2 Tim. 1:15 they in Asia be *t. a.*

TURNED back.
Jos. 8:20 peo. *t. b.* upon pursuers
11:10 Joshua at that time *t. b.*
1 Sam. 15:11 Saul *t. b.* from S.
2 Sam. 1:22 bow of Jon. *t.* not *b.*
1 K. 18:37 hast *t.* their heart *b.*
22:33 not king of Is. they *t. b.*
1 Chr. 12:9 messengers *t. b.* from
2 Chr. 20:27 Jehos. *t. b.* every m.
9:24 *t. b.* and looked on them
13:20 king of Assyria *t. b.* stay,
2 Chr. 21:20 Orn. *t. b.* saw angel
Job 34:27 bec. they *t. b.* from him
Ps. 9:3 mine enemies are *t. b.*
44:18 our heart is not *t. b.* from
78:9 Ephr. *t. b.* in day of battle
41 *t. b.* and tempted God, 57
129:5 let th. be *t. b.* that hate Z.
Is. 42:17 *t. back* trust in images
Jer. 4:8 anger of Lord is not *t. b.*
11:10 they are *t. b.* to iniquities
40:21 they are *t. b.* fled away
Lam. 1:13 he hath *t.* me *b.* made
Lam. 3:14 they are *t. b.* from Lord
Luke 2:45 *t. b.* again to Jerusa.
8:55 and her spirit came again
17:15 he *t. b.* and with loud vo.
Acts 7:39 in hea. *t. b.* ag. into E.

TURNED in.
Gen. 19:3 angels *t. in* unto Lot
38:1 Ju. *t. in* to Hirah the Adu.
Jud. 4:18 Sisera *t. in* unto Jael
18:3 the Danites *t. in* thither
2 K. 4:8 Elisha *t. in* thither
11 ho *t. into* the chamber

TURNEST.
1 K. 2:3 prosper whither. thou *t.*
Job 15:13 *t.* thy spirit ag. God
Ps. 90:3 thou *t.* man to destruct.

TURNETH.
Lev. 20:6 soul th. *t.* after wizards
Deut. 28:18 whose heart *t.* away
Jos. 7:8 when Is. *t.* their backs ?
Job 39:22 the horse *t.* not back.
Ps. 107:33 *t.* rivers into a wildern.
38 *t.* wilderness into water
146:9 wicked he *t.* upside down
Prov. 15:1 soft ans. *t.* away wra.
21:1 *t.* king's heart whither.
26:14 as door *t.* upon his hinges
28:9 *t.* away his ear fr. hearing
30:30 lion *t.* not away for any
Cant. 1:7 sho. I be as one that *t.* ?
Is. 9:13 the people *t.* not to him
44:25 Lord *t.* earth upside down
41:25 *t.* wise men backward
Jer. 14:8 that *t.* aside to tarry
49:24 Damascus *t.* herself to flee

CRUDEN'S CONCORDANCE.

TWE

Lam. 1:6 she sigheth and *t.* bac.
3:3 he *t.* his hand against me
Ezek. 18:44 righteous *t.* away fr.
his righteousness. 26; 33:18
27 wick. mau *t.* aw. 26; 33:12
Amos 5:8 *t.* shadow of death into

TURNING.
2 *K.* 21:13 wipe Jer. as a dish, *t.*
2 *Chr.* 36:13 hardened heart fr. *t.*
Prov. 1:32 the *t.* away of simple
Is. 29:16 your *t.* of things upside
Mic. 2:4 *t.* away he hath divided
Acts 3:26 to bless you in *t.* you
Jam. 1:17 wi. wh. is no sha. of *t.*
Jude 4 *t.* grace of G. into lasciv.

TURTLE, S.
Gen. 15:9 take a *t.* dove and a yo.
Lev. 5:7 he sh. bri. two *t.* doves,
14:8; 14:22, 30; 15:14, 29
11 if not able to br. two *t.* dov.
12:6 she shall bring a *t.* dove
Num. 6:10 on 8th day sh. bri. 2 *t.*
Ps. 74:19 deliver not soul of *t.* d.
Cant. 2:12 voice of the *t.* is hea.
Jer. 8:7 *t.* and crane observe time
Luke 2:24 sacri. pair of *t.* doves

TUTORS.
Gal. 4:2 a child is under *t.* and

TWAIN.
1 **Sam.** 18:21 son-in-law one of *t.*
2 *K.* 4:33 shut the door on th. *t.*
Is. 6:2 with *t.* he cover. his face,
with *t.* he cover. feet, with *t.*
Jer. 34:18 they cut the calf in *t.*
Ezek. 21:19 both *t.* sh. come out
Mat. 5:41 a mile, go with him *t.*
19:5 they *t.* shall be one flesh
6 are no more *t.*, Mark 10:8
21:31 who. of *t.* did will of faith, ?
27:21 who. of *t.* will I release?
51 veil rent in *t.* Mark 15:38
Eph. 2:15 make in himself of *t.*

TWELFTH.
1 *K.* 19:19 oxen, he with the *t.*
Rev. 21:20 *t.* founda. was ameth.
See MONTH.

TWELVE.
Gen. 14:4 *t.* years they served C.
17:20 *t.* princes sh. Ishm. 25:16
35:22 the sons of Jacob were *t.*
42:13 thy serv. are *t.* breth. 32
49:28 these are *t.* tribes of Isr.
Ex. 15:27 Elim, where were *t.*
24:4 *t.* pillars acc. to *t.* tribes
28:21 *t.* precious stones, 39:14
Lev. 24:5 thou sh. bake *t.* cakes
Deut. 1:23 I took *t.* men of you
Jos. 3:12 take ye *t.* men, 4:2
4:3 *t.* stones out of Jor. 8, 9, 20
2 *Sam.* 2:15 th. arose *t.* of Benja-
min, and *t.* servants of Dav.
1 *K.* 7:25 the sea stood on *t.* oxen,
44; 2 *Chr.* 4:15
10:20 *t.* lions on side, 2 *Chr.* 9:19
11:30 Ah. rent garm, in *t.* pieces
Neh. 5:14 *t.* years not eat. bread
Mat. 9:20 a wom. was discased *t.*
years, *Mark* 5:25; *Luke* 8:43
10:2 names of *t.* apos. *Luke* 6:13
26:20 he sat down with the *t.*
Mark 14:17; *Luke* 22:14
Mark 5:42 age of *t.* yrs. *Luke* 8:42
14:20 it is one of *t.* that dippeth
Luke 2:42 when Je. was *t.* years
John 6:70 have I not cho. you *t.*
11:9 are th. not *t.* hours in day
1 *Cor.* 15:5 seen of C. then of *t.*, ?
Rev. 12:1 on head cro. of *t.* stars
21:12 city had *t.* gates, at gat. *t.*
14 wall of city had *t.* founda!
In them names of *t.* apostles
21 the *t.* gates were *t.* pearls
22 tr. bare *t.* manner of fruits
See HUNDRED, THOUSAND.

TWENTY.
Gen. 18:31 be found *t.* there, I
will not destroy it for *t.* sake
31:38 *t.* yo. I have been with, 41
37:28 sold J. for *t.* pieces silver
Ex. 30:14 fr. *t.* old, 38:26; *Num.*
13, etc.
Lev. 27:3 estim. of males fr. *t.* y.
K. 4:13 brought man *t.* loaves
Ezr. 8:27 weighed *t.* bas. of gold
Zec. 5:2 length of roll *t.* cubits

TWENTY-TWO.
Jud. 10:3 Jair judged Is. *t.-t.* ye.
1 *Chr.* 12:28 house *t.-t.* captains
2 *Chr.* 13:21 Abi. begat *t.-t.* sons

TWENTY-THREE.
Jud. 10:2 T. judged Is. *t.-t.* ye.

TWENTY-FOUR.
2 *Sam.* 21:30 fing. and toes, *t.-f.*

TWO

Rev. 4:4 about throne were *t.-f.*
seats, I saw *t.-f.* elders sit.
5:8 *t.-f.* elders fell, 11:16; 19:4

TWENTY-FIVE.
Num. 8:24 from *t.-five* years old
Neh. 6:5 wall finished in *t.-f.* day

TWENTY-SIXTH.
1 *K.* 16:8 in *t.-s.* year of Asa Elah

TWENTY-SEVENTH.
Gen. 8:14 *t.-s.* day of sec. month

TWENTY-EIGHT.
Ex. 26:2 curtain *t.-e.* cubits, 36:9

TWENTY-NINE.
Gen. 11:24 Nahor lived *t.-n.* yea.
See THOUSAND.

TWICE.
Gen. 41:32 dream was doubled *t.*
Ex. 16:5 shall be *t.* as much, 22
1 *K.* 11:9 had appeared to him *t.*
9 *K.* 6:10 saved not once nor *t.*
Neh. 13:20 with. Jeru. once or *t.*
Job 33:14 God speak. once, yea *t.*
40:5 yea *t.* but I will proceed no
42:10 Lord gave Job *t.* as much
Ps. 62:11 *t.* have I heard, power
Luke 18:12 I fast *t.* in the week
Jude 12 *t.* dead, pluck. up by ro.

TWIGS.
Ezek. 17:4 he cropped off top of *t.*
22 crop of *t.* top of young *t.*

TWILIGHT.
1 **Sam.** 30:17 Da. smote th. fr. *t.*
2 *K.* 7:5 lepers rose in *t.* to go
7 Syrians arose and fled in *t.*
Job 3:9 let stars of the *t.* be dark
24:15 eye of adul. waiteth for *t.*
Prov. 7:9 went to her house in *t.*
Ezek. 12:6 sh. carry it forth in *t.*
7 and brought it forth in the *t.*
12 prince shall bear it in the *t.*

TWINED. *See FINE.*

TWINKLING.
1 *Cor.* 15:52 changed in *t.* of eye

TWINS.
Gen. 25:24 Reb. had *t.* 38:27 Ta.
Cant. 4:5 every one bear *t.* 6:6
5 like two roes that are *t.* 7:3

TWO.
Gen. 4:19 Lamech took *t.* wives
6:19 *t.* of ev. sort bring into ark
7:2 beasts not clean by *t.* 9:15
25:23 *t.* nations are in thy womb
32:10 I am become *t.* bands
Ex. 21:21 if he continue day or *t.*
Lev. 5:7 shall bring *t.* doves or *t.*
pigeons, 12:8; 14:22; 15:14,
29; *Num.* 6:10
Deut. 21:15 if man have *t.* wives
32:30 *t.* put 10,000 to flight
Jud. 5:30 *t.* *t.* tribes, 4; 21:16
21:25 wi. her suburbs, *t.* cities
Jud. 3:80 ev. man a damsel or *t.*
11:37 let me alone *t.* months
they shall not prevail, *t.* sh. wither,
19:8 Elkanah had *t.* wives
Ex. 21:21 if he continue day or *t.*
Lev. 5:7 shall bring *t.* doves or *t.*
1 *K.* 3:18 none save *t.* in house
16:21 halt ye flock. *t.* opinions?
Job 13:20 do not *t.* thi. unto me
42:7 wra. is kind. ag. *t.* friends
Prov. 30:7 *t.* things I required
Ec. 4:9 *t.* are better than one
11 if *t.* lie toget. th. have heat
12 if *t.* these *t.* things sh. come
Amos 3:3 peo. commit? *t.* evils
3:14 one of a city, *t.* of a family
Cant. 4:5 a walk together
Mat. 6:24 no man can serve *t.*
masters. *Luke* 16:13
18:8 *t.* ha. or *t.* feet, *Mark* 9:43
9 having *t.* eyes, *Mark* 9:47
10 take wi. thee one or *t.* more
19 if *t.* of you agree on earth
20 wh. *t.* or three are gathered
21:40 then shall *t.* be in field
Mark 6:7 send them by *t.* and *t.*
9 shoes, nor put on *t.* coats
Luke 9:3 take neither have *t.* coats
John 6:16 *t.* be one fl. *Eph.* 5:31
14:27 by *t.* or at most by three
Phil. 1:23 in a strait betwixt *t.*

See DAUGHTERS, DAYS, KIDNEYS,
LAMBS, SONS.

TWO men.
Num. 11:26 roma. *t.* m. in camp
Jos. 2:1 sent out *t.* men to spy
2 *Sam.* 12:1 *t. m.* by sepulc.
Ec. 4:10 if one fall *t.* m.* in one city
Mat. 9:32 fell on *t.* m.* righteous
21:30 sent *t.* m.* before Nab, 13

UNB

Mat. 9:27 *t.* blind men followed
Luke 7:30 talked with him *t.* m.*
17:34 *t.* men in bed; 36 *t.* men
in field
18:10 *t.* m.* went up to temple
John 8:17 testimony of *t.* m.* true
Acts 9:38 they sent *t.* m.* to Peter

TWO tables.
Ex. 31:18 gave to Moses *t.* tables
34:1 *t. t.* of stone, *Deut.* 10:1
4 hewed *t.* tables, *Deut.* 10:3
42:13 wrote upon *t.* *t.* 5:22
9:10 Lord deliv. unto me *t.* *t.* 11
1 *K.* 8:9 nothing in ark save *t.* *t.*
of stone, 2 *Chr.* 5:10
Ezek. 40:39 *t.* *t.* on side; 40 *t.* *t.*

TWO years.
Gen. 11:10 Arph. *t.* y. after flood
2 *Chr.* 21:19 aft. *t.* y. bowels fell
Jer. 28:3 in *t.* y. I'll bring vea. 11
Amos 1:1 *t.* y. before earthquake
Mat. 2:16 slew children fr. *t.* y.
Acts 19:10 *t.* y. in As. heard word
28:30 P. dwelt *t.* y. in his house

TWOFOLD.
Mat. 23:15 *t.* more child of hell

TYCHICUS.
Acts 20:4 T. accompanied Paul
Eph. 6:21 T. shall make known
Col. 4:7 sh. T. declare unto you
2 *Tim.* 4:12 T. sent to Ephesus
Tit. 3:12 I send T. unto thee

TYRANNUS.
Acts 19:9 disput. in school of T.

TYRE, or TYRUS.
Jos. 19:29 coast turn. to city T.
2 *Sam.* 24:7 to strong-hold of T.
1 *K.* 7:13 fetched Hira. out of T.
I was a man of T. 2 *Chr.* 2:14
9:12 Hiram came out from T. to
Ezr. 3:7 meat and drink to them
of T.
Neh. 13:16 dw. men of T. therein
Ps. 45:12 daughter of T. shall be
83:7 with the inhabitants of T.
87:4 Philistia and T. Ze. 23:1
Is. 23:5 pain. at the report of T.
8 who ha. taken coun. ag. T.?
15 T. shall be forgotten, 17
Jer. 25:22 made kings of T. dri.
27:3 send the yokes to king of T.
47:4 to cut off from T. and Zid.
Ezek. 26:2 T. said ag. Jerusalem
3 I am against thee, O T.
27:2 take up lamentation for T.
32 city like T. like destroyed?
28:2 say to prince of T.
12 lamentation on king of T.
29:18 serve great service ag. T.
Joel 3:4 ye to do with me, O T.?
Amos 1:9 three transgres. of T.
10 I will send fire on wall of T.
Zec. 9:2 T. and Zidon, though it
3 T. built herself a strong ho.
Mat. 11:21 if mighty works had
been done in T. *Luke* 10:13
Acts 12:20 displeas. wi. th. of T.

U.

UCAL.
Prov. 30:1 spoke to Ithiel and U.

UNACCUSTOMED.
Jer. 31:18 as a bullock u. to yoke

UNADVISEDLY.
Ps. 106:33 spake u. with his lips

UNAWARES.
Gen. 31:20 Jacob stole away u. 26
Num. 35:11 killeth any person u.
15; *Deut.* 4:42; *Jos.* 20:3, 9
Ps. 35:8 destru. come on him u.
Luke 21:34 day come on you u.
Gal. 2:4 false breth. u. brought
Jud. 4 cert. men crept in u.

UNBELIEF.
Mat. 13:58 works, because of u.
17:20 not cast out bec. of yo. u.
Mark 6:6 marvel. bec. of their u.
9:24 I believe, help in. mine u.
16:14 upbraid. them with u.
Rom. 3:3 sh. u. make faith with.
4:20 he staggered not through u.
11:20 bec. of u. they were brok.
23 if they abide not still in u.
30 obtained mercy through u.
32 G. concluded them all in u.
1 *Tim.* 1:13 did it ignorant. in u.
Heb. 3:12 an evil heart of u.
19 could not enter bec. of u. 4:6
4:11 after same example of u.

UNBELIEVERS.
Luke 12:46 appoi. portion wi. u.

UNC

1 *Cor.* 6:6 goeth to law before u.
14:23 come in those that are u.
2 *Cor.* 6:14 unequal. yoked wi. u.

UNBELIEVING.
Acts 14:2 u. Jews stirr. Gentiles
1 *Cor.* 7:14 u. husband sanctified
15 u. if depart, let him depart
Tit. 1:15 unto u. is nothing pure
Rev. 21:8 u. have th. part in lake

UNBLAMABLE, Y.
Col. 1:22 to present you holy, u.
1 *Thes.* 2:10 how u. we behaved
3:13 may stablish your hearts u.

UNCERTAIN, LY.
1 *Cor.* 9:26 run, not as u. so fight
14:8 if trumpet give an u. sound
1 *Tim.* 6:17 nor trust in u. riches

UNCHANGEABLE.
Heb. 7:24 hath an u. priesthood

UNCIRCUMCISED.
Gen. 17:14 u. man-child shall be
cut off
34:14 cannot give our sist. to u.
Ex. 6:12 who am of u. lips, 30
12:48 no u. person eat passover
Lev. 19:23 count fruit u. 3 years
26:41 if th. u. hearts be humbl.
Jos. 5:7 circumcised, th. wav u.
Jud. 14:3 pieces to take wife of u.
15:18 sh. I fall into hands of u.
1 *Sam.* 17:26 who is th. u. P. ? 23
31:4 lest ith. u. come, 1 *Chr.* 10:4
2 *Sam.* 1:20 daugh. of u. triumph
Is. 52:1 no more come to thee u.
Jer. 6:10 their ear is u. th. cann.
9:25 punish circumcised with u.
26 nations u. house of Israel u.
Ezek. 28:10 shalt die death of u.
31:18 sh. lie in midst of u. 32:19,
21, 24, 25, 26, 27, 28, 29, 30, 32
44:7 stranu. u. in heart, and u.
Acts 7:51 stiff-necked, u. in hea.
11:3 thou wentest in to men u.
Rom. 4:11 faith he had bef. u. 12
1 *Cor.* 7:18 let him not become u.

UNCIRCUMCISION.
Rom. 2:25 circumcis. is made u.
26 if u. keep righteous, of law
27 shall not u. judge thee?
3:30 shall justify u. through fai.
4:9 bless. on circumcision or u.
10 wh. he was in circu. or u. ?
1 *Cor.* 7:18 any man called in u.
19 circumce. nothing, u. noth.
Gal. 2:7 gospel of u. committed
5:6 circum. avail. nor u. 6:15
Eph. 2:11 who are called u. by
(by. 2:13 dead in u. of flesh
9:11 circumcis-ion nor u. but C.

UNCLE.
Lev. 10:4 Uzziel, the u. of Aaron
20:20 if a man lie with u. wife
25:49 u. or u. son may redeem
1 *Sam.* 10:14 Saul's u. said to, 15
10:15 Saul's u. son of Ner, Saul's u.
1 *Chr.* 27:32 Jonathan David's u.
Est. 2:7 brought u. daughter, 15
Jer. 32:7 son of Shallum thine u.
8 my u. son ca. unto me, 9, 12
Amos 6:10 a man's u. take him

UNCLEAN.
Lev. 5:2 if soul touch any u. thi.
care. of u. cattle, be u. 11:26
10:10 diff. betw. u. clean, 11:47
11:4-8; 5, 6, 7, 8; *Deut.* 14:10
24 for these ye sh. be u. 25-40;
14:46; 15:5-27; 17:15; 22:5;
Num. 19:7-22
12:2 be u. seven days; 5; 15:25
13:45 in wh. plague is, cry u. u.
14:40 cast them into u. pl. 41, 45
57 touch wh. u. and wh. clean
22:5 whereby may be made u.
Num. 6:7 sh. not make-hims. u.
9:6 that were u. could not ke. 7
7 ye are, why are we kept u.?
10 if any man be u. 29; 15:22
Jos. 22:19 if your possessl. be u.
Ec. 9:2 one event to clean and u.
Is. 35:8 I am a man of u. lips, in
midst of a people of u. lips
52:11 depart ye, it is u. de.
64:6 we are all as u. thing
Ezek. 22:26 between cican and u.
44:23 discern betw. clean and u.
Hag. 2:13 they u. touch it, be u.
14:58 u. hath a spirit of u. devil
Acts 10:28 not call any man com-
mon or u. 11:8
Rom. 14:14 noth. u. of itself,
thing to u. to him it is u.
1 *Cor.* 7:14 else children were u.

CRUDEN'S CONCORDANCE. 1065

UND

2 *Cor.* 6:17 touch not *u.* thing
Eph. 5:3 no *u.* person hath inhe.
Heb. 9:13 of heifer sprinkling *u.*
Rev. 18.2 bec. a cage of *u.* bird
See BEAST, SPIRIT, THING.

UNCLEAN Spirits.
Mat. 10:1 power against *u.*
  spirits, *Mark* 6:7
Mark 1:27 com. *u. s. Luke* 4:36
3:11 *u. s.* when they saw him
5:13 *u. s.* went out and cut. swine
Acts 5:16 were vexed with *u. s.*
8:7 *u. s.* came out of possessed
Rev. 16:13 saw 3 *u. s.* like frogs

UNCLEANNESS.
Lev. 5:3 if he touch *u.* of man,
  whatsoever *u.* 7:21; 22:5
7:23 having his *u.* on him, 22:3
15:31 separate Is. from their *u.*
18:19 as she is put apart for *u.*
Num. 5:19 not gone aside to *u.*
19:13 uncl. *u.* is yet upon him
Deut. 23:10 by reason of *u.* that
24:1 hath found some *u.* in her
2 *Sam.* 11:4 purified from her *u.*
2 *Chr.* 29:16 priests broug. out *u.*
Ezr. 9:11 filled the land with *u.*
Ezek. 36:17 as *u.* of removed wo.
39:24 according to their *u.*
Zec. 13:1 fountain opened for *u.*
Mat. 23:27 full of bones and *u.*
Rom. 1:24 O, also gave th. to *u.*
6:19 yielded members ser. to *u.*
2 *Cor.* 12:21 not repented of *u.*
Gal. 5:19 works of flesh are *u.*
Eph. 4:19 to work *u.* wl. greedi.
5:3 *u.* let it not once be named
Col. 3:5 mortify fornication, *u.*
1 *Thes.* 2:3 exhortation not of *u.*
4:7 God hath not called us to *u.*
2 *Pet.* 2:10 that walk in lust of *u.*

UNCLEANNESSES.
Ezek. 36:29 I will save you fr. *u.*

UNCLOTHED.
2 *Cor.* 5:4 not that we wo. be *u.*

UNCOMELY.
1 *Cor.* 7:36 beha. *u.* tow. virgin
12:23 *u.* parts have comeliness

UNCONDEMNED.
Acts 16:37 beaten us openly *u.*
22:25 that Is a Roman and *u.*

UNCORRUPTNESS.
Tit. 2:7 in doctrine showing *u.*

UNCOVER.
Lev. 10:6 *u.* not your heads
1:36 not *u.* nakedn. of near kin
7 nakedness of fa. shalt not *u.*
8 not *u.* father's wife; 9 sister
10 thy son's daug. shalt not *u.*
11 father's wife's dau. not *u.*
12 not *u.* nak. of fath.'s sister
13 not *u.* moth.'s sister, 20:19
14 not *u.* nakedn. of fath.'s br.
15 daug.-in-law; 16 brother's
17 not *u. a* woman and daugh.
19 *ch.* not *u.* thy wife's sister
20 not *u.* wo. put apart, 20:18
21:10 high priest not *u.* head
Num. 5:18 priest *u.* wom.'s head
Ruth 3:4 sh. go in and *u.* his feet
Is. 47:2 *u.* thy locks, *u.* thigh

UNCOVERED.
Gen. 9:21 Noah was *u.* in his te.
Lev. 20:11 *u.* his father's naked.
17 *u.* sister's; 20 *u.* his uncle's
18 she hath *u.* founta. of blood
Ruth 3:7 came softly and *u.* feet
2 *Sam.* 6:20 *u.* hims. as vain foi.
22:8 quiver, and Kir *u.* shield
4:5:3 thy nakedness shall be *u.*
Jer. 49:10 I *u.* his secret places
Ezek. 4:7 thine arm shall be *u.*
Hab. 2:10 let thy foreskin be *u.*
Mark 2:4 they *u.* roof wh. he was
1 *Cor.* 11:5 prophe. with head *u.*
13 is it comely fa. wo. pray *u.?*

UNCOVERETH.
Lev. 20:19 for he *u.* his near kin
Deut. 27:20 *u.* his father's skirt
2 *Sam.* 6:20 vain follows *u.* him.

UNCTION.
1 *John* 2:20 ye have *u.* fr. holy O.

UNDEFILED.
Ps. 119:1 blessed are *u.* in way
Cant. 5:2 love, my dove, my *u.*
6:9 my dove, my *u.* is one
Heb. 7:26 priest, holy, harml. *u.*
13:4 marriage honorable, bed *u.*
Jam. 1:27 pure religion and *u.*
1 *Pet.* 1:4 inher. incorruptible, *u.*

UNDER.
Mat. 2:16 fr. two yea. old and *u.*

UND

Mat. 8:9 I am *u.* authority, hav.
Lk. b. 7:11 *u.* it poo. received law
See FEET.

UNDERGIRDING.
Acts 27:17 used helps, *u.* the ship

UNDERNEATH.
Deut. 33:27 *u.* are everlast, arms

UNDERSETTERS.
1 *K.* 7:30 four corners had *u.* 34

UNDERSTAND.
Gen. 11:7 not *u.* anoth.'s speech
41:15 I heard th. canst *u.* dream
Num. 16:30 *u.* these provoked L.
Deut. 28:49 tong. thou sh. not *u.*
2 *K.* 18:26 speak to servants' in
  Syr. langu. we *u.* it, *Is.* 36:11
1 *Chr.* 28:19 Lord made me *u.*
Neh. 8:3 before those th. could *u.*
7 people to *u.* law, 8, 13
Job 6:24 cause me to *u.* wherein
23:5 I would *u.* what he say
26:14 thunder of power who *u.?*
32:9 neither do aged *u.* judgm.
36:29 can any *u.* spr. of clouds?
Ps. 14:2 if any that did *u.* 53:2
19:12 who can *u.* his errors?
58:5 nor. neither will they *u.*
92:6 neither doth a fool *u.* th.is
94:8 *u.* ye brutish among peop.
107:43 sh. *u.* lovingkind. of L.
119:27 make me *u.* thy precepts
100 I *u.* more than ancients
Prov. 2:5 then *u.* fear of the Lord
9 shalt thou *u.* righteousness
8:5 O ye simple, *u.* wisdom
14:8 wisd. of prudent to *u.* way
19:25 and he will *u.* knowledge
20:24 how can man *u.* his way?
28:5 evil men *u.* not judgment,
  they that seek L. *u.* all thin.
29:19 tho' he *u.* will not answer
Is. 6:9 hear ye indeed, *u.* not
28:9 whom make to *u.* doctri. ?
19 be vexation only to *u.* repo.
32:4 heart of rash *u.* knowledge
33:19 tongue thou canst not *u.*
41:20 *u.* together ha. hn. done th.
43:10 may know and *u.* I am he
44:18 shut hearts, th. cannot *u.*
56:11 shepherds that cannot *u.*
Jer. 9:12 who is wise that may *u.*
Ezek. 3:6 words th. canst not *u.*
Dan. 8:16 make this man *u.* vis.
17 said to me, *u.* O son of man
9:13 *u.* truth ; 23 *u.* matter, 25
10:12 didst set thy heart to *u.*
11 I am come to make thee *u.*
11:33 they that *u.* shall instruct
12:10 wicked not *u.* wise sh. *u.*
Hos. 4:14 peo. doth not *u.* sh. fa.
14:9 wise? *he* shall *u.* these thi.
Mic. 4:12 neither *u.* counsel of L.
Mat. 13:13 not, neith. do they *u.*
14 and shall not *u.*
15:10 hear and *u. Mark* 7:14
17 do not ye *u.?* 16:9, 11;
  Mark 8:21, 31
24:15 let him *u. Mark* 13:14
Mark 4:12 hear, they may hear,
  not *u. Luke* 8:10 ; *Acts* 28:26
14:68 nor *u.* I what thou sayest
Luke 24:45 might *u.* scriptures
John 8:43 why not *u.* my speech ?
Rom. 15:21 have not heard sh. *u.*
1 *Cor.* 13:2 tho' I *u.* all mysteries
Ib. 14:16 *u.* at the evil of thi. they *u.* not

UNDERSTANDEST.
Job 15:9 what *u.* thou, which is
Ps. 139:2 thou *u.* my thoughts
Jer. 5:15 neither *u.* what th. say
Acts 8:30 *u.* thou wh. th. readest ?

UNDERSTANDETH.
1 *Chr.* 28:9 Lord *u.* Imaginations
Job 28:23 God *u.* the way thereof
Ps. 49:20 man in honor *u.* not
Prov. 8:9 all plain to him that *u.*
14:6 knowl. easy to him that *u.*
Jer. 9:24 glory in this, that he *u.*
Mat. 13:19 heart. word. *u.* it not,
21 that have endur. word. *u.*
Rom. 3:11 there is none that *u.*
1 *Cor.* 14:2 to men, for no man *u.*
16 he *u.* not what thou sayest

UND

2 *Chr.* 2:12 a wise son prid. wi. *u.*
26:5 Zachari. had *u.* in visions
Ezr. 8:16 Joi. and El. men of *u.*
Neh. 8:2 that could hear with *u.*
10:28 ev. one hav. know. and *u.*
Job 12:3 I have *u.* as well as you
12 length of days *u.* 13 hath *u.*
20 he taketh away *u.* of aged
17:4 hast hid their heart from *u.*
20:3 my *u.* caus. me to answer
26:12 by his *u.* he smiteth thro'
28:12 where is place of *u. ?* 20
28 said, To depart fr. evil Is *u.*
32:8 Almighty giveth them *u.*
34:10 hearken to me, men of *u.*
16 if now thou hast *u.* hear this
31 let men of *u.* tell me
38:4 declare, if thou hast *u.*
36 who hath given *u.* to heart?
39:17 neither imparted to her *u.*
Ps. 32:9 as mule that hath no *u.*
47:7 King, sing praises with *u.*
49:3 medita. of heart shall be *u.*
119:34 give *u.* 73, 125, 144, 169
99 I have *u.* 130 word giveth *u.*
104 thro' thy precepts I get *u.*
147:5 great our L. *u.* is infinite
Prov. 1:2 to perceive words of *u.*
2:2 thou applyi. th. heart to *u.*
3 if thou liftest up voice for *u.*
6 out of his mouth cometh *u.*
11 discretion pres. thee, *u. d.*
3:5 lean not to thine own *u.*
13 happy is man th. getteth *u.*
19 by *u.* he establish. heavens
4:1 attend to kn. *u.* get *u. 7*
5 how thine ear to my *u.*
6:33 commit. adult. lacketh *u.*
7:4 and call *v.* thy kinswoman
8:1 doth not *u.* put forth voice?
14 I am *u.* 9:6 in way of *u.*
9:4 him that wanteth *u. 16*
10 knowledge of the holy is *u.*
10:13 that hath *u.* wisd. is found
14:29 is slow to wrath is of *u.*
33 wisdom in him that hath *u.*
15:14 heart of him that hath *u.*
32 that heareth reproof get. *u.*
16:16 better to get *u.* than silv.
22 *u.* is a well-spring of life to
17:24 wisd. bef. him that ha. *u.*
18:2 fool hath no delight in *u.*
19:8 he that keepeth *u.* sh. find
25 reprove one that hath *u.*
21:16 wander. out of way of *u.*
30 there is no *u.* nor counsel
23:23 buy also instruct. and *u.*
24:3 by *u.* house is establish'd
28:11 poor that hath *u.* search.
16 prince that wanteth *u.*
30:2 have not the *u.* of a matter
Ex. 9:11 nor rich. to men of *u.*
Is. 11:2 sp. of *u.* shall rest upon
3 make him of quick *u.*
27:11 for it is a people of no *u.*
29:14 *u.* of their prudent men
16 framed it, he had no *u.?*
24 erred in spir. sh. come to *u.*
40:14 showed him way of *u. 7*
28 there is no search of his *u.*
41:19 neither knowledge nor *u.*
44:19 none cousi. sh. *u.* nor *u.*
56:11 stretched out heaven hy *u.*
Dan. 1:17 Dan. had *u.* in visions
20 in matters of *u.* he found
2:21 give to them that know *u.*
4:34 mine *u.* returned to me
5:11 light, *u.* and wisdom fou.
12 excellent *u.* was in him
14 *u.* is found in thee
8:23 I am come to give thee *u.*
10:1 Daniel had *u.* of vision
11:35 some of th. of *u.* shall fall
Hos. 13:2 made idols acc. to th. *u.*
Ob. 7 there Is no *u.* in him
8 sh. I not destroy *u.* out of E.
Mat. 15:16 ye wit. *u. ? Mark* 7:18
Mark 12:33 to love him with *u.*
Luke 1:3 having had perfect *u.*
2:47 were astonished at his *u.*
24:45 then opened he their *u.*
Rom. 1:31 without *u.* covenbr.
1 Cor. 1:19 bring to noth. the *u.*
14:14 sp. prayeth, *u.* Is unfruit.
15 I pray with wi. sing with *u.*
19 in church five words with *u.*
20 not child. in *u.* in *u.* be men
Eph. 1:18 eyes of *u.* being enlig.
4:18 having the *u.* darkened
Phil. 4:7 peace of G. passeth all *u.*
Col. 1:9 filled with all spiritu. *u.*
2:2 rich. of full assurance of *u.*
1 *John* 5:20 G. hath giv. us an *u.*
Rev. 13:18 him that hath *u.*
See GOOD.

UNG

Man of UNDERSTANDING.
Ezr. 8:18 they brong. a *m. of u.*
Prov. 1:5 a *m. of u.* shall attain
10:23 a *m. of u.* hath wisdom
11:12 a *m. of u.* hath. his peace
15:21 a *m. of u.* walk. uprightly
17:27 a *m. of u.* is of an excell.
28 shutteth lips is a *m. of u.*
20:5 a *m. of u.* will dr. counsel
28:2 by a *m. of u.* state shall be

Void of UNDERSTANDING.
Prov. 7:7 a young man *v. of u.*
10:13 a rod for him th. is *v. of u.*
12:11 follow vain per. is *v. of u.*
17:18 a man *v. of u.* strik. han.
24:30 vineyard of man *v. of u.*

UNDERSTANDING, Adj.
Deut. 1:13 take wise men and *u.*
4:6 this nation Is an *u.* people
1 *K.* 3:9 servant an *u.* heart
12 lo, I have given thee an *u.*
Prov. 8:5 be of an *u.* heart
Dan. 1:4 *u.* science ; 8:23 *u.* dark
Eph. 5:17 *u.* what the will of L. is
1 *Tim.* 1:7 *u.* neit. what they say

UNDERSTOOD.
Gen. 42:23 knew not Jos. *u.* th.
Deut. 32:29 were wise, they *u.*
1 *Sam.* 4:6 they *u.* ark of L. was
26:4 Da. *u.* that Saul was come
2 *Sam.* 3:37 *u.* it was not of D.
Neh. 8:12 had *u.* words that were
13:7 I *u.* of the evil Elia-shib did
Job 13:1 mine ear heard and *u.* it
42:3 I uttered that I *u.* not
Ps. 73:17 then *u.* I their end
81:5 heard langu. that I *u.* not
106:7 our fath. *u.* not thy won.
Is. 40:21 ha. ye not *u.* fr. founda.
41:18 nor *u.* for he shut th. ey.es
Dan. 8:27 astonished, but none *u.*
9:2 Dan. *u.* by books; 10:1 ha *u.*
12:8 I heard, but I *u.* not, then
Mat. 13:51 have ye *u.* these thi.?
16:12 then *u.* they how he had
17:13 they *u.* that he spake of J.
Mark 9:32 *u.* not that sayi. *Luke*
  9:50 ; 9:45 ; *John* 8:27 ; 10:6
John 12:16 he supposed they *u.* L.
Acts 7:25 he supposed they *u.* G.
  would deliver th. they *u.* not
23:27 hav. *u.* he was a Roman
34 when I *u.* he was of Cilicia
Rom. 1:20 being *u.* by the things
1 *Cor.* 13:11 I *u.* as a child
11:9 ut. by tongue wor. to be *u.*
2 *Pet.* 3:16 some of th. hard to be *u.*

UNDERTAKE.
Is. 38:14 I am oppress. *u.* for me

UNDERTOOK.
Est. 9:23 Jews *u.* to do as they

UNDO.
Is. 58:6 the fast ? to *u.* burdens
Zep. 3:19 I will *u.* all that afflict

UNDONE.
Num. 21:29 thou art *u.* O people
Jos. 11:15 Joshua left nothing *u.*
Is. 6:5 woe Is me, for I am *u.*
Mat. 23:23 len. oth. *u. Lu.* 11:42

UNDRESSED.
Lev. 25:5 grapes of thy vine *u.* 11

UNEQUAL, LY.
Ezek. 18:25 *u.* not my ways *u. ?* 29
2 *Cor.* 6:14 be not *u.* yoked with

UNFAITHFUL, LY.
Ps. 78:57 they dealt *u.* like fath.
Prov. 25:19 confid. in an *u.* man

UNFEIGNED.
2 *Cor.* 6:6 by H. Ghost, by love *u.*
1 *Tim.* 1:5 pure heart, faith *u.*
2 *Tim.* 1:5 I call to remembr. *u.*
1 *Pet.* 1:22 thro' Spi. unto *u.* love

UNFRUITFUL.
Mat. 13:22 becom. *u. Mark* 4:19
1 *Cor.* 14:14 my understand, is *u.*
Eph. 5:11 no fellowship with *u.*
Tit. 3:14 that they be not *u.*
2 *Pet.* 1:8 neith. be barren nor *u.*

UNGIRDED.
Gen. 24:32 man *u.* the camels

UNGODLINESS.
Rom. 1:18 is wrath of God agal. *u.*
11:26 sh. turn away *u.* fr. Ja.
2 *Tim.* 2:16 will increase unto *u.*
Tit. 2:12 denying *u.* and worldly

UNGODLY.
2 *Sam.* 22:5 floods of *u.* men me.
  affraid. *Ps.* 18:1
2 *Chr.* 19:2 shouldest *u.* thou help *u.*
Job 16:11 G. h. deliv. me to the *u.*
34:18 is it fit to say, Ye are *u. ?*
Ps. 1:1 walk. not in couns. of *u.*

CRUDEN'S CONCORDANCE.

UNM

Ps. 1;4 *u.* are not so ; 5 *v.* not sin.
ii the way of the *u.* shall perish
3:7 hast broken the teeth of *u.*
4:4 i pl. my cause ag. *u.* nation
72:13 these are *u.* who prosper
Prov. 10:27 *v.* man dig. up evil
19:28 *u.* witness scorneth judg.
Rom. 4:5 him that justifieth *u.*
5:6 in due time Chr. died for *u.*
1 *Tim.* 1:9 the law is for the *u.*
1 *Pet.* 4:18 where shall *u.* appear ?
2 *Pet.* 2:5 bringing the flood on *u.*
6 those who after should live *u.*
3:7 judgment and perdi. of *u.*
Jude 4 *u.* men turn. grace of God
15 convince *u.* of th. *u.* deeds
18 who walk after th. *u.* lusts

UNHOLY.
Lev. 10:10 differ. bet. holy and *u.*
1 *Tim.* 1:9 law was made for *u.*
2 *Tim.* 3:2 men be unthankful, *u.*
Heb. 10:29 counted blood of *u.*

UNICORN.
Num. 23:22 strength of *u.* 24:8
Job 39:9 will the *u.* serve thee ?
10 canst bind *u.* in the furrow ?
Ps. 29:6 Leb. and Sirion like *u.*
92:10 shall exalt like horn of *u.*

UNICORNS.
Deut. 33:17 horns like horns of *u.*
Ps. 22:21 heard from horns of *u.*
Is. 34:7 the *u.* shall come down

UNITE, D.
Gen. 49:6 mine honor be not *u.*
Ps. 86:11 *u.* my heart to fear

UNITY.
Ps. 133:1 for bre. to dwell in *u.*
Eph. 4:3 endeavoring to keep *u.*
13 till we come in the *u.* of

UNJUST.
Ps. 43:1 deliv. me from *u.* man
Prov. 11:7 hope of *u.* men peris.
28:8 who by *u.* gain increaseth
29:27 an *u.* man is an abomina.
Zep. 3:5 *u.* knoweth no shame
Mat. 5:45 sen. rai. on just and *u.*
Luke 16:8 L. commend. *u.* stew.
18:6 hear what *u.* judge saith
11 I am not as oth. men are, *u.*
Acts 24:15 resurrec. of just and *u.*
1 *Cor.* 6:1 any go to law bef. *u.*
1 *Pet.* 3:18 Christ suf. just for *u.*
2 *Pet.* 2:9 res. *u.* to day of judg.
Rev. 22:11 th. is *u.* let him be *u.* st.

UNJUSTLY.
Ps. 82:2 how lo. will ye judge *u.*
Is. 26:10 in land of upri. deal *u.*

UNKNOWN.
Acts 17:23 inscript. To the *u.* G.
1 *Cor.* 14:2 sp. in *u.* tong. 4, 13, 27
19 I pray in *u.* tongue
19 10,000 words in *u.* tongue
2 *Cor.* 6:9 as *u.* yet well known
Gal. 1:22 *u.* by face unto the

UNLADE.
Acts 21:3 ship was to *u.* burden

UNLAWFUL.
Acts 10:28 an *u.* thing for a man
2 *Pet.* 2:8 vexed his soul with *u.*

UNLEARNED.
Acts 4:13 perceived they were *u.*
2 *Tim.* 2:23 foolish and *u.* quest
2 *Pet.* 3:16 they that are *u.* wrest

UNLEAVENED.
Ex. 12:39 they baked *u.* cakes
Lev. 2:4 au *u.* cake of fine flour
7:12 *u.* cakes mingled with oil
8:26 Moses took one *u.* cake
Num. 6:19 priest take one *u.* cake
Jos. 5:11 eat old corn of land *u.*
Jud. 6:19 Gid. made rea. *u.* cakes
20 take the flesh and *u.* cakes
21 ang. touc. flesh and *u.* cakes
1 *Chr.* 23:29 flour and *u.* cakes
1 *Cor.* 5:7 new lump, as ye are *u.*
See BREAD.

UNLOOSE.
Mark 1:7 shoes I am not worthy
to *u.* *Luke* 3:16; *John* 1:27

UNMARRIED.
1 *Cor.* 7:8 the *u.* 11 remain *u.*
32 he that is *u.* 34 *u.* woman

UNMERCIFUL.
Rom. 1:31 without affection, *u.*

UNMINDFUL.
Deut. 32:18 rock th. begat th. *u.*

UNMOVABLE.
Acts 27:41 forep. of ship rema. *u.*
1 *Cor.* 15:58 bret. be steadfast, *u.*

UNS

UNOCCUPIED.
Jud. 5:6 Sha. highways were *u.*

UNPERFECT.
Ps. 139:16 substan. yet being *u.*

UNPREPARED.
2 *Cor.* 9:4 if come and find you *u.*

UNPROFITABLE.
Job 15:3 sh. reason with *u.* talk
Mat. 25:30 cast *u.* ser. into dark.
Luke 17:10 say, We are *u.* serv.
Rom. 3:12 are altogether bec. *u.*
Tit. 3:9 genealogies, *u.* and vain
Phile. 11 in time past was *u.*
Heb. 13:17 not wi. grief, th. is *u.*

UNPROFITABLENESS.
Heb. 7:18 the weakness and *u.*

UNPUNISHED.
Prov. 11:21 wicked sh. not be *u.*
16:5 the proud shall not be *u.*
17:5 glad at calamities not be *u.*
19:5 false witness not be *u.* 9
Jer. 25:29 utterly *u.* sh. not be *u.*
30:11 not leave thee altoget. *u.*
46:28 not leave thee wholly *u.*
49:12 sh. thou go *u.* ? not go *u.*

UNQUENCHABLE.
Mat. 3:12 but burn the chaff with
u. fire, *Luke* 3:17

UNREASONABLE.
Acts 25:27 it seemeth *u.* to send
2 *Thes.* 3:2 delivered fr. *u.* men

UNREBUKABLE.
1 *Tim.* 6:14 keep this comm. *u.*

UNREPROVABLE.
Col. 1:22 to present you holy, *u.*

UNRIGHTEOUS.
Ex. 23:1 put not hand to be *u.*
Job 27:7 riseth ag. me be as *u.*
Ps. 71:4 deli. out of hand of *u.*
Is. 10:1 woe to th. that decree *u.*
55:7 *u.* man forsake thoughts
Luke 16:11 not faithful in *u.* ma.
Rom. 3:5 is G. *u.* who tak. ven.?
1 *Cor.* 6:9 the *u.* shall not inherit
Heb. 6:10 God is not *u.* to forget

UNRIGHTEOUSLY.
Deut. 25:16 all that do *u.* are ab.

UNRIGHTEOUSNESS.
Lev. 19:15 do no *u.* in judgm. 35
Ps. 92:15 there is no *u.* in him
Jer. 22:13 buildeth house by *u.*
Luke 16:9 friends of mam. of *u.*
John 7:18 true, no *u.* in him
Rom. 1:18 *u.* of men who hold
the truth in *u.*
29 filled with all *u.* fornication
2:8 them that obey *u.* indigna.
3:5 if our *u.* commend righte.
6:13 yield mem. as instru. of *u.*
9:14 is there *u.* with God ?
2 *Cor.* 6:14 with. fellow. with *u.* ?
2 *Thes.* 2:10 with deceivab. of *u.*
12 beli. not, had pleasure in *u.*
Heb. 8:12 be merciful to their *u.*
2 *Pet.* 2:13 shall receive rew. of *u.*
15 Bal. who loved wages of *u.*
1 *John* 1:9 cleanse us from all *u.*
5:17 all *u.* is sin ; th. is a sin not

UNRIPE.
Job 15:33 shall shake off *u.* grape

UNRULY.
1 *Thes.* 5:14 warn th. that are *u.*
Tit. 1:6 not accused of riot, or *u.*
10 there are many *u.* and vain
Jam. 3:8 the tongue is an *u.* evil

UNSATIABLE.
Ezek. 16:28 because thou wast *u.*

UNSAVORY.
Job 6:6 *u.* be eaten with. salt ?

UNSEARCHABLE.
Job 5:9 G. doeth great th. and *u.*
Ps. 145:3 L. his greatness is *u.*
Prov. 25:3 heart of kings is *u.*
Rom. 11:33 how *u.* are his judg.
Eph. 3:8 preach *u.* riches of Ch.

UNSEEMLY.
Rom. 1:27 work. that which is *u.*
1 *Cor.* 13:5 doth not behave *u.*

UNSHOD.
Jer. 2:25 withhold from being *u.*

UNSKILFUL.
Heb. 5:13 babe is *u.* in the word

UNSPEAKABLE.
2 *Cor.* 9:15 thanks to G. for his *u.*
12:4 cau. up and heard *u.* words
1 *Pet.* 1:8 rejoice with joy *u.* full

UNSPOTTED.
Jam. 1:27 to keep himself *u.* from

UNSTABLE.
Gen. 49:4 *u.* as water, not excel

UPP

Jam. 1:8 doubleminded. man is *u.*
2 *Pet.* 2:14 beguiling *u.* souls
3:16 are unlearned and *u.* wrest

UNSTOPPED.
Is. 35:7 ears of the deaf sh. be *u.*

UNTAKEN.
2 *Cor.* 3:14 remain. veil *u.* away

UNTEMPERED.
Ezek. 13:10 others daubed it with
u. mortar, 11, 14, 15 ; 22:28

UNTHANKFUL.
Luke 6:35 he is kind to the *u.*
2 *Tim.* 3:2 blasphem. *u.* unholy

UNTIMELY.
Job 3:16 or as a hidden *u.* birth
Ps. 58:8 like *u.* birth of a woman
Ec. 6:3 an *u.* birth is better than
Rev. 6:13 as fig-trees cast. *u.* figs

UNTOWARD.
Acts 2:40 save from *u.* generation

UNWALLED.
Deut. 3:5 cities, beside *u.* towns
Est. 9:19 Jews div. in *u.* towns
Ezek. 38:11 I will go to land of *u.*

UNWASHEN.
Mat. 15:20 to eat with *u.* hands,
Mark 7:2, 5

UNWEIGHED.
1 *K.* 7:47 Solomon left vessels *u.*

UNWISE.
Deut. 32:6 thus requi. L. *u.* peo.
Hos. 13:13 *u.* son, sh. not stay
Rom. 1:14 debtor to wise and *u.*
Eph. 5:17 be not *u.* but underst.

UNWITTINGLY.
Lev. 22:14 if eat of holy things *u.*
Jos. 20:3 that killeth person *u.* 5

UNWORTHY, ILY.
Acts 13:46 judge yourselves *u.* of
1 *Cor.* 6:2 are ye *u.* to judge the ?
11:27 drink this cup of the L. *u.*
29 he that eateth and drink. *u.*

UP, *interjectional.*
Gen. 19:14 L. said, *u.* get ye out
44:4 Joseph said, *u.* follow after
Ex. 32:1 *u.* make us gods that
Jos. 7:13 *u.* sanctify the people
Jud. 4:14 *u.* for this is the day
8:20 to first-born, *u.* slay them
9:32 *u.* thou and the people that
19:29 *u.* and let us he going
1 *Sam.* 9:26 *u.* that I may send
See DOWN.

UPBRAID, ED, ETH.
Jud. 8:15 with wh. ye did *u.* me
Mat. 11:20 then began he to *u.*
Mark 16:14 he *u.* th. with unbel.
Jam. 1:5 giveth liberally, *u.* not

UPHARSIN.
Dan. 5:25 Mene, Mene, Tekel, U.

UPHAZ.
Jer. 10:9 gold is brought from U.
Dan. 10:5 girded with gold of U.

UPHELD.
Ps. 63:5 and my fury it *u.* me

UPHOLD.
Ps. 51:12 *u.* me with thy free Sp.
54:4 L. with th. that *u.* my soul
119:116 *u.* me according to word
Prov. 29:23 honor sh. *v.* humble
Is. 41:10 I will *u.* thee with right.
42:1 my servant whom I *u.*
63:5 I wondered was none to *u.*
Ezek. 30:6 that *u.* Egypt sh. fall

UPHOLDEN.
Job 4:4 thy words have *u.* him
Prov. 20:28 throne is *u.* by mercy

UPHOLDEST, ETH.
Ps. 37:17 Lord *u.* the righteous
24 Lord *u.* him with his hand
41:12 thou *u.* me in mine integ.
63:8 follow, thy right hand *u.*
145:14 the Lord *u.* all that fall

UPHOLDING.
Heb. 1:3 *u.* all things by word of

UPP

UPPER.
Ex. 12:7 blood on *u.* door-posts
Lev. 13:45 put a cover. on *u.* lip
Deut. 24:6 no man take *u.* millet.
Jos. 15:19 gave *u.* spri. *Jud.* 1:15
Mat. 14:15 will show you an *u.*
room, *Luke* 22:12
Acts 1:13 went up into *u.* room
19:1 P. passed through *u.* coasts
See CHAMBER.

UPS

UPPERMOST.
Gen. 40:17 *u.* basket bakemeats
Is. 17:6 in top of the *u.* bough
9 cities sh. be as an *u.* branch
Mat. 23:6 they love the *u.* rooms,
Mark 12:39 ; *Luke* 11:43

UPRIGHT.
Gen. 37:7 my sheaf. arose, sto. *u.*
43 and made you go *u.*
1 *Sam.* 29:6 thou hast been *u.*
with me, 2 *Chr.* 29:34
26 wi. *u.* show thy. *v. Ps.* 18:25
3 *Chr.* 29:34 Levites were mor. *u.*
Job 1:1 perf. and *u.* man, 8 ; 2:3
8:6 if *u.* he wou. awake for thee
12:4 *u.* man is laughed to scorn
17:8 *u.* men shall be astonished
Ps. 11:7 countenance behold *u.*
19:13 then sh. I be *u.* innocent
25:8 Lord is good and *u.* 92:15
32:1 for praise is comely for *u.*
37:14 as be of *u.* conversation
18 Lord knoweth days of the *u.*
37 perfect man, behold the *u.*
49:14 *v.* sh. have dominion over
111:1 praise L. in assemb. of *u.*
112:2 generation of *u.* be bless.
4 to *u.* ariseth light in darkn.
119:137 *u.* are thy judgments
125:4 do good to the *u.* in heart
140:13 *u.* shall dwell in thy presence
Prov. 2:21 *u.* shall dwell in land
10:29 way of L. is strength to *u.*
11:3 integ. of *u.* sh. guide them
6 righteousness of *u.* deli. them
11 by bless. of *u.* city exalted
20 *v.* in their way are his deli.
12:6 mouth of *u.* shall deli. them
13:6 righteousness keep. the *u.*
14:11 taberna. of *u.* sh. flourish
15:8 prayer of *u.* is his delight
16:17 way of *u.* to dep. fr. evil
21:18 transg. be ransom for *u.*
29 as for *u.* he direct his way
28:10 *u.* hn. good in possession
29:10 bloodthirsty hate the *u.*
27 *u.* is an abomina. to wicked
Ec. 7:29 found G. made man *u.*
12:10 written *u.* words of truth
Cant. 1:4 rememb. *u.* love thee
Is. 26:7 *u.* weigh path of just
Jer. 10:5 they are *u.* as palm-tr.
24:6 I touched and set me *u.*
11:17 enter and *u.* ones wi. him
Mic. 7:2 is none *u.* among men
4 *u.* sharper th. a thorn hedge
Hab. 2:4 lifted, not *u.* in him
See HEART, STAND, STOOD.

UPRIGHTLY.
Ps. 15:2 walketh *u.* shall abide
58:1 ye judge *u.* ? 75:2 judge *u.*
84:11 good fr. them that walk *u.*
Prov. 2:7 buckler to th. walk *u.*
10:9 walketh *u.* walketh surely
15:21 man of underst. walk. *u.*
28:18 whoso walk. *u.* be saved
Is. 33:15 speak. *u.* sh. dwell high
Amos 5:10 him that speaketh *u.*
Mic. 2:7 to him that walketh *u.*
Gal. 2:14 that th. walked not *u.*

UPRIGHTNESS.
1 *K.* 3:6 walked before thee in *u.*
1 *Chr.* 29:17 hast pleasure in *u.*
Job 4:6 and the *u.* of thy ways ?
33:23 to show unto man his *u.*
Ps. 9:8 judgment to people in *u.*
25:21 and *u.* preserve me
111:8 st. fast and are done in *u.*
143:10 lead me into land of *u.*
Prov. 2:13 who leave paths of *u.*
14:2 walketh in *u.* feareth Lord
28:6 better is poor walketh in *u.*
Is. 26:7 way of just is *u.*
10 in land of *u.* deal unjustly
57:2 each one walking in his *u.*
See HEART.

UPRISING.
Ps. 139:2 my down-sitt. and *u.*

UPROAR.
1 *K.* 1:41 city being in an *u.*
Mat. 26:5 lest th. be *u.* *Mark* 14:2
Acts 17:5 Jews set city on an *u.*
19:40 question for this day's *u.*
20:1 after *u.* was ceased, Paul
21:31 Jerusalem was in an *u.*
38 Egypt. who madest an *u.* ?

UPSIDE *down.*
2 *K.* 21:13 dish, turning it *u. d.*
Ps. 146:9 wicked he turn. *u. d.*
Is. 24:1 L. turneth earth *u. d.*
29:16 your turning of th. *u. d.*
Acts 17:6 have turn. world *u. d.*

CRUDEN'S CONCORDANCE. 1067

USE

UPWARD.
Num. 8:24 from 25 years old and *u.* 1 *Chr.* 23:3
1 *Sam.* 9:4 from should. *u.* 10:23
2 *K.* 19:30 bear fruit *u. Is.* 37:31
2 *Chr.* 31:16 fr. 3 years old and *u.*
Job 5:7 to trouble as sparks fly *u.*
Ez. 3:01 spirit of man goeth *u.*
Is. 8:21 curse God, and look *u.*
38:14 mine eyes fail looking *u.*
Ezek. 1:27 app. of loins *v.* 8:2
41:7 a winding about still *v.*
Hag. 2:15 fr. this day and *u.* 13

US.
Gen. 11:23 before his father in *U.*
13:7 bro. thee out of *U. Neh.* 9:7
1 *Chr.* 11:35 Eliphal the son of *U.*

URGE, D.
Gen. 33:11 Jacob *u.* Esau, and he
Jud. 16:16 Delilah *u.* Samson
19:7 depart, his father-in-law *u.*
2 *K.* 3:17 *u.* him till ashamed
5:16 *u.* Elisha ; 23 he *u.* Gehazi
Luke 11:53 Pharisees began to *v.*

URGENT.
Ex. 12:33 Egypt. were *v.* on peo.
Dan. 3:22 king's commmand. *u.*

UR.
Ex. 31:2 D. son of *U.* 35:30; 38:22;
1 *Chr.* 2:20 ; 2 *Chr.* 1:5
1 *K.* 4:19 son of *U.* was in Gile.
Ezr. 10:24 Telem, and *U.* porters

URIAH, or **URIJAH,**
2 *Sam.* 11:3 Bathseb. wife of *U.*?
6 say, Send me *U.* the Hittite
11 went it by *U.* 21 *U.* is dead
12 hast killed *U.* with sword
23:39 *U.* one of David's worthies
1 *K.* 15:5 only in matter of *U.*
1 *Chr.* 11:41 *U.* the Hittite
Ezr. 8:33 weighed by son of *U.*
Neh. 3:4 next repaired son of *U.*
21 Meremoth, son of *U.*
8:4 *U.* on his right hand
Is. 8:2 I took faithful witnes. *U.*
Mat. 1:6 Solomon of wife of *U.*

URIJAH.
2 *K.* 16:10 king *U.* fashion of alt.
16 did *U.* as king A. comman.
Jer. 21:20 *U.* prophesied against
23 *U.* fled into Egypt

URIM.
Ex. 28:30 *u.* and thum. *Lev.* 8:8
Num. 27:21 coun. aft. judg. of *u.*
Deut. 33:8 let *u.* be with thy O.
1 *Sam.* 28:6 by *u.* nor prophets
Ezr. 2:63 prie. with *u. Neh.* 7:65

Against US.
Mark 9:40 he that is not *a. u.* is on our part, *Luke* 9:50
Rom. 8:31 O. for us, who *a. u.* ?

For US.
2 *Chr.* 13:10 as *f. u.* L. is our G.
Mat. 17:4 L. it is good *f. r. u.* to be here, *Mark* 9:5 ; *L.u.* 9:33

From US.
1 *John* 2:19 they went out *fr. u.*
See DEPART.

Of US.
1 *John* 2:19 Us, were not *of u.* for if they had been *of u.* they

To US-WARD.
Ps. 40:5 though, wh. are to *u.-w.*
Eph. 1:19 gre. of power *to u.-w.*
2 *Pet.* 3:9 long suffering *to u.-w.*

With US.
Mat. 1:23 interpret. is, G. *w. u.*

USE, Substantive.
Lev. 7:24 be used in any other *u.*
Deut. 20:14 aught for unclean *u.*
8 *Sam.* 1:18 teach Ju. *u.* of how
1 *Chr.* 28:15 to *u.* of candlestick
Rom. 1:26 did change natural *u.*
Eph. 4:29 good to *u.* of edifying
2 *Tim.* 2:21 meet for master's *u.*
Heb. 5:14 by *u.* ha. senses exer.

USES.
Tit. 3:11 works for necessary *u.*

USE, Verb.
Lev. 19:26 neither *u.* enchantm.
Num. 10:2 *u.* trumpe. for calling
15:39 ye *u.* to go a whoring
1 *Chr.* 12:2 could *u.* right hand
Jer. 23:31 *u.* th. tongues and say
31:23 shall *u.* this speech in J.
46:11 vain *u.* many medicines
Ezek. 12:23 no more *u.* it a prov.
16:11 shall *u.* proverb ag. thee
18:2 that ye *u.* this proverb ?
3 not have occasion to *u.* pro.
21:21 stood to *u.* divination
Mat. 6:7 *u.* not vain repetitions

UTT

Acts 14:5 to *u.* apostles despitef-
1 *Cor.* 7:21 made free, *u.* it rath-
31 *u.* this world as not abus. it
2 *Cor.* 1:17 did I *u.* lightness
3:12 we *u.* great plai. of speech
13:10 present, I should *u.* sharp
Gal. 5:13 *u.* not liberty for occa.
1 *Tim.* 1:8 if a man *u.* it lawfully
3:10 let th. *u.* office of a deacon
5:23 *u.* wine for stomach's sake
1 *Pet.* 4:9 *u.* hospitality one to

USED.
Ex. 21:36 if ox hath *u.* to push
Lev. 7:24 may be *u.* in any use
Jud. 14:10 so *u.* you, men to do
20 wh. Samson *u.* as his friend
2 *K.* 17:17 *u.* enchantments, 21:6
Jer. 2:24 ass *u.* to the wilderness
22:20 people *u.* oppression
33:11 easy which thou hast *u.*
Hos. 12:10 *u.* similitud. by prop.
Mark 2:18 disc. of John *u.* to fa.
Acts 19:19 which *u.* curious arts
Rom. 3:13 with tongues *u.* deceit
1 *Cor.* 9:13 not *u.* this pow.
15 I ha. *u.* none of these things
1 *Thes.* 2:5 *u.* we flattering wor.
1 *Tim.* 3:13 ha. *u.* office of deac.
Heb. 10:33 companio. were so *u.*

USEST.
Ps. 119:132 *u.* to those that love

USETH.
Deut. 18:10 any th. *u.* divination
22:8 apparel king *u.* to wear
Prov. 15:2 the wise *u.* knowledg.
18:23 the poor *u.* entreat, rich
Jer. 22:13 *u.* service with wages
Ezek. 16:44 that *u.* proverbs shall
Heb. 5:13 every one that *u.* milk

USING.
Col. 2:22 wh. are to perish wi. *u.*
1 *Pet.* 2:16 not *u.* liberty for clo.

USURP.
1 *Tim.* 2:12 wom. to *u.* authority

USURER.
Ex. 22:25 shalt not be as a *u.*

USURY.
Ex. 22:25 thou lay upon him *u.*
Lev. 25:36 take no *u.* of him, 37
Deut. 23:19 lend on *u.* to brother
20 thou mayest lend upon *u.*
Neh. 5:7 exact *u.* 10 leave off *u.*
13:25 putteth his money to *u.*
Prov. 28:8 *u.* increas. substance
Is. 24:2 tak. of *u.* so wi. gi. of *u.*
Jer. 15:10 neither lent on *u.* nor have men lent to me on *u.*
Ezek. 18:8 not giv. forth on *u.* 17
13 given on *u.* 22:12 taken *u.*
Mat. 25:27 own wi. *u. Luke* 19:23

UTMOST, or OUTMOST.
Gen. 49:26 *u.* bound of the hills
Num. 22:41 see *u.* of peop. 23:13
Deut. 3:24 driven to *u.* parts
Jer. 9:26 *u.* corners, 25:23 ; 49:32
Luke 11:31 who came fr. *u.* parts

UTTER, Verb.
Lev. 5:1 if he do not *u.* it hear
Jos. 2:14 our life if ye *u.* not this
20 if thou *u.* it, we will be quit
Jud. 5:12 Debor. *u.* song, Arise
Job 8:10 shall th. not *u.* words ?
15:2 wise man *u.* vain knowl. ?
27:4 nor shall tongue *u.* deceit
33:3 my lips shall *u.* knowledge
Ps. 78:2 I will *u.* dark sayings
94:4 long shall *u.* hard things ?
106:2 who can *u.* mighty acts ?
119:171 my lips shall *u.* praise
145:7 shall *u.* memory of goodn.
Prov. 23:33 heart shall *u.* perv. things
Ec. 1:8 labor, man cannot *u.* it
5:2 not hasty to *u.* before God
Is. 32:6 vile person will *u.* error
48:20 *u.* it even to end of earth
Jer. 1:16 I will *u.* my judgments
25:30 *u.* voice from holy habita.
Ezek. 24:3 *u.* a parab. unto rebel
Joel 2:11 Lord shall *u.* his voice
3:16 *u.* voice fr. Jerus. *Amos* 1:2
Mat. 13:35 I will *u.* things kept
1 *Cor.* 14:9 *u.* words easy under.
2 *Cor.* 12:4 not law. for man to *u.*

UTTER, Adjective.
Num. 17:13 I appointed to *u.* des.
Nah. 1:8 make *u.* end of place
1 *Cor.* 14:11 no more *u.* incer.

UTTERANCE.
Acts 2:4 spake as Spirit gave *u.*
1 *Cor.* 1:5 ye are abound in *u.* and
Eph. 6:19 pray, that *u.* be given
Col. 4:3 G. wo. open a door of *u.*

VAI

UTTERED.
Num. 30:6 husba. wh. she *u.* 8
Jud. 11:11 Jephtah *u.* his words
2 *Sam.* 22:14 Most High *u.* his voice, *Ps.* 46:6
Job 26:4 to whom hast *u.* words ?
42:3 I *u.* that I understood not
Ps. 66:14 lips *v.* when in trouble
Hab. 3:10 deep *u.* his voice and
Rom. 8:26 groan. wh. can. be *u.*
2 *Cor.* 12:4 not lawful for man to *u.*
Heb. 5:11 many th. hard to be *u.*
Rev. 10:3 seven thun. *u.* voices
4 when seven thunders had *u.*

UTTERETH.
Job 15:5 thy mouth *u.* iniquities
Ps. 19:2 day unto day *u.* speech
Prov. 1:20 wisdom *u.* her voice
21 she *u.* her words, saying
10:18 that *u.* slander is a fool
Mic. 7:3 great man *u.* his desire

UTTERING.
Is. 59:13 *u.* from heart words

UTTERLY.
Ex. 17:14 *u.* put out remembran.
Jud. 15:2 I thou. hadst *u.* hated
4:17 our eyes failed for *v.* help
22:19 *u.* destroy eve. male
1 *Sam.* 15:3 *v.* dest. Amalekites
Is. 2:18 idols he shall *u.* abolish
6:11 until land be *u.* desolate
24:3 *v.* emptied ; 19 *u.* broken
Jer. 14:2 I will *u.* take th. away
Mic. 2:10 a fool *u.* All his mind, but
Mic. 2:4 is *u.* spoiled, beauty *v.*
Ec. 6:12 all days of his *v.* life
Is. 1:13 br. no more *v.* oblations
56:5 they are *u.* words
Jer. 23 vanity, are become *v.*
4:14 how long thy *v.* thoughts ?
10:3 customs of the peop. are *v.*
14:22 *v.* prophets make you *v.* th.
Lam. 2:14 prophets have seen *v.*
Ezek. 12:24 no more any *v.* vision
13:7 have ye not seen *v.* vision
Mat. 3:14 if is *v.* to serve God
Mat. 6:7 use not *v.* repetitions
Rom. 1:21 bec. *v.* in imagination.
1 *Cor.* 3:20 thoug. of wise are *v.*
15:14 is our preaching *v.* and your faith is also *v.* 17
Eph. 5:6 decei. you wi. *v.* words
Col. 2:8 spoil you thro' *v.* deceit
1 *Tim.* 1:10 unruly and *v.* talkers
3:9 they are unprofitable and *v.*
Jam. 1:26 this man's religion is *v.*
2 *Pet.* 2:18 when speak *v.* wo.
1 *Pet.* 1:18 redeemed fr. *v.* conv.

In VAIN.
Ex. 20:7 not take name of Lord in *v. Deut.* 5:11
Lev. 26:16 ye shall sow seed in *v.*
Job 9:29 why then labor I *in v.* ?
35:16 doth Job open mouth *in v.*
39:16 her labor is *in v.* without
41:9 behold, ho. of him is *in v.*
Ps. 39:47 hast lift. m. men *in v.* ?
127:1 *in v.* watch, wak. *in v.*
Prov. 30:9 take name of G. *in v.*
Is. 45:19 seed of Jac. seek *in v.*
19 I have labored *in v.* spent strength for naught *in v.*
Jer. 2:30 *in v.* have I smit. chil.
4:30 *in v.* sh. make thyself fair
46:11 go up *in v.* to Gilead
Ezek. 6:10 kn. have not said *in v.*
Nah. 1:14 beer, not sowed *in v.*
1 *Cor.* 15:2 unless ye belie. *in v.*
2 *Cor.* 6:1 not grace of G. *in v.*
Gal. 2:2 lest I should run *in v.*
21 then Christ is dead *in v.*
1 *Thes.* 2:5 and our labor be *in v.*
Jam. 4:5 think scri. saith *in v.* ?

VAIN-GLORY.
Gal. 5:26 not be desirous of *v.-g.*
Phil. 2:3 noth. be done thro' *v.-g.*

VAINLY.
Col. 2:18 *v.* puffed up by fleshly

VALE.
Gen. 14:3 kings in *v.* of Siddi. 8
10 *v.* of Siddim was full of pits
37:14 he sent Joseph out of *v.*
Deut. 1:7 in hills and in the *v.*
Jos. 10:40 *v.* smote country of *v.*
Jer. 12:27 redare m. sycamores trees *in v.* 2 *Chr.* 1:15
Jer. 33:13 in cit. of *v.* sh. flocks

VALIANT.
1 *Sam.* 14:52 when S. saw *v.* man
son of J. a mighty *v.* man
18:17 be *v.* for me, and fight
26:15 Art not thou a *v.* man ?
2 *Sam.* 2:7 be *v.* 13:28 ; 17:10 is *v.*
11:16 he knew that *v.* men were
23:20 Benaiah, son of a *v.* man
of Kabzeel, 1 *Chr.* 11:22
1 *K.* 1:42 for thou art a *v.* man
1 *Chr.* 7:2 sons of T. we *v.* men
26:6 for they were *v.* men
Cant. 8:7 threescore *v.* men about B, of the *v.* of Israel
Is. 10:13 put down Inhab. like *v.*
33:7 th. *v.* ones sh. cry without
Jer. 9:3 are not *v.* for the truth
46:15 are *v.* men, sw. away ?

VAN

Neh. 2:3 r. men are in scarlet
Heb. 11:34 through faith wax. r.

VALIANTEST.
Jud. 21:10 12,000 men of the v.

VALIANTLY.
Num. 24:18 and Israel shall do r.
1 *Chr.* 19:13 and let us behave r.
Ps. 60:12 we shall do r. 108:13
118:15 hand of Lord doeth r. 16

VALLEY.
Gen. 14:17 king of Sod. met at r.
Num. 32:9 went to r. of Eshcol
Deut. 1:24 came to r. of Eshcol
21:4 bring heifer to a rough r.
34:3 the plain of r. of Jericho
G he buried Moses in a r. in
Jos. 7:24 broug. them to r. of A.
12:13 moon, in r. of Ajalon
15:8 which is at end of the r.
Jud. 1:19 drive out inhabit. of r.
7:3 host of Midian was in r. 12
10:1 a woman in the r. of Sorek
1 *Sam.* 6:13 reap. wheat-ha. in r.
21:9 whom th. slowest in the r.
2 *Sam.* 5:18 spread themselves in
r. of Rephaim, 22; 23:13
8:13 smi. Syrians in r. of salt
2 *K.* 2:16 Spirit cast him into r.
3:16 make this r. full of ditches
14:7 he slew of Edom in r. of
salt. 1 *Chr.* 18:12
2 *Chr.* 25:23 fight in v. of Megid.
Job 21:23 clods of r. sh. be sweet
32:21 paweth in r. and rejoiceth
Ps. 23:4 I walk thro' r. of death
60:6 mete r. of Succoth, 108:7
84:6 passi'ng through r. of Baca
Prov. 30:17 ravens of r. pick out
Cant. 6:11 went to see fruit. of r.
Is. 17:5 gathereth in v. of Reph.
22:1 burden of the r. of vision
5 day of trouble in r. of vision
28:1 beauty on head of fat r.
21 sh. he wroth as in r. of Gi.
40:4 every r. shall be exalted
63:10 r. of Ac. a place of herds
Jer. 2:23 see thy way in the r.
7:32 r. of Tl. r. of slaughtr. 19:6
21:13 eg. thee, O inhabita. of r.
49:4 r. perish, plain destroyed
49:1 why gloriest in flowi. r. /
Ezek. 37:1 in r. full of bones
2:13 give r. of A. door of hope
Joel 3:2 br. into r. of Jehoshap.
14 multitudes in the r. of dec.
18 fountain shall water r. of S.
Zec. 12:11 mourning in r. of M.
14:4 there shall be a great r.
5 shall flee to r. of mountains
Luke 3:5 every r. shall be filled
See GATE.

VALLEYS.
Num. 24:6 as r. are they spread
Deut. 8:7 depths springing out of r.
11:11 a land of hills and r.
1 *K.* 20:28 but he is not G. of r.
Job 30:6 to dwell in clifts of r.
39:10 he harrow r. after thee ?
Ps. 65:13 r. covered with corn
104:8 go down by r. unto place
10 sendeth springs into the r.
Cant. 2:1 rose of Shar, lily of r.
Is. 22:7 thy r. full of chariots
28:1 which are on head of fat r.
41:18 open fount. in midst of r.
57:5 slaying the children in r.
Jer. 49:4 whereof, glori. thou in r.
Ezek. 6:3 saith L. to r. 36:4, 6
7:16 on moun. like doves of r.

VALOR.
Jud. 3:29 slew 10,000 men of r.
6:12 with th. mighty man of r.
11:1 Jephtah, mighty man of r.
1 *K.* 11:28 Jeroboam, a man of r.
2 *K.* 5:1 Naa. mighty man in r.
1 *Chr.* 12:28 Zadok, a man of r.
2 *Chr.* 17:17 Eliada, a man of r.
See Mighty MEN.

VALUE.
J. 13:4 ye are physici. of no r.
Mat. 10:31 more r. than than
many sparrows, *Luke* 12:7

VALUE, ST.
Le. 27:8 the priest shall r. him
12 as thou r. it who art priest
Mat. 27:9 whom they of I. did r.

VALUED.
Le. 27:16 barley r. at 50 shekels
Job 28:16 wisdom cannot be r.
15 nei. shall it be r. with gold
Mat. 27:9 pri. of him that was r.

VANISH, ED, ETH.
Job 6:17 they wax warm, they r.

VEH

Job 7:9 as cloud is consumed, r.
Jer. 49:7 is their wisdom r. /
Luke 24:31 r. out of their sight
1 *Cor.* 13:8 knowledge, it shall r.
Heb. 8:13 wax, old, ready to r.
Jam. 4:14 life is a vapor that r.

VANITY.
2 *K.* 17:15 followed r. beca. vain
Job 7:3 ma. possess months of r.
7 let me alone, days are r.
15:31 let not him that is deceiv.
trust in r. r. sh. be recomp.
35 mischief, and bring forth r.
31:5 if I walked with r. or hast.
33:13 sare G. will not hear r.
Ps. 4:2 how long will ye love r. /
12:7 under his tongue misc. r.
12:8 they speak r. every one to
24:4 hath not lifted up soul to r.
39:5 best estate is altogether r.
11 man is r. 04:11 thoughts r.
41:6 he speaketh r. 144:8, 11
62:9 are r. and lighter than r.
78:33 days did he consume in r.
119:37 turn eyes from behold, r.
144:4 man is like to r. a shadow
Prov. 13:11 wealth gotten by r.
21:6 treas. by lying tong, is r.
22:8 soweth iniq. shall reap r.
30:8 remove from me r. and lies
Ec. 1:2 r. of vanities, saith the preacher, all is r. 14; 3:19;
12:8; 12:8
2:11 this is also r. 15, 19, 21, 23;
4:8, 16; 5:10; 6:2, 9; 7:6;
8:10, 14
11 beh. all was r. 17, 26; 4:4
4:7 I saw r. 6:4 cometh with r.
6:11 many things that there. r.
7:15 thi. I ha. seen in days of r.
8:14 a r. that is done on earth
9:9 with wife all the days of r.
11:10 childhood and youth are r.
Is. 5:18 r. iniq. with cords of r.
32:23 sift nations wi. sieve of r.
41:17 nations to him counted r.
29 maketh judges of earth as r.
41:29 behold, they are all r. 4:10
57:13 wind carry, r. take them
58:9 take away r. 59:4 tru. in r.
Jer. 2:5 th. have walked after r.
1 *K.* 17:15 they are r. errors, 51:18
10:19 fathers have inherited r.
16:13 people burnt incense to r.
Zec. 13:6 th. have seen r. 02:23
5 because ye have spoken r.
9 prophets that see r. 21:29
23 sh. see no more r. nor div.
Hos. 12:11 r. they sacri. bullocks
Hab. 2:13 weary themsel. for r.
Zec. 10:2 for idols have spok. r.
Rom. 8:20 creature subject to r.
Eph. 4:17 as Gentiles walk, in r.
2 *Pet.* 2:18 speak gre. words of r.

VANITIES.
Deut. 32:21 prove. me with their
r. 1 *K.* 16:13,26; *Jer.* 8:19
Ps. 31:6 that regard lying r.
Ec. 1:2 vanity of r. saith, 12:8
5:7 in multi. of dreams are r.
Jer. 10:8 stock is doctrine of r.
14:22 any an. r. can cause rain /
Jon. 2:8 that observe lying r.
Acts 14:15 ye should turn from r.

VAPOR, S.
Job 36:27 pour rain accord. to r.
32 cattle also concerning the r.
Ps. 135:7 causeth r. to ascend
148:8 and r. fulfilling his word
Jam. 2:19 signs in earth, r.
Jam. 4:14 what is your life / a r.

VARIABLENESS.
Jam. 1:17 lights, wi. wh. is no r.

VARIANCE.
Mat. 10:35 set a man at r. ag. fa.
Gal. 5:20 works of flesh, hat. r.

VASHTI.
Est. 1:9 V. queen made a feast
19 V. come no more bef. king
2:17 made her queen inst. of V.

VAUNT, ETH.
Jud. 7:2 lest Isr. r. against me
1 *Cor.* 13:4 charity r. not itself

VEHEMENT.
Cant. 8:6 love, th. ha. a r. flame
Jon. 4:8 G. prepared a r. wind
2 *Cor.* 7:11 r. desire it wrought

VEHEMENTLY.
Mark 14:31 Peter spake more r.
Luke 6:48 beat r. on house, 49
11:53 Pha. began to urge him r.
23:10 stood and r. accused him

VER

VEIL.
Gen. 24:65 Rebekah took a r.
38:14 Tam. covered here, with r.
Ex. 20:31 sh. make a r. of blue
34:33 Moses put a r. on face, 35
30:35 r. of blue, 2 *Chr.* 3:14
Lev. 16:2 come not within the r.
15 bring his blood within r.
24:3 without r. sh. Aaron order
Ruth 3:15 bring r. th. hast upon
Cant. 5:7 keep. took away my r.
Is. 25:7 destroy r. spread over
Mat. 27:51 r. of temple was rent,
Mark 15:38; *Luke* 23:45
2 *Cor.* 3:13 M. put a r. over face
14 same r. untaken away, wh
r. is done away in Christ
15 to this day r. Is upon heart
16 the r. shall be taken away
Heb. 6:19 wh. entereth within r.
9:3 aft. second r. the tabernacle
10:20 thro' the r. that is to say

VEILS.
Is. 3:23 L. will take away the r.

VEIN.
Job 28:1 there is a r. for silver

VENGEANCE.
Gen. 4:15 r. sh. be taken on him
Deut. 32:35 to me belongeth r.
and, *Ps.* 94:1 ; *Heb.* 10:30
Jer. 11:20 Lord hath taken r.
Ps. 58:10 rejoice wh. he seeth r.
99:8 took. r. of their inventions
149:7 execute r. upon heathen
Prov. 6:34 not spare in day of r.
Is. 34:8 day of r. 61:2 ; *Jer.* 51:6
35:4 your God will come with r.
47:3 I will take r. *Jer.* 51:36
59:17 he put on garments of r.
63:4 for day of r. is in my heart
Jer. 11:20 let see thy r. 20:12
46:10 day of r. 46:15 r. of the Lord, 28
50:28 r. of L. r. of temp. 51:11
Lam. 3:60 hast seen all their r.
Ezek. 25:12 by taking r. hath offended
14 r. on Edom by hand of Isr.
15 beca. Philistines have tak. r.
17 when I lay r. on Philistines
Mic. 5:15 execute r. *Ezek.* 25:17
Nah. 1:2 Lord will take r. on his adversaries
Luke 21:22 for these be days of r.
Acts 28:4 r. suffereth not to live
Rom. 3:5 unrigh. who tak. r. /
12:19 r. is mine, saith the Lord
2 *Thes.* 1:8 flaming fire, taking r.
Jude 7 suffering r. of eternal fire

VENISON.
Gen. 25:28 because he eat of r.
19 arise, and eat of my r. 31
21 I may eat r. that my soul
Rev. 2:27 as a r. of potter be brok.

VENOM.
Deut. 32:33 wine is r. of asps

VENOMOUS.
Acts 28:4 barbarians saw r. beast

VENT.
Job 32:19 as wine wh. hath no r.

VENTURE.
1 *K.* 22:34 a certain man drew a bow at a r. 2 *Chr.* 18:33

VERIFIED.
Gen. 42:20 so sh. your words be r.
K. 8:26 and let thy word be r.
2 *Chr.* 6:17

VERILY.
Gen. 42:21 we are r. guilty
Mat. 5:83 r. I say unto you, 6:2,
5, 16; 8:10; 10:15, 23, 42;
11, 19:17; 18:28; 17:20;
18:3, 13, 18; 19:23, 28; 21:21,
31; 23:36; 24:2, 34; *Mark* 3:28;
40, 48; *Mat.* 3:28;
Luke 6:18; 9:1, 41; 10:15, 24;
11:51; 12:43; 13:30; 14:9, 18,
25; *Luke* 4:24; 11:51; 12:37;
18:17, 29; 21:32; 23:43
Mark 14:30; *Luke* 23:43
Acts 22:3 am r. a Jew born in T.
1 *Cor.* 3:3 I r. as absent in body
Ezek. 8:9 I r. will r. hearts of peo.
Heb. 2:7 not wake that is that r. ?
John 3:3 hin r. is love of G.
Acts 12:11 Herod did r. the church

VERILY, VERILY.
John 1:51 v. r. I say unto you,
3:10, 24, 25 ; 6:26, 32, 47, 53 ;
8:34, 51, 58; 10:1, 7; 12:21;
13:16, 20, 21; 14:14; 10:20, 23
John 3:3 r. r. I say unto thee,
5:11; 13:33 ; 21:18

VEX

Ps. 111:7 works of hands are r.
1 *Tim.* 2:7 tench. in faith and r.

VERMILION.
Jer. 22:14 and painted with r.
Ezek. 23:14 C. portrayed with r.

VERY.
Gen. 27:21 thou be my r. son E.
9:16 in r. deed for this I
Deut. 30:14 word is r. nigh to th.
1 *Sam.* 25:34 in r. deed exc. thou
26:4 Saul was come in r. deed
Prov. 17:9 be separat. r. friends
John 7:26 this is r. Ch. *Acts* 9:22
8:4 taken in adultery, in r. act
1 *Thes.* 5:23 r. G. of peace sane.

VESSEL.
Deut. 23:24 not put any in thy r.
1 *Sam.* 21:5 sancti. this day in r.
1 *K.* 17:10 fetch me water in r.
2 *K.* 4:6 bring r. not a r. more
Ps. 2:9 pieces like a potter's r.
31:12 I am like a broken r.
Jer. 18:4 r. mar. in hand of pot.
22:28 r. wher. is no pleasure
25:34 ye sh. fall like r. pleas. r.
48:11 M. not emptied fr. r. to r.
38 I have broken M. like a r.
51:34 Neb. made me empty r.
Ezek. 4:9 put them in one r. and
15:3 a pin of it to hang any v. ?
Hos. 8:8 covereth candle wi. r.
Acts 9:15 a chosen r. unto me
10:11 Pe. saw a certain r. 11:5
Rom. 9:21 make one r. to honor
1 *Thes.* 4:4 his r. in sanctificati.
1 *Pet.* 3:7 to wife as to weaker r.

VESSELS.
Gen. 43:11 best fruits in your r.
Ex. 40:10 anoint r. *Lev.* 8:11
Num. 18:3 nigh r. of sanctuary
1 *Sam.* 9:7 bread spent in our r.
21:5 r. of young men are holy
2 *K.* 4:3 go, borrow r. abroad
1 *Chr.* 22:19 r. A. did cast away
Ezr. 1:7 Cyrus brought forth r.
5:15 take r. 7:19 r. given thee
Neh. 13:9 thither brought I r.
Is. 18:2 in r. of bulrushes
22:24 r. of small quantity, r. of
34:16 be clean that hear r. of L.
65:4 abominable things is in r.
Jer. 14:3 returned with r. empty
27:16 r. of L.'s house, 28:3
Dan. 5:23 brought r. of house
11:8 carry captive r. of gold
Hag. 2:16 dr. fifty r. out of press
Mat. 13:48 gathered good into r.
25:4 but wise took oil in their r.
Rom. 9:22 r. of wr. 23 r. of mercy
Rev. 2:27 as r. of potter be brok.
See BRASS, EARTHEN, GOLD, SILVER.

VESTMENTS.
2 *K.* 10:22 r. for worshippers
22 *K.* 10:22 said to him over r.

VESTRY.
2 *K.* 10:22 said to him over r.

VESTURE, S.
Gen. 41:42 arrayed Joseph in r.
Deut. 22:12 fringes on thy r.
Ps. 22:18 they cast lots upon my
r. *Mat.* 27:35 ; *John* 19:24
102:26 as a r. sh. thou fold th.
Heb. 1:12 as a r. sh. thou fold th.
Rev. 19:13 clothed with r. dipt
16 on his r. and thigh a name

VEX.
Ex. 22:21 and thou shalt not r. a stranger, *Lev.* 19:33
Lev. 18:18 wife to sister to r. her
Num. 25:17 r. the Midianites
18 they r. you with their wiles
33:55 ye let remain sh. r. you
2 *Sam.* 12:18 how will he r. him.
2 *Chr.* 15:6 God did r. them
Job 19:2 how long will ye r. soul
Ps. 2:5 r. th. in his displeasure
Is. 7:6 let us go ag. J. and r. it
11:13 Judah shall not r. Ephr.
Ezek. 32:9 I will r. hearts of peo.
Hab. 2:7 not wake that is that r. ?
Acts 12:1 Herod did r. the church

CRUDEN'S CONCORDANCE. 1069

VIL

Is. 9:1 not such as was in her v.
28:19 a v. to understand report
65:14 ye sh. howl for v. of spirit

VEXED.
Num. 20:15 Egyptians v. us and
Jud. 2:18 of them that v. them
10:8 that year Ammonites v. Is.
16:16 his soul was v. unto death
1 *Sam.* 14:47 Saul v. his enemies
2 *Sam.* 13:2 Amnon v. fell sick
2 *K.* 4:27 alone, for his soul is v.
Neh. 8:27 enemies who v. them
Job 27:2 Almighty v. my soul
Ps. 6:2 my bones v. 3 soul v.
10 let enemies be asha. and v.
Is. 63:10 they rebelled and v. Sp.
Ezek. 22:5 infamous and much v.
7 v. fatherless; 29 v. the poor
Mat. 15:22 daugh. is v. wi. devil
17:15 he is lunatic and sore v.
Luke 6:18 they that were v. with
unclean spirits. *Acts* 5:16
2 *Pet.* 2:7 Lot v. with conversat.
8 v. his righteous soul fr. day by

VIAL.
1 *Sam.* 10:1 Sam. took a v. of oil
Rev. 16:2 first angel pour. his v.
3 second v. on sea; 4 third v.
5 fourth v. 10 fifth v. on beast
12 sixth v. 17 sev. v. into air

VIALS.
Rev. 5:8 golden v. full of odors
15:7 gave seven angels seven v.
16:1 pour out v. of wrath of G.
17:1 angels wh. had 7 v. 21:9

VICTORY.
2 *Sam.* 19:2 v. th. day was turn.
23:10 L. wrought a great v. 12
1 *Chr.* 29:11 thine, O L. is the v.
Ps. 98:1 arm hath gotten him v.
Is. 25:8 will swallow up death in
v. 1 *Cor.* 15:54
Mat. 12:20 send judgm. unto v.
1 *Cor.* 15:55 O gra. where thy v. ?
57 to God, who giv. us the v.
1 *John* 5:4 this is the v. even fal.
Rev. 15:2 had got. v. over beast

VICTUAL, S.
Gen. 14:11 good v. of Sod. and v.
Ex. 12:39 nei. had prepared v.
Lev. 25:37 nor lend him thy v.
Deut. 23:19 usury of v. of any th.
Jos. 1:11 prepare v. 9:11 take v.
9:14 the men took of their v.
Jud. 17:10 will gi. apparel and v.
1 *Sam.* 22:10 gave v. and sword
1 *K.* 4:7 provided v. for king, 27
11:18 Pharaoh appointed him v.
Neh. 10:31 peo. bring v. on sab.
13:15 ag. th. in day they sold v.
Jer. 40:5 capt. gave Jeremiah v.
41:17 then had we plenty of v.
Mat. 14:15 to buy v. *Luke* 9:12

VIEW, ED.
Jos. 2:1 v. land ; 7:2 v. country
7:2 v. Ai ; *Ezr.* 8:15 v. people
2 *K.* 2:7 prophets stood to v. 15
Neh. 2:13 I v. walls of Jerus. 15

VIGILANT.
1 *Tim.* 3:2 a bishop must be v.
1 *Pet.* 5:8 bo v. bec. your advers.

VILE.
Deut. 25:3 lest thy brot. seem v.
Jud. 19:24 do not so, a thing
1 *Sam.* 3:13 sons made thems. v.
15:9 every thing that was v.
2 *Sam.* 6:22 I will yet be more v.
Job 18:3 why are we reputed v. ?
40:4 I am v. what shall I ans. ?
Ps. 15:4 v. person is contemned
Is. 32:5 v. person be no more
6 v. person will speak villany
Jer. 15:19 take prec. from the v.
29:17 I will make them v. figs
Lam. 1:11 O L. for I am bec. v.
Dan. 11:21 sh. stand a v. person
Nah. 1:14 make grave, th. art v.
3:6 cast filth on th. make thee v.
Rom. 1:26 G. gave them up to v.
Phil. 3:21 shall change v. body
Jam. 2:2 a poor man in v. rai.

VILELY.
2 *Sam.* 1:21 shield v. cast away

VILER, VILEST.
Job 30:8 they were v. than earth
Ps. 12:8 when v. men are exalted

VILLAGE.
Mat. 21:2 go into v. over ag. you,
Mark 11:2; *Luke* 19:30
Luke 21:13 two of th. went to v.

VILLAGES.
Lev. 25:31 houses of v. counted
Jud. 5:7 inhabitants of v. ceased

VIN

Neh. 6:2 meet in one of the v.
Est. 9:19 J. of v. made 14th day
Cant. 7:11 let us lodge in v.
Ezek. 38:11 to land of unwall. v.
Hab. 3:14 strike head of his v.
Mat. 14:15 they may go into the
the v. and buy, *Mark* 6:36

See CITIES.

VILLANY.
Is. 32:6 vile person will speak v.
Jer. 29:23 committed v. in Israel

VINE.
Gen. 40:9 a v. was before me
10 in v. were three branches
40:11 Judah binding his foal to
v. his ass's colt to choice v.
Lev. 25:5 nor gra. grapes of v. 11
Num. 6:4 eat nothing made of v.
Deut. 32:32 their v. is v. of Sod.
Jud. 9:12 trees said to v. reign
13:14 not eat that cometh of v.
1 *K.* 4:25 ev. man under his v.
2 *K.* 4:39 found a wild v. gather.
18:31 eat of own v. *Is.* 36:16
Job 15:33 sha. off grape as the v.
Ps. 80:8 hast bro. v. out of Eg.
14 look down, and visit this v.
128:3 wife sh. be as a fruitful v.
Cant. 6:11 who. v. flourish. 7:12
7:8 breasts as clusters of the v.
Is. 5:2 plant. it with choicest v.
16:8 v. of Sibmah languisheth
9 bewail v. of Sib. *Jer.* 48:32
24:7 wine mourneth, v. langui.
32:12 sh. lament for fruitful v.
34:4 as leaf falleth from the v.
Jer. 2:21 I planted th. a noble v.
how turned into strange v. ?
6:9 glean remnant of Is. as a v.
8:13 no grapes on v. nor figs
Ezek. 15:2 v. more th. any tree ?
6 v. which I have given for fuel
17:6 it became a spreading v.
7 v. did bend roots towards
19:10 moth. is like v. in blood
Joel 1:7 he laid my v. waste
12 v. is dried up, the fig-tree
2:22 fig-tree and v. yield stren.
Mic. 4:4 sit ev. man under his v.
Hag. 2:19 v. hath not bro. forth
Zec. 3:10 call ev. man under v.
8:12 the v. shall give her fruit
Mal. 3:11 nei. v. cast her fruit
Mat. 26:29 not drink of fruit of v.
Mark 14:25; *Luke* 22:18
John 15:1 I am the true v. 5
4 bear fruit, exc. it abide in v.
Jam. 3:12 can a v. bear figs ?
Rev. 14:18 ga. clusters of v. 19

VINES.
Num. 20:5 no pl. of v. or pome.
Deut. 8:8 a land of wheat and v.
Ps. 78:47 he destroyed their v.
105:33 smote th. v. and fig-trees
Cant. 2:13 v. give a good smell
15 foxes, that spoil the v. our
v. have tender grapes
Is. 7:23 th. were a thousand v.
Jer. 5:17 they shall eat up thy v.
31:5 plant v. on mountains
Hos. 2:12 I will destroy her v.
Hab. 3:17 nei. fruit be in the v.

VINE-DRESSERS.
2 *K.* 25:12 left the poor of land to
be v. *et.* *Jer.* 52:16
2 *Chr.* 26:10 Uzziah had v.-d.
Is. 61:5 sons of alien your v.-d.
Joel 1:11 be ashamed, O ye v.-d.

VINEGAR.
Num. 6:3 Naz. shall drink no v.
Ruth 2:14 dip thy morsel in v.
Ps. 69:21 gave v. *Mat.* 27:34
Prov. 10:26 as v. to the teeth
25:20 as v. upon nitre, so is he
Mat. 27:48 took a sponge and
filled it with v. *Mark* 15:36 ;
Luke 23:36 ; *John* 19:29, 30

VINEYARD.
Gen. 9:20 Noah planted a v. and
Ex. 22:5 if cause v. to be eaten
23:11 thou sh. deal with thy v.
Lev. 19:10 shalt not glean thy v.
25:3 six years sh. prune thy v.
4 sev. sow v. field, nor prune v.
Deut. 20:6 what man planted v. ?
22:9 not sow v. with div. seeds
23:24 comest into neighbor's v.
24:21 when gather. grapes of v.
28:30 plant v. not gath. grapes
1 *K.* 21:1 Nabo. had a v. beside
2 given me thy v. I will give
thee a better v. 6
7 I will give thee v. of Naboth

VIO

Ps. 80:15 v. thy ri. hand planted
Prov. 24:30 I went by v. of man
31:16 hand she planteth a v.
Cant. 1:6 own v. have I not kept
8:11 Solomon had a v. he let v.
12 my v. is bef. me, O Solom.
Is. 1:6 Z. is left as cottage in v.
3:14 for ye have eaten up the v.
5:1 my beloved touching his v.
7 v. of L. of hosts is hou. of Is.
10 ten acres of v. yi. one bath
27:2 sing to her, v. of red wine
Jer. 12:10 pastors destroy. my v.
35:7 Rechab. sh. not plant v. 9
Mic. 1:6 Samaria as plant. of v.
Mat. 20:1 hire labor. into his v.
2 agreed with laborers for v.
4 said, Go ye also into v. 7
21:28 go work to-day in my v.
33 certain householder planted
v. *Mark* 12:1 ; *Luke* 20:9
Luke 13:6 fig-tree planted in v.
7 said unto dresser of v.
1 *Cor.* 9:7 planteth v. eat. not ?

VINEYARDS.
Num. 16:14 not giv. inher. of v.
20:17 not pass through v. 21:22
22:24 angel stood in path of v.
Deut. 6:11 he sware to give thee
v. *Jos.* 24:13; *Neh.* 9:25
28:39 shalt plant v. dress them
Jud. 15:5 the foxes burnt up v.
21:20 go and lie in wait in v.
1 *Sam.* 8:14 take yo. fields and v.
22:7 will son of J. give you v. ?
1 *K.* 2:36 is 11 time to receive v. ?
18:32 I take you to a land of v.
19:29 in the third year plant v.
1 *Chr.* 27:27 over v. was Shimei
Neh. 5:3 have mortgaged our v.
11 restore v. and olive-yards
Ps. 107:37 sow fields, plant v.
Ec. 2:4 houses, I planted me v.
Cant. 1:6 made me keeper of v.
14 as cluster of camphire in v.
Is. 16:10 in v. sh. be no singing
65:21 shall plant v. and eat the
fruit of them, *Amos* 9:14
Jer. 32:15 v. sh. be possessed ag.
39:10 Nebuzar-ad. gave poor v.
Ezek. 28:26 build hous. and pl. v.
Hos. 2:15 I will give her her v.
Amos 4:9 palmer-worm devo. v.
5:11 ye have planted v.
Zep. 1:13 sh. plant v. not drink

VINTAGE.
Lev. 26:5 thresh. shall reach to
v. the v. reach to sowi. time
Jud. 8:2 better than v. of Abi. ?
Job 9:16 they gather v. of wick.
Is. 16:10 made v. shouti. to cease
Jer. 48:32 spoiler is fallen up. v.
Mic. 7:1 as grape-gleanings of v.
Zec. 11:2 for O. v. forest is down

VIOL.
Is. 5:12 harp and v. and wine
14:11 noise of v. brought down
Amos 5:23 not hear melody of v.
6:5 that chant to sound of v.

VIOLATED.
Ezek. 22:26 priests h. my law

VIOLENCE.
Gen. 6:11 earth filled with v. 13
Lev. 6:2 if lie in tak. taken by v.
2 *Sam.* 22:3 savest me from v.
Ps. 11:5 loveth v. his soul hateth
58:2 I have even v. and strife in
72:14 shall redeem th. soul fr. v.
73:6 v. covereth them as a gar.
Prov. 4:17 they drink wine of v.
10:6 v. covereth the mouth, 11
13:2 transgressors shall eat v.
26:17 man that doeth v. to blood
5:5:9 he had done no v.
59:6 act of v. is in their hands
60:18 v. shall no more be heard
Jer. 6:7 v. and spoil heard in her
20:8 I spoke, I cried v. and spoil
22:3 do no v. to the stranger
17 th. eyes, thy heart are for v.
51:35 v. done to me and flesh
Ezek. 7:11 v. risen up into a rod
23 for the city is full of v.
8:17 filled land with v. 28:16
12:19 because of the v. of them
Joel 3:19 Edom a wilder. for v.
Amos 3:10 store v. in palaces
6:3 cause seat of v. to come

VIR

Ob. 10 for v. shame shall cover
Jon. 3:8 turn every one from v.
Mic. 2:2 covet fields, take by v.
6:12 the rich men are full of v.
Hab. 1:2 I cry out to thee of v. ?
3 v. bef. me ; 9 come all for v.
2:8 and for the v. of the land
17 v. of Leba. cover thee, v. of
Zep. 1:9 fill mast. houses with v.
3:4 her priests have done v.
Mal. 2:16 covereth v. with garm.
Mat. 11:12 kingd. of hea. suff. v.
Luke 3:14 do v. to no man, nor
Acts 5:26 capt. bro. them with. v.
21:35 v. borne of soldiers for v.
27:41 was brok. for v. of waves
Heb. 11:34 quenched v. of fire
Rev. 18:21 with v. shall Babylon

VIOLENT.
2 *Sam.* 22:49 hast delivered me
from the v. man, *Ps.* 18:48
Ps. 7:16 his v. dealing come on
86:14 assemb. of v. men sought
140:1 preserve me fr. v. man, 4
11 evil shall hunt the v. man.
Prov. 16:29 v. man enticeth
neighbor
Ec. 5:8 if thou seest v. pervert.
Mat. 11:12 the v. take it by force

VIOLENTLY.
Lev. 6:4 sh. rest. that he took v.
Deut. 28:31 ass shall be v. taken
Job 20:19 hath v. taken a house
24:2 they v. take away flocks
Lam. 2:6 hath v. taken away tab.

VIPER.
Job 20:16 v. tongue sh. slay him
Is. 30:6 whenc. come v. and serp.
59:5 that is crushed br. into v.
Acts 28:3 v. fasten. on P.'s hand

VIPERS.
Mat. 3:7 O generation of v. 12:34 ;
23:33 ; *Luke* 3:7

VIRGIN.
Gen. 24:16 Rebekah was fair, v.
43 when the v. cometh to draw
Lev. 21:3 a v. for her he defiled
14 he shall take a v. to wife
Deut. 22:19 evil name upon a v.
23 v. betroth. 28 f. not betro.
32:25 destroy young man and v.
2 *K.* 19:21 the v. the daughter of
Zi. laughed to scorn, *Is.* 37:22
Is. 7:14 v. sh. conceiv. *Mat.* 1:23
23:12 rejoice, O th. oppressed v.
47:1 sit in the dust, O v. of Ba.
62:5 as a yo. man marrieth a v.
Jer. 14:17 the v. dau. is broken
18:13 v. of Is. ha. done horrible
31:4 shalt be built, O v. of Israel
13 then sh. v. rejoice in dance
21 turn, O v. of Is. to thy cit.
46:11 O v. daughter of Egypt
Lam. 1:15 L. hath trod. v. of Ju.
2:13 comfort thee, O v. of Zion
Joel 1:8 lament like a v. girded
Amos 5:2 v. of Israel is fallen
Luke 1:27 angel was sent to a v.
1 *Cor.* 7:28 if a v. marry, not sin.
34 difference betw. wife and v.
37 that he will keep his v.
2 *Cor.* 11:2 pres. you as chaste v.

VIRGINS.
2 *Sam.* 13:18 were king's dau. v.
18:2 wi. her compaions
Cant. 1:3 therefore do v. love thee
6:8 queens, v. without number
Ps. 45:14 her v. be brought to
Lam. 1:4 her v. are afflicted
2:10 v. of Jer. hang their heads
21 my v. and my young men
Amos 8:13 that day shall the fair v.
Mat. 25:1 ten v. went forth
7 virgins arose, trimmed lamps
11 other v. came, saying, Lord
Acts 21:9 four daugh. v. proph.
1 *Cor.* 7:25 concern. v. I have not
Rev. 14:4 not defiled, they are v.

Young VIRGINS.
Jud. 21:12 were four hund. v.
1 K. 1:2 sought for king, a v.
Est. 2:2 sought for king
3 gather together the fair y. v.

VIRGINITY.
Lev. 21:13 take a wife in her v.
Deut. 22:15 bring tok. of v. 17, 20
Jud. 11:37 may bewail my v. 38
Ezek. 23:3 bruised there fr. v. 8
Luke 2:36 lived 7 years fr. v.

VIRTUE.
Mark 5:30 v. had gone out of
him, *Luke* 6:19 ; 8:46
Phil. 4:8 if there be any v.

CRUDEN'S CONCORDANCE.

VIS

2 *Pet.* 1:3 called us to glo. and *v.*
5 add to faith *v.* to *v.* knowl.

VIRTUOUS, LY.
Ruth 3:11 thou art a *v.* woman
Prov. 12:4 a *v.* wom, is a crown
31:10 who can find a *v.* wom. ?
29 many daugh. have done *v.*

VISAGE.
Is. 52:14 his *v.* was marred
Lam. 4:8 *v.* is blacker th. a coal
Dan. 3:19 form of *v.* changed

VISIBLE.
Col. 1:16 all things created, *v.*

VISION.
Num. 24:4 *v.* of Almighty, 16
1 *Sam.* 3:1 there was no open *v.*
15 S. feared to show Eli the *v.*
2 *Sam.* 7:17 accord. to this *v.* did
  Nathan speak, 1 *Chr.* 17:15
2 *Chr.* 32:32 written in *v.* of Isa.
Job 33:8 he chased away as a *v.*
Ps. 89:19 spakest in *v.* to H. O.
Prov. 29:18 wh. no *v.* peo. perish
Is. 1:1 the *v.* of Isa. son of Amoz
21:2 a grievous *v.* is declared
22:1 burden of valley of *v.* 5
23:7 they err in *v.* stumble in
23:7 be as a dream of a night *v.*
11 *v.* is become as a book seal,
Jer. 14:14 they proph. a false *v.*
23:16 sp. a *v.* of their own heart
Lam. 3:9 proph. find no *v.* fr. L.
Ezek. 7:13 *v.* is touching whole
28 they seek a *v.* of prophet
8:4 according to *v.* 11:24; 43:3
12:22 days are prolonged *v.* fail.
23 the effect of ev. *v.* is at hand
24 no more vain *v.* nor divina.
27 *v.* he seeth is for days
13:7 ha. ye not seen a vain *v.* ?
Dan. 2:19 revealed to D. in a *v.*
7:2 in my *v.* four winds strove
8:1 a *v.* appeared unto me
15 make this man understa. *v.*
26 shut up *v.* 27 astonish. at *v.*
9:21 whom I had seen in *v.* 23
13:1 he had understanding of *v.*
7 I saw *v.* men saw not *v.* 8
11 yet the *v.* is for many days
16 by *v.* my sorrows are turn.
11:14 exalt themsel. to estab. *v.*
Ob. 1 the *v.* of Obadiah
Mic. 3:6 ye shall not have a *v.*
Nah. 1:1 book of *v.* of Nahum
Hab. 2:2 write *v.* make it plain
3 *v.* is for an appointed time
Zec. 13:4 prophets asha. of his *v.*
Mat. 17:9 tell the *v.* to no man
Luke 1:22 perc. he had seen a *v.*
21:23 had seen a *v.* of angels
Acts 10:17 Peter doubted of *v.* 19
11:5 I saw a *v.* a vessel descend
12:9 but thought he saw a *v.*
16:9 *v.* appeared to Paul, 18:9
26:19 I was not disobedi. to *v.*
Rev. 9:17 I saw horses in the *v.*

In a **VISION.**
Gen. 15:1 L. came to Ab. in a *v.*
Num. 12:6 make myself kn. in *v.*
Ezek. 11:24 brought me in a *v.*
Dan. 8:2 I saw in a *v.* by river
Acts 9:10 to An. said L. in a *v.*
12 S. hath seen in a *v.* a man
10:3 Cor. saw in a *v.* an angel

VISIONS.
Gen. 46:2 God spake to Is. in *v.*
2 *Chr.* 9:29 written in *v.* of Iddo
26:5 Z. had understanding in *v.*
Job 4:13 thoughts fr. *v.* of night
7:14 thou terrifest me thro' *v.*
Ezek. 1:1 I saw the *v.* of God
8:3 he bro. me in *v.* of G. to J.
13:16 which see *v.* of peace
43:2 in *v.* bro. he me to land of
Dan. 1:17 D. had underst. in *v.*
2:28 *v.* of thy head on thy bed
4:5 *v.* of my head troubled me
7:1 D. had *v.* of his head upon
7 I saw in night *v.* behold, 13
15 *v.* of my head troubled me
Ezek. 12:10 I have multiplied *v.*
Joel 2:28 men dream *v. Acts* 2:17
2 *Cor.* 12:1 come to *v.* and revela.

VISIT.
Gen. 50:24 will *v.* 25; *Ex.* 13:19
Ex. 32:34 when I *v.* I will *v.* sin
Lev. 18:25 I do *v.* iniq. thereof
Job 5:24 shalt *v.* thy habitation
7:18 that thou shouldest *v.* him
Ps. 59:5 awake, to *v.* the heath.
80:14 look down and *v.* this vine
89:32 th. will I *v.* transgression
106:4 O *v.* me wi. thy salvation
Is. 23:17 the Lord will *v.* Tyre
Jer. 3:16 they shall *v.* ark of L.

VOI

Jer. 5:9 shall I not *v.* ? 29 ; 9:9
6:15 *v.* them, shall be cast down
14:10 rememb. iniq. and *v.* sins
15:15 than kno. remem. and *v.*
29:2 *v.* on you evil of doings
27:22 there sh. they be till I *v.*
29:10 *v.* you and perf. my word
32:5 th. shall he be till I *v.* him
49:8 will *v.* Esau; 50:31 *v.* Baby.
Lam. 4:22 he will *v.* thine iniq.
Hos. 2:13 *v.* on her days of Baal.
8:13 now will he *v.* th. sins, 9:9
Amos 3:14 I will *v.* alt. of Beth-el
Zep. 2:7 L. shall *v.* turn captiv.
Zec. 11:16 not *v.* th. that be cut

VISITATION.
Acts 7:23 into heart in *v.* his br.
13:14 decla. how G. did *v.* Gent.
36 let us go and *v.* our breth.
Jam. 1:27 *v.* father. and widows

VISITATION.
Num. 16:29 if visit. aft. *v.* of men
Job 10:12 thy *v.* preser. my spir.
Is. 10:3 what do in day of *v.* ?
Jer. 6:15 in time of *v.* cast down
10:15 in time of *v.* perish, 51:18
11:23 in year of *v.* 23:12 ; 48:44
40:21 time of th. *v.* come, 50:27
Hos. 9:7 the days of *v.* are come
Mic. 7:4 thy *v.* cometh, perplex.
Luke 19:44 knew. not time of *v.*
1 *Pet.* 2:13 glorify G. in day of *v.*

VISITED.
Gen. 21:1 Lord *v.* Sar. as he said
Ex. 3:16 I have surely *v.* you
4:31 heard that Lord had *v.* Is.
Ruth 1:6 heard how L. *v.* people
1 *Sam.* 2:21 the Lord *v.* Hannah
Job 35:15 he hath *v.* in his anger
Ps. 17:3 thou hast *v.* me, thou
Prov. 19:23 aft. may they *v.* it.
Is. 24:22 after many days be *v.*
26:14 thercf. hast thou *v.* them
16 Lord in trouble have they *v.*
29:6 thou sh. be *v.* with thund.
Ezek. 38:8 after many days be *v.*
Zec. 10:3 L. of hosts *v.* his flock
Mat. 25:36 *v.* me; 43 *v.* me not
Luke 1:68 *v.* and redeemed peop.
78 the day-spring hath *v.* us
7:16 God hath *v.* his people

VISITEST, ETH, ING.
Ex. 20:5 *v.* iniquity of fathers,
34:7; *Num.* 14:18 ; *Deut.* 5:9
Job 31:14 *v.* what sh. I answer ?
Ps. 8:4 thou *v.* him, *Heb.* 2:6
65:9 thou *v.* earth, waterest it

VOCATION.
Eph. 4:1 walk worthy of the *v.*

VOICE.
Gen. 4:10 *v.* of thy broth.'s blood
27:22 *v.* is Jacob's *v.* but hands
38:15 heard that I lift. up my *v.*
Ex. 4:8 believe *v.* of latter sign
19:19 God answered with one *v.*
23:21 bewa. of him, obey his *v.*
24:3 people answered with one *v.*
Num. 14:1 congr. lifted their *v.*
Deut. 4:30 if thou be obedi. to *v.*
8:20 would not be obedi. to *v.*
Jud. 18:3 nor make noise wi. *v.*
Jud. 18:3 they knew *v.* of Levite
Sam. 24:16 is this thy *v.* my
  son David ? 26:17
2 *Sam.* 22:14 M. High uttered *v.*
1 *K.* 18:26 was no *v.* nor any, 29
19:12 after fire a still small *v.*
2 *K.* 4:31 neither *v.* nor hearing
7:10 there was no *v.* of man
19:22 ag. wh. exalt. *v.* ? *Is.* 37:23
1 *Chr.* 15:16 lifting up *v.* wi. joy
Job 2:12 Job's friends lift. up *v.*
3:7 let no joyful *v.* come there
30:31 the *v.* of them that weep
37:4 a *v.* roareth, he thundereth
5 God thundereth with his *v.*
30 and thunb. with a *v.* like him ?
Ps. 19:19 the Highest gave his *v.*
26:7 publish with *v.* of thanksg.
31:22 heardest *v.* of supplicat.
42:4 went to house of G. wi. *v.*
44:16 *v.* of him th. reprocheth
47:1 shout to G. wi. *v.* of triam.
66:10 attend. to *v.* of my prayer
68:33 send. out *v.* th. a mighty *v.*
74:23 forget not *v.* of enemies
77:1 cried unto G. with my *v.*
18 *v.* of thy thunder in heaven
93:6 attend to *v.* of my suppli.
93:3 floods have lifted up th. *v.*
98:5 sing to L. with *v.* of psalm

VOI

Ps. 102:5 by reas. of *v.* of groan,
103:20 hearkening to *v.* of word
104:7 at *v.* of thund. th. hasted
118:15 *v.* of rejoic. in tabernac.
141:1 give ear to my *v.*
Prov. 1:20 uttereth *v.* in streets
2:3 if liftest up *v.* for understa.
5:13 not obeyed *v.* of my touch.
8:1 understand, put forth her *v.*
Ec. 5:3 a fool's *v.* is known by
6 sho. G. be angry at thy *v.* ?
10:20 bird of air sh. carry the *v.*
12:4 he shall rise at *v.* of bird
Cant. 2:8 the *v.* of my beloved
12 *v.* of turtle is heard in land
5:2 it is *v.* of beloved knocketh
Is. 6:4 posts moved at *v.* of him
13:2 exalt the *v.* shake the hand
29:4 *v.* as one that hath a spirit
30:19 graci. to thee at *v.* of cry
31:4 lion not afraid of their *v.*
40:3 *v.* th. crieth in wilder. *Mat.*
  3:3 ; *Mark* 1:3 ; *Luke* 3:4
6 *v.* said, Cry ; 48:20 *v.* of sing.
50:10 obeyeth *v.* of his servant
51:3 thanksgiving, *v.* of melody
52:8 wi. *v.* together sh. th. sing
65:19 *v.* of weeping shall be no
more heard, nor *v.* of crying
66:6 a *v.* of noise, a *v.* fr. temp.
Jer. 4:15 *v.* declareth from Dan
16 give their *v.* ag. cities of J.
6:23 3. roareth like sea, 50:42
7:34 *v.* of mirth, *v.* of gladness
v. of the bridegroom, 16:9 ;
25:10 ; 33:11
8:19 *v.* of cry of dau. of people
10:13 when he uttereth *v.* 51:16
25:36 a *v.* of cry of shepherds
30:19 *v.* of th. that make merry
31:15 a *v.* was heard in Ram, 16
46:22 *v.* thereof go like a serp.
48:3 a *v.* of crying from Horon.
50:28 *v.* of them that flee
51:55 destro. out of her great *v.*
Ezek. 1:24 I heard *v.* of Almighty
10:5 as the *v.* of Almighty God
31:42 a *v.* of multitude at ease
33:32 one that hath a pleas. *v.*
43:2 *v.* li. noise of wat. *Rev.* 1:15
Dan. 4:31 there fell *v.* fr. heaven
6:20 cried with a lamentable *v.*
7:11 because of *v.* of words
Joel 2:11 L. utter *v.* before army
3:16 utter *v.* from J. *Amos* 1:2
Jon. 2:9 with *v.* of thanksgiving
Nah. 2:7 lead as with *v.* of doves
Mat. 3:17 a *v.* fr. heaven, *Mark*
  1:11 ; *Luke* 3:22
17:5 a *v.* out of cloud, this is
  my S. *Mark* 9:7; *Lu.* 9:35, 36
Luke 1:44 *v.* of saluta. sounded
John 1:23 *v.* of one cry. in wild.
10:4 follow. for they kn. his *v.*
5 knew not *v.* of strangers
12:28 then came a *v.* saying, I
30 *v.* came not because of me
18:37 that is of truth hear. my *v.*
Acts 9:7 hear. *v.* seeing no man
10:13 a *v.* say. Rise, 15 ; 11:9
19:34 when *v.* knew Peter's *v.*
22 it is *v.* of a god, not of man
22:9 heard not *v.* of him, 26:14
24:21 exc. it be for this one *v.*
26:10 I gave my *v.* again, them
1 *Cor.* 14:11 know not mean of *v.*
19 by my *v.* I might teach oth.
Gal. 4:20 I des. to change my *v.*
1 *Thes.* 4:16 with *v.* of archangel
Heb. 12:26 whose *v.* shook earth
2 *Pet.* 1:17 *v.* fr. excellent glory
2:16 ass speaking with man's *v.*
Rev. 1:12 I turned to see the *v.*
16:17 there came a great *v.*

VOICE, with hear.
Gen. 4:23 *hear* my *v.* ye wives
Deut. 4:33 did people *h. v.* of G.
36 he made thee to *hear* his *v.*
5:25 if we *h. v.* of God, we die
33:7 *hear*, Lord, the *v.* of Judah
1 *Sam.* 19:35 I *h. v.* of singing ?
22:7 did A. my *v.* out of temple
Job 3:18 *h.* not *v.* of oppressor
37:2 *h.* attentive, noise of his *v.*
Ps. 5:3 my *v.* shalt thou *hear*
27:7 *hear*, O Lord, when I cry
wi. my *v.* 64:1 ; 119:149 ;
130:2 ; 140:6
55:3 *h.* because of *v.* of enemy
17 cry aloud, he shall *h.* my *v.*
103:7 to-day if ye will *hear* his *v.*
Heb. 3:7, 15 ; 4:7
Cant. 2:14 let me *h.* *v.* my voice
Is. 32:9 A. my *v.* ye careless dan.
Jer. 9:10 can men *h. v.* of cattle
12:19 neither any A. his *v.*

VOW

John 5:25 dead *h. v.* of Son, 28
10:3 sheep *hear* his *v.* 16, 27
Acts 22:14 shouldst *h. v.* of mouth
Rev. 3:20 if any man *hear* my *v.*
See **HEARD.**

VOICE, with hearken, ed.
Gen. 3:17 hast A. to *v.* of wife
16:2 Abram *h.* to the *v.* of Sarai
Ex. 3:18 they shall *h.* to thy *v.*
4:8 nor A. to *v.* of the first sign
12:26 if diligently A. to *v.* of L.
18:19 A. to my *v.* I give counsel
24 and Moses *h.* to *v.* of Jethro
Num. 14:22 they have not *h.* to
  my *v. Deut.* 9:23 ; 28:45
21:3 Lord A. to the *v.* of Israel
Deut. 1:45 L. would not *h.* to *v.*
13:5 if thou carefully *h.* to *v.* of
L. 26:17 ; 28:1, 2 ; 30:10
28:15 if th. wilt not *h.* to *v.* of L.
Jos. 10:14 L. *h.* to *v.* of a man
Jud. 2:20 people not *h.* to my *v.*
13:9 God A. to *v.* of Manoah
20:13 B. would not *h.* to *v.* of Is.
1 *Sam.* 2:25 *h.* not to *v.* of father
8:7 *h.* to the *v.* of people, 9:22
9:17 I have A. to your *v.* in all
22:33 go in peace, I *h.* to thy *v.*
28:22 *h.* thou to *v.* of thy hand
2 *Sam.* 12:18 wo. not *h.* to our *v.*
1 *K.* 10:6 if ye will *h.* to my *v.*
20:9:16 hell. he had *h.* to my *v.*
Job 34:16 *hearken* to *v.* of my words
Ps. 5:2 *h.* to the *v.* of my cry
58:5 not A. to *v.* of charmers
81:11 peo. would not *h.* to my *v.*
Cant. 8:13 compan. A. to thy *v.*
Jer. 18:19 A. to *v.* of them that
See **LIFT, LOUD, LOUD, OBEY, OBEYED.**

VOICES.
Luke 17:13 lepers lifted up th. *v.*
23:23 the *v.* of priests prevailed
Acts 13:27 knew not *v.* of proph.
22:22 lift up their *v.* and said
1 *Cor.* 14:10 so many *v.* in world
Rev. 4:5 throne proceed. *v.* 16:18
8:5 into earth, and there were *v.*
10:3 *v.* of other *v.* of trump.
11:15 there were *v.* in heaven
19 temple opened, th. were *v.*

VOID.
Gen. 1:2 earth was without form and *v.*
Num. 30:12 husb. hath made it *v.* 15
Deut. 32:28 people *v.* of counsel
1 *K.* 22:10 in a *v.* place, 2 *Chr.* 18:9
Ps. 89:39 made *v.* the covenant
119:126 have made *v.* thy law
Prov. 11:12 *v.* of wisd. despiseth
Is. 55:11 word not ret. ret. to me *v.*
Jer. 4:23 earth with. form and *v.*
19:7 I will make *v.* counsel of J.
Nah. 2:10 Nineveh is empty, *v.*
Acts 24:16 conscien. *v.* of offence
Rom. 3:31 do we make *v.* law ?
4:14 be heirs, faith is made *v.*
1 *Cor.* 9:15 make any glorying *v.*
See **UNDERSTANDING.**

VOLUME.
Ps. 40:7 in *v.* it is writ. *Heb.* 10:7

VOLUNTARY.
Lev. 1:3 off. it of his own *v.* will
7:16 a *v.* offering shall be eaten
Ezek. 46:12 prepare *v.* burnt-off.
Col. 2:18 a *v.* humility, worship

VOLUNTARILY.
Ezek. 46:12 prepare offerings *v.*

VOMIT, ED, ETH.
Lev. 18:25 land *v.* inhabitants
Job 20:15 swallo. riches, *v.* them
Prov. 23:8 morsel eaten shalt *v.*
25:16 filled with honey and *v.* it
Jon. 2:10 the fish *v.* out Jonah

VOMIT, Substantive.
Prov. 26:11 dog return, to his *v.*
Is. 19:14 man stagger. in his *v.*
28:8 tables are full of *v.* filth.
Jer. 43:26 Moab sh. wallow in *v.*
2 *Pet.* 2:22 dog is turned to his *v.*

VOW.
Gen. 28:20 Ja. vowed a *v.* 31:13
Lev. 7:16 sacri. be a *v.* 22:18, 21
Num. 6:2 when a man make a singular *v.*
Num. 6:5 when a man vow a *v.*
21:2 Israel vowed a *v.* to Lord
30:2 if man vow *v.* 3 wo. vow a *v.*
Deut. 23:18 fer. price of dog for *v.*
Jud. 11:30 Jephthah vowed a *v.*
Ps. 65:1 unto thee sh. *v.* be per.
Ec. 5:4 defer not to pay *v.*
Is. 19:21 *v.* a *v.* unto the Lord
Jer. 44:25 we will surely perform our *v.*
Acts 18:18 had shorn head, he had a *v.*
21:23 we have four men which have a *v.*

CRUDEN'S CONCORDANCE. 1071

WAI

1 *Sam.* 1:11 Hannah vowed a v.
21 Elka. went to offer L. his v.
2 *Sam.* 15:7 let go and pay my v.
8 thy servant vowed a v. at G.
Ps. 65:1 to thee v. be performed
Ec. 5:4 when thou vowest a v.
Is. 19:21 they sh. vow a v. to L.
Acts 18:18 head, for he had a v.
21:23 which have a v. on them

VOWS.
Lev. 22:18 off. oblation for his v.
23:38 and beside all your v.
Num. 29:39 th. do beside your v.
30:5 not any of v. stand, 8, 12
Deut. 12:6 thi. bring v. 11, 17, 26
23:23 thou shalt pay thy v.
Ps. 22:25 I will pay my v. 66:13;
116:14, 18
50:14 pay v. 56:12 v. are on me
61:5 th. O G. hast heard my v.
8 that I may daily perf. my v.
Prov. 7:14 this day I paid my v.
20:25 snare after v. to make inq.
31:2 what the son of my v.?
Jer. 44:25 will surely perf. our v.
Jon. 1:16 men fear. L. made v.
Nah. 1:15 keep feasts, perform v.

VOW, EST, ETH.
Num. 6:2 sepa. themselves to v.
Deut. 23:22 if forbear to v. no sin
Ps. 76:11 v. and pay to the Lord
Ec. 5:4 when thou v. a vow
5 better thou shouldest not v.
Mal. 1:14 v. to L. corrupt thing

VOWED.
Gen. 28:20 Jacob v. a vow, 31:13
Lev. 27:8 accord. to ability th. v.
Num. 6:21 law of N. who hath v.
21:2 Is. v. a vow to L. and said
30:6 a husband when she v. 10
Deut. 23:23 accord. as th. hast v.
Jud. 11:30 Jephthah v. a vow
Ps. 132:2 v. to the mighty God
Ec. 5:4 pay th. wh. thou hast v.
Jon. 2:9 I will pay that that I v.

VOYAGE.
Acts 27:10 v. will be with hurt

VULTURE.
Lev. 11:14 the v. and kite, *Deut.* 14:13
Job 28:7 path v. eye ha. not seen
Is. 34:15 there sh. v. be gathered

W.

WAFER, S.
Ex. 16:31 the taste was like w.
29:2 w. unleav. anoint, with oil
23 w. out of basket, *Lev.* 8:26
Lev. 2:4 w. anointed with oil,
7:12; *Num.* 6:15
Num. 6:19 one w. on hands of N.

WAG.
Jer. 18:16 passeth sh. w. head
Lam. 2:15 w. heads at diss. of J.
Zep. 2:15 ev. one passeth sh. w.

WAGES.
Gen. 29:15 wh. shall thy w. be?
30:28 app. thy w. I will give it
31:7 changed my w. ten tim. 41
8 the speckled shall be thy w.
Ex. 2:9 child, I will gi. thee w.
Lev. 19:13 w. of hired not abide
Jer. 22:13 neigh.'s serv. with. w.
Ezek. 28:18 had no w. nor army
19 her spoil wh. be w. for army
Hag. 1:6 earn. w. to put into bag
Mal. 3:5 oppress hireling in w.
Luke 3:14 be cont. with your w.
John 4:36 that reapeth receiv. w.
Rom. 6:23 the w. of sin is death
2 *Cor.* 11:8 taking w. of them
2 *Pet.* 2:15 D. lov. w. of unright.

WAGGING.
Mat. 27:39 th. passed by reviled him, w. heads, *Mark* 15:29

WAGON, S.
Gen. 45:19 take w. out of Eg. 21
27 Jacob saw w. Jos. had sent
Num. 7:3 w. for two of princes
7 two w. 4 oxen to sons of G. 8
Ezek. 23:24 come ag. th. with w.

WAIL, ED.
Ezek. 32:18 w. for multit. of Eg.
Mic. 1:8 I will w. and howl
Mark 5:38 he seeth them th. w.
Rev. 1:7 kindr. of earth shall w.

WAILING.
Est. 4:3 whi. decree came was w.
Jer. 9:10 for mount. will I ta. w.
18 let them take up w. for us
19 a voice of w. heard out of Z.
20 teach your daughters w.
Ezek. 7:11 neither be w. for them

WAK

Ezek. 27:31 they sh. weep wi. w.
Amos 5:16 w. sh. be in all streets
17 in all vineyards shall be w.
Mic. 1:8 I will make w. like dra.
Mat. 13:42 w. and gna. teeth, 50
Rev. 18:15 merchants stand w. 19

WAIT, Noun.
Num. 35:20 if hurl by lay. of w.
22 cast on him with. laying w.
Jer. 9:8 in his heart he lay. his w.

WAIT, Verb.
Num. 8:10 Aa. and sons shall w. on priest's office, 8:24 ; 1 *Chr.* 23:28; 2 *Chr.* 5:11; 13:10
2 *K.* 6:33 sho. I w. for the L.?
Job 14:14 I will w. till change
17:13 if I w. grave is my house
Ps. 25:3 let none that w. 69:6
5 on thee do I w. all the day
21 preserve me, for I w. on th.
27:14 w. on the Lord, 37:34;
Prov. 20:22
37:7 w. patiently; 7 w. 29:9 will w.
9 that w. on Lord shall inherit
39:7 no. I for ; 62:5 w. on God
56:6 when they w. for my soul
59:9 bec. of strength will I w.
69:3 mine eyes fail while I w.
104:27 th. w. upon thee, 145:15
123:2 our eyes w. on the L. God
130:5 I w. for Lord, soul doth w.
Is. 8:17 I will w. on the Lord
30:18 L. w. to be grac. blessed are they that w. for him
40:31 th. w. on L. shall renew
42:4 isles shall w. 51:5; 2 *Chr.* 5:17
49:23 not asham. that w. for me
51:5 the isles shall w. upon me
59:9 we w. for light, but behold
60:9 the isles shall w. for me
Jer. 14:22 we will w. upon thee
Lam. 3:25 L. good to them th. w.
26 a man hope and quietly w.
Hos. 6:9 as troops of robbers w.
12:6 keep mercy and w. on God
Mic. 7:7 I will w. for God
Hab. 2:3 tarry, w. for it, it will
Zep. 3:8 m. upon me, saith Lord
Mark 3:9 small ship would w.
Luke 12:36 like men that w.
Acts 1:4 w. for promise of Father
Rom. 8:25 we with patience w.
12:7 let us w. on our ministeri.
1 *Cor.* 9:13 which w. at the altar
Gal. 5:5 we through the Sp. w.
1 *Thes.* 1:10 and to w. for his Son

See LAY, LAID, LYING.

WAITED.
Gen. 49:18 I ha. w. for thy salva.
2 *K.* 5:2 profit w. for thy salva. w.
2 *K.* 5:2 maid w. on Naa.'s wife
1 *Chr.* 6:32 they w. on office, 33
Neh. 12:44 priests and L. that w.
Job 6:19 companies of Sheba w.
15:22 he is w. for of the sword
29:21 to me men gave ear, w.
23 w. for me as for the rain
30:26 I w. for light, dark. came
32:4 Elihu w. till J. had spoken
Ps. 40:1 I w. patiently for Lord
106:13 they w. not for counsel
119:95 wicked have w. for me
Is. 25:9 our God, we w. for him
26:8 in way of judg. have we w.
33:2 be gracious, we w. for thee
Ezek. 19:5 saw that she had w.
Mic. 1:12 inhabit. of Maroth w.
Zec. 11:11 poor of flock that w.
Luke 1:21 peo. w. for Zacharias
Acts 10:7 Corn. called sol. th. w.
17:16 while P. w. his spirit was
Rom. 2:20 long-suffer. of G. w.

WAITETH.
Job 24:15 eye of the adulterer w.
Ps. 33:20 our soul w. for Lord
62:1 my soul w. upon G. 130:6
65:1 praise w. for thee, O God
Prov. 27:18 he that w. on master
Is. 64:4 prepared for him that w.
Dan. 12:12 blessed is he that w.
Mic. 5:7 as showers that w. not
Rom. 8:19 ev. for manifestation
Jam. 5:7 husbandman w. for fru.

WAITING.
Num. 8:25 fr. age of 50 cease w.
Prov. 8:34 w. at gates, w. posts
Luke 2:25 Simeon w. for consol.
John 5:3 w. for moving of water
Rom. 8:23 we earnestly. groan. w.
1 *Cor.* 1:7 w. for coming of our L.
1 *Thes.* 3:5 to patient w. for C.

WAKE, ED.
Ps. 139:18 when I w. I am still
Jer. 51:39 perp. sleep and not w.
Joel 3:9 w. up the mighty men

WAL

Zec. 4:1 angel came and w. me
1 *Thes.* 5:10 whether w. or sleep

WAKENED, ETH.
Is. 50:4 w. morning by morning, he w. mine ear to hear
Joel 3:12 let heathen be w. and
Zec. 4:1 as a man that is w.

WAKETH. ING.
Ps. 77:4 th. holdest mine eyes w.
127:1 watchman w. in vain
Cant. 5:2 I sleep but my hea. w.

WALK, Verb.
Gen. 21:40 L. before whom I w.
48:15 bef. wh. my fathers did w.
Ex. 16:4 whe. they w. in my law
18:20 way wherein th. must w.
21:19 if he w. abroad, that smote
Lev. 18:3 nor w. in ordin. 20:23
26:3 if ye w. in my statut. 1 *K.* 6:12; *Ezek.* 33:15; *Zec.* 3:7
12 I will w. am. you, be ye, O.
21 if w. contrary to me, 24, 27
24 I w. contrary to you, 28
Deut. 5:33 shall w. in ways of L.
13:4; 28:9; *Zech.* 3:7
8:19 if ye w. after other gods
23:19 I w. in imagina. of heart
Jos. 22:5 take heed w. in ways
Jud. 5:10 ye that w. by the way
1 *Sam.* 2:30 house sh. w. bef. me
35 wh. w. before mine anointed
8:5 thy sons w. not in thy ways
1 *K.* 3:14 if wilt w. to keep my comman. as Da. did w. 6:85;
9:4; 11:38; 2 *Chr.* 7:17
8:23 servants that w. before thee, 2 *Chr.* 6:14
36 teach them way wherein they should w. 2 *Chr.* 6:27
12:28 wicked w. on every side
28:4 though I so. thro' the val.
39:11 will w. in mine integrity
56:13 may w. before G. in light
82:5 they w. on in darkness
84:11 no good if. th. th. w. upr.
86:11 w. in light of countena.
89:15 sh. w. in light of countena.
101:2 will w. in my house
115:7 feet have they, but w. not
116:9 will w. before the Lord
119:3 do no iniquity, w. in ways
45 I will w. at liberty, I seek
138:7 I walk in midst of trouble
143:8 cause me to kn. way I sh. w.
Prov. 2:7 buckler to th. that w.
20 may. w. in way of good men
2:13 who leave paths up. to w.
4:12 when thou w. in thy steps
6 let us w. in light of the Lord
3:10 w. with stretched necks
8:11 not w. in way of this peo.
9:2 ha redeemed sh. w. there
40:31 that wait on L. shall w.
42:5 giv. spirit to them that w.
50:5 I would not w. in his ways
59:9 but we w. in darkness
18 Judah shall w. with Israel
65:4 said, We will not w. there.
7:6 if ye w. not after other gods
8:1 neigh. will w. wi. slanders
13:10 peo. which w. in imagina.
of heart, w. 16:12; 18:12
28:11 commit adult. w. in lies
42:3 G. may show whic. way
Ezek. 11:20 they w. in my statu.
Dan. 4:37 w. in pride he is able
Mic. 4:5 we will w. in his name
Nah. 2:11 then w. the bood
Hab. 3:19 make me to w. on high
Zec. 1:10 sent to w. to and fro
3:7 to w. am. these th. stand by
Mat. 15:31 saw the lame to w.
Luke 20:46 desire to w. in robes
Acts 3:12 made this man to w.
1:16 nations to w. th. in. ways
21:21 nor to w. after customs
1 *John* 2:6 to w. as he walked

WALKED.
Gen. 6:20 Enoch w. wi. God. 24
6:9 a just man, and w. with G.
Ex. 14:29 Is. w. upon dry land
Lev. 26:10 th. w. contrary to L.
Jos. 5:6 Is. w. 40 years in wild.
24:3 I w. father Abrah. through
1 *Sam.* 8:3 w. not in his ways
12:2 I am old, and have w.
17:39 David w. on, pul' it off
Jer. 18:15 to w. in paths
2804 not hearken to w.
31:9 cause th. to w. in strai. way
Mic. 6:16 for ye w. in counsel
Luke 1:6 w. in all com. blameless
John 7:1 Jesus w. in Galilee
11:54 no more w. am. the Jews
Acts 3:8 and w. with them to. L.
14:8 sat, never had w. 10
Rom. 4:12 w. in steps of faith
2 *Cor.* 10:2 think we w. ac. flesh
3 tho' we w. in flesh, not war

WAL

Gal. 6:16 as many as w. accord.
Eph. 2:10 we should w. in them
4:1 w. worthy of the vocation
17 ye w. not as other Gentiles
5:15 see ye w. circumspectly
Phil. 3:17 mark them which w.
18 many of wh. I told you
Col. 1:10 that ye mi. w. worthy of Lord, 1 *Thes.* 2:12
1 *Thes.* 4:12 ye may w. honestly
2 *Thes.* 3:11 which w. disorderly
2 *Pet.* 2:10 th. that w. after flesh
1 *John* 1:6 and w. in darkness
7 if w. in light as he in light
2 *John* 6 w. after his commandm.
3 *John* 4 children w. in the truth
Jude 18 mock. w. after their lus.
Rev. 3:4 they shall w. with me
9:20 cannot see, hear, nor w.
16:15 watch, lest he w. naked
21:24 nations w. in light of city

WALK, *imperatively.*
Gen. 13:17 ro. thru. land, *Jos.* 18:8
17:1 w. before me, be perfect
Ps. 48:12 w. about Z. go round
Prov. 1:15 w. not in way wi. th.
Ec. 11:9 w. in ways of thy heart
Is. 2:5 let us w. in hight of Lord
30:21 this is the way, w. in it
50:11 w. in light of your fire
Jer. 6:16 good way, w. therein
25 go not into fields, nor w. by
7:23 if. in ways I command, you
Ezek. 20:18 w. ye not in stat. of
Zec. 6:7 might w. to and fro
Mat. 9:5 say, Rise, and w. *Mark* 2:9; *Luke* 5:33; *John* 5:8, 11, 12; *Acts* 3:6
John 12:35 w. wh. ye have light
Rom. 13:13 let us w. honestly
1 *Cor.* 7:17 ev. one, so let him w.
Gal. 5:16 w. in the Spirit, 25
Eph. 5:2 w. in love, C. loved us
8 w. as children of light
Phil. 3:16 let us w. by same rule
Col. 2:6 received C. so w. in him
4:5 w. in wisdom toward them

To WALK.
Lev. 18:4 to w. in my ordinances
Deut. 8:6 to w. in his ways, 10:12;
11:22; 19:9; 26:17; 31:16;
2:3; 8:53; 2 *Chr.* 6:31
1 *K.* 2:4 take heed to w. in truth
8:61 to w. to statutes, *Ezek.* 36:27
16:31 to w. in sins of Jeroboam
2 *K.* 10:31 no need to w. in law
23:3 Josiah made a coven. to w. after the Lord, 2 *Chr.* 34:31
2 *Chr.* 6:16 to heed to w. in law
Neh. 5:9 not to w. in fear of G.?
10:23 an oath to w. in G.'s l w.
Ps. 78:10 refu. to w. in his law
Prov. 2:13 to w. in ways of dark.
6:28 know. to w. hot coals
Jer. 18:15 to w. in paths
26:4 not hearken to w.
31:9 cause th. to w. in strai. way
Mic. 6:8 to w. humbly with thy C.
Hab. 3:19 make me to w. on high
Zec. 1:10 sent to w. to and fro
3:7 to w. am. these th. stand by
Mat. 15:31 saw the lame to w.
Luke 20:46 desire to w. in robes
Acts 3:12 made this man to w.
1:16 nations to w. th. in. ways
21:21 nor to w. after customs
1 *John* 2:6 to w. as he walked

WALKED.
Gen. 5:22 Enoch w. wi. God, 24
6:9 a just man, and w. with G.
Ex. 14:29 Is. w. upon dry land
Lev. 26:10 th. w. contrary to L.
Jos. 5:6 Is. w. 40 years in wild.
24:3 I w. father Abrah. through
1 *Sam.* 8:3 w. not in his ways
12:2 I am old, and have w.
17:39 David w. on, pul' it off
2 *Chr.* 6:16; 7:17
11:33 not w. in my ways, *Ps.* 8:1
13:23 w. in way of Jerob.
31 Baasha w. in way of Jerob.
16:2; 2 *K.* 13:6; 17:22
2 *K.* 4:35 w. in house to and fro
in statutes of heath.
21:22 w. not in way of L. *Jer.* 12:13; 44:10; 23

WAL

2 K. 22:2 Josiah w. in ways of David, 2 Chr. 34:2
2 Chr. 11:17 w. in way of David
17:4 Jn. w. in G.'s commandm.
21:12 not w. in ways of Jehosh.
Job 23:3 I w. through darkness
31:7 if my heart w. after eyes
Ps. 55:14 we w. to house of God
81:13 w. in their own counsels
12 O th. I had w. in my ways
142:3 in way I w. th. laid snare
Is. 9:2 people th. w. in darkness
20:3 Isaiah w. naked for a sign
Jer. 2:5 they w. after vanity, 8
7:24 w. in couns. of heart, 11:8
8:2 after wh. th. w. 9:14; 16:11
Ezek. 16:47 not w. after th. ways
15:9 hath w. in my statutes, 17
23:31 w. in way of thy sister
23:14 hast w. in midst of stones
Amos 2.4 which t'eir fathers w.
Nah. 2:11 even the old lion w.
Zec. 1:11 we w. to and fro, 6:7
Mal. 3:14 what profit we w. mournfully?
Mark 16:12 J. appear. as they w.
John 6:66 disciples w. no more
11:54 Jesus w. no more openly
Acts 3:8 leap, stood and w. 14:10
14:8 cripple, who never had w.
2 Cor. 10:2 we w. accord. to flesh
12:18 w. we not in same spirit? w. we not in same steps?
Gal. 2:14 they w. not uprightly
Eph. 2:2 time past ye w. Col. 3:7
1 Pet. 4:3 we w. in lasciviousness

He WALKED.

1 K. 3:6 as he w. before thee
13:3 Abijam w. in all sins of his father, 2 K. 21:21
16:26 he w. in ways of Jeroboam
22:43 for he w. in all ways of Asa, 2 Chr. 20:32
2 K. 8:18 he w. in ways of kings of Is. 16:3; 2 Chr. 21:6; 28:2
27 he w. in way of kings, as did house of A. 2 Chr. 22:3, 5
2 Chr. 17:3 he w. in ways of Da.
Dan. 4:29 Nebuch. w. in palace
Hos. 5:11 he w. aft. commandm.
Mal. 2:6 he w. with me in peace
Mat. 14:29 Peter w. on the water
1 John 2:6 ought to walk as he w.

I have WALKED.

Lev. 26:41 I h. w. contr. to them
1 Sam. 12:2 I have w. before you
2 Sam. 7:6 I have w. in a tent
7 places wher. I h. w. with Is.
2 K. 20:3 how I h. w. befo. thee
Job 31:5 If I have w. with vanity
Ps. 26:1 for I h. w. in integrity
3 J h. w. in thy truth, Is. 38:3

WALKEDST.

John 21:18 w. whit. th. wouldest

WALKEST.

Deut. 6:7 talk wh. thou w. 11:19
1 K. 2:42 day thou w. abroad
Is. 43:2 when thou w. thro' fire
Acts 21:21 thou thyself w. orderly
Rom. 14:15 w. not charitably
3 John 3 even as thou w. in truth

WALKETH.

Gen. 24:65 wh. man w. in field?
Deut. 23:14 w. in midst of camp
1 Sam. 12:2 king w. before you
Job 18:8 and he w. on a snare
22:14 he w. in circuit of heaven
34:8 and w. with wicked men
Ps. 1:1 w. not in couns. of ungo.
15:2 he that w. uprightly shall
39:6 ev. man w. in a vain show
73:9 their tongue w. thro' earth
91:6 pestilence that w. in dark.
101:6 w. in perf. way serve me
104:3 w. upon wings of wind
128:1 bles. ev. one th. w. in ways
Prov. 6:12 w. with frow. mouth
10:9 w. uprigh. w. surely, 28:18
13:20 that w. with wise be wise
14:2 w. in upright. feareth L.
15:21 understand. w. uprightly
19:1 poor w. in integrity, 28:6
20:7 just man w. in his integr.
28:26 whoso w. wisely be deliv.
Ec. 2:14 but fool w. in darkness
10:3 he that is a fool w. by way
Is. 33:15 w. right. dw. on high
50:10 w. in dark. hath no light
65:2 which w. in way not good
Jer. 10:23 it w. not in man to direct his steps
23:17 w. after imagina. of heart
Ezek. 11:21 heart w. after del. th.
Mic. 2:7 to him that w. upright.
Mat. 12:43 spirit is gone out, w. thro' dry places, Luke 11:24
John 12:35 that w. in darkness

WAL

2 Thes. 2:6 brother w. disorderly
1 Pet. 5:8 devil w. about seeking
1 John 2:11 hate. bro. w. in dark.
Rev. 2:1 w. in midst of candlest.

WALKING.

Gen. 3:9 voice of L. w. in garden
Deut. 2:7 Lord knoweth thy w.
1 K. 3:3 Sol. loved L. w. as Dav.
16:19 Zimri w. in way of Jerob.
Job 1:7 fr. w. up and down, 2:2
31:26 beheld moon w. in bright.
Ec. 10:7 princes w. as servants
Is. 3:16 w. and mino. as they go
20:2 so, w. naked and barefoot
57:2 each w. in his uprightness
Jer. 6:23 revolters, w. with sland.
Dan. 3:25 men loose, w. in fire
Mic. 2:11 if a man w. in spirit
Mat. 14:25 Jesus went w. on sea
2 i saw him w. Mark 6:48
Mark 8:24 I see men as trees w.
Luke 1:6 w. in all commandm.
Acts 3:8 lame man w. leaping, 9
9:31 w. in the fear of the Lord
1 Cor. 4:2 not w. in craftiness
1 Pet. 2:1 w. after lusts, Jude 16
3 John 4 thy children w. in truth

WALL.

Gen. 40:6 they digged down a w.
22 whose branches ran over w.
Ex. 14:22 waters were a w. to
Lev. 14:37 If plague lower th. w.
Num. 22:24 w. on th. side, a w.
25 was crushed D.'s foot ag. w.
Jos. 2:15 Rah. dwelt on town-w.
6:5 w. of city shall fall flat, 20
1 Sam. 18:11 smi. D. to w. 19:10
25:22 king sat on seat by the w.
25:16 they were a w. by night
22 if I leave any th. pisseth ag. the w. 34; 1 K. 14:10; 16:11; 21:21; 2 K. 9:8
21:10 fastened Saul's body to w.
2 Sam. 11:20 they w. shoot fr. w.
21 fr. w. why went ye nigh w.?
20:15 the people battered the w.
21 head sh. he thrown over w.
22:30 I have leaped w. Ps. 18:29
1 K. 4:33 hyssop th. springs of w.
20:30 a w. fell on 27,000 men
21:23 dogs eat Jez. by w.
2 K. 3:27 for burnt-offering on w.
4:10 a little chamber on w.
6:26 king of Isr. pass. by on w.
9:33 Jezebel's blood was on w.
18:26 people on the w. Is. 36:11
23:8 Hezekiah turned his face to the w. Is. 38:2
2 Chr. 25:23 Joash brake down w.
32:19 Nebuchad. brake down w.
Ezr. 5:3 who com. to make a w.?
9:9 give us a w. in Ju. and Jer.
Neh. 1:3 w. of J. is broken down
2:15 I viewed w. 17 build w.
4:3 fox sh. break their stone w.
6 so built we w. all w. joined
15 w. returned all of us to w.
6:6 for wh. cause th. build. w.
15 w. was finished in month E.
12:27 dedication of w. of Jerus.
13:21 why lodge ye about w.? Ps. 62:3 a bowing w. shall ye be
Prov. 18:11 as high in h. conceit
24:31 stone w. was broken down
Cant. 2:9 belov. stand. behind w.
8:9 if she be a w. 10 I am a w.
Is. 9:13 day of L. on fenced w.
5:5 I will break down the w.
25:4 as a storm against the w.
30:13 as a breach in a high w.
59:10 grope for the w. like blind
Jer. 15:20 make thee a fenced w.
47:3 as a bird that w. from nest, so is a man that w.
Lam. 2:8 honey not him that w.
Jer. 2:20 under ev. green tree w.
40:5 none wi. gather him that w.
Ezek. 4:3 for w. of iron between
8:7 hole in w. 8 dig in w. 12:5
10 idols of Is. portrayed on w.
13:12 w. is full, 15; 22:20 ev. w.
15 accomplish my wrath on w.
41:5 measured w. of the house
43:8 setting w. betw. me and th.
Dan. 5:5 fingers wrote on the w.
9:25 street sh. be built, and w.
Hos. 2:6 I will make a w.
Joel 2:7 they shall climb the w.
9 they shall run upon the w.
Amos 1:7 I will send a fire on w.
10 w. of Tyrus; 14 w. of Rab.
5:19 leaned his hand on the w.
7:7 Lord stood upon a w. made
Nah. 2:5 shall make haste to w.
Hab. 2:11 stone sh. cry out of w.
Acts 9:25 let Saul down by the w. in a basket, 2 Cor. 11:33
23:3 G. sh. smite thee, whited w.

WAN

Eph. 2:14 Ch. ha. brok. down w.
Rev. 21:14 w. of city had 12 fou.
18 the w. of it was of Jasper
See BUILT.

WALLED.

Lev. 25:29 sell house in w. city
30 w. city shall be established
Num. 13:28 w. great, Deut. 1:28

WALLOW, ED.

2 Sam. 20:12 Amasa w. in blood
Jer. 6:26 gird with sackcloth, w.
25:34 w. yourselves in ashes
48:26 M. shall w. in his vomit
Ezek. 27:30 they sh. w. in ashes
Mark 9:20 he fell on ground, w.

WALLOWING.

2 Pet. 2:22 sow washed to w.

WALLS.

Lev. 14:37 If plague be in w. 39
25:31 the villages having no w.
Deut. 3:5 cit. fenced with high w.
28:52 till high w. come down
2 K. 25:4 men fled between 2 w.
10 Chaldees brake down the w. of Jerusalem, Jer. 52:8
Ezr. 4:13 if city to built, w. 16
5:8 finsh. ha w. work goeth fast
Neh. 4:7 w. of Jer. were made up
Job 24:11 make oil within th. w.
Ps. 51:18 build thy w. of Jerus.
55:10 they go about on w.
122:7 peace be within thy w.
Prov. 25:28 city broken, with. w.
Cant. 5:7 keepers of w. took veil
Is. 22:5 a day of break. down w.
25:12 thy w. sh. he bring down
26:1 salvati. will G. app. for w.
49:16 thy w. are contin. bef. me
60:5 within thy w. a place
60:10 strang. shall build thy w.
18 thou shalt call thy w. salva.
62:6 I have set watchman on w.
Jer. 1:15 set thrones ag. w. of J.
5:10 go upon her w. destroy
50:15 Bab.'s w. are down, 51:58
Ezek. 26:4 destroy w. Tyrus, 12
27:11 men of Arv. were upon w.
33:30 talking against thee by w.
38:11 all dwelling without w. or
Mic. 7:11 in day thy w. are built
Zec. 2:4 inhabit. towns with. w.
Heb. 11:30 w. of Jeri. fell down

WANDER.

Gen. 20:13 God caused me to w.
Num. 14:33 your chil. shall w. in wilderness 32:13; Ps. 107:40
Deut. 27:18 causeth blind to w.
Job 15:23 he casteth them to w.
38:41 ravens w. for lack of meat
Ps. 59:15 let them wand. f. up and down
119:10 let me not w. fr. comm.
Is. 47:15 they shall w. every one
Jer. 14:10 thus they loved to w.
48:12 wanderers th. cause to w.
Amos 8:12 shall f. fr. sea to sea

WANDERERS.

Jer. 48:12 I will send to him w.
Hos. 9:17 be w. am. the nations

WANDERED.

Gen. 22:14 Hagar w. in wildern.
Ps. 107:4 w. in wildern. Is. 16:3
Lam. 4:14 have w. as blind men
Ezek. 34:6 my sheep w. through
Amos 4:8 three cities w. to 1 city
Heb. 11:37 w. about in sheepsk.
38 they w. in deserts, in moun.

WANDEREST, ETH.

Job 15:23 he w. abroad for bread
Prov. 21:16 w. out of way
27:8 as a bird that w. from nest, so is a man that w.
Is. 16:3 bewray not him that w.
Jer. 2:20 under ev. green tree w.
40:5 none wi. gather him that w.

WANDERING.

Gen. 37:15 he was w. in the field
Prov. 26:2 w. as swallow by fly
Ec. 6:9 bet. sight of eyes th. w.
Is. 16:2 it shall be as a w. bird
1 Tim. 5:13 w. fr. house to house
Jude 13 w. stars to wh. is reser.

WANDERINGS.

Ps. 56:8 thou tellest my w. put

WANT, Substantive.

Deut. 28:48 serve thy ene. in w.
57 she shall eat them for w.
Jud. 18:10 where is no w. 19:19
Job 24:8 they embrace rock for w.
30:3 for w. they were solitary
31:19 seen any perish for w.
Ps. 34:9 no w. to them that fear
Prov. 6:11 w. as arm. man, 24:34
10:21 fools die for w. of wisdom

WAR

Prov. 13:23 destr. for w. of judg.
14:28 in w. of people is destruc.
21:5 that is hasty only to w.
22:16 giv. to rich eh. come to w.
Lam. 4:9 strlc. thro' w. of fruits
Amos 4:6 I have giv. w. of bread
Mark 12:44 of her w. cast in all
Luke 15:14 he began to be in w.
2 Cor. 8:14 abundance for th. w.
9:12 supplieth w. of the saints
Phil. 4:11 not that I speak of w.

WANTS.

Jud. 19:20 all thy w. lie on me
Phil. 2:25 Ep. ministered to w.

WANT, Verb.

Ps. 23:1 shepherd, I shall not w.
34:10 that seek Lord shall not w.
Prov. 13:25 belly of wicked sh. w.
Jer. 34:16 none shall w. her mate
33:17 D. not w. a man to sit
18 Lev. not w. 35:19 J. not w.
Ezek. 4:17 th. they may w. bread

WANTED.

Jer. 44:19 we have w. all things
John 2:3 w. wine, mother of Je.
2 Cor. 11:9 wh. I w. I was charg.

WANTETH.

Deut. 15:8 lend him in th. he w.
Prov. 9:4 th. w. understand. 16
10:19 in words there w. not sin
28:16 prince that w. understand.
Ec. 6:2 he w. noth. for his soul
Cant. 7:2 like goblet that w. not

WANTING.

2 K. 10:19 proph. of D. let none
be w. whoso be w. not live
Prov. 19:7 pursu. wi. wor. yet w.
Ec. 1:15 w. cannot be numbered
Dan. 5:27 weighed and found w.
Tit. 1:5 set in order the things w.
3:13 that noth. be w. unto them
Jam. 1:4 and entire, w. nothing

WANTON.

Is. 3:16 daught. walk wi. w. eyes
1 Tim. 5:11 wax w. ag. Christ
Jam. 5:5 have lived and been w.

WANTONNESS.

Rom. 13:13 not in chamb. and w.
2 Pet. 2:18 allure thro' much w.

WAR.

Ex. 1:10 when there is w. they
17:16 L. will have w. with Ama.
32:17 a noise of w. in the camp
Num. 1:3 all th. are able to go to w. 20:22; 26:2; Deut. 3:18
32:6 shall your breth. go to w.?
20 go before the Lord to w. 27
Deut. 4:34 G. assa. by w. to take
21:10 wh. thou goest forth to w.
Jos. 11:23 land rest. fr. w. 14:15
14:11 so is my strength for w.
Jud. 3:2 Is. might teach th. w.
5:8 then was w. in the gates
21:22 reserved not his wife in w.
1 Sam. 14:52 w. ag. Philist. 19:8
2 Sam. 3:1 w. bet. house of S. and
11:7 Da. demand. how w. prosp.
1 K. 2:5 shed the blood of w. put the blood of w.
11:30 w. bet. Re. and Jer. 13:6
13:7 w. bet. Abijam and Jerob.
16 w. bet. Asa and Baa-sha. 32
20:18 come for w. take th. alive
22:1 contin. 3 years without w.
2 K. 18:20 and strength for w.
1 Chr. 5:10 made w. with 11. 19
22 slain, bec. w. was of God
2 Chr. 15:19 no w. till 35th year
35:21 house wherewith I ha. w.
Job 5:20 in w. redeem fr. sword
10:17 changes and w. are ag.
38:23 reserved against day of w.
Ps. 27:3 tho' w. rise against me
55:21 but w. was in his heart
68:30 scatter peo. th. deli. in w.
120:7 wh. I speak th. are for w.
140:2 continual. are gath. for w.
Prov. 20:18 with advice make w.
24:6 by counsel th. sh. make w.
Ec. 3:8 time of w. time of peace
8:8 th. is no discharge in th. w.
Is. 2:4 nor learn w. Mic. 4:3
21:15 mighty shall fall in the w.
Jer. 4:10 hast heard alarm of w.
6:4 prepare ye w. against her
23 as men for w. against thee
21:2 Nebuch. maketh w. ag. us
42:14 where we shall see no w.
48:14 are mighty men for w.?
Ezek. 17:17 nor Phar. make in w.

CRUDEN'S CONCORDANCE. 1073

WAR
Dan. 7:21 made w. with saints
9:26 to end of w. are desolation
Joel 3:9 prepare w. wake up men
Mic. 2:8 as men averse from w.
3:5 even prepare w. against him
Luke 14:31 king going to ma. w.
Rev. 11:7 beast made w. ag. th.
12:7 w. in heaven ag. dragon
17 make w. with rem. of seed
13:4 able to make w. wi. beast?
7 to make w. wi. saints, 17:14
19:11 in righteousness make w.
19 kings gathered to make w.
See EXPERT, MAN, MEN.

Weapons of WAR.
Deut. 1:41 ye girded on w. of w.
Jud. 18:11 600 wi. w. of. 16, 17
2 Sam. 1:27 how are w. of w. per.
Jer. 21:4 turn back w. of w.
51:20 battle-axe and w. of w.
Ezek. 32:27 do. to hell wi. w. of w.

WAR, Verb.
2 Sam. 22:35 Lord teacheth my
  hands to w. Ps. 18:34; 144:1
2 K. 16:5 to w. against it, Is. 7:1
2 Chr. 6:34 if peo. w. ag. enemy
Is. 41:12 w. ag. thee be as noth.
2 Cor. 10:3 do not w. after flesh
1 Tim. 1:18 mightest w. a warf.
Jam. 4:1 lusts that w. in memb.
2 fight and w. yet ye have not
1 Pet. 2:11 lusts wh. w. ag. soul

WARRED, ETH.
Num. 31:7 w. against Midianites
Jos. 24:9 Balak w. against Israel
1 K. 14:19 how he w. and reigned
22:45 Jehoash, how he w. writ.
2 K. 6:8 king of Syria w. ag. Is.
2 Chr. 26:6 Uzziah w. ag. Philist.
2 Tim. 2:4 w. entangl. himself

WARRING.
2 K. 19:8 w. ag. Libnah, Is. 37:8
Rom. 7:23 a law in my memb. w.

WARRIOR, S.
1 K. 12:21 who were w. 2 Ch. 11:1
Is. 9:5 battle of w. is with noise

WARS.
Num. 21:14 in book of w. of Lord
Jud. 3:1 not known w. of Canaan
1 Chr. 22:8 great w. sh. not build
2 Chr. 16:9 hencef. shalt have w.
Ps. 46:9 he maketh w. to cease
Mat. 24:6 hear of w. and rumors
  of w. Mark 13:7; Luke 21:9
Jam. 4:1 from whence come w.?

WARD.
Gen. 40:3 put in w. 4, 7; 41:10
42:7 Joseph put brethren in w.
Lev. 24:12 put blasphemer in w.
Num. 15:34 gath. of sticks in w.
2 Sam. 2:8 on concubin. in w.
1 Chr. 12:29 had kept so. of Saul
23:8 cast lots, w. against w.
25:8 cast lots, w. against w.
Neh. 12:24 thanks w. against w.
25 porters keep. w. at gates, 45
Is. 21:8 I am set in my w.
Jer. 37:13 capt. of w. w. there
Ezek. 19:9 they put Zedek. in w.
Acts 12:10 first and second w.

WARDS.
1 Chr. 9:23 house of taber. by w.
26:12 hav. w. one ag. another
Neh. 13:30 appoint. w. of priests

WARDROBE.
2 K. 22:14 Shallum the keeper
  of the w. 2 Chr. 34:22

WARE.
Luke 8:27 man w. no clothes

WARE.
Acts 14:6 w. of it, fled to Lys.
2 Tim. 4:15 of coppersmith be w.

WARE, S.
Neh. 10:31 if peo. bri. w. on sab.
13:16 men of Tyre brought w.
20 merchants and sellers of w.
Jer. 10:17 gath. up w. out of land
Ezek. 27:16 by reas. of w. 18, 33
Jon. 1:5 mariners cast forth w.

WARFARE.
1 Sam. 28:1 gath. armies for w.
Is. 40:2 her w. is accomplished
1 Chr. 9:7 goeth a w. any time
2 Cor. 10:4 weap. of w. not carnal
1 Tim. 1:18 might. war a good w.

WARM.
2 K. 4:31 flesh of child waxed w.
Job 6:17 th. wax w. they vanish
37:17 how garm. are w. when
Ec. 4:11 how can one be w.?
Is. 44:15 take ther. and w. hims.

WAS
Is. 47:14 sh. not be a coal to w.
Hag. 1:6 but there is none w.

WARMED, ETH, ING.
Job 31:20 were not w. wi. fleece
39:14 ostrich w. eggs in dust
Mark 14:54 w. himself, and saith
14:67 and Pet. w. himself,
John 18:18, 25
67 when she saw P. w. himself
Jam. 2:16 depart in peace, be w.

WARN.
2 Chr. 19:10 sh. w. they tresp. not
Ezek. 3:18 to w. the wicked, 33:8
19 yet if thou w. wicked, 33:9
21 w. righteous; 33:3 w. peo. 7
1 Cor. 4:14 beloved sons I w. you
1 Thes. 5:14 w. that are unruly

WARNED.
2 K. 6:10 man of God w. him
Ps. 19:11 by them is servant w.
Ezek. 3:21 live, because he is w.
33:6 and the people be not w.
Mat. 2:12 Joseph being w. of G.
3:7 O generation of vipers, who
  hath w. you? Luke 3:7
Acts 10:22 Cornelius w. from G.
Heb. 11:7 Noah w. prepared ark

WARNING.
Jer. 6:10 to whom sh. I give to. ?
Ezek. 3:17 and give them w.
18 thou givest him not w. 20
33:4 tak. not w. 5 took not w.
Col. 1:28 w. every man, teaching

WARP.
Lev. 13:48 pla. in w. 49, 51, 57, 59
53 burn w. 53 rend w. 58 wash.

WAS.
Gen. 5:24 walked with G. w. not
Rev. 1:1 is and which w. 8; 4:8
17:8 beast th. saw. w. is not, 11

It WAS.
Ex. 16:15 wist not what it w.
Is. 48:16 his it w. 19 thus it w.
Ezek. 16:15 his it w. 19 thus it w.
Gen. 18:4 w. y. feet, 19:2; 24:32
Ex. 2:5 daught. of P. came to w.
30:19 Aa. w. 30:19, 21; 40:12
Lev. 6:27 shalt w. that whereon
13:54 w. thi. wherein plague is
14:8 w. himself, Deut. 23:11
9 w. his flesh in water, 15:16;
  16:1, 21; 22:6
17:15 if he w. not sh. bear iniq.
Deut. 21:6 w. hands over heifer
Ruth 3:3 w. thyself, and anoint
1 Sam. 25:41 servant to w. feet
2 Sam. 2:14 men of war were w.
2 K. 5:10 go w. in Jordan 7 times
12 may I not w. and be clean?
13 saith to thee, w. be clean?
2 Chr. 4:6 lavers to w. in, sea for
Job 9:30 if I w. myself wi. water
Ps. 26:6 I will w. my hands in
51:2 w. me from mine iniquity
7 w. me and I sh. be whiter th.
58:10 w. feet in blood of wicked
Is. 1:16 w. ye, make you clean
Jer. 2:22 tho' thou w. with nitre
4:14 w. thy heart from wickedn.
Ezek. 23:40 thou didst w. thyself
Mat. 6:17 when fastest, w. face
15:2 they w. not, when they eat
Mark 7:3 exc. they w. eat not, 4
Luke 7:38 began to w. his feet
John 9:7 in pool of Siloam, 11
13:5 began to w. disciples' feet
6 Lord, dost thou w. my feet?
8 never w. my feet, if I w. not
10 ought to w. one anoth. feet
Acts 22:16 and w. away thy sins
See CLOTHES, FEET.

WASHED.
Gen. 43:24 water, they w. feet
31 Joseph w. face and went out
49:11 Ju. w. garments in wine
Ex. 40:32 in. all w. commanded
Lev. 13:55 plague aft. it is w. 58
14:47 he that lay in house w.
15:11 whomsoever toucheth w.
2 Sam. 12:20 David arose and w.
1 K. 22:38 one w. chariot in pool
Job 29:6 I w. steps with butter
Ps. 73:13 I w. hands in innocen.
Prov. 30:12 not w. fr. filthiness
Cant. 5:3 I have w. my feet
12 his eyes are w. with milk.
Is. 4:4 away filth of daughters
Ezek. 16:4 nor wast w. in water
9 I thorou. w. away thy blood
Mat. 27:24 Pilate w. his hands
Luke 7:44 she hath w. my feet
11:38 marvelled he had not w.
John 9:7 he went and w. 11, 15

WAT
John 13:10 is w. need. not save to
  14 Master have w. your feet
Acts 9:37 wh. when they had w.
  16:33 he took them, w. stripes
1 Cor. 6:11 ye are w. sanctified
1 Tim. 5:10 if she w. saints' feet
Heb. 10:22 having our bodies w.
2 Pet. 2:22 sow w. to wallowing
Rev. 1:5 that w. us fr. our sins
7:14 have w. their robes white
See CLOTHES.

WASHEST, ING.
2 Sam. 11:2 Da. saw a woman w.
Job 14:19 w. away thi. wh. grow
Luke 5:2 fishermen were w. nets

WASHING, S.
Lev. 13:56 plague dark after w.
Neh. 4:23 ev. one put off for w.
Cant. 4:2 sheep came fr. w. 6:6
Mark 7:4 w. of cups and tables, 8
Eph. 5:26 cleanse wi. w. of wat.
Tit. 3:5 saved us by w. of regen.
Heb. 9:10 stood in meats and w.

WASHPOT.
Ps. 60:8 Moab is my w. 108:9

WAST.
Ob. 11 thou w. as one of them
Rev. 11:17 who art, and w. art

WASTE, Substantive.
Jer. 49:13 Bozrah shall bec. a w.
Mat. 26:8 to what purpose is this
  w. ? Mark 14:4

WASTE, Adjective.
Deut. 32:10 found him in w. wi.
Job 30:3 fleeing into the w. wil.
38:27 to satisfy desol. w. ground
Is. 24:1 Lord maketh earth w.
42:15 I will make w. mountains
13:17 that made w. sh. go forth
Jer. 2:15 lions made his land w.
46:19 Noph shall be w. and des.
Ezek. 5:14 I will makest Jerusal. w.
29:9 Eg. shall be w. 10; 30:12
38:8 mountains been always w.
Nah. 2:10 Ninev. is void and w.
Zep. 3:6 I have made streets w.
Mal. 1:9 because my house is w.
See CITIES, LAY, LAID, PLACES.

WASTE, Verb.
1 K. 17:14 barrel of meal not w.
1 Chr. 17:9 no childr. of wick. w.
Ps. 80:13 boar of wood doth w.
Jer. 50:21 w. inhabitants of Pek.
Mic. 5:6 they sh. w. land of Assy.

WASTED.
Num. 14:33 till carcasses be w.
24:22 the Kenite shall be w.
Deut. 2:14 men of war were w.
1 K. 17:16 barrel of meal w. not
1 Chr. 20:1 J. w. country of Am.
Ps. 137:3 that w. required mirth
Is. 6:11 till cities be w. without
19:5 river sh. be w. dried up
60:12 nations sh. be utterly w.
Jer. 44:6 are w. and desolate as
Joel 1:10 field is w. corn is w.
Luke 15:13 prodig. w. substance
16:1 accused that he w. goods
Gal. 1:13 persecu. church and w.

WASTENESS.
Zep. 1:15 day of w. desolation

WASTETH.
Prov. 18:9 brother to a great w.
Is. 51:16 created w. to destroy

WASTES.
Is. 61:4 they shall build old w.
49:19 Boz. sh. be perpet. w.
Ezek. 33:24 that inhab. w. of Is.
27 they in the w. shall fall
36:4 thus saith L. to desolate w.
10 the w. shall be builded, 33

WASTETH.
Job 14:10 man dieth, w. away
Ps. 91:6 nor destruction that w.
Prov. 19:26 he that w. father

WASTING.
Is. 59:7 w. and destruction not in
60:18 not heard w. nor destruc.

WATCH, Substantive.
Ex. 14:24 in morn. w. L. looked
Jud. 7:19 middle w. had set w.
1 Sam. 11:11 S. came in morn. w.
Job 7:12 am I a sea, that set. w.?
Ps. 63:4 a thous. years as a w.
119:148 prevent night w. eyes
141:3 set, O L. w. before my mouth
Jer. 51:12 make w. strong
Hab. 2:1 I will stand upon w.
Mat. 14:25 fourth w. of ni. Jesus
24:43 what w. thief wo. come
27:65 ye have a w. go your way
66 seal. stone and setting a w.
28:11 some of w. came into ci.
Luke 2:8 shepherds keeping w.
12:38 if he come in second w.

WATCHES.
Neh. 12:9 over against th. in w.
Ps. 63:6 when I meditate in w.
119:148 mine eyes prev. night w.
Lam. 2:19 in beginning of the w.

WATCH, Verb.
Gen. 31:49 Lord w. between me
1 Sam. 19:11 Saul sent to w. Da.
Ezr. 8:29 w. ye, keep vessels till
Job 14:16 not w. over my sin?
Ps. 102:7 I w. am as sparrow
130:6 more than they that w.
Is. 21:5 no. lie in the watch-tower
29:20 all that w. for iniquity
Jer. 5:6 a leop. sh. w. over cities
31:28 so will I w. over them
44:27 I will w. over them
Nah. 2:1 keep munit. w. way
Hab. 2:1 I will w. to see what he
Mat. 24:42 w. therefore, 25:13;
  Mark 13:35; Luke 21:36;
Acts 20:31
26:38 Jesus said, w. with me
40 could ye not w. ? Mark
  14:34, 37
41 w. and pray, Mark 13:33;
  14:38; Col. 4:2
13:34 command. porter to
  w. 37 I say unto all, w.
1 Cor. 16:13 w. stand in faith
2 Tim. 4:5 w. th. in all things
Heb. 13:17 th. w. for your souls

WATCHED.
Jer. 20:10 familiars w. for halt.
31:28 as I have w. over them
Lam. 4:17 w. for a nation that
Dan. 9:14 Lord w. upon the evil
Mat. 24:43 man of house would
have w. Luke 12:39
27:36 sitting down they w. him
Mark 3:2 w. whether he would
heal on sab. Luke 6:7; 14:1
Luke 20:20 lie. w. and sent spies
Acts 9:24 w. gates day and night

WATCHER, S.
Jer. 4:16 publishers w. for halt.
Dan. 4:13 w. and holy one came
17 degree of w. 23 king saw w.

WATCHETH.
Ps. 37:32 wicked w. righteous
Ezek. 7:6 it w. for th. it is come
Rev. 16:15 blessed is he that w.

WATCHFUL.
Rev. 3:2 be w. strengthen things

WATCHING, S.
1 Sam. 4:13 E. sat by way-si. w.
Prov. 8:34 heareth me, w. daily
Lam. 4:17 in w. we w. a nation
Mat. 27:54 centurion w. Jesus
Luke 12:37 L. when com. find w.
2 Cor. 6:5 in labors, in w. in fast.
11:27 w. often, in hunger, thirst
Eph. 6:18 w. with perseverance

WATCHMAN.
2 Sam. 18:25 w. cried, told king
25 w. saw anoth. man running
2 K. 9:18 w. told, cometh not, 20
Ps. 127:1 w. waketh but in vain
Is. 21:11 w. what of the
  night ?
Jer. 51:12 set ye the w. prepare
Ezek. 3:17 son of ma. a w. 33:7
33:2 if w. see him up for th. w.
6 if w. see him up for th. w.
Hos. 9:8 w. of Eph. was with G.

WATCHMEN.
Cant. 3:3 w. go about city, 5:7
Is. 52:8 thy w. shall lift voice
56:10 his w. are blind, ignorant
62:6 I have set w. on thy walls
Jer. 6:17 set w. over you, say.
31:6 a day w. on mount Ephr.
Mic. 7:4 day of w. is cometh

WATCH-TOWER.
2 Chr. 20:24 Ju. came toward w.
Is. 21:5 watch in w. eat, drink
8 I stand continually on the w.

WATER, Substantive.
Gen. 16:7 ang. found her w.
21:14 Abra. took a bot le of w.
21:25 Zalem gave the man w.
24:13 I stand by a well of w.
17 give me to drink
32 camels, w. to wash his feet
43:24 I unstable as w. sh. not excel
49:12 our wonder with w.
Ex. 12:9 nor sodden with w.
17:6 ball come w. out of rock

CRUDEN'S CONCORDANCE. 1075

WAY

Luke 12:23 hags wh. *w.* not old
1 *Tim.* 5:11 be;un to *w.* wanton
2 *Tim.* 3:13 seduce. sh. *w.* worse

WAXED.
Gen. 26:13 Isaac *w.* great
41:56 famine *w.* sore in Egypt
Ex. 1:7 Israel *w.* mighty, 20
19:21 when sun *w.* hot
32:19 Moses' anger *w.* hot
Num. 11:23 L.'s hand *w.* short ?
Deut. 8:4 their raiment *w.* not old, 29:5 ; *Neh.* 9:21
32:15 Jeshur. *w.* fat and kicked
Jos. 23:1 Joshua *w.* old, stricken
1 *Sam.* 3:2 had child. is *w.* feeble
2 *Sam.* 3:1 but Dav. *w.* stronger,
1 *Chr.* 11:9
21:15 David fought, *w.* faint
2 *K.* 4:34 flesh of child *w.* warm
2 *Chr.* 13:21 Abijah *w.* mighty
17:12 Jehoshaphat *w.* great
24:15 Jehoi. *w.* old full of days
Est. 9:4 Mordecai *w.* greater
Ps. 32:3 silence my bones *w.* old
Jer. 49:24 Damascus *w.* feeble
50:43 king of Baby.'s hands *w.*
Dan. 8:8 he-goat *w.* very great
9 lit. horn *w.* exceed. great, 10
Mat. 13:15 this people's heart *w.* gross, *Acts* 28:27
Luke 1:80 child *w.* strong, 2:40
13:19 mustard seed *w.* great tree
Acts 13:46 P. and Barn. *w.* bold
Heb. 11:34 *w.* valiant in fight
Rev. 18:3 merchants *w.* rich

WAXEN, WAXED.
Gen. 18:12 after I am *w.* old
19:13 cry of Sod. was *w.* great
Lev. 25:35 bro. be *w.* poor, 33, 39
Deut. 31:20 *w.* fat, turn to other
Jos. 17:13 child. of Is. *w.* strong
Jer. 5:27 hec. great and *w.* rich
28 they are *w.* fat, they shine
Ezek. 16:7 increased and *w.* great

WAXETH, ING.
Ps. 6:7 mine eye *w.* old because
Heb. 8:13 *w.* old, ready to vanish
Phil. 1:14 brethren *w.* confident

WAY.
Gen. 24:42 if thou prosper my *w.*
Ex. 13:17 through *w.* of Philist.
18 led people thro' *w.* of wild.
21 pillar of cloud to lead the *w.*
18:20 thou shalt show them the *w. Neh.* 9:19 ; *Ps.* 107:4
Num. 21:4 discouraged bec. of *w.*
22:26 there was no *w.* to turn
Deut. 1:22 by what *w. Jos.* 3:4
8:2 remember *w.* Lord led you
11:24 if *w.* be too long for thee
17:16 return no more that *w.*
19:3 prepare a *w.* G *w.* is long
28:25 shalt go out one *w.* ag. th.
31:29 turn from *w.* I command
Jos. 23:14 I am going *w.* of earth
24:17 present. us in *w.* we went
Jud. 2:19 ceased not fr. their *w.*
9:25 they rob. all came that *w.*
18:5 whether *w.* be prosperous
6 Lord is your *w.* wher. ye go
19:9 to-morrow get on your *w.*
1 *Sam.* 9:6 he can show us our *w.*
8 man of God to tell us *w.*
12:23 I will teach you good *w.*
15:20 have gone *w.* L. sent me
2 *Sam.* 19:36 go little *w.* over J.
1 *K.* 2:2 I will go *w.* of all earth
8:36 teach th. good way to walk
13:9 turn ag. by *w.* thou camest
10 another *w.* 12 what *w. w.*
19:4 Ahab went one *w.* Obadi.
22:21 which *w.* went Spirit of Lord ? 2 *Chr.* 18:23
2 *K.* 3:8 which *w.* shall we go?
5:19 departed fr. him a little *w.*
2 *Chr.* 6:27 taught them good *w.*
Ezr. 8:21 seek of him *w.* for us
Job 3:23 a man whose *w.* is hid
12:24 wander in a wilderness wh. there is no *w. Ps.* 107:40
16:22 go *w.* whence not return
22:15 hast thou marked old *w.*
23:10 he knoweth *w.* that I take
28:23 G. understandeth *w.* thereof
38:19 wh. is *w.* light dwell h ?
Ps. 1:6 L. knoweth *w.* of righteo
2:12 kiss Son, lest perish fr. *w.*
36:4 set. himself in *w.* not good
78:50 he made a *w.* to his anger
101:2 behave wisely in perf. *w.*
119:27 underst. *w.* of precepts
29 remove from me *w.* of lying
30 I have chosen *w.* of truth
32 I will run *w.* of thy comma.
33 teach me *w.* of statu. 143:8
104 I hate every false *w.* 128

WAY

Ps. 139:24 if there be wicked *w.*
146:9 *w.* of the wicked he turns
Prov. 2:8 preserveth *w.* of saints
12 deliv. thee fr. *w.* of evil man
4:19 *w.* of wicked is as darkness
6:23 *w.* of life, 15:24 ; *Jer.* 21:8
7:8 he went the *w.* to her house
27 her house is the *w.* to hell
12:15 *w.* of fool rig. in own eyes
26 *w.* of wick. seduceth them
13:15 *w.* of transgressors hard
14:12 *w.* whi. seem. right, 16:25
15:9 *w.* of wicked is abominati.
10 griev. to him th. forsak. *w.*
19 *w.* of slothf. man is a hedge
16:29 lead, him into *w.* not good
21:8 *w.* of man is froward and
16 *w.* of eagle, of serpent
30 such *w.* of adulterous wom.
Ec. 11:5 knowest not *w.* of Spirit
Is. 3:12 to err and destroy tho *w.*
26:7 *w.* of just is uprightness
35:8 a *w.* called *w.* of holiness
40:14 who show. *w.* of unders. ?
48:15 L. mak, a *w.* in sea, 51:10
19 I will make *w.* in wildern.
48:11 make my mountains a *w.*
57:14 prepare *w.* 62:10 high *w.*
59:8 *w.* of peace they know not,
Rom. 3:17
Jer. 9:16 whore is the good *w.*
10 *w.* of man is not in himself
12:1 doth *w.* of wicked prosp. ?
18:15 paths, in a *w.* not cast up
32:39 give th. one heart, one *w.*
50:5 thy G. may show us *w.*
Lam. 3:9 my paths hath she *w.* to 2
23:13 I saw th. both took one *w.*
43:2 glory came from *w.* of east
Amos 2:7 turn aside *w.* the meek
8:14 thy G. may show us *w.*
Mic. 2:13 breaker is come before me
Mal. 7:13 broad is *w.* to destruc.
14 narrow is *w.* lead, unto life
8:28 no man mi. pass by that *w.*
10:5 go not into *w.* of Gentiles
22:16 teach. *w.* of God in truth,
Mark 12:14 ; *Luke* 20:21
Luke 5:19 by what *w.* bring him
10:31 there came a priest th. *w.*
15:30 wh. he was a great *w.* off
19:4 Z. to see him, pass that *w.*
John 14:5 know; G I am the *w.*
14:4 *w.* ye know ; G I am the *w.*
5 Lord, how can we know *w.* ?
Acts 16:17 shew us *w.* of salvati.
18:26 expound. to him *w.* of G.
19:9 but spake evil of that *w.*
23 arose no small stir about *w.*
21:14 after *w.* they call heresy
Rom. 14:13 to fall in brother's *w.*
1 *Cor.* 10:13 make a *w.* to escape
12:31 a more excellent *w.*
1 *Thes.* 3:11 L. Je. direct our *w.*
Heb. 9:8 the *w.* into the holiest
10:20 living *w.* he consecrated
Jam. 2:25 sent them out ano. *w.*
2 *Pet.* 2:2 *w.* of truth evil spo. of
15 have forsaken right *w.* and are following *w.* of Balaam
21 not known *w.* of righteous.
Rev. 16:12 *w.* of kings be prepar.
By the WAY.
Gen. 42:38 if mischi. befall by t. *w.*
45:24 fall not out by the *w.*
Num. 14:25 by t. *w.* of Red sea,
21:4 ; *Deut.* 1:2, 40 ; 2:1
21:22 we will go by t. *w. Sam.* 15:2
28:68 L. sh. bring thee by t. *w.*
Jos. 5:7 not circum. them by t. *w.*
1 *K.* 13:9 not turn ag. by t. *w.* 17
20:36 prophet waited by the *w.*
Ezr. 8:22 ash. to require by the *w.*
19:24 I will turn th. back by the *w.* thou camest, *Is.* 37:29, 34
Ezr. 8:31 lay in wait by the *w.*
Job 21:29 not only, by the *w.*
Ps. 110:1 th. who pass by the *w.*
85:41 that pass by the *w.* spoil
Is. 10:9 fools walk by the *w.*
42:16 bring blind by the *w.*
48:17 God leadeth thee by *t. w.*
Jer. 3:17 he led thee by the *w.*
6:25 walk not by *t. w.* for sword
Ezek. 43:4 glory of L. came by *w.*
41:3 shall enter by *t. w.* 46:3, 8
46:9 he that entereth by the *w.*
Hos. 13:7 as a leopard by the *w.*
Mark 8:3 they faint by the *w.*
9:31 that ye disputed by *w.* ? 34
Luke 12:52 talked wi. us by *t. w.*
1 *Cor.* 16:7 not see you by the *w.*
Every WAY.
Ps. 119:101 refrain fr, e, evil *w.*

WAY.

Ps. 119:104 I hate e, false *w.* 128
Ezek. 16:25 thou hast built thy *w.*
Eccl. 12:5 every *w.* of man right
Ezek. 16:31 build. place in e. *w.*
Rom. 3:2 much e. to. bec. to th.
Phil. 1:18 e *w.* whe. in pretence
See EVIL.

His WAY.
Gen. 6:12 flesh had corrup. *h. w.*
2 *Sam.* 22:31 as for God, *his w.* is perfect, *Ps.* 18:30
1 *K.* 8:32 to bring *his w.* on his own head, 2 *Chr.* 6:23
Job 8:19 this is the joy of *his w.*
17:9 righteo. shall hold on *his w.*
21:31 wh. shall declare *his w.* ?
23:11 *his w.* have I kept
36:23 who enjoined him *his w.* ?
Ps. 25:9 meek will he teach *h. w.*
37:7 him who prosper. in *his w.*
23 and he delighteth in *his w.*
34 wait on L. and keep *his w.*
119:9 wh. young man clea. *h. w.*
Prov. 8:22 in be-ginning of *h. w.*
11:5 righ. of perfect direct *h. w.*
14:8 prudent is to unders. *h. w.*
16:9 a man's heart devis. *his w.*
17 that keepeth *his w.* preser.
19:3 foolish, of man perv. *h. w.*
20:14 when he is upon *his w.*
21:29 upright, directeth *his w.*
Is. 43:16 make *his w.* prospero.
55:7 let wicked forsake *his w.*
Jer. 4:7 destroyer of G. on *h. w.*
Ezek. 3:18 warn wicked fr. *h. w.*
19 turn not from *h. w.* 33:8, 9
13:22 sho. not return fr. *his w.*
Nah. 1:3 L. hath *h. w.* in whirlw.
Jam. 1:24 beholdeth, goeth *h. w.*
In the WAY.
Gen. 24:27 I being in *the w.*
45 who led me *in the w.*
35:3 L. was with me *in the w.*
Ex. 5:20 M. and A. stood *in t. w.*
23:20 to keep thee *in the w.*
Deut. 1:33 who went *in the w.*
1 *K.* 11:29 Ahijah found J. *in t. w.*
22:43 walked *in the w.* of Asa, 22:52
18:7 as Obadiah was *in the w.*
Ezr. 8:18 he walked *in the w.* of the kings of Israel, 16:3 ;
2 *Chr.* 21:6, 13
27 he walked *in the w.* of Aha.
2 *Chr.* 17:17 three years *in t. w.*
20:32 he walked *in the w.* of A.
Ezr. 8:22 the enemy *in the w.*
Job 3:14 to give th. light *in w.*
16 depart. not to tread *in t. w.*
Job 18:10 snare and trap *in t. w.*
Ps. 1:1 nor standeth *in the w.*
25:8 teach sinners *in the w.*
12 shall he teach *in the w.* 32:8
85:13 set. us *in the w.* of steps
102:23 weak, strength *in the w.*
110:7 drink of brook *in the w.*
110:1 bless. are undefiled *in t. w.*
14 I have rejoiced *in the w.* of
Prov. 1:15 walk not thou *in t. w.*
2:20 thou mayest walk *in t. w.*
4:11 I ha. taught thee *in the w.*
14 go not *in t. w.* of evil men
8:20 I lead *in t. w.* of righteous.
9:6 go *in the w.* of understand.
10:17 he is *in the w.* of life
12:28 *in the w.* of righteousness
13:6 him that is upright *in t. w.*
16:31 if it be found *in the w.*
22:5 thorns and snares *in the w.*
6 train up a child *in the w.*
23:19 guide thy heart *in the w.*
Ec. 12:5 afraid, and *in the w.* of
Is. 8:11 not walk *in the w.* of peo.
26:8 *in the w.* of thy judgments
57:17 went on *in the w.* of heart
Jer. 2:18 wh. to do *in t. w.* of E. ?
what to do *in t. w.* of Assy. ?
Ezek. 23:31 walk. *in t. w.* of sis.
Hos. 6:9 priests murder *in the w.*
Mal. 2:8 ye have caused to stumb.
Mat. 5:25 agree whil. art *in the w.*
21:32 J. came *in the w.* of right.
Mark 8:3 if worn. garments *in t. w.*
Mat. 11:10 prepare *t. w.* before thee, *Mark* 1:2 ; *Luke* 7:27
Luke 1:79 guide our feet *in t. w.*
12:58 as thou art *in the w.* give
Acts 9:17 J. that appeared *in w.*
27 he had seen the Lord *in w.*
Jude 11 have gone *in the w.* of C.
See LORD.
My WAY.
Gen. 24:56 Lord prospered *my w.*

WAY

2 *Sam.* 22:33 maketh *my w.* perfect, *Ps.* 19:32
Job 19:8 fenced *my w.* that I can
Is. 40:27 s:yest *my w.* is hid ?
Ezek. 1:25 is not *my w.* equal ?
John 8:21 I go *my w.* ye sh. seek
Rom. 15:21 bright on *my w.*
2 *Cor.* 1:16 be brought on *my w.*
Out of the WAY.
Ex. 22:8 turned aside *o. of the w.*
Deut. 9:12, 17 ; *Jud.* 2:17
Deut. 11:28 if ye turn *o. of the w.*
12:5 thrust thee *out of the w.*
27:18 blind wander *out of the w.*
Job 24:4 turn needy *out of the w.*
21 they are taken *out of the w.*
31:7 if my step turned *o. of t. w.*
Prov. 21:16 wand. *out of the w.*
28:10 causeth righteo. go *o. of w.*
Is. 28:7 thro' drink erred *o. of w.*
57:14 take stumbling-bl. *o. of w.*
Mal. 2:8 departed *out of the w.*
Rom. 3:12 all gone *out of the w.*
2 2:14 took handwrit. *o. of w.*
2 *Thes.* 2:7 be taken *out of the w.*
Heb. 5:2 comp. on them *o. of w.*
12:13 lame be turned *o. of t. w.*
Own WAY.
Prov. 1:31 eat fruit of their *o. w.*
20:24 ean man anders. his *o w.*
Is. 53:6 turn. every one to *o. w.*
56:11 they all look to their *o. w.*
Ezek. 22:31 *o. w.* have I recomp.
80:17 defiled 1sr. by their *o. w.*
WAY-SIDE.
Gen. 38:21 har. th. was by *w.-s.* ?
1 *Sam.* 4:13 Eli sat by a *w.-s.*
Ps. 140:5 proud spr. net by *w.-s.*
Mat. 13:4 seeds fell by *w.-s.* 19 ;
Mark 4:4, 15 ; *Luke* 8:5, 12
20:30 blind men sitting by *w.-s.*
Mark 10:46 blind Bartimeus sat by *w.-s.* begging, *Luke* 18:35
Their WAY.
1 *K.* 2:4 if children take heed to *t. w.* 8:25 ; 2 *Chr.* 6:16
19:3 troops raise up *t. w.* ar.
2 2:29 I chose out *t. w.* sat chief
Ps. 35:6 let *their w.* be dark
40:13 this *their w.* is their folly
Jer. 3:21 they have pervert. *t. w.*
6:27 mayest know and try *t. w.*
Ezek. 7:27 I will do to them after *their w.* 9:10 ; 11:21
14:22 ye sh. see *t. w.* and doings
32:7 as for th. *t. w.* is not equal
19 accord. to *t. w.* and doings
Acts 15:3 bro. on *t. w.* by church
See WENT.
This WAY.
Gen. 28:20 will keep me in *t. w.*
Ezr. 2:12 Moses looked *t. w.* and
Jos. 8:20 no power to flee *t. w.*
1 *K.* 6:39 Elisha said, *t. w.* nor
Ps. 80:21 this is *t. w.* walk ye in it
Acts 9:2 if he found any of *t. w.*
22:4 I persecu. *t. w.* unto death
Thy WAY.
Gen. 24:40 L. will prosper *t. w.*
Ex. 33:13 I pray, show me *t. w.*
Num. 22:32 bee. *t. w.* is perverse
Jos. 1:8 sh. make *t. w.* prosper.
1 *K.* 19:15 return on *t. w.* to Wil.
Ps. 5:8 make *t. w.* straight bef.
27:11 teach me *t. w.* O L. 86:11
37:5 commit *t. w.* unto the L.
40:13 tell, declined from *t. w.*
67:2 that *thy w.* may be known
77:13 *t. w.* O G. is in sanctuary
13 and guide me in *t. w.*
Prov. 3:23 sh. thou walk in *t. w.*
Is. remove *t. w.* far from her
Is. 57:10 in greatness of *t. w.*
85 why triim *t. w.* to seek love
80 why prid. to change *t. w.* ?
Ezek. 36:1 will because *t. w.*
16:43 fret *t. w.* on thy head
Mat. 8:13 as believed so *t. w.*
22:4 I perceive *t. w.* unto death
Thy WAY.
Gen. 24:40 L. will prosper *t. w.*
WAYS.
Gen. 19:2 early, go on your *w.*
Deut. 5:33 walk in *w.* Lord com.
8:6 sh. walked in *w.* of Moy.
28:7 he walked in *w.* of David,
2 *Chr.* 21:12 walk, not in *w.* of J.
2 Chr. 17:3 walked in *w.* of Ahaz
Ps. walked in *w.* of king, of Is.

CRUDEN'S CONCORDANCE.

WAY

Job 21:13 they kn. not w. of light
30:12 raise up w. of destruction
34:21 eyes are upon w. of man
40:19 Behe. is chief of w. of G.
Ps. 84:5 in heart are w. of them
Prov. 1:19 so w. of ev. one greedy
2:13 to walk in w. of darkness
15 whose w. are crooked, fro.
3:17 wisd.'s w. are w. of pleas.
5:6 her w. are movable
21 w. of man are bef. eyes of L.
6:6 go to ant, consider her w.
7:25 let not heart decl. to her w.
14:12 end the. w. of death, 16:25
16:2 w. of a man cl. in his eyes
7 when a man's w. please L.
17:23 gift to perv. w. of judgm.
31:27 looketh to w. of househ.
Ec. 11:9 walk in w. of thy heart
Is. 49:9 food in w. and pastures
Jer. 2:23 dromedary travers. w.
3:2 in w. hast thou sat as Arab.
6:16 stand in w. and see, ask
7:3 amend your w. 3; 26:13
23 walk in w. I command. yon
12:16 diligently learn w. of peo.
18:11 make w. and doings good
32:19 eyes open on w. of men
Lam. 1:4 w. of Zion do mourn
3:40 let us search and try our w.
Ezek. 18:25 are not w. unequ. ? 23
27:43 remember your w. doings
41 not acc. to your wicked w.
21:19 son of man appol. two w.
21 stood at head of two w.
Hag. 1:5 consider your w. 7
Zec. 1:6 do according to our w.
Luke 3:5 rough w. made smooth
Acts 2:28 known to me w. of life.

Any WAYS.

Lev. 20:4 do A. w. hide their eyes
Num. 37:15 any w. make void
1 Chr. 32:13 A. w. able to deliver
See BY-WAYS, EVIL, HIGH.

His WAYS.

Deut. 8:6 to walk in h. w. 26:17;
28:9; 30:16; 1 K. 2:3
10:12 walk in all his w. 11:22;
Jos. 22:5; 1 K. 8:58
19:9 love L. walk ever in his w.
32:4 A. w. are judgm. Dan. 4:37
1 Sam. 8:3 walked not in his w.
18:14 D. behav. wisely in his w.
1 K. 8:39 give every man accord-
ing to his w. 2 Chr. 6:30
2 Chr. 13:22 his w. are written
27:6 Jotham prepared his w.
7 h. w. are writ. in book, 28:26
Job 26:14 these are parts of h. w.
31:11 mn find accord. to h. w.
27 would not cons. any of h. w.
Ps. 10:5 his w. always grievous
103:7 made known h. w. to Mo.
119:3 iniq. they walk in his w.
128:1 blessed that walk. in h. w.
145:17 Lord is right. in all h. w.
Prov. 3:31 choose none of his w.
10:9 perverteth h. w. be known
14:2 perverse in h. w. despi. L.
19:16 despiseth his w. shall die
22:25 lest thou learn his w.
23:6 he that is perverse in h. w.
18 perverse in his w. shall fall
Is. 2:3 teach us his w. Mic. 4:2
42:24 would not walk in his w.
45:13 I will direct h. w. saith L.
57:18 I have seen his w.
Jer. 17:10 accord. to his w. 32:19
Ezek. 18:23 sho. return fr. his w.
30 judge is. acc. to h. w. 33:20
Hos. 9:8 snare of fowler in h. w.
12:2 punish Jac. accord. to h. w.
Joel 2:7 march ev. one in his w.
Hab. 3:6 his w. are everlasting
Luke 1:76 bef. L. to prep. his w.
Rom. 11:33 his w. past finding
Jam. 1:8 is unsta'ble in all his w.
11 rich man fade w. in his w.
See LORD.

My WAYS.

1 K. 3:14 if thou wilt walk in my
w. 11:33; Zec. 3:7
Job 13:4 shall not be see my w.
Jv. 38:1 will take heed to my w.
51:13 O is. walk. in my w. /
65:10 not kno. my w. Heb. 3:10
119:5 O that my w. were direct.
26 I have declared my w. and
59 I thought on my w. turned
168 all my w. are before thee
133:3 acquainted wi. all my w.
Prov. 8:32 bles. that keep my w.
23:26 to thine eyes obs. my w.
Is. 55:8 nei. your ways my w.
9 my w. higher th. your ways
58:2 delight to know my w.

WEA

Lam. 3:9 hath inclosed my w.
11 he turned aside my w.
Ezek. 18:29 are not my w. equ. ?
Zec. 3:7 if wilt walk in my w.
Mal. 2:9 have not kept my w.
1 Cor. 4:17 remember. of my w.

Own WAYS.

Job 13:15 I will maint. my o. w.
Prov. 14:14 filled with his o. w.
Is. 58:13 not doing thine o. w.
66:3 th. have chosen their o. w.
Ezek. 36:31 remember your o. w.
32 be ashamed for your o. w.
Acts 14:16 natl. to walk in o. w.

Their WAYS.

2 Chr. 7:14 turn fr. t. wicked w.
Job 24:23 his eyes are upon t. w.
Ps. 125:5 turn to t. crooked w.
Prov. 9:15 who go right on t. w.
Jer. 15:7 return not from t. w.
10:17 mine eyes upon all t. w.
18:15 caused to stumble in t. w.
Ezek. 14:23 when ye see t. w.
16:47 hast not walk. after t. w.
Hos. 4:9 punish them for t. w.
Rom. 3:16 misery are in their w.
2 Pet. 2:2 follow t. pernicious w.

Thy WAYS.

Deut. 28:29 not prosper in thy w.
1 Sam. 8:3 walk not in thy w.
2 Chr. 6:31 fear to walk in thy w.
Job 4:6 the uprightness of thy w.
21:14 not knowledge of thy w.
22:3 gain that mak. t. w. perf. ?
28 light sh. shine upon thy w.
Ps. 25:4 show me thy w. O Lord
51:13 teach transgressors t. w.
91:11 to keep thee in all thy w.
119:15 will ha. respect to thy w.
Prov. 3:6 in t. w. acknowl. him
4:26 let all t. w. be established
31:3 not t. w. to that wh. destr.
Is. 64:17 made us err from t. w.
64:5 that remembr. thee in t. w.
Jer. 2:33 hast taught wick. t. w.
3:13 thou hast scattered thy w.
Ezek. 7:3 accord. to thy w. 4, 8, 9
16:47 corrupted more in thy w.
61 remember t. w. be ashamed
24:14 according to t. w. Lord
28:15 thou wast perfect in t. w.
Dan. 5:21 in wh. hand are t. w.
Rev. 15:3 just and true are t. w.

WAYFARING.

Jud. 19:17 a w. man in street
2 Sam. 12:4 flock to dress for w.
Is. 33:8 the w. man ceaseth
35:8 w. men sh. not err therein
Jer. 9:2 a lodg.-place of w. men
14:8 why should. be as w. man ?

WAY-MARKS.

Jer. 31:21 set thee up w.-m. make

WEAK.

Num. 13:18 whether strong or w.
Jud. 16:7 st. as oth. men, 11, 17
2 Sam. 3:39 I am w. tho' anoint.
2 Chr. 15:7 let not hands be w.
Job 4:3 strengthened w. hands
Ps. 6:2 I am w. O L. heal me
I. 14:10 art thou bec. w. as we ?
35:3 strengthen ye the w. hands
Ezek. 7:17 knees w. as wat. 21:7
16:30 w. is thy heart, saith Lord
Joel 3:10 let w. say, I am strong
Mat. 26:41 flesh w. Mark 14:38
Acts 20:35 ye ought to supp. w.
Rom. 4:19 being not w. in faith
8:3 law was w. through flesh
14:1 that is w. in faith receiv. ye
2 another who is w. eat. herbs
21 broth. stumb. or is made w.
15:1 ought to bear infirm. of w.
1 Cor. 1:27 w. things to confound
4:10 we are w. 8:7 being w. 10
8:12 wound their w. conscience
9:22 to the w. I became w. that
11:30 for this cause many are w.
2 Cor. 10:10 bodily presence is w.
11:21 I speak as we had been w.
29 who is w. and I am not w. ?
12:10 when I am w. then strong
13:3 wh. to you-ward in not w.
4 we are w. in him, but sh. live
9 wh. we are w. and ye strong
Gal. 4:9 turn ye to w. elements ?
1 Thes. 5:14 support w. be pati.

WEAK-HANDED.

2 Sam. 17:2 come wh. he is w-h.

WEAKEN.

Is. 14:12 wh. didst w. nations ?

WEAKENED, ETH.

Ezr. 4:4 people of land w. Judah
Neh. 6:9 their hands shall be w.
Job 12:21 he w. stren. of mighty

WEA

Ps. 102:23 w. my strength in way
Jer. 38:4 w. hands of men of war

WEAKER.

2 Sam. 3:1 S.'s house w. and w.
1 Pet. 3:7 honor wife as w. vessel

WEAKNESS.

1 Cor. 1:25 w. of God is stronger
2:3 I was with you in w.
15:43 sown in w. raised in pow.
2 Cor. 12:9 strength is perf. in w.
13:4 though crucified thro' w.
Heb. 7:18 going before for the w.
11:34 out of w. were made stro.

WEALTH.

Gen. 34:29 sons of Ja. took th. w.
Deut. 8:17 hand got me this w.
18 L. giv. thee power to get w.
Ruth 2:1 a kinsman, man of w.
1 Sam. 2:32 see enemy in all w.
2 K. 15:20 exacted of men of w.
2 Chr. 1:11 th. hast not asked w.
12 I will give th. riches and w.
Ezr. 9:12 nor seek peace or w.
Est. 10:3 M. seeking w. of peo.
Job 31:25 spend their days in w.
31:25 if I rejoiced bec. w. great
Ps. 44:12 dost not increase w.
49:6 trust in w. boast in riches
10 and leave their w. to others
112:3 w. and riches in his house
Prov. 5:10 lest stra. be fill. wi. w.
10:15 man's w. is his city, 13:11
13:11 w. gotton by vanity sh. be
22 w. of sinner is laid up
19:4 w. maketh many friends
Ec. 5:19 God hath given w. 6:2
Zec. 14:14 w. of heathen shall
Acts 19:25 by this craft have w.
1 Cor. 10:24 seek every man an-
other's w.

WEALTHY.

P. 66:12 thou bro. us into w.
Jer. 49:31 get up unto w. nation

WEANED.

Gen. 21:8 Isaac grew and was w.
1 Sam. 1:22 not go till chi. be w.
1 K. 11:20 whom Taphenes w.
Ps. 131:2 w. of moth. soul as w.
v. 11:8 w. child put his hand
28:9 them th. are w. from milk
Hos. 1:8 wh. she w. Lo-ruhama

WEAPON.

Deut. 23:13 a paddle upon w.
Neh. 4:17 other hand held a w.
Job 20:24 shall flee from iron w.
Is. 54:17 no w. form. sh. prosper
Ezek. 9:1 with his destroy. w. 2

WEAPONS.

Gen. 27:3 take 1 pray, thy w.
1 Sam. 21:8 neither sword nor w.
2 K. 11:8 every man with his w.
in hand, 11; 2 Chr. 23:7, 10
Is. 13:5 L. cometh and the w. of
his indignation, Jer. 50:25
Jer. 22:7 prepare ev. one with w.
Ezek. 39:9 set on fire, burn w. 10
John 18:3 Judas cometh with w.
2 Cor. 10:4 w. of warf. not carnal
See WAR.

WEAR.

Ex. 18:18 wilt surely w. away
Deut. 22:5 woman not w. what
31 not w. garm. of divers sorts
1 Sam. 2:28 w. an ephod before
22:18 pers. that did w. an ephod
Job 14:19 waters w. the stones
Is. 4:1 eat our bread, w. apparel
Dan. 7:25 w. out saints of M. H.
Zec. 18:4 nor w. a rough gsrm.
Mat. 11:8 that w. soft clothing
Luke 9:12 day began to w. away

WEARETH, ING.

1 Sam. 14:3 priest w. an ephod
John 19:5 Jesus came w. purple
1 Pet. 3:3 let it not be w. of gold
Jam. 2:3 him that w. gay cloth.

WEARY.

Gen. 27:27 Rebek. said, I am w.
Deut. 25:18 Amalek sm. when w.
Jud. 4:21 J. smote Sis. when w.
8:15 bread to men that are w.
2 Sam. 16:14 and people came w.
17:2 come upon him whilst w.
23:10 smote Philist. till was w.
Job 3:17 wicked cease, w. at rest
10:1 my soul is w. of my life
16:7 he hath made me w. deso.
22:7 not given wat. to w. to dr.
Ps. 6:6 I am w. with groaning
68:9 confirm thy inher. when w.
Prov. 3:11 be not w. of h. corr.
25:17 lest he be w. of thee
Is. 1:14 feasts are trouble, am w.

WEE

Is. 5:27 none sh. be w. nor stum.
7:13 is it small thing to w. men
16:12 when it is seen M. is w.
28:12 wherewi. cause w. to rest
32:3 shadow of rock to w. land
40:28 G. fainteth not, nei. is w.
30 youths shall faint and be w.
31 that wait on L. sh. not be w.
43:22 thou hast been w. of me
46:1 a burden to the w. beast
50:4 spe. a word to him th. is w.
Jer. 2:24 th. seek her will not w.
6:11 I am w. with holding in
9:5 they w. thems. to commit
15:6 I am w. with repenting
20:9 I was w. with forbearing
31:25 I have satiated w. soul
51:58 folk shall labor and be w.
64 B. sink and they shall be w.
Hab. 2:13 peo. sh. w. themselves
Luke 18:5 by contin. com. shew.
Gal. 6:9 let us not be w. in well-
doing, 2 Thes. 3:13

WEARIED.

Gen. 19:11 w. themselves to find
Is. 43:23 nor have I w. thee
24 hast w. me with thine iniq.
47:13 art w. in multitude
57:10 w. in greatness of way
Jer. 4:31 soul is w. bec. of murd.
12:5 if run and they w. thee. if
in land of peace they w. th.
Ezek. 24:12 w. herself with lies
Mic. 6:3 wherein have I w. thee
Mal. 2:17 w. Lord, wherein have
we w. him ?
John 4:6 J. being w. sat on well
Heb. 12:3 lest ye be w. and faint

WEARIETH.

Job 37:11 he w. the thick cloud
Ec. 10:15 labor of foolish w.

WEARINESS.

Ec. 12:12 study is a w. of the flesh
Mal. 1:13 said, What a w. is it !
2 Cor. 11:27 w. and painfulness

WEARISOME.

Job 7:3 w. nights are appointed

WEASEL.

Lev. 11:20 w. and mouse, uncl.

WEATHER.

Job 37:22 fair w. com. out of nor.
Prov. 25:20 tak. a gar. in cold w.
Mat. 16:2 fair w. for sky is red
3 in morning it will be foul w.

WEAVE, EST.

Jud. 16:13 if th. w. seven locks
Is. 19:9 they that w. net-works
59:5 they w. a spider's web

WEAVER.

Ex. 35:35 work the work of w.
1 Sam. 17:7 staff of Goli.'s spear
like a w. beam. 2 Sam. 21:19;
1 Chr. 11:23; 20:5
Job 7:6 days swift. th. w. shuttle
Is. 38:12 I have cut off like a w.

WEB, s.

Jud. 16:13 if thou wearest seven
locks with the w. 14
Job 8:14 shall be a spider's w.
Is. 59:5 they weave spider's w.
6 w. sh. not become garments

WEDDING.

Mat. 22:3 were bidden to w. 8, 10
11 man had not on a w. garm.
Luke 12:36 will return from w.
14:8 when th. art bidden to a w.

WEDGE.

Jos. 7:21 Achan saw a w. of gold
24 Joshua took Achan and w.
Is. 13:12 more precious than
golden w. of Ophir

WEDLOCK.

Ezek. 16:38 as women th. br. w.

WEEDS.

Jon. 2:5 w. were about my head

WEEK.

Gen. 29:27 fulfil her w. we will
28 Jacob did so, fulfill. her w.
Dan. 9:27 one w. in midst of w.
Mat. 28:1 1st day of w. Mark 16:2,
9; Luke 24:1 ; John 20:1, 19
Luke 18:12 I fast twice in the w.
Acts 20:7 first day of w. Paul
preached
1 Cor. 16:2 on first day of w. let

WEEKS.

Lev. 12:5 child, be unclean 2 w.
Num. 28:26 hrt. offering after w.
Jer. 5:24 reserveth to us of harvest
Dan. 9:24 seventy w. are detor.
25 after threescore and 2 w. 26
10:2 I Dan. was mourning 3 w.

WEI

Dan. 10:3 nor ano. thys. till 3 w.
See FEAST, SEVEN.

WEEP.

Gen. 23:2 A. ca. to mourn and w.
43:30 Jos. sought where to w.
Num. 11:10 Moses heard peo. w.
13 they w. unto me, saying
1 *Sam.* 11:5 what ail. peo. th. w. ?
30:4 had no more power to w.
2 *Sam.* 1:24 daugh. of Is. w. over
12:21 thou didst w. for the child
2 *Chr.* 34:27 rend thy clothes, w.
Neh. 8:9 holy, mourn not, nor w.
Job 27:15 his widows sh. not w.
30:25 did I not w. for him
31 into voice of them that w.
Ps. 2:4 a time to w. a time to
Is. 13:2 gone to high places to w.
22:4 I will w. bitterly, labor not
33:19 thou shalt w. no more
33:7 ambassad. of peace sh. w.
Jer. 9:1 that I might w. day and
13:17 my soul shall w. in secret
places, mine eyes shall w.
22:10 w. not for the dead, nor
bemo. him, w. sore for him
48:32 O vine. I will w. for thee
Lam. 1:16 for these things I w.
Ezek. 24:16 thou mou. nor w. 23
27:31 sh. w. for thee with bitter.
Joel 1:5 drunkards, w. and howl
2:17 priests w. between porch
Mic. 1:10 declare it not, w. not
Zec. 7:3 sho. I w. in 5th month
Mark 5:39 why make ado and w.
Luke 6:21 blessed are ye that w.
23 woe to you th. laugh. sh. w.
7:13 w. not; 8:52; *Rev.* 5:5
23:28 w. not for me, w. for you.
John 11:31 goeth to grave to w.
16:20 ye sh. w. world sh. rejoice
Acts 21:13 what mean ye to w.
Rom. 12:15 w. wi. them that w.
1 *Cor.* 7:30 th. w. as though they
Jam. 4:9 afflicted, mourn, and w.
5:1 ye rich men, w. and howl
Rev. 18:11 merchants shall w.

WEEPEST.

1 *Sam.* 1:5 Han. why w. thou ?
John 20:13 wom. why w. th. ? 15

WEEPETH.

2 *Sam.* 10:1 behold the king w.
2 *K.* 8:12 Hazael said, Why w. ?
Ps. 126:6 goeth forth and w.
Lam. 1:2 she w. sore in the night

WEEPING.

Num. 25:6 w. bef. door of taber.
Deut. 34:8 days of w. for Moses
2 *Sam.* 3:16 husband with her w.
15:30 w. as they went up
Ezr. 3:13 not discern joy fr. w.
10:1 E. prayed and confess. w.
Est. 4:3 in ev. province was w.
Job 16:16 my face is foul with w.
Ps. 6:8 L. heard voice of my w.
30:5 w. may endure for a night
102:9 I mingl. my drink w. w.
Is. 15:3 in their streets howl, w.
16:9 I will bewail with w. of Ja.
vine of Sibmah, *Jer.* 48:32
22:12 did L. of hosts call to w.
65:19 voice of w. no more heard
Jer. 3:21 w. of Is. heard on high
9:10 for mountains I take up w.
31:9 they shall come with w.
15 lamentation and w. Rachel
w. for her childr. *Mat.* 2:18
16 restrain thy voice from w.
41:6 Ish. went to meet them w.
48:5 continual w. shall go up
for Judah going w. to seek L.
Ezek. 8:14 wom. w. for Tammuz
Joel 2:12 turn wi. fasting and w.
Mal. 2:13 covering altar with w.
Mat. 8:12 there sh. be w. 22:13;
24:51; 25:30; *Luke* 13:28
Luke 7:38 wom. stood at feet w.
John 11:33 when Je. saw her w.
20:11 Mary stood without w.
Acts 9:39 widow. stood by him w.
Phil. 3:18 told you often, now w.
Rev. 18:15 merch. shall stand w.
19 shipmaster and sailors, w.

WEIGH.

1 *Chr.* 20:2 crown to w. a talent
Ezr. 8:29 keep until ye w. them
Ps. 58:2 w. violence of hands
Is. 26:7 labor of w. path of just

WEIGHED.

Gen. 23:16 A. to Ephron silver
1 *Sam.* 2:3 by L. actions are w.
17:7 his spear's head w. 600
shekels, 2 *Sam.* 21:16
2 *Sam.* 14:26 Ab. w. hair of head
Ezr. 8:25 priests w. sil. and gold

WEL

Ezr. 8:26 w. into han. silver, 33
Job 6:2 oh that my grief were w.
28:15 nor shall silver be w. for
31:6 let me be w. in even bala.
Is. 40:12 who hath w. mount. ?
Jer. 32:9 Jeremi. w. him money
Dan. 5:27 thou art w. in balance
Zec. 11:12 they w. thirty pieces

WEIGHETH.

Job 28:25 he w. waters by meas.
Prov. 16:2 the Lord w. spirits

WEIGHING.

Num. 7:85 each w. 86 spoons w.

WEIGHT.

Gen. 43:21 money in sack full w.
Ex. 30:34 of each a like w.
Lev. 19:35 do no unright. in w.
26:26 deliver your bread by w.
Deut. 25:15 thou sh. have just w.
Jud. 8:26 w. of golden ear-rings
2 *Sam.* 12:30 w. of king's crown
1 *K.* 7:47 was w. of brass found
out, 2 *K.* 25:16
1 *Chr.* 28:14 he gave gold by w.
for candlesticks, w. for the winds
Prov. 11:1 a just w. is his delight
16:11 a just w. and bal. are L.'s
Ezek. 4:10 thy meat sh. be by w.
16 they shall eat bread by w.
Zec. 5:8 w. of lead on month
1 *Cor.* 4:17 a more exceeding w.
Heb. 12:1 let us lay aside ev. w.
Rev. 16:21 stone of hail w. of tal.

WEIGHTS.

Lev. 19:36 just w. shall ye have
Deut. 25:13 sh. not ha. divers w.
Prov. 16:11 w. of bag his work
20:10 divers w. are abomina. 23
Mic. 6:11 wi. bag of deceitful w.

WEIGHTY.

Prov. 27:3 stone heavy, sand w.
2 *Cor.* 10:10 lot. say they, are w.

WEIGHTIER.

Mat. 23:23 omitted w. matters

WELFARE.

Gen. 43:27 asked th. of their w.
Ex. 18:7 asked each other of w.
1 *Chr.* 18:10 sent to Jos. of his w.
Job 30:15 my w. passeth away
Ps. 69:22 also, let them be for w.
Jer. 38:4 seeketh not w. of peo.

WELL, Substantive.

Gen. 21:19 she saw a w. of water
30 witness I have dig. this w.
24:13 I stand here by w. 43
Num. 21:16 w. whereof L. spake
17 spring up, O w. 18 dig. w.
2 *Sam.* 17:18 map that had w.
23:15 give me drink of water of
w. of Beth. 1 *Chr.* 11:17, 18
Ps. 84:6 passing Baca make it w.
Prov. 5:15 wat. of thine own w.
10:11 a righte. man is w. of life
Cant. 4:15 a w. of waters fr. L.
John 4:6 Jacob's w. w. was there
11 w. is deep ; 12 J. gave us w.
11 sh. be in him a w. of water

WELLS.

Gen. 26:15 ye. Abr.'s serv. digg.
18 Isaac digged up. w. of water
Ex. 15:27 where were twelve w.
Num. 16:21 drink of water of w.
Deut. 6:11 ga. thee digged w. not
2 *K.* 3:19 ye sh. stop up. w. water
25 they stopped all w. of wat.
2 *Chr.* 26:10 towers and dig. w.
Is. 12:3 draw out of w. of salvat.
2 *Pet.* 2:17 are w. without water

WELL-SPRING.

Prov. 16:22 und. is a w-s. of life
18:4 w-s. of wisdom as a brook

WELL, Adverb.

Gen. 4:7 if thou doest not w. sin
12:13 that it may be w. wi. me
29:6 Ja. said, Is he w. ? he is w.
40:14 it shall be w. with thee
43:27 is your father w. ? he is w.
Ex. 4:14 I kn. he can speak w.
Deut. 1:23 saying pleased me w.
3:20 rest to breth. as w. as you.
4:40 that it may go w. with th.
5:16; 6:3, 18; 12:25, 28; 19:13;
22:7; *Ruth* 3:1 ; *Eph.* 6:3
5:29 it might be w. with them
33 that it may be w. with them
15:16 however he be w. wi. thee
Jud. 9:17 fa. w. a whoring, 8:33
Ps. 106:39 *ru.* g. it w. with Moses
Jer. 15:11 w. with rem. 22:15, 16
16:25 whereof ye not com. with

WEN

2 *Chr.* 12:12 in J. things went w.
Ps. 40:18 th. doest so. to thyself
Ec. 8:12 w. with them fear God
Jer. 22:15 it was w. with him, 16
40:4 and I will look w. to thee
42:6 that it may be w. with us
Ezek. 33:32 one that can play w.
Mat. 25:21 w. done, th. good and
faithful serv. 23; *Luke* 19:17
Luke 20:39 Master, thou hast w.
said, *John* 4:17
1 *Tim.* 3:17 elders that rule w.
be counted worthy
See DO, FAVORED, PLEASED.

WELL-BELOVED.

Cant. 1:13 myrrh is my w.-b.
Is. 5:1 will I sing to my w.-b.
Mark 12:6 he sent his w.-b. son
Rom. 16:5 salute w.-b. Epenetus
3 *John* 1 elder to the w.-b. Gaius

Very WELL.

Acts 25:10 as thou r. w. knowest
2 *Tim.* 1:18 thou knowest w. w.

WELL-NIGH.

Ps. 73:2 steps had w.-n. slipped

WEN.

Lev. 22:22 having a w. or scurvy

WENCH.

2 *Sam.* 17:17 a w. told Jonathan

WENT.

Gen. 25:2 L. wi. me in way I w.
Num. 1:31 bare th. in way ye w.
20. 24:17 present. in way w. w.
Jud. 1:17 Judah w. wi. Simeon
1 *Sam.* 10:14 said, What way w. he ?
Mat. 21:30 I go, sir, but w. not

WENT about.

Num. 11:8 people w. a. gath. it
2 *K.* 3:23 slinger w. a. smote it
2 *Chr.* 17:9 they w. about. taught
Ec. 2:20 I w. a. to cause my hea.
Cant. 5:7 watchmen that w. a.
Mat. 4:23 Jesus w. about teach-
ing, 9:35; *Mark* 6:6
Acts 9:29 they w. a. to slay him,
21:31; 26:21
10:38 Jesus w. about doing good
13:11 he w. a. seeking some to

WENT aside.

Luke 9:10 and w. aside privately
Acts 23:19 chief captain w. aside

WENT astray.

1 *Tim.* 19:27 before afflicted I w. a.
Ezek. 44:10 when Israel w. a. 15
48:11 priests wh. w. not astray
Mat. 18:13 which w. not astray

WENT away.

Mat. 19:22 he w. away sorrow-
ful, *Mark* 10:22
22 w. a. third time, *Mark* 14:39
1 *K.* 13:19 so he w. back and eat
Acts 3:26 many disciples w. back

WENT before.

Ex. 13:21 L. w. b. them in cloud
1 *Tim.* 1:18 prophecies wh. w. b.

WENT down.

Num. 16:33 w. d. alive into pit
Acts 8:38 th. both w. d. into wat.

WENT forth.

2 *Sam.* 20:8 as he w. f. it fell out

WENT out.

Gen. 44:28 one w. out from me
2 *Sam.* 13:9 they w. o. from him
John 13:30 received son. w. out
1 *John* 2:19 they w. out from us

WENT over.

2 *K.* 2:14 smote waters, w. over

WENT their way.

Num. 24:25 Balaam w. his w.
Jer. 10:2 w. t. w. ye a buck
Mat. 8:33 fled, and w. their way
20:4 you, and they w. th. way
22 heard words they w. t. way

WENT a whoring.

Jud. 2:17 brn. w. a. out of S.
2 *Sam.* 16:17 why w. thou not
19:25 wheref. w. thou not with

WHA

WEPT.

Gen. 21:16 Hag. w. 27:39 Es. w.
29:11 and Jacob w. 33:4; 37:35;
Hos. 12:4
42:24 Joseph w. 43:30; 45:2, 14,
15; 46:29; 50:1, 17
Ex. 2:6 behold, the babe w.
Num. 11:4 child. of Is. w. 13, 20;
14:1; *Deut.* 1:45; 34:8; *Jud.*
2:4; 20:23, 26; 21:2
Jud. 14:16 Samson's wife w.
Ruth 1:9 kissed daughters, w. 14
1 *Sam.* 1:7 Hannah w. not eat, 10
11:4 people w. 2 *Sam.* 3:32, 34
20:41 Jonathan and David w.
31:16 S. lifted up his v. and w.
30:4 and David w. 2 *Sam.* 1:12
2 *Sam.* 3:32 Da. w. at grave of A.
12:22 child alive, I fast. and w.
13:30 servants w. for Amnon
15:23 countrey w. 30 w. as he w.
18:33 moved, and w. for Absal.
2 *K.* 8:11 the man of God w.
13:14 Joash w. over Elisha
22:19 king of Judah w. bef. me
Ezr. 3:12 priests seen 1st ho. w.
10:1 peo. w. very sore. *Neh.* 8:9
Neh. 1:4 wh. I heard words I w.
Job 2:12 friends lift. voice and w.
Ps. 69:10 when I w. and chasten.
137:1 by rivers of Baby. we w.
Mat. 26:75 P. w. bitterly, *Mark*
14:72 ; *Luke* 22:62
Mark 5:38 them th. w. *Luke* 8:52
16:10 Mary told them as th. w.
Luke 7:32 mourned ye ha. not w.
19:41 beheld city and w. over it
John 11:35 Jesus w. 20:11 M. w.
Acts 20:37 te. fell on P.'s neck
1 *Cor.* 7:30 weep as tho' w. not
Rev. 5:4 so. because no man was

As it WEPT.

Is. 15:5 we hid as if w. one faces
Luke 22:44 as if w. drops of blo.
John 7:10 but as if w. in secret
Rev. 10:1 h's face as if w. sun
19:3 one of heads as if w. month,
14:3 sung as if w. a new song
15:2 I saw as if w. a sea of glass

WEST.

Gen. 28:14 shalt spread abroad
to w.
Deut. 33:23 possess w. and south
1 *K.* 7:25 three oxen towards w.
1 *Chr.* 9:24 porters tow. east, w.
north and south, 2 *Chr.* 4:4
10:15 to flight tow. east and w.
Ps. 75:6 promot. not from the w.
103:12 e. far as east is from w.
107:3 south, them fr. east and w.
Is. 11:14 fly on Philist. tow. w.
43:5 gather thee from the w.
45:6 that they may know fr. w.
49:12 come from north and w.
59:19 shall fear the L. from w.
Ezek. 48:1 his sides east and w.
Dan. 8:5 a he-goat came from w.
Hos. 11:10 children tremb. fr. w.
11:1 mount of O. cleave tow. w.
Mat. 8:11 many shall come from
east and w. *Luke* 13:20
24:27 as lightning shineth to w.
Luke 12:54 cloud rise out of w.
Rev. 21:13 and on w. three gates

WEST border.

Num. 34:6 this shall be w. bord.
Jos. 15:12 w. b. was to great sea
Ezek. 45:7 to the w. b. a portion

WESTERN.

Num. 34:6 as for the w. border

WEST quarter.

Jos. 18:14 this was w. quarter

WEST side.

Ex. 27:12 w. s. fifty cubits, 38:12
Num. 2:18 on w. s. stand. of Ep.
35:5 meas. on w. s. Lev.'s cities
Ezek. 45:7 for priests on w. s.
Ezek. 48:1 w. s. to east side, 2-7
a portion for
Naphtali, 4, 5, 6, 7, 8, 23, 24

WESTWARD.

Gen. 13:14 A. looked west. and e.
28:14 spread abroad w. and e.
Deut. 3:27 lift thine eyes w.
Ezek. 48:18 resi. sh. be 10,000 w.
Dan. 8:4 I saw ram pushing w.

WEST wind.

Ex. 10:19 w. w. took away locu.

WET.

Job 24:8 are w. with showers
4:15 let it be w. with dew
of heaven, 21, 25, 33; 5:21

WHALE.

Job 7:12 am I a sea or a w. that

1078 CRUDEN'S CONCORDANCE.

WHE
Ezek. 32:2 Phar. thou art as a w.
Mat. 12:40 Jo. was 3 days in w.

WHALES.
Gen. 1:21 God created great w.

WHAT.
Ezr. 13:14 wh. son ask, w. this?
16:7 w. are we that ye murm.?
15 they wist not w. it was
Deut. 20:5 w. man is th. ? 6, 7, 8
Jud. 18:8 w. say ye? 18 w. do?
24 w. have? more? w. is this?
w. aileth thee?

WHATSOEVER.
Gen. 31:16 w. G. said unto thee
Num. 22:17 I will do w. th. say.
Deut. 12:32 w. I command, ths.
Jud. 10:15 do th. w. 1 Sam. 14:36
Ps. 115:3 God hath done w. he
pleased, 135:6; Ec. 8:3
Ec. 3:14 w. G. doeth, it sh. be
Mat. 5:37 w. is more than these
7:12 w. ye would men sho. do
17:12 done w. listed, Mark 9:13
20:4 w. right I will give you, 7
John 15:16 w. ye shall ask, 16:23

WHEAT.
Gen. 30:14 R. found mand. in w.
Ex. 9:32 w. and rye were not
34:22 first-fr. of w. Num. 18:12
Deut. 32:14 fat of kidneys of w.
Jud. 6:11 Gideon threshed w.
15:1 time of w. harvest Samson
Ruth 2:23 to end of w. harvest
1 Sam. 6:13 Beth-she. reaping w.
12:17 is it not w. harv.-to-day?
2 Sam. 4:6 they wo. ha. fetch. w.
1 K. 5:11 Solom. gave Hiram w.
1 Chr. 21:23 w. for meat-offering
Ezr. 6:9 need of, w. salt, wine
7:22 a hundred measures of w.
Job 31:40 thistles grow ins. of w.
Ps. 81:16 fed th. wi. finest of w.
147:14 fill. thee with finest of w.
Prov. 27:22 bray a fool among w.
Cant. 7:2 belly like a heap of w.
Jer. 12:13 they have sown w.
23:28 what is chaff to the w.
31:12 flow together for w.
Ezek. 27:17 Judah traded in w.
Joel 2:24 floors shall be full of w.
Amos 5:11 take fr. him bur. of w.
8:5 that we may set forth w.
6 buy poor, sell refuse of w.
Mat. 3:12 gath. his w. Luke 3:17
13:25 enemy sowed tares am. w.
29 lest ye root up w. wi. them
30 gather the w. into my barn
Luke 16:7 said 100 meas. of w.
22:31 Satan may sift you as w.
John 12:24 exc. w. fall to ground
Acts 27:38 cast w. into the sea
1 Cor. 15:37 it may chance of w.
Rev. 6:6 meas. of w. for a penny
18:13 merchand. of w. depart.
See BARLEY.

WHEATEN.
Ex. 29:2 wafers made of w. flour

WHEEL.
Ps. 83:13 O G. make th. like w.
Prov. 20:26 king bringeth w. ov.
Ec. 12:6 or w. broken at cistern
Is. 28:28 nor break with w.
Ezek. 1:15 one w. upon the earth
16 a w. in midst of a w. 10:10
10:13 cried to the wheels, O w.

WHEELS.
Ex. 14:25 took off th. chariot w.
Jud. 5:28 why tarry w. of chari.
Is. 5:28 their w. like a whirlwind
Jer. 18:3 he wrought work on w.
47:3 at the rumbling of his w.
Ezek. 1:16 appearance of the w.
3:13 at noise of w. over against
10:10 w. were beside th. 1:18
23:24 S. come ag. thee with w.
26:10 walls shake at noise of w.
Dan. 7:9 his w. a burning fire
Nah. 3:2 noise of rattling of w.

WHELP.
Gen. 49:9 Judah is a lion's w.
Deut. 33:22 Dan is a lion's w.

WHELPS.
2 Sam. 17:8 as bear robbed of w.
Prov. 17:12 a bear robbed of w.
Ezek. 19:2 nourish. w. am, lions
3 she brought up one of her w.
Hos. 13:8 a bear bereaved of w.
Nah. 2:12 lion did tear for his w.
See LIONS.

WHEN.
Ps. 90:8 w. will ye be wise?
Ec. 8:7 who can tell w. it be?

WHENCE.
Gen. 42:7 w. come ye? Jos. 9:8
Jud. 17:9 M. said, w. comest th.?
19:17; 2 Sam. 1:3; 2 K. 5:25;
Job 1:7; 2:2; Jon. 1:8

WHI
Job 10:21 I go w. not ret. 16:22
John 7:35 and ye know w. I am
8:14 ye cannot tell w. I come
9:29 know not from w. he is, 30

WHENSOEVER.
Mark 14:7 w. ye may do th. good

WHERE.
Gen. 3:9 Lord said, w. art thou?
Ex. 2:20 w. is he? 2 Sam. 9:4
Job 9:24 if not, w. who is he?
14:10 the ghost, and w. is he?
38:4 w. wast thou wh. I laid. ?
Luke 17:37 w. Lord?
John 7:11 w. is he? 9:12
31 w. I am, 12:26; 14:3; 17:24

WHEREABOUT.
1 Sam. 21:2 let no man know w.

WHEREAS.
1 K. 8:18 w. it was in thy heart
Ezek. 13:7 w. ye say, L. saith it

WHEREFORE.
2 Sam. 18:19 say, w. done so?
Mat. 26:50 w. art thou come?

WHERETO.
Is. 55:11 sh. prosper w. I sent it

WHEREWITH.
Jud. 6:15 w. shall I save Israel?
1 K. 22:22 Lord said, w. 2 Chr. 18:20
Mic. 6:6 w. come before Lord?

WHEREWITHAL.
Mat. 6:31 w. shall we be clothed?

WHET.
Deut. 32:41 I w. my glit. sword
Ps. 7:12 he will w. his sword
64:3 who w. tongue like sword
Ec. 10:10 and he do w. not edge

WHILE.
Ps. 49:18 w. he lived, he blessed
63:4 bless thee w. I live, 146:2
Jer. 40:5 w. he was not go. back

A WHILE.
Gen. 46:29 Jos. wept a good w.
1 Sam. 9:27 S. said to S. st. a. w.
2 Sam. 7:19 hast spok. a great as.
Mat. 13:21 root, durcth for a. w.
Luke 8:13 which for a w. believe
18:4 he would not for a w.
1 Pet. 5:10 after suffered a w.

All the WHILE.
1 Sam. 22:4 a. t. w. Da. was in
25:7 none missing all the w. 16
27:11 will he his man. all the w.
Job 27:3 all t. w. breath is in me

Long WHILE.
Acts 20:11 had talked a long w.

WHIP.
Prov. 26:3 a w. for the horse
Nah. 3:2 noise of a w. noise of

WHIPS.
1 K. 12:11 my fath. chastis. you
with w. 14; 2 Chr. 10:11, 14

WHIRLETH.
Ec. 1:6 wind w. continually

WHIRLWIND.
2 K. 2:1 take up Elijah by a w. 11
Job 37:9 out of south cometh w.
38:1 L. answ. Job out of w. 40:6
Ps. 58:9 hath ta. away as in a w.
Prov. 10:25; Hos. 13:3
Prov. 1:27 destruction com. as w.
Is. 5:28 their wheels like a w.
40:24 w. shall take them away
41:16 the w. shall scatter them
66:15 chariots like w. Jer. 4:13
Jer. 23:19 a w. of L. is gone forth
23:20 w. great so. sh. be raised
30:23 a w. shall fall on wicked
Ezek. 1:4 a w. came out of north
47:10 come aga. him from w.
Hos. 8:7 sown wind, shall reap w.
Amos 1:14 devour in day of w.
Nah. 1:3 L. hath his way in w.
Hab. 3:14 they came out as a w.
Zec. 7:14 I scattered th. with w.

WHIRLWINDS.
Is. 21:1 as in south pass thro'
Zec. 9:14 Lord go forth with w.

WHISPER, ED.
2 Sam. 12:19 Da. saw servants w.
Ps. 41:7 all that hate me w.
Is. 29:4 speech w. out of dust

WHISPERER, S.
Prov. 16:28 a w. separat. friends
Rom. 1:29 debate, deceit, w.

WHIT.
1 Sam. 3:18 S. told Eli every w.
John 7:23 man every w. whole

WHO
John 13:10 but is clean every w.
2 Cor. 11:5 not a w. behind apo.

WHITE.
Gen. 30:37 Jacob made w. appear
49:12 his teeth be w. with milk
Ex. 16:31 like coriander-seed, w.
Lev. 13:3 turned w. 4, 20, 21, 25
Num. 12:10 leprous, w. as snow
Jud. 5:10 that ride on w. asses
2 K. 5:27 went out a leper, w.
2 Chr. 5:12 Levites arrayed in w.
Est. 8:15 Mord. went out in w.
Job 6:6 any taste in w. of egg?
Ps. 68:14 it was w. as snow in
Ec. 9:8 let thy garments be w.
Cant. 5:10 beloved is w. ruddy
Is. 1:18 sins sh. be w. as snow
Lam. 4:7 Naz. were w. than milk
Dan. 7:9 garm. was w. as wool
11:35 some fall to make them w.
12:10 many purifi. and made w.
Joel 1:7 branches thereof are w.
Zec. 1:8 horses speckled and w.
Mat. 5:36 make hair w. or black
17:2 his raim. was w. Luke 9:29
28:3 raim. w. as snow, Acts 1:10
Mark 16:5 a man clothed in w.
John 4:35 fields are w. to harvest
Rev. 1:14 head and hairs were w.
2:17 give him a w. stone, name
3:4 shall walk with me in w.
5 clothed in w. raiment, 4:4;
7:9, 13; 15:6; 19:8, 14
18 buy w. raiment, he clothed
6:2 behold, a w. horse, 19:11
7:14 made them w. in blood
14:14 w. cloud; 20:11 w. throne

WHITE, D.
Mat. 23:27 scribes like w. sepul.
Mark 9:3 no fuller can w. them
Acts 23:3 smite thee, thou w. wall

WHITER.
Ps. 51:7 I shall be w. than snow
Lam. 4:7 Nazarites w. th. milk

WHITHER.
1 Sam. 10:14 said, w. went ye?
Ruth 1:16 w. thou goest I will go,
2 K. 5:25 thy servant went no w.
Heb. 11:8 went, not knowing w.
See GO, GOEST, GOETH.

WHITHERSOEVER.
Prov. 17:8 w. it turn. it prosper.
21:1 king's heart w. he will
Mat. 8:19 fol. w. goest, Luke 9:57
Rev. 14:4 follow L. w. he goeth

WHOLE.
2 Sam. 1:9 my life is yet w.
2 Chr. 15:15 sou. with w. desire
1 Cor. 12:17 if w. body were eye
See CONGREGATION, HEART.

WHOLE, for sound.
Jos. 5:8 abode in camp till w.
Job 5:18 and his hands make w.
Mat. 9:12 th. that be w. need not
a physic. Mark 2:17; Lu. 5:31
21 I shall be w. Mark 5:28
12:13 and his hand was made w.
Mark 3:5; Luke 6:10
15:28 her daugh. was made w.
31 wond. saw maimed to be w.
Mark 5:34 faith hath made th. w.
go, be w. Luke 8:48; 17:19
Luke 7:10 found the servant w.
John 5:6 wilt th. be made w.? 11
7:23 made a man every whit w.
Acts 4:10 by what means he is w.
9:34 J. Christ maketh thee w.

WHOLLY.
Num. 32:11 not w. followed me
Deut. 1:36 hec. Caleb w. followed
Lord, Jos. 14:8, 9, 14
Jer. 46:28 leave thee w. unpunis.
1 Thes. 5:23 God sanctify you w.
1 Tim. 4:15 give thy. w. to them

WHOLESOME.
Prov. 15:4 w. tongue tree of life
1 Tim. 6:3 cons. not to w. words

WHOM.
1 K. 20:14 Ahab said, By w. ? 22:8
Ezr. 10:44; Rom. 1:5; 9:3, 17
See BEFORE.

WHOMSOEVER.
Dan. 4:17 he giveth to w. he will,
25, 32; 5:21

WHORE.
Lev. 19:29 not cause to be a w.
21:7 not take wife that is a w.
Deut. 22:21 play w. in father's—
23:17 there shall be no w. of Is.
18 not bring hire of a w.
Jud. 19:2 concubine played w.
Prov. 23:27 a w. is a deep ditch
Is. 57:3 seed of adulterer and w.

WIC
Jer. 3:3 thou hast a w. forehead
Ezek. 16:28 thou hast played w.
Rev. 17:1 judgm. of great w. 19:2
15 waters where w. sitteth, 16

WHORES.
Ezek. 16:33 they give gifts to w.
Hos. 4:14 are separated with w.

WHOREDOM.
Gen. 38:24 Ta. is wi. child by w.
Lev. 19:29 lost land fall to w.
Jer. 3:2 polluted w. with thy w.
13:27 seen lewdness of thy w.
Ezek. 16:33 may come for thy w.
23:8 they pour. their w. on her
17 Babylon defiled her with w.
43:7 not defile my holy n. by w.
9 let them put their w. fr. me
Hos. 4:11 w. and wine take heart
5:3 O Ephraim, th. commit. w.
6:10 there is the w. of Ephraim

WHOREDOMS.
Num. 14:33 wander and bear w.
2 K. 9:22 w. of thy mother Jezeb.
2 Chr. 21:13 w. of house of Ahab
Ezek. 16:20 is w. a small matter?
22 in w. not remember, youth
25 multiplied w. 26 increas, w.
34 contrary from women in w.
23:35 bear thy lewdness and w.
Hos. 1:2 wife and children of w.
Nah. 3:4 w. sellcth hat, thro' w.

WHOREMONGER, S.
Eph. 5:5 no w. hath any inherit.
1 Tim. 1:10 law made for w. liars
Heb. 13:4 w. and adulterers God
Rev. 21:8 w. have th. part in lake
22:15 without are w. murderers

WHORING. See GO, GONE, WENT.

WHORISH.
Prov. 6:26 by means of a w. wom.
6:9 break. with her w. heart
16:30 an imperious w. woman

WHOSE.
John 20:23 w. sin remit. w. sins

WHOSOEVER.
Mat. 11:6 bles. w. not be offend.
19:12 w. hath, to him be given
Gal. 5:10 bear judgm. w. he be
Rev. 22:17 w. will, let him take

WHY.
Jer. 25:13 turn ye, w. will ye die? Ezek. 18:31; 33:11
Luke 2:48 w. thus dealt with us?
Acts 14:13 w. do ye these things?

WICKED.
Ex. 18:23 righteous wi. w. ? 25
33:7 Ex. w. to ea. Ex. 9:27 people are w.
Ex. 23:7 I will not justify w.
Lev. 20:17 it is a w. thing
Deut. 15:9 not from. in w. heart
17:5 committed that w. thing
23:9 keep thee from ev. w. thing
25:1 condemn w. 1 K. 8:32
1 Sam. 2:9 w. be silent in darkn.
24:13 wick. proceedeth from w.
2 K. 17:11 Is. wrought w. things
2 Chr. 6:23 judge by requitl. w.
7:14 if my peo. turn fr. th. w.
ways, Ezek. 18:21; 33:11, 19
21:7 Athaliah that w. woman
Neh. 9:35 nor turned fr. w. ways,
Ezek. 3:19; 13:22
Est. 7:6 adversary is w. Haman
8:3 put away the mischief of w.
9:25 Haman's w. device sh. ret.
9:25 w. comes from cometh on w.
9:24 destroyeth perfect ra! w.
20 if I be w. why labor, 10:15
10:7 knowest that I am not w.
21:7 wherefore do the w. live?
30 w. reserv. to-day of destruc.
27:7 let mine enemy be as w.
34:18 say to king, Thou art w. ?
36:13 w. might be shaken out of
15 from w. light is withholden
40:12 tread down w. in th. place
Ps. 7:11 God is angry with w.
9:5 thou hast destroyed the w.
16 w. snared in work of hands
10:2 w. in pride persecute poor
3 w. boastcth, w. not seck G.
4 wherefore doth w. cont. G. ?
11:2 w. bend their bow, make
5 but the w. his soul hateth
6 upon w. he shall rain snares
12:8 w. walk on every side
17:9 keep me fr. w. that oppress

CRUDEN'S CONCORDANCE. 1079

CRUDEN'S CONCORDANCE.

WIF

Luke 18:3 th. was a w. in th. city
5 because this w. troubl. me
1 Tim. 5:4 If any w. have child.
5 she is a w. ind. tru-t. in God
9 let not w. be taken into num.
Rev. 18:7 I sit as a queen, no w.

WIDOWS.
Ex. 22:24 your wives shall be w.
Job 22:9 hast sent w. aw. empty
27:15 hur. in death, w. not weep
Ps. 68:5 judge of fatherl, and w.
146:9 their w. made so lament.
Is. 9:17 neither ha. mercy on w.
10:2 w. may be their prey, rob
Jer. 15:8 their w. are increased
13:21 let their wives be w. men
49:11 child. let w. trust in me
Lam. 5:3 our mothers are as w.
Ezek. 22:25 have made many w.
Mat. 23:14 ye devour w. houses
Mark 12:40; Luke 20:47
Luke 4:25 were many w. in Isr.
Acts 6:1 bec. w. were neglected
9:39 w. stood by him weeping
41 he had called saints and w.
1 Cor. 7:8 I said to w. It is good
1 Tim. 5:3 honor w. that are w.
11 but the younger w. refuse
16 if any have w. relieve them
Jam. 1:27 religion is to visit w.

WIDOWHOOD.
Gen. 38:19 put on garments of w.
2 Sam. 20:3 shut up, living in w.
Is. 47:9 loss of children and w.
54:4 remeumb. reproach of thy w.

WIFE.
Gen. 11:29 Abram's w. was Sarai, 31; 12:17, 20; 20:18; 24:36
20:3 hast taken is a man's w.
21:21 Hag. took w. for Ishmael
23:1 Abraham took w. Keturah
27:6 Jac. take w. of daughter's
33:6 Judah took a w. for Er his
8 go in unto thy brother's w.
Ex. 20:17 thou shalt not covet thy neighbor's w. Deut. 5:21
21:4 master ha. given him a w.
10 if he take him another w.
Lev. 18:8 father's w. sh. thou not uncover, 20:11; Deut. 27:20
18 won's w. 16 bro.'s w. 23:21
16 unc. take a w. to her sister
21:14 if man take a w. and her
21:7 priests not take w. a whore
13 high-priest take w. in virg.
Num. 5:12 if man's w. go asi, 29
30:8 he w. to one family of tribe
Deut. 13:6 if w. of bosom entice
21:7 betrothed w. not taken her
22:13 if a man take w. hate her
24 he humbleth neighbor's w.
30 a man not take his fa.'s w.
24:1 taken w. find uncleanness
5 hath taken a new w. not war
25:5 w. of dead not marry strau.
9 then sh. his bro.'s w. come
11 w. of one draweth near to
28:30 betroth w. another lie wi.
54 his eye be evil toward w.
Jud. 4:4 Debor. w. of Lapidoth
17 Jael, w. of Heber, 21; 5:21
14:3 take a w. of uncircumcised
16 Samson's w. went bef. him
20 w. was given to his compan.
21:18 that giveth a w. to Benj.
Ruth 4:5 buy it of R. w. of dead
2 Sam. 12:10 hast taken w. of U.
1 K. 14:2 known to be w. of Jer.
6 come in, thou w. of Jerobo.
2 K. 5:3 waited on Naaman's w.
2 Chr. 22:11 w. of Jehoi. hid him
Prov. 5:18 rej. with w. of youth
6:29 goeth in to neighbor's w.
18:22 a w. findeth a good thing
19:13 contentions of w. dropp.
14 a prudent w. is from the L.
Ec. 9:9 joyfully with w. of youth
Is. 54:1 children of married w.
6 called thee as a w. of youth
Jer. 3:20 surely as a w. departeth
5:8 neighed after neighbor's w.
6:11 husb. and w. sh. be taken
16:2 shalt not take thee a w.
Ezek. 16:32 as w. commit. adult.
18:11 and defiled his neighbor's w. 22:11; 33:26
Hos. 1:2 take a w. of whoredoms
12:12 Israel served for a w. kept
Mic. 2:14 witness bet. th. and w.
15 none deal treach. against w.
Mat. 1:6 that had been w. of U.
14:3 H. bound J. for Philip's w.
19:29 hath forsaken w. or child.
Mark 10:29; Luke 18:29
22:25 seven breth. married a w.
Mark 12:23; Luke 20:29

WIF

Luke 14:20 I have married a w.
17:32 remember Lot's w.
1 Cor. 5:1 should have faith.'s w.
7:3 husb. render to w. due ben.
nevolence, likew. w. to hus.
4 w. hath not power over body
10 let not w. depart from hus.
14 w. is sanctified by husband
16 what knowest thou, O w.
27 loosed fr. w. seek not a w.
34 difference bet. w. and virgin
39 w. is bound as long as hus.
Eph. 5:33 husband is head of w.
33 let every one love his w.
and w. see she rever. husb.
1 Tim. 3:2 hus. of 1 w. 12; Tit. 1:6
3:9 the w. of one man
1 Pet. 3:7 giving honor to w. as
Rev. 21:9 bride, the Lamb's w.

His WIFE.
Gen. 2:24 a man sh. cleave to his w. Mat. 19:5; Mark 10:7
25 both naked, man and his w.
12:12 this is his w. will kill me
19:16 laid hold on hand of his w.
26 his w. look. back fr. behind
20:7 restore the man his w.
21:67 hho hoc. h. w. 1 Sam. 25:42
25:21 Isa. entreated L. for h. w.
26:7 men asked him of his w.
31 touch. man or his w. sh. die
39:9 kept book, thou art his w.
Ex. 21:5 his w. shall go wi. him
21:16 sh. endow her to be h. w.
Lev. 18:14 shalt not appro. his w.
20:14 if he be jealous of his w.
30:16 statu. bet. man and his w.
Deut. 22:19 sho shall be his w. 25
24:5 he shall cheer up his w.
Jud. 13:11 Man. went after h. w.
15:1 Samson visited his w.
21:21 catch you ov. man his w.
2 K. 8:18 dan. of Ahab was h. w.
Est. 5:10 Haman called his w.
Ps. 109:9 let his w. be a widow
Jer. 3:1 if a man put away his w. Mat. 5:31, 34; 19:9; Mark 10:11; Luke 16:18
Mat. 8:14 saw his w. mother sick
10:3 is it lawful for a man to put away his w. ? Mark 10:2
10 if the case of the man be so with his w.
22:25 left his w. to his brother, Mark 19:19; Luke 20:28
Luke 1:26 and hate not his w.
18:2 Aquila with his w. Priscill.
24:24 Felix came with his w. D.
1 Cor. 7:2 let ev. man have h. w.
11 let not husb. put away h. w.
33 how he may please his w.
Eph. 5:23 loveth h. w. lov. hims.
31 join. to h. w. 33 love his w.
Rev. 19:7 his w. made herself ready

My WIFE.
Gen. 20:11 will st. me for my w.
13 here, my w. 26:7 is my w.
29:21 Jacob said, Give me my w.
Ex. 21:5 I love my w. and chill,
Jud. 13:1 I will go in to my w.
Sam. 3:14 deliver me my w. M.
11:11 sh. I go to lie with my w.
Job 19:17 breath is stra. to my w.
31:10 let my w. grind unto ano.
Ezek. 24:18 at even my w. died
Hos. 2:2 she is not my w. her
Luke 1:18 my w. is strick. in yrs.

Thy WIFE.
Gen. 3:17 heark. to voice of t. w.
12:18 why d'st tell me that she was thy w. ?
19 behold thy w. take her, go
17:15 t. w. sh. bear a son, 18:10
19:15 take thy w. and two dau.
20:3 man of a surety she is thy w.
10 one cui. have him with t. w.
Deut. 21:11 wool. ha. her to t. w.
13 go in to her, shall bo thy w.
2 Sam. 19:10 wife of t. w. to bd.
Ps. 128:3 t. w. sh. be fruitf. vine
Amos 7:17 t. w. shall be a harlot
1 Cor. 7:16 thou sh. save thy w.

To WIFE.
Gen. 12:19 taken her to me to w.
34:4 get me this damsel to w.
8 I pray, give her to him to w. 12
34:12 take a virgin to w.
Deut. 22:16 I gave my dau. to w.
Jos. 15:16 give Achsah my daug. to w. 17; Jud. 1:12, 13

WIL

Jud. 14:2 get her for me to w.
1 Sam. 18:17 her will I gi. th. to w.
1 K. 2:17 give me Abishag to w.
K. 14:9 thistle said, Give thy daughter, to w. 2 Chr. 25:18
2 Chr. 21:6 had daugh. of A. to w.
Mark 12:23 the seven had her to w. Luke 20:33

WILD.
Gen. 16:12 Ishm. will be w. man
Rom. 11:24 olive-tree, w. by nat.
See ASS, BEAST, BEASTS.

WILDERNESS.
Ex. 14:3 w. hath shut them in
Num. 14:2 wo. G. we died in w.
29 carcas. shall fall in w. 32:35
Deut. 1:19 went through w. 8:15
32:10 found him in howling w.
1 K. 19:15 retu. on thy way to w.
Job 24:5 w. yieldeth food for th.
Ps. 106:9 led through depths as thro' w. 136:16; Amos 2:10
107:35 turn. w. into stand. water
Cant. 3:6 cometh out of w. ? 8:5
Is. 14:17 that made world as w. ?
32:15 till Sp. poured upon them
41:18 I will make the w. a pool
42:11 let w. and cities lift voice
50:2 at rebuke I make riv. a w.
51:3 he will make her w. like E.
64:10 cities are a w. Zion is w.
Jer. 2:31 ha. I been to. unto Is. ?
4:26 the fruitful place was a w.
12:10 made pleas. portion a w.
23:6 make thee s. w. Hos. 2:3
Ezek. 6:14 laid more deso. th. w.
Joel 2:3 behind them a deser. w.
3:19 Edom sh. be a desolate w.
Zep. 2:13 make Ninev. like a w.

In the WILDERNESS.
Num. 14:22 mir. wh. I did in t. w.
32:15 he will yet leave them in the w. Ezek. 28:5
Deut. 8:2 forty years in the w.
9:25; Jos. 5:6; 14:10
16 fed thee in t. w. wi. manna ?
Neh. 9:21 didst sust. them in t. w.
Ps. 95:8 day of tempta. in t. w.
Prov. 21:19 better dwell in t. w.
Is. 35:6 judgm. sh. dwell in w.
35:6 in w. shall waters of him that crieth in the w. Mat. 3:3; Mark 1:3; Luke 3:4; John 1:23
41:19 I will plant in t. w. cedar
43:19 will make a way in the w.
22 went, after me in the w.
9:2 oh that I had in t. w. a lodg.
31:2 peo. found grace in the w.
48:6 be like the heath. in the w.
Lam. 4:19 laid wait for us in t. w.
Ezek. 19:13 she is planted in w.
20:15 I. rebelled bc. me in t. w.
15 lifted my hand in the w. 23
34:25 shall dwell safely in t. w.
Hos. 9:10 I found Israel in the w.
13:5 I did know thee in the w.
Mat. 3:1 John preaching in t. w.
15:33 whe. so much bread in w. to fill multitude ? Mark 8:4
Luke 15:4 leave 99 sheep in t. w.
2 Cor. 11:26 in perils in the w.

Into the WILDERNESS.
Lev. 16:10 by a fit man i. the w.
22 sh. let go the goat i. the w.
Eze. 20:10 I bro. them i. the w.
23 I will bring you into the w.
Hos. 2:14 I will bri. her in. the w.
Mat. 11:7 what went ye out into the w. to see ? Luke 7:24
Acts 19:38 led. ofJew drove i. t. w.
21:28 4,000 men
17:3 so he carried me into i. w.

WILES.
Num. 25:18 in. vex you with w.
Eph. 6:11 able to stand ag. w.

WILILY.
Jos. 9:4 Gibeonites did work w.
Deut. 33:16 for good w. of him
Ps. 27:12 deliver me not to w. of
41:2 not deliver to w. of enem.
Ezek. 16:27 delivered thee to w.
Mat. 6:10 thy w. be done in e.
Mark 3:35 whosoe. sh. do w. of G.
Rom. 1:10 pros. jour. by w. of G.
8:27 interce. accor. to w. of G.
12:2 accepta. and perf w. of G.
15:32 come with joy by w. of G.
1 Cor. 1:1 Paul an apostle by w. of G. 2 Cor. 1:1; Eph. 1:1
2 Cor. 8:3 ga. thems. by w. of G.
Gal. 1:4 deli. fr. evil by w. of G.
Eph. 6:6 doing the w. of God
Col. 4:12 complete in w. of God
1 Thes. 4:3 this is w. of God, 5:18
Heb. 10:36 have done w. of God
1 Pet. 2:15 so is the w. of God
3:17 better if w. of God be so
4:2 live not to lusts, to w. of G.
19 suffer according to w. of G.
1 John 2:17 he that doeth w. of G.

His WILL.
Dan. 4:35 doeth accord. to his w.
8:4 he did according to his w.
11:3 do accord. to his w. 16, 36
Luke 12:47 nei. accord. to his w.
John 7:17 if any do h. w. sh. kn.
Acts 22:14 shouldest know h. w.
Rom. 2:18 and knowest his w.
9:19 who hath resisted his w.
1 Cor. 7:37 hath power over h. w.
16:12 his w. not at all to come
Eph. 1:5 good pleasure of his w.
9 kn. to us mystery of his w.
11 wh. worketh knowledge of h. w.
2 Tim. 2:26 taken capt. at his w.
Heb. 13:21 good work to do h. w.
1 John 5:14 ask accord. to his w.
Rev. 17:17 hearts to fulfil his w.

My WILL.
Luke 22:42 not my w. but thine
Acts 13:22 shall fulfil all my w.
1 Cor. 9:17 if I do this ag. my w.

Own WILL.
Lev. 1:3 shall offer it of his o. w.
19:5 as your own w. 22:19, 29
Dan. 11:16 according to his o. w.
John 5:30 I seek not mine o. w.
6:38 to do mine own w.
Eph. 1:11 counsel of his own w.
Heb. 2:4 according to his own w.
Jam. 1:18 of his o. w. begat he us

Thy WILL.
Ps. 40:8 I delight to do thy w.
143:10 teach me to do thy w.
Mat. 6:10 t. w. be done, Luke 11:2
26:42 not pass, thy w. be done
Heb. 10:7 I come to do thy w. 9

WILL, Verb.
Job 13:13 let come on me what ye
Prov. 21:1 heart whither. he w.
Dan. 4:17 giveth it to whomsoever he w. 25, 32; 5:21
Mat. 8:3 and said, I w. be thou clean, Mark 1:41; Luke 5:13
Mark 14:7 when. w. may do good
15:12 what w. ye I should do ?
Luke 4:6 to whomsoever I w.
12:49 what w. I, if it be kindl. ?
John 13:7 ask what ye w.
17:24 I w. that they be with me
21:22 if I w. that he tarry, 23
Rom. 7:18 to w. is pres. with me
Phil. 2:13 Ch. worketh both to w.
1 Tim. 5:14 I w. women marry
Jam. 4:15 if L. w. we sh. do this

WILL not.
Ezek. 20:3 I re. n. be inquired of
Mat. 21:29 he answered, I w. not
John 5:40 ye w. not come to me

WILLETH.
Rom. 9:16 it is not of him th. w.

WILFULLY.
Heb. 10:26 if we sin w. after we

WILLING.
Gen. 24:5 w. to follow
Ex. 35:5 whosoever is of a w. heart, 21, 22, 29
1 Chr. 28:9 serve G. wi. w. mind
29:5 who is w. to consecrate his
Ps. 110:3 thy people shall be w.
Is. 1:19 if ye. sh. eat good of land

CRUDEN'S CONCORDANCE.

WIN

Mat. 1:19 not w. to make her a
26:41 spirit is w. flesh is weak
Luke 10:29 w. to justify himself
22:42 if thou be w. remove cup
John 5:35 ye were w. to rejoice
Rom. 2:23 if G. w. to shew wrath
2 Cor. 5:8 w. rather to be absent
6:3 they were w. of themselves
12 if there be first a w. mind
1 Thes. 2:8 w. to have imparted
Heb. 6:17 w. to shew heirs of pro.
2 Pet. 3:9 not w. any sho. perish

WILLINGLY.
Ex. 25:2 ev. man that gives w.
Jud. 5:2 people w. offered, 9
1 Chr. 29:6 rulers off. w. 9, 14, 17;
2 Chr. 35:8; Ezr. 1:6; 3:5
2 Chr. 17:16 Amaziah w. himself
Neh. 11:2 that w. offered thems.
Prov. 31:13 work. w. with hands
Lam. 3:33 he doth not afflict w.
Hos. 5:11 Ephr. w. walked after
John 6:21 they w. received him
Rom. 8:20 subj. to vanity not w.
2 Cor. 9:17 if I do this w. a rew.
Phile. 14 not as of necessity, but w. 1 Pet. 5:2
2 Pet. 3:5 they are w. ignorant

WILLOWS.
Lev. 23:40 shall take w. of brook
Job 40:22 w. of brook comp. him
Ps. 137:2 hanged harps on the
Is. 15:7 car. riches to brook of w.
44:4 they shall spring up as w.

WILLOW-TREE
Ezek. 17:5 he has set it as a w.-t.

WILL-WORSHIP.
Col. 2:23 show of wisd. in w.-w.

WILT.
Jud. 1:14 wh. w. thou ? Est. 5:3;
Mat. 20:21; Mark 10:51; Lu. 18:41
Ps. 60:10 w. not thou, O God?
108:11
Mat. 15:28 be it to th. as thou w.
17:4 if th. w. let us make taber.
26:39 not as I will, but as thou
w. Mark 14:36

WIMPLES.
Is. 3:22 take aw. mantles and w.

WIN, NETH.
2 Chr. 32:1 he thought to w. th.
Prov. 11:30 he that w. souls
Phil. 3:8 that I may w. Christ

WIND.
Gen. 8:1 God made a w. to pass
Ex. 15:10 didst blow with thy w.
Num. 11:31 w. brought quails
2 Sam. 22:11 was seen on wings
of w. Ps. 18:10; 104:3
1 K. 18:45 heaven black with w.
19:11 strong w. rent mountains
2 K. 3:17 shall not see w. nor rain
Job 1:19 came w. from wildern.
6:26 speeches which are as w.
7:7 O remem. that my life is w.
8:2 words of thy mouth like w.
21:18 they are as stubble bef. w.
30:15 ter. pursue my soul as w.
37:21 w. passeth, Ps. 103:16
Ps. 1:4 which w. driveth away
78:39 w. that passeth away
135:7 bringeth w. out of treas.
147:18 causeth his w. to blow
Prov. 11:29 he shall inherit w.
25:14 clouds and w. with. rain
23 north w. driveth away rain
27:16 whoso hid. her, hideth w.
30:4 who gath. wind in his fists
Ec. 1:6 w. goeth toward south
5:16 what profit, laboured for w.
11:4 he that observ. w. not sow
Cant. 4:16 awake, O north w.
Is. 7:2 trees are moved with w.
11:15 with w. shake his hand
26:18 as it were brou. forth w.
27:8 he stayeth his rough w.
41:16 as a ridding-place from w.
41:29 w. carry them away, 57:13
29 their molten images are w.
64:6 like w. have taken us away
Jer. 4:12 a w. from those places
5:13 prophets shall become w.
10:13 w. out of his treas. 51:16
22:22 w. shall eat up thy past.
Ezek. 5:2 thou shalt scatter in w.
12:14 scatter tow. w. about him
37:9 prophesy to w. say to w.
Dan. 2:35 w. carried them away
4:19 w. hath bound her up
8:7 move it, shall reap whirlw.
12:1 Ephraim feedeth on w.
Amos 4:13 he that createth w.
Jon. 1:11 w. sent a great w. to sea

WIN

Zec. 5:9 w. was in their wings
Mat. 11:7 a reed shaken with the w. Luke 7:24
14:24 w. was contrary, Mark 6:48; Acts 27:4
32 w. ceased, Mark 4:39; 6:51
John 3:8 w. blow. where it listeth
Acts 2:2 sound as of a mighty w.
Eph. 4:14 car. about with ev. w.
Jam. 1:6 like wave driven wi. w.
Rev. 6:13 wh. she is shaken of w.
7:1 w. should not blow on earth

WINDS.
Job 28:25 to make weight for w.
Ezek. 37:9 come from the four w.
Mat. 7:25 w. blew, beat house, 27
8:26 rebuked the w. Luke 8:24
27 even the w. and sea obey him ? Mark 4:41 ; Luke 8:25
24:31 gather from four w. Mark 13:27
Jam. 3:4 ships driven of fierce w.
Jude 12 clouds carri. about of w.
See EAST, FOUR, SCATTER, STORMY.

WINDY.
Ps. 55:8 hasten from w. storm

WINDOW.
Gen. 6:16 a w. shalt thou make
26:8 king of Gerar looked out w.
Jos. 2:15 Rah. let spies thro' w.
18 w. bound scarlet line in w.
Jud. 5:28 moth. looked out of w.
2 Sam. 6:16 M. looked thro' w.
2 K. 9:30 and look out at a w.
13:17 he said, Open w. eastward
Prov. 7:6 at w. I looked through
Acts 20:9 sat in w. a young man
2 Cor. 11:33 thro' a w. let down

WINDOWS.
Gen. 7:11 w. of heav. were open.
8:2 w. of heaven were stopped
2 K. 7:2 if L. make w. in hea. 19
Ec. 12:3 that look out of w.
Cant. 2:9 my beloved look, at w.
Is. 24:18 w. fr. on high are open
54:12 I will ma. thy w. of agates
60:8 flee as doves to their w.
Jer. 9:21 death is co. into our w.
22:14 that cutteth him out w.
Dan. 6:10 his w. being open
Joel 2:9 enter in at w. like thief
Zep. 2:14 voice shall sing in w.
Mal. 3:10 if I will not open w. of

WINE.
Gen. 9:24 Noah awoke fr. his w.
14:18 Melchizedek brought w.
27:1 washed his garments in w.
42 his eyes were red with w.
Ex. 29:40 fourth part of a hin of w. Le. 23:13; Num. 15:5
Num. 6:3 separate himself fr. w.
28:7 cause strong w. to be pour.
Deut. 32:33 w. is poison of drag.
Jud. 9:13 leave w. wh. cheereth
19:19 th. is bread and w. for me
1 Sam. 1:14 put away w. fr. thee
25:37 when w. gone out of Nab.
2 Sam. 13:29 flesh, and a flagon of w. 1 Chr. 16:3
13:28 Am. heart merry with w.
Neh. 2:1 the w. was before him
5:15 gover. taken bread and w.
18 once in ten days st. of all w.
13:15 lad. asses with w. grapes
Est. 1:7 they gave them royal w.
10 heart of king merry with w.
5:6 king said to Esth. at w. 7:2
7:7 arising from banquet of w.
Job 1:13 w. in th. bro. house, 18
32:19 my belly, till w. hath no vent
Ps. 75:8 w. is red, full of mixture
78:65 shouteth by reason of w.
104:15 w. that mak. glad heart
Prov. 9:2 hath mingled her w.
20:1 w. is a mocker, stro. drink
23:30 they that tarry long at w.
31 look not on w. wh. it is red
31:6 gi. w. to th. of heavy heart
Ec. 2:3 to give myself to w.
10:19 w. maketh merry, money
Cant. 1:2 love better th. w. 4:10
5:1 I have drunk my w.
8:2 cause thee to drink spiced w.
Is. 1:22 thy w. mixed with water
5:11 night, till w. inflame them
12 pipe and w. are in th. feasts
22:13 eating flesh and drink. w.
24:11 there is a crying for w.
27:2 red w. 55:1 come, buy w.

WIN

Jer. 25:15 take w. of fury at my hand
35:5 full of w. 40:12 gathered w.
48:33 I have caused w. to fail
51:7 nations drunken of her w.
Ezek. 27:18 Damascus trad. in w.
Dan. 1:5 king gave of w.
8 not to defile himself with w.
5:1 Belshazzar drank w. bef. 4
2 he tasted w. 23 drunk w.
10:3 neither came w. nor flesh
Hos. 2:9 take away my w. in sea
3:1 gods, and love flagons of w.
14:7 scent he as w. of Lebanon
Joel 1:5 howl, ye drinkers of w.
Mic. 2:11 I will prophesy of w.
Hab. 2:5 he transgresseth by w.
Zec. 9:15 make noise, as thro' w.
10:7 hearts rejoice, as thro' w.
Luke 7:33 J. neither drinking w.
John 2:3 saith, They have no w.
9 tasted water made w. 4:46
10 at begin. set forth good w.
Eph. 5:18 be not drunk with w.
1 Tim. 3:3 and not given to w. 8; Tit. 1:7; 2:3
5:23 use w. for stomach's sake
1 Pet. 4:3 walked in excess of w.
Rev. 16:19 give cup of w. of wrath
17:2 drunk with w. of forni. 18:3
See BOTTLE, CORN, DRINK, NEW, OFFERINGS, OIL, SWEET.

WINE-BIBBER, S.
Prov. 23:20 be not am. w.-b.
Mat. 11:19 man a w.-b. Luke 7:34

WINE-BOTTLES.
Jos. 9:4 Gibeonites took w.-bot.
13 b. of w. which we filled

WINE-CELLARS.
1 Chr. 27:27 over w.-c. was Zabdi

WINE-FAT.
Is. 63:2 like him treadeth w.-f.
Mark 12:1 dig. a place for w.-f.

WINE-PRESS.
Num. 18:27 fulness of w.-p. 30
Deut. 15:11 furnish out of w.-p.
Jud. 6:11 thres. wheat by w.-p.
7:25 they slew at w.-p. of Zeeb
2 K. 6:27 help thee out of w.-p. ?
Is. 5:2 made a w.-p. therein
63:3 I have trodden w.-p. alone
Lam. 1:15 trodden w.-p. as in
Hos. 9:2 w.-p. sh. not feed them
Mat. 21:33 digged a w.-p. in vi.
Rev. 14:19 cast w. into w.-p.
20 w.-p. trodden without city
19:15 he treadeth w.-p. of wrath

WINE-PRESSES.
Neh. 13:15 treading w.-p. on sab.
Job 24:11 tread their w.-p.
Jer. 48:33 wine to fail from w.-p.
Zec. 14:10 upon king's w.-p.

WINES.
Is. 25:6 make feast of w. on lees

WING.
2 K. 6:24 w. of cherub. 5 cubits
other w. 27; 2 Chr. 3:11, 12
Is. 14:4 none that moved the w.
Ezek. 17:23 ev. fowl of every w.

WINGS.
Ex. 19:4 bare you on eagle's w.
25:20 covering mercy-seat with their w. 37:9; 1 K. 8:7
Lev. 1:17 cleave it with w. ther.
Mat. 23:11 eagle spread, her w.
Ruth 2:12 under wh. w. thou art
2 Sam. 22:11 upon w. of wind
Job 39:13 gavest w. to peacock ?
Ps. 17:8 hide me under thy w.
18:10 fly on w. of wind, 104:3
36:7 put th. trust under shadow of thy w. 57:1 ; 61:4 ; 63:7
55:6 O that I had w. like a dove
63:7 in shadow of thy w. I rej.
68:13 lie among pots, w. of dove
91:4 shalt thou trust, w. truth
Prov. 23:5 riches make themse. w.
Ec. 10:20 wid. hath w. shall tell
Is. 6:2 each one had six w.
8:8 stretch. out his w. fill land
18:1 woe to land shadow. wi. w.
40:31 mount up with w. eagles
Jer. 38:9 give w. to M. may fly
40 he sh. spread his w. over M.
49:22 he sh. spread w. over Boz.
Ezek. 1:6 every one had four w.
6 were joined ; 10:12 w. full of eyes
24 I heard the noise of their w. 3:13; 10:5, 23
17:3 a great eagle with great w. 7
7 another great eagle with w.
Dan. 7:4 like lion, had eagle's w.
6 w. having on back four w.

WIS

Hos. 4:19 bou. her up in her w.
Zec. 5:9 wind was in their w.
Mal. 4:2 with healing in his w.
Mat. 23:37 as a hen gathereth her chick. under w. Luke 13:34
Rev. 9:9 sound of th. w. as horses
12:14 to wom. were giv. two w.

WINGED.
Gen. 1:21 G. created ev. w. fowl
Deut. 4:17 liken. of any w. fowl
Ezek. 17:3 great eagle, long-w.

WINK, ED, ETH.
Job 15:12 wh. do thi. eyes w. at ?
Ps. 35:19 neither let them w.
Prov. 6:13 a wicked man w.
10:10 he th. w. causeth sorrow
Acts 17:30 ignorance God w. at

WINNOWED, ETH.
Ruth 3:2 ho. w. barley to-night
Is. 30:24 hath been w. wi. shovel

WINTER.
Gen. 8:22 and w. shall not cease
Ps. 74:17 made summer and w.
Cant. 2:11 for lo, the w. is past
Zec. 14:8 in summer and w.
Mat. 24:20 pray that your flight be not in w. Mark 13:18
John 10:22 feast of dedicat. in w.
2 Tim. 4:21 to come before w.

WINTER-HOUSE.
Jer. 36:22 the king sat in w.-h.

WINTER, Verb.
Is. 18:6 beasts shall w. on them
Acts 27:12 not commod. to w. in
1 Cor. 16:6 abide, w. with you
Tit. 3:12 I determin. there to w.

WINTERED.
Acts 28:11 ship which w. in isle

WIPE.
2 K. 21:13 w. Jerusalem as a dish
Neh. 13:14 w. not out good deeds
Is. 25:8 Lord will w. away tears fr. all faces, Rev. 7:17; 21:4
Luke 7:38 woman did w. th. with hairs, 44; John 11:2; 12:3
John 13:5 began to w. their feet

WIPED, ETH, ING.
2 K. 21:13 w. it as a man w. dish
Prov. 6:33 reproach not w. way
30:20 she w. calteth, w. her mouth

WIRES.
Ex. 39:3 cut gold plates into w.

WISDOM.
Ex. 31:3 I have filled him wi. Sp. of God in w. 6; 35:31, 35
35:26 stirred them in w. 36:1, 2
Deut. 4:6 for this is your w. and
2 Sam. 14:20 acco. to w. of angel
1 K. 2:6 do accord. to w. do
3:28 saw w. of G. was in h.
4:29 God gave Solomon w. 5:12
2 Chr. 1:12
30 Solomon's w. excelled w. of Egypt, 34; 7:14; 10:4, 23, 24; 2 Chr. 9:22, 23
1 Chr. 22:12 Lord give thee w.
Job 4:21 die, even without w.
12:2 peo. w. shall die with you
12 with ancient is w. 13:12
13:5 hold your peace, be your w.
15 Is not this your w. to, thy ?
26:3 coun. him th. hath no w. ?
28:12 where shall w. be found ?
20 whence cometh w. where
32:7 multitude of years teach w.
13 say, We have found out w.
33:33 and I shall teach thee w.
38:36 who's word serve with, w.
39:17 hath deprived her of w.
Ps. 37:30 mouth of righ. speak w.
49:3 shall make me to know w.
90:12 apply our hearts to w.
104:24 in w. hast th. made wor.
Prov. 1:2 kn. w. ? 3 to rec. inst. w.
20 w. crieth, 8:1; 1:2 car to w.
2:6 Lord giveth w. 3:13
7 he layeth up w. for righteous
10 when w. entereth into heart
3:13 happy man that findeth w.
19 Lord by w. founded earth
4:5 get w. 7; 5:1 atte. to my w.
7 I say to w. Thou art my sister
8:5 unders. w. 11 w. better th.
14 counsel is mine, sound w.
10:13 man of underst. hath w.
10:23 sport to fool to do mis.
13:10 by pride cometh w.

WIS

Prov. 14:6 scorner seeketh *w.* fin.
8 *w.* of prudent is to understa.
33 *w.* resteth in heart of him
16:16 better to get *w.* than gold
17:16 in hand of fool to get *w.*
18:1 man intermeddleth with *w.*
19:8 that getteth *w.* loveth soul
21:30 there is no *w.* against L.
23:4 rich, cea. from thy own *w.*
9 a fool will despise *w.* of wor.
23 buy *w.* 24:3 thro' *w.* house
29:3 whoso loveth *w.* rejoiceth
15 the rod and reproof give *w.*
30:3 I nei. learned *w.* nor have
31:26 openeth her mouth wi. *w.*
Ec. 1:13 I gave my heart to *w.*
16 I have more *w.* than all
17 I gave my heart to know *w.*
18 for much *w.* is much grief
2:3 acquaint. my heart with *w.*
9 my *w.* remained with me
12 I turned myself to beho. *w.*
13 *w.* excel. folly; 21 lab. in *w.*
26 G. give. *w.* 7:12 *w.* giv. life
7:19 *w.* strengtheneth the wise
23 all this I have proved by *w.*
25 I applied heart to seek *w.*
8:1 man's *w.* mak. face to shine
16 I appli. my heart to kn. *w.*
9:10 there is no *w.* in the grave
13 *w.* have I seen under sun
15 poor man by *w.* deliv. city
10:1 that is in reputation for *w.*
3 *w.* falleth him, he is a fool
Is. 10:13 by my *w.* I have done it
29:14 *w.* of their wise sh. perish
33:6 *w.* be stability of thy times
Jer. 9:23 let not wise glory in *w.*
10:12 establi. world by *w.* 51:15
Dan. 1:4 chil. skilful in all *w.*
2:14 answ. with counsel and *w.*
20 blessed be G. *w.* and might
21 he giveth *w.* to the wise
23 God, who hast given me *w.*
30 not revealed for any *w.*
5:11 *w.* of gods found in him
Mat. 12:42 came fr. utterm. parts
to hear *w.* of Sol. *Luke* 11:31
13:54 whence ha. this man *w.?*
Luke 1:17 turn disobedient to *w.*
2:40 Jesus filled with *w.*
52 increased in *w.* and stature
11:49 also said the *w.* of God
21:15 give you a mouth and *w.*
Acts 6:3 seven men full of *w.*
10 *w.* not able to resist the *w.*
7:10 God gave Joseph *w.* in the
22 learned in *w.* of the Egypt.
1 *Cor.* 1:17 not with *w.* of words
19 destroy the *w.* of the wise
20 God made foolish the *w.* of
21 in the *w.* of God the world
by *w.* knew not G. it pleas.
22 and Greeks seek after *w.*
24 C. power of G. and *w.* of G.
30 God is made to us *w.* and
2:4 not with words of man's *w.*
5 not stand in the *w.* of men
6 speak *w.* 7 speak *w.* of God
13 which man's *w.* teacheth
3:19 for the *w.* of this world is
2 *Cor.* 1:12 not with fleshly *w.*
Eph. 1:8 abound. toward us in *w.*
3:10 the manifold *w.* of God
Col. 1:9 mi. be filled with all *w.*
28 teaching eve. man in all *w.*
3:16 words dw. in you in all *w.*
4:5 walk in *w.* tow. them that
Jam. 1:5 any lack *w.* let him ask
3:15 this *w.* descendeth not from
2 *Pet.* 3:15 according to *w.* given
Rev. 5:12 the Lamb to receive *w.*
7:12 glory, and *w.* be to our God
17:9 the mind which hath *w.*

WISDOM, joined with is.
Job 6:13 and *is w.* driven quite
12:12 with ancient *is w.* 13:16
28:18 *w. is* abo. rubi. *Prov.* 8:11
28 fear of the Lord that *is w.*
Prov. 4:7 *w.* is principal thing
10:13 with him that hath understanding, *w. is* found
11:2 but with the lowly *is w.*
13:10 with well-advised *is w.*
14:8 the *w.* of the prudent *is* to
17:24 *w. is* before him that hath
24:7 *w. is* too high for a fool, he
Ec. 1:18 in much *w. is* much
7:11 *w. is* good with an inherit.
12 *w. is* a defence, and money
9:16 *w. is* better than strength;
the poor man's *w. is* despis.
18 *w. is* better than weapons
10:10 *w. is* profitable to direct
Jer. 8:9 lo, th. have rejected the
word, what *w. is* in them?
49:7 *is w.* no more in Teman?

WIS

Dan. 5:14 excellent *w. is* found
Mat. 11:19 but *w. is* justified of
her children, *Luke* 7:35
Mark 6:2 wh. *w. is* giv. to him?
Jam. 3:17 *w.* from above *is* pure
Rev. 13:18 here *is w.* let him that

Of WISDOM.
Job 11:6 show thee secrets *of w.*
28:18 price *of w.* is above rubies
Ps. 49:3 speak *of w.* and medita.
111:10 fear of the Lord is the
beginning *of w. Prov.* 9:10
Prov. 1:3 instruct. *of w.* justice
4:11 in the way *of w.* have led
10:21 fools die for want *of w.*
11:12 he that is void *of w.* des.
13:21 to him that is desti. *of w.*
33 fear of L. is instruct. *of w.*
18:1 spring *of w.* as flow. brook
24:14 knowle. *of w.* to thy soul
Ezek. 28:12 the sum full *of w.*
Dan. 1:20 matters *of w.* he fou.
Mic. 6:9 the man *of w.* shall see
Rom. 11:33 depth *of w.* of God
1 *Cor.* 2:1 of speech *or of w.*
12:8 by Spirit the word *of w.*
Col. 2:3 are hid all treas. *of w.*
23 have indeed a show *of w.*
Jam. 3:13 show with meek. *of w.*

See SPIRIT.

Thy WISDOM.
1 *K.* 2:6 according to *thy w.*
10:6 true report I heard of *t. w.*
7 *thy w.* and prosperity exce.
8 hear *thy w.* 2 *Chr.* 9:5, 7
2 *Chr.* 9:6 *t. w.* was not told me
Job 39:26 (h hawk fly by *t. w.*)
Is. 47:10 *thy w.* perverted thee
Ezek. 28:4 *t. w.* and understanding hast got. thee riches, 5
17 corrupted *thy w.* by bright.

WISE.
Gen. 3:6 a tree to make one *w.*
41:30 none discreet and *w.* as
Ex. 23:8 for the gift blindeth the *w. Deut.* 16:19
Deut. 4:6 this nation is a *w.* peo.
32:29 O that they were *w.*
Jud. 5:29 her *w.* ladies answered
2 *Sam.* 14:20 my lord is *w.* accor.
1 *K.* 3:12 given thee a *w.* heart
5:7 blessed L. that hath given
David a *w.* son, 2 *Chr.* 2:12
1 *Chr.* 26:14 Zec. a *w.* counsellor
Job 5:13 taketh *w.* in own crafti.
9:4 he is *w.* in heart and stern.
11:12 vain man would be *w.*
22:2 he that is *w.* may be profi.
32:9 great men are not alw. *w.*
37:24 he respecteth not any that are *w.* of heart
Ps. 2:10 be *w.* now, O ye kings
19:7 making *w.* the simple
36:3 left off to be *w.* do good
94:8 fools, when will ye be *w.?*
107:43 whoso is *w.* and will obs.
Prov. 1:5 *w.* man att. *w.* counsel
6 understand *w.* and sayings
3:7 be not *w.* in thine own eyes
35 the *w.* shall inherit glory
6:6 be *w.* 8:33; 23:19; 27:11
9:12 be *w.* thou shalt be *w.* for
10:1 a *w.* son maketh a glad father, 15:20
5 gathereth in summer is *w.*
8 *w.* receive commandments
19 he that redrai. his lips is *w.*
12:18 servant to the *w.* in heart
80 he that winneth souls is *w.*
12:15 hearken. to counsel is *w.*
18 tongue of the *w.* is health
13:1 a *w.* son heareth instruct.
14 law of *w.* is a fount. of life
20 walk. with *w.* men sh. be *w.*
14:3 lips of the *w.* preserve th.
24 crown of the *w.* is th. riches
35 favor is toward *w.* servant
15:2 the tongue of the *w.* useth knowledge aright.
7 lips of *w.* dispo. knowledge
12 a scorner will not go to *w.*
31 way of life is above to *w.*
81 reproof abideth among *w.*
16:21 *w.* in heart called prudent
23 heart of *w.* teach. his mouth
17:2 *w.* serv. shall rule over son
28 hol. his peace is counted *w.*
18:15 the *w.* seeketh knowledge
19:20 be *w.* in thy latter end
20:1 deceived thereby, is not *w.*
26 *w.* king scattereth wicked
21:11 simple is made *w.* when
20 oil in the dwelling of the *w.*
23:17 hear the words of the *w.*

WIS

Prov. 23:15 be *w.* my hea. sh. rej.
24 begetteth a *w.* son have joy
24:6 by *w.* coun. make thy war
23 these things belong to *w.*
25:12 *w.* reprover on obedi. ear
26:5 answer a fool, lest he be *w.*
12 a man *w.* in his own conceit
28:7 whoso keep. law is *w.* son
11 rich is *w.* in his own conceit
30:24 be four things that are *w.*
Ec. 2:15 why was I more *w.?*
16 th. is no remembrance of *w.*
19 wherein I show. myself *w.*
4:13 better *w.* child than foolish
6:8 wh. hath *w.* more th. fool?
7:4 heart of *w.* house of mourn.
5 better to hear rebuke of *w.*
16 neither make thys. over *w.*
19 *w.* strengtheneth the *w.*
23 I will be *w.* far from me
9:1 *w.* are in the hand of God
11 I saw that her. is not to *w.*
12:9 preacher was *w.* he taught
11 words of *w.* are as goads
Is. 5:21 woe to them that are *w.*
19:11 counsellors of Pha. *w.*
31:2 yet he is also *w.* bring evil
Jer. 4:22 they are *w.* to do evil
8:8 how do ye say, We are *w.*
18:18 nor counsel perish fr. *w.*
Ezek. 28:3 art *w.* than Daniel
Ob. 8 destroy *w.* men out of E.
Hos. 14:9 *w.* undert. th. things
Zec. 9:2 Tyrus and Zidon be *w.*
Mat. 10:16 be ye *w.* as serpents
11:25 because th. hast hid these
things from *w. Luke* 10:21
24:45 who is faith. and *w.* serv.?
25:2 five virgins *w.* five foolish
4 *w.* took oil in their vessels
Luke 12:42 who is that *w.* stew.
Rom. 1:14 I am debtor to the *w.*
22 professs. thems. *w.* be. fools
11:25 lest ye be *w.* in your conc.
12:16 be not *w.* in your own
16:19 *w.* to that which is good
27 to God only *w.* be glory,
1 *Tim.* 1:17; *Jude* 25
1 *Cor.* 1:19 destroy wisdom of *w.*
20 where is the *w.?*
27 chosen foolish th. to confo.
3:10 as *w.* master-builder I lay
18 be *w.* let him become fool
19 taketh *w.* in their craftiness
20 knows thoughts of the *w.*
4:10 but ye are *w.* in Christ
2 *Cor.* 10:12 compar. are not *w.*
Eph. 5:15 not as fools, but as *w.*
2 *Tim.* 3:15 scrip. able to ma. *w.*

Any WISE.
Lev. 19:17 shall in a. *w.* rebuke
See MAN, MEN.

WISE-HEARTED.
Ex. 28:3 speak to all *w.-hearted*
31:6 I put wisdom in *w.-hearted*
35:10 every *w.-hearted* am. you
25 women *w.-hearted* did spin
36:1 wrought every *w. A.* man
8 ev. *w.-h.* man made 10 curta.

WISE men.
Gen. 41:8 Phar. called for magicians and *w.* men, *Ex.* 7:11

In no WISE.
Mat. 5:18 shall in *no w.* pass
10:42 he shall in *no w.* lose rew.
Luke 18:17 he shall *in no w.* enter therein, *Rev.* 21:27
John 6:37 will *in no w.* cast out
Rom. 3:9 are we bet. ? *in no w.*

On this WISE.
Mat. 1:18 birth of C. was on *t. w.*
Acts 13:34 he said *on t. w.* I will
Heb. 4:4 spake *of* 7th day *on t. w.*

WISE woman.
2 *Sam.* 11:2 Joab fetched *w. wo.*
20:16 cried a *w.* out of city
Prov. 14:1 *w.* bu. built. house

WISELY.
Ex. 1:10 let us deal *w.* with them
1 *Sam.* 18:5 behav. *w.* 14, 15, 30
2 *Chr.* 11:23 Rehoboam dealt *w.*
Ps. 58:5 charming never so *w.*
64:9 shall *w.* cons. of his doings
101:2 I will behave myself *w.*
Prov. 16:20 handleth a matter *w.*
21:12 he *w.* considereth wicked
28:26 who walk. *w.* sh. be deliv.
Ec. 7:10 thou dost not inquire *w.*
Luke 16:8 becau. he had done *w.*

WISER.
1 *K.* 4:31 Sol. was *w.* th. all men
Job 35:11 mak. us *w.* than fowls
Ps. 119:98 made me *w.* th. enem.

WIT

Prov. 9:9 and he will be yet *w.*
26:16 sing. is *w.* in his conceit
Ezek. 28:3 thou art *w.* th. Daniel
Luke 16:8 in their generation *w.*
1 *Cor.* 1:25 fool. of G. *w.* th. men

WISH.
Job 33:6 lo thy *w.* in God's stead
Ps. 40:14 put to sha. that *w.* evil
73:7 more than heart could *w.*
Rom. 9:3 co. *w.* myself accursed
2 *Cor.* 13:9 we *w.* even your per.
3 *John* 2 I *w.* th. mayest prosper

WISHED.
Jon. 4:8 and *w.* himself to die
Acts 27:29 cast anch. *w.* for day

WISHING.
Job 31:30 *w.* a curse to his soul

WIST.
Ex. 16:15 th. *w.* not what it was
34:29 Mo. *w.* not his face shone
Jud. 10:20 *w.* not Lord departed
Mark 9:6 he *w.* not what to say
Luke 2:49 *w.* ye not I must he
about my Father's business
Acts 12:9 *w.* it not true wh. was
23:5 *w.* not he was high-priest

To WIT.
Gen. 24:21 *to w.* wheth. L. made
Ex. 2:4 *to w.* what won. he done
2 *Cor.* 5:19 *to w.* th. G. in C. rec.
8:1 we do you *to w.* of gr. of G.

WITCH.
Ex. 22:18 not suffer a *w.* to live
Deut. 18:10 not be an *w.* among

WITCHCRAFT.
1 *Sam.* 15:23 rebelli. as sin of *w.*
2 *Chr.* 33:6 Manasseh used *w.*
Gal. 5:20 works of flesh are *w.*

WITCHCRAFTS.
2 *K.* 9:22 Jezebel's *w.* are many
Mic. 5:12 cut off *w.* out of hand
Nah. 3:4 mist. of *w.* selleth nati.

WITHAL.
1 *K.* 19:1 *w.* Elij. slain prophets
Acts 25:27 not *w.* to sigul. crimes

WITHDRAW.
1 *Sam.* 14:19 S. said to priest *w.*
Job 9:13 if God will not *w.* anger
13:21 *w.* thy hand far from me
33:17 that he may *w.* hand from
Prov. 25:17 *w.* fr. neigh.'s house
Ec. 7:18 fr. this *w.* not thy hand
Is. 60:20 neit. thy moon *w.* itself
Joel 2:10 stars *w.* shining, 3:15
2 *Thes.* 3:6 *w.* from every brother
1 *Tim.* 6:5 cor. minds *w.* thyself

WITHDRAWN.
Deut. 13:13 have *w.* inhabitants
Cant. 5:6 my beloved had *w.*
Lam. 2:8 hath not *w.* his hand
Ezek. 22:41 man's *w.* hand from iniq.
Hos. 5:6 L. *w.* himself from them
Luke 22:41 *w.* fr. them a stone's cast

WITHDRAWEST, ETH.
Ps. 74:11 why *w.* thy rig. hand?
Job 36:7 *w.* not from righteous

WITHDREW.
Neh. 9:29 *w.* and would not hear
Ezek. 20:22 I *w.* my hand
Mat. 12:15 J. know. *w.* himself
Mark 3:7 J. *w.* fr. them. *Lu.* 5:16
Gal. 2:12 when they come, he *w.*

WITHER.
Ps. 1:3 his leaf also shall not *w.*
37:2 shall *w.* as the green herb
Is. 19:6 reeds and flags shall *w.*
7 thing sown by brooks sh. *w.*
40:24 blow upon them, shall *w.*
Jer. 12:4 shall herbs of field *w.?*
Ezek. 17:9 cut off fruit that it *w.*
10 shall it not utterly *w.?*
Amos 1:2 top of Carmel shall *w.*

WITHERED.
Gen. 41:23 seven ears *w.*
Ps. 102:4 heart is *w.* 11 I am *w.*
Is. 15:6 the hay is *w.* away
27:11 boughs are *w.* broken off
Lam. 4:8 Nazarite's skin is *w.*
Joel 1:12 vine is *w.* and consum.
17 barns broken down, corn *w.*
Amos 4:7 where it rained not *w.*
Jon. 4:7 smote gourd that it *w.*
Mat. 12:10 man wh. had his hand
w. Mark 3:1, 3; *Luke* 6:6, 8
13:6 hav. no root, *w. Mark* 4:6
Mark 5:29 fig-tree *w.* 20; *Mark* 11:21
John 5:3 blind, halt, *w.*
15:6 cast fo. as a branch and *w.*

WITHERETH.
Job 8:12 flag so. before any herb
Ps. 90:6 even. cut down and *w.*

CRUDEN'S CONCORDANCE. 1083

WIT

Ps. 139:6 gra. w. bef. groweth up
Is. 40:7 grass w. the flower fad-
eth, 8 ; 1 Pet. 1:24
Jam. 1:11 the sun w. the grass
Jude 12 trees w. without fruit

WITHHELD, EST.
Gen. 23:6 l w. thee from sinning
22:12 thou hast not w. son
30:2 w. fr. thee, fruit of womb?
Neh. 9:20 w. not manna
Job 31:16 have w. poor fr. desire
Ec. 2:10 I w. not my heart

WITHHOLD.
Gen. 23:6 none sh. w. his sepulc.
2 Sam. 13:13 he will not w. me
Job 4:2 who can w. himself from
Ps. 40:11 w. not thy mercies
84:11 no good thing will be w.
Prov. 3:27 w. not good
23:13 w. not correct. from child
Ec. 11:6 even. w. not thy hand
Jer. 2:25 w. foot ft. being unsh

WITHHOLDEN.
1 Sam. 25:26 w. th. from reveng.
Job 22:7 w. bread from hungry
38:15 from wicked light is w.
42:2 no thought w. from thee
Ps. 21:2 hast not w. request
Jer. 3:3 showers have been w.
5:25 sins have w. good things
Ezek. 18:16 hath not w. pledge
Joel 1:13 drink-off. w. from God
Amos 4:7 I have w. rain from you

WITHHOLDETH.
Job 12:15 behold he w. waters
Prov. 11:24 w. more than meet
26 he that w. corn, peo. curse
2 Thes. 2:6 now ye kn. what w.

WITHIN.
Ec. 9:14 little city, few men w.
Luke 11:7 he from w. sh. answer

WITHOUT.
Gen. 24:31 wheref. stan. th. w. ?
Prov. 7:12 now she is w.
22:13 there is a lion w.
1 Cor. 5:13 but them that are w.

WITHOUT, with within.
Lev. 13:55 if garm. bare w. or w.
Ezek. 2:10 was written w. and w.

WITHS.
Jud. 16:7 bind with 7 green w.
8 brought w. 9 brake the w.

WITHSTAND.
Num. 22:32 angel went to w. Ra.
2 Chr. 13:7 it could not w. them
8 ye think to w. kingdom of L.
20:6 none is able to w. thee
Est. 9:2 no man can co. w. Jews
Ec. 4:12 one prevail, two sh. w.
Dan. 11:15 his people sh. not w.
Acts 11:17 that I could w. God ?
Eph. 6:13 able to w. in evil day

WITHSTOOD.
2 Chr. 26:18 w. Uzziah the king
Dan. 10:13 prince of Pers. w. me
Acts 13:8 Elymas sorcerer so. th.
Gal. 2:11 I w. Peter to the face
2 Tim. 3:8 James and J. w. Mo.
4:15 hath greatly w. our words

WITNESS.
Gen. 21:30 a w. that I dig. well
31:44 covenant be a w. betw. us
44 this heap a w. pillar a w. 52
50 God is w. between me and
thee, 1 Thes. 2:5
Ex. 22:13 if torn br. it for a w.
22:1 be not an unrighteous w.
Lev. 5:1 a soul sin and w. of w.
Num. 5:13 if ch. be no w. ag. her
35:30 one w. sh. shall not testify.
Deut. 17:6 ; 19:15
Deut. 31:19 song be a w. 21, 26
Jos. 22:27 altar w. het. us, 28, 34
24:27 this stone shall be a w.
Jud. 11:10 L. w. bet. us, Jer. 42:5
1 Sam. 12:5 L. w. against you
Job 16:8 my wrinkles w. ag. me
19 w. in heaven record on high
16:11 eye saw me it gave w.
Ps. 89:37 a faithful w. in heaven
Prov. 14:5 faithf. w. will not lie
25 a true w. delivereth souls
19:28 ungodly w. scorn. judgm.
21:28 he that w. ag. thy neighb.
Is. 19:20 a w. to the L. of hosts
55:4 given him for a w. to people
Jer. 29:23 and am a w. saith L.
42:5 L. faithful w. between us
Ec. 1:2 let L. G. be w. ag. you
Mic. 1:2 L. w. ag. thee and w.
2:5 swift w. against sorcerers
Mat. 24:14 preached for a w. to na.
Mark 14:55 sought for w. ag. Je.
56 w. agreed not together, 59

WIV

Luke 22:71 need we further w. ?
John 1:7 came for a w. to bear w.
3:11 ye receive not our w.
25 whom bear. w. same bapti.
5:31 if bear w. mys. w. not true
32 w. he witness. of me is true
36 I have greater w. than John
37 Father hath borne w. of me
Acts 1:22 one ordained to be w.
4:33 gave w. of re-urrect. of L.
10:43 all proph. w. whose beh.
14:17 left not himself without w.
22:15 thou shalt be his w. to all
26:16 make thee minister and w.
Rom. 1:9 God is my w. I serve
2:15 conscience bearing w. 9:1
Tit. 1:13 this w. is true. rebuke
Heb. 2:4 God bear. w. with signs
10:15 the Holy Ghost is w. to us
11:4 Abel obtained w. righteous
Jam. 5:3 rust shall be w. ag. you
1 Pet. 5:1 P. a w. of suffer. of C.
1 John 5:9 if we receive w. of m.
10 he th. bell. hath w. in hims.
1 John 5:9 w. on oath, of thy charity
Rev. 1:5 Jesus Ch. the faithf. w.
3:14 write th. thi. saith true w.
20:4 were beheaded for w. of J.
See BARE, BEAR, BEARETH,
FALSE, TABERNACLE.

WITNESSES.
Num. 35:30 put to death by w.
Deut. 17:6 at mouth of two or
three w. shall he be put to
death, 19:15 ; 2 Cor. 13:1
7 hands of w. be first on him
Jos. 24:22 Josh. said. Ye are w.
Ruth 4:9 ye are w. I have bou. 10
Job 10:17 renew. thy w. ag. me
Is. 8:2 I took faithful w. to rec.
43:9 all nations bring their w.
10 my w. saith the L. 12 ; 44:8
44:9 they are their own w.
Jer. 32:10 I seal, took wit. 12
25 buy field, take w. 44
Mat. 18:16 mou. of two or th. w.
23:31 ye be to w. to yourselves
26:65 need of w. ? Mark 14:63
Luke 24:48 ye are w. of th. thin.
Acts 1:8 ye sh. be w. in Jerusal.
2:32 Jesus G. raised up, whereof we are w. 3:15
5:32 w. of these things, 10:39
7:58 w. laid th. clothes at S.'s f.
10:41 unto w. chosen of G. to us
13:31 are his w. unto the people
Jer. 14:9 forgot. wicked. of y. w.
25 ye and your w. to. have spoken
Ezek. 5:23 love prey ur. Col. 3:19
Heb. 10:28 died under 2 or 3 w.
12:1 compassed with cloud of w.
Rev. 11:3 give power to my w.

See FALSE.

WITNESS, Verb.
Deut. 4:26 I call heaven and earth
to w. against you
1 Sam. 12:3 here I am, w. ag. me
Is. 3:9 countenance w. ag. them
Lam. 2:13 wh. thi. I take to w. ?
Mat. 26:62 what is it w. these
w. against thee? Mark 14:60
27:13 how many things they w.
against thee? Mark 15:4

WITNESSED, ETH, ING.
1 K. 21:13 men of B. w. ag. Nab.
John 5:32 witness w. of me
Acts 20:23 H. G. w. in every city
26:22 w. both to small and great
Rom. 3:21 being w. by law
1 Tim. 6:13 bef. P. w. good conf.
Heb. 7:8 of whom it is w. he liv.

WITS.
Ps. 107:27 stag. at their w. end

WITTY.
Prov. 8:12 I find out w. inventi.

WITTINGLY.
Gen. 48:14 Is. guid. his hands w.

WIVES.
Gen. 4:19 Lamech took two w.
6:2 took them w. wh. they cho.
30:26 give me my w. and child.
31:50 if thou take other w.
Num. 14:3 w. and chil. be a prey
Deut. 17:17 nor multi. w. to him.
21:15 if a man have two w.
Jud. 8:30 Gideon had many w.
21:7 how do for w. for them? (6
18 not give them w. of daught.
1 Sam. 27:3 they were Da.'s w.
2 Sam. 5:13 David took more w.
12:8 I gave thee w. into thy
1 K. 11:3 Solomon had 700 w.
4 his w. turn. his heart wh. old
2:25 sent for my w. and childr.

WOE

2 Chr. 11:21 Ma. above all his w.
23 he desired many w.
24:3 Jehoi. took for him two w.
29:9 our w. in captivity for tha.
Ezr. 10:3 a cov. to put aw. w. 44
Neh. 13:43 w. and chil. rejoiced
12:23 Jews married w. of Ashd.
Est. 1:20 w. give husbands hon.
Jer. 29:6 take w. and w. for sons
35:8 d. no wine, nor w. nor sons
Dan. 5:2 his w. drink therein, 3
Luke 17:27 eat, drank, marri. w.
Acts 21:5 on our way, with w.
1 Cor. 7:29 ba. w. be as bad none
Eph. 5:22 w. submit to your hus-
bands as unto the Lord, Col.
3:18 ; 1 Pet. 3:1
24 so let w. be to th. husbands
Luke 17:19 put away their w.
1 Pet. 3:1 won by conversa. of w.

S : s STRANGE.
Gen. 34:29 t. w. capt. 1 Sam. 30:3
Jud. 3:6 took daught. to be t. w.
2 Chr. 20:13 Ju. with t. w. stood
Ezr. 10:19 put away their w.
Neh. 5:1 cry of people and th. w.
10:28 t. w. entered into an oath
Is. 13:16 houses spoil. w. ravish.
Jer. 6:12 t. w. turned to oth. 8:10
14:16 none to bury their w.
18:21 t. w. be bereaved of child.
44:9 forgotten wicked. of t. w.
15 men knew t. w. burnt ince.
Ezek. 44:22 nor take for t. w. wi.
Dan. 6:24 cast t. w. into den of l.
Zec. 12:12 t. w. mourn, 13, 14
Eph. 5:28 love t. w. as th. bodies
1 Tim. 3:11 so must t. w. be gra.

Thy WIVES.
2 Sam. 12:11 take t. w. bef. eyes
19:5 who sav. ed lives of t. w.
1 K. 20:3 gold is mine and t. w.
5 deliver me thy w. and child.
2 Chr. 21:14 L. will smite t. w.
Jer. 38:23 bring thy w. and chil.
23 t w. thy tin have drunk wine
Mat. 24:19 w. to t. wh. are with
chi. Mark 13:17 ; Luke 21:23

Your WIVES.
Ex. 19:15 come not at your w.
32:2 your w. shall be widows
Deut. 3:19 y. w. and little ones
remain in cities. Jos. 1:14
29:11 y. w. enter coven. with L.
Jer. 44:9 forgot. wicked. of y. w.
25 ye and your w. have spoken
Eph. 5:25 love your w. Col. 3:19

WIZARD, s.
Lev. 19:31 not seek after w.
20:6 turns after w. I will cut off
27 that w. shall be put to death
Deut. 18:11 sh. not be am. you w.
1 Sam. 28:3 Saul put w. out of l.
2 K. 21:6 dealt with w. 2 Chr.
33:6
23:24 Josiah put tr. out of land
Is. 8:19 w. that peep and mutter
19:3 shall seek to idols and w.

WOE.

1 Sam. 4:7 w. unto v. 8 ; Jer.
4:13 ; 6:4 ; Lam. 5:16
Prov. 23:29 hath w. ? hath sor. ?
Ec. 4:10 w. to him that falls
10:16 w. to th. O land, wh. king
Is. 3:9 w. to their soul
11 w. to wick. sh. be ill wi. h.
17:12 w. to multi. of many peo.
18:1 w. to the land with wings
24:16 w. unto me
30 w. to pride, to drunkards
29:1 w. to Ariel ; 33:1 w. to thee
30:1 w. to rebellious children
43:9 w. to him striv. wi. Maker
Jer. 13:27 w. unto thee, O Jerus.
22:13 w. to him that builds
23:1 w. to pastors destroy sheep
48:1 w. to Nebo
45:3 w. to foolish prophets
16 w. to wom. th. sew pillows
16:23 w. w. unto thee, saith L.
21:6 w. to bloody city, Nah. 3:1
32:2 based, w. worth the day
31:2 w. be to the shepherds
Amos 5:18 w. to you de. day of L.
Hab. 2:6 w. to him that increas.
9 w. to him that build a town
12 w. to him that build a town
15 w. to him giveth neigh. drink
19 w. to him saith wood awake
Zep. 2:5 w. to inh. of sea coasts
3:1 w. to her that is polluted
Zec. 11:17 w. to idol shepherd

WOM

Mat. 11:21 w. to thee, Chora. w.
to thee, Bethsaida. Lu. 10:13
18:7 w. to the world because of
offences, Luke 17:1
23:13 w. unto you scribes and
Pharisees, 14, 15, 23, 25, 27,
29 ; Luke 11:44
16 w. unto you, blind guides
26:24 w. to man by whom Son
of man is betrayed, Mark
14:21 ; Luke 22:22
Luke 6:24 w. unto you are rich
25 w. to you that are full
26 w. to you wh. all speak well
11:42 w. unto you, Pharisees, 43
46 w. to you, ye lawyers, 4, 52
Rev. 8:13 w. w. w. to the inhabi-
ters of the earth, 12:12
9:12 one w. past ; 11:14 sec. w.

WOE is me.
Ps. 120:5 w. is me tha. I sojourn
Is. 6:5 w. is me, I am undone
Jer. 4:31 w. is me, soul wearied
10:19 w. is me, for my hurt
15:10 w. is me, moth. hast borne
45:3 w. is me, for L. added grief
Mic. 7:1 w. is me, I am as fruit

WOE unto me.
Job 10:15 if I be wicked, w. u. me
Jer. 24:16 my leavenness, w. u. me
1 Cor. 9:16 w. u. me if I preach

WOE to them.
Is. 5:8 w. to them that join house
11 w. to t. that rise in morning
18 w. to them that draw iniqu.
20 w. to t. that call evil good
21 w. to them wise in own eyes
22 w. to them that drink wine
10:1 w. to t. decree unright. dec.
29:15 w. to t. that seek counsel
31:1 w. to t. th. go down to Eg.
Jer. 50:27 w. to t. have fled fr. me
2:12 w. to t. depart from them
Amos 6:1 w. to t. at ease in Zion
Hos. 7:13 w. to t. have fled fr. me
9:12 w. to t. when I depart
Mat. Mark 13:17 ; Luke 21:23
chi. Mark 13:17 ; Luke 21:23
Jude 11 w. to t. gone way of Cain

WOES.
Rev. 9:12 two w. more hereafter

WOFUL.
Jer. 17:16 neither desired w. day

WOLF.
Gen. 49:27 Benja. ravin as a w.
Is. 11:6 w. sh. dwell with lamb
65:25 w. and lamb feed together
Jer. 5:6 w. of evening spoil them
John 10:12 bird. seeth w. coming

WOLVES.
Ezek. 22:27 her prince, are like w.
Hab. 1:8 horses fiercer than w.
Zep. 3:3 her judges evening w.
Luke 10:3 send you forth am. w.
Acts 20:29 w. sh. ent. among you

WOMAN.
Gen. 2:22 rib of man made he w.
23 sh. shall be called w.
3:1 seemly between th. and w.
2:15 perdition, w. not come, 29
41 let same be w. L. appointed
Ex. 21:22 hurt a w. with child
Lev. 12:28 her w. stand bef. beast
18:13 be with man's. as with w.
Num. 5:18 set w. before Lord, 30
27 w. be curse among her peo.
25:6 brought Midianitish w.
Deut. 17:5 bring out that w.
21:11 kill ev. w. beth know, man
Deut. 22:5 w. shall not wear
Jos. 2:4 w. took men, hid them
6:22 bring out thence w. Rahab
Jud. 4:9 Sisera into hand of w.
9:54 cr. ont aslew. in. Abime-
lech's head, 2 Sam. 11:21
51 may out of me. w. my people?
19:26 came w. in the dawning
Ruth 3:11 w. is a virtuous w.
4:11 L. make w. like Rachel
4:22 forf. of of sorrow ful sp
Sam. 1:15 I am a w. of sorrowful spi.
9:14 not a man had family
2 Sam. 11:2 Da. saw w. washing
14:2 put this w. out, bolt door
17:18 w. spread cover. on well
20:22 then w. to. all people
1 K. 3:17 I and this w. dwell
1:24 liken herself to the w.
17:17 son of w. fell sick, died
1 K. 4:8 where was a great w.

CRUDEN'S CONCORDANCE.

CRUDEN'S CONCORDANCE.

WOR

Ex. 7:21 no heed to a. t. w. spo.
Jr. 11:8 bring all t. w. of coven.
2:2 I speak all t. w. I command
3:4 write all t. w. spoken, 36:2
39:4 Ba. wrote a. t. w. of L. 32
43:1 J. had ended all t. w. of L.
Acts 5:20 speak to peo. all tha w.

WORDS of God.
Num. 24:4 wh. heard w. of G. 16
1 *Chr.* 25:5 kl.'s seer in w. of G.
Ezr. 9:4 trembleth at w. of G.
Ps. 107:11 rebelled ag. w. of God
John 3:34 G. sent speak. w. of G.
8:47 that is of G. hear. w. of G.
Rev. 17:17 until w. of G. be fulf.
See HEARD.

His WORDS.
Gen. 37:8 th. hated him for h. w.
Deut. 4:36 heard A. w. out of fire
Jud. 11:11 Jephth. uttered h. w.
1 *Sam.* 3:19 let none of h. w. fall
2 *Chr.* 36:16 they despised his w.
Job 22:22 lay up his w. in heart
34:34 not directed h. w. ag. me
34:35 his w. were without wisd.
37 he multiplieth his w. ag. G.
Ps. 55:21 his w. softer than oil
106:12 then believed they his w.
Prov. 17:27 knowl. spareth his w.
22:20 man th. is hasty in h. w. ?
30:6 add thou not unto his w.
Is. 31:2 Lord not call back his w.
Jer. 18:18 not give heed to h. w.
Jere. 9:12 he hath confirm. h. w.
Amos 7:10 not able to bear h. w.
Mark 10:24 astonished at his w.
12:13 to catch him in his w.
Luke 20:20
Luke 20:20 not take hold of h. w.
24:8 they remembered his w.
See LORD.

My WORDS.
Num. 12:6 hear my w. *Job* 34:2
Deut. 4:10 make th. hear my w.
11:18 lay up my w. in yo. heart
18:18 I will put my w. in mouth
19 whoso. will not heark. to my
w. I requ. *Jer.* 23:19 ; 33:13
Neh. 6:19 uttered my w. to him
Job 6:3 my w. are swallowed up
19:23 O that my w. were written
23:12 my w. they spake not
33:1 hearken to all my w. 34:16
Acts 2:14
3 my w. shall be of uprl. 36:4
Ps. 5:1 give ear to my w. O Lord
50:17 steteth my w. behind th.
56:5 every day th. wrest my w.
141:6 they shall hear my w.
Prov. 1:23 make kn. m. w. to you
2:1 if thou wilt receive my w.
4:1 let thy heart retain my w.
20 my son, attend to my w.
7:1 my son, keep my w.
Is. 51:16 I have put my w. in thy
mouth, *Jer.* 1:9
59:21 my w. wh. I put in mouth
Jer. 5:14 my w. in thy mouth
6:19 not hearkened to my w.
11:10 refused to hear my w.
18:2 cause thee to hear my w.
19:15 they nei. not hear my w.
23:22 caused peo. to hear my w.
23:8 ye have not heard my w.
13 bring upon that land my w.
3:16 bring my w. on this city
44:29 you may know my w.
Ezek. 2:7 speak my w. 3:4, 10
12:28 none of my w. be prolon.
Mic. 2:7 do not my w. do good to
Zec. 1:6 my w. did they n.t take
Mark 8:38 ashamed of my w. of
him sou he a-sha. *Luke* 9:26
13:31 my w. shall not pass away,
Luke 21:33
Luke 1:20 thou believ. not my w.
John 3:47 believe my w. ?
14:47 if any man hear my w.
48 he that receiveth not my w.
14:23 keep my w. 15:7 abide

Their WORDS.
Gen. 34:18 t. w. pleased Hamor
2 *Chr.* 9:6 I believed not their w.
Ps. 19:4 their w. to the end of the
world, *Rom.* 10:18
Ezek. 2:6 be not afraid of their w.
Luke 24:11 t. w. seemed as tales

These WORDS.
Ex. 19:6 t. w. th. shalt speak, 7
20:1 God spake t. w. *Deut.* 5:22
24:37 write these w. *Deut.* 27:8
35:1 these are the w. which Lord
commanded, *Deut.* 6:6 ; 29:1
Num. 16:31 end of these w. *Deut.*
32:47; 1 *Sam.* 24:16

WOR

Deut. 12:28 all these w. *Zec.* 8:9
1 *Sam.* 21:12 David laid up t. w.
2 *K.* 23:16 man proclaimed t. w.
Jer. 3:12 procl. t. w. tow. north
7:27 speak t. w. unto th. 26:15
16:10 sh. t. w. 25:30 proph. t. w.
38:24 let no man know of t. w.
43:1 wh. he had writ. t. w. 51:60
51:61 when thou shalt read t. w.
Luke 24:44 t. are the w. I spake
John 9:22 t. w. spake his parents
10:21 there are not w. of a devil
Acts 2:22 men of Israel hear t. w.
10:44 while Pet. yet spake t. w.
13:42 t. w. might be preached
26:25 said t. w. Jews departed
1 *Thes.* 4:18 comfort one another
with these w.
Rev. 21:5 t. w. true and faithful

Thy WORDS.
Deut. 33:3 ev. one sh. rec. of t. w.
Jos. 1:18 wh. not heark. to t. w.
Jud. 11:10 if do not acc. to t. w.
13:12 let thy w. come to pass
1 *Sam.* 15:24 I have transg. t. w.
28:21 I have hearkened to t. w.
2 *Sam.* 7:21 for thy w. sake
28 that God and thy w. be true
K. 1:14 come and confirm t. w.
22:13 th. hast performed t. w.
Job 4:4 t. w. upheld him th. was
Ps. 119:57 said I wo. keep t. w.
103 sweet t. w. to my taste!
130 entrance of t. w. giv. light
139 zeal hath consumed me t. w.
147 1 hoped in thy w.
Prov. 23:8 shalt lose t. sweet w.
9 he will despise wisd. of t. w.
Ec. 5:2 not rash, let t. w. be few
Jer. 15:16 thy w. were found
Ezek. 33:31 hear thy w. 32
Dan. 10:12 Daniel, thy w. heard
Mat. 12:37 by t. w. shalt be just.

Your WORDS.
Gen. 42:16 in prison y. w. be pro.
44:10 accord. to y. w. *Jos.* 2:21
Deut. 1:34 Lord heard y. w. 5:28
Job 32:11 I waited for your w.
Is. 41:26 none heareth your w.
Jer. 42:4 I will pray acc. to y. w.
Ezek. 35:13 I have multiplied y. w.
Mal. 2:17 wearied L. with y. w.
3:13 y. w. been ag. me. saith L.
Act. 10:14 not rec. nor hear y. w.

WORK.

Ex. 5:9 more w. laid on the men
12:16 no manner of w. shall be
done, 20:10; *Lev.* 16:29, 23:3,
28, 51; *Num.* 29:7
18:20 show the w. they must do
31:14 whoso doeth any w. thor.
sh. be cut off, 15; *Lev.* 23:30
Ex. 23:24 days w. be done, 20:9
36:7 sufficient for all the w.
Lev. 23:7 do no servile w. therein,
8, 21, 25, 35, 36; *Num.* 28:18,
25, 26; 29:1, 12, 35
Deut. 4:28 w. of men's hands.
27:15; 1 *K.* 19:18; 2 *Chr.*
32:19; *Ps.* 115:4; 135:15
5:14 sabbath, in it thou shalt
not w. 16:8; *Jer.* 17:24, 31
31:29 to provoke him thro' w.
of hands, 1 *K.* 16:7; *Jer.* 32:30
33:11 bless L. acc. w. of his ha'nl.
1 *K.* 5:16 officers over w. 9:23
7:8 house had court of like w.
K. 16:11 into han. did w. 22:5, 9
1 *Chr.* 9:33 in that w. day and ni.
16:37 minister as day's w. requ.
29:1 the w. is great, *Neh.* 4:19
2 *Chr.* 31:21 ev. w. he began did it
34:13 men did the w. faithfully
Ezr. 4:24 then ceased the w.
5:8 this w. goeth fast on
6:7 let w. of house of G. alone
22 stren. hands in w. of house
10:13 nei. a w. of one day or two
Neh. 3:5 nob. put not necks to w.
4:11 slay th. cause w. to cease
6:3 why should tha w. cease
16 they perc. this w. was of G.
7:70 the fathers gave to the w.
Job 1:10 blessed w. of his hands
10:3 despise w. of thy hands
14:15 desire to w. of thy hands
24:5 as asses go they to their w.
31:11 for w. of a man shall he
render to him, 1 *Pet.* 1:17
19 they are all w. of his hands
36:9 he showeth w. and transg.
Ps. 8:3 I consil. w. of th. fingers
9:16 snared in w. of his hands
19:1 firmament show. handy w.
28:4 after the w. of their hands
44:1 heard what w. thou didst
90:17 establish w. of our hands

WOR

Ps. 95:9 fa. proved me, saw my w.
101:3 I hate the w. of them that
102:25 heav. are w. of thy hands
143:5 I muse on w. of thy hands
Prov. 11:18 worketh deceitful w.
Ec. 3:17 a time for every w.
5:6 sh. G. destroy w. of hands?
8:9 I applied my heart to ev. w.
14 happen acc. to w. of wicked
9:10 there is no w. in grave
12:14 G. will bri. ev. into judg.
Cant. 7:1 w. of a cun. workman
Is. 3:38 they worship w. of their
own hands, 37:19; *Jer.* 1:16;
10:3, 9, 15; 51:18
17:8 not look to w. of his hands
19:15 nei. be any w. for Egypt
25 Assyria the w. of my hands
29:21 that he may do his w.
29:16 sh. w. say of him made it
23 children, the w. of my hands
32:17 w. of righteousness, peace
45:11 concerni. w. of my hands
49:4 surely my w. is with my G.
60:21 inherit w. of my hands
61:8 I will direct th. w. in truth
64:8 we are the w. of thy hands
65:22 elect enjoy w. of th. hands
Jer. 32:19 great and mighty in w.
50:29 recompense her according
to w. *Lam.* 3:64
Ezek. 13:3 shall wood do any w. ?
4 is it meet for w. ? 5 for w.
16:30 w. of a whorish woman
Hos. 13:2 the w. of craftsmen
14:3 say no more to w. of hands
Mic. 5:13 no more w. of hands
Hab. 1:5 work a w. in your days
Hag. 2:14 so is w. w. of hands
Mark 6:5 there do no mighty w.
John 7:21 done one w. ye marvel.
17:4 finished the w. thou gavest
Acts 5:38 if this w. be of men
13:2 w. whereunto I called them
41 I work a w. in your day
14:26 w. which they fulfilled
15:38 went not with them to w.
Rom. 2:15 show w. of law writ.
9:28 short w. L. make up. earth
11:6 otherwise w. is no more w.
1 *Cor.* 3:13 ev. man's w. be manif.
14 if w. abide ; 15 if w. burnt
9:1 are not ye my w. in Lord ?
Eph. 4:12 saine for w. of minis.
Phil. 1:6 who ha. begun good w.
2 *Thes.* 1:11 God fulfil w. of faith
2:17 sta'blish you in ev. good w.
2 *Tim.* 4:5 w. of an evangelist
Jam. 1:4 let patience ha. perf. w.
25 a doer of w. sh. be blessed
See EVIL.

WORK, 8 of God.
Ex. 32:16 tables were w. of God
Job 37:14 wondrous w. of God
Ps. 64:9 all declare the w. of G.
66:5 come and see w. of God
78:7 might not forget w. of God
Jer. 7:13 consider the w. of God
8:17 I behold all the w. of God
11:5 thou knowest not w. of G.
John 6:28 might work w. of God
29 this is w. of God he ye manif.
Acts 3:11 hear th. speak w. of G.
Rom. 14:20 for meat destroy not
the w. of God
See GOOD, GREAT.

His WORK.
Gen. 2:2 G. ended h. w. 3 rested
Ex. 36:4 every man from his w.
Deut. 32:4 his w. is perfect
Jud. 19:16 old man ca. fr. h. w.
1 *Sam.* 8:16 take asses to his w.
1 *K.* 7:14 Hiram wrought his w.
1 *Chr.* 4:23 dw. wi. king for h. w.
Neh. 4:15 returu. ev. man to h. w.
Job 7:2 looketh for rew. of h. w.
34:34 rem. thou magnify his w.
Ps. 62:12 renderest to ev. man
according to h. w. *Prov.* 24:29
104:23 man goeth to his w.
111:3 h. w. is honorable,glorious
Prov. 16:11 weights of bag h. w.
20:11 whether his w. be puro
21:8 for the pure h. w. is right
Is. 5:19 let him hasten his w.
10:12 L. performed h. whole w.
28:21 brin. to pass. h. w. h. 29:15
40:10 his w. is before him, 62:11
54:16 bring, an instru. for h. w.
Jer. 22:13 giveth not for his w.
48:10 keepeth not h. from h. w.
Hab. 2:18 maker of h. w. trusteth
Mark 13:34 gave ev. man his w.

WOR

John 4:34 my meat is to fin. h. w.
Gal. 6:4 every man prove his w.
Rev. 22:12 to every man as h. w.
See LORD, NEEDLE.

Our WORK.
Gen. 5:29 this sh. comfort our w.

Thy WORK.
Ex. 20:9 six days do all thy w.
23:12 ; *Deut.* 5:13
Ruth 2:12 L. recompense thy w.
Ps. 77:12 I will meditate thy w.
90:16 let t. w. ap. unto thy serv.
92:4 made me glad thro' thy w.
Prov. 24:27 prep. thy w. without
Is. 45:9 w. hath no hands ?
Jer. 31:16 thy w. sh. be rewarded
Hab. 3:2 revive thy w. in years

Your WORK.
Ex. 5:11 not aught of y. w. dim.
13 ; *Dent.* 13:7 y. w. sh. be rewarded
Is. 41:24 your w. is of naught
1 *Thes.* 1:3 remember y. w. faith
Heb. 6:10 to forget y. w. of faith

WORK-FELLOW.
Rom. 16:21 my w. f. salute you

WORK, Verb.
Ex. 5:18 go therefore now and w.
34:21 six days thou shalt w.
35:2 whoso w. ther. put to death
1 *Sam.* 14:6 may be Lord will w.
1 *K.* 21:20 sold thys. to w. evil, 25
Neh. 4:6 people had a mind to w.
Job 23:9 on left hand wh. he w.
Ps. 58:2 in heart you w. wicked.
119:126 it is time for Lord to w.
Prov. 11:18 wick. w. decei. work
Is. 5:19 they that w. in flax
43:13 I will w. who shall let it
Ezek. 33:26 ye w. abomination
Dan. 11:23 he sh. w. deceitfully
Mic. 2:1 woe to them that w. evil
Hab. 1:5 I will w. a work in your
days, *Acts* 13:41
Hag. 2:4 w. for I am with you
Mal. 3:15 w. wicked. are set up
Mat. 21:28 go w. in my vineyard
25:16 same, and w. men ought to w.
John 5:17 Father worketh, I w.
6:28 might w. the works of God
9:4 I must work the w. of him
30 said, What dost thou w. ?
9:4 I must w. the works of him
Rom. 7:5 sin did w. in me mem.
8:28 all thi. w. togeth. for good
Eph. 4:19 to w. uncleanness with
Phil. 2:12 w. out your salvation
1 *Thes.* 4:11 to w. with hands
2 *Thes.* 2:7 mys. of iniq. doth w.
3:10 not w. neit. should he eat
12 that with quietness they w.
See INIQUITY.

WORKER.
1 *K.* 7:14 was a w. in brass

WORKERS.
2 *K.* 23:24 w. wi. familiar spirits
1 *Cor.* 6:1 w. together with him
11:13 false apostles, deceitful w.
Phil. 3:2 dogs, beware of evil w.
See INIQUITY.

WORKS.
Ex. 5:13 fulfil your w. and tasks
Num. 16:28 sent me to do th. w.
Deut. 2:7 blos. thee in w. 16:15
Jud. 2:10 which knew not w.
1 *Sam.* 8:8 acc. to w. they have
1 *K.* 13:11 told w. man of G. did
2 *K.* 22:17 provoked me to anger
with w. of hands, 2 *Chr.* 34:25
Neh. 9:35 nor turned fr. wick. w.
10:1 done abominable w.
17:4 concerning the w. of men
92:4 triumph in w. of thy hands
111:2 w. of the Lord are great
7 w. of hands, verity and jud.
138:8 forsake not w. of thy ha.
141:4 to practice wicked w.
Prov. 31:31 let her w. praise her
Ec. 1:14 I have seen w. done, 2:11
Ec. 2:12 wrought our w. in us
Jer. 7:13 Lord, ye have done w.
25:6 provo. not with w. 7; 44:8
14 recompense them according
to w. of hands, *Rev.* 2:23
Ezek. 6:6 your w. be abolished
16:30 how weak is thy heart
Mic. 6:16 w. of house of A. kept
Mat. 11:2 John heard ro. of Chr.
John 5:20 show him greater w.
36 w. Father hath given me
7:3 may see the w. thou doest
8:39 I testify w. thereof are evil
9:3 would do w. of Abraham
9:4 I must work the w. of him
10:25 w. I do in Father's name
32 for wh. of w. do ye sto. me?

WOR

John 10:37 if I do not w. 38 believe w.
14:10 doeth w. 11 believe for w.
12 w. that I do, shall he do, gr.
15:24 if I had not done the w.
Acts 7:41 rejoiced in w. of hands
26:20 do w. meet for repentance
Rom. 3:27 by what law ? of w. ?
4:2 if Ab. were justified by w.
6 G. imputeth right. with. w.
9:11 not of w. but of him that
32 but as it were by w. of law
11:6 if by grace, no more of w.
13:12 cast off w. of darkness
Gal. 2:16 man is not justi. by w.
3:3 receiv. ye Sp. by w. of law ?
5 doeth he it by w. of the law
10 as many as are of w. of law
5:19 w. of the flesh are manifest
Eph. 2:9 not of w. lest any boast
5:11 wi. unfruitful w. of darkn.
Col. 1:21 enemies by wicked w.
1 Thes. 5:13 esteem for w. sake
2 Tim. 1:9 saved us, not according to our w. Tit. 3:5
Tit. 1:16 but in w. they deny G.
Heb. 1:10 heav. w. of thy hands
2:7 set him ov. w. of thy hands
3:9 your fathers saw my w.
4:3 although w. were finished
6:1 repentance from dead w.
9:14 purge conse. from dead w.
Jam. 2:14 not w. can faith save ?
17 faith with. w. is dead, 20:26
18 show me thy faith with. w.
21 was not Abr. justi. by w. ?
22 by w. was faith made perf.
24 by w. a man is justified
25 was not R. justified by w. ?
2 Pet. 2:10 w. therein burnt up
1 John 3:8 mi. destroy w. of devil
Rev. 2:26 that keepeth w. to end
9:20 repented not of w. of hands
18:6 double, according to her w.

See EVIL, GOOD, WORK *of* God.

His WORKS.

1 Sam. 19:4 his w. to thee good
2 Chr. 32:30 Hez. prosp. in h. w.
Ps. 33:4 h. w. are done in truth
78:11 forgat his w. wond. 106:13
103:22 bless the Lord, all his w.
104:31 L. shall rejoice in his w.
107:24 declare h. w. with rejoic.
111:6 show. peo. power of h. w.
115:9 his mercies are over h. w.
17 Lord is holy in all his w.
Prov. 8:22 pos. me before his w.
21:14 render to ev. man ac. to h. w. ? Mat. 16:27 ; 2 Tim. 4:14
Ec. 3:22 man sh. rejoice in h. w.
Dan. 9:14 G. is right. in his w.
Heb. 4:4 rest. on 7th day fr. h. w.
10 hath ceased from h. own w.
Jam. 3:13 faith wro. with h. w. ?
3:13 of a good conversat. his w.

See LORD, MARVELLOUS, MIGHTY.

Their WORKS.

Ex. 5:1 let people from their w.
23:24 shalt not do after their w.
Neh. 6:14 accord. to these t. w.
Job 34:25 therof. he know. t. w.
Ps. 33:15 he considereth their w.
106:35 they learned their w.
39 thus defiled with t. own w.
Ec. 9:1 t. w. are in hand of God
Is. 29:15 t. w. are in the dark
41:29 vanity, t. w. are nothing
59:6 nor cover thems. wi. t. w.
66:18 I kn. t. w. and thoughts
Amos 8:7 nev. forg. any of t. w.
Jon. 3:10 G. saw t. w. th. turned
Mat. 23:3 do not ye seen of them
5 t. w. do to be seen of men
2 Cor. 11:15 end accord. to t. w.
Rev. 14:13 t. w. do follow them
20:12 judged accord. to t. w. 13

Thy WORKS.

Deut. 3:24 according to thy w. ?
Le. 10 L. sh. bless thee in t. w.
2 Chr. 30:37 L. hath broken t. w.
Ps. 26:7 tell of t. wond. w. 145. 1
66:3 how terri. art thou in t. w.
73:28 that I may declare thy w.
86:8 neither are any works like unto thy w.
92:5 O L. how great are thy w.
104:13 earth satisfied with the fruit of thy w.
24 how manifold are thy w. !
143:5 remem. I meditate on t. w.
145:10 thy w. shall praise thee
Prov. 16:3 commit t. w. to Lord
Ec. 9:7 God accepteth thy w.
Is. 57:12 I will declare thy w.
Jer. 48:7 t. trusted in thy w.

WOR

Jam. 2:18 sh. faith without t. w.
Rev. 2, 3 I know thy w. 9, 13, 19;
3:1, 8, 15
3:2 I have not found t. w. perf.

Wonderful WORKS.

Ps. 40:5 many are thy wond. w.
78:4 showing his wonderful w.
107:8 praise L. for his w. w. to children of men, 15, 21, 31
111:4 made his w. w. rememb.
Mat. 7:22 in thy na. done w. w.
Acts 2:11 hear in tongues w. w.

See WONDROUS.

WORKETH.

Job 33:29 these w. God for man
Ps. 15:2 w. righteousness, dwell
101:7 w. deceit shall not dwell
Prov. 11:18 wicked w. deceitful
26:28 flattering mouth w. ruin
31:13 she w. with her hands
Ez. 3:9 what profit he that w. ?
4. 44:12 the smith w. in coals
64:5 meetest him th. w. right.
Dan. 6:27 w. signs and wonders
John 5:17 my Fath. w. hitherto
Acts 10:35 he that w. righteous.
Rom. 2:10 to every one w. good
4:4 to him that w. is reward
5 him that w. not, but believ.
15 because the law w. wrath
5:3 tribulation w. patience
13:10 love w. no ill to neighbor
1 Cor. 12:6 it is same G. that w.
11 those w. that one and same
16:10 for he w. the work of L.
2 Cor. 4:12 then death w. in us
17 w. for us more weight of gl.
7:10 godly sor. w. repentance
Gal. 3:5 he that w. miracles
5:6 but faith which w. by love
Eph. 1:11 who w. all things
2:2 spirit that w. in disobed.
3:20 according to power w. in us
Phil. 2:13 it is God w. in you
Col. 1:29 wh. w. in me mightily
1 Thes. 2:13 effectually w. in you
Jam. 1:3 try. of faith w. patience
20 wrath of man w. not right.
Rev. 21:27 whosoe. w. abomina.

WORKING, Participle.

Ps. 52:2 like a razor w. deceit.
74:12 w. salvation in the earth
Ezek. 46:1 gate shut six w. days
Mark 16:20 Lord w. with them
Rom. 1:27 w. that w. unseemly
7:13 sin w. death in me by good
1 Cor. 4:12 w. with our hands
Eph. 4:28 w. thing that is good
1 Thes. 3:11 w. not, busybodies
Heb. 13:21 w. th. wh. is plea ing
Rev. 16:14 spir. of devils w. mira.

WORKING, Substantive.

Is. 28:29 Lord excellent in w.
1 Cor. 9:6 power to forbear w. ?
12:10 another hw. of miracles
Eph. 1:19 accord. to w. of power
3:7 giv. me by w. of his power
4:16 accord. to w. of every part
Phil. 3:21 accord. to w. thereby
Col. 1:29 his w. wh. worketh in me
2 Thes. 2:9 after the w. of Satan

WORKMAN.

Ex. 35:35 work of cun. w. 38:23
Cant. 7:1 work of a cunning w.
Is. 40:19 w. melteth an image
20 seeketh to him a cun. w.
Jer. 10:3 work of w. with axe
Hos. 8:6 w. made it, not of God
Mat. 10:10 w. is worthy of meat
2 Tim. 2:15 a w. not to be asha.

WORKMANSHIP.

Ex. 31:3 and all manner of w.
5; 35:31
Eph. 2:10 his w. accord. to w. thereof
Nah. 38:10 w. of tabrets proper.
Eph. 2:10 we are his w. in C. Je.

2 K. 12:14 they gave that to the w. 15; 2 Chr. 34:10, 17
1 Chr. 22:15 w. with th. in abun.
25:1 the number of the w.
2 Chr. 24:13 so the w. wrought
Ezr. 3:9 set w. in house of God
Is. 44:11 the w. they are of men
Acts 19:25 with w. of like occup.

WORLD.

1 Sam. 2:8 he set the w. upon them
2 Sam. 22:16 the foundations of the w. appeared, Ps. 18:15
1 Chr. 16:30 st. sh. not be moved
Job 18:18 sh. not have disposed
37:12 may do on the face of w.
Ps. 9:8 he shall judge the w. in righteousness, 96:13; 98:9

WOR

Ps. 17:14 deliver from men of the w.
19:4 to end of w. Rom. 10:18
22:27 ends of w. shall remember
24:1 the earth and the w. is the Lord's, 89:11; Nah. 1:5
33:8 inhabit. of w. stand in awe
49:1 give ear, inhabitants of w.
50:12 for the w. is mine
77:18 lightnings flash. w. 97:4
89:11 founded w. and its fulness
90:2 form. the earth and the w.
93:1 the w. also is established
96:10 w. also sh. be established
Prov. 8:26 not made dust of w.
Ec. 3:11 set w. in their heart
Is. 13:11 I will punish w. for evil
14:17 is this he made w. wild. ?
24 nor fill face of w. wi. cities
26:9 w. will learn righteousness
18 we have, as it were, brought forth wind: neither have we wrought
27:6 Is. sh. fill the w. with fruit
34:1 let world hear, and all that
43:17 not confusn. w. with. end
Mat. 4:8 the devil showeth him all kingd. of the w. Luke 4:5
5:14 ye are the light of the w.
13:38 field is w. good seed chil.
40 so shall it be in end of w. 49
16:26 wind profit, gain w. lose soul ? Mark 8:36; Luke 9:25
18:7 woe to w. bec. of offences
24:14 sh. be preached in all the w. for witness, Mark 14:9
Luke 1:70 who has. been since w. began, Acts 3:21
2:1 decree that w. sh. be taxed
9:25 worthy to obtain that w.
John 1:10 he was in w. the w. was
9:32 since w. began was it not
12:19 the w. is gone after him
14:17 bec. w. cannot receive
19 the w. seeth me no more
22 how manifest thyself unto us and not unto the w. ?
27 I give, not as the w. giveth
31 the w. may know I love Fa.
15:18 w. hate you, I John 3:18
19 of w. the w. love his own
16:20 but the w. shall rejoice
28 I leave w. and go to Father
33 I have overcome the w.
17:5 glory I had before w. was
6 name to men gav. out of w.
9 I pray not for w. but for them
14 w. hated them, bec. not of w.
15 not take them out of w.
16 not of w. as I am not of w.
21 that the w. may believe th. hast sent me, 23
25 the w. hath not known me
18:20 I spake openly to w.
21:25 w. could not cont. books
Acts 17:6 turned w. upside down
24:5 a mover of sedit. thro' w.
Rom. 1:8 faith is spo. of thro' w.
19 w. may bec. guilty bef. G.
4:13 he should be heir of w.
11:12 fall of th. be riches of w.
15 if casting away of them be reconciling of w.
1 Cor. 1:21 w. by wis. kn. not G.
27 G. hath chosen foolish of w. to confound wise in t. w.
2:12 not received spirit of w.
3:22 w. or life, or death, yours
4:9 we are made a spectacle to w.
13 we are made as filth of w.
5:10 then must ye go out of w.
6:2 kn. th. saints sh. judge w. ?
7:31 careth for things of w. 31
8:4 an idol is noth. w. stand.
11:32 not be condemned with w.
1 Cor. 2:8 whi. none of princes of this w. knew
3:19 w. by wisdom knew not G.
4:10 fools for C. sake 1:27
6:14 saith, Lord, how can I be brighter
7:33 careth for things of this w.
14 if even the w. to come
6 destroy this body
21:26 and w. shall cover them
Mic. 7:17 out of holes like w.
Acts 12:23 he eaten of w.

WORMWOOD.

Deut. 28:8 a root that beareth w.
Prov. 5:4 her end is bitter as w.
Jer. 9:15 feed them with w. 23:15

WOR

1 John 3:1 the w. knoweth us not
4:5 they are of the w.
5:1 born of G. overcometh w.
19 whole w. lieth in wicked.
Rev. 3:10 temptation come on w.
12:9 Satan, deceiveth whole w.
13:3 w. wondered after the beast

See FOUNDATION.

In, *or* **into the WORLD.**

Ps. 73:12 ungod. wh. prosp. i. t. w.
Mat. 26:13 this gospel be preached in the whole w.
Mark 10:30 and in the w. to come eternal life, Luke 18:30
John 1:9 man that comes i. the w.
10 he was in the w.
3:17 sent not his Son into the w.
19 light is come into the w.
6:14 should come i. t. w. 11:27
9:5 as long as I am in the w.
12:46 I am come a light i. t. w.
16:33 i. w. ye sh. have tribula.
17:11 I am no more in the w.
12 while I was in w. I kept th.
18:37 for this came I into the w.
Rom. 5:12 sin entered into the w.
13 until law, sin was in the w.
1 Cor. 8:4 an idol is noth. in t. w.
Eph. 2:12 without God in the w.
Col. 1:6 as it is in all the w.
1 Tim. 1:15 Christ Jesus came into the w. to save sinners
3:16 and believed on in the w.
Heb. 10:5 when he cometh i. t. w.
1 Pet. 5:9 afflict. that are in t. w.
1 John 2:15 love not that. in t. w.
4:1 false prophets gone i. t. w.
3 now already is it in the w.
4 greater th. he that is in t. w.
5 sent his Son into the w. that
3 John 7 many deceivers i. t. w.

This WORLD.

Mat. 12:32 not forgi. him in t. w.
13:22 cares of this w. choke the word, Mark 4:19
Luke 16:8 children of this w. are wiser in their gen. than childr. of light
20:34 children of this w. marry
John 8:23 ye are of this w.
18:36 my kingdom is not of this w.
12:25 that hateth life in this w.
31 now is judgment of this w.
13:1 should depart out of this w.
14:30 prince of this w. cometh
16:11 prince of this w. is judged
18:36 kingdom is not of this w.
Rom. 12:2 not conformed to t. w.
1 Cor. 1:20 wh. is disp. of t. w. ?
2:6 speak not wisdom of this w.
3:18 if man seem. wise in t. w.
19 wisd. of t. w. foolish. wi. G.
5:10 not with fornicat. of t. w.
7:31 use t. w. as not abusing it
2 Cor. 4:4 god of t. w. blinded
Gal. 1:4 deli. us fr. t. present w.
Eph. 1:21 not only in t. w. but
2:2 according to course of t. w.
6:12 against rulers of this w.
1 Tim. 6:7 bro. nothing in t. w.
17 those that are rich in t. w.
2 Tim. 4:10 De. loved t. pres. w.
Tit. 2:12 live godly in t. pres. w.
Jam. 2:5 chosen poor of this w.
4:4 friendship w. is enmity w. G.
1 John 3:17 hath t. w. good
4:17 as he is, so we in t. w. w.

WORLDLY.

Tit. 2:12 ungodlin. and w. lusts
Heb. 9:1 first cov. had w. sanct.

WORMS.

Heb. 1:2 by whom he made w.
11:3 w. were fram. by word of G.

WORM.

Ex. 16:24 neither any w. therein
Job 17:14 said to w. my mother
24:20 w. feed sweetly on him
25:6 man is a w. son of man
Ps. 22:6 I am a w. and no man
Is. 41:14 w. is spread under thee
49:14 four not thou w. Jacob
51:8 w. sh. eat them like wool
66:24 their w. sh. not die, Mark 9:44, 46, 48
Jon. 4:7 a w. smote the gourd

WORMS.

Ex. 16:20 bred w. and stank
Deut. 28:39 w. sh. eat them
Job 7:5 clothed with w. and dust
19:26 tho' w. destroy this body
21:26 and w. shall cover them
Mic. 7:17 out of holes like w.
Acts 12:23 he was eaten of w.

WORMWOOD.

Deut. 29:18 a root that beareth w.
Prov. 5:4 her end is bitter as w.
Jer. 9:15 feed them with w. 23:15

WOR

Lam. 3:15 made drunken with w.
19 my misery, the w. and gall
Amos 5:7 who turn judgm. to w.
Rev. 8:11 name of star called W.

WORSE.

Gen. 19:9 deal w. with thee than
2 *Sam.* 19:7 w. th. all that befell
2 *K.* 14:12 Judah was put to the w. 2 *Chr.* 25:22
1 *Chr.* 19:16 Syrians put to w. 19
2 *Chr.* 6:24 if people be put to w.
33:9 Manasseh made Jer. do w.
Jer. 7:26 w. th. their fath. 16:12
Dan. 1:10 see faces w. liking ?
Mat. 12:45 last state of that man is w. than first, *Luke* 11:26
27:64 last error w. than the first
John 5:14 a w. thi. come unto th.
1 *Cor.* 8:8 if eat not are we w.
11:17 not for better but for w.
2 *Tim.* 3:13 seducers sh. wax w.
2 *Pet.* 2:20 latter end is w. with

WORSHIP.

Gen. 22:5 I and the lad will go and w.
Ex. 34:1 and w. ye afar off
34:14 thou shalt w. no other G.
Deut. 4:19 lest th. be driven to w.
8:19 if thou w. other gods, 11:16; 30:17
28:10 and w. before the L. thy God, *Ps.* 22:27, 29; 86:9
1 *Sam.* 1:3 man went up to w..
15:25 that I may w. Lord, 30
1 *K.* 12:30 the people went to w.
2 *K.* 5:18 to. in house of Rimmon
17:36 L. ye fear, him sh. ye w.
18:22 shall w. bef. this altar in Jer., 2 *Chr.* 32:12; *Is.* 36:7
1 *Chr.* 16:29 w. L. in the beauty of holiness, *Ps.* 29:2; 66:4; 96:9; *Mat.* 4:10; *Luke* 4:8
Ps. 5:7 w. tow. thy temple 138:2
45:11 he is thy L. w. thou him
81:9 neither w. any strange god
95:6 let us w. and bow down
97:7 w. him all ye gods
9:5 w. at his footstool, 132:7
9 and w. at his holy hill
Is. 2:8 w. work of hands, 20; 46:6
27:13 w. Lord in holy mount
49:7 princes also shall w.
60:23 all flesh w. before me
Jer. 7:2 enter th. gates to w. 26:2
13:10 w. other gods be as girdle
22:9 go not after oth. gods to w.
44:19 did we w. her with. men ?
Ezek. 46:2 he sh. w. at threshold
3 people of land sh. w. at door
w entereth to w. by north gate
Dan. 3:5 w. golden image, 10, 15
12 not w. fm. 18:14; 15 if ye w.
11 do not ye w. ima. I set up ?
Mic. 5:13 thou shalt no more w. work of thine hands
Zep. 1:5 that w. host of heaven
2:11 men sh. w. him, every one
Zec. 14:16 w. Lord of hosts, 17
Mal. a:2 and come to w. him
s that I may come and w. him
4:9 if thou wilt w. me, *Lu.* 4:7
15:9 but in vain they do w. me
John 4:20 in Jerusal. is the place wh. men ou,. to w. *Mark* 7:7
22 ye w. ye know not what
23 w. the Father in spirit, 24
12:20 Greeks ca. to w. at feast
Acts 7:42 gave th. to w. host, 43
8:27 eunuch came to Jer. to w.
17:23 whom ye ignorantly w.
18:13 persuaded men to w. God
24:11 Paul came to Jerus. to w.
14 so w. I God of my fathers
1 *Cor.* 11:25 he will w. God
Phil. 3:3 which w. God in spirit
Heb. 1:6 let angels of G. w. him
Rev. 3:9 and w. before thy feet
4:10 w. him that liveth for ever
9:20 they should not w. devils
13:8 all that dwell on earth shall w. beast, 12
15 th. would not w. the image
14:7 w. him that made heaven
9 if any man w. beast and im.
11 who w. beast, have no rest
15:4 nations come, w. bef. him
19:10 I fell at his feet to w. 22:8;
22:9 w. God

WORSHIPPED.

Gen. 24:26 Abraham w. Lord, 48
52 Abraham's servant w. Lord
Ex. 4:31 Israel w. 12:27; 33:10
32:8 they made a calf, and w. *Ps.* 106:19
34:8 Mos. w. Jud. 7:15 Old. w.

WOR

Deut. 17:3 served other gods, and w. 29:26; 1 *K.* 9:9; 2 *K.* 21:21; 2 *Chr.* 7:22; *Jer.* 1:16; 8:2; 16:11; 22:9
1 *Sam.* 1:19 Hannah w, before L.
28 Samuel w. 15:31; 8. w. Lord
2 *Sam.* 12:20 D. arose w. 15:32
1 *K.* 11:33 forsaken me, w. Ash.
10:31 served Baal, w. him, 22:53
2 *K.* 17:16 they w. host of heaven, 21:3, 2 *Chr.* 33:3
1 *Chr.* 29:20 cong. bowed, and w. L. 2 *Chr.* 7:3; 29:28, 29, 30
Neh. 8:6 all people w. Lord, 9:3
Job 1:20 Job w. *Ezek.* 8:16 w. sun
Dan. 2:46 king w. 3:7 w. image
Mat. 2:11 wise men fell, w. Christ
8:2 leper w. him, 9:18 a ruler w.
11:33 that were in ship w. him
15:25 woman of Canaan w. him
18:26 servant fell, w. his lord
28:9 held him by feet, w. him
17 disciples w. him, *Lu.* 24:52
Mark 5:6 ran out of tombs, w.
15:19 spit on him, bowing, w.
John 4:20 our fath. w. in mount.
Acts 10:25 Cornelius w. Peter
17:25 neither is w. with hands
Rom. 1:25 cr. creature more than
2 *Thes.* 2:4 exalteth above all w.
Heb. 11:21 Jacob w. *Rev.* 7:11 w. God
Rev. 5:14 twenty-four elders w. 11:16; 19:4
13:4 they w. dragon, w. beast
14:2 sore fell on them w. image
19:20 deceiv. that w. his image
20:4 souls that had not w. beast

WORSHIPPER, S.

K. 10:19 destroy w. of Baal
21 all w. of B. came, none left
23 none but the w. of Baal only
John 4:23 w. sh. worship in spirit
9:31 if any man be a w. of God
Acts 19:35 Ephesus is w. of D
Heb. 10:2 because w. once purged

WORSHIPPETH.

Neh. 9:6 host of heaven w. thou
Is. 44:15 maketh god. w. it, 17
Dan. 3:6 falleth not and w. 11
Acts 19:27 Asia and the world w.

WORSHIPPING.

2 *K.* 19:37 as he was w. in house of Nisroch, *Is.* 37:38
2 *Chr.* 20:18 Ju. fell down, w. L.
Mat. 20:20 Zeb's chil. came w.
Col. 2:18 begu. you in w. of ang.

WORST.

Ezek. 7:24 bri. w. of the heathen

WORTH.

Gen. 23:9 for as much money as it is w.
Job 24:25 make speech noth. w.
Prov. 10:20 heart of wick. lit. w.
Ezek. 30:2 say, howl, woe w. day

WORTHY.

Gen. 32:10 I am not w. of mercl.
1 *Sam.* 1:5 he gave a w. portion
26:16 as L. liv, ye are w. to die
2 *Sam.* 22:4 who is w. to be praised, *Ps.* 18:3
1 *K.* 1:52 show himself a w. man
2:26 Abia, L. not w. to die; 16 is not w.
Mat. 3:11 I am not w. to bear
8:8 Lord, I am not w. *Luke* 7:6
10:11 inquire who in it is w. 13
37 loveth more, he is not w. 38
9:23 which were bidden not w.
Mark 1:7 not w. to unloose, *Lu.* 3:16; *John* 1:27; *Acts* 13:25
Luke 3:9 fruits w. of repentance
7:1 w. for whom he should w.
7 nor thought I myself w.
10:7 laborer is w. of his hire
10:10 no more w. to be son, 21
Acts 28:14 w. deeds done to nat.
Rom. 8:18 not w. to be compared
Eph. 4:1 th. ye walk w. of vocat.
Col. 1:10 ye might walk w. of L.
1 *Thes.* 2:12 ye would walk w.
1 *Tim.* 1:15 w. of acceptati. 4:9
5:18 laborer is w. of his reward
Heb. 11:38 world was not w.
Jam. 2:7 blasph. that w. name ?
Rev. 3:4 walk in white, are w.
4:11 w. to receive glory, 5:9
5:2 who is w. to open the book
4 no man fo. w. to open book
8 thou art w. to take book
10:6 to drink, for they are w.

See COUNT, COUNTED, DEATH.

WORTHIES.

Nah. 2:5 he shall recount his w.

WOU

WORTHILY.
Ruth 4:11 do thou w. in Ephrat.

WOT, WOTTETH.

Gen. 21:26 I w. not who done
39:8 w. not what is with me
44:15 w. ye not I can divine ?
Ex. 32:1 we w. not what is become of him, 23; *Acts* 7:40
Num. 22:6 w. he wh. thou bless.
Jos. 2:5 whither the men went I w. not
Acts 3:17 I w. thro' ignor. ye did
Rom. 11:2 w. ye not what scrip.
Phil. 1:22 what choose I w. not

WOVE.

2 *K.* 23:7 women wove hangings

WOVEN.

Ex. 28:32 hab. of w. work, 39:22
39:27 linen, w. work for Aaron
John 19:23 coat without seam, w.

WOULD.

Neh. 9:24 do with th. as they w.
Ps. 81:11 Israel w. none of me
Prov. 1:25 ye w. none of reproof
Mark 10:36 what w. ye ? *Mr.* do
Rom. 7:15 what w. that I do not
19 the good that I w. I do not

WOULD God.

Ex. 16:3 w. God we had died in Egypt, *Num.* 11:2
Num. 11:29 w. G. people proph.
22:1 w. God we died wh. breth.
Deut. 28:67 w. God it were even
Jos. 7:7 w. God we dw. on side
Jud. 9:29 w. G. peo. under hand
Jam. 18:33 w. G. I died for th.
2 *K.* 5:3 w. G. lord with prophet
Acts 26:29 w. G. all such as I am
1 *Cor.* 4:8 I w. God ye did reign
2 *Cor.* 11:1 w. to G. bear wi. me

WOULD not.

1 *Sam.* 2R:9 w. not t let thee?
Is. 30:15 and ye w. not, *Mat.* 23:37; *Luke* 13:34
Rom. 7:16 do that wh. I w. not
19 evil that I w. not that I do
2 *Cor.* 12:30 such us ye w. not

WOULDEST.

Jos. 15:18 and Caleb said, What w. thou ? 1 *K.* 1:16

WOULDEST not.

John 21:18 carry whi. thou w. n.

WOUND.

Ex. 21:25 w. for w. stripe
1 *K.* 22:35 blood ran out of w.
Job 34:6 my w. is incurable
Prov. 6:33 a w. and dishonor
20:30 blueness of w. cleanseth
Is. 30:26 heal. stroke of their w.
Jer. 10:19 for my w. is grievous
15:18 why is my w. incurable?
30:12 w. is grievous, *Nah.* 3:19
14 I wounded thee with w.
Hos. 5:13 Jud. saw his w. could
Ob. 7 have laid a w. under thee
Mic. 1:9 her w. is incurable
Rev. 13:3 w. was healed, 12, 14

WOUNDS.

2 *K.* 8:29 king J. went to be heal. of the w. 9:15; 2 *Chr.* 22:6
Job 9:17 he multiplied my w.
Ps. 38:5 my w. stink, corrupt
147:3 and bindeth up their w.
Prov. 18:8 talebearer as w. 26:22
23:29 hath w. without cause?
27:6 faithful are w. of a friend
Is. 1:6 no soundness in it, but w.
Jer. 6:7 before me is grief and w.
3:17 I will heal thee of thy w.
Zec. 13:6 are th. w. in thy hands?
Luke 10:34 Samari. bound up w.

WOUND, Verb.

Deut. 32:39 I w. and I heal
Ps. 68:21 God sh. w. his enemies
110:0 w. heads o. many countr.
1 *Cor.* 8:12 ye w. their conscience

WOUND.

John 19:40 th. w. body of Jesus
Acts 5:6 yo. men w. up Ananias

WOUNDED.

Deut. 23:1 he that is w. in stones
1 *Sam.* 17:52 w. of Philistines
2 *Sam.* 22:29 I have w. mine enemies, *Ps.* 18:38
1 *K.* 20:37 in smiting he was w.
22:34 for I am w. 2 *Chr.* 18:33
2 *Chr.* 35:23 for I am sore w.
Job 21:2 soul of w. crieth out
21:7 suddenly sh. they be w.
26:36 grief of those th. hast w.
109:22 my heart is w. within me
Prov. 7:26 cast down many w.
13:14 a w. spirit who can bear ?

WRA

Cant. 5:7 found me, they w. me
Is. 51:9 art not it that w. drag. ?
53:5 he was w. for our transgr.
Jer. 30:14 I w. thee with wound
58:10 th. remained but w. men
51:52 thro' land w. shall groan
Lam. 2:12 they swooned as w.
Ezek. 26:15 when the w. cry
28:23 w. be judged in the midst
30:24 groanings of a w. man
Zec. 13:6 w. in house of my frie.
Mark 12:4 w. him, *Luke* 20:12
Luke 10:30 am. thieves, w. him
Acts 19:16 fled out house nak. w.
Rev. 13:3 his heads as it were, w.

WOUNDEDST, ETH.

Job 5:18 w. hands make whole
Hab. 3:13 thou w. head of wick.

WOUNDING.

Gen. 4:23 slain a man to my w.

WRAP.

Is. 28:20 he can w. himself in it
Mic. 7:3 reward, so they w. it up

WRAPPED, or WRAPT.

1 *Sam.* 21:9 sword is w. in cloth
1 *K.* 19:13 Elijah w. his face
2 *K.* 2:8 mantle, w. it together
Job 8:17 roots are w. about heap
40:17 sinews of stones w. togeth.
Ezek. 21:15 swo. is w. for slaug.
Jon. 2:5 weeds w. about head
Mat. 27:59 Jos. w. body in linen, *Mark* 15:16; *Luke* 23:53
Luke 2:7 Mary w. him in clothes
12 babe w. in swaddl. clothes
John 20:7 napkin w. together

WRATH.

Gen. 49:7 cursed be their w.
Num. 1:53 no w. be on cong. 18:5
16:46 there is w. gone out fr. L.
Deut. 9:7 provokedst L. to w. 22
29:24 rooted them out to w.
32:27 were it not I feared w.
Jos. 9:20 lest w. be upon us
22:20 w. fell on all the congre.
2 *Sam.* 11:20 if king's w. arise
2 *K.* 23:26 L. turned not from w.
Chr. 27:24 because th. fell w.
2 *Chr.* 19:2 theref. is w. on thee
10 and so w. come upon you
24:18 came on Ju. for tresp.
28:13 there is fierce w. ag. Isr.
29:9 w. of L. upon Judah, *Jer.* 32:25 theref. th. was w. on him
Ezr. 5:12 had provoked G. to w.
7:23 why sho. be w. ag. realm?
Neh. 13:15 bri. more w. on Isr.
Est. 1:18 th. arise too much an.
3:1 w. of king was appeased
3:5 bowed not, Ham. full of w.
7:10 then was king's w. pacified
Job 5:2 for w. killeth foolish man
19:29 for w. brings punishments
20:23 drink of w. of Almighty
21:33 hypocri. in heart heap w.
32:2 because there is w. beware
Ps. 37:8 forsake w. 78:5 w. hate
Prov. 11:23 exp. of wicked is w.
12:16 fool's w. presently known
14:29 slow to w. of great under.
18:1 soft answer turn. away w.
19:11 of king be messeng. of
19:12 king's w. as roar. of lion
19 man of w. suffer punishm.
21:14 rew. in bosom pacifieth w.
24 scorner, who dealeth in w.
27:3 fool's w. heavier than both
4 w. is cruel, anger is outrage.
29:8 wise men turn away w.
30:33 forcing of w. bring, strife
Ec. 5:17 moreo. w. with sickness
Is. 13:9 Day of L. cometh with w.
14:6 who smote the people in w.
54:8 in a little w. I hid my face
Jer. 27:5 fight against you in w.
32:37 driven them in great w.
44:8 provoke me to w. wi. idols
Ezek. 7:19 w. is on all multitude
Nah. 1:2 reserv. w. for enemies
Hab. 3:2 in w. remember mercy
Zec. 1:15 God not deliver to w.
Mat. 3:7 flee from w. to come, *Luke* 3:7
Luke 4:28 all, wi. w. *Acts* 19:28
21:23 th. sh. be w. on this peo.
Rom. 2:5 treasurest up w. agai.
8 to them th. obey upright, w.
4:15 because law worketh w.
5:9 be saved from w. thro' Lam

CRUDEN'S CONCORDANCE. 1089

WRA

Rom. 9:22 ves. of *w.* fit. to destr.
12:19 rather give place to *w.*
13:4 minister of G. to execu. *w.*
5 ye be subject, not only for *w.*
Gal. 5:20 works of flesh are *w.*
Eph. 2:3 by nature childr. of *w.*
4:26 let not sun go do. upon *w.*
31 let all *w.* anger, and clamor
6:4 provoke not your chil. to *w.*
Col. 3:8 put off these, *w.* malice
1 Thes. 1:10 delivered us from *w.*
2:16 for *w.* is come on them
5:9 G. hath not appoi. us to *w.*
1 Tim. 2:8 lift. hands without *w.*
Heb. 11:27 not fearing *w.* of king
Jam. 1:19 slow to spe. slow to *w.*
20 *w.* of man work. not right.
Rev. 6:16 hide us fr. *w.* of Lamb
12:12 devil come, hav. great *w.*
14:8 nations drink of *w.* 16:3

Day of WRATH.
Job 20:28 flow away in d. of *w.*
21:30 wicked brou. to day of *w.*
Ps. 110:5 strike kings in d. of *w.*
Prov. 11:4 riches profit not in the day of *w.*
Zep. 1:15 that day is a day of *w.*
Rom. 2:5 treasu. w. ag. d. of *w.*
Rev. 6:17 great d. of *w.* is come

WRATH of God.
2 Chr. 28:11 *w.* of God upon you
Ezr. 10:14 *w.* of God he turned
Ps. 78:31 *w.* of God ca. on them
John 3:36 *w.* of G. abid. on him
Rom. 1:18 *w.* of God is revealed
Eph. 5:6 *w.* of God cometh, *Col.* 3:6
Rev. 14:10 dr. wine of *w.* of G.
19 into wine-press of *w.* of G.
15:1 for th. is filled up *w.* of G.
7 seven vials full of *w.* of God
Rev. 19:1 pour vial of *w.* of God
19:15 tread. wine-pr. of *w.* of G.

His WRATH.
Deut. 29:23 L. overthr. in *his w.*
1 Sam. 28:18 execu. *h. w.* on A.
2 K. 23:26 L. turned not fr. *h. w.*
2 Chr. 29:10 *his* fierce *w.* may turn from us, 30:8
Ezr. 8:22 *his w.* is against them
7:28 from banquet in *his w.*
Job 16:9 no teareth me in *his w.*
20:23 cast fury of *his w.* on him
Ps. 2:5 speak to them in *his w.*
21:9 swallow them up in *his w.*
58:9 take them away in *his w.*
78:38 did not stir up all *his w.*
49 cast on th. fierceness of *h. w.*
106:23 Mo. stood to turn *his w.*
Prov. 14:35 *his w.* ag. him that
24:18 lest L. turn *his w.* fr. him
Is. 19:0 Moab's pride and *his w.*
Jer. 7:29 L. forsak. gen. of *h. w.*
10:10 at *his w.* earth sh. tremble
48:30 I know *his w.* saith Lord
Lam. 2:2 thrown down in *his w.*
3:1 affliction by rod of *his w.*
Amos 1:11 kept *his w.* for ever
Rom. 5:22 G. will, to show *h. w.*
Rev. 16:19 cup of wine of *his w.*
See KINDLED, *Wrath of the* LORD.

My WRATH.
Ex. 22:24 *my w.* shall wax hot
32:10 that *my w.* may wax hot
Num. 25:11 hath turned *my w.*
2 Chr. 12:7 *my w.* shall not be poured out
Ps. 95:11 I sware in *my w.*
Is. 10:6 against people of *my w.*
60:10 for in *my w.* I smote thee
Ezek. 7:14 *my w.* to accomplish
13:16 thus will I accomp. *my w.*
21:31 in fire of *my w.* 22:21
22:31 I consu. them with *my w.*
38:19 in fire of *my w.* h. I spo.
Hos. 5:10 I will pour *my w.* on
13:11 I took him away in *my w.*
Heb. 3:11 I sware in *my w.* they
4:3 as I have sworn in *my w.*

Thy WRATH.
Ex. 15:7 thou sentest *thy w.*
32:11 why doth *t. w.* wax hot?
12 turn from *t. w.* and repent
Job 14:13 until *thy w.* be past
40:11 cast abroad rage of *thy w.*
Ps. 38:1 rebuke me not in *t. w.*
78:6 pour out *t. w.* on heathen
85:3 thou hast taken away *t. w.*
88:7 *thy w.* lieth hard on me
16 *thy* fierce *w.* goeth over me
89:46 how long shall *thy w.* burn like fire?
90:7 by *thy w.* are we troubled
9 days are passed away in *t. w.*
11 ac. to *thy* fear, so is *t. w.*
102:10 beg. of indigna. and *t. w.*

WRI

Jer. 18:20 to turn *thy w.* fr. them
Hab. 3:8 was *thy w.* ag. the sea
Rev. 11:18 *t. w.* is come, time of

WRATHFUL.
Ps. 69:24 let *w.* anger take hold
Prov. 15:18 a *w.* man stir. strife

WRATHS.
2 Cor. 12:20 envyings, *w.* strifes

WREATH, S.
1 K. 7:17 *w.* for the chapiters
2 Chr. 4:2 two *w.* to cover the two pommels
13 400 pomegranates on two *w.*
two rows of pomeg. on *w.*

WREATHED, EN.
Ex. 28:14 two chains at ends of *w.* work, 24, 34, 25; 39:15-18
2 K. 25:17 pillar of *w.* work he
Lam. 1:14 my trangress. are *w.*

WREST.
Eph. 6:19 we *w.* not against flesh

WRESTLED.
Gen. 30:8 have I *w.* with sister
32:24 there *w.* a man with him
25 thigh out of joint as he *w.*

WRESTLINGS.
Gen. 30:8 wi. *w.* have I wrestled

WRETCHED.
Rom. 7:24 O *w.* man that I am
Rev. 3:17 know. not thou art *w.*

WRETCHEDNESS.
Num. 11:15 let me not see my *w.*

WRING, ED.
Lev. 1:15 priest *w.* off head, 5:8
Jud. 6:38 Gide. *w.* dew of fleece
Ps. 75:8 wicked sh. *w.* them out

WRINGING.
Prov. 30:33 *w.* of nose bri. blood

WRINKLE, S.
Job 16:8 hast filled me with *w.*
Eph. 5:27 not having spot or *w.*

WRITE.
Ex. 34:1 will *w.* on ta. *Deut.* 10:2
27 L. said to Mo. *w.* th. words
Num. 17:2 *w.* every man's name
3 *w.* Aaron's name on rod of L.
Deut. 6:9 *w.* them on posts, 11:30
24:1 let him *w.* her a bill of divorcement, 3; *Mark* 10:4
27:3 *w.* the words of the law, 8
31:19 *w.* ye this song for you
2 Chr. 20:32 acts of *D.* did Is. *w.*
Neh. 9:38 sure covon. and *w.* it
Ezr. 8:21 in great roll wi. a pen
Prov. 3:3 *w.* on tab. of heart, 7:3
Is. 8:1 *w.* in great roll wi. a pen
10:1 *w.* grievousness prescribed
19 that a child may *w.* them
30:8 *w.* it before them in a table
Jer. 22:30 *w.* ye this man childl.
30:2 *w.* the words I have spok. en, 36:2, 17, 28
31:33 *w.* in th. hearts, *Heb.* 8:10
Ezek. 24:2 *w.* the na. of the day
37:16 *w.* for Judah and Israel
43:11 *w.* it in their sight
Hab. 2:2 *w.* the vision on tables
Luke 1:3 it seem. good to *w.* th.
16:6 *w.* fifty ; 7 *w.* fourscore
John 1:45 Mos. and proph. did *w.*
19:21 *w.* not, King of the Jews
Acts 15:20 *w.* that th. abstain fr.
25:26 no cert. thi. to *w.* my lord
1 Cor. 4:14 I *w.* not to sha. you
14:37 things I *w.* are command.
2 *Cor.* 1:13 *w.* no. none other thi.
2:9 I *w.* that I might know
9:1 it is superfluous to *w.* you
13:2 I *w.* to th. wh. have sinned
10 *w.* these thi. being absent
Gal. 1:20 things I *w.* unto you
Phil. 3:1 to *w.* the same things
1 *Thes.* 4:9 not that I *w.* 5:1
2 *Thes.* 3:17 is the token ; so I *w.*
1 *Tim.* 3:14 these th. I unto thee
Heb. 10:16 in minds will I *w.*
2 *Pet.* 3:1 *w.* to you, 1 *John* 2:1
1 *John* 1:4 thi. that *w.* we to you
2:7 I *w.* no new commandment
8 a new commandm. I *w.* you
12 I *w.* to you, lit. children, 13
13 I *w.* to you, fathers
2 *John* 12 many th. to *w.* to you
3 *John* 13 not wi. ink and pen *w.*
Rev. 1:11 what seest *w.* 19

WRI

Rev. 2:1 angel of ch. of Ephe. *w.*
8 angel of chur. of Smyrna *w.*
12 angel of chu. in Pergam. *w.*
18 angel of chu. in Thyatira *w.*
3:1 angel of church in Sardis *w.*
7 angel of chu. in Philadel. *w.*
12 I will *w.* on him new name
14 angel in ch. of Laodicea *w.*
10:4 sko. to *w.* voice said *w.* not
14:13 *w.* bles. are dead die in L.
19:9 *w.* bles. are called to sup.
21:5 *w.* words true and faithful

See BOOK.

WRITER.
Jud. 5:14 that handle pen of *w.*
Ps. 45:1 long. is pen of ready *w.*
Ezek. 9:3 *w.* inkhorn by his si. 3

WRITEST, ETH.
Job 13:26 thou *w.* bitter things
Ps. 87:6 shall count wh. he *w.* up
Ezek. 37:20 sticks whereon th. *w.*

WRITING.
Ex. 32:16 tho *w.* was *w.* of God
39:30 on plate of holy cro. a *w.*
Deut. 10:4 wrote acco. to first *w.*
31:24 wh. Mos. made end of *w.*
1 Chr. 28:19 L. made me und. *w.*
2 Chr. 2:11 Hur. answered in *w.*
21:12 a *w.* from Eli. to Jehoram
35:4 prepare accord. to *w.* of D.
36:22 Cyrus put the proclamation in *w.*, *Ezr.* 1:1
Ezr. 4:7 *w.* of letter in Sy. tong.
Est. 1:22 sent letters accordi. to *w.* whereof, 3:12 ; 8:9 ; 9:27
3:14 copy of *w.* published to all
4:8 Mord. gave Haia. copy of *w.*
8:8 the *w.* in the king's name
13 the *w.* of Hezekiah
Ezek. 13:9 not in *w.* of ho. of Is.
Dan. 5:7 whoso sh. read this *w.*
8 they could not read the *w.*
15 th. they should read this *w.*
16 if thou canst read the *w.*
17 I will read *w.* to the king
24 this is *w.* that was writ. 25
6:8 establ. decree, and sign *w.*
9 Darius signed *w.* and decree
10 Daniel knew *w.* was signed
Mat. 5:31 let him give her a *w.* of divorcement, 19
John 19:19 *w.* was, Jesus of Naz.

WRITING-TABLE.
Luke 1:63 Zacha. asked for *w.-t.*

WRITINGS.
John 5:47 if ye believe not his *w.*

WRITTEN.
Ex. 31:18 *w.* with the finger of God, *Deut.* 9:10
1 *K.* 21:11 elders did writ as *w.*
1 *Chr.* 4:41 *w.* by name en. tents
2 *Chr.* 30:5 not kept passo. as *w.*
Ezr. 8:31 weight of ves. was *w.*
Neh. 6:6 sent letter wh. was *w.*
8:14 found *w.* in law of L. by M.
Est. 1:19 *w.* ame. laws of Medes
3:9 let it be *w.* that they may be
12 name of Ahasue. was it *w.*
8:5 *w.* to reverse Ham.'s letters
9:23 not *w.* with righteous
102:18 ac. for generat. to come
13:9 unto execute judgment *w.*
Prov. 22:20 have not I *w.* to thee
Jer. 17:13 depart from me be *w.*
36:29 in. king of Baby. sh. come
Ezek. 2:10 *w.* within and withou.
13:9 *w.* in writ. of house of Isr.
Dan. 5:24 *w.* writing was *w.* 25
Mal. 3:16 book of remem. was *w.*
Mark 1:1:17 *w.* my hou. he called
15:26 his accusation was *w.* K.
Luke 21:22 th. *w.* may be fulfilled
24:44 *w.* in law of Moses
John 2:17 *w.* zeal of th. house
20:30 your names are *w.* in hea.
22 *w.* to be accompli. 22:37
John 2:17 remembered it was *w.*
10:34 is it not *w.* in your law
20:31 *w.* that ye might believe
21:25 if should be *w.* every one
Acts 18:29 fulfill. all that was *w.*
21:25 touching Ge. we have *w.*
Rom. 2:15 work of the law *w.*
4:23 not *w.* for his sake alone
15:4 *w.* for our admonit.
1 Cor. 10:11 ex. for our admonit.
2 *Cor.* 3:2 epistle *w.* in hearts
3 *w.* not with ink, but S. of G.
7 minist. of death *w.* in stones
Phile. 19 I Paul have *w.*
12:23 church of first-born *w.*
Rev. 5:1 things *w.* within and *w.*
2:17 in stone a new name *w.*
13:8 whoso names are not *w.*
14:1 Fa.'s name *w.* in foreheads

WRO

Rev. 17:5 up. head was *w.* Myst.
19:12 name *w.* on his thigh, 16
21:12 names *w.* on the gates

Is WRITTEN.
Jos. 1:8 do all that *is w.* therein
K. 22:13 wh. *is w.* concern. us
Est. 8:8 *is w.* in king's name
Is. 4:3 that *is w.* among living
Dan. 9:11 curse that *is w.* in law
Luke 10:26 what *is w.* in law ?
20:17 what is this that *is w. ?*
22:37 *is w.* must be accomplish.
John 15:25 bo fulfilled that *is w.*
1 *Cor.* 4:6 to think ab. that *is w.*
9:10 for our sakes this *is w.*
15:54 he bro. to pass that *is w.*

It is WRITTEN.
Jos. 8:31 as *it w.* in the law of Moses, 1 *K.* 2:3 ; 2 *Chr.* 23:18 ;
23:4 ; 31:3 ; 35:12 *Ezr.* 3:2, 4 ;
6:18 ; *Neh.* 8:15 ; 10:34, 36 ;
Dan. 9:13
Ps. 40:7 in book *it is w.* of me, *Heb.* 10:7
Is. 65:6 *it is w.* before me
Mat. 2:5 thus *it is w. Luke* 24:46
11:10 of whom *it is w. Luke* 7:27
26:24 as *it is w.* of him, *Mark*
9:13 ; 14:21, 27
Luke 4:8 ; *Acts* 23:5
Mark 9:12 *it is w.* of Son of man
Luke 2:23 *it is w.* in law of Lord
Rom. 11:8 according as *it is w.*
1 *Cor.* 1:31 ; 2 *Cor.* 4:13
Gal. 3:10 ; 4:11 ; *Gal.* 3:10
15:3 pleas. not himself, *it is w.*
1 *Pet.* 1:16 *it is w.* be ye holy

I have, or have I WRITTEN.
Hos. 8:12 *I have w.* of my law
John 19:22 what *I ha. w. I h. w.*
1 *John* 2:14 *I h. w.* to you fath.
26 these things *have I w.* 5:13

Were WRITTEN.
Num. 11:26 they were of them that *were w.*
Job 19:23 O that my words *w. w.*
Luke 24:44 be fulfilled wh. *w. w.*
Rom. 15:16 thi. thi. wr. of *w. w.*
15:4 whatsoever thi. *w. w.*
See BOOK.

WRONG.
Gen. 16:5 my *w.* be upon thee
Ex. 2:13 to him that did the *w.*
Deut. 19:16 to testify what is *w.*
Jud. 11:27 *w.* to war against me
1 *Chr.* 12:17 no *w.* in my hands
10:21 he suffered no man to do *w. Ps.* 105:14
Est. 1:16 not done *w.* to king
Job 19:7 cry out of *w.* not heard
Jer. 22:3 do no *w.* to the stranger
13 that buildeth chambers *w.*
Lam. 3:59 thou hast seen my *w.*
Hab. 1:4 *w.* judgment proceed.
Mat. 20:13 frie. I do thee no *w.*
Acts 7:24 see. one of th. suffer *w.*
26 why do ye *w.* one to anot. ?
27 he that did his neighbor *w.*
18:14 a matter of *w.* or lewdness
25:10 P. said, Have I done no *w.*
1 *Cor.* 6:7 why do ye not rather take *w. ?*
8 ye do *w.* defraud brethren
2 *Cor.* 7:12 his cause th. done *w.*
12:13 burdensome, forg. this *w.*
Col. 3:25 doth *w.* receive for *w.*

WRONGED.
2 Cor. 7:2 we have *w.* no man
Phile. 18 if he hath *w.* thee

WRONGFULLY.
Job 21:27 devices ye *w.* imagine
Ps. 35:19 let mi. enemi. *w.* rejoi.
38:19 that hate me *w.* multipli.
09:4 being mine enemies *w.*
119:80 they persecuto me *w.*
Ezek. 22:29 oppressed strang. *w.*
1 *Pet.* 2:19 grief, suffering *w.*

WROTE.
Ex. 24:4 Moses *w.* all the words of the law, *Deut.* 31:9
34:28 L. *w.* on tables words of coven. *Deut.* 4:13 ; 5:22 ; 9:1
Num. 33:2 Moses *w.* their goings
48 Moses *w.* this song
1 *Sam.* 10:25 Sam. *w.* manner of
2 *Sam.* 11:14 Dav. *w.* a letter, 15
2 *K.* 4:18 Jezebel *w.* letters, 8
11 *w.* and Jehu *w.* letters, 8
Chr. 36:8 Shemaiah *w.* bef. king
2 *Chr.* 30:1 Hezekiah *w.* to Eph.
Ezr. 4:9 accusation acu. *Jud.*
8 Rehum *w.* a letter *Jer.* 9

CRUDEN'S CONCORDANCE.

WRO

Est. 8:5 Haman *w.* to destroy J.
Jer. 51:60 Jerem. *w.* all the evil
Dan. 5:5 man's hand *w.* on wall
7:1 dream, and he *w.* the dream
Mark 10:5 Moses *w.* this precept
12:19 Moses *w.* to us, *Luke* 20:28
Luke 1:63 Zacharias *w.* saying
John 5:46 for Moses *w.* of me
8:6 wh. his fing. *w.* on ground, 8
10:19 Pilate *w.* title, and put it
21:24 John *w.* of these things
Acts 15:23 apostles *w.* let. by th.
18:27 brethren *w.* exhorting
23:25 Lysias *w.* after this man.
Rom. 16:22 I Tertl. who *w.* this
1 *Cor.* 5:9 Paul *w.* in an epistle,
2 *Cor.* 2:3, 4; 7:12; *Eph.* 3:3;
Phile. 21
7:1 things whereof ye *w.* to me
2 *John* 5 not as th. I *w.* new com.
3 *John* 9 I *w.* to the church

WROTH.
Gen. 4:5 and Cain was very *w.*
6 L. sa. to C. Why art th. *w.?*
31:36 Jacob was *w.* 34:7 sons *w.*
40:2 Pharaoh was *w.* 41:10
Ex. 16:20 and Moses was very *w.*
Num. 16:15; 31:14
16:22 wilt thou be *w.* with
Deut. 1:34 L. heard, was *w.* 3:26;
9:19; 2 *Sam.* 22:8; 2 *Chr.*
28:9; *Ps.* 18:7; 78:21, 59, 62
1 *Sam.* 18:8 S. was very *w.* 20:7
20:4 prince of Ph. *w.* with him
2 *Sam.* 3:8 Abner *w.* 13:21 D. *w.*
2 *K.* 5:11 but Naaman was *w.*
13:19 man of God *w.* with him
2 *Chr.* 16:10 Asa *w.* 26:19 Uz. *w.*
Neh. 4:1 Sanballat was *w.* took
Est. 1:12 thereof, the king was *w.*
2:21 Bigthan and Teresh *w.*
Ps. 80:38 been *w.* with anointed
Is. 28:31 *w.* as in val. of of Gibe.
47:6 I was *w.* with my people
51:9 I would not be *w.* with th.
57:16 nor will I be always *w.*
17 for iniquity of his covetousness was I *w.*
64:5 thou art *w.* we have sinned
9 be not *w.* very sore, O Lord
Jer. 37:15 the princes were *w.*
Lam. 5:32 th. art very *w.* ag. us
Mat. 2:16 Iler. was exceeding *w.*
18:34 his lord was *w.* and deliv.
22:7 and the king was very *w.*
Rev. 12:17 the dragon was *w.*

WROUGHT, actively.
Gen. 34:7 Shechem *w.* folly in Is.
Ex. 10:2 what things I *w.* in E.
36:1 then *w.* Bezaleel and Ahol.
4 wise men *w.* work, 8; 39:6
Num. 23:23 what hath God *w.?*
Deut. 17:2 hath *w.* folly in Israel,
Jos. 7:15; *Jud.* 20:10
31:18 for evils they sh. have *w.*
Ruth 2:19 show. with wh. she *w.*
1 *Sam.* 6:6 L. had *w.* wonderful,
11:13 hath *w.* salva. in Isr. 19:5
14:45 Jonathan hath *w.* with G.
2 *Sam.* 23:10 L. *w.* great vict. 12
1 *K.* 5:16 ov. people that *w.* 9:23
4 *K.* 17:11 Is. *w.* wick. *Neh.* 9:18
21:6 Manasseh *w.* much wickedness, 2 *Chr.* 33:6
2 *Chr.* 24:12 hir. such as *w.* iron
13 workmen *w.* work. 34:10, 13
Neh. 4:16 my serv. *w.* to work
17 every one with hand *w.*
Job 12:9 hand of L. hath *w.* this
36:23 say, thou hast *w.* iniqu.?
Ps. 31:19 hast *w.* for them that
68:28 strength, th. thou hast *w.*
78:43 had *w.* his signs in Egypt
Ec. 2:11 works my hands *w.*
Is. 20:12 th. hast *w.* works in us
18 ha. not *w.* any deliverance
41:4 who hath *w.* and done it?
Jer. 18:3 he *w.* a work on wheels
Ezek. 20:9 I *w.* for my name's sake, 14, 22, 44
29:20 because they *w.* for me
Dan. 4:2 won. that God hath *w.*
Jon. 1:11 sea *w.* tempestuous, 13
Zep. 2:3 *w.* his judgment
Mat. 20:12 have *w.* the one hour
26:10 she hath *w.* a good work on me, *Mark* 14:6
Acts 15:12 wonders God *w.* 21:19
18:3 abode with Aquila and *w.*
Rom. 15:18 Ch. ha. not *w.* by me
2 *Cor.* 5:5 *w.* us for same thing, G.
Gal. 2:8 *w.* effectually in Pet.
Eph. 1:20 which he *w.* in Christ
Jam. 2:22 faith *w.* with works?
1 *Pet.* 4:3 to have *w.* will of Gen.
2 *John* 8 lose not thi. we have *w.*

YEA

WROUGHT, *passively.*
Num. 31:51 took of them *w.* jew.
Deut. 21:3 heifer ha. not been *w.*
Neh. 6:16 this work was *w.* of G.
Ps. 45:13 her clothing of *w.* gold
139:15 in secret, curiously *w.*
Ec. 2:17 work *w.* under sun
John 3:21 manif. th. are *w.* in G.
Acts 5:12 wonders *w.* am. people

WROUGHTEST.
Ruth 2:19 sa. to her, wh. *w.* th.?

WRUNG.
Lev. 1:15 blood sh. be *w.* out, 5:9
Ps. 73:10 wat. of cup *w.* to them
Is. 51:17 ha. *w.* out dregs of cup

Y.

YARN.
1 *K.* 10:28 Solomon had linen *y.* out of Egypt, 2 *Chr.* 1:16

YEA.
Mat. 5:37 conve. be *y. Jam.* 5:12
2 *Cor.* 1:17 sho. be *y. y.* and nay
18 word toward you was not *y.*
19 for Son of God was not *y.*
20 promises of G. in him are *y.*

YEAR.
Gen. 17:21 Sar. shall bear next *y.*
Ex. 12:2 first month of the *y.*
23:14 keep feast in *y. Lev.* 23:41
29 not drive them out in oney.
Lev. 16:34 atonement once a *y.*
25:5 a *y.* of rest; 30 within a *y.*
Num. 9:22 if *y.* that cloud tarried
14:34 for a *y.* sh. ye bear iniqu.
Jos. 5:12 eat fruit of Can. that *y.*
Jud. 10:8 that *y.* Am. vexed Isr.
11:40 to lament four days in *y.*
17:10 give thee ten shek. by *y.*
1 *Sam.* 27:7 David dwelt *y.* and
1 *K.* 9:25 in a *y.* did Solom. offer
Ex. 10:29 oat this *y.* such things as grow of themsel. *Is.* 37:30
Est. 9:27 keep two days every *y.*
Ps. 65:11 crowned *y.* with goodn.
Is. 6:1 in the *y.* that Uzziah died
21:16 in a *y.* glory of Kedar fail
61:2 procl. acc. *y.* of L. *Lu.* 4:19
63:4 *y.* of my redeemed is come
Jer. 11:23 *y.* of visit. 23:12; 48:44
17:8 not careful in *y.* of drought
28:16 saith I. th. *y.* th. shalt die
51:46 rumor both come in one *y.*
Ezek. 4:6 appoin. each day for *y.*
46:17 be his to the *y.* of liberty
Luke 2:41 went to Jerusal. ev. *y.*
13:8 Lord, let it alone this *y.*
9 if it bear fruit, be forward a *y.* ago
Acts 11:26 whole *y.* they assem.
2 *Cor.* 8:10 to be forward a *y.* ago
9:2 Achala was ready a *y.* ago
Heb. 9:7 pri. went in once a *y.* 25
10:3 remembrance of sins ev. *y.*
Jam. 4:13 continue there a *y.*
Rev. 9:15 prepare for month, a *y.*

YEAR after YEAR.
2 *Sam.* 21:1 fam. 3 years *y. a. y.*

YEAR by YEAR.
Deut. 14:22 tithe inc. of thy seed field bringeth forth *y. by y.*
15:20 eat before Lord *y. by y.*
1 *Sam.* 1:7 as he did so *y. by y.*
1 K. 10:25 they brought a rate *y. by y.* 2 *Chr.* 9:24
2 *K.* 17:4 as he had done *y. by y.*
Neh. 10:34 wood-offering *y. by y.*
Heb. 10:1 they offered *y. by y.*

YEAR to YEAR.
Ex. 13:10 ordinance from *y. to y.*
1 *Sam.* 2:19 brou. coat fr. *y. to y.*
7:16 Samuel went from *y. to y.*
1 Chr. 24:5 rep. house fr. *y. to y.*
Is. 20:1 add ye *y. to y.* let them
Zec. 14:16 fr. *y. to y.* to worship
See SECOND, THIRD, SEVENTH.

YEARLY.
Lev. 25:53 a *y.* serv. shall he be
Jud. 11:40 went *y.* to lament
21:19 a feast of L. in Shiloh *y.*
1 *Sam.* 1:3 E. went *y.* to worship
21 went to offer *y.* sacrif. 2:19
20:6 a *y.* sacrifice for family
Est. 9:21 keep 15th of same *y.*

YEARS.
Gen. 1:14 for seasons, days, *y.*
25:7 days of the *y.* of Abraham
8 Abraham died full of *y.*
47:9 evil have *y.* of my life been
Ex. 34:22 feast at the *y.* end
Lev. 25:15 accord. to *y.* th. sell, 50
27:18 accord. to *y.* that remain
Deut. 32:7 *y.* of many generations
Jos. 13:1 Josh. was stricken in *y.*
1 *Sam.* 29:3 Da. been with th. *y.*
1 *Chr.* 1:1 David was stricken in *y.*

YIE

1 *K.* 17:1 not dew nor rain th. *y.*
2 *Chr.* 14:6 and Asa had no war in those *y.*
Job 10:5 thy *y.* as man's days
15:20 nutu. of *y.* hid. to oppres.
16:22 when a few *y.* are come
32:7 multit. of *y.* teach wisdom
36:11 spend their *y.* in pleasure
26 nor can his *y.* be searched
Ps. 31:10 up *y.* spent with sigh.
61:6 prol. *y.* as many generatio.
77:5 the *y.* of ancient times
10 the *y.* of the right hand
78:33 their *y.* did he consume
90:4 a thous. *y.* in thy sight are but as yesterday, 2 *Pet.* 3:8
9 sp. our *y.* as a tale th. is told
10 *y.* are threescore *y.* and ten
15 *y.* wherein we ha. seen evil
102:24 *y.* throughout all genera.
27 thy *y.* shall have no end
Prov. 4:10 *y.* of life many, 9:11
5:9 lest thou give *y.* unto cruel
10:27 *y.* of wicked sh. be short.
Ec. 12:1 nor *y.* draw nigh
Is. 21:16 accord. to *y.* of hireling
38:10 I am deprived of my *y.*
15 I shall go softly all my *y.*
Ezek. 4:5 on thee *y.* of th. iniq.
22:4 thou art come unto thy *y.*
38:8 latter *y.* th. come into land
Dan. 9:2 I underst. number of *y.*
11:6 end of *y.* they join togeth.
8 more *y.* than king of north
13 king of north shall come after certain *y.*
Joel 2:2 *y.* of many generations
25 restore *y.* locust hath eaten
Hab. 3:2 thy work in midst of *y.*
Mal. 3:4 offerings as in former *y.*
Luke 1:7 both were stri. in *y.* 18
Gal. 4:10 ye obse. months and *y.*
Heb. 1:12 thy *y.* shall not fail
11:24 M. wh. come to *y.* refused
Rev. 20:2 bound Satan a thou. *y.*
3 till thousand *y.* be fulfilled, 4
7 when thousand *y.* are expir.

See Numeral *words in their places,* as HUNDRED, MANY, TWO, THREE, SIX, OLD.

YELL, ED.
Jer. 51:38 like lions, they sh. *y.*
2:15 lions roared and *y.* on him

YELLOW.
Lev. 13:30 if th. be in it a *y.* hair
39 if th. be in it no *y.* hair, 36
32 covered with *y.* gold
Ps. 68:13 covered with *y.* gold

YEARN, ED.
Gen. 43:30 for his bowels did *y.*
1 *K.* 3:26 her bowels *y.* upon son

YESTERDAY.
Ex. 5:14 why not fulfil. task *y.?*
20:20 shall *y.* sort of J. to meet *y.*
2 *Sam.* 15:20 thou camest but *y.*
2 *K.* 9:26 seen *y.* blood of Naboth
Job 8:9 we are of *y.* know noth.
Ps. 90:4 a thousand *y.* are as *y.*
John 4:52 *y.* the fever left him
Acts 7:28 kill me as Egyptian *y.*
Heb. 13:8 same *y.* and for ever

YESTERNIGHT.
Gen. 19:34 I lay *y.* with my fath.
31:29 G. of your father spake *y.*
42 affliction, rebuked thee *y.*

YIELD.
Gen. 4:12 earth not *y.* her stren.
49:20 shall *y.* royal dainties
20 your land not *y.* her increase
2 *Chr.* 30:8 *y.* yourself. to the L.
Ps. 67:6 land *y.* her incre. 85:12
107:37 may *y.* fruits of increase
Prov. 7:21 fair speech cau. him *y.*
Is. 5:10 ten acres sh. *y.* one bath
Hos. 8:7 the bud shall *y.* no meal
Joel 2:22 fig-tree *y.* strength
Hab. 3:17 altho' fields *y.* no meat
Acts 23:21 do not th. *y.* unto th.
Rom. 6:13 *y.* yourselves to God
16 that to whom ye *y.* yourself.
19 *y.* members to righteousn.
Jam. 3:12 no fount, *y.* salt water

YIELDED.
Gen. 49:33 Jacob *y.* up the ghost
Num. 17:8 rod of Aa. *y.* almonds
Dan. 3:28 *y.* th. bodies that they
Mat. 27:50 Jesus *y.* up the ghost
Rom. 6:19 ye have *y.* your mem.

YIELDETH.
Neh. 9:37 *y.* increase to kings
34:25 wildern. *y.* food for th.
Heb. 12:11 *y.* fruit of righteousness

YOU

YIELDING.
Gen. 1:11 forth herb *y.* seed, 12
20 given you every tree *y.* seed
Ec. 10:4 *y.* pacifie. great offences
See FRUIT.

YOKE.
Gen. 27:40 break his *y. Jer.* 30:8
Lev. 26:13 I have broken the bands of your *y. Ezek.* 34:27
Num. 10:2 heif. on which never came *y. Deut.* 21:3; 1 *Sa.* 6:7
Deut. 28:48 he sh. put a *y.* of iron upon thy neck, *Jer.* 28:14
1 *Sam.* 11:7 S. took a *y.* of oxen
14:14 wh. a *y.* of oxen mi. plow
1 *K.* 12:14 thy father made our *y.* griev. 10, 11, 14; 2 *Chr.* 10:4
19:19 plowing wi. 12 *y.* of oxen
21 took a *y.* of oxen, slew them
Job 1:3 Job had 500 *y.* of oxen
42:12 had a thousand *y.* of oxen
Is. 9:4 thon hast broken the *y.* of his burden, 10:27; 14:25
47:6 hast very heavi. laid thy *y.*
58:6 and that *y.* break every *y.*
Jer. 2:20 of old time brok. thy *y.*
5:5 these have broken thy *y.*
27:8 will not put neck under *y.*
11 bring their neck under *y.* 12
28:2 broken *y.* of king of B. 4, 11
12 H. has broken *y.* from Jer.
31:18 bullock unaccustom. to *y.*
51:23 break husband. and his *y.*
Lam. 1:14 *y.* of my transgressions is bound
3:27 good for a man to bear *y.*
Hos. 11:4 as they that take off *y.*
Nah. 1:13 now will I break his *y.*
Mal. 11:29 take my *y.* upon you
30 my *y.* is easy, burden light
Luke 14:19 I bought 5 *y.* of oxen
Acts 15:10 put *y.* on the disciples' neck
Gal. 5:1 be not entangled with *y.*
1 *Tim.* 6:1 as many as under *y.*

YOKES.
Jer. 27:2 make bonds and *y.*
28:13 hast broken *y.* of wood
Ezek. 30:18 when I brake *y.* of E.

YOKED.
2 *Cor.* 6:14 be not unequally *y.*

YOKE-FELLOW.
Phil. 4:3 I entreat thee, true *y.-f.*

YONDER.
Gen. 22:5 I and the lad will go *y.*
Num. 16:37 scatter th. the fire *y.*
23:15 stand here, I meet Lord *y.*
Mat. 17:20 say, Rem. to *y.* place

YOUNG.
Gen. 31:38 she-goats not cast *y.*
33:13 flocks with *y.* are with me
Ex. 23:26 nothing cast their *y.*
Lev. 22:28 shall not kill it and *y.*
Deut. 22:6 not take dam with *y.*
7 let the dam go and take the *y.*
28:50 not show favor to the *y.*
32:11 as the eagle over her *y.*
1 *Chr.* 29:5 S. my son is *y.* 29:1
2 *Chr.* 13:6 when Rehob. was *y.*
34:3 Josiah, while he was yet *y.*
Ps. 78:71 ewe great with *y.*
84:3 where she may lay her *y.*
Is. 40:11 those that are with *y.*
Jer. 31:12 together for *y.* of flock
Ezek. 17:4 cropped *y.* twigs, 22
Mark 7:25 *y.* dau. unclean spirit
John 21:18 *y.* thou girt. thyself
See OLD.

YOUNG ass, *or* **asses.**
Is. 30:6 carry riches on *y. asses*
24 *y. a.* sh. eat clean provender
John 12:14 when he found a *y. a.*
See BULLOCK.

YOUNG bullocks.
Num. 28:11 offer two *y. b.* 19, 27
Ezr. 6:9 gi. what th. need, *y. b.*

YOUNG calf.
Lev. 9:2 take *y. c.* for sin-offering
See CHILD, CHILDREN.

YOUNG cow.
Is. 7:21 man sh. nourish a *y. cow*

YOUNG dromedaries.
Est. 8:10 lett. by riders on *y. d.*

YOUNG eagles.
Prov. 30:17 *y. eagles* shall eat it

YOUNG hart.
Cant. 2:9 belo. like *y. h.* 17; 8:14
See LION, LIONS, MAN, MEN.

YOUNG one.
Deut. 28:57 evil toward her *y. o.*
Zec. 11:16 neither seek *y. one*

CRUDEN'S CONCORDANCE. 1091

YOU

YOUNG ones.
Deut. 22:6 whether y. o. or eggs
Job 38:41 when his y. o. cry to G.
39:3 they bring forth their y. o.
4 their y. o. are in good liking
16 ostrich is harden. ags. y. o.
30 eagles' y. o. suck up blood
Is. 11:7 y. o. lie down together
Lam. 4:3 give suck to their y. o.

YOUNG pigeon.
Gen. 15:9 turtle-dove and y. p.
Lev. 12:6 bring y. p. for sin-offer.

YOUNG pigeons.
Lep. 1:14 bring his offer. of y. p.
5:7 he sh. bring two y. *pigeons*,
12:8; 14:22, 30; 15:14, 29;
Num. 6:10; *Luke* 2:24
11 if not able to bring 2 y. p.

YOUNG ravens.
Ps. 147:9 he giveth food to y. r.

YOUNG roes.
Cant. 4:5 breasts like y. roes, 7:3

YOUNG virgin.
1 *K.* 1:2 let there be sought y. v.

YOUNG virgins.
Jud. 21:12 were found 400 y. v.
Est. 2:2 let y. v. be sou. for king
3 may gather together y. v.

YOUNG unicorn.
Ps. 29:6 and Sirion like a y. u.

YOUNG woman.
Ruth 4:12 L. give th. of this y. w.

YOUNG women.
Tit. 2:4 teach y. w. to be sober

YOUNGER.
Gen. 9:24 know what y. son done
19:31 first-born said to the y. 34
38 the y. bare a son Ben-ammi
25:23 elder serve y. *Rom.* 9:12
29:18 I will serve 7 years for y.
26 it must not be so, to give y.
43:29 is this your y. brother of
48:14 Is. laid right ha. on the y.
19 y. brother be greater tha. he
Jud. 1:13 y. brother took it, 3:9
15:2 is not her y. sister fairer?
1 *Sam.* 14:49 Saul's y. daughter
1 *Chr.* 24:31 against y. brethren
Job 30:1 that are y. than I, have
Ezek. 16:46 thy y. sister is Sodom
Luke 15:12 y. said, Gi. me portion
13 y. gathered all, took journ.
22:26 greatest, let him be as y.
1 *Tim.* 5:1 entreat y. as brethren
2 the y. women as sisters, with
11 y. widows refuse, for when
14 I will that y. women marry
1 *Pet.* 5:5 y. submit to the elder

YOUNGEST.
Gen. 42:13 y. is with our fath. 32
15 except your y. brother com.
20, 34; 44:23, 26
43:33 y. according to his youth
44:8 cup in sack's mouth of y.
Jos. 6:26 in his y. son set up gates, 1 *K.* 16:34
Jud. 9:5 Jotham, y. son, was left
1 *Sam.* 16:11 there remains yet y.
17:14 David was y. the eldest
2 *Chr.* 21:17 none left save the y.
22:1 made Ahaz. his y. son king

YOURS.
2 *Chr.* 20:15 battle not y. God's
2 *Cor.* 12:14 I seek not y. but you

YOUTH.
Gen. 8:21 imagina. evil fr. his y.
43:33 youngest accord. to his y.
46:34 from our y. even till now
Lev. 22:13 in fa. 's house as in y.
Num. 30:3 in fa. 's house in y. 16
Jud. 8:20 the y. drew not sword
1 *Sam.* 17:33 a man of war fr. y.
42 a y. of fair countenance
55 said, Whose son is this y.?
2 *Sam.* 19:7 evil befell thee fr. y.
1 *K.* 18:12 I fear Lord from y.
Job 13:26 possess iniqu. of my y.
20:11 bones full of sins of his y.
29:4 as I was in days of my y.
30:12 on my right hand rise y.
31:18 fr. y. he was brought up
33:25 shall return to days of y.
36:14 hypocrites die in y. their
Ps. 25:7 remember not sins of y.
71:5 art my trust from my y.
17 hast taught me from my y.
88:15 ready to die from my y.
103:5 thy y. renew. like eagle's
110:3 th. hast the dew of thy y.
127:4 so are children of thy y.
129:1 have afflicted me fr. my y.
144:12 as plants grown up in y.

ZAR

Prov. 2:17 forsak. guide of her y.
5:18 rejoice with wife of thy y.
Ec. 11:9 rejoi. O man, in thy y.
10 childhood and y. are vanity
12:1 remember thy Creator in y.
Is. 47:12 has labored from y.
15 thy merchants fr. y. wander
54:4 forget shame of thy y.
6 Lord called thee as wife of y.
Jer. 2:2 I remember kindn. of y.
3:4 thou art the guide of my y.
24 labor of our fathers from y.
25 our fathers from y. elmed
22:21 thy manner from thy y.
31:19 I did bear reproa. of my y.
32:30 only done evil fr. their y.
48:11 Moab been at ease from y.
Lam. 3:27 he bear yoke in his y.
Ezek. 4:14 not polluted fr. my y.
16:22 not remem. days of y. 43
60 remem. my covenant in y.
23:3 committed whored. in y.
3 in y. they lay with her
19 call to remembrn. her y. 21
Hos. 2:15 sing as in days of y.
Joel 1:8 as virgin for husb. of y.
Zec. 13:5 to keep cattle fr. my y.
Mal. 2:14 and the wife of thy y.
15 treach. again, wife of his y.
Mat. 19:20 th. have I kept fr. my y. *Mark* 10:20; *Luke* 18:21
Acts 26:4 manner of life fr. my y.
1 *Tim.* 4:12 no man desp. thy y.

YOUTHS.
Prov. 7:7 among y. a young man
Is. 40:30 oven the y. shall faint,

YOUTHFUL.
2 *Tim.* 2:22 flee also y. lusts, but

Z.

ZACCHEUS.
Luke 19:5 Z. haste, come down

ZACHARIAH, ZECHA-RIAH.
2 *K.* 14:29 Z. reigned, 15:8, 11
18:2 Abi dau. of Z. 2 *Chr.* 29:1
1 *Chr.* 5:7 of Reubeni. Jeiel, Z.
9:21 Z. of Levit. 15:18, 24; 26:2
37 Geder, Ahio, Z. and Mickl.
15:5 to Asaph, Z. 24:25 Iseh. Z.
26:11 Z. the 4th son of Hosah
14 Z. son of Shelemiah, wise
27:21 ruler was Iddo son of Z.
2 *Chr.* 17:7 Jehoshap. sent to Z.
20:14 Jahaziel son of Z. came
21:2 Jehiel and Z. sons of Jeho.
24:20 Spirit of G. came upon Z.
26:5 sought G. in the days of Z.
29:13 Asaph, Z. sancti. himself
34:12 Z. of the Kohathites was
35:8 Hilkiah, Z. rulers of house
Ezr. 5:1 Z. son of Iddo prophes.
to J. in Jud. 6:14; *Neh.* 12:16
8:3 of Pharo. Z. 11 of Bebai, Z.
16 Z. chief men, 10:26
Neh. 8:4 Ezra's left ha. stood Z.
11:5 Z. son of Shiloni; 12 Pash.
12:35 Z. son of Jonathan, 41
Is. 8:2 Z. the son of Jeberechiah
Zec. 1:1 Z. son of Barachiah, 7:1
Mat. 23:35; *Luke* 11:51
Luke 1:5 Z. a priest of the course
13 fear not Z. 40 called him Z.

ZADOK.
2 *Sam.* 8:17 Z. and Ahim. priests
15:25 Z. carried the ark of God
35 hast not with thee Z. ?
20:25 Z. and Abiathar, 1 *K.* 4:4
1 *K.* 1:8 but Z. was not with, 26
45 Z. and Nathan have anoint.
2:35 Z. the priest, 1 *Chr.* 29:22
4:2 Azariah son of Z. the priest
2 *K.* 15:33 dau. of Z. 2 *Chr.* 27:1
1 *Chr.* 6:8 Ahitub begat Z. 12, 53
12:28 Z. a yo. man, mighty man
24:3 both Z. sons of El. and Ah.
27:17 of Aaronites Z. was capt.
Ezr. 7:2 son of Shall. son of Z.
Neh. 3:4 Z. repaired, 29; 10:21
11:11 the son of Z. Meshullam
13:13 I made Z. scribe treasurer
Ezek. 40:46 the sons of Z. 43:19; 44:15
48:11 priests sanc. of sons of Z.

ZALMUNNA.
Jud. 8:5 pursu. aft. Zeba and Z.
6 hands of Zeba and Z. in, 15
21 Gideon slew Zeba and Z.
Ps. 83:11 make as Zeba and Z.

ZARAH.
Gen. 38:30 son called Z. 46:12
1 *Chr.* 2:4 Phares and Z. *Mat.* 1:3
6 sons of Z. Zimri, and Ethan
See ZERAH.

ZEP

ZAREPHATH.
1 *K.* 17:9 get thee to Z. 10
Ob. 20 of Israel sh. possess to Z.

ZEAL.
2 *Sam.* 21:2 slay them in his z.
2 *K.* 10:16 see my z. for the Lord
19:31 z. of Ld. do this, *Is.* 37:32
Ps. 69:9 the z. of thy house hath eaten me up, *John* 2:17
119:139 my z. hath consum. me
Is. 9:7 z. of L. will perform this
59:17 was clad wi. z. as a cloak
63:15 wh. is thy z. and stren. ?
Ezek. 5:13 I have spoken it in z.
Rom. 10:2 they have a z. of God
2 *Cor.* 7:11 what z. ? 9:2 your z.
Phil. 3:6 concerning z. persecut.
Col. 4:13 hath a great z. for you

ZEALOUS.
Num. 25:11 was z. for my sake
13 he was z. for his God, made
Acts 21:20 they are all z. of law
22:3 z. towards God, *Gal.* 1:14
1 *Cor.* 14:12 z. of spiritual gifts
Tit. 2:14 people, z. of good works
Rev. 3:19 be z. therefore, and repent

ZEALOUSLY.
Gal. 4:17 they z. affect you, not
18 it is good to be z. affected

ZEDAH. *See* ZALMUNNA.

ZEDEKIAH.
Mat. 4:21 in ship with Z. father
10:2 James and John; James of Z.
26:37; *Mark* 1:19; 3:17; 10:35;
Luke 5:10; *John* 21:2
John 21:2 mother of Z. children, 27:56
Mark 1:20 their father Z. in ship

ZEDOIM.
Gen. 14:2 king of Z. *Deut.* 29:23
1 *Sam.* 13:18 valley of Z. to the
Neh. 11:34 of Benja. dwelt at Z.
1 *Chr.* 8:18 shall I exit thee as Z.

ZEBUL.
Jud. 9:28 Jerubba. Z. his officer
41 Z. thrust out Baal and bre.

ZEBULUN.
Gen. 30:20 L. called his name Z.
35:23 Reuben, Simeon, Jud. Z.
46:14 the sons of Z. *Num.* 1:30;
1 *Chr.* 2:1
49:13 Z. shall dwell at haven
Num. 1:9 of Z. 2:7; 7:24; 10:16
Deut. 27:13 curse; Reu. Gad, Z.
33:18 of Z. be said, Rejoice Z.
Jos. 19:10 lot came up for Z.
Jud. 1:30 Z. drive out inhabita.
4:10 Barak called Z. and Naphtali
5:14 out of Z. that handle pen
18 Z. and Naphtali jeoparded
6:35 he sent messengers to Z.
12:12 Z. buried in country of Z.
Ps. 68:27 the princes of Z. and
Is. 9:1 lightly afflicted land of Z.
Ezek. 48:26 Z. a portion; 33 gate
Mat. 4:13 in the borders of Z.
15 land of Z. and Nephthalim
Tribe of ZEBULUN.
Num. 1:31 numbered of t. of Z.
2:7 t. of Z. Eliab captain, 10:16
13:10 of t. of Z. Gaddiel to spy
34:25 prince of t. of Z. to divide
Jos. 21:7 of t. Z. 34; 1 *Chr.* 6:77
Rev. 7:8 of t. of Z. sealed 12,000

ZEDEKIAH.
1 *K.* 22:11 Z. made, 2 *Chr.* 18:10
24 Z. smote Micai. 2 *Chr.* 18:23
2 *K.* 24:17 changed name to Z.
25:7 of Z. *Jer.* 39:6, 7; 52:11
1 *Chr.* 3:15 son of Josiah, Z. 16
Neh. 10:1 made Z. his br. king
Jer. 21:7 deliver Z. and his men,
29:22 Lord make thee like Z.
27:3 send yoke to Z. by hand
5 shall lend Z. to Babylon
Jer. 39:5 army overtook Z. 52:8

ZELOPHEHAD.
Num. 26:33 had no sons, *Jos.* 17:3
27:7 daught. of Z. speak right
36:11 daughters of Z. married

ZELZAH.
1 *Sam.* 10:2 men by sepulc. at Z.

ZENAS.
Tit. 3:13 bring Z. on his journey

ZEPHANIAH.
Jer. 21:1 whom Zedekiah sent Z.
29:25 letters in thy name to Z.
21 Z. read this letter in ears
37:3 Z. son of Maaseiah priest
Zep. 1:1 the word came to Z.

ZIO

Zec. 6:10 house of Jos. son of Z.
14 sh. be to Hen the son of Z.

ZERAH.
Gen. 36:13 sons of Reuel, Z.
1 *Chr.* 1:37, 44
31 Jobab the son of Z. reigned
Num. 26:13 of Z. family of, 20
Jos. 7:1 son of Zabdi, son of Z.
22:20 son of Z. commit a trespass
1 *Chr.* 4:24 sons of Sim. were Z.
6:21 Z. son of Iddo, 41 son of Z.
9:6 of sons of Z. Jeuel dwelt in
2 *Chr.* 14:9 Z. Ethiopian came
Neh. 11:24 Pethah. of chil. of Z.

ZERESH.
Est. 5:10 called for Z. his wife

ZERUBBABEL.
1 *Chr.* 3:19 son of Pedaiah, Z.
Ezr. 2:2 ca. up wi. Z. *Neh.* 12:1
3:2 Z. son of Shealtiel, 8; 5:2
Neh. 12:47 days of Z. gave port.
Hag. 1:1 word of the Lord to Z.
12 then Z. obeyed the voice of
14 Lord stirred up spirit of Z.
2:4 yet now be strong, O Z. 21
Zec. 4:6 word of Lord unto Z.
7 before Z. sh. become a plain
9 the hands of Z. have laid the

ZERUIAH.
2 *Sam.* 2:18 three sons of Z.
3:39 sons of Z. too hard for me
8:16 Joab son of Z. 1 *Chr.* 18:15
16:10 what have I to do with you, ye sons of Z. ? 19:22
1 *Chr.* 2:16 whose sisters were Z.

ZIDA.
2 *Sam.* 9:2 art thou Z. ? 10 Z. had
16:4 thine are all that pertain
19:29 thou and Z. divide land

ZIDDON.
Gen. 30:2 Anah daugh. of Z. 11
24 these are the children of Z.
1 *Chr.* 1:40 fed seven of Z. 29

ZIDON.
Gen. 49:13 border shall he to Z.
Jos. 11:8 chased th. to great Z.
19:28 Kanah, even unto great Z.
Jud. 10:6 and served gods of Z.
18:28 because it was far from Z.
K. 17:9 which belongeth to Z.
Ezr. 3:7 drink unto them of Z.
4 O Z. the sea hath spoken
12 O thou virgin, daught. of Z.
Jer. 25:22 kings of Z. shall drink
27:3 and yokes to king of Z.
47:4 Tyre and Z. every helper
Ezek. 27:8 the inhabitants of Z.
28:21 set thy face against Z.
22 behold, I am ag. thee, O Z.
Joel 3:4 with me, O Tyre and Z.
9:2 Tyrus and Z. though it

ZIDONIANS.
Jud. 10:12 Z. and Amalekites
18:7 careless, after manner of Z.
1 *K.* 11:1 Sol. loved women of Z.
33 Ashtoreth, goddess of Z.
Ezek. 32:30 Z. th. are gone down

ZIF.
1 *K.* 6:1 month of Z. is second
37 foundation laid in month Z.

ZIKLAG.
1 *Sam.* 27:6 Achish gave Z. to D.
30:14 we burnt Z. with fire
2 *Sam.* 1:1 D. abode 2 days in Z.
4:10 I slew him Z. 1 *Chr.* 11:28
12:1 came to David to Z. 20

ZILPAH.
Gen. 29:24 Lab. gave to Leah Z.
30:9 Leah gave Z. her maid to
35:26 Z. bare Jacob a son, 12
37:2 lad was with the sons of Z.

ZIMRI.
Num. 25:14 was slain was Z.
1 *K.* 16:9 Z. conspired against, 16
20 Z. reigned 7 days in Tirzah
2 *K.* 9:31 had Z. peace, who ?
1 *Chr.* 2:6 sons of Zerah, Z. and
8:36 Z. son of Jehoaddah, 9:42
Jer. 25:25 I made kings of Z. dr.

ZIN.
Num. 13:21 from wildern. of Z.
I came to desert of Z. 33:36
27:14 in desert of Z. *Deut.* 32:51

ZION.
2 *Sam.* 5:7 David took strong-hold of Z. 1 *Chr.* 11:5
1 *K.* 8:1 which is Z. 2 *Chr.* 5:2
Ps. 2:6 on my holy hill of Z.
48:12 walk about Z. go round about her

ZIO

Ps. 51:18 thy good pleas., unto Z.
69:35 for God will save Z. and
87:2 the Lord loveth gates of Z.
5 said of Z. this and that man
97:8 Z. heard and was glad
102:13 and have mercy on Z.
16 when Lord shall build up Z.
126:1 L. turned captivity of Z.
129:5 be turned back th. hate Z.
132:13 the Lord hath chosen Z.
133:3 as dew on mountains of Z.
137:1 when we remembered Z.
3 sing us one of the son. of Z.
146:10 the Lord shall reign, O Z.
147:12 praise thy God, O Z.
149:2 let children of Z. be joyful
Is. 1:27 Z. shall be redeemed
12:6 shout, th. inhabitant of Z.
14:32 that Lord hath founded Z.
33:5 hath filled Z. with judgm.
34:8 for controversy of Z.
40:9 O Z. bringest good tidings
41:27 sh. say to Z. behold them
40:14 Z. said, L. hath forsaken
51:3 the Lord shall comfort Z.
11 sh. come with singing to Z.
16 say unto Z. Th. art my peo.
52:1 put on thy strength, O Z.
7 saith unto Z. Thy G. reigneth
8 Lord shall bring again Z.
59:20 Redeemer sh. come to Z.
60:14 Z. of the Holy One of Is.
62:1 for Z. sake will I not hold
64:10 Z. is a wilderness, Jerusa.
66:8 as soon as Z, travailed, she
Jer. 3:14 I will bring you to Z.
4:6 set up standard towards Z.
14:19 hath thy soul loathed Z.?
26:18 Z. shall be plow. Mic. 3:12

ZIO

Jer. 30:17 Z, whom no man seek.
31:6 let us go up to Z. to the
12 and sing in height of Z.
50:5 they sh. ask the way to Z.
51:35 shall the inhabitant of Z.
Lam. 1:4 ways of Z. do mourn
17 Z. spreads forth her hands
4:2 sons of Z. compara. to gold
5:18 mountain of Z. is desolate
Joel 2:23 be glad, ye child. of Z.
Amos 1:2 Lord will roar from Z.
Mic. 3:10 th. build Z. with blood
4:2 for law shall go forth of Z.
11 let our eye look upon Z.
Zec. 1:14 I am jealous for Z. with
17 Lord shall yet comfort Z.
2:7 deliver thyself, O Z. 8:2
8:3 Lord, I am returned to Z.
9:13 raised up thy sons, O Z.

See DAUGHTER, DAUGHTERS.

In ZION.

Ps. 9:11 sing praises to L. who dwell. in Z. 76:2; Joel 3:21
65:1 praise for thee, O G. in Z.
84:7 every one in Z. appeareth
99:2 L. is great in Z. he is high
102:21 decl. name of Lord in Z.
Is. 4:3 that is left in Z. shall be
10:24 O my peo. dwellest in Z.
28:16 beh. I lay in Z. for a foundation, a tried st. 1 Pet. 2:6
30:19 people shall dwell in Z.
31:9 the L. whose fire is in Z.
33:14 sinners in Z. are afraid
46:13 I will place salva. in Z.
61:3 them that mourn in Z.
Jer. 8:19 is not the Lord in Z.?
50:28 declare in Z. vengeance
51:10 let us decl. in Z. the work

ZIP

Jer. 51:24 evil that they have done in Z.
Lam. 2:6 sabbaths forgot. in Z.
4:11 L. hath kindled fire in Z.
5:11 they ravished women in Z.
Joel 2:1 blow the trumpet in Z.
3:17 your God dwelling in Z.
Amos 6:1 that are at ease in Z.
Rom. 9:33 in Z. a stumbl. stone

Mount ZION.

2 K. 19:31 a remnant, they that escape out of mount Z. Is. 37:32
Ps. 48:2 joy of earth is mount Z.
11 m. Z. rejoice; 78:68 m. Z.
74:2 m. Z. wherein thou hast
125:1 as m. Z. cannot be remo.
Is. 4:5 dwelling-place of m. Z.
8:18 which dwell. in mo. Z. 18:7
10:12 perform. work upon m. Z.
24:23 Lord shall reign in m. Z.
29:8 fight aga. m. Z. 31:4 for
Joel 2:32 in m. Z. deliver. Ob. 17
Ob. 21 shall come up on m. Z.
Mic. 4:7 reign over th. in m. Z.
Hab. 12:22 are come unto m. Z.
Rev. 14:1 Lamb stood on m. Z.

Out of ZION.

Ps. 14:7 come out of Z. 53:6
20:2 streng. thee o. of Z. 110:2
128:5 bless thee o. of Z. 134:3
135:21 blessed be Lord o. of Z.
Is. 2:3 out of Z. shall go forth
Jer. 9:19 wail. is heard out of Z.
Joel 3:16 L. shall roar out of Z.
Rom. 11:26 come out of Z. deliv.

ZIPPORAH.

Ex. 2:21 Jethro gave Moses Z.
4:25 Z. took sharp stone, 18:2

ZUZ

ZOAN.

Num. 13:22 seven years bef. Z.
Ps. 78:12 things did he in Z. 43
Is. 19:11 princes of Z. fools, 13
30:4 for his princes were at Z.
Ezek. 30:14 I will set fire in Z.

ZOAR.

Gen. 14:2 of Bela, which is Z. 8
19:22 name of city was called Z.
Deut. 34:3 city of palm-tr. to Z.
Is. 15:5 fugitives sh. flee unto Z.
Jer. 48:34 uttered th. voice fr. Z.

ZOBAH.

1 Sam. 14:47 against kings of Z,
2 Sam. 8:3 Da. smote king of Z.
1 K. 11:24; 1 Chr. 18:3, 9
23:36 Igal son of Nathan of Z.
1 K. 11:23 fled from king of Z.

ZOPHAR.

Job 2:11 Z. Naamath. 11:1; 42:9

ZORAH.

Jos. 19:41 inheritance of Dan, Z.
Jud. 13:2 a certain man of Z.
25 Sams. bet Z. and Eshtaol
16:31 bur. Samson bet. Z. and
18:2 Danites sent from Z. to
8 came unto their breth. to Z.
2 Chr. 11:10 Rehoboam built Z.

ZOROBABEL.

Mat. 1:12 Salathiel begat Z. 13
Luke 3:27 Rhesa was son of Z.

ZUR.

Num. 25:15 daughter of Z. slain
31:8 Z. prince slain, Jos. 13:21
1 Chr. 8:30 Z. son of Gib. 9:36

ZUZIM.

Gen. 14:5 kings smote Z. in H.

www.ingramcontent.com/pod-product-compliance
Lightning Source LLC
Chambersburg PA
CBHW031851220426
43663CB00006B/579